Presented to

_____

by

_____

on

_____

_____

about
2100 BC

Creation

Noah and the Flood

Abraham travels
to Canaan

about
1250 BC

about
1200 BC

about
1200–1000 BC

The Exodus

The Israelites enter
the Promised Land

Judges
lead Israel

530 BC

30 AD

The Return

Jesus's Birth

Jesus's Baptism
by John

Crucifixion

before
1650 BC

about
1650–1250 BC

about
1350 BC

Joseph's family
moves to Egypt

Hebrews
become slaves

Moses is born

1000–900 BC

700 BC

700 BC

United
Kingdom

Divided
Kingdom

End of the
Northern
Kingdom

The Exile

30 AD

after
30 AD

about
40-50 AD

about
60–90 AD

Resurrection

Pentecost

Paul's Letters

The Gospels

Temple
(2 Chronicles 3)

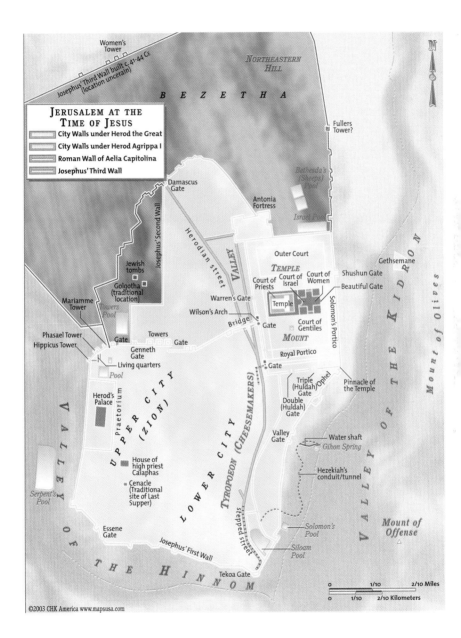

JERUSALEM AT THE TIME OF JESUS

- City Walls under Herod the Great
- City Walls under Herod Agrippa I
- Roman Wall of Aelia Capitolina
- Josephus' Third Wall

Women's Tower

Josephus' Third Wall built c. 41-44 CE (location uncertain)

NORTHEASTERN HILL

B E Z E T H A

Fullers Tower?

Bethesda's (Sheeps) Pool

Damascus Gate

Antonia Fortress

Israel Pool

Josephus' Second Wall

Herodian street

VALLEY

Outer Court

TEMPLE

Gethsemane

Jewish tombs

Court of Priests

Court of Israel

Court of Women

Shushun Gate

Golgotha (traditional location)

Warren's Gate

Temple

Beautiful Gate

Mariamme Tower

Towers Pool

Wilson's Arch

Bridge

Gate

Court of Gentiles

Solomon's Portico

Phasael Tower
Hippicus Tower

Towers

Gate

Gate

MOUNT

Mount of Olives

Genneth Gate

Royal Portico

Living quarters

Pool

Gate

Mount of Olives

Herod's Palace

UPPER CITY (ZION)

Praetorium

Triple (Huldah) Gate

Ophel

Pinnacle of the Temple

Double (Huldah) Gate

VALLEY OF THE KIDRON

House of high priest Caiaphas

TYROPOEON (CHEESEMAKERS)

Valley Gate

Water shaft

Gihon Spring

Cenacle (Traditional site of Last Supper)

Hezekiah's conduit/tunnel

LOWER CITY

Serpent's Pool

VALLEY OF

Solomon's Pool

Mount of Offense

Essene Gate

stepped street

Josephus' First Wall

Siloam Pool

THE HINNOM

Tekoa Gate

0   1/10   2/10 Miles
0   1/10   2/10 Kilometers

©2003 CHK America www.mapsusa.com

God is with us and always hears our prayers. Sometimes when we pray, we use our bodies to match the feelings behind our words. Here are some different positions, or postures, that you can use when you pray!

Standing with hands raised upward
1 Timothy 2:8
1 Kings 8:22

Standing
Mark 11:25

Kneeling
Luke 22:41
Daniel 6:10

Kneeling with outstretched hands
1 Kings 8:54

Bowing
Exodus 34:8

Sitting quietly in a favorite place
Matthew 14:23

ICON LEGEND

As you journey through the pages
of this Bible, you'll discover the
story of God and the message
of Jesus! Watch for these small,
blue signs to help you learn more:

God's Path—
Discover who God is and how
God wants you to live!

Finding the Path—
Learn how to apply the truths
in the Bible to your life!

Light on the Path—
Memorize key verses that you can
use now and remember forever!

Points along the Path—
Explore the people and
places of the Bible!

THE NRSV
CHILDREN'S BIBLE

THE NRSV CHILDREN'S BIBLE

containing the
Old and New Testaments

New Revised Standard Version

Abingdon Press
Nashville

THE NRSV CHILDREN'S BIBLE

Copyright © 2006 Abingdon Press

Library of Congress Cataloging-in-Publication Data

Bible. English. New Revised Standard. 2006.
  The NRSV children's Bible : containing the Old and New Testaments : New Revised Standard Version.
    p. cm.
    ISBN 0-687-49416-8 (9780687494163 : Noah hard cover)
    ISBN 0-687-05400-1 (9780687054008 : blue/green hard cover)
    ISBN 0-687-33245-1 (9780687332458 : gift and award burgundy imitation leather)

BS191.5.A12006 N37 2006
220.5'20434—dc22

2006004347

06 07 08 09 10 11 12 13 14 15—10 09 08 07 06 05 04 03 02 01

This book is printed on recycled, acid-free paper.

MANUFACTURED IN THE UNITED STATES OF AMERICA

Acknowledgments

Interior illustrations are by Dennis Jones.

"Contemporary Lord's Prayer" is from *Everyday Prayers for Teens* by Barry L. Culbertson © 1994 Dimensions for Living.

"Prayer Positions" is adapted from *Hey, God, Let's Talk!* by Charles L. Terrell, Jr. © 2000 Abingdon Press.

"Bible Basics" is adapted from *Learning to Use My Bible—Teachers Guide* by Joyce Brown © 1999 Abingdon Press.

Dictionary is adapted from *Young Reader's Bible Dictionary, Revised Edition* © 2000 Abingdon Press.

Cover art for the Noah's Ark hardcover version is based on the painting "The Promise" by Mary Singleton.

Welcome to the NRSV Children's Bible!

The NRSV Children's Bible was designed for you! It is a tool that will help you stay on God's path as you journey through the pages. Look for these special features:

Introduction pages

The blue introduction pages at the beginning of each book of the Bible give you information about who wrote the book, when it was written, and what it is about. Each of these pages also contains a picture that illustrates a story or theme from the book. You can find out more about the story or theme by using the blue verse reference next to the picture.

Icons

The small blue signs throughout the pages of this Bible will help you:
- discover who God is
- learn how God wants you to live
- understand the message of Jesus
- find out about the people and places of the Bible
- memorize Bible verses

For more information about these icons and what they mean, check out the icon legend in the front pages of the Bible. Watch for the icons as you read!

Color pages

Look for the two sections of full-color pages!

The first section is at the front of the Bible and contains the following pages: Presentation Page, Pictorial Timeline, Temple Cut-away, Map of Jerusalem, Prayer Positions, and Icon Legend.

The second section is between the Old and New Testaments and contains the following pages: Pictures of Bible Objects, Contemporary Lord's Prayer, Contemporary Beatitudes, Lesser-known Bible Folks, and the Christian Year.

Dictionary

The dictionary at the back of this Bible contains definitions of more than four hundred words. If there is a word in the Bible that you do not understand, look in the dictionary to see if you can find a definition.

Maps

The full-color maps at the back of the Bible will help you understand the part of the world where the stories of the Bible took place!

Bible Basics

On the next eight pages, you will find answers to the following questions:

- What is the Bible?
- Who wrote the Bible, and when was it written?
- Why is the Bible important to people today?
- How can I find my way through the Bible?
- How can I find a specific Bible verse or passage?
- What is a good way for me to begin reading the Bible?

Bible Basics

What is the Bible?

The Bible is a very special collection of books filled with stories of God's love for people. It is a library you can hold in your hand! The sixty-six books of the Bible tell about God, the Creator of the universe, who made people and wanted them to follow God's ways. They tell about God's great love and that God sent Jesus to be the Savior of the people of the whole world. The Bible is a special book that shows us what God is like and how we can know God. The Bible comes from God, who inspired people to write down God's teachings, and who inspires us to read and understand God's teachings. Throughout history, the Bible has changed many people's lives. Through the Bible, God speaks to us today.

Who wrote the Bible, and when was it written?

The Bible is a collection of books that were written by many different people. Long ago, before there were written Bible stories, people told the stories from memory. Parents told them to their children, who told them to their children. God helped the people remember the stories and teachings. Later, people began to write the stories and teachings down. We believe that God inspired people to write the Bible teachings. (*Inspire* means that God's spirit helps us know the right thing to do.)

The stories and teachings of the Old Testament were told for hundreds of years before they were written. About 950 BC people began to write down some of the Old Testament stories. The Old Testament was first written in the Hebrew language.

The stories and teachings of the New Testament were also told for many years before they were written. Some of the New Testament letters were written about twenty-five years after Jesus died. Then, about thirty years after Jesus died, people began to write down the stories and teachings of Jesus that are included in the four Gospel books—Matthew, Mark, Luke, and John. The New Testament was first written in the Greek language.

The stories and teachings of our Bible have been told for thousands of years. The Bible message spread to many lands and into many languages. Jesus told his followers to go into all the world to preach, baptize, and teach. They obeyed, and the Good News of Jesus spread from town to town, from country to country, and from continent to continent. It took many people and thousands of years for the stories, songs, and messages of the Bible to be written. Today, the Bible is read in almost two thousand languages and in hundreds of countries.

Why is the Bible important to people today?

The Bible message is a gift to us from God. It is also a gift to us from many people. It took many years and many people to give us this gift! As we read our Bibles, we learn more about God's great love for all people and how Jesus taught us to live. The

Bible shows us how awesome our God is and how we can know God! God inspires us to read and to understand the Bible today.

How can I find my way through the Bible?

The Bible looks like one big book, but really it is a lot of small books gathered together. It is like a library full of books! Each Bible book has its own name and place in the Bible library. Different books in the Bible library have different kinds of writings. Some give God's laws. Some tell stories of history. Some are songs or poems. Some have warnings. Some tell about Jesus. Some are letters.

The two main parts of the Bible are the Old Testament and the New Testament. Each of these two parts contains a large group of books. There are thirty-nine books in the Old Testament and twenty-seven books in the New Testament.

The Old Testament covers a period of several thousand years. It tells the story of Israel, a Jewish nation in the Middle East. The Old Testament contains many stories about God's love and mighty acts—creating the world, saving the Israelite people from slavery in Egypt, providing food for the people while they wandered for forty years in the wilderness, giving special laws to the people to help them live the way God wanted them to live, and leading them to the promised land of Canaan. The Scriptures Jesus learned as a child were Old Testament Scriptures. (The New Testament was not written until many years after Jesus lived on earth.)

The New Testament covers a period of about one hundred years. It tells about Jesus and those who told the story of Jesus to others. After Jesus rose from the dead, he told his followers to go into all the world to preach, baptize, and teach all that he had taught them. Jesus promised to be with them and to send the Holy Spirit to help them in this work. After Jesus returned to God, his followers carried on his work. They taught others what Jesus had said. They healed people in the name of Jesus. They told others how Jesus had shown them what God is like. Soon followers of Jesus Christ were called Christians.

Old Testament books:

Law—The first five books of the Old Testament contain the history of God's people from the creation of the world to Joseph's leadership of the Israelite people. These books contain the laws, or rules, God gave the people to help them live the way God wanted them to live.

History—The twelve history books tell us that the people often broke God's laws. So God chose leaders—first judges, then kings—to help them. These books are filled with stories about those leaders. They tell the history of God's people from Joshua's leadership to their return from exile in Babylon.

Wisdom—The five books of wisdom contain poetry and songs that express deep human emotions. Some are filled with wise sayings, and some are filled with words of praise to God.

Prophecy—There are seventeen books of prophecy in the Old Testament. When the Israelites forgot God's rules for living, God called prophets to speak God's message to the people.

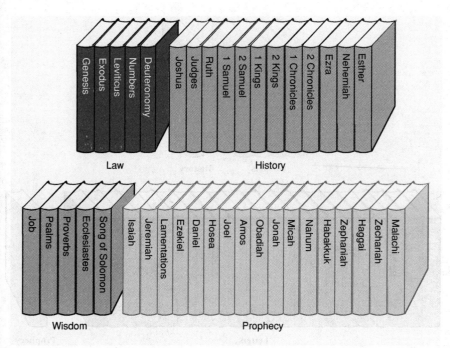

Law   History

Wisdom   Prophecy

New Testament books:

Gospels—The first four books of the New Testament are called "Gospels." These books tell the story of Jesus's life, death, and resurrection.

History—The fifth book, Acts, is about the actions of Jesus's followers and the beginning of the Christian church.

Letters—Twenty-one books are letters written by early Christian leaders to help others become faithful followers of Jesus.

Prophecy—The last book, Revelation, describes God's victory at the end of the world.

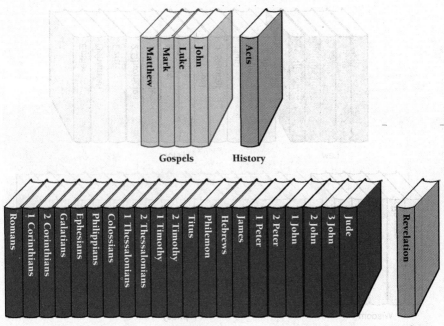

Gospels   History

Letters   Prophecy

How can I find a specific Bible verse or passage?

A **Bible reference** tells you where to look to find part of a book in the Bible. The first thing a Bible reference tells you is which **book** in the Bible to look up. At the beginning of this Bible, you will find a page with a list of the names and order of the books of the Bible. This list will help you find the page on which each book begins.

Most of the books of the Bible have been divided into large parts called **chapters**. The beginning of each chapter is marked with a big number. In a Bible reference, the first number after the name of the book tells you which chapter to look in.

To make it easier to find things in the Bible, the chapters have been divided into small parts called **verses**. Each verse has been given a small number. A verse ends when you come to the next verse number or when you come to the end of a section.

Remember, each **book** in the Bible is divided into **chapters**, and each chapter is divided into **verses**. To find a verse, you need to know the **book**, the **chapter**, and the **verse**:

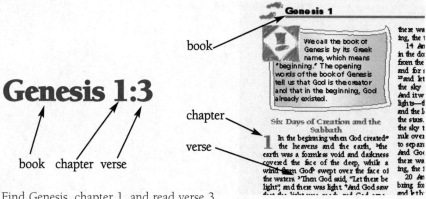

Find Genesis, chapter 1, and read verse 3.
(note: The number for verse 1 is not printed in most Bibles. In the Bible, every chapter begins with verse 1, even if the number is not printed there.)

A reference with a hyphen looks like this:

Genesis 1:3–5

Find Genesis, chapter 1, and read from the beginning of verse 3 to the end of verse 5.

A reference with a comma looks like this:

Genesis 1:26–27, 31

Find Genesis, chapter 1. Read verses 26 and 27. Skip verses 28, 29, and 30. Then read verse 31.

A reference for a whole chapter looks like this:

Genesis 1

Find Genesis chapter 1. Read from the beginning of the first verse to the end of the last verse.

Sometimes you will see small letters next to certain words or verses. These little letters mean "look at the bottom of the page" if you want to learn more. At the bottom of the page is a matching letter with more information. This extra information at the bottom of the page is called a footnote.

What is a good way for me to begin reading the Bible?

The more you read your Bible, the more you will learn to treasure God's word. Here are some places you can turn to find stories:

Old Testament Stories

The first Creation story
  (Genesis 1:1–2:4*a*)
The second Creation story
  (Genesis 2:4*b*–25)
The Flood
  (Genesis 6:5–8:22)
The call of Abram (Abraham)
  (Genesis 12:1–5*a*)
Jacob's ladder
  (Genesis 28:10–17)
Joseph's special robe
  (Genesis 37:1–36)
Moses and the burning bush
  (Exodus 3:1–22)
The Passover
  (Exodus 11:1–12:51)
The Exodus (parting of the sea)
  (Exodus 14:1–31)
Balaam and the donkey
  (Numbers 22:21–35)
Rahab and the spies
  (Joshua 2:1–24)
Joshua and the battle of Jericho
  (Joshua 6:1–20)
Ruth and Naomi
  (Ruth 1:6–22)
Hannah and the birth of Samuel
  (1 Samuel 1:9–28)
Call of Samuel
  (1 Samuel 3:1–20)
Anointing of David
  (1 Samuel 16:1–13)
David and Goliath
  (1 Samuel 17:1–54)
Elijah and the widow at Zarephath
  (1 Kings 17:8–24)
Elijah and the prophets of Baal
  (1 Kings 18:20–39)

Esther goes before the king
  (Esther 5:1–8)
Isaiah's vision
  (Isaiah 6:1–8)
The fiery furnace
  (Daniel 3:1–28)
Daniel in the lions' den
  (Daniel 6:1–23)
Jonah and the large fish
  (Jonah 1:1–3:10)

New Testament Gospel Stories

The Temptation of Jesus
  (Matthew 4:1–11)
Jesus heals a leper
  (Matthew 8:1–4)
Jesus walks on water
  (Matthew 14:22–33)
The triumphant entry
  (Matthew 21:1–11)
The crucifixion of Jesus
  (Matthew 27:32–56)
The resurrection of Jesus
  (Matthew 28:1–10)
Jesus calls the first disciples
  (Mark 1:16–20)
Jesus heals a sick woman
  (Mark 5:21–34)
Jesus blesses the children
  (Mark 10:13–16)
The rich young ruler
  (Mark 10:17–31)
Peter's denials of Jesus
  (Mark 14:66–72)
Jesus's trial before Pilate
  (Mark 15:1–15)
The birth of Jesus
  (Luke 2:1–7)

The shepherds and the angels
at the birth of Jesus
(Luke 2:8–20)
Jesus at the Temple
(Luke 2:39–52)
Jesus visits Mary and Martha
(Luke 10:38–42)
Jesus heals a crippled woman
(Luke 13:10–17)
Zacchaeus the tax collector
(Luke 19:1–10)
The Last Supper
(Luke 22:7–30)
Jesus's betrayal and arrest
(Luke 22:47–53)
The ascension of Jesus
(Luke 24:50–53)
Jesus turns water into wine
(John 2:1–11)
The woman at the well
(John 4:1–42)
Jesus feeds the multitude
(John 6:1–14)
Jesus heals the blind man
(John 9:1–41)
Jesus raises Lazarus
(John 11:1–44)
Mary anoints Jesus at Bethany
(John 12:1–8)
Jesus washes his disciples' feet
(John 13:1–20)

Parables of Jesus

The wise and foolish builders
(Matthew 7:24–27)
The mustard seed
(Matthew 13:31–32)
The pearl of great price
(Matthew 13:45–46)

The laborers in the vineyard
(Matthew 20:1–16)
The great banquet
(Matthew 22:1–10)
The ten bridesmaids
(Matthew 25:1–13)
The ten talents
(Matthew 25:14–30)
The sower
(Mark 4:3–9)
The two debtors
(Luke 7:41–43)
The good Samaritan
(Luke 10:25–37)
The rich fool
(Luke 12:16–21)
The lost sheep
(Luke 15:4–7)
The lost coin
(Luke 15:8–10)
The prodigal son
(Luke 15:11–32)

Acts of the Apostles

Peter and John heal at the Temple
(Acts 3:1–10)
Philip and the man from Ethiopia
(Acts 8:26–39)
Saul's conversion
(Acts 9:1–19)
Peter and Cornelius
(Acts 10:1–48)
Peter rescued from prison
(Acts 12:6–17)
The conversion of Lydia
(Acts 16:11–15)
Paul and Silas in prison
(Acts 16:16–40)

Names and Order of
the Books of the Bible

The Old Testament

The New Testament

Alphabetical Book Listing

To the Reader

This preface is addressed to you by the Committee of translators, who wish to explain, as briefly as possible, the origin and character of our work. The publication of our revision is yet another step in the long, continual process of making the Bible available in the form of the English language that is most widely current in our day. To summarize in a single sentence: the New Revised Standard Version of the Bible is an authorized revision of the Revised Standard Version, published in 1952, which was a revision of the American Standard Version, published in 1901, which, in turn, embodied earlier revisions of the King James Version, published in 1611.

In the course of time, the King James Version came to be regarded as "the Authorized Version." With good reason it has been termed "the noblest monument of English prose," and it has entered, as no other book has, into the making of the personal character and the public institutions of the English-speaking peoples. We owe to it an incalculable debt.

Yet the King James Version has serious defects. By the middle of the nineteenth century, the development of biblical studies and the discovery of many biblical manuscripts more ancient than those on which the King James Version was based made it apparent that these defects were so many as to call for revision. The task was begun, by authority of the Church of England, in 1870. The (British) Revised Version of the Bible was published in 1881–1885; and the American Standard Version, its variant embodying the preferences of the American scholars associated with the work, was published, as was mentioned above, in 1901. In 1928 the copyright of the latter was acquired by the International Council of Religious Education and thus passed into the ownership of the churches of the United States and Canada that were associated in this Council through their boards of education and publication.

The Council appointed a committee of scholars to have charge of the text of the American Standard Version and to undertake inquiry concerning the need for further revision. After studying the questions whether or not revision should be undertaken, and if so, what its nature and extent should be, in 1937 the Council authorized a revision. The scholars who served as members of the Committee worked in two sections, one dealing with the Old Testament and one with the New Testament. In 1946 the Revised Standard Version of the New Testament was published. The publication of the Revised Standard Version of the Bible, containing the Old and New Testaments, took place on September 30, 1952. A translation of the Apocryphal/Deuterocanonical Books of the Old Testament followed in 1957. In 1977 this collection was issued in an expanded edition, containing three additional texts received by Eastern Orthodox communions (3 and 4 Maccabees and Psalm 151). Thereafter the Revised Standard Version gained the distinction of being officially authorized for use by all major Christian churches: Protestant, Anglican, Roman Catholic, and Eastern Orthodox.

The Revised Standard Version Bible Committee is a continuing body, comprising about thirty members, both men and women. Ecumenical in representation, it includes scholars affiliated with various Protestant denominations, as well as several Roman Catholic members, an Eastern Orthodox member, and a Jewish member who serves in the Old Testament section. For a period of time the Committee included several members from Canada and from England.

Because no translation of the Bible is perfect or is acceptable to all groups of readers, and because discoveries of older manuscripts and further investigation of linguistic features of the text continue to become available, renderings of the Bible have proliferated. During the years following the publication of the Revised Standard Version, twenty-six other English translations and revisions of the Bible were produced by committees and by individual scholars—not to mention twenty-five other translations and revisions of the New Testament alone. One of the latter was the second edition of the RSV New Testament, issued in 1971, twenty-five years after its initial publication.

Following the publication of the RSV Old Testament in 1952, significant advances were made in the discovery and interpretation of documents in Semitic languages related to Hebrew. In addition to the information that had become available in the late 1940s from the Dead Sea texts of Isaiah and Habakkuk, subsequent acquisitions from the same area brought to light many other early copies of all the books of the Hebrew Scriptures (except Esther), though most of these copies are fragmentary. During the same period early Greek manuscript copies of books of the New Testament also became available.

In order to take these discoveries into account, along with recent studies of documents in Semitic languages related to Hebrew, in 1974 the Policies Committee of the Revised Standard Version, which is a standing committee of the National Council of the Churches of Christ in the U.S.A., authorized the preparation of a revision of the entire RSV Bible.

For the Old Testament the Committee has made use of the *Biblia Hebraica Stuttgartensia* (1977; ed. sec. emendata, 1983). This is an edition of the Hebrew and Aramaic text as current early in the Christian era and fixed by Jewish scholars (the "Masoretes") of the sixth to the ninth centuries. The vowel signs, which were added by the Masoretes, are accepted in the main, but where a more probable and convincing reading can be obtained by assuming different vowels, this has been done. No notes are given in such cases, because the vowel points are less ancient and reliable than the consonants. When an alternative reading given by the Masoretes is translated in a footnote, this is identified by the words "Another reading is."

Departures from the consonantal text of the best manuscripts have been made only where it seems clear that errors in copying had been made before the text was standardized. Most of the corrections adopted are based on the ancient versions (translations into Greek, Aramaic, Syriac, and Latin), which were made prior to the time of the work of the Masoretes and which therefore may reflect earlier forms of the Hebrew text. In such instances a footnote specifies the version or versions from which the correction has been derived and also gives a translation of the Masoretic Text. Where it was deemed appropriate to do so, information is supplied in footnotes from subsidiary Jewish traditions concerning other textual readings (the *Tiqqune Sopherim*, "emendations of the scribes"). These are identified in the footnotes as "Ancient Heb tradition."

Occasionally it is evident that the text has suffered in transmission and that none of the versions provides a satisfactory restoration. Here we can only follow the best judgment of competent scholars as to the most probable reconstruction of the original text. Such reconstructions are indicated in footnotes by the abbreviation Cn ("Correction"), and a translation of the Masoretic Text is added.

For the Apocryphal/Deuterocanonical Books of the Old Testament the Committee has made use of a number of texts. For most of these books the basic Greek text from which the present translation was made is the edition of the Septuagint prepared by Alfred Rahlfs and published by the Württemberg Bible Society (Stuttgart, 1935). For several of the books the more recently published individual volumes of the Göttingen Septuagint project were utilized. For the book of Tobit it was decided to follow the form of the Greek text found in codex Sinaiticus (supported as it is by evidence from Qumran); where this text is defective, it was supplemented and corrected by other Greek manuscripts. For the three Additions to Daniel (namely, Susanna, the Prayer of Azariah and the Song of the Three Jews, and Bel and the Dragon) the Committee continued to use the Greek version attributed to Theodotion (the so-called "Theodotion-Daniel"). In translating Ecclesiasticus (Sirach), while constant reference was made to the Hebrew fragments of a large portion of this book (those discovered at Qumran and Masada as well as those recovered from the Cairo Geniza), the Committee generally followed the Greek text (including verse numbers) published by Joseph Ziegler in the Göttingen Septuagint (1965). But in many places the Committee has translated the Hebrew text when this provides a reading that is clearly superior to the Greek; the Syriac and Latin versions were also consulted throughout and occasionally adopted. The basic text adopted in rendering 2 Esdras is the Latin version given in *Biblia Sacra*, edited by Robert Weber (Stuttgart, 1971). This was supplemented by consulting the Latin text as edited by R. L. Bensly (1895) and by Bruno Violet (1910), as well as by taking into account the several Oriental versions of 2 Esdras, namely, the Syriac, Ethiopic, Arabic (two forms, referred to as Arabic 1 and Arabic 2), Armenian, and Georgian versions. Finally, since the Additions to the Book of Esther are disjointed and quite unintelligible as they stand in most editions of the Apocrypha, we have provided them with their original context by translating the whole of the Greek version of Esther from Robert Hanhart's Göttingen edition (1983).

For the New Testament the Committee has based its work on the most recent edition of *The Greek New Testament*, prepared by an interconfessional and international committee and published by the United Bible Societies (1966; 3rd ed. corrected, 1983; information concerning changes to be introduced into the critical apparatus of the forthcoming 4th edition was available to the Committee). As in that edition, double brackets are used to enclose a few passages that are generally regarded to be later additions to the text, but that we have retained because of their evident antiquity and their importance in the textual tradition. Only in very rare instances have we replaced the text or the punctuation of the Bible Societies' edition by an alternative that seemed to us to be superior. Here and there in the footnotes the phrase, "Other ancient authorities read," identifies alternative readings preserved by Greek manuscripts and early versions. In both Testaments, alternative renderings of the text are indicated by the word "Or."

As for the style of English adopted for the present revision, among the mandates given to the Committee in 1980 by the Division of Education and Ministry of the National Council of Churches of Christ (which now holds the copyright of the RSV Bible) was the directive to continue in the tradition of the King James Bible, but to introduce such changes as are warranted on the basis of accuracy, clarity, euphony, and current English usage. Within the constraints set by the original texts and by the mandates of the Division, the Committee has followed the maxim, "As literal as possible, as free as necessary." As a consequence, the New Revised Standard Version (NRSV) remains essentially a literal translation. Paraphrastic renderings have been adopted only sparingly, and then chiefly to compensate for a deficiency in the English language—the lack of a common-gender third-person singular pronoun.

During the almost half a century since the publication of the RSV, many in the churches have become sensitive to the danger of linguistic sexism arising from the inherent bias of the English language towards the masculine gender, a bias that in the case of the Bible has often restricted or obscured the meaning of the original text. The mandates from the Division specified that, in references to men and women, masculine-oriented language should be eliminated as far as this can be done without altering passages that reflect the historical situation of ancient patriarchal culture. As can be appreciated, more than once the Committee found that the several mandates stood in tension and even in conflict. The various concerns had to be balanced case by case in order to provide a faithful and acceptable rendering without using contrived English. Only very occasionally has the pronoun "he" or "him" been retained in passages where the reference may have been to a woman as well as to a man, for example, in several legal texts in Leviticus and Deuteronomy. In such instances of formal, legal language, the options of either putting the passage in the plural or of introducing additional nouns to avoid masculine pronouns in English seemed to the Committee to obscure the historic structure and literary character of the original. In the vast majority of cases, however, inclusiveness has been attained by simple rephrasing or by introducing plural forms when this does not distort the meaning of the passage. Of course, in narrative and in parable no attempt was made to generalize the sex of individual persons.

Another aspect of style will be detected by readers who compare the more stately English rendering of the Old Testament with the less formal rendering adopted for the New Testament. For example, the traditional distinction between *shall* and *will* in English has been retained in the Old Testament as appropriate in rendering a document that embodies what may be termed the classic form of Hebrew, while in the New Testament the abandonment of such distinctions in the usage of the future tense in English reflects the more colloquial nature of the koine Greek used by most New Testament authors except when they are quoting the Old Testament.

Careful readers will notice that here and there in the Old Testament the word LORD (or in certain cases GOD) is printed in capital letters. This represents the traditional manner in English versions of rendering the Divine Name, the "Tetragrammaton" (see the notes on Exodus 3.14, 15), following the precedent of the ancient Greek and Latin translators and the long-established practice in the reading of the Hebrew Scriptures in the synagogue. While it is almost if not quite certain that the Name was originally pronounced "Yahweh," this pronunciation was not indicated when the Masoretes added vowel sounds to the consonantal Hebrew text. To the four consonants YHWH of the Name, which had come to be regarded as too sacred to be pronounced, *they* attached vowel signs indicating that in its place should be read the Hebrew word *Adonai* meaning "Lord" (or *Elohim* meaning "God"). Ancient Greek translators employed the word *Kyrios* ("Lord") for the Name. The Vulgate likewise used the Latin word *Dominus* ("Lord"). The form "Jehovah" is of late medieval origin; it is a combination of the consonants of the Divine Name and the vowels attached to it by the Masoretes but belonging to an entirely different word. Although the American Standard Version (1901) had used "Jehovah" to render the Tetragrammaton (the sound of Y being represented by J and the sound of W by V, as in Latin), for two reasons the Committees that produced the RSV and the NRSV returned to the more familiar usage of the King James Version. (1) The word "Jehovah" does not accurately represent any form of the Name ever used in Hebrew. (2) The use of any proper name for the one and only God, as though there were other gods from whom the true God had to be distinguished, began to be discontinued in Judaism before the Christian era and is inappropriate for the universal faith of the Christian Church.

It will be seen that in the Psalms and in other prayers addressed to God the archaic second-person singular pronouns (*thee, thou, thine*) and verb forms (*art, hast, hadst*) are no longer used. Although some readers may regret this change, it should be pointed out that in the original languages neither the Old Testament nor the New makes any linguistic distinction between addressing a human being and addressing the Deity. Furthermore, in the tradition of the King James Version one will not expect to find the use of capital letters for pronouns that refer to the Deity—such capitalization is an unnecessary innovation that has only recently been introduced into a few English translations of the Bible. Finally, we have left to the discretion of the licensed publishers such matters as section headings, cross-references, and clues to the pronunciation of proper names.

This new version seeks to preserve all that is best in the English Bible as it has been known and used through the years. It is intended for use in public reading and congregational worship, as well as in private study, instruction, and meditation. We have resisted the temptation to introduce terms and phrases that merely reflect current moods, and have tried to put the message of the Scriptures in simple, enduring words and expressions that are worthy to stand in the great tradition of the King James Bible and its predecessors.

In traditional Judaism and Christianity, the Bible has been more than a historical document to be preserved or a classic of literature to be cherished and admired; it is recognized as the unique record of God's dealings with people over the ages. The Old Testament sets forth the call of a special people to enter into covenant relation with the God of justice and steadfast love and to bring God's law to the nations. The New Testament records the life and work of Jesus Christ, the one in whom "the Word became flesh," as well as describes the rise and spread of the early Christian Church. The Bible carries its full message, not to those who regard it simply as a noble literary heritage of the past or who wish to use it to enhance political purposes and advance otherwise desirable goals, but to all persons and communities who read it so that they may discern and understand what God is saying to them. That message must not be disguised in phrases that are no longer clear, or hidden under words that have changed or lost their meaning; it must be presented in language that is direct and plain and meaningful to people today. It is the hope and prayer of the translators that this version of the Bible may continue to hold a large place in congregational life and to speak to all readers, young and old alike, helping them to understand and believe and respond to its message.

For the Committee,
BRUCE M. METZGER

THE HEBREW SCRIPTURES
commonly called

THE OLD TESTAMENT

New Revised Standard Version

Genesis

People have always wondered about how the world began. Hundreds of years ago, God helped a special group of people understand that God had planned and made the world and all that is within the world. Most importantly, God made human beings to live good lives as the children of God.

The people wanted these accounts to be handed down to their grandchildren and great-grandchildren. So several hundred years before Jesus Christ was born, people began to write down their stories. At different times, others added to the writings, and the entire story was finally finished about three or four hundred years before Jesus was born. Genesis, along with the books of Exodus, Leviticus, Numbers, and Deuteronomy, tells the story of the beginning of the Israelite people.

The book of Genesis opens by telling that God made the earth and everything in it. God made people to live as God's human family. God loved this human family very much, even during the times when they did not live as God wanted them to live. Genesis tells the stories of some of these family member. In particular, it tells about the family of Abraham. The book ends with the story of Joseph and his brothers, who all went to Egypt.

The most important thing to remember as you read Genesis and the other books that follow is that the Bible is a library of books about the people's connection to God. These books tell of God's love and care. As we read these stories, we learn not only about God but also about God's plan for us. Reading these stories helps us to live as faithful members of God's family. Because God inspired its writing, the Bible is called the Word of God.

Genesis 6:9–22

We call the book of Genesis by its Greek name, which means "beginning." The opening words of the book of Genesis tell us that God is the creator and that in the beginning, God already existed.

Six Days of Creation and the Sabbath

1 In the beginning when God created[a] the heavens and the earth, [2]the earth was a formless void and darkness covered the face of the deep, while a wind from God[b] swept over the face of the waters. [3]Then God said, "Let there be light"; and there was light. [4]And God saw that the light was good; and God separated the light from the darkness. [5]God called the light Day, and the darkness he called Night. And there was evening and there was morning, the first day.

6 And God said, "Let there be a dome in the midst of the waters, and let it separate the waters from the waters." [7]So God made the dome and separated the waters that were under the dome from the waters that were above the dome. And it was so. [8]God called the dome Sky. And there was evening and there was morning, the second day.

9 And God said, "Let the waters under the sky be gathered together into one place, and let the dry land appear." And it was so. [10]God called the dry land Earth, and the waters that were gathered together he called Seas. And God saw that it was good. [11]Then God said, "Let the earth put forth vegetation: plants yielding seed, and fruit trees of every kind on earth that bear fruit with the seed in it." And it was so. [12]The earth brought forth vegetation: plants yielding seed of every kind, and trees of every kind bearing fruit with the seed in it. And God saw that it was good. [13]And there was evening and there was morning, the third day.

14 And God said, "Let there be lights in the dome of the sky to separate the day from the night; and let them be for signs and for seasons and for days and years, [15]and let them be lights in the dome of the sky to give light upon the earth." And it was so. [16]God made the two great lights—the greater light to rule the day and the lesser light to rule the night—and the stars. [17]God set them in the dome of the sky to give light upon the earth, [18]to rule over the day and over the night, and to separate the light from the darkness. And God saw that it was good. [19]And there was evening and there was morning, the fourth day.

20 And God said, "Let the waters bring forth swarms of living creatures, and let birds fly above the earth across the dome of the sky." [21]So God created the great sea monsters and every living creature that moves, of every kind, with which the waters swarm, and every winged bird of every kind. And God saw that it was good. [22]God blessed them, saying, "Be fruitful and multiply and fill the waters in the seas, and let birds multiply on the earth." [23]And there was evening and there was morning, the fifth day.

24 And God said, "Let the earth bring forth living creatures of every kind: cattle and creeping things and wild animals of the earth of every kind." And it was so. [25]God made the wild animals of the

The more we learn about nature, the universe, or human beings, the more we are amazed by the miracle of God's creation. Because God said, "Let there be light, sky, seas, dry land, plants, sun, moon, stars, fish, birds, animals, and people," we have an awesome world!

[a] Or *when God began to create* or *In the beginning God created*   [b] Or *while the spirit of God* or *while a mighty wind*

earth of every kind, and the cattle of every kind, and everything that creeps upon the ground of every kind. And God saw that it was good.

26 Then God said, "Let us make humankind[c] in our image, according to our likeness; and let them have dominion over the fish of the sea, and over the birds of the air, and over the cattle, and over all the wild animals of the earth,[d] and over every creeping thing that creeps upon the earth."

27 So God created humankind[c] in his image,

in the image of God he created them;[e]

male and female he created them.

Because we are created in God's image, we are similar to God in our hearts, in our minds, and in our feelings. We are God's hands and feet here on earth!

28God blessed them, and God said to them, "Be fruitful and multiply, and fill the earth and subdue it; and have dominion over the fish of the sea and over the birds of the air and over every living thing that moves upon the earth." 29God said, "See, I have given you every plant yielding seed that is upon the face of all the earth, and every tree with seed in its fruit; you shall have them for food. 30And to every beast of the earth, and to every bird of the air, and to everything that creeps on the earth, everything that has the breath of life, I have given every green plant for food." And it was so. 31God saw everything that he had made, and indeed, it was very good. And there was evening and there was morning, the sixth day.

"God saw everything that he had made, and indeed, it was very good."
Genesis 1:31a

2 Thus the heavens and the earth were finished, and all their multitude. 2And on the seventh day God finished the work that he had done, and he rested on the seventh day from all the work that he had done. 3So God blessed the seventh day and hallowed it, because on it God rested from all the work that he had done in creation.

4 These are the generations of the heavens and the earth when they were created.

Another Account of the Creation

In the day that the LORD God made the earth and the heavens, 5when no plant of the field was yet in the earth and no herb of the field had yet sprung up—for the LORD God had not caused it to rain upon the earth, and there was no one to till the ground; 6but a stream would rise from the earth, and water the whole face of the ground— 7then the LORD God formed man from the dust of the ground,[f] and breathed into his nostrils the breath of life; and the man became a living being. 8And the LORD God planted a garden in Eden, in the east; and there he put the man whom he had formed. 9Out of the ground the LORD God made to grow every tree that is pleasant to the sight and good for food, the tree of life also in the midst of the garden, and the tree of the knowledge of good and evil.

10 A river flows out of Eden to water the garden, and from there it divides and becomes four branches. 11The name of the first is Pī´shon; it is the one that flows around the whole land of Hav´-i·lah, where there is gold; 12and the gold of that land is good; bdellium and onyx stone are there. 13The name of the second river is Gī´hon; it is the one that flows around the whole land of Cush. 14The name of the third river is Tigris, which flows east of Assyria. And the fourth river is the Euphrates.

c Heb *adam*   d Syr: Heb *and over all the earth*
e Heb *him*   g Or *formed a man* (Heb *adam*) *of dust from the ground* (Heb *adamah*)

15 The LORD God took the man and put him in the garden of Eden to till it and keep it. [16]And the LORD God commanded the man, "You may freely eat of every tree of the garden; [17]but of the tree of the knowledge of good and evil you shall not eat, for in the day that you eat of it you shall die."

18 Then the LORD God said, "It is not good that the man should be alone; I will make him a helper as his partner." [19]So out of the ground the LORD God formed every animal of the field and every bird of the air, and brought them to the man to see what he would call them; and whatever the man called every living creature, that was its name. [20]The man gave names to all cattle, and to the birds of the air, and to every animal of the field; but for the man[g] there was not found a helper as his partner. [21]So the LORD God caused a deep sleep to fall upon the man, and he slept; then he took one of his ribs and closed up its place with flesh. [22]And the rib that the LORD God had taken from the man he made into a woman and brought her to the man. [23]Then the man said,

"This at last is bone of my bones
  and flesh of my flesh;
this one shall be called Woman,[h]
  for out of Man[i] this one was taken."

[24]Therefore a man leaves his father and his mother and clings to his wife, and they become one flesh. [25]And the man and his wife were both naked, and were not ashamed.

The First Sin and Its Punishment

3 Now the serpent was more crafty than any other wild animal that the LORD God had made. He said to the woman, "Did God say, 'You shall not eat from any tree in the garden'?" [2]The woman said to the serpent, "We may eat of the fruit of the trees in the garden; [3]but God said, 'You shall not eat of the fruit of the tree that is in the middle of the garden, nor shall you touch it, or you shall die.' " [4]But the serpent said to the woman, "You will not die; [5]for God knows that when you eat of it your eyes will be opened, and you will be like God,[j] knowing good and evil." [6]So when the woman saw that the tree was good for food, and that it was a delight to the eyes, and that the tree was to be desired to make one wise, she took of its fruit and ate; and she also gave some to her husband, who was with her, and he ate. [7]Then the eyes of both were opened, and they knew that they were naked; and they sewed fig leaves together and made loincloths for themselves.

8 They heard the sound of the LORD God walking in the garden at the time of the evening breeze, and the man and his wife hid themselves from the presence of the LORD God among the trees of the garden. [9]But the LORD God called to the man, and said to him, "Where are you?" [10]He said, "I heard the sound of you in the garden, and I was afraid, because I was naked; and I hid myself." [11]He said, "Who told you that you were naked? Have you eaten from the tree of which I commanded you not to eat?" [12]The man said, "The woman whom you gave to be with me, she gave me fruit from the tree, and I ate." [13]Then the LORD God said to the woman, "What is this that you have done?" The woman said, "The serpent tricked me, and I ate." [14]The LORD God said to the serpent,

God gave people, including Adam and Eve, the freedom to make choices. But in the story we read in Genesis 3, Adam and Eve did not make a good choice. Even though God must have been very sad, God did not turn away from them. Even when we choose not to follow God's ways, God still loves us and cares for us.

[g] Or for Adam [h] Heb ishshah [i] Heb ish [j] Or gods

"Because you have done this,
  cursed are you among all animals
  and among all wild creatures;
upon your belly you shall go,
  and dust you shall eat
  all the days of your life.
[15] I will put enmity between you and
      the woman,
  and between your offspring and
      hers;
he will strike your head,
  and you will strike his heel."
[16] To the woman he said,
"I will greatly increase your pangs in
      childbearing;
  in pain you shall bring forth
      children,
yet your desire shall be for your
      husband,
  and he shall rule over you."
[17] And to the man[k] he said,
"Because you have listened to the
      voice of your wife,
  and have eaten of the tree
about which I commanded you,
  'You shall not eat of it,'
cursed is the ground because of you;
  in toil you shall eat of it all the
      days of your life;
[18] thorns and thistles it shall bring
      forth for you;
  and you shall eat the plants of the
      field.
[19] By the sweat of your face
  you shall eat bread
until you return to the ground,
  for out of it you were taken;
you are dust,
  and to dust you shall return."
20 The man named his wife Eve,[l]
because she was the mother of all living.
[21]And the LORD God made garments of
skins for the man[m] and for his wife, and
clothed them.
22 Then the LORD God said, "See, the
man has become like one of us, knowing
good and evil; and now, he might reach
out his hand and take also from the tree
of life, and eat, and live forever"—

[23]therefore the LORD God sent him forth
from the garden of Eden, to till the
ground from which he was taken. [24]He
drove out the man; and at the east of the
garden of Eden he placed the cherubim,
and a sword flaming and turning to
guard the way to the tree of life.

Cain and Abel were
the sons of Adam and
Eve. Cain was the
older brother, and Abel was the
younger brother. Cain became
jealous of Abel and killed him.
Cain was punished by being
exiled from his land, but God
promised to never leave him.

Cain Murders Abel

4 Now the man knew his wife Eve,
and she conceived and bore Cain,
saying, "I have produced[n] a man with the
help of the LORD." [2]Next she bore his
brother Abel. Now Abel was a keeper of
sheep, and Cain a tiller of the ground.
[3]In the course of time Cain brought to
the LORD an offering of the fruit of the
ground, [4]and Abel for his part brought
of the firstlings of his flock, their fat
portions. And the LORD had regard for
Abel and his offering, [5]but for Cain and
his offering he had no regard. So Cain
was very angry, and his countenance fell.
[6]The LORD said to Cain, "Why are you
angry, and why has your countenance
fallen? [7]If you do well, will you not be
accepted? And if you do not do well, sin
is lurking at the door; its desire is for
you, but you must master it."

8 Cain said to his brother Abel, "Let
us go out to the field."[o] And when they
were in the field, Cain rose up against
his brother Abel, and killed him. [9]Then
the LORD said to Cain, "Where is your

---

[k] Or to Adam   [l] In Heb Eve resembles the word
for living   [m] Or for Adam   [n] The verb in Heb
resembles the word for Cain   [o] Sam Gk Syr
Compare Vg; MT lacks Let us go out to the field

brother Abel?" He said, "I do not know; am I my brother's keeper?" [10]And the LORD said, "What have you done? Listen; your brother's blood is crying out to me from the ground! [11]And now you are cursed from the ground, which has opened its mouth to receive your brother's blood from your hand. [12]When you till the ground, it will no longer yield to you its strength; you will be a fugitive and a wanderer on the earth." [13]Cain said to the LORD, "My punishment is greater than I can bear! [14]Today you have driven me away from the soil, and I shall be hidden from your face; I shall be a fugitive and a wanderer on the earth, and anyone who meets me may kill me." [15]Then the LORD said to him, "Not so![p] Whoever kills Cain will suffer a sevenfold vengeance." And the LORD put a mark on Cain, so that no one who came upon him would kill him. [16]Then Cain went away from the presence of the LORD, and settled in the land of Nod,[q] east of Eden.

Beginnings of Civilization

17 Cain knew his wife, and she conceived and bore Ē´noch; and he built a city, and named it Ē´noch after his son Ē´noch. [18]To Ē´noch was born Ī´rad; and Ī´rad was the father of Me·hū´ja·el, and Me·hū´ja·el the father of Me·thū´sha·el, and Me·thū´sha·el the father of Lā´mech. [19]Lā´mech took two wives; the name of the one was Ā´dah, and the name of the other Zil´lah. [20]Ā´dah bore Jā´bal; he was the ancestor of those who live in tents and have livestock. [21]His brother's name was Jū´bal; he was the ancestor of all those who play the lyre and pipe. [22]Zil´lah bore Tū´bal-cāin, who made all kinds of bronze and iron tools. The sister of Tū´bal-cāin was Nā´a·mah.

23 Lā´mech said to his wives:
"Ā´dah and Zil´lah, hear my voice;
    you wives of Lā´mech, listen to
    what I say:
I have killed a man for wounding me,
    a young man for striking me.

[24] If Cain is avenged sevenfold,
    truly Lā´mech seventy-sevenfold."

25 Adam knew his wife again, and she bore a son and named him Seth, for she said, "God has appointed[r] for me another child instead of Abel, because Cain killed him." [26]To Seth also a son was born, and he named him Ē´nosh. At that time people began to invoke the name of the LORD.

Adam's Descendants to Noah and His Sons

5 This is the list of the descendants of Adam. When God created humankind,[s] he made them[t] in the likeness of God. [2]Male and female he created them, and he blessed them and named them "Humankind"[s] when they were created.

3 When Adam had lived one hundred thirty years, he became the father of a son in his likeness, according to his image, and named him Seth. [4]The days of Adam after he became the father of Seth were eight hundred years; and he had other sons and daughters. [5]Thus all the days that Adam lived were nine hundred thirty years; and he died.

6 When Seth had lived one hundred five years, he became the father of Ē´nosh. [7]Seth lived after the birth of Ē´nosh eight hundred seven years, and had other sons and daughters. [8]Thus all the days of Seth were nine hundred twelve years; and he died.

9 When Ē´nosh had lived ninety years, he became the father of Kē´nan. [10]Ē´nosh lived after the birth of Kē´nan eight hundred fifteen years, and had other sons and daughters. [11]Thus all the days of Ē´nosh were nine hundred five years; and he died.

12 When Kē´nan had lived seventy years, he became the father of Ma·hal´a·lel. [13]Kē´nan lived after the birth of Ma·hal´a·lel eight hundred and forty years, and had other sons and daughters. [14]Thus all

[p] Gk Syr Vg: Heb *Therefore*   [q] That is *Wandering*
[r] The verb in Heb resembles the word for *Seth*
[s] Heb *adam*   [t] Heb *him*

the days of Kē´nan were nine hundred and ten years; and he died.

15 When Ma·hal´a·lel had lived sixty-five years, he became the father of Jar´ed. ¹⁶Ma·hal´a·lel lived after the birth of Jar´ed eight hundred thirty years, and had other sons and daughters. ¹⁷Thus all the days of Ma·hal´a·lel were eight hundred ninety-five years; and he died.

18 When Jar´ed had lived one hundred sixty-two years he became the father of Ē´noch. ¹⁹Jar´ed lived after the birth of Ē´noch eight hundred years, and had other sons and daughters. ²⁰Thus all the days of Jar´ed were nine hundred sixty-two years; and he died.

21 When Ē´noch had lived sixty-five years, he became the father of Me·thū´se·lah. ²²Ē´noch walked with God after the birth of Me·thū´se·lah three hundred years, and had other sons and daughters. ²³Thus all the days of Ē´noch were three hundred sixty-five years. ²⁴Ē´noch walked with God; then he was no more, because God took him.

> **Check it out!**
> Methuselah lived for 969 years. He is the oldest person in the Bible. How old is the oldest person in your family?

25 When Me·thū´se·lah had lived one hundred eighty-seven years, he became the father of Lā´mech. ²⁶Me·thū´se·lah lived after the birth of Lā´mech seven hundred eighty-two years, and had other sons and daughters. ²⁷Thus all the days of Me·thū´se·lah were nine hundred sixty-nine years; and he died.

28 When Lā´mech had lived one hundred eighty-two years, he became the father of a son; ²⁹he named him Noah, saying, "Out of the ground that the LORD has cursed this one shall bring us relief from our work and from the toil of our hands." ³⁰Lā´mech lived after the

birth of Noah five hundred ninety-five years, and had other sons and daughters. ³¹Thus all the days of Lā´mech were seven hundred seventy-seven years; and he died.

32 After Noah was five hundred years old, Noah became the father of Shem, Ham, and Jā´pheth.

The Wickedness of Humankind

6 When people began to multiply on the face of the ground, and daughters were born to them, ²the sons of God saw that they were fair; and they took wives for themselves of all that they chose. ³Then the LORD said, "My spirit shall not abide*ᵘ* in mortals forever, for they are flesh; their days shall be one hundred twenty years." ⁴The Neph´i·lim were on the earth in those days—and also afterward—when the sons of God went in to the daughters of humans, who bore children to them. These were the heroes that were of old, warriors of renown.

5 The LORD saw that the wickedness of humankind was great in the earth, and that every inclination of the thoughts of their hearts was only evil continually. ⁶And the LORD was sorry that he had made humankind on the earth, and it grieved him to his heart. ⁷So the LORD said, "I will blot out from the earth the human beings I have created— people together with animals and creeping things and birds of the air, for I am sorry that I have made them." ⁸But Noah found favor in the sight of the LORD.

Noah tried his best to live the way God wanted him to live. He obeyed and honored God. This is why Genesis 6:9 tells us that Noah walked with God.

Noah Pleases God

9 These are the descendants of Noah. Noah was a righteous man, blameless in

ᵘ Meaning of Heb uncertain

his generation; Noah walked with God. ¹⁰And Noah had three sons, Shem, Ham, and Jā′pheth.

11 Now the earth was corrupt in God's sight, and the earth was filled with violence. ¹²And God saw that the earth was corrupt; for all flesh had corrupted its ways upon the earth. ¹³And God said to Noah, "I have determined to make an end of all flesh, for the earth is filled with violence because of them; now I am going to destroy them along with the earth. ¹⁴Make yourself an ark of cypressᵛ wood; make rooms in the ark, and cover it inside and out with pitch. ¹⁵This is how you are to make it: the length of the ark three hundred cubits, its width fifty cubits, and its height thirty cubits.

Measurements in the Bible are given in cubits. One cubit is about 18 inches. That would mean the ark was a rectangle about 450 feet long, 75 feet wide, and 45 feet high.

¹⁶Make a roofʷ for the ark, and finish it to a cubit above; and put the door of the ark in its side; make it with lower, second, and third decks. ¹⁷For my part, I am going to bring a flood of waters on the earth, to destroy from under heaven all flesh in which is the breath of life; everything that is on the earth shall die. ¹⁸But I will establish my covenant with you; and you shall come into the ark, you, your sons, your wife, and your sons' wives with you. ¹⁹And of every living thing, of all flesh, you shall bring two of every kind into the ark, to keep them alive with you; they shall be male and female. ²⁰Of the birds according to their kinds, and of the animals according to their kinds, of every creeping thing of the ground according to its kind, two of every kind shall come in to you, to keep them alive. ²¹Also take with you every

kind of food that is eaten, and store it up; and it shall serve as food for you and for them." ²²Noah did this; he did all that God commanded him.

The Great Flood

7 Then the LORD said to Noah, "Go into the ark, you and all your household, for I have seen that you alone are righteous before me in this generation. ²Take with you seven pairs of all clean animals, the male and its mate; and a pair of the animals that are not clean, the male and its mate; ³and seven pairs of the birds of the air also, male and female, to keep their kind alive on the face of all the earth. ⁴For in seven days I will send rain on the earth for forty days and forty nights; and every living thing that I have made I will blot out from the face of the ground." ⁵And Noah did all that the LORD had commanded him.

6 Noah was six hundred years old when the flood of waters came on the earth. ⁷And Noah with his sons and his wife and his sons' wives went into the ark to escape the waters of the flood. ⁸Of clean animals, and of animals that are not clean, and of birds, and of everything that creeps on the ground, ⁹two and two, male and female, went into the ark with Noah, as God had commanded Noah. ¹⁰And after seven days the waters of the flood came on the earth.

11 In the six hundredth year of Noah's life, in the second month, on the seventeenth day of the month, on that day all the fountains of the great deep burst forth, and the windows of the

When God saw that the people on the earth were not following God's ways, God was sad. But instead of starting over, God chose the best of creation and set it apart for a special purpose. God gave humanity a second chance.

ᵛ Meaning of Heb uncertain   ʷ Or *window*

heavens were opened. ¹²The rain fell on the earth forty days and forty nights. ¹³On the very same day Noah with his sons, Shem and Ham and Jā´pheth, and Noah's wife and the three wives of his sons entered the ark, ¹⁴they and every wild animal of every kind, and all domestic animals of every kind, and every creeping thing that creeps on the earth, and every bird of every kind— every bird, every winged creature. ¹⁵They went into the ark with Noah, two and two of all flesh in which there was the breath of life. ¹⁶And those that entered, male and female of all flesh, went in as God had commanded him; and the LORD shut him in.

17 The flood continued forty days on the earth; and the waters increased, and bore up the ark, and it rose high above the earth. ¹⁸The waters swelled and increased greatly on the earth; and the ark floated on the face of the waters. ¹⁹The waters swelled so mightily on the earth that all the high mountains under the whole heaven were covered; ²⁰the waters swelled above the mountains, covering them fifteen cubits deep. ²¹And all flesh died that moved on the earth, birds, domestic animals, wild animals, all swarming creatures that swarm on the earth, and all human beings; ²²everything on dry land in whose nostrils was the breath of life died. ²³He blotted out every living thing that was on the face of the ground, human beings and animals and creeping things and birds of the air; they were blotted out from the earth. Only Noah was left, and those that were with him in the ark. ²⁴And the waters swelled on the earth for one hundred fifty days.

The Flood Subsides

8 But God remembered Noah and all the wild animals and all the domestic animals that were with him in the ark. And God made a wind blow over the earth, and the waters subsided; ²the fountains of the deep and the win-

dows of the heavens were closed, the rain from the heavens was restrained, ³and the waters gradually receded from the earth. At the end of one hundred fifty days the waters had abated; ⁴and in the seventh month, on the seventeenth day of the month, the ark came to rest on the mountains of Ar´a·rat. ⁵The waters continued to abate until the tenth month; in the tenth month, on the first day of the month, the tops of the mountains appeared.

6 At the end of forty days Noah opened the window of the ark that he had made ⁷and sent out the raven; and it went to and fro until the waters were dried up from the earth. ⁸Then he sent out the dove from him, to see if the waters had subsided from the face of the ground; ⁹but the dove found no place to set its foot, and it returned to him to the ark, for the waters were still on the face of the whole earth. So he put out his hand and took it and brought it into the ark with him. ¹⁰He waited another seven days, and again he sent out the dove from the ark; ¹¹and the dove came back to him in the evening, and there in its beak was a freshly plucked olive leaf; so Noah knew that the waters had subsided from the earth. ¹²Then he waited another seven days, and sent out the dove; and it did not return to him any more.

13 In the six hundred first year, in the first month, the first day of the month, the waters were dried up from the earth; and Noah removed the covering of the ark, and looked, and saw that the face of the ground was drying. ¹⁴In the second month, on the twenty-seventh day of the month, the earth was dry. ¹⁵Then God said to Noah, ¹⁶"Go out of the ark, you and your wife, and your sons and your sons' wives with you. ¹⁷Bring out with you every living thing that is with you of all flesh—birds and animals and every creeping thing that creeps on the earth—so that they may abound on the earth, and be fruitful and

As soon as Noah left the ark, he built an altar so that he could worship God. God blessed Noah's family and promised that a flood would never again destroy all living things.

multiply on the earth." ¹⁸So Noah went out with his sons and his wife and his sons' wives. ¹⁹And every animal, every creeping thing, and every bird, everything that moves on the earth, went out of the ark by families.

God's Promise to Noah

20 Then Noah built an altar to the Lord, and took of every clean animal and of every clean bird, and offered burnt offerings on the altar. ²¹And when the Lord smelled the pleasing odor, the Lord said in his heart, "I will never again curse the ground because of humankind, for the inclination of the human heart is evil from youth; nor will I ever again destroy every living creature as I have done.

²² As long as the earth endures,
　　seedtime and harvest, cold and
　　　　heat,
　　summer and winter, day and night,
　　　　shall not cease."

The Covenant with Noah

9 God blessed Noah and his sons, and said to them, "Be fruitful and multiply, and fill the earth. ²The fear and dread of you shall rest on every animal of the earth, and on every bird of the air, on everything that creeps on the ground, and on all the fish of the sea; into your hand they are delivered. ³Every moving thing that lives shall be food for you; and just as I gave you the green plants, I give you everything. ⁴Only, you shall not eat flesh with its life, that is, its blood. ⁵For your own lifeblood I will surely require a reckoning: from every animal I will require it and from human beings, each

one for the blood of another, I will require a reckoning for human life.
⁶ Whoever sheds the blood of a human,
　　by a human shall that person's
　　　　blood be shed;
　　for in his own image
　　　　God made humankind.
⁷And you, be fruitful and multiply, abound on the earth and multiply in it."

A covenant is an important promise. "Covenant" is the word we use for the special relationship God had made between God and humanity.

8 Then God said to Noah and to his sons with him, ⁹"As for me, I am establishing my covenant with you and your descendants after you, ¹⁰and with every living creature that is with you, the birds, the domestic animals, and every animal of the earth with you, as many as came out of the ark.ˣ ¹¹I establish my covenant with you, that never again shall all flesh be cut off by the waters of a flood, and never again shall there be a flood to destroy the earth." ¹²God said, "This is the sign of the covenant that I make between me and you and every living creature that is with you, for all future generations: ¹³I have set my bow in the clouds, and it shall be a sign of the covenant between me and the earth. ¹⁴When I bring clouds over the earth and the bow is seen in the clouds, ¹⁵I will remember my covenant that is between me and you and every living creature of all flesh; and the waters shall never again become a flood to destroy all flesh. ¹⁶When the bow is in the

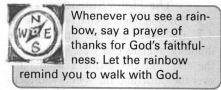

Whenever you see a rainbow, say a prayer of thanks for God's faithfulness. Let the rainbow remind you to walk with God.

ˣ Gk: Heb adds *every animal of the earth*

"When the bow is in the clouds, I will see it and remember the everlasting covenant between God and every living creature of all flesh that is on the earth."
Genesis 9:16

clouds, I will see it and remember the everlasting covenant between God and every living creature of all flesh that is on the earth." ¹⁷God said to Noah, "This is the sign of the covenant that I have established between me and all flesh that is on the earth."

Noah and His Sons

18 The sons of Noah who went out of the ark were Shem, Ham, and Jāʹpheth. Ham was the father of Cāʹnaan. ¹⁹These three were the sons of Noah; and from these the whole earth was peopled.

20 Noah, a man of the soil, was the first to plant a vineyard. ²¹He drank some of the wine and became drunk, and he lay uncovered in his tent. ²²And Ham, the father of Cāʹnaan, saw the nakedness of his father, and told his two brothers outside. ²³Then Shem and Jāʹpheth took a garment, laid it on both their shoulders, and walked backward and covered the nakedness of their father; their faces were turned away, and they did not see their father's nakedness. ²⁴When Noah awoke from his wine and knew what his youngest son had done to him, ²⁵he said,

"Cursed be Cāʹnaan;
lowest of slaves shall he be to his
brothers."
²⁶ He also said,
"Blessed by the LORD my God be Shem;
and let Cāʹnaan be his slave.
²⁷ May God make space forʸ Jāʹpheth,
and let him live in the tents of Shem;
and let Cāʹnaan be his slave."

28 After the flood Noah lived three hundred fifty years. ²⁹All the days of Noah were nine hundred fifty years; and he died.

Nations Descended from Noah

10 These are the descendants of Noah's sons, Shem, Ham, and Jāʹpheth; children were born to them after the flood.

2 The descendants of Jāʹpheth: Gōʹmer, Māʹgog, Māʹdaī, Jāʹvan, Tūʹbal, Mēʹshech, and Tīʹras. ³The descendants of Gōʹmer: Ashʹkeʹnaz, Rīʹphath, and Tōʹgarʹmah. ⁴The descendants of Jāʹvan: Eʹliʹshah, Tarʹshish, Kitʹtim, and Rodʹaʹnim.ᶻ ⁵From these the coastland peoples spread. These are the descendants of Jāʹpethᵃ in their lands, with their own language, by their families, in their nations.

6 The descendants of Ham: Cush, Egypt, Put, and Cāʹnaan. ⁷The descendants of Cush: Sēʹba, Havʹiʹlah, Sabʹtah, Rāʹaʹmah, and Sabʹteʹca. The descendants of Rāʹaʹmah: Shēʹba and Dēʹdan. ⁸Cush became the father of Nimʹrod; he was the first on earth to become a mighty warrior. ⁹He was a mighty hunter before the LORD; therefore it is said, "Like Nimʹrod a mighty hunter before the LORD." ¹⁰The beginning of his kingdom was Bāʹbel, Eʹrech, and Acʹcad, all of them in the land of Shīʹnar. ¹¹From that land he went into Assyria, and built Ninʹeʹveh, Reʹhōʹbothʹir, Cāʹlah, and ¹²Rēʹsen between Ninʹeʹveh and Cāʹlah; that is the great city. ¹³Egypt became the father of Lūʹdim, Anʹaʹmim, Leʹhāʹbim, Naphʹtūʹhim, ¹⁴Pathʹrūʹsim, Casʹlūʹhim, and Caphʹtoʹrim, from which the Phiʹlisʹtines come.ᵇ

15 Cāʹnaan became the father of Sīʹdon his firstborn, and Heth, ¹⁶and the Jebʹūʹsites, the Amʹoʹrītes, the Girʹgaʹshītes, ¹⁷the Hīʹvītes, the Arʹkītes, the Sīʹnites, ¹⁸the Arʹvadʹites, the Zemʹaʹrītes, and the Hāʹmathʹites. Afterward the families of the Cāʹnaanʹites spread abroad. ¹⁹And the territory of the Cāʹnaanʹites extended from Sīʹdon, in the direction of

ʸ Heb *yapht,* a play on *Japheth*   ᶻ Heb Mss Sam Gk See 1 Chr 1.7: MT *Dodanim*   ᵃ Compare verses 20, 31. Heb lacks *These are the descendants of Japheth*   ᵇ Cn: Heb *Casluhim, from which the Philistines come, and Caphtorim*

Gē´rar, as far as Gā´za, and in the direction of Sod´om, Go·mor´rah, Ad´mah, and Ze·boi´im, as far as Lā´sha. ²⁰These are the descendants of Ham, by their families, their languages, their lands, and their nations.

21 To Shem also, the father of all the children of Ē´ber, the elder brother of Jā´pheth, children were born. ²²The descendants of Shem: Ē´lam, As´shur, Ar·pach´shad, Lud, and Ar´am. ²³The descendants of Ar´am: Uz, Hul, Gē´ther, and Mash. ²⁴Ar·pach´shad became the father of Shē´lah; and Shē´lah became the father of Ē´ber. ²⁵To Ē´ber were born two sons: the name of the one was Pē´leg,ᶜ for in his days the earth was divided, and his brother's name was Jok´tan. ²⁶Jok´tan became the father of Al·mō´dad, Shē´leph, Hā·zar·mā´veth, Jē´rah, ²⁷Ha·dor´am, Ū´zal, Dik´lah, ²⁸Ō´bal, A·bim´a·el, Shē´ba, ²⁹Ō´phir, Hav´i·lah, and Jō´bab; all these were the descendants of Jok´tan. ³⁰The territory in which they lived extended from Mē´sha in the direction of Sē´phar, the hill country of the east. ³¹These are the descendants of Shem, by their families, their languages, their lands, and their nations.

32 These are the families of Noah's sons, according to their genealogies, in their nations; and from these the nations spread abroad on the earth after the flood.

The Tower of Babel

11 Now the whole earth had one language and the same words. ²And as they migrated from the east,ᵈ they came upon a plain in the land of Shī´nar and settled there. ³And they said to one another, "Come, let us make bricks, and burn them thoroughly." And they had brick for stone, and bitumen for mortar. ⁴Then they said, "Come, let us build ourselves a city, and a tower with its top in the heavens, and let us make a name for ourselves; otherwise we shall be scattered abroad upon the face of the whole earth." ⁵The LORD came

The people decided to build a tower that would reach to heaven. The word *babel* comes from a Hebrew word meaning "to mix." So God "mixed" their languages so that they could no longer understand each other. God then scattered the people across the earth.

down to see the city and the tower, which mortals had built. ⁶And the LORD said, "Look, they are one people, and they have all one language; and this is only the beginning of what they will do; nothing that they propose to do will now be impossible for them. ⁷Come, let us go down, and confuse their language there, so that they will not understand one another's speech." ⁸So the LORD scattered them abroad from there over the face of all the earth, and they left off building the city. ⁹Therefore it was called Bā´bel, because there the LORD confusedᵉ the language of all the earth; and from there the LORD scattered them abroad over the face of all the earth.

Descendants of Shem

10 These are the descendants of Shem. When Shem was one hundred years old, he became the father of Ar·pach´shad two years after the flood; ¹¹and Shem lived after the birth of Ar·pach´shad five hundred years, and had other sons and daughters.

12 When Ar·pach´shad had lived thirty-five years, he became the father of Shē´lah; ¹³and Ar·pach´shad lived after the birth of Shē´lah four hundred three years, and had other sons and daughters.

14 When Shē´lah had lived thirty years, he became the father of Ē´ber; ¹⁵and Shē´lah lived after the birth of Ē´ber four hundred three years, and had other sons and daughters.

ᶜ That is *Division*   ᵈ Or *migrated eastward*
ᵉ Heb *balal*, meaning *to confuse*

16 When Ē´ber had lived thirty-four years, he became the father of Pē´leg; ¹⁷and Ē´ber lived after the birth of Pē´leg four hundred thirty years, and had other sons and daughters.

18 When Pē´leg had lived thirty years, he became the father of Rē´u; ¹⁹and Pē´leg lived after the birth of Rē´u two hundred nine years, and had other sons and daughters.

20 When Rē´u had lived thirty-two years, he became the father of Sē´rug; ²¹and Rē´u lived after the birth of Sē´rug two hundred seven years, and had other sons and daughters.

22 When Sē´rug had lived thirty years, he became the father of Nā´hor; ²³and Sē´rug lived after the birth of Nā´hor two hundred years, and had other sons and daughters.

24 When Nā´hor had lived twenty-nine years, he became the father of Tē´rah; ²⁵and Nā´hor lived after the birth of Tē´rah one hundred nineteen years, and had other sons and daughters.

26 When Tē´rah had lived seventy years, he became the father of Abram, Nā´hor, and Har´an.

Descendants of Terah

27 Now these are the descendants of Tē´rah. Tē´rah was the father of Abram, Nā´hor, and Har´an; and Har´an was the father of Lot. ²⁸Har´an died before his father Tē´rah in the land of his birth, in Ūr of the Chal·dē´ans. ²⁹Abram and Nā´hor took wives; the name of Abram's wife was Sar´aī, and the name of Nā´hor's wife was Mil´cah. She was the daughter of Har´an the father of Mil´cah and Is´cah. ³⁰Now Sar´aī was barren; she had no child.

31 Tē´rah took his son Abram and his grandson Lot son of Har´an, and his daughter-in-law Sar´aī, his son Abram's wife, and they went out together from Ūr of the Chal·dē´ans to go into the land of Cā´naan; but when they came to Har´an, they settled there. ³²The days of Tē´rah were two hundred five years; and Tē´rah died in Har´an.

Abraham (who was at first called Abram) is known as the father of the Israelites. Christians also trace their spiritual roots back to Abraham. Abraham wandered with his family close to Haran. Obeying God, he left Haran and led his family to Canaan, the Land of Promise. God made a covenant (or promise), with Abraham and promised he would be the father of a great nation. God promised that through Abraham all the families of the earth would be blessed.

The Call of Abram

12 Now the LORD said to Abram, "Go from your country and your kindred and your father's house to the land that I will show you. ²I will make of you a great nation, and I will bless you, and make your name great, so that you will be a blessing. ³I will bless those who bless you, and the one who curses you I will curse; and in you all the families of the earth shall be blessed."ᶠ

4 So Abram went, as the LORD had told him; and Lot went with him. Abram was seventy-five years old when he departed from Har´an. ⁵Abram took his wife Sar´aī and his brother's son Lot, and all the possessions that they had gathered, and the persons whom they had acquired in Har´an; and they set forth to go to the land of Cā´naan. When they had come to the land of Cā´naan, ⁶Abram passed through the land to the place at Shē´chem, to the oakᵍ of Mō´reh. At that time the Cā´naan·ītes were in the land. ⁷Then the LORD appeared to Abram, and said, "To your offspringʰ I will give this land." So he built there an altar to the LORD, who had appeared to

ᶠ Or by you all the families of the earth shall bless themselves   ᵍ Or terebinth   ʰ Heb seed him. [8]From there he moved on to the hill country on the east of Beth´el, and pitched his tent, with Beth´el on the west and Aī on the east; and there he built an altar to the LORD and invoked the name of the LORD. [9]And Abram journeyed on by stages toward the Neg´eb.

Abram and Sarai in Egypt

10 Now there was a famine in the land. So Abram went down to Egypt to reside there as an alien, for the famine was severe in the land. [11]When he was about to enter Egypt, he said to his wife Sar´aī, "I know well that you are a woman beautiful in appearance; [12]and when the Egyptians see you, they will say, 'This is his wife'; then they will kill me, but they will let you live. [13]Say you are my sister, so that it may go well with me because of you, and that my life may be spared on your account." [14]When Abram entered Egypt the Egyptians saw that the woman was very beautiful. [15]When the officials of Pharaoh saw her, they praised her to Pharaoh. And the woman was taken into Pharaoh's house. [16]And for her sake he dealt well with Abram; and he had sheep, oxen, male donkeys, male and female slaves, female donkeys, and camels.

17 But the LORD afflicted Pharaoh and his house with great plagues because of Sar´aī, Abram's wife. [18]So Pharaoh called Abram, and said, "What is this you have done to me? Why did you not tell me that she was your wife? [19]Why did you say, 'She is my sister,' so that I took her for my wife? Now then, here is your wife, take her, and be gone." [20]And Pharaoh gave his men orders concerning him; and they set him on the way, with his wife and all that he had.

Abram and Lot Separate

13 So Abram went up from Egypt, he and his wife, and all that he had, and Lot with him, into the Neg´eb.

2 Now Abram was very rich in livestock, in silver, and in gold. [3]He jour-

> "Then Abram said to Lot, 'Let there be no strife between you and me...for we are kindred.'" Genesis 13:8

neyed on by stages from the Neg´eb as far as Beth´el, to the place where his tent had been at the beginning, between Beth´el and Aī, [4]to the place where he had made an altar at the first; and there Abram called on the name of the LORD. [5]Now Lot, who went with Abram, also had flocks and herds and tents, [6]so that the land could not support both of them living together; for their possessions were so great that they could not live together, [7]and there was strife between the herders of Abram's livestock and the herders of Lot's livestock. At that time the Cā´naan·ītes and the Per´iz·zītes lived in the land.

8 Then Abram said to Lot, "Let there be no strife between you and me, and between your herders and my herders; for we are kindred. [9]Is not the whole land before you? Separate yourself from me. If you take the left hand, then I will go to the right; or if you take the right hand, then I will go to the left." [10]Lot looked about him, and saw that the plain of the Jordan was well watered every-

Abraham acted out of love and generosity. For Abraham, staying friends with his family and following God was more important than being sure he had the best of the land God had to offer.

Are there ever disagreements in your family? Are there times when people are jealous or selfish? Are there times when you just can't get along with someone? What can you do about it? Pray for peace for each member of your family, starting with yourself.

where like the garden of the Lord, like the land of Egypt, in the direction of Zṓar; this was before the Lord had destroyed Sod'om and Go·mor'rah. [11]So Lot chose for himself all the plain of the Jordan, and Lot journeyed eastward; thus they separated from each other. [12]Abram settled in the land of Cā'naan, while Lot settled among the cities of the Plain and moved his tent as far as Sod'om. [13]Now the people of Sod'om were wicked, great sinners against the Lord.

14 The Lord said to Abram, after Lot had separated from him, "Raise your eyes now, and look from the place where you are, northward and southward and eastward and westward; [15]for all the land that you see I will give to you and to your offspring[i] forever. [16]I will make your offspring like the dust of the earth; so that if one can count the dust of the earth, your offspring also can be counted. [17]Rise up, walk through the length and the breadth of the land, for I will give it to you." [18]So Abram moved his tent, and came and settled by the oaks[j] of Mam're, which are at Hē'bron; and there he built an altar to the Lord.

In early Old Testament times an altar was usually a mound of earth or a block of stone supported by a pile of smaller stones. People made offerings to God on the altar. In later Old Testament times, altars were bigger and more elaborate.

Lot's Captivity and Rescue

14 In the days of King Am'ra·phel of Shī'nar, King Ar'i·och of El·lā'sar, King Ched·or·la·ō'mer of Ē'lam, and King Tī'dal of Goi'im, [2]these kings made war with King Bē'ra of Sod'om, King Bir'sha of Go·mor'rah, King Shī'nab of Ad'mah, King Shem·ē'ber of Ze·boi'im, and the king of Bē'la (that is, Zṓar). [3]All these joined forces in the Valley of Sid'dim (that is, the Dead Sea).[k] [4]Twelve years they had served Ched·or·la·ō'mer, but in the thirteenth year they rebelled. [5]In the fourteenth year Ched·or·la·ō'mer and the kings who were with him came and subdued the Reph'a·im in Ash'-te·roth-kar·nā'im, the Zū'zim in Ham, the Ē'mim in Shā'veh-kir·i·a·thā'im, [6]and the Hor'ites in the hill country of Sē'ir as far as El-par'an on the edge of the wilderness; [7]then they turned back and came to En-mish'pat (that is, Kā'desh), and subdued all the country of the A·mal'e·kītes, and also the Am'o·rītes who lived in Haz'a·zon-tā'mar. [8]Then the king of Sod'om, the king of Go·mor'rah, the king of Ad'mah, the king of Ze·boi'im, and the king of Bē'la (that is, Zṓar) went out, and they joined battle in the Valley of Sid'dim [9]with King Ched·-or·la·ō'mer of Ē'lam, King Tī'dal of Goi'im, King Am'ra·phel of Shī'nar, and King Ar'i·och of El·lā'sar, four kings against five. [10]Now the Valley of Sid'dim was full of bitumen pits; and as the kings of Sod'om and Go·mor'rah fled, some fell into them, and the rest fled to the hill country. [11]So the enemy took all the goods of Sod'om and Go·mor'rah, and all their provisions, and went their way; [12]they also took Lot, the son of Abram's brother, who lived in Sod'om, and his goods, and departed.

13 Then one who had escaped came and told Abram the Hebrew, who was living by the oaks[l] of Mam're the Am'-o·rīte, brother of Esh'col and of Ā'ner; these were allies of Abram. [14]When Abram heard that his nephew had been taken captive, he led forth his trained men, born in his house, three hundred eighteen of them, and went in pursuit as far as Dan. [15]He divided his forces against them by night, he and his servants, and routed them and pursued them to Hō'bah, north of Damascus.

[i] Heb *seed*   [j] Or *terebinths*   [k] Heb *Salt Sea*
[l] Or *terebinths*

¹⁶Then he brought back all the goods, and also brought back his nephew Lot with his goods, and the women and the people.

Abram Blessed by Melchizedek

17 After his return from the defeat of Ched·or·la·ō′mer and the kings who were with him, the king of Sod′om went out to meet him at the Valley of Shā′veh (that is, the King's Valley). ¹⁸And King Mel·chiz′e·dek of Salem brought out bread and wine; he was priest of God Most High.ᵐ ¹⁹He blessed him and said,

"Blessed be Abram by God Most High,ᵐ
maker of heaven and earth;
²⁰ and blessed be God Most High,ᵐ
who has delivered your enemies
into your hand!"

And Abram gave him one-tenth of everything. ²¹Then the king of Sod′om said to Abram, "Give me the persons, but take the goods for yourself." ²²But Abram said to the king of Sod′om, "I have sworn to the LORD, God Most High,ᵐ maker of heaven and earth, ²³that I would not take a thread or a sandal-thong or anything that is yours, so that you might not say, 'I have made Abram rich.' ²⁴I will take nothing but what the young men have eaten, and the share of the men who went with me— Ā′ner, Esh′col, and Mam′re. Let them take their share."

Melchizedek was a Canaanite king and priest of Salem (Jerusalem) who prepared a meal for Abraham and blessed him. Melchizedek had both royal and priestly power in the city of Salem before the Israelites came. David claimed to be his successor. Melchizedek became the symbol of an ideal priest-king. Read Psalm 110:4.

"He [God] brought him outside and said, 'Look toward heaven and count the stars, if you are able to count them.' Then he said to him, 'So shall your descendants be.' And he believed the LORD; and the LORD reckoned it to him as righteousness."
Genesis 15:5–6

God's Covenant with Abram

15 After these things the word of the LORD came to Abram in a vision, "Do not be afraid, Abram, I am your shield; your reward shall be very great." ²But Abram said, "O Lord GOD, what will you give me, for I continue childless, and the heir of my house is El·i·ē′-zer of Damascus?"ⁿ ³And Abram said, "You have given me no offspring, and so a slave born in my house is to be my heir." ⁴But the word of the LORD came to him, "This man shall not be your heir; no one but your very own issue shall be your heir." ⁵He brought him outside and said, "Look toward heaven and count the stars, if you are able to count them." Then he said to him, "So shall your descendants be." ⁶And he believed the LORD; and the LORDᵒ reckoned it to him as righteousness.

> To be righteous means to be free from wrong or sin and to do what is right.

7 Then he said to him, "I am the LORD who brought you from Ūr of the Chal·dē′-ans, to give you this land to possess." ⁸But he said, "O Lord GOD, how am I to know that I shall possess it?" ⁹He said to him, "Bring me a heifer three years old, a female goat three years old, a ram three years old, a turtledove, and a young pigeon." ¹⁰He brought him all these and cut them in two, laying each half over against the other; but he did not cut the birds in two. ¹¹And when birds of prey came down on the carcasses, Abram drove them away.

ᵐ Heb *El Elyon*   ⁿ Meaning of Heb uncertain
ᵒ Heb *he*

12 As the sun was going down, a deep sleep fell upon Abram, and a deep and terrifying darkness descended upon him. [13]Then the LORD[p] said to Abram, "Know this for certain, that your offspring shall be aliens in a land that is not theirs, and shall be slaves there, and they shall be oppressed for four hundred years; [14]but I will bring judgment on the nation that they serve, and afterward they shall come out with great possessions. [15]As for yourself, you shall go to your ancestors in peace; you shall be buried in a good old age. [16]And they shall come back here in the fourth generation; for the iniquity of the Am´o·rītes is not yet complete."

17 When the sun had gone down and it was dark, a smoking fire pot and a flaming torch passed between these pieces. [18]On that day the LORD made a covenant with Abram, saying, "To your descendants I give this land, from the river of Egypt to the great river, the river Euphrates, [19]the land of the Ken´ītes, the Ken´iz·zītes, the Kad´mon·ītes, [20]the Hit´tītes, the Per´iz·zītes, the Reph´a·im, [21]the Am´o·rītes, the Cā´naan·ītes, the Gir´ga·shītes, and the Jeb´ū·sītes."

God had a special relationship with the family of Abraham, which was to become the people of Israel. God was to be their God, and they were to be God's people. This was the meaning of the original covenant God made with Abraham. When Jesus lived on earth, he spoke of a new covenant. The earliest Christians thought of their relationships to one another and to Jesus as a covenant that kept them together.

Read about God's covenant with Abraham in Genesis 12. Read what Jesus said in Matthew 26:28 and Mark 14:24.

The Birth of Ishmael

16 Now Sar´aī, Abram's wife, bore him no children. She had an Egyptian slave-girl whose name was Hā´gar, [2]and Sar´aī said to Abram, "You see that the LORD has prevented me from bearing children; go in to my slave-girl; it may be that I shall obtain children by her." And Abram listened to the voice of Sar´aī. [3]So, after Abram had lived ten years in the land of Cā´naan, Sar´aī, Abram's wife, took Hā´gar the Egyptian, her slave-girl, and gave her to her husband Abram as a wife. [4]He went in to Hā´gar, and she conceived; and when she saw that she had conceived, she looked with contempt on her mistress. [5]Then Sar´aī said to Abram, "May the wrong done to me be on you! I gave my slave-girl to your embrace, and when she saw that she had conceived, she looked on me with contempt. May the LORD judge between you and me!" [6]But Abram said to Sar´aī, "Your slave-girl is in your power; do to her as you please." Then Sar´aī dealt harshly with her, and she ran away from her.

7 The angel of the LORD found her by a spring of water in the wilderness, the spring on the way to Shur. [8]And he said, "Hā´gar, slave-girl of Sar´aī, where have you come from and where are you going?" She said, "I am running away from my mistress Sar´aī." [9]The angel of the LORD said to her, "Return to your mistress, and submit to her." [10]The angel of the LORD also said to her, "I will so greatly multiply your offspring that they cannot be counted for multitude." [11]And the angel of the LORD said to her,

"Now you have conceived and shall
    bear a son;
  you shall call him Ish´ma·el,[q]
  for the LORD has given heed to your
    affliction.
12 He shall be a wild ass of a man,
  with his hand against everyone,
    and everyone's hand against him;
  and he shall live at odds with all his kin."

[p] Heb *he*   [q] That is *God hears*

Sarah began to believe she would never give birth to a child and suggested that Abraham have a child with her serving woman, Hagar. This was a custom in Bible times. So Hagar gave birth to a son named Ishmael. Later, after Sarah gave birth to a son named Isaac, she became jealous of Ishmael and angry with Hagar. Sarah forced Abraham to send Hagar and Ishmael into the wilderness of Paran. Ishmael grew up in the wilderness, and God took care of his mother and him.

[13]So she named the LORD who spoke to her, "You are El-roi";[r] for she said, "Have I really seen God and remained alive after seeing him?"[s] [14]Therefore the well was called Be´er-la´haï-roi;[t] it lies between Kā´-desh and Bē´red.

15 Hā´gar bore Abram a son; and Abram named his son, whom Hā´gar bore, Ish´ma·el. [16]Abram was eighty-six years old when Hā´gar bore him[u] Ish´ma·el.

The Sign of the Covenant

17 When Abram was ninety-nine years old, the LORD appeared to Abram, and said to him, "I am God Almighty;[v] walk before me, and be blameless. [2]And I will make my covenant between me and you, and will make you exceedingly numerous." [3]Then Abram fell on his face; and God said to him, [4]"As for me, this is my covenant with you: You shall be the ancestor of a multitude of nations. [5]No longer shall your name be Abram,[w] but your name shall be Abraham;[x] for I have made you the ancestor of a multitude of nations. [6]I will make you exceedingly fruitful; and I will make nations of you, and kings shall come from you. [7]I will establish my covenant between me and

you, and your offspring after you throughout their generations, for an everlasting covenant, to be God to you and to your offspring[y] after you. [8]And I will give to you, and to your offspring after you, the land where you are now an alien, all the land of Cā´naan, for a perpetual holding; and I will be their God."

9 God said to Abraham, "As for you, you shall keep my covenant, you and your offspring after you throughout their generations. [10]This is my covenant, which you shall keep, between me and you and your offspring after you: Every male among you shall be circumcised. [11]You shall circumcise the flesh of your foreskins, and it shall be a sign of the covenant between me and you. [12]Throughout your generations every male among you shall be circumcised when he is eight days old, including the slave born in your house and the one bought with your money from any foreigner who is not of your offspring. [13]Both the slave born in your house and the one bought with your money must be circumcised. So shall my covenant be in your flesh an everlasting covenant. [14]Any uncircumcised male who is not circumcised in the flesh of his foreskin shall be cut off from his people; he has broken my covenant."

15 God said to Abraham, "As for Sar´aï your wife, you shall not call her Sar´aï, but Sarah shall be her name. [16]I will bless her, and moreover I will give you a son by her. I will bless her, and she shall give rise to nations; kings of peoples shall come from her." [17]Then Abraham fell on his face and laughed, and said to himself, "Can a child be born to a man who is a hundred years old? Can Sarah, who is ninety years old, bear a child?" [18]And Abraham said to God, "O that Ish´ma·el might live in your

---

[r] Perhaps *God of seeing* or *God who sees*
[s] Meaning of Heb uncertain   [t] That is *the Well of the Living One who sees me*   [u] Heb *Abram*
[v] Traditional rendering of Heb *El Shaddai*   [w] That is *exalted ancestor*   [x] Here taken to mean *ancestor of a multitude*   [y] Heb *seed*

sight!" [19]God said, "No, but your wife Sarah shall bear you a son, and you shall name him Isaac.[z] I will establish my covenant with him as an everlasting covenant for his offspring after him. [20]As for Ish′ma·el, I have heard you; I will bless him and make him fruitful and exceedingly numerous; he shall be the father of twelve princes, and I will make him a great nation. [21]But my covenant I will establish with Isaac, whom Sarah shall bear to you at this season next year." [22]And when he had finished talking with him, God went up from Abraham.

23 Then Abraham took his son Ish′-ma·el and all the slaves born in his house or bought with his money, every male among the men of Abraham's house, and he circumcised the flesh of their foreskins that very day, as God had said to him. [24]Abraham was ninety-nine years old when he was circumcised in the flesh of his foreskin. [25]And his son Ish′ma·el was thirteen years old when he was circumcised in the flesh of his foreskin. [26]That very day Abraham and his son Ish′ma·el were circumcised; [27]and all the men of his house, slaves born in the house and those bought with money from a foreigner, were circumcised with him.

A Son Promised to Abraham and Sarah

18 The LORD appeared to Abraham[a] by the oaks[b] of Mam′re, as he sat at the entrance of his tent in the heat of the day. [2]He looked up and saw three men standing near him. When he saw them, he ran from the tent entrance to meet them, and bowed down to the ground. [3]He said, "My lord, if I find favor with you, do not pass by your servant. [4]Let a little water be brought, and wash your feet, and rest yourselves under the tree. [5]Let me bring a little bread, that you may refresh yourselves, and after that you may pass on—since you have come to your servant." So they said, "Do as you have said." [6]And Abraham hastened into the tent to Sarah, and said, "Make ready quickly three measures[c] of choice flour, knead it, and make cakes." [7]Abraham ran to the herd, and took a calf, tender and good, and gave it to the servant, who hastened to prepare it. [8]Then he took curds and milk and the calf that he had prepared, and set it before them; and he stood by them under the tree while they ate.

9 They said to him, "Where is your wife Sarah?" And he said, "There, in the tent." [10]Then one said, "I will surely return to you in due season, and your wife Sarah shall have a son." And Sarah was listening at the tent entrance behind him. [11]Now Abraham and Sarah were old, advanced in age; it had ceased to be with Sarah after the manner of women. [12]So Sarah laughed to herself, saying, "After I have grown old, and my husband is old, shall I have pleasure?" [13]The LORD said to Abraham, "Why did Sarah laugh, and say, 'Shall I indeed bear a child, now that I am old?' [14]Is anything too wonderful for the LORD? At the set time I will return to you, in due season, and Sarah shall have a son." [15]But Sarah denied, saying, "I did not laugh"; for she was afraid. He said, "Oh yes, you did laugh."

Judgment Pronounced on Sodom

16 Then the men set out from there, and they looked toward Sod′om; and Abraham went with them to set them on their way. [17]The LORD said, "Shall I hide from Abraham what I am about to do, [18]seeing that Abraham shall become a great and mighty nation, and all the

When Abraham welcomed the three strangers, he found that he had welcomed and entertained God. Have you or your family ever done something nice for someone you didn't even know?

[z] That is *he laughs*   [a] Heb *him*   [b] Or *terebinths*
[c] Heb *seahs*

nations of the earth shall be blessed in him?[d] [19]No, for I have chosen[e] him, that he may charge his children and his household after him to keep the way of the LORD by doing righteousness and justice; so that the LORD may bring about for Abraham what he has promised him." [20]Then the LORD said, "How great is the outcry against Sod'om and Go·mor'rah and how very grave their sin! [21]I must go down and see whether they have done altogether according to the outcry that has come to me; and if not, I will know."

[22] So the men turned from there, and went toward Sod'om, while Abraham remained standing before the LORD.[f] [23]Then Abraham came near and said, "Will you indeed sweep away the righteous with the wicked? [24]Suppose there are fifty righteous within the city; will you then sweep away the place and not forgive it for the fifty righteous who are in it? [25]Far be it from you to do such a thing, to slay the righteous with the wicked, so that the righteous fare as the wicked! Far be that from you! Shall not the Judge of all the earth do what is just?" [26]And the LORD said, "If I find at Sod'om fifty righteous in the city, I will forgive the whole place for their sake." [27]Abraham answered, "Let me take it upon myself to speak to the Lord, I who am but dust and ashes. [28]Suppose five of the fifty righteous are lacking? Will you destroy the whole city for lack of five?" And he said, "I will not destroy it if I find forty-five there." [29]Again he spoke to him, "Suppose forty are found there." He answered, "For the sake of forty I will not do it." [30]Then he said, "Oh do not let the Lord be angry if I speak. Suppose thirty are found there." He answered, "I will not do it, if I find thirty there." [31]He said, "Let me take it upon myself to speak to the Lord. Suppose twenty are found there." He answered, "For the sake of twenty I will not destroy it." [32]Then he said, "Oh do not let the Lord be angry if

I speak just once more. Suppose ten are found there." He answered, "For the sake of ten I will not destroy it." [33]And the LORD went his way, when he had finished speaking to Abraham; and Abraham returned to his place.

The Depravity of Sodom

19 The two angels came to Sod'om in the evening, and Lot was sitting in the gateway of Sod'om. When Lot saw them, he rose to meet them, and bowed down with his face to the ground. [2]He said, "Please, my lords, turn aside to your servant's house and spend the night, and wash your feet; then you can rise early and go on your way." They said, "No; we will spend the night in the square." [3]But he urged them strongly; so they turned aside to him and entered his house; and he made them a feast, and baked unleavened bread, and they ate. [4]But before they lay down, the men of the city, the men of Sod'om, both young and old, all the people to the last man, surrounded the house; [5]and they called to Lot, "Where are the men who came to you tonight? Bring them out to us, so that we may know them." [6]Lot went out of the door to the men, shut the door after him, [7]and said, "I beg you, my brothers, do not act so wickedly. [8]Look, I have two daughters who have not known a man; let me bring them out to you, and do to them as you please; only do nothing to these men, for they have come under the shelter of my roof." [9]But they replied, "Stand back!" And they said, "This fellow came here as an alien, and he would play the judge! Now we will deal worse with you than with them." Then they pressed hard against the man Lot, and came near the door to break it down. [10]But the men inside reached out their hands and brought Lot into the house with them, and shut the

---

[d] Or *and all the nations of the earth shall bless themselves by him*   [e] Heb *known*   [f] Another ancient tradition reads *while the LORD remained standing before Abraham*

door. [11]And they struck with blindness the men who were at the door of the house, both small and great, so that they were unable to find the door.

Sodom and Gomorrah Destroyed

12 Then the men said to Lot, "Have you anyone else here? Sons-in-law, sons, daughters, or anyone you have in the city—bring them out of the place. [13]For we are about to destroy this place, because the outcry against its people has become great before the LORD, and the LORD has sent us to destroy it." [14]So Lot went out and said to his sons-in-law, who were to marry his daughters, "Up, get out of this place; for the LORD is about to destroy the city." But he seemed to his sons-in-law to be jesting.

15 When morning dawned, the angels urged Lot, saying, "Get up, take your wife and your two daughters who are here, or else you will be consumed in the punishment of the city." [16]But he lingered; so the men seized him and his wife and his two daughters by the hand, the LORD being merciful to him, and they brought him out and left him outside the city. [17]When they had brought them outside, they[g] said, "Flee for your life; do not look back or stop anywhere in the Plain; flee to the hills, or else you will be consumed." [18]And Lot said to them, "Oh, no, my lords; [19]your servant has found favor with you, and you have shown me great kindness in saving my life; but I cannot flee to the hills, for fear the disaster will overtake me and I die. [20]Look, that city is near enough to flee to, and it is a little one. Let me escape there—is it

not a little one?—and my life will be saved!" [21]He said to him, "Very well, I grant you this favor too, and will not overthrow the city of which you have spoken. [22]Hurry, escape there, for I can do nothing until you arrive there." Therefore the city was called Zo̅'ar.[h] [23]The sun had risen on the earth when Lot came to Zo̅'ar.

24 Then the LORD rained on Sod'om and Go·mor'rah sulfur and fire from the LORD out of heaven; [25]and he overthrew those cities, and all the Plain, and all the inhabitants of the cities, and what grew on the ground. [26]But Lot's wife, behind him, looked back, and she became a pillar of salt.

27 Abraham went early in the morning to the place where he had stood before the LORD; [28]and he looked down toward Sod'om and Go·mor'rah and toward all the land of the Plain and saw the smoke of the land going up like the smoke of a furnace.

29 So it was that, when God destroyed the cities of the Plain, God remembered Abraham, and sent Lot out of the midst of the overthrow, when he overthrew the cities in which Lot had settled.

The Shameful Origin of Moab and Ammon

30 Now Lot went up out of Zo̅'ar and settled in the hills with his two daughters, for he was afraid to stay in Zo̅'ar; so he lived in a cave with his two daughters. [31]And the firstborn said to the younger, "Our father is old, and there is not a man on earth to come in to us after the manner of all the world. [32]Come, let us make our father drink wine, and we will lie with him, so that we may preserve offspring through our father." [33]So they made their father drink wine that night; and the firstborn went in, and lay with her father; he did not know when she lay down or when she rose. [34]On the

People think that the cities of Sodom and Gomorrah were near the southern end of the Dead Sea. They were known for their wickedness, and were destroyed by fire.

[g] Gk Syr Vg: Heb *he*   [h] That is *Little*

next day, the firstborn said to the younger, "Look, I lay last night with my father; let us make him drink wine tonight also; then you go in and lie with him, so that we may preserve offspring through our father." 35So they made their father drink wine that night also; and the younger rose, and lay with him; and he did not know when she lay down or when she rose. 36Thus both the daughters of Lot became pregnant by their father. 37The firstborn bore a son, and named him Mō′ab; he is the ancestor of the Mō′ab·ītes to this day. 38The younger also bore a son and named him Ben-am′mī; he is the ancestor of the Am′mon·ītes to this day.

Abraham and Sarah at Gerar

20 From there Abraham journeyed toward the region of the Neg′eb, and settled between Kā′desh and Shur. While residing in Gē′rar as an alien, 2Abraham said of his wife Sarah, "She is my sister." And King A·bim′-e·lech of Gē′rar sent and took Sarah. 3But God came to A·bim′e·lech in a dream by night, and said to him, "You are about to die because of the woman whom you have taken; for she is a married woman." 4Now A·bim′e·lech had not approached her; so he said, "Lord, will you destroy an innocent people? 5Did he not himself say to me, 'She is my sister'? And she herself said, 'He is my brother.' I did this in the integrity of my heart and the innocence of my hands." 6Then God said to him in the dream, "Yes, I know that you did this in the integrity of your heart; furthermore it was I who kept you from sinning against me. Therefore I did not let you touch her. 7Now then, return the man's wife; for he is a prophet, and he will pray for you and you shall live. But if you do not restore her, know that you shall surely die, you and all that are yours."

8 So A·bim′e·lech rose early in the morning, and called all his servants and told them all these things; and the men

were very much afraid. 9Then A·bim′-e·lech called Abraham, and said to him, "What have you done to us? How have I sinned against you, that you have brought such great guilt on me and my kingdom? You have done things to me that ought not to be done." 10And A·bim′-e·lech said to Abraham, "What were you thinking of, that you did this thing?" 11Abraham said, "I did it because I thought, There is no fear of God at all in this place, and they will kill me because of my wife. 12Besides, she is indeed my sister, the daughter of my father but not the daughter of my mother; and she became my wife. 13And when God caused me to wander from my father's house, I said to her, 'This is the kindness you must do me: at every place to which we come, say of me, He is my brother.'" 14Then A·bim′e·lech took sheep and oxen, and male and female slaves, and gave them to Abraham, and restored his wife Sarah to him. 15A·bim′e·lech said, "My land is before you; settle where it pleases you." 16To Sarah he said, "Look, I have given your brother a thousand pieces of silver; it is your exoneration before all who are with you; you are completely vindicated." 17Then Abraham prayed to God; and God healed A·bim′e·lech, and also healed his wife and female slaves so that they bore children. 18For the LORD had closed fast all the wombs of the house of A·bim′e·lech because of Sarah, Abraham's wife.

The Birth of Isaac

21 The LORD dealt with Sarah as he had said, and the LORD did for Sarah as he had promised. 2Sarah conceived and bore Abraham a son in his old age, at the time of which God had spoken to him. 3Abraham gave the name Isaac to his son whom Sarah bore him. 4And Abraham circumcised his son Isaac when he was eight days old, as God had commanded him. 5Abraham was a hundred years old when his son Isaac was born to him. 6Now Sarah said, "God has brought laughter for me; everyone who

Bible stories are about people who had doubts and questions, just like we do. Abraham and Sarah had doubts and questions. They waited a long time to have the child God had promised them. They laughed at the idea of having a baby in their old age (read Genesis 17:7 and 18:12), but God kept the promise! When Sarah gave birth to their son, they named him Isaac, which means "he laughs."

hears will laugh with me." [7]And she said, "Who would ever have said to Abraham that Sarah would nurse children? Yet I have borne him a son in his old age."

Hagar and Ishmael Sent Away

8 The child grew, and was weaned; and Abraham made a great feast on the day that Isaac was weaned. [9]But Sarah saw the son of Hā´gar the Egyptian, whom she had borne to Abraham, playing with her son Isaac.[i] [10]So she said to Abraham, "Cast out this slave woman with her son; for the son of this slave woman shall not inherit along with my son Isaac." [11]The matter was very distressing to Abraham on account of his son. [12]But God said to Abraham, "Do not be distressed because of the boy and because of your slave woman; whatever Sarah says to you, do as she tells you, for it is through Isaac that offspring shall be named for you. [13]As for the son of the slave woman, I will make a nation of him also, because he is your offspring." [14]So Abraham rose early in the morning, and took bread and a skin of water, and gave it to Hā´gar, putting it on her shoulder, along with the child, and sent her away. And she departed, and wandered about in the wilderness of Bē´er-shē´ba.

15 When the water in the skin was gone, she cast the child under one of the bushes. [16]Then she went and sat down opposite him a good way off, about the distance of a bowshot; for she said, "Do not let me look on the death of the child." And as she sat opposite him, she lifted up her voice and wept. [17]And God heard the voice of the boy; and the angel of God called to Hā´gar from heaven, and said to her, "What troubles you, Hā´gar? Do not be afraid; for God has heard the voice of the boy where he is. [18]Come, lift up the boy and hold him fast with your hand, for I will make a great nation of him." [19]Then God opened her eyes and she saw a well of water. She went, and filled the skin with water, and gave the boy a drink.

20 God was with the boy, and he grew up; he lived in the wilderness, and became an expert with the bow. [21]He lived in the wilderness of Par´an; and his mother got a wife for him from the land of Egypt.

Abraham and Abimelech Make a Covenant

22 At that time A·bim´e·lech, with Phi´col the commander of his army, said to Abraham, "God is with you in all that you do; [23]now therefore swear to me here by God that you will not deal falsely with me or with my offspring or with my posterity, but as I have dealt loyally with you, you will deal with me and with the land where you have resided as an alien." [24]And Abraham said, "I swear it."

25 When Abraham complained to A·bim´e·lech about a well of water that A·bim´e·lech's servants had seized, [26]A·bim´e·lech said, "I do not know who has done this; you did not tell me, and I have not heard of it until today." [27]So Abraham took sheep and oxen and gave them to A·bim´e·lech, and the two men made a covenant. [28]Abraham set apart seven ewe lambs of the flock. [29]And A·bim´e·lech said to Abraham, "What is the meaning of these seven ewe lambs that you have set apart?" [30]He said, "These seven ewe lambs you shall accept from my

---

[i] Gk Vg: Heb lacks *with her son Isaac*

hand, in order that you may be a witness for me that I dug this well." [31]Therefore that place was called Bē′er-shē′ba;[j] because there both of them swore an oath. [32]When they had made a covenant at Bē′er-shē′ba, A·bim′e·lech, with Phī′col the commander of his army, left and returned to the land of the Phi·lis′tines. [33]Abraham[k] planted a tamarisk tree in Bē′er-shē′ba, and called there on the name of the LORD, the Everlasting God.[l] [34]And Abraham resided as an alien many days in the land of the Phi·lis′tines.

The Command to Sacrifice Isaac

22 After these things God tested Abraham. He said to him, "Abraham!" And he said, "Here I am." [2]He said, "Take your son, your only son Isaac, whom you love, and go to the land of Mō·rī′ah, and offer him there as a burnt offering on one of the mountains that I shall show you." [3]So Abraham rose early in the morning, saddled his donkey, and took two of his young men with him, and his son Isaac; he cut the wood for the burnt offering, and set out and went to the place in the distance that God had shown him. [4]On the third day Abraham looked up and saw the place far away. [5]Then Abraham said to his young men, "Stay here with the donkey; the boy and I will go over there; we will worship, and then we will come back to you." [6]Abraham took the wood of the burnt offering and laid it on his son Isaac, and he himself carried the fire and the knife. So the two of them walked on together. [7]Isaac said to his

Abraham's faith was tested when God commanded him to return Isaac to God by sacrificing him. At the moment when Abraham was about to kill his son, he was stopped by an angel of the Lord. God loves people too much to ask for them to be killed.

father Abraham, "Father!" And he said, "Here I am, my son." He said, "The fire and the wood are here, but where is the lamb for a burnt offering?" [8]Abraham said, "God himself will provide the lamb for a burnt offering, my son." So the two of them walked on together.

9 When they came to the place that God had shown him, Abraham built an altar there and laid the wood in order. He bound his son Isaac, and laid him on the altar, on top of the wood. [10]Then Abraham reached out his hand and took the knife to kill[m] his son. [11]But the angel of the LORD called to him from heaven, and said, "Abraham, Abraham!" And he said, "Here I am." [12]He said, "Do not lay your hand on the boy or do anything to him; for now I know that you fear God, since you have not withheld your son, your only son, from me." [13]And Abraham looked up and saw a ram, caught in a thicket by its horns. Abraham went and took the ram and offered it up as a burnt offering instead of his son. [14]So Abraham called that place "The LORD will provide";[n] as it is said to this day, "On the mount of the LORD it shall be provided."[o]

15 The angel of the LORD called to Abraham a second time from heaven, [16]and said, "By myself I have sworn, says the LORD: Because you have done this, and have not withheld your son, your only son, [17]I will indeed bless you, and I will make your offspring as numerous as the stars of heaven and as the sand that is on the seashore. And your offspring shall possess the gate of their enemies, [18]and by your offspring shall all the nations of the earth gain blessing for themselves, because you have obeyed my voice." [19]So Abraham returned to his young men, and they arose and went together to Bē′er-shē′ba; and Abraham lived at Bē′er-shē′ba.

[j] That is *Well of seven* or *Well of the oath*   [k] Heb *He*   [l] Or *the LORD, El Olam*   [m] Or *to slaughter*   [n] Or *will see*; Heb traditionally transliterated *Jehovah Jireh*   [o] Or *he shall be seen*

The Children of Nahor

20 Now after these things it was told Abraham, "Mil´cah also has borne children, to your brother Nā´hor: ²¹Uz the firstborn, Buz his brother, Ke·mu´el the father of Ar´am, ²²Chē´sed, Hā´zō, Pil´dash, Jid´laph, and Be·thu´el." ²³Be·thu´el became the father of Rebekah. These eight Milcah bore to Nā´hor, Abraham's brother. ²⁴Moreover, his concubine, whose name was Re·u´mah, bore Tē´bah, Gā´ham, Tā´hash, and Mā´a·cah.

Sarah's Death and Burial

23 Sarah lived one hundred twenty-seven years; this was the length of Sarah's life. ²And Sarah died at Kir´i·ath-ar´ba (that is, Hē´bron) in the land of Cā´naan; and Abraham went in to mourn for Sarah and to weep for her. ³Abraham rose up from beside his dead, and said to the Hit´tītes, ⁴"I am a stranger and an alien residing among you; give me property among you for a burying place, so that I may bury my dead out of my sight." ⁵The Hit´tītes answered Abraham, ⁶"Hear us, my lord; you are a mighty prince among us. Bury your dead in the choicest of our burial places; none of us will withhold from you any burial ground for burying your dead." ⁷Abraham rose and bowed to the Hit´tītes, the people of the land. ⁸He said to them, "If you are willing that I should bury my dead out of my sight, hear me, and entreat for me Ē´phron son of Zō´har, ⁹so that he may give me the cave of Mach·pē´lah, which he owns; it is at the end of his field. For the full price let him give it to me in your presence as a possession for a burying place." ¹⁰Now Ē´phron was sitting among the Hit´tītes; and Ē´phron the Hit´tīte answered Abraham in the hearing of the Hit´tītes, of all who went in at the gate of his city, ¹¹"No, my lord, hear me; I give you the field, and I give you the cave that is in it; in the presence of my people I give it to you; bury your dead." ¹²Then Abraham bowed down before the people of the land. ¹³He said to Ē´phron in the hearing of the people of the land, "If you only will listen to me! I will give the price of the field; accept it from me, so that I may bury my dead there." ¹⁴Ē´phron answered Abraham, ¹⁵"My lord, listen to me; a piece of land worth four hundred shekels of silver—what is that between you and me? Bury your dead." ¹⁶Abraham agreed with Ē´phron; and Abraham weighed out for Ē´phron the silver that he had named in the hearing of the Hit´tītes, four hundred shekels of silver, according to the weights current among the merchants.

17 So the field of Ē´phron in Mach·pē´lah, which was to the east of Mam´re, the field with the cave that was in it and all the trees that were in the field, throughout its whole area, passed ¹⁸to Abraham as a possession in the presence of the Hit´tītes, in the presence of all who went in at the gate of his city. ¹⁹After this, Abraham buried Sarah his wife in the cave of the field of Mach·pē´lah facing Mam´re (that is, Hē´bron) in the land of Cā´naan. ²⁰The field and the cave that is in it passed from the Hit´tītes into Abraham's possession as a burying place.

The Marriage of Isaac and Rebekah

24 Now Abraham was old, well advanced in years; and the LORD had blessed Abraham in all things. ²Abraham said to his servant, the oldest of his house, who had charge of all that he had, "Put your hand under my thigh ³and I will make you swear by the LORD, the God of heaven and earth, that you will not get a wife for my son from the daughters of the Cā´naan·ites, among whom I live, ⁴but will go to my country and to my kindred and get a wife for my son Isaac." ⁵The servant said to him, "Perhaps the woman may not be willing to follow me to this land; must I then take your son back to the land from which you came?" ⁶Abraham said to him, "See to it that you do not take my son back there. [7]The LORD, the God of heaven, who took me from my father's house and from the land of my birth, and who spoke to me and swore to me, 'To your offspring I will give this land,' he will send his angel before you, and you shall take a wife for my son from there. [8]But if the woman is not willing to follow you, then you will be free from this oath of mine; only you must not take my son back there." [9]So the servant put his hand under the thigh of Abraham his master and swore to him concerning this matter.

10 Then the servant took ten of his master's camels and departed, taking all kinds of choice gifts from his master; and he set out and went to Ar'am-nā·ha·rā'im, to the city of Nā'hor. [11]He made the camels kneel down outside the city by the well of water; it was toward evening, the time when women go out to draw water. [12]And he said, "O LORD, God of my master Abraham, please grant me success today and show steadfast love to my master Abraham. [13]I am standing here by the spring of water, and the daughters of the townspeople are coming out to draw water. [14]Let the girl to whom I shall say, 'Please offer your jar that I may drink,' and who shall say, 'Drink, and I will water your camels'— let her be the one whom you have appointed for your servant Isaac. By this I shall know that you have shown steadfast love to my master."

15 Before he had finished speaking, there was Rebekah, who was born to Be·thu'el son of Mil'cah, the wife of Nā'-hor, Abraham's brother, coming out with her water jar on her shoulder. [16]The girl was very fair to look upon, a virgin, whom no man had known. She went down to the spring, filled her jar, and came up. [17]Then the servant ran to meet her and said, "Please let me sip a little water from your jar." [18]"Drink, my lord," she said, and quickly lowered her jar upon her hand and gave him a drink.

When Rebekah gave water to Abraham's chief servant and to his camels, she was showing hospitality. People treated guests as if they were members of their own families. They gave guests food, shelter, protection, and much more.

Today, we also show hospitality. How do you treat guests? What are their needs? How can you show loving care to them?

[19]When she had finished giving him a drink, she said, "I will draw for your camels also, until they have finished drinking." [20]So she quickly emptied her jar into the trough and ran again to the well to draw, and she drew for all his camels. [21]The man gazed at her in silence to learn whether or not the LORD had made his journey successful.

22 When the camels had finished drinking, the man took a gold nose-ring weighing a half shekel, and two bracelets for her arms weighing ten gold shekels, [23]and said, "Tell me whose daughter you are. Is there room in your father's house for us to spend the night?" [24]She said to him, "I am the daughter of Be·thu'el son of Mil'cah, whom she bore to Nā'hor." [25]She added, "We have plenty of straw and fodder and a place to spend the night." [26]The man bowed his head and worshiped the LORD [27]and said, "Blessed be the LORD, the God of my master Abraham, who has not forsaken his steadfast love and his faithfulness toward my master. As for me, the LORD has led me on the way to the house of my master's kin."

28 Then the girl ran and told her mother's household about these things. [29]Rebekah had a brother whose name was Lā'ban; and Lā'ban ran out to the man, to the spring. [30]As soon as he had seen the nose-ring, and the bracelets on his sister's arms, and when he heard the words of his sister Rebekah, "Thus the

man spoke to me," he went to the man; and there he was, standing by the camels at the spring. [31]He said, "Come in, O blessed of the LORD. Why do you stand outside when I have prepared the house and a place for the camels?" [32]So the man came into the house; and La'ban unloaded the camels, and gave him straw and fodder for the camels, and water to wash his feet and the feet of the men who were with him. [33]Then food was set before him to eat; but he said, "I will not eat until I have told my errand." He said, "Speak on."

34 So he said, "I am Abraham's servant. [35]The LORD has greatly blessed my master, and he has become wealthy; he has given him flocks and herds, silver and gold, male and female slaves, camels and donkeys. [36]And Sarah my master's wife bore a son to my master when she was old; and he has given him all that he has. [37]My master made me swear, saying, 'You shall not take a wife for my son from the daughters of the Ca'naan-ites, in whose land I live; [38]but you shall go to my father's house, to my kindred, and get a wife for my son.' [39]I said to my master, 'Perhaps the woman will not follow me.' [40]But he said to me, 'The LORD, before whom I walk, will send his angel with you and make your way successful. You shall get a wife for my son from my kindred, from my father's house. [41]Then you will be free from my oath, when you come to my kindred; even if they will not give her to you, you will be free from my oath.'

42 "I came today to the spring, and said, 'O LORD, the God of my master Abraham, if now you will only make successful the way I am going! [43]I am standing here by the spring of water; let the young woman who comes out to draw, to whom I shall say, "Please give me a little water from your jar to drink," [44]and who will say to me, "Drink, and I will draw for your camels also"—let her be the woman whom the LORD has appointed for my master's son.'

45 "Before I had finished speaking in my heart, there was Rebekah coming out with her water jar on her shoulder; and she went down to the spring, and drew. I said to her, 'Please let me drink.' [46]She quickly let down her jar from her shoulder, and said, 'Drink, and I will also water your camels.' So I drank, and she also watered the camels. [47]Then I asked her, 'Whose daughter are you?' She said, 'The daughter of Be-thu'el, Na'hor's son, whom Mil'cah bore to him.' So I put the ring on her nose, and the bracelets on her arms. [48]Then I bowed my head and worshiped the LORD, and blessed the LORD, the God of my master Abraham, who had led me by the right way to obtain the daughter of my master's kinsman for his son. [49]Now then, if you will deal loyally and truly with my master, tell me; and if not, tell me, so that I may turn either to the right hand or to the left."

50 Then La'ban and Be-thu'el answered, "The thing comes from the LORD; we cannot speak to you anything bad or good. [51]Look, Rebekah is before you, take her and go, and let her be the wife of your master's son, as the LORD has spoken."

52 When Abraham's servant heard their words, he bowed himself to the ground before the LORD. [53]And the servant brought out jewelry of silver and of gold, and garments, and gave them to Rebekah; he also gave to her brother and to her mother costly ornaments. [54]Then he and the men who were with him ate and drank, and they spent the night there. When they rose in the morning, he said, "Send me back to my master." [55]Her brother and her mother said, "Let the girl remain with us a while, at least ten days; after that she may go." [56]But he said to them, "Do not delay me, since the LORD has made my journey successful; let me go that I may go to my master." [57]They said, "We will call the girl, and ask her." [58]And they called Rebekah, and said to her, "Will you go with this man?" She said, "I will." [59]So they sent away their sister

Rebekah married Isaac, son of Abraham, and the line of God's people from Abraham continued.

Rebekah and her nurse along with Abraham's servant and his men. ⁶⁰And they blessed Rebekah and said to her,

"May you, our sister, become
thousands of myriads;
may your offspring gain possession
of the gates of their foes."

⁶¹Then Rebekah and her maids rose up, mounted the camels, and followed the man; thus the servant took Rebekah, and went his way.

62 Now Isaac had come from*ᵖ* Bḗer-la-haī́ roi, and was settled in the Neg´eb. ⁶³Isaac went out in the evening to walk*�q* in the field; and looking up, he saw camels coming. ⁶⁴And Rebekah looked up, and when she saw Isaac, she slipped quickly from the camel, ⁶⁵and said to the servant, "Who is the man over there, walking in the field to meet us?" The servant said, "It is my master." So she took her veil and covered herself. ⁶⁶And the servant told Isaac all the things that he had done. ⁶⁷Then Isaac brought her into his mother Sarah's tent. He took Rebekah, and she became his wife; and he loved her. So Isaac was comforted after his mother's death.

Abraham Marries Keturah

25 Abraham took another wife, whose name was Ke·tū´rah. ²She bore him Zim´ran, Jok´shan, Mē´dan, Mid´i·an, Ish´bak, and Shū´ah. ³Jok´shan was the father of Shē´ba and Dē´dan. The sons of Dē´dan were As·shū´rim, Le·tū´shim, and Le·um´mim. ⁴The sons of Mid´i·an were Ē´phah, Ē´pher, Hā´noch, A·bī´da, and El·dā´ah. All these were the children of Ke·tū´rah. ⁵Abraham gave all he had to Isaac. ⁶But to the sons of his concubines Abraham gave gifts, while he was still living, and he

sent them away from his son Isaac, eastward to the east country.

The Death of Abraham

7 This is the length of Abraham's life, one hundred seventy-five years. ⁸Abraham breathed his last and died in a good old age, an old man and full of years, and was gathered to his people. ⁹His sons Isaac and Ish´ma·el buried him in the cave of Mach·pē´lah, in the field of Ē´phron son of Zō´har the Hit´tīte, east of Mam´re, ¹⁰the field that Abraham purchased from the Hit´tītes. There Abraham was buried, with his wife Sarah. ¹¹After the death of Abraham God blessed his son Isaac. And Isaac settled at Bḗer-la´haī-roi.

God never forgets one of God's children! Ishmael and his mother, Hagar, had been sent to live in the wilderness of Paran, but the list of his twelve sons in Genesis 25:13–15 shows that God had a plan for his life. His descendants, called Ishmaelites, lived in camps in the desert of Arabia and became caravan traders and camel herders.

Ishmael's Descendants

12 These are the descendants of Ish´ma·el, Abraham's son, whom Hā´gar the Egyptian, Sarah's slave-girl, bore to Abraham. ¹³These are the names of the sons of Ish´ma·el, named in the order of their birth: Ne·bā´i·oth, the firstborn of Ish´ma·el; and Kē´dar, Ad´bē·el, Mib´sam, ¹⁴Mish´ma, Dū´mah, Mas´sa, ¹⁵Hā´dad, Tē´ma, Jē´tur, Nā´phish, and Ked´e·mah. ¹⁶These are the sons of Ish´ma·el and these are their names, by their villages and by their encampments, twelve princes according to their tribes. ¹⁷(This is the length of the life of Ish´ma·el, one hundred thirty-seven years; he breathed

ᵖ Syr Tg: Heb *from coming to*   *q* Meaning of Heb word is uncertain his last and died, and was gathered to his people.) [18]They settled from Hav′-i·lah to Shur, which is opposite Egypt in the direction of Assyria; he settled down[r] alongside of[s] all his people.

The Birth and Youth of Esau and Jacob

19 These are the descendants of Isaac, Abraham's son: Abraham was the father of Isaac, [20]and Isaac was forty years old when he married Rebekah, daughter of Be·thū′el the Ar·a·mē′an of Pad′dan-ar′am, sister of Lā′ban the Ar·a·mē′an. [21]Isaac prayed to the LORD for his wife, because she was barren; and the LORD granted his prayer, and his wife Rebekah conceived. [22]The children struggled together within her; and she said, "If it is to be this way, why do I live?"[t] So she went to inquire of the LORD. [23]And the LORD said to her,

"Two nations are in your womb,
    and two peoples born of you shall
        be divided;
the one shall be stronger than the
        other,
    the elder shall serve the younger."

[24]When her time to give birth was at hand, there were twins in her womb. [25]The first came out red, all his body like a hairy mantle; so they named him Esau. [26]Afterward his brother came out, with his hand gripping Esau's heel; so he was named Jacob.[u] Isaac was sixty years old when she bore them.

Isaac and Rebekah had twin sons named Jacob and Esau. Jacob's name is like the Hebrew word for "heel," and Esau's name is like the Hebrew words for "hairy" and "red." Jacob farmed, and Esau hunted. Farming and hunting led the brothers to live different kinds of lives.

27 When the boys grew up, Esau was a skillful hunter, a man of the field, while Jacob was a quiet man, living in tents. [28]Isaac loved Esau, because he was fond of game; but Rebekah loved Jacob.

Esau Sells His Birthright

29 Once when Jacob was cooking a stew, Esau came in from the field, and he was famished. [30]Esau said to Jacob, "Let me eat some of that red stuff, for I am famished!" (Therefore he was called Ē′dom.[v]) [31]Jacob said, "First sell me your birthright." [32]Esau said, "I am about to die; of what use is a birthright to me?" [33]Jacob said, "Swear to me first."[w] So he swore to him, and sold his birthright to Jacob. [34]Then Jacob gave Esau bread and lentil stew, and he ate and drank, and rose and went his way. Thus Esau despised his birthright.

The birthright is a difficult custom for us to understand today. In some cultures, the oldest son would receive twice as much of his father's inheritance as the other sons. Esau, the oldest son, was supposed to get the birthright. But he gave his birthright to his younger brother Jacob in exchange for a bowl of soup.

Isaac and Abimelech

26 Now there was a famine in the land, besides the former famine that had occurred in the days of Abraham. And Isaac went to Gē′rar, to King A·bim′e·lech of the Phi·lis′tines. [2]The LORD appeared to Isaac[x] and said, "Do not go down to Egypt; settle in the land that I shall show you. [3]Reside in

[p] Heb *he fell*   [q] Or *down in opposition to*   [r] Syr: Meaning of Heb uncertain   [s] That is *He takes by the heel* or *He supplants*   [t] That is *Red*   [u] Heb *today*   [v] Heb *him*

this land as an alien, and I will be with you, and will bless you; for to you and to your descendants I will give all these lands, and I will fulfill the oath that I swore to your father Abraham. [4]I will make your offspring as numerous as the stars of heaven, and will give to your offspring all these lands; and all the nations of the earth shall gain blessing for themselves through your offspring, [5]because Abraham obeyed my voice and kept my charge, my commandments, my statutes, and my laws."

6 So Isaac settled in Ge´rar. [7]When the men of the place asked him about his wife, he said, "She is my sister"; for he was afraid to say, "My wife," thinking, "or else the men of the place might kill me for the sake of Rebekah, because she is attractive in appearance." [8]When Isaac had been there a long time, King A·bim´e·lech of the Phi·lis´tines looked out of a window and saw him fondling his wife Rebekah. [9]So A·bim´e·lech called for Isaac, and said, "So she is your wife! Why then did you say, 'She is my sister'?" Isaac said to him, "Because I thought I might die because of her." [10]A·bim´e·lech said, "What is this you have done to us? One of the people might easily have lain with your wife, and you would have brought guilt upon us." [11]So A·bim´e·lech warned all the people, saying, "Whoever touches this man or his wife shall be put to death."

12 Isaac sowed seed in that land, and in the same year reaped a hundredfold. The LORD blessed him, [13]and the man became rich; he prospered more and more until he became very wealthy. [14]He had possessions of flocks and herds, and a great household, so that the Phi·lis´tines envied him. [15](Now the Phi·lis´tines had stopped up and filled with earth all the wells that his father's servants had dug in the days of his father Abraham.) [16]And A·bim´e·lech said to Isaac, "Go away from us; you have become too powerful for us."

17 So Isaac departed from there and camped in the valley of Ge´rar and settled there. [18]Isaac dug again the wells of water that had been dug in the days of his father Abraham; for the Phi·lis´tines had stopped them up after the death of Abraham; and he gave them the names that his father had given them. [19]But when Isaac's servants dug in the valley and found there a well of spring water, [20]the herders of Ge´rar quarreled with Isaac's herders, saying, "The water is ours." So he called the well E¯´sek,[y] because they contended with him. [21]Then they dug another well, and they quarreled over that one also; so he called it Sit´nah.[z] [22]He moved from there and dug another well, and they did not quarrel over it; so he called it Re·ho¯´both,[a] saying, "Now the LORD has made room for us, and we shall be fruitful in the land."

23 From there he went up to Be´er-she´ba. [24]And that very night the LORD appeared to him and said, "I am the God of your father Abraham; do not be afraid, for I am with you and will bless you and make your offspring numerous for my servant Abraham's sake." [25]So he built an altar there, called on the name of the LORD, and pitched his tent there. And there Isaac's servants dug a well.

26 Then A·bim´e·lech went to him from Ge´rar, with A·huz´zath his adviser and Phi´col the commander of his army. [27]Isaac said to them, "Why have you come to me, seeing that you hate me and have sent me away from you?" [28]They said, "We see plainly that the LORD has been with you; so we say, let there be an oath between you and us, and let us make a covenant with you [29]so that you will do us no harm, just as we have not touched you and have done to you nothing but good and have sent you away in peace. You are now the blessed of the LORD." [30]So he made them a feast, and they ate and drank. [31]In the morning they rose early and exchanged oaths; and Isaac set them on their way,

[y] That is *Contention*   [z] That is *Enmity*   [a] That is *Broad places* or *Room*

and they departed from him in peace. ³²That same day Isaac's servants came and told him about the well that they had dug, and said to him, "We have found water!" ³³He called it Shī´bah;[b] therefore the name of the city is Bē´er-shē´ba[c] to this day.

Esau's Hittite Wives

34 When Esau was forty years old, he married Judith daughter of Be·ē´rī the Hit´tīte, and Bas´e·math daughter of Ē´lon the Hit´tīte; ³⁵and they made life bitter for Isaac and Rebekah.

A blessing gave the promise of good health, long life, prosperity, many children, and security to the person who received it. Once a blessing had been given, it could not be taken back. Jacob tricked his father into giving him the blessing that belonged to his older brother Esau.

Isaac Blesses Jacob

27 When Isaac was old and his eyes were dim so that he could not see, he called his elder son Esau and said to him, "My son"; and he answered, "Here I am." ²He said, "See, I am old; I do not know the day of my death. ³Now then, take your weapons, your quiver and your bow, and go out to the field, and hunt game for me. ⁴Then prepare for me savory food, such as I like, and bring it to me to eat, so that I may bless you before I die."

5 Now Rebekah was listening when Isaac spoke to his son Esau. So when Esau went to the field to hunt for game and bring it, ⁶Rebekah said to her son Jacob, "I heard your father say to your brother Esau, ⁷'Bring me game, and prepare for me savory food to eat, that I may bless you before the LORD before I die.' ⁸Now therefore, my son, obey my word as I command you. ⁹Go to the flock, and get me two choice kids, so that I may prepare from them savory food for your father, such as he likes; ¹⁰and you shall take it to your father to eat, so that he may bless you before he dies." ¹¹But Jacob said to his mother Rebekah, "Look, my brother Esau is a hairy man, and I am a man of smooth skin. ¹²Perhaps my father will feel me, and I shall seem to be mocking him, and bring a curse on myself and not a blessing." ¹³His mother said to him, "Let your curse be on me, my son; only obey my word, and go, get them for me." ¹⁴So he went and got them and brought them to his mother; and his mother prepared savory food, such as his father loved. ¹⁵Then Rebekah took the best garments of her elder son Esau, which were with her in the house, and put them on her younger son Jacob; ¹⁶and she put the skins of the kids on his hands and on the smooth part of his neck. ¹⁷Then she handed the savory food, and the bread that she had prepared, to her son Jacob.

18 So he went in to his father, and said, "My father"; and he said, "Here I am; who are you, my son?" ¹⁹Jacob said to his father, "I am Esau your firstborn. I have done as you told me; now sit up and eat of my game, so that you may bless me." ²⁰But Isaac said to his son, "How is it that you have found it so quickly, my son?" He answered, "Because the LORD your God granted me success." ²¹Then Isaac said to Jacob, "Come near, that I may feel you, my son, to know whether you are really my son Esau or not." ²²So Jacob went up to his father Isaac, who felt him and said, "The voice is Jacob's voice, but the hands are the hands of Esau." ²³He did not recognize him, because his hands were hairy like his brother Esau's hands; so he blessed him. ²⁴He said, "Are you really my son Esau?"

[b] A word resembling the word for *oath*   [c] That is *Well of the oath* or *Well of seven*

He answered, "I am." ²⁵Then he said, "Bring it to me, that I may eat of my son's game and bless you." So he brought it to him, and he ate; and he brought him wine, and he drank. ²⁶Then his father Isaac said to him, "Come near and kiss me, my son." ²⁷So he came near and kissed him; and he smelled the smell of his garments, and blessed him, and said,

"Ah, the smell of my son
   is like the smell of a field that the
       LORD has blessed.
²⁸ May God give you of the dew of
       heaven,
   and of the fatness of the earth,
   and plenty of grain and wine.
²⁹ Let peoples serve you,
   and nations bow down to you.
Be lord over your brothers,
   and may your mother's sons bow
       down to you.
Cursed be everyone who curses you,
   and blessed be everyone who
       blesses you!"

Esau's Lost Blessing

30 As soon as Isaac had finished blessing Jacob, when Jacob had scarcely gone out from the presence of his father Isaac, his brother Esau came in from his hunting. ³¹He also prepared savory food, and brought it to his father. And he said to his father, "Let my father sit up and eat of his son's game, so that you may bless me." ³²His father Isaac said to him, "Who are you?" He answered, "I am your firstborn son, Esau." ³³Then Isaac trembled violently, and said, "Who was it then that hunted game and brought it to me, and I ate it all^d before you came,

and I have blessed him?—yes, and blessed he shall be!" ³⁴When Esau heard his father's words, he cried out with an exceedingly great and bitter cry, and said to his father, "Bless me, me also, father!" ³⁵But he said, "Your brother came deceitfully, and he has taken away your blessing." ³⁶Esau said, "Is he not rightly named Jacob?^e For he has supplanted me these two times. He took away my birthright; and look, now he has taken away my blessing." Then he said, "Have you not reserved a blessing for me?" ³⁷Isaac answered Esau, "I have already made him your lord, and I have given him all his brothers as servants, and with grain and wine I have sustained him. What then can I do for you, my son?" ³⁸Esau said to his father, "Have you only one blessing, father? Bless me, me also, father!" And Esau lifted up his voice and wept.

39 Then his father Isaac answered him:

"See, away from^f the fatness of the
       earth shall your home be,
   and away from^g the dew of heaven
       on high.
⁴⁰ By your sword you shall live,
   and you shall serve your brother;
but when you break loose,^h
   you shall break his yoke from
       your neck."

Jacob Escapes Esau's Fury

41 Now Esau hated Jacob because of the blessing with which his father had blessed him, and Esau said to himself, "The days of mourning for my father are approaching; then I will kill my brother Jacob." ⁴²But the words of her elder son Esau were told to Rebekah; so she sent and called her younger son Jacob and said to him, "Your brother Esau is consoling himself by planning to kill you. ⁴³Now therefore, my son, obey my voice; flee at once to my brother Lā´ban in Har´an, ⁴⁴and stay with him a while,

After Jacob stole his father's blessing from his brother Esau, he ran in fear for his life. He planned to make his way to Haran, where his mother's family still lived.

^d Cn: Heb of all   ^e That is He supplants or He takes by the heel   ^f Or See, of   ^g Or and of
^h Meaning of Heb uncertain

until your brother's fury turns away—
[45]until your brother's anger against you turns away, and he forgets what you have done to him; then I will send, and bring you back from there. Why should I lose both of you in one day?"

46 Then Rebekah said to Isaac, "I am weary of my life because of the Hit'tīte women. If Jacob marries one of the Hit'tīte women such as these, one of the women of the land, what good will my life be to me?"

28 Then Isaac called Jacob and blessed him, and charged him, "You shall not marry one of the Cā'-naan·īte women. [2]Go at once to Pad'-dan-ar'am to the house of Be·thū'el, your mother's father; and take as wife from there one of the daughters of Lā'ban, your mother's brother. [3]May God Almighty[i] bless you and make you fruitful and numerous, that you may become a company of peoples. [4]May he give to you the blessing of Abraham, to you and to your offspring with you, so that you may take possession of the land where you now live as an alien—land that God gave to Abraham." [5]Thus Isaac sent Jacob away; and he went to Pad'dan-ar'am, to Lā'ban son of Be·thū'el the Ar·a·mē'an, the brother of Rebekah, Jacob's and Esau's mother.

Esau Marries Ishmael's Daughter

6 Now Esau saw that Isaac had blessed Jacob and sent him away to Pad'dan-ar'am to take a wife from there, and that as he blessed him he charged him, "You shall not marry one of the Cā'-naan·īte women," [7]and that Jacob had obeyed his father and his mother and gone to Pad'dan-ar'am. [8]So when Esau saw that the Cā'naan·īte women did not please his father Isaac, [9]Esau went to Ish'ma·el and took Mā'ha·lath daughter of Abraham's son Ish'ma·el, and sister of Ne·bā'i·oth, to be his wife in addition to the wives he had.

Jacob's Dream at Bethel

10 Jacob left Bē'er-shē'ba and went toward Har'an. [11]He came to a certain place and stayed there for the night, because the sun had set. Taking one of the stones of the place, he put it under his head and lay down in that place. [12]And he dreamed that there was a ladder[j] set up on the earth, the top of it reaching to heaven; and the angels of God were ascending and descending on it. [13]And the LORD stood beside him[k] and said, "I am the LORD, the God of Abraham your father and the God of Isaac; the land on which you lie I will give to you and to your offspring; [14]and your offspring shall be like the dust of the earth, and you shall spread abroad to the west and to the east and to the north and to the south; and all the families of the earth shall be blessed[l] in you and in your offspring. [15]Know that I am with you and will keep you wherever you go, and will bring you back to this land; for I will not leave you until I have done what I have promised you." [16]Then Jacob woke from his sleep and said, "Surely the LORD is in this place—and I did not know it!" [17]And he was afraid, and said, "How awesome is this place! This is none other than the house of God, and this is the gate of heaven."

18 So Jacob rose early in the morning, and he took the stone that he had put under his head and set it up for a pillar and poured oil on the top of it. [19]He called that place Beth'el;[m] but the

Jacob met God at a place he called Bethel, which means "house of God." God had a plan for Jacob. The covenant that began with Abraham continued through Jacob. God chose Jacob to continue to keep God's promise.

[i] Traditional rendering of Heb El Shaddai   [j] Or stairway or ramp   [k] Or stood above it   [l] Or shall bless themselves   [m] That is House of God

name of the city was Luz at the first. [20]Then Jacob made a vow, saying, "If God will be with me, and will keep me in this way that I go, and will give me bread to eat and clothing to wear, [21]so that I come again to my father's house in peace, then the LORD shall be my God, [22]and this stone, which I have set up for a pillar, shall be God's house; and of all that you give me I will surely give one-tenth to you."

Jacob Meets Rachel

29 Then Jacob went on his journey, and came to the land of the people of the east. [2]As he looked, he saw a well in the field and three flocks of sheep lying there beside it; for out of that well the flocks were watered. The stone on the well's mouth was large, [3]and when all the flocks were gathered there, the shepherds would roll the stone from the mouth of the well, and water the sheep, and put the stone back in its place on the mouth of the well.

4 Jacob said to them, "My brothers, where do you come from?" They said, "We are from Har'an." [5]He said to them, "Do you know La'ban son of Na'hor?" They said, "We do." [6]He said to them, "Is it well with him?" "Yes," they replied, "and here is his daughter Rachel, coming with the sheep." [7]He said, "Look, it is still broad daylight; it is not time for the animals to be gathered together. Water the sheep, and go, pasture them." [8]But they said, "We cannot until all the flocks are gathered together, and the stone is rolled from the mouth of the well; then we water the sheep."

9 While he was still speaking with them, Rachel came with her father's sheep; for she kept them. [10]Now when Jacob saw Rachel, the daughter of his mother's brother La'ban, and the sheep of his mother's brother La'ban, Jacob went up and rolled the stone from the well's mouth, and watered the flock of his mother's brother La'ban. [11]Then Jacob kissed Rachel, and wept aloud. [12]And Jacob told Rachel that he was her father's kinsman, and that he was Rebekah's son; and she ran and told her father.

13 When La'ban heard the news about his sister's son Jacob, he ran to meet him; he embraced him and kissed him, and brought him to his house. Jacob[n] told La'ban all these things, [14]and La'ban said to him, "Surely you are my bone and my flesh!" And he stayed with him a month.

Jacob Marries Laban's Daughters

15 Then La'ban said to Jacob, "Because you are my kinsman, should you therefore serve me for nothing? Tell me, what shall your wages be?" [16]Now La'ban had two daughters; the name of the elder was Leah, and the name of the younger was Rachel. [17]Leah's eyes were lovely,[o] and Rachel was graceful and beautiful. [18]Jacob loved Rachel; so he said, "I will serve you seven years for your younger daughter Rachel." [19]La'ban said, "It is better that I give her to you than that I should give her to any other man; stay with me." [20]So Jacob served seven years for Rachel, and they seemed to him but a few days because of the love he had for her.

21 Then Jacob said to La'ban, "Give me my wife that I may go in to her, for my time is completed." [22]So La'ban gathered together all the people of the place, and made a feast. [23]But in the evening he took his daughter Leah and brought her to Jacob; and he went in to her. [24](La'ban gave his maid Zil'pah to his daughter Leah to be her maid.) [25]When morning came, it was Leah! And Jacob said to La'ban, "What is this you have done to me? Did I not serve with you for Rachel? Why then have you deceived me?" [26]La'ban said, "This is not done in our country—giving the younger before the firstborn. [27]Complete the week of this one, and we will give you the other also in return for serving me another seven

[n] Heb *He* [o] Meaning of Heb uncertain

years." [28]Jacob did so, and completed her week; then Lā´ban gave him his daughter Rachel as a wife. [29](Lā´ban gave his maid Bil´hah to his daughter Rachel to be her maid.) [30]So Jacob went in to Rachel also, and he loved Rachel more than Leah. He served Lā´ban[p] for another seven years.

31 When the LORD saw that Leah was unloved, he opened her womb; but Rachel was barren. [32]Leah conceived and bore a son, and she named him Reuben;[q] for she said, "Because the LORD has looked on my affliction; surely now my husband will love me." [33]She conceived again and bore a son, and said, "Because the LORD has heard[r] that I am hated, he has given me this son also"; and she named him Sim´e·on. [34]Again she conceived and bore a son, and said, "Now this time my husband will be joined[s] to me, because I have borne him three sons"; therefore he was named Levi. [35]She conceived again and bore a son, and said, "This time I will praise[t] the LORD"; therefore she named him Judah; then she ceased bearing.

30 When Rachel saw that she bore Jacob no children, she envied her sister; and she said to Jacob, "Give me children, or I shall die!" [2]Jacob became very angry with Rachel and said, "Am I in the place of God, who has withheld from you the fruit of the womb?" [3]Then she said, "Here is my maid Bil´hah; go in to her, that she may bear upon my knees and that I too may have children through her." [4]So she gave him her maid Bil´hah as a wife; and Jacob went in to her. [5]And Bil´hah conceived and bore Jacob a son. [6]Then Rachel said, "God has judged me, and has also heard my voice and given me a son"; therefore she named him Dan.[u] [7]Rachel's maid Bil´hah conceived again and bore Jacob a second son. [8]Then Rachel said, "With mighty wrestlings I have wrestled[v] with my sister, and have prevailed"; so she named him Naph´ta·lī.

9 When Leah saw that she had ceased bearing children, she took her maid Zil´pah and gave her to Jacob as a wife. [10]Then Leah's maid Zil´pah bore Jacob a son. [11]And Leah said, "Good fortune!" so she named him Gad.[w] [12]Leah's maid Zil´pah bore Jacob a second son. [13]And Leah said, "Happy am I! For the women will call me happy"; so she named him Ash´er.[x]

14 In the days of wheat harvest Reuben went and found mandrakes in the field, and brought them to his mother Leah. Then Rachel said to Leah, "Please give me some of your son's mandrakes." [15]But she said to her, "Is it a small matter that you have taken away my husband? Would you take away my son's mandrakes also?" Rachel said, "Then he may lie with you tonight for your son's mandrakes." [16]When Jacob came from the field in the evening, Leah went out to meet him, and said, "You must come in to me; for I have hired you with my son's mandrakes." So he lay with her that night. [17]And God heeded Leah, and she conceived and bore Jacob a fifth son. [18]Leah said, "God has given me my hire[y] because I gave my maid to my husband"; so she named him Is´sa·char. [19]And Leah conceived again, and she bore Jacob a sixth son. [20]Then Leah said, "God has endowed me with a good dowry; now my husband will honor[z] me, because I have borne him six sons"; so she named him Zeb´ū·lun. [21]Afterwards she bore a daughter, and named her Dī´nah.

22 Then God remembered Rachel, and God heeded her and opened her womb. [23]She conceived and bore a son, and said, "God has taken away my reproach"; [24]and she named him Joseph,[a] saying, "May the LORD add to me another son!"

---

[p] Heb *him*   [q] That is *See, a son*   [r] Heb *shama*
[s] Heb *lawah*   [t] Heb *hodah*   [u] That is *He judged*   [v] Heb *niphtal*   [w] That is *Fortune*
[x] That is *Happy*   [y] Heb *sakar*   [z] Heb *zabal*
[a] That is *He adds*

Jacob Prospers at Laban's Expense

25 When Rachel had borne Joseph, Jacob said to Lā´ban, "Send me away, that I may go to my own home and country. ²⁶Give me my wives and my children for whom I have served you, and let me go; for you know very well the service I have given you." ²⁷But Lā´ban said to him, "If you will allow me to say so, I have learned by divination that the LORD has blessed me because of you; ²⁸name your wages, and I will give it." ²⁹Jacob said to him, "You yourself know how I have served you, and how your cattle have fared with me. ³⁰For you had little before I came, and it has increased abundantly; and the LORD has blessed you wherever I turned. But now when shall I provide for my own household also?" ³¹He said, "What shall I give you?" Jacob said, "You shall not give me anything; if you will do this for me, I will again feed your flock and keep it: ³²let me pass through all your flock today, removing from it every speckled and spotted sheep and every black lamb, and the spotted and speckled among the goats; and such shall be my wages. ³³So my honesty will answer for me later, when you come to look into my wages with you. Every one that is not speckled and spotted among the goats and black among the lambs, if found with me, shall be counted stolen." ³⁴Lā´ban said, "Good! Let it be as you have said." ³⁵But that day Lā´ban removed the male goats that were striped and spotted, and all the female goats that were speckled and spotted, every one that had white on it, and every lamb that was black, and put them in charge of his sons; ³⁶and he set a distance of three days' journey between himself and Jacob, while Jacob was pasturing the rest of Lā´ban's flock.

37 Then Jacob took fresh rods of poplar and almond and plane, and peeled white streaks in them, exposing the white of the rods. ³⁸He set the rods that he had peeled in front of the flocks in the troughs, that is, the watering places, where the flocks came to drink. And since they bred when they came to drink, ³⁹the flocks bred in front of the rods, and so the flocks produced young that were striped, speckled, and spotted. ⁴⁰Jacob separated the lambs, and set the faces of the flocks toward the striped and the completely black animals in the flock of Lā´ban; and he put his own droves apart, and did not put them with Lā´ban's flock. ⁴¹Whenever the stronger of the flock were breeding, Jacob laid the rods in the troughs before the eyes of the flock, that they might breed among the rods, ⁴²but for the feebler of the flock he did not lay them there; so the feebler were Lā´ban's, and the stronger Jacob's. ⁴³Thus the man grew exceedingly rich, and had large flocks, and male and female slaves, and camels and donkeys.

Jacob Flees with Family and Flocks

31 Now Jacob heard that the sons of Lā´ban were saying, "Jacob has taken all that was our father's; he has gained all this wealth from what belonged to our father." ²And Jacob saw that Lā´ban did not regard him as favorably as he did before. ³Then the LORD said to Jacob, "Return to the land of your ancestors and to your kindred, and I will be with you." ⁴So Jacob sent and called Rachel and Leah into the field where his flock was, ⁵and said to them, "I see that your father does not regard me as favorably as he did before. But the God of my father has been with me. ⁶You know that I have served your father with all my strength; ⁷yet your father has cheated me and changed my wages ten times, but God did not permit him to harm me. ⁸If he said, 'The speckled shall be your wages,' then all the flock bore speckled; and if he said, 'The striped shall be your wages,' then all the flock bore striped. ⁹Thus God has taken away the livestock of your father, and given them to me.

10 During the mating of the flock I once had a dream in which I looked up and saw that the male goats that leaped upon the flock were striped, speckled, and mottled. [11]Then the angel of God said to me in the dream, 'Jacob,' and I said, 'Here I am!' [12]And he said, 'Look up and see that all the goats that leap on the flock are striped, speckled, and mottled; for I have seen all that Lā´ban is doing to you. [13]I am the God of Beth´el,[b] where you anointed a pillar and made a vow to me. Now leave this land at once and return to the land of your birth.' " [14]Then Rachel and Leah answered him, "Is there any portion or inheritance left to us in our father's house? [15]Are we not regarded by him as foreigners? For he has sold us, and he has been using up the money given for us. [16]All the property that God has taken away from our father belongs to us and to our children; now then, do whatever God has said to you."

17 So Jacob arose, and set his children and his wives on camels; [18]and he drove away all his livestock, all the property that he had gained, the livestock in his possession that he had acquired in Pad´dan-ar´am, to go to his father Isaac in the land of Cā´naan.

19 Now Lā´ban had gone to shear his sheep, and Rachel stole her father's household gods. [20]And Jacob deceived Lā´ban the Ar·a·mē´an, in that he did not tell him that he intended to flee. [21]So he fled with all that he had; starting out he crossed the Euphrates,[c] and set his face toward the hill country of Gil´e·ad.

Laban Overtakes Jacob

22 On the third day Lā´ban was told that Jacob had fled. [23]So he took his kinsfolk with him and pursued him for seven days until he caught up with him in the hill country of Gil´e·ad. [24]But God came to Lā´ban the Ar·a·mē´an in a dream by night, and said to him, "Take heed that you say not a word to Jacob, either good or bad."

25 Lā´ban overtook Jacob. Now Jacob had pitched his tent in the hill country, and Lā´ban with his kinsfolk camped in the hill country of Gil´e·ad. [26]Lā´ban said to Jacob, "What have you done? You have deceived me, and carried away my daughters like captives of the sword. [27]Why did you flee secretly and deceive me and not tell me? I would have sent you away with mirth and songs, with tambourine and lyre. [28]And why did you not permit me to kiss my sons and my daughters farewell? What you have done is foolish. [29]It is in my power to do you harm; but the God of your father spoke to me last night, saying, 'Take heed that you speak to Jacob neither good nor bad.' [30]Even though you had to go because you longed greatly for your father's house, why did you steal my gods?" [31]Jacob answered Lā´ban, "Because I was afraid, for I thought that you would take your daughters from me by force. [32]But anyone with whom you find your gods shall not live. In the presence of our kinsfolk, point out what I have that is yours, and take it." Now Jacob did not know that Rachel had stolen the gods.[d]

33 So Lā´ban went into Jacob's tent, and into Leah's tent, and into the tent of the two maids, but he did not find them. And he went out of Leah's tent, and entered Rachel's. [34]Now Rachel had taken the household gods and put them in the camel's saddle, and sat on them. Lā´ban felt all about in the tent, but did not find them. [35]And she said to her father, "Let not my lord be angry that I cannot rise before you, for the way of women is upon me." So he searched, but did not find the household gods.

36 Then Jacob became angry, and upbraided Lā´ban. Jacob said to Lā´ban, "What is my offense? What is my sin, that you have hotly pursued me? [37]Although you have felt about through

[b] Cn: Meaning of Heb uncertain　　[c] Heb *the river*
[d] Heb *them*

all my goods, what have you found of all your household goods? Set it here before my kinsfolk and your kinsfolk, so that they may decide between us two. ³⁸These twenty years I have been with you; your ewes and your female goats have not miscarried, and I have not eaten the rams of your flocks. ³⁹That which was torn by wild beasts I did not bring to you; I bore the loss of it myself; of my hand you required it, whether stolen by day or stolen by night. ⁴⁰It was like this with me: by day the heat consumed me, and the cold by night, and my sleep fled from my eyes. ⁴¹These twenty years I have been in your house; I served you fourteen years for your two daughters, and six years for your flock, and you have changed my wages ten times. ⁴²If the God of my father, the God of Abraham and the Fear *e* of Isaac, had not been on my side, surely now you would have sent me away empty-handed. God saw my affliction and the labor of my hands, and rebuked you last night."

Laban and Jacob Make a Covenant

43 Then Lā'ban answered and said to Jacob, "The daughters are my daughters, the children are my children, the flocks are my flocks, and all that you see is mine. But what can I do today about these daughters of mine, or about their children whom they have borne? ⁴⁴Come now, let us make a covenant, you and I; and let it be a witness between you and me." ⁴⁵So Jacob took a stone, and set it up as a pillar. ⁴⁶And Jacob said to his kinsfolk, "Gather stones," and they took stones, and made a heap; and they ate there by the heap. ⁴⁷Lā'ban called it Jē·gar-sā·ha·dū'tha;*f* but Jacob called it Gal'e·ed.*g* ⁴⁸Lā'ban said, "This heap is a witness between you and me today." Therefore he called it Gal'e·ed, ⁴⁹and the pillar*h* Miz'pah,*i* for he said, "The LORD watch between you and me, when we are absent one from the other. ⁵⁰If you ill-treat my daughters, or if you take wives in addition to my daughters, though no one else is with us, remember that God is witness between you and me."

51 Then Lā'ban said to Jacob, "See this heap and see the pillar, which I have set between you and me. ⁵²This heap is a witness, and the pillar is a witness, that I will not pass beyond this heap to you, and you will not pass beyond this heap and this pillar to me, for harm. ⁵³May the God of Abraham and the God of Nā'hor"—the God of their father—"judge between us." So Jacob swore by the Fear*e* of his father Isaac, ⁵⁴and Jacob offered a sacrifice on the height and called his kinsfolk to eat bread; and they ate bread and tarried all night in the hill country.

55*j* Early in the morning Lā'ban rose up, and kissed his grandchildren and his daughters and blessed them; then he departed and returned home.

32 Jacob went on his way and the angels of God met him; ²and when Jacob saw them he said, "This is God's camp!" So he called that place Mā·ha·nā'im.*k*

Jacob Sends Presents to Appease Esau

3 Jacob sent messengers before him to his brother Esau in the land of Sē'ir, the country of Ē'dom, ⁴instructing them, "Thus you shall say to my lord Esau: Thus says your servant Jacob, 'I have lived with Lā'ban as an alien, and stayed until now; ⁵and I have oxen, donkeys, flocks, male and female slaves; and I have sent to tell my lord, in order that I may find favor in your sight.' "

6 The messengers returned to Jacob, saying, "We came to your brother Esau, and he is coming to meet you, and four hundred men are with him." ⁷Then Jacob was greatly afraid and distressed; and he

---

e Meaning of Heb uncertain   *j* In Aramaic *The heap of witness*   *g* In Hebrew *The heap of witness*   *h* Compare Sam: MT lacks *the pillar*   *i* That is *Watchpost*   *j* Ch 32.1 in Heb   *k* Here taken to mean *Two camps*

Jacob knew that God was gracious and merciful. He prayed for God's help in dealing with his brother Esau. Just as God heard Jacob's prayer, we know that God hears our prayers too. During times when we are afraid, we can pray to God for help.

divided the people that were with him, and the flocks and herds and camels, into two companies, [8]thinking, "If Esau comes to the one company and destroys it, then the company that is left will escape."

9 And Jacob said, "O God of my father Abraham and God of my father Isaac, O LORD who said to me, 'Return to your country and to your kindred, and I will do you good,' [10]I am not worthy of the least of all the steadfast love and all the faithfulness that you have shown to your servant, for with only my staff I crossed this Jordan; and now I have become two companies. [11]Deliver me, please, from the hand of my brother, from the hand of Esau, for I am afraid of him; he may come and kill us all, the mothers with the children. [12]Yet you have said, 'I will surely do you good, and make your offspring as the sand of the sea, which cannot be counted because of their number.' "

13 So he spent that night there, and from what he had with him he took a present for his brother Esau, [14]two hundred female goats and twenty male goats, two hundred ewes and twenty rams, [15]thirty milch camels and their colts, forty cows and ten bulls, twenty female donkeys and ten male donkeys. [16]These he delivered into the hand of his servants, every drove by itself, and said to his servants, "Pass on ahead of me, and put a space between drove and drove." [17]He instructed the foremost, "When Esau my brother meets you, and asks you, 'To whom do you belong? Where are you going? And whose are

these ahead of you?' [18]then you shall say, 'They belong to your servant Jacob; they are a present sent to my lord Esau; and moreover he is behind us.' " [19]He likewise instructed the second and the third and all who followed the droves, "You shall say the same thing to Esau when you meet him, [20]and you shall say, 'Moreover your servant Jacob is behind us.' " For he thought, "I may appease him with the present that goes ahead of me, and afterwards I shall see his face; perhaps he will accept me." [21]So the present passed on ahead of him; and he himself spent that night in the camp.

Jacob Wrestles at Peniel

22 The same night he got up and took his two wives, his two maids, and his eleven children, and crossed the ford of the Jab'bok. [23]He took them and sent them across the stream, and likewise everything that he had. [24]Jacob was left alone; and a man wrestled with him until daybreak. [25]When the man saw that he did not prevail against Jacob, he struck him on the hip socket; and Jacob's hip was put out of joint as he wrestled with him. [26]Then he said, "Let me go, for the day is breaking." But Jacob said, "I will not let you go, unless you bless me." [27]So

As he waited to cross into Canaan, God came to Jacob in the form of a man who wrestled with Jacob all night. God blessed Jacob and changed his name to Israel, a word that means "one who struggles with God."

The name Israel later came to refer to the descendants of Jacob and their land. After the kingdoms of Israel and Judah were destroyed, those who were left behind became a people rather than a nation.

he said to him, "What is your name?" And he said, "Jacob." [28]Then the man[l] said, "You shall no longer be called Jacob, but Israel,[m] for you have striven with God and with humans,[n] and have prevailed." [29]Then Jacob asked him, "Please tell me your name?" But he said, "Why is it that you ask my name?" And there he blessed him. [30]So Jacob called the place Pe·niʹel,[o] saying, "For I have seen God face to face, and yet my life is preserved." [31]The sun rose upon him as he passed Pe·nuʹel, limping because of his hip. [32]Therefore to this day the Israelites do not eat the thigh muscle that is on the hip socket, because he struck Jacob on the hip socket at the thigh muscle.

Jacob and Esau Meet

33 Now Jacob looked up and saw Esau coming, and four hundred men with him. So he divided the children among Leah and Rachel and the two maids. [2]He put the maids with their children in front, then Leah with her children, and Rachel and Joseph last of all. [3]He himself went on ahead of them, bowing himself to the ground seven times, until he came near his brother.

4 But Esau ran to meet him, and embraced him, and fell on his neck and kissed him, and they wept. [5]When Esau looked up and saw the women and children, he said, "Who are these with you?" Jacob said, "The children whom God has graciously given your servant." [6]Then the maids drew near, they and their children, and bowed down; [7]Leah likewise and her children drew near and bowed down; and finally Joseph and Rachel drew near, and they bowed down. [8]Esau said, "What do you mean by all this company that I met?" Jacob answered, "To find favor with my lord." [9]But Esau said, "I have enough, my brother; keep what you have for yourself." [10]Jacob said, "No, please; if I find favor with you, then accept my present from my hand; for truly to see your face is like seeing the face of God—since you have received

> "If I find favor with you, then accept my present from my hand; for truly to see your face is like seeing the face of God—since you have received me with such favor."
> Genesis 33:10

me with such favor. [11]Please accept my gift that is brought to you, because God has dealt graciously with me, and because I have everything I want." So he urged him, and he took it.

12 Then Esau said, "Let us journey on our way, and I will go alongside you." [13]But Jacob said to him, "My lord knows that the children are frail and that the flocks and herds, which are nursing, are a care to me; and if they are overdriven for one day, all the flocks will die. [14]Let my lord pass on ahead of his servant, and I will lead on slowly, according to the pace of the cattle that are before me and according to the pace of the children, until I come to my lord in Seʹir."

15 So Esau said, "Let me leave with you some of the people who are with me." But he said, "Why should my lord be so kind to me?" [16]So Esau returned that day on his way to Seʹir. [17]But Jacob journeyed to Sucʹcoth,[p] and built himself a house, and made booths for his cattle; therefore the place is called Sucʹcoth.

Jacob Reaches Shechem

18 Jacob came safely to the city of Sheʹchem, which is in the land of Caʹnaan, on his way from Padʹdan-arʹam; and he camped before the city. [19]And from the sons of Haʹmor, Sheʹchem's father, he bought for one hundred pieces of money[q] the plot of land on which he had pitched his tent. [20]There he erected an altar and called it El-E̅·loʹhe-Is·raʹel.[r]

---

[l] Heb *he*   [m] That is *The one who strives with God* or *God strives*   [n] Or *with divine and human beings*   [o] That is *The face of God*   [p] That is *Booths*   [q] Heb *one hundred qesitah*   [r] That is *God, the God of Israel*

The Rape of Dinah

34 Now Dī´nah the daughter of Leah, whom she had borne to Jacob, went out to visit the women of the region. [2]When Shē´chem son of Hā´mor the Hī´vīte, prince of the region, saw her, he seized her and lay with her by force. [3]And his soul was drawn to Dī´nah daughter of Jacob; he loved the girl, and spoke tenderly to her. [4]So Shē´chem spoke to his father Hā´mor, saying, "Get me this girl to be my wife."

5 Now Jacob heard that Shē´chem[s] had defiled his daughter Dī´nah; but his sons were with his cattle in the field, so Jacob held his peace until they came. [6]And Hā´mor the father of Shē´chem went out to Jacob to speak with him, [7]just as the sons of Jacob came in from the field. When they heard of it, the men were indignant and very angry, because he had committed an outrage in Israel by lying with Jacob's daughter, for such a thing ought not to be done.

8 But Hā´mor spoke with them, saying, "The heart of my son Shē´chem longs for your daughter; please give her to him in marriage. [9]Make marriages with us; give your daughters to us, and take our daughters for yourselves. [10]You shall live with us; and the land shall be open to you; live and trade in it, and get property in it." [11]Shē´chem also said to her father and to her brothers, "Let me find favor with you, and whatever you say to me I will give. [12]Put the marriage present and gift as high as you like, and I will give whatever you ask me; only give me the girl to be my wife."

13 The sons of Jacob answered Shē´chem and his father Hā´mor deceitfully, because he had defiled their sister Dī´nah. [14]They said to them, "We cannot do this thing, to give our sister to one who is uncircumcised, for that would be a disgrace to us. [15]Only on this condition will we consent to you: that you will become as we are and every male among you be circumcised. [16]Then we will give our daughters to you, and we will take your daughters for ourselves, and we will live among you and become one people. [17]But if you will not listen to us and be circumcised, then we will take our daughter and be gone."

18 Their words pleased Hā´mor and Hā´mor's son Shē´chem. [19]And the young man did not delay to do the thing, because he was delighted with Jacob's daughter. Now he was the most honored of all his family. [20]So Hā´mor and his son Shē´chem came to the gate of their city and spoke to the men of their city, saying, [21]"These people are friendly with us; let them live in the land and trade in it, for the land is large enough for them; let us take their daughters in marriage, and let us give them our daughters. [22]Only on this condition will they agree to live among us, to become one people: that every male among us be circumcised as they are circumcised. [23]Will not their livestock, their property, and all their animals be ours? Only let us agree with them, and they will live among us." [24]And all who went out of the city gate heeded Hā´mor and his son Shē´chem; and every male was circumcised, all who went out of the gate of his city.

Dinah's Brothers
Avenge Their Sister

25 On the third day, when they were still in pain, two of the sons of Jacob, Sim´e·on and Levi, Dī´nah's brothers, took their swords and came against the city unawares, and killed all the males. [26]They killed Hā´mor and his son Shē´chem with the sword, and took Dī´nah out of Shē´chem's house, and went away. [27]And the other sons of Jacob came upon the slain, and plundered the city, because their sister had been defiled. [28]They took their flocks and their herds, their donkeys, and whatever was in the city and in the field. [29]All their wealth,

[s] Heb *he*

all their little ones and their wives, all that was in the houses, they captured and made their prey. ³⁰Then Jacob said to Sim´ē·on and Levi, "You have brought trouble on me by making me odious to the inhabitants of the land, the Cā´naan-ītes and the Per´iz·zītes; my numbers are few, and if they gather themselves against me and attack me, I shall be destroyed, both I and my household." ³¹But they said, "Should our sister be treated like a whore?"

Jacob Returns to Bethel

35 God said to Jacob, "Arise, go up to Beth´el, and settle there. Make an altar there to the God who appeared to you when you fled from your brother Esau." ²So Jacob said to his household and to all who were with him, "Put away the foreign gods that are among you, and purify yourselves, and change your clothes; ³then come, let us go up to Beth´el, that I may make an altar there to the God who answered me in the day of my distress and has been with me wherever I have gone." ⁴So they gave to Jacob all the foreign gods that they had, and the rings that were in their ears; and Jacob hid them under the oak that was near Shē´chem.

5 As they journeyed, a terror from God fell upon the cities all around them, so that no one pursued them. ⁶Jacob came to Luz (that is, Beth´el), which is in the land of Cā´naan, he and all the people who were with him, ⁷and there he built an altar and called the place El-beth´el,ᵗ because it was there that God had revealed himself to him when he fled from his brother. ⁸And Deb´or·ah, Rebekah's nurse, died, and she was buried under an oak below Beth´el. So it was called Al´lon-bac´uth.ᵘ

9 God appeared to Jacob again when he came from Pad´dan-ar´am, and he blessed him. ¹⁰God said to him, "Your name is Jacob; no longer shall you be called Jacob, but Israel shall be your name." So he was called Israel. ¹¹God said to him, "I am God Almighty:ᵛ be fruitful and multiply; a nation and a company of nations shall come from you, and kings shall spring from you. ¹²The land that I gave to Abraham and Isaac I will give to you, and I will give the land to your offspring after you." ¹³Then God went up from him at the place where he had spoken with him. ¹⁴Jacob set up a pillar in the place where he had spoken with him, a pillar of stone; and he poured out a drink offering on it, and poured oil on it. ¹⁵So Jacob called the place where God had spoken with him Beth´el.

The Birth of Benjamin and the Death of Rachel

16 Then they journeyed from Beth´el; and when they were still some distance from Eph´rath, Rachel was in childbirth, and she had hard labor. ¹⁷When she was in her hard labor, the midwife said to her, "Do not be afraid; for now you will have another son." ¹⁸As her soul was departing (for she died), she named him Ben-ō´ni;ʷ but his father called him Benjamin.ˣ ¹⁹So Rachel died, and she was buried on the way to Eph´rath (that is, Bethlehem), ²⁰and Jacob set up a pillar at her grave; it is the pillar of Rachel's tomb, which is there to this day. ²¹Israel journeyed on, and pitched his tent beyond the tower of Ē´der.

22 While Israel lived in that land, Reuben went and lay with Bil´hah his father's concubine; and Israel heard of it.

Now the sons of Jacob were twelve. ²³The sons of Leah: Reuben (Jacob's firstborn), Sim´ē·on, Levi, Judah, Is´sa·char, and Zeb´ū·lun. ²⁴The sons of Rachel: Joseph and Benjamin. ²⁵The sons of Bil´hah, Rachel's maid: Dan and Naph´ta·lī. ²⁶The sons of Zil´pah, Leah's maid: Gad and Ash´er. These were the sons of Jacob who were born to him in Pad´dan-ar´am.

ᵗ That is God of Bethel ᵘ That is Oak of weeping
ᵛ Traditional rendering of Heb El Shaddai
ʷ That is Son of my sorrow ˣ That is Son of the right hand or Son of the South

The Death of Isaac

27Jacob came to his father Isaac at Mam´re, or Kir´i·ath-ar´ba (that is, Hē´bron), where Abraham and Isaac had resided as aliens. 28Now the days of Isaac were one hundred eighty years. 29And Isaac breathed his last; he died and was gathered to his people, old and full of days; and his sons Esau and Jacob buried him.

Esau's Descendants

36 These are the descendants of Esau (that is, Ē´dom). 2Esau took his wives from the Cā´naan·ites: Ā´dah daughter of Ē´lon the Hit´tīte, Ō·hol·i·bā´mah daughter of An´ah son[y] of Zib´ē·on the Hī´vīte, 3and Bas´e·math, Ish´ma·el's daughter, sister of Ne·bā´i·oth. 4Ā´dah bore E·lī´phaz to Esau; Bas´e·math bore Reū´el; 5and Ō·hol·i·bā´mah bore Jē´ush, Jā´lam, and Kō´rah. These are the sons of Esau who were born to him in the land of Cā´naan.

6 Then Esau took his wives, his sons, his daughters, and all the members of his household, his cattle, all his livestock, and all the property he had acquired in the land of Cā´naan; and he moved to a land some distance from his brother Jacob. 7For their possessions were too great for them to live together; the land where they were staying could not support them because of their livestock. 8So Esau settled in the hill country of Sē´ir; Esau is Ē´dom.

9 These are the descendants of Esau, ancestor of the Ē´dom·ītes, in the hill country of Sē´ir. 10These are the names of Esau's sons: E·lī´phaz son of Ā´dah the wife of Esau; Reū´el, the son of Esau's wife Bas´e·math. 11The sons of E·lī´phaz were Tē´man, Ō´mar, Zē´phō, Gā´tam, and Kē´naz. 12(Tim´na was a concubine of E·lī´phaz, Esau's son; she bore Am´a·lek to E·lī´phaz.) These were the sons of Ā´dah, Esau's wife. 13These were the sons of Reū´el: Nā´hath, Zē´rah, Sham´mah, and Miz´zah. These were the sons of Esau's wife, Bas´e·math.

14These were the sons of Esau's wife Ō·hol·i·bā´mah, daughter of An´ah son[y] of Zib´ē·on: she bore to Esau Jē´ush, Jā´lam, and Kō´rah.

Clans and Kings of Edom

15 These are the clans[z] of the sons of Esau. The sons of E·lī´phaz the firstborn of Esau: the clans[z] Tē´man, Ō´mar, Zē´phō, Kē´naz, 16Kō´rah, Gā´tam, and Am´a·lek; these are the clans[z] of E·lī´phaz in the land of Ē´dom; they are the sons of Ā´dah. 17These are the sons of Esau's son Reū´el: the clans[z] Nā´hath, Zē´rah, Sham´mah, and Miz´zah; these are the clans[z] of Reū´el in the land of Ē´dom; they are the sons of Esau's wife Bas´e·math. 18These are the sons of Esau's wife Ō·hol·i·bā´mah: the clans[z] Jē´ush, Jā´lam, and Kō´rah; these are the clans[z] born of Esau's wife Ō·hol·i·bā´mah, the daughter of An´ah. 19These are the sons of Esau (that is, Ē´dom), and these are their clans.[z]

20 These are the sons of Sē´ir the Hor´īte, the inhabitants of the land: Lō´tan, Shō´bal, Zib´ē·on, An´ah, 21Dī´shon, Ē´zer, and Dī´shan; these are the clans[z] of the Hor´ītes, the sons of Sē´ir in the land of Ē´dom. 22The sons of Lō´tan were Hō´rī and Hē´man; and Lō´tan's sister was Tim´na. 23These are the sons of Shō´bal: Al´van, Man´a·hath, Ē´bal, Shē´phō, and Ō´nam. 24These are the sons of Zib´ē·on: Ā´i·ah and An´ah; he is the An´ah who found the springs[a] in the wilderness, as he pastured the donkeys of his father Zib´ē·on. 25These are the children of An´ah: Dī´shon and Ō·hol·i·bā´mah daughter of An´ah. 26These are the sons of Dī´shon: Hem´dan, Esh´ban, Ith´ran, and Chē´ran. 27These are the sons of Ē´zer: Bil´han, Zā´a·van, and Ā´kan. 28These are the sons of Dī´shan: Uz and Ar´an. 29These are the clans[z] of the Hor´ītes: the clans[z] Lō´tan, Shō´bal, Zib´ē·on,

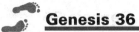
An´ah, ³⁰Dī´shon, Ē´zer, and Dī´shan; these are the clans^b of the Hor´ites, clan by clan^c in the land of Sē´ir.

31 These are the kings who reigned in the land of Ē´dom, before any king reigned over the Israelites. ³²Bē´la son of Bē´or reigned in Ē´dom, the name of his city being Din´ha·bah. ³³Bē´la died, and Jō´bab son of Zē´rah of Boz´rah succeeded him as king. ³⁴Jō´bab died, and Hū´sham of the land of the Tē´man·ites succeeded him as king. ³⁵Hū´sham died, and Hā´dad son of Bē´dad, who defeated Mid´i·an in the country of Mō´ab, succeeded him as king, the name of his city being Ā´vith. ³⁶Hā´dad died, and Sam´lah of Mas·rē´kah succeeded him as king. ³⁷Sam´lah died, and Shā´ul of Re·hō´both on the Euphrates succeeded him as king. ³⁸Shā´ul died, and Bā´al-hā´nan son of Ach´bor succeeded him as king. ³⁹Bā´al-hā´nan son of Ach´bor died, and Hā´dar succeeded him as king, the name of his city being Pā´u; his wife's name was Me·het´a·bel, the daughter of Mā´tred, daughter of Me-za·hab´.

40 These are the names of the clans^b of Esau, according to their families and their localities by their names: the clans^b Tim´na, Al´vah, Jē´theth, ⁴¹Ō·hol·i·bā´-mah, Ē´lah, Pī´non, ⁴²Kē´naz, Tē´man, Mib´zar, ⁴³Mag´di·el, and Ī´ram; these are the clans^b of Ē´dom (that is, Esau, the father of Ē´dom), according to their settlements in the land that they held.

Jacob had twelve sons, but only two of them were also the sons of his beloved wife Rachel, and he loved them more than the others. He loved Joseph best and gave him a special robe. We often call it a coat of many colors, but we don't really know what it looked like. The robe set Joseph apart from his brothers, who were often jealous of him.

Joseph Dreams of Greatness

37 Jacob settled in the land where his father had lived as an alien, the land of Cā´naan. ²This is the story of the family of Jacob.

Joseph, being seventeen years old, was shepherding the flock with his brothers; he was a helper to the sons of Bil´hah and Zil´pah, his father's wives; and Joseph brought a bad report of them to their father. ³Now Israel loved Joseph more than any other of his children, because he was the son of his old age; and he had made him a long robe with sleeves.^d ⁴But when his brothers saw that their father loved him more than all his brothers, they hated him, and could not speak peaceably to him.

5 Once Joseph had a dream, and when he told it to his brothers, they hated him even more. ⁶He said to them, "Listen to this dream that I dreamed. ⁷There we were, binding sheaves in the field. Suddenly my sheaf rose and stood upright; then your sheaves gathered around it, and bowed down to my sheaf." ⁸His brothers said to him, "Are you indeed to reign over us? Are you indeed to have dominion over us?" So they hated him even more because of his dreams and his words.

9 He had another dream, and told it to his brothers, saying, "Look, I have had another dream: the sun, the moon, and eleven stars were bowing down to me." ¹⁰But when he told it to his father and to his brothers, his father rebuked him, and said to him, "What kind of dream is this that you have had? Shall we indeed come, I and your mother and your brothers, and bow to the ground before you?" ¹¹So his brothers were jealous of him, but his father kept the matter in mind.

Joseph Is Sold by His Brothers

12 Now his brothers went to pasture their father's flock near Shē´chem. ¹³And

^b Or *chiefs*   ^c Or *chief by chief*   ^d Traditional rendering (compare Gk): *a coat of many colors*; Meaning of Heb uncertain

Israel said to Joseph, "Are not your brothers pasturing the flock at Shē′-chem? Come, I will send you to them." He answered, "Here I am." [14]So he said to him, "Go now, see if it is well with your brothers and with the flock; and bring word back to me." So he sent him from the valley of Hē′bron.

He came to Shē′chem, [15]and a man found him wandering in the fields; the man asked him, "What are you seeking?" [16]"I am seeking my brothers," he said; "tell me, please, where they are pasturing the flock." [17]The man said, "They have gone away, for I heard them say, 'Let us go to Dō′than.'" So Joseph went after his brothers, and found them at Dō′than. [18]They saw him from a distance, and before he came near to them, they conspired to kill him. [19]They said to one another, "Here comes this dreamer. [20]Come now, let us kill him and throw him into one of the pits; then we shall say that a wild animal has devoured him, and we shall see what will become of his dreams." [21]But when Reuben heard it, he delivered him out of their hands, saying, "Let us not take his life." [22]Reuben said to them, "Shed no blood; throw him into this pit here in the wilderness, but lay no hand on him"—that he might rescue him out of their hand and restore him to his father. [23]So when Joseph came to his brothers, they stripped him of his robe, the long robe with sleeves[e] that he wore; [24]and they took him and threw him into a pit. The pit was empty; there was no water in it.

25 Then they sat down to eat; and looking up they saw a caravan of Ish′-ma·el·ītes coming from Gil′e·ad, with their camels carrying gum, balm, and resin, on their way to carry it down to Egypt. [26]Then Judah said to his brothers, "What profit is it if we kill our brother and conceal his blood? [27]Come, let us sell him to the Ish′ma·el·ītes, and not lay our hands on him, for he is our brother, our own flesh." And his brothers agreed. [28]When some Mid′i·an·īte traders passed by, they drew Joseph up, lifting him out of the pit, and sold him to the Ish′ma·el·ītes for twenty pieces of silver. And they took Joseph to Egypt.

29 When Reuben returned to the pit and saw that Joseph was not in the pit, he tore his clothes. [30]He returned to his brothers, and said, "The boy is gone; and I, where can I turn?" [31]Then they took Joseph's robe, slaughtered a goat, and dipped the robe in the blood. [32]They had the long robe with sleeves[f] taken to their father, and they said, "This we have found; see now whether it is your son's robe or not." [33]He recognized it, and said, "It is my son's robe! A wild animal has devoured him; Joseph is without doubt torn to pieces." [34]Then Jacob tore his garments, and put sackcloth on his loins, and mourned for his son many days. [35]All his sons and all his daughters sought to comfort him; but he refused to be comforted, and said, "No, I shall go down to Shē′ōl to my son, mourning." Thus his father bewailed him. [36]Meanwhile the Mid′i·an·ītes had sold him in Egypt to Pot′i·phar, one of Pharaoh's officials, the captain of the guard.

Judah and Tamar

38 It happened at that time that Judah went down from his brothers and settled near a certain A·dul′lam·īte whose name was Hī′rah. [2]There Judah saw the daughter of a certain Cā′naan·īte whose name was Shū′a;

A caravan was a group of people who traveled together. Caravan routes crisscrossed the ancient world. Donkeys and camels were used to carry goods. Joseph's brothers sold him to a caravan of merchants that was headed for Egypt.

[e] See note on 37.3   [f] See note on 37.3

Judah probably saved Joseph's life by suggesting the brothers sell him to the passing caravan. He was the fourth son of Jacob and became the leader of the tribe descended from him, which took his name. In the Old Testament, King David was the most famous descendant of the tribe. The New Testament lists Judah as Jesus's ancestor.

he married her and went in to her. ³She conceived and bore a son; and he named him Er. ⁴Again she conceived and bore a son whom she named Ō´nan. ⁵Yet again she bore a son, and she named him Shē´-lah. She^g was in Chē´zib when she bore him. ⁶Judah took a wife for Er his firstborn; her name was Tā´mar. ⁷But Er, Judah's firstborn, was wicked in the sight of the LORD, and the LORD put him to death. ⁸Then Judah said to Ō´nan, "Go in to your brother's wife and perform the duty of a brother-in-law to her; raise up offspring for your brother." ⁹But since Ō´nan knew that the offspring would not be his, he spilled his semen on the ground whenever he went in to his brother's wife, so that he would not give offspring to his brother. ¹⁰What he did was displeasing in the sight of the LORD, and he put him to death also. ¹¹Then Judah said to his daughter-in-law Tā´-mar, "Remain a widow in your father's house until my son Shē´lah grows up"— for he feared that he too would die, like his brothers. So Tā´mar went to live in her father's house.

12 In course of time the wife of Judah, Shū´a's daughter, died; when Judah's time of mourning was over,^h he went up to Tim´nah to his sheepshearers, he and his friend Hī´rah the A·dul´lam·īte. ¹³When Tā´mar was told, "Your father-in-law is going up to

Tim´nah to shear his sheep," ¹⁴she put off her widow's garments, put on a veil, wrapped herself up, and sat down at the entrance to E·nā´im, which is on the road to Tim´nah. She saw that Shē´lah was grown up, yet she had not been given to him in marriage. ¹⁵When Judah saw her, he thought her to be a prostitute, for she had covered her face. ¹⁶He went over to her at the roadside, and said, "Come, let me come in to you," for he did not know that she was his daughter-in-law. She said, "What will you give me, that you may come in to me?" ¹⁷He answered, "I will send you a kid from the flock." And she said, "Only if you give me a pledge, until you send it." ¹⁸He said, "What pledge shall I give you?" She replied, "Your signet and your cord, and the staff that is in your hand." So he gave them to her, and went in to her, and she conceived by him. ¹⁹Then she got up and went away, and taking off her veil she put on the garments of her widowhood.

20 When Judah sent the kid by his friend the A·dul´lam·īte, to recover the pledge from the woman, he could not find her. ²¹He asked the townspeople, "Where is the temple prostitute who was at E·nā´im by the wayside?" But they said, "No prostitute has been here." ²²So he returned to Judah, and said, "I have not found her; moreover the townspeople said, 'No prostitute has been here.' " ²³Judah replied, "Let her keep the things as her own, otherwise we will be laughed at; you see, I sent this kid, and you could not find her."

24 About three months later Judah was told, "Your daughter-in-law Tā´mar has played the whore; moreover she is pregnant as a result of whoredom." And Judah said, "Bring her out, and let her be burned." ²⁵As she was being brought out, she sent word to her father-in-law, "It was the owner of these who made me pregnant." And she said, "Take note, please, whose these are, the signet and

^g Gk: Heb He   ^h Heb when Judah was comforted

the cord and the staff." ²⁶Then Judah acknowledged them and said, "She is more in the right than I, since I did not give her to my son Shē′lah." And he did not lie with her again.

27 When the time of her delivery came, there were twins in her womb. ²⁸While she was in labor, one put out a hand; and the midwife took and bound on his hand a crimson thread, saying, "This one came out first." ²⁹But just then he drew back his hand, and out came his brother; and she said, "What a breach you have made for yourself!" Therefore he was named Per′ez.ʲ ³⁰Afterward his brother came out with the crimson thread on his hand; and he was named Zē′rah.ˡ

Joseph and Potiphar's Wife

39 Now Joseph was taken down to Egypt, and Pot′i·phar, an officer of Pharaoh, the captain of the guard, an Egyptian, bought him from the Ish′-ma·el·ītes who had brought him down there. ²The LORD was with Joseph, and he became a successful man; he was in the house of his Egyptian master. ³His master saw that the LORD was with him, and that the LORD caused all that he did to prosper in his hands. ⁴So Joseph found favor in his sight and attended him; he made him overseer of his house and put him in charge of all that he had. ⁵From the time that he made him overseer in his house and over all that he had, the LORD blessed the Egyptian's house for Joseph's sake; the blessing of the LORD was on all that he had, in house and field. ⁶So he left all that he had in Joseph's charge; and, with him there, he had no concern for anything but the food that he ate.

Now Joseph was handsome and good-looking. ⁷And after a time his master's wife cast her eyes on Joseph and said, "Lie with me." ⁸But he refused and said to his master's wife, "Look, with me here, my master has no concern about anything in the house, and he has put

everything that he has in my hand. ⁹He is not greater in this house than I am, nor has he kept back anything from me except yourself, because you are his wife. How then could I do this great wickedness, and sin against God?" ¹⁰And although she spoke to Joseph day after day, he would not consent to lie beside her or to be with her. ¹¹One day, however, when he went into the house to do his work, and while no one else was in the house, ¹²she caught hold of his garment, saying, "Lie with me!" But he left his garment in her hand, and fled and ran outside. ¹³When she saw that he had left his garment in her hand and had fled outside, ¹⁴she called out to the members of her household and said to them, "See, my husbandᵏ has brought among us a Hebrew to insult us! He came in to me to lie with me, and I cried out with a loud voice; ¹⁵and when he heard me raise my voice and cry out, he left his garment beside me, and fled outside." ¹⁶Then she kept his garment by her until his master came home, ¹⁷and she told him the same story, saying, "The Hebrew servant, whom you have brought among us, came in to me to insult me; ¹⁸but as soon as I raised my voice and cried out, he left his garment beside me, and fled outside."

19 When his master heard the words that his wife spoke to him, saying, "This is the way your servant treated me," he

An Egyptian official named Potiphar bought Joseph from the merchants. Later, he had Joseph put into prison. Even in prison, God was with Joseph. The Bible is full of stories about God taking care of people in hard times! When we have problems, we can remember these stories and know that God is with us too.

ˡ That is *A breach* ʲ That is *Brightness*; perhaps alluding to the crimson thread ᵏ Heb *he* became enraged. ²⁰And Joseph's master took him and put him into the prison, the place where the king's prisoners were confined; he remained there in prison. ²¹But the LORD was with Joseph and showed him steadfast love; he gave him favor in the sight of the chief jailer. ²²The chief jailer committed to Joseph's care all the prisoners who were in the prison, and whatever was done there, he was the one who did it. ²³The chief jailer paid no heed to anything that was in Joseph's care, because the LORD was with him; and whatever he did, the LORD made it prosper.

The Dreams of Two Prisoners

40 Some time after this, the cupbearer of the king of Egypt and his baker offended their lord the king of Egypt. ²Pharaoh was angry with his two officers, the chief cupbearer and the chief baker, ³and he put them in custody in the house of the captain of the guard, in the prison where Joseph was confined. ⁴The captain of the guard charged Joseph with them, and he waited on them; and they continued for some time in custody. ⁵One night they both dreamed—the cupbearer and the baker of the king of Egypt, who were confined in the prison—each his own dream, and each dream with its own meaning. ⁶When Joseph came to them in the morning, he saw that they were troubled. ⁷So he asked Pharaoh's officers, who were with him in custody in his master's house, "Why are your faces downcast today?" ⁸They said to him, "We have had dreams, and there is no one to interpret them." And Joseph said to them, "Do not interpretations belong to God? Please tell them to me."

9 So the chief cupbearer told his dream to Joseph, and said to him, "In my dream there was a vine before me, ¹⁰and on the vine there were three branches. As soon as it budded, its blossoms came out and the clusters ripened into grapes. ¹¹Pharaoh's cup was in my hand; and I took the grapes and pressed them into Pharaoh's cup, and placed the cup in Pharaoh's hand." ¹²Then Joseph said to him, "This is its interpretation: the three branches are three days; ¹³within three days Pharaoh will lift up your head and restore you to your office; and you shall place Pharaoh's cup in his hand, just as you used to do when you were his cupbearer. ¹⁴But remember me when it is well with you; please do me the kindness to make mention of me to Pharaoh, and so get me out of this place. ¹⁵For in fact I was stolen out of the land of the Hebrews; and here also I have done nothing that they should have put me into the dungeon."

16 When the chief baker saw that the interpretation was favorable, he said to Joseph, "I also had a dream: there were three cake baskets on my head, ¹⁷and in the uppermost basket there were all sorts of baked food for Pharaoh, but the birds were eating it out of the basket on my head." ¹⁸And Joseph answered, "This is its interpretation: the three baskets are three days; ¹⁹within three days Pharaoh will lift up your head—from you!—and hang you on a pole; and the birds will eat the flesh from you."

20 On the third day, which was Pharaoh's birthday, he made a feast for all his servants, and lifted up the head of the chief cupbearer and the head of the chief baker among his servants. ²¹He restored the chief cupbearer to his cupbearing, and he placed the cup in Pharaoh's hand; ²²but the chief baker he hanged, just as Joseph had interpreted to them. ²³Yet the chief cupbearer did not remember Joseph, but forgot him.

Joseph Interprets Pharaoh's Dream

41 After two whole years, Pharaoh dreamed that he was standing by the Nile, ²and there came up out of the Nile seven sleek and fat cows, and they grazed in the reed grass. ³Then seven other cows, ugly and thin, came up out of the Nile after them, and stood by the other cows on the bank of the Nile. ⁴The ugly and thin cows ate up the seven sleek and fat cows. And Pharaoh awoke. ⁵Then he fell asleep and dreamed a second time; seven ears of grain, plump and good, were growing on one stalk. ⁶Then seven ears, thin and blighted by the east wind, sprouted after them. ⁷The thin ears swallowed up the seven plump and full ears. Pharaoh awoke, and it was a dream. ⁸In the morning his spirit was troubled; so he sent and called for all the magicians of Egypt and all its wise men. Pharaoh told them his dreams, but there was no one who could interpret them to Pharaoh.

9 Then the chief cupbearer said to Pharaoh, "I remember my faults today. ¹⁰Once Pharaoh was angry with his servants, and put me and the chief baker in custody in the house of the captain of the guard. ¹¹We dreamed on the same night, he and I, each having a dream with its own meaning. ¹²A young Hebrew was there with us, a servant of the captain of the guard. When we told him, he interpreted our dreams to us, giving an interpretation to each according to his dream. ¹³As he interpreted to us, so it turned out; I was restored to my office, and the baker was hanged."

14 Then Pharaoh sent for Joseph, and he was hurriedly brought out of the dungeon. When he had shaved himself and changed his clothes, he came in before Pharaoh. ¹⁵And Pharaoh said to Joseph, "I have had a dream, and there is no one who can interpret it. I have heard it said of you that when you hear a dream you can interpret it." ¹⁶Joseph answered Pharaoh, "It is not I; God will give Pharaoh a favorable answer." ¹⁷Then Pharaoh said to Joseph, "In my dream I was standing on the banks of the Nile; ¹⁸and seven cows, fat and sleek, came up out of the Nile and fed in the reed grass. ¹⁹Then seven other cows came up after

them, poor, very ugly, and thin. Never had I seen such ugly ones in all the land of Egypt. ²⁰The thin and ugly cows ate up the first seven fat cows, ²¹but when they had eaten them no one would have known that they had done so, for they were still as ugly as before. Then I awoke. ²²I fell asleep a second time[l] and I saw in my dream seven ears of grain, full and good, growing on one stalk, ²³and seven ears, withered, thin, and blighted by the east wind, sprouting after them; ²⁴and the thin ears swallowed up the seven good ears. But when I told it to the magicians, there was no one who could explain it to me."

25 Then Joseph said to Pharaoh, "Pharaoh's dreams are one and the same; God has revealed to Pharaoh what he is about to do. ²⁶The seven good cows are seven years, and the seven good ears are seven years; the dreams are one. ²⁷The seven lean and ugly cows that came up after them are seven years, as are the seven empty ears blighted by the east wind. They are seven years of famine. ²⁸It is as I told Pharaoh; God has shown to Pharaoh what he is about to do. ²⁹There will come seven years of great plenty

A famine is a period of time when there is not enough food to eat. A famine can happen if there is not enough rain for the crops to grow. Famines can also be caused by insects, war, disasters, and disease of grain or cattle. God warned Joseph about a famine that would happen. Joseph helped the country of Egypt get ready by storing up extra grain during the years before the famine. He not only saved the people of Egypt, but also his family.

---

l Gk Syr Vg: Heb lacks *I fell asleep a second time*

throughout all the land of Egypt. ³⁰After them there will arise seven years of famine, and all the plenty will be forgotten in the land of Egypt; the famine will consume the land. ³¹The plenty will no longer be known in the land because of the famine that will follow, for it will be very grievous. ³²And the doubling of Pharaoh's dream means that the thing is fixed by God, and God will shortly bring it about. ³³Now therefore let Pharaoh select a man who is discerning and wise, and set him over the land of Egypt. ³⁴Let Pharaoh proceed to appoint overseers over the land, and take one-fifth of the produce of the land of Egypt during the seven plenteous years. ³⁵Let them gather all the food of these good years that are coming, and lay up grain under the authority of Pharaoh for food in the cities, and let them keep it. ³⁶That food shall be a reserve for the land against the seven years of famine that are to befall the land of Egypt, so that the land may not perish through the famine."

Joseph's Rise to Power

37 The proposal pleased Pharaoh and all his servants. ³⁸Pharaoh said to his servants, "Can we find anyone else like this—one in whom is the spirit of God?" ³⁹So Pharaoh said to Joseph, "Since God has shown you all this, there is no one so discerning and wise as you. ⁴⁰You shall be over my house, and all my people shall order themselves as you command; only with regard to the throne will I be greater than you." ⁴¹And Pharaoh said to Joseph, "See, I have set you over all the land of Egypt." ⁴²Removing his signet ring from his hand, Pharaoh put it on Joseph's hand; he arrayed him in garments of fine linen, and put a gold chain around his neck. ⁴³He had him ride in the chariot of his second-in-command; and they cried out in front of him, "Bow the knee!"ᵐ Thus he set him over all the land of Egypt. ⁴⁴Moreover Pharaoh said to Joseph, "I am Pharaoh, and without your consent no one shall lift up hand or

foot in all the land of Egypt." ⁴⁵Pharaoh gave Joseph the name Zaph·e·nath-pa·ně′ah; and he gave him As′e·nath daughter of Pō·ti′phe·ra, priest of On, as his wife. Thus Joseph gained authority over the land of Egypt.

46 Joseph was thirty years old when he entered the service of Pharaoh king of Egypt. And Joseph went out from the presence of Pharaoh, and went through all the land of Egypt. ⁴⁷During the seven plenteous years the earth produced abundantly. ⁴⁸He gathered up all the food of the seven years when there was plentyⁿ in the land of Egypt, and stored up food in the cities; he stored up in every city the food from the fields around it. ⁴⁹So Joseph stored up grain in such abundance—like the sand of the sea—that he stopped measuring it; it was beyond measure.

50 Before the years of famine came, Joseph had two sons, whom As′e·nath daughter of Pō·ti′phe·ra, priest of On, bore to him. ⁵¹Joseph named the firstborn Ma·nas′seh,ᵒ "For," he said, "God has made me forget all my hardship and all my father's house." ⁵²The second he named Ē′phra·im,ᵖ "For God has made me fruitful in the land of my misfortunes."

53 The seven years of plenty that prevailed in the land of Egypt came to an end; ⁵⁴and the seven years of famine began to come, just as Joseph had said. There was famine in every country, but throughout the land of Egypt there was bread. ⁵⁵When all the land of Egypt was famished, the people cried to Pharaoh for bread. Pharaoh said to all the Egyptians, "Go to Joseph; what he says to you, do." ⁵⁶And since the famine had spread over all the land, Joseph opened all the storehouses,�q and sold to the Egyptians, for the famine was severe in

ᵐ *Abrek*, apparently an Egyptian word similar in sound to the Hebrew word meaning *to kneel*
ⁿ Sam Gk: MT *the seven years that were*   ᵒ That is *Making to forget*   ᵖ From a Hebrew word meaning *to be fruitful*   q Gk Vg Compare Syr: Heb *opened all that was in* (or, *among*) *them*

the land of Egypt. 57Moreover, all the world came to Joseph in Egypt to buy grain, because the famine became severe throughout the world.

Joseph's Brothers Go to Egypt

42 When Jacob learned that there was grain in Egypt, he said to his sons, "Why do you keep looking at one another? 2I have heard," he said, "that there is grain in Egypt; go down and buy grain for us there, that we may live and not die." 3So ten of Joseph's brothers went down to buy grain in Egypt. 4But Jacob did not send Joseph's brother Benjamin with his brothers, for he feared that harm might come to him. 5Thus the sons of Israel were among the other people who came to buy grain, for the famine had reached the land of Cā´naan.

6 Now Joseph was governor over the land; it was he who sold to all the people of the land. And Joseph's brothers came and bowed themselves before him with their faces to the ground. 7When Joseph saw his brothers, he recognized them, but he treated them like strangers and spoke harshly to them. "Where do you come from?" he said. They said, "From the land of Cā´naan, to buy food." 8Although Joseph had recognized his brothers, they did not recognize him. 9Joseph also remembered the dreams that he had dreamed about them. He said to them, "You are spies; you have come to see the nakedness of the land!" 10They said to him, "No, my lord; your servants have come to buy food. 11We are all sons of one man; we are honest men; your servants have never been spies." 12But he said to them, "No, you have come to see the nakedness of the land!" 13They said, "We, your servants, are twelve brothers, the sons of a certain man in the land of Cā´naan; the youngest, however, is now with our father, and one is no more." 14But Joseph said to them, "It is just as I have said to you; you are spies! 15Here is how you shall be

tested: as Pharaoh lives, you shall not leave this place unless your youngest brother comes here! 16Let one of you go and bring your brother, while the rest of you remain in prison, in order that your words may be tested, whether there is truth in you; or else, as Pharaoh lives, surely you are spies." 17And he put them all together in prison for three days.

When Joseph was a teenager, his brothers had sold him as a slave and told their father that a wild animal killed him. When they arrived in Egypt, Joseph was an adult.

18 On the third day Joseph said to them, "Do this and you will live, for I fear God: 19if you are honest men, let one of your brothers stay here where you are imprisoned. The rest of you shall go and carry grain for the famine of your households, 20and bring your youngest brother to me. Thus your words will be verified, and you shall not die." And they agreed to do so. 21They said to one another, "Alas, we are paying the penalty for what we did to our brother; we saw his anguish when he pleaded with us, but we would not listen. That is why this anguish has come upon us." 22Then Reuben answered them, "Did I not tell you not to wrong the boy? But you would not listen. So now there comes a reckoning for his blood." 23They did not know that Joseph understood them, since he spoke with them through an interpreter. 24He turned away from them and wept; then he returned and spoke to them. And he picked out Sim´e·on and had him bound before their eyes. 25Joseph then gave orders to fill their bags with grain, to return every man's money to his sack, and to give them provisions for their journey. This was done for them.

Joseph's Brothers
Return to Canaan

26 They loaded their donkeys with their grain, and departed. [27]When one of them opened his sack to give his donkey fodder at the lodging place, he saw his money at the top of the sack. [28]He said to his brothers, "My money has been put back; here it is in my sack!" At this they lost heart and turned trembling to one another, saying, "What is this that God has done to us?"

29 When they came to their father Jacob in the land of Cā'naan, they told him all that had happened to them, saying, [30]"The man, the lord of the land, spoke harshly to us, and charged us with spying on the land. [31]But we said to him, 'We are honest men, we are not spies. [32]We are twelve brothers, sons of our father; one is no more, and the youngest is now with our father in the land of Cā'naan.' [33]Then the man, the lord of the land, said to us, 'By this I shall know that you are honest men: leave one of your brothers with me, take grain for the famine of your households, and go your way. [34]Bring your youngest brother to me, and I shall know that you are not spies but honest men. Then I will release your brother to you, and you may trade in the land.' "

35 As they were emptying their sacks, there in each one's sack was his bag of money. When they and their father saw their bundles of money, they were dismayed. [36]And their father Jacob said to them, "I am the one you have bereaved of children: Joseph is no more, and Sim'ē·on is no more, and now you would take Benjamin. All this has happened to me!" [37]Then Reuben said to his father, "You may kill my two sons if I do not bring him back to you. Put him in my hands, and I will bring him back to you." [38]But he said, "My son shall not go down with you, for his brother is dead, and he alone is left. If harm should come to him on the journey that you are to

make, you would bring down my gray hairs with sorrow to Shē'ōl."

The Brothers Come Again,
Bringing Benjamin

43 Now the famine was severe in the land. [2]And when they had eaten up the grain that they had brought from Egypt, their father said to them, "Go again, buy us a little more food." [3]But Judah said to him, "The man solemnly warned us, saying, 'You shall not see my face unless your brother is with you.' [4]If you will send our brother with us, we will go down and buy you food; [5]but if you will not send him, we will not go down, for the man said to us, 'You shall not see my face, unless your brother is with you.' " [6]Israel said, "Why did you treat me so badly as to tell the man that you had another brother?" [7]They replied, "The man questioned us carefully about ourselves and our kindred, saying, 'Is your father still alive? Have you another brother?' What we told him was in answer to these questions. Could we in any way know that he would say, 'Bring your brother down'?" [8]Then Judah said to his father Israel, "Send the boy with me, and let us be on our way, so that we may live and not die—you and we and also our little ones. [9]I myself will be surety for him; you can hold me accountable for him. If I do not bring him back to you and set him before you, then let me bear the blame forever. [10]If we had not delayed, we would now have returned twice."

11 Then their father Israel said to them, "If it must be so, then do this: take some of the choice fruits of the land in your bags, and carry them down as a present to the man—a little balm and a little honey, gum, resin, pistachio nuts, and almonds. [12]Take double the money with you. Carry back with you the money that was returned in the top of your sacks; perhaps it was an oversight. [13]Take your brother also, and be on your

way again to the man; [14]may God Almighty[r] grant you mercy before the man, so that he may send back your other brother and Benjamin. As for me, if I am bereaved of my children, I am bereaved." [15]So the men took the present, and they took double the money with them, as well as Benjamin. Then they went on their way down to Egypt, and stood before Joseph.

16 When Joseph saw Benjamin with them, he said to the steward of his house, "Bring the men into the house, and slaughter an animal and make ready, for the men are to dine with me at noon." [17]The man did as Joseph said, and brought the men to Joseph's house. [18]Now the men were afraid because they were brought to Joseph's house, and they said, "It is because of the money, replaced in our sacks the first time, that we have been brought in, so that he may have an opportunity to fall upon us, to make slaves of us and take our donkeys." [19]So they went up to the steward of Joseph's house and spoke with him at the entrance to the house. [20]They said, "Oh, my lord, we came down the first time to buy food; [21]and when we came to the lodging place we opened our sacks, and there was each one's money in the top of his sack, our money in full weight. So we have brought it back with us. [22]Moreover we have brought down with us additional money to buy food. We do not know who put our money in our sacks." [23]He replied, "Rest assured, do not be afraid; your God and the God of your father must have put treasure in your sacks for you; I received your money." Then he brought Sim′e·on out to them. [24]When the steward[s] had brought the men into Joseph's house, and given them water, and they had washed their feet, and when he had given their donkeys fodder, [25]they made the present ready for Joseph's coming at noon, for they had heard that they would dine there.

26 When Joseph came home, they brought him the present that they had carried into the house, and bowed to the ground before him. [27]He inquired about their welfare, and said, "Is your father well, the old man of whom you spoke? Is he still alive?" [28]They said, "Your servant our father is well; he is still alive." And they bowed their heads and did obeisance. [29]Then he looked up and saw his brother Benjamin, his mother's son, and said, "Is this your youngest brother, of whom you spoke to me? God be gracious to you, my son!" [30]With that, Joseph hurried out, because he was overcome with affection for his brother, and he was about to weep. So he went into a private room and wept there. [31]Then he washed his face and came out; and controlling himself he said, "Serve the meal." [32]They served him by himself, and them by themselves, and the Egyptians who ate with him by themselves, because the Egyptians could not eat with the Hebrews, for that is an abomination to the Egyptians. [33]When they were seated before him, the firstborn according to his birthright and the youngest according to his youth, the men looked at one another in amazement. [34]Portions were taken to them from Joseph's table, but Benjamin's portion was five times as much as any of theirs. So they drank and were merry with him.

Joseph Detains Benjamin

44 Then he commanded the steward of his house, "Fill the men's sacks with food, as much as they can carry, and put each man's money in the top of his sack. [2]Put my cup, the silver cup, in the top of the sack of the youngest, with his money for the grain." And he did as Joseph told him. [3]As soon as the morning was light, the men were sent away with their donkeys. [4]When

[r] Traditional rendering of Heb *El Shaddai*   [s] Heb *the man*

they had gone only a short distance from the city, Joseph said to his steward, "Go, follow after the men; and when you overtake them, say to them, 'Why have you returned evil for good? Why have you stolen my silver cup?'[t] ⁵Is it not from this that my lord drinks? Does he not indeed use it for divination? You have done wrong in doing this.' "

6 When he overtook them, he repeated these words to them. ⁷They said to him, "Why does my lord speak such words as these? Far be it from your servants that they should do such a thing! ⁸Look, the money that we found at the top of our sacks, we brought back to you from the land of Cāʹnaan; why then would we steal silver or gold from your lord's house? ⁹Should it be found with any one of your servants, let him die; moreover the rest of us will become my lord's slaves." ¹⁰He said, "Even so; in accordance with your words, let it be: he with whom it is found shall become my slave, but the rest of you shall go free." ¹¹Then each one quickly lowered his sack to the ground, and each opened his sack. ¹²He searched, beginning with the eldest and ending with the youngest; and the cup was found in Benjamin's sack. ¹³At this they tore their clothes. Then each one loaded his donkey, and they returned to the city.

14 Judah and his brothers came to Joseph's house while he was still there; and they fell to the ground before him. ¹⁵Joseph said to them, "What deed is this that you have done? Do you not know that one such as I can practice divination?" ¹⁶And Judah said, "What can we say to my lord? What can we speak? How can we clear ourselves? God has found out the guilt of your servants; here we are then, my lord's slaves, both we and also the one in whose possession the cup has been found." ¹⁷But he said, "Far be it from me that I should do so! Only the one in whose possession the cup was found shall be my slave; but as for you, go up in peace to your father."

Judah Pleads for Benjamin's Release

18 Then Judah stepped up to him and said, "O my lord, let your servant please speak a word in my lord's ears, and do not be angry with your servant; for you are like Pharaoh himself. ¹⁹My lord asked his servants, saying, 'Have you a father or a brother?' ²⁰And we said to my lord, 'We have a father, an old man, and a young brother, the child of his old age. His brother is dead; he alone is left of his mother's children, and his father loves him.' ²¹Then you said to your servants, 'Bring him down to me, so that I may set my eyes on him.' ²²We said to my lord, 'The boy cannot leave his father, for if he should leave his father, his father would die.' ²³Then you said to your servants, 'Unless your youngest brother comes down with you, you shall see my face no more.' ²⁴When we went back to your servant my father we told him the words of my lord. ²⁵And when our father said, 'Go again, buy us a little food,' ²⁶we said, 'We cannot go down. Only if our youngest brother goes with us, will we go down; for we cannot see the man's face unless our youngest brother is with us.' ²⁷Then your servant my father said to us, 'You know that my wife bore me two sons; ²⁸one left me, and I said, Surely he has been torn to pieces; and I have never seen him since. ²⁹If you take this one also from me, and harm comes to him, you will bring down my gray hairs in sorrow to Sheʹōl.' ³⁰Now therefore, when I come to your servant my father and the boy is not with us, then, as his life is bound up in the boy's life, ³¹when he sees that the boy is not with us, he will die; and your servants will bring down the gray hairs of your servant our father with sorrow to Sheʹōl. ³²For your servant became surety for the boy to my father, saying, 'If I do not bring him back to you, then I will

[t] Gk Compare Vg: Heb lacks *Why have you stolen my silver cup?*

bear the blame in the sight of my father all my life.' ³³Now therefore, please let your servant remain as a slave to my lord in place of the boy; and let the boy go back with his brothers. ³⁴For how can I go back to my father if the boy is not with me? I fear to see the suffering that would come upon my father."

Joseph Reveals Himself to His Brothers

45 Then Joseph could no longer control himself before all those who stood by him, and he cried out, "Send everyone away from me." So no one stayed with him when Joseph made himself known to his brothers. ²And he wept so loudly that the Egyptians heard it, and the household of Pharaoh heard it. ³Joseph said to his brothers, "I am Joseph. Is my father still alive?" But his brothers could not answer him, so dismayed were they at his presence.

4 Then Joseph said to his brothers, "Come closer to me." And they came closer. He said, "I am your brother, Joseph, whom you sold into Egypt. ⁵And now do not be distressed, or angry with yourselves, because you sold me here; for God sent me before you to preserve life. ⁶For the famine has been in the land these two years; and there are five more years in which there will be neither plowing nor harvest. ⁷God sent me before you to preserve for you a remnant on earth, and to keep alive for you many survivors. ⁸So it was not you who sent me here, but God; he has made me a father to Pharaoh, and lord of all his house and ruler over all the land of Egypt. ⁹Hurry and go up to my father and say to him, 'Thus says your son Joseph, God has made me lord of all Egypt; come down to me, do not delay. ¹⁰You shall settle in the land of Gō´shen, and you shall be near me, you and your children and your children's children, as well as your flocks, your herds, and all that you have. ¹¹I will provide for you there—since there are five more years of famine to come—so that you and your

Because Joseph was not ready to tell his brothers who he was, he used an interpreter to translate what they were saying. But because he really understood everything they said, he knew that they were truly sorry for what they had done. He knew that they loved and cared for their father and were concerned for their father, rather than for themselves.

household, and all that you have, will not come to poverty.' ¹²And now your eyes and the eyes of my brother Benjamin see that it is my own mouth that speaks to you. ¹³You must tell my father how greatly I am honored in Egypt, and all that you have seen. Hurry and bring my father down here." ¹⁴Then he fell upon his brother Benjamin's neck and wept, while Benjamin wept upon his neck. ¹⁵And he kissed all his brothers and wept upon them; and after that his brothers talked with him.

16 When the report was heard in Pharaoh's house, "Joseph's brothers have come," Pharaoh and his servants were pleased. ¹⁷Pharaoh said to Joseph, "Say to your brothers, 'Do this: load your animals and go back to the land of Cā´naan. ¹⁸Take your father and your households and come to me, so that I may give you the best of the land of Egypt, and you may enjoy the fat of the land.' ¹⁹You are further charged to say, 'Do this: take wagons from the land of Egypt for your little ones and for your wives, and bring your father, and come. ²⁰Give no thought to your possessions, for the best of all the land of Egypt is yours.' "

21 The sons of Israel did so. Joseph gave them wagons according to the instruction of Pharaoh, and he gave them provisions for the journey. ²²To each one of them he gave a set of garments; but to Benjamin he gave three hundred pieces of silver and five sets of

garments. ²³To his father he sent the following: ten donkeys loaded with the good things of Egypt, and ten female donkeys loaded with grain, bread, and provision for his father on the journey. ²⁴Then he sent his brothers on their way, and as they were leaving he said to them, "Do not quarrelᵘ along the way."

25 So they went up out of Egypt and came to their father Jacob in the land of Cā´naan. ²⁶And they told him, "Joseph is still alive! He is even ruler over all the land of Egypt." He was stunned; he could not believe them. ²⁷But when they told him all the words of Joseph that he had said to them, and when he saw the wagons that Joseph had sent to carry him, the spirit of their father Jacob revived. ²⁸Israel said, "Enough! My son Joseph is still alive. I must go and see him before I die."

Jacob Brings His Whole Family to Egypt

46 When Israel set out on his journey with all that he had and came to Bē´er-shē´ba, he offered sacrifices to the God of his father Isaac. ²God spoke to Israel in visions of the night, and said, "Jacob, Jacob." And he said, "Here I am." ³Then he said, "I am God,ᵛ the God of your father; do not be afraid to go down to Egypt, for I will make of you a great nation there. ⁴I myself will go down with you to Egypt, and I will also bring you up again; and Joseph's own hand shall close your eyes."

5 Then Jacob set out from Bē´er-shē´ba; and the sons of Israel carried their father Jacob, their little ones, and their wives, in the wagons that Pharaoh had sent to carry him. ⁶They also took their livestock and the goods that they had acquired in the land of Cā´naan, and they came into Egypt, Jacob and all his offspring with him, ⁷his sons, and his sons' sons with him, his daughters, and his sons' daughters; all his offspring he brought with him into Egypt.

8 Now these are the names of the Israelites, Jacob and his offspring, who came to Egypt. Reuben, Jacob's firstborn, ⁹and the children of Reuben: Hā´noch, Pal´lū, Hez´ron, and Car´mī. ¹⁰The children of Sim´ē·on: Je·mū´el, Jā´min, Ō´had, Jā´chin, Zō´har, and Shā´ūl,ʷ the son of a Cā´naan·īte woman. ¹¹The children of Levi: Ger´shon, Kō´hath, and Me·rar´ī. ¹²The children of Judah: Er, Ō´nan, Shē´lah, Per´ez, and Zē´rah (but Er and Ō´nan died in the land of Cā´naan); and the children of Per´ez were Hez´ron and Hā´mul. ¹³The children of Is´sa·char: Tō´la, Pū´vah, Jash´ub,ˣ and Shim´ron. ¹⁴The children of Zeb´ū·lun: Sē´red, Ē´lon, and Jah´lē·el ¹⁵(these are the sons of Leah, whom she bore to Jacob in Pad´dan-ar´am, together with his daughter Dī´nah; in all his sons and his daughters numbered thirty-three). ¹⁶The children of Gad: Ziph´i·on, Hag´gī, Shū´nī, Ez´bon, Ē´rī, A·rō´dī, and A·rē´lī. ¹⁷The children of Ash´er: Im´nah, Ish´vah, Ish´vī, Bē·rī´ah, and their sister Sē´rah. The children of Bē·rī´ah: Hē´ber and Mal´chi·el ¹⁸(these are the children of Zil´pah, whom Lā´ban gave to his daughter Leah; and these she bore to Jacob—sixteen persons). ¹⁹The children of Jacob's wife Rachel: Joseph and Benjamin. ²⁰To Joseph in the land of Egypt were born Ma·nas´seh and Ē´phra·im, whom As´e·nath daughter of Pō·ti´phe·ra, priest of On, bore to him. ²¹The children of Benjamin: Bē´la, Bē´cher, Ash´bel, Gē´ra, Nā´a·man, Ē´hī, Rosh, Mup´pim, Hup´pim, and Ard ²²(these are the children of Rachel, who were born to Jacob—fourteen persons in all). ²³The children of Dan: Hā´shum.ʸ ²⁴The children of Naph´ta·lī: Jah´zē·el, Gū´nī, Jē´zer, and Shil´lem ²⁵(these are the children of Bil´hah, whom Lā´ban gave to his daughter Rachel, and these she bore to Jacob—seven persons in all).

ᵘ Or *be agitated*   ᵛ Heb *the God*   ʷ Or *Saul*
ˣ Compare Sam Gk Num 26.24; 1 Chr 7.1: MT *Iob*   ʸ Gk: Heb *Hushim*

²⁶All the persons belonging to Jacob who came into Egypt, who were his own offspring, not including the wives of his sons, were sixty-six persons in all. ²⁷The children of Joseph, who were born to him in Egypt, were two; all the persons of the house of Jacob who came into Egypt were seventy.

Jacob Settles in Goshen

28 Israel: sent Judah ahead to Joseph to lead the way before him into Gō′shen. When they came to the land of Gō′shen, ²⁹Joseph made ready his chariot and went up to meet his father Israel in Gō′shen. He presented himself to him, fell on his neck, and wept on his neck a good while. ³⁰Israel said to Joseph, "I can die now, having seen for myself that you are still alive." ³¹Joseph said to his brothers and to his father's household, "I will go up and tell Pharaoh, and will say to him, 'My brothers and my father's household, who were in the land of Cā′naan, have come to me. ³²The men are shepherds, for they have been keepers of livestock; and they have brought their flocks, and their herds, and all that they have.' ³³When Pharaoh calls you, and says, 'What is your occupation?' ³⁴you shall say, 'Your servants have been keepers of livestock from our youth even until now, both we and our ancestors'— in order that you may settle in the land of Gō′shen, because all shepherds are abhorrent to the Egyptians."

47 So Joseph went and told Pharaoh, "My father and my brothers, with their flocks and herds and all that they possess, have come from the land of Cā′naan; they are now in the land of Gō′shen." ²From among his brothers he took five men and presented them to Pharaoh. ³Pharaoh said to his brothers, "What is your occupation?" And they said to Pharaoh, "Your servants are shepherds, as our ancestors were." ⁴They said to Pharaoh, "We have come to reside as aliens in the land; for there is no pasture for your servants' flocks because the famine is severe in the land of Cā′naan. Now, we ask you, let your servants settle in the land of Gō′shen." ⁵Then Pharaoh said to Joseph, "Your father and your brothers have come to you. ⁶The land of Egypt is before you; settle your father and your brothers in the best part of the land; let them live in the land of Gō′shen; and if you know that there are capable men among them, put them in charge of my livestock."

7 Then Joseph brought in his father Jacob, and presented him before Pharaoh, and Jacob blessed Pharaoh. ⁸Pharaoh said to Jacob, "How many are the years of your life?" ⁹Jacob said to Pharaoh, "The years of my earthly sojourn are one hundred thirty; few and hard have been the years of my life. They do not compare with the years of the life of my ancestors during their long sojourn." ¹⁰Then Jacob blessed Pharaoh, and went out from the presence of Pharaoh. ¹¹Joseph settled his father and his brothers, and granted them a holding in the land of Egypt, in the best part of the land, in the land of Ram′e·sēs, as Pharaoh had instructed. ¹²And Joseph provided his father, his brothers, and all his father's household with food, according to the number of their dependents.

The Famine in Egypt

13 Now there was no food in all the land, for the famine was very severe. The land of Egypt and the land of Cā′naan languished because of the famine. ¹⁴Joseph collected all the money to be found in the land of Egypt and in the land of Cā′naan, in exchange for the grain that they bought; and Joseph brought the money into Pharaoh's house. ¹⁵When the money from the land of Egypt and from the land of Cā′naan was spent, all the Egyptians came to Joseph, and said, "Give us food! Why should we die before your eyes? For our

ᶻ Heb *He*

money is gone." ¹⁶And Joseph answered, "Give me your livestock, and I will give you food in exchange for your livestock, if your money is gone." ¹⁷So they brought their livestock to Joseph; and Joseph gave them food in exchange for the horses, the flocks, the herds, and the donkeys. That year he supplied them with food in exchange for all their livestock. ¹⁸When that year was ended, they came to him the following year, and said to him, "We can not hide from my lord that our money is all spent; and the herds of cattle are my lord's. There is nothing left in the sight of my lord but our bodies and our lands. ¹⁹Shall we die before your eyes, both we and our land? Buy us and our land in exchange for food. We with our land will become slaves to Pharaoh; just give us seed, so that we may live and not die, and that the land may not become desolate."

20 So Joseph bought all the land of Egypt for Pharaoh. All the Egyptians sold their fields, because the famine was severe upon them; and the land became Pharaoh's. ²¹As for the people, he made slaves of them*ᵃ* from one end of Egypt to the other. ²²Only the land of the priests he did not buy; for the priests had a fixed allowance from Pharaoh, and lived on the allowance that Pharaoh gave them; therefore they did not sell their land. ²³Then Joseph said to the people, "Now that I have this day bought you and your land for Pharaoh, here is seed for you; sow the land. ²⁴And at the harvests you shall give one-fifth to Pharaoh, and four-fifths shall be your own, as seed for the field and as food for yourselves and your households, and as food for your little ones." ²⁵They said, "You have saved our lives; may it please my lord, we will be slaves to Pharaoh." ²⁶So Joseph made it a statute concerning the land of Egypt, and it stands to this day, that Pharaoh should have the fifth. The land of the priests alone did not become Pharaoh's.

The Last Days of Jacob

27 Thus Israel settled in the land of Egypt, in the region of Gōʹshen; and they gained possessions in it, and were fruitful and multiplied exceedingly. ²⁸Jacob lived in the land of Egypt seventeen years; so the days of Jacob, the years of his life, were one hundred forty-seven years.

29 When the time of Israel's death drew near, he called his son Joseph and said to him, "If I have found favor with you, put your hand under my thigh and promise to deal loyally and truly with me. Do not bury me in Egypt. ³⁰When I lie down with my ancestors, carry me out of Egypt and bury me in their burial place." He answered, "I will do as you have said." ³¹And he said, "Swear to me"; and he swore to him. Then Israel bowed himself on the head of his bed.

Jacob Blesses Joseph's Sons

48 After this Joseph was told, "Your father is ill." So he took with him his two sons, Ma·nasʹseh and Eʹphra·im. ²When Jacob was told, "Your son Joseph has come to you," heᵇ summoned his strength and sat up in bed. ³And Jacob said to Joseph, "God Almightyᶜ appeared to me at Luz in the land of Cāʹnaan, and he blessed me, ⁴and said to me, 'I am going to make you fruitful and increase your numbers; I will make of you a company of peoples, and will give this land to your offspring after you for a perpetual holding.' ⁵Therefore your two sons, who were born to you in the land of Egypt before I came to you in Egypt, are now mine; Eʹphra·im and Ma·nasʹseh shall be mine, just as Reuben and Simʹe·on are. ⁶As for the offspring born to you after them, they shall be yours. They shall be recorded under the names of their brothers with regard to their inheritance. ⁷For when I came from Padʹdan, Rachel, alas, died in

---

the land of Cā´naan on the way, while there was still some distance to go to Eph´rath; and I buried her there on the way to Eph´rath" (that is, Bethlehem).

8 When Israel saw Joseph's sons, he said, "Who are these?" 9Joseph said to his father, "They are my sons, whom God has given me here." And he said, "Bring them to me, please, that I may bless them." 10Now the eyes of Israel were dim with age, and he could not see well. So Joseph brought them near him; and he kissed them and embraced them. 11Israel said to Joseph, "I did not expect to see your face; and here God has let me see your children also." 12Then Joseph removed them from his father's knees,[d] and he bowed himself with his face to the earth. 13Joseph took them both, Ē´phra·im in his right hand toward Israel's left, and Ma·nas´seh in his left hand toward Israel's right, and brought them near him. 14But Israel stretched out his right hand and laid it on the head of Ē´phra·im, who was the younger, and his left hand on the head of Ma·nas´seh, crossing his hands, for Ma·nas´seh was

the firstborn. 15He blessed Joseph, and said,

"The God before whom my ancestors
    Abraham and Isaac walked,
the God who has been my shep-
    herd all my life to this day,
16 the angel who has redeemed me
    from all harm, bless the boys;
and in them let my name be per-
    petuated, and the name of my
    ancestors Abraham and Isaac;
and let them grow into a multitude
    on the earth."

17 When Joseph saw that his father laid his right hand on the head of Ē´phra·im, it displeased him; so he took his father's hand, to remove it from Ē´phra·im's head to Ma·nas´seh's head. 18Joseph said to his father, "Not so, my father! Since this one is the firstborn, put your right hand on his head." 19But his father refused, and said, "I know, my son, I know; he also shall become a people, and he also shall be great. Nevertheless his younger brother shall be greater than he, and his offspring shall become a multitude of nations." 20So he blessed them that day, saying,

"By you[e] Israel will invoke blessings,
    saying,
'God make you[e] like Ē´phra·im and
    like Ma·nas´seh.'"

So he put Ē´phra·im ahead of Ma·nas´seh. 21Then Israel said to Joseph, "I am about to die, but God will be with you and will bring you again to the land of your ancestors. 22I now give to you one portion[f] more than to your brothers, the portion[f] that I took from the hand of the Am´or·ites with my sword and with my bow."

Jacob's Last Words to His Sons

49 Then Jacob called his sons, and said: "Gather around, that I may tell you what will happen to you in days to come.

Knowing that his father would not live much longer, Joseph took his two sons, Manasseh and Ephraim, to see their grandfather Jacob. Just as Jacob's father Isaac had begun to go blind when he was older, Jacob was losing his sight as well. Joseph put his younger son, Ephraim, by Jacob's left hand and his older son, Manasseh, by Jacob's right hand. When Jacob gave the blessing, he crossed his hands, placing his right hand on Ephraim and his left hand on Manasseh. Ephraim, the younger son, received the blessing.

[d] Heb *from his knees*   [e] *you* here is singular in Heb
[f] Or *mountain slope* (Heb *shekem*, a play on the name of the town and district of Shechem)

2 Assemble and hear, O sons of Jacob;
   listen to Israel your father.

3 Reuben, you are my firstborn,
   my might and the first fruits of
      my vigor,
   excelling in rank and excelling in
      power.
4 Unstable as water, you shall no
      longer excell
   because you went up onto your
      father's bed;
   then you defiled it—you[g] went up
      onto my couch!

5 Sim′e·on and Levi are brothers;
   weapons of violence are their swords.
6 May I never come into their council;
   may I not be joined to their com-
      pany—for in their anger they
      killed men,
   and at their whim they hamstrung
      oxen.
7 Cursed be their anger, for it is fierce,
   and their wrath, for it is cruel!
   I will divide them in Jacob,
   and scatter them in Israel.

8 Judah, your brothers shall praise you;
   your hand shall be on the neck of
      your enemies;
   your father's sons shall bow down
      before you.
9 Judah is a lion's whelp;
   from the prey, my son, you have
      gone up.
   He crouches down, he stretches out
      like a lion,
   like a lioness—who dares rouse
      him up?
10 The scepter shall not depart from
      Judah,
   nor the ruler's staff from between
      his feet,
   until tribute comes to him;[h]
   and the obedience of the peoples
      is his.
11 Binding his foal to the vine
   and his donkey's colt to the choice
      vine,

he washes his garments in wine
   and his robe in the blood of grapes;
12 his eyes are darker than wine,
   and his teeth whiter than milk.
13 Zeb′u·lun shall settle at the shore of
      the sea;
   he shall be a haven for ships,
   and his border shall be at Si′don.

14 Is′sa·char is a strong donkey,
   lying down between the sheepfolds;
15 he saw that a resting place was good,
   and that the land was pleasant;
   so he bowed his shoulder to the
      burden,
   and became a slave at forced labor.

16 Dan shall judge his people
   as one of the tribes of Israel.
17 Dan shall be a snake by the roadside,
   a viper along the path,
   that bites the horse's heels
   so that its rider falls backward.

18 I wait for your salvation, O LORD.

19 Gad shall be raided by raiders,
   but he shall raid at their heels.

20 Ash′er's[i] food shall be rich,
   and he shall provide royal
      delicacies.
21 Naph′ta·li is a doe let loose
   that bears lovely fawns.[j]

22 Joseph is a fruitful bough,
   a fruitful bough by a spring;
   his branches run over the wall.[k]
23 The archers fiercely attacked him;
   they shot at him and pressed him
      hard.
24 Yet his bow remained taut,
   and his arms[l] were made agile
   by the hands of the Mighty One of
      Jacob,

g Gk Syr Tg: Heb he   h Or until Shiloh comes or
until he comes to Shiloh or (with Syr) until he comes
to whom it belongs   i Gk Vg Syr: Heb From Asher
j Or that gives beautiful words   k Meaning of Heb
uncertain   l Heb the arms of his hands

by the name of the Shepherd, the
Rock of Israel,
25 by the God of your father, who will
help you,
by the Almighty[m] who will bless
you
with blessings of heaven above,
blessings of the deep that lies
beneath,
blessings of the breasts and of the
womb.
26 The blessings of your father
are stronger than the blessings of
the eternal mountains,
the bounties[n] of the everlasting
hills;
may they be on the head of Joseph,
on the brow of him who was set
apart from his brothers.

27 Benjamin is a ravenous wolf,
in the morning devouring the prey,
and at evening dividing the
spoil."

28 All these are the twelve tribes of
Israel, and this is what their father said
to them when he blessed them, blessing each one of them with a suitable
blessing.

Jacob's Death and Burial

29 Then he charged them, saying to
them, "I am about to be gathered to my
people. Bury me with my ancestors—in
the cave in the field of Ē′phron the Hit′tīte,
30 in the cave in the field at Mach·pē′lah,
near Mam′re, in the land of Cā′naan, in
the field that Abraham bought from
Ē′phron the Hit′tīte as a burial site.
31 There Abraham and his wife Sarah
were buried; there Isaac and his wife
Rebekah were buried; and there I buried
Leah— 32 the field and the cave that is in
it were purchased from the Hit′tītes."
33 When Jacob ended his charge to his
sons, he drew up his feet into the bed,
breathed his last, and was gathered to
his people.

50 Then Joseph threw himself on
his father's face and wept over
him and kissed him. 2 Joseph commanded the physicians in his service to
embalm his father. So the physicians
embalmed Israel; 3 they spent forty days
in doing this, for that is the time
required for embalming. And the Egyptians wept for him seventy days.

4 When the days of weeping for him
were past, Joseph addressed the household of Pharaoh, "If now I have found
favor with you, please speak to Pharaoh
as follows: 5 My father made me swear an
oath; he said, 'I am about to die. In the
tomb that I hewed out for myself in the
land of Cā′naan, there you shall bury
me.' Now therefore let me go up, so that
I may bury my father; then I will return."
6 Pharaoh answered, "Go up, and bury
your father, as he made you swear to do."

7 So Joseph went up to bury his
father. With him went up all the servants
of Pharaoh, the elders of his household,
and all the elders of the land of Egypt,
8 as well as all the household of Joseph,
his brothers, and his father's household.
Only their children, their flocks, and
their herds were left in the land of Gō′-
shen. 9 Both chariots and charioteers
went up with him. It was a very great
company. 10 When they came to the
threshing floor of Ā′tad, which is beyond
the Jordan, they held there a very great
and sorrowful lamentation; and he
observed a time of mourning for his
father seven days. 11 When the Cā′naan·īte
inhabitants of the land saw the mourning on the threshing floor of Ā′tad, they
said, "This is a grievous mourning on the
part of the Egyptians." Therefore the
place was named Ā′bel-miz′ra·im;[o] it is
beyond the Jordan. 12 Thus his sons did
for him as he had instructed them.
13 They carried him to the land of Cā′-
naan and buried him in the cave of the

m Traditional rendering of Heb *Shaddai*   n Cn
Compare Gk: Heb *of my progenitors to the boundaries*   o That is *mourning* (or *meadow*) *of Egypt*

field at Mach·pe'lah, the field near Mam're, which Abraham bought as a burial site from E'phron the Hit'tite. [14]After he had buried his father, Joseph returned to Egypt with his brothers and all who had gone up with him to bury his father.

Joseph Forgives His Brothers

15 Realizing that their father was dead, Joseph's brothers said, "What if Joseph still bears a grudge against us and pays us back in full for all the wrong that we did to him?" [16]So they approached[p] Joseph, saying, "Your father gave this instruction before he died, [17]'Say to Joseph: I beg you, forgive the crime of your brothers and the wrong they did in harming you.' Now therefore please forgive the crime of the servants of the God of your father." Joseph wept when they spoke to him. [18]Then his brothers also wept,[q] fell down before him, and said, "We are here as your slaves." [19]But Joseph said to them, "Do not be afraid! Am I in the place of God? [20]Even though you intended to do harm to me, God intended it for good, in order to preserve a numerous people, as he is doing today. [21]So have no fear; I myself will provide for you and your little ones." In this way he reassured them, speaking kindly to them.

Joseph's Last Days and Death

22 So Joseph remained in Egypt, he and his father's household; and Joseph lived one hundred ten years. [23]Joseph saw E'phra·im's children of the third generation; the children of Ma'chir son of Ma·nas'seh were also born on Joseph's knees.

24 Then Joseph said to his brothers, "I am about to die; but God will surely come to you, and bring you up out of this land to the land that he swore to Abraham, to Isaac, and to Jacob." [25]So Joseph made the Israelites swear, saying, "When God comes to you, you shall carry up my bones from here." [26]And Joseph died, being one hundred ten years old; he was embalmed and placed in a coffin in Egypt.

> Joseph and his family (or tribe) lived in a part of Egypt called Goshen. They lived there until Moses led them out of Egypt.

[p] Gk Syr: Heb *they commanded*   [q] Cn: Heb *also came*

Exodus

In Genesis, God made two promises to Abraham—that he would have many descendants and that from him would come a great nation that would bless all people. By the time the book of Exodus opens, the first promise has been kept.

The Greek word *exodus* means "going out." This book tells of the going out, or deliverance, of the Hebrews from Egypt, where they had become slaves. Abraham's descendants had moved to Egypt to escape a great famine. His great-grandson Joseph helped them do well in Egypt, and there were now many Hebrews. The Egyptians became worried about the number of Hebrews and made them slaves so they could control them. The pharaohs, or rulers, of Egypt became cruel masters, and the Hebrews prayed to God for freedom.

Exodus tells the thrilling story of how God prepared a great man, Moses, to be the leader of God's people. In answer to their prayers, God helped Moses bring the Hebrews out of slavery in Egypt and into the freedom of Canaan, the land promised to Abraham. Moses worshiped God truly and listened to God faithfully. Through Moses, God gave people the great rules for living that we call the Ten Commandments (Exodus 20:1–17).

Exodus 2:1–10

1 These are the names of the sons of Israel who came to Egypt with Jacob, each with his household: ²Reuben, Sim´e·on, Levi, and Judah, ³Is´sa·char, Zeb´u·lun, and Benjamin, ⁴Dan and Naph´ta·li, Gad and Ash´er. ⁵The total number of people born to Jacob was seventy. Joseph was already in Egypt. ⁶Then Joseph died, and all his brothers, and that whole generation. ⁷But the Israelites were fruitful and prolific; they multiplied and grew exceedingly strong, so that the land was filled with them.

The Egyptian word *pharaoh* first meant "the great house" and "the palace." The king lived in the "pharaoh," so in later years, he became known as "pharaoh." The Egyptians thought the pharaoh (or, king) was a god. They believed that the land and the people of Egypt belonged to him.

The Israelites Are Oppressed

8 Now a new king arose over Egypt, who did not know Joseph. ⁹He said to his people, "Look, the Israelite people are more numerous and more powerful than we. ¹⁰Come, let us deal shrewdly with them, or they will increase and, in the event of war, join our enemies and fight against us and escape from the land." ¹¹Therefore they set taskmasters over them to oppress them with forced labor. They built supply cities, Pi´thom and Ram´e·ses, for Pharaoh. ¹²But the more they were oppressed, the more they multiplied and spread, so that the Egyptians came to dread the Israelites. ¹³The Egyptians became ruthless in imposing tasks on the Israelites, ¹⁴and made their lives bitter with hard service in mortar and brick and in every kind of field labor. They were ruthless in all the tasks that they imposed on them.

15 The king of Egypt said to the Hebrew midwives, one of whom was named Shiph´rah and the other Pu´ah, ¹⁶"When you act as midwives to the Hebrew women, and see them on the birthstool, if it is a boy, kill him; but if it is a girl, she shall live." ¹⁷But the midwives feared God; they did not do as the king of Egypt commanded them, but they let the boys live. ¹⁸So the king of Egypt summoned the midwives and said to them, "Why have you done this, and allowed the boys to live?" ¹⁹The midwives said to Pharaoh, "Because the Hebrew women are not like the Egyptian women; for they are vigorous and give birth before the midwife comes to them." ²⁰So God dealt well with the midwives; and the people multiplied and became very strong. ²¹And because the midwives feared God, he gave them families. ²²Then Pharaoh commanded all his people, "Every boy that is born to the Hebrews*ᵃ* you shall throw into the Nile, but you shall let every girl live."

The Nile River, the main river of Egypt, is nearly 3,500 miles long. That's the same as driving from Los Angeles to New York and then to Chicago—that's a long way! The Nile begins in east central Africa and ends in the Mediterranean Sea. Each year the Nile River floods, spreading soil that is good for growing crops over the land on both sides of the river. Egypt needs this flood, and in ancient times the Egyptians celebrated the flood each year.

Birth and Youth of Moses

2 Now a man from the house of Levi went and married a Le´vite woman. ²The woman conceived and bore a

ᵃ *Sam Gk Tg: Heb lacks* to the Hebrews

Jacob had twelve sons, and one of his sons was named Levi. Levi and his family (called Levites) were priests with special duties in the Tabernacle. They took care of the Tabernacle by cleaning the holy objects, preparing the offerings, and carrying out the service of praise.

son; and when she saw that he was a fine baby, she hid him three months. ³When she could hide him no longer she got a papyrus basket for him, and plastered it with bitumen and pitch; she put the

When Moses was a baby, Pharaoh wanted to kill him, so Moses' mother made a plan to save his life. She created a basket by tying together flat, bending leaves called papyrus reeds. To seal the basket so water could not leak in, she used bitumen and pitch—sticky material like the tar we use on roofs and roads!

Moses' mother wrapped up Moses in some blankets, put him in the basket, and set it along the banks of the Nile River. The plan worked, and the tiny boat made of papyrus kept Moses safe.

Moses had a brother called Aaron and a sister called Miriam. Do you have any brothers and sisters?

When Moses' mother put him in a basket in the Nile River, his big sister Miriam watched to see what would happen. When she found a chance, she brought the whole family together again. Although Miriam was a young girl, her courage and care for her brother Moses helped keep him safe.

child in it and placed it among the reeds on the bank of the river. ⁴His sister stood at a distance, to see what would happen to him.

5 The daughter of Pharaoh came down to bathe at the river, while her attendants walked beside the river. She saw the basket among the reeds and sent her maid to bring it. ⁶When she opened it, she saw the child. He was crying, and she took pity on him. "This must be one of the Hebrews' children," she said. ⁷Then his sister said to Pharaoh's daughter, "Shall I go and get you a nurse from the Hebrew women to nurse the child for you?" ⁸Pharaoh's daughter said to her, "Yes." So the girl went and called the child's mother. ⁹Pharaoh's daughter said to her, "Take this child and nurse it for me, and I will give you your wages." So the woman took the child and nursed it. ¹⁰When the child grew up, she brought him to Pharaoh's daughter, and she took him as her son. She named him Moses,ᵇ "because," she said, "I drew him outᶜ of the water."

Have you heard of Moses, the baby rescued from the Nile River? He became an important person in the history of Israel. He was a prophet, a priest, a judge, and a lawgiver. He helped God's people understand and live by God's laws.

Moses Flees to Midian

11 One day, after Moses had grown up, he went out to his people and saw their forced labor. He saw an Egyptian beating a Hebrew, one of his kinsfolk. ¹²He looked this way and that, and seeing no one he killed the Egyptian and hid him in the sand. ¹³When he went out the next day, he saw two Hebrews fighting; and he said to the one who was in the wrong, "Why do

ᵇ Heb *Mosheh*   ᶜ Heb *mashah*

"Then he said, 'Come no closer! Remove the sandals from your feet, for the place on which you are standing is holy ground.'"
Exodus 3:5

you strike your fellow Hebrew?" ¹⁴He answered, "Who made you a ruler and judge over us? Do you mean to kill me as you killed the Egyptian?" Then Moses was afraid and thought, "Surely the thing is known." ¹⁵When Pharaoh heard of it, he sought to kill Moses.

But Moses fled from Pharaoh. He settled in the land of Mid´i·an, and sat down by a well. ¹⁶The priest of Mid´i·an had seven daughters. They came to draw water, and filled the troughs to water their father's flock. ¹⁷But some shepherds came and drove them away. Moses got up and came to their defense and watered their flock. ¹⁸When they returned to their father Reü´el, he said, "How is it that you have come back so soon today?" ¹⁹They said, "An Egyptian helped us against the shepherds; he even drew water for us and watered the flock." ²⁰He said to his daughters, "Where is he? Why did you leave the man? Invite him to break bread." ²¹Moses agreed to stay with the man, and he gave Moses his daughter Zip·pō´rah in marriage. ²²She bore a son, and he named him Ger´shom; for he said, "I have

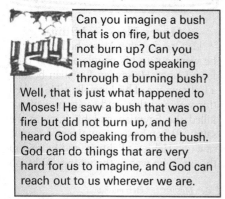

Can you imagine a bush that is on fire, but does not burn up? Can you imagine God speaking through a burning bush? Well, that is just what happened to Moses! He saw a bush that was on fire but did not burn up, and he heard God speaking from the bush. God can do things that are very hard for us to imagine, and God can reach out to us wherever we are.

been an alien[d] residing in a foreign land."

23 After a long time the king of Egypt died. The Israelites groaned under their slavery, and cried out. Out of the slavery their cry for help rose up to God. ²⁴God heard their groaning, and God remembered his covenant with Abraham, Isaac, and Jacob. ²⁵God looked upon the Israelites, and God took notice of them.

Moses at the Burning Bush

3 Moses was keeping the flock of his father-in-law Jeth´rō, the priest of Mid´i·an; he led his flock beyond the wilderness, and came to Hō´reb, the mountain of God. ²There the angel of the LORD appeared to him in a flame of fire out of a bush; he looked, and the bush was blazing, yet it was not consumed. ³Then Moses said, "I must turn aside and look at this great sight, and see why the bush is not burned up." ⁴When the LORD saw that he had turned aside to see, God called to

God spoke in a voice from the burning bush and told Moses to take off his shoes because he was standing on holy ground. Even today, in many places around the world people take off their shoes before they go into a place of worship. They do this to show respect, and to separate worship from the world outside.

him out of the bush, "Moses, Moses!" And he said, "Here I am." ⁵Then he said, "Come no closer! Remove the sandals from your feet, for the place on which you are standing is holy ground." ⁶He said further, "I am the God of your father, the God of Abraham, the God of Isaac, and the God of Jacob." And Moses hid his face, for he was afraid to look at God.

7 Then the LORD said, "I have observed the misery of my people who are in Egypt; I have heard their cry on

[d] Heb *ger*

Do you have a pair of sandals? Moses probably wore sandals that he tied onto his feet. There were no buckles or elastic back then. In Moses' time, people who were poor or in mourning did not wear sandals. Wearing sandals was a sign of being ready for a journey.

account of their taskmasters. Indeed, I know their sufferings, [8]and I have come down to deliver them from the Egyptians, and to bring them up out of that land to a good and broad land, a land flowing with milk and honey, to the country of the Cā́naan·ītes, the Hit´tītes, the Am´o·rītes, the Per´iz·zītes, the Hī´vītes, and the Jeb´u·sītes. [9]The cry of the Israelites has now come to me; I have also seen how the Egyptians oppress them. [10]So come, I will send you to Pharaoh to bring my people, the Israelites, out of Egypt." [11]But Moses said to God, "Who am I that I should go to Pharaoh, and bring the Israelites out of Egypt?" [12]He said, "I will be with you; and this shall be the sign for you that it is I who sent you: when you have brought the people out of Egypt, you shall worship God on this mountain."

The Divine Name Revealed

13 But Moses said to God, "If I come to the Israelites and say to them, 'The God of your ancestors has sent me to you,' and they ask me, 'What is his name?' what shall I say to them?" [14]God said to Moses, "I AM WHO I AM."[e] He said further, "Thus you shall say to the Israelites, 'I AM has sent me to you.'" [15]God also said to Moses, "Thus you shall say to the Israelites, 'The LORD,[f] the God of your ancestors, the God of Abraham, the God of Isaac, and the God of Jacob, has sent me to you':

This is my name forever, and this
    my title for all generations.
[16]Go and assemble the elders of Israel, and say to them, 'The LORD, the God of your ancestors, the God of Abraham, of Isaac, and of Jacob, has appeared to me, saying: I have given heed to you and to what has been done to you in Egypt. [17]I declare that I will bring you up out of the misery of Egypt, to the land of the Cā́naan·ītes, the Hit´tītes, the Am´o·rītes, the Per´iz·zītes, the Hī´vītes, and the Jeb´ū·sītes, a land flowing with milk and honey.' [18]They will listen to your voice; and you and the elders of Israel shall go to the king of Egypt and say to him, 'The LORD, the God of the Hebrews, has met with us; let us now go a three days' journey into the wilderness, so that we may sacrifice to the LORD our God.' [19]I know, however, that the king of Egypt will not let you go unless compelled by a mighty hand.[g] [20]So I will stretch out my hand and strike Egypt with all my wonders that I will perform in it; after that he will let you go. [21]I will bring this people into such favor with the Egyptians that, when you go, you will not go empty-handed; [22]each woman shall ask

People in Bible times did not use exact measures for distance as we do today. Back then, "one day's journey" was between eighteen and twenty-five miles. "One day's journey" meant the distance a person could travel by walking from sunrise to sunset, so the actual distance depended on the strength of the person traveling and the type of road.

[e] Or *I AM WHAT I AM or I WILL BE WHAT I WILL BE*
[f] The word "LORD" when spelled with capital letters stands for the divine name, *YHWH,* which is here connected with the verb *hayah,* "to be"   [g] Gk Vg: Heb *no, not by a mighty han*

her neighbor and any woman living in the neighbor's house for jewelry of silver and of gold, and clothing, and you shall put them on your sons and on your daughters; and so you shall plunder the Egyptians."

Moses' Miraculous Power

4 Then Moses answered, "But suppose they do not believe me or listen to me, but say, 'The LORD did not appear to you.'" ²The LORD said to him, "What is that in your hand?" He said, "A staff." ³And he said, "Throw it on the ground." So he threw the staff on the ground, and it became a snake; and Moses drew back from it. ⁴Then the LORD said to Moses, "Reach out your hand, and seize it by the tail"—so he reached out his hand and grasped it, and it became a staff in his hand— ⁵"so that they may believe that the LORD, the God of their ancestors, the God of Abraham, the God of Isaac, and the God of Jacob, has appeared to you."

6 Again, the LORD said to him, "Put your hand inside your cloak." He put his hand into his cloak; and when he took it out, his hand was leprous,ʰ as white as snow. ⁷Then God said, "Put your hand back into your cloak"—so he put his hand back into his cloak, and when he took it out, it was restored like the rest of his body— ⁸"If they will not believe you or heed the first sign, they may believe the second sign. ⁹If they will not believe even these two signs or heed you, you shall take some water from the Nile and pour it on

the dry ground; and the water that you shall take from the Nile will become blood on the dry ground."

10 But Moses said to the LORD, "O my Lord, I have never been eloquent, neither in the past nor even now that you have spoken to your servant; but I am slow of speech and slow of tongue." ¹¹Then the LORD said to him, "Who gives speech to mortals? Who makes them mute or deaf, seeing or blind? Is it not I, the LORD? ¹²Now go, and I will be with your mouth and teach you what you are to speak." ¹³But he said, "O my Lord, please send someone else." ¹⁴Then the anger of the LORD was kindled against Moses and he said, "What of your brother Aaron the Lēʹvīte? I know that he can speak fluently; even now he is coming out to meet you, and when he sees you his heart will be glad. ¹⁵You shall speak to him and put the words in his mouth; and I will be with your mouth and with his mouth, and will teach you what you shall do. ¹⁶He indeed shall speak for you to the people; he shall serve as a mouth for you, and you shall serve as God for him. ¹⁷Take in your hand this staff, with which you shall perform the signs."

Moses Returns to Egypt

18 Moses went back to his father-in-law Jethʹrō and said to him, "Please let me go back to my kindred in Egypt and see whether they are still living." And Jethʹrō said to Moses, "Go in peace." ¹⁹The LORD said to Moses in Midʹi·an, "Go back to Egypt; for all those who were seeking your life are dead." ²⁰So Moses took his wife and his sons, put them on a donkey, and went back to the land of Egypt; and Moses carried the staff of God in his hand.

21 And the LORD said to Moses, "When you go back to Egypt, see that you perform before Pharaoh all the

Moses set apart his brother Aaron and Aaron's sons to be priests. This was a very high honor and a very special duty for Aaron's family. Only the high priest could enter the holy of holies once a year to offer sacrifices to God for the sins of the people.

ʰ A term for several skin diseases; precise meaning uncertain wonders that I have put in your power; but I will harden his heart, so that he will not let the people go. ²²Then you shall say to Pharaoh, 'Thus says the LORD: Israel is my firstborn son. ²³I said to you, "Let my son go that he may worship me." But you refused to let him go; now I will kill your firstborn son.' "

24 On the way, at a place where they spent the night, the LORD met him and tried to kill him. ²⁵But Zip·pō´rah took a flint and cut off her son's foreskin, and touched Moses'ⁱ feet with it, and said, "Truly you are a bridegroom of blood to me!" ²⁶So he let him alone. It was then she said, "A bridegroom of blood by circumcision."

27 The LORD said to Aaron, "Go into the wilderness to meet Moses." So he went; and he met him at the mountain of God and kissed him. ²⁸Moses told Aaron all the words of the LORD with which he had sent him, and all the signs with which he had charged him. ²⁹Then Moses and Aaron went and assembled all the elders of the Israelites. ³⁰Aaron spoke all the words that the LORD had spoken to Moses, and performed the signs in the sight of the people. ³¹The people believed; and when they heard that the LORD had given heed to the Israelites and that he had seen their misery, they bowed down and worshiped.

Bricks without Straw

5 Afterward Moses and Aaron went to Pharaoh and said, "Thus says the LORD, the God of Israel, 'Let my people go, so that they may celebrate a festival to me in the wilderness.' " ²But

> Many buildings in Bible lands were made of brick. People made bricks by mixing soft clay with straw, which helped hold the clay together. They formed the clay into blocks and dried the blocks in the sun. While they were in Egypt, the Hebrews had to make bricks for the pharaoh. When the pharaoh became angry with them, he made it harder for them to get the straw they needed, but said that they had to make the same number of bricks each day.

Pharaoh said, "Who is the LORD, that I should heed him and let Israel go? I do not know the LORD, and I will not let Israel go." ³Then they said, "The God of the Hebrews has revealed himself to us; let us go a three days' journey into the wilderness to sacrifice to the LORD our God, or he will fall upon us with pestilence or sword." ⁴But the king of Egypt said to them, "Moses and Aaron, why are you taking the people away from their work? Get to your labors!" ⁵Pharaoh continued, "Now they are more numerous than the people of the landʲ and yet you want them to stop working!" ⁶That same day Pharaoh commanded the taskmasters of the people, as well as their supervisors, ⁷"You shall no longer give the people straw to make bricks, as before; let them go and gather straw for themselves. ⁸But you shall require of them the same quantity of bricks as they have made previously; do not diminish it, for they are lazy; that is why they cry, 'Let us go and offer sacrifice to our God.' ⁹Let heavier work be laid on them; then they will labor at it and pay no attention to deceptive words."

10 So the taskmasters and the supervisors of the people went out and said to

> The people believed; and when they heard that the LORD had given heed to the Israelites and that he had seen their misery, they bowed down and worshiped.
> Exodus 4:31

ⁱ Heb *his*   ʲ Sam: Heb *The people of the land are now many* the people, "Thus says Pharaoh, 'I will not give you straw. [11]Go and get straw yourselves, wherever you can find it; but your work will not be lessened in the least.' " [12]So the people scattered throughout the land of Egypt, to gather stubble for straw. [13]The taskmasters were urgent, saying, "Complete your work, the same daily assignment as when you were given straw." [14]And the supervisors of the Israelites, whom Pharaoh's taskmasters had set over them, were beaten, and were asked, "Why did you not finish the required quantity of bricks yesterday and today, as you did before?"

15 Then the Israelite supervisors came to Pharaoh and cried, "Why do you treat your servants like this? [16]No straw is given to your servants, yet they say to us, 'Make bricks!' Look how your servants are beaten! You are unjust to your own people."[k] [17]He said, "You are lazy, lazy; that is why you say, 'Let us go and sacrifice to the LORD.' [18]Go now, and work; for no straw shall be given you, but you shall still deliver the same number of bricks." [19]The Israelite supervisors saw that they were in trouble when they were told, "You shall not lessen your daily number of bricks." [20]As they left Pharaoh, they came upon Moses and Aaron who were waiting to meet them. [21]They said to them, "The LORD look upon you and judge! You have brought us into bad odor with Pharaoh and his officials, and have put a sword in their hand to kill us."

22 Then Moses turned again to the LORD and said, "O LORD, why have you mistreated this people? Why did you ever send me? [23]Since I first came to Pharaoh to speak in your name, he has mistreated this people, and you have done nothing at all to deliver your people."

Israel's Deliverance Assured

6 Then the LORD said to Moses, "Now you shall see what I will do to Pharaoh: Indeed, by a mighty hand he will let them go; by a mighty hand he will drive them out of his land."

2 God also spoke to Moses and said to him: "I am the LORD. [3]I appeared to Abraham, Isaac, and Jacob as God Almighty,[l] but by my name 'The LORD'[m] I did not make myself known to them. [4]I also established my covenant with them, to give them the land of Cā´naan, the land in which they resided as aliens. [5]I have also heard the groaning of the Israelites whom the Egyptians are holding as slaves, and I have remembered my covenant. [6]Say therefore to the Israelites, 'I am the LORD, and I will free you from the burdens of the Egyptians and deliver you from slavery to them. I will redeem you with an outstretched arm and with mighty acts of judgment. [7]I will take you as my people, and I will be your God. You shall know that I am the LORD your God, who has freed you from the burdens of the Egyptians. [8]I will bring you into the land that I swore to give to Abraham, Isaac, and Jacob; I will give it to you for a possession. I am the LORD.' " [9]Moses told this to the Israelites; but they would not listen to Moses, because of their broken spirit and their cruel slavery.

10 Then the LORD spoke to Moses, [11]"Go and tell Pharaoh king of Egypt to let the Israelites go out of his land." [12]But Moses spoke to the LORD, "The Israelites have not listened to me; how then shall Pharaoh listen to me, poor speaker that I am?"[n] [13]Thus the LORD spoke to Moses and Aaron, and gave them orders regarding the Israelites and Pharaoh king of Egypt, charging them to free the Israelites from the land of Egypt.

The Genealogy of Moses and Aaron

14 The following are the heads of their ancestral houses: the sons of Reuben, the firstborn of Israel: Hā´noch,

[k] Gk Compare Syr Vg: Heb *beaten, and the sin of your people* [l] Traditional rendering of Heb *El Shaddai* [m] Heb *YHWH*; see note at 3.15 [n] Heb *me? I am uncircumcised of lips*

Pal´lū, Hez´ron, and Car´mī; these are the families of Reuben. ¹⁵The sons of Sim´ē·on: Je·mū´el, Jā´min, Ō´had, Jā´-chin, Zō´har, and Shā´ūl,ᵒ the son of a Cā-naan·īte woman; these are the families of Sim´ē·on. ¹⁶The following are the names of the sons of Levi according to their genealogies: Ger´shon,ᵖ Kō´hath, and Me·rar´ī, and the length of Levi's life was one hundred thirty-seven years. ¹⁷The sons of Ger´shon:ᵖ Lib´nī and Shim´ē·ī, by their families. ¹⁸The sons of Kō´hath: Am´ram, Iz´har, Hē´bron, and Uz´zi·el, and the length of Kō´hath's life was one hundred thirty-three years. ¹⁹The sons of Me·rar´ī: Mah´lī and Mū´shī. These are the families of the Lē´vītes according to their genealogies. ²⁰Am´ram married Joch´e·bed his father's sister and she bore him Aaron and Moses, and the length of Am´ram's life was one hundred thirty-seven years. ²¹The sons of Iz´har: Kō´rah, Nē´pheg, and Zich´rī. ²²The sons of Uz´-zi·el: Mish´a·el, El´za·phan, and Sith´rī. ²³Aaron married E·lish´e·ba, daughter of Am·min´a·dab and sister of Nah´shon, and she bore him Nā´dab, A·bī´hū, El·ē·ā´-zar, and Ith´a·mar. ²⁴The sons of Kō´rah: As´sir, El·kā´nah, and A·bī´a·saph; these are the families of the Kō´ra·hītes. ²⁵Aaron's son El·ē·ā´zar married one of the daughters of Pū´ti·el, and she bore him Phin´e·has. These are the heads of the ancestral houses of the Lē´vītes by their families.

26 It was this same Aaron and Moses to whom the LORD said, "Bring the Israelites out of the land of Egypt, company by company." ²⁷It was they who spoke to Pharaoh king of Egypt to bring the Israelites out of Egypt, the same Moses and Aaron.

Moses and Aaron Obey God's Commands

28 On the day when the LORD spoke to Moses in the land of Egypt, ²⁹he said to him, "I am the LORD; tell Pharaoh king of Egypt all that I am speaking to you." ³⁰But Moses said in the LORD's presence,

"Since I am a poor speaker,�q why would Pharaoh listen to me?"

7 The LORD said to Moses, "See, I have made you like God to Pharaoh, and your brother Aaron shall be your prophet. ²You shall speak all that I command you, and your brother Aaron shall tell Pharaoh to let the Israelites go out of his land. ³But I will harden Pharaoh's heart, and I will multiply my signs and wonders in the land of Egypt. ⁴When Pharaoh does not listen to you, I will lay my hand upon Egypt and bring my people the Israelites, company by company, out of the land of Egypt by great acts of judgment. ⁵The Egyptians shall know that I am the LORD, when I stretch out my hand against Egypt and bring the Israelites out from among them." ⁶Moses and Aaron did so; they did just as the LORD commanded them. ⁷Moses was eighty years old and Aaron eighty-three when they spoke to Pharaoh.

Aaron's Miraculous Rod

8 The LORD said to Moses and Aaron, ⁹"When Pharaoh says to you, 'Perform a wonder,' then you shall say to Aaron, 'Take your staff and throw it down before Pharaoh, and it will become a snake.' " ¹⁰So Moses and Aaron went to Pharaoh and did as the LORD had

When Moses asked the pharaoh to let God's people leave Egypt, the pharaoh said no. So God sent plagues, or disasters, upon Egypt. In the first plague, the water in the Nile River turned to blood, and the fish all died. The Egyptians needed the Nile for bathing, for food, and to water their animals and crops, but they could not use it for a while after this plague.

ᵒ Or *Saul*   ᵖ Also spelled *Gershom*; see 2.22
q Heb *am uncircumcised of lips*; see 6.12

commanded; Aaron threw down his staff before Pharaoh and his officials, and it became a snake. [11]Then Pharaoh summoned the wise men and the sorcerers; and they also, the magicians of Egypt, did the same by their secret arts. [12]Each one threw down his staff, and they became snakes; but Aaron's staff swallowed up theirs. [13]Still Pharaoh's heart was hardened, and he would not listen to them, as the Lord had said.

The First Plague:
Water Turned to Blood

14 Then the Lord said to Moses, "Pharaoh's heart is hardened; he refuses to let the people go. [15]Go to Pharaoh in the morning, as he is going out to the water; stand by at the river bank to meet him, and take in your hand the staff that was turned into a snake. [16]Say to him, 'The Lord, the God of the Hebrews, sent me to you to say, "Let my people go, so that they may worship me in the wilderness." But until now you have not listened. [17]Thus says the Lord, "By this you shall know that I am the Lord." See, with the staff that is in my hand I will strike the water that is in the Nile, and it shall be turned to blood. [18]The fish in the river shall die, the river itself shall stink, and the Egyptians shall be unable to drink water from the Nile.' " [19]The Lord said to Moses, "Say to Aaron, 'Take your staff and stretch out your hand over the waters of Egypt—over its rivers, its canals, and its ponds, and all its pools of water—so that they may become blood; and there shall be blood throughout the whole land of Egypt, even in vessels of wood and in vessels of stone.' "

20 Moses and Aaron did just as the Lord commanded. In the sight of Pharaoh and of his officials he lifted up the staff and struck the water in the river, and all the water in the river was turned into blood, [21]and the fish in the river died. The river stank so that the Egyptians could not drink its water, and there was blood throughout the whole land of Egypt. [22]But the magicians of Egypt did the same by their secret arts; so Pharaoh's heart remained hardened, and he would not listen to them, as the Lord had said. [23]Pharaoh turned and went into his house, and he did not take even this to heart. [24]And all the Egyptians had to dig along the Nile for water to drink, for they could not drink the water of the river.

25 Seven days passed after the Lord had struck the Nile.

The Second Plague: Frogs

8[r] Then the Lord said to Moses, "Go to Pharaoh and say to him, 'Thus says the Lord: Let my people go, so that they may worship me. [2]If you refuse to let them go, I will plague your whole country with frogs. [3]The river shall swarm with frogs; they shall come up into your palace, into your bedchamber and your bed, and into the houses of your officials and of your people,[s] and into your ovens and your kneading bowls. [4]The frogs shall come up on you and on your people and on all your officials.' " [5t]And the Lord said to Moses, "Say to Aaron, 'Stretch out your hand with your staff over the rivers, the canals, and the pools, and make frogs come up on the land of Egypt.' " [6]So Aaron stretched out his hand over the waters of Egypt; and the frogs came up and covered the land of Egypt. [7]But the magicians did the same by their secret arts, and brought frogs up on the land of Egypt.

8 Then Pharaoh called Moses and Aaron, and said, "Pray to the Lord to take away the frogs from me and my people, and I will let the people go to sacrifice to the Lord." [9]Moses said to Pharaoh, "Kindly tell me when I am to pray for you and for your officials and for your people, that the frogs may be removed from you and your houses and be left only in the Nile." [10]And he said,

---

[r] Ch 7.26 in Heb   [s] Gk: Heb *upon your people*
[t] Ch 8.1 in Heb

"Tomorrow." Moses said, "As you say! So that you may know that there is no one like the LORD our God, [11]the frogs shall leave you and your houses and your officials and your people; they shall be left only in the Nile." [12]Then Moses and Aaron went out from Pharaoh; and Moses cried out to the LORD concerning the frogs that he had brought upon Pharaoh.[u] [13]And the LORD did as Moses requested: the frogs died in the houses, the courtyards, and the fields. [14]And they gathered them together in heaps, and the land stank. [15]But when Pharaoh saw that there was a respite, he hardened his heart, and would not listen to them, just as the LORD had said.

The Third Plague: Gnats

16 Then the LORD said to Moses, "Say to Aaron, 'Stretch out your staff and strike the dust of the earth, so that it may become gnats throughout the whole land of Egypt.'" [17]And they did so; Aaron stretched out his hand with his staff and struck the dust of the earth, and gnats came on humans and animals alike; all the dust of the earth turned into gnats throughout the whole land of Egypt. [18]The magicians tried to produce gnats by their secret arts, but they could not. There were gnats on both humans and animals. [19]And the magicians said to Pharaoh, "This is the finger of God!" But Pharaoh's heart was hardened, and he would not listen to them, just as the LORD had said.

The Fourth Plague: Flies

20 Then the LORD said to Moses, "Rise early in the morning and present yourself before Pharaoh, as he goes out to the water, and say to him, 'Thus says the LORD: Let my people go, so that they may worship me. [21]For if you will not let my people go, I will send swarms of flies on you, your officials, and your people, and into your houses; and the houses of the Egyptians shall be filled with swarms of flies; so also the land where they live. [22]But on that day I will set apart the land

of Go'shen, where my people live, so that no swarms of flies shall be there, that you may know that I the LORD am in this land. [23]Thus I will make a distinction[v] between my people and your people. This sign shall appear tomorrow.'" [24]The LORD did so, and great swarms of flies came into the house of Pharaoh and into his officials' houses; in all of Egypt the land was ruined because of the flies.

25 Then Pharaoh summoned Moses and Aaron, and said, "Go, sacrifice to your God within the land." [26]But Moses said, "It would not be right to do so; for the sacrifices that we offer to the LORD our God are offensive to the Egyptians. If we offer in the sight of the Egyptians sacrifices that are offensive to them, will they not stone us? [27]We must go a three days' journey into the wilderness and sacrifice to the LORD our God as he commands us." [28]So Pharaoh said, "I will let you go to sacrifice to the LORD your God in the wilderness, provided you do not go very far away. Pray for me." [29]Then Moses said, "As soon as I leave you, I will pray to the LORD that the swarms of flies may depart tomorrow from Pharaoh, from his officials, and from his people; only do not let Pharaoh again deal falsely by not letting the people go to sacrifice to the LORD."

30 So Moses went out from Pharaoh and prayed to the LORD. [31]And the LORD did as Moses asked: he removed the swarms of flies from Pharaoh, from his officials, and from his people; not one remained. [32]But Pharaoh hardened his heart this time also, and would not let the people go.

The Fifth Plague: Livestock Diseased

9 Then the LORD said to Moses, "Go to Pharaoh, and say to him, 'Thus says the LORD, the God of the Hebrews: Let my people go, so that they may

---

[u] Or *frogs, as he had agreed with Pharaoh*   [v] Gk Vg: Heb *will set redemption*

worship me. [2]For if you refuse to let them go and still hold them, [3]the hand of the LORD will strike with a deadly pestilence your livestock in the field: the horses, the donkeys, the camels, the herds, and the flocks. [4]But the LORD will make a distinction between the livestock of Israel and the livestock of Egypt, so that nothing shall die of all that belongs to the Israelites.'" [5]The LORD set a time, saying, "Tomorrow the LORD will do this thing in the land." [6]And on the next day the LORD did so; all the livestock of the Egyptians died, but of the livestock of the Israelites not one died. [7]Pharaoh inquired and found that not one of the livestock of the Israelites was dead. But the heart of Pharaoh was hardened, and he would not let the people go.

The Sixth Plague: Boils

8 Then the LORD said to Moses and Aaron, "Take handfuls of soot from the kiln, and let Moses throw it in the air in the sight of Pharaoh. [9]It shall become fine dust all over the land of Egypt, and shall cause festering boils on humans and animals throughout the whole land of Egypt." [10]So they took soot from the kiln, and stood before Pharaoh, and Moses threw it in the air, and it caused festering boils on humans and animals. [11]The magicians could not stand before Moses because of the boils, for the boils afflicted the magicians as well as all the Egyptians. [12]But the LORD hardened the heart of Pharaoh, and he would not listen to them, just as the LORD had spoken to Moses.

The Seventh Plague: Thunder and Hail

13 Then the LORD said to Moses, "Rise early in the morning and present yourself before Pharaoh, and say to him, 'Thus says the LORD, the God of the Hebrews: Let my people go, so that they may worship me. [14]For this time I will send all my plagues upon you yourself, and upon your officials, and upon your people, so that you may know that there is no one like me in all the earth. [15]For by now I could have stretched out my hand and struck you and your people with pestilence, and you would have been cut off from the earth. [16]But this is why I have let you live: to show you my power, and to make my name resound through all the earth. [17]You are still exalting yourself against my people, and will not let them go. [18]Tomorrow at this time I will cause the heaviest hail to fall that has ever fallen in Egypt from the day it was founded until now. [19]Send, therefore, and have your livestock and everything that you have in the open field brought to a secure place; every human or animal that is in the open field and is not brought under shelter will die when the hail comes down upon them.'" [20]Those officials of Pharaoh who feared the word of the LORD hurried their slaves and livestock off to a secure place. [21]Those who did not regard the word of the LORD left their slaves and livestock in the open field.

22 The LORD said to Moses, "Stretch out your hand toward heaven so that hail may fall on the whole land of Egypt, on humans and animals and all the plants of the field in the land of Egypt." [23]Then Moses stretched out his staff toward heaven, and the LORD sent thunder and hail, and fire came down on the earth. And the LORD rained hail on the land of Egypt; [24]there was hail with fire flashing continually in the midst of it, such heavy hail as had never fallen in all the land of Egypt since it became a nation. [25]The hail struck down everything that was in the open field throughout all the land of Egypt, both human and animal; the hail also struck down all the plants of the field, and shattered every tree in the field. [26]Only in the land of Gōshen, where the Israelites were, there was no hail.

27 Then Pharaoh summoned Moses and Aaron, and said to them, "This time

I have sinned; the LORD is in the right, and I and my people are in the wrong. 28Pray to the LORD! Enough of God's thunder and hail! I will let you go; you need stay no longer." 29Moses said to him, "As soon as I have gone out of the city, I will stretch out my hands to the LORD; the thunder will cease, and there will be no more hail, so that you may know that the earth is the LORD's. 30But as for you and your officials, I know that you do not yet fear the LORD God." 31(Now the flax and the barley were ruined, for the barley was in the ear and the flax was in bud. 32But the wheat and the spelt were not ruined, for they are late in coming up.) 33So Moses left Pharaoh, went out of the city, and stretched out his hands to the LORD; then the thunder and the hail ceased, and the rain no longer poured down on the earth. 34But when Pharaoh saw that the rain and the hail and the thunder had ceased, he sinned once more and hardened his heart, he and his officials. 35So the heart of Pharaoh was hardened, and he would not let the Israelites go, just as the LORD had spoken through Moses.

The Eighth Plague: Locusts

10 Then the LORD said to Moses, "Go to Pharaoh; for I have hardened his heart and the heart of his officials, in order that I may show these signs of mine among them, 2and that you may tell your children and grandchildren how I have made fools of the Egyptians and what signs I have done among them—so that you may know that I am the LORD."

3 So Moses and Aaron went to Pharaoh, and said to him, "Thus says the LORD, the God of the Hebrews, 'How long will you refuse to humble yourself before me? Let my people go, so that they may worship me. 4For if you refuse to let my people go, tomorrow I will bring locusts into your country. 5They shall cover the surface of the land, so that no one will be able to see the land.

They shall devour the last remnant left you after the hail, and they shall devour every tree of yours that grows in the field. 6They shall fill your houses, and the houses of all your officials and of all the Egyptians—something that neither your parents nor your grandparents have seen, from the day they came on earth to this day.' " Then he turned and went out from Pharaoh.

7 Pharaoh's officials said to him, "How long shall this fellow be a snare to us? Let the people go, so that they may worship the LORD their God; do you not yet understand that Egypt is ruined?" 8So Moses and Aaron were brought back to Pharaoh, and he said to them, "Go, worship the LORD your God! But which ones are to go?" 9Moses said, "We will go with our young and our old; we will go with our sons and daughters and with our flocks and herds, because we have the LORD's festival to celebrate." 10He said to them, "The LORD indeed will be with you, if ever I let your little ones go with you! Plainly, you have some evil purpose in mind. 11No, never! Your men may go and worship the LORD, for that is what you are asking." And they were driven out from Pharaoh's presence.

12 Then the LORD said to Moses, "Stretch out your hand over the land of Egypt, so that the locusts may come upon it and eat every plant in the land, all that the hail has left." 13So Moses stretched out his staff over the land of Egypt, and the LORD brought an east wind upon the land all that day and all that night; when morning came, the east wind had brought the locusts. 14The locusts came upon all the land of Egypt and settled on the whole country of Egypt, such a dense swarm of locusts as had never been before, nor ever shall be again. 15They covered the surface of the whole land, so that the land was black; and they ate all the plants in the land and all the fruit of the trees that the hail had left; nothing green was left, no tree,

no plant in the field, in all the land of Egypt. ¹⁶Pharaoh hurriedly summoned Moses and Aaron and said, "I have sinned against the LORD your God, and against you. ¹⁷Do forgive my sin just this once, and pray to the LORD your God that at the least he remove this deadly thing from me." ¹⁸So he went out from Pharaoh and prayed to the LORD. ¹⁹The LORD changed the wind into a very strong west wind, which lifted the locusts and drove them into the Red Sea;^w not a single locust was left in all the country of Egypt. ²⁰But the LORD hardened Pharaoh's heart, and he would not let the Israelites go.

The Ninth Plague: Darkness

21 Then the LORD said to Moses, "Stretch out your hand toward heaven so that there may be darkness over the land of Egypt, a darkness that can be felt." ²²So Moses stretched out his hand toward heaven, and there was dense darkness in all the land of Egypt for three days. ²³People could not see one another, and for three days they could not move from where they were; but all the Israelites had light where they lived. ²⁴Then Pharaoh summoned Moses, and said, "Go, worship the LORD. Only your flocks and your herds shall remain behind. Even your children may go with you." ²⁵But Moses said, "You must also let us have sacrifices and burnt offerings to sacrifice to the LORD our God. ²⁶Our livestock also must go with us; not a hoof shall be left behind, for we must choose some of them for the worship of the LORD our God, and we will not know what to use to worship the LORD until we arrive there." ²⁷But the LORD hardened Pharaoh's heart, and he was unwilling to let them go. ²⁸Then Pharaoh said to him, "Get away from me! Take care that you do not see my face again, for on the day you see my face you shall die." ²⁹Moses said, "Just as you say! I will never see your face again."

Warning of the Final Plague

11 The LORD said to Moses, "I will bring one more plague upon Pharaoh and upon Egypt; afterwards he will let you go from here; indeed, when he lets you go, he will drive you away. ²Tell the people that every man is to ask his neighbor and every woman is to ask her neighbor for objects of silver and gold." ³The LORD gave the people favor in the sight of the Egyptians. Moreover, Moses himself was a man of great importance in the land of Egypt, in the sight of Pharaoh's officials and in the sight of the people.

4 Moses said, "Thus says the LORD: About midnight I will go out through Egypt. ⁵Every firstborn in the land of Egypt shall die, from the firstborn of Pharaoh who sits on his throne to the firstborn of the female slave who is behind the handmill, and all the firstborn of the livestock. ⁶Then there will be a loud cry throughout the whole land of Egypt, such as has never been or will ever be again. ⁷But not a dog shall growl at any of the Israelites—not at people, not at animals—so that you may know that the LORD makes a distinction between Egypt and Israel. ⁸Then all these officials of yours shall come down to me, and bow low to me, saying, 'Leave us, you and all the people who follow you.' After that I will leave." And in hot anger he left Pharaoh.

9 The LORD said to Moses, "Pharaoh will not listen to you, in order that my wonders may be multiplied in the land of Egypt." ¹⁰Moses and Aaron performed all these wonders before Pharaoh; but the LORD hardened Pharaoh's heart, and he did not let the people of Israel go out of his land.

The First Passover Instituted

12 The LORD said to Moses and Aaron in the land of Egypt: ²This month shall mark for you the

^w Or *Sea of Reeds*

"This day shall be a day of remembrance for you. You shall celebrate it as a festival to the LORD; throughout your generations you shall observe it as a perpetual ordinance." Exodus 12:14

beginning of months; it shall be the first month of the year for you. ³Tell the whole congregation of Israel that on the tenth of this month they are to take a lamb for each family, a lamb for each household. ⁴If a household is too small for a whole lamb, it shall join its closest neighbor in obtaining one; the lamb shall be divided in proportion to the number of people who eat of it. ⁵Your lamb shall be without blemish, a year-old male; you may take it from the sheep or from the goats. ⁶You shall keep it until the fourteenth day of this month; then the whole assembled congregation of Israel shall slaughter it at twilight. ⁷They shall take some of the blood and put it on the two doorposts and the lintel of the houses in which they eat it. ⁸They shall eat the lamb that same night; they shall eat it roasted over the fire with unleavened bread and bitter herbs. ⁹Do not eat any of it raw or boiled in water, but roasted over the fire, with its head, legs, and inner organs. ¹⁰You shall let none of it remain until the morning; anything that remains until the morning you shall burn. ¹¹This is how you shall eat it: your loins girded, your sandals on your feet, and your staff in your hand; and you shall eat it hurriedly. It is the passover of the LORD. ¹²For I will pass through the land of Egypt that night, and I will strike down every firstborn in the land of Egypt, both human beings and animals; on all the gods of Egypt I will execute judgments: I am the LORD. ¹³The blood shall be a sign for you on the houses where you live: when I see the blood, I will pass over you, and no plague shall destroy you when I strike the land of Egypt.

14 This day shall be a day of remembrance for you. You shall celebrate it as a festival to the LORD; throughout your generations you shall observe it as a perpetual ordinance. ¹⁵Seven days you shall eat unleavened bread; on the first day you shall remove leaven from your houses, for whoever eats leavened bread from the first day until the seventh day shall be cut off from Israel. ¹⁶On the first day you shall hold a solemn assembly, and on the seventh day a solemn assembly; no work shall be done on those days; only what everyone must eat, that alone may be prepared by you. ¹⁷You shall observe the festival of unleavened bread, for on this very day I brought your companies out of the land of Egypt: you shall observe this day throughout your generations as a perpetual ordinance. ¹⁸In the first month, from the evening of the fourteenth day until the evening of the twenty-first day, you shall eat unleavened bread. ¹⁹For seven days no leaven shall be found in your houses; for whoever eats what is leavened shall be cut off from the congregation of Israel, whether an alien or a native of the land. ²⁰You shall eat nothing leavened; in all your settlements you shall eat unleavened bread.

21 Then Moses called all the elders of Israel and said to them, "Go, select lambs for your families, and slaughter the passover lamb. ²²Take a bunch of hyssop, dip it in the blood that is in the basin, and touch the lintel and the two doorposts with the blood in the basin. None of you shall go outside the door of your house until morning. ²³For the LORD will pass through to strike down the Egyptians; when he sees the blood on the lintel and on the two doorposts, the LORD will pass over that door and will not allow the destroyer to enter your houses to strike you down. ²⁴You shall observe this rite as a perpetual ordinance

for you and your children. ²⁵When you come to the land that the LORD will give you, as he has promised, you shall keep this observance. ²⁶And when your children ask you, 'What do you mean by this observance?' ²⁷you shall say, 'It is the passover sacrifice to the LORD, for he passed over the houses of the Israelites in Egypt, when he struck down the Egyptians but spared our houses.' " And the people bowed down and worshiped.

28 The Israelites went and did just as the LORD had commanded Moses and Aaron.

The Tenth Plague:
Death of the Firstborn

29 At midnight the LORD struck down all the firstborn in the land of Egypt, from the firstborn of Pharaoh who sat on his throne to the firstborn of the prisoner who was in the dungeon, and all the firstborn of the livestock. ³⁰Pharaoh arose in the night, he and all his officials and all the Egyptians; and there was a loud cry in Egypt, for there was not a house without someone dead. ³¹Then he summoned Moses and Aaron in the night, and said, "Rise up, go away from my people, both you and the Israelites! Go, worship the LORD, as you said. ³²Take your flocks and your herds, as you said, and be gone. And bring a blessing on me too!"

The Exodus:
From Rameses to Succoth

33 The Egyptians urged the people to hasten their departure from the land, for they said, "We shall all be dead." ³⁴So the people took their dough before it was leavened, with their kneading bowls wrapped up in their cloaks on their shoulders. ³⁵The Israelites had done as Moses told them; they had asked the Egyptians for jewelry of silver and gold, and for clothing, ³⁶and the LORD had given the people favor in the sight of the Egyptians, so that they let them have what they asked. And so they plundered the Egyptians.

37 The Israelites journeyed from Ram´e·sēs to Suc´coth, about six hundred thousand men on foot, besides children. ³⁸A mixed crowd also went up with them, and livestock in great numbers, both flocks and herds. ³⁹They baked unleavened cakes of the dough that they had brought out of Egypt; it was not leavened, because they were driven out of Egypt and could not wait, nor had they prepared any provisions for themselves.

40 The time that the Israelites had lived in Egypt was four hundred thirty years. ⁴¹At the end of four hundred thirty years, on that very day, all the companies of the LORD went out from the land of Egypt. ⁴²That was for the LORD a night of vigil, to bring them out of the land of Egypt. That same night is a vigil to be kept for the LORD by all the Israelites throughout their generations.

Directions for the Passover

43 The LORD said to Moses and Aaron: This is the ordinance for the passover: no foreigner shall eat of it, ⁴⁴but any slave who has been purchased may eat of it after he has been circumcised; ⁴⁵no bound or hired servant may eat of it. ⁴⁶It shall be eaten in one house; you shall not take any of the animal outside the house, and you shall not break any of its bones. ⁴⁷The whole congregation of Israel shall celebrate it. ⁴⁸If an alien who resides with you wants to celebrate the passover to the LORD, all his males shall be circumcised; then he may draw near to celebrate it; he shall be regarded as a native of the land. But no uncircumcised person shall eat of it; ⁴⁹there shall be one law for the native and for the alien who resides among you.

50 All the Israelites did just as the LORD had commanded Moses and Aaron. ⁵¹That very day the LORD brought the Israelites out of the land of Egypt, company by company.

"The LORD went in front of them in a pillar of cloud by day, to lead them along the way, and in a pillar of fire by night, to give them light, so that they might travel by day and by night."

Exodus 13:21

13 The LORD said to Moses: ²Consecrate to me all the firstborn; whatever is the first to open the womb among the Israelites, of human beings and animals, is mine.

The Festival of Unleavened Bread

3 Moses said to the people, "Remember this day on which you came out of Egypt, out of the house of slavery, because the LORD brought you out from there by strength of hand; no leavened bread shall be eaten. ⁴Today, in the month of Āʹbib, you are going out. ⁵When the LORD brings you into the land of the Cāʹnaan·ites, the Hitʹtītes, the Amʹo·rītes, the Hīʹvītes, and the Jebʹū·sītes, which he swore to your ancestors to give you, a land flowing with milk and honey, you shall keep this observance in this month. ⁶Seven days you shall eat unleavened bread, and on the seventh day there shall be a festival to the LORD. ⁷Unleavened bread shall be eaten for seven days; no leavened bread shall be seen in your possession, and no leaven shall be seen among you in all your territory. ⁸You shall tell your child on that day, 'It is because of what the LORD did for me when I came out of Egypt.' ⁹It shall serve for you as a sign on your hand and as a reminder on your forehead, so that the teaching of the LORD may be on your lips; for with a strong hand the LORD brought you out of Egypt. ¹⁰You shall keep this ordinance at its proper time from year to year.

The Consecration of the Firstborn

11 "When the LORD has brought you into the land of the Cāʹnaan·ites, as he swore to you and your ancestors, and has given it to you, ¹²you shall set apart to the LORD all that first opens the womb. All the firstborn of your livestock that are males shall be the LORD's. ¹³But every firstborn donkey you shall redeem with a sheep; if you do not redeem it, you must break its neck. Every firstborn male among your children you shall redeem. ¹⁴When in the future your child asks you, 'What does this mean?' you shall answer, 'By strength of hand the LORD brought us out of Egypt, from the house of slavery. ¹⁵When Pharaoh stubbornly refused to let us go, the LORD killed all the firstborn in the land of Egypt, from human firstborn to the firstborn of animals. Therefore I sacrifice to the LORD every male that first opens the womb, but every firstborn of my sons I redeem.' ¹⁶It shall serve as a sign on your hand and as an emblemˣ on your forehead that by strength of hand the LORD brought us out of Egypt."

The Pillars of Cloud and Fire

17 When Pharaoh let the people go, God did not lead them by way of the land of the Phi·lisʹtines, although that was nearer; for God thought, "If the people face war, they may change their minds and return to Egypt." ¹⁸So God led the people by the roundabout way of the wilderness toward the Red Sea.ʸ The Israelites went up out of the land of Egypt prepared for battle. ¹⁹And Moses took with him the bones of Joseph who had required a solemn oath of the Israelites, saying, "God will surely take notice of you, and then you must carry my bones with you from here." ²⁰They set out from Sucʹcoth, and camped at Ēʹtham, on the edge of the wilderness. ²¹The LORD went in front of them in a

ˣ Or *as a frontlet*; Meaning of Heb uncertain
ʸ Or *Sea of Reeds*

pillar of cloud by day, to lead them along the way, and in a pillar of fire by night, to give them light, so that they might travel by day and by night. [22]Neither the pillar of cloud by day nor the pillar of fire by night left its place in front of the people.

Crossing the Red Sea

14 Then the LORD said to Moses: [2]Tell the Israelites to turn back and camp in front of Pī-ha·hī′roth, between Mig′dōl and the sea, in front of Bā′al-zē′phon; you shall camp opposite it, by the sea. [3]Pharaoh will say of the Israelites, 'They are wandering aimlessly in the land; the wilderness has closed in on them.' [4]I will harden Pharaoh's heart, and he will pursue them, so that I will gain glory for myself over Pharaoh and all his army; and the Egyptians shall know that I am the LORD. And they did so.

5 When the king of Egypt was told that the people had fled, the minds of Pharaoh and his officials were changed toward the people, and they said, "What have we done, letting Israel leave our service?" [6]So he had his chariot made ready, and took his army with him; [7]he took six hundred picked chariots and all the other chariots of Egypt with officers over all of them. [8]The LORD hardened the heart of Pharaoh king of Egypt and he pursued the Israelites, who were going out boldly. [9]The Egyptians pursued them, all Pharaoh's horses and chariots, his chariot drivers and his army; they overtook them camped by the sea, by Pī-ha·hī′-roth, in front of Bā′al-zē′phon.

10 As Pharaoh drew near, the Israelites looked back, and there were the Egyptians advancing on them. In great fear the Israelites cried out to the LORD. [11]They said to Moses, "Was it because there were no graves in Egypt that you have taken us away to die in the wilderness? What have you done to us, bringing us out of Egypt? [12]Is this not the very thing we told you in Egypt, 'Let us alone and let us serve the Egyptians'? For it would have been better for us to serve the Egyptians than to die in

the wilderness." [13]But Moses said to the people, "Do not be afraid, stand firm, and see the deliverance that the LORD will accomplish for you today; for the Egyptians whom you see today you shall never see again. [14]The LORD will fight for you, and you have only to keep still."

15 Then the LORD said to Moses, "Why do you cry out to me? Tell the Israelites to go forward. [16]But you lift up your staff, and stretch out your hand over the sea and divide it, that the Israelites may go into the sea on dry ground. [17]Then I will harden the hearts of the Egyptians so that they will go in after them; and so I will gain glory for myself over Pharaoh and all his army, his chariots, and his chariot drivers. [18]And the Egyptians shall know that I am the LORD, when I have gained glory for myself over Pharaoh, his chariots, and his chariot drivers."

19 The angel of God who was going before the Israelite army moved and went behind them; and the pillar of cloud moved from in front of them and took its place behind them. [20]It came between the army of Egypt and the army of Israel. And so the cloud was there with the darkness, and it lit up the night; one did not come near the other all night.

21 Then Moses stretched out his hand over the sea. The LORD drove the sea back by a strong east wind all night, and turned the sea into dry land; and the waters were divided. [22]The Israelites went into the sea on dry ground, the waters forming a wall for them on their right and on their left. [23]The Egyptians pursued, and went into the sea after them, all of Pharaoh's horses, chariots, and chariot drivers. [24]At the morning watch the LORD in the pillar of fire and cloud looked down upon the Egyptian army, and threw the Egyptian army into panic. [25]He clogged[z] their chariot wheels so that they turned with difficulty. The Egyptians said, "Let us flee from the Israelites, for the LORD is fighting for them against Egypt."

[z] Sam Gk Syr: MT *removed*

The Pursuers Drowned

26 Then the LORD said to Moses, "Stretch out your hand over the sea, so that the water may come back upon the Egyptians, upon their chariots and chariot drivers." ²⁷So Moses stretched out his hand over the sea, and at dawn the sea returned to its normal depth. As the Egyptians fled before it, the LORD tossed the Egyptians into the sea. ²⁸The waters returned and covered the chariots and the chariot drivers, the entire army of Pharaoh that had followed them into the sea; not one of them remained. ²⁹But the Israelites walked on dry ground through the sea, the waters forming a wall for them on their right and on their left.

30 Thus the LORD saved Israel that day from the Egyptians; and Israel saw the Egyptians dead on the seashore. ³¹Israel saw the great work that the LORD did against the Egyptians. So the people feared the LORD and believed in the LORD and in his servant Moses.

The Song of Moses

15 Then Moses and the Israelites sang this song to the LORD:

"I will sing to the LORD, for he has
    triumphed gloriously;
  horse and rider he has thrown into
    the sea.
² The LORD is my strength and my
    might,ᵃ
  and he has become my salvation;
this is my God, and I will praise him,
  my father's God, and I will exalt him.
³ The LORD is a warrior;
  the LORD is his name.

⁴ "Pharaoh's chariots and his army he
    cast into the sea;
  his picked officers were sunk in the
    Red Sea.ᵇ
⁵ The floods covered them;
  they went down into the depths like
    a stone.
⁶ Your right hand, O LORD, glorious in
    power—

> "The LORD is my strength and my might, and he has become my salvation; this is my God, and I will praise him, my father's God, and I will exalt him." Exodus 15:2

your right hand, O LORD, shattered
  the enemy.
⁷ In the greatness of your majesty you
    overthrew your adversaries;
  you sent out your fury, it consumed
    them like stubble.
⁸ At the blast of your nostrils the waters
    piled up,
  the floods stood up in a heap;
  the deeps congealed in the heart of
    the sea.
⁹ The enemy said, 'I will pursue, I will
    overtake,
  I will divide the spoil, my desire
    shall have its fill of them.
  I will draw my sword, my hand
    shall destroy them.'
¹⁰ You blew with your wind, the sea
    covered them;
  they sank like lead in the mighty
    waters.

¹¹ "Who is like you, O LORD, among the
    gods?
  Who is like you, majestic in holiness,
    awesome in splendor, doing
    wonders?
¹² You stretched out your right hand,
  the earth swallowed them.

¹³ "In your steadfast love you led the
    people whom you redeemed;
  you guided them by your strength
    to your holy abode.
¹⁴ The peoples heard, they trembled;
  pangs seized the inhabitants of
    Phi·lis′ti·a.
¹⁵ Then the chiefs of Ē′dom were
    dismayed;
  trembling seized the leaders of Mō′ab;

ᵃ Or *song*   ᵇ Or *Sea of Reeds*

all the inhabitants of Cā´naan melted away.

[16] Terror and dread fell upon them;
by the might of your arm, they
became still as a stone
until your people, O LORD, passed by,
until the people whom you acquired
passed by.
[17] You brought them in and planted them
on the mountain of your own
possession,
the place, O LORD, that you made
your abode,
the sanctuary, O LORD, that your
hands have established.
[18] The LORD will reign forever and ever."

19 When the horses of Pharaoh with his chariots and his chariot drivers went into the sea, the LORD brought back the waters of the sea upon them; but the Israelites walked through the sea on dry ground.

Once God's people were safely across the Red Sea, Moses' sister Miriam (who was a prophet) sang a song of victory, praising God because she knew that God had led the people to safety. As she sang, she played a tambourine. The early Israelites liked to honor and thank God with songs of praise, and we still sing songs of praise today. Besides singing, what other ways can you honor and give thanks to God?

The Song of Miriam

20 Then the prophet Miriam, Aaron's sister, took a tambourine in her hand; and all the women went out after her with tambourines and with dancing. [21]And Miriam sang to them:

"Sing to the LORD, for he has
triumphed gloriously;
horse and rider he has thrown into
the sea."

Have you ever been really hungry? In the desert, the people began to complain that they didn't have enough food. God told Moses that the people did not need to worry because they would soon have enough. The next morning, the people found bread, or "manna," on the ground. Manna appeared each morning as a direct action of God, sent so God's wandering people wouldn't suffer.

Bitter Water Made Sweet

22 Then Moses ordered Israel to set out from the Red Sea,[c] and they went into the wilderness of Shur. They went three days in the wilderness and found no water. [23]When they came to Mar´ah, they could not drink the water of Mar´ah because it was bitter. That is why it was called Mar´ah.[d] [24]And the people complained against Moses, saying, "What shall we drink?" [25]He cried out to the LORD; and the LORD showed him a piece of wood;[e] he threw it into the water, and the water became sweet.

There the LORD[f] made for them a statute and an ordinance and there he put them to the test. [26]He said, "If you will listen carefully to the voice of the LORD your God, and do what is right in his sight, and give heed to his commandments and keep all his statutes, I will not bring upon you any of the diseases that I brought upon the Egyptians; for I am the LORD who heals you."

27 Then they came to Ē´lim, where there were twelve springs of water and seventy palm trees; and they camped there by the water.

Bread from Heaven

16 The whole congregation of the Israelites set out from Ē´lim; and

[c] Or *Sea of Reeds*   [d] That is *Bitterness*   [e] Or a *tree*   [f] Heb *he*

Israel came to the wilderness of Sin, which is between Ē′lim and Sinai, on the fifteenth day of the second month after they had departed from the land of Egypt. [2]The whole congregation of the Israelites complained against Moses and Aaron in the wilderness. [3]The Israelites said to them, "If only we had died by the hand of the LORD in the land of Egypt, when we sat by the fleshpots and ate our fill of bread; for you have brought us out into this wilderness to kill this whole assembly with hunger."

4 Then the LORD said to Moses, "I am going to rain bread from heaven for you, and each day the people shall go out and gather enough for that day. In that way I will test them, whether they will follow my instruction or not. [5]On the sixth day, when they prepare what they bring in, it will be twice as much as they gather on other days." [6]So Moses and Aaron said to all the Israelites, "In the evening you shall know that it was the LORD who brought you out of the land of Egypt, [7]and in the morning you shall see the glory of the LORD, because he has heard your complaining against the LORD. For what are we, that you complain against us?" [8]And Moses said, "When the LORD gives you meat to eat in the evening and your fill of bread in the morning, because the LORD has heard the complaining that you utter against him—what are we? Your complaining is not against us but against the LORD."

9 Then Moses said to Aaron, "Say to the whole congregation of the Israelites, 'Draw near to the LORD, for he has heard your complaining.' " [10]And as Aaron spoke to the whole congregation of the Israelites, they looked toward the wilderness, and the glory of the LORD appeared in the cloud. [11]The LORD spoke to Moses and said, [12]"I have heard the complaining of the Israelites; say to them, 'At twilight you shall eat meat, and in the morning you shall have your fill of bread; then you shall know that I am the LORD your God.' "

13 In the evening quails came up and covered the camp; and in the morning there was a layer of dew around the camp. [14]When the layer of dew lifted, there on the surface of the wilderness was a fine flaky substance, as fine as frost on the ground. [15]When the Israelites saw it, they said to one another, "What is it?"[g] For they did not know what it was. Moses said to them, "It is the bread that the LORD has given you to eat. [16]This is what the LORD has commanded: 'Gather as much of it as each of you needs, an omer to a person according to the number of persons, all providing for those in their own tents.' " [17]The Israelites did so, some gathering more, some less. [18]But when they measured it with an omer, those who gathered much had nothing over, and those who gathered little had no shortage; they gathered as much as each of them needed. [19]And Moses said to them, "Let no one leave any of it over until morning." [20]But they did not listen to Moses; some left part of it until morning, and it bred worms and became foul. And Moses was angry with them. [21]Morning by morning they gathered it, as much as each needed; but when the sun grew hot, it melted.

22 On the sixth day they gathered twice as much food, two omers apiece. When all the leaders of the congregation came and told Moses, [23]he said to them, "This is what the LORD has commanded: 'Tomorrow is a day of solemn rest, a holy sabbath to the LORD; bake what you want to bake and boil what you want to boil, and all that is left over put aside to be kept until morning.' " [24]So they put it aside until morning, as Moses commanded them; and it did not become foul, and there were no worms in it. [25]Moses said, "Eat it today, for today is a sabbath to the LORD; today you will not find it in the field. [26]Six days you shall gather it; but on the seventh day, which is a sabbath, there will be none."

[g] Or "It is manna" (Heb man hu, see verse 31)

27 On the seventh day some of the people went out to gather, and they found none. ²⁸The LORD said to Moses, "How long will you refuse to keep my commandments and instructions? ²⁹See! The LORD has given you the sabbath, therefore on the sixth day he gives you food for two days; each of you stay where you are; do not leave your place on the seventh day." ³⁰So the people rested on the seventh day.

31 The house of Israel called it manna; it was like coriander seed, white, and the taste of it was like wafers made with honey. ³²Moses said, "This is what the LORD has commanded: 'Let an omer of it be kept throughout your generations, in order that they may see the food with which I fed you in the wilderness, when I brought you out of the land of Egypt.'" ³³And Moses said to Aaron, "Take a jar, and put an omer of manna in it, and place it before the LORD, to be kept throughout your generations." ³⁴As the LORD commanded Moses, so Aaron placed it before the covenant,ʰ for safe-keeping. ³⁵The Israelites ate manna forty years, until they came to a habitable land; they ate manna, until they came to the border of the land of Cā´naan. ³⁶An omer is a tenth of an ephah.

Water from the Rock

17 From the wilderness of Sin the whole congregation of the Israelites journeyed by stages, as the LORD commanded. They camped at Reph´i·dim, but there was no water for the people to drink. ²The people quarreled with Moses, and said, "Give us water to drink." Moses said to them, "Why do you quarrel with me? Why do you test the LORD?" ³But the people thirsted there for water; and the people complained against Moses and said, "Why did you bring us out of Egypt, to kill us and our children and livestock with thirst?" ⁴So Moses cried out to the LORD, "What shall I do with this people?

They are almost ready to stone me." ⁵The LORD said to Moses, "Go on ahead of the people, and take some of the elders of Israel with you; take in your hand the staff with which you struck the Nile, and go. ⁶I will be standing there in front of you on the rock at Hō´reb. Strike the rock, and water will come out of it, so that the people may drink." Moses did so, in the sight of the elders of Israel. ⁷He called the place Mas´sahⁱ and Mer´i·bah,ʲ because the Israelites quarreled and tested the LORD, saying, "Is the LORD among us or not?"

> Find the story of Esau in Genesis 25–28, 33, 36. The Amalekites were the family of Esau, and they were a danger to the Israelites. Once, when Israel fought against the Amalekites, Moses stood on a nearby hill with his arms raised up to God. As long as he kept his arms up, Joshua and the soldiers would win. When his arms began to get tired, Aaron and Hur came and stood with him to hold his arms in the air. And so Israel won the battle!

Amalek Attacks Israel and Is Defeated

8 Then Am´a·lek came and fought with Israel at Reph´i·dim. ⁹Moses said to Joshua, "Choose some men for us and go out, fight with Am´a·lek. Tomorrow I will stand on the top of the hill with the staff of God in my hand." ¹⁰So Joshua did as Moses told him, and fought with Am´a·lek, while Moses, Aaron, and Hur went up to the top of the hill. ¹¹Whenever Moses held up his hand, Israel prevailed; and whenever he lowered his hand, Am´a·lek prevailed. ¹²But Moses' hands

ʰ Or *treaty* or *testimony*; Heb *eduth*   ⁱ That is *Test*   ʲ That is *Quarrel* grew weary; so they took a stone and put it under him, and he sat on it. Aaron and Hur held up his hands, one on one side, and the other on the other side; so his hands were steady until the sun set. [13]And Joshua defeated Am´a·lek and his people with the sword.

14 Then the LORD said to Moses, "Write this as a reminder in a book and recite it in the hearing of Joshua: I will utterly blot out the remembrance of Am´a·lek from under heaven." [15]And Moses built an altar and called it, The LORD is my banner. [16]He said, "A hand upon the banner of the LORD![k] The LORD will have war with Am´a·lek from generation to generation."

An altar is a place set aside for offerings and a place to have ceremonies. When God's people were wandering in the wilderness, they built altars by piling up dirt or by putting a block of stone onto a pile of smaller stones. Altars today are usually wooden or stone tables at the front of the church.

Jethro's Advice

18 Jeth´rō, the priest of Mid´i·an, Moses' father-in-law, heard of all that God had done for Moses and for his people Israel, how the LORD had brought Israel out of Egypt. [2]After Moses had sent away his wife Zip·pō´rah, his father-in-law Jeth´rō took her back, [3]along with her two sons. The name of the one was Ger´shom (for he said, "I have been an alien[l] in a foreign land"), [4]and the name of the other, El·i·e´zer[m] (for he said, "The God of my father was my help, and delivered me from the sword of Pharaoh"). [5]Jeth´rō, Moses' father-in-law, came into the wilderness where Moses was encamped at the mountain of God, bringing Moses' sons

and wife to him. [6]He sent word to Moses, "I, your father-in-law Jeth´rō, am coming to you, with your wife and her two sons." [7]Moses went out to meet his father-in-law; he bowed down and kissed him; each asked after the other's welfare, and they went into the tent. [8]Then Moses told his father-in-law all that the LORD had done to Pharaoh and to the Egyptians for Israel's sake, all the hardship that had beset them on the way, and how the LORD had delivered them. [9]Jeth´rō rejoiced for all the good that the LORD had done to Israel, in delivering them from the Egyptians.

10 Jeth´rō said, "Blessed be the LORD, who has delivered you from the Egyptians and from Pharaoh. [11]Now I know that the LORD is greater than all gods, because he delivered the people from the Egyptians,[n] when they dealt arrogantly with them." [12]And Jeth´rō, Moses' father-in-law, brought a burnt offering and sacrifices to God; and Aaron came with all the elders of Israel to eat bread with Moses' father-in-law in the presence of God.

13 The next day Moses sat as judge for the people, while the people stood around him from morning until evening. [14]When Moses' father-in-law saw all that he was doing for the people, he said, "What is this that you are doing for the people? Why do

Moses' father-in-law, Jethro, saw that Moses was trying to do too much himself and said that he should train other leaders to help. When we are tired or scared, it is good to ask a family member for help. Sometimes just talking about a problem will make it seem smaller and easier to deal with.

---

[k] Cn: Meaning of Heb uncertain   [l] Heb *ger*   [m] Heb *Eli,* my God; *ezer,* help   [n] The clause *because . . . Egyptians* has been transposed from verse 10

you sit alone, while all the people stand around you from morning until evening?" ¹⁵Moses said to his father-in-law, "Because the people come to me to inquire of God. ¹⁶When they have a dispute, they come to me and I decide between one person and another, and I make known to them the statutes and instructions of God." ¹⁷Moses' father-in-law said to him, "What you are doing is not good. ¹⁸You will surely wear yourself out, both you and these people with you. For the task is too heavy for you; you cannot do it alone. ¹⁹Now listen to me. I will give you counsel, and God be with you! You should represent the people before God, and you should bring their cases before God; ²⁰teach them the statutes and instructions and make known to them the way they are to go and the things they are to do. ²¹You should also look for able men among all the people, men who fear God, are trustworthy, and hate dishonest gain; set such men over them as officers over thousands, hundreds, fifties and tens. ²²Let them sit as judges for the people at all times; let them bring every important case to you, but decide every minor case themselves. So it will be easier for you, and they will bear the burden with you. ²³If you do this, and God so commands you, then you will be able to endure, and all these people will go to their home in peace."

24 So Moses listened to his father-in-law and did all that he had said. ²⁵Moses chose able men from all Israel and appointed them as heads over the people, as officers over thousands, hundreds, fifties, and tens. ²⁶And they judged the people at all times; hard cases they brought to Moses, but any minor case they decided themselves. ²⁷Then Moses let his father-in-law depart, and he went off to his own country.

The Israelites Reach Mount Sinai

19 On the third new moon after the Israelites had gone out of the land of Egypt, on that very day, they came into the wilderness of Sinai. ²They had journeyed from Reph´i·dim, entered the wilderness of Sinai, and camped in the wilderness; Israel camped there in front of the mountain. ³Then Moses went up to God; the LORD called to him from the mountain, saying, "Thus you shall say to the house of Jacob, and tell the Israelites: ⁴You have seen what I did to the Egyptians, and how I bore you on eagles' wings and brought you to myself. ⁵Now therefore, if you obey my voice and keep my covenant, you shall be my treasured possession out of all the peoples. Indeed, the whole earth is mine, ⁶but you shall be for me a priestly kingdom and a holy nation. These are the words that you shall speak to the Israelites."

7 So Moses came, summoned the elders of the people, and set before them all these words that the LORD had commanded him. ⁸The people all answered as one: "Everything that the LORD has spoken we will do." Moses reported the words of the people to the LORD. ⁹Then the LORD said to Moses, "I am going to come to you in a dense cloud, in order that the people may hear when I speak with you and so trust you ever after."

The People Consecrated

When Moses had told the words of the people to the LORD, ¹⁰the LORD said to Moses: "Go to the people and consecrate them today and tomorrow. Have them wash their clothes ¹¹and prepare for the third day, because on the third

On Mount Sinai, God appeared to Moses and made a special promise to the Israelites. Today, we are no longer sure which mountain is Mount Sinai, but the exact place does not matter. We rejoice because the promises God made to care for the Israelites are promises made to care for us as well.

God spoke from Mount Sinai through fire, thunder, and the sound of a trumpet. Today, God speaks to us through the Bible, God's holy Word, and through men and women who share with us what they know about the Bible.

day the LORD will come down upon Mount Sinai in the sight of all the people. ¹²You shall set limits for the people all around, saying, 'Be careful not to go up the mountain or to touch the edge of it. Any who touch the mountain shall be put to death. ¹³No hand shall touch them, but they shall be stoned or shot with arrows;⁰ whether animal or human being, they shall not live.' When the trumpet sounds a long blast, they may go up on the mountain." ¹⁴So Moses went down from the mountain to the people. He consecrated the people, and they washed their clothes. ¹⁵And he said to the people, "Prepare for the third day; do not go near a woman."

16 On the morning of the third day there was thunder and lightning, as well as a thick cloud on the mountain, and a blast of a trumpet so loud that all the people who were in the camp trembled. ¹⁷Moses brought the people out of the camp to meet God. They took their stand at the foot of the mountain. ¹⁸Now Mount Sinai was wrapped in smoke, because the LORD had descended upon it in fire; the smoke went up like the smoke of a kiln, while the whole mountain shook violently. ¹⁹As the blast of the trumpet grew louder and louder, Moses would speak and God would answer him in thunder. ²⁰When the LORD descended upon Mount Sinai, to the top of the mountain, the LORD summoned Moses to the top of the mountain, and Moses went up. ²¹Then the LORD said to Moses, "Go down and warn the people not to break through to the LORD to look; otherwise many of them will perish. ²²Even

the priests who approach the LORD must consecrate themselves or the LORD will break out against them." ²³Moses said to the LORD, "The people are not permitted to come up to Mount Sinai; for you yourself warned us, saying, 'Set limits around the mountain and keep it holy.'" ²⁴The LORD said to him, "Go down, and come up bringing Aaron with you; but do not let either the priests or the people break through to come up to the LORD; otherwise he will break out against them." ²⁵So Moses went down to the people and told them.

The Ten Commandments showed God's people how they were supposed to treat God and each other. Today, the Ten Commandments are still used as a guide for living God's way. The first four commandments have to do with our relationship to God, and the last six deal with our relationships to other people.

The Ten Commandments

20 Then God spoke all these words:

2 I am the LORD your God, who brought you out of the land of Egypt, out of the house of slavery; ³you shall have no other gods before^p me.

4 You shall not make for yourself an idol, whether in the form of anything that is in heaven above, or that is on the earth beneath, or that is in the water under the earth. ⁵You shall not bow down to them or worship them; for I the LORD your God am a jealous God, punishing children for the iniquity of parents, to the third and the fourth generation of those who reject me, ⁶but showing steadfast love to the thousandth generation^q of those who love me and keep my commandments.

⁰ Heb lacks *with arrows*   ^p Or *besides*   ^q Or *to thousands*

7 You shall not make wrongful use of the name of the LORD your God, for the LORD will not acquit anyone who misuses his name.

8 Remember the sabbath day, and keep it holy. ⁹Six days you shall labor and do all your work. ¹⁰But the seventh day is a sabbath to the LORD your God; you shall not do any work—you, your son or your daughter, your male or female slave, your livestock, or the alien resident in your towns. ¹¹For in six days the LORD made heaven and earth, the sea, and all that is in them, but rested the seventh day; therefore the LORD blessed the sabbath day and consecrated it.

12 Honor your father and your mother, so that your days may be long in the land that the LORD your God is giving you.

13 You shall not murder.ʳ

14 You shall not commit adultery.

15 You shall not steal.

16 You shall not bear false witness against your neighbor.

17 You shall not covet your neighbor's house; you shall not covet your neighbor's wife, or male or female slave, or ox, or donkey, or anything that belongs to your neighbor.

18 When all the people witnessed the thunder and lightning, the sound of the trumpet, and the mountain smoking, they were afraidˢ and trembled and stood at a distance, ¹⁹and said to Moses, "You speak to us, and we will listen; but do not let God speak to us, or we will die." ²⁰Moses said to the people, "Do not be afraid; for God has come only to test you and to put the fear of him upon you so that you do not sin." ²¹Then the people stood at a distance, while Moses drew near to the thick darkness where God was.

The Law concerning the Altar

22 The LORD said to Moses: Thus you shall say to the Israelites: "You have seen for yourselves that I spoke with you from heaven. ²³You shall not make gods of silver alongside me, nor shall you make for yourselves gods of gold. ²⁴You need make for me only an altar of earth and sacrifice on it your burnt offerings and your offerings of well-being, your sheep and your oxen; in every place where I cause my name to be remembered I will come to you and bless you. ²⁵But if you make for me an altar of stone, do not build it of hewn stones; for if you use a chisel upon it you profane it. ²⁶You shall not go up by steps to my altar, so that your nakedness may not be exposed on it."

The Law concerning Slaves

21 These are the ordinances that you shall set before them:

2 When you buy a male Hebrew slave, he shall serve six years, but in the seventh he shall go out a free person, without debt. ³If he comes in single, he shall go out single; if he comes in married, then his wife shall go out with him. ⁴If his master gives him a wife and she bears him sons or daughters, the wife and her children shall be her master's and he shall go out alone. ⁵But if the slave declares, "I love my master, my wife, and my children; I will not go out a free person," ⁶then his master shall bring him before God.ᵗ He shall be brought to the door or the doorpost; and his master shall pierce his ear with an awl; and he shall serve him for life.

7 When a man sells his daughter as a slave, she shall not go out as the male slaves do. ⁸If she does not please her master, who designated her for himself, then he shall let her be redeemed; he shall have no right to sell her to a foreign people, since he has dealt unfairly with her. ⁹If he designates her for his son, he shall deal with her as with a daughter. ¹⁰If he takes another wife to himself, he shall not diminish the food, clothing, or marital rights of the first wife.ᵘ ¹¹And if

ʳ Or kill   ˢ Sam Gk Syr Vg: MT they saw   ᵗ Or
to the judges   ᵘ Heb of her

he does not do these three things for her, she shall go out without debt, without payment of money.

The Law concerning Violence

12 Whoever strikes a person mortally shall be put to death. [13]If it was not premeditated, but came about by an act of God, then I will appoint for you a place to which the killer may flee. [14]But if someone willfully attacks and kills another by treachery, you shall take the killer from my altar for execution.

15 Whoever strikes father or mother shall be put to death.

16 Whoever kidnaps a person, whether that person has been sold or is still held in possession, shall be put to death.

17 Whoever curses father or mother shall be put to death.

18 When individuals quarrel and one strikes the other with a stone or fist so that the injured party, though not dead, is confined to bed, [19]but recovers and walks around outside with the help of a staff, then the assailant shall be free of liability, except to pay for the loss of time, and to arrange for full recovery.

20 When a slaveowner strikes a male or female slave with a rod and the slave dies immediately, the owner shall be punished. [21]But if the slave survives a day or two, there is no punishment; for the slave is the owner's property.

22 When people who are fighting injure a pregnant woman so that there is a miscarriage, and yet no further harm follows, the one responsible shall be fined what the woman's husband demands, paying as much as the judges determine. [23]If any harm follows, then you shall give life for life, [24]eye for eye, tooth for tooth, hand for hand, foot for foot, [25]burn for burn, wound for wound, stripe for stripe.

26 When a slaveowner strikes the eye of a male or female slave, destroying it, the owner shall let the slave go, a free person, to compensate for the eye. [27]If the owner knocks out a tooth of a male or female slave, the slave shall be let go, a free person, to compensate for the tooth.

Laws concerning Property

28 When an ox gores a man or a woman to death, the ox shall be stoned, and its flesh shall not be eaten; but the owner of the ox shall not be liable. [29]If the ox has been accustomed to gore in the past, and its owner has been warned but has not restrained it, and it kills a man or a woman, the ox shall be stoned, and its owner also shall be put to death. [30]If a ransom is imposed on the owner, then the owner shall pay whatever is imposed for the redemption of the victim's life. [31]If it gores a boy or a girl, the owner shall be dealt with according to this same rule. [32]If the ox gores a male or female slave, the owner shall pay to the slaveowner thirty shekels of silver, and the ox shall be stoned.

33 If someone leaves a pit open, or digs a pit and does not cover it, and an ox or a donkey falls into it, [34]the owner of the pit shall make restitution, giving money to its owner, but keeping the dead animal.

35 If someone's ox hurts the ox of another, so that it dies, then they shall sell the live ox and divide the price of it; and the dead animal they shall also divide. [36]But if it was known that the ox was accustomed to gore in the past, and its owner has not restrained it, the owner shall restore ox for ox, but keep the dead animal.

Laws of Restitution

22 [v]When someone steals an ox or a sheep, and slaughters it or sells it, the thief shall pay five oxen for an ox, and four sheep for a sheep.[w] The thief shall make restitution, but if unable to do so, shall be sold for the theft. [4]When the animal, whether ox or donkey or sheep, is found alive in the thief's possession, the thief shall pay double.

---

[v] Ch 21.37 in Heb   [w] Verses 2, 3, and 4 rearranged thus: 3b, 4, 2, 3a

2[x] If a thief is found breaking in, and is beaten to death, no bloodguilt is incurred; [3]but if it happens after sunrise, bloodguilt is incurred.

5 When someone causes a field or vineyard to be grazed over, or lets livestock loose to graze in someone else's field, restitution shall be made from the best in the owner's field or vineyard.

6 When fire breaks out and catches in thorns so that the stacked grain or the standing grain or the field is consumed, the one who started the fire shall make full restitution.

7 When someone delivers to a neighbor money or goods for safekeeping, and they are stolen from the neighbor's house, then the thief, if caught, shall pay double. [8]If the thief is not caught, the owner of the house shall be brought before God,[y] to determine whether or not the owner had laid hands on the neighbor's goods.

9 In any case of disputed ownership involving ox, donkey, sheep, clothing, or any other loss, of which one party says, "This is mine," the case of both parties shall come before God;[y] the one whom God condemns[z] shall pay double to the other.

10 When someone delivers to another a donkey, ox, sheep, or any other animal for safekeeping, and it dies or is injured or is carried off, without anyone seeing it, [11]an oath before the LORD shall decide between the two of them that the one has not laid hands on the property of the other; the owner shall accept the oath, and no restitution shall be made. [12]But if it was stolen, restitution shall be made to its owner. [13]If it was mangled by beasts, let it be brought as evidence; restitution shall not be made for the mangled remains.

14 When someone borrows an animal from another and it is injured or dies, the owner not being present, full restitution shall be made. [15]If the owner was present, there shall be no restitution; if it was hired, only the hiring fee is due.

Social and Religious Laws

16 When a man seduces a virgin who is not engaged to be married, and lies with her, he shall give the bride-price for her and make her his wife. [17]But if her father refuses to give her to him, he shall pay an amount equal to the bride-price for virgins.

18 You shall not permit a female sorcerer to live.

19 Whoever lies with an animal shall be put to death.

20 Whoever sacrifices to any god, other than the LORD alone, shall be devoted to destruction.

21 You shall not wrong or oppress a resident alien, for you were aliens in the land of Egypt. [22]You shall not abuse any widow or orphan. [23]If you do abuse them, when they cry out to me, I will surely heed their cry; [24]my wrath will burn, and I will kill you with the sword, and your wives shall become widows and your children orphans.

25 If you lend money to my people, to the poor among you, you shall not deal with them as a creditor; you shall not exact interest from them. [26]If you take your neighbor's cloak in pawn, you shall restore it before the sun goes down; [27]for it may be your neighbor's only clothing to use as cover; in what else shall that person sleep? And if your neighbor cries out to me, I will listen, for I am compassionate.

28 You shall not revile God, or curse a leader of your people.

29 You shall not delay to make offerings from the fullness of your harvest and from the outflow of your presses.[a] The firstborn of your sons you shall give to me. [30]You shall do the same with your oxen and with your sheep: seven days it shall remain with its mother; on the eighth day you shall give it to me.

31 You shall be people consecrated to me; therefore you shall not eat any meat

[x] Ch 22.1 in Heb [y] Or *before the judges* [z] Or *the judges condemn* [a] Meaning of Heb uncertain

The laws in Exodus 23:1–9 showed the Hebrew people how to treat one another fairly. God wanted the people to act with love and care. God wants us to do the same! What are some ways you can care for your friends and family? What are some ways you can care for people others seem to forget? What are some ways you can care for the people you have trouble getting along with? Read what Jesus said in Matthew 5:43–48 and Matthew 7:12.

that is mangled by beasts in the field; you shall throw it to the dogs.

Justice for All

23 You shall not spread a false report. You shall not join hands with the wicked to act as a malicious witness. ²You shall not follow a majority in wrongdoing; when you bear witness in a lawsuit, you shall not side with the majority so as to pervert justice; ³nor shall you be partial to the poor in a lawsuit.

4 When you come upon your enemy's ox or donkey going astray, you shall bring it back.

5 When you see the donkey of one who hates you lying under its burden and you would hold back from setting it free, you must help to set it free.[b]

6 You shall not pervert the justice due to your poor in their lawsuits. ⁷Keep far from a false charge, and do not kill the innocent and those in the right, for I will not acquit the guilty. ⁸You shall take no bribe, for a bribe blinds the officials, and subverts the cause of those who are in the right.

9 You shall not oppress a resident alien; you know the heart of an alien, for you were aliens in the land of Egypt.

Sabbatical Year and Sabbath

10 For six years you shall sow your land and gather in its yield; ¹¹but the seventh year you shall let it rest and lie fallow, so that the poor of your people may eat; and what they leave the wild animals may eat. You shall do the same with your vineyard, and with your olive orchard.

12 Six days you shall do your work, but on the seventh day you shall rest, so that your ox and your donkey may have relief, and your homeborn slave and the resident alien may be refreshed. ¹³Be attentive to all that I have said to you. Do not invoke the names of other gods; do not let them be heard on your lips.

The Annual Festivals

14 Three times in the year you shall hold a festival for me. ¹⁵You shall observe the festival of unleavened bread; as I commanded you, you shall eat unleavened bread for seven days at the appointed time in the month of A'bib, for in it you came out of Egypt.

No one shall appear before me empty-handed.

16 You shall observe the festival of harvest, of the first fruits of your labor, of what you sow in the field. You shall observe the festival of ingathering at the end of the year, when you gather in from the field the fruit of your labor. ¹⁷Three times in the year all your males shall appear before the Lord GOD.

18 You shall not offer the blood of my sacrifice with anything leavened, or let the fat of my festival remain until the morning.

19 The choicest of the first fruits of your ground you shall bring into the house of the LORD your God.

You shall not boil a kid in its mother's milk.

The Conquest
of Canaan Promised

20 I am going to send an angel in front of you, to guard you on the way

_____
[b] Meaning of Heb uncertain

and to bring you to the place that I have prepared. [21]Be attentive to him and listen to his voice; do not rebel against him, for he will not pardon your transgression; for my name is in him.

22 But if you listen attentively to his voice and do all that I say, then I will be an enemy to your enemies and a foe to your foes.

23 When my angel goes in front of you, and brings you to the Am'o·rītes, the Hit'tītes, the Per'iz·zītes, the Cā'naan·ītes, the Hī'vītes, and the Jeb'ū·sītes, and I blot them out, [24]you shall not bow down to their gods, or worship them, or follow their practices, but you shall utterly demolish them and break their pillars in pieces. [25]You shall worship the LORD your God, and I[c] will bless your bread and your water; and I will take sickness away from among you. [26]No one shall miscarry or be barren in your land; I will fulfill the number of your days. [27]I will send my terror in front of you, and will throw into confusion all the people against whom you shall come, and I will make all your enemies turn their backs to you. [28]And I will send the pestilence[d] in front of you, which shall drive out the Hī'vītes, the Cā'naan·ītes, and the Hit'tītes from before you. [29]I will not drive them out from before you in one year, or the land would become desolate and the wild animals would multiply against you. [30]Little by little I will drive them out from before you, until you have increased and possess the land. [31]I will set your borders from the Red Sea[e] to the sea of the Phi·lis'tines, and from the wilderness to the Euphrates; for I will hand over to you the inhabitants of the land, and you shall drive them out before you. [32]You shall make no covenant with them and their gods. [33]They shall not live in your land, or they will make you sin against me; for if you worship their gods, it will surely be a snare to you.

The Blood of the Covenant

24 Then he said to Moses, "Come up to the LORD, you and Aaron, Nā'dab, and A·bī'hū, and seventy of the elders of Israel, and worship at a distance. [2]Moses alone shall come near the LORD; but the others shall not come near, and the people shall not come up with him."

3 Moses came and told the people all the words of the LORD and all the ordinances; and all the people answered with one voice, and said, "All the words that the LORD has spoken we will do." [4]And Moses wrote down all the words of the LORD. He rose early in the morning, and built an altar at the foot of the mountain, and set up twelve pillars, corresponding to the twelve tribes of Israel. [5]He sent young men of the people of Israel, who offered burnt offerings and sacrificed oxen as offerings of well-being to the LORD. [6]Moses took half of the blood and put it in basins, and half of the blood he dashed against the altar. [7]Then he took the book of the covenant, and read it in the hearing of the people; and they said, "All that the LORD has spoken we will do, and we will be obedient." [8]Moses took the blood and dashed it on the people, and said, "See the blood of the covenant that the LORD has made with you in accordance with all these words."

On the Mountain with God

9 Then Moses and Aaron, Nā'dab, and A·bī'hū, and seventy of the elders of Israel went up, [10]and they saw the God of Israel. Under his feet there was something like a pavement of sapphire stone, like the very heaven for clearness. [11]God[f] did not lay his hand on the chief men of the people of Israel; also they beheld God, and they ate and drank.

12 The LORD said to Moses, "Come up to me on the mountain, and wait there; and I will give you the tablets of

[c] Gk Vg: Heb *He* [d] Or *hornets*: Meaning of Heb uncertain [e] Or *Sea of Reeds* [f] Heb *He*

stone, with the law and the commandment, which I have written for their instruction." [13]So Moses set out with his assistant Joshua, and Moses went up into the mountain of God. [14]To the elders he had said, "Wait here for us, until we come to you again; for Aaron and Hur are with you; whoever has a dispute may go to them."

15 Then Moses went up on the mountain, and the cloud covered the mountain. [16]The glory of the LORD settled on Mount Sinai, and the cloud covered it for six days; on the seventh day he called to Moses out of the cloud. [17]Now the appearance of the glory of the LORD was like a devouring fire on the top of the mountain in the sight of the people of Israel. [18]Moses entered the cloud, and went up on the mountain. Moses was on the mountain for forty days and forty nights.

Offerings for the Tabernacle

25 The LORD said to Moses: [2]Tell the Israelites to take for me an offering; from all whose hearts prompt them to give you shall receive the offering for me. [3]This is the offering that you shall receive from them: gold, silver, and bronze, [4]blue, purple, and crimson yarns and fine linen, goats' hair, [5]tanned rams' skins, fine leather,[g] acacia wood, [6]oil for the lamps, spices for the anointing oil and for the fragrant incense, [7]onyx stones and gems to be set in the ephod and for the breastpiece. [8]And have them make me a sanctuary, so that I may dwell among them. [9]In accordance with all that I show you concerning the pattern of the tabernacle and of all its furniture, so you shall make it.

The Ark of the Covenant

10 They shall make an ark of acacia wood; it shall be two and a half cubits long, a cubit and a half wide, and a cubit and a half high. [11]You shall overlay it with pure gold, inside and outside you shall overlay it, and you shall make a

molding of gold upon it all around. [12]You shall cast four rings of gold for it and put them on its four feet, two rings on the one side of it, and two rings on the other side. [13]You shall make poles of acacia wood, and overlay them with gold. [14]And you shall put the poles into the rings on the sides of the ark, by which to carry the ark. [15]The poles shall remain in the rings of the ark; they shall not be taken from it. [16]You shall put into the ark the covenant[h] that I shall give you.

The Tabernacle was a place of worship that could be moved—like church in a tent. For many years, the Hebrews wandered in the desert. Everywhere they went, they took this tent with them so they could always have a place to worship God. Have you ever been to church in a tent or outside?

God told the people to build a box made of wood and gold and to put the stone tablets that the Ten Commandments were written on inside this box. The name for this special box is the ark of the covenant. (Do you remember when God told Noah to build a special box? Find the story of Noah's ark in Genesis 6–9!) The ark was too holy to be touched, so the priests carried it with poles. The Israelites carried the ark with them the whole time they wandered in the wilderness and also when they went into battle. Later Solomon built the Temple in Jerusalem and put the ark inside it.

[g] Meaning of Heb uncertain [h] Or treaty, or testimony; Heb eduth

17 Then you shall make a mercy seat[i] of pure gold; two cubits and a half shall be its length, and a cubit and a half its width. [18]You shall make two cherubim of gold; you shall make them of hammered work, at the two ends of the mercy seat.[i] [19]Make one cherub at the one end, and one cherub at the other; of one piece with the mercy seat[i] you shall make the cherubim at its two ends. [20]The cherubim shall spread out their wings above, overshadowing the mercy seat[i] with their wings. They shall face one to another; the faces of the cherubim shall be turned toward the mercy seat.[i] [21]You shall put the mercy seat[i] on the top of the ark; and in the ark you shall put the covenant[j] that I shall give you. [22]There I will meet with you, and from above the mercy seat,[i] from between the two cherubim that are on the ark of the covenant,[j] I will deliver to you all my commands for the Israelites.

The Table for the Bread of the Presence

23 You shall make a table of acacia wood, two cubits long, one cubit wide, and a cubit and a half high. [24]You shall overlay it with pure gold, and make a molding of gold around it. [25]You shall make around it a rim a handbreadth wide, and a molding of gold around the rim. [26]You shall make for it four rings of gold, and fasten the rings to the four corners at its four legs. [27]The rings that hold the poles used for carrying the table shall be close to the rim. [28]You shall make the poles of acacia wood, and overlay them with gold, and the table shall be carried with these. [29]You shall make its plates and dishes for incense, and its flagons and bowls with which to pour drink offerings; you shall make them of pure gold. [30]And you shall set the bread of the Presence on the table before me always.

The Lampstand

31 You shall make a lampstand of pure gold. The base and the shaft of the lampstand shall be made of hammered work; its cups, its calyxes, and its petals shall be of one piece with it; [32]and there shall be six branches going out of its sides, three branches of the lampstand out of one side of it and three branches of the lampstand out of the other side of it; [33]three cups shaped like almond blossoms, each with calyx and petals, on one branch, and three cups shaped like almond blossoms, each with calyx and petals, on the other branch—so for the six branches going out of the lampstand. [34]On the lampstand itself there shall be four cups shaped like almond blossoms, each with its calyxes and petals. [35]There shall be a calyx of one piece with it under the first pair of branches, a calyx of one piece with it under the next pair of branches, and a calyx of one piece with it under the last pair of branches—so for the six branches that go out of the lampstand. [36]Their calyxes and their branches shall be of one piece with it, the whole of it one hammered piece of pure gold. [37]You shall make the seven lamps for it; and the lamps shall be set up so as to give light on the space in front of it. [38]Its snuffers and trays shall be of pure gold. [39]It, and all these utensils, shall be made from a talent of pure gold. [40]And see that you make them according to the pattern for them, which is being shown you on the mountain.

The Tabernacle

26 Moreover you shall make the tabernacle with ten curtains of fine twisted linen, and blue, purple, and crimson yarns; you shall make them with cherubim skillfully worked into them. [2]The length of each curtain shall be twenty-eight cubits, and the width of each curtain four cubits; all the curtains shall be of the same size. [3]Five curtains shall be joined to one another; and the

---

[i] Or *a cover*   [j] Or *treaty*, or *testimony*; Heb *eduth*

other five curtains shall be joined to one another. ⁴You shall make loops of blue on the edge of the outermost curtain in the first set; and likewise you shall make loops on the edge of the outermost curtain in the second set. ⁵You shall make fifty loops on the one curtain, and you shall make fifty loops on the edge of the curtain that is in the second set; the loops shall be opposite one another. ⁶You shall make fifty clasps of gold, and join the curtains to one another with the clasps, so that the tabernacle may be one whole.

7 You shall also make curtains of goats' hair for a tent over the tabernacle; you shall make eleven curtains. ⁸The length of each curtain shall be thirty cubits, and the width of each curtain four cubits; the eleven curtains shall be of the same size. ⁹You shall join five curtains by themselves, and six curtains by themselves, and the sixth curtain you shall double over at the front of the tent. ¹⁰You shall make fifty loops on the edge of the curtain that is outermost in one set, and fifty loops on the edge of the curtain that is outermost in the second set.

11 You shall make fifty clasps of bronze, and put the clasps into the loops, and join the tent together, so that it may be one whole. ¹²The part that remains of the curtains of the tent, the half curtain that remains, shall hang over the back of the tabernacle. ¹³The cubit on the one side, and the cubit on the other side, of what remains in the length of the curtains of the tent, shall hang over the sides of the tabernacle, on this side and that side, to cover it. ¹⁴You shall make for the tent a covering of tanned rams' skins and an outer covering of fine leather.ᵏ

The Framework

15 You shall make upright frames of acacia wood for the tabernacle. ¹⁶Ten cubits shall be the length of a frame, and a cubit and a half the width of each frame. ¹⁷There shall be two pegs in each frame to fit the frames together; you shall make these for all the frames of the tab-

ernacle. ¹⁸You shall make the frames for the tabernacle: twenty frames for the south side; ¹⁹and you shall make forty bases of silver under the twenty frames, two bases under the first frame for its two pegs, and two bases under the next frame for its two pegs; ²⁰and for the second side of the tabernacle, on the north side twenty frames, ²¹and their forty bases of silver, two bases under the first frame, and two bases under the next frame; ²²and for the rear of the tabernacle westward you shall make six frames. ²³You shall make two frames for corners of the tabernacle in the rear; ²⁴they shall be separate beneath, but joined at the top, at the first ring; it shall be the same with both of them; they shall form the two corners. ²⁵And so there shall be eight frames, with their bases of silver, sixteen bases; two bases under the first frame, and two bases under the next frame.

26 You shall make bars of acacia wood, five for the frames of the one side of the tabernacle, ²⁷and five bars for the frames of the other side of the tabernacle, and five bars for the frames of the side of the tabernacle at the rear westward. ²⁸The middle bar, halfway up the frames, shall pass through from end to end. ²⁹You shall overlay the frames with gold, and shall make their rings of gold to hold the bars; and you shall overlay the bars with gold. ³⁰Then you shall erect the tabernacle according to the plan for it that you were shown on the mountain.

The Curtain

31 You shall make a curtain of blue, purple, and crimson yarns, and of fine twisted linen; it shall be made with cherubim skillfully worked into it. ³²You shall hang it on four pillars of acacia overlaid with gold, which have hooks of gold and rest on four bases of silver. ³³You shall hang the curtain under the clasps, and bring the ark of the covenantˡ in there, within the curtain; and the

ᵏ Meaning of Heb uncertain   ˡ Or treaty, or testimony; Heb eduth curtain shall separate for you the holy place from the most holy. [34]You shall put the mercy seat[m] on the ark of the covenant[n] in the most holy place. [35]You shall set the table outside the curtain, and the lampstand on the south side of the tabernacle opposite the table; and you shall put the table on the north side.

36 You shall make a screen for the entrance of the tent, of blue, purple, and crimson yarns, and of fine twisted linen, embroidered with needlework. [37]You shall make for the screen five pillars of acacia, and overlay them with gold; their hooks shall be of gold, and you shall cast five bases of bronze for them.

The Altar of Burnt Offering

27 You shall make the altar of acacia wood, five cubits long and five cubits wide; the altar shall be square, and it shall be three cubits high. [2]You shall make horns for it on its four corners; its horns shall be of one piece with it, and you shall overlay it with bronze. [3]You shall make pots for it to receive its ashes, and shovels and basins and forks and firepans; you shall make all its utensils of bronze. [4]You shall also make for it a grating, a network of bronze; and on the net you shall make four bronze rings at its four corners. [5]You shall set it under the ledge of the altar so that the net shall extend halfway down the altar. [6]You shall make poles for the altar, poles of acacia wood, and overlay them with bronze; [7]the poles shall be put through the rings, so that the poles shall be on the two sides of the altar when it is carried. [8]You shall make it hollow, with boards. They shall be made just as you were shown on the mountain.

The Court and Its Hangings

9 You shall make the court of the tabernacle. On the south side the court shall have hangings of fine twisted linen one hundred cubits long for that side; [10]its twenty pillars and their twenty bases shall be of bronze, but the hooks of the pillars and their bands shall be of silver. [11]Likewise for its length on the north side there shall be hangings one hundred cubits long, their pillars twenty and their bases twenty, of bronze, but the hooks of the pillars and their bands shall be of silver. [12]For the width of the court on the west side there shall be fifty cubits of hangings, with ten pillars and ten bases. [13]The width of the court on the front to the east shall be fifty cubits. [14]There shall be fifteen cubits of hangings on the one side, with three pillars and three bases. [15]There shall be fifteen cubits of hangings on the other side, with three pillars and three bases. [16]For the gate of the court there shall be a screen twenty cubits long, of blue, purple, and crimson yarns, and of fine twisted linen, embroidered with needlework; it shall have four pillars and with them four bases. [17]All the pillars around the court shall be banded with silver; their hooks shall be of silver, and their bases of bronze. [18]The length of the court shall be one hundred cubits, the width fifty, and the height five cubits, with hangings of fine twisted linen and bases of bronze. [19]All the utensils of the tabernacle for every use, and all its pegs and all the pegs of the court, shall be of bronze.

The Oil for the Lamp

20 You shall further command the Israelites to bring you pure oil of beaten olives for the light, so that a lamp may be set up to burn regularly. [21]In the tent of meeting, outside the curtain that is before the covenant,[n] Aaron and his sons shall tend it from evening to morning before the LORD. It shall be a perpetual ordinance to be observed throughout their generations by the Israelites.

Vestments for the Priesthood

28 Then bring near to you your brother Aaron, and his sons with him, from among the Israelites, to

[m] Or *the cover*   [n] Or *treaty*, or *testimony*; Heb *eduth*

serve me as priests—Aaron and Aaron's sons, Nā´dab and A·bī´hū, El·ē·āzar and Ith´a·mar. ²You shall make sacred vestments for the glorious adornment of your brother Aaron. ³And you shall speak to all who have ability, whom I have endowed with skill, that they make Aaron's vestments to consecrate him for my priesthood. ⁴These are the vestments that they shall make: a breastpiece, an ephod, a robe, a checkered tunic, a turban, and a sash. When they make these sacred vestments for your brother Aaron and his sons to serve me as priests, ⁵they shall use gold, blue, purple, and crimson yarns, and fine linen.

> The high priest wore special clothes when he served in the sanctuary. Part of his outfit was a breastplate, which was like a shield made of gold and fine cloth with twelve jewels, one for each of the twelve tribes of Israel. The breastplate attached to the front of his shirt with golden rings.

The Ephod

6 They shall make the ephod of gold, of blue, purple, and crimson yarns, and of fine twisted linen, skillfully worked. ⁷It shall have two shoulder-pieces attached to its two edges, so that it may be joined together. ⁸The decorated band on it shall be of the same workmanship and materials, of gold, of blue, purple, and crimson yarns, and of fine twisted linen. ⁹You shall take two onyx stones, and engrave on them the names of the sons of Israel, ¹⁰six of their names on the one stone, and the names of the remaining six on the other stone, in the order of their birth. ¹¹As a gem-cutter engraves signets, so you shall engrave the two stones with the names of the sons of Israel; you shall mount them in settings of gold filigree. ¹²You shall set the two stones on the shoulder-pieces of the ephod, as stones of remembrance for the sons of Israel; and Aaron shall bear their names before the LORD on his two shoulders for remembrance. ¹³You shall make settings of gold filigree, ¹⁴and two chains of pure gold, twisted like cords; and you shall attach the corded chains to the settings.

The Breastplate

15 You shall make a breastpiece of judgment, in skilled work; you shall make it in the style of the ephod; of gold, of blue and purple and crimson yarns, and of fine twisted linen you shall make it. ¹⁶It shall be square and doubled, a span in length and a span in width. ¹⁷You shall set in it four rows of stones. A row of carnelian,ᵒ chrysolite, and emerald shall be the first row; ¹⁸and the second row a turquoise, a sapphireᵖ and a moonstone; ¹⁹and the third row a jacinth, an agate, and an amethyst; ²⁰and the fourth row a beryl, an onyx, and a jasper; they shall be set in gold filigree. ²¹There shall be twelve stones with names corresponding to the names of the sons of Israel; they shall be like signets, each engraved with its name, for the twelve tribes. ²²You shall make for the breastpiece chains of pure gold, twisted like cords; ²³and you shall make for the breastpiece two rings of gold, and put the two rings on the two edges of the breastpiece. ²⁴You shall put the two cords of gold in the two rings at the edges of the breastpiece; ²⁵the two ends of the two cords you shall attach to the two settings, and so attach it in front to the shoulder-pieces of the ephod. ²⁶You shall make two rings of gold, and put them at the two ends of the breastpiece, on its inside edge next to the ephod. ²⁷You shall make two rings of gold, and attach them in front to the lower part of the two shoulder-pieces of the ephod, at

ᵒ The identity of several of these stones is uncertain   ᵖ Or *lapis lazuli* its joining above the decorated band of the ephod. ²⁸The breastpiece shall be bound by its rings to the rings of the ephod with a blue cord, so that it may lie on the decorated band of the ephod, and so that the breastpiece shall not come loose from the ephod. ²⁹So Aaron shall bear the names of the sons of Israel in the breastpiece of judgment on his heart when he goes into the holy place, for a continual remembrance before the LORD. ³⁰In the breastpiece of judgment you shall put the Ūrim and the Thum′mim, and they shall be on Aaron's heart when he goes in before the LORD; thus Aaron shall bear the judgment of the Israelites on his heart before the LORD continually.

Other Priestly Vestments

31 You shall make the robe of the ephod all of blue. ³²It shall have an opening for the head in the middle of it, with a woven binding around the opening, like the opening in a coat of mail,^q so that it may not be torn. ³³On its lower hem you shall make pomegranates of blue, purple, and crimson yarns, all around the lower hem, with bells of gold between them all around— ³⁴a golden bell and a pomegranate alternating all around the lower hem of the robe. ³⁵Aaron shall wear it when he ministers, and its sound shall be heard when he goes into the holy place before the LORD, and when he comes out, so that he may not die.

36 You shall make a rosette of pure gold, and engrave on it, like the engraving of a signet, "Holy to the LORD." ³⁷You shall fasten it on the turban with a blue cord; it shall be on the front of the turban. ³⁸It shall be on Aaron's forehead, and Aaron shall take on himself any guilt incurred in the holy offering that the Israelites consecrate as their sacred donations; it shall always be on his forehead, in order that they may find favor before the LORD.

39 You shall make the checkered tunic of fine linen, and you shall make a turban of fine linen, and you shall make a sash embroidered with needlework.

40 For Aaron's sons you shall make tunics and sashes and headdresses; you shall make them for their glorious adornment. ⁴¹You shall put them on your brother Aaron, and on his sons with him, and shall anoint them and ordain them and consecrate them, so that they may serve me as priests. ⁴²You shall make for them linen undergarments to cover their naked flesh; they shall reach from the hips to the thighs; ⁴³Aaron and his sons shall wear them when they go into the tent of meeting, or when they come near the altar to minister in the holy place; or they will bring guilt on themselves and die. This shall be a perpetual ordinance for him and for his descendants after him.

The Ordination of the Priests

29 Now this is what you shall do to them to consecrate them, so that they may serve me as priests. Take one young bull and two rams without blemish, ²and unleavened bread, unleavened cakes mixed with oil, and unleavened wafers spread with oil. You shall make them of choice wheat flour. ³You shall put them in one basket and bring them in the basket, and bring the bull and the two rams. ⁴You shall bring Aaron and his sons to the entrance of the tent of meeting, and wash them with water. ⁵Then you shall take the vestments, and put on Aaron the tunic and the robe of the ephod, and the ephod, and the breastpiece, and gird him with the decorated band of the ephod; ⁶and you shall set the turban on his head, and put the holy diadem on the turban. ⁷You shall take the anointing oil, and pour it on his head and anoint him. ⁸Then you shall bring his sons, and put tunics on them, ⁹and you shall gird them with sashes^r and tie headdresses on them; and the priesthood shall be theirs by a

^q Meaning of Heb uncertain   ^r Gk: Heb sashes, Aaron and his sons

perpetual ordinance. You shall then ordain Aaron and his sons.

10 You shall bring the bull in front of the tent of meeting. Aaron and his sons shall lay their hands on the head of the bull, [11]and you shall slaughter the bull before the LORD, at the entrance of the tent of meeting, [12]and shall take some of the blood of the bull and put it on the horns of the altar with your finger, and all the rest of the blood you shall pour out at the base of the altar. [13]You shall take all the fat that covers the entrails, and the appendage of the liver, and the two kidneys with the fat that is on them, and turn them into smoke on the altar. [14]But the flesh of the bull, and its skin, and its dung, you shall burn with fire outside the camp; it is a sin offering.

15 Then you shall take one of the rams, and Aaron and his sons shall lay their hands on the head of the ram, [16]and you shall slaughter the ram, and shall take its blood and dash it against all sides of the altar. [17]Then you shall cut the ram into its parts, and wash its entrails and its legs, and put them with its parts and its head, [18]and turn the whole ram into smoke on the altar; it is a burnt offering to the LORD; it is a pleasing odor, an offering by fire to the LORD.

19 You shall take the other ram; and Aaron and his sons shall lay their hands on the head of the ram, [20]and you shall slaughter the ram, and take some of its blood and put it on the lobe of Aaron's right ear and on the lobes of the right ears of his sons, and on the thumbs of their right hands, and on the big toes of their right feet, and dash the rest of the blood against all sides of the altar. [21]Then you shall take some of the blood that is on the altar, and some of the anointing oil, and sprinkle it on Aaron and his vestments and on his sons and his sons' vestments with him; then he and his vestments shall be holy, as well as his sons and his sons' vestments.

22 You shall also take the fat of the ram, the fat tail, the fat that covers the entrails, the appendage of the liver, the two kidneys with the fat that is on them, and the right thigh (for it is a ram of ordination), [23]and one loaf of bread, one cake of bread made with oil, and one wafer, out of the basket of unleavened bread that is before the LORD; [24]and you shall place all these on the palms of Aaron and on the palms of his sons, and raise them as an elevation offering before the LORD. [25]Then you shall take them from their hands, and turn them into smoke on the altar on top of the burnt offering of pleasing odor before the LORD; it is an offering by fire to the LORD.

26 You shall take the breast of the ram of Aaron's ordination and raise it as an elevation offering before the LORD; and it shall be your portion. [27]You shall consecrate the breast that was raised as an elevation offering and the thigh that was raised as an elevation offering from the ram of ordination, from that which belonged to Aaron and his sons. [28]These things shall be a perpetual ordinance for Aaron and his sons from the Israelites, for this is an offering; and it shall be an offering by the Israelites from their sacrifice of offerings of well-being, their offering to the LORD.

29 The sacred vestments of Aaron shall be passed on to his sons after him; they shall be anointed in them and ordained in them. [30]The son who is priest in his place shall wear them seven days, when he comes into the tent of meeting to minister in the holy place.

31 You shall take the ram of ordination, and boil its flesh in a holy place; [32]and Aaron and his sons shall eat the flesh of the ram and the bread that is in the basket, at the entrance of the tent of meeting. [33]They themselves shall eat the food by which atonement is made, to ordain and consecrate them, but no one else shall eat of them, because they are holy. [34]If any of the flesh for the ordination, or of the bread, remains until the morning, then you shall burn the

remainder with fire; it shall not be eaten, because it is holy.

35 Thus you shall do to Aaron and to his sons, just as I have commanded you; through seven days you shall ordain them. [36]Also every day you shall offer a bull as a sin offering for atonement. Also you shall offer a sin offering for the altar, when you make atonement for it, and shall anoint it, to consecrate it. [37]Seven days you shall make atonement for the altar, and consecrate it, and the altar shall be most holy; whatever touches the altar shall become holy.

The Daily Offerings

38 Now this is what you shall offer on the altar: two lambs a year old regularly each day. [39]One lamb you shall offer in the morning, and the other lamb you shall offer in the evening; [40]and with the first lamb one-tenth of a measure of choice flour mixed with one-fourth of a hin of beaten oil, and one-fourth of a hin of wine for a drink offering. [41]And the other lamb you shall offer in the evening, and shall offer with it a grain offering and its drink offering, as in the morning, for a pleasing odor, an offering by fire to the LORD. [42]It shall be a regular burnt offering throughout your generations at the entrance of the tent of meeting before the LORD, where I will meet with you, to speak to you there. [43]I will meet with the Israelites there, and it shall be sanctified by my glory; [44]I will consecrate the tent of meeting and the altar; Aaron also and his sons I will consecrate, to serve me as priests. [45]I will dwell among the Israelites, and I will be their God. [46]And they shall know that I am the LORD their God, who brought them out of the land of Egypt that I might dwell among them; I am the LORD their God.

The Altar of Incense

30 You shall make an altar on which to offer incense; you shall make it of acacia wood. [2]It shall be one cubit long, and one cubit wide; it shall be square, and shall be two cubits high; its horns shall be of one piece with it. [3]You shall overlay it with pure gold, its top, and its sides all around and its horns; and you shall make for it a molding of gold all around. [4]And you shall make two golden rings for it; under its molding on two opposite sides of it you shall make them, and they shall hold the poles with which to carry it. [5]You shall make the poles of acacia wood, and overlay them with gold. [6]You shall place it in front of the curtain that is above the ark of the covenant,[s] in front of the mercy seat[t] that is over the covenant,[s] where I will meet with you. [7]Aaron shall offer fragrant incense on it; every morning when he dresses the lamps he shall offer it, [8]and when Aaron sets up the lamps in the evening, he shall offer it, a regular incense offering before the LORD throughout your generations. [9]You shall not offer unholy incense on it, or a burnt offering, or a grain offering; and you shall not pour a drink offering on it. [10]Once a year Aaron shall perform the rite of atonement on its horns. Throughout your generations he shall perform the atonement for it once a year with the blood of the atoning sin offering. It is most holy to the LORD.

The priests burned incense in the Tabernacle and later in the Temple. Incense, which is made from herbs and minerals, burns slowly like a candle and makes a sweet-smelling smoke. As the smell of the burning incense floated up toward the sky, the people understood that God was hearing their prayers.

[s] Or *treaty*, or *testimony*; Heb *eduth*   [t] Or *the cover*

The Half Shekel for the Sanctuary

11 The LORD spoke to Moses: [12]When you take a census of the Israelites to register them, at registration all of them shall give a ransom for their lives to the LORD, so that no plague may come upon them for being registered. [13]This is what each one who is registered shall give: half a shekel according to the shekel of the sanctuary (the shekel is twenty gerahs), half a shekel as an offering to the LORD. [14]Each one who is registered, from twenty years old and upward, shall give the LORD's offering. [15]The rich shall not give more, and the poor shall not give less, than the half shekel, when you bring this offering to the LORD to make atonement for your lives. [16]You shall take the atonement money from the Israelites and shall designate it for the service of the tent of meeting; before the LORD it will be a reminder to the Israelites of the ransom given for your lives.

The Bronze Basin

17 The LORD spoke to Moses: [18]You shall make a bronze basin with a bronze stand for washing. You shall put it between the tent of meeting and the altar, and you shall put water in it; [19]with the water[u] Aaron and his sons shall wash their hands and their feet. [20]When they go into the tent of meeting, or when they come near the altar to minister, to make an offering by fire to the LORD, they shall wash with water, so that they may not die. [21]They shall wash their hands and their feet, so that they may not die: it shall be a perpetual ordinance for them, for him and for his descendants throughout their generations.

The Anointing Oil and Incense

22 The LORD spoke to Moses: [23]Take the finest spices: of liquid myrrh five hundred shekels, and of sweet-smelling cinnamon half as much, that is, two hundred fifty, and two hundred fifty of aromatic cane, [24]and five hundred of cassia—measured by the sanctuary shekel—and a hin of olive oil; [25]and you shall make of these a sacred anointing oil blended as by the perfumer; it shall be a holy anointing oil. [26]With it you shall anoint the tent of meeting and the ark of the covenant,[v] [27]and the table and all its utensils, and the lampstand and its utensils, and the altar of incense, [28]and the altar of burnt offering with all its utensils, and the basin with its stand; [29]you shall consecrate them, so that they may be most holy; whatever touches them will become holy. [30]You shall anoint Aaron and his sons, and consecrate them, in order that they may serve me as priests. [31]You shall say to the Israelites, "This shall be my holy anointing oil throughout your generations. [32]It shall not be used in any ordinary anointing of the body, and you shall make no other like it in composition; it is holy, and it shall be holy to you. [33]Whoever compounds any like it or whoever puts any of it on an unqualified person shall be cut off from the people."

34 The LORD said to Moses: Take sweet spices, stacte, and onycha, and galbanum, sweet spices with pure frankincense (an equal part of each), [35]and make an incense blended as by the perfumer, seasoned with salt, pure and holy; [36]and you shall beat some of it into powder, and put part of it before the covenant[v] in the tent of meeting where I shall meet with you; it shall be for you most holy. [37]When you make incense according to this composition, you shall not make it for yourselves; it shall be regarded by you as holy to the LORD. [38]Whoever makes any like it to use as perfume shall be cut off from the people.

Bezalel and Oholiab

31 The LORD spoke to Moses: [2]See, I have called by name Bez·a·lel son of Ū·rī son of Hur, of the tribe of

[u] Heb it   [v] Or treaty, or testimony; Heb eduth

Judah: [3]and I have filled him with divine spirit,[w] with ability, intelligence, and knowledge in every kind of craft, [4]to devise artistic designs, to work in gold, silver, and bronze, [5]in cutting stones for setting, and in carving wood, in every kind of craft. [6]Moreover, I have appointed with him Ō·hŏ′li·ab son of A·his′a·mach, of the tribe of Dan; and I have given skill to all the skillful, so that they may make all that I have commanded you: [7]the tent of meeting, and the ark of the covenant,[x] and the mercy seat[y] that is on it, and all the furnishings of the tent, [8]the table and its utensils, and the pure lampstand with all its utensils, and the altar of incense, [9]and the altar of burnt offering with all its utensils, and the basin with its stand, [10]and the finely worked vestments, the holy vestments for the priest Aaron and the vestments of his sons, for their service as priests, [11]and the anointing oil and the fragrant incense for the holy place. They shall do just as I have commanded you.

The Sabbath Law

12 The LORD said to Moses: [13]You yourself are to speak to the Israelites: "You shall keep my sabbaths, for this is a sign between me and you throughout your generations, given in order that you may know that I, the LORD, sanctify you. [14]You shall keep the sabbath, because it is holy for you; everyone who profanes it shall be put to death; whoever does any work on it shall be cut off from among the people. [15]Six days shall work be done, but the seventh day is a sabbath of solemn rest, holy to the LORD; whoever does any work on the sabbath day shall be put to death. [16]Therefore the Israelites shall keep the sabbath, observing the sabbath throughout their generations, as a perpetual covenant. [17]It is a sign forever between me and the people of Israel that in six days the LORD made heaven and earth, and on the seventh day he rested, and was refreshed."

The Two Tablets of the Covenant

18 When God[z] finished speaking with Moses on Mount Sinai, he gave him the two tablets of the covenant,[x] tablets of stone, written with the finger of God.

During Bible times, many people worshiped idols made from clay or gold. God's people began to wish that they had a god they could see. They asked Moses' brother Aaron to melt down their gold and make a "god" for them. Aaron made a golden calf, and the people began to worship it.

The Golden Calf

32 When the people saw that Moses delayed to come down from the mountain, the people gathered around Aaron, and said to him, "Come, make gods for us, who shall go before us; as for this Moses, the man who brought us up out of the land of Egypt, we do not know what has become of him." [2]Aaron said to them, "Take off the gold rings that are on the ears of your wives, your sons, and your daughters, and bring them to me." [3]So all the people took off the gold rings from their ears, and brought them to Aaron. [4]He took the gold from them, formed it in a mold,[a] and cast an image of a calf; and they said, "These are your gods, O Israel, who brought you up out of the land of Egypt!" [5]When Aaron saw this, he built an altar before it; and Aaron made proclamation and said, "Tomorrow shall be a festival to the LORD." [6]They rose early the next day, and offered burnt offerings and brought sacrifices of well-being; and the people sat down to eat and drink, and rose up to revel.

[w] Or *with the spirit of God* [x] Or *treaty*, or *testimony*; Heb *eduth* [y] Or *the cover* [z] Heb *he* [a] Or *fashioned it with a graving tool*; Meaning of Heb uncertain

7 The LORD said to Moses, "Go down at once! Your people, whom you brought up out of the land of Egypt, have acted perversely; [8]they have been quick to turn aside from the way that I commanded them; they have cast for themselves an image of a calf, and have worshiped it and sacrificed to it, and said, 'These are your gods, O Israel, who brought you up out of the land of Egypt!' " [9]The LORD said to Moses, "I have seen this people, how stiff-necked they are. [10]Now let me alone, so that my wrath may burn hot against them and I may consume them; and of you I will make a great nation."

11 But Moses implored the LORD his God, and said, "O LORD, why does your wrath burn hot against your people, whom you brought out of the land of Egypt with great power and with a mighty hand? [12]Why should the Egyptians say, 'It was with evil intent that he brought them out to kill them in the mountains, and to consume them from the face of the earth'? Turn from your fierce wrath; change your mind and do not bring disaster on your people. [13]Remember Abraham, Isaac, and Israel, your servants, how you swore to them by your own self, saying to them, 'I will multiply your descendants like the stars of heaven, and all this land that I have promised I will give to your descendants, and they shall inherit it forever.' " [14]And the LORD changed his mind about the disaster that he planned to bring on his people.

15 Then Moses turned and went down from the mountain, carrying the two tablets of the covenant[b] in his hands, tablets that were written on both sides, written on the front and on the back. [16]The tablets were the work of God, and the writing was the writing of God, engraved upon the tablets. [17]When Joshua heard the noise of the people as they shouted, he said to Moses, "There is a noise of war in the camp." [18]But he said,

"It is not the sound made by victors,
    or the sound made by losers;
it is the sound of revelers that I hear."
[19]As soon as he came near the camp and saw the calf and the dancing, Moses' anger burned hot, and he threw the tablets from his hands and broke them at the foot of the mountain. [20]He took the calf that they had made, burned it with fire, ground it to powder, scattered it on the water, and made the Israelites drink it.

21 Moses said to Aaron, "What did this people do to you that you have brought so great a sin upon them?" [22]And Aaron said, "Do not let the anger of my lord burn hot; you know the people, that they are bent on evil. [23]They said to me, 'Make us gods, who shall go before us; as for this Moses, the man who brought us up out of the land of Egypt, we do not know what has become of him.' [24]So I said to them, 'Whoever has gold, take it off'; so they gave it to me, and I threw it into the fire, and out came this calf!"

25 When Moses saw that the people were running wild (for Aaron had let them run wild, to the derision of their enemies), [26]then Moses stood in the gate of the camp, and said, "Who is on the LORD's side? Come to me!" And all the sons of Levi gathered around him. [27]He said to them, "Thus says the LORD, the God of Israel, 'Put your sword on your side, each of you! Go back and forth from gate to gate throughout the camp, and each of you kill your brother, your friend, and your neighbor.' " [28]The sons of Levi did as Moses commanded, and about three thousand of the people fell on that day. [29]Moses said, "Today you have ordained yourselves[c] for the service of the LORD, each one at the cost of a son or a brother, and so have brought a blessing on yourselves this day."

30 On the next day Moses said to the people, "You have sinned a great sin. But

---

[b] Or *treaty*, or *testimony*; Heb *eduth*   [c] Gk Vg Compare Tg: Heb *Today ordain yourselves*

now I will go up to the LORD; perhaps I can make atonement for your sin." ³¹So Moses returned to the LORD and said, "Alas, this people has sinned a great sin; they have made for themselves gods of gold. ³²But now, if you will only forgive their sin—but if not, blot me out of the book that you have written." ³³But the LORD said to Moses, "Whoever has sinned against me I will blot out of my book. ³⁴But now go, lead the people to the place about which I have spoken to you; see, my angel shall go in front of you. Nevertheless, when the day comes for punishment, I will punish them for their sin."

35 Then the LORD sent a plague on the people, because they made the calf—the one that Aaron made.

The Command to Leave Sinai

33 The LORD said to Moses, "Go, leave this place, you and the people whom you have brought up out of the land of Egypt, and go to the land of which I swore to Abraham, Isaac, and Jacob, saying, 'To your descendants I will give it.' ²I will send an angel before you, and I will drive out the Cā́naan·ītes, the Am´o·rītes, the Hit´tītes, the Per´iz·zītes, the Hī´vītes, and the Jeb´ū·sītes. ³Go up to a land flowing with milk and honey; but I will not go up among you, or I would consume you on the way, for you are a stiff-necked people."

4 When the people heard these harsh words, they mourned, and no one put on ornaments. ⁵For the LORD had said to Moses, "Say to the Israelites, 'You are a stiff-necked people; if for a single moment I should go up among you, I would consume you. So now take off your ornaments, and I will decide what to do to you.'" ⁶Therefore the Israelites stripped themselves of their ornaments, from Mount Hṓreb onward.

The Tent outside the Camp

7 Now Moses used to take the tent and pitch it outside the camp, far off from the camp; he called it the tent of meeting. And everyone who sought the LORD would go out to the tent of meeting, which was outside the camp. ⁸Whenever Moses went out to the tent, all the people would rise and stand, each of them, at the entrance of their tents and watch Moses until he had gone into the tent. ⁹When Moses entered the tent, the pillar of cloud would descend and stand at the entrance of the tent, and the LORD would speak with Moses. ¹⁰When all the people saw the pillar of cloud standing at the entrance of the tent, all the people would rise and bow down, all of them, at the entrance of their tent. ¹¹Thus the LORD used to speak to Moses face to face, as one speaks to a friend. Then he would return to the camp; but his young assistant, Joshua son of Nun, would not leave the tent.

Moses' Intercession

12 Moses said to the LORD, "See, you have said to me, 'Bring up this people'; but you have not let me know whom you will send with me. Yet you have said, 'I know you by name, and you have also found favor in my sight.' ¹³Now if I have found favor in your sight, show me your ways, so that I may know you and find favor in your sight. Consider too that this nation is your people." ¹⁴He said, "My presence will go with you, and I will give you rest." ¹⁵And he said to him, "If your presence will not go, do not carry us up from here. ¹⁶For how shall it be known that I have found favor in your sight, I and your people, unless you go with us? In this way, we shall be distinct, I and your people, from every people on the face of the earth."

17 The LORD said to Moses, "I will do the very thing that you have asked; for you have found favor in my sight, and I know you by name." ¹⁸Moses said, "Show me your glory, I pray." ¹⁹And he said, "I will make all my

goodness pass before you, and will proclaim before you the name, 'The LORD';[d] and I will be gracious to whom I will be gracious, and will show mercy on whom I will show mercy. [20]But," he said, "you cannot see my face; for no one shall see me and live." [21]And the LORD continued, "See, there is a place by me where you shall stand on the rock; [22]and while my glory passes by I will put you in a cleft of the rock, and I will cover you with my hand until I have passed by; [23]then I will take away my hand, and you shall see my back; but my face shall not be seen."

Moses Makes New Tablets

34 The LORD said to Moses, "Cut two tablets of stone like the former ones, and I will write on the tablets the words that were on the former tablets, which you broke. [2]Be ready in the morning, and come up in the morning to Mount Sinai and present yourself there to me, on the top of the mountain. [3]No one shall come up with you, and do not let anyone be seen throughout all the mountain; and do not let flocks or herds graze in front of that mountain." [4]So Moses cut two tablets of stone like the former ones; and he rose early in the morning and went up on Mount Sinai, as the LORD had commanded him, and took in his hand the two tablets of stone. [5]The LORD descended in the cloud and stood with him there, and proclaimed the name, "The LORD."[d] [6]The LORD passed before him, and proclaimed,

"The LORD, the LORD,
a God merciful and gracious,
slow to anger,
and abounding in steadfast love and
faithfulness,
[7] keeping steadfast love for the
thousandth generation,[e]
forgiving iniquity and transgression
and sin,
yet by no means clearing the guilty,

but visiting the iniquity of the parents
upon the children
and the children's children,
to the third and the fourth generation."
[8]And Moses quickly bowed his head toward the earth, and worshiped. [9]He said, "If now I have found favor in your sight, O Lord, I pray, let the Lord go with us. Although this is a stiff-necked people, pardon our iniquity and our sin, and take us for your inheritance."

The Covenant Renewed

10 He said: I hereby make a covenant. Before all your people I will perform marvels, such as have not been performed in all the earth or in any nation; and all the people among whom you live shall see the work of the LORD; for it is an awesome thing that I will do with you.

11 Observe what I command you today. See, I will drive out before you the Am′o·rites, the Cā′naan·ites, the Hit′tites, the Per′iz·zites, the Hī′vites, and the Jeb′u·sites. [12]Take care not to make a covenant with the inhabitants of the land to which you are going, or it will become a snare among you. [13]You shall tear down their altars, break their pillars, and cut down their sacred poles[f] [14](for you shall worship no other god, because the LORD, whose name is Jealous, is a jealous God). [15]You shall not make a covenant with the inhabitants of the

When Moses came down from the mountain with the Ten Commandments that God had written on two stone tablets, he found the people worshiping an idol. Moses became so angry that he threw the tablets on the ground and broke them. He had to return to the mountain to get new tablets from God.

[d] Heb *YHWH*; see note at 3.15   [e] Or *for thousands*   [f] Heb *Asherim*

land, for when they prostitute themselves to their gods and sacrifice to their gods, someone among them will invite you, and you will eat of the sacrifice. [16]And you will take wives from among their daughters for your sons, and their daughters who prostitute themselves to their gods will make your sons also prostitute themselves to their gods.

17 You shall not make cast idols.

18 You shall keep the festival of unleavened bread. Seven days you shall eat unleavened bread, as I commanded you, at the time appointed in the month of A´bib; for in the month of A´bib you came out from Egypt.

19 All that first opens the womb is mine, all your male[g] livestock, the firstborn of cow and sheep. [20]The firstborn of a donkey you shall redeem with a lamb, or if you will not redeem it you shall break its neck. All the firstborn of your sons you shall redeem.

No one shall appear before me emptyhanded.

21 Six days you shall work, but on the seventh day you shall rest; even in plowing time and in harvest time you shall rest. [22]You shall observe the festival of weeks, the first fruits of wheat harvest, and the festival of ingathering at the turn of the year. [23]Three times in the year all your males shall appear before the LORD God, the God of Israel. [24]For I will cast out nations before you, and enlarge your borders; no one shall covet your land when you go up to appear before the LORD your God three times in the year.

25 You shall not offer the blood of my sacrifice with leaven, and the sacrifice of the festival of the passover shall not be left until the morning.

26 The best of the first fruits of your ground you shall bring to the house of the LORD your God.

You shall not boil a kid in its mother's milk.

27 The LORD said to Moses: Write these words; in accordance with these words I have made a covenant with you and with Israel. [28]He was there with the LORD forty days and forty nights; he neither ate bread nor drank water. And he wrote on the tablets the words of the covenant, the ten commandments.[h]

The Shining Face of Moses

29 Moses came down from Mount Sinai. As he came down from the mountain with the two tablets of the covenant[i] in his hand, Moses did not know that the skin of his face shone because he had been talking with God. [30]When Aaron and all the Israelites saw Moses, the skin of his face was shining, and they were afraid to come near him. [31]But Moses called to them; and Aaron and all the leaders of the congregation returned to him, and Moses spoke with them. [32]Afterward all the Israelites came near, and he gave them in commandment all that the LORD had spoken with him on Mount Sinai. [33]When Moses had finished speaking with them, he put a veil on his face; [34]but whenever Moses went in before the LORD to speak with him, he would take the veil off, until he came out; and when he came out, and told the Israelites what he had been commanded, [35]the Israelites would see the face of Moses, that the skin of his face was shining; and Moses would put the veil on his face again, until he went in to speak with him.

Sabbath Regulations

35 Moses assembled all the congregation of the Israelites and said to them: These are the things that the LORD has commanded you to do:

2 Six days shall work be done, but on the seventh day you shall have a holy sabbath of solemn rest to the LORD; whoever does any work on it shall be put to death. [3]You shall kindle no fire in all your dwellings on the sabbath day.

[g] Gk Theodotion Vg Tg: Meaning of Heb uncertain [h] Heb words [i] Or treaty, or testimony; Heb eduth

Preparations for Making the Tabernacle

4 Moses said to all the congregation of the Israelites: This is the thing that the LORD has commanded: [5]Take from among you an offering to the LORD; let whoever is of a generous heart bring the LORD's offering: gold, silver, and bronze; [6]blue, purple, and crimson yarns, and fine linen; goats' hair, [7]tanned rams' skins, and fine leather;[j] acacia wood, [8]oil for the light, spices for the anointing oil and for the fragrant incense, [9]and onyx stones and gems to be set in the ephod and the breastpiece.

"Let the people bring offerings," God told Moses. And that is what they did! The people brought gifts of gold, silver, and bronze. They brought yarn, leather, and fine cloth. They brought wood, stones, spices, and oils. The people provided everything that was needed to build the Tabernacle. They were glad to be able to build a sanctuary where they could worship God together.

10 All who are skillful among you shall come and make all that the LORD has commanded: the tabernacle, [11]its tent and its covering, its clasps and its frames, its bars, its pillars, and its bases; [12]the ark with its poles, the mercy seat,[k] and the curtain for the screen; [13]the table with its poles and all its utensils, and the bread of the Presence; [14]the lampstand also for the light, with its utensils and its lamps, and the oil for the light; [15]and the altar of incense, with its poles, and the anointing oil and the fragrant incense, and the screen for the entrance, the entrance of the tabernacle; [16]the altar of burnt offering, with its grating of bronze, its poles, and all its utensils, the basin with its stand; [17]the hangings of the court, its pillars and its bases, and the screen for the gate of the court; [18]the pegs of the tabernacle and the pegs of the court, and their cords; [19]the finely worked vestments for ministering in the holy place, the holy vestments for the priest Aaron, and the vestments of his sons, for their service as priests.

Offerings for the Tabernacle

20 Then all the congregation of the Israelites withdrew from the presence of Moses. [21]And they came, everyone whose heart was stirred, and everyone whose spirit was willing, and brought the LORD's offering to be used for the tent of meeting, and for all its service, and for the sacred vestments. [22]So they came, both men and women; all who were of a willing heart brought brooches and earrings and signet rings and pendants, all sorts of gold objects, everyone bringing an offering of gold to the LORD. [23]And everyone who possessed blue or purple or crimson yarn or fine linen or goats' hair or tanned rams' skins or fine leather,[j] brought them. [24]Everyone who could make an offering of silver or bronze brought it as the LORD's offering; and everyone who possessed acacia wood of any use in the work, brought it. [25]All the skillful women spun with their hands, and brought what they had spun in blue and purple and crimson yarns and fine linen; [26]all the women whose hearts moved them to use their skill spun the goats' hair. [27]And the leaders brought onyx stones and gems to be set in the ephod and the breastpiece, [28]and spices and oil for the light, and for the anointing oil, and for the fragrant incense. [29]All the Israelite men and women whose hearts made them willing to bring anything for the work that the LORD had commanded by Moses to be done, brought it as a freewill offering to the LORD.

Bezalel and Oholiab

30 Then Moses said to the Israelites: See, the LORD has called by name

[j] Meaning of Heb uncertain   [k] Or *the cover*

A talented man named Bezalel was in charge of making the Tabernacle and all the things that went in it—the Ark of the Covenant, altars, tables, and other things. He used gold, silver, bronze, stone, and wood to design the worship space.

Bez´a·lel son of Ū´rī son of Hur, of the tribe of Judah; ³¹he has filled him with divine spirit,ᶦ with skill, intelligence, and knowledge in every kind of craft, ³²to devise artistic designs, to work in gold, silver, and bronze, ³³in cutting stones for setting, and in carving wood, in every kind of craft. ³⁴And he has inspired him to teach, both him and Ō·hō´li·ab son of A·hisʹa·mach, of the tribe of Dan. ³⁵He has filled them with skill to do every kind of work done by an artisan or by a designer or by an embroiderer in blue, purple, and crimson yarns, and in fine linen, or by a weaver—by any sort of artisan or skilled designer.

36 Bez´a·lel and Ō·hō´li·ab and every skillful one to whom the LORD has given skill and understanding to know how to do any work in the construction of the sanctuary shall work in accordance with all that the LORD has commanded.

2 Moses then called Bez´a·lel and Ō·hō´li·ab and every skillful one to whom the LORD had given skill, everyone whose heart was stirred to come to do the work; ³and they received from Moses all the freewill offerings that the Israelites had brought for doing the work on the sanctuary. They still kept bringing him freewill offerings every morning, ⁴so that all the artisans who were doing every sort of task on the sanctuary came, each from the task being performed, ⁵and said to Moses, "The people are bringing much more than enough for doing the work that the LORD has commanded us to do." ⁶So

Moses gave command, and word was proclaimed throughout the camp: "No man or woman is to make anything else as an offering for the sanctuary." So the people were restrained from bringing; ⁷for what they had already brought was more than enough to do all the work.

Construction of the Tabernacle

8 All those with skill among the workers made the tabernacle with ten curtains; they were made of fine twisted linen, and blue, purple, and crimson yarns, with cherubim skillfully worked into them. ⁹The length of each curtain was twenty-eight cubits, and the width of each curtain four cubits; all the curtains were of the same size.

10 He joined five curtains to one another, and the other five curtains he joined to one another. ¹¹He made loops of blue on the edge of the outermost curtain of the first set; likewise he made them on the edge of the outermost curtain of the second set; ¹²he made fifty loops on the one curtain, and he made fifty loops on the edge of the curtain that was in the second set; the loops were opposite one another. ¹³And he made fifty clasps of gold, and joined the curtains one to the other with clasps; so the tabernacle was one whole.

14 He also made curtains of goats' hair for a tent over the tabernacle; he made eleven curtains. ¹⁵The length of each curtain was thirty cubits, and the width of each curtain four cubits; the eleven curtains were of the same size. ¹⁶He joined five curtains by themselves, and six curtains by themselves. ¹⁷He made fifty loops on the edge of the outermost curtain of the one set, and fifty loops on the edge of the other connecting curtain. ¹⁸He made fifty clasps of bronze to join the tent together so that it might be one whole. ¹⁹And he made for the tent a covering of tanned rams' skins and an outer covering of fine leather.ᵐ

ᶦ Or *the spirit of God*   ᵐ Meaning of Heb uncertain

20 Then he made the upright frames for the tabernacle of acacia wood. ²¹Ten cubits was the length of a frame, and a cubit and a half the width of each frame. ²²Each frame had two pegs for fitting together; he did this for all the frames of the tabernacle. ²³The frames for the tabernacle he made in this way: twenty frames for the south side; ²⁴and he made forty bases of silver under the twenty frames, two bases under the first frame for its two pegs, and two bases under the next frame for its two pegs. ²⁵For the second side of the tabernacle, on the north side, he made twenty frames ²⁶and their forty bases of silver, two bases under the first frame and two bases under the next frame. ²⁷For the rear of the tabernacle westward he made six frames. ²⁸He made two frames for corners of the tabernacle in the rear. ²⁹They were separate beneath, but joined at the top, at the first ring; he made two of them in this way, for the two corners. ³⁰There were eight frames with their bases of silver: sixteen bases, under every frame two bases.

31 He made bars of acacia wood, five for the frames of the one side of the tabernacle, ³²and five bars for the frames of the other side of the tabernacle, and five bars for the frames of the tabernacle at the rear westward. ³³He made the middle bar to pass through from end to end halfway up the frames. ³⁴And he overlaid the frames with gold, and made rings of gold for them to hold the bars, and overlaid the bars with gold.

The Ark of the Covenant was built from the wood of an acacia tree. Acacia trees have soft green leaves and sweet-smelling yellow flowers. The wood is orange-brown. These trees are still found in deserts today.

35 He made the curtain of blue, purple, and crimson yarns, and fine twisted linen, with cherubim skillfully worked into it. ³⁶For it he made four pillars of acacia, and overlaid them with gold; their hooks were of gold, and he cast for them four bases of silver. ³⁷He also made a screen for the entrance to the tent, of blue, purple, and crimson yarns, and fine twisted linen, embroidered with needlework; ³⁸and its five pillars with their hooks. He overlaid their capitals and their bases with gold, but their five bases were of bronze.

Making the Ark of the Covenant

37 Bez´a·lel made the ark of acacia wood; it was two and a half cubits long, a cubit and a half wide, and a cubit and a half high. ²He overlaid it with pure gold inside and outside, and made a molding of gold around it. ³He cast for it four rings of gold for its four feet, two rings on its one side and two rings on its other side. ⁴He made poles of acacia wood, and overlaid them with gold, ⁵and put the poles into the rings on the sides of the ark, to carry the ark. ⁶He made a mercy seat[n] of pure gold; two cubits and a half was its length, and a cubit and a half its width. ⁷He made two cherubim of hammered gold; at the two ends of the mercy seat[o] he made them, ⁸one cherub at the one end, and one cherub at the other end; of one piece with the mercy seat[o] he made the cherubim at its two ends. ⁹The cherubim spread out their wings above, overshadowing the mercy seat[o] with their wings. They faced one another; the faces of the cherubim were turned toward the mercy seat.[o]

Making the Table for the Bread of the Presence

10 He also made the table of acacia wood, two cubits long, one cubit wide, and a cubit and a half high. ¹¹He overlaid it with pure gold, and made a molding of gold around it. ¹²He made around it a rim a handbreadth wide, and made a

[n] Or *a cover*   [o] Or *the cover*

In the first room of the Tabernacle was the altar of incense. On the right side of this room was a golden lampstand with seven lamps that were never allowed to go out. On the left side of the room was a table. Once a week, twelve loaves of bread (one for each of the twelve tribes of Israel) were placed on the table.

molding of gold around the rim. ¹³He cast for it four rings of gold, and fastened the rings to the four corners at its four legs. ¹⁴The rings that held the poles used for carrying the table were close to the rim. ¹⁵He made the poles of acacia wood to carry the table, and overlaid them with gold. ¹⁶And he made the vessels of pure gold that were to be on the table, its plates and dishes for incense, and its bowls and flagons with which to pour drink offerings.

Making the Lampstand

17 He also made the lampstand of pure gold. The base and the shaft of the lampstand were made of hammered work; its cups, its calyxes, and its petals were of one piece with it. ¹⁸There were six branches going out of its sides, three branches of the lampstand out of one side of it and three branches of the lampstand out of the other side of it; ¹⁹three cups shaped like almond blossoms, each with calyx and petals, on one branch, and three cups shaped like almond blossoms, each with calyx and petals, on the other branch—so for the six branches going out of the lampstand. ²⁰On the lampstand itself there were four cups shaped like almond blossoms, each with its calyxes and petals. ²¹There was a calyx of one piece with it under the first pair of branches, a calyx of one piece with it under the next pair of branches, and a calyx of one piece with it under the last pair of branches. ²²Their calyxes and their branches were of one piece with it, the whole of it one hammered piece of pure gold. ²³He made its seven lamps and its snuffers and its trays of pure gold. ²⁴He made it and all its utensils of a talent of pure gold.

Making the Altar of Incense

25 He made the altar of incense of acacia wood, one cubit long, and one cubit wide; it was square, and was two cubits high; its horns were of one piece with it. ²⁶He overlaid it with pure gold, its top, and its sides all around, and its horns; and he made for it a molding of gold all around, ²⁷and made two golden rings for it under its molding, on two opposite sides of it, to hold the poles with which to carry it. ²⁸And he made the poles of acacia wood, and overlaid them with gold.

Making the Anointing Oil and the Incense

29 He made the holy anointing oil also, and the pure fragrant incense, blended as by the perfumer.

Making the Altar of Burnt Offering

38 He made the altar of burnt offering also of acacia wood; it was five cubits long, and five cubits wide; it was square, and three cubits high. ²He made horns for it on its four corners; its horns were of one piece with it, and he overlaid it with bronze. ³He made all the utensils of the altar, the pots, the shovels, the basins, the forks, and the firepans: all its utensils he made of bronze. ⁴He made for the altar a grating, a network of bronze, under its ledge, extending halfway down. ⁵He cast four rings on the four corners of the bronze grating to hold the poles; ⁶he made the poles of acacia wood, and overlaid them with bronze. ⁷And he put the poles through the rings on the sides of the altar, to carry it with them; he made it hollow, with boards.

8 He made the basin of bronze with its stand of bronze, from the mirrors of the women who served at the entrance to the tent of meeting.

Making the Court of the Tabernacle

9 He made the court; for the south side the hangings of the court were of fine twisted linen, one hundred cubits long; [10]its twenty pillars and their twenty bases were of bronze, but the hooks of the pillars and their bands were of silver. [11]For the north side there were hangings one hundred cubits long; its twenty pillars and their twenty bases were of bronze, but the hooks of the pillars and their bands were of silver. [12]For the west side there were hangings fifty cubits long, with ten pillars and ten bases; the hooks of the pillars and their bands were of silver. [13]And for the front to the east, fifty cubits. [14]The hangings for one side of the gate were fifteen cubits, with three pillars and three bases. [15]And so for the other side; on each side of the gate of the court were hangings of fifteen cubits, with three pillars and three bases. [16]All the hangings around the court were of fine twisted linen. [17]The bases for the pillars were of bronze, but the hooks of the pillars and their bands were of silver; the overlaying of their capitals was also of silver, and all the pillars of the court were banded with silver. [18]The screen for the entrance to the court was embroidered with needlework in blue, purple, and crimson yarns and fine twisted linen. It was twenty cubits long and, along the width of it, five cubits high, corresponding to the hangings of the court. [19]There were four pillars; their four bases were of bronze, their hooks of silver, and the overlaying of their capitals and their bands of silver. [20]All the pegs for the tabernacle and for the court all around were of bronze.

Materials of the Tabernacle

21 These are the records of the tabernacle, the tabernacle of the covenant[p] which were drawn up at the commandment of Moses, the work of the Lē´vītes being under the direction of Ith´a·mar son of the priest Aaron. [22]Bez´a·lel son of Ū´rī son of Hur, of the tribe of Judah, made all that the Lord commanded Moses; [23]and with him was Ō·hō´li·ab son of A·his´a·mach, of the tribe of Dan, engraver, designer, and embroiderer in blue, purple, and crimson yarns, and in fine linen.

24 All the gold that was used for the work, in all the construction of the sanctuary, the gold from the offering, was twenty-nine talents and seven hundred thirty shekels, measured by the sanctuary shekel. [25]The silver from those of the congregation who were counted was one hundred talents and one thousand seven hundred seventy-five shekels, measured by the sanctuary shekel; [26]a beka a head (that is, half a shekel, measured by the sanctuary shekel), for everyone who was counted in the census, from twenty years old and upward, for six hundred three thousand, five hundred fifty men. [27]The hundred talents of silver were for casting the bases of the sanctuary, and the bases of the curtain; one hundred bases for the hundred talents, a talent for a base. [28]Of the thousand seven hundred

Around the courtyard of the Tabernacle was a large cloth wall that helped keep sand and animals out of the holy place. Inside the entrance to the courtyard was a large altar for burnt offerings. In front of the altar was a bronze bowl of water where the priests would wash their hands and feet before they entered the Tabernacle or offered a sacrifice to God.

[p] Or *treaty*, or *testimony*; Heb *eduth*

seventy-five shekels he made hooks for the pillars, and overlaid their capitals and made bands for them. ²⁹The bronze that was contributed was seventy talents, and two thousand four hundred shekels; ³⁰with it he made the bases for the entrance of the tent of meeting, the bronze altar and the bronze grating for it and all the utensils of the altar, ³¹the bases all around the court, and the bases of the gate of the court, all the pegs of the tabernacle, and all the pegs around the court.

Making the Vestments for the Priesthood

39 Of the blue, purple, and crimson yarns they made finely worked vestments, for ministering in the holy place; they made the sacred vestments for Aaron; as the LORD had commanded Moses.

2 He made the ephod of gold, of blue, purple, and crimson yarns, and of fine twisted linen. ³Gold leaf was hammered out and cut into threads to work into the blue, purple, and crimson yarns and into the fine twisted linen, in skilled design. ⁴They made for the ephod shoulder-pieces, joined to it at its two edges. ⁵The decorated band on it was of the same materials and workmanship, of gold, of blue, purple, and crimson yarns, and of fine twisted linen; as the LORD had commanded Moses.

6 The onyx stones were prepared, enclosed in settings of gold filigree and engraved like the engravings of a signet, according to the names of the sons of Israel. ⁷He set them on the shoulder-pieces of the ephod, to be stones of remembrance for the sons of Israel; as the LORD had commanded Moses.

8 He made the breastpiece, in skilled work, like the work of the ephod, of gold, of blue, purple, and crimson yarns, and of fine twisted linen. ⁹It was square; the breastpiece was made double, a span in length and a span in width when doubled. ¹⁰They set in it four rows of stones.

A row of carnelian,^q chrysolite, and emerald was the first row; ¹¹and the second row, a turquoise, a sapphire,^r and a moonstone; ¹²and the third row, a jacinth, an agate, and an amethyst; ¹³and the fourth row, a beryl, an onyx, and a jasper; they were enclosed in settings of gold filigree. ¹⁴There were twelve stones with names corresponding to the names of the sons of Israel; they were like signets, each engraved with its name, for the twelve tribes. ¹⁵They made on the breastpiece chains of pure gold, twisted like cords; ¹⁶and they made two settings of gold filigree and two gold rings, and put the two rings on the two edges of the breastpiece; ¹⁷and they put the two cords of gold in the two rings at the edges of the breastpiece. ¹⁸Two ends of the two cords they had attached to the two settings of filigree; in this way they attached it in front to the shoulder-pieces of the ephod. ¹⁹Then they made two rings of gold, and put them at the two ends of the breastpiece, on its inside edge next to the ephod. ²⁰They made two rings of gold, and attached them in front to the lower part of the two shoulder-pieces of the ephod, at its joining above the decorated band of the ephod. ²¹They bound the breastpiece by its rings to the rings of the ephod with a blue cord, so that it should lie on the decorated band of the ephod, and that the breastpiece should not come loose from the ephod; as the LORD had commanded Moses.

22 He also made the robe of the ephod woven all of blue yarn; ²³and the opening of the robe in the middle of it was like the opening in a coat of mail,^s with a binding around the opening, so that it might not be torn. ²⁴On the lower hem of the robe they made pomegranates of blue, purple, and crimson yarns, and of fine twisted linen. ²⁵They also made bells of pure gold, and put the

^q The identification of several of these stones is uncertain   ^r Or *lapis lazuli*   ^s Meaning of Heb uncertain

bells between the pomegranates on the lower hem of the robe all around, between the pomegranates; 26a bell and a pomegranate, a bell and a pomegranate all around on the lower hem of the robe for ministering; as the LORD had commanded Moses.

27 They also made the tunics, woven of fine linen, for Aaron and his sons, 28and the turban of fine linen, and the head-dresses of fine linen, and the linen undergarments of fine twisted linen, 29and the sash of fine twisted linen, and of blue, purple, and crimson yarns, embroidered with needlework; as the LORD had commanded Moses.

30 They made the rosette of the holy diadem of pure gold, and wrote on it an inscription, like the engraving of a signet, "Holy to the LORD." 31They tied to it a blue cord, to fasten it on the turban above; as the LORD had commanded Moses.

The Work Completed

32 In this way all the work of the tabernacle of the tent of meeting was finished; the Israelites had done everything just as the LORD had commanded Moses. 33Then they brought the tabernacle to Moses, the tent and all its utensils, its hooks, its frames, its bars, its pillars, and its bases; 34the covering of tanned rams' skins and the covering of fine leather,^{t} and the curtain for the screen; 35the ark of the covenant^u with its poles and the mercy seat;^{v} 36the table with all its utensils, and the bread of the Presence; 37the pure lampstand with its lamps set on it and all its utensils, and the oil for the light; 38the golden altar, the anointing oil and the fragrant incense, and the screen for the entrance of the tent; 39the bronze altar, and its grating of bronze, its poles, and all its utensils; the basin with its stand; 40the hangings of the court, its pillars, and its bases, and the screen for the gate of the court, its cords, and its pegs; and all the utensils for the service of the tabernacle, for the tent of meeting;

41the finely worked vestments for ministering in the holy place, the sacred vestments for the priest Aaron, and the vestments of his sons to serve as priests. 42The Israelites had done all of the work just as the LORD had commanded Moses. 43When Moses saw that they had done all the work just as the LORD had commanded, he blessed them.

The Tabernacle Erected and Its Equipment Installed

40 The LORD spoke to Moses: 2On the first day of the first month you shall set up the tabernacle of the tent of meeting. 3You shall put in it the ark of the covenant,^{u} and you shall screen the ark with the curtain. 4You shall bring in the table, and arrange its setting; and you shall bring in the lampstand, and set up its lamps. 5You shall put the golden altar for incense before the ark of the covenant,^{u} and set up the screen for the entrance of the tabernacle. 6You shall set the altar of burnt offering before the entrance of the tabernacle of the tent of meeting, 7and place the basin between the tent of meeting and the altar, and put water in it. 8You shall set up the court all around, and hang up the screen for the gate of the court. 9Then you shall take the anointing oil, and anoint the tabernacle and all that is in it, and consecrate it and all its furniture, so that it shall become holy. 10You shall also

At the back of the Tabernacle, a curtain hung between the first room and the second room. The second room was a small, special place that held the Ark of the Covenant. The high priest was the only person who could go into this room, and he could only go once a year. This was the most holy place.

^{t} Meaning of Heb uncertain ^{u} Or *treaty*, or *testimony*; Heb *eduth* ^{v} Or *the cover* anoint the altar of burnt offering and all its utensils, and consecrate the altar, so that the altar shall be most holy. [11]You shall also anoint the basin with its stand, and consecrate it. [12]Then you shall bring Aaron and his sons to the entrance of the tent of meeting, and shall wash them with water, [13]and put on Aaron the sacred vestments, and you shall anoint him and consecrate him, so that he may serve me as priest. [14]You shall bring his sons also and put tunics on them, [15]and anoint them, as you anointed their father, that they may serve me as priests: and their anointing shall admit them to a perpetual priesthood throughout all generations to come.

16 Moses did everything just as the LORD had commanded him. [17]In the first month in the second year, on the first day of the month, the tabernacle was set up. [18]Moses set up the tabernacle; he laid its bases, and set up its frames, and put in its poles, and raised up its pillars; [19]and he spread the tent over the tabernacle, and put the covering of the tent over it; as the LORD had commanded Moses. [20]He took the covenant[w] and put it into the ark, and put the poles on the ark, and set the mercy seat[x] above the ark; [21]and he brought the ark into the tabernacle, and set up the curtain for screening, and screened the ark of the covenant;[w] as the LORD had commanded Moses. [22]He put the table in the tent of meeting, on the north side of the tabernacle, outside the curtain, [23]and set the bread in order on it before the LORD; as the LORD had commanded Moses. [24]He put the lampstand in the tent of meeting, opposite the table on the south side of the tabernacle, [25]and set up the lamps before the LORD; as the LORD had

commanded Moses. [26]He put the golden altar in the tent of meeting before the curtain, [27]and offered fragrant incense on it; as the LORD had commanded Moses. [28]He also put in place the screen for the entrance of the tabernacle. [29]He set the altar of burnt offering at the entrance of the tabernacle of the tent of meeting, and offered on it the burnt offering and the grain offering as the LORD had commanded Moses. [30]He set the basin between the tent of meeting and the altar, and put water in it for washing, [31]with which Moses and Aaron and his sons washed their hands and their feet. [32]When they went into the tent of meeting, and when they approached the altar, they washed; as the LORD had commanded Moses. [33]He set up the court around the tabernacle and the altar, and put up the screen at the gate of the court. So Moses finished the work.

The Cloud and the Glory

34 Then the cloud covered the tent of meeting, and the glory of the LORD filled the tabernacle. [35]Moses was not able to enter the tent of meeting because the cloud settled upon it, and the glory of the LORD filled the tabernacle. [36]Whenever the cloud was taken up from the tabernacle, the Israelites would set out on each stage of their journey; [37]but if the cloud was not taken up, then they did not set out until the day that it was taken up. [38]For the cloud of the LORD was on the tabernacle by day, and fire was in the cloud[y] by night, before the eyes of all the house of Israel at each stage of their journey.

[w] Or *treaty*, or *testimony;* Heb *eduth*   [x] Or *the cover*   [y] Heb *it*

Leviticus

The book of Leviticus gets its name from the Levites, who were an order of Israelite priests. Leviticus contains detailed instructions for worship and for other tasks that the priests would perform. It tells how they were to offer certain animals as sacrifices to God. Such a custom seems strange to us today, but in those days it was how the Israelites showed God they were thankful or asked for God's help.

Leviticus shows the Israelites how to live a holy life. This book describes many rules and customs of the day, including rules about how people should act toward one another. When people broke the rules, the book of Leviticus gave laws that told what their punishment was to be. Leviticus is a book of laws that helped to govern the young nation of God's people.

The books we call the Old Testament were the Scriptures that Jesus read and used. He was quoting from Leviticus when he said, "You shall love your neighbor as yourself" (Leviticus 19:18). This rule for living is as good today as when it was first given to the people of God.

Leviticus 8:1-36

God told the people to offer the very best animals from their flocks and herds as sacrifices. What we offer to God today should be our very best too, whether it is our time, our talents, or our resources. What are some ways that you can honor God by giving God your very best?

The Burnt Offering

1 The LORD summoned Moses and spoke to him from the tent of meeting, saying: ²Speak to the people of Israel and say to them: When any of you bring an offering of livestock to the LORD, you shall bring your offering from the herd or from the flock.

3 If the offering is a burnt offering from the herd, you shall offer a male without blemish; you shall bring it to the entrance of the tent of meeting, for acceptance in your behalf before the LORD. ⁴You shall lay your hand on the head of the burnt offering, and it shall be acceptable in your behalf as atonement for you. ⁵The bull shall be slaughtered before the LORD; and Aaron's sons the priests shall offer the blood, dashing the blood against all sides of the altar that is at the entrance of the tent of meeting. ⁶The burnt offering shall be flayed and cut up into its parts. ⁷The sons of the priest Aaron shall put fire on the altar and arrange wood on the fire. ⁸Aaron's sons the priests shall arrange the parts, with the head and the suet, on the wood that is on the fire on the altar; ⁹but its entrails and its legs shall be washed with water. Then the priest shall turn the whole into smoke on the altar as a burnt offering, an offering by fire of pleasing odor to the LORD.

10 If your gift for a burnt offering is from the flock, from the sheep or goats, your offering shall be a male without blemish. ¹¹It shall be slaughtered on the north side of the altar before the LORD, and Aaron's sons the priests shall dash its blood against all sides of the altar. ¹²It shall be cut up into its parts, with its head and its suet, and the priest shall arrange them on the wood that is on the fire on the altar; ¹³but the entrails and the legs shall be washed with water. Then the priest shall offer the whole and turn it into smoke on the altar; it is a burnt offering, an offering by fire of pleasing odor to the LORD.

14 If your offering to the LORD is a burnt offering of birds, you shall choose your offering from turtledoves or pigeons. ¹⁵The priest shall bring it to the altar and wring off its head, and turn it into smoke on the altar; and its blood shall be drained out against the side of the altar. ¹⁶He shall remove its crop with its contents[a] and throw it at the east side of the altar, in the place for ashes. ¹⁷He shall tear it open by its wings without severing it. Then the priest shall turn it into smoke on the altar, on the wood that is on the fire; it is a burnt offering, an offering by fire of pleasing odor to the LORD.

Grain Offerings

2 When anyone presents a grain offering to the LORD, the offering shall be of choice flour; the worshiper shall pour oil on it, and put frankincense

During Bible times, people ate meals together as a sign of friendship. If the food was seasoned with salt, it meant that the friendship was very special. When God told the people to offer salt with their sacrifices of grain, God wanted them to remember that they were joined to God in a special way. The next time you see a salt shaker on the table, you can remember that you too are a special friend of God!

---

[a] Meaning of Heb uncertain

on it, ²and bring it to Aaron's sons the priests. After taking from it a handful of the choice flour and oil, with all its frankincense, the priest shall turn this token portion into smoke on the altar, an offering by fire of pleasing odor to the LORD. ³And what is left of the grain offering shall be for Aaron and his sons, a most holy part of the offerings by fire to the LORD.

4 When you present a grain offering baked in the oven, it shall be of choice flour: unleavened cakes mixed with oil, or unleavened wafers spread with oil. ⁵If your offering is grain prepared on a griddle, it shall be of choice flour mixed with oil, unleavened; ⁶break it in pieces, and pour oil on it; it is a grain offering. ⁷If your offering is grain prepared in a pan, it shall be made of choice flour in oil. ⁸You shall bring to the LORD the grain offering that is prepared in any of these ways; and when it is presented to the priest, he shall take it to the altar. ⁹The priest shall remove from the grain offering its token portion and turn this into smoke on the altar, an offering by fire of pleasing odor to the LORD. ¹⁰And what is left of the grain offering shall be for Aaron and his sons; it is a most holy part of the offerings by fire to the LORD.

11 No grain offering that you bring to the LORD shall be made with leaven, for you must not turn any leaven or honey into smoke as an offering by fire to the LORD. ¹²You may bring them to the LORD as an offering of choice products, but they shall not be offered on the altar for a pleasing odor. ¹³You shall not omit from your grain offerings the salt of the covenant with your God; with all your offerings you shall offer salt.

14 If you bring a grain offering of first fruits to the LORD, you shall bring as the grain offering of your first fruits coarse new grain from fresh ears, parched with fire. ¹⁵You shall add oil to it and lay frankincense on it; it is a grain offering. ¹⁶And the priest shall turn a token portion of it into smoke—some of the coarse grain and oil with all its frankincense; it is an offering by fire to the LORD.

Offerings of Well-Being

3 If the offering is a sacrifice of well-being, if you offer an animal of the herd, whether male or female, you shall offer one without blemish before the LORD. ²You shall lay your hand on the head of the offering and slaughter it at the entrance of the tent of meeting; and Aaron's sons the priests shall dash the blood against all sides of the altar. ³You shall offer from the sacrifice of well-being, as an offering by fire to the LORD, the fat that covers the entrails and all the fat that is around the entrails; ⁴the two kidneys with the fat that is on them at the loins, and the appendage of the liver, which he shall remove with the kidneys. ⁵Then Aaron's sons shall turn these into smoke on the altar, with the burnt offering that is on the wood on the fire, as an offering by fire of pleasing odor to the LORD.

6 If your offering for a sacrifice of well-being to the LORD is from the flock, male or female, you shall offer one without blemish. ⁷If you present a sheep as your offering, you shall bring it before the LORD ⁸and lay your hand on the head of the offering. It shall be slaughtered before the tent of meeting, and Aaron's sons shall dash its blood against all sides of the altar. ⁹You shall present its fat from the sacrifice of well-being, as an offering by fire to the LORD: the whole broad tail, which shall be removed close to the backbone, the fat that covers the entrails, and all the fat that is around the entrails; ¹⁰the two kidneys with the fat that is on them at the loins, and the appendage of the liver, which you shall remove with the kidneys. ¹¹Then the priest shall turn these into smoke on the altar as a food offering by fire to the LORD.

12 If your offering is a goat, you shall bring it before the LORD ¹³and lay your hand on its head; it shall be slaughtered before the tent of meeting; and the sons

of Aaron shall dash its blood against all sides of the altar. [14]You shall present as your offering from it, as an offering by fire to the LORD, the fat that covers the entrails, and all the fat that is around the entrails; [15]the two kidneys with the fat that is on them at the loins, and the appendage of the liver, which you shall remove with the kidneys. [16]Then the priest shall turn these into smoke on the altar as a food offering by fire for a pleasing odor.

All fat is the LORD's. [17]It shall be a perpetual statute throughout your generations, in all your settlements: you must not eat any fat or any blood.

Sin Offerings

4 The LORD spoke to Moses, saying, [2]Speak to the people of Israel, saying: When anyone sins unintentionally in any of the LORD's commandments about things not to be done, and does any one of them:

3 If it is the anointed priest who sins, thus bringing guilt on the people, he shall offer for the sin that he has committed a bull of the herd without blemish as a sin offering to the LORD. [4]He shall bring the bull to the entrance of the tent of meeting before the LORD and lay his hand on the head of the bull; the bull shall be slaughtered before the LORD. [5]The anointed priest shall take some of the blood of the bull and bring it into the tent of meeting. [6]The priest shall dip his finger in the blood and sprinkle some of the blood seven times before the LORD in front of the curtain of the sanctuary. [7]The priest shall put some of the blood on the horns of the altar of fragrant incense that is in the tent of meeting before the LORD; and the rest of the blood of the bull he shall pour out at the base of the altar of burnt offering, which is at the entrance of the tent of meeting. [8]He shall remove all the fat from the bull of sin offering: the fat that covers the entrails and all the fat that is around the entrails; [9]the two kidneys with the fat

that is on them at the loins; and the appendage of the liver, which he shall remove with the kidneys, [10]just as these are removed from the ox of the sacrifice of well-being. The priest shall turn them into smoke upon the altar of burnt offering. [11]But the skin of the bull and all its flesh, as well as its head, its legs, its entrails, and its dung— [12]all the rest of the bull—he shall carry out to a clean place outside the camp, to the ash heap, and shall burn it on a wood fire; at the ash heap it shall be burned.

13 If the whole congregation of Israel errs unintentionally and the matter escapes the notice of the assembly, and they do any one of the things that by the LORD's commandments ought not to be done and incur guilt; [14]when the sin that they have committed becomes known, the assembly shall offer a bull of the herd for a sin offering and bring it before the tent of meeting. [15]The elders of the congregation shall lay their hands on the head of the bull before the LORD, and the bull shall be slaughtered before the LORD. [16]The anointed priest shall bring some of the blood of the bull into the tent of meeting, [17]and the priest shall dip his finger in the blood and sprinkle it seven times before the LORD, in front of the curtain. [18]He shall put some of the blood on the horns of the altar that is before the LORD in the tent of meeting; and the rest of the blood he shall pour out at the base of the altar of burnt offering that is at the entrance of the tent of meeting. [19]He shall remove all its fat and turn it into smoke on the altar. [20]He shall do with the bull just as is done with the bull of sin offering; he shall do the same with this. The priest shall make atonement for them, and they shall be forgiven. [21]He shall carry the bull outside the camp, and burn it as he burned the first bull; it is the sin offering for the assembly.

22 When a ruler sins, doing unintentionally any one of all the things that by commandments of the LORD his God

ought not to be done and incurs guilt, [23]once the sin that he has committed is made known to him, he shall bring as his offering a male goat without blemish. [24]He shall lay his hand on the head of the goat; it shall be slaughtered at the spot where the burnt offering is slaughtered before the Lord; it is a sin offering. [25]The priest shall take some of the blood of the sin offering with his finger and put it on the horns of the altar of burnt offering, and pour out the rest of its blood at the base of the altar of burnt offering. [26]All its fat he shall turn into smoke on the altar, like the fat of the sacrifice of well-being. Thus the priest shall make atonement on his behalf for his sin, and he shall be forgiven.

27 If anyone of the ordinary people among you sins unintentionally in doing any one of the things that by the Lord's commandments ought not to be done and incurs guilt, [28]when the sin that you have committed is made known to you, you shall bring a female goat without blemish as your offering, for the sin that you have committed. [29]You shall lay your hand on the head of the sin offering; and the sin offering shall be slaughtered at the place of the burnt offering. [30]The priest shall take some of its blood with his finger and put it on the horns of the altar of burnt offering, and he shall pour out the rest of its blood at the base of the altar. [31]He shall remove all its fat, as the fat is removed from the offering of well-being, and the priest shall turn it into smoke on the altar for a pleasing odor to the Lord. Thus the priest shall make atonement on your behalf, and you shall be forgiven.

32 If the offering you bring as a sin offering is a sheep, you shall bring a female without blemish. [33]You shall lay your hand on the head of the sin offering; and it shall be slaughtered as a sin offering at the spot where the burnt offering is slaughtered. [34]The priest shall take some of the blood of the sin offering

with his finger and put it on the horns of the altar of burnt offering, and pour out the rest of its blood at the base of the altar. [35]You shall remove all its fat, as the fat of the sheep is removed from the sacrifice of well-being, and the priest shall turn it into smoke on the altar, with the offerings by fire to the Lord. Thus the priest shall make atonement on your behalf for the sin that you have committed, and you shall be forgiven.

5 When any of you sin in that you have heard a public adjuration to testify and—though able to testify as one who has seen or learned of the matter—does not speak up, you are subject to punishment. [2]Or when any of you touch any unclean thing—whether the carcass of an unclean beast or the carcass of unclean livestock or the carcass of an unclean swarming thing—and are unaware of it, you have become unclean, and are guilty. [3]Or when you touch human uncleanness—any uncleanness by which one can become unclean—and are unaware of it, when you come to know it, you shall be guilty. [4]Or when any of you utter aloud a rash oath for a bad or a good purpose, whatever people utter in an oath, and are unaware of it, when you come to know it, you shall in any of these be guilty. [5]When you realize your guilt in any of these, you shall confess the sin that you have committed. [6]And you shall bring to the Lord, as your penalty for the sin that you have committed, a female from the flock, a sheep or a goat, as a sin offering; and the priest shall make atonement on your behalf for your sin.

7 But if you cannot afford a sheep, you shall bring to the Lord, as your penalty for the sin that you have committed, two turtledoves or two pigeons, one for a sin offering and the other for a burnt offering. [8]You shall bring them to the priest, who shall offer first the one for the sin offering, wringing its head at the nape without severing it. [9]He shall sprinkle

some of the blood of the sin offering on the side of the altar, while the rest of the blood shall be drained out at the base of the altar; it is a sin offering. [10]And the second he shall offer for a burnt offering according to the regulation. Thus the priest shall make atonement on your behalf for the sin that you have committed, and you shall be forgiven.

11 But if you cannot afford two turtledoves or two pigeons, you shall bring as your offering for the sin that you have committed one-tenth of an ephah of choice flour for a sin offering; you shall not put oil on it or lay frankincense on it, for it is a sin offering. [12]You shall bring it to the priest, and the priest shall scoop up a handful of it as its memorial portion, and turn this into smoke on the altar, with the offerings by fire to the LORD; it is a sin offering. [13]Thus the priest shall make atonement on your behalf for whichever of these sins you have committed, and you shall be forgiven. Like the grain offering, the rest shall be for the priest.

Offerings with Restitution

14 The LORD spoke to Moses, saying: [15]When any of you commit a trespass and sin unintentionally in any of the holy things of the LORD, you shall bring, as your guilt offering to the LORD, a ram without blemish from the flock, convertible into silver by the sanctuary shekel; it is a guilt offering. [16]And you shall make restitution for the holy thing in which you were remiss, and shall add one-fifth to it and give it to the priest. The priest shall make atonement on your behalf with the ram of the guilt offering, and you shall be forgiven.

17 If any of you sin without knowing it, doing any of the things that by the LORD's commandments ought not to be done, you have incurred guilt, and are subject to punishment. [18]You shall bring to the priest a ram without blemish from the flock, or the equivalent, as a guilt

offering; and the priest shall make atonement on your behalf for the error that you committed unintentionally, and you shall be forgiven. [19]It is a guilt offering; you have incurred guilt before the LORD.

6 [b]The LORD spoke to Moses, saying: [2]When any of you sin and commit a trespass against the LORD by deceiving a neighbor in a matter of a deposit or a pledge, or by robbery, or if you have defrauded a neighbor, [3]or have found something lost and lied about it—if you swear falsely regarding any of the various things that one may do and sin thereby— [4]when you have sinned and realize your guilt, and would restore what you took by robbery or by fraud or the deposit that was committed to you, or the lost thing that you found, [5]or anything else about which you have sworn falsely, you shall repay the principal amount and shall add one-fifth to it. You shall pay it to its owner when you realize your guilt. [6]And you shall bring to the priest, as your guilt offering to the LORD, a ram without blemish from the flock, or its equivalent, for a guilt offering. [7]The priest shall make atonement on your behalf before the LORD, and you shall be forgiven for any of the things that one may do and incur guilt thereby.

Instructions concerning Sacrifices

8[c] The LORD spoke to Moses, saying: [9]Command Aaron and his sons, saying: This is the ritual of the burnt offering. The burnt offering itself shall remain on the hearth upon the altar all night until the morning, while the fire on the altar shall be kept burning. [10]The priest shall put on his linen vestments after putting on his linen undergarments next to his body; and he shall take up the ashes to which the fire has reduced the burnt offering on the altar, and place them beside the altar. [11]Then he shall take off his vestments and put on other garments,

[b] Ch 5.20 in Heb   [c] Ch 6.1 in Heb

and carry the ashes out to a clean place outside the camp. ¹²The fire on the altar shall be kept burning; it shall not go out. Every morning the priest shall add wood to it, lay out the burnt offering on it, and turn into smoke the fat pieces of the offerings of well-being. ¹³A perpetual fire shall be kept burning on the altar; it shall not go out.

14 This is the ritual of the grain offering: The sons of Aaron shall offer it before the LORD, in front of the altar. ¹⁵They shall take from it a handful of the choice flour and oil of the grain offering, with all the frankincense that is on the offering, and they shall turn its memorial portion into smoke on the altar as a pleasing odor to the LORD. ¹⁶Aaron and his sons shall eat what is left of it; it shall be eaten as unleavened cakes in a holy place; in the court of the tent of meeting they shall eat it. ¹⁷It shall not be baked with leaven. I have given it as their portion of my offerings by fire; it is most holy, like the sin offering and the guilt offering. ¹⁸Every male among the descendants of Aaron shall eat of it, as their perpetual due throughout your generations, from the LORD's offerings by fire; anything that touches them shall become holy.

19 The LORD spoke to Moses, saying: ²⁰This is the offering that Aaron and his sons shall offer to the LORD on the day when he is anointed: one-tenth of an ephah of choice flour as a regular offering, half of it in the morning and half in the evening. ²¹It shall be made with oil on a griddle; you shall bring it well soaked, as a grain offering of baked[d] pieces, and you shall present it as a pleasing odor to the LORD. ²²And so the priest, anointed from among Aaron's descendants as a successor, shall prepare it; it is the LORD's—a perpetual due—to be turned entirely into smoke. ²³Every grain offering of a priest shall be wholly burned; it shall not be eaten.

24 The LORD spoke to Moses, saying: ²⁵Speak to Aaron and his sons, saying:

This is the ritual of the sin offering. The sin offering shall be slaughtered before the LORD at the spot where the burnt offering is slaughtered; it is most holy. ²⁶The priest who offers it as a sin offering shall eat of it; it shall be eaten in a holy place, in the court of the tent of meeting. ²⁷Whatever touches its flesh shall become holy; and when any of its blood is spattered on a garment, you shall wash the bespattered part in a holy place. ²⁸An earthen vessel in which it was boiled shall be broken; but if it is boiled in a bronze vessel, that shall be scoured and rinsed in water. ²⁹Every male among the priests shall eat of it; it is most holy. ³⁰But no sin offering shall be eaten from which any blood is brought into the tent of meeting for atonement in the holy place; it shall be burned with fire.

7 This is the ritual of the guilt offering. It is most holy; ²at the spot where the burnt offering is slaughtered, they shall slaughter the guilt offering, and its blood shall be dashed against all sides of the altar. ³All its fat shall be offered: the broad tail, the fat that covers the entrails, ⁴the two kidneys with the fat that is on them at the loins, and the appendage of the liver, which shall be removed with the kidneys. ⁵The priest shall turn them into smoke on the altar as an offering by fire to the LORD; it is a guilt offering. ⁶Every male among the priests shall eat of it; it shall be eaten in a holy place; it is most holy.

7 The guilt offering is like the sin offering, there is the same ritual for them; the priest who makes atonement with it shall have it. ⁸So, too, the priest who offers anyone's burnt offering shall keep the skin of the burnt offering that he has offered. ⁹And every grain offering baked in the oven, and all that is prepared in a pan or on a griddle, shall belong to the priest who offers it. ¹⁰But every other grain offering, mixed with

---

[d] Meaning of Heb uncertain

oil or dry, shall belong to all the sons of Aaron equally.

Further Instructions

11 This is the ritual of the sacrifice of the offering of well-being that one may offer to the LORD. ¹²If you offer it for thanksgiving, you shall offer with the thank offering unleavened cakes mixed with oil, unleavened wafers spread with oil, and cakes of choice flour well soaked in oil. ¹³With your thanksgiving sacrifice of well-being you shall bring your offering with cakes of leavened bread. ¹⁴From this you shall offer one cake from each offering, as a gift to the LORD; it shall belong to the priest who dashes the blood of the offering of well-being. ¹⁵And the flesh of your thanksgiving sacrifice of well-being shall be eaten on the day it is offered; you shall not leave any of it until morning. ¹⁶But if the sacrifice you offer is a votive offering or a freewill offering, it shall be eaten on the day that you offer your sacrifice, and what is left of it shall be eaten the next day; ¹⁷but what is left of the flesh of the sacrifice shall be burned up on the third day. ¹⁸If any of the flesh of your sacrifice of well-being is eaten on the third day, it shall not be acceptable, nor shall it be credited to the one who offers it; it shall be an abomination, and the one who eats of it shall incur guilt.

19 Flesh that touches any unclean thing shall not be eaten; it shall be burned up. As for other flesh, all who are clean may eat such flesh. ²⁰But those who eat flesh from the LORD's sacrifice of well-being while in a state of uncleanness shall be cut off from their kin. ²¹When any one of you touches any unclean thing—human uncleanness or an unclean animal or any unclean creature—and then eats flesh from the LORD's sacrifice of well-being, you shall be cut off from your kin.

22 The LORD spoke to Moses, saying: ²³Speak to the people of Israel, saying: You shall eat no fat of ox or sheep or goat. ²⁴The fat of an animal that died or was torn by wild animals may be put to any other use, but you must not eat it. ²⁵If any one of you eats the fat from an animal of which an offering by fire may be made to the LORD, you who eat it shall be cut off from your kin. ²⁶You must not eat any blood whatever, either of bird or of animal, in any of your settlements. ²⁷Any one of you who eats any blood shall be cut off from your kin.

28 The LORD spoke to Moses, saying: ²⁹Speak to the people of Israel, saying: Any one of you who would offer to the LORD your sacrifice of well-being must yourself bring to the LORD your offering from your sacrifice of well-being. ³⁰Your own hands shall bring the LORD's offering by fire; you shall bring the fat with the breast, so that the breast may be raised as an elevation offering before the LORD. ³¹The priest shall turn the fat into smoke on the altar, but the breast shall belong to Aaron and his sons. ³²And the right thigh from your sacrifices of well-being you shall give to the priest as an offering; ³³the one among the sons of Aaron who offers the blood and fat of the offering of well-being shall have the right thigh for a portion. ³⁴For I have taken the breast of the elevation offering, and the thigh that is offered, from the people of Israel, from their sacrifices of well-being, and have given them to Aaron the priest and to his sons, as a perpetual due from the people of Israel. ³⁵This is the portion allotted to Aaron and to his sons from the offerings made by fire to the LORD, once they have been brought forward to serve the LORD as priests; ³⁶these the LORD commanded to be given them, when he anointed them, as a perpetual due from the people of Israel throughout their generations.

37 This is the ritual of the burnt offering, the grain offering, the sin offering, the guilt offering, the offering of

ordination, and the sacrifice of well-being, [38]which the LORD commanded Moses on Mount Sinai, when he commanded the people of Israel to bring their offerings to the LORD, in the wilderness of Sinai.

The Rites of Ordination

8 The LORD spoke to Moses, saying: [2]Take Aaron and his sons with him, the vestments, the anointing oil, the bull of sin offering, the two rams, and the basket of unleavened bread; [3]and assemble the whole congregation at the entrance of the tent of meeting. [4]And Moses did as the LORD commanded him. When the congregation was assembled at the entrance of the tent of meeting, [5]Moses said to the congregation, "This is what the LORD has commanded to be done."

6 Then Moses brought Aaron and his sons forward, and washed them with water. [7]He put the tunic on him, fastened the sash around him, clothed him with the robe, and put the ephod on him. He then put the decorated band of the ephod around him, tying the ephod to him with it. [8]He placed the breastpiece on him, and in the breastpiece he put the Ūrim and the Thum´mim. [9]And he set the turban on his head, and on the turban, in front, he set the golden ornament, the holy crown, as the LORD commanded Moses.

10 Then Moses took the anointing oil and anointed the tabernacle and all that was in it, and consecrated them. [11]He sprinkled some of it on the altar seven times, and anointed the altar and all its utensils, and the basin and its base, to consecrate them. [12]He poured some of the anointing oil on Aaron's head and anointed him, to consecrate him. [13]And Moses brought forward Aaron's sons, and clothed them with tunics, and fastened sashes around them, and tied headdresses on them, as the LORD commanded Moses.

14 He led forward the bull of sin offering; and Aaron and his sons laid their hands upon the head of the bull of sin offering, [15]and it was slaughtered. Moses took the blood and with his finger put some on each of the horns of the altar, purifying the altar; then he poured out the blood at the base of the altar. Thus he consecrated it, to make atonement for it. [16]Moses took all the fat that was around the entrails, and the appendage of the liver, and the two kidneys with their fat, and turned them into smoke on the altar. [17]But the bull itself, its skin and flesh and its dung, he burned with fire outside the camp, as the LORD commanded Moses.

18 Then he brought forward the ram of burnt offering. Aaron and his sons laid their hands on the head of the ram, [19]and it was slaughtered. Moses dashed the blood against all sides of the altar. [20]The ram was cut into its parts, and Moses turned into smoke the head and the parts and the suet. [21]And after the entrails and the legs were washed with water, Moses turned into smoke the whole ram on the altar; it was a burnt offering for a pleasing odor, an offering by fire to the LORD, as the LORD commanded Moses.

22 Then he brought forward the second ram, the ram of ordination. Aaron

Have you ever played a game in which you roll dice? In Old Testament times, the priests used objects called Urim and Thummim to figure out answers to questions they asked God. These objects may have been stones or pieces of metal. The priests would shake them in a container and throw them on the ground like dice. How the Urim and the Thummim landed would tell the priests what to do.

and his sons laid their hands on the head of the ram, [23]and it was slaughtered. Moses took some of its blood and put it on the lobe of Aaron's right ear and on the thumb of his right hand and on the big toe of his right foot. [24]After Aaron's sons were brought forward, Moses put some of the blood on the lobes of their right ears and on the thumbs of their right hands and on the big toes of their right feet; and Moses dashed the rest of the blood against all sides of the altar. [25]He took the fat—the broad tail, all the fat that was around the entrails, the appendage of the liver, and the two kidneys with their fat—and the right thigh. [26]From the basket of unleavened bread that was before the LORD, he took one cake of unleavened bread, one cake of bread with oil, and one wafer, and placed them on the fat and on the right thigh. [27]He placed all these on the palms of Aaron and on the palms of his sons, and raised them as an elevation offering before the LORD. [28]Then Moses took them from their hands and turned them into smoke on the altar with the burnt offering. This was an ordination offering for a pleasing odor, an offering by fire to the LORD. [29]Moses took the breast and raised it as an elevation offering before the LORD; it was Moses' portion of the ram of ordination, as the LORD commanded Moses.

30 Then Moses took some of the anointing oil and some of the blood that was on the altar and sprinkled them on Aaron and his vestments, and also on his sons and their vestments. Thus he consecrated Aaron and his vestments, and also his sons and their vestments.

31 And Moses said to Aaron and his sons, "Boil the flesh at the entrance of the tent of meeting, and eat it there with the bread that is in the basket of ordination offerings, as I was commanded, 'Aaron and his sons shall eat it'; [32]and what remains of the flesh and the bread you shall burn with fire. [33]You shall not go outside the entrance of the tent of meeting for seven days, until the day when your period of ordination is completed. For it will take seven days to ordain you; [34]as has been done today, the LORD has commanded to be done to make atonement for you. [35]You shall remain at the entrance of the tent of meeting day and night for seven days, keeping the LORD's charge so that you do not die; for so I am commanded." [36]Aaron and his sons did all the things that the LORD commanded through Moses.

Aaron's Priesthood Inaugurated

9 On the eighth day Moses summoned Aaron and his sons and the elders of Israel. [2]He said to Aaron, "Take a bull calf for a sin offering and a ram for a burnt offering, without blemish, and offer them before the LORD. [3]And say to the people of Israel, 'Take a male goat for a sin offering; a calf and a lamb, yearlings without blemish, for a burnt offering; [4]and an ox and a ram for an offering of well-being to sacrifice before the LORD; and a grain offering mixed with oil. For today the LORD will appear to you.' " [5]They brought what Moses commanded to the front of the tent of meeting; and the whole congregation drew near and stood before the LORD. [6]And Moses said, "This is the thing that the LORD commanded you to do, so that the glory of the LORD may appear to you." [7]Then Moses said to Aaron, "Draw near to the altar and sacrifice your sin offering and your burnt offering, and make atonement for yourself and for the people; and sacrifice the offering of the people, and make atonement for them; as the LORD has commanded."

8 Aaron drew near to the altar, and slaughtered the calf of the sin offering, which was for himself. [9]The sons of Aaron presented the blood to him, and he dipped his finger in the blood and put it on the horns of the altar; and the rest of the blood he poured out at the base of the altar. [10]But the fat, the kidneys, and the appendage of the liver

from the sin offering he turned into smoke on the altar, as the LORD commanded Moses; ¹¹and the flesh and the skin he burned with fire outside the camp.

12 Then he slaughtered the burnt offering. Aaron's sons brought him the blood, and he dashed it against all sides of the altar. ¹³And they brought him the burnt offering piece by piece, and the head, which he turned into smoke on the altar. ¹⁴He washed the entrails and the legs and, with the burnt offering, turned them into smoke on the altar.

15 Next he presented the people's offering. He took the goat of the sin offering that was for the people, and slaughtered it, and presented it as a sin offering like the first one. ¹⁶He presented the burnt offering, and sacrificed it according to regulation. ¹⁷He presented the grain offering, and, taking a handful of it, he turned it into smoke on the altar, in addition to the burnt offering of the morning.

18 He slaughtered the ox and the ram as a sacrifice of well-being for the people. Aaron's sons brought him the blood, which he dashed against all sides of the altar, ¹⁹and the fat of the ox and of the ram—the broad tail, the fat that covers the entrails, the two kidneys and the fat on them,ᵉ and the appendage of the liver. ²⁰They first laid the fat on the breasts, and the fat was turned into smoke on the altar; ²¹and the breasts and the right thigh Aaron raised as an elevation offering before the LORD, as Moses had commanded.

22 Aaron lifted his hands toward the people and blessed them; and he came down after sacrificing the sin offering, the burnt offering, and the offering of well-being. ²³Moses and Aaron entered the tent of meeting, and then came out and blessed the people; and the glory of the LORD appeared to all the people. ²⁴Fire came out from the LORD and consumed the burnt offering and the fat on the altar; and when all the people saw it, they shouted and fell on their faces.

Nadab and Abihu were priests who chose to do things their own way instead of following the rules for worship. Our parents, teachers, and communities make rules to keep us safe and to help us treat each other like we should. Sometimes, even when we know better, we choose to break the rules. When this happens, the best thing to do is ask for forgiveness from our families, our friends, and God. What are some rules that you have been asked to follow? Can you think of some reasons why these rules are good for you? What could happen if you broke them?

Nadab and Abihu

10 Now Aaron's sons, Nā´dab and A·bī´hu, each took his censer, put fire in it, and laid incense on it; and they offered unholy fire before the LORD, such as he had not commanded them. ²And fire came out from the presence of the LORD and consumed them, and they died before the LORD. ³Then Moses said to Aaron, "This is what the LORD meant when he said,

'Through those who are near me
    I will show myself holy,
and before all the people
    I will be glorified.' "

And Aaron was silent.

4 Moses summoned Mish´a·el and El´za·phan, sons of Uz´zi·el the uncle of Aaron, and said to them, "Come forward, and carry your kinsmen away from the front of the sanctuary to a place outside the camp." ⁵They came forward and carried them by their tunics out of the camp, as Moses had ordered. ⁶And Moses said to Aaron and to his sons El·ē·á´zar and Ith´a·mar, "Do not dishevel your hair, and do not tear

ᵉ Gk: Heb *the broad tail, and that which covers, and the kidneys* your vestments, or you will die and wrath will strike all the congregation; but your kindred, the whole house of Israel, may mourn the burning that the LORD has sent. [7]You shall not go outside the entrance of the tent of meeting, or you will die; for the anointing oil of the LORD is on you." And they did as Moses had ordered.

8 And the LORD spoke to Aaron: [9]Drink no wine or strong drink, neither you nor your sons, when you enter the tent of meeting, that you may not die; it is a statute forever throughout your generations. [10]You are to distinguish between the holy and the common, and between the unclean and the clean; [11]and you are to teach the people of Israel all the statutes that the LORD has spoken to them through Moses.

12 Moses spoke to Aaron and to his remaining sons, El·e·a´zar and Ith´a·mar: Take the grain offering that is left from the LORD's offerings by fire, and eat it unleavened beside the altar, for it is most holy; [13]you shall eat it in a holy place, because it is your due and your sons' due, from the offerings by fire to the LORD; for so I am commanded. [14]But the breast that is elevated and the thigh that is raised, you and your sons and daughters as well may eat in any clean place; for they have been assigned to you and your children from the sacrifices of the offerings of well-being of the people of Israel. [15]The thigh that is raised and the breast that is elevated they shall bring, together with the offerings by fire of the fat, to raise for an elevation offering before the LORD; they are to be your due and that of your children forever, as the LORD has commanded.

16 Then Moses made inquiry about the goat of the sin offering, and—it had already been burned! He was angry with El·e·a´zar and Ith´a·mar, Aaron's remaining sons, and said, [17]"Why did you not eat the sin offering in the sacred area? For it is most holy, and God[f] has given it to you

that you may remove the guilt of the congregation, to make atonement on their behalf before the LORD. [18]Its blood was not brought into the inner part of the sanctuary. You should certainly have eaten it in the sanctuary, as I commanded." [19]And Aaron spoke to Moses, "See, today they offered their sin offering and their burnt offering before the LORD; and yet such things as these have befallen me! If I had eaten the sin offering today, would it have been agreeable to the LORD?" [20]And when Moses heard that, he agreed.

Clean and Unclean Foods

11 The LORD spoke to Moses and Aaron, saying to them: [2]Speak to the people of Israel, saying:

From among all the land animals, these are the creatures that you may eat. [3]Any animal that has divided hoofs and is cleft-footed and chews the cud—such you may eat. [4]But among those that chew the cud or have divided hoofs, you shall not eat the following: the camel, for even though it chews the cud, it does not have divided hoofs; it is unclean for you. [5]The rock badger, for even though it chews the cud, it does not have divided hoofs; it is unclean for you. [6]The hare, for even though it chews the cud, it does not have divided hoofs; it is unclean for you. [7]The pig, for even though it has divided hoofs and is cleft-footed, it does not chew the cud; it is unclean for you. [8]Of their flesh you shall not eat, and their carcasses you shall not touch; they are unclean for you.

9 These you may eat, of all that are in the waters. Everything in the waters that has fins and scales, whether in the seas or in the streams—such you may eat. [10]But anything in the seas or the streams that does not have fins and scales, of the swarming creatures in the waters and among all the other living creatures that are in the waters—they are detestable to you [11]and detestable they shall remain. Of their flesh you shall not eat, and their

[f] Heb *he*

carcasses you shall regard as detestable. [12]Everything in the waters that does not have fins and scales is detestable to you.

13 These you shall regard as detestable among the birds. They shall not be eaten; they are an abomination: the eagle, the vulture, the osprey, [14]the buzzard, the kite of any kind; [15]every raven of any kind; [16]the ostrich, the nighthawk, the sea gull, the hawk of any kind; [17]the little owl, the cormorant, the great owl, [18]the water hen, the desert owl,[g] the carrion vulture, [19]the stork, the heron of any kind, the hoopoe, and the bat.[h]

20 All winged insects that walk upon all fours are detestable to you. [21]But among the winged insects that walk on all fours you may eat those that have jointed legs above their feet, with which to leap on the ground. [22]Of them you may eat: the locust according to its kind, the bald locust according to its kind, the cricket according to its kind, and the grasshopper according to its kind. [23]But all other winged insects that have four feet are detestable to you.

Unclean Animals

24 By these you shall become unclean; whoever touches the carcass of any of them shall be unclean until the evening, [25]and whoever carries any part of the carcass of any of them shall wash his clothes and be unclean until the evening. [26]Every animal that has divided hoofs but is not cleft-footed or does not chew the cud is unclean for you; everyone who touches one of them shall be unclean. [27]All that walk on their paws, among the animals that walk on all fours, are unclean for you; whoever touches the carcass of any of them shall be unclean until the evening, [28]and the one who carries the carcass shall wash his clothes and be unclean until the evening; they are unclean for you.

29 These are unclean for you among the creatures that swarm upon the earth: the weasel, the mouse, the great lizard according to its kind, [30]the gecko, the land crocodile, the lizard, the sand lizard, and the chameleon. [31]These are unclean for you among all that swarm; whoever touches one of them when they are dead shall be unclean until the evening. [32]And anything upon which any of them falls when they are dead shall be unclean, whether an article of wood or cloth or skin or sacking, any article that is used for any purpose; it shall be dipped into water, and it shall be unclean until the evening, and then it shall be clean. [33]And if any of them falls into any earthen vessel, all that is in it shall be unclean, and you shall break the vessel. [34]Any food that could be eaten shall be unclean if water from any such vessel comes upon it; and any liquid that could be drunk shall be unclean if it was in any such vessel. [35]Everything on which any part of the carcass falls shall be unclean; whether an oven or stove, it shall be broken in pieces; they are unclean, and shall remain unclean for you. [36]But a spring or a cistern holding water shall be clean, while whatever touches the carcass in it shall be unclean. [37]If any part of their carcass falls upon any seed set aside for sowing, it is clean; [38]but if water is put on the seed and any part of their carcass falls on it, it is unclean for you.

39 If an animal of which you may eat dies, anyone who touches its carcass shall be unclean until the evening. [40]Those who eat of its carcass shall wash their clothes and be unclean until the evening; and those who carry the carcass shall wash their clothes and be unclean until the evening.

41 All creatures that swarm upon the earth are detestable; they shall not be eaten. [42]Whatever moves on its belly, and whatever moves on all fours, or whatever has many feet, all the creatures that swarm upon the earth, you shall not eat; for they are detestable. [43]You shall not make yourselves detestable with any creature that

[g] Or *pelican*   [h] Identification of several of the birds in verses 13-19 is uncertain

swarms; you shall not defile yourselves with them, and so become unclean. ⁴⁴For I am the LORD your God; sanctify yourselves therefore, and be holy, for I am holy. You shall not defile yourselves with any swarming creature that moves on the earth. ⁴⁵For I am the LORD who brought you up from the land of Egypt, to be your God; you shall be holy, for I am holy.

46 This is the law pertaining to land animal and bird and every living creature that moves through the waters and every creature that swarms upon the earth, ⁴⁷to make a distinction between the unclean and the clean, and between the living creature that may be eaten and the living creature that may not be eaten.

Purification of Women after Childbirth

12 The LORD spoke to Moses, saying: ²Speak to the people of Israel, saying:

If a woman conceives and bears a male child, she shall be ceremonially unclean seven days; as at the time of her menstruation, she shall be unclean. ³On the eighth day the flesh of his foreskin shall be circumcised. ⁴Her time of blood purification shall be thirty-three days; she shall not touch any holy thing, or come into the sanctuary, until the days of her purification are completed. ⁵If she bears a female child, she shall be unclean two weeks, as in her menstruation; her time of blood purification shall be sixty-six days.

6 When the days of her purification are completed, whether for a son or for a daughter, she shall bring to the priest at the entrance of the tent of meeting a lamb in its first year for a burnt offering, and a pigeon or a turtledove for a sin offering. ⁷He shall offer it before the LORD, and make atonement on her behalf; then she shall be clean from her flow of blood. This is the law for her who bears a child, male or female. ⁸If she cannot afford a sheep, she shall take two turtledoves or two pigeons, one for a burnt

offering and the other for a sin offering; and the priest shall make atonement on her behalf, and she shall be clean.

Leprosy, Varieties and Symptoms

13 The LORD spoke to Moses and Aaron, saying:

2 When a person has on the skin of his body a swelling or an eruption or a spot, and it turns into a leprous[i] disease on the skin of his body, he shall be brought to Aaron the priest or to one of his sons the priests. ³The priest shall examine the disease on the skin of his body, and if the hair in the diseased area has turned white and the disease appears to be deeper than the skin of his body, it is a leprous[i] disease; after the priest has examined him he shall pronounce him ceremonially unclean. ⁴But if the spot is white in the skin of his body, and appears no deeper than the skin, and the hair in it has not turned white, the priest shall confine the diseased person for seven days. ⁵The priest shall examine him on the seventh day, and if he sees that the disease is checked and the disease has not spread in the skin, then the priest shall confine him seven days more. ⁶The priest shall examine him again on the seventh

When people in Bible times had a spot or a rash, they went to the priest to figure out if they had leprosy. Leprosy was a serious skin disease, and people who had it were thought to be unclean. They could not live with their families, and had to stay away from everyone who did not have the disease. It was a very hard life. Today leprosy is called Hansen's Disease, and there are ways to treat some forms.

---

[i] A term for several skin diseases; precise meaning uncertain

day, and if the disease has abated and the disease has not spread in the skin, the priest shall pronounce him clean; it is only an eruption; and he shall wash his clothes, and be clean. [7]But if the eruption spreads in the skin after he has shown himself to the priest for his cleansing, he shall appear again before the priest. [8]The priest shall make an examination, and if the eruption has spread in the skin, the priest shall pronounce him unclean; it is a leprous[j] disease.

9 When a person contracts a leprous[j] disease, he shall be brought to the priest. [10]The priest shall make an examination, and if there is a white swelling in the skin that has turned the hair white, and there is quick raw flesh in the swelling, [11]it is a chronic leprous[j] disease in the skin of his body. The priest shall pronounce him unclean; he shall not confine him, for he is unclean. [12]But if the disease breaks out in the skin, so that it covers all the skin of the diseased person from head to foot, so far as the priest can see, [13]then the priest shall make an examination, and if the disease has covered all his body, he shall pronounce him clean of the disease; since it has all turned white, he is clean. [14]But if raw flesh ever appears on him, he shall be unclean; [15]the priest shall examine the raw flesh and pronounce him unclean. Raw flesh is unclean, for it is a leprous[j] disease. [16]But if the raw flesh again turns white, he shall come to the priest; [17]the priest shall examine him, and if the disease has turned white, the priest shall pronounce the diseased person clean. He is clean.

18 When there is on the skin of one's body a boil that has healed, [19]and in the place of the boil there appears a white swelling or a reddish-white spot, it shall be shown to the priest. [20]The priest shall make an examination, and if it appears deeper than the skin and its hair has turned white, the priest shall pronounce him unclean; this is a leprous[j] disease, broken out in the boil. [21]But if the priest examines it and the hair on it is not white, nor is it deeper than the skin but has abated, the priest shall confine him seven days. [22]If it spreads in the skin, the priest shall pronounce him unclean; it is diseased. [23]But if the spot remains in one place and does not spread, it is the scar of the boil; the priest shall pronounce him clean.

24 Or, when the body has a burn on the skin and the raw flesh of the burn becomes a spot, reddish-white or white, [25]the priest shall examine it. If the hair in the spot has turned white and it appears deeper than the skin, it is a leprous[j] disease; it has broken out in the burn, and the priest shall pronounce him unclean. This is a leprous[j] disease. [26]But if the priest examines it and the hair in the spot is not white, and it is no deeper than the skin but has abated, the priest shall confine him seven days. [27]The priest shall examine him the seventh day; if it is spreading in the skin, the priest shall pronounce him unclean. This is a leprous[j] disease. [28]But if the spot remains in one place and does not spread in the skin but has abated, it is a swelling from the burn, and the priest shall pronounce him clean; for it is the scar of the burn.

29 When a man or woman has a disease on the head or in the beard, [30]the priest shall examine the disease. If it appears deeper than the skin and the hair in it is yellow and thin, the priest shall pronounce him unclean; it is an itch, a leprous[j] disease of the head or the beard. [31]If the priest examines the itching disease, and it appears no deeper than the skin and there is no black hair in it, the priest shall confine the person with the itching disease for seven days. [32]On the seventh day the priest shall examine the itch; if the itch has not spread, and there is no yellow hair in it,

[j] A term for several skin diseases; precise meaning uncertain

and the itch appears to be no deeper than the skin, ³³he shall shave, but the itch he shall not shave. The priest shall confine the person with the itch for seven days more. ³⁴On the seventh day the priest shall examine the itch; if the itch has not spread in the skin and it appears to be no deeper than the skin, the priest shall pronounce him clean. He shall wash his clothes and be clean. ³⁵But if the itch spreads in the skin after he was pronounced clean, ³⁶the priest shall examine him. If the itch has spread in the skin, the priest need not seek for the yellow hair; he is unclean. ³⁷But if in his eyes the itch is checked, and black hair has grown in it, the itch is healed, he is clean; and the priest shall pronounce him clean.

38 When a man or a woman has spots on the skin of the body, white spots, ³⁹the priest shall make an examination, and if the spots on the skin of the body are of a dull white, it is a rash that has broken out on the skin; he is clean.

40 If anyone loses the hair from his head, he is bald but he is clean. ⁴¹If he loses the hair from his forehead and temples, he has baldness of the forehead but he is clean. ⁴²But if there is on the bald head or the bald forehead a reddish-white diseased spot, it is a leprous[k] disease breaking out on his bald head or his bald forehead. ⁴³The priest shall examine him; if the diseased swelling is reddish-white on his bald head or on his bald forehead, which resembles a leprous[k] disease in the skin of the body, ⁴⁴he is leprous,[k] he is unclean. The priest shall pronounce him unclean; the disease is on his head.

45 The person who has the leprous[k] disease shall wear torn clothes and let the hair of his head be disheveled; and he shall cover his upper lip and cry out, "Unclean, unclean." ⁴⁶He shall remain unclean as long as he has the disease; he is unclean. He shall live alone; his dwelling shall be outside the camp.

47 Concerning clothing: when a leprous[k] disease appears in it, in woolen or linen cloth, ⁴⁸in warp or woof of linen or wool, or in a skin or in anything made of skin, ⁴⁹if the disease shows greenish or reddish in the garment, whether in warp or woof or in skin or in anything made of skin, it is a leprous[k] disease and shall be shown to the priest. ⁵⁰The priest shall examine the disease, and put the diseased article aside for seven days. ⁵¹He shall examine the disease on the seventh day. If the disease has spread in the cloth, in warp or woof, or in the skin, whatever be the use of the skin, this is a spreading leprous[k] disease; it is unclean. ⁵²He shall burn the clothing, whether diseased in warp or woof, woolen or linen, or anything of skin, for it is a spreading leprous[k] disease; it shall be burned in fire.

53 If the priest makes an examination, and the disease has not spread in the clothing, in warp or woof or in anything of skin, ⁵⁴the priest shall command them to wash the article in which the disease appears, and he shall put it aside seven days more. ⁵⁵The priest shall examine the diseased article after it has been washed. If the diseased spot has not changed color, though the disease has not spread, it is unclean; you shall burn it in fire, whether the leprous[k] spot is on the inside or on the outside.

56 If the priest makes an examination, and the disease has abated after it is washed, he shall tear the spot out of the cloth, in warp or woof, or out of skin. ⁵⁷If it appears again in the garment, in warp or woof, or in anything of skin, it is spreading; you shall burn with fire that in which the disease appears. ⁵⁸But the cloth, warp or woof, or anything of skin from which the disease disappears when you have washed it, shall then be washed a second time, and it shall be clean.

59 This is the ritual for a leprous[k]

[k] A term for several skin diseases; precise meaning uncertain

disease in a cloth of wool or linen, either in warp or woof, or in anything of skin, to decide whether it is clean or unclean.

Purification of Lepers and Leprous Houses

14 The LORD spoke to Moses, saying: [2]This shall be the ritual for the leprous[l] person at the time of his cleansing:

He shall be brought to the priest; [3]the priest shall go out of the camp, and the priest shall make an examination. If the disease is healed in the leprous[l] person, [4]the priest shall command that two living clean birds and cedarwood and crimson yarn and hyssop be brought for the one who is to be cleansed. [5]The priest shall command that one of the birds be slaughtered over fresh water in an earthen vessel. [6]He shall take the living bird with the cedarwood and the crimson yarn and the hyssop, and dip them and the living bird in the blood of the bird that was slaughtered over the fresh water. [7]He shall sprinkle it seven times upon the one who is to be cleansed of the leprous[l] disease; then he shall pronounce him clean, and he shall let the living bird go into the open field. [8]The one who is to be cleansed shall wash his clothes, and shave off all his hair, and bathe himself in water, and he shall be clean. After that he shall come into the camp, but shall live outside his tent seven days. [9]On the seventh day he shall shave all his hair: of head, beard, eyebrows; he shall shave all his hair. Then he shall wash his clothes, and bathe his body in water, and he shall be clean.

10 On the eighth day he shall take two male lambs without blemish, and one ewe lamb in its first year without blemish, and a grain offering of three-tenths of an ephah of choice flour mixed with oil, and one log[m] of oil. [11]The priest who cleanses shall set the person to be cleansed, along with these things, before the LORD, at the entrance of the tent of meeting. [12]The priest shall take one of the lambs, and offer it as a guilt offering, along with the log[m] of oil, and raise them as an elevation offering before the LORD. [13]He shall slaughter the lamb in the place where the sin offering and the burnt offering are slaughtered in the holy place; for the guilt offering, like the sin offering, belongs to the priest: it is most holy. [14]The priest shall take some of the blood of the guilt offering and put it on the lobe of the right ear of the one to be cleansed, and on the thumb of the right hand, and on the big toe of the right foot. [15]The priest shall take some of the log[m] of oil and pour it into the palm of his own left hand, [16]and dip his right finger in the oil that is in his left hand and sprinkle some oil with his finger seven times before the LORD. [17]Some of the oil that remains in his hand the priest shall put on the lobe of the right ear of the one to be cleansed, and on the thumb of the right hand, and on the big toe of the right foot, on top of the blood of the guilt offering. [18]The rest of the oil that is in the priest's hand he shall put on the head of the one to be cleansed. Then the priest shall make atonement on his behalf before the LORD: [19]the priest shall offer the sin offering, to make atonement for the one to be cleansed from his uncleanness. Afterward he shall slaughter the burnt offering; [20]and the priest shall offer the burnt offering and the grain offering on the altar. Thus the priest shall make atonement on his behalf and he shall be clean.

21 But if he is poor and cannot afford so much, he shall take one male lamb for a guilt offering to be elevated, to make atonement on his behalf, and one-tenth of an ephah of choice flour mixed with oil for a grain offering and a log[m] of oil; [22]also two turtledoves or two pigeons, such as he can afford, one for a sin offering and the other for a burnt offering. [23]On the eighth day he shall bring them

[l] A term for several skin diseases; precise meaning uncertain   [m] A liquid measure

for his cleansing to the priest, to the entrance of the tent of meeting, before the LORD; [24]and the priest shall take the lamb of the guilt offering and the log[n] of oil, and the priest shall raise them as an elevation offering before the LORD. [25]The priest shall slaughter the lamb of the guilt offering and shall take some of the blood of the guilt offering, and put it on the lobe of the right ear of the one to be cleansed, and on the thumb of the right hand, and on the big toe of the right foot. [26]The priest shall pour some of the oil into the palm of his own left hand, [27]and shall sprinkle with his right finger some of the oil that is in his left hand seven times before the LORD. [28]The priest shall put some of the oil that is in his hand on the lobe of the right ear of the one to be cleansed, and on the thumb of the right hand, and the big toe of the right foot, where the blood of the guilt offering was placed. [29]The rest of the oil that is in the priest's hand he shall put on the head of the one to be cleansed, to make atonement on his behalf before the LORD. [30]And he shall offer, of the turtle-doves or pigeons such as he can afford, [31]one[o] for a sin offering and the other for a burnt offering, along with a grain offering; and the priest shall make atonement before the LORD on behalf of the one being cleansed. [32]This is the ritual for the one who has a leprous[p] disease, who cannot afford the offerings for his cleansing.

33 The LORD spoke to Moses and Aaron, saying:

34 When you come into the land of Cā′naan, which I give you for a possession, and I put a leprous[p] disease in a house in the land of your possession, [35]the owner of the house shall come and tell the priest, saying, "There seems to me to be some sort of disease in my house." [36]The priest shall command that they empty the house before the priest goes to examine the disease, or all that is in the house will become unclean; and afterward the priest shall go in to inspect the house. [37]He shall examine the disease; if the disease is in the walls of the house with greenish or reddish spots, and if it appears to be deeper than the surface, [38]the priest shall go outside to the door of the house and shut up the house seven days. [39]The priest shall come again on the seventh day and make an inspection; if the disease has spread in the walls of the house, [40]the priest shall command that the stones in which the disease appears be taken out and thrown into an unclean place outside the city. [41]He shall have the inside of the house scraped thoroughly, and the plaster that is scraped off shall be dumped in an unclean place outside the city. [42]They shall take other stones and put them in the place of those stones, and take other plaster and plaster the house.

43 If the disease breaks out again in the house, after he has taken out the stones and scraped the house and plastered it, [44]the priest shall go and make inspection; if the disease has spread in the house, it is a spreading leprous[p] disease in the house; it is unclean. [45]He shall have the house torn down, its stones and timber and all the plaster of the house, and taken outside the city to an unclean place. [46]All who enter the house while it is shut up shall be unclean until the evening; [47]and all who sleep in the house shall wash their clothes; and all who eat in the house shall wash their clothes.

48 If the priest comes and makes an inspection, and the disease has not spread in the house after the house was plastered, the priest shall pronounce the house clean; the disease is healed. [49]For the cleansing of the house he shall take two birds, with cedarwood and crimson yarn and hyssop, [50]and shall slaughter one of the birds over fresh water in an earthen vessel, [51]and shall take the cedarwood and

---

[n] A liquid measure   [o] Gk Syr: Heb *afford,* [31]*such as he can afford, one*   [p] A term for several skin diseases; precise meaning uncertain

Hyssop was a small, bushy plant the Israelites used like a brush in cleaning ceremonies. During the Passover in Egypt, the Hebrews used hyssop to mark their doorways with streaks of blood from the sacrificial lamb. You can read this really cool story about how God protected the people in Exodus 12!

the hyssop and the crimson yarn, along with the living bird, and dip them in the blood of the slaughtered bird and the fresh water, and sprinkle the house seven times. [52]Thus he shall cleanse the house with the blood of the bird, and with the fresh water, and with the living bird, and with the cedarwood and hyssop and crimson yarn; [53]and he shall let the living bird go out of the city into the open field; so he shall make atonement for the house, and it shall be clean.

54 This is the ritual for any leprous[q] disease: for an itch, [55]for leprous[q] diseases in clothing and houses, [56]and for a swelling or an eruption or a spot, [57]to determine when it is unclean and when it is clean. This is the ritual for leprous[q] diseases.

Concerning Bodily Discharges

15 The LORD spoke to Moses and Aaron, saying: [2]Speak to the people of Israel and say to them:

When any man has a discharge from his member,[r] his discharge makes him ceremonially unclean. [3]The uncleanness of his discharge is this: whether his member[r] flows with his discharge, or his member[r] is stopped from discharging, it is uncleanness for him. [4]Every bed on which the one with the discharge lies shall be unclean; and everything on which he sits shall be unclean. [5]Anyone who touches his bed shall wash his clothes, and bathe in water, and be

unclean until the evening. [6]All who sit on anything on which the one with the discharge has sat shall wash their clothes, and bathe in water, and be unclean until the evening. [7]All who touch the body of the one with the discharge shall wash their clothes, and bathe in water, and be unclean until the evening. [8]If the one with the discharge spits on persons who are clean, then they shall wash their clothes, and bathe in water, and be unclean until the evening. [9]Any saddle on which the one with the discharge rides shall be unclean. [10]All who touch anything that was under him shall be unclean until the evening, and all who carry such a thing shall wash their clothes, and bathe in water, and be unclean until the evening. [11]All those whom the one with the discharge touches without his having rinsed his hands in water shall wash their clothes, and bathe in water, and be unclean until the evening. [12]Any earthen vessel that the one with the discharge touches shall be broken; and every vessel of wood shall be rinsed in water.

13 When the one with a discharge is cleansed of his discharge, he shall count seven days for his cleansing; he shall wash his clothes and bathe his body in fresh water, and he shall be clean. [14]On the eighth day he shall take two turtledoves or two pigeons and come before the LORD to the entrance of the tent of meeting and give them to the priest. [15]The priest shall offer them, one for a sin offering and the other for a burnt offering; and the priest shall make atonement on his behalf before the LORD for his discharge.

16 If a man has an emission of semen, he shall bathe his whole body in water, and be unclean until the evening. [17]Everything made of cloth or of skin on which the semen falls shall be washed with water, and be unclean until the

[q] A term for several skin diseases; precise meaning uncertain   [r] Heb *flesh*

evening. ¹⁸If a man lies with a woman and has an emission of semen, both of them shall bathe in water, and be unclean until the evening.

19 When a woman has a discharge of blood that is her regular discharge from her body, she shall be in her impurity for seven days, and whoever touches her shall be unclean until the evening. ²⁰Everything upon which she lies during her impurity shall be unclean; everything also upon which she sits shall be unclean. ²¹Whoever touches her bed shall wash his clothes, and bathe in water, and be unclean until the evening. ²²Whoever touches anything upon which she sits shall wash his clothes, and bathe in water, and be unclean until the evening; ²³whether it is the bed or anything upon which she sits, when he touches it he shall be unclean until the evening. ²⁴If any man lies with her, and her impurity falls on him, he shall be unclean seven days; and every bed on which he lies shall be unclean.

25 If a woman has a discharge of blood for many days, not at the time of her impurity, or if she has a discharge beyond the time of her impurity, all the days of the discharge she shall continue in uncleanness; as in the days of her impurity, she shall be unclean. ²⁶Every bed on which she lies during all the days of her discharge shall be treated as the bed of her impurity; and everything on which she sits shall be unclean, as in the uncleanness of her impurity. ²⁷Whoever touches these things shall be unclean, and shall wash his clothes, and bathe in water, and be unclean until the evening. ²⁸If she is cleansed of her discharge, she shall count seven days, and after that she shall be clean. ²⁹On the eighth day she shall take two turtledoves or two pigeons and bring them to the priest to the entrance of the tent of meeting. ³⁰The priest shall offer one for a sin offering and the other for a burnt offering; and the priest shall make atonement

on her behalf before the LORD for her unclean discharge.

31 Thus you shall keep the people of Israel separate from their uncleanness, so that they do not die in their uncleanness by defiling my tabernacle that is in their midst.

32 This is the ritual for those who have a discharge: for him who has an emission of semen, becoming unclean thereby, ³³for her who is in the infirmity of her period, for anyone, male or female, who has a discharge, and for the man who lies with a woman who is unclean.

The Day of Atonement

16 The LORD spoke to Moses after the death of the two sons of Aaron, when they drew near before the LORD and died. ²The LORD said to Moses: Tell your brother Aaron not to come just at any time into the sanctuary inside the curtain before the mercy seatˢ that is upon the ark, or he will die; for I appear in the cloud upon the mercy seat.ˢ ³Thus shall Aaron come into the holy place: with a young bull for a sin offering and a ram for a burnt offering. ⁴He shall put on the holy linen tunic, and shall have the linen undergarments next to his

Sin separates people from God. One day each year, the Hebrew people would give two goats as an offering. The high priest would sacrifice one goat and sprinkle its blood in the most holy place of the temple. Then he would put his hands on the head of the second goat, confess the sins of the people, and send the goat away into the wilderness. These goats were a symbol that the people had been forgiven of their sins. This day was called the Day of Atonement (or, Yom Kippur). It is still a most holy day for Jews everywhere.

ˢ Or the cover

body, fasten the linen sash, and wear the linen turban; these are the holy vestments. He shall bathe his body in water, and then put them on. [5]He shall take from the congregation of the people of Israel two male goats for a sin offering, and one ram for a burnt offering.

6 Aaron shall offer the bull as a sin offering for himself, and shall make atonement for himself and for his house. [7]He shall take the two goats and set them before the LORD at the entrance of the tent of meeting; [8]and Aaron shall cast lots on the two goats, one lot for the LORD and the other lot for Az·a·zel.[t] [9]Aaron shall present the goat on which the lot fell for the LORD, and offer it as a sin offering; [10]but the goat on which the lot fell for Az·a·zel[t] shall be presented alive before the LORD to make atonement over it, that it may be sent away into the wilderness to Az·a·zel.[t]

11 Aaron shall present the bull as a sin offering for himself, and shall make atonement for himself and for his house; he shall slaughter the bull as a sin offering for himself. [12]He shall take a censer full of coals of fire from the altar before the LORD, and two handfuls of crushed sweet incense, and he shall bring it inside the curtain [13]and put the incense on the fire before the LORD, that the cloud of the incense may cover the mercy seat[u] that is upon the covenant,[v] or he will die. [14]He shall take some of the blood of the bull, and sprinkle it with his finger on the front of the mercy seat,[u] and before the mercy seat[u] he shall sprinkle the blood with his finger seven times.

15 He shall slaughter the goat of the sin offering that is for the people and bring its blood inside the curtain, and do with its blood as he did with the blood of the bull, sprinkling it upon the mercy seat[u] and before the mercy seat.[u] [16]Thus he shall make atonement for the sanctuary, because of the uncleannesses of the people of Israel, and because of their

> An offering is a gift that people give to God as an act of worship. During Bible times, the Israelites would offer food, drink, incense, money, and animals to God. These gifts showed that a person was giving of himself or herself. There were extra offerings at special times like sabbaths and holy days. One way that people today give offerings to God is by putting money in the offering plate at church. There are many ways we can give to God.

transgressions, all their sins; and so he shall do for the tent of meeting, which remains with them in the midst of their uncleannesses. [17]No one shall be in the tent of meeting from the time he enters to make atonement in the sanctuary until he comes out and has made atonement for himself and for his house and for all the assembly of Israel. [18]Then he shall go out to the altar that is before the LORD and make atonement on its behalf, and shall take some of the blood of the bull and of the blood of the goat, and put it on each of the horns of the altar. [19]He shall sprinkle some of the blood on it with his finger seven times, and cleanse it and hallow it from the uncleannesses of the people of Israel.

20 When he has finished atoning for the holy place and the tent of meeting and the altar, he shall present the live goat. [21]Then Aaron shall lay both his hands on the head of the live goat, and confess over it all the iniquities of the people of Israel, and all their transgressions, all their sins, putting them on the head of the goat, and sending it away

[t] Traditionally rendered *a scapegoat*   [u] Or *the cover*   [v] Or *treaty,* or *testament;* Heb *eduth*

During special cere-
monies, the Israelites
sacrificed animals as
offerings to God. They
would give part of the
animal to God, and then the priest
and the people would eat part of
the animal. This meal reminded
the people that they were in a special family relationship with God.

into the wilderness by means of someone designated for the task.ʷ ²²The goat
shall bear on itself all their iniquities to a
barren region; and the goat shall be set
free in the wilderness.

23 Then Aaron shall enter the tent of
meeting, and shall take off the linen
vestments that he put on when he went
into the holy place, and shall leave them
there. ²⁴He shall bathe his body in water
in a holy place, and put on his vestments; then he shall come out and offer
his burnt offering and the burnt offering
of the people, making atonement for
himself and for the people. ²⁵The fat of
the sin offering he shall turn into smoke
on the altar. ²⁶The one who sets the goat
free for Azʹa·zelˣ shall wash his clothes
and bathe his body in water, and afterward may come into the camp. ²⁷The
bull of the sin offering and the goat of
the sin offering, whose blood was
brought in to make atonement in the
holy place, shall be taken outside the
camp; their skin and their flesh and their
dung shall be consumed in fire. ²⁸The
one who burns them shall wash his
clothes and bathe his body in water, and
afterward may come into the camp.

29 This shall be a statute to you forever: In the seventh month, on the tenth
day of the month, you shall deny yourselves,ʸ and shall do no work, neither
the citizen nor the alien who resides
among you. ³⁰For on this day atonement
shall be made for you, to cleanse you;
from all your sins you shall be clean
before the LORD. ³¹It is a sabbath of com-

plete rest to you, and you shall deny
yourselves;ʸ it is a statute forever. ³²The
priest who is anointed and consecrated
as priest in his father's place shall make
atonement, wearing the linen vestments,
the holy vestments. ³³He shall make
atonement for the sanctuary, and he shall
make atonement for the tent of meeting
and for the altar, and he shall make
atonement for the priests and for all the
people of the assembly. ³⁴This shall be an
everlasting statute for you, to make
atonement for the people of Israel once
in the year for all their sins. And Moses
did as the LORD had commanded him.

The Slaughtering of Animals

17 The LORD spoke to Moses:
2 Speak to Aaron and his sons
and to all the people of Israel and say to
them: This is what the LORD has commanded. ³If anyone of the house of
Israel slaughters an ox or a lamb or a
goat in the camp, or slaughters it outside
the camp, ⁴and does not bring it to the
entrance of the tent of meeting, to present it as an offering to the LORD before
the tabernacle of the LORD, he shall be
held guilty of bloodshed; he has shed
blood, and he shall be cut off from the
people. ⁵This is in order that the people
of Israel may bring their sacrifices that
they offer in the open field, that they
may bring them to the LORD, to the
priest at the entrance of the tent of meeting, and offer them as sacrifices of well-
being to the LORD. ⁶The priest shall dash
the blood against the altar of the LORD at
the entrance of the tent of meeting, and
turn the fat into smoke as a pleasing
odor to the LORD, ⁷so that they may no
longer offer their sacrifices for goat-
demons, to whom they prostitute themselves. This shall be a statute forever to
them throughout their generations.

8 And say to them further: Anyone of
the house of Israel or of the aliens who

ʷ Meaning of Heb uncertain   ˣ Traditionally rendered *a scapegoat*   ʸ Or *shall fast*

reside among them who offers a burnt offering or sacrifice, [9]and does not bring it to the entrance of the tent of meeting, to sacrifice it to the LORD, shall be cut off from the people.

Eating Blood Prohibited

10 If anyone of the house of Israel or of the aliens who reside among them eats any blood, I will set my face against that person who eats blood, and will cut that person off from the people. [11]For the life of the flesh is in the blood; and I have given it to you for making atonement for your lives on the altar; for, as life, it is the blood that makes atonement. [12]Therefore I have said to the people of Israel: No person among you shall eat blood, nor shall any alien who resides among you eat blood. [13]And anyone of the people of Israel, or of the aliens who reside among them, who hunts down an animal or bird that may be eaten shall pour out its blood and cover it with earth.

14 For the life of every creature—its blood is its life; therefore I have said to the people of Israel: You shall not eat the blood of any creature, for the life of every creature is its blood; whoever eats it shall be cut off. [15]All persons, citizens or aliens, who eat what dies of itself or what has been torn by wild animals, shall wash their clothes, and bathe themselves in water, and be unclean until the evening; then they shall be clean. [16]But if they do not wash themselves or bathe their body, they shall bear their guilt.

Sexual Relations

18 The LORD spoke to Moses, saying: 2 Speak to the people of Israel and say to them: I am the LORD your God. [3]You shall not do as they do in the land of Egypt, where you lived, and you shall not do as they do in the land of Cā́-naan, to which I am bringing you. You shall not follow their statutes. [4]My ordinances you shall observe and my

statutes you shall keep, following them: I am the LORD your God. [5]You shall keep my statutes and my ordinances; by doing so one shall live: I am the LORD.

6 None of you shall approach anyone near of kin to uncover nakedness: I am the LORD. [7]You shall not uncover the nakedness of your father, which is the nakedness of your mother; she is your mother, you shall not uncover her nakedness. [8]You shall not uncover the nakedness of your father's wife; it is the nakedness of your father. [9]You shall not uncover the nakedness of your sister, your father's daughter or your mother's daughter, whether born at home or born abroad. [10]You shall not uncover the nakedness of your son's daughter or of your daughter's daughter, for their nakedness is your own nakedness. [11]You shall not uncover the nakedness of your father's wife's daughter, begotten by your father, since she is your sister. [12]You shall not uncover the nakedness of your father's sister; she is your father's flesh. [13]You shall not uncover the nakedness of your mother's sister, for she is your mother's flesh. [14]You shall not uncover the nakedness of your father's brother, that is, you shall not approach his wife; she is your aunt. [15]You shall not uncover the nakedness of your daughter-in-law: she is your son's wife; you shall not uncover her nakedness. [16]You shall not uncover the nakedness of your brother's wife; it is your brother's nakedness. [17]You shall not uncover the nakedness of a woman and her daughter, and you shall not take[z] her son's daughter or her daughter's daughter to uncover her nakedness; they are your[a] flesh; it is depravity. [18]And you shall not take[z] a woman as a rival to her sister, uncovering her nakedness while her sister is still alive.

19 You shall not approach a woman to uncover her nakedness while she is in her menstrual uncleanness. [20]You shall not have sexual relations with your kins-

[z] Or *marry*   [a] Gk: Heb lacks *your*

man's wife, and defile yourself with her. [21]You shall not give any of your offspring to sacrifice them[b] to Mōʹlech, and so profane the name of your God: I am the LORD. [22]You shall not lie with a male as with a woman; it is an abomination. [23]You shall not have sexual relations with any animal and defile yourself with it, nor shall any woman give herself to an animal to have sexual relations with it: it is perversion.

24 Do not defile yourselves in any of these ways, for by all these practices the nations I am casting out before you have defiled themselves. [25]Thus the land became defiled; and I punished it for its iniquity, and the land vomited out its inhabitants. [26]But you shall keep my statutes and my ordinances and commit none of these abominations, either the citizen or the alien who resides among you [27](for the inhabitants of the land, who were before you, committed all of these abominations, and the land became defiled); [28]otherwise the land will vomit you out for defiling it, as it vomited out the nation that was before you. [29]For whoever commits any of these abominations shall be cut off from their people. [30]So keep my charge not to commit any of these abominations that were done before you, and not to defile yourselves by them: I am the LORD your God.

Ritual and Moral Holiness

19 The LORD spoke to Moses, saying: 2 Speak to all the congregation of the people of Israel and say to them: You shall be holy, for I the LORD your God am holy. [3]You shall each revere your mother and father, and you shall keep my sabbaths: I am the LORD your God. [4]Do not turn to idols or make cast images for yourselves: I am the LORD your God.

5 When you offer a sacrifice of well-being to the LORD, offer it in such a way that it is acceptable on your behalf. [6]It shall be eaten on the same day you offer it, or on the next day; and anything left over until the third day shall be consumed in fire. [7]If it is eaten at all on the third day, it is an abomination; it will not be acceptable. [8]All who eat it shall be subject to punishment, because they have profaned what is holy to the LORD; and any such person shall be cut off from the people.

9 When you reap the harvest of your land, you shall not reap to the very edges of your field, or gather the gleanings of your harvest. [10]You shall not strip your vineyard bare, or gather the fallen grapes of your vineyard; you shall leave them for the poor and the alien: I am the LORD your God.

11 You shall not steal; you shall not deal falsely; and you shall not lie to one another. [12]And you shall not swear falsely by my name, profaning the name of your God: I am the LORD.

13 You shall not defraud your neighbor; you shall not steal; and you shall not keep for yourself the wages of a laborer until morning. [14]You shall not revile the deaf or put a stumbling block before the blind; you shall fear your God: I am the LORD.

15 You shall not render an unjust judgment; you shall not be partial to the poor or defer to the great: with justice you shall judge your neighbor. [16]You shall not go around as a slanderer[c] among your people, and you shall not profit by the blood[d] of your neighbor: I am the LORD.

17 You shall not hate in your heart anyone of your kin; you shall reprove your neighbor, or you will incur guilt yourself. [18]You shall not take vengeance or bear a grudge against any of your people, but you shall love your neighbor as yourself: I am the LORD.

19 You shall keep my statutes. You shall not let your animals breed with a

---

[b] Heb *to pass them over*   [c] Meaning of Heb uncertain   [d] Heb *stand against the blood*

different kind; you shall not sow your field with two kinds of seed; nor shall you put on a garment made of two different materials.

20 If a man has sexual relations with a woman who is a slave, designated for another man but not ransomed or given her freedom, an inquiry shall be held. They shall not be put to death, since she has not been freed; ²¹but he shall bring a guilt offering for himself to the LORD, at the entrance of the tent of meeting, a ram as guilt offering. ²²And the priest shall make atonement for him with the ram of guilt offering before the LORD for his sin that he committed; and the sin he committed shall be forgiven him.

23 When you come into the land and plant all kinds of trees for food, then you shall regard their fruit as forbidden;^e three years it shall be forbidden^f to you, it must not be eaten. ²⁴In the fourth year all their fruit shall be set apart for rejoicing in the LORD. ²⁵But in the fifth year you may eat of their fruit, that their yield may be increased for you: I am the LORD your God.

26 You shall not eat anything with its blood. You shall not practice augury or witchcraft. ²⁷You shall not round off the hair on your temples or mar the edges of your beard. ²⁸You shall not make any gashes in your flesh for the dead or tattoo any marks upon you: I am the LORD.

29 Do not profane your daughter by making her a prostitute, that the land not become prostituted and full of depravity. ³⁰You shall keep my sabbaths and reverence my sanctuary: I am the LORD.

31 Do not turn to mediums or wizards; do not seek them out, to be defiled by them: I am the LORD your God.

32 You shall rise before the aged, and defer to the old; and you shall fear your God: I am the LORD.

33 When an alien resides with you in your land, you shall not oppress the alien. ³⁴The alien who resides with you shall be to you as the citizen among you; you shall love the alien as yourself, for you were aliens in the land of Egypt: I am the LORD your God.

35 You shall not cheat in measuring length, weight, or quantity. ³⁶You shall have honest balances, honest weights, an honest ephah, and an honest hin: I am the LORD your God, who brought you out of the land of Egypt. ³⁷You shall keep all my statutes and all my ordinances, and observe them: I am the LORD.

Penalties for Violations of Holiness

20 The LORD spoke to Moses, saying: ²Say further to the people of Israel:

Any of the people of Israel, or of the aliens who reside in Israel, who give any of their offspring to Mŏʹlech shall be put to death; the people of the land shall stone them to death. ³I myself will set my face against them, and will cut them off from the people, because they have given of their offspring to Mŏʹlech, defiling my sanctuary and profaning my holy name. ⁴And if the people of the land should ever close their eyes to them, when they give of their offspring to Mŏʹlech, and do not put them to death, ⁵I myself will set my face against them and against their family, and will cut them off from among their people, them and all who follow them in prostituting themselves to Mŏʹlech.

6 If any turn to mediums and wizards, prostituting themselves to them, I will set my face against them, and will cut them off from the people. ⁷Consecrate yourselves therefore, and be holy; for I am the LORD your God. ⁸Keep my statutes, and observe them; I am the LORD; I sanctify you. ⁹All who curse father or mother shall be put to death; having cursed father or mother, their blood is upon them.

^e Heb as their uncircumcision   ^f Heb uncircumcision

10 If a man commits adultery with the wife of[g] his neighbor, both the adulterer and the adulteress shall be put to death. [11]The man who lies with his father's wife has uncovered his father's nakedness; both of them shall be put to death; their blood is upon them. [12]If a man lies with his daughter-in-law, both of them shall be put to death; they have committed perversion, their blood is upon them. [13]If a man lies with a male as with a woman, both of them have committed an abomination; they shall be put to death; their blood is upon them. [14]If a man takes a wife and her mother also, it is depravity; they shall be burned to death, both he and they, that there may be no depravity among you. [15]If a man has sexual relations with an animal, he shall be put to death; and you shall kill the animal. [16]If a woman approaches any animal and has sexual relations with it, you shall kill the woman and the animal; they shall be put to death, their blood is upon them.

17 If a man takes his sister, a daughter of his father or a daughter of his mother, and sees her nakedness, and she sees his nakedness, it is a disgrace, and they shall be cut off in the sight of their people; he has uncovered his sister's nakedness, he shall be subject to punishment. [18]If a man lies with a woman having her sickness and uncovers her nakedness, he has laid bare her flow and she has laid bare her flow of blood; both of them shall be cut off from their people. [19]You shall not uncover the nakedness of your mother's sister or of your father's sister, for that is to lay bare one's own flesh; they shall be subject to punishment. [20]If a man lies with his uncle's wife, he has uncovered his uncle's nakedness; they shall be subject to punishment; they shall die childless. [21]If a man takes his brother's wife, it is impurity; he has uncovered his brother's nakedness; they shall be childless.

22 You shall keep all my statutes and all my ordinances, and observe them, so that the land to which I bring you to settle in may not vomit you out. [23]You shall not follow the practices of the nation that I am driving out before you. Because they did all these things, I abhorred them. [24]But I have said to you: You shall inherit their land, and I will give it to you to possess, a land flowing with milk and honey. I am the LORD your God; I have separated you from the peoples. [25]You shall therefore make a distinction between the clean animal and the unclean, and between the unclean bird and the clean; you shall not bring abomination on yourselves by animal or by bird or by anything with which the ground teems, which I have set apart for you to hold unclean. [26]You shall be holy to me; for I the LORD am holy, and I have separated you from the other peoples to be mine.

27 A man or a woman who is a medium or a wizard shall be put to death; they shall be stoned to death, their blood is upon them.

The Holiness of Priests

21 The LORD said to Moses: Speak to the priests, the sons of Aaron, and say to them:

No one shall defile himself for a dead person among his relatives, [2]except for his nearest kin: his mother, his father, his son, his daughter, his brother; [3]likewise, for a virgin sister, close to him because she has had no husband, he may defile himself for her. [4]But he shall not defile himself as a husband among his people and so profane himself. [5]They shall not make bald spots upon their heads, or shave off the edges of their beards, or make any gashes in their flesh. [6]They shall be holy to their God, and not profane the name of their God; for they offer the LORD's offerings by fire, the food of their God; therefore they

[g] Heb repeats *if a man commits adultery with the wife of*

shall be holy. [7]They shall not marry a prostitute or a woman who has been defiled; neither shall they marry a woman divorced from her husband. For they are holy to their God, [8]and you shall treat them as holy, since they offer the food of your God; they shall be holy to you, for I the LORD, I who sanctify you, am holy. [9]When the daughter of a priest profanes herself through prostitution, she profanes her father; she shall be burned to death.

10 The priest who is exalted above his fellows, on whose head the anointing oil has been poured and who has been consecrated to wear the vestments, shall not dishevel his hair, nor tear his vestments. [11]He shall not go where there is a dead body; he shall not defile himself even for his father or mother. [12]He shall not go outside the sanctuary and thus profane the sanctuary of his God; for the consecration of the anointing oil of his God is upon him: I am the LORD. [13]He shall marry only a woman who is a virgin. [14]A widow, or a divorced woman, or a woman who has been defiled, a prostitute, these he shall not marry. He shall marry a virgin of his own kin, [15]that he may not profane his offspring among his kin; for I am the LORD; I sanctify him.

16 The LORD spoke to Moses, saying: [17]Speak to Aaron and say: No one of your offspring throughout their generations who has a blemish may approach to offer the food of his God. [18]For no one who has a blemish shall draw near, one who is blind or lame, or one who has a mutilated face or a limb too long, [19]or one who has a broken foot or a broken hand, [20]or a hunchback, or a dwarf, or a man with a blemish in his eyes or an itching disease or scabs or crushed testicles. [21]No descendant of Aaron the priest who has a blemish shall come near to offer the LORD's offerings by fire; since he has a blemish, he shall not come near to offer the food of his God. [22]He may eat the food of his God, of the most holy as

well as of the holy. [23]But he shall not come near the curtain or approach the altar, because he has a blemish, that he may not profane my sanctuaries; for I am the LORD; I sanctify them. [24]Thus Moses spoke to Aaron and to his sons and to all the people of Israel.

The Use of Holy Offerings

22 The LORD spoke to Moses, saying: [2]Direct Aaron and his sons to deal carefully with the sacred donations of the people of Israel, which they dedicate to me, so that they may not profane my holy name; I am the LORD. [3]Say to them: If anyone among all your offspring throughout your generations comes near the sacred donations, which the people of Israel dedicate to the LORD, while he is in a state of uncleanness, that person shall be cut off from my presence: I am the LORD. [4]No one of Aaron's offspring who has a leprous[h] disease or suffers a discharge may eat of the sacred donations until he is clean. Whoever touches anything made unclean by a corpse or a man who has had an emission of semen, [5]and whoever touches any swarming thing by which he may be made unclean or any human being by whom he may be made unclean—whatever his uncleanness may be— [6]the person who touches any such shall be unclean until evening and shall not eat of the sacred donations unless he has washed his body in water. [7]When the sun sets he shall be clean; and afterward he may eat of the sacred donations, for they are his food. [8]That which died or was torn by wild animals he shall not eat, becoming unclean by it: I am the LORD. [9]They shall keep my charge, so that they may not incur guilt and die in the sanctuary[i] for having profaned it: I am the LORD; I sanctify them.

10 No lay person shall eat of the sacred donations. No bound or hired servant of the priest shall eat of the

[h] A term for several skin diseases; precise meaning uncertain   [i] Vg: Heb *incur guilt for it and die in it*

sacred donations; [11]but if a priest acquires anyone by purchase, the person may eat of them; and those that are born in his house may eat of his food. [12]If a priest's daughter marries a layman, she shall not eat of the offering of the sacred donations; [13]but if a priest's daughter is widowed or divorced, without offspring, and returns to her father's house, as in her youth, she may eat of her father's food. No lay person shall eat of it. [14]If a man eats of the sacred donation unintentionally, he shall add one-fifth of its value to it, and give the sacred donation to the priest. [15]No one shall profane the sacred donations of the people of Israel, which they offer to the LORD, [16]causing them to bear guilt requiring a guilt offering, by eating their sacred donations: for I am the LORD; I sanctify them.

Acceptable Offerings

17 The LORD spoke to Moses, saying: [18]Speak to Aaron and his sons and all the people of Israel and say to them: When anyone of the house of Israel or of the aliens residing in Israel presents an offering, whether in payment of a vow or as a freewill offering that is offered to the LORD as a burnt offering, [19]to be acceptable in your behalf it shall be a male without blemish, of the cattle or the sheep or the goats. [20]You shall not offer anything that has a blemish, for it will not be acceptable in your behalf.

21 When anyone offers a sacrifice of well-being to the LORD, in fulfillment of a vow or as a freewill offering, from the herd or from the flock, to be acceptable it must be perfect; there shall be no blemish in it. [22]Anything blind, or injured, or maimed, or having a discharge or an itch or scabs—these you shall not offer to the LORD or put any of them on the altar as offerings by fire to the LORD. [23]An ox or a lamb that has a limb too long or too short you may present for a freewill offering; but it will not be accepted for a vow. [24]Any animal that

Sheep were important animals to the Israelites. They used sheep for food, such as meat, milk, and cheese. They also used sheep wool to make clothes. A lamb, or young sheep, was something of great value. When the people offered a lamb as a sacrifice to God, they were giving God their very best.

has its testicles bruised or crushed or torn or cut, you shall not offer to the LORD; such you shall not do within your land, [25]nor shall you accept any such animals from a foreigner to offer as food to your God; since they are mutilated, with a blemish in them, they shall not be accepted in your behalf.

26 The LORD spoke to Moses, saying: [27]When an ox or a sheep or a goat is born, it shall remain seven days with its mother, and from the eighth day on it shall be acceptable as the LORD's offering by fire. [28]But you shall not slaughter, from the herd or the flock, an animal with its young on the same day. [29]When you sacrifice a thanksgiving offering to the LORD, you shall sacrifice it so that it may be acceptable in your behalf. [30]It shall be eaten on the same day; you shall not leave any of it until morning: I am the LORD.

31 Thus you shall keep my commandments and observe them: I am the LORD. [32]You shall not profane my holy name, that I may be sanctified among the people of Israel: I am the LORD; I sanctify you, [33]I who brought you out of the land of Egypt to be your God: I am the LORD.

Appointed Festivals

23 The LORD spoke to Moses, saying: [2]Speak to the people of Israel and say to them: These are the appointed festivals of the LORD that you

Barley is a plant that looks like tall grass. People in Bible times used barley as food for themselves and their animals. Barley was very important to the poor because it was their main food. Every year when it was time to gather the barley, the people would give what they gathered first as an offering to God.

shall proclaim as holy convocations, my appointed festivals.

The Sabbath, Passover, and Unleavened Bread

3 Six days shall work be done; but the seventh day is a sabbath of complete rest, a holy convocation; you shall do no work: it is a sabbath to the LORD throughout your settlements.

4 These are the appointed festivals of the LORD, the holy convocations, which you shall celebrate at the time appointed for them. [5]In the first month, on the fourteenth day of the month, at twilight,[j] there shall be a passover offering to the LORD, [6]and on the fifteenth day of the same month is the festival of unleavened bread to the LORD; seven days you shall eat unleavened bread. [7]On the first day you shall have a holy convocation; you shall not work at your occupations. [8]For seven days you shall present the LORD's offerings by fire; on the seventh day there shall be a holy convocation: you shall not work at your occupations.

The Offering of First Fruits

9 The LORD spoke to Moses: [10]Speak to the people of Israel and say to them: When you enter the land that I am giving you and you reap its harvest, you shall bring the sheaf of the first fruits of your harvest to the priest. [11]He shall raise the sheaf before the LORD, that you may find acceptance; on the day after the sabbath

the priest shall raise it. [12]On the day when you raise the sheaf, you shall offer a lamb a year old, without blemish, as a burnt offering to the LORD. [13]And the grain offering with it shall be two-tenths of an ephah of choice flour mixed with oil, an offering by fire of pleasing odor to the LORD; and the drink offering with it shall be of wine, one-fourth of a hin. [14]You shall eat no bread or parched grain or fresh ears until that very day, until you have brought the offering of your God: it is a statute forever throughout your generations in all your settlements.

The Festival of Weeks

15 And from the day after the sabbath, from the day on which you bring the sheaf of the elevation offering, you shall count off seven weeks; they shall be complete. [16]You shall count until the day after the seventh sabbath, fifty days; then you shall present an offering of new grain to the LORD. [17]You shall bring from your settlements two loaves of bread as an elevation offering, each made of two-tenths of an ephah; they shall be of choice flour, baked with leaven, as first fruits to the LORD. [18]You shall present with the bread seven lambs a year old without blemish, one young bull, and two rams; they shall be a burnt offering to the LORD, along with their grain offering and their drink offerings, an offering

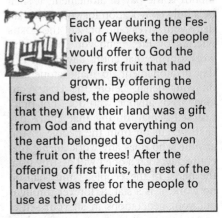

Each year during the Festival of Weeks, the people would offer to God the very first fruit that had grown. By offering the first and best, the people showed that they knew their land was a gift from God and that everything on the earth belonged to God—even the fruit on the trees! After the offering of first fruits, the rest of the harvest was free for the people to use as they needed.

[j] Heb *between the two evenings*

by fire of pleasing odor to the LORD. [19]You shall also offer one male goat for a sin offering, and two male lambs a year old as a sacrifice of well-being. [20]The priest shall raise them with the bread of the first fruits as an elevation offering before the LORD, together with the two lambs; they shall be holy to the LORD for the priest. [21]On that same day you shall make proclamation; you shall hold a holy convocation; you shall not work at your occupations. This is a statute forever in all your settlements throughout your generations.

22 When you reap the harvest of your land, you shall not reap to the very edges of your field, or gather the gleanings of your harvest; you shall leave them for the poor and for the alien: I am the LORD your God.

The Festival of Trumpets

23 The LORD spoke to Moses, saying: [24]Speak to the people of Israel, saying: In the seventh month, on the first day of the month, you shall observe a day of complete rest, a holy convocation commemorated with trumpet blasts. [25]You shall not work at your occupations; and you shall present the LORD's offering by fire.

The Day of Atonement

26 The LORD spoke to Moses, saying: [27]Now, the tenth day of this seventh month is the day of atonement; it shall be a holy convocation for you: you shall deny yourselves[k] and present the LORD's offering by fire; [28]and you shall do no work during that entire day; for it is a day of atonement, to make atonement on your behalf before the LORD your God. [29]For anyone who does not practice self-denial[l] during that entire day shall be cut off from the people. [30]And anyone who does any work during that entire day, such a one I will destroy from the midst of the people. [31]You shall do no work: it is a statute forever throughout your generations in all your settlements. [32]It shall be to you a sabbath of

The people of Israel celebrated the Feast of Booths every year. Each family built a booth out of branches and vines when it was almost harvest time. The father and oldest son slept in the booth to guard the grain as it finished growing. During the feast, the family ate meals in the booth for seven days. The Feast of Booths reminded the people of their long journey from Egypt to the promised land of Canaan.

complete rest, and you shall deny yourselves;[l] on the ninth day of the month at evening, from evening to evening you shall keep your sabbath.

The Festival of Booths

33 The LORD spoke to Moses, saying: [34]Speak to the people of Israel, saying: On the fifteenth day of this seventh month, and lasting seven days, there shall be the festival of booths[m] to the LORD. [35]The first day shall be a holy convocation; you shall not work at your occupations. [36]Seven days you shall present the LORD's offerings by fire; on the eighth day you shall observe a holy convocation and present the LORD's offerings by fire; it is a solemn assembly; you shall not work at your occupations.

37 These are the appointed festivals of the LORD, which you shall celebrate as times of holy convocation, for presenting to the LORD offerings by fire—burnt offerings and grain offerings, sacrifices and drink offerings, each on its proper day— [38]apart from the sabbaths of the LORD, and apart from your gifts, and apart from all your votive offerings, and apart from all your freewill offerings, which you give to the LORD.

[k] Or *shall fast*   [l] Or *does not fast*   [m] Or *tabernacles*: Heb *succoth*

39 Now, the fifteenth day of the seventh month, when you have gathered in the produce of the land, you shall keep the festival of the LORD, lasting seven days; a complete rest on the first day, and a complete rest on the eighth day. [40]On the first day you shall take the fruit of majestic[n] trees, branches of palm trees, boughs of leafy trees, and willows of the brook; and you shall rejoice before the LORD your God for seven days. [41]You shall keep it as a festival to the LORD seven days in the year; you shall keep it in the seventh month as a statute forever throughout your generations. [42]You shall live in booths for seven days; all that are citizens in Israel shall live in booths, [43]so that your generations may know that I made the people of Israel live in booths when I brought them out of the land of Egypt: I am the LORD your God.

44 Thus Moses declared to the people of Israel the appointed festivals of the LORD.

The Lamp

24 The LORD spoke to Moses, saying: [2]Command the people of Israel to bring you pure oil of beaten olives for the lamp, that a light may be kept burning regularly. [3]Aaron shall set it up in the tent of meeting, outside the curtain of the covenant,[o] to burn from evening to morning before the LORD regularly; it shall be a statute forever throughout your generations. [4]He shall set up the lamps on the lampstand of pure gold[p] before the LORD regularly.

The Bread for the Tabernacle

5 You shall take choice flour, and bake twelve loaves of it; two-tenths of an ephah shall be in each loaf. [6]You shall place them in two rows, six in a row, on the table of pure gold.[q] [7]You shall put pure frankincense with each row, to be a token offering for the bread, as an offering by fire to the LORD. [8]Every sabbath day Aaron shall set them in order before the LORD regularly as a commitment of the people of Israel, as a covenant forever. [9]They shall be for Aaron and his descendants, who shall eat them in a holy place, for they are most holy portions for him from the offerings by fire to the LORD, a perpetual due.

Blasphemy and Its Punishment

10 A man whose mother was an Israelite and whose father was an Egyptian came out among the people of Israel; and the Israelite woman's son and a certain Israelite began fighting in the camp. [11]The Israelite woman's son blasphemed the Name in a curse. And they brought him to Moses—now his mother's name was She·lō'mith, daughter of Dib'rī, of the tribe of Dan— [12]and they put him in custody, until the decision of the LORD should be made clear to them.

13 The LORD said to Moses, saying: [14]Take the blasphemer outside the camp; and let all who were within hearing lay their hands on his head, and let the whole congregation stone him. [15]And speak to the people of Israel, saying: Anyone who curses God shall bear the sin. [16]One who blasphemes the name of the LORD shall be put to death; the whole congregation shall stone the blasphemer. Aliens as well as citizens, when they blaspheme the Name, shall be put to death. [17]Anyone who kills a human being shall be put to death. [18]Anyone who kills an animal shall make restitution for it, life for life. [19]Anyone who maims another shall suffer the same injury in return: [20]fracture for fracture, eye for eye, tooth for tooth; the injury inflicted is the injury to be suffered. [21]One who kills an animal shall make restitution for it; but one who kills a human being shall be put to death. [22]You shall have one law for the alien and for the citizen: for I am the LORD your God. [23]Moses spoke thus to the people of Israel; and they took the blasphemer outside the camp, and stoned him to death. The people of Israel did as the LORD had commanded Moses.

[n] Meaning of Heb uncertain   [o] Or *treaty,* or *testament;* Heb *eduth*   [p] Heb *pure lampstand*   [q] Heb *pure table*

A jubilee is a time of celebration! God told the people that every fifty years they were supposed to free all slaves, cancel all debts, and give all land back to the people who owned it first. This was called the "year of jubilee."

The Sabbatical Year

25 The LORD spoke to Moses on Mount Sinai, saying: ²Speak to the people of Israel and say to them: When you enter the land that I am giving you, the land shall observe a sabbath for the LORD. ³Six years you shall sow your field, and six years you shall prune your vineyard, and gather in their yield; ⁴but in the seventh year there shall be a sabbath of complete rest for the land, a sabbath for the LORD: you shall not sow your field or prune your vineyard. ⁵You shall not reap the aftergrowth of your harvest or gather the grapes of your unpruned vine: it shall be a year of complete rest for the land. ⁶You may eat what the land yields during its sabbath—you, your male and female slaves, your hired and your bound laborers who live with you; ⁷for your livestock also, and for the wild animals in your land all its yield shall be for food.

The Year of Jubilee

8 You shall count off seven weeks^r of years, seven times seven years, so that the period of seven weeks of years gives forty-nine years. ⁹Then you shall have the trumpet sounded loud; on the tenth day of the seventh month—on the day of atonement—you shall have the trumpet sounded throughout all your land. ¹⁰And you shall hallow the fiftieth year and you shall proclaim liberty throughout the land to all its inhabitants. It shall be a jubilee for you: you shall return, every one of you, to your property and every one of you to your family. ¹¹That fiftieth

year shall be a jubilee for you: you shall not sow, or reap the aftergrowth, or harvest the unpruned vines. ¹²For it is a jubilee; it shall be holy to you: you shall eat only what the field itself produces.

13 In this year of jubilee you shall return, every one of you, to your property. ¹⁴When you make a sale to your neighbor or buy from your neighbor, you shall not cheat one another. ¹⁵When you buy from your neighbor, you shall pay only for the number of years since the jubilee; the seller shall charge you only for the remaining crop years. ¹⁶If the years are more, you shall increase the price, and if the years are fewer, you shall diminish the price; for it is a certain number of harvests that are being sold to you. ¹⁷You shall not cheat one another, but you shall fear your God; for I am the LORD your God.

18 You shall observe my statutes and faithfully keep my ordinances, so that you may live on the land securely. ¹⁹The land will yield its fruit, and you will eat your fill and live on it securely. ²⁰Should you ask, "What shall we eat in the seventh year, if we may not sow or gather in our crop?" ²¹I will order my blessing for you in the sixth year, so that it will yield a crop for three years. ²²When you sow in the eighth year, you will be eating from the old crop; until the ninth year, when its produce comes in, you shall eat the old. ²³The land shall not be sold in perpetuity, for the land is mine; with me you are but aliens and tenants. ²⁴Throughout the land that you hold, you shall provide for the redemption of the land.

25 If anyone of your kin falls into difficulty and sells a piece of property, then the next of kin shall come and redeem what the relative has sold. ²⁶If the person has no one to redeem it, but then prospers and finds sufficient means to do so, ²⁷the years since its sale shall be computed and the difference shall be refunded to the person to whom it was sold, and the property shall be returned.

^{r} Or *sabbaths*

²⁸But if there are not sufficient means to recover it, what was sold shall remain with the purchaser until the year of jubilee; in the jubilee it shall be released, and the property shall be returned.

29 If anyone sells a dwelling house in a walled city, it may be redeemed until a year has elapsed since its sale; the right of redemption shall be one year. ³⁰If it is not redeemed before a full year has elapsed, a house that is in a walled city shall pass in perpetuity to the purchaser, throughout the generations; it shall not be released in the jubilee. ³¹But houses in villages that have no walls around them shall be classed as open country; they may be redeemed, and they shall be released in the jubilee. ³²As for the cities of the Lĕʹvītes, the Lĕʹvītes shall forever have the right of redemption of the houses in the cities belonging to them. ³³Such property as may be redeemed from the Lĕʹvītes— houses sold in a city belonging to them— shall be released in the jubilee; because the houses in the cities of the Lĕʹvītes are their possession among the people of Israel. ³⁴But the open land around their cities may not be sold; for that is their possession for all time.

35 If any of your kin fall into difficulty and become dependent on you,ˢ you shall support them; they shall live with you as though resident aliens. ³⁶Do not take interest in advance or otherwise make a profit from them, but fear your God; let them live with you. ³⁷You shall not lend them your money at interest taken in advance, or provide them food at a profit. ³⁸I am the LORD your God, who brought you out of the land of Egypt, to give you the land of Cāʹnaan, to be your God.

39 If any who are dependent on you become so impoverished that they sell themselves to you, you shall not make them serve as slaves. ⁴⁰They shall remain with you as hired or bound laborers. They shall serve with you until the year of the jubilee. ⁴¹Then they and their children with them shall be free from your author-

ity; they shall go back to their own family and return to their ancestral property. ⁴²For they are my servants, whom I brought out of the land of Egypt; they shall not be sold as slaves are sold. ⁴³You shall not rule over them with harshness, but shall fear your God. ⁴⁴As for the male and female slaves whom you may have, it is from the nations around you that you may acquire male and female slaves. ⁴⁵You may also acquire them from among the aliens residing with you, and from their families that are with you, who have been born in your land; and they may be your property. ⁴⁶You may keep them as a possession for your children after you, for them to inherit as property. These you may treat as slaves, but as for your fellow Israelites, no one shall rule over the other with harshness.

47 If resident aliens among you prosper, and if any of your kin fall into difficulty with one of them and sell themselves to an alien, or to a branch of the alien's family, ⁴⁸after they have sold themselves they shall have the right of redemption; one of their brothers may redeem them, ⁴⁹or their uncle or their uncle's son may redeem them, or anyone of their family who is of their own flesh may redeem them; or if they prosper they may redeem themselves. ⁵⁰They shall compute with the purchaser the total from the year when they sold themselves to the alien until the jubilee year; the price of the sale shall be applied to the number of years: the time they were with the owner shall be rated as the time of a hired laborer. ⁵¹If many years remain, they shall pay for their redemption in proportion to the purchase price; ⁵²and if few years remain until the jubilee year, they shall compute thus: according to the years involved they shall make payment for their redemption. ⁵³As a laborer hired by the year they shall be under the alien's authority, who shall not, however, rule with harshness over them in your sight. ⁵⁴And if they have not been redeemed in any of these ways, they and

ˢ Meaning of Heb uncertain

"I am the LORD your God who brought you out of the land of Egypt, to be their slaves no more; I have broken the bars of your yoke and made you walk erect." Leviticus 26:13

their children with them shall go free in the jubilee year. ⁵⁵For to me the people of Israel are servants; they are my servants whom I brought out from the land of Egypt: I am the LORD your God.

Rewards for Obedience

26 You shall make for yourselves no idols and erect no carved images or pillars, and you shall not place figured stones in your land, to worship at them; for I am the LORD your God. ²You shall keep my sabbaths and reverence my sanctuary: I am the LORD.

3 If you follow my statutes and keep my commandments and observe them faithfully, ⁴I will give you your rains in their season, and the land shall yield its produce, and the trees of the field shall yield their fruit. ⁵Your threshing shall overtake the vintage, and the vintage shall overtake the sowing; you shall eat your bread to the full, and live securely in your land. ⁶And I will grant peace in the land, and you shall lie down, and no one shall make you afraid; I will remove dangerous animals from the land, and no sword shall go through your land. ⁷You shall give chase to your enemies, and they shall fall before you by the sword. ⁸Five of you shall give chase to a hundred, and a hundred of you shall give chase to ten thousand; your enemies shall fall before you by the sword. ⁹I will look with favor upon you and make you fruitful and multiply you; and I will maintain my covenant with you. ¹⁰You shall eat old grain long stored, and you shall have to clear out the old to make way for the new. ¹¹I will place my dwelling in your midst, and I shall not abhor you.

¹²And I will walk among you, and will be your God, and you shall be my people. ¹³I am the LORD your God who brought you out of the land of Egypt, to be their slaves no more; I have broken the bars of your yoke and made you walk erect.

Penalties for Disobedience

14 But if you will not obey me, and do not observe all these commandments, ¹⁵if you spurn my statutes, and abhor my ordinances, so that you will not observe all my commandments, and you break my covenant, ¹⁶I in turn will do this to you: I will bring terror on you; consumption and fever that waste the eyes and cause life to pine away. You shall sow your seed in vain, for your enemies shall eat it. ¹⁷I will set my face against you, and you shall be struck down by your enemies; your foes shall rule over you, and you shall flee though no one pursues you. ¹⁸And if in spite of this you will not obey me, I will continue to punish you sevenfold for your sins. ¹⁹I will break your proud glory, and I will make your sky like iron and your earth like copper. ²⁰Your strength shall be spent to no purpose: your land shall not yield its produce, and the trees of the land shall not yield their fruit.

21 If you continue hostile to me, and will not obey me, I will continue to plague you sevenfold for your sins. ²²I will let loose wild animals against you, and they shall bereave you of your children and destroy your livestock; they shall make you few in number, and your roads shall be deserted.

23 If in spite of these punishments you have not turned back to me, but continue hostile to me, ²⁴then I too will continue hostile to you: I myself will strike you sevenfold for your sins. ²⁵I will bring the sword against you, executing vengeance for the covenant; and if you withdraw within your cities, I will send pestilence among you, and you shall be delivered into enemy hands. ²⁶When I break your staff of bread, ten

women shall bake your bread in a single oven, and they shall dole out your bread by weight; and though you eat, you shall not be satisfied.

27 But if, despite this, you disobey me, and continue hostile to me, ²⁸I will continue hostile to you in fury; I in turn will punish you myself sevenfold for your sins. ²⁹You shall eat the flesh of your sons, and you shall eat the flesh of your daughters. ³⁰I will destroy your high places and cut down your incense altars; I will heap your carcasses on the carcasses of your idols. I will abhor you. ³¹I will lay your cities waste, will make your sanctuaries desolate, and I will not smell your pleasing odors. ³²I will devastate the land, so that your enemies who come to settle in it shall be appalled at it. ³³And you I will scatter among the nations, and I will unsheathe the sword against you; your land shall be a desolation, and your cities a waste.

34 Then the land shall enjoy[t] its sabbath years as long as it lies desolate, while you are in the land of your enemies; then the land shall rest, and enjoy[t] its sabbath years. ³⁵As long as it lies desolate, it shall have the rest it did not have on your sabbaths when you were living on it. ³⁶And as for those of you who survive, I will send faintness into their hearts in the lands of their enemies; the sound of a driven leaf shall put them to flight, and they shall flee as one flees from the sword, and they shall fall though no one pursues. ³⁷They shall stumble over one another, as if to escape a sword, though no one pursues; and you shall have no power to stand against your enemies. ³⁸You shall perish among the nations, and the land of your enemies shall devour you. ³⁹And those of you who survive shall languish in the land of your enemies because of their iniquities; also they shall languish because of the iniquities of their ancestors.

40 But if they confess their iniquity and the iniquity of their ancestors, in that they committed treachery against me and, moreover, that they continued hostile to me— ⁴¹so that I, in turn, continued hostile to them and brought them into the land of their enemies; if then their uncircumcised heart is humbled and they make amends for their iniquity, ⁴²then will I remember my covenant with Jacob; I will remember also my covenant with Isaac and also my covenant with Abraham, and I will remember the land. ⁴³For the land shall be deserted by them, and enjoy[t] its sabbath years by lying desolate without them, while they shall make amends for their iniquity, because they dared to spurn my ordinances, and they abhorred my statutes. ⁴⁴Yet for all that, when they are in the land of their enemies, I will not spurn them, or abhor them so as to destroy them utterly and break my covenant with them; for I am the LORD their God; ⁴⁵but I will remember in their favor the covenant with their ancestors whom I brought out of the land of Egypt in the sight of the nations, to be their God: I am the LORD.

46 These are the statutes and ordinances and laws that the LORD established between himself and the people of Israel on Mount Sinai through Moses.

Votive Offerings

27 The LORD spoke to Moses, saying: ²Speak to the people of Israel and say to them: When a person makes an explicit vow to the LORD concerning the equivalent for a human being, ³the equivalent for a male shall be: from twenty to sixty years of age the equivalent shall be fifty shekels of silver by the sanctuary shekel. ⁴If the person is a female, the equivalent is thirty shekels. ⁵If the age is from five to twenty years of age, the equivalent is twenty shekels for a male and ten shekels for a female. ⁶If the age is from one month to five years, the equivalent for a male is five shekels of silver, and for a female the equivalent is three shekels

_____
[t] Or make up for

of silver. [7]And if the person is sixty years old or over, then the equivalent for a male is fifteen shekels, and for a female ten shekels. [8]If any cannot afford the equivalent, they shall be brought before the priest and the priest shall assess them; the priest shall assess them according to what each one making a vow can afford.

9 If it concerns an animal that may be brought as an offering to the LORD, any such that may be given to the LORD shall be holy. [10]Another shall not be exchanged or substituted for it, either good for bad or bad for good; and if one animal is substituted for another, both that one and its substitute shall be holy. [11]If it concerns any unclean animal that may not be brought as an offering to the LORD, the animal shall be presented before the priest. [12]The priest shall assess it: whether good or bad, according to the assessment of the priest, so it shall be. [13]But if it is one-fifth must be added to the assessment.

14 If a person consecrates a house to the LORD, the priest shall assess it: whether good or bad, as the priest assesses it, so it shall stand. [15]And if the one who consecrates the house wishes to redeem it, one-fifth shall be added to its assessed value, and it shall revert to the original owner.

16 If a person consecrates to the LORD any inherited landholding, its assessment shall be in accordance with its seed requirements: fifty shekels of silver to a homer of barley seed. [17]If the person consecrates the field as of the year of jubilee, that assessment shall stand; [18]but if the field is consecrated after the jubilee, the priest shall compute the price for it according to the years that remain until the year of jubilee, and the assessment shall be reduced. [19]And if the one who consecrates the field wishes to redeem it, then one-fifth shall be added to its assessed value, and it shall revert to the original owner; [20]but if the field is not redeemed, or if it has been sold to some-

one else, it shall no longer be redeemable. [21]But when the field is released in the jubilee, it shall be holy to the LORD as a devoted field; it becomes the priest's holding. [22]If someone consecrates to the LORD a field that has been purchased, which is not a part of the inherited landholding, [23]the priest shall compute for it the proportionate assessment up to the year of jubilee, and the assessment shall be paid as of that day, a sacred donation to the LORD. [24]In the year of jubilee the field shall return to the one from whom it was bought, whose holding the land is. [25]All assessments shall be by the sanctuary shekel: twenty gerahs shall make a shekel.

26 A firstling of animals, however, which as a firstling belongs to the LORD, cannot be consecrated by anyone; whether ox or sheep, it is the LORD's. [27]If it is an unclean animal, it shall be ransomed at its assessment, with one-fifth added; if it is not redeemed, it shall be sold at its assessment.

28 Nothing that a person owns that has been devoted to destruction for the LORD, be it human or animal, or inherited landholding, may be sold or redeemed; every devoted thing is most holy to the LORD. [29]No human beings who have been devoted to destruction can be ransomed; they shall be put to death.

30 All tithes from the land, whether the seed from the ground or the fruit from the tree, are the LORD's; they are holy to the LORD. [31]If persons wish to redeem any of their tithes, they must add one-fifth to them. [32]All tithes of herd and flock, every tenth one that passes under the shepherd's staff, shall be holy to the LORD. [33]Let no one inquire whether it is good or bad, or make substitution for it; if one makes substitution for it, then both it and the substitute shall be holy and cannot be redeemed.

34 These are the commandments that the LORD gave to Moses for the people of Israel on Mount Sinai.

Numbers

The book of Numbers gets its name from the "numbering," or census, of the Israelites that was taken not long after they escaped from Egypt, where they had been slaves. It includes many stories from the early days of the Israelites. Many believe the book was completed about 400 BC along with Genesis, Exodus, Leviticus, and Deuteronomy, but it tells of events that happened long before.

Numbers tells about many of the adventures of God's people as they wandered in the wilderness to the south and east of the land of Canaan. One of the most familiar stories is the one in which Moses sent spies into Canaan, the land promised to Abraham. Most of the spies came back discouraged and afraid, but Joshua and Caleb came back saying that with God's help, they could live in the land. Numbers shows how God led the people through many hard times. In this way, the people came to depend on God.

Numbers 26:1–51

Reuben 43,730

Simeon 22,200

Gad 40,500

Issachar 64,300

Judah 76,500

Manasseh 52,700

Zebulun 60,500

Benjamin 45,600

Dan 64,400

Asher 53,400

Naphtali 45,400

Ephraim 32,500

The First Census of Israel

1 The LORD spoke to Moses in the wilderness of Sinai, in the tent of meeting, on the first day of the second month, in the second year after they had come out of the land of Egypt, saying: ²Take a census of the whole congregation of Israelites, in their clans, by ancestral houses, according to the number of names, every male individually; ³from twenty years old and upward, everyone in Israel able to go to war. You and Aaron shall enroll them, company by company. ⁴A man from each tribe shall be with you, each man the head of his ancestral house. ⁵These are the names of the men who shall assist you:

From Reuben, E·lī´zur son of She´de·ur.

⁶ From Sim´e·on, She·lū´mi·el son of Zū·ri·shad´daī.

⁷ From Judah, Nah´shon son of Am·min´a·dab.

⁸ From Is´sa·char, Ne·than´el son of Zū-ar.

⁹ From Zeb´ū·lun, E·lī´ab son of Hē´lon.

¹⁰ From the sons of Joseph:
from Ē´phra·im, E·lish´a·ma son of Am·mī´hud;
from Ma·nas´seh, Ga·mā´li·el son of Pe·dah´zur.

¹¹ From Benjamin, A·bī´dan son of Gid·e·ō´ni.

¹² From Dan, Ā·hī·e´zer son of Am·mi·shad´daī.

¹³ From Ash´er, Pā´gi·el son of Ōch´ran.

¹⁴ From Gad, E·lī´a·saph son of Deū´el.

¹⁵ From Naph´ta·lī, A·hī´ra son of Ē´nan.

¹⁶These were the ones chosen from the congregation, the leaders of their ancestral tribes, the heads of the divisions of Israel.

17 Moses and Aaron took these men who had been designated by name, ¹⁸and on the first day of the second month they assembled the whole congregation together. They registered themselves in their clans, by their ancestral houses, according to the number of names from twenty years old and upward, individually, ¹⁹as the LORD com-manded Moses. So he enrolled them in the wilderness of Sinai.

20 The descendants of Reuben, Israel's firstborn, their lineage, in their clans, by their ancestral houses, according to the number of names, individually, every male from twenty years old and upward, everyone able to go to war: ²¹those enrolled of the tribe of Reuben were forty-six thousand five hundred.

22 The descendants of Sim´e·on, their lineage, in their clans, by their ancestral houses, those of them that were numbered, according to the number of names, individually, every male from twenty years old and upward, everyone able to go to war: ²³those enrolled of the tribe of Sim´e·on were fifty-nine thousand three hundred.

24 The descendants of Gad, their lineage, in their clans, by their ancestral houses, according to the number of the names, from twenty years old and upward, everyone able to go to war: ²⁵those enrolled of the tribe of Gad were forty-five thousand six hundred fifty.

26 The descendants of Judah, their lineage, in their clans, by their ancestral houses, according to the number of names, from twenty years old and upward, everyone able to go to war: ²⁷those enrolled of the tribe of Judah were seventy-four thousand six hundred.

28 The descendants of Is´sa·char, their lineage, in their clans, by their ancestral houses, according to the number of names, from twenty years old and upward, everyone able to go to war: ²⁹those enrolled of the tribe of Is´sa·char were fifty-four thousand four hundred.

30 The descendants of Zeb´ū·lun, their lineage, in their clans, by their ancestral houses, according to the number of names, from twenty years old and upward, everyone able to go to war: ³¹those enrolled of the tribe of Zeb´ū·lun were fifty-seven thousand four hundred.

32 The descendants of Joseph, namely, the descendants of Ē´phra·im,

their lineage, in their clans, by their ancestral houses, according to the number of names, from twenty years old and upward, everyone able to go to war: [33]those enrolled of the tribe of Ēʹphra·im were forty thousand five hundred.

34 The descendants of Ma·nasʹseh, their lineage, in their clans, by their ancestral houses, according to the number of names, from twenty years old and upward, everyone able to go to war: [35]those enrolled of the tribe of Ma·nasʹseh were thirty-two thousand two hundred.

36 The descendants of Benjamin, their lineage, in their clans, by their ancestral houses, according to the number of names, from twenty years old and upward, everyone able to go to war: [37]those enrolled of the tribe of Benjamin were thirty-five thousand four hundred.

38 The descendants of Dan, their lineage, in their clans, by their ancestral houses, according to the number of names, from twenty years old and upward, everyone able to go to war: [39]those enrolled of the tribe of Dan were sixty-two thousand seven hundred.

40 The descendants of Ashʹer, their lineage, in their clans, by their ancestral houses, according to the number of names, from twenty years old and upward, everyone able to go to war: [41]those enrolled of the tribe of Ashʹer were forty-one thousand five hundred.

42 The descendants of Naphʹta·li, their lineage, in their clans, by their ancestral houses, according to the number of names, from twenty years old and upward, everyone able to go to war: [43]those enrolled of the tribe of Naphʹta·li were fifty-three thousand four hundred.

44 These are those who were enrolled, whom Moses and Aaron enrolled with the help of the leaders of Israel, twelve men, each representing his ancestral house. [45]So the whole number of the Israelites, by their ancestral houses, from twenty years old and upward, everyone able to go to war in Israel— [46]their whole number was six hundred three thousand five hundred fifty. [47]The Lēʹvites, however, were not numbered by their ancestral tribe along with them.

A census is a count of all people in a land. The first census of Israel counted 603,550 adult men who could serve in the military. This number does not include any women, children, men who were not in the military, or members of the tribe of Levi, who served in the Tabernacle. There were a lot of people!

48 The LORD had said to Moses: [49]Only the tribe of Levi you shall not enroll, and you shall not take a census of them with the other Israelites. [50]Rather you shall appoint the Lēʹvites over the tabernacle of the covenant,[a] and over all its equipment, and over all that belongs to it; they are to carry the tabernacle and all its equipment, and they shall tend it, and shall camp around the tabernacle. [51]When the tabernacle is to set out, the Lēʹvites shall take it down; and when the tabernacle is to be pitched, the Lēʹvites shall set it up. And any outsider who comes near shall be put to death. [52]The other Israelites shall camp in their respective regimental camps, by companies; [53]but the Lēʹvites shall camp around the tabernacle of the covenant,[a] that there may be no wrath on the congregation of the Israelites; and the Lēʹvites shall perform the guard duty of the tabernacle of the covenant.[a] [54]The Israelites did so; they did just as the LORD commanded Moses.

The Order of Encampment and Marching

2 The LORD spoke to Moses and Aaron, saying: [2]The Israelites shall camp each in their respective regiments,

---

[a] Or treaty, or testimony; Heb eduth

During their time in the wilderness, the Israelites lived in a camp surrounding the Tabernacle, or tent of worship. This was a symbol of God being with them. Around the Tabernacle was an inner circle formed by the tribe of Levi, whose members served as priests. The twelve tribes of Israel surrounded the inner circle.

under ensigns by their ancestral houses; they shall camp facing the tent of meeting on every side. ³Those to camp on the east side toward the sunrise shall be of the regimental encampment of Judah by companies. The leader of the people of Judah shall be Nah´shon son of Am·min´a·dab, ⁴with a company as enrolled of seventy-four thousand six hundred. ⁵Those to camp next to him shall be the tribe of Is´sa·char. The leader of the Is´sa·char·ites shall be Ne·than´el son of Zū´ar, ⁶with a company as enrolled of fifty-four thousand four hundred. ⁷Then the tribe of Zeb´ū·lun: The leader of the Zeb´ū·lun·ites shall be E·lī´ab son of Hē´lon, ⁸with a company as enrolled of fifty-seven thousand four hundred. ⁹The total enrollment of the camp of Judah, by companies, is one hundred eighty-six thousand four hundred. They shall set out first on the march.

10 On the south side shall be the regimental encampment of Reuben by com-

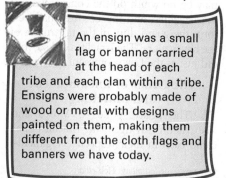

An ensign was a small flag or banner carried at the head of each tribe and each clan within a tribe. Ensigns were probably made of wood or metal with designs painted on them, making them different from the cloth flags and banners we have today.

panies. The leader of the Reū´ben·ites shall be E·lī´zur son of She·dē´ur, ¹¹with a company as enrolled of forty-six thousand five hundred. ¹²And those to camp next to him shall be the tribe of Sim´ē·on. The leader of the Sim´ē·on·ites shall be She·lū´mi·el son of Zū·ri·shad´daī, ¹³with a company as enrolled of fifty-nine thousand three hundred. ¹⁴Then the tribe of Gad: The leader of the Gad´ites shall be E·lī´a·saph son of Reū´el, ¹⁵with a company as enrolled of forty-five thousand six hundred fifty. ¹⁶The total enrollment of the camp of Reuben, by companies, is one hundred fifty-one thousand four hundred fifty. They shall set out second.

17 The tent of meeting, with the camp of the Lē´vītes, shall set out in the center of the camps; they shall set out just as they camp, each in position, by their regiments.

18 On the west side shall be the regimental encampment of Ē´phra·im by companies. The leader of the people of Ē´phra·im shall be E·lish´a·ma son of Am·mī´hud, ¹⁹with a company as enrolled of forty thousand five hundred. ²⁰Next to him shall be the tribe of Ma·nas´seh. The leader of the people of Ma·nas´seh shall be Ga·mā´li·el son of Pe·dah´zur, ²¹with a company as enrolled of thirty-two thousand two hundred. ²²Then the tribe of Benjamin: The leader of the Ben·ja·min·ites shall be A·bī´dan son of Gid·ē·ō´ni, ²³with a company as enrolled of thirty-five thousand four hundred. ²⁴The total enrollment of the camp of Ē´phra·im, by companies, is one hundred eight thousand one hundred. They shall set out third on the march.

25 On the north side shall be the regimental encampment of Dan by companies. The leader of the Dan´ites shall be Ā·hī·ē´zer son of Am·mi·shad´daī, ²⁶with a company as enrolled of sixty-two thousand seven hundred. ²⁷Those to camp next to him shall be the tribe of Ash´er. The leader of the Ash´er·ites shall be Pā´gi·el son

of Ōch′ran, [28]with a company as enrolled of forty-one thousand five hundred. [29]Then the tribe of Naph′ta·lī: The leader of the Naph′ta·lītes shall be A·hī′ra son of Ē′nan, [30]with a company as enrolled of fifty-three thousand four hundred. [31]The total enrollment of the camp of Dan is one hundred fifty-seven thousand six hundred. They shall set out last, by companies.[b]

32 This was the enrollment of the Israelites by their ancestral houses; the total enrollment in the camps by their companies was six hundred three thousand five hundred fifty. [33]Just as the LORD had commanded Moses, the Lē′vītes were not enrolled among the other Israelites.

34 The Israelites did just as the LORD had commanded Moses: They camped by regiments, and they set out the same way, everyone by clans, according to ancestral houses.

The Sons of Aaron

3 This is the lineage of Aaron and Moses at the time when the LORD spoke with Moses on Mount Sinai. [2]These are the names of the sons of Aaron: Nā′dab the firstborn, and A·bī′hū, El·ē·ā′zar, and Ith′a·mar; [3]these are the names of the sons of Aaron, the anointed priests, whom he ordained to minister as priests. [4]Nā′dab and A·bī′hū died before the LORD when they offered unholy fire before the LORD in the wilderness of Sinai, and they had no children. El·ē·ā′zar and Ith′a·mar served as priests in the lifetime of their father Aaron.

The Duties of the Levites

5 Then the LORD spoke to Moses, saying: [6]Bring the tribe of Levi near, and set them before Aaron the priest, so that they may assist him. [7]They shall perform duties for him and for the whole congregation in front of the tent of meeting, doing service at the tabernacle; [8]they shall be in charge of all the furnishings of the tent of meeting, and attend to the duties for the Israelites as they do service at the tabernacle. [9]You shall give the Lē′vītes to Aaron and his descendants; they are unreservedly given to him from among the Israelites. [10]But you shall make a register of Aaron and his descendants; it is they who shall attend to the priesthood, and any outsider who comes near shall be put to death.

11 Then the LORD spoke to Moses, saying: [12]I hereby accept the Lē′vītes from among the Israelites as substitutes for all the firstborn that open the womb among the Israelites. The Lē′vītes shall be mine, [13]for all the firstborn are mine; when I killed all the firstborn in the land of Egypt, I consecrated for my own all the firstborn in Israel, both human and animal; they shall be mine. I am the LORD.

A Census of the Levites

14 Then the LORD spoke to Moses in the wilderness of Sinai, saying: [15]Enroll the Lē′vītes by ancestral houses and by clans. You shall enroll every male from a month old and upward. [16]So Moses enrolled them according to the word of the LORD, as he was commanded. [17]The following were the sons of Levi, by their names: Ger′shon, Kō′hath, and Me·rar′ī. [18]These are the names of the sons of

Think of the people of Israel as one big family made of many smaller tribes. And think of each tribe as a family made of many smaller clans. The family of Aaron was set apart to be the priests for the Israelites; the tribe of Levi had the responsibility to help the priests and perform special duties for worship. Different families and tribes had different responsibilities. Is there something you do to help your family that no one else in your family does?

[b] Compare verses 9, 16, 24: Heb *by their regiments*

Ger´shon by their clans: Lib´ni and Shim´-ē·i. ¹⁹The sons of Kō´hath by their clans: Am´ram, Iz´har, Hē´bron, and Uz´zi·el. ²⁰The sons of Me·rar´i by their clans: Mah´li and Mū´shi. These are the clans of the Lē´vites, by their ancestral houses.

21 To Ger´shon belonged the clan of the Lib´nites and the clan of the Shim´ē·ites; these were the clans of the Ger´shon·ites. ²²Their enrollment, counting all the males from a month old and upward, was seven thousand five hundred. ²³The clans of the Ger´shon·ites were to camp behind the tabernacle on the west, ²⁴with E·li´a·saph son of Lā´el as head of the ancestral house of the Ger´shon·ites. ²⁵The responsibility of the sons of Ger´shon in the tent of meeting was to be the tabernacle, the tent with its covering, the screen for the entrance of the tent of meeting, ²⁶the hangings of the court, the screen for the entrance of the court that is around the tabernacle and the altar, and its cords—all the service pertaining to these.

27 To Kō´hath belonged the clan of the Am´ram·ites, the clan of the Iz´har·ites, the clan of the Hē´bron·ites, and the clan of the Uz´zi·el·ites; these are the clans of the Kō´hath·ites. ²⁸Counting all the males, from a month old and upward, there were eight thousand six hundred, attending to the duties of the sanctuary. ²⁹The clans of the Kō´hath·ites were to camp on the south side of the tabernacle, ³⁰with E·li·zā´phan son of Uz´zi·el as head of the ancestral house of the clans of the Kō´hath·ites. ³¹Their responsibility was to be the ark, the table, the lampstand, the altars, the vessels of the sanctuary with which the priests minister, and the screen—all the service pertaining to these. ³²El·e·ā´zar son of Aaron the priest was to be chief over the leaders of the Lē´vites, and to have oversight of those who had charge of the sanctuary.

33 To Me·rar´i belonged the clan of the Mah´lites and the clan of the Mū´shites: these are the clans of Me·rar´i. ³⁴Their enrollment, counting all the males from a month old and upward, was six thousand two hundred. ³⁵The head of the ancestral house of the clans of Me·rar´i was Zū´ri·el son of Ab·i·hā´il; they were to camp on the north side of the tabernacle. ³⁶The responsibility assigned to the sons of Me·rar´i was to be the frames of the tabernacle, the bars, the pillars, the bases, and all their accessories—all the service pertaining to these; ³⁷also the pillars of the court all around, with their bases and pegs and cords.

38 Those who were to camp in front of the tabernacle on the east—in front of the tent of meeting toward the east—were Moses and Aaron and Aaron's sons, having charge of the rites within the sanctuary, whatever had to be done for the Israelites; and any outsider who came near was to be put to death. ³⁹The total enrollment of the Lē´vites whom Moses and Aaron enrolled at the commandment of the LORD, by their clans, all the males from a month old and upward, was twenty-two thousand.

The Redemption of the Firstborn

40 Then the LORD said to Moses: Enroll all the firstborn males of the Israelites, from a month old and upward, and count their names. ⁴¹But you shall accept the Lē´vites for me—I am the LORD—as substitutes for all the firstborn among the Israelites, and the livestock of the Lē´vites as substitutes for all the firstborn among the livestock of the Israelites. ⁴²So Moses enrolled all the firstborn among the Israelites, as the LORD commanded him. ⁴³The total enrollment, all the firstborn males from a month old and upward, counting the number of names, was twenty-two thousand two hundred seventy-three.

44 Then the LORD spoke to Moses, saying: ⁴⁵Accept the Lē´vites as substitutes for all the firstborn among the Israelites, and the livestock of the Lē´vites as substitutes for their livestock; and the

Lē´vītes shall be mine. I am the LORD. ⁴⁶As the price of redemption of the two hundred seventy-three of the firstborn of the Israelites, over and above the number of the Lē´vītes, ⁴⁷you shall accept five shekels apiece, reckoning by the shekel of the sanctuary, a shekel of twenty gerahs. ⁴⁸Give to Aaron and his sons the money by which the excess number of them is redeemed. ⁴⁹So Moses took the redemption money from those who were over and above those redeemed by the Lē´vītes; ⁵⁰from the firstborn of the Israelites he took the money, one thousand three hundred sixty-five shekels, reckoned by the shekel of the sanctuary; ⁵¹and Moses gave the redemption money to Aaron and his sons, according to the word of the LORD, as the LORD had commanded Moses.

The Kohathites

4 The LORD spoke to Moses and Aaron, saying: ²Take a census of the Kō´hath·ītes separate from the other Lē´vītes, by their clans and their ancestral houses, ³from thirty years old up to fifty years old, all who qualify to do work relating to the tent of meeting. ⁴The service of the Kō´hath·ītes relating to the tent of meeting concerns the most holy things.

5 When the camp is to set out, Aaron and his sons shall go in and take down the screening curtain, and cover the ark of the covenant[c] with it; ⁶then they shall put on it a covering of fine leather,[d] and spread over that a cloth all of blue, and shall put its poles in place. ⁷Over the table of the bread of the Presence they shall spread a blue cloth, and put on it the plates, the dishes for incense, the bowls, and the flagons for the drink offering; the regular bread also shall be on it; ⁸then they shall spread over them a crimson cloth, and cover it with a covering of fine leather,[d] and shall put its poles in place. ⁹They shall take a blue cloth, and cover the lampstand for the light, with its lamps, its snuffers, its trays, and all the vessels for oil with which it is supplied; ¹⁰and they shall put it with all its

utensils in a covering of fine leather,[d] and put it on the carrying frame. ¹¹Over the golden altar they shall spread a blue cloth, and cover it with a covering of fine leather,[d] and shall put its poles in place; ¹²and they shall take all the utensils of the service that are used in the sanctuary, and put them in a blue cloth, and cover them with a covering of fine leather,[d] and put them on the carrying frame. ¹³They shall take away the ashes from the altar, and spread a purple cloth over it; ¹⁴and they shall put on it all the utensils of the altar, which are used for the service there, the firepans, the forks, the shovels, and the basins, all the utensils of the altar; and they shall spread on it a covering of fine leather,[d] and shall put its poles in place. ¹⁵When Aaron and his sons have finished covering the sanctuary and all the furnishings of the sanctuary, as the camp sets out, after that the Kō´hath·ītes shall come to carry these, but they must not touch the holy things, or they will die. These are the things of the tent of meeting that the Kō´hath·ītes are to carry.

16 El·ē·ā´zar son of Aaron the priest shall have charge of the oil for the light, the fragrant incense, the regular grain offering, and the anointing oil, the oversight of all the tabernacle and all that is in it, in the sanctuary and in its utensils.

17 Then the LORD spoke to Moses and Aaron, saying: ¹⁸You must not let the tribe of the clans of the Kō´hath·ītes be destroyed from among the Lē´vītes. ¹⁹This is how you must deal with them in order that they may live and not die when they come near to the most holy things: Aaron and his sons shall go in and assign each to a particular task or burden. ²⁰But the Kō´hath·ītes[e] must not go in to look on the holy things even for a moment; otherwise they will die.

---

[c] Or *treaty*, or *testimony* ; Heb *eduth*   [d] Meaning of Heb uncertain   [e] Heb *they*

The Gershonites and Merarites

21 Then the LORD spoke to Moses, saying: [22]Take a census of the Ger'shon·ites also, by their ancestral houses and by their clans; [23]from thirty years old up to fifty years old you shall enroll them, all who qualify to do work in the tent of meeting. [24]This is the service of the clans of the Ger'shon·ites, in serving and bearing burdens: [25]They shall carry the curtains of the tabernacle, and the tent of meeting with its covering, and the outer covering of fine leather[f] that is on top of it, and the screen for the entrance of the tent of meeting, [26]and the hangings of the court, and the screen for the entrance of the gate of the court that is around the tabernacle and the altar, and their cords, and all the equipment for their service; and they shall do all that needs to be done with regard to them. [27]All the service of the Ger'shon·ites shall be at the command of Aaron and his sons, in all that they are to carry, and in all that they have to do; and you shall assign to their charge all that they are to carry. [28]This is the service of the clans of the Ger'shon·ites relating to the tent of meeting, and their responsibilities are to be under the oversight of Ith'a·mar son of Aaron the priest.

29 As for the Me·rar'ites, you shall enroll them by their clans and their ancestral houses; [30]from thirty years old up to fifty years old you shall enroll them, everyone who qualifies to do the work of the tent of meeting. [31]This is what they are charged to carry, as the whole of their service in the tent of meeting: the frames of the tabernacle, with its bars, pillars, and bases, [32]and the pillars of the court all around with their bases, pegs, and cords, with all their equipment and all their related service; and you shall assign by name the objects that they are required to carry. [33]This is the service of the clans of the Me·rar'ites, the whole of their service relating to the tent of meeting, under the hand of Ith'a·mar son of Aaron the priest.

Census of the Levites

34 So Moses and Aaron and the leaders of the congregation enrolled the Kō'hath·ites, by their clans and their ancestral houses, [35]from thirty years old up to fifty years old, everyone who qualified for work relating to the tent of meeting; [36]and their enrollment by clans was two thousand seven hundred fifty. [37]This was the enrollment of the clans of the Kō'hath·ites, all who served at the tent of meeting, whom Moses and Aaron enrolled according to the commandment of the LORD by Moses.

38 The enrollment of the Ger'shon·ites, by their clans and their ancestral houses, [39]from thirty years old up to fifty years old, everyone who qualified for work relating to the tent of meeting— [40]their enrollment by their clans and their ancestral houses was two thousand six hundred thirty. [41]This was the enrollment of the clans of the Ger'shon·ites, all who served at the tent of meeting, whom Moses and Aaron enrolled according to the commandment of the LORD.

42 The enrollment of the clans of the Me·rar'ites, by their clans and their ancestral houses, [43]from thirty years old up to fifty years old, everyone who qualified for work relating to the tent of meeting— [44]their enrollment by their clans was three thousand two hundred. [45]This is the enrollment of the clans of the Me·rar'ites, whom Moses and Aaron enrolled according to the commandment of the LORD by Moses.

46 All those who were enrolled of the Lē'vites, whom Moses and Aaron and the leaders of Israel enrolled, by their clans and their ancestral houses, [47]from thirty years old up to fifty years old, everyone who qualified to do the work of service and the work of bearing burdens relating to the tent of meeting, [48]their enrollment was eight thousand five hundred eighty. [49]According to the commandment of the LORD through Moses they were appointed to their

several tasks of serving or carrying; thus they were enrolled by him, as the LORD commanded Moses.

Unclean Persons

5 The LORD spoke to Moses, saying: [2]Command the Israelites to put out of the camp everyone who is leprous,[f] or has a discharge, and everyone who is unclean through contact with a corpse; [3]you shall put out both male and female, putting them outside the camp; they must not defile their camp, where I dwell among them. [4]The Israelites did so, putting them outside the camp; as the LORD had spoken to Moses, so the Israelites did.

Confession and Restitution

5 The LORD spoke to Moses, saying: [6]Speak to the Israelites: When a man or a woman wrongs another, breaking faith with the LORD, that person incurs guilt [7]and shall confess the sin that has been committed. The person shall make full restitution for the wrong, adding one fifth to it, and giving it to the one who was wronged. [8]If the injured party has no next of kin to whom restitution may be made for the wrong, the restitution for wrong shall go to the LORD for the priest, in addition to the ram of atonement with which atonement is made for the guilty party. [9]Among all the sacred donations of the Israelites, every gift that they bring to the priest shall be his. [10]The sacred donations of all are their own; whatever anyone gives to the priest shall be his.

Concerning an Unfaithful Wife

11 The LORD spoke to Moses, saying: [12]Speak to the Israelites and say to them: If any man's wife goes astray and is unfaithful to him, [13]if a man has had intercourse with her but it is hidden from her husband, so that she is undetected though she has defiled herself, and there is no witness against her since she was not caught in the act; [14]if a spirit of jealousy comes on him, and he is jealous of his wife who has defiled herself; or if a spirit of jealousy comes on him, and he is jealous of his wife, though she has not defiled herself; [15]then the man shall bring his wife to the priest. And he shall bring the offering required for her, one-tenth of an ephah of barley flour. He shall pour no oil on it and put no frankincense on it, for it is a grain offering of jealousy, a grain offering of remembrance, bringing iniquity to remembrance.

16 Then the priest shall bring her near, and set her before the LORD; [17]the priest shall take holy water in an earthen vessel, and take some of the dust that is on the floor of the tabernacle and put it into the water. [18]The priest shall set the woman before the LORD, dishevel the woman's hair, and place in her hands the grain offering of remembrance, which is the grain offering of jealousy. In his own hand the priest shall have the water of bitterness that brings the curse. [19]Then the priest shall make her take an oath, saying, "If no man has lain with you, if you have not turned aside to uncleanness while under your husband's authority, be immune to this water of bitterness that brings the curse. [20]But if you have gone astray while under your husband's authority, if you have defiled yourself and some man other than your husband has had intercourse with you," [21]—let the priest make the woman take the oath of the curse and say to the woman—"the LORD make you an execration and an oath among your people, when the LORD makes your uterus drop, your womb discharge; [22]now may this water that brings the curse enter your bowels and make your womb discharge, your uterus drop!" And the woman shall say, "Amen. Amen."

23 Then the priest shall put these curses in writing, and wash them off into the water of bitterness. [24]He shall make the woman drink the water of bitterness

---

[f] A term for several skin diseases; precise meaning uncertain

that brings the curse, and the water that brings the curse shall enter her and cause bitter pain. ²⁵The priest shall take the grain offering of jealousy out of the woman's hand, and shall elevate the grain offering before the LORD and bring it to the altar; ²⁶and the priest shall take a handful of the grain offering, as its memorial portion, and turn it into smoke on the altar, and afterward shall make the woman drink the water. ²⁷When he has made her drink the water, then, if she has defiled herself and has been unfaithful to her husband, the water that brings the curse shall enter into her and cause bitter pain, and her womb shall discharge, her uterus drop, and the woman shall become an execration among her people. ²⁸But if the woman has not defiled herself and is clean, then she shall be immune and be able to conceive children.

29 This is the law in cases of jealousy, when a wife, while under her husband's authority, goes astray and defiles herself, ³⁰or when a spirit of jealousy comes on a man and he is jealous of his wife; then he shall set the woman before the LORD, and the priest shall apply this entire law to her. ³¹The man shall be free from iniquity, but the woman shall bear her iniquity.

The Nazirites

6 The LORD spoke to Moses, saying: ²Speak to the Israelites and say to them: When either men or women make a special vow, the vow of a nazirite,ᵍ to separate themselves to the LORD, ³they shall separate themselves from wine and strong drink; they shall drink no wine vinegar or other vinegar, and shall not drink any grape juice or eat grapes, fresh or dried. ⁴All their days as nazirites^h they shall eat nothing that is produced by the grapevine, not even the seeds or the skins.

5 All the days of their nazirite vow no razor shall come upon the head; until the time is completed for which they separate themselves to the LORD, they

In Bible times, people called Nazirites promised God that they would follow certain rules. They did not cut their hair, drink wine, or have anything to do with dead bodies. Nazirites followed these rules in order to set themselves apart for special service to God. Samson, Samuel, and John the Baptist were all Nazirites.

shall be holy; they shall let the locks of the head grow long.

6 All the days that they separate themselves to the LORD they shall not go near a corpse. ⁷Even if their father or mother, brother or sister, should die, they may not defile themselves; because their consecration to God is upon the head. ⁸All their days as nazirites^h they are holy to the LORD.

9 If someone dies very suddenly nearby, defiling the consecrated head, then they shall shave the head on the day of their cleansing; on the seventh day they shall shave it. ¹⁰On the eighth day they shall bring two turtledoves or two young pigeons to the priest at the entrance of the tent of meeting, ¹¹and the priest shall offer one as a sin offering and the other as a burnt offering, and make atonement for them, because they incurred guilt by reason of the corpse. They shall sanctify the head that same day, ¹²and separate themselves to the LORD for their days as nazirites,^h and bring a male lamb a year old as a guilt offering. The former time shall be void, because the consecrated head was defiled.

13 This is the law for the nazirites^h when the time of their consecration has been completed: they shall be brought to the entrance of the tent of meeting, ¹⁴and they shall offer their gift to the LORD, one male lamb a year old without blemish as a burnt offering, one ewe

ᵍ That is *one separated* or *one consecrated*   ^h That is *those separated* or *those consecrated*

"The LORD bless you and keep you; the LORD make his face to shine upon you, and be gracious to you; the LORD lift up his countenance upon you, and give you peace." Numbers 6:24–26

lamb a year old without blemish as a sin offering, one ram without blemish as an offering of well-being, [15]and a basket of unleavened bread, cakes of choice flour mixed with oil and unleavened wafers spread with oil, with their grain offering and their drink offerings. [16]The priest shall present them before the LORD and offer their sin offering and burnt offering, [17]and shall offer the ram as a sacrifice of well-being to the LORD, with the basket of unleavened bread; the priest also shall make the accompanying grain offering and drink offering. [18]Then the nazirites[i] shall shave the consecrated head at the entrance of the tent of meeting, and shall take the hair from the consecrated head and put it on the fire under the sacrifice of well-being. [19]The priest shall take the shoulder of the ram, when it is boiled, and one unleavened cake out of the basket, and one unleavened wafer, and shall put them in the palms of the nazirites,[i] after they have shaved the consecrated head. [20]Then the priest shall elevate them as an elevation offering before the LORD; they are a holy portion for the priest, together with the breast that is elevated and the thigh that is offered. After that the nazirites[i] may drink wine.

21 This is the law for the nazirites[i] who take a vow. Their offering to the LORD must be in accordance with the nazirite[j] vow, apart from what else they can afford. In accordance with whatever vow they take, so they shall do, following the law for their consecration.

The Priestly Benediction

22 The LORD spoke to Moses, saying:

[23]Speak to Aaron and his sons, saying, Thus you shall bless the Israelites: You shall say to them,

[24] The LORD bless you and keep you;

[25] the LORD make his face to shine upon you, and be gracious to you;

[26] the LORD lift up his countenance upon you, and give you peace.

27 So they shall put my name on the Israelites, and I will bless them.

God gave Aaron a special blessing to give the people, letting them know that God promised to treat them with love and compassion. Today we can be sure that God loves us and cares for us.

Offerings of the Leaders

7 On the day when Moses had finished setting up the tabernacle, and had anointed and consecrated it with all its furnishings, and had anointed and consecrated the altar with all its utensils, [2]the leaders of Israel, heads of their ancestral houses, the leaders of the tribes, who were over those who were enrolled, made offerings. [3]They brought their offerings before the LORD, six covered wagons and twelve oxen, a wagon for every two of the leaders, and for each one an ox; they presented them before the tabernacle. [4]Then the LORD said to Moses: [5]Accept these from them, that they may be used in doing the service of the tent of meeting, and give them to the Lē′vītes, to each according to his service. [6]So Moses took the wagons and the oxen, and gave them to the Lē′vītes. [7]Two wagons and four oxen he gave to the Ger′shon·ītes, according to their service; [8]and four wagons and eight oxen he gave to the Me·rar′-ītes, according to their service, under the direction of Ith′a·mar son of Aaron the priest. [9]But to the Kō′hath·ītes he gave

[i] That is *those separated* or *those consecrated*
[j] That is *one separated* or *one consecrated*

When the Tabernacle was finished, the leader of each tribe offered gifts to God. Every day for twelve days, one leader would bring the gifts from his tribe. The gifts from each tribe were exactly the same—no one gift was better or worse than any other gift. Together, they made an awesome offering to God's sanctuary. Think about the things you have. What could you give to God as a gift?

none, because they were charged with the care of the holy things that had to be carried on the shoulders.

10 The leaders also presented offerings for the dedication of the altar at the time when it was anointed; the leaders presented their offering before the altar. [11]The LORD said to Moses: They shall present their offerings, one leader each day, for the dedication of the altar.

12 The one who presented his offering the first day was Nah′shon son of Am·min′a·dab, of the tribe of Judah; [13]his offering was one silver plate weighing one hundred thirty shekels, one silver basin weighing seventy shekels, according to the shekel of the sanctuary, both of them full of choice flour mixed with oil for a grain offering; [14]one golden dish weighing ten shekels, full of incense; [15]one young bull, one ram, one male lamb a year old, for a burnt offering; [16]one male goat for a sin offering; [17]and for the sacrifice of well-being, two oxen, five rams, five male goats, and five male lambs a year old. This was the offering of Nah′shon son of Am·min′a·dab.

18 On the second day Ne·than′el son of Zū′ar, the leader of Is′sa·char, presented an offering; [19]he presented for his offering one silver plate weighing one hundred thirty shekels, one silver basin weighing seventy shekels, according to the shekel of the sanctuary, both of them full of choice flour mixed with oil for a grain offering; [20]one golden dish weigh-

ing ten shekels, full of incense; [21]one young bull, one ram, one male lamb a year old, as a burnt offering; [22]one male goat as a sin offering; [23]and for the sacrifice of well-being, two oxen, five rams, five male goats, and five male lambs a year old. This was the offering of Ne·than′el son of Zū′ar.

24 On the third day E·lī′ab son of Hē′lon, the leader of the Zeb′ū·lun·ites: [25]his offering was one silver plate weighing one hundred thirty shekels, one silver basin weighing seventy shekels, according to the shekel of the sanctuary, both of them full of choice flour mixed with oil for a grain offering; [26]one golden dish weighing ten shekels, full of incense; [27]one young bull, one ram, one male lamb a year old, for a burnt offering; [28]one male goat for a sin offering; [29]and for the sacrifice of well-being, two oxen, five rams, five male goats, and five male lambs a year old. This was the offering of E·lī′ab son of Hē′lon.

30 On the fourth day E·lī′zur son of Shed′e·ur, the leader of the Reū′ben·ites: [31]his offering was one silver plate weighing one hundred thirty shekels, one silver basin weighing seventy shekels, according to the shekel of the sanctuary, both of them full of choice flour mixed with oil for a grain offering; [32]one golden dish weighing ten shekels, full of incense; [33]one young bull, one ram, one male lamb a year old, for a burnt offering; [34]one male goat for a sin offering; [35]and for the sacrifice of well-being, two oxen, five rams, five male goats, and five male lambs a year old. This was the offering of E·lī′zur son of Shed′e·ur.

36 On the fifth day She·lū′mi·el son of Zū′ri·shad′dai, the leader of the Sim′e·on·ites: [37]his offering was one silver plate weighing one hundred thirty shekels, one silver basin weighing seventy shekels, according to the shekel of the sanctuary, both of them full of choice flour mixed with oil for a grain offering; [38]one golden dish weighing ten shekels, full of incense;

³⁹one young bull, one ram, one male lamb a year old, for a burnt offering; ⁴⁰one male goat for a sin offering; ⁴¹and for the sacrifice of well-being, two oxen, five rams, five male goats, and five male lambs a year old. This was the offering of She·lūʹmi·el son of Zūʹri·shadʹdaī.

42 On the sixth day E·liʹa·saph son of Deūʹel, the leader of the Gadʹites: ⁴³his offering was one silver plate weighing one hundred thirty shekels, one silver basin weighing seventy shekels, according to the shekel of the sanctuary, both of them full of choice flour mixed with oil for a grain offering; ⁴⁴one golden dish weighing ten shekels, full of incense; ⁴⁵one young bull, one ram, one male lamb a year old, for a burnt offering; ⁴⁶one male goat for a sin offering; ⁴⁷and for the sacrifice of well-being, two oxen, five rams, five male goats, and five male lambs a year old. This was the offering of E·liʹa·saph son of Deūʹel.

48 On the seventh day E·lishʹa·ma son of Am·miʹhud, the leader of the Eʹphra·im·ites: ⁴⁹his offering was one silver plate weighing one hundred thirty shekels, one silver basin weighing seventy shekels, according to the shekel of the sanctuary, both of them full of choice flour mixed with oil for a grain offering; ⁵⁰one golden dish weighing ten shekels, full of incense; ⁵¹one young bull, one ram, one male lamb a year old, for a burnt offering; ⁵²one male goat for a sin offering; ⁵³and for the sacrifice of well-being, two oxen, five rams, five male goats, and five male lambs a year old. This was the offering of E·lishʹa·ma son of Am·miʹhud.

54 On the eighth day Ga·māʹli·el son of Pe·dahʹzur, the leader of the Ma·nasʹsites: ⁵⁵his offering was one silver plate weighing one hundred thirty shekels, one silver basin weighing seventy shekels, according to the shekel of the sanctuary, both of them full of choice flour mixed with oil for a grain offering; ⁵⁶one golden dish weighing ten shekels, full of in-

cense; ⁵⁷one young bull, one ram, one male lamb a year old, for a burnt offering; ⁵⁸one male goat for a sin offering; ⁵⁹and for the sacrifice of well-being, two oxen, five rams, five male goats, and five male lambs a year old. This was the offering of Ga·māʹli·el son of Pe·dahʹzur.

60 On the ninth day A·bīʹdan son of Gid·e·ōʹni, the leader of the Benʹja·min·ites: ⁶¹his offering was one silver plate weighing one hundred thirty shekels, one silver basin weighing seventy shekels, according to the shekel of the sanctuary, both of them full of choice flour mixed with oil for a grain offering; ⁶²one golden dish weighing ten shekels, full of incense; ⁶³one young bull, one ram, one male lamb a year old, for a burnt offering; ⁶⁴one male goat for a sin offering; ⁶⁵and for the sacrifice of well-being, two oxen, five rams, five male goats, and five male lambs a year old. This was the offering of A·bīʹdan son of Gid·e·ōʹni.

66 On the tenth day Āʹhi·eʹzer son of Am·mi·shadʹdaī, the leader of the Danʹites: ⁶⁷his offering was one silver plate weighing one hundred thirty shekels, one silver basin weighing seventy shekels, according to the shekel of the sanctuary, both of them full of choice flour mixed with oil for a grain offering; ⁶⁸one golden dish weighing ten shekels, full of incense; ⁶⁹one young bull, one ram, one male lamb a year old, for a burnt offering; ⁷⁰one male goat for a sin offering; ⁷¹and for the sacrifice of well-being, two oxen, five rams, five male goats, and five male lambs a year old. This was the offering of Āʹhi·eʹzer son of Am·mi·shadʹdaī.

72 On the eleventh day Pāʹgi·el son of Ōchʹran, the leader of the Ashʹer·ites: ⁷³his offering was one silver plate weighing one hundred thirty shekels, one silver basin weighing seventy shekels, according to the shekel of the sanctuary, both of them full of choice flour mixed with oil for a grain offering; ⁷⁴one golden dish weighing ten shekels, full of incense; ⁷⁵one young bull, one ram, one

male lamb a year old, for a burnt offering; [76]one male goat for a sin offering; [77]and for the sacrifice of well-being, two oxen, five rams, five male goats, and five male lambs a year old. This was the offering of Pā´gi·el son of Ōch´ran.

78 On the twelfth day A·hī´ra son of Ē´nan, the leader of the Naph´ta·lites: [79]his offering was one silver plate weighing one hundred thirty shekels, one silver basin weighing seventy shekels, according to the shekel of the sanctuary, both of them full of choice flour mixed with oil for a grain offering; [80]one golden dish weighing ten shekels, full of incense; [81]one young bull, one ram, one male lamb a year old, for a burnt offering; [82]one male goat for a sin offering; [83]and for the sacrifice of well-being, two oxen, five rams, five male goats, and five male lambs a year old. This was the offering of A·hī´ra son of Ē´nan.

84 This was the dedication offering for the altar, at the time when it was anointed, from the leaders of Israel: twelve silver plates, twelve silver basins, twelve golden dishes, [85]each silver plate weighing one hundred thirty shekels and each basin seventy, all the silver of the vessels two thousand four hundred shekels according to the shekel of the sanctuary, [86]the twelve golden dishes, full of incense, weighing ten shekels apiece according to the shekel of the sanctuary, all the gold of the dishes being one hundred twenty shekels; [87]all the livestock for the burnt offering twelve bulls, twelve rams, twelve male lambs a year old, with their grain offering; and twelve male goats for a sin offering; [88]and all the livestock for the sacrifice of well-being twenty-four bulls, the rams sixty, the male goats sixty, the male lambs a year old sixty. This was the dedication offering for the altar, after it was anointed.

89 When Moses went into the tent of meeting to speak with the LORD,[k] he would hear the voice speaking to him from above the mercy seat[l] that was on the ark of the covenant[m] from between the two cherubim; thus it spoke to him.

The Seven Lamps

8 The LORD spoke to Moses, saying: [2]Speak to Aaron and say to him: When you set up the lamps, the seven lamps shall give light in front of the lampstand. [3]Aaron did so; he set up its lamps to give light in front of the lampstand, as the LORD had commanded Moses. [4]Now this was how the lampstand was made, out of hammered work of gold. From its base to its flowers, it was hammered work; according to the pattern that the LORD had shown Moses, so he made the lampstand.

Consecration and Service of the Levites

5 The LORD spoke to Moses, saying: [6]Take the Lē´vites from among the Israelites and cleanse them. [7]Thus you shall do to them, to cleanse them: sprinkle the water of purification on them, have them shave their whole body with a razor and wash their clothes, and so cleanse themselves. [8]Then let them take a young bull and its grain offering of choice flour mixed with oil, and you shall take another young bull for a sin offering. [9]You shall bring the Lē´vites before the tent of meeting, and assemble the whole congregation of the Israelites. [10]When you bring the Lē´vites before the LORD, the Israelites shall lay their hands on the Lē´vites, [11]and Aaron shall present the Lē´vites before the LORD as an elevation offering from the Israelites, that they may do the service of the LORD. [12]The Lē´vites shall lay their hands on the heads of the bulls, and he shall offer the one for a sin offering and the other for a burnt offering to the LORD, to make atonement for the Lē´vites. [13]Then you shall have the Lē´vites stand before Aaron and his sons, and you shall present them as an elevation offering to the LORD.

[k] Heb him   [l] Or the cover   [m] Or treaty, or testimony; Heb eduth

14 Thus you shall separate the Lĕʹvītes from among the other Israelites, and the Lĕʹvītes shall be mine. [15]Thereafter the Lĕʹvītes may go in to do service at the tent of meeting, once you have cleansed them and presented them as an elevation offering. [16]For they are unreservedly given to me from among the Israelites; I have taken them for myself, in place of all that open the womb, the firstborn of all the Israelites. [17]For all the firstborn among the Israelites are mine, both human and animal. On the day that I struck down all the firstborn in the land of Egypt I consecrated them for myself, [18]but I have taken the Lĕʹvītes in place of all the firstborn among the Israelites. [19]Moreover, I have given the Lĕʹvītes as a gift to Aaron and his sons from among the Israelites, to do the service for the Israelites at the tent of meeting, and to make atonement for the Israelites, in order that there may be no plague among the Israelites for coming too close to the sanctuary.

20 Moses and Aaron and the whole congregation of the Israelites did with the Lĕʹvītes accordingly; the Israelites did with the Lĕʹvītes just as the LORD had commanded Moses concerning them. [21]The Lĕʹvītes purified themselves from sin and washed their clothes; then Aaron presented them as an elevation offering before the LORD, and Aaron made atonement for them to cleanse them. [22]Thereafter the Lĕʹvītes went in to do their service in the tent of meeting in attendance on Aaron and his sons. As the LORD had commanded Moses concerning the Lĕʹvītes, so they did with them.

23 The LORD spoke to Moses, saying: [24]This applies to the Lĕʹvītes: from twenty-five years old and upward they shall begin to do duty in the service of the tent of meeting; [25]and from the age of fifty years they shall retire from the duty of the service and serve no more. [26]They may assist their brothers in the tent of meeting in carrying out their duties, but they shall perform no service.

Thus you shall do with the Lĕʹvītes in assigning their duties.

The Passover at Sinai

9 The LORD spoke to Moses in the wilderness of Sinai, in the first month of the second year after they had come out of the land of Egypt, saying: [2]Let the Israelites keep the passover at its appointed time. [3]On the fourteenth day of this month, at twilight,[nn] you shall keep it at its appointed time; according to all its statutes and all its regulations you shall keep it. [4]So Moses told the Israelites that they should keep the passover. [5]They kept the passover in the first month, on the fourteenth day of the month, at twilight,[n] in the wilderness of Sinai. Just as the LORD had commanded Moses, so the Israelites did. [6]Now there were certain people who were unclean through touching a corpse, so that they could not keep the passover on that day. They came before Moses and Aaron on that day, [7]and said to him, "Although we are unclean through touching a corpse, why must we be kept from presenting the LORD's offering at its appointed time among the Israelites?" [8]Moses spoke to them, "Wait, so that I may hear what the LORD will command concerning you."

9 The LORD spoke to Moses, saying: [10]Speak to the Israelites, saying: Anyone of you or your descendants who is unclean through touching a corpse, or is away on a journey, shall still keep the passover to the LORD. [11]In the second month on the fourteenth day, at twilight,[n] they shall keep it; they shall eat it with unleavened bread and bitter herbs. [12]They shall leave none of it until morning, nor break a bone of it; according to all the statute for the passover they shall keep it. [13]But anyone who is clean and is not on a journey, and yet refrains from keeping the passover, shall be cut off from the people for not presenting the LORD's offering at its appointed time;

[n] Heb *between the two evenings*

such a one shall bear the consequences for the sin. [14]Any alien residing among you who wishes to keep the passover to the LORD shall do so according to the statute of the passover and according to its regulation; you shall have one statute for both the resident alien and the native.

The Cloud and the Fire

15 On the day the tabernacle was set up, the cloud covered the tabernacle, the tent of the covenant;[o] and from evening until morning it was over the tabernacle, having the appearance of fire. [16]It was always so: the cloud covered it by day[p] and the appearance of fire by night. [17]Whenever the cloud lifted from over the tent, then the Israelites would set out; and in the place where the cloud settled down, there the Israelites would camp. [18]At the command of the LORD the Israelites would set out, and at the command of the LORD they would camp. As long as the cloud rested over the tabernacle, they would remain in camp. [19]Even when the cloud continued over the tabernacle many days, the Israelites would keep the charge of the LORD, and would not set out. [20]Sometimes the cloud would remain a few days over the tabernacle, and according to the command of the LORD they would remain in camp; then according to the command of the LORD they would set out. [21]Sometimes the cloud would remain from evening until morning; and when the cloud lifted in the morning, they would set out, or if it continued for a day and a night, when the cloud lifted they would set out. [22]Whether it was two days, or a month, or a longer time, that the cloud continued over the tabernacle, resting upon it, the Israelites would remain in camp and would not set out; but when it lifted they would set out. [23]At the command of the LORD they would camp, and at the command of the LORD they would set out. They kept the charge of the LORD, at the command of the LORD by Moses.

The Silver Trumpets

10 The LORD spoke to Moses, saying: [2]Make two silver trumpets; you shall make them of hammered work; and you shall use them for summoning the congregation, and for breaking camp. [3]When both are blown, the whole congregation shall assemble before you at the entrance of the tent of meeting. [4]But if only one is blown, then the leaders, the heads of the tribes of Israel, shall assemble before you. [5]When you blow an alarm, the camps on the east side shall set out; [6]when you blow a second alarm, the camps on the south side shall set out. An alarm is to be blown whenever they are to set out. [7]But when the assembly is to be gathered, you shall blow, but you shall not sound an alarm. [8]The sons of Aaron, the priests, shall blow the trumpets; this shall be a perpetual institution for you throughout your generations. [9]When you go to war in your land against the adversary who oppresses you, you shall sound an alarm with the trumpets, so that you may be remembered before the LORD your God and be saved from your enemies. [10]Also on your days of rejoicing, at your appointed festivals, and at the beginnings of your months, you shall blow the trumpets over your burnt offerings and over your sacrifices of well-being; they shall serve as a reminder on your behalf before the LORD your God: I am the LORD your God.

Departure from Sinai

11 In the second year, in the second month, on the twentieth day of the month, the cloud lifted from over the tabernacle of the covenant.[o] [12]Then the Israelites set out by stages from the wilderness of Sinai, and the cloud settled down in the wilderness of Par'an. [13]They set out for the first time at the command of the LORD by Moses. [14]The standard of the camp of

---

[o] Or *treaty*, or *testimony*; Heb *eduth*   [p] Gk Syr Vg: Heb lacks *by day*

Judah set out first, company by company, and over the whole company was Nah´shon son of Am·min´a·dab. [15]Over the company of the tribe of Is´sa·char was Ne·than´el son of Zū´ar; [16]and over the company of the tribe of Zeb´ū·lun was E·lī´-ab son of Hē´lon.

17 Then the tabernacle was taken down, and the Ger´shon·ītes and the Me·rar´ītes, who carried the tabernacle, set out. [18]Next the standard of the camp of Reuben set out, company by company; and over the whole company was E·lī´zur son of Shed´ē·ur. [19]Over the company of the tribe of Sim´ē·on was She·lū´mi·el son of Zū´ri·shad´daī, [20]and over the company of the tribe of Gad was E·lī´a·saph son of Deū´el.

21 Then the Kō´hath·ītes, who carried the holy things, set out; and the tabernacle was set up before their arrival. [22]Next the standard of the Ē´phra·im·īte camp set out, company by company, and over the whole company was E·lish´a·ma son of Am·mī´hud. [23]Over the company of the tribe of Ma·nas´seh was Ga·mā´li·el son of Pe·dah´zur, [24]and over the company of the tribe of Benjamin was A·bī´dan son of Gid·ē·ō´ni.

25 Then the standard of the camp of Dan, acting as the rear guard of all the camps, set out, company by company, and over the whole company was Ā·hī´ē´zer son of Am·mi·shad´daī. [26]Over the company of the tribe of Ash´er was Pā´gi·el son of Ōch´ran, [27]and over the company of the tribe of Naph´ta·lī was A·hī´ra son of Ē´nan. [28]This was the order of march of the Israelites, company by company, when they set out.

29 Moses said to Hō´bab son of Reū´el the Mid´i·an·īte, Moses' father-in-law, "We are setting out for the place of which the LORD said, 'I will give it to you'; come with us, and we will treat you well; for the LORD has promised good to Israel." [30]But he said to him, "I will not go, but I will go back to my own land and to my kindred." [31]He said, "Do not leave us, for you know

where we should camp in the wilderness, and you will serve as eyes for us. [32]Moreover, if you go with us, whatever good the LORD does for us, the same we will do for you."

33 So they set out from the mount of the LORD three days' journey with the ark of the covenant of the LORD going before them three days' journey, to seek out a resting place for them, [34]the cloud of the LORD being over them by day when they set out from the camp.

35 Whenever the ark set out, Moses would say,

"Arise, O LORD, let your enemies
　　be scattered,
and your foes flee before you."
[36] And whenever it came to rest, he
　　would say,
"Return, O LORD of the ten thou-
　　sand thousands of Israel."[q]

Complaining in the Desert

11 Now when the people complained in the hearing of the LORD about their misfortunes, the LORD heard it and his anger was kindled. Then the fire of the LORD burned against them, and consumed some outlying parts of the camp. [2]But the people cried out to Moses; and Moses prayed to the LORD, and the fire abated. [3]So that place was called Tab´e·rah,[r] because the fire of the LORD burned against them.

4 The rabble among them had a strong craving; and the Israelites also wept again, and said, "If only we had meat to eat! [5]We remember the fish we used to eat in Egypt for nothing, the cucumbers, the melons, the leeks, the onions, and the garlic; [6]but now our strength is dried up, and there is nothing at all but this manna to look at."

7 Now the manna was like coriander seed, and its color was like the color of gum resin. [8]The people went around and gathered it, ground it in mills or beat it in mortars, then boiled it in pots and

---

[q] Meaning of Heb uncertain　　[r] That is *Burning*

made cakes of it; and the taste of it was like the taste of cakes baked with oil. ⁹When the dew fell on the camp in the night, the manna would fall with it.

10 Moses heard the people weeping throughout their families, all at the entrances of their tents. Then the LORD became very angry, and Moses was displeased. ¹¹So Moses said to the LORD, "Why have you treated your servant so badly? Why have I not found favor in your sight, that you lay the burden of all this people on me? ¹²Did I conceive all this people? Did I give birth to them, that you should say to me, 'Carry them in your bosom, as a nurse carries a sucking child,' to the land that you promised on oath to their ancestors? ¹³Where am I to get meat to give to all this people? For they come weeping to me and say, 'Give us meat to eat!' ¹⁴I am not able to carry all this people alone, for they are too heavy for me. ¹⁵If this is the way you are going to treat me, put me to death at once—if I have found favor in your sight—and do not let me see my misery."

The Seventy Elders

16 So the LORD said to Moses, "Gather for me seventy of the elders of Israel, whom you know to be the elders of the people and officers over them; bring them to the tent of meeting, and have them take their place there with you. ¹⁷I will come down and talk with you there; and I will take some of the spirit that is on you and put it on them; and they shall bear the burden of the people along with you so that you will not bear it all by yourself. ¹⁸And say to the people: Consecrate yourselves for tomorrow, and you shall eat meat; for you have wailed in the hearing of the LORD, saying, 'If only we had meat to eat! Surely it was better for us in Egypt.' Therefore the LORD will give you meat, and you shall eat. ¹⁹You shall eat not only one day, or two days, or five days, or ten days, or twenty days, ²⁰but for a whole month—until it comes out of

When the Israelites wandered in the desert, they complained about eating the manna that God had given them. They wanted to eat meat. Because of their grumbling, God said they would have so much meat that it would come out of their noses! This was a way of saying they would eat so much meat that they would be too full to eat more. God wanted the people to trust that God would take care of them and to be thankful for what they had been given. God wants us to trust and be thankful too!

your nostrils and becomes loathsome to you—because you have rejected the LORD who is among you, and have wailed before him, saying, 'Why did we ever leave Egypt?' " ²¹But Moses said, "The people I am with number six hundred thousand on foot; and you say, 'I will give them meat, that they may eat for a whole month'! ²²Are there enough flocks and herds to slaughter for them? Are there enough fish in the sea to catch for them?" ²³The LORD said to Moses, "Is the LORD's power limited?ˢ Now you shall see whether my word will come true for you or not."

24 So Moses went out and told the people the words of the LORD; and he gathered seventy elders of the people, and placed them all around the tent. ²⁵Then the LORD came down in the cloud and spoke to him, and took some of the spirit that was on him and put it on the seventy elders; and when the spirit rested upon them, they prophesied. But they did not do so again.

26 Two men remained in the camp, one named El'dad, and the other named Me'dad, and the spirit rested on them; they were among those registered, but they had not gone out to the tent, and so they prophesied in the camp. ²⁷And a

ˢ Heb LORD's hand too short

young man ran and told Moses, "El´dad and Mē´dad are prophesying in the camp." [28]And Joshua son of Nun, the assistant of Moses, one of his chosen men,[t] said, "My lord Moses, stop them!" [29]But Moses said to him, "Are you jealous for my sake? Would that all the LORD's people were prophets, and that the LORD would put his spirit on them!" [30]And Moses and the elders of Israel returned to the camp.

The Quails

31 Then a wind went out from the LORD, and it brought quails from the sea and let them fall beside the camp, about a day's journey on this side and a day's journey on the other side, all around the camp, about two cubits deep on the ground. [32]So the people worked all that day and night and all the next day, gathering the quails; the least anyone gathered was ten homers; and they spread them out for themselves all around the camp. [33]But while the meat was still between their teeth, before it was consumed, the anger of the LORD was kindled against the people, and the LORD struck the people with a very great plague. [34]So that place was called Kib´roth-hat·tā´a·vah,[u] because there they buried the people who had the craving. [35]From Kib´roth-hat·tā´a·vah the people journeyed to Ha·zē´roth.

Aaron and Miriam Jealous of Moses

12 While they were at Ha·zē´roth, Miriam and Aaron spoke against Moses because of the Cū´shīte woman whom he had married (for he had indeed married a Cū´shīte woman); [2]and they said, "Has the LORD spoken only through Moses? Has he not spoken through us also?" And the LORD heard it. [3]Now the man Moses was very humble,[v] more so than anyone else on the face of the earth. [4]Suddenly the LORD said to Moses, Aaron, and Miriam, "Come out, you three, to the tent of meeting." So the

three of them came out. [5]Then the LORD came down in a pillar of cloud, and stood at the entrance of the tent, and called Aaron and Miriam; and they both came forward. [6]And he said, "Hear my words:

When there are prophets among you,
    I the LORD make myself known to
        them in visions;
    I speak to them in dreams.
[7] Not so with my servant Moses;
    he is entrusted with all my house.
[8] With him I speak face to face—
        clearly, not in riddles;
    and he beholds the form of the LORD.

Why then were you not afraid to speak against my servant Moses?" [9]And the anger of the LORD was kindled against them, and he departed.

10 When the cloud went away from over the tent, Miriam had become leprous,[w] as white as snow. And Aaron turned towards Miriam and saw that she was leprous. [11]Then Aaron said to Moses, "Oh, my lord, do not punish us[x] for a sin that we have so foolishly committed. [12]Do not let her be like one stillborn, whose flesh is half consumed when it comes out of its mother's womb." [13]And Moses cried to the LORD, "O God, please heal her." [14]But the LORD said to Moses, "If her father had but spit in her face, would she not bear her shame for seven days? Let her be shut out of the camp for seven days, and after that she may be brought in again." [15]So Miriam was shut out of the camp for seven days; and the people did not set out on the march until Miriam had been brought in again. [16]After that the people set out from Ha·zē´roth, and camped in the wilderness of Par´an.

Spies Sent into Canaan

13 The LORD said to Moses, [2]"Send men to spy out the land of Cā´naan, which I am giving to the Israelites;

[t] Or of Moses from his youth   [u] That is Graves of craving   [v] Or devout   [w] A term for several skin diseases; precise meaning uncertain   [x] Heb do not lay sin upon us

Canaan, sometimes called the Promised Land or the Land of Promise, was the land that God promised to Abraham. After the Israelites left Egypt and crossed through the desert, they took control of Canaan. The area today includes parts of the countries of Israel, Lebanon, and Jordan. See if you can find these countries on a map of the world!

they live in is good or bad, and whether the towns that they live in are unwalled or fortified, ²⁰and whether the land is rich or poor, and whether there are trees in it or not. Be bold, and bring some of the fruit of the land." Now it was the season of the first ripe grapes.

21 So they went up and spied out the land from the wilderness of Zin to Rē′-hob, near Lē′bō-hā′math. ²²They went up into the Neg′eb, and came to Hē′-bron; and A·hī′man, Shē′shaī, and Tal′maī, the An′a·kītes, were there. (Hē′-bron was built seven years before Zō′an in Egypt.) ²³And they came to the Wadi Esh′col, and cut down from there a branch with a single cluster of grapes, and they carried it on a pole between two of them. They also brought some pomegranates and figs. ²⁴That place was called the Wadi Esh′col,ʸ because of the cluster that the Israelites cut down from there.

The Report of the Spies

25 At the end of forty days they returned from spying out the land. ²⁶And they came to Moses and Aaron

from each of their ancestral tribes you shall send a man, every one a leader among them." ³So Moses sent them from the wilderness of Par′an, according to the command of the LORD, all of them leading men among the Israelites. ⁴These were their names: From the tribe of Reuben, Sham′mū·a son of Zac′cur; ⁵from the tribe of Sim′e·on, Shā′phat son of Hō′-rī; ⁶from the tribe of Judah, Caleb son of Je·phūn′neh; ⁷from the tribe of Is′-sa·char, Ī′gal son of Joseph; ⁸from the tribe of Ē′phra·im, Hō·shē′a son of Nun; ⁹from the tribe of Benjamin, Pal′tī son of Rā′phū; ¹⁰from the tribe of Zeb′ū·lun, Gad′di·el son of Sō′dī; ¹¹from the tribe of Joseph (that is, from the tribe of Ma·nas′seh), Gad′dī son of Sū′sī; ¹²from the tribe of Dan, Am′mi·el son of Ge·mal′lī; ¹³from the tribe of Ash′er, Seth′ur son of Michael; ¹⁴from the tribe of Naph′ta·lī, Nah′bī son of Voph′sī; ¹⁵from the tribe of Gad, Ge·ū′el son of Mā′chī. ¹⁶These were the names of the men whom Moses sent to spy out the land. And Moses changed the name of Hō·shē′a son of Nun to Joshua.

17 Moses sent them to spy out the land of Cā′naan, and said to them, "Go up there into the Neg′eb, and go up into the hill country, ¹⁸and see what the land is like, and whether the people who live in it are strong or weak, whether they are few or many, ¹⁹and whether the land

God's people were finally close to the land that God had promised to them! Moses sent twelve spies to find out about the land. Ten came back and said the people of the land were much too big and strong for the Israelites. Only Caleb and Joshua were faithful and believed. They said that with God on their side, the Israelites could take the land. But no one listened to them, so God decided that none of the adults would be allowed to enter the land. The Israelites continued to live in the wilderness next to Canaan until they died. Of all the men over the age of twenty, only Joshua and Caleb were allowed to enter the Promised Land.

ʸ That is *Cluster*

and to all the congregation of the Israelites in the wilderness of Par´an, at Kā´desh; they brought back word to them and to all the congregation, and showed them the fruit of the land. [27]And they told him, "We came to the land to which you sent us; it flows with milk and honey, and this is its fruit. [28]Yet the people who live in the land are strong, and the towns are fortified and very large; and besides, we saw the descendants of Ā´nak there. [29]The A·mal´e·kītes live in the land of the Neg´eb; the Hit´tītes, the Jeb´ū·sītes, and the Am´o·rītes live in the hill country; and the Cā´naan·ītes live by the sea, and along the Jordan."

30 But Caleb quieted the people before Moses, and said, "Let us go up at once and occupy it, for we are well able to overcome it." [31]Then the men who had gone up with him said, "We are not able to go up against this people, for they are stronger than we." [32]So they brought to the Israelites an unfavorable report of the land that they had spied out, saying, "The land that we have gone through as spies is a land that devours its inhabitants; and all the people that we saw in it are of great size. [33]There we saw the Neph´i·lim (the An´a·kītes come from the Neph´i·lim); and to ourselves we seemed like grasshoppers, and so we seemed to them."

The People Rebel

14 Then all the congregation raised a loud cry, and the people wept that night. [2]And all the Israelites complained against Moses and Aaron; the whole congregation said to them, "Would that we had died in the land of Egypt! Or would that we had died in this wilderness! [3]Why is the LORD bringing us into this land to fall by the sword? Our wives and our little ones will become booty; would it not be better for us to go back to Egypt?" [4]So they said to one another, "Let us choose a captain, and go back to Egypt."

5 Then Moses and Aaron fell on their faces before all the assembly of the congregation of the Israelites. [6]And Joshua son of Nun and Caleb son of Je·phun´neh, who were among those who had spied out the land, tore their clothes [7]and said to all the congregation of the Israelites, "The land that we went through as spies is an exceedingly good land. [8]If the LORD is pleased with us, he will bring us into this land and give it to us, a land that flows with milk and honey. [9]Only, do not rebel against the LORD; and do not fear the people of the land, for they are no more than bread for us; their protection is removed from them, and the LORD is with us; do not fear them." [10]But the whole congregation threatened to stone them.

Then the glory of the LORD appeared at the tent of meeting to all the Israelites. [11]And the LORD said to Moses, "How long will this people despise me? And how long will they refuse to believe in me, in spite of all the signs that I have done among them? [12]I will strike them with pestilence and disinherit them, and I will make of you a nation greater and mightier than they."

Moses Intercedes for the People

13 But Moses said to the LORD, "Then the Egyptians will hear of it, for in your might you brought up this people from among them, [14]and they will tell the inhabitants of this land. They have heard that you, O LORD, are in the midst of this people; for you, O LORD, are seen face to face, and your cloud stands over them and you go in front of them, in a pillar of cloud by day and in a pillar of fire by night. [15]Now if you kill this people all at one time, then the nations who have heard about you will say, [16]'It is because the LORD was not able to bring this people into the land he swore to give to them that he has slaughtered them in the wilderness.' [17]And now, therefore, let the power of the LORD be great in the way that you promised when you spoke, saying,

18 'The LORD is slow to anger,
and abounding in steadfast love,
forgiving iniquity and transgression,
but by no means clearing the guilty,
visiting the iniquity of the parents
upon the children
to the third and the fourth generation.'
19Forgive the iniquity of this people according to the greatness of your steadfast love, just as you have pardoned this people, from Egypt even until now."

20 Then the LORD said, "I do forgive, just as you have asked; 21nevertheless—as I live, and as all the earth shall be filled with the glory of the LORD—22none of the people who have seen my glory and the signs that I did in Egypt and in the wilderness, and yet have tested me these ten times and have not obeyed my voice, 23shall see the land that I swore to give to their ancestors; none of those who despised me shall see it. 24But my servant Caleb, because he has a different spirit and has followed me wholeheartedly, I will bring into the land into which he went, and his descendants shall possess it. 25Now, since the A·mal´-e·kītes and the Cā´naan·ītes live in the valleys, turn tomorrow and set out for the wilderness by the way to the Red Sea."z

An Attempted Invasion
Is Repulsed

26 And the LORD spoke to Moses and to Aaron, saying: 27How long shall this wicked congregation complain against me? I have heard the complaints of the Israelites, which they complain against me. 28Say to them, "As I live," says the LORD, "I will do to you the very things I heard you say: 29your dead bodies shall fall in this very wilderness; and of all your number, included in the census, from twenty years old and upward, who have complained against me, 30not one of you shall come into the land in which I swore to settle you, except Caleb son of Je·phūn´-neh and Joshua son of Nun. 31But your little ones, who you said would become

booty, I will bring in, and they shall know the land that you have despised. 32But as for you, your dead bodies shall fall in this wilderness. 33And your children shall be shepherds in the wilderness for forty years, and shall suffer for your faithlessness, until the last of your dead bodies lies in the wilderness. 34According to the number of the days in which you spied out the land, forty days, for every day a year, you shall bear your iniquity, forty years, and you shall know my displeasure." 35I the LORD have spoken; surely I will do thus to all this wicked congregation gathered together against me: in this wilderness they shall come to a full end, and there they shall die.

36 And the men whom Moses sent to spy out the land, who returned and made all the congregation complain against him by bringing a bad report about the land—37the men who brought an unfavorable report about the land died by a plague before the LORD. 38But Joshua son of Nun and Caleb son of Je·phūn´neh alone remained alive, of those men who went to spy out the land.

39 When Moses told these words to all the Israelites, the people mourned greatly. 40They rose early in the morning and went up to the heights of the hill country, saying, "Here we are. We will go up to the place that the LORD has promised, for we have sinned." 41But Moses said, "Why do you continue to transgress the command of the LORD? That will not succeed. 42Do not go up, for the LORD is not with you; do not let yourselves be struck down before your enemies. 43For the A·mal´e·kītes and the Cā´naan·ītes will confront you there, and you shall fall by the sword; because you have turned back from following the LORD, the LORD will not be with you." 44But they presumed to go up to the heights of the hill country, even though the ark of the covenant of the LORD, and Moses, had not left the camp. 45Then the

z Or Sea of Reeds

A·mal´e·kītes and the Cā´naan·ītes who lived in that hill country came down and defeated them, pursuing them as far as Hor´mah.

Various Offerings

15 The LORD spoke to Moses, saying: [2]Speak to the Israelites and say to them: When you come into the land you are to inhabit, which I am giving you, [3]and you make an offering by fire to the LORD from the herd or from the flock—whether a burnt offering or a sacrifice, to fulfill a vow or as a freewill offering or at your appointed festivals—to make a pleasing odor for the LORD, [4]then whoever presents such an offering to the LORD shall present also a grain offering, one-tenth of an ephah of choice flour, mixed with one-fourth of a hin of oil. [5]Moreover, you shall offer one-fourth of a hin of wine as a drink offering with the burnt offering or the sacrifice, for each lamb. [6]For a ram, you shall offer a grain offering, two-tenths of an ephah of choice flour mixed with one-third of a hin of oil; [7]and as a drink offering you shall offer one-third of a hin of wine, a pleasing odor to the LORD. [8]When you offer a bull as a burnt offering or a sacrifice, to fulfill a vow or as an offering of well-being to the LORD, [9]then you shall present with the bull a grain offering, three-tenths of an ephah of choice flour, mixed with half a hin of oil, [10]and you shall present as a drink offering half a hin of wine, as an offering by fire, a pleasing odor to the LORD.

11 Thus it shall be done for each ox or ram, or for each of the male lambs or the kids. [12]According to the number that you offer, so you shall do with each and every one. [13]Every native Israelite shall do these things in this way, in presenting an offering by fire, a pleasing odor to the LORD. [14]An alien who lives with you, or who takes up permanent residence among you, and wishes to offer an offering by fire, a pleasing odor to the LORD, shall do as you do. [15]As for the assembly, there shall be for both you and the resident alien a single statute, a perpetual statute throughout your generations; you and the alien shall be alike before the LORD. [16]You and the alien who resides with you shall have the same law and the same ordinance.

17 The LORD spoke to Moses, saying: [18]Speak to the Israelites and say to them: After you come into the land to which I am bringing you, [19]whenever you eat of the bread of the land, you shall present a donation to the LORD. [20]From your first batch of dough you shall present a loaf as a donation; you shall present it just as you present a donation from the threshing floor. [21]Throughout your generations you shall give to the LORD a donation from the first of your batch of dough.

22 But if you unintentionally fail to observe all these commandments that the LORD has spoken to Moses— [23]everything that the LORD has commanded you by Moses, from the day the LORD gave commandment and thereafter, throughout your generations— [24]then if it was done unintentionally without the knowledge of the congregation, the whole congregation shall offer one young bull for a burnt offering, a pleasing odor to the LORD, together with its grain offering and its drink offering, according to the ordinance, and one male goat for a sin offering. [25]The priest shall make atonement for all the congregation of the Israelites, and they shall be forgiven; it was unintentional, and they have brought their offering, an offering by fire to the LORD, and their sin offering before the LORD, for their error. [26]All the congregation of the Israelites shall be forgiven, as well as the aliens residing among them, because the whole people was involved in the error.

27 An individual who sins unintentionally shall present a female goat a year old for a sin offering. [28]And the priest shall make atonement before the LORD for the one who commits an error, when it is unintentional, to make atonement for the person, who then shall be forgiven. [29]For

both the native among the Israelites and the alien residing among them—you shall have the same law for anyone who acts in error. ³⁰But whoever acts high-handedly, whether a native or an alien, affronts the LORD, and shall be cut off from among the people. ³¹Because of having despised the word of the LORD and broken his commandment, such a person shall be utterly cut off and bear the guilt.

Penalty for Violating the Sabbath

32 When the Israelites were in the wilderness, they found a man gathering sticks on the sabbath day. ³³Those who found him gathering sticks brought him to Moses, Aaron, and to the whole congregation. ³⁴They put him in custody, because it was not clear what should be done to him. ³⁵Then the LORD said to Moses, "The man shall be put to death; all the congregation shall stone him outside the camp." ³⁶The whole congregation brought him outside the camp and stoned him to death, just as the LORD had commanded Moses.

Fringes on Garments

37 The LORD said to Moses: ³⁸Speak to the Israelites, and tell them to make fringes on the corners of their garments throughout their generations and to put a blue cord on the fringe at each corner. ³⁹You have the fringe so that, when you see it, you will remember all the commandments of the LORD and do them, and not follow the lust of your own heart and your own eyes. ⁴⁰So you shall remember and do all my commandments, and you shall be holy to your God. ⁴¹I am the LORD your God, who brought you out of the land of Egypt, to be your God: I am the LORD your God.

Revolt of Korah, Dathan, and Abiram

16 Now Kōʹrah son of Izʹhar son of Kōʹhath son of Levi, along with Dāʹthan and A·biʹram sons of E·liʹab, and

God had already decided that Aaron's family would serve as priests. Other families would be faithful in other ways. But Korah did not want to follow God's rules. He argued with Moses, saying that all the Israelite families were holy and could be religious leaders. Because Korah refused to listen, he was punished. The family and followers of Korah were swallowed up by the earth!

On son of Pēʹleth—descendants of Reuben—took ²two hundred fifty Israelite men, leaders of the congregation, chosen from the assembly, well-known men,ᵃ and they confronted Moses. ³They assembled against Moses and against Aaron, and said to them, "You have gone too far! All the congregation are holy, every one of them, and the LORD is among them. So why then do you exalt yourselves above the assembly of the LORD?" ⁴When Moses heard it, he fell on his face. ⁵Then he said to Kōʹrah and all his company, "In the morning the LORD will make known who is his, and who is holy, and who will be allowed to approach him; the one whom he will choose he will allow to approach him. ⁶Do this: take censers, Kōʹrah and all yourᵇ company, ⁷and tomorrow put fire in them, and lay incense on them before the LORD; and the man whom the LORD chooses shall be the holy one. You Lēʹvītes have gone too far!" ⁸Then Moses said to Kōʹrah, "Hear now, you Lēʹvītes! ⁹Is it too little for you that the God of Israel has separated you from the congregation of Israel, to allow you to approach him in order to perform the duties of the LORD's tabernacle, and to

---

ᵃ Cn: Heb *and they confronted Moses, and two hundred fifty men . . . well-known men*   ᵇ Heb *his* stand before the congregation and serve them? [10]He has allowed you to approach him, and all your brother Lē´vītes with you; yet you seek the priesthood as well! [11]Therefore you and all your company have gathered together against the LORD. What is Aaron that you rail against him?"

12 Moses sent for Dā´than and A·bī´-ram sons of E·lī´ab; but they said, "We will not come! [13]Is it too little that you have brought us up out of a land flowing with milk and honey to kill us in the wilderness, that you must also lord it over us? [14]It is clear you have not brought us into a land flowing with milk and honey, or given us an inheritance of fields and vineyards. Would you put out the eyes of these men? We will not come!"

15 Moses was very angry and said to the LORD, "Pay no attention to their offering. I have not taken one donkey from them, and I have not harmed any one of them." [16]And Moses said to Kō´-rah, "As for you and all your company, be present tomorrow before the LORD, you and they and Aaron; [17]and let each one of you take his censer, and put incense on it, and each one of you present his censer before the LORD, two hundred fifty censers; you also, and Aaron, each his censer." [18]So each man took his censer, and they put fire in the censers and laid incense on them, and they stood at the entrance of the tent of meeting with Moses and Aaron. [19]Then Kō´-rah assembled the whole congregation against them at the entrance of the tent of meeting. And the glory of the LORD appeared to the whole congregation.

20 Then the LORD spoke to Moses and to Aaron, saying: [21]Separate yourselves from this congregation, so that I may consume them in a moment. [22]They fell on their faces, and said, "O God, the God of the spirits of all flesh, shall one person sin and you become angry with the whole congregation?"

23 And the LORD spoke to Moses, saying: [24]Say to the congregation: Get away from the dwellings of Kō´rah, Dā´-than, and A·bī´ram. [25]So Moses got up and went to Dā´than and A·bī´ram; the elders of Israel followed him. [26]He said to the congregation, "Turn away from the tents of these wicked men, and touch nothing of theirs, or you will be swept away for all their sins." [27]So they got away from the dwellings of Kō´rah, Dā´than, and A·bī´ram; and Dā´than and A·bī´ram came out and stood at the entrance of their tents, together with their wives, their children, and their little ones. [28]And Moses said, "This is how you shall know that the LORD has sent me to do all these works; it has not been of my own accord: [29]If these people die a natural death, or if a natural fate comes on them, then the LORD has not sent me. [30]But if the LORD creates something new, and the ground opens its mouth and swallows them up, with all that belongs to them, and they go down alive into Shē´-ōl, then you shall know that these men have despised the LORD."

31 As soon as he finished speaking all these words, the ground under them was split apart. [32]The earth opened its mouth and swallowed them up, along with their households—everyone who belonged to Kō´rah and all their goods. [33]So they with all that belonged to them went down alive into Shē´ōl; the earth closed over them, and they perished from the midst of the assembly. [34]All Israel around them fled at their outcry, for they said, "The earth will swallow us too!" [35]And fire came out from the LORD and consumed the two hundred fifty men offering the incense.

36[c] Then the LORD spoke to Moses, saying: [37]Tell El·ē·ā´zar son of Aaron the priest to take the censers out of the blaze; then scatter the fire far and wide. [38]For the censers of these sinners have become holy at the cost of their lives. Make them into hammered plates as a covering for the

[c] Ch 17.1 in Heb

altar, for they presented them before the LORD and they became holy. Thus they shall be a sign to the Israelites. [39]So El·e·a'-zar the priest took the bronze censers that had been presented by those who were burned; and they were hammered out as a covering for the altar— [40]a reminder to the Israelites that no outsider, who is not of the descendants of Aaron, shall approach to offer incense before the LORD, so as not to become like Kō'rah and his company—just as the LORD had said to him through Moses.

41 On the next day, however, the whole congregation of the Israelites rebelled against Moses and against Aaron, saying, "You have killed the people of the LORD." [42]And when the congregation had assembled against them, Moses and Aaron turned toward the tent of meeting; the cloud had covered it and the glory of the LORD appeared. [43]Then Moses and Aaron came to the front of the tent of meeting, [44]and the LORD spoke to Moses, saying, [45]"Get away from this congregation, so that I may consume them in a moment." And they fell on their faces. [46]Moses said to Aaron, "Take your censer, put fire on it from the altar and lay incense on it, and carry it quickly to the congregation and make atonement for them. For wrath has gone out from the LORD; the plague has begun." [47]So Aaron took it as Moses had ordered, and ran into the middle of the assembly, where the plague had already begun among the people. He put on the incense, and made atonement for the people. [48]He stood between the dead and the living; and the plague was stopped. [49]Those who died by the plague were fourteen thousand seven hundred, besides those who died in the affair of Kō'rah. [50]When the plague was stopped, Aaron returned to Moses at the entrance of the tent of meeting.

The Budding of Aaron's Rod

17 [d] The LORD spoke to Moses, saying: [2]Speak to the Israelites, and get twelve staffs from them, one for each ancestral house, from all the leaders of their ancestral houses. Write each man's name on his staff, [3]and write Aaron's name on the staff of Levi. For there shall be one staff for the head of each ancestral house. [4]Place them in the tent of meeting before the covenant,[e] where I meet with you. [5]And the staff of the man whom I choose shall sprout; thus I will put a stop to the complaints of the Israelites that they continually make against you. [6]Moses spoke to the Israelites; and all their leaders gave him staffs, one for each leader, according to their ancestral houses, twelve staffs; and the staff of Aaron was among theirs. [7]So Moses placed the staffs before the LORD in the tent of the covenant.[e]

8 When Moses went into the tent of the covenant[f] on the next day, the staff of Aaron for the house of Levi had sprouted. It put forth buds, produced blossoms, and bore ripe almonds. [9]Then Moses brought out all the staffs from before the LORD to all the Israelites; and they looked, and each man took his staff. [10]And the LORD said to Moses, "Put back the staff of Aaron before the covenant,[e] to be kept as a warning to rebels, so that you may make an end of their complaints against me, or else they will die." [11]Moses did so; just as the LORD commanded him, so he did.

12 The Israelites said to Moses, "We are perishing; we are lost, all of us are lost! [13]Everyone who approaches the tabernacle of the LORD will die. Are we all to perish?"

Responsibility of Priests and Levites

18 The LORD said to Aaron: You and your sons and your ancestral house with you shall bear responsibility for offenses connected with the sanctuary, while you and your sons alone shall bear responsibility for

---

[d] Ch 17.16 in Heb   [e] Or *treaty*, or *testimony*; Heb *eduth*

offenses connected with the priesthood. [2]So bring with you also your brothers of the tribe of Levi, your ancestral tribe, in order that they may be joined to you, and serve you while you and your sons with you are in front of the tent of the covenant.[f] [3]They shall perform duties for you and for the whole tent. But they must not approach either the utensils of the sanctuary or the altar, otherwise both they and you will die. [4]They are attached to you in order to perform the duties of the tent of meeting, for all the service of the tent; no outsider shall approach you. [5]You yourselves shall perform the duties of the sanctuary and the duties of the altar, so that wrath may never again come upon the Israelites. [6]It is I who now take your brother Lē´vītes from among the Israelites; they are now yours as a gift, dedicated to the LORD, to perform the service of the tent of meeting. [7]But you and your sons with you shall diligently perform your priestly duties in all that concerns the altar and the area behind the curtain. I give your priesthood as a gift;[g] any outsider who approaches shall be put to death.

The Priests' Portion

8 The LORD spoke to Aaron: I have given you charge of the offerings made to me, all the holy gifts of the Israelites; I have given them to you and your sons as a priestly portion due you in perpetuity. [9]This shall be yours from the most holy things, reserved from the fire: every offering of theirs that they render to me as a most holy thing, whether grain offering, sin offering, or guilt offering, shall belong to you and your sons. [10]As a most holy thing you shall eat it; every male may eat it; it shall be holy to you. [11]This also is yours: I have given to you, together with your sons and daughters, as a perpetual due, whatever is set aside from the gifts of all the elevation offerings of the Israelites; everyone who is clean in your house may eat them. [12]All the best of the oil and all

the best of the wine and of the grain, the choice produce that they give to the LORD, I have given to you. [13]The first fruits of all that is in their land, which they bring to the LORD, shall be yours; everyone who is clean in your house may eat of it. [14]Every devoted thing in Israel shall be yours. [15]The first issue of the womb of all creatures, human and animal, which is offered to the LORD, shall be yours; but the first-born of human beings you shall redeem, and the firstborn of unclean animals you shall redeem. [16]Their redemption price, reckoned from one month of age, you shall fix at five shekels of silver, according to the shekel of the sanctuary (that is, twenty gerahs). [17]But the firstborn of a cow, or the firstborn of a sheep, or the firstborn of a goat, you shall not redeem; they are holy. You shall dash their blood on the altar, and shall turn their fat into smoke as an offering by fire for a pleasing odor to the LORD; [18]but their flesh shall be yours, just as the breast that is elevated and as the right thigh are yours. [19]All the holy offerings that the Israelites present to the LORD I have given to you, together with your sons and daughters, as a perpetual due; it is a covenant of salt forever before the LORD for you and your descendants as well. [20]Then the LORD said to Aaron: You shall have no allotment in their land, nor shall you have any share among them; I am your share and your possession among the Israelites.

21 To the Lē´vītes I have given every tithe in Israel for a possession in return for the service that they perform, the service in the tent of meeting. [22]From now on the Israelites shall no longer approach the tent of meeting, or else they will incur guilt and die. [23]But the Lē´vītes shall perform the service of the tent of meeting, and they shall bear responsibility for their own offenses; it shall be a perpetual statute throughout your generations. But among the Israelites they shall have no allotment,

---

[f] Or treaty, or testimony; Heb eduth   [g] Heb as a service of gift

²⁴because I have given to the Lē´vītes as their portion the tithe of the Israelites, which they set apart as an offering to the LORD. Therefore I have said of them that they shall have no allotment among the Israelites.

25 Then the LORD spoke to Moses, saying: ²⁶You shall speak to the Lē´vītes, saying: When you receive from the Israelites the tithe that I have given you from them for your portion, you shall set apart an offering from it to the LORD, a tithe of the tithe. ²⁷It shall be reckoned to you as your gift, the same as the grain of the threshing floor and the fullness of the wine press. ²⁸Thus you also shall set apart an offering to the LORD from all the tithes that you receive from the Israelites; and from them you shall give the LORD's offering to the priest Aaron. ²⁹Out of all the gifts to you, you shall set apart every offering due to the LORD; the best of all of them is the part to be consecrated. ³⁰Say also to them: When you have set apart the best of it, then the rest shall be reckoned to the Lē´vītes as produce of the threshing floor, and as produce of the wine press. ³¹You may eat it in any place, you and your households; for it is your payment for your service in the tent of meeting. ³²You shall incur no guilt by reason of it, when you have offered the best of it. But you shall not profane the holy gifts of the Israelites, on pain of death.

Ceremony of the Red Heifer

19 The LORD spoke to Moses and Aaron, saying: ²This is a statute of the law that the LORD has commanded: Tell the Israelites to bring you a red heifer without defect, in which there is no blemish and on which no yoke has been laid. ³You shall give it to the priest El·ē·ā´zar, and it shall be taken outside the camp and slaughtered in his presence. ⁴The priest El·ē·ā´zar shall take some of its blood with his finger and sprinkle it seven times towards the front of the tent of meeting. ⁵Then the heifer shall be burned in his sight; its skin, its flesh, and its blood, with its dung, shall be burned. ⁶The priest shall take cedarwood, hyssop, and crimson material, and throw them into the fire in which the heifer is burning. ⁷Then the priest shall wash his clothes and bathe his body in water, and afterwards he may come into the camp; but the priest shall remain unclean until evening. ⁸The one who burns the heifer[h] shall wash his clothes in water and bathe his body in water; he shall remain unclean until evening. ⁹Then someone who is clean shall gather up the ashes of the heifer, and deposit them outside the camp in a clean place; and they shall be kept for the congregation of the Israelites for the water for cleansing. It is a purification offering. ¹⁰The one who gathers the ashes of the heifer shall wash his clothes and be unclean until evening.

This shall be a perpetual statute for the Israelites and for the alien residing among them. ¹¹Those who touch the dead body of any human being shall be unclean seven days. ¹²They shall purify themselves with the water on the third day and on the seventh day, and so be clean; but if they do not purify themselves on the third day and on the seventh day, they will not become clean. ¹³All who touch a corpse, the body of a human being who has died, and do not purify themselves, defile the tabernacle of the LORD; such persons shall be cut off from Israel. Since water for cleansing was not dashed on them, they remain unclean; their uncleanness is still on them.

14 This is the law when someone dies in a tent: everyone who comes into the tent, and everyone who is in the tent, shall be unclean seven days. ¹⁵And every open vessel with no cover fastened on it is unclean. ¹⁶Whoever in the open field touches one who has been killed by a sword, or who has died naturally,[i] or a

[h] Heb *it*   [i] Heb lacks *naturally*

human bone, or a grave, shall be unclean seven days. [17]For the unclean they shall take some ashes of the burnt purification offering, and running water shall be added in a vessel; [18]then a clean person shall take hyssop, dip it in the water, and sprinkle it on the tent, on all the furnishings, on the persons who were there, and on whoever touched the bone, the slain, the corpse, or the grave. [19]The clean person shall sprinkle the unclean ones on the third day and on the seventh day, thus purifying them on the seventh day. Then they shall wash their clothes and bathe themselves in water, and at evening they shall be clean. [20]Any who are unclean but do not purify themselves, those persons shall be cut off from the assembly, for they have defiled the sanctuary of the LORD. Since the water for cleansing has not been dashed on them, they are unclean.

21 It shall be a perpetual statute for them. The one who sprinkles the water for cleansing shall wash his clothes, and whoever touches the water for cleansing shall be unclean until evening. [22]Whatever the unclean person touches shall be unclean, and anyone who touches it shall be unclean until evening.

The Waters of Meribah

20 The Israelites, the whole congregation, came into the wilderness of Zin in the first month, and the people stayed in Ka'desh. Miriam died there, and was buried there.

2 Now there was no water for the congregation; so they gathered together against Moses and against Aaron. [3]The people quarreled with Moses and said, "Would that we had died when our kindred died before the LORD! [4]Why have you brought the assembly of the LORD into this wilderness for us and our livestock to die here? [5]Why have you brought us up out of Egypt, to bring us to this wretched place? It is no place for grain, or figs, or vines, or pomegranates; and there is no water to drink." [6]Then

Moses and Aaron went away from the assembly to the entrance of the tent of meeting; they fell on their faces, and the glory of the LORD appeared to them. [7]The LORD spoke to Moses, saying: [8]Take the staff, and assemble the congregation, you and your brother Aaron, and command the rock before their eyes to yield its water. Thus you shall bring water out of the rock for them; thus you shall provide drink for the congregation and their livestock.

9 So Moses took the staff from before the LORD, as he had commanded him. [10]Moses and Aaron gathered the assembly together before the rock, and he said to them, "Listen, you rebels, shall we bring water for you out of this rock?" [11]Then Moses lifted up his hand and struck the rock twice with his staff; water came out abundantly, and the congregation and their livestock drank. [12]But the LORD said to Moses and Aaron, "Because you did not trust in me, to show my holiness before the eyes of the Israelites, therefore you shall not bring this assembly into the land that I have given them." [13]These are the waters of Mer'i·bah,[j] where the people of Israel quarreled with the LORD, and by which he showed his holiness.

Passage through Edom Refused

14 Moses sent messengers from Ka'-desh to the king of E'dom, "Thus says your brother Israel: You know all the adversity that has befallen us: [15]how our ancestors went down to Egypt, and we lived in Egypt a long time; and the Egyptians oppressed us and our ancestors; [16]and when we cried to the LORD, he heard our voice, and sent an angel and brought us out of Egypt; and here we are in Ka'desh, a town on the edge of your territory. [17]Now let us pass through your land. We will not pass through field or vineyard, or drink water from any well; we will go along the King's Highway, not turning aside to the right hand or to the left until we have

[j] That is *Quarrel*

passed through your territory."

18 But Ē′dom said to him, "You shall not pass through, or we will come out with the sword against you." ¹⁹The Israelites said to him, "We will stay on the highway; and if we drink of your water, we and our livestock, then we will pay for it. It is only a small matter; just let us pass through on foot." ²⁰But he said, "You shall not pass through." And Ē′dom came out against them with a large force, heavily armed. ²¹Thus Ē′dom refused to give Israel passage through their territory; so Israel turned away from them.

The Death of Aaron

22 They set out from Kā′desh, and the Israelites, the whole congregation, came to Mount Hor. ²³Then the LORD said to Moses and Aaron at Mount Hor, on the border of the land of Ē′dom, ²⁴"Let Aaron be gathered to his people. For he shall not enter the land that I have given to the Israelites, because you rebelled against my command at the waters of Mer′i·bah. ²⁵Take Aaron and his son El·ē·ā′zar, and bring them up Mount Hor; ²⁶strip Aaron of his vestments, and put them on his son El·ē·ā′zar. But Aaron shall be gathered to his people,ᵏ and shall die there." ²⁷Moses did as the LORD had commanded; they went up Mount Hor in the sight of the whole congregation. ²⁸Moses stripped Aaron of his vestments, and put them on his son El·ē·ā′zar; and Aaron died there on the top of the mountain. Moses and El·ē·ā′zar came down from the mountain. ²⁹When all the congregation saw that Aaron had died, all the house of Israel mourned for Aaron thirty days.

The Bronze Serpent

21 When the Cā′naan·īte, the king of Ar′ad, who lived in the Neg′eb, heard that Israel was coming by the way of Ath′a·rim, he fought against Israel and took some of them captive. ²Then Israel made a vow to the LORD and said, "If you will indeed give this people

The Israelites were very impatient as they waited to enter the land of Canaan. They whined and complained against God. As punishment, their camp was filled with poisonous snakes that bit the people. When Moses asked God for help, God told him to make a snake out of bronze and put it on a pole. Everyone who looked at the bronze snake was healed. Even though they were not patient and did not trust, God healed and took care of the people.

into our hands, then we will utterly destroy their towns." ³The LORD listened to the voice of Israel, and handed over the Cā′naan·ītes; and they utterly destroyed them and their towns; so the place was called Hor′mah.ˡ

4 From Mount Hor they set out by the way to the Red Sea,ᵐ to go around the land of Ē′dom; but the people became impatient on the way. ⁵The people spoke against God and against Moses, "Why have you brought us up out of Egypt to die in the wilderness? For there is no food and no water, and we detest this miserable food." ⁶Then the LORD sent poisonousⁿ serpents among the people, and they bit the people, so that many Israelites died. ⁷The people came to Moses and said, "We have sinned by speaking against the LORD and against you; pray to the LORD to take away the serpents from us." So Moses prayed for the people. ⁸And the LORD said to Moses, "Make a poisonousᵒ serpent, and set it on a pole; and everyone who is bitten shall look at it and live." ⁹So Moses made a serpent of bronze, and put it upon a pole; and whenever a serpent bit someone, that person would look at the serpent of bronze and live.

ᵏ Heb lacks *to his people*   ˡ Heb *Destruction*
ᵐ Or *Sea of Reeds*   ⁿ Or *fiery;* Heb *seraphim*
ᵒ Or *fiery;* Heb *seraph*

The Journey to Moab

10 The Israelites set out, and camped in Ō´both. [11]They set out from Ō´both, and camped at Ī´ye-ab´a·rim, in the wilderness bordering Mō´ab toward the sunrise. [12]From there they set out, and camped in the Wadi Zē´red. [13]From there they set out, and camped on the other side of the Ar´non, in[p] the wilderness that extends from the boundary of the Am´o·rītes; for the Ar´non is the boundary of Mō´ab, between Mō´ab and the Am´o·rītes. [14]Wherefore it is said in the Book of the Wars of the LORD,

"Wa´heb in Sū´phah and the wadis.
The Ar´non [15]and the slopes of the
    wadis
    that extend to the seat of Ar,
and lie along the border of Mō´ab."[q]

16 From there they continued to Bē´er;[r] that is the well of which the LORD said to Moses, "Gather the people together, and I will give them water." [17]Then Israel sang this song:

"Spring up, O well!—Sing to it!—
[18] the well that the leaders sank,
    that the nobles of the people dug,
    with the scepter, with the staff."

From the wilderness to Mat´ta·nah, [19]from Mat´ta·nah to Na·hal´i·el, from Na·hal´i·el to Bā´moth, [20]and from Bā´moth to the valley lying in the region of Mō´ab by the top of Pis´gah that overlooks the wasteland.[s]

King Sihon Defeated

21 Then Israel sent messengers to King Sī´hon of the Am´o·rītes, saying, [22]"Let me pass through your land; we will not turn aside into field or vineyard; we will not drink the water of any well; we will go by the King's Highway until we have passed through your territory." [23]But Sī´hon would not allow Israel to pass through his territory. Sī´hon gathered all his people together, and went out against Israel to the wilderness; he came to Jā´haz, and fought against Israel. [24]Israel put him to the sword, and took possession of his land

from the Ar´non to the Jab´bok, as far as to the Am´mon·ītes; for the boundary of the Am´mon·ītes was strong. [25]Israel took all these towns, and Israel settled in all the towns of the Am´o·rītes, in Hesh´bon, and in all its villages. [26]For Hesh´bon was the city of King Sī´hon of the Am´o·rītes, who had fought against the former king of Mō´ab and captured all his land as far as the Ar´non. [27]Therefore the ballad singers say,

"Come to Hesh´bon, let it be built;
    let the city of Sī´hon be established.
[28] For fire came out from Hesh´bon,
    flame from the city of Sī´hon.
It devoured Ar of Mō´ab,
    and swallowed up[t] the heights of
        the Ar´non.
[29] Woe to you, O Mō´ab!
    You are undone, O people of Chē´-
        mosh!
He has made his sons fugitives,
    and his daughters captives,
    to an Am´o·rīte king, Sī´hon.
[30] So their posterity perished
    from Hesh´bon[u] to Dī´bon,
    and we laid waste until fire spread
        to Med´e·ba."[v]

31 Thus Israel settled in the land of the Am´o·rītes. [32]Moses sent to spy out Jā´zer; and they captured its villages, and dispossessed the Am´o·rītes who were there.

King Og Defeated

33 Then they turned and went up the road to Bā´shan; and King Og of Bā´shan came out against them, he and all his people, to battle at Ed´rē·ī. [34]But the LORD said to Moses, "Do not be afraid of him; for I have given him into your hand, with all his people, and all his land. You shall do to him as you did to King Sī´hon of the Am´o·rītes, who ruled in Hesh´bon." [35]So they killed him, his sons, and all his people, until there was no survivor left; and they took possession of his land.

---

[p] Gk: Heb *which is in*   [q] Meaning of Heb uncertain   [r] That is *Well*   [s] Or *Jeshimon*   [t] Gk: Heb *and the lords of*   [u] Gk: Heb *we have shot at them; Heshbon has perished*   [v] Compare Sam Gk: Meaning of MT uncertain

Balak Summons Balaam to Curse Israel

22 The Israelites set out, and camped in the plains of Mō′ab across the Jordan from Jericho. ²Now Bā′lak son of Zip′por saw all that Israel had done to the Am′o·rītes. ³Mō′ab was in great dread of the people, because they were so numerous; Mō′ab was overcome with fear of the people of Israel. ⁴And Mō′ab said to the elders of Mid′i·an, "This horde will now lick up all that is around us, as an ox licks up the grass of the field." Now Bā′lak son of Zip′por was king of Mō′ab at that time. ⁵He sent messengers to Bā′laam son of Bē′or at Pē′thor, which is on the Euphrates, in the land of Ā′maw,ʷ to summon him, saying, "A people has come out of Egypt; they have spread over the face of the earth, and they have settled next to me. ⁶Come now, curse this people for me, since they are stronger than I; perhaps I shall be able to defeat them and drive them from the land; for I know that whomever you bless is blessed, and whomever you curse is cursed."

7 So the elders of Mō′ab and the elders of Mid′i·an departed with the fees for divination in their hand; and they came to Bā′laam, and gave him Bā′lak's message. ⁸He said to them, "Stay here tonight, and I will bring back word to you, just as the LORD speaks to me"; so the officials of Mō′ab stayed with Bā′laam. ⁹God came to Bā′laam and said, "Who are these men with you?" ¹⁰Bā′laam said to God, "King Bā′lak son of Zip′por of Mō′ab, has sent me this message: ¹¹'A people has come out of Egypt and has spread over the face of the earth; now come, curse them for me; perhaps I shall be able to fight against them and drive them out.' " ¹²God said to Bā′laam, "You shall not go with them; you shall not curse the people, for they are blessed." ¹³So Bā′laam rose in the morning, and said to the officials of Bā′lak, "Go to your own land, for the LORD has

Have you ever heard an animal talk? Once God used a talking donkey to get someone's attention! When Balak, king of Moab, was afraid of the Israelites, he told Balaam to curse them. As Balaam traveled to the Israelites' camp, the angel of the Lord blocked the road. Balaam didn't see the angel, but his donkey did. The donkey tried to turn away three times, and Balaam was angry. Finally the donkey was given the power to speak! Imagine how Balaam must have felt! In the same way that God opened the donkey's mouth, God opened Balaam's eyes. Balaam did what God commanded him to do, and he blessed Israel.

refused to let me go with you." ¹⁴So the officials of Mō′ab rose and went to Bā′lak, and said, "Bā′laam refuses to come with us."

15 Once again Bā′lak sent officials, more numerous and more distinguished than these. ¹⁶They came to Bā′laam and said to him, "Thus says Bā′lak son of Zip′por: 'Do not let anything hinder you from coming to me; ¹⁷for I will surely do you great honor, and whatever you say to me I will do; come, curse this people for me.' " ¹⁸But Bā′laam replied to the servants of Bā′lak, "Although Bā′lak were to give me his house full of silver and gold, I could not go beyond the command of the LORD my God, to do less or more. ¹⁹You remain here, as the others did, so that I may learn what more the LORD may say to me." ²⁰That night God came to Bā′laam and said to him, "If the men have come to summon you, get up and go with them; but do only what I tell you to do." ²¹So Bā′laam got up in the morning, saddled his donkey, and went with the officials of Mō′ab.

ʷ Or *land of his kinsfolk*

Balaam, the Donkey, and the Angel

22 God's anger was kindled because he was going, and the angel of the LORD took his stand in the road as his adversary. Now he was riding on the donkey, and his two servants were with him. ²³The donkey saw the angel of the LORD standing in the road, with a drawn sword in his hand; so the donkey turned off the road, and went into the field; and Bā'laam struck the donkey, to turn it back onto the road. ²⁴Then the angel of the LORD stood in a narrow path between the vineyards, with a wall on either side. ²⁵When the donkey saw the angel of the LORD, it scraped against the wall, and scraped Bā'laam's foot against the wall; so he struck it again. ²⁶Then the angel of the LORD went ahead, and stood in a narrow place, where there was no way to turn either to the right or to the left. ²⁷When the donkey saw the angel of the LORD, it lay down under Bā'laam; and Bā'laam's anger was kindled, and he struck the donkey with his staff. ²⁸Then the LORD opened the mouth of the donkey, and it said to Bā'laam, "What have I done to you, that you have struck me these three times?" ²⁹Bā'laam said to the donkey, "Because you have made a fool of me! I wish I had a sword in my hand! I would kill you right now!" ³⁰But the donkey said to Bā'laam, "Am I not your donkey, which you have ridden all your life to this day? Have I been in the habit of treating you this way?" And he said, "No."

31 Then the LORD opened the eyes of Bā'laam, and he saw the angel of the LORD standing in the road, with his drawn sword in his hand; and he bowed down, falling on his face. ³²The angel of the LORD said to him, "Why have you struck your donkey these three times? I have come out as an adversary, because your way is perverse[x] before me. ³³The donkey saw me, and turned away from me these three times. If it had not turned away from me, surely just now I would

have killed you and let it live." ³⁴Then Bā'laam said to the angel of the LORD, "I have sinned, for I did not know that you were standing in the road to oppose me. Now therefore, if it is displeasing to you, I will return home." ³⁵The angel of the LORD said to Bā'laam, "Go with the men; but speak only what I tell you to speak." So Bā'laam went on with the officials of Bā'lak.

36 When Bā'lak heard that Bā'laam had come, he went out to meet him at Ir-mō'ab, on the boundary formed by the Ar'non, at the farthest point of the boundary. ³⁷Bā'lak said to Bā'laam, "Did I not send to summon you? Why did you not come to me? Am I not able to honor you?" ³⁸Bā'laam said to Bā'lak, "I have come to you now, but do I have power to say just anything? The word God puts in my mouth, that is what I must say." ³⁹Then Bā'laam went with Bā'lak, and they came to Kir'i-ath-hū'zoth. ⁴⁰Bā'lak sacrificed oxen and sheep, and sent them to Bā'laam and to the officials who were with him.

Balaam's First Oracle

41 On the next day Bā'lak took Bā'laam and brought him up to Bā'moth-bā'-al; and from there he could see part of the people of Israel.[y] ¹Then Bā'laam said to Bā'lak, "Build me seven altars here, and prepare seven bulls and seven rams for me." ²Bā'lak did as Bā'laam had said; and Bā'lak and Bā'laam offered a bull and a ram on each altar. ³Then Bā'laam said to Bā'lak, "Stay here beside your burnt offerings while I go aside. Perhaps the LORD will come to meet me. Whatever he shows me I will tell you." And he went to a bare height.

4 Then God met Bā'laam; and Bā'laam said to him, "I have arranged the seven altars, and have offered a bull and a ram on each altar." ⁵The LORD put a word in Bā'laam's mouth, and said, "Return to Bā'lak, and this is what you

---

[x] Meaning of Heb uncertain   [y] Heb lacks *of Israel*

must say." ⁶So he returned to Bāʹlak,ᶻ who was standing beside his burnt offerings with all the officials of Mōʹab. ⁷Then Bāʹlaamᵃ uttered his oracle, saying:

"Bāʹlak has brought me from Arʹam,
the king of Mōʹab from the eastern mountains:
'Come, curse Jacob for me;
Come, denounce Israel!'
⁸ How can I curse whom God has not cursed?
How can I denounce those whom the LORD has not denounced?
⁹ For from the top of the crags I see him,
from the hills I behold him;
Here is a people living alone,
and not reckoning itself among the nations!
¹⁰ Who can count the dust of Jacob,
or number the dust-cloudᵇ of Israel?
Let me die the death of the upright,
and let my end be like his!"

11 Then Bāʹlak said to Bāʹlaam, "What have you done to me? I brought you to curse my enemies, but now you have done nothing but bless them." ¹²He answered, "Must I not take care to say what the LORD puts into my mouth?"

Balaam's Second Oracle

13 So Bāʹlak said to him, "Come with me to another place from which you may see them; you shall see only part of them, and shall not see them all; then curse them for me from there." ¹⁴So he took him to the field of Zōʹphim, to the top of Pisʹgah. He built seven altars, and offered a bull and a ram on each altar. ¹⁵Bāʹlaam said to Bāʹlak, "Stand here beside your burnt offerings, while I meet the LORD over there." ¹⁶The LORD met Bāʹlaam, put a word into his mouth, and said, "Return to Bāʹlak, and this is what you shall say." ¹⁷When he came to him, he was standing beside his burnt offerings with the officials of Mōʹab. Bāʹlak said to him, "What has the LORD said?"

¹⁸Then Bāʹlaam uttered his oracle, saying:
"Rise, Bāʹlak, and hear;
listen to me, O son of Zipʹpor:
¹⁹ God is not a human being, that he should lie,
or a mortal, that he should change his mind.
Has he promised, and will he not do it?
Has he spoken, and will he not fulfill it?
²⁰ See, I received a command to bless;
he has blessed, and I cannot revoke it.
²¹ He has not beheld misfortune in Jacob;
nor has he seen trouble in Israel.
The LORD their God is with them,
acclaimed as a king among them.
²² God, who brings them out of Egypt,
is like the horns of a wild ox for them.
²³ Surely there is no enchantment against Jacob,
no divination against Israel;
now it shall be said of Jacob and Israel,
'See what God has done!'
²⁴ Look, a people rising up like a lioness,
and rousing itself like a lion!
It does not lie down until it has eaten the prey
and drunk the blood of the slain."

25 Then Bāʹlak said to Bāʹlaam, "Do not curse them at all, and do not bless them at all." ²⁶But Bāʹlaam answered Bāʹlak, "Did I not tell you, 'Whatever the LORD says, that is what I must do'?"

27 So Bāʹlak said to Bāʹlaam, "Come now, I will take you to another place;

"God is not a human being, that he should lie, or a mortal, that he should change his mind. Has he promised, and will he not do it? Has he spoken and will he not fulfill it?" Numbers 23:19

ᶻ Heb *him*   ᵃ Heb *he*   ᵇ Or *fourth part*

perhaps it will please God that you may curse them for me from there." ²⁸So Bā´lak took Bā´laam to the top of Pē´or, which overlooks the wasteland.^c ²⁹Bā-laam said to Bā´lak, "Build me seven altars here, and prepare seven bulls and seven rams for me." ³⁰So Bā´lak did as Bā´laam had said, and offered a bull and a ram on each altar.

Balaam's Third Oracle

24 Now Bā´laam saw that it pleased the LORD to bless Israel, so he did not go, as at other times, to look for omens, but set his face toward the wilderness. ²Bā´laam looked up and saw Israel camping tribe by tribe. Then the spirit of God came upon him, ³and he uttered his oracle, saying:

"The oracle of Bā´laam son of Bē´or,
   the oracle of the man whose eye is
     clear,^d
⁴ the oracle of one who hears the
     words of God,
  who sees the vision of the Almighty,^e
  who falls down, but with eyes
     uncovered:
⁵ how fair are your tents, O Jacob,
   your encampments, O Israel!
⁶ Like palm groves that stretch far away,
   like gardens beside a river,
  like aloes that the LORD has planted,
  like cedar trees beside the waters.
⁷ Water shall flow from his buckets,
   and his seed shall have abundant
     water,
  his king shall be higher than Ā´gag,
   and his kingdom shall be exalted.
⁸ God who brings him out of Egypt,
   is like the horns of a wild ox for him;
  he shall devour the nations that are
     his foes
   and break their bones.
  He shall strike with his arrows.^f
⁹ He crouched, he lay down like a lion,
   and like a lioness; who will rouse
     him up?
  Blessed is everyone who blesses you,
   and cursed is everyone who
     curses you."

¹⁰ Then Bā´lak's anger was kindled against Bā´laam, and he struck his hands together. Bā´lak said to Bā´laam, "I summoned you to curse my enemies, but instead you have blessed them these three times. ¹¹Now be off with you! Go home! I said, 'I will reward you richly,' but the LORD has denied you any reward." ¹²And Bā´laam said to Bā´lak, "Did I not tell your messengers whom you sent to me, ¹³'If Bā´lak should give me his house full of silver and gold, I would not be able to go beyond the word of the LORD, to do either good or bad of my own will; what the LORD says, that is what I will say'? ¹⁴So now, I am going to my people; let me advise you what this people will do to your people in days to come."

Balaam's Fourth Oracle

¹⁵ So he uttered his oracle, saying:
"The oracle of Bā´laam son of Bē´or,
   the oracle of the man whose eye is
     clear,^g
¹⁶ the oracle of one who hears the
     words of God,
  and knows the knowledge of the
     Most High,^g
  who sees the vision of the Almighty^h
  who falls down, but with his eyes
     uncovered:
¹⁷ I see him, but not now;
   I behold him, but not near—
  a star shall come out of Jacob,
   and a scepter shall rise out of
     Israel;
  it shall crush the borderlandsⁱ of Mō´ab,
   and the territoryⁱ of all the Sheth´-
     ītes.
¹⁸ Ē´dom will become a possession,
   Sē´ir a possession of its enemies,^j
    while Israel does valiantly.
¹⁹ One out of Jacob shall rule,
   and destroy the survivors of Ir."

^c Or *overlooks Jeshimon*   ^d Or *closed* or *open*
^e Traditional rendering of Heb *Shaddai*   ^f Meaning of Heb uncertain   ^g Or *of Elyon*   ^h Or *forehead*   ⁱ Some Mss read *skull*   ^j Heb *Seir, its enemies, a possession*

20 Then he looked on Amʹa·lek, and uttered his oracle, saying:

"First among the nations was Amʹa·lek, but its end is to perish forever."

21 Then he looked on the Kenʹīte, and uttered his oracle, saying:

"Enduring is your dwelling place, and your nest is set in the rock;

22 yet Kāin is destined for burning.

How long shall Asʹshur take you away captive?"

23 Again he uttered his oracle, saying:

"Alas, who shall live when God does this?

24 But ships shall come from Kitʹtim and shall afflict Asʹshur and Ēʹber;

and he also shall perish forever."

25 Then Bāʹlaam got up and went back to his place, and Bāʹlak also went his way.

Worship of Baal of Peor

25 While Israel was staying at Shitʹtim, the people began to have sexual relations with the women of Mōʹab. ²These invited the people to the sacrifices of their gods, and the people ate and bowed down to their gods. ³Thus Israel yoked itself to the Bāʹal of Pēʹor, and the LORD's anger was kindled against Israel. ⁴The LORD said to Moses, "Take all the chiefs of the people, and impale them in the sun before the LORD, in order that the fierce anger of the LORD may turn away from Israel." ⁵And Moses said to the judges of Israel, "Each of you shall kill any of your people who have yoked themselves to the Bāʹal of Pēʹor."

6 Just then one of the Israelites came and brought a Midʹi·an·īte woman into his family, in the sight of Moses and in the sight of the whole congregation of the Israelites, while they were weeping at the entrance of the tent of meeting. ⁷When Phinʹe·has son of El·ē·āʹzar, son of Aaron the priest, saw it, he got up and left the congregation. Taking a spear in his hand, ⁸he went after the Israelite man into the tent, and pierced the two of them, the Israelite and the woman, through the belly. So the plague was stopped among the people of Israel. ⁹Nevertheless those that died by the plague were twenty-four thousand.

10 The LORD spoke to Moses, saying: ¹¹"Phinʹe·has son of El·ē·āʹzar, son of Aaron the priest, has turned back my wrath from the Israelites by manifesting such zeal among them on my behalf that in my jealousy I did not consume the Israelites. ¹²Therefore say, 'I hereby grant him my covenant of peace. ¹³It shall be for him and for his descendants after him a covenant of perpetual priesthood, because he was zealous for his God, and made atonement for the Israelites.' "

14 The name of the slain Israelite man, who was killed with the Midʹi·an·īte woman, was Zimʹrī son of Saʹlū, head of an ancestral house belonging to the Simʹē·on·ītes. ¹⁵The name of the Midʹi·an·īte woman who was killed was Cōzʹbī daughter of Zur, who was the head of a clan, an ancestral house in Midʹi·an.

16 The LORD said to Moses, ¹⁷"Harass the Midʹi·an·ītes, and defeat them; ¹⁸for they have harassed you by the trickery with which they deceived you in the affair of Pēʹor, and in the affair of Cōzʹbī, the daughter of a leader of Midʹi·an, their sister; she was killed on the day of the plague that resulted from Pēʹor."

A Census of the New Generation

26 After the plague the LORD said to Moses and to El·ē·āʹzar son of Aaron the priest, ²"Take a census of the whole congregation of the Israelites, from twenty years old and upward, by their ancestral houses, everyone in Israel able to go to war." ³Moses and El·ē·āʹzar the priest spoke with them in the plains of Mōʹab by the Jordan opposite Jericho, saying, ⁴"Take a census of the people,ᵏ from twenty years old and upward," as the LORD commanded Moses.

ᵏ Heb lacks *take a census of the people:* Compare verse 2

God told Moses to take a second census, so Moses counted the Israelite men and gave land to each of them. This list did not include anyone from the older people who were counted in the first census (see Numbers 1). From those people, only Caleb and Joshua were allowed to enter Canaan.

The Israelites, who came out of the land of Egypt, were:

5 Reuben, the firstborn of Israel. The descendants of Reuben: of Hā´noch, the clan of the Hā´noch·ītes; of Pal´lū, the clan of the Pal´lū·ītes; [6]of Hez´ron, the clan of the Hez´ron·ītes; of Car´mī, the clan of the Car´mītes. [7]These are the clans of the Reū´ben·ītes; the number of those enrolled was forty-three thousand seven hundred thirty. [8]And the descendants of Pal´lū E·lī´ab. [9]The descendants of E·lī´ab: Nem´ū·el, Dā´than, and A·bī´ram. These are the same Dā´than and A·bī´ram, chosen from the congregation, who rebelled against Moses and Aaron in the company of Kō´rah, when they rebelled against the LORD, [10]and the earth opened its mouth and swallowed them up along with Kō´rah, when that company died, when the fire devoured two hundred fifty men; and they became a warning. [11]Notwithstanding, the sons of Kō´rah did not die.

12 The descendants of Sim´ē·on by their clans: of Nem´ū·el, the clan of the Nem´ū·el·ītes; of Jā´min, the clan of the Jā´min·ītes; of Jā´chin, the clan of the Jā´chin·ītes; [13]of Zē´rah, the clan of the Zē´ra·hītes; of Shā´ūl, the clan of the Shā´ūl·ītes.[1] [14]These are the clans of the Sim´ē·on·ītes, twenty-two thousand two hundred.

15 The children of Gad by their clans: of Zē´phon, the clan of the Zē´phon·ītes; of Hag´gī, the clan of the Hag´gītes; of Shū´nī, the clan of the Shū´nītes; [16]of Oz´nī, the clan of the Oz´nītes; of Ē´rī, the clan of the Ē´rītes; [17]of Ar´od, the clan of the Ar´od·ītes; of A·rē´lī, the clan of the A·rē´lītes. [18]These are the clans of the Gad´ītes: the number of those enrolled was forty thousand five hundred.

19 The sons of Judah: Er and Ō´nan; Er and Ō´nan died in the land of Cā´naan. [20]The descendants of Judah by their clans were: of Shē´lah, the clan of the Shē´lan·ītes; of Per´ez, the clan of the Per´e·zītes; of Zē´rah, the clan of the Zē´ra·hītes. [21]The descendants of Per´ez were: of Hez´ron, the clan of the Hez´ron·ītes; of Hā´mul, the clan of the Hā´mul·ītes. [22]These are the clans of Judah: the number of those enrolled was seventy-six thousand five hundred.

23 The descendants of Is´sa·char by their clans: of Tō´la, the clan of the Tō´la·ītes; of Pū´vah, the clan of the Pū´nītes; [24]of Jash´ub, the clan of the Jash´ub·ītes; of Shim´ron, the clan of the Shim´ron·ītes. [25]These are the clans of Is´sa·char: sixty-four thousand three hundred enrolled.

26 The descendants of Zeb´ū·lun by their clans: of Sē´red, the clan of the Sē´red·ītes; of Ē´lon, the clan of the Ē´lon·ītes; of Jah´lē·el, the clan of the Jah´lē·el·ītes. [27]These are the clans of the Zeb´ū·lun·ītes; the number of those enrolled was sixty thousand five hundred.

28 The sons of Joseph by their clans: Ma·nas´seh and Ē´phra·im. [29]The descendants of Ma·nas´seh: of Mā´chir, the clan of the Mā´chir·ītes; and Mā´chir was the father of Gil´e·ad; of Gil´e·ad, the clan of the Gil´e·ad·ītes. [30]These are the descendants of Gil´e·ad: of Ī´e´zer, the clan of the Ī´e´zer·ītes; of Hē´lek, the clan of the Hē´lek·ītes; [31]and of As´ri·el, the clan of the As´ri·el·ītes; and of Shē´chem, the clan of the Shē´chem·ītes; [32]and of She·mī´da, the clan of the She·mī´da·ītes; and of Hē´pher, the clan of the Hē´pher·ītes. [33]Now Ze·loph´e·had son of Hē´pher had no sons, but daughters: and the names of

[1] Or Saul . . . Saulites

the daughters of Ze·loph´e·had were Mah´lah, Noah, Hog´lah, Mil´cah, and Tir´zah. [34]These are the clans of Ma·nas´seh; the number of those enrolled was fifty-two thousand seven hundred.

35 These are the descendants of E´phra·im according to their clans: of Shū·thē´lah, the clan of the Shū·the·lā´hītes; of Bē´cher, the clan of the Bē´cher·ītes; of Tā´han, the clan of the Tā´ha·nītes. [36]And these are the descendants of Shū·thē´lah: of E´ran, the clan of the E´ran·ītes. [37]These are the clans of the E´phra·im·ītes: the number of those enrolled was thirty-two thousand five hundred. These are the descendants of Joseph by their clans.

38 The descendants of Benjamin by their clans: of Bē´la, the clan of the Bē´la·ītes; of Ash´bel, the clan of the Ash´bel·ītes; of A·hī´ram, the clan of the A·hī´ram·ītes; [39]of She·phū´pham, the clan of the She·phū´pham·ītes; of Hū´pham, the clan of the Hū´pham·ītes. [40]And the sons of Bē´la were Ard and Nā´a·man: of Ard, the clan of the Ard´ītes; of Nā´a·man, the clan of the Nā´a·mītes. [41]These are the descendants of Benjamin by their clans; the number of those enrolled was forty-five thousand six hundred.

42 These are the descendants of Dan by their clans: of Shū´ham, the clan of the Shū´ham·ītes. These are the clans of Dan by their clans. [43]All the clans of the Shū´ham·ītes: sixty-four thousand four hundred enrolled.

44 The descendants of Ash´er by their families: of Im´nah, the clan of the Im´nītes; of Ish´vī, the clan of the Ish´vītes; of Bē·rī´ah, the clan of the Bē·rī´ītes. [45]Of the descendants of Bē·rī´ah: of Hē´ber, the clan of the Hē´ber·ītes; of Mal´chi·el, the clan of the Mal´chi·el·ītes. [46]And the name of the daughter of Ash´er was Sē´rah. [47]These are the clans of the Ash´er·ītes: the number of those enrolled was fifty-three thousand four hundred.

48 The descendants of Naph´ta·lī by their clans: of Jah´zē·el, the clan of the Jah´zē·el·ītes; of Gū´nī, the clan of the Gū´nītes; [49]of Jē´zer, the clan of the Jē´zer·ītes; of Shil´lem, the clan of the Shil´lem·ītes. [50]These are the Naph´ta·lītes[m] by their clans: the number of those enrolled was forty-five thousand four hundred.

51 This was the number of the Israelites enrolled: six hundred and one thousand seven hundred thirty.

52 The LORD spoke to Moses, saying: [53]To these the land shall be apportioned for inheritance according to the number of names. [54]To a large tribe you shall give a large inheritance, and to a small tribe you shall give a small inheritance; every tribe shall be given its inheritance according to its enrollment. [55]But the land shall be apportioned by lot; according to the names of their ancestral tribes they shall inherit. [56]Their inheritance shall be apportioned according to lot between the larger and the smaller.

57 This is the enrollment of the Lē´vītes by their clans: of Ger´shon, the clan of the Ger´shon·ītes; of Kō´hath, the clan of the Kō´hath·ītes; of Me·rar´ī, the clan of the Me·rar´ītes. [58]These are the clans of Levi: the clan of the Lib´nītes, the clan of the Hē´bron·ītes, the clan of the Mah´lītes, the clan of the Mū´shītes, the clan of the Kō´ra·hītes. Now Kō´hath was the father of Am´ram. [59]The name of Am´ram's wife was Joch´e·bed daughter of Levi, who was born to Levi in Egypt; and she bore to Am´ram: Aaron, Moses, and their sister Miriam. [60]To Aaron were born Nā´dab, A·bī´hū, El·e·ā´zar, and Ith´a·mar. [61]But Nā´dab and A·bī´hū died when they offered unholy fire before the LORD. [62]The number of those enrolled was twenty-three thousand, every male one month old and upward; for they were not enrolled among the Israelites because there was no allotment given to them among the Israelites.

63 These were those enrolled by Moses and El·e·ā´zar the priest, who enrolled the Israelites in the plains of Mō´ab

[m] Heb *clans of Naphtali*

by the Jordan opposite Jericho. [64]Among these there was not one of those enrolled by Moses and Aaron the priest, who had enrolled the Israelites in the wilderness of Sinai. [65]For the LORD had said of them, "They shall die in the wilderness." Not one of them was left, except Caleb son of Je·phŭn´neh and Joshua son of Nun.

A man named Zelophehad had five daughters, but no sons. After he died, Zelophehad's daughters asked for his property. At that time, women did not usually inherit land. But when Moses asked God, God said that these daughters should have their father's property.

The Daughters of Zelophehad

27 Then the daughters of Ze·loph´e·had came forward. Ze·loph´e·had was son of Hē´pher son of Gil´e·ad son of Mā´chir son of Ma·nas´seh son of Joseph, a member of the Ma·nas´sīte clans. The names of his daughters were: Mah´lah, Noah, Hog´lah, Mil´cah, and Tir´zah. [2]They stood before Moses, El·ē·ā´zar the priest, the leaders, and all the congregation, at the entrance of the tent of meeting, and they said, [3]"Our father died in the wilderness; he was not among the company of those who gathered themselves together against the LORD in the company of Kō´rah, but died for his own sin; and he had no sons. [4]Why should the name of our father be taken away from his clan because he had no son? Give to us a possession among our father's brothers."

[5] Moses brought their case before the LORD. [6]And the LORD spoke to Moses, saying: [7]The daughters of Ze·loph´e·had are right in what they are saying; you shall indeed let them possess an inheritance among their father's brothers and

pass the inheritance of their father on to them. [8]You shall also say to the Israelites, "If a man dies, and has no son, then you shall pass his inheritance on to his daughter. [9]If he has no daughter, then you shall give his inheritance to his brothers. [10]If he has no brothers, then you shall give his inheritance to his father's brothers. [11]And if his father has no brothers, then you shall give his inheritance to the nearest kinsman of his clan, and he shall possess it. It shall be for the Israelites a statute and ordinance, as the LORD commanded Moses."

Joshua Appointed Moses' Successor

[12] The LORD said to Moses, "Go up this mountain of the Ab´a·rim range, and see the land that I have given to the Israelites. [13]When you have seen it, you also shall be gathered to your people, as your brother Aaron was, [14]because you rebelled against my word in the wilderness of Zin when the congregation quarreled with me.[n] You did not show my holiness before their eyes at the waters." (These are the waters of Mer´i·bath-kā´desh in the wilderness of Zin.) [15]Moses spoke to the LORD, saying, [16]"Let the LORD, the God of the spirits of all flesh, appoint someone over the congregation [17]who shall go out before them and come in before them, who shall lead them out and bring them in, so that the

Before Moses died, he chose Joshua to be the next leader. Joshua had great military skill and was faithful to God and God's promises. Think of some people you know who are good leaders for God's people today—maybe your mom or dad, a teacher, a pastor, or a friend. How do they show their faithfulness to God? What can you learn from them?

[n] Heb lacks *with me*

congregation of the LORD may not be like sheep without a shepherd." ¹⁸So the LORD said to Moses, "Take Joshua son of Nun, a man in whom is the spirit, and lay your hand upon him; ¹⁹have him stand before El·ē·ā´zar the priest and all the congregation, and commission him in their sight. ²⁰You shall give him some of your authority, so that all the congregation of the Israelites may obey. ²¹But he shall stand before El·ē·ā´zar the priest, who shall inquire for him by the decision of the Ū´rim before the LORD; at his word they shall go out, and at his word they shall come in, both he and all the Israelites with him, the whole congregation." ²²So Moses did as the LORD commanded him. He took Joshua and had him stand before El·ē·ā´zar the priest and the whole congregation; ²³he laid his hands on him and commissioned him— as the LORD had directed through Moses.

Daily Offerings

28 The LORD spoke to Moses, saying: ²Command the Israelites, and say to them: My offering, the food for my offerings by fire, my pleasing odor, you shall take care to offer to me at its appointed time. ³And you shall say to them, This is the offering by fire that you shall offer to the LORD: two male lambs a year old without blemish, daily, as a regular offering. ⁴One lamb you shall offer in the morning, and the other lamb you shall offer at twilight;ᵒ ⁵also one-tenth of an ephah of choice flour for a grain offering, mixed with one-fourth of a hin of beaten oil. ⁶It is a regular burnt offering, ordained at Mount Sinai for a pleasing odor, an offering by fire to the LORD. ⁷Its drink offering shall be one-fourth of a hin for each lamb; in the sanctuary you shall pour out a drink offering of strong drink to the LORD. ⁸The other lamb you shall offer at twilightᵒ with a grain offering and a drink offering like the one in the morning; you shall offer it as an offering by fire, a pleasing odor to the LORD.

Sabbath Offerings

9 On the sabbath day: two male lambs a year old without blemish, and two-tenths of an ephah of choice flour for a grain offering, mixed with oil, and its drink offering— ¹⁰this is the burnt offering for every sabbath, in addition to the regular burnt offering and its drink offering.

Monthly Offerings

11 At the beginnings of your months you shall offer a burnt offering to the LORD: two young bulls, one ram, seven male lambs a year old without blemish; ¹²also three-tenths of an ephah of choice flour for a grain offering, mixed with oil, for each bull; and two-tenths of choice flour for a grain offering, mixed with oil, for the one ram; ¹³and one-tenth of choice flour mixed with oil as a grain offering for every lamb—a burnt offering of pleasing odor, an offering by fire to the LORD. ¹⁴Their drink offerings shall be half a hin of wine for a bull, one-third of a hin for a ram, and one-fourth of a hin for a lamb. This is the burnt offering of every month throughout the months of the year. ¹⁵And there shall be one male goat for a sin offering to the LORD; it shall be offered in addition to the regular burnt offering and its drink offering.

Offerings at Passover

16 On the fourteenth day of the first month there shall be a passover offering to the LORD. ¹⁷And on the fifteenth day of this month is a festival; seven days shall unleavened bread be eaten. ¹⁸On the first day there shall be a holy convocation. You shall not work at your occupations. ¹⁹You shall offer an offering by fire, a burnt offering to the LORD: two young bulls, one ram, and seven male lambs a year old; see that they are without blemish. ²⁰Their grain offering shall be of choice flour mixed with oil: three-tenths of an ephah shall you offer for a bull, and two-tenths for a ram; ²¹one-tenth shall you offer for each of the

ᵒ Heb *between the two evenings*

seven lambs; ²²also one male goat for a sin offering, to make atonement for you. ²³You shall offer these in addition to the burnt offering of the morning, which belongs to the regular burnt offering. ²⁴In the same way you shall offer daily, for seven days, the food of an offering by fire, a pleasing odor to the LORD; it shall be offered in addition to the regular burnt offering and its drink offering. ²⁵And on the seventh day you shall have a holy convocation; you shall not work at your occupations.

Offerings at the Festival of Weeks

26 On the day of the first fruits, when you offer a grain offering of new grain to the LORD at your festival of weeks, you shall have a holy convocation; you shall not work at your occupations. ²⁷You shall offer a burnt offering, a pleasing odor to the LORD: two young bulls, one ram, seven male lambs a year old. ²⁸Their grain offering shall be of choice flour mixed with oil, three-tenths of an ephah for each bull, two-tenths for one ram, ²⁹one-tenth for each of the seven lambs; ³⁰with one male goat, to make atonement for you. ³¹In addition to the regular burnt offering with its grain offering, you shall offer them and their drink offering. They shall be without blemish.

Offerings at the Festival of Trumpets

29 On the first day of the seventh month you shall have a holy convocation; you shall not work at your occupations. It is a day for you to blow the trumpets, ²and you shall offer a burnt offering, a pleasing odor to the LORD: one young bull, one ram, seven male lambs a year old without blemish. ³Their grain offering shall be of choice flour mixed with oil, three-tenths of one ephah for the bull, two-tenths for the ram, ⁴and one-tenth for each of the seven lambs; ⁵with one male goat for a

sin offering, to make atonement for you. ⁶These are in addition to the burnt offering of the new moon and its grain offering, and the regular burnt offering and its grain offering, and their drink offerings, according to the ordinance for them, a pleasing odor, an offering by fire to the LORD.

Offerings on the Day of Atonement

7 On the tenth day of this seventh month you shall have a holy convocation, and deny yourselves;^p you shall do no work. ⁸You shall offer a burnt offering to the LORD, a pleasing odor: one young bull, one ram, seven male lambs a year old. They shall be without blemish. ⁹Their grain offering shall be of choice flour mixed with oil, three-tenths of an ephah for the bull, two-tenths for the one ram, ¹⁰one-tenth for each of the seven lambs; ¹¹with one male goat for a sin offering, in addition to the sin offering of atonement, and the regular burnt offering and its grain offering, and their drink offerings.

Offerings at the Festival of Booths

12 On the fifteenth day of the seventh month you shall have a holy convocation; you shall not work at your occupations. You shall celebrate a festival to the LORD seven days. ¹³You shall offer a burnt offering, an offering by fire, a pleasing odor to the LORD: thirteen young bulls, two rams, fourteen male lambs a year old. They shall be without blemish. ¹⁴Their grain offering shall be of choice flour mixed with oil, three-tenths of an ephah for each of the thirteen bulls, two-tenths for each of the two rams, ¹⁵and one-tenth for each of the fourteen lambs; ¹⁶also one male goat for a sin offering, in addition to the regular burnt offering, its grain offering and its drink offering.

p Or and fast

17 On the second day: twelve young bulls, two rams, fourteen male lambs a year old without blemish, [18]with the grain offering and the drink offerings for the bulls, for the rams, and for the lambs, as prescribed in accordance with their number; [19]also one male goat for a sin offering, in addition to the regular burnt offering and its grain offering, and their drink offerings.

20 On the third day: eleven bulls, two rams, fourteen male lambs a year old without blemish, [21]with the grain offering and the drink offerings for the bulls, for the rams, and for the lambs, as prescribed in accordance with their number; [22]also one male goat for a sin offering, in addition to the regular burnt offering and its grain offering and its drink offering.

23 On the fourth day: ten bulls, two rams, fourteen male lambs a year old without blemish, [24]with the grain offering and the drink offerings for the bulls, for the rams, and for the lambs, as prescribed in accordance with their number; [25]also one male goat for a sin offering, in addition to the regular burnt offering, its grain offering and its drink offering.

26 On the fifth day: nine bulls, two rams, fourteen male lambs a year old without blemish, [27]with the grain offering and the drink offerings for the bulls, for the rams, and for the lambs, as prescribed in accordance with their number; [28]also one male goat for a sin offering, in addition to the regular burnt offering and its grain offering and its drink offering.

29 On the sixth day: eight bulls, two rams, fourteen male lambs a year old without blemish, [30]with the grain offering and the drink offerings for the bulls, for the rams, and for the lambs, as prescribed in accordance with their number; [31]also one male goat for a sin offering, in addition to the regular burnt offering, its grain offering, and its drink offerings.

32 On the seventh day: seven bulls, two rams, fourteen male lambs a year old

without blemish, [33]with the grain offering and the drink offerings for the bulls, for the rams, and for the lambs, as prescribed in accordance with their number; [34]also one male goat for a sin offering, besides the regular burnt offering, its grain offering, and its drink offering.

35 On the eighth day you shall have a solemn assembly; you shall not work at your occupations. [36]You shall offer a burnt offering, an offering by fire, a pleasing odor to the LORD: one bull, one ram, seven male lambs a year old without blemish, [37]and the grain offering and the drink offerings for the bull, for the ram, and for the lambs, as prescribed in accordance with their number; [38]also one male goat for a sin offering, in addition to the regular burnt offering and its grain offering and its drink offering.

39 These you shall offer to the LORD at your appointed festivals, in addition to your votive offerings and your freewill offerings, as your burnt offerings, your grain offerings, your drink offerings, and your offerings of well-being.

40[q] So Moses told the Israelites everything just as the LORD had commanded Moses.

Vows Made by Women

30 Then Moses said to the heads of the tribes of the Israelites: This is what the LORD has commanded. [2]When a man makes a vow to the LORD, or swears an oath to bind himself by a pledge, he shall not break his word; he shall do according to all that proceeds out of his mouth.

3 When a woman makes a vow to the LORD, or binds herself by a pledge, while within her father's house, in her youth, [4]and her father hears of her vow or her pledge by which she has bound herself, and says nothing to her; then all her vows shall stand, and any pledge by which she has bound herself shall stand. [5]But if her father expresses disapproval

[q] Ch 30.1 in Heb

to her at the time that he hears of it, no vow of hers, and no pledge by which she has bound herself, shall stand; and the LORD will forgive her, because her father had expressed to her his disapproval.

6 If she marries, while obligated by her vows or any thoughtless utterance of her lips by which she has bound herself, ⁷and her husband hears of it and says nothing to her at the time that he hears, then her vows shall stand, and her pledges by which she has bound herself shall stand. ⁸But if, at the time that her husband hears of it, he expresses disapproval to her, then he shall nullify the vow by which she was obligated, or the thoughtless utterance of her lips, by which she bound herself; and the LORD will forgive her. ⁹(But every vow of a widow or of a divorced woman, by which she has bound herself, shall be binding upon her.) ¹⁰And if she made a vow in her husband's house, or bound herself by a pledge with an oath, ¹¹and her husband heard it and said nothing to her, and did not express disapproval to her, then all her vows shall stand, and any pledge by which she bound herself shall stand. ¹²But if her husband nullifies them at the time that he hears them, then whatever proceeds out of her lips concerning her vows, or concerning her pledge of herself, shall not stand. Her husband has nullified them, and the LORD will forgive her. ¹³Any vow or any binding oath to deny herself,ʳ her husband may allow to stand, or her husband may nullify. ¹⁴But if her husband says nothing to her from day to day,ˢ then he validates all her vows, or all her pledges, by which she is obligated; he has validated them, because he said nothing to her at the time that he heard of them. ¹⁵But if he nullifies them some time after he has heard of them, then he shall bear her guilt.

16 These are the statutes that the LORD commanded Moses concerning a husband and his wife, and a father and his daughter while she is still young and in her father's house.

War against Midian

31 The LORD spoke to Moses, saying, ²"Avenge the Israelites on the Mid·i·an·ites; afterward you shall be gathered to your people." ³So Moses said to the people, "Arm some of your number for the war, so that they may go against Mid·i·an, to execute the LORD's vengeance on Mid·i·an. ⁴You shall send a thousand from each of the tribes of Israel to the war." ⁵So out of the thousands of Israel, a thousand from each tribe were conscripted, twelve thousand armed for battle. ⁶Moses sent them to the war, a thousand from each tribe, along with Phin´e·has son of El·e·a´zar the priest,ᵗ with the vessels of the sanctuary and the trumpets for sounding the alarm in his hand. ⁷They did battle against Mid´i·an, as the LORD had commanded Moses, and killed every male. ⁸They killed the kings of Mid´i·an: Ē´vī, Rē´kem, Zur, Hur, and Rē´ba, the five kings of Mid´i·an, in addition to others who were slain by them; and they also killed Bā´laam son of Bē´or with the sword. ⁹The Israelites took the women of Mid´i·an and their little ones captive; and they took all their cattle, their flocks, and all their goods as booty. ¹⁰All their towns where they had settled, and all their encampments, they burned, ¹¹but they took all the spoil and all the booty, both people and animals. ¹²Then they brought the captives and the booty and the spoil to Moses, to El·e·a´zar the priest, and to the congregation of the Israelites, at the camp on the plains of Mō´ab by the Jordan at Jericho.

Return from the War

13 Moses, El·e·a´zar the priest, and all the leaders of the congregation went to meet them outside the camp. ¹⁴Moses became angry with the officers of the army, the commanders of thousands and the commanders of hundreds, who had come from service in the war. ¹⁵Moses

ʳ Or to fast　ˢ Or from that day to the next　ᵗ Gk: Heb adds to the war said to them, "Have you allowed all the women to live? [16]These women here, on Bā´laam's advice, made the Israelites act treacherously against the LORD in the affair of Pē´or, so that the plague came among the congregation of the LORD. [17]Now therefore, kill every male among the little ones, and kill every woman who has known a man by sleeping with him. [18]But all the young girls who have not known a man by sleeping with him, keep alive for yourselves. [19]Camp outside the camp seven days; whoever of you has killed any person or touched a corpse, purify yourselves and your captives on the third and on the seventh day. [20]You shall purify every garment, every article of skin, everything made of goats' hair, and every article of wood."

21 El·ē·ā´zar the priest said to the troops who had gone to battle: "This is the statute of the law that the LORD has commanded Moses: [22]gold, silver, bronze, iron, tin, and lead— [23]everything that can withstand fire, shall be passed through fire, and it shall be clean. Nevertheless it shall also be purified with the water for purification; and whatever cannot withstand fire, shall be passed through the water. [24]You must wash your clothes on the seventh day, and you shall be clean; afterward you may come into the camp."

Disposition of Captives and Booty

25 The LORD spoke to Moses, saying, [26]"You and El·ē·ā´zar the priest and the heads of the ancestral houses of the congregation make an inventory of the booty captured, both human and animal. [27]Divide the booty into two parts, between the warriors who went out to battle and all the congregation. [28]From the share of the warriors who went out to battle, set aside as tribute for the LORD, one item out of every five hundred, whether persons, oxen, donkeys, sheep, or goats. [29]Take it from their half and give it to El·ē·ā´zar the priest as an

offering to the LORD. [30]But from the Israelites' half you shall take one out of every fifty, whether persons, oxen, donkeys, sheep, or goats—all the animals— and give them to the Lē´vītes who have charge of the tabernacle of the LORD."

31 Then Moses and El·ē·ā´zar the priest did as the LORD had commanded Moses: 32 The booty remaining from the spoil that the troops had taken totaled six hundred seventy-five thousand sheep, [33]seventy-two thousand oxen, [34]sixty-one thousand donkeys, [35]and thirty-two thousand persons in all, women who had not known a man by sleeping with him. 36 The half-share, the portion of those who had gone out to war, was in number three hundred thirty-seven thousand five hundred sheep and goats, [37]and the LORD's tribute of sheep and goats was six hundred seventy-five. [38]The oxen were thirty-six thousand, of which the LORD's tribute was seventy-two. [39]The donkeys were thirty thousand five hundred, of which the LORD's tribute was sixty-one. [40]The persons were sixteen thousand, of which the LORD's tribute was thirty-two persons. [41]Moses gave the tribute, the offering for the LORD, to El·ē·ā´zar the priest, as the LORD had commanded Moses.

42 As for the Israelites' half, which Moses separated from that of the troops, [43]the congregation's half was three hundred thirty-seven thousand five hundred sheep and goats, [44]thirty-six thousand oxen, [45]thirty thousand five hundred donkeys, [46]and sixteen thousand persons. [47]From the Israelites' half Moses took one of every fifty, both of persons and of animals, and gave them to the Lē´vītes who had charge of the tabernacle of the LORD; as the LORD had commanded Moses.

48 Then the officers who were over the thousands of the army, the commanders of thousands and the commanders of hundreds, approached Moses, [49]and said to Moses, "Your servants have counted the warriors who are

under our command, and not one of us is missing. ⁵⁰And we have brought the LORD's offering, what each of us found, articles of gold, armlets and bracelets, signet rings, earrings, and pendants, to make atonement for ourselves before the LORD." ⁵¹Moses and El·e·a´zar the priest received the gold from them, all in the form of crafted articles. ⁵²And all the gold of the offering that they offered to the LORD, from the commanders of thousands and the commanders of hundreds, was sixteen thousand seven hundred fifty shekels. ⁵³(The troops had all taken plunder for themselves.) ⁵⁴So Moses and El·e·a´zar the priest received the gold from the commanders of thousands and of hundreds, and brought it into the tent of meeting as a memorial for the Israelites before the LORD.

Conquest and Division of Transjordan

32 Now the Reu̅´ben·ites and the Gad´ites owned a very great number of cattle. When they saw that the land of Ja´zer and the land of Gil´e·ad was a good place for cattle, ²the Gad´ites and the Reu̅´ben·ites came and spoke to Moses, to El·e·a´zar the priest, and to the leaders of the congregation, saying, ³"At´a·roth, Di´bon, Ja´zer, Nim´rah, Hesh´bon, E̅·le·a´leh, Se̅´bam, Ne̅´bo, and Be̅´on— ⁴the land that the LORD subdued before the congregation of Israel—is a land for cattle; and your servants have cattle." ⁵They continued, "If we have found favor in your sight, let this land be given to your servants for a possession; do not make us cross the Jordan."

6 But Moses said to the Gad´ites and to the Reu̅´ben·ites, "Shall your brothers go to war while you sit here? ⁷Why will you discourage the hearts of the Israelites from going over into the land that the LORD has given them? ⁸Your fathers did this, when I sent them from Ka̅´desh-bar´ne̅·a to see the land. ⁹When they went up to the Wadi Esh´col and saw the land, they discour-

aged the hearts of the Israelites from going into the land that the LORD had given them. ¹⁰The LORD's anger was kindled on that day and he swore, saying, ¹¹"Surely none of the people who came up out of Egypt, from twenty years old and upward, shall see the land that I swore to give to Abraham, to Isaac, and to Jacob, because they have not unreservedly followed me— ¹²none except Caleb son of Je·phun´neh the Ken´iz·zite and Joshua son of Nun, for they have unreservedly followed the LORD.' ¹³And the LORD's anger was kindled against Israel, and he made them wander in the wilderness for forty years, until all the generation that had done evil in the sight of the LORD had disappeared. ¹⁴And now you, a brood of sinners, have risen in place of your fathers, to increase the LORD's fierce anger against Israel! ¹⁵If you turn away from following him, he will again abandon them in the wilderness; and you will destroy all this people."

16 Then they came up to him and said, "We will build sheepfolds here for our flocks, and towns for our little ones, ¹⁷but we will take up arms as a vanguardᵘ before the Israelites, until we have brought them to their place. Meanwhile our little ones will stay in the fortified towns because of the inhabitants of the land. ¹⁸We will not return to our homes until all the Israelites have obtained their inheritance. ¹⁹We will not inherit with them on the other side of the Jordan and beyond, because our inheritance has come to us on this side of the Jordan to the east."

20 So Moses said to them, "If you do this—if you take up arms to go before the LORD for the war, ²¹and all those of you who bear arms cross the Jordan before the LORD, until he has driven out his enemies from before him ²²and the land is subdued before the LORD—then after that you may return and be free of obligation to the LORD and to Israel, and this land shall be your possession before the LORD.

ᵘ Cn: heb *hurrying*

²³But if you do not do this, you have sinned against the LORD; and be sure your sin will find you out. ²⁴Build towns for your little ones, and folds for your flocks; but do what you have promised."

25 Then the Gadʹites and the Reūʹben·ites said to Moses, "Your servants will do as my lord commands. ²⁶Our little ones, our wives, our flocks, and all our livestock shall remain there in the towns of Gilʹe·ad; ²⁷but your servants will cross over, everyone armed for war, to do battle for the LORD, just as my lord orders."

28 So Moses gave command concerning them to El·ē·aʹzar the priest, to Joshua son of Nun, and to the heads of the ancestral houses of the Israelite tribes. ²⁹And Moses said to them, "If the Gadʹites and the Reūʹben·ites, everyone armed for battle before the LORD, will cross over the Jordan with you and the land shall be subdued before you, then you shall give them the land of Gilʹe·ad for a possession; ³⁰but if they will not cross over with you armed, they shall have possessions among you in the land of Cāʹnaan." ³¹The Gadʹites and the Reūʹben·ites answered, "As the LORD has spoken to your servants, so we will do. ³²We will cross over armed before the LORD into the land of Cāʹnaan, but the possession of our inheritance shall remain with us on this side of ᵛ the Jordan."

33 Moses gave to them—to the Gadʹites and to the Reūʹben·ites and to the half-tribe of Ma·nasʹseh son of Joseph—the kingdom of King Sīʹhon of the Amʹo·rītes and the kingdom of King Og of Bāʹshan, the land and its towns, with the territories of the surrounding towns. ³⁴And the Gadʹites rebuilt Dīʹbon, Atʹa·roth, A·rōʹer, ³⁵Atʹroth-shōʹphan, Jāʹzer, Jogʹbe·hah, ³⁶Beth-nimʹrah, and Beth-harʹan, fortified cities, and folds for sheep. ³⁷And the Reūʹben·ites rebuilt Heshʹbon, Ē·le·āʹleh, Kir·i·a·thāʹim, ³⁸Nēʹbō, and Bāʹal-mēʹon (some names being changed), and Sibʹmah; and they gave names to the towns that they rebuilt. ³⁹The descendants of Māʹchir son of Ma·nasʹseh went to Gilʹe·ad, captured it, and dispossessed the Amʹo·rītes who were there; ⁴⁰so Moses gave Gilʹe·ad to Māʹchir son of Ma·nasʹseh, and he settled there. ⁴¹Jāʹir son of Ma·nasʹseh went and captured their villages, and renamed them Havʹvoth-jāʹir.ʷ ⁴²And Nōʹbah went and captured Kēʹnath and its villages, and renamed it Nōʹbah after himself.

The Stages of Israel's Journey from Egypt

33 These are the stages by which the Israelites went out of the land of Egypt in military formation under the leadership of Moses and Aaron. ²Moses wrote down their starting points, stage by stage, by command of the LORD; and these are their stages according to their starting places. ³They set out from Ramʹe·sēs in the first month, on the fifteenth day of the first month; on the day after the passover the Israelites went out boldly in the sight of all the Egyptians, ⁴while the Egyptians were burying all their firstborn, whom the LORD had struck down among them. The LORD executed judgments even against their gods.

5 So the Israelites set out from Ramʹe·sēs, and camped at Sucʹcoth. ⁶They set out from Sucʹcoth, and camped at Ēʹtham, which is on the edge of the wilderness. ⁷They set out from Ēʹtham, and turned back to Pī-ha·hīʹroth, which faces Bāʹal-zēʹphon; and they camped before Migʹdōl. ⁸They set out from Pī-ha·hīʹroth, passed through the sea into the wilderness, went a three days' journey in the wilderness of Ēʹtham, and camped at Marʹah. ⁹They set out from Marʹah and came to Ēʹlim; at Ēʹlim there were twelve springs of water and seventy palm trees, and they camped there. ¹⁰They set out from Ēʹlim and camped by the Red Sea.ˣ ¹¹They set out from the Red Seaˣ and camped in the wilderness of Sin. ¹²They set out from the wilderness of Sin and camped at Dophʹkah. ¹³They set

---

ᵛ Heb *beyond*   ʷ That is *the villages of Jair*   ˣ Or *Sea of Reeds* out from Doph′kah and camped at Ā′lush. [14]They set out from Ā′lush and camped at Reph′i·dim, where there was no water for the people to drink. [15]They set out from Reph′i·dim and camped in the wilderness of Sinai. [16]They set out from the wilderness of Sinai and camped at Kib′roth-hat·tā′a·vah. [17]They set out from Kib′roth-hat·tā′a·vah and camped at Ha·zē′roth. [18]They set out from Ha·zē′- roth and camped at Rith′mah. [19]They set out from Rith′mah and camped at Rim′mon-per′ez. [20]They set out from Rim′mon-per′ez and camped at Lib′nah. [21]They set out from Lib′nah and camped at Ris′sah. [22]They set out from Ris′sah and camped at Kē·he·lā′thah. [23]They set out from Kē·he·lā′thah and camped at Mount Shē′pher. [24]They set out from Mount Shē′pher and camped at Ha·-rā′dah. [25]They set out from Ha·rā′dah and camped at Mak·hē′loth. [26]They set out from Mak·hē′loth and camped at Tā′hath. [27]They set out from Tā′hath and camped at Tē′rah. [28]They set out from Tē′rah and camped at Mith′kah. [29]They set out from Mith′kah and camped at Hash·mō′nah. [30]They set out from Hash·mō′nah and camped at Mō·sē′roth. [31]They set out from Mō·sē′roth and camped at Ben′ē-jā′a·kan. [32]They set out from Ben′ē-jā′a·kan and camped at Hor-hag·gid′gad. [33]They set out from Hor-hag·gid′gad and camped at Jot′ba·thah. [34]They set out from Jot′-ba·thah and camped at A·brō′nah. [35]They set out from A·brō′nah and camped at Ē′zi·on-gē′ber. [36]They set out from Ē′zi·on-gē′ber and camped in the wilderness of Zin (that is, Kā′desh). [37]They set out from Kā′-desh and camped at Mount Hor, on the edge of the land of Ē′dom.

38 Aaron the priest went up Mount Hor at the command of the LORD and died there in the fortieth year after the Israelites had come out of the land of Egypt, on the first day of the fifth month. [39]Aaron was one hundred twenty-three years old when he died on Mount Hor.

40 The Cā′naan·īte, the king of Ar′ad, who lived in the Neg′eb in the land of Cā′naan, heard of the coming of the Israelites.

41 They set out from Mount Hor and camped at Zal·mō′nah. [42]They set out from Zal·mō′nah and camped at Pū′non. [43]They set out from Pū′non and camped at Ō′both. [44]They set out from Ō′both and camped at Ī′ye-ab′ar·im, in the territory of Mō′ab. [45]They set out from Ī′yim and camped at Dī′bon-gad. [46]They set out from Dī′bon-gad and camped at Al′mon-dib·la·thā′im. [47]They set out from Al′mon-dib·la·thā′im and camped in the mountains of Ab′a·rim, before Nē′bō. [48]They set out from the mountains of Ab′a·rim and camped in the plains of Mō′ab by the Jordan at Jericho; [49]they camped by the Jordan from Beth-jesh′i·moth as far as Ā′bel-shit′tim in the plains of Mō′ab.

Directions for the Conquest of Canaan

50 In the plains of Mō′ab by the Jordan at Jericho, the LORD spoke to Moses, saying: [51]Speak to the Israelites, and say to them: When you cross over the Jordan into the land of Cā′naan, [52]you shall drive out all the inhabitants of the land from before you, destroy all their figured stones, destroy all their cast images, and demolish all their high places. [53]You shall take possession of the land and settle in it, for I have given you the land to possess. [54]You shall apportion the land by lot according to your clans; to a large one you shall give a large inheritance, and to a small one you shall give a small inheritance; the inheritance shall belong to the person on whom the lot falls; according to your ancestral tribes you shall inherit. [55]But if you do not drive out the inhabitants of the land from before you, then those whom you let remain shall be as barbs in your eyes and thorns in your sides; they shall trouble you in the land where you are settling. [56]And I will do to you as I thought to do to them.

The Boundaries of the Land

34 The LORD spoke to Moses, saying: ²Command the Israelites, and say to them: When you enter the land of Cā´naan (this is the land that shall fall to you for an inheritance, the land of Cā´naan, defined by its boundaries), ³your south sector shall extend from the wilderness of Zin along the side of Ē´dom. Your southern boundary shall begin from the end of the Dead Sea[y] on the east; ⁴your boundary shall turn south of the ascent of Ak·rab´bim, and cross to Zin, and its outer limit shall be south of Kā´desh-bar´nē·a; then it shall go on to Hā´zar-ad´dar, and cross to Az´mon; ⁵the boundary shall turn from Az´mon to the Wadi of Egypt, and its termination shall be at the Sea.

6 For the western boundary, you shall have the Great Sea and its[z] coast; this shall be your western boundary.

7 This shall be your northern boundary: from the Great Sea you shall mark out your line to Mount Hor; ⁸from Mount Hor you shall mark it out to Lē´-bō-hā´math, and the outer limit of the boundary shall be at Zē´dad; ⁹then the boundary shall extend to Ziph´ron, and its end shall be at Hā´zar-ē´nan; this shall be your northern boundary.

10 You shall mark out your eastern boundary from Hā´zar-ē´nan to Shē´-pham; ¹¹and the boundary shall continue down from Shē´pham to Rib´lah on the east side of Ā´in; and the boundary shall go down, and reach the eastern slope of the sea of Chin´ne·reth; ¹²and the boundary shall go down to the Jordan, and its end shall be at the Dead Sea.[y] This shall be your land with its boundaries all around.

13 Moses commanded the Israelites, saying: This is the land that you shall inherit by lot, which the LORD has commanded to give to the nine tribes and to the half-tribe; ¹⁴for the tribe of the Reū´-ben·ītes by their ancestral houses and the tribe of the Gad´ītes by their ancestral houses have taken their inheritance, and also the half-tribe of Ma·nas´seh; ¹⁵the two tribes and the half-tribe have taken their inheritance beyond the Jordan at Jericho eastward, toward the sunrise.

Tribal Leaders

16 The LORD spoke to Moses, saying: ¹⁷These are the names of the men who shall apportion the land to you for inheritance: the priest El·ē·ā´zar and Joshua son of Nun. ¹⁸You shall take one leader of every tribe to apportion the land for inheritance. ¹⁹These are the names of the men: Of the tribe of Judah, Caleb son of Je·phūn´neh. ²⁰Of the tribe of the Sim´ē·on·ītes, She·mū´el son of Am·mī´hud. ²¹Of the tribe of Benjamin, Ē·lī´dad son of Chis´lon. ²²Of the tribe of the Dan´ītes a leader, Buk´kī son of Jog´lī. ²³Of the Jō´-seph·ītes: of the tribe of the Ma·nas´sītes a leader, Han´ni·el son of Ē´phod, ²⁴and of the tribe of the Ē´phra·im·ītes a leader, Ke·mū´el son of Shiph´tan. ²⁵Of the tribe of the Zeb´ū·lun·ītes a leader, Ē·lī·zā´phan son of Par´nach. ²⁶Of the tribe of the Is´sa·char·ītes a leader, Pal´ti·el son of Az´-zan. ²⁷And of the tribe of the Ash´er·ītes a leader, A·hī´hud son of She·lō´mī. ²⁸Of the tribe of the Naph´ta·lītes a leader, Pe·dah´el son of Am·mī´hud. ²⁹These were the ones whom the LORD commanded to apportion the inheritance for the Israelites in the land of Cā´naan.

Cities for the Levites

35 In the plains of Mō´ab by the Jordan at Jericho, the LORD spoke to Moses, saying: ²Command the Israelites to give, from the inheritance that they possess, towns for the Lē´vītes to live in; you shall also give to the Lē´vītes pasture lands surrounding the towns. ³The towns shall be theirs to live in, and their pasture lands shall be for their cattle, for their livestock, and for all their animals. ⁴The pasture lands of the towns, which you shall give to the Lē´-vītes, shall reach from the wall of the

[y] Heb *Salt Sea*   [z] Syr: Heb lacks *it*

town outward a thousand cubits all around. [5]You shall measure, outside the town, for the east side two thousand cubits, for the south side two thousand cubits, for the west side two thousand cubits, and for the north side two thousand cubits, with the town in the middle; this shall belong to them as pasture land for their towns.

6 The towns that you give to the Lē´vītes shall include the six cities of refuge, where you shall permit a slayer to flee, and in addition to them you shall give forty-two towns. [7]The towns that you give to the Lē´vītes shall total forty-eight, with their pasture lands. [8]And as for the towns that you shall give from the possession of the Israelites, from the larger tribes you shall take many, and from the smaller tribes you shall take few; each, in proportion to the inheritance that it obtains, shall give of its towns to the Lē´vītes.

Cities of Refuge

9 The Lord spoke to Moses, saying: [10]Speak to the Israelites, and say to them: When you cross the Jordan into the land of Cā´naan, [11]then you shall select cities to be cities of refuge for you, so that a slayer who kills a person without intent may flee there. [12]The cities shall be for you a refuge from the avenger, so that the slayer may not die until there is a trial before the congregation.

13 The cities that you designate shall be six cities of refuge for you: [14]you shall designate three cities beyond the Jordan, and three cities in the land of Cā´naan, to be cities of refuge. [15]These six cities shall serve as refuge for the Israelites, for the resident or transient alien among them, so that anyone who kills a person without intent may flee there.

Concerning Murder and Blood Revenge

16 But anyone who strikes another with an iron object, and death ensues, is a murderer; the murderer shall be put to death. [17]Or anyone who strikes another with a stone in hand that could cause death, and death ensues, is a murderer; the murderer shall be put to death. [18]Or anyone who strikes another with a weapon of wood in hand that could cause death, and death ensues, is a murderer; the murderer shall be put to death. [19]The avenger of blood is the one who shall put the murderer to death; when they meet, the avenger of blood shall execute the sentence. [20]Likewise, if someone pushes another from hatred, or hurls something at another, lying in wait, and death ensues, [21]or in enmity strikes another with the hand, and death ensues, then the one who struck the blow shall be put to death; that person is a murderer; the avenger of blood shall put the murderer to death, when they meet.

22 But if someone pushes another suddenly without enmity, or hurls any object without lying in wait, [23]or, while handling any stone that could cause death, unintentionally[a] drops it on another and death ensues, though they were not enemies, and no harm was intended, [24]then the congregation shall judge between the slayer and the avenger of blood, in accordance with these ordinances; [25]and the congregation shall rescue the slayer from the avenger of blood. Then the congregation shall send the slayer back to the original city of refuge. The slayer shall live in it until the death of the high priest who was

When the people crossed into the land of Canaan, six cities were safe places for people who had accidentally killed someone. These cities were called cities of refuge. In each of these cities, people who had killed someone were protected until the community found out if the killing was an accident or if it had been done on purpose.

[a] Heb *without seeing*

anointed with the holy oil. ²⁶But if the slayer shall at any time go outside the bounds of the original city of refuge, ²⁷and is found by the avenger of blood outside the bounds of the city of refuge, and is killed by the avenger, no bloodguilt shall be incurred. ²⁸For the slayer must remain in the city of refuge until the death of the high priest; but after the death of the high priest the slayer may return home.

29 These things shall be a statute and ordinance for you throughout your generations wherever you live.

30 If anyone kills another, the murderer shall be put to death on the evidence of witnesses; but no one shall be put to death on the testimony of a single witness. ³¹Moreover you shall accept no ransom for the life of a murderer who is subject to the death penalty; a murderer must be put to death. ³²Nor shall you accept ransom for one who has fled to a city of refuge, enabling the fugitive to return to live in the land before the death of the high priest. ³³You shall not pollute the land in which you live; for blood pollutes the land, and no expiation can be made for the land, for the blood that is shed in it, except by the blood of the one who shed it. ³⁴You shall not defile the land in which you live, in which I also dwell; for I the LORD dwell among the Israelites.

Marriage of Female Heirs

36 The heads of the ancestral houses of the clans of the descendants of Gil·e·ad son of Mā′chir son of Ma·nas′seh, of the Jō′seph·īte clans, came forward and spoke in the presence of Moses and the leaders, the heads of the ancestral houses of the Israelites; ²they said, "The LORD commanded my lord to give the land for inheritance by lot to the Israelites; and my lord was commanded by the LORD to give the inheritance of our brother Ze·loph′e·had to his daughters. ³But if they are married into another Israelite tribe, then their inheritance will be taken from the inheritance of our ancestors and added to the inheritance of the tribe into which they marry; so it will be taken away from the allotted portion of our inheritance. ⁴And when the jubilee of the Israelites comes, then their inheritance will be added to the inheritance of the tribe into which they have married; and their inheritance will be taken from the inheritance of our ancestral tribe."

5 Then Moses commanded the Israelites according to the word of the LORD, saying, "The descendants of the tribe of Joseph are right in what they are saying. ⁶This is what the LORD commands concerning the daughters of Ze·loph′e·had, 'Let them marry whom they think best; only it must be into a clan of their father's tribe that they are married, ⁷so that no inheritance of the Israelites shall be transferred from one tribe to another; for all Israelites shall retain the inheritance of their ancestral tribes. ⁸Every daughter who possesses an inheritance in any tribe of the Israelites shall marry one from the clan of her father's tribe, so that all Israelites may continue to possess their ancestral inheritance. ⁹No inheritance shall be transferred from one tribe to another; for each of the tribes of the Israelites shall retain its own inheritance.' "

10 The daughters of Ze·loph′e·had did as the LORD had commanded Moses. ¹¹Mah′lah, Tir′zah, Hog′lah, Mil′cah, and Noah, the daughters of Ze·loph′e·had, married sons of their father's brothers. ¹²They were married into the clans of the descendants of Ma·nas′seh son of Joseph, and their inheritance remained in the tribe of their father's clan.

13 These are the commandments and the ordinances that the LORD commanded through Moses to the Israelites in the plains of Mō′ab by the Jordan at Jericho.

Deuteronomy

The book of Deuteronomy gets its name from two Greek words that mean "second law" because it lists again the Ten Commandments, which appear in the book of Exodus. Deuteronomy also contains many new rules that the Israelites were supposed to follow. Written about 650 BC, the book was probably made longer about 400 BC.

Deuteronomy continues the story of God's people wandering in the desert. It tells how Moses finally had to give up as leader and send the people on their journey without him. Because Moses was their greatest hero and lawgiver, this whole book is written as if it were a long goodbye speech that Moses gave to the people just before they entered the Promised Land. Deuteronomy was lost for many years after it was written. In chapters 22 and 23 of Second Kings, we read how it was found when the Judahites were repairing the Temple in Jerusalem in 621 BC. Finding these scrolls helped King Josiah and the people change some of their sinful ways and return to the right way of living.

Deuteronomy 6:1–3

Events at Horeb Recalled

1 These are the words that Moses spoke to all Israel beyond the Jordan—in the wilderness, on the plain opposite Sūph, between Par´an and Tō´phel, Lā´ban, Ha·zē´roth, and Di·za·hab´. ²(By the way of Mount Sē´ir it takes eleven days to reach Kā´desh-bar´nē·a from Hō´reb.) ³In the fortieth year, on the first day of the eleventh month, Moses spoke to the Israelites just as the LORD had commanded him to speak to them. ⁴This was after he had defeated King Sī´hon of the Am´o·rītes, who reigned in Hesh´bon, and King Og of Bā´shan, who reigned in Ash´ta·roth and*a* in Ed´rē·ī. ⁵Beyond the Jordan in the land of Mō´ab, Moses undertook to expound this law as follows:

6 The LORD our God spoke to us at Hō´reb, saying, "You have stayed long enough at this mountain. ⁷Resume your journey, and go into the hill country of the Am´o·rītes as well as into the neighboring regions—the Ar´a·bah, the hill country, the She·phē´lah, the Neg´eb, and the seacoast—the land of the Cā´naan·ītes and the Lebanon, as far as the great river, the river Euphrates. ⁸See, I have set the land before you; go in and take possession of the land that I*b* swore to your ancestors, to Abraham, to Isaac, and to Jacob, to give to them and to their descendants after them."

Appointment of Tribal Leaders

9 At that time I said to you, "I am unable by myself to bear you. ¹⁰The LORD your God has multiplied you, so that today you are as numerous as the stars of heaven. ¹¹May the LORD, the God of your ancestors, increase you a thousand times more and bless you, as he has promised you! ¹²But how can I bear the heavy burden of your disputes all by myself? ¹³Choose for each of your tribes individuals who are wise, discerning, and reputable to be your leaders." ¹⁴You answered me, "The plan you have proposed is a good one." ¹⁵So I took the leaders of your tribes, wise and reputable individuals, and installed them as leaders over you, commanders of thousands, commanders of hundreds, commanders of fifties, commanders of tens, and officials, throughout your tribes. ¹⁶I charged your judges at that time: "Give the members of your community a fair hearing, and judge rightly between one person and another, whether citizen or resident alien. ¹⁷You must not be partial in judging: hear out the small and the great alike; you shall not be intimidated by anyone, for the judgment is God's. Any case that is too hard for you, bring to me, and I will hear it." ¹⁸So I charged you at that time with all the things that you should do.

Israel's Refusal to Enter the Land

19 Then, just as the LORD our God had ordered us, we set out from Hō´reb and went through all that great and terrible wilderness that you saw, on the way to the hill country of the Am´o·rītes, until we reached Kā´desh-bar´nē·a. ²⁰I said to you, "You have reached the hill country of the Am´o·rītes, which the LORD our God is giving us. ²¹See, the LORD your God has given the land to you; go up, take possession, as the LORD, the God of your ancestors, has promised you; do not fear or be dismayed."

22 All of you came to me and said, "Let us send men ahead of us to explore the land for us and bring back a report to us regarding the route by which we should go up and the cities we will come to." ²³The plan seemed good to me, and I selected twelve of you, one from each tribe. ²⁴They set out and went up into the hill country, and when they reached the Valley of Esh´col they spied it out ²⁵and gathered some of the land's produce, which they brought down to us.

a Gk Syr Vg Compare Josh 12.4: Heb lacks *and*
b Sam Gk: MT *the* LORD

They brought back a report to us, and said, "It is a good land that the LORD our God is giving us."

26 But you were unwilling to go up. You rebelled against the command of the LORD your God; [27]you grumbled in your tents and said, "It is because the LORD hates us that he has brought us out of the land of Egypt, to hand us over to the Am′o·rītes to destroy us. [28]Where are we headed? Our kindred have made our hearts melt by reporting, 'The people are stronger and taller than we; the cities are large and fortified up to heaven! We actually saw there the offspring of the An′a·kim!' " [29]I said to you, "Have no dread or fear of them. [30]The LORD your God, who goes before you, is the one who will fight for you, just as he did for you in Egypt before your very eyes, [31]and in the wilderness, where you saw how the LORD your God carried you, just as one carries a child, all the way that you traveled until you reached this place. [32]But in spite of this, you have no trust in the LORD your God, [33]who goes before you on the way to seek out a place for you to camp, in fire by night, and in the cloud by day, to show you the route you should take."

The Penalty for Israel's Rebellion

34 When the LORD heard your words, he was wrathful and swore: [35]"Not one of these—not one of this evil generation—shall see the good land that I swore to give to your ancestors, [36]except Caleb son of Je·phŭn′neh. He shall see it, and to him and to his descendants I will give the land on which he set foot, because of his complete fidelity to the LORD." [37]Even with me the LORD was angry on your account, saying, "You also shall not enter there. [38]Joshua son of Nun, your assistant, shall enter there; encourage him, for he is the one who will secure Israel's possession of it. [39]And as for your little ones, who you thought would become booty, your children, who today do not yet know right from wrong, they shall enter there; to them I will give it, and they shall take possession of it. [40]But as for you, journey back into the wilderness, in the direction of the Red Sea."[c]

41 You answered me, "We have sinned against the LORD! We are ready to go up and fight, just as the LORD our God commanded us." So all of you strapped on your battle gear, and thought it easy to go up into the hill country. [42]The LORD said to me, "Say to them, 'Do not go up and do not fight, for I am not in the midst of you; otherwise you will be defeated by your enemies.' " [43]Although I told you, you would not listen. You rebelled against the command of the LORD and presumptuously went up into the hill country. [44]The Am′o·rītes who lived in that hill country then came out against you and chased you as bees do. They beat you down in Sē′ir as far as Hor′mah. [45]When you returned and wept before the LORD, the LORD would neither heed your voice nor pay you any attention.

On their way to Canaan, the Israelites went through a country called Edom. Edom means "the red region" and was named for its red rocks and soil. The people who lived in the land were called Edomites. They came from the family of Esau, who had reddish-colored skin or hair. Read about Esau and his brother Jacob in Genesis 25–36.

The Desert Years

46 After you had stayed at Kā′desh as many days as you did, [1]we journeyed back into the wilderness, in the

2 direction of the Red Sea,[c] as the LORD had told me and skirted Mount Sē′ir

[c] Or *Sea of Reeds*

for many days. [2]Then the LORD said to me: [3]"You have been skirting this hill country long enough. Head north, [4]and charge the people as follows: You are about to pass through the territory of your kindred, the descendants of Esau, who live in Sē´ir. They will be afraid of you, so, be very careful [5]not to engage in battle with them, for I will not give you even so much as a foot's length of their land, since I have given Mount Sē´ir to Esau as a possession. [6]You shall purchase food from them for money, so that you may eat; and you shall also buy water from them for money, so that you may drink. [7]Surely the LORD your God has blessed you in all your undertakings; he knows your going through this great wilderness. These forty years the LORD your God has been with you; you have lacked nothing." [8]So we passed by our kin, the descendants of Esau who live in Sē´ir, leaving behind the route of the Ar´a·bah, and leaving behind Ē´lath and Ē´zi·on·gē´ber.

When we had headed out along the route of the wilderness of Mō´ab, [9]the LORD said to me: "Do not harass Mō´ab or engage them in battle, for I will not give you any of its land as a possession, since I have given Ar as a possession to the descendants of Lot." [10](The Ē´mim— a large and numerous people, as tall as the An´a·kim—had formerly inhabited it. [11]Like the An´a·kim, they are usually reckoned as Reph´a·im, though the Mō´-ab·ītes call them Ē´mim. [12]Moreover, the Hō´rim had formerly inhabited Sē´ir, but the descendants of Esau dispossessed them, destroying them and settling in their place, as Israel has done in the land that the LORD gave them as a posses-sion.) [13]"Now then, proceed to cross over the Wadi Zē´red."

So we crossed over the Wadi Zē´red. [14]And the length of time we had traveled from Kā´desh-bar´nē·a until we crossed the Wadi Zē´red was thirty-eight years, until the entire generation of warriors had perished from the camp, as the LORD

had sworn concerning them. [15]Indeed, the LORD's own hand was against them, to root them out from the camp, until all had perished.

16 Just as soon as all the warriors had died off from among the people, [17]the LORD spoke to me, saying, [18]"Today you are going to cross the boundary of Mō´ab at Ar. [19]When you approach the frontier of the Am´mon·ītes, do not harass them or engage them in battle, for I will not give the land of the Am´mon·ītes to you as a possession, because I have given it to the descendants of Lot." [20](It also is usually reckoned as a land of Reph´a·im. Reph´a·im formerly inhabited it, though the Am´mon·ītes call them Zam·zum´-mim, [21]a strong and numerous people, as tall as the An´a·kim. But the LORD destroyed them from before the Am´-mon·ītes so that they could dispossess them and settle in their place. [22]He did the same for the descendants of Esau, who live in Sē´ir, by destroying the Hō´-rim before them so that they could dis-possess them and settle in their place even to this day. [23]As for the Av´vim, who had lived in settlements in the vicinity of Gā´za, the Caph´to·rim, who came from Caph´tor, destroyed them and settled in their place.) [24]"Proceed on your journey and cross the Wadi Ar´non. See, I have handed over to you King Sī´hon the Am´-o·rīte of Hesh´bon, and his land. Begin to take possession by engaging him in bat-tle. [25]This day I will begin to put the dread and fear of you upon the peoples everywhere under heaven; when they hear report of you, they will tremble and be in anguish because of you."

Defeat of King Sihon

26 So I sent messengers from the wilderness of Ked´e·moth to King Sī´hon of Hesh´bon with the following terms of peace: [27]"If you let me pass through your land, I will travel only along the road; I will turn aside neither to the right nor to the left. [28]You shall sell me food for

money, so that I may eat, and supply me water for money, so that I may drink. Only allow me to pass through on foot— [29]just as the descendants of Esau who live in Sē´ir have done for me and likewise the Mō´ab·ītes who live in Ar— until I cross the Jordan into the land that the LORD our God is giving us." [30]But King Sī´hon of Hesh´bon was not willing to let us pass through, for the LORD your God had hardened his spirit and made his heart defiant in order to hand him over to you, as he has now done.

31 The LORD said to me, "See, I have begun to give Sī´hon and his land over to you. Begin now to take possession of his land." [32]So when Sī´hon came out against us, he and all his people for battle at Jā´haz, [33]the LORD our God gave him over to us; and we struck him down, along with his offspring and all his people. [34]At that time we captured all his towns, and in each town we utterly destroyed men, women, and children. We left not a single survivor. [35]Only the livestock we kept as spoil for ourselves, as well as the plunder of the towns that we had captured. [36]From A·rō´er on the edge of the Wadi Ar´non (including the town that is in the wadi itself) as far as Gil´e·ad, there was no citadel too high for us. The LORD our God gave everything to us. [37]You did not encroach, however, on the land of the Am´mon·ites, avoiding the whole upper region of the Wadi Jab´bok as well as the towns of the hill country, just as[d] the LORD our God had charged.

Bashan was a wide, flat land that was good for growing wheat and raising cattle. The poetry in the Bible refers to Bashan as a beautiful place. While they were in the wilderness, the Israelites took Bashan and divided it among their tribes.

The Jordan River is an important river in the history of God's people. The name means "stream that goes down." The river curves and twists so much that it is two hundred miles long. People cannot use the Jordan for travel, but there are many shallow places where they can cross over the river. The Israelites had to cross over the Jordan River to enter the land of Canaan.

Defeat of King Og

3 When we headed up the road to Bā´shan, King Og of Bā´shan came out against us, he and all his people, for battle at Ed´rē·ī. [2]The LORD said to me, "Do not fear him, for I have handed him over to you, along with his people and his land. Do to him as you did to King Sī´hon of the Am´o·rītes, who reigned in Hesh´bon." [3]So the LORD our God also handed over to us King Og of Bā´shan and all his people. We struck him down until not a single survivor was left. [4]At that time we captured all his towns; there was no citadel that we did not take from them— sixty towns, the whole region of Ar´gob, the kingdom of Og in Bā´shan. [5]All these were fortress towns with high walls, double gates, and bars, besides a great many villages. [6]And we utterly destroyed them, as we had done to King Sī´hon of Hesh´bon, in each city utterly destroying men, women, and children. [7]But all the livestock and the plunder of the towns we kept as spoil for ourselves.

8 So at that time we took from the two kings of the Am´o·rītes the land beyond the Jordan, from the Wadi Ar´non to Mount Hermon [9](the Sī·dō´ni·ans call Hermon Sir´i·on, while the Am´o·rītes call it Sē´nir), [10]all the towns of the tableland, the whole of Gil´e·ad,

[d] Gk Tg: Heb *and all*

King Og, from the land of Bashan, was a giant man with a giant bed. His bed was about thirteen feet long and six feet wide. A person would have to be pretty big to fit on a bed that size—it's about twice as big as the twin-size beds we have today! The Israelites defeated King Og in a battle. This was important and helped them move closer to the land of Canaan.

and all of Bā´shan, as far as Sal´e·cah and Ed´rē·ī, towns of Og's kingdom in Bā´shan. ¹¹(Now only King Og of Bā´shan was left of the remnant of the Reph´a·im. In fact his bed, an iron bed, can still be seen in Rab´bah of the Am´mon·ītes. By the common cubit it is nine cubits long and four cubits wide.) ¹²As for the land that we took possession of at that time, I gave to the Reū´ben·ītes and Gad´ītes the territory north of A·rō´er,ᵉ that is on the edge of the Wadi Ar´non, as well as half the hill country of Gil´e·ad with its towns, ¹³and I gave to the half-tribe of Ma·nas´seh the rest of Gil´e·ad and all of Bā´shan, Og's kingdom. (The whole region of Ar´gob: all that portion of Bā´shan used to be called a land of Reph´a·im;) ¹⁴Jā´ir the Ma·nas´sīte acquired the whole region of Ar´gob as far as the border of the Gesh´ū·rītes and the Mā´a·ca·thītes, and he named them—that is, Bā´shan—after himself, Hav´voth-jā´ir,ᶠ as it is to this day.) ¹⁵To Mā´chir I gave Gil´e·ad. ¹⁶And to the Reū´ben·ītes and the Gad´ītes I gave the territory from Gil´e·ad as far as the Wadi Ar´non, with the middle of the wadi as a boundary, and up to the Jab´bok, the wadi being boundary of the Am´mon·ītes; ¹⁷the Ar´a·bah also, with the Jordan and its banks, from Chin´ne·reth down to the sea of the Ar´a·bah, the Dead Sea,ᵍ with the lower slopes of Pis´gah on the east.

18 At that time, I charged you as follows: "Although the LORD your God has given you this land to occupy, all your troops shall cross over armed as the vanguard of your Israelite kin. ¹⁹Only your wives, your children, and your livestock— I know that you have much livestock— shall stay behind in the towns that I have given to you. ²⁰When the LORD gives rest to your kindred, as to you, and they too have occupied the land that the LORD your God is giving them beyond the Jordan, then each of you may return to the property that I have given to you." ²¹And I charged Joshua as well at that time, saying: "Your own eyes have seen everything that the LORD your God has done to these two kings; so the LORD will do to all the kingdoms into which you are about to cross. ²²Do not fear them, for it is the LORD your God who fights for you."

Moses Views Canaan from Pisgah

23 At that time, too, I entreated the LORD, saying: ²⁴"O Lord GOD, you have only begun to show your servant your greatness and your might; what god in heaven or on earth can perform deeds and mighty acts like yours! ²⁵Let me cross over to see the good land beyond the Jordan, that good hill country and the Lebanon." ²⁶But the LORD was angry with me on your account and would not heed me. The LORD said to me, "Enough from you! Never speak to me of this matter again! ²⁷Go up to the top of Pis´gah and look around you to the west, to the north, to the south, and to the east. Look well, for you shall not cross over this Jordan. ²⁸But charge Joshua, and encourage and strengthen him, because it is he who shall cross over at the head of this people and who shall secure their possession of the land that you will see." ²⁹So we remained in the valley opposite Beth-pē´or.

ᵉ Heb territory from Aroer   ᶠ That is Settlement of Jair   ᵍ Heb Salt Sea

Moses Commands Obedience

4 So now, Israel, give heed to the statutes and ordinances that I am teaching you to observe, so that you may live to enter and occupy the land that the LORD, the God of your ancestors, is giving you. [2]You must neither add anything to what I command you nor take away anything from it, but keep the commandments of the LORD your God with which I am charging you. [3]You have seen for yourselves what the LORD did with regard to the Bā'al of Pē'or—how the LORD your God destroyed from among you everyone who followed the Bā'al of Pē'or, [4]while those of you who held fast to the LORD your God are all alive today.

5 See, just as the LORD my God has charged me, I now teach you statutes and ordinances for you to observe in the land that you are about to enter and occupy. [6]You must observe them diligently, for this will show your wisdom and discernment to the peoples, who, when they hear all these statutes, will say, "Surely this great nation is a wise and discerning people!" [7]For what other great nation has a god so near to it as the LORD our God is whenever we call to him? [8]And what other great nation has statutes and ordinances as just as this entire law that I am setting before you today?

9 But take care and watch yourselves closely, so as neither to forget the things that your eyes have seen nor to let them slip from your mind all the days of your life; make them known to your children and your children's children— [10]how you once stood before the LORD your God at Hō'reb, when the LORD said to me, "Assemble the people for me, and I will let them hear my words, so that they may learn to fear me as long as they live on the earth, and may teach their children so"; [11]you approached and stood at the foot of the mountain while the mountain was blazing up to the very heavens, shrouded in dark clouds. [12]Then the LORD spoke to you out of the

The Canaanites called their chief god "Baal," a word that meant "lord." They believed in many less important gods also called Baals. The Canaanites built altars to their gods on high spots and named many places of the land with the word "Baal." They believed that these places belonged to their gods. Moses told the Israelites not to turn away from the one true God to worship the idols of the Canaanites. God had given them rules to obey so they could live in the right way with God and each other.

fire. You heard the sound of words but saw no form; there was only a voice. [13]He declared to you his covenant, which he charged you to observe, that is, the ten commandments;[h] and he wrote them on two stone tablets. [14]And the LORD charged me at that time to teach you statutes and ordinances for you to observe in the land that you are about to cross into and occupy.

15 Since you saw no form when the LORD spoke to you at Hō'reb out of the fire, take care and watch yourselves closely, [16]so that you do not act corruptly by making an idol for yourselves, in the form of any figure—the likeness of male or female, [17]the likeness of any animal that is on the earth, the likeness of any winged bird that flies in the air, [18]the likeness of anything that creeps on the ground, the likeness of any fish that is in the water under the earth. [19]And when you look up to the heavens and see the sun, the moon, and the stars, all the host of heaven, do not be led astray and bow down to them and serve them, things that the LORD your God has allotted to all the peoples everywhere under heaven. [20]But the LORD has taken you and brought you out of the iron-smelter, out of Egypt, to become a people of his

[h] Heb *the ten words*

very own possession, as you are now.

21 The LORD was angry with me because of you, and he vowed that I should not cross the Jordan and that I should not enter the good land that the LORD your God is giving for your possession. [22]For I am going to die in this land without crossing over the Jordan, but you are going to cross over to take possession of that good land. [23]So be careful not to forget the covenant that the LORD your God made with you, and not to make for yourselves an idol in the form of anything that the LORD your God has forbidden you. [24]For the LORD your God is a devouring fire, a jealous God.

25 When you have had children and children's children, and become complacent in the land, if you act corruptly by making an idol in the form of anything, thus doing what is evil in the sight of the LORD your God, and provoking him to anger, [26]I call heaven and earth to witness against you today that you will soon utterly perish from the land that you are crossing the Jordan to occupy; you will not live long on it, but will be utterly destroyed. [27]The LORD will scatter you among the peoples; only a few of you will be left among the nations where the LORD will lead you. [28]There you will serve other gods made by human hands, objects of wood and stone that neither see, nor hear, nor eat, nor smell. [29]From there you will seek the LORD your God, and you will find him if you search after him with all your heart and soul. [30]In

your distress, when all these things have happened to you in time to come, you will return to the LORD your God and heed him. [31]Because the LORD your God is a merciful God, he will neither abandon you nor destroy you; he will not forget the covenant with your ancestors that he swore to them.

32 For ask now about former ages, long before your own, ever since the day that God created human beings on the earth; ask from one end of heaven to the other: has anything so great as this ever happened or has its like ever been heard of? [33]Has any people ever heard the voice of a god speaking out of a fire, as you have heard, and lived? [34]Or has any god ever attempted to go and take a nation for himself from the midst of another nation, by trials, by signs and wonders, by war, by a mighty hand and an outstretched arm, and by terrifying displays of power, as the LORD your God did for you in Egypt before your very eyes? [35]To you it was shown so that you would acknowledge that the LORD is God; there is no other besides him. [36]From heaven he made you hear his voice to discipline you. On earth he showed you his great fire, while you heard his words coming out of the fire. [37]And because he loved your ancestors, he chose their descendants after them. He brought you out of Egypt with his own presence, by his great power, [38]driving out before you nations greater and mightier than yourselves, to bring you in, giving you their land for a possession, as it is still today. [39]So acknowledge today and take to heart that the LORD is God in heaven above and on the earth beneath; there is no other. [40]Keep his statutes and his commandments, which I am commanding you today for your own well-being and that of your descendants after you, so that you may long remain in the land that the LORD your God is giving you for all time.

As a military word, "host" means "a body of men organized for war." In the Bible, God is often called "God of hosts." The "host of heaven" includes the sun, moon, stars, and particularly angels. These forces are at God's command to carry out God's purpose for the world.

Cities of Refuge East of the Jordan

41 Then Moses set apart on the east side of the Jordan three cities [42]to which a homicide could flee, someone who unintentionally kills another person, the two not having been at enmity before; the homicide could flee to one of these cities and live: [43]Bē′zer in the wilderness on the tableland belonging to the Reŭ-ben·ītes, Rā′moth in Gil′e·ad belonging to the Gad′ītes, and Gō′lan in Bā′shan belonging to the Ma·nas′sītes.

Transition to the Second Address

44 This is the law that Moses set before the Israelites. [45]These are the decrees and the statutes and ordinances that Moses spoke to the Israelites when they had come out of Egypt, [46]beyond the Jordan in the valley opposite Beth-pē′-or, in the land of King Sī′hon of the Am′o·rītes, who reigned at Hesh′bon, whom Moses and the Israelites defeated when they came out of Egypt. [47]They occupied his land and the land of King Og of Bā′shan, the two kings of the Am′o·rītes on the eastern side of the Jordan: [48]from A·rō′er, which is on the edge of the Wadi Ar′non, as far as Mount Sir′i·on[i] (that is, Hermon), [49]together with all the Ar′a·bah on the east side of the Jordan as far as the Sea of the Ar′a·bah, under the slopes of Pis′gah.

The Ten Commandments

5 Moses convened all Israel, and said to them:

Hear, O Israel, the statutes and ordinances that I am addressing to you today; you shall learn them and observe them diligently. [2]The LORD our God made a covenant with us at Hō′reb. [3]Not with our ancestors did the LORD make this covenant, but with us, who are all of us here alive today. [4]The LORD spoke with you face to face at the mountain, out of the fire. [5](At that time I was standing between the LORD and you to declare

to you the words[j] of the LORD; for you were afraid because of the fire and did not go up the mountain.) And he said:

6 I am the LORD your God, who brought you out of the land of Egypt, out of the house of slavery; [7]you shall have no other gods before[k] me.

8 You shall not make for yourself an idol, whether in the form of anything that is in heaven above, or that is on the earth beneath, or that is in the water under the earth. [9]You shall not bow down to them or worship them; for I the LORD your God am a jealous God, punishing children for the iniquity of parents, to the third and fourth generation of those who reject me, [10]but showing steadfast love to the thousandth generation[l] of those who love me and keep my commandments.

11 You shall not make wrongful use of the name of the LORD your God, for the LORD will not acquit anyone who misuses his name.

12 Observe the sabbath day and keep it holy, as the LORD your God commanded you. [13]Six days you shall labor and do all your work. [14]But the seventh day is a sabbath to the LORD your God; you shall not do any work—you, or your son or your daughter, or your male or female slave, or your ox or your donkey, or any of your livestock, or the resident alien in your towns, so that your male and female slave may rest as well as you. [15]Remember that you were a slave in the

Moses called the Israelite people together to listen to the rules that God had given them. These rules are called the Ten Commandments, and they show people how to live God's way. Can you think of another place in the Bible where you can find the Ten Commandments? Try Exodus 20!

---

[i] Syr: Heb *Sion*   [j] Q Mss Sam Gk Syr Vg Tg: MT *word*   [k] Or *besides*   [l] Or *to thousands*

land of Egypt, and the LORD your God brought you out from there with a mighty hand and an outstretched arm; therefore the LORD your God commanded you to keep the sabbath day.

16 Honor your father and your mother, as the LORD your God commanded you, so that your days may be long and that it may go well with you in the land that the LORD your God is giving you.

17 You shall not murder.[m]

18 Neither shall you commit adultery.

19 Neither shall you steal.

20 Neither shall you bear false witness against your neighbor.

21 Neither shall you covet your neighbor's wife.

Neither shall you desire your neighbor's house, or field, or male or female slave, or ox, or donkey, or anything that belongs to your neighbor.

Moses the Mediator of God's Will

22 These words the LORD spoke with a loud voice to your whole assembly at the mountain, out of the fire, the cloud, and the thick darkness, and he added no more. He wrote them on two stone tablets, and gave them to me. 23When

The fourth commandment says to "observe the sabbath day by keeping it holy." The word "sabbath" means "to cease" or "to be at an end." God told the people that the last day of the week should be a day of rest. On this day, the people stopped all ordinary work and activity. The laws that said what could and could not be done on this day were very specific. The sabbath was a day of joy that the people used to worship God.

you heard the voice out of the darkness, while the mountain was burning with fire, you approached me, all the heads of your tribes and your elders; 24and you said, "Look, the LORD our God has shown us his glory and greatness, and we have heard his voice out of the fire. Today we have seen that God may speak to someone and the person may still live. 25So now why should we die? For this great fire will consume us; if we hear the voice of the LORD our God any longer, we shall die. 26For who is there of all flesh that has heard the voice of the living God speaking out of fire, as we have, and remained alive? 27Go near, you yourself, and hear all that the LORD our God will say. Then tell us everything that the LORD our God tells you, and we will listen and do it."

28 The LORD heard your words when you spoke to me, and the LORD said to me: "I have heard the words of this people, which they have spoken to you; they are right in all that they have spoken. 29If only they had such a mind as this, to fear me and to keep all my commandments always, so that it might go well with them and with their children forever! 30Go say to them, 'Return to your tents.' 31But you, stand here by me, and I will tell you all the commandments, the statutes and the ordinances, that you shall teach them, so that they may do them in the land that I am giving them to possess." 32You must therefore be careful to do as the LORD your God has commanded you; you shall not turn to the right or to the left. 33You must follow exactly the path that the LORD your God has commanded you, so that you may live, and that it may go well with you, and that you may live long in the land that you are to possess.

The Great Commandment

6 Now this is the commandment— the statutes and the ordinances— that the LORD your God charged me to teach you to observe in the land that you

[m] Or kill

> "You shall love the LORD your God with all your heart, and with all your soul, and with all your might." Deuteronomy 6:5

are about to cross into and occupy, [2]so that you and your children and your children's children, may fear the LORD your God all the days of your life, and keep all his decrees and his commandments that I am commanding you, so that your days may be long. [3]Hear therefore, O Israel, and observe them diligently, so that it may go well with you, and so that you may multiply greatly in a land flowing with milk and honey, as the LORD, the God of your ancestors, has promised you.

4 Hear, O Israel: The LORD is our God, the LORD alone.[n] [5]You shall love the LORD your God with all your heart, and with all your soul, and with all your might. [6]Keep these words that I am commanding you today in your heart. [7]Recite them to your children and talk about them when you are at home and when you are away, when you lie down and when you rise. [8]Bind them as a sign on your hand, fix them as an emblem[o] on your forehead, [9]and write them on the doorposts of your house and on your gates.

Caution against Disobedience

10 When the LORD your God has brought you into the land that he swore

> "Keep these words that I am commanding you today in your heart. Recite them to your children and talk about them when you are at home and when you are away, when you lie down and when you rise. Bind them as a sign on your hand, fix them as an emblem on your forehead, and write them on the doorposts of your house and on your gates." Deuteronomy 6:6–9

to your ancestors, to Abraham, to Isaac, and to Jacob, to give you—a land with fine, large cities that you did not build, [11]houses filled with all sorts of goods that you did not fill, hewn cisterns that you did not hew, vineyards and olive groves that you did not plant—and when you have eaten your fill, [12]take care that you do not forget the LORD, who brought you out of the land of Egypt, out of the house of slavery. [13]The LORD your God you shall fear; him you shall serve, and by his name alone you shall swear. [14]Do not follow other gods, any of the gods of the peoples who are all around you, [15]because the LORD your God, who is present with you, is a jealous God. The anger of the LORD your God would be kindled against you and he would destroy you from the face of the earth.

16 Do not put the LORD your God to the test, as you tested him at Mas'sah. [17]You must diligently keep the commandments of the LORD your God, and his decrees, and his statutes that he has commanded you. [18]Do what is right and good in the sight of the LORD, so that it may go well with you, and so that you may go in and occupy the good land that the LORD swore to your ancestors to give you, [19]thrusting out all your enemies from before you, as the LORD has promised.

20 When your children ask you in time to come, "What is the meaning of the decrees and the statutes and the ordinances that the LORD our God has commanded you?" [21]then you shall say to your children, "We were Pharaoh's slaves in Egypt, but the LORD brought us out of Egypt with a mighty hand. [22]The LORD displayed before our eyes great and awesome signs and wonders against Egypt, against Pharaoh and all his household. [23]He brought us out from there in order to bring us in, to give us the land that he promised on oath to our

[n] Or *The LORD our God is one LORD*, or *The LORD our God, the LORD is one*, or *The LORD is our God, the LORD is one*   [o] Or *as a frontlet*

ancestors. ²⁴Then the LORD commanded us to observe all these statutes, to fear the LORD our God, for our lasting good, so as to keep us alive, as is now the case. ²⁵If we diligently observe this entire commandment before the LORD our God, as he has commanded us, we will be in the right."

A Chosen People

7 When the LORD your God brings you into the land that you are about to enter and occupy, and he clears away many nations before you—the Hit′tites, the Gir′ga·shites, the Am′o·rites, the Cā′naan·ites, the Per′iz·zites, the Hī′vites, and the Jeb′ū·sites, seven nations mightier and more numerous than you—²and when the LORD your God gives them over to you and you defeat them, then you must utterly destroy them. Make no covenant with them and show them no mercy. ³Do not intermarry with them, giving your daughters to their sons or taking their daughters for your sons, ⁴for that would turn away your children from following me, to serve other gods. Then the anger of the LORD would be kindled against you, and he would destroy you quickly. ⁵But this is how you must deal with them: break down their altars, smash their pillars, hew down their sacred poles,^p and burn their idols with fire. ⁶For you are a people holy to the LORD your God; the LORD your God has chosen you out of all the peoples on earth to be his people, his treasured possession.

7 It was not because you were more numerous than any other people that the LORD set his heart on you and chose you—for you were the fewest of all peoples. ⁸It was because the LORD loved you and kept the oath that he swore to your ancestors, that the LORD has brought you out with a mighty hand, and redeemed you from the house of slavery, from the hand of Pharaoh king of Egypt. ⁹Know therefore that the LORD your God is God, the faithful God who maintains covenant

loyalty with those who love him and keep his commandments, to a thousand generations, ¹⁰and who repays in their own person those who reject him. He does not delay but repays in their own person those who reject him. ¹¹Therefore, observe diligently the commandment— the statutes and the ordinances—that I am commanding you today.

Blessings for Obedience

12 If you heed these ordinances, by diligently observing them, the LORD your God will maintain with you the covenant loyalty that he swore to your ancestors; ¹³he will love you, bless you, and multiply you; he will bless the fruit of your womb and the fruit of your ground, your grain and your wine and your oil, the increase of your cattle and the issue of your flock, in the land that he swore to your ancestors to give you. ¹⁴You shall be the most blessed of peoples, with neither sterility nor barrenness among you or your livestock. ¹⁵The LORD will turn away from you every illness; all the dread diseases of Egypt that you experienced, he will not inflict on you, but he will lay them on all who hate you. ¹⁶You shall devour all the peoples that the LORD your God is giving over to you, showing them no pity; you shall not serve their gods, for that would be a snare to you.

17 If you say to yourself, "These nations are more numerous than I; how can I dispossess them?" ¹⁸do not be afraid of them. Just remember what the LORD your God did to Pharaoh and to all Egypt, ¹⁹the great trials that your eyes saw, the signs and wonders, the mighty hand and the outstretched arm by which the LORD your God brought you out. The LORD your God will do the same to all the peoples of whom you are afraid. ²⁰Moreover, the LORD your God will send the pestilence^q against them, until even

^p Heb Asherim   ^q Or hornets: Meaning of Heb uncertain

the survivors and the fugitives are destroyed. [21]Have no dread of them, for the Lord your God, who is present with you, is a great and awesome God. [22]The Lord your God will clear away these nations before you little by little; you will not be able to make a quick end of them, otherwise the wild animals would become too numerous for you. [23]But the Lord your God will give them over to you, and throw them into great panic, until they are destroyed. [24]He will hand their kings over to you and you shall blot out their name from under heaven; no one will be able to stand against you, until you have destroyed them. [25]The images of their gods you shall burn with fire. Do not covet the silver or the gold that is on them and take it for yourself, because you could be ensnared by it; for it is abhorrent to the Lord your God. [26]Do not bring an abhorrent thing into your house, or you will be set apart for destruction like it. You must utterly detest and abhor it, for it is set apart for destruction.

A Warning Not to Forget God in Prosperity

8 This entire commandment that I command you today you must diligently observe, so that you may live and increase, and go in and occupy the land that the Lord promised on oath to your ancestors. [2]Remember the long way that the Lord your God has led you these forty years in the wilderness, in order to humble you, testing you to know what was in your heart, whether or not you would keep his commandments. [3]He humbled you by letting you hunger, then by feeding you with manna, with which neither you nor your ancestors were acquainted, in order to make you understand that one does not live by bread alone, but by every word that comes from the mouth of the Lord.[r] [4]The clothes on your back did not wear out and your feet did not swell these forty years. [5]Know then in your heart that as a parent disciplines a child so the Lord

your God disciplines you. [6]Therefore keep the commandments of the Lord your God, by walking in his ways and by fearing him. [7]For the Lord your God is bringing you into a good land, a land with flowing streams, with springs and underground waters welling up in valleys and hills, [8]a land of wheat and barley, of vines and fig trees and pomegranates, a land of olive trees and honey, [9]a land where you may eat bread without scarcity, where you will lack nothing, a land whose stones are iron and from whose hills you may mine copper. [10]You shall eat your fill and bless the Lord your God for the good land that he has given you.

11 Take care that you do not forget the Lord your God, by failing to keep his commandments, his ordinances, and his statutes, which I am commanding you today. [12]When you have eaten your fill and have built fine houses and live in them, [13]and when your herds and flocks have multiplied, and your silver and gold is multiplied, and all that you have is multiplied, [14]then do not exalt yourself, forgetting the Lord your God, who brought you out of the land of Egypt, out of the house of slavery, [15]who led you through the great and terrible wilderness, an arid wasteland with poisonous[s] snakes and scorpions. He made water flow for you from flint rock, [16]and fed you in the wilderness with manna that your ancestors did not know, to humble you and to test you, and in the end to do you good. [17]Do not say to yourself, "My power and the might of my own hand have gotten me this wealth." [18]But remember the Lord your God, for it is he who gives you power to get wealth, so that he may confirm his covenant that he swore to your ancestors, as he is doing today. [19]If you do forget the Lord your God and follow other gods to serve and worship them, I solemnly warn you today that you shall

[r] Or by anything that the Lord decrees   [s] Or fiery; Heb seraph

surely perish. [20]Like the nations that the LORD is destroying before you, so shall you perish, because you would not obey the voice of the LORD your God.

The Consequences of Rebelling against God

9 Hear, O Israel! You are about to cross the Jordan today, to go in and dispossess nations larger and mightier than you, great cities, fortified to the heavens, [2]a strong and tall people, the offspring of the An′a·kim, whom you know. You have heard it said of them, "Who can stand up to the An′a·kim?" [3]Know then today that the LORD your God is the one who crosses over before you as a devouring fire; he will defeat them and subdue them before you, so that you may dispossess and destroy them quickly, as the LORD has promised you.

4 When the LORD your God thrusts them out before you, do not say to yourself, "It is because of my righteousness that the LORD has brought me in to occupy this land"; it is rather because of the wickedness of these nations that the LORD is dispossessing them before you. [5]It is not because of your righteousness or the uprightness of your heart that you are going in to occupy their land; but because of the wickedness of these nations the LORD your God is dispossessing them before you, in order to fulfill the promise that the LORD made on oath to your ancestors, to Abraham, to Isaac, and to Jacob.

6 Know, then, that the LORD your God is not giving you this good land to occupy because of your righteousness; for you are a stubborn people. [7]Remember and do not forget how you provoked the LORD your God to wrath in the wilderness; you have been rebellious against the LORD from the day you came out of the land of Egypt until you came to this place.

8 Even at Hō′reb you provoked the LORD to wrath, and the LORD was so angry with you that he was ready to destroy you. [9]When I went up the mountain to receive the stone tablets, the tablets of the covenant that the LORD made with you, I remained on the mountain forty days and forty nights; I neither ate bread nor drank water. [10]And the LORD gave me the two stone tablets written with the finger of God; on them were all the words that the LORD had spoken to you at the mountain out of the fire on the day of the assembly. [11]At the end of forty days and forty nights the LORD gave me the two stone tablets, the tablets of the covenant. [12]Then the LORD said to me, "Get up, go down quickly from here, for your people whom you have brought from Egypt have acted corruptly. They have been quick to turn from the way that I commanded them; they have cast an image for themselves." [13]Furthermore the LORD said to me, "I have seen that this people is indeed a stubborn people. [14]Let me alone that I may destroy them and blot out their name from under heaven; and I will make of you a nation mightier and more numerous than they."

15 So I turned and went down from the mountain, while the mountain was ablaze; the two tablets of the covenant were in my two hands. [16]Then I saw that you had indeed sinned against the LORD your God, by casting for yourselves an image of a calf; you had been quick to turn from the way that the LORD had commanded you. [17]So I took hold of the two tablets and flung them from my two hands, smashing them before your eyes. [18]Then I lay prostrate before the LORD as before, forty days and forty nights; I neither ate bread nor drank water, because of all the sin you had committed, provoking the LORD by doing what was evil in his sight. [19]For I was afraid that the anger that the LORD bore against you was so fierce that he would destroy you. But the LORD listened to me that time also. [20]The LORD was so angry with Aaron that

he was ready to destroy him, but I interceded also on behalf of Aaron at that same time. ²¹Then I took the sinful thing you had made, the calf, and burned it with fire and crushed it, grinding it thoroughly, until it was reduced to dust; and I threw the dust of it into the stream that runs down the mountain.

22 At Tab´e·rah also, and at Mas´sah, and at Kib´roth-hat·ta´a·vah, you provoked the LORD to wrath. ²³And when the LORD sent you from Ka´desh-bar´ne·a, saying, "Go up and occupy the land that I have given you," you rebelled against the command of the LORD your God, neither trusting him nor obeying him. ²⁴You have been rebellious against the LORD as long as he has⁽ᵗ⁾ known you.

25 Throughout the forty days and forty nights that I lay prostrate before the LORD when the LORD intended to destroy you, ²⁶I prayed to the LORD and said, "Lord GOD, do not destroy the people who are your very own possession, whom you redeemed in your greatness, whom you brought out of Egypt with a mighty hand. ²⁷Remember your servants, Abraham, Isaac, and Jacob; pay no attention to the stubbornness of this people, their wickedness and their sin, ²⁸otherwise the land from which you have brought us might say, 'Because the LORD was not able to bring them into the land that he promised them, and because he hated them, he has brought them out to let them die in the wilderness.' ²⁹For they are the people of your very own possession, whom you brought out by your great power and by your outstretched arm."

The Second Pair of Tablets

10 At that time the LORD said to me, "Carve out two tablets of stone like the former ones, and come up to me on the mountain, and make an ark of wood. ²I will write on the tablets the words that were on the former tablets, which you smashed, and you shall put them in the ark." ³So I made an ark of

acacia wood, cut two tablets of stone like the former ones, and went up the mountain with the two tablets in my hand. ⁴Then he wrote on the tablets the same words as before, the ten commandments⁽ᵘ⁾ that the LORD had spoken to you on the mountain out of the fire on the day of the assembly; and the LORD gave them to me. ⁵So I turned and came down from the mountain, and put the tablets in the ark that I had made; and there they are, as the LORD commanded me.

6 (The Israelites journeyed from Be·er´oth Ben·e´-ja´a·kan⁽ᵛ⁾ to Mo·se´rah. There Aaron died, and there he was buried; his son El·e·a´zar succeeded him as priest. ⁷From there they journeyed to Gud´go·dah, and from Gud´go·dah to Jot´ba·thah, a land with flowing streams. ⁸At that time the LORD set apart the tribe of Levi to carry the ark of the covenant of the LORD, to stand before the LORD to minister to him, and to bless in his name, to this day. ⁹Therefore Levi has no allotment or inheritance with his kindred; the LORD is his inheritance, as the LORD your God promised him.)

10 I stayed on the mountain forty days and forty nights, as I had done the first time. And once again the LORD listened to me. The LORD was unwilling to destroy you. ¹¹The LORD said to me, "Get up, go on your journey at the head of the people, that they may go in and occupy the land that I swore to their ancestors to give them."

The Essence of the Law

12 So now, O Israel, what does the LORD your God require of you? Only to fear the LORD your God, to walk in all his ways, to love him, to serve the LORD your God with all your heart and with all your soul, ¹³and to keep the commandments of the LORD your God⁽ʷ⁾ and his decrees that I am commanding you today, for your own well-being.

ᵗ Sam Gk: MT *I have*   ᵘ Heb *the ten words*   ᵛ Or *the wells of the Bene-jaakan*   ʷ Q Ms Gk Syr: MT lacks *your God*

[14]Although heaven and the heaven of heavens belong to the LORD your God, the earth with all that is in it, [15]yet the LORD set his heart in love on your ancestors alone and chose you, their descendants after them, out of all the peoples, as it is today. [16]Circumcise, then, the foreskin of your heart, and do not be stubborn any longer. [17]For the LORD your God is God of gods and Lord of lords, the great God, mighty and awesome, who is not partial and takes no bribe, [18]who executes justice for the orphan and the widow, and who loves the strangers, providing them food and clothing. [19]You shall also love the stranger, for you were strangers in the land of Egypt. [20]You shall fear the LORD your God; him alone you shall worship; to him you shall hold fast, and by his name you shall swear. [21]He is your praise; he is your God, who has done for you these great and awesome things that your own eyes have seen. [22]Your ancestors went down to Egypt seventy persons; and now the LORD your God has made you as numerous as the stars in heaven.

Rewards for Obedience

11 You shall love the LORD your God, therefore, and keep his charge, his decrees, his ordinances, and his commandments always. [2]Remember today that it was not your children (who have not known or seen the discipline of the LORD your God), but it is you who must acknowledge his greatness, his mighty hand and his outstretched arm, [3]his signs and his deeds that he did in Egypt to Pharaoh, the king of Egypt, and to all his land; [4]what he did to the Egyptian army, to their horses and chariots, how he made the water of the Red Sea[x] flow over them as they pursued you, so that the LORD has destroyed them to this day; [5]what he did to you in the wilderness, until you came to this place; [6]and what he did to Dā´than and A·bī´ram, sons of E·lī´ab son of Reuben, how in the midst of all Israel the earth opened its

From the time of Moses until today, Jewish people have written the verses from Deuteronomy 6:4–9 and 11:13–21 on a small scroll. They place the scroll in a small cylinder and attach it to the doorpost of their house. Every time they go in or out of their house, they are reminded that they are the people of the one true God.

mouth and swallowed them up, along with their households, their tents, and every living being in their company; [7]for it is your own eyes that have seen every great deed that the LORD did.

8 Keep, then, this entire commandment that I am commanding you today, so that you may have strength to go in and occupy the land that you are crossing over to occupy, [9]and so that you may live long in the land that the LORD swore to your ancestors to give them and to their descendants, a land flowing with milk and honey. [10]For the land that you are about to enter to occupy is not like the land of Egypt, from which you have come, where you sow your seed and irrigate by foot like a vegetable garden. [11]But the land that you are crossing over to occupy is a land of hills and valleys, watered by rain from the sky, [12]a land that the LORD your God looks after. The eyes of the LORD your God are always on it, from the beginning of the year to the end of the year.

13 If you will only heed his every commandment[y] that I am commanding you today—loving the LORD your God, and serving him with all your heart and with all your soul— [14]then he[z] will give the rain for your land in its season, the early rain and the later rain, and you will gather in your grain, your wine, and your oil; [15]and he[z] will give grass in your fields for your livestock, and you will eat

---

[x] Or *Sea of Reeds*   [y] Compare Gk: Heb *my commandments*   [z] Sam Gk Vg: MT *I*

According to Jewish custom, men wear small leather boxes tied to their foreheads and arms. These boxes, called phylacteries, hold verses from the Hebrew Scriptures. The head phylactery has four small parts that contain copies of Exodus 13:1–6 and Deuteronomy 6:4–9; 11:13–21. These boxes help remind them of the greatest commandment —to love and serve God. How do you remember this commandment? What can you use as a reminder?

your fill. ¹⁶Take care, or you will be seduced into turning away, serving other gods and worshiping them, ¹⁷for then the anger of the LORD will be kindled against you and he will shut up the heavens, so that there will be no rain and the land will yield no fruit; then you will perish quickly off the good land that the LORD is giving you.

18 You shall put these words of mine in your heart and soul, and you shall bind them as a sign on your hand, and fix them as an emblem*a* on your forehead. ¹⁹Teach them to your children, talking about them when you are at home and when you are away, when you lie down and when you rise. ²⁰Write them on the doorposts of your house and on your gates, ²¹so that your days and the days of your children may be multiplied in the land that the LORD swore to your ancestors to give them, as long as the heavens are above the earth.

22 If you will diligently observe this entire commandment that I am commanding you, loving the LORD your God, walking in all his ways, and holding fast to him, ²³then the LORD will drive out all these nations before you, and you will dispossess nations larger and mightier than yourselves. ²⁴Every place on which you set foot shall be yours; your territory shall extend from the wilderness to the Lebanon and from the River, the river Euphrates, to the Western Sea. ²⁵No one will be able to stand against you; the LORD your God will put the fear and dread of you on all the land on which you set foot, as he promised you.

26 See, I am setting before you today a blessing and a curse: ²⁷the blessing, if you obey the commandments of the LORD your God that I am commanding you today; ²⁸and the curse, if you do not obey the commandments of the LORD your God, but turn from the way that I am commanding you today, to follow other gods that you have not known.

29 When the LORD your God has brought you into the land that you are entering to occupy, you shall set the blessing on Mount Ger′i·zim and the curse on Mount Ē′bal. ³⁰As you know, they are beyond the Jordan, some distance to the west, in the land of the Cā′naan·ītes who live in the Ar′a·bah, opposite Gil′gal, beside the oak*b* of Mŏ′reh. 31 When you cross the Jordan to go in to occupy the land that the LORD your God is giving you, and when you occupy it and live in it, ³²you must diligently observe all the statutes and ordinances that I am setting before you today.

Pagan Shrines to Be Destroyed

12 These are the statutes and ordinances that you must diligently observe in the land that the LORD, the God of your ancestors, has given you to occupy all the days that you live on the earth. 2 You must demolish completely all the places where the nations whom you are about to dispossess served their gods, on the mountain heights, on the hills, and under every leafy tree. ³Break down their altars, smash their pillars, burn their sacred poles*c* with fire, and hew down the idols of their gods, and thus blot out their name from their places. ⁴You shall not worship the LORD

a Or *as a frontlet*   *b* Gk Syr: Compare Gen 12.6;
Heb *oaks* or *terebinths*   *c* Heb *Asherim*

your God in such ways. ⁵But you shall seek the place that the LORD your God will choose out of all your tribes as his habitation to put his name there. You shall go there, ⁶bringing there your burnt offerings and your sacrifices, your tithes and your donations, your votive gifts, your freewill offerings, and the firstlings of your herds and flocks. ⁷And you shall eat there in the presence of the LORD your God, you and your households together, rejoicing in all the undertakings in which the LORD your God has blessed you.

8 You shall not act as we are acting here today, all of us according to our own desires, ⁹for you have not yet come into the rest and the possession that the LORD your God is giving you. ¹⁰When you cross over the Jordan and live in the land that the LORD your God is allotting to you, and when he gives you rest from your enemies all around so that you live in safety, ¹¹then you shall bring everything that I command you to the place that the LORD your God will choose as a dwelling for his name: your burnt offerings and your sacrifices, your tithes and your donations, and all your choice votive gifts that you vow to the LORD. ¹²And you shall rejoice before the LORD your God, you together with your sons and your daughters, your male and female slaves, and the Lē′vītes who reside in your towns (since they have no allotment or inheritance with you).

A Prescribed Place of Worship

13 Take care that you do not offer your burnt offerings at any place you happen to see. ¹⁴But only at the place that the LORD will choose in one of your tribes—there you shall offer your burnt offerings and there you shall do everything I command you.

15 Yet whenever you desire you may slaughter and eat meat within any of your towns, according to the blessing that the LORD your God has given you; the unclean and the clean may eat of it, as they would of gazelle or deer. ¹⁶The

blood, however, you must not eat; you shall pour it out on the ground like water. ¹⁷Nor may you eat within your towns the tithe of your grain, your wine, and your oil, the firstlings of your herds and your flocks, any of your votive gifts that you vow, your freewill offerings, or your donations; ¹⁸these you shall eat in the presence of the LORD your God at the place that the LORD your God will choose, you together with your son and your daughter, your male and female slaves, and the Lē′vītes resident in your towns, rejoicing in the presence of the LORD your God in all your undertakings. ¹⁹Take care that you do not neglect the Lē′vīte as long as you live in your land.

20 When the LORD your God enlarges your territory, as he has promised you, and you say, "I am going to eat some meat," because you wish to eat meat, you may eat meat whenever you have the desire. ²¹If the place where the LORD your God will choose to put his name is too far from you, and you slaughter as I have commanded you any of your herd or flock that the LORD has given you, then you may eat within your towns whenever you desire. ²²Indeed, just as gazelle or deer is eaten, so you may eat it; the unclean and the clean alike may eat it. ²³Only be sure that you do not eat the blood; for the blood is the life, and you shall not eat the life with the meat. ²⁴Do not eat it; you shall pour it out on the ground like water. ²⁵Do not eat it, so that all may go well with you and your children after you, because you do what is right in the sight of the LORD. ²⁶But the sacred donations that are due from you, and your votive gifts, you shall bring to the place that the LORD will choose. ²⁷You shall present your burnt offerings, both the meat and the blood, on the altar of the LORD your God; the blood of your other sacrifices shall be poured out beside*ᵈ* the altar of the LORD your God, but the meat you may eat.

28 Be careful to obey all these words

ᵈ Or *on*

that I command you today,[c] so that it may go well with you and with your children after you forever, because you will be doing what is good and right in the sight of the LORD your God.

Warning against Idolatry

29 When the LORD your God has cut off before you the nations whom you are about to enter to dispossess them, when you have dispossessed them and live in their land, [30]take care that you are not snared into imitating them, after they have been destroyed before you: do not inquire concerning their gods, saying, "How did these nations worship their gods? I also want to do the same." [31]You must not do the same for the LORD your God, because every abhorrent thing that the LORD hates they have done for their gods. They would even burn their sons and their daughters in the fire to their gods. [32][j] You must diligently observe everything that I command you; do not add to it or take anything from it.

13 [g] If prophets or those who divine by dreams appear among you and promise you omens or portents, [2]and the omens or the portents declared by them take place, and they say, "Let us follow other gods" (whom you have not known) "and let us serve them," [3]you must not heed the words of those prophets or those who divine by dreams; for the LORD your God is testing you, to know whether you indeed love the LORD your God with all your heart and soul. [4]The LORD your God you shall follow, him alone you shall fear, his commandments you shall keep, his voice you shall obey, him you shall serve, and to him you shall hold fast. [5]But those prophets or those who divine by dreams shall be put to death for having spoken treason against the LORD your God—who brought you out of the land of Egypt and redeemed you from the house of slavery—to turn you from the way in which the LORD your God

commanded you to walk. So you shall purge the evil from your midst.

6 If anyone secretly entices you—even if it is your brother, your father's son or[h] your mother's son, or your own son or daughter, or the wife you embrace, or your most intimate friend—saying, "Let us go worship other gods," whom neither you nor your ancestors have known, [7]any of the gods of the peoples that are around you, whether near you or far away from you, from one end of the earth to the other, [8]you must not yield to or heed any such persons. Show them no pity or compassion and do not shield them. [9]But you shall surely kill them; your own hand shall be first against them to execute them, and afterwards the hand of all the people. [10]Stone them to death for trying to turn you away from the LORD your God, who brought you out of the land of Egypt, out of the house of slavery. [11]Then all Israel shall hear and be afraid, and never again do any such wickedness.

12 If you hear it said about one of the towns that the LORD your God is giving you to live in, [13]that scoundrels from among you have gone out and led the inhabitants of the town astray, saying, "Let us go and worship other gods," whom you have not known, [14]then you shall inquire and make a thorough investigation. If the charge is established that such an abhorrent thing has been done among you, [15]you shall put the inhabitants of that town to the sword, utterly destroying it and everything in it—even putting its livestock to the sword. [16]All of its spoil you shall gather into its public square; then burn the town and all its spoil with fire, as a whole burnt offering to the LORD your God. It shall remain a perpetual ruin, never to be rebuilt. [17]Do not let anything devoted to destruction stick to your

---

[c] Gk Sam Syr: MT lacks *today*   [j] Ch 13.1 in Heb
[g] Ch 13.2 in Heb   [h] Sam Gk Compare Tg: MT lacks *your father's son or*

hand, so that the LORD may turn from his fierce anger and show you compassion, and in his compassion multiply you, as he swore to your ancestors, [18]if you obey the voice of the LORD your God by keeping all his commandments that I am commanding you today, doing what is right in the sight of the LORD your God.

Pagan Practices Forbidden

14 You are children of the LORD your God. You must not lacerate yourselves or shave your forelocks for the dead. [2]For you are a people holy to the LORD your God; it is you the LORD has chosen out of all the peoples on earth to be his people, his treasured possession.

Clean and Unclean Foods

3 You shall not eat any abhorrent thing. [4]These are the animals you may eat: the ox, the sheep, the goat, [5]the deer, the gazelle, the roebuck, the wild goat, the ibex, the antelope, and the mountain-sheep. [6]Any animal that divides the hoof and has the hoof cleft in two, and chews the cud, among the animals, you may eat. [7]Yet of those that chew the cud or have the hoof cleft you shall not eat these: the camel, the hare, and the rock badger, because they chew the cud but do not divide the hoof; they are unclean for you. [8]And the pig, because it divides the hoof but does not chew the cud, is unclean for you. You shall not eat their meat, and you shall not touch their carcasses.

9 Of all that live in water you may eat these: whatever has fins and scales you may eat. [10]And whatever does not have fins and scales you shall not eat; it is unclean for you.

11 You may eat any clean birds. [12]But these are the ones that you shall not eat: the eagle, the vulture, the osprey, [13]the buzzard, the kite, of any kind; [14]every raven of any kind; [15]the ostrich, the nighthawk, the sea gull, the hawk, of any kind; [16]the little owl and the great owl, the water hen [17]and the desert owl,[i] the carrion vulture and the cormorant, [18]the stork, the heron of any kind; the hoopoe and the bat.[j] [19]And all winged insects are unclean for you; they shall not be eaten. [20]You may eat any clean winged creature.

21 You shall not eat anything that dies of itself; you may give it to aliens residing in your towns for them to eat, or you may sell it to a foreigner. For you are a people holy to the LORD your God.

You shall not boil a kid in its mother's milk.

Regulations concerning Tithes

22 Set apart a tithe of all the yield of your seed that is brought in yearly from the field. [23]In the presence of the LORD your God, in the place that he will choose as a dwelling for his name, you shall eat the tithe of your grain, your wine, and your oil, as well as the firstlings of your herd and flock, so that you may learn to fear the LORD your God always. [24]But if, when the LORD your God has blessed you, the distance is so great that you are unable to transport it, because the place where the LORD your God will choose to set his

Did you know that a camel can drink thirty-five gallons of water at one time? That's a lot of water! People use camels to carry heavy objects and help them travel through the desert. Camels have flat feet to keep them from sinking in the desert sand. Although the Israelites did not eat camel meat, they drank camel milk and wove camel hair into wool for tents and clothing. You may have seen camels with two humps, but the type of camel we read about in the Bible is mostly the one-humped Arabian camel.

[i] Or *pelican*   [j] Identification of several of the birds in verses 12-18 is uncertain

name is too far away from you, ²⁵then you may turn it into money. With the money secure in hand, go to the place that the LORD your God will choose; ²⁶spend the money for whatever you wish—oxen, sheep, wine, strong drink, or whatever you desire. And you shall eat there in the presence of the LORD your God, you and your household rejoicing together. ²⁷As for the Lē´vītes resident in your towns, do not neglect them, because they have no allotment or inheritance with you.

28 Every third year you shall bring out the full tithe of your produce for that year, and store it within your towns; ²⁹the Lē´vītes, because they have no allotment or inheritance with you, as well as the resident aliens, the orphans, and the widows in your towns, may come and eat their fill so that the LORD your God may bless you in all the work that you undertake.

Laws concerning the Sabbatical Year

15 Every seventh year you shall grant a remission of debts. ²And this is the manner of the remission: every creditor shall remit the claim that is held against a neighbor, not exacting it of a neighbor who is a member of the community, because the LORD's remission has been proclaimed. ³Of a foreigner you may exact it, but you must remit your claim on whatever any member of your community owes you. ⁴There will, however, be no one in need among you, because the LORD is sure to bless you in the land that the LORD your God is giving you as a possession to occupy, ⁵if only you will obey the LORD your God by diligently observing this entire commandment that I command you today. ⁶When the LORD your God has blessed you, as he promised you, you will lend to many nations, but you will not borrow; you will rule over many nations, but they will not rule over you.

7 If there is among you anyone in need, a member of your community in

any of your towns within the land that the LORD your God is giving you, do not be hard-hearted or tight-fisted toward your needy neighbor. ⁸You should rather open your hand, willingly lending enough to meet the need, whatever it may be. ⁹Be careful that you do not entertain a mean thought, thinking, "The seventh year, the year of remission, is near," and therefore view your needy neighbor with hostility and give nothing; your neighbor might cry to the LORD against you, and you would incur guilt. ¹⁰Give liberally and be ungrudging when you do so, for on this account the LORD your God will bless you in all your work and in all that you undertake. ¹¹Since there will never cease to be some in need on the earth, I therefore command you, "Open your hand to the poor and needy neighbor in your land."

12 If a member of your community, whether a Hebrew man or a Hebrew woman, is sold^k to you and works for you six years, in the seventh year you shall set that person free. ¹³And when you send a male slave^l out from you a free person, you shall not send him out empty-handed. ¹⁴Provide liberally out of your flock, your threshing floor, and your wine press, thus giving to him some of the bounty with which the LORD your God has blessed you. ¹⁵Remember that you were a slave in the land of Egypt, and the LORD your God redeemed you; for this reason I lay this command upon you today. ¹⁶But if he says to you, "I will not go out from you," because he loves you and your household, since he is well off with you, ¹⁷then you shall take an awl and thrust it through his earlobe into the door, and he shall be your slave^m forever.

You shall do the same with regard to your female slave.ⁿ

18 Do not consider it a hardship when you send them out from you free persons, because for six years they have given you services worth the wages of

^k Or *sells himself or herself*   ^l Heb *him*   ^m Or *bondman*   ⁿ Or *bondwoman*

hired laborers; and the LORD your God will bless you in all that you do.

The Firstborn of Livestock

19 Every firstling male born of your herd and flock you shall consecrate to the LORD your God; you shall not do work with your firstling ox nor shear the firstling of your flock. ²⁰You shall eat it, you together with your household, in the presence of the LORD your God year by year at the place that the LORD will choose. ²¹But if it has any defect—any serious defect, such as lameness or blindness—you shall not sacrifice it to the LORD your God; ²²within your towns you may eat it, the unclean and the clean alike, as you would a gazelle or deer. ²³Its blood, however, you must not eat; you shall pour it out on the ground like water.

The Passover Reviewed

16 Observe the month° of Āʹbib by keeping the passover for the LORD your God, for in the month of Āʹbib the LORD your God brought you out of Egypt by night. ²You shall offer the passover sacrifice to the LORD your God, from the flock and the herd, at the place that the LORD will choose as a dwelling for his name. ³You must not eat with it anything leavened. For seven days you shall eat unleavened bread with it—the bread of affliction—because you came out of the land of Egypt in great haste, so that all the days of your life you may remember the day of your departure from the land of Egypt. ⁴No leaven shall be seen with you in all your territory for seven days; and none of the meat of what you slaughter on the evening of the first day shall remain until morning. ⁵You are not permitted to offer the passover sacrifice within any of your towns that the LORD your God is giving you. ⁶But at the place that the LORD your God will choose as a dwelling for his name, only there shall you offer the passover sacrifice, in the evening at sun-

set, the time of day when you departed from Egypt. ⁷You shall cook it and eat it at the place that the LORD your God will choose; the next morning you may go back to your tents. ⁸For six days you shall continue to eat unleavened bread, and on the seventh day there shall be a solemn assembly for the LORD your God, when you shall do no work.

The Festival of Weeks Reviewed

9 You shall count seven weeks; begin to count the seven weeks from the time the sickle is first put to the standing grain. ¹⁰Then you shall keep the festival of weeks to the LORD your God, contributing a freewill offering in proportion to the blessing that you have received from the LORD your God. ¹¹Rejoice before the LORD your God—you and your sons and your daughters, your male and female slaves, the Lēʹvītes resident in your towns, as well as the strangers, the orphans, and the widows who are among you—at the place that the LORD your God will choose as a dwelling for his name. ¹²Remember that you were a slave in Egypt, and diligently observe these statutes.

Yeast is an ingredient that makes bread rise into a loaf. Yeast is also called leaven. When the Israelite people left Egypt, where they had been slaves, they needed to leave quickly! They did not stop to bake bread because it would have taken too much time to rise. Each year during the Feast of Unleavened Bread, the Israelites ate bread made without yeast. This flat bread reminded them of the time God saved their ancestors from slavery. Today, Jews eat unleavened bread during Passover.

° Or *new moon*

The Festival of Booths Reviewed

13 You shall keep the festival of booths[p] for seven days, when you have gathered in the produce from your threshing floor and your wine press. [14]Rejoice during your festival, you and your sons and your daughters, your male and female slaves, as well as the Lē´vītes, the strangers, the orphans, and the widows resident in your towns. [15]Seven days you shall keep the festival to the LORD your God at the place that the LORD will choose; for the LORD your God will bless you in all your produce and in all your undertakings, and you shall surely celebrate.

16 Three times a year all your males shall appear before the LORD your God at the place that he will choose: at the festival of unleavened bread, at the festival of weeks, and at the festival of booths.[p] They shall not appear before the LORD empty-handed; [17]all shall give as they are able, according to the blessing of the LORD your God that he has given you.

Municipal Judges and Officers

18 You shall appoint judges and officials throughout your tribes, in all your towns that the LORD your God is giving you, and they shall render just decisions for the people. [19]You must not distort justice; you must not show partiality; and you must not accept bribes, for a bribe blinds the eyes of the wise and subverts the cause of those who are in the right. [20]Justice, and only justice, you shall pursue, so that you may live and occupy the land that the LORD your God is giving you.

Forbidden Forms of Worship

21 You shall not plant any tree as a sacred pole[q] beside the altar that you make for the LORD your God; [22]nor shall you set up a stone pillar—things that the LORD your God hates.

17 You must not sacrifice to the LORD your God an ox or a sheep that has a defect, anything seriously wrong; for that is abhorrent to the LORD your God.

2 If there is found among you, in one of your towns that the LORD your God is giving you, a man or woman who does what is evil in the sight of the LORD your God, and transgresses his covenant [3]by going to serve other gods and worshiping them—whether the sun or the moon or any of the host of heaven, which I have forbidden— [4]and if it is reported to you or you hear of it, and you make a thorough inquiry, and the charge is proved true that such an abhorrent thing has occurred in Israel, [5]then you shall bring out to your gates that man or that woman who has committed this crime and you shall stone the man or woman to death. [6]On the evidence of two or three witnesses the death sentence shall be executed; a person must not be put to death on the evidence of only one witness. [7]The hands of the witnesses shall be the first raised against the person to execute the death penalty, and afterward the hands of all the people. So you shall purge the evil from your midst.

Legal Decisions by Priests and Judges

8 If a judicial decision is too difficult for you to make between one kind of bloodshed and another, one kind of legal right and another, or one kind of assault and another—any such matters of dispute in your towns—then you shall immediately go up to the place that the LORD your God will choose, [9]where you shall consult with the levitical priests and the judge who is in office in those days; they shall announce to you the decision in the case. [10]Carry out exactly the decision that they announce to you from the place that the LORD will choose, diligently observing everything they instruct you. [11]You must carry out fully the law that they interpret for you or the ruling that they announce to you; do not turn aside from the decision that they announce to you, either to the right or to

---

[p] Or *tabernacles;* Heb *succoth*   [q] Heb *Asherah*

the left. [12]As for anyone who presumes to disobey the priest appointed to minister there to the LORD your God, or the judge, that person shall die. So you shall purge the evil from Israel. [13]All the people will hear and be afraid, and will not act presumptuously again.

Limitations of Royal Authority

14 When you have come into the land that the LORD your God is giving you, and have taken possession of it and settled in it, and you say, "I will set a king over me, like all the nations that are around me," [15]you may indeed set over you a king whom the LORD your God will choose. One of your own community you may set as king over you; you are not permitted to put a foreigner over you, who is not of your own community. [16]Even so, he must not acquire many horses for himself, or return the people to Egypt in order to acquire more horses, since the LORD has said to you, "You must never return that way again." [17]And he must not acquire many wives for himself, or else his heart will turn away; also silver and gold he must not acquire in great quantity for himself. [18]When he has taken the throne of his kingdom, he shall have a copy of this law written for him in the presence of the levitical priests. [19]It shall remain with him and he shall read in it all the days of his life, so that he may learn to fear the LORD his God, diligently observing all the words of this law and these statutes, [20]neither exalting himself above other members of the community nor turning aside from the commandment, either to the right or to the left, so that he and his descendants may reign long over his kingdom in Israel.

Privileges of Priests and Levites

18 The levitical priests, the whole tribe of Levi, shall have no allotment or inheritance within Israel. They may eat the sacrifices that are the LORD's portion[r] [2]but they shall have no inheri-

tance among the other members of the community; the LORD is their inheritance, as he promised them.

3 This shall be the priests' due from the people, from those offering a sacrifice, whether an ox or a sheep: they shall give to the priest the shoulder, the two jowls, and the stomach. [4]The first fruits of your grain, your wine, and your oil, as well as the first of the fleece of your sheep, you shall give him. [5]For the LORD your God has chosen Levi[s] out of all your tribes, to stand and minister in the name of the LORD, him and his sons for all time.

6 If a Lḗvīte leaves any of your towns, from wherever he has been residing in Israel, and comes to the place that the LORD will choose (and he may come whenever he wishes), [7]then he may minister in the name of the LORD his God, like all his fellow Lḗvītes who stand to minister there before the LORD. [8]They shall have equal portions to eat, even though they have income from the sale of family possessions.[r]

Child-Sacrifice, Divination, and Magic Prohibited

9 When you come into the land that the LORD your God is giving you, you must not learn to imitate the abhorrent practices of those nations. [10]No one shall be found among you who makes a son or daughter pass through fire, or who practices divination, or is a soothsayer, or an augur, or a sorcerer, [11]or one who casts spells, or who consults ghosts or spirits, or who seeks oracles from the dead. [12]For whoever does these things is abhorrent to the LORD; it is because of such abhorrent practices that the LORD your God is driving them out before you. [13]You must remain completely loyal to the LORD your God. [14]Although these nations that you are about to dispossess do give heed to soothsayers and diviners, as for you, the LORD your God does not permit you to do so.

[r] Meaning of Heb uncertain   [s] Heb him

A New Prophet Like Moses

15 The LORD your God will raise up for you a prophet[t] like me from among your own people; you shall heed such a prophet.[u] 16This is what you requested of the LORD your God at Hō'reb on the day of the assembly when you said: "If I hear the voice of the LORD my God any more, or ever again see this great fire, I will die." 17Then the LORD replied to me: "They are right in what they have said. 18I will raise up for them a prophet[t] like you from among their own people; I will put my words in the mouth of the prophet,[v] who shall speak to them everything that I command. 19Anyone who does not heed the words that the prophet[w] shall speak in my name, I myself will hold accountable. 20But any prophet who speaks in the name of other gods, or who presumes to speak in my name a word that I have not commanded the prophet to speak—that prophet shall die." 21You may say to yourself, "How can we recognize a word that the LORD has not spoken?" 22If a prophet speaks in the name of the LORD but the thing does not take place or prove true, it is a word that the LORD has not spoken. The prophet has spoken it presumptuously; do not be frightened by it.

Laws concerning the Cities of Refuge

19 When the LORD your God has cut off the nations whose land the LORD your God is giving you, and you have dispossessed them and settled in their towns and in their houses, 2you shall set apart three cities in the land that the LORD your God is giving you to possess. 3You shall calculate the distances[x] and divide into three regions the land that the LORD your God gives you as a possession, so that any homicide can flee to one of them.

4 Now this is the case of a homicide who might flee there and live, that is, someone who has killed another person unintentionally when the two had not been at enmity before: 5Suppose someone goes into the forest with another to cut wood, and when one of them swings the ax to cut down a tree, the head slips from the handle and strikes the other person who then dies; the killer may flee to one of these cities and live. 6But if the distance is too great, the avenger of blood in hot anger might pursue and overtake and put the killer to death, although a death sentence was not deserved, since the two had not been at enmity before. 7Therefore I command you: You shall set apart three cities.

8 If the LORD your God enlarges your territory, as he swore to your ancestors— and he will give you all the land that he promised your ancestors to give you, 9provided you diligently observe this entire commandment that I command you today, by loving the LORD your God and walking always in his ways—then you shall add three more cities to these three, 10so that the blood of an innocent person may not be shed in the land that the LORD your God is giving you as an inheritance, thereby bringing bloodguilt upon you.

If someone killed an innocent person, even by accident, he or she had guilt that was called bloodguilt. The whole community shared in the bloodguilt, and so everyone helped find out the reason for the killing. If it had been done on purpose, the murderer had to die. If the killing was an accident, the person responsible could live for a while in a city of refuge. Read more about these cities in Numbers 35:9–34.

[t] Or prophets [u] Or such prophets [v] Or mouths of the prophets [w] Heb he [x] Or prepare roads to them

11 But if someone at enmity with another lies in wait and attacks and takes the life of that person, and flees into one of these cities, 12then the elders of the killer's city shall send to have the culprit taken from there and handed over to the avenger of blood to be put to death. 13Show no pity; you shall purge the guilt of innocent blood from Israel, so that it may go well with you.

Property Boundaries

14 You must not move your neighbor's boundary marker, set up by former generations, on the property that will be allotted to you in the land that the LORD your God is giving you to possess.

Law concerning Witnesses

15 A single witness shall not suffice to convict a person of any crime or wrongdoing in connection with any offense that may be committed. Only on the evidence of two or three witnesses shall a charge be sustained. 16If a malicious witness comes forward to accuse someone of wrongdoing, 17then both parties to the dispute shall appear before the LORD, before the priests and the judges who are in office in those days, 18and the judges shall make a thorough inquiry. If the witness is a false witness, having testified falsely against another, 19then you shall do to the false witness just as the false witness had meant to do to the other. So you shall purge the evil from your midst. 20The rest shall hear and be afraid, and a crime such as this shall never again be committed among you. 21Show no pity: life for life, eye for eye, tooth for tooth, hand for hand, foot for foot.

Rules of Warfare

20 When you go out to war against your enemies, and see horses and chariots, an army larger than your own, you shall not be afraid of them; for the LORD your God is with you, who brought you up from the land of Egypt. 2Before you engage in battle, the priest shall come forward and speak to the troops, 3and shall say to them: "Hear, O Israel! Today you are drawing near to do battle against your enemies. Do not lose heart, or be afraid, or panic, or be in dread of them; 4for it is the LORD your God who goes with you, to fight for you against your enemies, to give you victory." 5Then the officials shall address the troops, saying, "Has anyone built a new house but not dedicated it? He should go back to his house, or he might die in the battle and another dedicate it. 6Has anyone planted a vineyard but not yet enjoyed its fruit? He should go back to his house, or he might die in the battle and another be first to enjoy its fruit. 7Has anyone become engaged to a woman but not yet married her? He should go back to his house, or he might die in the battle and another marry her." 8The officials shall continue to address the troops, saying, "Is anyone afraid or disheartened? He should go back to his house, or he might cause the heart of his comrades to melt like his own." 9When the officials have finished addressing the troops, then the commanders shall take charge of them.

10 When you draw near to a town to fight against it, offer it terms of peace. 11If it accepts your terms of peace and surrenders to you, then all the people in it shall serve you at forced labor. 12If it does not submit to you peacefully, but makes war against you, then you shall besiege it; 13and when the LORD your God gives it into your hand, you shall put all its males to the sword. 14You may, however, take as your booty the women, the children, livestock, and everything else in the town, all its spoil. You may enjoy the spoil of your enemies, which the LORD your God has given you. 15Thus you shall treat all the towns that are very far from you, which are not towns of the nations here. 16But as for the towns of these peoples that the LORD your God is giving you as an inheritance, you must not let anything that breathes

remain alive. [17]You shall annihilate them—the Hīt´tītes and the Am´o·rītes, the Cā´naan·ītes and the Per´iz·zītes, the Hī´vītes and the Jeb´ū·sītes—just as the LORD your God has commanded, [18]so that they may not teach you to do all the abhorrent things that they do for their gods, and you thus sin against the LORD your God.

19 If you besiege a town for a long time, making war against it in order to take it, you must not destroy its trees by wielding an ax against them. Although you may take food from them, you must not cut them down. Are trees in the field human beings that they should come under siege from you? [20]You may destroy only the trees that you know do not produce food; you may cut them down for use in building siegeworks against the town that makes war with you, until it falls.

Law concerning Murder by Persons Unknown

21 If, in the land that the LORD your God is giving you to possess, a body is found lying in open country, and it is not known who struck the person down, [2]then your elders and your judges shall come out to measure the distances to the towns that are near the body. [3]The elders of the town nearest the body shall take a heifer that has never been worked, one that has not pulled in the yoke; [4]the elders of that town shall bring the heifer down to a wadi with running water, which is neither plowed nor sown, and shall break the heifer's neck there in the wadi. [5]Then the priests, the sons of Levi, shall come forward, for the LORD your God has chosen them to minister to him and to pronounce blessings in the name of the LORD, and by their decision all cases of dispute and assault shall be settled. [6]All the elders of that town nearest the body shall wash their hands over the heifer whose neck was broken in the wadi, [7]and

they shall declare: "Our hands did not shed this blood, nor were we witnesses to it. [8]Absolve, O LORD, your people Israel, whom you redeemed; do not let the guilt of innocent blood remain in the midst of your people Israel." Then they will be absolved of bloodguilt. [9]So you shall purge the guilt of innocent blood from your midst, because you must do what is right in the sight of the LORD.

Female Captives

10 When you go out to war against your enemies, and the LORD your God hands them over to you and you take them captive, [11]suppose you see among the captives a beautiful woman whom you desire and want to marry, [12]and so you bring her home to your house: she shall shave her head, pare her nails, [13]discard her captive's garb, and shall remain in your house a full month, mourning for her father and mother; after that you may go in to her and be her husband, and she shall be your wife. [14]But if you are not satisfied with her, you shall let her go free and not sell her for money. You must not treat her as a slave, since you have dishonored her.

The Right of the Firstborn

15 If a man has two wives, one of them loved and the other disliked, and if both the loved and the disliked have borne him sons, the firstborn being the son of the one who is disliked, [16]then on the day when he wills his possessions to his sons, he is not permitted to treat the son of the loved as the firstborn in preference to the son of the disliked, who is the firstborn. [17]He must acknowledge as firstborn the son of the one who is disliked, giving him a double portion[y] of all that he has; since he is the first issue of his virility, the right of the firstborn is his.

Rebellious Children

18 If someone has a stubborn and rebellious son who will not obey his

[y] Heb *two-thirds*

father and mother, who does not heed them when they discipline him, [19]then his father and his mother shall take hold of him and bring him out to the elders of his town at the gate of that place. [20]They shall say to the elders of his town, "This son of ours is stubborn and rebellious. He will not obey us. He is a glutton and a drunkard." [21]Then all the men of the town shall stone him to death. So you shall purge the evil from your midst; and all Israel will hear, and be afraid.

Miscellaneous Laws

22 When someone is convicted of a crime punishable by death and is executed, and you hang him on a tree, [23]his corpse must not remain all night upon the tree; you shall bury him that same day, for anyone hung on a tree is under God's curse. You must not defile the land that the LORD your God is giving you for possession.

22 You shall not watch your neighbor's ox or sheep straying away and ignore them; you shall take them back to their owner. [2]If the owner does not reside near you or you do not know who the owner is, you shall bring it to your own house, and it shall remain with you until the owner claims it; then you shall return it. [3]You shall do the same with a neighbor's donkey; you shall do the same with a neighbor's garment; and you shall do the same with anything else that your neighbor loses and you find. You may not withhold your help.

4 You shall not see your neighbor's donkey or ox fallen on the road and ignore it; you shall help to lift it up.

5 A woman shall not wear a man's apparel, nor shall a man put on a woman's garment; for whoever does such things is abhorrent to the LORD your God.

6 If you come on a bird's nest, in any tree or on the ground, with fledglings or eggs, with the mother sitting on the fledglings or on the eggs, you shall not take the mother with the young. [7]Let the mother go, taking only the young for

yourself, in order that it may go well with you and you may live long.

8 When you build a new house, you shall make a parapet for your roof; otherwise you might have bloodguilt on your house, if anyone should fall from it.

9 You shall not sow your vineyard with a second kind of seed, or the whole yield will have to be forfeited, both the crop that you have sown and the yield of the vineyard itself.

10 You shall not plow with an ox and a donkey yoked together.

11 You shall not wear clothes made of wool and linen woven together.

12 You shall make tassels on the four corners of the cloak with which you cover yourself.

Moses told the Israelites to attach tassels to the corners of their cloak so that they would remember the commandments of God each time they wore it. Today we often use symbols in church to remind us of God. The next time you are in your church building, look around to see what symbols are there. You might see a lamb, a shepherd, or a cross. Think about your house. Is there a symbol you could put in your room to remind you that God cares for you and wants you to care for others?

Laws concerning Sexual Relations

13 Suppose a man marries a woman, but after going in to her, he dislikes her [14]and makes up charges against her, slandering her by saying, "I married this woman; but when I lay with her, I did not find evidence of her virginity." [15]The father of the young woman and her mother shall then submit the evidence of the young woman's virginity to the elders of the city at the gate. [16]The father

of the young woman shall say to the elders: "I gave my daughter in marriage to this man but he dislikes her; [17]now he has made up charges against her, saying, 'I did not find evidence of your daughter's virginity.' But here is the evidence of my daughter's virginity." Then they shall spread out the cloth before the elders of the town. [18]The elders of that town shall take the man and punish him; [19]they shall fine him one hundred shekels of silver (which they shall give to the young woman's father) because he has slandered a virgin of Israel. She shall remain his wife; he shall not be permitted to divorce her as long as he lives.

20 If, however, this charge is true, that evidence of the young woman's virginity was not found, [21]then they shall bring the young woman out to the entrance of her father's house and the men of her town shall stone her to death, because she committed a disgraceful act in Israel by prostituting herself in her father's house. So you shall purge the evil from your midst.

22 If a man is caught lying with the wife of another man, both of them shall die, the man who lay with the woman as well as the woman. So you shall purge the evil from Israel.

23 If there is a young woman, a virgin already engaged to be married, and a man meets her in the town and lies with her, [24]you shall bring both of them to the gate of that town and stone them to death, the young woman because she did not cry for help in the town and the man because he violated his neighbor's wife. So you shall purge the evil from your midst.

25 But if the man meets the engaged woman in the open country, and the man seizes her and lies with her, then only the man who lay with her shall die. [26]You shall do nothing to the young woman; the young woman has not committed an offense punishable by death, because this case is like that of someone who attacks and murders a neighbor. [27]Since he found her in the open country, the engaged woman may have cried for help, but there was no one to rescue her.

28 If a man meets a virgin who is not engaged, and seizes her and lies with her, and they are caught in the act, [29]the man who lay with her shall give fifty shekels of silver to the young woman's father, and she shall become his wife. Because he violated her he shall not be permitted to divorce her as long as he lives.

30[z] A man shall not marry his father's wife, thereby violating his father's rights.[a]

Those Excluded from the Assembly

23 No one whose testicles are crushed or whose penis is cut off shall be admitted to the assembly of the LORD.

2 Those born of an illicit union shall not be admitted to the assembly of the LORD. Even to the tenth generation, none of their descendants shall be admitted to the assembly of the LORD.

3 No Am′mon·ite or Mŏ′ab·ite shall be admitted to the assembly of the LORD. Even to the tenth generation, none of their descendants shall be admitted to the assembly of the LORD, [4]because they did not meet you with food and water on your journey out of Egypt, and because they hired against you Bā′laam son of Bē′or, from Pē′thor of Mes·o·po·tā′mi·a, to curse you. [5](Yet the LORD your God refused to heed Bā′laam; the LORD your God turned the curse into a blessing for you, because the LORD your God loved you.) [6]You shall never promote their welfare or their prosperity as long as you live.

7 You shall not abhor any of the Ē′dom·ites, for they are your kin. You shall not abhor any of the Egyptians, because you were an alien residing in their land. [8]The children of the third

z Ch 23.1 in Heb   a Heb *uncovering his father's skirt*

Although they were relatives, the Israelites and the Edomites often fought against each other. The people of Edom were called Edomites. The Edomites came from the family of Esau, and the Israelites came from the family of his twin brother Jacob. You can read more about Jacob and Esau in Genesis 25–36.

generation that are born to them may be admitted to the assembly of the LORD.

Sanitary, Ritual, and Humanitarian Precepts

9 When you are encamped against your enemies you shall guard against any impropriety.

10 If one of you becomes unclean because of a nocturnal emission, then he shall go outside the camp; he must not come within the camp. [11]When evening comes, he shall wash himself with water, and when the sun has set, he may come back into the camp.

12 You shall have a designated area outside the camp to which you shall go. [13]With your utensils you shall have a trowel; when you relieve yourself outside, you shall dig a hole with it and then cover up your excrement. [14]Because the LORD your God travels along with your camp, to save you and to hand over your enemies to you, therefore your camp must be holy, so that he may not see anything indecent among you and turn away from you.

15 Slaves who have escaped to you from their owners shall not be given back to them. [16]They shall reside with you, in your midst, in any place they choose in any one of your towns, wherever they please; you shall not oppress them.

17 None of the daughters of Israel shall be a temple prostitute; none of the sons of Israel shall be a temple prostitute. [18]You shall not bring the fee of a prostitute or the wages of a male prostitute[b] into the house of the LORD your God in payment for any vow, for both of these are abhorrent to the LORD your God.

19 You shall not charge interest on loans to another Israelite, interest on money, interest on provisions, interest on anything that is lent. [20]On loans to a foreigner you may charge interest, but on loans to another Israelite you may not charge interest, so that the LORD your God may bless you in all your undertakings in the land that you are about to enter and possess.

21 If you make a vow to the LORD your God, do not postpone fulfilling it; for the LORD your God will surely require it of you, and you would incur guilt. [22]But if you refrain from vowing, you will not incur guilt. [23]Whatever your lips utter you must diligently perform, just as you have freely vowed to the LORD your God with your own mouth.

24 If you go into your neighbor's vineyard, you may eat your fill of grapes, as many as you wish, but you shall not put any in a container.

25 If you go into your neighbor's standing grain, you may pluck the ears with your hand, but you shall not put a sickle to your neighbor's standing grain.

Laws concerning Marriage and Divorce

24 Suppose a man enters into marriage with a woman, but she does not please him because he finds something objectionable about her, and so he writes her a certificate of divorce, puts it in her hand, and sends her out of his house; she then leaves his house [2]and goes off to become another man's wife. [3]Then suppose the second man dislikes her, writes her a bill of divorce, puts it in her hand, and sends her out of his house

[b] Heb a dog

(or the second man who married her dies); ⁴her first husband, who sent her away, is not permitted to take her again to be his wife after she has been defiled; for that would be abhorrent to the LORD, and you shall not bring guilt on the land that the LORD your God is giving you as a possession.

Miscellaneous Laws

5 When a man is newly married, he shall not go out with the army or be charged with any related duty. He shall be free at home one year, to be happy with the wife whom he has married.

6 No one shall take a mill or an upper millstone in pledge, for that would be taking a life in pledge.

7 If someone is caught kidnaping another Israelite, enslaving or selling the Israelite, then that kidnaper shall die. So you shall purge the evil from your midst.

8 Guard against an outbreak of a leprousᶜ skin disease by being very careful; you shall carefully observe whatever the levitical priests instruct you, just as I have commanded them. ⁹Remember what the LORD your God did to Miriam on your journey out of Egypt.

10 When you make your neighbor a loan of any kind, you shall not go into the house to take the pledge. ¹¹You shall wait outside, while the person to whom

you are making the loan brings the pledge out to you. ¹²If the person is poor, you shall not sleep in the garment given you asᵈ the pledge. ¹³You shall give the pledge back by sunset, so that your neighbor may sleep in the cloak and bless you; and it will be to your credit before the LORD your God.

14 You shall not withhold the wages of poor and needy laborers, whether other Israelites or aliens who reside in your land in one of your towns. ¹⁵You shall pay them their wages daily before sunset, because they are poor and their livelihood depends on them; otherwise they might cry to the LORD against you, and you would incur guilt.

16 Parents shall not be put to death for their children, nor shall children be put to death for their parents; only for their own crimes may persons be put to death.

17 You shall not deprive a resident alien or an orphan of justice; you shall not take a widow's garment in pledge. ¹⁸Remember that you were a slave in Egypt and the LORD your God redeemed you from there; therefore I command you to do this.

19 When you reap your harvest in your field and forget a sheaf in the field, you shall not go back to get it; it shall be left for the alien, the orphan, and the widow, so that the LORD your God may bless you in all your undertakings. ²⁰When you beat your olive trees, do not strip what is left; it shall be for the alien, the orphan, and the widow.

21 When you gather the grapes of your vineyard, do not glean what is left; it shall be for the alien, the orphan, and the widow. ²²Remember that you were a slave in the land of Egypt; therefore I am commanding you to do this.

25 Suppose two persons have a dispute and enter into litigation, and the judges decide between them, declaring one to be in the right

Did you know that many people all over the world do not have enough food to eat? Moses told the Israelites how to take care of the poor. At harvest time the people were supposed to leave behind grain in the fields, olives in the olive grove, and grapes in the vineyard. This leftover food was for the poor. God cares for the poor and wanted the Israelites to make sure they had food to eat. God wants us to care for those who have less than we do.

ᶜ A term for several skin diseases; precise meaning uncertain   ᵈ Heb lacks *the garment given you as* and the other to be in the wrong. ²If the one in the wrong deserves to be flogged, the judge shall make that person lie down and be beaten in his presence with the number of lashes proportionate to the offense. ³Forty lashes may be given but not more; if more lashes than these are given, your neighbor will be degraded in your sight.

4 You shall not muzzle an ox while it is treading out the grain.

Levirate Marriage

5 When brothers reside together, and one of them dies and has no son, the wife of the deceased shall not be married outside the family to a stranger. Her husband's brother shall go in to her, taking her in marriage, and performing the duty of a husband's brother to her, ⁶and the firstborn whom she bears shall succeed to the name of the deceased brother, so that his name may not be blotted out of Israel. ⁷But if the man has no desire to marry his brother's widow, then his brother's widow shall go up to the elders at the gate and say, "My husband's brother refuses to perpetuate his brother's name in Israel; he will not perform the duty of a husband's brother to me." ⁸Then the elders of his town shall summon him and speak to him. If he persists, saying, "I have no desire to marry her," ⁹then his brother's wife shall go up to him in the presence of the elders, pull his sandal off his foot, spit in his face, and declare, "This is what is done to the man who does not build up his brother's house." ¹⁰Throughout Israel his family shall be known as "the house of him whose sandal was pulled off."

Various Commands

11 If men get into a fight with one another, and the wife of one intervenes to rescue her husband from the grip of his opponent by reaching out and seizing his genitals, ¹²you shall cut off her hand; show no pity.

13 You shall not have in your bag two kinds of weights, large and small. ¹⁴You shall not have in your house two kinds of measures, large and small. ¹⁵You shall have only a full and honest weight; you shall have only a full and honest measure, so that your days may be long in the land that the LORD your God is giving you. ¹⁶For all who do such things, all who act dishonestly, are abhorrent to the LORD your God.

17 Remember what Am·a·lek did to you on your journey out of Egypt, ¹⁸how he attacked you on the way, when you were faint and weary, and struck down all who lagged behind you; he did not fear God. ¹⁹Therefore when the LORD your God has given you rest from all your enemies on every hand, in the land that the LORD your God is giving you as an inheritance to possess, you shall blot out the remembrance of Am·a·lek from under heaven; do not forget.

First Fruits and Tithes

26 When you have come into the land that the LORD your God is giving you as an inheritance to possess, and you possess it, and settle in it, ²you shall take some of the first of all the fruit of the ground, which you harvest from the land that the LORD your God is giving you, and you shall put it in a basket and go to the place that the LORD your God will choose as a dwelling for his name. ³You shall go to the priest who is in office at that time, and say to him, "Today I declare to the LORD your God that I have come into the land that the LORD swore to our ancestors to give us." ⁴When the priest takes the basket from your hand and sets it down before the altar of the LORD your God, ⁵you shall make this response before the LORD your God: "A wandering Ar·a·me·an was my ancestor; he went down into Egypt and lived there as an alien, few in number, and there he became a great nation, mighty and populous. ⁶When the Egyptians treated us harshly and afflicted us, by imposing hard labor on us, [7]we cried to the LORD, the God of our ancestors; the LORD heard our voice and saw our affliction, our toil, and our oppression. [8]The LORD brought us out of Egypt with a mighty hand and an outstretched arm, with a terrifying display of power, and with signs and wonders; [9]and he brought us into this place and gave us this land, a land flowing with milk and honey. [10]So now I bring the first of the fruit of the ground that you, O LORD, have given me." You shall set it down before the LORD your God and bow down before the LORD your God. [11]Then you, together with the Lēʹvītes and the aliens who reside among you, shall celebrate with all the bounty that the LORD your God has given to you and to your house.

12 When you have finished paying all the tithe of your produce in the third year (which is the year of the tithe), giving it to the Lēʹvītes, the aliens, the orphans, and the widows, so that they may eat their fill within your towns, [13]then you shall say before the LORD your God: "I have removed the sacred portion from the house, and I have given it to the Lēʹvītes, the resident aliens, the orphans, and the widows, in accordance with your entire commandment that you commanded me; I have neither transgressed nor forgotten any of your commandments: [14]I have not eaten of it while in mourning; I have not removed any of it while I was unclean; and I have not offered any of it to the dead. I have obeyed the LORD my God, doing just as you commanded me. [15]Look down from your holy habitation, from heaven, and bless your people Israel and the ground that you have given us, as you swore to our ancestors—a land flowing with milk and honey."

Concluding Exhortation

16 This very day the LORD your God is commanding you to observe these statutes and ordinances; so observe them diligently with all your heart and with all your soul. [17]Today you have obtained the LORD's agreement: to be your God; and for you to walk in his ways, to keep his statutes, his commandments, and his ordinances, and to obey him. [18]Today the LORD has obtained your agreement: to be his treasured people, as he promised you, and to keep his commandments; [19]for him to set you high above all nations that he has made, in praise and in fame and in honor; and for you to be a people holy to the LORD your God, as he promised.

The Inscribed Stones and Altar on Mount Ebal

27 Then Moses and the elders of Israel charged all the people as follows: Keep the entire commandment that I am commanding you today. [2]On the day that you cross over the Jordan into the land that the LORD your God is giving you, you shall set up large stones and cover them with plaster. [3]You shall write on them all the words of this law when you have crossed over, to enter the land that the LORD your God is giving you, a land flowing with milk and honey, as the LORD, the God of your ancestors, promised you. [4]So when you have crossed over the Jordan, you shall set up these stones, about which I am commanding you today, on Mount Eʹbal, and you shall cover them with plaster. [5]And you shall build an altar there to the LORD your God, an altar of stones on which you have not used an iron tool. [6]You must build the altar of the LORD your God of unhewnᵉ stones. Then offer up burnt offerings on it to the LORD your God, [7]make sacrifices of well-being, and eat them there, rejoicing before the LORD your God. [8]You shall write on the stones all the words of this law very clearly.

9 Then Moses and the levitical priests spoke to all Israel, saying: Keep silence and hear, O Israel! This very day you have become the people of the LORD your God.

ᵉ Heb *whole*

Moses gave the people a list of rules for how to act when they entered Canaan. Each said that those who did not follow would be cursed, or punished. After each rule, the people said "amen" to show that they agreed. "Amen" is a Hebrew word that means "truly" or "surely." Today we say "amen" at the end of prayers or songs to say that we really mean what we have said or sung.

[10]Therefore obey the LORD your God, observing his commandments and his statutes that I am commanding you today.

Twelve Curses

11 The same day Moses charged the people as follows: [12]When you have crossed over the Jordan, these shall stand on Mount Ger′i·zim for the blessing of the people: Sim′e·on, Levi, Judah, Is′sa·char, Joseph, and Benjamin. [13]And these shall stand on Mount E′bal for the curse: Reuben, Gad, Ash′er, Zeb′u·lun, Dan, and Naph′ta·li. [14]Then the Le′vites shall declare in a loud voice to all the Israelites:

15 "Cursed be anyone who makes an idol or casts an image, anything abhorrent to the LORD, the work of an artisan, and sets it up in secret." All the people shall respond, saying, "Amen!"

16 "Cursed be anyone who dishonors father or mother." All the people shall say, "Amen!"

17 "Cursed be anyone who moves a neighbor's boundary marker." All the people shall say, "Amen!"

18 "Cursed be anyone who misleads a blind person on the road." All the people shall say, "Amen!"

19 "Cursed be anyone who deprives the alien, the orphan, and the widow of justice." All the people shall say, "Amen!"

20 "Cursed be anyone who lies with his father's wife, because he has violated his father's rights."[j] All the people shall say, "Amen!"

21 "Cursed be anyone who lies with any animal." All the people shall say, "Amen!"

22 "Cursed be anyone who lies with his sister, whether the daughter of his father or the daughter of his mother." All the people shall say, "Amen!"

23 "Cursed be anyone who lies with his mother-in-law." All the people shall say, "Amen!"

24 "Cursed be anyone who strikes down a neighbor in secret." All the people shall say, "Amen!"

25 "Cursed be anyone who takes a bribe to shed innocent blood." All the people shall say, "Amen!"

26 "Cursed be anyone who does not uphold the words of this law by observing them." All the people shall say, "Amen!"

Blessings for Obedience

28 If you will only obey the LORD your God, by diligently observing all his commandments that I am commanding you today, the LORD your God will set you high above all the nations of the earth; [2]all these blessings shall come upon you and overtake you, if you obey the LORD your God:

God's people had a choice, said Moses. They could choose to obey God's laws and live a blessed life. Or, they could choose to disobey God's laws and face the consequences. We also are free to make our own choices. When we make bad choices, we have to live with the consequences. If we stay up too late at night, we may be tired and cranky the next day. If we talk back to our parents, we may get in trouble. Just as God wanted the Israelites to obey and make good choices, God wants us to do the same.

[j] Heb *uncovered his father's skirt*

3 Blessed shall you be in the city, and blessed shall you be in the field.

4 Blessed shall be the fruit of your womb, the fruit of your ground, and the fruit of your livestock, both the increase of your cattle and the issue of your flock.

5 Blessed shall be your basket and your kneading bowl.

6 Blessed shall you be when you come in, and blessed shall you be when you go out.

7 The LORD will cause your enemies who rise against you to be defeated before you; they shall come out against you one way, and flee before you seven ways. ⁸The LORD will command the blessing upon you in your barns, and in all that you undertake; he will bless you in the land that the LORD your God is giving you. ⁹The LORD will establish you as his holy people, as he has sworn to you, if you keep the commandments of the LORD your God and walk in his ways. ¹⁰All the peoples of the earth shall see that you are called by the name of the LORD, and they shall be afraid of you. ¹¹The LORD will make you abound in prosperity, in the fruit of your womb, in the fruit of your livestock, and in the fruit of your ground in the land that the LORD swore to your ancestors to give you. ¹²The LORD will open for you his rich storehouse, the heavens, to give the rain of your land in its season and to bless all your undertakings. You will lend to many nations, but you will not borrow. ¹³The LORD will make you the head, and not the tail; you shall be only at the top, and not at the bottom—if you obey the commandments of the LORD your God, which I am commanding you today, by diligently observing them, ¹⁴and if you do not turn aside from any of the words that I am commanding you today, either to the right or to the left, following other gods to serve them.

Warnings against Disobedience

15 But if you will not obey the LORD your God by diligently observing all his commandments and decrees, which I am commanding you today, then all these curses shall come upon you and overtake you:

16 Cursed shall you be in the city, and cursed shall you be in the field.

17 Cursed shall be your basket and your kneading bowl.

18 Cursed shall be the fruit of your womb, the fruit of your ground, the increase of your cattle and the issue of your flock.

19 Cursed shall you be when you come in, and cursed shall you be when you go out.

20 The LORD will send upon you disaster, panic, and frustration in everything you attempt to do, until you are destroyed and perish quickly, on account of the evil of your deeds, because you have forsaken me. ²¹The LORD will make the pestilence cling to you until it has consumed you off the land that you are entering to possess. ²²The LORD will afflict you with consumption, fever, inflammation, with fiery heat and drought, and with blight and mildew; they shall pursue you until you perish. ²³The sky over your head shall be bronze, and the earth under you iron. ²⁴The LORD will change the rain of your land into powder, and only dust shall come down upon you from the sky until you are destroyed.

25 The LORD will cause you to be defeated before your enemies; you shall go out against them one way and flee before them seven ways. You shall become an object of horror to all the kingdoms of the earth. ²⁶Your corpses shall be food for every bird of the air and animal of the earth, and there shall be no one to frighten them away. ²⁷The LORD will afflict you with the boils of Egypt, with ulcers, scurvy, and itch, of which you cannot be healed. ²⁸The LORD will afflict you with madness, blindness, and confusion of mind; ²⁹you shall grope about at noon as blind people grope in darkness, but you shall be unable to find your way; and you shall be continually

abused and robbed, without anyone to help. [30]You shall become engaged to a woman, but another man shall lie with her. You shall build a house, but not live in it. You shall plant a vineyard, but not enjoy its fruit. [31]Your ox shall be butchered before your eyes, but you shall not eat of it. Your donkey shall be stolen in front of you, and shall not be restored to you. Your sheep shall be given to your enemies, without anyone to help you. [32]Your sons and daughters shall be given to another people, while you look on; you will strain your eyes looking for them all day but be powerless to do anything. [33]A people whom you do not know shall eat up the fruit of your ground and of all your labors; you shall be continually abused and crushed, [34]and driven mad by the sight that your eyes shall see. [35]The LORD will strike you on the knees and on the legs with grievous boils of which you cannot be healed, from the sole of your foot to the crown of your head. [36]The LORD will bring you, and the king whom you set over you, to a nation that neither you nor your ancestors have known, where you shall serve other gods, of wood and stone. [37]You shall become an object of horror, a proverb, and a byword among all the peoples where the LORD will lead you.

38 You shall carry much seed into the field but shall gather little in, for the locust shall consume it. [39]You shall plant vineyards and dress them, but you shall neither drink the wine nor gather the grapes, for the worm shall eat them. [40]You shall have olive trees throughout all your territory, but you shall not anoint yourself with the oil, for your olives shall drop off. [41]You shall have sons and daughters, but they shall not remain yours, for they shall go into captivity. [42]All your trees and the fruit of your ground the cicada shall take over. [43]Aliens residing among you shall ascend above you higher and higher, while you shall descend lower and lower. [44]They

shall lend to you but you shall not lend to them; they shall be the head and you shall be the tail.

45 All these curses shall come upon you, pursuing and overtaking you until you are destroyed, because you did not obey the LORD your God, by observing the commandments and the decrees that he commanded you. [46]They shall be among you and your descendants as a sign and a portent forever.

47 Because you did not serve the LORD your God joyfully and with gladness of heart for the abundance of everything, [48]therefore you shall serve your enemies whom the LORD will send against you, in hunger and thirst, in nakedness and lack of everything. He will put an iron yoke on your neck until he has destroyed you. [49]The LORD will bring a nation from far away, from the end of the earth, to swoop down on you like an eagle, a nation whose language you do not understand, [50]a grim-faced nation showing no respect to the old or favor to the young. [51]It shall consume the fruit of your livestock and the fruit of your ground until you are destroyed, leaving you neither grain, wine, and oil, nor the increase of your cattle and the issue of your flock, until it has made you perish. [52]It shall besiege you in all your towns until your high and fortified walls, in which you trusted, come down throughout your land; it shall besiege you in all your towns throughout the land that the LORD your God has given you. [53]In the desperate straits to which the enemy siege reduces you, you will eat the fruit of your womb, the flesh of your own sons and daughters whom the LORD your God has given you. [54]Even the most refined and gentle of men among you will begrudge food to his own brother, to the wife whom he embraces, and to the last of his remaining children, [55]giving to none of them any of the flesh of his children whom he is eating, because nothing else remains to him, in

the desperate straits to which the enemy siege will reduce you in all your towns. [56]She who is the most refined and gentle among you, so gentle and refined that she does not venture to set the sole of her foot on the ground, will begrudge food to the husband whom she embraces, to her own son, and to her own daughter, [57]begrudging even the afterbirth that comes out from between her thighs, and the children that she bears, because she is eating them in secret for lack of anything else, in the desperate straits to which the enemy siege will reduce you in your towns.

58 If you do not diligently observe all the words of this law that are written in this book, fearing this glorious and awesome name, the LORD your God, [59]then the LORD will overwhelm both you and your offspring with severe and lasting afflictions and grievous and lasting maladies. [60]He will bring back upon you all the diseases of Egypt, of which you were in dread, and they shall cling to you. [61]Every other malady and affliction, even though not recorded in the book of this law, the LORD will inflict on you until you are destroyed. [62]Although once you were as numerous as the stars in heaven, you shall be left few in number, because you did not obey the LORD your God. [63]And just as the LORD took delight in making you prosperous and numerous, so the LORD will take delight in bringing you to ruin and destruction; you shall be plucked off the land that you are entering to possess. [64]The LORD will scatter you among all peoples, from one end of the earth to the other; and there you shall serve other gods, of wood and stone, which neither you nor your ancestors have known. [65]Among those nations you shall find no ease, no resting place for the sole of your foot. There the LORD will give you a trembling heart, failing eyes, and a languishing spirit. [66]Your life shall hang in doubt before you; night and day you shall be in dread,

with no assurance of your life. [67]In the morning you shall say, "If only it were evening!" and at evening you shall say, "If only it were morning!"—because of the dread that your heart shall feel and the sights that your eyes shall see. [68]The LORD will bring you back in ships to Egypt, by a route that I promised you would never see again; and there you shall offer yourselves for sale to your enemies as male and female slaves, but there will be no buyer.

29 [g] These are the words of the covenant that the LORD commanded Moses to make with the Israelites in the land of Mō'ab, in addition to the covenant that he had made with them at Hō'reb.

The Covenant Renewed in Moab

2[h] Moses summoned all Israel and said to them: You have seen all that the LORD did before your eyes in the land of Egypt, to Pharaoh and to all his servants and to all his land, [3]the great trials that your eyes saw, the signs, and those great wonders. [4]But to this day the LORD has not given you a mind to understand, or eyes to see, or ears to hear. [5]I have led you forty years in the wilderness. The clothes on your back have not worn out, and the sandals on your feet have not worn out; [6]you have not eaten bread, and you have not drunk wine or strong drink—so that you may know that I am the LORD your God. [7]When you came to this place, King Sī'hon of Hesh'bon and King Og of Bā'shan came out against us for battle, but we defeated them. [8]We took their land and gave it as an inheritance to the Reū'ben-ī tes, the Gad'ītes, and the half-tribe of Ma·nas'seh. [9]Therefore diligently observe the words of this covenant, in order that you may succeed[i] in everything that you do.

10 You stand assembled today, all of you, before the LORD your God—the

[g] Ch 28.69 in Heb   [h] Ch 29.1 in Heb   [i] Or *deal wisely*

leaders of your tribes,[j] your elders, and your officials, all the men of Israel, [11]your children, your women, and the aliens who are in your camp, both those who cut your wood and those who draw your water— [12]to enter into the covenant of the LORD your God, sworn by an oath, which the LORD your God is making with you today; [13]in order that he may establish you today as his people, and that he may be your God, as he promised you and as he swore to your ancestors, to Abraham, to Isaac, and to Jacob. [14]I am making this covenant, sworn by an oath, not only with you who stand here with us today before the LORD our God, [15]but also with those who are not here with us today. [16]You know how we lived in the land of Egypt, and how we came through the midst of the nations through which you passed. [17]You have seen their detestable things, the filthy idols of wood and stone, of silver and gold, that were among them. [18]It may be that there is among you a man or woman, or a family or tribe, whose heart is already turning away from the LORD our God to serve the gods of those nations. It may be that there is among you a root sprouting poisonous and bitter growth. [19]All who hear the words of this oath and bless themselves, thinking in their hearts, "We are safe even though we go our own stubborn ways" (thus bringing disaster on moist and dry alike)[k]— [20]the LORD will be unwilling to pardon them, for the LORD's anger and passion will smoke against them. All the curses written in this book will descend on them, and the LORD will blot out their names from under heaven. [21]The LORD will single them out from all the tribes of Israel for calamity, in accordance with all the curses of the covenant written in this book of the law. [22]The next generation, your children who rise up after you, as well as the foreigner who comes from a distant country, will see the devastation of that land and the afflictions with

which the LORD has afflicted it— [23]all its soil burned out by sulfur and salt, nothing planted, nothing sprouting, unable to support any vegetation, like the destruction of Sod´om and Go·mor´rah, Ad´mah and Ze·boi´im, which the LORD destroyed in his fierce anger— [24]they and indeed all the nations will wonder, "Why has the LORD done thus to this land? What caused this great display of anger?" [25]They will conclude, "It is because they abandoned the covenant of the LORD, the God of their ancestors, which he made with them when he brought them out of the land of Egypt. [26]They turned and served other gods, worshiping them, gods whom they had not known and whom he had not allotted to them; [27]so the anger of the LORD was kindled against that land, bringing on it every curse written in this book. [28]The LORD uprooted them from their land in anger, fury, and great wrath, and cast them into another land, as is now the case." [29]The secret things belong to the LORD our God, but the revealed things belong to us and to our children forever, to observe all the words of this law.

God's Fidelity Assured

30 When all these things have happened to you, the blessings and the curses that I have set before you, if you call them to mind among all the nations where the LORD your God has driven you, [2]and return to the LORD your God, and you and your children obey him with all your heart and with all your soul, just as I am commanding you today, [3]then the LORD your God will restore your fortunes and have compassion on you, gathering you again from all the peoples among whom the LORD your God has scattered you. [4]Even if you are exiled to the ends of the world,[l] from there the LORD your God will gather you, and from there he will bring you back. [5]The LORD your God will bring you into the land that your ances-

[j] Gk Syr: Heb *your leaders, your tribes*
[k] Meaning of Heb uncertain   [l] Heb *of heaven*

tors possessed, and you will possess it; he will make you more prosperous and numerous than your ancestors.

6 Moreover, the LORD your God will circumcise your heart and the heart of your descendants, so that you will love the LORD your God with all your heart and with all your soul, in order that you may live. [7]The LORD your God will put all these curses on your enemies and on the adversaries who took advantage of you. [8]Then you shall again obey the LORD, observing all his commandments that I am commanding you today, [9]and the LORD your God will make you abundantly prosperous in all your undertakings, in the fruit of your body, in the fruit of your livestock, and in the fruit of your soil. For the LORD will again take delight in prospering you, just as he delighted in prospering your ancestors, [10]when you obey the LORD your God by observing his commandments and decrees that are written in this book of the law, because you turn to the LORD your God with all your heart and with all your soul.

Exhortation to Choose Life

11 Surely, this commandment that I am commanding you today is not too hard for you, nor is it too far away. [12]It is not in heaven, that you should say, "Who will go up to heaven for us, and get it for us so that we may hear it and observe it?" [13]Neither is it beyond the sea, that you should say, "Who will cross to the other side of the sea for us, and get it for us so that we may hear it and observe it?" [14]No, the word is very near to you; it is in your mouth and in your heart for you to observe.

15 See, I have set before you today life and prosperity, death and adversity. [16]If you obey the commandments of the LORD your God[m] that I am commanding you today, by loving the LORD your God, walking in his ways, and observing his commandments, decrees, and ordinances, then you shall live and become numerous,

and the LORD your God will bless you in the land that you are entering to possess. [17]But if your heart turns away and you do not hear, but are led astray to bow down to other gods and serve them, [18]I declare to you today that you shall perish; you shall not live long in the land that you are crossing the Jordan to enter and possess. [19]I call heaven and earth to witness against you today that I have set before you life and death, blessings and curses. Choose life so that you and your descendants may live, [20]loving the LORD your God, obeying him, and holding fast to him; for that means life to you and length of days, so that you may live in the land that the LORD swore to give to your ancestors, to Abraham, to Isaac, and to Jacob.

Joshua Becomes Moses' Successor

31 When Moses had finished speaking all[n] these words to all Israel, [2]he said to them: "I am now one hundred twenty years old. I am no longer able to get about, and the LORD has told me, 'You shall not cross over this Jordan.' [3]The LORD your God himself will cross over before you. He will destroy these nations before you, and you shall dispossess them. Joshua also will cross over before you, as the LORD promised. [4]The LORD will do to them as he did to Sī-hon and Og, the kings of the Am´o·rītes, and to their land, when he destroyed them. [5]The LORD will give them over to you and you shall deal with them in full accord with the command that I have given to you. [6]Be strong and bold; have no fear or dread of them, because it is the LORD your God who goes with you; he will not fail you or forsake you."

7 Then Moses summoned Joshua and said to him in the sight of all Israel: "Be strong and bold, for you are the one who will go with this people into the land that the LORD has sworn to their

---

[m] Gk: Heb lacks *If you obey the commandments of the LORD your God*   [n] Q Ms Gk: MT *Moses went and spoke*

ancestors to give them; and you will put them in possession of it. ⁸It is the LORD who goes before you. He will be with you; he will not fail you or forsake you. Do not fear or be dismayed."

The Law to Be Read Every Seventh Year

9 Then Moses wrote down this law, and gave it to the priests, the sons of Levi, who carried the ark of the covenant of the LORD, and to all the elders of Israel. ¹⁰Moses commanded them: "Every seventh year, in the scheduled year of remission, during the festival of booths,ᵒ ¹¹when all Israel comes to appear before the LORD your God at the place that he will choose, you shall read this law before all Israel in their hearing. ¹²Assemble the people—men, women, and children, as well as the aliens residing in your towns—so that they may hear and learn to fear the LORD your God and to observe diligently all the words of this law, ¹³and so that their children, who have not known it, may hear and learn to fear the LORD your God, as long as you live in the land that you are crossing over the Jordan to possess."

Moses and Joshua Receive God's Charge

14 The LORD said to Moses, "Your time to die is near; call Joshua and present yourselves in the tent of meeting, so that I may commission him." So Moses and Joshua went and presented themselves in the tent of meeting, ¹⁵and the LORD appeared at the tent in a pillar of cloud; the pillar of cloud stood at the entrance to the tent.

16 The LORD said to Moses, "Soon you will lie down with your ancestors. Then this people will begin to prostitute themselves to the foreign gods in their midst, the gods of the land into which they are going; they will forsake me, breaking my covenant that I have made with them. ¹⁷My anger will be kindled against them in that day. I will forsake them and hide my face from them; they will become easy

prey, and many terrible troubles will come upon them. In that day they will say, 'Have not these troubles come upon us because our God is not in our midst?' ¹⁸On that day I will surely hide my face on account of all the evil they have done by turning to other gods. ¹⁹Now therefore write this song, and teach it to the Israelites; put it in their mouths, in order that this song may be a witness for me against the Israelites. ²⁰For when I have brought them into the land flowing with milk and honey, which I promised on oath to their ancestors, and they have eaten their fill and grown fat, they will turn to other gods and serve them, despising me and breaking my covenant. ²¹And when many terrible troubles come upon them, this song will confront them as a witness, because it will not be lost from the mouths of their descendants. For I know what they are inclined to do even now, before I have brought them into the land that I promised them on oath." ²²That very day Moses wrote this song and taught it to the Israelites.

23 Then the LORD commissioned Joshua son of Nun and said, "Be strong and bold, for you shall bring the Israelites into the land that I promised them; I will be with you."

24 When Moses had finished writing down in a book the words of this law to the very end, ²⁵Moses commanded the Lē′vītes who carried the ark of the covenant of the LORD, saying, ²⁶"Take this book of the law and put it beside the ark of the covenant of the LORD your God; let it remain there as a witness against you. ²⁷For I know well how rebellious and stubborn you are. If you already have been so rebellious toward the LORD while I am still alive among you, how much more after my death! ²⁸Assemble to me all the elders of your tribes and your officials, so that I may recite these words in their hearing and call heaven and earth to witness against them.

ᵒ Or *tabernacles*; Heb *succoth*

²⁹For I know that after my death you will surely act corruptly, turning aside from the way that I have commanded you. In time to come trouble will befall you, because you will do what is evil in the sight of the LORD, provoking him to anger through the work of your hands."

The Song of Moses

30 Then Moses recited the words of this song, to the very end, in the hearing of the whole assembly of Israel:

32 Give ear, O heavens, and I will speak;
  let the earth hear the words of my mouth.

² May my teaching drop like the rain,
  my speech condense like the dew;
like gentle rain on grass,
  like showers on new growth.

³ For I will proclaim the name of the LORD;
  ascribe greatness to our God!

⁴ The Rock, his work is perfect,
  and all his ways are just.
A faithful God, without deceit,
  just and upright is he;

⁵ yet his degenerate children have
  dealt falsely with him,ᵖ
  a perverse and crooked generation.

⁶ Do you thus repay the LORD,
  O foolish and senseless people?
Is not he your father, who created you,
  who made you and established you?

⁷ Remember the days of old,
  consider the years long past;
ask your father, and he will inform you;
  your elders, and they will tell you.

⁸ When the Most High�q apportioned the nations,
  when he divided humankind,
he fixed the boundaries of the peoples
  according to the number of the gods;ʳ

⁹ the LORD's own portion was his people,
  Jacob his allotted share.

¹⁰ He sustainedˢ him in a desert land,
  in a howling wilderness waste;

he shielded him, cared for him,
  guarded him as the apple of his eye.

¹¹ As an eagle stirs up its nest,
  and hovers over its young;
as it spreads its wings, takes them up,
  and bears them aloft on its pinions,

¹² the LORD alone guided him;
  no foreign god was with him.

¹³ He set him atop the heights of the land,
  and fed him withᵗ produce of the field;
he nursed him with honey from the crags,
  with oil from flinty rock;

¹⁴ curds from the herd, and milk from the flock,
  with fat of lambs and rams;
Bā´shan bulls and goats,
  together with the choicest wheat—
you drank fine wine from the blood of grapes.

¹⁵ Jacob ate his fill;ᵘ
Jesh´ū·run grew fat, and kicked.
  You grew fat, bloated, and gorged!
He abandoned God who made him,
  and scoffed at the Rock of his salvation.

¹⁶ They made him jealous with strange gods,
  with abhorrent things they provoked him.

¹⁷ They sacrificed to demons, not God,
  to deities they had never known,
to new ones recently arrived,
  whom your ancestors had not feared.

¹⁸ You were unmindful of the Rock that bore you;ᵛ
  you forgot the God who gave you birth.

¹⁹ The LORD saw it, and was jealousʷ
  he spurnedˣ his sons and daughters.

ᵖ Meaning of Heb uncertain q Traditional rendering of Heb *Elyon* ʳ Q Ms Compare Gk Tg: MT *the Israelites* ˢ Sam Gk Compare Tg: MT *found* ᵗ Sam Gk Syr Tg: MT *he ate* ᵘ Q Mss Sam Gk: MT lacks *Jacob ate his fill* ᵛ Or *that begot you* ʷ Q Mss Gk: MT lacks *was jealous* ˣ Cn: Heb *he spurned because of provocation*

20 He said: I will hide my face from
them,
I will see what their end will be;
for they are a perverse generation,
children in whom there is no
faithfulness.
21 They made me jealous with what is
no god,
provoked me with their idols.
So I will make them jealous with
what is no people,
provoke them with a foolish
nation.
22 For a fire is kindled by my anger,
and burns to the depths of Shēʹōl;
it devours the earth and its increase,
and sets on fire the foundations of
the mountains.
23 I will heap disasters upon them,
spend my arrows against them:
24 wasting hunger,
burning consumption,
bitter pestilence.
The teeth of beasts I will send against
them,
with venom of things crawling in
the dust.
25 In the street the sword shall bereave,
and in the chambers terror,
for young man and woman alike,
nursing child and old gray head.
26 I thought to scatter them*y*
and blot out the memory of them
from humankind;
27 but I feared provocation by the enemy,
for their adversaries might
misunderstand
and say, "Our hand is triumphant;
it was not the LORD who did all
this."

28 They are a nation void of sense;
there is no understanding in them.
29 If they were wise, they would
understand this;
they would discern what the end
would be.
30 How could one have routed a
thousand,

and two put a myriad to flight,
unless their Rock had sold them,
the LORD had given them up?
31 Indeed their rock is not like our Rock;
our enemies are fools.*y*
32 Their vine comes from the vinestock
of Sodʹom,
from the vineyards of Go·morʹrah;
their grapes are grapes of poison,
their clusters are bitter;
33 their wine is the poison of serpents,
the cruel venom of asps.

34 Is not this laid up in store with me,
sealed up in my treasuries?
35 Vengeance is mine, and recompense,
for the time when their foot shall
slip;
because the day of their calamity is at
hand,
their doom comes swiftly.
36 Indeed the LORD will vindicate his people,
have compassion on his servants,
when he sees that their power is gone,
neither bond nor free remaining.
37 Then he will say: Where are their
gods,
the rock in which they took refuge,
38 who ate the fat of their sacrifices,
and drank the wine of their
libations?
Let them rise up and help you,
let them be your protection!
39 See now that I, even I, am he;
there is no god besides me.
I kill and I make alive;
I wound and I heal;
and no one can deliver from my
hand.

"Happy are you, O Israel! Who is
like you, a people saved by the
LORD, the shield of your
help, and the sword of
your triumph!"
Deuteronomy 33:29*a*

---

y Gk: Meaning of Heb uncertain

⁴⁰ For I lift up my hand to heaven,
    and swear: As I live forever,
⁴¹ when I whet my flashing sword,
    and my hand takes hold on
        judgment;
    I will take vengeance on my
        adversaries,
    and will repay those who hate me.
⁴² I will make my arrows drunk with
        blood,
    and my sword shall devour flesh—
    with the blood of the slain and the
        captives,
    from the long-haired enemy.

⁴³ Praise, O heavens,ᵉ his people,
    worship him, all you gods!ᵃ
    For he will avenge the blood of his
        children,ᵇ
    and take vengeance on his
        adversaries;
    he will repay those who hate him,ᵃ
    and cleanse the land for his people.ᶜ

44 Moses came and recited all the words of this song in the hearing of the people, he and Joshuaᵈ son of Nun. ⁴⁵When Moses had finished reciting all these words to all Israel, ⁴⁶he said to them: "Take to heart all the words that I am giving in witness against you today; give them as a command to your children, so that they may diligently observe all the words of this law. ⁴⁷This is no trifling matter for you, but rather your very life; through it you may live long in the land that you are crossing over the Jordan to possess."

Moses' Death Foretold

48 On that very day the LORD addressed Moses as follows: ⁴⁹"Ascend this mountain of the Ab´a·rim, Mount Nē´bō, which is in the land of Mō´ab, across from Jericho, and view the land of Cā´naan, which I am giving to the Israelites for a possession; ⁵⁰you shall die there on the mountain that you ascend and shall be gathered to your kin, as your brother Aaron died on Mount Hor and was gathered to his kin; ⁵¹because both of you

broke faith with me among the Israelites at the waters of Mer´i·bath-kā´desh in the wilderness of Zin, by failing to maintain my holiness among the Israelites. ⁵²Although you may view the land from a distance, you shall not enter it—the land that I am giving to the Israelites."

Moses' Final Blessing on Israel

33 This is the blessing with which Moses, the man of God, blessed the Israelites before his death. ²He said:
    The LORD came from Sinai,
        and dawned from Sē´ir upon us;ᵉ
        he shone forth from Mount Par´an.
    With him were myriads of holy ones;ᶠ
        at his right, a host of his own.ᵍ
³ Indeed, O favorite amongʰ peoples,
    all his holy ones were in your charge;
    they marched at your heels,
    accepted direction from you.
⁴ Moses charged us with the law,
    as a possession for the assembly of
        Jacob.
⁵ There arose a king in Jesh´ū·run,
    when the leaders of the people
        assembled—
    the united tribes of Israel.

⁶ May Reuben live, and not die out,
    even though his numbers are few.

⁷And this he said of Judah:
    O LORD, give heed to Judah,
    and bring him to his people;
    strengthen his hands for him,ⁱ
    and be a help against his adversaries.

⁸And of Levi he said:
    Give to Leviʲ your Thum´mim,
    and your Ū´rim to your loyal one,
    whom you tested at Mas´sah,

ᵉ Q Ms Gk: MT *nations*   ᵃ Q Ms Gk: MT lacks this line   ᵇ Q Ms Gk: MT *his servants*   ᶜ Q Ms Sam Gk Vg: MT *his land his people*   ᵈ Sam Gk Syr Vg: MT *Hoshea*   ᵉ Gk Syr Vg Compare Tg: Heb *upon them*   ᶠ Cn Compare Gk Sam Syr Vg: MT *He came from Ribeboth-kodesh,*   ᵍ Cn Compare Gk: meaning of Heb uncertain   ʰ Or *O lover of the*   ⁱ Cn: Heb *with his hands he contended*   ʲ Q Ms Gk: MT lacks *Give to Levi*

with whom you contended at the
  waters of Mer´i·bah;
[9] who said of his father and mother,
  "I regard them not";
he ignored his kin,
  and did not acknowledge his children.
For they observed your word,
  and kept your covenant.
[10] They teach Jacob your ordinances,
  and Israel your law;
they place incense before you,
  and whole burnt offerings on your
    altar.
[11] Bless, O LORD, his substance,
  and accept the work of his hands;
crush the loins of his adversaries,
  of those that hate him, so that they
    do not rise again.

[12]Of Benjamin he said:
  The beloved of the LORD rests in
    safety—
  the High God[k] surrounds him all day
    long—
  the beloved[l] rests between his
    shoulders.

[13]And of Joseph he said:
  Blessed by the LORD be his land,
    with the choice gifts of heaven
      above,
    and of the deep that lies beneath;
[14] with the choice fruits of the sun,
  and the rich yield of the months;
[15] with the finest produce of the ancient
    mountains,
  and the abundance of the
    everlasting hills;
[16] with the choice gifts of the earth and
    its fullness,
  and the favor of the one who
    dwells on Sinai.[m]
Let these come on the head of Joseph,
  on the brow of the prince among
    his brothers.
[17] A firstborn[n] bull—majesty is his!
  His horns are the horns of a wild ox;
  with them he gores the peoples,

driving them to[o] the ends of the
  earth;
such are the myriads of E´phra·im,
  such the thousands of Ma·nas´seh.

[18]And of Zeb´u·lun he said:
  Rejoice, Zeb´u·lun, in your going out;
    and Is´sa·char, in your tents.
[19] They call peoples to the mountain;
  there they offer the right sacrifices;
for they suck the affluence of the seas
  and the hidden treasures of the sand.

[20]And of Gad he said:
  Blessed be the enlargement of Gad!
    Gad lives like a lion;
    he tears at arm and scalp.
[21] He chose the best for himself,
  for there a commander's allotment
    was reserved;
he came at the head of the people,
  he executed the justice of the LORD,
  and his ordinances for Israel.

[22]And of Dan he said:
  Dan is a lion's whelp
    that leaps forth from Ba´shan.

[23]And of Naph´ta·lī he said:
  O Naph´ta·lī, sated with favor,
    full of the blessing of the LORD,
    possess the west and the south.

[24]And of Ash´er he said:
  Most blessed of sons be Ash´er;
    may he be the favorite of his
      brothers,
    and may he dip his foot in oil.
[25] Your bars are iron and bronze;
  and as your days, so is your
    strength.

[26] There is none like God, O Jesh´u·run,
  who rides through the heavens to
    your help,
  majestic through the skies.

---

[k] Heb *above him*   [l] Heb *he*   [m] Cn: Heb *in the bush*
[n] Q Ms Gk Syr Vg: MT *His firstborn*   [o] Cn: Heb
the peoples, together

27 He subdues the ancient gods,[p]
    shatters[q] the forces of old;[r]
he drove out the enemy before you,
    and said, "Destroy!"
28 So Israel lives in safety,
    untroubled is Jacob's abode[s]
in a land of grain and wine,
    where the heavens drop down dew.
29 Happy are you, O Israel! Who is like
        you,
    a people saved by the LORD,
the shield of your help,
    and the sword of your triumph!
Your enemies shall come fawning to
        you,
    and you shall tread on their backs.

Moses Dies and Is Buried in the Land of Moab

34 Then Moses went up from the plains of Mŏ´ab to Mount Nē´-bō, to the top of Pis´gah, which is opposite Jericho, and the LORD showed him the whole land: Gil´e·ad as far as Dan, 2all Naph´ta·lī, the land of Ē´phra·im and Ma·nas´seh, all the land of Judah as far as the Western Sea, 3the Ne´geb, and the Plain—that is, the valley of Jericho, the city of palm trees—as far as Zŏ´ar. 4The LORD said to him, "This is the land of which I swore to Abraham, to Isaac, and to Jacob, saying, 'I will give it to your descendants'; I have let you see it with your eyes, but you shall not cross over there." 5Then Moses, the servant of the LORD, died there in the land of Mŏ´ab, at the LORD's command. 6He was buried in a valley in the land of Mŏ´ab, opposite Beth-pē´or, but no one knows his burial place to this day. 7Moses was one hundred twenty years old when he died; his sight was unimpaired and his vigor had not abated. 8The Israelites wept for Moses in the plains of Mŏ´ab thirty days; then the period of mourning for Moses was ended.

9 Joshua son of Nun was full of the spirit of wisdom, because Moses had laid his hands on him; and the Israelites obeyed him, doing as the LORD had commanded Moses.

10 Never since has there arisen a prophet in Israel like Moses, whom the LORD knew face to face. 11He was unequaled for all the signs and wonders that the LORD sent him to perform in the land of Egypt, against Pharaoh and all his servants and his entire land, 12and for all the mighty deeds and all the terrifying displays of power that Moses performed in the sight of all Israel.

---

[p] Or *The eternal God is a dwelling place*   [q] Cn: Heb *from underneath*   [r] Or *the everlasting arms*   [s] Or *fountain*

Joshua

The first five books of the Bible tell the stories of God's creation of the world and of the beginnings of the Israelite people. They tell about the slavery of the Israelites, their escape from Egypt, and their troubles in serving the one true God. They tell how the people got the Ten Commandments and wandered in the desert for many years.

The book of Joshua begins a new series of stories about how the Israelites crossed the Jordan River, captured the city of Jericho, and began to take over Canaan, the land promised to Abraham.

This book is named for Joshua, who became the leader of the Israelite tribes after Moses. Joshua led the people in the conquest of the Promised Land.

The Canaanites, who were farmers, lived very differently from the Israelites, who were wanderers. The Israelites found that Canaanites, the people already living in Canaan, worshiped other gods. The book of Joshua shows how the Israelites were tempted to disobey God and how close they came to not living by the laws they had been given.

Joshua 6:2–5

"I hereby command you: Be strong and courageous; do not be frightened or dismayed, for the LORD your God is with you wherever you go." Joshua 1:9

God's Commission to Joshua

1 After the death of Moses the servant of the LORD, the LORD spoke to Joshua son of Nun, Moses' assistant, saying, ²"My servant Moses is dead. Now proceed to cross the Jordan, you and all this people, into the land that I am giving to them, to the Israelites. ³Every place that the sole of your foot will tread upon I have given to you, as I promised to Moses. ⁴From the wilderness and the Lebanon as far as the great river, the river Euphrates, all the land of the Hit´tītes, to the Great Sea in the west shall be your territory. ⁵No one shall be able to stand against you all the days of your life. As I was with Moses, so I will be with you; I will not fail you or forsake you. ⁶Be strong and courageous; for you shall put this people in possession of the land that I swore to their ancestors to give them. ⁷Only be strong and very courageous, being careful to act in accordance with all the law that my servant Moses commanded you; do not turn from it to the right hand or to the left, so that you may be successful wherever you go. ⁸This book of the law shall not depart out of your mouth; you shall meditate on it day and night, so that you may be careful to act in accordance with all that is written in it. For then you shall make your way prosperous, and then you shall be successful. ⁹I hereby command you: Be strong and courageous; do not be frightened or dismayed, for the LORD your God is with you wherever you go."

Preparations for the Invasion

10 Then Joshua commanded the officers of the people, ¹¹"Pass through the camp, and command the people: 'Prepare your provisions; for in three days you are to cross over the Jordan, to go in to take possession of the land that the LORD your God gives you to possess.' "

12 To the Reū´ben·ites, the Gad´ītes, and the half-tribe of Ma·nas´seh Joshua said, ¹³"Remember the word that Moses the servant of the LORD commanded you, saying, 'The LORD your God is providing you a place of rest, and will give you this land.' ¹⁴Your wives, your little ones, and your livestock shall remain in the land that Moses gave you beyond the Jordan. But all the warriors among you shall cross over armed before your kindred and shall help them, ¹⁵until the LORD gives rest to your kindred as well as to you, and they too take possession of the land that the LORD your God is giving them. Then you shall return to your own land and take possession of it, the land that Moses the servant of the LORD gave you beyond the Jordan to the east."

16 They answered Joshua: "All that you have commanded us we will do, and wherever you send us we will go. ¹⁷Just as we obeyed Moses in all things, so we will obey you. Only may the LORD your God be with you, as he was with Moses! ¹⁸Whoever rebels against your orders and disobeys your words, whatever you command, shall be put to death. Only be strong and courageous."

Spies Sent to Jericho

2 Then Joshua son of Nun sent two men secretly from Shit´tim as spies, saying, "Go, view the land, especially Jericho." So they went, and entered the house of a prostitute whose name was Rā´hab, and spent the night there. ²The king of Jericho was told, "Some Israelites have come here tonight to search out the land." ³Then the king of Jericho sent orders to Rā´hab, "Bring out the men who have come to you, who entered your house, for they have come only to search out the whole land." ⁴But the woman took the two men and hid

Rahab was a woman who lived in Jericho. She had heard how God protected the Israelites as they traveled to Canaan. Because of this, she too protected God's people! When Joshua sent spies into Jericho, they had to run for their lives. Rahab hid the spies under stalks of flax that were drying on the flat roof of her home. (Flax is a plant people used to make cloth.) Because Rahab helped the spies to escape, Joshua saved her life when the Israelites took Jericho. Rahab is named as one of the ancestors of Jesus in Matthew 1:5.

them. Then she said, "True, the men came to me, but I did not know where they came from. ⁵And when it was time to close the gate at dark, the men went out. Where the men went I do not know. Pursue them quickly, for you can overtake them." ⁶She had, however, brought them up to the roof and hidden them with the stalks of flax that she had laid out on the roof. ⁷So the men pursued them on the way to the Jordan as far as the fords. As soon as the pursuers had gone out, the gate was shut.

8 Before they went to sleep, she came up to them on the roof ⁹and said to the men: "I know that the LORD has given you the land, and that dread of you has fallen on us, and that all the inhabitants of the land melt in fear before you. ¹⁰For we have heard how the LORD dried up the water of the Red Sea[a] before you when you came out of Egypt, and what you did to the two kings of the Am′o·rītes that were beyond the Jordan, to Sī′hon and Og, whom you utterly destroyed. ¹¹As soon as we heard it, our hearts melted, and there was no courage left in any of us because of you. The LORD your God is indeed God in heaven above and on earth below. ¹²Now then, since I have dealt kindly with you, swear to me by

the LORD that you in turn will deal kindly with my family. Give me a sign of good faith ¹³that you will spare my father and mother, my brothers and sisters, and all who belong to them, and deliver our lives from death." ¹⁴The men said to her, "Our life for yours! If you do not tell this business of ours, then we will deal kindly and faithfully with you when the LORD gives us the land."

15 Then she let them down by a rope through the window, for her house was on the outer side of the city wall and she resided within the wall itself. ¹⁶She said to them, "Go toward the hill country, so that the pursuers may not come upon you. Hide yourselves there three days, until the pursuers have returned; then afterward you may go your way." ¹⁷The men said to her, "We will be released from this oath that you have made us swear to you ¹⁸if we invade the land and you do not tie this crimson cord in the window through which you let us down, and you do not gather into your house your father and mother, your brothers, and all your family. ¹⁹If any of you go out of the doors of your house into the street, they shall be responsible for their own death, and we shall be innocent; but if a hand is laid upon any who are with you in the house, we shall bear the responsibility for their death. ²⁰But if you tell this business of ours, then we shall be released from this oath that you made us swear to you." ²¹She said, "According to your words, so be it." She sent them away and they departed. Then she tied the crimson cord in the window.

22 They departed and went into the hill country and stayed there three days, until the pursuers returned. The pursuers had searched all along the way and found nothing. ²³Then the two men came down again from the hill country. They crossed over, came to Joshua son of Nun, and told him all that had happened to them. ²⁴They said to Joshua,

[a] Or Sea of Reeds

"Truly the Lord has given all the land into our hands; moreover all the inhabitants of the land melt in fear before us."

Israel Crosses the Jordan

3 Early in the morning Joshua rose and set out from Shit´tim with all the Israelites, and they came to the Jordan. They camped there before crossing over. ²At the end of three days the officers went through the camp ³and commanded the people, "When you see the ark of the covenant of the Lord your God being carried by the levitical priests, then you shall set out from your place. Follow it, ⁴so that you may know the way you should go, for you have not passed this way before. Yet there shall be a space between you and it, a distance of about two thousand cubits; do not come any nearer to it." ⁵Then Joshua said to the people, "Sanctify yourselves; for tomorrow the Lord will do wonders among you." ⁶To the priests Joshua said, "Take up the ark of the covenant, and pass on in front of the people." So they took up the ark of the covenant and went in front of the people.

7 The Lord said to Joshua, "This day I will begin to exalt you in the sight of all Israel, so that they may know that I will be with you as I was with Moses. ⁸You are the one who shall command the priests who bear the ark of the covenant, 'When you come to the edge of the waters of the Jordan, you shall stand still in the Jordan.'" ⁹Joshua then said to the Israelites, "Draw near and hear the words of the Lord your God." ¹⁰Joshua said, "By this you shall know that among you is the living God who without fail will drive out from before you the Cā´naan·ites, Hit´tites, Hi´vites, Per´iz·zites, Gir´ga·shites, Am´o·rites, and Jeb´ū·sites: ¹¹the ark of the covenant of the Lord of all the earth is going to pass before you into the Jordan. ¹²So now select twelve men from the tribes of Israel, one from each tribe. ¹³When the soles of the feet of the priests who bear the ark of the Lord, the Lord of all the earth, rest in the waters

of the Jordan, the waters of the Jordan flowing from above shall be cut off; they shall stand in a single heap."

14 When the people set out from their tents to cross over the Jordan, the priests bearing the ark of the covenant were in front of the people. ¹⁵Now the Jordan overflows all its banks throughout the time of harvest. So when those who bore the ark had come to the Jordan, and the feet of the priests bearing the ark were dipped in the edge of the water, ¹⁶the waters flowing from above stood still, rising up in a single heap far off at Adam, the city that is beside Zar´e·than, while those flowing toward the sea of the Ar´a·bah, the Dead Sea,ᵇ were wholly cut off. Then the people crossed over opposite Jericho. ¹⁷While all Israel were crossing over on dry ground, the priests who bore the ark of the covenant of the Lord stood on dry ground in the middle of the Jordan, until the entire nation finished crossing over the Jordan.

Twelve Stones Set Up at Gilgal

4 When the entire nation had finished crossing over the Jordan, the Lord said to Joshua: ²"Select twelve men from the people, one from each tribe, ³and command them, 'Take twelve stones from

Joshua had been with the Israelites when they left Egypt and crossed the Red Sea. Later in his life, he stood at the edge of the Jordan River. God said this was the time to enter the Promised Land. Joshua trusted God, and God made it possible for the people to cross the river. The Levites picked up the Ark of the Covenant and walked out into the water. As soon as their feet touched the water, the river stopped flowing. The Levites carried the Ark across the river on dry ground, and all the people followed.

ᵇ Heb *Salt Sea*

As the people passed through the river on dry ground, Joshua told the head of each tribe to pick up a large stone to take to the other side. There they piled the stones together to remember that God had been with them and had blessed them. As time went by their children would ask about the stones and would hear the story of God's faithfulness. Today we can read this story because people took time to write down the stories of God and God's people. You can do the same! Write your favorite Bible story in your own words. Tell the story to someone in your family or to someone younger than you.

here out of the middle of the Jordan, from the place where the priests' feet stood, carry them over with you, and lay them down in the place where you camp tonight.' " ⁴Then Joshua summoned the twelve men from the Israelites, whom he had appointed, one from each tribe. ⁵Joshua said to them, "Pass on before the ark of the LORD your God into the middle of the Jordan, and each of you take up a stone on his shoulder, one for each of the tribes of the Israelites, ⁶so that this may be a sign among you. When your children ask in time to come, 'What do those stones mean to you?' ⁷then you shall tell them that the waters of the Jordan were cut off in front of the ark of the covenant of the LORD. When it crossed over the Jordan, the waters of the Jordan were cut off. So these stones shall be to the Israelites a memorial forever."

8 The Israelites did as Joshua commanded. They took up twelve stones out of the middle of the Jordan, according to the number of the tribes of the Israelites, as the LORD told Joshua, carried them over with them to the place where they camped, and laid them down there.

⁹(Joshua set up twelve stones in the middle of the Jordan, in the place where the feet of the priests bearing the ark of the covenant had stood; and they are there to this day.)

10 The priests who bore the ark remained standing in the middle of the Jordan, until everything was finished that the LORD commanded Joshua to tell the people, according to all that Moses had commanded Joshua. The people crossed over in haste. ¹¹As soon as all the people had finished crossing over, the ark of the LORD, and the priests, crossed over in front of the people. ¹²The Reū·ben·ites, the Gad·ites, and the half-tribe of Ma·nas´seh crossed over armed before the Israelites, as Moses had ordered them. ¹³About forty thousand armed for war crossed over before the LORD to the plains of Jericho for battle.

14 On that day the LORD exalted Joshua in the sight of all Israel; and they stood in awe of him, as they had stood in awe of Moses, all the days of his life.

15 The LORD said to Joshua, ¹⁶"Command the priests who bear the ark of the covenant,ᶜ to come up out of the Jordan." ¹⁷Joshua therefore commanded the priests, "Come up out of the Jordan." ¹⁸When the priests bearing the ark of the covenant of the LORD came up from the middle of the Jordan, and the soles of the priests' feet touched dry ground, the waters of the Jordan returned to their place and overflowed all its banks, as before.

19 The people came up out of the Jordan on the tenth day of the first month, and they camped in Gil´gal on the east border of Jericho. ²⁰Those twelve stones, which they had taken out of the Jordan, Joshua set up in Gil´gal, ²¹saying to the Israelites, "When your children ask their parents in time to come, 'What do these stones mean?' ²²then you shall let your children know, 'Israel crossed over the Jordan here on dry ground.' ²³For the

ᶜ Or *treaty*, or *testimony*; Heb *eduth*

Lord your God dried up the waters of the Jordan for you until you crossed over, as the Lord your God did to the Red Sea,[d] which he dried up for us until we crossed over, [24]so that all the peoples of the earth may know that the hand of the Lord is mighty, and so that you may fear the Lord your God forever."

The New Generation Circumcised

5 When all the kings of the Am´o·rītes beyond the Jordan to the west, and all the kings of the Cā´naan·ītes by the sea, heard that the Lord had dried up the waters of the Jordan for the Israelites until they had crossed over, their hearts melted, and there was no longer any spirit in them, because of the Israelites.

2 At that time the Lord said to Joshua, "Make flint knives and circumcise the Israelites a second time." [3]So Joshua made flint knives, and circumcised the Israelites at Gib´ē·ath-ha·ar´a·loth.[e] [4]This is the reason why Joshua circumcised them: all the males of the people who came out of Egypt, all the warriors, had died during the journey through the wilderness after they had come out of Egypt. [5]Although all the people who came out had been circumcised, yet all the people born on the journey through the wilderness after they had come out of Egypt had not been circumcised. [6]For the Israelites traveled forty years in the wilderness, until all the nation, the warriors who came out of Egypt, perished, not having listened to the voice of the Lord. To them the Lord swore that he would not let them see the land that he had sworn to their ancestors to give us, a land flowing with milk and honey. [7]So it was their children, whom he raised up in their place, that Joshua circumcised; for they were uncircumcised, because they had not been circumcised on the way.

8 When the circumcising of all the nation was done, they remained in their places in the camp until they were healed. [9]The Lord said to Joshua, "Today I have rolled away from you the disgrace of Egypt." And so that place is called Gil´gal[f] to this day.

The Passover at Gilgal

10 While the Israelites were camped in Gil´gal they kept the passover in the evening on the fourteenth day of the month in the plains of Jericho. [11]On the day after the passover, on that very day, they ate the produce of the land, unleavened cakes and parched grain. [12]The manna ceased on the day they ate the produce of the land, and the Israelites no longer had manna; they ate the crops of the land of Cā´naan that year.

Joshua's Vision

13 Once when Joshua was by Jericho, he looked up and saw a man standing before him with a drawn sword in his hand. Joshua went to him and said to him, "Are you one of us, or one of our adversaries?" [14]He replied, "Neither; but as commander of the army of the Lord I have now come." And Joshua fell on his face to the earth and worshiped, and he said to him, "What do you command your servant, my lord?" [15]The commander of the army of the Lord said to Joshua, "Remove the sandals from your feet, for the place where you stand is holy." And Joshua did so.

Jericho Taken and Destroyed

6 Now Jericho was shut up inside and out because of the Israelites; no one came out and no one went in. [2]The Lord said to Joshua, "See, I have handed Jericho over to you, along with its king and soldiers. [3]You shall march around the city, all the warriors circling the city once. Thus you shall do for six days, [4]with seven priests bearing seven trumpets of rams' horns before the ark. On the seventh day you shall march around the city seven times, the priests blowing the trumpets. [5]When they make a long blast with the ram's horn, as soon

---

[d] Or *Sea of Reeds*   [e] That is *the Hill of the Foreskins*   [f] Related to Heb *galal* to roll

Jericho was a strong, protected city that stood in the path of the Israelites as they entered Canaan. The people did what God told them to do, and they marched around the walls of the city once a day for six days. On the seventh day, they marched around the walls seven times, and the priests blew rams' horns like trumpets. When the horns sounded, the walls crumbled, and the city of Jericho fell to the Israelites.

as you hear the sound of the trumpet, then all the people shall shout with a great shout; and the wall of the city will fall down flat, and all the people shall charge straight ahead." ⁶So Joshua son of Nun summoned the priests and said to them, "Take up the ark of the covenant, and have seven priests carry seven trumpets of rams' horns in front of the ark of the LORD." ⁷To the people he said, "Go forward and march around the city; have the armed men pass on before the ark of the LORD."

8 As Joshua had commanded the people, the seven priests carrying the seven trumpets of rams' horns before the LORD went forward, blowing the trumpets, with the ark of the covenant of the LORD following them. ⁹And the armed men went before the priests who blew the trumpets; the rear guard came after the ark, while the trumpets blew continually. ¹⁰To the people Joshua gave this command: "You shall not shout or let your voice be heard, nor shall you utter a word, until the day I tell you to shout. Then you shall shout." ¹¹So the ark of the LORD went around the city, circling it once; and they came into the camp, and spent the night in the camp.

12 Then Joshua rose early in the morning, and the priests took up the ark of the LORD. ¹³The seven priests carrying the seven trumpets of rams' horns before

the ark of the LORD passed on, blowing the trumpets continually. The armed men went before them, and the rear guard came after the ark of the LORD, while the trumpets blew continually. ¹⁴On the second day they marched around the city once and then returned to the camp. They did this for six days.

15 On the seventh day they rose early, at dawn, and marched around the city in the same manner seven times. It was only on that day that they marched around the city seven times. ¹⁶And at the seventh time, when the priests had blown the trumpets, Joshua said to the people, "Shout! For the LORD has given you the city. ¹⁷The city and all that is in it shall be devoted to the LORD for destruction. Only Raʹhab the prostitute and all who are with her in her house shall live because she hid the messengers we sent. ¹⁸As for you, keep away from the things devoted to destruction, so as not to covet⁸ and take any of the devoted things and make the camp of Israel an object for destruction, bringing trouble upon it. ¹⁹But all silver and gold, and vessels of bronze and iron, are sacred to the LORD; they shall go into the treasury of the LORD." ²⁰So the people shouted, and the trumpets were blown. As soon as the people heard the sound of the trumpets, they raised a great shout, and the wall fell down flat; so the people charged straight ahead into the city and captured it. ²¹Then they devoted to destruction by the edge of the sword all in the city, both men and women, young and old, oxen, sheep, and donkeys.

22 Joshua said to the two men who had spied out the land, "Go into the prostitute's house, and bring the woman out of it and all who belong to her, as you swore to her." ²³So the young men who had been spies went in and brought Raʹhab out, along with her father, her mother, her brothers, and all who belonged to her— they brought all her kindred out—and set them outside the camp of Israel. ²⁴They

⁸ Gk: Heb *devote to destruction* Compare 7.21

burned down the city, and everything in it; only the silver and gold, and the vessels of bronze and iron, they put into the treasury of the house of the LORD. 25But Rā'hab the prostitute, with her family and all who belonged to her, Joshua spared. Her family[h] has lived in Israel ever since. For she hid the messengers whom Joshua sent to spy out Jericho.

26 Joshua then pronounced this oath, saying,

"Cursed before the LORD be anyone who tries
   to build this city—this Jericho!
At the cost of his firstborn he shall
   lay its foundation,
   and at the cost of his youngest he
   shall set up its gates!"

27 So the LORD was with Joshua; and his fame was in all the land.

The Sin of Achan and Its Punishment

7 But the Israelites broke faith in regard to the devoted things: Ā'chan son of Car'mī son of Zab'dī son of Zē'rah, of the tribe of Judah, took some of the devoted things; and the anger of the LORD burned against the Israelites.

2 Joshua sent men from Jericho to Aī, which is near Beth-ā'ven, east of Beth'el, and said to them, "Go up and spy out the land." And the men went up and spied out Aī. 3Then they returned to Joshua and said to him, "Not all the people need go up; about two or three thousand men should go up and attack Aī. Since they are so few, do not make the whole people toil up there." 4So about three thousand of the people went up there; and they fled before the men of Aī. 5The men of Aī killed about thirty-six of them, chasing them from outside the gate as far as Sheb'a·rim and killing them on the slope. The hearts of the people melted and turned to water.

6 Then Joshua tore his clothes, and fell to the ground on his face before the ark of the LORD until the evening, he and the elders of Israel; and they put dust on their heads. 7Joshua said, "Ah, Lord GOD! Why have you brought this people across the Jordan at all, to hand us over to the Am'o·rītes so as to destroy us? Would that we had been content to settle beyond the Jordan! 8O Lord, what can I say, now that Israel has turned their backs to their enemies! 9The Cā'naan·ītes and all the inhabitants of the land will hear of it, and surround us, and cut off our name from the earth. Then what will you do for your great name?"

10 The LORD said to Joshua, "Stand up! Why have you fallen upon your face? 11Israel has sinned; they have transgressed my covenant that I imposed on them. They have taken some of the devoted things; they have stolen, they have acted deceitfully, and they have put them among their own belongings. 12Therefore the Israelites are unable to stand before their enemies; they turn their backs to their enemies, because they have become a thing devoted for destruction themselves. I will be with you no more, unless you destroy the devoted things from among you. 13Proceed to sanctify the people, and say, 'Sanctify yourselves for tomorrow; for thus says the LORD, the God of Israel, "There are devoted things among you, O Israel; you will be unable to stand before your enemies until you take away the devoted things from among you." 14In the morning therefore you shall come forward tribe by tribe. The tribe that the LORD takes shall come near by clans, the clan that the LORD takes shall come near by households, and the household that the LORD takes shall come near one by one. 15And the one who is taken as having the devoted things shall be burned with fire, together with all that he has, for having transgressed the covenant of the LORD, and for having done an outrageous thing in Israel.' "

16 So Joshua rose early in the morning, and brought Israel near tribe by tribe,

[h] Heb *She*

and the tribe of Judah was taken. [17]He brought near the clans of Judah, and the clan of the Zē´ra·hītes was taken; and he brought near the clan of the Zē´ra·hītes, family by family,[i] and Zab´dī was taken. [18]And he brought near his household one by one, and Ā´chan son of Car´mī son of Zab´dī son of Zē´rah, of the tribe of Judah, was taken. [19]Then Joshua said to Ā´chan, "My son, give glory to the LORD God of Israel and make confession to him. Tell me now what you have done; do not hide it from me." [20]And Ā´chan answered Joshua, "It is true; I am the one who sinned against the LORD God of Israel. This is what I did: [21]when I saw among the spoil a beautiful mantle from Shī´nar, and two hundred shekels of silver, and a bar of gold weighing fifty shekels, then I coveted them and took them. They now lie hidden in the ground inside my tent, with the silver underneath."

22 So Joshua sent messengers, and they ran to the tent; and there it was, hidden in his tent with the silver underneath. [23]They took them out of the tent and brought them to Joshua and all the Israelites; and they spread them out before the LORD. [24]Then Joshua and all Israel with him took Ā´chan son of Zē´rah, with the silver, the mantle, and the bar of gold, with his sons and daughters, with his oxen, donkeys, and sheep, and his tent and all that he had; and they brought them up to the Valley of Ā´chor. [25]Joshua said, "Why did you bring trouble on us? The LORD is bringing trouble on you today." And all Israel stoned him to death; they burned them with fire, cast stones on them, [26]and raised over him a great heap of stones that remains to this day. Then the LORD turned from his burning anger. Therefore that place to this day is called the Valley of Ā´chor.[j]

Ai Captured by a Stratagem and Destroyed

8 Then the LORD said to Joshua, "Do not fear or be dismayed; take all the fighting men with you, and go up now to Aī. See, I have handed over to you the king of Aī with his people, his city, and his land. [2]You shall do to Aī and its king as you did to Jericho and its king; only its spoil and its livestock you may take as booty for yourselves. Set an ambush against the city, behind it."

3 So Joshua and all the fighting men set out to go up against Aī. Joshua chose thirty thousand warriors and sent them out by night [4]with the command, "You shall lie in ambush against the city, behind it; do not go very far from the city, but all of you stay alert. [5]I and all the people who are with me will approach the city. When they come out against us, as before, we shall flee from them. [6]They will come out after us until we have drawn them away from the city; for they will say, 'They are fleeing from us, as before.' While we flee from them, [7]you shall rise up from the ambush and seize the city; for the LORD your God will give it into your hand. [8]And when you have taken the city, you shall set the city on fire, doing as the LORD has ordered; see, I have commanded you." [9]So Joshua sent them out; and they went to the place of ambush, and lay between Beth´el and Aī, to the west of Aī; but Joshua spent that night in the camp.[k]

10 In the morning Joshua rose early and mustered the people, and went up, with the elders of Israel, before the people to Aī. [11]All the fighting men who were with him went up, and drew near before the city, and camped on the north side of Aī, with a ravine between them and Aī. [12]Taking about five thousand men, he set them in ambush between Beth´el and Aī, to the west of the city. [13]So they stationed the forces, the main encampment that was north of the city and its rear guard west of the city. But Joshua spent that night in the valley. [14]When the king of Aī saw this, he and

[i] Mss Syr: MT *man by man*   [j] That is *Trouble*
[k] Heb *among the people*

The Arabah, one of the main regions of Israel, is south of the Sea of Galilee. It contains the Jordan Valley and the Dead Sea. See if you can find this area on one of the maps in the back of this Bible! The southern part of the Arabah was one of the areas the Israelites traveled through on their journey from Egypt to Canaan.

all his people, the inhabitants of the city, hurried out early in the morning to the meeting place facing the Ar´a·bah to meet Israel in battle; but he did not know that there was an ambush against him behind the city. ¹⁵And Joshua and all Israel made a pretense of being beaten before them, and fled in the direction of the wilderness. ¹⁶So all the people who were in the city were called together to pursue them, and as they pursued Joshua they were drawn away from the city. ¹⁷There was not a man left in Aī or Beth´el who did not go out after Israel; they left the city open, and pursued Israel.

18 Then the Lord said to Joshua, "Stretch out the sword that is in your hand toward Aī; for I will give it into your hand." And Joshua stretched out the sword that was in his hand toward the city. ¹⁹As soon as he stretched out his hand, the troops in ambush rose quickly out of their place and rushed forward. They entered the city, took it, and at once set the city on fire. ²⁰So when the men of Aī looked back, the smoke of the city was rising to the sky. They had no power to flee this way or that, for the people who fled to the wilderness turned back against the pursuers. ²¹When Joshua and all Israel saw that the ambush had taken the city and that the smoke of the city was rising, then they turned back and struck down the men of Aī. ²²And the others came out from the city against

them; so they were surrounded by Israelites, some on one side, and some on the other; and Israel struck them down until no one was left who survived or escaped. ²³But the king of Aī was taken alive and brought to Joshua.

24 When Israel had finished slaughtering all the inhabitants of Aī in the open wilderness where they pursued them, and when all of them to the very last had fallen by the edge of the sword, all Israel returned to Aī, and attacked it with the edge of the sword. ²⁵The total of those who fell that day, both men and women, was twelve thousand—all the people of Aī. ²⁶For Joshua did not draw back his hand, with which he stretched out the sword, until he had utterly destroyed all the inhabitants of Aī. ²⁷Only the livestock and the spoil of that city Israel took as their booty, according to the word of the Lord that he had issued to Joshua. ²⁸So Joshua burned Aī, and made it forever a heap of ruins, as it is to this day. ²⁹And he hanged the king of Aī on a tree until evening; and at sunset Joshua commanded, and they took his body down from the tree, threw it down at the entrance of the gate of the city, and raised over it a great heap of stones, which stands there to this day.

After the Israelites entered Canaan, Joshua led them in a ceremony in which they agreed to obey God's commandments. Six tribes stood in front of Mt. Ebal, and six stood in front of Mt. Gerizim. The Ark of the Covenant was placed between them. The tribes standing before Mt. Ebal cursed all who failed to keep the commandments. The tribes standing before Mt. Gerizim announced the blessings that would come to those who served the Lord.

Joshua Renews the Covenant

30 Then Joshua built on Mount Ē´bal an altar to the LORD, the God of Israel, [31]just as Moses the servant of the LORD had commanded the Israelites, as it is written in the book of the law of Moses, "an altar of unhewn[l] stones, on which no iron tool has been used"; and they offered on it burnt offerings to the LORD, and sacrificed offerings of well-being. [32]And there, in the presence of the Israelites, Joshua[m] wrote on the stones a copy of the law of Moses, which he had written. [33]All Israel, alien as well as citizen, with their elders and officers and their judges, stood on opposite sides of the ark in front of the levitical priests who carried the ark of the covenant of the LORD, half of them in front of Mount Ger´i·zim and half of them in front of Mount Ē´bal, as Moses the servant of the LORD had commanded at the first, that they should bless the people of Israel. [34]And afterward he read all the words of the law, blessings and curses, according to all that is written in the book of the law. [35]There was not a word of all that Moses commanded that Joshua did not read before all the assembly of Israel, and the women, and the little ones, and the aliens who resided among them.

The Gibeonites Save Themselves by Trickery

9 Now when all the kings who were beyond the Jordan in the hill country and in the lowland all along the coast of the Great Sea toward Lebanon—the Hit´tites, the Am´o·rites, the Cā´naanītes, the Per´iz·zītes, the Hī´vītes, and the Jeb´ū·sītes—heard of this, [2]they gathered together with one accord to fight Joshua and Israel.

3 But when the inhabitants of Gib´ē·on heard what Joshua had done to Jericho and to Ai, [4]they on their part acted with cunning: they went and prepared provisions,[n] and took worn-out sacks for their donkeys, and wineskins, worn-out

and torn and mended, [5]with worn-out, patched sandals on their feet, and worn-out clothes; and all their provisions were dry and moldy. [6]They went to Joshua in the camp at Gil´gal, and said to him and to the Israelites, "We have come from a far country; so now make a treaty with us." [7]But the Israelites said to the Hī´vītes, "Perhaps you live among us; then how can we make a treaty with you?" [8]They said to Joshua, "We are your servants." And Joshua said to them, "Who are you? And where do you come from?" [9]They said to him, "Your servants have come from a very far country, because of the name of the LORD your God; for we have heard a report of him, of all that he did in Egypt, [10]and of all that he did to the two kings of the Am´o·rītes who were beyond the Jordan, King Sī´hon of Hesh´bon, and King Og of Bā´shan who lived in Ash´ta·roth. [11]So our elders and all the inhabitants of our country said to us, 'Take provisions in your hand for the journey; go to meet them, and say to them, "We are your servants; come now, make a treaty with us." ' [12]Here is our bread; it was still warm when we took it from our houses as our food for the journey, on the day we set out to come to you, but now, see, it is dry and moldy; [13]these wineskins were new when we filled them, and see, they are burst; and these garments and sandals of ours are worn out from the very long journey." [14]So the leaders[o] partook of their provisions, and did not ask direction from the LORD. [15]And Joshua made peace with them, guaranteeing their lives by a treaty; and the leaders of the congregation swore an oath to them.

16 But when three days had passed after they had made a treaty with them, they heard that they were their neighbors and were living among them. [17]So the Israelites set out and reached their cities on the third day. Now their cities

---

[l] Heb *whole*   [m] Heb *he*   [n] Cn: Meaning of Heb uncertain   [o] Gk: Heb *men*

were Gib´e·on, Chē·phī´rah, Be·er´oth, and Kir´i·ath-jē´a·rim. ¹⁸But the Israelites did not attack them, because the leaders of the congregation had sworn to them by the LORD, the God of Israel. Then all the congregation murmured against the leaders. ¹⁹But all the leaders said to all the congregation, "We have sworn to them by the LORD, the God of Israel, and now we must not touch them. ²⁰This is what we will do to them: We will let them live, so that wrath may not come upon us, because of the oath that we swore to them." ²¹The leaders said to them, "Let them live." So they became hewers of wood and drawers of water for all the congregation, as the leaders had decided concerning them.

22 Joshua summoned them, and said to them, "Why did you deceive us, saying, 'We are very far from you,' while in fact you are living among us? ²³Now therefore you are cursed, and some of you shall always be slaves, hewers of wood and drawers of water for the house of my God." ²⁴They answered Joshua, "Because it was told to your servants for a certainty that the LORD your God had commanded his servant Moses to give you all the land, and to destroy all the inhabitants of the land before you; so we were in great fear for our lives because of you, and did this thing. ²⁵And now we are in your hand: do as it seems good and right in your sight to do to us." ²⁶This is what he did for them: he saved them from the Israelites; and they did not kill them. ²⁷But on that day Joshua made them hewers of wood and drawers of water for the congregation and for the altar of the LORD, to continue to this day, in the place that he should choose.

The Sun Stands Still

10 When King A·dō´ni-ze´dek of Jerusalem heard how Joshua had taken Aī, and had utterly destroyed it, doing to Aī and its king as he had done to Jericho and its king, and how

the inhabitants of Gib´e·on had made peace with Israel and were among them, ²he[p] became greatly frightened, because Gib´e·on was a large city, like one of the royal cities, and was larger than Aī, and all its men were warriors. ³So King A·dō´ni-ze´dek of Jerusalem sent a message to King Hō´ham of Hē´bron, to King Pī´ram of Jar´muth, to King Ja·phī´a of Lā´chish, and to King Dē´bir of Eg´lon, saying, ⁴"Come up and help me, and let us attack Gib´e·on; for it has made peace with Joshua and with the Israelites." ⁵Then the five kings of the Am´o·rītes— the king of Jerusalem, the king of Hē´-bron, the king of Jar´muth, the king of Lā´chish, and the king of Eg´lon—gathered their forces, and went up with all their armies and camped against Gib´e·on, and made war against it.

6 And the Gib´e·on·ītes sent to Joshua at the camp in Gil´gal, saying, "Do not abandon your servants; come up to us quickly, and save us, and help us; for all the kings of the Am´o·rītes who live in the hill country are gathered against us." ⁷So Joshua went up from Gil´gal, he and all the fighting force with him, all the mighty warriors. ⁸The LORD said to Joshua, "Do not fear them, for I have handed them over to you; not one of them shall stand before you." ⁹So Joshua came upon them suddenly, having marched up all night from Gil´gal. ¹⁰And the LORD threw them into a panic before Israel, who inflicted a great slaughter on them at Gib´e·on, chased them by the way of the ascent of Beth-hō´ron, and struck them down as far as A·ze´kah and Mak·kē´dah. ¹¹As they fled before Israel, while they were going down the slope of Beth-hō´ron, the LORD threw down huge stones from heaven on them as far as A·ze´kah, and they died; there were more who died because of the hailstones than the Israelites killed with the sword.

12 On the day when the LORD gave the Am´o·rītes over to the Israelites,

p Heb they

Joshua spoke to the LORD; and he said in the sight of Israel,

"Sun, stand still at Gib´e·on,
    and Moon, in the valley of Aī´ja·lon."
[13] And the sun stood still, and the
    moon stopped,
        until the nation took vengeance
        on their enemies.

Is this not written in the Book of Jash´ar? The sun stopped in midheaven, and did not hurry to set for about a whole day. [14]There has been no day like it before or since, when the LORD heeded a human voice; for the LORD fought for Israel.

15 Then Joshua returned, and all Israel with him, to the camp at Gil´gal.

Five Kings Defeated

16 Meanwhile, these five kings fled and hid themselves in the cave at Mak·ke´dah. [17]And it was told Joshua, "The five kings have been found, hidden in the cave at Mak·ke´dah." [18]Joshua said, "Roll large stones against the mouth of the cave, and set men by it to guard them; [19]but do not stay there yourselves; pursue your enemies, and attack them from the rear. Do not let them enter their towns, for the LORD your God has given them into your hand." [20]When Joshua and the Israelites had finished inflicting a very great slaughter on them, until they were wiped out, and when the survivors had entered into the fortified towns, [21]all the people returned safe to Joshua in the camp at Mak·ke´dah; no one dared to speak[q] against any of the Israelites.

22 Then Joshua said, "Open the mouth of the cave, and bring those five kings out to me from the cave." [23]They did so, and brought the five kings out to him from the cave, the king of Jerusalem, the king of He´bron, the king of Jar´muth, the king of La´chish, and the king of Eg´lon. [24]When they brought the kings out to Joshua, Joshua summoned all the Israelites, and said to the chiefs of the warriors who had gone with him, "Come near, put your feet on the necks of these kings." Then they came near

and put their feet on their necks. [25]And Joshua said to them, "Do not be afraid or dismayed; be strong and courageous; for thus the LORD will do to all the enemies against whom you fight." [26]Afterward Joshua struck them down and put them to death, and he hung them on five trees. And they hung on the trees until evening. [27]At sunset Joshua commanded, and they took them down from the trees and threw them into the cave where they had hidden themselves; they set large stones against the mouth of the cave, which remain to this very day.

28 Joshua took Mak·ke´dah on that day, and struck it and its king with the edge of the sword; he utterly destroyed every person in it; he left no one remaining. And he did to the king of Mak·ke´dah as he had done to the king of Jericho.

29 Then Joshua passed on from Mak·ke´dah, and all Israel with him, to Lib´nah, and fought against Lib´nah. [30]The LORD gave it also and its king into the hand of Israel; and he struck it with the edge of the sword, and every person in it; he left no one remaining in it; and he did to its king as he had done to the king of Jericho.

31 Next Joshua passed on from Lib´nah, and all Israel with him, to La´chish, and laid siege to it, and assaulted it. [32]The LORD gave La´chish into the hand of Israel, and he took it on the second day, and struck it with the edge of the sword, and every person in it, as he had done to Lib´nah.

33 Then King Hō´ram of Ge´zer came up to help La´chish; and Joshua struck him and his people, leaving him no survivors.

34 From La´chish Joshua passed on with all Israel to Eg´lon; and they laid siege to it, and assaulted it; [35]and they took it that day, and struck it with the edge of the sword; and every person in it he utterly destroyed that day, as he had done to La´chish.

[q] Heb *moved his tongue*

36 Then Joshua went up with all Israel from Eg′lon to He̅′bron; they assaulted it, ³⁷and took it, and struck it with the edge of the sword, and its king and its towns, and every person in it; he left no one remaining, just as he had done to Eg′lon, and utterly destroyed it with every person in it.

38 Then Joshua, with all Israel, turned back to De̅′bir and assaulted it, ³⁹and he took it with its king and all its towns; they struck them with the edge of the sword, and utterly destroyed every person in it; he left no one remaining; just as he had done to He̅′bron, and, as he had done to Lib′nah and its king, so he did to De̅′bir and its king.

40 So Joshua defeated the whole land, the hill country and the Neg′eb and the lowland and the slopes, and all their kings; he left no one remaining, but utterly destroyed all that breathed, as the LORD God of Israel commanded. ⁴¹And Joshua defeated them from Ka̅′desh-bar′ne̅·a to Ga̅′za, and all the country of Go̅′shen, as far as Gib′e̅·on. ⁴²Joshua took all these kings and their land at one time, because the LORD God of Israel fought for Israel. ⁴³Then Joshua returned, and all Israel with him, to the camp at Gil′gal.

The United Kings of Northern Canaan Defeated

11 When King Ja̅′bin of Ha̅′zor heard of this, he sent to King Jo̅′bab of Ma̅′don, to the king of Shim′ron, to the king of Ach′shaph, ²and to the kings who were in the northern hill country, and in the Ar′a·bah south of Chin′ne·roth, and in the lowland, and in Na̅′photh-dor on the west, ³to the Ca̅′naan-ites in the east and the west, the Am′o·rites, the Hit′tites, the Per′iz-zites, and the Jeb′u·sites in the hill country, and the Hi̅′vites under Hermon in the land of Miz′pah. ⁴They came out, with all their troops, a great army, in number like the sand on the seashore, with very many horses and chariots. ⁵All these kings joined their forces, and came and camped together at the waters of Me̅′rom, to fight with Israel.

6 And the LORD said to Joshua, "Do not be afraid of them, for tomorrow at this time I will hand over all of them, slain, to Israel; you shall hamstring their horses, and burn their chariots with fire." ⁷So Joshua came suddenly upon them with all his fighting force, by the waters of Me̅′rom, and fell upon them. ⁸And the LORD handed them over to Israel, who attacked them and chased them as far as Great Si̅′don and Mis′re̅-photh-ma̅′im, and eastward as far as the valley of Miz′peh. They struck them down, until they had left no one remaining. ⁹And Joshua did to them as the LORD commanded him; he hamstrung their horses, and burned their chariots with fire.

10 Joshua turned back at that time, and took Ha̅′zor, and struck its king down with the sword. Before that time Ha̅′zor was the head of all those kingdoms. ¹¹And they put to the sword all who were in it, utterly destroying them; there was no one left who breathed, and he burned Ha̅′zor with fire. ¹²And all the towns of those kings, and all their kings, Joshua took, and struck them with the edge of the sword, utterly destroying them, as Moses the servant of the LORD had commanded. ¹³But Israel burned none of the towns that stood on mounds except Ha̅′zor, which Joshua did burn. ¹⁴All the spoil of these towns, and the livestock, the Israelites took for their booty; but all the people they struck down with the edge of the sword, until they had destroyed them, and they did not leave any who breathed. ¹⁵As the LORD had commanded his servant Moses, so Moses commanded Joshua, and so Joshua did; he left nothing undone of all that the LORD had commanded Moses.

Summary of Joshua's Conquests

16 So Joshua took all that land: the hill country and all the Neg´eb and all the land of Gō´shen and the lowland and the Ar´a·bah and the hill country of Israel and its lowland, [17]from Mount Hā´lak, which rises toward Sē´ir, as far as Bā´al-gad in the valley of Lebanon below Mount Hermon. He took all their kings, struck them down, and put them to death. [18]Joshua made war a long time with all those kings. [19]There was not a town that made peace with the Israelites, except the Hī´vites, the inhabitants of Gib´ē·on; all were taken in battle. [20]For it was the LORD's doing to harden their hearts so that they would come against Israel in battle, in order that they might be utterly destroyed, and might receive no mercy, but be exterminated, just as the LORD had commanded Moses.

21 At that time Joshua came and wiped out the An´a·kim from the hill country, from Hē´bron, from Dē´bir, from Ā´nab, and from all the hill country of Judah, and from all the hill country of Israel; Joshua utterly destroyed them with their towns. [22]None of the An´a·kim was left in the land of the Israelites; some remained only in Gā´za, in Gath, and in Ash´dod. [23]So Joshua took the whole land, according to all that the LORD had spoken to Moses; and Joshua gave it for an inheritance to Israel according to their tribal allotments. And the land had rest from war.

The Kings Conquered by Moses

12 Now these are the kings of the land, whom the Israelites defeated, whose land they occupied beyond the Jordan toward the east, from the Wadi Ar´non to Mount Hermon, with all the Ar´a·bah eastward: [2]King Sī´hon of the Am´o·rītes who lived at Hesh´bon, and ruled from A·rō´er, which is on the edge of the Wadi Ar´non, and from the middle of the valley as far as the river Jab´bok, the boundary of the

Canaan was the land promised by God to Abraham and his descendants. After the Israelites entered Canaan and defeated the kings of the area, pieces of land were given to each of the tribes descended from Jacob. These pieces were called allotments. The Israelites had a very special feeling toward their land because they believed that it belonged to God. God owned the land, and the people thought of God as their landlord.

Am´mon·ītes, that is, half of Gil´e·ad, [3]and the Ar´a·bah to the Sea of Chin´ne·roth eastward, and in the direction of Beth-jesh´i·moth, to the sea of the Ar´a·bah, the Dead Sea,[r] southward to the foot of the slopes of Pis´gah; [4]and King Og[s] of Bā´shan, one of the last of the Reph´a·im, who lived at Ash´ta·roth and at Ed´re·ī [5]and ruled over Mount Hermon and Sal´e·cah and all Bā´shan to the boundary of the Gesh´ū·rītes and the Mā´a·ca·thītes, and over half of Gil´e·ad to the boundary of King Sī´hon of Hesh´bon. [6]Moses, the servant of the LORD, and the Israelites defeated them; and Moses the servant of the LORD gave their land for a possession to the Reū´ben·ītes and the Gad´ītes and the half-tribe of Ma·nas´seh.

The Kings Conquered by Joshua

7 The following are the kings of the land whom Joshua and the Israelites defeated on the west side of the Jordan, from Bā´al-gad in the valley of Lebanon to Mount Hā´lak, that rises toward Sē´ir (and Joshua gave their land to the tribes of Israel as a possession according to their allotments, [8]in the hill country, in the lowland, in the Ar´a·bah, in the slopes, in the wilderness, and in the Neg´eb, the land of the Hit´tītes, Am´o·rītes, Cā´naan·ītes, Per´iz·zītes, Hī´vītes, and Jeb´ū·sītes):

[r] Heb Salt Sea　　[s] Gk: Heb the boundary of King Og

⁹ the king of Jericho — one
the king of Aī,
which is next to Beth´el — one
¹⁰ the king of Jerusalem — one
the king of Hē´bron — one
¹¹ the king of Jar´muth — one
the king of Lā´chish — one
¹² the king of Eg´lon — one
the king of Gē´zer — one
¹³ the king of Dē´bir — one
the king of Gē´der — one
¹⁴ the king of Hor´mah — one
the king of Ar´ad — one
¹⁵ the king of Lib´nah — one
the king of A·dul´lam — one
¹⁶ the king of Mak·kē´dah — one
the king of Beth´el — one
¹⁷ the king of Tap´pū·ah — one
the king of Hē´pher — one
¹⁸ the king of Ā´phek — one
the king of La·shar´on — one
¹⁹ the king of Mā´don — one
the king of Hā´zor — one
²⁰ the king of Shim´ron-mē´ron — one
the king of Ach´shaph — one
²¹ the king of Tā´a·nach — one
the king of Me·gid´dō — one
²² the king of Kē´desh — one
the king of Jok´nē·am in Car´mel — one
²³ the king of Dor in
Nā´phath-dor — one
the king of Goi´im in Galilee,ᵗ — one
²⁴ the king of Tir´zah — one
thirty-one kings in all.

The Parts of Canaan Still Unconquered

13 Now Joshua was old and advanced in years; and the LORD said to him, "You are old and advanced in years, and very much of the land still remains to be possessed. ²This is the land that still remains: all the regions of the Phi·lis´tines, and all those of the Gesh´ū·rītes ³(from the Shī´hor, which is east of Egypt, northward to the boundary of Ek´ron, it is reckoned as Cā´naan·īte; there are five rulers of the Phi·lis´tines, those of Gā´za, Ash´dod, Ash´ke·lon, Gath, and Ek´ron), and those of

Joshua defeated the king of Adullam during the conquest of Canaan. The town later became part of the land of the tribe of Judah. David hid from Saul in a cave near Adullam. You can read about David's adventure in 1 Samuel 22.

the Av´vim ⁴in the south; all the land of the Cā´naan·ītes, and Mear´ah that belongs to the Sī·dō´ni·ans, to Ā´phek, to the boundary of the Am´o·rītes, ⁵and the land of the Gē´bal·ītes, and all Lebanon, toward the east, from Bā´al-gad below Mount Hermon to Lē·bō-hā´math, ⁶all the inhabitants of the hill country from Lebanon to Mis´rē·photh-mā´im, even all the Sī·dō´ni·ans. I will myself drive them out from before the Israelites; only allot the land to Israel for an inheritance, as I have commanded you. ⁷Now therefore divide this land for an inheritance to the nine tribes and the half-tribe of Ma·nas´seh."

The Territory East of the Jordan

8 With the other half-tribe of Manas´-sehᵘ the Reū´ben·ītes and the Gad´ītes received their inheritance, which Moses gave them, beyond the Jordan eastward, as Moses the servant of the LORD gave them: ⁹from A·rō´er, which is on the edge of the Wadi Ar´non, and the town that is in the middle of the valley, and all the tableland fromᵛ Med´e·ba as far as

The Philistines lived along the coast and in the eastern part of Canaan when the Israelites arrived in the land. The Philistines and the Israelites were almost always at war.

ᵗ Gk: Heb *Gilgal*   ᵘ Cn: Heb *With it*   ᵛ Compare Gk: Heb lacks *from*

Dĭ´bon; ¹⁰and all the cities of King Sī´-hon of the Am´o·rītes, who reigned in Hesh´bon, as far as the boundary of the Am´mon·ītes; ¹¹and Gil´e·ad, and the region of the Gesh´ū·rītes and Mā´a·ca·thītes, and all Mount Hermon, and all Bā´shan to Sal´e·cah; ¹²all the kingdom of Og in Bā´shan, who reigned in Ash´ta·roth and in Ed´rē·ī (he alone was left of the survivors of the Reph´a·im); these Moses had defeated and driven out. ¹³Yet the Israelites did not drive out the Gesh´ū·rītes or the Mā´a·ca·thītes; but Gē´shur and Mā´a·cath live within Israel to this day.

14 To the tribe of Levi alone Moses gave no inheritance; the offerings by fire to the LORD God of Israel are their inheritance, as he said to them.

The Territory of Reuben

15 Moses gave an inheritance to the tribe of the Reū´ben·ītes according to their clans. ¹⁶Their territory was from A·rō´er, which is on the edge of the Wadi Ar´non, and the town that is in the middle of the valley, and all the tableland by Med´e·ba; ¹⁷with Hesh´bon, and all its towns that are in the tableland; Dī´bon, and Bā´moth-bā´al, and Beth-bā´al-mē´on, ¹⁸and Jā´haz, and Ked´e·moth, and Meph´a·ath, ¹⁹and Kir·i·a·thā´im, and Sib´mah, and Zē´reth-shā´har on the hill of the valley, ²⁰and Beth-pē´or, and the slopes of Pis´gah, and Beth-jesh´i·moth, ²¹that is, all the towns of the tableland, and all the kingdom of King Sī´hon of the Am´o·rītes, who reigned in Hesh´bon, whom Moses defeated with the leaders of Mid´i·an, Ē´vī and Rē´kem and Zur and Hur and Rē´ba, as princes of Sī´hon, who lived in the land. ²²Along with the rest of those they put to death, the Israelites also put to the sword Bā´laam son of Bē´or, who practiced divination. ²³And the border of the Reū´ben·ītes was the Jordan and its banks. This was the inheritance of the Reū´ben·ītes according to their families with their towns and villages.

The Territory of Gad

24 Moses gave an inheritance also to the tribe of the Gad´ītes, according to their families. ²⁵Their territory was Jā´zer, and all the towns of Gil´e·ad, and half the land of the Am´mon·ītes, to A·rō´er, which is east of Rab´bah, ²⁶and from Hesh´bon to Rā´math-miz´peh and Bet´-ō·nim, and from Mā·ha·nā´im to the territory of Dē´bir,ʷ ²⁷and in the valley Beth-hā´ram, Beth-nim´rah, Suc´coth, and Zā´phon, the rest of the kingdom of King Sī´hon of Hesh´bon, the Jordan and its banks, as far as the lower end of the Sea of Chin´ne·reth, eastward beyond the Jordan. ²⁸This is the inheritance of the Gad´ītes according to their clans, with their towns and villages.

The Territory of the Half-Tribe of Manasseh (East)

29 Moses gave an inheritance to the half-tribe of Ma·nas´seh; it was allotted to the half-tribe of the Ma·nas´sītes according to their families. ³⁰Their territory extended from Mā·ha·nā´im, through all Bā´shan, the whole kingdom of King Og of Bā´shan, and all the settlements of Jā´ir, which are in Bā´shan, sixty towns, ³¹and half of Gil´e·ad, and Ash´ta·roth, and Ed´rē·ī, the towns of the kingdom of Og in Bā´shan; these were allotted to the people of Mā´chir son of Ma·nas´seh according to their clans—for half the Mā´chir·ītes.

32 These are the inheritances that Moses distributed in the plains of Mō´ab, beyond the Jordan east of Jericho. ³³But to the tribe of Levi Moses gave no inheritance; the LORD God of Israel is their inheritance, as he said to them.

The Distribution of Territory West of the Jordan

14 These are the inheritances that the Israelites received in the land of Cā´naan, which the priest El·ē·ā´-zar, and Joshua son of Nun, and the heads of the families of the tribes of the

ʷ Gk Syr Vg: Heb *Lidebir*

Israelites distributed to them. ²Their inheritance was by lot, as the LORD had commanded Moses for the nine and one-half tribes. ³For Moses had given an inheritance to the two and one-half tribes beyond the Jordan; but to the Lḗvītes he gave no inheritance among them. ⁴For the people of Joseph were two tribes, Ma·nas´seh and Ē´phra·im; and no portion was given to the Lē´vītes in the land, but only towns to live in, with their pasture lands for their flocks and herds. ⁵The Israelites did as the LORD commanded Moses; they allotted the land.

Hebron Allotted to Caleb

6 Then the people of Judah came to Joshua at Gil´gal; and Caleb son of Je·phun´neh the Ken´iz·zīte said to him, "You know what the LORD said to Moses the man of God in Kā´desh-bar´nē·a concerning you and me. ⁷I was forty years old when Moses the servant of the LORD sent me from Kā´desh-bar´nē·a to spy out the land; and I brought him an honest report. ⁸But my companions who went up with me made the heart of the people melt; yet I wholeheartedly followed the LORD my God. ⁹And Moses swore on that day, saying, 'Surely the land on which your foot has trodden shall be an inheritance for you and your children forever, because you have wholeheartedly followed the LORD my God.' ¹⁰And now, as you see, the LORD has kept me alive, as he said, these forty-five years since the time that the LORD spoke this word to Moses, while Israel was journeying through the wilderness; and here I am today, eighty-five years old. ¹¹I am still as strong today as I was on the day that Moses sent me; my strength now is as my strength was then, for war, and for going and coming. ¹²So now give me this hill country of which the LORD spoke on that day; for you heard on that day how the An´a·kim were there, with great fortified cities; it may be that the LORD will be with me, and I shall drive them out, as the LORD said."

Eleazar, the son of Aaron, took over the priestly duties after his father's death. He was Moses' helper on the journey to the land of Canaan. Along with Joshua, Eleazar divided the land by lots among the tribes of Israel.

13 Then Joshua blessed him, and gave Hē´bron to Caleb son of Je·phun´neh for an inheritance. ¹⁴So Hē´bron became the inheritance of Caleb son of Je·phun´neh the Ken´iz·zīte to this day, because he wholeheartedly followed the LORD, the God of Israel. ¹⁵Now the name of Hē´bron formerly was Kir´i·ath-ar´ba;ˣ this Ar´ba wasʸ the greatest man among the An´a·kim. And the land had rest from war.

The Territory of Judah

15 The lot for the tribe of the people of Judah according to their families reached southward to the boundary of Ē´dom, to the wilderness of Zin at the farthest south. ²And their south boundary ran from the end of the Dead Sea,ᶻ from the bay that faces southward; ³it goes out southward of the ascent of Ak·rab´bim, passes along to Zin, and goes up south of Kā´desh-bar´nē·a, along by Hez´ron, up to Ad´dar, makes a turn to Kar´ka, ⁴passes along to Az´mon, goes out by the Wadi of Egypt, and comes to its end at the sea. This shall be your south boundary. ⁵And the east boundary is the Dead Sea,ᶻ to the mouth of the Jordan. And the boundary on the north side runs from the bay of the sea at the mouth of the Jordan; ⁶and the boundary goes up to Beth-hog´lah, and passes along north of Beth-ar´a·bah; and the boundary goes up to the Stone of Bō´han, Reuben's son; ⁷and the boundary goes up to Dē´bir from the Valley of

ˣ That is *the city of Arba*   ʸ Heb lacks *this Arba was*   ᶻ Heb *Salt Sea*

Ā´chor, and so northward, turning toward Gil´gal, which is opposite the ascent of A·dum´mim, which is on the south side of the valley; and the boundary passes along to the waters of En-shē´-mesh, and ends at En-rō´gel; [8]then the boundary goes up by the valley of the son of Hin´nom at the southern slope of the Jeb´ū·sītes (that is, Jerusalem); and the boundary goes up to the top of the mountain that lies over against the valley of Hin´nom, on the west, at the northern end of the valley of Reph´a·im; [9]then the boundary extends from the top of the mountain to the spring of the Waters of Neph·tō´ah, and from there to the towns of Mount Ē´phron; then the boundary bends around to Bā´a·lah (that is, Kir´i·ath-jē´a·rim); [10]and the boundary circles west of Bā´a·lah to Mount Sē´ir, passes along to the northern slope of Mount Jē´a·rim (that is, Ches´a·lon), and goes down to Beth-shē´mesh, and passes along by Tim´nah; [11]the boundary goes out to the slope of the hill north of Ek´ron, then the boundary bends around to Shik´ke·ron, and passes along to Mount Bā´a·lah, and goes out to Jab´nē·el; then the boundary comes to an end at the sea. [12]And the west boundary was the Mediterranean with its coast. This is the boundary surrounding the people of Judah according to their families.

Caleb Occupies His Portion

13 According to the commandment of the LORD to Joshua, he gave to Caleb son of Je·phūn´neh a portion among the people of Judah, Kir´i·ath-ar´ba,[a] that is, Hē´-bron (Ar´ba was the father of Ā´nak). [14]And Caleb drove out from there the three sons of Ā´nak: Shē´shaī, A·hī´man, and Tal´maī, the descendants of Ā´nak. [15]From there he went up against the inhabitants of Dē´bir; now the name of Dē´bir formerly was Kir´i·ath-sē´pher. [16]And Caleb said, "Whoever attacks Kir´i·ath-sē´pher and takes it, to him I will give my daughter Ach´sah as wife." [17]Oth´ni·el son of Kē´naz, the brother of Caleb, took it; and he gave him his daughter Ach´sah as wife. [18]When she came to him, she urged him to ask her father for a field. As she dismounted from her donkey, Caleb said to her, "What do you wish?" [19]She said to him, "Give me a present; since you have set me in the land of the Neg´eb, give me springs of water as well." So Caleb gave her the upper springs and the lower springs.

The Towns of Judah

20 This is the inheritance of the tribe of the people of Judah according to their families. [21]The towns belonging to the tribe of the people of Judah in the extreme south, toward the boundary of Ē´dom, were Kab´zē·el, Ē´der, Jā´gur, [22]Kī´-nah, Di·mō´nah, A·dā´dah, [23]Kē´desh, Hā´-zor, Ith´nan, [24]Ziph, Tē´lem, Be·ā´loth, [25]Hā´zor-ha·dat´tah, Ker´i·oth-hez´ron (that is, Hā´zor), [26]Ā´mam, Shē´ma, Mō´-la·dah, [27]Hā´zar-gad´dah, Hesh´mon, Beth-pel´et, [28]Hā´zar-shū´al, Bē´er-shē´ba, Biz·i·o·thī´ah, [29]Bā´a·lah, Ī´im, Ē´zem, [30]El·tō´lad, Chē´sil, Hor´mah, [31]Zik´lag, Mad·man´nah, San·san´nah, [32]Leba´oth, Shil´him, Ā´in, and Rim´mon: in all, twenty-nine towns, with their villages.

33 And in the lowland, Esh·tā·ol, Zō´-rah, Ash´nah, [34]Za·nō´ah, En-gan´nim, Tap´pū·ah, Ē´nam, [35]Jar´muth, A·dul´-lam, Sō´cōh, A·zē´kah, [36]Shā·a·rā´im, Ad·i·thā´im, Ge·dē´rah, Ged·e·rō·thā´im: fourteen towns with their villages.

37 Zē´nan, Ha·dash´ah, Mig´dal-gad, [38]Dil´an, Miz´peh, Jok´thē-el, [39]Lā´chish, Boz´kath, Eg´lon, [40]Cab´bon, Lah´mam, Chit´lish, [41]Ge·dē´roth, Beth-dā´gon, Nā´-a·mah, and Mak·kē´dah: sixteen towns with their villages.

42 Lib´nah, Ē´ther, Ā´shan, [43]Iph´tah, Ash´nah, Nē´zib, [44]Kē·ī´lah, Ach´zib, and Ma·rē´shah: nine towns with their villages.

45 Ek´ron, with its dependencies and its villages; [46]from Ek´ron to the sea, all that were near Ash´dod, with their villages.

[a] That is *the city of Arba*

47 Ash′dod, its towns and its villages; Gā′za, its towns and its villages; to the Wadi of Egypt, and the Great Sea with its coast.

48 And in the hill country, Shā′mir, Jat′tir, Sō′cōh, ⁴⁹Dan′nah, Kir′i·ath-san′nah (that is, Dē′bir), ⁵⁰Ā′nab, Esh′te·mōh, Ā′nim, ⁵¹Gō′shen, Hō′lon, and Gī′lōh: eleven towns with their villages.

52 A′rab, Dū′mah, Ē′shan, ⁵³Jā′nim, Beth-tap·pū′ah, A·phē′kah, ⁵⁴Hum′tah, Kir′i·ath-ar′ba (that is, Hē′bron), and Zī′or: nine towns with their villages.

55 Mā′on, Car′mel, Ziph, Jut′tah, ⁵⁶Jez′rē·el, Jok′dē·am, Za·nō′ah, ⁵⁷Kāin, Gib′ē·ah, and Tim′nah: ten towns with their villages.

58 Hal′hul, Beth-zur, Gē′dor, ⁵⁹Mā′a·rath, Beth-ā′noth, and El′tē·kon: six towns with their villages.

60 Kir′i·ath-bā′al (that is, Kir′i·ath-jē′a·rim) and Rab′bah: two towns with their villages.

61 In the wilderness, Beth-ar′a·bah, Mid′din, Se·cā′cah, ⁶²Nib′shan, the City of Salt, and En-ge′di: six towns with their villages.

63 But the people of Judah could not drive out the Jeb′ū·sītes, the inhabitants of Jerusalem; so the Jeb′ū·sītes live with the people of Judah in Jerusalem to this day.

The Territory of Ephraim

16 The allotment of the Jō′seph·ītes went from the Jordan by Jericho, east of the waters of Jericho, into the wilderness, going up from Jericho into the hill country to Beth′el; ²then going from Beth′el to Luz, it passes along to At′a·roth, the territory of the Ar′chītes; ³then it goes down westward to the territory of the Japh′let·ītes, as far as the territory of Lower Beth-hō′ron, then to Gē′zer, and it ends at the sea.

4 The Jō′seph·ītes—Ma·nas′seh and Ē′phra·im—received their inheritance.

5 The territory of the Ē′phra·im·ītes by their families was as follows: the boundary of their inheritance on the east was At′a·roth-ad′dar as far as Upper Beth-hō′ron, ⁶and the boundary goes from there to the sea; on the north is Mich·mē′thath; then on the east the boundary makes a turn toward Tā′a·nath-shī′lōh, and passes along beyond it on the east to Ja·nō′ah, ⁷then it goes down from Ja·nō′ah to At′a·roth and to Nā′a·rah, and touches Jericho, ending at the Jordan. ⁸From Tap·pū′ah the boundary goes westward to the Wadi Kā′nah, and ends at the sea. Such is the inheritance of the tribe of the Ē′phra·im·ītes by their families, ⁹together with the towns that were set apart for the Ē′phra·im·ītes within the inheritance of the Ma·nas′sītes, all those towns with their villages. ¹⁰They did not, however, drive out the Cā′naan·ītes who lived in Gē′zer: so the Cā′naan·ītes have lived within Ē′phra·im to this day but have been made to do forced labor.

The Other Half-Tribe of Manasseh (West)

17 Then allotment was made to the tribe of Ma·nas′seh, for he was the firstborn of Joseph. To Mā′chir the firstborn of Ma·nas′seh, the father of Gil′e·ad, were allotted Gil′e·ad and Bā′shan, because he was a warrior. ²And allotments were made to the rest of the tribe of Ma·nas′seh, by their families, Ā·bi·ē′zer, Hē′lek, As′ri·el, Shē′chem, Hē′pher, and She·mī′da; these were the male descendants of Ma·nas′seh son of Joseph, by their families.

3 Now Ze·loph′e·had son of Hē′pher son of Gil′e·ad son of Mā′chir son of Ma·nas′seh had no sons, but only daughters; and these are the names of his daughters: Mah′lah, Noah, Hog′lah, Mil′cah, and Tir′zah. ⁴They came before the priest El·e·ā′zar and Joshua son of Nun and the leaders, and said, "The LORD commanded Moses to give us an inheritance along with our male kin." So according to the commandment of the LORD he gave them an inheritance

among the kinsmen of their father. 5Thus there fell to Ma·nas´seh ten portions, besides the land of Gil´e·ad and Bā´-shan, which is on the other side of the Jordan, 6because the daughters of Ma·nas´seh received an inheritance along with his sons. The land of Gil´e·ad was allotted to the rest of the Ma·nas´sītes.

7 The territory of Ma·nas´seh reached from Ash´er to Mich·mē´thath, which is east of Shē´chem; then the boundary goes along southward to the inhabitants of En-tap´pū·ah. 8The land of Tap´pū·ah belonged to Ma·nas´seh, but the town of Tap´pū·ah on the boundary of Ma·nas´seh belonged to the Ē´phra·im·ītes. 9Then the boundary went down to the Wadi Kā´-nah. The towns here, to the south of the wadi, among the towns of Ma·nas´seh, belong to Ē´phra·im. Then the boundary of Ma·nas´seh goes along the north side of the wadi and ends at the sea. 10The land to the south is Ē´phra·im's and that to the north is Ma·nas´seh's, with the sea forming its boundary; on the north Ash´er is reached, and on the east Is´sa·char. 11Within Is´sa·char and Ash´er, Ma·nas´seh had Beth-shē´an and its villages, Ib´lē·am and its villages, the inhabitants of Dor and its villages, the inhabitants of En-dor and its villages, the inhabitants of Tā´a·nach and its villages, and the inhabitants of Me·gid´dō and its villages (the third is Nā´phath).b 12Yet the Ma·nas´sītes could not take possession of those towns; but the Cā´-naan·ītes continued to live in that land. 13But when the Israelites grew strong, they put the Cā·naan·ītes to forced labor, but did not utterly drive them out.

The Tribe of Joseph Protests

14 The tribe of Joseph spoke to Joshua, saying, "Why have you given me but one lot and one portion as an inheritance, since we are a numerous people, whom all along the LORD has blessed?" 15And Joshua said to them, "If you are a numerous people, go up to the forest,

and clear ground there for yourselves in the land of the Per´iz·zītes and the Reph´a·im, since the hill country of Ē´phra·im is too narrow for you." 16The tribe of Joseph said, "The hill country is not enough for us; yet all the Cā´naan·ītes who live in the plain have chariots of iron, both those in Beth-shē´an and its villages and those in the Valley of Jez´rē·el." 17Then Joshua said to the house of Joseph, to Ē´phra·im and Ma·nas´seh, "You are indeed a numerous people, and have great power; you shall not have one lot only, 18but the hill country shall be yours, for though it is a forest, you shall clear it and possess it to its farthest borders; for you shall drive out the Cā´-naan·ītes, though they have chariots of iron, and though they are strong."

The Territories of the Remaining Tribes

18 Then the whole congregation of the Israelites assembled at Shī´-lōh, and set up the tent of meeting there. The land lay subdued before them.

2 There remained among the Israelites seven tribes whose inheritance had not yet been apportioned. 3So Joshua said to the Israelites, "How long will you be slack about going in and taking possession of the land that the LORD, the God of your ancestors, has given you? 4Provide three men from each tribe, and I will send them out that they may begin to go throughout the land, writing a description of it with a view to their inheritances. Then come back to me. 5They shall divide it into seven portions, Judah continuing in its territory on the south, and the house of Joseph in their territory on the north. 6You shall describe the land in seven divisions and bring the description here to me; and I will cast lots for you here before the LORD our God. 7The Lē´vītes have no portion among you, for the priesthood of the LORD is their heritage; and Gad

b Meaning of Heb uncertain

and Reuben and the half-tribe of Ma·nas′seh have received their inheritance beyond the Jordan eastward, which Moses the servant of the LORD gave them."

8 So the men started on their way; and Joshua charged those who went to write the description of the land, saying, "Go throughout the land and write a description of it, and come back to me; and I will cast lots for you here before the LORD in Shī′lōh." ⁹So the men went and traversed the land and set down in a book a description of it by towns in seven divisions; then they came back to Joshua in the camp at Shī′lōh, ¹⁰and Joshua cast lots for them in Shī′lōh before the LORD; and there Joshua apportioned the land to the Israelites, to each a portion.

The Territory of Benjamin

11 The lot of the tribe of Benjamin according to its families came up, and the territory allotted to it fell between the tribe of Judah and the tribe of Joseph. ¹²On the north side their boundary began at the Jordan; then the boundary goes up to the slope of Jericho on the north, then up through the hill country westward; and it ends at the wilderness of Beth-ā′ven. ¹³From there the boundary passes along southward in the direction of Luz, to the slope of Luz (that is, Beth′el), then the boundary goes down to At′a·roth-ad′dar, on the mountain that lies south of Lower Beth-hō′ron. ¹⁴Then the boundary goes in another direction, turning on the western side southward from the mountain that lies to the south, opposite Beth-hō′ron, and it ends at Kir′i·ath-bā′al (that is, Kir′i·ath-jē′a·rim), a town belonging to the tribe of Judah. This forms the western side. ¹⁵The southern side begins at the outskirts of Kir′i·ath-jē′a·rim; and the boundary goes from there to Ē′phron,ᶜ to the spring of the Waters of Neph·tō′ah; ¹⁶then the boundary goes down to the border of the mountain that overlooks the valley of the son of Hin′nom, which is at the north end of the valley of Reph′a·im;

and it then goes down the valley of Hin′nom, south of the slope of the Jeb′ū·sītes, and downward to En-rō′gel; ¹⁷then it bends in a northerly direction going on to En-shē′mesh, and from there goes to Ge·lī′loth, which is opposite the ascent of A·dum′mim; then it goes down to the Stone of Bō′han, Reuben's son; ¹⁸and passing on to the north of the slope of Beth-ar′a·bahᵈ it goes down to the Ar′a·bah; ¹⁹then the boundary passes on to the north of the slope of Beth-hog′lah; and the boundary ends at the northern bay of the Dead Sea,ᵉ at the south end of the Jordan: this is the southern border. ²⁰The Jordan forms its boundary on the eastern side. This is the inheritance of the tribe of Benjamin, according to its families, boundary by boundary all around.

21 Now the towns of the tribe of Benjamin according to their families were Jericho, Beth-hog′lah, Ē′mek-kē′ziz, ²²Beth-ara′·bah, Zem·a·rā′im, Beth′el, ²³Av′vim, Par′ah, Oph′rah, ²⁴Chē′phar-am′mo·nī, Oph′nī, and Gē′ba—twelve towns with their villages: ²⁵Gib′ē·on, Rā′mah, Be·er′oth, ²⁶Miz′peh, Chē·phī′rah, Mō′zah, ²⁷Rē′kem, Ir′pē·el, Tar′a·lah, ²⁸Zē′la, Ha·ē′leph, Jē′bus꟩ (that is, Jerusalem), Gib′ē·ahᵍ and Kir′i·ath-jē′a·rimʰ—fourteen towns with their villages. This is the inheritance of the tribe of Benjamin according to its families.

The Territory of Simeon

19 The second lot came out for Sim′ē·on, for the tribe of Sim′ē·on, according to its families; its inheritance lay within the inheritance of the tribe of Judah. ²It had for its inheritance Bē′er-shē′ba, Shē′ba, Mō′la·dah, ³Hā′zar-shū′al, Bā′lah, Ē′zem, ⁴El′tō·lad, Bē′thul, Hor′mah, ⁵Zik′lag, Beth-mar′ca·both, Hā′zar-sū′sah, ⁶Beth-le·bā′oth, and Sha·rū′hen—thirteen towns with their villages; ⁷Ā′in, Rim′mon, Ē′ther, and

---

ᶜ Cn: See 15.9. Heb *westward* ᵈ Gk: Heb *to the slope over against the Arabah* ᵉ Heb *Salt Sea* ꟩ Gk Syr Vg: Heb *the Jebusite* ᵍ Heb *Gibeath* ʰ Gk: Heb *Kiriath*

Ā´shan—four towns with their villages; [8]together with all the villages all around these towns as far as Bā´a·lath-bē´er, Rā´mah of the Neg´eb. This was the inheritance of the tribe of Sim´ē·on according to its families. [9]The inheritance of the tribe of Sim´ē·on formed part of the territory of Judah; because the portion of the tribe of Judah was too large for them, the tribe of Sim´ē·on obtained an inheritance within their inheritance.

The Territory of Zebulun

10 The third lot came up for the tribe of Zeb´ū·lun, according to its families. The boundary of its inheritance reached as far as Sā´rid; [11]then its boundary goes up westward, and on to Mar´a·lah, and touches Dab´be·sheth, then the wadi that is east of Jok´nē·am; [12]from Sā´rid it goes in the other direction eastward toward the sunrise to the boundary of Chis´loth-tā´bor; from there it goes to Dab´e·rath, then up to Ja·phī´a; [13]from there it passes along on the east toward the sunrise to Gath-hē´pher, to Eth-kā´zin, and going on to Rim´mon it bends toward Nē´ah; [14]then on the north the boundary makes a turn to Han··na´thon, and it ends at the valley of Iph´-tah-el; [15]and Kat´tath, Na·hal´al, Shim´ron, I´da·lah, and Bethlehem—twelve towns with their villages. [16]This is the inheritance of the tribe of Zeb´ū·lun, according to its families—these towns with their villages.

The Territory of Issachar

17 The fourth lot came out for Is´sa·char, for the tribe of Is´sa·char, according to its families. [18]Its territory included Jez´rē·el, Che·sul´loth, Shū´nem, [19]Haph·a·rā´im, Shī´-on, A·nā´ha·rath, [20]Rab´bith, Kish´i·on, Ē´bez, [21]Rē´meth, En-gan´nim, En-had´dah, Beth-paz´zez; [22]the boundary also touches Tā´bor, Sha·ha·zū´mah, and Beth-shē´mesh, and its boundary ends at the Jordan—sixteen towns with their villages. [23]This is the inheritance of the tribe of Is´sa·char, according to its families—the towns with their villages.

The Territory of Asher

24 The fifth lot came out for the tribe of Ash´er according to its families. [25]Its boundary included Hel´kath, Hā´lī, Bē´ten, Ach´shaph, [26]Al·lam´me·lech, Ā´mad, and Mī´shal; on the west it touches Car´mel and Shī·hor-lib´nath, [27]then it turns eastward, goes to Beth-dā´gon, and touches Zeb´ū·lun and the valley of Iph´tah-el northward to Beth-ē´mek and Nē·ī´el; then it continues in the north to Cā´bul, [28]Ē´bron, Rē´hob, Ham´mon, Kā´nah, as far as Great Sī´don; [29]then the boundary turns to Rā´mah, reaching to the fortified city of Tyre; then the boundary turns to Hō´sah, and it ends at the sea; Ma·hā´lab,[i] Ach´zib, [30]Um´mah, Ā´phek, and Rē´hob—twenty-two towns with their villages. [31]This is the inheritance of the tribe of Ash´er according to its families—these towns with their villages.

The Territory of Naphtali

32 The sixth lot came out for the tribe of Naph´ta·lī, for the tribe of Naph´ta·lī, according to its families. [33]And its boundary ran from Hē´leph, from the oak in Zā·a·nan´nim, and Ad´ami-nek´eb and Jab´nē·el, as far as Lak´kum; and it ended at the Jordan; [34]then the boundary turns westward to Az´noth-tā´bor, and goes from there to Huk´kok, touching Zeb´-ū·lun at the south, and Ash´er on the west, and Judah on the east at the Jordan. [35]The fortified towns are Zid´dim, Zer, Ham´-math, Rak´kath, Chin´ne·reth, [36]Ad´-a·mah, Rā´mah, Hā´zor, [37]Kē´desh, Ed´rē·ī, En-hā´zor, [38]Ī´ron, Mig´dal-el, Hō´rem, Beth-ā´nath, and Beth-shē´mesh—nineteen towns with their villages. [39]This is the inheritance of the tribe of Naph´ta·lī according to its families—the towns with their villages.

The Territory of Dan

40 The seventh lot came out for the tribe of Dan, according to its families. [41]The territory of its inheritance included

---

[i] Cn Compare Gk: Heb *Mehebel*

Zō′rah, Esh′tā·ol, Ir-she′mesh, [42]Shāa·lab′-bin, Aī′ja·lon, Ith′lah, [43]Ē′lon, Tim′nah, Ek′ron, [44]El′tē·keh, Gib′be·thon, Bā-a·lath, [45]Jē′hud, Ben·ē-bē′rak, Gath-rim′mon, [46]Me-jar′kon, and Rak′kon at the border opposite Jop′pa. [47]When the territory of the Dan′ites was lost to them, the Dan′ites went up and fought against Le′shem, and after capturing it and putting it to the sword, they took possession of it and settled in it, calling Le′shem, Dan, after their ancestor Dan. [48]This is the inheritance of the tribe of Dan, according to their families—these towns with their villages.

Joshua's Inheritance

49 When they had finished distributing the several territories of the land as inheritances, the Israelites gave an inheritance among them to Joshua son of Nun. [50]By command of the LORD they gave him the town that he asked for, Tim′nath-se′rah in the hill country of Ē′phra·im; he rebuilt the town, and settled in it.

51 These are the inheritances that the priest El·e·ā′zar and Joshua son of Nun and the heads of the families of the tribes of the Israelites distributed by lot at Shī′-lōh before the LORD, at the entrance of the tent of meeting. So they finished dividing the land.

The Cities of Refuge

20 Then the LORD spoke to Joshua, saying, [2]"Say to the Israelites, 'Appoint the cities of refuge, of which I spoke to you through Moses, [3]so that anyone who kills a person without intent or by mistake may flee there; they shall be for you a refuge from the avenger of blood. [4]The slayer shall flee to one of these cities and shall stand at the entrance of the gate of the city, and explain the case to the elders of that city; then the fugitive shall be taken into the city, and given a place, and shall remain with them. [5]And if the avenger of blood is in pursuit, they shall not give up the slayer, because the neighbor was killed by mistake, there having been no enmity between them before. [6]The slayer shall remain in that city until there is a trial before the congregation, until the death of the one who is high priest at the time: then the slayer may return home, to the town in which the deed was done.' "

7 So they set apart Ke′desh in Galilee in the hill country of Naph′ta·li, and She′-chem in the hill country of Ē′phra·im, and Kir′i·ath-ar′ba (that is, He′bron) in the hill country of Judah. [8]And beyond the Jordan east of Jericho, they appointed Be′zer in the wilderness on the tableland, from the tribe of Reuben, and Rā′moth in Gil′e·ad, from the tribe of Gad, and Gō′lan in Bā′shan, from the tribe of Ma·nas′seh. [9]These were the cities designated for all the Israelites, and for the aliens residing among them, that anyone who killed a person without intent could flee there, so as not to die by the hand of the avenger of blood, until there was a trial before the congregation.

Cities Allotted to the Levites

21 Then the heads of the families of the Le′vites came to the priest El·e·ā′zar and to Joshua son of Nun and to the heads of the families of the tribes of the Israelites; [2]they said to them at Shī′lōh in the land of Cā′naan, "The LORD commanded through Moses that we be given towns to live in, along with their pasture lands for our livestock." [3]So by command of the LORD the Israelites gave to the Le′vites the following towns and pasture lands out of their inheritance.

4 The lot came out for the families of the Kō′hath·ites. So those Le′vites who were descendants of Aaron the priest received by lot thirteen towns from the tribes of Judah, Sim′e·on, and Benjamin.

5 The rest of the Kō′hath·ites received by lot ten towns from the families of the tribe of Ē′phra·im, from the tribe of Dan, and the half-tribe of Ma·nas′seh.

6 The Ger′shon·ites received by lot

thirteen towns from the families of the tribe of Is´sa·char, from the tribe of Ash´er, from the tribe of Naph´ta·lī, and from the half-tribe of Ma·nas´seh in Bā´shan.

7 The Me·rar´ītes according to their families received twelve towns from the tribe of Reuben, the tribe of Gad, and the tribe of Zeb´ū·lun.

8 These towns and their pasture lands the Israelites gave by lot to the Lē´vītes, as the LORD had commanded through Moses.

9 Out of the tribe of Judah and the tribe of Sim´e·on they gave the following towns mentioned by name, ¹⁰which went to the descendants of Aaron, one of the families of the Kō´hath·ītes who belonged to the Lē´vītes, since the lot fell to them first. ¹¹They gave them Kir´i·ath-ar´ba (Ar´ba being the father of Ā´nak), that is Hē´bron, in the hill country of Judah, along with the pasture lands around it. ¹²But the fields of the town and its villages had been given to Caleb son of Je·phūn´neh as his holding.

13 To the descendants of Aaron the priest they gave Hē´bron, the city of refuge for the slayer, with its pasture lands, Lib´nah with its pasture lands, ¹⁴Jat´tir with its pasture lands, Esh·te·mō´a with its pasture lands, ¹⁵Hŏ´lon with its pasture lands, Dē´bir with its pasture lands, ¹⁶Ā´in with its pasture lands, Jut´tah with its pasture lands, and Beth-shĕ´mesh with its pasture lands—nine towns out of these two tribes. ¹⁷Out of the tribe of Benjamin: Gib´ē·on with its pasture lands, Gē´ba with its pasture lands, ¹⁸An´a·thoth with its pasture lands, and Al´mon with its pasture lands—four towns. ¹⁹The towns of the descendants of Aaron—the priests—were thirteen in all, with their pasture lands.

20 As to the rest of the Kō´hath·ītes belonging to the Kō´hath·īte families of the Lē´vītes, the towns allotted to them were out of the tribe of Ē´phra·im. ²¹To them were given Shĕ´chem, the city of refuge for the slayer, with its pasture lands in the hill country of Ē´phra·im, Gē´zer with its pasture lands, ²²Kib´zā·im with its pasture lands, and Beth-hŏ´ron with its pasture lands—four towns. ²³Out of the tribe of Dan: El´tē·ke with its pasture lands, Gib´be·thon with its pasture lands, ²⁴Aī´ja·lon with its pasture lands, Gath-rim´mon with its pasture lands—four towns. ²⁵Out of the half-tribe of Ma·nas´seh: Tā´a·nach with its pasture lands, and Gath-rim´mon with its pasture lands—two towns. ²⁶The towns of the families of the rest of the Kō´hath·ītes were ten in all, with their pasture lands.

27 To the Ger´shon·ītes, one of the families of the Lē´vītes, were given out of the half-tribe of Ma·nas´seh, Gō´lan in Bā´shan with its pasture lands, the city of refuge for the slayer, and Be·esh·tē´rah with its pasture lands—two towns. ²⁸Out of the tribe of Is´sa·char: Kish´i·on with its pasture lands, Dab´e·rath with its pasture lands, ²⁹Jar´muth with its pasture lands, En-gan´nim with its pasture lands—four towns. ³⁰Out of the tribe of Ash´er: Mī´shal with its pasture lands, Ab´don with its pasture lands, ³¹Hel´kath with its pasture lands, and Rē´hob with its pasture lands—four towns. ³²Out of the tribe of Naph´ta·lī: Kē´desh in Galilee with its pasture lands, the city of refuge for the slayer, Ham´moth-dor with its pasture lands, and Kar´tan with its pasture lands—three towns. ³³The towns of the several families of the Ger´shon·ītes were in all thirteen, with their pasture lands.

34 To the rest of the Lē´vītes—the Me·rar´īte families—were given out of the tribe of Zeb´ū·lun: Jok´nē·am with its pasture lands, Kar´tah with its pasture lands, ³⁵Dim´nah with its pasture lands, Na·hal´al with its pasture lands—four towns. ³⁶Out of the tribe of Reuben: Bē´zer with its pasture lands, Jah´zah with its pasture lands, ³⁷Ked´e·moth with its pasture lands, and Meph´a·ath with its pasture lands—four towns. ³⁸Out of the tribe of Gad: Rā´moth in Gil´e·ad with its

"Not one of all the good promises that the LORD had made to the house of Israel had failed; all had come to pass."

Joshua 21:45

pasture lands, the city of refuge for the slayer, Mā·ha·nā´im with its pasture lands, ³⁹Hesh´bon with its pasture lands, Jā´zer with its pasture lands—four towns in all. ⁴⁰As for the towns of the several Me·rar´īte families, that is, the remainder of the families of the Lē´vītes, those allotted to them were twelve in all.

41 The towns of the Lē´vītes within the holdings of the Israelites were in all forty-eight towns with their pasture lands. ⁴²Each of these towns had its pasture lands around it; so it was with all these towns.

43 Thus the LORD gave to Israel all the land that he swore to their ancestors that he would give them; and having taken possession of it, they settled there. ⁴⁴And the LORD gave them rest on every side just as he had sworn to their ancestors; not one of all their enemies had withstood them, for the LORD had given all their enemies into their hands. ⁴⁵Not one of all the good promises that the LORD had made to the house of Israel had failed; all came to pass.

The Eastern Tribes Return to Their Territory

22 Then Joshua summoned the Reū´ben·ītes, the Gad´ītes, and the half-tribe of Ma·nas´seh, ²and said to them, "You have observed all that Moses the servant of the LORD commanded you, and have obeyed me in all that I have commanded you; ³you have not forsaken your kindred these many days, down to this day, but have been careful to keep the charge of the LORD your God. ⁴And now the LORD your God has given rest to your kindred, as he promised them; therefore turn and go to your tents in the land where your possession lies, which Moses the servant of the LORD gave you on the other side

of the Jordan. ⁵Take good care to observe the commandment and instruction that Moses the servant of the LORD commanded you, to love the LORD your God, to walk in all his ways, to keep his commandments, and to hold fast to him, and to serve him with all your heart and with all your soul." ⁶So Joshua blessed them and sent them away, and they went to their tents.

7 Now to the one half of the tribe of Ma·nas´seh Moses had given a possession in Bā´shan; but to the other half Joshua had given a possession beside their fellow Israelites in the land west of the Jordan. And when Joshua sent them away to their tents and blessed them, ⁸he said to them, "Go back to your tents with much wealth, and with very much livestock, with silver, gold, bronze, and iron, and with a great quantity of clothing; divide the spoil of your enemies with your kindred." ⁹So the Reū´ben·ītes and the Gad´ītes and the half-tribe of Ma·nas´seh returned home, parting from the Israelites at Shī´lōh, which is in the land of Cā´naan, to go to the land of Gil´e·ad, their own land of which they had taken possession by command of the LORD through Moses.

A Memorial Altar East of the Jordan

10 When they came to the region^j near the Jordan that lies in the land of Cā´naan, the Reū´ben·ītes and the Gad´ītes and the half-tribe of Ma·nas´seh built there an altar by the Jordan, an altar of great size. ¹¹The Israelites heard that the Reū´ben·ītes and the Gad´ītes and the half-tribe of Ma·nas´seh had built an altar at the frontier of the land of Cā´naan, in the region^k near the Jordan, on the side that belongs to the Israelites. ¹²And when the people of Israel heard of it, the whole assembly of the Israelites gathered at Shī´lōh, to make war against them.

13 Then the Israelites sent the priest

^j Or *to Geliloth* ^k Or *at Geliloth*

Phin′e·has son of El·ē·ā′zar to the Reū-
ben·ītes and the Gad′ītes and the half-
tribe of Ma·nas′seh, in the land of
Gil′e·ad, [14]and with him ten chiefs, one
from each of the tribal families of Israel,
every one of them the head of a family
among the clans of Israel. [15]They came to
the Reū·ben·ītes, the Gad′ītes, and the
half-tribe of Ma·nas′seh, in the land of
Gil′e·ad, and they said to them, [16]"Thus
says the whole congregation of the LORD,
'What is this treachery that you have
committed against the God of Israel in
turning away today from following the
LORD, by building yourselves an altar
today in rebellion against the LORD?
[17]Have we not had enough of the sin at
Pē′or from which even yet we have not
cleansed ourselves, and for which a
plague came upon the congregation of
the LORD, [18]that you must turn away
today from following the LORD! If you
rebel against the LORD today, he will be
angry with the whole congregation of
Israel tomorrow. [19]But now, if your land is
unclean, cross over into the LORD's land
where the LORD's tabernacle now stands,
and take for yourselves a possession
among us; only do not rebel against the
LORD, or rebel against us[l] by building
yourselves an altar other than the altar of
the LORD our God. [20]Did not Ā′chan son
of Zē′rah break faith in the matter of the
devoted things, and wrath fell upon all
the congregation of Israel? And he did not
perish alone for his iniquity!' "

21 Then the Reū·ben·ītes, the Gad′ītes,
and the half-tribe of Ma·nas′seh said in
answer to the heads of the families of
Israel, [22]"The LORD, God of gods! The
LORD, God of gods! He knows; and let
Israel itself know! If it was in rebellion or
in breach of faith toward the LORD, do
not spare us today [23]for building an altar
to turn away from following the LORD; or
if we did so to offer burnt offerings or
grain offerings or offerings of well-being
on it, may the LORD himself take vengeance. [24]No! We did it from fear that in

When the Israelites
camped in the wilder-
ness, they were called a
congregation. Later, the
word "congregation" meant any
gathering of the people, especially
if they came together to worship
God or for judgment. Today we call
people who meet together as a
church a congregation. Can you
think of some reasons why it is
important to gather together with
others to worship God?

time to come your children might say to
our children, 'What have you to do with
the LORD, the God of Israel? [25]For the
LORD has made the Jordan a boundary
between us and you, you Reū·ben·ītes
and Gad′ītes; you have no portion in the
LORD.' So your children might make our
children cease to worship the LORD.
[26]Therefore we said, 'Let us now build an
altar, not for burnt offering, nor for sacrifice, [27]but to be a witness between us
and you, and between the generations
after us, that we do perform the service
of the LORD in his presence with our
burnt offerings and sacrifices and offerings of well-being; so that your children
may never say to our children in time to
come, "You have no portion in the
LORD." ' [28]And we thought, If this should
be said to us or to our descendants in
time to come, we could say, 'Look at this
copy of the altar of the LORD, which our
ancestors made, not for burnt offerings,
nor for sacrifice, but to be a witness
between us and you.' [29]Far be it from us
that we should rebel against the LORD,
and turn away this day from following
the LORD by building an altar for burnt
offering, grain offering, or sacrifice, other
than the altar of the LORD our God that
stands before his tabernacle!"

30 When the priest Phin′e·has and
the chiefs of the congregation, the heads

---

[l] Or *make rebels of us*

of the families of Israel who were with him, heard the words that the Reū́ben·ītes and the Gad́ītes and the Ma·naśsītes spoke, they were satisfied. ³¹The priest Phin´e·has son of El·ē·ā́zar said to the Reū́ben·ītes and the Gad́ītes and the Ma·naśsītes, "Today we know that the LORD is among us, because you have not committed this treachery against the LORD; now you have saved the Israelites from the hand of the LORD."

32 Then the priest Phin´e·has son of El·ē·ā́zar and the chiefs returned from the Reū́ben·ītes and the Gad́ītes in the land of Gil´e·ad to the land of Cā́naan, to the Israelites, and brought back word to them. ³³The report pleased the Israelites; and the Israelites blessed God and spoke no more of making war against them, to destroy the land where the Reū́ben·ītes and the Gad́ītes were settled. ³⁴The Reū́ben·ītes and the Gad́ītes called the altar Witness;ᵐ "For," said they, "it is a witness between us that the LORD is God."

Joshua Exhorts the People

23 A long time afterward, when the LORD had given rest to Israel from all their enemies all around, and Joshua was old and well advanced in years, ²Joshua summoned all Israel, their elders and heads, their judges and officers, and said to them, "I am now old and well advanced in years; ³and you have seen all that the LORD your God has done to all these nations for your sake, for it is the LORD your God who has fought for you. ⁴I have allotted to you as an inheritance for your tribes those nations that remain, along with all the nations that I have already cut off, from the Jordan to the Great Sea in the west. ⁵The LORD your God will push them back before you, and drive them out of your sight; and you shall possess their land, as the LORD your God promised you. ⁶Therefore be very steadfast to observe and do all that is written in the book of the law of Moses, turning aside from it neither to the right nor to the left, ⁷so that you may not be mixed with these nations left here among you, or make mention of the names of their gods, or swear by them, or serve them, or bow yourselves down to them, ⁸but hold fast to the LORD your God, as you have done to this day. ⁹For the LORD has driven out before you great and strong nations; and as for you, no one has been able to withstand you to this day. ¹⁰One of you puts to flight a thousand, since it is the LORD your God who fights for you, as he promised you. ¹¹Be very careful, therefore, to love the LORD your God. ¹²For if you turn back, and join the survivors of these nations left here among you, and intermarry with them, so that you marry their women and they yours, ¹³know assuredly that the LORD your God will not continue to drive out these nations before you; but they shall be a snare and a trap for you, a scourge on your sides, and thorns in your eyes, until you perish from this good land that the LORD your God has given you.

14 "And now I am about to go the way of all the earth, and you know in your hearts and souls, all of you, that not one thing has failed of all the good things that the LORD your God promised concerning you; all have come to pass for you, not one of them has failed. ¹⁵But just as all the good things that the LORD your God promised concerning you have been fulfilled for you, so the LORD will bring upon you all the bad things, until he has destroyed you from this good land that the LORD your God has given you. ¹⁶If you transgress the covenant of the LORD your God, which he enjoined on you, and go and serve other gods and bow down to them, then the anger of the LORD will be kindled against you, and you shall perish quickly from the good land that he has given to you."

ᵐ Cn Compare Syr: Heb lacks *Witness*

The Tribes Renew the Covenant

24 Then Joshua gathered all the tribes of Israel to Shē´chem, and summoned the elders, the heads, the judges, and the officers of Israel; and they presented themselves before God. [2]And Joshua said to all the people, "Thus says the LORD, the God of Israel: Long ago your ancestors—Tē´rah and his sons Abraham and Nā´hor—lived beyond the Euphrates and served other gods. [3]Then I took your father Abraham from beyond the River and led him through all the land of Cā´naan and made his offspring many. I gave him Isaac; [4]and to Isaac I gave Jacob and Esau. I gave Esau the hill country of Sē´ir to possess, but Jacob and his children went down to Egypt. [5]Then I sent Moses and Aaron, and I plagued Egypt with what I did in its midst; and afterwards I brought you out. [6]When I brought your ancestors out of Egypt, you came to the sea; and the Egyptians pursued your ancestors with chariots and horsemen to the Red Sea.[n] [7]When they cried out to the LORD, he put darkness between you and the Egyptians, and made the sea come upon them and cover them; and your eyes saw what I did to Egypt. Afterwards you lived in the wilderness a long time. [8]Then I brought you to the land of the Am´o-rītes, who lived on the other side of the Jordan; they fought with you, and I handed them over to you, and you took possession of their land, and I destroyed them before you. [9]Then King Bā´lak son of Zip´por of Mō´ab, set out to fight against Israel. He sent and invited Bā´laam son of Bē´or to curse you, [10]but I would not listen to Bā´laam; therefore he blessed you; so I rescued you out of his hand. [11]When you went over the Jordan and came to Jericho, the citizens of Jericho fought against you, and also the Am´o-rītes, the Per´iz-zītes, the Cā´naan-ites, the Hit´tītes, the Gir´ga-shītes, the Hī´vītes, and the Jeb´u-sītes; and I handed them over to you. [12]I sent the hor-

> "Now if you are unwilling to serve the LORD, choose this day whom you will serve ... but as for me and my household, we will serve the LORD." Joshua 24:15

net[o] ahead of you, which drove out before you the two kings of the Am´o-rītes; it was not by your sword or by your bow. [13]I gave you a land on which you had not labored, and towns that you had not built, and you live in them; you eat the fruit of vineyards and oliveyards that you did not plant.

14 "Now therefore revere the LORD, and serve him in sincerity and in faithfulness; put away the gods that your ancestors served beyond the River and in Egypt, and serve the LORD. [15]Now if you are unwilling to serve the LORD, choose this day whom you will serve, whether the gods your ancestors served in the region beyond the River or the gods of the Am´o-rītes in whose land you are living; but as for me and my household, we will serve the LORD."

16 Then the people answered, "Far be it from us that we should forsake the LORD to serve other gods; [17]for it is the LORD our God who brought us and our ancestors up from the land of Egypt, out of the house of slavery, and who did those great signs in our sight. He protected us along all the way that we went, and among all the peoples through whom we passed; [18]and the LORD drove out before us all the peoples, the Am´o-rītes who lived in the land. Therefore we also will serve the LORD, for he is our God."

19 But Joshua said to the people, "You cannot serve the LORD, for he is a holy God. He is a jealous God; he will not forgive your transgressions or your sins. [20]If you forsake the LORD and serve foreign gods, then he will turn and do you harm, and consume you, after

---

[n] Or *Sea of Reeds*   [o] Meaning of Heb uncertain

having done you good." ²¹And the people said to Joshua, "No, we will serve the LORD!" ²²Then Joshua said to the people, "You are witnesses against yourselves that you have chosen the LORD, to serve him." And they said, "We are witnesses." ²³He said, "Then put away the foreign gods that are among you, and incline your hearts to the LORD, the God of Israel." ²⁴The people said to Joshua, "The LORD our God we will serve, and him we will obey." ²⁵So Joshua made a covenant with the people that day, and made statutes and ordinances for them at Shē´chem. ²⁶Joshua wrote these words in the book of the law of God; and he took a large stone, and set it up there under the oak in the sanctuary of the LORD. ²⁷Joshua said to all the people, "See, this stone shall be a witness against us; for it has heard all the words of the LORD that he spoke to us; therefore it shall be a witness against you, if you deal falsely with your God." ²⁸So Joshua sent the people away to their inheritances.

Death of Joshua and Eleazar

29 After these things Joshua son of Nun, the servant of the LORD, died, being one hundred ten years old. ³⁰They buried him in his own inheritance at Tim´nath-sē´rah, which is in the hill country of Ē´phra·im, north of Mount Gā´ash.

31 Israel served the LORD all the days of Joshua, and all the days of the elders who outlived Joshua and had known all the work that the LORD did for Israel.

32 The bones of Joseph, which the Israelites had brought up from Egypt, were buried at Shē´chem, in the portion of ground that Jacob had bought from the children of Hā´mor, the father of Shē´-chem, for one hundred pieces of money;ᵖ it became an inheritance of the descendants of Joseph.

33 El·ē·ā´zar son of Aaron died; and they buried him at Gib´ē·ah, the town of his son Phin´e·has, which had been given him in the hill country of Ē´phra·im.

ᵖ Heb *one hundred qesitah*

Judges

After Joshua died, the Israelites did not have one strong leader to keep them together. Instead, they followed several different leaders called "judges." The judges were people God had chosen to help lead the people of Israel. The judges were similar to military leaders. Sometimes they led the people in battles with the Canaanites, who had been living in the land before the Israelites moved there.

The book of Judges was written around the sixth century BC. The book tells of the Israelites' struggle to stay faithful to God. Often, the people were sinful, doing what they wanted to do instead of what God wanted them to do. The people began to worship the gods of the Canaanites (called Baals and Asherahs), and began to live in ways that were wrong. Over and over again "the Israelites did what was evil in the sight of the LORD" (Judges 2:11). Through all of this, God remained faithful to the the Israelites and forgave them many times. But even though God was faithful, the people continued to sin. The book of Judges finishes with these words, "In those days there was no king in Israel; all the people did what was right in their own eyes" (Judges 21:25).

Judges 4:4–5

Israel's Failure to Complete the Conquest of Canaan

1 After the death of Joshua, the Israelites inquired of the LORD, "Who shall go up first for us against the Cā´naan·ītes, to fight against them?" ²The LORD said, "Judah shall go up. I hereby give the land into his hand." ³Judah said to his brother Sim´e·on, "Come up with me into the territory allotted to me, that we may fight against the Cā´naan·ītes; then I too will go with you into the territory allotted to you." So Sim´e·on went with him. ⁴Then Judah went up and the LORD gave the Cā´naan·ītes and the Per´iz·zītes into their hand; and they defeated ten thousand of them at Bē´zek. ⁵They came upon A·dō´ni-bē´zek at Bē´zek, and fought against him, and defeated the Cā´naan·ītes and the Per´iz·zītes. ⁶A·dō´ni-bē´zek fled; but they pursued him, and caught him, and cut off his thumbs and big toes. ⁷A·dō´ni-bē´zek said, "Seventy kings with their thumbs and big toes cut off used to pick up scraps under my table; as I have done, so God has paid me back." They brought him to Jerusalem, and he died there.

8 Then the people of Judah fought against Jerusalem and took it. They put it to the sword and set the city on fire. ⁹Afterward the people of Judah went down to fight against the Cā´naan·ītes who lived in the hill country, in the Neg´eb, and in the lowland. ¹⁰Judah went against the Cā´naan·ītes who lived in Hē´bron (the name of Hē´bron was formerly Kir´i·ath-ar´ba); and they defeated Shē´shaī and A·hī´man and Tal´maī.

11 From there they went against the inhabitants of Dē´bir (the name of Dē´bir was formerly Kir´i·ath-sē´pher). ¹²Then Caleb said, "Whoever attacks Kir´i·ath-sē´-pher and takes it, I will give him my daughter Ach´sah as wife." ¹³And Oth´ni·el son of Kē´naz, Caleb's younger brother, took it; and he gave him his daughter Ach´sah as wife. ¹⁴When she came to him, she urged him to ask her father for a field. As she dismounted from her donkey, Caleb said to her, "What do you wish?" ¹⁵She said to him, "Give me a present; since you have set me in the land of the Neg´eb, give me also Gul´loth-māy´im."ᵃ So Caleb gave her Upper Gul´loth and Lower Gul´loth.

A palm tree is a tall, thin tree with a group of branches at the top. Palm trees grew in most parts of Bible lands. People ate the palm's fruit, called dates, and they wove mats from its leaves. They often used the palm tree as a symbol for righteousness. There were carvings of palm trees on the walls, doors, and other parts of Solomon's Temple.

16 The descendants of Hō´babᵇ the Ken´īte, Moses' father-in-law, went up with the people of Judah from the city of palms into the wilderness of Judah, which lies in the Neg´eb near Ar´ad. Then they went and settled with the A·mal´e·kītes.ᶜ ¹⁷Judah went with his brother Sim´e·on, and they defeated the Cā´naan·ītes who inhabited Zē´phath, and devoted it to destruction. So the city was called Hor´mah. ¹⁸Judah took Gā´za with its territory, Ash´ke·lon with its territory, and Ek´ron with its territory. ¹⁹The LORD was with Judah, and he took possession of the hill country, but could not drive out the inhabitants of the plain, because they had chariots of iron. ²⁰Hē´bron was given to Caleb, as Moses had said; and he drove out from it the three sons of Ā´nak. ²¹But the Ben´-ja·min·ītes did not drive out the Jeb´u·sītes who lived in Jerusalem; so the Jeb´u·sītes have lived in Jerusalem among the Ben´ja·min·ītes to this day.

ᵃ That is *Basins of Water*   ᵇ Gk: Heb lacks *Hobab*
ᶜ See 1 Sam 15.6: Heb *people*

Gaza was an important city because people traveled through it to buy and trade things. Gaza was one the five main cities of the Philistines, and its people fought against the Israelites. Did you know that the city of Gaza still exists today? Look at a map and see if you can find it! (Hint: Gaza is by the Mediterranean Sea, close to Egypt and Israel.)

22 The house of Joseph also went up against Beth´el; and the LORD was with them. ²³The house of Joseph sent out spies to Beth´el (the name of the city was formerly Luz). ²⁴When the spies saw a man coming out of the city, they said to him, "Show us the way into the city, and we will deal kindly with you." ²⁵So he showed them the way into the city; and they put the city to the sword, but they let the man and all his family go. ²⁶So the man went to the land of the Hit´tites and built a city, and named it Luz; that is its name to this day.

27 Ma·nas´seh did not drive out the inhabitants of Beth-she´an and its villages, or Ta´a·nach and its villages, or the inhabitants of Dor and its villages, or the inhabitants of Ib´le·am and its villages, or the inhabitants of Me·gid´do and its villages; but the Ca´naan·ites continued to live in that land. ²⁸When Israel grew strong, they put the Ca´naan·ites to forced labor, but did not in fact drive them out.

29 And E´phra·im did not drive out the Ca´naan·ites who lived in Ge´zer; but the Ca´naan·ites lived among them in Ge´zer.

30 Zeb´u·lun did not drive out the inhabitants of Kit´ron, or the inhabitants of Na·hal´ol; but the Ca´naan·ites lived among them, and became subject to forced labor.

31 Ash´er did not drive out the inhabitants of Ac´co, or the inhabitants of Si´don, or of Ah´lab, or of Ach´zib, or of Hel´bah, or of A´phik, or of Re´hob; ³²but the Ash´er·ites lived among the Ca´naan·ites, the inhabitants of the land; for they did not drive them out.

33 Naph´ta·li did not drive out the inhabitants of Beth-she´mesh, or the inhabitants of Beth-a´nath, but lived among the Ca´naan·ites, the inhabitants of the land; nevertheless the inhabitants of Beth-she´mesh and of Beth-a´nath became subject to forced labor for them.

34 The Am´o·rites pressed the Dan´-ites back into the hill country; they did not allow them to come down to the plain. ³⁵The Am´o·rites continued to live in Har-he´res, in Ai´ja·lon, and in Sha-al´-bim, but the hand of the house of Joseph rested heavily on them, and they became subject to forced labor. ³⁶The border of the Am´o·rites ran from the ascent of Ak·rab´bim, from Se´la and upward.

Israel's Disobedience

2 Now the angel of the LORD went up from Gil´gal to Bo´chim, and said, "I brought you up from Egypt, and brought you into the land that I had promised to your ancestors. I said, 'I will never break my covenant with you. ²For your part, do not make a covenant with the inhabitants of this land; tear down their altars.' But you have not obeyed my command. See what you have done! ³So now I say, I will not drive them out before you; but they shall become adversaries[d] to you, and their gods shall be a snare to you." ⁴When the angel of the LORD spoke these words to all the Israelites, the people lifted up their voices and wept. ⁵So they named that place Bo´chim,[e] and there they sacrificed to the LORD.

Death of Joshua

6 When Joshua dismissed the people, the Israelites all went to their own

[d] OL Vg Compare Gk: Heb *sides*   [e] That is *Weepers*

inheritances to take possession of the land. [7]The people worshiped the LORD all the days of Joshua, and all the days of the elders who outlived Joshua, who had seen all the great work that the LORD had done for Israel. [8]Joshua son of Nun, the servant of the LORD, died at the age of one hundred ten years. [9]So they buried him within the bounds of his inheritance in Tim′nath-hē′rēs, in the hill country of Ē′phra·im, north of Mount Gā′ash. [10]Moreover, that whole generation was gathered to their ancestors, and another generation grew up after them, who did not know the LORD or the work that he had done for Israel.

Israel's Unfaithfulness

11 Then the Israelites did what was evil in the sight of the LORD and worshiped the Bā′als; [12]and they abandoned the LORD, the God of their ancestors, who had brought them out of the land of Egypt; they followed other gods, from among the gods of the peoples who were all around them, and bowed down to them; and they provoked the LORD to anger. [13]They abandoned the LORD, and worshiped Bā′al and the As·tar′tēs. [14]So the anger of the LORD was kindled against Israel, and he gave them over to plunderers who plundered them, and he sold them into the power of their enemies all around, so that they could no longer withstand their enemies. [15]Whenever they marched out, the hand of the LORD was against them to bring misfortune, as the LORD had warned them and sworn to them; and they were in great distress.

16 Then the LORD raised up judges, who delivered them out of the power of those who plundered them. [17]Yet they did not listen even to their judges; for they lusted after other gods and bowed down to them. They soon turned aside from the way in which their ancestors had walked, who had obeyed the commandments of the LORD; they did not follow their example. [18]Whenever the LORD raised up judges

Between the time of Joshua and David, the judges of Israel were military leaders who saved the people from their enemies. After the people had a king, he would often act as judge or choose others to act as judge. "Judge" is also a title for God, who is the Judge of all the earth.

for them, the LORD was with the judge, and he delivered them from the hand of their enemies all the days of the judge; for the LORD would be moved to pity by their groaning because of those who persecuted and oppressed them. [19]But whenever the judge died, they would relapse and behave worse than their ancestors, following other gods, worshiping them and bowing down to them. They would not drop any of their practices or their stubborn ways. [20]So the anger of the LORD was kindled against Israel; and he said, "Because this people have transgressed my covenant that I commanded their ancestors, and have not obeyed my voice, [21]I will no longer drive out before them any of the nations that Joshua left when he died." [22]In order to test Israel, whether or not they would take care to walk in the way of the LORD as their ancestors did, [23]the LORD had left those nations, not driving them out at once, and had not handed them over to Joshua.

Nations Remaining in the Land

3 Now these are the nations that the LORD left to test all those in Israel who had no experience of any war in Cā′naan [2](it was only that successive generations of Israelites might know war, to teach those who had no experience of it before): [3]the five lords of the Phi·lis′tines, and all the Cā′naan·ites, and the Sī·dō′ni·ans, and the Hī′vītes who lived on Mount Lebanon, from Mount Bā′al-her′mon as far as Lē′bō-hā′math. [4]They were

for the testing of Israel, to know whether Israel would obey the commandments of the LORD, which he commanded their ancestors by Moses. ⁵So the Israelites lived among the Cā´naan·ītes, the Hit´tītes, the Am´o·rītes, the Per´iz·zītes, the Hī´vītes, and the Jeb´ū·sītes; ⁶and they took their daughters as wives for themselves, and their own daughters they gave to their sons; and they worshiped their gods.

> In Canaan, the Israelites forgot God's goodness in bringing them out of Egypt and began to worship the gods of the people around them. The king of Aram ruled them for eight years until they cried out to God for help. God chose Othniel to deliver the people. Othniel was one of four judges (the other three were Gideon, Jephthah, and Samson) of whom the Scripture says, "the Spirit of Lord came upon him" (3:10).

Othniel

7 The Israelites did what was evil in the sight of the LORD, forgetting the LORD their God, and worshiping the Bā´als and the A·shē´rahs. ⁸Therefore the anger of the LORD was kindled against Israel, and he sold them into the hand of King Cū´shan-rish·a·thā´im of Ar´am Nā·ha·rā´im; and the Israelites served Cū´shan-rish·a·thā´im eight years. ⁹But when the Israelites cried out to the LORD, the LORD raised up a deliverer for the Israelites, who delivered them, Oth´ni·el son of Kē´naz, Caleb's younger brother. ¹⁰The spirit of the LORD came upon him, and he judged Israel; he went out to war, and the LORD gave King Cū´shan-rish·a·thā´im of Ar´am into his hand; and his hand prevailed over Cū´shan-rish·a·thā´im. ¹¹So the land had rest forty years. Then Oth´ni·el son of Kē´naz died.

Ehud

12 The Israelites again did what was evil in the sight of the LORD; and the LORD strengthened King Eg´lon of Mō´ab against Israel, because they had done what was evil in the sight of the LORD. ¹³In alliance with the Am´mon·ītes and the A·mal´e·kītes, he went and defeated Israel; and they took possession of the city of palms. ¹⁴So the Israelites served King Eg´lon of Mō´ab eighteen years.

15 But when the Israelites cried out to the LORD, the LORD raised up for them a deliverer, Ē´hud son of Gē´ra, the Ben´ja·min·īte, a left-handed man. The Israelites sent tribute by him to King Eg´lon of Mō´ab. ¹⁶Ē´hud made for himself a sword with two edges, a cubit in length; and he fastened it on his right thigh under his clothes. ¹⁷Then he presented the tribute to King Eg´lon of Mō´ab. Now Eg´lon was a very fat man. ¹⁸When Ē´hud had finished presenting the tribute, he sent the people who carried the tribute on their way. ¹⁹But he himself turned back at the sculptured stones near Gil´gal, and said, "I have a secret message for you, O king." So the king said,ᶠ "Silence!" and all his attendants went out from his presence. ²⁰Ē´hud came to him, while he was sitting alone in his cool roof chamber, and said, "I have a message from God for you." So he rose from his seat. ²¹Then Ē´hud reached with his left hand, took the sword from his right thigh, and thrust it into Eg´lon'sᵍ belly; ²²the hilt also went in after the blade, and the fat closed over the blade, for he did not draw the sword out of his belly; and the dirt came out.ʰ ²³Then Ē´hud went out into the vestibule,ⁱ and closed the doors of the roof chamber on him, and locked them.

24 After he had gone, the servants came. When they saw that the doors of the roof chamber were locked, they thought, "He must be relieving himselfʲ in the cool chamber." ²⁵So they waited until they were embarrassed. When he still did not open

---

ᶠ Heb *he said*   ᵍ Heb *his*   ʰ With Tg Vg: Meaning of Heb uncertain   ⁱ Meaning of Heb uncertain   ʲ Heb *covering his feet* the doors of the roof chamber, they took the key and opened them. There was their lord lying dead on the floor.

26 Ē′hud escaped while they delayed, and passed beyond the sculptured stones, and escaped to Sē·ī′rah. [27]When he arrived, he sounded the trumpet in the hill country of Ē′phra·im; and the Israelites went down with him from the hill country, having him at their head. [28]He said to them, "Follow after me; for the LORD has given your enemies the Mō′ab·ītes into your hand." So they went down after him, and seized the fords of the Jordan against the Mō′ab·ītes, and allowed no one to cross over. [29]At that time they killed about ten thousand of the Mō′ab·ītes, all strong, able-bodied men; no one escaped. [30]So Mō′ab was subdued that day under the hand of Israel. And the land had rest eighty years.

Shamgar

31 After him came Sham′gar son of Ā′nath, who killed six hundred of the Phi·lis′tines with an oxgoad. He too delivered Israel.

An oxgoad was a pointed stick used to guide oxen.

Deborah and Barak

4 The Israelites again did what was evil in the sight of the LORD, after Ē′hud died. [2]So the LORD sold them into the hand of King Jā′bin of Cā′naan, who reigned in Hā′zor; the commander of his army was Sis′e·ra, who lived in Ha·rō′sheth-ha-goi′im. [3]Then the Israelites cried out to the LORD for help; for he had nine hundred chariots of iron, and had oppressed the Israelites cruelly twenty years.

4 At that time Deb′or·ah, a prophetess, wife of Lap′pi·doth, was judging Israel. [5]She used to sit under the palm of Deb′or·ah between Rā′mah and Beth′el in the hill country of Ē′phra·im; and the

Deborah was one of the early judges of ancient Israel. She was a wise leader and a great woman! Deborah called the tribes of Israel to fight against the Canaanites, and the Israelites grew stronger. Read about what she did in the poem called "The Song of Deborah" (Judges 5). Can you think of someone you know who obeys God and tries to live out his or her faith? Write that person a note, saying thanks for the qualities you admire. Mail or e-mail the note so that person can know what a difference he or she has made in your life!

Israelites came up to her for judgment. [6]She sent and summoned Bar′ak son of A·bin′ō·am from Kē′desh in Naph′ta·lī, and said to him, "The LORD, the God of Israel, commands you, 'Go, take position at Mount Tā′bor, bringing ten thousand from the tribe of Naph′ta·lī and the tribe of Zeb′ū·lun. [7]I will draw out Sis′e·ra, the general of Jā′bin's army, to meet you by the Wadi Kī′shon with his chariots and his troops; and I will give him into your hand.'" [8]Bar′ak said to her, "If you will go with me, I will go; but if you will not go with me, I will not go." [9]And she said, "I will surely go with you; nevertheless, the road on which you are going will not lead to your glory, for the LORD will sell Sis′e·ra into the hand of a woman." Then Deb′or·ah got

Iron is very strong metal. When the Israelites came to Canaan, the Canaanites and Philistines were using iron to make chariots and weapons. "Iron" is used in the Bible as a symbol for hardness, strength, and harshness.

Along with Deborah, Barak led the Israelite army in victory against the Canaanites. Look in Hebrews 11 to see Barak listed as a person of great faith.

up and went with Barʹak to Keʹdesh. ¹⁰Barʹak summoned Zebʹu·lun and Naphʹta·li to Keʹdesh; and ten thousand warriors went up behind him; and Debʹor·ah went up with him.

11 Now Heʹber the Kenʹite had separated from the other Kenʹites,ᵏ that is, the descendants of Hoʹbab the father-in-law of Moses, and had encamped as far away as Eʹlon-be·zaʹa·nanʹnim, which is near Keʹdesh.

12 When Sisʹe·ra was told that Barʹak son of A·binʹo·am had gone up to Mount Taʹbor, ¹³Sisʹe·ra called out all his chariots, nine hundred chariots of iron, and all the troops who were with him, from Ha·roʹsheth-ha-goiʹim to the Wadi Kiʹshon. ¹⁴Then Debʹor·ah said to Barʹak, "Up! For this is the day on which the LORD has given Sisʹe·ra into your hand. The LORD is indeed going out before you." So Barʹak went down from Mount Taʹbor with ten thousand warriors following him. ¹⁵And the LORD threw Sisʹe·ra and all his chariots and all his army into a panicˡ before Barʹak; Sisʹe·ra got down from his chariot and fled away on foot, ¹⁶while Barʹak pursued the chariots and the army to Ha·roʹsheth-ha-goiʹim. All the army of Sisʹe·ra fell by the sword; no one was left.

17 Now Sisʹe·ra had fled away on foot to the tent of Jaʹel wife of Heʹber the Kenʹite; for there was peace between King Jaʹbin of Haʹzor and the clan of Heʹber the Kenʹite. ¹⁸Jaʹel came out to meet Sisʹe·ra, and said to him, "Turn aside, my lord, turn aside to me; have no fear." So he turned aside to her into the tent, and

she covered him with a rug. ¹⁹Then he said to her, "Please give me a little water to drink; for I am thirsty." So she opened a skin of milk and gave him a drink and covered him. ²⁰He said to her, "Stand at the entrance of the tent, and if anybody comes and asks you, 'Is anyone here?' say, 'No.' " ²¹But Jaʹel wife of Heʹber took a tent peg, and took a hammer in her hand, and went softly to him and drove the peg into his temple, until it went down into the ground—he was lying fast asleep from weariness—and he died. ²²Then, as Barʹak came in pursuit of Sisʹe·ra, Jaʹel went out to meet him, and said to him, "Come, and I will show you the man whom you are seeking." So he went into her tent; and there was Sisʹe·ra lying dead, with the tent peg in his temple.

23 So on that day God subdued King Jaʹbin of Caʹnaan before the Israelites. ²⁴Then the hand of the Israelites bore harder and harder on King Jaʹbin of Caʹnaan, until they destroyed King Jaʹbin of Caʹnaan.

After losing a battle against the Israelites, Sisera, the Canaanite commander, ran to the tent of Heber. Heber was probably a metal smith who did not take sides in a battle but gave weapons to both sides. Sisera thought he would be safe in Heber's tent. But Jael, Heber's wife, sided with the Israelites. She gave Sisera some milk to drink, let him fall asleep, and then drove a tent peg through his head.

The Song of Deborah

5 Then Debʹor·ah and Barʹak son of A·binʹo·am sang on that day, saying:
² "When locks are long in Israel,

ᵏ Heb from the Kain   ˡ Heb adds to the sword; compare verse 16

> "Hear, O kings; give ear, O princes; to the LORD I will sing, I will make melody to the LORD, the God of Israel."
>
> Judges 5:3

when the people offer themselves
willingly—
bless[m] the LORD!

3 "Hear, O kings; give ear, O princes;
to the LORD I will sing,
I will make melody to the LORD,
the God of Israel.

4 "LORD, when you went out from Sēʹir,
when you marched from the
region of Ēʹdom,
the earth trembled,
and the heavens poured,
the clouds indeed poured water.
5 The mountains quaked before the
LORD, the One of Sinai,
before the LORD, the God of Israel.

6 "In the days of Shamʹgar son of
Āʹnath,
in the days of Jāʹel, caravans ceased
and travelers kept to the byways.
7 The peasantry prospered in Israel,
they grew fat on plunder,
because you arose, Debʹor·ah,
arose as a mother in Israel.
8 When new gods were chosen,
then war was in the gates.

A caravan is a group of people who travel together. People traveled together through the desert because they felt safer in larger numbers. Caravan routes crisscrossed the ancient world. The people used donkeys and camels to transport goods, and they sometimes traveled with guards who rode on horses.

Was shield or spear to be seen
among forty thousand in Israel?
9 My heart goes out to the commanders of Israel
who offered themselves willingly
among the people.
Bless the LORD.

10 "Tell of it, you who ride on white
donkeys,
you who sit on rich carpets[n]
and you who walk by the way.
11 To the sound of musicians[n] at the
watering places,
there they repeat the triumphs of
the LORD,
the triumphs of his peasantry in
Israel.

"Then down to the gates marched
the people of the LORD.

12 "Awake, awake, Debʹor·ah!
Awake, awake, utter a song!
Arise, Barʹak, lead away your captives,
O son of A·bin´ō·am.
13 Then down marched the remnant of
the noble;
the people of the LORD marched
down for him[o] against the
mighty.
14 From Ēʹphra·im they set out[p] into
the valley,[q]
following you, Benjamin, with
your kin;
from Māʹchir marched down the
commanders,
and from Zebʹū·lun those who
bear the marshal's staff;
15 the chiefs of Isʹsa·char came with
Debʹor·ah,
and Isʹsa·char faithful to Barʹak;
into the valley they rushed out at
his heels.
Among the clans of Reuben
there were great searchings of
heart.

m Or You who offer yourselves willingly among the
people, bless   n Meaning of Heb uncertain
o Gk: Heb me   p Cn: Heb From Ephraim their root
q Gk: Heb in Amalek

16 Why did you tarry among the sheepfolds,
to hear the piping for the flocks?
Among the clans of Reuben
there were great searchings of heart.
17 Gil´e·ad stayed beyond the Jordan;
and Dan, why did he abide with
the ships?
Ash´er sat still at the coast of the sea,
settling down by his landings.
18 Zeb´u·lun is a people that scorned
death;
Naph´ta·lī too, on the heights of
the field.

19 "The kings came, they fought;
then fought the kings of Cā´naan,
at Tā´a·nach, by the waters of
Me·gid´dō;
they got no spoils of silver.
20 The stars fought from heaven,
from their courses they fought
against Sis´e·ra.
21 The torrent Kī´shon swept them away,
the onrushing torrent, the torrent
Kī´shon.
March on, my soul, with might!

22 "Then loud beat the horses' hoofs
with the galloping, galloping of
his steeds.

23 "Curse Me´roz, says the angel of the
LORD,
curse bitterly its inhabitants,
because they did not come to the
help of the LORD,
to the help of the LORD against the
mighty.
24 "Most blessed of women be Jā´el,
the wife of Hē´ber the Ken´īte,
of tent-dwelling women most
blessed.
25 He asked water and she gave him milk,
she brought him curds in a lordly
bowl.
26 She put her hand to the tent peg
and her right hand to the workmen's mallet;

> "So perish all your ene-
> mies, O LORD! But may
> your friends be like the
> sun as it rises in its
> might."   Judges 5:31

she struck Sis´e·ra a blow,
she crushed his head,
she shattered and pierced his temple.
27 He sank, he fell,
he lay still at her feet;
at her feet he sank, he fell;
where he sank, there he fell dead.

28 "Out of the window she peered,
the mother of Sis´e·ra gazed[r]
through the lattice:
'Why is his chariot so long in coming?
Why tarry the hoofbeats of his
chariots?'
29 Her wisest ladies make answer,
indeed, she answers the question
herself:
30 'Are they not finding and dividing
the spoil?—
A girl or two for every man;
spoil of dyed stuffs for Sis´e·ra,
spoil of dyed stuffs embroidered,
two pieces of dyed work embroidered for my neck as spoil?'

31 "So perish all your enemies, O LORD!
But may your friends be like the
sun as it rises in its might."

And the land had rest forty years.

The Midianite Oppression

6 The Israelites did what was evil in
the sight of the LORD, and the LORD
gave them into the hand of Mid´i·an
seven years. 2The hand of Mid´i·an prevailed over Israel; and because of
Mid´i·an the Israelites provided for
themselves hiding places in the mountains, caves and strongholds. 3For whenever the Israelites put in seed, the
Mid´i·an·ītes and the A·mal´e·kītes and

_____
r Gk Compare Tg: Heb *exclaimed*

the people of the East would come up against them. ⁴They would encamp against them and destroy the produce of the land, as far as the neighborhood of Gā´za, and leave no sustenance in Israel, and no sheep or ox or donkey. ⁵For they and their livestock would come up, and they would even bring their tents, as thick as locusts; neither they nor their camels could be counted; so they wasted the land as they came in. ⁶Thus Israel was greatly impoverished because of Mid´i·an; and the Israelites cried out to the LORD for help.

7 When the Israelites cried to the LORD on account of the Mid´i·an·ites, ⁸the LORD sent a prophet to the Israelites; and he said to them, "Thus says the LORD, the God of Israel: I led you up from Egypt, and brought you out of the house of slavery; ⁹and I delivered you from the hand of the Egyptians, and from the hand of all who oppressed you, and drove them out before you, and gave you their land; ¹⁰and I said to you, 'I am the LORD your God; you shall not pay reverence to the gods of the Am´or·ites, in whose land you live.' But you have not given heed to my voice."

The Midianites would ride into the Israelites' land to ruin and steal their animals and crops. With their food destroyed, the Israelite people were starving. When the people cried out to God, God called Gideon to deliver them. The angel of the Lord told Gideon to rescue the people from the Midianites.

The Call of Gideon

11 Now the angel of the LORD came and sat under the oak at Oph´rah, which belonged to Jō´ash the Ā·bi·ez´rīte, as his son Gideon was beating out wheat in the wine press, to hide it from the Mid´i·an·ites. ¹²The angel of the LORD appeared to him and said to him, "The LORD is with you, you mighty warrior." ¹³Gideon answered him, "But sir, if the LORD is with us, why then has all this happened to us? And where are all his wonderful deeds that our ancestors recounted to us, saying, 'Did not the LORD bring us up from Egypt?' But now the LORD has cast us off, and given us into the hand of Mid´i·an." ¹⁴Then the LORD turned to him and said, "Go in this might of yours and deliver Israel from the hand of Mid´i·an; I hereby commission you." ¹⁵He responded, "But sir, how can I deliver Israel? My clan is the weakest in Ma·nas´seh, and I am the least in my family." ¹⁶The LORD said to him, "But I will be with you, and you shall strike down the Mid´i·an·ites, every one of them." ¹⁷Then he said to him, "If now I have found favor with you, then show me a sign that it is you who speak with me. ¹⁸Do not depart from here until I come to you, and bring out my present, and set it before you." And he said, "I will stay until you return."

19 So Gideon went into his house and prepared a kid, and unleavened cakes from an ephah of flour; the meat he put in a basket, and the broth he put in a pot, and brought them to him under the oak and presented them. ²⁰The angel of God said to him, "Take the meat and the unleavened cakes, and put them on this rock, and pour out the broth." And he did so. ²¹Then the angel of the LORD reached out the tip of the staff that was in his hand, and touched the meat and the unleavened cakes; and fire sprang up from the rock and consumed the meat and the unleavened cakes; and the angel of the LORD vanished from his sight. ²²Then Gideon perceived that it was the angel of the LORD; and Gideon said, "Help me, Lord GOD! For I have seen the angel of the LORD face to face." ²³But the LORD said to him, "Peace be to you; do not fear, you shall not die." ²⁴Then Gideon built an altar there to the LORD, and called it, The LORD is peace. To this day it still stands at Oph´rah, which belongs to the Ā·bi·ez´rītes.

Gideon took down the altar that had been built to honor Baal and built in its place an altar to honor God. When the people found out, they wanted to kill Gideon, but his father said that if Baal truly had power, he could have defended himself. The people began to call Gideon Jerubbaal because he had won against Baal. What are some ways that you can honor God?

25 That night the LORD said to him, "Take your father's bull, the second bull seven years old, and pull down the altar of Bā´al that belongs to your father, and cut down the sacred pole⁵ that is beside it; ²⁶and build an altar to the LORD your God on the top of the stronghold here, in proper order; then take the second bull, and offer it as a burnt offering with the wood of the sacred pole⁵ that you shall cut down." ²⁷So Gideon took ten of his servants, and did as the LORD had told him; but because he was too afraid of his family and the townspeople to do it by day, he did it by night.

Gideon Destroys the Altar of Baal

28 When the townspeople rose early in the morning, the altar of Bā´al was broken down, and the sacred pole⁵ beside it was cut down, and the second bull was offered on the altar that had been built. ²⁹So they said to one another, "Who has done this?" After searching and inquiring, they were told, "Gideon son of Jō´ash did it." ³⁰Then the townspeople said to Jō´ash, "Bring out your son, so that he may die, for he has pulled down the altar of Bā´al and cut down the sacred pole⁵ beside it." ³¹But Jō´ash said to all who were arrayed against him, "Will you contend for Bā´al? Or will you defend his cause? Whoever contends for him shall be put to death by morning. If he is a god, let him contend for himself,

because his altar has been pulled down." ³²Therefore on that day Gideon^t was called Jer·ub·bā´al, that is to say, "Let Bā´al contend against him," because he pulled down his altar.

33 Then all the Mid´i·an·ītes and the A·mal´e·kītes and the people of the East came together, and crossing the Jordan they encamped in the Valley of Jez´rē·el. ³⁴But the spirit of the LORD took possession of Gideon; and he sounded the trumpet, and the A·bi·ez´rītes were called out to follow him. ³⁵He sent messengers throughout all Ma·nas´seh, and they too were called out to follow him. He also sent messengers to Ash´er, Zeb´ū·lun, and Naph´ta·lī, and they went up to meet them.

God called Gideon to lead the people against the Midianites, but Gideon did not have faith. He tested God twice by putting a wool fleece on the floor overnight. The first night he asked God to let the fleece be wet and to let the ground around it be dry. The second night he asked God to let the fleece be dry and to let the ground around it be wet. Read Judges 6:36–40 to see what happened.

The Sign of the Fleece

36 Then Gideon said to God, "In order to see whether you will deliver Israel by my hand, as you have said, ³⁷I am going to lay a fleece of wool on the threshing floor; if there is dew on the fleece alone, and it is dry on all the ground, then I shall know that you will deliver Israel by my hand, as you have said." ³⁸And it was so. When he rose early next morning and squeezed the fleece, he wrung enough dew from the fleece to fill a bowl with water. ³⁹Then Gideon said to God, "Do not let your

⁵ Heb Asherah   ᵗ Heb he

anger burn against me, let me speak one more time; let me, please, make trial with the fleece just once more; let it be dry only on the fleece, and on all the ground let there be dew." [40]And God did so that night. It was dry on the fleece only, and on all the ground there was dew.

Gideon raised an army of 32,000 men to fight the Midianites, but God told him that was too many men. If they won with that many soldiers, the Israelites would think they had saved themselves by their own strength. With only 300 men, the Israelites completely defeated the Midianites. (Read Judges 7:2–7 to see how God chose the men who would go as soldiers.)

Gideon Surprises and Routs the Midianites

7 Then Jer·ub·ba̅´al (that is, Gideon) and all the troops that were with him rose early and encamped beside the spring of Har´od; and the camp of Mid´i·an was north of them, below[u] the hill of Mo̅´reh, in the valley.

2 The LORD said to Gideon, "The troops with you are too many for me to give the Mid´i·an·ites into their hand. Israel would only take the credit away from me, saying, 'My own hand has delivered me.' [3]Now therefore proclaim this in the hearing of the troops, 'Whoever is fearful and trembling, let him return home.'" Thus Gideon sifted them out;[v] twenty-two thousand returned, and ten thousand remained.

4 Then the LORD said to Gideon, "The troops are still too many; take them down to the water and I will sift them out for you there. When I say, 'This one shall go with you,' he shall go with you; and when I say, 'This one shall not go with you,' he shall not go." [5]So he brought the troops down to the water; and the LORD said to Gideon, "All those who lap the water with their tongues, as a dog laps, you shall put to one side; all those who kneel down to drink, putting their hands to their mouths,[w] you shall put to the other side." [6]The number of those that lapped was three hundred; but all the rest of the troops knelt down to drink water. [7]Then the LORD said to Gideon, "With the three hundred that lapped I will deliver you, and give the Mid´i·an·ites into your hand. Let all the others go to their homes." [8]So he took the jars of the troops from their hands,[x] and their trumpets; and he sent all the rest of Israel back to their own tents, but retained the three hundred. The camp of Mid´i·an was below him in the valley.

9 That same night the LORD said to him, "Get up, attack the camp; for I have given it into your hand. [10]But if you fear to attack, go down to the camp with your servant Pu̅´rah; [11]and you shall hear what they say, and afterward your hands shall be strengthened to attack the camp." Then he went down with his servant Pu̅´rah to the outposts of the armed men that were in the camp. [12]The Mid´i·an·ites and the A·mal´e·kites and all the people of the East lay along the valley as thick as locusts; and their camels were without number, countless as the sand on the seashore. [13]When Gideon arrived, there was a man telling a dream to his comrade; and he said, "I had a dream, and in it a cake of barley bread tumbled into the camp of Mid´-i·an, and came to the tent, and struck it so that it fell; it turned upside down, and the tent collapsed." [14]And his comrade answered, "This is no other than the sword of Gideon son of Jo̅´ash, a man of Israel; into his hand God has given Mid´i·an and all the army."

15 When Gideon heard the telling of

---

[u] Heb from [v] Cn: Heb home, and depart from Mount Gilead'" [w] Heb places the words putting their hands to their mouths after the word lapped in verse 6 [x] Cn: Heb So the people took provisions in their hands

the dream and its interpretation, he worshiped; and he returned to the camp of Israel, and said, "Get up; for the LORD has given the army of Mid′i·an into your hand." ¹⁶After he divided the three hundred men into three companies, and put trumpets into the hands of all of them, and empty jars, with torches inside the jars, ¹⁷he said to them, "Look at me, and do the same; when I come to the outskirts of the camp, do as I do. ¹⁸When I blow the trumpet, I and all who are with me, then you also blow the trumpets around the whole camp, and shout, 'For the LORD and for Gideon!' "

19 So Gideon and the hundred who were with him came to the outskirts of the camp at the beginning of the middle watch, when they had just set the watch; and they blew the trumpets and smashed the jars that were in their hands. ²⁰So the three companies blew the trumpets and broke the jars, holding in their left hands the torches, and in their right hands the trumpets to blow; and they cried, "A sword for the LORD and for Gideon!" ²¹Every man stood in his place all around the camp, and all the men in camp ran; they cried out and fled. ²²When they blew the three hundred trumpets, the LORD set every man's sword against his fellow and against all the army; and the army fled as far as Beth-shit′tah toward Zer′e·rah,ʸ as far as the border of A′bel-me·hō′lah, by Tab′bath. ²³And the men of Israel were called out from Naph′ta·li and from Ash′er and from all Ma·nas′seh, and they pursued after the Mid′i·an·ites.

24 Then Gideon sent messengers throughout all the hill country of E′phra·im, saying, "Come down against the Mid′i·an·ites and seize the waters against them, as far as Beth-bar′ah, and also the Jordan." So all the men of E′phra·im were called out, and they seized the waters as far as Beth-bar′ah, and also the Jordan. ²⁵They captured the two captains of Mid′i·an, Or′eb and Zē′eb; they killed Or′eb at the rock of Or′eb, and Zē′eb they killed at the wine press of Zē′eb, as they pursued the Mid′i·an·ites. They brought the heads of Or′eb and Zē′eb to Gideon beyond the Jordan.

Gideon's Triumph and Vengeance

8 Then the E′phra·im·ites said to him, "What have you done to us, not to call us when you went to fight against the Mid′i·an·ites?" And they upbraided him violently. ²So he said to them, "What have I done now in comparison with you? Is not the gleaning of the grapes of E′phra·im better than the vintage of A·bi·e′zer? ³God has given into your hands the captains of Mid′i·an, Or′eb and Zē′eb; what have I been able to do in comparison with you?" When he said this, their anger against him subsided.

4 Then Gideon came to the Jordan and crossed over, he and the three hundred who were with him, exhausted and famished.ᶻ ⁵So he said to the people of Suc′coth, "Please give some loaves of bread to my followers, for they are exhausted, and I am pursuing Zē′bah and Zal·mun′na, the kings of Mid′i·an." ⁶But the officials of Suc′coth said, "Do you already have in your possession the hands of Zē′bah and Zal·mun′na, that we should give bread to your army?" ⁷Gideon replied, "Well then, when the LORD has given Zē′bah and Zal·mun′na into my hand, I will trample your flesh on the thorns of the wilderness and on briers." ⁸From there he went up to Pe·nū′el, and made the same request of them; and the people of Pe·nū′el answered him as the people of Suc′coth had answered. ⁹So he said to the people of Pe·nū′el, "When I come back victorious, I will break down this tower."

10 Now Zē′bah and Zal·mun′na were in Kar′kor with their army, about fifteen thousand men, all who were left of all the army of the people of the East; for

ʸ Another reading is *Zeredah*   ᶻ Gk: Heb *pursuing*

one hundred twenty thousand men bearing arms had fallen. ¹¹So Gideon went up by the caravan route east of Nō´bah and Jog´be·hah, and attacked the army; for the army was off its guard. ¹²Zē´bah and Zal·mun´na fled; and he pursued them and took the two kings of Mid´i·an, Zē´bah and Zal·mun´na, and threw all the army into a panic.

13 When Gideon son of Jō´ash returned from the battle by the ascent of Heres, ¹⁴he caught a young man, one of the people of Suc´coth, and questioned him; and he listed for him the officials and elders of Suc´coth, seventy-seven people. ¹⁵Then he came to the people of Suc´coth, and said, "Here are Zē´bah and Zal·mun´na, about whom you taunted me, saying, 'Do you already have in your possession the hands of Zē´bah and Zal·mun´na, that we should give bread to your troops who are exhausted?' " ¹⁶So he took the elders of the city and he took thorns of the wilderness and briers and with them he trampled*ᵃ* the people of Suc´coth. ¹⁷He also broke down the tower of Pe·nū´el, and killed the men of the city.

18 Then he said to Zē´bah and Zal·mun´na, "What about the men whom you killed at Tā´bor?" They answered, "As you are, so were they, every one of them; they resembled the sons of a king." ¹⁹And he replied, "They were my brothers, the sons of my mother; as the LORD lives, if you had saved them alive, I would not kill you." ²⁰So he said to Jether his firstborn, "Go kill them!" But the boy did not draw his sword, for he was afraid, because he was still a boy. ²¹Then Zē´bah and Zal·mun´na said, "You come and kill us; for as the man is, so is his strength." So Gideon proceeded to kill Zē´bah and Zal·mun´na; and he took the crescents that were on the necks of their camels.

Gideon's Idolatry

22 Then the Israelites said to Gideon, "Rule over us, you and your son and your grandson also; for you have delivered us out of the hand of Mid´i·an." ²³Gideon said to them, "I will not rule over you, and my son will not rule over you; the LORD will rule over you." ²⁴Then Gideon said to them, "Let me make a request of you; each of you give me an earring he has taken as booty." (For the enemy*ᵇ* had golden earrings, because they were Ish´ma·el·ītes.) ²⁵"We will willingly give them," they answered. So they spread a garment, and each threw into it an earring he had taken as booty. ²⁶The weight of the golden earrings that he requested was one thousand seven hundred shekels of gold (apart from the crescents and the pendants and the purple garments worn by the kings of Mid´i·an, and the collars that were on the necks of their camels). ²⁷Gideon made an ephod of it and put it in his town, in Oph´rah; and all Israel prostituted themselves to it there, and it became a snare to Gideon and to his family. ²⁸So Mid´i·an was subdued before the Israelites, and they lifted up their heads no more. So the land had rest forty years in the days of Gideon.

Death of Gideon

29 Jer·ub·bā´al son of Jō´ash went to live in his own house. ³⁰Now Gideon had seventy sons, his own offspring, for he had many wives. ³¹His concubine who was in Shē´chem also bore him a son, and he named him A·bim´e·lech. ³²Then Gideon son of Jō´ash died at a good old age, and was buried in the tomb of his father Jō´ash at Oph´rah of the Ā·bi·ez´rītes.

33 As soon as Gideon died, the Israelites relapsed and prostituted themselves with the Bā´als, making Bā´al-bē´rith their god. ³⁴The Israelites did not remember the LORD their God, who had rescued them from the hand of all their enemies on every side; ³⁵and they did not exhibit loyalty to the house of Jer·ub·bā´al

ᵃ With verse 7, Compare Gk: Heb he taught
ᵇ Heb they

(that is, Gideon) in return for all the good that he had done to Israel.

> An allegory is a story with two meanings. In the Bible there are some stories that have one clear meaning but also a hidden meaning. Judges 9:7–15 is an example of an allegory. Here, the trees try to choose a king. The olive, the fig, and the vine refuse to be king because they have no need for power—what they give to people is their reward. But the bramble (a tree not useful for people) accepts the offer to be king. The hidden meaning of this story is that Abimelech's kingship has been founded on theft and murder instead of on good faith and honor.

Abimelech Attempts to Establish a Monarchy

9 Now A·bim´e·lech son of Jer·ub·bā´al went to Shē´chem to his mother's kinsfolk and said to them and to the whole clan of his mother's family, ²"Say in the hearing of all the lords of Shē´chem, 'Which is better for you, that all seventy of the sons of Jer·ub·bā´al rule over you, or that one rule over you?' Remember also that I am your bone and your flesh." ³So his mother's kinsfolk spoke all these words on his behalf in the hearing of all the lords of Shē´chem; and their hearts inclined to follow A·bim´e·lech, for they said, "He is our brother." ⁴They gave him seventy pieces of silver out of the temple of Bā´al-bē´rith with which A·bim´e·lech hired worthless and reckless fellows, who followed him. ⁵He went to his father's house at Oph´rah, and killed his brothers the sons of Jer·ub·bā´al, seventy men, on one stone; but Jō´tham, the youngest son of Jer·ub·bā´al, survived, for he hid himself. ⁶Then all the lords of Shē´chem and

all Beth-mil´lō came together, and they went and made A·bim´e·lech king, by the oak of the pillar*c* at Shē´chem.

The Parable of the Trees

7 When it was told to Jō´tham, he went and stood on the top of Mount Ger´i·zim, and cried aloud and said to them, "Listen to me, you lords of Shē´chem, so that God may listen to you.
⁸ The trees once went out
    to anoint a king over themselves.
  So they said to the olive tree,
    'Reign over us.'
⁹ The olive tree answered them,
    'Shall I stop producing my rich oil
      by which gods and mortals are honored,
    and go to sway over the trees?'
¹⁰ Then the trees said to the fig tree,
    'You come and reign over us.'
¹¹ But the fig tree answered them,
    'Shall I stop producing my sweetness
      and my delicious fruit,
    and go to sway over the trees?'
¹² Then the trees said to the vine,
    'You come and reign over us.'
¹³ But the vine said to them,
    'Shall I stop producing my wine
      that cheers gods and mortals,
    and go to sway over the trees?'
¹⁴ So all the trees said to the bramble,
    'You come and reign over us.'

> In biblical times anointing was part of a religious ceremony showing that a person had been set apart for the service of the Lord. When a king was crowned, he was also anointed by a priest or a prophet. Read 1 Samuel 16 to learn about a young shepherd boy who was anointed to be king.

c Cn: Meaning of Heb uncertain

¹⁵ And the bramble said to the trees,
  'If in good faith you are anointing
    me king over you,
    then come and take refuge in
     my shade;
  but if not, let fire come out of the
    bramble
    and devour the cedars of
     Lebanon.'

16 "Now therefore, if you acted in good faith and honor when you made A·bim´e·lech king, and if you have dealt well with Jer·ub·ba´al and his house, and have done to him as his actions deserved— ¹⁷for my father fought for you, and risked his life, and rescued you from the hand of Mid´i·an; ¹⁸but you have risen up against my father's house this day, and have killed his sons, seventy men on one stone, and have made A·bim´e·lech, the son of his slave woman, king over the lords of Shĕ´-chem, because he is your kinsman— ¹⁹if, I say, you have acted in good faith and honor with Jer·ub·ba´al and with his house this day, then rejoice in A·bim´-e·lech, and let him also rejoice in you; ²⁰but if not, let fire come out from A·bim´e·lech, and devour the lords of Shĕ´-chem, and Beth-mil´lo; and let fire come out from the lords of Shĕ´chem, and from Beth-mil´lo, and devour A·bim´e·lech." ²¹Then Jo´tham ran away and fled, going to Bĕ´er, where he remained for fear of his brother A·bim´e·lech.

The Downfall of Abimelech

22 A·bim´e·lech ruled over Israel three years. ²³But God sent an evil spirit between A·bim´e·lech and the lords of Shĕ´chem; and the lords of Shĕ´chem dealt treacherously with A·bim´e·lech. ²⁴This happened so that the violence done to the seventy sons of Jer·ub·ba´al might be avenged[d] and their blood be laid on their brother A·bim´e·lech, who killed them, and on the lords of Shĕ´chem, who strengthened his hands to kill his brothers. ²⁵So, out of hostility to him, the lords of Shĕ´chem set ambushes on the mountain tops. They robbed all who passed by them along that way; and it was reported to A·bim´e·lech.

26 When Ga´al son of E´bed moved into Shĕ´chem with his kinsfolk, the lords of Shĕ´chem put confidence in him. ²⁷They went out into the field and gathered the grapes from their vineyards, trod them, and celebrated. Then they went into the temple of their god, ate and drank, and ridiculed A·bim´-e·lech. ²⁸Ga´al son of E´bed said, "Who is A·bim´e·lech, and who are we of Shĕ´-chem, that we should serve him? Did not the son of Jer·ub·ba´al and Zĕ´bul his officer serve the men of Ha´mor father of Shĕ´chem? Why then should we serve him? ²⁹If only this people were under my command! Then I would remove A·bim´e·lech; I would say[e] to him, 'Increase your army, and come out.' "

30 When Zĕ´bul the ruler of the city heard the words of Ga´al son of E´bed, his anger was kindled. ³¹He sent messengers to A·bim´e·lech at A·ru´mah,[f] saying, "Look, Ga´al son of E´bed and his kinsfolk have come to Shĕ´chem, and they are stirring up[g] the city against you. ³²Now therefore, go by night, you and the troops that are with you, and lie in wait in the fields. ³³Then early in the morning, as soon as the sun rises, get up and rush on the city; and when he and the troops that are with him come out against you, you may deal with them as best you can."

34 So A·bim´e·lech and all the troops with him got up by night and lay in wait against Shĕ´chem in four companies. ³⁵When Ga´al son of E´bed went out and stood in the entrance of the gate of the city, A·bim´e·lech and the troops with him rose from the ambush. ³⁶And when Ga´al saw them, he said to Zĕ´bul, "Look, people are coming down from the mountain tops!" And Zĕ´bul said to him, "The shadows on the mountains look

---

[d] Heb *might come*   [e] Gk: Heb *and he said*   [f] Cn
See 9.41. Heb *Tormah*   [g] Cn: Heb *are besieging*

like people to you." [37]Gā′al spoke again and said, "Look, people are coming down from Tab·bū·re′rez, and one company is coming from the direction of E′lon-me·on′e·nim."[h] [38]Then Zē′bul said to him, "Where is your boast[i] now, you who said, 'Who is A·bim′e·lech, that we should serve him?' Are not these the troops you made light of? Go out now and fight with them." [39]So Gā′al went out at the head of the lords of Shē′chem, and fought with A·bim′e·lech. [40]A·bim′-e·lech chased him, and he fled before him. Many fell wounded, up to the entrance of the gate. [41]So A·bim′e·lech resided at A·rū′mah; and Zē′bul drove out Gā′al and his kinsfolk, so that they could not live on at Shē′chem.

42 On the following day the people went out into the fields. When A·bim′-e·lech was told, [43]he took his troops and divided them into three companies, and lay in wait in the fields. When he looked and saw the people coming out of the city, he rose against them and killed them. [44]A·bim′e·lech and the company that was[j] with him rushed forward and stood at the entrance of the gate of the city, while the two companies rushed on all who were in the fields and killed them. [45]A·bim′e·lech fought against the city all that day; he took the city, and killed the people that were in it; and he razed the city and sowed it with salt.

46 When all the lords of the Tower of Shē′chem heard of it, they entered the stronghold of the temple of El-bē′rith. [47]A·bim′e·lech was told that all the lords of the Tower of Shē′chem were gathered together. [48]So A·bim′e·lech went up to Mount Zal′mon, he and all the troops that were with him. A·bim′e·lech took an ax in his hand, cut down a bundle of brushwood, and took it up and laid it on his shoulder. Then he said to the troops with him, "What you have seen me do, do quickly, as I have done." [49]So every one of the troops cut down a bundle and following A·bim′e·lech put it against the stronghold, and they set the stronghold on fire over them, so that all the people of the Tower of Shē′chem also died, about a thousand men and women.

50 Then A·bim′e·lech went to Thē′-bez, and encamped against Thē′bez, and took it. [51]But there was a strong tower within the city, and all the men and women and all the lords of the city fled to it and shut themselves in; and they went to the roof of the tower. [52]A·bim′-e·lech came to the tower, and fought against it, and came near to the entrance of the tower to burn it with fire. [53]But a certain woman threw an upper millstone on A·bim′e·lech's head, and crushed his skull. [54]Immediately he called to the young man who carried his armor and said to him, "Draw your sword and kill me, so people will not say about me, 'A woman killed him.' " So the young man thrust him through, and he died. [55]When the Israelites saw that A·bim′-e·lech was dead, they all went home. [56]Thus God repaid A·bim′e·lech for the crime he committed against his father in killing his seventy brothers; [57]and God also made all the wickedness of the people of Shē′chem fall back on their heads, and on them came the curse of Jō′tham son of Jer·ub·bā′al.

Have you ever crushed something between two rocks? That's how people long ago made flour to cook with! They used millstones—hard, rough stones used to grind grain. People would hold one stone in their hand and push it back and forth against another, crushing the grain between them. Because they were heavy and strong, millstones could also be used as weapons.

[h] That is *Diviners' Oak*   [i] Heb *mouth*   [j] Vg and some Gk Mss: Heb *companies that were*

Tola and Jair

10 After A·bim´e·lech, Tō´la son of Pū´ah son of Dō´dō, a man of Is´sa·char, who lived at Shā´mir in the hill country of Ē´phra·im, rose to deliver Israel. ²He judged Israel twenty-three years. Then he died, and was buried at Shā´mir.

3 After him came Jā´ir the Gil´e·ad·īte, who judged Israel twenty-two years. ⁴He had thirty sons who rode on thirty donkeys; and they had thirty towns, which are in the land of Gil´e·ad, and are called Hav´voth-jā´ir to this day. ⁵Jā´ir died, and was buried in Kā´mon.

Oppression by the Ammonites

6 The Israelites again did what was evil in the sight of the LORD, worshiping the Bā´als and the As·tar´tēs, the gods of Ar´am, the gods of Sī´don, the gods of Mō´ab, the gods of the Am´mon·ītes, and the gods of the Phi·lis´tines. Thus they abandoned the LORD, and did not worship him. ⁷So the anger of the LORD was kindled against Israel, and he sold them into the hand of the Phi·lis´tines and into the hand of the Am´mon·ītes, ⁸and they crushed and oppressed the Israelites that year. For eighteen years they oppressed all the Israelites that were beyond the Jordan in the land of the Am´o·rītes, which is in Gil´e·ad. ⁹The Am´mon·ītes also crossed the Jordan to fight against Judah and against Benjamin and against the house of Ē´phra·im; so that Israel was greatly distressed.

10 So the Israelites cried to the LORD, saying, "We have sinned against you, because we have abandoned our God and have worshiped the Bā´als." ¹¹And the LORD said to the Israelites, "Did I not deliver you[k] from the Egyptians and from the Am´o·rītes, from the Am´mon·ītes and from the Phi·lis´tines? ¹²The Sī´do·ni·ans also, and the A·mal´e·kītes, and the Mā´on·ītes, oppressed you; and you cried to me, and I delivered you out of their hand. ¹³Yet you have abandoned

me and worshiped other gods; therefore I will deliver you no more. ¹⁴Go and cry to the gods whom you have chosen; let them deliver you in the time of your distress." ¹⁵And the Israelites said to the LORD, "We have sinned; do to us whatever seems good to you; but deliver us this day!" ¹⁶So they put away the foreign gods from among them and worshiped the LORD; and he could no longer bear to see Israel suffer.

17 Then the Am´mon·ītes were called to arms, and they encamped in Gil´e·ad; and the Israelites came together, and they encamped at Miz´pah. ¹⁸The commanders of the people of Gil´e·ad said to one another, "Who will begin the fight against the Am´mon·ītes? He shall be head over all the inhabitants of Gil´e·ad."

Jephthah

11 Now Jeph´thah the Gil´e·ad·īte, the son of a prostitute, was a mighty warrior. Gil´e·ad was the father of Jeph´thah. ²Gil´e·ad's wife also bore him sons; and when his wife's sons grew up, they drove Jeph´thah away, saying to him, "You shall not inherit anything in our father's house; for you are the son of another woman." ³Then Jeph´thah fled from his brothers and lived in the land of Tob. Outlaws collected around Jeph´thah and went raiding with him.

4 After a time the Am´mon·ītes made war against Israel. ⁵And when the Am´mon·ītes made war against Israel, the elders of Gil´e·ad went to bring Jeph´thah from the land of Tob. ⁶They said to Jeph´thah, "Come and be our commander, so that we may fight with the Am´mon·ītes." ⁷But Jeph´thah said to the elders of Gil´e·ad, "Are you not the very ones who rejected me and drove me out of my father's house? So why do you come to me now when you are in trouble?" ⁸The elders of Gil´e·ad said to Jeph´thah, "Nevertheless, we have now turned back to you, so that you may go

---

[k] Heb lacks *Did I not deliver you*

with us and fight with the Am´mon·ītes, and become head over us, over all the inhabitants of Gil´e·ad." Jeph´thah said to the elders of Gil´e·ad, "If you bring me home again to fight with the Am´mon·ītes, and the LORD gives them over to me, I will be your head." ¹⁰And the elders of Gil´e·ad said to Jeph´thah, "The LORD will be witness between us; we will surely do as you say." ¹¹So Jeph´thah went with the elders of Gil´e·ad, and the people made him head and commander over them; and Jeph´thah spoke all his words before the LORD at Miz´pah.

12 Then Jeph´thah sent messengers to the king of the Am´mon·ītes and said, "What is there between you and me, that you have come to me to fight against my land?" ¹³The king of the Am´mon·ītes answered the messengers of Jeph´thah, "Because Israel, on coming from Egypt, took away my land from the Ar´non to the Jab´bok and to the Jordan; now therefore restore it peaceably." ¹⁴Once again Jeph´thah sent messengers to the king of the Am´mon·ītes ¹⁵and said to him: "Thus says Jeph´thah: Israel did not take away the land of Mō´ab or the land of the Am´mon·ītes, ¹⁶but when they came up from Egypt, Israel went through the wilderness to the Red Seaˡ and came to Kā´desh. ¹⁷Israel then sent messengers to the king of Ē´dom, saying, 'Let us pass through your land'; but the king of Ē´dom would not listen. They also sent to the king of Mō´ab, but he would not consent. So Israel remained at Kā´desh. ¹⁸Then they journeyed through the wilderness, went around the land of Ē´dom and the land of Mō´ab, arrived on the east side of the land of Mō´ab, and camped on the other side of the Ar´non. They did not enter the territory of Mō´ab, for the Ar´non was the boundary of Mō´ab. ¹⁹Israel then sent messengers to King Sī´hon of the Am´o·rītes, king of Hesh´bon; and Israel said to him, 'Let us pass through your land to our country.' ²⁰But Sī´hon did not trust Israel to pass

through his territory; so Sī´hon gathered all his people together, and encamped at Jā´haz, and fought with Israel. ²¹Then the LORD, the God of Israel, gave Sī´hon and all his people into the hand of Israel, and they defeated them; so Israel occupied all the land of the Am´o·rītes, who inhabited that country. ²²They occupied all the territory of the Am´o·rītes from the Ar´non to the Jab´bok and from the wilderness to the Jordan. ²³So now the LORD, the God of Israel, has conquered the Am´o·rītes for the benefit of his people Israel. Do you intend to take their place? ²⁴Should you not possess what your god Chē´mosh gives you to possess? And should we not be the ones to possess everything that the LORD our God has conquered for our benefit? ²⁵Now are you any better than King Bā´lak son of Zip´por of Mō´ab? Did he ever enter into conflict with Israel, or did he ever go to war with them? ²⁶While Israel lived in Hesh´bon and its villages, and in A·rō´er and its villages, and in all the towns that are along the Ar´non, three hundred years, why did you not recover them within that time? ²⁷It is not I who have sinned against you, but you are the one who does me wrong by making war on me. Let the LORD, who is judge, decide today for the Israelites or for the Am´mon·ītes." ²⁸But the king of the Am´mon·ītes did not heed the message that Jeph´thah sent him.

Jephthah's Vow

29 Then the spirit of the LORD came upon Jeph´thah, and he passed through Gil´e·ad and Ma·nas´seh. He passed on to Miz´pah of Gil´e·ad, and from Miz´pah of Gil´e·ad he passed on to the Am´mon·ītes. ³⁰And Jeph´thah made a vow to the LORD, and said, "If you will give the Am´mon·ītes into my hand, ³¹then whoever comes out of the doors of my house to meet me, when I return victorious from the Am´mon·ītes, shall be the LORD's, to be offered up by me as a burnt

---

ˡ Or *Sea of Reeds*

offering." ³²So Jeph′thah crossed over to the Am′mon·ītes to fight against them; and the LORD gave them into his hand. ³³He inflicted a massive defeat on them from A·rō′er to the neighborhood of Min′nith, twenty towns, and as far as Ā·bel-ker′a·mim. So the Am′mon·ītes were subdued before the people of Israel.

Jephthah's Daughter

34 Then Jeph′thah came to his home at Miz′pah; and there was his daughter coming out to meet him with timbrels and with dancing. She was his only child; he had no son or daughter except her. ³⁵When he saw her, he tore his clothes, and said, "Alas, my daughter! You have brought me very low; you have become the cause of great trouble to me. For I have opened my mouth to the LORD, and I cannot take back my vow." ³⁶She said to him, "My father, if you have opened your mouth to the LORD, do to me according to what has gone out of your mouth, now that the LORD has given you vengeance against your enemies, the Am′mon·ītes." ³⁷And she said to her father, "Let this thing be done for me: Grant me two months, so that I may go and wander^m on the mountains, and bewail my virginity, my companions and I." ³⁸"Go," he said and sent her away for two months. So she departed, she and her companions, and bewailed her virginity on the mountains. ³⁹At the end of two months, she returned to her father, who did with her according to the vow he had made. She had never slept with a man. So there arose an Israelite custom that ⁴⁰for four days every year the daughters of Israel would go out to lament the daughter of Jeph′thah the Gil′e·ad·īte.

Intertribal Dissension

12 The men of Ē′phra·im were called to arms, and they crossed to Zā′phon and said to Jeph′thah, "Why did you cross over to fight against the Am′mon·ītes, and did not call us to go with you? We will burn your house down

over you!" ²Jeph′thah said to them, "My people and I were engaged in conflict with the Am′mon·ītes who oppressed us^n severely. But when I called you, you did not deliver me from their hand. ³When I saw that you would not deliver me, I took my life in my hand, and crossed over against the Am′mon·ītes, and the LORD gave them into my hand. Why then have you come up to me this day, to fight against me?" ⁴Then Jeph′thah gathered all the men of Gil′e·ad and fought with Ē′phra·im; and the men of Gil′e·ad defeated Ē′phra·im, because they said, "You are fugitives from Ē′phra·im, you Gil′-e·ad·ītes—in the heart of Ē′phra·im and Ma·nas′seh."^{o} ⁵Then the Gil′e·ad·ītes took the fords of the Jordan against the Ē′phra·im·ītes. Whenever one of the fugitives of Ē′phra·im said, "Let me go over," the men of Gil′e·ad would say to him, "Are you an Ē′phra·im·īte?" When he said, "No," ⁶they said to him, "Then say Shib′-bo·leth," and he said, "Sib′bo·leth," for he could not pronounce it right. Then they seized him and killed him at the fords of the Jordan. Forty-two thousand of the Ē′phra·im·ītes fell at that time.

7 Jeph′thah judged Israel six years. Then Jeph′thah the Gil′e·ad·īte died, and was buried in his town in Gil′e·ad.^{p}

Ibzan, Elon, and Abdon

8 After him Ib′zan of Bethlehem judged Israel. ⁹He had thirty sons. He gave his thirty daughters in marriage outside his clan and brought in thirty young women from outside for his sons. He judged Israel seven years. ¹⁰Then Ib′zan died, and was buried at Bethlehem.

11 After him Ē′lon the Zeb′ū·lun·īte judged Israel; and he judged Israel ten years. ¹²Then Ē′lon the Zeb′ū·lun·īte died, and was buried at Aī′ja·lon in the land of Zeb′ū·lun.

---

^{m} Cn: Heb *go down*　　^{n} Gk OL, Syr H: Heb lacks *who oppressed us*　　^{o} Meaning of Heb uncertain: Gk omits *because . . . Manasseh*　　^{p} Gk: Heb *in the towns of Gilead*

13 After him Ab´don son of Hil´lel the Pir´a·thon·ite judged Israel. ¹⁴He had forty sons and thirty grandsons, who rode on seventy donkeys; he judged Israel eight years. ¹⁵Then Ab´don son of Hil´lel the Pir´a·thon·ite died, and was buried at Pir´a·thon in the land of E´phra·im, in the hill country of the A·mal´e·kites.

The Birth of Samson

13 The Israelites again did what was evil in the sight of the LORD, and the LORD gave them into the hand of the Phi·lis´tines forty years.

2 There was a certain man of Zo´rah, of the tribe of the Dan´ites, whose name was Ma·no´ah. His wife was barren, having borne no children. ³And the angel of the LORD appeared to the woman and said to her, "Although you are barren, having borne no children, you shall conceive and bear a son. ⁴Now be careful not to drink wine or strong drink, or to eat anything unclean, ⁵for you shall conceive and bear a son. No razor is to come on his head, for the boy shall be a nazirite^q to God from birth. It is he who shall begin to deliver Israel from the hand of the Phi·lis´tines." ⁶Then the woman came and told her husband, "A man of God came to me, and his appearance was like that of an angel^r of God, most awe-inspiring; I did not ask him where he came from, and he did not tell me his name; ⁷but he said to me, 'You shall conceive and bear a son. So then drink no wine or strong drink, and eat nothing unclean, for the boy shall be a nazirite^q to God from birth to the day of his death.' "

8 Then Ma·no´ah entreated the LORD, and said, "O LORD, I pray, let the man of God whom you sent come to us again and teach us what we are to do concerning the boy who will be born." ⁹God listened to Ma·no´ah, and the angel of God came again to the woman as she sat in the field; but her husband Ma·no´ah was not with her. ¹⁰So the woman ran quickly and told her husband, "The man who came to me

the other day has appeared to me." ¹¹Ma·no´ah got up and followed his wife, and came to the man and said to him, "Are you the man who spoke to this woman?" And he said, "I am." ¹²Then Ma·no´ah said, "Now when your words come true, what is to be the boy's rule of life; what is he to do?" ¹³The angel of the LORD said to Ma·no´ah, "Let the woman give heed to all that I said to her. ¹⁴She may not eat of anything that comes from the vine. She is not to drink wine or strong drink, or eat any unclean thing. She is to observe everything that I commanded her."

15 Ma·no´ah said to the angel of the LORD, "Allow us to detain you, and prepare a kid for you." ¹⁶The angel of the LORD said to Ma·no´ah, "If you detain me, I will not eat your food; but if you want to prepare a burnt offering, then offer it to the LORD." (For Ma·no´ah did not know that he was the angel of the LORD.) ¹⁷Then Ma·no´ah said to the angel of the LORD, "What is your name, so that we may honor you when your words come true?" ¹⁸But the angel of the LORD said to him, "Why do you ask my name? It is too wonderful."

19 So Ma·no´ah took the kid with the grain offering, and offered it on the rock to the LORD, to him who works^s wonders.^t ²⁰When the flame went up toward

Samson was a judge from the Israelite tribe of Dan. He was famous for his great strength. When he was born, Samson was dedicated as a Nazirite, which meant that he promised never to cut his hair. His long hair was the secret of his strength. Do you know what happened to Samson when his hair was cut? Read chapter 16 to find out!

^q That is *one separated* or *one consecrated* ^r Or *the angel* ^s Gk Vg: Heb *and working* ^t Heb *wonders, while Manoah and his wife looked on* heaven from the altar, the angel of the LORD ascended in the flame of the altar while Ma·nō´ah and his wife looked on; and they fell on their faces to the ground. ²¹The angel of the LORD did not appear again to Ma·nō´ah and his wife. Then Ma·nō´ah realized that it was the angel of the LORD. ²²And Ma·nō´ah said to his wife, "We shall surely die, for we have seen God." ²³But his wife said to him, "If the LORD had meant to kill us, he would not have accepted a burnt offering and a grain offering at our hands, or shown us all these things, or now announced to us such things as these."

24 The woman bore a son, and named him Samson. The boy grew, and the LORD blessed him. ²⁵The spirit of the LORD began to stir him in Mā´ha·neh-dan, between Zō´rah and Esh´tā·ol.

Samson's Marriage

14 Once Samson went down to Tim´nah, and at Tim´nah he saw a Phi·lis´tine woman. ²Then he came up, and told his father and mother, "I saw a Phi·lis´tine woman at Tim´nah; now get her for me as my wife." ³But his father and mother said to him, "Is there not a woman among your kin, or among all our^u people, that you must go to take a wife from the uncircumcised Phi·lis´-tines?" But Samson said to his father, "Get her for me, because she pleases me." ⁴His father and mother did not know that this was from the LORD; for he was seeking a pretext to act against the Phi·lis´tines. At that time the Phi·lis´tines had dominion over Israel.

5 Then Samson went down with his father and mother to Tim´nah. When he came to the vineyards of Tim´nah, suddenly a young lion roared at him. ⁶The spirit of the LORD rushed on him, and he tore the lion apart barehanded as one might tear apart a kid. But he did not tell his father or his mother what he had done. ⁷Then he went down and talked with the woman, and she pleased

What words would you use to describe a lion? Beautiful? Strong? Scary? Lions were a common animal in Bible times. We read in the Bible that both David and Samson killed a lion. Shepherds kept a close watch for lions, because a lion could quickly destroy a flock of sheep. Israelite poetry writers used the lion as a symbol of both strength and cruelty.

Samson. ⁸After a while he returned to marry her, and he turned aside to see the carcass of the lion, and there was a swarm of bees in the body of the lion, and honey. ⁹He scraped it out into his hands, and went on, eating as he went. When he came to his father and mother, he gave some to them, and they ate it. But he did not tell them that he had taken the honey from the carcass of the lion.

10 His father went down to the woman, and Samson made a feast there as the young men were accustomed to do. ¹¹When the people saw him, they brought thirty companions to be with him. ¹²Samson said to them, "Let me now put a riddle to you. If you can explain it to me within the seven days of the feast, and find it out, then I will give you thirty linen garments and thirty

Do you like puzzles, riddles, and games? People in Bible times had fun trying to solve riddles, often at meal times. Even kings and queens enjoyed them. The Queen of Sheba used riddles to test Solomon's wisdom. Read 1 Kings 10 to learn about her visit to Solomon.

^u Cn: Heb *my*

festal garments. ¹³But if you cannot explain it to me, then you shall give me thirty linen garments and thirty festal garments." So they said to him, "Ask your riddle; let us hear it." ¹⁴He said to them,

"Out of the eater came something to eat.
Out of the strong came something sweet."

But for three days they could not explain the riddle.

15 On the fourth^v day they said to Samson's wife, "Coax your husband to explain the riddle to us, or we will burn you and your father's house with fire. Have you invited us here to impoverish us?" ¹⁶So Samson's wife wept before him, saying, "You hate me; you do not really love me. You have asked a riddle of my people, but you have not explained it to me." He said to her, "Look, I have not told my father or my mother. Why should I tell you?" ¹⁷She wept before him the seven days that their feast lasted; and because she nagged him, on the seventh day he told her. Then she explained the riddle to her people. ¹⁸The men of the town said to him on the seventh day before the sun went down,

"What is sweeter than honey?
What is stronger than a lion?"

And he said to them,

"If you had not plowed with my heifer,
you would not have found out my riddle."

¹⁹Then the spirit of the LORD rushed on him, and he went down to Ash′ke·lon. He killed thirty men of the town, took their spoil, and gave the festal garments to those who had explained the riddle. In hot anger he went back to his father's house. ²⁰And Samson's wife was given to his companion, who had been his best man.

Samson Defeats the Philistines

15 After a while, at the time of the wheat harvest, Samson

went to visit his wife, bringing along a kid. He said, "I want to go into my wife's room." But her father would not allow him to go in. ²Her father said, "I was sure that you had rejected her; so I gave her to your companion. Is not her younger sister prettier than she? Why not take her instead?" ³Samson said to them, "This time, when I do mischief to the Phi·lis′tines, I will be without blame." ⁴So Samson went and caught three hundred foxes, and took some torches; and he turned the foxes^w tail to tail, and put a torch between each pair of tails. ⁵When he had set fire to the torches, he let the foxes go into the standing grain of the Phi·lis′tines, and burned up the shocks and the standing grain, as well as the vineyards and^x olive groves. ⁶Then the Phi·lis′tines asked, "Who has done this?" And they said, "Samson, the son-in-law of the Tim′nīte, because he has taken Samson's wife and given her to his companion." So the Phi·lis′tines came up, and burned her and her father. ⁷Samson said to them, "If this is what you do, I swear I will not stop until I have taken revenge on you." ⁸He struck them down hip and thigh with great slaughter; and he went down and stayed in the cleft of the rock of Ē′tam.

9 Then the Phi·lis′tines came up and encamped in Judah, and made a raid on Lē′hī. ¹⁰The men of Judah said, "Why have you come up against us?" They said, "We have come up to bind Samson, to do to him as he did to us." ¹¹Then three thousand men of Judah went down to the cleft of the rock of Ē′tam, and they said to Samson, "Do you not know that the Phi·lis′tines are rulers over us? What then have you done to us?" He replied, "As they did to me, so I have done to them." ¹²They said to him, "We have come down to bind you, so that we may give you into the hands of the Philistines." Samson answered them,

^v Gk Syr: Heb *seventh*   ^w Heb *them*   ^x Gk Tg Vg: Heb lacks *and*

"Swear to me that you yourselves will not attack me." ¹³They said to him, "No, we will only bind you and give you into their hands; we will not kill you." So they bound him with two new ropes, and brought him up from the rock.

14 When he came to Lē′hī, the Phi·lis′-tines came shouting to meet him; and the spirit of the LORD rushed on him, and the ropes that were on his arms became like flax that has caught fire, and his bonds melted off his hands. ¹⁵Then he found a fresh jawbone of a donkey, reached down and took it, and with it he killed a thousand men. ¹⁶And Samson said,

"With the jawbone of a donkey,
    heaps upon heaps,
with the jawbone of a donkey
    I have slain a thousand men."

¹⁷When he had finished speaking, he threw away the jawbone; and that place was called Rā′math-lē′hī.ʸ

18 By then he was very thirsty, and he called on the LORD, saying, "You have granted this great victory by the hand of your servant. Am I now to die of thirst, and fall into the hands of the uncircumcised?" ¹⁹So God split open the hollow place that is at Lē′hī, and water came from it. When he drank, his spirit returned, and he revived. Therefore it was named En-hak·kor′ē,ᶻ which is at Lē′hī to this day. ²⁰And he judged Israel in the days of the Phi·lis′tines twenty years.

Samson and Delilah

16 Once Samson went to Gā′za, where he saw a prostitute and went in to her. ²The Gā′zītes were told,ᵃ "Samson has come here." So they circled around and lay in wait for him all night at the city gate. They kept quiet all night, thinking, "Let us wait until the light of the morning; then we will kill him." ³But Samson lay only until midnight. Then at midnight he rose up, took hold of the doors of the city gate and the two posts, pulled them up, bar and all, put them on his shoulders, and carried them to the

Samson fell in love with Delilah, and she tricked him. After she tried three times to get Samson to tell her the secret of his great strength, he finally gave in. Delilah learned that Samson's hair was the secret of his power, and she had it cut off while he was sleeping. He woke up to find he was no stronger than an ordinary man. The Philistines captured him, poked out his eyes, and put him in prison. Read 16:23–31 to find out how Samson got back at them.

top of the hill that is in front of Hē′bron.

4 After this he fell in love with a woman in the valley of Sō′rek, whose name was Dē·lī′lah. ⁵The lords of the Phi·lis′tines came to her and said to her, "Coax him, and find out what makes his strength so great, and how we may overpower him, so that we may bind him in order to subdue him; and we will each give you eleven hundred pieces of silver." ⁶So Dē·lī′lah said to Samson, "Please tell me what makes your strength so great, and how you could be bound, so that one could subdue you." ⁷Samson said to her, "If they bind me with seven fresh bowstrings that are not dried out, then I shall become weak, and be like anyone else." ⁸Then the lords of the Phi·lis′tines brought her seven fresh bowstrings that had not dried out, and she bound him with them. ⁹While men were lying in wait in an inner chamber, she said to him, "The Phi·lis′tines are upon you, Samson!" But he snapped the bowstrings, as a strand of fiber snaps when it touches the fire. So the secret of his strength was not known.

ʸ That is *The Hill of the Jawbone*   ᶻ That is *The Spring of the One who Called*   ᵃ Gk: Heb lacks *were told*

10 Then Dē·lī´lah said to Samson, "You have mocked me and told me lies; please tell me how you could be bound." [11]He said to her, "If they bind me with new ropes that have not been used, then I shall become weak, and be like anyone else." [12]So Dē·lī´lah took new ropes and bound him with them, and said to him, "The Phi·lis´tines are upon you, Samson!" (The men lying in wait were in an inner chamber.) But he snapped the ropes off his arms like a thread.

13 Then Dē·lī´lah said to Samson, "Until now you have mocked me and told me lies; tell me how you could be bound." He said to her, "If you weave the seven locks of my head with the web and make it tight with the pin, then I shall become weak, and be like anyone else." [14]So while he slept, Dē·lī´lah took the seven locks of his head and wove them into the web,[b] and made them tight with the pin. Then she said to him, "The Phi·lis´tines are upon you, Samson!" But he awoke from his sleep, and pulled away the pin, the loom, and the web.

15 Then she said to him, "How can you say, 'I love you,' when your heart is not with me? You have mocked me three times now and have not told me what makes your strength so great." [16]Finally, after she had nagged him with her words day after day, and pestered him, he was tired to death. [17]So he told her his whole secret, and said to her, "A razor has never come upon my head; for I have been a nazirite[c] to God from my mother's womb. If my head were shaved, then my strength would leave me; I would become weak, and be like anyone else."

18 When Dē·lī´lah realized that he had told her his whole secret, she sent and called the lords of the Phi·lis´tines, saying, "This time come up, for he has told his whole secret to me." Then the lords of the Phi·lis´tines came up to her, and brought the money in their hands. [19]She let him fall asleep on her lap; and she called a man, and had him shave off the seven locks of his head. He began to weaken,[d] and his strength left him. [20]Then she said, "The Phi·lis´tines are upon you, Samson!" When he awoke from his sleep, he thought, "I will go out as at other times, and shake myself free." But he did not know that the LORD had left him. [21]So the Phi·lis´tines seized him and gouged out his eyes. They brought him down to Gā´za and bound him with bronze shackles; and he ground at the mill in the prison. [22]But the hair of his head began to grow again after it had been shaved.

Samson's Death

23 Now the lords of the Phi·lis´tines gathered to offer a great sacrifice to their god Dā´gon, and to rejoice; for they said, "Our god has given Samson our enemy into our hand." [24]When the people saw him, they praised their god; for they said, "Our god has given our enemy into our hand, the ravager of our country, who has killed many of us." [25]And when their hearts were merry, they said, "Call Samson, and let him entertain us." So they called Samson out of the prison, and he performed for them. They made him stand between the pillars; [26]and Samson said to the attendant who held him by the hand, "Let me feel the pillars on which the house rests, so that I may lean against them." [27]Now the house was full of men and women; all the lords of the Phi·lis´tines were there, and on the roof there were about three thousand men and women, who looked on while Samson performed.

28 Then Samson called to the LORD and said, "Lord GOD, remember me and strengthen me only this once, O God, so that with this one act of revenge I may pay back the Phi·lis´tines for my two eyes."[e] [29]And Samson grasped the two

b Compare Gk: in verses 13-14, Heb lacks and make it tight . . . into the web   c That is one separated or one consecrated   d Gk: Heb She began to torment him   e Or so that I may be avenged upon the Philistines for one of my two eyes middle pillars on which the house rested, and he leaned his weight against them, his right hand on the one and his left hand on the other. [30]Then Samson said, "Let me die with the Phi·lis´tines." He strained with all his might; and the house fell on the lords and all the people who were in it. So those he killed at his death were more than those he had killed during his life. [31]Then his brothers and all his family came down and took him and brought him up and buried him between Zō´rah and Esh´tā·ol in the tomb of his father Ma·nō´ah. He had judged Israel twenty years.

The Sanctuary and Idolatry of Dan

17 There was a man in the hill country of Ē´phra·im whose name was Mī´cah. [2]He said to his mother, "The eleven hundred pieces of silver that were taken from you, about which you uttered a curse, and even spoke it in my hearing,—that silver is in my possession; I took it; but now I will return it to you."[f] And his mother said, "May my son be blessed by the LORD!" [3]Then he returned the eleven hundred pieces of silver to his mother; and his mother said, "I consecrate the silver to the LORD from my hand for my son, to make an idol of cast metal." [4]So when he returned the money to his mother, his mother took two hundred pieces of silver, and gave it to the silversmith, who made it into an idol of cast metal; and it was in the house of Mī´cah. [5]This man Mī´cah had a shrine, and he made an ephod and teraphim, and installed one of his sons, who became his priest. [6]In those days there was no king in Israel; all the people did what was right in their own eyes.

7 Now there was a young man of Bethlehem in Judah, of the clan of Judah. He was a Lē´vīte residing there. [8]This man left the town of Bethlehem in Judah, to live wherever he could find a place. He came to the house of Mī´cah in the hill country of Ē´phra·im to carry on his work.[g] [9]Mī´cah said to him, "From where do you come?" He replied, "I am a Lē´vīte of Bethlehem in Judah, and I am going to live wherever I can find a place." [10]Then Mī´cah said to him, "Stay with me, and be to me a father and a priest, and I will give you ten pieces of silver a year, a set of clothes, and your living."[h] [11]The Lē´vīte agreed to stay with the man; and the young man became to him like one of his sons. [12]So Mī´cah installed the Lē´vīte, and the young man became his priest, and was in the house of Mī´cah. [13]Then Mī´cah said, "Now I know that the LORD will prosper me, because the Lē´vīte has become my priest."

The Migration of Dan

18 In those days there was no king in Israel. And in those days the tribe of the Dan´ītes was seeking for itself a territory to live in; for until then no territory among the tribes of Israel had been allotted to them. [2]So the Dan´ītes sent five valiant men from the whole number of their clan, from Zō´rah and from Esh´tā·ol, to spy out the land and to explore it; and they said to them, "Go, explore the land." When they came to the hill country of Ē´phra·im, to the house of Mī´cah, they stayed there. [3]While they were at Mī´cah's house, they recognized the voice of the young Lē´vīte; so they went over and asked him, "Who brought you here? What are you doing in this place? What is your business here?" [4]He said to them, "Mī´cah did such and such for me, and he hired me, and I have become his priest." [5]Then they said to him, "Inquire of God that we may know whether the mission we are undertaking will succeed." [6]The priest replied, "Go in peace. The mission you are on is under the eye of the LORD."

[f] The words *but now I will return it to you* are transposed from the end of verse 3 in Heb
[g] Or *Ephraim, continuing his journey*   [h] Heb *living, and the Levite went*

7 The five men went on, and when they came to Lā´ish, they observed the people who were there living securely, after the manner of the Sī·dō´ni·ans, quiet and unsuspecting, lacking[i] nothing on earth, and possessing wealth.[j] Furthermore, they were far from the Sī·dō´ni·ans and had no dealings with Ar´am.[k] 8When they came to their kinsfolk at Zō´rah and Esh´tā·ol, they said to them, "What do you report?" 9They said, "Come, let us go up against them; for we have seen the land, and it is very good. Will you do nothing? Do not be slow to go, but enter in and possess the land. 10When you go, you will come to an unsuspecting people. The land is broad—God has indeed given it into your hands—a place where there is no lack of anything on earth."

11 Six hundred men of the Dan´ite clan, armed with weapons of war, set out from Zō´rah and Esh´tā·ol, 12and went up and encamped at Kir´i·ath-jē´a·rim in Judah. On this account that place is called Mā´ha·neh-dan[l] to this day; it is west of Kir´i·ath-jē´a·rim. 13From there they passed on to the hill country of Ē´phra·im, and came to the house of Mī´cah.

14 Then the five men who had gone to spy out the land (that is, Lā´ish) said to their comrades, "Do you know that in these buildings there are an ephod, teraphim, and an idol of cast metal? Now therefore consider what you will do." 15So they turned in that direction and came to the house of the young Lē´vīte, at the home of Mī´cah, and greeted him. 16While the six hundred men of the Dan´ites, armed with their weapons of war, stood by the entrance of the gate, 17the five men who had gone to spy out the land proceeded to enter and take the idol of cast metal, the ephod, and the teraphim.[m] The priest was standing by the entrance of the gate with the six hundred men armed with weapons of war. 18When the men went into Mī´cah's house and took the idol of cast metal, the ephod, and the teraphim, the priest said to them, "What are you doing?" 19They said to him, "Keep quiet! Put your hand over your mouth, and come with us, and be to us a father and a priest. Is it better for you to be priest to the house of one person, or to be priest to a tribe and clan in Israel?" 20Then the priest accepted the offer. He took the ephod, the teraphim, and the idol, and went along with the people.

21 So they resumed their journey, putting the little ones, the livestock, and the goods in front of them. 22When they were some distance from the home of Mī´cah, the men who were in the houses near Mī´cah's house were called out, and they overtook the Dan´ites. 23They shouted to the Dan´ites, who turned around and said to Mī´cah, "What is the matter that you come with such a company?" 24He replied, "You take my gods that I made, and the priest, and go away, and what have I left? How then can you ask me, 'What is the matter?' " 25And the Dan´ites said to him, "You had better not let your voice be heard among us or else hot-tempered fellows will attack you, and you will lose your life and the lives of your household." 26Then the Dan´ites went their way. When Mī´cah saw that they were too strong for him, he turned and went back to his home.

The Danites Settle in Laish

27 The Dan´ites, having taken what Mī´cah had made, and the priest who belonged to him, came to Lā´ish, to a people quiet and unsuspecting, put them to the sword, and burned down the city. 28There was no deliverer, because it was far from Sī´don and they had no dealings with Ar´am.[n] It was in the valley that belongs to Beth-rē´hob. They rebuilt the city, and lived in it. 29They named the city Dan, after their

---

[i] Cn: Compare 18.10: Meaning of Heb uncertain
[j] Meaning of Heb uncertain   [k] Symmachus: Heb *with anyone*   [l] That is *Camp of Dan*   [m] Compare 17.4, 5; 18.14: Heb *teraphim and the cast metal*   [n] Cn: Compare verse 7: Heb *with anyone*

ancestor Dan, who was born to Israel; but the name of the city was formerly Lā´ish. [30]Then the Dan´ītes set up the idol for themselves. Jonathan son of Ger´shom, son of Moses,[o] and his sons were priests to the tribe of the Dan´ītes until the time the land went into captivity. [31]So they maintained as their own Mī´-cah's idol that he had made, as long as the house of God was at Shī´loh.

The Levite's Concubine

19 In those days, when there was no king in Israel, a certain Lē´vīte, residing in the remote parts of the hill country of Ē´phra·im, took to himself a concubine from Bethlehem in Judah. [2]But his concubine became angry with[p] him, and she went away from him to her father's house at Bethlehem in Judah, and was there some four months. [3]Then her husband set out after her, to speak tenderly to her and bring her back. He had with him his servant and a couple of donkeys. When he reached[q] her father's house, the girl's father saw him and came with joy to meet him. [4]His father-in-law, the girl's father, made him stay, and he remained with him three days; so they ate and drank, and he[r] stayed there. [5]On the fourth day they got up early in the morning, and he prepared to go; but the girl's father said to his son-in-law, "Fortify yourself with a bit of food, and after that you may go." [6]So the two men sat and ate and drank together; and the girl's father said to the man, "Why not spend the night and enjoy yourself?" [7]When the man got up to go, his father-in-law kept urging him until he spent the night there again. [8]On the fifth day he got up early in the morning to leave; and the girl's father said, "Fortify yourself." So they lingered[s] until the day declined, and the two of them ate and drank.[t] [9]When the man with his concubine and his servant got up to leave, his father-in-law, the girl's father, said to him, "Look, the day has worn on until it

is almost evening. Spend the night. See, the day has drawn to a close. Spend the night here and enjoy yourself. Tomorrow you can get up early in the morning for your journey, and go home."

10 But the man would not spend the night; he got up and departed, and arrived opposite Jē´bus (that is, Jerusalem). He had with him a couple of saddled donkeys, and his concubine was with him. [11]When they were near Jē´bus, the day was far spent, and the servant said to his master, "Come now, let us turn aside to this city of the Jeb´ū·sītes, and spend the night in it." [12]But his master said to him, "We will not turn aside into a city of foreigners, who do not belong to the people of Israel; but we will continue on to Gib´ē·ah." [13]Then he said to his servant, "Come, let us try to reach one of these places, and spend the night at Gib´ē·ah or at Rā´mah." [14]So they passed on and went their way; and the sun went down on them near Gib´ē·ah, which belongs to Benjamin. [15]They turned aside there, to go in and spend the night at Gib´ē·ah. He went in and sat down in the open square of the city, but no one took them in to spend the night.

16 Then at evening there was an old man coming from his work in the field. The man was from the hill country of Ē´phra·im, and he was residing in Gib´ē·ah. (The people of the place were Ben´-ja·min·ītes.) [17]When the old man looked up and saw the wayfarer in the open square of the city, he said, "Where are you going and where do you come from?" [18]He answered him, "We are passing from Bethlehem in Judah to the remote parts of the hill country of Ē´phra·im, from which I come. I went to Bethlehem in Judah; and I am going to my home.[u] Nobody has offered to take

[o] Another reading is *son of Manasseh*　[p] Gk OL: Heb *prostituted herself against*　[q] Gk: Heb *she brought him*　[r] Compare verse 7 and Gk: Heb *they*　[s] Cn: Heb *Linger*　[t] Gk: Heb lacks *and drank*　[u] Gk Compare 19.29. Heb *to the house of the LORD*

me in. ¹⁹We your servants have straw and fodder for our donkeys, with bread and wine for me and the woman and the young man along with us. We need nothing more." ²⁰The old man said, "Peace be to you. I will care for all your wants; only do not spend the night in the square." ²¹So he brought him into his house, and fed the donkeys; they washed their feet, and ate and drank.

Gibeah's Crime

22 While they were enjoying themselves, the men of the city, a perverse lot, surrounded the house, and started pounding on the door. They said to the old man, the master of the house, "Bring out the man who came into your house, so that we may have intercourse with him." ²³And the man, the master of the house, went out to them and said to them, "No, my brothers, do not act so wickedly. Since this man is my guest, do not do this vile thing. ²⁴Here are my virgin daughter and his concubine; let me bring them out now. Ravish them and do whatever you want to them; but against this man do not do such a vile thing." ²⁵But the men would not listen to him. So the man seized his concubine, and put her out to them. They wantonly raped her, and abused her all through the night until the morning. And as the dawn began to break, they let her go. ²⁶As morning appeared, the woman came and fell down at the door of the man's house where her master was, until it was light.

27 In the morning her master got up, opened the doors of the house, and when he went out to go on his way, there was his concubine lying at the door of the house, with her hands on the threshold. ²⁸"Get up," he said to her, "we are going." But there was no answer. Then he put her on the donkey; and the man set out for his home. ²⁹When he had entered his house, he took a knife, and grasping his concubine he cut her into

twelve pieces, limb by limb, and sent her throughout all the territory of Israel. ³⁰Then he commanded the men whom he sent, saying, "Thus shall you say to all the Israelites, 'Has such a thing ever happened^v since the day that the Israelites came up from the land of Egypt until this day? Consider it, take counsel, and speak out.' "

The Other Tribes Attack Benjamin

20 Then all the Israelites came out, from Dan to Bē´er-shē´ba, including the land of Gil´e·ad, and the congregation assembled in one body before the LORD at Miz´pah. ²The chiefs of all the people, of all the tribes of Israel, presented themselves in the assembly of the people of God, four hundred thousand foot-soldiers bearing arms. ³(Now the Ben´ja·min·ites heard that the people of Israel had gone up to Miz´pah.) And the Israelites said, "Tell us, how did this criminal act come about?" ⁴The Lē´vīte, the husband of the woman who was murdered, answered, "I came to Gib´ē·ah that belongs to Benjamin, I and my concubine, to spend the night. ⁵The lords of Gib´ē·ah rose up against me, and surrounded the house at night. They intended to kill me, and they raped my concubine until she died. ⁶Then I took my concubine and cut her into pieces, and sent her throughout the whole extent of Israel's territory; for they have committed a vile outrage in Israel. ⁷So now, you Israelites, all of you, give your advice and counsel here."

8 All the people got up as one, saying, "We will not any of us go to our tents, nor will any of us return to our houses. ⁹But now this is what we will do to Gib´ē·ah: we will go up^w against it by lot. ¹⁰We will take ten men of a hundred throughout all the tribes of Israel, and a hundred of a thou-

---

^{v} Compare Gk: Heb ³⁰And all who saw it said, "Such a thing has not happened or been seen ^{w} Gk: Heb lacks we will go up sand, and a thousand of ten thousand, to bring provisions for the troops, who are going to repay[x] Gib´e·ah of Benjamin for all the disgrace that they have done in Israel." [11]So all the men of Israel gathered against the city, united as one.

12 The tribes of Israel sent men through all the tribe of Benjamin, saying, "What crime is this that has been committed among you? [13]Now then, hand over those scoundrels in Gib´e·ah, so that we may put them to death, and purge the evil from Israel." But the Ben´ja·min·ītes would not listen to their kinsfolk, the Israelites. [14]The Ben´ja·min·ītes came together out of the towns to Gib´e·ah, to go out to battle against the Israelites. [15]On that day the Ben´ja·min·ītes mustered twenty-six thousand armed men from their towns, besides the inhabitants of Gib´e·ah. [16]Of all this force, there were seven hundred picked men who were left-handed; every one could sling a stone at a hair, and not miss. [17]And the Israelites, apart from Benjamin, mustered four hundred thousand armed men, all of them warriors.

18 The Israelites proceeded to go up to Beth´el, where they inquired of God, "Which of us shall go up first to battle against the Ben´ja·min·ītes?" And the LORD answered, "Judah shall go up first."

19 Then the Israelites got up in the morning, and encamped against Gib´e·ah. [20]The Israelites went out to battle against Benjamin; and the Israelites drew up the battle line against them at Gib´e·ah. [21]The Ben´ja·min·ītes came out of Gib´e·ah, and struck down on that day twenty-two thousand of the Israelites. [23][y] The Israelites went up and wept before the LORD until the evening; and they inquired of the LORD, "Shall we again draw near to battle against our kinsfolk the Ben´ja·min·ītes?" And the LORD said, "Go up against them." [22]The Israelites took courage, and again formed the battle line in the same place where they had formed it on the first day.

24 So the Israelites advanced against the Ben´ja·min·ītes the second day. [25]Benjamin moved out against them from Gib´e·ah the second day, and struck down eighteen thousand of the Israelites, all of them armed men. [26]Then all the Israelites, the whole army, went back to Beth´el and wept, sitting there before the LORD; they fasted that day until evening. Then they offered burnt offerings and sacrifices of well-being before the LORD. [27]And the Israelites inquired of the LORD (for the ark of the covenant of God was there in those days, [28]and Phin´e·has son of El·e·a´zar, son of Aaron, ministered before it in those days), saying, "Shall we go out once more to battle against our kinsfolk the Ben´ja·min·ītes, or shall we desist?" The LORD answered, "Go up, for tomorrow I will give them into your hand."

29 So Israel stationed men in ambush around Gib´e·ah. [30]Then the Israelites went up against the Ben´ja·min·ītes on the third day, and set themselves in array against Gib´e·ah, as before. [31]When the Ben´ja·min·ītes went out against the army, they were drawn away from the city. As before they began to inflict casualties on the troops, along the main roads, one of which goes up to Beth´el and the other to Gib´e·ah, as well as in the open country, killing about thirty men of Israel. [32]The Ben´ja·min·ītes thought, "They are being routed before us, as previously." But the Israelites said, "Let us retreat and draw them away from the city toward the roads." [33]The main body of the Israelites drew back its battle line to Ba´al-ta´mar, while those Israelites who were in ambush rushed out of their place west[z] of Ge´ba. [34]There came against Gib´e·ah ten thousand picked men out of all Israel, and the battle was fierce. But the Ben´ja·min·ītes did not realize that disaster was close upon them.

35 The LORD defeated Benjamin before Israel; and the Israelites destroyed

[x] Compare Gk: Meaning of Heb uncertain
[y] Verses 22 and 23 are transposed   [z] Gk Vg: Heb *in the plain*

twenty-five thousand one hundred men of Benjamin that day, all of them armed.

36 Then the Ben´ja·min·ites saw that they were defeated.[a]

The Israelites gave ground to Benjamin, because they trusted to the troops in ambush that they had stationed against Gib´e·ah. [37]The troops in ambush rushed quickly upon Gib´e·ah. Then they put the whole city to the sword. [38]Now the agreement between the main body of Israel and the men in ambush was that when they sent up a cloud of smoke out of the city [39]the main body of Israel should turn in battle. But Benjamin had begun to inflict casualties on the Israelites, killing about thirty of them; so they thought, "Surely they are defeated before us, as in the first battle." [40]But when the cloud, a column of smoke, began to rise out of the city, the Ben´ja·min·ites looked behind them—and there was the whole city going up in smoke toward the sky! [41]Then the main body of Israel turned, and the Ben´ja·min·ites were dismayed, for they saw that disaster was close upon them. [42]Therefore they turned away from the Israelites in the direction of the wilderness; but the battle overtook them, and those who came out of the city[b] were slaughtering them in between.[c] [43]Cutting down[d] the Ben´ja·min·ites, they pursued them from Nō´hah[e] and trod them down as far as a place east of Gib´e·ah. [44]Eighteen thousand Ben´ja·min·ites fell, all of them courageous fighters. [45]When they turned and fled toward the wilderness to the rock of Rim´mon, five thousand of them were cut down on the main roads, and they were pursued as far as Gi´dom, and two thousand of them were slain. [46]So all who fell that day of Benjamin were twenty-five thousand arms-bearing men, all of them courageous fighters. [47]But six hundred turned and fled toward the wilderness to the rock of Rim´mon, and remained at the rock of Rim´mon for four months.

[48]Meanwhile, the Israelites turned back against the Ben´ja·min·ites, and put them to the sword—the city, the people, the animals, and all that remained. Also the remaining towns they set on fire.

The Benjaminites Saved from Extinction

21 Now the Israelites had sworn at Miz´pah, "No one of us shall give his daughter in marriage to Benjamin." [2]And the people came to Beth´el, and sat there until evening before God, and they lifted up their voices and wept bitterly. [3]They said, "O LORD, the God of Israel, why has it come to pass that today there should be one tribe lacking in Israel?" [4]On the next day, the people got up early, and built an altar there, and offered burnt offerings and sacrifices of well-being. [5]Then the Israelites said, "Which of all the tribes of Israel did not come up in the assembly to the LORD?" For a solemn oath had been taken concerning whoever did not come up to the LORD to Miz´pah, saying, "That one shall be put to death." [6]But the Israelites had compassion for Benjamin their kin, and said, "One tribe is cut off from Israel this day. [7]What shall we do for wives for those who are left, since we have sworn by the LORD that we will not give them any of our daughters as wives?"

8 Then they said, "Is there anyone from the tribes of Israel who did not come up to the LORD to Miz´pah?" It turned out that no one from Jā´besh-gil´e·ad had come to the camp, to the assembly. [9]For when the roll was called among the people, not one of the inhabitants of Jā´besh-gil´e·ad was there. [10]So the congregation sent twelve thousand soldiers there and commanded them, "Go, put the inhabitants of Jā´besh-gil´e·ad

---

[a] This sentence is continued by verse 45.
[b] Compare Vg and some Gk Mss: Heb *cities*
[c] Compare Syr: Meaning of Heb uncertain
[d] Gk: Heb *Surrounding*   [e] Gk: Heb *pursued them at their resting place*

to the sword, including the women and the little ones. [11]This is what you shall do; every male and every woman that has lain with a male you shall devote to destruction." [12]And they found among the inhabitants of Jā′besh-gil′ē·ad four hundred young virgins who had never slept with a man and brought them to the camp at Shī′loh, which is in the land of Cā′naan.

13 Then the whole congregation sent word to the Ben′ja·min·ītes who were at the rock of Rim′mon, and proclaimed peace to them. [14]Benjamin returned at that time; and they gave them the women whom they had saved alive of the women of Jā′besh-gil′ē·ad; but they did not suffice for them.

15 The people had compassion on Benjamin because the LORD had made a breach in the tribes of Israel. [16]So the elders of the congregation said, "What shall we do for wives for those who are left, since there are no women left in Benjamin?" [17]And they said, "There must be heirs for the survivors of Benjamin, in order that a tribe may not be blotted out from Israel. [18]Yet we cannot give any of our daughters to them as wives." For the Israelites had sworn, "Cursed be anyone who gives a wife to Benjamin." [19]So they said, "Look, the yearly festival of the LORD is taking place at Shī′loh, which is north of Beth′el, on the east of the highway that goes up from Beth′el to Shē′chem, and south of Le·bō′nah." [20]And they instructed the Ben′ja·min·ītes, saying, "Go and lie in wait in the vineyards, [21]and watch; when the young women of Shī′loh come out to dance in the dances, then come out of the vineyards and each of you carry off a wife for himself from the young women of Shī′loh, and go to the land of Benjamin. [22]Then if their fathers or their brothers come to complain to us, we will say to them, 'Be generous and allow us to have them; because we did not capture in battle a wife for each man. But neither did you incur guilt by giving your daughters to them.' " [23]The Ben′ja·min·ītes did so; they took wives for each of them from the dancers whom they abducted. Then they went and returned to their territory, and rebuilt the towns, and lived in them. [24]So the Israelites departed from there at that time by tribes and families, and they went out from there to their own territories.

25 In those days there was no king in Israel; all the people did what was right in their own eyes.

Ruth

The book of Ruth is about the relationship between a mother (in-law) and a daughter (in-law). This book tells the story of Ruth the Moabite who left Moab and her family to follow her mother-in-law, Naomi, to Bethlehem. Because Ruth trusted Naomi's God, she found a new home for herself and Naomi by marrying an Israelite named Boaz. The book of Ruth was written about 400 BC, after the Jews who had been living in Babylon returned to Judah.

When Ruth was written, some leaders believed that Jews should not marry people from other cultures. The books of Ezra and Nehemiah show this belief. Other books show the tradition of caring for family, widows, and foreigners (Deuteronomy 24:19 and Leviticus 19:9–10; 25:25–34, 47–55). The author of the book of Ruth used the story of Ruth's marriage to Boaz to show that marriage with foreigners had long been accepted. This book is a call for people to treat one another with kindness and love. The writer used the story of Ruth to show the people that they needed to accept everyone and treat them with love.

God took care of Ruth and her mother-in-law, Naomi. Ruth and Boaz became the great-grandparents of the best-loved king of Israel and Judah, King David. The Gospel of Matthew, the first book in the New Testament, names the family of Jesus through David, and also through Ruth and Boaz.

Ruth 2:8–9

The people who lived in Moab were descendants of Abraham's nephew Lot. Although they were related to the Israelites, they fought against God's people who were traveling to Canaan. From the time of the Exodus to the fall of Jerusalem, Moab was often against Israel and Judah.

Elimelech's Family Goes to Moab

1 In the days when the judges ruled, there was a famine in the land, and a certain man of Bethlehem in Judah went to live in the country of Mō´ab, he and his wife and two sons. ²The name of the man was Ē·lim´e·lech and the name of his wife Nā´o·mī, and the names of his two sons were Mah´lon and Chil´i·on; they were Eph´ra·thītes from Bethlehem in Judah. They went into the country of Mō´ab and remained there. ³But Ē·lim´-e·lech, the husband of Nā´o·mī, died, and she was left with her two sons. ⁴These took Mō´ab·īte wives; the name of the one was Or´pah and the name of the other Ruth. When they had lived there about ten years, ⁵both Mah´lon and Chil´i·on also died, so that the woman was left without her two sons and her husband.

When there was no food in Israel, Naomi went with her husband and their two sons to live in Moab. Her sons married women from Moab, but soon her husband and both sons died. Life was very hard for a widow in that time. Widows were often very poor and had to depend on the kindness of other people. Because she had no family in Moab to care for her, Naomi decided to return to Bethlehem, and her daughter-in-law Ruth went with her.

Naomi and Her Moabite Daughters-in-Law

6 Then she started to return with her daughters-in-law from the country of Mō´ab, for she had heard in the country of Mō´ab that the LORD had considered his people and given them food. ⁷So she set out from the place where she had been living, she and her two daughters-in-law, and they went on their way to go back to the land of Judah. ⁸But Nā´o·mī said to her two daughters-in-law, "Go back each of you to your mother's house. May the LORD deal kindly with you, as

Instead of going with Naomi, Ruth could have gone back to her family in Moab. A widow did not usually stay with her mother-in-law, but Ruth cared deeply for Naomi. Her actions showed loyalty beyond what was expected. Ruth's love and care for Naomi are like God's love and care for us. Think of a time when someone did something totally unexpected for you. Say a prayer of thanksgiving for that person. Think of something you can do to show love to someone else.

you have dealt with the dead and with me. ⁹The LORD grant that you may find security, each of you in the house of your husband." Then she kissed them, and they wept aloud. ¹⁰They said to her, "No, we will return with you to your people." ¹¹But Nā´o·mī said, "Turn back, my daughters, why will you go with me? Do I still have sons in my womb that they may become your husbands? ¹²Turn back, my daughters, go your way, for I am too old to have a husband. Even if I thought there was hope for me, even if I should have a husband tonight and bear sons, ¹³would you then wait until they were grown? Would you then refrain from marrying? No, my daughters, it has

"Where you go, I will go; Where you lodge, I will lodge; your people shall be my people, and your God my God." Ruth 1:16

been far more bitter for me than for you, because the hand of the LORD has turned against me." [14]Then they wept aloud again. Or'pah kissed her mother-in-law, but Ruth clung to her.

15 So she said, "See, your sister-in-law has gone back to her people and to her gods; return after your sister-in-law." [16]But Ruth said,

"Do not press me to leave you
    or to turn back from following you!
Where you go, I will go;
    where you lodge, I will lodge;
your people shall be my people,
    and your God my God.
[17] Where you die, I will die—
    there will I be buried.
May the LORD do thus and so to me,
    and more as well,
if even death parts me from you!"
[18]When Nā′o·mī saw that she was determined to go with her, she said no more to her.

19 So the two of them went on until they came to Bethlehem. When they came to Bethlehem, the whole town was stirred because of them; and the women said, "Is this Nā′o·mī?" [20]She said to them,

"Call me no longer Nā′o·mī,[a]
    call me Mar′a,[b]
    for the Almighty[c] has dealt bitterly
        with me.

Naomi was very angry and blamed God for her troubles. Because the name Naomi means "sweet," she asked her friends to call her Mara, which sounds like the Hebrew word for "bitter."

[21] I went away full,
    but the LORD has brought me
        back empty;
why call me Nā′o·mī
    when the LORD has dealt harshly
        with[d] me,
    and the Almighty[c] has brought
        calamity upon me?"

22 So Nā′o·mī returned together with Ruth the Mō′ab·īte, her daughter-in-law, who came back with her from the country of Mō′ab. They came to Bethlehem at the beginning of the barley harvest.

Every year during harvest time, the people would gather stalks of grain from the fields. God's law made sure that the poor did not go hungry. The people gathering the grain had to leave some in the corners of the fields, and they also had to leave behind any they dropped. The poor would come behind them to pick up the leftover grain. This was called "gleaning," and it was one way God took care of all people.

Ruth Meets Boaz

2 Now Nā′o·mī had a kinsman on her husband's side, a prominent rich man, of the family of Ē·lim′e·lech, whose name was Bō′az. [2]And Ruth the Mō′ab·īte said to Nā′o·mī, "Let me go to the field and glean among the ears of grain, behind someone in whose sight I may find favor." She said to her, "Go, my daughter." [3]So she went. She came and gleaned in the field behind the reapers. As it happened, she came to the part of the field belonging to Bō′az, who was of the family of Ē·lim′e·lech. [4]Just then Bō′az came from Bethlehem. He said to the reapers, "The LORD be with you." They answered, "The LORD bless you." [5]Then

[a] That is Pleasant   [b] That is Bitter   [c] Traditional rendering of Heb Shaddai   [d] Or has testified against

Bō′az said to his servant who was in charge of the reapers, "To whom does this young woman belong?" 6The servant who was in charge of the reapers answered, "She is the Mō′ab·īte who came back with Nā′o·mī from the country of Mō′ab. 7She said, 'Please, let me glean and gather among the sheaves behind the reapers.' So she came, and she has been on her feet from early this morning until now, without resting even for a moment."*e*

8 Then Bō′az said to Ruth, "Now listen, my daughter, do not go to glean in another field or leave this one, but keep close to my young women. 9Keep your eyes on the field that is being reaped, and follow behind them. I have ordered the young men not to bother you. If you get thirsty, go to the vessels and drink from what the young men have drawn." 10Then she fell prostrate, with her face to the ground, and said to him, "Why have I found favor in your sight, that you should take notice of me, when I am a foreigner?" 11But Bō′az answered her, "All that you have done for your mother-in-law since the death of your husband has been fully told me, and how you left your father and mother and your native land and came to a people that you did not know before. 12May the LORD reward you for your deeds, and may you have a full reward from the LORD, the God of Israel, under whose wings you have come for refuge!" 13Then she said, "May I continue to find favor in your sight, my lord, for you have comforted me and spoken kindly to your servant, even though I am not one of your servants."

14 At mealtime Bō′az said to her, "Come here, and eat some of this bread, and dip your morsel in the sour wine." So she sat beside the reapers, and he heaped up for her some parched grain. She ate until she was satisfied, and she had some left over. 15When she got up to glean, Bō′az instructed his young men, "Let her glean even among the standing sheaves, and do not reproach her. 16You must also pull out some handfuls for her

People in Bible times stored water in large pots or jars to keep it cool and fresh. When Boaz told Ruth to help herself to water, he was treating her with kindness. What are some ways that you can be kind to others?

from the bundles, and leave them for her to glean, and do not rebuke her."

17 So she gleaned in the field until evening. Then she beat out what she had gleaned, and it was about an ephah of barley. 18She picked it up and came into the town, and her mother-in-law saw how much she had gleaned. Then she took out and gave her what was left over after she herself had been satisfied. 19Her mother-in-law said to her, "Where did you glean today? And where have you worked? Blessed be the man who took notice of you." So she told her mother-in-law with whom she had worked, and said, "The name of the man with whom I worked today is Bō′az." 20Then Nā′o·mī said to her daughter-in-law, "Blessed be he by the LORD, whose kindness has not forsaken the living or the dead!" Nā′o·mī also said to her, "The man is a relative of ours, one of our nearest kin."*f* 21Then Ruth the Mō′ab·īte said, "He even said to me, 'Stay close by my servants, until they have finished all my harvest.'" 22Nā′o·mī said to Ruth, her daughter-in-law, "It is better, my daughter, that you go out with his young women, otherwise you might be bothered in another field." 23So she stayed close to the young women of Bō′az, gleaning until the end of the barley and wheat harvests; and she lived with her mother-in-law.

Ruth and Boaz at the Threshing Floor

3 Nā′o·mī her mother-in-law said to her, "My daughter, I need to seek some security for you, so that it may be

e Compare Gk Vg: Meaning of Heb uncertain
f Or *one with the right to redeem*

well with you. ²Now here is our kinsman Bōʻaz, with whose young women you have been working. See, he is winnowing barley tonight at the threshing floor. ³Now wash and anoint yourself, and put on your best clothes and go down to the threshing floor; but do not make yourself known to the man until he has finished eating and drinking. ⁴When he lies down, observe the place where he lies; then, go and uncover his feet and lie down; and he will tell you what to do." ⁵She said to her, "All that you tell me I will do."

6 So she went down to the threshing floor and did just as her mother-in-law had instructed her. ⁷When Bōʻaz had eaten and drunk, and he was in a contented mood, he went to lie down at the end of the heap of grain. Then she came stealthily and uncovered his feet, and lay down. ⁸At midnight the man was startled, and turned over, and there, lying at his feet, was a woman! ⁹He said, "Who are you?" And she answered, "I am Ruth, your servant; spread your cloak over your servant, for you are next-of-kin."ᵍ ¹⁰He said, "May you be blessed by the LORD, my daughter; this last instance of your loyalty is better than the first; you have not gone after young men, whether poor or rich. ¹¹And now, my daughter, do not be afraid, I will do for you all that you ask, for all the assembly of my people know that you are a worthy woman. ¹²But now, though it is true that I am a near kinsman, there is another kinsman more closely related than I. ¹³Remain this night, and in the morning, if he will act as next-of-kinᵍ for you, good; let him do it. If he is not willing to act as next-of-kinᵍ for you, then, as the LORD lives, I will act as next-of-kinᵍ for you. Lie down until the morning."

14 So she lay at his feet until morning, but got up before one person could recognize another; for he said, "It must not be known that the woman came to the threshing floor." ¹⁵Then he said, "Bring the cloak you are wearing and hold it out." So she held it, and he measured out six

When the barley was taken from the fields to the threshing floor, it was tossed into the air with a tool called a winnowing fork. The stalks blew away, and the grain fell to the ground. Farmers did this work in the evening because it was often cooler and windier than in the day, helping them to do a better job. The farmer or a trusted servant slept at the threshing floor to protect the grain from being stolen.

measures of barley, and put it on her back; then he went into the city. ¹⁶She came to her mother-in-law, who said, "How did things go with you,ʰ my daughter?" Then she told her all that the man had done for her, ¹⁷saying, "He gave me these six measures of barley, for he said, 'Do not go back to your mother-in-law empty-handed.'" ¹⁸She replied, "Wait, my daughter, until you learn how the matter turns out, for the man will not rest, but will settle the matter today."

Boaz did not have to marry Ruth. He knew that she could have married someone closer to her own age. He also knew that only a male relative of Naomi's husband, Elimelech, could take over Elimelech's responsibilities. Those responsibilities included the care of Naomi and Ruth. Because Ruth was willing to marry Boaz, he knew that she was loyal to Naomi.

The Marriage of Boaz and Ruth

4 No sooner had Bōʻaz gone up to the gate and sat down there than the next-of-kin,ᵍ of whom Bōʻaz had spoken, came passing by. So Bōʻaz said, "Come

ᵍ Or "Who are you,   ʰ Or one with the right to redeem

> "He shall be to you a restorer of life and a nourisher of your old age; for your daughter-in-law who loves you, who is more to you than seven sons, has borne him."
>
> Ruth 4:15

over, friend; sit down here." And he went over and sat down. [2]Then Bōʹaz took ten men of the elders of the city, and said, "Sit down here"; so they sat down. [3]He then said to the next-of-kin,[i] "Nāʹo·mī, who has come back from the country of Mōʹab, is selling the parcel of land that belonged to our kinsman Ēʹlim·eʹe·lech. [4]So I thought I would tell you of it, and say: Buy it in the presence of those sitting here, and in the presence of the elders of my people. If you will redeem it, redeem it; but if you will not, tell me, so that I may know; for there is no one prior to you to redeem it, and I come after you." So he said, "I will redeem it." [5]Then Bōʹaz said, "The day you acquire the field from the hand of Nāʹo·mī, you are also acquiring Ruth[j] the Mōʹab·īte, the widow of the dead man, to maintain the dead man's name on his inheritance." [6]At this, the next-of-kin[i] said, "I cannot redeem it for myself without damaging my own inheritance. Take my right of redemption yourself, for I cannot redeem it."

[7] Now this was the custom in former times in Israel concerning redeeming and exchanging: to confirm a transaction, the one took off a sandal and gave it to the other; this was the manner of attesting in Israel. [8]So when the next-of-kin[i] said to Bōʹaz, "Acquire it for yourself," he took off his sandal. [9]Then Bōʹaz said to the elders and all the people, "Today you are witnesses that I have acquired from the hand of Nāʹo·mī all that belonged to Ēʹlim·eʹe·lech and all that belonged to Chilʹi·on and Mahʹlon. [10]I have also acquired Ruth the Mōʹab·īte, the wife of Mahʹlon, to be my wife, to maintain the dead man's name on his inheritance, in order that the name of the dead may not be cut off from his kindred

and from the gate of his native place; today you are witnesses." [11]Then all the people who were at the gate, along with the elders, said, "We are witnesses. May the LORD make the woman who is coming into your house like Rachel and Leah, who together built up the house of Israel. May you produce children in Ephʹra·thah and bestow a name in Bethlehem; [12]and, through the children that the LORD will give you by this young woman, may your house be like the house of Perʹez, whom Tāʹmar bore to Judah."

The Genealogy of David

[13] So Bōʹaz took Ruth and she became his wife. When they came together, the LORD made her conceive, and she bore a son. [14]Then the women said to Nāʹo·mī, "Blessed be the LORD, who has not left you this day without next-of-kin;[i] and may his name be renowned in Israel! [15]He shall be to you a restorer of life and a nourisher of your old age; for your daughter-in-law who loves you, who is more to you than seven sons, has borne him." [16]Then Nāʹo·mī took the child and laid him in her bosom, and became his nurse. [17]The women of the neighborhood gave him a name, saying, "A son has been born to Nāʹo·mī." They named him Ōʹbed; he became the father of Jesse, the father of David.

[18] Now these are the descendants of Perʹez: Perʹez became the father of Hezʹron, [19]Hezʹron of Ram, Ram of Am·min·ʹa·dab, [20]Am·min·ʹa·dab of Nahʹshon, Nahʹshon of Salʹmon, [21]Salʹmon of Bōʹaz, Bōʹaz of Ōʹbed, [22] Ōʹbed of Jesse, and Jesse of David.

Giving up his sandal meant that the closer relative was willing to give up his right to own Elimelech's property.

---

[i] Or *one with the right to redeem*   [j] OL Vg: Heb *from the hand of Naomi and from Ruth*

1 Samuel

The book of First Samuel tells about the struggles Israel faced as they became a people ruled by kings. The book tells stories about Samuel, Saul, and David. Samuel, the last judge of the Israelites, was a great leader who lived about 1000 BC. God used Samuel to anoint Saul as the first king of Israel. But because Saul did not follow God's ways, God chose David as the next king of Israel. Just as he had done for Saul, Samuel anointed David as king. Even though David and Saul argued, David still loved Saul and his son Jonathan. He respected that God

appointed Saul king first. David honored Saul and Jonathan.

Like most of the history books of the Bible, First Samuel was not finished until many years after the things it tells about. The book is named for one of its most important characters, Samuel, who lived about 450 years before the book was finished in the sixth century BC. Second Samuel continues the story started in this book. The two books are really one long story about the early Israelite kingdom.

1 Samuel 17

When Joshua led the people into Canaan, no one was living in the land near the city of Shiloh. Joshua chose Shiloh as his headquarters, and it became an important religious center for the Israelites. The ark of the covenant and the tabernacle were kept at Shiloh until the time of Samuel. Samuel was dedicated at Shiloh as a child. Shiloh was also one of the cities of refuge—a place a person could go if he had killed someone without meaning to.

Samuel's Birth and Dedication

1 There was a certain man of Rā·ma·thā´-im, a Zuph´īte*[a]* from the hill country of Ē´phra·im, whose name was El·kā´nah son of Je·rō´ham son of E·lī´hū son of Tō´-hū son of Zuph, an Ē´phra·im·īte. ²He had two wives; the name of the one was Hannah, and the name of the other Pe·nin´nah. Pe·nin´nah had children, but Hannah had no children.

3 Now this man used to go up year by year from his town to worship and to sacrifice to the LORD of hosts at Shī´lōh, where the two sons of Ē´lī, Hoph´nī and Phin´e·has, were priests of the LORD. ⁴On the day when El·kā´nah sacrificed, he would give portions to his wife Pe·nin´-nah and to all her sons and daughters; ⁵but to Hannah he gave a double portion,*[b]* because he loved her, though the LORD had closed her womb. ⁶Her rival used to provoke her severely, to irritate her, because the LORD had closed her womb. ⁷So it went on year by year; as often as she went up to the house of the LORD, she used to provoke her. Therefore Hannah wept and would not eat. ⁸Her husband El·kā´nah said to her, "Hannah, why do you weep? Why do you not eat? Why is your heart sad? Am I not more to you than ten sons?"

9 After they had eaten and drunk at Shī´lōh, Hannah rose and presented herself before the LORD.*[c]* Now Ē´lī the priest was sitting on the seat beside the doorpost of the temple of the LORD. ¹⁰She was deeply distressed and prayed to the LORD, and wept bitterly. ¹¹She made this vow: "O LORD of hosts, if only you will look on the misery of your servant, and remember me, and not forget your servant, but will give to your servant a male child, then I will set him before you as a nazirite*[d]* until the day of his death. He shall drink neither wine nor intoxicants,*[e]* and no razor shall touch his head."

12 As she continued praying before the LORD, Ē´lī observed her mouth. ¹³Hannah was praying silently; only her lips moved, but her voice was not heard; therefore Ē´lī thought she was drunk. ¹⁴So Ē´lī said to her, "How long will you make a drunken spectacle of yourself? Put away your wine." ¹⁵But Hannah answered, "No, my lord, I am a woman deeply troubled; I have drunk neither wine nor strong drink, but I have been pouring out my soul before the LORD. ¹⁶Do not regard your servant as a worth-

Have you ever waited a very long time for something? Hannah and her husband, Elkanah, waited many years for a child. Hannah prayed for a son and promised to dedicate him to God. God answered her prayer, and Hannah gave birth to a son named Samuel. When he was old enough, she took him to serve in the sanctuary at Shiloh. Samuel grew up to be one of the great judges of Israel.

[a] Compare Gk and 1 Chr 6.35-36: Heb *Ramathaim-zophim* *[b]* Syr: Meaning of Heb uncertain
[c] Gk: Heb lacks *and presented herself before the LORD* *[d]* That is *one separated* or *one consecrated*
[e] Cn: Compare Gk Q Ms 1.22: MT *then I will give him to the LORD all the days of his life*

less woman, for I have been speaking out of my great anxiety and vexation all this time." [17]Then Ē′lī answered, "Go in peace; the God of Israel grant the petition you have made to him." [18]And she said, "Let your servant find favor in your sight." Then the woman went to her quarters,[f] ate and drank with her husband,[g] and her countenance was sad no longer.[h]

19 They rose early in the morning and worshiped before the LORD; then they went back to their house at Rā′mah. El·kā′nah knew his wife Hannah, and the LORD remembered her. [20]In due time Hannah conceived and bore a son. She named him Samuel, for she said, "I have asked him of the LORD."

21 The man El·kā′nah and all his household went up to offer to the LORD the yearly sacrifice, and to pay his vow. [22]But Hannah did not go up, for she said to her husband, "As soon as the child is weaned, I will bring him, that he may appear in the presence of the LORD, and remain there forever; I will offer him as a nazirite[i] for all time."[j] [23]Her husband El·kā′nah said to her, "Do what seems best to you, wait until you have weaned him; only—may the LORD establish his word."[k] So the woman remained and nursed her son, until she weaned him. [24]When she had weaned him, she took him up with her, along with a three-year-old bull,[l] an ephah of flour, and a skin of wine. She brought him to the house of the LORD at Shī′lōh; and the child was young. [25]Then they slaughtered the bull, and they brought the child to Ē′lī. [26]And she said, "Oh, my lord! As you live, my lord, I am the woman who was standing here in your presence, praying to the LORD. [27]For this child I prayed; and the LORD has granted me the petition that I made to him. [28]Therefore I have lent him to the LORD; as long as he lives, he is given to the LORD."

She left him there for[m] the LORD.

> "There is no Holy One like the LORD, no one besides you; there is no Rock like our God."
>
> 1 Samuel 2:2

Hannah's Prayer

2 Hannah prayed and said,
"My heart exults in the LORD;
my strength is exalted in my God.[n]
My mouth derides my enemies,
because I rejoice in my[o] victory.

2 "There is no Holy One like the LORD,
no one besides you;
there is no Rock like our God.
3 Talk no more so very proudly,
let not arrogance come from your mouth;
for the LORD is a God of knowledge,
and by him actions are weighed.
4 The bows of the mighty are broken,
but the feeble gird on strength.
5 Those who were full have hired themselves out for bread,
but those who were hungry are fat with spoil.
The barren has borne seven,
but she who has many children is forlorn.
6 The LORD kills and brings to life;
he brings down to Shē′ōl and raises up.
7 The LORD makes poor and makes rich;
he brings low, he also exalts.
8 He raises up the poor from the dust;
he lifts the needy from the ash heap,
to make them sit with princes
and inherit a seat of honor.[p]

[f] Gk: Heb went her way   [g] Gk: Heb lacks and drank with her husband   [h] Gk: Meaning of Heb uncertain   [i] That is one separated or one consecrated   [j] Cn: Compare Q Ms: MT lacks I will offer him as a nazirite for all time   [k] MT: Q Ms Gk Compare Syr that which goes out of your mouth   [l] Q Ms Gk Syr: MT three bulls   [m] Gk (Compare Q Ms) and Gk at 2.11: MT And he (that is, Elkanah) worshiped there before   [n] Gk: Heb the LORD   [o] Q Ms: MT your   [p] Gk (Compare Q Ms) adds He grants the vow of the one who vows, and blesses the years of the just

For the pillars of the earth are the
LORD's,
and on them he has set the world.

[9] "He will guard the feet of his faithful
ones,
but the wicked shall be cut off in
darkness;
for not by might does one prevail.
[10] The LORD! His adversaries shall be
shattered;
the Most High[q] will thunder in
heaven.
The LORD will judge the ends of the
earth;
he will give strength to his king,
and exalt the power of his
anointed."

Eli's Wicked Sons

[11] Then El·kā´nah went home to Rā´-
mah, while the boy remained to minister
to the LORD, in the presence of the priest
Ē´lī.

[12] Now the sons of Ē´lī were scoundrels; they had no regard for the LORD
[13]or for the duties of the priests to the
people. When anyone offered sacrifice,
the priest's servant would come, while
the meat was boiling, with a three-
pronged fork in his hand, [14]and he
would thrust it into the pan, or kettle,
or caldron, or pot; all that the fork
brought up the priest would take for
himself.[r] This is what they did at Shī´lōh
to all the Israelites who came there.
[15]Moreover, before the fat was burned,
the priest's servant would come and say
to the one who was sacrificing, "Give
meat for the priest to roast; for he will
not accept boiled meat from you, but
only raw." [16]And if the man said to him,
"Let them burn the fat first, and then
take whatever you wish," he would say,
"No, you must give it now; if not, I will
take it by force." [17]Thus the sin of the
young men was very great in the sight of
the LORD; for they treated the offerings
of the LORD with contempt.

The Child Samuel at Shiloh

[18] Samuel was ministering before
the LORD, a boy wearing a linen ephod.
[19]His mother used to make for him a
little robe and take it to him each year,
when she went up with her husband to
offer the yearly sacrifice. [20]Then Ē´lī
would bless El·kā´nah and his wife,
and say, "May the LORD repay[s] you with
children by this woman for the gift that
she made to[t] the LORD"; and then they
would return to their home.

[21] And[u] the LORD took note of Hannah; she conceived and bore three sons
and two daughters. And the boy Samuel
grew up in the presence of the LORD.

Prophecy against Eli's Household

[22] Now Ē´lī was very old. He heard all
that his sons were doing to all Israel, and
how they lay with the women who served
at the entrance to the tent of meeting.
[23]He said to them, "Why do you do such
things? For I hear of your evil dealings
from all these people. [24]No, my sons; it is
not a good report that I hear the people of
the LORD spreading abroad. [25]If one person sins against another, someone can
intercede for the sinner with the LORD;[v]
but if someone sins against the LORD, who
can make intercession?" But they would
not listen to the voice of their father; for it
was the will of the LORD to kill them.

[26] Now the boy Samuel continued to
grow both in stature and in favor with
the LORD and with the people.

[27] A man of God came to Ē´lī and said
to him, "Thus the LORD has said, 'I revealed[w] myself to the family of your ancestor in Egypt when they were slaves[x] to the
house of Pharaoh. [28]I chose him out of all
the tribes of Israel to be my priest, to go up
to my altar, to offer incense, to wear an
ephod before me; and I gave to the family

[q] Cn: Heb *against him he*   [r] Gk Syr Vg: Heb *with
it*   [s] Q Ms Gk: MT *give*   [t] Q Ms Gk: MT *for
the petition that she asked of*   [u] Q Ms Gk: MT
When   [v] Gk Compare Q Ms: MT *another, God
will mediate for him*   [w] Gk Tg Syr: Heb *Did I reveal*
[x] Q Ms Gk: MT lacks *slaves*

of your ancestor all my offerings by fire from the people of Israel. [29]Why then look with greedy eye[y] at my sacrifices and my offerings that I commanded, and honor your sons more than me by fattening yourselves on the choicest parts of every offering of my people Israel?' [30]Therefore the LORD the God of Israel declares: 'I promised that your family and the family of your ancestor should go in and out before me forever'; but now the LORD declares: 'Far be it from me; for those who honor me I will honor, and those who despise me shall be treated with contempt. [31]See, a time is coming when I will cut off your strength and the strength of your ancestor's family, so that no one in your family will live to old age. [32]Then in distress you will look with greedy eye[z] on all the prosperity that shall be bestowed upon Israel; and no one in your family shall ever live to old age. [33]The only one of you whom I shall not cut off from my altar shall be spared to weep out his[a] eyes and grieve his[b] heart; all the members of your household shall die by the sword.[c] [34]The fate of your two sons, Hoph·ni and Phin·e·has, shall be the sign to you—both of them shall die on the same day. [35]I will raise up for myself a faithful priest, who shall do according to what is in my heart and in my mind. I will build him a sure house, and he shall go in and out before my anointed one forever. [36]Everyone who is left in your family shall come to implore him for a piece of silver or a loaf of bread, and shall say, Please put me in one of the priest's places, that I may eat a morsel of bread.' "

Samuel's Calling and Prophetic Activity

3 Now the boy Samuel was ministering to the LORD under E·li. The word of the LORD was rare in those days; visions were not widespread.

2 At that time E·li, whose eyesight had begun to grow dim so that he could not see, was lying down in his room; [3]the lamp of God had not yet gone out,

Eli was the priest of the sanctuary at Shiloh and the judge of Israel for forty years. Eli trained Samuel to help him work in the sanctuary. Eli realized that the voice Samuel heard calling in the night was the voice of God. Samuel began serving God as a child. You can do that too! Every church needs greeters to welcome those who come to church and to show visitors where to go. You can serve God in your church by being a greeter. Can you think of other ways you can serve God in your church?

and Samuel was lying down in the temple of the LORD, where the ark of God was. [4]Then the LORD called, "Samuel! Samuel!"[d] and he said, "Here I am!" [5]and ran to E·li, and said, "Here I am, for you called me." But he said, "I did not call; lie down again." So he went and lay down. [6]The LORD called again, "Samuel!" Samuel got up and went to E·li, and said, "Here I am, for you called me." But he said, "I did not call, my son; lie down again." [7]Now Samuel did not yet know the LORD, and the word of the LORD had not yet been revealed to him. [8]The LORD

In the middle of the night, Samuel woke up when he heard someone calling his name. He thought Eli was calling him, so he hurried to Eli's side. After the third time this happened, Eli realized that God was calling Samuel and told him to answer. God was calling Samuel to special service as a priest and a prophet to God's people. As he grew up, God was with Samuel. God is with us too!

[y] Q Ms Gk: MT *then kick*   [z] Q Ms Gk: MT *will kick*   [a] Q Ms Gk: MT *your*   [b] Q Ms Gk: Heb *your*   [c] Q Ms See Gk: MT *die like mortals*   [d] Q Ms Gk See 3.10: MT *the LORD called Samuel*

called Samuel again, a third time. And he got up and went to Ēʹlī, and said, "Here I am, for you called me." Then Ēʹlī perceived that the LORD was calling the boy. [9]Therefore Ēʹlī said to Samuel, "Go, lie down; and if he calls you, you shall say, 'Speak, LORD, for your servant is listening.' " So Samuel went and lay down in his place.

10 Now the LORD came and stood there, calling as before, "Samuel! Samuel!" And Samuel said, "Speak, for your servant is listening." [11]Then the LORD said to Samuel, "See, I am about to do something in Israel that will make both ears of anyone who hears of it tingle. [12]On that day I will fulfill against Ēʹlī all that I have spoken concerning his house, from beginning to end. [13]For I have told him that I am about to punish his house forever, for the iniquity that he knew, because his sons were blaspheming God,[e] and he did not restrain them. [14]Therefore I swear to the house of Ēʹlī that the iniquity of Eli's house shall not be expiated by sacrifice or offering forever."

15 Samuel lay there until morning; then he opened the doors of the house of the LORD. Samuel was afraid to tell the vision to Ēʹlī. [16]But Ēʹlī called Samuel and said, "Samuel, my son." He said, "Here I am." [17]Ēʹlī said, "What was it that he told you? Do not hide it from me. May God do so to you and more also, if you hide anything from me of all that he told you." [18]So Samuel told him everything and hid nothing from him. Then he said, "It is the LORD; let him do what seems good to him."

19 As Samuel grew up, the LORD was with him and let none of his

> Dan was at the northern end of Israel, and Beersheba was at the southern end. The phrase *from Dan to Beersheba* meant the entire length of the land.

> "As Samuel grew up, the LORD was with him and let none of his words fall to the ground. And all Israel from Dan to Beersheba knew that Samuel was a trustworthy prophet of the LORD." 1 Samuel 3:19-20

words fall to the ground. [20]And all Israel from Dan to Bēʹer-shēʹba knew that Samuel was a trustworthy prophet of the LORD. [21]The LORD continued to appear at Shīʹlōh, for the LORD revealed himself to Samuel at Shīʹlōh by the word of the LORD.

> Ebenezer was a place where the Israelites fought against the Philistines. Here, the Philistines captured the ark. The word *Ebenezer* is also the name of a stone that was set up to remember a victory over the Philistines (see 1 Samuel 7:12). The stone reminded the people that God had helped them. The Israelites believed that the hand of God was in all their victories and defeats. They believed that God was in every part of their lives.

4 [1]And the word of Samuel came to all Israel.

The Ark of God Captured

In those days the Phi·lisʹtines mustered for war against Israel,[f] and Israel went out to battle against them;[g] they encamped at Eb·e·nēʹzer, and the Phi·lisʹtines encamped at Āʹphek. [2]The Phi·lisʹtines drew up in line against Israel, and when the battle was joined,[h] Israel was defeated by the Phi·lisʹtines,

[e] Another reading is *for themselves*　　[f] Gk: Heb lacks *In those days the Philistines mustered for war against Israel*　　[g] Gk: Heb *against the Philistines*　　[h] Meaning of Heb uncertain

who killed about four thousand men on the field of battle. [3]When the troops came to the camp, the elders of Israel said, "Why has the LORD put us to rout today before the Phi·lis′tines? Let us bring the ark of the covenant of the LORD here from Shī′lōh, so that he may come among us and save us from the power of our enemies." [4]So the people sent to Shī′lōh, and brought from there the ark of the covenant of the LORD of hosts, who is enthroned on the cherubim. The two sons of E′lī, Hoph′nī and Phin′e·has, were there with the ark of the covenant of God.

5 When the ark of the covenant of the LORD came into the camp, all Israel gave a mighty shout, so that the earth resounded. [6]When the Phi·lis′tines heard the noise of the shouting, they said, "What does this great shouting in the camp of the Hebrews mean?" When they learned that the ark of the LORD had come to the camp, [7]the Phi·lis′tines were afraid; for they said, "Gods have[i] come into the camp." They also said, "Woe to us! For nothing like this has happened before. [8]Woe to us! Who can deliver us from the power of these mighty gods? These are the gods who struck the Egyptians with every sort of plague in the wilderness. [9]Take courage, and be men, O Phi·lis′tines, in order not to become slaves to the Hebrews as they have been to you; be men and fight."

10 So the Phi·lis′tines fought; Israel was defeated, and they fled, everyone to his home. There was a very great slaughter, for there fell of Israel thirty thousand foot soldiers. [11]The ark of God was captured; and the two sons of E′lī, Hoph′nī and Phin′e·has, died.

Death of Eli

12 A man of Benjamin ran from the battle line, and came to Shī′lōh the same day, with his clothes torn and with earth upon his head. [13]When he arrived, E′lī was sitting upon his seat by the road watching, for his heart trembled for the ark of God. When the man came into the

city and told the news, all the city cried out. [14]When E′lī heard the sound of the outcry, he said, "What is this uproar?" Then the man came quickly and told E′lī. [15]Now E′lī was ninety-eight years old and his eyes were set, so that he could not see. [16]The man said to E′lī, "I have just come from the battle; I fled from the battle today." He said, "How did it go, my son?" [17]The messenger replied, "Israel has fled before the Phi·lis′tines, and there has also been a great slaughter among the troops; your two sons also, Hoph′nī and Phin′e·has, are dead, and the ark of God has been captured." [18]When he mentioned the ark of God, E′lī[j] fell over backward from his seat by the side of the gate; and his neck was broken and he died, for he was an old man, and heavy. He had judged Israel forty years.

19 Now his daughter-in-law, the wife of Phin′e·has, was pregnant, about to give birth. When she heard the news that the ark of God was captured, and that her father-in-law and her husband were dead, she bowed and gave birth; for her labor pains overwhelmed her. [20]As she was about to die, the women attending her said to her, "Do not be afraid, for you have borne a son." But she did not answer or give heed. [21]She named the child Ich′a·bod, meaning, "The glory has departed from Israel," because the ark of God had been captured and because of her father-in-law and her husband. [22]She said, "The glory has departed from Israel, for the ark of God has been captured."

The Philistines and the Ark

5 When the Phi·lis′tines captured the ark of God, they brought it from Eb·e·ne′zer to Ash′dod; [2]then the Phi·lis′tines took the ark of God and brought it into the house of Dā′gon and placed it beside Dā′gon. [3]When the people of Ash′dod rose early the next day, there was Dā′gon, fallen on his face

[i] Or A god has   [j] Heb he

The Philistines were people who lived on the coast. Their name comes from an Egyptian word meaning "people of the sea." The Philistines were often at war with the Israelites. They had large armies with chariots and weapons made of iron. Their chief cities were Gath, Gaza, Ashkelon, Ashdod, and Ekron.

to the ground before the ark of the LORD. So they took Dā´gon and put him back in his place. [4]But when they rose early on the next morning, Dā´gon had fallen on his face to the ground before the ark of the LORD, and the head of Dā´gon and both his hands were lying cut off upon the threshold; only the trunk of[k] Dā´gon was left to him. [5]This is why the priests of Dā´gon and all who enter the house of Dā´gon do not step on the threshold of Dā´gon in Ash´dod to this day.

6 The hand of the LORD was heavy upon the people of Ash´dod, and he terrified and struck them with tumors, both in Ash´dod and in its territory. [7]And when the inhabitants of Ash´dod saw how things were, they said, "The ark of the God of Israel must not remain with us; for his hand is heavy on us and on our god Dā´gon." [8]So they sent and gathered together all the lords of the Phi·lis´tines, and said, "What shall we do with the ark of the God of Israel?" The inhabitants of Gath replied, "Let the ark of God be moved on to us."[l] So they moved the ark of the God of Israel to Gath.[m] [9]But after they had brought it to Gath,[n] the hand of the LORD was against the city, causing a very great panic; he struck the inhabitants of the city, both young and old, so that tumors broke out on them. [10]So they sent the ark of the God of Israel[o] to Ek´ron. But when the ark of God came to Ek´ron, the people of

Ek´ron cried out, "Why[p] have they brought around to us[q] the ark of the God of Israel to kill us[q] and our[r] people?" [11]They sent therefore and gathered together all the lords of the Phi·lis´tines, and said, "Send away the ark of the God of Israel, and let it return to its own place, that it may not kill us and our people." For there was a deathly panic[s] throughout the whole city. The hand of God was very heavy there; [12]those who did not die were stricken with tumors, and the cry of the city went up to heaven.

The Ark Returned to Israel

6 The ark of the LORD was in the country of the Phi·lis´tines seven months. [2]Then the Phi·lis´tines called for the priests and the diviners and said, "What shall we do with the ark of the LORD? Tell us what we should send with it to its place." [3]They said, "If you send away the ark of the God of Israel, do not send it empty, but by all means return him a guilt offering. Then you will be healed and will be ransomed;[t] will not his hand then turn from you?" [4]And they said, "What is the guilt offering that we shall return to him?" They answered, "Five gold tumors and five gold mice, according to the number of the lords of the Phi·lis´tines; for the same plague was upon all of you and upon your lords. [5]So you must make images of your tumors and images of your mice that ravage the land, and give glory to the God of Israel; perhaps he will lighten his hand on you and your gods and your land. [6]Why should you harden your hearts as the Egyptians and Pharaoh hardened their hearts? After he had made fools of them, did they not let the people go, and they departed? [7]Now then, get ready a new cart and two milch cows that have never borne

[k] Heb lacks *the trunk of*   [l] Gk Compare Q Ms: MT *They answered, "Let the ark of the God of Israel be brought around to Gath."*   [m] Gk: Heb lacks *to Gath*   [n] Q Ms: MT lacks *to Gath*   [o] Q Ms Gk: MT lacks *of Israel*   [p] Q Ms Gk: MT lacks *Why*   [q] Heb *me*   [r] Heb *my*   [s] Q Ms reads *a panic from the LORD*   [t] Q Ms Gk: MT *and it will be known to you*

a yoke, and yoke the cows to the cart, but take their calves home, away from them. [8]Take the ark of the LORD and place it on the cart, and put in a box at its side the figures of gold, which you are returning to him as a guilt offering. Then send it off, and let it go its way. [9]And watch; if it goes up on the way to its own land, to Beth-shē´-mesh, then it is he who has done us this great harm; but if not, then we shall know that it is not his hand that struck us; it happened to us by chance."

10 The men did so; they took two milch cows and yoked them to the cart, and shut up their calves at home. [11]They put the ark of the LORD on the cart, and the box with the gold mice and the images of their tumors. [12]The cows went straight in the direction of Beth-shē´mesh along one highway, lowing as they went; they turned neither to the right nor to the left, and the lords of the Phi·lis´tines went after them as far as the border of Beth-shē´mesh.

13 Now the people of Beth-shē´mesh were reaping their wheat harvest in the valley. When they looked up and saw the ark, they went with rejoicing to meet it.[u] [14]The cart came into the field of Joshua of Beth-shē´mesh, and stopped there. A large stone was there; so they split up the wood of the cart and offered the cows as a burnt offering to the LORD. [15]The Lē´vītes took down the ark of the LORD and the box that was beside it, in which were the gold objects, and set them upon the large stone. Then the people of Beth-shē´mesh offered burnt offerings and presented sacrifices on that day to the LORD. [16]When the five lords of the Phi·lis´tines saw it, they returned that day to Ek´ron.

17 These are the gold tumors, which the Phi·lis´tines returned as a guilt offering to the LORD: one for Ash´dod, one for Gā´za, one for Ash´ke·lon, one for Gath, one for Ek´ron; [18]also the gold mice, according to the number of all the cities of the Phi·lis´tines belonging to the five lords, both fortified cities and unwalled

villages. The great stone, beside which they set down the ark of the LORD, is a witness to this day in the field of Joshua of Beth-shē´mesh.

The Ark at Kiriath-jearim

19 The descendants of Jec·o·nī´ah did not rejoice with the people of Beth-shē´-mesh when they greeted[v] the ark of the LORD; and he killed seventy men of them.[w] The people mourned because the LORD had made a great slaughter among the people. [20]Then the people of Beth-shē´-mesh said, "Who is able to stand before the LORD, this holy God? To whom shall he go so that we may be rid of him?" [21]So they sent messengers to the inhabitants of Kir´i·ath-jē´a·rim, saying, "The Phi·lis´tines have returned the ark of the LORD. Come down and take it up to you."

7 [1]And the people of Kir´i·ath-jē´-a·rim came and took up the ark of the LORD, and brought it to the house of A·bin´a·dab on the hill. They consecrated his son, El·ē·ā´zar, to have charge of the ark of the LORD.

2 From the day that the ark was lodged at Kir´i·ath-jē´a·rim, a long time passed, some twenty years, and all the house of Israel lamented[x] after the LORD.

Samuel as Judge

3 Then Samuel said to all the house of Israel, "If you are returning to the LORD with all your heart, then put away the foreign gods and the As·tar´tēs from among you. Direct your heart to the LORD, and serve him only, and he will deliver you out of the hand of the Phi·lis´tines." [4]So Israel put away the Bā´als and the As·tar´tēs, and they served the LORD only.

5 Then Samuel said, "Gather all Israel at Miz´pah, and I will pray to the LORD for you." [6]So they gathered at Miz´pah,

---

[u] Gk: Heb *rejoiced to see it* [v] Gk: Heb *And he killed some of the people of Beth-shemesh, because they looked into* [w] Heb *killed seventy men, fifty thousand men* [x] Meaning of Heb uncertain[v] Gk: Heb *And he killed some of the people of Beth-shemesh, because they looked into*

and drew water and poured it out before the LORD. They fasted that day, and said, "We have sinned against the LORD." And Samuel judged the people of Israel at Miz'pah.

7 When the Phi·lis'tines heard that the people of Israel had gathered at Miz'pah, the lords of the Phi·lis'tines went up against Israel. And when the people of Israel heard of it they were afraid of the Phi·lis'tines. ⁸The people of Israel said to Samuel, "Do not cease to cry out to the LORD our God for us, and pray that he may save us from the hand of the Phi·lis'tines." ⁹So Samuel took a sucking lamb and offered it as a whole burnt offering to the LORD; Samuel cried out to the LORD for Israel, and the LORD answered him. ¹⁰As Samuel was offering up the burnt offering, the Phi·lis'tines drew near to attack Israel; but the LORD thundered with a mighty voice that day against the Phi·lis'tines and threw them into confusion; and they were routed before Israel. ¹¹And the men of Israel went out of Miz'pah and pursued the Phi·lis'tines, and struck them down as far as beyond Beth-car.

12 Then Samuel took a stone and set it up between Miz'pah and Je·sha'nah,ʸ and named it Eb·e·ne'zer;ᶻ for he said, "Thus far the LORD has helped us." ¹³So the Phi·lis'tines were subdued and did not again enter the territory of Israel; the hand of the LORD was against the Phi·lis'tines all the days of Samuel. ¹⁴The towns that the Phi·lis'tines had taken from Israel were restored to Israel, from Ek'ron to Gath; and Israel recovered their territory from the hand of the Phi·lis'tines. There was peace also between Israel and the Am'o·rītes.

15 Samuel judged Israel all the days of his life. ¹⁶He went on a circuit year by year to Beth'el, Gil'gal, and Miz'pah; and he judged Israel in all these places. ¹⁷Then he would come back to Rā'mah, for his home was there; he administered justice there to Israel, and built there an altar to the LORD.

Israel Demands a King

8 When Samuel became old, he made his sons judges over Israel. ²The name of his firstborn son was Jō'el, and the name of his second, Ab·ī'jah; they were judges in Bē'er-shē'ba. ³Yet his sons did not follow in his ways, but turned aside after gain; they took bribes and perverted justice.

4 Then all the elders of Israel gathered together and came to Samuel at Rā'mah, ⁵and said to him, "You are old and your sons do not follow in your ways; appoint for us, then, a king to govern us, like other nations." ⁶But the thing displeased Samuel when they said, "Give us a king to govern us." Samuel prayed to the LORD, ⁷and the LORD said to Samuel, "Listen to the voice of the people in all that they say to you; for they have not rejected you, but they have rejected me from being king over them. ⁸Just as they have done to me,ᵃ from the day I brought them up out of Egypt to this day, forsaking me and serving other gods, so also they are doing to you. ⁹Now then, listen to their voice; only— you shall solemnly warn them, and show them the ways of the king who shall reign over them."

10 So Samuel reported all the words of the LORD to the people who were asking him for a king. ¹¹He said, "These will be the ways of the king who will reign

Gilgal was the first place the Israelites camped after they crossed the Jordan River to enter Canaan. At Gilgal, the people set up twelve memorial stones taken from the Jordan. Gilgal became the base city for the Israelites' battles against the Canaanites. The Israelites built a great sanctuary there.

ʸ Gk Syr: Heb *Shen*   ᶻ That is *Stone of Help*
ᵃ Gk: Heb lacks *to me*

over you: he will take your sons and appoint them to his chariots and to be his horsemen, and to run before his chariots; [12]and he will appoint for himself commanders of thousands and commanders of fifties, and some to plow his ground and to reap his harvest, and to make his implements of war and the equipment of his chariots. [13]He will take your daughters to be perfumers and cooks and bakers. [14]He will take the best of your fields and vineyards and olive orchards and give them to his courtiers. [15]He will take one-tenth of your grain and of your vineyards and give it to his officers and his courtiers. [16]He will take your male and female slaves, and the best of your cattle[b] and donkeys, and put them to his work. [17]He will take one-tenth of your flocks, and you shall be his slaves. [18]And in that day you will cry out because of your king, whom you have chosen for yourselves; but the LORD will not answer you in that day."

Israel's Request for a King Granted

19 But the people refused to listen to the voice of Samuel; they said, "No! but we are determined to have a king over us, [20]so that we also may be like other nations, and that our king may govern us and go out before us and fight our battles." [21]When Samuel had heard all the words of the people, he repeated them in the ears of the LORD. [22]The LORD said to Samuel, "Listen to their voice and set a king over them." Samuel then said to the people of Israel, "Each of you return home."

Saul Chosen to Be King

9 There was a man of Benjamin whose name was Kish son of A·bi′-el son of Zē′ror son of Be·cō′rath son of A·phī′ah, a Ben′ja·min·ite, a man of wealth. [2]He had a son whose name was Saul, a handsome young man. There was not a man among the people of Israel more handsome than he; he stood head and shoulders above everyone else.

3 Now the donkeys of Kish, Saul's father, had strayed. So Kish said to his son Saul, "Take one of the boys with you; go and look for the donkeys." [4]He passed through the hill country of Ē′phra·im and passed through the land of Shal′i·shah, but they did not find them. And they passed through the land of Shā′a·lim, but they were not there. Then he passed through the land of Benjamin, but they did not find them.

5 When they came to the land of Zuph, Saul said to the boy who was with him, "Let us turn back, or my father will stop worrying about the donkeys and worry about us." [6]But he said to him, "There is a man of God in this town; he is a man held in honor. Whatever he says always comes true. Let us go there now; perhaps he will tell us about the journey on which we have set out." [7]Then Saul replied to the boy, "But if we go, what can we bring the man? For the bread in our sacks is gone, and there is no present to bring to the man of God. What have we?" [8]The boy answered Saul again, "Here, I have with me a quarter shekel of silver; I will give it to the man of God, to tell us our way." [9](Formerly in Israel, anyone who went to inquire of God would say, "Come, let us go to the seer"; for the one who is now called a prophet was formerly called a seer.) [10]Saul said to the boy, "Good; come, let us go." So they went to the town where the man of God was.

11 As they went up the hill to the town, they met some girls coming out to draw water, and said to them, "Is the seer here?" [12]They answered, "Yes, there he is just ahead of you. Hurry; he has come just now to the town, because the people have a sacrifice today at the shrine. [13]As soon as you enter the town, you will find him, before he goes up to the shrine to eat. For the people will not eat until he comes, since he must bless the sacrifice; afterward those eat who are invited. Now

---

[b] Gk: Heb *young men*

Can you think of some words that have more than one meaning? How about "left" or "note"? The word "Israel" is sort of like that. The name "Israel" was used for the people as a whole and also for their land. When the twelve tribes were united, the name "Israel" was used for the kingdom. The kingdom was called Israel under the rule of Saul, David, and Solomon. After Solomon died, the kingdom divided into two parts, north and south. The northern kingdom was called Israel until it was overthrown by Assyria about 722 BC.

go up, for you will meet him immediately." [14]So they went up to the town. As they were entering the town, they saw Samuel coming out toward them on his way up to the shrine.

15 Now the day before Saul came, the LORD had revealed to Samuel: [16]"Tomorrow about this time I will send to you a man from the land of Benjamin, and you shall anoint him to be ruler over my people Israel. He shall save my people from the hand of the Phi·lis′tines; for I have seen the suffering of[c] my people, because their outcry has come to me." [17]When Samuel saw Saul, the LORD told him, "Here is the man of whom I spoke to you. He it is who shall rule over my people." [18]Then Saul approached Samuel inside the gate, and said, "Tell me, please, where is the house of the seer?" [19]Samuel answered Saul, "I am the seer; go up before me to the shrine, for today you shall eat with me, and in the morning I will let you go and will tell you all that is on your mind. [20]As for your donkeys that were lost three days ago, give no further thought to them, for they have been found. And on whom is all Israel's desire fixed, if not on you and on all your ancestral house?" [21]Saul answered, "I am

only a Ben′ja·min·īte, from the least of the tribes of Israel, and my family is the humblest of all the families of the tribe of Benjamin. Why then have you spoken to me in this way?"

22 Then Samuel took Saul and his servant-boy and brought them into the hall, and gave them a place at the head of those who had been invited, of whom there were about thirty. [23]And Samuel said to the cook, "Bring the portion I gave you, the one I asked you to put aside." [24]The cook took up the thigh and what went with it[d] and set them before Saul. Samuel said, "See, what was kept is set before you. Eat; for it is set[e] before you at the appointed time, so that you might eat with the guests."[f]

So Saul ate with Samuel that day. [25]When they came down from the shrine into the town, a bed was spread for Saul[g] on the roof, and he lay down to sleep.[h] [26]Then at the break of dawn[i] Samuel called to Saul upon the roof, "Get up, so that I may send you on your way." Saul got up, and both he and Samuel went out into the street.

Sometimes we want to be like someone else instead of being ourselves. The people of Israel wanted to be like the people who lived around them, so they asked Samuel for a king. Samuel told them having a king would cause trouble because God was their king. But the people insisted (see 1 Samuel 8). God told Samuel to anoint Saul. Samuel poured special oil on Saul's head as a sign that God had chosen him.

[c] Gk: Heb lacks the suffering of   [d] Meaning of Heb uncertain   [e] Q Ms Gk: MT it was kept   [f] Cn: Heb it was kept for you, saying, I have invited the people   [g] Gk: Heb and he spoke with Saul   [h] Gk: Heb lacks and he lay down to sleep   [i] Gk: Heb and they arose early and at break of dawn

Samuel Anoints Saul

27 As they were going down to the outskirts of the town, Samuel said to Saul, "Tell the boy to go on before us, and when he has passed on, stop here yourself for a while, that I may make known to you the word of God."

10 [1]Samuel took a vial of oil and poured it on his head, and kissed him; he said, "The LORD has anointed you ruler over his people Israel. You shall reign over the people of the LORD and you will save them from the hand of their enemies all around. Now this shall be the sign to you that the LORD has anointed you ruler[j] over his heritage: [2]When you depart from me today you will meet two men by Rachel's tomb in the territory of Benjamin at Zel′zah; they will say to you, 'The donkeys that you went to seek are found, and now your father has stopped worrying about them and is worrying about you, saying: What shall I do about my son?' [3]Then you shall go on from there further and come to the oak of Ta′bor; three men going up to God at Beth′el will meet you there, one carrying three kids, another carrying three loaves of bread, and another carrying a skin of wine. [4]They will greet you and give you two loaves of bread, which you shall accept from them. [5]After that you shall come to Gib′e·ath-e·lo′him,[k] at the place where the Phi·lis′tine garrison is; there, as you come to the town, you will meet a band of prophets coming down from the shrine with harp, tambourine, flute, and lyre playing in front of them; they will be in a prophetic frenzy. [6]Then the spirit of the LORD will possess you, and you will be in a prophetic frenzy along with them and be turned into a different person. [7]Now when these signs meet you, do whatever you see fit to do, for God is with you. [8]And you shall go down to Gil′gal ahead of me; then I will come down to you to present burnt offerings and offer sacrifices of well-being. Seven days you shall wait, until I come to you and show you what you shall do."

Saul Prophesies

9 As he turned away to leave Samuel, God gave him another heart; and all these signs were fulfilled that day. [10]When they were going from there[l] to Gib′e·ah,[m] a band of prophets met him; and the spirit of God possessed him, and he fell into a prophetic frenzy along with them. [11]When all who knew him before saw how he prophesied with the prophets, the people said to one another, "What has come over the son of Kish? Is Saul also among the prophets?" [12]A man of the place answered, "And who is their father?" Therefore it became a proverb, "Is Saul also among the prophets?" [13]When his prophetic frenzy had ended, he went home.[n]

14 Saul's uncle said to him and to the boy, "Where did you go?" And he replied, "To seek the donkeys; and when we saw they were not to be found, we went to Samuel." [15]Saul's uncle said, "Tell me what Samuel said to you." [16]Saul said to his uncle, "He told us that the donkeys had been found." But about the matter of the kingship, of which Samuel had spoken, he did not tell him anything.

Saul Proclaimed King

17 Samuel summoned the people to the LORD at Miz′pah [18]and said to them,[o] "Thus says the LORD, the God of Israel, 'I brought up Israel out of Egypt, and I rescued you from the hand of the Egyptians and from the hand of all the kingdoms that were oppressing you.' [19]But today you have rejected your God, who saves you from all your calamities and your distresses; and you have said, 'No! but set a king over us.' Now therefore present yourselves before the LORD by your tribes and by your clans."

[j] Gk: Heb lacks *over his people Israel. You shall . . . anointed you ruler*   [k] Or *the Hill of God*   [l] Gk: Heb *they came there*   [m] Or *the hill*   [n] Cn: Heb *he came to the shrine*   [o] Heb *to the people of Israel*

20 Then Samuel brought all the tribes of Israel near, and the tribe of Benjamin was taken by lot. ²¹He brought the tribe of Benjamin near by its families, and the family of the Mā´trītes was taken by lot. Finally he brought the family of the Mā´trītes near man by man,ᵖ and Saul the son of Kish was taken by lot. But when they sought him, he could not be found. ²²So they inquired again of the LORD, "Did the man come here?"�q and the LORD said, "See, he has hidden himself among the baggage." ²³Then they ran and brought him from there. When he took his stand among the people, he was head and shoulders taller than any of them. ²⁴Samuel said to all the people, "Do you see the one whom the LORD has chosen? There is no one like him among all the people." And all the people shouted, "Long live the king!"

25 Samuel told the people the rights and duties of the kingship; and he wrote them in a book and laid it up before the LORD. Then Samuel sent all the people back to their homes. ²⁶Saul also went to his home at Gib´ē·ah, and with him went warriors whose hearts God had touched. ²⁷But some worthless fellows said, "How can this man save us?" They despised him and brought him no present. But he held his peace.

Now Nā´hash, king of the Am´mon·ītes, had been grievously oppressing the Gad´ītes and the Reū´ben·ītes. He would gouge out the right eye of each of them and would not grant Israel a deliverer. No one was left of the Israelites across the Jordan whose right eye Nā´hash, king of the Am´mon·ītes, had not gouged out. But there were seven thousand men who had escaped from the Am´mon·ītes and had entered Jā´besh-gil´ē·ad.ʳ

Saul Defeats the Ammonites

11 About a month later,ˢ Nā´hash the Am´mon·īte went up and besieged Jā´besh-gil´ē·ad; and all the men of Jā´besh said to Nā´hash, "Make a treaty with us, and we will serve you." ²But Nā-

hash the Am´mon·īte said to them, "On this condition I will make a treaty with you, namely that I gouge out everyone's right eye, and thus put disgrace upon all Israel." ³The elders of Jā´besh said to him, "Give us seven days' respite that we may send messengers through all the territory of Israel. Then, if there is no one to save us, we will give ourselves up to you." ⁴When the messengers came to Gib´ē·ah of Saul, they reported the matter in the hearing of the people; and all the people wept aloud.

5 Now Saul was coming from the field behind the oxen; and Saul said, "What is the matter with the people, that they are weeping?" So they told him the message from the inhabitants of Jā´besh. ⁶And the spirit of God came upon Saul in power when he heard these words, and his anger was greatly kindled. ⁷He took a yoke of oxen, and cut them in pieces and sent them throughout all the territory of Israel by messengers, saying, "Whoever does not come out after Saul and Samuel, so shall it be done to his oxen!" Then the dread of the LORD fell upon the people, and they came out as one. ⁸When he mustered them at Bē´zek, those from Israel were three hundred thousand, and those from Judah seventyᵗ thousand. ⁹They said to the messengers who had come, "Thus shall you say to the inhabitants of Jā´-besh-gil´ē·ad: 'Tomorrow, by the time the sun is hot, you shall have deliverance.'" When the messengers came and told the inhabitants of Jā´besh, they rejoiced. ¹⁰So the inhabitants of Jā´besh said, "Tomorrow we will give ourselves up to you, and you may do to us whatever seems good to you." ¹¹The next day Saul put the people in three companies. At the morning watch they came into the camp and cut down the Am´mon·ītes until the heat of the day; and

---

ᵖ Gk: Heb lacks *Finally . . . man by man*　　�q Gk: Heb *Is there yet a man to come here?*　　ʳ Q Ms Compare Josephus, *Antiquities* VI.v.1 (68-71): MT lacks *Now Nahash . . . entered Jabesh-gilead.*　　ˢ Q Ms Gk: MT lacks *About a month later*　　ᵗ Q Ms Gk: MT *thirty* those who survived were scattered, so that no two of them were left together.

12 The people said to Samuel, "Who is it that said, 'Shall Saul reign over us?' Give them to us so that we may put them to death." ¹³But Saul said, "No one shall be put to death this day, for today the LORD has brought deliverance to Israel."

14 Samuel said to the people, "Come, let us go to Gil´gal and there renew the kingship." ¹⁵So all the people went to Gil´gal, and there they made Saul king before the LORD in Gil´gal. There they sacrificed offerings of well-being before the LORD, and there Saul and all the Israelites rejoiced greatly.

Samuel's Farewell Address

12 Samuel said to all Israel, "I have listened to you in all that you have said to me, and have set a king over you. ²See, it is the king who leads you now; I am old and gray, but my sons are with you. I have led you from my youth until this day. ³Here I am; testify against me before the LORD and before his anointed. Whose ox have I taken? Or whose donkey have I taken? Or whom have I defrauded? Whom have I oppressed? Or from whose hand have I taken a bribe to blind my eyes with it? Testify against me*ᵘ* and I will restore it to you." ⁴They said, "You have not defrauded us or oppressed us or taken anything from the hand of anyone." ⁵He said to them, "The LORD is witness against you, and his anointed is witness this day, that you have not found anything in my hand." And they said, "He is witness."

6 Samuel said to the people, "The LORD is witness, who*ᵛ* appointed Moses and Aaron and brought your ancestors up out of the land of Egypt. ⁷Now therefore take your stand, so that I may enter into judgment with you before the LORD, and I will declare to you*ʷ* all the saving deeds of the LORD that he performed for you and for your ancestors. ⁸When Jacob went into Egypt and the Egyptians oppressed them,*ˣ* then your ancestors cried to the LORD and the LORD sent Moses and Aaron, who brought forth your ancestors out of Egypt, and settled them in this place. ⁹But they forgot the LORD their God; and he sold them into the hand of Sis´e·ra, commander of the army of King Ja´bin of*ʸ* Ha´zor, and into the hand of the Phi·lis´tines, and into the hand of the king of Mo´ab; and they fought against them. ¹⁰Then they cried to the LORD, and said, 'We have sinned, because we have forsaken the LORD, and have served the Ba´als and the As·tar´tes; but now rescue us out of the hand of our enemies, and we will serve you.' ¹¹And the LORD sent Jer·ub·ba´al and Bar´ak,*ᶻ* and Jeph´thah, and Samson,*ᵃ* and rescued you out of the hand of your enemies on every side; and you lived in safety. ¹²But when you saw that King Na´hash of the Am´mon·ites came against you, you said to me, 'No, but a king shall reign over us,' though the LORD your God was your king. ¹³See, here is the king whom you have chosen, for whom you have asked; see, the LORD has set a king over you. ¹⁴If you will fear the LORD and serve him and heed his voice and not rebel against the commandment of the LORD, and if both you and the king who reigns over you will follow the LORD your God, it will be well; ¹⁵but if you will not heed the voice of the LORD, but rebel against the commandment of the LORD, then the hand of the LORD will be against you and your king.*ᵇ* ¹⁶Now therefore take your stand and see this great thing that the LORD will do before your eyes. ¹⁷Is it not the wheat harvest today? I will call upon the LORD, that he may send thunder and rain; and you shall know and see that the wickedness that you have done in the sight of the LORD is great in demanding a

ᵘ Gk: Heb lacks *Testify against me*   *ᵛ* Gk: Heb lacks *is witness, who*   *ʷ* Gk: Heb lacks *and I will declare to you*   *ˣ* Gk: Heb lacks *and the Egyptians oppressed them*   *ʸ* Gk: Heb lacks *King Jabin of*   *ᶻ* Gk Syr: Heb *Bedan*   *ᵃ* Gk: Heb *Samuel*   *ᵇ* Gk: Heb *and your ancestors* king for yourselves." [18]So Samuel called upon the LORD, and the LORD sent thunder and rain that day; and all the people greatly feared the LORD and Samuel.

19 All the people said to Samuel, "Pray to the LORD your God for your servants, so that we may not die; for we have added to all our sins the evil of demanding a king for ourselves." [20]And Samuel said to the people, "Do not be afraid; you have done all this evil, yet do not turn aside from following the LORD, but serve the LORD with all your heart; [21]and do not turn aside after useless things that cannot profit or save, for they are useless. [22]For the LORD will not cast away his people, for his great name's sake, because it has pleased the LORD to make you a people for himself. [23]Moreover as for me, far be it from me that I should sin against the LORD by ceasing to pray for you; and I will instruct you in the good and the right way. [24]Only fear the LORD, and serve him faithfully with all your heart; for consider what great things he has done for you. [25]But if you still do wickedly, you shall be swept away, both you and your king."

Saul's Unlawful Sacrifice

13 Saul was . . .[c] years old when he began to reign; and he reigned . . . and two[d] years over Israel.

2 Saul chose three thousand out of Israel; two thousand were with Saul in Mich´mash and the hill country of Beth´el, and a thousand were with Jonathan in Gib´e·ah of Benjamin; the rest of the people he sent home to their tents. [3]Jonathan defeated the garrison of the Phi·lis´tines that was at Gẽ´ba; and the Phi·lis´tines heard of it. And Saul blew the trumpet throughout all the land, saying, "Let the Hebrews hear!" [4]When all Israel heard that Saul had defeated the garrison of the Phi·lis´tines, and also that Israel had become odious to the Phi·lis´tines, the people were called out to join Saul at Gil´gal.

5 The Phi·lis´tines mustered to fight with Israel, thirty thousand chariots, and six thousand horsemen, and troops like the sand on the seashore in multitude; they came up and encamped at Mich´mash, to the east of Beth-a´ven. [6]When the Israelites saw that they were in distress (for the troops were hard pressed), the people hid themselves in caves and in holes and in rocks and in tombs and in cisterns. [7]Some Hebrews crossed the Jordan to the land of Gad and Gil´e·ad. Saul was still at Gil´gal, and all the people followed him trembling.

8 He waited seven days, the time appointed by Samuel; but Samuel did not come to Gil´gal, and the people began to slip away from Saul.[e] [9]So Saul said, "Bring the burnt offering here to me, and the offerings of well-being." And he offered the burnt offering. [10]As soon as he had finished offering the burnt offering, Samuel arrived; and Saul went out to meet him and salute him. [11]Samuel said, "What have you done?" Saul replied, "When I saw that the people were slipping away from me, and that you did not come within the days appointed, and that the Phi·lis´tines were mustering at Mich´mash, [12]I said, 'Now the Phi·lis´tines will come down upon me at Gil´gal, and I have not entreated the favor of the LORD'; so I forced myself, and offered the burnt offering."

Jonathan was the oldest son of King Saul. He was a warrior who helped his father in many battles. Jonathan was also a good friend to David. You can read about their friendship in chapters 18–20. Jonathan died with his father and brothers in a battle against the Philistines at Gilboa.

[c] The number is lacking in the Heb text (the verse is lacking in the Septuagint).   [d] *Two* is not the entire number; something has dropped out.   [e] Heb *him*

¹³Samuel said to Saul, "You have done foolishly; you have not kept the commandment of the LORD your God, which he commanded you. The LORD would have established your kingdom over Israel forever, ¹⁴but now your kingdom will not continue; the LORD has sought out a man after his own heart; and the LORD has appointed him to be ruler over his people, because you have not kept what the LORD commanded you." ¹⁵And Samuel left and went on his way from Gil'gal.ᶠ The rest of the people followed Saul to join the army; they went up from Gil'gal toward Gib'ē·ah of Benjamin.ᵍ

Preparations for Battle

Saul counted the people who were present with him, about six hundred men. ¹⁶Saul, his son Jonathan, and the people who were present with them stayed in Gē'ba of Benjamin; but the Phi·lis'tines encamped at Mich'mash. ¹⁷And raiders came out of the camp of the Phi·lis'tines in three companies; one company turned toward Oph'rah, to the land of Shū'al, ¹⁸another company turned toward Beth-hō'ron, and another company turned toward the mountainʰ that looks down upon the valley of Ze·bō'im toward the wilderness.

19 Now there was no smith to be found throughout all the land of Israel; for the Phi·lis'tines said, "The Hebrews must not make swords or spears for themselves"; ²⁰so all the Israelites went down to the Phi·lis'tines to sharpen their plowshares, mattocks, axes, or sickles;ⁱ ²¹The charge was two-thirds of a shekelʲ for the plowshares and for the mattocks, and one-third of a shekel for sharpening the axes and for setting the goads.ᵏ ²²So on the day of the battle neither sword nor spear was to be found in the possession of any of the people with Saul and Jonathan; but Saul and his son Jonathan had them.

Jonathan Surprises and Routs the Philistines

23 Now a garrison of the Phi·lis'tines had gone out to the pass of Mich'mash.

14 ¹One day Jonathan son of Saul said to the young man who carried his armor, "Come, let us go over to the Phi·lis'tine garrison on the other side." But he did not tell his father. ²Saul was staying in the outskirts of Gib'ē·ah under the pomegranate tree that is at Mig'ron; the troops that were with him were about six hundred men, ³along with A·hī'jah son of A·hī'tub, Ich'a·bod's brother, son of Phin'e·has son of Ē'li, the priest of the LORD in Shī'lōh, carrying an ephod. Now the people did not know that Jonathan had gone. ⁴In the pass,ˡ by which Jonathan tried to go over to the Phi·lis'tine garrison, there was a rocky crag on one side and a rocky crag on the other; the name of the one was Bō'zez, and the name of the other Sē'neh. ⁵One crag rose on the north in front of Mich'mash, and the other on the south in front of Gē'ba.

6 Jonathan said to the young man who carried his armor, "Come, let us go over to the garrison of these uncircumcised; it may be that the LORD will act for us; for nothing can hinder the LORD from saving by many or by few." ⁷His armor-bearer said to him, "Do all that your mind inclines to.ᵐ I am with you; as your mind is, so is mine."ⁿ ⁸Then Jonathan said, "Now we will cross over to those men and will show ourselves to them. ⁹If they say to us, 'Wait until we come to you,' then we will stand still in our place, and we will not go up to them. ¹⁰But if they say, 'Come up to us,' then we will go up; for the LORD has given them into our hand. That will be the sign for us." ¹¹So both of them showed themselves to the garrison of the Phi·lis'tines; and the Phi·lis'tines said, "Look, Hebrews are coming out of the

---

ᶠ Gk: Heb *went up from Gilgal to Gibeah of Benjamin* ᵍ Gk: Heb lacks *The rest . . . of Benjamin* ʰ Cn: Compare Gk: Heb *toward the border* ⁱ Gk: Heb *plowshare* ʲ Heb *was a pim* ᵏ Cn: Meaning of Heb uncertain ˡ Heb *Between the passes* ᵐ Gk: Heb *Do all that is in your mind. Turn*   ⁿ Gk: Heb lacks *so is mine* holes where they have hidden themselves." [12]The men of the garrison hailed Jonathan and his armor-bearer, saying, "Come up to us, and we will show you something." Jonathan said to his armor-bearer, "Come up after me; for the LORD has given them into the hand of Israel." [13]Then Jonathan climbed up on his hands and feet, with his armor-bearer following after him. The Phi·lis·tines[o] fell before Jonathan, and his armor-bearer, coming after him, killed them. [14]In that first slaughter Jonathan and his armor-bearer killed about twenty men within an area about half a furrow long in an acre[p] of land. [15]There was a panic in the camp, in the field, and among all the people; the garrison and even the raiders trembled; the earth quaked; and it became a very great panic.

16 Saul's lookouts in Gib´e·ah of Benjamin were watching as the multitude was surging back and forth.[q] [17]Then Saul said to the troops that were with him, "Call the roll and see who has gone from us." When they had called the roll, Jonathan and his armor-bearer were not there. [18]Saul said to A·hi´jah, "Bring the ark[r] of God here." For at that time the ark[r] of God went with the Israelites. [19]While Saul was talking to the priest, the tumult in the camp of the Phi·lis´tines increased more and more; and Saul said to the priest, "Withdraw your hand." [20]Then Saul and all the people who were with him rallied and went into the battle; and every sword was against the other, so that there was very great confusion. [21]Now the Hebrews who previously had been with the Phi·lis´tines and had gone up with them into the camp turned and joined the Israelites who were with Saul and Jonathan. [22]Likewise, when all the Israelites who had gone into hiding in the hill country of E´phra·im heard that the Phi·lis´tines were fleeing, they too followed closely after them in the battle. [23]So the LORD gave Israel the victory that day.

The battle passed beyond Beth-a´ven, and the troops with Saul numbered altogether about ten thousand men. The battle spread out over the hill country of E´phra·im.

Saul's Rash Oath

24 Now Saul committed a very rash act on that day.[s] He had laid an oath on the troops, saying, "Cursed be anyone who eats food before it is evening and I have been avenged on my enemies." So none of the troops tasted food. [25]All the troops[t] came upon a honeycomb; and there was honey on the ground. [26]When the troops came upon the honeycomb, the honey was dripping out; but they did not put their hands to their mouths, for they feared the oath. [27]But Jonathan had not heard his father charge the troops with the oath; so he extended the staff that was in his hand, and dipped the tip of it in the honeycomb, and put his hand to his mouth; and his eyes brightened. [28]Then one of the soldiers said, "Your father strictly charged the troops with an oath, saying, 'Cursed be anyone who eats food this day.' And so the troops are faint." [29]Then Jonathan said, "My father has troubled the land; see how my eyes have brightened because I tasted a little of this honey. [30]How much better if today the troops had eaten freely of the spoil taken from their enemies; for now the slaughter among the Phi·lis´tines has not been great."

31 After they had struck down the Phi·lis´tines that day from Mich´mash to Ai´ja·lon, the troops were very faint; [32]so the troops flew upon the spoil, and took sheep and oxen and calves, and slaughtered them on the ground; and the troops ate them with the blood. [33]Then it was reported to Saul, "Look, the troops are sinning against the LORD by eating with the blood." And he said, "You have dealt treacherously; roll a

---

[o] Heb They   [p] Heb yoke   [q] Gk: Heb they went and there   [r] Gk the ephod   [s] Gk: Heb The Israelites were distressed that day   [t] Heb land   [u] Gk: Heb me this day

large stone before me here."ᵘ ³⁴Saul said, "Disperse yourselves among the troops, and say to them, 'Let all bring their oxen or their sheep, and slaughter them here, and eat; and do not sin against the LORD by eating with the blood.'" So all of the troops brought their oxen with them that night, and slaughtered them there. ³⁵And Saul built an altar to the LORD; it was the first altar that he built to the LORD.

Jonathan in Danger of Death

36 Then Saul said, "Let us go down after the Phi·lis′tines by night and despoil them until the morning light; let us not leave one of them." They said, "Do whatever seems good to you." But the priest said, "Let us draw near to God here." ³⁷So Saul inquired of God, "Shall I go down after the Phi·lis′tines? Will you give them into the hand of Israel?" But he did not answer him that day. ³⁸Saul said, "Come here, all you leaders of the people; and let us find out how this sin has arisen today. ³⁹For as the LORD lives who saves Israel, even if it is in my son Jonathan, he shall surely die!" But there was no one among all the people who answered him. ⁴⁰He said to all Israel, "You shall be on one side, and I and my son Jonathan will be on the other side." The people said to Saul, "Do what seems good to you." ⁴¹Then Saul said, "O LORD God of Israel, why have you not answered your servant today? If this guilt is in me or in my son Jonathan, O LORD God of Israel, give Ū′rim; but if this guilt is in your people Israel,ᵛ give Thum′mim." And Jonathan and Saul were indicated by the lot, but the people were cleared. ⁴²Then Saul said, "Cast the lot between me and my son Jonathan." And Jonathan was taken.

43 Then Saul said to Jonathan, "Tell me what you have done." Jonathan told him, "I tasted a little honey with the tip of the staff that was in my hand; here I am, I will die." ⁴⁴Saul said, "God do so to me and more also; you shall surely die, Jonathan!" ⁴⁵Then the people said to Saul, "Shall Jonathan die, who has accomplished this great victory in Israel? Far from it! As the LORD lives, not one hair of his head shall fall to the ground; for he has worked with God today." So the people ransomed Jonathan, and he did not die. ⁴⁶Then Saul withdrew from pursuing the Phi·lis′tines; and the Phi·lis′tines went to their own place.

Saul's Continuing Wars

47 When Saul had taken the kingship over Israel, he fought against all his enemies on every side—against Mō′ab, against the Am′mon·ites, against Ē′dom, against the kings of Zō′bah, and against the Phi·lis′tines; wherever he turned he routed them. ⁴⁸He did valiantly, and struck down the A·mal′e·kītes, and rescued Israel out of the hands of those who plundered them.

49 Now the sons of Saul were Jonathan, Ish′vī, and Mal·chī·shū′a; and the names of his two daughters were these: the name of the firstborn was Mē′rab, and the name of the younger, Mī′chal. ⁵⁰The name of Saul's wife was A·hin′o·am daughter of A·him′a·az. And the name of the commander of his army was Abner son of Ner, Saul's uncle; ⁵¹Kish was the father of Saul, and Ner the father of Abner was the son of A·bī′el.

52 There was hard fighting against the Phi·lis′tines all the days of Saul; and when Saul saw any strong or valiant warrior, he took him into his service.

Saul Defeats the Amalekites but Spares Their King

15 Samuel said to Saul, "The LORD sent me to anoint you king over his people Israel; now therefore listen to the words of the LORD. ²Thus says the LORD of hosts, 'I will punish the A·mal′e·kītes for what they did in opposing the Israelites when they came

ᵛ Vg Compare Gk: Heb ⁴¹*Saul said to the LORD, the God of Israel* up out of Egypt. ³Now go and attack Am·a·lek, and utterly destroy all that they have; do not spare them, but kill both man and woman, child and infant, ox and sheep, camel and donkey.' "

4 So Saul summoned the people, and numbered them in Te·lā´im, two hundred thousand foot soldiers, and ten thousand soldiers of Judah. ⁵Saul came to the city of the A·mal´e·kītes and lay in wait in the valley. ⁶Saul said to the Ken´ītes, "Go! Leave! Withdraw from among the A·mal´e·kītes, or I will destroy you with them; for you showed kindness to all the people of Israel when they came up out of Egypt." So the Ken´ītes withdrew from the A·mal´e·kītes. ⁷Saul defeated the A·mal´e·kītes, from Hav´i·lah as far as Shur, which is east of Egypt. ⁸He took King Ā´gag of the A·mal´e·kītes alive, but utterly destroyed all the people with the edge of the sword. ⁹Saul and the people spared Ā´gag, and the best of the sheep and of the cattle and of the fatlings, and the lambs, and all that was valuable, and would not utterly destroy them; all that was despised and worthless they utterly destroyed.

Saul Rejected as King

10 The word of the LORD came to Samuel: ¹¹"I regret that I made Saul king, for he has turned back from following me, and has not carried out my commands." Samuel was angry; and he cried out to the LORD all night. ¹²Samuel rose early in the morning to meet Saul, and Samuel was told, "Saul went to Car´mel, where he set up a monument for himself, and on returning he passed on down to Gil´gal." ¹³When Samuel came to Saul, Saul said to him, "May you be blessed by the LORD; I have carried out the command of the LORD." ¹⁴But Samuel said, "What then is this bleating of sheep in my ears, and the lowing of cattle that I hear?" ¹⁵Saul said, "They have brought them from the A·mal´e·kītes; for the people spared the best of

the sheep and the cattle, to sacrifice to the LORD your God; but the rest we have utterly destroyed." ¹⁶Then Samuel said to Saul, "Stop! I will tell you what the LORD said to me last night." He replied, "Speak."

17 Samuel said, "Though you are little in your own eyes, are you not the head of the tribes of Israel? The LORD anointed you king over Israel. ¹⁸And the LORD sent you on a mission, and said, 'Go, utterly destroy the sinners, the A·mal´e·kītes, and fight against them until they are consumed.' ¹⁹Why then did you not obey the voice of the LORD? Why did you swoop down on the spoil, and do what was evil in the sight of the LORD?" ²⁰Saul said to Samuel, "I have obeyed the voice of the LORD, I have gone on the mission on which the LORD sent me, I have brought Ā´gag the king of Am´a·lek, and I have utterly destroyed the A·mal´e·kītes. ²¹But from the spoil the people took sheep and cattle, the best of the things devoted to destruction, to sacrifice to the LORD your God in Gil´gal." ²²And Samuel said,

"Has the LORD as great delight in
　　burnt offerings and sacrifices,
　as in obedience to the voice of the
　　LORD?
Surely, to obey is better than sacrifice,
　and to heed than the fat of rams.
²³ For rebellion is no less a sin than
　　divination,
　and stubbornness is like iniquity and
　　idolatry.
Because you have rejected the word
　　of the LORD,
　he has also rejected you from
　　being king."

24 Saul said to Samuel, "I have sinned; for I have transgressed the commandment of the LORD and your words, because I feared the people and obeyed their voice. ²⁵Now therefore, I pray, pardon my sin, and return with me, so that I may worship the LORD." ²⁶Samuel said to Saul, "I will not return with you;

for you have rejected the word of the LORD, and the LORD has rejected you from being king over Israel." 27As Samuel turned to go away, Saul caught hold of the hem of his robe, and it tore. 28And Samuel said to him, "The LORD has torn the kingdom of Israel from you this very day, and has given it to a neighbor of yours, who is better than you. 29Moreover the Glory of Israel will not recant[w] or change his mind; for he is not a mortal, that he should change his mind." 30Then Saul[x] said, "I have sinned; yet honor me now before the elders of my people and before Israel, and return with me, so that I may worship the LORD your God." 31So Samuel turned back after Saul; and Saul worshiped the LORD.

32 Then Samuel said, "Bring Āʹgag king of the Aʹmalʹeʹkītes here to me." And Āʹgag came to him haltingly.[y] Āʹgag said, "Surely this is the bitterness of death."[z] 33But Samuel said,

"As your sword has made women childless,
so your mother shall be childless among women."

And Samuel hewed Āʹgag in pieces before the LORD in Gilʹgal.

34 Then Samuel went to Rāʹmah; and Saul went up to his house in Gibʹeʹah of Saul. 35Samuel did not see Saul again until the day of his death, but Samuel grieved over Saul. And the LORD was sorry that he had made Saul king over Israel.

David Anointed as King

16 The LORD said to Samuel, "How long will you grieve over Saul? I have rejected him from being king over Israel. Fill your horn with oil and set out; I will send you to Jesse the Bethʹleʹhemʹite, for I have provided for myself a king among his sons." 2Samuel said, "How can I go? If Saul hears of it, he will kill me." And the LORD said, "Take a heifer with you, and say, 'I have come to sacrifice to the LORD.' 3Invite

"For the LORD does not see as mortals see; they look on the outward appearance, but the LORD looks on the heart."

1 Samuel 16:7b

Jesse to the sacrifice, and I will show you what you shall do; and you shall anoint for me the one whom I name to you." 4Samuel did what the LORD commanded, and came to Bethlehem. The elders of the city came to meet him trembling, and said, "Do you come peaceably?" 5He said, "Peaceably; I have come to sacrifice to the LORD; sanctify yourselves and come with me to the sacrifice." And he sanctified Jesse and his sons and invited them to the sacrifice.

6 When they came, he looked on Ēʹlīʹab and thought, "Surely the LORD's anointed is now before the LORD."[a] 7But the LORD said to Samuel, "Do not look on his appearance or on the height of his stature, because I have rejected him; for the LORD does not see as mortals see; they look on the outward appearance,

David grew up in Bethlehem, the same city where Jesus was born many years later! As the youngest son, David spent most of his time watching the sheep while his older brothers were away fighting the Philistines. He took good care of the sheep and showed great courage by saving them from a lion and a bear. When God rejected Saul as king, Samuel went to Bethlehem to anoint one of Jesse's sons as king. God told Samuel to pass over the older, stronger brothers and anoint the youngest and smallest! God chose David to be king.

but the LORD looks on the heart." [8]Then Jesse called A·bin´a·dab, and made him pass before Samuel. He said, "Neither has the LORD chosen this one." [9]Then Jesse made Sham´mah pass by. And he said, "Neither has the LORD chosen this one." [10]Jesse made seven of his sons pass before Samuel, and Samuel said to Jesse, "The LORD has not chosen any of these." [11]Samuel said to Jesse, "Are all your sons here?" And he said, "There remains yet the youngest, but he is keeping the sheep." And Samuel said to Jesse, "Send and bring him; for we will not sit down until he comes here." [12]He sent and brought him in. Now he was ruddy, and had beautiful eyes, and was handsome. The LORD said, "Rise and anoint him; for this is the one." [13]Then Samuel took the horn of oil, and anointed him in the presence of his brothers; and the spirit of the LORD came mightily upon David from that day forward. Samuel then set out and went to Ra´mah.

David Plays the Lyre for Saul

14 Now the spirit of the LORD departed from Saul, and an evil spirit from the LORD tormented him. [15]And Saul's servants said to him, "See now, an evil spirit from God is tormenting you. [16]Let our lord now command the servants who attend you to look for someone who is skillful in playing the lyre; and when the evil spirit from God is upon you, he will play it, and you will feel better." [17]So Saul said to his servants, "Provide for me someone who can play well, and bring him to me." [18]One of the young men answered, "I have seen a son of Jesse the Beth´le·hem·ite who is skillful in playing, a man of valor, a warrior, prudent in speech, and a man of good presence; and the LORD is with him." [19]So Saul sent messengers to Jesse, and said, "Send me your son David who is with the sheep." [20]Jesse took a donkey loaded with bread, a skin of wine, and a kid, and sent them by his son David to Saul. [21]And David came to Saul, and entered his service. Saul loved him greatly, and he became his armor-bearer. [22]Saul sent to Jesse, saying, "Let David remain in my service, for he has found favor in my sight." [23]And whenever the evil spirit from God came upon Saul, David took the lyre and played it with his hand, and Saul would be relieved and feel better, and the evil spirit would depart from him.

David and Goliath

17 Now the Phi·lis´tines gathered their armies for battle; they were gathered at Sō´cōh, which belongs to Judah, and encamped between Sō´cōh and A·zē´kah, in Ē´phes-dam´mim. [2]Saul and the Israelites gathered and encamped in the valley of Ē´lah, and formed ranks against the Phi·lis´tines. [3]The Phi·lis´tines stood on the mountain on the one side, and Israel stood on the mountain on the other side, with a valley between them. [4]And there came out from the camp of the Phi·lis´tines a champion named Goliath, of Gath, whose height was six[b] cubits and a span. [5]He had a helmet of bronze on his head, and he was armed with a coat of mail; the weight of the coat was five thousand shekels of bronze. [6]He had greaves of bronze on his legs and a javelin of bronze slung between his shoulders.

Goliath was the Philistine champion who teased the Israelite army. He was probably about 9½ feet tall! Even though Goliath was big and had strong armor, the young boy David fought him with a slingshot. He shot a rounded stone that hit Goliath in the head and knocked him down. David trusted in God, and God helped him to win against the giant!

[b] MT: Q Ms Gk *four*

⁷The shaft of his spear was like a weaver's beam, and his spear's head weighed six hundred shekels of iron; and his shield-bearer went before him. ⁸He stood and shouted to the ranks of Israel, "Why have you come out to draw up for battle? Am I not a Phi·lis′tine, and are you not servants of Saul? Choose a man for yourselves, and let him come down to me. ⁹If he is able to fight with me and kill me, then we will be your servants; but if I prevail against him and kill him, then you shall be our servants and serve us." ¹⁰And the Phi·lis′tine said, "Today I defy the ranks of Israel! Give me a man, that we may fight together." ¹¹When Saul and all Israel heard these words of the Phi·lis′tine, they were dismayed and greatly afraid.

12 Now David was the son of an Eph′ra·thīte of Bethlehem in Judah, named Jesse, who had eight sons. In the days of Saul the man was already old and advanced in years.ᶜ ¹³The three eldest sons of Jesse had followed Saul to the battle; the names of his three sons who went to the battle were E·lī′ab the firstborn, and next to him A·bin′a·dab, and the third Sham′mah. ¹⁴David was the youngest; the three eldest followed Saul, ¹⁵but David went back and forth from Saul to feed his father's sheep at Bethlehem. ¹⁶For forty days the Phi·lis′tine came forward and took his stand, morning and evening.

17 Jesse said to his son David, "Take for your brothers an ephah of this parched grain and these ten loaves, and carry them quickly to the camp to your brothers; ¹⁸also take these ten cheeses to the commander of their thousand. See how your brothers fare, and bring some token from them."

19 Now Saul, and they, and all the men of Israel, were in the valley of Ē′lah, fighting with the Phi·lis′tines. ²⁰David rose early in the morning, left the sheep with a keeper, took the provisions, and went as Jesse had commanded him. He came to the encampment as the army was going forth to the battle line, shouting the war cry. ²¹Israel and the Phi·lis′tines drew up for battle, army against army. ²²David left the things in charge of the keeper of the baggage, ran to the ranks, and went and greeted his brothers. ²³As he talked with them, the champion, the Phi·lis′tine of Gath, Goliath by name, came up out of the ranks of the Phi·lis′tines, and spoke the same words as before. And David heard him.

24 All the Israelites, when they saw the man, fled from him and were very much afraid. ²⁵The Israelites said, "Have you seen this man who has come up? Surely he has come up to defy Israel. The king will greatly enrich the man who kills him, and will give him his daughter and make his family free in Israel." ²⁶David said to the men who stood by him, "What shall be done for the man who kills this Phi·lis′tine, and takes away the reproach from Israel? For who is this uncircumcised Phi·lis′tine that he should defy the armies of the living God?" ²⁷The people answered him in the same way, "So shall it be done for the man who kills him."

28 His eldest brother E·lī′ab heard him talking to the men; and Eliab's anger was kindled against David. He said, "Why have you come down? With whom have you left those few sheep in the wilderness? I know your presumption and the evil of your heart; for you have come down just to see the battle." ²⁹David said, "What have I done now? It was only a question." ³⁰He turned away from him toward another and spoke in the same way; and the people answered him again as before.

31 When the words that David spoke were heard, they repeated them before Saul; and he sent for him. ³²David said to Saul, "Let no one's heart fail because of him; your servant will go and fight with this Phi·lis′tine." ³³Saul said to David, "You are not able to go against

ᶜ Gk Syr: Heb *among men*

this Phi·lis′tine to fight with him; for you are just a boy, and he has been a warrior from his youth." ³⁴But David said to Saul, "Your servant used to keep sheep for his father; and whenever a lion or a bear came, and took a lamb from the flock, ³⁵I went after it and struck it down, rescuing the lamb from its mouth; and if it turned against me, I would catch it by the jaw, strike it down, and kill it. ³⁶Your servant has killed both lions and bears; and this uncircumcised Phi·lis′tine shall be like one of them, since he has defied the armies of the living God." ³⁷David said, "The LORD, who saved me from the paw of the lion and from the paw of the bear, will save me from the hand of this Phi·lis′tine." So Saul said to David, "Go, and may the LORD be with you!"

38 Saul clothed David with his armor; he put a bronze helmet on his head and clothed him with a coat of mail. ³⁹David strapped Saul's sword over the armor, and he tried in vain to walk, for he was not used to them. Then David said to Saul, "I cannot walk with these; for I am not used to them." So David removed them. ⁴⁰Then he took his staff in his hand, and chose five smooth stones from the wadi, and put them in his shepherd's bag, in the pouch; his sling was in his hand, and he drew near to the Phi·lis′tine.

41 The Phi·lis′tine came on and drew near to David, with his shield-bearer in front of him. ⁴²When the Phi·lis′tine looked and saw David, he disdained him, for he was only a youth, ruddy and handsome in appearance. ⁴³The Phi·lis′tine said to David, "Am I a dog, that you come to me with sticks?" And the Phi·lis′tine cursed David by his gods. ⁴⁴The Phi·lis′tine said to David, "Come to me, and I will give your flesh to the birds of the air and to the wild animals of the field." ⁴⁵But David said to the Phi·lis′tine, "You come to me with sword and spear and javelin; but I come to you in the name of the LORD of hosts, the God of the armies

Have you ever used a slingshot? David's sling was made of two pieces of leather or cloth joined to a pouch-shaped piece of leather that held a stone. He would tie one end of the sling to his wrist and hold the other end with his hand. He would swing the stone over his head in a circle and then let it go. David had practiced his skill with the sling while protecting his father's sheep. The Israelite army also had soldiers who fought with slingshots. These soldiers, called slingers or slingmen, could fight from far away. Read about the Benjamites' left-handed slingers in Judges 20:16.

of Israel, whom you have defied. ⁴⁶This very day the LORD will deliver you into my hand, and I will strike you down and cut off your head; and I will give the dead bodies of the Phi·lis′tine army this very day to the birds of the air and to the wild animals of the earth, so that all the earth may know that there is a God in Israel, ⁴⁷and that all this assembly may know that the LORD does not save by sword and spear; for the battle is the LORD's and he will give you into our hand."

48 When the Phi·lis′tine drew nearer to meet David, David ran quickly toward the battle line to meet the Phi·lis′tine. ⁴⁹David put his hand in his bag, took out a stone, slung it, and struck the Phi·lis′tine on his forehead; the stone sank into his forehead, and he fell face down on the ground.

50 So David prevailed over the Phi·lis′tine with a sling and a stone, striking down the Phi·lis′tine and killing him; there was no sword in David's hand. ⁵¹Then David ran and stood over the Phi·lis′tine; he grasped his sword, drew it out of its sheath, and killed him; then he cut off his head with it.

When the Phi·lis′tines saw that their champion was dead, they fled. ⁵²The troops of Israel and Judah rose up with a shout and pursued the Phi·lis′tines as far as Gath[d] and the gates of Ek′ron, so that the wounded Phi·lis′tines fell on the way from Shā·a·rā′im as far as Gath and Ek′ron. ⁵³The Israelites came back from chasing the Phi·lis′tines, and they plundered their camp. ⁵⁴David took the head of the Phi·lis′tine and brought it to Jerusalem; but he put his armor in his tent.

55 When Saul saw David go out against the Phi·lis′tine, he said to Abner, the commander of the army, "Abner, whose son is this young man?" Abner said, "As your soul lives, O king, I do not know." ⁵⁶The king said, "Inquire whose son the stripling is." ⁵⁷On David's return from killing the Phi·lis′tine, Abner took him and brought him before Saul, with the head of the Phi·lis′tine in his hand. ⁵⁸Saul said to him, "Whose son are you, young man?" And David answered, "I am the son of your servant Jesse the Beth′le·hem·īte."

Jonathan's Covenant with David

18 When David[e] had finished speaking to Saul, the soul of Jonathan was bound to the soul of David, and Jonathan loved him as his own soul. ²Saul took him that day and would not let him return to his father's house. ³Then Jonathan made a covenant with David, because he loved him as his own soul. ⁴Jonathan stripped himself of the robe that he was wearing, and gave it to David, and his armor, and even his sword and his bow and his belt. ⁵David went out and was successful wherever Saul sent him; as a result, Saul set him over the army. And all the people, even the servants of Saul, approved.

6 As they were coming home, when David returned from killing the Phi·lis′tine, the women came out of all the towns of Israel, singing and dancing, to meet King Saul, with tambourines, with songs of joy, and with musical instruments.[f] ⁷And the women sang to one another as they made merry,

"Saul has killed his thousands,
and David his ten thousands."

⁸Saul was very angry, for this saying displeased him. He said, "They have ascribed to David ten thousands, and to me they have ascribed thousands; what more can he have but the kingdom?" ⁹So Saul eyed David from that day on.

Saul Tries to Kill David

10 The next day an evil spirit from God rushed upon Saul, and he raved within his house, while David was playing the lyre, as he did day by day. Saul had his spear in his hand; ¹¹and Saul threw the spear, for he thought, "I will pin David to the wall." But David eluded him twice.

12 Saul was afraid of David, because the LORD was with him but had departed from Saul. ¹³So Saul removed him from his presence, and made him a commander of a thousand; and David marched out and came in, leading the army. ¹⁴David had success in all his undertakings; for the LORD was with him. ¹⁵When Saul saw that he had great success, he stood in awe of him. ¹⁶But all Israel and Judah loved David; for it was he who marched out and came in leading them.

David Marries Michal

17 Then Saul said to David, "Here is my elder daughter Mĕ′rab; I will give her to you as a wife; only be valiant for me and fight the LORD's battles." For Saul thought, "I will not raise a hand against him; let the Phi·lis′tines deal with him." ¹⁸David said to Saul, "Who am I and who are my kinsfolk, my father's family in Israel, that I should be son-in-law to the king?" ¹⁹But at the time when Saul's daughter Mĕ′rab should have been given to David, she was given to Ā′dri·el the Me·hō′la·thīte as a wife.

[d] Gk Syr: Heb *Gai*   [e] Heb *he*   [f] Or *triangles*, or *three-stringed instruments*

20 Now Saul's daughter Mī'chal loved David. Saul was told, and the thing pleased him. [21]Saul thought, "Let me give her to him that she may be a snare for him and that the hand of the Phi·lis'tines may be against him." Therefore Saul said to David a second time,[g] "You shall now be my son-in-law." [22]Saul commanded his servants, "Speak to David in private and say, 'See, the king is delighted with you, and all his servants love you; now then, become the king's son-in-law.'" [23]So Saul's servants reported these words to David in private. And David said, "Does it seem to you a little thing to become the king's son-in-law, seeing that I am a poor man and of no repute?" [24]The servants of Saul told him, "This is what David said." [25]Then Saul said, "Thus shall you say to David, 'The king desires no marriage present except a hundred foreskins of the Phi·lis'tines, that he may be avenged on the king's enemies.'" Now Saul planned to make David fall by the hand of the Phi·lis'tines. [26]When his servants told David these words, David was well pleased to be the king's son-in-law. Before the time had expired, [27]David rose and went, along with his men, and killed one hundred[h] of the Phi·lis'tines; and David brought their foreskins, which were given in full number to the king, that he might become the king's son-in-law. Saul gave him his daughter Mī'chal as a wife. [28]But when Saul realized that the LORD was with David, and that Saul's daughter Mī'-chal loved him, [29]Saul was still more afraid of David. So Saul was David's enemy from that time forward.

30 Then the commanders of the Phi·lis'tines came out to battle; and as often as they came out, David had more success than all the servants of Saul, so that his fame became very great.

Jonathan Intercedes for David

19 Saul spoke with his son Jonathan and with all his servants about killing David. But Saul's son Jonathan took great delight in David. [2]Jonathan told David, "My father Saul is trying to kill you; therefore be on guard tomorrow morning; stay in a secret place and hide yourself. [3]I will go out and stand beside my father in the field where you are, and I will speak to my father about you; if I learn anything I will tell you." [4]Jonathan spoke well of David to his father Saul, saying to him, "The king should not sin against his servant David, because he has not sinned against you, and because his deeds have been of good service to you; [5]for he took his life in his hand when he attacked the Phi·lis'tine, and the LORD brought about a great victory for all Israel. You saw it, and rejoiced; why then will you sin against an innocent person by killing David without cause?" [6]Saul heeded the voice of Jonathan; Saul swore, "As the LORD lives, he shall not be put to death." [7]So Jonathan called David and related all these things to him. Jonathan then brought David to Saul, and he was in his presence as before.

Michal Helps David Escape from Saul

8 Again there was war, and David went out to fight the Phi·lis'tines. He launched a heavy attack on them, so that they fled before him. [9]Then an evil spirit from the LORD came upon Saul, as he sat in his house with his spear in his hand, while David was playing music. [10]Saul sought to pin David to the wall with the spear; but he eluded Saul, so that he struck the spear into the wall. David fled and escaped that night.

11 Saul sent messengers to David's house to keep watch over him, planning to kill him in the morning. David's wife Mī'chal told him, "If you do not save your life tonight, tomorrow you will be killed." [12]So Mī'chal let David down through the window; he fled away and escaped.

g Heb *by two*   h Gk Compare 2 Sam 3.14: Heb *two hundred*

¹³Mī́chal took an idolⁱ and laid it on the bed; she put a net^j of goats' hair on its head, and covered it with the clothes. ¹⁴When Saul sent messengers to take David, she said, "He is sick." ¹⁵Then Saul sent the messengers to see David for themselves. He said, "Bring him up to me in the bed, that I may kill him." ¹⁶When the messengers came in, the idol^k was in the bed, with the covering^j of goats' hair on its head. ¹⁷Saul said to Mī́chal, "Why have you deceived me like this, and let my enemy go, so that he has escaped?" Mī́chal answered Saul, "He said to me, 'Let me go; why should I kill you?' "

David Joins Samuel in Ramah

18 Now David fled and escaped; he came to Samuel at Rā́mah, and told him all that Saul had done to him. He and Samuel went and settled at Naī́oth. ¹⁹Saul was told, "David is at Naī́oth in Rā́mah." ²⁰Then Saul sent messengers to take David. When they saw the company of the prophets in a frenzy, with Samuel standing in charge of^j them, the spirit of God came upon the messengers of Saul, and they also fell into a prophetic frenzy. ²¹When Saul was told, he sent other messengers, and they also fell into a frenzy. Saul sent messengers again the third time, and they also fell into a frenzy. ²²Then he himself went to Rā́mah. He came to the great well that is in Sḗcū;^l he asked, "Where are Samuel and David?" And someone said, "They are at Naī́oth in Rā́mah." ²³He went there, toward Naī́oth in Rā́mah; and the spirit of God came upon him. As he was going, he fell into a prophetic frenzy, until he came to Naī́oth in Rā́mah. ²⁴He too stripped off his clothes, and he too fell into a frenzy before Samuel. He lay naked all that day and all that night. Therefore it is said, "Is Saul also among the prophets?"

The Friendship of David and Jonathan

20 David fled from Naī́oth in Rā́mah. He came before Jonathan and said, "What have I done? What is my guilt? And what is my sin against your father that he is trying to take my life?" ²He said to him, "Far from it! You shall not die. My father does nothing either great or small without disclosing it to me; and why should my father hide this from me? Never!" ³But David also swore, "Your father knows well that you like me; and he thinks, 'Do not let Jonathan know this, or he will be grieved.' But truly, as the LORD lives and as you yourself live, there is but a step between me and death." ⁴Then Jonathan said to David, "Whatever you say, I will do for you." ⁵David said to Jonathan, "Tomorrow is the new moon, and I should not fail to sit with the king at the meal; but let me go, so that I may hide in the field until the third evening. ⁶If your father misses me at all, then say, 'David earnestly asked leave of me to run to Bethlehem his city; for there is a yearly sacrifice there for all the family.' ⁷If he says, 'Good!' it will be well with your servant; but if he is angry, then know that evil has been determined by him. ⁸Therefore deal kindly with your servant, for you have brought your servant into a sacred covenant^m with you. But if there is guilt in me, kill me yourself; why should you bring me to your father?" ⁹Jonathan said, "Far be it from you! If I knew that it was decided by my father that evil should come upon you, would I not tell you?" ¹⁰Then David said to Jonathan, "Who will tell me if your father answers you harshly?" ¹¹Jonathan replied to David, "Come, let us go out into the field." So they both went out into the field.

12 Jonathan said to David, "By the LORD, the God of Israel! When I have sounded out my father, about this time tomorrow, or on the third day, if he is well disposed toward David, shall I not

ⁱ Heb took the teraphim   ^j Meaning of Heb uncertain   ^k Heb the teraphim   ^l Gk reads to the well of the threshing floor on the bare height   ^m Heb a covenant of the LORD

Jonathan knew that his father might hurt his friend David, so he told David to hide. Jonathan came up with a plan to get a secret message to David. He took his servant to the field with him while he practiced with his bow and arrow. He told David that if he said, "Look, the arrows are on this side of you," then David would be safe. But if he said, "Look, the arrows are beyond you," then David would know that he had to run for his life. David heard Jonathan's words and knew that he had to leave. David and Jonathan said goodbye, but they promised each other they would always be friends.

then send and disclose it to you? [13]But if my father intends to do you harm, the LORD do so to Jonathan, and more also, if I do not disclose it to you, and send you away, so that you may go in safety. May the LORD be with you, as he has been with my father. [14]If I am still alive, show me the faithful love of the LORD; but if I die,[n] [15]never cut off your faithful love from my house, even if the LORD were to cut off every one of the enemies of David from the face of the earth." [16]Thus Jonathan made a covenant with the house of David, saying, "May the LORD seek out the enemies of David." [17]Jonathan made David swear again by his love for him; for he loved him as he loved his own life.

18 Jonathan said to him, "Tomorrow is the new moon; you will be missed, because your place will be empty. [19]On the day after tomorrow, you shall go a long way down; go to the place where you hid yourself earlier, and remain beside the stone there.[n] [20]I will shoot three arrows to the side of it, as though I shot at a mark. [21]Then I will send the boy, saying, 'Go, find the arrows.' If I say to the boy, 'Look, the arrows are on this side of you, collect them,' then you are to come, for, as the LORD lives, it is safe for you and there is no danger. [22]But if I say to the young man, 'Look, the arrows are beyond you,' then go; for the LORD has sent you away. [23]As for the matter about which you and I have spoken, the LORD is witness[o] between you and me forever."

24 So David hid himself in the field. When the new moon came, the king sat at the feast to eat. [25]The king sat upon his seat, as at other times, upon the seat by the wall. Jonathan stood, while Abner sat by Saul's side; but David's place was empty.

26 Saul did not say anything that day; for he thought, "Something has befallen him; he is not clean, surely he is not clean." [27]But on the second day, the day after the new moon, David's place as empty. And Saul said to his son Jonathan, "Why has the son of Jesse not come to the feast, either yesterday or today?" [28]Jonathan answered Saul, "David earnestly asked leave of me to go to Bethlehem; [29]he said, 'Let me go; for our family is holding a sacrifice in the city, and my brother has commanded me to be there. So now, if I have found favor in your sight, let me get away, and see my brothers.' For this reason he has not come to the king's table."

30 Then Saul's anger was kindled against Jonathan. He said to him, "You son of a perverse, rebellious woman! Do I not know that you have chosen the son of Jesse to your own shame, and to the shame of your mother's nakedness? [31]For as long as the son of Jesse lives upon the earth, neither you nor your kingdom shall be established. Now send and bring him to me, for he shall surely die." [32]Then Jonathan answered his father Saul, "Why should he be put to death? What has he done?" [33]But Saul threw his spear at him to strike him; so

[n] Meaning of Heb uncertain   [o] Gk: Heb lacks *witness*

Jonathan knew that it was the decision of his father to put David to death. ³⁴Jonathan rose from the table in fierce anger and ate no food on the second day of the month, for he was grieved for David, and because his father had disgraced him.

35 In the morning Jonathan went out into the field to the appointment with David, and with him was a little boy. ³⁶He said to the boy, "Run and find the arrows that I shoot." As the boy ran, he shot an arrow beyond him. ³⁷When the boy came to the place where Jonathan's arrow had fallen, Jonathan called after the boy and said, "Is the arrow not beyond you?" ³⁸Jonathan called after the boy, "Hurry, be quick, do not linger." So Jonathan's boy gathered up the arrows and came to his master. ³⁹But the boy knew nothing; only Jonathan and David knew the arrangement. ⁴⁰Jonathan gave his weapons to the boy and said to him, "Go and carry them to the city." ⁴¹As soon as the boy had gone, David rose from beside the stone heap^p and prostrated himself with his face to the ground. He bowed three times, and they kissed each other, and wept with each other; David wept the more.^{q} ⁴²Then Jonathan said to David, "Go in peace, since both of us have sworn in the name of the LORD, saying, 'The LORD shall be between me and you, and between my descendants and your descendants, forever.' " He got up and left; and Jonathan went into the city.^{r}

David and the Holy Bread

21 ^{s} David came to Nob to the priest A·him′e·lech. A·him′e·lech came trembling to meet David, and said to him, "Why are you alone, and no one with you?" ²David said to the priest A·him′e·lech, "The king has charged me with a matter, and said to me, 'No one must know anything of the matter about which I send you, and with which I have charged you.' I have made an appointment^t with the young men for such and such a place. ³Now then, what have you at hand? Give me five loaves of bread, or whatever is here." ⁴The priest answered David, "I have no ordinary bread at hand, only holy bread—provided that the young men have kept themselves from women." ⁵David answered the priest, "Indeed women have been kept from us as always when I go on an expedition; the vessels of the young men are holy even when it is a common journey; how much more today will their vessels be holy?" ⁶So the priest gave him the holy bread; for there was no bread there except the bread of the Presence, which is removed from before the LORD, to be replaced by hot bread on the day it is taken away.

7 Now a certain man of the servants of Saul was there that day, detained before the LORD; his name was Dō′eg the Ē′dom·ite, the chief of Saul's shepherds.

8 David said to A·him′e·lech, "Is there no spear or sword here with you? I did not bring my sword or my weapons with me, because the king's business required haste." ⁹The priest said, "The sword of Goliath the Phi·lis′tine, whom you killed in the valley of Ē′lah, is here wrapped in a cloth behind the ephod; if you will take that, take it, for there is none here except that one." David said, "There is none like it; give it to me."

David Flees to Gath

10 David rose and fled that day from Saul; he went to King Ā′chish of Gath. ¹¹The servants of Ā′chish said to him, "Is this not David the king of the land? Did they not sing to one another of him in dances,

'Saul has killed his thousands,
     and David his ten thousands'?"

¹²David took these words to heart and was very much afraid of King Ā′chish of Gath. ¹³So he changed his behavior before them; he pretended to be mad

^{p} Gk: Heb *from beside the south* ^{q} Vg: Meaning of Heb uncertain ^{r} This sentence is 21.1 in Heb ^{s} Ch 21.2 in Heb ^{t} Q Ms Vg Compare Gk: Meaning of MT uncertain when in their presence.[u] He scratched marks on the doors of the gate, and let his spittle run down his beard. [14]Ā´chish said to his servants, "Look, you see the man is mad; why then have you brought him to me? [15]Do I lack madmen, that you have brought this fellow to play the madman in my presence? Shall this fellow come into my house?"

David and His Followers at Adullam

22 David left there and escaped to the cave of A·dul´lam; when his brothers and all his father's house heard of it, they went down there to him. [2]Everyone who was in distress, and everyone who was in debt, and everyone who was discontented gathered to him; and he became captain over them. Those who were with him numbered about four hundred.

3 David went from there to Miz´peh of Mō´ab. He said to the king of Mō´ab, "Please let my father and mother come[v] to you, until I know what God will do for me." [4]He left them with the king of Mō´ab, and they stayed with him all the time that David was in the stronghold. [5]Then the prophet Gad said to David, "Do not remain in the stronghold; leave, and go into the land of Judah." So David left, and went into the forest of Hē´reth.

Saul Slaughters the Priests at Nob

6 Saul heard that David and those who were with him had been located. Saul was sitting at Gib´ē·ah, under the tamarisk tree on the height, with his spear in his hand, and all his servants were standing around him. [7]Saul said to his servants who stood around him, "Hear now, you Ben´ja·min·ītes; will the son of Jesse give every one of you fields and vineyards, will he make you all commanders of thousands and commanders of hundreds? [8]Is that why all of you have conspired against me? No one discloses to me when my son makes a

league with the son of Jesse, none of you is sorry for me or discloses to me that my son has stirred up my servant against me, to lie in wait, as he is doing today." [9]Dō´eg the Ē´dom·īte, who was in charge of Saul's servants, answered, "I saw the son of Jesse coming to Nob, to A·him´e·lech son of A·hī´tub; [10]he inquired of the LORD for him, gave him provisions, and gave him the sword of Goliath the Phi·lis´tine."

11 The king sent for the priest A·him´e·lech son of A·hī´tub and for all his father's house, the priests who were at Nob; and all of them came to the king. [12]Saul said, "Listen now, son of A·hī´tub." He answered, "Here I am, my lord." [13]Saul said to him, "Why have you conspired against me, you and the son of Jesse, by giving him bread and a sword, and by inquiring of God for him, so that he has risen against me, to lie in wait, as he is doing today?"

14 Then A·him´e·lech answered the king, "Who among all your servants is so faithful as David? He is the king's son-in-law, and is quick[w] to do your bidding, and is honored in your house. [15]Is today the first time that I have inquired of God for him? By no means! Do not let the king impute anything to his servant or to any member of my father's house; for your servant has known nothing of all this, much or little." [16]The king said, "You shall surely die, A·him´e·lech, you and all your father's house." [17]The king said to the guard who stood around him, "Turn and kill the priests of the LORD, because their hand also is with David; they knew that he fled, and did not disclose it to me." But the servants of the king would not raise their hand to attack the priests of the LORD. [18]Then the king said to Dō´eg, "You, Dō´eg, turn and attack the priests." Dō´eg the Ē´dom·īte turned and attacked the priests; on that day he killed eighty-five who wore the

[u] Heb *in their hands*　　[v] Syr Vg: Heb *come out*
[w] Heb *and turns aside*

linen ephod. [19]Nob, the city of the priests, he put to the sword; men and women, children and infants, oxen, donkeys, and sheep, he put to the sword.

20 But one of the sons of A·him´e·lech son of A·hī´tub, named A·bī´a·thar, escaped and fled after David. [21] A·bī´a·thar told David that Saul had killed the priests of the LORD. [22]David said to A·bī´a·thar, "I knew on that day, when Dō´eg the Ē´dom·īte was there, that he would surely tell Saul. I am responsible[x] for the lives of all your father's house. [23]Stay with me, and do not be afraid; for the one who seeks my life seeks your life; you will be safe with me."

David Saves the City of Keilah

23 Now they told David, "The Phi·lis´tines are fighting against Kē·ī´lah, and are robbing the threshing floors." [2]David inquired of the LORD, "Shall I go and attack these Phi·lis´tines?" The LORD said to David, "Go and attack the Phi·lis´tines and save Kē·ī´lah." [3]But David's men said to him, "Look, we are afraid here in Judah; how much more then if we go to Kē·ī´lah against the armies of the Phi·lis´tines?" [4]Then David inquired of the LORD again. The LORD answered him, "Yes, go down to Kē·ī´lah; for I will give the Phi·lis´tines into your hand." [5]So David and his men went to Kē·ī´lah, fought with the Phi·lis´tines, brought away their livestock, and dealt them a heavy defeat. Thus David rescued the inhabitants of Kē·ī´lah.

6 When A·bī´a·thar son of A·him´e·lech fled to David at Kē·ī´lah, he came down with an ephod in his hand. [7]Now it was told Saul that David had come to Kē·ī´lah. And Saul said, "God has given[y] him into my hand; for he has shut himself in by entering a town that has gates and bars." [8]Saul summoned all the people to war, to go down to Kē·ī´lah, to besiege David and his men. [9]When David learned that Saul was plotting evil against him, he said to the priest A·bī´-

a·thar, "Bring the ephod here." [10]David said, "O LORD, the God of Israel, your servant has heard that Saul seeks to come to Kē·ī´lah, to destroy the city on my account. [11]And now, will[z] Saul come down as your servant has heard? O LORD, the God of Israel, I beseech you, tell your servant." The LORD said, "He will come down." [12]Then David said, "Will the men of Kē·ī´lah surrender me and my men into the hand of Saul?" The LORD said, "They will surrender you." [13]Then David and his men, who were about six hundred, set out and left Kē·ī´lah; they wandered wherever they could go. When Saul was told that David had escaped from Kē·ī´lah, he gave up the expedition. [14]David remained in the strongholds in the wilderness, in the hill country of the Wilderness of Ziph. Saul sought him every day, but the LORD[a] did not give him into his hand.

David Eludes Saul in the Wilderness

15 David was in the Wilderness of Ziph at Hō´resh when he learned that[b] Saul had come out to seek his life. [16]Saul's son Jonathan set out and came to David at Hō´resh; there he strengthened his hand through the LORD.[c] [17]He said to him, "Do not be afraid; for the hand of my father Saul shall not find you; you shall be king over Israel, and I shall be second to you; my father Saul also knows that this is so." [18]Then the two of them made a covenant before the LORD; David remained at Hō´resh, and Jonathan went home.

19 Then some Ziph´ītes went up to Saul at Gib´ē·ah and said, "David is hiding among us in the strongholds of Hō´resh, on the hill of Ha·chī´lah, which is south of Jē´shī·mon. [20]Now, O king, whenever you wish to come down, do so; and our part

---

[x] Gk Vg: Meaning of Heb uncertain   [y] Gk Tg: Heb *made a stranger of*   [z] Q Ms Compare Gk: MT *Will the men of Keilah surrender me into his hand? Will*   [a] Q Ms Gk: MT *God*   [b] Or *saw that*   [c] Compare Q Ms Gk: MT *God*

will be to surrender him into the king's hand." ²¹Saul said, "May you be blessed by the LORD for showing me compassion! ²²Go and make sure once more; find out exactly where he is, and who has seen him there; for I am told that he is very cunning. ²³Look around and learn all the hiding places where he lurks, and come back to me with sure information. Then I will go with you; and if he is in the land, I will search him out among all the thousands of Judah." ²⁴So they set out and went to Ziph ahead of Saul.

Even though King Saul wanted to kill him, David was a good man who remembered Saul's kindness in earlier times. David also knew that God had once chosen Saul to be king. Several times David had the chance to kill Saul, but he always let Saul go free.

David and his men were in the wilderness of Māʹon, in the Arʹaʹbah to the south of Jeʹshīʹmon. ²⁵Saul and his men went to search for him. When David was told, he went down to the rock and stayed in the wilderness of Māʹon. When Saul heard that, he pursued David into the wilderness of Māʹon. ²⁶Saul went on one side of the mountain, and David and his men on the other side of the mountain. David was hurrying to get away from Saul, while Saul and his men were closing in on David and his men to capture them. ²⁷Then a messenger came to Saul, saying, "Hurry and come; for the Phiʹlisʹtines have made a raid on the land." ²⁸So Saul stopped pursuing David, and went against the Phiʹlisʹtines; therefore that place was called the Rock of Escape.ᵈ ²⁹ᵉDavid then went up from there, and lived in the strongholds of En-geʹdi.

David Spares Saul's Life

24 When Saul returned from following the Phiʹlisʹtines, he was told, "David is in the wilderness of Enʹgeʹdi." ²Then Saul took three thousand chosen men out of all Israel, and went to look for David and his men in the direction of the Rocks of the Wild Goats. ³He came to the sheepfolds beside the road, where there was a cave; and Saul went in to relieve himself.ᶠ Now David and his men were sitting in the innermost parts of the cave. ⁴The men of David said to him, "Here is the day of which the LORD said to you, 'I will give your enemy into your hand, and you shall do to him as it seems good to you.' " Then David went and stealthily cut off a corner of Saul's cloak. ⁵Afterward David was stricken to the heart because he had cut off a corner of Saul's cloak. ⁶He said to his men, "The LORD forbid that I should do this thing to my lord, the LORD's anointed, to raise my hand against him; for he is the LORD's anointed." ⁷So David scolded his men severely and did not permit them to attack Saul. Then Saul got up and left the cave, and went on his way.

8 Afterwards David also rose up and went out of the cave and called after Saul, "My lord the king!" When Saul looked behind him, David bowed with his face to the ground, and did obeisance. ⁹David said to Saul, "Why do you listen to the words of those who say, 'David seeks to do you harm'? ¹⁰This very day your eyes have seen how the LORD gave you into my hand in the cave; and some urged me to kill you, but I sparedᵍ you. I said, 'I will not raise my hand against my lord; for he is the LORD's anointed.' ¹¹See, my father, see the corner of your cloak in my hand; for by the fact that I cut off the corner of your cloak, and did not kill you, you may know for certain that there is no wrong

ᵈ Or *Rock of Division*; Meaning of Heb uncertain
ᵉ Ch 24.1 in Heb   ᶠ Heb *to cover his feet*   ᵍ Gk
Syr Tg Vg: Heb *it* (my eye) *spared*

or treason in my hands. I have not sinned against you, though you are hunting me to take my life. [12]May the LORD judge between me and you! May the LORD avenge me on you; but my hand shall not be against you. [13]As the ancient proverb says, 'Out of the wicked comes forth wickedness'; but my hand shall not be against you. [14]Against whom has the king of Israel come out? Whom do you pursue? A dead dog? A single flea? [15]May the LORD therefore be judge, and give sentence between me and you. May he see to it, and plead my cause, and vindicate me against you."

16 When David had finished speaking these words to Saul, Saul said, "Is this your voice, my son David?" Saul lifted up his voice and wept. [17]He said to David, "You are more righteous than I; for you have repaid me good, whereas I have repaid you evil. [18]Today you have explained how you have dealt well with me, in that you did not kill me when the LORD put me into your hands. [19]For who has ever found an enemy, and sent the enemy safely away? So may the LORD reward you with good for what you have done to me this day. [20]Now I know that you shall surely be king, and that the kingdom of Israel shall be established in your hand. [21]Swear to me therefore by the LORD that you will not cut off my descendants after me, and that you will not wipe out my name from my father's house." [22]So David swore this to Saul. Then Saul went home; but David and his men went up to the stronghold.

Death of Samuel

25 Now Samuel died; and all Israel assembled and mourned for him. They buried him at his home in Rā´mah.

Then David got up and went down to the wilderness of Pa´ran.

David and the Wife of Nabal

2 There was a man in Mā´on, whose property was in Car´mel. The man was very rich; he had three thousand sheep and a thousand goats. He was shearing his sheep in Car´mel. [3]Now the name of the man was Nā´bal, and the name of his wife Ab´i·gāil. The woman was clever and beautiful, but the man was surly and mean; he was a Cā´leb·īte. [4]David heard in the wilderness that Nā´bal was shearing his sheep. [5]So David sent ten young men; and David said to the young men, "Go up to Car´mel, and go to Nā´bal, and greet him in my name. [6]Thus you shall salute him: 'Peace be to you, and peace be to your house, and peace be to all that you have. [7]I hear that you have shearers; now your shepherds have been with us, and we did them no harm, and they missed nothing, all the time they were in Car´mel. [8]Ask your young men, and they will tell you. Therefore let my young men find favor in your sight; for we have come on a feast day. Please give whatever you have at hand to your servants and to your son David.' "

9 When David's young men came, they said all this to Nā´bal in the name of David; and then they waited. [10]But Nā´bal answered David's servants, "Who is David? Who is the son of Jesse? There are many servants today who are breaking away from their masters. [11]Shall I take my bread and my water and the meat that I have butchered for my shearers, and give it to men who come from I do not know where?" [12]So David's young men turned away, and came back and told him all this. [13]David said to his men, "Every man strap on his sword!" And every one of them strapped on his sword; David also strapped on his sword; and about four hundred men went up after David, while two hundred remained with the baggage.

14 But one of the young men told Ab´i·gāil, Nā´bal's wife, "David sent messengers out of the wilderness to salute our master; and he shouted insults at them. [15]Yet the men were very good to us, and we suffered no harm, and we

never missed anything when we were in the fields, as long as we were with them; [16]they were a wall to us both by night and by day, all the while we were with them keeping the sheep. [17]Now therefore know this and consider what you should do; for evil has been decided against our master and against all his house; he is so ill-natured that no one can speak to him."

18 Then Ab´i·gail hurried and took two hundred loaves, two skins of wine, five sheep ready dressed, five measures of parched grain, one hundred clusters of raisins, and two hundred cakes of figs. She loaded them on donkeys [19]and said to her young men, "Go on ahead of me; I am coming after you." But she did not tell her husband Na´bal. [20]As she rode on the donkey and came down under cover of the mountain, David and his men came down toward her; and she met them. [21]Now David had said, "Surely it was in vain that I protected all that this fellow has in the wilderness, so that nothing was missed of all that belonged to him; but he has returned me evil for good. [22]God do so to David[h] and more also, if by morning I leave so much as one male of all who belong to him."

23 When Ab´i·gail saw David, she hurried and alighted from the donkey, and fell before David on her face, bowing to the ground. [24]She fell at his feet and said, "Upon me alone, my lord, be the guilt; please let your servant speak in your ears, and hear the words of your servant. [25]My lord, do not take seriously this ill-natured fellow, Na´bal; for as his name is, so is he; Na´bal[i] is his name, and folly is with him; but I, your servant, did not see the young men of my lord, whom you sent.

26 "Now then, my lord, as the LORD lives, and as you yourself live, since the LORD has restrained you from bloodguilt and from taking vengeance with your own hand, now let your enemies and those who seek to do evil to my lord be like Na´bal. [27]And now let this present that your

Hospitality is treating guests with kindness. In Bible times people sometimes had to welcome guests they had never even met! Hospitality meant giving food and shelter to anyone who came along. Guests might be family members, or they might be enemies! Whoever the guests were, they had to be treated nicely. What about you? How can you show hospitality in your neighborhood? If a new family moves in, you might take them some cookies you've made or some flowers in a pot you've painted. (Be sure to take a parent with you when you go.) Don't forget to tell them where you go to church and invite them to go with you!

servant has brought to my lord be given to the young men who follow my lord. [28]Please forgive the trespass of your servant; for the LORD will certainly make my lord a sure house, because my lord is fighting the battles of the LORD; and evil shall not be found in you so long as you live. [29]If anyone should rise up to pursue you and to seek your life, the life of my lord shall be bound in the bundle of the living under the care of the LORD your God; but the lives of your enemies he shall sling out as from the hollow of a sling. [30]When the LORD has done to my lord according to all the good that he has spoken concerning you, and has appointed you prince over Israel, [31]my lord shall have no cause of grief, or pangs of conscience, for having shed blood without cause or for having saved himself. And when the LORD has dealt well with my lord, then remember your servant."

32 David said to Ab´i·gail, "Blessed be the LORD, the God of Israel, who sent you to meet me today! [33]Blessed be your good sense, and blessed be you, who

[h] Gk Compare Syr: Heb *the enemies of David*
[i] That is *Fool*

have kept me today from bloodguilt and from avenging myself by my own hand! [34]For as surely as the LORD the God of Israel lives, who has restrained me from hurting you, unless you had hurried and come to meet me, truly by morning there would not have been left to Nā´bal so much as one male." [35]Then David received from her hand what she had brought him; he said to her, "Go up to your house in peace; see, I have heeded your voice, and I have granted your petition."

36 Ab´i·gāil came to Nā´bal; he was holding a feast in his house, like the feast of a king. Nā´bal's heart was merry within him, for he was very drunk; so she told him nothing at all until the morning light. [37]In the morning, when the wine had gone out of Nā´bal, his wife told him these things, and his heart died within him; he became like a stone. [38]About ten days later the LORD struck Nā´bal, and he died.

39 When David heard that Nā´bal was dead, he said, "Blessed be the LORD who has judged the case of Nā´bal's insult to me, and has kept back his servant from evil; the LORD has returned the evildoing of Nā´bal upon his own head." Then David sent and wooed Ab´i·gāil, to make her his wife. [40]When David's servants came to Ab´i·gāil at Car´mel, they said to her, "David has sent us to you to take you to him as his wife." [41]She rose and bowed down, with her face to the ground, and said, "Your servant is a slave to wash the feet of the servants of my lord." [42]Ab´i·gāil got up hurriedly and rode away on a donkey; her five maids attended her. She went after the messengers of David and became his wife.

43 David also married A·hin´ō·am of Jez´rē·el; both of them became his wives. [44]Saul had given his daughter Mī´chal, David's wife, to Pal´tī son of Lā´ish, who was from Gal´lim.

David Spares Saul's Life a Second Time

26 Then the Ziph´ītes came to Saul at Gib´ē·ah, saying, "David is in hiding on the hill of Ha·chī´lah, which is opposite Jē·shī´mon."[j] [2]So Saul rose and went down to the Wilderness of Ziph, with three thousand chosen men of Israel, to seek David in the Wilderness of Ziph. [3]Saul encamped on the hill of Ha·chī´lah, which is opposite Jē·shī´mon[j] beside the road. But David remained in the wilderness. When he learned that Saul had come after him into the wilderness, [4]David sent out spies, and learned that Saul had indeed arrived. [5]Then David set out and came to the place where Saul had encamped; and David saw the place where Saul lay, with Abner son of Ner, the commander of his army. Saul was lying within the encampment, while the army was encamped around him.

6 Then David said to A·him´e·lech the Hit´tīte, and to Jō´ab's brother A·bi´shaī son of Ze·rū´i·ah, "Who will go down with me into the camp to Saul?" A·bi´shaī said, "I will go down with you." [7]So David and A·bi´shaī went to the army by night; there Saul lay sleeping within the encampment, with his spear stuck in the ground at his head; and Abner and the army lay around him. [8]A·bi´shaī said to David, "God has given your enemy into your hand today; now therefore let me pin him to the ground with one stroke of the spear; I will not strike him twice." [9]But David said to A·bi´shaī, "Do not destroy him; for who can raise his hand against the LORD's anointed, and be guiltless?" [10]David said, "As the LORD lives, the LORD will strike him down; or his day will come to die; or he will go down into battle and perish. [11]The LORD forbid that I should raise my hand against the LORD's anointed; but now take the spear that is at his head, and the water jar, and let us go." [12]So David took the spear that was at Saul's head and the water jar, and they went away. No one saw it, or knew it, nor did anyone awake; for they were all asleep, because a deep sleep from the LORD had fallen upon them.

[j] Or *opposite the wasteland*

13 Then David went over to the other side, and stood on top of a hill far away, with a great distance between them. [14]David called to the army and to Abner son of Ner, saying, "Abner! Will you not answer?" Then Abner replied, "Who are you that calls to the king?" [15]David said to Abner, "Are you not a man? Who is like you in Israel? Why then have you not kept watch over your lord the king? For one of the people came in to destroy your lord the king. [16]This thing that you have done is not good. As the LORD lives, you deserve to die, because you have not kept watch over your lord, the LORD's anointed. See now, where is the king's spear, or the water jar that was at his head?"

17 Saul recognized David's voice, and said, "Is this your voice, my son David?" David said, "It is my voice, my lord, O king." [18]And he added, "Why does my lord pursue his servant? For what have I done? What guilt is on my hands? [19]Now therefore let my lord the king hear the words of his servant. If it is the LORD who has stirred you up against me, may he accept an offering; but if it is mortals, may they be cursed before the LORD, for they have driven me out today from my share in the heritage of the LORD, saying, 'Go, serve other gods.' [20]Now therefore, do not let my blood fall to the ground, away from the presence of the LORD; for the king of Israel has come out to seek a single flea, like one who hunts a partridge in the mountains."

21 Then Saul said, "I have done wrong; come back, my son David, for I will never harm you again, because my life was precious in your sight today; I have been a fool, and have made a great mistake." [22]David replied, "Here is the spear, O king! Let one of the young men come over and get it. [23]The LORD rewards everyone for his righteousness and his faithfulness; for the LORD gave you into my hand today, but I would not raise my hand against the LORD's anointed. [24]As your life was precious today in my sight, so may my life be precious in the sight of the LORD, and may he rescue me from all tribulation." [25]Then Saul said to David, "Blessed be you, my son David! You will do many things and will succeed in them." So David went his way, and Saul returned to his place.

David Serves King Achish of Gath

27 David said in his heart, "I shall now perish one day by the hand of Saul; there is nothing better for me than to escape to the land of the Phi·lis′tines; then Saul will despair of seeking me any longer within the borders of Israel, and I shall escape out of his hand." [2]So David set out and went over, he and the six hundred men who were with him, to King Ā′chish son of Mā′och of Gath. [3]David stayed with Ā′chish at Gath, he and his troops, every man with his household, and David with his two wives, A·hin′ō·am of Jez′rē·el, and Ab′i·gāil of Car′mel, Nā′bal's widow. [4]When Saul was told that David had fled to Gath, he no longer sought for him.

5 Then David said to Ā′chish, "If I have found favor in your sight, let a place be given me in one of the country towns, so that I may live there; for why should your servant live in the royal city with you?" [6]So that day Ā′chish gave him Zik′lag; therefore Zik′lag has belonged to the kings of Judah to this day. [7]The length of time that David lived in the country of the Phi·lis′tines was one year and four months.

8 Now David and his men went up and made raids on the Gesh′ū·rītes, the Gir′zītes, and the A·mal′e·kītes; for these were the landed settlements from Tē′lam[k] on the way to Shur and on to the land of Egypt. [9]David struck the land, leaving neither man nor woman alive, but took away the sheep, the oxen, the donkeys, the camels, and the clothing, and came back to Ā′chish. [10]When Ā′chish asked, "Against whom[l] have you

[k] Compare Gk 15.4: Heb *from of old*   [l] Q Ms Gk Vg: MT lacks *whom*

made a raid today?" David would say, "Against the Neg´eb of Judah," or "Against the Neg´eb of the Je·rah´mē·el·ītes," or, "Against the Neg´eb of the Ken´ītes." [11]David left neither man nor woman alive to be brought back to Gath, thinking, "They might tell about us, and say, 'David has done so and so.'" Such was his practice all the time he lived in the country of the Phi·lis´tines. [12]Ā´chish trusted David, thinking, "He has made himself utterly abhorrent to his people Israel; therefore he shall always be my servant."

28

In those days the Phi·lis´tines gathered their forces for war, to fight against Israel. Ā´chish said to David, "You know, of course, that you and your men are to go out with me in the army." [2]David said to Ā´chish, "Very well, then you shall know what your servant can do." Ā´chish said to David, "Very well, I will make you my bodyguard for life."

Saul Consults a Medium

3 Now Samuel had died, and all Israel had mourned for him and buried him in Rā´mah, his own city. Saul had expelled the mediums and the wizards from the land. [4]The Phi·lis´tines assembled, and came and encamped at Shū´nem. Saul gathered all Israel, and they encamped at Gil·bō´a. [5]When Saul saw the army of the Phi·lis´tines, he was afraid, and his heart trembled greatly. [6]When Saul inquired of the LORD, the LORD did not answer him, not by dreams, or by U´rim, or by prophets. [7]Then Saul said to his servants, "Seek out for me a woman who is a medium, so that I may go to her and inquire of her." His servants said to him, "There is a medium at En´dor."

8 So Saul disguised himself and put on other clothes and went there, he and two men with him. They came to the woman by night. And he said, "Consult a spirit for me, and bring up for me the one whom I name to you." [9]The woman said to him, "Surely you know what Saul has done,

how he has cut off the mediums and the wizards from the land. Why then are you laying a snare for my life to bring about my death?" [10]But Saul swore to her by the LORD, "As the LORD lives, no punishment shall come upon you for this thing." [11]Then the woman said, "Whom shall I bring up for you?" He answered, "Bring up Samuel for me." [12]When the woman saw Samuel, she cried out with a loud voice; and the woman said to Saul, "Why have you deceived me? You are Saul!" [13]The king said to her, "Have no fear; what do you see?" The woman said to Saul, "I see a divine being[m] coming up out of the ground." [14]He said to her, "What is his appearance?" She said, "An old man is coming up; he is wrapped in a robe." So Saul knew that it was Samuel, and he bowed with his face to the ground, and did obeisance.

15 Then Samuel said to Saul, "Why have you disturbed me by bringing me up?" Saul answered, "I am in great distress, for the Phi·lis´tines are warring against me, and God has turned away from me and answers me no more, either by prophets or by dreams; so I have summoned you to tell me what I should do." [16]Samuel said, "Why then do you ask me, since the LORD has turned from you and become your enemy? [17]The LORD has done to you just as he spoke by me; for the LORD has torn the kingdom out of your hand, and given it to your neighbor, David. [18]Because you did not obey the voice of the LORD, and did not carry out his fierce wrath against Am´a·lek, therefore the LORD has done this thing to you today. [19]Moreover the LORD will give Israel along with you into the hands of the Phi·lis´tines; and tomorrow you and your sons shall be with me; the LORD will also give the army of Israel into the hands of the Phi·lis´tines."

20 Immediately Saul fell full length on the ground, filled with fear because of the words of Samuel; and there was no strength in him, for he had eaten nothing

_____

[m] Or a god; or gods

all day and all night. [21]The woman came to Saul, and when she saw that he was terrified, she said to him, "Your servant has listened to you; I have taken my life in my hand, and have listened to what you have said to me. [22]Now therefore, you also listen to your servant; let me set a morsel of bread before you. Eat, that you may have strength when you go on your way." [23]He refused, and said, "I will not eat." But his servants, together with the woman, urged him; and he listened to their words. So he got up from the ground and sat on the bed. [24]Now the woman had a fatted calf in the house. She quickly slaughtered it, and she took flour, kneaded it, and baked unleavened cakes. [25]She put them before Saul and his servants, and they ate. Then they rose and went away that night.

The Philistines Reject David

29 Now the Phi·lis´tines gathered all their forces at A̅´phek, while the Israelites were encamped by the fountain that is in Jez´re·el. [2]As the lords of the Phi·lis´tines were passing on by hundreds and by thousands, and David and his men were passing on in the rear with A̅´chish, [3]the commanders of the Phi·lis´tines said, "What are these Hebrews doing here?" A̅´chish said to the commanders of the Phi·lis´tines, "Is this not David, the servant of King Saul of Israel, who has been with me now for days and years? Since he deserted to me I have found no fault in him to this day." [4]But the commanders of the Phi·lis´tines were angry with him; and the commanders of the Phi·lis´tines said to him, "Send the man back, so that he may return to the place that you have assigned to him; he shall not go down with us to battle, or else he may become an adversary to us in the battle. For how could this fellow reconcile himself to his lord? Would it not be with the heads of the men here? [5]Is this not David, of whom they sing to one another in dances,

'Saul has killed his thousands,
　　and David his ten thousands'?"

6 Then A̅´chish called David and said to him, "As the LORD lives, you have been honest, and to me it seems right that you should march out and in with me in the campaign; for I have found nothing wrong in you from the day of your coming to me until today. Nevertheless the lords do not approve of you. [7]So go back now; and go peaceably; do nothing to displease the lords of the Phi·lis´tines." [8]David said to A̅´chish, "But what have I done? What have you found in your servant from the day I entered your service until now, that I should not go and fight against the enemies of my lord the king?" [9]A̅´chish replied to David, "I know that you are as blameless in my sight as an angel of God; nevertheless, the commanders of the Phi·lis´tines have said, 'He shall not go up with us to the battle.' [10]Now then rise early in the morning, you and the servants of your lord who came with you, and go to the place that I appointed for you. As for the evil report, do not take it to heart, for you have done well before me.[n] Start early in the morning, and leave as soon as you have light." [11]So David set out with his men early in the morning, to return to the land of the Phi·lis´tines. But the Phi·lis´tines went up to Jez´re·el.

David Avenges the Destruction of Ziklag

30 Now when David and his men came to Zik´lag on the third day, the A·mal´e·kites had made a raid on the Neg´eb and on Zik´lag. They had attacked Zik´lag, burned it down, [2]and taken captive the women and all[o] who were in it, both small and great; they killed none of them, but carried them off, and went their way. [3]When David and his men came to the city, they found it burned down, and their wives and sons and daughters taken captive. [4]Then David and the people who were with him raised their voices and wept, until they

---

[n] Gk: Heb lacks *and go to the place . . . done well before me*　[o] Gk: Heb lacks *and all*

had no more strength to weep. [5]David's two wives also had been taken captive, A·hin´ō·am of Jez´rē·el, and Ab´i·gail the widow of Nā´bal of Car´mel. [6]David was in great danger; for the people spoke of stoning him, because all the people were bitter in spirit for their sons and daughters. But David strengthened himself in the LORD his God.

7 David said to the priest A·bī´a·thar son of A·him´e·lech, "Bring me the ephod." So A·bī´a·thar brought the ephod to David. [8]David inquired of the LORD, "Shall I pursue this band? Shall I overtake them?" He answered him, "Pursue; for you shall surely overtake and shall surely rescue." [9]So David set out, he and the six hundred men who were with him. They came to the Wadi Bē´sor, where those stayed who were left behind. [10]But David went on with the pursuit, he and four hundred men; two hundred stayed behind, too exhausted to cross the Wadi Bē´sor.

11 In the open country they found an Egyptian, and brought him to David. They gave him bread and he ate; they gave him water to drink; [12]they also gave him a piece of fig cake and two clusters of raisins. When he had eaten, his spirit revived; for he had not eaten bread or drunk water for three days and three nights. [13]Then David said to him, "To whom do you belong? Where are you from?" He said, "I am a young man of Egypt, servant to an A·mal´e·kīte. My master left me behind because I fell sick three days ago. [14]We had made a raid on the Neg´eb of the Cher´e·thītes and on that which belongs to Judah and on the Neg´eb of Caleb; and we burned Zik´lag down." [15]David said to him, "Will you take me down to this raiding party?" He said, "Swear to me by God that you will not kill me, or hand me over to my master, and I will take you down to them."

16 When he had taken him down, they were spread out all over the ground, eating and drinking and dancing, because of the great amount of spoil they had taken from the land of the Phi·lis´tines and from the land of Judah. [17]David attacked them from twilight until the evening of the next day. Not one of them escaped, except four hundred young men, who mounted camels and fled. [18]David recovered all that the A·mal´e·kītes had taken; and David rescued his two wives. [19]Nothing was missing, whether small or great, sons or daughters, spoil or anything that had been taken; David brought back everything. [20]David also captured all the flocks and herds, which were driven ahead of the other cattle; people said, "This is David's spoil."

21 Then David came to the two hundred men who had been too exhausted to follow David, and who had been left at the Wadi Bē´sor. They went out to meet David and to meet the people who were with him. When David drew near to the people he saluted them. [22]Then all the corrupt and worthless fellows among the men who had gone with David said, "Because they did not go with us, we will not give them any of the spoil that we have recovered, except that each man may take his wife and children, and leave." [23]But David said, "You shall not do so, my brothers, with what the LORD

In Bible times, an army that won a battle took all the possessions of the army that lost. The winning army had the right to take anything that belonged to the enemy. This included cattle, clothes, metal, and even people. These belongings were called spoil, and there were rules for dividing the spoil. One of David's rules was that the soldiers who guarded his army's possessions received the same amount of spoils as the soldiers who fought in the battle.

has given us; he has preserved us and handed over to us the raiding party that attacked us. ²⁴Who would listen to you in this matter? For the share of the one who goes down into the battle shall be the same as the share of the one who stays by the baggage; they shall share alike." ²⁵From that day forward he made it a statute and an ordinance for Israel; it continues to the present day.

26 When David came to Zik´lag, he sent part of the spoil to his friends, the elders of Judah, saying, "Here is a present for you from the spoil of the enemies of the LORD"; ²⁷it was for those in Beth´-el, in Rā´moth of the Neg´eb, in Jat´tir, ²⁸in A·rō´er, in Siph´moth, in Esh·te·mō´a, ²⁹in Rā´cal, in the towns of the Je·rah´-mē·el·ītes, in the towns of the Ken´ītes, ³⁰in Hor´mah, in Bor-ash´an, in Ā´thach, ³¹in Hē´bron, all the places where David and his men had roamed.

Mount Gilboa is a group of hills close to the Mediterranean Sea. Many battles took place on these hills. King Saul and his son Jonathan died at Mount Gilboa in a battle against the Philistines. King Saul defended Israel even though he knew he would die (see 1 Samuel 28:19).

The Death of Saul and His Sons

31 Now the Phi·lis´tines fought against Israel; and the men of Israel fled before the Phi·lis´tines, and many fellᵖ on Mount Gil·bō´a. ²The Phi·lis´tines overtook Saul and his sons; and the Phi·lis´tines killed Jonathan and A·bin´-a·dab and Mal·chī·shū´a, the sons of Saul. ³The battle pressed hard upon Saul; the archers found him, and he was badly wounded by them. ⁴Then Saul said to his armor-bearer, "Draw your sword and

thrust me through with it, so that these uncircumcised may not come and thrust me through, and make sport of me." But his armor-bearer was unwilling; for he was terrified. So Saul took his own sword and fell upon it. ⁵When his armor-bearer saw that Saul was dead, he also fell upon his sword and died with him. ⁶So Saul and his three sons and his armor-bearer and all his men died together on the same day. ⁷When the men of Israel who were on the other side of the valley and those beyond the Jordan saw that the men of Israel had fled and that Saul and his sons were dead, they forsook their towns and fled; and the Phi·lis´tines came and occupied them.

8 The next day, when the Phi·lis´tines came to strip the dead, they found Saul and his three sons fallen on Mount Gil·bō´a. ⁹They cut off his head, stripped off his armor, and sent messengers throughout the land of the Phi·lis´tines to carry the good news to the houses of their idols and to the people. ¹⁰They put his armor in the temple of As·tar´te;�q and they fastened his body to the wall of Beth-shan. ¹¹But when the inhabitants of Jā´besh-gil´ē·ad heard what the Phi·lis´tines had done to Saul, ¹²all the valiant men set out, traveled all night long, and took the body of Saul and the bodies of his sons from the wall of Beth-shan. They came to Jā´besh and burned them there. ¹³Then they took their bones and buried them under the tamarisk tree in Jā´besh, and fasted seven days.

The tamarisk tree is a desert shrub with small leaves on feathery branches. Some types of these trees have a sugary juice, which some people think is like the manna the Israelites ate as they traveled through the wilderness.

ᵖ Heb *and they fell slain*   �q Heb plural

2 Samuel

Second Samuel continues the story started in First Samuel—the story of Israel's struggles as they became a people ruled by kings. These two books, which were finished in the sixth century BC, are really one long story about the early Israelite kingdom. Although Second Samuel is named after Samuel, the book tells about David as the king of Israel.

The book of Second Samuel tells how David first was anointed king of Judah and later was anointed king over all Israel. As king of Israel, David captured the city of Jerusalem and made it the capital city. He also brought the ark of the covenant back to Jerusalem. God helped David do many good things for God's people. King David often made wrong choices, but he also asked for God's forgiveness. David was a great and powerful king. Under David's rule, the kingdom of Israel became very strong, and the people thought of him as their ideal king. David's most outstanding quality was his devotion to God.

2 Samuel 6:1–15

David Mourns for Saul and Jonathan

1 After the death of Saul, when David had returned from defeating the A·mal´e·kītes, David remained two days in Zik´lag. ²On the third day, a man came from Saul's camp, with his clothes torn and dirt on his head. When he came to David, he fell to the ground and did obeisance. ³David said to him, "Where have you come from?" He said to him, "I have escaped from the camp of Israel." ⁴David said to him, "How did things go? Tell me!" He answered, "The army fled from the battle, but also many of the army fell and died; and Saul and his son Jonathan also died." ⁵Then David asked the young man who was reporting to him, "How do you know that Saul and his son Jonathan died?" ⁶The young man reporting to him said, "I happened to be on Mount Gil·bō´a; and there was Saul leaning on his spear, while the chariots and the horsemen drew close to him. ⁷When he looked behind him, he saw me, and called to me. I answered, 'Here sir.' ⁸And he said to me, 'Who are you?' I answered him, 'I am an A·mal´e·kīte.' ⁹He said to me, 'Come, stand over me and kill me; for convulsions have seized me, and yet my life still lingers.' ¹⁰So I stood over him, and killed him, for I knew that he could not live after he had fallen. I took the crown that was on his head and the armlet that was on his arm, and I have brought them here to my lord."

11 Then David took hold of his clothes and tore them; and all the men who were with him did the same. ¹²They mourned and wept, and fasted until evening for Saul and for his son Jonathan, and for the army of the LORD and for the house of Israel, because they had fallen by the sword. ¹³David said to the young man who had reported to him, "Where do you come from?" He answered, "I am the son of a resident alien, an A·mal´e·kīte." ¹⁴David said to him, "Were you not afraid to lift your hand to destroy the LORD's

David was the second and greatest king of Israel. He ruled from about 1000 to 965 BC. David was a shepherd boy living in Bethlehem when he was chosen to serve King Saul. He soon became a favorite of the court because he had many talents. He was a great poet and musician who probably wrote many of the psalms. He was also an excellent, courageous soldier. After Saul's death, David became a great and powerful king.

anointed?" ¹⁵Then David called one of the young men and said, "Come here and strike him down." So he struck him down and he died. ¹⁶David said to him, "Your blood be on your head; for your own mouth has testified against you, saying, 'I have killed the LORD's anointed.'"

17 David intoned this lamentation over Saul and his son Jonathan. ¹⁸(He ordered that The Song of the Bow[a] be taught to the people of Judah; it is written in the Book of Jash´ar.) He said:

¹⁹ Your glory, O Israel, lies slain upon
    your high places!
  How the mighty have fallen!
²⁰ Tell it not in Gath,
    proclaim it not in the streets of
      Ash´ke·lon;
  or the daughters of the Phi·lis´tines
    will rejoice,
  the daughters of the uncircumcised will exult.
²¹ You mountains of Gil·bō´a,
    let there be no dew or rain upon
      you,
    nor bounteous fields![b]
  For there the shield of the mighty
    was defiled,
    the shield of Saul, anointed with
      oil no more.

---

[a] Heb *that The Bow* [b] Meaning of Heb uncertain

²² From the blood of the slain,
　　from the fat of the mighty,
the bow of Jonathan did not turn back,
　　nor the sword of Saul return empty.

²³ Saul and Jonathan, beloved and lovely!
　　In life and in death they were not
　　　　divided;
they were swifter than eagles,
　　they were stronger than lions.

²⁴ O daughters of Israel, weep over Saul,
　　who clothed you with crimson, in
　　　　luxury,
who put ornaments of gold on
　　your apparel.

²⁵ How the mighty have fallen
　　in the midst of the battle!
Jonathan lies slain upon your high
　　places.
²⁶ I am distressed for you, my
　　brother Jonathan;
greatly beloved were you to me;
　　your love to me was wonderful,
　　passing the love of women.

²⁷ How the mighty have fallen,
　　and the weapons of war perished!

David Anointed King of Judah

2 After this David inquired of the LORD, "Shall I go up into any of the cities of Judah?" The LORD said to him, "Go up." David said, "To which shall I go up?" He said, "To Hē´bron." ²So David went up there, along with his two wives, A·hin´-ō·am of Jez´rē·el, and Ab´i·gāil the widow of Nā´bal of Car´mel. ³David brought up the men who were with him, every one with his household; and they settled in the towns of Hē´bron. ⁴Then the people of Judah came, and there they anointed David king over the house of Judah.

When they told David, "It was the people of Jā´besh-gil´ē·ad who buried Saul," ⁵David sent messengers to the people of Jā´besh-gil´ē·ad, and said to them, "May you be blessed by the LORD, because you showed this loyalty to Saul your lord, and buried him! ⁶Now may the LORD show steadfast love and faithfulness to you!

And I too will reward you because you have done this thing. ⁷Therefore let your hands be strong, and be valiant; for Saul your lord is dead, and the house of Judah has anointed me king over them."

Ishbaal King of Israel

8 But Abner son of Ner, commander of Saul's army, had taken Ish´bā·al^c son of Saul, and brought him over to Mā·ha·nā´im. ⁹He made him king over Gil´e·ad, the Ash´ur-ītes, Jez´rē·el, Ē´phra·im, Benjamin, and over all Israel. ¹⁰Ish´bā·al,^c Saul's son, was forty years old when he began to reign over Israel, and he reigned two years. But the house of Judah followed David. ¹¹The time that David was king in Hē´bron over the house of Judah was seven years and six months.

The Battle of Gibeon

12 Abner son of Ner, and the servants of Ish´bā·al^c son of Saul, went out from Mā·ha·nā´im to Gib´e·on. ¹³Jō´ab son of Ze·rū´i·ah, and the servants of David, went out and met them at the pool of Gib´e·on. One group sat on one side of the pool, while the other sat on the other side of the pool. ¹⁴Abner said to Jō´ab, "Let the young men come forward and have a contest before us." Jō´ab said, "Let them come forward." ¹⁵So they came forward and were counted as they passed by, twelve for Benjamin and Ish´bā·al^c son of Saul, and

Hebron is a city that is close to Jerusalem. The Israelites conquered and destroyed Hebron, but they later rebuilt the city. Hebron was David's capital during the first years of his reign as king. Today, Hebron is still an important city. Can you imagine a city that has been around for so long? See if you can find it on a map or globe!

---

^c Gk Compare 1 Chr 8.33; 9.39: Heb *Ish-bosheth*, "man of shame"

Abner was in charge of the Israelite army when Saul was king. Abner fought in many battles against the Philistines. After Saul died, Abner chose Saul's son Ishbosheth to be king. Eleven of the tribes followed Ishbosheth as king, but the tribe of Judah followed David as king. After a while, Abner told all the tribes of Israel to follow David. Soon after, Abner was killed.

twelve of the servants of David. [16]Each grasped his opponent by the head, and thrust his sword in his opponent's side; so they fell down together. Therefore that place was called Hel′kath-haz·zū′rim,[d] which is at Gib′e·on. [17]The battle was very fierce that day; and Abner and the men of Israel were beaten by the servants of David.

18 The three sons of Ze·rū′i·ah were there, Jō′ab, A·bi′shaī, and As′a·hel. Now As′a·hel was as swift of foot as a wild gazelle. [19]As′a·hel pursued Abner, turning neither to the right nor to the left as he followed him. [20]Then Abner looked back and said, "Is it you, As′a·hel?" He answered, "Yes, it is." [21]Abner said to him, "Turn to your right or to your left, and seize one of the young men, and take his spoil." But As′a·hel would not turn away from following him. [22]Abner said again to As′a·hel, "Turn away from following me; why should I strike you to the ground? How then could I show my face to your brother Jō′ab?" [23]But he refused to turn away. So Abner struck him in the stomach with the butt of his spear, so that the spear came out at his back. He fell there, and died where he lay. And all those who came to the place where As′a·hel had fallen and died, stood still.

24 But Jō′ab and A·bi′shaī pursued Abner. As the sun was going down they came to the hill of Am′mah, which lies before Gī′ah on the way to the wilderness of Gib′e·on. [25]The Ben·ja·min·ites rallied around Abner and formed a single band; they took their stand on the top of a hill. [26]Then Abner called to Jō′ab, "Is the sword to keep devouring forever? Do you not know that the end will be bitter? How long will it be before you order your people to turn from the pursuit of their kinsmen?" [27]Jō′ab said, "As God lives, if you had not spoken, the people would have continued to pursue their kinsmen, not stopping until morning." [28]Jō′ab sounded the trumpet and all the people stopped; they no longer pursued Israel or engaged in battle any further.

29 Abner and his men traveled all that night through the Ar′a·bah; they crossed the Jordan, and, marching the whole forenoon,[e] they came to Mā·ha·nā′-im. [30]Jō′ab returned from the pursuit of Abner; and when he had gathered all the people together, there were missing of David's servants nineteen men besides As′a·hel. [31]But the servants of David had killed of Benjamin three hundred sixty of Abner's men. [32]They took up As′a·hel and buried him in the tomb of his father, which was at Bethlehem. Jō′ab and his men marched all night, and the day broke upon them at Hē′bron.

Abner Defects to David

3 There was a long war between the house of Saul and the house of David; David grew stronger and stronger, while the house of Saul became weaker and weaker.

2 Sons were born to David at Hē′bron: his firstborn was Am′non, of A·hin′ō·am of Jez′re·el; [3]his second, Chi′le·ab, of Ab′i·gāil the widow of Nā′bal of Car′mel; the third, Ab′sa·lom son of Mā′a·cah, daughter of King Tal′maī of Gē′shur; [4]the fourth, Ad·o·nī′jah son of Hag′gith; the fifth, Sheph·a·tī′ah son of A·bī′tal; [5]and the

[d] That is *Field of Sword-edges*   [e] Meaning of Heb uncertain

sixth, Ith′rē·am, of David's wife Eg′lah. These were born to David in Hē′bron.

6 While there was war between the house of Saul and the house of David, Abner was making himself strong in the house of Saul. [7]Now Saul had a concubine whose name was Riz′pah daughter of Āi·ah. And Ish′bā·al[f] said to Abner, "Why have you gone in to my father's concubine?" [8]The words of Ish′bā·al[g] made Abner very angry; he said, "Am I a dog's head for Judah? Today I keep showing loyalty to the house of your father Saul, to his brothers, and to his friends, and have not given you into the hand of David; and yet you charge me now with a crime concerning this woman. [9]So may God do to Abner and so may he add to it! For just what the LORD has sworn to David, that will I accomplish for him, [10]to transfer the kingdom from the house of Saul, and set up the throne of David over Israel and over Judah, from Dan to Bē′er-shē′ba." [11]And Ish′bā·al[f] could not answer Abner another word, because he feared him.

12 Abner sent messengers to David at Hē′bron,[h] saying, "To whom does the land belong? Make your covenant with me, and I will give you my support to bring all Israel over to you." [13]He said, "Good; I will make a covenant with you. But one thing I require of you: you shall never appear in my presence unless you bring Saul's daughter Mī′chal when you come to see me." [14]Then David sent messengers to Saul's son Ish′bā·al,[i] saying, "Give me my wife Mī′chal, to whom I became engaged at the price of one hundred foreskins of the Phi·lis′tines." [15]Ish′bā·al[i] sent and took her from her husband Pal′ti·el the son of Lā′ish. [16]But her husband went with her, weeping as he walked behind her all the way to Ba·hū′rim. Then Abner said to him, "Go back home!" So he went back.

17 Abner sent word to the elders of Israel, saying, "For some time past you have been seeking David as king over you. [18]Now then bring it about; for the LORD has promised David: Through my servant David I will save my people Israel from the hand of the Phi·lis′tines, and from all their enemies." [19]Abner also spoke directly to the Ben′ja·min·ites; then Abner went to tell David at Hē′bron all that Israel and the whole house of Benjamin were ready to do.

20 When Abner came with twenty men to David at Hē′bron, David made a feast for Abner and the men who were with him. [21]Abner said to David, "Let me go and rally all Israel to my lord the king, in order that they may make a covenant with you, and that you may reign over all that your heart desires." So David dismissed Abner, and he went away in peace.

Abner Is Killed by Joab

22 Just then the servants of David arrived with Jō′ab from a raid, bringing much spoil with them. But Abner was not with David at Hē′bron, for David[j] had dismissed him, and he had gone away in peace. [23]When Jō′ab and all the army that was with him came, it was told Jō′ab, "Abner son of Ner came to the king, and he has dismissed him, and he has gone away in peace." [24]Then Jō′ab went to the king and said, "What have you done? Abner came to you; why did you dismiss him, so that he got away? [25]You know that Abner son of Ner came to deceive you, and to learn your comings and goings and to learn all that you are doing."

26 When Jō′ab came out from David's presence, he sent messengers after Abner, and they brought him back from the cistern of Sī′rah; but David did not know about it. [27]When Abner returned to Hē′bron, Jō′ab took him aside in the gateway to speak with him privately, and there he stabbed him in the stomach. So he died for shedding[k] the blood of As′a·hel, Jō′ab's[l] brother. [28]Afterward, when David heard of it, he

[f] Heb And he   [g] Gk Compare 1 Chr 8.33; 9.39: Heb Ish-bosheth, "man of shame"   [h] Gk: Heb where he was   [i] Heb Ish-bosheth   [j] Heb he   [k] Heb lacks shedding   [l] Heb his

said, "I and my kingdom are forever guiltless before the LORD for the blood of Abner son of Ner. [29]May the guilt[m] fall on the head of Jō´ab, and on all his father's house; and may the house of Jō´ab never be without one who has a discharge, or who is leprous,[n] or who holds a spindle, or who falls by the sword, or who lacks food!" [30]So Jō´ab and his brother A·bi´shaī murdered Abner because he had killed their brother As´a·hel in the battle at Gib´ē·on.

31 Then David said to Jō´ab and to all the people who were with him, "Tear your clothes, and put on sackcloth, and mourn over Abner." And King David followed the bier. [32]They buried Abner at Hē´bron. The king lifted up his voice and wept at the grave of Abner, and all the people wept. [33]The king lamented for Abner, saying,

"Should Abner die as a fool dies?
[34] Your hands were not bound,
　　your feet were not fettered;
　as one falls before the wicked
　　you have fallen."

And all the people wept over him again. [35]Then all the people came to persuade David to eat something while it was still day; but David swore, saying, "So may God do to me, and more, if I taste bread or anything else before the sun goes down!" [36]All the people took notice of it, and it pleased them; just as everything the king did pleased all the people. [37]So all the people and all Israel understood that day that the king had no part in the killing of Abner son of Ner. [38]And the king said to his servants, "Do you not know that a prince and a great man has fallen this day in Israel? [39]Today I am powerless, even though anointed king; these men, the sons of Ze·rū´i·ah, are too violent for me. The LORD pay back the one who does wickedly in accordance with his wickedness!"

Ishbaal Assassinated

4 When Saul's son Ish´bā·al[o] heard that Abner had died at Hē´bron, his courage failed, and all Israel was dismayed. [2]Saul's son had two captains of raiding bands; the name of the one was Bā´a·nah,

and the name of the other Rē´chab. They were sons of Rim´mon a Ben´ja·min·īte from Be·er´oth—for Be·er´oth is considered to belong to Benjamin. [3](Now the people of Be·er´oth had fled to Git´ta·im and are there as resident aliens to this day).

4 Saul's son Jonathan had a son who was crippled in his feet. He was five years old when the news about Saul and Jonathan came from Jez´rē·el. His nurse picked him up and fled; and, in her haste to flee, it happened that he fell and became lame. His name was Me·phib´o·sheth.[p]

5 Now the sons of Rim´mon the Be·er´oth·īte, Rē´chab and Bā´an·ah, set out, and about the heat of the day they came to the house of Ish´bā·al,[q] while he was taking his noonday rest. [6]They came inside the house as though to take wheat, and they struck him in the stomach; then Rē´chab and his brother Bā´an·ah escaped.[r] [7]Now they had come into the house while he was lying on his couch in his bedchamber; they attacked him, killed him, and beheaded him. Then they took his head and traveled by way of the Ar´a·bah all night long. [8]They brought the head of Ish´bā·al[q] to David at Hē´bron and said to the king, "Here is the head of Ish´bā·al,[q] son of Saul, your enemy, who sought your life; the LORD has avenged my lord the king this day on Saul and on his offspring."

9 David answered Rē´chab and his brother Bā´a·nah, the sons of Rim´mon the Be·er´oth·īte, "As the LORD lives, who has redeemed my life out of every adversity, [10]when the one who told me, 'See, Saul is dead,' thought he was bringing good news, I seized him and killed him at Zik´lag— this was the reward I gave him for his news. [11]How much more then, when wicked men have killed a righteous man on his bed in his own house! And now shall I not require his blood at your hand, and destroy you from the earth?" [12]So

---

[m] Heb *May it*　　[n] A term for several skin diseases; precise meaning uncertain　　[o] Heb lacks *Ishbaal*　　[p] In 1 Chr 8.34 and 9.40, *Merib-baal*　　[q] Heb *Ish-bosheth*　　[r] Meaning of Heb of verse 6

David commanded the young men, and they killed them; they cut off their hands and feet, and hung their bodies beside the pool at Hēʹbron. But the head of Ishʹbaʹalˢ they took and buried in the tomb of Abner at Hēʹbron.

David Anointed King of All Israel

5 Then all the tribes of Israel came to David at Hēʹbron, and said, "Look, we are your bone and flesh. ²For some time, while Saul was king over us, it was you who led out Israel and brought it in. The LORD said to you: It is you who shall be shepherd of my people Israel, you who shall be ruler over Israel." ³So all the elders of Israel came to the king at Hēʹbron; and King David made a covenant with them at Hēʹbron before the LORD, and they anointed David king over Israel. ⁴David was thirty years old when he began to reign, and he reigned forty years. ⁵At Hēʹbron he reigned over Judah seven years and six months; and at Jerusalem he reigned over all Israel and Judah thirty-three years.

Jerusalem Made Capital of the United Kingdom

6 The king and his men marched to Jerusalem against the Jebʹū·sītes, the inhabitants of the land, who said to David, "You will not come in here, even the blind and the lame will turn you back"—thinking, "David cannot come in here." ⁷Nevertheless David took the stronghold of Zion, which is now the city of David. ⁸David had said on that day, "Whoever would strike down the Jebʹū·sītes, let him get up the water shaft to attack the lame and the blind, those whom David hates."ᵗ Therefore it is said, "The blind and the lame shall not come into the house." ⁹David occupied the stronghold, and named it the city of David. David built the city all around from the Milʹlō inward. ¹⁰And David became greater and greater, for the LORD, the God of hosts, was with him.

11 King Hiram of Tyre sent messengers to David, along with cedar trees, and carpenters and masons who built David a house. ¹²David then perceived that the LORD had established him king over Israel, and that he had exalted his kingdom for the sake of his people Israel.

13 In Jerusalem, after he came from Hēʹbron, David took more concubines and wives; and more sons and daughters were born to David. ¹⁴These are the names of those who were born to him in Jerusalem: Shamʹmū·a, Shōʹbab, Nathan, Solomon, ¹⁵Ibʹhar, E·lishʹū·a, Nēʹpheg, Ja·phīʹa, ¹⁶E·lishʹa·ma, E·līʹa·da, and E·liphʹe·let.

Philistine Attack Repulsed

17 When the Phi·lisʹtines heard that David had been anointed king over Israel, all the Phi·lisʹtines went up in search of David; but David heard about it and went down to the stronghold. ¹⁸Now the Phi·lisʹtines had come and spread out in the valley of Rephʹa·im. ¹⁹David inquired of the LORD, "Shall I go up against the Phi·lisʹtines? Will you give them into my hand?" The LORD said to David, "Go up; for I will certainly give the Phi·lisʹtines into

In the Bible, the city of Jerusalem is also called Salem, Zion, city of David, and Jebus. When David was king, he captured Jerusalem from the Jebusites and made it his capital city. When he brought the ark to Jerusalem, the city became the religious center of the Israelites. David's son Solomon built the Temple there, and Jerusalem became a holy city. After Solomon's death when the kingdom was divided, Jerusalem was the capital of the southern kingdom, Judah. Many nations threatened Jerusalem. The city was finally conquered and burned by Nebuchadnezzar, and its important leaders were taken to Babylon.

ˢ Heb *Ish-bosheth*   ᵗ Another reading is *those who hate David* your hand." [20]So David came to Bāʹal-pe-rāʹ-zim, and David defeated them there. He said, "The LORD has burst forth against[u] my enemies before me, like a bursting flood." Therefore that place is called Bāʹal-pe-rāʹ-zim.[v] [21]The Phi·lisʹtines abandoned their idols there, and David and his men carried them away.

[22] Once again the Phi·lisʹtines came up, and were spread out in the valley of Rephʹa·im. [23]When David inquired of the LORD, he said, "You shall not go up; go around to their rear, and come upon them opposite the balsam trees. [24]When you hear the sound of marching in the tops of the balsam trees, then be on the alert; for then the LORD has gone out before you to strike down the army of the Phi·lisʹtines." [25]David did just as the LORD had commanded him; and he struck down the Phi·lisʹtines from Gēʹba all the way to Gēʹzer.

David brought the Ark of the Covenant to Jerusalem with a big celebration. He built a special tent for the Ark and offered sacrifices to God. The Ark stayed in the tent until the Temple was built.

David Brings the Ark to Jerusalem

6 David again gathered all the chosen men of Israel, thirty thousand. [2]David and all the people with him set out and went from Bāʹa·lē-jūʹdah, to bring up from there the ark of God, which is called by the name of the LORD of hosts who is enthroned on the cherubim. [3]They carried the ark of God on a new cart, and brought it out of the house of A·binʹa·dab, which was on the hill. Uzʹzah and A·hīʹō,[w] the sons of A·binʹa·dab, were driving the new cart [4]with the ark of God;[x] and A·hīʹō[w] went in front of the ark. [5]David and all the house of Israel were dancing before the LORD with all their might, with songs[y] and lyres

and harps and tambourines and castanets and cymbals.

[6] When they came to the threshing floor of Naʹcon, Uzʹzah reached out his hand to the ark of God and took hold of it, for the oxen shook it. [7]The anger of the LORD was kindled against Uzʹzah; and God struck him there because he reached out his hand to the ark;[z] and he died there beside the ark of God. [8]David was angry because the LORD had burst forth with an outburst upon Uzʹzah; so that place is called Perʹez-uzʹzah,[a] to this day. [9]David was afraid of the LORD that day; he said, "How can the ark of the LORD come into my care?" [10]So David was unwilling to take the ark of the LORD into his care in the city of David; instead David took it to the house of Ōʹbed-ēʹdom the Gitʹtīte. [11]The ark of the LORD remained in the house of Ōʹbed-ēʹdom the Gitʹtīte three months; and the LORD blessed Ōʹbed-ēʹdom and all his household.

[12] It was told King David, "The LORD has blessed the household of Ōʹbed-ēʹdom and all that belongs to him, because of the ark of God." So David went and brought up the ark of God from the house of Ōʹbed-ēʹdom to the city of David with rejoicing; [13]and when those who bore the ark of the LORD had gone six paces, he sacrificed an ox and a fatling. [14]David danced before the LORD with all his might; David was girded with a linen ephod. [15]So David and all the house of Israel brought up the ark of the LORD with shouting, and with the sound of the trumpet.

[16] As the ark of the LORD came into the city of David, Mīʹchal daughter of Saul looked out of the window, and saw King David leaping and dancing before the LORD; and she despised him in her heart.

[u] Heb *paraz*   [v] That is *Lord of Bursting Forth*
[w] Or *and his brother*   [x] Compare Gk: Heb *and brought it out of the house of Abinadab, which was on the hill with the ark of God*   [y] Q Ms Gk 1 Chr 13.8: Heb *fir trees*   [z] 1 Chr 13.10 Compare Q Ms: Meaning of Heb uncertain   [a] That is *Bursting Out Against Uzzah*

17 They brought in the ark of the LORD, and set it in its place, inside the tent that David had pitched for it; and David offered burnt offerings and offerings of well-being before the LORD. ¹⁸When David had finished offering the burnt offerings and the offerings of well-being, he blessed the people in the name of the LORD of hosts, ¹⁹and distributed food among all the people, the whole multitude of Israel, both men and women, to each a cake of bread, a portion of meat,ᵇ and a cake of raisins. Then all the people went back to their homes.

20 David returned to bless his household. But Mī´chal the daughter of Saul came out to meet David, and said, "How the king of Israel honored himself today, uncovering himself today before the eyes of his servants' maids, as any vulgar fellow might shamelessly uncover himself!" ²¹David said to Mī´chal, "It was before the LORD, who chose me in place of your father and all his household, to appoint me as prince over Israel, the people of the LORD, that I have danced before the LORD. ²²I will make myself yet more contemptible than this, and I will be abased in my own eyes; but by the maids of whom you have spoken, by them I shall be held in honor." ²³And Mī´chal the daughter of Saul had no child to the day of her death.

God's Covenant with David

7 Now when the king was settled in his house, and the LORD had given him rest from all his enemies around him, ²the king said to the prophet Nathan, "See now, I am living in a house of cedar, but the ark of God stays in a tent." ³Nathan said to the king, "Go, do all that you have in mind; for the LORD is with you."

4 But that same night the word of the LORD came to Nathan: ⁵Go and tell my servant David: Thus says the LORD: Are you the one to build me a house to live in? ⁶I have not lived in a house since the day I brought up the people of Israel from Egypt to this day, but I have been moving about in a tent and a tabernacle. ⁷Wherever I have moved about among all the people of Israel, did I ever speak a word with any of the tribal leadersᶜ of Israel, whom I commanded to shepherd my people Israel, saying, "Why have you not built me a house of cedar?" ⁸Now therefore thus you shall say to my servant David: Thus says the LORD of hosts: I took you from the pasture, from following the sheep to be prince over my people Israel; ⁹and I have been with you wherever you went, and have cut off all your enemies from before you; and I will make for you a great name, like the name of the great ones of the earth. ¹⁰And I will appoint a place for my people Israel and will plant them, so that they may live in their own place, and be disturbed no more; and evildoers shall afflict them no more, as formerly, ¹¹from the time that I appointed judges over my people Israel; and I will give you rest from all your enemies. Moreover the LORD declares to you that the LORD will make you a house. ¹²When your days are fulfilled and you lie down with your ancestors, I will raise up your offspring after you, who shall come forth from your body, and I will establish his kingdom. ¹³He shall build a house for my name, and I will establish the throne of his kingdom forever. ¹⁴I will be a father to him, and he shall be a son to me. When he commits iniquity, I will punish him with a rod such as mortals use, with blows inflicted by human beings. ¹⁵But I will not takeᵈ my steadfast love from him, as I took it from Saul, whom I put away from before you. ¹⁶Your house and your kingdom shall be made sure forever before me;ᵉ your throne shall be established forever. ¹⁷In accordance with all these words and with all this vision, Nathan spoke to David.

David's Prayer

18 Then King David went in and sat before the LORD, and said, "Who am I, O

ᵇ Vg: Meaning of Heb uncertain   ᶜ Or *any of the tribes*   ᵈ Gk Syr Vg 1 Chr 17.13: Heb *shall not depart*   ᵉ Gk Heb Mss: MT *before you*; Compare 2 Sam 7.26, 29

"Therefore you are great, O LORD God; for there is no one like you, and there is no God besides you, according to all that we have heard with our ears."

2 Samuel 7:22

Lord GOD, and what is my house, that you have brought me thus far? [19]And yet this was a small thing in your eyes, O Lord GOD; you have spoken also of your servant's house for a great while to come. May this be instruction for the people,[f] O Lord GOD! [20]And what more can David say to you? For you know your servant, O Lord GOD! [21]Because of your promise, and according to your own heart, you have wrought all this greatness, so that your servant may know it. [22]Therefore you are great, O LORD God; for there is no one like you, and there is no God besides you, according to all that we have heard with our ears. [23]Who is like your people, like Israel? Is there another[g] nation on earth whose God went to redeem it as a people, and to make a name for himself, doing great and awesome things for them,[h] by driving out[i] before his people nations and their gods?[j] [24]And you established your people Israel for yourself to be your people forever; and you, O LORD, became their God. [25]And now, O LORD God, as for the word that you have spoken concerning your servant and concerning his house, confirm it forever; do as you have promised. [26]Thus your name will be magnified forever in the saying, 'The LORD of hosts is God over Israel'; and the house of your servant David will be established before you. [27]For you, O LORD of hosts, the God of Israel, have made this revelation to your servant, saying, 'I will build you a house'; therefore your servant has found courage to pray this prayer to you. [28]And now, O Lord GOD, you are God, and your words are true, and you have promised this good thing to your servant; [29]now therefore may

it please you to bless the house of your servant, so that it may continue forever before you; for you, O Lord GOD, have spoken, and with your blessing shall the house of your servant be blessed forever."

David's Wars

8 Some time afterward, David attacked the Phi·lis′tines and subdued them; David took Meth′eg-am′mah out of the hand of the Phi·lis′tines.

2 He also defeated the Mō′ab·ītes and, making them lie down on the ground, measured them off with a cord; he measured two lengths of cord for those who were to be put to death, and one length[k] for those who were to be spared. And the Mō′ab·ītes became servants to David and brought tribute.

3 David also struck down King Had·a·dē′zer son of Rē′hob of Zō′bah, as he went to restore his monument[l] at the river Euphrates. [4]David took from him one thousand seven hundred horsemen, and twenty thousand foot soldiers. David hamstrung all the chariot horses, but left enough for a hundred chariots. [5]When the Ar·a·mē′ans of Damascus came to help King Had·a·dē′zer of Zō′bah, David killed twenty-two thousand men of the Ar·a·mē′ans. [6]Then David put garrisons among the Ar·a·mē′ans of Damascus; and the Ar·a·mē′ans became servants to David and brought

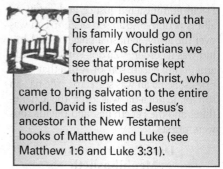

God promised David that his family would go on forever. As Christians we see that promise kept through Jesus Christ, who came to bring salvation to the entire world. David is listed as Jesus's ancestor in the New Testament books of Matthew and Luke (see Matthew 1:6 and Luke 3:31).

[f] Meaning of Heb uncertain   [g] Gk: Heb *one*
[h] Heb *you*   [i] Gk 1 Chr 17.21: Heb *for your land*
[j] Cn: Heb *before your people, whom you redeemed for yourself from Egypt, nations and its gods*   [k] Heb *one full length*   [l] Compare 1 Sam 15.12 and 2 Sam 18.18

tribute. The LORD gave victory to David wherever he went. [7]David took the gold shields that were carried by the servants of Had·a·dē′zer, and brought them to Jerusalem. [8]From Bē′tah and from Be·rō′thaī, towns of Had·a·dē′zer, King David took a great amount of bronze.

9 When King Tō′ī of Hā′math heard that David had defeated the whole army of Had·a·dē′zer, [10]Tō′ī sent his son Jō′ram to King David, to greet him and to congratulate him because he had fought against Had·a·dē′zer and defeated him. Now Had·a·dē′zer had often been at war with Tō′ī. Jō′ram brought with him articles of silver, gold, and bronze; [11]these also King David dedicated to the LORD, together with the silver and gold that he dedicated from all the nations he subdued, [12]from Ē′dom, Mō′ab, the Am′mon·ītes, the Phi·lis′tines, Am′a·lek, and from the spoil of King Had·a·dē′zer son of Rē′hob of Zō′bah.

13 David won a name for himself. When he returned, he killed eighteen thousand Ē′dom·ītes[m] in the Valley of Salt. [14]He put garrisons in Ē′dom; throughout all Ē′dom he put garrisons, and all the Ē′dom·ītes became David's servants. And the LORD gave victory to David wherever he went.

David's Officers

15 So David reigned over all Israel; and David administered justice and equity to all his people. [16]Jō′ab son of Ze·rū′i·ah was over the army; Je·hosh′a·phat son of A·hī′lud was recorder; [17]Zā′dok son of A·hī′tub and A·him′e·lech son of A·bī′a·thar were priests; Se·rāi′ah was secretary; [18]Be·nā′i·ah son of Je·hoi′a·da was over[n] the Cher′e·thītes and the Pel′eth·ītes; and David's sons were priests.

David's Kindness to Mephibosheth

9 David asked, "Is there still anyone left of the house of Saul to whom I may show kindness for Jonathan's sake?" [2]Now there was a servant of the house of Saul whose name was Zī′ba, and he was

summoned to David. The king said to him, "Are you Zī′ba?" And he said, "At your service!" [3]The king said, "Is there anyone remaining of the house of Saul to whom I may show the kindness of God?" Zī′ba said to the king, "There remains a son of Jonathan; he is crippled in his feet." [4]The king said to him, "Where is he?" Zī′ba said to the king, "He is in the house of Mā′chir son of Am′mi·el, at Lō-dē′bar." [5]Then King David sent and brought him from the house of Mā′chir son of Am′mi·el, at Lō-dē′bar. [6]Me·phib′o·sheth[o] son of Jonathan son of Saul came to David, and fell on his face and did obeisance. David said, "Me·phib′o·sheth!"[o] He answered, "I am your servant." [7]David said to him, "Do not be afraid, for I will show you kindness for the sake of your father Jonathan; I will restore to you all the land of your grandfather Saul, and you yourself shall eat at my table always." [8]He did obeisance and said, "What is your servant, that you should look upon a dead dog such as I?"

9 Then the king summoned Saul's servant Zī′ba, and said to him, "All that belonged to Saul and to all his house I have given to your master's grandson. [10]You and your sons and your servants shall till the land for him, and shall bring in the produce, so that your master's grandson may have food to eat; but your master's grandson Me·phib′o·sheth[o] shall always eat at my table." Now Zī′ba had fifteen sons and twenty servants. [11]Then Zī′ba said to the king, "According to all that my lord the king commands his servant, so your servant will do." Me·phib′o·sheth[o] ate at David's[p] table, like one of the king's sons. [12]Me·phib′o·sheth[o] had a young son whose name was Mī′ca. And all who lived in Zī′ba's house became Me·phib′o·sheth's[q] servants. [13]Me·phib′o·sheth[o] lived in Jerusalem, for he always ate at the king's table. Now he was lame in both his feet.

[m] Gk: Heb *returned from striking down eighteen thousand Arameans* [n] Syr Tg Vg 20.23; 1 Chr 18.17: Heb lacks *was over* [o] Or *Merib-baal* : See 4.4 note [p] Gk: Heb *my* [q] Or *Merib-baal's*: See 4.4 note

When Jonathan was killed, his son Mephibosheth was injured as his nurse rushed him to safety. When King David learned about Mephibosheth, he took him into his own household in memory of his promise to Jonathan. From then on, Mephibosheth ate regularly at the king's table. This was a very special honor.

The Ammonites and Arameans Are Defeated

10 Some time afterward, the king of the Am´mon·ītes died, and his son Hā´nun succeeded him. ²David said, "I will deal loyally with Hā´nun son of Nā´hash, just as his father dealt loyally with me." So David sent envoys to console him concerning his father. When David's envoys came into the land of the Am´mon·ītes, ³the princes of the Am´mon·ītes said to their lord Hā´nun, "Do you really think that David is honoring your father just because he has sent messengers with condolences to you? Has not David sent his envoys to you to search the city, to spy it out, and to overthrow it?" ⁴So Hā´nun seized David's envoys, shaved off half the beard of each, cut off their garments in the middle at their hips, and sent them away. ⁵When David was told, he sent to meet them, for the men were greatly ashamed. The king said, "Remain at Jericho until your beards have grown, and then return."

6 When the Am´mon·ītes saw that they had become odious to David, the Am´mon·ītes sent and hired the Ar·a·mē´-ans of Beth-rē´hob and the Ar·a·mē´ans of Zō´bah, twenty thousand foot soldiers, as well as the king of Mā´a·cah, one thousand men, and the men of Tob, twelve thousand men. ⁷When David heard of it, he sent Jō´ab and all the army with the warriors. ⁸The Am´mon·ītes came out and drew up in battle array at the entrance of the gate; but the Ar·a·mē´-ans of Zō´bah and of Rē´hob, and the men of Tob and Mā´a·cah, were by themselves in the open country.

9 When Jō´ab saw that the battle was set against him both in front and in the rear, he chose some of the picked men of Israel, and arrayed them against the Ar·a·mē´ans; ¹⁰the rest of his men he put in the charge of his brother A·bi´shaī, and he arrayed them against the Am´-mon·ītes. ¹¹He said, "If the Ar·a·mē´ans are too strong for me, then you shall help me; but if the Am´mon·ītes are too strong for you, then I will come and help you. ¹²Be strong, and let us be courageous for the sake of our people, and for the cities of our God; and may the LORD do what seems good to him." ¹³So Jō´ab and the people who were with him moved forward into battle against the Ar·a·mē´ans; and they fled before him. ¹⁴When the Am´mon·ītes saw that the Ar·a·mē´ans fled, they likewise fled before A·bi´shaī, and entered the city. Then Jō´ab returned from fighting against the Am´mon·ītes, and came to Jerusalem.

15 But when the Ar·a·mē´ans saw that they had been defeated by Israel, they gathered themselves together. ¹⁶Had·a·dē´zer sent and brought out the Ar·a·mē´ans who were beyond the Euphrates; and they came to Hē´lam, with Shō´bach the commander of the army of Had·a·dē´zer at their head. ¹⁷When it was told David, he gathered all Israel together, and crossed the Jordan, and came to Hē´lam. The Ar·a·mē´ans arrayed themselves against David and fought with him. ¹⁸The Ar·a·mē´ans fled before Israel; and David killed of the Ar·a·mē´-ans seven hundred chariot teams, and forty thousand horsemen,ʳ and wounded Shō´bach the commander of their army, so that he died there. ¹⁹When all the kings who were servants of Had·a·dē´-zer saw that they had been defeated by

ʳ 1 Chr 19.18 and some Gk Mss read *foot soldiers*

Israel, they made peace with Israel, and became subject to them. So the A·ra·mē'ans were afraid to help the Am'mon·ites any more.

David Commits Adultery with Bathsheba

11 In the spring of the year, the time when kings go out to battle, David sent Jō'ab with his officers and all Israel with him; they ravaged the Am'mon·ites, and besieged Rab'bah. But David remained at Jerusalem.

2 It happened, late one afternoon, when David rose from his couch and was walking about on the roof of the king's house, that he saw from the roof a woman bathing; the woman was very beautiful. ³David sent someone to inquire about the woman. It was reported, "This is Bath·shē'ba daughter of Ē·lī'am, the wife of Ū·rī'ah the Hit'tīte." ⁴So David sent messengers to get her, and she came to him, and he lay with her. (Now she was purifying herself after her period.) Then she returned to her house. ⁵The woman conceived; and she sent and told David, "I am pregnant."

6 So David sent word to Jō'ab, "Send me Ū·rī'ah the Hit'tīte." And Jō'ab sent Ū·rī'ah to David. ⁷When Ū·rī'ah came to him, David asked how Jō'ab and the people fared, and how the war was going. ⁸Then David said to Ū·rī'ah, "Go down to your house, and wash your feet." Ū·rī'ah went out of the king's house, and there followed him a present from the king. ⁹But Ū·rī'ah slept at the entrance of the king's house with all the servants of his lord, and did not go down to his house. ¹⁰When they told David, "Ū·rī'ah did not go down to his house," David said to Ū·rī'ah, "You have just come from a journey. Why did you not go down to your house?" ¹¹ Ū·rī'ah said to David, "The ark and Israel and Judah remain in booths;ˢ and my lord Jō'ab and the servants of my lord are camping in the open field; shall I then go to my house, to eat and to drink, and to lie with my wife?

As you live, and as your soul lives, I will not do such a thing." ¹²Then David said to Ū·rī'ah, "Remain here today also, and tomorrow I will send you back." So Ū·rī'ah remained in Jerusalem that day. On the next day, ¹³David invited him to eat and drink in his presence and made him drunk; and in the evening he went out to lie on his couch with the servants of his lord, but he did not go down to his house.

David Has Uriah Killed

14 In the morning David wrote a letter to Jō'ab, and sent it by the hand of Ū·rī'ah. ¹⁵In the letter he wrote, "Set Ū·rī'ah in the forefront of the hardest fighting, and then draw back from him, so that he may be struck down and die." ¹⁶As Jō'ab was besieging the city, he assigned Ū·rī'ah to the place where he knew there were valiant warriors. ¹⁷The men of the city came out and fought with Jō'ab; and some of the servants of David among the people fell. Ū·rī'ah the Hit'tīte was killed as well. ¹⁸Then Jō'ab sent and told David all the news about the fighting; ¹⁹and he instructed the messenger, "When you have finished telling the king all the news about the fighting, ²⁰then, if the king's anger rises, and if he says to you, 'Why did you go so near the city to fight? Did you not know that they would shoot from the wall? ²¹Who killed A·bim'e·lech son of Jer·ub·bā'al?ᵗ Did not a woman throw an upper millstone on him from the wall, so that he died at Thē'bez? Why did you go so near the wall?' then you shall say, 'Your servant Ūrī'ah the Hit'tīte is dead too.' "

22 So the messenger went, and came and told David all that Jō'ab had sent him to tell. ²³The messenger said to David, "The men gained an advantage over us, and came out against us in the field; but we drove them back to the entrance of the gate. ²⁴Then the archers shot at your servants from the wall; some of the king's servants are dead; and your servant Ū·rī'ah the Hit'tīte is dead

ˢ Or at Succoth   ᵗ Gk Syr Judg 7.1: Heb Jerubbesheth

also." ²⁵David said to the messenger, "Thus you shall say to Jō´ab, 'Do not let this matter trouble you, for the sword devours now one and now another; press your attack on the city, and overthrow it.' And encourage him."

26 When the wife of Ū·rī´ah heard that her husband was dead, she made lamentation for him. ²⁷When the mourning was over, David sent and brought her to his house, and she became his wife, and bore him a son.

Nathan Condemns David

12 But the thing that David had done displeased the LORD, ¹and the LORD sent Nathan to David. He came to him, and said to him, "There were two men in a certain city, the one rich and the other poor. ²The rich man had very many flocks and herds; ³but the poor man had nothing but one little ewe lamb, which he had bought. He brought it up, and it grew up with him and with his children; it used to eat of his meager fare, and drink from his cup, and lie in his bosom, and it was like a daughter to him. ⁴Now there came a traveler to the rich man, and he was loath to take one of his own flock or herd to prepare for the wayfarer who had come to him, but he took the poor man's lamb, and prepared that for the guest who had come to him." ⁵Then David's anger was greatly kindled against the man. He said to Nathan, "As the LORD lives, the man who has done this deserves to die; ⁶he shall restore the lamb fourfold, because he did this thing, and because he had no pity."

7 Nathan said to David, "You are the man! Thus says the LORD, the God of Israel: I anointed you king over Israel, and I rescued you from the hand of Saul; ⁸I gave you your master's house, and your master's wives into your bosom, and gave you the house of Israel and of Judah; and if that had been too little, I would have added as much more. ⁹Why have you despised the word of the LORD, to do what is evil in his sight? You have struck

down Ū·rī´ah the Hit´tīte with the sword, and have taken his wife to be your wife, and have killed him with the sword of the Am´mon·ītes. ¹⁰Now therefore the sword shall never depart from your house, for you have despised me, and have taken the wife of Ū·rī´ah the Hit´tīte to be your wife. ¹¹Thus says the LORD: I will raise up trouble against you from within your own house; and I will take your wives before your eyes, and give them to your neighbor, and he shall lie with your wives in the sight of this very sun. ¹²For you did it secretly; but I will do this thing before all Israel, and before the sun." ¹³David said to Nathan, "I have sinned against the LORD." Nathan said to David, "Now the LORD has put away your sin; you shall not die. ¹⁴Nevertheless, because by this deed you have utterly scorned the LORD,^u the child that is born to you shall die." ¹⁵Then Nathan went to his house.

Bathsheba's Child Dies

The LORD struck the child that Ū·rī´ah's wife bore to David, and it became very ill. ¹⁶David therefore pleaded with God for the child; David fasted, and went in and lay all night on the ground. ¹⁷The elders of his house stood beside him, urging him to rise from the ground; but he would not, nor

> King David committed a sin in taking Bathsheba and then having her husband killed. When the prophet Nathan brought David a message from God, the king repented with all his heart and asked God's forgiveness. When we do things that are hurtful to other people, we too need to ask for God's forgiveness. If you have hurt someone with your words or actions, pray and ask God for forgiveness. If someone has hurt you, pray and ask God to help you forgive that person.

^u Ancient scribal tradition: Compare 1 Sam 25.22
note: Heb *scorned the enemies of the* LORD

did he eat food with them. ¹⁸On the seventh day the child died. And the servants of David were afraid to tell him that the child was dead; for they said, "While the child was still alive, we spoke to him, and he did not listen to us; how then can we tell him the child is dead? He may do himself some harm." ¹⁹But when David saw that his servants were whispering together, he perceived that the child was dead; and David said to his servants, "Is the child dead?" They said, "He is dead."

20 Then David rose from the ground, washed, anointed himself, and changed his clothes. He went into the house of the LORD, and worshiped; he then went to his own house; and when he asked, they set food before him and he ate. ²¹Then his servants said to him, "What is this thing that you have done? You fasted and wept for the child while it was alive; but when the child died, you rose and ate food." ²²He said, "While the child was still alive, I fasted and wept; for I said, 'Who knows? The LORD may be gracious to me, and the child may live.' ²³But now he is dead; why should I fast? Can I bring him back again? I shall go to him, but he will not return to me."

Solomon Is Born

24 Then David consoled his wife Bath·she̅´ba, and went to her, and lay with her; and she bore a son, and he named him Solomon. The LORD loved him, ²⁵and sent a message by the prophet Nathan; so he named him Jed·i·di̅´ah,ᵛ because of the LORD.

The Ammonites Crushed

26 Now Jo̅´ab fought against Rab´bah of the Am´mon·ites, and took the royal city. ²⁷Jo̅´ab sent messengers to David, and said, "I have fought against Rab´bah; moreover, I have taken the water city. ²⁸Now, then, gather the rest of the people together, and encamp against the city, and take it; or I myself will take the city, and it will be called by my name." ²⁹So David gathered all the people together and went to Rab´bah, and fought against it and took it.

³⁰He took the crown of Mil´comʷ from his head; the weight of it was a talent of gold, and in it was a precious stone; and it was placed on David's head. He also brought forth the spoil of the city, a very great amount. ³¹He brought out the people who were in it, and set them to work with saws and iron picks and iron axes, or sent them to the brickworks. Thus he did to all the cities of the Am´mon·ites. Then David and all the people returned to Jerusalem.

Amnon and Tamar

13 Some time passed. David's son Ab´sa·lom had a beautiful sister whose name was Ta̅´mar; and David's son Am´non fell in love with her. ²Am´non was so tormented that he made himself ill because of his sister Ta̅´mar, for she was a virgin and it seemed impossible to Am´non to do anything to her. ³But Am´non had a friend whose name was Jon´a·dab, the son of David's brother Shim´e̅·ah; and Jon´a·dab was a very crafty man. ⁴He said to him, "O son of the king, why are you so haggard morning after morning? Will you not tell me?" Am´non said to him, "I love Ta̅´mar, my brother Ab´sa·lom's sister." ⁵Jon´a·dab said to him, "Lie down on your bed, and pretend to be ill; and when your father comes to see you, say to him, 'Let my sister Ta̅´mar come and give me something to eat, and prepare the food in my sight, so that I may see it and eat it from her hand.'" ⁶So Am´non lay down, and pretended to be ill; and when the king came to see him, Am´non said to the king, "Please let my sister Ta̅´mar come and make a couple of cakes in my sight, so that I may eat from her hand."

7 Then David sent home to Ta̅´mar, saying, "Go to your brother Am´non's house, and prepare food for him." ⁸So Ta̅´mar went to her brother Amnon's house, where he was lying down. She took dough, kneaded it, made cakes in his sight, and baked the cakes. ⁹Then she

ᵛ That is *Beloved of the LORD*   ʷ Gk See 1 Kings 11.5, 33: Heb *their kings* took the pan and set them[x] out before him, but he refused to eat. Am´non said, "Send out everyone from me." So everyone went out from him. [10]Then Am´non said to Tā´mar, "Bring the food into the chamber, so that I may eat from your hand." So Tā´mar took the cakes she had made, and brought them into the chamber to Am´non her brother. [11]But when she brought them near him to eat, he took hold of her, and said to her, "Come, lie with me, my sister." [12]She answered him, "No, my brother, do not force me; for such a thing is not done in Israel; do not do anything so vile! [13]As for me, where could I carry my shame? And as for you, you would be as one of the scoundrels in Israel. Now therefore, I beg you, speak to the king; for he will not withhold me from you." [14]But he would not listen to her; and being stronger than she, he forced her and lay with her.

15 Then Am´non was seized with a very great loathing for her; indeed, his loathing was even greater than the lust he had felt for her. Am´non said to her, "Get out!" [16]But she said to him, "No, my brother;[y] for this wrong in sending me away is greater than the other that you did to me." But he would not listen to her. [17]He called the young man who served him and said, "Put this woman out of my presence, and bolt the door after her." [18](Now she was wearing a long robe with sleeves; for this is how the virgin daughters of the king were clothed in earlier times.[z]) So his servant put her out, and bolted the door after her. [19]But Tā´mar put ashes on her head, and tore the long robe that she was wearing; she put her hand on her head, and went away, crying aloud as she went.

20 Her brother Ab´sa·lom said to her, "Has Am´non your brother been with you? Be quiet for now, my sister; he is your brother; do not take this to heart." So Tā´mar remained, a desolate woman, in her brother Ab´sa·lom's house. [21]When King David heard of all these things, he

became very angry, but he would not punish his son Am´non, because he loved him, for he was his firstborn.[a] [22]But Ab´sa·lom spoke to Am´non neither good nor bad; for Ab´sa·lom hated Am´non, because he had raped his sister Tā´mar.

Absalom Avenges the Violation of His Sister

23 After two full years Ab´sa·lom had sheepshearers at Bā´al-hā´zor, which is near Ē´phra·im, and Ab´sa·lom invited all the king's sons. [24]Ab´sa·lom came to the king, and said, "Your servant has sheepshearers; will the king and his servants please go with your servant?" [25]But the king said to Ab´sa·lom, "No, my son, let us not all go, or else we will be burdensome to you." He pressed him, but he would not go but gave him his blessing. [26]Then Ab´sa·lom said, "If not, please let my brother Am´non go with us." The king said to him, "Why should he go with you?" [27]But Ab´sa·lom pressed him until he let Am´non and all the king's sons go with him. Ab´sa·lom made a feast like a king's feast.[b] [28]Then Ab´sa·lom commanded his servants, "Watch when Am´non's heart is merry with wine, and when I say to you, 'Strike Am´non,' then kill him. Do not be afraid; have I not myself commanded you? Be courageous and valiant." [29]So the servants of Ab´sa·lom did to Am´non as Ab´sa·lom had commanded. Then all the king's sons rose, and each mounted his mule and fled.

30 While they were on the way, the report came to David that Ab´sa·lom had killed all the king's sons, and not one of them was left. [31]The king rose, tore his garments, and lay on the ground; and all his servants who were standing by tore their garments. [32]But Jon´a·dab, the son of David's brother Shim´ē·ah, said, "Let not my lord suppose that they have killed all the young men the king's sons;

---

[x] Heb *and poured*   [y] Cn: Compare Gk Vg: Meaning of Heb uncertain   [z] Cn: Heb *were clothed in robes*   [a] Q Ms Gk: MT lacks *but he would not punish . . . firstborn*   [b] Gk Compare Q Ms: MT lacks *Absalom made a feast like a king's feast*

Am'non alone is dead. This has been determined by Ab'sa·lom from the day Am'non*c* raped his sister Ta'mar. ³³Now therefore, do not let my lord the king take it to heart, as if all the king's sons were dead; for Am'non alone is dead."

34 But Ab'sa·lom fled. When the young man who kept watch looked up, he saw many people coming from the Hor·ō·na'im road*d* by the side of the mountain. ³⁵Jon'a·dab said to the king, "See, the king's sons have come; as your servant said, so it has come about." ³⁶As soon as he had finished speaking, the king's sons arrived, and raised their voices and wept; and the king and all his servants also wept very bitterly.

37 But Ab'sa·lom fled, and went to Tal'mai son of Am·mī'hud, king of Gē'-shur. David mourned for his son day after day. ³⁸Ab'sa·lom, having fled to Gē'-shur, stayed there three years. ³⁹And the heart of*e* the king went out, yearning for Ab'sa·lom; for he was now consoled over the death of Am'non.

Absalom Returns to Jerusalem

14 Now Jō'ab son of Ze·rū'i·ah perceived that the king's mind was on Ab'sa·lom. ²Jō'ab sent to Te·kō'a and brought from there a wise woman. He said to her, "Pretend to be a mourner; put on mourning garments, do not anoint yourself with oil, but behave like a woman who has been mourning many days for the dead. ³Go to the king and speak to him as follows." And Jō'ab put the words into her mouth.

4 When the woman of Te·kō'a came to the king, she fell on her face to the ground and did obeisance, and said, "Help, O king!" ⁵The king asked her, "What is your trouble?" She answered, "Alas, I am a widow; my husband is dead. ⁶Your servant had two sons, and they fought with one another in the field; there was no one to part them, and one struck the other and killed him. ⁷Now the whole family has risen against your servant. They say, 'Give

up the man who struck his brother, so that we may kill him for the life of his brother whom he murdered, even if we destroy the heir as well.' Thus they would quench my one remaining ember, and leave to my husband neither name nor remnant on the face of the earth."

8 Then the king said to the woman, "Go to your house, and I will give orders concerning you." ⁹The woman of Te·kō'a said to the king, "On me be the guilt, my lord the king, and on my father's house; let the king and his throne be guiltless." ¹⁰The king said, "If anyone says anything to you, bring him to me, and he shall never touch you again." ¹¹Then she said, "Please, may the king keep the LORD your God in mind, so that the avenger of blood may kill no more, and my son not be destroyed." He said, "As the LORD lives, not one hair of your son shall fall to the ground."

12 Then the woman said, "Please let your servant speak a word to my lord the king." He said, "Speak." ¹³The woman said, "Why then have you planned such a thing against the people of God? For in giving this decision the king convicts himself, inasmuch as the king does not bring his banished one home again. ¹⁴We must all die; we are like water spilled on the ground, which cannot be gathered up. But God will not take away a life; he will devise plans so as not to keep an outcast banished forever from his presence.*f* ¹⁵Now I have come to say this to my lord the king because the people have made me afraid; your servant thought, 'I will speak to the king; it may be that the king will perform the request of his servant. ¹⁶For the king will hear, and deliver his servant from the hand of the man who would cut both me and my son off from the heritage of God.' ¹⁷Your servant thought, 'The word of my lord the king will set me at rest'; for my lord the king

c Heb *he*   *d* Cn: Compare Gk: Heb *the road behind him*   *e* Q Ms Gk: MT *And David*
f Meaning of Heb uncertain

is like the angel of God, discerning good and evil. The LORD your God be with you!"

18 Then the king answered the woman, "Do not withhold from me anything I ask you." The woman said, "Let my lord the king speak." ¹⁹The king said, "Is the hand of Jŏ′ab with you in all this?" The woman answered and said, "As surely as you live, my lord the king, one cannot turn right or left from anything that my lord the king has said. For it was your servant Jŏ′ab who commanded me; it was he who put all these words into the mouth of your servant. ²⁰In order to change the course of affairs your servant Jŏ′ab did this. But my lord has wisdom like the wisdom of the angel of God to know all things that are on the earth."

21 Then the king said to Jŏ′ab, "Very well, I grant this; go, bring back the young man Ab′sa·lom." ²² Jŏ′ab prostrated himself with his face to the ground and did obeisance, and blessed the king; and Jŏ′ab said, "Today your servant knows that I have found favor in your sight, my lord the king, in that the king has granted the request of his servant." ²³So Jŏ′ab set off, went to Gĕ′shur, and brought Ab′sa·lom to Jerusalem. ²⁴The king said, "Let him go to his own house; he is not to come into my presence." So Ab′sa·lom went to his own house, and did not come into the king's presence.

David Forgives Absalom

25 Now in all Israel there was no one to be praised so much for his beauty as Ab′sa·lom; from the sole of his foot to the crown of his head there was no blemish in him. ²⁶When he cut the hair of his head (for at the end of every year he used to cut it; when it was heavy on him, he cut it), he weighed the hair of his head, two hundred shekels by the king's weight. ²⁷There were born to Ab′sa·lom three sons, and one daughter whose name was Tā′mar; she was a beautiful woman.

28 So Ab′sa·lom lived two full years in Jerusalem, without coming into the king's presence. ²⁹Then Ab′sa·lom sent for Jŏ′ab to send him to the king; but Jŏ′ab would not come to him. He sent a second time, but Jŏ′ab would not come. ³⁰Then he said to his servants, "Look, Jŏ′ab's field is next to mine, and he has barley there; go and set it on fire." So Ab′sa·lom's servants set the field on fire. ³¹Then Jŏ′ab rose and went to Ab′sa·lom at his house, and said to him, "Why have your servants set my field on fire?" ³²Ab′sa·lom answered Jŏ′ab, "Look, I sent word to you: Come here, that I may send you to the king with the question, 'Why have I come from Gĕ′shur? It would be better for me to be there still.' Now let me go into the king's presence; if there is guilt in me, let him kill me!" ³³Then Jŏ′ab went to the king and told him; and he summoned Ab′sa·lom. So he came to the king and prostrated himself with his face to the ground before the king; and the king kissed Ab′sa·lom.

Absalom Usurps the Throne

15 After this Ab′sa·lom got himself a chariot and horses, and fifty men to run ahead of him. ²Ab′sa·lom used to rise early and stand beside the road into the gate; and when anyone brought a suit before the king for judgment, Ab′sa·lom would call out and say, "From what city are you?" When the person said, "Your servant is of such and such a tribe in Israel," ³Ab′sa·lom would say, "See, your claims are good and right; but there is no one deputed by the king to hear you." ⁴Ab′sa·lom said moreover, "If only I were judge in the land! Then all who had a suit or cause might come to me, and I would give them justice." ⁵Whenever people came near to do obeisance to him, he would put out his hand and take hold of them, and kiss them. ⁶Thus Ab′sa·lom did to every Israelite who came to the king for judgment; so Ab′sa·lom stole the hearts of the people of Israel.

7 At the end of four[g] years Ab′sa·lom said to the king, "Please let me go to Hē′bron and pay the vow that I have made to the LORD. [8]For your servant made a vow while I lived at Gē′shur in Ar′am: If the LORD will indeed bring me back to Jerusalem, then I will worship the LORD in Hē′bron."[h] [9]The king said to him, "Go in peace." So he got up, and went to Hē′bron. [10]But Ab′sa·lom sent secret messengers throughout all the tribes of Israel, saying, "As soon as you hear the sound of the trumpet, then shout: Ab′sa·lom has become king at Hē′bron!" [11]Two hundred men from Jerusalem went with Ab′sa·lom; they were invited guests, and they went in their innocence, knowing nothing of the matter. [12]While Ab′sa·lom was offering the sacrifices, he sent for[i] A·hith′o·phel the Gī′lo·nīte, David's counselor, from his city Gī′lōh. The conspiracy grew in strength, and the people with Ab′sa·lom kept increasing.

David Flees from Jerusalem

13 A messenger came to David, saying, "The hearts of the Israelites have gone after Ab′sa·lom." [14]Then David said to all his officials who were with him at Jerusalem, "Get up! Let us flee, or there will be no escape for us from Ab′sa·lom. Hurry, or he will soon overtake us, and bring disaster down upon us, and attack the city with the edge of the sword." [15]The king's officials said to the king, "Your servants are ready to do whatever our lord the king decides." [16]So the king left, followed by all his household, except ten concubines whom he left behind to look after the house. [17]The king left, followed by all the people; and they stopped at the last house. [18]All his officials passed by him; and all the Cher′e·thītes, and all the Pel′eth·ītes, and all the six hundred Git′tītes who had followed him from Gath, passed on before the king.

19 Then the king said to It′taī the Git′tīte, "Why are you also coming with us? Go back, and stay with the king; for you are a foreigner, and also an exile from your home. [20]You came only yesterday, and shall I today make you wander about with us, while I go wherever I can? Go back, and take your kinsfolk with you; and may the LORD show[j] steadfast love and faithfulness to you." [21]But It′taī answered the king, "As the LORD lives, and as my lord the king lives, wherever my lord the king may be, whether for death or for life, there also your servant will be." [22]David said to It′taī, "Go then, march on." So It′taī the Git′tīte marched on, with all his men and all the little ones who were with him. [23]The whole country wept aloud as all the people passed by; the king crossed the Wadi Kid′ron, and all the people moved on toward the wilderness.

24 A·bī′a·thar came up, and Zā′dok also, with all the Lē′vītes, carrying the ark of the covenant of God. They set down the ark of God, until the people had all passed out of the city. [25]Then the king said to Zā′dok, "Carry the ark of God back into the city. If I find favor in the eyes of the LORD, he will bring me back and let me see both it and the place where it stays. [26]But if he says, 'I take no pleasure in you,' here I am, let him do to me what seems good to him." [27]The king also said to the priest Zā′dok, "Look,[k] go back to the city in peace, you and A·bī′a·thar,[l] with your two sons, A·him′a·az your son, and Jonathan son of A·bī′a·thar. [28]See, I will wait at the fords of the wilderness until word comes from you to inform me." [29]So Zā′dok and A·bī′a·thar carried the ark of God back to Jerusalem, and they remained there.

30 But David went up the ascent of the Mount of Olives, weeping as he went, with his head covered and walking barefoot; and all the people who

---

[g] Gk Syr: Heb forty   [h] Gk Mss: Heb lacks in Hebron   [i] Or he sent   [j] Gk Compare 2.6: Heb lacks may the LORD show   [k] Gk: Heb Are you a seer or Do you see?   [l] Cn: Heb lacks and Abi-

were with him covered their heads and went up, weeping as they went. [31]David was told that A·hith′o·phel was among the conspirators with Ab′sa·lom. And David said, "O LORD, I pray you, turn the counsel of A·hith′o·phel into foolishness."

Hushai Becomes David's Spy

32 When David came to the summit, where God was worshiped, Hū′shai the Ar′chīte came to meet him with his coat torn and earth on his head. [33]David said to him, "If you go on with me, you will be a burden to me. [34]But if you return to the city and say to Ab′sa·lom, 'I will be your servant, O king; as I have been your father's servant in time past, so now I will be your servant,' then you will defeat for me the counsel of A·hith′o·phel. [35]The priests Zā′dok and A·bī′a·thar will be with you there. So whatever you hear from the king's house, tell it to the priests Zā′dok and A·bī′a·thar. [36]Their two sons are with them there, Zā′dok's son A·him′a·az and A·bī′a·thar's son Jonathan; and by them you shall report to me everything you hear." [37]So Hū′shai, David's friend, came into the city, just as Ab′sa·lom was entering Jerusalem.

David's Adversaries

16 When David had passed a little beyond the summit, Zī′ba the servant of Me·phib′o·sheth[m] met him, with a couple of donkeys saddled, carrying two hundred loaves of bread, one hundred bunches of raisins, one hundred of summer fruits, and one skin of wine. [2]The king said to Zī′ba, "Why have you brought these?" Zī′ba answered, "The donkeys are for the king's household to ride, the bread and summer fruit for the young men to eat, and the wine is for those to drink who faint in the wilderness." [3]The king said, "And where is your master's son?" Zī′ba said to the king, "He remains in Jerusalem; for he said, 'Today the house of Israel will give me back my grandfather's kingdom.' " [4]Then the king said to Zī′ba, "All that belonged to Me·phib′o·sheth[m] is now

yours." Zī′ba said, "I do obeisance; let me find favor in your sight, my lord the king."

Shimei Curses David

5 When King David came to Ba·hū′rim, a man of the family of the house of Saul came out whose name was Shim′e·ī son of Gē′ra; he came out cursing. [6]He threw stones at David and at all the servants of King David; now all the people and all the warriors were on his right and on his left. [7]Shim′e·ī shouted while he cursed, "Out! Out! Murderer! Scoundrel! [8]The LORD has avenged on all of you the blood of the house of Saul, in whose place you have reigned; and the LORD has given the kingdom into the hand of your son Ab′sa·lom. See, disaster has overtaken you; for you are a man of blood."

9 Then A·bi′shai son of Ze·rū′i·ah said to the king, "Why should this dead dog curse my lord the king? Let me go over and take off his head." [10]But the king said, "What have I to do with you, you sons of Ze·rū′i·ah? If he is cursing because the LORD has said to him, 'Curse David,' who then shall say, 'Why have you done so?' " [11]David said to A·bi′shai and to all his servants, "My own son seeks my life; how much more now may this Ben′ja·min·īte! Let him alone, and let him curse; for the LORD has bidden him. [12]It may be that the LORD will look on my distress,[n] and the LORD will repay me with good for this cursing of me today." [13]So David and his men went on the road, while Shim′e·ī went along on the hillside opposite him and cursed as he went, throwing stones and flinging dust at him. [14]The king and all the people who were with him arrived weary at the Jordan;[o] and there he refreshed himself.

The Counsel of Ahithophel

15 Now Ab′sa·lom and all the Israelites[p] came to Jerusalem; A·hith′o·phel was with him. [16]When Hū′shai the Ar′chīte,

---

[m] Or Merib-baal: See 4.4 note　[n] Gk Vg: Heb iniquity　[o] Gk: Heb lacks at the Jordan　[p] Gk: Heb all the people, the men of Israela

David's friend, came to Ab·sa·lom, Hū´shaī said to Ab·sa·lom, "Long live the king! Long live the king!" ¹⁷Ab·sa·lom said to Hū´shaī, "Is this your loyalty to your friend? Why did you not go with your friend?" ¹⁸Hū´shaī said to Ab·sa·lom, "No; but the one whom the LORD and this people and all the Israelites have chosen, his I will be, and with him I will remain. ¹⁹Moreover, whom should I serve? Should it not be his son? Just as I have served your father, so I will serve you."

20 Then Ab·sa·lom said to A·hith´-o·phel, "Give us your counsel; what shall we do?" ²¹A·hith´o·phel said to Ab·sa·lom, "Go in to your father's concubines, the ones he has left to look after the house; and all Israel will hear that you have made yourself odious to your father, and the hands of all who are with you will be strengthened." ²²So they pitched a tent for Ab·sa·lom upon the roof; and Ab·sa·lom went in to his father's concubines in the sight of all Israel. ²³Now in those days the counsel that A·hith´o·phel gave was as if one consulted the oracle*q* of God; so all the counsel of A·hith´o·phel was esteemed, both by David and by Ab·sa·lom.

17 Moreover A·hith´o·phel said to Ab·sa·lom, "Let me choose twelve thousand men, and I will set out and pursue David tonight. ²I will come upon him while he is weary and discouraged, and throw him into a panic; and all the people who are with him will flee. I will strike down only the king, ³and I will bring all the people back to you as a bride comes home to her husband. You seek the life of only one man,*r* and all the people will be at peace." ⁴The advice pleased Ab·sa·lom and all the elders of Israel.

The Counsel of Hushai

5 Then Ab·sa·lom said, "Call Hū´shaī the Ar´chīte also, and let us hear too what he has to say." ⁶When Hū´shaī came to Ab·sa·lom, Ab·sa·lom said to him, "This is what A·hith´o·phel has said; shall we do as he advises? If not, you tell us." ⁷Then Hū´-shaī said to Ab·sa·lom, "This time the counsel that A·hith´o·phel has given is not good." ⁸Hū´shaī continued, "You know that your father and his men are warriors, and that they are enraged, like a bear robbed of her cubs in the field. Besides, your father is expert in war; he will not spend the night with the troops. ⁹Even now he has hidden himself in one of the pits, or in some other place. And when some of our troops*s* fall at the first attack, whoever hears it will say, 'There has been a slaughter among the troops who follow Ab·sa·lom.' ¹⁰Then even the valiant warrior, whose heart is like the heart of a lion, will utterly melt with fear; for all Israel knows that your father is a warrior, and that those who are with him are valiant warriors. ¹¹But my counsel is that all Israel be gathered to you, from Dan to Bē´er-shē´-ba, like the sand by the sea for multitude, and that you go to battle in person. ¹²So we shall come upon him in whatever place he may be found, and we shall light on him as the dew falls on the ground; and he will not survive, nor will any of those with him. ¹³If he withdraws into a city, then all Israel will bring ropes to that city, and we shall drag it into the valley, until not even a pebble is to be found there." ¹⁴Ab·sa·lom and all the men of Israel said, "The counsel of Hū´shaī the Ar´chīte is better than the counsel of A·hith´o·phel." For the LORD had ordained to defeat the good counsel of A·hith´-o·phel, so that the LORD might bring ruin on Ab·sa·lom.

Hushai Warns David to Escape

15 Then Hū´shaī said to the priests Zā´dok and A·bī´a·thar, "Thus and so did A·hith´o·phel counsel Ab·sa·lom and the elders of Israel; and thus and so I have counseled. ¹⁶Therefore send quickly and tell David, 'Do not lodge tonight at the fords of the wilderness, but by all means cross over; otherwise the king and all the people who are with him will be swal-

q Heb *word*   *r* Gk: Heb *like the return of the whole (is) the man whom you seek*   *s* Gk Mss: Heb *some of them* lowed up.' " [17]Jonathan and A·him´a·az were waiting at En-rō´gel; a servant-girl used to go and tell them, and they would go and tell King David; for they could not risk being seen entering the city. [18]But a boy saw them, and told Ab´sa·lom; so both of them went away quickly, and came to the house of a man at Ba·hū´rim, who had a well in his courtyard; and they went down into it. [19]The man's wife took a covering, stretched it over the well's mouth, and spread out grain on it; and nothing was known of it. [20]When Ab´sa·lom's servants came to the woman at the house, they said, "Where are A·him´a·az and Jonathan?" The woman said to them, "They have crossed over the brook[t] of water." And when they had searched and could not find them, they returned to Jerusalem.

21 After they had gone, the men came up out of the well, and went and told King David. They said to David, "Go and cross the water quickly; for thus and so has A·hith´o·phel counseled against you." [22]So David and all the people who were with him set out and crossed the Jordan; by daybreak not one was left who had not crossed the Jordan.

23 When A·hith´o·phel saw that his counsel was not followed, he saddled his donkey and went off home to his own city. He set his house in order, and hanged himself; he died and was buried in the tomb of his father.

24 Then David came to Mā·ha·nā´im, while Ab´sa·lom crossed the Jordan with all the men of Israel. [25]Now Ab´sa·lom had set A·mā´sa over the army in the place of Jō´ab. A·mā´sa was the son of a man named Ith´ra the Ish´ma·el·īte,[u] who had married Ab´i·gāl daughter of Nā´hash, sister of Ze·rū´i·ah, Jō´ab's mother. [26]The Israelites and Ab´sa·lom encamped in the land of Gil´e·ad.

27 When David came to Mā·ha·nā´im, Shō´bī son of Nā´hash from Rab´bah of the Am´mon·ītes, and Mā´chir son of Am´mi·el from Lō-dē´bar, and Bar·zil´laī the Gil´-

e·ad·īte from Rō´ge·lim, [28]brought beds, basins, and earthen vessels, wheat, barley, meal, parched grain, beans and lentils,[v] [29]honey and curds, sheep, and cheese from the herd, for David and the people with him to eat; for they said, "The troops are hungry and weary and thirsty in the wilderness."

> Curds were a thick food made by churning fresh milk in a goatskin. In Old Testament times curds were part of the everyday food.

The Defeat and Death of Absalom

18 Then David mustered the men who were with him, and set over them commanders of thousands and commanders of hundreds. [2]And David divided the army into three groups:[w] one third under the command of Jō´ab, one third under the command of A·bi´shaī son of Ze·rū´i·ah, Jō´ab's brother, and one third under the command of It´taī the Git´tīte. The king said to the men, "I myself will also go out with you." [3]But the men said, "You shall not go out. For if we flee, they will not care about us. If half of us die, they will not care about us. But you are worth ten thousand of us;[x] therefore it is better that you send us help from the city." [4]The king said to them, "Whatever seems best to you I will do." So the king stood at the side of the gate, while all the army marched out by hundreds and by thousands. [5]The king ordered Jō´ab and A·bi´shaī and It´taī, saying, "Deal gently for my sake with the young man Ab´sa·lom." And all the people heard when the king gave orders to all the commanders concerning Ab´sa·lom.

6 So the army went out into the field against Israel; and the battle was fought in the forest of E̅´phra·im. [7]The men of

---

[t] Meaning of Heb uncertain   [u] 1 Chr 2.17: Heb *Israelite*   [v] Heb *and lentils and parched grain*   [w] Gk: Heb *sent forth the army*   [x] Gk Vg Symmachus: Heb *for now there are ten thousand such as*

Israel were defeated there by the servants of David, and the slaughter there was great on that day, twenty thousand men. ⁸The battle spread over the face of all the country; and the forest claimed more victims that day than the sword.

9 Ab´sa·lom happened to meet the servants of David. Ab´sa·lom was riding on his mule, and the mule went under the thick branches of a great oak. His head caught fast in the oak, and he was left hanging^y between heaven and earth, while the mule that was under him went on. ¹⁰A man saw it, and told Jō´ab, "I saw Ab´sa·lom hanging in an oak." ¹¹Jō´ab said to the man who told him, "What, you saw him! Why then did you not strike him there to the ground? I would have been glad to give you ten pieces of silver and a belt." ¹²But the man said to Jō´ab, "Even if I felt in my hand the weight of a thousand pieces of silver, I would not raise my hand against the king's son; for in our hearing the king commanded you and A·bi´shaī and It´taī, saying: For my sake protect the young man Ab´sa·lom! ¹³On the other hand, if I had dealt treacherously against his life^z (and there is nothing hidden from the king), then you yourself would have stood aloof." ¹⁴Jō´ab said, "I will not waste time like this with you." He took three spears in his hand, and thrust them into the heart of Ab´sa·lom, while he was still alive in the oak. ¹⁵And ten young men, Jō´ab's armorbearers, surrounded Ab´sa·lom and struck him, and killed him.

16 Then Jō´ab sounded the trumpet, and the troops came back from pursuing Israel, for Jō´ab restrained the troops. ¹⁷They took Ab´sa·lom, threw him into a great pit in the forest, and raised over him a very great heap of stones. Meanwhile all the Israelites fled to their homes. ¹⁸Now Ab´sa·lom in his lifetime had taken and set up for himself a pillar that is in the King's Valley, for he said, "I have no son to keep my name in remembrance"; he called the pillar by his own name. It is called Ab´sa·lom's Monument to this day.

David Hears of Absalom's Death

19 Then A·him´a·az son of Zā´dok said, "Let me run, and carry tidings to the king that the LORD has delivered him from the power of his enemies." ²⁰Jō´ab said to him, "You are not to carry tidings today; you may carry tidings another day, but today you shall not do so, because the king's son is dead." ²¹Then Jō´ab said to a Cū´shīte, "Go, tell the king what you have seen." The Cū´shīte bowed before Jō´ab, and ran. ²²Then A·him´a·az son of Zā´dok said again to Jō´ab, "Come what may, let me also run after the Cū´shīte." And Jō´ab said, "Why will you run, my son, seeing that you have no reward^a for the tidings?" ²³"Come what may," he said, "I will run." So he said to him, "Run." Then A·him´-a·az ran by the way of the Plain, and outran the Cū´shīte.

24 Now David was sitting between the two gates. The sentinel went up to the roof of the gate by the wall, and when he looked up, he saw a man running alone. ²⁵The sentinel shouted and

In Bible times, many cities had walls around them. These walls were very thick and strong. Since the armies of other nations would first try to enter a city through the city gates, the people took special care to make the gates strong and secure. Sometimes we build "walls" around ourselves to keep others from getting to know us. Can you think of ways that you build walls between yourself and others? Pray that God will show you how to open the gates so that you can live happily with your family and friends. If there is one person you have "walled out" of your life, ask God to show you the way to be a friend to that person.

^y Gk Syr Tg: Heb *was put*   ^z Another reading is *at the risk of my life*   ^a Meaning of Heb uncertain

told the king. The king said, "If he is alone, there are tidings in his mouth." He kept coming, and drew near. ²⁶Then the sentinel saw another man running; and the sentinel called to the gatekeeper and said, "See, another man running alone!" The king said, "He also is bringing tidings." ²⁷The sentinel said, "I think the running of the first one is like the running of A·him´a·az son of Zā´dok." The king said, "He is a good man, and comes with good tidings."

28 Then A·him´a·az cried out to the king, "All is well!" He prostrated himself before the king with his face to the ground, and said, "Blessed be the LORD your God, who has delivered up the men who raised their hand against my lord the king." ²⁹The king said, "Is it well with the young man Ab´sa·lom?" A·him´a·az answered, "When Jō´ab sent your servant,[b] I saw a great tumult, but I do not know what it was." ³⁰The king said, "Turn aside, and stand here." So he turned aside, and stood still.

31 Then the Cū´shīte came; and the Cū´shīte said, "Good tidings for my lord the king! For the LORD has vindicated you this day, delivering you from the power of all who rose up against you." ³²The king said to the Cū´shīte, "Is it well with the young man Ab´sa·lom?" The Cū´shīte answered, "May the enemies of my lord the king, and all who rise up to do you harm, be like that young man."

David Mourns for Absalom

33[c] The king was deeply moved, and went up to the chamber over the gate, and wept; and as he went, he said, "O my son Ab´sa·lom, my son, my son Ab´sa·lom! Would I had died instead of you, O Ab´sa·lom, my son, my son!"

19 It was told Jō´ab, "The king is weeping and mourning for Ab´sa·lom." ²So the victory that day was turned into mourning for all the troops; for the troops heard that day, "The king is grieving for his son." ³The troops stole

into the city that day as soldiers steal in who are ashamed when they flee in battle. ⁴The king covered his face, and the king cried with a loud voice, "O my son Ab´sa·lom, O Ab´sa·lom, my son, my son!" ⁵Then Jō´ab came into the house to the king, and said, "Today you have covered with shame the faces of all your officers who have saved your life today, and the lives of your sons and your daughters, and the lives of your wives and your concubines, ⁶for love of those who hate you and for hatred of those who love you. You have made it clear today that commanders and officers are nothing to you; for I perceive that if Ab´sa·lom were alive and all of us were dead today, then you would be pleased. ⁷So go out at once and speak kindly to your servants; for I swear by the LORD, if you do not go, not a man will stay with you this night; and this will be worse for you than any disaster that has come upon you from your youth until now."

Absalom was King David's third son. He led a revolt against his father and tried to take over the throne. In spite of this, David loved Absalom and told his soldiers not to hurt him. But when Absalom tried to run away following a battle, his hair got caught in some tree branches and one of David's commanders killed him. David cried bitterly, "O my son Absalom, my son, my son Absalom! Would I had died instead of you, O Absalom, my son, my son!" Although David had gone alone to grieve, all the people heard him and mourned with him. His words are some of the saddest in the Bible.

[b] Heb *the king's servant, your servant*   [c] Ch 19.1 in Heb

[8]Then the king got up and took his seat in the gate. The troops were all told, "See, the king is sitting in the gate"; and all the troops came before the king.

David Recalled to Jerusalem

Meanwhile, all the Israelites had fled to their homes. [9]All the people were disputing throughout all the tribes of Israel, saying, "The king delivered us from the hand of our enemies, and saved us from the hand of the Phi·lis′tines; and now he has fled out of the land because of Ab′sa·lom. [10]But Ab′sa·lom, whom we anointed over us, is dead in battle. Now therefore why do you say nothing about bringing the king back?"

11 King David sent this message to the priests Za′dok and A·bi′a·thar, "Say to the elders of Judah, 'Why should you be the last to bring the king back to his house? The talk of all Israel has come to the king.[d] [12]You are my kin, you are my bone and my flesh; why then should you be the last to bring back the king?' [13]And say to A·ma′sa, 'Are you not my bone and my flesh? So may God do to me, and more, if you are not the commander of my army from now on, in place of Jo′ab.' " [14]A·ma′sa[e] swayed the hearts of all the people of Judah as one, and they sent word to the king, "Return, both you and all your servants." [15]So the king came back to the Jordan; and Judah came to Gil′gal to meet the king and to bring him over the Jordan.

16 Shim′e·i son of Ge′ra, the Ben′-ja·min·ite, from Ba·hu′rim, hurried to come down with the people of Judah to meet King David; [17]with him were a thousand people from Benjamin. And Zi′ba, the servant of the house of Saul, with his fifteen sons and his twenty servants, rushed down to the Jordan ahead of the king, [18]while the crossing was taking place,[f] to bring over the king's household, and to do his pleasure.

David's Mercy to Shimei

Shim′e·i son of Ge′ra fell down before the king, as he was about to cross the Jordan, [19]and said to the king, "May my lord not hold me guilty or remember how your servant did wrong on the day my lord the king left Jerusalem; may the king not bear it in mind. [20]For your servant knows that I have sinned; therefore, see, I have come this day, the first of all the house of Joseph to come down to meet my lord the king." [21]A·bi′shai son of Ze·ru′i·ah answered, "Shall not Shim′-e·i be put to death for this, because he cursed the LORD's anointed?" [22]But David said, "What have I to do with you, you sons of Ze·ru′i·ah, that you should today become an adversary to me? Shall anyone be put to death in Israel this day? For do I not know that I am this day king over Israel?" [23]The king said to Shim′e·i, "You shall not die." And the king gave him his oath.

David and Mephibosheth Meet

24 Me·phib′o·sheth[g] grandson of Saul came down to meet the king; he had not taken care of his feet, or trimmed his beard, or washed his clothes, from the day the king left until the day he came back in safety. [25]When he came from Jerusalem to meet the king, the king said to him, "Why did you not go with me, Me·phib′-o·sheth?"[g] [26]He answered, "My lord, O king, my servant deceived me; for your servant said to him, 'Saddle a donkey for me,[h] so that I may ride on it and go with the king.' For your servant is lame. [27]He has slandered your servant to my lord the king. But my lord the king is like the angel of God; do therefore what seems good to you. [28]For all my father's house were doomed to death before my lord the king; but you set your servant among those who eat at your table. What further right have I, then, to appeal to the king?" [29]The king said to him, "Why speak any more of your affairs? I have decided: you and Zi′ba shall divide the land." [30]Me·phib′o·sheth[g] said to

---

[d] Gk: Heb to the king, to his house   [e] Heb He   [f] Cn: Heb the ford crossed   [g] Or Merib-baal : See 4.4 note   [h] Gk Syr Vg: Heb said, 'I will saddle a donkey for myself

the king, "Let him take it all, since my lord the king has arrived home safely."

David's Kindness to Barzillai

31 Now Bar·zil′lai the Gil′e·ad·īte had come down from Rŏ′ge·lim; he went on with the king to the Jordan, to escort him over the Jordan. [32]Bar·zil′lai was a very aged man, eighty years old. He had provided the king with food while he stayed at Mā·ha·nā′im, for he was a very wealthy man. [33]The king said to Bar·zil′lai, "Come over with me, and I will provide for you in Jerusalem at my side." [34]But Bar·zil′lai said to the king, "How many years have I still to live, that I should go up with the king to Jerusalem? [35]Today I am eighty years old; can I discern what is pleasant and what is not? Can your servant taste what he eats or what he drinks? Can I still listen to the voice of singing men and singing women? Why then should your servant be an added burden to my lord the king? [36]Your servant will go a little way over the Jordan with the king. Why should the king recompense me with such a reward? [37]Please let your servant return, so that I may die in my own town, near the graves of my father and my mother. But here is your servant Chim′ham; let him go over with my lord the king; and do for him whatever seems good to you." [38]The king answered, "Chim′ham shall go over with me, and I will do for him whatever seems good to you and all that you desire of me I will do for you." [39]Then all the people crossed over the Jordan, and the king crossed over; the king kissed Bar·zil′lai and blessed him, and he returned to his own home. [40]The king went on to Gil′gal, and Chim′ham went on with him; all the people of Judah, and also half the people of Israel, brought the king on his way.

41 Then all the people of Israel came to the king, and said to him, "Why have our kindred the people of Judah stolen you away, and brought the king and his household over the Jordan, and all David's men with him?" [42]All the people of Judah answered the people of Israel, "Because the king is near of kin to us. Why then are you angry over this matter? Have we eaten at all at the king's expense? Or has he given us any gift?" [43]But the people of Israel answered the people of Judah, "We have ten shares in the king, and in David also we have more than you. Why then did you despise us? Were we not the first to speak of bringing back our king?" But the words of the people of Judah were fiercer than the words of the people of Israel.

The Rebellion of Sheba

20 Now a scoundrel named Shē′ba son of Bich′rī, a Ben′ja·min·īte, happened to be there. He sounded the trumpet and cried out,

"We have no portion in David,
   no share in the son of Jesse!
Everyone to your tents, O Israel!"

[2]So all the people of Israel withdrew from David and followed Shē′ba son of Bich′rī; but the people of Judah followed their king steadfastly from the Jordan to Jerusalem.

3 David came to his house at Jerusalem; and the king took the ten concubines whom he had left to look after the house, and put them in a house under guard, and provided for them, but did not go in to them. So they were shut up until the day of their death, living as if in widowhood.

4 Then the king said to A·mā′sa, "Call the men of Judah together to me within three days, and be here yourself." [5]So A·mā′sa went to summon Judah; but he delayed beyond the set time that had been appointed him. [6]David said to A·bi′shai, "Now Shē′ba son of Bich′rī will do us more harm than Ab′sa·lom; take your lord's servants and pursue him, or he will find fortified cities for himself, and escape from us." [7]Jō′ab's men went out after him, along with the Cher′e·thītes, the Pel′eth·ītes, and all the warriors; they went out from Jerusalem to pursue Shē′ba son of Bich′rī. [8]When

they were at the large stone that is in Gib´-ē·on, A·ma´sa came to meet them. Now Jō´ab was wearing a soldier's garment and over it was a belt with a sword in its sheath fastened at his waist; as he went forward it fell out. [9]Jō´ab said to A·ma´sa, "Is it well with you, my brother?" And Jō´ab took A·ma´sa by the beard with his right hand to kiss him. [10]But A·ma´sa did not notice the sword in Jō´ab's hand; Jō´ab struck him in the belly so that his entrails poured out on the ground, and he died. He did not strike a second blow.

A sheath is a case or covering for a sword.

Then Jō´ab and his brother A·bi´shaī pursued Shē´ba son of Bich´rī. [11]And one of Jō´ab's men took his stand by A·ma´sa, and said, "Whoever favors Jō´ab, and whoever is for David, let him follow Jō´ab." [12]A·ma´sa lay wallowing in his blood on the highway, and the man saw that all the people were stopping. Since he saw that all who came by him were stopping, he carried A·ma´sa from the highway into a field, and threw a garment over him. [13]Once he was removed from the highway, all the people went on after Jō´ab to pursue Shē´ba son of Bich´rī.

14 Shē´ba[i] passed through all the tribes of Israel to Abel of Beth-ma´a·cah;[j] and all the Bich´rītes[k] assembled, and followed him inside. [15] Jō´ab's forces[l] came and besieged him in Abel of Beth-ma´a·cah; they threw up a siege ramp against the city, and it stood against the rampart. Jō´ab's forces were battering the wall to break it down. [16]Then a wise woman called from the city, "Listen! Listen! Tell Jō´ab, 'Come here, I want to speak to you.' " [17]He came near her; and the woman said, "Are you Jō´ab?" He answered, "I am." Then she said to him, "Listen to the words of your servant." He answered, "I am listening." [18]Then she said, "They used to say in the old days, 'Let them inquire at Abel'; and so they would

Joab came to Amasa as if he were a friend. As part of a normal greeting in those times, Joab reached out to touch Amasa's beard as if to kiss him. This was usually a sign of friendship. But Joab was no friend! He suddenly grasped Amasa's beard and stabbed him to death.

settle a matter. [19]I am one of those who are peaceable and faithful in Israel; you seek to destroy a city that is a mother in Israel; why will you swallow up the heritage of the LORD?" [20]Jō´ab answered, "Far be it from me, far be it, that I should swallow up or destroy! [21]That is not the case! But a man of the hill country of Ē´phra·im, called Shē´ba son of Bich´rī, has lifted up his hand against King David; give him up alone, and I will withdraw from the city." The woman said to Jō´ab, "His head shall be thrown over the wall to you." [22]Then the woman went to all the people with her wise plan. And they cut off the head of Shē´ba son of Bich´rī, and threw it out to Jō´ab. So he blew the trumpet, and they dispersed from the city, and all went to their homes, while Jō´ab returned to Jerusalem to the king.

When an army wanted to take over a city, it used several different tools. A battering ram was a large pole on wheels that people pushed very hard against the gates and walls of a city to break them down. Armies would also build a ramp outside the walls. From this ramp, armies could throw arrows and stones over the wall and could eventually climb the wall.

[i] Heb *He*   [j] Compare 20.15: Heb *and Beth-maacah*
[k] Compare Gk Vg: Heb *Berites*   [l] Heb *They*

23 Now Jō´ab was in command of all the army of Israel;[m] Be·nā´i·ah son of Je·hoi´a·da was in command of the Cher´e·thītes and the Pel´eth·ītes; [24]A·dor´am was in charge of the forced labor; Je·hosh´a·phat son of A·hī´lud was the recorder; [25]Shē´va was secretary; Zā´dok and A·bī´a·thar were priests; [26]and Ira the Jā´i·rīte was also David's priest.

David Avenges the Gibeonites

21 Now there was a famine in the days of David for three years, year after year; and David inquired of the LORD. The LORD said, "There is bloodguilt on Saul and on his house, because he put the Gib´ē·on·ītes to death." [2]So the king called the Gib´ē·on·ītes and spoke to them. (Now the Gib´ē·on·ītes were not of the people of Israel, but of the remnant of the Am´o·rītes; although the people of Israel had sworn to spare them, Saul had tried to wipe them out in his zeal for the people of Israel and Judah.) [3]David said to the Gib´ē·on·ītes, "What shall I do for you? How shall I make expiation, that you may bless the heritage of the LORD?" [4]The Gib´ē·on·ītes said to him, "It is not a matter of silver or gold between us and Saul or his house; neither is it for us to put anyone to death in Israel." He said, "What do you say that I should do for you?" [5]They said to the king, "The man who consumed us and planned to destroy us, so that we should have no place in all the territory of Israel— [6]let seven of his sons be handed over to us, and we will impale them before the LORD at Gib´ē·on on the mountain of the LORD."[n] The king said, "I will hand them over."

7 But the king spared Me·phib´o·sheth,[o] the son of Saul's son Jonathan, because of the oath of the LORD that was between them, between David and Jonathan son of Saul. [8]The king took the two sons of Riz´pah daughter of Ā´i·ah, whom she bore to Saul, Ar·mō´nī and Me·phib´o·sheth;[o] and the five sons of Mē´rab[p] daughter of Saul, whom she bore to Ā´dri·el son of Bar·zil´lai the Me·hō´la·thīte; [9]he gave them into the hands of

the Gib´ē·on·ītes, and they impaled them on the mountain before the LORD. The seven of them perished together. They were put to death in the first days of harvest, at the beginning of barley harvest.

10 Then Riz´pah the daughter of Ā´i·ah took sackcloth, and spread it on a rock for herself, from the beginning of harvest until rain fell on them from the heavens; she did not allow the birds of the air to come on the bodies[q] by day, or the wild animals by night. [11]When David was told what Riz´pah daughter of Ā´i·ah, the concubine of Saul, had done, [12]David went and took the bones of Saul and the bones of his son Jonathan from the people of Jā´besh-gil´ē·ad, who had stolen them from the public square of Beth-shan, where the Phi·lis´tines had hung them up, on the day the Phi·lis´tines killed Saul on Gil·bō´a. [13]He brought up from there the bones of Saul and the bones of his son Jonathan; and they gathered the bones of those who had been impaled. [14]They buried the bones of Saul and of his son Jonathan in the land of Benjamin in Zē´la, in the tomb of his father Kish; they did all that the king commanded. After that, God heeded supplications for the land.

Exploits of David's Men

15 The Phi·lis´tines went to war again with Israel, and David went down together with his servants. They fought against the Phi·lis´tines, and David grew weary. [16]Ish´bi-bē´nob, one of the descendants of the giants, whose spear weighed three hundred shekels of bronze, and who was fitted out with new weapons,[r] said he would kill David. [17]But A·bi´shai son of Ze·rū´i·ah came to his aid, and attacked the Phi·lis´tine and killed him. Then David's men swore to him, "You shall not go out with us to

---

[m] Cn: Heb *Joab to all the army, Israel*   [n] Cn: Compare Gk and 21.9: Heb *at Gibeah of Saul, the chosen of the LORD*   [o] Or *Merib-baal:* See 4.4 note   [p] Two Heb Mss Syr Compare Gk: MT *Michal*   [q] Heb *them*   [r] Heb *was belted anew*

battle any longer, so that you do not quench the lamp of Israel."

18 After this a battle took place with the Phi·lis′tines, at Gob; then Sib′be·caī the Hū′sha·thīte killed Saph, who was one of the descendants of the giants. ¹⁹Then there was another battle with the Phi·lis′tines at Gob; and El·hā′nan son of Jā′a·rē-or′e·gim, the Beth′le·hem·īte, killed Goliath the Git′tīte, the shaft of whose spear was like a weaver's beam. ²⁰There was again war at Gath, where there was a man of great size, who had six fingers on each hand, and six toes on each foot, twenty-four in number; he too was descended from the giants. ²¹When he taunted Israel, Jonathan son of David's brother Shim′ē·ī, killed him. ²²These four were descended from the giants in Gath; they fell by the hands of David and his servants.

David's Song of Thanksgiving

22 David spoke to the LORD the words of this song on the day when the LORD delivered him from the hand of all his enemies, and from the hand of Saul. ²He said:

The LORD is my rock, my fortress, and my deliverer,
3 my God, my rock, in whom I take refuge,
my shield and the horn of my salvation,
my stronghold and my refuge,
my savior; you save me from violence.
⁴ I call upon the LORD, who is worthy to be praised,
and I am saved from my enemies.

⁵ For the waves of death encompassed me,
the torrents of perdition assailed me;
⁶ the cords of Shē′ōl entangled me,
the snares of death confronted me.

⁷ In my distress I called upon the LORD;
to my God I called.
From his temple he heard my voice,
and my cry came to his ears.

⁸ Then the earth reeled and rocked;
the foundations of the heavens trembled
and quaked, because he was angry.
⁹ Smoke went up from his nostrils,
and devouring fire from his mouth;
glowing coals flamed forth from him.
¹⁰ He bowed the heavens, and came down;
thick darkness was under his feet.
¹¹ He rode on a cherub, and flew;
he was seen upon the wings of the wind.
¹² He made darkness around him a canopy,
thick clouds, a gathering of water.
¹³ Out of the brightness before him
coals of fire flamed forth.
¹⁴ The LORD thundered from heaven;
the Most High uttered his voice.
¹⁵ He sent out arrows, and scattered them
—lightning, and routed them.
¹⁶ Then the channels of the sea were seen,
the foundations of the world were laid bare
at the rebuke of the LORD,
at the blast of the breath of his nostrils.

¹⁷ He reached from on high, he took me,
he drew me out of mighty waters.
¹⁸ He delivered me from my strong enemy,
from those who hated me;
for they were too mighty for me.
¹⁹ They came upon me in the day of my calamity,
but the LORD was my stay.
²⁰ He brought me out into a broad place;
he delivered me, because he delighted in me.
²¹ The LORD rewarded me according to my righteousness;
according to the cleanness of my hands he recompensed me.

²² For I have kept the ways of the LORD,
  and have not wickedly departed
    from my God.
²³ For all his ordinances were before me,
  and from his statutes I did not turn
    aside.
²⁴ I was blameless before him,
  and I kept myself from guilt.
²⁵ Therefore the LORD has recompensed
  me according to my
    righteousness,
  according to my cleanness in his
    sight.

²⁶ With the loyal you show yourself loyal;
  with the blameless you show
    yourself blameless;
²⁷ with the pure you show yourself pure,
  and with the crooked you show
    yourself perverse.
²⁸ You deliver a humble people,
  but your eyes are upon the haughty
    to bring them down.
²⁹ Indeed, you are my lamp, O LORD,
  the LORD lightens my darkness.
³⁰ By you I can crush a troop,
  and by my God I can leap over a
    wall.

³¹ This God—his way is perfect;
  the promise of the LORD proves true;
  he is a shield for all who take refuge
    in him.

³² For who is God, but the LORD?
  And who is a rock, except our God?
³³ The God who has girded me with
    strength[s]
  has opened wide my path.[t]
³⁴ He made my[u] feet like the feet of deer,
  and set me secure on the heights.
³⁵ He trains my hands for war,
  so that my arms can bend a bow of
    bronze.
³⁶ You have given me the shield of your
    salvation,
  and your help[v] has made me great.
³⁷ You have made me stride freely,
  and my feet do not slip;
³⁸ I pursued my enemies and destroyed
    them,

> "The LORD lives! Blessed
> be my rock, and exalted
> be my God, the rock of
> my salvation."
> **2 Samuel 22:47**

and did not turn back until they
    were consumed.
³⁹ I consumed them; I struck them
    down, so that they did not rise;
  they fell under my feet.
⁴⁰ For you girded me with strength for
    the battle;
  you made my assailants sink under
    me.
⁴¹ You made my enemies turn their backs
    to me,
  those who hated me, and I
    destroyed them.
⁴² They looked, but there was no one to
    save them;
  they cried to the LORD, but he did
    not answer them.
⁴³ I beat them fine like the dust of the
    earth,
  I crushed them and stamped them
    down like the mire of the streets.

⁴⁴ You delivered me from strife with the
    peoples;[w]
  you kept me as the head of the
    nations;
  people whom I had not known
    served me.
⁴⁵ Foreigners came cringing to me;
  as soon as they heard of me, they
    obeyed me.
⁴⁶ Foreigners lost heart,
  and came trembling out of their
    strongholds.

⁴⁷ The LORD lives! Blessed be my rock,
  and exalted be my God, the rock of
    my salvation,
⁴⁸ the God who gave me vengeance
  and brought down peoples under me,

---

[s] Q Ms Gk Syr Vg Compare Ps 18.32: MT *God is
my strong refuge*   [t] Meaning of Heb uncertain
[u] Another reading is *his*   [v] Q Ms: MT *your
answering*   [w] Gk: Heb *from strife with my people*

> David and others often used the symbol of a rock, cliff, or cave to give praise for God's care. Stones formed shelters for travelers and warriors. David saw God as a shelter from the storms of life. Say a prayer of thanks to God for being your shelter!

49 who brought me out from my enemies;
　　you exalted me above my
　　　adversaries,
　　you delivered me from the violent.

50 For this I will extol you, O LORD,
　　among the nations,
　　and sing praises to your name.
51 He is a tower of salvation for his king,
　　and shows steadfast love to his
　　　anointed,
　　to David and his descendants forever.

The Last Words of David

23 Now these are the last words of David:
The oracle of David, son of Jesse,
　　the oracle of the man whom God
　　　exalted,ˣ
　the anointed of the God of Jacob,
　　the favorite of the Strong One of
　　　Israel:
2 The spirit of the LORD speaks through
　　me,
　　his word is upon my tongue.
3 The God of Israel has spoken,
　　the Rock of Israel has said to me:
　One who rules over people justly,
　　ruling in the fear of God,
4 is like the light of morning,
　　like the sun rising on a cloudless
　　　morning,

"One who rules over the people justly, ruling in the fear of God, is like the light of morning, like the sun rising on a cloudless morning, gleaming from the rain on the grassy land." 2 Samuel 23:3-4

gleaming from the rain on the
　　grassy land.
5 Is not my house like this with God?
　For he has made with me an ever-
　　lasting covenant,
　　ordered in all things and secure.
　Will he not cause to prosper
　　all my help and my desire?
6 But the godless areʸ all like thorns
　　that are thrown away;
　for they cannot be picked up with
　　the hand;
7 to touch them one uses an iron bar
　　or the shaft of a spear.
　And they are entirely consumed in
　　fire on the spot.ᶻ

David's Mighty Men

8 These are the names of the warriors whom David had: Jō′sheb-bas·shē′beth a Tah·chē′mo·nīte; he was chief of the Three;ᵃ he wielded his spearᵇ against eight hundred whom he killed at one time.

9 Next to him among the three warriors was El·ē·ā′zar son of Dō′dō son of A·hō′hī. He was with David when they defied the Phi·lis′tines who were gathered there for battle. The Israelites withdrew, 10but he stood his ground. He struck down the Phi·lis′tines until his arm grew weary, though his hand clung to the sword. The LORD brought about a great victory that day. Then the people came back to him—but only to strip the dead.

11 Next to him was Sham′mah son of A′gee, the Har′a·rīte. The Phi·lis′tines gathered together at Lē′hī, where there was a plot of ground full of lentils; and the army fled from the Phi·lis′tines. 12But he took his stand in the middle of the plot, defended it, and killed the Phi·lis′tines; and the LORD brought about a great victory.

13 Towards the beginning of harvest three of the thirtyᶜ chiefs went down to join David at the cave of A·dul′lam,

ˣ Q Ms: MT *who was raised on high*　ʸ Heb *But worthlessness*　ᶻ Heb *in sitting*　ᵃ Gk Vg Compare 1 Chr 11.11: Meaning of Heb uncertain　ᵇ 1 Chr 11.11: Meaning of Heb uncertain　ᶜ Heb adds *head* while a band of Phi·lis′tines was encamped in the valley of Reph′a·im. [14]David was then in the stronghold; and the garrison of the Phi·lis′tines was then at Bethlehem. [15]David said longingly, "O that someone would give me water to drink from the well of Bethlehem that is by the gate!" [16]Then the three warriors broke through the camp of the Phi·lis′tines, drew water from the well of Bethlehem that was by the gate, and brought it to David. But he would not drink of it; he poured it out to the LORD, [17]for he said, "The LORD forbid that I should do this. Can I drink the blood of the men who went at the risk of their lives?" Therefore he would not drink it. The three warriors did these things.

18 Now A·bi′shai son of Ze·ru′i·ah, the brother of Jo′ab, was chief of the Thirty.[d] With his spear he fought against three hundred men and killed them, and won a name beside the Three. [19]He was the most renowned of the Thirty,[e] and became their commander; but he did not attain to the Three.

20 Be·na′i·ah son of Je·hoi′a·da was a valiant warrior[f] from Kab′ze·el, a doer of great deeds; he struck down two sons of Ar′i·el[g] of Mo′ab. He also went down and killed a lion in a pit on a day when snow had fallen. [21]And he killed an Egyptian, a handsome man. The Egyptian had a spear in his hand; but Be·na′i·ah went against him with a staff, snatched the spear out of the Egyptian's hand, and killed him with his own spear. [22]Such were the things Be·na′i·ah son of Je·hoi′a·da did, and won a name beside the three warriors. [23]He was renowned among the Thirty, but he did not attain to the Three. And David put him in charge of his bodyguard.

24 Among the Thirty were As′a·hel brother of Jo′ab; El·ha′nan son of Do′do of Bethlehem; [25]Sham′mah of Har′od; E·li′ka of Har′od; [26]He′lez the Pal′tite; Ira son of Ik′kesh of Te·ko′a; [27]A·bi·e′zer of An′a·thoth; Me·bun′nai the Hu′sha·thite; [28]Zal′mon the A·ho′hite; Ma′ha·rai of

Ne·toph′ah; [29]He′leb son of Ba′a·nah of Ne·toph′ah; It′tai son of Ri′bai of Gib′e·ah of the Ben′ja·min·ites; [30]Be·na′i·ah of Pir′a·thon; Hid′dai of the torrents of Ga′ash; [31]A′bi·al′bon the Ar′ba·thite; Az′ma·veth of Ba·hu′rim; [32]E·li′ah·ba of Sha·al′bon; the sons of Ja′shen: Jonathan [33]son of[h] Sham′mah the Har′a·rite; A·hi′am son of Shar′ar the Har′a·rite; [34]E·liph′e·let son of A·has′bai of Ma′a·cah; E·li′am son of A·hith′o·phel the Gi′lo·nite; [35]Hez·ro′[i] of Car′mel; Pa′a·rai the Ar′bite; [36]I′gal son of Nathan of Zo′bah; Ba′ni the Gad′ite; [37]Ze′lek the Am′mon·ite; Na′ha·rai of Be·er′oth, the armor-bearer of Jo′ab son of Ze·ru′i·ah; [38]Ira the Ith′rite; Ga′reb the Ith′rite; [39]U·ri′ah the Hit′tite—thirty-seven in all.

David's Census of Israel and Judah

24 Again the anger of the LORD was kindled against Israel, and he incited David against them, saying, "Go, count the people of Israel and Judah." [2]So the king said to Jo′ab and the commanders of the army,[j] who were with him, "Go through all the tribes of Israel, from Dan to Be′er-she′ba, and take a census of the people, so that I may know how many there are." [3]But Jo′ab said to the king, "May the LORD your God increase the number of the people a hundredfold, while the eyes of my lord the king can still see it! But why does my lord the king want to do this?" [4]But the king's word prevailed against Jo′ab and the commanders of the army. So Jo′ab and the commanders of the army went out from the presence of the king to take a census of the people of Israel. [5]They crossed the Jordan, and began from[k] A·ro′er and from the city that is in the middle

[d] Two Heb Mss Syr: MT *Three*   [e] Syr Compare 1 Chr 11.25: Heb *Was he the most renowned of the Three?*   [f] Another reading is *the son of Ish-hai*   [g] Gk: Heb lacks *sons of*   [h] Gk: Heb lacks *son of*   [i] Another reading is *Hezrai*   [j] 1 Chr 21.2 Gk: Heb *to Joab the commander of the army*   [k] Gk Mss: Heb *encamped in Aroer south of*

of the valley, toward Gad and on to Jā´-zer. [6]Then they came to Gil´e·ad, and to Kā´desh in the land of the Hit´tītes;[l] and they came to Dan, and from Dan[m] they went around to Sī´don, [7]and came to the fortress of Tyre and to all the cities of the Hī´vītes and Cā´naan·ītes; and they went out to the Neg´eb of Judah at Bē´er-she´ba. [8]So when they had gone through all the land, they came back to Jerusalem at the end of nine months and twenty days. [9]Jō-ab reported to the king the number of those who had been recorded: in Israel there were eight hundred thousand soldiers able to draw the sword, and those of Judah were five hundred thousand.

Judgment on David's Sin

10 But afterward, David was stricken to the heart because he had numbered the people. David said to the LORD, "I have sinned greatly in what I have done. But now, O LORD, I pray you, take away the guilt of your servant; for I have done very foolishly." [11]When David rose in the morning, the word of the LORD came to the prophet Gad, David's seer, saying, [12]"Go and say to David: Thus says the LORD: Three things I offer[n] you; choose one of them, and I will do it to you." [13]So Gad came to David and told him; he asked him, "Shall three[o] years of famine come to you on your land? Or will you flee three months before your foes while they pursue you? Or shall there be three days' pestilence in your land? Now consider, and decide what answer I shall return to the one who sent me." [14]Then David said to Gad, "I am in great distress; let us fall into the hand of the LORD, for his mercy is great; but let me not fall into human hands."

15 So the LORD sent a pestilence on Israel from that morning until the appointed time; and seventy thousand of the people died, from Dan to Bē´er-she´ba. [16]But when the angel stretched out his hand toward Jerusalem to destroy it, the LORD relented concerning the evil, and

said to the angel who was bringing destruction among the people, "It is enough; now stay your hand." The angel of the LORD was then by the threshing floor of A·rau´nah the Jeb´ū·sīte. [17]When David saw the angel who was destroying the people, he said to the LORD, "I alone have sinned, and I alone have done wickedly; but these sheep, what have they done? Let your hand, I pray, be against me and against my father's house."

A threshing sledge was a machine made of two boards turned up a little at the front. Heavy stones weighed down the machine, and there were sharp stones set in holes in the bottom. Animals pulled the sledge over the grain, and the sharp stones collected the straw to separate it from the grain.

David's Altar on the Threshing Floor

18 That day Gad came to David and said to him, "Go up and erect an altar to the LORD on the threshing floor of A·rau´nah the Jeb´ū·sīte." [19]Following Gad's instructions, David went up, as the LORD had commanded. [20]When A·rau´nah looked down, he saw the king and his servants coming toward him; and A·rau´nah went out and prostrated himself before the king with his face to the ground. [21]A·rau´nah said, "Why has my lord the king come to his servant?" David said, "To buy the threshing floor from you in order to build an altar to the LORD, so that the plague may be averted from the people." [22]Then A·rau´nah said to David, "Let my lord the king take and offer up what seems good to him; here are the oxen for the burnt offering, and the threshing sledges and the yokes of the

[l] Gk: Heb *to the land of Tahtim-hodshi*   [m] Cn: Compare Gk: Heb *they came to Dan-jaan and*   [n] Or *hold over*   [o] 1 Chr 21:12 Gk: Heb *seven*

oxen for the wood. [23]All this, O king, A·rau´nah gives to the king." And A·rau´-nah said to the king, "May the LORD your God respond favorably to you."

24 But the king said to A·rau´nah, "No, but I will buy them from you for a price; I will not offer burnt offerings to the LORD my God that cost me nothing."

So David bought the threshing floor and the oxen for fifty shekels of silver. [25]David built there an altar to the LORD, and offered burnt offerings and offerings of well-being. So the LORD answered his supplication for the land, and the plague was averted from Israel.

1 Kings

The book of First Kings begins with David as an old man about to die. After David's death, his son Solomon became king. Solomon built many fine buildings in Jerusalem, including the Temple for worship. To pay for these expensive things, King Solomon made the people pay heavy taxes. He also forced them to work on his building projects. The writer of First Kings believed that in spite of his many faults, Solomon had been given much wisdom from God.

After King Solomon's death, the Israelite people argued about the high taxes and about other matters. As a result, the people were divided into two small rival kingdoms. Judah, in the south, was ruled by Solomon's son Rehoboam. Israel, in the north, was ruled by a popular hero named Jeroboam. The rest of First Kings tells about the many kings who ruled each of these two kingdoms.

The books of First and Second Kings are really one long story that has been divided into two parts. In the sixth century BC, God inspired someone to write down this story. As we read this history, we can see that the writer was teaching that it was important for the king and the people to obey only God.

1 Kings 6:1–22

The Struggle for the Succession

1 King David was old and advanced in years; and although they covered him with clothes, he could not get warm. ²So his servants said to him, "Let a young virgin be sought for my lord the king, and let her wait on the king, and be his attendant; let her lie in your bosom, so that my lord the king may be warm." ³So they searched for a beautiful girl throughout all the territory of Israel, and found Ab′i·shag the Shū′nam·mīte, and brought her to the king. ⁴The girl was very beautiful. She became the king's attendant and served him, but the king did not know her sexually.

5 Now Ad·o·nī′jah son of Hag′gith exalted himself, saying, "I will be king"; he prepared for himself chariots and horsemen, and fifty men to run before him. ⁶His father had never at any time displeased him by asking, "Why have you done thus and so?" He was also a very handsome man, and he was born next after Ab′sa·lom. ⁷He conferred with Jō′ab son of Ze·rū′i·ah and with the priest A·bī′a·thar, and they supported Ad·o·nī′jah. ⁸But the priest Zā′dok, and Be·nā′i·ah son of Je·hoi′a·da, and the prophet Nathan, and Shim′e·ī, and Rē′ī, and David's own warriors did not side with Ad·o·nī′jah.

9 Ad·o·nī′jah sacrificed sheep, oxen, and fatted cattle by the stone Zō′he·leth, which is beside En-rō′gel, and he invited all his brothers, the king's sons, and all the royal officials of Judah, ¹⁰but he did not invite the prophet Nathan or Be·nā′i·ah or the warriors or his brother Solomon.

11 Then Nathan said to Bath·shē′ba, Solomon's mother, "Have you not heard that Ad·o·nī′jah son of Hag′gith has become king and our lord David does not know it? ¹²Now therefore come, let me give you advice, so that you may save your own life and the life of your son Solomon. ¹³Go in at once to King David, and say to him, 'Did you not, my lord the king, swear to your servant, saying:

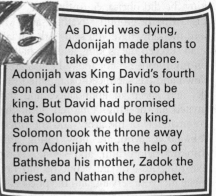

As David was dying, Adonijah made plans to take over the throne. Adonijah was King David's fourth son and was next in line to be king. But David had promised that Solomon would be king. Solomon took the throne away from Adonijah with the help of Bathsheba his mother, Zadok the priest, and Nathan the prophet.

Your son Solomon shall succeed me as king, and he shall sit on my throne? Why then is Ad·o·nī′jah king?' ¹⁴Then while you are still there speaking with the king, I will come in after you and confirm your words."

15 So Bath·shē′ba went to the king in his room. The king was very old; Ab′i·shag the Shū′nam·mīte was attending the king. ¹⁶Bath·shē′ba bowed and did obeisance to the king, and the king said, "What do you wish?" ¹⁷She said to him, "My lord, you swore to your servant by the LORD your God, saying: Your son Solomon shall succeed me as king, and he shall sit on my throne. ¹⁸But now suddenly Ad·o·nī′jah has become king, though you, my lord the king, do not know it. ¹⁹He has sacrificed oxen, fatted cattle, and sheep in abundance, and has invited all the children of the king, the priest A·bī′a·thar, and Jō′ab the commander of the army; but your servant Solomon he has not invited. ²⁰But you, my lord the king—the eyes of all Israel are on you to tell them who shall sit on the throne of my lord the king after him. ²¹Otherwise it will come to pass, when my lord the king sleeps with his ancestors, that my son Solomon and I will be counted offenders."

22 While she was still speaking with the king, the prophet Nathan came in. ²³The king was told, "Here is the prophet Nathan." When he came in before the

king, he did obeisance to the king, with his face to the ground. [24]Nathan said, "My lord the king, have you said, 'Ad·o·nī´jah shall succeed me as king, and he shall sit on my throne'? [25]For today he has gone down and has sacrificed oxen, fatted cattle, and sheep in abundance, and has invited all the king's children, Jō´ab the commander[a] of the army, and the priest A·bī´a·thar, who are now eating and drinking before him, and saying, 'Long live King Ad·o·nī´jah!' [26]But he did not invite me, your servant, and the priest Zā´dok, and Be·nā´i·ah son of Je·hoi´a·da, and your servant Solomon. [27]Has this thing been brought about by my lord the king and you have not let your servants know who should sit on the throne of my lord the king after him?"

The Accession of Solomon

28 King David answered, "Summon Bath·shē´ba to me." So she came into the king's presence, and stood before the king. [29]The king swore, saying, "As the LORD lives, who has saved my life from every adversity, [30]as I swore to you by the LORD, the God of Israel, 'Your son Solomon shall succeed me as king, and he shall sit on my throne in my place,' so will I do this day." [31]Then Bath·shē´ba bowed with her face to the ground, and did obeisance to the king, and said, "May my lord King David live forever!"

32 King David said, "Summon to me the priest Zā´dok, the prophet Nathan, and Be·nā´i·ah son of Je·hoi´a·da." When they came before the king, [33]the king said to them, "Take with you the servants of your lord, and have my son Solomon ride on my own mule, and bring him down to Gī´hon. [34]There let the priest Zā´dok and the prophet Nathan anoint him king over Israel; then blow the trumpet, and say, 'Long live King Solomon!' [35]You shall go up following him. Let him enter and sit on my throne; he shall be king in my place; for I have appointed him to be ruler over Israel and over Judah." [36]Be·nā´i·ah son of Je·hoi´a·da

Solomon was famous for his wisdom. Read about one of his most famous decisions in 1 Kings 3:16–28. While he was king, Solomon created a strong government and began a large building program. He built a temple for the Lord and also a palace for himself. He created a large army, started a navy, and increased Israel's trade with foreign countries. Solomon made the Israelites pay taxes for his expensive projects and also forced them to work on his buildings. This upset the people and started a fight in Israel.

answered the king, "Amen! May the LORD, the God of my lord the king, so ordain. [37]As the LORD has been with my lord the king, so may he be with Solomon, and make his throne greater than the throne of my lord King David."

38 So the priest Zā´dok, the prophet Nathan, and Be·nā´i·ah son of Je·ho´i·ada, and the Cher´e·thītes and the Pel´eth·ītes, went down and had Solomon ride on King David's mule, and led him to Gī´hon. [39]There the priest Zā´dok took the horn of oil from the tent and anointed Solomon. Then they blew the trumpet, and all the people said, "Long live King Solomon!" [40]And all the people went up following him, playing on pipes and rejoicing with great joy, so that the earth quaked at their noise.

41 Ad·o·nī´jah and all the guests who were with him heard it as they finished feasting. When Jō´ab heard the sound of the trumpet, he said, "Why is the city in an uproar?" [42]While he was still speaking, Jonathan son of the priest A·bī´a·thar arrived. Ad·o·nī´jah said, "Come

---

[a] Gk: Heb *the commanders*

in, for you are a worthy man and surely you bring good news." ⁴³Jonathan answered Ad·o·nīʹjah, "No, for our lord King David has made Solomon king; ⁴⁴the king has sent with him the priest Zāʹdok, the prophet Nathan, and Be·naʹi·ah son of Je·hoiʹa·da, and the Cherʹe·thītes and the Pelʹeth·ites; and they had him ride on the king's mule; ⁴⁵the priest Zāʹdok and the prophet Nathan have anointed him king at Gīʹhon; and they have gone up from there rejoicing, so that the city is in an uproar. This is the noise that you heard. ⁴⁶Solomon now sits on the royal throne. ⁴⁷Moreover the king's servants came to congratulate our lord King David, saying, 'May God make the name of Solomon more famous than yours, and make his throne greater than your throne.' The king bowed in worship on the bed ⁴⁸and went on to pray thus, 'Blessed be the LORD, the God of Israel, who today has granted one of my offspring*ᵇ* to sit on my throne and permitted me to witness it.' "

49 Then all the guests of Ad·o·nīʹjah got up trembling and went their own ways. ⁵⁰ Ad·o·nīʹjah, fearing Solomon, got up and went to grasp the horns of the altar. ⁵¹Solomon was informed, "Ad·o·nīʹjah is afraid of King Solomon; see, he has laid hold of the horns of the altar, saying, 'Let King Solomon swear to me first that he will not kill his servant with the sword.' " ⁵²So Solomon responded, "If he proves to be a worthy man, not one of his hairs shall fall to the ground; but if wickedness is found in him, he shall die." ⁵³Then King Solomon sent to have him brought down from the altar. He came to do obeisance to King Solomon; and Solomon said to him, "Go home."

David's Instruction to Solomon

2 When David's time to die drew near, he charged his son Solomon, saying: ²"I am about to go the way of all the earth. Be strong, be courageous, ³and keep the charge of the LORD your God,

> "Be strong, be courageous, and keep the charge of the LORD your God, walking in his ways and keeping his statutes, his commandments, his ordinances, and his testimonies, as it is written in the law of Moses, so that you may prosper in all that you do and wherever you turn." 1 Kings 2:2–3

walking in his ways and keeping his statutes, his commandments, his ordinances, and his testimonies, as it is written in the law of Moses, so that you may prosper in all that you do and wherever you turn. ⁴Then the LORD will establish his word that he spoke concerning me: 'If your heirs take heed to their way, to walk before me in faithfulness with all their heart and with all their soul, there shall not fail you a successor on the throne of Israel.'

5 "Moreover you know also what Jōʹab son of Ze·rūʹi·ah did to me, how he dealt with the two commanders of the armies of Israel, Abner son of Ner, and A·māʹsa son of Jēʹther, whom he murdered, retaliating in time of peace for blood that had been shed in war, and putting the blood of war on the belt around his waist, and on the sandals on his feet. ⁶Act therefore according to your wisdom, but do not let his gray head go down to Shēʹōl in peace. ⁷Deal loyally, however, with the sons of Bar·zilʹlaī the Gilʹe·ad·īte, and let them be among those who eat at your table; for with such loyalty they met me when I fled from your brother Abʹsa·lom. ⁸There is also with you Shimʹe·ī son of Gēʹra, the Benʹja·min·īte from Ba·hūʹrim, who cursed me with a terrible curse on the day when I went to Mā·ha·nāʹim; but when he came down to meet me at the Jordan, I swore to him by the LORD, 'I will not put you to death with the

---

ᵇ Gk: Heb *one*

sword.' ⁹Therefore do not hold him guiltless, for you are a wise man; you will know what you ought to do to him, and you must bring his gray head down with blood to Shĕ´ol."

Death of David

10 Then David slept with his ancestors, and was buried in the city of David. ¹¹The time that David reigned over Israel was forty years; he reigned seven years in Hĕ´bron, and thirty-three years in Jerusalem. ¹²So Solomon sat on the throne of his father David; and his kingdom was firmly established.

Solomon Consolidates His Reign

13 Then Ad·o·nī´jah son of Hag´gith came to Bath·shĕ´ba, Solomon's mother. She asked, "Do you come peaceably?" He said, "Peaceably." ¹⁴Then he said, "May I have a word with you?" She said, "Go on." ¹⁵He said, "You know that the kingdom was mine, and that all Israel expected me to reign; however, the kingdom has turned about and become my brother's, for it was his from the LORD. ¹⁶And now I have one request to make of you; do not refuse me." She said to him, "Go on." ¹⁷He said, "Please ask King Solomon—he will not refuse you—to give me Ab´i·shag the Shū´nam·mīte as my wife." ¹⁸Bath·shĕ´ba said, "Very well; I will speak to the king on your behalf."

19 So Bath·shĕ´ba went to King Solomon, to speak to him on behalf of Ad·o·nī´jah. The king rose to meet her, and bowed down to her; then he sat on his throne, and had a throne brought for the king's mother, and she sat on his right. ²⁰Then she said, "I have one small request to make of you; do not refuse me." And the king said to her, "Make your request, my mother; for I will not refuse you." ²¹She said, "Let Ab´i·shag the Shū´nam·mīte be given to your brother Ad·o·nī´jah as his wife." ²²King Solomon answered his mother, "And why do you ask Ab´i·shag the Shū´nam·mīte for Ad·o·nī´jah? Ask for him

the kingdom as well! For he is my elder brother; ask not only for him but also for the priest A·bī´a·thar and for Jō´ab son of Ze·rū´i·ah!" ²³Then King Solomon swore by the LORD, "So may God do to me, and more also, for Ad·o·nī´jah has devised this scheme at the risk of his life! ²⁴Now therefore as the LORD lives, who has established me and placed me on the throne of my father David, and who has made me a house as he promised, today Ad·o·nī´jah shall be put to death." ²⁵So King Solomon sent Be·nā´i·ah son of Je·hoi´a·da; he struck him down, and he died.

26 The king said to the priest A·bī´a·thar, "Go to An´a·thoth, to your estate; for you deserve death. But I will not at this time put you to death, because you carried the ark of the Lord GOD before my father David, and because you shared in all the hardships my father endured." ²⁷So Solomon banished A·bī´a·thar from being priest to the LORD, thus fulfilling the word of the LORD that he had spoken concerning the house of Ē´lī in Shī´lōh.

28 When the news came to Jō´ab—for Jō´ab had supported Ad·o·nī´jah though he had not supported Ab´sa·lom—Jō´ab fled to the tent of the LORD and grasped the horns of the altar. ²⁹When it was told King Solomon, "Jō´ab has fled to the tent of the LORD and now is beside the altar," Solomon sent Be·nā´i·ah son of Je·hoi´a·da, saying, "Go, strike him down." ³⁰So Be·nā´i·ah came to the tent of the LORD and said to him, "The king commands, 'Come out.'" But he said, "No, I will die here." Then Be·nā´i·ah brought the king word again, saying, "Thus said Jō´ab, and thus he answered me." ³¹The king replied to him, "Do as he has said, strike him down and bury him; and thus take away from me and from my father's house the guilt for the blood that Jō´ab shed without cause. ³²The LORD will bring back his bloody deeds on his own head, because, without the knowledge of my father

David, he attacked and killed with the sword two men more righteous and better than himself, Abner son of Ner, commander of the army of Israel, and A·mā′sa son of Jĕ′ther, commander of the army of Judah. [33]So shall their blood come back on the head of Jŏ′ab and on the head of his descendants forever; but to David, and to his descendants, and to his house, and to his throne, there shall be peace from the LORD forevermore." [34]Then Be·nā′i·ah son of Je·hoi′a·da went up and struck him down and killed him; and he was buried at his own house near the wilderness. [35]The king put Be·nā′i·ah son of Je·hoi′a·da over the army in his place, and the king put the priest Zā′dok in the place of A·bī′a·thar.

36 Then the king sent and summoned Shim′e·ī, and said to him, "Build yourself a house in Jerusalem, and live there, and do not go out from there to any place whatever. [37]For on the day you go out, and cross the Wadi Kid′ron, know for certain that you shall die; your blood shall be on your own head." [38]And Shim′e·ī said to the king, "The sentence is fair; as my lord the king has said, so will your servant do." So Shim′e·ī lived in Jerusalem many days.

39 But it happened at the end of three years that two of Shim′e·ī′s slaves ran away to King Ā′chish son of Mā′a·cah of Gath. When it was told Shim′e·ī, "Your slaves are in Gath," [40]Shim′e·ī arose and saddled a donkey, and went to Ā′chish in Gath, to search for his slaves; Shim′e·ī went and brought his slaves from Gath. [41]When Solomon was told that Shim′e·ī had gone from Jerusalem to Gath and returned, [42]the king sent and summoned Shim′e·ī, and said to him, "Did I not make you swear by the LORD, and solemnly adjure you, saying, 'Know for certain that on the day you go out and go to any place whatever, you shall die'? And you said to me, 'The sentence is fair; I accept.' [43]Why then have you not kept your oath to the LORD and the

commandment with which I charged you?" [44]The king also said to Shim′e·ī, "You know in your own heart all the evil that you did to my father David; so the LORD will bring back your evil on your own head. [45]But King Solomon shall be blessed, and the throne of David shall be established before the LORD forever." [46]Then the king commanded Be·nā′i·ah son of Je·hoi′a·da; and he went out and struck him down, and he died.

So the kingdom was established in the hand of Solomon.

Solomon's Prayer for Wisdom

3 Solomon made a marriage alliance with Pharaoh king of Egypt; he took Pharaoh's daughter and brought her into the city of David, until he had finished building his own house and the house of the LORD and the wall around Jerusalem. [2]The people were sacrificing at the high places, however, because no house had yet been built for the name of the LORD.

3 Solomon loved the LORD, walking in the statutes of his father David; only, he sacrificed and offered incense at the high places. [4]The king went to Gib′e·on to sacrifice there, for that was the principal high place; Solomon used to offer a thousand burnt offerings on that altar. [5]At Gib′e·on the LORD appeared to Solomon in a dream by night; and God said, "Ask what I should give you." [6]And Solomon said, "You have shown great and steadfast love to your servant my father David, because he walked before you in faithfulness, in righteousness, and in uprightness of heart toward you;

The Canaanites had built places to worship their gods on hilltops. God told the Israelites to destroy these "high places" when they entered Canaan, but the people did not obey. Instead, they often joined in the Canaanite worship of false gods.

and you have kept for him this great and steadfast love, and have given him a son to sit on his throne today. 7And now, O LORD my God, you have made your servant king in place of my father David, although I am only a little child; I do not know how to go out or come in. 8And your servant is in the midst of the people whom you have chosen, a great people, so numerous they cannot be numbered or counted. 9Give your servant therefore an understanding mind to govern your people, able to discern between good and evil; for who can govern this your great people?"

10 It pleased the Lord that Solomon had asked this. 11God said to him, "Because you have asked this, and have not asked for yourself long life or riches, or for the life of your enemies, but have asked for yourself understanding to discern what is right, 12I now do according to your word. Indeed I give you a wise and discerning mind; no one like you has been before you and no one like you shall arise after you. 13I give you also what you have not asked, both riches and honor all your life; no other king shall compare with you. 14If you will walk in my ways, keeping my statutes and my commandments, as your father David walked, then I will lengthen your life."

15 Then Solomon awoke; it had been a dream. He came to Jerusalem where he stood before the ark of the covenant of the LORD. He offered up burnt offerings and offerings of well-being, and provided a feast for all his servants.

Solomon's Wisdom in Judgment

16 Later, two women who were prostitutes came to the king and stood before him. 17The one woman said, "Please, my lord, this woman and I live in the same house; and I gave birth while she was in the house. 18Then on the third day after I gave birth, this woman also gave birth. We were together; there was no one else with us in the house, only the two of us were in the house. 19Then this woman's son died in the night, because she lay on him. 20She got up in the middle of the night and took my son from beside me while your servant slept. She laid him at her breast, and laid her dead son at my breast. 21When I rose in the morning to nurse my son, I saw that he was dead; but when I looked at him closely in the morning, clearly it was not the son I had borne." 22But the other woman said, "No, the living son is mine, and the dead son is yours." The first said, "No, the dead son is yours, and the living son is mine." So they argued before the king.

23 Then the king said, "The one says, 'This is my son that is alive, and your son is dead'; while the other says, 'Not so! Your son is dead, and my son is the living one.' " 24So the king said, "Bring me a sword," and they brought a sword before the king. 25The king said, "Divide the living boy in two; then give half to the one, and half to the other." 26But the woman whose son was alive said to the king—because compassion for her son burned within her—"Please, my lord, give her the living boy; certainly do not kill him!" The other said, "It shall be neither mine nor yours; divide it." 27Then the king responded: "Give the first woman the living boy; do not kill him. She is his mother." 28All Israel heard of the judgment that the king had rendered; and they stood in awe of the king, because they perceived that the wisdom of God was in him, to execute justice.

Solomon's Administrative Officers

4 King Solomon was king over all Israel, 2and these were his high officials: Az·a·rī´ah son of Zā´dok was the priest; 3El·i·hōr´eph and A·hī´jah sons of Shī´sha were secretaries; Je·hosh´a·phat son of A·hī´lud was recorder; 4Be·nā´i·ah son of Je·hoi´a·da was in command of the army; Zā´dok and A·bī´a·thar were priests; 5Aza·rī´ah son of Nathan was over the officials; Zā´bud son of Nathan was priest and king's friend; 6A·hī´shar

was in charge of the palace; and Ad·o·nī´-ram son of Ab´da was in charge of the forced labor.

7 Solomon had twelve officials over all Israel, who provided food for the king and his household; each one had to make provision for one month in the year. [8]These were their names: Ben-hur, in the hill country of Ē´phra·im; [9]Ben-dē´ker, in Mā´-kaz, Shā·al´bim, Beth-shē´mesh, and Ē´lon-beth-hā´nan; [10]Ben-hē´sed, in A·rūb´both (to him belonged Sō´cōh and all the land of Hē´pher); [11]Ben-a·bin´a·dab, in all Nā´-phath-dor (he had Tā´phath, Solomon's daughter, as his wife); [12]Bā´a·na son of A·hī´-lud, in Tā´a·nach, Me·gid´dō, and all Beth-shē´an, which is beside Zar´e·than below Jez´rē·el, and from Beth-shē´an to Ā´bel-me·hō´lah, as far as the other side of Jok´-mē·am; [13]Ben-gē´ber, in Rā´moth-gil´e·ad (he had the villages of Jā´ir son of Ma·nas´seh, which are in Gil´e·ad, and he had the region of Ar´gob, which is in Bā´-shan, sixty great cities with walls and bronze bars); [14]A·hin´a·dab son of Id´dō, in Mā·ha·nā´im; [15]A·him´a·az, in Naph´ta·lī (he had taken Bas´e·math, Solomon's daughter, as his wife); [16]Bā´a·na son of Hū´-shaī, in Ash´er and Be·ā´loth; [17]Je·hosh´-a·phat son of Pa·rū´ah, in Is´sa·char; [18]Shim´ē·ī son of Ē´la, in Benjamin; [19]Gē´-ber son of Ū´rī, in the land of Gil´e·ad, the country of King Sī´hon of the Am´o·rītes and of King Og of Bā´shan. And there was one official in the land of Judah.

Magnificence of Solomon's Rule

20 Judah and Israel were as numerous as the sand by the sea; they ate and drank and were happy. [21c] Solomon was sovereign over all the kingdoms from the Euphrates to the land of the Phi·lis´tines, even to the border of Egypt; they brought tribute and served Solomon all the days of his life.

22 Solomon's provision for one day was thirty cors of choice flour, and sixty cors of meal, [23]ten fat oxen, and twenty pasture-fed cattle, one hundred sheep, besides deer, gazelles, roebucks, and fatted fowl. [24]For he had dominion over all the region west of the Euphrates from Tiph´sah to Gā´za, over all the kings west of the Euphrates; and he had peace on all sides. [25]During Solomon's lifetime Judah and Israel lived in safety, from Dan even to Bē´er-shē´ba, all of them under their vines and fig trees. [26]Solomon also had forty thousand stalls of horses for his chariots, and twelve thousand horsemen. [27]Those officials supplied provisions for King Solomon and for all who came to King Solomon's table, each one in his month; they let nothing be lacking. [28]They also brought to the required place barley and straw for the horses and swift steeds, each according to his charge.

Fame of Solomon's Wisdom

29 God gave Solomon very great wisdom, discernment, and breadth of understanding as vast as the sand on the seashore, [30]so that Solomon's wisdom surpassed the wisdom of all the people of the east, and all the wisdom of Egypt. [31]He was wiser than anyone else, wiser than Ē´than the Ez´ra·hīte, and Hē´man, Cal´col, and Dar´da, children of Mā´hol; his fame spread throughout all the surrounding nations. [32]He composed three thousand proverbs, and his songs numbered a thousand and five. [33]He would speak of trees, from the cedar that is in the Lebanon to the hyssop that grows in the wall; he would speak of animals, and birds, and reptiles, and fish. [34]People came from all the nations to hear the wisdom of Solomon; they came from all the kings of the earth who had heard of his wisdom.

Preparations and Materials for the Temple

5 [d] Now King Hiram of Tyre sent his servants to Solomon, when he heard that they had anointed him king in place of his father; for Hiram had

---

[c] Ch 5.1 in Heb   [d] Ch 5.15 in Heb

always been a friend to David. ²Solomon sent word to Hiram, saying, ³"You know that my father David could not build a house for the name of the LORD his God because of the warfare with which his enemies surrounded him, until the LORD put them under the soles of his feet.ᵉ ⁴But now the LORD my God has given me rest on every side; there is neither adversary nor misfortune. ⁵So I intend to build a house for the name of the LORD my God, as the LORD said to my father David, 'Your son, whom I will set on your throne in your place, shall build the house for my name.' ⁶Therefore command that cedars from the Lebanon be cut for me. My servants will join your servants, and I will give you whatever wages you set for your servants; for you know that there is no one among us who knows how to cut timber like the Sī·dō´ni·ans."

7 When Hiram heard the words of Solomon, he rejoiced greatly, and said, "Blessed be the LORD today, who has given to David a wise son to be over this great people." ⁸Hiram sent word to Solomon, "I have heard the message that you have sent to me; I will fulfill all your needs in the matter of cedar and cypress timber. ⁹My servants shall bring it down to the sea from the Lebanon; I will make it into rafts to go by sea to the place you indicate. I will have them broken up there for you to take away. And you shall meet my needs by providing food for my household." ¹⁰So Hiram supplied Solomon's every need for timber of cedar and cypress. ¹¹Solomon in turn gave Hiram twenty thousand cors of wheat as food for his household, and twenty cors of fine oil. Solomon gave this to Hiram year by year. ¹²So the LORD gave Solomon wisdom, as he promised him. There was peace between Hiram and Solomon; and the two of them made a treaty.

13 King Solomon conscripted forced labor out of all Israel; the levy numbered thirty thousand men. ¹⁴He sent them to the Lebanon, ten thousand a month in shifts; they would be a month in the Lebanon and two months at home; Ad·o·nī´ram was in charge of the forced labor. ¹⁵Solomon also had seventy thousand laborers and eighty thousand stonecutters in the hill country, ¹⁶besides Solomon's three thousand three hundred supervisors who were over the work, having charge of the people who did the work. ¹⁷At the king's command, they quarried out great, costly stones in order to lay the foundation of the house with dressed stones. ¹⁸So Solomon's builders and Hiram's builders and the Geb´alītes did the stonecutting and prepared the timber and the stone to build the house.

Solomon Builds the Temple

6 In the four hundred eightieth year after the Israelites came out of the land of Egypt, in the fourth year of

The Temple was called the house of God, or the house of the Lord. King Solomon built the first Temple in Jerusalem on the land chosen by his father David. Solomon brought in skilled builders and spent a lot of money! It took seven years to build the Temple. The Temple had three rooms: (1) the porch or vestibule, (2) the holy place where the golden candlestick, the bread of the Presence, and the altar of incense were kept, (3) the holy of holies, where there were two cherubim and the Ark of the Covenant to symbolize God's presence.

In the courtyard outside the Temple, there was a great altar of burnt offerings and a brass basin (called the molten sea), which held water for the priests to wash themselves and the offerings and vessels.

ᵉ Gk Tg Vg: Heb *my feet* or *his feet*

Solomon's reign over Israel, in the month of Ziv, which is the second month, he began to build the house of the LORD. [2]The house that King Solomon built for the LORD was sixty cubits long, twenty cubits wide, and thirty cubits high. [3]The vestibule in front of the nave of the house was twenty cubits wide, across the width of the house. Its depth was ten cubits in front of the house. [4]For the house he made windows with recessed frames.[f] [5]He also built a structure against the wall of the house, running around the walls of the house, both the nave and the inner sanctuary; and he made side chambers all around. [6]The lowest story[g] was five cubits wide, the middle one was six cubits wide, and the third was seven cubits wide; for around the outside of the house he made offsets on the wall in order that the supporting beams should not be inserted into the walls of the house.

7 The house was built with stone finished at the quarry, so that neither hammer nor ax nor any tool of iron was heard in the temple while it was being built.

8 The entrance for the middle story was on the south side of the house: one went up by winding stairs to the middle story, and from the middle story to the third. [9]So he built the house, and finished it; he roofed the house with beams and planks of cedar. [10]He built the structure against the whole house, each story[h] five cubits high, and it was joined to the house with timbers of cedar.

11 Now the word of the LORD came to Solomon, [12]"Concerning this house that you are building, if you will walk in my statutes, obey my ordinances, and keep all my commandments by walking in them, then I will establish my promise with you, which I made to your father David. [13]I will dwell among the children of Israel, and will not forsake my people Israel."

14 So Solomon built the house, and finished it. [15]He lined the walls of the house on the inside with boards of cedar; from the floor of the house to the rafters of the ceiling, he covered them on the inside with wood; and he covered the floor of the house with boards of cypress. [16]He built twenty cubits of the rear of the house with boards of cedar from the floor to the rafters, and he built this within as an inner sanctuary, as the most holy place. [17]The house, that is, the nave in front of the inner sanctuary, was forty cubits long. [18]The cedar within the house had carvings of gourds and open flowers; all was cedar, no stone was seen. [19]The inner sanctuary he prepared in the innermost part of the house, to set there the ark of the covenant of the LORD. [20]The interior of the inner sanctuary was twenty cubits long, twenty cubits wide, and twenty cubits high; he overlaid it with pure gold. He also overlaid the altar with cedar.[i] [21]Solomon overlaid the inside of the house with pure gold, then he drew chains of gold across, in front of the inner sanctuary, and overlaid it with gold. [22]Next he overlaid the whole house with gold, in order that the whole house might be perfect; even the whole altar that belonged to the inner sanctuary he overlaid with gold.

The Furnishings of the Temple

23 In the inner sanctuary he made two cherubim of olivewood, each ten cubits high. [24]Five cubits was the length of one wing of the cherub, and five cubits the length of the other wing of the cherub; it was ten cubits from the tip of one wing to the tip of the other. [25]The other cherub also measured ten cubits; both cherubim had the same measure and the same form. [26]The height of one cherub was ten cubits, and so was that of the other cherub. [27]He put the cherubim in the innermost part of the house; the

---

[f] Gk: Meaning of Heb uncertain　　[g] Gk: Heb structure　　[h] Heb lacks *each story*　　[i] Meaning of Heb uncertain

wings of the cherubim were spread out so that a wing of one was touching the one wall, and a wing of the other cherub was touching the other wall; their other wings toward the center of the house were touching wing to wing. 28He also overlaid the cherubim with gold.

29 He carved the walls of the house all around about with carved engravings of cherubim, palm trees, and open flowers, in the inner and outer rooms. 30The floor of the house he overlaid with gold, in the inner and outer rooms.

31 For the entrance to the inner sanctuary he made doors of olivewood; the lintel and the doorposts were five-sided.*j* 32He covered the two doors of olivewood with carvings of cherubim, palm trees, and open flowers; he overlaid them with gold, and spread gold on the cherubim and on the palm trees.

33 So also he made for the entrance to the nave doorposts of olivewood, four-sided each, 34and two doors of cypress wood; the two leaves of the one door were folding, and the two leaves of the other door were folding. 35He carved cherubim, palm trees, and open flowers, overlaying them with gold evenly applied upon the carved work. 36He built the inner court with three courses of dressed stone to one course of cedar beams.

37 In the fourth year the foundation of the house of the LORD was laid, in the month of Ziv. 38In the eleventh year, in the month of Bul, which is the eighth month, the house was finished in all its parts, and according to all its specifications. He was seven years in building it.

Solomon's Palace and Other Buildings

7 Solomon was building his own house thirteen years, and he finished his entire house.

2 He built the House of the Forest of the Lebanon one hundred cubits long, fifty cubits wide, and thirty cubits high, built on four rows of cedar pillars, with cedar beams on the pillars. 3It was roofed with cedar on the forty-five rafters, fifteen in each row, which were on the pillars. 4There were window frames in the three rows, facing each other in the three rows. 5All the doorways and doorposts had four-sided frames, opposite, facing each other in the three rows.

6 He made the Hall of Pillars fifty cubits long and thirty cubits wide. There was a porch in front with pillars, and a canopy in front of them.

7 He made the Hall of the Throne where he was to pronounce judgment, the Hall of Justice, covered with cedar from floor to floor.

8 His own house where he would reside, in the other court back of the hall, was of the same construction. Solomon also made a house like this hall for Pharaoh's daughter, whom he had taken in marriage.

9 All these were made of costly stones, cut according to measure, sawed with saws, back and front, from the foundation to the coping, and from outside to the great court. 10The foundation was of costly stones, huge stones, stones of eight and ten cubits. 11There were costly stones above, cut to measure, and cedarwood. 12The great court had three courses of dressed stone to one layer of cedar beams all around; so had the inner court of the house of the LORD, and the vestibule of the house.

Cedar is a beautiful wood that comes from cedar trees. The wood smells good and lasts a long time. Cedar trees usually grow about 20 feet tall, but the cedars that grew on the mountains of Lebanon were 120 to 140 feet tall! The Israelites used cedar wood for many of Solomon's building projects, including the Temple and his palace.

j Meaning of Heb uncertain

Products of Hiram the Bronzeworker

13 Now King Solomon invited and received Hiram from Tyre. [14]He was the son of a widow of the tribe of Naph'ta·lī, whose father, a man of Tyre, had been an artisan in bronze; he was full of skill, intelligence, and knowledge in working bronze. He came to King Solomon, and did all his work.

15 He cast two pillars of bronze. Eighteen cubits was the height of the one, and a cord of twelve cubits would encircle it; the second pillar was the same[k] [16]He also made two capitals of molten bronze, to set on the tops of the pillars; the height of the one capital was five cubits, and the height of the other capital was five cubits. [17]There were nets of checker work with wreaths of chain work for the capitals on the tops of the pillars; seven[l] for the one capital, and seven[l] for the other capital. [18]He made the columns with two rows around each latticework to cover the capitals that were above the pomegranates; he did the same with the other capital. [19]Now the capitals that were on the tops of the pillars in the vestibule were of lily-work, four cubits high. [20]The capitals were on the two pillars and also above the rounded projection that was beside the latticework; there were two hundred pomegranates in rows all around; and so with the other capital. [21]He set up the pillars at the vestibule of the temple; he set up the pillar on the south and called it Jā'chin; and he set up the pillar on the north and called it Bō'az. [22]On the tops of the pillars was lily-work. Thus the work of the pillars was finished.

23 Then he made the molten sea; it was round, ten cubits from brim to brim, and five cubits high. A line of thirty cubits would encircle it completely. [24]Under its brim were panels all around it, each of ten cubits, surrounding the sea; there were two rows of panels, cast when it was cast. [25]It stood on twelve oxen, three facing north, three facing west, three facing south, and three facing east; the sea was set on them. The hindquarters of each were toward the inside. [26]Its thickness was a handbreadth; its brim was made like the brim of a cup, like the flower of a lily; it held two thousand baths.[m]

27 He also made the ten stands of bronze; each stand was four cubits long, four cubits wide, and three cubits high. [28]This was the construction of the stands: they had borders; the borders were within the frames; [29]on the borders that were set in the frames were lions, oxen, and cherubim. On the frames, both above and below the lions and oxen, there were wreaths of beveled work. [30]Each stand had four bronze wheels and axles of bronze; at the four corners were supports for a basin. The supports were cast with wreaths at the side of each. [31]Its opening was within the crown whose height was one cubit; its opening was round, as a pedestal is made; it was a cubit and a half wide. At its opening there were carvings; its borders were four-sided, not round. [32]The four wheels were underneath the borders; the axles of the wheels were in the stands; and the height of a wheel was a cubit and a half. [33]The wheels were made like a chariot wheel; their axles, their rims, their spokes, and their hubs were all cast. [34]There were four supports at the four corners of each stand; the supports were of one piece with the stands. [35]On the top of the stand there was a round band half a cubit high; on the top of the stand, its stays and its borders were of one piece with it. [36]On the surfaces of its stays and on its borders he carved cherubim, lions, and palm trees, where each had space, with wreaths all around. [37]In this way he made the ten stands; all of them were cast alike, with the same size and the same form.[m]

[k] Cn: Heb *and a cord of twelve cubits encircled the second pillar* ; Compare Jer 52.21   [l] Heb: Gk *a net*   [m] A Heb measure of volume

38 He made ten basins of bronze; each basin held forty baths,[n] each basin measured four cubits; there was a basin for each of the ten stands. [39]He set five of the stands on the south side of the house, and five on the north side of the house; he set the sea on the southeast corner of the house.

40 Hiram also made the pots, the shovels, and the basins. So Hiram finished all the work that he did for King Solomon on the house of the LORD: [41]the two pillars, the two bowls of the capitals that were on the tops of the pillars, the two latticeworks to cover the two bowls of the capitals that were on the tops of the pillars; [42]the four hundred pomegranates for the two latticeworks, two rows of pomegranates for each latticework, to cover the two bowls of the capitals that were on the pillars; [43]the ten stands, the ten basins on the stands; [44]the one sea, and the twelve oxen underneath the sea.

45 The pots, the shovels, and the basins, all these vessels that Hiram made for King Solomon for the house of the LORD were of burnished bronze. [46]In the plain of the Jordan the king cast them, in the clay ground between Suc´coth and Zar´e·than. [47]Solomon left all the vessels unweighed, because there were so many of them; the weight of the bronze was not determined.

48 So Solomon made all the vessels that were in the house of the LORD: the golden altar, the golden table for the bread of the Presence, [49]the lampstands of pure gold, five on the south side and five on the north, in front of the inner sanctuary; the flowers, the lamps, and the tongs, of gold; [50]the cups, snuffers, basins, dishes for incense, and firepans, of pure gold; the sockets for the doors of the innermost part of the house, the most holy place, and for the doors of the nave of the temple, of gold.

51 Thus all the work that King Solomon did on the house of the LORD was finished. Solomon brought in the things that his father David had dedicated, the silver, the gold, and the vessels, and stored them in the treasuries of the house of the LORD.

Dedication of the Temple

8 Then Solomon assembled the elders of Israel and all the heads of the tribes, the leaders of the ancestral houses of the Israelites, before King Solomon in Jerusalem, to bring up the ark of the covenant of the LORD out of the city of David, which is Zion. [2]All the people of Israel assembled to King Solomon at the festival in the month Eth´a·nim, which is the seventh month. [3]And all the elders of Israel came, and the priests carried the ark. [4]So they brought up the ark of the LORD, the tent of meeting, and all the holy vessels that were in the tent; the priests and the Lē´vītes brought them up. [5]King Solomon and all the congregation of Israel, who had assembled before him, were with him before the ark, sacrificing so many sheep and oxen that they could not be counted or numbered. [6]Then the priests brought the ark of the covenant of the LORD to its place, in the inner sanctuary of the house, in the most holy place, underneath the wings of the

The bread of the Presence, also called showbread, always had to be in the Temple. This bread was twelve loaves of bread set on a table as an offering to God. The number twelve reminded the people of the twelve tribes of Israel. Each sabbath, the priests ate the old loaves, and fresh loaves were brought in. King David once ate the bread when he was running away from Saul (1 Samuel 21:1–9). Read what Jesus had to say about that story in Matthew 12:1–4.

[n] A Heb measure of volume

> "O LORD, God of Israel, there is no God like you in heaven above or on earth beneath, keeping covenant and steadfast love for your servants who walk before you with all their heart." 1 Kings 8:23

cherubim. [7]For the cherubim spread out their wings over the place of the ark, so that the cherubim made a covering above the ark and its poles. [8]The poles were so long that the ends of the poles were seen from the holy place in front of the inner sanctuary; but they could not be seen from outside; they are there to this day. [9]There was nothing in the ark except the two tablets of stone that Moses had placed there at Hōʹreb, where the LORD made a covenant with the Israelites, when they came out of the land of Egypt. [10]And when the priests came out of the holy place, a cloud filled the house of the LORD, [11]so that the priests could not stand to minister because of the cloud; for the glory of the LORD filled the house of the LORD.

[12] Then Solomon said,
"The LORD has said that he would dwell in thick darkness.
[13] I have built you an exalted house, a place for you to dwell in forever."

Solomon's Speech

[14] Then the king turned around and blessed all the assembly of Israel, while all the assembly of Israel stood. [15]He said, "Blessed be the LORD, the God of Israel, who with his hand has fulfilled what he promised with his mouth to my father David, saying, [16]'Since the day that I brought my people Israel out of Egypt, I have not chosen a city from any of the tribes of Israel in which to build a house, that my name might be there; but I chose David to be over my people Israel.' [17]My father David had it in mind to build a house for the name of the LORD, the God of Israel. [18]But the LORD said to my father David, 'You did well to consider building a house for my name; [19]nevertheless you shall not build the house, but your son who shall be born to you shall build the house for my name.' [20]Now the LORD has upheld the promise that he made; for I have risen in the place of my father David; I sit on the throne of Israel, as the LORD promised, and have built the house for the name of the LORD, the God of Israel. [21]There I have provided a place for the ark, in which is the covenant of the LORD that he made with our ancestors when he brought them out of the land of Egypt."

Solomon's Prayer of Dedication

[22] Then Solomon stood before the altar of the LORD in the presence of all the assembly of Israel, and spread out his hands to heaven. [23]He said, "O LORD, God of Israel, there is no God like you in heaven above or on earth beneath, keeping covenant and steadfast love for your servants who walk before you with all their heart, [24]the covenant that you kept for your servant my father David as you declared to him; you promised with your mouth and have this day fulfilled with your hand. [25]Therefore, O LORD, God of Israel, keep for your servant my father David that which you promised him, saying, 'There shall never fail you a successor before me to sit on the throne of Israel, if only your children look to their way, to walk before me as you have walked before me.' [26]Therefore, O God of Israel, let your word be confirmed, which you promised to your servant my father David.

[27] "But will God indeed dwell on the earth? Even heaven and the highest heaven cannot contain you, much less this house that I have built! [28]Regard your servant's prayer and his plea, O LORD my God, heeding the cry and the prayer that your servant prays to you today; [29]that your eyes may be open night and day toward this house, the

place of which you said, 'My name shall be there,' that you may heed the prayer that your servant prays toward this place. [30]Hear the plea of your servant and of your people Israel when they pray toward this place; O hear in heaven your dwelling place; heed and forgive.

31 "If someone sins against a neighbor and is given an oath to swear, and comes and swears before your altar in this house, [32]then hear in heaven, and act, and judge your servants, condemning the guilty by bringing their conduct on their own head, and vindicating the righteous by rewarding them according to their righteousness.

33 "When your people Israel, having sinned against you, are defeated before an enemy but turn again to you, confess your name, pray and plead with you in this house, [34]then hear in heaven, forgive the sin of your people Israel, and bring them again to the land that you gave to their ancestors.

35 "When heaven is shut up and there is no rain because they have sinned against you, and then they pray toward this place, confess your name, and turn from their sin, because you punish[o] them, [36]then hear in heaven, and forgive the sin of your servants, your people Israel, when you teach them the good way in which they should walk; and grant rain on your land, which you have given to your people as an inheritance.

37 "If there is famine in the land, if there is plague, blight, mildew, locust, or caterpillar; if their enemy besieges them in any[p] of their cities; whatever plague, whatever sickness there is; [38]whatever prayer, whatever plea there is from any individual or from all your people Israel, all knowing the afflictions of their own hearts so that they stretch out their hands toward this house; [39]then hear in heaven your dwelling place, forgive, act, and render to all whose hearts you know—according to all their ways, for only you know what is in every human heart— [40]so that they may fear you all the days that they live in the land that you gave to our ancestors.

41 "Likewise when a foreigner, who is not of your people Israel, comes from a distant land because of your name [42]— for they shall hear of your great name, your mighty hand, and your outstretched arm—when a foreigner comes and prays toward this house, [43]then hear in heaven your dwelling place, and do according to all that the foreigner calls to you, so that all the peoples of the earth may know your name and fear you, as do your people Israel, and so that they may know that your name has been invoked on this house that I have built.

44 "If your people go out to battle against their enemy, by whatever way you shall send them, and they pray to the LORD toward the city that you have chosen and the house that I have built for your name, [45]then hear in heaven their prayer and their plea, and maintain their cause.

46 "If they sin against you—for there is no one who does not sin—and you are angry with them and give them to an enemy, so that they are carried away captive to the land of the enemy, far off or near; [47]yet if they come to their senses in the land to which they have been taken captive, and repent, and plead with you in the land of their captors, saying, 'We have sinned, and have done wrong; we have acted wickedly'; [48]if they repent with all their heart and soul in the land of their enemies, who took them captive, and pray to you toward their land, which you gave to their ancestors, the city that you have chosen, and the house that I have built for your name; [49]then hear in heaven your dwelling place their prayer and their plea, maintain their cause [50]and forgive your people who have sinned against you, and all their transgressions that they have committed against you; and grant them compassion

[o] Or when you answer   [p] Gk Syr: Heb in the land

in the sight of their captors, so that they may have compassion on them [51](for they are your people and heritage, which you brought out of Egypt, from the midst of the iron-smelter). [52]Let your eyes be open to the plea of your servant, and to the plea of your people Israel, listening to them whenever they call to you. [53]For you have separated them from among all the peoples of the earth, to be your heritage, just as you promised through Moses, your servant, when you brought our ancestors out of Egypt, O Lord GOD."

Solomon Blesses the Assembly

54 Now when Solomon finished offering all this prayer and this plea to the LORD, he arose from facing the altar of the LORD, where he had knelt with hands outstretched toward heaven; [55]he stood and blessed all the assembly of Israel with a loud voice:

56 "Blessed be the LORD, who has given rest to his people Israel according to all that he promised; not one word has failed of all his good promise, which he spoke through his servant Moses. [57]The LORD our God be with us, as he was with our ancestors; may he not leave us or abandon us, [58]but incline our hearts to him, to walk in all his ways, and to keep his commandments, his statutes, and his ordinances, which he commanded our ancestors. [59]Let these words of mine, with which I pleaded before the LORD, be near to the LORD our God day and night, and may he maintain the cause of his servant and the cause of his people Israel, as each day requires; [60]so that all the peoples of the earth may know that the LORD is God; there is no other. [61]Therefore devote yourselves completely to the LORD our God, walking in his statutes and keeping his commandments, as at this day."

Solomon Offers Sacrifices

62 Then the king, and all Israel with him, offered sacrifice before the LORD. [63]Solomon offered as sacrifices of well-being to the LORD twenty-two thousand oxen and one hundred twenty thousand sheep. So the king and all the people of Israel dedicated the house of the LORD. [64]The same day the king consecrated the middle of the court that was in front of the house of the LORD; for there he offered the burnt offerings and the grain offerings and the fat pieces of the sacrifices of well-being, because the bronze altar that was before the LORD was too small to receive the burnt offerings and the grain offerings and the fat pieces of the sacrifices of well-being.

65 So Solomon held the festival at that time, and all Israel with him—a great assembly, people from Lĕ′bō-hā′math to the Wadi of Egypt—before the LORD our God, seven days.[q] [66]On the eighth day he sent the people away; and they blessed the king, and went to their tents, joyful and in good spirits because of all the goodness that the LORD had shown to his servant David and to his people Israel.

God Appears Again to Solomon

9 When Solomon had finished building the house of the LORD and the king's house and all that Solomon desired to build, [2]the LORD appeared to Solomon a second time, as he had appeared to him at Gib′e·on. [3]The LORD said to him, "I have heard your prayer and your plea, which you made before me; I have consecrated this house that you have built, and put my name there forever; my eyes and my heart will be there for all time. [4]As for you, if you will walk before me, as David your father walked, with integrity of heart and uprightness, doing according to all that I have commanded you, and keeping my statutes and my ordinances, [5]then I will establish your royal throne over Israel forever, as I promised your father David, saying, 'There shall not fail you a successor on the throne of Israel.'

[q] Compare Gk: Heb *seven days and seven days, fourteen days*

6 "If you turn aside from following me, you or your children, and do not keep my commandments and my statutes that I have set before you, but go and serve other gods and worship them, [7]then I will cut Israel off from the land that I have given them; and the house that I have consecrated for my name I will cast out of my sight; and Israel will become a proverb and a taunt among all peoples. [8]This house will become a heap of ruins;[r] everyone passing by it will be astonished, and will hiss; and they will say, 'Why has the LORD done such a thing to this land and to this house?' [9]Then they will say, 'Because they have forsaken the LORD their God, who brought their ancestors out of the land of Egypt, and embraced other gods, worshiping them and serving them; therefore the LORD has brought this disaster upon them.' "

10 At the end of twenty years, in which Solomon had built the two houses, the house of the LORD and the king's house, [11]King Hiram of Tyre having supplied Solomon with cedar and cypress timber and gold, as much as he desired, King Solomon gave to Hiram twenty cities in the land of Galilee. [12]But when Hiram came from Tyre to see the cities that Solomon had given him, they did not please him. [13]Therefore he said, "What kind of cities are these that you have given me, my brother?" So they are called the land of Cā´bul[s] to this day. [14]But Hiram had sent to the king one hundred twenty talents of gold.

Other Acts of Solomon

15 This is the account of the forced labor that King Solomon conscripted to build the house of the LORD and his own house, the Mil´lo and the wall of Jerusalem, Hā´zor, Me·gid´do, Gē´zer [16](Pharaoh king of Egypt had gone up and captured Gē´zer and burned it down, had killed the Cā´naan·ites who lived in the city, and had given it as dowry to his daughter, Solomon's wife; [17]so Solomon rebuilt Gē´zer), Lower Beth-hō´ron, [18]Bā´al·ath, Tā´mar in the wilderness, within the land, [19]as well as all of Solomon's storage cities, the cities for his chariots, the cities for his cavalry, and whatever Solomon desired to build, in Jerusalem, in Lebanon, and in all the land of his dominion. [20]All the people who were left of the Am´o·rites, the Hit´tites, the Per´iz·zites, the Hī´vites, and the Jeb´u·sites, who were not of the people of Israel— [21]their descendants who were still left in the land, whom the Israelites were unable to destroy completely—these Solomon conscripted for slave labor, and so they are to this day. [22]But of the Israelites Solomon made no slaves; they were the soldiers, they were his officials, his commanders, his captains, and the commanders of his chariotry and cavalry.

23 These were the chief officers who were over Solomon's work: five hundred fifty, who had charge of the people who carried on the work.

24 But Pharaoh's daughter went up from the city of David to her own house that Solomon had built for her; then he built the Mil´lo.

25 Three times a year Solomon used to offer up burnt offerings and sacrifices of well-being on the altar that he built for the LORD, offering incense[t] before the LORD. So he completed the house.

Solomon's Commercial Activity

26 King Solomon built a fleet of ships at Ē´zi·on-gē´ber, which is near Ē´loth on the shore of the Red Sea,[u] in the land of Ē´dom. [27]Hiram sent his servants with the fleet, sailors who were familiar with the sea, together with the servants of Solomon. [28]They went to Ō´phir, and imported from there four hundred twenty talents of gold, which they delivered to King Solomon.

[r] Syr Old Latin: Heb *will become high* [s] Perhaps meaning *a land good for nothing* [t] Gk: Heb *offering incense with it that was* [u] Or *Sea of Reeds*

No one knows for sure where the Queen of Sheba ruled or why she came to visit Solomon. She tested him with riddles (hard questions) and found that he was very wise. Read Matthew 12:42 to see what Jesus had to say about her.

Visit of the Queen of Sheba

10 When the queen of Shē′ba heard of the fame of Solomon (fame due to[v] the name of the LORD), she came to test him with hard questions. ²She came to Jerusalem with a very great retinue, with camels bearing spices, and very much gold, and precious stones; and when she came to Solomon, she told him all that was on her mind. ³Solomon answered all her questions; there was nothing hidden from the king that he could not explain to her. ⁴When the queen of Shē′ba had observed all the wisdom of Solomon, the house that he had built, ⁵the food of his table, the seating of his officials, and the attendance of his servants, their clothing, his valets, and his burnt offerings that he offered at the house of the LORD, there was no more spirit in her.

6 So she said to the king, "The report was true that I heard in my own land of your accomplishments and of your wisdom, ⁷but I did not believe the reports until I came and my own eyes had seen it. Not even half had been told me; your wisdom and prosperity far surpass the report that I had heard. ⁸Happy are your wives![w] Happy are these your servants, who continually attend you and hear your wisdom! ⁹Blessed be the LORD your God, who has delighted in you and set you on the throne of Israel! Because the LORD loved Israel forever, he has made you king to execute justice and righteousness." ¹⁰Then she gave the king one hundred twenty talents of gold, a great

quantity of spices, and precious stones; never again did spices come in such quantity as that which the queen of Shē′ba gave to King Solomon.

11 Moreover, the fleet of Hiram, which carried gold from Ō′phir, brought from Ō′phir a great quantity of almug wood and precious stones. ¹²From the almug wood the king made supports for the house of the LORD, and for the king's house, lyres also and harps for the singers; no such almug wood has come or been seen to this day.

Almug was a special kind of sweet-scented wood used to make musical instruments such as lyres and harps. It was also used in the building of Solomon's Temple.

13 Meanwhile King Solomon gave to the queen of Shē′ba every desire that she expressed, as well as what he gave her out of Solomon's royal bounty. Then she returned to her own land, with her servants.

14 The weight of gold that came to Solomon in one year was six hundred sixty-six talents of gold, ¹⁵besides that which came from the traders and from the business of the merchants, and from all the kings of Arabia and the governors of the land. ¹⁶King Solomon made two hundred large shields of beaten gold; six hundred shekels of gold went into each large shield; ¹⁷He made three hundred shields of beaten gold; three minas of gold went into each shield; and the king put them in the House of the Forest of Lebanon. ¹⁸The king also made a great ivory throne, and overlaid it with the finest gold. ¹⁹The throne had six steps. The top of the throne was rounded in the back, and on each side of the seat were arm rests and two lions standing

v Meaning of Heb uncertain   w Gk Syr: Heb *men*

Ivory is a white bone-like substance that makes up the tusks of elephants and walruses! In Bible times, people carved ivory to make decorations for thrones and houses. Ivory was a sign of great wealth. Solomon's throne was covered with ivory and gold.

beside the arm rests, ²⁰while twelve lions were standing, one on each end of a step on the six steps. Nothing like it was ever made in any kingdom. ²¹All King Solomon's drinking vessels were of gold, and all the vessels of the House of the Forest of Lebanon were of pure gold; none were of silver—it was not considered as anything in the days of Solomon. ²²For the king had a fleet of ships of Tar′shish at sea with the fleet of Hiram. Once every three years the fleet of ships of Tar′shish used to come bringing gold, silver, ivory, apes, and peacocks.^x

23 Thus King Solomon excelled all the kings of the earth in riches and in wisdom. ²⁴The whole earth sought the presence of Solomon to hear his wisdom, which God had put into his mind. ²⁵Every one of them brought a present, objects of silver and gold, garments, weaponry, spices, horses, and

For a long time, the Israelites did not use the coast of the Mediterranean Sea as a place to buy and sell things. There were no good harbors on the coast of Palestine, and the Philistines controlled the coast for many years. But in the time of Solomon, the Israelites built and sailed many ships. Hiram, king of Tyre, sent sailors to train the men for Solomon's ships.

mules, so much year by year.

26 Solomon gathered together chariots and horses; he had fourteen hundred chariots and twelve thousand horses, which he stationed in the chariot cities and with the king in Jerusalem. ²⁷The king made silver as common in Jerusalem as stones, and he made cedars as numerous as the sycamores of the She·phe′lah. ²⁸Solomon's import of horses was from Egypt and Kū′e, and the king's traders received them from Kū′e at a price. ²⁹A chariot could be imported from Egypt for six hundred shekels of silver, and a horse for one hundred fifty; so through the king's traders they were exported to all the kings of the Hit′tītes and the kings of Ar′am.

Chariots were two-wheeled vehicles pulled by horses. People in Bible times, especially kings and officials, used chariots for travel. They also used chariots for war. Armies that used chariots had a great advantage over armies that did not. The hilly land of Judah kept the Judeans from making good use of chariots in war, but King Solomon had hundreds and built chariot cities like Megiddo.

Solomon's Errors

11 King Solomon loved many foreign women along with the daughter of Pharaoh: Mō′ab·īte, Am′mon·īte, Ē′dom·īte, Sī·dō′ni·an, and Hit′tīte women, ²from the nations concerning which the LORD had said to the Israelites, "You shall not enter into marriage with them, neither shall they with you; for they will surely incline your heart to follow their gods"; Solomon clung to these in love. ³Among his wives were seven hundred princesses and three hundred concubines; and his

^x Or *baboons*

wives turned away his heart. ⁴For when Solomon was old, his wives turned away his heart after other gods; and his heart was not true to the LORD his God, as was the heart of his father David. ⁵For Solomon followed As·tar′tē the goddess of the Sī·dō′ni·ans, and Mil′com the abomination of the Am′mon·ītes. ⁶So Solomon did what was evil in the sight of the LORD, and did not completely follow the LORD, as his father David had done. ⁷Then Solomon built a high place for Chē′mosh the abomination of Mō′ab, and for Mō′lech the abomination of the Am′mon·ītes, on the mountain east of Jerusalem. ⁸He did the same for all his foreign wives, who offered incense and sacrificed to their gods.

9 Then the LORD was angry with Solomon, because his heart had turned away from the LORD, the God of Israel, who had appeared to him twice, ¹⁰and had commanded him concerning this matter, that he should not follow other gods; but he did not observe what the LORD commanded. ¹¹Therefore the LORD said to Solomon, "Since this has been your mind and you have not kept my covenant and my statutes that I have commanded you, I will surely tear the kingdom from you and give it to your servant. ¹²Yet for the sake of your father David I will not do it in your lifetime; I will tear it out of the hand of your son. ¹³I will not, however, tear away the entire kingdom; I will give one tribe to your son, for the sake of my servant David and for the sake of Jerusalem, which I have chosen."

Adversaries of Solomon

14 Then the LORD raised up an adversary against Solomon, Hā′dad the Ē′dom·īte; he was of the royal house in Ē′dom. ¹⁵For when David was in Ē′dom, and Jō′ab the commander of the army went up to bury the dead, he killed every male in Ē′dom ¹⁶(for Jō′ab and all Israel remained there six months, until he had eliminated every male in Ē′dom);

¹⁷but Hā′dad fled to Egypt with some Ē′dom·ītes who were servants of his father. He was a young boy at that time. ¹⁸They set out from Mid′i·an and came to Par′an; they took people with them from Par′an and came to Egypt, to Pharaoh king of Egypt, who gave him a house, assigned him an allowance of food, and gave him land. ¹⁹Hā′dad found great favor in the sight of Pharaoh, so that he gave him his sister-in-law for a wife, the sister of Queen Tah′pe·nēs. ²⁰The sister of Tah′pe·nēs gave birth by him to his son Ge·nū′bath, whom Tah′pe·nēs weaned in Pharaoh's house; Ge·nū′bath was in Pharaoh's house among the children of Pharaoh. ²¹When Hā′dad heard in Egypt that David slept with his ancestors and that Jō′ab the commander of the army was dead, Hā′dad said to Pharaoh, "Let me depart, that I may go to my own country." ²²But Pharaoh said to him, "What do you lack with me that you now seek to go to your own country?" And he said, "No, do let me go."

23 God raised up another adversary against Solomon,ʸ Rē′zon son of E·lī′a·da,

After the death of Solomon (when the kingdom was split into two parts), Jeroboam was chosen as king by the ten northern tribes. He was the first king of the northern kingdom of Israel, ruling from about 922–901 BC. Jeroboam did not follow the ways of God. He broke God's rules for worship. He even had golden calves made so that the people could worship them. After his death, other kings of Israel who did not follow God were compared to Jeroboam, who caused Israel to sin.

ʸ Heb him

who had fled from his master, King Had·a·dē´zer of Zō´bah. [24]He gathered followers around him and became leader of a marauding band, after the slaughter by David; they went to Damascus, settled there, and made him king in Damascus. [25]He was an adversary of Israel all the days of Solomon, making trouble as Hā´dad did; he despised Israel and reigned over Ar´am.

Jeroboam's Rebellion

26 Jer·o·bō´am son of Nē´bat, an Ē´phra·im·īte of Zer´e·dah, a servant of Solomon, whose mother's name was Ze·rū´ah, a widow, rebelled against the king. [27]The following was the reason he rebelled against the king. Solomon built the Mil´lō, and closed up the gap in the wall[z] of the city of his father David. [28]The man Jer·o·bō´am was very able, and when Solomon saw that the young man was industrious he gave him charge over all the forced labor of the house of Joseph. [29]About that time, when Jer·o·bō´am was leaving Jerusalem, the prophet A·hī´jah the Shī´lo·nīte found him on the road. A·hī´jah had clothed himself with a new garment. The two of them were alone in the open country [30]when A·hī´jah laid hold of the new garment he was wearing and tore it into twelve pieces. [31]He then said to Jer·o·bō´am: Take for yourself ten pieces; for thus says the LORD, the God of Israel, "See, I am about to tear the kingdom from the hand of Solomon, and will give you ten tribes. [32]One tribe will

remain his, for the sake of my servant David and for the sake of Jerusalem, the city that I have chosen out of all the tribes of Israel. [33]This is because he has[a] forsaken me, worshiped As·tar´tē the goddess of the Sī·dō´ni·ans, Chē´mosh the god of Mō´ab, and Mil´com the god of the Am´mon·ītes, and has[z] not walked in my ways, doing what is right in my sight and keeping my statutes and my ordinances, as his father David did. [34]Nevertheless I will not take the whole kingdom away from him but will make him ruler all the days of his life, for the sake of my servant David whom I chose and who did keep my commandments and my statutes; [35]but I will take the kingdom away from his son and give it to you—that is, the ten tribes. [36]Yet to his son I will give one tribe, so that my servant David may always have a lamp before me in Jerusalem, the city where I have chosen to put my name. [37]I will take you, and you shall reign over all that your soul desires; you shall be king over Israel. [38]If you will listen to all that I command you, walk in my ways, and do what is right in my sight by keeping my statutes and my commandments, as David my servant did, I will be with you, and will build you an enduring house, as I built for David, and I will give Israel to you. [39]For this reason I will punish the descendants of David, but not forever." [40]Solomon sought therefore to kill Jer·o·bō´am; but Jer·o·bō´am promptly fled to Egypt, to King Shī´shak of Egypt, and remained in Egypt until the death of Solomon.

Death of Solomon

41 Now the rest of the acts of Solomon, all that he did as well as his wisdom, are they not written in the Book of the Acts of Solomon? [42]The time that Solomon reigned in Jerusalem over all Israel was forty years. [43]Solomon slept with his ancestors and was buried in the city of his father David; and his son Rē·ho·bō´am succeeded him.

Ahijah was a priest and prophet from the town of Shiloh. He told about one of the most important events in the history of Israel before it ever happened! When he met Jeroboam on the road outside Jerusalem, Ahijah told him that Israel would be divided into two separate kingdoms.

[z] Heb lacks *in the wall*   [a] Gk Syr Vg: Heb *they have*

The Northern Tribes Secede

12 Rē·ho·bō′am went to Shē′chem, for all Israel had come to Shē′chem to make him king. ²When Jer·o·bō′am son of Nē′bat heard of it (for he was still in Egypt, where he had fled from King Solomon), then Jer·o·bō′am returned from^b Egypt. ³And they sent and called him; and Jer·o·bō′am and all the assembly of Israel came and said to Rē·ho·bō′am, ⁴"Your father made our yoke heavy. Now therefore lighten the hard service of your father and his heavy yoke that he placed on us, and we will serve you." ⁵He said to them, "Go away for three days, then come again to me." So the people went away.

6 Then King Rē·ho·bō′am took counsel with the older men who had attended his father Solomon while he was still alive, saying, "How do you advise me to answer this people?" ⁷They answered him, "If you will be a servant to this people today and serve them, and speak good words to them when you answer them, then they will be your servants forever." ⁸But he disregarded the advice that the older men gave him, and consulted with the young men who had grown up with him and now attended him. ⁹He said to them, "What do you advise that we answer this people who have said to me, 'Lighten the yoke that your father put on us'?" ¹⁰The young men who had grown up with him said to him, "Thus you should say to this people who spoke to you, 'Your father made our yoke heavy, but you must lighten it for us'; thus you should say to them, 'My little finger is thicker than my father's loins. ¹¹Now, whereas my father laid on you a heavy yoke, I will add to your yoke. My father disciplined you with whips, but I will discipline you with scorpions.' "

12 So Jer·o·bō′am and all the people came to Rē·ho·bō′am the third day, as the king had said, "Come to me again the third day." ¹³The king answered the

Solomon made the people pay high taxes to pay for his rich lifestyle. His son Rehoboam became king after Solomon died. The people asked Rehoboam for lower taxes. They said that Solomon's taxes and forced labor were too much. Rehoboam asked the older men who had served his father what he should do, and they told him to give the people what they wanted. Rehoboam didn't like their answer so he asked the younger men. They told him to tell the people to be ready for even harsher treatment. This is why the kingdom split into two parts.

people harshly. He disregarded the advice that the older men had given him ¹⁴and spoke to them according to the advice of the young men, "My father made your yoke heavy, but I will add to your yoke; my father disciplined you with whips, but I will discipline you with scorpions." ¹⁵So the king did not listen to the people, because it was a turn of affairs brought about by the LORD that he might fulfill his word, which the LORD had spoken by A·hī′jah the Shī′lo·nīte to Jer·o·bō′am son of Nē′bat.

16 When all Israel saw that the king would not listen to them, the people answered the king,

"What share do we have in David?
　We have no inheritance in the son
　　of Jesse.
To your tents, O Israel!
　Look now to your own house,
　　O David."

So Israel went away to their tents. ¹⁷But Rē·ho·bō′am reigned over the Israelites who were living in the towns of Judah. ¹⁸When King Rē·ho·bō′am sent A·dor′am,

^b Gk Vg Compare 2 Chr 10.2: Heb *lived in*

who was taskmaster over the forced labor, all Israel stoned him to death. King Rē·ho·bŏ´am then hurriedly mounted his chariot to flee to Jerusalem. ¹⁹So Israel has been in rebellion against the house of David to this day.

First Dynasty: Jeroboam Reigns over Israel

20 When all Israel heard that Jer·o·bŏ´am had returned, they sent and called him to the assembly and made him king over all Israel. There was no one who followed the house of David, except the tribe of Judah alone.

21 When Rē·ho·bŏ´am came to Jerusalem, he assembled all the house of Judah and the tribe of Benjamin, one hundred eighty thousand chosen troops to fight against the house of Israel, to restore the kingdom to Rē·ho·bŏ´am son of Solomon. ²²But the word of God came to She·māi´ah the man of God: ²³Say to King Rē·ho·bŏ´am of Judah, son of Solomon, and to all the house of Judah and Benjamin, and to the rest of the people, ²⁴"Thus says the LORD, You shall not go up or fight against your kindred the people of Israel. Let everyone go home, for this thing is from me." So they heeded the word of the LORD and went home again, according to the word of the LORD.

Jeroboam's Golden Calves

25 Then Jer·o·bŏ´am built Shē´chem in the hill country of Ē´phra·im, and resided there; he went out from there and built Pe·nū´el. ²⁶Then Jer·o·bŏ´am said to himself, "Now the kingdom may well revert to the house of David. ²⁷If this people continues to go up to offer sacrifices in the house of the LORD at Jerusalem, the heart of this people will turn again to their master, King Rē·ho·bŏ´am of Judah; they will kill me and return to King Rē·ho·bŏ´am of Judah." ²⁸So the king took counsel, and made two calves of gold. He said to the people,ᶜ "You have gone up to Jerusalem long enough. Here

are your gods, O Israel, who brought you up out of the land of Egypt." ²⁹He set one in Beth´el, and the other he put in Dan. ³⁰And this thing became a sin, for the people went to worship before the one at Beth´el and before the other as far as Dan.ᵈ ³¹He also made housesᵉ on high places, and appointed priests from among all the people, who were not Lē´vites. ³²Jer·o·bŏ´am appointed a festival on the fifteenth day of the eighth month like the festival that was in Judah, and he offered sacrifices on the altar; so he did in Beth´el, sacrificing to the calves that he had made. And he placed in Beth´el the priests of the high places that he had made. ³³He went up to the altar that he had made in Beth´el on the fifteenth day in the eighth month, in the month that he alone had devised; he appointed a festival for the people of Israel, and he went up to the altar to offer incense.

A Man of God from Judah

13 While Jer·o·bŏ´am was standing by the altar to offer incense, a man of God came out of Judah by the word of the LORD to Beth´el ²and proclaimed against the altar by the word of the LORD, and said, "O altar, altar, thus says the LORD: 'A son shall be born to the house of David, Jo·sī´ah by name; and he shall sacrifice on you the priests of the high places who offer incense on you, and human bones shall be burned on you.'" ³He gave a sign the same day, saying, "This is the sign that the LORD has spoken: 'The altar shall be torn down, and the ashes that are on it shall be poured out.'" ⁴When the king heard what the man of God cried out against the altar at Beth´el, Jer·o·bŏ´am stretched out his hand from the altar, saying, "Seize him!" But the hand that he stretched out against him withered so that he could not draw it back to himself. ⁵The altar also was torn

ᶜ Gk: Heb to them   ᵈ Compare Gk: Heb went to
the one as far as Dan   ᵉ Gk Vg Compare 13.32:
Heb a house

down, and the ashes poured out from the altar, according to the sign that the man of God had given by the word of the LORD. ⁶The king said to the man of God, "Entreat now the favor of the LORD your God, and pray for me, so that my hand may be restored to me." So the man of God entreated the LORD; and the king's hand was restored to him, and became as it was before. ⁷Then the king said to the man of God, "Come home with me and dine, and I will give you a gift." ⁸But the man of God said to the king, "If you give me half your kingdom, I will not go in with you; nor will I eat food or drink water in this place. ⁹For thus I was commanded by the word of the LORD: You shall not eat food, or drink water, or return by the way that you came." ¹⁰So he went another way, and did not return by the way that he had come to Beth´el.

11 Now there lived an old prophet in Beth´el. One of his sons came and told him all that the man of God had done that day in Beth´el; the words also that he had spoken to the king, they told to their father. ¹²Their father said to them, "Which way did he go?" And his sons showed him the way that the man of God who came from Judah had gone. ¹³Then he said to his sons, "Saddle a donkey for me." So they saddled a donkey for him, and he mounted it. ¹⁴He went after the man of God, and found him sitting under an oak tree. He said to him, "Are you the man of God who came from Judah?" He answered, "I am." ¹⁵Then he said to him, "Come home with me and eat some food." ¹⁶But he said, "I cannot return with you, or go in with you; nor will I eat food or drink water with you in this place; ¹⁷for it was said to me by the word of the LORD: You shall not eat food or drink water there, or return by the way that you came." ¹⁸Then the other^f said to him, "I also am a prophet as you are, and an angel spoke to me by the word of the LORD: Bring him back with you into your house so

that he may eat food and drink water." But he was deceiving him. ¹⁹Then the man of God^f went back with him, and ate food and drank water in his house.

20 As they were sitting at the table, the word of the LORD came to the prophet who had brought him back; ²¹and he proclaimed to the man of God who came from Judah, "Thus says the LORD: Because you have disobeyed the word of the LORD, and have not kept the commandment that the LORD your God commanded you, ²²but have come back and have eaten food and drunk water in the place of which he said to you, 'Eat no food, and drink no water,' your body shall not come to your ancestral tomb." ²³After the man of God^f had eaten food and had drunk, they saddled for him a donkey belonging to the prophet who had brought him back. ²⁴Then as he went away, a lion met him on the road and killed him. His body was thrown in the road, and the donkey stood beside it; the lion also stood beside the body. ²⁵People passed by and saw the body thrown in the road, with the lion standing by the body. And they came and told it in the town where the old prophet lived.

26 When the prophet who had brought him back from the way heard of it, he said, "It is the man of God who disobeyed the word of the LORD; therefore the LORD has given him to the lion, which has torn him and killed him according to the word that the LORD spoke to him." ²⁷Then he said to his sons, "Saddle a donkey for me." So they saddled one, ²⁸and he went and found the body thrown in the road, with the donkey and the lion standing beside the body. The lion had not eaten the body or attacked the donkey. ²⁹The prophet took up the body of the man of God, laid it on the donkey, and brought it back to the city,^g to mourn and to bury him. ³⁰He laid the body in his own grave; and they mourned over him, saying, "Alas, my

---

^f Heb *he*   ^g Gk: Heb *he came to the town of the old prophet* brother!" [31]After he had buried him, he said to his sons, "When I die, bury me in the grave in which the man of God is buried; lay my bones beside his bones. [32]For the saying that he proclaimed by the word of the LORD against the altar in Beth´el, and against all the houses of the high places that are in the cities of Sa·mār´-i·a, shall surely come to pass."

33 Even after this event Jer·o·bō´am did not turn from his evil way, but made priests for the high places again from among all the people; any who wanted to be priests he consecrated for the high places. [34]This matter became sin to the house of Jer·o·bō´am, so as to cut it off and to destroy it from the face of the earth.

Judgment on the House of Jeroboam

14 At that time A·bī´jah son of Jer·o·bō´am fell sick. [2]Jer·o·bō´am said to his wife, "Go, disguise yourself, so that it will not be known that you are the wife of Jer·o·bō´am, and go to Shī´lōh; for the prophet A·hī´jah is there, who said of me that I should be king over this people. [3]Take with you ten loaves, some cakes, and a jar of honey, and go to him; he will tell you what shall happen to the child."

4 Jer·o·bō´am's wife did so; she set out and went to Shī´lōh, and came to the house of A·hī´jah. Now A·hī´jah could not see, for his eyes were dim because of his age. [5]But the LORD said to A·hī´jah, "The wife of Jer·o·bō´am is coming to inquire of you concerning her son; for he is sick. Thus and thus you shall say to her."

When she came, she pretended to be another woman. [6]But when A·hī´jah heard the sound of her feet, as she came in at the door, he said, "Come in, wife of Jer·o·bō´am; why do you pretend to be another? For I am charged with heavy tidings for you. [7]Go, tell Jer·o·bō´am, 'Thus says the LORD, the God of Israel: Because I exalted you from among the people, made you leader over my people Israel, [8]and tore the

kingdom away from the house of David to give it to you; yet you have not been like my servant David, who kept my commandments and followed me with all his heart, doing only that which was right in my sight, [9]but you have done evil above all those who were before you and have gone and made for yourself other gods, and cast images, provoking me to anger, and have thrust me behind your back; [10]therefore, I will bring evil upon the house of Jer·o·bō´am. I will cut off from Jer·o·bō´am every male, both bond and free in Israel, and will consume the house of Jer·o·bō´am, just as one burns up dung until it is all gone. [11]Anyone belonging to Jer·o·bō´am who dies in the city, the dogs shall eat; and anyone who dies in the open country, the birds of the air shall eat; for the LORD has spoken.' [12]Therefore set out, go to your house. When your feet enter the city, the child shall die. [13]All Israel shall mourn for him and bury him; for he alone of Jer·o·bō´am's family shall come to the grave, because in him there is found something pleasing to the LORD, the God of Israel, in the house of Jer·o·bō´am. [14]Moreover the LORD will raise up for himself a king over Israel, who shall cut off the house of Jer·o·bō´am today, even right now![h]

15 "The LORD will strike Israel, as a reed is shaken in the water; he will root up Israel out of this good land that he gave to their ancestors, and scatter them beyond the Euphrates, because they have made their sacred poles,[i] provoking the LORD to anger. [16]He will give Israel up because of the sins of Jer·o·bō´am, which he sinned and which he caused Israel to commit."

17 Then Jer·o·bō´am's wife got up and went away, and she came to Tir´zah. As she came to the threshold of the house, the child died. [18]All Israel buried him and mourned for him, according to the word of the LORD, which he spoke by his servant the prophet A·hī´jah.

[h] Meaning of Heb uncertain   [i] Heb Asherim

Death of Jeroboam

19 Now the rest of the acts of Jer·o·bō´am, how he warred and how he reigned, are written in the Book of the Annals of the Kings of Israel. [20]The time that Jer·o·bō´am reigned was twenty-two years; then he slept with his ancestors, and his son Nā´dab succeeded him.

Rehoboam Reigns over Judah

21 Now Rē·ho·bō´am son of Solomon reigned in Judah. Rē·ho·bō´am was forty-one years old when he began to reign, and he reigned seventeen years in Jerusalem, the city that the LORD had chosen out of all the tribes of Israel, to put his name there. His mother's name was Nā´a·mah the Am´mon·īte. [22]Judah did what was evil in the sight of the LORD; they provoked him to jealousy with their sins that they committed, more than all that their ancestors had done. [23]For they also built for themselves high places, pillars, and sacred poles[j] on every high hill and under every green tree; [24]there were also male temple prostitutes in the land. They committed all the abominations of the nations that the LORD drove out before the people of Israel.

25 In the fifth year of King Rē·ho·bō´am, King Shī´shak of Egypt came up against Jerusalem; [26]he took away the treasures of the house of the LORD and the treasures of the king's house; he took everything. He also took away all the shields of gold that Solomon had made; [27]so King Rē·ho·bō´am made shields of bronze instead, and committed them to the hands of the officers of the guard, who kept the door of the king's house. [28]As often as the king went into the house of the LORD, the guard carried them and brought them back to the guardroom.

29 Now the rest of the acts of Rē·ho·bō´am, and all that he did, are they not written in the Book of the Annals of the Kings of Judah? [30]There was war between Rē·ho·bō´am and Jer·o·bō´am continually. [31] Rē·ho·bō´am slept with his ancestors and was buried with his ances-

tors in the city of David. His mother's name was Nā´a·mah the Am´mon·īte. His son A·bī´jam succeeded him.

Abijam Reigns over Judah: Idolatry and War

15 Now in the eighteenth year of King Jer·o·bō´am son of Nē´bat, A·bī´jam began to reign over Judah. [2]He reigned for three years in Jerusalem. His mother's name was Mā´a·cah daughter of A·bish´a·lom. [3]He committed all the sins that his father did before him; his heart was not true to the LORD his God, like the heart of his father David. [4]Nevertheless for David's sake the LORD his God gave him a lamp in Jerusalem, setting up his son after him, and establishing Jerusalem; [5]because David did what was right in the sight of the LORD, and did not turn aside from anything that he commanded him all the days of his life, except in the matter of Ū·rī´ah the Hit´tīte. [6]The war begun between Rē·ho·bō´am and Jer·o·bō´am continued all the days of his life. [7]The rest of the acts of A·bī´jam, and all that he did, are they not written in the Book of the Annals of the Kings of Judah? There was war between A·bī´jam and Jer·o·bō´am. [8] A·bī´jam slept with his ancestors, and they buried him in the city of David. Then his son Asa succeeded him.

Asa Reigns over Judah

9 In the twentieth year of King Jer·o·bō´am of Israel, Asa began to reign over Judah; [10]he reigned forty-one years

Asa ruled as king of Judah from about 913–873 BC. Asa was faithful to God and tried to do what God wanted him to do. Asa took idols out of the land and again made the worship of God very important to the Judeans.

[j] Heb *Asherim*

in Jerusalem. His mother's name was Māʹ-a·cah daughter of A·bishʹa·lom. [11]Asa did what was right in the sight of the LORD, as his father David had done. [12]He put away the male temple prostitutes out of the land, and removed all the idols that his ancestors had made. [13]He also removed his mother Māʹa·cah from being queen mother, because she had made an abominable image for A·sheʹrah; Asa cut down her image and burned it at the Wadi Kidʹron. [14]But the high places were not taken away. Nevertheless the heart of Asa was true to the LORD all his days. [15]He brought into the house of the LORD the votive gifts of his father and his own votive gifts—silver, gold, and utensils.

Baasha ruled as king of the northern kingdom of Israel from about 900–877 BC. He became king after Nadab, whom he murdered during a battle against the Philistines.

Alliance with Aram against Israel

16 There was war between Asa and King Bāʹa·sha of Israel all their days. [17]King Bāʹa·sha of Israel went up against Judah, and built Rāʹmah, to prevent anyone from going out or coming in to King Asa of Judah. [18]Then Asa took all the silver and the gold that were left in the treasures of the house of the LORD and the treasures of the king's house, and gave them into the hands of his servants. King Asa sent them to King Ben-haʹdad son of Tab·rimʹmon son of Hēʹzi·on of Arʹam, who resided in Damascus, saying, [19]"Let there be an alliance between me and you, like that between my father and your father: I am sending you a present of silver and gold; go, break your alliance with King Bāʹa·sha of Israel, so that he may withdraw from me." [20]Ben-haʹdad listened to King Asa, and sent the com-

manders of his armies against the cities of Israel. He conquered Iʹjon, Dan, Āʹbel-beth-māʹa·cah, and all Chinʹne·roth, with all the land of Naphʹta·li. [21]When Bāʹa·sha heard of it, he stopped building Rāʹmah and lived in Tirʹzah. [22]Then King Asa made a proclamation to all Judah, none was exempt: they carried away the stones of Rāʹmah and its timber, with which Bāʹa·sha had been building; with them King Asa built Geʹba of Benjamin and Mizʹpah. [23]Now the rest of all the acts of Asa, all his power, all that he did, and the cities that he built, are they not written in the Book of the Annals of the Kings of Judah? But in his old age he was diseased in his feet. [24]Then Asa slept with his ancestors, and was buried with his ancestors in the city of his father David; his son Je·hoshʹ-a·phat succeeded him.

Nadab Reigns over Israel

25 Nāʹdab son of Jer·o·bōʹam began to reign over Israel in the second year of King Asa of Judah; he reigned over Israel two years. [26]He did what was evil in the sight of the LORD, walking in the way of his ancestor and in the sin that he caused Israel to commit.

27 Bāʹa·sha son of A·hīʹjah, of the house of Isʹsa·char, conspired against him; and Bāʹa·sha struck him down at Gibʹbe·thon, which belonged to the Phi·lisʹtines; for Nāʹdab and all Israel were laying siege to Gibʹbe·thon. [28]So Bāʹa·sha killed Nāʹdab[k] in the third year of King Asa of Judah, and succeeded him. [29]As soon as he was king, he killed all the house of Jer·o·bōʹam; he left to the house of Jer·o·bōʹam not one that breathed, until he had destroyed it, according to the word of the LORD that he spoke by his servant A·hīʹjah the Shīʹ-lo·nīte— [30]because of the sins of Jer·o·bō ʹam that he committed and that he caused Israel to commit, and because of the anger to which he provoked the LORD, the God of Israel.

[k] Heb him

31 Now the rest of the acts of Nā´dab, and all that he did, are they not written in the Book of the Annals of the Kings of Israel? ³²There was war between Asa and King Bā´a·sha of Israel all their days.

Second Dynasty: Baasha Reigns over Israel

33 In the third year of King Asa of Judah, Bā´a·sha son of A·hī´jah began to reign over all Israel at Tir´zah; he reigned twenty-four years. ³⁴He did what was evil in the sight of the LORD, walking in the way of Jer·o·bō´am and in the sin that he caused Israel to commit.

16 The word of the LORD came to Jē´hū son of Ha·nā´nī against Bā´a·sha, saying, ²"Since I exalted you out of the dust and made you leader over my people Israel, and you have walked in the way of Jer·o·bō´am, and have caused my people Israel to sin, provoking me to anger with their sins, ³therefore, I will consume Bā´a·sha and his house, and I will make your house like the house of Jer·o·bō´am son of Nē´bat. ⁴Anyone belonging to Bā´a·sha who dies in the city the dogs shall eat; and anyone of his who dies in the field the birds of the air shall eat."

5 Now the rest of the acts of Bā´a·sha, what he did, and his power, are they not written in the Book of the Annals of the Kings of Israel? ⁶Bā´a·sha slept with his ancestors, and was buried at Tir´zah; and his son Ē´lah succeeded him. ⁷Moreover the word of the LORD came by the prophet Jē´hū son of Ha·nā´nī against Bā´a·sha and his house, both because of all the evil that he did in the sight of the LORD, provoking him to anger with the work of his hands, in being like the house of Jer·o·bō´am, and also because he destroyed it.

Elah Reigns over Israel

8 In the twenty-sixth year of King Asa of Judah, Ē´lah son of Bā´a·sha began to reign over Israel in Tir´zah; he reigned two years. ⁹But his servant Zim´rī, commander of half his chariots, conspired against him. When he was at Tir´zah, drinking himself drunk in the house of Ar´za, who was in charge of the palace at Tir´zah, ¹⁰Zim´rī came in and struck him down and killed him, in the twenty-seventh year of King Asa of Judah, and succeeded him.

11 When he began to reign, as soon as he had seated himself on his throne, he killed all the house of Bā´a·sha; he did not leave him a single male of his kindred or his friends. ¹²Thus Zim´rī destroyed all the house of Bā´a·sha, according to the word of the LORD, which he spoke against Bā´a·sha by the prophet Jē´hū— ¹³because of all the sins of Bā´a·sha and the sins of his son Ē´lah that they committed, and that they caused Israel to commit, provoking the LORD God of Israel to anger with their idols. ¹⁴Now the rest of the acts of Ē´lah, and all that he did, are they not written in the Book of the Annals of the Kings of Israel?

Third Dynasty: Zimri Reigns over Israel

15 In the twenty-seventh year of King Asa of Judah, Zim´rī reigned seven days in Tir´zah. Now the troops were encamped against Gib´be·thon, which belonged to the Phi·lis´tines, ¹⁶and the troops who were encamped heard it said, "Zim´rī has conspired, and he has killed the king"; therefore all Israel made Om´rī, the commander of the army, king over Israel that day in the camp. ¹⁷So Om´rī went up from Gib´be·thon, and all Israel with him, and they besieged Tir´zah. ¹⁸When Zim´rī saw that the city was taken, he went into the citadel of the king's house; he burned down the king's house over himself with fire, and died— ¹⁹because of the sins that he committed, doing evil in the sight of the LORD, walking in the way of Jer·o·bō´am, and for the sin that he committed, causing Israel to sin. ²⁰Now the rest of the acts of Zim´rī, and the conspiracy that he made, are they not written in the Book of the Annals of the Kings of Israel?

Fourth Dynasty: Omri Reigns over Israel

21 Then the people of Israel were divided into two parts; half of the people followed Tib´nī son of Gī´nath, to make him king, and half followed Om´rī. ²²But the people who followed Om´rī overcame the people who followed Tib´nī son of Gī´nath; so Tib´nī died, and Om´rī became king. ²³In the thirty-first year of King Asa of Judah, Om´rī began to reign over Israel; he reigned for twelve years, six of them in Tir´zah.

Samaria the New Capital

24 He bought the hill of Sa·mār´i·a from Shē´mer for two talents of silver; he fortified the hill, and called the city that he built, Sa·mār´i·a, after the name of Shē´mer, the owner of the hill.

25 Om´rī did what was evil in the sight of the LORD; he did more evil than all who were before him. ²⁶For he walked in all the way of Jer·o·bō´am son of Nē´bat, and in the sins that he caused Israel to commit, provoking the LORD, the God of Israel, to anger by their idols. ²⁷Now the rest of the acts of Om´rī that he did, and the power that he showed, are they not written in the Book of the Annals of the Kings of Israel? ²⁸Om´rī slept with his ancestors, and was buried in Sa·mār´i·a; his son Ā´hab succeeded him.

Ahab Reigns over Israel

29 In the thirty-eighth year of King Asa of Judah, Ā´hab son of Om´rī began

Ahab reigned over Israel about 869–850 BC. During most of his reign, he was at war with the Assyrians. Ahab built a temple and an altar for Baal and worshiped this false god. The prophet Elijah told Ahab that he was wrong to worship Baal. Eventually, Ahab was wounded in a battle and died in his capital city, Samaria.

to reign over Israel; Ā´hab son of Om´rī reigned over Israel in Sa·mār´i·a twenty-two years. ³⁰Ā´hab son of Om´rī did evil in the sight of the LORD more than all who were before him.

Jezebel was a princess from Phoenicia who became the wife of King Ahab. Jezebel was a strong, clever woman who led Ahab and the people of Israel to turn away from God and worship Baal. The prophet Elijah spoke out against Jezebel. Jezebel scared Elijah away, but he won a great victory over the prophets of Baal.

Ahab Marries Jezebel and Worships Baal

31 And as if it had been a light thing for him to walk in the sins of Jer·o·bō´am son of Nē´bat, he took as his wife Jez´e·bel daughter of King Eth·bā´al of the Sī·dō´ni·ans, and went and served Bā´al, and worshiped him. ³²He erected an altar for Bā´al in the house of Bā´al, which he built in Sa·mār´i·a. ³³Ā´hab also made a sacred pole.[l] Ā´hab did more to provoke the anger of the LORD, the God of Israel, than had all the kings of Israel who were before him. ³⁴In his days Hī´el of Beth´el built Jericho; he laid its foundation at the cost of A·bī´ram his firstborn, and set up its gates at the cost of his youngest son Sē´gub, according to the word of the LORD, which he spoke by Joshua son of Nun.

Elijah Predicts a Drought

17 Now E·lī´jah the Tish´bīte, of Tish´bē[m] in Gil´e·ad, said to Ā´hab, "As the LORD the God of Israel lives, before whom I stand, there shall be neither dew nor rain these years, except by my word." ²The word of the LORD came to him, saying, ³"Go from here and

[l] Heb *Asherah*   [m] Gk: Heb *of the settlers*

Ravens are large, purple-black birds that travel in flocks. Ravens attack small, helpless animals, and they also eat dead flesh. For this reason, the Hebrew people thought of ravens as unclean and did not use them for food. God used a raven to feed Elijah when he was hiding from Jezebel.

turn eastward, and hide yourself by the Wadi Chĕ´rith, which is east of the Jordan. ⁴You shall drink from the wadi, and I have commanded the ravens to feed you there." ⁵So he went and did according to the word of the LORD; he went and lived by the Wadi Chĕ´rith, which is east of the Jordan. ⁶The ravens brought him bread and meat in the morning, and bread and meat in the evening; and he drank from the wadi. ⁷But after a while the wadi dried up, because there was no rain in the land.

The Widow of Zarephath

8 Then the word of the LORD came to him, saying, ⁹"Go now to Zar´e·phath, which belongs to Sī´don, and live there; for I have commanded a widow there to feed you." ¹⁰So he set out and went to Zar´e·phath. When he came to the gate of the town, a widow was there gathering sticks; he called to her and said, "Bring me a little water in a vessel, so that I may drink." ¹¹As she was going to bring it, he called to her and said, "Bring me a morsel of bread in your hand." ¹²But she said, "As the LORD your God lives, I have nothing baked, only a handful of meal in a jar, and a little oil in a jug; I am now gathering a couple of sticks, so that I may go home and prepare it for myself and my son, that we may eat it, and die." ¹³E·lī´jah said to her, "Do not be afraid; go and do as you have said; but first make me a little cake of it and bring it to me, and afterwards make

something for yourself and your son. ¹⁴For thus says the LORD the God of Israel: The jar of meal will not be emptied and the jug of oil will not fail until the day that the LORD sends rain on the earth." ¹⁵She went and did as E·lī´jah said, so that she as well as he and her household ate for many days. ¹⁶The jar of meal was not emptied, neither did the jug of oil fail, according to the word of the LORD that he spoke by E·lī´jah.

Elijah Revives the Widow's Son

17 After this the son of the woman, the mistress of the house, became ill; his illness was so severe that there was no breath left in him. ¹⁸She then said to E·lī´jah, "What have you against me, O man of God? You have come to me to bring my sin to remembrance, and to cause the death of my son!" ¹⁹But he said to her, "Give me your son." He took him from her bosom, carried him up into the upper chamber where he was lodging, and laid him on his own bed. ²⁰He cried out to the LORD, "O LORD my God, have you brought calamity even upon the widow with whom I am staying, by killing her son?" ²¹Then he stretched

In Bible times, widows were often very poor and had to depend on the care of others. But God told a widow to feed Elijah and sent him to her house. Even though she thought she had nothing to give, she did what God asked. God took care of the widow, and she had enough to feed herself, her son, and Elijah.

Ask your parents if they can remember a time when they got help from someone they never thought would be able to help. Write a family prayer giving thanks for God's care and compassion and for God's workers here on earth who help to carry them out.

himself upon the child three times, and cried out to the LORD, "O LORD my God, let this child's life come into him again." ²²The LORD listened to the voice of E·lī´-jah; the life of the child came into him again, and he revived. ²³E·lī´jah took the child, brought him down from the upper chamber into the house, and gave him to his mother; then E·lī´jah said, "See, your son is alive." ²⁴So the woman said to E·lī´jah, "Now I know that you are a man of God, and that the word of the LORD in your mouth is truth."

Elijah was a prophet in the northern kingdom of Israel in the ninth century BC. Elijah opposed King Ahab and his wife Jezebel because they worshiped Baal and wanted Israel to worship Baal too. Elijah performed many miracles. He once challenged 450 prophets of Baal to a great contest. The Baal prophets prepared a sacrifice, but their god did not respond. Elijah also prepared a sacrifice, and the one true God responded! Read the exciting story of that contest in chapter 18:20–31.

Elijah's Message to Ahab

18 After many days the word of the LORD came to E·lī´jah, in the third year of the drought,[n] saying, "Go, present yourself to Ā´hab; I will send rain on the earth." ²So E·lī´jah went to present himself to Ā´hab. The famine was severe in Sa·mār´i·a. ³Ā´hab summoned Ō·ba·dī´ah, who was in charge of the palace. (Now Ō·ba·dī´ah revered the LORD greatly; ⁴when Jez´e·bel was killing off the prophets of the LORD, Ō·ba·dī´ah took a hundred prophets, hid them fifty to a cave, and provided them with bread and water.) ⁵Then Ā´hab said to Ō·ba·dī´-ah, "Go through the land to all the springs of water and to all the wadis; perhaps we may find grass to keep the

horses and mules alive, and not lose some of the animals." ⁶So they divided the land between them to pass through it; Ā´hab went in one direction by himself, and Ō·ba·dī´ah went in another direction by himself.

7 As Ō·ba·dī´ah was on the way, E·lī´jah met him; Ō·ba·dī´ah recognized him, fell on his face, and said, "Is it you, my lord E·lī´jah?" ⁸He answered him, "It is I. Go, tell your lord that E·lī´jah is here." ⁹And he said, "How have I sinned, that you would hand your servant over to Ā´hab, to kill me? ¹⁰As the LORD your God lives, there is no nation or kingdom to which my lord has not sent to seek you; and when they would say, 'He is not here,' he would require an oath of the kingdom or nation, that they had not found you. ¹¹But now you say, 'Go, tell your lord that E·lī´jah is here.' ¹²As soon as I have gone from you, the spirit of the LORD will carry you I know not where; so, when I come and tell Ā´hab and he cannot find you, he will kill me, although I your servant have revered the LORD from my youth. ¹³Has it not been told my lord what I did when Jez´e·bel killed the prophets of the LORD, how I hid a hundred of the LORD's prophets fifty to a cave, and provided them with bread and water? ¹⁴Yet now you say, 'Go, tell your lord that E·lī´jah is here'; he will surely kill me." ¹⁵E·lī´jah said, "As the LORD of hosts lives, before whom I stand, I will surely show myself to him today." ¹⁶So Ō·ba·dī´ah went to meet Ā´hab, and told him; and Ā´hab went to meet E·lī´jah.

17 When Ā´hab saw E·lī´jah, Ā´hab said to him, "Is it you, you troubler of Israel?" ¹⁸He answered, "I have not troubled Israel; but you have, and your father's house, because you have forsaken the commandments of the LORD and followed the Bā´als. ¹⁹Now therefore have all Israel assemble for me at Mount Car´mel, with the four hundred fifty

[n] Heb lacks *of the drought*

prophets of Bāʹal and the four hundred prophets of A·sheʹrah, who eat at Jezʹe·belʹs table."

Elijah's Triumph over the Priests of Baal

20 So Āʹhab sent to all the Israelites, and assembled the prophets at Mount Carʹmel. 21E·līʹjah then came near to all the people, and said, "How long will you go limping with two different opinions? If the LORD is God, follow him; but if Bāʹal, then follow him." The people did not answer him a word. 22Then E·līʹjah said to the people, "I, even I only, am left a prophet of the LORD; but Bāʹalʹs prophets number four hundred fifty. 23Let two bulls be given to us; let them choose one bull for themselves, cut it in pieces, and lay it on the wood, but put no fire to it; I will prepare the other bull and lay it on the wood, but put no fire to it. 24Then you call on the name of your god and I will call on the name of the LORD; the god who answers by fire is indeed God." All the people answered, "Well spoken!" 25Then E·līʹjah said to the prophets of Bāʹal, "Choose for yourselves one bull and prepare it first, for you are many; then call on the name of your god, but put no fire to it." 26So they took the bull that was given them, prepared it, and called on the name of Bāʹal from morning until noon, crying, "O Bāʹal, answer us!" But there was no voice, and no answer. They limped about the altar that they had made. 27At noon E·līʹjah mocked them, saying, "Cry aloud! Surely he is a god; either he is meditating, or he has wandered away, or he is on a journey, or perhaps he is asleep and must be awakened." 28Then they cried aloud and, as was their custom, they cut themselves with swords and lances until the blood gushed out over them. 29As midday passed, they raved on until the time of the offering of the oblation, but there was no voice, no answer, and no response.

30 Then E·līʹjah said to all the people, "Come closer to me"; and all the

people came closer to him. First he repaired the altar of the LORD that had been thrown down; 31 E·līʹjah took twelve stones, according to the number of the tribes of the sons of Jacob, to whom the word of the LORD came, saying, "Israel shall be your name"; 32with the stones he built an altar in the name of the LORD. Then he made a trench around the altar, large enough to contain two measures of seed. 33Next he put the wood in order, cut the bull in pieces, and laid it on the wood. He said, "Fill four jars with water and pour it on the burnt offering and on the wood." 34Then he said, "Do it a second time"; and they did it a second time. Again he said, "Do it a third time"; and they did it a third time, 35so that the water ran all around the altar, and filled the trench also with water.

36 At the time of the offering of the oblation, the prophet E·līʹjah came near and said, "O LORD, God of Abraham, Isaac, and Israel, let it be known this day that you are God in Israel, that I am your servant, and that I have done all these things at your bidding. 37Answer me, O LORD, answer me, so that this people may know that you, O LORD, are God, and that you have turned their hearts back." 38Then the fire of the LORD fell and consumed the burnt offering, the wood, the stones, and the dust, and even licked up the water that was in the trench. 39When all the people saw it, they fell on their faces and said, "The LORD indeed is God; the LORD indeed is God." 40E·līʹjah said to them, "Seize the prophets of Bāʹal; do not let one of them escape." Then they seized them; and E·līʹjah brought them down to the Wadi Kīʹshon, and killed them there.

The Drought Ends

41 E·līʹjah said to Āʹhab, "Go up, eat and drink; for there is a sound of rushing rain." 42So Āʹhab went up to eat and to drink. E·līʹjah went up to the top of Carʹmel; there he bowed himself down

upon the earth and put his face between his knees. ⁴³He said to his servant, "Go up now, look toward the sea." He went up and looked, and said, "There is nothing." Then he said, "Go again seven times." ⁴⁴At the seventh time he said, "Look, a little cloud no bigger than a person's hand is rising out of the sea." Then he said, "Go say to Ā´hab, 'Harness your chariot and go down before the rain stops you.' " ⁴⁵In a little while the heavens grew black with clouds and wind; there was a heavy rain. Ā´hab rode off and went to Jez´rē·el. ⁴⁶But the hand of the LORD was on E·lī´jah; he girded up his loins and ran in front of Ā´hab to the entrance of Jez´rē·el.

A girdle was a piece of clothing like a belt or a sash. People used girdles to hold in their long, flowing robes. They also used girdles to carry money pouches and weapons. Messengers and travelers who wanted to move more easily would bring their robe through their legs toward the front and tuck it into their girdle. This was called "girding up the loins."

Elijah Flees from Jezebel

19 Ā´hab told Jez´e·bel all that E·lī´jah had done, and how he had killed all the prophets with the sword. ²Then Jez´e·bel sent a messenger to E·lī´jah, saying, "So may the gods do to me, and more also, if I do not make your life like the life of one of them by this time tomorrow." ³Then he was afraid; he got up and fled for his life, and came to Bē´er-shē´ba, which belongs to Judah; he left his servant there.

4 But he himself went a day's journey into the wilderness, and came and sat down under a solitary broom tree. He asked that he might die: "It is enough; now, O LORD, take away my life, for I am no better than my ancestors." ⁵Then he lay down under the broom tree and fell asleep. Suddenly an angel touched him and said to him, "Get up and eat." ⁶He looked, and there at his head was a cake baked on hot stones, and a jar of water. He ate and drank, and lay down again. ⁷The angel of the LORD came a second time, touched him, and said, "Get up and eat, otherwise the journey will be too much for you." ⁸He got up, and ate and drank; then he went in the strength of that food forty days and forty nights to Hō´reb the mount of God. ⁹At that place he came to a cave, and spent the night there.

Then the word of the LORD came to him, saying, "What are you doing here, E·lī´jah?" ¹⁰He answered, "I have been very zealous for the LORD, the God of hosts; for the Israelites have forsaken your covenant, thrown down your altars, and killed your prophets with the sword. I alone am left, and they are seeking my life, to take it away."

Elijah Meets God at Horeb

11 He said, "Go out and stand on the mountain before the LORD, for the LORD is about to pass by." Now there was a great wind, so strong that it was splitting mountains and breaking rocks in pieces before the LORD, but the LORD was not in the wind; and after the wind an earthquake, but the LORD was not in the earthquake; ¹²and after the earthquake a fire, but the LORD was not in the fire; and after

Elijah felt very low. He had tried to live life as God wanted him to and to lead God's people back to true worship, but it seemed everyone was against him. He cried out to God, and God did a wonderful thing. On Mt. Horab, God revealed himself to Elijah—not in a loud way, but with silence. God let Elijah understand that God is in all things and that God is always with us.

the fire a sound of sheer silence. ¹³When E·lī′jah heard it, he wrapped his face in his mantle and went out and stood at the entrance of the cave. Then there came a voice to him that said, "What are you doing here, E·lī′jah?" ¹⁴He answered, "I have been very zealous for the LORD, the God of hosts; for the Israelites have forsaken your covenant, thrown down your altars, and killed your prophets with the sword. I alone am left, and they are seeking my life, to take it away." ¹⁵Then the LORD said to him, "Go, return on your way to the wilderness of Damascus; when you arrive, you shall anoint Haz′a·el as king over Ar′am. ¹⁶Also you shall anoint Jē′hū son of Nim′shī as king over Israel; and you shall anoint E·lī′sha son of Shā′-phat of Ā′bel-me·hō′lah as prophet in your place. ¹⁷Whoever escapes from the sword of Haz′a·el, Jē′hū shall kill; and whoever escapes from the sword of Jē′hū, E·lī′sha shall kill. ¹⁸Yet I will leave seven thousand in Israel, all the knees that have not bowed to Bā′al, and every mouth that has not kissed him."

Elisha Becomes Elijah's Disciple

19 So he set out from there, and found E·lī′sha son of Shā′phat, who was plowing. There were twelve yoke of oxen ahead of him, and he was with the twelfth. E·lī′jah passed by him and threw his mantle over him. ²⁰He left the oxen, ran after E·lī′jah, and said, "Let me kiss my father and my mother, and then I will follow you." Then Elī′jah^o said to him, "Go back again; for what have I done to you?" ²¹He returned from following him, took the yoke of oxen, and slaughtered them; using the equipment from the oxen, he boiled their flesh, and gave it to the people, and they ate. Then he set out and followed E·lī′jah, and became his servant.

Ahab's Wars with the Arameans

20 King Ben-hā′dad of Ar′am gathered all his army together; thirty-two kings were with him, along with horses and chariots. He marched against Sa·mā′r·ia, laid siege to it, and attacked it. ²Then he sent messengers into the city to King Ā′hab of Israel, and said to him: "Thus says Ben-hā′dad: ³Your silver and gold are mine; your fairest wives and children also are mine." ⁴The king of Israel answered, "As you say, my lord, O king, I am yours, and all that I have." ⁵The messengers came again and said: "Thus says Ben-hā′dad: I sent to you, saying, 'Deliver to me your silver and gold, your wives and children'; ⁶nevertheless I will send my servants to you tomorrow about this time, and they shall search your house and the houses of your servants, and lay hands on whatever pleases them,^p and take it away."

7 Then the king of Israel called all the elders of the land, and said, "Look now! See how this man is seeking trouble; for he sent to me for my wives, my children, my silver, and my gold; and I did not refuse him." ⁸Then all the elders and all the people said to him, "Do not listen or consent." ⁹So he said to the messengers of Ben-hā′dad, "Tell my lord the king: All that you first demanded of your servant I will do; but this thing I cannot do." The messengers left and brought him word again. ¹⁰Ben-hā′dad sent to him and said, "The gods do so to me, and more also, if the dust of Sa·mā′r·i·a will provide a handful for each of the people who follow me." ¹¹The king of Israel answered, "Tell him: One who puts on armor should not brag like one who takes it off." ¹²When Ben-hā′dad heard this message—now he had been drinking with the kings in the booths—he said to his men, "Take your positions!" And they took their positions against the city.

Prophetic Opposition to Ahab

13 Then a certain prophet came up to King Ā′hab of Israel and said, "Thus says the LORD, Have you seen all this great multitude? Look, I will give it into

^o Heb *he*   ^p Gk Syr Vg: Heb *you*

your hand today; and you shall know that I am the LORD." ¹⁴A̅hab said, "By whom?" He said, "Thus says the LORD, By the young men who serve the district governors." Then he said, "Who shall begin the battle?" He answered, "You." ¹⁵Then he mustered the young men who served the district governors, two hundred thirty-two; after them he mustered all the people of Israel, seven thousand.

16 They went out at noon, while Ben-ha̅dad was drinking himself drunk in the booths, he and the thirty-two kings allied with him. ¹⁷The young men who served the district governors went out first. Ben-ha̅dad had sent out scouts,�q and they reported to him, "Men have come out from Sa·ma̅rʹi·a." ¹⁸He said, "If they have come out for peace, take them alive; if they have come out for war, take them alive."

19 But these had already come out of the city: the young men who served the district governors, and the army that followed them. ²⁰Each killed his man; the Ar·a·me̅ʹans fled and Israel pursued them, but King Ben-ha̅dad of Arʹam escaped on a horse with the cavalry. ²¹The king of Israel went out, attacked the horses and chariots, and defeated the Ar·a·me̅ʹans with a great slaughter.

22 Then the prophet approached the king of Israel and said to him, "Come, strengthen yourself, and consider well what you have to do; for in the spring the king of Arʹam will come up against you."

The Arameans Are Defeated

23 The servants of the king of Arʹam said to him, "Their gods are gods of the hills, and so they were stronger than we; but let us fight against them in the plain, and surely we shall be stronger than they. ²⁴Also do this: remove the kings, each from his post, and put commanders in place of them; ²⁵and muster an army like the army that you have lost, horse for horse, and chariot for chariot; then we will fight against them in the plain, and surely we shall be stronger than they." He heeded their voice, and did so.

26 In the spring Ben-ha̅dad mustered the Ar·a·me̅ʹans and went up to A̅ʹphek to fight against Israel. ²⁷After the Israelites had been mustered and provisioned, they went out to engage them; the people of Israel encamped opposite them like two little flocks of goats, while the Ar·a·me̅ʹans filled the country. ²⁸A man of God approached and said to the king of Israel, "Thus says the LORD: Because the Ar·a·me̅ʹans have said, 'The LORD is a god of the hills but he is not a god of the valleys,' therefore I will give all this great multitude into your hand, and you shall know that I am the LORD." ²⁹They encamped opposite one another seven days. Then on the seventh day the battle began; the Israelites killed one hundred thousand Ar·a·me̅ʹan foot soldiers in one day. ³⁰The rest fled into the city of A̅ʹphek; and the wall fell on twenty-seven thousand men that were left.

Ben-ha̅dad also fled, and entered the city to hide. ³¹His servants said to him, "Look, we have heard that the kings of the house of Israel are merciful kings; let us put sackcloth around our waists and ropes on our heads, and go out to the king of Israel; perhaps he will spare your life." ³²So they tied sackcloth around their waists, put ropes on their heads, went to the king of Israel, and said, "Your servant Ben-ha̅dad says, 'Please let me live.' " And he said, "Is he still alive? He is my brother." ³³Now the men were watching for an omen; they quickly took it up from him and said, "Yes, Ben-ha̅dad is your brother." Then he said, "Go and bring him." So Ben-ha̅dad came out to him; and he had him come up into the chariot. ³⁴Ben-ha̅dadʳ said to him, "I will restore the towns that my father took from your father; and you may establish bazaars for yourself in Damascus, as my father did in Sa·ma̅rʹi·a." The king of Israel responded,ˢ "I will let you go on those terms." So he made a treaty with him and let him go.

q Heb lacks *scouts* ʳ Heb *He* ˢ Heb lacks *The king of Israel responded*

A Prophet Condemns Ahab

35 At the command of the LORD a certain member of a company of prophets[t] said to another, "Strike me!" But the man refused to strike him. [36]Then he said to him, "Because you have not obeyed the voice of the LORD, as soon as you have left me, a lion will kill you." And when he had left him, a lion met him and killed him. [37]Then he found another man and said, "Strike me!" So the man hit him, striking and wounding him. [38]Then the prophet departed, and waited for the king along the road, disguising himself with a bandage over his eyes. [39]As the king passed by, he cried to the king and said, "Your servant went out into the thick of the battle; then a soldier turned and brought a man to me, and said, 'Guard this man; if he is missing, your life shall be given for his life, or else you shall pay a talent of silver.' [40]While your servant was busy here and there, he was gone." The king of Israel said to him, "So shall your judgment be; you yourself have decided it." [41]Then he quickly took the bandage away from his eyes. The king of Israel recognized him as one of the prophets. [42]Then he said to him, "Thus says the LORD, 'Because you have let the man go whom I had devoted to destruction, therefore your life shall be for his life, and your people for his people.' " [43]The king of Israel set out toward home, resentful and sullen, and came to Sa·mar´i·a.

Naboth's Vineyard

21 Later the following events took place: Na´both the Jez´re·el·ite had a vineyard in Jez´re·el, beside the palace of King A´hab of Sa·mar´i·a. [2]And A´hab said to Na´both, "Give me your vineyard, so that I may have it for a vegetable garden, because it is near my house; I will give you a better vineyard for it; or, if it seems good to you, I will give you its value in money." [3]But Na´both said to A´hab, "The LORD forbid

Do you like to eat grapes? A vineyard is a field of grapes. In Bible times, the people planted grapevines on hillsides. Grapes were worth money because they were used to make wine and food.

Naboth owned a vineyard close to King Ahab's palace. The king wanted the vineyard and offered to buy it, but Naboth did not want to sell his land. Israelite law did not allow people to sell the land because it belonged to God (Leviticus 25:23), so Ahab's wife Jezebel came up with a plan to get the land. She had some men say false things about Naboth. Naboth was stoned to death, and King Ahab got his land.

that I should give you my ancestral inheritance." [4]A´hab went home resentful and sullen because of what Na´both the Jez´re·el·ite had said to him; for he had said, "I will not give you my ancestral inheritance." He lay down on his bed, turned away his face, and would not eat.

5 His wife Jez´e·bel came to him and said, "Why are you so depressed that you will not eat?" [6]He said to her, "Because I spoke to Na´both the Jez´re·el·ite and said to him, 'Give me your vineyard for money; or else, if you prefer, I will give you another vineyard for it'; but he answered, 'I will not give you my vineyard.' " [7]His wife Jez´e·bel said to him, "Do you now govern Israel? Get up, eat some food, and be cheerful; I will give you the vineyard of Na´both the Jez´re·el·ite."

8 So she wrote letters in A´hab's name and sealed them with his seal; she sent the letters to the elders and the nobles who lived with Na´both in his city. [9]She wrote

[t] Heb *of the sons of the prophets*

in the letters, "Proclaim a fast, and seat Nā́-both at the head of the assembly; ¹⁰seat two scoundrels opposite him, and have them bring a charge against him, saying, 'You have cursed God and the king.' Then take him out, and stone him to death." ¹¹The men of his city, the elders and the nobles who lived in his city, did as Jeźe·bel had sent word to them. Just as it was written in the letters that she had sent to them, ¹²they proclaimed a fast and seated Nā́both at the head of the assembly. ¹³The two scoundrels came in and sat opposite him; and the scoundrels brought a charge against Nā́both, in the presence of the people, saying, "Nā́both cursed God and the king." So they took him outside the city, and stoned him to death. ¹⁴Then they sent to Jeźe·bel, saying, "Nā́both has been stoned; he is dead."

15 As soon as Jeźe·bel heard that Nā́-both had been stoned and was dead, Jeźe·bel said to Ā́hab, "Go, take possession of the vineyard of Nā́both the Jeź-rē·el·ite, which he refused to give you for money; for Nā́both is not alive, but dead." ¹⁶As soon as Ā́hab heard that Nā́-both was dead, Ā́hab set out to go down to the vineyard of Nā́both the Jeź-rē·el·ite, to take possession of it.

Elijah Pronounces God's Sentence

17 Then the word of the LORD came to E·lī́jah the Tish́bīte, saying: ¹⁸Go down to meet King Ā́hab of Israel, who rules[u] in Sa·māŕi·a; he is now in the vineyard of Nā́both, where he has gone to take possession. ¹⁹You shall say to him, "Thus says the LORD: Have you killed, and also taken possession?" You shall say to him, "Thus says the LORD: In the place where dogs licked up the blood of Nā́both, dogs will also lick up your blood." 20 Ā́hab said to E·lī́jah, "Have you found me, O my enemy?" He answered, "I have found you. Because you have sold yourself to do what is evil in the sight of the LORD, ²¹I will bring disaster on you; I

will consume you, and will cut off from Ā́hab every male, bond or free, in Israel; ²²and I will make your house like the house of Jer·o·bṓam son of Nḗbat, and like the house of Bā́a·sha son of A·hī́jah, because you have provoked me to anger and have caused Israel to sin. ²³Also concerning Jeźe·bel the LORD said, 'The dogs shall eat Jeźe·bel within the bounds of Jeźrē·el.' ²⁴Anyone belonging to Ā́hab who dies in the city the dogs shall eat; and anyone of his who dies in the open country the birds of the air shall eat."

25 (Indeed, there was no one like Ā́hab, who sold himself to do what was evil in the sight of the LORD, urged on by his wife Jeźe·bel. ²⁶He acted most abominably in going after idols, as the Aḿo·rītes had done, whom the LORD drove out before the Israelites.)

27 When Ā́hab heard those words, he tore his clothes and put sackcloth over his bare flesh; he fasted, lay in the sackcloth, and went about dejectedly. ²⁸Then the word of the LORD came to E·lī́-jah the Tish́bīte: ²⁹"Have you seen how Ā́hab has humbled himself before me? Because he has humbled himself before me, I will not bring the disaster in his days; but in his son's days I will bring the disaster on his house."

Joint Campaign with Judah against Aram

22 For three years Aŕam and Israel continued without war. ²But in the third year King Je·hosh́a·phat of Judah came down to the king of Israel. ³The king of Israel said to his servants, "Do you know that Rā́moth-giĺē·ad belongs to us, yet we are doing nothing to take it out of the hand of the king of Aŕam?" ⁴He said to Je·hosh́a·phat, "Will you go with me to battle at Rā́moth-giĺ-ē·ad?" Je·hosh́a·phat replied to the king of Israel, "I am as you are; my people are your people, my horses are your horses."

5 But Je·hosh́a·phat also said to the

u Heb *who is*

king of Israel, "Inquire first for the word of the LORD." [6]Then the king of Israel gathered the prophets together, about four hundred of them, and said to them, "Shall I go to battle against Rā′moth-gil′ē·ad, or shall I refrain?" They said, "Go up; for the LORD will give it into the hand of the king." [7]But Je·hosh′a·phat said, "Is there no other prophet of the LORD here of whom we may inquire?" [8]The king of Israel said to Je·hosh′-a·phat, "There is still one other by whom we may inquire of the LORD, Mī·cāi′ah son of Im′lah; but I hate him, for he never prophesies anything favorable about me, but only disaster." Je·hosh′-a·phat said, "Let the king not say such a thing." [9]Then the king of Israel summoned an officer and said, "Bring quickly Mī·cāi′ah son of Im′lah." [10]Now the king of Israel and King Je·hosh′-a·phat of Judah were sitting on their thrones, arrayed in their robes, at the threshing floor at the entrance of the gate of Sa·mār′i·a; and all the prophets were prophesying before them. [11]Zed-e·kī′ah son of Che·nā′a·nah made for himself horns of iron, and he said, "Thus says the LORD: With these you shall gore the Ar·a·mē′ans until they are destroyed." [12]All the prophets were prophesying the same and saying, "Go up to Rā′moth-gil′ē·ad and triumph; the LORD will give it into the hand of the king."

Micaiah Predicts Failure

13 The messenger who had gone to summon Mī·cāi′ah said to him, "Look, the words of the prophets with one accord are favorable to the king; let your word be like the word of one of them, and speak favorably." [14]But Mī·cāi′ah said, "As the LORD lives, whatever the LORD says to me, that I will speak."

15 When he had come to the king, the king said to him, "Mī·cāi′ah, shall we go to Rā′moth-gil′ē·ad to battle, or shall we refrain?" He answered him, "Go up and triumph; the LORD will give it into

the hand of the king." [16]But the king said to him, "How many times must I make you swear to tell me nothing but the truth in the name of the LORD?" [17]Then Mī·cāi′ah[v] said, "I saw all Israel scattered on the mountains, like sheep that have no shepherd; and the LORD said, 'These have no master; let each one go home in peace.'" [18]The king of Israel said to Je·hosh′a·phat, "Did I not tell you that he would not prophesy anything favorable about me, but only disaster?"

19 Then Mī·cāi′ah[v] said, "Therefore hear the word of the LORD: I saw the LORD sitting on his throne, with all the host of heaven standing beside him to the right and to the left of him. [20]And the LORD said, 'Who will entice Ā′hab, so that he may go up and fall at Rā′moth-gil′ē·ad?' Then one said one thing, and another said another, [21]until a spirit came forward and stood before the LORD, saying, 'I will entice him.' [22]'How?' the LORD asked him. He replied, 'I will go out and be a lying spirit in the mouth of all his prophets.' Then the LORD[v] said, 'You are to entice him, and you shall succeed; go out and do it.' [23]So you see, the LORD has put a lying spirit in the mouth of all these your prophets; the LORD has decreed disaster for you."

24 Then Zed·e·kī′ah son of Che·nā′-a·nah came up to Mī·cāi′ah, slapped him on the cheek, and said, "Which way did the spirit of the LORD pass from me to speak to you?" [25]Mī·cāi′ah replied, "You will find out on that day when you go in to hide in an inner chamber." [26]The king of Israel then ordered, "Take Mī·cāi′ah, and return him to Ā′mon the governor of the city and to Jō′ash the king's son, [27]and say, 'Thus says the king: Put this fellow in prison, and feed him on reduced rations of bread and water until I come in peace.'" [28]Mī·cāi′ah said, "If you return in peace, the LORD has not spoken by me." And he said, "Hear, you peoples, all of you!"

[v] Heb *he*

Defeat and Death of Ahab

29 So the king of Israel and King Je·hosh´a·phat of Judah went up to Rā-moth-gil´e·ad. ³⁰The king of Israel said to Je·hosh´a·phat, "I will disguise myself and go into battle, but you wear your robes." So the king of Israel disguised himself and went into battle. ³¹Now the king of Ar´am had commanded the thirty-two captains of his chariots, "Fight with no one small or great, but only with the king of Israel." ³²When the captains of the chariots saw Je·hosh´a·phat, they said, "It is surely the king of Israel." So they turned to fight against him; and Je·hosh´a·phat cried out. ³³When the captains of the chariots saw that it was not the king of Israel, they turned back from pursuing him. ³⁴But a certain man drew his bow and unknowingly struck the king of Israel between the scale armor and the breastplate; so he said to the driver of his chariot, "Turn around, and carry me out of the battle, for I am wounded." ³⁵The battle grew hot that day, and the king was propped up in his chariot facing the Ar·a·mē´ans, until at evening he died; the blood from the wound had flowed into the bottom of the chariot. ³⁶Then about sunset a shout went through the army, "Every man to his city, and every man to his country!"

37 So the king died, and was brought to Sa·mār´i·a; they buried the king in Sa·mār´i·a. ³⁸They washed the chariot by the pool of Sa·mār´i·a; the dogs licked up his blood, and the prostitutes washed themselves in it,ʷ according to the word of the LORD that he had spoken. ³⁹Now the rest of the acts of Ā´hab, and all that he did, and the ivory house that he built, and all the cities that he built, are they not written in the Book of the Annals of the Kings of Israel? ⁴⁰So Ā´hab slept with his ancestors; and his son A·ha·zī´ah succeeded him.

Jehoshaphat Reigns over Judah

41 Je·hosh´a·phat son of Asa began to reign over Judah in the fourth year of King Ā´hab of Israel. ⁴²Je·hosh´a·phat was thirty-five years old when he began to reign, and he reigned twenty-five years in Jerusalem. His mother's name was A·zū´bah daughter of Shil´hī. ⁴³He walked in all the way of his father Asa; he did not turn aside from it, doing what was right in the sight of the LORD; yet the high places were not taken away, and the people still sacrificed and offered incense on the high places. ⁴⁴ Je·hosh´a·phat also made peace with the king of Israel.

45 Now the rest of the acts of Je·hosh´a·phat, and his power that he showed, and how he waged war, are they not written in the Book of the Annals of the Kings of Judah? ⁴⁶The remnant of the male temple prostitutes who were still in the land in the days of his father Asa, he exterminated.

47 There was no king in Ē´dom; a deputy was king. ⁴⁸Je·hosh´a·phat made ships of the Tar´shish type to go to Ō´phir for gold; but they did not go, for the ships were wrecked at Ē´zi·on-gē´ber. ⁴⁹Then A·ha·zī´ah son of Ā´hab said to Je·hosh´a·phat, "Let my servants go with your servants in the ships," but Je·hosh´a·phat was not willing. ⁵⁰Je·hosh´a·phat slept with his ancestors and was buried with his ancestors in the city of his father David; his son Je·hō´ram succeeded him.

Ahaziah Reigns over Israel

51 A·ha·zī´ah son of Ā´hab began to reign over Israel in Sa·mār´i·a in the seventeenth year of King Je·hosh´a·phat of Judah; he reigned two years over Israel. ⁵²He did what was evil in the sight of the LORD, and walked in the way of his father and mother, and in the way of Jer·o·bō´am son of Nē´bat, who caused Israel to sin. ⁵³He served Bā´al and worshiped him; he provoked the LORD, the God of Israel, to anger, just as his father had done.

ʷ Heb lacks in it

2 Kings

The book of Second Kings was written at the same time as the book of First Kings—in the sixth century BC. It continues with stories about the prophets Elijah and Elisha and their many wonderful deeds.

Second Kings tells about many kings of Israel and Judah who ruled during a period of over one hundred years. During this time, the kingdom of Assyria was growing stronger and stronger. In 722 BC Assyrian armies attacked and destroyed Samaria, the capital city of the northern kingdom of Israel. The Assyrians carried away 27,000 Israelites as captives of war.

These people never came back to their homes, so they are sometimes called "the ten lost tribes of Israel."

During these years the kingdom of Babylon was growing in power. Babylon conquered Assyria about 695 BC, so they controlled the southern kingdom of Judah. In 597 BC and again in 587 BC, the Babylonian armies conquered the city of Jerusalem and sent the rulers, officers, and leaders of the Judeans to Babylonia, sometimes called Chaldea. Some people were left behind, and others moved to Egypt. This was the sad end of the southern kingdom of Judah, but it was not the end of God's people.

2 Kings 12:1-16

Elijah Denounces Ahaziah

1 After the death of Āʹhab, Mōʹab rebelled against Israel.

2 A·ha·zīʹah had fallen through the lattice in his upper chamber in Sa·mārʹi·a, and lay injured; so he sent messengers, telling them, "Go, inquire of Bāʹal-zēʹbub, the god of Ekʹron, whether I shall recover from this injury." [3]But the angel of the LORD said to E·līʹjah the Tishʹbīte, "Get up, go to meet the messengers of the king of Sa·mārʹi·a, and say to them, 'Is it because there is no God in Israel that you are going to inquire of Bāʹal-zēʹbub, the god of Ekʹron?' [4]Now therefore thus says the LORD, 'You shall not leave the bed to which you have gone, but you shall surely die.' " So E·līʹjah went.

5 The messengers returned to the king, who said to them, "Why have you returned?" [6]They answered him, "There came a man to meet us, who said to us, 'Go back to the king who sent you, and say to him: Thus says the LORD: Is it because there is no God in Israel that you are sending to inquire of Bāʹal-zēʹbub, the god of Ekʹron? Therefore you shall not leave the bed to which you have gone, but shall surely die.' " [7]He said to them, "What sort of man was he who came to meet you and told you these things?" [8]They answered him, "A hairy man, with a leather belt around his waist." He said, "It is E·līʹjah the Tishʹbīte."

9 Then the king sent to him a captain of fifty with his fifty men. He went up to E·līʹjah, who was sitting on the top of a hill, and said to him, "O man of God, the king says, 'Come down.' " [10]But E·līʹjah answered the captain of fifty, "If I am a man of God, let fire come down from heaven and consume you and your fifty." Then fire came down from heaven, and consumed him and his fifty.

11 Again the king sent to him another captain of fifty with his fifty. He went up[a] and said to him, "O man of God, this is the king's order: Come down

quickly!" [12]But E·līʹjah answered them, "If I am a man of God, let fire come down from heaven and consume you and your fifty." Then the fire of God came down from heaven and consumed him and his fifty.

13 Again the king sent the captain of a third fifty with his fifty. So the third captain of fifty went up, and came and fell on his knees before E·līʹjah, and entreated him, "O man of God, please let my life, and the life of these fifty servants of yours, be precious in your sight. [14]Look, fire came down from heaven and consumed the two former captains of fifty men with their fifties; but now let my life be precious in your sight." [15]Then the angel of the LORD said to E·līʹjah, "Go down with him; do not be afraid of him." So he set out and went down with him to the king, [16]and said to him, "Thus says the LORD: Because you have sent messengers to inquire of Bāʹal-zēʹbub, the god of Ekʹron,—is it because there is no God in Israel to inquire of his word?—therefore you shall not leave the bed to which you have gone, but you shall surely die."

Death of Ahaziah

17 So he died according to the word of the LORD that E·līʹjah had spoken. His brother,[b] Je·hōʹram succeeded him as king in the second year of King Je·hōʹram son of Je·hoshʹa·phat of Judah, because A·ha·zīʹah had no son. [18]Now the rest of the acts of A·ha·zīʹah that he did, are they not written in the Book of the Annals of the Kings of Israel?

Elijah Ascends to Heaven

2 Now when the LORD was about to take E·līʹjah up to heaven by a whirlwind, E·līʹjah and E·līʹsha were on their way from Gilʹgal. [2]E·līʹjah said to E·līʹsha, "Stay here; for the LORD has sent me as far as Bethʹel." But E·līʹsha said, "As the LORD lives, and as you yourself

---

[a] Gk Compare verses 9, 13: Heb *He answered*
[b] Gk Syr: Heb lacks *His brother*

live, I will not leave you." So they went down to Beth′el. ³The company of prophets[c] who were in Beth′el came out to E·li′sha, and said to him, "Do you know that today the LORD will take your master away from you?" And he said, "Yes, I know; keep silent."

4 E·li′jah said to him, "E·li′sha, stay here; for the LORD has sent me to Jericho." But he said, "As the LORD lives, and as you yourself live, I will not leave you." So they came to Jericho. ⁵The company of prophets[c] who were at Jericho drew near to E·li′sha, and said to him, "Do you know that today the LORD will take your master away from you?" And he answered, "Yes, I know; be silent."

6 Then E·li′jah said to him, "Stay here; for the LORD has sent me to the Jordan." But he said, "As the LORD lives, and as you yourself live, I will not leave you." So the two of them went on. ⁷Fifty men of the company of prophets[c] also went, and stood at some distance from them, as they both were standing by the Jordan. ⁸Then E·li′jah took his mantle and rolled it up, and struck the water; the water was parted to the one side and to the other, until the two of them crossed on dry ground.

9 When they had crossed, E·li′jah said to E·li′sha, "Tell me what I may do for you, before I am taken from you." E·li′sha said, "Please let me inherit a double share of your spirit." ¹⁰He responded, "You have asked a hard thing; yet, if you see me as I am being taken from you, it will be granted you; if not, it will not." ¹¹As they continued walking and talking, a chariot of fire and horses of fire separated the two of them, and E·li′jah ascended in a whirlwind into heaven. ¹²E·li′sha kept watching and crying out, "Father, father! The chariots of Israel and its horsemen!" But when he could no longer see him, he grasped his own clothes and tore them in two pieces.

Have you ever been sad because a friend moved far away from you? Elijah and Elisha both knew that God was calling Elijah to heaven, but they must have been surprised when a fiery chariot came down and took Elijah away. Although Elisha knew Elijah would be leaving, he was still sad because his friend and teacher was gone.

Elisha Succeeds Elijah

13 He picked up the mantle of E·li′jah that had fallen from him, and went back and stood on the bank of the Jordan. ¹⁴He took the mantle of E·li′jah that had fallen from him, and struck the water, saying, "Where is the LORD, the God of E·li′jah?" When he had struck the water, the water was parted to the one side and to the other, and E·li′sha went over.

15 When the company of prophets[c] who were at Jericho saw him at a distance, they declared, "The spirit of E·li′jah rests on E·li′sha." They came to meet him and bowed to the ground before him. ¹⁶They said to him, "See now, we have fifty strong men among your servants; please let them go and seek your master; it may be that the spirit of the LORD has caught him up and thrown

A mantle was a long coat. Elijah's mantle would have been made of rough hair to show others he was a prophet. When he went up to heaven, the mantle fell to earth, and Elisha put it on to show that he would continue the work started by Elijah.

[c] Heb *sons of the prophets*

him down on some mountain or into some valley." He responded, "No, do not send them." [17]But when they urged him until he was ashamed, he said, "Send them." So they sent fifty men who searched for three days but did not find him. [18]When they came back to him (he had remained at Jericho), he said to them, "Did I not say to you, Do not go?"

Elisha Performs Miracles

19 Now the people of the city said to E·li´sha, "The location of this city is good, as my lord sees; but the water is bad, and the land is unfruitful." [20]He said, "Bring me a new bowl, and put salt in it." So they brought it to him. [21]Then he went to the spring of water and threw the salt into it, and said, "Thus says the LORD, I have made this water wholesome; from now on neither death nor miscarriage shall come from it." [22]So the water has been wholesome to this day, according to the word that E·li´sha spoke.

23 He went up from there to Beth´el; and while he was going up on the way, some small boys came out of the city and jeered at him, saying, "Go away, bald-head! Go away, baldhead!" [24]When he turned around and saw them, he cursed them in the name of the LORD. Then two she-bears came out of the woods and mauled forty-two of the boys. [25]From there he went on to Mount Car´mel, and then returned to Sa·mar´i·a.

Jehoram Reigns over Israel

3 In the eighteenth year of King Je·hosh´a·phat of Judah, Je·ho´ram son of A´hab became king over Israel in Sa·mar´i·a; he reigned twelve years. [2]He did what was evil in the sight of the LORD, though not like his father and mother, for he removed the pillar of Ba´al that his father had made. [3]Nevertheless he clung to the sin of Jer·o·bo´am son of Ne´bat, which he caused Israel to commit; he did not depart from it.

War with Moab

4 Now King Me´sha of Mo´ab was a sheep breeder, who used to deliver to the king of Israel one hundred thousand lambs, and the wool of one hundred thousand rams. [5]But when A´hab died, the king of Mo´ab rebelled against the king of Israel. [6]So King Je·ho´ram marched out of Sa·mar´i·a at that time and mustered all Israel. [7]As he went he sent word to King Je·hosh´a·phat of Judah, "The king of Mo´ab has rebelled against me; will you go with me to battle against Mo´ab?" He answered, "I will; I am with you, my people are your people, my horses are your horses." [8]Then he asked, "By which way shall we march?" Je·ho´ram answered, "By the way of the wilderness of E´dom."

9 So the king of Israel, the king of Judah, and the king of E´dom set out; and when they had made a roundabout march of seven days, there was no water for the army or for the animals that were with them. [10]Then the king of Israel said, "Alas! The LORD has summoned us, three kings, only to be handed over to Mo´ab." [11]But Je·hosh´a·phat said, "Is there no prophet of the LORD here, through whom we may inquire of the LORD?" Then one of the servants of the king of Israel answered, "E·li´sha son of Sha´phat, who used to pour water on the hands of E·li´jah, is here." [12]Je·hosh´-a·phat said, "The word of the LORD is with him." So the king of Israel and Je·hosh´a·phat and the king of E´dom went down to him.

13 E·li´sha said to the king of Israel, "What have I to do with you? Go to your

Elisha continued to fight the worship of Baal. He gave advice and tried to guide the kings of Israel for fifty years. Elisha wanted the kings and the people to follow God's ways.

father's prophets or to your mother's."
But the king of Israel said to him, "No; it
is the LORD who has summoned us, three
kings, only to be handed over to Mō′ab."
¹⁴E·lī′sha said, "As the LORD of hosts
lives, whom I serve, were it not that I
have regard for King Je·hosh′a·phat of
Judah, I would give you neither a look
nor a glance. ¹⁵But get me a musician."
And then, while the musician was playing, the power of the LORD came on him.
¹⁶And he said, "Thus says the LORD, 'I
will make this wadi full of pools.' ¹⁷For
thus says the LORD, 'You shall see neither
wind nor rain, but the wadi shall be filled
with water, so that you shall drink, you,
your cattle, and your animals.' ¹⁸This is
only a trifle in the sight of the LORD, for
he will also hand Mō′ab over to you.
¹⁹You shall conquer every fortified city
and every choice city; every good tree
you shall fell, all springs of water you
shall stop up, and every good piece of
land you shall ruin with stones." ²⁰The
next day, about the time of the morning
offering, suddenly water began to flow
from the direction of Ē′dom, until the
country was filled with water.

21 When all the Mō′ab·ites heard that
the kings had come up to fight against
them, all who were able to put on armor,
from the youngest to the oldest, were
called out and were drawn up at the frontier. ²²When they rose early in the morning, and the sun shone upon the water,
the Mō′ab·ites saw the water opposite
them as red as blood. ²³They said, "This is
blood; the kings must have fought
together, and killed one another. Now
then, Mō′ab, to the spoil!" ²⁴But when
they came to the camp of Israel, the Israelites rose up and attacked the Mō′ab·ites,
who fled before them; as they entered Mō′-
ab they continued the attack.[d] ²⁵The cities
they overturned, and on every good piece
of land everyone threw a stone, until it
was covered; every spring of water they
stopped up, and every good tree they
felled. Only at Kir-har′e·seth did the stone

walls remain, until the slingers surrounded and attacked it. ²⁶When the king
of Mō′ab saw that the battle was going
against him, he took with him seven hundred swordsmen to break through, opposite the king of Ē′dom; but they could not.
²⁷Then he took his firstborn son who was
to succeed him, and offered him as a
burnt offering on the wall. And great
wrath came upon Israel, so they withdrew
from him and returned to their own land.

Elisha and the Widow's Oil

4 Now the wife of a member of the
company of prophets[e] cried to
E·lī′sha, "Your servant my husband is
dead; and you know that your servant
feared the LORD, but a creditor has
come to take my two children as
slaves." ²E·lī′sha said to her, "What
shall I do for you? Tell me, what do you
have in the house?" She answered,
"Your servant has nothing in the house,
except a jar of oil." ³He said, "Go outside, borrow vessels from all your
neighbors, empty vessels and not just a
few. ⁴Then go in, and shut the door
behind you and your children, and
start pouring into all these vessels;
when each is full, set it aside." ⁵So she
left him and shut the door behind her

In Bible times, if someone owed another person money but could not pay, his or her children could be taken as slaves. That is exactly what was about to happen to a widow who came to Elisha! By a miracle, she used the one jar of oil she had in her house to fill all of the empty jars in the neighborhood. Elisha told her to sell these jars of oil to pay what she owed. God showed love and care to provide for this widow and her children.

[d] Compare Gk Syr: Meaning of Heb uncertain
[e] Heb the sons of the prophets

The Shunammite woman knew that Elisha was a man of God. She wanted to do something to honor Elisha, so she and her husband built a small room for him on the roof of their house. When Elisha asked how he could repay her, she said that she was happy with her life. But Elisha knew that she did not have a son, and he promised her that she would have one.

and her children; they kept bringing vessels to her, and she kept pouring. [6]When the vessels were full, she said to her son, "Bring me another vessel." But he said to her, "There are no more." Then the oil stopped flowing. [7]She came and told the man of God, and he said, "Go sell the oil and pay your debts, and you and your children can live on the rest."

Elisha Raises the Shunammite's Son

8 One day E·lī´sha was passing through Shū´nem, where a wealthy woman lived, who urged him to have a meal. So whenever he passed that way, he would stop there for a meal. [9]She said to her husband, "Look, I am sure that this man who regularly passes our way is a holy man of God. [10]Let us make a small roof chamber with walls, and put there for him a bed, a table, a chair, and a lamp, so that he can stay there whenever he comes to us."

11 One day when he came there, he went up to the chamber and lay down there. [12]He said to his servant Ge·hā´zī, "Call the Shū´nam·mīte woman." When he had called her, she stood before him. [13]He said to him, "Say to her, Since you have taken all this trouble for us, what may be done for you? Would you have a word spoken on your behalf to the king

or to the commander of the army?" She answered, "I live among my own people." [14]He said, "What then may be done for her?" Ge·hā´zī answered, "Well, she has no son, and her husband is old." [15]He said, "Call her." When he had called her, she stood at the door. [16]He said, "At this season, in due time, you shall embrace a son." She replied, "No, my lord, O man of God; do not deceive your servant."

17 The woman conceived and bore a son at that season, in due time, as E·lī´sha had declared to her.

18 When the child was older, he went out one day to his father among the reapers. [19]He complained to his father, "Oh, my head, my head!" The father said to his servant, "Carry him to his mother." [20]He carried him and brought him to his mother; the child sat on her lap until noon, and he died. [21]She went up and laid him on the bed of the man of God, closed the door on him, and left. [22]Then she called to her husband, and said, "Send me one of the servants and one of the donkeys, so that I may quickly go to the man of God and come back again." [23]He said, "Why go to him today? It is neither new moon nor sabbath." She said, "It will be all right." [24]Then she saddled the donkey and said to her servant, "Urge the animal on; do not hold back for me unless I tell you." [25]So she set out, and came to the man of God at Mount Car´mel.

When the man of God saw her coming, he said to Ge·hā´zī his servant, "Look, there is the Shū´nam·mīte woman; [26]run

When the Shunammite woman's son died, Elisha came and breathed his own breath into the young boy. The boy sneezed seven times and then opened his eyes. The number seven is used to show that the action came from God.

at once to meet her, and say to her, Are you all right? Is your husband all right? Is the child all right?" She answered, "It is all right." [27]When she came to the man of God at the mountain, she caught hold of his feet. Ge·ha´zī approached to push her away. But the man of God said, "Let her alone, for she is in bitter distress; the LORD has hidden it from me and has not told me." [28]Then she said, "Did I ask my lord for a son? Did I not say, Do not mislead me?" [29]He said to Ge·ha´zī, "Gird up your loins, and take my staff in your hand, and go. If you meet anyone, give no greeting, and if anyone greets you, do not answer; and lay my staff on the face of the child." [30]Then the mother of the child said, "As the LORD lives, and as you yourself live, I will not leave without you." So he rose up and followed her. [31]Ge·ha´zī went on ahead and laid the staff on the face of the child, but there was no sound or sign of life. He came back to meet him and told him, "The child has not awakened."

32 When E·lī´sha came into the house, he saw the child lying dead on his bed. [33]So he went in and closed the door on the two of them, and prayed to the LORD. [34]Then he got up on the bed[f] and lay upon the child, putting his mouth upon his mouth, his eyes upon his eyes, and his hands upon his hands; and while he lay bent over him, the flesh of the child became warm. [35]He got down, walked once to and fro in the room, then got up again and bent over him; the child sneezed seven times, and the child opened his eyes. [36]E·lī´sha[g] summoned Ge·ha´zī and said, "Call the Shū´nam·mīte woman." So he called her. When she came to him, he said, "Take your son." [37]She came and fell at his feet, bowing to the ground; then she took her son and left.

Elisha Purifies the Pot of Stew

38 When E·lī´sha returned to Gil´gal, there was a famine in the land. As the company of prophets was[h] sitting before him, he said to his servant, "Put the large pot on, and make some stew for the com-

pany of prophets."[i] [39]One of them went out into the field to gather herbs; he found a wild vine and gathered from it a lapful of wild gourds, and came and cut them up into the pot of stew, not knowing what they were. [40]They served some for the men to eat. But while they were eating the stew, they cried out, "O man of God, there is death in the pot!" They could not eat it. [41]He said, "Then bring some flour." He threw it into the pot, and said, "Serve the people and let them eat." And there was nothing harmful in the pot.

Elisha Feeds One Hundred Men

42 A man came from Bā´al-shal´i·shah, bringing food from the first fruits to the man of God: twenty loaves of barley and fresh ears of grain in his sack. E·lī´sha said, "Give it to the people and let them eat." [43]But his servant said, "How can I set this before a hundred people?" So he repeated, "Give it to the people and let them eat, for thus says the LORD, 'They shall eat and have some left.'" [44]He set it before them, they ate, and had some left, according to the word of the LORD.

Naaman heard about the prophet Elisha from a young Israelite girl serving in his house. Although she had been taken away from her home and people, she remembered the things she had been taught.

Is there a Bible verse that has special meaning for you? Make a poster with that verse, and hang it on your wall. Read the verse every day, and soon you will be able to say it without even looking at the poster! Some good verses to remember are: Psalm 23:1–3, John 3:16, Hebrews 11:1, and James 4:8. Maybe you could design a Bible-verse poster for a friend or an older person you know!

---

[f] Heb lacks *on the bed*   [g] Heb *he*   [h] Heb *sons*
of the prophets were   [i] Heb *sons of the prophets*

The Healing of Naaman

5 Nā·a·man, commander of the army of the king of Ar´am, was a great man and in high favor with his master, because by him the LORD had given victory to Ar´am. The man, though a mighty warrior, suffered from leprosy. ²Now the Ar·a·mē´ans on one of their raids had taken a young girl captive from the land of Israel, and she served Nā·a·man's wife. ³She said to her mistress, "If only my lord were with the prophet who is in Sa·mār´i·a! He would cure him of his leprosy."⁴So Nā´a·man[k] went in and told his lord just what the girl from the land of Israel had said. ⁵And the king of Ar´am said, "Go then, and I will send along a letter to the king of Israel."

He went, taking with him ten talents of silver, six thousand shekels of gold, and ten sets of garments. ⁶He brought the letter to the king of Israel, which read, "When this letter reaches you, know that I have sent to you my servant Nā´a·man, that you may cure him of his leprosy."[j] ⁷When the king of Israel read the letter, he tore his clothes and said, "Am I God, to give death or life, that this man sends word to me to cure a man of his leprosy?[j] Just look and see how he is trying to pick a quarrel with me."

8 But when E·lī´sha the man of God heard that the king of Israel had torn his clothes, he sent a message to the king, "Why have you torn your clothes? Let him come to me, that he may learn that there is a prophet in Israel." ⁹So Nā´a·man came with his horses and chariots, and halted at the entrance of E·lī´sha's house. ¹⁰E·lī´sha sent a messenger to him, saying, "Go, wash in the Jordan seven times, and your flesh shall be restored and you shall be clean." ¹¹But Nā·a·man became angry and went away, saying, "I thought that for me he would surely come out, and stand and call on the name of the LORD his God, and would wave his hand over the spot, and cure the leprosy!"[j] ¹²Are not A·bā´na[l] and Phar´par, the rivers of Damascus, better than all the waters of Israel? Could I not wash in them, and be clean?" He turned and went away in a rage. ¹³But his servants approached and said to him, "Father, if the prophet had commanded you to do something difficult, would you not have done it? How much more, when all he said to you was, 'Wash, and be clean'?" ¹⁴So he went down and immersed himself seven times in the Jordan, according to the word of the man of God; his flesh was restored like the flesh of a young boy, and he was clean.

15 Then he returned to the man of God, he and all his company; he came and stood before him and said, "Now I know that there is no God in all the earth except in Israel; please accept a present from your servant." ¹⁶But he said, "As the LORD lives, whom I serve, I will accept nothing!" He urged him to accept, but he refused. ¹⁷Then Nā´a·man said, "If not, please let two muleloads of earth be given to your servant; for your servant will no longer offer burnt offering or sacrifice to any god except the LORD. ¹⁸But may the LORD pardon your servant on one count: when my master goes into the house of Rim´mon to worship there, leaning on my arm, and I bow down in the house of Rim´mon, when I do bow down in the

Naaman was a commander of the Syrian army who went to see the prophet Elisha to be cured of leprosy. At first, Naaman did not want to follow Elisha's instructions. But when he did what Elisha told him to do, he was healed. Read Elisha's instructions in 2 Kings 5:9–14.

---

[j] A term for several skin diseases; precise meaning uncertain   [k] Heb he   [l] Another reading is Amana

house of Rim´mon, may the LORD pardon your servant on this one count." [19]He said to him, "Go in peace."

Gehazi's Greed

But when Nā´a·man had gone from him a short distance, [20]Ge·hā´zī, the servant of E·lī´sha the man of God, thought, "My master has let that Ar·a·mē´an Nā´a·man off too lightly by not accepting from him what he offered. As the LORD lives, I will run after him and get something out of him." [21]So Ge·hā´zī went after Nā´a·man. When Nā´a·man saw someone running after him, he jumped down from the chariot to meet him and said, "Is everything all right?" [22]He replied, "Yes, but my master has sent me to say, 'Two members of a company of prophets[m] have just come to me from the hill country of Ē´phra·im; please give them a talent of silver and two changes of clothing.' " [23]Nā´a·man said, "Please accept two talents." He urged him, and tied up two talents of silver in two bags, with two changes of clothing, and gave them to two of his servants, who carried them in front of Ge·hā´zī.[n] [24]When he came to the citadel, he took the bags[o] from them, and stored them inside; he dismissed the men, and they left.

[25] He went in and stood before his master; and E·lī´sha said to him, "Where have you been, Ge·hā´zī?" He answered, "Your servant has not gone anywhere at all." [26]But he said to him, "Did I not go with you in spirit when someone left his chariot to meet you? Is this a time to accept money and to accept clothing, olive orchards and vineyards, sheep and oxen, and male and female slaves? [27]Therefore the leprosy[p] of Nā´a·man shall cling to you, and to your descendants forever." So he left his presence leprous,[p] as white as snow.

The Miracle of the Ax Head

6 Now the company of prophets[m] said to E·lī´sha, "As you see, the place where we live under your charge is too small for us. [2]Let us go to the Jordan, and let us collect logs there, one for each of us, and build a place there for us to live." He answered, "Do so." [3]Then one of them said, "Please come with your servants." And he answered, "I will." [4]So he went with them. When they came to the Jordan, they cut down trees. [5]But as one was felling a log, his ax head fell into the water; he cried out, "Alas, master! It was borrowed." [6]Then the man of God said, "Where did it fall?" When he showed him the place, he cut off a stick, and threw it in there, and made the iron float. [7]He said, "Pick it up." So he reached out his hand and took it.

The Aramean Attack Is Thwarted

[8] Once when the king of Ar´am was at war with Israel, he took counsel with his officers. He said, "At such and such a place shall be my camp." [9]But the man of God sent word to the king of Israel, "Take care not to pass this place, because the Ar·a·mē´ans are going down there." [10]The king of Israel sent word to the place of which the man of God spoke. More than once or twice he warned such a place[q] so that it was on the alert.

[11] The mind of the king of Ar´am

Read the exciting story of the floating ax head in 2 Kings 6:1–7. A servant had borrowed an ax head to use to cut trees. The ax head fell into a river while he was working, and he was afraid because it was very expensive and did not belong to him. By a miracle, Elisha gave him another ax head. Through Elisha, God worked miracles for all kinds of people—rich women, kings and princes, and poor people in need. God's love is for all people. God cares for everyone.

[m] Heb *sons of the prophets*   [n] Heb *him*   [o] Heb lacks *the bags*   [p] A term for several skin diseases; precise meaning uncertain   [q] Heb *warned it*

was greatly perturbed because of this; he called his officers and said to them, "Now tell me who among us sides with the king of Israel?" [12]Then one of his officers said, "No one, my lord king. It is E·li′sha, the prophet in Israel, who tells the king of Israel the words that you speak in your bedchamber." [13]He said, "Go and find where he is; I will send and seize him." He was told, "He is in Do′than." [14]So he sent horses and chariots there and a great army; they came by night, and surrounded the city.

15 When an attendant of the man of God rose early in the morning and went out, an army with horses and chariots was all around the city. His servant said, "Alas, master! What shall we do?" [16]He replied, "Do not be afraid, for there are more with us than there are with them." [17]Then E·li′sha prayed: "O LORD, please open his eyes that he may see." So the LORD opened the eyes of the servant, and he saw; the mountain was full of horses and chariots of fire all around E·li′sha. [18]When the Ar·a·me′ans[r] came down against him, E·li′sha prayed to the LORD, and said, "Strike this people, please, with blindness." So he struck them with blindness as E·li′sha had asked. [19]E·li′sha said to them, "This is not the way, and this is not the city; follow me, and I will bring you to the man whom you seek." And he led them to Sa·mar′i·a.

20 As soon as they entered Sa·mar′i·a, E·li′sha said, "O LORD, open the eyes of these men so that they may see." The LORD opened their eyes, and they saw that they were inside Sa·mar′i·a. [21]When the king of Israel saw them he said to E·li′sha, "Father, shall I kill them? Shall I kill them?" [22]He answered, "No! Did you capture with your sword and your bow those whom you want to kill? Set food and water before them so that they may eat and drink; and let them go to their master." [23]So he prepared for them a great feast; after they ate and drank, he sent them on their way, and they went to their

master. And the Ar·a·me′ans no longer came raiding into the land of Israel.

Ben-hadad's Siege of Samaria

24 Some time later King Ben-ha′dad of Ar′am mustered his entire army; he marched against Sa·mar′i·a and laid siege to it. [25]As the siege continued, famine in Sa·mar′i·a became so great that a donkey's head was sold for eighty shekels of silver, and one-fourth of a kab of dove's dung for five shekels of silver. [26]Now as the king of Israel was walking on the city wall, a woman cried out to him, "Help, my lord king!" [27]He said, "No! Let the LORD help you. How can I help you? From the threshing floor or from the wine press?" [28]But then the king asked her, "What is your complaint?" She answered, "This woman said to me, 'Give up your son; we will eat him today, and we will eat my son tomorrow.' [29]So we cooked my son and ate him. The next day I said to her, 'Give up your son and we will eat him.' But she has hidden her son." [30]When the king heard the words of the woman he tore his clothes—now since he was walking on the city wall, the people could see that he had sackcloth on his body underneath— [31]and he said, "So may God do to me, and more, if the head of E·li′sha son of Sha′phat stays on his shoulders today." [32]So he dispatched a man from his presence.

Now E·li′sha was sitting in his house, and the elders were sitting with him. Before the messenger arrived, E·li′sha said to the elders, "Are you aware that this murderer has sent someone to take off my head? When the messenger comes, see that you shut the door and hold it closed against him. Is not the sound of his master's feet behind him?" [33]While he was still speaking with them, the king[s] came down to him and said, "This trouble is from the LORD! Why should I hope in the LORD any longer?"

[r]Heb *they* [s]See 7.2: Heb *messenger*

7 [1]But E·li-'sha said, "Hear the word of the Lord: thus says the Lord, Tomorrow about this time a measure of choice meal shall be sold for a shekel, and two measures of barley for a shekel, at the gate of Sa·ma-ri·a." 2Then the captain on whose hand the king leaned said to the man of God, "Even if the Lord were to make windows in the sky, could such a thing happen?" But he said, "You shall see it with your own eyes, but you shall not eat from it."

The Arameans Flee

3 Now there were four leprous[t] men outside the city gate, who said to one another, "Why should we sit here until we die? [4]If we say, 'Let us enter the city,' the famine is in the city, and we shall die there; but if we sit here, we shall also die. Therefore, let us desert to the Ar·a·mē'an camp; if they spare our lives, we shall live; and if they kill us, we shall but die." [5]So they arose at twilight to go to the Ar·a·mē'an camp; but when they came to the edge of the Ar·a·mē'an camp, there was no one there at all. [6]For the Lord had caused the Ar·a·mē'an army to hear the sound of chariots, and of horses, the sound of a great army, so that they said to one another, "The king of Israel has hired the kings of the Hit'-tītes and the kings of Egypt to fight against us." [7]So they fled away in the twilight and abandoned their tents, their horses, and their donkeys leaving the camp just as it was, and fled for their lives. [8]When these leprous[t] men had come to the edge of the camp, they went into a tent, ate and drank, carried off silver, gold, and clothing, and went and hid them. Then they came back, entered another tent, carried off things from it, and went and hid them.

9 Then they said to one another, "What we are doing is wrong. This is a day of good news; if we are silent and wait until the morning light, we will be found guilty; therefore let us go and tell the king's household." [10]So they came and called to the gatekeepers of the city, and told them, "We went to the Ar·a·mē'-an camp, but there was no one to be seen or heard there, nothing but the horses tied, the donkeys tied, and the tents as they were." [11]Then the gatekeepers called out and proclaimed it to the king's household. [12]The king got up in the night, and said to his servants, "I will tell you what the Ar·a·mē'ans have prepared against us. They know that we are starving; so they have left the camp to hide themselves in the open country, thinking, 'When they come out of the city, we shall take them alive and get into the city.'" [13]One of his servants said, "Let some men take five of the remaining horses, since those left here will suffer the fate of the whole multitude of Israel that have perished already;[u] let us send and find out." [14]So they took two mounted men, and the king sent them after the Ar·a·mē'an army, saying, "Go and find out." [15]So they went after them as far as the Jordan; the whole way was littered with garments and equipment that the Ar·a·mē'ans had thrown away in their haste. So the messengers returned, and told the king.

16 Then the people went out, and plundered the camp of the Ar·a·mē'ans. So a measure of choice meal was sold for a shekel, and two measures of barley for a shekel, according to the word of the LORD. [17]Now the king had appointed the captain on whose hand he leaned to have charge of the gate; the people trampled him to death in the gate, just as the man of God had said when the king came down to him. [18]For when the man of God had said to the king, "Two measures of barley shall be sold for a shekel, and a measure of choice meal for a shekel, about this time tomorrow in the gate of Sa·mār'i·a," [19]the captain had

---

[t] A term for several skin diseases; precise meaning uncertain   [u] Compare Gk Syr Vg: Meaning of Heb uncertain

answered the man of God, "Even if the LORD were to make windows in the sky, could such a thing happen?" And he had answered, "You shall see it with your own eyes, but you shall not eat from it." [20]It did indeed happen to him; the people trampled him to death in the gate.

The Shunammite Woman's Land Restored

8 Now E·li'sha had said to the woman whose son he had restored to life, "Get up and go with your household, and settle wherever you can; for the LORD has called for a famine, and it will come on the land for seven years." [2]So the woman got up and did according to the word of the man of God; she went with her household and settled in the land of the Phi·lis'tines seven years. [3]At the end of the seven years, when the woman returned from the land of the Phi·lis'tines, she set out to appeal to the king for her house and her land. [4]Now the king was talking with Ge·ha'zi the servant of the man of God, saying, "Tell me all the great things that E·li'sha has done." [5]While he was telling the king how E·li'sha had restored a dead person to life, the woman whose son he had restored to life appealed to the king for her house and her land. Ge·ha'zi said, "My lord king, here is the woman, and here is her son whom E·li'sha restored to life." [6]When the king questioned the woman, she told him. So the king appointed an official for her, saying, "Restore all that was hers, together with all the revenue of the fields from the day that she left the land until now."

Death of Ben-hadad

7 E·li'sha went to Damascus while King Ben-ha'dad of Ar'am was ill. When it was told him, "The man of God has come here," [8]the king said to Haz'a·el, "Take a present with you and go to meet the man of God. Inquire of the LORD through him, whether I shall recover from this illness." [9]So Haz'a·el went to

meet him, taking a present with him, all kinds of goods of Damascus, forty camel loads. When he entered and stood before him, he said, "Your son King Ben-ha'dad of Ar'am has sent me to you, saying, 'Shall I recover from this illness?'" [10]E·li'sha said to him, "Go, say to him, 'You shall certainly recover'; but the LORD has shown me that he shall certainly die." [11]He fixed his gaze and stared at him, until he was ashamed. Then the man of God wept. [12]Haz'a·el asked, "Why does my lord weep?" He answered, "Because I know the evil that you will do to the people of Israel; you will set their fortresses on fire, you will kill their young men with the sword, dash in pieces their little ones, and rip up their pregnant women." [13]Haz'a·el said, "What is your servant, who is a mere dog, that he should do this great thing?" E·li'sha answered, "The LORD has shown me that you are to be king over Ar'am." [14]Then he left E·li'sha, and went to his master Ben-ha'dad,[v] who said to him, "What did E·li'sha say to you?" And he answered, "He told me that you would certainly recover." [15]But the next day he took the bed-cover and dipped it in water and spread it over the king's face, until he died. And Haz'a·el succeeded him.

Hazael took over the throne of Damascus when he murdered the king. He ruled from about 841–798 BC. Hazael was a mighty warrior and builder who often invaded the kingdoms of Israel and Judah. The prophet Elisha knew that these terrible things would happen before they did, and so he cried. Elisha viewed Hazael's attacks as the anger of God turned against the people because of their sins.

[v] Heb lacks *Ben-hadad*

Jehoram Reigns over Judah

16 In the fifth year of King Jō´ram son of Ā´hab of Israel,ʷ Je·hō´ram son of King Je·hosh´a·phat of Judah began to reign. [17]He was thirty-two years old when he became king, and he reigned eight years in Jerusalem. [18]He walked in the way of the kings of Israel, as the house of Ā´hab had done, for the daughter of Ā´hab was his wife. He did what was evil in the sight of the LORD. [19]Yet the LORD would not destroy Judah, for the sake of his servant David, since he had promised to give a lamp to him and to his descendants forever.

20 In his days Ē´dom revolted against the rule of Judah, and set up a king of their own. [21]Then Jō´ram crossed over to Zā´ir with all his chariots. He set out by night and attacked the Ē´dom·ites and their chariot commanders who had surrounded him;ˣ but his army fled home. [22]So Ē´dom has been in revolt against the rule of Judah to this day. Lib´nah also revolted at the same time. [23]Now the rest of the acts of Jō´ram, and all that he did, are they not written in the Book of the Annals of the Kings of Judah? [24]So Jō´ram slept with his ancestors, and was buried with them in the city of David; his son A·ha·zī´ah succeeded him.

Ahaziah Reigns over Judah

25 In the twelfth year of King Jō´ram son of Ā´hab of Israel, A·ha·zī´ah son of King Je·hō´ram of Judah began to reign. [26]A·ha·zī´ah was twenty-two years old when he began to reign; he reigned one year in Jerusalem. His mother's name was Ath·a·lī´ah, a granddaughter of King Om´rī of Israel. [27]He also walked in the way of the house of Ā´hab, doing what was evil in the sight of the LORD, as the house of Ā´hab had done, for he was son-in-law to the house of Ā´hab.

28 He went with Jō´ram son of Ā´hab to wage war against King Haz´a·el of Ar´am at Rā´moth-gil´ē·ad, where the Ar·a·mē´ans wounded Jō´ram. [29]King Jō-

ram returned to be healed in Jez´rē·el of the wounds that the Ar·a·mē´ans had inflicted on him at Rā´mah, when he fought against King Haz´a·el of Ar´am. King A·ha·zī´ah son of Je·hō´ram of Judah went down to see Jō´ram son of Ā´hab in Jez´rē·el, because he was wounded.

Anointing of Jehu

9 Then the prophet E·lī´sha called a member of the company of prophetsʸ and said to him, "Gird up your loins; take this flask of oil in your hand, and go to Rā´moth-gil´ē·ad. [2]When you arrive, look there for Jē´hū son of Je·hosh´a·phat, son of Nim´shī; go in and get him to leave his companions, and take him into an inner chamber. [3]Then take the flask of oil, pour it on his head, and say, 'Thus says the LORD: I anoint you king over Israel.' Then open the door and flee; do not linger."

4 So the young man, the young prophet, went to Rā´moth-gil´ē·ad. [5]He arrived while the commanders of the army were in council, and he announced, "I have a message for you, commander." "For which one of us?" asked Jē´hū. "For you, commander." [6]So Jē´hūᶻ got up and went inside; the young man poured the oil on his head, saying to him, "Thus says the LORD the God of Israel: I anoint you king over the people of the LORD, over Israel. [7]You shall strike down the house of your master Ā´hab, so that I may avenge on Jez´e·bel the blood of my servants the prophets, and the blood of all the servants of the LORD. [8]For the whole house of Ā´hab shall perish; I will cut off from Ā´hab every male, bond or free, in Israel. [9]I will make the house of Ā´hab like the house of Jer·o·bō´am son of Nē´bat, and like the house of Bā´a·sha son of A·hī´jah. [10]The dogs shall eat Jez´e·bel in the territory of Jez´rē·el, and no one shall bury her." Then he opened the door and fled.

ʷ Gk Syr: Heb adds *Jehoshaphat being king of Judah,*   ˣ Meaning of Heb uncertain   ʸ Heb *sons of the prophets*   ᶻ Heb *he*

11 When Jē′hū came back to his master's officers, they said to him, "Is everything all right? Why did that madman come to you?" He answered them, "You know the sort and how they babble." ¹²They said, "Liar! Come on, tell us!" So he said, "This is just what he said to me: 'Thus says the LORD, I anoint you king over Israel.'" ¹³Then hurriedly they all took their cloaks and spread them for him on the bare[a] steps; and they blew the trumpet, and proclaimed, "Jē′hū is king."

Joram of Israel Killed

14 Thus Jē′hū son of Je·hosh′a·phat son of Nim′shī conspired against Jō′ram. Jō′ram with all Israel had been on guard at Rā′moth-gil′e·ad against King Haz′a·el of Ar′am; ¹⁵but King Jō′ram had returned to be healed in Jez′re·el of the wounds that the Ar·a·me′ans had inflicted on him, when he fought against King Haz′a·el of Ar′am. So Jē′hū said, "If this is your wish, then let no one slip out of the city to go and tell the news in Jez′re·el." ¹⁶Then Jē′hū mounted his chariot and went to Jez′re·el, where Jō′ram was lying ill. King A·ha·zī′ah of Judah had come down to visit Jō′ram.

17 In Jez′re·el, the sentinel standing on the tower spied the company of Jē′hū arriving, and said, "I see a company." Jō′ram said, "Take a horseman; send him to meet them, and let him say, 'Is it peace?'" ¹⁸So the horseman went to meet him; he said, "Thus says the king, 'Is it peace?'" Jē′hū responded, "What have you to do with peace? Fall in behind me." The sentinel reported, saying, "The messenger reached them, but he is not coming back." ¹⁹Then he sent out a second horseman, who came to them and said, "Thus says the king, 'Is it peace?'" Jē′hū answered, "What have you to do with peace? Fall in behind me." ²⁰Again the sentinel reported, "He reached them, but he is not coming back. It looks like the driving of Jē′hū son of Nim′shī; for he drives like a maniac."

21 Jō′ram said, "Get ready." And they got his chariot ready. Then King Jō′ram of Israel and King A·ha·zī′ah of Judah set out, each in his chariot, and went to meet Jē′hū; they met him at the property of Nā′both the Jez′re·el·ite. ²²When Jō′ram saw Jē′hū, he said, "Is it peace, Jē′hū?" He answered, "What peace can there be, so long as the many whoredoms and sorceries of your mother Jez′e·bel continue?" ²³Then Jō′ram reined about and fled, saying to A·ha·zī′ah, "Treason, A·ha·zī′ah!" ²⁴Jē′hū drew his bow with all his strength, and shot Jō′ram between the shoulders, so that the arrow pierced his heart; and he sank in his chariot. ²⁵Jē′hū said to his aide Bid′kar, "Lift him out, and throw him on the plot of ground belonging to Nā′both the Jez′re·el·ite; for remember, when you and I rode side by side behind his father Ā′hab how the LORD uttered this oracle against him: ²⁶'For the blood of Nā′both and for the blood of his children that I saw yesterday, says the LORD, I swear I will repay you on this very plot of ground.' Now therefore lift him out and throw him on the plot of ground, in accordance with the word of the LORD."

Ahaziah of Judah Killed

27 When King A·ha·zī′ah of Judah saw this, he fled in the direction of Beth-hag′gan. Jē′hū pursued him, saying, "Shoot him also!" And they shot him[b] in the chariot at the ascent to Gur, which is by Ib′le·am. Then he fled to Me·gid′dō, and died there. ²⁸His officers carried him in a chariot to Jerusalem, and buried him in his tomb with his ancestors in the city of David.

29 In the eleventh year of Jō′ram son of Ā′hab, A·ha·zī′ah began to reign over Judah.

Jezebel's Violent Death

30 When Jē′hū came to Jez′re·el, Jez′e·bel heard of it; she painted her

---

[a] Meaning of Heb uncertain   [b] Syr Vg Compare Gk: Heb lacks *and they shot him*

eyes, and adorned her head, and looked out of the window. [31]As Jē´hū entered the gate, she said, "Is it peace, Zim´rī, murderer of your master?" [32]He looked up to the window and said, "Who is on my side? Who?" Two or three eunuchs looked out at him. [33]He said, "Throw her down." So they threw her down; some of her blood spattered on the wall and on the horses, which trampled on her. [34]Then he went in and ate and drank; he said, "See to that cursed woman and bury her; for she is a king's daughter." [35]But when they went to bury her, they found no more of her than the skull and the feet and the palms of her hands. [36]When they came back and told him, he said, "This is the word of the LORD, which he spoke by his servant E·lī´jah the Tish´bīte, 'In the territory of Jez´rē·el the dogs shall eat the flesh of Jez´e·bel; [37]the corpse of Jez´e·bel shall be like dung on the field in the territory of Jez´rē·el, so that no one can say, This is Jez´e·bel.' "

Massacre of Ahab's Descendants

10 Now Ā´hab had seventy sons in Sa·mār´i·a. So Jē´hū wrote letters and sent them to Sa·mār´i·a, to the rulers of Jez´rē·el,[c] to the elders, and to the guardians of the sons of[d] Ā´hab, saying, [2]"Since your master's sons are with you and you have at your disposal chariots and horses, a fortified city, and weapons, [3]select the son of your master who is the best qualified, set him on his father's throne, and fight for your master's house." [4]But they were utterly terrified and said, "Look, two kings could not withstand him; how then can we stand?" [5]So the steward of the palace, and the governor of the city, along with the elders and the guardians, sent word to Jē´hū: "We are your servants; we will do anything you say. We will not make anyone king; do whatever you think right." [6]Then he wrote them a second letter, saying, "If you are on my side, and if you are ready to obey me, take the heads of

your master's sons and come to me at Jez´rē·el tomorrow at this time." Now the king's sons, seventy persons, were with the leaders of the city, who were charged with their upbringing. [7]When the letter reached them, they took the king's sons and killed them, seventy persons; they put their heads in baskets and sent them to him at Jez´rē·el. [8]When the messenger came and told him, "They have brought the heads of the king's sons," he said, "Lay them in two heaps at the entrance of the gate until the morning." [9]Then in the morning when he went out, he stood and said to all the people, "You are innocent. It was I who conspired against my master and killed him; but who struck down all these? [10]Know then that there shall fall to the earth nothing of the word of the LORD, which the LORD spoke concerning the house of Ā´hab; for the LORD has done what he said through his servant E·lī´jah." [11]So Jē´hū killed all who were left of the house of Ā´hab in Jez´rē·el, all his leaders, close friends, and priests, until he left him no survivor.

[12] Then he set out and went to Sa·mār´i·a. On the way, when he was at Beth-ek´ed of the Shepherds, [13]Jē´hū met relatives of King A·ha·zī´ah of Judah and said, "Who are you?" They answered, "We are kin of A·ha·zī´ah; we have come down to visit the royal princes and the sons of the queen mother." [14]He said, "Take them alive." They took them alive, and slaughtered them at the pit of Beth-ek´ed, forty-two in all; he spared none of them.

[15] When he left there, he met Je·hon´a·dab son of Rē´chab coming to meet him; he greeted him, and said to him, "Is your heart as true to mine as mine is to yours?"[e] Je·hon´a·dab answered, "It is." Jē´hū said,[f] "If it is, give me your hand." So he gave him his hand. Jē´hū took him up with him into

c Or *of the city;* Vg Compare Gk   d Gk: Heb lacks *of the sons of*   e Gk: Heb *Is it right with your heart, as my heart is with your heart?*   f Gk: Heb lacks *Jehu said* the chariot. ¹⁶He said, "Come with me, and see my zeal for the LORD." So he^g had him ride in his chariot. ¹⁷When he came to Sa·mār´i·a, he killed all who were left to A´hab in Sa·mār´i·a, until he had wiped them out, according to the word of the LORD that he spoke to E·lī´jah.

Slaughter of Worshipers of Baal

18 Then Jē´hū assembled all the people and said to them, "A´hab offered Bā´al small service; but Jē´hū will offer much more. ¹⁹Now therefore summon to me all the prophets of Bā´al, all his worshipers, and all his priests; let none be missing, for I have a great sacrifice to offer to Bā´al; whoever is missing shall not live." But Jē´hū was acting with cunning in order to destroy the worshipers of Bā´al. ²⁰Jē´hū decreed, "Sanctify a solemn assembly for Bā´al." So they proclaimed it. ²¹Jē´hū sent word throughout all Israel; all the worshipers of Bā´al came, so that there was no one left who did not come. They entered the temple of Bā´al, until the temple of Bā´al was filled from wall to wall. ²²He said to the keeper of the wardrobe, "Bring out the vestments for all the worshipers of Bā´al." So he brought out the vestments for them. ²³Then Jē´hū entered the temple of Bā´al with Je·hon´a·dab son of Rē´chab; he said to the worshipers of Bā´al, "Search and see that there is no worshiper of the LORD here among you, but only worshipers of Bā´al." ²⁴Then they proceeded to offer sacrifices and burnt offerings.

Now Jē´hū had stationed eighty men outside, saying, "Whoever allows any of those to escape whom I deliver into your hands shall forfeit his life." ²⁵As soon as he had finished presenting the burnt offering, Jē´hū said to the guards and to the officers, "Come in and kill them; let no one escape." So they put them to the sword. The guards and the officers threw them out, and then went into the citadel of the temple of Bā´al. ²⁶They brought

out the pillar^h that was in the temple of Bā´al, and burned it. ²⁷Then they demolished the pillar of Bā´al, and destroyed the temple of Bā´al, and made it a latrine to this day.

28 Thus Jē´hū wiped out Bā´al from Israel. ²⁹But Jē´hū did not turn aside from the sins of Jer·o·bō´am son of Nē´bat, which he caused Israel to commit—the golden calves that were in Beth´el and in Dan. ³⁰The LORD said to Jē´hū, "Because you have done well in carrying out what I consider right, and in accordance with all that was in my heart have dealt with the house of A´hab, your sons of the fourth generation shall sit on the throne of Israel." ³¹But Jē´hū was not careful to follow the law of the LORD the God of Israel with all his heart; he did not turn from the sins of Jer·o·bō´am, which he caused Israel to commit.

Death of Jehu

32 In those days the LORD began to trim off parts of Israel. Haz´a·el defeated them throughout the territory of Israel: ³³from the Jordan eastward, all the land of Gil´e·ad, the Gad´ītes, the Reū´ben·ītes, and the Ma·nas´sītes, from A·rō´er, which is by the Wadi Ar´non, that is, Gil´e·ad and Bā´shan. ³⁴Now the rest of the acts of Jē´hū, all that he did, and all his power, are they not written in the Book of the Annals of the Kings of Israel? ³⁵So Jē´hū slept with his ancestors, and they buried him in Sa·mār´i·a. His son Je·hō´a·haz succeeded him. ³⁶The time that Jē´hū reigned over Israel in Sa·mār´i·a was twenty-eight years.

Athaliah Reigns over Judah

11 Now when Ath·a·lī´ah, A·ha·zī´ah's mother, saw that her son was dead, she set about to destroy all the royal family. ²But Je·hosh´e·ba, King Jō´ram's daughter, A·ha·zī´ah's sister, took Jō´ash son of A·ha·zī´ah, and stole him away from among the king's chil-

^g Gk Syr Tg: Heb *they*   ^h Gk Vg Syr Tg: Heb *pillars*

dren who were about to be killed; she put[i] him and his nurse in a bedroom. Thus she[j] hid him from Ath·a·lī′ah, so that he was not killed; [3]he remained with her six years, hidden in the house of the LORD, while Ath·a·lī′ah reigned over the land.

Jehoiada Anoints the Child Joash

4 But in the seventh year Je·hoi′a·da summoned the captains of the Cār′ītes and of the guards and had them come to him in the house of the LORD. He made a covenant with them and put them under oath in the house of the LORD; then he showed them the king's son. [5]He commanded them, "This is what you are to do: one-third of you, those who go off duty on the sabbath and guard the king's house [6](another third being at the gate Sur and a third at the gate behind the guards), shall guard the palace; [7]and your two divisions that come on duty in force on the sabbath and guard the house of the LORD[k] [8]shall surround the king, each with weapons in hand; and whoever approaches the ranks is to be killed. Be with the king in his comings and goings."

9 The captains did according to all that the priest Je·hoi′a·da commanded; each brought his men who were to go off duty on the sabbath, with those who were to come on duty on the sabbath, and came to the priest Je·hoi′a·da. [10]The priest delivered to the captains the spears and shields that had been King David's, which were in the house of the LORD; [11]the guards stood, every man with his weapons in his hand, from the south side of the house to the north side of the house, around the altar and the house, to guard the king on every side. [12]Then he brought out the king's son, put the crown on him, and gave him the covenant;[l] they proclaimed him king, and anointed him; they clapped their hands and shouted, "Long live the king!"

Death of Athaliah

13 When Ath·a·lī′ah heard the noise of the guard and of the people, she went into the house of the LORD to the people; [14]when she looked, there was the king standing by the pillar, according to custom, with the captains and the trumpeters beside the king, and all the people of the land rejoicing and blowing trumpets. Ath·a·lī′ah tore her clothes and cried, "Treason! Treason!" [15]Then the priest Je·hoi′a·da commanded the captains who were set over the army, "Bring her out between the ranks, and kill with the sword anyone who follows her." For the priest said, "Let her not be killed in the house of the LORD." [16]So they laid hands on her; she went through the horses' entrance to the king's house, and there she was put to death.

17 Je·hoi′a·da made a covenant between the LORD and the king and people, that they should be the LORD's people; also between the king and the people. [18]Then all the people of the land went to the house of Bā′al, and tore it down; his altars and his images they broke in pieces, and they killed Mat′tan, the priest of Bā′al, before the altars. The priest posted guards over the house of the LORD. [19]He took the captains, the Cār′ītes, the guards, and all the people of the land; then they brought the king down from the house of the LORD, marching through the gate of the guards to the king's house. He took his seat on the throne of the kings. [20]So all the people of the land rejoiced; and the city was quiet after Ath·a·lī′ah had been killed with the sword at the king's house.

21[m] Je·hō′ash[n] was seven years old when he began to reign.

The Temple Repaired

12 In the seventh year of Jē′hū, Je·hō′ash began to reign; he reigned forty years in Jerusalem. His

---

[i] With 2 Chr 22.11: Heb lacks *she put*   [j] Gk Syr Vg Compare 2 Chr 22.11: Heb *they*   [k] Heb *the LORD to the king*   [l] Or *treaty* or *testimony*; Heb *eduth*   [m] Ch 12.1 in Heb   [n] Another spelling is *Joash*; see verse 19

Jehoash was only seven years old when he became king. He ruled for forty years in Jerusalem. 2 Kings 12:2 says that he did what was right in the sight of the Lord all his days. Jehoash was a king who followed the ways of God.

mother's name was Zib·i·ah of Bē´er-shē´ba. ²Je·hō´ash did what was right in the sight of the LORD all his days, because the priest Je·hoi´a·da instructed him. ³Nevertheless the high places were not taken away; the people continued to sacrifice and make offerings on the high places.

4 Je·hō´ash said to the priests, "All the money offered as sacred donations that is brought into the house of the LORD, the money for which each person is assessed—the money from the assessment of persons—and the money from the voluntary offerings brought into the house of the LORD, ⁵let the priests receive from each of the donors; and let them repair the house wherever any need of repairs is discovered." ⁶But by the twenty-third year of King Je·hō´ash the priests had made no repairs on the house. ⁷Therefore King Je·hō´ash summoned the priest Je·hoi´a·da with the other priests and said to them, "Why are you not repairing the house? Now therefore do not accept any more money from your donors but hand it over for the repair of the house." ⁸So the priests agreed that they would neither accept more money from the people nor repair the house.

9 Then the priest Je·hoi´a·da took a chest, made a hole in its lid, and set it beside the altar on the right side as one entered the house of the LORD; the priests who guarded the threshold put in it all the money that was brought into the house of the LORD. ¹⁰Whenever they saw that there was a great deal of money

in the chest, the king's secretary and the high priest went up, counted the money that was found in the house of the LORD, and tied it up in bags. ¹¹They would give the money that was weighed out into the hands of the workers who had the oversight of the house of the LORD; then they paid it out to the carpenters and the builders who worked on the house of the LORD, ¹²to the masons and the stonecutters, as well as to buy timber and quarried stone for making repairs on the house of the LORD, as well as for any outlay for repairs of the house. ¹³But for the house of the LORD no basins of silver, snuffers, bowls, trumpets, or any vessels of gold, or of silver, were made from the money that was brought into the house of the LORD, ¹⁴for that was given to the workers who were repairing the house of the LORD with it. ¹⁵They did not ask an accounting from those into whose hand they delivered the money to pay out to the workers, for they dealt honestly. ¹⁶The money from the guilt offerings and the money from the sin offerings was not brought into the house of the LORD; it belonged to the priests.

Hazael Threatens Jerusalem

17 At that time King Haz´a·el of Ar´am went up, fought against Gath, and took it. But when Haz´a·el set his face to go up against Jerusalem, ¹⁸King Je·hō´ash of Judah took all the votive gifts that Je·hosh´a·phat, Je·hō´ram, and A·ha·zī´-ah, his ancestors, the kings of Judah, had dedicated, as well as his own votive gifts, all the gold that was found in the treasuries of the house of the LORD and of the king's house, and sent these to King Haz´a·el of Ar´am. Then Haz´a·el withdrew from Jerusalem.

Death of Joash

19 Now the rest of the acts of Jō´ash, and all that he did, are they not written in the Book of the Annals of the Kings of Judah? ²⁰His servants arose, devised a conspiracy, and killed Jō´ash in the

house of Mil·lo, on the way that goes down to Sil·la. ²¹It was Jo̅´za·car son of Shim´ē·ath and Je·ho̅´za·bad son of Sho̅´mer, his servants, who struck him down, so that he died. He was buried with his ancestors in the city of David; then his son Am·a·zi̅´ah succeeded him.

Jehoahaz Reigns over Israel

13 In the twenty-third year of King Jo̅´ash son of A·ha·zi̅´ah of Judah, Je·ho̅´a·haz son of Jē´hū began to reign over Israel in Sa·mār´i·a; he reigned seventeen years. ²He did what was evil in the sight of the LORD, and followed the sins of Jer·o·bo̅´am son of Nē´bat, which he caused Israel to sin; he did not depart from them. ³The anger of the LORD was kindled against Israel, so that he gave them repeatedly into the hand of King Haz´a·el of Ar´am, then into the hand of Ben-hā´dad son of Haz´a·el. ⁴But Je·ho̅´a·haz entreated the LORD, and the LORD heeded him; for he saw the oppression of Israel, how the king of Ar´am oppressed them. ⁵Therefore the LORD gave Israel a savior, so that they escaped from the hand of the Ar·a·mē´ans; and the people of Israel lived in their homes as formerly. ⁶Nevertheless they did not depart from the sins of the house of Jer·o·bo̅´am, which he caused Israel to sin, but walked° in them; the sacred poleᵖ also remained in Sa·mār´i·a. ⁷So Je·ho̅´a·haz was left with an army of not more than fifty horsemen, ten chariots and ten thousand footmen; for the king of Ar´am had destroyed them and made them like the dust at threshing. ⁸Now the rest of the acts of Je·ho̅´a·haz and all that he did, including his might, are they not written in the Book of the Annals of the Kings of Israel? ⁹So Je·ho̅´a·haz slept with his ancestors, and they buried him in Sa·mār´i·a; then his son Jo̅´ash succeeded him.

Jehoash Reigns over Israel

10 In the thirty-seventh year of King Jo̅´ash of Judah, Je·ho̅´ash son of Je·ho̅´a·haz began to reign over Israel in Sa·mār´-

i·a; he reigned sixteen years. ¹¹He also did what was evil in the sight of the LORD; he did not depart from all the sins of Jer·o·bo̅´am son of Nē´bat, which he caused Israel to sin, but he walked in them. ¹²Now the rest of the acts of Jo̅´ash, and all that he did, as well as the might with which he fought against King Am·a·zi̅´ah of Judah, are they not written in the Book of the Annals of the Kings of Israel? ¹³So Jo̅´ash slept with his ancestors, and Jer·o·bo̅´am sat upon his throne; Jo̅´ash was buried in Sa·mār´i·a with the kings of Israel.

Death of Elisha

14 Now when E·li̅´sha had fallen sick with the illness of which he was to die, King Jo̅´ash of Israel went down to him, and wept before him, crying, "My father, my father! The chariots of Israel and its horsemen!" ¹⁵E·li̅´sha said to him, "Take a bow and arrows"; so he took a bow and arrows. ¹⁶Then he said to the king of Israel, "Draw the bow"; and he drew it. E·li̅´sha laid his hands on the king's hands. ¹⁷Then he said, "Open the window eastward"; and he opened it. E·li̅´sha said, "Shoot"; and he shot. Then he said, "The LORD's arrow of victory, the arrow of victory over Ar´am! For you shall fight the Ar·a·mē´ans in A̅´phek until you have made an end of them." ¹⁸He continued, "Take the arrows"; and he took them. He said to the king of Israel, "Strike the ground with them"; he struck three times, and stopped. ¹⁹Then the man of God was angry with him, and said, "You should have struck five or six times; then you would have struck down Ar´am until you had made an end of it, but now you will strike down Ar´am only three times."

20 So E·li̅´sha died, and they buried him. Now bands of Mo̅´ab·ites used to invade the land in the spring of the year. ²¹As a man was being buried, a marauding band was seen and the man was

° Gk Syr Tg Vg: Heb *he walked*   ᵖ Heb *Asherah*

thrown into the grave of E·lī´sha; as soon as the man touched the bones of E·lī´sha, he came to life and stood on his feet.

Israel Recaptures Cities from Aram

22 Now King Haz´a·el of Ar´am oppressed Israel all the days of Je·hō´a·haz. [23]But the LORD was gracious to them and had compassion on them; he turned toward them, because of his covenant with Abraham, Isaac, and Jacob, and would not destroy them; nor has he banished them from his presence until now.

24 When King Haz´a·el of Ar´am died, his son Ben-hā´dad succeeded him. [25]Then Je·hō´ash son of Je·hō´a·haz took again from Ben-hā´dad son of Haz´a·el the towns that he had taken from his father Je·hō´a·haz in war. Three times Jō´ash defeated him and recovered the towns of Israel.

Amaziah Reigns over Judah

14 In the second year of King Jō´ash son of Jō´a·haz of Israel, King Am·a·zī´ah son of Jō´ash of Judah, began to reign. [2]He was twenty-five years old when he began to reign, and he reigned twenty-nine years in Jerusalem. His mother's name was Je·hō·ad´din of Jerusalem. [3]He did what was right in the sight of the LORD, yet not like his ancestor David; in all things he did as his father Jō´ash had done. [4]But the high places were not removed; the people still sacrificed and made offerings on the high places. [5]As soon as the royal power was firmly in his hand he killed his servants who had murdered his father the king. [6]But he did not put to death the children of the murderers; according to what is written in the book of the law of Moses, where the LORD commanded, "The parents shall not be put to death for the children, or the children be put to death for the parents; but all shall be put to death for their own sins."

7 He killed ten thousand E´dom·ites in the Valley of Salt and took Sē´la by storm; he called it Jok´thē-el, which is its name to this day.

8 Then Am·a·zī´ah sent messengers to King Je·hō´ash son of Je·hō´a·haz, son of Jē´hū, of Israel, saying, "Come, let us look one another in the face." [9]King Je·hō´ash of Israel sent word to King Am·a·zī´ah of Judah, "A thornbush on Lebanon sent to a cedar on Lebanon, saying, 'Give your daughter to my son for a wife'; but a wild animal of Lebanon passed by and trampled down the thornbush. [10]You have indeed defeated E´dom, and your heart has lifted you up. Be content with your glory, and stay at home; for why should you provoke trouble so that you fall, you and Judah with you?"

11 But Am·a·zī´ah would not listen. So King Je·hō´ash of Israel went up; he and King Am·a·zī´ah of Judah faced one another in battle at Beth-shē´mesh, which belongs to Judah. [12]Judah was defeated by Israel; everyone fled home. [13]King Je·hō´ash of Israel captured King Am·a·zī´ah of Judah son of Je·hō´ash, son of A·ha·zī´ah, at Beth-shē´mesh; he came to Jerusalem, and broke down the wall of Jerusalem from the E´phra·im Gate to the Corner Gate, a distance of four hundred cubits. [14]He seized all the gold and silver, and all the vessels that were found in the house of the LORD and in the treasuries of the king's house, as well as hostages; then he returned to Sa·mār´i·a.

15 Now the rest of the acts that Je·hō´ash did, his might, and how he fought with King Am·a·zī´ah of Judah, are they not written in the Book of the Annals of the Kings of Israel? [16]Je·hō´ash slept with his ancestors, and was buried in Sa·mār´i·a with the kings of Israel; then his son Jer·o·bō´am succeeded him.

17 King Am·a·zī´ah son of Jō´ash of Judah lived fifteen years after the death of King Je·hō´ash son of Je·hō´a·haz of Israel. [18]Now the rest of the deeds of Am·a·zī´ah, are they not written in the Book of the Annals of the Kings of Judah? [19]They made a conspiracy against

him in Jerusalem, and he fled to Lā′chish. But they sent after him to Lā′chish, and killed him there. ²⁰They brought him on horses; he was buried in Jerusalem with his ancestors in the city of David. ²¹All the people of Judah took Az·a·rī′ah, who was sixteen years old, and made him king to succeed his father Am·a·zī′ah. ²²He rebuilt Ē′lath and restored it to Judah, after King Am·a·zī′ah�q slept with his ancestors.

Jeroboam II Reigns over Israel

23 In the fifteenth year of King Am·a·zī′ah son of Jō′ash of Judah, King Jer·o·bō′am son of Jō′ash of Israel began to reign in Sa·mār′i·a; he reigned forty-one years. ²⁴He did what was evil in the sight of the LORD; he did not depart from all the sins of Jer·o·bō′am son of Nē′bat, which he caused Israel to sin. ²⁵He restored the border of Israel from Lē′bo-hā′math as far as the Sea of the Ar′a·bah, according to the word of the LORD, the God of Israel, which he spoke by his servant Jonah son of A·mit′tai, the prophet, who was from Gath-hē′pher. ²⁶For the LORD saw that the distress of Israel was very bitter; there was no one left, bond or free, and no one to help Israel. ²⁷But the LORD had not said that he would blot out the name of Israel from under heaven, so he saved them by the hand of Jer·o·bō′am son of Jō′ash.

28 Now the rest of the acts of Jer·o·bō′am, and all that he did, and his might, how he fought, and how he recovered for Israel Damascus and Hā′math, which had belonged to Judah, are they not written in the Book of the Annals of the Kings of Israel? ²⁹Jer·o·bō′am slept with his ancestors, the kings of Israel; his son Zech·a·rī′ah succeeded him.

Azariah Reigns over Judah

15 In the twenty-seventh year of King Jer·o·bō′am of Israel King Az·a·rī′ah son of Am·a·zī′ah of Judah began to reign. ²He was sixteen years old when he began to reign, and he reigned fifty-two years in Jerusalem. His mother's name was Jec·o·lī′ah of Jerusalem. ³He did what was right in the sight of the LORD, just as his father Am·a·zī′ah had done. ⁴Nevertheless the high places were not taken away; the people still sacrificed and made offerings on the high places. ⁵The LORD struck the king, so that he was leprousʳ to the day of his death, and lived in a separate house. Jō′tham the king's son was in charge of the palace, governing the people of the land. ⁶Now the rest of the acts of Az·a·rī′ah, and all that he did, are they not written in the Book of the Annals of the Kings of Judah? ⁷Az·a·rī′ah slept with his ancestors; they buried him with his ancestors in the city of David; his son Jō′tham succeeded him.

Zechariah Reigns over Israel

8 In the thirty-eighth year of King Az·a·rī′ah of Judah, Zech·a·rī′ah son of Jer·o·bō′am reigned over Israel in Sa·mār′i·a six months. ⁹He did what was evil in the sight of the LORD, as his ancestors had done. He did not depart from the sins of Jer·o·bō′am son of Nē′bat, which caused Israel to sin. ¹⁰Shal′lum son of Jā′besh conspired against him, and struck him down in public and killed him, and reigned in place of him. ¹¹Now the rest of the deeds of Zech·a·rī′ah are written in the Book of the Annals of the Kings of Israel. ¹²This was the promise of the LORD that he gave to Jē′hū, "Your sons shall sit on the throne of Israel to the fourth generation." And so it happened.

Shallum Reigns over Israel

13 Shal′lum son of Jā′besh began to reign in the thirty-ninth year of King Uz·zī′ah of Judah; he reigned one month in Sa·mār′i·a. ¹⁴Then Men′a·hem son of Gā′di came up from Tir′zah and came to Sa·mār′i·a; he struck down Shal′lum son of Jā′besh in Sa·mār′i·a and killed him; he reigned in place of him. ¹⁵Now the rest of the deeds of Shal′lum, including the conspiracy that he made, are written in the

---

�q Heb *the king*   ʳ A term for several skin diseases; precise meaning uncertain

Book of the Annals of the Kings of Israel. ¹⁶At that time Men·a·hem sacked Tiph·sah, all who were in it and its territory from Tir´zah on; because they did not open it to him, he sacked it. He ripped open all the pregnant women in it.

Menahem Reigns over Israel

17 In the thirty-ninth year of King Az·a·rī´ah of Judah, Men´a·hem son of Gā´dī began to reign over Israel; he reigned ten years in Sa·mār´i·a. ¹⁸He did what was evil in the sight of the LORD; he did not depart all his days from any of the sins of Jer·o·bō´am son of Ne´bat, which he caused Israel to sin. ¹⁹King Pūl of Assyria came against the land; Men´a·hem gave Pūl a thousand talents of silver, so that he might help him confirm his hold on the royal power. ²⁰Men´a·hem exacted the money from Israel, that is, from all the wealthy, fifty shekels of silver from each one, to give to the king of Assyria. So the king of Assyria turned back, and did not stay there in the land. ²¹Now the rest of the deeds of Men´a·hem, and all that he did, are they not written in the Book of the Annals of the Kings of Israel? ²²Men´a·hem slept with his ancestors, and his son Pek·a·hī´-ah succeeded him.

Pekahiah Reigns over Israel

23 In the fiftieth year of King Az·a·rī´-ah of Judah, Pek·a·hī´ah son of Men´a·hem began to reign over Israel in Sa·mār´i·a; he reigned two years. ²⁴He did what was evil in the sight of the LORD; he did not turn away from the sins of Jer·o·bō´am son of Ne´bat, which he caused Israel to sin. ²⁵Pē´kah son of Rem·a·lī´ah, his captain, conspired against him with fifty of the Gil´e·ad·ītes, and attacked him in Sa·mār´i·a, in the citadel of the palace along with Ar´gob and A·ri´eh; he killed him, and reigned in place of him. ²⁶Now the rest of the deeds of Pek·a·hī´ah, and all that he did, are written in the Book of the Annals of the Kings of Israel.

Pekah Reigns over Israel

27 In the fifty-second year of King Az·a·rī´ah of Judah, Pē´kah son of Rem·a·lī´ah began to reign over Israel in Sa·mār´i·a; he reigned twenty years. ²⁸He did what was evil in the sight of the LORD; he did not depart from the sins of Jer·o·bō´am son of Ne´bat, which he caused Israel to sin.

29 In the days of King Pē´kah of Israel, King Tig´lath-pī·lē´ser of Assyria came and captured I´jon, Ā´bel-beth-mā´a·cah, Ja·nō´ah, Kē´desh, Hā´zor, Gil´e·ad, and Galilee, all the land of Naph´ta·lī; and he carried the people captive to Assyria. ³⁰Then Hō·shē´a son of Ē´lah made a conspiracy against Pē´-kah son of Rem·a·lī´ah, attacked him, and killed him; he reigned in place of him, in the twentieth year of Jō´tham son of Uz·zī´ah. ³¹Now the rest of the acts of Pē´-kah, and all that he did, are written in the Book of the Annals of the Kings of Israel.

Jotham Reigns over Judah

32 In the second year of King Pē´kah son of Rem·a·lī´ah of Israel, King Jō´tham son of Uz·zī´ah of Judah began to reign. ³³He was twenty-five years old when he began to reign and reigned sixteen years in Jerusalem. His mother's name was Je·rū´sha daughter of Zā´dok. ³⁴He did what was right in the sight of the LORD, just as his father Uz·zī´ah had done. ³⁵Nevertheless the high places were not removed; the people still sacrificed and made offerings on the high places. He built the upper gate of the house of the LORD. ³⁶Now the rest of the acts of Jō´tham, and all that he did, are they not written in the Book of the Annals of the Kings of Judah? ³⁷In those days the LORD began to send King Rē´zin of Ar´am and Pē´kah son of Rem·a·lī´ah against Judah. ³⁸Jō´tham slept with his ancestors, and was buried with his ancestors in the city of David, his ancestor; his son Ā´haz succeeded him.

Ahaz Reigns over Judah

16 In the seventeenth year of Pēkah son of Rem·a·lī'ah, King Ā'haz son of Jō'tham of Judah began to reign. ²Ā'haz was twenty years old when he began to reign; he reigned sixteen years in Jerusalem. He did not do what was right in the sight of the LORD his God, as his ancestor David had done, ³but he walked in the way of the kings of Israel. He even made his son pass through fire, according to the abominable practices of the nations whom the LORD drove out before the people of Israel. ⁴He sacrificed and made offerings on the high places, on the hills, and under every green tree.

5 Then King Rē'zin of Ar'am and King Pē'kah son of Rem·a·lī'ah of Israel came up to wage war on Jerusalem; they besieged Ā'haz but could not conquer him. ⁶At that time the king of Ē'dom[s] recovered Ē'lath for Ē'dom,[t] and drove the Judeans from Ē'lath; and the Ē'dom·ītes came to Ē'lath, where they live to this day. ⁷Ā'haz sent messengers to King Tig'lath-pī·lē'ser of Assyria, saying, "I am your servant and your son. Come up, and rescue me from the hand of the king of Ar'am and from the hand of the king of Israel, who are attacking me." ⁸Ā'haz also took the silver and gold found in the house of the LORD and in the treasures of the king's house, and sent a present to the king of Assyria. ⁹The king of Assyria listened to him; the king of Assyria marched up against Damascus, and took it, carrying its people captive to Kir; then he killed Rē'zin.

10 When King Ā'haz went to Damascus to meet King Tig'lath-pī·lē'ser of Assyria, he saw the altar that was at Damascus. King Ā'haz sent to the priest Ū·rī'ah a model of the altar, and its pattern, exact in all its details. ¹¹The priest Ū·rī'ah built the altar; in accordance with all that King Ā'haz had sent from Damascus, just so did the priest Ū·rī'ah build it, before King Ā'haz arrived from Damascus. ¹²When the king came from Damascus, the king viewed the altar. Then the king drew near to the altar, went up on it, ¹³and offered his burnt offering and his grain offering, poured his drink offering, and dashed the blood of his offerings of well-being against the altar. ¹⁴The bronze altar that was before the LORD he removed from the front of the house, from the place between his altar and the house of the LORD, and put it on the north side of his altar. ¹⁵King Ā'haz commanded the priest Ū·rī'ah, saying, "Upon the great altar offer the morning burnt offering, and the evening grain offering, and the king's burnt offering, and his grain offering, with the burnt offering of all the people of the land, their grain offering, and their drink offering; then dash against it all the blood of the burnt offering, and all the blood of the sacrifice; but the bronze altar shall be for me to inquire by." ¹⁶The priest Ū·rī'ah did everything that King Ā'haz commanded.

17 Then King Ā'haz cut off the frames of the stands, and removed the laver from them; he removed the sea from the bronze oxen that were under it, and put it on a pediment of stone. ¹⁸The covered portal for use on the sabbath that had been built inside the palace, and the outer entrance for the king he removed from[u] the house of the LORD. He did this because of the king of Assyria. ¹⁹Now the rest of the acts of Ā'haz that he did, are they not written in the Book of the Annals of the Kings of Judah? ²⁰Ā'haz slept with his ancestors, and was buried with his ancestors in the city of David; his son Hez·e·kī'ah succeeded him.

Hoshea Reigns over Israel

17 In the twelfth year of King Ā'haz of Judah, Hō·shē'a son of Ē'lah began to reign in Sa·mār'i·a over Israel; he reigned nine years. ²He did what was

---

[s] Cn: Heb *King Rezin of Aram*   [t] Cn: Heb *Aram*
[u] Cn: Heb lacks *from*

evil in the sight of the LORD, yet not like the kings of Israel who were before him. [3]King Shal·ma·nē´ser of Assyria came up against him; Hō·shē´a became his vassal, and paid him tribute. [4]But the king of Assyria found treachery in Hō·shē´a; for he had sent messengers to King So of Egypt, and offered no tribute to the king of Assyria, as he had done year by year; therefore the king of Assyria confined him and imprisoned him.

Israel Carried Captive to Assyria

5 Then the king of Assyria invaded all the land and came to Sa·mār´i·a; for three years he besieged it. [6]In the ninth year of Hō·shē´a the king of Assyria captured Sa·mār´i·a; he carried the Israelites away to Assyria. He placed them in Hā´lah, on the Hā´bor, the river of Gō´zan, and in the cities of the Mēdes.

7 This occurred because the people of Israel had sinned against the LORD their God, who had brought them up out of the land of Egypt from under the hand of Pharaoh king of Egypt. They had worshiped other gods [8]and walked in the customs of the nations whom the LORD drove out before the people of Israel, and in the customs that the kings of Israel had introduced.[v] [9]The people of Israel secretly did things that were not right against the LORD their God. They built for themselves high places at all their towns, from watchtower to fortified city; [10]they set up for themselves pillars and sacred poles[w] on every high hill and under every green tree; [11]there they made offerings on all the high places, as the nations did whom the LORD carried away before them. They did wicked things, provoking the LORD to anger; [12]they served idols, of which the LORD had said to them, "You shall not do this." [13]Yet the LORD warned Israel and Judah by every prophet and every seer, saying, "Turn from your evil ways and keep my commandments and my statutes, in accordance with all the law that I commanded your ancestors and that I sent to you by my servants the prophets." [14]They would not listen but were stubborn, as their ancestors had been, who did not believe in the LORD their God. [15]They despised his statutes, and his covenant that he made with their ancestors, and the warnings that he gave them. They went after false idols and became false; they followed the nations that were around them, concerning whom the LORD had commanded them that they should not do as they did. [16]They rejected all the commandments of the LORD their God and made for themselves cast images of two calves; they made a sacred pole,[x] worshiped all the host of heaven, and served Bā´al. [17]They made their sons and their daughters pass through fire; they used divination and augury; and they sold themselves to do evil in the sight of the LORD, provoking him to anger. [18]Therefore the LORD was very angry with Israel and removed them out of his sight; none was left but the tribe of Judah alone.

19 Judah also did not keep the commandments of the LORD their God but walked in the customs that Israel had introduced. [20]The LORD rejected all the descendants of Israel; he punished them and gave them into the hand of plunderers, until he had banished them from his presence.

21 When he had torn Israel from the house of David, they made Jer·o·bō´am son of Nē´bat king. Jer·o·bō´am drove Israel from following the LORD and made them commit great sin. [22]The people of Israel continued in all the sins that Jer·o·bō´am committed; they did not depart from them [23]until the LORD removed Israel out of his sight, as he had foretold through all his servants the prophets. So Israel was exiled from their own land to Assyria until this day.

[v] Meaning of Heb uncertain   [w] Heb *Asherim*
[x] Heb *Asherah*

Assyria Resettles Samaria

24 The king of Assyria brought people from Babylon, Cū´thah, Av´va, Hā´math, and Seph·ar·vā´im, and placed them in the cities of Sa·mār´i·a in place of the people of Israel; they took possession of Sa·mār´i·a, and settled in its cities. ²⁵When they first settled there, they did not worship the LORD; therefore the LORD sent lions among them, which killed some of them. ²⁶So the king of Assyria was told, "The nations that you have carried away and placed in the cities of Sa·mār´i·a do not know the law of the god of the land; therefore he has sent lions among them; they are killing them, because they do not know the law of the god of the land." ²⁷Then the king of Assyria commanded, "Send there one of the priests whom you carried away from there; let him^y go and live there, and teach them the law of the god of the land." ²⁸So one of the priests whom they had carried away from Sa·mār´i·a came and lived in Beth´el; he taught them how they should worship the LORD.

29 But every nation still made gods of its own and put them in the shrines of the high places that the people of Sa·mār´i·a had made, every nation in the cities in which they lived; ³⁰the people of Babylon made Suc´coth-be´noth, the people of Cuth made Ner´gal, the people of Hā´math made A·shī´ma; ³¹the Av´vites made Nib´haz and Tar´tak; the Se·phar´vites burned their children in the fire to A·dram´me·lech and A·nam´me·lech, the gods of Seph·ar·vā´im. ³²They also worshiped the LORD and appointed from among themselves all sorts of people as priests of the high places, who sacrificed for them in the shrines of the high places. ³³So they worshiped the LORD but also served their own gods, after the manner of the nations from among whom they had been carried away. ³⁴To this day they continue to practice their former customs.

They do not worship the LORD and they do not follow the statutes or the ordinances or the law or the commandment that the LORD commanded the children of Jacob, whom he named Israel. ³⁵The LORD had made a covenant with them and commanded them, "You shall not worship other gods or bow yourselves to them or serve them or sacrifice to them, ³⁶but you shall worship the LORD, who brought you out of the land of Egypt with great power and with an outstretched arm; you shall bow yourselves to him, and to him you shall sacrifice. ³⁷The statutes and the ordinances and the law and the commandment that he wrote for you, you shall always be careful to observe. You shall not worship other gods; ³⁸you shall not forget the covenant that I have made with you. You shall not worship other gods, ³⁹but you shall worship the LORD your God; he will deliver you out of the hand of all your enemies." ⁴⁰They would not listen, however, but they continued to practice their former custom.

41 So these nations worshiped the LORD, but also served their carved images; to this day their children and their children's children continue to do as their ancestors did.

Hezekiah's Reign over Judah

18 In the third year of King Hō·shē´a son of E´lah of Israel, Hez·e·kī´ah son of King Ā´haz of Judah began to reign. ²He was twenty-five years old when he began to reign; he reigned twenty-nine years in Jerusalem. His mother's name was Ā´bī daughter of Zech·a·rī´ah. ³He did what was right in the sight of the LORD just as his ancestor David had done. ⁴He removed the high places, broke down the pillars, and cut down the sacred pole.^z He broke in pieces the bronze serpent that Moses had made, for until those days the people of Israel had made offerings to it; it was called Ne·hush´tan. ⁵He trusted in the LORD the God of Israel; so that there

^y Syr Vg: Heb *them*   ^z Heb *Asherah*

Hezekiah was twenty-five years old when he became king of Judah at a very important time in Judah's history. The nation was weak from fighting wars and from paying money to the kingdom of Assyria. The people had turned away from God to worship idols. Hezekiah destroyed the idols and tore down the high places where these idols were worshiped. He cleaned and reopened the Temple and restored the true worship of God. He made the city walls stronger and built a tunnel to bring in water from another city so that the people of Jerusalem would have water during an attack. That tunnel is still there today! Hezekiah is remembered as a great and good king who followed God's ways.

was no one like him among all the kings of Judah after him, or among those who were before him. 6For he held fast to the LORD; he did not depart from following him but kept the commandments that the LORD commanded Moses. 7The LORD was with him; wherever he went, he prospered. He rebelled against the king of Assyria and would not serve him. 8He attacked the Phi·lis´tines as far as Gā´za and its territory, from watchtower to fortified city.

9 In the fourth year of King Hez·e·kī´-ah, which was the seventh year of King Hō·shē´a son of Ē´lah of Israel, King Shal·man·ē´ser of Assyria came up against Sa·mār´i·a, besieged it, 10and at the end of three years, took it. In the sixth year of Hez·e·kī´ah, which was the ninth year of King Hō·shē´a of Israel, Sa·mār´i·a was taken. 11The king of Assyria carried the Israelites away to Assyria, settled them in Hā´lah, on the Hā´bor, the river of Gō´zan, and in the cities

of the Mēdes, 12because they did not obey the voice of the LORD their God but transgressed his covenant—all that Moses the servant of the LORD had commanded; they neither listened nor obeyed.

Sennacherib Invades Judah

13 In the fourteenth year of King Hez·e·kī´ah, King Sen·nach´e·rib of Assyria came up against all the fortified cities of Judah and captured them. 14King Hez·e·kī´ah of Judah sent to the king of Assyria at Lā´chish, saying, "I have done wrong; withdraw from me; whatever you impose on me I will bear." The king of Assyria demanded of King Hez·e·kī´ah of Judah three hundred talents of silver and thirty talents of gold. 15Hez·e·kī´ah gave him all the silver that was found in the house of the LORD and in the treasuries of the king's house. 16At that time Hez·e·kī´ah stripped the gold from the doors of the temple of the LORD, and from the doorposts that King Hez·e·kī´ah of Judah had overlaid and gave it to the king of Assyria. 17The king of Assyria sent the Tar´tan, the Rab-sar´-is, and the Rab´sha·keh with a great army from Lā´chish to King Hez·e·kī´ah at Jerusalem. They went up and came to Jerusalem. When they arrived, they came and stood by the conduit of the upper pool, which is on the highway to the Fuller's Field. 18When they called for the king, there came out to them E·lī´a·kim son of Hil·kī´ah, who was in charge of the palace, and Sheb´nah the secretary, and Jō´ah son of Ā´saph, the recorder.

19 The Rab´sha·keh said to them, "Say to Hez·e·kī´ah: Thus says the great king, the king of Assyria: On what do you base this confidence of yours? 20Do you think that mere words are strategy and power for war? On whom do you now rely, that you have rebelled against me? 21See, you are relying now on Egypt, that broken reed of a staff, which will pierce the hand of anyone who leans on

it. Such is Pharaoh king of Egypt to all who rely on him. ²²But if you say to me, 'We rely on the LORD our God,' is it not he whose high places and altars Hez·e·kī´-ah has removed, saying to Judah and to Jerusalem, 'You shall worship before this altar in Jerusalem'? ²³Come now, make a wager with my master the king of Assyria: I will give you two thousand horses, if you are able on your part to set riders on them. ²⁴How then can you repulse a single captain among the least of my master's servants, when you rely on Egypt for chariots and for horsemen? ²⁵Moreover, is it without the LORD that I have come up against this place to destroy it? The LORD said to me, Go up against this land, and destroy it."

26 Then E·lī´a·kim son of Hil·kī´ah, and Sheb´nah, and Jō´ah said to the Rab´sha·keh, "Please speak to your servants in the Ar·a·mā´ic language, for we understand it; do not speak to us in the language of Judah within the hearing of the people who are on the wall." ²⁷But the Rab´sha·keh said to them, "Has my master sent me to speak these words to your master and to you, and not to the people sitting on the wall, who are doomed with you to eat their own dung and to drink their own urine?"

28 Then the Rab´sha·keh stood and called out in a loud voice in the language of Judah, "Hear the word of the great king, the king of Assyria! ²⁹Thus says the king: 'Do not let Hez·e·kī´ah deceive you, for he will not be able to deliver you out of my hand. ³⁰Do not let Hez·e·kī´ah make you rely on the LORD by saying, The LORD will surely deliver us, and this city will not be given into the hand of the king of Assyria.' ³¹Do not listen to Hez·e·kī´ah; for thus says the king of Assyria: 'Make your peace with me and come out to me; then every one of you will eat from your own vine and your own fig tree, and drink water from your own cistern, ³²until I come and take you away to a land like your own

land, a land of grain and wine, a land of bread and vineyards, a land of olive oil and honey, that you may live and not die. Do not listen to Hez·e·kī´ah when he misleads you by saying, The LORD will deliver us. ³³Has any of the gods of the nations ever delivered its land out of the hand of the king of Assyria? ³⁴Where are the gods of Hā´math and Ar´pad? Where are the gods of Seph·ar·vā´im, Hē´na, and Iv´vah? Have they delivered Sa·mār´i·a out of my hand? ³⁵Who among all the gods of the countries have delivered their countries out of my hand, that the LORD should deliver Jerusalem out of my hand?' "

36 But the people were silent and answered him not a word, for the king's command was, "Do not answer him." ³⁷Then E·lī´a·kim son of Hil·kī´ah, who was in charge of the palace, and Sheb´na the secretary, and Jō´ah son of Ā´saph, the recorder, came to Hez·e·kī´ah with their clothes torn and told him the words of the Rab´sha·keh.

Hezekiah Consults Isaiah

19 When King Hez·e·kī´ah heard it, he tore his clothes, covered himself with sackcloth, and went into the house of the LORD. ²And he sent E·lī´a·kim, who was in charge of the palace, and Sheb´na the secretary, and the senior priests, covered with sackcloth, to the prophet Ī·sāi´ah son of Ā´moz. ³They said to him, "Thus says Hez·e·kī´ah, This day is a day of distress, of rebuke, and of disgrace; children have come to the birth, and there is no strength to bring them forth. ⁴It may be that the LORD your God heard all the words of the Rab´sha·keh, whom his master the king of Assyria has sent to mock the living God, and will rebuke the words that the LORD your God has heard; therefore lift up your prayer for the remnant that is left." ⁵When the servants of King Hez·e·kī´ah came to Ī·sāi´ah, ⁶Ī·sāi´ah said to them, "Say to your master, 'Thus says the LORD:

Do not be afraid because of the words that you have heard, with which the servants of the king of Assyria have reviled me. ⁷I myself will put a spirit in him, so that he shall hear a rumor and return to his own land; I will cause him to fall by the sword in his own land.'"

Sennacherib's Threat

8 The Rab´sha·keh returned, and found the king of Assyria fighting against Lib´nah; for he had heard that the king had left La´chish. ⁹When the king[a] heard concerning King Tir·ha´kah of Ethiopia,[b] "See, he has set out to fight against you," he sent messengers again to Hez·e·ki´ah, saying, ¹⁰"Thus shall you speak to King Hez·e·ki´ah of Judah: Do not let your God on whom you rely deceive you by promising that Jerusalem will not be given into the hand of the king of Assyria. ¹¹See, you have heard what the kings of Assyria have done to all lands, destroying them utterly. Shall you be delivered? ¹²Have the gods of the nations delivered them, the nations that my predecessors destroyed, Go´zan, Ha´ran, Re´zeph, and the people of Eden who were in Te·las´sar? ¹³Where is the king of Ha´math, the king of Ar´pad, the king of the city of Seph·ar·va´im, the king of He´na, or the king of Iv´vah?"

Hezekiah's Prayer

14 Hez·e·ki´ah received the letter from the hand of the messengers and read it; then Hez·e·ki´ah went up to the house of the LORD and spread it before the LORD. ¹⁵And Hez·e·ki´ah prayed before the LORD, and said: "O LORD the God of Israel, who are enthroned above the cherubim, you are God, you alone, of all the kingdoms of the earth; you have made heaven and earth. ¹⁶Incline your ear, O LORD, and hear; open your eyes, O LORD, and see; hear the words of Sen·nach´e·rib, which he has sent to mock the living God. ¹⁷Truly, O LORD, the kings of Assyria have laid waste the nations and their lands, ¹⁸and have

"O LORD the God of Israel, who are enthroned above the cherubim, you are God, you alone, of all the kingdoms of the earth; you have made heaven and earth. Incline your ear, O LORD, and hear; open your eyes, O LORD, and see." 2 Kings 19:15–16

hurled their gods into the fire, though they were no gods but the work of human hands—wood and stone—and so they were destroyed. ¹⁹So now, O LORD our God, save us, I pray you, from his hand, so that all the kingdoms of the earth may know that you, O LORD, are God alone."

20 Then I·sai´ah son of A´moz sent to Hez·e·ki´ah, saying, "Thus says the LORD, the God of Israel: I have heard your prayer to me about King Sen·nach´-e·rib of Assyria. ²¹This is the word that the LORD has spoken concerning him:

She despises you, she scorns you—
  virgin daughter Zion;
she tosses her head—behind your
    back,
    daughter Jerusalem.

²² "Whom have you mocked and reviled?
  Against whom have you raised your
    voice
and haughtily lifted your eyes?
  Against the Holy One of Israel!
²³ By your messengers you have mocked
    the Lord,
  and you have said, 'With my many
    chariots
I have gone up the heights of the
    mountains,
  to the far recesses of Lebanon;
I felled its tallest cedars,
  its choicest cypresses;
I entered its farthest retreat,
  its densest forest.
²⁴ I dug wells
  and drank foreign waters,

---

a Heb *he*   *b* Or *Nubia*; Heb *Cush*

I dried up with the sole of my foot
all the streams of Egypt.'

25 "Have you not heard
　　that I determined it long ago?
I planned from days of old
　　what now I bring to pass,
that you should make fortified cities
　　crash into heaps of ruins,
26 while their inhabitants, shorn of
　　　strength,
　　are dismayed and confounded;
they have become like plants of the
　　　field
　　and like tender grass,
like grass on the housetops,
　　blighted before it is grown.

27 "But I know your rising* and your
　　　sitting,
　　your going out and coming in,
　　and your raging against me.
28 Because you have raged against me
　　and your arrogance has come to my
　　　ears,
I will put my hook in your nose
　　and my bit in your mouth;
I will turn you back on the way
　　by which you came.

29 "And this shall be the sign for you:
This year you shall eat what grows of
itself, and in the second year what springs
from that; then in the third year sow,
reap, plant vineyards, and eat their fruit.
30The surviving remnant of the house of
Judah shall again take root downward,
and bear fruit upward; 31for from
Jerusalem a remnant shall go out, and
from Mount Zion a band of survivors.
The zeal of the LORD of hosts will do this.

32 "Therefore thus says the LORD concerning the king of Assyria: He shall not
come into this city, shoot an arrow there,
come before it with a shield, or cast up a
siege-ramp against it. 33By the way that
he came, by the same he shall return; he
shall not come into this city, says the
LORD. 34For I will defend this city to save

it, for my own sake and for the sake of
my servant David."

Sennacherib's Defeat and Death

35 That very night the angel of the
LORD set out and struck down one hundred eighty-five thousand in the camp of
the Assyrians; when morning dawned,
they were all dead bodies. 36Then King
Sen·nach´e·rib of Assyria left, went home,
and lived at Nin´e·veh. 37As he was worshiping in the house of his god Nis´roch,
his sons A·dram´me·lech and Sha·rē´zer
killed him with the sword, and they
escaped into the land of Ar´a·rat. His son
E´sar-had´don succeeded him.

Hezekiah's Illness

20 In those days Hez·e·kī´ah
became sick and was at the
point of death. The prophet I·sāi´ah son
of A´moz came to him, and said to him,
"Thus says the LORD: Set your house in
order, for you shall die; you shall not
recover." 2Then Hez·e·kī´ah turned his
face to the wall and prayed to the LORD:
3"Remember now, O LORD, I implore
you, how I have walked before you in
faithfulness with a whole heart, and have
done what is good in your sight."
Hez·e·kī´ah wept bitterly. 4Before I·sāi´ah
had gone out of the middle court, the
word of the LORD came to him: 5"Turn
back, and say to Hez·e·kī´ah prince of
my people, Thus says the LORD, the God
of your ancestor David: I have heard
your prayer, I have seen your tears;
indeed, I will heal you; on the third day
you shall go up to the house of the LORD.
6I will add fifteen years to your life. I will
deliver you and this city out of the hand
of the king of Assyria; I will defend this
city for my own sake and for my servant
David's sake." 7Then I·sāi´ah said, "Bring
a lump of figs. Let them take it and apply
it to the boil, so that he may recover."

8 Hez·e·kī´ah said to I·sāi´ah, "What
shall be the sign that the LORD will heal

_____
ᶜ Gk Compare Isa 37.27 Q Ms: MT lacks *rising*

me, and that I shall go up to the house of the LORD on the third day?" [9]I·sāi´ah said, "This is the sign to you from the LORD, that the LORD will do the thing that he has promised: the shadow has now advanced ten intervals; shall it retreat ten intervals?" [10]Hez·e·kī´ah answered, "It is normal for the shadow to lengthen ten intervals; rather let the shadow retreat ten intervals." [11]The prophet Ī·sāi´ah cried to the LORD; and he brought the shadow back the ten intervals, by which the sun[d] had declined on the dial of Ā´haz.

Envoys from Babylon

12 At that time King Mer´o·dach-bal´-a·dan son of Bal´a·dan of Babylon sent envoys with letters and a present to Hez·e·kī´ah, for he had heard that Hez·e·kī´ah had been sick. [13]Hez·e·kī´ah welcomed them;[e] he showed them all his treasure house, the silver, the gold, the spices, the precious oil, his armory, all that was found in his storehouses; there was nothing in his house or in all his realm that Hez·e·kī´ah did not show them. [14]Then the prophet Ī·sāi´ah came to King Hez·e·kī´ah, and said to him, "What did these men say? From where did they come to you?" Hez·e·kī´ah answered, "They have come from a far country, from Babylon." [15]He said, "What have they seen in your house?" Hez·e·kī´ah answered, "They have seen all that is in my house; there is nothing in my storehouses that I did not show them."

16 Then Ī·sāi´ah said to Hez·e·kī´ah, "Hear the word of the LORD: [17]Days are coming when all that is in your house, and that which your ancestors have stored up until this day, shall be carried to Babylon; nothing shall be left, says the LORD. [18]Some of your own sons who are born to you shall be taken away; they shall be eunuchs in the palace of the king of Babylon." [19]Then Hez·e·kī´ah said to Ī·sāi´ah, "The word of the LORD that you have spoken is good." For he thought, "Why not, if there will be peace and security in my days?"

Death of Hezekiah

20 The rest of the deeds of Hez·e·kī´ah, all his power, how he made the pool and the conduit and brought water into the city, are they not written in the Book of the Annals of the Kings of Judah? [21]Hez·e·kī´ah slept with his ancestors; and his son Ma·nas´seh succeeded him.

Manasseh Reigns over Judah

21 Ma·nas´seh was twelve years old when he began to reign; he reigned fifty-five years in Jerusalem. His mother's name was Heph´zi·bah. [2]He did what was evil in the sight of the LORD, following the abominable practices of the nations that the LORD drove out before the people of Israel. [3]For he rebuilt the high places that his father Hez·e·kī´ah had destroyed; he erected altars for Bā´al, made a sacred pole,[f] as King Ā´hab of Israel had done, worshiped all the host of heaven, and served them. [4]He built altars in the house of the LORD, of which the LORD had said, "In Jerusalem I will put my name." [5]He built altars for all the host of heaven in the two courts of the house of the LORD. [6]He made his son pass through fire; he practiced soothsaying and augury, and dealt with mediums and with wizards. He did much evil in the sight of the LORD, provoking him to anger. [7]The carved image of A·shē´rah that he had made he set in the house of which the LORD said to David and to his son Solomon, "In this house, and in Jerusalem, which I have chosen out of all the tribes of Israel, I will put my name forever; [8]I will not cause the feet of Israel to wander any more out of the land that I gave to their ancestors, if only they will be careful to do according to all that I have commanded them, and according to all the law that my servant Moses commanded

[d] Syr See Isa 38.8 and Tg: Heb *it*　　[e] Gk Vg Syr: Heb *When Hezekiah heard about them*　　[f] Heb *Asherah*

them." ⁹But they did not listen; Ma·nas´-seh misled them to do more evil than the nations had done that the LORD destroyed before the people of Israel.

10 The LORD said by his servants the prophets, ¹¹"Because King Ma·nas´seh of Judah has committed these abominations, has done things more wicked than all that the Am´o·rītes did, who were before him, and has caused Judah also to sin with his idols; ¹²therefore thus says the LORD, the God of Israel, I am bringing upon Jerusalem and Judah such evil that the ears of everyone who hears of it will tingle. ¹³I will stretch over Jerusalem the measuring line for Sa·mār´i·a, and the plummet for the house of Ā´hab; I will wipe Jerusalem as one wipes a dish, wiping it and turning it upside down. ¹⁴I will cast off the remnant of my heritage, and give them into the hand of their enemies; they shall become a prey and a spoil to all their enemies, ¹⁵because they have done what is evil in my sight and have provoked me to anger, since the day their ancestors came out of Egypt, even to this day."

16 Moreover Ma·nas´seh shed very much innocent blood, until he had filled Jerusalem from one end to another, besides the sin that he caused Judah to sin so that they did what was evil in the sight of the LORD.

17 Now the rest of the acts of Ma·nas´seh, all that he did, and the sin that he committed, are they not written in the Book of the Annals of the Kings of Judah? ¹⁸Ma·nas´seh slept with his ancestors, and was buried in the garden of his house, in the garden of Uz´za. His son Ā´mon succeeded him.

Amon Reigns over Judah

19 Ā´mon was twenty-two years old when he began to reign; he reigned two years in Jerusalem. His mother's name was Me·shul´le·meth daughter of Hā´ruz of Jot´bah. ²⁰He did what was evil in the sight of the LORD, as his father Ma·nas´seh had

done. ²¹He walked in all the way in which his father walked, served the idols that his father served, and worshiped them; ²²he abandoned the LORD, the God of his ancestors, and did not walk in the way of the LORD. ²³The servants of Ā´mon conspired against him, and killed the king in his house. ²⁴But the people of the land killed all those who had conspired against King Ā´mon, and the people of the land made his son Jō·sī´ah king in place of him. ²⁵Now the rest of the acts of Ā´mon that he did, are they not written in the Book of the Annals of the Kings of Judah? ²⁶He was buried in his tomb in the garden of Uz´za; then his son Jō·sī´ah succeeded him.

Josiah Reigns over Judah

22 Jō·sī´ah was eight years old when he began to reign; he reigned thirty-one years in Jerusalem. His mother's name was Je·dī´dah daughter of A·dāi´ah of Boz´kath. ²He did what was right in the sight of the LORD, and walked in all the way of his father David; he did not turn aside to the right or to the left.

Hilkiah Finds the Book of the Law

3 In the eighteenth year of King Jō·sī´ah, the king sent Shā´phan son of Az·a·lī´ah, son of Me·shul´lam, the secretary, to the house of the LORD, saying, ⁴"Go up to the high priest Hil·kī´ah, and have him count the entire sum of the money that has been brought into the house of the LORD, which the keepers of the threshold have collected from the people; ⁵let it be given into the hand of the workers who have the oversight of the house of the LORD; let them give it to the workers who are at the house of the LORD, repairing the house, ⁶that is, to the carpenters, to the builders, to the masons; and let them use it to buy timber and quarried stone to repair the house. ⁷But no accounting shall be asked from them for the money that is delivered into their hand, for they deal honestly."

8 The high priest Hil·kī´ah said to Shā´phan the secretary, "I have found the

book of the law in the house of the LORD." When Hil·kī´ah gave the book to Shā´phan, he read it. ⁹Then Shā´phan the secretary came to the king, and reported to the king, "Your servants have emptied out the money that was found in the house, and have delivered it into the hand of the workers who have oversight of the house of the LORD." ¹⁰Shā´phan the secretary informed the king, "The priest Hil·kī´ah has given me a book." Shā´phan then read it aloud to the king.

11 When the king heard the words of the book of the law, he tore his clothes. ¹²Then the king commanded the priest Hil·kī´ah, A·hī´kam son of Shā´phan, Ach´bor son of Mī·cāi´ah, Shā´phan the secretary, and the king's servant A·sāi´ah, saying, ¹³"Go, inquire of the LORD for me, for the people, and for all Judah, concerning the words of this book that has been found; for great is the wrath of the LORD that is kindled against us, because our ancestors did not obey the words of this book, to do according to all that is written concerning us."

14 So the priest Hil·kī´ah, A·hī´kam, Ach´bor, Shā´phan, and A·sāi´ah went to the prophetess Hul´dah the wife of Shal´lum son of Tik´vah, son of Har´has, keeper of the wardrobe; she resided in Jerusalem in the Second Quarter, where they consulted her. ¹⁵She declared to them, "Thus says the LORD, the God of Israel: Tell the man who sent you to me, ¹⁶Thus says the LORD, I will indeed bring disaster on this place and on its inhabitants—all the words of the book that the king of Judah has read. ¹⁷Because they have abandoned me and have made offerings to other gods, so that they have provoked me to anger with all the work of their hands, therefore my wrath will be kindled against this place, and it will not be quenched. ¹⁸But as to the king of Judah, who sent you to inquire of the LORD, thus shall you say to him, Thus says the LORD, the God of Israel: Regarding the words that you have heard,

Hilkiah was a high priest when Josiah was king of Judah (about 641–609 BC). While the Temple was being repaired, Hilkiah found the scrolls of the book of the law (which most people believe is part of Deuteronomy) and took them to Josiah. When King Josiah heard what was written in these scrolls, he was very sad because he knew the people were not following the ways of God. Josiah, along with Hilkiah, helped the people go back to living the way God wanted them to live. He got rid of idols and altars, and he tore down the high places that were used to worship other gods. Josiah wanted the people to worship only God.

¹⁹because your heart was penitent, and you humbled yourself before the LORD, when you heard how I spoke against this place, and against its inhabitants, that they should become a desolation and a curse, and because you have torn your clothes and wept before me, I also have heard you, says the LORD. ²⁰Therefore, I will gather you to your ancestors, and you shall be gathered to your grave in peace; your eyes shall not see all the disaster that I will bring on this place." They took the message back to the king.

Josiah's Reformation

23 Then the king directed that all the elders of Judah and Jerusalem should be gathered to him. ²The king went up to the house of the LORD, and with him went all the people of Judah, all the inhabitants of Jerusalem, the priests, the prophets, and all the people, both small and great; he read in their hearing all the words of the book of the covenant that had been found in the house of the LORD. ³The king stood by the pillar and made a covenant before the LORD, to follow the LORD, keeping his commandments, his decrees, and his statutes, with all his heart and all his soul, to perform the words of this covenant that were written in this book. All the people joined in the covenant.

4 The king commanded the high priest Hil·kī´ah, the priests of the second order, and the guardians of the threshold, to bring out of the temple of the LORD all the vessels made for Bā´al, for A·shē´rah, and for all the host of heaven; he burned them outside Jerusalem in the fields of the Kid´ron, and carried their ashes to Beth´el. ⁵He deposed the idolatrous priests whom the kings of Judah had ordained to make offerings in the high places at the cities of Judah and around Jerusalem; those also who made offerings to Bā´al, to the sun, the moon, the constellations, and all the host of the heavens. ⁶He brought out the image of⁸ A·shē´rah from the house of the LORD, outside Jerusalem, to the Wadi Kid´ron, burned it at the Wadi Kid´ron, beat it to dust and threw the dust of it upon the graves of the common people. ⁷He broke down the houses of the male temple prostitutes that were in the house of the LORD, where the women did weaving for A·shē´-rah. ⁸He brought all the priests out of the towns of Judah, and defiled the high places where the priests had made offerings, from Gē´ba to Bē´er-shē´ba; he broke down the high places of the gates that were at the entrance of the gate of Joshua the governor of the city, which were on the left at the gate of the city. ⁹The priests of the high places, however, did not come up to the altar of the LORD in Jerusalem, but ate unleavened bread among their kindred. ¹⁰He defiled Tō´pheth, which is in the valley of Ben-hin´nom, so that no one would make a son or a daughter pass through fire as an offering to Mō´lech. ¹¹He removed the horses that the kings of Judah had dedicated to the sun, at the entrance to the house of the LORD, by the chamber of the eunuch Nā´than-mē´lech,

which was in the precincts;ʰ then he burned the chariots of the sun with fire. ¹²The altars on the roof of the upper chamber of Ā´haz, which the kings of Judah had made, and the altars that Ma·nas´seh had made in the two courts of the house of the LORD, he pulled down from there and broke in pieces, and threw the rubble into the Wadi Kid´ron. ¹³The king defiled the high places that were east of Jerusalem, to the south of the Mount of Destruction, which King Solomon of Israel had built for As·tar´tē the abomination of the Sī·dō´ni·ans, for Chē´mosh the abomination of Mō´ab, and for Mil´com the abomination of the Am´mon·ītes. ¹⁴He broke the pillars in pieces, cut down the sacred poles,ⁱ and covered the sites with human bones.

15 Moreover, the altar at Beth´el, the high place erected by Jer·o·bō´am son of Nē´bat, who caused Israel to sin—he pulled down that altar along with the high place. He burned the high place, crushing it to dust; he also burned the sacred pole.ʲ ¹⁶As Jō·sī´ah turned, he saw the tombs there on the mount; and he sent and took the bones out of the tombs, and burned them on the altar, and defiled it, according to the word of the LORD that the man of God proclaimed,ᵏ when Jer·o·bō´am stood by the altar at the festival; he turned and looked up at the tomb of the man of God who had predicted these things. ¹⁷Then he said, "What is that monument that I see?" The people of the city told him, "It is the tomb of the man of God who came from Judah and predicted these things that you have done against the altar at Beth´el." ¹⁸He said, "Let him rest; let no one move his bones." So they let his bones alone, with the bones of the prophet who came out of Sa·mār´i·a. ¹⁹Moreover, Jō·sī´ah removed all the shrines of the high places that were in

⁸ Heb lacks *image of* ʰ Meaning of Heb uncertain ⁱ Heb *Asherim* ʲ Heb *Asherah* ᵏ Gk: Heb *proclaimed, who had predicted these things*

the towns of Sa·mār′i·a, which kings of Israel had made, provoking the LORD to anger; he did to them just as he had done at Beth′el. [20]He slaughtered on the altars all the priests of the high places who were there, and burned human bones on them. Then he returned to Jerusalem.

The Passover Celebrated

21 The king commanded all the people, "Keep the passover to the LORD your God as prescribed in this book of the covenant." [22]No such passover had been kept since the days of the judges who judged Israel, or during all the days of the kings of Israel or of the kings of Judah; [23]but in the eighteenth year of King Jō·sī′ah this passover was kept to the LORD in Jerusalem.

24 Moreover Jō·sī′ah put away the mediums, wizards, teraphim,[1] idols, and all the abominations that were seen in the land of Judah and in Jerusalem, so that he established the words of the law that were written in the book that the priest Hil·kī′ah had found in the house of the LORD. [25]Before him there was no king like him, who turned to the LORD with all his heart, with all his soul, and with all his might, according to all the law of Moses; nor did any like him arise after him.

26 Still the LORD did not turn from the fierceness of his great wrath, by which his anger was kindled against Judah, because of all the provocations with which Ma·nas′seh had provoked him. [27]The LORD said, "I will remove Judah also out of my sight, as I have removed Israel; and I will reject this city that I have chosen, Jerusalem, and the house of which I said, My name shall be there."

Josiah Dies in Battle

28 Now the rest of the acts of Jō·sī′ah, and all that he did, are they not written in the Book of the Annals of the Kings of Judah? [29]In his days Pharaoh Nē′cō king of Egypt went up to the king of Assyria to the river Euphrates. King Jō·sī′ah went to meet him; but when Pharaoh Nē′cō met him at Me·gid′dō, he killed him. [30]His servants carried him dead in a chariot from Me·gid′dō, brought him to Jerusalem, and buried him in his own tomb. The people of the land took Je·hō′a·haz son of Jō·sī′ah, anointed him, and made him king in place of his father.

Reign and Captivity of Jehoahaz

31 Je·hō′a·haz was twenty-three years old when he began to reign; he reigned three months in Jerusalem. His mother's name was Ha·mū′tal daughter of Jer·e·mī′ah of Lib′nah. [32]He did what was evil in the sight of the LORD, just as his ancestors had done. [33]Pharaoh Nē′cō confined him at Rib′lah in the land of Hā′math, so that he might not reign in Jerusalem, and imposed tribute on the land of one hundred talents of silver and a talent of gold. [34]Pharaoh Nē′cō made E·lī′a·kim son of Jō·sī′ah king in place of his father Jo·sī′ah, and changed his name to Je·hoi′a·kim. But he took Je·hō′a·haz away; he came to Egypt, and died there. [35]Je·hoi′a·kim gave the silver and the gold to Pharaoh, but he taxed the land in order to meet Pharaoh's demand for money. He exacted the silver and the gold from the people of the land, from all according to their assessment, to give it to Pharaoh Nē′cō.

Jehoiakim Reigns over Judah

36 Je·hoi′a·kim was twenty-five years old when he began to reign; he reigned eleven years in Jerusalem. His mother's name was Ze·bī′dah daughter of Pe·dāi′ah of Rū′mah. [37]He did what was evil in the sight of the LORD, just as all his ancestors had done.

Judah Overrun by Enemies

24 In his days King Ne·bū·chad·nez′zar of Babylon came up; Je·hoi′a·kim became his servant for three years; then he turned and rebelled against him. [2]The LORD sent against him bands of

---

[1] Or *household gods*

Nebuchadnezzar was king of Babylon from 605–562 BC. During the many years he ruled, gates and temples were built in Babylon, and huge walls were constructed around the city. Nebuchadnezzar conquered many kingdoms, including Judah. He destroyed Jerusalem and sent many people away from their land to live in Babylon.

the Chal·dē´ans, bands of the Ar·a·mē´ans, bands of the Mō´ab·ītes, and bands of the Am´mon·ītes; he sent them against Judah to destroy it, according to the word of the LORD that he spoke by his servants the prophets. ³Surely this came upon Judah at the command of the LORD, to remove them out of his sight, for the sins of Ma·nas´seh, for all that he had committed, ⁴and also for the innocent blood that he had shed; for he filled Jerusalem with innocent blood, and the LORD was not willing to pardon. ⁵Now the rest of the deeds of Je·hoi´a·kim, and all that he did, are they not written in the Book of the Annals of the Kings of Judah? ⁶So Je·hoi´a·kim slept with his ancestors; then his son Je·hoi´a·chin succeeded him. ⁷The king of Egypt did not come again out of his land, for the king of Babylon had taken over all that belonged to the king of Egypt from the Wadi of Egypt to the River Euphrates.

Reign and Captivity of Jehoiachin

8 Je·hoi´a·chin was eighteen years old when he began to reign; he reigned three months in Jerusalem. His mother's name was Ne·hush´ta daughter of El·nā´than of Jerusalem. ⁹He did what was evil in the sight of the LORD, just as his father had done.

10 At that time the servants of King Ne·bū·chad·nez´zar of Babylon came up to Jerusalem, and the city was besieged. ¹¹King Ne·bū·chad·nez´zar of Babylon came to the city, while his servants were besieging it; ¹²King Je·hoi´a·chin of Judah gave himself up to the king of Babylon, himself, his mother, his servants, his officers, and his palace officials. The king of Babylon took him prisoner in the eighth year of his reign.

Capture of Jerusalem

13 He carried off all the treasures of the house of the LORD, and the treasures of the king's house; he cut in pieces all the vessels of gold in the temple of the LORD, which King Solomon of Israel had made, all this as the LORD had foretold. ¹⁴He carried away all Jerusalem, all the officials, all the warriors, ten thousand captives, all the artisans and the smiths; no one remained, except the poorest people of the land. ¹⁵He carried away Je·hoi´a·chin to Babylon; the king's mother, the king's wives, his officials, and the elite of the land, he took into captivity from Jerusalem to Babylon. ¹⁶The king of Babylon brought captive to Babylon all the men of valor, seven thousand, the artisans and the smiths, one thousand, all of them strong and fit for war. ¹⁷The king of Babylon made Mat·ta·nī´ah, Je·hoi´a·chin's uncle, king in his place, and changed his name to Zed·e·kī´ah.

Zedekiah Reigns over Judah

18 Zed·e·kī´ah was twenty-one years old when he began to reign; he reigned eleven years in Jerusalem. His mother's name was Ha·mū´tal daughter of Jer·e·mī´ah of Lib´nah. ¹⁹He did what was evil in the sight of the LORD, just as Je·hoi´a·kim had done. ²⁰Indeed, Jerusalem and Judah so angered the LORD that he expelled them from his presence.

The Fall and Captivity of Judah

Zed·e·kī´ah rebelled against the king of Babylon.

25 And in the ninth year of his reign, in the tenth month, on the tenth day of the month, King Ne·bu·chad·nez′zar of Babylon came with all his army against Jerusalem, and laid siege to it; they built siegeworks against it all around. ²So the city was besieged until the eleventh year of King Zed·e·kī′ah. ³On the ninth day of the fourth month the famine became so severe in the city that there was no food for the people of the land. ⁴Then a breach was made in the city wall;ᵐ the king with all the soldiers fledⁿ by night by the way of the gate between the two walls, by the king's garden, though the Chal·dē′ans were all around the city. They went in the direction of the Ar′a·bah. ⁵But the army of the Chal·dē′ans pursued the king, and overtook him in the plains of Jericho; all his army was scattered, deserting him. ⁶Then they captured the king and brought him up to the king of Babylon at Rib′lah, who passed sentence on him. ⁷They slaughtered the sons of Zed·e·kī′ah before his eyes, then put out the eyes of Zed·e·kī′ah; they bound him in fetters and took him to Babylon.

8 In the fifth month, on the seventh day of the month—which was the nineteenth year of King Ne·bu·chad·nez′zar, king of Babylon—Ne·bu·za·rad′an, the captain of the bodyguard, a servant of the king of Babylon, came to Jerusalem. ⁹He burned the house of the LORD, the king's house, and all the houses of Jerusalem; every great house he burned down. ¹⁰All the army of the Chal·dē′ans who were with the captain of the guard broke down the walls around Jerusalem. ¹¹Ne·bu·za·rad′an the captain of the guard carried into exile the rest of the people who were left in the city and the deserters who had defected to the king of Babylon—all the rest of the population. ¹²But the captain of the guard left some of the poorest people of the land to be vinedressers and tillers of the soil.

13 The bronze pillars that were in the house of the LORD, as well as the stands and the bronze sea that were in the house of the LORD, the Chal·dē′ans broke in pieces, and carried the bronze to Babylon. ¹⁴They took away the pots, the shovels, the snuffers, the dishes for incense, and all the bronze vessels used in the temple service, ¹⁵as well as the firepans and the basins. What was made of gold the captain of the guard took away for the gold, and what was made of silver, for the silver. ¹⁶As for the two pillars, the one sea, and the stands, which Solomon had made for the house of the LORD, the bronze of all these vessels was beyond weighing. ¹⁷The height of the one pillar was eighteen cubits, and on it was a bronze capital; the height of the capital was three cubits; latticework and pomegranates, all of bronze, were on the capital all around. The second pillar had the same, with the latticework.

18 The captain of the guard took the chief priest Se·rāi′ah, the second priest Zeph·a·nī′ah, and the three guardians of the threshold; ¹⁹from the city he took an officer who had been in command of the soldiers, and five men of the king's council who were found in the city; the secretary who was the commander of the army who mustered the people of the land; and sixty men of the people of the land who were found in the city. ²⁰Ne·bu·za·rad′an the captain of the guard took them, and brought them to the king of Babylon at Rib′lah. ²¹The king of Babylon struck them down and put them to death at Rib′lah in the land of Hā′math. So Judah went into exile out of its land.

Gedaliah Made Governor of Judah

22 He appointed Ged·a·lī′ah son of A·hī′kam son of Shaa′phan as governor over the people who remained in the land

---

ᵐ Heb lacks *wall*   ⁿ Gk Compare Jer 39.4; 52.7: Heb lacks *the king* and lacks *fled* of Judah, whom King Ne·bū·chad·nez´zar of Babylon had left. ²³Now when all the captains of the forces and their men heard that the king of Babylon had appointed Ged·a·lī´ah as governor, they came with their men to Ged·a·lī´ah at Miz´pah, namely, Ish´ma·el son of Neth·a·nī´ah, Jō·hā´-nan son of Ka·rē´ah, Se·rāi´ah son of Tan´hu·meth the Ne·toph´a·thīte, and Jā·az·a·nī´ah son of the Mā´a·ca·thīte. ²⁴Ged·a·lī´ah swore to them and their men, saying, "Do not be afraid because of the Chal·dē´an officials; live in the land, serve the king of Babylon, and it shall be well with you." ²⁵But in the seventh month, Ish´ma·el son of Neth·a·nī´ah son of E·lish´a·ma, of the royal family, came with ten men; they struck down Ged·a·lī´-ah so that he died, along with the Judeans and Chal·dē´ans who were with him at Miz´pah. ²⁶Then all the people, high and low,ᵒ and the captains of the forces set out and went to Egypt; for they were afraid of the Chal·dē´ans.

Jehoiachin Released from Prison

27 In the thirty-seventh year of the exile of King Je·hoi´a·chin of Judah, in the twelfth month, on the twenty-seventh day of the month, King Ē´vil-me·rō´dach of Babylon, in the year that he began to reign, released King Je·hoi´a·chin of Judah from prison; ²⁸he spoke kindly to him, and gave him a seat above the other seats of the kings who were with him in Babylon. ²⁹So Je·hoi´a·chin put aside his prison clothes. Every day of his life he dined regularly in the king's presence. ³⁰For his allowance, a regular allowance was given him by the king, a portion every day, as long as he lived.

ᵒ Or *young and old*

1 Chronicles

First Chronicles is the first of a group of four books of history that includes First and Second Chronicles, Ezra, and Nehemiah. We can't be absolutely sure when these books were written, but scholars believe they were written about the fourth century BC after the people returned from Babylonia. The author of First Chronicles, whose name is not known, is called the Chronicler. His purpose was to write about the people—their achievements, their worship, and their kings.

The Chronicler, or writer, believed that when the people were faithful to God and to Temple worship, they were blessed. He taught that when they did not obey and became careless in their worship, God punished them. The writer used stories from First Samuel, Second Samuel, First Kings, and Second Kings. These rewritten stories told the people to support their nation and look to Jerusalem and the rebuilt Temple as their national religious center and symbol of unity.

Like the series of books from Genesis through Second Kings, this set of books begins with Adam and Eve. The story-teller goes into great detail when the story reaches the rule of King David. He shows David as the one who helped unify the people with strong leadership, by planning the Temple worship and music, and by setting aside the Levites to be priests.

1 Chronicles 29:22–25

From Adam to Abraham

1 Adam, Seth, Ē´nosh; [2]Kē´nan, Ma·hal´-a·lel, Jar´ed; [3]Ē´noch, Me·thū´se·lah, Lā´mech; [4]Noah, Shem, Ham, and Jā´pheth.

5 The descendants of Jā´pheth: Gō´mer, Mā´gog, Mā´daī, Jā´van, Tū´bal, Mē´shech, and Tī´ras. [6]The descendants of Gō´mer: Ash´ke·naz, Dī´phath,[a] and Tō·gar´mah. [7]The descendants of Jā´van: E·li´shah, Tar´shish, Kit´tim, and Rod´a·nim.[b]

8 The descendants of Ham: Cush, Egypt, Put, and Cā´naan. [9]The descendants of Cush: Sē´ba, Hav´i·lah, Sab´ta, Rā´a·ma, and Sab´te·ca. The descendants of Rā´a·mah: Shē´ba and Dē´dan. [10]Cush became the father of Nim´rod; he was the first to be a mighty one on the earth.

11 Egypt became the father of Lū´dim, An´a·mim, Le·hā´bim, Naph´tū·him, [12]Path·rū´sim, Cas·lū´him, and Caph´to·rim, from whom the Phi·lis´tines come.[c]

13 Cā´naan became the father of Sī´don his firstborn, and Heth, [14]and the Jeb´ū·sītes, the Am´o·rītes, the Gir´ga·shītes, [15]the Hī´vītes, the Ar´kītes, the Sī´nītes, [16]the Ar´vad·ītes, the Zem´a·rītes, and the Hā´math·ītes.

17 The descendants of Shem: Ē´lam, As´shur, Ar·pach´shad, Lud, Ar´am, Uz, Hul, Gē´ther, and Mē´shech.[d] [18]Ar·pach´shad became the father of Shē´lah; and Shē´lah became the father of Ē´ber. [19]To Ē´ber were born two sons: the name of the one was Pē´leg (for in his days the earth was divided), and the name of his brother Jok´tan. [20]Jok´tan became the father of Al·mō´dad, Shē´leph, Hā·zar·mā´veth, Jē´rah, [21]Ha·dor´am, Ū´zal, Dik´lah, [22]Ē´bal, A·bim´a·el, Shē´ba, [23]Ō´phir, Hav´i·lah, and Jō´bab; all these were the descendants of Jok´tan.

24 Shem, Ar·pach´shad, Shē´lah; [25]Ē´ber, Pē´leg, Rē´ū; [26]Sē´rug, Nā´hor, Tē´rah; [27]Abram, that is, Abraham.

From Abraham to Jacob

28 The sons of Abraham: Isaac and Ish´ma·el. [29]These are their genealogies: the firstborn of Ish´ma·el, Ne·bā´i·oth; and Kē´dar, Ad´bē·el, Mib´sam, [30]Mish´ma, Dū´mah, Mas´sa, Hā´dad, Tē´ma, [31]Jē´tur, Nā´phish, and Ked´e·mah. These are the sons of Ish´ma·el. [32]The sons of Ke·tū´rah, Abraham's concubine: she bore Zim´ran, Jok´shan, Mē´dan, Mid´i·an, Ish´bak, and Shū´ah. The sons of Jok´shan: Shē´ba and Dē´dan. [33]The sons of Mid´i·an: Ē´phah, Ē´pher, Hā´noch, A·bī´da, and El·dā´ah. All these were the descendants of Ke·tū´rah.

34 Abraham became the father of Isaac. The sons of Isaac: Esau and Israel. [35]The sons of Esau: E·lī´phaz, Reū´el, Jē´ush, Jā´lam, and Kō´rah. [36]The sons of E·lī´phaz: Tē´man, Ō´mar, Zē´phī, Gā´tam, Kē´naz, Tim´na, and Am´a·lek. [37]The sons of Reū´el: Nā´hath, Zē´rah, Sham´mah, and Miz´zah.

38 The sons of Sē´ir: Lō´tan, Shō´bal, Zib´ē·on, An´ah, Dī´shon, Ē´zer, and Dī´shan. [39]The sons of Lō´tan: Hō´rī and Hō´mam; and Lō´tan's sister was Tim´na. [40]The sons of Shō´bal: Al´i·an, Man´a·hath, Ē´bal, Shē´phī, and Ō´nam. The sons of Zib´ē·on: Ā´i·ah and An´ah. [41]The sons of An´ah: Dī´shon. The sons of Dī´shon: Ham´ran, Esh´ban, Ith´ran, and

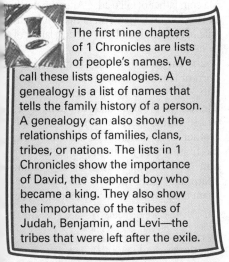

The first nine chapters of 1 Chronicles are lists of people's names. We call these lists genealogies. A genealogy is a list of names that tells the family history of a person. A genealogy can also show the relationships of families, clans, tribes, or nations. The lists in 1 Chronicles show the importance of David, the shepherd boy who became a king. They also show the importance of the tribes of Judah, Benjamin, and Levi—the tribes that were left after the exile.

[a] Gen 10.3 *Ripath;* See Gk Vg   [b] Gen 10.4 *Dodanim;* See Syr Vg   [c] Heb *Casluhim, from which the Philistines come, Caphtorim;* See Am 9.7, Jer 47.4   [d] *Mash* in Gen 10.23

Chē′ran. ⁴²The sons of Ē′zer: Bil′han, Zā·a·van, and Jā′a·kan.ᵉ The sons of Dī′shan:ʲ Uz and Ar′an.

43 These are the kings who reigned in the land of Ē′dom before any king reigned over the Israelites: Bē′la son of Bē′or, whose city was called Din′ha·bah. ⁴⁴When Bē′la died, Jō′bab son of Zē′rah of Boz′rah succeeded him. ⁴⁵When Jō′bab died, Hū′sham of the land of the Tē′man·ites succeeded him. ⁴⁶When Hū′sham died, Hā′dad son of Bē′dad, who defeated Mid′i·an in the country of Mō′ab, succeeded him; and the name of his city was Ā′vith. ⁴⁷When Hā′dad died, Sam′lah of Mas·rē′kah succeeded him. ⁴⁸When Sam′lah died, Shā′ūlᵍ of Re·hō′both on the Euphrates succeeded him. ⁴⁹When Shā′ūlᵍ died, Bā′al-hā′nan son of Ach′bor succeeded him. ⁵⁰When Bā′al-hā′nan died, Hā′dad succeeded him; the name of his city was Pā′ī, and his wife's name Me·het′a·bel daughter of Mā′tred, daughter of Me-za-hab′. ⁵¹And Hā′dad died.

The clansʰ of Ē′dom were: clansʰ Tim′na, Al′i·ah,ⁱ Jē′theth, ⁵²Ō·hol·i·bā′mah, Ē′lah, Pī′non, ⁵³Kē′naz, Tē′man, Mib′zar, ⁵⁴Mag′di·el, and Ī′ram; these are the clansʰ of Ē′dom.

The Sons of Israel and the Descendants of Judah

2 These are the sons of Israel: Reuben, Sim′ē·on, Levi, Judah, Is′sa·char, Zeb′ū·lun, ²Dan, Joseph, Benjamin, Naph′ta·lī, Gad, and Ash′er. ³The sons of Judah: Er, Ō′nan, and Shē′lah; these three the Cā′naan·ite woman Bath-shū′a bore to him. Now Er, Judah's firstborn, was wicked in the sight of the LORD, and he put him to death. ⁴His daughter-in-law Tā′mar also bore him Per′ez and Zē′rah. Judah had five sons in all.

5 The sons of Per′ez: Hez′ron and Hā′mul. ⁶The sons of Zē′rah: Zim′rī, Ē′than, Hē′man, Cal′col, and Dar′a,ʲ five in all. ⁷The sons of Car′mī: Ā′char, the troubler of Israel, who transgressed in the matter of the devoted thing; ⁸and Ē′than's son was Aza·rī′ah.

9 The sons of Hez′ron, who were born to him: Je·rah′mē·el, Ram, and Che·lū′baī. ¹⁰Ram became the father of Am·min′a·dab, and Am·min′a·dab became the father of Nah′shon, prince of the sons of Judah. ¹¹Nah′shon became the father of Sal′ma, Sal′ma of Bō′az, ¹²Bō′az of Ō′bed, Ō′bed of Jesse. ¹³Jesse became the father of E·lī′ab his firstborn, A·bin′a·dab the second, Shim′ē·a the third, ¹⁴Ne·than′el the fourth, Rad′daī the fifth, ¹⁵Ō′zem the sixth, David the seventh; ¹⁶and their sisters were Ze·rū′i·ah and Ab′i·gāil. The sons of Ze·rū′i·ah: A·bi′shaī, Jō′ab, and As′a·hel, three. ¹⁷Ab′i·gāil bore A·mā′sa, and the father of A·mā′sa was Jē′ther the Ish·ma·el·īte.

18 Caleb son of Hez′ron had children by his wife A·zū′bah, and by Jer′i·oth; these were her sons: Jē′sher, Shō′bab, and Ar′don. ¹⁹When A·zū′bah died, Caleb married Eph′rath, who bore him Hur. ²⁰Hur became the father of Ū′rī, and Ū′rī became the father of Bez′a·lel.

21 Afterward Hez′ron went in to the daughter of Mā′chir father of Gil′e·ad, whom he married when he was sixty years old; and she bore him Sē′gub; ²²and Sē′gub became the father of Jā′ir, who had twenty-three towns in the land of Gil′e·ad. ²³But Gē′shur and Ar′am took from them Hav′voth-jā′ir, Kē′nath and its villages, sixty towns. All these were descendants of Mā′chir, father of Gil′e·ad. ²⁴After the death of Hez′ron, in Cā′leb-eph′ra·thah, A·bī′jah wife of Hez′ron bore him Ash′hur, father of Te·kō′a.

25 The sons of Je·rah′mē·el, the firstborn of Hez′ron: Ram his firstborn, Bū′nah, Ō′ren, Ō′zem, and A·hī′jah. ²⁶Je·rah′mē·el also had another wife, whose name was At′a·rah; she was the mother of Ō′nam. ²⁷The sons of Ram, the firstborn of Je·rah′mē·el: Mā′az, Jā′min, and Ē′ker. ²⁸The sons of Ō′nam: Sham′maī and Jā′da. The sons of Sham′maī: Nā′dab and A·bī′shur. ²⁹The

---

ᵉ Or and Akan; See Gen 36.27   ʲ See 1.38: Heb Dishon   ᵍ Or Saul   ʰ Or chiefs   ⁱ Or Alvah; See Gen 36.40   ʲ Or Darda; Compare Syr Tg some Gk Mss; See 1 Kings 4.31

name of A·bi´shur's wife was Ab·i·ha´il, and she bore him Ah´ban and Mō´lid. ³⁰The sons of Na´dab: Sē´led and Ap´pa·im; and Sē´led died childless. ³¹The son^k of Ap´pa·im: Ish´i. The son^k of Ish´i: She´shan. The son^k of She´shan: Ah´lai. ³²The sons of Ja´da, Sham´mai's brother: Jē´ther and Jonathan; and Jē´-ther died childless. ³³The sons of Jonathan: Pē´leth and Za´za. These were the descendants of Je·rah´mē·el. ³⁴Now She´shan had no sons, only daughters; but She´shan had an Egyptian slave, whose name was Jar´ha. ³⁵So She´shan gave his daughter in marriage to his slave Jar´ha; and she bore him At´tai. ³⁶At´tai became the father of Nathan, and Nathan of Za´-bad. ³⁷Za´bad became the father of Eph´lal, and Eph´lal of Ō´bed. ³⁸Ō´bed became the father of Jē´hū, and Jē´hū of Az·a·ri´ah. ³⁹Az·a·ri´ah became the father of Hē´lez, and Hē´lez of El·e·a´sah. ⁴⁰El·e·a´sah became the father of Sis´·mai, and Sis´·mai of Shal´lum. ⁴¹Shal´lum became the father of Jek·a·mi´ah, and Jek·a·mi´ah of E·lish´-a·ma.

42 The sons of Caleb brother of Je·rah´-mē·el: Mē´sha^l his firstborn, who was father of Ziph. The sons of Ma·rē´shah father of Hē´bron. ⁴³The sons of Hē´bron: Kō´rah, Tap´pū·ah, Rē´kem, and Shē´ma. ⁴⁴Shē´ma became father of Rā´ham, father of Jor´kē·am; and Rē´kem became the father of Sham´mai. ⁴⁵The son of Sham´-mai: Ma´on; and Ma´on was the father of Beth-zur. ⁴⁶Ē´phah also, Caleb's concubine, bore Har´an, Mō´za, and Ga´zez; and Har´an became the father of Ga´zez. ⁴⁷The sons of Jah´dai: Rē´gem, Jō´tham, Gē´shan, Pē´let, Ē´phah, and Sha´aph. ⁴⁸Ma´a·cah, Caleb's concubine, bore Shē´ber and Tir´ha·nah. ⁴⁹She also bore Sha´aph father of Mad·man´nah, Shē´va father of Machbē´-nah and father of Gib´ē·a; and the daughter of Caleb was Ach´sah. ⁵⁰These were the descendants of Caleb.

The sons^m of Hur the firstborn of Eph´-ra·thah: Shō´bal father of Kir·i·ath-jē´a·rim, ⁵¹Sal´ma father of Bethlehem, and Har´-eph father of Beth-ga´der. ⁵²Shō´bal father of Kir·i·ath-jē´a·rim had other sons: Ha·rō´eh, half of the Me·nū´hoth. ⁵³And the families of Kir·i·ath-jē´a·rim: the Ith´rītes, the Pū´thītes, the Shū´ma·thītes, and the Mish´ra·ītes; from these came the Zō´ra·thītes and the Esh´ta·o·lītes. ⁵⁴The sons of Sal´ma: Bethlehem, the Ne·toph´a·thītes, At´roth-beth-jō´ab, and half of the Man·a·hā´thītes, the Zō´rītes. ⁵⁵The families also of the scribes that lived at Ja´bez: the Tī´ra·thītes, the Shim´ē·a·-thītes, and the Sū´ca·thītes. These are the Ken´ītes who came from Ham´math, father of the house of Rē´chab.

Descendants of David and Solomon

3 These are the sons of David who were born to him in Hē´bron: the firstborn Am´non, by A·hin´ō·am the Jez´rē·el·īte; the second Daniel, by Ab´i·gāil the Car´mel·īte; ²the third Ab´sa·lom, son of Ma´a·cah, daughter of King Tal´mai of Gē´shur; the fourth Ad·o·ni´jah, son of Hag´gith; ³the fifth Sheph·a·tī´ah, by A·bi´tal; the sixth Ith´-rē·am, by his wife Eg´lah; ⁴six were born to him in Hē´bron, where he reigned for seven years and six months. And he reigned thirty-three years in Jerusalem. ⁵These were born to him in Jerusalem: Shim´ē·a, Shō´bab, Nathan, and Solo-mon, four by Bath-shū´a, daughter of Am´mi·el; ⁶then Ib´har, E·lish´a·ma, E·liph´e·let, ⁷Nō´gah, Nē´pheg, Ja·phi´a, ⁸E·lish´a·ma, E·li´a·da, and E·liph´e·let, nine. ⁹All these were David's sons, besides the sons of the concubines; and Ta´mar was their sister.

10 The descendants of Solomon: Rē·ho·bō´am, A·bi´jah his son, Asa his son, Je·hosh´a·phat his son, ¹¹Jō´ram his son, A·ha·zī´ah his son, Jō´ash his son, ¹²Am·a·zī´ah his son, Az·a·ri´ah his son, Jō´tham his son, ¹³Ā´haz his son, Hez·-e·kī´ah his son, Ma·nas´seh his son,

---

^k Heb *sons*   ^l Gk reads *Mareshah*   ^m Gk Vg: Heb *son*

¹⁴Āʹmon his son, Jō·sīʹah his son. ¹⁵The sons of Jō·sīʹah: Jō·hāʹnan the firstborn, the second Je·hoiʹa·kim, the third Zed·e·kīʹah, the fourth Shalʹlum. ¹⁶The descendants of Je·hoiʹa·kim: Jec·o·nīʹah his son, Zed·e·kīʹah his son; ¹⁷and the sons of Jec·o·nīʹah, the captive: She·alʹti·el his son, ¹⁸Mal·chīʹram, Pe·dāiʹah, Shen·azʹzar, Jek·a·mīʹah, Hoshʹa·ma, and Ned·a·bīʹah; ¹⁹The sons of Pe·dāiʹah: Ze·rubʹba·bel and Shimʹē·ī; and the sons of Ze·rubʹba·bel: Me·shulʹlam and Han·a·nīʹah, and She·lōʹmith was their sister; ²⁰and Ha·shūʹbah, Ōʹhel, Ber·e·chīʹah, Has·a·dīʹah, and Jūʹshab-hēʹsed, five. ²¹The sons of Han·a·nīʹah: Pel·a·tīʹah and Je·shāʹi·ah, his son[n] Reph·aīʹah, his son[n] Arʹnan, his son[n] Ō·ba·dīʹah, his son[n] Shec·a·nīʹah. ²²The son[o] of Shec·a·nīʹah: She·māiʹah. And the sons of She·māiʹah: Hatʹtush, Īʹgal, Ba·rīʹah, Nē·a·rīʹah, and Shāʹphat, six. ²³The sons of Nē·a·rīʹah: El·i·ō·ēʹnai, Hiz·kīʹah, and Az·rīʹkam, three. ²⁴The sons of El·i·ō·ēʹnai: Hod·a·vīʹah, E·līʹa·shib, Pe·lāiʹah, Akʹkub, Jō·hāʹnan, De·laīʹah, and A·naʹnī, seven.

Descendants of Judah

4 The sons of Judah: Perʹez, Hezʹron, Carʹmī, Hur, and Shōʹbal. ²Rē·āiʹah son of Shōʹbal became the father of Jāʹhath, and Jāʹhath became the father of A·hūʹmāi and Lāʹhad. These were the families of the Zōʹra·thītes. ³These were the sons[p] of Ēʹtam: Jezʹrē·el, Ishʹma, and Idʹbash; and the name of their sister was Haz·ze·lel·pōʹnī, ⁴and Pe·nūʹel was the father of Gēʹdor, and Ēʹzer the father of Hūʹshah. These were the sons of Hur, the firstborn of Ephʹra·thah, the father of Bethlehem. ⁵Ashʹhur father of Te·kōʹa had two wives, Hēʹlah and Nāʹa·rah; ⁶Nāʹa·rah bore him A·huzʹzam, Hēʹpher, Tēʹme·nī, and Hā·a·hashʹta·rī.[q] These were the sons of Nāʹa·rah. ⁷The sons of Hēʹlah: Zēʹreth, Izʹhar,[r] and Ethʹnan. ⁸Koz became the father of Āʹnub, Zō·bēʹbah, and the families of A·harʹhel son of Harʹum. ⁹Jāʹbez was honored more than

his brothers; and his mother named him Jāʹbez, saying, "Because I bore him in pain." ¹⁰Jāʹbez called on the God of Israel, saying, "Oh that you would bless me and enlarge my border, and that your hand might be with me, and that you would keep me from hurt and harm!" And God granted what he asked. ¹¹Chēʹlub the brother of Shūʹhah became the father of Mēʹhir, who was the father of Eshʹton. ¹²Eshʹton became the father of Beth-rāʹpha, Pa·sēʹah, and Te·hinʹnah the father of Ir·nāʹhash. These are the men of Rēʹcah. ¹³The sons of Kēʹnaz: Othʹni·el and Se·rāiʹah; and the sons of Othʹni·el: Hāʹthath and Me·ōʹno·thai.[s] ¹⁴Me·ōʹno·thai became the father of Ophʹrah; and Se·rāiʹah became the father of Jōʹab father of Gē·harʹa·shim,[t] so-called because they were artisans. ¹⁵The sons of Caleb son of Je·phunʹneh: Īʹrū, Ēʹlah, and Nāʹam; and the son[o] of Ēʹlah: Kēʹnaz. ¹⁶The sons of Je·halʹle·lel: Ziph, Zīʹphah, Tirʹi·a, and Asʹa·rel. ¹⁷The sons of Ezʹrah: Jēʹther, Mēʹred, Ēʹpher, and Jāʹlon. These are the sons of Bithʹi·ah, daughter of Pharaoh, whom Mēʹred married;[u] and she conceived and bore[v] Miriam, Shamʹmāi, and Ishʹbah father of Esh·te·mōʹa. ¹⁸And his Judean wife bore Jēʹred father of Gēʹdor, Hēʹber father of Sōʹcō, and Je·kūʹthi·el father of Za·nōʹah. ¹⁹The sons of the wife of Hō·dīʹah, the sister of Nāʹham, were the fathers of Kē·īʹlah the Garʹmīte and Esh·te·mōʹa the Mā·a·ca·thīte. ²⁰The sons of Shīʹmon: Amʹnon, Rinʹnah, Ben-hāʹnan, and Tiʹlon. The sons of Ishʹī: Zōʹheth and Ben-zōʹheth. ²¹The sons of Shēʹlah son of Judah: Er father of Lēʹcah, Lāʹa·dah father of Ma·rēʹshah, and the families of the guild of linen workers at Beth-ash·bēʹa; ²²and Jōʹkim, and the men of Cō·zēʹba, and Jōʹash, and Sarʹaph, who married into Mōʹab

[n] Gk Compare Syr Vg: Heb *sons of*   [o] Heb *sons*
[p] Gk Compare Vg: Heb *the father*   [q] Or *Ahashtari*
[r] Another reading is *Zohar*   [s] Gk Vg: Heb lacks *and Meonothai*   [t] That is *Valley of artisans*
[u] The clause: *These are . . . married* is transposed from verse 18   [v] Heb lacks *and bore*

but returned to Le̅′hem[w] (now the records[x] are ancient). [23]These were the potters and inhabitants of Ne·ta̅′im and Ge·de̅′- rah; they lived there with the king in his service.

Descendants of Simeon

24 The sons of Sim′e·on: Nem′u̅·el, Ja̅′- min, Ja̅′rib, Ze̅′rah, Sha′ul;[y] [25]Shal′lum was his son, Mib′sam his son, Mish′ma his son. [26]The sons of Mish′ma: Ham′mu̅·el his son, Zac′cur his son, Shim′e·ī his son. [27]Shim′e·ī had sixteen sons and six daughters; but his brothers did not have many children, nor did all their family multiply like the Judeans. [28]They lived in Be̅′er-she̅′ba, Mo̅′la·dah, Ha̅′zar-shu̅′al, [29]Bil′hah, E̅′zem, To̅′lad, [30]Be·thu̅′el, Hor′- mah, Zik′lag, [31]Beth-mar′ca·both, Ha̅′zar- su̅′sim, Beth-bi′rī, and Sha̅·a·ra̅′im. These were their towns until David became king. [32]And their villages were E̅′tam, A̅′in, Rim′mon, To̅′chen, and A̅′shan, five towns, [33]along with all their villages that were around these towns as far as Ba̅′- al. These were their settlements. And they kept a genealogical record.

34 Me·sho̅′bab, Jam′lech, Jo̅′shah son of Am·a·zi̅′ah, [35]Jo̅′el, Je̅′hū son of Josh′- i·bi̅′ah son of Se·ra̅i′ah son of As′i·el, [36]El·i·o̅·e̅′naī, Ja̅·a·ko̅′bah, Jesh·o̅·ha̅i′ah, A·sa̅i′ah, Ad′i·el, Jesim′i·el, Be·na̅i′ah, [37]Zī′- za son of Shī′phī son of Al′lon son of Je·da̅i′- ah son of Shim′rī son of She·ma̅i′ah— [38]these mentioned by name were leaders in their families, and their clans increas- ed greatly. [39]They journeyed to the entrance of Ge̅′dor, to the east side of the valley, to seek pasture for their flocks, [40]where they found rich, good pasture, and the land was very broad, quiet, and peaceful; for the former inhabitants there belonged to Ham. [41]These, registered by name, came in the days of King Hez·e·kī′- ah of Judah, and attacked their tents and the Me·u̅′nim who were found there, and exterminated them to this day, and set- tled in their place, because there was pas- ture there for their flocks. [42]And some of

them, five hundred men of the Sim′- e·on·ītes, went to Mount Se̅′ir, having as their leaders Pel·a·tī′ah, Ne̅·a·rī′ah, Reph·a̅i′- ah, and Uz′zi·el, sons of Ish′ī; [43]they de- stroyed the remnant of the A·mal′e·kītes that had escaped, and they have lived there to this day.

Descendants of Reuben

5 The sons of Reuben the firstborn of Israel. (He was the firstborn, but because he defiled his father's bed his birthright was given to the sons of Joseph son of Israel, so that he is not enrolled in the genealogy according to the birthright; [2]though Judah became prominent among his brothers and a ruler came from him, yet the birthright belonged to Joseph.) [3]The sons of Reuben, the firstborn of Israel: Ha̅′noch, Pal′lū, Hez′ron, and Car′mī. [4]The sons of Jo̅′el: She·ma̅i′ah his son, Gog his son, Shim′e·ī his son, [5]Mī′cah his son, Re̅·a̅i′- ah his son, Ba̅′al his son, [6]Be·er′ah his son, whom King Til′gath-pil·ne̅′ser of Assyria carried away into exile; he was a chieftain of the Reu̅′ben·ītes. [7]And his kindred by their families, when the genealogy of their generations was reck- oned: the chief, Je·ī′el, and Zech·a·rī′ah, [8]and Be̅′la son of A̅′zaz, son of She̅′ma, son of Jo̅′el, who lived in A·ro̅′er, as far as Ne̅′bō and Ba̅′al-me̅′on. [9]He also lived to the east as far as the beginning of the desert this side of the Euphrates, because their cattle had multiplied in the land of Gil′e·ad. [10]And in the days of Saul they made war on the Hag′rītes, who fell by their hand; and they lived in their tents throughout all the region east of Gil′e·ad.

Descendants of Gad

11 The sons of Gad lived beside them in the land of Ba̅′shan as far as Sal′e·cah: [12]Jo̅′el the chief, Sha̅′pham the second, Ja̅′naī, and Sha̅′phat in Ba̅′shan. [13]And their kindred according to their clans: Michael, Me·shul′lam, She̅′ba, Jo̅′raī,

[w] Vg Compare Gk: Heb *and Jashubi-lahem*　　[x] Or *matters*　　[y] Or *Saul*

Jā´can, Zī´a, and Ē´ber, seven. ¹⁴These were the sons of Ab·i·hā´il son of Hū´rī, son of Ja·rō´ah, son of Gil´e·ad, son of Michael, son of Je·shish´aī, son of Jah´dō, son of Buz; ¹⁵Ā´hī son of Ab´di·el, son of Gū´nī, was chief in their clan; ¹⁶and they lived in Gil´e·ad, in Bā´shan and in its towns, and in all the pasture lands of Sharon to their limits. ¹⁷All of these were enrolled by genealogies in the days of King Jō´tham of Judah, and in the days of King Jer·o·bō´am of Israel.

18 The Reu´ben·ites, the Gad´ites, and the half-tribe of Ma·nas´seh had valiant warriors, who carried shield and sword, and drew the bow, expert in war, forty-four thousand seven hundred sixty, ready for service. ¹⁹They made war on the Hag´rītes, Jē´tur, Nā´phish, and Nō´dab; ²⁰and when they received help against them, the Hag´rītes and all who were with them were given into their hands, for they cried to God in the battle, and he granted their entreaty because they trusted in him. ²¹They captured their livestock: fifty thousand of their camels, two hundred fifty thousand sheep, two thousand donkeys, and one hundred thousand captives. ²²Many fell slain, because the war was of God. And they lived in their territory until the exile.

The Half-Tribe of Manasseh

23 The members of the half-tribe of Ma·nas´seh lived in the land; they were very numerous from Bā´shan to Bā´al-her´mon, Sē´nir, and Mount Hermon. ²⁴These were the heads of their clans: Ē´pher,ᶻ Ish´ī, E·lī´el, Az´ri·el, Jer·e·mī´ah, Hod·a·vī´ah, and Jah´di·el, mighty warriors, famous men, heads of their clans. ²⁵But they transgressed against the God of their ancestors, and prostituted themselves to the gods of the peoples of the land, whom God had destroyed before them. ²⁶So the God of Israel stirred up the spirit of King Pūl of Assyria, the spirit of King Til´gath-pil·nē´ser of Assyria, and he carried them away, namely, the Reū´ben·ites, the Gad´ites, and the half-tribe of Ma·nas´seh, and brought them to Hā´lah, Hā´bor, Hār´a, and the river Gō´zan, to this day.

Descendants of Levi

6ᵃ The sons of Levi: Ger´shom,ᵇ Kō´hath, and Me·rar´ī. ²The sons of Kō´hath: Am´ram, Iz´har, Hē´bron, and Uz´zi·el. ³The children of Am´ram: Aaron, Moses, and Miriam. The sons of Aaron: Nā´dab, A·bī´hū, El·e·ā´zar, and Ith´a·mar. ⁴El·e·ā´zar became the father of Phin´e·has, Phin´e·has of Ab·i·shū´a, ⁵Ab·i·shū´a of Buk´kī, Buk´kī of Uz´zī, ⁶Uz´zī of Zer·a·hī´ah, Zer·a·hī´ah of Me·rā´i·oth, ⁷Me·rā´i·oth of Am·a·rī´ah, Am·a·rī´ah of A·hī´tub, ⁸A·hī´tub of Zā´dok, Zā´dok of A·him´a·az, ⁹A·him´a·az of Az·a·rī´ah, Az·a·rī´ah of Jō·hā´nan, ¹⁰and Jō·hā´nan of Az·a·rī´ah (it was he who served as priest in the house that Solomon built in Jerusalem). ¹¹Az·a·rī´ah became the father of Am·a·rī´ah, Am·a·rī´ah of A·hī´tub, ¹²A·hī´tub of Zā´dok, Zā´dok of Shal´lum, ¹³Shal´lum of Hil·kī´ah, Hil·kī´ah of Az·a·rī´ah, ¹⁴Az·a·rī´ah of Se·rāī´ah, Se·rāī´ah of Je·hoz´a·dak; ¹⁵and Je·hoz´a·dak went into exile when the LORD sent Judah and Jerusalem into exile by the hand of Ne·bū·chad·nez´zar.

16ᶜ The sons of Levi: Ger´shom, Kō´hath, and Me·rar´ī. ¹⁷These are the names of the sons of Ger´shom: Lib´nī and Shim´e·ī. ¹⁸The sons of Kō´hath: Am´ram, Iz´har, Hē´bron, and Uz´zi·el. ¹⁹The sons of Me·rar´ī: Mah´lī and Mū´shī. These are the clans of the Lē´vītes according to their ancestry. ²⁰Of Ger´shom: Lib´nī his son, Jā´hath his son, Zim´mah his son, ²¹Jō´ah his son, Id´dō his son, Zē´rah his son, Je·ath´e·raī his son. ²²The sons of Kō´hath: Am·min´a·dab his son, Kō´rah his son, As´sir his son, ²³El·kā´nah his son, E·bī´a·saph his son, As´sir his son, ²⁴Tā´hath his son, Ū·rī´el his son, Uz·zī´ah his son, and Shā´ul

---

ᶻ Gk Vg: Heb and Epher ᵃ Ch 5.27 in Heb
ᵇ Heb Gershon, variant of Gershom; See 6.16
ᶜ Ch 6.1 in Heb

his son. ²⁵The sons of El·kā´nah: A·mā´-sai and A·hī´moth, ²⁶El·kā´nah his son, Zō´phai his son, Nā´hath his son, ²⁷E·lī´-ab his son, Je·rō´ham his son, El·kā´nah his son. ²⁸The sons of Samuel: Jō´el[d] his firstborn, the second A·bī´jah.[e] ²⁹The sons of Me·rar´ī: Mah´lī, Lib´nī his son, Shim´e·ī his son, Uz´zah his son, ³⁰Shim´e·a his son, Hag·gī´ah his son, and A·sāi´ah his son.

Men from the tribe of Levi were chosen to lead music in the Tabernacle and later in the Temple. We can all praise God by singing. Pay special attention to the hymns and songs you sing in church. If there are words you don't under-stand, ask an adult to explain them to you. If there is a Bible reference given with the hymn or song, find and read those verses!

Musicians Appointed by David

31 These are the men whom David put in charge of the service of song in the house of the LORD, after the ark came to rest there. ³²They ministered with song before the tabernacle of the tent of meeting, until Solomon had built the house of the LORD in Jerusalem; and they performed their service in due order. ³³These are the men who served; and their sons were: Of the Kō´hath·ites: Hē´-man, the singer, son of Jō´el, son of Samuel, ³⁴son of El·kā´nah, son of Je·rō´-ham, son of E·lī´el, son of Tō´ah, ³⁵son of Zuph, son of El·kā´nah, son of Mā´hath, son of A·mā´sai, ³⁶son of El·kā´nah, son of Jō´el, son of Az·a·rī´ah, son of Zeph·a·nī´ah, ³⁷son of Tā´hath, son of As´sir, son of E·bī´a·saph, son of Kō´rah, ³⁸son of Iz´har, son of Kō´hath, son of Levi, son of Israel; ³⁹and his brother Ā´saph, who stood on his right, namely, Ā´saph son of Ber·e·chī´ah, son of Shim´e·a, ⁴⁰son of Michael, son of Bā·a·sē´i·ah, son

of Mal·chī´jah, ⁴¹son of Eth´nī, son of Zē´-rah, son of A·dāi´ah, ⁴²son of Ē´than, son of Zim´mah, son of Shim´e·ī, ⁴³son of Jā´hath, son of Ger´shom, son of Levi. ⁴⁴On the left were their kindred the sons of Me·rar´ī: Ē´than son of Kish´ī, son of Ab´-dī, son of Mal´luch, ⁴⁵son of Hash·a·bī´-ah, son of Am·a·zī´ah, son of Hil·kī´ah, ⁴⁶son of Am´zī, son of Bā´nī, son of Shē´mer, ⁴⁷son of Mah´lī, son of Mū´shī, son of Me·rar´ī, son of Levi; ⁴⁸and their kindred the Lē´vītes were appointed for all the service of the tabernacle of the house of God.

49 But Aaron and his sons made offerings on the altar of burnt offering and on the altar of incense, doing all the work of the most holy place, to make atonement for Israel, according to all that Moses the servant of God had com-manded. ⁵⁰These are the sons of Aaron: El·ē·ā´zar his son, Phin´e·has his son, Ab·i·shū´a his son, ⁵¹Buk´kī his son, Uz´zī his son, Zer·a·hī´ah his son, ⁵²Me·rā´i·oth his son, Am·a·rī´ah his son, A·hī´tub his son, ⁵³Zā´dok his son, A·him´a·az his son.

The people knew that their sins separated them from God. Through Aaron and his family, they made sacrifices and offerings to the Lord to bring them back into a right relationship with God. People offered sacrifices as a symbol of their hearts not being right with God and of their wish to be united with God.

When we do something wrong, we often feel that we have messed up our relationship with God. But we no longer have to make a sacri-fice to make the relationship good again. We pray and ask for God's forgiveness. God is always willing to forgive us!

^d Gk Syr Compare verse 33 and 1 Sam 8.2: Heb lacks *Joel*   ^e Heb reads *Vashni, and Abijah* for *the second Abijah*, taking *the second* as a proper name

Settlements of the Levites

54 These are their dwelling places according to their settlements within their borders: to the sons of Aaron of the families of Kōʹhath·ītes—for the lot fell to them first— [55]to them they gave Hēʹbron in the land of Judah and its surrounding pasture lands, [56]but the fields of the city and its villages they gave to Caleb son of Je·phunʹneh. [57]To the sons of Aaron they gave the cities of refuge: Hēʹbron, Libʹnah with its pasture lands, Jatʹtir, Esh·te·mōʹa with its pasture lands, [58]Hīʹlen[f] with its pasture lands, Dēʹbir with its pasture lands, [59]Āʹshan with its pasture lands, and Beth-sheʹmesh with its pasture lands. [60]From the tribe of Benjamin, Gēʹba with its pasture lands, Alʹe·meth with its pasture lands, and Anʹa·thoth with its pasture lands. All their towns throughout their families were thirteen.

61 To the rest of the Kōʹhath·ītes were given by lot out of the family of the tribe, out of the half-tribe, the half of Ma·nasʹseh, ten towns. [62]To the Gerʹshom·ītes according to their families were allotted thirteen towns out of the tribes of Isʹsa·char, Ashʹer, Naphʹta·lī, and Ma·nasʹseh in Bāʹshan. [63]To the Me·rarʹītes according to their families were allotted twelve towns out of the tribes of Reuben, Gad, and Zebʹū·lun. [64]So the people of Israel gave the Lēʹvītes the towns with their pasture lands. [65]They also gave them by lot out of the tribes of Judah, Simʹe·on, and Benjamin these towns that are mentioned by name.

66 And some of the families of the sons of Kōʹhath had towns of their territory out of the tribe of Ēʹphra·im. [67]They were given the cities of refuge: Sheʹchem with its pasture lands in the hill country of Ēʹphra·im, Gēʹzer with its pasture lands, [68]Jokʹmē·am with its pasture lands, Beth-hōʹron with its pasture lands, [69]Aīʹja·lon with its pasture lands, Gath-rimʹmon with its pasture lands; [70]and out of the half-tribe of Ma·nasʹseh, Āʹner with its pasture lands, and Bilʹē·am with its pasture lands, for the rest of the families of the Kōʹhath·ītes.

71 To the Gerʹshom·ītes: out of the half-tribe of Ma·nasʹseh: Gōʹlan in Bāʹshan with its pasture lands and Ashʹta·roth with its pasture lands; [72]and out of the tribe of Isʹsa·char: Kēʹdesh with its pasture lands, Dabʹe·rath[g] with its pasture lands, [73]Rāʹmoth with its pasture lands, and Āʹnem with its pasture lands; [74]out of the tribe of Ashʹer: Māʹshal with its pasture lands, Abʹdon with its pasture lands, [75]Hūʹkok with its pasture lands, and Rēʹhob with its pasture lands; [76]and out of the tribe of Naphʹta·lī: Kēʹdesh in Galilee with its pasture lands, Hamʹmon with its pasture lands, and Kir·i·a·thāʹim with its pasture lands. [77]To the rest of the Me·rarʹītes out of the tribe of Zebʹū·lun: Rimʹmo·nō with its pasture lands, Tāʹbor with its pasture lands, [78]and across the Jordan from Jericho, on the east side of the Jordan, out of the tribe of Reuben: Bēʹzer in the steppe with its pasture lands, Jahʹzah with its pasture lands, [79]Kedʹe·moth with its pasture lands, and Mephʹa·ath with its pasture lands; [80]and out of the tribe of Gad: Rāʹmoth in Gilʹe·ad with its pasture lands, Māʹha·nāʹim with its pasture lands, [81]Heshʹbon with its pasture lands, and Jāʹzer with its pasture lands.

Descendants of Issachar

7 The sons[h] of Isʹsa·char: Tōʹla, Pūʹah, Jashʹub, and Shimʹron, four. [2]The sons of Tōʹla: Uzʹzī, Reph·āiʹah, Jēʹri·el, Jahʹmai, Ibʹsam, and She·mūʹel, heads of their ancestral houses, namely of Tōʹla, mighty warriors of their generations, their number in the days of David being twenty-two thousand six hundred. [3]The son[i] of Uzʹzī: Iz·ra·hīʹah. And the sons of Iz·ra·hīʹah: Michael, Ō·ba·dīʹah, Jōʹel, and Is·shīʹah, five, all of them chiefs; [4]and along with them, by their genera-

[f] Other readings *Hilez, Holon;* See Josh 21.15   [g] Or *Dobrath*   [h] Syr Compare Vg: Heb *And to the sons*   [i] Heb *sons*

tions, according to their ancestral houses, were units of the fighting force, thirty-six thousand, for they had many wives and sons. [5]Their kindred belonging to all the families of Is·sa·char were in all eighty-seven thousand mighty warriors, enrolled by genealogy.

Descendants of Benjamin

6 The sons of Benjamin: Bē´la, Bē´cher, and Je·dī´a·el, three. [7]The sons of Bē´la: Ez´bon, Uz´zī, Uz´zi·el, Jer´i·moth, and Ī´rī, five, heads of ancestral houses, mighty warriors; and their enrollment by genealogies was twenty-two thousand thirty-four. [8]The sons of Bē´cher: Ze·mī´rah, Jō´ash, El·i·ē´zer, El·i·ō·ē´nai, Om´rī, Jer´e·moth, A·bī´jah, An´a·thoth, and Al´e·meth. All these were the sons of Bē´cher; [9]and their enrollment by genealogies, according to their generations, as heads of their ancestral houses, mighty warriors, was twenty thousand two hundred. [10]The sons of Je·dī´a·el: Bil´han. And the sons of Bil´han: Jē´ush, Benjamin, Ē´hud, Che·nā´a·nah, Zē´than, Tar´shish, and A·hish´a·har. [11]All these were the sons of Je·dī´a·el according to the heads of their ancestral houses, mighty warriors, seventeen thousand two hundred, ready for service in war. [12]And Shup´pim and Hup´pim were the sons of Ir, Hū´shim the son[j] of Ā´her.

Descendants of Naphtali

13 The descendants of Naph´ta·lī: Jah´zī·el, Gū´nī, Jē´zer, and Shal´lum, the descendants of Bil´hah.

Descendants of Manasseh

14 The sons of Ma·nas´seh: As´ri·el, whom his Ar·a·mē´an concubine bore; she bore Mā´chir the father of Gil´e·ad. [15]And Mā´chir took a wife for Hup´pim and for Shup´pim. The name of his sister was Mā´a·cah. And the name of the second was Ze·loph´e·had; and Ze·loph´e·had had daughters. [16]Mā´a·cah the wife of Mā´chir bore a son, and she named him Pē´resh; the name of his brother was Shē´resh; and

his sons were Ū´lam and Rē´kem. [17]The son[j] of Ū´lam: Bē´dan. These were the sons of Gil´e·ad son of Mā´chir, son of Ma·nas´seh. [18]And his sister Ham·mō´le·cheth bore Ish´hod, Ā´bi·ē´zer, and Mah´lah. [19]The sons of She·mī´da were A·hī´an, Shē´chem, Lik´hī, and A·nī´am.

Descendants of Ephraim

20 The sons of Ē´phra·im: Shū·thē´lah, and Bē´red his son, Tā´hath his son, El·ē´a·dah his son, Tā´hath his son, [21]Zā´bad his son, Shū·thē´lah his son, and Ē´zer and Ē´lē·ad. Now the people of Gath, who were born in the land, killed them, because they came down to raid their cattle. [22]And their father Ē´phra·im mourned many days, and his brothers came to comfort him. [23]Ē´phra·im[k] went in to his wife, and she conceived and bore a son; and he named him Bē·rī´ah, because disaster[l] had befallen his house. [24]His daughter was Shē´e·rah, who built both Lower and Upper Beth-hō´ron, and Uz´zen-shē´e·rah. [25]Rē´phah was his son, Rē´sheph his son, Tē´lah his son, Tā´han his son, [26]Lā´dan his son, Am·mī´hud his son, E·lish´a·ma his son, [27]Nun[m] his son, Joshua his son. [28]Their possessions and settlements were Beth´el and its towns, and eastward Nā´a·ran, and westward Gē´zer and its towns, Shē´chem and its towns, as far as Āy´yah and its towns; [29]also along the borders of the Ma·nas´sītes, Beth-shē´an and its towns, Tā´a·nach and its towns, Me·gid´dō and its towns, Dor and its towns. In these lived the sons of Joseph son of Israel.

Descendants of Asher

30 The sons of Ash´er: Im´nah, Ish´vah, Ish´vī, Bē·rī´ah, and their sister Sē´rah. [31]The sons of Bē·rī´ah: Hē´ber and Mal´chi·el, who was the father of Bir´zā·ith. [32]Hē´ber became the father of Japh´let, Shō´mer, Hō´tham, and their sister Shū´a. [33]The sons of Japh´let: Pā´sach, Bim´hal, and Ash´vath. These are

[j] Heb sons [k] Heb He [l] Heb beraah [m] Here spelled Non; see Exod 33:11

the sons of Japh′let. ³⁴The sons of Shē′-mer: Ā′hī, Rōh′gah, Hub′bah, and Ar′am. ³⁵The sons of Hē′lem[n] his brother: Zō′phah, Im′na, Shē′lesh, and Ā′mal. ³⁶The sons of Zō′phah: Sū′ah, Har′ne·pher, Shū′al, Bē′rī, Im′rah, ³⁷Bē′-zer, Hod, Sham′ma, Shil′shah, Ith′ran, and Be·ē′ra. ³⁸The sons of Jē′ther: Je·phūn′-neh, Pis′pa, and Ar′a. ³⁹The sons of Ul′la: Ā′rah, Han′ni·el, and Rī·zī′a. ⁴⁰All of these were men of Ash′er, heads of ancestral houses, select mighty warriors, chief of the princes. Their number enrolled by genealogies, for service in war, was twenty-six thousand men.

Descendants of Benjamin

8 Benjamin became the father of Bē′la his firstborn, Ash′bel the second, A′har·ah the third, ²Nō′hah the fourth, and Rā′pha the fifth. ³And Bē′la had sons: Ad′dar, Gē′ra, A·bī′hud,[o] ⁴Ab·i·shū′a, Nā′-a·man, A·hō′ah, ⁵Gē′ra, She·phū′phan, and Hū′ram. ⁶These are the sons of Ē′hud (they were heads of ancestral houses of the inhabitants of Gē′ba, and they were carried into exile to Man′a·hath): ⁷Nā′-a·man,[p] A·hī′jah, and Gē′ra, that is, Heg′lam,[q] who became the father of Uz′za and A·hī′hud. ⁸And Shā·ha·rā′im had sons in the country of Mō′ab after he had sent away his wives Hū′shim and Bā′a·ra. ⁹He had sons by his wife Hō′desh: Jō′bab, Zib′i·a, Mē′sha, Mal′cam, ¹⁰Jē′uz, Sa·chī′a, and Mir′mah. These were his sons, heads of ancestral houses. ¹¹He also had sons by Hū′shim: A·bī′tub and El·pā′al. ¹²The sons of El·pā′al: Ē′ber, Mī′sham, and Shē′med, who built Ō′nō and Lod with its towns, ¹³and Bē·rī′ah and Shē′ma (they were heads of ancestral houses of the inhabitants of Aī′ja·lon, who put to flight the inhabitants of Gath); ¹⁴and A·hī′ō, Shā′-shak, and Jer′e·moth. ¹⁵Zeb·a·dī′ah, Ar′ad, Ē′der, ¹⁶Michael, Ish′pah, and Jō′ha were sons of Bē·rī′ah. ¹⁷Zeb·a·dī′ah, Me·shul′-lam, Hiz′kī, Hē′ber, ¹⁸Ish′me·raī, Iz·lī′ah, and Jō′bab were the sons of El·pā′al. ¹⁹Jā′-kim, Zich′rī, Zab′dī, ²⁰E·li·ē′naī, Zil′le·thaī,

E·lī′el, ²¹A·daī′ah, Be·rā′i·ah, and Shim′-rath were the sons of Shim·ē′·ī. ²²Ish′pan, Ē′ber, E·lī′el, ²³Ab′don, Zich′rī, Hā′nan, ²⁴Han·a·nī′ah, Ē′lam, An·tho·thī′jah, ²⁵Iphde·ī·ah, and Pe·nū′el were the sons of Shā′shak. ²⁶Sham′she·raī, Shē·ha·rī′ah, Ath·a·lī′ah, ²⁷Jā·ar·eshī′ah, E·lī′jah, and Zich′rī were the sons of Je·rō′ham. ²⁸These were the heads of ancestral houses, according to their generations, chiefs. These lived in Jerusalem.

29 Je·ī′el[r] the father of Gib′e·on lived in Gib′e·on, and the name of his wife was Mā′a·cah. ³⁰His firstborn son: Ab′don, then Zur, Kish, Bā′al,[s] Nā′dab, ³¹Gē′dor, A·hī′ō, Zē′cher, ³²and Mik′loth, who became the father of Shim·ē′ah. Now these also lived opposite their kindred in Jerusalem, with their kindred. ³³Ner became the father of Kish, Kish of Saul,[t] Saul[t] of Jonathan, Mal·chī·shū′a, A·bin′-a·dab, and Esh-bā′al; ³⁴and the son of Jonathan was Mer·ib-bā′al; and Mer·ib-bā′-al became the father of Mī′cah. ³⁵The sons of Mī′cah: Pī′thon, Mē′lech, Ta·rē′a, and Ā′haz. ³⁶Ā′haz became the father of Je·hō′-ad·dah; and Je·hō′ad·dah became the father of Al′e·meth, Az′ma·veth, and Zim′rī; Zim′rī became the father of Mō′za. ³⁷Mō′za became the father of Bin′e·a; Rā′-phah was his son, El·e·ā′sah his son, Ā′zel his son. ³⁸Ā′zel had six sons, and these are their names: Az·rī′kam, Bō′che·rū, Ish′-ma·el, Shē·a·rī′ah, Ō·ba·dī′ah, and Hā′nan; all these were the sons of Ā′zel. ³⁹The sons of his brother Ē′shek: Ū′lam his firstborn, Jē′ush the second, and E·liph′e·let the third. ⁴⁰The sons of Ū′lam were mighty warriors, archers, having many children and grandchildren, one hundred fifty. All these were Ben′ja·min·ītes.

9 So all Israel was enrolled by genealogies; and these are written in the Book of the Kings of Israel. And

---

[n] Or *Hotham;* see 7.32   [o] Or *father of Ehud;* see 8.6   [p] Heb *and Naaman*   [q] Or *he carried them into exile*   [r] Compare 9.35: Heb lacks *Jeiel*   [s] Gk Ms adds *Ner;* Compare 8.33 and 9.36   [t] Or *Shaul*

Judah was taken into exile in Babylon because of their unfaithfulness. ²Now the first to live again in their possessions in their towns were Israelites, priests, Lě·vītes, and temple servants.

Inhabitants of Jerusalem after the Exile

3 And some of the people of Judah, Benjamin, Ē´phra·im, and Ma·nas´seh lived in Jerusalem: ⁴Ū´thaī son of Am·mī´hud, son of Om´rī, son of Im´rī, son of Bā´nī, from the sons of Pe´rez son of Judah. ⁵And of the Shī´lo·nītes: A·saī´ah the firstborn, and his sons. ⁶Of the sons of Zē´rah: Je·ū´el and their kin, six hundred ninety. ⁷Of the Ben´ja·min·ītes: Sal´lū son of Me·shul´lam, son of Hod·a·vī´ah, son of Has·se·nū´ah, ⁸Ib·nē´i·ah son of Je·rō´ham, Ē´lah son of Uz´zī, son of Mich´rī, and Me·shul´lam son of Sheph·a·tī´ah, son of Reū´el, son of Ib·nī´jah; ⁹and their kindred according to their generations, nine hundred fifty-six. All these were heads of families according to their ancestral houses.

Priestly Families

10 Of the priests: Je·daī´ah, Je·hoi´a·rib, Jā´chin, ¹¹and Az·a·rī´ah son of Hil·kī´ah, son of Me·shul´lam, son of Zā´dok, son of Me·rā´i·oth, son of A·hī´tub, the chief officer of the house of God; ¹²and A·daī´ah son of Je·rō´ham, son of Pash´hur, son of Mal·chī´jah, and Mā´a·saī son of Ad´i·el, son of Jah´ze·rah, son of Me·shul´lam, son of Me·shil´le·mith, son of Im´mer; ¹³besides their kindred, heads of their ancestral houses, one thousand seven hundred sixty, qualified for the work of the service of the house of God.

Levitical Families

14 Of the Lě´vītes: She·maī´ah son of Has´shub, son of Az·rī´kam, son of Hash·a·bī´ah, of the sons of Me·rar´ī; ¹⁵and Bak·bak´kar, Hē´resh, Gā´lal, and Mat·ta·nī´ah son of Mī´ca, son of Zich´rī, son of Ā´saph; ¹⁶and Ō·ba·dī´ah son of She·maī´ah, son of Gā´lal, son of Je·dū´thun, and Ber·e·chī´ah son of Asa, son of El·kā´nah, who lived in the villages of the Ne·toph´a·thītes.

17 The gatekeepers were: Shal´lum, Ak´kub, Tal´mon, A·hī´man; and their kindred Shal´lum was the chief, ¹⁸stationed previously in the king's gate on the east side. These were the gatekeepers of the camp of the Lě´vītes. ¹⁹Shal´lum son of Kō´re, son of E·bī´a·saph, son of Kō´rah, and his kindred of his ancestral house, the Kō´ra·hītes, were in charge of the work of the service, guardians of the thresholds of the tent, as their ancestors had been in charge of the camp of the LORD, guardians of the entrance. ²⁰And Phin´e·has son of El·ē·ā´zar was chief over them in former times; the LORD was with him. ²¹Zech·a·rī´ah son of Me·shel´e·mī´ah was gatekeeper at the entrance of the tent of meeting. ²²All these, who were chosen as gatekeepers at the thresholds, were two hundred twelve. They were enrolled by genealogies in their villages. David and the seer Samuel established them in their office of trust. ²³So they and their descendants were in charge of the gates of the house of the LORD, that is, the house of the tent, as guards. ²⁴The gatekeepers were on the four sides, east, west, north, and south; ²⁵and their kindred who were in their villages were obliged to come in every seven days, in turn, to be with them; ²⁶for the four chief gatekeepers, who were Lě´vītes, were in charge of the chambers and the treasures of the house of God. ²⁷And they would spend the night near the house of God; for on them lay the duty of watching, and they had charge of opening it every morning.

28 Some of them had charge of the utensils of service, for they were required to count them when they were brought in and taken out. ²⁹Others of them were appointed over the furniture, and over all the holy utensils, also over the choice flour, the wine, the oil, the

incense, and the spices. ³⁰Others, of the sons of the priests, prepared the mixing of the spices, ³¹and Mat·ti·thī´ah, one of the Lē´vītes, the firstborn of Shal´lum the Kō´ra·hīte, was in charge of making the flat cakes. ³²Also some of their kindred of the Kō´hath·ītes had charge of the rows of bread, to prepare them for each sabbath.

33 Now these are the singers, the heads of ancestral houses of the Lē´vītes, living in the chambers of the temple free from other service, for they were on duty day and night. ³⁴These were heads of ancestral houses of the Lē´vītes, according to their generations; these leaders lived in Jerusalem.

The Kohathites were in charge of making the Bread of the Presence (also called showbread). This was twelve loaves of bread made of fine flour, set in the Temple as an offering to God. These twelve loaves were a symbol of the twelve tribes of Israel. Because this bread always had to be in the Temple, fresh loaves were brought each Sabbath, and the priests ate the old loaves.

Have you ever paid attention to the bread your church uses in the Communion (or Lord's Supper) service? Is it a loaf of bread or wafers? Ask an adult at your church who prepares the bread and juice for communion, and thank that person for his or her special service.

The Family of King Saul

35 In Gib´e·on lived the father of Gib´e·on, Je·ī´el, and the name of his wife was Mā´a·cah. ³⁶His firstborn son was Ab´don, then Zur, Kish, Bā´al, Ner, Nā´dab, ³⁷Gē´dor, A·hī´ō, Zech·a·rī´ah, and Mik´loth; ³⁸and Mik´loth became the father of Shim´ē·am; and these also lived

opposite their kindred in Jerusalem, with their kindred. ³⁹Ner became the father of Kish, Kish of Saul, Saul of Jonathan, Mal·chī·shū´a, A·bin´a·dab, and Esh-bā´al; ⁴⁰and the son of Jonathan was Mer´ib-bā´al; and Mer´ib-bā´al became the father of Mī´cah. ⁴¹The sons of Mī´cah: Pī´thon, Mē´lech, Tah·rē´a, and Ā´haz;ᵘ ⁴²and Ā´haz became the father of Jar´ah, and Jar´ah of Al´e·meth, Az´ma·veth, and Zim´rī; and Zim´rī became the father of Mō´za. ⁴³Mō´za became the father of Bin´e·a; and Reph·āi´ah was his son, El·e·ā´sah his son, Ā´zel his son. ⁴⁴Ā´zel had six sons, and these are their names: Az·rī´kam, Bō´che·rū, Ish´ma·el, Shē·a·rī´ah, Ō·ba·dī´ah, and Hā´nan; these were the sons of Ā´zel.

Death of Saul and His Sons

10 Now the Phi·lis´tines fought against Israel; and the men of Israel fled before the Phi·lis´tines, and fell slain on Mount Gil·bō´a. ²The Phi·lis´tines overtook Saul and his sons; and the Phi·lis´tines killed Jonathan and A·bin´a·dab and Mal·chī·shū´a, sons of Saul. ³The battle pressed hard on Saul; and the archers found him, and he was wounded by the archers. ⁴Then Saul said to his armor-bearer, "Draw your sword, and thrust me through with it, so that these uncircumcised may not come and make sport of me." But his armor-bearer was unwilling, for he was terrified. So Saul took his own sword and fell on it. ⁵When his armor-bearer saw that Saul was dead, he also fell on his sword and died. ⁶Thus Saul died; he and his three sons and all his house died together. ⁷When all the men of Israel who were in the valley saw that the armyᵛ had fled and that Saul and his sons were dead, they abandoned their towns and fled; and the Phi·lis´tines came and occupied them.

8 The next day when the Phi·lis´tines came to strip the dead, they found Saul and his sons fallen on Mount Gil·bō´a.

ᵘ Compare 8.35: Heb lacks *and Ahaz*   ᵛ Heb *they*

⁹They stripped him and took his head and his armor, and sent messengers throughout the land of the Phi·lis′tines to carry the good news to their idols and to the people. ¹⁰They put his armor in the temple of their gods, and fastened his head in the temple of Dā′gon. ¹¹But when all Jā′besh-gil′ē·ad heard everything that the Phi·lis′tines had done to Saul, ¹²all the valiant warriors got up and took away the body of Saul and the bodies of his sons, and brought them to Jā′besh. Then they buried their bones under the oak in Jā′besh, and fasted seven days.

13 So Saul died for his unfaithfulness; he was unfaithful to the LORD in that he did not keep the command of the LORD; moreover, he had consulted a medium, seeking guidance, ¹⁴and did not seek guidance from the LORD. Therefore the LORDᵂ put him to death and turned the kingdom over to David son of Jesse.

David Anointed King of All Israel

11 Then all Israel gathered together to David at Hē′bron and said, "See, we are your bone and flesh. ²For some time now, even while Saul was king, it was you who commanded the army of Israel. The LORD your God said to you: It is you who shall be shepherd of my people Israel, you who shall be ruler over my people Israel." ³So all the elders of Israel came to the king at Hē′bron, and David made a covenant with them at Hē′bron before the LORD. And they anointed David king over Israel, according to the word of the LORD by Samuel.

Jerusalem Captured

4 David and all Israel marched to Jerusalem, that is Jē′bus, where the Jeb′ū·sītes were, the inhabitants of the land. ⁵The inhabitants of Jē′bus said to David, "You will not come in here." Nevertheless David took the stronghold of Zion, now the city of David. ⁶David had said, "Whoever attacks the Jeb′ū·sītes first

shall be chief and commander." And Jō′ab son of Ze·rū′i·ah went up first, so he became chief. ⁷David resided in the stronghold; therefore it was called the city of David. ⁸He built the city all around, from the Mil′lō in complete circuit; and Jō′ab repaired the rest of the city. ⁹And David became greater and greater, for the LORD of hosts was with him.

David's Mighty Men and Their Exploits

10 Now these are the chiefs of David's warriors, who gave him strong support in his kingdom, together with all Israel, to make him king, according to the word of the LORD concerning Israel. ¹¹This is an account of David's mighty warriors: Ja·shō′bē·am, son of Hach′mo·nī,ˣ was chief of the Three;ʸ he wielded his spear against three hundred whom he killed at one time.

12 And next to him among the three warriors was El·ē·ā′zar son of Dō′dō, the A·hō′hīte. ¹³He was with David at Pasdam′mim when the Phi·lis′tines were gathered there for battle. There was a plot of ground full of barley. Now the people had fled from the Phi·lis′tines, ¹⁴but he and David took their stand in the middle of the plot, defended it, and killed the Phi·lis′tines; and the LORD saved them by a great victory.

15 Three of the thirty chiefs went down to the rock to David at the cave of A·dul′lam, while the army of Phi·lis′tines was encamped in the valley of Reph′a·im. ¹⁶David was then in the stronghold; and the garrison of the Phi·lis′tines was then at Bethlehem. ¹⁷David said longingly, "O that someone would give me water to drink from the well of Bethlehem that is by the gate!" ¹⁸Then the Three broke through the camp of the Phi·lis′tines, and drew water from the well of Bethlehem that was by the gate, and they brought it to David. But David

---

ᵂ Heb *he*   ˣ Or *a Hachmonite*   ʸ Compare 2 Sam 23.8: Heb *Thirty* or *captains* would not drink of it; he poured it out to the LORD, [19]and said, "My God forbid that I should do this. Can I drink the blood of these men? For at the risk of their lives they brought it." Therefore he would not drink it. The three warriors did these things.

20 Now A·bi´shai,[z] the brother of Jō´ab, was chief of the Thirty.[a] With his spear he fought against three hundred and killed them, and won a name beside the Three. [21]He was the most renowned[b] of the Thirty,[a] and became their commander; but he did not attain to the Three.

22 Be·nā´i·ah son of Je·hoi´a·da was a valiant man[c] of Kab´ze·el, a doer of great deeds; he struck down two sons of[d] Ar´i·el of Mō´ab. He also went down and killed a lion in a pit on a day when snow had fallen. [23]And he killed an Egyptian, a man of great stature, five cubits tall. The Egyptian had in his hand a spear like a weaver's beam; but Be·nā´i·ah went against him with a staff, snatched the spear out of the Egyptian's hand, and killed him with his own spear. [24]Such were the things Be·nā´i·ah son of Je·hoi´a·da did, and he won a name beside the three warriors. [25]He was renowned among the Thirty, but he did not attain to the Three. And David put him in charge of his bodyguard.

26 The warriors of the armies were As´a·hel brother of Jō´ab, El·hā´nan son of Dō´dō of Bethlehem, [27]Sham´moth of Har´od,[e] Hē´lez the Pel´o·nīte, [28]Ira son of Ik´kesh of Te·kō´a, A·bi·e´zer of An´a·thoth, [29]Sib´be·caī the Hū´sha·thīte, I´lai the A·hō´hīte, [30]Mā´ha·raī of Ne·toph´ah, Hē´led son of Bā´a·nah of Ne·toph´ah, [31]Ith´aī son of Rī´bai of Gib´e·ah of the Ben´ja·min·ītes, Be·nā´i·ah of Pir´a·thon, [32]Hū´raī of the wadis of Gā´ash, A·bī´el the Ar´ba·thīte, [33]Az´ma·veth of Ba·hā´rum, Ē·lī´ah·ba of Shā·al´bon, [34]Hā´shem[f] the Gī´zo·nīte, Jonathan son of Shā´gee the Har´a·rīte, [35]A·hī´am son of Sā´char the Har´a·rīte, E·lī´phal son of Ūr, [36]Hē´pher the Me·chē´ra·thīte, A·hī´jah the Pel´o·nīte, [37]Hez´rō of Car´mel, Nā´a·raī son of Ez´bai, [38]Jō´el the brother of Nathan, Mib´har son of Hag´rī, [39]Zē´lek the Am´mon·īte, Na´ha·raī of Be·er´oth, the armor-bearer of Jō´ab son of Ze·rū´i·ah, [40]Ira the Ith´rīte, Gā´reb the Ith´rīte, [41]Ū·rī´ah the Hit´tīte, Zā´bad son of Ah´lai, [42]Ad´i·na son of Shī´za the Reū´ben·īte, a leader of the Reū´ben·ītes, and thirty with him, [43]Hā´nan son of Mā´a·cah, and Josh´a·phat the Mith´nīte, [44]Uz·zī´a the Ash´te·ra·thīte, Shā´ma and Je·ī´el sons of Hō´tham the A·rō´er·īte, [45]Je·dī´a·el son of Shim´rī, and his brother Jō´ha the Tī´zīte, [46]E·lī´el the Mā´ha·vīte, and Jer´i·bai and Josh·a·vī´ah sons of El´nā·am, and Ith´mah the Mō´ab·īte, [47]E·lī´el, and Ō´bed, and Jā·a·sī´el the Me·zō´ba·īte.

David's Followers in the Wilderness

12 The following are those who came to David at Zik´lag, while he could not move about freely because of Saul son of Kish; they were among the mighty warriors who helped him in war. [2]They were archers, and could shoot arrows and sling stones with either the right hand or the left; they were Ben´ja·min·ītes, Saul's kindred. [3]The chief was Ā·hi·e´zer, then Jō´ash, both sons of She·mā´ah of Gib´e·ah; also Jē´zi·el and Pē´let sons of Az´ma·veth; Ber´a·cah, Jē´hū of An´a·thoth, [4]Ish·mā´i·ah of Gib´e·on, a warrior among the Thirty and a leader over the Thirty; Jer·e·mī´ah,[g] Ja·hā´zi·el, Jō·hā´nan, Joz´a·bad of Ge·dē´rah, [5]E·lū´zai,[h] Jer´i·moth, Be·a·lī´ah, Shem´a·rī´ah, Sheph·a·tī´ah the Ha·rū´phite; [6]El·kā´nah, Is·shī´ah, Az´a·rel, Jo·e´zer, and Ja·shō´be·am, the Kō´ra·hītes; [7]and

[z] Gk Vg Tg Compare 2 Sam 23.18: Heb *Abshai*
[a] Syr: Heb *Three*   [b] Compare 2 Sam 23.19: Heb *more renowned among the two*   [c] Syr: Heb *the son of a valiant man*   [d] See 2 Sam 23.20: Heb lacks *sons of*   [e] Compare 2 Sam 23.25: Heb *the Harorite*
[f] Compare Gk and 2 Sam 23.32: Heb *the sons of Hashem*   [g] Heb verse 5   [h] Heb verse 6

Jō·ē'lah and Zeb·a·dī'ah, sons of Je·rō'-ham of Gē'dor.

8 From the Gad'ites there went over to David at the stronghold in the wilderness mighty and experienced warriors, expert with shield and spear, whose faces were like the faces of lions, and who were swift as gazelles on the mountains: [9]Ē'zer the chief, Ō·ba·dī'ah second, E·lī'ab third, [10]Mish·man'nah fourth, Jer·e·mī'ah fifth, [11]At'tai sixth, E·lī'el seventh, [12]Jō·hā'nan eighth, El·zā'bad ninth, [13]Jer·e·mī'ah tenth, Mach'ban·nai eleventh. [14]These Gad'ites were officers of the army, the least equal to a hundred and the greatest to a thousand. [15]These are the men who crossed the Jordan in the first month, when it was overflowing all its banks, and put to flight all those in the valleys, to the east and to the west.

16 Some Ben'ja·min·ites and Jū'dah·ites came to the stronghold to David. [17]David went out to meet them and said to them, "If you have come to me in friendship, to help me, then my heart will be knit to you; but if you have come to betray me to my adversaries, though my hands have done no wrong, then may the God of our ancestors see and give judgment." [18]Then the spirit came upon A·mā'sai, chief of the Thirty, and he said,

"We are yours, O David;
  and with you, O son of Jesse!
Peace, peace to you,
  and peace to the one who helps
    you!
For your God is the one who
  helps you."

Then David received them, and made them officers of his troops.

19 Some of the Ma·nas'sites deserted to David when he came with the Phi·lis'tines for the battle against Saul. (Yet he did not help them, for the rulers of the Phi·lis'tines took counsel and sent him away, saying, "He will desert to his master Saul at the cost of our heads.")

> "Peace, peace to you, and peace to the one who helps you! For your God is the one who helps you!"
> 1 Chronicles 12:18b

[20]As he went to Zik'lag these Ma·nas'sites deserted to him: Ad'nah, Joz'a·bad, Je·dī'a·el, Michael, Joz'a·bad, E·lī'hū, and Zil'le·thai, chiefs of the thousands in Ma·nas'seh. [21]They helped David against the band of raiders,[i] for they were all warriors and commanders in the army. [22]Indeed from day to day people kept coming to David to help him, until there was a great army, like an army of God.

David's Army at Hebron

23 These are the numbers of the divisions of the armed troops who came to David in Hē'bron to turn the kingdom of Saul over to him, according to the word of the LORD. [24]The people of Judah bearing shield and spear numbered six thousand eight hundred armed troops. [25]Of the Sim'e·on·ites, mighty warriors, seven thousand one hundred. [26]Of the Lē'vites four thousand six hundred. [27]Je·hoi'a·da, leader of the house of Aaron, and with him three thousand seven hundred. [28]Zā'dok, a young warrior, and twenty-two commanders from his own ancestral house. [29]Of the Ben'ja·min·ites, the kindred of Saul, three thousand, of whom the majority had continued to keep their allegiance to the house of Saul. [30]Of the Ē'phra·im·ites, twenty thousand eight hundred, mighty warriors, notables in their ancestral houses. [31]Of the half-tribe of Ma·nas'seh, eighteen thousand, who were expressly named to come and make David king. [32]Of Is'sa·char, those who had understanding of the times, to know what Israel ought to do, two hundred chiefs, and all their kindred under their command. [33]Of Zeb'ū·lun, fifty thousand seasoned troops, equipped for battle with all the weapons of war, to help David[j]

[i] Or *as officers of his troops* [j] Gk: Heb lacks *David*

with singleness of purpose. ³⁴Of Naph′ta·li, a thousand commanders, with whom there were thirty-seven thousand armed with shield and spear. ³⁵Of the Dan′ites, twenty-eight thousand six hundred equipped for battle. ³⁶Of Ash′er, forty thousand seasoned troops ready for battle. ³⁷Of the Reū′ben·ites and Gad′ites and the half-tribe of Ma·nas′seh from beyond the Jordan, one hundred twenty thousand armed with all the weapons of war.

38 All these, warriors arrayed in battle order, came to Hē′bron with full intent to make David king over all Israel; likewise all the rest of Israel were of a single mind to make David king. ³⁹They were there with David for three days, eating and drinking, for their kindred had provided for them. ⁴⁰And also their neighbors, from as far away as Is′sa·char and Zeb′ū·lun and Naph′ta·li, came bringing food on donkeys, camels, mules, and oxen— abundant provisions of meal, cakes of figs, clusters of raisins, wine, oil, oxen, and sheep, for there was joy in Israel.

We sometimes celebrate special events like holidays and birthdays by eating a big meal with our families. People in Bible times did the same thing! When the people came to Hebron to make David king over all Israel, they ate a great feast. They enjoyed cakes of figs and clusters of raisins. Because figs and raisins were common, these foods had been a part of meals for many years.

The Ark Brought from Kiriath-jearim

13 David consulted with the commanders of the thousands and of the hundreds, with every leader. ²David said to the whole assembly of Israel, "If it seems good to you, and if it is the will of the LORD our God, let us send abroad to our kindred who remain in all the land of Israel, including the priests and Lē′vites in the cities that have pasture lands, that they may come together to us. ³Then let us bring again the ark of our God to us; for we did not turn to it in the days of Saul." ⁴The whole assembly agreed to do so, for the thing pleased all the people.

5 So David assembled all Israel from the Shī′hor of Egypt to Lē′bō-hā′math, to bring the ark of God from Kir′i·ath-jē′a·rim. ⁶And David and all Israel went up to Bā′a·lah, that is, to Kir′i·ath-jē′a·rim, which belongs to Judah, to bring up from there the ark of God, the LORD, who is enthroned on the cherubim, which is called by his^k name. ⁷They carried the ark of God on a new cart, from the house of A·bin′a·dab, and Uz′zah and A·hī′o^l were driving the cart. ⁸David and all Israel were dancing before God with all their might, with song and lyres and harps and tambourines and cymbals and trumpets.

9 When they came to the threshing floor of Chī′don, Uz′zah put out his hand to hold the ark, for the oxen shook it. ¹⁰The anger of the LORD was kindled against Uz′zah; he struck him down because he put out his hand to the ark; and he died there before God. ¹¹David was angry because the LORD had burst out against Uz′zah; so that place is called Per′ez-uz′zah^m to this day. ¹²David was afraid of God that day; he said, "How can I bring the ark of God into my care?" ¹³So David did not take the ark into his care into the city of David; he took it instead to the house of Ō′bed-ē′dom the Git′tite. ¹⁴The ark of God remained with the household of Ō′bed-ē′dom in his house three months, and the LORD blessed the household of Ō′bed-ē′dom and all that he had.

^k Heb lacks his   ^l Or and his brother   ^m That is Bursting Out Against Uzzah

David Established at Jerusalem

14 King Hiram of Tyre sent messengers to David, along with cedar logs, and masons and carpenters to build a house for him. ²David then perceived that the LORD had established him as king over Israel, and that his kingdom was highly exalted for the sake of his people Israel.

3 David took more wives in Jerusalem, and David became the father of more sons and daughters. ⁴These are the names of the children whom he had in Jerusalem: Sham´mū·a, Shō´bab, and Nathan; Solomon, ⁵Ib´har, E·lish´ū·a, and El´pe·let; ⁶Nō´gah, Nē´pheg, and Ja·phī´a; ⁷E·lish´a·ma, Bē·e·lī´a·da, and E·liph´e·let.

Defeat of the Philistines

8 When the Phi·lis´tines heard that David had been anointed king over all Israel, all the Phi·lis´tines went up in search of David; and David heard of it and went out against them. ⁹Now the Phi·lis´tines had come and made a raid in the valley of Reph´a·im. ¹⁰David inquired of God, "Shall I go up against the Phi·lis´tines? Will you give them into my hand?" The LORD said to him, "Go up, and I will give them into your hand." ¹¹So he went up to Bā´al-pe·rā´zim, and David defeated them there. David said, "God has burst out[n] against my enemies by my hand, like a bursting flood." Therefore that place is called Bā´al-pe·rā´zim.[o] ¹²They abandoned their gods there, and at David's command they were burned.

13 Once again the Phi·lis´tines made a raid in the valley. ¹⁴When David again inquired of God, God said to him, "You shall not go up after them; go around and come on them opposite the balsam trees. ¹⁵When you hear the sound of marching in the tops of the balsam trees, then go out to battle; for God has gone out before you to strike down the army of the Phi·lis´tines." ¹⁶David did as God had commanded him, and they struck down the Phi·lis´tine army from Gib-

e·on to Gē´zer. ¹⁷The fame of David went out into all lands, and the LORD brought the fear of him on all nations.

One of the first things David did as king was make plans to bring the ark to Jerusalem. He made a special place for it. He asked the chiefs of the Levites to choose singers and musicians to go before the ark. What a joyful parade it must have been!

The Ark Brought to Jerusalem

15 David[p] built houses for himself in the city of David, and he prepared a place for the ark of God and pitched a tent for it. ²Then David commanded that no one but the Lē´vītes were to carry the ark of God, for the LORD had chosen them to carry the ark of the LORD and to minister to him forever. ³David assembled all Israel in Jerusalem to bring up the ark of the LORD to its place, which he had prepared for it. ⁴Then David gathered together the descendants of Aaron and the Lē´vītes: ⁵of the sons of Kō´hath, Ū·rī´el the chief, with one hundred twenty of his kindred; ⁶of the sons of Me·rar´ī, A·sāi´ah the chief, with two hundred twenty of his kindred; ⁷of the sons of Ger´shom, Jō´el the chief, with one hundred thirty of his kindred; ⁸of the sons of E·li·zā´phan, She·māi´ah the chief, with two hundred of his kindred; ⁹of the sons of Hē´bron, E·lī´el the chief, with eighty of his kindred; ¹⁰of the sons of Uz´zi·el, Am·min´-a·dab the chief, with one hundred twelve of his kindred.

11 David summoned the priests Zā´dok and A·bī´a·thar, and the Lē´vītes Ū·rī´el, A·sāi´ah, Jō´el, She·māi´ah, E·lī´el, and Am·min´a·dab. ¹²He said to them,

---

[n] Heb *paraz*   [o] That is *Lord of Bursting Out*
[p] Heb *He*

"You are the heads of families of the Lĕ́vītes; sanctify yourselves, you and your kindred, so that you may bring up the ark of the LORD, the God of Israel, to the place that I have prepared for it. ¹³Because you did not carry it the first time,�q the LORD our God burst out against us, because we did not give it proper care." ¹⁴So the priests and the Lĕ́vītes sanctified themselves to bring up the ark of the LORD, the God of Israel. ¹⁵And the Lĕ́vītes carried the ark of God on their shoulders with the poles, as Moses had commanded according to the word of the LORD.

16 David also commanded the chiefs of the Lĕ́vītes to appoint their kindred as the singers to play on musical instruments, on harps and lyres and cymbals, to raise loud sounds of joy. ¹⁷So the Lĕ́vītes appointed Hḗman son of Jṓel; and of his kindred Ā́saph son of Ber·e·chī́·ah; and of the sons of Me·rar´ī, their kindred, Ḗthan son of Kū·shā´i·ah; ¹⁸and with them their kindred of the second order, Zech·a·rī́ah, Ja·ā·zi·el, She·mir´a·moth, Je·hī́el, Un´nī, E·lī́ab, Be·nā́i·ah, Mā·a·sēi´ah, Mat·ti·thī́ah, E·liph´e·le·hū, and Mik·nḗi·ah, and the gatekeepers Ṓbed-ḗdom and Je·ī́el. ¹⁹The singers Hḗman, Ā́saph, and Ḗthan were to sound bronze cymbals; ²⁰Zech·a·rī́ah, Ā́zi·el, Shemir´a·moth, Je·hī́el, Un´nī, E·lī́ab, Mā·a·sēi´ah, and Be·nā́i·ah were to play harps according to Al´a·moth; ²¹but Mat·ti·thī́ah, E·liph´e·le·hū, Mik·nḗi·ah, Ṓbed-ḗdom, Je·ī́el, and Az·a·zī́ah were to lead with lyres according to the Shem´i·nith. ²²Chen·a·nī́ah, leader of the Lĕ́vītes in music, was to direct the music, for he understood it. ²³Ber·e·chī́ah and El·kā́nah were to be gatekeepers for the ark. ²⁴Sheb·a·nī́ah, Josh´a·phat, Ne·than´el, A·mā́saī, Zech·a·rī́ah, Be·nā́i·ah, and El·i·ḗzer, the priests, were to blow the trumpets before the ark of God. Ṓbed-ḗdom and Je·hī́ah also were to be gatekeepers for the ark.

What is your favorite musical instrument? There were many different instruments in Bible times. There were stringed instruments, such as the harp (small enough to be held in the hand) and the lute. There were wind instruments, such as the flute (made from reed pipes). There were horns (made from an animal horn) and trumpets (made of metal). And there were noisemakers, such as bells, tambourines, timbrels, cymbals, castanets, and gongs. People used all these different instruments to praise God!

25 So David and the elders of Israel, and the commanders of the thousands, went to bring up the ark of the covenant of the LORD from the house of Ṓbed-ḗdom with rejoicing. ²⁶And because God helped the Lĕ́vītes who were carrying the ark of the covenant of the LORD, they sacrificed seven bulls and seven rams. ²⁷David was clothed with a robe of fine linen, as also were all the Lĕ́vītes who were carrying the ark, and the singers, and Chen·a·nī́ah the leader of the music of the singers; and David wore a linen ephod. ²⁸So all Israel brought up the ark of the covenant of the LORD with shouting, to the sound of the horn, trumpets, and cymbals, and made loud music on harps and lyres.

29 As the ark of the covenant of the LORD came to the city of David, Mī́chal daughter of Saul looked out of the window, and saw King David leaping and dancing; and she despised him in her heart.

The Ark Placed in the Tent

16 They brought in the ark of God, and set it inside the tent that David had pitched for it; and they offered burnt offerings and offerings of

q Meaning of Heb uncertain

well-being before God. ²When David had finished offering the burnt offerings and the offerings of well-being, he blessed the people in the name of the LORD; ³and he distributed to every person in Israel—man and woman alike—to each a loaf of bread, a portion of meat,ʳ and a cake of raisins.

4 He appointed certain of the Lē′vītes as ministers before the ark of the LORD, to invoke, to thank, and to praise the LORD, the God of Israel. ⁵A′saph was the chief, and second to him Zech·a·rī′ah, Je·ī′el, She·mir′a·moth, Je·hī′el, Mat·ti·thī′ah, E·lī′ab, Be·nā′i·ah, Ō′bed-ē′dom, and Je·ī′el, with harps and lyres; A′saph was to sound the cymbals, ⁶and the priests Be·nā′i·ah and Ja·hā′zi·el were to blow trumpets regularly, before the ark of the covenant of God.

David's Psalm of Thanksgiving

7 Then on that day David first appointed the singing of praises to the LORD by A′saph and his kindred.

⁸ O give thanks to the LORD, call on his name,
    make known his deeds among the peoples.
⁹ Sing to him, sing praises to him,
    tell of all his wonderful works.
¹⁰ Glory in his holy name;
    let the hearts of those who seek the LORD rejoice.
¹¹ Seek the LORD and his strength,
    seek his presence continually.
¹² Remember the wonderful works he has done,
    his miracles, and the judgments he uttered,
¹³ O offspring of his servant Israel,ˢ
    children of Jacob, his chosen ones.
¹⁴ He is the LORD our God;
    his judgments are in all the earth.
¹⁵ Remember his covenant forever,
    the word that he commanded, for a thousand generations,
¹⁶ the covenant that he made with Abraham,

    his sworn promise to Isaac,
¹⁷ which he confirmed to Jacob as a statute,
    to Israel as an everlasting covenant,
¹⁸ saying, "To you I will give the land of Cā′naan
    as your portion for an inheritance."

¹⁹ When they were few in number,
    of little account, and strangers in the land,ᵗ
²⁰ wandering from nation to nation,
    from one kingdom to another people,
²¹ he allowed no one to oppress them;
    he rebuked kings on their account,
²² saying, "Do not touch my anointed ones;
    do my prophets no harm."
²³ Sing to the LORD, all the earth.
    Tell of his salvation from day to day.
²⁴ Declare his glory among the nations,
    his marvelous works among all the peoples.
²⁵ For great is the LORD, and greatly to be praised;
    he is to be revered above all gods.
²⁶ For all the gods of the peoples are idols,
    but the LORD made the heavens.
²⁷ Honor and majesty are before him;
    strength and joy are in his place.

²⁸ Ascribe to the LORD, O families of the peoples,
    ascribe to the LORD glory and strength.
²⁹ Ascribe to the LORD the glory due his name;
    bring an offering, and come before him.
    Worship the LORD in holy splendor;
³⁰   tremble before him, all the earth.
    The world is firmly established; it shall never be moved.
³¹ Let the heavens be glad, and let the earth rejoice,

ʳ Compare Gk Syr Vg: Meaning of Heb uncertain
ˢ Another reading is *Abraham* (compare Ps 105.6)
ᵗ Heb *in it*

and let them say among the
nations, "The LORD is king!"
32 Let the sea roar, and all that fills it;
let the field exult, and everything
in it.
33 Then shall the trees of the forest sing
for joy
before the LORD, for he comes to
judge the earth.
34 O give thanks to the LORD, for he is
good;
for his steadfast love endures
forever.
35Say also:
"Save us, O God of our salvation,
and gather and rescue us from
among the nations,
that we may give thanks to your
holy name,
and glory in your praise.
36 Blessed be the LORD, the God of
Israel,
from everlasting to everlasting."
Then all the people said "Amen!" and
praised the LORD.

Regular Worship Maintained

37 David left Ā′saph and his kinsfolk
there before the ark of the covenant of
the LORD to minister regularly before the
ark as each day required, 38and also
Ō′bed-ē′dom and his[u] sixty-eight kinsfolk; while Ō′bed-ē′dom son of Je·dū′-
thun and Hō′sah were to be gatekeepers. 39And he left the priest Zā′dok
and his kindred the priests before the
tabernacle of the LORD in the high place
that was at Gib′ē·on, 40to offer burnt
offerings to the LORD on the altar of
burnt offering regularly, morning and
evening, according to all that is written
in the law of the LORD that he commanded Israel. 41With them were Hē′-
man and Je·dū′thun, and the rest of
those chosen and expressly named to
render thanks to the LORD, for his steadfast love endures forever. 42Hē′man and
Je·dū′thun had with them trumpets and
cymbals for the music, and instruments

for sacred song. The sons of Je·dū′thun
were appointed to the gate.
43 Then all the people departed to
their homes, and David went home to
bless his household.

King David knew that God had richly blessed the people of Israel, so he decided to build a Temple to hold the Ark of the Covenant. But God had other plans and sent him a message through the prophet Nathan that the Ark should stay in the tent.

God's Covenant with David

17 Now when David settled in
his house, David said to the
prophet Nathan, "I am living in a house
of cedar, but the ark of the covenant of
the LORD is under a tent." 2Nathan said
to David, "Do all that you have in mind,
for God is with you."
3 But that same night the word of the
LORD came to Nathan, saying: 4Go and
tell my servant David: Thus says the
LORD: You shall not build me a house to
live in. 5For I have not lived in a house
since the day I brought out Israel to this
very day, but I have lived in a tent and a
tabernacle.[v] 6Wherever I have moved
about among all Israel, did I ever speak
a word with any of the judges of Israel,
whom I commanded to shepherd my
people, saying, Why have you not built
me a house of cedar? 7Now therefore
thus you shall say to my servant David:
Thus says the LORD of hosts: I took you
from the pasture, from following the
sheep, to be ruler over my people Israel;
8and I have been with you wherever you
went, and have cut off all your enemies
before you; and I will make for you a
name, like the name of the great ones of
the earth. 9I will appoint a place for my

u Gk Syr Vg: Heb *their*   v Gk 2 Sam 7.6: Heb
but I have been from tent to tent and from tabernacle

people Israel, and will plant them, so that they may live in their own place, and be disturbed no more; and evildoers shall wear them down no more, as they did formerly, [10]from the time that I appointed judges over my people Israel; and I will subdue all your enemies.

Moreover I declare to you that the LORD will build you a house. [11]When your days are fulfilled to go to be with your ancestors, I will raise up your offspring after you, one of your own sons, and I will establish his kingdom. [12]He shall build a house for me, and I will establish his throne forever. [13]I will be a father to him, and he shall be a son to me. I will not take my steadfast love from him, as I took it from him who was before you, [14]but I will confirm him in my house and in my kingdom forever, and his throne shall be established forever. [15]In accordance with all these words and all this vision, Nathan spoke to David.

David's Prayer

16 Then King David went in and sat before the LORD, and said, "Who am I, O LORD God, and what is my house, that you have brought me thus far? [17]And even this was a small thing in your sight, O God; you have also spoken of your servant's house for a great while to come. You regard me as someone of high rank,[w] O LORD God! [18]And what more can David say to you for honoring your servant? You know your servant. [19]For your servant's sake, O LORD, and according to your own heart, you have done all these great deeds, making known all these great things. [20]There is no one like you, O LORD, and there is no God besides you, according to all that we have heard with our ears. [21]Who is like your people Israel, one nation on the earth whom God went to redeem to be his people, making for yourself a name for great and terrible things, in driving out nations before your people whom you redeemed from Egypt? [22]And you made your peo-

ple Israel to be your people forever; and you, O LORD, became their God.

23 "And now, O LORD, as for the word that you have spoken concerning your servant and concerning his house, let it be established forever, and do as you have promised. [24]Thus your name will be established and magnified forever in the saying, 'The LORD of hosts, the God of Israel, is Israel's God'; and the house of your servant David will be established in your presence. [25]For you, my God, have revealed to your servant that you will build a house for him; therefore your servant has found it possible to pray before you. [26]And now, O LORD, you are God, and you have promised this good thing to your servant; [27]therefore may it please you to bless the house of your servant, that it may continue forever before you. For you, O LORD, have blessed and are blessed[x] forever."

David's Kingdom Established and Extended

18 Some time afterward, David attacked the Phi·lis′tines and subdued them; he took Gath and its villages from the Phi·lis′tines.

2 He defeated Mō′ab, and the Mō′ab·ītes became subject to David and brought tribute.

3 David also struck down King Had·a·dē′zer of Zō′bah, toward Hā′math,[y] as he went to set up a monument at the river Euphrates. [4]David took from him one thousand chariots, seven thousand cavalry, and twenty thousand foot soldiers. David hamstrung all the chariot horses, but left one hundred of them. [5]When the Ar·a·mē′ans of Damascus came to help King Had·a·dē′zer of Zō′bah, David killed twenty-two thousand Ar·a·mē′ans. [6]Then David put garrisons[z] in Ar′am of Damascus; and the Ar·a·mē′ans became subject to David, and brought tribute. The LORD gave victory

---

[w] Meaning of Heb uncertain   [x] Or and it is blessed   [y] Meaning of Heb uncertain   [z] Gk Vg 2 Sam 8.6 Compare Syr: Heb lacks garrisons

to David wherever he went. ⁷David took the gold shields that were carried by the servants of Had·a·dē´zer, and brought them to Jerusalem. ⁸From Tib´hath and from Cūn, cities of Had·a·dē´zer, David took a vast quantity of bronze; with it Solomon made the bronze sea and the pillars and the vessels of bronze.

9 When King Tō´u of Hā´math heard that David had defeated the whole army of King Had·a·dē´zer of Zō´bah, ¹⁰he sent his son Ha·dor´am to King David, to greet him and to congratulate him, because he had fought against Had·a·dē´zer and defeated him. Now Had·a·dē´zer had often been at war with Tō´u. He sent all sorts of articles of gold, of silver, and of bronze; ¹¹these also King David dedicated to the LORD, together with the silver and gold that he had carried off from all the nations, from Ē´dom, Mō´ab, the Am´-mon·ītes, the Phi·lis´tines, and Am´a·lek.

12 A·bi´shaī son of Ze·rū´i·ah killed eighteen thousand Ē´dom·ītes in the Valley of Salt. ¹³He put garrisons in Ē´dom; and all the Ē´dom·ītes became subject to David. And the LORD gave victory to David wherever he went.

David's Administration

14 So David reigned over all Israel; and he administered justice and equity to all his people. ¹⁵Jō´ab son of Ze·rū´i·ah was over the army; Je·hosh´a·phat son of A·hī´lud was recorder; ¹⁶Zā´dok son of A·hī´tub and A·him´e·lech son of A·bī´a·thar were priests; Shav´sha was secretary; ¹⁷Be·nā´i·ah son of Je·hoi´a·da was over the Cher´e·thītes and the Pel´eth·ītes; and David's sons were the chief officials in the service of the king.

Defeat of the Ammonites and Arameans

19 Some time afterward, King Nā´-hash of the Am´mon·ītes died, and his son succeeded him. ²David said, "I will deal loyally with Hā´nun son of Nā´hash, for his father dealt loyally with me." So David sent messengers to con-

sole him concerning his father. When David's servants came to Hā´nun in the land of the Am´mon·ītes, to console him, ³the officials of the Am´mon·ītes said to Hā´nun, "Do you think, because David has sent consolers to you, that he is honoring your father? Have not his servants come to you to search and to overthrow and to spy out the land?" ⁴So Hā´nun seized David's servants, shaved them, cut off their garments in the middle at their hips, and sent them away; ⁵and they departed. When David was told about the men, he sent messengers to them, for they felt greatly humiliated. The king said, "Remain at Jericho until your beards have grown, and then return."

6 When the Am´mon·ītes saw that they had made themselves odious to David, Hā´nun and the Am´mon·ītes sent a thousand talents of silver to hire chariots and cavalry from Mes·o·po·tā´-mia, from Ar´am-mā´a·cah and from Zō´-bah. ⁷They hired thirty-two thousand chariots and the king of Mā´a·cah with his army, who came and camped before Med´e·ba. And the Am´mon·ītes were mustered from their cities and came to battle. ⁸When David heard of it, he sent Jō´ab and all the army of the warriors. ⁹The Am´mon·ītes came out and drew up in battle array at the entrance of the city, and the kings who had come were by themselves in the open country.

10 When Jō´ab saw that the line of battle was set against him both in front and in the rear, he chose some of the picked men of Israel and arrayed them against the Ar·a·mē´ans; ¹¹the rest of his troops he put in the charge of his brother A·bi´shaī, and they were arrayed against the Am´mon·ītes. ¹²He said, "If the Ar·a·mē´ans are too strong for me, then you shall help me; but if the Am´mon·ītes are too strong for you, then I will help you. ¹³Be strong, and let us be courageous for our people and for the cities of our God; and may the LORD do what seems good to him." ¹⁴So Jō´ab and the troops who were with him advanced

toward the Ar·a·mē´ans for battle; and they fled before him. [15]When the Am´mon·ītes saw that the Ar·a·mē´ans fled, they likewise fled before A·bi´shaī, Jō´ab's brother, and entered the city. Then Jō´ab came to Jerusalem.

16 But when the Ar·a·mē´ans saw that they had been defeated by Israel, they sent messengers and brought out the Ar·a·mē´ans who were beyond the Euphrates, with Shō´phach the commander of the army of Had·a·dē´zer at their head. [17]When David was informed, he gathered all Israel together, crossed the Jordan, came to them, and drew up his forces against them. When David set the battle in array against the Ar·a·mē´ans, they fought with him. [18]The Ar·a·mē´ans fled before Israel; and David killed seven thousand Ar·a·mē´an charioteers and forty thousand foot soldiers, and also killed Shō´phach the commander of their army. [19]When the servants of Had·a·dē´zer saw that they had been defeated by Israel, they made peace with David, and became subject to him. So the Ar·a·mē´ans were not willing to help the Am´mon·ītes any more.

Siege and Capture of Rabbah

20 In the spring of the year, the time when kings go out to battle, Jō´ab led out the army, ravaged the country of the Am´mon·ītes, and came and besieged Rab´bah. But David remained at Jerusalem. Jō´ab attacked Rab´bah, and overthrew it. [2]David took the crown of Mil´com[a] from his head; he found that it weighed a talent of gold, and in it was a precious stone; and it was placed on David's head. He also brought out the booty of the city, a very great amount. [3]He brought out the people who were in it, and set them to work[b] with saws and iron picks and axes.[c] Thus David did to all the cities of the Am´mon·ītes. Then David and all the people returned to Jerusalem.

Exploits against the Philistines

4 After this, war broke out with the Phi·lis´tines at Gē´zer; then Sib´be·caī the Hū´sha·thīte killed Sip´paī, who was one of the descendants of the giants; and the Phi·lis´tines were subdued. [5]Again there was war with the Phi·lis´tines; and El·hā´nan son of Jā´ir killed Lah´mī the brother of Goliath the Git´tīte, the shaft of whose spear was like a weaver's beam. [6]Again there was war at Gath, where there was a man of great size, who had six fingers on each hand, and six toes on each foot, twenty-four in number; he also was descended from the giants. [7]When he taunted Israel, Jonathan son of Shim´ē·a, David's brother, killed him. [8]These were descended from the giants in Gath; they fell by the hand of David and his servants.

The Census and Plague

21 Satan stood up against Israel, and incited David to count the people of Israel. [2]So David said to Jō´ab and the commanders of the army, "Go, number Israel, from Bē´er-shē´ba to Dan, and bring me a report, so that I may know their number." [3]But Jō´ab said, "May the LORD increase the number of his people a hundredfold! Are they not, my lord the king, all of them my lord's servants? Why then should my lord require this? Why should he bring guilt on Israel?" [4]But the king's word prevailed against Jō´ab. So Jō´ab departed and went throughout all Israel, and came back to Jerusalem. [5]Jō´ab gave the total count of the people to David. In all Israel there were one million one hundred thousand men who drew the sword, and in Judah four hundred seventy thousand who drew the sword. [6]But he did not include Levi and Benjamin in the numbering, for the king's command was abhorrent to Jō´ab.

7 But God was displeased with this thing, and he struck Israel. [8]David said to God, "I have sinned greatly in that I have done this thing. But now, I pray

---

[a] Gk Vg See 1 Kings 11.5, 33: MT *of their king*
[b] Compare 2 Sam 12.31: Heb *and he sawed*
[c] Compare 2 Sam 12.31: Heb *saws*

you, take away the guilt of your servant; for I have done very foolishly." [9]The LORD spoke to Gad, David's seer, saying, [10]"Go and say to David, 'Thus says the LORD: Three things I offer you; choose one of them, so that I may do it to you.' " [11]So Gad came to David and said to him, "Thus says the LORD, 'Take your choice: [12]either three years of famine; or three months of devastation by your foes, while the sword of your enemies overtakes you; or three days of the sword of the LORD, pestilence on the land, and the angel of the LORD destroying throughout all the territory of Israel.' Now decide what answer I shall return to the one who sent me." [13]Then David said to Gad, "I am in great distress; let me fall into the hand of the LORD, for his mercy is very great; but let me not fall into human hands."

14 So the LORD sent a pestilence on Israel; and seventy thousand persons fell in Israel. [15]And God sent an angel to Jerusalem to destroy it; but when he was about to destroy it, the LORD took note and relented concerning the calamity; he said to the destroying angel, "Enough! Stay your hand." The angel of the LORD was then standing by the threshing floor of Or'nan the Jeb'u·site. [16]David looked up and saw the angel of the LORD standing between earth and heaven, and in his hand a drawn sword stretched out over Jerusalem. Then David and the elders, clothed in sackcloth, fell on their faces. [17]And David said to God, "Was it not I who gave the command to count the people? It is I who have sinned and done very wickedly. But these sheep, what have they done? Let your hand, I pray, O LORD my God, be against me and against my father's house; but do not let your people be plagued!"

David's Altar and Sacrifice

18 Then the angel of the LORD commanded Gad to tell David that he should go up and erect an altar to the LORD on the threshing floor of Or'nan the Jeb'u·site. [19]So David went up following Gad's instructions, which he had spoken in the name of the LORD. [20]Or'nan turned and saw the angel; and while his four sons who were with him hid themselves, Or'nan continued to thresh wheat. [21]As David came to Or'nan, Or'nan looked and saw David; he went out from the threshing floor, and did obeisance to David with his face to the ground. [22]David said to Or'nan, "Give me the site of the threshing floor that I may build on it an altar to the LORD—give it to me at its full price—so that the plague may be averted from the people." [23]Then Or'nan said to David, "Take it; and let my lord the king do what seems good to him; see, I present the oxen for burnt offerings, and the threshing sledges for the wood, and the wheat for a grain offering. I give it all." [24]But King David said to Or'nan, "No; I will buy them for the full price. I will not take for the LORD what is yours, nor offer burnt offerings that cost me nothing." [25]So David paid Or'nan six hundred shekels of gold by weight for the site. [26]David built there an altar to the LORD and presented burnt offerings and offerings of well-being. He called upon the LORD, and he answered him with fire from heaven on the altar of burnt offering. [27]Then the LORD commanded the angel, and he put his sword back into its sheath.

The Place Chosen for the Temple

28 At that time, when David saw that the LORD had answered him at the threshing floor of Or'nan the Jeb'u·site, he made his sacrifices there. [29]For the tabernacle of the LORD, which Moses had made in the wilderness, and the altar of burnt offering were at that time in the high place at Gib'e·on; [30]but David could not go before it to inquire of God, for he was afraid of the sword of the angel of the LORD. [1]Then David said,

22 "Here shall be the house of the LORD God and here the altar of burnt offering for Israel."

David Prepares to Build the Temple

2 David gave orders to gather together the aliens who were residing in the land of Israel, and he set stonecutters to prepare dressed stones for building the house of God. ³David also provided great stores of iron for nails for the doors of the gates and for clamps, as well as bronze in quantities beyond weighing, ⁴and cedar logs without number—for the Sī·dō′ni·ans and Tȳ′ri·ans brought great quantities of cedar to David. ⁵For David said, "My son Solomon is young and inexperienced, and the house that is to be built for the LORD must be exceedingly magnificent, famous and glorified throughout all lands; I will therefore make preparation for it." So David provided materials in great quantity before his death.

David's Charge to Solomon and the Leaders

6 Then he called for his son Solomon and charged him to build a house for the LORD, the God of Israel. ⁷David said to Solomon, "My son, I had planned to build a house to the name of the LORD my God. ⁸But the word of the LORD came to me, saying, 'You have shed much blood and have waged great wars; you shall not build a house to my name, because you have shed so much blood in my sight on the earth. ⁹See, a son shall be born to you; he shall be a man of peace. I will give him peace from all his enemies on every side; for his name shall be Solomon,[d] and I will give peace[e] and quiet to Israel in his days. ¹⁰He shall build a house for my name. He shall be a son to me, and I will be a father to him, and I will establish his royal throne in Israel forever.' ¹¹Now, my son, the LORD be with you, so that you may succeed in building the house of the LORD your God, as he has spoken concerning you. ¹²Only, may the LORD grant you discretion and understanding, so that when he gives you charge over Israel you may keep the law of the LORD your God. ¹³Then you will prosper if you are careful to observe the statutes and the ordinances that the LORD commanded Moses for Israel. Be strong and of good courage. Do not be afraid or dismayed. ¹⁴With great pains I have provided for the house of the LORD one hundred thousand talents of gold, one million talents of silver, and bronze and iron beyond weighing, for there is so much of it; timber and stone too I have provided. To these you must add more. ¹⁵You have an abundance of workers: stonecutters, masons, carpenters, and all kinds of artisans without number, skilled in working ¹⁶gold, silver, bronze, and iron. Now begin the work, and the LORD be with you."

17 David also commanded all the leaders of Israel to help his son Solomon, saying, ¹⁸"Is not the LORD your God with you? Has he not given you peace on every side? For he has delivered the inhabitants of the land into my hand; and the land is subdued before the LORD and his people. ¹⁹Now set your mind and heart to seek the LORD your God. Go and build the sanctuary of the LORD God so that the ark of the covenant of the LORD and the holy vessels of God may be brought into a house built for the name of the LORD."

Families of the Levites and Their Functions

23 When David was old and full of days, he made his son Solomon king over Israel.

2 David assembled all the leaders of Israel and the priests and the Lē′vītes.

> **"Now set your mind and heart to seek the Lord your God."**
> **1 Chronicles 22:19a**

---

[d] Heb *Shelomoh*   [e] Heb *shalom*

³The Lē´vītes, thirty years old and upward, were counted, and the total was thirty-eight thousand. ⁴"Twenty-four thousand of these," David said, "shall have charge of the work in the house of the LORD, six thousand shall be officers and judges, ⁵four thousand gatekeepers, and four thousand shall offer praises to the LORD with the instruments that I have made for praise." ⁶And David organized them in divisions corresponding to the sons of Levi: Ger´shon,ᶠ Kō´hath, and Me·rar´ī.

7 The sons of Ger´shonᵍ were Lā´dan and Shim´ē·ī. ⁸The sons of Lā´dan: Je·hī´el the chief, Zē´tham, and Jō´el, three. ⁹The sons of Shim´ē·ī: She·lō´moth, Hā´zi·el, and Har´an, three. These were the heads of families of Lā´dan. ¹⁰And the sons of Shim´ē·ī: Jā´hath, Zī´na, Jē´ush, and Bē·rī´ah. These four were the sons of Shim´ē·ī. ¹¹Jā´hath was the chief, and Zī´zah the second; but Jē´ush and Bē·rī´ah did not have many sons, so they were enrolled as a single family.

12 The sons of Kō´hath: Am´ram, Iz´har, Hē´bron, and Uz´zi·el, four. ¹³The sons of Am´ram: Aaron and Moses. Aaron was set apart to consecrate the most holy things, so that he and his sons forever should make offerings before the LORD, and minister to him and pronounce blessings in his name forever; ¹⁴but as for Moses the man of God, his sons were to be reckoned among the tribe of Levi. ¹⁵The sons of Moses: Ger´shom and El·i·ē´zer. ¹⁶The sons of Ger´shom: She·bū´el the chief. ¹⁷The sons of El·i·ē´zer: Rē·ha·bī´ah the chief; El·i·ē´zer had no other sons, but the sons of Rē·ha·bī´ah were very numerous. ¹⁸The sons of Iz´har: She·lō´mith the chief. ¹⁹The sons of Hē´bron: Je·rī´ah the chief, Am·a·rī´ah the second, Ja·hā´zi·el the third, and Jek·a·mē´am the fourth. ²⁰The sons of Uz´zi·el: Mī´cah the chief and Is·shī´ah the second.

21 The sons of Me·rar´ī: Mah´lī and Mū´shī. The sons of Mah´lī: El·e·ā´zar and Kish. ²²El·e·ā´zar died having no sons, but only daughters; their kindred, the sons of Kish, married them. ²³The sons of Mū´shī: Mah´lī, Ē´der, and Jer´e·moth, three.

24 These were the sons of Levi by their ancestral houses, the heads of families as they were enrolled according to the number of the names of the individuals from twenty years old and upward who were to do the work for the service of the house of the LORD. ²⁵For David said, "The LORD, the God of Israel, has given rest to his people; and he resides in Jerusalem forever. ²⁶And so the Lē´vītes no longer need to carry the tabernacle or any of the things for its service"— ²⁷for according to the last words of David these were the number of the Lē´vītes from twenty years old and upward— ²⁸"but their duty shall be to assist the descendants of Aaron for the service of the house of the LORD, having the care of the courts and the chambers, the cleansing of all that is holy, and any work for the service of the house of God; ²⁹to assist also with the rows of bread, the choice flour for the grain offering, the wafers of unleavened bread, the baked offering, the offering mixed with oil, and all measures of quantity or size. ³⁰And they shall stand every morning, thanking and praising the LORD, and likewise at evening, ³¹and whenever burnt offerings are offered to the LORD on sabbaths, new moons, and appointed festivals, according to the number required of them, regularly before the LORD. ³²Thus they shall keep charge of the tent of meeting and the sanctuary, and shall attend the descendants of Aaron, their kindred, for the service of the house of the LORD."

Divisions of the Priests

24 The divisions of the descendants of Aaron were these. The sons of Aaron: Nā´dab, A·bī´hū, El·e·ā´zar,

---

ᶠ Or *Gershom;* See 1 Chr 6.1, note, and 23.15
ᵍ Vg Compare Gk Syr: Heb *to the Gershonite*

and Ith·a´mar. ²But Na´dab and A·bi´hu died before their father, and had no sons; so El·e·a´zar and Ith´a·mar became the priests. ³Along with Za´dok of the sons of El·e·a´zar, and A·him´e·lech of the sons of Ith´a·mar, David organized them according to the appointed duties in their service. ⁴Since more chief men were found among the sons of El·e·a´zar than among the sons of Ith´a·mar, they organized them under sixteen heads of ancestral houses of the sons of El·e·a´zar, and eight of the sons of Ith´a·mar. ⁵They organized them by lot, all alike, for there were officers of the sanctuary and officers of God among both the sons of El·e·a´zar and the sons of Ith´a·mar. ⁶The scribe She·mai´ah son of Ne·than´el, a Le´vite, recorded them in the presence of the king, and the officers, and Za´dok the priest, and A·him´e·lech son of A·bi´a·thar, and the heads of ancestral houses of the priests and of the Le´vites; one ancestral house being chosen for El·e·a´zar and one chosen for Ith´a·mar.

7 The first lot fell to Je·hoi´a·rib, the second to Je·dai´ah, ⁸the third to Ha´rim, the fourth to Se·o´rim, ⁹the fifth to Mal·chi´-jah, the sixth to Mij´a·min, ¹⁰the seventh to Hak´koz, the eighth to A·bi´jah, ¹¹the ninth to Jesh´u·a, the tenth to Shec·a·ni´ah, ¹²the eleventh to E·li´a·shib, the twelfth to Ja´-kim, ¹³the thirteenth to Hup´pah, the fourteenth to Je·sheb´e·ab, ¹⁴the fifteenth to Bil´gah, the sixteenth to Im´mer, ¹⁵the seventeenth to He´zir, the eighteenth to Hap´piz·zez, ¹⁶the nineteenth to Peth·a·hi´-ah, the twentieth to Je·hez´kel, ¹⁷the twenty-first to Ja´chin, the twenty-second to Ga´mul, ¹⁸the twenty-third to De·lai´ah, the twenty-fourth to Ma·a·zi´ah. ¹⁹These had as their appointed duty in their service to enter the house of the Lord according to the procedure established for them by their ancestor Aaron, as the Lord God of Israel had commanded him.

Other Levites

20 And of the rest of the sons of Levi: of the sons of Am´ram, Shu´ba·el; of the sons of Shu´ba·el, Jeh·de´i·ah. ²¹Of Re·ha·bi´ah:

of the sons of Re·ha·bi´ah, Is·shi´ah the chief. ²²Of the Iz´har·ites, She·lo´moth; of the sons of She·lo´moth, Ja´hath. ²³The sons of He´bron:ʰ Je·ri´ah the chief,ⁱ Am·a·ri´ah the second, Ja·ha´zi·el the third, Jek·a·me´am the fourth. ²⁴The sons of Uz´zi·el, Mi´cah; of the sons of Mi´cah, Sha´-mir. ²⁵The brother of Mi´cah, Is·shi´ah; of the sons of Is·shi´ah, Zech·a·ri´ah. ²⁶The sons of Me·rar´i: Mah´li and Mu´shi. The sons of Ja·a·zi´ah: Be´no.ʲ ²⁷The sons of Me·rar´i: of Ja·a·zi´ah, Be´no,ʲ Sho´ham, Zac´cur, and Ib´ri. ²⁸Of Mah´li: El·e·a´zar, who had no sons. ²⁹Of Kish, the sons of Kish: Je·rah´me·el. ³⁰The sons of Mu´shi: Mah´li, E´der, and Jer´i·moth. These were the sons of the Le´vites according to their ancestral houses. ³¹These also cast lots corresponding to their kindred, the descendants of Aaron, in the presence of King David, Za´dok, A·him´e·lech, and the heads of ancestral houses of the priests and of the Le´vites, the chief as well as the youngest brother.

The Temple Musicians

25 David and the officers of the army also set apart for the service the sons of A´saph, and of He´man, and of Je·du´thun, who should prophesy with lyres, harps, and cymbals. The list of those who did the work and of their duties was: ²Of the sons of A´saph: Zac´cur, Joseph, Neth·a·ni´ah, and As·a·re´lah, sons of A´saph, under the direction of A´saph, who prophesied under the direction of the king. ³Of Je·du´thun, the sons of Je·du´thun: Ged·a·li´ah, Ze´ri, Je·shai´ah, Shim´e·i,ᵏ Hash·a·bi´ah, and Mat·ti·thi´ah, six, under the direction of their father Je·du´-thun, who prophesied with the lyre in thanksgiving and praise to the Lord. ⁴Of He´man, the sons of He´man: Buk·ki´ah, Mat·ta·ni´ah, Uz´zi·el, She·bu´el, and Jer´i·moth, Han·a·ni´ah, Ha·na´ni, E·li´-a·thah, Gid·dal´ti, and Ro·mam´ti-e´zer,

---

ʰ See 23.19: Heb lacks *Hebron*   ⁱ See 23.19: Heb lacks *the chief*   ʲ Or *his son*: Meaning of Heb uncertain   ᵏ One Ms: Gk: MT lacks *Shimei*

Josh·be·kash´ah, Mal·lō´thī, Hō´thir, Ma·hā´zi·oth. [5]All these were the sons of Hē´man the king's seer, according to the promise of God to exalt him; for God had given Hē´man fourteen sons and three daughters. [6]They were all under the direction of their father for the music in the house of the LORD with cymbals, harps, and lyres for the service of the house of God. Ā´saph, Je·dū´thun, and Hē´man were under the order of the king. [7]They and their kindred, who were trained in singing to the LORD, all of whom were skillful, numbered two hundred eighty-eight. [8]And they cast lots for their duties, small and great, teacher and pupil alike.

9 The first lot fell for Ā´saph to Joseph; the second to Ged·a·lī´ah, to him and his brothers and his sons, twelve; [10]the third to Zac´cur, his sons and his brothers, twelve; [11]the fourth to Iz´rī, his sons and his brothers, twelve; [12]the fifth to Neth·a·nī´ah, his sons and his brothers, twelve; [13]the sixth to Buk·kī´ah, his sons and his brothers, twelve; [14]the seventh to Jes·a·rē´lah,[l] his sons and his brothers, twelve; [15]the eighth to Je·shā´i·ah, his sons and his brothers, twelve; [16]the ninth to Mat·ta·nī´ah, his sons and his brothers, twelve; [17]the tenth to Shim´ē·ī, his sons and his brothers, twelve; [18]the eleventh to Az´a·rel, his sons and his brothers, twelve; [19]the twelfth to Hash·a·bī´ah, his sons and his brothers, twelve; [20]to the thirteenth, Shū´ba·el, his sons and his brothers, twelve; [21]to the fourteenth, Matti·thī´ah, his sons and his brothers, twelve; [22]to the fifteenth, to Jer´e·moth, his sons and his brothers, twelve; [23]to the sixteenth, to Han·a·nī´ah, his sons and his brothers, twelve; [24]to the seventeenth, to Josh·be··kash´ah, his sons and his brothers, twelve; [25]to the eighteenth, to Ha·nā´nī, his sons and his brothers, twelve; [26]to the nineteenth, to Mal·lō´thī, his sons and his brothers, twelve; [27]to the twentieth, to E·lī´a·thah, his sons and his

brothers, twelve; [28]to the twenty-first, to Hō´thir, his sons and his brothers, twelve; [29]to the twenty-second, to Gid·dal´tī, his sons and his brothers, twelve; [30]to the twenty-third, to Ma·hā´zi·oth, his sons and his brothers, twelve; [31]to the twenty-fourth, to Rō·mam´ti-ē´zer, his sons and his brothers, twelve.

The Gatekeepers

26 As for the divisions of the gatekeepers: of the Kō´ra·hītes, Me·shel·e·mī´ah son of Kō´re, of the sons of Ā´saph. [2]Me·shel·e·mī´ah had sons: Zech·a·rī´ah the firstborn, Je·dī´a·el the second, Zeb·a·dī´ah the third, Jath´ni·el the fourth, [3]Ē´lam the fifth, Jē·hō·hā´nan the sixth, El·i·ē·hō·ē´naī the seventh. [4]Ō´bed-ē´dom had sons: She·māi´ah the firstborn, Je·hō´za·bad the second, Jō´ah the third, Sā´char the fourth, Ne·than´el the fifth, [5]Am´mi·el the sixth, Is´sa·char the seventh, Pe·ul´le·thaī the eighth; for God blessed him. [6]Also to his son She·māi´ah sons were born who exercised authority in their ancestral houses, for they were men of great ability. [7]The sons of She·māi´ah: Oth´nī, Reph´a·el, Ō´bed, and El·zā´bad, whose brothers were able men, E·lī´hū and Sem·a·chī´ah. [8]All these, sons of Ō´bed-ē´dom with their sons and brothers, were able men qualified for the service; sixty-two of Ō´bed-ē´dom. [9]Me·shel·e·mī´ah had sons and brothers, able men, eighteen. [10]Hō´sah, of the sons of Me·rar´ī, had sons: Shim´rī the chief (for though he was not the firstborn, his father made him chief), [11]Hil·kī´ah the second, Teb·a·lī´ah the third, Zech·a·rī´ah the fourth: all the sons and brothers of Hō´sah totaled thirteen.

12 These divisions of the gatekeepers, corresponding to their leaders, had duties, just as their kindred did, ministering in the house of the LORD; [13]and they cast lots by ancestral houses, small and great alike, for their gates. [14]The lot for the east fell to Shel·e·mī´ah. They

[l] Or *Asarelah*; see 25.2

Many places in the Bible, we read that the people cast lots to make choices. Casting lots was similar to throwing dice today. Instead of dice, the people used small stones or animal bones. They would throw these stones onto the ground. How they landed would help the people figure out the will of God, determine which priest would serve at a certain time, and divide land and property. In 1 Chronicles 26:12–16, casting lots helped the people decide which Levites would serve at which gate (or entrance) to the Tabernacle.

cast lots also for his son Zech·a·rī´ah, a prudent counselor, and his lot came out for the north. [15] Ō´bed-ē´dom's came out for the south, and to his sons was allotted the storehouse. [16]For Shup´pim and Hō´sah it came out for the west, at the gate of Shal´le·cheth on the ascending road. Guard corresponded to guard. [17]On the east there were six Lē´vītes each day,[m] on the north four each day, on the south four each day, as well as two and two at the storehouse; [18]and for the colonnade[n] on the west there were four at the road and two at the colonnade.[n] [19]These were the divisions of the gatekeepers among the Kō´ra·hītes and the sons of Me·rar´ī.

The Treasurers, Officers, and Judges

[20] And of the Lē´vītes, A·hī´jah had charge of the treasuries of the house of God and the treasuries of the dedicated gifts. [21]The sons of Lā´dan, the sons of the Ger´shon·ītes belonging to Lā´dan, the heads of families belonging to Lā´dan the Ger´shon·īte: Je·hī´e·lī.[o]

[22] The sons of Je·hī´e·lī, Zē´tham and his brother Jō´el, were in charge of the treasuries of the house of the LORD. [23]Of

the Am´ram·ītes, the Iz´har·ītes, the Hē´bron·ītes, and the Uz´zi·el·ītes: [24]She·bū´el son of Ger´shom, son of Moses, was chief officer in charge of the treasuries. [25]His brothers: from El·i·ē´zer were his son Rē·ha·bī´ah, his son Je·shā´i·ah, his son Jō´ram, his son Zich´rī, and his son She·lō´moth. [26]This She·lō´moth and his brothers were in charge of all the treasuries of the dedicated gifts that King David, and the heads of families, and the officers of the thousands and the hundreds, and the commanders of the army, had dedicated. [27]From booty won in battles they dedicated gifts for the maintenance of the house of the LORD. [28]Also all that Samuel the seer, and Saul son of Kish, and Abner son of Ner, and Jō´ab son of Ze·rū´i·ah had dedicated—all dedicated gifts were in the care of She·lō´moth[p] and his brothers.

[29] Of the Iz´har·ītes, Chen·a·nī´ah and his sons were appointed to outside duties for Israel, as officers and judges. [30]Of the Hē´bron·ītes, Hash·a·bī´ah and his brothers, one thousand seven hundred men of ability, had the oversight of Israel west of the Jordan for all the work of the LORD and for the service of the king. [31]Of the Hē´bron·ītes, Je·rī´jah was chief of the Hē´bron·ītes. (In the fortieth year of David's reign search was made, of whatever genealogy or family, and men of great ability among them were found at Jā´zer in Gil´e·ad.) [32]King David appointed him and his brothers, two thousand seven hundred men of ability, heads of families, to have the oversight of the Reū´ben·ītes, the Gad´ītes, and the half-tribe of the Ma·nas´sītes for everything pertaining to God and for the affairs of the king.

The Military Divisions

27 [1] This is the list of the people of Israel, the heads of families, the

[m] Gk: Heb lacks *each day*　　[n] Heb *parbar*: meaning uncertain　　[o] The Hebrew text of verse 21 is confused　　[p] Gk Compare 26.28: Heb *Shelomith*

commanders of the thousands and the hundreds, and their officers who served the king in all matters concerning the divisions that came and went, month after month throughout the year, each division numbering twenty-four thousand:

2 Ja·sho´bē·am son of Zab´di·el was in charge of the first division in the first month; in his division were twenty-four thousand. ³He was a descendant of Per´ez, and was chief of all the commanders of the army for the first month. ⁴Do´dai the A·ho´hite was in charge of the division of the second month; Mik´loth was the chief officer of his division. In his division were twenty-four thousand. ⁵The third commander, for the third month, was Be·na´i·ah son of the priest Je·hoi´a·da, as chief; in his division were twenty-four thousand. ⁶This is the Be·na´i·ah who was a mighty man of the Thirty and in command of the Thirty; his son Am·miz´a·bad was in charge of his division.�q ⁷As´a·hel brother of Jo´ab was fourth, for the fourth month, and his son Zeb·a·di´ah after him; in his division were twenty-four thousand. ⁸The fifth commander, for the fifth month, was Sham´huth, the Iz´ra·hīte; in his division were twenty-four thousand. ⁹Sixth, for the sixth month, was Ira son of Ik´kesh the Te·ko´ite; in his division were twenty-four thousand. ¹⁰Seventh, for the seventh month, was He´lez the Pel´o·nīte, of the E´phra·im·ītes; in his division were twenty-four thousand. ¹¹Eighth, for the eighth month, was Sib´be·cai the Hu´sha·thite, of the Ze´ra·hītes; in his division were twenty-four thousand. ¹²Ninth, for the ninth month, was A´bi·e´zer of An´a·thoth, a Ben´ja·min·ite; in his division were twenty-four thousand. ¹³Tenth, for the tenth month, was Ma´ha·rai of Ne·toph´ah, of the Ze´ra·hītes; in his division were twenty-four thousand. ¹⁴Eleventh, for the eleventh month, was Be·na´i·ah of Pir´a·thon, of the E´phra·im·ītes; in his division were twenty-four thousand. ¹⁵Twelfth, for the twelfth

month, was Hel´dai the Ne·toph´a·thīte, of Oth´ni·el; in his division were twenty-four thousand.

Leaders of Tribes

16 Over the tribes of Israel, for the Reu´ben·ītes, El·i·e´zer son of Zich´rī was chief officer; for the Sim´e·on·ītes, Sheph·a·tī´ah son of Ma´a·cah; ¹⁷for Levi, Hash·a·bī´ah son of Ke·mu´el; for Aaron, Za´dok; ¹⁸for Judah, E·lī´hu, one of David's brothers; for Is´sa·char, Om´rī son of Michael; ¹⁹for Zeb´u·lun, Ish·ma´i·ah son of O´ba·dī´ah; for Naph´ta·lī, Jer´i·moth son of Az´ri·el; ²⁰for the E´phra·im·ītes, Ho·she´a son of Az·a·zī´ah; for the half-tribe of Ma·nas´seh, Jo´el son of Pe·dai´ah; ²¹for the half-tribe of Ma·nas´seh in Gil´e·ad, Id´do son of Zech·a·rī´ah; for Benjamin, Ja·a·sī´el son of Abner; ²²for Dan, Az´a·rel son of Je·ro´ham. These were the leaders of the tribes of Israel. ²³David did not count those below twenty years of age, for the LORD had promised to make Israel as numerous as the stars of heaven. ²⁴Jo´ab son of Ze·ru´i·ah began to count them, but did not finish; yet wrath came upon Israel for this, and the number was not entered into the account of the Annals of King David.

Other Civic Officials

25 Over the king's treasuries was Az´ma·veth son of Ad´i·el. Over the treasuries in the country, in the cities, in the villages and in the towers, was Jonathan son of Uz·zī´ah. ²⁶Over those who did the work of the field, tilling the soil, was Ez´rī son of Che´lub. ²⁷Over the vineyards was Shim´e·i the Ra´ma·thīte. Over the produce of the vineyards for the wine cellars was Zab´dī the Shiph´mīte. ²⁸Over the olive and sycamore trees in the She·phe´lah was Ba´al-ha´nan the Ge·de´rīte. Over the stores of oil was Jo´ash. ²⁹Over the herds that pastured in Sharon was Shit´rai the Shar´on·īte. Over the herds in the valleys was Sha´phat son of Ad·la´i. ³⁰Over the camels was O´bil

---

�q Gk Vg: Heb *Ammizabad was his division*

the Ish´ma·el·īte. Over the donkeys was Jeh·dē´i·ah the Me·ron´o·thīte. Over the flocks was Jā´ziz the Hag´rīte. ³¹All these were stewards of King David's property.

32 Jonathan, David's uncle, was a counselor, being a man of understanding and a scribe; Je·hī´el son of Hach´mo·nī attended the king's sons. ³³A·hith´o·phel was the king's counselor, and Hū´shaī the Ar´chīte was the king's friend. ³⁴After A·hith´o·phel came Je·hoi´a·da son of Be·nā´i·ah, and A·bī´a·thar. Jō´ab was commander of the king's army.

Solomon Instructed to Build the Temple

28 David assembled at Jerusalem all the officials of Israel, the officials of the tribes, the officers of the divisions that served the king, the commanders of the thousands, the commanders of the hundreds, the stewards of all the property and cattle of the king and his sons, together with the palace officials, the mighty warriors, and all the warriors. ²Then King David rose to his feet and said: "Hear me, my brothers and my people. I had planned to build a house of rest for the ark of the covenant of the LORD, for the footstool of our God; and I made preparations for building. ³But God said to me, 'You shall not build a house for my name, for you are a warrior and have shed blood.' ⁴Yet the LORD God of Israel chose me from all my ancestral house to be king over Israel forever; for he chose Judah as leader, and in the house of Judah my father's house, and among my father's sons he took delight in making me king over all Israel. ⁵And of all my sons, for the LORD has given me many, he has chosen my son Solomon to sit upon the throne of the kingdom of the LORD over Israel. ⁶He said to me, 'It is your son Solomon who shall build my house and my courts, for I have chosen him to be a son to me, and I will be a father to him. ⁷I will establish his kingdom forever if he continues resolute in keeping my commandments and my ordinances, as he is today.' ⁸Now therefore in the sight of all Israel, the assembly of the LORD, and in the hearing of our God, observe and search out all the commandments of the LORD your God; that you may possess this good land, and leave it for an inheritance to your children after you forever.

9 "And you, my son Solomon, know the God of your father, and serve him with single mind and willing heart; for the LORD searches every mind, and understands every plan and thought. If you seek him, he will be found by you; but if you forsake him, he will abandon you forever. ¹⁰Take heed now, for the LORD has chosen you to build a house as the sanctuary; be strong, and act."

11 Then David gave his son Solomon the plan of the vestibule of the temple, and of its houses, its treasuries, its upper rooms, and its inner chambers, and of the room for the mercy seat;ʳ ¹²and the plan of all that he had in mind: for the courts of the house of the LORD, all the surrounding chambers, the treasuries of the house of God, and the treasuries for dedicated gifts; ¹³for the divisions of the priests and of the Lē´vītes, and all the work of the service in the house of the LORD; for all the vessels for the service in the house of the LORD, ¹⁴the weight of gold for all golden vessels for each service, the weight of silver vessels for each service, ¹⁵the weight of the golden lampstands and their lamps, the weight of gold for each lampstand and its lamps, the weight of silver for a lampstand and its lamps, according to the use of each in the service, ¹⁶the weight of gold for each table for the rows of bread, the silver for the silver tables, ¹⁷and pure gold for the forks, the basins, and the cups; for the golden bowls and the weight of each; for the silver bowls and the weight of each; ¹⁸for the altar of incense made of refined gold, and its weight; also his plan for the golden chariot of the cherubim that spread their

ʳ Or *the cover*

wings and covered the ark of the covenant of the LORD.

19 "All this, in writing at the LORD's direction, he made clear to me—the plan of all the works."

20 David said further to his son Solomon, "Be strong and of good courage, and act. Do not be afraid or dismayed; for the LORD God, my God, is with you. He will not fail you or forsake you, until all the work for the service of the house of the LORD is finished. ²¹Here are the divisions of the priests and the Lēʹvītes for all the service of the house of God; and with you in all the work will be every volunteer who has skill for any kind of service; also the officers and all the people will be wholly at your command."

Offerings for Building the Temple

29 King David said to the whole assembly, "My son Solomon, whom alone God has chosen, is young and inexperienced, and the work is great; for the temple⁵ will not be for mortals but for the LORD God. ²So I have provided for the house of my God, so far as I was able, the gold for the things of gold, the silver for the things of silver, and the bronze for the things of bronze, the iron for the things of iron, and wood for the things of wood, besides great quantities of onyx and stones for setting, antimony, colored stones, all sorts of precious stones, and marble in abundance. ³Moreover, in addition to all that I have provided for the holy house, I have a treasure of my own of gold and silver, and because of my devotion to the house of my God I give it to the house of my God: ⁴three thousand talents of gold, of the gold of Ōʹphir, and seven thousand talents of refined silver, for overlaying the walls of the house, ⁵and for all the work to be done by artisans, gold for the things of gold and silver for the things of silver. Who then will offer willingly, consecrating themselves today to the LORD?"

6 Then the leaders of ancestral houses made their freewill offerings, as did also the leaders of the tribes, the commanders of the thousands and of the hundreds, and the officers over the king's work. ⁷They gave for the service of the house of God five thousand talents and ten thousand darics of gold, ten thousand talents of silver, eighteen thousand talents of bronze, and one hundred thousand talents of iron. ⁸Whoever had precious stones gave them to the treasury of the house of the LORD, into the care of Je·hīʹel the Gerʹshon·īte. ⁹Then the people rejoiced because these had given willingly, for with single mind they had offered freely to the LORD; King David also rejoiced greatly.

"Blessed are you, O LORD, the God of our ancestor Israel, forever and ever. Yours, O LORD, are the greatness, the power, the glory, the victory, and the majesty; for all that is in the heavens and on the earth is yours; yours is the kingdom, O LORD, and you are exalted as head above all. Riches and honor come from you, and you rule over all. In your hand are power and might; and it is in your hand to make great and to give strength to all. And now, our God, we give thanks to you and praise your glorious name."   1 Chronicles 29:10–13

David's Praise to God

10 Then David blessed the LORD in the presence of all the assembly; David said: "Blessed are you, O LORD, the God of our ancestor Israel, forever and ever. ¹¹Yours, O LORD, are the greatness, the power, the glory, the victory, and the majesty; for all that is in the heavens and on the earth is yours; yours is the kingdom, O LORD, and you are exalted as head above all. ¹²Riches and honor come from you, and you rule over all. In your hand

⁵ Heb *fortress*

are power and might; and it is in your hand to make great and to give strength to all. ¹³And now, our God, we give thanks to you and praise your glorious name.

14 "But who am I, and what is my people, that we should be able to make this freewill offering? For all things come from you, and of your own have we given you. ¹⁵For we are aliens and transients before you, as were all our ancestors; our days on the earth are like a shadow, and there is no hope. ¹⁶O LORD our God, all this abundance that we have provided for building you a house for your holy name comes from your hand and is all your own. ¹⁷I know, my God, that you search the heart, and take pleasure in uprightness; in the uprightness of my heart I have freely offered all these things, and now I have seen your people, who are present here, offering freely and joyously to you. ¹⁸O LORD, the God of Abraham, Isaac, and Israel, our ancestors, keep forever such purposes and thoughts in the hearts of your people, and direct their hearts toward you. ¹⁹Grant to my son Solomon that with single mind he may keep your commandments, your decrees, and your statutes, performing all of them, and that he may build the temple*t* for which I have made provision."

20 Then David said to the whole assembly, "Bless the LORD your God." And all the assembly blessed the LORD, the God of their ancestors, and bowed their heads and prostrated themselves before the LORD and the king. ²¹On the next day they offered sacrifices and burnt offerings to the LORD, a thousand bulls, a thousand rams, and a thousand lambs, with their libations, and sacrifices in abundance for all Israel; ²²and they ate and drank before the LORD on that day with great joy.

Solomon Anointed King

They made David's son Solomon king a second time; they anointed him as the LORD's prince, and Zā´dok as priest. ²³Then Solomon sat on the throne of the LORD, succeeding his father David as king; he prospered, and all Israel obeyed him. ²⁴All the leaders and the mighty warriors, and also all the sons of King David, pledged their allegiance to King Solomon. ²⁵The LORD highly exalted Solomon in the sight of all Israel, and bestowed upon him such royal majesty as had not been on any king before him in Israel.

Summary of David's Reign

26 Thus David son of Jesse reigned over all Israel. ²⁷The period that he reigned over Israel was forty years; he reigned seven years in Hē´bron, and thirty-three years in Jerusalem. ²⁸He died in a good old age, full of days, riches, and honor; and his son Solomon succeeded him. ²⁹Now the acts of King David, from first to last, are written in the records of the seer Samuel, and in the records of the prophet Nathan, and in the records of the seer Gad, ³⁰with accounts of all his rule and his might and of the events that befell him and Israel and all the kingdoms of the earth.

t Heb *fortress*

2 Chronicles

First Chronicles closes with an account of the end of King David's reign. Second Chronicles begins with the reign of his son Solomon. This book tells about the building and dedication of the Temple and about other events of Solomon's reign. Second Chronicles 10 begins the story of how the kingdom divided after King Solomon's death. Second Chronicles was written by the same writer and at the same time as First Chronicles—in the fourth century BC.

The Chronicler, or writer, was so interested in the southern kingdom of Judah and the city of Jerusalem (where the Temple and its priests were located)

that he told very little about the northern kingdom of Israel. Like First Chronicles, Second Chronicles says it is important for God's people to be faithful to God. When God's people were faithful to the worship of God at the Temple, they were blessed. When they became careless and did not follow God, they were punished.

Second Chronicles closes by telling how the Babylonians (also called Chaldeans) finally conquered Judah and took many of its people to the land of Babylon. These people stayed there until Cyrus of Persia conquered Babylonia and let them return to their homeland about 538 BC.

2 Chronicles 1:1

Solomon Requests Wisdom

1 Solomon son of David established himself in his kingdom; the LORD his God was with him and made him exceedingly great.

2 Solomon summoned all Israel, the commanders of the thousands and of the hundreds, the judges, and all the leaders of all Israel, the heads of families. ³Then Solomon, and the whole assembly with him, went to the high place that was at Gib·e·on; for God's tent of meeting, which Moses the servant of the LORD had made in the wilderness, was there. ⁴(But David had brought the ark of God up from Kir´i·ath-je´a·rim to the place that David had prepared for it; for he had pitched a tent for it in Jerusalem.) ⁵Moreover the bronze altar that Bez´a·lel son of U´ri, son of Hur, had made, was there in front of the tabernacle of the LORD. And Solomon and the assembly inquired at it. ⁶Solomon went up there to the bronze altar before the LORD, which was at the tent of meeting, and offered a thousand burnt offerings on it.

7 That night God appeared to Solomon, and said to him, "Ask what I should give you." ⁸Solomon said to God, "You have shown great and steadfast love to my father David, and have made me succeed him as king. ⁹O LORD God, let your promise to my father David now be fulfilled, for you have made me king over a people as numerous as the dust of the earth. ¹⁰Give me now wisdom and knowledge to go out and come in before this people, for who can rule this great people of yours?" ¹¹God answered Solomon, "Because this was in your heart, and you have not asked for possessions, wealth, honor, or the life of those who hate you, and have not even asked for long life, but have asked for wisdom and knowledge for yourself that you may rule my people over whom I have made you king, ¹²wisdom and knowledge are granted to you. I will also give you riches, possessions, and honor,

> "O LORD God, let your promise to my father David now be fulfilled, for you have made me king over a people as numerous as the dust of the earth. Give me now wisdom and knowledge to go out and come in before this people, for who can rule this great people of yours?" 2 Chronicles 1:9–10

such as none of the kings had who were before you, and none after you shall have the like." ¹³So Solomon came from*ᵃ* the high place at Gib´e·on, from the tent of meeting, to Jerusalem. And he reigned over Israel.

Solomon's Military and Commercial Activity

14 Solomon gathered together chariots and horses; he had fourteen hundred chariots and twelve thousand horses, which he stationed in the chariot cities and with the king in Jerusalem. ¹⁵The king made silver and gold as common in Jerusalem as stone, and he made cedar as plentiful as the sycamore of the She·phe´lah. ¹⁶Solomon's horses were imported from Egypt and Ku´e; the king's traders received them from Ku´e at the prevailing price. ¹⁷They imported from Egypt, and then exported, a chariot for six hundred shekels of silver, and a horse for one hundred fifty; so through them these were exported to all the kings of the Hit´tites and the kings of Ar´am.

God came to Solomon and asked what God could give him. Solomon asked for knowledge and wisdom so that he could rule wisely. God gave Solomon what he asked for, and God gave him riches, possessions, and honor as well.

ᵃ Gk Vg: Heb *to*

Solomon asked for wisdom to rule the large number of people (read 2 Chronicles 1:9–10). Long ago, God made a covenant with Abraham and promised that he would have as many descendants as there are grains of sand in the desert. God's part of the covenant had been kept! Solomon set about keeping the people's part of the covenant as he prepared to build a permanent temple where the people could worship God.

Preparations for Building the Temple

2 [b] Solomon decided to build a temple for the name of the LORD, and a royal palace for himself. 2[c] Solomon conscripted seventy thousand laborers and eighty thousand stonecutters in the hill country, with three thousand six hundred to oversee them.

Alliance with Huram of Tyre

3 Solomon sent word to King Hū´ram of Tȳre: "Once you dealt with my father David and sent him cedar to build himself a house to live in. 4I am now about to build a house for the name of the LORD my God and dedicate it to him for offering fragrant incense before him, and for the regular offering of the rows of bread, and for burnt offerings morning and evening, on the sabbaths and the new moons and the appointed festivals of the LORD our God, as ordained forever for Israel. 5The house that I am about to build will be great, for our God is greater than other gods. 6But who is able to build him a house, since heaven, even highest heaven, cannot contain him? Who am I to build a house for him, except as a place to make offerings before him? 7So now send me an artisan skilled to work in gold, sil-

ver, bronze, and iron, and in purple, crimson, and blue fabrics, trained also in engraving, to join the skilled workers who are with me in Judah and Jerusalem, whom my father David provided. 8Send me also cedar, cypress, and algum timber from Lebanon, for I know that your servants are skilled in cutting Lebanon timber. My servants will work with your servants 9to prepare timber for me in abundance, for the house I am about to build will be great and wonderful. 10I will provide for your servants, those who cut the timber, twenty thousand cors of crushed wheat, twenty thousand cors of barley, twenty thousand baths[d] of wine, and twenty thousand baths of oil."

11 Then King Hū´ram of Tȳre answered in a letter that he sent to Solomon, "Because the LORD loves his people he has made you king over them." 12Hū´ram also said, "Blessed be the LORD God of Israel, who made heaven and earth, who has given King David a wise son, endowed with discretion and understanding, who will build a temple for the LORD, and a royal palace for himself.

13 "I have dispatched Hū´ram-ā´bī, a skilled artisan, endowed with understand-

King Huram of Tyre (called King Hiram in 1 Kings) was a friend of King Solomon. They traded with each other to get things they needed. Solomon needed skilled workers for his building program, especially for the Temple. Huram needed agricultural products and olive oil. Huram helped Solomon by giving him ships and sailors for his merchant fleet. Later Solomon owed Huram so much money for these goods that he was forced to sell twenty cities of Galilee to him.

[b] Ch 1.18 in Heb   [c] Ch 2.1 in Heb
[d] A Hebrew measure of volume

ing, [14]the son of one of the Dan′ite women, his father a Ty̆′ri·an. He is trained to work in gold, silver, bronze, iron, stone, and wood, and in purple, blue, and crimson fabrics and fine linen, and to do all sorts of engraving and execute any design that may be assigned him, with your artisans, the artisans of my lord, your father David. [15]Now, as for the wheat, barley, oil, and wine, of which my lord has spoken, let him send them to his servants. [16]We will cut whatever timber you need from Lebanon, and bring it to you as rafts by sea to Jop′pa; you will take it up to Jerusalem."

17 Then Solomon took a census of all the aliens who were residing in the land of Israel, after the census that his father David had taken; and there were found to be one hundred fifty-three thousand six hundred. [18]Seventy thousand of them he assigned as laborers, eighty thousand as stonecutters in the hill country, and three thousand six hundred as overseers to make the people work.

Solomon Builds the Temple

3 Solomon began to build the house of the LORD in Jerusalem on Mount Mō·rī′ah, where the LORD had appeared to his father David, at the place that David had designated, on the threshing floor of Or′nan the Jeb′ū·sīte. [2]He began to build on the second day of the second month of the fourth year of his reign. [3]These are Solomon's measurements[c] for building the house of God: the length, in cubits of the old standard, was sixty cubits, and the width twenty cubits. [4]The vestibule in front of the nave of the house was twenty cubits long, across the width of the house;[f] and its height was one hundred twenty cubits. He overlaid it on the inside with pure gold. [5]The nave he lined with cypress, covered it with fine gold, and made palms and chains on it. [6]He adorned the house with settings of precious stones. The gold was gold from Par·vā′im. [7]So he lined the house with

We can't be absolutely sure what the cherubim looked like. They were lost with the ark of the covenant, and there are no pictures. We do know that they were made of wood and covered with gold. One cherubim sat on each side of the mercy seat (which was a symbol of the throne of God), and their wings stretched out to touch above it.

gold—its beams, its thresholds, its walls, and its doors; and he carved cherubim on the walls.

8 He made the most holy place; its length, corresponding to the width of the house, was twenty cubits, and its width was twenty cubits; he overlaid it with six hundred talents of fine gold. [9]The weight of the nails was fifty shekels of gold. He overlaid the upper chambers with gold.

10 In the most holy place he made two carved cherubim and overlaid[g] them with gold. [11]The wings of the cherubim together extended twenty cubits: one wing of the one, five cubits long, touched the wall of the house, and its other wing, five cubits long, touched the wing of the other cherub; [12]and of this cherub, one wing, five cubits long, touched the wall of the house, and the other wing, also five cubits long, was joined to the wing of the first cherub. [13]The wings of these cherubim extended twenty cubits; the cherubim[h] stood on their feet, facing the nave. [14]And Solomon[i] made the curtain of blue and purple and crimson fabrics and fine linen, and worked cherubim into it.

15 In front of the house he made two pillars thirty-five cubits high, with a capital of five cubits on the top of each. [16]He

c Syr: Heb *foundations*   f Compare 1 Kings 6.3: Meaning of Heb uncertain   g Heb *they overlaid*   h Heb *they*   i Heb *he* made encircling chains and put them on the tops of the pillars; and he made one hundred pomegranates, and put them on the chains. [17]He set up the pillars in front of the temple, one on the right, the other on the left; the one on the right he called Jā'chin, and the one on the left, Bō'az.

Furnishings of the Temple

4 He made an altar of bronze, twenty cubits long, twenty cubits wide, and ten cubits high. [2]Then he made the molten sea; it was round, ten cubits from rim to rim, and five cubits high. A line of thirty cubits would encircle it completely. [3]Under it were panels all around, each of ten cubits, surrounding the sea; there were two rows of panels, cast when it was cast. [4]It stood on twelve oxen, three facing north, three facing west, three facing south, and three facing east; the sea was set on them. The hindquarters of each were toward the inside. [5]Its thickness was a handbreadth; its rim was made like the rim of a cup, like the flower of a lily; it held three thousand baths.[k] [6]He also made ten basins in which to wash, and set five on the right side, and five on the left. In these they were to rinse what was used for the burnt offering. The sea was for the priests to wash in.

[7] He made ten golden lampstands as prescribed, and set them in the temple, five on the south side and five on the north. [8]He also made ten tables and placed them in the temple, five on the right side and five on the left. And he made one hundred basins of gold. [9]He made the court of the priests, and the great court, and doors for the court; he overlaid their doors with bronze. [10]He set the sea at the southeast corner of the house.

[11] And Hū'ram made the pots, the shovels, and the basins. Thus Hū'ram finished the work that he did for King Solomon on the house of God: [12]the two pillars, the bowls, and the two capitals on the top of the pillars; and the two lat-

ticeworks to cover the two bowls of the capitals that were on the top of the pillars; [13]the four hundred pomegranates for the two latticeworks, two rows of pomegranates for each latticework, to cover the two bowls of the capitals that were on the pillars. [14]He made the stands, the basins on the stands, [15]the one sea, and the twelve oxen underneath it. [16]The pots, the shovels, the forks, and all the equipment for these Hū'ram-ā'bī made of burnished bronze for King Solomon for the house of the LORD. [17]In the plain of the Jordan the king cast them, in the clay ground between Suc'coth and Zer'e·dah. [18]Solomon made all these things in great quantities, so that the weight of the bronze was not determined.

[19] So Solomon made all the things that were in the house of God: the golden altar, the tables for the bread of the Presence, [20]the lampstands and their lamps of pure gold to burn before the inner sanctuary, as prescribed; [21]the flowers, the lamps, and the tongs, of purest gold; [22]the snuffers, basins, ladles, and firepans, of pure gold. As for the entrance to the temple: the inner doors to the most holy place and the doors of the nave of the temple were of gold.

5 Thus all the work that Solomon did for the house of the LORD was finished. Solomon brought in the things that his father David had dedicated, and stored the silver, the gold, and all the vessels in the treasuries of the house of God.

The Ark Brought into the Temple

[2] Then Solomon assembled the elders of Israel and all the heads of the tribes, the leaders of the ancestral houses of the people of Israel, in Jerusalem, to bring up the ark of the covenant of the LORD out of the city of David, which is Zion. [3]And all the Israelites assembled before the king at the festival that is in the seventh

[j] Cn: Heb *in the inner sanctuary*   [k] A Hebrew measure of volume

month. ⁴And all the elders of Israel came, and the Lēʹvītes carried the ark. ⁵So they brought up the ark, the tent of meeting, and all the holy vessels that were in the tent; the priests and the Lēʹvītes brought them up. ⁶King Solomon and all the congregation of Israel, who had assembled before him, were before the ark, sacrificing so many sheep and oxen that they could not be numbered or counted. ⁷Then the priests brought the ark of the covenant of the Lord to its place, in the inner sanctuary of the house, in the most holy place, underneath the wings of the cherubim. ⁸For the cherubim spread out their wings over the place of the ark, so that the cherubim made a covering above the ark and its poles. ⁹The poles were so long that the ends of the poles were seen from the holy place in front of the inner sanctuary; but they could not be seen from outside; they are there to this day. ¹⁰There was nothing in the ark except the two tablets that Moses put there at Hōʹreb, where the Lord made a covenant[1] with the people of Israel after they came out of Egypt.

11 Now when the priests came out of the holy place (for all the priests who were present had sanctified themselves, without regard to their divisions), ¹²and all the levitical singers, Āʹsaph, Hēʹman, and Je·dūʹthun, their sons and kindred, arrayed in fine linen, with cymbals, harps, and lyres, stood east of the altar with one hundred twenty priests who were trumpeters. ¹³It was the duty of the trumpeters and singers to make themselves heard in unison in praise and thanksgiving to the Lord, and when the song was raised, with trumpets and cymbals and other musical instruments, in praise to the Lord,

"For he is good,
    for his steadfast love endures
      forever,"

the house, the house of the Lord, was filled with a cloud, ¹⁴so that the priests

could not stand to minister because of the cloud; for the glory of the Lord filled the house of God.

Dedication of the Temple

6 Then Solomon said, "The Lord has said that he would reside in thick darkness. ²I have built you an exalted house, a place for you to reside in forever."

3 Then the king turned around and blessed all the assembly of Israel, while all the assembly of Israel stood. ⁴And he said, "Blessed be the Lord, the God of Israel, who with his hand has fulfilled what he promised with his mouth to my father David, saying, ⁵'Since the day that I brought my people out of the land of Egypt, I have not chosen a city from any of the tribes of Israel in which to build a house, so that my name might be there, and I chose no one as ruler over my people Israel; ⁶but I have chosen Jerusalem in order that my name may be there, and I have chosen David to be over my people Israel.' ⁷My father David had it in mind to build a house for the name of the Lord, the God of Israel. ⁸But the Lord said to my father David, 'You did well to consider building a house for my name; ⁹nevertheless you shall not build the house, but your son who shall be born to you shall build the house for my name.' ¹⁰Now the Lord has fulfilled his promise that he made; for I have succeeded my father David, and sit on the throne of Israel, as the Lord promised, and have built the house for the name of the Lord, the God of Israel. ¹¹There I have set the ark, in which is the covenant of the Lord that he made with the people of Israel."

Solomon's Prayer of Dedication

12 Then Solomon[m] stood before the altar of the Lord in the presence of the whole assembly of Israel, and spread out his hands. ¹³Solomon had made a bronze platform five cubits long, five cubits wide, and three cubits high, and

[1] Heb lacks *a covenant*   [m] Heb *he*

"O LORD, God of Israel, there is no God like you, in heaven or on earth, keeping covenant in steadfast love with your servants who walk before you with all their heart." 2 Chronicles 6:14

had set it in the court; and he stood on it. Then he knelt on his knees in the presence of the whole assembly of Israel, and spread out his hands toward heaven. ¹⁴He said, "O LORD, God of Israel, there is no God like you, in heaven or on earth, keeping covenant in steadfast love with your servants who walk before you with all their heart— ¹⁵you who have kept for your servant, my father David, what you promised to him. Indeed, you promised with your mouth and this day have fulfilled with your hand. ¹⁶Therefore, O LORD, God of Israel, keep for your servant, my father David, that which you promised him, saying, 'There shall never fail you a successor before me to sit on the throne of Israel, if only your children keep to their way, to walk in my law as you have walked before me.' ¹⁷Therefore, O LORD, God of Israel, let your word be confirmed, which you promised to your servant David.

18 "But will God indeed reside with mortals on earth? Even heaven and the highest heaven cannot contain you, how much less this house that I have built! ¹⁹Regard your servant's prayer and his plea, O LORD my God, heeding the cry and the prayer that your servant prays to you. ²⁰May your eyes be open day and night toward this house, the place where you promised to set your name, and may you heed the prayer that your servant prays toward this place. ²¹And hear the plea of your servant and of your people Israel, when they pray toward this place; may you hear from heaven your dwelling place; hear and forgive.

22 "If someone sins against another and is required to take an oath and comes and swears before your altar in this house, ²³may you hear from heaven, and act, and judge your servants, repaying the guilty by bringing their conduct on their own head, and vindicating those who are in the right by rewarding them in accordance with their righteousness.

24 "When your people Israel, having sinned against you, are defeated before an enemy but turn again to you, confess your name, pray and plead with you in this house, ²⁵may you hear from heaven, and forgive the sin of your people Israel, and bring them again to the land that you gave to them and to their ancestors.

26 "When heaven is shut up and there is no rain because they have sinned against you, and then they pray toward this place, confess your name, and turn from their sin, because you punish them, ²⁷may you hear in heaven, forgive the sin of your servants, your people Israel, when you teach them the good way in which they should walk; and send down rain upon your land, which you have given to your people as an inheritance.

28 "If there is famine in the land, if there is plague, blight, mildew, locust, or caterpillar; if their enemies besiege them in any of the settlements of the lands; whatever suffering, whatever sickness there is; ²⁹whatever prayer, whatever plea from any individual or from all your people Israel, all knowing their own suffering and their own sorrows so that they stretch out their hands toward this house; ³⁰may you hear from heaven, your dwelling place, forgive, and render to all whose heart you know, according to all their ways, for only you know the human heart. ³¹Thus may they fear you and walk in your ways all the days that they live in the land that you gave to our ancestors.

32 "Likewise when foreigners, who are not of your people Israel, come from a distant land because of your great

name, and your mighty hand, and your outstretched arm, when they come and pray toward this house, ³³may you hear from heaven your dwelling place, and do whatever the foreigners ask of you, in order that all the peoples of the earth may know your name and fear you, as do your people Israel, and that they may know that your name has been invoked on this house that I have built.

34 "If your people go out to battle against their enemies, by whatever way you shall send them, and they pray to you toward this city that you have chosen and the house that I have built for your name, ³⁵then hear from heaven their prayer and their plea, and maintain their cause.

36 "If they sin against you—for there is no one who does not sin—and you are angry with them and give them to an enemy, so that they are carried away captive to a land far or near; ³⁷then if they come to their senses in the land to which they have been taken captive, and repent, and plead with you in the land of their captivity, saying, 'We have sinned, and have done wrong; we have acted wickedly'; ³⁸if they repent with all their heart and soul in the land of their captivity, to which they were taken captive, and pray toward their land, which you gave to their ancestors, the city that you have chosen, and the house that I have built for your name, ³⁹then hear from heaven your dwelling place their prayer and their pleas, maintain their cause and forgive your people who have sinned against you. ⁴⁰Now, O my God, let your eyes be open and your ears attentive to prayer from this place.

⁴¹ "Now rise up, O Lᴏʀᴅ God, and go to
your resting place,
you and the ark of your might.
Let your priests, O Lᴏʀᴅ God,
be clothed with salvation,
and let your faithful rejoice in
your goodness.
⁴² O Lᴏʀᴅ God, do not reject your

anointed one.
Remember your steadfast love for
your servant David."

Solomon Dedicates the Temple

7 When Solomon had ended his prayer, fire came down from heaven and consumed the burnt offering and the sacrifices; and the glory of the Lᴏʀᴅ filled the temple. ²The priests could not enter the house of the Lᴏʀᴅ, because the glory of the Lᴏʀᴅ filled the Lᴏʀᴅ's house. ³When all the people of Israel saw the fire come down and the glory of the Lᴏʀᴅ on the temple, they bowed down on the pavement with their faces to the ground, and worshiped and gave thanks to the Lᴏʀᴅ, saying,

"For he is good,
for his steadfast love endures
forever."

4 Then the king and all the people offered sacrifice before the Lᴏʀᴅ. ⁵King Solomon offered as a sacrifice twenty-two thousand oxen and one hundred twenty thousand sheep. So the king and all the people dedicated the house of God. ⁶The priests stood at their posts; the Lēʹvites also, with the instruments for music to the Lᴏʀᴅ that King David had made for giving thanks to the Lᴏʀᴅ—for his steadfast love endures forever—whenever David offered praises by their ministry. Opposite them the priests sounded trumpets; and all Israel stood.

7 Solomon consecrated the middle of the court that was in front of the house of the Lᴏʀᴅ; for there he offered the burnt offerings and the fat of the offerings of well-being because the bronze altar Solomon had made could not hold the burnt offering and the grain offering and the fat parts.

8 At that time Solomon held the festival for seven days, and all Israel with him, a very great congregation, from Lēʹ-bō-hāʹmath to the Wadi of Egypt. ⁹On the eighth day they held a solemn assembly; for they had observed the

dedication of the altar seven days and the festival seven days. [10]On the twenty-third day of the seventh month he sent the people away to their homes, joyful and in good spirits because of the goodness that the LORD had shown to David and to Solomon and to his people Israel.

11 Thus Solomon finished the house of the LORD and the king's house; all that Solomon had planned to do in the house of the LORD and in his own house he successfully accomplished.

God's Second Appearance to Solomon

12 Then the LORD appeared to Solomon in the night and said to him: "I have heard your prayer, and have chosen this place for myself as a house of sacrifice. [13]When I shut up the heavens so that there is no rain, or command the locust to devour the land, or send pestilence among my people, [14]if my people who are called by my name humble themselves, pray, seek my face, and turn from their wicked ways, then I will hear from heaven, and will forgive their sin and heal their land. [15]Now my eyes will be open and my ears attentive to the prayer that is made in this place. [16]For now I have chosen and consecrated this house so that my name may be there forever; my eyes and my heart will be there for all time. [17]As for you, if you walk before me, as your father David walked, doing according to all that I have commanded you and keeping my statutes and my ordinances, [18]then I will establish your royal throne, as I made covenant with your father David saying, 'You shall never lack a successor to rule over Israel.'

19 "But if you[n] turn aside and forsake my statutes and my commandments that I have set before you, and go and serve other gods and worship them, [20]then I will pluck you[o] up from the land that I have given you;[o] and this house, which I have consecrated for my name, I will cast out of my sight, and will make it a proverb and a byword among all peoples. [21]And regarding this house, now exalted, everyone passing by will be astonished, and say, 'Why has the LORD done such a thing to this land and to this house?' [22]Then they will say, 'Because they abandoned the LORD the God of their ancestors who brought them out of the land of Egypt, and they adopted other gods, and worshiped them and served them; therefore he has brought all this calamity upon them.' "

Various Activities of Solomon

8 At the end of twenty years, during which Solomon had built the house of the LORD and his own house, [2]Solomon rebuilt the cities that Hū′ram had given to him, and settled the people of Israel in them.

3 Solomon went to Hā′math-zō′bah, and captured it. [4]He built Tad′mor in the wilderness and all the storage towns that he built in Hā′math. [5]He also built Upper Beth-hō′ron and Lower Beth-hō′ron, fortified cities, with walls, gates, and bars, [6]and Bā′a·lath, as well as all Solomon's storage towns, and all the towns for his chariots, the towns for his cavalry, and whatever Solomon desired to build, in Jerusalem, in Lebanon, and in all the land of his dominion. [7]All the people who were left of the Hit′tītes, the Am′o·rītes, the Per′iz·zītes, the Hī′vītes, and the Jeb′ū·sītes, who were not of Israel, [8]from their descendants who were still left in the land, whom the people of Israel had not destroyed—these Solomon

"If my people who are called by my name humble themselves, pray, seek my face, and turn from their wicked ways, then I will hear from heaven, and will forgive their sin and heal their land."
2 Chronicles 7:14

---

[n] The word *you* in this verse is plural   [o] Heb *them*

conscripted for forced labor, as is still the case today. [9]But of the people of Israel Solomon made no slaves for his work; they were soldiers, and his officers, the commanders of his chariotry and cavalry. [10]These were the chief officers of King Solomon, two hundred fifty of them, who exercised authority over the people.

11 Solomon brought Pharaoh's daughter from the city of David to the house that he had built for her, for he said, "My wife shall not live in the house of King David of Israel, for the places to which the ark of the LORD has come are holy."

12 Then Solomon offered up burnt offerings to the LORD on the altar of the LORD that he had built in front of the vestibule, [13]as the duty of each day required, offering according to the commandment of Moses for the sabbaths, the new moons, and the three annual festivals—the festival of unleavened bread, the festival of weeks, and the festival of booths. [14]According to the ordinance of his father David, he appointed the divisions of the priests for their service, and the Lēʹvītes for their offices of praise and ministry alongside the priests as the duty of each day required, and the gatekeepers in their divisions for the several gates; for so David the man of God had commanded. [15]They did not turn away from what the king had commanded the priests and Lēʹvītes regarding anything at all, or regarding the treasuries.

16 Thus all the work of Solomon was accomplished from[p] the day the foundation of the house of the LORD was laid until the house of the LORD was finished completely.

17 Then Solomon went to Ēʹzion-gēʹber and Ēʹloth on the shore of the sea, in the land of Ēʹdom. [18]Hūʹram sent him, in the care of his servants, ships and servants familiar with the sea. They went to Ōʹphir, together with the servants of Solomon, and imported from there four hundred fifty talents of gold and brought it to King Solomon.

The Queen of Sheba had heard that Solomon was very wise, but she didn't know how wise he was until she came to visit him. He answered all of her "hard questions." Talk with your family about people you think are wise. If there is someone you know who has answered hard questions about God or about the Bible for you or a family member, write that person a thank-you note.

Visit of the Queen of Sheba

9 When the queen of Shēʹba heard of the fame of Solomon, she came to Jerusalem to test him with hard questions, having a very great retinue and camels bearing spices and very much gold and precious stones. When she came to Solomon, she discussed with him all that was on her mind. [2]Solomon answered all her questions; there was nothing hidden from Solomon that he could not explain to her. [3]When the queen of Shēʹba had observed the wisdom of Solomon, the house that he had built, [4]the food of his table, the seating of his officials, and the attendance of his servants, and their clothing, his valets, and their clothing, and his burnt offerings[q] that he offered at the house of the LORD, there was no more spirit left in her.

Ophir was a region known for its gold and for the wood that came from its almug trees. The wood smelled good, and the people used it to make musical instruments. They also used it to make a red dye that gave rich color to fabric.

[p] Gk Syr Vg: Heb to   [q] Gk Syr Vg 1 Kings 10.5: Heb ascent

5 So she said to the king, "The report was true that I heard in my own land of your accomplishments and of your wisdom, [6]but I did not believe the[r] reports until I came and my own eyes saw it. Not even half of the greatness of your wisdom had been told to me; you far surpass the report that I had heard. [7]Happy are your people! Happy are these your servants, who continually attend you and hear your wisdom! [8]Blessed be the LORD your God, who has delighted in you and set you on his throne as king for the LORD your God. Because your God loved Israel and would establish them forever, he has made you king over them, that you may execute justice and righteousness." [9]Then she gave the king one hundred twenty talents of gold, a very great quantity of spices, and precious stones: there were no spices such as those that the queen of Shē′ba gave to King Solomon.

10 Moreover the servants of Hū′ram and the servants of Solomon who brought gold from O′phir brought algum wood and precious stones. [11]From the algum wood, the king made steps[s] for the house of the LORD and for the king's house, lyres also and harps for the singers; there never was seen the like of them before in the land of Judah.

12 Meanwhile King Solomon granted the queen of Shē′ba every desire that she expressed, well beyond what she had brought to the king. Then she returned to her own land, with her servants.

Solomon's Great Wealth

13 The weight of gold that came to Solomon in one year was six hundred sixty-six talents of gold, [14]besides that which the traders and merchants brought; and all the kings of Arabia and the governors of the land brought gold and silver to Solomon. [15]King Solomon made two hundred large shields of beaten gold; six hundred shekels of beaten gold went into each large shield. [16]He made three hundred shields of beaten gold; three hundred shekels of gold went into each shield; and the king put them in the House of the Forest of Lebanon. [17]The king also made a great ivory throne, and overlaid it with pure gold. [18]The throne had six steps and a footstool of gold, which were attached to the throne, and on each side of the seat were arm rests and two lions standing beside the arm rests, [19]while twelve lions were standing, one on each end of a step on the six steps. The like of it was never made in any kingdom. [20]All King Solomon's drinking vessels were of gold, and all the vessels of the House of the Forest of Lebanon were of pure gold; silver was not considered as anything in the days of Solomon. [21]For the king's ships went to Tar′shish with the servants of Hū′ram; once every three years the ships of Tar′shish used to come bringing gold, silver, ivory, apes, and peacocks.[t]

22 Thus King Solomon excelled all the kings of the earth in riches and in wisdom. [23]All the kings of the earth sought the presence of Solomon to hear his wisdom, which God had put into his mind. [24]Every one of them brought a present, objects of silver and gold, garments, weaponry, spices, horses, and mules, so much year by year. [25]Solomon had four thousand stalls for horses and chariots, and twelve thousand horses, which he stationed in the chariot cities and with the king in Jerusalem. [26]He ruled over all the kings from the Euphrates to the land of the Phi·lis′tines, and to the border of Egypt. [27]The king

People used the sweet-smelling leaves, roots, and gums of certain herbs and vegetables to make makeup, oil, incense, and perfume. They also used these things to prepare a body for burial.

[r] Heb *their*   [s] Gk Vg: Meaning of Heb uncertain
[t] Or *baboons*

made silver as common in Jerusalem as stone, and cedar as plentiful as the sycamore of the She·phe'lah. [28]Horses were imported for Solomon from Egypt and from all lands.

Death of Solomon

29 Now the rest of the acts of Solomon, from first to last, are they not written in the history of the prophet Nathan, and in the prophecy of A·hi'jah the Shi'lo·nite, and in the visions of the seer Id'do concerning Jer·o·bo'am son of Ne'bat? [30]Solomon reigned in Jerusalem over all Israel forty years. [31]Solomon slept with his ancestors and was buried in the city of his father David; and his son Re·ho·bo'am succeeded him.

The Revolt against Rehoboam

10 Re·ho·bo'am went to She'chem, for all Israel had come to She'chem to make him king. [2]When Jer·o·bo'am son of Ne'bat heard of it (for he was in Egypt, where he had fled from King Solomon), then Jer·o·bo'am returned from Egypt. [3]They sent and called him; and Jer·o·bo'am and all Israel came and said to Re·ho·bo'am, [4]"Your father made our yoke heavy. Now therefore lighten the hard service of your father and his heavy yoke that he placed on us, and we will serve you." [5]He said to them, "Come to me again in three days." So the people went away.

6 Then King Re·ho·bo'am took counsel with the older men who had attended his father Solomon while he was still alive, saying, "How do you advise me to answer this people?" [7]They answered him, "If you will be kind to this people and please them, and speak good words to them, then they will be your servants forever." [8]But he rejected the advice that the older men gave him, and consulted the young men who had grown up with him and now attended him. [9]He said to them, "What do you advise that we answer this people who have said to me, 'Lighten the yoke that your father put on us'?" [10]The young men who had grown up with him said to him, "Thus should you speak to the people who said to you, 'Your father made our yoke heavy, but you must lighten it for us'; tell them, 'My little finger is thicker than my father's loins. [11]Now, whereas my father laid on you a heavy yoke, I will add to your yoke. My father disciplined you with whips, but I will discipline you with scorpions.'"

12 So Jer·o·bo'am and all the people came to Re·ho·bo'am the third day, as the king had said, "Come to me again the third day." [13]The king answered them harshly. King Re·ho·bo'am rejected the advice of the older men; [14]he spoke to them in accordance with the advice of the young men, "My father made your yoke heavy, but I will add to it; my father disciplined you with whips, but I will discipline you with scorpions." [15]So the king did not listen to the people, because it was a turn of affairs brought about by God so that the LORD might fulfill his word, which he had spoken by A·hi'jah the Shi'lo·nite to Jer·o·bo'am son of Ne'bat.

16 When all Israel saw that the king would not listen to them, the people answered the king,

"What share do we have in David?
We have no inheritance in the son of Jesse.
Each of you to your tents, O Israel!
Look now to your own house, O David."

So all Israel departed to their tents. [17]But Re·ho·bo'am reigned over the people of Israel who were living in the cities of Judah. [18]When King Re·ho·bo'am sent Ha·do'ram, who was taskmaster over the forced labor, the people of Israel stoned him to death. King Re·ho·bo'am hurriedly mounted his chariot to flee to Jerusalem. [19]So Israel has been in rebellion against the house of David to this day.

Judah and Benjamin Fortified

11 When Re·ho·bo'am came to Jerusalem, he assembled one hundred eighty thousand chosen troops of the house of Judah and Benjamin to fight against Israel, to restore the kingdom to Rē·ho·bō´am. ²But the word of the LORD came to She·māi´ah the man of God: ³Say to King Rē·ho·bō´am of Judah, son of Solomon, and to all Israel in Judah and Benjamin, ⁴"Thus says the LORD: You shall not go up or fight against your kindred. Let everyone return home, for this thing is from me." So they heeded the word of the LORD and turned back from the expedition against Jer·o·bō´am.

5 Rē·ho·bō´am resided in Jerusalem, and he built cities for defense in Judah. ⁶He built up Bethlehem, Ē´tam, Te·kō´a, ⁷Beth-zur, Sō´cō, A·dul´lam, ⁸Gath, Ma·rē´shah, Ziph, ⁹Ad·o·rā´im, Lā´chish, A·zē´kah, ¹⁰Zō´rah, Aī´ja·lon, and Hē´bron, fortified cities that are in Judah and in Benjamin. ¹¹He made the fortresses strong, and put commanders in them, and stores of food, oil, and wine. ¹²He also put large shields and spears in all the cities, and made them very strong. So he held Judah and Benjamin.

Priests and Levites Support Rehoboam

13 The priests and the Lē´vītes who were in all Israel presented themselves to him from all their territories. ¹⁴The Lē´vītes had left their common lands and their holdings and had come to Judah and Jerusalem, because Jer·o·bō´am and his sons had prevented them from serving as priests of the LORD, ¹⁵and had appointed his own priests for the high places, and for the goat-demons, and for the calves that he had made. ¹⁶Those who had set their hearts to seek the LORD God of Israel came after them from all the tribes of Israel to Jerusalem to sacrifice to the LORD, the God of their ancestors. ¹⁷They strengthened the kingdom of Judah, and for three years they made Rē·ho·bō´am son of Solomon secure, for they walked for three years in the way of David and Solomon.

Rehoboam's Marriages

18 Rē·ho·bō´am took as his wife Mā´ha·lath daughter of Jer´i·moth son of David, and of Ab·i·hā´il daughter of E·lī´ab son of Jesse. ¹⁹She bore him sons: Jē´ush, Shem·a·rī´ah, and Zā´ham. ²⁰After her he took Mā´a·cah daughter of Ab´sa·lom, who bore him A·bī´jah, At´taī, Zī´za, and She·lō´mith. ²¹Rē·ho·bō´am loved Mā´a·cah daughter of Ab´sa·lom more than all his other wives and concubines (he took eighteen wives and sixty concubines, and became the father of twenty-eight sons and sixty daughters). ²²Rē·ho·bō´am appointed A·bī´jah son of Mā´a·cah as chief prince among his brothers, for he intended to make him king. ²³He dealt wisely, and distributed some of his sons through all the districts of Judah and Benjamin, in all the fortified cities; he gave them abundant provisions, and found many wives for them.

Egypt Attacks Judah

12 When the rule of Rē·ho·bō´am was established and he grew strong, he abandoned the law of the LORD, he and all Israel with him. ²In the fifth year of King Rē·ho·bō´am, because they had been unfaithful to the LORD, King Shī´shak of Egypt came up against Jerusalem ³with twelve hundred chariots and sixty thousand cavalry. A countless army came with him from Egypt— Libyans, Suk´ki·im, and Ethiopians.ᵘ ⁴He took the fortified cities of Judah and came as far as Jerusalem. ⁵Then the prophet She·māi´ah came to Rē·ho·bō´am and to the officers of Judah, who had gathered at Jerusalem because of Shī´shak, and said to them, "Thus says the LORD: You abandoned me, so I have abandoned you to the hand of Shī´shak." ⁶Then the officers of Israel and the king humbled themselves and said, "The LORD is in the right." ⁷When the LORD saw that they humbled themselves, the word of the LORD came to She·māi´ah,

---

ᵘ Or *Nubians*; Heb *Cushites*

saying: "They have humbled themselves; I will not destroy them, but I will grant them some deliverance, and my wrath shall not be poured out on Jerusalem by the hand of Shī´shak. [8]Nevertheless they shall be his servants, so that they may know the difference between serving me and serving the kingdoms of other lands."

9 So King Shī´shak of Egypt came up against Jerusalem; he took away the treasures of the house of the LORD and the treasures of the king's house; he took everything. He also took away the shields of gold that Solomon had made; [10]but King Rē·ho·bō´am made in place of them shields of bronze, and committed them to the hands of the officers of the guard, who kept the door of the king's house. [11]Whenever the king went into the house of the LORD, the guard would come along bearing them, and would then bring them back to the guardroom. [12]Because he humbled himself the wrath of the LORD turned from him, so as not to destroy them completely; moreover, conditions were good in Judah.

Death of Rehoboam

13 So King Rē·ho·bō´am established himself in Jerusalem and reigned. Rē·ho·bō´am was forty-one years old when he began to reign; he reigned seventeen years in Jerusalem, the city that the LORD had chosen out of all the tribes of Israel to put his name there. His mother's name was Nā´a·m·ah the Am´mon·īte. [14]He did evil, for he did not set his heart to seek the LORD.

15 Now the acts of Rē·ho·bō´am, from first to last, are they not written in the records of the prophet She·māi´ah and of the seer Id´dō, recorded by genealogy? There were continual wars between Rē·ho·bō´am and Jer·o·bō´am. [16]Rē·ho·bō´am slept with his ancestors and was buried in the city of David; and his son A·bī´jah succeeded him.

Abijah Reigns over Judah

13 In the eighteenth year of King Jer·o·bō´am, A·bī´jah began to reign over Judah. [2]He reigned for three years in Jerusalem. His mother's name was Mi·cāi´ah daughter of Ū·rī´el of Gib´ē·ah.

Now there was war between A·bī´jah and Jer·o·bō´am. [3]A·bī´jah engaged in battle, having an army of valiant warriors, four hundred thousand picked men; and Jer·o·bō´am drew up his line of battle against him with eight hundred thousand picked mighty warriors. [4]Then A·bī´jah stood on the slope of Mount Zem·a·rā´im that is in the hill country of Ē´phra·im, and said, "Listen to me, Jer·o·bō´am and all Israel! [5]Do you not know that the LORD God of Israel gave the kingship over Israel forever to David and his sons by a covenant of salt? [6]Yet Jer·o·bō´am son of Nē´bat, a servant of Solomon son of David, rose up and rebelled against his lord; [7]and certain worthless scoundrels gathered around him and defied Rē·ho·bō´am son of Solomon, when Rē·ho·bō´am was young and irresolute and could not withstand them.

8 "And now you think that you can withstand the kingdom of the LORD in the hand of the sons of David, because you are a great multitude and have with you the golden calves that Jer·o·bō´am made as gods for you. [9]Have you not driven out the priests of the LORD, the descendants of Aaron, and the Lē´vītes, and made priests for yourselves like the peoples of other lands? Whoever comes to be consecrated with a young bull or seven rams becomes a priest of what are no gods. [10]But as for us, the LORD is our God, and we have not abandoned him. We have priests ministering to the LORD who are descendants of Aaron, and Lē´vītes for their service. [11]They offer to the LORD every morning and every evening burnt offerings and fragrant incense, set out the rows of bread on the table of pure gold, and care for the golden lamp-

stand so that its lamps may burn every evening; for we keep the charge of the LORD our God, but you have abandoned him. [12]See, God is with us at our head, and his priests have their battle trumpets to sound the call to battle against you. O Israelites, do not fight against the LORD, the God of your ancestors; for you cannot succeed."

13 Jer·o·bo′am had sent an ambush around to come on them from behind; thus his troops[v] were in front of Judah, and the ambush was behind them. [14]When Judah turned, the battle was in front of them and behind them. They cried out to the LORD, and the priests blew the trumpets. [15]Then the people of Judah raised the battle shout. And when the people of Judah shouted, God defeated Jer·o·bo′am and all Israel before A·bi′jah and Judah. [16]The Israelites fled before Judah, and God gave them into their hands. [17]A·bi′jah and his army defeated them with great slaughter; five hundred thousand picked men of Israel fell slain. [18]Thus the Israelites were subdued at that time, and the people of Judah prevailed, because they relied on the LORD, the God of their ancestors. [19]A·bi′jah pursued Jer·o·bo′am, and took cities from him: Beth′el with its villages and Je·sha′nah with its villages and E′phron[w] with its villages. [20]Jer·o·bo′am did not recover his power in the days of A·bi′jah; the LORD struck him down, and he died. [21]But A·bi′jah grew strong. He took fourteen wives, and became the father of twenty-two sons and sixteen daughters. [22]The rest of the acts of A·bi′-jah, his behavior and his deeds, are written in the story of the prophet Id′do.

Asa Reigns

14[x] So A·bi′jah slept with his ancestors, and they buried him in the city of David. His son Asa succeeded him. In his days the land had rest for ten years. [2][y]Asa did what was good and right in the sight of the LORD his God. [3]He took away the foreign altars and the high places, broke down the pillars, hewed down the sacred poles,[z] [4]and commanded Judah to seek the LORD, the God of their ancestors, and to keep the law and the commandment. [5]He also removed from all the cities of Judah the high places and the incense altars. And the kingdom had rest under him. [6]He built fortified cities in Judah while the land had rest. He had no war in those years, for the LORD gave him peace. [7]He said to Judah, "Let us build these cities, and surround them with walls and towers, gates and bars; the land is still ours because we have sought the LORD our God; we have sought him, and he has given us peace on every side." So they built and prospered. [8]Asa had an army of three hundred thousand from Judah, armed with large shields and spears, and two hundred eighty thousand troops from Benjamin who carried shields and drew bows; all these were mighty warriors.

Ethiopian Invasion Repulsed

9 Ze′rah the Ethiopian[a] came out against them with an army of a million men and three hundred chariots, and came as far as Ma·re′shah. [10]Asa went out to meet him, and they drew up their lines of battle in the valley of Zeph′a·thah at Ma·re′shah. [11]Asa cried to the LORD his God, "O LORD, there is no difference for you between helping the mighty and the weak. Help us, O LORD our God, for we rely on you, and in your name we have come against this multitude. O LORD, you are our God; let no mortal prevail against you." [12]So the LORD defeated the Ethiopians[b] before Asa and before Judah, and the Ethiopians[b] fled. [13]Asa and the army with him pursued them as far as Ge′rar, and the Ethiopians[b] fell until no one remained alive; for they were broken

---

[v] Heb *they*   [w] Another reading is *Ephrain*   [x] Ch 13.23 in Heb   [y] Ch 14.1 in Heb   [z] Heb *Asherim*   [a] Or *Nubian*; Heb *Cushite*   [b] Or *Nubians*; Heb *Cushites*   [c] Heb *They*

before the L ORD and his army. The people of Judah[c] carried away a great quantity of booty. [14]They defeated all the cities around Gē′rar, for the fear of the L ORD was on them. They plundered all the cities; for there was much plunder in them. [15]They also attacked the tents of those who had livestock,[d] and carried away sheep and goats in abundance, and camels. Then they returned to Jerusalem.

15 The spirit of God came upon Az·a·rī′ah son of Ō′ded. [2]He went out to meet Asa and said to him, "Hear me, Asa, and all Judah and Benjamin: The L ORD is with you, while you are with him. If you seek him, he will be found by you, but if you abandon him, he will abandon you. [3]For a long time Israel was without the true God, and without a teaching priest, and without law; [4]but when in their distress they turned to the L ORD, the God of Israel, and sought him, he was found by them. [5]In those times it was not safe for anyone to go or come, for great disturbances afflicted all the inhabitants of the lands. [6]They were broken in pieces, nation against nation and city against city, for God troubled them with every sort of distress. [7]But you, take courage! Do not let your hands be weak, for your work shall be rewarded."

8 When Asa heard these words, the prophecy of Az·a·rī′ah son of Ō′ded,[e] he took courage, and put away the abominable idols from all the land of Judah and Benjamin and from the towns that he had taken in the hill country of Ē′phra·im. He repaired the altar of the L ORD that was in front of the vestibule of the house of the L ORD.[f] [9]He gathered all Judah and Benjamin, and those from Ē′phra·im, Ma·nas′seh, and Sim′e·on who were residing as aliens with them, for great numbers had deserted to him from Israel when they saw that the L ORD his God was with him. [10]They were gathered at Jerusalem in the third month of the fifteenth year of the reign of Asa.

[11]They sacrificed to the L ORD on that day, from the booty that they had brought, seven hundred oxen and seven thousand sheep. [12]They entered into a covenant to seek the L ORD, the God of their ancestors, with all their heart and with all their soul. [13]Whoever would not seek the L ORD, the God of Israel, should be put to death, whether young or old, man or woman. [14]They took an oath to the L ORD with a loud voice, and with shouting, and with trumpets, and with horns. [15]All Judah rejoiced over the oath; for they had sworn with all their heart, and had sought him with their whole desire, and he was found by them, and the L ORD gave them rest all around.

16 King Asa even removed his mother Mā′a·cah from being queen mother because she had made an abominable image for A·shē′rah. Asa cut down her image, crushed it, and burned it at the Wadi Kid′ron. [17]But the high places were not taken out of Israel. Nevertheless the heart of Asa was true all his days. [18]He brought into the house of God the votive gifts of his father and his own votive gifts—silver, gold, and utensils. [19]And there was no more war until the thirty-fifth year of the reign of Asa.

A votive offering was a gift a person gave to God as part of a promise.

Alliance with Aram Condemned

16 In the thirty-sixth year of the reign of Asa, King Bā·a′sha of Israel went up against Judah, and built Rā′mah, to prevent anyone from going out or coming into the territory of[g] King Asa of Judah. [2]Then Asa took silver and gold from the treasures of the house of the L ORD and the king's house, and sent

---

[d] Meaning of Heb uncertain   [e] Compare Syr Vg: Heb *the prophecy, the prophet Obed*   [f] Heb *the vestibule of the L ORD*   [g] Heb lacks *the territory of*

them to King Ben-hā´dad of Ar´am, who resided in Damascus, saying, ³"Let there be an alliance between me and you, like that between my father and your father; I am sending to you silver and gold; go, break your alliance with King Bā·a´sha of Israel, so that he may withdraw from me." ⁴Ben-hā´dad listened to King Asa, and sent the commanders of his armies against the cities of Israel. They conquered Ī´jon, Dan, Ā´bel-mā´im, and all the store-cities of Naph´ta·lī. ⁵When Bā´a-sha heard of it, he stopped building Rā´-mah, and let his work cease. ⁶Then King Asa brought all Judah, and they carried away the stones of Rā´mah and its timber, with which Bā·a´sha had been building, and with them he built up Gē´ba and Miz´pah.

7 At that time the seer Ha·nā´nī came to King Asa of Judah, and said to him, "Because you relied on the king of Ar´am, and did not rely on the LORD your God, the army of the king of Ar´am has escaped you. ⁸Were not the Ethiopians[h] and the Libyans a huge army with exceedingly many chariots and cavalry? Yet because you relied on the LORD, he gave them into your hand. ⁹For the eyes of the LORD range throughout the entire earth, to strengthen those whose heart is true to him. You have done foolishly in this; for from now on you will have wars." ¹⁰Then Asa was angry with the seer, and put him in the stocks, in prison, for he was in a rage with him because of this. And Asa inflicted cruelties on some of the people at the same time.

Asa's Disease and Death

11 The acts of Asa, from first to last, are written in the Book of the Kings of Judah and Israel. ¹²In the thirty-ninth year of his reign Asa was diseased in his feet, and his disease became severe; yet even in his disease he did not seek the LORD, but sought help from physicians. ¹³Then Asa slept with his ancestors, dying in the forty-first year of his reign. ¹⁴They buried him in the tomb that he had hewn out for himself in the city of David. They laid him on a bier that had been filled with various kinds of spices prepared by the perfumer's art; and they made a very great fire in his honor.

Jehoshaphat's Reign

17 His son Je·hosh´a·phat succeeded him, and strengthened himself against Israel. ²He placed forces in all the fortified cities of Judah, and set garrisons in the land of Judah, and in the cities of Ē´phra·im that his father Asa had taken. ³The LORD was with Je·hosh´-a·phat, because he walked in the earlier ways of his father;[i] he did not seek the Bā´als, ⁴but sought the God of his father and walked in his commandments, and not according to the ways of Israel. ⁵Therefore the LORD established the kingdom in his hand. All Judah brought tribute to Je·hosh´a·phat, and he had great riches and honor. ⁶His heart was courageous in the ways of the LORD; and furthermore he removed the high places and the sacred poles[j] from Judah.

7 In the third year of his reign he sent his officials, Ben-hā´il, Ō´ba·dī´ah, Zech·a·rī´ah, Ne·than´el, and Mī·cāi´ah, to teach in the cities of Judah. ⁸With them were the Lē´vītes, She·māi´ah, Neth·a·nī´-ah, Zeb·a·dī´ah, As´a·hel, She·mir´-a·moth, Je·hon´a·than, Ad·o·nī´jah, Tō´bi´-jah, and Tob-ad·o·nī´jah; and with these Lē´vītes, the priests E·lish´a·ma and Je·hō´-ram. ⁹They taught in Judah, having the book of the law of the LORD with them; they went around through all the cities of Judah and taught among the people.

10 The fear of the LORD fell on all the kingdoms of the lands around Judah, and they did not make war against Je·hosh´a·phat. ¹¹Some of the Phi·lis´-tines brought Je·hosh´a·phat presents, and silver for tribute; and the Arabs also brought him seven thousand seven hun-

---

[h] Or *Nubians;* Heb *Cushites*   [i] Another reading is *his father David*   [j] Heb *Asherim*

dred rams and seven thousand seven hundred male goats. ¹²Je·hosh´a·phat grew steadily greater. He built fortresses and storage cities in Judah. ¹³He carried out great works in the cities of Judah. He had soldiers, mighty warriors, in Jerusalem. ¹⁴This was the muster of them by ancestral houses: Of Judah, the commanders of the thousands: Ad´nah the commander, with three hundred thousand mighty warriors, ¹⁵and next to him Jē·hō·hā´nan the commander, with two hundred eighty thousand, ¹⁶and next to him Am·a·si´ah son of Zich´ri, a volunteer for the service of the LORD, with two hundred thousand mighty warriors. ¹⁷Of Benjamin: E·lī´a·da, a mighty warrior, with two hundred thousand armed with bow and shield, ¹⁸and next to him Je·hō´za·bad with one hundred eighty thousand armed for war. ¹⁹These were in the service of the king, besides those whom the king had placed in the fortified cities throughout all Judah.

Micaiah Predicts Failure

18 Now Je·hosh´a·phat had great riches and honor; and he made a marriage alliance with A´hab. ²After some years he went down to A´hab in Sa·mār´i·a. A´hab slaughtered an abundance of sheep and oxen for him and for the people who were with him, and induced him to go up against Rā´moth-gil´e·ad. ³King A´hab of Israel said to King Je·hosh´a·phat of Judah, "Will you go with me to Rā´moth-gil´e·ad?" He answered him, "I am with you, my people are your people. We will be with you in the war."

4 But Je·hosh´a·phat also said to the king of Israel, "Inquire first for the word of the LORD." ⁵Then the king of Israel gathered the prophets together, four hundred of them, and said to them, "Shall we go to battle against Rā´moth-gil´e·ad, or shall I refrain?" They said, "Go up; for God will give it into the hand of the king." ⁶But Je·hosh´a·phat said, "Is there no other prophet of the LORD here of whom we may inquire?" ⁷The king of Israel said to Je·hosh´a·phat, "There is still one other by whom we may inquire of the LORD, Mī·cāi´ah son of Im´lah; but I hate him, for he never prophesies anything favorable about me, but only disaster." Je·hosh´a·phat said, "Let the king not say such a thing." ⁸Then the king of Israel summoned an officer and said, "Bring quickly Mī·cāi´ah son of Im´lah." ⁹Now the king of Israel and King Je·hosh´a·phat of Judah were sitting on their thrones, arrayed in their robes; and they were sitting at the threshing floor at the entrance of the gate of Sa·mār´i·a; and all the prophets were prophesying before them. ¹⁰Zed·e·kī´ah son of Che·nā´a·nah made for himself horns of iron, and he said, "Thus says the LORD: With these you shall gore the Ar·a·mē´ans until they are destroyed." ¹¹All the prophets were prophesying the same and saying, "Go up to Rā´moth-gil´e·ad and triumph; the LORD will give it into the hand of the king."

12 The messenger who had gone to summon Mī·cāi´ah said to him, "Look, the words of the prophets with one accord are favorable to the king; let your word be like the word of one of them, and speak favorably." ¹³But Mī·cāi´ah said, "As the LORD lives, whatever my God says, that I will speak."

14 When he had come to the king, the king said to him, "Mī·cāi´ah, shall we go to Rā´moth-gil´e·ad to battle, or shall I refrain?" He answered, "Go up and triumph; they will be given into your hand." ¹⁵But the king said to him, "How many times must I make you swear to tell me nothing but the truth in the name of the LORD?" ¹⁶Then Mī·cāi´ah[k] said, "I saw all Israel scattered on the mountains, like sheep without a shepherd; and the LORD said, 'These have no master; let each one go home in peace.' " ¹⁷The king of Israel said to Je·hosh´a·phat, "Did I not tell you that he would not prophesy anything favorable about me, but only disaster?"

[k] Heb *he*

18 Then Mī·cāi´ah[k] said, "Therefore hear the word of the LORD: I saw the LORD sitting on his throne, with all the host of heaven standing to the right and to the left of him. ¹⁹And the LORD said, 'Who will entice King Ā´hab of Israel, so that he may go up and fall at Rā´moth-gil´ē·ad?' Then one said one thing, and another said another, ²⁰until a spirit came forward and stood before the LORD, saying, 'I will entice him.' The LORD asked him, 'How?' ²¹He replied, 'I will go out and be a lying spirit in the mouth of all his prophets.' Then the LORD[k] said, 'You are to entice him, and you shall succeed; go out and do it.' ²²So you see, the LORD has put a lying spirit in the mouth of these your prophets; the LORD has decreed disaster for you."

23 Then Zed·e·kī´ah son of Che·nā´-a·nah came up to Mī·cāi´ah, slapped him on the cheek, and said, "Which way did the spirit of the LORD pass from me to speak to you?" ²⁴Mī·cāi´ah replied, "You will find out on that day when you go in to hide in an inner chamber." ²⁵The king of Israel then ordered, "Take Mī·cāi´ah, and return him to Ā´mon the governor of the city and to Jō´ash the king's son; ²⁶and say, 'Thus says the king: Put this fellow in prison, and feed him on reduced rations of bread and water until I return in peace.' " ²⁷Mī·cāi´ah said, "If you return in peace, the LORD has not spoken by me." And he said, "Hear, you peoples, all of you!"

Defeat and Death of Ahab

28 So the king of Israel and King Je·hosh´a·phat of Judah went up to Rā´-moth-gil´ē·ad. ²⁹The king of Israel said to Je·hosh´a·phat, "I will disguise myself and go into battle, but you wear your robes." So the king of Israel disguised himself, and they went into battle. ³⁰Now the king of Ar´am had commanded the captains of his chariots, "Fight with no one small or great, but only with the king of Israel." ³¹When the captains of the chariots saw Je·hosh´-a·phat, they said, "It is the king of Israel." So they turned to fight against

him; and Je·hosh´a·phat cried out, and the LORD helped him. God drew them away from him, ³²for when the captains of the chariots saw that it was not the king of Israel, they turned back from pursuing him. ³³But a certain man drew his bow and unknowingly struck the king of Israel between the scale armor and the breastplate; so he said to the driver of his chariot, "Turn around, and carry me out of the battle, for I am wounded." ³⁴The battle grew hot that day, and the king of Israel propped himself up in his chariot facing the Ar·a·mē´ans until evening; then at sunset he died.

19 King Je·hosh´a·phat of Judah returned in safety to his house in Jerusalem. ²Jē´hū son of Ha·nā´nī the seer went out to meet him and said to King Je·hosh´a·phat, "Should you help the wicked and love those who hate the LORD? Because of this, wrath has gone out against you from the LORD. ³Nevertheless, some good is found in you, for you destroyed the sacred poles[l] out of the land, and have set your heart to seek God."

The Reforms of Jehoshaphat

4 Je·hosh´a·phat resided at Jerusalem; then he went out again among the people, from Bē´er-shē´ba to the hill country of Ē´phra·im, and brought them back to the LORD, the God of their ancestors. ⁵He appointed judges in the land in all the fortified cities of Judah, city by city, ⁶and said to the judges, "Consider what you are doing, for you judge not on behalf of human beings but on the LORD's behalf; he is with you in giving judgment. ⁷Now, let the fear of the LORD be upon you; take care what you do, for there is no perversion of justice with the LORD our God, or partiality, or taking of bribes."

8 Moreover in Jerusalem Je·hosh´-a·phat appointed certain Lē´vītes and priests and heads of families of Israel, to give judgment for the LORD and to decide disputed cases. They had their seat at Jerusalem. ⁹He charged them:

[k] Heb *he*   [l] Heb *Asheroth*

The word "fear" can mean panic, worry, or dread, but it can also mean something else. "Fear of God" and "fear of the Lord" mean having awe, respect, love, trust, and faith. This sort of fear recognizes God's holiness.

"This is how you shall act: in the fear of the LORD, in faithfulness, and with your whole heart; ¹⁰whenever a case comes to you from your kindred who live in their cities, concerning bloodshed, law or commandment, statutes or ordinances, then you shall instruct them, so that they may not incur guilt before the LORD and wrath may not come on you and your kindred. Do so, and you will not incur guilt. ¹¹See, Am·a·rī´ah the chief priest is over you in all matters of the LORD; and Zeb·a·dī´ah son of Ish´ma·el, the governor of the house of Judah, in all the king's matters; and the Lē´vītes will serve you as officers. Deal courageously, and may the LORD be with the good!"

Invasion from the East

20 After this the Mō´ab·ītes and Am´mon·ītes, and with them some of the Me·ū´nītes,ᵐ came against Je·hosh´a·phat for battle. ²Messengersⁿ came and told Je·hosh´a·phat, "A great multitude is coming against you from Ē´dom,º from beyond the sea; already they are at Haz´a·zon-tā´mar" (that is, En-ge´di). ³Je·hosh´a·phat was afraid; he set himself to seek the LORD, and proclaimed a fast throughout all Judah. ⁴Judah assembled to seek help from the LORD; from all the towns of Judah they came to seek the LORD.

Jehoshaphat's Prayer and Victory

5 Je·hosh´a·phat stood in the assembly of Judah and Jerusalem, in the house of the LORD, before the new court, ⁶and said, "O LORD, God of our ancestors, are you not God in heaven? Do you not rule over all the kingdoms of the nations? In your hand are power and might, so that no one is able to withstand you. ⁷Did you not, O our God, drive out the inhabitants of this land before your people Israel, and give it forever to the descendants of your friend Abraham? ⁸They have lived in it, and in it have built you a sanctuary for your name, saying, ⁹'If disaster comes upon us, the sword, judgment,ᵖ or pestilence, or famine, we will stand before this house, and before you, for your name is in this house, and cry to you in our distress, and you will hear and save.' ¹⁰See now, the people of Am´mon, Mō´ab, and Mount Sē´ir, whom you would not let Israel invade when they came from the land of Egypt, and whom they avoided and did not destroy— ¹¹they reward us by coming to drive us out of your possession that you have given us to inherit. ¹²O our God, will you not execute judgment upon them? For we are powerless against this great multitude that is coming against us. We do not know what to do, but our eyes are on you."

13 Meanwhile all Judah stood before the LORD, with their little ones, their wives, and their children. ¹⁴Then the spirit of the LORD came upon Ja·hā´zi·el son of Zech·a·rī´ah, son of Be·nā´i·ah, son of Je·ī´el, son of Mat·ta·nī´ah, a Lē´vīte of the sons of Ā´saph, in the middle of the assembly. ¹⁵He said, "Listen, all Judah and inhabitants of Jerusalem, and King Je·hosh´a·phat: Thus says the LORD to you: 'Do not fear or be dismayed at this great multitude; for the battle is not yours but God's. ¹⁶Tomorrow go down against them; they will come up by the ascent of Ziz; you will find them at the end of the valley, before the wilderness of Je·rū´el. ¹⁷This battle is not for you to fight; take your position, stand still, and see the vic-

---

ᵐ Compare 26.7: Heb *Ammonites* ⁿ Heb *They*
º One Ms: MT *Aram* ᵖ Or *the sword of judgment*

tory of the LORD on your behalf, O Judah and Jerusalem.' Do not fear or be dismayed; tomorrow go out against them, and the LORD will be with you."

18 Then Je·hosh´a·phat bowed down with his face to the ground, and all Judah and the inhabitants of Jerusalem fell down before the LORD, worshiping the LORD. ¹⁹And the Lē´vītes, of the Kō´hath·ītes and the Kō´ra·hītes, stood up to praise the LORD, the God of Israel, with a very loud voice.

20 They rose early in the morning and went out into the wilderness of Te·kō´a; and as they went out, Je·hosh´-a·phat stood and said, "Listen to me, O Judah and inhabitants of Jerusalem! Believe in the LORD your God and you will be established; believe his prophets." ²¹When he had taken counsel with the people, he appointed those who were to sing to the LORD and praise him in holy splendor, as they went before the army, saying,

"Give thanks to the LORD,
　for his steadfast love endures
　　forever."

²²As they began to sing and praise, the LORD set an ambush against the Am´mon·ītes, Mō´ab, and Mount Sē´ir, who had come against Judah, so that they were routed. ²³For the Am´mon·ītes and Mō´ab attacked the inhabitants of Mount Sē´ir, destroying them utterly; and when they had made an end of the inhabitants of Sē´ir, they all helped to destroy one another.

24 When Judah came to the watchtower of the wilderness, they looked toward the multitude; they were corpses lying on the ground; no one had escaped. ²⁵When Je·hosh´a·phat and his people came to take the booty from them, they found livestock*q* in great numbers, goods, clothing, and precious things, which they took for themselves until they could carry no more. They spent three days taking the booty, because of its abundance. ²⁶On the fourth day they assembled in the Val-

ley of Ber´a·cah, for there they blessed the LORD; therefore that place has been called the Valley of Ber´a·cah*r* to this day. ²⁷Then all the people of Judah and Jerusalem, with Je·hosh´a·phat at their head, returned to Jerusalem with joy, for the LORD had enabled them to rejoice over their enemies. ²⁸They came to Jerusalem, with harps and lyres and trumpets, to the house of the LORD. ²⁹The fear of God came on all the kingdoms of the countries when they heard that the LORD had fought against the enemies of Israel. ³⁰And the realm of Je·hosh´a·phat was quiet, for his God gave him rest all around.

The End of Jehoshaphat's Reign

31 So Je·hosh´a·phat reigned over Judah. He was thirty-five years old when he began to reign; he reigned twenty-five years in Jerusalem. His mother's name was A·zū´bah daughter of Shil´hī. ³²He walked in the way of his father Asa and did not turn aside from it, doing what was right in the sight of the LORD. ³³Yet the high places were not removed; the people had not yet set their hearts upon the God of their ancestors.

34 Now the rest of the acts of Je·hosh´a·phat, from first to last, are written in the Annals of Jē´hū son of Ha·nā´nī, which are recorded in the Book of the Kings of Israel.

35 After this King Je·hosh´a·phat of Judah joined with King A·ha·zī´ah of Israel, who did wickedly. ³⁶He joined him in building ships to go to Tar´shish; they built the ships in Ē´zi·on·gē´ber. ³⁷Then El·i·ē´zer son of Dō·dav´a·hū of Ma·rē´shah prophesied against Je·hosh´a·phat, saying, "Because you have joined with A·ha·zī´ah, the LORD will destroy what you have made." And the ships were wrecked and were not able to go to Tar´shish.

Jehoram's Reign

21 Je·hosh´a·phat slept with his ancestors and was buried with his ancestors in the city of David; his son

---

q Gk: Heb *among them*　　*r* That is *Blessing*

Je·ho´ram succeeded him. [2]He had brothers, the sons of Je·hosh´a·phat: Az·a·rī´ah, Je·hī´el, Zech·a·rī´ah, Az·a·rī´ah, Michael, and Sheph·a·tī´ah; all these were the sons of King Je·hosh´a·phat of Judah.[s] [3]Their father gave them many gifts, of silver, gold, and valuable possessions, together with fortified cities in Judah; but he gave the kingdom to Je·ho´ram, because he was the firstborn. [4]When Je·ho´ram had ascended the throne of his father and was established, he put all his brothers to the sword, and also some of the officials of Israel. [5]Je·ho´ram was thirty-two years old when he began to reign; he reigned eight years in Jerusalem. [6]He walked in the way of the kings of Israel, as the house of A´hab had done; for the daughter of A´hab was his wife. He did what was evil in the sight of the LORD. [7]Yet the LORD would not destroy the house of David because of the covenant that he had made with David, and since he had promised to give a lamp to him and to his descendants forever.

Revolt of Edom

8 In his days E´dom revolted against the rule of Judah and set up a king of their own. [9]Then Je·ho´ram crossed over with his commanders and all his chariots. He set out by night and attacked the E´dom·ites, who had surrounded him and his chariot commanders. [10]So E´dom has been in revolt against the rule of Judah to this day. At that time Lib´nah also revolted against his rule, because he had forsaken the LORD, the God of his ancestors.

Elijah's Letter

11 Moreover he made high places in the hill country of Judah, and led the inhabitants of Jerusalem into unfaithfulness, and made Judah go astray. [12]A letter came to him from the prophet E·lī´jah, saying: "Thus says the LORD, the God of your father David: Because you have not walked in the ways of your father Je·hosh´a·phat or in the ways of King Asa of Judah, [13]but have walked in the way of the kings of Israel, and have led Judah and the inhabitants of Jerusalem into unfaithfulness, as the house of A´hab led Israel into unfaithfulness, and because you also have killed your brothers, members of your father's house, who were better than yourself, [14]see, the LORD will bring a great plague on your people, your children, your wives, and all your possessions, [15]and you yourself will have a severe sickness with a disease of your bowels, until your bowels come out, day after day, because of the disease."

16 The LORD aroused against Je·ho´ram the anger of the Phi·lis´tines and of the Arabs who are near the Ethiopians.[t] [17]They came up against Judah, invaded it, and carried away all the possessions they found that belonged to the king's house, along with his sons and his wives, so that no son was left to him except Je·ho´a·haz, his youngest son.

Disease and Death of Jehoram

18 After all this the LORD struck him in his bowels with an incurable disease. [19]In course of time, at the end of two years, his bowels came out because of the disease, and he died in great agony. His people made no fire in his honor, like the fires made for his ancestors. [20]He was thirty-two years old when he began to reign; he reigned eight years in Jerusalem. He departed with no one's regret. They buried him in the city of David, but not in the tombs of the kings.

Ahaziah's Reign

22 The inhabitants of Jerusalem made his youngest son A·ha·zī´ah king as his successor; for the troops who came with the Arabs to the camp had killed all the older sons. So A·ha·zī´ah son of Je·ho´ram reigned as king of Judah. [2]A·ha·zī´ah was forty-two years old when he began to reign; he reigned one year in

[s] Gk Syr: Heb *Israel*   [t] Or *Nubians*; Heb *Cushites*

Jerusalem. His mother's name was Ath·a·lī´ah, a granddaughter of Om´rī. ³He also walked in the ways of the house of Ā´hab, for his mother was his counselor in doing wickedly. ⁴He did what was evil in the sight of the LORD, as the house of Ā´hab had done; for after the death of his father they were his counselors, to his ruin. ⁵He even followed their advice, and went with Je·hō´ram son of King Ā´hab of Israel to make war against King Haz´a·el of Ar´am at Rā´moth-gil´ē·ad. The Ar·a·mē´ans wounded Jō´ram, ⁶and he returned to be healed in Jez´rē·el of the wounds that he had received at Rā´mah, when he fought King Haz´a·el of Ar´am. And A·ha·zī´ah son of King Je·hō´ram of Judah went down to see Jō´ram son of Ā´hab in Jez´rē·el, because he was sick.

7 But it was ordained by God that the downfall of A·ha·zī´ah should come about through his going to visit Jō´ram. For when he came there he went out with Je·hō´ram to meet Jē´hū son of Nim´shī, whom the LORD had anointed to destroy the house of Ā´hab. ⁸When Jē´hū was executing judgment on the house of Ā´hab, he met the officials of Judah and the sons of A·ha·zī´ah's brothers, who attended A·ha·zī´ah, and he killed them. ⁹He searched for A·ha·zī´ah, who was captured while hiding in Sa·mār´i·a and was brought to Jē´hū, and put to death. They buried him, for they said, "He is the grandson of Je·hosh´a·phat, who sought the LORD with all his heart." And the house of A·ha·zī´ah had no one able to rule the kingdom.

Athaliah Seizes the Throne

10 Now when Ath·a·lī´ah, A·ha·zī´ah's mother, saw that her son was dead, she set about to destroy all the royal family of the house of Judah. ¹¹But Jē·hō·shab´e·ath, the king's daughter, took Jō´ash son of A·ha·zī´ah, and stole him away from among the king's children who were about to be killed; she put him and his nurse in a bedroom. Thus Jē·hō·shab´-

e·ath, daughter of King Je·hō´ram and wife of the priest Je·hoi´a·da—because she was a sister of A·ha·zī´ah—hid him from Ath·a·lī´ah, so that she did not kill him; ¹²he remained with them six years, hidden in the house of God, while Ath·a·lī´ah reigned over the land.

23 But in the seventh year Je·hoi´a·da took courage, and entered into a compact with the commanders of the hundreds, Az·a·rī´ah son of Je·rō´ham, Ish´ma·el son of Jē·hō·hā´nan, Az·a·rī´ah son of Ō´bed, Mā·a·sēi´ah son of A·dāi´ah, and El·i·shā´phat son of Zich´rī. ²They went around through Judah and gathered the Lē´vītes from all the towns of Judah, and the heads of families of Israel, and they came to Jerusalem. ³Then the whole assembly made a covenant with the king in the house of God. Je·hoi´a·daᵘ said to them, "Here is the king's son! Let him reign, as the LORD promised concerning the sons of David. ⁴This is what you are to do: one third of you, priests and Lē´vītes, who come on duty on the sabbath, shall be gatekeepers, ⁵one third shall be at the king's house, and one third at the Gate of the Foundation; and all the people shall be in the courts of the house of the LORD. ⁶Do not let anyone enter the house of the LORD except the priests and ministering Lē´vītes; they may enter, for they are holy, but all the otherᵛ people shall observe the instructions of the LORD. ⁷The Lē´vītes shall surround the king, each with his weapons in his hand; and whoever enters the house shall be killed. Stay with the king in his comings and goings."

Joash Crowned King

8 The Lē´vītes and all Judah did according to all that the priest Je·hoi´a·da commanded; each brought his men, who were to come on duty on the sabbath, with those who were to go off duty on the sabbath; for the priest Je·hoi´a·da

ᵘ Heb *He*   ᵛ Heb lacks *other*

did not dismiss the divisions. ⁹The priest Je·hoi′a·da delivered to the captains the spears and the large and small shields that had been King David's, which were in the house of God; ¹⁰and he set all the people as a guard for the king, everyone with weapon in hand, from the south side of the house to the north side of the house, around the altar and the house. ¹¹Then he brought out the king's son, put the crown on him, and gave him the covenant;ʷ they proclaimed him king, and Je·hoi′a·da and his sons anointed him; and they shouted, "Long live the king!"

Athaliah Murdered

12 When Ath·a·lī′ah heard the noise of the people running and praising the king, she went into the house of the LORD to the people; ¹³and when she looked, there was the king standing by his pillar at the entrance, and the captains and the trumpeters beside the king, and all the people of the land rejoicing and blowing trumpets, and the singers with their musical instruments leading in the celebration. Ath·a·lī′ah tore her clothes, and cried, "Treason! Treason!" ¹⁴Then the priest Je·hoi′a·da brought out the captains who were set over the army, saying to them, "Bring her out between the ranks; anyone who follows her is to be put to the sword." For the priest said, "Do not put her to death in the house of the LORD." ¹⁵So they laid hands on her; she went into the entrance of the Horse Gate of the king's house, and there they put her to death.

16 Je·hoi′a·da made a covenant between himself and all the people and the king that they should be the LORD's people. ¹⁷Then all the people went to the house of Bā′al, and tore it down; his altars and his images they broke in pieces, and they killed Mat′tan, the priest of Bā′al, in front of the altars. ¹⁸Je·hoi′-a·da assigned the care of the house of the LORD to the levitical priests whom David had organized to be in charge of the house of the LORD, to offer burnt offerings to the LORD, as it is written in the

law of Moses, with rejoicing and with singing, according to the order of David. ¹⁹He stationed the gatekeepers at the gates of the house of the LORD so that no one should enter who was in any way unclean. ²⁰And he took the captains, the nobles, the governors of the people, and all the people of the land, and they brought the king down from the house of the LORD, marching through the upper gate to the king's house. They set the king on the royal throne. ²¹So all the people of the land rejoiced, and the city was quiet after Ath·a·lī′ah had been killed with the sword.

Joash Repairs the Temple

24 Jō′ash was seven years old when he began to reign; he reigned forty years in Jerusalem; his mother's name was Zib′i·ah of Bē′er-shē′-ba. ²Jō′ash did what was right in the sight of the LORD all the days of the priest Je·hoi′a·da. ³Je·hoi′a·da got two wives for him, and he became the father of sons and daughters.

4 Some time afterward Jō′ash decided to restore the house of the LORD. ⁵He assembled the priests and the Lē′vītes and said to them, "Go out to the cities of Judah and gather money from all Israel to repair the house of your God, year by year; and see that you act quickly." But the Lē′vītes did not act quickly. ⁶So the king summoned Je·hoi′a·da the chief, and said to him, "Why have you not required the Lē′vītes to bring in from Judah and Jerusalem the tax levied by Moses, the servant of the LORD, onˣ the congregation of Israel for the tent of the covenant?"ʷ ⁷For the children of Ath·a·lī′-ah, that wicked woman, had broken into the house of God, and had even used all the dedicated things of the house of the LORD for the Bā′als.

8 So the king gave command, and they made a chest, and set it outside the gate of the house of the LORD. ⁹A procla-

---

ʷ Or *treaty*, or *testimony*; Heb *eduth*   ˣ Compare Vg: Heb *and* mation was made throughout Judah and Jerusalem to bring in for the LORD the tax that Moses the servant of God laid on Israel in the wilderness. [10]All the leaders and all the people rejoiced and brought their tax and dropped it into the chest until it was full. [11]Whenever the chest was brought to the king's officers by the Lē´vī tes, when they saw that there was a large amount of money in it, the king's secretary and the officer of the chief priest would come and empty the chest and take it and return it to its place. So they did day after day, and collected money in abundance. [12]The king and Je·hoi´a·da gave it to those who had charge of the work of the house of the LORD, and they hired masons and carpenters to restore the house of the LORD, and also workers in iron and bronze to repair the house of the LORD. [13]So those who were engaged in the work labored, and the repairing went forward at their hands, and they restored the house of God to its proper condition and strengthened it. [14]When they had finished, they brought the rest of the money to the king and Je·hoi´a·da, and with it were made utensils for the house of the LORD, utensils for the service and for the burnt offerings, and ladles, and vessels of gold and silver. They offered burnt offerings in the house of the LORD regularly all the days of Je·hoi´a·da.

Apostasy of Joash

15 But Je·hoi´a·da grew old and full of days, and died; he was one hundred thirty years old at his death. [16]And they buried him in the city of David among the kings, because he had done good in Israel, and for God and his house.

17 Now after the death of Je·hoi´a·da the officials of Judah came and did obeisance to the king; then the king listened to them. [18]They abandoned the house of the LORD, the God of their ancestors, and served the sacred poles[y] and the idols. And wrath came upon Judah and Jerusalem for this guilt of theirs. [19]Yet he sent prophets among them to bring them back to the LORD; they testified against them, but they would not listen.

20 Then the spirit of God took possession of[z] Zech·a·rī´ah son of the priest Je·hoi´a·da; he stood above the people and said to them, "Thus says God: Why do you transgress the commandments of the LORD, so that you cannot prosper? Because you have forsaken the LORD, he has also forsaken you." [21]But they conspired against him, and by command of the king they stoned him to death in the court of the house of the LORD. [22]King Jō´ash did not remember the kindness that Je·hoi´-a·da, Zech·a·rī´ah's father, had shown him, but killed his son. As he was dying, he said, "May the LORD see and avenge!"

Death of Joash

23 At the end of the year the army of Ar´am came up against Jō´ash. They came to Judah and Jerusalem, and destroyed all the officials of the people from among them, and sent all the booty they took to the king of Damascus. [24]Although the army of Ar´am had come with few men, the LORD delivered into their hand a very great army, because they had abandoned the LORD, the God of their ancestors. Thus they executed judgment on Jō´ash.

25 When they had withdrawn, leaving him severely wounded, his servants conspired against him because of the blood of the son[a] of the priest Je·hoi´-a·da, and they killed him on his bed. So he died; and they buried him in the city of David, but they did not bury him in the tombs of the kings. [26]Those who conspired against him were Zā´bad son of Shim´ē·ath the Am´mon·īte, and Je·hō´za·bad son of Shim´rith the Mō´ab·īte. [27]Accounts of his sons, and of the many oracles against him, and of the rebuild-ing[b] of the house of God are written in the Commentary on the Book of the Kings. And his son Am·a·zī´ah succeeded him.

[y] Heb *Asherim*   [z] Heb *clothed itself with*   [a] Gk Vg: Heb *sons*   [b] Heb *founding*

Reign of Amaziah

25 Am·a·zi´ah was twenty-five years old when he began to reign, and he reigned twenty-nine years in Jerusalem. His mother's name was Jē·hō·ad´-dan of Jerusalem. [2]He did what was right in the sight of the LORD, yet not with a true heart. [3]As soon as the royal power was firmly in his hand he killed his servants who had murdered his father the king. [4]But he did not put their children to death, according to what is written in the law, in the book of Moses, where the LORD commanded, "The parents shall not be put to death for the children, or the children be put to death for the parents; but all shall be put to death for their own sins."

Slaughter of the Edomites

[5]Am·a·zi´ah assembled the people of Judah, and set them by ancestral houses under commanders of the thousands and of the hundreds for all Judah and Benjamin. He mustered those twenty years old and upward, and found that they were three hundred thousand picked troops fit for war, able to handle spear and shield. [6]He also hired one hundred thousand mighty warriors from Israel for one hundred talents of silver. [7]But a man of God came to him and said, "O king, do not let the army of Israel go with you, for the LORD is not with Israel—all these Ē´phra·im·ites. [8]Rather, go by yourself and act; be strong in battle, or God will fling you down before the enemy; for God has power to help or to overthrow." [9]Am·a·zi´ah said to the man of God, "But what shall we do about the hundred talents that I have given to the army of Israel?" The man of God answered, "The LORD is able to give you much more than this." [10]Then Am·a·zi´ah discharged the army that had come to him from Ē´phra·im, letting them go home again. But they became very angry with Judah, and returned home in fierce anger.

[11]Am·a·zi´ah took courage, and led out his people; he went to the Valley of Salt, and struck down ten thousand men of Sē´ir. [12]The people of Judah captured another ten thousand alive, took them to the top of Sē´la, and threw them down from the top of Sē´la, so that all of them were dashed to pieces. [13]But the men of the army whom Am·a·zi´ah sent back, not letting them go with him to battle, fell on the cities of Judah from Sa·mār´i·a to Beth-hō´ron; they killed three thousand people in them, and took much booty.

[14]Now after Am·a·zi´ah came from the slaughter of the Ē´dom·ītes, he brought the gods of the people of Sē´ir, set them up as his gods, and worshiped them, making offerings to them. [15]The LORD was angry with Am·a·zi´ah and sent to him a prophet, who said to him, "Why have you resorted to a people's gods who could not deliver their own people from your hand?" [16]But as he was speaking the king[c] said to him, "Have we made you a royal counselor? Stop! Why should you be put to death?" So the prophet stopped, but said, "I know that God has determined to destroy you, because you have done this and have not listened to my advice."

Israel Defeats Judah

[17]Then King Am·a·zi´ah of Judah took counsel and sent to King Jō´ash son of Je·hō´a·haz son of Jē´hū of Israel, saying, "Come, let us look one another in the face." [18]King Jō´ash of Israel sent word to King Am·a·zi´ah of Judah, "A thornbush on Lebanon sent to a cedar on Lebanon, saying, 'Give your daughter to my son for a wife'; but a wild animal of Lebanon passed by and trampled down the thorn bush. [19]You say, 'See, I have defeated Ē´dom,' and your heart has lifted you up in boastfulness. Now stay at home; why should you provoke trouble so that you fall, you and Judah with you?"

[c] Heb *he*

Uzziah was king of the southern kingdom of Judah from 783-742 BC. He is also called Azariah. Azariah may have been his personal name and Uzziah his throne name. He was sixteen years old when he became king. Uzziah was a strong ruler, adding to Judah's defenses and agricultural wealth. After he came down with leprosy, his son Jotham ruled in his place.

20 But Am·a·zī´ah would not listen—it was God's doing, in order to hand them over, because they had sought the gods of Ē´dom. ²¹So King Jō´ash of Israel went up; he and King Am·a·zī´ah of Judah faced one another in battle at Beth-shē´mesh, which belongs to Judah. ²²Judah was defeated by Israel; everyone fled home. ²³King Jō´ash of Israel captured King Am·a·zī´ah of Judah, son of Jō´ash, son of A·ha·zī´ah, at Beth-shē´-mesh; he brought him to Jerusalem, and broke down the wall of Jerusalem from the Ē´phra·im Gate to the Corner Gate, a distance of four hundred cubits. ²⁴He seized all the gold and silver, and all the vessels that were found in the house of God, and Ō´bed-ē´dom with them; he seized also the treasuries of the king's house, also hostages; then he returned to Sa·mār´i·a.

Death of Amaziah

25 King Am·a·zī´ah son of Jō´ash of Judah, lived fifteen years after the death of King Jō´ash son of Je·hō´a·haz of Israel. ²⁶Now the rest of the deeds of Am·a·zī´ah, from first to last, are they not written in the Book of the Kings of Judah and Israel?

"As long as he sought the Lord, God made him prosper." 2 Chronicles 26:5*b*

²⁷From the time that Am·a·zī´ah turned away from the LORD they made a conspiracy against him in Jerusalem, and he fled to Lā´chish. But they sent after him to Lā´chish, and killed him there. ²⁸They brought him back on horses; he was buried with his ancestors in the city of David.

Reign of Uzziah

26 Then all the people of Judah took Uz·zī´ah, who was sixteen years old, and made him king to succeed his father Am·a·zī´ah. ²He rebuilt Ē´loth and restored it to Judah, after the king slept with his ancestors. ³Uz·zī´ah was sixteen years old when he began to reign, and he reigned fifty-two years in Jerusalem. His mother's name was Jec·o·lī´ah of Jerusalem. ⁴He did what was right in the sight of the LORD, just as his father Am·a·zī´ah had done. ⁵He set himself to seek God in the days of Zech·a·rī´ah, who instructed him in the fear of God; and as long as he sought the LORD, God made him prosper.

6 He went out and made war against the Phi·lis´tines, and broke down the wall of Gath and the wall of Jab´neh and the wall of Ash´dod; he built cities in the territory of Ash´dod and elsewhere among the Phi·lis´tines. ⁷God helped him against the Phi·lis´tines, against the Arabs who lived in Gur-bā´al, and against the Me·ū´nītes. ⁸The Am´mon·ītes paid tribute to Uz·zī´ah, and his fame spread even to the border of Egypt, for he became very strong. ⁹Moreover Uz·zī´ah built towers in Jerusalem at the Corner Gate, at the Valley Gate, and at the Angle, and fortified them. ¹⁰He built towers in the wilderness and hewed out many cisterns, for he had large herds, both in the She·phē´lah and in the plain, and he had farmers and vinedressers in the hills and in the fertile lands, for he loved the soil. ¹¹Moreover Uz·zī´ah had an army of soldiers, fit for war, in divisions according to the numbers in the

muster made by the secretary Je·ĭ´el and the officer Mā·a·sēi´ah, under the direction of Han·a·nī´ah, one of the king's commanders. [12]The whole number of the heads of ancestral houses of mighty warriors was two thousand six hundred. [13]Under their command was an army of three hundred seven thousand five hundred, who could make war with mighty power, to help the king against the enemy. [14]Uz·zī´ah provided for all the army the shields, spears, helmets, coats of mail, bows, and stones for slinging. [15]In Jerusalem he set up machines, invented by skilled workers, on the towers and the corners for shooting arrows and large stones. And his fame spread far, for he was marvelously helped until he became strong.

Pride and Apostasy

16 But when he had become strong he grew proud, to his destruction. For he was false to the LORD his God, and entered the temple of the LORD to make offering on the altar of incense. [17]But the priest Az·a·rī´ah went in after him, with eighty priests of the LORD who were men of valor; [18]they withstood King Uz·zī´ah, and said to him, "It is not for you, Uz·zī´ah, to make offering to the LORD, but for the priests the descendants of Aaron, who are consecrated to make offering. Go out of the sanctuary; for you have done wrong, and it will bring you no honor from the LORD God." [19]Then Uz·zī´ah was angry. Now he had a censer in his hand to make offering, and when he became angry with the priests a leprous[d] disease broke out on his forehead, in the presence of the priests in the house of the LORD, by the altar of incense. [20]When the chief priest Az·a·rī´ah, and all the priests, looked at him, he was leprous[d] in his forehead. They hurried him out, and he himself hurried to get out, because the LORD had struck him. [21]King Uz·zī´ah was leprous[d] to the day of his death, and being leprous[d] lived in a separate house, for he was excluded from the house of the LORD. His son Jō´tham was in charge of the palace of the king, governing the people of the land.

22 Now the rest of the acts of Uz·zī´ah, from first to last, the prophet Ĭ·sāi´ah son of Ā´moz wrote. [23]Uz·zī´ah slept with his ancestors; they buried him near his ancestors in the burial field that belonged to the kings, for they said, "He is leprous."[d] His son Jō´tham succeeded him.

Reign of Jotham

27 Jō´tham was twenty-five years old when he began to reign; he reigned sixteen years in Jerusalem. His mother's name was Je·rū´shah daughter of Zā´dok. [2]He did what was right in the sight of the LORD just as his father Uz·zī´ah had done—only he did not invade the temple of the LORD. But the people still followed corrupt practices. [3]He built the upper gate of the house of the LORD, and did extensive building on the wall of Ō´phel. [4]Moreover he built cities in the hill country of Judah, and forts and towers on the wooded hills. [5]He fought with the king of the Am´mon·ites and prevailed against them. The Am´mon·ites gave him that year one hundred talents of silver, ten thousand cors of wheat and ten thousand of barley. The Am´mon·ites paid him the same amount in the second and the third years. [6]So Jō´tham became strong because he ordered his ways before the LORD his God. [7]Now the rest of the acts of Jō´tham, and all his wars and his ways, are written in the Book of the Kings of Israel and Judah. [8]He was twenty-five years old when he began to reign; he reigned sixteen years in Jerusalem. [9]Jō´tham slept with his ancestors, and they buried him in the city of David; and his son Ā´haz succeeded him.

Reign of Ahaz

28 Ā´haz was twenty years old when he began to reign; he reigned sixteen years in Jerusalem. He

[d] A term for several skin diseases; precise meaning uncertain

did not do what was right in the sight of the LORD, as his ancestor David had done, [2]but he walked in the ways of the kings of Israel. He even made cast images for the Ba'als; [3]and he made offerings in the valley of the son of Hin'nom, and made his sons pass through fire, according to the abominable practices of the nations whom the LORD drove out before the people of Israel. [4]He sacrificed and made offerings on the high places, on the hills, and under every green tree.

Aram and Israel Defeat Judah

5 Therefore the LORD his God gave him into the hand of the king of Ar'am, who defeated him and took captive a great number of his people and brought them to Damascus. He was also given into the hand of the king of Israel, who defeated him with great slaughter. [6]Pe'-kah son of Rem·a·li'ah killed one hundred twenty thousand in Judah in one day, all of them valiant warriors, because they had abandoned the LORD, the God of their ancestors. [7]And Zich'ri, a mighty warrior of E'phra·im, killed the king's son Ma·a·sei'ah, Az·ri'kam the commander of the palace, and El·ka'nah the next in authority to the king.

Intervention of Oded

8 The people of Israel took captive two hundred thousand of their kin, women, sons, and daughters; they also took much booty from them and brought the booty to Sa·mar'i·a. [9]But a prophet of the LORD was there, whose name was O'ded; he went out to meet the army that came to Sa·mar'i·a, and said to them, "Because the LORD, the God of your ancestors, was angry with Judah, he gave them into your hand, but you have killed them in a rage that has reached up to heaven. [10]Now you intend to subjugate the people of Judah and Jerusalem, male and female, as your slaves. But what have you except sins against the LORD your God? [11]Now hear

me, and send back the captives whom you have taken from your kindred, for the fierce wrath of the LORD is upon you." [12]Moreover, certain chiefs of the E'phra·im·ites, Az·a·ri'ah son of Jo·ha'-nan, Ber·e·chi'ah son of Me·shil'le·moth, Je·hiz·ki'ah son of Shal'lum, and A·ma'sa son of Had'lai, stood up against those who were coming from the war, [13]and said to them, "You shall not bring the captives in here, for you propose to bring on us guilt against the LORD in addition to our present sins and guilt. For our guilt is already great, and there is fierce wrath against Israel." [14]So the warriors left the captives and the booty before the officials and all the assembly. [15]Then those who were mentioned by name got up and took the captives, and with the booty they clothed all that were naked among them; they clothed them, gave them sandals, provided them with food and drink, and anointed them; and carrying all the feeble among them on donkeys, they brought them to their kindred at Jericho, the city of palm trees. Then they returned to Sa·mar'i·a.

Assyria Refuses to Help Judah

16 At that time King A'haz sent to the king[e] of Assyria for help. [17]For the E'dom·ites had again invaded and defeated Judah, and carried away captives. [18]And the Phi·lis'tines had made raids on the cities in the She·phe'lah and the Ne'geb of Judah, and had taken Beth-she'mesh, Ai'ja·lon, Ge·de'roth, So'-co with its villages, Tim'nah with its villages, and Gim'zo with its villages; and they settled there. [19]For the LORD brought Judah low because of King A'haz of Israel, for he had behaved without restraint in Judah and had been faithless to the LORD. [20]So King Til'gath-pil·ne'ser of Assyria came against him, and oppressed him instead of strengthening him. [21]For A'haz plundered the house of the LORD and the houses of the king

[e] Gk Syr Vg Compare 2 Kings 16.7: Heb *kings*

and of the officials, and gave tribute to the king of Assyria; but it did not help him.

Apostasy and Death of Ahaz

22 In the time of his distress he became yet more faithless to the LORD— this same King Ā´haz. ²³For he sacrificed to the gods of Damascus, which had defeated him, and said, "Because the gods of the kings of Ar´am helped them, I will sacrifice to them so that they may help me." But they were the ruin of him, and of all Israel. ²⁴Ā´haz gathered together the utensils of the house of God, and cut in pieces the utensils of the house of God. He shut up the doors of the house of the LORD and made himself altars in every corner of Jerusalem. ²⁵In every city of Judah he made high places to make offerings to other gods, provoking to anger the LORD, the God of his ancestors. ²⁶Now the rest of his acts and all his ways, from first to last, are written in the Book of the Kings of Judah and Israel. ²⁷Ā´haz slept with his ancestors, and they buried him in the city, in Jerusalem; but they did not bring him into the tombs of the kings of Israel. His son Hez·e·kī´ah succeeded him.

Reign of Hezekiah

29 Hez·e·kī´ah began to reign when he was twenty-five years old; he reigned twenty-nine years in Jerusalem. His mother's name was A·bī´jah daughter of Zech·a·rī´ah. ²He did what was right in the sight of the LORD, just as his ancestor David had done.

The Temple Cleansed

3 In the first year of his reign, in the first month, he opened the doors of the house of the LORD and repaired them. ⁴He brought in the priests and the Lē´vītes and assembled them in the square on the east. ⁵He said to them, "Listen to me, Lē´vītes! Sanctify yourselves, and sanctify the house of the LORD, the God of your ancestors, and carry out the filth from the holy place. ⁶For our ancestors have

been unfaithful and have done what was evil in the sight of the LORD our God; they have forsaken him, and have turned away their faces from the dwelling of the LORD, and turned their backs. ⁷They also shut the doors of the vestibule and put out the lamps, and have not offered incense or made burnt offerings in the holy place to the God of Israel. ⁸Therefore the wrath of the LORD came upon Judah and Jerusalem, and he has made them an object of horror, of astonishment, and of hissing, as you see with your own eyes. ⁹Our fathers have fallen by the sword and our sons and our daughters and our wives are in captivity for this. ¹⁰Now it is in my heart to make a covenant with the LORD, the God of Israel, so that his fierce anger may turn away from us. ¹¹My sons, do not now be negligent, for the LORD has chosen you to stand in his presence to minister to him, and to be his ministers and make offerings to him."

12 Then the Lē´vītes arose, Mā´hath son of A·mā´saī, and Jō´el son of Az·a·rī´-ah, of the sons of the Kō´hath·ītes; and of the sons of Me·rar´ī, Kish son of Ab´dī, and Az·a·rī´ah son of Je·hal´le·lel; and of the Ger´shon·ītes, Jō´ah son of Zim´mah, and Eden son of Jō´ah; ¹³and of the sons of E·li·zā´phan, Shim´rī and Je·ū´el; and of the sons of Ā´saph, Zech·a·rī´ah and Mat·ta·nī´ah; ¹⁴and of the sons of Hē´man, Jē·hū´el and Shim´ē·ī; and of the sons of Je·dū´thun, She·māi´ah and Uz´zi·el. ¹⁵They gathered their brothers, sanctified themselves, and went in as the king had commanded, by the words of the LORD, to cleanse the house of the LORD. ¹⁶The priests went into the inner part of the house of the LORD to cleanse it, and they brought out all the unclean things that they found in the temple of the LORD into the court of the house of the LORD; and the Lē´vītes took them and carried them out to the Wadi Kid´ron. ¹⁷They began to sanctify on the first day of the first month, and on the eighth day

of the month they came to the vestibule of the LORD; then for eight days they sanctified the house of the LORD, and on the sixteenth day of the first month they finished. ¹⁸Then they went inside to King Hez·e·kī´ah and said, "We have cleansed all the house of the LORD, the altar of burnt offering and all its utensils, and the table for the rows of bread and all its utensils. ¹⁹All the utensils that King Ā´haz repudiated during his reign when he was faithless, we have made ready and sanctified; see, they are in front of the altar of the LORD."

Temple Worship Restored

20 Then King Hez·e·kī´ah rose early, assembled the officials of the city, and went up to the house of the LORD. ²¹They brought seven bulls, seven rams, seven lambs, and seven male goats for a sin offering for the kingdom and for the sanctuary and for Judah. He commanded the priests the descendants of Aaron to offer them on the altar of the LORD. ²²So they slaughtered the bulls, and the priests received the blood and dashed it against the altar; they slaughtered the rams and their blood was dashed against the altar; they also slaughtered the lambs and their blood was dashed against the altar. ²³Then the male goats for the sin offering were brought to the king and the assembly; they laid their hands on them, ²⁴and the priests slaughtered them and made a sin offering with their blood at the altar, to make atonement for all Israel. For the king commanded that the burnt offering and the sin offering should be made for all Israel.

25 He stationed the Lē´vītes in the house of the LORD with cymbals, harps, and lyres, according to the commandment of David and of Gad the king's seer and of the prophet Nathan, for the commandment was from the LORD through his prophets. ²⁶The Lē´vītes stood with the instruments of David, and the priests with the trumpets. ²⁷Then Hez·e·kī´ah

Draw a picture of your church, and then compare it to the picture of the Temple at the beginning of First Kings. In what ways do they look alike? In what ways are they different? The church is a special place to worship God, but we know also that God is everywhere. We can worship God at any time and in any place. Hang up your picture in your room to remind you to be thankful to God who always cares for us.

commanded that the burnt offering be offered on the altar. When the burnt offering began, the song to the LORD began also, and the trumpets, accompanied by the instruments of King David of Israel. ²⁸The whole assembly worshiped, the singers sang, and the trumpeters sounded; all this continued until the burnt offering was finished. ²⁹When the offering was finished, the king and all who were present with him bowed down and worshiped. ³⁰King Hez·e·kī´ah and the officials commanded the Lē´vītes to sing praises to the LORD with the words of David and of the seer Ā´saph. They sang praises with gladness, and they bowed down and worshiped.

31 Then Hez·e·kī´ah said, "You have now consecrated yourselves to the LORD; come near, bring sacrifices and thank offerings to the house of the LORD." The assembly brought sacrifices and thank offerings; and all who were of a willing heart brought burnt offerings. ³²The number of the burnt offerings that the assembly brought was seventy bulls, one hundred rams, and two hundred lambs; all these were for a burnt offering to the LORD. ³³The consecrated offerings were six hundred bulls and three thousand sheep. ³⁴But the priests were too few and could not skin all the burnt offerings, so, until other priests had sanctified them-

Hezekiah commanded the priests to make a sin offering for all Israel. As the priests gave sacrifices, the people praised and worshiped God with gladness. Hezekiah told them that they were consecrated (which means set apart) for the Lord. He asked them to bring thank offerings to the Temple. The people were so joyful that they brought more sacrifices than the priests could handle! The priests asked the Levites for help with the sacrifices. All the people rejoiced and praised God for God's goodness.

selves, their kindred, the Lē´vītes, helped them until the work was finished—for the Lē´vītes were more conscientious[/] than the priests in sanctifying themselves. [35]Besides the great number of burnt offerings there was the fat of the offerings of well-being, and there were the drink offerings for the burnt offerings. Thus the service of the house of the LORD was restored. [36]And Hez·e·kī´ah and all the people rejoiced because of what God had done for the people; for the thing had come about suddenly.

The Great Passover

30 Hez·e·kī´ah sent word to all Israel and Judah, and wrote letters also to Ē´phra·im and Ma·nas´seh, that they should come to the house of the LORD at Jerusalem, to keep the passover to the LORD the God of Israel. [2]For the king and his officials and all the assembly in Jerusalem had taken counsel to keep the passover in the second month [3](for they could not keep it at its proper time because the priests had not sanctified themselves in sufficient number, nor had the people assembled in Jerusalem). [4]The plan seemed right to the king and all the assembly. [5]So they decreed to make a proclamation through-

out all Israel, from Bē´er-shē´ba to Dan, that the people should come and keep the passover to the LORD the God of Israel, at Jerusalem; for they had not kept it in great numbers as prescribed. [6]So couriers went throughout all Israel and Judah with letters from the king and his officials, as the king had commanded, saying, "O people of Israel, return to the LORD, the God of Abraham, Isaac, and Israel, so that he may turn again to the remnant of you who have escaped from the hand of the kings of Assyria. [7]Do not be like your ancestors and your kindred, who were faithless to the LORD God of their ancestors, so that he made them a desolation, as you see. [8]Do not now be stiff-necked as your ancestors were, but yield yourselves to the LORD and come to his sanctuary, which he has sanctified forever, and serve the LORD your God, so that his fierce anger may turn away from you. [9]For as you return to the LORD, your kindred and your children will find compassion with their captors, and return to this land. For the LORD your God is gracious and merciful, and will not turn away his face from you, if you return to him."

10 So the couriers went from city to

Sometimes God's people behaved in ways that God did not want them to. They were rebellious and stubborn. They chose not to follow God. When this happened, the prophets called the people "stiff-necked." The word "stiff-necked" came from they way that oxen sometimes refused to turn their necks when they were given direction. What about you? Do you try your best to do what God wants you to do? What are some ways you can choose to follow God?

[/] Heb upright in heart

city through the country of Ē′phra·im and Ma·nas′seh, and as far as Zeb′ū·lun; but they laughed them to scorn, and mocked them. ¹¹Only a few from Ash′er, Ma·nas′seh, and Zeb′ū·lun humbled themselves and came to Jerusalem. ¹²The hand of God was also on Judah to give them one heart to do what the king and the officials commanded by the word of the LORD.

13 Many people came together in Jerusalem to keep the festival of unleavened bread in the second month, a very large assembly. ¹⁴They set to work and removed the altars that were in Jerusalem, and all the altars for offering incense they took away and threw into the Wadi Kid′ron. ¹⁵They slaughtered the passover lamb on the fourteenth day of the second month. The priests and the Lē′vītes were ashamed, and they sanctified themselves and brought burnt offerings into the house of the LORD. ¹⁶They took their accustomed posts according to the law of Moses the man of God; the priests dashed the blood that they received^g from the hands of the Lē′vītes. ¹⁷For there were many in the assembly who had not sanctified themselves; therefore the Lē′vītes had to slaughter the passover lamb for everyone who was not clean, to make it holy to the LORD. ¹⁸For a multitude of the people, many of them from Ē′phra·im, Ma·nas′seh, Is′sa·char, and Zeb′ū·lun, had not cleansed themselves, yet they ate the passover otherwise than as prescribed. But Hez·e·kī′ah prayed for them, saying, "The good LORD pardon all ¹⁹who set their hearts to seek God, the LORD the God of their ancestors, even though not in accordance with the sanctuary's rules of cleanness." ²⁰The LORD heard Hez·e·kī′ah, and healed the people. ²¹The people of Israel who were present at Jerusalem kept the festival of unleavened bread seven days with great gladness; and the Lē′vītes and the priests praised the LORD day by day, accompanied by loud instruments for the LORD.

²²Hez·e·kī′ah spoke encouragingly to all the Lē′vītes who showed good skill in the service of the LORD. So the people ate the food of the festival for seven days, sacrificing offerings of well-being and giving thanks to the LORD the God of their ancestors.

23 Then the whole assembly agreed together to keep the festival for another seven days; so they kept it for another seven days with gladness. ²⁴For King Hez·e·kī′ah of Judah gave the assembly a thousand bulls and seven thousand sheep for offerings, and the officials gave the assembly a thousand bulls and ten thousand sheep. The priests sanctified themselves in great numbers. ²⁵The whole assembly of Judah, the priests and the Lē′vītes, and the whole assembly that came out of Israel, and the resident aliens who came out of the land of Israel, and the resident aliens who lived in Judah, rejoiced. ²⁶There was great joy in Jerusalem, for since the time of Solomon son of King David of Israel there had been nothing like this in Jerusalem. ²⁷Then the priests and the Lē′vītes stood up and blessed the people, and their voice was heard; their prayer came to his holy dwelling in heaven.

Pagan Shrines Destroyed

31 Now when all this was finished, all Israel who were present went out to the cities of Judah and broke down the pillars, hewed down the sacred poles,^h and pulled down the high places and the altars throughout all Judah and Benjamin, and in Ē′phra·im and Ma·nas′seh, until they had destroyed them all. Then all the people of Israel returned to their cities, all to their individual properties.

2 Hez·e·kī′ah appointed the divisions of the priests and of the Lē′vītes, division by division, everyone according to his service, the priests and the Lē′vītes, for burnt offerings and offerings of well-

^g Heb lacks *that they received*   ^h Heb *Asherim*

being, to minister in the gates of the camp of the LORD and to give thanks and praise. ³The contribution of the king from his own possessions was for the burnt offerings: the burnt offerings of morning and evening, and the burnt offerings for the sabbaths, the new moons, and the appointed festivals, as it is written in the law of the LORD. ⁴He commanded the people who lived in Jerusalem to give the portion due to the priests and the Lē´vītes, so that they might devote themselves to the law of the LORD. ⁵As soon as the word spread, the people of Israel gave in abundance the first fruits of grain, wine, oil, honey, and of all the produce of the field; and they brought in abundantly the tithe of everything. ⁶The people of Israel and Judah who lived in the cities of Judah also brought in the tithe of cattle and sheep, and the tithe of the dedicated things that had been consecrated to the LORD their God, and laid them in heaps. ⁷In the third month they began to pile up the heaps, and finished them in the seventh month. ⁸When Hez·e·kī´ah and the officials came and saw the heaps, they blessed the LORD and his people Israel. ⁹Hez·e·kī´ah questioned the priests and the Lē´vītes about the heaps. ¹⁰The chief priest Az·a·rī´ah, who was of the house of Zā´dok, answered him, "Since they began to bring the contributions into the house of the LORD, we have had enough to eat and have plenty to spare; for the LORD has blessed his people, so that we have this great supply left over."

Reorganization of Priests and Levites

11 Then Hez·e·kī´ah commanded them to prepare store-chambers in the house of the LORD; and they prepared them. ¹²Faithfully they brought in the contributions, the tithes and the dedicated things. The chief officer in charge of them was Con·a·nī´ah the Lē´vīte,

with his brother Shim´ē·ī as second; ¹³while Je·hī´el, Az·a·zī´ah, Nā´hath, As´a·hel, Jer´i·moth, Joz´a·bad, E·lī´el, Is·ma·chī´ah, Mā´hath, and Be·nā´i·ah were overseers assisting Con·a·nī´ah and his brother Shim´ē·ī, by the appointment of King Hez·e·kī´ah and of Az·a·rī´ah the chief officer of the house of God. ¹⁴Kō´re son of Im´nah the Lē´vīte, keeper of the east gate, was in charge of the freewill offerings to God, to apportion the contribution reserved for the LORD and the most holy offerings. ¹⁵Eden, Mi·nī´a·min, Jesh´ū·a, She·māi´ah, Am·a·rī´ah, and Shec·a·nī´ah were faithfully assisting him in the cities of the priests, to distribute the portions to their kindred, old and young alike, by divisions, ¹⁶except those enrolled by genealogy, males from three years old and upwards, all who entered the house of the LORD as the duty of each day required, for their service according to their offices, by their divisions. ¹⁷The enrollment of the priests was according to their ancestral houses; that of the Lē´vītes from twenty years old and upwards was according to their offices, by their divisions. ¹⁸The priests were enrolled with all their little children, their wives, their sons, and their daughters, the whole multitude; for they were faithful in keeping themselves holy. ¹⁹And for the descendants of Aaron, the priests, who were in the fields of common land belonging to their towns, town by town, the people designated by name were to distribute portions to every male among the priests and to everyone among the Lē´vītes who was enrolled.

20 Hez·e·kī´ah did this throughout all Judah; he did what was good and right and faithful before the LORD his God. ²¹And every work that he undertook in the service of the house of God, and in accordance with the law and the commandments, to seek his God, he did with all his heart; and he prospered.

Sennacherib's Invasion

32 After these things and these acts of faithfulness, King Sen·ʹnach·eʹrib of Assyria came and invaded Judah and encamped against the fortified cities, thinking to win them for himself. ²When Hez·e·kiʹah saw that Sen·ʹnach·eʹrib had come and intended to fight against Jerusalem, ³he planned with his officers and his warriors to stop the flow of the springs that were outside the city; and they helped him. ⁴A great many people were gathered, and they stopped all the springs and the wadi that flowed through the land, saying, "Why should the Assyrian kings come and find water in abundance?" ⁵Hez·e·kiʹahⁱ set to work resolutely and built up the entire wall that was broken down, and raised towers on it,ʲ and outside it he built another wall; he also strengthened the Milʹlo in the city of David, and made weapons and shields in abundance. ⁶He appointed combat commanders over the people, and gathered them together to him in the square at the gate of the city and spoke encouragingly to them, saying, ⁷"Be strong and of good courage. Do not be afraid or dismayed before the king of Assyria and all the horde that is with him; for there is one greater with us than with him. ⁸With him is an arm of flesh; but with us is the LORD our God, to help us and to fight our battles." The people were encouraged by the words of King Hez·e·kiʹah of Judah.

9 After this, while King Sen·nachʹe·rib of Assyria was at Laʹchish with all his forces, he sent his servants to Jerusalem to King Hez·e·kiʹah of Judah and to all the people of Judah that were in Jerusalem, saying, ¹⁰"Thus says King Sen·nachʹe·rib of Assyria: On what are you relying, that you undergo the siege of Jerusalem? ¹¹Is not Hez·e·kiʹah misleading you, handing you over to die by famine and by thirst, when he tells you, 'The LORD our God will save us from the hand of the king of Assyria'? ¹²Was it not this same Hez·e·kiʹah who took away his high places and his altars and commanded Judah and Jerusalem, saying, 'Before one altar you shall worship, and upon it you shall make your offerings'? ¹³Do you not know what I and my ancestors have done to all the peoples of other lands? Were the gods of the nations of those lands at all able to save their lands out of my hand? ¹⁴Who among all the gods of those nations that my ancestors utterly destroyed was able to save his people from my hand, that your God should be able to save you from my hand? ¹⁵Now therefore do not let Hez·e·kiʹah deceive you or mislead you in this fashion, and do not believe him, for no god of any nation or kingdom has been able to save his people from my hand or from the hand of my ancestors. How much less will your God save you out of my hand!"

16 His servants said still more against the Lord GOD and against his servant Hez·e·kiʹah. ¹⁷He also wrote letters to throw contempt on the LORD the God of Israel and to speak against him, saying, "Just as the gods of the nations in other lands did not rescue their people from my hands, so the God of Hez·e·kiʹah will not rescue his people from my hand." ¹⁸They shouted it with a loud voice in the language of Judah to the people of Jerusalem who were on the wall, to frighten and terrify them, in order that they might take the city. ¹⁹They spoke of the God of Jerusalem as if he were like the gods of the peoples of the earth, which are the work of human hands.

Sennacherib's Defeat and Death

20 Then King Hez·e·kiʹah and the prophet I·saiʹah son of Aʹmoz prayed because of this and cried to heaven. ²¹And the LORD sent an angel who cut off all the mighty warriors and commanders and officers in the camp of the king of Assyria. So he returned in disgrace to his own land. When he came into the house

---

ⁱ Heb *He*   ʲ Vg: Heb *and raised on the towers*

of his god, some of his own sons struck him down there with the sword. [22]So the LORD saved Hez·e·kī´ah and the inhabitants of Jerusalem from the hand of King Sen·nach´e·rib of Assyria and from the hand of all his enemies; he gave them rest[k] on every side. [23]Many brought gifts to the LORD in Jerusalem and precious things to King Hez·e·kī´ah of Judah, so that he was exalted in the sight of all nations from that time onward.

Hezekiah's Sickness

24 In those days Hez·e·kī´ah became sick and was at the point of death. He prayed to the LORD, and he answered him and gave him a sign. [25]But Hez·e·kī´ah did not respond according to the benefit done to him, for his heart was proud. Therefore wrath came upon him and upon Judah and Jerusalem. [26]Then Hez·e·kī´ah humbled himself for the pride of his heart, both he and the inhabitants of Jerusalem, so that the wrath of the LORD did not come upon them in the days of Hez·e·kī´ah.

Hezekiah's Prosperity and Achievements

27 Hez·e·kī´ah had very great riches and honor; and he made for himself treasuries for silver, for gold, for precious stones, for spices, for shields, and for all kinds of costly objects; [28]storehouses also for the yield of grain, wine, and oil; and stalls for all kinds of cattle, and sheepfolds.[l] [29]He likewise provided cities for himself, and flocks and herds in abundance; for God had given him very great possessions. [30]This same Hez·e·kī´ah closed the upper outlet of the waters of Gī´hon and directed them down to the west side of the city of David. Hez·e·kī´ah prospered in all his works. [31]So also in the matter of the envoys of the officials of Babylon, who had been sent to him to inquire about the sign that had been done in the land, God left him to himself, in order to test him and to know all that was in his heart.

32 Now the rest of the acts of Hez·e·kī´ah,

and his good deeds, are written in the vision of the prophet Ī·sāi´ah son of Ā´moz in the Book of the Kings of Judah and Israel. [33]Hez·e·kī´ah slept with his ancestors, and they buried him on the ascent to the tombs of the descendants of David; and all Judah and the inhabitants of Jerusalem did him honor at his death. His son Ma·nas´seh succeeded him.

Reign of Manasseh

33 Ma·nas´seh was twelve years old when he began to reign; he reigned fifty-five years in Jerusalem. [2]He did what was evil in the sight of the LORD, according to the abominable practices of the nations whom the LORD drove out before the people of Israel. [3]For he rebuilt the high places that his father Hez·e·kī´ah had pulled down, and erected altars to the Bā´als, made sacred poles,[m] worshiped all the host of heaven, and served them. [4]He built altars in the house of the LORD, of which the LORD had said, "In Jerusalem shall my name be forever." [5]He built altars for all the host of heaven in the two courts of the house of the LORD. [6]He made his son pass through fire in the valley of the son of Hin´nom, practiced soothsaying and augury and sorcery, and dealt with mediums and with wizards. He did much evil in the sight of the LORD, provoking him

Many people believed in magical powers and practiced different kinds of magic. They believed that these powers could be set into action by the use of certain words and acts. The laws of the Israelites did not allow magic, and the prophets spoke out against its use. Still, some people practiced magic instead of following God's laws.

[k] Gk Vg: Heb *guided them* [l] Gk Vg: Heb *flocks for folds* [m] Heb *Asheroth*

to anger. [7]The carved image of the idol that he had made he set in the house of God, of which God said to David and to his son Solomon, "In this house, and in Jerusalem, which I have chosen out of all the tribes of Israel, I will put my name forever; [8]I will never again remove the feet of Israel from the land that I appointed for your ancestors, if only they will be careful to do all that I have commanded them, all the law, the statutes, and the ordinances given through Moses." [9]Ma·nas´seh misled Judah and the inhabitants of Jerusalem, so that they did more evil than the nations whom the LORD had destroyed before the people of Israel.

Manasseh Restored after Repentance

10 The LORD spoke to Ma·nas´seh and to his people, but they gave no heed. [11]Therefore the LORD brought against them the commanders of the army of the king of Assyria, who took Ma·nas´seh captive in manacles, bound him with fetters, and brought him to Babylon. [12]While he was in distress he entreated the favor of the LORD his God and humbled himself greatly before the God of his ancestors. [13]He prayed to him, and God received his entreaty, heard his plea, and restored him again to Jerusalem and to his kingdom. Then Ma·nas´seh knew that the LORD indeed was God.

14 Afterward he built an outer wall for the city of David west of Gi´hon, in the valley, reaching the entrance at the Fish Gate; he carried it around O´phel, and raised it to a very great height. He also put commanders of the army in all the fortified cities in Judah. [15]He took away the foreign gods and the idol from the house of the LORD, and all the altars that he had built on the mountain of the house of the LORD and in Jerusalem, and he threw them out of the city. [16]He also restored the altar of the LORD and offered

on it sacrifices of well-being and of thanksgiving; and he commanded Judah to serve the LORD the God of Israel. [17]The people, however, still sacrificed at the high places, but only to the LORD their God.

Death of Manasseh

18 Now the rest of the acts of Ma·nas´-seh, his prayer to his God, and the words of the seers who spoke to him in the name of the LORD God of Israel, these are in the Annals of the Kings of Israel. [19]His prayer, and how God received his entreaty, all his sin and his faithlessness, the sites on which he built high places and set up the sacred poles[n] and the images, before he humbled himself, these are written in the records of the seers.[o] [20]So Ma·nas´seh slept with his ancestors, and they buried him in his house. His son A´mon succeeded him.

Amon's Reign and Death

21 A´mon was twenty-two years old when he began to reign; he reigned two years in Jerusalem. [22]He did what was evil in the sight of the LORD, as his father Ma·nas´seh had done. A´mon sacrificed to all the images that his father Ma·nas´-seh had made, and served them. [23]He did not humble himself before the LORD, as his father Ma·nas´seh had humbled himself, but this A´mon incurred more and more guilt. [24]His servants conspired against him and killed him in his house. [25]But the people of the land killed all those who had conspired against King A´mon; and the people of the land made his son Jo·si´ah king to succeed him.

Reign of Josiah

34 Jo·si´ah was eight years old when he began to reign; he reigned thirty-one years in Jerusalem. [2]He did what was right in the sight of the LORD, and walked in the ways of his ancestor David; he did not turn aside to the right or to the left. [3]For in the eighth

[n] Heb Asherim   [o] One Ms Gk: MT of Hozai

A recorder was a person who gave advice to and kept records for the king. Joah was the recorder when Josiah was king. He went with the secretary, Shaphan, to repair the Temple. During the repairs, the "book of the law" (which is part of the book of Deuteronomy) was found and brought to the king.

year of his reign, while he was still a boy, he began to seek the God of his ancestor David, and in the twelfth year he began to purge Judah and Jerusalem of the high places, the sacred poles,[p] and the carved and the cast images. [4]In his presence they pulled down the altars of the Bā'als; he demolished the incense altars that stood above them. He broke down the sacred poles[p] and the carved and the cast images; he made dust of them and scattered it over the graves of those who had sacrificed to them. [5]He also burned the bones of the priests on their altars, and purged Judah and Jerusalem. [6]In the towns of Ma·nas'seh, Ē'phra·im, and Sim'ē·on, and as far as Naph'ta·lī, in their ruins[q] all around, [7]he broke down the altars, beat the sacred poles[p] and the images into powder, and demolished all the incense altars throughout all the land of Israel. Then he returned to Jerusalem.

Discovery of the Book of the Law

8 In the eighteenth year of his reign, when he had purged the land and the house, he sent Shā'phan son of Az·a·lī'ah, Mā·a·sēī'ah the governor of the city, and Jō'ah son of Jō'a·haz, the recorder, to repair the house of the LORD his God. [9]They came to the high priest Hil·kī'ah and delivered the money that had been brought into the house of God, which the Lē'vītes, the keepers of the threshold, had collected from Man·as'seh and Ē'phra·im

and from all the remnant of Israel and from all Judah and Benjamin and from the inhabitants of Jerusalem. [10]They delivered it to the workers who had the oversight of the house of the LORD, and the workers who were working in the house of the LORD gave it for repairing and restoring the house. [11]They gave it to the carpenters and the builders to buy quarried stone, and timber for binders, and beams for the buildings that the kings of Judah had let go to ruin. [12]The people did the work faithfully. Over them were appointed the Lē'vītes Jā'hath and Ō·ba·dī'ah, of the sons of Me·rar'ī, along with Zech·a·rī'ah and Me·shul'lam, of the sons of the Kō'hath·ītes, to have oversight. Other Lē'vītes, all skillful with instruments of music, [13]were over the burden bearers and directed all who did work in every kind of service; and some of the Lē'vītes were scribes, and officials, and gatekeepers.

14 While they were bringing out the money that had been brought into the house of the LORD, the priest Hil·kī'ah found the book of the law of the LORD given through Moses. [15]Hil·kī'ah said to the secretary Shā'phan, "I have found the book of the law in the house of the LORD"; and Hil·kī'ah gave the book to Shā'phan. [16]Shā'phan brought the book to the king, and further reported to the king, "All that was committed to your servants they are doing. [17]They have emptied out the

A scribe was a person who wrote messages and kept records. The Old Testament scribes became a professional class of men. Scribes came from the families of priests. They probably wrote and gathered together many of Israel's sacred writings that make up the Old Testament we have today.

[p] Heb *Asherim*   [q] Meaning of Heb uncertain

Huldah was a prophet who was a woman. Even though most of the prophets mentioned in the Bible were men, God called both men and women. When the book of the law (which is part of the book of Deuteronomy) had been found in the Temple, King Josiah sent it to her to ask for advice.

money that was found in the house of the LORD and have delivered it into the hand of the overseers and the workers." ¹⁸The secretary Shā´phan informed the king, "The priest Hil·kī´ah has given me a book." Shā´phan then read it aloud to the king.

19 When the king heard the words of the law he tore his clothes. ²⁰Then the king commanded Hil·kī´ah, A·hī´kam son of Shā´phan, Ab´don son of Mī´cah, the secretary Shā´phan, and the king's servant A·sāi´ah: ²¹"Go, inquire of the LORD for me and for those who are left in Israel and in Judah, concerning the words of the book that has been found; for the wrath of the LORD that is poured out on us is great, because our ancestors did not keep the word of the LORD, to act in accordance with all that is written in this book."

The Prophet Huldah Consulted

22 So Hil·kī´ah and those whom the king had sent went to the prophet Hul´dah, the wife of Shal´lum son of Tok´hath son of Has´rah, keeper of the wardrobe (who lived in Jerusalem in the Second Quarter) and spoke to her to that effect. ²³She declared to them, "Thus says the LORD, the God of Israel: Tell the man who sent you to me, ²⁴Thus says the LORD: I will indeed bring disaster upon this place and upon its inhabitants, all the curses that are written in the book that was read before the king of Judah. ²⁵Because they have forsaken me and have made offerings to other gods,

so that they have provoked me to anger with all the works of their hands, my wrath will be poured out on this place and will not be quenched. ²⁶But as to the king of Judah, who sent you to inquire of the LORD, thus shall you say to him: Thus says the LORD, the God of Israel: Regarding the words that you have heard, ²⁷because your heart was penitent and you humbled yourself before God when you heard his words against this place and its inhabitants, and you have humbled yourself before me, and have torn your clothes and wept before me, I also have heard you, says the LORD. ²⁸I will gather you to your ancestors and you shall be gathered to your grave in peace; your eyes shall not see all the disaster that I will bring on this place and its inhabitants." They took the message back to the king.

The Covenant Renewed

29 Then the king sent word and gathered together all the elders of Judah and Jerusalem. ³⁰The king went up to the house of the LORD, with all the people of Judah, the inhabitants of Jerusalem, the priests and the Lē´vītes, all the people both great and small; he read in their hearing all the words of the book of the covenant that had been found in the house of the LORD. ³¹The king stood in his place and made a covenant before the LORD, to follow the LORD, keeping his commandments, his decrees, and his statutes, with all his heart and all his soul, to perform the words of the covenant that were written in this book. ³²Then he made all who were present in Jerusalem and in Benjamin pledge themselves to it. And the inhabitants of Jerusalem acted according to the covenant of God, the God of their ancestors. ³³Jō·sī´ah took away all the abominations from all the territory that belonged to the people of Israel, and made all who were in Israel worship the LORD their God. All his days they did not turn away from following the LORD the God of their ancestors.

Celebration of the Passover

35 Jō·sī'ah kept a passover to the LORD in Jerusalem; they slaughtered the passover lamb on the fourteenth day of the first month. [2]He appointed the priests to their offices and encouraged them in the service of the house of the LORD. [3]He said to the Lē'vītes who taught all Israel and who were holy to the LORD, "Put the holy ark in the house that Solomon son of David, king of Israel, built; you need no longer carry it on your shoulders. Now serve the LORD your God and his people Israel. [4]Make preparations by your ancestral houses by your divisions, following the written directions of King David of Israel and the written directions of his son Solomon. [5]Take position in the holy place according to the groupings of the ancestral houses of your kindred the people, and let there be Lē'vītes for each division of an ancestral house.[r] [6]Slaughter the passover lamb, sanctify yourselves, and on behalf of your kindred make preparations, acting according to the word of the LORD by Moses."

7 Then Jō·sī'ah contributed to the people, as passover offerings for all that were present, lambs and kids from the flock to the number of thirty thousand, and three thousand bulls; these were from the king's possessions. [8]His officials contributed willingly to the people, to the priests, and to the Lē'vītes. Hil·kī'ah, Zech·a·rī'ah, and Je·hī'el, the chief officers of the house of God, gave to the priests for the passover offerings two thousand six hundred lambs and kids and three hundred bulls. [9]Con·a·nī'ah also, and his brothers She·mā'iah and Ne·than'el, and Hash·a·bī'ah and Je·ī'el and Joz'a·bad, the chiefs of the Lē'vītes, gave to the Lē'vītes for the passover offerings five thousand lambs and kids and five hundred bulls.

10 When the service had been prepared for, the priests stood in their place, and the Lē'vītes in their divisions according to the king's command. [11]They slaughtered the passover lamb, and the priests dashed the blood that they received[s] from them, while the Lē'vītes did the skinning. [12]They set aside the burnt offerings so that they might distribute them according to the groupings of the ancestral houses of the people, to offer to the LORD, as it is written in the book of Moses. And they did the same with the bulls. [13]They roasted the passover lamb with fire according to the ordinance; and they boiled the holy offerings in pots, in caldrons, and in pans, and carried them quickly to all the people. [14]Afterward they made preparations for themselves and for the priests, because the priests the descendants of Aaron were occupied in offering the burnt offerings and the fat parts until night; so the Lē'vītes made preparations for themselves and for the priests, the descendants of Aaron. [15]The singers, the descendants of Ā'saph, were in their place according to the command of David, and Ā'saph, and Hē'man, and the king's seer Je·dū'thun. The gatekeepers were at each gate; they did not need to interrupt their service, for their kindred the Lē'vītes made preparations for them.

16 So all the service of the LORD was prepared that day, to keep the passover and to offer burnt offerings on the altar of the LORD, according to the command of King Jo·sī'ah. [17]The people of Israel who were present kept the passover at that time, and the festival of unleavened bread seven days. [18]No passover like it had been kept in Israel since the days of the prophet Samuel; none of the kings of Israel had kept such a passover as was kept by Jō·sī'ah, by the priests and the Lē'vītes, by all Judah and Israel who were present, and by the inhabitants of Jerusalem. [19]In the eighteenth year of the reign of Jō·sī'ah this passover was kept.

---

[r] Meaning of Heb uncertain　　[s] Heb lacks *that they received*

Defeat by Pharaoh Neco and Death of Josiah

20 After all this, when Jō·sī´ah had set the temple in order, King Nē´cō of Egypt went up to fight at Car´chem·ish on the Euphrates, and Jō·sī´ah went out against him. ²¹But Nē´cō[t] sent envoys to him, saying, "What have I to do with you, king of Judah? I am not coming against you today, but against the house with which I am at war; and God has commanded me to hurry. Cease opposing God, who is with me, so that he will not destroy you." ²²But Jō·sī´ah would not turn away from him, but disguised himself in order to fight with him. He did not listen to the words of Nē´cō from the mouth of God, but joined battle in the plain of Me·gid´dō. ²³The archers shot King Jō·sī´ah; and the king said to his servants, "Take me away, for I am badly wounded." ²⁴So his servants took him out of the chariot and carried him in his second chariot[u] and brought him to Jerusalem. There he died, and was buried in the tombs of his ancestors. All Judah and Jerusalem mourned for Jō·sī´ah. ²⁵Jer·e·mī´ah also uttered a lament for Jō·sī´ah, and all the singing men and singing women have spoken of Jō·sī´ah in their laments to this day. They made these a custom in Israel; they are recorded in the Laments. ²⁶Now the rest of the acts of Jō·sī´ah and his faithful deeds in accordance with what is written in the law of the LORD, ²⁷and his acts, first and last, are written in the Book of the Kings of Israel and Judah.

Reign of Jehoahaz

36 The people of the land took Je·hō´a·haz son of Jō·sī´ah and made him king to succeed his father in Jerusalem. ²Je·hō´a·haz was twenty-three years old when he began to reign; he reigned three months in Jerusalem. ³Then the king of Egypt deposed him in Jerusalem and laid on the land a tribute of one hundred talents of silver and one talent of gold. ⁴The king of Egypt made his brother E·lī´a·kim king over Judah and Jerusalem, and changed his name to Je·hoi´a·kim; but Nē´cō took his brother Je·hō´a·haz and carried him to Egypt.

Reign and Captivity of Jehoiakim

5 Je·hoi´a·kim was twenty-five years old when he began to reign; he reigned eleven years in Jerusalem. He did what was evil in the sight of the LORD his God. ⁶Against him King Ne·bū·chad·nez´zar of Babylon came up, and bound him with fetters to take him to Babylon. ⁷Ne·bū·chad·nez´zar also carried some of the vessels of the house of the LORD to Babylon and put them in his palace in Babylon. ⁸Now the rest of the acts of Je·hoi´a·kim, and the abominations that he did, and what was found against him, are written in the Book of the Kings of Israel and Judah; and his son Je·hoi´a·chin succeeded him.

Reign and Captivity of Jehoiachin

9 Je·hoi´a·chin was eight years old when he began to reign; he reigned three months and ten days in Jerusalem. He did what was evil in the sight of the LORD. ¹⁰In the spring of the year King Ne·bū·chad·nez´zar sent and brought him to Babylon, along with the precious vessels of the house of the LORD, and made his brother Zed·e·kī´ah king over Judah and Jerusalem.

Reign of Zedekiah

11 Zed·e·kī´ah was twenty-one years old when he began to reign; he reigned eleven years in Jerusalem. ¹²He did what was evil in the sight of the LORD his God.

A talent was a large weight used as a type of money before coins were made. Each talent probably weighed about seventy-five pounds.

---

[t] Heb *he*   [u] Or *the chariot of his deputy*

He did not humble himself before the prophet Jer·e·mī´ah who spoke from the mouth of the LORD. [13]He also rebelled against King Ne·bū·chad·nez´zar, who had made him swear by God; he stiffened his neck and hardened his heart against turning to the LORD, the God of Israel. [14]All the leading priests and the people also were exceedingly unfaithful, following all the abominations of the nations; and they polluted the house of the LORD that he had consecrated in Jerusalem.

The Fall of Jerusalem

15 The LORD, the God of their ancestors, sent persistently to them by his messengers, because he had compassion on his people and on his dwelling place; [16]but they kept mocking the messengers of God, despising his words, and scoffing at his prophets, until the wrath of the LORD against his people became so great that there was no remedy.

17 Therefore he brought up against them the king of the Chal·dē´ans, who killed their youths with the sword in the house of their sanctuary, and had no compassion on young man or young woman, the aged or the feeble; he gave them all into his hand. [18]All the vessels of the house of God, large and small, and the treasures of the house of the LORD, and the treasures of the king and of his officials, all these he brought to Babylon. [19]They burned the house of God, broke down the wall of Jerusalem, burned all its palaces with fire, and destroyed all its precious vessels. [20]He took into exile in Babylon those who had escaped from the sword, and they became servants to him and to his sons until the establishment of the kingdom of Persia, [21]to fulfill the word of the LORD by the mouth of Jer·e·mī´ah, until the land had made up for its sabbaths. All the days that it lay desolate it kept sabbath, to fulfill seventy years.

Cyrus Proclaims Liberty for the Exiles

22 In the first year of King Cyrus of Persia, in fulfillment of the word of the LORD spoken by Jer·e·mī´ah, the LORD stirred up the spirit of King Cyrus of Persia so that he sent a herald throughout all his kingdom and also declared in a written edict: [23]"Thus says King Cyrus of Persia: The LORD, the God of heaven, has given me all the kingdoms of the earth, and he has charged me to build him a house at Jerusalem, which is in Judah. Whoever is among you of all his people, may the LORD his God be with him! Let him go up."

The Exile refers to the time in biblical history when the Babylonians conquered the country of Judah and the city of Jerusalem. At that time, many of the people were sent to live in Babylonia. The first of the exiles left their homes in 597 BC. Others left in 586 and 582 BC. Many came home in 538 BC when Cyrus, the Persian king, conquered Babylonia and let them go free.

Ezra

The book of Ezra tells about the troubles of the Israelites who returned from exile to their homeland after Cyrus of Persia conquered Babylonia in 538 BC. Solomon's Temple had been destroyed many years earlier, in 586 BC, when their nation was conquered. After Ezra returned, he became chief priest. He spent most of his time telling the people and the priests about God's laws for their life and worship.

Ezra found that many of the Israelites had married foreigners. Therefore, he demanded that those who had married foreign women divorce them, even though this would cause suffering and unhappiness. He felt that these foreign wives would change the true worship of God with the pagan ideas and moral standards of the gods they worshiped. However, some of the men did not agree with Ezra and refused to leave their foreign wives. In fact, the book of Ruth seems to have been written to protest the divorcing of foreign wives.

The book of Ezra was probably written about 350 BC as part of the series of books that focus on Israelite history— First and Second Chronicles, Ezra, and Nehemiah. Like all these books of history, Ezra focuses on the importance of official Temple worship at Jerusalem.

Ezra 3:8–13

Ezra's story takes place in the part of the world that is now called Iran. See if you can find this country on a map or globe. In Bible times, the land was called Persia. After the Persians defeated the Babylonians in the sixth century BC, Persia became a great empire. King Cyrus named himself "king of the world." He let the people who had been exiled in Babylon go back to Jerusalem to rebuild the Temple and the walls of the city.

End of the Babylonian Captivity

1 In the first year of King Cyrus of Persia, in order that the word of the LORD by the mouth of Jer·e·mī´ah might be accomplished, the LORD stirred up the spirit of King Cyrus of Persia so that he sent a herald throughout all his kingdom, and also in a written edict declared:

2 "Thus says King Cyrus of Persia: The LORD, the God of heaven, has given me all the kingdoms of the earth, and he has charged me to build him a house at Jerusalem in Judah. ³Any of those among you who are of his people—may their God be with them!—are now permitted to go up to Jerusalem in Judah, and rebuild the house of the LORD, the God of Israel— he is the God who is in Jerusalem; ⁴and let all survivors, in whatever place they reside, be assisted by the people of their place with silver and gold, with goods and with animals, besides freewill offerings for the house of God in Jerusalem."

5 The heads of the families of Judah and Benjamin, and the priests and the Lē´- vītes—everyone whose spirit God had stirred—got ready to go up and rebuild the house of the LORD in Jerusalem. ⁶All their neighbors aided them with silver vessels, with gold, with goods, with ani- mals, and with valuable gifts, besides all that was freely offered. ⁷King Cyrus him-

self brought out the vessels of the house of the LORD that Ne·bū·chad·nez´zar had carried away from Jerusalem and placed in the house of his gods. ⁸King Cyrus of Persia had them released into the charge of Mith´re·dath the treasurer, who counted them out to Shesh·baz´zar the prince of Judah. ⁹And this was the inven- tory: gold basins, thirty; silver basins, one thousand; knives,ᵃ twenty-nine; ¹⁰gold bowls, thirty; other silver bowls, four hundred ten; other vessels, one thousand; ¹¹the total of the gold and sil- ver vessels was five thousand four hun- dred. All these Shesh·baz´zar brought up, when the exiles were brought up from Babylonia to Jerusalem.

List of the Returned Exiles

2 Now these were the people of the province who came from those cap- tive exiles whom King Ne·bū·chad·nez´zar of Babylon had carried captive to Babylo- nia; they returned to Jerusalem and Judah, all to their own towns. ²They came with Ze·rub´ba·bel, Jesh´ū·a, Nē·he·mī´ah, Se- rāi´ah, Rē·el·āi´ah, Mor´de·cai, Bil´shan, Mis´par, Big´vai, Rē´hum, and Bā´a·nah.

The number of the Israelite people: ³the descendants of Pā´rosh, two thousand one hundred seventy-two. ⁴Of Sheph·a·tī´ah, three hundred seventy-two. ⁵Of Ā´rah, seven hundred seventy-five. ⁶Of Pā´hath- mō´ab, namely the descendants of Jesh´ū·a

When the Temple was destroyed, Nebuchad- nezzar had taken the Temple vessels (things made of gold and silver) from Jerusalem. King Cyrus of Persia brought out these vessels so that they could be returned to the place where they belonged. In addition, some Persians gave many valuable gifts to help restore the Temple and to help the people on their journey.

ᵃ Vg: Meaning of Heb uncertain

and Jṓab, two thousand eight hundred twelve. [7]Of Ḗlam, one thousand two hundred fifty-four. [8]Of Zat́tū, nine hundred forty-five. [9]Of Zaćcai, seven hundred sixty. [10]Of Bā́ni, six hundred forty-two. [11]Of Bḗbai, six hundred twenty-three. [12]Of Aźgad, one thousand two hundred twenty-two. [13]Of Ad·o·ni´kam, six hundred sixty-six. [14]Of Biǵvai, two thousand fifty-six. [15]Of Ā́din, four hundred fifty-four. [16]Of Ā́ter, namely of Hez·e·ki´ah, ninety-eight. [17]Of Bḗzai, three hundred twenty-three. [18]Of Jṓrah, one hundred twelve. [19]Of Hā́shum, two hundred twenty-three. [20]Of Gib́bar, ninety-five. [21]Of Bethlehem, one hundred twenty-three. [22]The people of Ne·toph´ah, fifty-six. [23]Of An´a·thoth, one hundred twenty-eight. [24]The descendants of Az´ma·veth, forty-two. [25]Of Kir·i·ath·ar´im, Chē·phi´rah, and Be·er´oth, seven hundred forty-three. [26]Of Rā́mah and Gḗba, six hundred twenty-one. [27]The people of Mich́mas, one hundred twenty-two. [28]Of Beth́el and Aī, two hundred twenty-three. [29]The descendants of Nḗbo, fifty-two. [30]Of Maǵbish, one hundred fifty-six. [31]Of the other Ḗlam, one thousand two hundred fifty-four. [32]Of Hā́rim, three hundred twenty. [33]Of Lod, Hā́did, and Ṓno, seven hundred twenty-five. [34]Of Jericho, three hundred forty-five. [35]Of Se·nā́ah, three thousand six hundred thirty.

36 The priests: the descendants of Je·dai´ah, of the house of Jesh´u·a, nine hundred seventy-three. [37]Of Im´mer, one thousand fifty-two. [38]Of Pash´hur, one thousand two hundred forty-seven. [39]Of Hā́rim, one thousand seventeen.

40 The Lḗvites: the descendants of Jesh´u·a and Kad´mi·el, of the descendants of Hod·a·vi´ah, seventy-four. [41]The singers: the descendants of Ā́saph, one hundred twenty-eight. [42]The descendants of the gatekeepers: of Shal´lum, of Ā́ter, of Tal´mon, of Ak´kub, of Ha·ti´ta, and of Shṓbai, in all one hundred thirty-nine.

43 The temple servants: the descendants of Zī́ha, Ha·sū́pha, Tab·bā́oth, [44]Kḗros, Sī́a·ha, Pā́don, [45]Le·bā́nah, Hag´a·bah, Ak´kub, [46]Hā́gab, Sham´lai, Hā́nan, [47]Gid́del, Gā́har, Rē·ai´ah, [48]Rḗzin, Ne·kṓda, Gaźzam, [49]Uźza, Pa·sḗah, Bḗsai, [50]As´nah, Me·ū́nim, Ne·phi´sim, [51]Bak´buk, Ha·kū́pha, Har´hur, [52]Baz´luth, Me·hī́da, Har´sha, [53]Bar´kos, Sis·e´ra, Tḗmah, [54]Ne·zī́ah, and Ha·tī́pha.

55 The descendants of Solomon's servants: Sṓtai, Has·sṓphe·reth, Pe·rū́da, [56]Jā´a·lah, Dar´kon, Gid́del, [57]Sheph·a·tī´ah, Hat´til, Pṓche·reth-haz·ze·bā´im, and Ā́mi.

58 All the temple servants and the descendants of Solomon's servants were three hundred ninety-two.

59 The following were those who came up from Tel-mḗlah, Tel-har´sha, Chḗrub, Ad´dan, and Im´mer, though they could not prove their families or their descent, whether they belonged to Israel: [60]the descendants of De·lai´ah, Tō·bī́ah, and Ne·kṓda, six hundred fifty-two. [61]Also, of the descendants of the priests: the descendants of Ha·bai´ah, Hak´koz, and Bar·zil´lai (who had married one of the daughters of Bar·zil´lai the Gil´e·ad·īte, and was called by their name). [62]These looked for their entries in the genealogical records, but they were not found there, and so they were excluded from the priesthood as unclean; [63]the governor told them that they were not to partake of the most holy food, until there should be a priest to consult Ū́rim and Thum´mim.

64 The whole assembly together was forty-two thousand three hundred sixty, [65]besides their male and female servants, of whom there were seven thousand three hundred thirty-seven; and they had two hundred male and female singers. [66]They had seven hundred thirty-six horses, two hundred forty-five mules, [67]four hundred thirty-five camels, and six thousand seven hundred twenty donkeys.

68 As soon as they came to the house of the LORD in Jerusalem, some of the heads of families made freewill offerings for the house of God, to erect it on its site.

As soon as the people reached Jerusalem, the heads of some of the families gave an offering so the rebuilding of the Temple could begin. The gifts of gold may have weighed as much as 1,133 pounds, and the gifts of silver may have weighed as much as 6,250 pounds. This great offering shows how thankful the people were to be able to rebuild God's house.

[69]According to their resources they gave to the building fund sixty-one thousand darics of gold, five thousand minas of silver, and one hundred priestly robes.

70 The priests, the Lē´vītes, and some of the people lived in Jerusalem and its vicinity;[b] and the singers, the gatekeepers, and the temple servants lived in their towns, and all Israel in their towns.

Worship Restored at Jerusalem

3 When the seventh month came, and the Israelites were in the towns, the people gathered together in Jerusalem. [2]Then Jesh´ū·a son of Jō´-za·dak, with his fellow priests, and Ze·rub´ba·bel son of She·al´ti·el with his kin set out to build the altar of the God of Israel, to offer burnt offerings on it, as prescribed in the law of Moses the man of God. [3]They set up the altar on its foundation, because they were in dread of the neighboring peoples, and they offered burnt offerings upon it to the LORD, morning and evening. [4]And they kept the festival of booths,[c] as prescribed, and offered the daily burnt offerings by number according to the ordinance, as required for each day, [5]and after that the regular burnt offerings, the offerings at the new moon and at all the sacred festivals of the LORD, and the offerings of everyone who made a free-will offering to the LORD. [6]From the first day of the seventh month they began to

offer burnt offerings to the LORD. But the foundation of the temple of the LORD was not yet laid. [7]So they gave money to the masons and the carpenters, and food, drink, and oil to the Sī·dō´ni·ans and the Tỹ´ri·ans to bring cedar trees from Lebanon to the sea, to Jop´pa, according to the grant that they had from King Cyrus of Persia.

Foundation Laid for the Temple

8 In the second year after their arrival at the house of God at Jerusalem, in the second month, Ze·rub´ba·bel son of She·al´ti·el and Jesh´ū·a son of Jō´za·dak made a beginning, together with the rest of their people, the priests and the Lē´-vītes and all who had come to Jerusalem from the captivity. They appointed the Lē´vītes, from twenty years old and upward, to have the oversight of the work on the house of the LORD. [9]And Jesh´ū·a with his sons and his kin, and Kad´mi·el and his sons, Bin´nū·ī and Hod·a·vī´ah[d] along with the sons of Hen´a·dad, the Lē´vītes, their sons and

The work of rebuilding the Temple went slowly. The people set up an altar and made sacrifices on the site, but they did not lay the foundation until they had been in Jerusalem for two years. As the builders finished the foundation, the priests and Levites led a celebration! The people sang, giving praise and thanks to the Lord. They remembered and honored the past by singing to God as King David had sung, "For he is good, for his steadfast love endures forever toward Israel."

[b] 1 Esdras 5.46: Heb lacks *lived in Jerusalem and its vicinity*   [c] Or *tabernacles*; Heb *succoth*
[d] Compare 2.40; Neh 7.43; 1 Esdras 5.58: Heb *sons of Judah*

Of course we don't need a temple, a church, or a holiday to be thankful. We don't need a lot of money, clothes, or other things to be thankful either. We just need to remember that everything, from the air we breathe to the ground we walk on, is a gift from God.

One way we can honor God is by thanking the people who take care of God's house. Make a thank-you card for someone who cares for your church building, such as the person who cleans the building. Maybe there is someone who faithfully sets out beautiful flowers for each worship service. You may not know the names of some of these people, so ask an adult to help you.

kin, together took charge of the workers in the house of God.

10 When the builders laid the foundation of the temple of the LORD, the priests in their vestments were stationed to praise the LORD with trumpets, and the Lē'vītes, the sons of Ā'saph, with cymbals, according to the directions of King David of Israel; [11]and they sang responsively, praising and giving thanks to the LORD,

"For he is good,
for his steadfast love endures forever toward Israel."

And all the people responded with a great shout when they praised the LORD, because the foundation of the house of the LORD was laid. [12]But many of the priests and Lē'vītes and heads of families, old people who had seen the first house on its foundations, wept with a loud voice when they saw this house, though many shouted aloud for joy, [13]so that the people could not distinguish the sound of the joyful shout from the sound of the people's weeping, for the people shouted so loudly that the sound was heard far away.

Resistance to Rebuilding the Temple

4 When the adversaries of Judah and Benjamin heard that the returned exiles were building a temple to the LORD, the God of Israel, [2]they approached Ze·rub'ba·bel and the heads of families and said to them, "Let us build with you, for we worship your God as you do, and we have been sacrificing to him ever since the days of King Ē'sar-had'don of Assyria who brought us here." [3]But Ze·rub'ba·bel, Jesh'ū·a and the rest of the heads of families in Israel said to them, "You shall have no part with us in building a house to our God; but we alone will build to the LORD, the God of Israel, as King Cyrus of Persia has commanded us."

4 Then the people of the land discouraged the people of Judah, and made them afraid to build, [5]and they bribed officials to frustrate their plan throughout the reign of King Cyrus of Persia and until the reign of King Da·rī'us of Persia.

Rebuilding of Jerusalem Opposed

6 In the reign of A·has·ū·ē'rus, in his accession year, they wrote an accusation against the inhabitants of Judah and Jerusalem.

7 And in the days of Ar·ta·xerx'ēs, Bish'lam and Mith're·dath and Tā'bē·el and the rest of their associates wrote to King Ar·ta·xerx'ēs of Persia; the letter

Some people were not a part of the Israelites living in the land around Jerusalem. They complained about the rebuilding of the Temple, so work stopped for about fifteen years. But when Darius became king, he said that the rebuilding of the Temple must not be stopped. And so work began again.

was written in Ar·a·mā´ic and translated.[e] [8]Rē´hum the royal deputy and Shim´shaī the scribe wrote a letter against Jerusalem to King Ar·ta·xerx´ēs as follows [9](then Rē´hum the royal deputy, Shim´shaī the scribe, and the rest of their associates, the judges, the envoys, the officials, the Persians, the people of Ē´rech, the Babylonians, the people of Su´sa, that is, the Ē´lam·ītes, [10]and the rest of the nations whom the great and noble Os·nap´par deported and settled in the cities of Sa·mār´i·a and in the rest of the province Beyond the River wrote—and now [11]this is a copy of the letter that they sent):

"To King Ar·ta·xerx´ēs: Your servants, the people of the province Beyond the River, send greeting. And now [12]may it be known to the king that the Jews who came up from you to us have gone to Jerusalem. They are rebuilding that rebellious and wicked city; they are finishing the walls and repairing the foundations. [13]Now may it be known to the king that, if this city is rebuilt and the walls finished, they will not pay tribute, custom, or toll, and the royal revenue will be reduced. [14]Now because we share the salt of the palace and it is not fitting for us to witness the king's dishonor, therefore we send and inform the king, [15]so that a search may be made in the annals of your ancestors. You will discover in the annals that this is a rebellious city, hurtful to kings and provinces, and that sedition was stirred up in it from long ago. On that account this city was laid waste. [16]We make known to the king that, if this city is rebuilt and its walls finished, you will then have no possession in the province Beyond the River."

[17] The king sent an answer: "To Rē´hum the royal deputy and Shim´shaī the scribe and the rest of their associates who live in Sa·mār´i·a and in the rest of the province Beyond the River, greeting. And now [18]the letter that you sent to us has been read in translation before me.

[19]So I made a decree, and someone searched and discovered that this city has risen against kings from long ago, and that rebellion and sedition have been made in it. [20]Jerusalem has had mighty kings who ruled over the whole province Beyond the River, to whom tribute, custom, and toll were paid. [21]Therefore issue an order that these people be made to cease, and that this city not be rebuilt, until I make a decree. [22]Moreover, take care not to be slack in this matter; why should damage grow to the hurt of the king?"

[23] Then when the copy of King Ar·ta·xerx´ēs' letter was read before Rē´hum and the scribe Shim´shaī and their associates, they hurried to the Jews in Jerusalem and by force and power made them cease. [24]At that time the work on the house of God in Jerusalem stopped and

After a long time, Haggai and Zechariah (two prophets) got the work on the Temple started again. But it didn't go smoothly even then! Tattenai, governor of a place called Beyond the River, said they did not have the right to do the work. He wrote to King Darius to ask for his advice. Because the people said that Cyrus had given them permission and money to rebuild, Tattenai suggested that Darius look in the royal archives to see if this was true. Darius searched and found the decree. Immediately he said to those trying to stop the work: "Keep away! Let the work on this house of God go on. And not only that, but you help supply their needs!"

[e] Heb adds *in Aramaic*, indicating that 4.8-6.18 is in Aramaic. Another interpretation is *The letter was written in the Aramaic script and set forth in the Aramaic language*

was discontinued until the second year of the reign of King Da·rī′us of Persia.

Restoration of the Temple Resumed

5 Now the prophets, Hag′gaī[f] and Zech·a·rī′ah son of Id′dō, prophesied to the Jews who were in Judah and Jerusalem, in the name of the God of Israel who was over them. [2]Then Ze·rub′ba·bel son of She·al′ti·el and Jesh·ū′a son of Jō′za·dak set out to rebuild the house of God in Jerusalem; and with them were the prophets of God, helping them.

3 At the same time Tat′te·naī the governor of the province Beyond the River and Shē′thar-boz′e·naī and their associates came to them and spoke to them thus, "Who gave you a decree to build this house and to finish this structure?" [4]They[g] also asked them this, "What are the names of the men who are building this building?" [5]But the eye of their God was upon the elders of the Jews, and they did not stop them until a report reached Da·rī′us and then answer was returned by letter in reply to it.

6 The copy of the letter that Tat′te·naī the governor of the province Beyond the River and Shē′thar-boz′e·naī and his associates the envoys who were in the province Beyond the River sent to King Da·rī′us; [7]they sent him a report, in which was written as follows: "To Da·rī′us the king, all peace! [8]May it be known to the king that we went to the province of Judah, to the house of the great God. It is being built of hewn stone, and timber is laid in the walls; this work is being done diligently and prospers in their hands. [9]Then we spoke to those elders and asked them, 'Who gave you a decree to build this house and to finish this structure?' [10]We also asked them their names, for your information, so that we might write down the names of the men at their head. [11]This was their reply to us: 'We are the servants of the God of heaven and earth, and we are rebuilding the house that was built many years ago, which a great king of Israel built and finished. [12]But because our ancestors had angered the God of heaven, he gave them into the hand of King Ne·bū·chad·nez′zar of Babylon, the Chal·dē′an, who destroyed this house and carried away the people to Babylonia. [13]However, King Cyrus of Babylon, in the first year of his reign, made a decree that this house of God should be rebuilt. [14]Moreover, the gold and silver vessels of the house of God, which Ne·bū·chad·nez′zar had taken out of the temple in Jerusalem and had brought into the temple of Babylon, these King Cyrus took out of the temple of Babylon, and they were delivered to a man named Shesh·baz′zar, whom he had made governor. [15]He said to him, "Take these vessels; go and put them in the temple in Jerusalem, and let the house of God be rebuilt on its site." [16]Then this Shesh·baz′zar came and laid the foundations of the house of God in Jerusalem; and from that time until now it has been under construction, and it is not yet finished.' [17]And now, if it seems good to the king, have a search made in the royal archives there in Babylon, to see whether a decree was issued by King Cyrus for the rebuilding of this house of God in Jerusalem. Let the king send us his pleasure in this matter."

In Bible times, a decree was something a king would declare or proclaim. A decree was usually written down and then read aloud to the people to let them know what they were supposed to do.

The Decree of Darius

6 Then King Da·rī′us made a decree, and they searched the archives where the documents were stored in

---

[f] Aram adds *the prophet* [g] Gk Syr: Aram *We*

Babylon. [2]But it was in Ec·bat´a·na, the capital in the province of Mē´di·a, that a scroll was found on which this was written: "A record. [3]In the first year of his reign, King Cyrus issued a decree: Concerning the house of God at Jerusalem, let the house be rebuilt, the place where sacrifices are offered and burnt offerings are brought;[h] its height shall be sixty cubits and its width sixty cubits, [4]with three courses of hewn stones and one course of timber; let the cost be paid from the royal treasury. [5]Moreover, let the gold and silver vessels of the house of God, which Ne·bū·chad·nez´zar took out of the temple in Jerusalem and brought to Babylon, be restored and brought back to the temple in Jerusalem, each to its place; you shall put them in the house of God."

[6] "Now you, Tat´te·naī, governor of the province Beyond the River, Shē´thar-boz´e·naī, and you, their associates, the envoys in the province Beyond the River, keep away; [7]let the work on this house of God alone; let the governor of the Jews and the elders of the Jews rebuild this house of God on its site. [8]Moreover I make a decree regarding what you shall do for these elders of the Jews for the rebuilding of this house of God: the cost is to be paid to these people, in full and without delay, from the royal revenue, the tribute of the province Beyond the River. [9]Whatever is needed—young bulls, rams, or sheep for burnt offerings to the God of heaven, wheat, salt, wine, or oil, as the priests in Jerusalem require—let that be given to them day by day without fail, [10]so that they may offer pleasing sacrifices to the God of heaven, and pray for the life of the king and his children. [11]Furthermore I decree that if anyone alters this edict, a beam shall be pulled out of the house of the perpetrator, who then shall be impaled on it. The house shall be made a dunghill. [12]May the God who has established his name there over-throw any king or people that shall put forth a hand to alter this, or to destroy this house of God in Jerusalem. I, Da·rī´us, make a decree; let it be done with all diligence."

Completion and Dedication of the Temple

[13] Then, according to the word sent by King Da·rī´us, Tat´te·naī, the governor of the province Beyond the River, Shē´thar-boz´e·naī, and their associates did with all diligence what King Da·rī´us had ordered. [14]So the elders of the Jews built and prospered, through the prophesying of the prophet Hag´gaī and Zech·-a·rī´ah son of Id´dō. They finished their building by command of the God of Israel and by decree of Cyrus, Da·rī´us, and King Ar·ta·xerx´ēs of Persia; [15]and this house was finished on the third day of the month of Ā´dar, in the sixth year of the reign of King Da·rī´us.

[16] The people of Israel, the priests and the Lē´vītes, and the rest of the returned exiles, celebrated the dedication of this house of God with joy. [17]They offered at the dedication of this house of God one hundred bulls, two hundred rams, four hundred lambs, and as a sin offering for all Israel, twelve male goats, according to the number of the tribes of Israel. [18]Then they set the priests in their divisions and the Lē´vītes

At last the people finished working on the Temple, and they dedicated it once again to the Lord. For the first time in many years, the people celebrated the Passover. The priests killed the Passover lamb, which was eaten by those who returned from the exile and also by others of the community who had chosen to worship God.

[h] Meaning of Aram uncertain

"With joy they celebrated the festival of unleavened bread seven days; for the LORD had made them joyful."   Ezra 6:22

in their courses for the service of God at Jerusalem, as it is written in the book of Moses.

The Passover Celebrated

19 On the fourteenth day of the first month the returned exiles kept the passover. [20]For both the priests and the Lē′vītes had purified themselves; all of them were clean. So they killed the passover lamb for all the returned exiles, for their fellow priests, and for themselves. [21]It was eaten by the people of Israel who had returned from exile, and also by all who had joined them and separated themselves from the pollutions of the nations of the land to worship the LORD, the God of Israel. [22]With joy they celebrated the festival of unleavened bread seven days; for the LORD had made them joyful, and had turned the heart of the king of Assyria to them, so that he aided them in the work on the house of God, the God of Israel.

The Coming and Work of Ezra

7 After this, in the reign of King Ar·ta·xerx′ēs of Persia, Ezra son of Se·rāi′ah, son of Az·a·rī′ah, son of Hil·kī′ah, [2]son of Shal′lum, son of Zā′dok, son of A·hī′tub, [3]son of Am·a·rī′ah, son of Az·a·rī′ah, son of Me·rā′i·oth, [4]son of Zer·a·hī′ah, son of Uz′zī, son of Buk′kī, [5]son of Ab·i·shū′a, son of Phin′e·has, son of El·ē·ā′zar, son of the chief priest Aaron— [6]this Ezra went up from Babylonia. He was a scribe skilled in the law of Moses that the LORD the God of Israel had given; and the king granted him all that he asked, for the hand of the LORD his God was upon him.

7 Some of the people of Israel, and some of the priests and Lē′vītes, the singers and gatekeepers, and the temple servants also went up to Jerusalem, in the seventh year of King Ar·ta·xerx′ēs. [8]They came to Jerusalem in the fifth month, which was in the seventh year of the king. [9]On the first day of the first month the journey up from Babylon was begun, and on the first day of the fifth month he came to Jerusalem, for the gracious hand of his God was upon him. [10]For Ezra had set his heart to study the law of the LORD, and to do it, and to teach the statutes and ordinances in Israel.

The Letter of Artaxerxes to Ezra

11 This is a copy of the letter that King Ar·ta·xerx′ēs gave to the priest Ezra, the scribe, a scholar of the text of the commandments of the LORD and his statutes for Israel: [12]"Ar·ta·xerx′ēs, king of kings, to the priest Ezra, the scribe of the law of the God of heaven: Peace.[i] And now [13]I decree that any of the people of Israel or their priests or Lē′vītes in my kingdom who freely offers to go to Jerusalem may go with you. [14]For you are sent by the king and his seven counselors to make inquiries about Judah and Jerusalem according to the law of your God, which is in your hand, [15]and also to convey the silver and gold that the king and his counselors have freely offered to the God of Israel, whose dwelling is in Jerusalem, [16]with all the silver and gold that you shall find in the whole province of Babylonia, and with the freewill offerings of the people and the priests, given willingly for the house of

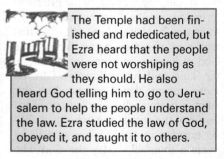

The Temple had been finished and rededicated, but Ezra heard that the people were not worshiping as they should. He also heard God telling him to go to Jerusalem to help the people understand the law. Ezra studied the law of God, obeyed it, and taught it to others.

[i] Syr Vg 1 Esdras 8.9: Aram *Perfect*

their God in Jerusalem. [17]With this money, then, you shall with all diligence buy bulls, rams, and lambs, and their grain offerings and their drink offerings, and you shall offer them on the altar of the house of your God in Jerusalem. [18]Whatever seems good to you and your colleagues to do with the rest of the silver and gold, you may do, according to the will of your God. [19]The vessels that have been given you for the service of the house of your God, you shall deliver before the God of Jerusalem. [20]And whatever else is required for the house of your God, which you are responsible for providing, you may provide out of the king's treasury.

21 "I, King Ar·ta·xerx´ēs, decree to all the treasurers in the province Beyond the River: Whatever the priest Ezra, the scribe of the law of the God of heaven, requires of you, let it be done with all diligence, [22]up to one hundred talents of silver, one hundred cors of wheat, one hundred baths[j] of wine, one hundred baths[j] of oil, and unlimited salt. [23]Whatever is commanded by the God of heaven, let it be done with zeal for the house of the God of heaven, or wrath will come upon the realm of the king and his heirs. [24]We also notify you that it shall not be lawful to impose tribute, custom, or toll on any of the priests, the Lē´vītes, the singers, the doorkeepers, the temple servants, or other servants of this house of God.

25 "And you, Ezra, according to the God-given wisdom you possess, appoint magistrates and judges who may judge all the people in the province Beyond the River who know the laws of your God; and you shall teach those who do not know them. [26]All who will not obey the law of your God and the law of the king, let judgment be strictly executed on them, whether for death or for banishment or for confiscation of their goods or for imprisonment."

27 Blessed be the LORD, the God of our ancestors, who put such a thing as this into the heart of the king to glorify the house of the LORD in Jerusalem, [28]and who extended to me steadfast love before the king and his counselors, and before all the king's mighty officers. I took courage, for the hand of the LORD my God was upon me, and I gathered leaders from Israel to go up with me.

Heads of Families Who Returned with Ezra

8 These are their family heads, and this is the genealogy of those who went up with me from Babylonia, in the reign of King Ar·ta·xerx´ēs: [2]Of the descendants of Phin´e·has, Ger´shom. Of Ith´a·mar, Daniel. Of David, Hat´tush, [3]of the descendants of Shec·a·nī´ah. Of Pā´rosh, Zech·a·rī´ah, with whom were registered one hundred fifty males. [4]Of the descendants of Pā´hath-mō´ab, El·i·ē·hō·ē´naī son of Zer·a·hī´ah, and with him two hundred males. [5]Of the descendants of Zat´tū,[k] Shec·a·nī´ah son of Ja·hā´zi·el, and with him three hundred males. [6]Of the descendants of Ā´din, Ē´bed son of Jonathan, and with him fifty males. [7]Of the descendants of Ē´lam, Je·shā´i·ah son of Ath·a·lī´ah, and with him seventy males. [8]Of the descendants of Sheph·a·tī´ah, Zeb·a·dī´ah son of Michael, and with him eighty males. [9]Of the descendants of Jō´ab, Ō·ba·dī´ah son of Je·hī´el, and with him two hundred eighteen males. [10]Of the descendants of Bā´nī,[l] She·lō´mith son of Jos·i·phī´ah, and with him one hundred sixty males. [11]Of the descendants of Bē´baī, Zech·a·rī´ah son of Bē´baī, and with him twenty-eight males. [12]Of the descendants of Az´gad, Jō·hā´nan son of Hak´ka·tan, and with him one hundred ten males. [13]Of the descendants of Ad·o·nī´kam, those who came later, their names being E·liph´e·let, Je·ū´el, and She·māi´ah, and with them sixty males. [14]Of the descendants of Big´vaī, Ū´thaī and Zac´cur, and with them seventy males.

[j] A Heb measure of volume   [k] Gk 1 Esdras 8.32: Heb lacks *of Zattu*   [l] Gk 1 Esdras 8.36: Heb lacks *Bani*

Servants for the Temple

15 I gathered them by the river that runs to A·ha´va, and there we camped three days. As I reviewed the people and the priests, I found there none of the descendants of Levi. [16]Then I sent for El·i·e´zer, Ar´i·el, She·mai´ah, El·na´than, Ja´rib, El·na´than, Nathan, Zech·a·ri´ah, and Me·shul´lam, who were leaders, and for Joi´a·rib and El·na´than, who were wise, [17]and sent them to Id´do, the leader at the place called Cas·i·phi´a, telling them what to say to Id´do and his colleagues the temple servants at Cas·i·phi´a, namely, to send us ministers for the house of our God. [18]Since the gracious hand of our God was upon us, they brought us a man of discretion, of the descendants of Mah´li son of Levi son of Israel, namely Sher·e·bi´ah, with his sons and kin, eighteen; [19]also Hash·a·bi´ah and with him Je·sha´i·ah of the descendants of Me·rar´i, with his kin and their sons, twenty; [20]besides two hundred twenty of the temple servants, whom David and his officials had set apart to attend the Le´vites. These were all mentioned by name.

Fasting and Prayer for Protection

21 Then I proclaimed a fast there, at the river A·ha´va, that we might deny ourselves[m] before our God, to seek from him a safe journey for ourselves, our children, and all our possessions. [22]For I was ashamed to ask the king for a band of soldiers and cavalry to protect us against the enemy on our way, since we had told the king that the hand of our God is gracious to all who seek him, but his power and his wrath are against all who forsake him. [23]So we fasted and petitioned our God for this, and he listened to our entreaty.

Gifts for the Temple

24 Then I set apart twelve of the leading priests: Sher·e·bi´ah, Hasha·bi´ah, and ten of their kin with them.

[25]And I weighed out to them the silver and the gold and the vessels, the offering for the house of our God that the king, his counselors, his lords, and all Israel there present had offered; [26]I weighed out into their hand six hundred fifty talents of silver, and one hundred silver vessels worth . . . talents,[n] and one hundred talents of gold, [27]twenty gold bowls worth a thousand darics, and two vessels of fine polished bronze as precious as gold. [28]And I said to them, "You are holy to the LORD, and the vessels are holy; and the silver and the gold are a freewill offering to the LORD, the God of your ancestors. [29]Guard them and keep them until you weigh them before the chief priests and the Le´vites and the heads of families in Israel at Jerusalem, within the chambers of the house of the LORD." [30]So the priests and the Le´vites took over the silver, the gold, and the vessels as they were weighed out, to bring them to Jerusalem, to the house of our God.

The Return to Jerusalem

31 Then we left the river A·ha´va on the twelfth day of the first month, to go to Jerusalem; the hand of our God was upon us, and he delivered us from the hand of the enemy and from ambushes along the way. [32]We came to Jerusalem and remained there three days. [33]On the fourth day, within the house of our God, the silver, the gold, and the vessels were weighed into the hands of the priest Mer´e·moth son of U·ri´ah, and with him was El·e·a´zar son of Phin´e·has, and with them were the Le´vites, Joz´a·bad son of Jesh´u·a and No·a·di´ah son of Bin´nu·i. [34]The total was counted and weighed, and the weight of everything was recorded.

35 At that time those who had come from captivity, the returned exiles, offered burnt offerings to the God of Israel, twelve bulls for all Israel, ninety-six rams, seventy-seven lambs, and as a sin offering twelve male goats; all this

[m] Or *might fast*   [n] The number of talents is lacking

was a burnt offering to the LORD. ³⁶They also delivered the king's commissions to the king's satraps and to the governors of the province Beyond the River; and they supported the people and the house of God.

Denunciation of Mixed Marriages

9 After these things had been done, the officials approached me and said, "The people of Israel, the priests, and the Lē´vītes have not separated themselves from the peoples of the lands with their abominations, from the Cā´-naan·ītes, the Hit´tītes, the Per´iz·zītes, the Jeb´ū·sītes, the Am´mon·ītes, the Mō´-ab·ītes, the Egyptians, and the Am´o·rītes. ²For they have taken some of their daughters as wives for themselves and for their sons. Thus the holy seed has mixed itself with the peoples of the lands, and in this faithlessness the officials and leaders have led the way." ³When I heard this, I tore my garment and my mantle, and pulled hair from my head and beard, and sat appalled. ⁴Then all who trembled at the words of the God of Israel, because of the faithlessness of the returned exiles, gathered around me while I sat appalled until the evening sacrifice.

Ezra's Prayer

5 At the evening sacrifice I got up from my fasting, with my garments and my mantle torn, and fell on my knees, spread out my hands to the LORD my God, ⁶and said,

"O my God, I am too ashamed and embarrassed to lift my face to you, my God, for our iniquities have risen higher than our heads, and our guilt has mounted up to the heavens. ⁷From the days of our ancestors to this day we have been deep in guilt, and for our iniquities we, our kings, and our priests have been handed over to the kings of the lands, to the sword, to captivity, to plundering, and to utter shame, as is now the case.

⁸But now for a brief moment favor has been shown by the LORD our God, who has left us a remnant, and given us a stake in his holy place, in order that he⁰ may brighten our eyes and grant us a little sustenance in our slavery. ⁹For we are slaves; yet our God has not forsaken us in our slavery, but has extended to us his steadfast love before the kings of Persia, to give us new life to set up the house of our God, to repair its ruins, and to give us a wall in Judea and Jerusalem.

10 "And now, our God, what shall we say after this? For we have forsaken your commandments, ¹¹which you commanded by your servants the prophets, saying, 'The land that you are entering to possess is a land unclean with the pollutions of the peoples of the lands, with their abominations. They have filled it from end to end with their uncleanness. ¹²Therefore do not give your daughters to their sons, neither take their daughters for your sons, and never seek their peace or prosperity, so that you may be strong and eat the good of the land and leave it for an inheritance to your children forever.' ¹³After all that has come upon us for our evil deeds and for our great guilt, seeing that you, our God, have punished us less than our iniquities deserved and have given us such a remnant as this, ¹⁴shall we break your commandments again and intermarry with the peoples who practice these abominations? Would you not be angry with us until you destroy us without remnant or survivor? ¹⁵O LORD, God of Israel, you are just, but we have escaped as a remnant, as is now the case. Here we are before you in our guilt, though no one can face you because of this."

The People's Response

10 While Ezra prayed and made confession, weeping and throwing himself down before the house of God, a very great assembly of men, women, and

⁰ Heb *our God*

children gathered to him out of Israel; the people also wept bitterly. [2]Shec·a·nī´ah son of Je·hī´el, of the descendants of Ē´lam, addressed Ezra, saying, "We have broken faith with our God and have married foreign women from the peoples of the land, but even now there is hope for Israel in spite of this. [3]So now let us make a covenant with our God to send away all these wives and their children, according to the counsel of my lord and of those who tremble at the commandment of our God; and let it be done according to the law. [4]Take action, for it is your duty, and we are with you; be strong, and do it." [5]Then Ezra stood up and made the leading priests, the Lē´vītes, and all Israel swear that they would do as had been said. So they swore.

Foreign Wives and Their Children Rejected

[6] Then Ezra withdrew from before the house of God, and went to the chamber of Jē·hō·hā´nan son of E·lī´a·shib, where he spent the night.[p] He did not eat bread or drink water, for he was mourning over the faithlessness of the exiles. [7]They made a proclamation throughout Judah and Jerusalem to all the returned exiles that they should assemble at Jerusalem, [8]and that if any did not come within three days, by order of the officials and the elders all their property should be forfeited, and they themselves banned from the congregation of the exiles.

[9] Then all the people of Judah and Benjamin assembled at Jerusalem within the three days; it was the ninth month, on the twentieth day of the month. All the people sat in the open square before the house of God, trembling because of this matter and because of the heavy rain. [10]Then Ezra the priest stood up and said to them, "You have trespassed and married foreign women, and so increased the guilt of Israel. [11]Now make confession to the LORD the God of your ancestors, and do his will; separate yourselves from the peoples of the land and

from the foreign wives." [12]Then all the assembly answered with a loud voice, "It is so; we must do as you have said. [13]But the people are many, and it is a time of heavy rain; we cannot stand in the open. Nor is this a task for one day or for two, for many of us have transgressed in this matter. [14]Let our officials represent the whole assembly, and let all in our towns who have taken foreign wives come at appointed times, and with them the elders and judges of every town, until the fierce wrath of our God on this account is averted from us." [15]Only Jonathan son of As´a·hel and Jah·zēi´ah son of Tīk´vah opposed this, and Me·shul´lam and Shab´be·thaī the Lē´vītes supported them.

[16] Then the returned exiles did so. Ezra the priest selected men,[q] heads of families, according to their families, each of them designated by name. On the first day of the tenth month they sat down to examine the matter. [17]By the first day of the first month they had come to the end of all the men who had married foreign women.

[18] There were found of the descendants of the priests who had married foreign women, of the descendants of Jesh´ū·a son of Jō´za·dak and his brothers: Mā·a·sēi´ah, El·i·ē´zer, Jā´rib, and Ged·a·lī´ah. [19]They pledged themselves to send away their wives, and their guilt offering was a ram of the flock for their guilt. [20]Of the descendants of Im´mer: Ha·nā´nī and Zeb·a·dī´ah. [21]Of the descendants of Hā´rim: Mā·a·sēi´ah, E·lī´jah, She·māi´ah, Je·hī´el, and Uz·zī´ah. [22]Of the descendants of Pash´hur: El·i·ō·ē´naī, Mā·a·sēi´ah, Ish´ma·el, Ne·than´el, Joz´a·bad, and El·ā´sah.

[23] Of the Lē´vītes: Joz´a·bad, Shim´ē·ī, Ke·lāi´ah (that is, Ke·lī´ta), Peth·a·hī´ah, Judah, and El·i·ē´zer. [24]Of the singers: E·lī´a·shib. Of the gatekeepers: Shal´lum, Tē´lem, and Ū´rī.

p 1 Esdras 9.2: Heb *where he went* q 1 Esdras 9.16: Syr: Heb *And there were selected Ezra,*

25 And of Israel: of the descendants of Pā′rosh: Ra·mī′ah, Iz·zī′ah, Mal·chī′jah, Mij′a·min, El·e·ā′zar, Hash·a·bī′ah,[r] and Be·nā′i·ah. [26]Of the descendants of Ē′lam: Mat·ta·nī′ah, Zech·a·rī′ah, Je·hī′el, Ab′dī, Jer′e·moth, and E·lī′jah. [27]Of the descendants of Zat′tū: El·i·ō·ē′naī, E·lī′a·shib, Mat·ta·nī′ah, Jer′e·moth, Zā′bad, and A·zī′za. [28]Of the descendants of Bē′baī: Jē·hō·hā′nan, Hana·nī′ah, Zab′baī, and Ath′laī. [29]Of the descendants of Bā′nī: Me·shul′lam, Mal′luch, A·dāi′ah, Jash′ub, Shē′al, and Jer′e·moth. [30]Of the descendants of Pā′hath-mō′ab: Ad′na, Chē′lal, Be·nā′i·ah, Mā·a·sēi′ah, Mat·ta·nī′ah, Bez′a·lel, Bin′nū·ī, and Ma·nas′seh. [31]Of the descendants of Hā′rim: El·i·ē′zer, Is·shī′jah, Mal·chī′jah, She·māi′ah, Shim′ē·on, [32]Benjamin, Mal′luch, and Shem·a·rī′ah. [33]Of the descendants of Hā′shum: Mat·tē′naī, Mat·tat′tah, Zā′bad, E·liph′e·let, Jer′e·maī, Ma·nas′seh, and Shim′ē·ī. [34]Of the descendants of Bā′nī: Mā·a·dā′ī, Am′ram, Ū′el, [35]Be·nā′i·ah, Bē′dēi′ah, Chel′ū·hī, [36]Va·nī′ah, Mer′e·moth, E·lī′a·shib, [37]Mat·ta·nī′ah, Mat·tē′naī, and Jā·a′sū. [38]Of the descendants of Bin·nū·ī:[s] Shim′ē·ī, [39]Shel·e·mī′ah, Nathan, A·dāi′ah, [40]Mach·nad′e·baī, Shā′shaī, Shā′raī, [41]Az′a·rel, Shel·e·mī′ah, Shem·a·rī′ah, [42]Shal′lum, Am·a·rī′ah, and Joseph. [43]Of the descendants of Nē′bō: Je·ī′el, Mat·ti·thī′ah, Zā′bad, Ze·bī′na, Jad′daī, Jō′el, and Be·nā′i·ah. [44]All these had married foreign women, and they sent them away with their children.[t]

[r] 1 Esdras 9.26 Gk: Heb *Malchijah*   [s] Gk: Heb *Bani, Binnui*   [t] 1 Esdras 9.36; Meaning of Heb uncertain

Nehemiah

The book of Nehemiah is one of four books (First and Second Chronicles, Ezra, and Nehemiah) that were written around the same time by the same person. These books date from about 350 BC, although part of Nehemiah was probably written about 444 BC. These books focus on Israelite history and on the importance of worshiping at the Temple in Jerusalem.

This book is about Nehemiah, an Israelite man who had come to be a trusted official of King Ar·ta·xerx´ēs of Persia. Jerusalem had been destroyed, and thousands of Israelites had been sent away as prisoners to Babylon about 597 and 586 BC. In 538 BC Babylon was conquered by Persia, and the Persian king, Cyrus, allowed the Israelites to return to their homeland of Judah. In 444 BC, with the permission and support of King Ar·ta·xerx´ēs, Nehemiah went to Jerusalem and helped the Israelites rebuild the city. Then Nehemiah returned to Persia.

Twelve years later, when Nehemiah came back to Jerusalem again, he found that the Israelites were not keeping God's laws and were marrying their foreign neighbors. He demanded changes that seem very strict to us. He felt that the people would lose their faith in God and their loyalty to their nation if they did not separate themselves from people of other tribes and nations. Not all Israelites liked this idea, as we see in the book of Ruth. The writer of Ruth pointed out that Ruth had been a Moabite foreigner who said to her Israelite mother-in-law, "Your people shall be my people, and your God my God."

Nehemiah 2:17–18

Nehemiah Prays for His People

1 The words of Nē·he·mī´ah son of Hac·a·lī´ah. In the month of Chis´lev, in the twentieth year, while I was in Su´sa the capital, ²one of my brothers, Ha·nā´nī, came with certain men from Judah; and I asked them about the Jews that survived, those who had escaped the captivity, and about Jerusalem. ³They replied, "The survivors there in the province who escaped captivity are in great trouble and shame; the wall of Jerusalem is broken down, and its gates have been destroyed by fire."

4 When I heard these words I sat down and wept, and mourned for days, fasting and praying before the God of heaven. ⁵I said, "O LORD God of heaven, the great and awesome God who keeps covenant and steadfast love with those who love him and keep his commandments; ⁶let your ear be attentive and your eyes open to hear the prayer of your servant that I now pray before you day and night for your servants, the people of Israel, confessing the sins of the people of Israel, which we have sinned against you. Both I and my family have sinned. ⁷We have offended you deeply, failing to keep the commandments, the statutes, and the ordinances that you commanded your servant Moses. ⁸Remember the word that you commanded your servant Moses, 'If you are unfaithful, I will scatter you among the peoples; ⁹but if you return to me and keep my commandments and do them, though your outcasts are under the farthest skies, I will gather them from there and bring them to the place at which I have chosen to establish my name.' ¹⁰They are your servants and your people, whom you redeemed by your great power and your strong hand. ¹¹O Lord, let your ear be attentive to the prayer of your servant, and to the prayer of your servants who delight in revering your name. Give success to your servant today, and grant him mercy in the sight of this man!"

At the time, I was cupbearer to the king.

Nehemiah was a cupbearer for King Arta·xer´xes of Persia. Cupbearers had a very high position among royal officials. They traveled with kings and served as keepers of royal treasure. Kings respected and trusted their cupbearers.

Nehemiah Sent to Judah

2 In the month of Nī´san, in the twentieth year of King Ar·ta·xerx´ēs, when wine was served him, I carried the wine and gave it to the king. Now, I had never been sad in his presence before. ²So the king said to me, "Why is your face sad, since you are not sick? This can only be sadness of the heart." Then I was very much afraid. ³I said to the king, "May the king live forever! Why should my face not be sad, when the city, the place of my ancestors' graves, lies waste, and its gates have been destroyed by fire?" ⁴Then the king said to me, "What do you request?" So I prayed to the God of heaven. ⁵Then I said to the king, "If it pleases the king, and if your servant has found favor with you, I ask that you send me to Judah, to the city of my ancestors' graves, so that I may rebuild it." ⁶The king said to me (the queen also was sitting beside him), "How long will you be gone, and when will you return?" So it pleased the king to send me, and I set him a date. ⁷Then I said to the king, "If it pleases the king, let letters be given me to

Artaxerxes was king of Persia during the fifth century BC. He gave Ezra permission to go to Jerusalem. Later he stopped the rebuilding of the Temple for a while. Read this part of the story in Ezra 4:11–13, 23–24 and Ezra 7:1, 7–8, 11–26.

the governors of the province Beyond the River, that they may grant me passage until I arrive in Judah; [8]and a letter to Ā´saph, the keeper of the king's forest, directing him to give me timber to make beams for the gates of the temple fortress, and for the wall of the city, and for the house that I shall occupy." And the king granted me what I asked, for the gracious hand of my God was upon me.

9 Then I came to the governors of the province Beyond the River, and gave them the king's letters. Now the king had sent officers of the army and cavalry with me. [10]When San·bal´lat the Hor´o·nīte and To·bī´ah the Am´mon·īte official heard this, it displeased them greatly that someone had come to seek the welfare of the people of Israel.

Nehemiah secretly inspected the walls and then gave his report to the people. The people said, "Let's start building!" Sometimes it takes only one person to get a project going. Ask your family members if they remember a time in your church when one person had an idea for a project that the whole church became involved in.

Nehemiah's Inspection of the Walls

11 So I came to Jerusalem and was there for three days. [12]Then I got up during the night, I and a few men with me; I told no one what my God had put into my heart to do for Jerusalem. The only animal I took was the animal I rode. [13]I went out by night by the Valley Gate past the Dragon's Spring and to the Dung Gate, and I inspected the walls of Jerusalem that had been broken down and its gates that had been destroyed by fire. [14]Then I went on to the Fountain Gate and to the King's Pool; but there was no place for the animal I was riding to continue. [15]So I went up by way of the valley by night and inspected the

wall. Then I turned back and entered by the Valley Gate, and so returned. [16]The officials did not know where I had gone or what I was doing; I had not yet told the Jews, the priests, the nobles, the officials, and the rest that were to do the work.

Decision to Restore the Walls

17 Then I said to them, "You see the trouble we are in, how Jerusalem lies in ruins with its gates burned. Come, let us rebuild the wall of Jerusalem, so that we may no longer suffer disgrace." [18]I told them that the hand of my God had been gracious upon me, and also the words that the king had spoken to me. Then they said, "Let us start building!" So they committed themselves to the common good. [19]But when San·bal´lat the Hor´o·nīte and Tō·bī´ah the Am´mon·īte official, and Gē´shem the Arab heard of it, they mocked and ridiculed us, saying, "What is this that you are doing? Are you rebelling against the king?" [20]Then I replied to them, "The God of heaven is the one who will give us success, and we his servants are going to start building; but you have no share or claim or historic right in Jerusalem."

Some leaders who lived nearby did not want to see the walls fixed. They accused Nehemiah and the Israelite people of rebelling against the king. But Nehemiah trusted in God and told these leaders that God would give them success.

Organization of the Work

3 Then the high priest E·lī´a·shib set to work with his fellow priests and rebuilt the Sheep Gate. They consecrated it and set up its doors; they consecrated it as far as the Tower of the Hundred and as far as the Tower of Ha·nan´el. [2]And the men of Jericho built next to him. And next to them[a] Zac´cur son of Im´rī built.

[a] Heb *him*

Ezra 3 tells about the work of rebuilding the walls of Jerusalem. The work was divided among the people—some rebuilt the gates and others made repairs to the walls. City walls were very thick, so they helped to protect against an enemy attack. A city with a strong wall had a strong defense.

3 The sons of Has·se·nā′ah built the Fish Gate; they laid its beams and set up its doors, its bolts, and its bars. ⁴Next to them Mer′e·moth son of Ū·rī′ah son of Hak′koz made repairs. Next to them Me·shul′lam son of Ber·e·chī′ah son of Me·shez′a·bel made repairs. Next to them Zā′dok son of Bā′a·na made repairs. ⁵Next to them the Te·kō′ites made repairs; but their nobles would not put their shoulders to the work of their Lord.ᵇ

6 Joi′a·da son of Pa·sē′ah and Me·shul′-lam son of Bes·o·dē′ah repaired the Old Gate; they laid its beams and set up its doors, its bolts, and its bars. ⁷Next to them repairs were made by Me·la·tī′ah the Gib′ē·on·īte and Jā′don the Me·ron′o·thī te—the men of Gib′ē·on and of Miz′pah—who were under the jurisdiction ofᶜ the governor of the province Beyond the River. ⁸Next to them Uz′zi·el son of Har·hai′ah, one of the goldsmiths, made repairs. Next to him Han·a·nī′ah, one of the perfumers, made repairs; and they restored Jerusalem as far as the Broad Wall. ⁹Next to them Reph·āi′ah son of Hur, ruler of half the district ofᵈ Jerusalem, made repairs. ¹⁰Next to them Je·dai′ah son of Har·ū′maph made repairs opposite his house; and next to him Hat′tush son of Hash·ab·nei′ah made repairs. ¹¹Mal·chī′jah son of Hā′rim and Has′shub son of Pā′hath-mō′ab repaired another section and the Tower of the Ovens. ¹²Next to him Shal′lum son of Hal·-lō′hesh, ruler of half the district ofᵈ Jerusalem, made repairs, he and his daughters.

13 Hā′nun and the inhabitants of Za·nō′ah repaired the Valley Gate; they rebuilt it and set up its doors, its bolts, and its bars, and repaired a thousand cubits of the wall, as far as the Dung Gate.

14 Mal·chī′jah son of Rē′chab, ruler of the district ofᵉ Beth-hac·chē′rem, repaired the Dung Gate; he rebuilt it and set up its doors, its bolts, and its bars.

15 And Shal′lum son of Col-hō′zeh, ruler of the district ofᵉ Miz′pah, repaired the Fountain Gate; he rebuilt it and covered it and set up its doors, its bolts, and its bars; and he built the wall of the Pool of Shē′lah of the king's garden, as far as the stairs that go down from the City of David. ¹⁶After him Nē·he·mī′ah son of Az′buk, ruler of half the district ofᵈ Beth-zur, repaired from a point opposite the graves of David, as far as the artificial pool and the house of the warriors. ¹⁷After him the Lē′-vītes made repairs: Rē′hum son of Bā′nī; next to him Hash·a·bī′ah, ruler of half the district ofᵈ Kē·ī′lah, made repairs for his district. ¹⁸After him their kin made repairs: Bin′nūī,ᶠ son of Hen′a·dad, ruler of half the district ofᵈ Kē·ī′lah; ¹⁹next to him Ē′zer son of Jesh′ū·a, rulerᵍ of Miz′pah, repaired another section opposite the ascent to the armory at the Angle. ²⁰After him Bar′uch son of Zab′bai repaired another section from the Angle to the door of the house of the high priest E·lī′a·shib. ²¹After him Mer′e·moth son of Ū·rī′ah son of Hak′koz repaired another section from the door of the house of E·lī′a·shib to the end of the house of E·lī′a·shib. ²²After him the priests, the men of the surrounding area, made repairs. ²³After them Benjamin and Has′-shub made repairs opposite their house. After them Az·a·rī′ah son of Mā·a·¯sēi′ah son of An·a·nī′ah made repairs beside his own house. ²⁴After him Bin′-nū·ī son of Hen′a·dad repaired another section, from the house of Az·a·rī′ah to the

ᵇ Or lords   ᶜ Meaning of Heb uncertain
ᵈ Or supervisor of half the portion assigned to
ᵉ Or supervisor of the portion assigned to   ᶠ Gk Syr
Compare verse 24, 10.9: Heb Bavvai   ᵍ Or
supervisor

Angle and to the corner. [25]Pā́lal son of Ū́zaī repaired opposite the Angle and the tower projecting from the upper house of the king at the court of the guard. After him Pe·dāi´ah son of Pā́rosh [26]and the temple servants living[h] on Ṓphel made repairs up to a point opposite the Water Gate on the east and the projecting tower. [27]After him the Te·ko´ītes repaired another section opposite the great projecting tower as far as the wall of Ṓphel.

28 Above the Horse Gate the priests made repairs, each one opposite his own house. [29]After them Zā́dok son of Im´mer made repairs opposite his own house. After him She·māi´ah son of Shec·a·nī´ah, the keeper of the East Gate, made repairs. [30]After him Han·a·nī´ah son of Shel·e·mī´-ah and Hā́nun sixth son of Zā́laph repaired another section. After him Me·-shul´lam son of Ber·e·chī´ah made repairs opposite his living quarters. [31]After him Mal·chī´jah, one of the goldsmiths, made repairs as far as the house of the temple servants and of the merchants, opposite the Muster Gate,[i] and to the upper room of the corner. [32]And between the upper room of the corner and the Sheep Gate the gold-smiths and the merchants made repairs.

Hostile Plots Thwarted

4 [j] Now when San·bal´lat heard that we were building the wall, he was angry and greatly enraged, and he mocked the Jews. [2]He said in the presence of his associates and of the army of Sa·mā́r·i·a, "What are these feeble Jews doing? Will they restore things? Will they sacrifice? Will they finish it in a day? Will they revive the stones out of the heaps of rubbish—and burned ones at that?" [3]Tō·bī´ah the Am´mon·ite was beside him, and he said, "That stone wall they are building—any fox going up on it would break it down!" [4]Hear, O our God, for we are despised; turn their taunt back on their own heads, and give them over as plunder in a land of captivity. [5]Do not cover their guilt, and

Have you ever tried to break apart a rock? It's not very easy! To cut stone in Bible times, workers called stonemasons would drill holes into a rock along the line they wanted to cut. Then they would hammer wooden pegs into the holes and soak the wood with water. The wet wood would expand, forcing the rock apart a little. Then the stonemasons would hammer the pegs further into the rock and wet the pegs again until the rock split open.

do not let their sin be blotted out from your sight; for they have hurled insults in the face of the builders.

6 So we rebuilt the wall, and all the wall was joined together to half its height; for the people had a mind to work.

7[k] But when San·bal´lat and Tō·bī´ah and the Arabs and the Am´mon·ites and the Ash´dod·ites heard that the repairing of the walls of Jerusalem was going forward and the gaps were beginning to be closed, they were very angry, [8]and all plotted together to come and fight against Jerusalem and to cause confusion in it. [9]So

Tribal leaders from the countryside made plans to stop the Israelites from rebuilding the walls of Jerusalem. When Nehemiah heard about their plans, he prayed to God. He also posted guards so that the people would know if their enemies came close. Nehemiah and his troops guarded the city all day and all night.

[h] Cn: Heb were living   [i] Or *Hammiphkad Gate*
[j] Ch 3.33 in Heb   [k] Ch 4.1 in Heb

we prayed to our God, and set a guard as a protection against them day and night.

10 But Judah said, "The strength of the burden bearers is failing, and there is too much rubbish so that we are unable to work on the wall." [11]And our enemies said, "They will not know or see anything before we come upon them and kill them and stop the work." [12]When the Jews who lived near them came, they said to us ten times, "From all the places where they live[l] they will come up against us."[m] [13]So in the lowest parts of the space behind the wall, in open places, I stationed the people according to their families,[n] with their swords, their spears, and their bows. [14]After I looked these things over, I stood up and said to the nobles and the officials and the rest of the people, "Do not be afraid of them. Remember the LORD, who is great and awesome, and fight for your kin, your sons, your daughters, your wives, and your homes."

15 When our enemies heard that their plot was known to us, and that God had frustrated it, we all returned to the wall, each to his work. [16]From that day on, half of my servants worked on construction, and half held the spears, shields, bows, and body-armor; and the leaders posted themselves behind the whole house of Judah, [17]who were building the wall. The burden bearers carried their loads in such a way that each labored on the work with one hand and with the other held a weapon. [18]And each of the builders had his sword strapped at his side while he built. The man who sounded the trumpet was beside me. [19]And I said to the nobles, the officials, and the rest of the people, "The work is great and widely spread out, and we are separated far from one another on the wall. [20]Rally to us wherever you hear the sound of the trumpet. Our God will fight for us."

21 So we labored at the work, and half of them held the spears from break of dawn until the stars came out. [22]I also said to the people at that time, "Let every man and his servant pass the night inside Jerusalem, so that they may be a guard for us by night and may labor by day." [23]So neither I nor my brothers nor my servants nor the men of the guard who followed me ever took off our clothes; each kept his weapon in his right hand.[o]

> Nehemiah was governor of Jerusalem from 445 to 433 BC. He not only turned down the food allowance he could have taken from taxes, but he also refused to take more property for himself. Nehemiah was generous to all people, especially the poor. He knew that everything he had came because of God's steadfast love.

Nehemiah Deals with Oppression

5 Now there was a great outcry of the people and of their wives against their Jewish kin. [2]For there were those who said, "With our sons and our daughters, we are many; we must get grain, so that we may eat and stay alive." [3]There were also those who said, "We are having to pledge our fields, our vineyards, and our houses in order to get grain during the famine." [4]And there were those who said, "We are having to borrow money on our fields and vineyards to pay the king's tax. [5]Now our flesh is the same as that of our kindred; our children are the same as their children; and yet we are forcing our sons and daughters to be slaves, and some of our daughters have been ravished; we are powerless, and our fields and vineyards now belong to others."

[l] Cn: Heb *you return*　[m] Compare Gk Syr: Meaning of Heb uncertain　[n] Meaning of Heb uncertain　[o] Cn: Heb *each his weapon the water*

6 I was very angry when I heard their outcry and these complaints. ⁷After thinking it over, I brought charges against the nobles and the officials; I said to them, "You are all taking interest from your own people." And I called a great assembly to deal with them, ⁸and said to them, "As far as we were able, we have bought back our Jewish kindred who had been sold to other nations; but now you are selling your own kin, who must then be bought back by us!" They were silent, and could not find a word to say. ⁹So I said, "The thing that you are doing is not good. Should you not walk in the fear of our God, to prevent the taunts of the nations our enemies? ¹⁰Moreover I and my brothers and my servants are lending them money and grain. Let us stop this taking of interest. ¹¹Restore to them, this very day, their fields, their vineyards, their olive orchards, and their houses, and the interest on money, grain, wine, and oil that you have been exacting from them." ¹²Then they said, "We will restore everything and demand nothing more from them. We will do as you say." And I called the priests, and made them take an oath to do as they had promised. ¹³I also shook out the fold of my garment and said, "So may God shake out everyone from house and from property who does not perform this promise. Thus may they be shaken out and emptied." And all the assembly said, "Amen," and praised the LORD. And the people did as they had promised.

The Generosity of Nehemiah

14 Moreover from the time that I was appointed to be their governor in the land of Judah, from the twentieth year to the thirty-second year of King Ar·ta·xerx´ēs, twelve years, neither I nor my brothers ate the food allowance of the governor. ¹⁵The former governors who were before me laid heavy burdens on the people, and took food and wine from them, besides forty shekels of silver. Even their servants lorded it over the people. But I did not do so, because of the fear of God. ¹⁶Indeed, I devoted myself to the work on this wall, and acquired no land; and all my servants were gathered there for the work. ¹⁷Moreover there were at my table one hundred fifty people, Jews and officials, besides those who came to us from the nations around us. ¹⁸Now that which was prepared for one day was one ox and six choice sheep; also fowls were prepared for me, and every ten days skins of wine in abundance; yet with all this I did not demand the food allowance of the governor, because of the heavy burden of labor on the people. ¹⁹Remember for my good, O my God, all that I have done for this people.

Intrigues of Enemies Foiled

6 Now when it was reported to San·bal´lat and Tō·bī´ah and to Gē´shem the Arab and to the rest of our enemies that I had built the wall and that there was no gap left in it (though up to that time I had not set up the doors in the gates), ²San·bal´lat and Gē´shem sent to me, saying, "Come and let us meet together in one of the villages in the plain of Ō´nō." But they intended to do me harm. ³So I sent messengers to them, saying, "I am doing a great work and I cannot come down. Why should the work stop while I leave it to come down to you?" ⁴They sent to me four times in this way, and I answered them

What are some of the good building blocks needed for living a faithful Christian life? God, Love, Trust, Loyalty, Jesus Christ, Strength, Joy, Hope, Peace, Patience, Holy Spirit. Which of these things are reflected in your life? What would you add to the list? Read the following verses and think of yourself as a living stone being shaped by God: Matthew 16:18, Luke 6:46–49, and 1 Peter 2:4–5.

in the same manner. ⁵In the same way San·bal´lat for the fifth time sent his servant to me with an open letter in his hand. ⁶In it was written, "It is reported among the nations—and Gē´shem*ᵖ* also says it—that you and the Jews intend to rebel; that is why you are building the wall; and according to this report you wish to become their king. ⁷You have also set up prophets to proclaim in Jerusalem concerning you, 'There is a king in Judah!' And now it will be reported to the king according to these words. So come, therefore, and let us confer together." ⁸Then I sent to him, saying, "No such things as you say have been done; you are inventing them out of your own mind"⁹—for they all wanted to frighten us, thinking, "Their hands will drop from the work, and it will not be done." But now, O God, strengthen my hands.

10 One day when I went into the house of She·mai´ah son of De·lai´ah son of Me·het´a·bel, who was confined to his house, he said, "Let us meet together in the house of God, within the temple, and let us close the doors of the temple, for they are coming to kill you;

indeed, tonight they are coming to kill you." ¹¹But I said, "Should a man like me run away? Would a man like me go into the temple to save his life? I will not go in!" ¹²Then I perceived and saw that God had not sent him at all, but he had pronounced the prophecy against me because Tō·bi´ah and San·bal´lat had hired him. ¹³He was hired for this purpose, to intimidate me and make me sin by acting in this way, and so they could give me a bad name, in order to taunt me. ¹⁴Remember Tō·bi´ah and San·bal´lat, O my God, according to these things that they did, and also the prophetess Nō·a·di´ah and the rest of the prophets who wanted to make me afraid.

The Wall Completed

15 So the wall was finished on the twenty-fifth day of the month Ē´lul, in fifty-two days. ¹⁶And when all our enemies heard of it, all the nations around us were afraid*�q* and fell greatly in their own esteem; for they perceived that this work had been accomplished with the help of our God. ¹⁷Moreover in those days the nobles of Judah sent many letters to Tō·bi´ah, and Tō·bi´ah's letters came to them. ¹⁸For many in Judah were bound by oath to him, because he was the son-in-law of Shec·a·ni´ah son of Ā´rah: and his son Je·hō·hā´nan had married the daughter of Me·shul´lam son of Ber·e·chi´ah. ¹⁹Also they spoke of his good deeds in my presence, and reported my words to him. And Tō·bi´ah sent letters to intimidate me.

7 Now when the wall had been built and I had set up the doors, and the gatekeepers, the singers, and the Lē´vites had been appointed, ²I gave my brother Ha·na´ni charge over Jerusalem, along with Han·a·ni´ah the commander of the citadel—for he was a faithful man and feared God more than many. ³And I said to them, "The gates of Jerusalem are not to be opened until the sun is hot; while

To keep the walls standing straight, the people used a reed (a straight cane about twenty feet long) and a plumb line (a lead cone attached by a line to a wooden rod). They strung a line from corner to corner as a guide for laying each layer of stone. The stones in the walls were fit together so tightly that there was no need for mortar (cement-like material)! The people worked together to finish the wall. Despite the threats from their enemies, they finished in only fifty-two days. After 150 years, Jerusalem was once again a city protected by strong walls.

ᵖ Heb *Gashmu*   *�q* Another reading is *saw*

the gatekeepers[r] are still standing guard, let them shut and bar the doors. Appoint guards from among the inhabitants of Jerusalem, some at their watch posts, and others before their own houses." [4]The city was wide and large, but the people within it were few and no houses had been built.

Lists of the Returned Exiles

5 Then my God put it into my mind to assemble the nobles and the officials and the people to be enrolled by genealogy. And I found the book of the genealogy of those who were the first to come back, and I found the following written in it:

6 These are the people of the province who came up out of the captivity of those exiles whom King Ne·bū·chad·nez′zar of Babylon had carried into exile; they returned to Jerusalem and Judah, each to his town. [7]They came with Ze·rub′ba·bel, Jesh′ū·a, Nē·he·mī′ah, Az·a·rī′ah, Rā·a·mī′ah, Nā·ham′a·nī, Mor′de·caī, Bil′shan, Mis′pe·reth, Big′vaī, Nē′hum, Bā′a·nah.

The number of the Israelite people: [8]the descendants of Pā′rosh, two thousand one hundred seventy-two. [9]Of Sheph·a·tī′ah, three hundred seventy-two. [10]Of Ā′rah, six hundred fifty-two. [11]Of Pā′hath-mō′ab, namely the descendants of Jesh′ū·a and Jō′ab, two thousand eight hundred eighteen. [12]Of Ē′lam, one thousand two hundred fifty-four. [13]Of Zat′tū, eight hundred forty-five. [14]Of Zac′caī, seven hundred sixty. [15]Of Bin′nū·ī, six hundred forty-eight. [16]Of Bē′baī, six hundred twenty-eight. [17]Of Az′gad, two thousand three hundred twenty-two. [18]Of Ad·o·nī′kam, six hundred sixty-seven. [19]Of Big′vaī, two thousand sixty-seven. [20]Of Ā′din, six hundred fifty-five. [21]Of Ā′ter, namely of Hez·e·kī′ah, ninety-eight. [22]Of Hā′shum, three hundred twenty-eight. [23]Of Be′zaī, three hundred twenty-four. [24]Of Ha′riph, one hundred twelve. [25]Of Gib′ē·on, ninety-five. [26]The people of Bethlehem and Ne·toph′ah, one hundred eighty-eight. [27]Of An′a·thoth, one hundred

twenty-eight. [28]Of Beth-az′ma·veth, forty-two. [29]Of Kir′i·ath-jē′a·rim, Chē·phī′rah, and Be·er′oth, seven hundred forty-three. [30]Of Rā′mah and Gē′ba, six hundred twenty-one. [31]Of Mich′mas, one hundred twenty-two. [32]Of Beth′el and Aī, one hundred twenty-three. [33]Of the other Nē′bō, fifty-two. [34]The descendants of the other Ē′lam, one thousand two hundred fifty-four. [35]Of Hā′rim, three hundred twenty. [36]Of Jericho, three hundred forty-five. [37]Of Lod, Hā′did, and Ō′nō, seven hundred twenty-one. [38]Of Se·nā′ah, three thousand nine hundred thirty.

39 The priests: the descendants of Je·daī′ah, namely the house of Jesh′ū·a, nine hundred seventy-three. [40]Of Im′mer, one thousand fifty-two. [41]Of Pash′hur, one thousand two hundred forty-seven. [42]Of Hā′rim, one thousand seventeen.

43 The Lē′vītes: the descendants of Jesh′ū·a, namely of Kad′mi·el of the descendants of Hō′de·vah, seventy-four. [44]The singers: the descendants of Ā′saph, one hundred forty-eight. [45]The gatekeepers: the descendants of Shal′lum, of Ā′ter, of Tal′mon, of Ak′kub, of Ha·tī′ta, of Shō′baī, one hundred thirty-eight.

46 The temple servants: the descendants of Zī′ha, of Ha·sū′pha, of Tab·bā′oth, [47]of Kē′ros, of Sī′a, of Pā′don, [48]of Le·bā′na, of Hag′a·ba, of Shal′maī, [49]of Hā′nan, of Gid′del, of Gā′har, [50]of Rē·aī′ah, of Rē′zin, of Ne·kō′da, [51]of Gaz′zam, of Uz′za, of Pa·sē′ah, [52]of Bē′saī, of Me·ū′nim, of Ne·phūsh′e·sim, [53]of Bak′buk, of Ha·kū′pha, of Har′hur, [54]of Baz′lith, of Me·hī′da, of Har′sha, [55]of Bar′kos, of Sis′e·ra, of Tē′mah, [56]of Ne·zī′ah, of Ha·tī′pha.

57 The descendants of Solomon's servants: of Sō′taī, of Sō′phe·reth, of Pe·rī′da, [58]of Jā′a·la, of Dar′kon, of Gid′del, [59]of Sheph·a·tī′ah, of Hat′til, of Pō′che·reth-haz·ze·bā′im, of Ā′mon.

60 All the temple servants and the descendants of Solomon's servants were three hundred ninety-two.

61 The following were those who came

[r] Heb *while they*

up from Tel-me´lah, Tel-har´sha, Che´rub, Ad´don, and Im´mer, but they could not prove their ancestral houses or their descent, whether they belonged to Israel: [62]the descendants of De·lai´ah, of To·bi´ah, of Ne·ko´da, six hundred forty-two. [63]Also, of the priests: the descendants of Ho·bai´ah, of Hak´koz, of Bar·zil´lai (who had married one of the daughters of Bar·zil´lai the Gil´e·ad·ite and was called by their name). [64]These sought their registration among those enrolled in the genealogies, but it was not found there, so they were excluded from the priesthood as unclean; [65]the governor told them that they were not to partake of the most holy food, until a priest with U´rim and Thum´mim should come.

66 The whole assembly together was forty-two thousand three hundred sixty, [67]besides their male and female slaves, of whom there were seven thousand three hundred thirty-seven; and they had two hundred forty-five singers, male and female. [68]They had seven hundred thirty-six horses, two hundred forty-five mules,[s] [69]four hundred thirty-five camels, and six thousand seven hundred twenty donkeys.

70 Now some of the heads of ancestral houses contributed to the work. The governor gave to the treasury one thousand darics of gold, fifty basins, and five hundred thirty priestly robes. [71]And some of the heads of ancestral houses gave into the building fund twenty thousand darics of gold and two thousand two hundred minas of silver. [72]And what the rest of the people gave was twenty thousand darics of gold, two thousand minas of silver, and sixty-seven priestly robes.

73 So the priests, the Le´vites, the gatekeepers, the singers, some of the people, the temple servants, and all Israel settled in their towns.

Ezra Summons the People to Obey the Law

When the seventh month came— the people of Israel being settled in their towns—[1]all the people gathered **8** together into the square before the Water Gate. They told the scribe Ezra to bring the book of the law of Moses, which the LORD had given to Israel. [2]Accordingly, the priest Ezra brought the law before the assembly, both men and women and all who could hear with understanding. This was on the first day of the seventh month. [3]He read from it facing the square before the Water Gate from early morning until midday, in the presence of the men and the women and those who could understand; and the ears of all the people were attentive to the book of the law. [4]The scribe Ezra stood on a wooden platform that had been made for the purpose; and beside him stood Mat·ti·thi´ah, She´ma, A·nai´ah, U·ri´ah, Hil·ki´ah, and Ma·a·sei´ah on his right hand; and Pe·dai´ah, Mish´a·el, Mal·chi´- jah, Ha´shum, Hash-bad´da·nah, Zech·a·ri´- ah, and Me·shul´lam on his left hand. [5]And Ezra opened the book in the sight of all the people, for he was standing above all the people; and when he opened it, all the people stood up. [6]Then Ezra blessed the LORD, the great God, and all the people answered, "Amen, Amen," lifting up their hands. Then they bowed their heads and

When the walls were finished, the people gathered together and listened for the first time in many years as Ezra read the book of the law. The Levites went out into the crowd and answered any questions the people had about what they were hearing. The people were sad because they realized how far they had moved from the way God wanted them to live and worship. Nehemiah told them not to be sad, but to celebrate! This was a holy day, and the people were returning to God's way of living.

s Ezra 2.66 and the margins of some Hebrew Mss: MT lacks *They had . . . forty-five mules* worshiped the LORD with their faces to the ground. ⁷Also Jesh´u·a, Bā´nī, Sher·e·bī´ah, Jā´min, Ak´kub, Shab´be·thaī, Hō·dī´ah, Mā·a·sēi´ah, Ke·lī´ta, Az·a·rī´ah, Joz´a·bad, Hā´nan, Pe·lāi´ah, the Lē´vītes,^t helped the people to understand the law, while the people remained in their places. ⁸So they read from the book, from the law of God, with interpretation. They gave the sense, so that the people understood the reading.

9 And Nē·he·mī´ah, who was the governor, and Ezra the priest and scribe, and the Lē´vītes who taught the people said to all the people, "This day is holy to the LORD your God; do not mourn or weep." For all the people wept when they heard the words of the law. ¹⁰Then he said to them, "Go your way, eat the fat and drink sweet wine and send portions of them to those for whom nothing is prepared, for this day is holy to our LORD; and do not be grieved, for the joy of the LORD is your strength." ¹¹So the Lē´vītes stilled all the people, saying, "Be quiet, for this day is holy; do not be grieved." ¹²And all the people went their way to eat and drink and to send portions and to make great rejoicing, because they had understood the words that were declared to them.

The Festival of Booths Celebrated

13 On the second day the heads of ancestral houses of all the people, with the priests and the Lē´vītes, came together to the scribe Ezra in order to study the words of the law. ¹⁴And they found it written in the law, which the LORD had commanded by Moses, that the people of Israel should live in booths^u during the festival of the seventh month, ¹⁵and that they should publish and proclaim in all their towns and in Jerusalem as follows, "Go out to the hills and bring branches of olive, wild olive, myrtle, palm, and other leafy trees to make booths,^u as it is written." ¹⁶So the people went out and brought them, and made booths^u for themselves, each on the roofs of their houses, and in their courts

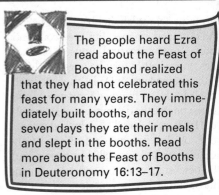

The people heard Ezra read about the Feast of Booths and realized that they had not celebrated this feast for many years. They immediately built booths, and for seven days they ate their meals and slept in the booths. Read more about the Feast of Booths in Deuteronomy 16:13–17.

and in the courts of the house of God, and in the square at the Water Gate and in the square at the Gate of Ē´phra·im. ¹⁷And all the assembly of those who had returned from the captivity made booths^u and lived in them; for from the days of Jesh´u·a son of Nun to that day the people of Israel had not done so. And there was very great rejoicing. ¹⁸And day by day, from the first day to the last day, he read from the book of the law of God. They kept the festival seven days; and on the eighth day there was a solemn assembly, according to the ordinance.

National Confession

9 Now on the twenty-fourth day of this month the people of Israel were assembled with fasting and in sackcloth, and with earth on their heads.^v ²Then those of Israelite descent separated themselves from all foreigners, and stood and confessed their sins and the iniquities of their ancestors. ³They stood up in their place and read from the book of the law of the LORD their God for a fourth part of the day, and for another fourth they made confession and worshiped the LORD their God. ⁴Then Jesh´u·a, Bā´nī, Kad´mi·el, Sheb·a·nī´ah, Bun´nī, Sher·e·bī´ah, Bā´nī, and Che·nā´nī stood on the stairs of the Lē´vītes and cried out with a loud voice to the LORD their God. ⁵Then the Lē´vītes, Jesh´u·a, Kad´mi·el, Bā´nī, Hash·ab·neī´ah, Sher·e·bī´ah, Hō·dī´ah, Sheb·a·nī´ah, and Peth·a·hī´ah, said, "Stand up and bless the LORD

^t 1 Esdras 9.48 Vg: Heb *and the Levites*   ^u Or *tabernacles*; Heb *succoth*   ^v Heb *on them*

"Stand up and bless the
LORD your God from ever-
lasting to everlasting.
Blessed be your glorious
name, which is exalted above all
blessing and praise." Nehemiah 9:5*b*

your God from everlasting to everlasting.
Blessed be your glorious name, which is
exalted above all blessing and praise."

6 And Ezra said:*w* "You are the LORD,
you alone; you have made heaven, the
heaven of heavens, with all their host, the
earth and all that is on it, the seas and all
that is in them. To all of them you give life,
and the host of heaven worships you.
⁷You are the LORD, the God who chose
Abram and brought him out of Ūr of the
Chal·dēʹans and gave him the name Abraham; ⁸and you found his heart faithful
before you, and made with him a
covenant to give to his descendants the
land of the Cāʹnaan·īte, the Hitʹtīte, the
Amʹo·rīte, the Perʹiz·zīte, the Jebʹu·sīte,
and the Girʹga·shīte; and you have fulfilled your promise, for you are righteous.
9 "And you saw the distress of our
ancestors in Egypt and heard their cry at
the Red Sea.*x* ¹⁰You performed signs and
wonders against Pharaoh and all his servants and all the people of his land, for
you knew that they acted insolently
against our ancestors. You made a name
for yourself, which remains to this day.
¹¹And you divided the sea before them, so
that they passed through the sea on dry
land, but you threw their pursuers into
the depths, like a stone into mighty
waters. ¹²Moreover, you led them by day
with a pillar of cloud, and by night with a
pillar of fire, to give them light on the way
in which they should go. ¹³You came
down also upon Mount Sinai, and spoke
with them from heaven, and gave them
right ordinances and true laws, good
statutes and commandments, ¹⁴and you
made known your holy sabbath to them
and gave them commandments and

statutes and a law through your servant
Moses. ¹⁵For their hunger you gave them
bread from heaven, and for their thirst
you brought water for them out of the
rock, and you told them to go in to possess the land that you swore to give them.
16 "But they and our ancestors acted
presumptuously and stiffened their
necks and did not obey your commandments; ¹⁷they refused to obey, and were
not mindful of the wonders that you
performed among them; but they stiffened their necks and determined to
return to their slavery in Egypt. But you
are a God ready to forgive, gracious and
merciful, slow to anger and abounding
in steadfast love, and you did not forsake
them. ¹⁸Even when they had cast an
image of a calf for themselves and said,
'This is your God who brought you up
out of Egypt,' and had committed great
blasphemies, ¹⁹you in your great mercies
did not forsake them in the wilderness;
the pillar of cloud that led them in the
way did not leave them by day, nor the
pillar of fire by night that gave them
light on the way by which they should
go. ²⁰You gave your good spirit to
instruct them, and did not withhold
your manna from their mouths, and
gave them water for their thirst. ²¹Forty
years you sustained them in the wilderness
so that they lacked nothing; their clothes
did not wear out and their feet did not
swell. ²²And you gave them kingdoms
and peoples, and allotted to them every
corner,*y* so they took possession of the
land of King Sīʹhon of Heshʹbon and the
land of King Og of Bāʹshan. ²³You multiplied their descendants like the stars of
heaven, and brought them into the land
that you had told their ancestors to enter
and possess. ²⁴So the descendants went in
and possessed the land, and you subdued
before them the inhabitants of the land,
the Cāʹnaan·ites, and gave them into their
hands, with their kings and the peoples of

w Gk: Heb lacks *And Ezra said*   *x* Or *Sea of Reeds*
y Meaning of Heb uncertain

the land, to do with them as they pleased. ²⁵And they captured fortress cities and a rich land, and took possession of houses filled with all sorts of goods, hewn cisterns, vineyards, olive orchards, and fruit trees in abundance; so they ate, and were filled and became fat, and delighted themselves in your great goodness.

26 "Nevertheless they were disobedient and rebelled against you and cast your law behind their backs and killed your prophets, who had warned them in order to turn them back to you, and they committed great blasphemies. ²⁷Therefore you gave them into the hands of their enemies, who made them suffer. Then in the time of their suffering they cried out to you and you heard them from heaven, and according to your great mercies you gave them saviors who saved them from the hands of their enemies. ²⁸But after they had rest, they again did evil before you, and you abandoned them to the hands of their enemies, so that they had dominion over them; yet when they turned and cried to you, you heard from heaven, and many times you rescued them according to your mercies. ²⁹And you warned them in order to turn them back to your law. Yet they acted presumptuously and did not obey your commandments, but sinned against your ordinances, by the observance of which a person shall live. They turned a stubborn shoulder and stiffened their neck and would not obey. ³⁰Many years you were patient with them, and warned them by your spirit through your prophets; yet they would not listen. Therefore you handed them over to the peoples of the lands. ³¹Nevertheless, in your great mercies you did not make an end of them or forsake them, for you are a gracious and merciful God.

32 "Now therefore, our God—the great and mighty and awesome God, keeping covenant and steadfast love—do not treat lightly all the hardship that has come upon us, upon our kings, our officials, our priests, our prophets, our ancestors, and

all your people, since the time of the kings of Assyria until today. ³³You have been just in all that has come upon us, for you have dealt faithfully and we have acted wickedly; ³⁴our kings, our officials, our priests, and our ancestors have not kept your law or heeded the commandments and the warnings that you gave them. ³⁵Even in their own kingdom, and in the great goodness you bestowed on them, and in the large and rich land that you set before them, they did not serve you and did not turn from their wicked works. ³⁶Here we are, slaves to this day—slaves in the land that you gave to our ancestors to enjoy its fruit and its good gifts. ³⁷Its rich yield goes to the kings whom you have set over us because of our sins; they have power also over our bodies and over our livestock at their pleasure, and we are in great distress."

Those Who Signed the Covenant

38^z Because of all this we make a firm agreement in writing, and on that sealed document are inscribed the names of our officials, our Lē′vītes, and our priests.

10 ^a Upon the sealed document are the names of Nē·he·mī′ah the governor, son of Hac·a·lī′ah, and Zed·e·kī′ah; ²Se·rāi′ah, Az·a·rī′ah, Jer·e·mī′ah, ³Pash′hur, Am·a·rī′ah, Mal·chī′jah, ⁴Hat′tush, Sheb·a·nī′ah, Mal′luch, ⁵Hā′rim, Mer′e·moth, Ō·ba·dī′ah, ⁶Daniel, Gin′ne·thon, Bar′uch, ⁷Me·shul′lam, A·bī′jah, Mij′a·min, ⁸Mā·a·zī′ah, Bil′gai, She·māi′ah; these are the priests. ⁹And the Lē′vītes: Jesh′ū·a son of Az·a·nī′ah, Bin′nū·ī of the sons of Hen′a·dad, Kad′mi·el; ¹⁰and their associates, Sheb·a·nī′ah, Hō·dī′ah, Ke·lī′ta, Pe·lāi′ah, Hā′nan, ¹¹Mī′ca, Rē′hob, Hash·a·bī′ah, ¹²Zac′cur, Sher·e·bī′ah, Sheb·a·nī′ah, ¹³Hō·dī′ah, Bā′nī, Be·nī′nū. ¹⁴The leaders of the people: Pā′rosh, Pā′hath-mō′ab, Ē′lam, Zat′tū, Bā′nī, ¹⁵Bun′nī, Az′gad, Bē′bai, ¹⁶Ad·o·nī′jah, Big′vai, Ā′din, ¹⁷Ā′ter, Hez·e·kī′ah, Az′zur, ¹⁸Hō·dī′ah, Hā′shum, Bē′zai,

[19]Hā´riph, An´a·thoth, Ne̅´ba̅i, [20]Mag´pi-ash, Me·shul´lam, He̅´zir, [21]Me·shez´a·bel, Zā´dok, Jad´du̅·a, [22]Pel·a·tī´ah, Hā´nan, A·naī´ah, [23]Hō·she̅´a, Han·a·nī´ah, Has´-shub, [24]Hal·lō´hesh, Pil´ha, Shō´bek, [25]Re̅´hum, Ha·shab´nah, Mā·a·sēi´ah, [26]A·hī´ah, Hā´nan, Ā´nan, [27]Mal´luch, Hā´rim, and Bā´a·nah.

Summary of the Covenant

28 The rest of the people, the priests, the Le̅´vītes, the gatekeepers, the singers, the temple servants, and all who have separated themselves from the peoples of the lands to adhere to the law of God, their wives, their sons, their daughters, all who have knowledge and understanding, [29]join with their kin, their nobles, and enter into a curse and an oath to walk in God's law, which was given by Moses the servant of God, and to observe and do all the commandments of the LORD our Lord and his ordinances and his statutes. [30]We will not give our daughters to the peoples of the land or take their daughters for our sons; [31]and if the peoples of the land bring in merchandise or any grain on the sabbath day to sell, we will not buy it from them on the sabbath or on a holy day; and we will forego the crops of the seventh year and the exaction of every debt.

32 We also lay on ourselves the obligation to charge ourselves yearly one-third of a shekel for the service of the house of our God: [33]for the rows of bread, the regular grain offering, the regular burnt offering, the sabbaths, the new moons, the appointed festivals, the sacred donations, and the sin offerings to make atonement for Israel, and for all the work of the house of our God. [34]We have also cast lots among the priests, the Le̅´vītes, and the people, for the wood offering, to bring it into the house of our God, by ancestral houses, at appointed times, year by year, to burn on the altar of the LORD our God, as it is written in the law. [35]We obligate ourselves to bring the first fruits of our soil and the first

fruits of all fruit of every tree, year by year, to the house of the LORD; [36]also to bring to the house of our God, to the priests who minister in the house of our God, the firstborn of our sons and of our livestock, as it is written in the law, and the firstlings of our herds and of our flocks; [37]and to bring the first of our dough, and our contributions, the fruit of every tree, the wine and the oil, to the priests, to the chambers of the house of our God; and to bring to the Le̅´vītes the tithes from our soil, for it is the Le̅´vītes who collect the tithes in all our rural towns. [38]And the priest, the descendant of Aaron, shall be with the Le̅´vītes when the Le̅´vītes receive the tithes; and the Le̅´vītes shall bring up a tithe of the tithes to the house of our God, to the chambers of the storehouse. [39]For the people of Israel and the sons of Levi shall bring the contribution of grain, wine, and oil to the storerooms where the vessels of the sanctuary are, and where the priests that minister, and the gatekeepers and the singers are. We will not neglect the house of our God.

Population of the City Increased

11 Now the leaders of the people lived in Jerusalem; and the rest of the people cast lots to bring one out of ten to live in the holy city Jerusalem, while nine-tenths remained in the other towns. [2]And the people blessed all those who willingly offered to live in Jerusalem.

3 These are the leaders of the province who lived in Jerusalem; but in the towns of Judah all lived on their property in their towns: Israel, the priests, the Le̅´vītes, the temple servants, and the descendants of Solomon's servants. [4]And in Jerusalem lived some of the Ju̅´dah·ītes and of the Ben´ja·min·ītes. Of the Ju̅´dah-ītes: A·thaī´ah son of Uz·zī´ah son of Zech·a·rī´ah son of Am·a·rī´ah son of Sheph·a·tī´ah son of Ma·hal´a·lel, of the descendants of Per´ez; [5]and Mā·a·sēi´ah son of Bar´uch son of Col·hō´zeh son of

Ha·zaī´ah son of A·dāi´ah son of Joi´a·rib son of Zech·a·rī´ah son of the Shī´lo·nīte. ⁶All the descendants of Per´ez who lived in Jerusalem were four hundred sixty-eight valiant warriors.

7 And these are the Ben´ja·min·ītes: Sal´lū son of Me·shul´lam son of Jō´ed son of Pe·dāi´ah son of Kō´laī´ah son of Mā·a·sēi´ah son of Ith´i·el son of Je·shā´i·ah. ⁸And his brothers*b* Gab·bā´ī, Sal´laī: nine hundred twenty-eight. ⁹Jō´el son of Zich´rī was their overseer; and Judah son of Has·se·nū´ah was second in charge of the city.

10 Of the priests: Je·daī´ah son of Joi´a·rib, Jā´chin, ¹¹Se·rāi´ah son of Hil·kī´ah son of Me·shul´lam son of Zā´dok son of Me·rā´i·oth son of A·hī´tub, officer of the house of God, ¹²and their associates who did the work of the house, eight hundred twenty-two; and A·dāi´ah son of Je·rō´ham son of Pel·a·lī´ah son of Am´zī son of Zech·a·rī´ah son of Pash´-hur son of Mal·chī´jah, ¹³and his associates, heads of ancestral houses, two hundred forty-two; and A·mash´sai son of Az´a·rel son of Ah´zaī son of Me·shil´le·moth son of Im´mer, ¹⁴and their associates, valiant warriors, one hundred twenty-eight; their overseer was Zab´di·el son of Hag·ge·dō´lim.

15 And of the Lē´vītes: She·māi´ah son of Has´shub son of Az·rī´kam son of Hash·a·bī´ah son of Bun´nī; ¹⁶and Shab´-be·thaī and Joz´a·bad, of the leaders of the Lē´vītes, who were over the outside work of the house of God; ¹⁷and Mat·ta·nī´ah son of Mī´ca son of Zab´dī son of Ā´saph, who was the leader to begin the thanksgiving in prayer, and Bak·bū·kī´ah, the second among his associates; and Ab´da son of Sham´mū·a son of Gā´lal son of Je·dū´thun. ¹⁸All the Lē´vītes in the holy city were two hundred eighty-four.

19 The gatekeepers, Ak´kub, Tal´-mon and their associates, who kept watch at the gates, were one hundred seventy-two. ²⁰And the rest of Israel, and of the priests and the Lē´vītes, were in all

the towns of Judah, all of them in their inheritance. ²¹But the temple servants lived on Ō´phel; and Zī´ha and Gish´pa were over the temple servants.

22 The overseer of the Lē´vītes in Jerusalem was Uz´zī son of Bā´nī son of Hash·a·bī´ah son of Mat·ta·nī´ah son of Mī´-ca, of the descendants of Ā´saph, the singers, in charge of the work of the house of God. ²³For there was a command from the king concerning them, and a settled provision for the singers, as was required every day. ²⁴And Peth·a·hī´ah son of Me·shez´a·bel, of the descendants of Zē´-rah son of Judah, was at the king's hand in all matters concerning the people.

Villages outside Jerusalem

25 And as for the villages, with their fields, some of the people of Judah lived in Kir´i·ath-ar´ba and its villages, and in Dī´bon and its villages, and in Je·kab´zē·el and its villages, ²⁶and in Jesh´ū·a and in Mō´la·dah and Beth-pel´et, ²⁷in Hā´zar-shū´al, in Bē´er-shē´ba and its villages, ²⁸in Zik´lag, in Mē·cō´nah and its villages, ²⁹in En-rim´mon, in Zō´rah, in Jar´-muth, ³⁰Za·nō´ah, A·dul´lam, and their villages, Lā´chish and its fields, and A·zē´-kah and its villages. So they camped from Bē´er-shē´ba to the valley of Hin´nom. ³¹The people of Benjamin also lived from Gē´ba onward, at Mich´mash, Āi´ja, Beth´el and its villages, ³²An´a·thoth, Nob, An·a·nī´ah, ³³Hā´zor, Rā´mah, Git´ta·im, ³⁴Hā´did, Ze·bō´im, Ne·bal´lat, ³⁵Lod, and Ō´nō, the valley of artisans. ³⁶And certain divisions of the Lē´vītes in Judah were joined to Benjamin.

A List of Priests and Levites

12 These are the priests and the Lē´-vītes who came up with Ze·rub´-ba·bel son of She·al´ti·el, and Jesh´ū·a: Se·rāi´ah, Jer·e·mī´ah, Ezra, ²Am·a·rī´ah, Mal´luch, Hat´tush, ³Shec·a·nī´ah, Rē´hum, Mer´e·moth, ⁴Id´dō, Gin´ne·thoi, A·bī´jah, ⁵Mij´a·min, Mā·a·dī´ah, Bil´gah, ⁶She·māi´ah, Joi´a·rib, Je·daī´ah, ⁷Sal´lū, Ā´mok,

b Gk Mss: Heb And after him

Hil·kī´ah, Je·daī´ah. These were the leaders of the priests and of their associates in the days of Jesh´ū·a.

8 And the Lē´vītes: Jesh´ū·a, Bin´nū·ī, Kad´mi·el, Sher·e·bī´ah, Judah, and Mat⁻ta·nī´ah, who with his associates was in charge of the songs of thanksgiving. ⁹And Bak·bū·kī´ah and Un´nō their associates stood opposite them in the service. ¹⁰Jesh´ū·a was the father of Joi´a·kim, Joi´a·kim the father of E·lī´a·shib, E·lī´a·shib the father of Joi´a·da, ¹¹Joi´a·da the father of Jonathan, and Jonathan the father of Jad´dū·a.

12 In the days of Joi´a·kim the priests, heads of ancestral houses, were: of Se·rāi´ah, Me·rāi´ah; of Je·re·mī´ah, Han·a·nī´ah; ¹³of Ezra, Me·shul´lam; of Am·a·rī´ah, Jē·hō·hā´nan; ¹⁴of Mal´lu·chī, Jonathan; of Sheb·a·nī´ah, Joseph; ¹⁵of Hā´rim, Ad´na; of Me·rāi´oth, Hel´kaī; ¹⁶of Id´dō, Zech·a·rī´ah; of Gin´ne·thon, Me·shul´lam; ¹⁷of A·bī´jah, Zich´rī; of Mi·nī´a·min, of Mō·a·dī´ah, Pil´taī; ¹⁸of Bil´gah, Sham·mū´a; of She·māi´ah, Je·hon´a·than; ¹⁹of Joi´a·rib, Mat·tē´naī; of Je·daī´ah, Uz´zī; ²⁰of Sal´laī, Kal´laī; of Ā´mok, Ē´ber; ²¹of Hil·kī´ah, Hash·a·bī´ah; of Je·daī´ah, Ne·than´el.

22 As for the Lē´vītes, in the days of E·lī´a·shib, Joi´a·da, Jō·hā´nan, and Jad´dū·a, there were recorded the heads of ancestral houses; also the priests until the reign of Da·rī´us the Persian. ²³The Lē´vītes, heads of ancestral houses, were recorded in the Book of the Annals until the days of Jō·hā´nan son of E·lī´a·shib. ²⁴And the leaders of the Lē´vītes: Hash·a·bī´ah, Sher·e·bī´ah, and Jesh´ū·a son of Kad´mi·el, with their associates over against them, to praise and to give thanks, according to the commandment of David the man of God, section opposite to section. ²⁵Mat·ta·nī´ah, Bak·bū·kī´ah, Ō·ba·dī´ah, Me·shul´lam, Tal´mon, and Ak´kub were gatekeepers standing guard at the storehouses of the gates. ²⁶These were in the days of Joi´a·kim son of Jesh´ū·a son of Jō´za·dak, and in the days of the governor Nē·he·mī´ah and of the priest Ezra, the scribe.

Dedication of the City Wall

27 Now at the dedication of the wall of Jerusalem they sought out the Lē´vītes in all their places, to bring them to Jerusalem to celebrate the dedication with rejoicing, with thanksgivings and with singing, with cymbals, harps, and lyres. ²⁸The companies of the singers gathered together from the circuit around Jerusalem and from the villages of the Ne·toph´a·thītes; ²⁹also from Beth-gil´gal and from the region of Gē´ba and Az´ma·veth; for the singers had built for themselves villages around Jerusalem. ³⁰And the priests and the Lē´vītes purified themselves; and they purified the people and the gates and the wall.

31 Then I brought the leaders of Judah up onto the wall, and appointed two great companies that gave thanks and went in procession. One went to the right on the wall to the Dung Gate; ³²and after them went Hō·shaī´ah and half the officials of Judah, ³³and Az·a·rī´ah, Ezra, Me·shul´lam, ³⁴Judah, Benjamin, She·māi´ah, and Je·re·mī´ah, ³⁵and some of the young priests with trumpets: Zech·a·rī´ah son of Jonathan son of She·māi´ah son of Mat·ta·nī´ah son of Mī·cāi´ah son of Zac´cur son of Ā´saph; ³⁶and his kindred, She·māi´ah, Az´a·rel, Mil´a·laī, Gil´a·laī, Mā´aī, Ne·than´el, Judah, and Ha·nā´nī, with the musical instruments of David the man of God; and the scribe Ezra went in front of them. ³⁷At the Fountain Gate, in front of them, they went straight up by

The Israelites dedicated the walls of Jerusalem with a great celebration! The Levites led the people as they rejoiced with singing and musical instruments. The people were very thankful, and people far away heard their rejoicing.

"The joy of Jerusalem was heard far away."
Nehemiah 12:43

the stairs of the city of David, at the ascent of the wall, above the house of David, to the Water Gate on the east.

38 The other company of those who gave thanks went to the left,[c] and I followed them with half of the people on the wall, above the Tower of the Ovens, to the Broad Wall, ³⁹and above the Gate of Ē′phra·im, and by the Old Gate, and by the Fish Gate and the Tower of Ha·nan′el and the Tower of the Hundred, to the Sheep Gate; and they came to a halt at the Gate of the Guard. ⁴⁰So both companies of those who gave thanks stood in the house of God, and I and half of the officials with me; ⁴¹and the priests E·lī′a·kim, Mā·a·sēi′ah, Mi·nī′a·min, Mī′cāi′ah, El·i·ō·ē′naī, Zech·a·rī′ah, and Han·a·nī′ah, with trumpets; ⁴²and Mā·a·sēi′ah, She·māi′ah, El·ē·ā′zar, Uz′zī, Jē·hō·hā′nan, Mal·chī′jah, Ē′lam, and Ē′zer. And the singers sang with Jez·ra·hī′ah as their leader. ⁴³They offered great sacrifices that day and rejoiced, for God had made them rejoice with great joy; the women and children also rejoiced. The joy of Jerusalem was heard far away.

Temple Responsibilities

44 On that day men were appointed over the chambers for the stores, the contributions, the first fruits, and the tithes, to gather into them the portions required by the law for the priests and for the Lē′vītes from the fields belonging to the towns; for Judah rejoiced over the priests and the Lē′vītes who ministered. ⁴⁵They performed the service of their God and the service of purification, as did the singers and the gatekeepers, according to the command of David and his son Solomon. ⁴⁶For in the days of David and Ā′saph long ago there was a leader of the singers, and there were songs of praise and thanksgiving to God. ⁴⁷In the days of

Ze·rub′ba·bel and in the days of Nē·he·mī′ah all Israel gave the daily portions for the singers and the gatekeepers. They set apart that which was for the Lē′vītes; and the Lē′vītes set apart that which was for the descendants of Aaron.

Foreigners Separated from Israel

13 On that day they read from the book of Moses in the hearing of the people; and in it was found written that no Am′mon·īte or Mō′ab·īte should ever enter the assembly of God, ²because they did not meet the Israelites with bread and water, but hired Bā′laam against them to curse them—yet our God turned the curse into a blessing. ³When the people heard the law, they separated from Israel all those of foreign descent.

The Reforms of Nehemiah

4 Now before this, the priest E·lī′a·shib, who was appointed over the chambers of the house of our God, and who was related to Tō·bī′ah, ⁵prepared for Tō·bī′ah a large room where they had previously put the grain offering, the frankincense, the vessels, and the tithes of grain, wine, and oil, which were given by commandment to the Lē′vītes, singers, and gatekeepers, and the contributions for the priests. ⁶While this was taking place I was not in Jerusalem, for in the thirty-second year of King Ar·ta·xerx′ēs of Babylon I went to the king. After some time I asked leave of the king ⁷and returned to Jerusalem. I then discovered the wrong that E·lī′a·shib had done on behalf of Tō·bī′ah, preparing a room for him in the courts of the house of God. ⁸And I was very angry, and I threw all the household furniture of Tō·bī′ah out of the room. ⁹Then I gave orders and they cleansed the chambers, and I brought back the vessels of the house of God, with the grain offering and the frankincense.

10 I also found out that the portions of the Lē′vītes had not been given to them; so that the Lē′vītes and the singers, who had

---

[c] Cn: Heb *opposite*

conducted the service, had gone back to their fields. [11]So I remonstrated with the officials and said, "Why is the house of God forsaken?" And I gathered them together and set them in their stations. [12]Then all Judah brought the tithe of the grain, wine, and oil into the storehouses. [13]And I appointed as treasurers over the storehouses the priest Shel·e·mī´ah, the scribe Zā´dok, and Pe·dāi´ah of the Lē´vītes, and as their assistant Hā´nan son of Zac´cur son of Mat·ta·nī´ah, for they were considered faithful; and their duty was to distribute to their associates. [14]Remember me, O my God, concerning this, and do not wipe out my good deeds that I have done for the house of my God and for his service.

Sabbath Reforms Begun

15 In those days I saw in Judah people treading wine presses on the sabbath, and bringing in heaps of grain and loading them on donkeys; and also wine, grapes, figs, and all kinds of burdens, which they brought into Jerusalem on the sabbath day; and I warned them at that time against selling food. [16]Tȳ´ri·ans also, who lived in the city, brought in fish and all kinds of merchandise and sold them on the sabbath to the people of Judah, and in Jerusalem. [17]Then I remonstrated with the nobles of Judah and said to them, "What is this evil thing that you are doing, profaning the sabbath day? [18]Did not your ancestors act in this way, and did not our God bring all this disaster on us and on this city? Yet you bring more wrath on Israel by profaning the sabbath."

19 When it began to be dark at the gates of Jerusalem before the sabbath, I commanded that the doors should be shut and gave orders that they should not be opened until after the sabbath. And I set some of my servants over the gates, to prevent any burden from being brought in on the sabbath day. [20]Then the merchants and sellers of all kinds of merchandise spent the night outside Jerusalem once or

twice. [21]But I warned them and said to them, "Why do you spend the night in front of the wall? If you do so again, I will lay hands on you." From that time on they did not come on the sabbath. [22]And I commanded the Lē´vītes that they should purify themselves and come and guard the gates, to keep the sabbath day holy. Remember this also in my favor, O my God, and spare me according to the greatness of your steadfast love.

Mixed Marriages Condemned

23 In those days also I saw Jews who had married women of Ash´dod, Am´mon, and Mō´ab; [24]and half of their children spoke the language of Ash´dod, and they could not speak the language of Judah, but spoke the language of various peoples. [25]And I contended with them and cursed them and beat some of them and pulled out their hair; and I made them take an oath in the name of God, saying, "You shall not give your daughters to their sons, or take their daughters for your sons or for yourselves. [26]Did not King Solomon of Israel sin on account of such women? Among the many nations there was no king like him, and he was beloved by his God, and God made him king over all Israel; nevertheless, foreign women made even him to sin. [27]Shall we then listen to you and do all this great evil and act treacherously against our God by marrying foreign women?"

28 And one of the sons of Je·hoi´a·da, son of the high priest E·lī´a·shib, was the son-in-law of San·bal´lat the Hor´o·nīte; I chased him away from me. [29]Remember them, O my God, because they have defiled the priesthood, the covenant of the priests and the Lē´vītes.

30 Thus I cleansed them from everything foreign, and I established the duties of the priests and Lē´vītes, each in his work; [31]and I provided for the wood offering, at appointed times, and for the first fruits. Remember me, O my God, for good.

Esther

The book of Esther was written in the second century BC. This book tells about a time several hundred years earlier, about 485–465 BC, when many of the Judahites were living in exile in Persia. They had been taken there as prisoners of war. Many scholars believe that Esther is not a real record of history but a story written to encourage the Judahites living in exile.

The reading of the dramatic story of Esther is a regular part of the Festival of Purim. This festival celebrates the Jews' hope that however much they suffer, their final victory is sure. Although she became a queen of Persia, the beautiful Esther was still loyal to her own people, the Jews. The story of her courage was meant to give strength to the Jewish people at any time they were in danger from their enemies.

Esther 5:1–2

What an exciting story! The book of Esther contains many twists and turns. As you read it, you may want to make a list of the characters so that you can keep them straight.

King Ahasuerus Deposes Queen Vashti

1 This happened in the days of A·has·u·e′rus, the same A·has·u·e′rus who ruled over one hundred twenty-seven provinces from India to Ethiopia.[a] [2]In those days when King A·has·u·e′rus sat on his royal throne in the citadel of Su′sa, [3]in the third year of his reign, he gave a banquet for all his officials and ministers. The army of Persia and Mēd′i·a and the nobles and governors of the provinces were present, [4]while he displayed the great wealth of his kingdom and the splendor and pomp of his majesty for many days, one hundred eighty days in all.

5 When these days were completed, the king gave for all the people present in the citadel of Su′sa, both great and small, a banquet lasting for seven days, in the court of the garden of the king's palace. [6]There were white cotton curtains and blue hangings tied with cords of fine linen and purple to silver rings[b] and marble pillars. There were couches of gold and silver on a mosaic pavement of porphyry, marble, mother-of-pearl, and colored stones. [7]Drinks were served in golden goblets, goblets of different kinds, and the royal wine was lavished according to the bounty of the king.

The king gave a banquet for the men of the kingdom. At the same time, Queen Vashti gave a separate banquet for the women. During the king's banquet, the men were allowed to drink as much wine as they wanted. Apparently King Ahasuerus drank a lot and then made a bad decision. He commanded Vashti to appear before the men so that they could see her beauty. But she refused. The king was embarrassed in front of his subjects, and so in the end he sent Vashti away.

Ahasuerus is the Emperor Xerxes, and the Hebrew name Ahasuerus means "mighty man." This is the title Ahasuerus used for himself. He liked to get huge groups of people together for banquets so that he could show off his power and great wealth. While the book says the first banquet lasted for 180 days, this is probably just a way for the writer to show us how unwise the king was. It is not likely that he could put the business of the empire on hold for half a year.

[8]Drinking was by flagons, without restraint; for the king had given orders to all the officials of his palace to do as each one desired. [9]Furthermore, Queen Vash′tī gave a banquet for the women in the palace of King A·has·u·e′rus.

10 On the seventh day, when the king was merry with wine, he commanded Me·hū′man, Biz′tha, Har·bō′na, Big′tha and A·bag′tha, Zē′thar and Car′kas, the seven eunuchs who attended him, [11]to bring Queen Vash′tī before the king, wearing the royal crown, in order to show the peoples and the officials her beauty; for she was fair to behold. [12]But Queen Vash′tī refused to come at the king's command conveyed by the eunuchs. At this

[a] Or Nubia; Heb Cush   [b] Or rods

the king was enraged, and his anger burned within him.

13 Then the king consulted the sages who knew the laws[c] (for this was the king's procedure toward all who were versed in law and custom, [14]and those next to him were Car·she̅′na, She̅′thar, Ad·ma̅′tha, Tar′shish, Me̅′re̅s, Mar·se̅′na, and Me̅·mu̅′can, the seven officials of Persia and Me̅d′i·a, who had access to the king, and sat first in the kingdom): [15]"According to the law, what is to be done to Queen Vash′ti̅ because she has not performed the command of King A·has·u̅·e̅′rus conveyed by the eunuchs?" [16]Then Me̅·mu̅′can said in the presence of the king and the officials, "Not only has Queen Vash′ti̅ done wrong to the king, but also to all the officials and all the peoples who are in all the provinces of King A·has·u̅·e̅′rus. [17]For this deed of the queen will be made known to all women, causing them to look with contempt on their husbands, since they will say, 'King A·has·u̅·e̅′rus commanded Queen Vash′ti̅ to be brought before him, and she did not come.' [18]This very day the noble ladies of Persia and Me̅d′i·a who have heard of the queen's behavior will rebel against[d] the king's officials, and there will be no end of contempt and wrath! [19]If it pleases the king, let a royal order go out from him, and let it be written among the laws of the Persians and the Me̅des so that it may not be altered, that Vash′ti̅ is never again to come before King A·has·u̅·e̅′rus; and let the king give her royal position to another who is better than she. [20]So when the decree made by the king is proclaimed throughout all his kingdom, vast as it is, all women will give honor to their husbands, high and low alike."

21 This advice pleased the king and the officials, and the king did as Me̅·mu̅′can proposed; [22]he sent letters to all the royal provinces, to every province in its own script and to every people in its own language, declaring that every man should be master in his own house.[e]

King Ahasuerus grew lonely without Queen Vashti. His servants suggested that they gather a large group of young women who were the right age to get married and let the king choose a new queen. Out of all the girls, Ahasuerus chose Esther to be the new queen. Esther was a Benjaminite from the family of Kish, King Saul's father.

Esther Becomes Queen

2 After these things, when the anger of King A·has·u̅·e̅′rus had abated, he remembered Vash′ti̅ and what she had done and what had been decreed against her. [2]Then the king's servants who attended him said, "Let beautiful young virgins be sought out for the king. [3]And let the king appoint commissioners in all the provinces of his kingdom to gather all the beautiful young virgins to the harem in the citadel of Su′sa under custody of Heg′ai̅, the king's eunuch, who is in charge of the women; let their cosmetic treatments be given them. [4]And let the girl who pleases the king be queen instead of Vash′ti̅." This pleased the king, and he did so.

5 Now there was a Jew in the citadel of Su′sa whose name was Mor′de·cai̅ son of Ja̅′ir son of Shim′e·i̅ son of Kish, a Ben′ja·min·i̅te. [6]Kish[f] had been carried away from Jerusalem among the captives carried away with King Jec·o·ni̅′ah of Judah, whom King Ne·bu̅·chad·nez′zar of Babylon had carried away. [7]Mor′de·cai̅[g] had brought up Ha·das′sah, that is Esther, his cousin, for she had neither father nor mother; the girl was fair and beautiful, and when her father and her mother died, Mor′de·cai̅ adopted her as his own daugh-

ter. [8]So when the king's order and his edict were proclaimed, and when many young women were gathered in the citadel of Su´sa in custody of Heg´aī, Esther also was taken into the king's palace and put in custody of Heg´aī, who had charge of the women. [9]The girl pleased him and won his favor, and he quickly provided her with her cosmetic treatments and her portion of food, and with seven chosen maids from the king's palace, and advanced her and her maids to the best place in the harem. [10]Esther did not reveal her people or kindred, for Mor´de·caī had charged her not to tell. [11]Every day Mor´de·caī would walk around in front of the court of the harem, to learn how Esther was and how she fared.

12 The turn came for each girl to go in to King A·has·ū·ē´rus, after being twelve months under the regulations for the women, since this was the regular period of their cosmetic treatment, six months with oil of myrrh and six months with perfumes and cosmetics for women. [13]When the girl went in to the king she was given whatever she asked for to take with her from the harem to the king's palace. [14]In the evening she went in; then in the morning she came back to the second harem in custody of Sha·ash´gaz, the king's eunuch, who was in charge of the concubines; she did not go in to the king again, unless the king delighted in her and she was summoned by name.

15 When the turn came for Esther daughter of Ab·i·hā´il the uncle of Mor´de·caī, who had adopted her as his own daughter, to go in to the king, she asked for nothing except what Heg´aī the king's eunuch, who had charge of the women, advised. Now Esther was admired by all who saw her. [16]When Esther was taken to King A·has·ū·ē´rus in his royal palace in the tenth month, which is the month of Tē´beth, in the seventh year of his reign, [17]the king loved Esther more than all the other women; of all the virgins she won his favor and devotion, so that he set the royal

crown on her head and made her queen instead of Vash´tī. [18]Then the king gave a great banquet to all his officials and ministers—"Esther's banquet." He also granted a holiday[h] to the provinces, and gave gifts with royal liberality.

> In Hebrew, Esther's name means "I will hide." And she did have something to hide! Because of her cousin Mordecai's advice, she kept secret the fact she was Jewish. While she was living in the king's palace with the other young women, she did not keep the Jewish dietary (eating) laws. Read a story in Daniel 1 about four friends who did keep the laws. Think about the courage it took in each of these stories. Talk with an adult about ways that you can stay faithful to God.

Mordecai Discovers a Plot

19 When the virgins were being gathered together,[i] Mor´de·caī was sitting at the king's gate. [20]Now Esther had not revealed her kindred or her people, as Mor´de·caī had charged her; for Esther obeyed Mor´de·caī just as when she was brought up by him. [21]In those days, while Mor´de·caī was sitting at the king's gate, Big´than and Tē´resh, two of the king's eunuchs, who guarded the threshold, became angry and conspired to assassinate[j] King A·has·ū·ē´rus. [22]But the matter came to the knowledge of Mor´de·caī, and he told it to Queen Esther, and Esther told the king in the name of Mor´de·caī. [23]When the affair was investigated and found to be so, both the men were hanged on the gallows. It was recorded in the book of the annals in the presence of the king.

Haman Undertakes to Destroy the Jews

3 After these things King A·has·ū·ē´rus promoted Hā´man son of Ham·me·dā´tha the Ag´ag·īte, and advanced him and

[h] Or *an amnesty*   [i] Heb adds *a second time*   [j] Heb *to lay hands on*

Haman was the king's prime minister. He was also an Agagite, a descendent of Saul's Amalakite enemy (read 1 Samuel 15). He was full of himself, and thought he was better than others. The king had commanded that all people living in the land must bow down to Haman just as they would to the king. Mordecai refused, which made Haman so angry that he planned to destroy not only Mordecai, but all the Jews!

Have you ever been so angry that you took your feelings out on the people around you who were not even involved in what was happening to you? Your parents or other adults may have told you to stop and count to ten before you act in anger. This is very good advice. Asking for God's help in difficult situations is even better. If you stay calm, pray silently, and listen for God's answer, you will find that you are better able to deal with any situation.

set his seat above all the officials who were with him. [2]And all the king's servants who were at the king's gate bowed down and did obeisance to Hā′man; for the king had so commanded concerning him. But Mor′de·caī did not bow down or do obeisance. [3]Then the king's servants who were at the king's gate said to Mor′de·caī, "Why do you disobey the king's command?" [4]When they spoke to him day after day and he would not listen to them, they told Hā′man, in order to see whether Mor′-de·caī's words would avail; for he had told them that he was a Jew. [5]When Hā′man saw that Mor′de·caī did not bow down or do obeisance to him, Hā′man was infuriated. [6]But he thought it beneath him to lay hands on Mor′de·caī alone. So, having been told who Mor′de·caī's people were, Hā′man plotted to destroy all the Jews, the people of Mor′de·caī, throughout the whole kingdom of A·has·ū·ē′rus.

7 In the first month, which is the month of Nī′san, in the twelfth year of King A·has·ū·ē′rus, they cast Pūr—which means "the lot"—before Hā′man for the day and for the month, and the lot fell on the thirteenth day[k] of the twelfth month, which is the month of Ā′dar. [8]Then Hā′man said to King A·has·ū·ē′rus, "There is a certain people scattered and separated among the peoples in all the provinces of your kingdom; their laws are different from those of every other people, and they do not keep the king's laws, so that it is not appropriate for the king to tolerate them. [9]If it pleases the king, let a decree be issued for their destruction, and I will pay ten thousand talents of silver into the hands of those who have charge of the king's business, so that they may put it into the king's treasuries." [10]So the king took his signet ring from his hand and gave it to Hā′man son of Ham·me·dā′tha the Ag′ag·īte, the enemy of the Jews. [11]The king said to Hā′man, "The money is given to you, and the people as well, to do with them as it seems good to you."

12 Then the king's secretaries were summoned on the thirteenth day of the first month, and an edict, according to all that Hā′man commanded, was written to the king's satraps and to the governors over all the provinces and to the officials of all the peoples, to every province in its own script and every people in its own language; it was written in the name of King A·has·ū·ē′rus and sealed with the king's ring. [13]Letters were sent by couriers to all the king's provinces, giving orders to destroy, to kill, and to annihilate all Jews, young and old, women and children, in one day, the thirteenth day of the twelfth month, which is the month of Ā′dar, and to plunder their goods. [14]A copy of the document was to be issued as a decree in every province by proclamation, calling

[k] Cn: Compare Gk and verse 13 below: Heb *the twelfth month*

"Perhaps you have come to royal dignity for just such a time as this." Esther 4:14*b*

on all the peoples to be ready for that day. [15]The couriers went quickly by order of the king, and the decree was issued in the citadel of Su´sa. The king and Hā´man sat down to drink; but the city of Su´sa was thrown into confusion.

Sackcloth was a rough cloth made of goat and camel hair. The people usually used this cloth to make bags. They also used it to make clothes. The people wore clothes made of sackcloth to show repentance or to show that they were mourning.

Esther Agrees to Help the Jews

4 When Mor´de·caī learned all that had been done, Mor´de·caī tore his clothes and put on sackcloth and ashes, and went through the city, wailing with a loud and bitter cry; [2]he went up to the entrance of the king's gate, for no one might enter the king's gate clothed with sackcloth. [3]In every province, wherever the king's command and his decree came, there was great mourning among the Jews, with fasting and weeping and lamenting, and most of them lay in sackcloth and ashes.

[4] When Esther's maids and her eunuchs came and told her, the queen was deeply distressed; she sent garments to clothe Mor´de·caī, so that he might take off his sackcloth; but he would not accept them. [5]Then Esther called for Hā´thach, one of the king's eunuchs, who had been appointed to attend her, and ordered him to go to Mor´de·caī to learn what was happening and why. [6]Hā´thach went out to Mor´de·caī in the open square of the city

in front of the king's gate, [7]and Mor´de·caī told him all that had happened to him, and the exact sum of money that Hā´man had promised to pay into the king's treasuries for the destruction of the Jews. [8]Mor´de·caī also gave him a copy of the written decree issued in Su´sa for their destruction, that he might show it to Esther, explain it to her, and charge her to go to the king to make supplication to him and entreat him for her people.

9 Hā´thach went and told Esther what Mor´de·caī had said. [10]Then Esther spoke to Hā´thach and gave him a message for Mor´de·caī, saying, [11]"All the king's servants and the people of the king's provinces know that if any man or woman goes to the king inside the inner court without being called, there is but one law—all alike are to be put to death. Only if the king holds out the golden scepter to someone, may that person live. I myself have not been called to come in to the king for thirty days." [12]When they told Mor´de·caī what Esther had said, [13]Mor´de·caī told them to reply to Esther, "Do not think that in the king's palace you will escape any more than all the other Jews. [14]For if you keep silence at such a time as this, relief and deliverance will rise for the Jews from another quarter, but you and your father's family will perish. Who knows? Perhaps you have come to royal dignity for just such a time as this." [15]Then Esther said in reply to Mor´de·caī, [16]"Go, gather all the Jews

Ask your parents if they have ever been asked to speak on behalf of a group of people. What gave them the courage to speak up? Read Romans 8:28 together. God is with us in all things. God is working for good. Pray that God will work through your life to accomplish good things.

When Mordecai asked Queen Esther to speak on behalf of her people, she knew that she might be killed. She asked all the Jews to fast with her before she went before the king. Although the story does not specifically mention prayer, we can assume that praying and asking for God's protection were a part of the fast.

How important do you think it is to pray before making a big decision? Talk with your family or with a leader at your church about the importance of prayer. The next time you are in church, listen carefully when the pastor prays. Can you identify what kind of help the pastor is asking from God?

to be found in Su´sa, and hold a fast on my behalf, and neither eat nor drink for three days, night or day. I and my maids will also fast as you do. After that I will go to the king, though it is against the law; and if I perish, I perish." [17]Mor´de·cai then went away and did everything as Esther had ordered him.

Esther's Banquet

5 On the third day Esther put on her royal robes and stood in the inner court of the king's palace, opposite the king's hall. The king was sitting on his royal throne inside the palace opposite the entrance to the palace. [2]As soon as the king saw Queen Esther standing in the court, she won his favor and he held out to her the golden scepter that was in his hand. Then Esther approached and touched the top of the scepter. [3]The king said to her, "What is it, Queen Esther? What is your request? It shall be given you, even to the half of my kingdom." [4]Then Esther said, "If it pleases the king, let the king and Ha´man come today to a banquet that I have prepared for the king." [5]Then the king said, "Bring Ha´man quickly, so that we may do

as Esther desires." So the king and Ha´man came to the banquet that Esther had prepared. [6]While they were drinking wine, the king said to Esther, "What is your petition? It shall be granted you. And what is your request? Even to the half of my kingdom, it shall be fulfilled." [7]Then Esther said, "This is my petition and request: [8]If I have won the king's favor, and if it pleases the king to grant my petition and fulfill my request, let the king and Ha´man come tomorrow to the banquet that I will prepare for them, and then I will do as the king has said."

Haman Plans to Have Mordecai Hanged

9 Ha´man went out that day happy and in good spirits. But when Ha´man saw Mor´de·cai in the king's gate, and observed that he neither rose nor trembled before him, he was infuriated with Mor´de·cai; [10]nevertheless Ha´man restrained himself and went home. Then he sent and called for his friends and his wife Ze´resh, [11]and Ha´man recounted to them the splendor of his riches, the number of his sons, all the promotions with which the king had honored him, and how he had advanced him above the officials and the ministers of the king. [12]Ha´man added, "Even Queen Esther let no one but myself come with the king to the banquet that she prepared. Tomorrow also I am invited by her, together with the king. [13]Yet all this does me no good so long as I see the Jew Mor´de·cai sitting at the king's gate." [14]Then his wife Ze´resh and all his friends said to him, "Let a gallows fifty cubits high be made, and in the morning tell the king to have Mor´de·cai hanged on it; then go with the king to the banquet in good spirits." This advice pleased Ha´man, and he had the gallows made.

The King Honors Mordecai

6 On that night the king could not sleep, and he gave orders to bring the book of records, the annals, and they

were read to the king. [2]It was found written how Mor´de·caī had told about Big·thā´na and Tē´resh, two of the king's eunuchs, who guarded the threshold, and who had conspired to assassinate[l] King A·has·u·ē´rus. [3]Then the king said, "What honor or distinction has been bestowed on Mor´de·caī for this?" The king's servants who attended him said, "Nothing has been done for him." [4]The king said, "Who is in the court?" Now Hā´man had just entered the outer court of the king's palace to speak to the king about having Mor´de·caī hanged on the gallows that he had prepared for him. [5]So the king's servants told him, "Hā´man is there, standing in the court." The king said, "Let him come in." [6]So Hā´man came in, and the king said to him, "What shall be done for the man whom the king wishes to honor?" Hā´man said to himself, "Whom would the king wish to honor more than me?" [7]So Hā´man said to the king, "For the man whom the king wishes to honor, [8]let royal robes be brought, which the king has worn, and a horse that the king has ridden, with a royal crown on its head. [9]Let the robes and the horse be handed over to one of the king's most noble officials; let him[m] robe the man whom the king wishes to honor, and let him[m] conduct the man on horseback through the open square of the city, proclaiming before him: 'Thus shall it be done for the man whom the king wishes to honor.'" [10]Then the king said to Hā´man, "Quickly, take the robes and the horse, as you have said, and do so to the Jew Mor´de·caī who sits at the king's gate. Leave out nothing that you have mentioned." [11]So Hā´man took the robes and the horse and robed Mor´de·caī and led him riding through the open square of the city, proclaiming, "Thus shall it be done for the man whom the king wishes to honor."

12 Then Mor´de·caī returned to the king's gate, but Hā´man hurried to his house, mourning and with his head cov-

ered. [13]When Hā´man told his wife Zē´resh and all his friends everything that had happened to him, his advisers and his wife Zē´resh said to him, "If Mor´de·caī, before whom your downfall has begun, is of the Jewish people, you will not prevail against him, but will surely fall before him."

Haman's Downfall and Mordecai's Advancement

14 While they were still talking with him, the king's eunuchs arrived and hurried Hā´man off to the banquet that Esther had prepared. [1]So the king and Hā´man went in to feast with Queen Esther. [2]On the second day, as they were drinking wine, the king again said to Esther, "What is your petition, Queen Esther? It shall be granted you. And what is your request? Even to the half of my kingdom, it shall be fulfilled." [3]Then Queen Esther answered, "If I have won your favor, O king, and if it pleases the king, let my life be given me—that is my petition—and the lives of my people—that is my request. [4]For we have been sold, I and my people, to be destroyed, to be killed, and to be annihilated. If we had been sold merely as slaves, men and women, I would have held my peace; but no enemy can compensate for this damage to the king."[n] [5]Then King A·has·u·ē´rus said to Queen Esther, "Who is he, and where is he, who has presumed to do this?" [6]Esther said, "A foe and enemy, this wicked Hā´man!" Then Hā´man was terrified before the king and the queen. [7]The king rose from the feast in wrath and went into the palace garden, but Hā´man stayed to beg his life from Queen Esther, for he saw that the king had determined to destroy him. [8]When the king returned from the palace garden to the banquet hall, Hā´man had thrown himself on the couch where Esther was

---

[l] Heb *to lay hands on*   [m] Heb *them*   [n] Meaning of Heb uncertain

reclining; and the king said, "Will he even assault the queen in my presence, in my own house?" As the words left the mouth of the king, they covered Hā´man's face. ⁹Then Har·bō´na, one of the eunuchs in attendance on the king, said, "Look, the very gallows that Hā´man has prepared for Mor´de·caī, whose word saved the king, stands at Hā´man's house, fifty cubits high." And the king said, "Hang him on that." ¹⁰So they hanged Hā´man on the gallows that he had prepared for Mor´de·caī. Then the anger of the king abated.

God used Esther and Mordecai to save the Jewish people! They defeated Haman's evil plan and gained everything that belonged to him. They regained the power that Saul had lost many years earlier.

Esther Saves the Jews

8 On that day King A·has·u·e´rus gave to Queen Esther the house of Hā´man, the enemy of the Jews; and Mor´de·caī came before the king, for Esther had told what he was to her. ²Then the king took off his signet ring, which he had taken from Hā´man, and gave it to Mor´de·caī. So Esther set Mor´de·caī over the house of Hā´man.

3 Then Esther spoke again to the king; she fell at his feet, weeping and pleading with him to avert the evil design of Hā´man the Ag´ag·īte and the plot that he had devised against the Jews. ⁴The king held out the golden scepter to Esther, ⁵and Esther rose and stood before the king. She said, "If it pleases the king, and if I have won his favor, and if the thing seems right before the king, and I have his approval, let an order be written to revoke the letters devised by Hā´man son of Ham·me·dā´tha the Ag´ag·īte, which he wrote giving orders to destroy the Jews who are in all the provinces of the king. ⁶For how can I bear to see the calamity that is coming on my people? Or how can I bear to see the destruction of my kindred?" ⁷Then King A·has·u·e´rus said to Queen Esther and to the Jew Mor´de·caī, "See, I have given Esther the house of Hā´man, and they have hanged him on the gallows, because he plotted to lay hands on the Jews. ⁸You may write as you please with regard to the Jews, in the name of the king, and seal it with the king's ring; for an edict written in the name of the king and sealed with the king's ring cannot be revoked."

9 The king's secretaries were summoned at that time, in the third month, which is the month of Sī´van, on the twenty-third day; and an edict was written, according to all that Mor´de·caī commanded, to the Jews and to the satraps and the governors and the officials of the provinces from India to Ethiopia,ᵒ one hundred twenty-seven provinces, to every province in its own script and to every people in its own language, and also to the Jews in their script and their language. ¹⁰He wrote letters in the name of King A·has·u·e´rus, sealed them with the king's ring, and sent them by mounted couriers riding on fast steeds bred from the royal herd.ᵖ ¹¹By these letters the king allowed the Jews who were in every city

Esther 8:9 is the longest verse in the Bible! It tells of all the places the king's messengers had to go to deliver a message to the Jews and all the Persian officials. The messengers rode on fast horses, sort of like the "Pony Express" from the early days of the United States. Look up "Pony Express" on the Internet or at the library. How long did it take to get a letter across our country?

ᵒ Or *Nubia*; Heb *Cush*   ᵖ Meaning of Heb uncertain

to assemble and defend their lives, to destroy, to kill, and to annihilate any armed force of any people or province that might attack them, with their children and women, and to plunder their goods ¹²on a single day throughout all the provinces of King A·has·u·e´rus, on the thirteenth day of the twelfth month, which is the month of Ā´dar. ¹³A copy of the writ was to be issued as a decree in every province and published to all peoples, and the Jews were to be ready on that day to take revenge on their enemies. ¹⁴So the couriers, mounted on their swift royal steeds, hurried out, urged by the king's command. The decree was issued in the citadel of Su´sa.

15 Then Mor´de·cai went out from the presence of the king, wearing royal robes of blue and white, with a great golden crown and a mantle of fine linen and purple, while the city of Su´sa shouted and rejoiced. ¹⁶For the Jews there was light and gladness, joy and honor. ¹⁷In every province and in every city, wherever the king's command and his edict came, there was gladness and joy among the Jews, a festival and a holiday. Furthermore, many of the peoples of the country professed to be Jews, because the fear of the Jews had fallen upon them.

Destruction of the Enemies of the Jews

9 Now in the twelfth month, which is the month of Ā´dar, on the thirteenth day, when the king's command and edict were about to be executed, on the very day when the enemies of the Jews hoped to gain power over them, but which had been changed to a day when the Jews would gain power over their foes, ²the Jews gathered in their cities throughout all the provinces of King A·has·u·e´rus to lay hands on those who had sought their ruin; and no one could withstand them, because the fear of them had fallen upon all peoples. ³All

the officials of the provinces, the satraps and the governors, and the royal officials were supporting the Jews, because the fear of Mor´de·cai had fallen upon them. ⁴For Mor´de·cai was powerful in the king's house, and his fame spread throughout all the provinces as the man Mor´de·cai grew more and more powerful. ⁵So the Jews struck down all their enemies with the sword, slaughtering, and destroying them, and did as they pleased to those who hated them. ⁶In the citadel of Su´sa the Jews killed and destroyed five hundred people. ⁷They killed Par·shan·da´tha, Dal´phon, As·pā´-tha, ⁸Pō·ra´thā, A·dā´li·a, Ar·i·dā´tha, ⁹Par·mash´ta, Ar´i·sai, Ar´i·dai, Vai·zā´-tha, ¹⁰the ten sons of Hā´man son of Ham·me·dā´tha, the enemy of the Jews; but they did not touch the plunder.

11 That very day the number of those killed in the citadel of Su´sa was reported to the king. ¹²The king said to Queen Esther, "In the citadel of Su´sa the Jews have killed five hundred people and also the ten sons of Hā´man. What have they done in the rest of the king's provinces? Now what is your petition? It shall be granted you. And what further is your request? It shall be fulfilled." ¹³Esther said, "If it pleases the king, let the Jews who are in Su´sa be allowed tomorrow also to do according to this day's edict, and let the ten sons of Hā´man be hanged on the gallows." ¹⁴So the king commanded this to be done; a decree was issued in Su´sa, and the ten sons of Hā´-man were hanged. ¹⁵The Jews who were in Su´sa gathered also on the fourteenth day of the month of Ā´dar and they killed three hundred persons in Su´sa; but they did not touch the plunder.

16 Now the other Jews who were in the king's provinces also gathered to defend their lives, and gained relief from their enemies, and killed seventy-five thousand of those who hated them; but they laid no hands on the plunder. ¹⁷This was on the thirteenth day of the

month of Ā́dar, and on the fourteenth day they rested and made that a day of feasting and gladness.

The Feast of Purim Inaugurated

18 But the Jews who were in Su′sa gathered on the thirteenth day and on the fourteenth, and rested on the fifteenth day, making that a day of feasting and gladness. ¹⁹Therefore the Jews of the villages, who live in the open towns, hold the fourteenth day of the month of Ā́dar as a day for gladness and feasting, a holiday on which they send gifts of food to one another.

20 Mor′de·caī recorded these things, and sent letters to all the Jews who were in all the provinces of King A·has·ū·ē′rus, both near and far, ²¹enjoining them that they should keep the fourteenth day of the month Ā́dar and also the fifteenth day of the same month, year by year, ²²as the days on which the Jews gained relief from their enemies, and as the month that had been turned for them from sorrow into gladness and from mourning into a holiday; that they should make them days of feasting and gladness, days for sending gifts of food to one another and presents to the poor. ²³So the Jews adopted as a custom what they had begun to do, as Mor′de·caī had written to them.

24 Hā′man son of Ham·me·dā′tha the Ag′ag·īte, the enemy of all the Jews, had plotted against the Jews to destroy them, and had cast Pūr—that is "the lot"—to crush and destroy them; ²⁵but when Esther came before the king, he gave orders in writing that the wicked plot that he had devised against the Jews should come upon his own head, and that he and his sons should be hanged on the gallows. ²⁶Therefore these days are called Pūr′im, from the word Pūr. Thus because of all that was written in this letter, and of what they had faced in this matter, and of what had happened to them, ²⁷the Jews established and accepted as a custom for themselves and their descendants and all who joined them, that without fail they would continue to observe these two days every

> Jewish people today still celebrate the Feast of Purim. It is a family tradition to go to the synagogue to hear the story of Esther. After the story, the celebration continues with fun and games. There is a Purim custom called *mishlo'ah manot*, which means giving sweet treats to friends and neighbors. Another custom, called *tzedakah*, means giving gifts to the poor. What customs does your family have? Do you eat meals together? Do you celebrate holidays together? Do you read Bible stories together?

year, as it was written and at the time appointed. ²⁸These days should be remembered and kept throughout every generation, in every family, province, and city; and these days of Pūr′im should never fall into disuse among the Jews, nor should the commemoration of these days cease among their descendants.

29 Queen Esther daughter of Ab·i·hā′il, along with the Jew Mor′de·caī, gave full written authority, confirming this second letter about Pūr′im. ³⁰Letters were sent wishing peace and security to all the Jews, to the one hundred twenty-seven provinces of the kingdom of A·has·ū·ē′rus, ³¹and giving orders that these days of Pūr′im should be observed at their appointed seasons, as the Jew Mor′de·caī and Queen Esther enjoined on the Jews, just as they had laid down for themselves and for their descendants regulations concerning their fasts and their lamentations. ³²The command of Queen Esther fixed these practices of Pūr′im, and it was recorded in writing.

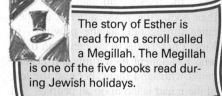

> The story of Esther is read from a scroll called a Megillah. The Megillah is one of the five books read during Jewish holidays.

10 King A·has·ū·ē´rus laid tribute on the land and on the islands of the sea. [2]All the acts of his power and might, and the full account of the high honor of Mor´de·caī, to which the king advanced him, are they not written in the annals of the kings of Mēd´i·a and Persia? [3]For Mor´de·caī the Jew was next in rank to King A·has·ū·ē´rus, and he was powerful among the Jews and popular with his many kindred, for he sought the good of his people and interceded for the welfare of all his descendants.

Job

The book of Job is a poetic drama or play that was written sometime between the seventh and fifth centuries BC. The plot of the book centers on one of the hardest questions humans have ever had to answer: Why do bad things happen to good people? Many of God's people believe that good people always do well and that bad people always suffer. The book of Job was written to show that this belief is not true.

In this play, three friends come to comfort Job. They claim that because he has so much sickness and trouble, he must be guilty of secret sins. Job says that although he is not perfect, he doesn't deserve to suffer this much. Even though the book does not explain why bad things happen to good people, it does make clear that we can trust God no matter what happens. The book of Job helps people who are in deep trouble continue to trust God even when they cannot understand all the reasons for the hard times of life.

Job 2:7–8

In Bible times, you could tell how rich people were by how many animals they owned. So Job was seen as a wealthy man because he owned a large number of animals.

Job and His Family

1 There was once a man in the land of Uz whose name was Jōb. That man was blameless and upright, one who feared God and turned away from evil. ²There were born to him seven sons and three daughters. ³He had seven thousand sheep, three thousand camels, five hundred yoke of oxen, five hundred donkeys, and very many servants; so that this man was the greatest of all the people of the east. ⁴His sons used to go and hold feasts in one another's houses in turn; and they would send and invite their three sisters to eat and drink with them. ⁵And when the feast days had run their course, Jōb would send and sanctify them, and he would rise early in the morning and offer burnt offerings according to the number of them all; for Jōb said, "It may be that my children have sinned, and cursed God in their hearts." This is what Jōb always did.

Attack on Job's Character

6 One day the heavenly beings[a] came to present themselves before the LORD, and Satan[b] also came among them. ⁷The LORD said to Satan,[b] "Where have you come from?" Satan[b] answered the LORD, "From going to and fro on the earth, and from walking up and down on it." ⁸The LORD said to Satan,[b] "Have you considered my servant Jōb? There is no one like him on the earth, a blameless and upright man who fears God and turns away from evil." ⁹Then Satan[b] answered the LORD, "Does Jōb fear God for nothing? ¹⁰Have you not put a fence around him and his house and all that he has, on every side? You have blessed the work of his hands, and his possessions have increased in the land. ¹¹But stretch out your hand now, and touch all that he has, and he will curse you to your face." ¹²The LORD said to Satan,[b] "Very well, all that he has is in your power; only do not stretch out your hand against him!" So Satan[b] went out from the presence of the LORD.

Job Loses Property and Children

13 One day when his sons and daughters were eating and drinking wine in the eldest brother's house, ¹⁴a messenger came to Jōb and said, "The oxen were plowing and the donkeys were feeding beside them, ¹⁵and the Sa·bē´ans fell on them and carried them off, and killed the servants with the edge of the sword; I alone have escaped to tell you." ¹⁶While he was still speaking, another came and said, "The fire of God fell from heaven and burned up the sheep and the servants, and consumed them; I alone have escaped to tell you." ¹⁷While he was still speaking, another came and said, "The Chal·dē´ans formed three columns, made a raid on the camels and carried them off, and killed the servants with the edge of the sword; I alone have escaped to tell you." ¹⁸While he was still speaking, another came and said, "Your sons and daughters were eating and drinking wine in their eldest brother's house, ¹⁹and suddenly a great wind came across the desert, struck the four corners of the house, and it fell on the young people, and they are dead; I alone have escaped to tell you."

20 Then Jōb arose, tore his robe, shaved his head, and fell on the ground and worshiped. ²¹He said, "Naked I came from my mother's womb, and naked shall I return there; the LORD gave, and the LORD has taken away; blessed be the name of the LORD."

[a] Heb *sons of God*   [b] Or *the Accuser;* Heb *ha-satan*

22 In all this Jōb did not sin or charge God with wrongdoing.

Attack on Job's Health

2 One day the heavenly beings[c] came to present themselves before the LORD, and Satan[d] also came among them to present himself before the LORD. [2]The LORD said to Satan,[d] "Where have you come from?" Satan[d] answered the LORD, "From going to and fro on the earth, and from walking up and down on it." [3]The LORD said to Satan,[d] "Have you considered my servant Jōb? There is no one like him on the earth, a blameless and upright man who fears God and turns away from evil. He still persists in his integrity, although you incited me against him, to destroy him for no reason." [4]Then Satan[d] answered the LORD, "Skin for skin! All that people have they will give to save their lives.[e] [5]But stretch out your hand now and touch his bone and his flesh, and he will curse you to your face." [6]The LORD said to Satan,[d] "Very well, he is in your power; only spare his life."

7 So Satan[d] went out from the presence of the LORD, and inflicted loathsome sores on Job from the sole of his foot to the crown of his head. [8]Jōb[f] took a potsherd with which to scrape himself, and sat among the ashes.

9 Then his wife said to him, "Do you still persist in your integrity? Curse[g] God, and die." [10]But he said to her, "You speak as any foolish woman would speak. Shall we receive the good at the hand of God, and not receive the bad?" In all this Jōb did not sin with his lips.

Job's Three Friends

11 Now when Job's three friends heard of all these troubles that had come upon him, each of them set out from his home—E·lī'phaz the Tē'man·ite, Bil'dad the Shū'hīte, and Zō'phar the Na'a·ma·-thīte. They met together to go and console and comfort him. [12]When they saw

In Bible times, a council was a group made up of men of authority. Here and in Job 15:8, there are references to the council of God, made up of God and the heavenly beings. Although we do not know exactly who the heavenly beings are, we know that the Hebrew title of one was Satan. This means "the accuser" and not the devil.

him from a distance, they did not recognize him, and they raised their voices and wept aloud; they tore their robes and threw dust in the air upon their heads. [13]They sat with him on the ground seven days and seven nights, and no one spoke a word to him, for they saw that his suffering was very great.

Job Curses the Day He Was Born

3 After this Jōb opened his mouth and cursed the day of his birth. [2] Jōb said:

[3] "Let the day perish in which I was born,
    and the night that said,
    'A man-child is conceived.'
[4] Let that day be darkness!
    May God above not seek it,
    or light shine on it.
[5] Let gloom and deep darkness claim it.
    Let clouds settle upon it;
    let the blackness of the day terrify it.
[6] That night—let thick darkness seize it!
    let it not rejoice among the days of the year;
    let it not come into the number of the months.

[c] Heb sons of God   [d] Or the Accuser; Heb ha-satan
[e] Or All that the man has he will give for his life
[f] Heb He   [g] Heb Bless

7 Yes, let that night be barren;
  let no joyful cry be heard[h] in it.
8 Let those curse it who curse the Sea,[i]
  those who are skilled to rouse up
    Le·vi´a·than.
9 Let the stars of its dawn be dark;
  let it hope for light, but have none;
  may it not see the eyelids of the
    morning—
10 because it did not shut the doors of
   my mother's womb,
   and hide trouble from my eyes.

11 "Why did I not die at birth,
   come forth from the womb and
     expire?
12 Why were there knees to receive me,
   or breasts for me to suck?
13 Now I would be lying down and quiet;
   I would be asleep; then I would be
     at rest
14 with kings and counselors of the earth
   who rebuild ruins for themselves,
15 or with princes who have gold,
   who fill their houses with silver.
16 Or why was I not buried like a
     stillborn child,
   like an infant that never sees the
     light?
17 There the wicked cease from
     troubling,
   and there the weary are at rest.
18 There the prisoners are at ease
     together;
   they do not hear the voice of the
     taskmaster.
19 The small and the great are there,
   and the slaves are free from their
     masters.

20 "Why is light given to one in misery,
   and life to the bitter in soul,
21 who long for death, but it does not
     come,
   and dig for it more than for hidden
     treasures;
22 who rejoice exceedingly,
   and are glad when they find the
     grave?

23 Why is light given to one who cannot
     see the way,
   whom God has fenced in?
24 For my sighing comes like[j] my bread,
   and my groanings are poured out
     like water.
25 Truly the thing that I fear comes upon
     me,
   and what I dread befalls me.
26 I am not at ease, nor am I quiet;
   I have no rest; but trouble comes."

Eliphaz Speaks: Job Has Sinned

4 Then E·li´phaz the Te´man·ite
  answered:
2 "If one ventures a word with you, will
     you be offended?
   But who can keep from speaking?
3 See, you have instructed many;
   you have strengthened the weak
     hands.
4 Your words have supported those
     who were stumbling,
   and you have made firm the feeble
     knees.
5 But now it has come to you, and you
     are impatient;
   it touches you, and you are
     dismayed.
6 Is not your fear of God your
     confidence,
   and the integrity of your ways your
     hope?
7 "Think now, who that was innocent
     ever perished?
   Or where were the upright cut off?
8 As I have seen, those who plow
     iniquity
   and sow trouble reap the same.
9 By the breath of God they perish,
   and by the blast of his anger they
     are consumed.
10 The roar of the lion, the voice of the
     fierce lion,
   and the teeth of the young lions are
     broken.

h Heb *come*   i Cn: Heb *day*   j Heb *before*

A vision is like a dream. In a vision, God reveals the presence of God or the will of God to someone. Prophets are the ones who have visions most often, but sometimes very ordinary people also have visions.

11 The strong lion perishes for lack of prey,
  and the whelps of the lioness are scattered.

12 "Now a word came stealing to me,
  my ear received the whisper of it.
13 Amid thoughts from visions of the night,
  when deep sleep falls on mortals,
14 dread came upon me, and trembling,
  which made all my bones shake.
15 A spirit glided past my face;
  the hair of my flesh bristled.
16 It stood still,
  but I could not discern its appearance.
  A form was before my eyes;
  there was silence, then I heard a voice:
17 'Can mortals be righteous before[k] God?
  Can human beings be pure before[k] their Maker?
18 Even in his servants he puts no trust,
  and his angels he charges with error;
19 how much more those who live in houses of clay,
  whose foundation is in the dust,
  who are crushed like a moth.
20 Between morning and evening they are destroyed;
  they perish forever without any regarding it.
21 Their tent-cord is plucked up within them,
  and they die devoid of wisdom.'

Job Is Corrected by God

5 "Call now; is there anyone who will answer you?
  To which of the holy ones will you turn?
2 Surely vexation kills the fool,
  and jealousy slays the simple.
3 I have seen fools taking root,
  but suddenly I cursed their dwelling.
4 Their children are far from safety,
  they are crushed in the gate,
  and there is no one to deliver them.
5 The hungry eat their harvest,
  and they take it even out of the thorns;[l]
  and the thirsty[m] pant after their wealth.
6 For misery does not come from the earth,
  nor does trouble sprout from the ground;
7 but human beings are born to trouble
  just as sparks[n] fly upward.

8 "As for me, I would seek God,
  and to God I would commit my cause.
9 He does great things and unsearchable,
  marvelous things without number.
10 He gives rain on the earth
  and sends waters on the fields;
11 he sets on high those who are lowly,
  and those who mourn are lifted to safety.
12 He frustrates the devices of the crafty,
  so that their hands achieve no success.
13 He takes the wise in their own craftiness;
  and the schemes of the wily are brought to a quick end.
14 They meet with darkness in the daytime,
  and grope at noonday as in the night.

k Or *more than* *l* Meaning of Heb uncertain *m* Aquila Symmachus Syr Vg: Heb *snare* *n* Or *birds*; Heb *sons of Resheph*

¹⁵ But he saves the needy from the sword
     of their mouth,
  from the hand of the mighty.
¹⁶ So the poor have hope,
  and injustice shuts its mouth.

¹⁷ "How happy is the one whom God
     reproves;
  therefore do not despise the
     discipline of the Almighty.ᵒ
¹⁸ For he wounds, but he binds up;
  he strikes, but his hands heal.
¹⁹ He will deliver you from six troubles;
  in seven no harm shall touch you.
²⁰ In famine he will redeem you from
     death,
  and in war from the power of the
     sword.
²¹ You shall be hidden from the scourge
     of the tongue,
  and shall not fear destruction when
     it comes.
²² At destruction and famine you shall
     laugh,
  and shall not fear the wild animals
     of the earth.
²³ For you shall be in league with the
     stones of the field,
  and the wild animals shall be at
     peace with you.
²⁴ You shall know that your tent is safe,
  you shall inspect your fold and miss
     nothing.
²⁵ You shall know that your descendants
     will be many,
  and your offspring like the grass of
     the earth.
²⁶ You shall come to your grave in ripe
     old age,
  as a shock of grain comes up to the
     threshing floor in its season.
²⁷ See, we have searched this out; it is
     true.
  Hear, and know it for yourself."

Job Replies:
My Complaint Is Just

6 Then Jōb answered:
² "O that my vexation were weighed,

  and all my calamity laid in the
     balances!
³ For then it would be heavier than the
     sand of the sea;
  therefore my words have been rash.
⁴ For the arrows of the Almightyᵒ are in
     me;
  my spirit drinks their poison;
  the terrors of God are arrayed
     against me.
⁵ Does the wild ass bray over its grass,
  or the ox low over its fodder?
⁶ Can that which is tasteless be eaten
     without salt,
  or is there any flavor in the juice of
     mallows?ᵖ
⁷ My appetite refuses to touch them;
  they are like food that is loathsome
     to me.ᵖ

⁸ "O that I might have my request,
  and that God would grant my
     desire;
⁹ that it would please God to crush me,
  that he would let loose his hand
     and cut me off!
¹⁰ This would be my consolation;
  I would even exultᵖ in unrelenting
     pain;
  for I have not denied the words of
     the Holy One.
¹¹ What is my strength, that I should
     wait?
  And what is my end, that I should
     be patient?
¹² Is my strength the strength of stones,
  or is my flesh bronze?
¹³ In truth I have no help in me,
  and any resource is driven from me.

¹⁴ "Those who withholdᑫ kindness
     from a friend
  forsake the fear of the Almighty.ʳ
¹⁵ My companions are treacherous like
     a torrent-bed,
  like freshets that pass away,

ᵒ Traditional rendering of Heb *Shaddai*
ᵖ Meaning of Heb uncertain   ᑫ Syr Vg Compare
Tg: Meaning of Heb uncertain   ʳ Traditional
rendering of Heb *Shaddai*

16 that run dark with ice,
   turbid with melting snow.
17 In time of heat they disappear;
   when it is hot, they vanish from
      their place.
18 The caravans turn aside from their
      course;
   they go up into the waste, and
      perish.
19 The caravans of Tē'ma look,
   the travelers of Shē'ba hope.
20 They are disappointed because they
      were confident;
   they come there and are
      confounded.
21 Such you have now become to me;[s]
   you see my calamity, and are afraid.
22 Have I said, 'Make me a gift'?
   Or, 'From your wealth offer a bribe
      for me'?
23 Or, 'Save me from an opponent's
      hand'?
   Or, 'Ransom me from the hand of
      oppressors'?
24 "Teach me, and I will be silent;
   make me understand how I have
      gone wrong.
25 How forceful are honest words!
   But your reproof, what does it
      reprove?
26 Do you think that you can reprove
      words,
   as if the speech of the desperate
      were wind?
27 You would even cast lots over the
      orphan,
   and bargain over your friend.
28 "But now, be pleased to look at me;
   for I will not lie to your face.
29 Turn, I pray, let no wrong be done.
   Turn now, my vindication is at stake.
30 Is there any wrong on my tongue?
   Cannot my taste discern calamity?

Job: My Suffering Is without End

7 "Do not human beings have a hard
   service on earth,

and are not their days like the days
   of a laborer?
2 Like a slave who longs for the shadow,
   and like laborers who look for their
      wages,
3 so I am allotted months of emptiness,
   and nights of misery are
      apportioned to me.
4 When I lie down I say, 'When shall I
      rise?'
   But the night is long,
   and I am full of tossing until dawn.
5 My flesh is clothed with worms and
      dirt;
   my skin hardens, then breaks out
      again.
6 My days are swifter than a weaver's
      shuttle,
   and come to their end without
      hope.[t]
7 "Remember that my life is a breath;
   my eye will never again see good.
8 The eye that beholds me will see me
      no more;
   while your eyes are upon me, I shall
      be gone.
9 As the cloud fades and vanishes,
   so those who go down to Shē'ōl do
      not come up;
10 they return no more to their houses,
   nor do their places know them any
      more.
11 "Therefore I will not restrain my
      mouth;
   I will speak in the anguish of my
      spirit;
   I will complain in the bitterness of
      my soul.
12 Am I the Sea, or the Dragon,
   that you set a guard over me?
13 When I say, 'My bed will comfort me,
   my couch will ease my
      complaint,'
14 then you scare me with dreams
   and terrify me with visions,

s Cn Compare Gk Syr: Meaning of Heb uncertain
t Or as the thread runs out

¹⁵ so that I would choose strangling
　　and death rather than this body.
¹⁶ I loathe my life; I would not live
　　forever.
　　Let me alone, for my days are a
　　　breath.
¹⁷ What are human beings, that you
　　make so much of them,
　　that you set your mind on them,
¹⁸ visit them every morning,
　　test them every moment?
¹⁹ Will you not look away from me for a
　　while,
　　let me alone until I swallow my
　　　spittle?
²⁰ If I sin, what do I do to you, you
　　watcher of humanity?
　　Why have you made me your
　　　target?
　　Why have I become a burden to
　　　you?
²¹ Why do you not pardon my
　　transgression
　　and take away my iniquity?
　　For now I shall lie in the earth;
　　you will seek me, but I shall not
　　　be."

Bildad Speaks:
Job Should Repent

8 Then Bil′dad the Shu′hite answered:
² "How long will you say these
　　things,
　　and the words of your mouth be
　　a great wind?
³ Does God pervert justice?
　　Or does the Almighty[u] pervert the
　　right?
⁴ If your children sinned against him,
　　he delivered them into the power
　　of their transgression.
⁵ If you will seek God
　　and make supplication to the
　　Almighty,[u]
⁶ if you are pure and upright,
　　surely then he will rouse himself
　　for you
　　and restore to you your rightful
　　place.

⁷ Though your beginning was small,
　　your latter days will be very great.
⁸ "For inquire now of bygone
　　generations,
　　and consider what their ancestors
　　have found;
⁹ for we are but of yesterday, and we
　　know nothing,
　　for our days on earth are but a
　　shadow.
¹⁰ Will they not teach you and tell you
　　and utter words out of their
　　understanding?
¹¹ "Can papyrus grow where there is
　　no marsh?
　　Can reeds flourish where there is
　　no water?
¹² While yet in flower and not cut
　　down,
　　they wither before any other
　　plant.
¹³ Such are the paths of all who forget
　　God;
　　the hope of the godless shall
　　perish.
¹⁴ Their confidence is gossamer,
　　a spider's house their trust.
¹⁵ If one leans against its house, it will
　　not stand;
　　if one lays hold of it, it will not
　　endure.
¹⁶ The wicked thrive[v] before the sun,
　　and their shoots spread over the
　　garden.
¹⁷ Their roots twine around the
　　stoneheap;
　　they live among the rocks.[w]
¹⁸ If they are destroyed from their
　　place,
　　then it will deny them, saying, 'I
　　have never seen you.'
¹⁹ See, these are their happy ways,[x]
　　and out of the earth still others
　　will spring.

[u] Traditional rendering of Heb *Shaddai*　　[v] Heb *He thrives*　　[w] Gk Vg: Meaning of Heb uncertain
[x] Meaning of Heb uncertain

"He will yet fill your mouth with laughter, and your lips with shouts of joy." Job 8:21

20 "See, God will not reject a blameless person,

nor take the hand of evildoers.

21 He will yet fill your mouth with laughter,

and your lips with shouts of joy.

22 Those who hate you will be clothed with shame,

and the tent of the wicked will be no more."

Job Replies:
There Is No Mediator

9 Then Jōb answered:

2 "Indeed I know that this is so;

but how can a mortal be just before God?

3 If one wished to contend with him,

one could not answer him once in a thousand.

4 He is wise in heart, and mighty in strength

—who has resisted him, and succeeded?—

5 he who removes mountains, and they do not know it,

when he overturns them in his anger;

6 who shakes the earth out of its place,

and its pillars tremble;

7 who commands the sun, and it does not rise;

who seals up the stars;

8 who alone stretched out the heavens

and trampled the waves of the Sea;ʸ

9 who made the Bear and Ō·rī′on,

the Plēi′a·dēs and the chambers of the south;

10 who does great things beyond understanding,

and marvelous things without number.

11 Look, he passes by me, and I do not see him;

he moves on, but I do not perceive him.

12 He snatches away; who can stop him?

Who will say to him, 'What are you doing?'

13 "God will not turn back his anger;

the helpers of Rā′hab bowed beneath him.

14 How then can I answer him,

choosing my words with him?

15 Though I am innocent, I cannot answer him;

I must appeal for mercy to my accuser.ᶻ

16 If I summoned him and he answered me,

I do not believe that he would listen to my voice.

17 For he crushes me with a tempest,

and multiplies my wounds without cause;

18 he will not let me get my breath,

but fills me with bitterness.

19 If it is a contest of strength, he is the strong one!

If it is a matter of justice, who can summon him?ᵃ

The Pleiades is a group of seven stars. Because the Pleiades shines so brightly, it is mentioned in the writings of many peoples throughout the world. The Bear and Orion are also groups of stars, which are called constellations.

Look up information about these constellations on the Internet or in a book about the stars. Wait for a clear night and take a walk with your family to see if you can find the Pleiades, the Bear, or Orion. Isn't it awesome to think that Job saw the same stars that we can see today?

ʸ Or *trampled the back of the sea dragon*   ᶻ Or *for my right*   ᵃ Compare Gk: Heb *me*

20 Though I am innocent, my own
   mouth would condemn me;
   though I am blameless, he would
   prove me perverse.
21 I am blameless; I do not know myself;
   I loathe my life.
22 It is all one; therefore I say,
   he destroys both the blameless and
   the wicked.
23 When disaster brings sudden death,
   he mocks at the calamity[b] of the
   innocent.
24 The earth is given into the hand of the
   wicked;
   he covers the eyes of its judges—
   if it is not he, who then is it?

25 "My days are swifter than a runner;
   they flee away, they see no good.
26 They go by like skiffs of reed,
   like an eagle swooping on the
   prey.
27 If I say, 'I will forget my complaint;
   I will put off my sad countenance
   and be of good cheer,'
28 I become afraid of all my suffering,
   for I know you will not hold me
   innocent.
29 I shall be condemned;
   why then do I labor in vain?
30 If I wash myself with soap
   and cleanse my hands with lye,
31 yet you will plunge me into filth,
   and my own clothes will abhor
   me.
32 For he is not a mortal, as I am, that I
   might answer him,
   that we should come to trial
   together.
33 There is no umpire[c] between us,
   who might lay his hand on us
   both.
34 If he would take his rod away from
   me,
   and not let dread of him terrify me,
35 then I would speak without fear of
   him,
   for I know I am not what I am
   thought to be.[d]

Job: I Loathe My Life

10 "I loathe my life;
   I will give free utterance to my
   complaint;
   I will speak in the bitterness of my
   soul.
2 I will say to God, Do not condemn
   me;
   let me know why you contend
   against me.
3 Does it seem good to you to oppress,
   to despise the work of your hands
   and favor the schemes of the
   wicked?
4 Do you have eyes of flesh?
   Do you see as humans see?
5 Are your days like the days of
   mortals,
   or your years like human years,
6 that you seek out my iniquity
   and search for my sin,
7 although you know that I am not
   guilty,
   and there is no one to deliver out of
   your hand?
8 Your hands fashioned and made me;
   and now you turn and destroy me.[e]
9 Remember that you fashioned me like
   clay;
   and will you turn me to dust
   again?
10 Did you not pour me out like milk
   and curdle me like cheese?
11 You clothed me with skin and flesh,
   and knit me together with bones
   and sinews.
12 You have granted me life and steadfast
   love,
   and your care has preserved my
   spirit.
13 Yet these things you hid in your heart;
   I know that this was your purpose.
14 If I sin, you watch me,
   and do not acquit me of my
   iniquity.

b Meaning of Heb uncertain   c Another reading
is *Would that there were an umpire*   d Cn: Heb *for
I am not so in myself*   e Cn Compare Gk Syr: Heb
made me together all around, and you destroy me

15 If I am wicked, woe to me!
    If I am righteous, I cannot lift up
      my head,
  for I am filled with disgrace
    and look upon my affliction.
16 Bold as a lion you hunt me;
    you repeat your exploits against
      me.
17 You renew your witnesses against me,
    and increase your vexation toward
      me;
    you bring fresh troops against me.ʲ

18 "Why did you bring me forth from the
      womb?
    Would that I had died before any
      eye had seen me,
19 and were as though I had not been,
    carried from the womb to the grave.
20 Are not the days of my life few?ᵍ
    Let me alone, that I may find a little
      comfortʰ
21 before I go, never to return,
    to the land of gloom and deep
      darkness,
22 the land of gloomⁱ and chaos,
    where light is like darkness."

Zophar Speaks: Job's Guilt Deserves Punishment

11 Then Zōʹphar the Naʹa·ma·thīte
    answered:
2 "Should a multitude of words go
      unanswered,
    and should one full of talk be
      vindicated?
3 Should your babble put others to
      silence,
    and when you mock, shall no one
      shame you?
4 For you say, 'My conductʲ is pure,
    and I am clean in God'sᵏ sight.'
5 But O that God would speak,
    and open his lips to you,
6 and that he would tell you the secrets
      of wisdom!
    For wisdom is many-sided.ˡ

Know then that God exacts of you less
    than your guilt deserves.
7 "Can you find out the deep things of
      God?
    Can you find out the limit of the
      Almighty?ᵐ
8 It is higher than heavenⁿ—what can
      you do?
    Deeper than Shēʹōl—what can you
      know?
9 Its measure is longer than the earth,
    and broader than the sea.
10 If he passes through, and imprisons,
    and assembles for judgment, who
      can hinder him?
11 For he knows those who are
      worthless;
    when he sees iniquity, will he not
      consider it?
12 But a stupid person will get
      understanding,
    when a wild ass is born human.ˡ

13 "If you direct your heart rightly,
    you will stretch out your hands
      toward him.
14 If iniquity is in your hand, put it far
      away,
    and do not let wickedness reside in
      your tents.
15 Surely then you will lift up your face
      without blemish;
    you will be secure, and will not fear.
16 You will forget your misery;
    you will remember it as waters that
      have passed away.
17 And your life will be brighter than the
      noonday;
    its darkness will be like the
      morning.
18 And you will have confidence,
    because there is hope;

ʲ Cn Compare Gk: Heb *toward me; changes and a
troop are with me*   ᵍ Cn Compare Gk Syr: Heb
Are not my days few? Let him cease!   ʰ Heb *that I
may brighten up a little*   ⁱ Heb *gloom as darkness,
deep darkness*   ʲ Gk: Heb *teaching*
ᵏ Heb *your*   ˡ Meaning of Heb uncertain
ᵐ Traditional rendering of Heb *Shaddai*   ⁿ Heb
The heights of heaven

you will be protected[o] and take your
rest in safety.
19 You will lie down, and no one will
make you afraid;
many will entreat your favor.
20 But the eyes of the wicked will fail;
all way of escape will be lost to
them,
and their hope is to breathe their
last."

Job Replies: I Am a Laughingstock

12 Then Jōb answered:
2 "No doubt you are the people,
and wisdom will die with you.
3 But I have understanding as well as
you;
I am not inferior to you.
Who does not know such things as
these?
4 I am a laughingstock to my friends;
I, who called upon God and he
answered me,
a just and blameless man, I am a
laughingstock.
5 Those at ease have contempt for
misfortune,[p]
but it is ready for those whose feet
are unstable.
6 The tents of robbers are at peace,
and those who provoke God are
secure,
who bring their god in their hands.[q]

7 "But ask the animals, and they will
teach you;
the birds of the air, and they will tell
you;
8 ask the plants of the earth,[r] and they
will teach you;
and the fish of the sea will declare
to you.
9 Who among all these does not know
that the hand of the Lord has done
this?
10 In his hand is the life of every living
thing

and the breath of every human
being.
11 Does not the ear test words
as the palate tastes food?
12 Is wisdom with the aged,
and understanding in length of
days?

13 "With God[s] are wisdom and strength;
he has counsel and understanding.
14 If he tears down, no one can rebuild;
if he shuts someone in, no one can
open up.
15 If he withholds the waters, they dry
up;
if he sends them out, they
overwhelm the land.
16 With him are strength and wisdom;
the deceived and the deceiver are
his.
17 He leads counselors away stripped,
and makes fools of judges.
18 He looses the sash of kings,
and binds a waistcloth on their
loins.
19 He leads priests away stripped,
and overthrows the mighty.
20 He deprives of speech those who are
trusted,
and takes away the discernment of
the elders.
21 He pours contempt on princes,
and looses the belt of the strong.
22 He uncovers the deeps out of
darkness,
and brings deep darkness to light.
23 He makes nations great, then destroys
them;
he enlarges nations, then leads them
away.
24 He strips understanding from the
leaders[t] of the earth,
and makes them wander in a
pathless waste.

---

[o] Or *you will look around*   [p] Meaning of Heb
uncertain   [q] Or *whom God brought forth by his
hand*; Meaning of Heb uncertain   [r] Or *speak to
the earth*   [s] Heb *him*   [t] Heb adds *of the people*

25 They grope in the dark without light;
    he makes them stagger like a
      drunkard.

13 "Look, my eye has seen all this,
    my ear has heard and
      understood it.
2 What you know, I also know;
    I am not inferior to you.
3 But I would speak to the Almighty,[u]
    and I desire to argue my case with
      God.
4 As for you, you whitewash with lies;
    all of you are worthless physicians.
5 If you would only keep silent,
    that would be your wisdom!
6 Hear now my reasoning,
    and listen to the pleadings of my lips.
7 Will you speak falsely for God,
    and speak deceitfully for him?
8 Will you show partiality toward him,
    will you plead the case for God?
9 Will it be well with you when he
      searches you out?
    Or can you deceive him, as one
      person deceives another?
10 He will surely rebuke you
    if in secret you show partiality.
11 Will not his majesty terrify you,
    and the dread of him fall upon you?
12 Your maxims are proverbs of ashes,
    your defenses are defenses of clay.

13 "Let me have silence, and I will speak,
    and let come on me what may.
14 I will take my flesh in my teeth,
    and put my life in my hand.[v]
15 See, he will kill me; I have no hope;[w]
    but I will defend my ways to his face.
16 This will be my salvation,
    that the godless shall not come
      before him.
17 Listen carefully to my words,
    and let my declaration be in your
      ears.
18 I have indeed prepared my case;
    I know that I shall be vindicated.
19 Who is there that will contend with
      me?
    For then I would be silent and die.

Job's Despondent Prayer

20 Only grant two things to me,
    then I will not hide myself from
      your face:
21 withdraw your hand far from me,
    and do not let dread of you terrify
      me.
22 Then call, and I will answer;
    or let me speak, and you reply to
      me.
23 How many are my iniquities and my
      sins?
    Make me know my transgression
      and my sin.
24 Why do you hide your face,
    and count me as your enemy?
25 Will you frighten a windblown leaf
    and pursue dry chaff?
26 For you write bitter things against me,
    and make me reap[x] the iniquities of
      my youth.
27 You put my feet in the stocks,
    and watch all my paths;
    you set a bound to the soles of my
      feet.
28 One wastes away like a rotten thing,
    like a garment that is moth-eaten.

14 "A mortal, born of woman, few
    of days and full of trouble,
2 comes up like a flower and
      withers,
    flees like a shadow and does not
      last.
3 Do you fix your eyes on such a one?
    Do you bring me into judgment
      with you?
4 Who can bring a clean thing out of
      an unclean?
    No one can.
5 Since their days are determined,
    and the number of their months
      is known to you,
    and you have appointed the
      bounds that they cannot pass,

---

[u] Traditional rendering of Heb *Shaddai*
Heb *Why should I take . . . in my hand?*
Though he kill me, yet I will trust in him
[v] Gk:
[w] Or
[x] Heb
inherit

6 look away from them, and desist,[y]
   that they may enjoy, like laborers,
     their days.

7 "For there is hope for a tree,
   if it is cut down, that it will
     sprout again,
   and that its shoots will not cease.
8 Though its root grows old in the
     earth,
   and its stump dies in the ground,
9 yet at the scent of water it will bud
   and put forth branches like a
     young plant.
10 But mortals die, and are laid low;
   humans expire, and where are
     they?
11 As waters fail from a lake,
   and a river wastes away and dries
     up,
12 so mortals lie down and do not rise
     again;
   until the heavens are no more,
     they will not awake
   or be roused out of their sleep.
13 O that you would hide me in She´ōl,
   that you would conceal me until
     your wrath is past,
   that you would appoint me a set
     time, and remember me!
14 If mortals die, will they live again?
   All the days of my service I would
     wait
   until my release should come.
15 You would call, and I would answer
     you;
   you would long for the work of
     your hands.
16 For then you would not[z] number my
     steps,
   you would not keep watch over my
     sin;
17 my transgression would be sealed up
     in a bag,
   and you would cover over my
     iniquity.

18 "But the mountain falls and crumbles
     away,

and the rock is removed from its
     place;
19 the waters wear away the stones;
   the torrents wash away the soil of
     the earth;
   so you destroy the hope of mortals.
20 You prevail forever against them, and
     they pass away;
   you change their countenance, and
     send them away.
21 Their children come to honor, and
     they do not know it;
   they are brought low, and it goes
     unnoticed.
22 They feel only the pain of their own
     bodies,
   and mourn only for themselves."

Eliphaz Speaks: Job Undermines Religion

15 Then Eli´phaz the Te´man·īte
     answered:
2 "Should the wise answer with windy
     knowledge,
   and fill themselves with the east
     wind?
3 Should they argue in unprofitable talk,
   or in words with which they can do
     no good?
4 But you are doing away with the fear
     of God,
   and hindering meditation before
     God.
5 For your iniquity teaches your mouth,
   and you choose the tongue of the
     crafty.
6 Your own mouth condemns you, and
     not I;
   your own lips testify against you.

7 "Are you the firstborn of the human
     race?
   Were you brought forth before the
     hills?
8 Have you listened in the council of
     God?

[y] Cn: Heb *that they may desist*   [z] Syr: Heb lacks *not*

And do you limit wisdom to
yourself?
9 What do you know that we do not
know?
What do you understand that is not
clear to us?
10 The gray-haired and the aged are on
our side,
those older than your father.
11 Are the consolations of God too small
for you,
or the word that deals gently with
you?
12 Why does your heart carry you away,
and why do your eyes flash,[a]
13 so that you turn your spirit against
God,
and let such words go out of your
mouth?
14 What are mortals, that they can be
clean?
Or those born of woman, that they
can be righteous?
15 God puts no trust even in his holy
ones,
and the heavens are not clean in his
sight;
16 how much less one who is
abominable and corrupt,
one who drinks iniquity like water!

17 "I will show you; listen to me;
what I have seen I will declare—
18 what sages have told,
and their ancestors have not
hidden,
19 to whom alone the land was given,
and no stranger passed among
them.
20 The wicked writhe in pain all their
days,
through all the years that are laid up
for the ruthless.
21 Terrifying sounds are in their ears;
in prosperity the destroyer will
come upon them.
22 They despair of returning from
darkness,
and they are destined for the sword.
23 They wander abroad for bread, saying,
'Where is it?'
They know that a day of darkness is
ready at hand;
24 distress and anguish terrify them;
they prevail against them, like a
king prepared for battle.
25 Because they stretched out their hands
against God,
and bid defiance to the Almighty,[b]
26 running stubbornly against him
with a thick-bossed shield;
27 because they have covered their faces
with their fat,
and gathered fat upon their loins,
28 they will live in desolate cities,
in houses that no one should inhabit,
houses destined to become heaps of
ruins;
29 they will not be rich, and their wealth
will not endure,
nor will they strike root in the
earth;[c]
30 they will not escape from darkness;
the flame will dry up their shoots,

In Job's time many of
the houses were built of
stones or mud bricks. Roofs
were made by covering
wooden beams with branches and
then adding a layer of earth. If no one
was living in the house to take care of
it, rain would soak into the layer of
earth, and the weight would break
down the roof. Once the roof fell, the
walls would easily fall, and then the
whole house would be nothing more
than a pile of mud.

Just as people need to take care of
their houses, they need to take care
of their bodies, hearts, and minds.
What are some ways that you take
care of yourself?

[a] Meaning of Heb uncertain   [b] Traditional rendering of Heb *Shaddai*   [c] Vg: Meaning of Heb uncertain   [d] Gk: Heb *mouth*

and their blossom^d will be swept
away^e by the wind.
³¹ Let them not trust in emptiness,
deceiving themselves;
for emptiness will be their
recompense.
³² It will be paid in full before their time,
and their branch will not be green.
³³ They will shake off their unripe grape,
like the vine,
and cast off their blossoms, like the
olive tree.
³⁴ For the company of the godless is
barren,
and fire consumes the tents of
bribery.
³⁵ They conceive mischief and bring
forth evil
and their heart prepares deceit."

Job Reaffirms His Innocence

16 Then Jōb answered:
² "I have heard many such
things;
miserable comforters are you all.
³ Have windy words no limit?
Or what provokes you that you
keep on talking?
⁴ I also could talk as you do,
if you were in my place;
I could join words together against
you,
and shake my head at you.
⁵ I could encourage you with my
mouth,

> The word "heaven"
> was used in two ways
> in the Bible. The first
> and most important meaning is
> the place where God lives. The
> second meaning is the sky. In
> Bible times, heaven (the sky),
> was thought to have "windows"
> to let the rain through. It was
> also called a "tent," a "curtain,"
> and a "mirror."

and the solace of my lips would
assuage your pain.
⁶ "If I speak, my pain is not assuaged,
and if I forbear, how much of it
leaves me?
⁷ Surely now God has worn me out;
he has^f made desolate all my
company.
⁸ And he has^f shriveled me up,
which is a witness against me;
my leanness has risen up against me,
and it testifies to my face.
⁹ He has torn me in his wrath, and
hated me;
he has gnashed his teeth at me;
my adversary sharpens his eyes
against me.
¹⁰ They have gaped at me with their
mouths;
they have struck me insolently on
the cheek;
they mass themselves together
against me.
¹¹ God gives me up to the ungodly,
and casts me into the hands of the
wicked.
¹² I was at ease, and he broke me in
two;
he seized me by the neck and
dashed me to pieces;
he set me up as his target;
¹³ his archers surround me.
He slashes open my kidneys, and
shows no mercy;
he pours out my gall on the
ground.
¹⁴ He bursts upon me again and again;
he rushes at me like a warrior.
¹⁵ I have sewed sackcloth upon my skin,
and have laid my strength in the
dust.
¹⁶ My face is red with weeping,
and deep darkness is on my
eyelids,
¹⁷ though there is no violence in my
hands,
and my prayer is pure.

^d Gk: Heb *mouth* ^e Cn: Heb *will depart* ^f Heb
you have

18 "O earth, do not cover my blood;
     let my outcry find no resting place.
19 Even now, in fact, my witness is in heaven,
     and he that vouches for me is on high.
20 My friends scorn me;
     my eye pours out tears to God,
21 that he would maintain the right of a mortal with God,
     as[g] one does for a neighbor.
22 For when a few years have come,
     I shall go the way from which I shall not return.

Job Prays for Relief

17 My spirit is broken, my days are extinct,
     the grave is ready for me.
2 Surely there are mockers around me,
     and my eye dwells on their provocation.
3 "Lay down a pledge for me with yourself;
     who is there that will give surety for me?
4 Since you have closed their minds to understanding,
     therefore you will not let them triumph.
5 Those who denounce friends for reward—
     the eyes of their children will fail.

6 "He has made me a byword of the peoples,
     and I am one before whom people spit.
7 My eye has grown dim from grief,
     and all my members are like a shadow.
8 The upright are appalled at this,
     and the innocent stir themselves up against the godless.
9 Yet the righteous hold to their way,
     and they that have clean hands grow stronger and stronger.
10 But you, come back now, all of you,

     and I shall not find a sensible person among you.
11 My days are past, my plans are broken off,
     the desires of my heart.
12 They make night into day;
     'The light,' they say, 'is near to the darkness.'[h]
13 If I look for Shē´ōl as my house,
     if I spread my couch in darkness,
14 if I say to the Pit, 'You are my father,'
     and to the worm, 'My mother,' or 'My sister,'
15 where then is my hope?
     Who will see my hope?
16 Will it go down to the bars of Shē´ōl?
     Shall we descend together into the dust?"

Bildad Speaks: God Punishes the Wicked

18 Then Bil´dad the Shū´hīte answered:
2 "How long will you hunt for words?
     Consider, and then we shall speak.
3 Why are we counted as cattle?
     Why are we stupid in your sight?
4 You who tear yourself in your anger—
     shall the earth be forsaken because of you,

Most people would rather live in the light than in the dark. It is hard to see things in the dark! Because there was no electricity in Bible times, people would keep a lamp burning all night long. Job spoke of his time of wealth as a time when God's light shined on him, and he also spoke of the light of the wicked being put out. Read Proverbs 13:9. What do you think this verse means? Look through the book of Psalms (the next book after Job). How many references to light and dark can you find?

[g] Syr Vg Tg: Heb *and*   [h] Meaning of Heb uncertain

or the rock be removed out of its
    place?
5 "Surely the light of the wicked is
    put out,
    and the flame of their fire does not
      shine.
6 The light is dark in their tent,
    and the lamp above them is put
      out.
7 Their strong steps are shortened,
    and their own schemes throw them
      down.
8 For they are thrust into a net by their
    own feet,
    and they walk into a pitfall.
9 A trap seizes them by the heel;
    a snare lays hold of them.
10 A rope is hid for them in the ground,
    a trap for them in the path.
11 Terrors frighten them on every side,
    and chase them at their heels.
12 Their strength is consumed by
    hunger,[i]
    and calamity is ready for their
      stumbling.
13 By disease their skin is consumed,[j]
    the firstborn of Death consumes
      their limbs.
14 They are torn from the tent in which
    they trusted,
    and are brought to the king of
      terrors.
15 In their tents nothing remains;
    sulfur is scattered upon their
      habitations.
16 Their roots dry up beneath,
    and their branches wither above.

People caught birds and animals using traps or snares. Traps in Bible times were nets, rope nooses, and pits covered with branches for camouflage. The words "trap" and "snare" are also figures of speech that describe disaster, sudden danger, or unexpected death.

17 Their memory perishes from the earth,
    and they have no name in the
      street.
18 They are thrust from light into
    darkness,
    and driven out of the world.
19 They have no offspring or descendant
    among their people,
    and no survivor where they used to
      live.
20 They of the west are appalled at their
    fate,
    and horror seizes those of the east.
21 Surely such are the dwellings of the
    ungodly,
    such is the place of those who do
      not know God."

Job Replies: I Know That My Redeemer Lives

19 Then Jōb answered:
2 "How long will you
    torment me,
    and break me in pieces with words?
3 These ten times you have cast
    reproach upon me;
    are you not ashamed to wrong me?
4 And even if it is true that I have erred,
    my error remains with me.
5 If indeed you magnify yourselves
    against me,
    and make my humiliation an
      argument against me,
6 know then that God has put me in the
    wrong,
    and closed his net around me.
7 Even when I cry out, 'Violence!' I am
    not answered;
    I call aloud, but there is no justice.
8 He has walled up my way so that I
    cannot pass,
    and he has set darkness upon my
      paths.
9 He has stripped my glory from me,
    and taken the crown from my
      head.

[i] Or *Disaster is hungry for them*   [j] Cn: Heb *It consumes the limbs of his skin*

"For I know that my Redeemer lives, and that at the last he will stand upon the earth."
Job 19:25

10 He breaks me down on every side,
and I am gone,
he has uprooted my hope like a
tree.
11 He has kindled his wrath against me,
and counts me as his adversary.
12 His troops come on together;
they have thrown up siegeworks[k]
against me,
and encamp around my tent.

13 "He has put my family far from me,
and my acquaintances are wholly
estranged from me.
14 My relatives and my close friends have
failed me;
15 the guests in my house have
forgotten me;
my serving girls count me as a
stranger;
I have become an alien in their eyes.
16 I call to my servant, but he gives me
no answer;
I must myself plead with him.
17 My breath is repulsive to my wife;
I am loathsome to my own family.
18 Even young children despise me;
when I rise, they talk against me.
19 All my intimate friends abhor me,
and those whom I loved have
turned against me.
20 My bones cling to my skin and to my
flesh,
and I have escaped by the skin of
my teeth.
21 Have pity on me, have pity on me, O
you my friends,
for the hand of God has touched
me!
22 Why do you, like God, pursue me,
never satisfied with my flesh?

23 "O that my words were written down!
O that they were inscribed in a
book!
24 O that with an iron pen and with lead
they were engraved on a rock
forever!
25 For I know that my Redeemer[l] lives,
and that at the last he[m] will stand
upon the earth;[n]
26 and after my skin has been thus
destroyed,
then in[o] my flesh I shall see God,[p]
27 whom I shall see on my side,[q]
and my eyes shall behold, and not
another.
My heart faints within me!
28 If you say, 'How we will persecute
him!'
and, 'The root of the matter is
found in him';
29 be afraid of the sword,
for wrath brings the punishment of
the sword,
so that you may know there is a
judgment."

Zophar Speaks: Wickedness Receives Just Retribution

20 Then Zŏ´phar the Nā´a·ma·thīte
answered:
2 "Pay attention! My thoughts urge me
to answer,
because of the agitation within me.
3 I hear censure that insults me,
and a spirit beyond my
understanding answers me.
4 Do you not know this from of old,
ever since mortals were placed on
earth,
5 that the exulting of the wicked is short,
and the joy of the godless is but for
a moment?
6 Even though they mount up high as
the heavens,
and their head reaches to the clouds,

[k] Cn: Heb *their way*   [l] Or *Vindicator*   [m] Or *that he the Last*   [n] Heb *dust*   [o] Or *without*
[p] Meaning of Heb of this verse uncertain   [q] Or *for myself*

⁷ they will perish forever like their own
    dung;
    those who have seen them will say,
        'Where are they?'
⁸ They will fly away like a dream, and
    not be found;
    they will be chased away like a vision
        of the night.
⁹ The eye that saw them will see them
    no more,
    nor will their place behold them
        any longer.
¹⁰ Their children will seek the favor of
    the poor,
    and their hands will give back their
        wealth.
¹¹ Their bodies, once full of youth,
    will lie down in the dust with them.

¹² "Though wickedness is sweet in their
    mouth,
    though they hide it under their
        tongues,
¹³ though they are loath to let it go,
    and hold it in their mouths,
¹⁴ yet their food is turned in their
    stomachs;
    it is the venom of asps within them.
¹⁵ They swallow down riches and vomit
    them up again;
    God casts them out of their bellies.
¹⁶ They will suck the poison of asps;
    the tongue of a viper will kill them.
¹⁷ They will not look on the rivers,
    the streams flowing with honey and
        curds.
¹⁸ They will give back the fruit of their
    toil,
    and will not swallow it down;
    from the profit of their trading
        they will get no enjoyment.
¹⁹ For they have crushed and abandoned
    the poor,
    they have seized a house that they
        did not build.

²⁰ "They knew no quiet in their bellies;
    in their greed they let nothing
        escape.

²¹ There was nothing left after they had
    eaten;
    therefore their prosperity will not
        endure.
²² In full sufficiency they will be in
    distress;
    all the force of misery will come
        upon them.
²³ To fill their belly to the full
    God*ʳ* will send his fierce anger into
        them,
    and rain it upon them as their food.*ˢ*
²⁴ They will flee from an iron weapon;
    a bronze arrow will strike them
        through.
²⁵ It is drawn forth and comes out of
    their body,
    and the glittering point comes out
        of their gall;
    terrors come upon them.
²⁶ Utter darkness is laid up for their
    treasures;
    a fire fanned by no one will devour
        them;
    what is left in their tent will be
        consumed.
²⁷ The heavens will reveal their iniquity,
    and the earth will rise up against
        them.
²⁸ The possessions of their house will be
    carried away,
    dragged off in the day of God's*ᵗ*
        wrath.
²⁹ This is the portion of the wicked from
    God,
    the heritage decreed for them by
        God."

Job Replies: The Wicked Often Go Unpunished

21 Then Job answered:
² "Listen carefully to my words,
    and let this be your consolation.
³ Bear with me, and I will speak;
    then after I have spoken, mock
        on.
⁴ As for me, is my complaint
    addressed to mortals?

ʳ Heb *he*   *ˢ* Cn: Meaning of Heb uncertain
ᵗ Heb *his*

Why should I not be impatient?
5 Look at me, and be appalled,
and lay your hand upon your
mouth.
6 When I think of it I am dismayed,
and shuddering seizes my flesh.
7 Why do the wicked live on,
reach old age, and grow mighty in
power?
8 Their children are established in their
presence,
and their offspring before their eyes.
9 Their houses are safe from fear,
and no rod of God is upon them.
10 Their bull breeds without fail;
their cow calves and never
miscarries.
11 They send out their little ones like a
flock,
and their children dance around.
12 They sing to the tambourine and the
lyre,
and rejoice to the sound of the pipe.
13 They spend their days in prosperity,
and in peace they go down to
Shē´ōl.
14 They say to God, 'Leave us alone!
We do not desire to know your ways.
15 What is the Almighty[u] that we should
serve him?
And what profit do we get if we
pray to him?'
16 Is not their prosperity indeed their
own achievement?[v]
The plans of the wicked are
repugnant to me.

17 "How often is the lamp of the wicked
put out?
How often does calamity come
upon them?
How often does God[w] distribute
pains in his anger?
18 How often are they like straw before
the wind,
and like chaff that the storm carries
away?
19 You say, 'God stores up their iniquity
for their children.'

Let it be paid back to them, so that
they may know it.
20 Let their own eyes see their
destruction,
and let them drink of the wrath of
the Almighty.[u]
21 For what do they care for their
household after them,
when the number of their months is
cut off?
22 Will any teach God knowledge,
seeing that he judges those that are
on high?
23 One dies in full prosperity,
being wholly at ease and secure,
24 his loins full of milk
and the marrow of his bones moist.
25 Another dies in bitterness of soul,
never having tasted of good.
26 They lie down alike in the dust,
and the worms cover them.

27 "Oh, I know your thoughts,
and your schemes to wrong me.
28 For you say, 'Where is the house of the
prince?
Where is the tent in which the
wicked lived?'
29 Have you not asked those who travel
the roads,
and do you not accept their
testimony,
30 that the wicked are spared in the day
of calamity,
and are rescued in the day of
wrath?
31 Who declares their way to their
face,
and who repays them for what they
have done?
32 When they are carried to the grave,
a watch is kept over their tomb.
33 The clods of the valley are sweet to
them;
everyone will follow after,
and those who went before are
innumerable.

[u] Traditional rendering of Heb *Shaddai*   [v] Heb *in their hand*   [w] Heb *he*

³⁴ How then will you comfort me with
empty nothings?
There is nothing left of your
answers but falsehood."

Eliphaz Speaks: Job's Wickedness Is Great

22 Then E·li'phaz the Te'man·ite
answered:
² "Can a mortal be of use to God?
Can even the wisest be of service to
him?
³ Is it any pleasure to the Almighty^x if
you are righteous,
or is it gain to him if you make your
ways blameless?
⁴ Is it for your piety that he reproves
you,
and enters into judgment with you?
⁵ Is not your wickedness great?
There is no end to your iniquities.
⁶ For you have exacted pledges from
your family for no reason,
and stripped the naked of their
clothing.
⁷ You have given no water to the weary
to drink,
and you have withheld bread from
the hungry.
⁸ The powerful possess the land,
and the favored live in it.
⁹ You have sent widows away empty-
handed,
and the arms of the orphans you
have crushed.^y
¹⁰ Therefore snares are around you,
and sudden terror overwhelms you,
¹¹ or darkness so that you cannot see;
a flood of water covers you.

¹² "Is not God high in the heavens?
See the highest stars, how lofty they
are!
¹³ Therefore you say, 'What does God
know?
Can he judge through the deep
darkness?
¹⁴ Thick clouds enwrap him, so that he
does not see,

and he walks on the dome of
heaven.'
¹⁵ Will you keep to the old way
that the wicked have trod?
¹⁶ They were snatched away before their
time;
their foundation was washed away
by a flood.
¹⁷ They said to God, 'Leave us alone,'
and 'What can the Almighty^x do to
us?'^z
¹⁸ Yet he filled their houses with good
things—
but the plans of the wicked are
repugnant to me.
¹⁹ The righteous see it and are glad;
the innocent laugh them to scorn,
²⁰ saying, 'Surely our adversaries are cut
off,
and what they left, the fire has
consumed.'

²¹ "Agree with God,^a and be at peace;
in this way good will come to you.
²² Receive instruction from his mouth,
and lay up his words in your heart.
²³ If you return to the Almighty,^x you will
be restored,
if you remove unrighteousness from
your tents,
²⁴ if you treat gold like dust,
and gold of O'phir like the stones of
the torrent-bed,
²⁵ and if the Almighty^x is your gold
and your precious silver,
²⁶ then you will delight yourself in the
Almighty,^x
and lift up your face to God.
²⁷ You will pray to him, and he will hear
you,
and you will pay your vows.
²⁸ You will decide on a matter, and it will
be established for you,
and light will shine on your ways.
²⁹ When others are humiliated, you say
it is pride;

^x Traditional rendering of Heb *Shaddai* ^y Gk
Syr Tg Vg: Heb *were crushed* ^z Gk Syr: Heb
them ^a Heb *him*

"If I go forward, he is not there; or backward, I cannot perceive him; on the left he hides, and I cannot behold him; I turn to the right, but I cannot see him. But he knows the way that I take; when he has tested me, I shall come out like gold."

Job 23:9–10

for he saves the humble.
30 He will deliver even those who are guilty;
they will escape because of the cleanness of your hands."[b]

Job Replies: My Complaint Is Bitter

23 Then Jōb answered:
2 "Today also my complaint is bitter;[c]
his[d] hand is heavy despite my groaning.
3 Oh, that I knew where I might find him,
that I might come even to his dwelling!
4 I would lay my case before him,
and fill my mouth with arguments.
5 I would learn what he would answer me,
and understand what he would say to me.
6 Would he contend with me in the greatness of his power?
No; but he would give heed to me.
7 There an upright person could reason with him,
and I should be acquitted forever by my judge.

8 "If I go forward, he is not there;
or backward, I cannot perceive him;
9 on the left he hides, and I cannot behold him;
I turn[e] to the right, but I cannot see him.

10 But he knows the way that I take;
when he has tested me, I shall come out like gold.
11 My foot has held fast to his steps;
I have kept his way and have not turned aside.
12 I have not departed from the commandment of his lips;
I have treasured in[f] my bosom the words of his mouth.
13 But he stands alone and who can dissuade him?
What he desires, that he does.
14 For he will complete what he appoints for me;
and many such things are in his mind.
15 Therefore I am terrified at his presence;
when I consider, I am in dread of him.
16 God has made my heart faint;
the Almighty[g] has terrified me;
17 If only I could vanish in darkness,
and thick darkness would cover my face![h]

Job Complains of Violence on the Earth

24 "Why are times not kept by the Almighty,[g]
and why do those who know him never see his days?
2 The wicked[i] remove landmarks;
they seize flocks and pasture them.
3 They drive away the donkey of the orphan;
they take the widow's ox for a pledge.
4 They thrust the needy off the road;
the poor of the earth all hide themselves.

[b] Meaning of Heb uncertain   [c] Syr Vg Tg: Heb rebellious   [d] Gk Syr: Heb my   [e] Syr Vg: Heb he turns   [f] Gk Vg: Heb from   [g] Traditional rendering of Heb Shaddai   [h] Or But I am not destroyed by the darkness; he has concealed the thick darkness from me   [i] Gk: Heb they

5 Like wild asses in the desert
  they go out to their toil,
scavenging in the wasteland
  food for their young.
6 They reap in a field not their own
  and they glean in the vineyard of
    the wicked.
7 They lie all night naked, without
    clothing,
  and have no covering in the cold.
8 They are wet with the rain of the
    mountains,
  and cling to the rock for want of
    shelter.

9 "There are those who snatch the
    orphan child from the breast,
  and take as a pledge the infant of
    the poor.
10 They go about naked, without
    clothing;
  though hungry, they carry the
    sheaves;
11 between their terraces[j] they press out
    oil;
  they tread the wine presses, but
    suffer thirst.
12 From the city the dying groan,
  and the throat of the wounded cries
    for help;
  yet God pays no attention to their
    prayer.

13 "There are those who rebel against the
    light,
  who are not acquainted with its
    ways,
  and do not stay in its paths.
14 The murderer rises at dusk
  to kill the poor and needy,
  and in the night is like a thief.
15 The eye of the adulterer also waits for
    the twilight,
  saying, 'No eye will see me';
  and he disguises his face.
16 In the dark they dig through houses;
  by day they shut themselves up;
  they do not know the light.
17 For deep darkness is morning to all of
    them;

  for they are friends with the terrors
    of deep darkness.

18 "Swift are they on the face of the
    waters;
  their portion in the land is cursed;
  no treader turns toward their
    vineyards.
19 Drought and heat snatch away the
    snow waters;
  so does Shĕʾōl those who have
    sinned.
20 The womb forgets them;
  the worm finds them sweet;
  they are no longer remembered;
  so wickedness is broken like a tree.

21 "They harm[k] the childless woman,
  and do no good to the widow.
22 Yet God[l] prolongs the life of the
    mighty by his power;
  they rise up when they despair of
    life.
23 He gives them security, and they are
    supported;
  his eyes are upon their ways.
24 They are exalted a little while, and
    then are gone;
  they wither and fade like the
    mallow;[m]
  they are cut off like the heads of
    grain.
25 If it is not so, who will prove me a
    liar,
  and show that there is nothing in
    what I say?"

> Job points out to his friends that although wicked people often seem to be powerful, they only have so long before they are cut down like a shrub (mallow) that grows in salt marshes.

[j] Meaning of Heb uncertain   [k] Gk Tg: Heb *feed on* or *associate with*   [l] Heb *he*   [m] Gk: Heb *like all others*

Bildad Speaks: How Can a Mortal Be Righteous Before God?

25 Then Bil'dad the Shū'hīte answered:

2 "Dominion and fear are with God;[n]
  he makes peace in his high heaven.

3 Is there any number to his armies?
  Upon whom does his light not arise?

4 How then can a mortal be righteous before God?
  How can one born of woman be pure?

5 If even the moon is not bright
  and the stars are not pure in his sight,

6 how much less a mortal, who is a maggot,
  and a human being, who is a worm!"

Job Replies: God's Majesty Is Unsearchable

26 Then Jōb answered:
  2 "How you have helped one who has no power!
  How you have assisted the arm that has no strength!

3 How you have counseled one who has no wisdom,
  and given much good advice!

4 With whose help have you uttered words,
  and whose spirit has come forth from you?

5 The shades below tremble,
  the waters and their inhabitants.

6 Shē'ōl is naked before God,
  and A·bad'don has no covering.

7 He stretches out Zā'phon[o] over the void,
  and hangs the earth upon nothing.

8 He binds up the waters in his thick clouds,
  and the cloud is not torn open by them.

9 He covers the face of the full moon,
  and spreads over it his cloud.

10 He has described a circle on the face of the waters,

at the boundary between light and darkness.

11 The pillars of heaven tremble,
  and are astounded at his rebuke.

12 By his power he stilled the Sea;
  by his understanding he struck down Rā'hab.

13 By his wind the heavens were made fair;
  his hand pierced the fleeing serpent.

14 These are indeed but the outskirts of his ways;
  and how small a whisper do we hear of him!
  But the thunder of his power who can understand?"

> Palestine has thunderstorms with flashes of lightning in the spring and fall. People in Bible times saw them as an act of divine power. Some passages in the Bible mention thunder as the voice of God and lightning as the spear or sword of God.

Job Maintains His Integrity

27 Jōb again took up his discourse and said:
  2 "As God lives, who has taken away my right,
  and the Almighty,[p] who has made my soul bitter,

3 as long as my breath is in me
  and the spirit of God is in my nostrils,

4 my lips will not speak falsehood,
  and my tongue will not utter deceit.

5 Far be it from me to say that you are right;
  until I die I will not put away my integrity from me.

6 I hold fast my righteousness, and will not let it go;

---

[n] Heb *him* [o] Or *the North* [p] Traditional rendering of Heb *Shaddai*

my heart does not reproach me for
  any of my days.

7 "May my enemy be like the wicked,
  and may my opponent be like the
  unrighteous.
8 For what is the hope of the godless
  when God cuts them off,
  when God takes away their lives?
9 Will God hear their cry
  when trouble comes upon them?
10 Will they take delight in the
  Almighty?q
  Will they call upon God at all
  times?
11 I will teach you concerning the hand
  of God;
  that which is with the Almightyq I
  will not conceal.
12 All of you have seen it yourselves;
  why then have you become
  altogether vain?
13 "This is the portion of the wicked with
  God,
  and the heritage that oppressors
  receive from the Almighty:q
14 If their children are multiplied, it is for
  the sword;
  and their offspring have not enough
  to eat.
15 Those who survive them the
  pestilence buries,
  and their widows make no
  lamentation.
16 Though they heap up silver like dust,
  and pile up clothing like clay—
17 they may pile it up, but the just will
  wear it,
  and the innocent will divide the
  silver.

18 They build their houses like nests,
  like booths made by sentinels of the
  vineyard.
19 They go to bed with wealth, but will
  do so no more;
  they open their eyes, and it is gone.
20 Terrors overtake them like a flood;
  in the night a whirlwind carries
  them off.
21 The east wind lifts them up and they
  are gone;
  it sweeps them out of their place.
22 Itr hurls at them without pity;
  they flee from itss power in headlong flight.
23 Itr claps itss hands at them,
  and hisses at them from itss place.

Interlude: Where Wisdom Is Found

28 "Surely there is a mine for
  silver,
  and a place for gold to be refined.
2 Iron is taken out of the earth,
  and copper is smelted from ore.
3 Miners putt an end to darkness,
  and search out to the farthest
  bound
  the ore in gloom and deep
  darkness.
4 They open shafts in a valley away
  from human habitation;
  they are forgotten by travelers,
  they sway suspended, remote from
  people.
5 As for the earth, out of it comes bread;
  but underneath it is turned up as by
  fire.
6 Its stones are the place of sapphires,u
  and its dust contains gold.

7 "That path no bird of prey knows,
  and the falcon's eye has not seen it.
8 The proud wild animals have not
  trodden it;

"Sentinel" is another word for "watchman." The watchman of a city patrolled the walls of the city at night. From time to time, he called out that everything was okay.

q Traditional rendering of Heb *Shaddai*
(that is, God)   s Or *his*   t Heb *He puts*   r Or *He*   u Or
lapis lazuli

the lion has not passed over it.

9 "They put their hand to the flinty
rock,
and overturn mountains by the
roots.
10 They cut out channels in the rocks,
and their eyes see every precious
thing.
11 The sources of the rivers they probe;ᵛ
hidden things they bring to light.

12 "But where shall wisdom be found?
And where is the place of
understanding?
13 Mortals do not know the way to it,ʷ
and it is not found in the land of
the living.
14 The deep says, 'It is not in me,'
and the sea says, 'It is not with me.'
15 It cannot be gotten for gold,
and silver cannot be weighed out as
its price.
16 It cannot be valued in the gold of
Ō′phir,
in precious onyx or sapphire.ˣ
17 Gold and glass cannot equal it,
nor can it be exchanged for jewels
of fine gold.
18 No mention shall be made of coral or
of crystal;
the price of wisdom is above pearls.
19 The chrysolite of Ethiopiaʸ cannot
compare with it,
nor can it be valued in pure gold.

20 "Where then does wisdom come
from?
And where is the place of
understanding?
21 It is hidden from the eyes of all living,
and concealed from the birds of the
air.
22 A·bad′don and Death say,
'We have heard a rumor of it with
our ears.'

23 "God understands the way to it,
and he knows its place.

24 For he looks to the ends of the earth,
and sees everything under the
heavens.
25 When he gave to the wind its weight,
and apportioned out the waters by
measure;
26 when he made a decree for the rain,
and a way for the thunderbolt;
27 then he saw it and declared it;
he established it, and searched it
out.
28 And he said to humankind,
'Truly, the fear of the Lord, that is
wisdom;
and to depart from evil is
understanding.' "

Job Finishes His Defense

29 Jōb again took up his discourse
and said:
2 "O that I were as in the months of old,
as in the days when God watched
over me;
3 when his lamp shone over my head,
and by his light I walked through
darkness;
4 when I was in my prime,
when the friendship of God was
upon my tent;
5 when the Almightyᶻ was still with me,
when my children were around me;
6 when my steps were washed with
milk,
and the rock poured out for me
streams of oil!
7 When I went out to the gate of the
city,
when I took my seat in the square,
8 the young men saw me and withdrew,
and the aged rose up and stood;
9 the nobles refrained from talking,
and laid their hands on their
mouths;
10 the voices of princes were hushed,
and their tongues stuck to the roof
of their mouths.

ᵛ Gk Vg: Heb *bind*   ʷ Gk: Heb *its price*
ˣ Or *lapis lazuli*   ʸ Or *Nubia;* Heb *Cush*
ᶻ Traditional rendering of Heb *Shaddai*

11 When the ear heard, it commended
me,
and when the eye saw, it approved;
12 because I delivered the poor who
cried,
and the orphan who had no helper.
13 The blessing of the wretched came
upon me,
and I caused the widow's heart to
sing for joy.
14 I put on righteousness, and it clothed
me;
my justice was like a robe and a
turban.
15 I was eyes to the blind,
and feet to the lame.
16 I was a father to the needy,
and I championed the cause of the
stranger.
17 I broke the fangs of the unrighteous,
and made them drop their prey
from their teeth.
18 Then I thought, 'I shall die in my nest,
and I shall multiply my days like
the phoenix;[a]
19 my roots spread out to the waters,
with the dew all night on my
branches;
20 my glory was fresh with me,
and my bow ever new in my hand.'

21 "They listened to me, and waited,
and kept silence for my counsel.
22 After I spoke they did not speak
again,
and my word dropped upon them
like dew.[b]
23 They waited for me as for the rain;
they opened their mouths as for the
spring rain.
24 I smiled on them when they had no
confidence;
and the light of my countenance
they did not extinguish.[c]
25 I chose their way, and sat as chief,
and I lived like a king among his
troops,
like one who comforts mourners.

30

"But now they make sport of me,
those who are younger than I,
whose fathers I would have disdained
to set with the dogs of my flock.
2 What could I gain from the strength of
their hands?
All their vigor is gone.
3 Through want and hard hunger
they gnaw the dry and desolate
ground,
4 they pick mallow and the leaves of
bushes,
and to warm themselves the roots of
broom.
5 They are driven out from society;
people shout after them as after a
thief.
6 In the gullies of wadis they must live,
in holes in the ground, and in the
rocks.
7 Among the bushes they bray;
under the nettles they huddle
together.
8 A senseless, disreputable brood,

Nettles are fast-growing
wild plants with thorns
that sting people who get
too close! Nettles grow
quickly in fields that are not taken care
of. In the Bible, nettles are often a sign
of extreme poverty and the destruction or desolation of an area. When
you drive around the city or the countryside near your home, see if there
are signs that wild plants are taking
over an area.

Sometimes people talk or write
about having nettles (or thorns) in their
hearts. This means that something has
hurt them or made them sad. Have
you ever felt like you might have a
"nettle" in your heart? If you have any
of those feelings now, talk to an adult
about them. Pray to God for help.

[a] Or *like sand*   [b] Heb lacks *like dew*   [c] Meaning
of Heb uncertain

they have been whipped out of the
    land.

9 "And now they mock me in song;
    I am a byword to them.
10 They abhor me, they keep aloof from
    me;
      they do not hesitate to spit at the
        sight of me.
11 Because God has loosed my bowstring
    and humbled me,
      they have cast off restraint in my
        presence.
12 On my right hand the rabble rise up;
    they send me sprawling,
    and build roads for my ruin.
13 They break up my path,
    they promote my calamity;
    no one restrains*d* them.
14 As through a wide breach they come;
    amid the crash they roll on.
15 Terrors are turned upon me;
    my honor is pursued as by the
      wind,
      and my prosperity has passed away
        like a cloud.

16 "And now my soul is poured out
    within me;
      days of affliction have taken hold of
        me.
17 The night racks my bones,
    and the pain that gnaws me takes
      no rest.
18 With violence he seizes my garment;*e*
    he grasps me by*f* the collar of my
      tunic.
19 He has cast me into the mire,
    and I have become like dust and
      ashes.
20 I cry to you and you do not answer me;
    I stand, and you merely look at me.
21 You have turned cruel to me;
    with the might of your hand you
      persecute me.
22 You lift me up on the wind, you make
    me ride on it,
      and you toss me about in the roar
        of the storm.

23 I know that you will bring me to
    death,
      and to the house appointed for all
        living.

24 "Surely one does not turn against the
    needy,*g*
      when in disaster they cry for help.*h*
25 Did I not weep for those whose day
    was hard?
      Was not my soul grieved for the
        poor?
26 But when I looked for good, evil
    came;
      and when I waited for light,
        darkness came.
27 My inward parts are in turmoil, and
    are never still;
      days of affliction come to meet me.
28 I go about in sunless gloom;
    I stand up in the assembly and cry
      for help.
29 I am a brother of jackals,
    and a companion of ostriches.
30 My skin turns black and falls from
    me,
      and my bones burn with heat.
31 My lyre is turned to mourning,
    and my pipe to the voice of those
      who weep.

31 "I have made a covenant with
      my eyes;
    how then could I look upon a
      virgin?
2 What would be my portion from God
    above,
      and my heritage from the Almighty*i*
        on high?
3 Does not calamity befall the
    unrighteous,
      and disaster the workers of iniquity?
4 Does he not see my ways,
    and number all my steps?

d Cn: Heb *helps*   *e* Gk: Heb *my garment is disfig-
ured*   *f* Heb *like*   *g* Heb *ruin*   *h* Cn: Meaning
of Heb uncertain   *i* Traditional rendering of Heb
Shaddai

5 "If I have walked with falsehood,
  and my foot has hurried to deceit—
6 let me be weighed in a just balance,
  and let God know my integrity!—
7 if my step has turned aside from the way,
  and my heart has followed my eyes,
  and if any spot has clung to my hands;
8 then let me sow, and another eat;
  and let what grows for me be rooted out.

9 "If my heart has been enticed by a woman,
  and I have lain in wait at my neighbor's door;
10 then let my wife grind for another,
  and let other men kneel over her.
11 For that would be a heinous crime;
  that would be a criminal offense;
12 for that would be a fire consuming down to A·bad´don,
  and it would burn to the root all my harvest.

13 "If I have rejected the cause of my male or female slaves,
  when they brought a complaint against me;
14 what then shall I do when God rises up?
  When he makes inquiry, what shall I answer him?
15 Did not he who made me in the womb make them?
  And did not one fashion us in the womb?

16 "If I have withheld anything that the poor desired,
  or have caused the eyes of the widow to fail,
17 or have eaten my morsel alone,
  and the orphan has not eaten from it—
18 for from my youth I reared the orphan[j] like a father,
  and from my mother's womb I guided the widow[k]—

19 if I have seen anyone perish for lack of clothing,
  or a poor person without covering,
20 whose loins have not blessed me,
  and who was not warmed with the fleece of my sheep;
21 if I have raised my hand against the orphan,
  because I saw I had supporters at the gate;
22 then let my shoulder blade fall from my shoulder,
  and let my arm be broken from its socket.
23 For I was in terror of calamity from God,
  and I could not have faced his majesty.

24 "If I have made gold my trust,
  or called fine gold my confidence;
25 if I have rejoiced because my wealth was great,
  or because my hand had gotten much;
26 if I have looked at the sun[l] when it shone,
  or the moon moving in splendor,
27 and my heart has been secretly enticed,
  and my mouth has kissed my hand;
28 this also would be an iniquity to be punished by the judges,
  for I should have been false to God above.

29 "If I have rejoiced at the ruin of those who hated me,
  or exulted when evil overtook them—
30 I have not let my mouth sin
  by asking for their lives with a curse—
31 if those of my tent ever said,
  'O that we might be sated with his flesh!'[m]—

[j] Heb him [k] Heb her [l] Heb the light
[m] Meaning of Heb uncertain

32 the stranger has not lodged in the
   street;
   I have opened my doors to the
      traveler—
33 if I have concealed my transgressions
      as others do,[n]
   by hiding my iniquity in my
      bosom,
34 because I stood in great fear of the
      multitude,
   and the contempt of families
      terrified me,
   so that I kept silence, and did not
      go out of doors—
35 O that I had one to hear me!
   (Here is my signature! Let the
      Almighty[o] answer me!)
   O that I had the indictment written
      by my adversary!
36 Surely I would carry it on my
      shoulder;
   I would bind it on me like a crown;
37 I would give him an account of all my
      steps;
   like a prince I would approach
      him.

38 "If my land has cried out against me,
   and its furrows have wept together;
39 if I have eaten its yield without
      payment,
   and caused the death of its owners;
40 let thorns grow instead of wheat,
   and foul weeds instead of barley."

The words of Job are ended.

Elihu Rebukes Job's Friends

32 So these three men ceased to
answer Jōb, because he was
righteous in his own eyes. ²Then E·lī′hū
son of Bar′a·chel the Būz′īte, of the family
of Ram, became angry. He was angry at
Jōb because he justified himself rather than
God; ³he was angry also at Job's three
friends because they had found no answer,
though they had declared Jōb to be in the
wrong.[p] ⁴Now E·lī′hū had waited to speak
to Jōb, because they were older than he.

⁵But when E·lī′hū saw that there was no
answer in the mouths of these three men,
he became angry.

6 E·lī′hū son of Bar′a·chel the Būz′īte
answered:

   "I am young in years,
      and you are aged;
   therefore I was timid and afraid
      to declare my opinion to you.
7 I said, 'Let days speak,
   and many years teach wisdom.'
8 But truly it is the spirit in a mortal,
   the breath of the Almighty,[o] that
      makes for understanding.
9 It is not the old[q] that are wise,
   nor the aged that understand what
      is right.
10 Therefore I say, 'Listen to me;
   let me also declare my opinion.'

11 "See, I waited for your words,
   I listened for your wise sayings,
   while you searched out what to say.
12 I gave you my attention,
   but there was in fact no one that
      confuted Jōb,
   no one among you that answered
      his words.
13 Yet do not say, 'We have found wisdom;
   God may vanquish him, not a
      human.'
14 He has not directed his words against
      me,
   and I will not answer him with
      your speeches.

15 "They are dismayed, they answer no
      more;
   they have not a word to say.
16 And am I to wait, because they do not
      speak,
   because they stand there, and
      answer no more?
17 I also will give my answer;
   I also will declare my opinion.

[n] Or *as Adam did*   [o] Traditional rendering of Heb
Shaddai   [p] Another ancient tradition reads
answer, and had put God in the wrong   [q] Gk Syr
Vg: Heb *many*

18 For I am full of words;
   the spirit within me constrains me.
19 My heart is indeed like wine that
      has no vent;
   like new wineskins, it is ready to
      burst.
20 I must speak, so that I may find
      relief;
   I must open my lips and answer.
21 I will not show partiality to any
      person
   or use flattery toward anyone.
22 For I do not know how to flatter—
   or my Maker would soon put an
      end to me!

Elihu Rebukes Job

33 "But now, hear my speech,
      O Jōb,
   and listen to all my words.
2 See, I open my mouth;
   the tongue in my mouth speaks.
3 My words declare the uprightness of
      my heart,
   and what my lips know they speak
      sincerely.
4 The spirit of God has made me,
   and the breath of the Almighty[r]
      gives me life.
5 Answer me, if you can;
   set your words in order before me;
      take your stand.
6 See, before God I am as you are;
   I too was formed from a piece of clay.
7 No fear of me need terrify you;
   my pressure will not be heavy on
      you.

8 "Surely, you have spoken in my
      hearing,
   and I have heard the sound of your
      words.
9 You say, 'I am clean, without
      transgression;
   I am pure, and there is no iniquity
      in me.
10 Look, he finds occasions against me,
   he counts me as his enemy;
11 he puts my feet in the stocks,

   and watches all my paths.'
12 "But in this you are not right. I will
      answer you:
   God is greater than any mortal.
13 Why do you contend against him,
   saying, 'He will answer none of my[s]
      words'?
14 For God speaks in one way,
   and in two, though people do not
      perceive it.
15 In a dream, in a vision of the night,
   when deep sleep falls on mortals,
   while they slumber on their beds,
16 then he opens their ears,
   and terrifies them with warnings,
17 that he may turn them aside from
      their deeds,
   and keep them from pride,
18 to spare their souls from the Pit,
   their lives from traversing the
      River.
19 They are also chastened with pain
      upon their beds,
   and with continual strife in their
      bones,
20 so that their lives loathe bread,
   and their appetites dainty food.
21 Their flesh is so wasted away that it
      cannot be seen;
   and their bones, once invisible, now
      stick out.
22 Their souls draw near the Pit,
   and their lives to those who bring
      death.
23 Then, if there should be for one of
      them an angel,
   a mediator, one of a thousand,
   one who declares a person upright,
24 and he is gracious to that person, and
      says,
   'Deliver him from going down into
      the Pit;
   I have found a ransom;
25 let his flesh become fresh with youth;
   let him return to the days of his
      youthful vigor';

[r] Traditional rendering of Heb *Shaddai*
[s] Compare Gk: Heb *his*

26 then he prays to God, and is accepted
 by him,
  he comes into his presence with
   joy,
 and God[t] repays him for his
  righteousness.
27   That person sings to others and
   says,
  'I sinned, and perverted what was
   right,
   and it was not paid back to me.
28 He has redeemed my soul from going
  down to the Pit,
  and my life shall see the light.'

29 "God indeed does all these things,
  twice, three times, with mortals,
30 to bring back their souls from the Pit,
  so that they may see the light of
   life.[u]
31 Pay heed, Jōb, listen to me;
  be silent, and I will speak.
32 If you have anything to say, answer
   me;
  speak, for I desire to justify you.
33 If not, listen to me;
  be silent, and I will teach you
   wisdom."

Elihu Proclaims God's Justice

34 Then E·lī´hū continued and
     said:
2 "Hear my words, you wise men,
  and give ear to me, you who know;
3 for the ear tests words
  as the palate tastes food.
4 Let us choose what is right;
  let us determine among ourselves
   what is good.
5 For Jōb has said, 'I am innocent,
  and God has taken away my right;
6 in spite of being right I am counted a
   liar;
  my wound is incurable, though I
   am without transgression.'
7 Who is there like Jōb,
  who drinks up scoffing like water,
8 who goes in company with evildoers
  and walks with the wicked?

9 For he has said, 'It profits one nothing
  to take delight in God.'

10 "Therefore, hear me, you who have
   sense,
  far be it from God that he should
   do wickedness,
  and from the Almighty[v] that he
   should do wrong.
11 For according to their deeds he will
   repay them,
  and according to their ways he will
   make it befall them.
12 Of a truth, God will not do wickedly,
  and the Almighty[v] will not pervert
   justice.
13 Who gave him charge over the earth
  and who laid on him[w] the whole
   world?
14 If he should take back his spirit[x] to
   himself,
  and gather to himself his breath,
15 all flesh would perish together,
  and all mortals return to dust.

16 "If you have understanding, hear this;
  listen to what I say.
17 Shall one who hates justice govern?
  Will you condemn one who is
   righteous and mighty,
18 who says to a king, 'You scoundrel!'
  and to princes, 'You wicked men!';
19 who shows no partiality to nobles,
  nor regards the rich more than the
   poor,
  for they are all the work of his
   hands?
20 In a moment they die;
  at midnight the people are shaken
   and pass away,
  and the mighty are taken away by
   no human hand.

21 "For his eyes are upon the ways of
   mortals,
  and he sees all their steps.

---

[t] Heb he   [u] Syr: Heb to be lighted with the light of
life   [v] Traditional rendering of Heb Shaddai
[w] Heb lacks on him   [x] Heb his heart his spirit

²² There is no gloom or deep darkness
 where evildoers may hide
 themselves.
²³ For he has not appointed a time^y for
 anyone
 to go before God in judgment.
²⁴ He shatters the mighty without
 investigation,
 and sets others in their place.
²⁵ Thus, knowing their works,
 he overturns them in the night, and
 they are crushed.
²⁶ He strikes them for their wickedness
 while others look on,
²⁷ because they turned aside from
 following him,
 and had no regard for any of his
 ways,
²⁸ so that they caused the cry of the poor
 to come to him,
 and he heard the cry of the
 afflicted—
²⁹ When he is quiet, who can condemn?
 When he hides his face, who can
 behold him,
 whether it be a nation or an
 individual?—
³⁰ so that the godless should not reign,
 or those who ensnare the people.

³¹ "For has anyone said to God,
 'I have endured punishment; I will
 not offend any more;
³² teach me what I do not see;
 if I have done iniquity, I will do it
 no more'?
³³ Will he then pay back to suit you,
 because you reject it?
 For you must choose, and not I;
 therefore declare what you know.^z
³⁴ Those who have sense will say to me,
 and the wise who hear me will say,
³⁵ 'Job speaks without knowledge,
 his words are without insight.'
³⁶ Would that Job were tried to the limit,
 because his answers are those of the
 wicked.
³⁷ For he adds rebellion to his sin;
 he claps his hands among us,

and multiplies his words against
 God."

Elihu Condemns Self-Righteousness

35 E·lī´hū continued and said:
² "Do you think this to be just?
 You say, 'I am in the right before
 God.'
³ If you ask, 'What advantage have I?
 How am I better off than if I had
 sinned?'
⁴ I will answer you
 and your friends with you.
⁵ Look at the heavens and see;
 observe the clouds, which are
 higher than you.
⁶ If you have sinned, what do you
 accomplish against him?
 And if your transgressions are
 multiplied, what do you do to
 him?
⁷ If you are righteous, what do you give
 to him;
 or what does he receive from your
 hand?
⁸ Your wickedness affects others like
 you,
 and your righteousness, other
 human beings.

⁹ "Because of the multitude of
 oppressions people cry out;
 they call for help because of the arm
 of the mighty.
¹⁰ But no one says, 'Where is God my
 Maker,
 who gives strength in the night,
¹¹ who teaches us more than the animals
 of the earth,
 and makes us wiser than the birds
 of the air?'
¹² There they cry out, but he does not
 answer,
 because of the pride of evildoers.
¹³ Surely God does not hear an empty
 cry,

^y Cn: Heb yet   ^z Meaning of Heb of verses 29-33
uncertain

nor does the Almighty*a* regard it.

¹⁴ How much less when you say that
you do not see him,
that the case is before him, and you
are waiting for him!

¹⁵ And now, because his anger does not
punish,
and he does not greatly heed
transgression,*b*

¹⁶ Jōb opens his mouth in empty talk,
he multiplies words without
knowledge."

Elihu Exalts God's Goodness

36 E·lī´hū continued and said:
² "Bear with me a little, and I
will show you,
for I have yet something to say on
God's behalf.

³ I will bring my knowledge from far
away,
and ascribe righteousness to my
Maker.

⁴ For truly my words are not false;
one who is perfect in knowledge is
with you.

⁵ "Surely God is mighty and does not
despise any;
he is mighty in strength of
understanding.

⁶ He does not keep the wicked alive,
but gives the afflicted their right.

⁷ He does not withdraw his eyes from
the righteous,
but with kings on the throne
he sets them forever, and they are
exalted.

⁸ And if they are bound in fetters
and caught in the cords of affliction,

⁹ then he declares to them their work
and their transgressions, that they
are behaving arrogantly.

¹⁰ He opens their ears to instruction,
and commands that they return
from iniquity.

¹¹ If they listen, and serve him,

they complete their days in
prosperity,
and their years in pleasantness.

¹² But if they do not listen, they shall
perish by the sword,
and die without knowledge.

¹³ "The godless in heart cherish anger;
they do not cry for help when he
binds them.

¹⁴ They die in their youth,
and their life ends in shame.*c*

¹⁵ He delivers the afflicted by their
affliction,
and opens their ear by adversity.

¹⁶ He also allured you out of distress
into a broad place where there was
no constraint,
and what was set on your table was
full of fatness.

¹⁷ "But you are obsessed with the case of
the wicked;
judgment and justice seize you.

¹⁸ Beware that wrath does not entice you
into scoffing,
and do not let the greatness of the
ransom turn you aside.

¹⁹ Will your cry avail to keep you from
distress,
or will all the force of your strength?

²⁰ Do not long for the night,
when peoples are cut off in their
place.

²¹ Beware! Do not turn to iniquity;
because of that you have been tried
by affliction.

²² See, God is exalted in his power;
who is a teacher like him?

²³ Who has prescribed for him his way,
or who can say, 'You have done
wrong'?

Elihu Proclaims God's Majesty

²⁴ "Remember to extol his work,

a Traditional rendering of Heb *Shaddai*   *b* Theodotion Symmachus Compare Vg: Meaning of Heb
uncertain   *c* Heb *ends among the temple prostitutes*

> "He draws up the drops of water; he distills his mist in rain, which the skies pour down and drop upon mortals abundantly."
> Job 36:27–28

of which mortals have sung.
25 All people have looked on it;
    everyone watches it from far away.
26 Surely God is great, and we do not
        know him;
    the number of his years is
        unsearchable.
27 For he draws up the drops of water;
    he distills^d his mist in rain,
28 which the skies pour down
    and drop upon mortals abundantly.
29 Can anyone understand the spreading
        of the clouds,
    the thunderings of his pavilion?
30 See, he scatters his lightning around
        him
    and covers the roots of the sea.
31 For by these he governs peoples;
    he gives food in abundance.
32 He covers his hands with the
        lightning,
    and commands it to strike the mark.
33 Its crashing^e tells about him;
    he is jealous^e with anger against
        iniquity.

37 "At this also my heart trembles,
    and leaps out of its place.
2 Listen, listen to the thunder of his
        voice
    and the rumbling that comes from
        his mouth.
3 Under the whole heaven he lets it
        loose,
    and his lightning to the corners of
        the earth.
4 After it his voice roars;
    he thunders with his majestic voice
    and he does not restrain the
        lightnings^f when his voice is
        heard.

5 God thunders wondrously with his
        voice;
    he does great things that we cannot
        comprehend.
6 For to the snow he says, 'Fall on the
        earth';
    and the shower of rain, his heavy
        shower of rain,
7 serves as a sign on everyone's hand,
    so that all whom he has made may
        know it.^g
8 Then the animals go into their lairs
    and remain in their dens.
9 From its chamber comes the
        whirlwind,
    and cold from the scattering winds.
10 By the breath of God ice is given,
    and the broad waters are frozen fast.
11 He loads the thick cloud with
        moisture;
    the clouds scatter his lightning.
12 They turn round and round by his
        guidance,
    to accomplish all that he commands
        them
    on the face of the habitable world.
13 Whether for correction, or for his
        land,
    or for love, he causes it to happen.

14 "Hear this, O Jōb;
    stop and consider the wondrous
        works of God.
15 Do you know how God lays his
        command upon them,
    and causes the lightning of his
        cloud to shine?
16 Do you know the balancings of the
        clouds,
    the wondrous works of the one
        whose knowledge is perfect,
17 you whose garments are hot
    when the earth is still because of
        the south wind?
18 Can you, like him, spread out the
        skies,

^d Cn: Heb *they distill*   ^e Meaning of Heb uncertain   ^f Heb *them*   ^g Meaning of Heb of verse 7 uncertain

hard as a molten mirror?
19 Teach us what we shall say to him;
we cannot draw up our case
because of darkness.
20 Should he be told that I want to
speak?
Did anyone ever wish to be
swallowed up?
21 Now, no one can look on the light
when it is bright in the skies,
when the wind has passed and
cleared them.
22 Out of the north comes golden
splendor;
around God is awesome majesty.
23 The Almighty[h]—we cannot find
him;
he is great in power and justice,
and abundant righteousness he
will not violate.
24 Therefore mortals fear him;
he does not regard any who are
wise in their own conceit."

The Lord Answers Job

38 Then the LORD answered Jōb
out of the whirlwind:
2 "Who is this that darkens counsel by
words without knowledge?
3 Gird up your loins like a man,
I will question you, and you shall
declare to me.

4 "Where were you when I laid the
foundation of the earth?
Tell me, if you have understanding.
5 Who determined its measurements—
surely you know!
Or who stretched the line upon it?
6 On what were its bases sunk,
or who laid its cornerstone
7 when the morning stars sang together
and all the heavenly beings[i] shouted
for joy?

8 "Or who shut in the sea with doors
when it burst out from the
womb?—
9 when I made the clouds its garment,

and thick darkness its swaddling
band,
10 and prescribed bounds for it,
and set bars and doors,
11 and said, 'Thus far shall you come,
and no farther,
and here shall your proud waves be
stopped'?

12 "Have you commanded the morning
since your days began,
and caused the dawn to know its
place,
13 so that it might take hold of the skirts
of the earth,
and the wicked be shaken out of it?
14 It is changed like clay under the seal,
and it is dyed[j] like a garment.
15 Light is withheld from the wicked,
and their uplifted arm is broken.

16 "Have you entered into the springs of
the sea,
or walked in the recesses of the
deep?
17 Have the gates of death been revealed
to you,
or have you seen the gates of deep
darkness?
18 Have you comprehended the expanse
of the earth?
Declare, if you know all this.

19 "Where is the way to the dwelling of
light,
and where is the place of darkness,
20 that you may take it to its territory
and that you may discern the paths
to its home?
21 Surely you know, for you were born
then,
and the number of your days is
great!

22 "Have you entered the storehouses of
the snow,

---

[h] Traditional rendering of Heb *Shaddai*   [i] Heb
sons of God   [j] Cn: Heb *and they stand forth*

or have you seen the storehouses of
the hail,
²³ which I have reserved for the time of
trouble,
for the day of battle and war?
²⁴ What is the way to the place where
the light is distributed,
or where the east wind is scattered
upon the earth?

²⁵ "Who has cut a channel for the
torrents of rain,
and a way for the thunderbolt,
²⁶ to bring rain on a land where no one
lives,
on the desert, which is empty of
human life,
²⁷ to satisfy the waste and desolate land,
and to make the ground put forth
grass?
²⁸ "Has the rain a father,
or who has begotten the drops of
dew?
²⁹ From whose womb did the ice come
forth,
and who has given birth to the
hoarfrost of heaven?
³⁰ The waters become hard like stone,
and the face of the deep is frozen.

³¹ "Can you bind the chains of the
Plēi´a·dēs,
or loose the cords of Ō·rī´on?
³² Can you lead forth the Maz´za·roth in
their season,
or can you guide the Bear with its
children?
³³ Do you know the ordinances of the
heavens?
Can you establish their rule on the
earth?

³⁴ "Can you lift up your voice to the
clouds,
so that a flood of waters may cover
you?
³⁵ Can you send forth lightnings, so that
they may go
and say to you, 'Here we are'?

³⁶ Who has put wisdom in the inward
parts,[k]
or given understanding to the
mind?[k]
³⁷ Who has the wisdom to number the
clouds?
Or who can tilt the waterskins of
the heavens,
³⁸ when the dust runs into a mass
and the clods cling together?

³⁹ "Can you hunt the prey for the lion,
or satisfy the appetite of the young
lions,
⁴⁰ when they crouch in their dens,
or lie in wait in their covert?
⁴¹ Who provides for the raven its prey,
when its young ones cry to God,
and wander about for lack of food?

39 "Do you know when the
mountain goats give birth?
Do you observe the calving of the
deer?
² Can you number the months that they
fulfill,
and do you know the time when
they give birth,
³ when they crouch to give birth to their
offspring,
and are delivered of their young?
⁴ Their young ones become strong, they
grow up in the open;
they go forth, and do not return to
them.

⁵ "Who has let the wild ass go free?
Who has loosed the bonds of the
swift ass,
⁶ to which I have given the steppe for
its home,
the salt land for its dwelling place?
⁷ It scorns the tumult of the city;
it does not hear the shouts of the
driver.
⁸ It ranges the mountains as its pasture,
and it searches after every green
thing.

[k] Meaning of Heb uncertain

9 "Is the wild ox willing to serve you?
  Will it spend the night at your crib?
10 Can you tie it in the furrow with
      ropes,
    or will it harrow the valleys after
      you?
11 Will you depend on it because its
      strength is great,
    and will you hand over your labor
      to it?
12 Do you have faith in it that it will
      return,
    and bring your grain to your
      threshing floor?*l*

13 "The ostrich's wings flap wildly,
    though its pinions lack plumage.*m*
14 For it leaves its eggs to the earth,
    and lets them be warmed on the
      ground,
15 forgetting that a foot may crush them,
    and that a wild animal may trample
      them.
16 It deals cruelly with its young, as if
      they were not its own;
    though its labor should be in vain,
      yet it has no fear;
17 because God has made it forget
      wisdom,
    and given it no share in
      understanding.
18 When it spreads its plumes aloft,*m*
    it laughs at the horse and its rider.

19 "Do you give the horse its might?
    Do you clothe its neck with mane?
20 Do you make it leap like the locust?
    Its majestic snorting is terrible.
21 It paws*n* violently, exults mightily;
    it goes out to meet the weapons.
22 It laughs at fear, and is not dismayed;
    it does not turn back from the
      sword.
23 Upon it rattle the quiver,
    the flashing spear, and the javelin.
24 With fierceness and rage it swallows
      the ground;
    it cannot stand still at the sound of
      the trumpet.

25 When the trumpet sounds, it says
      'Aha!'
    From a distance it smells the battle,
    the thunder of the captains, and the
      shouting.

26 "Is it by your wisdom that the hawk
      soars,
    and spreads its wings toward the
      south?
27 Is it at your command that the eagle
      mounts up
    and makes its nest on high?
28 It lives on the rock and makes its
      home
    in the fastness of the rocky crag.
29 From there it spies the prey;
    its eyes see it from far away.
30 Its young ones suck up blood;
    and where the slain are, there it is."

40 And the LORD said to Jōb:
  2 "Shall a faultfinder contend
      with the Almighty?*o*
    Anyone who argues with God
      must respond."

Job's Response to God

3 Then Job answered the LORD:
4 "See, I am of small account; what
      shall I answer you?
    I lay my hand on my mouth.
5 I have spoken once, and I will not
      answer;
    twice, but will proceed no further."

God's Challenge to Job

6 Then the LORD answered Jōb out of
  the whirlwind:
7 "Gird up your loins like a man;
    I will question you, and you declare
      to me.
8 Will you even put me in the wrong?
    Will you condemn me that you may
      be justified?

---

l Heb *your grain and your threshing floor*
m Meaning of Heb uncertain   *n* Gk Syr Vg: Heb
they dig   *o* Traditional rendering of Heb *Shaddai*

A reed is the flowering stem of several tall grasses that grow in marshy places. Reeds are sometimes called rushes. People in Bible times used reeds to make many things, including measuring rods, writing pens, baskets and mats.

9 Have you an arm like God,
    and can you thunder with a voice like his?

10 "Deck yourself with majesty and dignity;
    clothe yourself with glory and splendor.
11 Pour out the overflowings of your anger,
    and look on all who are proud, and abase them.
12 Look on all who are proud, and bring them low;
    tread down the wicked where they stand.
13 Hide them all in the dust together;
    bind their faces in the world below[p]
14 Then I will also acknowledge to you
    that your own right hand can give you victory.

15 "Look at Be′he·moth,
    which I made just as I made you;
    it eats grass like an ox.
16 Its strength is in its loins,
    and its power in the muscles of its belly.
17 It makes its tail stiff like a cedar;
    the sinews of its thighs are knit together.
18 Its bones are tubes of bronze,
    its limbs like bars of iron.

19 "It is the first of the great acts of God—
    only its Maker can approach it with the sword.
20 For the mountains yield food for it
    where all the wild animals play.

21 Under the lotus plants it lies,
    in the covert of the reeds and in the marsh.
22 The lotus trees cover it for shade;
    the willows of the wadi surround it.
23 Even if the river is turbulent, it is not frightened;
    it is confident though Jordan rushes against its mouth.
24 Can one take it with hooks[q]
    or pierce its nose with a snare?

41 [r] "Can you draw out
    Le·vi′a·than[s] with a fishhook,
    or press down its tongue with a cord?
2 Can you put a rope in its nose,
    or pierce its jaw with a hook?
3 Will it make many supplications to you?
    Will it speak soft words to you?
4 Will it make a covenant with you
    to be taken as your servant forever?
5 Will you play with it as with a bird,
    or will you put it on leash for your girls?
6 Will traders bargain over it?
    Will they divide it up among the merchants?
7 Can you fill its skin with harpoons,
    or its head with fishing spears?
8 Lay hands on it;
    think of the battle; you will not do it again!
9[t] Any hope of capturing it[u] will be disappointed;
    were not even the gods[v] overwhelmed at the sight of it?
10 No one is so fierce as to dare to stir it up.
    Who can stand before it?[w]
11 Who can confront it[w] and be safe?[x]
    —under the whole heaven, who?[y]

p Heb *the hidden place*   q Cn: Heb *in his eyes*
r Ch 40.25 in Heb   s Or *the crocodile*   t Ch 41.1
in Heb   u Heb *of it*   v Cn Compare Symmachus
Syr: Heb *one is*   w Heb *me*   x Gk: Heb *that I
shall repay*   y Heb *to me*

God tells Job that there is nothing God cannot do, including controling Leviathan, the giant sea monster that represents disorder and evil in the world. Human beings, God says, are not able to bring about order on their own.

12 "I will not keep silence concerning its limbs,
  or its mighty strength, or its splendid frame.

13 Who can strip off its outer garment?
  Who can penetrate its double coat of mail?[z]

14 Who can open the doors of its face?
  There is terror all around its teeth.

15 Its back[a] is made of shields in rows,
  shut up closely as with a seal.

16 One is so near to another
  that no air can come between them.

17 They are joined one to another;
  they clasp each other and cannot be separated.

18 Its sneezes flash forth light,
  and its eyes are like the eyelids of the dawn.

19 From its mouth go flaming torches;
  sparks of fire leap out.

20 Out of its nostrils comes smoke,
  as from a boiling pot and burning rushes.

21 Its breath kindles coals,
  and a flame comes out of its mouth.

22 In its neck abides strength,
  and terror dances before it.

23 The folds of its flesh cling together;
  it is firmly cast and immovable.

24 Its heart is as hard as stone,
  as hard as the lower millstone.

25 When it raises itself up the gods are afraid;

at the crashing they are beside themselves.

26 Though the sword reaches it, it does not avail,
  nor does the spear, the dart, or the javelin.

27 It counts iron as straw,
  and bronze as rotten wood.

28 The arrow cannot make it flee;
  slingstones, for it, are turned to chaff.

29 Clubs are counted as chaff;
  it laughs at the rattle of javelins.

30 Its underparts are like sharp potsherds;
  it spreads itself like a threshing sledge on the mire.

31 It makes the deep boil like a pot;
  it makes the sea like a pot of ointment.

32 It leaves a shining wake behind it;
  one would think the deep to be white-haired.

33 On earth it has no equal,
  a creature without fear.

34 It surveys everything that is lofty;
  it is king over all that are proud."

Job Is Humbled and Satisfied

42 Then Jōb answered the LORD:
  2 "I know that you can do all things,
  and that no purpose of yours can be thwarted.

3 'Who is this that hides counsel without knowledge?'
  Therefore I have uttered what I did not understand,
  things too wonderful for me, which I did not know.

4 'Hear, and I will speak;
  I will question you, and you declare to me.'

5 I had heard of you by the hearing of the ear,
  but now my eye sees you;

"I know that you can do all things, and that no purpose of yours can be thwarted." Job 42:2

z Gk: Heb *bridle*   a Cn Compare Gk Vg: Heb *pride*

⁶ therefore I despise myself,
  and repent in dust and ashes."

Job's Friends Are Humiliated

7 After the LORD had spoken these words to Jōb, the LORD said to E·lī´phaz the Tē´man·īte: "My wrath is kindled against you and against your two friends; for you have not spoken of me what is right, as my servant Jōb has. ⁸Now therefore take seven bulls and seven rams, and go to my servant Jōb, and offer up for yourselves a burnt offering; and my servant Jōb shall pray for you, for I will accept his prayer not to deal with you according to your folly; for you have not spoken of me what is right, as my servant Job has done." ⁹So E·lī´phaz the Tē´man·īte and Bil´dad the Shū´hīte and Zō´phar the Nā´a·ma·thīte went and did what the LORD had told them; and the LORD accepted Job's prayer.

Job's Fortunes Are Restored Twofold

10 And the LORD restored the fortunes of Jōb when he had prayed for his friends; and the LORD gave Jōb twice as much as he had before. ¹¹Then there came to him all his brothers and sisters and all who had known him before, and they ate bread with him in his house; they showed him sympathy and comforted him for all the evil that the LORD had brought upon him; and each of them gave him a piece of money*ᵇ* and a gold ring. ¹²The LORD blessed the latter days of Jōb more than his beginning; and he had fourteen thousand sheep, six thousand camels, a thousand yoke of oxen, and a thousand donkeys. ¹³He also had seven sons and three daughters. ¹⁴He named the first Je·mī´mah, the second Ke·zī´ah, and the third Ker´en-hap´-puch. ¹⁵In all the land there were no women so beautiful as Job's daughters; and their father gave them an inheritance along with their brothers. ¹⁶After this Jōb lived one hundred and forty years, and saw his children, and his children's children, four generations. ¹⁷And Jōb died, old and full of days.

ᵇ Heb *a qesitah*

Psalms

The book of Psalms is the hymnbook of the Hebrew people. Like the hymnals many churches use today, it contains songs by many different writers from many periods of history. It was completed about 100 BC. Psalms contains five collections of hymns, including "The Songs of David" and "the Songs of the Sons of Korah."

The book of Psalms contains hymns (or poems) of praise, repentance, thanksgiving, and petition. Some are very personal, while some were written on behalf of a whole congregation. Some were written so that the choir would sing one line and the congregation would sing the next line. Some were joyful songs to be sung by groups of friends as they walked along their way to Jerusalem for some great festival. Others are about the wonders of God's creation. The Hebrews did not have musical notes as we do in our songbooks, but some of the psalms include instructions to the musicians and singers.

Many of the psalms are among the most familiar and best-loved portions of the Bible. They are regularly used in Jewish and Christian worship as both hymns and responsive readings. Worshipers have loved these psalms for thousands of years because of the way they express our longings and prayers to God.

Psalm 42:1

The book of Psalms begins with the word "happy," which is used twenty-six times in Psalms and only twenty times in the rest of the Old Testament. The writers of these songs wanted their listeners to know that being in a right relationship with God leads to happiness and peace.

BOOK I

(Psalms 1–41)

Psalm 1

The Two Ways

1 Happy are those
    who do not follow the advice of
        the wicked,
or take the path that sinners tread,
    or sit in the seat of scoffers;
2 but their delight is in the law of the
        LORD,
    and on his law they meditate day
        and night.
3 They are like trees
    planted by streams of water,
which yield their fruit in its season,
    and their leaves do not wither.
In all that they do, they prosper.

4 The wicked are not so,
    but are like chaff that the wind
        drives away.
5 Therefore the wicked will not stand
        in the judgment,
    nor sinners in the congregation of
        the righteous;
6 for the LORD watches over the way of
        the righteous,
    but the way of the wicked will
        perish.

Psalm 2

God's Promise to His Anointed

1 Why do the nations conspire,
    and the peoples plot in vain?

2 The kings of the earth set themselves,
    and the rulers take counsel
        together,
    against the LORD and his anointed,
        saying,
3 "Let us burst their bonds asunder,
    and cast their cords from us."

4 He who sits in the heavens laughs;
    the LORD has them in derision.
5 Then he will speak to them in his
        wrath,
    and terrify them in his fury, saying,
6 "I have set my king on Zion, my
        holy hill."

7 I will tell of the decree of the LORD:
He said to me, "You are my son;
    today I have begotten you.
8 Ask of me, and I will make the
        nations your heritage,
    and the ends of the earth your
        possession.
9 You shall break them with a rod of
        iron,
    and dash them in pieces like a
        potter's vessel."

10 Now therefore, O kings, be wise;
    be warned, O rulers of the earth.
11 Serve the LORD with fear,
    with trembling 12kiss his feet,*a*
or he will be angry, and you will
        perish in the way;
    for his wrath is quickly kindled.

Happy are all who take refuge in him.

Chaff is the useless dry husks of grain blown away from the good seed in the process of winnowing. Many times in the Bible, the word "chaff" is used to mean someone or something worthless.

a Cn: Meaning of Heb of verses 11b and 12a is uncertain

"But you, O LORD, are a shield around me, my glory, and the one who lifts up my head. I cry aloud to the LORD, and he answers me from his holy hill." Psalm 3:3–4

Psalm 3

Trust in God under Adversity

A Psalm of David, when he fled from his son Ab´sa.lom.

1 O LORD, how many are my foes!
Many are rising against me;
2 many are saying to me,
"There is no help for you*b* in
God." *Sēlah*

3 But you, O Lord, are a shield around me,
my glory, and the one who lifts up my head.
4 I cry aloud to the LORD,
and he answers me from his holy hill. *Sēlah*

5 I lie down and sleep;
I wake again, for the Lord sustains me.
6 I am not afraid of ten thousands of people
who have set themselves against me all around.

7 Rise up, O LORD!
Deliver me, O my God!
For you strike all my enemies on the cheek;
you break the teeth of the wicked.

8 Deliverance belongs to the LORD;
may your blessing be on your people! *Sēlah*

Psalm 4

Confident Plea for Deliverance from Enemies

To the leader:
with stringed instruments.
A Psalm of David.

1 Answer me when I call, O God of my right!
You gave me room when I was in distress.
Be gracious to me, and hear my prayer.

2 How long, you people, shall my honor suffer shame?
How long will you love vain words, and seek after lies? *Sēlah*
3 But know that the LORD has set apart the faithful for himself;
the LORD hears when I call to him.

4 When you are disturbed,*c* do not sin;
ponder it on your beds, and be silent. *Sēlah*
5 Offer right sacrifices,
and put your trust in the LORD.

6 There are many who say, "O that we might see some good!
Let the light of your face shine on us, O LORD!"
7 You have put gladness in my heart
more than when their grain and wine abound.

8 I will both lie down and sleep in peace;
for you alone, O LORD, make me lie down in safety.

Psalm 5

Trust in God for Deliverance from Enemies

To the leader: for the flutes.
A Psalm of David.

1 Give ear to my words, O LORD;
give heed to my sighing.
2 Listen to the sound of my cry,
my King and my God,
for to you I pray.
3 O LORD, in the morning you hear my voice;
in the morning I plead my case to you, and watch.

b Syr: Heb *him*   *c* Or *are angry*

4 For you are not a God who delights
        in wickedness;
    evil will not sojourn with you.
5 The boastful will not stand before
        your eyes;
    you hate all evildoers.
6 You destroy those who speak lies;
        the Lord abhors the bloodthirsty
        and deceitful.

7 But I, through the abundance of
            your steadfast love,
    will enter your house,
    I will bow down toward your holy
        temple
    in awe of you.
8 Lead me, O Lord, in your
        righteousness
        because of my enemies;
        make your way straight before me.

9 For there is no truth in their
        mouths;
        their hearts are destruction;
    their throats are open graves;
        they flatter with their tongues.
10 Make them bear their guilt, O God;
        let them fall by their own counsels;
    because of their many transgressions
        cast them out,
        for they have rebelled against you.

11 But let all who take refuge in you
        rejoice;
        let them ever sing for joy.
    Spread your protection over them,
        so that those who love your name
        may exult in you.
12 For you bless the righteous, O Lord;
        you cover them with favor as with
        a shield.

Psalm 6

Prayer for Recovery from Grave Illness
To the leader: with stringed instruments;
    according to The Shem′i·nith.
            A Psalm of David.

1 O Lord, do not rebuke me in your
        anger,

or discipline me in your wrath.
2 Be gracious to me, O Lord, for I am
        languishing;
        O Lord, heal me, for my bones are
        shaking with terror.
3 My soul also is struck with terror,
        while you, O Lord—how long?

4 Turn, O Lord, save my life;
        deliver me for the sake of your
        steadfast love.
5 For in death there is no remembrance
        of you;
        in She′ōl who can give you praise?

6 I am weary with my moaning;
        every night I flood my bed with
        tears;
        I drench my couch with my weeping.
7 My eyes waste away because of grief;
        they grow weak because of all my
        foes.

8 Depart from me, all you workers of
        evil,
        for the Lord has heard the sound of
        my weeping.
9 The Lord has heard my supplication;
        the Lord accepts my prayer.
10 All my enemies shall be ashamed and
        struck with terror;
        they shall turn back, and in a
        moment be put to shame.

Psalm 7

Plea for Help against Persecutors
A Shig.ga-i′on of David, which he sang
    to the Lord concerning Cush,
            a Ben′ja·min·ī te.

1 O Lord my God, in you I take
        refuge;
        save me from all my pursuers, and
        deliver me,
2 or like a lion they will tear me apart;
        they will drag me away, with no
        one to rescue.

3 O Lord my God, if I have done this,
        if there is wrong in my hands,

⁴ if I have repaid my ally with harm
    or plundered my foe without cause,
⁵ then let the enemy pursue and
        over-take me,
    trample my life to the ground,
    and lay my soul in the dust.   *Sĕ'lah*

⁶ Rise up, O LORD, in your anger;
    lift yourself up against the fury of
        my enemies;
    awake, O my God;^d you have
        appointed a judgment.
⁷ Let the assembly of the peoples be
        gathered around you,
    and over it take your seat^e on high.
⁸ The LORD judges the peoples;
    judge me, O LORD, according to my
        righteousness
    and according to the integrity that is
        in me.

⁹ O let the evil of the wicked come to an
        end,
    but establish the righteous,
    you who test the minds and hearts,
        O righteous God.
¹⁰ God is my shield,
    who saves the upright in heart.
¹¹ God is a righteous judge,
    and a God who has indignation
        every day.

¹² If one does not repent, God^f will whet
        his sword;
    he has bent and strung his bow;
¹³ he has prepared his deadly weapons,
    making his arrows fiery shafts.
¹⁴ See how they conceive evil,
    and are pregnant with mischief,
    and bring forth lies.
¹⁵ They make a pit, digging it out,
    and fall into the hole that they have
        made.
¹⁶ Their mischief returns upon their own
        heads,
    and on their own heads their
        violence descends.

¹⁷ I will give to the LORD the thanks due
    to his righteousness,

and sing praise to the name of the
    LORD, the Most High.

A bulwark is a wall or barrier built to defend against enemies. In this psalm, the word is used to describe God's protection. Look up the words to the hymn "A Mighty Fortress Is Our God" in a hymnal or on the Internet. Do you think the hymn writer was thinking of Psalm 8 when he wrote this hymn?

Psalm 8

Divine Majesty and Human Dignity

To the leader: according to The Git'tith.
    A Psalm of David.

¹ O LORD, our Sovereign,
    how majestic is your name in all
        the earth!

You have set your glory above the
    heavens.
² Out of the mouths of babes and
        infants
you have founded a bulwark because
        of your foes,
    to silence the enemy and the
        avenger.

³ When I look at your heavens, the
        work of your fingers,
    the moon and the stars that you
        have established;
⁴ what are human beings that you are
        mindful of them,
    mortals^g that you care for them?

⁵ Yet you have made them a little
        lower than God,^h
    and crowned them with glory and
        honor.
⁶ You have given them dominion over
        the works of your hands;

^d Or *awake for me*   ^e Cn: Heb *return*   ^f Heb *he*
^g Heb *ben adam*, lit. *son of man*   ^h Or *than the
divine beings* or *angels:* Heb *elohim*

"I will give thanks to the
LORD with my whole
heart; I will tell of all
your wonderful deeds."
Psalm 9:1

you have put all things under
their feet,
⁷ all sheep and oxen,
and also the beasts of the field,
⁸ the birds of the air, and the fish
of the sea,
whatever passes along the paths of
the seas.

⁹ O LORD, our Sovereign,
how majestic is your name in all
the earth!

Psalm 9

God's Power and Justice
To the leader: according to
Muth-lab´ben.
A Psalm of David.

¹ I will give thanks to the LORD with
my whole heart;
I will tell of all your wonderful
deeds.
² I will be glad and exult in you;
I will sing praise to your name,
O Most High.

³ When my enemies turned back,
they stumbled and perished
before you.
⁴ For you have maintained my just cause;
you have sat on the throne giving
righteous judgment.

⁵ You have rebuked the nations, you
have destroyed the wicked;
you have blotted out their name
forever and ever.
⁶ The enemies have vanished in
ever-lasting ruins;
their cities you have rooted out;
the very memory of them has
perished.

⁷ But the LORD sits enthroned forever,
he has established his throne for
judgment.
⁸ He judges the world with
righteousness;
he judges the peoples with equity.

⁹ The LORD is a stronghold for the
oppressed,
a stronghold in times of trouble.
¹⁰ And those who know your name put
their trust in you,
for you, O LORD, have not
forsaken those who seek you.

¹¹ Sing praises to the LORD, who dwells
in Zion.
Declare his deeds among the
peoples.
¹² For he who avenges blood is
mindful of them;
he does not forget the cry of the
afflicted.

¹³ Be gracious to me, O LORD.
See what I suffer from those who
hate me;
you are the one who lifts me up
from the gates of death,
¹⁴ so that I may recount all your
praises,
and, in the gates of daughter Zion,
rejoice in your deliverance.

¹⁵ The nations have sunk in the pit
that they made;
in the net that they hid has their
own foot been caught.
¹⁶ The LORD has made himself known,
he has executed judgment;
the wicked are snared in the work
of their own hands.
Hig·gāi´on. Se̅´lah

¹⁷ The wicked shall depart to She̅´o̅l,
all the nations that forget God.

¹⁸ For the needy shall not always be
forgotten,
nor the hope of the poor perish
forever.

19 Rise up, O LORD! Do not let mortals
    prevail;
  let the nations be judged before you.
20 Put them in fear, O LORD;
  let the nations know that they are
    only human.   *Selah*

Psalm 10

Prayer for Deliverance from Enemies

1 Why, O LORD, do you stand far off?
  Why do you hide yourself in times
    of trouble?
2 In arrogance the wicked persecute the
    poor—
  let them be caught in the schemes
    they have devised.

3 For the wicked boast of the desires of
    their heart,
  those greedy for gain curse and
    renounce the LORD.
4 In the pride of their countenance the
    wicked say, "God will not seek it
    out";
  all their thoughts are, "There is no
    God."

5 Their ways prosper at all times;
  your judgments are on high, out of
    their sight;
  as for their foes, they scoff at them.
6 They think in their heart, "We shall
    not be moved;
  throughout all generations we shall
    not meet adversity."

7 Their mouths are filled with cursing
    and deceit and oppression;
  under their tongues are mischief and
    iniquity.
8 They sit in ambush in the villages;
  in hiding places they murder the
    innocent.

  Their eyes stealthily watch for the
    helpless;
9 they lurk in secret like a lion in its
    covert;
  they lurk that they may seize the poor;

  they seize the poor and drag them
    off in their net.
10 They stoop, they crouch,
  and the helpless fall by their might.
11 They think in their heart, "God has
    forgotten,
  he has hidden his face, he will never
    see it."

12 Rise up, O LORD; O God, lift up your
    hand;
  do not forget the oppressed.
13 Why do the wicked renounce God,
  and say in their hearts, "You will not
    call us to account"?

14 But you do see! Indeed you note
    trouble and grief,
  that you may take it into your hands;
  the helpless commit themselves to you;
  you have been the helper of the
    orphan.

15 Break the arm of the wicked and
    evildoers;
  seek out their wickedness until you
    find none.
16 The LORD is king forever and ever;
  the nations shall perish from his land.

17 O LORD, you will hear the desire of
    the meek;
  you will strengthen their heart,
  you will incline your ear
18 to do justice for the orphan and the
    oppressed,
  so that those from earth may
    strike terror no more.[i]

Psalm 11

Song of Trust in God
To the leader. Of David.

1 In the LORD I take refuge; how can
    you say to me,
  "Flee like a bird to the mountains;[j]

i Meaning of Heb uncertain   j Gk Syr Jerome Tg:
Heb *flee to your mountain, O bird*

2 for look, the wicked bend the bow,
    they have fitted their arrow to the
        string,
    to shoot in the dark at the upright in
        heart.
3 If the foundations are destroyed,
    what can the righteous do?"

4 The LORD is in his holy temple;
    the LORD's throne is in heaven.
    His eyes behold, his gaze examines
        humankind.
5 The LORD tests the righteous and the
        wicked,
    and his soul hates the lover of
        violence.
6 On the wicked he will rain coals of fire
        and sulfur;
    a scorching wind shall be the
        portion of their cup.
7 For the LORD is righteous;
  he loves righteous deeds;
    the upright shall behold his face.

Psalm 12

Plea for Help in Evil Times
To the leader:
according to The Shem´i·nith.
A Psalm of David.

1 Help, O LORD, for there is no longer
    anyone who is godly;
    the faithful have disappeared from
        humankind.
2 They utter lies to each other;
    with flattering lips and a double
        heart they speak.

3 May the LORD cut off all flattering lips,
    the tongue that makes great boasts,
4 those who say, "With our tongues we
        will prevail;
    our lips are our own—who is our
        master?"

5 "Because the poor are despoiled,
    because the needy groan,
  I will now rise up," says the LORD;
  "I will place them in the safety for
    which they long."

6 The promises of the LORD are promises
    that are pure,
    silver refined in a furnace on the
        ground,
    purified seven times.

7 You, O LORD, will protect us;
    you will guard us from this
        generation forever.
8 On every side the wicked prowl,
    as vileness is exalted among
        humankind.

Psalm 13

Prayer for Deliverance from Enemies
To the leader. A Psalm of David.

1 How long, O LORD? Will you forget me
    forever?
    How long will you hide your face
        from me?
2 How long must I bear pain[k] in my soul,
    and have sorrow in my heart all day
        long?
    How long shall my enemy be exalted
        over me?

3 Consider and answer me, O LORD my
    God!
    Give light to my eyes, or I will sleep
        the sleep of death,
4 and my enemy will say, "I have
        prevailed";
    my foes will rejoice because I am
        shaken.

5 But I trusted in your steadfast love;
    my heart shall rejoice in your
        salvation.
6 I will sing to the LORD,
    because he has dealt bountifully
        with me.

Psalm 14

Denunciation of Godlessness
To the leader. Of David.

1 Fools say in their hearts, "There is
    no God."

k Syr: Heb *hold counsels*

They are corrupt, they do
abominable deeds;
there is no one who does good.

2 The LORD looks down from heaven on
humankind
to see if there are any who are wise,
who seek after God.

3 They have all gone astray, they are all
alike perverse;
there is no one who does good,
no, not one.

4 Have they no knowledge, all the
evildoers
who eat up my people as they eat
bread,
and do not call upon the LORD?

5 There they shall be in great terror,
for God is with the company of the
righteous.
6 You would confound the plans of the
poor,
but the LORD is their refuge.

7 O that deliverance for Israel would
come from Zion!
When the LORD restores the fortunes
of his people,
Jacob will rejoice; Israel will be glad.

Psalm 15

Who Shall Abide in God's Sanctuary?
A Psalm of David.

1 O LORD, who may abide in your tent?
Who may dwell on your holy hill?

2 Those who walk blamelessly, and do
what is right,
and speak the truth from their heart;
3 who do not slander with their tongue,
and do no evil to their friends,
nor take up a reproach against their
neighbors;
4 in whose eyes the wicked are despised,
but who honor those who fear the
LORD;

who stand by their oath even to their
hurt;
5 who do not lend money at interest,
and do not take a bribe against the
innocent.

Those who do these things shall never
be moved.

Psalm 16

Song of Trust and Security in God
A Mik´tam of David.

1 Protect me, O God, for in you I take
refuge.
2 I say to the LORD, "You are my Lord;
I have no good apart from you."[l]

3 As for the holy ones in the land,
they are the noble,
in whom is all my delight.

4 Those who choose another god
multiply their sorrows;[m]
their drink offerings of blood I
will not pour out
or take their names upon my lips.

5 The LORD is my chosen portion and
my cup;
you hold my lot.
6 The boundary lines have fallen for
me in pleasant places;
I have a goodly heritage.

7 I bless the LORD who gives me counsel;
in the night also my heart
instructs me.
8 I keep the LORD always before me;
because he is at my right hand, I
shall not be moved.

9 Therefore my heart is glad, and my
soul rejoices;
my body also rests secure.
10 For you do not give me up to Shĕ´ōl,
or let your faithful one see the Pit.

11 You show me the path of life.
In your presence there is fullness
of joy;

l Jerome Tg: Meaning of Heb uncertain   *m* Cn:
Meaning of Heb uncertain

"You show me the path of life. In your presence there is fullness of joy; in your right hand are pleasures forevermore." Psalm 16:11

in your right hand are pleasures forevermore.

Psalm 17

Prayer for Deliverance from Persecutors
A Prayer of David.

[1] Hear a just cause, O LORD; attend to
my cry;
give ear to my prayer from lips free
of deceit.
[2] From you let my vindication come;
let your eyes see the right.

[3] If you try my heart, if you visit me by
night,
if you test me, you will find no
wickedness in me;
my mouth does not transgress.
[4] As for what others do, by the word of
your lips
I have avoided the ways of the
violent.
[5] My steps have held fast to your paths;
my feet have not slipped.

[6] I call upon you, for you will answer
me, O God;
incline your ear to me, hear my
words.
[7] Wondrously show your steadfast love,
O savior of those who seek refuge
from their adversaries at your right
hand.

[8] Guard me as the apple of the eye;
hide me in the shadow of your wings,
[9] from the wicked who despoil me,
my deadly enemies who surround me.
[10] They close their hearts to pity;
with their mouths they speak
arrogantly.

[11] They track me down;[n] now they
surround me;
they set their eyes to cast me to the
ground.
[12] They are like a lion eager to tear,
like a young lion lurking in ambush.

[13] Rise up, O LORD, confront them,
overthrow them!
By your sword deliver my life from
the wicked,
[14] from mortals—by your hand, O
LORD—
from mortals whose portion in life is
in this world.
May their bellies be filled with what
you have stored up for them;
may their children have more than
enough;
may they leave something over to
their little ones.

[15] As for me, I shall behold your face in
righteousness;
when I awake I shall be satisfied,
beholding your likeness.

Psalm 18

Royal Thanksgiving for Victory
To the leader. A Psalm of David the
servant of the LORD, who addressed the
words of this song to the LORD on the day
when the LORD delivered him from the
hand of all his enemies, and from the
hand of Saul. He said:

When danger threatens baby birds, the mother gathers them under her wings to protect them from harm. The psalmist knew that in times of danger, he could turn to God for protection. Today, we too can turn to God for protection, praying that God will help us and keep us safe.

[n] One Ms Compare Syr: MT *Our steps*

¹ I love you, O LORD, my strength.
² The LORD is my rock, my fortress,
   and my deliverer,
      my God, my rock in whom I take
      refuge,
      my shield, and the horn of my
      salvation, my stronghold.
³ I call upon the LORD, who is worthy
   to be praised,
      so I shall be saved from my enemies.

⁴ The cords of death encompassed me;
   the torrents of perdition assailed me;
⁵ the cords of Shē´ōl entangled me;
   the snares of death confronted me.

⁶ In my distress I called upon the LORD;
   to my God I cried for help.
From his temple he heard my voice,
   and my cry to him reached his ears.

⁷ Then the earth reeled and rocked;
   the foundations also of the
      mountains trembled
   and quaked, because he was angry.
⁸ Smoke went up from his nostrils,
   and devouring fire from his mouth;
   glowing coals flamed forth from him.
⁹ He bowed the heavens, and came down;
   thick darkness was under his feet.
¹⁰ He rode on a cherub, and flew;
   he came swiftly upon the wings of
      the wind.
¹¹ He made darkness his covering around
      him,
   his canopy thick clouds dark with
      water.
¹² Out of the brightness before him
   there broke through his clouds
   hailstones and coals of fire.
¹³ The LORD also thundered in the
      heavens,
   and the Most High uttered his voice.ᵒ
¹⁴ And he sent out his arrows, and
      scattered them;
   he flashed forth lightnings, and
      routed them.
¹⁵ Then the channels of the sea were
      seen,

Because animals use their horns as weapons, the Old Testament writers used the word "horn" as a symbol of power and might. The writer of Psalm 18 thought of God as the horn, or strength, of his salvation.

and the foundations of the world were
      laid bare
at your rebuke, O LORD,
   at the blast of the breath of your
      nostrils.

¹⁶ He reached down from on high, he
      took me;
   he drew me out of mighty waters.
¹⁷ He delivered me from my strong
      enemy,
   and from those who hated me;
   for they were too mighty for me.
¹⁸ They confronted me in the day of my
      calamity;
   but the LORD was my support.
¹⁹ He brought me out into a broad place;
   he delivered me, because he
      delighted in me.

²⁰ The LORD rewarded me according to
      my righteousness;
   according to the cleanness of my
      hands he recompensed me.
²¹ For I have kept the ways of the LORD,
   and have not wickedly departed
      from my God.
²² For all his ordinances were before me,
   and his statutes I did not put away
      from me.
²³ I was blameless before him,
   and I kept myself from guilt.
²⁴ Therefore the LORD has recompensed
      me according to my
      righteousness,

ᵒ Gk See 2 Sam 22.14: Heb adds *hailstones and
coals of fire*

according to the cleanness of my
hands in his sight.

25 With the loyal you show yourself loyal;
with the blameless you show
yourself blameless;
26 with the pure you show yourself pure;
and with the crooked you show
yourself perverse.
27 For you deliver a humble people,
but the haughty eyes you bring down.
28 It is you who light my lamp;
the LORD, my God, lights up my
darkness.
29 By you I can crush a troop,
and by my God I can leap over a
wall.
30 This God—his way is perfect;
the promise of the LORD proves
true;
he is a shield for all who take
refuge in him.

31 For who is God except the LORD?
And who is a rock besides our
God?—
32 the God who girded me with strength,
and made my way safe.
33 He made my feet like the feet of a deer,
and set me secure on the heights.
34 He trains my hands for war,
so that my arms can bend a bow
of bronze.
35 You have given me the shield of your
salvation,
and your right hand has
supported me;
your help^p has made me great.
36 You gave me a wide place for my
steps under me,
and my feet did not slip.
37 I pursued my enemies and overtook
them;
and did not turn back until they
were consumed.
38 I struck them down, so that they
were not able to rise;
they fell under my feet.

39 For you girded me with strength for
the battle;
you made my assailants sink
under me.
40 You made my enemies turn their
backs to me,
and those who hated me I
destroyed.
41 They cried for help, but there was
no one to save them;
they cried to the LORD, but he did
not answer them.
42 I beat them fine, like dust before the
wind;
I cast them out like the mire of
the streets.

43 You delivered me from strife with
the peoples;^q
you made me head of the nations;
people whom I had not known
served me.
44 As soon as they heard of me they
obeyed me;
foreigners came cringing to me.
45 Foreigners lost heart,
and came trembling out of their
strongholds.

46 The LORD lives! Blessed be my rock,
and exalted be the God of my
salvation,
47 the God who gave me vengeance
and subdued peoples under me;
48 who delivered me from my enemies;
indeed, you exalted me above my
adversaries;
you delivered me from the violent.

49 For this I will extol you, O LORD,
among the nations,
and sing praises to your name.
50 Great triumphs he gives to his king,
and shows steadfast love to his
anointed,
to David and his descendants
forever.

^p Or *gentleness*   ^q Gk Tg: Heb *people*

"Let the words of my mouth and the meditation of my heart be acceptable to you, O LORD, my rock and my redeemer."

Psalm 19:14

Psalm 19

God's Glory in Creation and the Law

To the leader. A Psalm of David.

1 The heavens are telling the glory of God;
   and the firmament[r] proclaims his handiwork.
2 Day to day pours forth speech,
   and night to night declares knowledge.
3 There is no speech, nor are there words;
   their voice is not heard;
4 yet their voice[s] goes out through all the earth,
   and their words to the end of the world.

In the heavens[t] he has set a tent for the sun,
5 which comes out like a bridegroom from his wedding canopy,
   and like a strong man runs its course with joy.
6 Its rising is from the end of the heavens,
   and its circuit to the end of them;
   and nothing is hid from its heat.

7 The law of the LORD is perfect,
   reviving the soul;
the decrees of the LORD are sure,
   making wise the simple;
8 the precepts of the LORD are right,
   rejoicing the heart;
the commandment of the LORD is clear,
   enlightening the eyes;
9 the fear of the LORD is pure,
   enduring forever;
the ordinances of the LORD are true
   and righteous altogether.
10 More to be desired are they than gold,
   even much fine gold;
   sweeter also than honey,
   and drippings of the honeycomb.

11 Moreover by them is your servant warned;
   in keeping them there is great reward.
12 But who can detect their errors?
   Clear me from hidden faults.
13 Keep back your servant also from the insolent;[u]
   do not let them have dominion over me.
Then I shall be blameless,
   and innocent of great transgression.

14 Let the words of my mouth and the meditation of my heart
   be acceptable to you,
   O LORD, my rock and my redeemer.

Psalm 20

Prayer for Victory

To the leader. A Psalm of David.

1 The LORD answer you in the day of trouble!
   The name of the God of Jacob protect you!
2 May he send you help from the sanctuary,
   and give you support from Zion.
3 May he remember all your offerings,
   and regard with favor your burnt sacrifices.   *Se'lah*

4 May he grant you your heart's desire,
   and fulfill all your plans.
5 May we shout for joy over your victory,
   and in the name of our God set up our banners.
May the LORD fulfill all your petitions.

---

r Or *dome*   s Gk Jerome Compare Syr: Heb *line*
t Heb *In them*   u Or *from proud thoughts*

6· Now I know that the LORD will help
his anointed;
he will answer him from his holy
heaven
with mighty victories by his right
hand.

7 Some take pride in chariots, and some
in horses,
but our pride is in the name of the
LORD our God.

8 They will collapse and fall,
but we shall rise and stand upright.

9 Give victory to the king, O LORD;
answer us when we call.[v]

Psalm 21

Thanksgiving for Victory
To the leader. A Psalm of David.

1 In your strength the king rejoices, O
LORD,
and in your help how greatly he
exults!

2 You have given him his heart's desire,
and have not withheld the request
of his lips.   *Sēlah*

3 For you meet him with rich blessings;
you set a crown of fine gold on his
head.

4 He asked you for life; you gave it to
him—
length of days forever and ever.

5 His glory is great through your help;
splendor and majesty you bestow on
him.

6 You bestow on him blessings forever;
you make him glad with the joy of
your presence.

7 For the king trusts in the LORD,
and through the steadfast love of the
Most High he shall not be
moved.

8 Your hand will find out all your
enemies;
your right hand will find out those
who hate you.

> In Bible times, horses and
> chariots were weapons
> used in war. Nations that
> had large numbers of
> chariots and horses felt very power-
> ful and strong. These nations were
> proud of their might, but the writer
> of Psalm 20 reminds God's people
> to trust only in God.

9 You will make them like a fiery furnace
when you appear.
The LORD will swallow them up in his
wrath,
and fire will consume them.

10 You will destroy their offspring from
the earth,
and their children from among
humankind.

11 If they plan evil against you,
if they devise mischief, they will not
succeed.

12 For you will put them to flight;
you will aim at their faces with your
bows.

13 Be exalted, O LORD, in your strength!
We will sing and praise your power.

Psalm 22

*Plea for Deliverance from Suffering and
Hostility*
To the leader: according to
The Deer of the Dawn.
A Psalm of David.

1 My God, my God, why have you
forsaken me?
Why are you so far from helping
me, from the words of my
groaning?

2 O my God, I cry by day, but you do
not answer;
and by night, but find no rest.

3 Yet you are holy,
enthroned on the praises of Israel.

[v] Gk: Heb *give victory, O LORD; let the King answer us
when we call*

Jesus said the opening words of Psalm 22 as he was being crucified. Read Matthew 27:46 and Mark 15:34.

4 In you our ancestors trusted;
    they trusted, and you delivered
      them.
5 To you they cried, and were saved;
    in you they trusted, and were not
      put to shame.

6 But I am a worm, and not human;
    scorned by others, and despised by
      the people.
7 All who see me mock at me;
    they make mouths at me, they shake
      their heads;
8 "Commit your cause to the LORD; let
    him deliver—
    let him rescue the one in whom he
      delights!"

9 Yet it was you who took me from the
    womb;
    you kept me safe on my mother's
      breast.
10 On you I was cast from my birth,
    and since my mother bore me you
      have been my God.
11 Do not be far from me,
    for trouble is near
    and there is no one to help.

12 Many bulls encircle me,
    strong bulls of Bā′shan surround
      me;
13 they open wide their mouths at me,
    like a ravening and roaring lion.

14 I am poured out like water,
    and all my bones are out of joint;
    my heart is like wax;
      it is melted within my breast;
15 my mouth[w] is dried up like a potsherd,
    and my tongue sticks to my jaws;
    you lay me in the dust of death.

16 For dogs are all around me;
    a company of evildoers encircles me.
    My hands and feet have shriveled;[x]
17 I can count all my bones.
    They stare and gloat over me;
18 they divide my clothes among
      themselves,
    and for my clothing they cast lots.

19 But you, O LORD, do not be far away!
    O my help, come quickly to my aid!
20 Deliver my soul from the sword,
    my life[y] from the power of the dog!
21   Save me from the mouth of the lion!

    From the horns of the wild oxen you
      have rescued[z] me.
22 I will tell of your name to my brothers
    and sisters;[a]
    in the midst of the congregation I
      will praise you:
23 You who fear the LORD, praise him!
    All you offspring of Jacob, glorify him;
    stand in awe of him, all you
      offspring of Israel!
24 For he did not despise or abhor
    the affliction of the afflicted;
    he did not hide his face from me,[b]
    but heard when I[c] cried to him.

25 From you comes my praise in the great
    congregation;
    my vows I will pay before those
      who fear him.

In the Bible, the word "dominion" is used to mean the supreme rule of God, humanity's rule over nature, or power gained by conquest. In the book of Psalms, the word "dominion" usually praises God for creating the world and for caring for that creation.

---

[w] Cn: Heb *strength*   [x] Meaning of Heb uncertain   [y] Heb *my only one*   [z] Heb *answered*   [a] Or *kindred*   [b] Heb *him*   [c] Heb *he*

²⁶ The poor^d shall eat and be satisfied;
  those who seek him shall praise the
    LORD.
  May your hearts live forever!

²⁷ All the ends of the earth shall remember
    and turn to the LORD;
  and all the families of the nations
    shall worship before him.^e
²⁸ For dominion belongs to the LORD,
    and he rules over the nations.

²⁹ To him,^f indeed, shall all who sleep in^g
    the earth bow down;
  before him shall bow all who go
    down to the dust,
  and I shall live for him.^h
³⁰ Posterity will serve him;
  future generations will be told about
    the Lord,
³¹ andⁱ proclaim his deliverance to a
    people yet unborn,
  saying that he has done it.

Psalm 23

The Divine Shepherd
A Psalm of David.

¹ The LORD is my shepherd, I shall not
    want.
²   He makes me lie down in green
      pastures;
  he leads me beside still waters;^j
³   he restores my soul.^k
  He leads me in right paths^l
    for his name's sake.

⁴ Even though I walk through the
      darkest valley,^m
    I fear no evil;
  for you are with me;
    your rod and your staff—
    they comfort me.

⁵ You prepare a table before me
    in the presence of my enemies;
  you anoint my head with oil;
    my cup overflows.
⁶ Surelyⁿ goodness and mercy^o shall
    follow me

Shepherds were constantly protecting sheep from wild animals such as lions, bears, and wolves. Sometimes robbers would try to steal the sheep. The shepherd would protect the sheep even if it meant he would die or be injured. If a sheep got hurt or tired, the shepherd would carry the sheep across his shoulders. Little lambs, however, he would carry in his arms, close to his heart. The psalmist saw God as a good shepherd, caring for the people just as the shepherd cared for his sheep.

  all the days of my life,
  and I shall dwell in the house of the
    LORD
    my whole life long.^p

Psalm 24

Entrance into the Temple
Of David. A Psalm.

¹ The earth is the LORD's and all that is
    in it,
  the world, and those who live in it;
² for he has founded it on the seas,
    and established it on the rivers.

Read the following Scriptures, and discover how God works as your shepherd: Psalm 23:1, Psalm 95:7, Isaiah 40:11, John 10:1–15, and John 10:27–30. What are some ways that someone you know has acted as a shepherd for you? What are some ways that you can act as a shepherd for someone else?

^d Or *afflicted*   ^e Gk Syr Jerome: Heb *you*   ^f Cn:
Heb *They have eaten and*   ^g Cn: Heb *all the fat ones*
^h Compare Gk Syr Vg: Heb *and he who cannot keep
himself alive*   ⁱ Compare Gk: Heb *it will be told about
the Lord to the generation,* ³¹*they will come and*   ^j Heb
waters of rest   ^k Or *life*   ^l Or *paths of righteousness*
^m Or *the valley of the shadow of death*   ⁿ Or *Only*
^o Or *kindness*   ^p Heb *for length of days*

3 Who shall ascend the hill of the LORD?
    And who shall stand in his holy
        place?
4 Those who have clean hands and pure
        hearts,
    who do not lift up their souls to
        what is false,
    and do not swear deceitfully.
5 They will receive blessing from the
        LORD,
    and vindication from the God of
        their salvation.
6 Such is the company of those who
        seek him,
    who seek the face of the God of
        Jacob.q   Sĕlah

7 Lift up your heads, O gates!
    and be lifted up, O ancient doors!
    that the King of glory may come in.
8 Who is the King of glory?
    The LORD, strong and mighty,
    the LORD, mighty in battle.
9 Lift up your heads, O gates!
    and be lifted up, O ancient doors!
    that the King of glory may come in.
10 Who is this King of glory?
    The LORD of hosts,
    he is the King of glory.   Sĕlah

Psalm 25

Prayer for Guidance and for Deliverance
            Of David.
1 To you, O LORD, I lift up my soul.
2 O my God, in you I trust;
    do not let me be put to shame;
    do not let my enemies exult over
        me.
3 Do not let those who wait for you be
        put to shame;
    let them be ashamed who are
        wantonly treacherous.

4 Make me to know your ways, O LORD;
    teach me your paths.
5 Lead me in your truth, and teach me,
    for you are the God of my salvation;
    for you I wait all day long.

6 Be mindful of your mercy, O LORD,
    and of your steadfast love,
    for they have been from of old.
7 Do not remember the sins of my youth
        or my transgressions;
    according to your steadfast love
        remember me,
    for your goodness' sake, O LORD!

8 Good and upright is the LORD;
    therefore he instructs sinners in the
        way.
9 He leads the humble in what is right,
    and teaches the humble his way.
10 All the paths of the LORD are steadfast
        love and faithfulness,
    for those who keep his covenant
        and his decrees.

11 For your name's sake, O LORD,
    pardon my guilt, for it is great.
12 Who are they that fear the LORD?
    He will teach them the way that
        they should choose.

13 They will abide in prosperity,
    and their children shall possess the
        land.
14 The friendship of the LORD is for those
        who fear him,
    and he makes his covenant known
        to them.
15 My eyes are ever toward the LORD,
    for he will pluck my feet out of the
        net.

16 Turn to me and be gracious to me,
    for I am lonely and afflicted.
17 Relieve the troubles of my heart,
    and bring mer out of my distress.
18 Consider my affliction and my
        trouble,
    and forgive all my sins.

19 Consider how many are my foes,
    and with what violent hatred they
        hate me.

q Gk Syr: Heb *your face, O Jacob*   r Or *The troubles
of my heart are enlarged; bring me*

20 O guard my life, and deliver me;
    do not let me be put to shame, for I
    take refuge in you.
21 May integrity and uprightness preserve
    me,
    for I wait for you.

22 Redeem Israel, O God,
    out of all its troubles.

Psalm 26

*Plea for Justice and Declaration of
Righteousness*
Of David.

1 Vindicate me, O LORD,
    for I have walked in my integrity,
    and I have trusted in the LORD
    without wavering.
2 Prove me, O LORD, and try me;
    test my heart and mind.
3 For your steadfast love is before my eyes,
    and I walk in faithfulness to you.[s]

4 I do not sit with the worthless,
    nor do I consort with hypocrites;
5 I hate the company of evildoers,
    and will not sit with the wicked.

6 I wash my hands in innocence,
    and go around your altar, O LORD,
7 singing aloud a song of thanksgiving,
    and telling all your wondrous deeds.

8 O LORD, I love the house in which you
    dwell,

In Bible times, people washed their hands before they worshiped God. Handwashing was a symbol of washing away their sins. Jesus reminded those who listened to him that the most important thing is to clean the heart—to pray for forgiveness and turn from sin to right living. The next time you wash your hands, remind yourself to clean your heart too!

and the place where your glory
    abides.
9 Do not sweep me away with sinners,
    nor my life with the bloodthirsty,
10 those in whose hands are evil devices,
    and whose right hands are full of
    bribes.

11 But as for me, I walk in my integrity;
    redeem me, and be gracious to me.
12 My foot stands on level ground;
    in the great congregation I will bless
    the LORD.

God is our light, our salvation, and our stronghold. We don't have to be afraid of anyone or anything! This psalm of trust reminds us that we can have confidence in God. God will protect and deliver us.

Psalm 27

Triumphant Song of Confidence
Of David.

1 The LORD is my light and my salvation;
    whom shall I fear?
    The LORD is the stronghold[t] of my life;
    of whom shall I be afraid?

2 When evildoers assail me
    to devour my flesh—
    my adversaries and foes—
    they shall stumble and fall.

3 Though an army encamp against me,
    my heart shall not fear;
    though war rise up against me,
    yet I will be confident.

4 One thing I asked of the LORD,
    that will I seek after:
    to live in the house of the LORD
    all the days of my life,
    to behold the beauty of the LORD,
    and to inquire in his temple.

s Or *in your faithfulness*   t Or *refuge*

5 For he will hide me in his shelter
  in the day of trouble;
he will conceal me under the cover of
    his tent;
  he will set me high on a rock.

6 Now my head is lifted up
    above my enemies all around me,
and I will offer in his tent
    sacrifices with shouts of joy;
  I will sing and make melody to the
    LORD.

7 Hear, O LORD, when I cry aloud,
    be gracious to me and answer me!
8 "Come," my heart says, "seek his face!"
    Your face, LORD, do I seek.
9   Do not hide your face from me.

  Do not turn your servant away in anger,
    you who have been my help.
  Do not cast me off, do not forsake me,
    O God of my salvation!
10 If my father and mother forsake me,
    the LORD will take me up.

11 Teach me your way, O LORD,
    and lead me on a level path
    because of my enemies.
12 Do not give me up to the will of my
    adversaries,
    for false witnesses have risen against
      me,
    and they are breathing out violence.

13 I believe that I shall see the goodness
    of the LORD
  in the land of the living.
14 Wait for the LORD;
    be strong, and let your heart take
      courage;
    wait for the LORD!

Psalm 28

Prayer for Help and Thanksgiving for It
Of David.

1 To you, O LORD, I call;
    my rock, do not refuse to hear me,
  for if you are silent to me,

I shall be like those who go down to
    the Pit.
2 Hear the voice of my supplication,
    as I cry to you for help,
  as I lift up my hands
    toward your most holy sanctuary.[u]

3 Do not drag me away with the wicked,
    with those who are workers of evil,
  who speak peace with their neighbors,
    while mischief is in their hearts.
4 Repay them according to their work,
    and according to the evil of their
      deeds;
  repay them according to the work of
      their hands;
    render them their due reward.
5 Because they do not regard the works
    of the LORD,
    or the work of his hands,
  he will break them down and build
      them up no more.

6 Blessed be the LORD,
    for he has heard the sound of my
      pleadings.
7 The LORD is my strength and my shield;
    in him my heart trusts;
  so I am helped, and my heart exults,
    and with my song I give thanks to
      him.

8 The LORD is the strength of his people;
    he is the saving refuge of his
      anointed.
9 O save your people, and bless your
    heritage;
    be their shepherd, and carry them
      forever.

Psalm 29

The Voice of God in a Great Storm
A Psalm of David.

1 Ascribe to the LORD, O heavenly
    beings,[v]
    ascribe to the LORD glory and
      strength.
2 Ascribe to the LORD the glory of his
    name;

[u] Heb *your innermost sanctuary*   [v] Heb *sons of gods*

"Weeping may linger for the night, but joy comes with the morning." Psalm 30:5*b*

worship the LORD in holy splendor.

3 The voice of the LORD is over the
waters;
the God of glory thunders,
the LORD, over mighty waters.
4 The voice of the LORD is powerful;
the voice of the LORD is full of
majesty.

5 The voice of the LORD breaks the
cedars;
the LORD breaks the cedars of
Lebanon.
6 He makes Lebanon skip like a calf,
and Sir´i·on like a young wild ox.

7 The voice of the LORD flashes forth
flames of fire.
8 The voice of the LORD shakes the
wilderness;
the LORD shakes the wilderness of
Kā´desh.
9 The voice of the LORD causes the oaks
to whirl,^{w}
and strips the forest bare;
and in his temple all say, "Glory!"

10 The LORD sits enthroned over the flood;
the LORD sits enthroned as king
forever.
11 May the LORD give strength to his
people!
May the LORD bless his people with
peace!

Psalm 30

*Thanksgiving for Recovery from Grave
Illness*

A Psalm. A Song at the dedication
of the temple. Of David.

1 I will extol you, O LORD, for you have
drawn me up,

and did not let my foes rejoice over
me.
2 O LORD my God, I cried to you for help,
and you have healed me.
3 O LORD, you brought up my soul from
Shē´ōl,
restored me to life from among
those gone down to the Pit.^{x}

4 Sing praises to the LORD, O you his
faithful ones,
and give thanks to his holy name.
5 For his anger is but for a moment;
his favor is for a lifetime.
Weeping may linger for the night,
but joy comes with the morning.

6 As for me, I said in my prosperity,
"I shall never be moved."
7 By your favor, O LORD,
you had established me as a strong
mountain;
you hid your face;
I was dismayed.

8 To you, O LORD, I cried,
and to the LORD I made
supplication:
9 "What profit is there in my death,
if I go down to the Pit?
Will the dust praise you?
Will it tell of your faithfulness?
10 Hear, O LORD, and be gracious to me!
O LORD, be my helper!"

11 You have turned my mourning into
dancing;
you have taken off my sackcloth
and clothed me with joy,
12 so that my soul^y may praise you and
not be silent.
O LORD my God, I will give thanks
to you forever.

Psalm 31

*Prayer and Praise for Deliverance from
Enemies*

To the leader. A Psalm of David.

^{w} Or *causes the deer to calve* ^{x} Or *that I should not
go down to the Pit* ^{y} Heb *that glory*

1 In you, O LORD, I seek refuge;
    do not let me ever be put to shame;
    in your righteousness deliver me.
2 Incline your ear to me;
    rescue me speedily.
  Be a rock of refuge for me,
    a strong fortress to save me.

3 You are indeed my rock and my
        fortress;
    for your name's sake lead me and
        guide me,
4 take me out of the net that is hidden
    for me,
    for you are my refuge.
5 Into your hand I commit my spirit;
    you have redeemed me, O LORD,
        faithful God.

6 You hate[z] those who pay regard to
        worthless idols,
    but I trust in the LORD.
7 I will exult and rejoice in your
        steadfast love,
    because you have seen my affliction;
    you have taken heed of my
        adversities,
8 and have not delivered me into the
        hand of the enemy;
    you have set my feet in a broad
        place.

9 Be gracious to me, O LORD, for I am in
        distress;
    my eye wastes away from grief,
    my soul and body also.
10 For my life is spent with sorrow,
    and my years with sighing;
    my strength fails because of my
        misery,[a]
    and my bones waste away.

11 I am the scorn of all my adversaries,
    a horror[b] to my neighbors,
    an object of dread to my acquaintances;
    those who see me in the street flee
        from me.
12 I have passed out of mind like one
        who is dead;

    I have become like a broken vessel.
13 For I hear the whispering of many—
        terror all around!—
    as they scheme together against me,
    as they plot to take my life.

14 But I trust in you, O LORD;
    I say, "You are my God."
15 My times are in your hand;
    deliver me from the hand of my
        enemies and persecutors.
16 Let your face shine upon your servant;
    save me in your steadfast love.
17 Do not let me be put to shame, O LORD,
    for I call on you;
    let the wicked be put to shame;
    let them go dumbfounded to Shĕ'ōl.
18 Let the lying lips be stilled
    that speak insolently against the
        righteous
    with pride and contempt.

19 O how abundant is your goodness
    that you have laid up for those who
        fear you,
    and accomplished for those who take
        refuge in you,
    in the sight of everyone!
20 In the shelter of your presence you
        hide them
    from human plots;
    you hold them safe under your shelter
    from contentious tongues.

21 Blessed be the LORD,
    for he has wondrously shown his
        steadfast love to me
    when I was beset as a city under
        siege.
22 I had said in my alarm,
    "I am driven far[c] from your sight."
    But you heard my supplications
    when I cried out to you for help.

23 Love the LORD, all you his saints.
    The LORD preserves the faithful,

---

z One Heb Ms Gk Syr Jerome: MT *I hate*   a Gk Syr:
Heb *my iniquity*   b Cn: Heb *exceedingly*
c Another reading is *cut off*

but abundantly repays the one
who acts haughtily.
24 Be strong, and let your heart take
courage,
all you who wait for the LORD.

Psalm 32

The Joy of Forgiveness

Of David. A Mas'kil.

1 Happy are those whose transgression
is forgiven,
whose sin is covered.
2 Happy are those to whom the LORD
imputes no iniquity,
and in whose spirit there is no deceit.

3 While I kept silence, my body
wasted away
through my groaning all day long.
4 For day and night your hand was
heavy upon me;
my strength was dried up[d] as by
the heat of summer.   *Sē'lah*

5 Then I acknowledged my sin to you,
and I did not hide my iniquity;
I said, "I will confess my
transgressions to the LORD,"
and you forgave the guilt of my
sin.   *Sē'lah*

6 Therefore let all who are faithful
offer prayer to you;
at a time of distress,[e] the rush of
mighty waters
shall not reach them.
7 You are a hiding place for me;
you preserve me from trouble;
you surround me with glad cries
of deliverance.   *Sē'lah*

8 I will instruct you and teach you the
way you should go;
I will counsel you with my eye
upon you.
9 Do not be like a horse or a mule,
without understanding,
whose temper must be curbed
with bit and bridle,
else it will not stay near you.

10 Many are the torments of the
wicked,
but steadfast love surrounds those
who trust in the LORD.
11 Be glad in the LORD and rejoice, O
righteous,
and shout for joy, all you upright
in heart.

Psalm 33

The Greatness and Goodness of God

1 Rejoice in the LORD, O you
righteous.
Praise befits the upright.
2 Praise the LORD with the lyre;
make melody to him with the
harp of ten strings.
3 Sing to him a new song;
play skillfully on the strings, with
loud shouts.

4 For the word of the LORD is upright,
and all his work is done in
faithfulness.
5 He loves righteousness and justice;
the earth is full of the steadfast
love of the LORD.

6 By the word of the LORD the heavens
were made,
and all their host by the breath of
his mouth.
7 He gathered the waters of the sea as
in a bottle;
he put the deeps in storehouses.

8 Let all the earth fear the LORD;
let all the inhabitants of the world
stand in awe of him.
9 For he spoke, and it came to be;
he commanded, and it stood firm.

10 The LORD brings the counsel of the
nations to nothing;
he frustrates the plans of the
peoples.

[d] Meaning of Heb uncertain   [e] Cn: Heb *at a time of finding only*

11 The counsel of the LORD stands
forever,
    the thoughts of his heart to all
generations.
12 Happy is the nation whose God is the
LORD,
    the people whom he has chosen as
his heritage.

13 The LORD looks down from heaven;
    he sees all humankind.
14 From where he sits enthroned he
watches
    all the inhabitants of the earth—
15 he who fashions the hearts of them all,
    and observes all their deeds.
16 A king is not saved by his great army;
    a warrior is not delivered by his
great strength.
17 The war horse is a vain hope for
victory,
    and by its great might it cannot save.

18 Truly the eye of the LORD is on those
who fear him,
    on those who hope in his steadfast
love,
19 to deliver their soul from death,
    and to keep them alive in famine.

20 Our soul waits for the LORD;
    he is our help and shield.
21 Our heart is glad in him,
    because we trust in his holy name.
22 Let your steadfast love, O LORD, be
upon us,
    even as we hope in you.

Psalm 34

Praise for Deliverance from Trouble

Of David, when he feigned madness
before A·bim′e·lech, so that he drove
him out, and he went away.

"I will bless the LORD at all
times; his praise shall continually be in my mouth."
Psalm 34:1

1 I will bless the LORD at all times;
    his praise shall continually be in my
mouth.
2 My soul makes its boast in the LORD;
    let the humble hear and be glad.
3 O magnify the LORD with me,
    and let us exalt his name together.

4 I sought the LORD, and he answered
me,
    and delivered me from all my fears.
5 Look to him, and be radiant;
    so your*f* faces shall never be
ashamed.
6 This poor soul cried, and was heard by
the LORD,
    and was saved from every trouble.
7 The angel of the LORD encamps
    around those who fear him, and
delivers them.
8 O taste and see that the LORD is good;
    happy are those who take refuge in
him.
9 O fear the LORD, you his holy ones,
    for those who fear him have no
want.
10 The young lions suffer want and
hunger,
    but those who seek the LORD lack
no good thing.

11 Come, O children, listen to me;
    I will teach you the fear of the LORD.
12 Which of you desires life,
    and covets many days to enjoy
good?
13 Keep your tongue from evil,
    and your lips from speaking deceit.
14 Depart from evil, and do good;
    seek peace, and pursue it.

15 The eyes of the LORD are on the
righteous,
    and his ears are open to their cry.
16 The face of the LORD is against
evildoers,
    to cut off the remembrance of
them from the earth.

f Gk Syr Jerome: Heb *their*

17 When the righteous cry for help, the
Lord hears,
and rescues them from all their
troubles.
18 The Lord is near to the
brokenhearted,
and saves the crushed in spirit.
19 Many are the afflictions of the
righteous,
but the Lord rescues them from
them all.

20 He keeps all their bones;
not one of them will be broken.
21 Evil brings death to the wicked,
and those who hate the righteous
will be condemned.
22 The Lord redeems the life of his
servants;
none of those who take refuge in
him will be condemned.

Psalm 35

Prayer for Deliverance from Enemies
Of David.
1 Contend, O Lord, with those who
contend with me;
fight against those who fight against
me!
2 Take hold of shield and buckler,
and rise up to help me!
3 Draw the spear and javelin
against my pursuers;
say to my soul,
"I am your salvation."

4 Let them be put to shame and dishonor
who seek after my life.
Let them be turned back and
confounded
who devise evil against me.
5 Let them be like chaff before the wind,
with the angel of the Lord driving
them on.
6 Let their way be dark and slippery,
with the angel of the Lord pursuing
them.

7 For without cause they hid their net[g]
for me;

without cause they dug a pit[h] for my
life.
8 Let ruin come on them unawares.
And let the net that they hid ensnare
them;
let them fall in it—to their ruin.

9 Then my soul shall rejoice in the
Lord,
exulting in his deliverance.
10 All my bones shall say,
"O Lord, who is like you?
You deliver the weak
from those too strong for them,
the weak and needy from those who
despoil them."

11 Malicious witnesses rise up;
they ask me about things I do not
know.
12 They repay me evil for good;
my soul is forlorn.
13 But as for me, when they were sick,
I wore sackcloth;
I afflicted myself with fasting.
I prayed with head bowed[i] on my
bosom,

The words "shield" and "buckler" refer to the same thing. In Bible times, a shield was made of leather or metal. A soldier would carry his shield in his hand or wear it on his arm and would carry his weapon in his other hand. With his shield, the soldier could protect parts of his body not covered with armor and could stop the blows and weapons of his enemies. In this psalm, the writer uses "shield and buckler" to speak of God's protection and God's truth.

g Heb *a pit, their net*   h The word *pit* is transposed from the preceding line   i Or *My prayer turned back*

14 as though I grieved for a friend or a
      brother;
   I went about as one who laments for a
      mother,
      bowed down and in mourning.

15 But at my stumbling they gathered in
      glee,
   they gathered together against me;
   ruffians whom I did not know
      tore at me without ceasing;
16 they impiously mocked more and
      more,[j]
      gnashing at me with their teeth.

17 How long, O LORD, will you look on?
   Rescue me from their ravages,
      my life from the lions!
18 Then I will thank you in the great
      congregation;
   in the mighty throng I will praise
      you.

19 Do not let my treacherous enemies
      rejoice over me,
   or those who hate me without cause
      wink the eye.
20 For they do not speak peace,
   but they conceive deceitful words
      against those who are quiet in the
      land.
21 They open wide their mouths against
      me;
   they say, "Aha, Aha,
      our eyes have seen it."

22 You have seen, O LORD; do not be
      silent!
   O Lord, do not be far from me!
23 Wake up! Bestir yourself for my
      defense,
   for my cause, my God and my Lord!
24 Vindicate me, O LORD, my God,
   according to your righteousness,
   and do not let them rejoice over me.
25 Do not let them say to themselves,
   "Aha, we have our heart's desire."
   Do not let them say, "We have
      swallowed you[k] up."

26 Let all those who rejoice at my calamity
   be put to shame and confusion;
   let those who exalt themselves against
      me
   be clothed with shame and
      dishonor.

27 Let those who desire my vindication
   shout for joy and be glad,
   and say evermore,
   "Great is the LORD,
      who delights in the welfare of his
      servant."
28 Then my tongue shall tell of your
      righteousness
   and of your praise all day long.

Psalm 36

Human Wickedness and Divine Goodness

   To the leader. Of David,
      the servant of the LORD.

1 Transgression speaks to the wicked
   deep in their hearts;
   there is no fear of God
      before their eyes.
2 For they flatter themselves in their
      own eyes
   that their iniquity cannot be found
      out and hated.
3 The words of their mouths are
      mischief and deceit;
   they have ceased to act wisely and
      do good.
4 They plot mischief while on their
      beds;
   they are set on a way that is not
      good;
   they do not reject evil.

5 Your steadfast love, O LORD, extends to
      the heavens,
   your faithfulness to the clouds.
6 Your righteousness is like the mighty
      mountains,
   your judgments are like the great
      deep;

[j] Cn Compare Gk: Heb *like the profanest of mockers of a cake*   [k] Heb *him*

you save humans and animals alike,
O LORD.

7 How precious is your steadfast love, O
    God!
  All people may take refuge in the
    shadow of your wings.
8 They feast on the abundance of your
    house,
  and you give them drink from the
    river of your delights.
9 For with you is the fountain of life;
  in your light we see light.

10 O continue your steadfast love to those
    who know you,
  and your salvation to the upright of
    heart!
11 Do not let the foot of the arrogant
    tread on me,
  or the hand of the wicked drive me
    away.
12 There the evildoers lie prostrate;
  they are thrust down, unable to rise.

The fountain referred to here is a spring of water flowing from an opening in a hillside or valley. In the dry Bible lands, a fountain was an important source of water, so villages were often located near a fountain. Here the word "fountain" is used as a figure of speech for the power and wisdom of God as the source of life and refreshment.

Psalm 37

Exhortation to Patience and Trust
Of David.

1 Do not fret because of the wicked;
  do not be envious of wrongdoers,
2 for they will soon fade like the grass,
  and wither like the green herb.

3 Trust in the LORD, and do good;
  so you will live in the land, and
    enjoy security.
4 Take delight in the LORD,
  and he will give you the desires of
    your heart.

5 Commit your way to the LORD;
  trust in him, and he will act.
6 He will make your vindication shine
    like the light,

and the justice of your cause like the
    noonday.

7 Be still before the LORD, and wait
    patiently for him;
  do not fret over those who prosper
    in their way,
  over those who carry out evil
    devices.

8 Refrain from anger, and forsake wrath.
  Do not fret—it leads only to evil.
9 For the wicked shall be cut off,
  but those who wait for the LORD
    shall inherit the land.

10 Yet a little while, and the wicked will
    be no more;
  though you look diligently for their
    place, they will not be there.
11 But the meek shall inherit the land,
  and delight themselves in abundant
    prosperity.

12 The wicked plot against the righteous,
  and gnash their teeth at them;
13 but the LORD laughs at the wicked,
  for he sees that their day is coming.

14 The wicked draw the sword and
    bend their bows
  to bring down the poor and
    needy,

"Commit your way to the LORD; trust in him, and he will act." Psalm 37:5

to kill those who walk uprightly;
¹⁵ their sword shall enter their own heart,
and their bows shall be broken.

¹⁶ Better is a little that the righteous
person has
than the abundance of many
wicked.
¹⁷ For the arms of the wicked shall be
broken,
but the LORD upholds the righteous.

¹⁸ The LORD knows the days of the
blameless,
and their heritage will abide forever;
¹⁹ they are not put to shame in evil times,
in the days of famine they have
abundance.

²⁰ But the wicked perish,
and the enemies of the LORD are like
the glory of the pastures;
they vanish—like smoke they vanish
away.

²¹ The wicked borrow, and do not pay
back,
but the righteous are generous and
keep giving;
²² for those blessed by the LORD shall
inherit the land,
but those cursed by him shall be cut
off.

²³ Our steps[l] are made firm by the LORD,
when he delights in our[m] way;
²⁴ though we stumble,[n] we[o] shall not fall
headlong,
for the LORD holds us[p] by the hand.

²⁵ I have been young, and now am old,
yet I have not seen the righteous
forsaken
or their children begging bread.
²⁶ They are ever giving liberally and
lending,
and their children become a
blessing.

²⁷ Depart from evil, and do good;
so you shall abide forever.
²⁸ For the LORD loves justice;
he will not forsake his faithful ones.

The righteous shall be kept safe forever,
but the children of the wicked shall
be cut off.
²⁹ The righteous shall inherit the land,
and live in it forever.

³⁰ The mouths of the righteous utter
wisdom,
and their tongues speak justice.
³¹ The law of their God is in their hearts;
their steps do not slip.

³² The wicked watch for the righteous,
and seek to kill them.
³³ The LORD will not abandon them to
their power,
or let them be condemned when
they are brought to trial.

³⁴ Wait for the LORD, and keep to his way,
and he will exalt you to inherit the
land;
you will look on the destruction of
the wicked.

³⁵ I have seen the wicked oppressing,
and towering like a cedar of
Lebanon.[q]
³⁶ Again I[r] passed by, and they were no
more;
though I sought them, they could
not be found.

³⁷ Mark the blameless, and behold the
upright,
for there is posterity for the
peaceable.
³⁸ But transgressors shall be altogether
destroyed;
the posterity of the wicked shall
be cut off.

[l] Heb *A man's steps*   [m] Heb *his*   [n] Heb *he stumbles*   [o] Heb *he*   [p] Heb *him*   [q] Gk: Meaning of
Heb uncertain   [r] Gk Syr Jerome: Heb *he*

39 The salvation of the righteous is from
the LORD;
he is their refuge in the time of trouble.
40 The LORD helps them and rescues
them;
he rescues them from the wicked,
and saves them,
because they take refuge in him.

Psalm 38

A Penitent Sufferer's Plea for Healing

A Psalm of David,
for the memorial offering.

1 O LORD, do not rebuke me in your
anger,
or discipline me in your wrath.
2 For your arrows have sunk into me,
and your hand has come down on
me.

3 There is no soundness in my flesh
because of your indignation;
there is no health in my bones
because of my sin.
4 For my iniquities have gone over my
head;
they weigh like a burden too heavy
for me.

5 My wounds grow foul and fester
because of my foolishness;
6 I am utterly bowed down and prostrate;
all day long I go around mourning.
7 For my loins are filled with burning,
and there is no soundness in my
flesh.
8 I am utterly spent and crushed;
I groan because of the tumult of my
heart.

9 O Lord, all my longing is known to
you;
my sighing is not hidden from you.
10 My heart throbs, my strength fails me;
as for the light of my eyes—it also
has gone from me.
11 My friends and companions stand
aloof from my affliction,
and my neighbors stand far off.

12 Those who seek my life lay their snares;
those who seek to hurt me speak of
ruin,
and meditate treachery all day long.

13 But I am like the deaf, I do not hear;
like the mute, who cannot speak.
14 Truly, I am like one who does not
hear,
and in whose mouth is no retort.

15 But it is for you, O LORD, that I wait;
it is you, O lord my God, who will
answer.
16 For I pray, "Only do not let them
rejoice over me,
those who boast against me when
my foot slips."

17 For I am ready to fall,
and my pain is ever with me.
18 I confess my iniquity;
I am sorry for my sin.
19 Those who are my foes without cause[s]
are mighty,
and many are those who hate me
wrongfully.
20 Those who render me evil for good
are my adversaries because I follow
after good.

21 Do not forsake me, O LORD;
O my God, do not be far from me;
22 make haste to help me,
O Lord, my salvation.

Psalm 39

Prayer for Wisdom and Forgiveness

To the leader: To Je·du'thun. A Psalm of
David.

1 I said, "I will guard my ways
that I may not sin with my tongue;
I will keep a muzzle on my mouth
as long as the wicked are in my
presence."
2 I was silent and still;
I held my peace to no avail;
my distress grew worse,

s Q Ms: MT *my living foes*

³ my heart became hot within me.
While I mused, the fire burned;
then I spoke with my tongue:

⁴ "LORD, let me know my end,
and what is the measure of my days;
let me know how fleeting my life is.
⁵ You have made my days a few
handbreadths,
and my lifetime is as nothing in
your sight.
Surely everyone stands as a mere
breath.   *Sĕlah*
⁶   Surely everyone goes about like a
shadow.
Surely for nothing they are in turmoil;
they heap up, and do not know
who will gather.

⁷ "And now, O Lord, what do I wait for?
My hope is in you.
⁸ Deliver me from all my transgressions.
Do not make me the scorn of the
fool.
⁹ I am silent; I do not open my mouth,
for it is you who have done it.
¹⁰ Remove your stroke from me;
I am worn down by the blows*ᵗ* of
your hand.

¹¹ "You chastise mortals
in punishment for sin,
consuming like a moth what is dear to
them;
surely everyone is a mere breath.
Sĕlah
¹² "Hear my prayer, O LORD,
and give ear to my cry;
do not hold your peace at my tears.
For I am your passing guest,
an alien, like all my forebears.
¹³ Turn your gaze away from me, that I
may smile again,
before I depart and am no more."

Psalm 40

*Thanksgiving for Deliverance and Prayer for
Help*

To the leader. Of David. A Psalm.

> "I delight to do your will, O
> my God; your law is within
> my heart." Psalm 40:8

¹ I waited patiently for the LORD;
he inclined to me and heard my cry.
² He drew me up from the desolate pit,*ᵘ*
out of the miry bog,
and set my feet upon a rock,
making my steps secure.
³ He put a new song in my mouth,
a song of praise to our God.
Many will see and fear,
and put their trust in the LORD.

⁴ Happy are those who make
the LORD their trust,
who do not turn to the proud,
to those who go astray after false
gods.
⁵ You have multiplied, O LORD my God,
your wondrous deeds and your
thoughts toward us;
none can compare with you.
Were I to proclaim and tell of them,
they would be more than can be
counted.

⁶ Sacrifice and offering you do not
desire,
but you have given me an open ear.*ᵛ*
Burnt offering and sin offering
you have not required.
⁷ Then I said, "Here I am;
in the scroll of the book it is written
of me.*ʷ*
⁸ I delight to do your will, O my God;
your law is within my heart."

⁹ I have told the glad news of deliverance
in the great congregation;
see, I have not restrained my lips,
as you know, O LORD.
¹⁰ I have not hidden your saving help
within my heart,
I have spoken of your faithfulness
and your salvation;

ᵗ Heb *hostility*   *ᵘ* Cn: Heb *pit of tumult*   *ᵛ* Heb
ears you have dug for me   *ʷ* Meaning of Heb
uncertain

I have not concealed your steadfast
love and your faithfulness
from the great congregation.

11 Do not, O LORD, withhold
your mercy from me;
let your steadfast love and your
faithfulness
keep me safe forever.
12 For evils have encompassed me
without number;
my iniquities have overtaken me,
until I cannot see;
they are more than the hairs of my
head,
and my heart fails me.

13 Be pleased, O LORD, to deliver me;
O LORD, make haste to help me.
14 Let all those be put to shame and
confusion
who seek to snatch away my life;
let those be turned back and brought
to dishonor
who desire my hurt.
15 Let those be appalled because of their
shame
who say to me, "Aha, Aha!"

16 But may all who seek you
rejoice and be glad in you;
may those who love your salvation
say continually, "Great is the LORD!"
17 As for me, I am poor and needy,
but the Lord takes thought for me.
You are my help and my deliverer;
do not delay, O my God.

Psalm 41

*Assurance of God's Help and a Plea for
Healing*

To the leader. A Psalm of David.
1 Happy are those who consider the
poor;ˣ
the LORD delivers them in the day of
trouble.
2 The LORD protects them and keeps
them alive;
they are called happy in the land.

You do not give them up to the will
of their enemies.
3 The LORD sustains them on their
sickbed;
in their illness you heal all their
infirmities.ʸ

4 As for me, I said, "O LORD, be gracious
to me;
heal me, for I have sinned against
you."
5 My enemies wonder in malice
when I will die, and my name
perish.
6 And when they come to see me, they
utter empty words,
while their hearts gather mischief;
when they go out, they tell it
abroad.
7 All who hate me whisper together
about me;
they imagine the worst for me.

8 They think that a deadly thing has
fastened on me,
that I will not rise again from where
I lie.
9 Even my bosom friend in whom I
trusted,
who ate of my bread, has lifted the
heel against me.
10 But you, O LORD, be gracious to me,
and raise me up, that I may repay
them.

11 By this I know that you are pleased
with me;
because my enemy has not
triumphed over me.
12 But you have upheld me because of
my integrity,
and set me in your presence forever.

13 Blessed be the LORD, the God of
Israel,
from everlasting to everlasting.
Amen and Amen.

ˣ Or *weak*   ʸ Heb *you change all his bed*

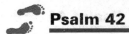

BOOK II
(Psalms 42–72)

Psalm 42

Longing for God and His Help in Distress

To the leader.
A Mas´kil of the Kō´ra·hītes.

[1] As a deer longs for flowing streams,
  so my soul longs for you, O God.
[2] My soul thirsts for God,
  for the living God.
When shall I come and behold
  the face of God?
[3] My tears have been my food
  day and night,
while people say to me continually,
  "Where is your God?"

[4] These things I remember,
  as I pour out my soul:
how I went with the throng,[z]
  and led them in procession to the
  house of God,
with glad shouts and songs of
  thanksgiving,
  a multitude keeping festival.
[5] Why are you cast down, O my soul,
  and why are you disquieted within
  me?
Hope in God; for I shall again praise
  him,
  my help [6]and my God.

My soul is cast down within me;
  therefore I remember you
from the land of Jordan and of
  Hermon,
  from Mount Mī´zar.
[7] Deep calls to deep
  at the thunder of your cataracts;
all your waves and your billows
  have gone over me.
[8] By day the LORD commands his
  steadfast love,
  and at night his song is with me,
  a prayer to the God of my life.

[9] I say to God, my rock,
  "Why have you forgotten me?

Why must I walk about mournfully
  because the enemy oppresses me?"
[10] As with a deadly wound in my body,
  my adversaries taunt me,
while they say to me continually,
  "Where is your God?"

[11] Why are you cast down, O my soul,
  and why are you disquieted within
  me?
Hope in God; for I shall again praise
  him,
  my help and my God.

Psalm 43

Prayer to God in Time of Trouble

[1] Vindicate me, O God, and defend my
  cause
  against an ungodly people;
from those who are deceitful and unjust
  deliver me!
[2] For you are the God in whom I take
  refuge;
  why have you cast me off?
Why must I walk about mournfully
  because of the oppression of the
  enemy?

[3] O send out your light and your truth;
  let them lead me;
let them bring me to your holy hill
  and to your dwelling.
[4] Then I will go to the altar of God,
  to God my exceeding joy;
and I will praise you with the harp,
  O God, my God.

[5] Why are you cast down, O my soul,
  and why are you disquieted within me?

"Deep" is a poetic term meaning ocean. The deepness of the ocean is used as a substitute word for the ocean itself.

---

[z] Meaning of Heb uncertain

Hope in God; for I shall again praise
  him,
  my help and my God.

Psalm 44

National Lament and Prayer for Help

To the leader.
Of the Kō′ra·hītes. A Mas′kil.

1 We have heard with our ears, O God,
  our ancestors have told us,
what deeds you performed in their
  days,
  in the days of old:
2 you with your own hand drove out the
  nations,
  but them you planted;
you afflicted the peoples,
  but them you set free;
3 for not by their own sword did they
  win the land,
  nor did their own arm give them
  victory;
but your right hand, and your arm,
  and the light of your countenance,
  for you delighted in them.

4 You are my King and my God;
  you command*ᵃ* victories for Jacob.
5 Through you we push down our foes;
  through your name we tread down
  our assailants.
6 For not in my bow do I trust,
  nor can my sword save me.
7 But you have saved us from our foes,
  and have put to confusion those
  who hate us.
8 In God we have boasted continually,
  and we will give thanks to your
  name forever.   *Sēlah*

9 Yet you have rejected us and abased
  us,
  and have not gone out with our
  armies.
10 You made us turn back from the foe,
  and our enemies have gotten spoil.
11 You have made us like sheep for
  slaughter,

and have scattered us among the
  nations.
12 You have sold your people for a trifle,
  demanding no high price for them.

13 You have made us the taunt of our
  neighbors,
  the derision and scorn of those
  around us.
14 You have made us a byword among
  the nations,
  a laughingstock*ᵇ* among the peoples.
15 All day long my disgrace is before me,
  and shame has covered my face
16 at the words of the taunters and
  revilers,
  at the sight of the enemy and the
  avenger.

17 All this has come upon us,
  yet we have not forgotten you,
  or been false to your covenant.
18 Our heart has not turned back,
  nor have our steps departed from
  your way,
19 yet you have broken us in the haunt
  of jackals,
  and covered us with deep darkness.

20 If we had forgotten the name of our
  God,
  or spread out our hands to a strange
  god,
21 would not God discover this?
  For he knows the secrets of the
  heart.
22 Because of you we are being killed
  all day long,
  and accounted as sheep for the
  slaughter.

23 Rouse yourself! Why do you sleep,
  O Lord?
  Awake, do not cast us off forever!
24 Why do you hide your face?
  Why do you forget our affliction
  and oppression?

ᵃ Gk Syr: Heb *You are my King, O God; command*
ᵇ Heb *a shaking of the head*

25 For we sink down to the dust;
  our bodies cling to the ground.
26 Rise up, come to our help.
  Redeem us for the sake of your
    steadfast love.

Psalm 45

Ode for a Royal Wedding

To the leader: according to Lilies.
Of the Kō′ra·hītes. A Mas′kil.
    A love song.
1 My heart overflows with a goodly
    theme;
  I address my verses to the king;
  my tongue is like the pen of a
    ready scribe.

2 You are the most handsome of men;
  grace is poured upon your lips;
  therefore God has blessed you
    forever.
3 Gird your sword on your thigh, O
    mighty one,
  in your glory and majesty.

4 In your majesty ride on victoriously
  for the cause of truth and to
    defend[c] the right;
  let your right hand teach you
    dread deeds.
5 Your arrows are sharp
  in the heart of the king's enemies;
  the peoples fall under you.

6 Your throne, O God,[d] endures
    forever and ever.
  Your royal scepter is a scepter of
    equity;
7 you love righteousness and hate
    wickedness.
  Therefore God, your God, has
    anointed you
  with the oil of gladness beyond
    your companions;
8 your robes are all fragrant with
    myrrh and aloes and cassia.
  From ivory palaces stringed
    instruments make you glad;

9 daughters of kings are among
  your ladies of honor;
  at your right hand stands the
    queen in gold of O̅phir.

10 Hear, O daughter, consider and
    incline your ear;
  forget your people and your
    father's house,
11 and the king will desire your
    beauty.
  Since he is your lord, bow to him;
12 the people[e] of Tyre will seek your
    favor with gifts,
  the richest of the people 13with all
    kinds of wealth.

The princess is decked in her
  chamber with gold-woven
    robes;[f]
14 in many-colored robes she is led
    to the king;
  behind her the virgins, her
    companions, follow.
15 With joy and gladness they are led
    along
  as they enter the palace of the
    king.

16 In the place of ancestors you, O
    king,[g] shall have sons;
  you will make them princes in all
    the earth.
17 I will cause your name to be
    celebrated in all generations;
  therefore the peoples will praise
    you forever and ever.

"God is our refuge and
strength, a very present help
in trouble." Psalm 46:1

[c] Cn: Heb *and the meekness of*   [d] Or *Your throne is
a throne of God, it*   [e] Heb *daughter*   [f] Or *people.*
13*All glorious is the princess within, gold embroidery is
her clothing*   [g] Heb lacks *O king*

Psalm 46

God's Defense of His City and People

To the leader. Of the Kó·ra·hītes.
According to Al´a·moth. A Song.

¹ God is our refuge and strength,
a very present[h] help in trouble.
² Therefore we will not fear, though the
earth should change,
though the mountains shake in the
heart of the sea;
³ though its waters roar and foam,
though the mountains tremble with
its tumult.　　　*Sĕ´lah*

⁴ There is a river whose streams make
glad the city of God,
the holy habitation of the Most
High.
⁵ God is in the midst of the city;[i] it shall
not be moved;
God will help it when the morning
dawns.
⁶ The nations are in an uproar, the
kingdoms totter;
he utters his voice, the earth melts.
⁷ The LORD of hosts is with us;
the God of Jacob is our refuge.[j]
　　　Sĕ´lah

⁸ Come, behold the works of the LORD;
see what desolations he has brought
on the earth.
⁹ He makes wars cease to the end of the
earth;
he breaks the bow, and shatters the
spear;
he burns the shields with fire.
¹⁰ "Be still, and know that I am God!
I am exalted among the nations,
I am exalted in the earth."

Take a few moments to be
completely still and silent.
Try not to move or talk. Use
this time to think of the
greatness and goodness of God! See
if you can spend a few moments
each day being still before God.

¹¹ The LORD of hosts is with us;
the God of Jacob is our refuge.[j]
　　　Sĕ´lah

"Clap your hands, all you
peoples; shout to God
with loud songs of joy."
Psalm 47:1

Psalm 47

God's Rule over the Nations

To the leader. Of the Kó·ra·hītes. A Psalm.

¹ Clap your hands, all you peoples;
shout to God with loud songs of joy.
² For the LORD, the Most High, is
awesome,
a great king over all the earth.
³ He subdued peoples under us,
and nations under our feet.
⁴ He chose our heritage for us,
the pride of Jacob whom he loves.
　　　Sĕ´lah

⁵ God has gone up with a shout,
the LORD with the sound of a
trumpet.
⁶ Sing praises to God, sing praises;
sing praises to our King, sing praises.
⁷ For God is the king of all the earth;
sing praises with a psalm.[k]

⁸ God is king over the nations;
God sits on his holy throne.
⁹ The princes of the peoples gather
as the people of the God of
Abraham.
For the shields of the earth belong to
God;
he is highly exalted.

Psalm 48

The Glory and Strength of Zion

A Song. A Psalm of the Kó·ra·hītes.

¹ Great is the LORD and greatly to be
praised
in the city of our God.

---

[h] Or *well proved*　　[i] Heb *of it*　　[j] Or *fortress*
[k] Heb *Maskil*

His holy mountain, ²beautiful in
elevation,
is the joy of all the earth,
Mount Zion, in the far north,
the city of the great King.
³ Within its citadels God
has shown himself a sure defense.

⁴ Then the kings assembled,
they came on together.
⁵ As soon as they saw it, they were
astounded;
they were in panic, they took to flight;
⁶ trembling took hold of them there,
pains as of a woman in labor,
⁷ as when an east wind shatters
the ships of Tarʹshish.
⁸ As we have heard, so have we seen
in the city of the LORD of hosts,
in the city of our God,
which God establishes forever.

Sēʹlah

⁹ We ponder your steadfast love, O God,
in the midst of your temple.
¹⁰ Your name, O God, like your praise,
reaches to the ends of the earth.
Your right hand is filled with victory.
¹¹ Let Mount Zion be glad,
let the towns[l] of Judah rejoice
because of your judgments.

¹² Walk about Zion, go all around it,
count its towers,
¹³ consider well its ramparts;
go through its citadels,
that you may tell the next generation
¹³ that this is God,
our God forever and ever.
He will be our guide forever.

Psalm 49

The Folly of Trust in Riches

To the leader. Of the Koʹra·hītes. A Psalm.
¹ Hear this, all you peoples;
give ear, all inhabitants of the world,
² both low and high,
rich and poor together.

A citadel is a strong
building or place of
safety within a city.
Citadels were sometimes
attached to a palace or temple
for the purpose of defense.

³ My mouth shall speak wisdom;
the meditation of my heart shall be
understanding.
⁴ I will incline my ear to a proverb;
I will solve my riddle to the music
of the harp.

⁵ Why should I fear in times of trouble,
when the iniquity of my persecutors
surrounds me,
⁶ those who trust in their wealth
and boast of the abundance of their
riches?
⁷ Truly, no ransom avails for one's life,[m]
there is no price one can give to
God for it.
⁸ For the ransom of life is costly,
and can never suffice,
⁹ that one should live on forever
and never see the grave.[n]

¹⁰ When we look at the wise, they die;
fool and dolt perish together
and leave their wealth to others.
¹¹ Their graves[o] are their homes forever,
their dwelling places to all generations,
though they named lands their own.
¹² Mortals cannot abide in their pomp;
they are like the animals that perish.

¹³ Such is the fate of the foolhardy,
the end of those[p] who are pleased
with their lot.   *Sēʹlah*
¹⁴ Like sheep they are appointed for
Shēʹōl;
Death shall be their shepherd;

---

[l] Heb *daughters*   [m] Another reading is *no one can
ransom a brother*   [n] Heb *the pit*   [o] Gk Syr
Compare Tg: Heb *their inward* (thought)   [p] Tg:
Heb *after them*   [q] Cn: Heb *the upright shall have
dominion over them in the morning*

straight to the grave they descend,^{q}
  and their form shall waste away;
  Shĕ´ōl shall be their home.^{r}
15 But God will ransom my soul from the
    power of Shĕ´ōl,
  for he will receive me.   *Sĕ´lah*

16 Do not be afraid when some become
    rich,
  when the wealth of their houses
    increases.
17 For when they die they will carry
    nothing away;
  their wealth will not go down after
    them.
18 Though in their lifetime they count
    themselves happy
  —for you are praised when you do
    well for yourself—
19 they^s will go to the company of their
    ancestors,
  who will never again see the light.
20 Mortals cannot abide in their pomp;
  they are like the animals that
    perish.

Psalm 50

The Acceptable Sacrifice

A Psalm of Ā´saph.
1 The mighty one, God the Lord,
  speaks and summons the earth
  from the rising of the sun to its
    setting.
2 Out of Zion, the perfection of beauty,
  God shines forth.

3 Our God comes and does not keep
    silence,
  before him is a devouring fire,
  and a mighty tempest all around
    him.
4 He calls to the heavens above
  and to the earth, that he may judge
    his people:
5 "Gather to me my faithful ones,
  who made a covenant with me by
    sacrifice!"
6 The heavens declare his righteousness,
  for God himself is judge.   *Sĕ´lah*

7 "Hear, O my people, and I will speak,
  O Israel, I will testify against you.
  I am God, your God.
8 Not for your sacrifices do I rebuke you;
  your burnt offerings are continually
    before me.
9 I will not accept a bull from your
    house,
  or goats from your folds.
10 For every wild animal of the forest is
    mine,
  the cattle on a thousand hills.
11 I know all the birds of the air,^{t}
  and all that moves in the field is
    mine.

12 "If I were hungry, I would not tell you,
  for the world and all that is in it is
    mine.
13 Do I eat the flesh of bulls,
  or drink the blood of goats?
14 Offer to God a sacrifice of
    thanksgiving,^{u}
  and pay your vows to the Most High.
15 Call on me in the day of trouble;
  I will deliver you, and you shall
    glorify me."

16 But to the wicked God says:
  "What right have you to recite my
    statutes,
  or take my covenant on your lips?
17 For you hate discipline,
  and you cast my words behind you.
18 You make friends with a thief when
    you see one,
  and you keep company with
    adulterers.

19 "You give your mouth free rein for
    evil,
  and your tongue frames deceit.
20 You sit and speak against your kin;
  you slander your own mother's
    child.

^{r} Meaning of Heb uncertain ^{s} Cn: Heb *you* ^{t} Gk
Syr Tg: Heb *mountains* ^{u} Or *make thanksgiving
your sacrifice to God*

21 These things you have done and I have
   been silent;
   you thought that I was one just like
   yourself.
   But now I rebuke you, and lay the
   charge before you.

22 "Mark this, then, you who forget God,
   or I will tear you apart, and there
   will be no one to deliver.
23 Those who bring thanksgiving as their
   sacrifice honor me;
   to those who go the right way[v]
   I will show the salvation of God."

Psalm 51

Prayer for Cleansing and Pardon

To the leader. A Psalm of David, when
   the prophet Nathan came to him,
   after he had gone in to Bath·she′ba.

1 Have mercy on me, O God,
   according to your steadfast love;
   according to your abundant mercy
   blot out my transgressions.
2 Wash me thoroughly from my iniquity,
   and cleanse me from my sin.

3 For I know my transgressions,
   and my sin is ever before me.
4 Against you, you alone, have I sinned,
   and done what is evil in your sight,
   so that you are justified in your
   sentence
   and blameless when you pass
   judgment.
5 Indeed, I was born guilty,
   a sinner when my mother conceived
   me.

6 You desire truth in the inward being;[w]
   therefore teach me wisdom in my
   secret heart.
7 Purge me with hyssop, and I shall be
   clean;
   wash me, and I shall be whiter than
   snow.
8 Let me hear joy and gladness;
   let the bones that you have crushed
   rejoice.

9 Hide your face from my sins,
   and blot out all my iniquities.

10 Create in me a clean heart, O God,
   and put a new and right[x] spirit
   within me.
11 Do not cast me away from your
   presence,
   and do not take your holy spirit
   from me.
12 Restore to me the joy of your salvation,
   and sustain in me a willing[y] spirit.

13 Then I will teach transgressors your
   ways,
   and sinners will return to you.
14 Deliver me from bloodshed, O God,
   O God of my salvation,
   and my tongue will sing aloud of
   your deliverance.

15 O Lord, open my lips,
   and my mouth will declare your
   praise.
16 For you have no delight in sacrifice;
   if I were to give a burnt offering, you
   would not be pleased.
17 The sacrifice acceptable to God[z] is a
   broken spirit;
   a broken and contrite heart, O God,
   you will not despise.

Psalm 51 is thought to be a
prayer of David after he
sinned against God. (Read
the story in 2 Samuel
11–12.) In this psalm, David prayed to
God for forgiveness, asking God to
clean his heart and give him a new
spirit. When we do something
wrong, we also need to ask God for
forgiveness. If there is someone you
have hurt with your words or your
actions, apologize to that person and
ask him or her for forgiveness. Just
as David did, pray to God and ask for
a clean heart.

---

v Heb *who set a way*   w Meaning of Heb uncertain
x Or *steadfast*   y Or *generous*   z Or *My sacrifice,
O God,*

"I will thank you forever, because of what you have done. In the presence of the faithful I will proclaim your name, for it is good."
Psalm 52:9

18 Do good to Zion in your good
  pleasure;
  rebuild the walls of Jerusalem,
19 then you will delight in right sacrifices,
  in burnt offerings and whole burnt
    offerings;
  then bulls will be offered on your
    altar.

Psalm 52

Judgment on the Deceitful

To the leader. A Mas´kil of David, when
  Dō´eg the Ē´dom·īte came to Saul
  and said to him, "David has come to
  the house of A·him´e·lech."
1 Why do you boast, O mighty one,
  of mischief done against the godly?*a*
  All day long 2you are plotting
    destruction.
  Your tongue is like a sharp razor,
  you worker of treachery.
3 You love evil more than good,
  and lying more than speaking the
    truth.   *Sē´lah*
4 You love all words that devour,
  O deceitful tongue.

5 But God will break you down forever;
  he will snatch and tear you from
    your tent;
  he will uproot you from the land of
    the living.   *Sē´lah*
6 The righteous will see, and fear,
  and will laugh at the evildoer,*b*
    saying,
7 "See the one who would not take
    refuge in God,
  but trusted in abundant riches,
  and sought refuge in wealth!"*c*

8 But I am like a green olive tree
  in the house of God.
  I trust in the steadfast love of God
    forever and ever.
9 I will thank you forever,
  because of what you have done.
  In the presence of the faithful
  I will proclaim*d* your name, for it is
    good.

Psalm 53

Denunciation of Godlessness

To the leader: according to Mā´ha·lath.
  A Mas´kil of David.
1 Fools say in their hearts, "There is no
    God."
  They are corrupt, they commit
    abominable acts;
  there is no one who does good.

2 God looks down from heaven on
    humankind
  to see if there are any who are wise,
  who seek after God.

3 They have all fallen away, they are all
    alike perverse;
  there is no one who does good,
  no, not one.

4 Have they no knowledge, those
    evildoers,
  who eat up my people as they eat
    bread,
  and do not call upon God?

5 There they shall be in great terror,
  in terror such as has not been.
  For God will scatter the bones of the
    ungodly;*e*
  they will be put to shame,*f* for God
    has rejected them.

6 O that deliverance for Israel would
    come from Zion!

a Cn Compare Syr: Heb *the kindness of God*   *b* Heb
him   *c* Syr Tg: Heb *in his destruction*   *d* Cn: Heb
wait for   *e* Cn Compare Gk Syr: Heb *him who
encamps against you*   *f* Gk: Heb *you have put
(them) to shame*

When God restores the fortunes
  of his people,
Jacob will rejoice; Israel will be glad.

Psalm 54

Prayer for Vindication

To the leader: with stringed instruments. A Mas′kil of David, when the
Ziph′ites went and told Saul, "David is
  in hiding among us."
[1] Save me, O God, by your name,
  and vindicate me by your might.
[2] Hear my prayer, O God;
  give ear to the words of my
    mouth.

[3] For the insolent have risen against
    me,
  the ruthless seek my life;
  they do not set God before them.
                                  Selah

[4] But surely, God is my helper;
  the Lord is the upholder of[g] my
    life.
[5] He will repay my enemies for their
    evil.
  In your faithfulness, put an end to
    them.

[6] With a freewill offering I will
    sacrifice to you;
  I will give thanks to your name, O
    Lord, for it is good.
[7] For he has delivered me from every
    trouble,
  and my eye has looked in triumph
    on my enemies.

Psalm 55

Complaint about a Friend's Treachery

To the leader:
  with stringed instruments.
  A Mas′kil of David.
[1] Give ear to my prayer, O God;
  do not hide yourself from my
    supplication.

[2] Attend to me, and answer me;
  I am troubled in my complaint.
I am distraught [3]by the noise of the
    enemy,
  because of the clamor of the
    wicked.
For they bring[h] trouble upon me,
  and in anger they cherish enmity
    against me.

[4] My heart is in anguish within me,
  the terrors of death have fallen
    upon me.
[5] Fear and trembling come upon me,
  and horror overwhelms me.
[6] And I say, "O that I had wings like a
    dove!
  I would fly away and be at rest;
[7] truly, I would flee far away;
  I would lodge in the wilderness;
                                  Selah
[8] I would hurry to find a shelter for
    myself
  from the raging wind and tempest."

[9] Confuse, O Lord, confound their
    speech;
  for I see violence and strife in the
    city.
[10] Day and night they go around it
    on its walls,
  and iniquity and trouble are within
    it;
[11] ruin is in its midst;
  oppression and fraud
    do not depart from its
      marketplace.

[12] It is not enemies who taunt me—
  I could bear that;
  it is not adversaries who deal
    insolently with me—
  I could hide from them.
[13] But it is you, my equal,
  my companion, my familiar
    friend,

g Gk Syr Jerome: Heb *is of those who uphold* or *is
with those who uphold*   h Cn Compare Gk: Heb
they cause to totter

¹⁴ with whom I kept pleasant company;
    we walked in the house of God with
      the throng.
¹⁵ Let death come upon them;
    let them go down alive to Shē′ōl;
    for evil is in their homes and in their
      hearts.

¹⁶ But I call upon God,
    and the LORD will save me.
¹⁷ Evening and morning and at noon
    I utter my complaint and moan,
    and he will hear my voice.
¹⁸ He will redeem me unharmed
    from the battle that I wage,
    for many are arrayed against me.
¹⁹ God, who is enthroned from of old,
                Sē′lah
    will hear, and will humble them—
because they do not change,
    and do not fear God.

²⁰ My companion laid hands on a friend
    and violated a covenant with me^i
²¹ with speech smoother than butter,
    but with a heart set on war;
with words that were softer than oil,
    but in fact were drawn swords.

²² Cast your burden^j on the LORD,
    and he will sustain you;
he will never permit
    the righteous to be moved.

²³ But you, O God, will cast them down
    into the lowest pit;
the bloodthirsty and treacherous
    shall not live out half their days.
But I will trust in you.

Psalm 56

Trust in God under Persecution

To the leader: according to The Dove on
Far-off Terebinths. Of David. A Mik′tam,
when the Phi·lis′tines seized him in Gath.
¹ Be gracious to me, O God, for people
    trample on me;
    all day long foes oppress me;

² my enemies trample on me all day
      long,
    for many fight against me.
O Most High, ³when I am afraid,
    I put my trust in you.
⁴ In God, whose word I praise,
    in God I trust; I am not afraid;
    what can flesh do to me?

⁵ All day long they seek to injure my
      cause;
    all their thoughts are against me for
      evil.
⁶ They stir up strife, they lurk,
    they watch my steps.
As they hoped to have my life,
⁷   so repay^k them for their crime;
    in wrath cast down the peoples, O
      God!

⁸ You have kept count of my tossings;
    put my tears in your bottle.
    Are they not in your record?
⁹ Then my enemies will retreat
    in the day when I call.
    This I know, that^l God is for me.
¹⁰ In God, whose word I praise,
    in the LORD, whose word I praise,
¹¹ in God I trust; I am not afraid.
    What can a mere mortal do to me?

¹² My vows to you I must perform, O
      God;
    I will render thank offerings to you.
¹³ For you have delivered my soul from
      death,
    and my feet from falling,
so that I may walk before God
    in the light of life.

Psalm 57

Praise and Assurance under Persecution

To the leader: Do Not Destroy.
Of David. A Mik′tam, when he fled
    from Saul, in the cave.
¹ Be merciful to me, O God, be
      merciful to me,
    for in you my soul takes refuge;

^i Heb lacks *with me*   ^j Or *Cast what he has given
you*

in the shadow of your wings I will take
refuge,
until the destroying storms pass by.
2 I cry to God Most High,
to God who fulfills his purpose for
me.
3 He will send from heaven and save
me,
he will put to shame those who
trample on me. *Sēlah*

God will send forth his steadfast love
and his faithfulness.

4 I lie down among lions
that greedily devour[m] human prey;
their teeth are spears and arrows,
their tongues sharp swords.

5 Be exalted, O God, above the heavens.
Let your glory be over all the earth.

6 They set a net for my steps;
my soul was bowed down.
They dug a pit in my path,
but they have fallen into it
themselves. *Sēlah*
7 My heart is steadfast, O God,
my heart is steadfast.
I will sing and make melody.
8 Awake, my soul!
Awake, O harp and lyre!
I will awake the dawn.
9 I will give thanks to you, O Lord,
among the peoples;
I will sing praises to you among the
nations.
10 For your steadfast love is as high as the
heavens;
your faithfulness extends to the
clouds.

11 Be exalted, O God, above the heavens.
Let your glory be over all the earth.

Psalm 58

Prayer for Vengeance

To the leader: Do Not Destroy.
Of David. A Mik´tam.

1 Do you indeed decree what is right,
you gods?[n]
Do you judge people fairly?
2 No, in your hearts you devise wrongs;
your hands deal out violence on
earth.

3 The wicked go astray from the womb;
they err from their birth, speaking lies.
4 They have venom like the venom of a
serpent,
like the deaf adder that stops its ear,
5 so that it does not hear the voice of
charmers
or of the cunning enchanter.

6 O God, break the teeth in their
mouths;
tear out the fangs of the young lions,
O Lord!
7 Let them vanish like water that runs
away;
like grass let them be trodden down[o]
and wither.
8 Let them be like the snail that dissolves
into slime;
like the untimely birth that never
sees the sun.
9 Sooner than your pots can feel the heat
of thorns,
whether green or ablaze, may he
sweep them away!

10 The righteous will rejoice when they
see vengeance done;
they will bathe their feet in the
blood of the wicked.
11 People will say, "Surely there is a
reward for the righteous;

"I will give thanks to you, O Lord,
among the peoples; I will sing
praises to you among the nations.
For your steadfast love is
as high as the heavens;
your faithfulness extends to
the clouds." Psalm 57:9–10

---

[m] Cn: Heb *are aflame for*   [n] Or *mighty lords*
[o] Cn: Meaning of Heb uncertain

"I will sing of your might;
I will sing aloud of your
steadfast love in the
morning." Psalm 59:16*a*

surely there is a God who judges on
 earth."

Psalm 59

Prayer for Deliverance from Enemies

To the leader: Do Not Destroy.
Of David. A Mik´tam, when Saul
ordered his house to be watched in
 order to kill him.

¹ Deliver me from my enemies, O my
 God;
  protect me from those who rise up
   against me.
² Deliver me from those who work evil;
  from the bloodthirsty save me.

³ Even now they lie in wait for my life;
  the mighty stir up strife against me.
 For no transgression or sin of mine, O
  LORD,
⁴   for no fault of mine, they run and
   make ready.

 Rouse yourself, come to my help and
  see!
⁵ You, LORD God of hosts, are God of
  Israel.
 Awake to punish all the nations;
  spare none of those who
   treacherously plot evil.   *Se´lah*

⁶ Each evening they come back,
  howling like dogs
  and prowling about the city.
⁷ There they are, bellowing with their
  mouths,
  with sharp words[p] on their lips—
  for "Who," they think,[q] "will hear
   us?"

⁸ But you laugh at them, O LORD;
  you hold all the nations in derision.
⁹ O my strength, I will watch for you;
  for you, O God, are my fortress.

¹⁰ My God in his steadfast love will meet
  me;
  my God will let me look in triumph
   on my enemies.

¹¹ Do not kill them, or my people may
  forget;
  make them totter by your power,
   and bring them down,
   O Lord, our shield.
¹² For the sin of their mouths, the words
  of their lips,
  let them be trapped in their pride.
 For the cursing and lies that they utter,
¹³   consume them in wrath;
  consume them until they are no more.
 Then it will be known to the ends of
   the earth
  that God rules over Jacob.   *Se´lah*

¹⁴ Each evening they come back,
  howling like dogs
  and prowling about the city.
¹⁵ They roam about for food,
  and growl if they do not get their fill.

¹⁶ But I will sing of your might;
  I will sing aloud of your steadfast
   love in the morning.
 For you have been a fortress for me
  and a refuge in the day of my
   distress.
¹⁷ O my strength, I will sing praises to
  you,
  for you, O God, are my fortress,
  the God who shows me steadfast love.

Psalm 60

Prayer for National Victory after Defeat

To the leader: according to the Lily of the
 Covenant. A Mik´tam of David; for
 instruction; when he struggled with
  Ar´am-nā·ha·rā´im and with
  Ar´am-zō´bah, and when Jō´ab
 on his return killed twelve thousand
  Ē´dom·ites in the Valley of Salt.

¹ O God, you have rejected us, broken
  our defenses;

---

p Heb *with swords*   *q* Heb lacks *they think*

you have been angry; now restore
us!

2 You have caused the land to quake;
you have torn it open;
repair the cracks in it, for it is
tottering.

3 You have made your people suffer hard
things;
you have given us wine to drink that
made us reel.

4 You have set up a banner for those
who fear you,
to rally to it out of bowshot.[r]
Sēlah

5 Give victory with your right hand, and
answer us,[s]
so that those whom you love may
be rescued.

6 God has promised in his sanctuary:[t]
"With exultation I will divide up
Shē´chem,
and portion out the Vale of
Suc´coth.

7 Gil´e·ad is mine, and Ma·nas´seh is
mine;
E´phra·im is my helmet;
Judah is my scepter.

8 Mō´ab is my washbasin;
on E´dom I hurl my shoe;
over Phi·lis´ti·a I shout in triumph."

9 Who will bring me to the fortified city?
Who will lead me to E´dom?

10 Have you not rejected us, O God?
You do not go out, O God, with our
armies.

11 O grant us help against the foe,
for human help is worthless.

12 With God we shall do valiantly;
it is he who will tread down our foes.

Psalm 61

Assurance of God's Protection

To the leader: with stringed instruments.
Of David.

1 Hear my cry, O God;
listen to my prayer.

2 From the end of the earth I call to you,
when my heart is faint.

Lead me to the rock
that is higher than I;

3 for you are my refuge,
a strong tower against the enemy.

4 Let me abide in your tent forever,
find refuge under the shelter of your
wings. *Sēlah*

5 For you, O God, have heard my vows;
you have given me the heritage of
those who fear your name.

6 Prolong the life of the king;
may his years endure to all
generations!

7 May he be enthroned forever before
God;
appoint steadfast love and
faithfulness to watch over him!

8 So I will always sing praises to your
name,
as I pay my vows day after day.

In Psalm 61, there are many words that describe God: refuge, tower, rock, and shelter. These words help us to understand that God is strong and powerful and that God wants to protect us. We can always cry out to God when we are afraid or in need of help.

Psalm 62

Song of Trust in God Alone

To the leader: according to Je·dū´thun.
A Psalm of David.

1 For God alone my soul waits in
silence;
from him comes my salvation.

2 He alone is my rock and my salvation,
my fortress; I shall never be shaken.

[r] Gk Syr Jerome: Heb *because of the truth*
[s] Another reading is *me*   [t] Or *by his holiness*

3 How long will you assail a person,
 will you batter your victim, all of
 you,
 as you would a leaning wall, a
 tottering fence?
4 Their only plan is to bring down a
 person of prominence.
 They take pleasure in falsehood;
they bless with their mouths,
 but inwardly they curse.   *Sĕʻlah*

5 For God alone my soul waits in silence,
 for my hope is from him.
6 He alone is my rock and my salvation,
 my fortress; I shall not be shaken.
7 On God rests my deliverance and my
 honor;
 my mighty rock, my refuge is in
 God.

8 Trust in him at all times, O people;
 pour out your heart before him;
 God is a refuge for us.   *Sĕʻlah*

9 Those of low estate are but a breath,
 those of high estate are a delusion;
in the balances they go up;
 they are together lighter than a
 breath.
10 Put no confidence in extortion,
 and set no vain hopes on robbery;
 if riches increase, do not set your
 heart on them.

11 Once God has spoken;
 twice have I heard this:
that power belongs to God,
12   and steadfast love belongs to you, O
 Lord.
 For you repay to all
 according to their work.

Psalm 63

Comfort and Assurance in God's Presence

A Psalm of David, when he
was in the Wilderness of Judah.
1 O God, you are my God, I seek you,
 my soul thirsts for you;

my flesh faints for you,
 as in a dry and weary land where
 there is no water.
2 So I have looked upon you in the
 sanctuary,
 beholding your power and glory.
3 Because your steadfast love is better
 than life,
 my lips will praise you.
4 So I will bless you as long as I live;
 I will lift up my hands and call on
 your name.

5 My soul is satisfied as with a rich
 feast,[u]
 and my mouth praises you with
 joyful lips
6 when I think of you on my bed,
 and meditate on you in the watches
 of the night;
7 for you have been my help,
 and in the shadow of your wings I
 sing for joy.
8 My soul clings to you;
 your right hand upholds me.

9 But those who seek to destroy my life
 shall go down into the depths of the
 earth;
10 they shall be given over to the power
 of the sword,
 they shall be prey for jackals.
11 But the king shall rejoice in God;
 all who swear by him shall exult,
 for the mouths of liars will be
 stopped.

Psalm 64

Prayer for Protection from Enemies

To the leader. A Psalm of David.
1 Hear my voice, O God, in my
 complaint;
 preserve my life from the dread
 enemy.
2 Hide me from the secret plots of the
 wicked,
 from the scheming of evildoers,

u Heb *with fat and fatness*

³ who whet their tongues like swords,
who aim bitter words like arrows,
⁴ shooting from ambush at the blameless;
they shoot suddenly and without
fear.
⁵ They hold fast to their evil purpose;
they talk of laying snares secretly,
thinking, "Who can see us?ᵛ
⁶ Who can search out our crimes?ʷ
We have thought out a cunningly
conceived plot."
For the human heart and mind are
deep.

⁷ But God will shoot his arrow at them;
they will be wounded suddenly.
⁸ Because of their tongue he will bring
them to ruin;ˣ
all who see them will shake with
horror.
⁹ Then everyone will fear;
they will tell what God has brought
about,
and ponder what he has done.

¹⁰ Let the righteous rejoice in the LORD
and take refuge in him.
Let all the upright in heart glory.

Psalm 65

Thanksgiving for Earth's Bounty

To the leader. A Psalm of David. A Song.
¹ Praise is due to you,
O God, in Zion;
and to you shall vows be performed,
² O you who answer prayer!
To you all flesh shall come.
³ When deeds of iniquity overwhelm us,
you forgive our transgressions.
⁴ Happy are those whom you choose
and bring near
to live in your courts.
We shall be satisfied with the goodness
of your house,
your holy temple.

⁵ By awesome deeds you answer us with
deliverance,

O God of our salvation;
you are the hope of all the ends of the
earth
and of the farthest seas.
⁶ By yourʸ strength you established the
mountains;
you are girded with might.
⁷ You silence the roaring of the seas,
the roaring of their waves,
the tumult of the peoples.
⁸ Those who live at earth's farthest
bounds are awed by your signs;
you make the gateways of the morning
and the evening shout for joy.

⁹ You visit the earth and water it,
you greatly enrich it;
the river of God is full of water;
you provide the people with grain,
for so you have prepared it.
¹⁰ You water its furrows abundantly,
settling its ridges,
softening it with showers,
and blessing its growth.
¹¹ You crown the year with your bounty;
your wagon tracks overflow with
richness.
¹² The pastures of the wilderness
overflow,
the hills gird themselves with joy,
¹³ the meadows clothe themselves with
flocks,
the valleys deck themselves with
grain,
they shout and sing together for joy.

Psalm 66

Praise for God's Goodness to Israel

To the leader. A Song. A Psalm.
¹ Make a joyful noise to God, all the
earth;
² sing the glory of his name;
give to him glorious praise.
³ Say to God, "How awesome are your
deeds!

ᵛ Syr: Heb *them*   ʷ Cn: Heb *They search out crimes*
ˣ Cn: Heb *They will bring him to ruin, their tongue
being against them*   ʸ Gk Jerome: Heb *his*

"Make a joyful noise to God, all the earth; sing the glory of his name; give to him glorious praise."
Psalm 66:1–2

Because of your great power, your
  enemies cringe before you.
⁴ All the earth worships you;
  they sing praises to you,
  sing praises to your name." *Sělah*

⁵ Come and see what God has done:
  he is awesome in his deeds among
    mortals.
⁶ He turned the sea into dry land;
  they passed through the river on foot.
  There we rejoiced in him,
⁷   who rules by his might forever,
  whose eyes keep watch on the
    nations—
  let the rebellious not exalt
    themselves. *Sělah*

⁸ Bless our God, O peoples,
  let the sound of his praise be heard,
⁹ who has kept us among the living,
  and has not let our feet slip.
¹⁰ For you, O God, have tested us;
  you have tried us as silver is tried.
¹¹ You brought us into the net;
  you laid burdens on our backs;
¹² you let people ride over our heads;
  we went through fire and through
    water;
  yet you have brought us out to a
    spacious place.ᶻ

¹³ I will come into your house with burnt
    offerings;
  I will pay you my vows,
¹⁴ those that my lips uttered
  and my mouth promised when I
    was in trouble.
¹⁵ I will offer to you burnt offerings of
    fatlings,
  with the smoke of the sacrifice of
    rams;

I will make an offering of bulls and
    goats. *Sělah*

¹⁶ Come and hear, all you who fear God,
  and I will tell what he has done for
    me.
¹⁷ I cried aloud to him,
  and he was extolled with my
    tongue.
¹⁸ If I had cherished iniquity in my heart,
  the Lord would not have listened.
¹⁹ But truly God has listened;
  he has given heed to the words of
    my prayer.

²⁰ Blessed be God,
  because he has not rejected my
    prayer
  or removed his steadfast love from
    me.

Psalm 67

The Nations Called to Praise God

To the leader: with stringed instruments.
    A Psalm. A Song.
¹ May God be gracious to us and bless
    us
  and make his face to shine upon us,
    Sělah
² that your way may be known upon
    earth,
  your saving power among all
    nations.
³ Let the peoples praise you, O God;
  let all the peoples praise you.

⁴ Let the nations be glad and sing for joy,
  for you judge the peoples with
    equity
  and guide the nations upon earth.
    Sělah
⁵ Let the peoples praise you, O God;
  let all the peoples praise you.

⁶ The earth has yielded its increase;
  God, our God, has blessed us.

ᶻ Cn Compare Gk Syr Jerome Tg: Heb *to a satura-tion*

⁷ May God continue to bless us;
  let all the ends of the earth revere
    him.

Psalm 68
Praise and Thanksgiving

To the leader. Of David. A Psalm. A Song.
¹ Let God rise up, let his enemies be
    scattered;
  let those who hate him flee before
    him.
² As smoke is driven away, so drive
    them away;
  as wax melts before the fire,
  let the wicked perish before God.
³ But let the righteous be joyful;
  let them exult before God;
  let them be jubilant with joy.

⁴ Sing to God, sing praises to his name;
  lift up a song to him who rides
    upon the clouds[a]—
  his name is the LORD—
  be exultant before him.

⁵ Father of orphans and protector of
    widows
  is God in his holy habitation.
⁶ God gives the desolate a home to live
    in;
  he leads out the prisoners to
    prosperity,
  but the rebellious live in a parched
    land.

⁷ O God, when you went out before
    your people,
  when you marched through the
    wilderness,   *Selah*
⁸ the earth quaked, the heavens poured
    down rain
  at the presence of God, the God of
    Sinai,
  at the presence of God, the God of
    Israel.
⁹ Rain in abundance, O God, you
    showered abroad;
  you restored your heritage when it
    languished;
¹⁰ your flock found a dwelling in it;

> "May God be gracious to us and bless us and make his face to shine upon us." Psalm 67:1

in your goodness, O God, you
  provided for the needy.

¹¹ The Lord gives the command;
  great is the company of those[b] who
    bore the tidings:
¹² "The kings of the armies, they flee,
    they flee!"
  The women at home divide the spoil,
¹³   though they stay among the
      sheepfolds—
  the wings of a dove covered with silver,
  its pinions with green gold.
¹⁴ When the Almighty[c] scattered kings
    there,
  snow fell on Zal′mon.

¹⁵ O mighty mountain, mountain of
    Ba′shan;
  O many-peaked mountain,
    mountain of Ba′shan!
¹⁶ Why do you look with envy, O
    many-peaked mountain,
  at the mount that God desired for
    his abode,
  where the LORD will reside forever?

¹⁷ With mighty chariotry, twice ten
    thousand,
  thousands upon thousands,
  the Lord came from Sinai into the
    holy place.[d]
¹⁸ You ascended the high mount,
  leading captives in your train
  and receiving gifts from people,
  even from those who rebel against the
    LORD God's abiding there.
¹⁹ Blessed be the Lord,
  who daily bears us up;
  God is our salvation.   *Selah*

---

[a] Or *cast up a highway for him who rides through the deserts*   [b] Or *company of the women*
[c] Traditional rendering of Heb *Shaddai*   [d] Cn: Heb *The Lord among them Sinai in the holy* (place)

20 Our God is a God of salvation,
   and to GOD, the Lord, belongs
      escape from death.

21 But God will shatter the heads of his
      enemies,
   the hairy crown of those who walk
      in their guilty ways.
22 The Lord said,
   "I will bring them back from Bā´shan,
   I will bring them back from the depths
      of the sea,
23 so that you may bathe^e your feet in
      blood,
   so that the tongues of your dogs may
      have their share from the foe."

24 Your solemn processions are seen,^f O
      God,
   the processions of my God, my
      King, into the sanctuary—
25 the singers in front, the musicians last,
   between them girls playing
      tambourines:
26 "Bless God in the great congregation,
   the LORD, O you who are of Israel's
      fountain!"
27 There is Benjamin, the least of them, in
      the lead,
   the princes of Judah in a body,
   the princes of Zeb´ū·lun, the princes
      of Naph´ta·lī.

28 Summon your might, O God;
   show your strength, O God, as you
      have done for us before.
29 Because of your temple at Jerusalem
   kings bear gifts to you.
30 Rebuke the wild animals that live
      among the reeds,
   the herd of bulls with the calves of
      the peoples.
   Trample^g under foot those who lust
      after tribute;
   scatter the peoples who delight in
      war.^h
31 Let bronze be brought from Egypt;
   let Ethiopia^i hasten to stretch out its
      hands to God.

32 Sing to God, O kingdoms of the earth;
   sing praises to the Lord,   Sē´lah
33 O rider in the heavens, the ancient
      heavens;
   listen, he sends out his voice, his
      mighty voice.
34 Ascribe power to God,
   whose majesty is over Israel;
   and whose power is in the skies.
35 Awesome is God in his^j sanctuary,
   the God of Israel;
   he gives power and strength to his
      people.

Blessed be God!

Psalm 69

Prayer for Deliverance from Persecution

To the leader: according to Lilies.
      Of David.
1 Save me, O God,
   for the waters have come up to my
      neck.
2 I sink in deep mire,
   where there is no foothold;
   I have come into deep waters,
   and the flood sweeps over me.
3 I am weary with my crying;
   my throat is parched.
   My eyes grow dim
   with waiting for my God.

4 More in number than the hairs of my
      head
   are those who hate me without
      cause;
   many are those who would destroy me,
   my enemies who accuse me falsely.
   What I did not steal
   must I now restore?
5 O God, you know my folly;
   the wrongs I have done are not
      hidden from you.

6 Do not let those who hope in you be
      put to shame because of me,

---

^e Gk Syr Tg: Heb *shatter*   ^f Or *have been seen*
^g Cn: Heb *Trampling*   ^h Meaning of Heb of verse 30
is uncertain   ^i Or *Nubia*; Heb *Cush*   ^j Gk: Heb
from your

O Lord GOD of hosts;
do not let those who seek you be
dishonored because of me,
O God of Israel.
7 It is for your sake that I have borne
reproach,
that shame has covered my face.
8 I have become a stranger to my
kindred,
an alien to my mother's children.

9 It is zeal for your house that has
consumed me;
the insults of those who insult you
have fallen on me.
10 When I humbled my soul with
fasting,[k]
they insulted me for doing so.
11 When I made sackcloth my clothing,
I became a byword to them.
12 I am the subject of gossip for those
who sit in the gate,
and the drunkards make songs
about me.

13 But as for me, my prayer is to you, O
LORD.
At an acceptable time, O God,
in the abundance of your steadfast
love, answer me.
With your faithful help 14rescue me
from sinking in the mire;
let me be delivered from my enemies
and from the deep waters.
15 Do not let the flood sweep over me,
or the deep swallow me up,
or the Pit close its mouth over me.

16 Answer me, O LORD, for your steadfast
love is good;
according to your abundant mercy,
turn to me.
17 Do not hide your face from your
servant,
for I am in distress—make haste to
answer me.
18 Draw near to me, redeem me,
set me free because of my enemies.

19 You know the insults I receive,
and my shame and dishonor;
my foes are all known to you.
20 Insults have broken my heart,
so that I am in despair.
I looked for pity, but there was none;
and for comforters, but I found none.
21 They gave me poison for food,
and for my thirst they gave me
vinegar to drink.

22 Let their table be a trap for them,
a snare for their allies.
23 Let their eyes be darkened so that they
cannot see,
and make their loins tremble
continually.
24 Pour out your indignation upon them,
and let your burning anger overtake
them.
25 May their camp be a desolation;
let no one live in their tents.
26 For they persecute those whom you
have struck down,
and those whom you have
wounded, they attack still more.[l]
27 Add guilt to their guilt;
may they have no acquittal from
you.
28 Let them be blotted out of the book of
the living;
let them not be enrolled among the
righteous.
29 But I am lowly and in pain;
let your salvation, O God, protect me.

30 I will praise the name of God with a
song;
I will magnify him with
thanksgiving.
31 This will please the LORD more than
an ox
or a bull with horns and hoofs.
32 Let the oppressed see it and be glad;
you who seek God, let your hearts
revive.

[k] Gk Syr: Heb *I wept, with fasting my soul*, or *I made
my soul mourn with fasting*   [l] Gk Syr: Heb *recount
the pain o*

³³ For the LORD hears the needy,
  and does not despise his own that
    are in bonds.

³⁴ Let heaven and earth praise him,
  the seas and everything that moves
    in them.
³⁵ For God will save Zion
  and rebuild the cities of Judah;
and his servants shall live[m] there and
    possess it;
³⁶ the children of his servants shall
      inherit it,
  and those who love his name shall
    live in it.

Psalm 70

Prayer for Deliverance from Enemies

To the leader. Of David,
  for the memorial offering.
¹ Be pleased, O God, to deliver me.
  O LORD, make haste to help me!
² Let those be put to shame and
    confusion
  who seek my life.
Let those be turned back and brought
    to dishonor
  who desire to hurt me.
³ Let those who say, "Aha, Aha!"
  turn back because of their shame.

⁴ Let all who seek you
  rejoice and be glad in you.
Let those who love your salvation
  say evermore, "God is great!"
⁵ But I am poor and needy;
  hasten to me, O God!
You are my help and my deliverer;
  O LORD, do not delay!

Psalm 71

Prayer for Lifelong Protection and Help

¹ In you, O LORD, I take refuge;
  let me never be put to shame.
² In your righteousness deliver me and
    rescue me;
  incline your ear to me and save me.
³ Be to me a rock of refuge,

a strong fortress,[n] to save me,
  for you are my rock and my fortress.

⁴ Rescue me, O my God, from the hand
    of the wicked,
  from the grasp of the unjust and cruel.
⁵ For you, O Lord, are my hope,
  my trust, O LORD, from my youth.
⁶ Upon you I have leaned from my
    birth;
  it was you who took me from my
    mother's womb.
My praise is continually of you.

⁷ I have been like a portent to many,
  but you are my strong refuge.
⁸ My mouth is filled with your praise,
  and with your glory all day long.
⁹ Do not cast me off in the time of old
    age;
  do not forsake me when my
    strength is spent.
¹⁰ For my enemies speak concerning me,
  and those who watch for my life
    consult together.
¹¹ They say, "Pursue and seize that person
    whom God has forsaken,
  for there is no one to deliver."

¹² O God, do not be far from me;
  O my God, make haste to help me!
¹³ Let my accusers be put to shame and
    consumed;
  let those who seek to hurt me
    be covered with scorn and disgrace.
¹⁴ But I will hope continually,
  and will praise you yet more and
    more.

 When things in our life are difficult, we can always ask God for help. Even when it seems God is very far away, or may have forgotten us, we can remember the ways God has taken care of God's people throughout all time.

---

[m] Syr: Heb *and they shall live*   [n] Gk Compare
31.3: Heb *to come continually you have commande*

15 My mouth will tell of your righteous
acts,
of your deeds of salvation all day long,
though their number is past my
knowledge.
16 I will come praising the mighty deeds
of the Lord GOD,
I will praise your righteousness,
yours alone.

17 O God, from my youth you have
taught me,
and I still proclaim your wondrous
deeds.
18 So even to old age and gray hairs,
O God, do not forsake me,
until I proclaim your might
to all the generations to come.*o*
Your power 19and your righteousness,
O God,
reach the high heavens.

You who have done great things,
O God, who is like you?
20 You who have made me see many
troubles and calamities
will revive me again;
from the depths of the earth
you will bring me up again.
21 You will increase my honor,
and comfort me once again.

22 I will also praise you with the harp
for your faithfulness, O my God;
I will sing praises to you with the lyre,
O Holy One of Israel.
23 My lips will shout for joy
when I sing praises to you;
my soul also, which you have rescued.
24 All day long my tongue will talk of
your righteous help,
for those who tried to do me harm
have been put to shame, and
disgraced.

> Psalm 72 is one of two
> psalms (the other is
> Psalm 127) thought to be
> a prayer of Solomon.

Psalm 72

Prayer for Guidance and Support for the King

Of Solomon.

1 Give the king your justice, O God,
and your righteousness to a king's
son.
2 May he judge your people with
righteousness,
and your poor with justice.
3 May the mountains yield prosperity for
the people,
and the hills, in righteousness.
4 May he defend the cause of the poor of
the people,
give deliverance to the needy,
and crush the oppressor.

5 May he live *p* while the sun endures,
and as long as the moon,
throughout all generations.
6 May he be like rain that falls on the
mown grass,
like showers that water the earth.
7 In his days may righteousness flourish
and peace abound, until the moon
is no more.

8 May he have dominion from sea to sea,
and from the River to the ends of
the earth.
9 May his foes*q* bow down before him,
and his enemies lick the dust.
10 May the kings of Tar´shish and of the
isles
render him tribute,
may the kings of Shē´ba and Sē´ba
bring gifts.
11 May all kings fall down before him,
all nations give him service.

12 For he delivers the needy when they
call,
the poor and those who have no
helper.
13 He has pity on the weak and the
needy,

o Gk Compare Syr: Heb *to a generation, to all that
come*   *p* Gk: Heb *may they fear you*   *q* Cn: Heb
those who live in the wilderness

and saves the lives of the needy.
¹⁴ From oppression and violence he
redeems their life;
and precious is their blood in his
sight.

¹⁵ Long may he live!
May gold of Shē′ba be given to him.
May prayer be made for him
continually,
and blessings invoked for him all
day long.
¹⁶ May there be abundance of grain in
the land;
may it wave on the tops of the
mountains;
may its fruit be like Lebanon;
and may people blossom in the cities
like the grass of the field.
¹⁷ May his name endure forever,
his fame continue as long as the
sun.
May all nations be blessed in him;[r]
may they pronounce him happy.

¹⁸ Blessed be the LORD, the God of Israel,
who alone does wondrous things.
¹⁹ Blessed be his glorious name forever;
may his glory fill the whole earth.
Amen and Amen.

²⁰ The prayers of David son of Jesse are
ended.

BOOK III
(Psalms 73–89)

Psalm 73
Plea for Relief from Oppressors
A Psalm of Ā′saph.
¹ Truly God is good to the upright,[s]
to those who are pure in heart.
² But as for me, my feet had almost
stumbled;
my steps had nearly slipped.
³ For I was envious of the arrogant;
I saw the prosperity of the wicked.

⁴ For they have no pain;
their bodies are sound and sleek.

⁵ They are not in trouble as others are;
they are not plagued like other
people.
⁶ Therefore pride is their necklace;
violence covers them like a garment.
⁷ Their eyes swell out with fatness;
their hearts overflow with follies.
⁸ They scoff and speak with malice;
loftily they threaten oppression.
⁹ They set their mouths against heaven,
and their tongues range over the
earth.

¹⁰ Therefore the people turn and praise
them,[t]
and find no fault in them.[u]
¹¹ And they say, "How can God know?
Is there knowledge in the Most
High?"
¹² Such are the wicked;
always at ease, they increase in
riches.
¹³ All in vain I have kept my heart clean
and washed my hands in innocence.
¹⁴ For all day long I have been plagued,
and am punished every morning.

¹⁵ If I had said, "I will talk on in this
way,"
I would have been untrue to the
circle of your children.
¹⁶ But when I thought how to
understand this,
it seemed to me a wearisome task,
¹⁷ until I went into the sanctuary of God;
then I perceived their end.
¹⁸ Truly you set them in slippery places;
you make them fall to ruin.
¹⁹ How they are destroyed in a moment,
swept away utterly by terrors!
²⁰ They are[v] like a dream when one
awakes;
on awaking you despise their
phantoms.

²¹ When my soul was embittered,
when I was pricked in heart,

---

[r] Or bless themselves by him   [s] Or good to Israel
[t] Cn: Heb his people return here   [u] Cn: Heb abundant waters are drained by them   [v] Cn: Heb Lord

²² I was stupid and ignorant;
    I was like a brute beast toward you.
²³ Nevertheless I am continually with
        you;
    you hold my right hand.
²⁴ You guide me with your counsel,
    and afterward you will receive me
        with honor.ʷ
²⁵ Whom have I in heaven but you?
    And there is nothing on earth that I
        desire other than you.
²⁶ My flesh and my heart may fail,
    but God is the strengthˣ of my heart
        and my portion forever.

²⁷ Indeed, those who are far from you
        will perish;
    you put an end to those who are
        false to you.
²⁸ But for me it is good to be near God;
    I have made the Lord God my
        refuge,
    to tell of all your works.

Psalm 74

*Plea for Help in Time of National
    Humiliation*

A Mas′kil of A′saph.

¹ O God, why do you cast us off forever?
    Why does your anger smoke against
        the sheep of your pasture?
² Remember your congregation, which
        you acquired long ago,
    which you redeemed to be the tribe
        of your heritage.
    Remember Mount Zion, where you
        came to dwell.
³ Direct your steps to the perpetual
        ruins;
    the enemy has destroyed everything
        in the sanctuary.

⁴ Your foes have roared within your holy
        place;
    they set up their emblems there.
⁵ At the upper entrance they hacked
    the wooden trellis with axes.ʸ
⁶ And then, with hatchets and hammers,
    they smashed all its carved work.

The dragons to which
the psalmist refers
were a type of sea
monster. These creatures were
frightening to look at and were
also very strong.

⁷ They set your sanctuary on fire;
    they desecrated the dwelling place
        of your name,
    bringing it to the ground.
⁸ They said to themselves, "We will
        utterly subdue them";
    they burned all the meeting places
        of God in the land.

⁹ We do not see our emblems;
    there is no longer any prophet,
    and there is no one among us who
        knows how long.
¹⁰ How long, O God, is the foe to scoff?
    Is the enemy to revile your name
        forever?
¹¹ Why do you hold back your hand;
    why do you keep your hand inᶻ
        your bosom?

¹² Yet God my King is from of old,
    working salvation in the earth.
¹³ You divided the sea by your might;
    you broke the heads of the dragons
        in the waters.
¹⁴ You crushed the heads of Le·vī′a·than;
    you gave him as foodᵃ for the
        creatures of the wilderness.
¹⁵ You cut openings for springs and
        torrents;
    you dried up ever-flowing streams.
¹⁶ Yours is the day, yours also the night;
    you established the luminariesᵇ
        and the sun.
¹⁷ You have fixed all the bounds of the
        earth;
    you made summer and winter.

ʷ Or *to glory*   ˣ Heb *rock*   ʸ Cn Compare Gk Syr:
Meaning of Heb uncertain   ᶻ Cn: Heb *do you consume your right hand from*   ᵃ Heb *food for the people*   ᵇ Or *moon;* Heb *light*

¹⁸ Remember this, O LORD, how the
    enemy scoffs,
    and an impious people reviles your
      name.
¹⁹ Do not deliver the soul of your dove to
    the wild animals;
    do not forget the life of your poor
      forever.

²⁰ Have regard for your*ᶜ* covenant,
    for the dark places of the land are
      full of the haunts of violence.
²¹ Do not let the downtrodden be put to
    shame;
    let the poor and needy praise your
      name.
²² Rise up, O God, plead your cause;
    remember how the impious scoff at
      you all day long.
²³ Do not forget the clamor of your foes,
    the uproar of your adversaries that
      goes up continually.

Psalm 75

Thanksgiving for God's Wondrous Deeds

To the leader: Do Not Destroy.
    A Psalm of Āʹsaph. A Song.
¹ We give thanks to you, O God;
    we give thanks; your name is near.
People tell of your wondrous deeds.

² At the set time that I appoint
    I will judge with equity.
³ When the earth totters, with all its
    inhabitants,
    it is I who keep its pillars steady.
                  Sēʹlah
⁴ I say to the boastful, "Do not boast,"
    and to the wicked, "Do not lift up
      your horn;
⁵ do not lift up your horn on high,
    or speak with insolent neck."

⁶ For not from the east or from the west
    and not from the wilderness comes
      lifting up;
⁷ but it is God who executes judgment,
    putting down one and lifting up
      another.

⁸ For in the hand of the LORD there is a
    cup
    with foaming wine, well mixed;
he will pour a draught from it,
    and all the wicked of the earth
    shall drain it down to the dregs.
⁹ But I will rejoiceᵈ forever;
    I will sing praises to the God of
      Jacob.

¹⁰ All the horns of the wicked I will cut
    off,
    but the horns of the righteous shall
      be exalted.

God created the heaven and the earth, and God cares for and protects all of creation. The psalmist reminds all the people of the earth to praise God for God's wonderful works.

Psalm 76

Israel's God—Judge of All the Earth

To the leader: with stringed instruments.
    A Psalm of Āʹsaph. A Song.
¹ In Judah God is known,
    his name is great in Israel.
² His abode has been established in
    Salem,
    his dwelling place in Zion.
³ There he broke the flashing arrows,
    the shield, the sword, and the
      weapons of war.   *Sēʹlah*

⁴ Glorious are you, more majestic
    than the everlasting mountains.ᵉ
⁵ The stouthearted were stripped of their
    spoil;
    they sank into sleep;
none of the troops
    was able to lift a hand.
⁶ At your rebuke, O God of Jacob,
    both rider and horse lay stunned.

⁷ But you indeed are awesome!

ᶜ Gk Syr: Heb *the*   ᵈ Gk: Heb *declare*   ᵉ Gk:
Heb *the mountains of prey*

Who can stand before you
　when once your anger is roused?
8 From the heavens you uttered
　judgment;
　the earth feared and was still
9 when God rose up to establish
　judgment,
　to save all the oppressed of the
　earth. *Selah*

10 Human wrath serves only to praise
　you,
　when you bind the last bit of your[f]
　wrath around you.
11 Make vows to the LORD your God, and
　perform them;
　let all who are around him bring
　gifts
　to the one who is awesome,
12 who cuts off the spirit of princes,
　who inspires fear in the kings of the
　earth.

Psalm 77

God's Mighty Deeds Recalled

To the leader: according to Je·dŭ́thun.
　　Of Ā́saph. A Psalm.
1 I cry aloud to God,
　aloud to God, that he may hear me.
2 In the day of my trouble I seek the
　Lord;
　in the night my hand is stretched
　out without wearying;
　my soul refuses to be comforted.
3 I think of God, and I moan;
　I meditate, and my spirit faints. *Selah*

4 You keep my eyelids from closing;
　I am so troubled that I cannot
　speak.
5 I consider the days of old,
　and remember the years of long ago.
6 I commune[g] with my heart in the
　night;
　I meditate and search my spirit:[h]
7 "Will the Lord spurn forever,
　and never again be favorable?
8 Has his steadfast love ceased forever?

Are his promises at an end for all
　time?
9 Has God forgotten to be gracious?
　Has he in anger shut up his
　compassion?" *Selah*
10 And I say, "It is my grief
　that the right hand of the Most High
　has changed."

11 I will call to mind the deeds of the
　LORD;
　I will remember your wonders of
　old.
12 I will meditate on all your work,
　and muse on your mighty deeds.
13 Your way, O God, is holy.
　What god is so great as our God?
14 You are the God who works wonders;
　you have displayed your might
　among the peoples.
15 With your strong arm you redeemed
　your people,
　the descendants of Jacob and
　Joseph. *Selah*

16 When the waters saw you, O God,
　when the waters saw you, they were
　afraid;
　the very deep trembled.
17 The clouds poured out water;
　the skies thundered;
　your arrows flashed on every side.
18 The crash of your thunder was in the
　whirlwind;
　your lightnings lit up the world;
　the earth trembled and shook.
19 Your way was through the sea,
　your path, through the mighty
　waters;
　yet your footprints were unseen.
20 You led your people like a flock
　by the hand of Moses and Aaron.

Psalm 78

God's Goodness and Israel's Ingratitude

A Mas´kil of Ā́saph.

f Heb lacks *your*　　g Gk Syr: Heb *My music*
h Syr Jerome: Heb *my spirit searches*

¹ Give ear, O my people, to my teaching;
  incline your ears to the words of my
    mouth.
² I will open my mouth in a parable;
  I will utter dark sayings from of old,
³ things that we have heard and known,
  that our ancestors have told us.
⁴ We will not hide them from their
    children;
  we will tell to the coming generation
  the glorious deeds of the LORD, and his
    might,
  and the wonders that he has done.

⁵ He established a decree in Jacob,
  and appointed a law in Israel,
  which he commanded our ancestors
  to teach to their children;
⁶ that the next generation might know
    them,
  the children yet unborn,
  and rise up and tell them to their
    children,
⁷ so that they should set their hope in
    God,
  and not forget the works of God,
  but keep his commandments;
⁸ and that they should not be like their
    ancestors,
  a stubborn and rebellious generation,
  a generation whose heart was not
    steadfast,
  whose spirit was not faithful to God.

⁹ The Ē'phra·im·ītes, armed withⁱ the
    bow,
  turned back on the day of battle.
¹⁰ They did not keep God's covenant,
  but refused to walk according to his
    law.
¹¹ They forgot what he had done,
  and the miracles that he had shown
    them.
¹² In the sight of their ancestors he
    worked marvels
  in the land of Egypt, in the fields of
    Zō'an.
¹³ He divided the sea and let them pass
    through it,

God's people often wandered away from God's teachings and even worshiped idols. But God continued to love them and care for them. Psalm 78 tells many of the miracles that God has done in the past and promises that God will continue to protect God's people.

and made the waters stand like a
    heap.
¹⁴ In the daytime he led them with a
    cloud,
  and all night long with a fiery light.
¹⁵ He split rocks open in the wilderness,
  and gave them drink abundantly as
    from the deep.
¹⁶ He made streams come out of the rock,
  and caused waters to flow down like
    rivers.

¹⁷ Yet they sinned still more against him,
  rebelling against the Most High in
    the desert.
¹⁸ They tested God in their heart
  by demanding the food they craved.
¹⁹ They spoke against God, saying,
  "Can God spread a table in the
    wilderness?
²⁰ Even though he struck the rock so that
    water gushed out
  and torrents overflowed,
  can he also give bread,
  or provide meat for his people?"

²¹ Therefore, when the LORD heard, he
    was full of rage;
  a fire was kindled against Jacob,
  his anger mounted against Israel,
²² because they had no faith in God,
  and did not trust his saving power.
²³ Yet he commanded the skies above,
  and opened the doors of heaven;

ⁱ Heb *armed with shooting*

24 he rained down on them manna to eat,
  and gave them the grain of heaven.
25 Mortals ate of the bread of angels;
  he sent them food in abundance.
26 He caused the east wind to blow in the
    heavens,
  and by his power he led out the
    south wind;
27 he rained flesh upon them like dust,
  winged birds like the sand of the seas;
28 he let them fall within their camp,
  all around their dwellings.
29 And they ate and were well filled,
  for he gave them what they craved.
30 But before they had satisfied their
    craving,
  while the food was still in their
    mouths,
31 the anger of God rose against them
  and he killed the strongest of them,
  and laid low the flower of Israel.

32 In spite of all this they still sinned;
  they did not believe in his wonders.
33 So he made their days vanish like a
    breath,
  and their years in terror.
34 When he killed them, they sought for
    him;
  they repented and sought God
    earnestly.
35 They remembered that God was their
    rock,
  the Most High God their redeemer.
36 But they flattered him with their
    mouths;
  they lied to him with their tongues.
37 Their heart was not steadfast toward
    him;
  they were not true to his covenant.
38 Yet he, being compassionate,
    forgave their iniquity,
  and did not destroy them;
  often he restrained his anger,
  and did not stir up all his wrath.
39 He remembered that they were but
    flesh,
  a wind that passes and does not
    come again.

40 How often they rebelled against him in
    the wilderness
  and grieved him in the desert!
41 They tested God again and again,
  and provoked the Holy One of
    Israel.
42 They did not keep in mind his power,
  or the day when he redeemed them
    from the foe;
43 when he displayed his signs in Egypt,
  and his miracles in the fields of Zŏ'an.
44 He turned their rivers to blood,
  so that they could not drink of their
    streams.
45 He sent among them swarms of flies,
    which devoured them,
  and frogs, which destroyed them.
46 He gave their crops to the caterpillar,
  and the fruit of their labor to the
    locust.
47 He destroyed their vines with hail,
  and their sycamores with frost.
48 He gave over their cattle to the hail,
  and their flocks to thunderbolts.
49 He let loose on them his fierce anger,
  wrath, indignation, and distress,
  a company of destroying angels.
50 He made a path for his anger;
  he did not spare them from death,
  but gave their lives over to the
    plague.
51 He struck all the firstborn in Egypt,
  the first issue of their strength in the
    tents of Ham.
52 Then he led out his people like sheep,
  and guided them in the wilderness
    like a flock.
53 He led them in safety, so that they
    were not afraid;
  but the sea overwhelmed their
    enemies.
54 And he brought them to his holy hill,
  to the mountain that his right hand
    had won.
55 He drove out nations before them;
  he apportioned them for a
    possession
  and settled the tribes of Israel in
    their tents.

⁵⁶ Yet they tested the Most High God,
  and rebelled against him.
  They did not observe his decrees,
⁵⁷ but turned away and were faithless like
    their ancestors;
  they twisted like a treacherous bow.
⁵⁸ For they provoked him to anger with
    their high places;
  they moved him to jealousy with
    their idols.
⁵⁹ When God heard, he was full of wrath,
  and he utterly rejected Israel.
⁶⁰ He abandoned his dwelling at Shīˊlōh,
  the tent where he dwelt among
    mortals,
⁶¹ and delivered his power to captivity,
  his glory to the hand of the foe.
⁶² He gave his people to the sword,
  and vented his wrath on his heritage.
⁶³ Fire devoured their young men,
  and their girls had no marriage
    song.
⁶⁴ Their priests fell by the sword,
  and their widows made no
    lamentation.
⁶⁵ Then the Lord awoke as from sleep,
  like a warrior shouting because of
    wine.
⁶⁶ He put his adversaries to rout;
  he put them to everlasting disgrace.

⁶⁷ He rejected the tent of Joseph,
  he did not choose the tribe of
    Ēˊphra·im;
⁶⁸ but he chose the tribe of Judah,
  Mount Zion, which he loves.
⁶⁹ He built his sanctuary like the high
    heavens,
  like the earth, which he has founded
    forever.
⁷⁰ He chose his servant David,
  and took him from the sheepfolds;
⁷¹ from tending the nursing ewes he
    brought him
  to be the shepherd of his people
    Jacob,
  of Israel, his inheritance.
⁷² With upright heart he tended them,
  and guided them with skillful hand.

Psalm 79

Plea for Mercy for Jerusalem

A Psalm of Āˊsaph.

¹ O God, the nations have come into
    your inheritance;
  they have defiled your holy temple;
  they have laid Jerusalem in ruins.
² They have given the bodies of your
    servants
  to the birds of the air for food,
  the flesh of your faithful to the wild
    animals of the earth.
³ They have poured out their blood like
    water
  all around Jerusalem,
  and there was no one to bury them.
⁴ We have become a taunt to our
    neighbors,
  mocked and derided by those
    around us.

⁵ How long, O LORD? Will you be angry
    forever?
  Will your jealous wrath burn like fire?
⁶ Pour out your anger on the nations
    that do not know you,
  and on the kingdoms
    that do not call on your name.
⁷ For they have devoured Jacob
  and laid waste his habitation.

⁸ Do not remember against us the
    iniquities of our ancestors;
  let your compassion come speedily
    to meet us,
  for we are brought very low.
⁹ Help us, O God of our salvation,
    for the glory of your name;
  deliver us, and forgive our sins,
    for your name's sake.
¹⁰ Why should the nations say,
    "Where is their God?"
  Let the avenging of the outpoured
    blood of your servants
  be known among the nations before
    our eyes.
¹¹ Let the groans of the prisoners come
    before you;

"Restore us, O LORD God
of hosts; let your face
shine, that we may be
saved." Psalm 80:19

according to your great power
  preserve those doomed to die.
¹² Return sevenfold into the bosom of
    our neighbors
  the taunts with which they taunted
    you, O Lord!
¹³ Then we your people, the flock of
    your pasture,
  will give thanks to you forever;
  from generation to generation we
    will recount your praise.

Psalm 80

Prayer for Israel's Restoration

To the leader: on Lilies, a Covenant.
  Of Āʹsaph. A Psalm.
¹ Give ear, O Shepherd of Israel,
  you who lead Joseph like a flock!
You who are enthroned upon the
    cherubim, shine forth
²   before Ēʹphra·im and Benjamin and
    Ma·nasʹseh.
Stir up your might,
  and come to save us!

³ Restore us, O God;
  let your face shine, that we may be
    saved.

⁴ O LORD God of hosts,
  how long will you be angry with
    your people's prayers?
⁵ You have fed them with the bread of
    tears,
  and given them tears to drink in full
    measure.
⁶ You make us the scornʲ of our
    neighbors;
  our enemies laugh among themselves.

⁷ Restore us, O God of hosts;
  let your face shine, that we may be
    saved.

⁸ You brought a vine out of Egypt;
  you drove out the nations and
    planted it.
⁹ You cleared the ground for it;
  it took deep root and filled the land.
¹⁰ The mountains were covered with its
    shade,
  the mighty cedars with its branches;
¹¹ it sent out its branches to the sea,
  and its shoots to the River.
¹² Why then have you broken down its
    walls,
  so that all who pass along the way
    pluck its fruit?
¹³ The boar from the forest ravages it,
  and all that move in the field feed
    on it.

¹⁴ Turn again, O God of hosts;
  look down from heaven, and see;
have regard for this vine,
¹⁵   the stock that your right hand
    planted.ᵏ
¹⁶ They have burned it with fire, they
    have cut it down;ˡ
  may they perish at the rebuke of
    your countenance.
¹⁷ But let your hand be upon the one at
    your right hand,
  the one whom you made strong for
    yourself.
¹⁸ Then we will never turn back from you;
  give us life, and we will call on your
    name.

¹⁹ Restore us, O LORD God of hosts;
  let your face shine, that we may be
    saved.

Psalm 81

God's Appeal to Stubborn Israel

To the leader: according to
  The Gitʹtith. Of Āʹsaph.
¹ Sing aloud to God our strength;
  shout for joy to the God of Jacob.
² Raise a song, sound the tambourine,
  the sweet lyre with the harp.

ʲ Syr: Heb *strife*   ᵏ Heb adds from verse 17 *and
upon the one whom you made strong for yourself*
ˡ Cn: Heb *it is cut down*

³ Blow the trumpet at the new moon,
　　at the full moon, on our festal day.
⁴ For it is a statute for Israel,
　　an ordinance of the God of Jacob.
⁵ He made it a decree in Joseph,
　　when he went out over^m the land of
　　　Egypt.

I hear a voice I had not known:
⁶ "I relieved your^n shoulder of the burden;
　　your^n hands were freed from the
　　　basket.
⁷ In distress you called, and I rescued
　　　you;
　　I answered you in the secret place of
　　　thunder;
　　I tested you at the waters of
　　　Mer′i·bah.　　　　　　Sē′lah
⁸ Hear, O my people, while I admonish
　　　you;
　　O Israel, if you would but listen to
　　　me!
⁹ There shall be no strange god among
　　　you;
　　you shall not bow down to a foreign
　　　god.
¹⁰ I am the LORD your God,
　　who brought you up out of the land
　　　of Egypt.
　　Open your mouth wide and I will
　　　fill it.

¹¹ "But my people did not listen to my
　　　voice;
　　Israel would not submit to me.
¹² So I gave them over to their stubborn
　　　hearts,
　　to follow their own counsels.
¹³ O that my people would listen to me,
　　that Israel would walk in my ways!
¹⁴ Then I would quickly subdue their
　　　enemies,
　　and turn my hand against their foes.
¹⁵ Those who hate the LORD would
　　　cringe before him,
　　and their doom would last forever.
¹⁶ I would feed you^o with the finest of the
　　　wheat,

and with honey from the rock I
　　would satisfy you."

Psalm 82

A Plea for Justice

A Psalm of Ā′saph.

¹ God has taken his place in the divine
　　council;
　　in the midst of the gods he holds
　　　judgment:
² "How long will you judge unjustly
　　and show partiality to the wicked?
　　　　　　　　　　　　　　Sē′lah
³ Give justice to the weak and the orphan;
　　maintain the right of the lowly and
　　　the destitute.
⁴ Rescue the weak and the needy;
　　deliver them from the hand of the
　　　wicked."

⁵ They have neither knowledge nor
　　understanding,
　　they walk around in darkness;
　　all the foundations of the earth are
　　　shaken.

⁶ I say, "You are gods,
　　children of the Most High, all of
　　　you;
⁷ nevertheless, you shall die like mortals,
　　and fall like any prince."^p

⁸ Rise up, O God, judge the earth;
　　for all the nations belong to you!

Psalm 83

Prayer for Judgment on Israel's Foes

A Song. A Psalm of Ā′saph.

¹ O God, do not keep silence;
　　do not hold your peace or be still, O
　　　God!
² Even now your enemies are in tumult;
　　those who hate you have raised
　　　their heads.
³ They lay crafty plans against your
　　　people;

^m Or *against*　　^n Heb *his*　　^o Cn Compare verse
16b: Heb *he would feed him*　　^p Or *fall as one man,
O princes*

they consult together against those
  you protect.
⁴ They say, "Come, let us wipe them out
  as a nation;
  let the name of Israel be
  remembered no more."
⁵ They conspire with one accord;
  against you they make a covenant—
⁶ the tents of Ēdom and the Ish´ma·el·ītes,
  Mō´ab and the Hag´rītes,
⁷ Gē´bal and Am´mon and Am´a·lek,
  Phi·lis´ti·a with the inhabitants of
  Ṫyre;
⁸ Assyria also has joined them;
  they are the strong arm of the
  children of Lot. *Sē´lah*

⁹ Do to them as you did to Mid´i·an,
  as to Sis´e·ra and Jā´bin at the Wadi
  Kī´shon,
¹⁰ who were destroyed at En-dor,
  who became dung for the ground.
¹¹ Make their nobles like Or´eb and
  Zē´eb,
  all their princes like Zē´bah and
  Zal·mun´na,
¹² who said, "Let us take the pastures of
  God
  for our own possession."

¹³ O my God, make them like whirling
  dust,�q
  like chaff before the wind.
¹⁴ As fire consumes the forest,
  as the flame sets the mountains
  ablaze,
¹⁵ so pursue them with your tempest
  and terrify them with your
  hurricane.
¹⁶ Fill their faces with shame,
  so that they may seek your name, O
  LORD.
¹⁷ Let them be put to shame and
  dismayed forever;
  let them perish in disgrace.
¹⁸ Let them know that you alone,
  whose name is the LORD,
  are the Most High over all the earth.

Psalm 84

The Joy of Worship in the Temple

To the leader: according to The Git´tith.
  Of the Kō´ra·hītes. A Psalm.
¹ How lovely is your dwelling place,
  O LORD of hosts!
² My soul longs, indeed it faints
  for the courts of the LORD;
  my heart and my flesh sing for joy
  to the living God.

³ Even the sparrow finds a home,
  and the swallow a nest for herself,
  where she may lay her young,
  at your altars, O LORD of hosts,
  my King and my God.
⁴ Happy are those who live in your
  house,
  ever singing your praise. *Sē´lah*

⁵ Happy are those whose strength is in
  you,
  in whose heart are the highways to
  Zion.ʳ
⁶ As they go through the valley of Bā´ca
  they make it a place of springs;
  the early rain also covers it with
  pools.
⁷ They go from strength to strength;
  the God of gods will be seen in
  Zion.

⁸ O LORD God of hosts, hear my prayer;
  give ear, O God of Jacob! *Sē´lah*
⁹ Behold our shield, O God;
  look on the face of your anointed.

¹⁰ For a day in your courts is better
  than a thousand elsewhere.
  I would rather be a doorkeeper in the
  house of my God
  than live in the tents of wickedness.
¹¹ For the LORD God is a sun and shield;
  he bestows favor and honor.
  No good thing does the LORD
  withhold
  from those who walk uprightly.

q Or *a tumbleweed*   r Heb lacks *to Zion*

A doorkeeper guarded the entrance of the Temple and collected money from the people. It probably didn't seem as important a job as being a priest, but it was a good way to serve God. The psalmist says that he would rather serve in a simple way in God's house than live a rich life somewhere else. Sometimes the simplest things we can do are the best. What are some simple things you can do to serve God?

12 O LORD of hosts,
　happy is everyone who trusts in
　you.

Psalm 85

Prayer for the Restoration of God's Favor

To the leader.
Of the Kō′ra·hītes. A Psalm.

1 LORD, you were favorable to your land;
　you restored the fortunes of Jacob.
2 You forgave the iniquity of your
　people;
　you pardoned all their sin.　　*Sĕ′lah*
3 You withdrew all your wrath;
　you turned from your hot anger.

4 Restore us again, O God of our
　salvation,
　and put away your indignation
　toward us.
5 Will you be angry with us forever?
　Will you prolong your anger to all
　generations?
6 Will you not revive us again,
　so that your people may rejoice in
　you?
7 Show us your steadfast love, O LORD,
　and grant us your salvation.

8 Let me hear what God the LORD will
　speak,
　for he will speak peace to his people,
　to his faithful, to those who turn to
　him in their hearts.[s]

9 Surely his salvation is at hand for those
　who fear him,
　that his glory may dwell in our land.
10 Steadfast love and faithfulness will
　meet;
　righteousness and peace will kiss
　each other.
11 Faithfulness will spring up from the
　ground,
　and righteousness will look down
　from the sky.
12 The LORD will give what is good,
　and our land will yield its increase.
13 Righteousness will go before him,
　and will make a path for his steps.

Psalm 86

Supplication for Help against Enemies

A Prayer of David.

1 Incline your ear, O LORD, and answer
　me,
　for I am poor and needy.
2 Preserve my life, for I am devoted to
　you;
　save your servant who trusts in you.
You are my God; 3be gracious to me, O
　Lord,
　for to you do I cry all day long.
4 Gladden the soul of your servant,
　for to you, O Lord, I lift up my soul.
5 For you, O Lord, are good and
　forgiving,
　abounding in steadfast love to all
　who call on you.
6 Give ear, O LORD, to my prayer;
　listen to my cry of supplication.
7 In the day of my trouble I call on you,
　for you will answer me.

8 There is none like you among the
　gods, O Lord,
　nor are there any works like yours.
9 All the nations you have made shall
　come
　and bow down before you, O
　Lord,
　and shall glorify your name.

─────────

s Gk: Heb *but let them not turn back to folly*

"I will give thanks to you, O Lord my God, with my whole heart, and I will glorify your name forever." Psalm 86:12

10 For you are great and do wondrous
    things;
        you alone are God.
11 Teach me your way, O LORD,
        that I may walk in your truth;
    give me an undivided heart to revere
        your name.
12 I give thanks to you, O Lord my God,
        with my whole heart,
    and I will glorify your name forever.
13 For great is your steadfast love toward
        me;
    you have delivered my soul from the
        depths of Shĕ´ōl.

14 O God, the insolent rise up against me;
        a band of ruffians seeks my life,
    and they do not set you before
        them.
15 But you, O Lord, are a God merciful
        and gracious,
    slow to anger and abounding in
        steadfast love and faithfulness.
16 Turn to me and be gracious to me;
        give your strength to your servant;
    save the child of your serving girl.
17 Show me a sign of your favor,
        so that those who hate me may see
            it and be put to shame,
    because you, LORD, have helped me
        and comforted me.

Psalm 87

The Joy of Living in Zion

Of the Kō´ra·hītes. A Psalm. A Song.
1 On the holy mount stands the city he
        founded;
2   the LORD loves the gates of Zion
    more than all the dwellings of Jacob.
3 Glorious things are spoken of you,
        O city of God. *Sĕ´lah*

4 Among those who know me I mention
        Rā´hab and Babylon;
    Phi·lis´ti·a too, and Tyre, with
        Ethiopia[t]—
    "This one was born there," they say.
5 And of Zion it shall be said,
        "This one and that one were born in
            it";
    for the Most High himself will
        establish it.
6 The LORD records, as he registers the
        peoples,
    "This one was born there." *Sĕ´lah*

7 Singers and dancers alike say,
        "All my springs are in you."

Psalm 88

Prayer for Help in Despondency

A Song. A Psalm of the Kō´ra·hītes.
To the leader: according to Mā´ha·lath
        Le·an´noth.
A Mas´kil of Hē´man the Ez´ra·hīte.
1 O LORD, God of my salvation,
        when, at night, I cry out in your
            presence,
2 let my prayer come before you;
        incline your ear to my cry.

3 For my soul is full of troubles,
        and my life draws near to Shĕ´ōl.
4 I am counted among those who go
        down to the Pit;
    I am like those who have no help,
5 like those forsaken among the dead,
    like the slain that lie in the grave,
    like those whom you remember no
        more,
    for they are cut off from your hand.
6 You have put me in the depths of the
        Pit,
    in the regions dark and deep.
7 Your wrath lies heavy upon me,
        and you overwhelm me with all
            your waves. *Sĕ´lah*

8 You have caused my companions to
        shun me;

t Or *Nubia*; Heb *Cush*

you have made me a thing of horror
    to them.
I am shut in so that I cannot escape;
9   my eye grows dim through sorrow.
Every day I call on you, O LORD;
    I spread out my hands to you.

10 Do you work wonders for the dead?
    Do the shades rise up to praise you?
                 Sĕlah

11 Is your steadfast love declared in the
    grave,
    or your faithfulness in A·bad′don?
12 Are your wonders known in the
    darkness,
    or your saving help in the land of
    forgetfulness?

13 But I, O LORD, cry out to you;
    in the morning my prayer comes
    before you.
14 O LORD, why do you cast me off?
    Why do you hide your face from me?
15 Wretched and close to death from my
    youth up,
    I suffer your terrors; I am desperate.[u]
16 Your wrath has swept over me;
    your dread assaults destroy me.
17 They surround me like a flood all day
    long;
    from all sides they close in on me.
18 You have caused friend and neighbor
    to shun me;
    my companions are in darkness.

Psalm 89

God's Covenant with David

A Mas′kil of Ē′than the Ez′ra·hīte.
1 I will sing of your steadfast love, O
    LORD,[v] forever;
    with my mouth I will proclaim your
    faithfulness to all generations.
2 I declare that your steadfast love is
    established forever;
    your faithfulness is as firm as the
    heavens.

3 You said, "I have made a covenant
    with my chosen one,
    I have sworn to my servant David:

"I will sing of your steadfast love, O LORD, forever; with my mouth I will proclaim your faithfulness to all generations." Psalm 89:1

4 'I will establish your descendants
    forever,
    and build your throne for all
    generations.'"   *Sĕlah*

5 Let the heavens praise your wonders,
    O LORD,
    your faithfulness in the assembly of
    the holy ones.
6 For who in the skies can be compared
    to the LORD?
    Who among the heavenly beings is
    like the LORD,
7 a God feared in the council of the holy
    ones,
    great and awesome[w] above all that
    are around him?
8 O LORD God of hosts,
    who is as mighty as you, O LORD?
    Your faithfulness surrounds you.
9 You rule the raging of the sea;
    when its waves rise, you still them.
10 You crushed Ra′hab like a carcass;
    you scattered your enemies with
    your mighty arm.
11 The heavens are yours, the earth also is
    yours;
    the world and all that is in it—you
    have founded them.
12 The north and the south[x]—you created
    them;
    Ta′bor and Hermon joyously praise
    your name.
13 You have a mighty arm;
    strong is your hand, high your right
    hand.
14 Righteousness and justice are the
    foundation of your throne;

u Meaning of Heb uncertain   v Gk: Heb *the*
steadfast love of the LORD   w Gk Syr: Heb *greatly*
awesome   x Or *Zaphon and Yamin*

steadfast love and faithfulness go
before you.

15 Happy are the people who know the
festal shout,
who walk, O LORD, in the light of
your countenance;

16 they exult in your name all day long,
and extol[y] your righteousness.

17 For you are the glory of their strength;
by your favor our horn is exalted.

18 For our shield belongs to the LORD,
our king to the Holy One of Israel.

19 Then you spoke in a vision to your
faithful one, and said:
"I have set the crown[z] on one who is
mighty,
I have exalted one chosen from the
people.

20 I have found my servant David;
with my holy oil I have anointed him;

21 my hand shall always remain with him;
my arm also shall strengthen him.

22 The enemy shall not outwit him,
the wicked shall not humble him.

23 I will crush his foes before him
and strike down those who hate
him.

24 My faithfulness and steadfast love shall
be with him;
and in my name his horn shall be
exalted.

25 I will set his hand on the sea
and his right hand on the rivers.

26 He shall cry to me, 'You are my Father,
my God, and the Rock of my
salvation!'

27 I will make him the firstborn,
the highest of the kings of the earth.

28 Forever I will keep my steadfast love
for him,
and my covenant with him will
stand firm.

29 I will establish his line forever,
and his throne as long as the
heavens endure.

30 If his children forsake my law
and do not walk according to my
ordinances,

31 if they violate my statutes
and do not keep my
commandments,

32 then I will punish their transgression
with the rod
and their iniquity with scourges;

33 but I will not remove from him my
steadfast love,
or be false to my faithfulness.

34 I will not violate my covenant,
or alter the word that went forth
from my lips.

35 Once and for all I have sworn by my
holiness;
I will not lie to David.

36 His line shall continue forever,
and his throne endure before me
like the sun.

37 It shall be established forever like the
moon,
an enduring witness in the skies."
Selah

38 But now you have spurned and
rejected him;
you are full of wrath against your
anointed.

39 You have renounced the covenant with
your servant;
you have defiled his crown in the
dust.

40 You have broken through all his walls;
you have laid his strongholds in
ruins.

41 All who pass by plunder him;
he has become the scorn of his
neighbors.

42 You have exalted the right hand of his
foes;
you have made all his enemies
rejoice.

43 Moreover, you have turned back the
edge of his sword,
and you have not supported him
in battle.

44 You have removed the scepter from
his hand,[a]

---

[y] Cn: Heb *are exalted in*   [z] Cn: Heb *help*   [a] Cn:
Heb *removed his cleanness*

and hurled his throne to the
ground.
45 You have cut short the days of his
youth;
you have covered him with shame.
Se̅lah

46 How long, O LORD? Will you hide
yourself forever?
How long will your wrath burn like
fire?
47 Remember how short my time is—[b]
for what vanity you have created all
mortals!
48 Who can live and never see death?
Who can escape the power of
She̅ol?   *Se̅lah*

49 Lord, where is your steadfast love of
old,
which by your faithfulness you
swore to David?
50 Remember, O Lord, how your servant
is taunted;
how I bear in my bosom the insults
of the peoples,[c]
51 with which your enemies taunt, O
LORD,
with which they taunted the
footsteps of your anointed.

52 Blessed be the LORD forever.
Amen and Amen.

BOOK IV
(Psalms 90–106)

Psalm 90
God's Eternity and Human Frailty

A Prayer of Moses, the man of God.
1 Lord, you have been our dwelling
place[d]
in all generations.
2 Before the mountains were brought
forth,
or ever you had formed the earth
and the world,
from everlasting to everlasting you
are God.

Psalm 90 is the only psalm thought to be a prayer of Moses. When we read this psalm, we should remember the stories of Moses and the people of God found in the books of Exodus, Leviticus, Numbers, and Deuteronomy.

3 You turn us[e] back to dust,
and say, "Turn back, you mortals."
4 For a thousand years in your sight
are like yesterday when it is past,
or like a watch in the night.

5 You sweep them away; they are like a
dream,
like grass that is renewed in the
morning;
6 in the morning it flourishes and is
renewed;
in the evening it fades and withers.

7 For we are consumed by your anger;
by your wrath we are overwhelmed.
8 You have set our iniquities before you,
our secret sins in the light of your
countenance.

9 For all our days pass away under your
wrath;
our years come to an end[f] like a sigh.
10 The days of our life are seventy years,
or perhaps eighty, if we are strong;
even then their span[g] is only toil and
trouble;
they are soon gone, and we fly away.

11 Who considers the power of your
anger?
Your wrath is as great as the fear that
is due you.

---

[b] Meaning of Heb uncertain   [c] Cn: Heb *bosom all of many peoples*   [d] Another reading is *our refuge*
[e] Heb *humankind*   [f] Syr: Heb *we bring our years to an end*   [g] Cn Compare Gk Syr Jerome Tg: Heb *pride*

¹² So teach us to count our days
   that we may gain a wise heart.

¹³ Turn, O LORD! How long?
   Have compassion on your servants!
¹⁴ Satisfy us in the morning with your
      steadfast love,
      so that we may rejoice and be glad
         all our days.
¹⁵ Make us glad as many days as you
      have afflicted us,
      and as many years as we have seen
         evil.
¹⁶ Let your work be manifest to your
      servants,
      and your glorious power to their
         children.
¹⁷ Let the favor of the Lord our God be
      upon us,
      and prosper for us the work of our
         hands—
      O prosper the work of our hands!

Psalm 91

Assurance of God's Protection

¹ You who live in the shelter of the Most
      High,
      who abide in the shadow of the
         Almighty,ʰ
² will say to the LORD, "My refuge and
      my fortress;
      my God, in whom I trust."
³ For he will deliver you from the snare
      of the fowler
      and from the deadly pestilence;
⁴ he will cover you with his pinions,
      and under his wings you will find
         refuge;
      his faithfulness is a shield and
         buckler.
⁵ You will not fear the terror of the night,
      or the arrow that flies by day,
⁶ or the pestilence that stalks in
      darkness,
      or the destruction that wastes at
         noonday.

⁷ A thousand may fall at your side,
   ten thousand at your right hand,

The word "almighty" is sometimes used as an adjective with "God" to describe God's greatness, power, and might. As a noun, the word "almighty" is a synonym for God, so "the Almighty" is often used in hymns and psalms in place of the word "God."

but it will not come near you.
⁸ You will only look with your eyes
   and see the punishment of the
      wicked.

⁹ Because you have made the LORD your
      refuge,ⁱ
      the Most High your dwelling place,
¹⁰ no evil shall befall you,
      no scourge come near your tent.

¹¹ For he will command his angels
      concerning you
      to guard you in all your ways.
¹² On their hands they will bear you up,
      so that you will not dash your foot
         against a stone.
¹³ You will tread on the lion and the
      adder,
      the young lion and the serpent you
         will trample under foot.

¹⁴ Those who love me, I will deliver;
      I will protect those who know my
         name.
¹⁵ When they call to me, I will answer
      them;
      I will be with them in trouble,
      I will rescue them and honor them.
¹⁶ With long life I will satisfy them,
      and show them my salvation.

Psalm 92

Thanksgiving for Vindication

A Psalm. A Song for the Sabbath Day.
¹ It is good to give thanks to the LORD,
      to sing praises to your name, O
         Most High;

ʰ Traditional rendering of Heb *Shaddai*   ⁱ Cn: Heb
Because you, LORD, are my refuge; you have made

"It is good to give thanks to the LORD, to sing praises to your name, O Most High." Psalm 92:1

2 to declare your steadfast love in the
morning,
and your faithfulness by night,
3 to the music of the lute and the harp,
to the melody of the lyre.
4 For you, O LORD, have made me glad
by your work;
at the works of your hands I sing for
joy.

5 How great are your works, O LORD!
Your thoughts are very deep!
6 The dullard cannot know,
the stupid cannot understand this:
7 though the wicked sprout like grass
and all evildoers flourish,
they are doomed to destruction
forever,
8 but you, O LORD, are on high
forever.
9 For your enemies, O LORD,
for your enemies shall perish;
all evildoers shall be scattered.

10 But you have exalted my horn like that
of the wild ox;
you have poured over me^j fresh oil.
11 My eyes have seen the downfall of my
enemies;
my ears have heard the doom of my
evil assailants.

12 The righteous flourish like the palm
tree,
and grow like a cedar in Lebanon.
13 They are planted in the house of the
LORD;
they flourish in the courts of our
God.
14 In old age they still produce fruit;
they are always green and full of sap,
15 showing that the LORD is upright;
he is my rock, and there is no
unrighteousness in him.

Psalm 93
The Majesty of God's Rule

1 The LORD is king, he is robed in
majesty;
the LORD is robed, he is girded with
strength.
He has established the world; it shall
never be moved;
2 your throne is established from of
old;
you are from everlasting.

3 The floods have lifted up, O LORD,
the floods have lifted up their voice;
the floods lift up their roaring.
4 More majestic than the thunders of
mighty waters,
more majestic than the waves^k of the
sea,
majestic on high is the LORD!

5 Your decrees are very sure;
holiness befits your house,
O LORD, forevermore.

Psalm 93 praises God as the creator and ruler of all things. There is no person or thing more powerful, majestic, and holy than God! We have a truly awesome God!

Psalm 94
God the Avenger of the Righteous

1 O LORD, you God of vengeance,
you God of vengeance, shine forth!
2 Rise up, O judge of the earth;
give to the proud what they deserve!
3 O LORD, how long shall the wicked,
how long shall the wicked exult?

4 They pour out their arrogant words;
all the evildoers boast.
5 They crush your people, O LORD,
and afflict your heritage.

^{j} Syr: Meaning of Heb uncertain ^{k} Cn: Heb *majestic are the waves*

⁶ They kill the widow and the stranger,
 they murder the orphan,
⁷ and they say, "The LORD does not see;
 the God of Jacob does not perceive."

⁸ Understand, O dullest of the people;
 fools, when will you be wise?
⁹ He who planted the ear, does he not
 hear?
 He who formed the eye, does he not
 see?
¹⁰ He who disciplines the nations,
 he who teaches knowledge to
 humankind,
 does he not chastise?
¹¹ The LORD knows our thoughts,¹
 that they are but an empty breath.

¹² Happy are those whom you discipline,
 O LORD,
 and whom you teach out of your law,
¹³ giving them respite from days of
 trouble,
 until a pit is dug for the wicked.
¹⁴ For the LORD will not forsake his
 people;
 he will not abandon his heritage;
¹⁵ for justice will return to the righteous,
 and all the upright in heart will
 follow it.

¹⁶ Who rises up for me against the
 wicked?
 Who stands up for me against
 evildoers?
¹⁷ If the LORD had not been my help,
 my soul would soon have lived in
 the land of silence.
¹⁸ When I thought, "My foot is slipping,"
 your steadfast love, O LORD, held
 me up.
¹⁹ When the cares of my heart are many,
 your consolations cheer my soul.
²⁰ Can wicked rulers be allied with you,
 those who contrive mischief by
 statute?
²¹ They band together against the life of
 the righteous,
 and condemn the innocent to death.

²² But the LORD has become my
 stronghold,
 and my God the rock of my refuge.
²³ He will repay them for their iniquity
 and wipe them out for their
 wickedness;
 the LORD our God will wipe them
 out.

Psalm 95

A Call to Worship and Obedience

¹ O come, let us sing to the LORD;
 let us make a joyful noise to the
 rock of our salvation!
² Let us come into his presence with
 thanksgiving;
 let us make a joyful noise to him
 with songs of praise!
³ For the LORD is a great God,
 and a great King above all gods.
⁴ In his hand are the depths of the earth;
 the heights of the mountains are his
 also.
⁵ The sea is his, for he made it,
 and the dry land, which his hands
 have formed.

⁶ O come, let us worship and bow
 down,
 let us kneel before the LORD, our
 Maker!

In the same way that a shepherd takes good care of sheep, God cares for people. The psalmist says that God is our shepherd and that we are the people of God's pasture. The psalmist invites us to come before God in worship and praise. We should always give thanks for the way God cares for us. Make a list of the ways God cares for you, and put this list in a place where you can see it every day. Pray, giving thanks for God's tender care.

¹ Heb *the thoughts of humankind*

⁷ For he is our God,
　and we are the people of his pasture,
　and the sheep of his hand.

O that today you would listen to his
　voice!
⁸ Do not harden your hearts, as at
　Mer´i·bah,
　as on the day at Mas´sah in the
　wilderness,
⁹ when your ancestors tested me,
　and put me to the proof, though
　they had seen my work.
¹⁰ For forty years I loathed that generation
　and said, "They are a people whose
　hearts go astray,
　and they do not regard my ways."
¹¹ Therefore in my anger I swore,
　"They shall not enter my rest."

Psalm 96

Praise to God Who Comes in Judgment

¹ O sing to the LORD a new song;
　sing to the LORD, all the earth.
² Sing to the LORD, bless his name;
　tell of his salvation from day to day.
³ Declare his glory among the nations,
　his marvelous works among all the
　peoples.
⁴ For great is the LORD, and greatly to be
　praised;
　he is to be revered above all gods.
⁵ For all the gods of the peoples are
　idols,
　but the LORD made the heavens.
⁶ Honor and majesty are before him;
　strength and beauty are in his
　sanctuary.

⁷ Ascribe to the LORD, O families of the
　peoples,
　ascribe to the LORD glory and
　strength.
⁸ Ascribe to the LORD the glory due his
　name;
　bring an offering, and come into his
　courts.
⁹ Worship the LORD in holy splendor;
　tremble before him, all the earth.

¹⁰ Say among the nations, "The LORD is
　king!
　The world is firmly established; it
　shall never be moved.
　He will judge the peoples with
　equity."
¹¹ Let the heavens be glad, and let the
　earth rejoice;
　let the sea roar, and all that fills it;
¹² let the field exult, and everything in
　it.
　Then shall all the trees of the forest
　sing for joy
¹³ before the LORD; for he is
　coming,
　for he is coming to judge the
　earth.
　He will judge the world with
　righteousness,
　and the peoples with his truth.

Psalm 97

The Glory of God's Reign

¹ The LORD is king! Let the earth
　rejoice;
　let the many coastlands be glad!
² Clouds and thick darkness are all
　around him;
　righteousness and justice are the
　foundation of his throne.
³ Fire goes before him,
　and consumes his adversaries on
　every side.
⁴ His lightnings light up the world;
　the earth sees and trembles.
⁵ The mountains melt like wax before
　the LORD,
　before the Lord of all the earth.
⁶ The heavens proclaim his
　righteousness;
　and all the peoples behold his
　glory.
⁷ All worshipers of images are put to
　shame,
　those who make their boast in
　worthless idols;
　all gods bow down before him.
⁸ Zion hears and is glad,

and the towns[m] of Judah rejoice,
because of your judgments, O God.
[9] For you, O LORD, are most high over
all the earth;
you are exalted far above all gods.

[10] The LORD loves those who hate[n] evil;
he guards the lives of his faithful;
he rescues them from the hand of
the wicked.
[11] Light dawns[o] for the righteous,
and joy for the upright in heart.
[12] Rejoice in the LORD, O you righteous,
and give thanks to his holy name!

Psalm 98

Praise the Judge of the World

A Psalm.

[1] O sing to the LORD a new song,
for he has done marvelous things.
His right hand and his holy arm
have gotten him victory.
[2] The LORD has made known his victory;
he has revealed his vindication in
the sight of the nations.
[3] He has remembered his steadfast love
and faithfulness
to the house of Israel.
All the ends of the earth have seen
the victory of our God.

[4] Make a joyful noise to the LORD, all the
earth;
break forth into joyous song and
sing praises.
[5] Sing praises to the LORD with the lyre,
with the lyre and the sound of
melody.
[6] With trumpets and the sound of the
horn
make a joyful noise before the King,
the LORD.

[7] Let the sea roar, and all that fills it;
the world and those who live in it.
[8] Let the floods clap their hands;
let the hills sing together for joy
[9] at the presence of the LORD, for he is
coming

"Make a joyful noise to the
LORD, all the earth."
Psalm 98:4a

to judge the earth.
He will judge the world with
righteousness,
and the peoples with equity.

Psalm 99

Praise to God for His Holiness

[1] The LORD is king; let the peoples
tremble!
He sits enthroned upon the
cherubim; let the earth quake!
[2] The LORD is great in Zion;
he is exalted over all the peoples.
[3] Let them praise your great and
awesome name.
Holy is he!
[4] Mighty King,[p] lover of justice,
you have established equity;
you have executed justice
and righteousness in Jacob.
[5] Extol the LORD our God;
worship at his footstool.
Holy is he!

[6] Moses and Aaron were among his
priests,
Samuel also was among those who
called on his name.
They cried to the LORD, and he
answered them.
[7] He spoke to them in the pillar of
cloud;
they kept his decrees,
and the statutes that he gave
them.

[8] O LORD our God, you answered
them;
you were a forgiving God to them,
but an avenger of their
wrongdoings.

[m] Heb *daughters*   [n] Cn: Heb *You who love the*
LORD *hate*   [o] Gk Syr Jerome: Heb *is sown*   [p] Cn:
Heb *And a king's strength*

⁹ Extol the Lord our God,
  and worship at his holy mountain;
  for the Lord our God is holy.

Psalm 100

All Lands Summoned to Praise God

A Psalm of thanksgiving.

¹ Make a joyful noise to the Lord, all the
  earth.
² Worship the Lord with gladness;
  come into his presence with singing.

³ Know that the Lord is God.
  It is he that made us, and we are his;ᑫ
  we are his people, and the sheep of
  his pasture.

⁴ Enter his gates with thanksgiving,
  and his courts with praise.
  Give thanks to him, bless his name.

⁵ For the Lord is good;
  his steadfast love endures forever,
  and his faithfulness to all
  generations.

Psalm 101

A Sovereign's Pledge of Integrity and Justice

Of David. A Psalm.

¹ I will sing of loyalty and of justice;
  to you, O Lord, I will sing.
² I will study the way that is blameless.
  When shall I attain it?

  I will walk with integrity of heart
  within my house;
³ I will not set before my eyes
  anything that is base.

  I hate the work of those who fall away;
  it shall not cling to me.
⁴ Perverseness of heart shall be far from
  me;
  I will know nothing of evil.

⁵ One who secretly slanders a neighbor
  I will destroy.
  A haughty look and an arrogant heart
  I will not tolerate.

⁶ I will look with favor on the faithful in
  the land,
  so that they may live with me;
  whoever walks in the way that is
  blameless
  shall minister to me.

⁷ No one who practices deceit
  shall remain in my house;
  no one who utters lies
  shall continue in my presence.

⁸ Morning by morning I will destroy
  all the wicked in the land,
  cutting off all evildoers
  from the city of the Lord.

Psalm 102

Prayer to the Eternal King for Help

A prayer of one afflicted, when faint
  and pleading before the Lord.

¹ Hear my prayer, O Lord;
  let my cry come to you.
² Do not hide your face from me
  in the day of my distress.
  Incline your ear to me;
  answer me speedily in the day when
  I call.

³ For my days pass away like smoke,
  and my bones burn like a furnace.
⁴ My heart is stricken and withered like
  grass;
  I am too wasted to eat my bread.
⁵ Because of my loud groaning
  my bones cling to my skin.
⁶ I am like an owl of the wilderness,
  like a little owl of the waste places.
⁷ I lie awake;
  I am like a lonely bird on the
  housetop.
⁸ All day long my enemies taunt me;
  those who deride me use my name
  for a curse.
⁹ For I eat ashes like bread,
  and mingle tears with my drink,
¹⁰ because of your indignation and anger;
  for you have lifted me up and
  thrown me aside.

ᑫ Another reading is *and not we ourselves*

¹¹ My days are like an evening shadow;
  I wither away like grass.

¹² But you, O LORD, are enthroned
    forever;
  your name endures to all generations.
¹³ You will rise up and have compassion
    on Zion,
  for it is time to favor it;
    the appointed time has come.
¹⁴ For your servants hold its stones dear,
  and have pity on its dust.
¹⁵ The nations will fear the name of the
    LORD,
  and all the kings of the earth your
    glory.
¹⁶ For the LORD will build up Zion;
  he will appear in his glory.
¹⁷ He will regard the prayer of the
    destitute,
  and will not despise their prayer.

¹⁸ Let this be recorded for a generation to
    come,
  so that a people yet unborn may
    praise the LORD:
¹⁹ that he looked down from his holy
    height,
  from heaven the LORD looked at the
    earth,
²⁰ to hear the groans of the prisoners,
  to set free those who were doomed
    to die;
²¹ so that the name of the LORD may be
    declared in Zion,
  and his praise in Jerusalem,
²² when peoples gather together,
  and kingdoms, to worship the LORD.

²³ He has broken my strength in
    midcourse;
  he has shortened my days.
²⁴ "O my God," I say, "do not take me
    away
  at the midpoint of my life,
  you whose years endure
    throughout all generations."

²⁵ Long ago you laid the foundation of
    the earth,

and the heavens are the work of
    your hands.
²⁶ They will perish, but you endure;
  they will all wear out like a garment.
You change them like clothing, and
    they pass away;
²⁷   but you are the same, and your
    years have no end.
²⁸ The children of your servants shall live
    secure;
  their offspring shall be established in
    your presence.

Psalm 103

Thanksgiving for God's Goodness
    Of David.
¹ Bless the LORD, O my soul,
  and all that is within me,
  bless his holy name.
² Bless the LORD, O my soul,
  and do not forget all his benefits—
³ who forgives all your iniquity,
  who heals all your diseases,
⁴ who redeems your life from the Pit,
  who crowns you with steadfast love
    and mercy,
⁵ who satisfies you with good as long as
    you liveʳ
  so that your youth is renewed like
    the eagle's.

⁶ The LORD works vindication
  and justice for all who are oppressed.

Writers of Hebrew poetry were impressed by eagles. These birds lived long lives, had a majestic appearance, nested in the tallest trees, and cared for their young. In this psalm, the writer suggests that living in a right relationship with God will renew a person's strength as if he or she were young again.

ʳ Meaning of Heb uncertain

⁷ He made known his ways to Moses,
his acts to the people of Israel.
⁸ The LORD is merciful and gracious,
slow to anger and abounding in
steadfast love.
⁹ He will not always accuse,
nor will he keep his anger forever.
¹⁰ He does not deal with us according to
our sins,
nor repay us according to our
iniquities.
¹¹ For as the heavens are high above the
earth,
so great is his steadfast love toward
those who fear him;
¹² as far as the east is from the west,
so far he removes our transgressions
from us.
¹³ As a father has compassion for his
children,
so the LORD has compassion for
those who fear him.
¹⁴ For he knows how we were made;
he remembers that we are dust.

¹⁵ As for mortals, their days are like grass;
they flourish like a flower of the
field;
¹⁶ for the wind passes over it, and it is
gone,
and its place knows it no more.
¹⁷ But the steadfast love of the LORD is
from everlasting to everlasting
on those who fear him,
and his righteousness to children's
children,
¹⁸ to those who keep his covenant
and remember to do his
commandments.

¹⁹ The LORD has established his throne in
the heavens,
and his kingdom rules over all.
²⁰ Bless the LORD, O you his angels,
you mighty ones who do his
bidding,
obedient to his spoken word.
²¹ Bless the LORD, all his hosts,
his ministers that do his will.

²² Bless the LORD, all his works,
in all places of his dominion.
Bless the LORD, O my soul.

Psalm 104

God the Creator and Provider

¹ Bless the LORD, O my soul.
O LORD my God, you are very great.
You are clothed with honor and
majesty,
² wrapped in light as with a garment.
You stretch out the heavens like a tent,
³ you set the beams of your^s
chambers on the waters,
you make the clouds your^s chariot,
you ride on the wings of the wind,
⁴ you make the winds your^s messengers,
fire and flame your^s ministers.

⁵ You set the earth on its foundations,
so that it shall never be shaken.
⁶ You cover it with the deep as with a
garment;
the waters stood above the
mountains.
⁷ At your rebuke they flee;
at the sound of your thunder they
take to flight.
⁸ They rose up to the mountains, ran
down to the valleys
to the place that you appointed for
them.
⁹ You set a boundary that they may not
pass,
so that they might not again cover
the earth.

¹⁰ You make springs gush forth in the
valleys;
they flow between the hills,
¹¹ giving drink to every wild animal;
the wild asses quench their thirst.
¹² By the streams^t the birds of the air
have their habitation;
they sing among the branches.
¹³ From your lofty abode you water the
mountains;

^{s} Heb *his* ^{t} Heb *By them*

the earth is satisfied with the fruit of
your work.

14 You cause the grass to grow for the
cattle,
and plants for people to use,ᵘ
to bring forth food from the earth,
15 and wine to gladden the human
heart,
oil to make the face shine,
and bread to strengthen the human
heart.
16 The trees of the LORD are watered
abundantly,
the cedars of Lebanon that he
planted.
17 In them the birds build their nests;
the stork has its home in the fir
trees.
18 The high mountains are for the wild
goats;
the rocks are a refuge for the coneys.
19 You have made the moon to mark the
seasons;
the sun knows its time for setting.
20 You make darkness, and it is night,
when all the animals of the forest
come creeping out.
21 The young lions roar for their prey,
seeking their food from God.
22 When the sun rises, they withdraw
and lie down in their dens.
23 People go out to their work
and to their labor until the evening.

24 O LORD, how manifold are your
works!
In wisdom you have made them all;
the earth is full of your creatures.
25 Yonder is the sea, great and wide,
creeping things innumerable are
there,
living things both small and great.
26 There go the ships,
and Le·vi´a·than that you formed to
sport in it.

27 These all look to you
to give them their food in due
season;
28 when you give to them, they gather it
up;
when you open your hand, they are
filled with good things.
29 When you hide your face, they are
dismayed;
when you take away their breath,
they die
and return to their dust.
30 When you send forth your spirit,ᵛ they
are created;
and you renew the face of the
ground.

31 May the glory of the LORD endure
forever;
may the LORD rejoice in his works—
32 who looks on the earth and it
trembles,
who touches the mountains and
they smoke.
33 I will sing to the LORD as long as I live;
I will sing praise to my God while I
have being.
34 May my meditation be pleasing to
him,
for I rejoice in the LORD.
35 Let sinners be consumed from the
earth,
and let the wicked be no more.
Bless the LORD, O my soul.
Praise the LORD!

Psalm 105

God's Faithfulness to Israel

1 O give thanks to the LORD, call on his
name,
make known his deeds among the
peoples.
2 Sing to him, sing praises to him;
tell of all his wonderful works.
3 Glory in his holy name;
let the hearts of those who seek
the LORD rejoice.
4 Seek the LORD and his strength;
seek his presence continually.
5 Remember the wonderful works he
has done,

ᵘ Or *to cultivate*   ᵛ Or *your breath*

his miracles, and the judgments he
　　has uttered,
6 O offspring of his servant Abraham,[w]
　　children of Jacob, his chosen ones.

7 He is the LORD our God;
　　his judgments are in all the earth.
8 He is mindful of his covenant forever,
　　of the word that he commanded, for
　　　a thousand generations,
9 the covenant that he made with
　　Abraham,
　　his sworn promise to Isaac,
10 which he confirmed to Jacob as a
　　statute,
　　to Israel as an everlasting covenant,
11 saying, "To you I will give the land of
　　Cā'naan
　　as your portion for an inheritance."

12 When they were few in number,
　　of little account, and strangers in it,
13 wandering from nation to nation,
　　from one kingdom to another people,
14 he allowed no one to oppress them;
　　he rebuked kings on their account,
15 saying, "Do not touch my anointed
　　ones;
　　do my prophets no harm."

16 When he summoned famine against
　　the land,
　　and broke every staff of bread,
17 he had sent a man ahead of them,
　　Joseph, who was sold as a slave.
18 His feet were hurt with fetters,
　　his neck was put in a collar of iron;
19 until what he had said came to pass,
　　the word of the LORD kept testing
　　him.
20 The king sent and released him;
　　the ruler of the peoples set him free.
21 He made him lord of his house,
　　and ruler of all his possessions,
22 to instruct[x] his officials at his pleasure,
　　and to teach his elders wisdom.

23 Then Israel came to Egypt;
　　Jacob lived as an alien in the land of
　　Ham.

Psalm 105 remembers the faithfulness of God to Israel throughout time. This poem tells the story of God's people from the call of Abraham to the time they entered the Promised Land. The poem reminds us that God was with the people to provide for them and guide them.

24 And the LORD made his people very
　　fruitful,
　　and made them stronger than their
　　foes,
25 whose hearts he then turned to hate
　　his people,
　　to deal craftily with his servants.

26 He sent his servant Moses,
　　and Aaron whom he had chosen.
27 They performed his signs among
　　them,
　　and miracles in the land of Ham.
28 He sent darkness, and made the land
　　dark;
　　they rebelled[y] against his words.
29 He turned their waters into blood,
　　and caused their fish to die.
30 Their land swarmed with frogs,
　　even in the chambers of their kings.
31 He spoke, and there came swarms of
　　flies,
　　and gnats throughout their
　　country.
32 He gave them hail for rain,
　　and lightning that flashed through
　　their land.
33 He struck their vines and fig trees,
　　and shattered the trees of their
　　country.
34 He spoke, and the locusts came,
　　and young locusts without
　　number;
35 they devoured all the vegetation in
　　their land,

w Another reading is *Israel* (compare 1 Chr 16.13)
x Gk Syr Jerome: Heb *to bind*　y Cn Compare Gk
Syr: Heb *they did not rebel*

and ate up the fruit of their ground.
³⁶ He struck down all the firstborn in
their land,
the first issue of all their strength.

³⁷ Then he brought Israel[z] out with silver
and gold,
and there was no one among their
tribes who stumbled.
³⁸ Egypt was glad when they departed,
for dread of them had fallen upon it.
³⁹ He spread a cloud for a covering,
and fire to give light by night.
⁴⁰ They asked, and he brought quails,
and gave them food from heaven in
abundance.
⁴¹ He opened the rock, and water gushed
out;
it flowed through the desert like a
river.
⁴² For he remembered his holy promise,
and Abraham, his servant.

⁴³ So he brought his people out with joy,
his chosen ones with singing.
⁴⁴ He gave them the lands of the nations,
and they took possession of the
wealth of the peoples,
⁴⁵ that they might keep his statutes
and observe his laws.
Praise the LORD!

Psalm 106

A Confession of Israel's Sins

¹ Praise the LORD!
O give thanks to the LORD, for he is
good;
for his steadfast love endures
forever.
² Who can utter the mighty doings of
the LORD,
or declare all his praise?
³ Happy are those who observe justice,
who do righteousness at all times.

⁴ Remember me, O LORD, when you
show favor to your people;
help me when you deliver them;

⁵ that I may see the prosperity of your
chosen ones,
that I may rejoice in the gladness of
your nation,
that I may glory in your heritage.

⁶ Both we and our ancestors have
sinned;
we have committed iniquity, have
done wickedly.
⁷ Our ancestors, when they were in
Egypt,
did not consider your wonderful
works;
they did not remember the abundance
of your steadfast love,
but rebelled against the Most High[a]
at the Red Sea.[b]
⁸ Yet he saved them for his name's sake,
so that he might make known his
mighty power.
⁹ He rebuked the Red Sea,[b] and it
became dry;
he led them through the deep as
through a desert.
¹⁰ So he saved them from the hand of the
foe,
and delivered them from the hand
of the enemy.
¹¹ The waters covered their adversaries;
not one of them was left.
¹² Then they believed his words;
they sang his praise.

¹³ But they soon forgot his works;
they did not wait for his counsel.
¹⁴ But they had a wanton craving in the
wilderness,
and put God to the test in the desert;
¹⁵ he gave them what they asked,
but sent a wasting disease among
them.

¹⁶ They were jealous of Moses in the
camp,
and of Aaron, the holy one of the
LORD.

[z] Heb *them*   [a] Cn Compare 78.17, 56: Heb
rebelled at the sea   [b] Or *Sea of Reeds*

17 The earth opened and swallowed up
Dā´than,
and covered the faction of
A·bī´ram.
18 Fire also broke out in their company;
the flame burned up the wicked.

19 They made a calf at Hō´reb
and worshiped a cast image.
20 They exchanged the glory of God[c]
for the image of an ox that eats
grass.
21 They forgot God, their Savior,
who had done great things in Egypt,
22 wondrous works in the land of Ham,
and awesome deeds by the Red Sea.[d]
23 Therefore he said he would destroy
them—
had not Moses, his chosen one,
stood in the breach before him,
to turn away his wrath from
destroying them.

24 Then they despised the pleasant land,
having no faith in his promise.
25 They grumbled in their tents,
and did not obey the voice of the
LORD.
26 Therefore he raised his hand and
swore to them
that he would make them fall in the
wilderness,
27 and would disperse[e] their descendants
among the nations,
scattering them over the lands.

28 Then they attached themselves to the
Bā´al of Pē´or,
and ate sacrifices offered to the dead;
29 they provoked the LORD to anger with
their deeds,
and a plague broke out among
them.
30 Then Phin´e·has stood up and
interceded,
and the plague was stopped.
31 And that has been reckoned to him as
righteousness

from generation to generation
forever.

32 They angered the LORD[f] at the waters
of Mer´i·bah,
and it went ill with Moses on their
account;
33 for they made his spirit bitter,
and he spoke words that were rash.

34 They did not destroy the peoples,
as the LORD commanded them,
35 but they mingled with the nations
and learned to do as they did.
36 They served their idols,
which became a snare to them.
37 They sacrificed their sons
and their daughters to the demons;
38 they poured out innocent blood,
the blood of their sons and
daughters,
whom they sacrificed to the idols of
Cā´naan;
and the land was polluted with
blood.
39 Thus they became unclean by their
acts,
and prostituted themselves in their
doings.

40 Then the anger of the LORD was
kindled against his people,
and he abhorred his heritage;
41 he gave them into the hand of the
nations,
so that those who hated them ruled
over them.
42 Their enemies oppressed them,
and they were brought into
subjection under their power.
43 Many times he delivered them,
but they were rebellious in their
purposes,
and were brought low through their
iniquity.

---

[c] Compare Gk Mss: Heb *exchanged their glory*
[d] Or *Sea of Reeds*   [e] Syr Compare Ezek 20.23:
Heb *cause to fall*   [f] Heb *him*

"O give thanks to the
LORD, for he is good; for
his steadfast love
endures forever."
Psalm 107:1

⁴⁴ Nevertheless he regarded their distress
when he heard their cry.
⁴⁵ For their sake he remembered his
covenant,
and showed compassion according
to the abundance of his steadfast
love.
⁴⁶ He caused them to be pitied
by all who held them captive.

⁴⁷ Save us, O LORD our God,
and gather us from among the
nations,
that we may give thanks to your holy
name
and glory in your praise.

⁴⁸ Blessed be the LORD, the God of Israel,
from everlasting to everlasting.
And let all the people say, "Amen."
Praise the LORD!

BOOK V

(Psalms 107–150)

Psalm 107

*Thanksgiving for Deliverance from Many
Troubles*

¹ O give thanks to the LORD, for he is
good;
for his steadfast love endures forever.
² Let the redeemed of the LORD say so,
those he redeemed from trouble,
³ and gathered in from the lands,
from the east and from the west,
from the north and from the south.^g

⁴ Some wandered in desert wastes,
finding no way to an inhabited
town;
⁵ hungry and thirsty,
their soul fainted within them.

⁶ Then they cried to the LORD in their
trouble,
and he delivered them from their
distress;
⁷ he led them by a straight way,
until they reached an inhabited
town.
⁸ Let them thank the LORD for his
steadfast love,
for his wonderful works to
humankind.
⁹ For he satisfies the thirsty,
and the hungry he fills with good
things.

¹⁰ Some sat in darkness and in gloom,
prisoners in misery and in irons,
¹¹ for they had rebelled against the words
of God,
and spurned the counsel of the Most
High.
¹² Their hearts were bowed down with
hard labor;
they fell down, with no one to help.
¹³ Then they cried to the LORD in their
trouble,
and he saved them from their
distress;
¹⁴ he brought them out of darkness and
gloom,
and broke their bonds asunder.
¹⁵ Let them thank the LORD for his
steadfast love,
for his wonderful works to
humankind.
¹⁶ For he shatters the doors of bronze,
and cuts in two the bars of iron.

¹⁷ Some were sick^h through their sinful
ways,
and because of their iniquities
endured affliction;
¹⁸ they loathed any kind of food,
and they drew near to the gates of
death.
¹⁹ Then they cried to the LORD in their
trouble,
and he saved them from their
distress;

^g Cn: Heb *sea*   ^h Cn: Heb *fools*

20 he sent out his word and healed them,
  and delivered them from destruction.
21 Let them thank the LORD for his
    steadfast love,
  for his wonderful works to
    humankind.
22 And let them offer thanksgiving
    sacrifices,
  and tell of his deeds with songs of
    joy.

23 Some went down to the sea in ships,
  doing business on the mighty
    waters;
24 they saw the deeds of the LORD,
  his wondrous works in the deep.
25 For he commanded and raised the
    stormy wind,
  which lifted up the waves of the sea.
26 They mounted up to heaven, they
    went down to the depths;
  their courage melted away in their
    calamity;
27 they reeled and staggered like
    drunkards,
  and were at their wits' end.
28 Then they cried to the LORD in their
    trouble,
  and he brought them out from their
    distress;
29 he made the storm be still,
  and the waves of the sea were
    hushed.
30 Then they were glad because they had
    quiet,
  and he brought them to their
    desired haven.
31 Let them thank the LORD for his
    steadfast love,
  for his wonderful works to
    humankind.
32 Let them extol him in the congregation
    of the people,
  and praise him in the assembly of
    the elders.

33 He turns rivers into a desert,
  springs of water into thirsty ground,
34 a fruitful land into a salty waste,

because of the wickedness of its
  inhabitants.
35 He turns a desert into pools of water,
  a parched land into springs of water.
36 And there he lets the hungry live,
  and they establish a town to live in;
37 they sow fields, and plant vineyards,
  and get a fruitful yield.
38 By his blessing they multiply greatly,
  and he does not let their cattle
    decrease.

39 When they are diminished and
    brought low
  through oppression, trouble, and
    sorrow,
40 he pours contempt on princes
  and makes them wander in trackless
    wastes;
41 but he raises up the needy out of
    distress,
  and makes their families like flocks.
42 The upright see it and are glad;
  and all wickedness stops its mouth.
43 Let those who are wise give heed to
    these things,
  and consider the steadfast love of
    the LORD.

Psalm 108

Praise and Prayer for Victory

A Song. A Psalm of David.
1 My heart is steadfast, O God, my
    heart is steadfast;[i]
  I will sing and make melody.
    Awake, my soul![j]
2 Awake, O harp and lyre!
  I will awake the dawn.
3 I will give thanks to you, O LORD,
    among the peoples,
  and I will sing praises to you
    among the nations.
4 For your steadfast love is higher than
    the heavens,
  and your faithfulness reaches to
    the clouds.

i Heb Mss Gk Syr: MT lacks *my heart is steadfast*
j Compare 57.8: Heb *also my soul*

5 Be exalted, O God, above the heavens,
   and let your glory be over all the
   earth.
6 Give victory with your right hand, and
   answer me,
     so that those whom you love may
     be rescued.

7 God has promised in his sanctuary:[k]
   "With exultation I will divide up
   Shĕ´chem,
     and portion out the Vale of
     Suc´coth.
8 Gil´e·ad is mine; Ma·nas´seh is mine;
   Ē´phra·im is my helmet;
     Judah is my scepter.
9 Mŏ´ab is my washbasin;
   on Ē´dom I hurl my shoe;
     over Phi·lis´ti·a I shout in triumph."

10 Who will bring me to the fortified
    city?
      Who will lead me to Ē´dom?
11 Have you not rejected us, O God?
      You do not go out, O God, with our
      armies.
12 O grant us help against the foe,
      for human help is worthless.
13 With God we shall do valiantly;
      it is he who will tread down our
      foes.

Psalm 109

Prayer for Vindication and Vengeance

To the leader. Of David. A Psalm.
1 Do not be silent, O God of my praise.
2 For wicked and deceitful mouths are
   opened against me,
     speaking against me with lying
     tongues.
3 They beset me with words of hate,
   and attack me without cause.
4 In return for my love they accuse me,
   even while I make prayer for them.[l]
5 So they reward me evil for good,
   and hatred for my love.

6 They say,[m] "Appoint a wicked man
   against him;

     let an accuser stand on his right.
7 When he is tried, let him be found
   guilty;
     let his prayer be counted as sin.
8 May his days be few;
     may another seize his position.
9 May his children be orphans,
     and his wife a widow.
10 May his children wander about and
    beg;
      may they be driven out of[n] the ruins
      they inhabit.
11 May the creditor seize all that he has;
      may strangers plunder the fruits of
      his toil.
12 May there be no one to do him a
    kindness,
      nor anyone to pity his orphaned
      children.
13 May his posterity be cut off;
      may his name be blotted out in the
      second generation.
14 May the iniquity of his father[o] be
      remembered before the LORD,
      and do not let the sin of his mother
      be blotted out.
15 Let them be before the LORD
    continually,
      and may his[p] memory be cut off
      from the earth.
16 For he did not remember to show
    kindness,
      but pursued the poor and needy
      and the brokenhearted to their
      death.
17 He loved to curse; let curses come on
    him.
      He did not like blessing; may it be
      far from him.
18 He clothed himself with cursing as his
    coat,
      may it soak into his body like water,
      like oil into his bones.
19 May it be like a garment that he wraps
      around himself,
      like a belt that he wears every day."

[k] Or *by his holiness*   [l] Syr: Heb *I prayer*   [m]
Heb lacks *They say*   [n] Gk: Heb *and seek*   [o] Cn:
Heb *fathers*   [p] Gk: Heb *their*

A footstool was the footrest for a king's throne or steps leading to the throne. Solomon's throne had a footstool of gold. The footstools of some ancient kings had carvings representing other peoples and nations. These kings believed that they walked over their captives or enemies as they walked to the throne. In the Bible, the earth is often referred to as the footstool of God. This shows the dominion, or authority, of God as king and ruler over all things.

20 May that be the reward of my accusers
from the LORD,
of those who speak evil against my
life.
21 But you, O LORD my Lord,
act on my behalf for your name's
sake;
because your steadfast love is good,
deliver me.
22 For I am poor and needy,
and my heart is pierced within me.
23 I am gone like a shadow at evening;
I am shaken off like a locust.
24 My knees are weak through fasting;
my body has become gaunt.
25 I am an object of scorn to my accusers;
when they see me, they shake their
heads.

26 Help me, O LORD my God!
Save me according to your steadfast
love.
27 Let them know that this is your hand;
you, O LORD, have done it.
28 Let them curse, but you will bless.
Let my assailants be put to shame;*q*
may your servant be glad.
29 May my accusers be clothed with
dishonor;

may they be wrapped in their own
shame as in a mantle.
30 With my mouth I will give great
thanks to the LORD;
I will praise him in the midst of the
throng.
31 For he stands at the right hand of the
needy,
to save them from those who would
condemn them to death.

Psalm 110

Assurance of Victory for God's Priest-King

Of David. A Psalm.
1 The LORD says to my lord,
"Sit at my right hand
until I make your enemies your
footstool."

2 The LORD sends out from Zion
your mighty scepter.
Rule in the midst of your foes.
3 Your people will offer themselves
willingly
on the day you lead your forces
on the holy mountains.*r*
From the womb of the morning,
like dew, your youth*s* will come to
you.
4 The LORD has sworn and will not
change his mind,
"You are a priest forever according to
the order of Mel·chiz′e·dek."*t*

5 The Lord is at your right hand;
he will shatter kings on the day of
his wrath.
6 He will execute judgment among the
nations,
filling them with corpses;
he will shatter heads
over the wide earth.
7 He will drink from the stream by the
path;
therefore he will lift up his head.

q Gk: Heb *They have risen up and have been put to*
shame   *r* Another reading is *in holy splendor*
s Cn: Heb *the dew of your youth*   *t* Or *forever, a*
rightful king by my edict

Psalm 111

Praise for God's Wonderful Works

¹ Praise the LORD!
I will give thanks to the LORD with my
whole heart,
in the company of the upright, in
the congregation.
² Great are the works of the LORD,
studied by all who delight in them.
³ Full of honor and majesty is his work,
and his righteousness endures
forever.
⁴ He has gained renown by his
wonderful deeds;
the LORD is gracious and merciful.
⁵ He provides food for those who fear
him;
he is ever mindful of his covenant.
⁶ He has shown his people the power of
his works,
in giving them the heritage of the
nations.
⁷ The works of his hands are faithful and
just;
all his precepts are trustworthy.
⁸ They are established forever and ever,
to be performed with faithfulness
and uprightness.
⁹ He sent redemption to his people;
he has commanded his covenant
forever.
Holy and awesome is his name.
¹⁰ The fear of the LORD is the beginning
of wisdom;
all those who practice it[u] have a
good understanding.
His praise endures forever.

Psalm 112

Blessings of the Righteous

¹ Praise the LORD!
Happy are those who fear the LORD,
who greatly delight in his
commandments.
² Their descendants will be mighty in
the land;
the generation of the upright will be
blessed.

> "Great are the works of the
> LORD, studied by all who
> delight in them."
> Psalm 111:2

³ Wealth and riches are in their houses,
and their righteousness endures
forever.
⁴ They rise in the darkness as a light for
the upright;
they are gracious, merciful, and
righteous.
⁵ It is well with those who deal
generously and lend,
who conduct their affairs with justice.
⁶ For the righteous will never be moved;
they will be remembered forever.
⁷ They are not afraid of evil tidings;
their hearts are firm, secure in the
LORD.
⁸ Their hearts are steady, they will not be
afraid;
in the end they will look in triumph
on their foes.
⁹ They have distributed freely, they have
given to the poor;
their righteousness endures forever;
their horn is exalted in honor.
¹⁰ The wicked see it and are angry;
they gnash their teeth and melt
away;
the desire of the wicked comes to
nothing.

Psalm 113

God the Helper of the Needy

¹ Praise the LORD!
Praise, O servants of the LORD;
praise the name of the LORD.
² Blessed be the name of the LORD
from this time on and forevermore.
³ From the rising of the sun to its setting
the name of the LORD is to be
praised.
⁴ The LORD is high above all nations,
and his glory above the heavens.

u Gk Syr: Heb *them*

⁵ Who is like the LORD our God,
  who is seated on high,
⁶ who looks far down
  on the heavens and the earth?
⁷ He raises the poor from the dust,
  and lifts the needy from the ash
    heap,
⁸ to make them sit with princes,
  with the princes of his people.
⁹ He gives the barren woman a home,
  making her the joyous mother of
    children.
Praise the LORD!

> God cares for the poor
> and needy, lifting them up
> from their troubles. This
> psalm reminds us that just
> as God helps people in need, God
> wants us to do the same.

Psalm 114

God's Wonders at the Exodus

¹ When Israel went out from Egypt,
  the house of Jacob from a people
  of strange language,
² Judah became God'sᵛ sanctuary,
  Israel his dominion.

³ The sea looked and fled;
  Jordan turned back.
⁴ The mountains skipped like rams,
  the hills like lambs.

⁵ Why is it, O sea, that you flee?
  O Jordan, that you turn back?
⁶ O mountains, that you skip like
    rams?
  O hills, like lambs?

⁷ Tremble, O earth, at the presence of
    the LORD,
  at the presence of the God of
    Jacob,
⁸ who turns the rock into a pool of
    water,
  the flint into a spring of water.

Psalm 115

*The Impotence of Idols and the Greatness of
God*

¹ Not to us, O LORD, not to us, but to
    your name give glory,
  for the sake of your steadfast love
  and your faithfulness.
² Why should the nations say,
  "Where is their God?"

³ Our God is in the heavens;
  he does whatever he pleases.
⁴ Their idols are silver and gold,
  the work of human hands.
⁵ They have mouths, but do not speak;
  eyes, but do not see.
⁶ They have ears, but do not hear;
  noses, but do not smell.
⁷ They have hands, but do not feel;
  feet, but do not walk;
  they make no sound in their throats.
⁸ Those who make them are like them;
  so are all who trust in them.

⁹ O Israel, trust in the LORD!
  He is their help and their shield.
¹⁰ O house of Aaron, trust in the LORD!
  He is their help and their shield.
¹¹ You who fear the LORD, trust in the
    LORD!
  He is their help and their shield.

¹² The LORD has been mindful of us; he
    will bless us;
  he will bless the house of Israel;
  he will bless the house of Aaron;
¹³ he will bless those who fear the LORD,
  both small and great.

¹⁴ May the LORD give you increase,
  both you and your children.
¹⁵ May you be blessed by the LORD,
  who made heaven and earth.

¹⁶ The heavens are the LORD's heavens,
  but the earth he has given to human
    beings.
¹⁷ The dead do not praise the LORD,
  nor do any that go down into
    silence.

ᵛ Heb *his*

18 But we will bless the LORD
  from this time on and forevermore.
Praise the LORD!

Psalm 116

Thanksgiving for Recovery from Illness

1 I love the LORD, because he has heard
  my voice and my supplications.
2 Because he inclined his ear to me,
  therefore I will call on him as long
    as I live.
3 The snares of death encompassed me;
  the pangs of Shḗōl laid hold on me;
  I suffered distress and anguish.
4 Then I called on the name of the LORD:
  "O LORD, I pray, save my life!"

5 Gracious is the LORD, and righteous;
  our God is merciful.
6 The LORD protects the simple;
  when I was brought low, he saved
    me.
7 Return, O my soul, to your rest,
  for the LORD has dealt bountifully
    with you.

8 For you have delivered my soul from
    death,
  my eyes from tears,
  my feet from stumbling.
9 I walk before the LORD
  in the land of the living.
10 I kept my faith, even when I said,
  "I am greatly afflicted";
11 I said in my consternation,
  "Everyone is a liar."

12 What shall I return to the LORD
  for all his bounty to me?
13 I will lift up the cup of salvation
  and call on the name of the LORD,
14 I will pay my vows to the LORD
  in the presence of all his people.
15 Precious in the sight of the LORD
  is the death of his faithful ones.
16 O LORD, I am your servant;
  I am your servant, the child of your
    serving girl.
  You have loosed my bonds.

17 I will offer to you a thanksgiving
    sacrifice
  and call on the name of the LORD.
18 I will pay my vows to the LORD
  in the presence of all his people,
19 in the courts of the house of the LORD,
  in your midst, O Jerusalem.
Praise the LORD!

Psalm 117

Universal Call to Worship

1 Praise the LORD, all you nations!
  Extol him, all you peoples!
2 For great is his steadfast love toward
    us,
  and the faithfulness of the LORD
    endures forever.
Praise the LORD!

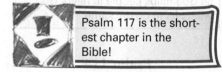

Psalm 117 is the short-
est chapter in the
Bible!

Psalm 118

A Song of Victory

1 O give thanks to the LORD, for he is
    good;
  his steadfast love endures forever!

2 Let Israel say,
  "His steadfast love endures forever."
3 Let the house of Aaron say,
  "His steadfast love endures forever."
4 Let those who fear the LORD say,
  "His steadfast love endures forever."

5 Out of my distress I called on the
    LORD;
  the LORD answered me and set me
    in a broad place.
6 With the LORD on my side I do not
    fear.
  What can mortals do to me?
7 The LORD is on my side to help
    me;
  I shall look in triumph on those
    who hate me.

⁸ It is better to take refuge in the LORD
  than to put confidence in mortals.
⁹ It is better to take refuge in the LORD
  than to put confidence in princes.

¹⁰ All nations surrounded me;
  in the name of the LORD I cut them
  off!
¹¹ They surrounded me, surrounded me
  on every side;
  in the name of the LORD I cut them
  off!
¹² They surrounded me like bees;
  they blazedʷ like a fire of thorns;
  in the name of the LORD I cut them
  off!
¹³ I was pushed hard,ˣ so that I was
  falling,
  but the LORD helped me.
¹⁴ The LORD is my strength and my
  might;
  he has become my salvation.

¹⁵ There are glad songs of victory in the
  tents of the righteous:
  "The right hand of the LORD does
  valiantly;
¹⁶ the right hand of the LORD is
  exalted;
  the right hand of the LORD does
  valiantly."
¹⁷ I shall not die, but I shall live,
  and recount the deeds of the LORD.
¹⁸ The LORD has punished me severely,
  but he did not give me over to
  death.

¹⁹ Open to me the gates of righteousness,
  that I may enter through them
  and give thanks to the LORD.

²⁰ This is the gate of the LORD;
  the righteous shall enter through it.

²¹ I thank you that you have answered me
  and have become my salvation.
²² The stone that the builders rejected
  has become the chief cornerstone.
²³ This is the LORD's doing;
  it is marvelous in our eyes.

²⁴ This is the day that the LORD has made;
  let us rejoice and be glad in it.ʸ
²⁵ Save us, we beseech you, O LORD!
  O LORD, we beseech you, give us
  success!

²⁶ Blessed is the one who comes in the
  name of the LORD.ᶻ
  We bless you from the house of the
  LORD.
²⁷ The LORD is God,
  and he has given us light.
  Bind the festal procession with
  branches,
  up to the horns of the altar.ᵃ

²⁸ You are my God, and I will give thanks
  to you;
  you are my God, I will extol you.

²⁹ O give thanks to the LORD, for he is
  good,
  for his steadfast love endures forever.

Psalm 119

The Glories of God's Law

¹ Happy are those whose way is
  blameless,
  who walk in the law of the LORD.
² Happy are those who keep his decrees,
  who seek him with their whole
  heart,

A cornerstone is the foundation of a wall. Without the cornerstone, the wall would fall down. Psalm 118:22 tells us that although some builders thought that a certain stone was useless, that same stone became the chief cornerstone. In the New Testament, we read that Jesus is the cornerstone for our lives. Read Matthew 21:42, Acts 4:11, Ephesians 2:20, and 1 Peter 2:7.

ʷ Gk: Heb *were extinguished*   ˣ Gk Syr Jerome:
Heb *You pushed me hard*   ʸ Or *in him*   ᶻ Or
Blessed in the name of the LORD is the one who comes
ᵃ Meaning of Heb uncertain

Psalm 119 is the longest psalm and the longest chapter in the whole Bible! This poem is based on the letters of the Hebrew alphabet. Each eight-line section of verses starts with a different letter of the alphabet. For example, verses 1–8 begin with the letter *Alef* (A), verses 9–16 begin with the letter *Bet* (B), and so on. This poem shows the importance of God's law for the people of God.

3 who also do no wrong,
   but walk in his ways.
4 You have commanded your precepts
   to be kept diligently.
5 O that my ways may be steadfast
   in keeping your statutes!
6 Then I shall not be put to shame,
   having my eyes fixed on all your
   commandments.
7 I will praise you with an upright
   heart,
   when I learn your righteous
   ordinances.
8 I will observe your statutes;
   do not utterly forsake me.

9 How can young people keep their way
   pure?
   By guarding it according to your
   word.
10 With my whole heart I seek you;
   do not let me stray from your
   commandments.
11 I treasure your word in my heart,
   so that I may not sin against you.
12 Blessed are you, O LORD;
   teach me your statutes.
13 With my lips I declare
   all the ordinances of your mouth.
14 I delight in the way of your decrees
   as much as in all riches.

15 I will meditate on your precepts,
   and fix my eyes on your ways.
16 I will delight in your statutes;
   I will not forget your word.

17 Deal bountifully with your servant,
   so that I may live and observe your
   word.
18 Open my eyes, so that I may behold
   wondrous things out of your law.
19 I live as an alien in the land;
   do not hide your commandments
   from me.
20 My soul is consumed with longing
   for your ordinances at all times.
21 You rebuke the insolent, accursed
   ones,
   who wander from your
   commandments;
22 take away from me their scorn and
   contempt,
   for I have kept your decrees.
23 Even though princes sit plotting
   against me,
   your servant will meditate on your
   statutes.
24 Your decrees are my delight,
   they are my counselors.

25 My soul clings to the dust;
   revive me according to your word.
26 When I told of my ways, you
   answered me;
   teach me your statutes.
27 Make me understand the way of your
   precepts,
   and I will meditate on your
   wondrous works.
28 My soul melts away for sorrow;
   strengthen me according to your
   word.
29 Put false ways far from me;
   and graciously teach me your law.
30 I have chosen the way of faithfulness;
   I set your ordinances before me.
31 I cling to your decrees, O LORD;
   let me not be put to shame.
32 I run the way of your
   commandments,

for you enlarge my understanding.

33 Teach me, O LORD, the way of your
     statutes,
     and I will observe it to the end.
34 Give me understanding, that I may
     keep your law
     and observe it with my whole heart.
35 Lead me in the path of your
     commandments,
     for I delight in it.
36 Turn my heart to your decrees,
     and not to selfish gain.
37 Turn my eyes from looking at vanities;
     give me life in your ways.
38 Confirm to your servant your promise,
     which is for those who fear you.
39 Turn away the disgrace that I dread,
     for your ordinances are good.
40 See, I have longed for your precepts;
     in your righteousness give me life.

41 Let your steadfast love come to me, O
     LORD,
     your salvation according to your
     promise.
42 Then I shall have an answer for those
     who taunt me,
     for I trust in your word.
43 Do not take the word of truth utterly
     out of my mouth,
     for my hope is in your ordinances.
44 I will keep your law continually,
     forever and ever.
45 I shall walk at liberty,
     for I have sought your precepts.
46 I will also speak of your decrees before
     kings,
     and shall not be put to shame;
47 I find my delight in your
     commandments,
     because I love them.
48 I revere your commandments, which I
     love,
     and I will meditate on your statutes.

49 Remember your word to your servant,
     in which you have made me hope.

50 This is my comfort in my distress,
     that your promise gives me life.
51 The arrogant utterly deride me,
     but I do not turn away from your
     law.
52 When I think of your ordinances from
     of old,
     I take comfort, O LORD.
53 Hot indignation seizes me because of
     the wicked,
     those who forsake your law.
54 Your statutes have been my songs
     wherever I make my home.
55 I remember your name in the night, O
     LORD,
     and keep your law.
56 This blessing has fallen to me,
     for I have kept your precepts.

57 The LORD is my portion;
     I promise to keep your words.
58 I implore your favor with all my heart;
     be gracious to me according to your
     promise.
59 When I think of your ways,
     I turn my feet to your decrees;
60 I hurry and do not delay
     to keep your commandments.
61 Though the cords of the wicked
     ensnare me,
     I do not forget your law.
62 At midnight I rise to praise you,
     because of your righteous
     ordinances.
63 I am a companion of all who fear you,
     of those who keep your precepts.
64 The earth, O LORD, is full of your
     steadfast love;
     teach me your statutes.
65 You have dealt well with your servant,
     O LORD, according to your word.
66 Teach me good judgment and
     knowledge,
     for I believe in your commandments.
67 Before I was humbled I went astray,
     but now I keep your word.
68 You are good and do good;
     teach me your statutes.
69 The arrogant smear me with lies,

but with my whole heart I keep
your precepts.
70 Their hearts are fat and gross,
but I delight in your law.
71 It is good for me that I was humbled,
so that I might learn your statutes.
72 The law of your mouth is better to me
than thousands of gold and silver
pieces.

73 Your hands have made and fashioned
me;
give me understanding that I may
learn your commandments.
74 Those who fear you shall see me and
rejoice,
because I have hoped in your word.
75 I know, O LORD, that your judgments
are right,
and that in faithfulness you have
humbled me.
76 Let your steadfast love become my
comfort
according to your promise to your
servant.
77 Let your mercy come to me, that I may
live;
for your law is my delight.
78 Let the arrogant be put to shame,
because they have subverted me
with guile;
as for me, I will meditate on your
precepts.
79 Let those who fear you turn to me,
so that they may know your decrees.
80 May my heart be blameless in your
statutes,
so that I may not be put to shame.

81 My soul languishes for your salvation;
I hope in your word.
82 My eyes fail with watching for your
promise;
I ask, "When will you comfort me?"
83 For I have become like a wineskin in
the smoke,
yet I have not forgotten your
statutes.
84 How long must your servant endure?

When will you judge those who
persecute me?
85 The arrogant have dug pitfalls for me;
they flout your law.
86 All your commandments are
enduring;
I am persecuted without cause; help
me!
87 They have almost made an end of me
on earth;
but I have not forsaken your
precepts.
88 In your steadfast love spare my life,
so that I may keep the decrees of
your mouth.

89 The LORD exists forever;
your word is firmly fixed in heaven.
90 Your faithfulness endures to all
generations;
you have established the earth, and
it stands fast.
91 By your appointment they stand today,
for all things are your servants.
92 If your law had not been my delight,
I would have perished in my misery.
93 I will never forget your precepts,
for by them you have given me life.
94 I am yours; save me,
for I have sought your precepts.
95 The wicked lie in wait to destroy me,
but I consider your decrees.
96 I have seen a limit to all perfection,
but your commandment is
exceedingly broad.

97 Oh, how I love your law!

When the psalmist
said he had become
"like a wineskin in the
smoke," he is referring
to the effects of suffering on his
body. In Bible times the people
hung wineskins in their tents,
and smoke from the fire made
the wineskins hard, wrinkled,
and shriveled.

It is my meditation all day long.
98 Your commandment makes me wiser
than my enemies,
for it is always with me.
99 I have more understanding than all my
teachers,
for your decrees are my meditation.
100 I understand more than the aged,
for I keep your precepts.
101 I hold back my feet from every evil
way,
in order to keep your word.
102 I do not turn away from your
ordinances,
for you have taught me.
103 How sweet are your words to my taste,
sweeter than honey to my mouth!
104 Through your precepts I get
understanding;
therefore I hate every false way.

105 Your word is a lamp to my feet
and a light to my path.
106 I have sworn an oath and confirmed it,
to observe your righteous
ordinances.
107 I am severely afflicted;
give me life, O LORD, according to
your word.
108 Accept my offerings of praise, O LORD,
and teach me your ordinances.
109 I hold my life in my hand continually,
but I do not forget your law.
110 The wicked have laid a snare for me,
but I do not stray from your
precepts.
111 Your decrees are my heritage forever;
they are the joy of my heart.
112 I incline my heart to perform your
statutes
forever, to the end.

113 I hate the double-minded,
but I love your law.
114 You are my hiding place and my shield;
I hope in your word.
115 Go away from me, you evildoers,
that I may keep the commandments
of my God.

"Your word is a lamp to
my feet and a light to
my path."
Psalm 119:105

116 Uphold me according to your promise,
that I may live,
and let me not be put to shame in
my hope.
117 Hold me up, that I may be safe
and have regard for your statutes
continually.
118 You spurn all who go astray from your
statutes;
for their cunning is in vain.
119 All the wicked of the earth you count
as dross;
therefore I love your decrees.
120 My flesh trembles for fear of you,
and I am afraid of your judgments.

121 I have done what is just and right;
do not leave me to my oppressors.
122 Guarantee your servant's well-being;
do not let the godless oppress me.
123 My eyes fail from watching for your
salvation,
and for the fulfillment of your
righteous promise.
124 Deal with your servant according to
your steadfast love,
and teach me your statutes.
125 I am your servant; give me
understanding,
so that I may know your decrees.
126 It is time for the LORD to act,
for your law has been broken.
127 Truly I love your commandments
more than gold, more than fine gold.
128 Truly I direct my steps by all your
precepts;[b]
I hate every false way.

129 Your decrees are wonderful;
therefore my soul keeps them.
130 The unfolding of your words gives light;
it imparts understanding to the
simple.

[b] Gk Jerome: Meaning of Heb uncertain

131 With open mouth I pant,
  because I long for your
   commandments.
132 Turn to me and be gracious to me,
  as is your custom toward those who
   love your name.
133 Keep my steps steady according to
   your promise,
  and never let iniquity have
   dominion over me.
134 Redeem me from human oppression,
  that I may keep your precepts.
135 Make your face shine upon your
   servant,
  and teach me your statutes.
136 My eyes shed streams of tears
  because your law is not kept.

137 You are righteous, O LORD,
  and your judgments are right.
138 You have appointed your decrees in
   righteousness
  and in all faithfulness.
139 My zeal consumes me
  because my foes forget your words.
140 Your promise is well tried,
  and your servant loves it.
141 I am small and despised,
  yet I do not forget your precepts.
142 Your righteousness is an everlasting
   righteousness,
  and your law is the truth.
143 Trouble and anguish have come upon
   me,
  but your commandments are my
   delight.
144 Your decrees are righteous forever;
  give me understanding that I may
   live.

145 With my whole heart I cry; answer
   me, O LORD.
  I will keep your statutes.
146 I cry to you; save me,
  that I may observe your decrees.
147 I rise before dawn and cry for help;
  I put my hope in your words.
148 My eyes are awake before each watch
  of the night,
   that I may meditate on your
    promise.
149 In your steadfast love hear my voice;
  O LORD, in your justice preserve my
   life.
150 Those who persecute me with evil
   purpose draw near;
  they are far from your law.
151 Yet you are near, O LORD,
  and all your commandments are
   true.
152 Long ago I learned from your decrees
  that you have established them
   forever.

153 Look on my misery and rescue me,
  for I do not forget your law.
154 Plead my cause and redeem me;
  give me life according to your
   promise.
155 Salvation is far from the wicked,
  for they do not seek your statutes.
156 Great is your mercy, O LORD;
  give me life according to your
   justice.
157 Many are my persecutors and my
   adversaries,
  yet I do not swerve from your
   decrees.
158 I look at the faithless with disgust,
  because they do not keep your
   commands.
159 Consider how I love your precepts;
  preserve my life according to your
   steadfast love.
160 The sum of your word is truth;
  and every one of your righteous
   ordinances endures forever.

161 Princes persecute me without cause,
  but my heart stands in awe of your
   words.
162 I rejoice at your word
  like one who finds great spoil.
163 I hate and abhor falsehood,
  but I love your law.
164 Seven times a day I praise you
  for your righteous ordinances.

¹⁶⁵ Great peace have those who love your law;
nothing can make them stumble.
¹⁶⁶ I hope for your salvation, O LORD,
and I fulfill your commandments.
¹⁶⁷ My soul keeps your decrees;
I love them exceedingly.
¹⁶⁸ I keep your precepts and decrees,
for all my ways are before you.
¹⁶⁹ Let my cry come before you, O LORD;
give me understanding according to your word.
¹⁷⁰ Let my supplication come before you;
deliver me according to your promise.
¹⁷¹ My lips will pour forth praise,
because you teach me your statutes.
¹⁷² My tongue will sing of your promise,
for all your commandments are right.
¹⁷³ Let your hand be ready to help me,
for I have chosen your precepts.
¹⁷⁴ I long for your salvation, O LORD,
and your law is my delight.
¹⁷⁵ Let me live that I may praise you,
and let your ordinances help me.
¹⁷⁶ I have gone astray like a lost sheep;
seek out your servant,
for I do not forget your commandments.

> The broom tree is a desert shrub or bush with pale pink flowers. It often grows large enough to offer shade. When burned, its roots and leaves get very hot and make a fine charcoal.

Psalm 120

Prayer for Deliverance from Slanderers

A Song of Ascents.

¹ In my distress I cry to the LORD,
that he may answer me:
² "Deliver me, O LORD,
from lying lips,
from a deceitful tongue."
³ What shall be given to you?

And what more shall be done to you,
you deceitful tongue?
⁴ A warrior's sharp arrows,
with glowing coals of the broom tree!

⁵ Woe is me, that I am an alien in Mē´shech,
that I must live among the tents of Kē´dar.
⁶ Too long have I had my dwelling
among those who hate peace.
⁷ I am for peace;
but when I speak,
they are for war.

> During times of trouble, we know that God will always help us. Psalm 121 is a song of trust in God, reminding us that God—the creator of heaven and earth—will watch over and protect us.

Psalm 121

Assurance of God's Protection

A Song of Ascents.

¹ I lift up my eyes to the hills—
from where will my help come?
² My help comes from the LORD,
who made heaven and earth.

³ He will not let your foot be moved;
he who keeps you will not slumber.
⁴ He who keeps Israel
will neither slumber nor sleep.

⁵ The LORD is your keeper;
the LORD is your shade at your right hand.
⁶ The sun shall not strike you by day,
nor the moon by night.

⁷ The LORD will keep you from all evil;
he will keep your life.
⁸ The LORD will keep
your going out and your coming in
from this time on and forevermore.

Psalm 122

Song of Praise and Prayer for Jerusalem

A Song of Ascents. Of David.

¹ I was glad when they said to me,
  "Let us go to the house of the
      LORD!"
² Our feet are standing
    within your gates, O Jerusalem.

³ Jerusalem—built as a city
    that is bound firmly together.
⁴ To it the tribes go up,
      the tribes of the LORD,
  as was decreed for Israel,
      to give thanks to the name of the
          LORD.
⁵ For there the thrones for judgment
      were set up,
    the thrones of the house of David.

⁶ Pray for the peace of Jerusalem:
    "May they prosper who love you.
⁷ Peace be within your walls,
    and security within your towers."
⁸ For the sake of my relatives and
      friends
    I will say, "Peace be within you."
⁹ For the sake of the house of the
      LORD our God,
    I will seek your good.

Psalm 123

Supplication for Mercy

A Song of Ascents.

¹ To you I lift up my eyes,
    O you who are enthroned in the
      heavens!
² As the eyes of servants
    look to the hand of their master,
  as the eyes of a maid
    to the hand of her mistress,
  so our eyes look to the LORD our God,
    until he has mercy upon us.

³ Have mercy upon us, O LORD, have
      mercy upon us,
    for we have had more than
      enough of contempt.

⁴ Our soul has had more than its fill
    of the scorn of those who are at
      ease,
  of the contempt of the proud.

Psalms 120–134 are called "Songs of Ascent." The Israelites sang these songs when they traveled to the city of Jerusalem at festival times or in procession going up to the Temple. Jerusalem was on a hill, and the only way to get to the Temple was to "ascend," or climb, the hill. The word "ascent" means "a going up."

Psalm 124

Thanksgiving for Israel's Deliverance

A Song of Ascents. Of David.

¹ If it had not been the LORD who was
      on our side
    —let Israel now say—
² if it had not been the LORD who was
      on our side,
    when our enemies attacked us,
³ then they would have swallowed us
      up alive,
    when their anger was kindled
      against us;
⁴ then the flood would have swept us
      away,
    the torrent would have gone over
      us;
⁵ then over us would have gone
      the raging waters.

⁶ Blessed be the LORD,
    who has not given us
      as prey to their teeth.
⁷ We have escaped like a bird
    from the snare of the fowlers;
  the snare is broken,
    and we have escaped.

⁸ Our help is in the name of the LORD,
    who made heaven and earth.

In the same way that mountains surrounded the city of Jerusalem, God surrounded God's people, and God surrounds us still today. God is always with us, and we can trust that God will protect us and keep us safe.

Psalm 125

The Security of God's People

A Song of Ascents.

¹ Those who trust in the LORD are like Mount Zion,
  which cannot be moved, but abides forever.
² As the mountains surround Jerusalem,
  so the LORD surrounds his people,
  from this time on and forevermore.
³ For the scepter of wickedness shall not rest
  on the land allotted to the righteous,
  so that the righteous might not stretch out
  their hands to do wrong.
⁴ Do good, O LORD, to those who are good,
  and to those who are upright in their hearts.
⁵ But those who turn aside to their own crooked ways
  the LORD will lead away with evildoers.
  Peace be upon Israel!

Psalm 126

A Harvest of Joy

A Song of Ascents.

¹ When the LORD restored the fortunes of Zion,ᶜ
  we were like those who dream.

"Unless the LORD builds the house, those who build it labor in vain. Unless the LORD guards the city, the guard keeps watch in vain."
Psalm 127:1

² Then our mouth was filled with laughter,
  and our tongue with shouts of joy;
  then it was said among the nations,
  "The LORD has done great things for them."
³ The LORD has done great things for us,
  and we rejoiced.

⁴ Restore our fortunes, O LORD,
  like the watercourses in the Neg´eb.
⁵ May those who sow in tears
  reap with shouts of joy.
⁶ Those who go out weeping,
  bearing the seed for sowing,
shall come home with shouts of joy,
  carrying their sheaves.

Psalm 127

God's Blessings in the Home

A Song of Ascents. Of Solomon.

¹ Unless the LORD builds the house,
  those who build it labor in vain.
Unless the LORD guards the city,
  the guard keeps watch in vain.
² It is in vain that you rise up early
  and go late to rest,
eating the bread of anxious toil;
  for he gives sleep to his beloved.ᵈ

³ Sons are indeed a heritage from the LORD,
  the fruit of the womb a reward.
⁴ Like arrows in the hand of a warrior
  are the sons of one's youth.
⁵ Happy is the man who has
  his quiver full of them.
He shall not be put to shame
  when he speaks with his enemies in the gate.

Psalm 128

The Happy Home of the Faithful

A Song of Ascents.

¹ Happy is everyone who fears the LORD,
  who walks in his ways.

ᶜ Or brought back those who returned to Zion   ᵈ Or for he provides for his beloved during sleep

2 You shall eat the fruit of the labor of
     your hands;
     you shall be happy, and it shall go
       well with you.

3 Your wife will be like a fruitful vine
     within your house;
     your children will be like olive shoots
       around your table.
4 Thus shall the man be blessed
     who fears the LORD.

5 The LORD bless you from Zion.
     May you see the prosperity of
       Jerusalem
     all the days of your life.
6 May you see your children's children.
     Peace be upon Israel!

Psalm 129

Prayer for the Downfall of Israel's Enemies

A Song of Ascents.
1 "Often have they attacked me from my
     youth"
     —let Israel now say—
2 "often have they attacked me from my
     youth,
     yet they have not prevailed against
       me.
3 The plowers plowed on my back;
     they made their furrows long."
4 The LORD is righteous;
     he has cut the cords of the wicked.
5 May all who hate Zion
     be put to shame and turned
       backward.

In Bible times, people made roofs by laying large beams side to side and covering these beams with branches. Then they spread earth or gravel on top of the branches. Grass would grow out of the layer of earth, but it would soon die because there was no place for it to put down roots

6 Let them be like the grass on the
     housetops
     that withers before it grows up,
7 with which reapers do not fill their
     hands
     or binders of sheaves their arms,
8 while those who pass by do not say,
     "The blessing of the LORD be upon
       you!
     We bless you in the name of the
       LORD!"

The psalmist says that if God remembered all the wrongs we have done, we wouldn't even be able to stand up. But God forgives us. All we need to do is ask, and our sins are forgotten. In the same way that God forgives us, so we must also forgive others. Think of a time when someone did something that hurt or upset you. Then, even if that person never apologized, forgive him or her. Pray to God for help with forgiveness, and thank God for always hearing us and forgiving our sins.

Psalm 130

Waiting for Divine Redemption

A Song of Ascents.
1 Out of the depths I cry to you, O LORD.
2   Lord, hear my voice!
     Let your ears be attentive
     to the voice of my supplications!

3 If you, O LORD, should mark iniquities,
     Lord, who could stand?
4 But there is forgiveness with you,
     so that you may be revered.

5 I wait for the LORD, my soul waits,
     and in his word I hope;
6 my soul waits for the Lord
     more than those who watch for the
       morning,
     more than those who watch for the
       morning.

⁷ O Israel, hope in the LORD!
    For with the LORD there is steadfast
    love,
    and with him is great power to
    redeem.
⁸ It is he who will redeem Israel
    from all its iniquities.

Psalm 131

Song of Quiet Trust

A Song of Ascents. Of David.

¹ O LORD, my heart is not lifted up,
    my eyes are not raised too high;
  I do not occupy myself with things
    too great and too marvelous for me.
² But I have calmed and quieted my
    soul,
    like a weaned child with its mother;
    my soul is like the weaned child that
    is with me.ᵉ

³ O Israel, hope in the LORD
    from this time on and forevermore.

Psalm 132

The Eternal Dwelling of God in Zion

A Song of Ascents.

¹ O LORD, remember in David's favor
    all the hardships he endured;
² how he swore to the LORD
    and vowed to the Mighty One of
    Jacob,
³ "I will not enter my house
    or get into my bed;
⁴ I will not give sleep to my eyes
    or slumber to my eyelids,
⁵ until I find a place for the LORD,
    a dwelling place for the Mighty One
    of Jacob."

⁶ We heard of it in Eph´ra·thah;
    we found it in the fields of Ja´ar.
⁷ "Let us go to his dwelling place;
    let us worship at his footstool."

⁸ Rise up, O LORD, and go to your
    resting place,
    you and the ark of your might.

⁹ Let your priests be clothed with
    righteousness,
    and let your faithful shout for joy.
¹⁰ For your servant David's sake
    do not turn away the face of your
    anointed one.

¹¹ The LORD swore to David a sure oath
    from which he will not turn back:
  "One of the sons of your body
    I will set on your throne.
¹² If your sons keep my covenant
    and my decrees that I shall teach
    them,
  their sons also, forevermore,
    shall sit on your throne."

¹³ For the LORD has chosen Zion;
    he has desired it for his habitation:
¹⁴ "This is my resting place forever;
    here I will reside, for I have desired it.
¹⁵ I will abundantly bless its provisions;
    I will satisfy its poor with bread.
¹⁶ Its priests I will clothe with salvation,
    and its faithful will shout for joy.
¹⁷ There I will cause a horn to sprout up
    for David;
    I have prepared a lamp for my
    anointed one.
¹⁸ His enemies I will clothe with disgrace,
    but on him, his crown will gleam."

Psalm 133

The Blessedness of Unity

A Song of Ascents.

¹ How very good and pleasant it is
    when kindred live together in unity!
² It is like the precious oil on the head,
    running down upon the beard,
  on the beard of Aaron,
    running down over the collar of his
    robes.

"How very good and
pleasant it is when kindred
live together in unity!"
Psalm 133:1

ᵉ Or *my soul within me is like a weaned child*

3 It is like the dew of Hermon,
  which falls on the mountains of Zion.
For there the LORD ordained his
    blessing,
  life forevermore.

Psalm 134

Praise in the Night

A Song of Ascents.

1 Come, bless the LORD, all you servants
  of the LORD,
  who stand by night in the house of
    the LORD!
2 Lift up your hands to the holy place,
  and bless the LORD.

3 May the LORD, maker of heaven and
    earth,
  bless you from Zion.

Psalm 135

Praise for God's Goodness and Might

1 Praise the LORD!
  Praise the name of the LORD;
  give praise, O servants of the LORD,
2 you that stand in the house of the
    LORD,
  in the courts of the house of our
    God.
3 Praise the LORD, for the LORD is good;
  sing to his name, for he is gracious.
4 For the LORD has chosen Jacob for
    himself,
  Israel as his own possession.

5 For I know that the LORD is great;
  our Lord is above all gods.
6 Whatever the LORD pleases he does,
  in heaven and on earth,
  in the seas and all deeps.
7 He it is who makes the clouds rise at
    the end of the earth;
  he makes lightnings for the rain
  and brings out the wind from his
    storehouses.

8 He it was who struck down the
    firstborn of Egypt,
  both human beings and animals;

9 he sent signs and wonders
  into your midst, O Egypt,
  against Pharaoh and all his servants.
10 He struck down many nations
  and killed mighty kings—
11 Sī′hon, king of the Am′o·rītes,
  and Og, king of Bā′shan,
  and all the kingdoms of Cā′naan—
12 and gave their land as a heritage,
  a heritage to his people Israel.

13 Your name, O LORD, endures forever,
  your renown, O LORD, throughout
    all ages.
14 For the LORD will vindicate his people,
  and have compassion on his
    servants.

15 The idols of the nations are silver and
    gold,
  the work of human hands.
16 They have mouths, but they do not
    speak;
  they have eyes, but they do not see;
17 they have ears, but they do not hear,
  and there is no breath in their
    mouths.
18 Those who make them
  and all who trust them
  shall become like them.

19 O house of Israel, bless the LORD!
  O house of Aaron, bless the LORD!
20 O house of Levi, bless the LORD!
  You that fear the LORD, bless the
    LORD!
21 Blessed be the LORD from Zion,
  he who resides in Jerusalem.
Praise the LORD!

Psalm 136

God's Work in Creation and in History

1 O give thanks to the LORD, for he is
    good,
  for his steadfast love endures forever.
2 O give thanks to the God of gods,
  for his steadfast love endures forever.

Every single verse of Psalm 136 ends with the words, "for his steadfast love endures forever." God will never stop loving and caring for this world. The love of God will last for all time.

³ O give thanks to the Lord of lords,
    for his steadfast love endures forever;

⁴ who alone does great wonders,
    for his steadfast love endures forever;
⁵ who by understanding made the
      heavens,
    for his steadfast love endures forever;
⁶ who spread out the earth on the
      waters,
    for his steadfast love endures forever;
⁷ who made the great lights,
    for his steadfast love endures forever;
⁸ the sun to rule over the day,
    for his steadfast love endures forever;
⁹ the moon and stars to rule over the
      night,
    for his steadfast love endures forever;

¹⁰ who struck Egypt through their
      firstborn,
    for his steadfast love endures forever;
¹¹ and brought Israel out from among
      them,
    for his steadfast love endures forever;
¹² with a strong hand and an
      outstretched arm,
    for his steadfast love endures forever;
¹³ who divided the Red Sea*ᶠ* in two,
    for his steadfast love endures forever;
¹⁴ and made Israel pass through the
      midst of it,
    for his steadfast love endures forever;
¹⁵ but overthrew Pharaoh and his army
      in the Red Sea,ᶠ
    for his steadfast love endures forever;
¹⁶ who led his people through the
      wilderness,
    for his steadfast love endures forever;

¹⁷ who struck down great kings,
    for his steadfast love endures forever;
¹⁸ and killed famous kings,
    for his steadfast love endures forever;
¹⁹ Sīʹhon, king of the Amʹo·rītes,
    for his steadfast love endures forever;
²⁰ and Og, king of Bāʹshan,
    for his steadfast love endures forever;
²¹ and gave their land as a heritage,
    for his steadfast love endures forever;
²² a heritage to his servant Israel,
    for his steadfast love endures forever.

²³ It is he who remembered us in our low
      estate,
    for his steadfast love endures forever;
²⁴ and rescued us from our foes,
    for his steadfast love endures forever;
²⁵ who gives food to all flesh,
    for his steadfast love endures forever.

²⁶ O give thanks to the God of heaven,
    for his steadfast love endures forever.

Psalm 137 talks about the loss of the great city of Jerusalem. Writing from exile in Babylon, the psalmist remembers the way things used to be and expresses sadness and anger to God. We too can express our honest feelings to God. Take some time right now to pray, telling God exactly how you feel.

Psalm 137

Lament over the Destruction of Jerusalem

¹ By the rivers of Babylon—
    there we sat down and there we
      wept
    when we remembered Zion.
² On the willowsᵍ there
    we hung up our harps.
³ For there our captors
    asked us for songs,

ᶠ Or *Sea of Reeds*   ᵍ Or *poplars*

and our tormentors asked for mirth,
saying,
"Sing us one of the songs of Zion!"

[4] How could we sing the LORD's song
in a foreign land?
[5] If I forget you, O Jerusalem,
let my right hand wither!
[6] Let my tongue cling to the roof of my
mouth,
if I do not remember you,
if I do not set Jerusalem
above my highest joy.

[7] Remember, O LORD, against the
Ē´dom·ites
the day of Jerusalem's fall,
how they said, "Tear it down! Tear it
down!
Down to its foundations!"
[8] O daughter Babylon, you devastator![h]
Happy shall they be who pay you
back
what you have done to us!
[9] Happy shall they be who take your
little ones
and dash them against the rock!

Psalm 138

Thanksgiving and Praise

Of David.
[1] I give you thanks, O LORD, with my
whole heart;
before the gods I sing your praise;
[2] I bow down toward your holy temple
and give thanks to your name for
your steadfast love and your
faithfulness;
for you have exalted your name and
your word
above everything.[i]
[3] On the day I called, you answered me,
you increased my strength of soul.[j]

[4] All the kings of the earth shall praise
you, O LORD,
for they have heard the words of
your mouth.

[5] They shall sing of the ways of the LORD,
for great is the glory of the LORD.
[6] For though the LORD is high, he
regards the lowly;
but the haughty he perceives from
far away.

[7] Though I walk in the midst of trouble,
you preserve me against the wrath
of my enemies;
you stretch out your hand,
and your right hand delivers me.
[8] The LORD will fulfill his purpose for me;
your steadfast love, O LORD, endures
forever.
Do not forsake the work of your
hands.

Psalm 139

The Inescapable God

To the leader. Of David. A Psalm.
[1] O LORD, you have searched me and
known me.
[2] You know when I sit down and
when I rise up;
you discern my thoughts from far
away.
[3] You search out my path and my lying
down,
and are acquainted with all my
ways.
[4] Even before a word is on my tongue,
O LORD, you know it completely.
[5] You hem me in, behind and before,
and lay your hand upon me.
[6] Such knowledge is too wonderful for
me;
it is so high that I cannot attain it.

[7] Where can I go from your spirit?
Or where can I flee from your
presence?
[8] If I ascend to heaven, you are there;
if I make my bed in Shē´ōl, you are
there.

[h] *Or you who are devastated*   [i] *Cn: Heb you have
exalted your word above all your name*   [j] *Syr
Compare Gk Tg: Heb you made me arrogant in my
soul with strength*

Is there anyone who knows everything there is to know about you? God does! God knows you inside and out—every thought, every word, and every action. God is with you everywhere you go. God never leaves or sleeps. God loves you and cares for you.

9 If I take the wings of the morning
  and settle at the farthest limits of the
    sea,
10 even there your hand shall lead me,
  and your right hand shall hold me
    fast.
11 If I say, "Surely the darkness shall
    cover me,
  and the light around me become
    night,"
12 even the darkness is not dark to you;
  the night is as bright as the day,
    for darkness is as light to you.

13 For it was you who formed my inward
    parts;
  you knit me together in my mother's
    womb.
14 I praise you, for I am fearfully and
    wonderfully made.
  Wonderful are your works;
    that I know very well.
15   My frame was not hidden from you,
  when I was being made in secret,
    intricately woven in the depths of
      the earth.
16 Your eyes beheld my unformed
    substance.
  In your book were written
    all the days that were formed for me,
      when none of them as yet existed.
17 How weighty to me are your thoughts,
    O God!
  How vast is the sum of them!
18 I try to count them—they are more
    than the sand;
  I come to the end[k]—I am still with
    you.

19 O that you would kill the wicked, O
    God,
  and that the bloodthirsty would
    depart from me—
20 those who speak of you maliciously,
  and lift themselves up against you
    for evil![l]
21 Do I not hate those who hate you, O
    LORD?
  And do I not loathe those who rise
    up against you?
22 I hate them with perfect hatred;
  I count them my enemies.
23 Search me, O God, and know my
    heart;
  test me and know my thoughts.
24 See if there is any wicked[m] way in
    me,
  and lead me in the way
    everlasting.[n]

Psalm 140

Prayer for Deliverance from Enemies

To the leader. A Psalm of David.
1 Deliver me, O LORD, from
    evildoers;
  protect me from those who are
    violent,
2 who plan evil things in their minds
  and stir up wars continually.
3 They make their tongue sharp as a
    snake's,
  and under their lips is the venom of
    vipers.   *Selah*

4 Guard me, O LORD, from the hands of
    the wicked;
  protect me from the violent
    who have planned my downfall.
5 The arrogant have hidden a trap for
    me,
  and with cords they have spread a
    net,[o]
  along the road they have set snares
    for me.   *Selah*

---

[k] Or *I awake*   [l] Cn: Meaning of Heb uncertain
[m] Heb *hurtful*   [n] Or *the ancient way.* Compare Jer
6.16   [o] Or *they have spread cords as a net*

6 I say to the LORD, "You are my God;
> give ear, O LORD, to the voice of my
> supplications."
7 O LORD, my Lord, my strong deliverer,
> you have covered my head in the
> day of battle.
8 Do not grant, O LORD, the desires of
> the wicked;
> do not further their evil plot.*p*

Sělah

9 Those who surround me lift up their
> heads;*q*
> let the mischief of their lips
> overwhelm them!
10 Let burning coals fall on them!
> Let them be flung into pits, no more
> to rise!
11 Do not let the slanderer be established
> in the land;
> let evil speedily hunt down the
> violent!

12 I know that the LORD maintains the
> cause of the needy,
> and executes justice for the poor.
13 Surely the righteous shall give thanks
> to your name;
> the upright shall live in your
> presence.

Psalm 141

Prayer for Preservation from Evil

A Psalm of David.

1 I call upon you, O LORD; come quickly
> to me;
> give ear to my voice when I call to
> you.
2 Let my prayer be counted as incense
> before you,
> and the lifting up of my hands as an
> evening sacrifice.

3 Set a guard over my mouth, O LORD;
> keep watch over the door of my lips.
4 Do not turn my heart to any evil,
> to busy myself with wicked deeds

in company with those who work
> iniquity;
> do not let me eat of their delicacies.
5 Let the righteous strike me;
> let the faithful correct me.
> Never let the oil of the wicked anoint
> my head,*r*
> for my prayer is continually*s* against
> their wicked deeds.
6 When they are given over to those
> who shall condemn them,
> then they shall learn that my words
> were pleasant.
7 Like a rock that one breaks apart and
> shatters on the land,
> so shall their bones be strewn at the
> mouth of Shě'ōl.*t*

8 But my eyes are turned toward you, O
> GOD, my Lord;
> in you I seek refuge; do not leave
> me defenseless.
9 Keep me from the trap that they have
> laid for me,
> and from the snares of evildoers.
10 Let the wicked fall into their own nets,
> while I alone escape.

Psalm 142

Prayer for Deliverance from Persecutors

A Maskil of David.
When he was in the cave. A Prayer.

1 With my voice I cry to the LORD;
> with my voice I make supplication
> to the LORD.
2 I pour out my complaint before him;
> I tell my trouble before him.
3 When my spirit is faint,
> you know my way.

In the path where I walk
> they have hidden a trap for me.

p Heb adds *they are exalted*   *q* Cn Compare Gk:
Heb *those who surround me are uplifted in head*; Heb
divides verses 8 and 9 differently   *r* Gk: Meaning
of Heb uncertain   *s* Cn: Heb *for continually and
my prayer*   *t* Meaning of Heb of verses 5-7 is
uncertain

⁴ Look on my right hand and see—
  there is no one who takes notice of
    me;
no refuge remains to me;
  no one cares for me.

⁵ I cry to you, O LORD;
  I say, "You are my refuge,
    my portion in the land of the living."
⁶ Give heed to my cry,
  for I am brought very low.

Save me from my persecutors,
  for they are too strong for me.
⁷ Bring me out of prison,
  so that I may give thanks to your
    name.
The righteous will surround me,
  for you will deal bountifully with me.

Psalm 143

Prayer for Deliverance from Enemies

A Psalm of David.
¹ Hear my prayer, O LORD;
  give ear to my supplications in your
    faithfulness;
  answer me in your righteousness.
² Do not enter into judgment with your
    servant,
  for no one living is righteous before
    you.
³ For the enemy has pursued me,
  crushing my life to the ground,
  making me sit in darkness like those
    long dead.
⁴ Therefore my spirit faints within me;
  my heart within me is appalled.
⁵ I remember the days of old,
  I think about all your deeds,
  I meditate on the works of your
    hands.
⁶ I stretch out my hands to you;
  my soul thirsts for you like a
    parched land.   *Selah*

⁷ Answer me quickly, O LORD;
  my spirit fails.
Do not hide your face from me,

> "Let me hear of your stead-
> fast love in the morning, for
> in you I put my trust. Teach
> me the way I should go, for
> to you I lift up my soul."
> **Psalm 143:8**

or I shall be like those who go down
  to the Pit.

⁸ Let me hear of your steadfast love in
    the morning,
  for in you I put my trust.
Teach me the way I should go,
  for to you I lift up my soul.
⁹ Save me, O LORD, from my enemies;
  I have fled to you for refuge.ᵘ
¹⁰ Teach me to do your will,
  for you are my God.
Let your good spirit lead me
  on a level path.

¹¹ For your name's sake, O LORD,
    preserve my life.
In your righteousness bring me out
  of trouble.
¹² In your steadfast love cut off my
    enemies,
  and destroy all my adversaries,
  for I am your servant.

Psalm 144

*Prayer for National Deliverance and
Security*

Of David.
¹ Blessed be the LORD, my rock,
  who trains my hands for war, and
    my fingers for battle;
² my rockᵛ and my fortress,
  my stronghold and my deliverer,
my shield, in whom I take refuge,
  who subdues the peoplesʷ under me.

³ O LORD, what are human beings that
    you regard them,
  or mortals that you think of them?

ᵘ One Heb Ms Gk: MT *to you I have hidden*
ᵛ With 18.2 and 2 Sam 22.2: Heb *my steadfast love*
ʷ Heb Mss Syr Aquila Jerome: MT *my people*

"Happy are the people whose God is the LORD."
Psalm 144:15*b*

⁴ They are like a breath;
their days are like a passing shadow.

⁵ Bow your heavens, O LORD, and come
down;
touch the mountains so that they
smoke.
⁶ Make the lightning flash and scatter
them;
send out your arrows and rout
them.
⁷ Stretch out your hand from on high;
set me free and rescue me from the
mighty waters,
from the hand of aliens,
⁸ whose mouths speak lies,
and whose right hands are false.

⁹ I will sing a new song to you,
O God;
upon a ten-stringed harp I will play
to you,
¹⁰ the one who gives victory to kings,
who rescues his servant David.
¹¹ Rescue me from the cruel sword,
and deliver me from the hand of
aliens,
whose mouths speak lies,
and whose right hands are false.

¹² May our sons in their youth
be like plants full grown,
our daughters like corner pillars,
cut for the building of a palace.
¹³ May our barns be filled,
with produce of every kind;
may our sheep increase by
thousands,
by tens of thousands in our fields,
¹⁴ and may our cattle be heavy with
young.
May there be no breach in the walls,^x
no exile,
and no cry of distress in our
streets.

¹⁵ Happy are the people to whom such
blessings fall;
happy are the people whose God is
the LORD.

Psalm 145

The Greatness and the Goodness of God

Praise. Of David.
¹ I will extol you, my God and King,
and bless your name forever and
ever.
² Every day I will bless you,
and praise your name forever and
ever.
³ Great is the LORD, and greatly to be
praised;
his greatness is unsearchable.

⁴ One generation shall laud your works
to another,
and shall declare your mighty
acts.
⁵ On the glorious splendor of your
majesty,
and on your wondrous works, I will
meditate.
⁶ The might of your awesome deeds
shall be proclaimed,
and I will declare your greatness.
⁷ They shall celebrate the fame of your
abundant goodness,
and shall sing aloud of your
righteousness.

⁸ The LORD is gracious and merciful,
slow to anger and abounding in
steadfast love.
⁹ The LORD is good to all,
and his compassion is over all that
he has made.

¹⁰ All your works shall give thanks to
you, O LORD,
and all your faithful shall bless
you.
¹¹ They shall speak of the glory of your
kingdom,
and tell of your power,

^x Heb lacks *in the walls*

The writer of Psalm 145 praises God for God's goodness and greatness. Read this psalm and make a list of the words and phrases used to describe God. Here are a few to help you get started: great, wondrous works, gracious, merciful, power, faithful, and kind. What other words in this psalm describe who God is?

¹² to make known to all people your^y
    mighty deeds,
    and the glorious splendor of your^z
      kingdom.
¹³ Your kingdom is an everlasting
    kingdom,
    and your dominion endures
      throughout allgenerations.
The LORD is faithful in all his words,
    and gracious in all his deeds.^a
¹⁴ The LORD upholds all who are falling,
    and raises up all who are bowed
      down.
¹⁵ The eyes of all look to you,
    and you give them their food in due
      season.
¹⁶ You open your hand,
    satisfying the desire of every living
      thing.
¹⁷ The LORD is just in all his ways,
    and kind in all his doings.
¹⁸ The LORD is near to all who call on
    him,
    to all who call on him in truth.
¹⁹ He fulfills the desire of all who fear
    him;
    he also hears their cry, and saves
      them.
²⁰ The LORD watches over all who love
    him,
    but all the wicked he will destroy.

²¹ My mouth will speak the praise of the
    LORD,
    and all flesh will bless his holy name
    forever and ever.

Psalm 146
Praise for God's Help

¹ Praise the LORD!
    Praise the LORD, O my soul!
² I will praise the LORD as long as I
    live;
    I will sing praises to my God all
      my life long

³ Do not put your trust in princes,
    in mortals, in whom there is no
      help.
⁴ When their breath departs, they
    return to the earth;
    on that very day their plans perish.

⁵ Happy are those whose help is the
    God of Jacob,
    whose hope is in the LORD their
      God,
⁶ who made heaven and earth,
    the sea, and all that is in them;
who keeps faith forever;
⁷   who executes justice for the
      oppressed;
    who gives food to the hungry.

The LORD sets the prisoners free;
⁸   the LORD opens the eyes of the
      blind.
The LORD lifts up those who are
    bowed down;
    the LORD loves the righteous.
⁹ The LORD watches over the strangers;
    he upholds the orphan and the
      widow,
    but the way of the wicked he brings
    to ruin.

What are some ways that God has helped you? What are some ways that God has helped your family and your friends? Our whole life long, we should always praise God, giving thanks for God's loving care.

^y Gk Jerome Syr: Heb *his*   ^z Heb *his*   ^a These two lines supplied by Q Ms Gk Syr

10 The LORD will reign forever,
  your God, O Zion, for all
    generations.
  Praise the LORD!

Psalm 147

Praise for God's Care for Jerusalem

1 Praise the LORD!
  How good it is to sing praises to our
    God;
  for he is gracious, and a song of
    praise is fitting.
2 The LORD builds up Jerusalem;
  he gathers the outcasts of Israel.
3 He heals the brokenhearted,
  and binds up their wounds.
4 He determines the number of the stars;
  he gives to all of them their names.
5 Great is our Lord, and abundant in
    power;
  his understanding is beyond
    measure.
6 The LORD lifts up the downtrodden;
  he casts the wicked to the ground.

7 Sing to the LORD with thanksgiving;
  make melody to our God on the
    lyre.
8 He covers the heavens with clouds,
  prepares rain for the earth,
  makes grass grow on the hills.
9 He gives to the animals their food,
  and to the young ravens when they
    cry.
10 His delight is not in the strength of the
    horse,
  nor his pleasure in the speed of a
    runner;[b]
11 but the LORD takes pleasure in those
    who fear him,
  in those who hope in his steadfast
    love.

12 Praise the LORD, O Jerusalem!
  Praise your God, O Zion!
13 For he strengthens the bars of your
    gates;
  he blesses your children within you.

14 He grants peace[c] within your borders;
  he fills you with the finest of wheat.
15 He sends out his command to the
    earth;
  his word runs swiftly.
16 He gives snow like wool;
  he scatters frost like ashes.
17 He hurls down hail like crumbs—
  who can stand before his cold?
18 He sends out his word, and melts them;
  he makes his wind blow, and the
    waters flow.
19 He declares his word to Jacob,
  his statutes and ordinances to Israel.
20 He has not dealt thus with any other
    nation;
  they do not know his ordinances.
  Praise the LORD!

Psalm 148

Praise for God's Universal Glory

1 Praise the LORD!
  Praise the LORD from the heavens;
  praise him in the heights!
2 Praise him, all his angels;
  praise him, all his host!

3 Praise him, sun and moon;
  praise him, all you shining stars!
4 Praise him, you highest heavens,
  and you waters above the heavens!

5 Let them praise the name of the LORD,
  for he commanded and they were
    created.
6 He established them forever and ever;
  he fixed their bounds, which
    cannot be passed.[d]

7 Praise the LORD from the earth,
  you sea monsters and all deeps,
8 fire and hail, snow and frost,
  stormy wind fulfilling his command!

9 Mountains and all hills,
  fruit trees and all cedars!

*b Heb legs of a person   c Or prosperity   d Or he
set a law that cannot pass away*

10 Wild animals and all cattle,
    creeping things and flying birds!

11 Kings of the earth and all peoples,
    princes and all rulers of the earth!
12 Young men and women alike,
    old and young together!

13 Let them praise the name of the LORD,
    for his name alone is exalted;
    his glory is above earth and heaven.
14 He has raised up a horn for his people,
    praise for all his faithful,
    for the people of Israel who are
        close to him.
    Praise the LORD!

Psalm 149

Praise for God's Goodness to Israel

1 Praise the LORD!
  Sing to the LORD a new song,
    his praise in the assembly of the
        faithful.
2 Let Israel be glad in its Maker;
    let the children of Zion rejoice in
        their King.
3 Let them praise his name with
        dancing,
    making melody to him with
        tambourine and lyre.
4 For the LORD takes pleasure in his
        people;
    he adorns the humble with victory.
5 Let the faithful exult in glory;
    let them sing for joy on their
        couches.
6 Let the high praises of God be in their
        throats
    and two-edged swords in their
        hands,

7 to execute vengeance on the nations
    and punishment on the peoples,
8 to bind their kings with fetters
    and their nobles with chains of iron,
9 to execute on them the judgment
    decreed.
    This is glory for all his faithful ones.
    Praise the LORD!

Psalm 150

Praise for God's Surpassing Greatness

1 Praise the LORD!
  Praise God in his sanctuary;
    praise him in his mighty firmament![e]
2 Praise him for his mighty deeds;
    praise him according to his
        surpassing greatness!

3 Praise him with trumpet sound;
    praise him with lute and harp!
4 Praise him with tambourine and dance;
    praise him with strings and pipe!
5 Praise him with clanging cymbals;
    praise him with loud clashing
        cymbals!
6 Let everything that breathes praise the
        LORD!
    Praise the LORD!

Cymbals in Bible times
looked very much like
the cymbals we use
today. They were made of two
circular plates of brass or other
metal. The people would strike
the two plates against each other
to make a loud clanging sound.

[e] Or *dome*

Proverbs

Proverbs is a collection of poetic sayings. Some chapters of Proverbs are long poems, while others contain many short and witty sayings. Because Solomon was thought to be a very wise king, many of these sayings are called proverbs of Solomon. These poetic sayings were collected at different times over hundreds of years.

Most of the proverbs are couplets—little poems of two lines each. Frequently, the second line of a couplet says the same thing as the first line, but in an opposite way, as this one does:

A soft answer turns away wrath,
     but a harsh word stirs up anger."
                              Proverbs 15:1

Proverbs 1:8–9

The writer of Proverbs often mentions the "fear of the Lord." We should always think of God with love, awe, and respect. Knowing how to think about God is the beginning of knowing lots of other things and will help us live our lives in the right way.

1 The proverbs of Solomon son of David, king of Israel:

Prologue

2 For learning about wisdom and instruction,
for understanding words of insight,
3 for gaining instruction in wise dealing,
righteousness, justice, and equity;
4 to teach shrewdness to the simple,
knowledge and prudence to the young—
5 let the wise also hear and gain in learning,
and the discerning acquire skill,
6 to understand a proverb and a figure,
the words of the wise and their riddles.

7 The fear of the Lord is the beginning of knowledge;
fools despise wisdom and instruction.

Warnings against Evil Companions

8 Hear, my child, your father's instruction,
and do not reject your mother's teaching;
9 for they are a fair garland for your head,
and pendants for your neck.
10 My child, if sinners entice you,
do not consent.
11 If they say, "Come with us, let us lie in wait for blood;
let us wantonly ambush the innocent;

12 like Shēʹōl let us swallow them alive
and whole, like those who go down to the Pit.
13 We shall find all kinds of costly things;
we shall fill our houses with booty.
14 Throw in your lot among us;
we will all have one purse"—
15 my child, do not walk in their way,
keep your foot from their paths;
16 for their feet run to evil,
and they hurry to shed blood.
17 For in vain is the net baited
while the bird is looking on;
18 yet they lie in wait—to kill themselves!
and set an ambush—for their own lives!
19 Such is the end[a] of all who are greedy for gain;
it takes away the life of its possessors.

The Call of Wisdom

20 Wisdom cries out in the street;
in the squares she raises her voice.
21 At the busiest corner she cries out;
at the entrance of the city gates she speaks:
22 "How long, O simple ones, will you love being simple?
How long will scoffers delight in their scoffing
and fools hate knowledge?
23 Give heed to my reproof;
I will pour out my thoughts to you;
I will make my words known to you.
24 Because I have called and you refused,
have stretched out my hand and no one heeded,
25 and because you have ignored all my counsel
and would have none of my reproof,
26 I also will laugh at your calamity;
I will mock when panic strikes you,
27 when panic strikes you like a storm,
and your calamity comes like a whirlwind,
when distress and anguish come upon you.

[a] Gk: Heb *are the ways*

> "Therefore walk in the way of the good, and keep to the paths of the just." Proverbs 2:20

28 Then they will call upon me, but I will
    not answer;
  they will seek me diligently, but will
    not find me.
29 Because they hated knowledge
    and did not choose the fear of the
    LORD,
30 would have none of my counsel,
    and despised all my reproof,
31 therefore they shall eat the fruit of their
    way
  and be sated with their own devices.
32 For waywardness kills the simple,
    and the complacency of fools
    destroys them;
33 but those who listen to me will be
    secure
  and will live at ease, without dread
    of disaster."

The Value of Wisdom

2 My child, if you accept my words
    and treasure up my command-
    ments within you,
2 making your ear attentive to wisdom
    and inclining your heart to
    understanding;
3 if you indeed cry out for insight,
    and raise your voice for
    understanding;
4 if you seek it like silver,
    and search for it as for hidden
    treasures—
5 then you will understand the fear of
    the LORD
  and find the knowledge of God.
6 For the LORD gives wisdom;
    from his mouth come knowledge
    and understanding;
7 he stores up sound wisdom for the
    upright;
  he is a shield to those who walk
    blamelessly,

8 guarding the paths of justice
    and preserving the way of his
    faithful ones.
9 Then you will understand
    righteousness and justice
    and equity, every good path;
10 for wisdom will come into your heart,
    and knowledge will be pleasant to
    your soul;
11 prudence will watch over you;
    and understanding will guard you.
12 It will save you from the way of evil,
    from those who speak perversely,
13 who forsake the paths of uprightness
    to walk in the ways of darkness,
14 who rejoice in doing evil
    and delight in the perverseness of
    evil;
15 those whose paths are crooked,
    and who are devious in their ways.

16 You will be saved from the loose[b]
    woman,
  from the adulteress with her smooth
    words,
17 who forsakes the partner of her youth
    and forgets her sacred covenant;
18 for her way[c] leads down to death,
    and her paths to the shades;
19 those who go to her never come back,
    nor do they regain the paths of life.

20 Therefore walk in the way of the good,
    and keep to the paths of the just.
21 For the upright will abide in the land,
    and the innocent will remain in it;
22 but the wicked will be cut off from the
    land,
  and the treacherous will be rooted
    out of it.

Admonition to Trust and Honor God

3 My child, do not forget my teaching,
    but let your heart keep my
    commandments;
2 for length of days and years of life

---

[b] Heb strange   [c] Cn: Heb house

and abundant welfare they will give
you.

³ Do not let loyalty and faithfulness
forsake you;
bind them around your neck,
write them on the tablet of your
heart.
⁴ So you will find favor and good repute
in the sight of God and of people.

⁵ Trust in the Lord with all your heart,
and do not rely on your own
insight.
⁶ In all your ways acknowledge him,
and he will make straight your
paths.
⁷ Do not be wise in your own eyes;
fear the Lord, and turn away from
evil.
⁸ It will be a healing for your flesh
and a refreshment for your body.

⁹ Honor the Lord with your substance
and with the first fruits of all your
produce;
¹⁰ then your barns will be filled with
plenty,
and your vats will be bursting with
wine.

¹¹ My child, do not despise the Lord's
discipline
or be weary of his reproof,
¹² for the Lord reproves the one he loves,
as a father the son in whom he
delights.

The True Wealth
¹³ Happy are those who find wisdom,
and those who get understanding,
¹⁴ for her income is better than silver,
and her revenue better than gold.
¹⁵ She is more precious than jewels,
and nothing you desire can compare
with her.
¹⁶ Long life is in her right hand;
in her left hand are riches and
honor.

> "Trust in the Lord with
> all your heart, and do
> not rely on your own
> insight. In all your ways
> acknowledge him, and he will
> make straight your paths."
> Proverbs 3:5–6

¹⁷ Her ways are ways of pleasantness,
and all her paths are peace.
¹⁸ She is a tree of life to those who lay
hold of her;
those who hold her fast are called
happy.

God's Wisdom in Creation
¹⁹ The Lord by wisdom founded the
earth;
by understanding he established the
heavens;
²⁰ by his knowledge the deeps broke
open,
and the clouds drop down the dew.

The True Security
²¹ My child, do not let these escape from
your sight:
keep sound wisdom and prudence,
²² and they will be life for your soul
and adornment for your neck.
²³ Then you will walk on your way
securely
and your foot will not stumble.
²⁴ If you sit down,ᵈ you will not be
afraid;
when you lie down, your sleep will
be sweet.
²⁵ Do not be afraid of sudden panic,
or of the storm that strikes the
wicked;
²⁶ for the Lord will be your confidence
and will keep your foot from being
caught.

²⁷ Do not withhold good from those to
whom it is due,ᵉ
when it is in your power to do it.

ᵈ Gk: Heb *lie down*   ᵉ Heb *from its owners*

28 Do not say to your neighbor, "Go, and come again,
   tomorrow I will give it"—when you have it with you.
29 Do not plan harm against your neighbor
   who lives trustingly beside you.
30 Do not quarrel with anyone without cause,
   when no harm has been done to you.
31 Do not envy the violent
   and do not choose any of their ways;
32 for the perverse are an abomination to the LORD,
   but the upright are in his confidence.
33 The LORD's curse is on the house of the wicked,
   but he blesses the abode of the righteous.
34 Toward the scorners he is scornful,
   but to the humble he shows favor.
35 The wise will inherit honor,
   but stubborn fools, disgrace.

Parental Advice

4 Listen, children, to a father's instruction,
   and be attentive, that you may gain*f* insight;
2 for I give you good precepts:
   do not forsake my teaching.
3 When I was a son with my father,
   tender, and my mother's favorite,
4 he taught me, and said to me,
   "Let your heart hold fast my words;
   keep my commandments, and live.
5 Get wisdom; get insight: do not forget,
   nor turn away
   from the words of my mouth.
6 Do not forsake her, and she will keep you;
   love her, and she will guard you.
7 The beginning of wisdom is this: Get wisdom,
   and whatever else you get, get insight.

8 Prize her highly, and she will exalt you;
   she will honor you if you embrace her.
9 She will place on your head a fair garland;
   she will bestow on you a beautiful crown."

Admonition to Keep to the Right Path

10 Hear, my child, and accept my words,
   that the years of your life may be many.
11 I have taught you the way of wisdom;
   I have led you in the paths of uprightness.
12 When you walk, your step will not be hampered;
   and if you run, you will not stumble.
13 Keep hold of instruction; do not let go;
   guard her, for she is your life.
14 Do not enter the path of the wicked,
   and do not walk in the way of evildoers.
15 Avoid it; do not go on it;
   turn away from it and pass on.
16 For they cannot sleep unless they have done wrong;
   they are robbed of sleep unless they have made someone stumble.
17 For they eat the bread of wickedness
   and drink the wine of violence.
18 But the path of the righteous is like the light of dawn,
   which shines brighter and brighter until full day.
19 The way of the wicked is like deep darkness;
   they do not know what they stumble over.
20 My child, be attentive to my words;
   incline your ear to my sayings.
21 Do not let them escape from your sight;
   keep them within your heart.
22 For they are life to those who find them,
   and healing to all their flesh.

f Heb *know*

23 Keep your heart with all vigilance,
    for from it flow the springs of life.
24 Put away from you crooked speech,
    and put devious talk far from you.
25 Let your eyes look directly forward,
    and your gaze be straight before
    you.
26 Keep straight the path of your feet,
    and all your ways will be sure.
27 Do not swerve to the right or to the left;
    turn your foot away from evil.

Warning against Impurity and Infidelity

5 My child, be attentive to my
    wisdom;
    incline your ear to my
    understanding,
2 so that you may hold on to prudence,
    and your lips may guard knowledge.
3 For the lips of a loose[g] woman drip
    honey,
    and her speech is smoother than oil;
4 but in the end she is bitter as
    wormwood,
    sharp as a two-edged sword.
5 Her feet go down to death;
    her steps follow the path to Shē'ōl.
6 She does not keep straight to the path
    of life;
    her ways wander, and she does not
    know it.

7 And now, my child,[h] listen to me,
    and do not depart from the words of
    my mouth.
8 Keep your way far from her,
    and do not go near the door of her
    house;
9 or you will give your honor to others,
    and your years to the merciless,
10 and strangers will take their fill of your
    wealth,
    and your labors will go to the house
    of an alien;
11 and at the end of your life you will
    groan,
    when your flesh and body are
    consumed,

12 and you say, "Oh, how I hated
    discipline,
    and my heart despised reproof!
13 I did not listen to the voice of my
    teachers
    or incline my ear to my instructors.
14 Now I am at the point of utter ruin
    in the public assembly."

15 Drink water from your own cistern,
    flowing water from your own well.
16 Should your springs be scattered
    abroad,
    streams of water in the streets?
17 Let them be for yourself alone,
    and not for sharing with strangers.
18 Let your fountain be blessed,
    and rejoice in the wife of your
    youth,
19   a lovely deer, a graceful doe.
    May her breasts satisfy you at all
    times;
    may you be intoxicated always by
    her love.
20 Why should you be intoxicated, my
    son, by another woman
    and embrace the bosom of an
    adulteress?
21 For human ways are under the eyes of
    the LORD,
    and he examines all their paths.
22 The iniquities of the wicked ensnare
    them,
    and they are caught in the toils of
    their sin.
23 They die for lack of discipline,
    and because of their great folly they
    are lost.

Practical Admonitions

6 My child, if you have given your
    pledge to your neighbor,
    if you have bound yourself to
    another,[i]
2 you are snared by the utterance of
    your lips,[j]

g Heb strange   h Gk Vg: Heb children   i Or a
stranger   j Cn: Compare Gk Syr: Heb the words
of your mouth

Did you ever make a promise you couldn't keep? How did you feel? The writer reminds us that we should never give our word (make a promise) lightly. We should be thoughtful and only make promises we know we can keep.

caught by the words of your mouth.
³ So do this, my child, and save yourself,
for you have come into your
neighbor's power:
go, hurry,[k] and plead with your
neighbor.
⁴ Give your eyes no sleep
and your eyelids no slumber;
⁵ save yourself like a gazelle from the
hunter,[l]
like a bird from the hand of the
fowler.

⁶ Go to the ant, you lazybones;
consider its ways, and be wise.
⁷ Without having any chief
or officer or ruler,
⁸ it prepares its food in summer,
and gathers its sustenance in harvest.
⁹ How long will you lie there, O
lazybones?
When will you rise from your sleep?
¹⁰ A little sleep, a little slumber,
a little folding of the hands to rest,
¹¹ and poverty will come upon you like a
robber,
and want, like an armed warrior.

¹² A scoundrel and a villain
goes around with crooked speech,
¹³ winking the eyes, shuffling the feet,
pointing the fingers,
¹⁴ with perverted mind devising evil,
continually sowing discord;
¹⁵ on such a one calamity will descend
suddenly;
in a moment, damage beyond repair.

¹⁶ There are six things that the LORD
hates,

seven that are an abomination to
him:
¹⁷ haughty eyes, a lying tongue,
and hands that shed innocent blood,
¹⁸ a heart that devises wicked plans,
feet that hurry to run to evil,
¹⁹ a lying witness who testifies falsely,
and one who sows discord in a
family.

²⁰ My child, keep your father's
commandment,
and do not forsake your mother's
teaching.
²¹ Bind them upon your heart always;
tie them around your neck.
²² When you walk, they[m] will lead you;
when you lie down, they[m] will
watch over you;
and when you awake, they[m] will talk
with you.
²³ For the commandment is a lamp and
the teaching a light,
and the reproofs of discipline are the
way of life,
²⁴ to preserve you from the wife of
another,[n]
from the smooth tongue of the
adulteress.
²⁵ Do not desire her beauty in your heart,
and do not let her capture you with
her eyelashes;
²⁶ for a prostitute's fee is only a loaf of
bread,[o]
but the wife of another stalks a
man's very life.

There are many wise sayings about the foolishness of living a lazy life. Read Proverbs 10:26; 12:24; 13:4; 15:19; 19:15; 20:4; 21:25; 22:13; 24:30–34 and 26:13–16. What do these proverbs have in common?

k Or *humble yourself*   l Cn: Heb *from the hand*
m Heb *it*   n Gk: MT *the evil woman*   o Cn
Compare Gk Syr Vg Tg: Heb *for because of a harlot
to a piece of bread*

²⁷ Can fire be carried in the bosom
  without burning one's clothes?
²⁸ Or can one walk on hot coals
  without scorching the feet?
²⁹ So is he who sleeps with his neighbor's
  wife;
  no one who touches her will go
  unpunished.
³⁰ Thieves are not despised who steal only
  to satisfy their appetite when they
  are hungry.
³¹ Yet if they are caught, they will pay
  sevenfold;
  they will forfeit all the goods of their
  house.
³² But he who commits adultery has no
  sense;
  he who does it destroys himself.
³³ He will get wounds and dishonor,
  and his disgrace will not be wiped
  away.
³⁴ For jealousy arouses a husband's fury,
  and he shows no restraint when he
  takes revenge.
³⁵ He will accept no compensation,
  and refuses a bribe no matter how
  great.

The False Attractions of Adultery

7 My child, keep my words
  and store up my commandments with you;
² keep my commandments and live,
  keep my teachings as the apple of
  your eye;
³ bind them on your fingers,
  write them on the tablet of your
  heart.

In Bible times, people wrote on tablets made of clay or wood. For this reason, the writer tells listeners to remember words of wisdom in their hearts as if their hearts were tablets on which they were writing the words.

⁴ Say to wisdom, "You are my sister,"
  and call insight your intimate friend,
⁵ that they may keep you from the loose[p]
  woman,
  from the adulteress with her smooth
  words.

⁶ For at the window of my house
  I looked out through my lattice,
⁷ and I saw among the simple ones,
  I observed among the youths,
  a young man without sense,
⁸ passing along the street near her
  corner,
  taking the road to her house
⁹ in the twilight, in the evening,
  at the time of night and darkness.

¹⁰ Then a woman comes toward him,
  decked out like a prostitute, wily of
  heart.[q]
¹¹ She is loud and wayward;
  her feet do not stay at home;
¹² now in the street, now in the squares,
  and at every corner she lies in
  wait.
¹³ She seizes him and kisses him,
  and with impudent face she says to
  him:
¹⁴ "I had to offer sacrifices,
  and today I have paid my vows;
¹⁵ so now I have come out to meet you,
  to seek you eagerly, and I have
  found you!
¹⁶ I have decked my couch with
  coverings,
  colored spreads of Egyptian linen;
¹⁷ I have perfumed my bed with myrrh,
  aloes, and cinnamon.
¹⁸ Come, let us take our fill of love until
  morning;
  let us delight ourselves with love.
¹⁹ For my husband is not at home;
  he has gone on a long journey.
²⁰ He took a bag of money with him;
  he will not come home until full
  moon."

[p] Heb strange   [q] Meaning of Heb uncertain

> "Take my instruction instead of silver, and knowledge rather than choice gold; for wisdom is better than jewels."
>
> Proverbs 8:10–11*a*

21 With much seductive speech she
　　persuades him;
　with her smooth talk she compels
　　him.
22 Right away he follows her,
　　and goes like an ox to the slaughter,
　or bounds like a stag toward the trap[r]
23 　　until an arrow pierces its entrails.
　He is like a bird rushing into a snare,
　　not knowing that it will cost him his
　　life.

24 And now, my children, listen to me,
　　and be attentive to the words of my
　　mouth.
25 Do not let your hearts turn aside to her
　　ways;
　do not stray into her paths.
26 for many are those she has laid low,
　　and numerous are her victims.
27 Her house is the way to Shĕ'ōl,
　　going down to the chambers of
　　death.

The Gifts of Wisdom

8 Does not wisdom call,
　　and does not understanding
　　raise her voice?
2 On the heights, beside the way,
　　at the crossroads she takes her
　　stand;
3 beside the gates in front of the town,
　　at the entrance of the portals she
　　cries out:
4 "To you, O people, I call,
　　and my cry is to all that live.
5 O simple ones, learn prudence;
　　acquire intelligence, you who lack
　　it.
6 Hear, for I will speak noble things,
　　and from my lips will come what is
　　right;

7 for my mouth will utter truth;
　　wickedness is an abomination to my
　　lips.
8 All the words of my mouth are
　　righteous;
　there is nothing twisted or crooked
　　in them.
9 They are all straight to one who
　　understands
　and right to those who find
　　knowledge.
10 Take my instruction instead of
　　silver,
　and knowledge rather than choice
　　gold;
11 for wisdom is better than jewels,
　　and all that you may desire cannot
　　compare with her.
12 I, wisdom, live with prudence,[s]
　　and I attain knowledge and
　　discretion.
13 The fear of the Lord is hatred of
　　evil.
　Pride and arrogance and the way of
　　evil
　and perverted speech I hate.
14 I have good advice and sound
　　wisdom;
　I have insight, I have strength.
15 By me kings reign,
　　and rulers decree what is just;
16 by me rulers rule,
　　and nobles, all who govern
　　rightly.
17 I love those who love me,
　　and those who seek me diligently
　　find me.
18 Riches and honor are with me,
　　enduring wealth and prosperity.
19 My fruit is better than gold, even fine
　　gold,
　and my yield than choice silver.
20 I walk in the way of righteousness,
　　along the paths of justice,
21 endowing with wealth those who love
　　me,
　and filling their treasuries.

[r] Cn: Compare Gk: Meaning of Heb uncertain
[s] Meaning of Heb uncertain

Wisdom's Part in Creation

22 The LORD created me at the beginning[t]
    of his work,[u]
  the first of his acts of long ago.
23 Ages ago I was set up,
    at the first, before the beginning of
    the earth.
24 When there were no depths I was
    brought forth,
  when there were no springs
    abounding with water.
25 Before the mountains had been
    shaped,
  before the hills, I was brought
    forth—
26 when he had not yet made earth and
    fields,[v]
  or the world's first bits of soil.
27 When he established the heavens, I
    was there,
  when he drew a circle on the face of
    the deep,
28 when he made firm the skies above,
  when he established the fountains of
    the deep,
29 when he assigned to the sea its limit,
    so that the waters might not
    transgress his command,
  when he marked out the foundations
    of the earth,
30   then I was beside him, like a master
    worker;[w]
  and I was daily his[x] delight,
    rejoicing before him always,
31 rejoicing in his inhabited world
    and delighting in the human race.

32 "And now, my children, listen to me:
    happy are those who keep my ways.
33 Hear instruction and be wise,
    and do not neglect it.
34 Happy is the one who listens to me,
    watching daily at my gates,
    waiting beside my doors.
35 For whoever finds me finds life
    and obtains favor from the LORD;
36 but those who miss me injure
    themselves;
  all who hate me love death."

Wisdom's Feast

9 Wisdom has built her house,
    she has hewn her seven pillars.
2 She has slaughtered her animals, she
    has mixed her wine,
  she has also set her table.
3 She has sent out her servant-girls, she
    calls
  from the highest places in the town,
4 "You that are simple, turn in here!"
    To those without sense she says,
5 "Come, eat of my bread
    and drink of the wine I have mixed.
6 Lay aside immaturity,[y] and live,
    and walk in the way of insight."

General Maxims

7 Whoever corrects a scoffer wins abuse;
    whoever rebukes the wicked gets
    hurt.
8 A scoffer who is rebuked will only
    hate you;
  the wise, when rebuked, will love
    you.
9 Give instruction[z] to the wise, and they
    will become wiser still;
  teach the righteous and they will
    gain in learning.
10 The fear of the LORD is the beginning
    of wisdom,
  and the knowledge of the Holy One
    is insight.
11 For by me your days will be multiplied,
    and years will be added to your life.
12 If you are wise, you are wise for
    yourself;
  if you scoff, you alone will bear it.

Folly's Invitation and Promise

13 The foolish woman is loud;
    she is ignorant and knows nothing.
14 She sits at the door of her house,
    on a seat at the high places of the
    town,
15 calling to those who pass by,
    who are going straight on their way,

---

[t] Or *me as the beginning*   [u] Heb *way*   [v] Meaning of Heb uncertain   [w] Another reading is *little child*   [x] Gk: Heb lacks *his*   [y] Or *simpleness*   [z] Heb lacks *instruction*

16 "You who are simple, turn in here!"
    And to those without sense she says,
17 "Stolen water is sweet,
    and bread eaten in secret is pleasant."
18 But they do not know that the dead[a]
    are there,
    that her guests are in the depths of
    Shĕ´ōl.

Wise Sayings of Solomon

10 The proverbs of Solomon.

1 A wise child makes a glad father,
    but a foolish child is a mother's grief.
2 Treasures gained by wickedness do not
    profit,
    but righteousness delivers from
    death.
3 The LORD does not let the righteous go
    hungry,
    but he thwarts the craving of the
    wicked.
4 A slack hand causes poverty,
    but the hand of the diligent makes
    rich.
5 A child who gathers in summer is
    prudent,
    but a child who sleeps in harvest
    brings shame.
6 Blessings are on the head of the
    righteous,
    but the mouth of the wicked
    conceals violence.
7 The memory of the righteous is a
    blessing,
    but the name of the wicked will rot.
8 The wise of heart will heed
    commandments,
    but a babbling fool will come to
    ruin.
9 Whoever walks in integrity walks
    securely,
    but whoever follows perverse ways
    will be found out.

"The blessing of the LORD
makes rich, and he adds
no sorrow with it."
Proverbs 10:22

10 Whoever winks the eye causes trouble,
    but the one who rebukes boldly
    makes peace.[b]
11 The mouth of the righteous is a
    fountain of life,
    but the mouth of the wicked
    conceals violence.
12 Hatred stirs up strife,
    but love covers all offenses.
13 On the lips of one who has
    understanding wisdom is found,
    but a rod is for the back of one who
    lacks sense.
14 The wise lay up knowledge,
    but the babbling of a fool brings
    ruin near.
15 The wealth of the rich is their fortress;
    the poverty of the poor is their ruin.
16 The wage of the righteous leads to life,
    the gain of the wicked to sin.
17 Whoever heeds instruction is on the
    path to life,
    but one who rejects a rebuke goes
    astray.
18 Lying lips conceal hatred,
    and whoever utters slander is a fool.
19 When words are many, transgression is
    not lacking,
    but the prudent are restrained in
    speech.
20 The tongue of the righteous is choice
    silver;
    the mind of the wicked is of little
    worth.
21 The lips of the righteous feed many,
    but fools die for lack of sense.
22 The blessing of the LORD makes rich,
    and he adds no sorrow with it.[c]
23 Doing wrong is like sport to a fool,
    but wise conduct is pleasure to a
    person of understanding.
24 What the wicked dread will come
    upon them,
    but the desire of the righteous will
    be granted.
25 When the tempest passes, the wicked
    are no more,

[a] Heb shades   [b] Gk: Heb but a babbling fool will
come to ruin   [c] Or and toil adds nothing to it

but the righteous are established
forever.
26 Like vinegar to the teeth, and smoke to
the eyes,
so are the lazy to their employers.
27 The fear of the LORD prolongs life,
but the years of the wicked will be
short.
28 The hope of the righteous ends in
gladness,
but the expectation of the wicked
comes to nothing.
29 The way of the LORD is a stronghold
for the upright,
but destruction for evildoers.
30 The righteous will never be
removed,
but the wicked will not remain in
the land.
31 The mouth of the righteous brings
forth wisdom,
but the perverse tongue will be cut
off.
32 The lips of the righteous know what is
acceptable,
but the mouth of the wicked what is
perverse.

11 A false balance is an
abomination to the LORD,
but an accurate weight is his delight.
2 When pride comes, then comes
disgrace;
but wisdom is with the humble.
3 The integrity of the upright guides
them,
but the crookedness of the
treacherous destroys them.
4 Riches do not profit in the day of
wrath,
but righteousness delivers from
death.
5 The righteousness of the blameless
keeps their ways straight,
but the wicked fall by their own
wickedness.
6 The righteousness of the upright saves
them,
but the treacherous are taken captive
by their schemes.

7 When the wicked die, their hope
perishes,
and the expectation of the godless
comes to nothing.
8 The righteous are delivered from
trouble,
and the wicked get into it
instead.
9 With their mouths the godless would
destroy their neighbors,
but by knowledge the righteous are
delivered.
10 When it goes well with the righteous,
the city rejoices;
and when the wicked perish, there
is jubilation.
11 By the blessing of the upright a city is
exalted,
but it is overthrown by the mouth of
the wicked.
12 Whoever belittles another lacks
sense,
but an intelligent person remains
silent.
13 A gossip goes about telling secrets,
but one who is trustworthy in spirit
keeps a confidence.
14 Where there is no guidance, a nation[d]
falls,
but in an abundance of counselors
there is safety.
15 To guarantee loans for a stranger
brings trouble,
but there is safety in refusing to do
so.
16 A gracious woman gets honor,
but she who hates virtue is covered
with shame.[e]
The timid become destitute,[f]
but the aggressive gain riches.
17 Those who are kind reward
themselves,
but the cruel do themselves harm.
18 The wicked earn no real gain,
but those who sow righteousness get
a true reward.

---

[d] Or *an army*   [e] Compare Gk Syr: Heb lacks *but
she . . . shame*   [f] Gk: Heb lacks *The timid . . .
destitute*

19 Whoever is steadfast in righteousness
will live,
but whoever pursues evil will die.
20 Crooked minds are an abomination to
the LORD,
but those of blameless ways are his
delight.
21 Be assured, the wicked will not go
unpunished,
but those who are righteous will
escape.
22 Like a gold ring in a pig's snout
is a beautiful woman without good
sense.
23 The desire of the righteous ends only
in good;
the expectation of the wicked in
wrath.
24 Some give freely, yet grow all the
richer;
others withhold what is due, and
only suffer want.
25 A generous person will be enriched,
and one who gives water will get
water.
26 The people curse those who hold back
grain,
but a blessing is on the head of
those who sell it.
27 Whoever diligently seeks good seeks
favor,
but evil comes to the one who
searches for it.
28 Those who trust in their riches will
wither,[g]
but the righteous will flourish like
green leaves.
29 Those who trouble their households
will inherit wind,
and the fool will be servant to the
wise.
30 The fruit of the righteous is a tree of
life,
but violence[h] takes lives away.
31 If the righteous are repaid on earth,
how much more the wicked and the
sinner!

12 Whoever loves discipline loves
knowledge,

but those who hate to be rebuked
are stupid.
2 The good obtain favor from the LORD,
but those who devise evil he
condemns.
3 No one finds security by wickedness,
but the root of the righteous will
never be moved.
4 A good wife is the crown of her
husband,
but she who brings shame is like
rottenness in his bones.
5 The thoughts of the righteous are just;
the advice of the wicked is
treacherous.
6 The words of the wicked are a deadly
ambush,
but the speech of the upright
delivers them.
7 The wicked are overthrown and are no
more,
but the house of the righteous will
stand.
8 One is commended for good sense,
but a perverse mind is despised.
9 Better to be despised and have a
servant,
than to be self-important and lack
food.
10 The righteous know the needs of their
animals,
but the mercy of the wicked is cruel.
11 Those who till their land will have
plenty of food,
but those who follow worthless
pursuits have no sense.
12 The wicked covet the proceeds of
wickedness,[i]
but the root of the righteous bears
fruit.
13 The evil are ensnared by the
transgression of their lips,
but the righteous escape from
trouble.
14 From the fruit of the mouth one is
filled with good things,
and manual labor has its reward.

g Cn: Heb *fall*　　h Cn: Compare Gk Syr: Heb *a wise man*　　i Or *covet the catch of the wicked*

¹⁵ Fools think their own way is right,
  but the wise listen to advice.
¹⁶ Fools show their anger at once,
  but the prudent ignore an insult.
¹⁷ Whoever speaks the truth gives honest
    evidence,
  but a false witness speaks deceitfully.
¹⁸ Rash words are like sword thrusts,
  but the tongue of the wise brings
    healing.
¹⁹ Truthful lips endure forever,
  but a lying tongue lasts only a
    moment.
²⁰ Deceit is in the mind of those who
    plan evil,
  but those who counsel peace have
    joy.
²¹ No harm happens to the righteous,
  but the wicked are filled with
    trouble.
²² Lying lips are an abomination to the
    LORD,
  but those who act faithfully are his
    delight.
²³ One who is clever conceals
    knowledge,
  but the mind of a fool ʲ broadcasts
    folly.
²⁴ The hand of the diligent will rule,
  while the lazy will be put to forced
    labor.
²⁵ Anxiety weighs down the human
    heart,
  but a good word cheers it up.
²⁶ The righteous gives good advice to
    friends,ᵏ
  but the way of the wicked leads
    astray.
²⁷ The lazy do not roastˡ their game,
  but the diligent obtain precious
    wealth.ˡ
²⁸ In the path of righteousness there is
    life,
  in walking its path there is no death.

13 A wise child loves discipline,ᵐ
  but a scoffer does not listen to
    rebuke.
² From the fruit of their words good
    persons eat good things,

In the Bible, the term
"discipline" refers to
training and instruc-
tion. It also means "correction"
and "punishment." This usually refers to the training of a
child, as here, but it is also
used to indicate God's discipline of people through fortune
and misfortune.

  but the desire of the treacherous is
    for wrongdoing.
³ Those who guard their mouths
    preserve their lives;
  those who open wide their lips
    come to ruin.
⁴ The appetite of the lazy craves, and
    gets nothing,
  while the appetite of the diligent is
    richly supplied.
⁵ The righteous hate falsehood,
  but the wicked act shamefully and
    disgracefully.
⁶ Righteousness guards one whose way
    is upright,
  but sin overthrows the wicked.
⁷ Some pretend to be rich, yet have
    nothing;
  others pretend to be poor, yet have
    great wealth.
⁸ Wealth is a ransom for a person's life,
  but the poor get no threats.

You may have heard peo-
ple say, "Sticks and
stones may break my
bones, but words can
never hurt me." That saying is not
at all true! Hateful words do hurt.
When we say ugly things to others,
two people get hurt—the person we
are talking to and also ourselves.

ʲ Heb *the heart of fools*   ᵏ Syr: Meaning of Heb
uncertain   ˡ Meaning of Heb uncertain
ᵐ Cn: Heb *A wise child the discipline of his father*

In a dry land, a natural fountain provides life-giving water. Wise teaching is like that life-giving water. It helps people to avoid trouble and live well.

9 The light of the righteous rejoices,
  but the lamp of the wicked goes out.
10 By insolence the heedless make strife,
  but wisdom is with those who take advice.
11 Wealth hastily gotten[n] will dwindle,
  but those who gather little by little will increase it.
12 Hope deferred makes the heart sick,
  but a desire fulfilled is a tree of life.
13 Those who despise the word bring destruction on themselves,
  but those who respect the commandment will be rewarded.
14 The teaching of the wise is a fountain of life,
  so that one may avoid the snares of death.
15 Good sense wins favor,
  but the way of the faithless is their ruin.[o]
16 The clever do all things intelligently,
  but the fool displays folly.
17 A bad messenger brings trouble,
  but a faithful envoy, healing.
18 Poverty and disgrace are for the one who ignores instruction,
  but one who heeds reproof is honored.
19 A desire realized is sweet to the soul,
  but to turn away from evil is an abomination to fools.
20 Whoever walks with the wise becomes wise,
  but the companion of fools suffers harm.
21 Misfortune pursues sinners,
  but prosperity rewards the righteous.

22 The good leave an inheritance to their children's children,
  but the sinner's wealth is laid up for the righteous.
23 The field of the poor may yield much food,
  but it is swept away through injustice.
24 Those who spare the rod hate their children,
  but those who love them are diligent to discipline them.
25 The righteous have enough to satisfy their appetite,
  but the belly of the wicked is empty.

An inheritance is money or property handed down from parents to their children. In the Bible, the word refers to material possessions such as land, cattle, and wealth.

14

The wise woman[p] builds her house,
  but the foolish tears it down with her own hands.
2 Those who walk uprightly fear the LORD,
  but one who is devious in conduct despises him.
3 The talk of fools is a rod for their backs,[q]
  but the lips of the wise preserve them.
4 Where there are no oxen, there is no grain;
  abundant crops come by the strength of the ox.
5 A faithful witness does not lie,
  but a false witness breathes out lies.

[n] Gk Vg: Heb *from vanity*   [o] Cn: Compare Gk Syr Vg Tg: Heb *is enduring*   [p] Heb *Wisdom of women*
[q] Cn: Heb *a rod of pride*

⁶ A scoffer seeks wisdom in vain,
  but knowledge is easy for one who
    understands.
⁷ Leave the presence of a fool,
  for there you do not find words of
    knowledge.
⁸ It is the wisdom of the clever to
    understand where they go,
  but the folly of fools misleads.
⁹ Fools mock at the guilt offering,ʳ
  but the upright enjoy God's favor.
¹⁰ The heart knows its own bitterness,
  and no stranger shares its joy.
¹¹ The house of the wicked is
    destroyed,
  but the tent of the upright flourishes.
¹² There is a way that seems right to a
    person,
  but its end is the way to death.ˢ
¹³ Even in laughter the heart is sad,
  and the end of joy is grief.
¹⁴ The perverse get what their ways
    deserve,
  and the good, what their deeds
    deserve.ᵗ
¹⁵ The simple believe everything,
  but the clever consider their steps.
¹⁶ The wise are cautious and turn away
    from evil,
  but the fool throws off restraint and
    is careless.
¹⁷ One who is quick-tempered acts
    foolishly,
  and the schemer is hated.
¹⁸ The simple are adorned withᵘ folly,
  but the clever are crowned with
    knowledge.
¹⁹ The evil bow down before the good,
  the wicked at the gates of the
    righteous.
²⁰ The poor are disliked even by their
    neighbors,
  but the rich have many friends.

²¹ Those who despise their neighbors are
    sinners,
  but happy are those who are kind to
    the poor.
²² Do they not err that plan evil?
  Those who plan good find loyalty
    and faithfulness.
²³ In all toil there is profit,
  but mere talk leads only to poverty.
²⁴ The crown of the wise is their
    wisdom,ᵛ
  but folly is the garlandʷ of fools.
²⁵ A truthful witness saves lives,
  but one who utters lies is a betrayer.
²⁶ In the fear of the LORD one has strong
    confidence,
  and one's children will have a refuge.
²⁷ The fear of the LORD is a fountain of
    life,
  so that one may avoid the snares of
    death.
²⁸ The glory of a king is a multitude of
    people;
  without people a prince is ruined.
²⁹ Whoever is slow to anger has great
    understanding,
  but one who has a hasty temper
    exalts folly.
³⁰ A tranquil mind gives life to the flesh,
  but passion makes the bones rot.
³¹ Those who oppress the poor insult
    their Maker,
  but those who are kind to the needy
    honor him.
³² The wicked are overthrown by their
    evildoing,
  but the righteous find a refuge in
    their integrity.ˣ
³³ Wisdom is at home in the mind of one
    who has understanding,
  but it is notʸ known in the heart of
    fools.
³⁴ Righteousness exalts a nation,
  but sin is a reproach to any people.

"Those who oppress the
poor insult their Maker,
but those who are kind to
the needy honor him."
Proverbs 14:31

ʳ Meaning of Heb uncertain   ˢ Heb *ways of death*
ᵗ Cn: Heb *from upon him*   ᵘ Or *inherit*
ᵛ Cn Compare Gk: Heb *riches*   ʷ Cn: Heb *is the*
folly   ˣ Gk Syr: Heb *in their death*   ʸ Gk Syr:
Heb lacks *not*

"Better is a dinner of vegetables where love is than a fatted ox and hatred with it."
Proverbs 15:17

³⁵ A servant who deals wisely has the king's favor,
but his wrath falls on one who acts shamefully.

15

A soft answer turns away wrath,
but a harsh word stirs up anger.

² The tongue of the wise dispenses knowledge,^z
but the mouths of fools pour out folly.

³ The eyes of the LORD are in every place,
keeping watch on the evil and the good.

⁴ A gentle tongue is a tree of life,
but perverseness in it breaks the spirit.

⁵ A fool despises a parent's instruction,
but the one who heeds admonition is prudent.

⁶ In the house of the righteous there is much treasure,
but trouble befalls the income of the wicked.

⁷ The lips of the wise spread knowledge;
not so the minds of fools.

⁸ The sacrifice of the wicked is an abomination to the LORD,
but the prayer of the upright is his delight.

⁹ The way of the wicked is an abomination to the LORD,
but he loves the one who pursues righteousness.

¹⁰ There is severe discipline for one who forsakes the way,
but one who hates a rebuke will die.

¹¹ Shē′ōl and A·bad′don lie open before the LORD,
how much more human hearts!

¹² Scoffers do not like to be rebuked;
they will not go to the wise.

¹³ A glad heart makes a cheerful countenance,
but by sorrow of heart the spirit is broken.

¹⁴ The mind of one who has understanding seeks knowledge,
but the mouths of fools feed on folly.

¹⁵ All the days of the poor are hard,
but a cheerful heart has a continual feast.

¹⁶ Better is a little with the fear of the LORD
than great treasure and trouble with it.

¹⁷ Better is a dinner of vegetables where love is
than a fatted ox and hatred with it.

¹⁸ Those who are hot-tempered stir up strife,
but those who are slow to anger calm contention.

¹⁹ The way of the lazy is overgrown with thorns,
but the path of the upright is a level highway.

²⁰ A wise child makes a glad father,
but the foolish despise their mothers.

²¹ Folly is a joy to one who has no sense,
but a person of understanding walks straight ahead.

²² Without counsel, plans go wrong,
but with many advisers they succeed.

²³ To make an apt answer is a joy to anyone,
and a word in season, how good it is!

A highway is a road built up higher than the land on either side.

^z Cn: Heb *makes knowledge good*

24 For the wise the path of life leads
   upward,
      in order to avoid Shē´ōl below.
25 The LORD tears down the house of the
   proud,
      but maintains the widow's
      boundaries.
26 Evil plans are an abomination to the
   LORD,
      but gracious words are pure.
27 Those who are greedy for unjust gain
   make trouble for their
   households,
      but those who hate bribes will live.
28 The mind of the righteous ponders
   how to answer,
      but the mouth of the wicked pours
      out evil.
29 The LORD is far from the wicked,
      but he hears the prayer of the
      righteous.
30 The light of the eyes rejoices the heart,
      and good news refreshes the body.
31 The ear that heeds wholesome
   admonition
      will lodge among the wise.
32 Those who ignore instruction despise
   themselves,
      but those who heed admonition
      gain understanding.
33 The fear of the LORD is instruction in
   wisdom,
      and humility goes before honor.

16 The plans of the mind belong to
   mortals,
      but the answer of the tongue is from
      the LORD.
2 All one's ways may be pure in one's
   own eyes,
      but the LORD weighs the spirit.
3 Commit your work to the LORD,
      and your plans will be established.
4 The LORD has made everything for its
   purpose,
      even the wicked for the day of
      trouble.
5 All those who are arrogant are an
   abomination to the LORD;

be assured, they will not go
      unpunished.
6 By loyalty and faithfulness iniquity is
   atoned for,
      and by the fear of the LORD one
      avoids evil.
7 When the ways of people please the
   LORD,
      he causes even their enemies to be
      at peace with them.
8 Better is a little with righteousness
      than large income with injustice.
9 The human mind plans the way,
      but the LORD directs the steps.
10 Inspired decisions are on the lips of a
   king;
      his mouth does not sin in judgment.
11 Honest balances and scales are the
   LORD's;
      all the weights in the bag are his work.
12 It is an abomination to kings to do evil,
      for the throne is established by
      righteousness.
13 Righteous lips are the delight of a king,
      and he loves those who speak what
      is right.
14 A king's wrath is a messenger of death,
      and whoever is wise will appease it.
15 In the light of a king's face there is life,
      and his favor is like the clouds that
      bring the spring rain.
16 How much better to get wisdom than
   gold!
      To get understanding is to be chosen
      rather than silver.
17 The highway of the upright avoids evil;
      those who guard their way preserve
      their lives.

A "way" is a path,
road, or street that
someone travels to
reach a destination. In
the Old Testament, the word
"way" often describes the
courses of nature and of a person's life. "Way" also describes
the paths of good and evil.

¹⁸ Pride goes before destruction,
  and a haughty spirit before a fall.
¹⁹ It is better to be of a lowly spirit
    among the poor
  than to divide the spoil with the
    proud.
²⁰ Those who are attentive to a matter
    will prosper,
  and happy are those who trust in
    the LORD.
²¹ The wise of heart is called perceptive,
  and pleasant speech increases
    persuasiveness.
²² Wisdom is a fountain of life to one
    who has it,
  but folly is the punishment of fools.
²³ The mind of the wise makes their
    speech judicious,
  and adds persuasiveness to their
    lips.
²⁴ Pleasant words are like a honeycomb,
  sweetness to the soul and health to
    the body.
²⁵ Sometimes there is a way that seems to
    be right,
  but in the end it is the way to death.
²⁶ The appetite of workers works for
    them;
  their hunger urges them on.
²⁷ Scoundrels concoct evil,
  and their speech is like a scorching
    fire.
²⁸ A perverse person spreads strife,
  and a whisperer separates close
    friends.
²⁹ The violent entice their neighbors,
  and lead them in a way that is not
    good.
³⁰ One who winks the eyes plans*a*
    perverse things;
  one who compresses the lips brings
    evil to pass.

³¹ Gray hair is a crown of glory;
  it is gained in a righteous life.
³² One who is slow to anger is better
    than the mighty,
  and one whose temper is controlled
    than one who captures a city.
³³ The lot is cast into the lap,
  but the decision is the LORD's alone.

17 Better is a dry morsel with quiet
    than a house full of feasting
    with strife.
² A slave who deals wisely will rule over
    a child who acts shamefully,
  and will share the inheritance as one
    of the family.
³ The crucible is for silver, and the
    furnace is for gold,
  but the LORD tests the heart.
⁴ An evildoer listens to wicked lips;
  and a liar gives heed to a
    mischievous tongue.
⁵ Those who mock the poor insult their
    Maker;
  those who are glad at calamity will
    not go unpunished.
⁶ Grandchildren are the crown of the
    aged,
  and the glory of children is their
    parents.
⁷ Fine speech is not becoming to a fool;
  still less is false speech to a ruler.*b*
⁸ A bribe is like a magic stone in the
    eyes of those who give it;
  wherever they turn they prosper.
⁹ One who forgives an affront fosters
    friendship,
  but one who dwells on disputes will
    alienate a friend.
¹⁰ A rebuke strikes deeper into a
    discerning person
  than a hundred blows into a fool.
¹¹ Evil people seek only rebellion,
  but a cruel messenger will be sent
    against them.
¹² Better to meet a she-bear robbed of its
    cubs
  than to confront a fool immersed in
    folly.

a Gk Syr Vg Tg: Heb *to plan*   *b* Or *a noble person*

"One who is slow to anger is better than the mighty, and one whose temper is controlled than one who captures a city."
Proverbs 16:32

¹³ Evil will not depart from the house
of one who returns evil for good.
¹⁴ The beginning of strife is like letting
out water;
so stop before the quarrel breaks out.
¹⁵ One who justifies the wicked and one
who condemns the righteous
are both alike an abomination to the
LORD.
¹⁶ Why should fools have a price in hand
to buy wisdom, when they have no
mind to learn?
¹⁷ A friend loves at all times,
and kinsfolk are born to share
adversity.
¹⁸ It is senseless to give a pledge,
to become surety for a neighbor.
¹⁹ One who loves transgression loves
strife;
one who builds a high threshold
invites broken bones.
²⁰ The crooked of mind do not prosper,
and the perverse of tongue fall into
calamity.
²¹ The one who begets a fool gets trouble;
the parent of a fool has no joy.
²² A cheerful heart is a good medicine,
but a downcast spirit dries up the
bones.
²³ The wicked accept a concealed bribe
to pervert the ways of justice.
²⁴ The discerning person looks to
wisdom,
but the eyes of a fool to the ends of
the earth.
²⁵ Foolish children are a grief to their
father
and bitterness to her who bore
them.
²⁶ To impose a fine on the innocent is not
right,
or to flog the noble for their
integrity.
²⁷ One who spares words is
knowledgeable;
one who is cool in spirit has
understanding.
²⁸ Even fools who keep silent are
considered wise;

A tower is a tall structure that is usually higher and narrower than things around it. In Bible times towers were common in cities, pastures, vineyards, and farmlands. Built of brick or stone, towers were used as refuge or defense against military attack. The word "tower" is also used as a symbol for God's protective power.

when they close their lips, they are
deemed intelligent.

18 The one who lives alone is
self-indulgent,
showing contempt for all who have
sound judgment.^c
² A fool takes no pleasure in
understanding,
but only in expressing personal
opinion.
³ When wickedness comes, contempt
comes also;
and with dishonor comes disgrace.
⁴ The words of the mouth are deep
waters;
the fountain of wisdom is a gushing
stream.
⁵ It is not right to be partial to the guilty,
or to subvert the innocent in
judgment.
⁶ A fool's lips bring strife,
and a fool's mouth invites a flogging.
⁷ The mouths of fools are their ruin,
and their lips a snare to themselves.
⁸ The words of a whisperer are like
delicious morsels;
they go down into the inner parts of
the body.
⁹ One who is slack in work
is close kin to a vandal.
¹⁰ The name of the LORD is a strong
tower;

"A friend loves at all times,
and kinsfolk are born to
share adversity."
Proverbs 17:17

^c Meaning of Heb uncertain

the righteous run into it and are safe.
11 The wealth of the rich is their strong
city;
in their imagination it is like a high
wall.
12 Before destruction one's heart is
haughty,
but humility goes before honor.
13 If one gives answer before hearing,
it is folly and shame.
14 The human spirit will endure sickness;
but a broken spirit—who can bear?
15 An intelligent mind acquires
knowledge,
and the ear of the wise seeks
knowledge.
16 A gift opens doors;
it gives access to the great.
17 The one who first states a case seems
right,
until the other comes and
cross-examines.
18 Casting the lot puts an end to disputes
and decides between powerful
contenders.
19 An ally offended is stronger than a
city;[d]
such quarreling is like the bars of a
castle.
20 From the fruit of the mouth one's
stomach is satisfied;
the yield of the lips brings
satisfaction.
21 Death and life are in the power of the
tongue,
and those who love it will eat its
fruits.
22 He who finds a wife finds a good
thing,
and obtains favor from the LORD.
23 The poor use entreaties,
but the rich answer roughly.
24 Some[e] friends play at friendship[f]

but a true friend sticks closer than
one's nearest kin.

19 Better the poor walking in
integrity
than one perverse of speech who is
a fool.
2 Desire without knowledge is not good,
and one who moves too hurriedly
misses the way.
3 One's own folly leads to ruin,
yet the heart rages against the LORD.
4 Wealth brings many friends,
but the poor are left friendless.
5 A false witness will not go
unpunished,
and a liar will not escape.
6 Many seek the favor of the generous,
and everyone is a friend to a giver of
gifts.
7 If the poor are hated even by their kin,
how much more are they shunned
by their friends!
When they call after them, they are not
there.[g]
8 To get wisdom is to love oneself;
to keep understanding is to prosper.
9 A false witness will not go unpunished,
and the liar will perish.
10 It is not fitting for a fool to live in
luxury,
much less for a slave to rule over
princes.
11 Those with good sense are slow to
anger,
and it is their glory to overlook an
offense.
12 A king's anger is like the growling of a
lion,
but his favor is like dew on the
grass.
13 A stupid child is ruin to a father,
and a wife's quarreling is a continual
dripping of rain.
14 House and wealth are inherited from
parents,

"Some friends play at
friendship but a true
friend sticks closer than
one's nearest kin."
Proverbs 18:24

---

[d] Gk Syr Vg Tg: Meaning of Heb uncertain
[e] Syr Tg: Heb *A man of*   [f] Cn Compare Syr Vg
Tg: Meaning of Heb uncertain   [g] Meaning of
Heb uncertain

but a prudent wife is from the LORD.
15 Laziness brings on deep sleep;
an idle person will suffer hunger.
16 Those who keep the commandment
will live;
those who are heedless of their ways
will die.
17 Whoever is kind to the poor lends to
the LORD,
and will be repaid in full.
18 Discipline your children while there is
hope;
do not set your heart on their
destruction.
19 A violent tempered person will pay
the penalty;
if you effect a rescue, you will only
have to do it again.[h]
20 Listen to advice and accept instruction,
that you may gain wisdom for the
future.
21 The human mind may devise many
plans,
but it is the purpose of the LORD
that will be established.
22 What is desirable in a person is loyalty,
and it is better to be poor than a liar.
23 The fear of the LORD is life indeed;
filled with it one rests secure
and suffers no harm.
24 The lazy person buries a hand in the
dish,
and will not even bring it back to
the mouth.
25 Strike a scoffer, and the simple will
learn prudence;
reprove the intelligent, and they will
gain knowledge.
26 Those who do violence to their father
and chase away their mother
are children who cause shame and
bring reproach.
27 Cease straying, my child, from the
words of knowledge,
in order that you may hear
instruction.
28 A worthless witness mocks at justice,
and the mouth of the wicked
devours iniquity.

29 Condemnation is ready for scoffers,
and flogging for the backs of fools.

20 Wine is a mocker, strong drink a
brawler,
and whoever is led astray by it is not
wise.
2 The dread anger of a king is like the
growling of a lion;
anyone who provokes him to anger
forfeits life itself.
3 It is honorable to refrain from strife,
but every fool is quick to quarrel.
4 The lazy person does not plow in
season;
harvest comes, and there is nothing
to be found.
5 The purposes in the human mind are
like deep water,
but the intelligent will draw them
out.
6 Many proclaim themselves loyal,
but who can find one worthy of
trust?
7 The righteous walk in integrity—
happy are the children who follow
them!
8 A king who sits on the throne of
judgment
winnows all evil with his eyes.
9 Who can say, "I have made my heart
clean;
I am pure from my sin"?
10 Diverse weights and diverse measures
are both alike an abomination to the
LORD.
11 Even children make themselves known
by their acts,
by whether what they do is pure
and right.
12 The hearing ear and the seeing eye—
the LORD has made them both.
13 Do not love sleep, or else you will
come to poverty;
open your eyes, and you will have
plenty of bread.
14 "Bad, bad," says the buyer,
then goes away and boasts.

[h] Meaning of Heb uncertain

> "To do righteousness and justice is more acceptable to the LORD than sacrifice."
> Proverbs 21:3

15 There is gold, and abundance of costly stones;
  but the lips informed by knowledge are a precious jewel.
16 Take the garment of one who has given surety for a stranger;
  seize the pledge given as surety for foreigners.
17 Bread gained by deceit is sweet,
  but afterward the mouth will be full of gravel.
18 Plans are established by taking advice;
  wage war by following wise guidance.
19 A gossip reveals secrets;
  therefore do not associate with a babbler.
20 If you curse father or mother,
  your lamp will go out in utter darkness.
21 An estate quickly acquired in the beginning
  will not be blessed in the end.
22 Do not say, "I will repay evil";
  wait for the LORD, and he will help you.
23 Differing weights are an abomination to the LORD,
  and false scales are not good.
24 All our steps are ordered by the LORD;
  how then can we understand our own ways?
25 It is a snare for one to say rashly, "It is holy,"
  and begin to reflect only after making a vow.
26 A wise king winnows the wicked,
  and drives the wheel over them.
27 The human spirit is the lamp of the LORD,
  searching every inmost part.

28 Loyalty and faithfulness preserve the king,
  and his throne is upheld by righteousness.[i]
29 The glory of youths is their strength,
  but the beauty of the aged is their gray hair.
30 Blows that wound cleanse away evil;
  beatings make clean the innermost parts.

21 The king's heart is a stream of water in the hand of the LORD;
  he turns it wherever he will.
2 All deeds are right in the sight of the doer,
  but the LORD weighs the heart.
3 To do righteousness and justice
  is more acceptable to the LORD than sacrifice.
4 Haughty eyes and a proud heart—
  the lamp of the wicked—are sin.
5 The plans of the diligent lead surely to abundance,
  but everyone who is hasty comes only to want.
6 The getting of treasures by a lying tongue
  is a fleeting vapor and a snare[j] of death.
7 The violence of the wicked will sweep them away,
  because they refuse to do what is just.
8 The way of the guilty is crooked,
  but the conduct of the pure is right.
9 It is better to live in a corner of the housetop
  than in a house shared with a contentious wife.
10 The souls of the wicked desire evil;
  their neighbors find no mercy in their eyes.
11 When a scoffer is punished, the simple become wiser;
  when the wise are instructed, they increase in knowledge.

i Gk: Heb loyalty   j Gk: Heb seekers

12 The Righteous One observes the
  house of the wicked;
    he casts the wicked down to ruin.
13 If you close your ear to the cry of the
  poor,
    you will cry out and not be heard.
14 A gift in secret averts anger;
    and a concealed bribe in the bosom,
    strong wrath.
15 When justice is done, it is a joy to the
  righteous,
    but dismay to evildoers.
16 Whoever wanders from the way of
  understanding
    will rest in the assembly of the dead.
17 Whoever loves pleasure will suffer
  want;
    whoever loves wine and oil will not
    be rich.
18 The wicked is a ransom for the
  righteous,
    and the faithless for the upright.
19 It is better to live in a desert land
    than with a contentious and fretful
    wife.
20 Precious treasure remains^k in the
  house of the wise,
    but the fool devours it.
21 Whoever pursues righteousness and
  kindness
    will find life^l and honor.
22 One wise person went up against a
  city of warriors
    and brought down the stronghold in
    which they trusted.
23 To watch over mouth and tongue
    is to keep out of trouble.
24 The proud, haughty person, named
  "Scoffer,"
    acts with arrogant pride.
25 The craving of the lazy person is fatal,
    for lazy hands refuse to labor.
26 All day long the wicked covet,^{m}
    but the righteous give and do not
    hold back.
27 The sacrifice of the wicked is an
  abomination;
    how much more when brought with
    evil intent.

28 A false witness will perish,
    but a good listener will testify
    successfully.
29 The wicked put on a bold face,
    but the upright give thought to^n
    their ways.
30 No wisdom, no understanding, no
  counsel,
    can avail against the LORD.
31 The horse is made ready for the day of
  battle,
    but the victory belongs to the LORD.

22 A good name is to be chosen
  rather than great riches,
    and favor is better than silver or
    gold.
2 The rich and the poor have this in
  common:
    the LORD is the maker of them all.
3 The clever see danger and hide;
    but the simple go on, and suffer for
    it.
4 The reward for humility and fear of the
  LORD
    is riches and honor and life.
5 Thorns and snares are in the way of
  the perverse;
    the cautious will keep far from
    them.
6 Train children in the right way,
    and when old, they will not stray.
7 The rich rule over the poor,
    and the borrower is the slave of the
    lender.
8 Whoever sows injustice will reap
  calamity,
    and the rod of anger will fail.
9 Those who are generous are blessed,
    for they share their bread with the
    poor.
10 Drive out a scoffer, and strife goes out;
    quarreling and abuse will cease.
11 Those who love a pure heart and are
  gracious in speech
    will have the king as a friend.

^{k} Gk: Heb *and oil* ^{l} Gk: Heb *life and righteousness*
^{m} Gk: Heb *all day long one covets covetously*
^{n} Another reading is *establish*

¹² The eyes of the LORD keep watch over knowledge,
  but he overthrows the words of the faithless.
¹³ The lazy person says, "There is a lion outside!
  I shall be killed in the streets!"
¹⁴ The mouth of a loose° woman is a deep pit;
  he with whom the LORD is angry falls into it.
¹⁵ Folly is bound up in the heart of a boy,
  but the rod of discipline drives it far away.
¹⁶ Oppressing the poor in order to enrich oneself,
  and giving to the rich, will lead only to loss.

Sayings of the Wise

¹⁷ The words of the wise:

Incline your ear and hear my words,ᵖ
  and apply your mind to my teaching;
¹⁸ for it will be pleasant if you keep them within you,
  if all of them are ready on your lips.
¹⁹ So that your trust may be in the LORD,
  I have made them known to you today—yes, to you.
²⁰ Have I not written for you thirty sayings
  of admonition and knowledge,
²¹ to show you what is right and true,
  so that you may give a true answer to those who sent you?

²² Do not rob the poor because they are poor,
  or crush the afflicted at the gate;
²³ for the LORD pleads their cause
  and despoils of life those who despoil them.
²⁴ Make no friends with those given to anger,
  and do not associate with hotheads,
²⁵ or you may learn their ways
  and entangle yourself in a snare.

²⁶ Do not be one of those who give pledges,
  who become surety for debts.
²⁷ If you have nothing with which to pay,
  why should your bed be taken from under you?
²⁸ Do not remove the ancient landmark
  that your ancestors set up.
²⁹ Do you see those who are skillful in their work?
  They will serve kings;
  they will not serve common people.

23 When you sit down to eat with a ruler,
  observe carefully what�q is before you,
² and put a knife to your throat
  if you have a big appetite.
³ Do not desire the ruler'sʳ delicacies,
  for they are deceptive food.
⁴ Do not wear yourself out to get rich;
  be wise enough to desist.
⁵ When your eyes light upon it, it is gone;
  for suddenly it takes wings to itself,
  flying like an eagle toward heaven.
⁶ Do not eat the bread of the stingy;
  do not desire their delicacies;

A landmark showed the boundaries of an area of land. In Bible times, people made landmarks by piling stones. These landmarks showed the border between the fields of one man and those of his neighbors. They also marked borders between districts and nations. Removing the landmarks was a serious offense.

° Heb *strange*   ᵖ Cn Compare Gk: Heb *Incline your ear, and hear the words of the wise*   q Or *who*   ʳ Heb *his*

7 for like a hair in the throat, so are they.ˢ
"Eat and drink!" they say to you;
but they do not mean it.
8 You will vomit up the little you have eaten,
and you will waste your pleasant words.
9 Do not speak in the hearing of a fool,
who will only despise the wisdom of your words.
10 Do not remove an ancient landmark
or encroach on the fields of orphans,
11 for their redeemer is strong;
he will plead their cause against you.
12 Apply your mind to instruction
and your ear to words of knowledge.
13 Do not withhold discipline from your children;
if you beat them with a rod, they will not die.
14 If you beat them with the rod,
you will save their lives from Shēʹōl.
15 My child, if your heart is wise,
my heart too will be glad.
16 My soul will rejoice
when your lips speak what is right.
17 Do not let your heart envy sinners,
but always continue in the fear of the LORD.
18 Surely there is a future,
and your hope will not be cut off.

19 Hear, my child, and be wise,
and direct your mind in the way.
20 Do not be among winebibbers,

"My child, if your heart is wise, my heart too will be glad. My soul will rejoice when your lips speak what is right."
Proverbs 23:15–16

or among gluttonous eaters of meat;
21 for the drunkard and the glutton will come to poverty,
and drowsiness will clothe them with rags.

22 Listen to your father who begot you,
and do not despise your mother when she is old.
23 Buy truth, and do not sell it;
buy wisdom, instruction, and understanding.
24 The father of the righteous will greatly rejoice;
he who begets a wise son will be glad in him.
25 Let your father and mother be glad;
let her who bore you rejoice.

26 My child, give me your heart,
and let your eyes observeᵗ my ways.
27 For a prostitute is a deep pit;
an adulteressᵘ is a narrow well.
28 She lies in wait like a robber
and increases the number of the faithless.

29 Who has woe? Who has sorrow?
Who has strife? Who has complaining?
Who has wounds without cause?
Who has redness of eyes?
30 Those who linger late over wine,
those who keep trying mixed wines.
31 Do not look at wine when it is red,
when it sparkles in the cup
and goes down smoothly.
32 At the last it bites like a serpent,

An eagle is a strong, powerful bird. The writer of Proverbs warns readers not to wear themselves out trying to get rich because wealth is gone as quickly as the eagle flies. Money can never make us happy, and being rich does not give us purpose or meaning. God wants us to be concerned with the things that really matter. What do you think those things are?

ˢ Meaning of Heb uncertain   ᵗ Another reading is *delight in*   ᵘ Heb *an alien woman* and stings like an adder.

33 Your eyes will see strange things,
  and your mind utter perverse
    things.
34 You will be like one who lies down in
    the midst of the sea,
  like one who lies on the top of a
    mast.ᵛ
35 "They struck me," you will say,ʷ "but I
    was not hurt;
  they beat me, but I did not feel it.
When shall I awake?
  I will seek another drink."

24 Do not envy the wicked,
    nor desire to be with them;
2 for their minds devise violence,
  and their lips talk of mischief.

3 By wisdom a house is built,
  and by understanding it is
    established;
4 by knowledge the rooms are filled
  with all precious and pleasant riches.
5 Wise warriors are mightier than strong
    ones,ˣ
  and those who have knowledge than
    those who have strength;
6 for by wise guidance you can wage
    your war,
  and in abundance of counselors
    there is victory.
7 Wisdom is too high for fools;
  in the gate they do not open their
    mouths.

8 Whoever plans to do evil
  will be called a mischief-maker.
9 The devising of folly is sin,
  and the scoffer is an abomination to
    all.

10 If you faint in the day of adversity,
  your strength being small;
11 if you hold back from rescuing those
    taken away to death,
  those who go staggering to the
    slaughter;
12 if you say, "Look, we did not know
    this"—

does not he who weighs the heart
    perceive it?
Does not he who keeps watch over
    your soul know it?
  And will he not repay all according
    to their deeds?

13 My child, eat honey, for it is good,
  and the drippings of the honeycomb
    are sweet to your taste.
14 Know that wisdom is such to your
    soul;
  if you find it, you will find a future,
  and your hope will not be cut off.

15 Do not lie in wait like an outlaw
    against the home of the
      righteous;
  do no violence to the place where
    the righteous live;
16 for though they fall seven times, they
    will rise again;
  but the wicked are overthrown by
    calamity.

17 Do not rejoice when your enemies
    fall,
  and do not let your heart be glad
    when they stumble,
18 or else the LORD will see it and be
    displeased,
  and turn away his anger from
    them.

19 Do not fret because of evildoers.
  Do not envy the wicked;
20 for the evil have no future;
  the lamp of the wicked will go out.

21 My child, fear the LORD and the king,
  and do not disobey either of them;ʸ
22 for disaster comes from them suddenly,
  and who knows the ruin that both
    can bring?

ᵛ Meaning of Heb uncertain   ʷ Gk Syr Vg Tg: Heb
lacks *you will say*   ˣ Gk Compare Syr Tg: Heb *A
wise man is strength*   ʸ Gk: Heb *do not associate
with those who change*

Further Sayings of the Wise

23 These also are sayings of the wise:

Partiality in judging is not good.
24 Whoever says to the wicked, "You are innocent,"
  will be cursed by peoples, abhorred by nations;
25 but those who rebuke the wicked will have delight,
  and a good blessing will come upon them.
26 One who gives an honest answer
  gives a kiss on the lips.

27 Prepare your work outside,
  get everything ready for you in the field;
  and after that build your house.

28 Do not be a witness against your neighbor without cause,
  and do not deceive with your lips.
29 Do not say, "I will do to others as they have done to me;
  I will pay them back for what they have done."

30 I passed by the field of one who was lazy,
  by the vineyard of a stupid person;
31 and see, it was all overgrown with thorns;
  the ground was covered with nettles,
  and its stone wall was broken down.
32 Then I saw and considered it;
  I looked and received instruction.
33 A little sleep, a little slumber,
  a little folding of the hands to rest,
34 and poverty will come upon you like a robber,
  and want, like an armed warrior.

Further Wise Sayings of Solomon

25 These are other proverbs of Solomon that the officials of King Hez·e·kī′ah of Judah copied.

2 It is the glory of God to conceal things,
  but the glory of kings is to search things out.
3 Like the heavens for height, like the earth for depth,
  so the mind of kings is unsearchable.
4 Take away the dross from the silver,
  and the smith has material for a vessel;
5 take away the wicked from the presence of the king,
  and his throne will be established in righteousness.
6 Do not put yourself forward in the king's presence
  or stand in the place of the great;
7 for it is better to be told, "Come up here,"
  than to be put lower in the presence of a noble.

What your eyes have seen
8   do not hastily bring into court;
for ͏ᶻ what will you do in the end,
  when your neighbor puts you to shame?
9 Argue your case with your neighbor directly,
  and do not disclose another's secret;
10 or else someone who hears you will bring shame upon you,
  and your ill repute will have no end.

11 A word fitly spoken
  is like apples of gold in a setting of silver.
12 Like a gold ring or an ornament of gold
  is a wise rebuke to a listening ear.
13 Like the cold of snow in the time of harvest
  are faithful messengers to those who send them;
  they refresh the spirit of their masters.

"A word fitly spoken is like apples of gold in a setting of silver."
Proverbs 25:11

ᶻ Cn: Heb *or else*

¹⁴ Like clouds and wind without rain
  is one who boasts of a gift never
    given.
¹⁵ With patience a ruler may be
    persuaded,
  and a soft tongue can break bones.
¹⁶ If you have found honey, eat only
    enough for you,
  or else, having too much, you will
    vomit it.
¹⁷ Let your foot be seldom in your
    neighbor's house,
  otherwise the neighbor will become
    weary of you and hate you.
¹⁸ Like a war club, a sword, or a sharp
    arrow
  is one who bears false witness
    against a neighbor.
¹⁹ Like a bad tooth or a lame foot
  is trust in a faithless person in time
    of trouble.
²⁰ Like vinegar on a wound*a*
  is one who sings songs to a heavy
    heart.
  Like a moth in clothing or a worm in
    wood,
  sorrow gnaws at the human heart.*b*
²¹ If your enemies are hungry, give them
    bread to eat;
  and if they are thirsty, give them
    water to drink;
²² for you will heap coals of fire on their
    heads,
  and the LORD will reward you.
²³ The north wind produces rain,
  and a backbiting tongue, angry
    looks.
²⁴ It is better to live in a corner of the
    housetop
  than in a house shared with a
    contentious wife.
²⁵ Like cold water to a thirsty soul,
  so is good news from a far country.
²⁶ Like a muddied spring or a polluted
    fountain
  are the righteous who give way
    before the wicked.
²⁷ It is not good to eat much honey,
  or to seek honor on top of honor.

²⁸ Like a city breached, without walls,
  is one who lacks self-control.

26 Like snow in summer or rain
    in harvest,
  so honor is not fitting for a fool.
² Like a sparrow in its flitting, like a
    swallow in its flying,
  an undeserved curse goes nowhere.
³ A whip for the horse, a bridle for the
    donkey,
  and a rod for the back of fools.
⁴ Do not answer fools according to their
    folly,
  or you will be a fool yourself.
⁵ Answer fools according to their folly,
  or they will be wise in their own eyes.
⁶ It is like cutting off one's foot and
    drinking down violence,
  to send a message by a fool.
⁷ The legs of a disabled person hang
    limp;
  so does a proverb in the mouth of a
    fool.
⁸ It is like binding a stone in a sling
  to give honor to a fool.
⁹ Like a thornbush brandished by the
    hand of a drunkard
  is a proverb in the mouth of a fool.
¹⁰ Like an archer who wounds everybody
  is one who hires a passing fool or
    drunkard.*c*

A sling in Bible times had a pouch-shaped piece of leather that held a stone. The sling would be swung over the head in a circle, and the stone would be released. If the stone were "bound" (or tied up) in the pouch, it would not go anywhere. It would be useless! The writer of Proverbs says honoring a fool is just as useless.

---

a Gk: Heb *Like one who takes off a garment on a cold day, like vinegar on lye*   *b* Gk Syr Tg: Heb lacks *Like a moth . . . human heart*   *c* Meaning of Heb uncertain

Can you think of some plants that have thorns? In hot, rocky soil, wild plants with thorns or thistles sometimes grow where other plants cannot grow. In the Bible, thorns are used as symbols of useless things that must be pulled up and destroyed.

¹¹ Like a dog that returns to its vomit
is a fool who reverts to his folly.
¹² Do you see persons wise in their own eyes?
There is more hope for fools than for them.
¹³ The lazy person says, "There is a lion in the road!
There is a lion in the streets!"
¹⁴ As a door turns on its hinges,
so does a lazy person in bed.
¹⁵ The lazy person buries a hand in the dish,
and is too tired to bring it back to the mouth.
¹⁶ The lazy person is wiser in self-esteem
than seven who can answer discreetly.
¹⁷ Like somebody who takes a passing dog by the ears
is one who meddles in the quarrel of another.
¹⁸ Like a maniac who shoots deadly firebrands and arrows,
¹⁹ so is one who deceives a neighbor
and says, "I am only joking!"
²⁰ For lack of wood the fire goes out,
and where there is no whisperer,
quarreling ceases.
²¹ As charcoal is to hot embers and wood to fire,
so is a quarrelsome person for kindling strife.
²² The words of a whisperer are like delicious morsels;
they go down into the inner parts of the body.

²³ Like the glaze[d] covering an earthen vessel
are smooth[e] lips with an evil heart.
²⁴ An enemy dissembles in speaking
while harboring deceit within;
²⁵ when an enemy speaks graciously, do not believe it,
for there are seven abominations concealed within;
²⁶ though hatred is covered with guile,
the enemy's wickedness will be exposed in the assembly.
²⁷ Whoever digs a pit will fall into it,
and a stone will come back on the one who starts it rolling.
²⁸ A lying tongue hates its victims,
and a flattering mouth works ruin.

27 Do not boast about tomorrow,
for you do not know what a day may bring.
² Let another praise you, and not your own mouth—
a stranger, and not your own lips.
³ A stone is heavy, and sand is weighty,
but a fool's provocation is heavier than both.
⁴ Wrath is cruel, anger is overwhelming,
but who is able to stand before jealousy?
⁵ Better is open rebuke
than hidden love.
⁶ Well meant are the wounds a friend inflicts,
but profuse are the kisses of an enemy.
⁷ The sated appetite spurns honey,
but to a ravenous appetite even the bitter is sweet.
⁸ Like a bird that strays from its nest
is one who strays from home.
⁹ Perfume and incense make the heart glad,
but the soul is torn by trouble.[f]
¹⁰ Do not forsake your friend or the friend of your parent;

[d] Cn: Heb *silver of dross* [e] Gk: Heb *burning*
[f] Gk: Heb *the sweetness of a friend is better than one's own counsel*

do not go to the house of your
kindred in the day of your
calamity.
Better is a neighbor who is nearby
than kindred who are far away.
11 Be wise, my child, and make my heart
glad,
so that I may answer whoever
reproaches me.
12 The clever see danger and hide;
but the simple go on, and suffer for it.
13 Take the garment of one who has
given surety for a stranger;
seize the pledge given as surety for
foreigners.[g]
14 Whoever blesses a neighbor with a
loud voice,
rising early in the morning,
will be counted as cursing.
15 A continual dripping on a rainy day
and a contentious wife are alike;
16 to restrain her is to restrain the wind
or to grasp oil in the right hand.[h]
17 Iron sharpens iron,
and one person sharpens the wits[i] of
another.
18 Anyone who tends a fig tree will eat its
fruit,
and anyone who takes care of a
master will be honored.
19 Just as water reflects the face,
so one human heart reflects another.
20 She´ol and A·bad´don are never
satisfied,
and human eyes are never satisfied.
21 The crucible is for silver, and the
furnace is for gold,
so a person is tested[j] by being
praised.
22 Crush a fool in a mortar with a pestle
along with crushed grain,
but the folly will not be driven out.

23 Know well the condition of your flocks,
and give attention to your herds;
24 for riches do not last forever,
nor a crown for all generations.
25 When the grass is gone, and new
growth appears,

and the herbage of the mountains is
gathered,
26 the lambs will provide your clothing,
and the goats the price of a field;
27 there will be enough goats' milk for
your food,
for the food of your household
and nourishment for your
servant-girls.

28

The wicked flee when no one
pursues,
but the righteous are as bold as a
lion.
2 When a land rebels
it has many rulers;
but with an intelligent ruler
there is lasting order.[h]
3 A ruler[k] who oppresses the poor
is a beating rain that leaves no food.
4 Those who forsake the law praise the
wicked,
but those who keep the law struggle
against them.
5 The evil do not understand justice,
but those who seek the LORD
understand it completely.
6 Better to be poor and walk in integrity
than to be crooked in one's ways
even though rich.
7 Those who keep the law are wise
children,
but companions of gluttons shame
their parents.
8 One who augments wealth by
exorbitant interest
gathers it for another who is kind to
the poor.
9 When one will not listen to the law,
even one's prayers are an abomination.
10 Those who mislead the upright into
evil ways
will fall into pits of their own making,
but the blameless will have a goodly
inheritance.
11 The rich is wise in self-esteem,

---

g Vg and 20.16: Heb *for a foreign woman*
h Meaning of Heb uncertain   i Heb *face*   j Heb
lacks *is tested*   k Cn: Heb *A poor person*

but an intelligent poor person sees
through the pose.

12 When the righteous triumph, there is
great glory,
but when the wicked prevail, people
go into hiding.

13 No one who conceals transgressions
will prosper,
but one who confesses and forsakes
them will obtain mercy.

14 Happy is the one who is never without
fear,
but one who is hard-hearted will fall
into calamity.

15 Like a roaring lion or a charging bear
is a wicked ruler over a poor people.

16 A ruler who lacks understanding is a
cruel oppressor;
but one who hates unjust gain will
enjoy a long life.

17 If someone is burdened with the
blood of another,
let that killer be a fugitive until
death;
let no one offer assistance.

18 One who walks in integrity will be safe,
but whoever follows crooked ways
will fall into the Pit.[1]

19 Anyone who tills the land will have
plenty of bread,
but one who follows worthless
pursuits will have plenty of
poverty.

20 The faithful will abound with blessings,
but one who is in a hurry to be rich
will not go unpunished.

21 To show partiality is not good—
yet for a piece of bread a person
may do wrong.

22 The miser is in a hurry to get rich
and does not know that loss is sure
to come.

23 Whoever rebukes a person will
afterward find more favor
than one who flatters with the
tongue.

24 Anyone who robs father or mother
and says, "That is no crime,"
is partner to a thug.

25 The greedy person stirs up strife,
but whoever trusts in the LORD will
be enriched.

26 Those who trust in their own wits are
fools;
but those who walk in wisdom
come through safely.

27 Whoever gives to the poor will lack
nothing,
but one who turns a blind eye will
get many a curse.

28 When the wicked prevail, people go
into hiding;
but when they perish, the righteous
increase.

29 One who is often reproved, yet
remains stubborn,
will suddenly be broken beyond
healing.

2 When the righteous are in authority,
the people rejoice;
but when the wicked rule, the
people groan.

3 A child who loves wisdom makes a
parent glad,
but to keep company with
prostitutes is to squander one's
substance.

4 By justice a king gives stability to the
land,
but one who makes heavy exactions
ruins it.

5 Whoever flatters a neighbor
is spreading a net for the neighbor's
feet.

6 In the transgression of the evil there is
a snare,
but the righteous sing and rejoice.

7 The righteous know the rights of the
poor;
the wicked have no such
understanding.

8 Scoffers set a city aflame,
but the wise turn away wrath.

9 If the wise go to law with fools,
there is ranting and ridicule without
relief.

[1] Syr: Heb *fall all at once*

10 The bloodthirsty hate the blameless,
   and they seek the life of the upright.
11 A fool gives full vent to anger,
   but the wise quietly holds it back.
12 If a ruler listens to falsehood,
   all his officials will be wicked.
13 The poor and the oppressor have this
      in common:
   the LORD gives light to the eyes of
      both.
14 If a king judges the poor with equity,
   his throne will be established
      forever.
15 The rod and reproof give wisdom,
   but a mother is disgraced by a
      neglected child.
16 When the wicked are in authority,
      transgression increases,
   but the righteous will look upon
      their downfall.
17 Discipline your children, and they will
      give you rest;
   they will give delight to your heart.
18 Where there is no prophecy, the
      people cast off restraint,
   but happy are those who keep the law.
19 By mere words servants are not
      disciplined,
   for though they understand, they
      will not give heed.
20 Do you see someone who is hasty in
      speech?
   There is more hope for a fool than
      for anyone like that.
21 A slave pampered from childhood
   will come to a bad end.*m*
22 One given to anger stirs up strife,
   and the hothead causes much
      transgression.
23 A person's pride will bring
      humiliation,
   but one who is lowly in spirit will
      obtain honor.
24 To be a partner of a thief is to hate
      one's own life;
   one hears the victim's curse, but
      discloses nothing.*n*
25 The fear of others*o* lays a snare,
   but one who trusts in the LORD is

secure.
26 Many seek the favor of a ruler,
   but it is from the LORD that one gets
      justice.
27 The unjust are an abomination to the
      righteous,
   but the upright are an abomination
      to the wicked.

Sayings of Agur

30 The words of Ā´gur son of Jā´keh.
      An oracle.

Thus says the man: I am weary, O God,
   I am weary, O God. How can I
      prevail?*p*
2 Surely I am too stupid to be human;
   I do not have human understanding.
3 I have not learned wisdom,
   nor have I knowledge of the holy
      ones.*q*
4 Who has ascended to heaven and
      come down?
   Who has gathered the wind in the
      hollow of the hand?
   Who has wrapped up the waters in a
      garment?
   Who has established all the ends of
      the earth?
   What is the person's name?
   And what is the name of the
      person's child?
   Surely you know!

5 Every word of God proves true;
   he is a shield to those who take
      refuge in him.
6 Do not add to his words,
   or else he will rebuke you, and you
      will be found a liar.

7 Two things I ask of you;
   do not deny them to me before I die:
8 Remove far from me falsehood and
      lying;
   give me neither poverty nor riches;
   feed me with the food that I need,

---

m Vg: Meaning of Heb uncertain   *n* Meaning of
Heb uncertain   *o* Or *human fear*   *p* Or *I am spent.*
Meaning of Heb uncertain   *q* Or *Holy One*

9 or I shall be full, and deny you,
   and say, "Who is the LORD?"
or I shall be poor, and steal,
   and profane the name of my God.

10 Do not slander a servant to a master,
   or the servant will curse you, and
      you will be held guilty.

11 There are those who curse their fathers
   and do not bless their mothers.
12 There are those who are pure in their
      own eyes
   yet are not cleansed of their filthiness.
13 There are those—how lofty are their
      eyes,
   how high their eyelids lift!—
14 there are those whose teeth are swords,
   whose teeth are knives,
to devour the poor from off the earth,
   the needy from among mortals.

15 The leech[r] has two daughters;
   "Give, give," they cry.
Three things are never satisfied;
   four never say, "Enough":
16 Shĕ´ōl, the barren womb,
   the earth ever thirsty for water,
   and the fire that never says,
      "Enough."[r]

17 The eye that mocks a father
   and scorns to obey a mother
will be pecked out by the ravens of the
      valley
   and eaten by the vultures.

18 Three things are too wonderful for me;
   four I do not understand:
19 the way of an eagle in the sky,
   the way of a snake on a rock,
the way of a ship on the high seas,
   and the way of a man with a girl.

20 This is the way of an adulteress:
   she eats, and wipes her mouth,
   and says, "I have done no wrong."

21 Under three things the earth trembles;
   under four it cannot bear up:

22 a slave when he becomes king,
   and a fool when glutted with food;
23 an unloved woman when she gets a
      husband,
   and a maid when she succeeds her
      mistress.

24 Four things on earth are small,
   yet they are exceedingly wise:
25 the ants are a people without strength,
   yet they provide their food in the
      summer;
26 the badgers are a people without power,
   yet they make their homes in the
      rocks;
27 the locusts have no king,
   yet all of them march in rank;
28 the lizard[s] can be grasped in the hand,
   yet it is found in kings' palaces.

29 Three things are stately in their stride;
   four are stately in their gait:
30 the lion, which is mightiest among
      wild animals
   and does not turn back before any;
31 the strutting rooster,[t] the he-goat,
   and a king striding before[r] his people.

32 If you have been foolish, exalting
      yourself,
   or if you have been devising evil,
   put your hand on your mouth.
33 For as pressing milk produces curds,
   and pressing the nose produces
      blood,
   so pressing anger produces strife.

The Teaching of King Lemuel's Mother

31 The words of King Lem´ū·el. An
      oracle that his mother taught him:

2 No, my son! No, son of my womb!
   No, son of my vows!
3 Do not give your strength to women,
   your ways to those who destroy kings.
4 It is not for kings, O Lem´ū·el,
   it is not for kings to drink wine,

---

[r] Meaning of Heb uncertain   [s] Or *spider*   [t] Gk
Syr Tg Compare Vg: Meaning of Heb uncertain

or for rulers to desire[u] strong drink;
5 or else they will drink and forget what
has been decreed,
and will pervert the rights of all the
afflicted.
6 Give strong drink to one who is
perishing,
and wine to those in bitter distress;
7 let them drink and forget their poverty,
and remember their misery no
more.
8 Speak out for those who cannot speak,
for the rights of all the destitute.[v]
9 Speak out, judge righteously,
defend the rights of the poor and
needy.

Ode to a Capable Wife

10 A capable wife who can find?
She is far more precious than jewels.
11 The heart of her husband trusts in her,
and he will have no lack of gain.
12 She does him good, and not harm,
all the days of her life.
13 She seeks wool and flax,
and works with willing hands.
14 She is like the ships of the merchant,
she brings her food from far away.
15 She rises while it is still night
and provides food for her household
and tasks for her servant-girls.
16 She considers a field and buys it;
with the fruit of her hands she
plants a vineyard.
17 She girds herself with strength,
and makes her arms strong.
18 She perceives that her merchandise is
profitable.
Her lamp does not go out at night.
19 She puts her hands to the distaff,
and her hands hold the spindle.
20 She opens her hand to the poor,
and reaches out her hands to the
needy.
21 She is not afraid for her household
when it snows,
for all her household are clothed in
crimson.

22 She makes herself coverings;
her clothing is fine linen and purple.
23 Her husband is known in the city
gates,
taking his seat among the elders of
the land.
24 She makes linen garments and sells
them;
she supplies the merchant with
sashes.
25 Strength and dignity are her clothing,
and she laughs at the time to come.
26 She opens her mouth with wisdom,
and the teaching of kindness is on
her tongue.
27 She looks well to the ways of her
household,
and does not eat the bread of
idleness.
28 Her children rise up and call her
happy;
her husband too, and he praises her:
29 "Many women have done excellently,
but you surpass them all."
30 Charm is deceitful, and beauty is vain,
but a woman who fears the LORD is
to be praised.
31 Give her a share in the fruit of her
hands,
and let her works praise her in the
city gates.

In early Bible times,
people made lamps
by filling a pottery
saucer with olive oil and resting a wick of twisted threads
on the edge. Later, covered
lamps with spouts for holding
the wick became popular. The
woman of this household
made sure that her lamp was
always filled with oil.

[u] Cn: Heb *where* [v] Heb *all children of passing away*

Ecclesiastes

The word "ecclesiastes" means "member or gatherer of the assembly," or "the teacher." The book of Ecclesiastes is said to have been written by "the Teacher, the son of David," but there is no other hint about who the writer was. The book was written around the third century BC.

Ecclesiastes tells about a man who tried to do many things in order to find meaning in life and to make himself happy. Some of the things he tried include making money, studying to become wise, and seeking pleasure. But no matter what he tried, nothing provided him real happiness. Instead, the man felt hopeless.

The book of Ecclesiastes shows over and over again that many of the things people try so hard to do or to get do not really matter. There are many doubts we have and many problems in life that we cannot solve. But the book ends by saying that in spite of every disappointment, we should always trust God.

Ecclesiastes 1:14

Reflections of a Royal Philosopher

1 The words of the Teacher,[a] the son of David, king in Jerusalem.

2 Vanity of vanities, says the Teacher,[a]
　vanity of vanities! All is vanity.

3 What do people gain from all the toil
　at which they toil under the sun?

4 A generation goes, and a generation comes,
　but the earth remains forever.

5 The sun rises and the sun goes down,
　and hurries to the place where it rises.

6 The wind blows to the south,
　and goes around to the north;
round and round goes the wind,
　and on its circuits the wind returns.

7 All streams run to the sea,
　but the sea is not full;
to the place where the streams flow,
　there they continue to flow.

8 All things[b] are wearisome;
　more than one can express;
the eye is not satisfied with seeing,
　or the ear filled with hearing.

9 What has been is what will be,
　and what has been done is what will be done;
　there is nothing new under the sun.

10 Is there a thing of which it is said,
　"See, this is new"?
It has already been,
　in the ages before us.

11 The people of long ago are not remembered,
　nor will there be any remembrance
of people yet to come
　by those who come after them.

The author of Ecclesiastes calls himself "the Teacher." "Teacher" might also mean "speaker before an assembly." We don't know exactly who the author was, but he must have been a wise man and a philosopher. Because Solomon was a wise man, the author wanted his readers to think of him as another Solomon. He explored life and wrote down what he thought was best for those who want to live good, satisfying lives that are pleasing to God.

The Futility of Seeking Wisdom

12 I, the Teacher,[a] when king over Israel in Jerusalem, 13applied my mind to seek and to search out by wisdom all that is done under heaven; it is an unhappy business that God has given to human beings to be busy with. 14I saw all the deeds that are done under the sun; and see, all is vanity and a chasing after wind.[c]

15 What is crooked cannot be made straight,
　and what is lacking cannot be counted.

16 I said to myself, "I have acquired great wisdom, surpassing all who were over Jerusalem before me; and my mind has had great experience of wisdom and knowledge." 17And I applied my mind to know wisdom and to know madness and folly. I perceived that this also is but a chasing after wind.[c]

18 For in much wisdom is much vexation,
　and those who increase knowledge increase sorrow.

The Futility of Self-Indulgence

2 I said to myself, "Come now, I will make a test of pleasure; enjoy yourself." But again, this also was vanity. 2I said of laughter, "It is mad," and of pleasure, "What use is it?" 3I searched with my mind how to cheer my body with wine—my mind still guiding me with wisdom—and how to lay hold on folly, until I might see what was good for mortals to do under heaven during the few days of their life.

---

[a] Heb Qoheleth, traditionally rendered Preacher
[b] Or words　　[c] Or a feeding on wind. See Hos 12.1

[4]I made great works; I built houses and planted vineyards for myself; [5]I made myself gardens and parks, and planted in them all kinds of fruit trees. [6]I made myself pools from which to water the forest of growing trees. [7]I bought male and female slaves, and had slaves who were born in my house; I also had great possessions of herds and flocks, more than any who had been before me in Jerusalem. [8]I also gathered for myself silver and gold and the treasure of kings and of the provinces; I got singers, both men and women, and delights of the flesh, and many concubines.[d]

9 So I became great and surpassed all who were before me in Jerusalem; also my wisdom remained with me. [10]Whatever my eyes desired I did not keep from them; I kept my heart from no pleasure, for my heart found pleasure in all my toil, and this was my reward for all my toil. [11]Then I considered all that my hands had done and the toil I had spent in doing it, and again, all was vanity and a chasing after wind,[e] and there was nothing to be gained under the sun.

Wisdom and Joy Given to One Who Pleases God

12 So I turned to consider wisdom and madness and folly; for what can the one do who comes after the king? Only what has already been done. [13]Then I saw that wisdom excels folly as light excels darkness.

[14] The wise have eyes in their head,
    but fools walk in darkness.

Yet I perceived that the same fate befalls all of them. [15]Then I said to myself, "What happens to the fool will happen to me also; why then have I been so very wise?" And I said to myself that this also is vanity. [16]For there is no enduring remembrance of the wise or of fools, seeing that in the days to come all will have been long forgotten. How can the wise die just like fools? [17]So I hated life, because what is done under the sun was grievous to me; for all is vanity and a chasing after wind.[e]

18 I hated all my toil in which I had toiled under the sun, seeing that I must leave it to those who come after me [19]— and who knows whether they will be wise or foolish? Yet they will be master of all for which I toiled and used my wisdom under the sun. This also is vanity. [20]So I turned and gave my heart up to despair concerning all the toil of my labors under the sun, [21]because sometimes one who has toiled with wisdom and knowledge and skill must leave all to be enjoyed by another who did not toil for it. This also is vanity and a great evil. [22]What do mortals get from all the toil and strain with which they toil under the sun? [23]For all their days are full of pain, and their work is a vexation; even at night their minds do not rest. This also is vanity.

24 There is nothing better for mortals than to eat and drink, and find enjoyment in their toil. This also, I saw, is from the hand of God; [25]for apart from him[f] who can eat or who can have enjoyment? [26]For to the one who pleases him God gives wisdom and knowledge and joy; but to the sinner he gives the work of gathering and heaping, only to give to one who pleases God. This also is vanity and a chasing after wind.[e]

Everything Has Its Time

3 For everything there is a season, and a time for every matter under heaven:

[2] a time to be born, and a time to die;
    a time to plant, and a time to pluck up
        what is planted;
[3] a time to kill, and a time to heal;
    a time to break down, and a time to
        build up;
[4] a time to weep, and a time to laugh;
    a time to mourn, and a time to dance;
[5] a time to throw away stones, and a
        time to gather stones together;
    a time to embrace, and a time to
        refrain from embracing;

---

[d] Meaning of Heb uncertain   [e] Or a feeding on wind. See Hos 12.1   [f] Gk Syr: Heb apart from me

⁶ a time to seek, and a time to lose;
   a time to keep, and a time to throw
      away;
⁷ a time to tear, and a time to sew;
   a time to keep silence, and a time to
      speak;
⁸ a time to love, and a time to hate;
   a time for war, and a time for peace.

The God-Given Task

9 What gain have the workers from their toil? ¹⁰I have seen the business that God has given to everyone to be busy with. ¹¹He has made everything suitable for its time; moreover he has put a sense of past and future into their minds, yet they cannot find out what God has done from the beginning to the end. ¹²I know that there is nothing better for them than to be happy and enjoy themselves as long as they live; ¹³moreover, it is God's gift that all should eat and drink and take pleasure in all their toil. ¹⁴I know that whatever God does endures forever; nothing can be added to it, nor anything taken from it; God has done this, so that all should stand in awe before him. ¹⁵That which is, already has been; that which is to be, already is; and God seeks out what has gone by.ᵍ

Judgment and the Future Belong to God

16 Moreover I saw under the sun that in the place of justice, wickedness was there, and in the place of righteousness, wickedness was there as well. ¹⁷I said in my heart, God will judge the righteous and the wicked, for he has appointed a time for every matter, and for every work. ¹⁸I said in my heart with regard to human beings that God is testing them to show that they are but animals. ¹⁹For the fate of humans and the fate of animals is the same; as one dies, so dies the other. They all have the same breath, and humans have no advantage over the animals; for all is vanity. ²⁰All go to one place; all are from the dust, and all turn to dust again. ²¹Who knows whether the human spirit goes upward and the spirit of animals goes downward to

> "I know that whatever God does endures forever; nothing can be added to it, nor anything taken from it."
> Ecclesiastes 3:14*a*

the earth? ²²So I saw that there is nothing better than that all should enjoy their work, for that is their lot; who can bring them to see what will be after them?

4 Again I saw all the oppressions that are practiced under the sun. Look, the tears of the oppressed—with no one to comfort them! On the side of their oppressors there was power—with no one to comfort them. ²And I thought the dead, who have already died, more fortunate than the living, who are still alive; ³but better than both is the one who has not yet been, and has not seen the evil deeds that are done under the sun.

4 Then I saw that all toil and all skill in work come from one person's envy of another. This also is vanity and a chasing after wind.ʰ

⁵ Fools fold their hands
   and consume their own flesh.
⁶ Better is a handful with quiet
   than two handfuls with toil,
      and a chasing after wind.ʰ

7 Again, I saw vanity under the sun: ⁸the case of solitary individuals, without sons or brothers; yet there is no end to all their toil, and their eyes are never satisfied with riches. "For whom am I toiling," they ask, "and depriving myself of pleasure?" This also is vanity and an unhappy business.

The Value of a Friend

9 Two are better than one, because they have a good reward for their toil. ¹⁰For if they fall, one will lift up the other; but woe to one who is alone and falls and does not have another to help. ¹¹Again, if two lie together, they keep warm; but how can one keep warm alone? ¹²And though one

ᵍ Heb *what is pursued*   ʰ Or *a feeding on wind.* See Hos 12.1

"Two are better than one, because they have a good reward for their toil. For if they fall, one will lift up the other; but woe to one who is alone and falls and does not have another to help."   Ecclesiastes 4:9

might prevail against another, two will withstand one. A threefold cord is not quickly broken.

13 Better is a poor but wise youth than an old but foolish king, who will no longer take advice. [14]One can indeed come out of prison to reign, even though born poor in the kingdom. [15]I saw all the living who, moving about under the sun, follow that[i] youth who replaced the king;[j] [16]there was no end to all those people whom he led. Yet those who come later will not rejoice in him. Surely this also is vanity and a chasing after wind.[k]

Reverence, Humility, and Contentment

5 [1]Guard your steps when you go to the house of God; to draw near to listen is better than the sacrifice offered by fools; for they do not know how to keep from doing evil.[m] [2n] Never be rash with your mouth, nor let your heart be quick to utter a word before God, for God is in heaven, and you upon earth; therefore let your words be few.

3 For dreams come with many cares, and a fool's voice with many words.

4 When you make a vow to God, do not delay fulfilling it; for he has no pleasure in fools. Fulfill what you vow. [5]It is better that you should not vow than that you should vow and not fulfill it. [6]Do not let your mouth lead you into sin, and do not say before the messenger that it was a mistake; why should God be angry at your words, and destroy the work of your hands?

7 With many dreams come vanities and a multitude of words;[o] but fear God.

8 If you see in a province the oppres-sion of the poor and the violation of justice and right, do not be amazed at the matter; for the high official is watched by a higher, and there are yet higher ones over them. [9]But all things considered, this is an advantage for a land: a king for a plowed field.[o]

10 The lover of money will not be satisfied with money; nor the lover of wealth, with gain. This also is vanity.

11 When goods increase, those who eat them increase; and what gain has their owner but to see them with his eyes?

12 Sweet is the sleep of laborers, whether they eat little or much; but the surfeit of the rich will not let them sleep.

13 There is a grievous ill that I have seen under the sun: riches were kept by their owners to their hurt, [14]and those riches were lost in a bad venture; though they are parents of children, they have nothing in their hands. [15]As they came from their mother's womb, so they shall go again, naked as they came; they shall take nothing for their toil, which they may carry away with their hands. [16]This also is a grievous ill: just as they came, so shall they go; and what gain do they have from toiling for the wind? [17]Besides, all their days they eat in darkness, in much vexation and sickness and resentment.

18 This is what I have seen to be good: it is fitting to eat and drink and find enjoyment in all the toil with which one toils under the sun the few days of the life God gives us; for this is our lot. [19]Likewise all to whom God gives wealth and possessions and whom he enables to enjoy them, and to accept their lot and find enjoyment in their toil—this is the gift of God. [20]For they will scarcely brood over the days of their lives, because God keeps them occupied with the joy of their hearts.

[i] Heb *the second*   [j] Heb *him*   [k] Or *a feeding on wind.* See Hos 12.1   [l] Ch 4.17 in Heb   [m] Cn: Heb *they do not know how to do evil*   [n] Ch 5.1 in Heb   [o] Meaning of Heb uncertain

The Frustration of Desires

6 There is an evil that I have seen under the sun, and it lies heavy upon humankind: ²those to whom God gives wealth, possessions, and honor, so that they lack nothing of all that they desire, yet God does not enable them to enjoy these things, but a stranger enjoys them. This is vanity; it is a grievous ill. ³A man may beget a hundred children, and live many years; but however many are the days of his years, if he does not enjoy life's good things, or has no burial, I say that a stillborn child is better off than he. ⁴For it comes into vanity and goes into darkness, and in darkness its name is covered; ⁵moreover it has not seen the sun or known anything; yet it finds rest rather than he. ⁶Even though he should live a thousand years twice over, yet enjoy no good—do not all go to one place?

7 All human toil is for the mouth, yet the appetite is not satisfied. ⁸For what advantage have the wise over fools? And what do the poor have who know how to conduct themselves before the living? ⁹Better is the sight of the eyes than the wandering of desire; this also is vanity and a chasing after wind.*

10 Whatever has come to be has already been named, and it is known what human beings are, and that they are not able to dispute with those who are stronger. ¹¹The more words, the more vanity, so how is one the better? ¹²For who knows what is good for mortals while they live the few days of their vain life, which they pass like a shadow? For who can tell them what will be after them under the sun?

A Disillusioned View of Life

7 A good name is better than precious ointment,
and the day of death,
than the day of birth.
² It is better to go to the house of mourning
than to go to the house of feasting;
for this is the end of everyone,

and the living will lay it to heart.
³ Sorrow is better than laughter,
for by sadness of countenance the heart is made glad.
⁴ The heart of the wise is in the house of mourning;
but the heart of fools is in the house of mirth.
⁵ It is better to hear the rebuke of the wise
than to hear the song of fools.
⁶ For like the crackling of thorns under a pot,
so is the laughter of fools;
this also is vanity.
⁷ Surely oppression makes the wise foolish,
and a bribe corrupts the heart.
⁸ Better is the end of a thing than its beginning;
the patient in spirit are better than the proud in spirit.
⁹ Do not be quick to anger,
for anger lodges in the bosom of fools.
¹⁰ Do not say, "Why were the former days better than these?"
For it is not from wisdom that you ask this.
¹¹ Wisdom is as good as an inheritance,
an advantage to those who see the sun.
¹² For the protection of wisdom is like the protection of money,
and the advantage of knowledge is that wisdom gives life to the one who possesses it.
¹³ Consider the work of God;
who can make straight what he has made crooked?

14 In the day of prosperity be joyful, and in the day of adversity consider; God has made the one as well as the other, so that mortals may not find out anything that will come after them.

The Riddles of Life

15 In my vain life I have seen everything; there are righteous people who per-

p Or *a feeding on wind.* See Hos 12.1

ish in their righteousness, and there are wicked people who prolong their life in their evildoing. [16]Do not be too righteous, and do not act too wise; why should you destroy yourself? [17]Do not be too wicked, and do not be a fool; why should you die before your time? [18]It is good that you should take hold of the one, without letting go of the other; for the one who fears God shall succeed with both.

19 Wisdom gives strength to the wise more than ten rulers that are in a city.

20 Surely there is no one on earth so righteous as to do good without ever sinning.

21 Do not give heed to everything that people say, or you may hear your servant cursing you; [22]your heart knows that many times you have yourself cursed others.

23 All this I have tested by wisdom; I said, "I will be wise," but it was far from me. [24]That which is, is far off, and deep, very deep; who can find it out? [25]I turned my mind to know and to search out and to seek wisdom and the sum of things, and to know that wickedness is folly and that foolishness is madness. [26]I found more bitter than death the woman who is a trap, whose heart is snares and nets, whose hands are fetters; one who pleases God escapes her, but the sinner is taken by her. [27]See, this is what I found, says the Teacher,[q] adding one thing to another to find the sum, [28]which my mind has sought repeatedly, but I have not found. One man among a thousand I found, but a woman among all these I have not found. [29]See, this alone I found, that God made human beings straightforward, but they have devised many schemes.

Obey the King and Enjoy Yourself

8 Who is like the wise man?
And who knows the interpretation of
a thing?
Wisdom makes one's face shine,
and the hardness of one's countenance is changed.
2 Keep[r] the king's command because

of your sacred oath. [3]Do not be terrified; go from his presence, do not delay when the matter is unpleasant, for he does whatever he pleases. [4]For the word of the king is powerful, and who can say to him, "What are you doing?" [5]Whoever obeys a command will meet no harm, and the wise mind will know the time and way. [6]For every matter has its time and way, although the troubles of mortals lie heavy upon them. [7]Indeed, they do not know what is to be, for who can tell them how it will be? [8]No one has power over the wind[s] to restrain the wind,[s] or power over the day of death; there is no discharge from the battle, nor does wickedness deliver those who practice it. [9]All this I observed, applying my mind to all that is done under the sun, while one person exercises authority over another to the other's hurt.

God's Ways Are Inscrutable

10 Then I saw the wicked buried; they used to go in and out of the holy place, and were praised in the city where they had done such things.[t] This also is vanity. [11]Because sentence against an evil deed is not executed speedily, the human heart is fully set to do evil. [12]Though sinners do evil a hundred times and prolong their lives, yet I know that it will be well with those who fear God, because they stand in fear before him, [13]but it will not be well with the wicked, neither will they prolong their days like a shadow, because they do not stand in fear before God.

14 There is a vanity that takes place on earth, that there are righteous people who are treated according to the conduct of the wicked, and there are wicked people who are treated according to the conduct of the righteous. I said that this also is vanity. [15]So I commend enjoyment, for there is nothing better for people under the sun than to eat, and drink, and enjoy themselves, for this will go with them in their toil through

---

[q] *Qoheleth*, traditionally rendered *Preacher*   [r] Heb I keep   [s] Or *breath*   [t] Meaning of Heb uncertain

the days of life that God gives them under the sun.

16 When I applied my mind to know wisdom, and to see the business that is done on earth, how one's eyes see sleep neither day nor night, [17]then I saw all the work of God, that no one can find out what is happening under the sun. However much they may toil in seeking, they will not find it out; even though those who are wise claim to know, they cannot find it out.

Take Life as It Comes

9 All this I laid to heart, examining it all, how the righteous and the wise and their deeds are in the hand of God; whether it is love or hate one does not know. Everything that confronts them [2]is vanity[u] since the same fate comes to all, to the righteous and the wicked, to the good and the evil,[v] to the clean and the unclean, to those who sacrifice and those who do not sacrifice. As are the good, so are the sinners; those who swear are like those who shun an oath. [3]This is an evil in all that happens under the sun, that the same fate comes to everyone. Moreover, the hearts of all are full of evil; madness is in their hearts while they live, and after that they go to the dead. [4]But whoever is joined with all the living has hope, for a living dog is better than a dead lion. [5]The living know that they will die, but the dead know nothing; they have no more reward, and even the memory of them is lost. [6]Their love and their hate and their envy have already perished; never again will they have any share in all that happens under the sun.

7 Go, eat your bread with enjoyment, and drink your wine with a merry heart; for God has long ago approved what you do. [8]Let your garments always be white; do not let oil be lacking on your head. [9]Enjoy life with the wife whom you love, all the days of your vain life that are given you under the sun, because that is your portion in life and in your toil at which you toil under the sun. [10]Whatever your hand

finds to do, do with your might; for there is no work or thought or knowledge or wisdom in Shĕʾōl, to which you are going.

11 Again I saw that under the sun the race is not to the swift, nor the battle to the strong, nor bread to the wise, nor riches to the intelligent, nor favor to the skillful; but time and chance happen to them all. [12]For no one can anticipate the time of disaster. Like fish taken in a cruel net, and like birds caught in a snare, so mortals are snared at a time of calamity, when it suddenly falls upon them.

Wisdom Superior to Folly

13 I have also seen this example of wisdom under the sun, and it seemed great to me. [14]There was a little city with few people in it. A great king came against it and besieged it, building great siegeworks against it. [15]Now there was found in it a poor wise man, and he by his wisdom delivered the city. Yet no one remembered that poor man. [16]So I said, "Wisdom is better than might; yet the poor man's wisdom is despised, and his words are not heeded."

We often use the color red as a symbol for love. Can you think of some other colors that we use as symbols? In the Bible, the color white can be a symbol for purity. Saying "let your garments (clothes) be white" is a way of saying "stay pure." In Daniel 7:9, God is described as wearing white clothes. In Matthew 17:2, Jesus's clothes became as white as snow when he was transfigured. In John 20:12, the angels were dressed in white when the disciples visited the tomb of our risen Lord. And in Revelation 7:9, the redeemed are said to be clothed in white.

[u] Syr Compare Gk: Heb *Everything that confronts them* [2]*is everything*   [v] Gk Syr Vg: Heb lacks *and the evil*

Have you ever heard the expression "look before you leap"? The Teacher is saying much the same thing in Ecclesiastes 10:10. Stop and think before you act! You will get the job done faster, easier, and safer. This is true for the way we act toward others and also for the things we say.

17 The quiet words of the wise are more
    to be heeded
      than the shouting of a ruler among
        fools.
18 Wisdom is better than weapons of war,
      but one bungler destroys much good.

Miscellaneous Observations

10 Dead flies make the perfumer's
    ointment give off a foul odor;
  so a little folly outweighs wisdom
    and honor.
2 The heart of the wise inclines to the
    right,
  but the heart of a fool to the left.
3 Even when fools walk on the road,
    they lack sense,
  and show to everyone that they are
    fools.
4 If the anger of the ruler rises against
    you, do not leave your post,
  for calmness will undo great
    offenses.
5 There is an evil that I have seen under
the sun, as great an error as if it proceeded
from the ruler: 6folly is set in many high
places, and the rich sit in a low place. 7I
have seen slaves on horseback, and princes
walking on foot like slaves.
8 Whoever digs a pit will fall into it;
    and whoever breaks through a wall
      will be bitten by a snake.
9 Whoever quarries stones will be hurt
    by them;
    and whoever splits logs will be
      endangered by them.
10 If the iron is blunt, and one does not
    whet the edge,

then more strength must be exerted;
    but wisdom helps one to succeed.
11 If the snake bites before it is charmed,
      there is no advantage in a charmer.

12 Words spoken by the wise bring them
      favor,
    but the lips of fools consume them.
13 The words of their mouths begin in
      foolishness,
    and their talk ends in wicked mad-
      ness;
14 yet fools talk on and on.
    No one knows what is to happen,
      and who can tell anyone what the
        future holds?
15 The toil of fools wears them out,
    for they do not even know the way
      to town.
16 Alas for you, O land, when your king
      is a servant,w
    and your princes feast in the morning!
17 Happy are you, O land, when your
      king is a nobleman,
    and your princes feast at the proper
      time—
    for strength, and not for drunken-
      ness!
18 Through sloth the roof sinks in,
    and through indolence the house
      leaks.
19 Feasts are made for laughter;
    wine gladdens life,
    and money meets every need.
20 Do not curse the king, even in your
      thoughts,
    or curse the rich, even in your bed-
      room;
  for a bird of the air may carry your
      voice,
    or some winged creature tell the
      matter.

The Value of Diligence

11 Send out your bread upon the
    waters,
  for after many days you
    will get it back.

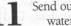

w Or *a child*

"Sending out bread upon the waters" seems to refer to acting with goodness and charity. When we give without expecting a reward, we are often surprised at the result. God always acts with love toward us and wants us to act the same toward others.

2 Divide your means seven ways, or
even eight,
for you do not know what disaster
may happen on earth.
3 When clouds are full,
they empty rain on the earth;
whether a tree falls to the south or to
the north,
in the place where the tree falls,
there it will lie.
4 Whoever observes the wind will not
sow;
and whoever regards the clouds will
not reap.

5 Just as you do not know how the breath comes to the bones in the mother's womb, so you do not know the work of God, who makes everything.

6 In the morning sow your seed, and at evening do not let your hands be idle; for you do not know which will prosper, this or that, or whether both alike will be good.

Youth and Old Age

7 Light is sweet, and it is pleasant for the eyes to see the sun.

8 Even those who live many years should rejoice in them all; yet let them remember that the days of darkness will be many. All that comes is vanity.

9 Rejoice, young man, while you are young, and let your heart cheer you in the days of your youth. Follow the inclination of your heart and the desire of your eyes, but know that for all these things God will bring you into judgment.

10 Banish anxiety from your mind, and put away pain from your body; for youth and the dawn of life are vanity.

"Remember your creator in the days of your youth."
Ecclesiastes 12:1*a*

12 Remember your creator in the days of your youth, before the days of trouble come, and the years draw near when you will say, "I have no pleasure in them"; [2]before the sun and the light and the moon and the stars are darkened and the clouds return with[x] the rain; [3]in the day when the guards of the house tremble, and the strong men are bent, and the women who grind cease working because they are few, and those who look through the windows see dimly; [4]when the doors on the street are shut, and the sound of the grinding is low, and one rises up at the sound of a bird, and all the daughters of song are brought low; [5]when one is afraid of heights, and terrors are in the road; the almond tree blossoms, the grasshopper drags itself along[y] and desire fails; because all must go to their eternal home, and the mourners will go about the streets; [6]before the silver cord is snapped,[z] and the golden bowl is broken, and the pitcher is broken

A goad is a pointed stick (sometimes with nails set in the end) that people in Bible times used to guide cattle where they needed to go. The goad would spur, or push, the cattle to action.

Listening to the words of wise people can push us on to better behavior. Think of someone you know who is very wise. Has that person given you any advice that has helped you? Ask your parents who they look to for advice. Say a family prayer together, thanking God for the wise people in your lives.

x Or *after* ; Heb '*ahar* y Or *is a burden* z Syr Vg
Compare Gk: Heb *is removed*

"The end of the matter; all has been heard. Fear God, and keep his commandments; for that is the whole duty of everyone."
Ecclesiastes 12:13

at the fountain, and the wheel broken at the cistern, [7]and the dust returns to the earth as it was, and the breath[a] returns to God who gave it. [8]Vanity of vanities, says the Teacher;[b] all is vanity.

Epilogue

9 Besides being wise, the Teacher[c] also taught the people knowledge, weighing and studying and arranging many proverbs. [10]The Teacher[c] sought to find pleasing words, and he wrote words of truth plainly.

11 The sayings of the wise are like goads, and like nails firmly fixed are the collected sayings that are given by one shepherd.[d] [12]Of anything beyond these, my child, beware. Of making many books there is no end, and much study is a weariness of the flesh.

13 The end of the matter; all has been heard. Fear God, and keep his commandments; for that is the whole duty of everyone. [14]For God will bring every deed into judgment, including[e] every secret thing, whether good or evil.

[a] Or *the spirit*   [b] *Qoheleth*, traditionally rendered *Preacher*   [c] *Qoheleth*, traditionally rendered *Preacher*   [d] Meaning of Heb uncertain   [e] Or *into the judgment on*

The Song of Solomon

The Song of Solomon is a series of ancient Near Eastern wedding songs. It includes parts for the bride, the groom, and the chorus of villagers to sing during the wedding festivities. Although Solomon's name was given to the book, we do not know who wrote it. Scholars think that the songs in this book were put together about 300 BC and were probably used in the wedding celebrations of the Jews. There are many cultures today that still have these types of weddings with singing and dancing.

The Song of Solomon celebrates the joyful love that a groom and a bride have for each other. The songs in this book describe that love as something beautiful and good. It is something to be celebrated! The Song of Solomon also is said to be a description of the love between God (the Bridegroom) and God's people (the Bride).

Song of Solomon 8:6–7

> The young woman describes several oils used as perfume for the body, clothing, or sheets. Nard was an expensive, fragrant oil prepared from the roots and stems of the spikenard plant.

1

The Song of Songs, which is Solomon's.

Colloquy of Bride and Friends

2 Let him kiss me with the kisses of his
    mouth!
For your love is better than wine,
3   your anointing oils are fragrant,
your name is perfume poured out;
    therefore the maidens love you.
4 Draw me after you, let us make haste.
    The king has brought me into his
    chambers.
We will exult and rejoice in you;
    we will extol your love more than
    wine;
    rightly do they love you.

5 I am black and beautiful,
    O daughters of Jerusalem,
like the tents of Kē'dar,
    like the curtains of Solomon.
6 Do not gaze at me because I am dark,
    because the sun has gazed on me.
My mother's sons were angry with me;
    they made me keeper of the
    vineyards,
    but my own vineyard I have not
    kept!
7 Tell me, you whom my soul loves,
    where you pasture your flock,
    where you make it lie down at
    noon;
for why should I be like one who is
    veiled
    beside the flocks of your
    companions?

8 If you do not know,
    O fairest among women,
follow the tracks of the flock,
    and pasture your kids
    beside the shepherds' tents.

Colloquy of Bridegroom, Friends, and Bride

9 I compare you, my love,
    to a mare among Pharaoh's chariots.
10 Your cheeks are comely with
    ornaments,
    your neck with strings of jewels.
11 We will make you ornaments of gold,
    studded with silver.

12 While the king was on his couch,
    my nard gave forth its fragrance.
13 My beloved is to me a bag of myrrh
    that lies between my breasts.
14 My beloved is to me a cluster of henna
    blossoms
    in the vineyards of En-ge'di.

15 Ah, you are beautiful, my love;
    ah, you are beautiful;
    your eyes are doves.
16 Ah, you are beautiful, my beloved,
    truly lovely.
Our couch is green;
17   the beams of our house are cedar,
    our rafters[a] are pine.

2

I am a rose[b] of Sharon,
    a lily of the valleys.

> Many springtime flowers that grew in Bible lands were called lilies. The rose of Sharon was a type of flower that grew on the Plain of Sharon, which was known for its marshes and forests. What kinds of flowers grow in the springtime where you live?

[a] Meaning of Heb uncertain   [b] Heb crocus

2 As a lily among brambles,
  so is my love among maidens.
3 As an apple tree among the trees of
    the wood,
  so is my beloved among young
    men.
With great delight I sat in his shadow,
  and his fruit was sweet to my taste.
4 He brought me to the banqueting
    house,
  and his intention toward me was
    love.
5 Sustain me with raisins,
  refresh me with apples;
  for I am faint with love.
6 O that his left hand were under my
    head,
  and that his right hand embraced
    me!
7 I adjure you, O daughters of
    Jerusalem,
  by the gazelles or the wild does:
do not stir up or awaken love
  until it is ready!

Springtime Rhapsody

8 The voice of my beloved!
  Look, he comes,
leaping upon the mountains,
  bounding over the hills.
9 My beloved is like a gazelle
  or a young stag.
Look, there he stands
  behind our wall,
gazing in at the windows,
  looking through the lattice.
10 My beloved speaks and says to me:
"Arise, my love, my fair one,
  and come away;
11 for now the winter is past,
  the rain is over and gone.

Figs were very important in Bible times. Fig trees provided shade from the sun, and their fruit was a source of food. People also used fig cakes as medication. In addition, people could sew together the leaves of fig trees to serve as wrappings for fruits and vegetables taken to market.

12 The flowers appear on the earth;
  the time of singing has come,
and the voice of the turtledove
  is heard in our land.
13 The fig tree puts forth its figs,
  and the vines are in blossom;
  they give forth fragrance.
Arise, my love, my fair one,
  and come away.
14 O my dove, in the clefts of the rock,
  in the covert of the cliff,
let me see your face,
  let me hear your voice;
for your voice is sweet,
  and your face is lovely.
15 Catch us the foxes,
  the little foxes,
that ruin the vineyards—
  for our vineyards are in blossom."

16 My beloved is mine and I am his;
  he pastures his flock among the
    lilies.
17 Until the day breathes
  and the shadows flee,
turn, my beloved, be like a gazelle
  or a young stag on the cleft
    mountains.[c]

Love's Dream

3 Upon my bed at night
    I sought him whom my soul loves;
  I sought him, but found him not;
    I called him, but he gave no
      answer.[d]

The dove is a gentle bird that is faithful to its mate. Because of these qualities, the dove was a favorite of those who wrote poetry and love songs.

[c] Or *on the mountains of Bether*: meaning of Heb uncertain   [d] Gk: Heb lacks this line

A palanquin is a covered couch used to carry passengers. Strong poles were fastened to the palanquin so that slaves, mules, or horses could carry it. Solomon's palanquin was magnificent, made of richly carved woodwork and decorated with ornaments of gold, silver, and precious stones. It may have had a canopy of silk or satin to shade the king from the sun.

2 "I will rise now and go about the city,
  in the streets and in the squares;
I will seek him whom my soul loves."
  I sought him, but found him not.
3 The sentinels found me,
  as they went about in the city.
"Have you seen him whom my soul
    loves?"
4 Scarcely had I passed them,
  when I found him whom my soul
    loves.
I held him, and would not let him go
  until I brought him into my
    mother's house,
  and into the chamber of her that
    conceived me.
5 I adjure you, O daughters of
    Jerusalem,
  by the gazelles or the wild does:
do not stir up or awaken love
  until it is ready!

The Groom and His Party Approach

6 What is that coming up from the
    wilderness,
  like a column of smoke,
perfumed with myrrh and frankincense,
  with all the fragrant powders of the
    merchant?
7 Look, it is the litter of Solomon!
Around it are sixty mighty men
  of the mighty men of Israel,

8 all equipped with swords
    and expert in war,
  each with his sword at his thigh
    because of alarms by night.
9 King Solomon made himself a
    palanquin
  from the wood of Lebanon.
10 He made its posts of silver,
    its back of gold, its seat of purple;
  its interior was inlaid with love.ᵉ
    Daughters of Jerusalem,
11   come out.
  Look, O daughters of Zion,
    at King Solomon,
  at the crown with which his mother
    crowned him
    on the day of his wedding,
    on the day of the gladness of his
      heart.

The Bride's Beauty Extolled

4 How beautiful you are, my love,
    how very beautiful!
Your eyes are doves
  behind your veil.
Your hair is like a flock of goats,
  moving down the slopes of Gil′e·ad.
2 Your teeth are like a flock of shorn ewes
  that have come up from the washing,
all of which bear twins,
  and not one among them is
    bereaved.
3 Your lips are like a crimson thread,
  and your mouth is lovely.
Your cheeks are like halves of a
    pomegranate
  behind your veil.

A veil is a head covering worn usually by women. We are not certain what these were like in Bible times, but most scholars agree that they were more for decoration than for hiding the face.

ᵉ Meaning of Heb uncertain

4 Your neck is like the tower of David,
   built in courses;
on it hang a thousand bucklers,
   all of them shields of warriors.
5 Your two breasts are like two fawns,
   twins of a gazelle,
   that feed among the lilies.
6 Until the day breathes
   and the shadows flee,
I will hasten to the mountain of myrrh
   and the hill of frankincense.
7 You are altogether beautiful, my love;
   there is no flaw in you.
8 Come with me from Lebanon, my
   bride;
   come with me from Lebanon.
Depart[f] from the peak of A·ma´na,
   from the peak of Se´nir and
      Hermon,
from the dens of lions,
   from the mountains of leopards.

9 You have ravished my heart, my sister,
   my bride,
   you have ravished my heart with a
      glance of your eyes,
   with one jewel of your necklace.
10 How sweet is your love, my sister, my
   bride!
   how much better is your love than
      wine,
   and the fragrance of your oils than
      any spice!
11 Your lips distill nectar, my bride;
   honey and milk are under your
      tongue;
   the scent of your garments is like
      the scent of Lebanon.
12 A garden locked is my sister, my bride,
   a garden locked, a fountain sealed.
13 Your channel[g] is an orchard of
      pomegranates
   with all choicest fruits,
   henna with nard,
14 nard and saffron, calamus and
      cinnamon,
   with all trees of frankincense,
myrrh and aloes,
   with all chief spices——

15 a garden fountain, a well of living
      water,
   and flowing streams from Lebanon.

16 Awake, O north wind,
   and come, O south wind!
Blow upon my garden
   that its fragrance may be wafted
      abroad.
Let my beloved come to his garden,
   and eat its choicest fruits.

5 I come to my garden, my sister,
   my bride;
I gather my myrrh with my spice,
I eat my honeycomb with my honey,
I drink my wine with my milk.

Eat, friends, drink,
   and be drunk with love.

Another Dream
2 I slept, but my heart was awake.
Listen! my beloved is knocking.
"Open to me, my sister, my love,
   my dove, my perfect one;
for my head is wet with dew,
   my locks with the drops of the
      night."
3 I had put off my garment;
   how could I put it on again?
I had bathed my feet;
   how could I soil them?
4 My beloved thrust his hand into the
      opening,
   and my inmost being yearned for
      him.
5 I arose to open to my beloved,
   and my hands dripped with myrrh,
my fingers with liquid myrrh,
   upon the handles of the bolt.
6 I opened to my beloved,
   but my beloved had turned and was
      gone.
My soul failed me when he spoke.
I sought him, but did not find him;
   I called him, but he gave no answer.

[f] Or Look   [g] Meaning of Heb uncertain

7 Making their rounds in the city
  the sentinels found me;
they beat me, they wounded me,
  they took away my mantle,
  those sentinels of the walls.
8 I adjure you, O daughters of Jerusalem,
  if you find my beloved,
tell him this:
  I am faint with love.

Colloquy of Friends and Bride

9 What is your beloved more than
    another beloved,
  O fairest among women?
What is your beloved more than
    another beloved,
  that you thus adjure us?

10 My beloved is all radiant and ruddy,
    distinguished among ten thousand.
11 His head is the finest gold;
  his locks are wavy,
  black as a raven.
12 His eyes are like doves
    beside springs of water,
  bathed in milk,
  fitly set.[h]
13 His cheeks are like beds of spices,
    yielding fragrance.
  His lips are lilies,
    distilling liquid myrrh.
14 His arms are rounded gold,
    set with jewels.
  His body is ivory work,[h]
    encrusted with sapphires.[i]
15 His legs are alabaster columns,
    set upon bases of gold.
  His appearance is like Lebanon,
    choice as the cedars.
16 His speech is most sweet,
    and he is altogether desirable.
  This is my beloved and this is my
    friend,
  O daughters of Jerusalem.

6 Where has your beloved gone,
    O fairest among women?
Which way has your beloved turned,
  that we may seek him with you?

2 My beloved has gone down to his
    garden,
  to the beds of spices,
  to pasture his flock in the gardens,
    and to gather lilies.
3 I am my beloved's and my beloved is
    mine;
  he pastures his flock among the
    lilies.

Tirzah was a town in Canaan, conquered by Joshua, that later became the capital of the northern kingdom of Israel. Because the root meaning of the word Tirzah is "pleasant," the young man is using it to describe his beloved.

The Bride's Matchless Beauty

4 You are beautiful as Tir´zah, my love,
    comely as Jerusalem,
  terrible as an army with banners.
5 Turn away your eyes from me,
    for they overwhelm me!
  Your hair is like a flock of goats,
    moving down the slopes of Gil´e·ad.
6 Your teeth are like a flock of ewes,
    that have come up from the
      washing;
  all of them bear twins,
    and not one among them is
      bereaved.
7 Your cheeks are like halves of a
    pomegranate
  behind your veil.

A banner was a sign or symbol held high on a pole as the emblem of a tribe. Soldiers used banners like flags to rally the troops. They sounded trumpets when the banners were raised.

[h] Meaning of Heb uncertain   [i] Heb lapis lazuli

Design a banner for your family. Think about the hobbies and interests of everyone in your family. Ask your parents where your ancestors came from, and look at the flags of those countries. Add a favorite Bible verse. Hang your banner where the members of your family can see and enjoy it.

8 There are sixty queens and eighty concubines,
and maidens without number.
9 My dove, my perfect one, is the only one,
the darling of her mother,
flawless to her that bore her.
The maidens saw her and called her happy;
the queens and concubines also, and they praised her.
10 "Who is this that looks forth like the dawn,
fair as the moon, bright as the sun,
terrible as an army with banners?"

11 I went down to the nut orchard,
to look at the blossoms of the valley,
to see whether the vines had budded,
whether the pomegranates were in bloom.
12 Before I was aware, my fancy set me
in a chariot beside my prince.[j]

13[k] Return, return, O Shū´lam·mīte!
Return, return, that we may look upon you.

Why should you look upon the Shū´lam·mīte,
as upon a dance before two armies?[l]

Expressions of Praise

7 How graceful are your feet in sandals,
O queenly maiden!
Your rounded thighs are like jewels,
the work of a master hand.

2 Your navel is a rounded bowl
that never lacks mixed wine.
Your belly is a heap of wheat,
encircled with lilies.
3 Your two breasts are like two fawns,
twins of a gazelle.
4 Your neck is like an ivory tower.
Your eyes are pools in Hesh´bon,
by the gate of Bath-rab´bim.
Your nose is like a tower of Lebanon,
overlooking Damascus.
5 Your head crowns you like Car´mel,
and your flowing locks are like purple;
a king is held captive in the tresses.[m]

6 How fair and pleasant you are,
O loved one, delectable maiden![n]
7 You are stately[o] as a palm tree,
and your breasts are like its clusters.
8 I say I will climb the palm tree
and lay hold of its branches.
O may your breasts be like clusters of the vine,
and the scent of your breath like apples,
9 and your kisses[p] like the best wine
that goes down[q] smoothly,
gliding over lips and teeth.[r]

10 I am my beloved's,
and his desire is for me.
11 Come, my beloved,
let us go forth into the fields,
and lodge in the villages;
12 let us go out early to the vineyards,
and see whether the vines have budded,
whether the grape blossoms have opened
and the pomegranates are in bloom.
There I will give you my love.
13 The mandrakes give forth fragrance,
and over our doors are all choice fruits,

[j] Cn: Meaning of Heb uncertain   [k] Ch 7.1 in Heb
[l] Or *dance of Mahanaim*   [m] Meaning of Heb uncertain   [n] Syr: Heb *in delights*   [o] Heb *This your stature is*   [p] Heb *palate*   [q] Heb *down for my lover*
[r] Gk Syr Vg: Heb *lips of sleepers*

new as well as old,
    which I have laid up for you, O my
        beloved.

8 O that you were like a brother to me,
    who nursed at my mother's breast!
If I met you outside, I would kiss you,
    and no one would despise me.
2 I would lead you and bring you
        into the house of my mother,
        and into the chamber of the one
            who bore me.[s]
    I would give you spiced wine to drink,
        the juice of my pomegranates.
3 O that his left hand were under my
        head,
    and that his right hand embraced me!
4 I adjure you, O daughters of
        Jerusalem,
    do not stir up or awaken love
        until it is ready!

Homecoming

5 Who is that coming up from the
        wilderness,
    leaning upon her beloved?

Under the apple tree I awakened you.
There your mother was in labor with
        you;
    there she who bore you was in
        labor.

6 Set me as a seal upon your heart,
    as a seal upon your arm;
for love is strong as death,
    passion fierce as the grave.
Its flashes are flashes of fire,
    a raging flame.
7 Many waters cannot quench love,
    neither can floods drown it.
If one offered for love

all the wealth of his house,
    it would be utterly scorned.

8 We have a little sister,
    and she has no breasts.
What shall we do for our sister,
    on the day when she is spoken for?
9 If she is a wall,
    we will build upon her a battlement
        of silver;
but if she is a door,
    we will enclose her with boards of
        cedar.
10 I was a wall,
    and my breasts were like towers;
then I was in his eyes
    as one who brings[t] peace.
11 Solomon had a vineyard at
        Bā´al-hā´mon;
    he entrusted the vineyard to
        keepers;
    each one was to bring for its fruit a
        thousand pieces of silver.
12 My vineyard, my very own, is for
        myself;
    you, O Solomon, may have the
        thousand,
    and the keepers of the fruit two
        hundred!

13 O you who dwell in the gardens,
    my companions are listening for
        your voice;
    let me hear it.

14 Make haste, my beloved,
    and be like a gazelle
or a young stag
    upon the mountains of spices!

[s] Gk Syr: Heb *my mother; she* (or *you*) *will teach me*
[t] Or *finds*

Isaiah

One of the greatest prophets of Israel lived from 740 to 700 BC. His name was Isaiah, and his messages are found in Isaiah 1–39. The book of Isaiah also contains other writings that were added later.

Isaiah was from an influential family, so the rulers paid attention to his advice, even though what he told them was not always pleasant to hear. In the first chapter of Isaiah, he spoke out against the sins and injustices of the people. He warned that God would not let such evil go unchallenged. He pleaded with the people and their leaders to repent of their sins. Isaiah said that God would forgive them if they were truly sorry.

The sermons and poems of Isaiah 40–55 were written by an unknown prophet of the Jewish exiles in Babylon about 540 BC. People often speak of these chapters as "Second Isaiah" because they were written about 150 years after the prophet who wrote the first thirty-nine chapters. Still others probably wrote chapters 56–66.

No matter who wrote which part, this book teaches that God wanted the Israelites to help all nations by leading them to love and serve the one true God. Israel was to be a servant of God that was willing to suffer in order to help achieve God's purpose for humankind.

Isaiah 11:6–7

Ahaz was king of the southern kingdom of Judah from about 732 to 716 BC. His reign had important and long-lasting results for the religious and political life of Judah and also Israel. When the kings of Israel and Syria joined together to invade Judah, Ahaz turned to the king of Assyria for help. The Assyrian king responded quickly and finally destroyed the northern kingdom of Israel. Judah, however, was then forced to pay heavy tribute (taxes) to the Assyrians. Ahaz also introduced Assyrian worship into the Temple.

1 The vision of Ī·saī´ah son of Ā´moz, which he saw concerning Judah and Jerusalem in the days of Uz·zī´ah, Jō´tham, Ā´haz, and Hez·e·kī´ah, kings of Judah.

Long ago God created everything that exists, including people. God is humankind's heavenly parent, and God's children have been disobedient. They have acted as though they did not even know God! But because of God's great love, God wanted to forgive the people of Judah and Jerusalem. When we do wrong things, God wants to forgive us, too.

The Wickedness of Judah

2 Hear, O heavens, and listen, O earth;
    for the LORD has spoken:
I reared children and brought them
        up,
    but they have rebelled against me.
3 The ox knows its owner,
    and the donkey its master's crib;
but Israel does not know,
    my people do not understand.

4 Ah, sinful nation,
    people laden with iniquity,
offspring who do evil,
    children who deal corruptly,
who have forsaken the LORD,
    who have despised the Holy One of
        Israel,
    who are utterly estranged!

5 Why do you seek further beatings?
    Why do you continue to rebel?
The whole head is sick,
    and the whole heart faint.
6 From the sole of the foot even to the
        head,
    there is no soundness in it,
but bruises and sores
    and bleeding wounds;
they have not been drained, or bound
        up,
    or softened with oil.

7 Your country lies desolate,
    your cities are burned with fire;
in your very presence
    aliens devour your land;
    it is desolate, as overthrown by
        foreigners.
8 And daughter Zion is left
    like a booth in a vineyard,
like a shelter in a cucumber field,
    like a besieged city.
9 If the LORD of hosts
    had not left us a few survivors,
we would have been like Sod´om,
    and become like Go·mor´rah.

10 Hear the word of the LORD,
    you rulers of Sod´om!
Listen to the teaching of our God,
    you people of Go·mor´rah!
11 What to me is the multitude of your
        sacrifices?
    says the LORD;
I have had enough of burnt offerings
        of rams
    and the fat of fed beasts;
I do not delight in the blood of bulls,
    or of lambs, or of goats.

"Come now, let us argue it out, says the LORD: though your sins are like scarlet, they shall be like snow; though they are red like crimson, they shall become like wool."

Isaiah 1:18

12 When you come to appear before me,[a]
    who asked this from your hand?
    Trample my courts no more;
13 bringing offerings is futile;
    incense is an abomination to me.
New moon and sabbath and calling of
        convocation—
    I cannot endure solemn assemblies
        with iniquity.
14 Your new moons and your appointed
        festivals
    my soul hates;
    they have become a burden to me,
    I am weary of bearing them.
15 When you stretch out your hands,
    I will hide my eyes from you;
    even though you make many prayers,
    I will not listen;
    your hands are full of blood.
16 Wash yourselves; make yourselves clean;
    remove the evil of your doings
        from before my eyes;
    cease to do evil,
17   learn to do good;
    seek justice,
        rescue the oppressed,
    defend the orphan,
        plead for the widow.

18 Come now, let us argue it out,
    says the LORD:
    though your sins are like scarlet,
        they shall be like snow;
    though they are red like crimson,
        they shall become like wool.
19 If you are willing and obedient,
    you shall eat the good of the land;
20 but if you refuse and rebel,
    you shall be devoured by the sword;
    for the mouth of the LORD has
        spoken.

The Degenerate City

21 How the faithful city
        has become a whore!
    She that was full of justice,
righteousness lodged in her—
        but now murderers!
22 Your silver has become dross,
        your wine is mixed with water.
23   Your princes are rebels
    and companions of thieves.
Everyone loves a bribe
    and runs after gifts.
They do not defend the orphan,
    and the widow's cause does not
        come before them.

24 Therefore says the Sovereign, the LORD
        of hosts, the Mighty One of
        Israel:
    Ah, I will pour out my wrath on my
        enemies,
        and avenge myself on my foes!
25 I will turn my hand against you;
    I will smelt away your dross as with
        lye
    and remove all your alloy.
26 And I will restore your judges as at the
        first,
    and your counselors as at the
        beginning.
Afterward you shall be called the city
        of righteousness,
    the faithful city.

27 Zion shall be redeemed by justice,
    and those in her who repent, by
        righteousness.
28 But rebels and sinners shall be
        destroyed together,
    and those who forsake the LORD
        shall be consumed.
29 For you shall be ashamed of the oaks
        in which you delighted;
    and you shall blush for the gardens
        that you have chosen.
30 For you shall be like an oak
        whose leaf withers,
    and like a garden without water.

[a] Or see my face

[31] The strong shall become like tinder,
  and their work[b] like a spark;
they and their work shall burn
    together,
  with no one to quench them.

The Future House of God

2 The word that I·saiʾah son of Āʾmoz
  saw concerning Judah and Jerusalem.

[2] In days to come
  the mountain of the LORD's house
shall be established as the highest of
    the mountains,
  and shall be raised above the hills;
all the nations shall stream to it.
[3]   Many peoples shall come and say,
"Come, let us go up to the mountain
    of the LORD,
  to the house of the God of Jacob;
that he may teach us his ways
  and that we may walk in his paths."
For out of Zion shall go forth
    instruction,
  and the word of the LORD from
    Jerusalem.
[4] He shall judge between the nations,
  and shall arbitrate for many peoples;
they shall beat their swords into
    plowshares,
  and their spears into pruning hooks;
nation shall not lift up sword against
    nation,
  neither shall they learn war any
    more.

Judgment Pronounced on Arrogance

[5] O house of Jacob,
  come, let us walk
  in the light of the LORD!
[6] For you have forsaken the ways of[c]
    your people,
  O house of Jacob.
Indeed they are full of diviners[d] from
    the east
  and of soothsayers like the
    Phi·lisʾtines,
  and they clasp hands with foreigners.
[7] Their land is filled with silver and

A plowshare was a piece of iron used to prepare soil for planting. A plowshare looked like a short sword. When peace comes, says Isaiah, people will no longer need to use iron pieces as weapons but will instead use them for plowing or pruning vines.

    gold,
  and there is no end to their treasures;
their land is filled with horses,
  and there is no end to their chariots.
[8] Their land is filled with idols;
  they bow down to the work of their
    hands,
  to what their own fingers have
    made.
[9] And so people are humbled,
  and everyone is brought low—
  do not forgive them!
[10] Enter into the rock,
  and hide in the dust
from the terror of the LORD,
  and from the glory of his majesty.
[11] The haughty eyes of people shall be
    brought low,
  and the pride of everyone shall be
    humbled;
and the LORD alone will be exalted on
    that day.
[12] For the LORD of hosts has a day
  against all that is proud and lofty,
  against all that is lifted up and high;[e]
[13] against all the cedars of Lebanon,
  lofty and lifted up;
  and against all the oaks of Bāʾshan;
[14] against all the high mountains,
  and against all the lofty hills;
[15] against every high tower,
  and against every fortified wall;
[16] against all the ships of Tarʾshish,
  and against all the beautiful craft.[f]

---

[b] Or *its makers*   [c] Heb lacks *the ways of*   [d] Cn:
Heb lacks *of diviners*   [e] Cn Compare Gk: Heb *low*
[f] Compare Gk: Meaning of Heb uncertain

¹⁷ The haughtiness of people shall be
   humbled,
   and the pride of everyone shall be
      brought low;
   and the LORD alone will be exalted
      on that day.
¹⁸ The idols shall utterly pass away.
¹⁹ Enter the caves of the rocks
   and the holes of the ground,
from the terror of the LORD,
   and from the glory of his majesty,
   when he rises to terrify the earth.
²⁰ On that day people will throw away
   to the moles and to the bats
their idols of silver and their idols of
      gold,
   which they made for themselves to
      worship,
²¹ to enter the caverns of the rocks
   and the clefts in the crags,
from the terror of the LORD,
   and from the glory of his majesty,
   when he rises to terrify the earth.
²² Turn away from mortals,
   who have only breath in their
      nostrils,
   for of what account are they?

3 For now the Sovereign, the LORD of
   hosts, is taking away from Jerusalem and from Judah
support and staff—
   all support of bread,
   and all support of water—
² warrior and soldier,
   judge and prophet,
   diviner and elder,
³ captain of fifty
   and dignitary,
counselor and skillful magician
   and expert enchanter.
⁴ And I will make boys their princes,
   and babes shall rule over them.
⁵ The people will be oppressed,
   everyone by another
   and everyone by a neighbor;
the youth will be insolent to the elder,
   and the base to the honorable.

⁶ Someone will even seize a relative,

a member of the clan, saying,
"You have a cloak;
   you shall be our leader,
and this heap of ruins
   shall be under your rule."
⁷ But the other will cry out on that day,
   saying,
"I will not be a healer;
   in my house there is neither bread
      nor cloak;
you shall not make me
   leader of the people."
⁸ For Jerusalem has stumbled
   and Judah has fallen,
because their speech and their deeds
   are against the LORD,
   defying his glorious presence.

⁹ The look on their faces bears witness
      against them;
   they proclaim their sin like Sod´om,
   they do not hide it.
Woe to them!
   For they have brought evil on
      themselves.
¹⁰ Tell the innocent how fortunate they
      are,
   for they shall eat the fruit of their
      labors.
¹¹ Woe to the guilty! How unfortunate
      they are,
   for what their hands have done shall
      be done to them.
¹² My people—children are their
      oppressors,
   and women rule over them.
O my people, your leaders mislead you,
   and confuse the course of your paths.

¹³ The LORD rises to argue his case;
   he stands to judge the peoples.
¹⁴ The LORD enters into judgment
   with the elders and princes of his
      people:
It is you who have devoured the
      vineyard;
   the spoil of the poor is in your houses.
¹⁵ What do you mean by crushing my
      people,

by grinding the face of the poor?
says the Lord GOD of hosts.

[16] The LORD said:
Because the daughters of Zion are
haughty
and walk with outstretched necks,
glancing wantonly with their eyes,
mincing along as they go,
tinkling with their feet;
[17] the Lord will afflict with scabs
the heads of the daughters of Zion,
and the LORD will lay bare their
secret parts.

18 In that day the Lord will take away
the finery of the anklets, the headbands,
and the crescents; [19]the pendants, the
bracelets, and the scarfs; [20]the headdresses,
the armlets, the sashes, the perfume boxes,
and the amulets; [21]the signet rings and
nose rings; [22]the festal robes, the mantles,
the cloaks, and the handbags; [23]the
garments of gauze, the linen garments, the
turbans, and the veils.
[24] Instead of perfume there will be a
stench;
and instead of a sash, a rope;
and instead of well-set hair, baldness;
and instead of a rich robe, a binding
of sackcloth;
instead of beauty, shame.[g]
[25] Your men shall fall by the sword
and your warriors in battle.
[26] And her gates shall lament and mourn;
ravaged, she shall sit upon the
ground.

4 Seven women shall take hold of one
man in that day, saying,
"We will eat our own bread and wear
our own clothes;
just let us be called by your name;
take away our disgrace."

The Future Glory of the Survivors in Zion

2 On that day the branch of the LORD
shall be beautiful and glorious, and the
fruit of the land shall be the pride and
glory of the survivors of Israel. [3]Whoever is
left in Zion and remains in Jerusalem will
be called holy, everyone who has been
recorded for life in Jerusalem, [4]once the
Lord has washed away the filth of the
daughters of Zion and cleansed the blood-
stains of Jerusalem from its midst by a
spirit of judgment and by a spirit of burning. [5]Then the LORD will create over the
whole site of Mount Zion and over its
places of assembly a cloud by day and
smoke and the shining of a flaming fire by
night. Indeed over all the glory there will
be a canopy. [6]It will serve as a pavilion, a
shade by day from the heat, and a refuge
and a shelter from the storm and rain.

The Song of the Unfruitful Vineyard

5 Let me sing for my beloved
my love-song concerning his
vineyard:
My beloved had a vineyard
on a very fertile hill.
[2] He dug it and cleared it of stones,
and planted it with choice vines;
he built a watchtower in the midst of it,
and hewed out a wine vat in it;
he expected it to yield grapes,
but it yielded wild grapes.

[3] And now, inhabitants of Jerusalem
and people of Judah,
judge between me
and my vineyard.
[4] What more was there to do for my
vineyard
that I have not done in it?
When I expected it to yield grapes,
why did it yield wild grapes?

[5] And now I will tell you
what I will do to my vineyard.
I will remove its hedge,
and it shall be devoured;
I will break down its wall,
and it shall be trampled down.
[6] I will make it a waste;
it shall not be pruned or hoed,

g Q Ms: MT lacks *shame*

and it shall be overgrown with briers
and thorns;
I will also command the clouds
that they rain no rain upon it.

⁷ For the vineyard of the LORD of hosts
is the house of Israel,
and the people of Judah
are his pleasant planting;
he expected justice,
but saw bloodshed;
righteousness,
but heard a cry!

Social Injustice Denounced

⁸ Ah, you who join house to house,
who add field to field,
until there is room for no one but you,
and you are left to live alone
in the midst of the land!
⁹ The LORD of hosts has sworn in my
hearing:
Surely many houses shall be desolate,
large and beautiful houses, without
inhabitant.
¹⁰ For ten acres of vineyard shall yield
but one bath,
and a homer of seed shall yield a
mere ephah.ʰ

¹¹ Ah, you who rise early in the morning
in pursuit of strong drink,
who linger in the evening
to be inflamed by wine,
¹² whose feasts consist of lyre and harp,
tambourine and flute and wine,
but who do not regard the deeds of the
LORD,
or see the work of his hands!
¹³ Therefore my people go into exile
without knowledge;
their nobles are dying of hunger,
and their multitude is parched with
thirst.

¹⁴ Therefore Shē´ōl has enlarged its
appetite
and opened its mouth beyond
measure;

the nobility of Jerusalemⁱ and her
multitude go down,
her throng and all who exult in her.
¹⁵ People are bowed down, everyone is
brought low,
and the eyes of the haughty are
humbled.
¹⁶ But the LORD of hosts is exalted by
justice,
and the Holy God shows himself
holy by righteousness.
¹⁷ Then the lambs shall graze as in their
pasture,
fatlings and kidsʲ shall feed among
the ruins.

¹⁸ Ah, you who drag iniquity along with
cords of falsehood,
who drag sin along as with cart ropes,
¹⁹ who say, "Let him make haste,
let him speed his work
that we may see it;
let the plan of the Holy One of Israel
hasten to fulfillment,
that we may know it!"
²⁰ Ah, you who call evil good
and good evil,
who put darkness for light
and light for darkness,
who put bitter for sweet
and sweet for bitter!
²¹ Ah, you who are wise in your own
eyes,
and shrewd in your own sight!
²² Ah, you who are heroes in drinking
wine
and valiant at mixing drink,
²³ who acquit the guilty for a bribe,
and deprive the innocent of their
rights!

Foreign Invasion Predicted

²⁴ Therefore, as the tongue of fire devours
the stubble,
and as dry grass sinks down in the
flame,

ʰ The Heb *bath, homer,* and *ephah* are measures of
quantity   ⁱ Heb *her nobility*   ʲ Cn Compare Gk:
Heb *aliens*

so their root will become rotten,
  and their blossom go up like dust;
for they have rejected the instruction
    of the LORD of hosts,
  and have despised the word of the
    Holy One of Israel.

25 Therefore the anger of the LORD was
      kindled against his people,
  and he stretched out his hand
      against them and struck them;
  the mountains quaked,
and their corpses were like refuse
    in the streets.
For all this his anger has not turned
      away,
  and his hand is stretched out still.

26 He will raise a signal for a nation far
      away,
  and whistle for a people at the ends
    of the earth;
here they come, swiftly, speedily!
27 None of them is weary, none stumbles,
    none slumbers or sleeps,
  not a loincloth is loose,
    not a sandal-thong broken;
28 their arrows are sharp,
    all their bows bent,
  their horses' hoofs seem like flint,
    and their wheels like the whirlwind.
29 Their roaring is like a lion,
    like young lions they roar;
  they growl and seize their prey,
    they carry it off, and no one can
      rescue.
30 They will roar over it on that day,
    like the roaring of the sea.
And if one look to the land—
    only darkness and distress;
  and the light grows dark with clouds.

A Vision of God in the Temple

6 In the year that King Uz·zī´ah died, I
saw the Lord sitting on a throne,
high and lofty; and the hem of his robe
filled the temple. ²Seraphs were in attendance above him; each had six wings: with
two they covered their faces, and with two

> "Then I heard the voice of
> the Lord saying, 'Whom
> shall I send, and who will
> go for us?' And I said,
> 'Here I am; send me!'"
>
> Isaiah 6:8

they covered their feet, and with two they
flew. ³And one called to another and said:
  "Holy, holy, holy is the LORD of hosts;
    the whole earth is full of his glory."
⁴The pivots*ᵏ* on the thresholds shook at the
voices of those who called, and the house
filled with smoke. ⁵And I said: "Woe is me!
I am lost, for I am a man of unclean lips,
and I live among a people of unclean lips;
yet my eyes have seen the King, the LORD
of hosts!"

6 Then one of the seraphs flew to me,
holding a live coal that had been taken
from the altar with a pair of tongs. ⁷The
seraph*ˡ* touched my mouth with it and
said: "Now that this has touched your lips,
your guilt has departed and your sin is
blotted out." ⁸Then I heard the voice of the
Lord saying, "Whom shall I send, and who
will go for us?" And I said, "Here am I;
send me!" ⁹And he said, "Go and say to
this people:
  'Keep listening, but do not
      comprehend;
    keep looking, but do not understand.'
10 Make the mind of this people dull,
    and stop their ears,
    and shut their eyes,
  so that they may not look with their
      eyes,
    and listen with their ears,
  and comprehend with their minds,
    and turn and be healed."
11 Then I said, "How long, O Lord?" And
    he said:
  "Until cities lie waste
    without inhabitant,
  and houses without people,
    and the land is utterly desolate;

ᵏ Meaning of Heb uncertain   *ˡ* Heb *He*

12 until the LORD sends everyone far
away,
and vast is the emptiness in the
midst of the land.
13 Even if a tenth part remain in it,
it will be burned again,
like a terebinth or an oak
whose stump remains standing
when it is felled."^m
The holy seed is its stump.

Isaiah Reassures King Ahaz

7 In the days of Ā´haz son of Jō´tham
son of Uz·zī´ah, king of Judah, King
Rē´zin of Ar´am and King Pē´kah son of
Rem·a·lī´ah of Israel went up to attack
Jerusalem, but could not mount an attack
against it. ²When the house of David heard
that A´ram had allied itself with Ē´phra·im,
the heart of Ā´haz^n and the heart of his
people shook as the trees of the forest
shake before the wind.

3 Then the LORD said to Ī·saī´ah, Go out
to meet Ā´haz, you and your son Shē´-
ar·jash´ub,^o at the end of the conduit of the
upper pool on the highway to the Fuller's
Field, ⁴and say to him, Take heed, be quiet,
do not fear, and do not let your heart be
faint because of these two smoldering
stumps of firebrands, because of the fierce
anger of Rē´zin and Ar´am and the son of
Rem·a·lī´ah. ⁵Because Ar´am—with Ē´phra-
im and the son of Rem·a·lī´ah—has plotted
evil against you, saying, ⁶Let us go up
against Judah and cut off Jerusalem^p and
conquer it for ourselves and make the son
of Tā´bē·el king in it; ⁷therefore thus says
the Lord GOD:
It shall not stand,
and it shall not come to pass.
8 For the head of Ar´am is Damascus,
and the head of Damascus is Rē´zin.
(Within sixty-five years Ē´phra·im will
be shattered, no longer a people.)
9 The head of Ē´phra·im is Sa·mār´i·a,
and the head of Sa·mār´i·a is the son
of Rem·a·lī´ah.
If you do not stand firm in faith,
you shall not stand at all.

The name Immanuel
means "God is with
us." Isaiah 7:14 has
been an important verse to
Christians, and many have seen
it as a reference to the birth of
Jesus.

Isaiah Gives Ahaz
the Sign of Immanuel

10 Again the LORD spoke to Ā´haz, saying, ¹¹Ask a sign of the LORD your God; let
it be deep as Shē´ōl or high as heaven.
¹²But Ā´haz said, I will not ask, and I will
not put the LORD to the test. ¹³Then Ī·saī´-
ah^q said: "Hear then, O house of David! Is
it too little for you to weary mortals, that
you weary my God also? ¹⁴Therefore the
Lord himself will give you a sign. Look, the
young woman^r is with child and shall bear
a son, and shall name him Im·man´ū·el.^s
¹⁵He shall eat curds and honey by the time
he knows how to refuse the evil and
choose the good. ¹⁶For before the child
knows how to refuse the evil and choose
the good, the land before whose two kings
you are in dread will be deserted. ¹⁷The
LORD will bring on you and on your people and on your ancestral house such days
as have not come since the day that
Ē´phra·im departed from Judah—the king
of Assyria."

18 On that day the LORD will whistle
for the fly that is at the sources of the
streams of Egypt, and for the bee that is in
the land of Assyria. ¹⁹And they will all
come and settle in the steep ravines, and in
the clefts of the rocks, and on all the thorn-
bushes, and on all the pastures.

20 On that day the Lord will shave with
a razor hired beyond the River—with the
king of Assyria—the head and the hair of
the feet, and it will take off the beard as
well.

---

^m Meaning of Heb uncertain   ^n Heb his heart
^o That is A remnant shall return   ^p Heb cut it off
^q Heb he   ^r Gk the virgin   ^s That is God is with us

Both hunters and warriors used bows and arrows. In Bible times, bows were made of wood or bone with a gut or hide string. Arrows were made of a shaft of reed or light wood and had heads of flint, bone, or metal. Sometimes the arrows were given barbs or were dipped in poison to make them more painful or deadly.

21 On that day one will keep alive a young cow and two sheep, 22and will eat curds because of the abundance of milk that they give; for everyone that is left in the land shall eat curds and honey.

23 On that day every place where there used to be a thousand vines, worth a thousand shekels of silver, will become briers and thorns. 24With bow and arrows one will go there, for all the land will be briers and thorns; 25and as for all the hills that used to be hoed with a hoe, you will not go there for fear of briers and thorns; but they will become a place where cattle are let loose and where sheep tread.

Isaiah's Son a Sign of the Assyrian Invasion

8 Then the Lord said to me, Take a large tablet and write on it in common characters, "Belonging to Mā·her-shal´al-hash-baz,"[t] 2and have it attested[u] for me by reliable witnesses, the priest Ū·rī´ah and Zech·a·rī´ah son of Je·ber·e·chī´ah. 3And I went to the prophetess, and she conceived and bore a son. Then the Lord said to me, Name him Mā´her-shal´al-hash-baz; 4for before the child knows how to call "My father" or "My mother," the wealth of Damascus and the spoil of Sa·mār´i·a will be carried away by the king of Assyria.

5 The Lord spoke to me again: 6Because this people has refused the waters of Shī·lō´ah that flow gently, and melt in fear before[v] Rē´zin and the son of Rem·a·lī´ah; 7therefore, the Lord is bringing up against it the mighty flood waters of the River, the king of Assyria and all his glory; it will rise above all its channels and overflow all its banks; 8it will sweep on into Judah as a flood, and, pouring over, it will reach up to the neck; and its outspread wings will fill the breadth of your land, O Im·man´u·el.

9 Band together, you peoples, and be dismayed;
  listen, all you far countries;
 gird yourselves and be dismayed;
  gird yourselves and be dismayed!
10 Take counsel together, but it shall be brought to naught;
  speak a word, but it will not stand,
  for God is with us.[w]

11 For the Lord spoke thus to me while his hand was strong upon me, and warned me not to walk in the way of this people, saying: 12Do not call conspiracy all that this people calls conspiracy, and do not fear what it fears, or be in dread. 13But the Lord of hosts, him you shall regard as holy; let him be your fear, and let him be your dread. 14He will become a sanctuary, a stone one strikes against; for both houses of Israel he will become a rock one stumbles over—a trap and a snare for the inhabitants of Jerusalem. 15And many among them shall stumble; they shall fall and be broken; they shall be snared and taken.

Disciples of Isaiah

16 Bind up the testimony, seal the teaching among my disciples. 17I will wait for the Lord, who is hiding his face from the house of Jacob, and I will hope in him. 18See, I and the children whom the Lord has given me are signs and portents in Israel from the Lord of hosts, who dwells

---

[t] That is *The spoil speeds, the prey hastens* [u] Q Ms Gk Syr: MT *and I caused to be attested* [v] Cn: Meaning of Heb uncertain [w] Heb *immanu el*

"The people who walked in darkness have seen a great light; those who lived in a land of deep darkness—on them light has shined." Isaiah 9:2

on Mount Zion. [19]Now if people say to you, "Consult the ghosts and the familiar spirits that chirp and mutter; should not a people consult their gods, the dead on behalf of the living, [20]for teaching and for instruction?" surely, those who speak like this will have no dawn! [21]They will pass through the land,[x] greatly distressed and hungry; when they are hungry, they will be enraged and will curse[y] their king and their gods. They will turn their faces upward, [22]or they will look to the earth, but will see only distress and darkness, the gloom of anguish; and they will be thrust into thick darkness.[z]

The Righteous Reign of the Coming King

9 [a]But there will be no gloom for those who were in anguish. In the former time he brought into contempt the land of Zeb′u·lun and the land of Naph′ta·li, but in the latter time he will make glorious the way of the sea, the land beyond the Jordan, Galilee of the nations.

[2b] The people who walked in darkness
    have seen a great light;
those who lived in a land of deep
    darkness—
      on them light has shined.
[3] You have multiplied the nation,
    you have increased its joy;
they rejoice before you
    as with joy at the harvest,
    as people exult when dividing
      plunder.
[4] For the yoke of their burden,
    and the bar across their shoulders,
    the rod of their oppressor,
    you have broken as on the day of
      Mid′i·an.

[5] For all the boots of the tramping
    warriors
    and all the garments rolled in blood
    shall be burned as fuel for the fire.
[6] For a child has been born for us,
    a son given to us;
authority rests upon his shoulders;
    and he is named
Wonderful Counselor, Mighty God,
    Everlasting Father, Prince of Peace.
[7] His authority shall grow continually,
    and there shall be endless peace
for the throne of David and his
    kingdom.
He will establish and uphold it
with justice and with righteousness
    from this time onward and
      forevermore.
The zeal of the LORD of hosts will do
    this.

Long before Jesus's birth, Isaiah told the Israelites about God's promise to send a messiah, or savior. The Israelites, who had been oppressed for centuries, found hope in the promise of a savior. As Christians we believe that this promise has been fulfilled in the birth of Jesus.

Have you ever felt discouraged? What gives you comfort and hope for the future? Talk with an adult about any problems you may have and ask this adult to pray with you.

Judgment on Arrogance and Oppression

[8] The Lord sent a word against Jacob,
    and it fell on Israel;
[9] and all the people knew it—
    E′phra·im and the inhabitants of
      Sa·mar′i·a—
    but in pride and arrogance of heart
      they said:

[x] Heb it   [y] Or curse by   [z] Meaning of Heb
uncertain   [a] Ch 8.23 in Heb   [b] Ch 9.1 in Heb

10 "The bricks have fallen,
  but we will build with dressed
    stones;
the sycamores have been cut down,
  but we will put cedars in their
    place."
11 So the LORD raised adversaries[c] against
    them,
  and stirred up their enemies,
12 the Ar·a·mē´ans on the east and the
    Phi·lis´tines on the west,
  and they devoured Israel with open
    mouth.
For all this his anger has not turned
    away;
  his hand is stretched out still.

13 The people did not turn to him who
    struck them,
  or seek the LORD of hosts.
14 So the LORD cut off from Israel head
    and tail,
  palm branch and reed in one day—
15 elders and dignitaries are the head,
  and prophets who teach lies are the
    tail;
16 for those who led this people led them
    astray,
  and those who were led by them
    were left in confusion.
17 That is why the Lord did not have pity
    on[d] their young people,
  or compassion on their orphans and
    widows;
for everyone was godless and an
    evildoer,
  and every mouth spoke folly.
For all this his anger has not turned
    away;
  his hand is stretched out still.

18 For wickedness burned like a fire,
    consuming briers and thorns;
  it kindled the thickets of the forest,
    and they swirled upward in a
      column of smoke.
19 Through the wrath of the LORD of hosts
    the land was burned,
  and the people became like fuel for the
    fire;

no one spared another.
20 They gorged on the right, but still were
    hungry,
  and they devoured on the left, but
    were not satisfied;
they devoured the flesh of their own
    kindred;[e]
21 Ma·nas´seh devoured Ē´phra·im, and
    Ē´phra·im Ma·nas´seh,
  and together they were against
    Judah.
For all this his anger has not turned
    away;
  his hand is stretched out still.

A decree was a declaration or proclamation issued by a king and read to the people to inform, instruct, or command them about what was to be done. The decree was usually written down and then carried to villages and cities by a herald. Isaiah warned the kingdom of Judah not to make decrees that were unjust, especially to the poor, the widows, and orphans.

10 Ah, you who make iniquitous decrees, who write oppressive statutes,
2 to turn aside the needy from justice
  and to rob the poor of my people of
    their right,
that widows may be your spoil,
  and that you may make the orphans
    your prey!
3 What will you do on the day of
    punishment,
  in the calamity that will come from
    far away?
To whom will you flee for help,
  and where will you leave your
    wealth,

---

[c] Cn: Heb *the adversaries of Rezin*   [d] Q Ms: MT
rejoice over   [e] Or *arm*

⁴ so as not to crouch among the prisoners
or fall among the slain?
For all this his anger has not turned
away;
his hand is stretched out still.

Arrogant Assyria Also Judged

⁵ Ah, Assyria, the rod of my anger—
the club in their hands is my fury!
⁶ Against a godless nation I send him,
and against the people of my wrath I
command him,
to take spoil and seize plunder,
and to tread them down like the
mire of the streets.
⁷ But this is not what he intends,
nor does he have this in mind;
but it is in his heart to destroy,
and to cut off nations not a few.
⁸ For he says:
"Are not my commanders all kings?
⁹ Is not Cal′nō like Car′chem·ish?
Is not Hā′math like Ar′pad?
Is not Sa·mār′i·a like Damascus?
¹⁰ As my hand has reached to the
kingdoms of the idols
whose images were greater than those
of Jerusalem and Sa·mār′i·a,
¹¹ shall I not do to Jerusalem and her
idols
what I have done to Sa·mār′i·a and
her images?"

12 When the Lord has finished all his
work on Mount Zion and on Jerusalem,
he*f* will punish the arrogant boasting of the
king of Assyria and his haughty pride.
¹³For he says:
"By the strength of my hand I have
done it,
and by my wisdom, for I have
understanding;
I have removed the boundaries of
peoples,
and have plundered their treasures;
like a bull I have brought down
those who sat on thrones.
¹⁴ My hand has found, like a nest,
the wealth of the peoples;

and as one gathers eggs that have been
forsaken,
so I have gathered all the earth;
and there was none that moved a wing,
or opened its mouth, or chirped."

¹⁵ Shall the ax vaunt itself over the one
who wields it,
or the saw magnify itself against the
one who handles it?
As if a rod should raise the one who
lifts it up,
or as if a staff should lift the one
who is not wood!
¹⁶ Therefore the Sovereign, the LORD of
hosts,
will send wasting sickness among
his stout warriors,
and under his glory a burning will be
kindled,
like the burning of fire.
¹⁷ The light of Israel will become a fire,
and his Holy One a flame;
and it will burn and devour
his thorns and briers in one day.
¹⁸ The glory of his forest and his fruitful
land
the LORD will destroy, both soul and
body,
and it will be as when an invalid
wastes away.
¹⁹ The remnant of the trees of his forest
will be so few
that a child can write them down.

The Repentant Remnant of Israel

20 On that day the remnant of Israel
and the survivors of the house of Jacob will
no more lean on the one who struck them,
but will lean on the LORD, the Holy One of
Israel, in truth. ²¹A remnant will return,
the remnant of Jacob, to the mighty God.
²²For though your people Israel were like
the sand of the sea, only a remnant of them
will return. Destruction is decreed, overflowing with righteousness. ²³For the Lord
GOD of hosts will make a full end, as
decreed, in all the earth.*g*

f Heb I   *g* Or land

24 Therefore thus says the Lord GOD of hosts: O my people, who live in Zion, do not be afraid of the Assyrians when they beat you with a rod and lift up their staff against you as the Egyptians did. 25For in a very little while my indignation will come to an end, and my anger will be directed to their destruction. 26The LORD of hosts will wield a whip against them, as when he struck Mid·i·an at the rock of Or´eb; his staff will be over the sea, and he will lift it as he did in Egypt. 27On that day his burden will be removed from your shoulder, and his yoke will be destroyed from your neck.

He has gone up from Rim´mon,[h]
28   he has come to Ai´ath;
  he has passed through Mig´ron,
    at Mich´mash he stores his baggage;
29 they have crossed over the pass,
    at Ge´ba they lodge for the night;
  Ra´mah trembles,
    Gib´e·ah of Saul has fled.
30 Cry aloud, O daughter Gal´lim!
  Listen, O La´i·shah!
  Answer her, O An´a·thoth!
31 Mad·me´nah is in flight,
  the inhabitants of Ge´bim flee for safety.
32 This very day he will halt at Nob,
  he will shake his fist
    at the mount of daughter Zion,
    the hill of Jerusalem.

33 Look, the Sovereign, the LORD of hosts,
  will lop the boughs with terrifying power;
  the tallest trees will be cut down,
    and the lofty will be brought low.
34 He will hack down the thickets of the forest with an ax,
  and Lebanon with its majestic trees[i] will fall.

The Peaceful Kingdom

11 A shoot shall come out from the stump of Jesse,
  and a branch shall grow out of his roots.

2 The spirit of the LORD shall rest on him,
  the spirit of wisdom and understanding,
  the spirit of counsel and might,
  the spirit of knowledge and the fear of the LORD.
3 His delight shall be in the fear of the LORD.

He shall not judge by what his eyes see,
  or decide by what his ears hear;
4 but with righteousness he shall judge the poor,
  and decide with equity for the meek of the earth;
  he shall strike the earth with the rod of his mouth,
  and with the breath of his lips he shall kill the wicked.
5 Righteousness shall be the belt around his waist,
  and faithfulness the belt around his loins.

6 The wolf shall live with the lamb,
  the leopard shall lie down with the kid,
  the calf and the lion and the fatling together,
  and a little child shall lead them.
7 The cow and the bear shall graze,
  their young shall lie down together;

Jesse was the father of King David, the greatest king of Israel. Jesse, who was part of the tribe of Judah, lived in Bethlehem. Christians trace the ancestry of Jesus back to Jesse, and we see in him the Savior that Isaiah promised. Look for Jesse's name in the genealogy of Jesus found in Matthew 1.

[h] Cn: Heb *and his yoke from your neck, and a yoke will be destroyed because of fatness* [i] Cn Compare Gk Vg: Heb *with a majestic one*

and the lion shall eat straw like the
ox.
8 The nursing child shall play over the
hole of the asp,
and the weaned child shall put its
hand on the adder's den.
9 They will not hurt or destroy
on all my holy mountain;
for the earth will be full of the
knowledge of the LORD
as the waters cover the sea.

Return of the Remnant of Israel and Judah

10 On that day the root of Jesse shall
stand as a signal to the peoples; the nations
shall inquire of him, and his dwelling shall
be glorious.

11 On that day the Lord will extend his
hand yet a second time to recover the remnant that is left of his people, from Assyria,
from Egypt, from Path′ros, from Ethiopia,ʲ
from E′lam, from Shī′nar, from Hā′math,
and from the coastlands of the sea.

12 He will raise a signal for the nations,
and will assemble the outcasts of
Israel,
and gather the dispersed of Judah
from the four corners of the earth.

Biblical writers used the word "earth" to mean dry land. The Israelites pictured the earth as a flat strip of land sitting over the ocean. They pictured a domelike canopy, called the firmament, over the dry land. The stars showed through the openings in the firmament, and the rain and snow came through the windows in the firmament. Heaven was above the firmament. There are many references throughout the Bible to the four corners of the earth. Here, God is promising to gather the Israelites scattered throughout the nations and bring them home.

13 The jealousy of E′phra·im shall depart,
the hostility of Judah shall be cut off;
E′phra·im shall not be jealous of
Judah,
and Judah shall not be hostile
towards E′phra·im.
14 But they shall swoop down on the
backs of the Phi·lis′tines in the
west,
together they shall plunder the
people of the east.
They shall put forth their hand against
E′dom and Mō′ab,
and the Am′mon·ītes shall obey them.
15 And the LORD will utterly destroy
the tongue of the sea of Egypt;
and will wave his hand over the River
with his scorching wind;
and will split it into seven channels,
and make a way to cross on foot;
16 so there shall be a highway from
Assyria
for the remnant that is left of his
people,
as there was for Israel
when they came up from the land of
Egypt.

Thanksgiving and Praise

12 You will say in that day:
I will give thanks to you, O LORD,
for though you were angry with me,
your anger turned away,
and you comforted me.

2 Surely God is my salvation;
I will trust, and will not be afraid,
for the LORD GODᵏ is my strength and
my might;
he has become my salvation.

3 With joy you will draw water from
the wells of salvation. 4And you
will say in that day:
Give thanks to the LORD,
call on his name;
make known his deeds among the
nations;
proclaim that his name is exalted.

ʲ Or *Nubia*; Heb *Cush*   ᵏ Heb *for Yah, the* LORD

5 Sing praises to the Lord, for he has
  done gloriously;
  let this be known[l] in all the earth.
6 Shout aloud and sing for joy, O royal[m]
  Zion,
  for great in your midst is the Holy
  One of Israel.

Proclamation against Babylon

13 The oracle concerning Babylon
that I·saiʹah son of Aʹmoz saw.

2 On a bare hill raise a signal,
  cry aloud to them;
  wave the hand for them to enter
  the gates of the nobles.
3 I myself have commanded my
  consecrated ones,
  have summoned my warriors, my
  proudly exulting ones,
  to execute my anger.

4 Listen, a tumult on the mountains
  as of a great multitude!
  Listen, an uproar of kingdoms,
  of nations gathering together!
  The Lord of hosts is mustering
  an army for battle.
5 They come from a distant land,
  from the end of the heavens,
  the Lord and the weapons of his
  indignation,
  to destroy the whole earth.

6 Wail, for the day of the Lord is near;
  it will come like destruction from
  the Almighty![n]
7 Therefore all hands will be feeble,
  and every human heart will melt,
8 and they will be dismayed.
  Pangs and agony will seize them;
  they will be in anguish like a
  woman in labor.
  They will look aghast at one another;
  their faces will be aflame.
9 See, the day of the Lord comes,
  cruel, with wrath and fierce anger,
  to make the earth a desolation,
  and to destroy its sinners from it.

10 For the stars of the heavens and their
  constellations
  will not give their light;
  the sun will be dark at its rising,
  and the moon will not shed its light.
11 I will punish the world for its evil,
  and the wicked for their iniquity;
  I will put an end to the pride of the
  arrogant,
  and lay low the insolence of tyrants.
12 I will make mortals more rare than fine
  gold,
  and humans than the gold of Oʹphir.
13 Therefore I will make the heavens
  tremble,
  and the earth will be shaken out of
  its place,
  at the wrath of the Lord of hosts
  in the day of his fierce anger.
14 Like a hunted gazelle,
  or like sheep with no one to gather
  them,
  all will turn to their own people,
  and all will flee to their own lands.
15 Whoever is found will be thrust
  through,
  and whoever is caught will fall by
  the sword.
16 Their infants will be dashed to pieces
  before their eyes;
  their houses will be plundered,
  and their wives ravished.
17 See, I am stirring up the Mēdes against
  them,
  who have no regard for silver
  and do not delight in gold.
18 Their bows will slaughter the young
  men;
  they will have no mercy on the fruit
  of the womb;
  their eyes will not pity children.
19 And Babylon, the glory of kingdoms,
  the splendor and pride of the
  Chal·deʹans,
  will be like Sodʹom and Go·morʹrah
  when God overthrew them.

l Or this is made known   m Or O inhabitant of
n Traditional rendering of Heb Shaddai

20 It will never be inhabited
　　or lived in for all generations;
　Arabs will not pitch their tents there,
　　shepherds will not make their flocks
　　　lie down there.
21 But wild animals will lie down there,
　　and its houses will be full of
　　　howling creatures;
　there ostriches will live,
　　and there goat-demons will dance.
22 Hyenas will cry in its towers,
　　and jackals in the pleasant palaces;
　its time is close at hand,
　　and its days will not be prolonged.

Restoration of Judah

14 But the LORD will have compassion on Jacob and will again choose Israel, and will set them in their own land; and aliens will join them and attach themselves to the house of Jacob. 2And the nations will take them and bring them to their place, and the house of Israel will possess the nations*o* as male and female slaves in the LORD's land; they will take captive those who were their captors, and rule over those who oppressed them.

Downfall of the King of Babylon

3 When the LORD has given you rest from your pain and turmoil and the hard service with which you were made to serve, 4you will take up this taunt against the king of Babylon:

How the oppressor has ceased!
　How his insolence*p* has ceased!
5 The LORD has broken the staff of the
　　wicked,
　the scepter of rulers,
6 that struck down the peoples in wrath
　　with unceasing blows,
　that ruled the nations in anger
　　with unrelenting persecution.
7 The whole earth is at rest and quiet;
　　they break forth into singing.
8 The cypresses exult over you,
　　the cedars of Lebanon, saying,
　"Since you were laid low,
　　no one comes to cut us down."

9 Shĕ´ōl beneath is stirred up
　　to meet you when you come;
　it rouses the shades to greet you,
　　all who were leaders of the earth;
　it raises from their thrones
　　all who were kings of the nations.
10 All of them will speak
　　and say to you:
　"You too have become as weak as we!
　　You have become like us!"
11 Your pomp is brought down to Shĕ´ōl,
　　and the sound of your harps;
　maggots are the bed beneath you,
　　and worms are your covering.

12 How you are fallen from heaven,
　　O Day Star, son of Dawn!
　How you are cut down to the ground,
　　you who laid the nations low!
13 You said in your heart,
　　"I will ascend to heaven;
　I will raise my throne
　　above the stars of God;
　I will sit on the mount of assembly
　　on the heights of Zā´phon;*q*
14 I will ascend to the tops of the clouds,
　　I will make myself like the Most
　　　High."
15 But you are brought down to Shĕ´ōl,
　　to the depths of the Pit.
16 Those who see you will stare at you,
　　and ponder over you:
　"Is this the man who made the earth
　　　tremble,
　　who shook kingdoms,
17 who made the world like a desert
　　and overthrew its cities,
　who would not let his prisoners go
　　　home?"
18 All the kings of the nations lie in glory,
　　each in his own tomb;
19 but you are cast out, away from your
　　　grave,
　like loathsome carrion,*r*
　clothed with the dead, those pierced
　　　by the sword,

o Heb *them*　　*p* Q Ms Compare Gk Syr Vg: Meaning of MT uncertain　　*q* Or *assembly in the far north*
r Cn Compare Gk: Heb *like a loathed branch*

who go down to the stones of the
  Pit,
  like a corpse trampled underfoot.
²⁰ You will not be joined with them in
  burial,
  because you have destroyed your
    land,
  you have killed your people.

May the descendants of evildoers
  nevermore be named!
²¹ Prepare slaughter for his sons
  because of the guilt of their father.ˢ
  Let them never rise to possess the
    earth
  or cover the face of the world with
    cities.

22 I will rise up against them, says the
LORD of hosts, and will cut off from
Babylon name and remnant, offspring and
posterity, says the LORD. ²³And I will make
it a possession of the hedgehog, and pools
of water, and I will sweep it with the
broom of destruction, says the LORD of
hosts.

An Oracle concerning Assyria
²⁴ The LORD of hosts has sworn:
  As I have designed,
    so shall it be;
  and as I have planned,
    so shall it come to pass:
²⁵ I will break the Assyrian in my land,
  and on my mountains trample him
    under foot;
  his yoke shall be removed from them,
    and his burden from their shoulders.
²⁶ This is the plan that is planned
    concerning the whole earth;
  and this is the hand that is stretched out
    over all the nations.
²⁷ For the LORD of hosts has planned,
    and who will annul it?
  His hand is stretched out,
    and who will turn it back?

An Oracle concerning Philistia
²⁸ In the year that King Āʹhaz died this
  oracle came:

²⁹ Do not rejoice, all you Phi·lisʹtines,
    that the rod that struck you is
      broken,
  for from the root of the snake will
    come forth an adder,
  and its fruit will be a flying fiery
    serpent.
³⁰ The firstborn of the poor will graze,
    and the needy lie down in safety;
  but I will make your root die of
    famine,
  and your remnant Iᵗ will kill.
³¹ Wail, O gate; cry, O city;
    melt in fear, O Phi·lisʹti·a, all of you!
  For smoke comes out of the north,
    and there is no straggler in its ranks.

³² What will one answer the messengers
    of the nation?
  "The LORD has founded Zion,
    and the needy among his people
    will find refuge in her."

An Oracle concerning Moab
15 An oracle concerning Mōʹab.
    Because Ar is laid waste in a
      night,
  Mōʹab is undone;
  because Kir is laid waste in a night,
    Mōʹab is undone.
² Dīʹbonᵘ has gone up to the temple,
    to the high places to weep;
  over Nēʹbō and over Medʹe·ba
    Mōʹab wails.
  On every head is baldness,
    every beard is shorn;
³ in the streets they bind on sackcloth;
    on the housetops and in the squares
    everyone wails and melts in tears.
⁴ Heshʹbon and Ē·le·āʹleh cry out,
    their voices are heard as far as Jāʹhaz;
  therefore the loins of Mōʹab quiver;ᵛ
    his soul trembles.
⁵ My heart cries out for Mōʹab;
    his fugitives flee to Zōʹar,
    to Egʹlath-she·lishʹi·yah.

ˢ Syr Compare Gk: Heb *fathers*   ᵗ Q Ms Vg: MT *he*
ᵘ Cn: Heb *the house and Dibon*   ᵛ Cn Compare Gk
Syr: Heb *the armed men of Moab cry aloud*

For at the ascent of Lu´hith
they go up weeping;
on the road to Hor·o·na´im
they raise a cry of destruction;
⁶ the waters of Nim´rim
are a desolation;
the grass is withered, the new growth
fails,
the verdure is no more.
⁷ Therefore the abundance they have
gained
and what they have laid up
they carry away
over the Wadi of the Willows.
⁸ For a cry has gone
around the land of Mo´ab;
the wailing reaches to Eg·la´im,
the wailing reaches to Be´er-e´lim.
⁹ For the waters of Di´bonʷ are full of
blood;
yet I will bring upon Di´bonʷ even
more—
a lion for those of Mo´ab who escape,
for the remnant of the land.

16 Send lambs
to the ruler of the land,
from Se´la, by way of the desert,
to the mount of daughter Zion.
² Like fluttering birds,
like scattered nestlings,
so are the daughters of Mo´ab
at the fords of the Arnon.
³ "Give counsel,
grant justice;
make your shade like night
at the height of noon;
hide the outcasts,
do not betray the fugitive;
⁴ let the outcasts of Mo´ab
settle among you;
be a refuge to them
from the destroyer."

When the oppressor is no more,
and destruction has ceased,
and marauders have vanished from the
land,
⁵ then a throne shall be established in
steadfast love

in the tent of David,
and on it shall sit in faithfulness
a ruler who seeks justice
and is swift to do what is right.

⁶ We have heard of the pride of Mo´ab
—how proud he is!—
of his arrogance, his pride, and his
insolence;
his boasts are false.
⁷ Therefore let Mo´ab wail,
let everyone wail for Mo´ab.
Mourn, utterly stricken,
for the raisin cakes of Kir-har´e·seth.

⁸ For the fields of Hesh´bon languish,
and the vines of Sib´mah,
whose clusters once made drunk
the lords of the nations,
reached to Ja´zer
and strayed to the desert;
their shoots once spread abroad
and crossed over the sea.
⁹ Therefore I weep with the weeping of
Ja´zer
for the vines of Sib´mah;
I drench you with my tears,
O Hesh´bon and E·le·a´leh;
for the shout over your fruit harvest
and your grain harvest has ceased.
¹⁰ Joy and gladness are taken away
from the fruitful field;
and in the vineyards no songs are sung,
no shouts are raised;
no treader treads out wine in the presses;
the vintage-shout is hushed.ˣ

Many people like to
sing as they work in
the fields. The
Israelites were especially joyful
at the time of the grape harvest.
They gathered the grapes with
shouts of joy, and they sang
while they crushed them in the
wine press.

ʷ Q Ms Vg Compare Syr: MT *Dimon*   ˣ Gk: Heb *I
have hushed*

11 Therefore my heart throbs like a harp
for Mŏ´ab,
and my very soul for Kir-hē´res.

12 When Mŏ´ab presents himself,
when he wearies himself upon the high
place, when he comes to his sanctuary to
pray, he will not prevail.

13 This was the word that the LORD
spoke concerning Mŏ´ab in the past. 14But
now the LORD says, In three years, like the
years of a hired worker, the glory of Mŏ´ab
will be brought into contempt, in spite of
all its great multitude; and those who survive will be very few and feeble.

An Oracle concerning Damascus

17 An oracle concerning Damascus.

See, Damascus will cease to be a city,
and will become a heap of ruins.
2 Her towns will be deserted forever;[y]
they will be places for flocks,
which will lie down, and no one
will make them afraid.
3 The fortress will disappear from
Ē´phra·im,
and the kingdom from Damascus;
and the remnant of Ar´am will be
like the glory of the children of Israel,
says the LORD of hosts.

4 On that day
the glory of Jacob will be brought
low,
and the fat of his flesh will grow
lean.
5 And it shall be as when reapers gather
standing grain
and their arms harvest the ears,
and as when one gleans the ears of
grain
in the Valley of Reph´a·im.
6 Gleanings will be left in it,
as when an olive tree is beaten—
two or three berries
in the top of the highest bough,
four or five
on the branches of a fruit tree,
says the LORD God of Israel.

7 On that day people will regard their
Maker, and their eyes will look to the Holy
One of Israel; 8they will not have regard for
the altars, the work of their hands, and
they will not look to what their own fingers have made, either the sacred poles[z] or
the altars of incense.

9 On that day their strong cities will be
like the deserted places of the Hī´vītes and
the Am´o·rītes,[a] which they deserted
because of the children of Israel, and there
will be desolation.

For the Israelites, every
person's name represented
who he or she was inside. It
was the same for the name
of God. This name expressed power
and holiness. The fact that God had
revealed this name to the Israelites
was a sign of God's special care for
them. They thought of the divine
name with great reverence and did
not use it carelessly. Advice and
prophecies given in the name of God
had God's authority.

There are many names in the Bible
that refer to God. Some of these
include: Lord, Holy One, Rock, Father,
Savior, King, Judge, Shepherd,
Creator, Redeemer, Maker, and
Almighty. There are also descriptive
expressions such as the Living God,
the First and the Last, the Ancient of
Days, the God of our Fathers, and the
God of Abraham.

Use the names above to make a
poster showing the names we use
when we think or speak of God. Share
the poster with your family. Can you
or your family think of other names
that are used to speak or write about
God? What is your favorite in the list
above or the list you made? Why?
What is it about that name that makes
you think of God?

y Cn Compare Gk: Heb *the cities of Aroer are deserted*
z Heb *Asherim*   a Cn Compare Gk: Heb *places of
the wood and the highest bough*

10 For you have forgotten the God of
  your salvation,
 and have not remembered the Rock
  of your refuge;
therefore, though you plant pleasant
  plants
 and set out slips of an alien god,
11 though you make them grow on the
  day that you plant them,
 and make them blossom in the
  morning that you sow;
yet the harvest will flee away
 in a day of grief and incurable pain.

12 Ah, the thunder of many peoples,
 they thunder like the thundering of
  the sea!
Ah, the roar of nations,
 they roar like the roaring of mighty
  waters!
13 The nations roar like the roaring of
  many waters,
 but he will rebuke them, and they
  will flee far away,
chased like chaff on the mountains
  before the wind
 and whirling dust before the storm.
14 At evening time, lo, terror!
 Before morning, they are no more.
This is the fate of those who despoil us,
 and the lot of those who plunder us.

An Oracle concerning Ethiopia

18 Ah, land of whirring wings
  beyond the rivers of Ethiopia,[b]
2 sending ambassadors by the Nile
 in vessels of papyrus on the waters!
Go, you swift messengers,
 to a nation tall and smooth,
to a people feared near and far,
 a nation mighty and conquering,
 whose land the rivers divide.

3 All you inhabitants of the world,
 you who live on the earth,
when a signal is raised on the
  mountains, look!
 When a trumpet is blown, listen!
4 For thus the LORD said to me:

I will quietly look from my dwelling
 like clear heat in sunshine,
 like a cloud of dew in the heat of
  harvest.
5 For before the harvest, when the
  blossom is over
 and the flower becomes a ripening
  grape,
he will cut off the shoots with pruning
  hooks,
 and the spreading branches he will
  hew away.
6 They shall all be left
 to the birds of prey of the mountains
 and to the animals of the earth.
And the birds of prey will summer on
  them,
 and all the animals of the earth will
  winter on them.

7 At that time gifts will be brought to
the LORD of hosts from[c] a people tall and
smooth, from a people feared near and far,
a nation mighty and conquering, whose
land the rivers divide, to Mount Zion, the
place of the name of the LORD of hosts.

An Oracle concerning Egypt

19 An oracle concerning Egypt.

See, the LORD is riding on a swift cloud
 and comes to Egypt;
the idols of Egypt will tremble at his
  presence,
 and the heart of the Egyptians will
  melt within them.
2 I will stir up Egyptians against
  Egyptians,
 and they will fight, one against the
  other,
neighbor against neighbor,
 city against city, kingdom against
  kingdom;
3 the spirit of the Egyptians within them
  will be emptied out,
 and I will confound their plans;
they will consult the idols and the
  spirits of the dead

---

b Or Nubia; Heb Cush   c Q Ms Gk Vg: MT of

and the ghosts and the familiar
spirits;

4 I will deliver the Egyptians
into the hand of a hard master;
a fierce king will rule over them,
says the Sovereign, the LORD of
hosts.

5 The waters of the Nile will be dried
up,
and the river will be parched and
dry;

6 its canals will become foul,
and the branches of Egypt's Nile will
diminish and dry up,
reeds and rushes will rot away.

7 There will be bare places by the Nile,
on the brink of the Nile;
and all that is sown by the Nile will
dry up,
be driven away, and be no more.

8 Those who fish will mourn;
all who cast hooks in the Nile will
lament,
and those who spread nets on the
water will languish.

9 The workers in flax will be in despair,
and the carders and those at the
loom will grow pale.

10 Its weavers will be dismayed,
and all who work for wages will be
grieved.

11 The princes of Zōʹan are utterly foolish;
the wise counselors of Pharaoh give
stupid counsel.
How can you say to Pharaoh,
"I am one of the sages,
a descendant of ancient kings"?

12 Where now are your sages?
Let them tell you and make known
what the LORD of hosts has planned
against Egypt.

13 The princes of Zōʹan have become
fools,
and the princes of Memphis are
deluded;
those who are the cornerstones of its
tribes

have led Egypt astray.

14 The LORD has poured into them[d]
a spirit of confusion;
and they have made Egypt stagger in
all its doings
as a drunkard staggers around in
vomit.

15 Neither head nor tail, palm branch or
reed,
will be able to do anything for Egypt.

16 On that day the Egyptians will be
like women, and tremble with fear before
the hand that the LORD of hosts raises
against them. 17And the land of Judah will
become a terror to the Egyptians; everyone
to whom it is mentioned will fear because
of the plan that the LORD of hosts is planning against them.

Egypt, Assyria, and Israel Blessed

18 On that day there will be five cities
in the land of Egypt that speak the language of Caʹnaan and swear allegiance to
the LORD of hosts. One of these will be
called the City of the Sun.

19 On that day there will be an altar to
the LORD in the center of the land of Egypt,
and a pillar to the LORD at its border. 20It
will be a sign and a witness to the LORD of
hosts in the land of Egypt; when they cry
to the LORD because of oppressors, he will
send them a savior, and will defend and
deliver them. 21The LORD will make himself known to the Egyptians; and the
Egyptians will know the LORD on that day,
and will worship with sacrifice and burnt
offering, and they will make vows to the
LORD and perform them. 22The LORD will
strike Egypt, striking and healing; they will
return to the LORD, and he will listen to
their supplications and heal them.

23 On that day there will be a highway
from Egypt to Assyria, and the Assyrian
will come into Egypt, and the Egyptian
into Assyria, and the Egyptians will worship with the Assyrians.

d Gk Compare Tg: Heb it

24 On that day Israel will be the third with Egypt and Assyria, a blessing in the midst of the earth, ²⁵whom the LORD of hosts has blessed, saying, "Blessed be Egypt my people, and Assyria the work of my hands, and Israel my heritage."

Isaiah Dramatizes the Conquest of Egypt and Ethiopia

20 In the year that the commander-in-chief, who was sent by King Sar´gon of Assyria, came to Ash´dod and fought against it and took it— ²at that time the LORD had spoken to Ī·sāi´ah son of Ā´moz, saying, "Go, and loose the sackcloth from your loins and take your sandals off your feet," and he had done so, walking naked and barefoot. ³Then the LORD said, "Just as my servant Ī·sāi´ah has walked naked and barefoot for three years as a sign and a portent against Egypt and Ethiopia,ᵉ ⁴so shall the king of Assyria lead away the Egyptians as captives and the Ethiopiansᶠ as exiles, both the young and the old, naked and barefoot, with buttocks uncovered, to the shame of Egypt. ⁵And they shall be dismayed and confounded because of Ethiopiaᵉ their hope and of Egypt their boast. ⁶In that day the inhabitants of this coastland will say, 'See, this is what has happened to those in whom we hoped and to whom we fled for help and deliverance from the king of Assyria! And we, how shall we escape?'"

Oracles concerning Babylon, Edom, and Arabia

21 The oracle concerning the wilderness of the sea.

As whirlwinds in the Neg´eb sweep on,
    it comes from the desert,
    from a terrible land.
² A stern vision is told to me;
    the betrayer betrays,
    and the destroyer destroys.
Go up, O Ē´lam,
    lay siege, O Mēd´i·a;
all the sighing she has caused
    I bring to an end.

³ Therefore my loins are filled with
        anguish;
    pangs have seized me,
    like the pangs of a woman in labor;
I am bowed down so that I cannot
        hear,
    I am dismayed so that I cannot see.
⁴ My mind reels, horror has appalled
        me;
    the twilight I longed for
    has been turned for me into
        trembling.
⁵ They prepare the table,
    they spread the rugs,
    they eat, they drink.
Rise up, commanders,
    oil the shield!
⁶ For thus the Lord said to me:
"Go, post a lookout,
    let him announce what he sees.
⁷ When he sees riders, horsemen in
        pairs,
    riders on donkeys, riders on camels,
let him listen diligently,
    very diligently."
⁸ Then the watcherᵍ called out:
"Upon a watchtower I stand, O Lord,
    continually by day,
and at my post I am stationed
    throughout the night.
⁹ Look, there they come, riders,
        horsemen in pairs!"
Then he responded,
    "Fallen, fallen is Babylon;
and all the images of her gods
    lie shattered on the ground."
¹⁰ O my threshed and winnowed one,
    what I have heard from the LORD of
        hosts,
    the God of Israel, I announce to
        you.

¹¹ The oracle concerning Dū´mah.

One is calling to me from Sē´ir,
    "Sentinel, what of the night?
    Sentinel, what of the night?"

ᵉ Or *Nubia;* Heb *Cush*   ᶠ Or *Nubians;* Heb *Cushites*
ᵍ Q Ms: MT *a lion*

¹² The sentinel says:
"Morning comes, and also the night.
    If you will inquire, inquire;
    come back again."

¹³ The oracle concerning the desert plain.

In the scrub of the desert plain you
        will lodge,
    O caravans of Ded′an·ītes.
¹⁴ Bring water to the thirsty,
    meet the fugitive with bread,
    O inhabitants of the land of Tē′ma.
¹⁵ For they have fled from the swords,
    from the drawn sword,
from the bent bow,
    and from the stress of battle.

16 For thus the Lord said to me: Within a year, according to the years of a hired worker, all the glory of Kē′dar will come to an end; ¹⁷and the remaining bows of Kē′dar's warriors will be few; for the LORD, the God of Israel, has spoken.

A Warning of Destruction of Jerusalem

22 The oracle concerning the valley of vision.

What do you mean that you have
        gone up,
    all of you, to the housetops,
² you that are full of shoutings,
    tumultuous city, exultant town?
Your slain are not slain by the sword,
    nor are they dead in battle.
³ Your rulers have all fled together;
    they were captured without the use
        of a bow.ʰ
All of you who were found were
        captured,
    though they had fled far away.ⁱ
⁴ Therefore I said:
Look away from me,
    let me weep bitter tears;
do not try to comfort me
    for the destruction of my beloved
        people.

⁵ For the Lord GOD of hosts has a day
    of tumult and trampling and confusion

in the valley of vision,
    a battering down of walls
    and a cry for help to the mountains.
⁶ Ē′lam bore the quiver
    with chariots and cavalry,ʲ
    and Kir uncovered the shield.
⁷ Your choicest valleys were full of
        chariots,
    and the cavalry took their stand at
        the gates.
⁸ He has taken away the covering of
        Judah.

On that day you looked to the weapons of the House of the Forest, ⁹and you saw that there were many breaches in the city of David, and you collected the waters of the lower pool. ¹⁰You counted the houses of Jerusalem, and you broke down the houses to fortify the wall. ¹¹You made a reservoir between the two walls for the water of the old pool. But you did not look to him who did it, or have regard for him who planned it long ago.

¹² In that day the Lord GOD of hosts
        called to weeping and mourning,
    to baldness and putting on
        sackcloth;
¹³ but instead there was joy and festivity,
    killing oxen and slaughtering sheep,
    eating meat and drinking wine.
"Let us eat and drink,
    for tomorrow we die."
¹⁴ The LORD of hosts has revealed himself
        in my ears:
    Surely this iniquity will not be forgiven
        you until you die,
    says the Lord GOD of hosts.

Denunciation of Self-Seeking Officials

15 Thus says the Lord GOD of hosts: Come, go to this steward, to Sheb′na, who is master of the household, and say to him: ¹⁶What right do you have here? Who are your relatives here, that you have cut out a

---

ʰ Or *without their bows*   ⁱ Gk Syr Vg: Heb *fled from far away*   ʲ Meaning of Heb uncertain tomb here for yourself, cutting a tomb on the height, and carving a habitation for yourself in the rock? [17]The LORD is about to hurl you away violently, my fellow. He will seize firm hold on you, [18]whirl you round and round, and throw you like a ball into a wide land; there you shall die, and there your splendid chariots shall lie, O you disgrace to your master's house! [19]I will thrust you from your office, and you will be pulled down from your post.

20 On that day I will call my servant E·lī´a·kim son of Hil·kī´ah, [21]and will clothe him with your robe and bind your sash on him. I will commit your authority to his hand, and he shall be a father to the inhabitants of Jerusalem and to the house of Judah. [22]I will place on his shoulder the key of the house of David; he shall open, and no one shall shut; he shall shut, and no one shall open. [23]I will fasten him like a peg in a secure place, and he will become a throne of honor to his ancestral house. [24]And they will hang on him the whole weight of his ancestral house, the offspring and issue, every small vessel, from the cups to all the flagons. [25]On that day, says the LORD of hosts, the peg that was fastened in a secure place will give way; it will be cut down and fall, and the load that was on it will perish, for the LORD has spoken.

> Flagons were large pitchers made of pottery or metal. People used them to store oil, wine, and other liquids. They usually had a cover to keep insects out.

An Oracle concerning Tyre

23

The oracle concerning Tyre.

Wail, O ships of Tar´shish,
  for your fortress is destroyed.[k]
When they came in from Cyprus
  they learned of it.
[2] Be still, O inhabitants of the coast,
  O merchants of Sī´don,
your messengers crossed over the sea[l]

[3] and were on the mighty waters;
your revenue was the grain of Shī´hor,
  the harvest of the Nile;
  you were the merchant of the
    nations.
[4] Be ashamed, O Sī´don, for the sea has
    spoken,
  the fortress of the sea, saying:
"I have neither labored nor given birth,
  I have neither reared young men
  nor brought up young women."
[5] When the report comes to Egypt,
  they will be in anguish over the
    report about Tyre.
[6] Cross over to Tar´shish—
  wail, O habitants of the coast!
[7] Is this your exultant city
  whose origin is from days of old,
  whose feet carried her
    to settle far away?
[8] Who has planned this
    against Tyre, the bestower of crowns,
  whose merchants were princes,
    whose traders were the honored of
      the earth?
[9] The LORD of hosts has planned it—
  to defile the pride of all glory,
  to shame all the honored of the
    earth.
[10] Cross over to your own land,
  O ships of[m] Tar´shish;
  this is a harbor[n] no more.
[11] He has stretched out his hand over the
    sea,
  he has shaken the kingdoms;
the LORD has given command
    concerning Cā´naan
  to destroy its fortresses.
[12] He said:
You will exult no longer,
  O oppressed virgin daughter Sī´don;
rise, cross over to Cyprus—
  even there you will have no rest.

13 Look at the land of the Chal·dē´ans!

---

[k] Cn Compare verse 14: Heb *for it is destroyed, without houses*   [l] Q Ms: MT *crossing over the sea, they replenished you*   [m] Cn Compare Gk: Heb *like the Nile, daughter*   [n] Cn: Heb *restraint*

This is the people; it was not Assyria. They destined Tyre for wild animals. They erected their siege towers, they tore down her palaces, they made her a ruin.[o]

¹⁴ Wail, O ships of Tar'shish,
  for your fortress is destroyed.

¹⁵From that day Tyre will be forgotten for seventy years, the lifetime of one king. At the end of seventy years, it will happen to Tyre as in the song about the prostitute:

¹⁶ Take a harp,
    go about the city,
    you forgotten prostitute!
  Make sweet melody,
    sing many songs,
    that you may be remembered.

¹⁷At the end of seventy years, the LORD will visit Tyre, and she will return to her trade, and will prostitute herself with all the kingdoms of the world on the face of the earth. ¹⁸Her merchandise and her wages will be dedicated to the LORD; her profits[p] will not be stored or hoarded, but her merchandise will supply abundant food and fine clothing for those who live in the presence of the LORD.

Impending Judgment on the Earth

24 Now the LORD is about to lay
    waste the earth
    and make it desolate,
  and he will twist its surface and
    scatter its inhabitants.

² And it shall be, as with the people, so
    with the priest;
  as with the slave, so with his master;
  as with the maid, so with her
    mistress;
  as with the buyer, so with the seller;
  as with the lender, so with the
    borrower;
  as with the creditor, so with the
    debtor.

³ The earth shall be utterly laid waste
    and utterly despoiled;
  for the LORD has spoken this word.

⁴ The earth dries up and withers,
  the world languishes and withers;
  the heavens languish together with
    the earth.

⁵ The earth lies polluted
    under its inhabitants;
  for they have transgressed laws,
    violated the statutes,
    broken the everlasting covenant.

⁶ Therefore a curse devours the earth,
    and its inhabitants suffer for their
      guilt;
  therefore the inhabitants of the earth
    dwindled,
    and few people are left.

⁷ The wine dries up,
    the vine languishes,
    all the merry-hearted sigh.

⁸ The mirth of the timbrels is stilled,
    the noise of the jubilant has ceased,
    the mirth of the lyre is stilled.

⁹ No longer do they drink wine with
    singing;
  strong drink is bitter to those who
    drink it.

¹⁰ The city of chaos is broken down,
    every house is shut up so that no
      one can enter.

¹¹ There is an outcry in the streets for
    lack of wine;
  all joy has reached its eventide;
    the gladness of the earth is banished.

¹² Desolation is left in the city,
    the gates are battered into ruins.

¹³ For thus it shall be on the earth
    and among the nations,
  as when an olive tree is beaten,
    as at the gleaning when the grape
      harvest is ended.

¹⁴ They lift up their voices, they sing for
    joy;
  they shout from the west over the
    majesty of the LORD.

¹⁵ Therefore in the east give glory to the
    LORD;
  in the coastlands of the sea glorify
    the name of the LORD, the God of
      Israel.

---

[o] Meaning of Heb uncertain   [p] Heb it

16 From the ends of the earth we hear
  songs of praise,
  of glory to the Righteous One.
But I say, I pine away,
  I pine away. Woe is me!
For the treacherous deal treacherously,
  the treacherous deal very
  treacherously.

17 Terror, and the pit, and the snare
  are upon you, O inhabitant of the
  earth!
18 Whoever flees at the sound of the terror
  shall fall into the pit;
and whoever climbs out of the pit
  shall be caught in the snare.
For the windows of heaven are opened,
  and the foundations of the earth
  tremble.
19 The earth is utterly broken,
  the earth is torn asunder,
  the earth is violently shaken.
20 The earth staggers like a drunkard,
  it sways like a hut;
its transgression lies heavy upon it,
  and it falls, and will not rise again.

21 On that day the LORD will punish
  the host of heaven in heaven,
  and on earth the kings of the earth.
22 They will be gathered together
  like prisoners in a pit;
they will be shut up in a prison,
  and after many days they will be
  punished.
23 Then the moon will be abashed,
  and the sun ashamed;
for the LORD of hosts will reign
  on Mount Zion and in Jerusalem,
and before his elders he will manifest
  his glory.

Praise for Deliverance
from Oppression

25 O LORD, you are my God;
  I will exalt you, I will praise your
  name;
for you have done wonderful things,
  plans formed of old, faithful and
  sure.

"O LORD, you are my God; I will exalt you, I will praise your name; for you have done wonderful things, plans formed of old, faithful and sure." Isaiah 25:1

2 For you have made the city a heap,
  the fortified city a ruin;
the palace of aliens is a city no more,
  it will never be rebuilt.
3 Therefore strong peoples will glorify
  you;
  cities of ruthless nations will fear you.
4 For you have been a refuge to the
  poor,
  a refuge to the needy in their
  distress,
  a shelter from the rainstorm and a
  shade from the heat.
When the blast of the ruthless was like
  a winter rainstorm,
5   the noise of aliens like heat in a dry
  place,
you subdued the heat with the shade
  of clouds;
  the song of the ruthless was stilled.

6 On this mountain the LORD of hosts
  will make for all peoples
  a feast of rich food, a feast of
  well-aged wines,
  of rich food filled with marrow, of
  well-aged wines strained clear.
7 And he will destroy on this mountain
  the shroud that is cast over all
  peoples,
  the sheet that is spread over all
  nations;
8   he will swallow up death forever.
Then the Lord GOD will wipe away the
  tears from all faces,
  and the disgrace of his people he
  will take away from all the earth,
  for the LORD has spoken.
9 It will be said on that day,
  Lo, this is our God; we have
  waited for him, so that he
  might save us.

This is the LORD for whom we have
    waited;
    let us be glad and rejoice in his
        salvation.
10 For the hand of the LORD will rest on
    this mountain.

The Mō'ab·ites shall be trodden down
    in their place
    as straw is trodden down in a
        dung-pit.
11 Though they spread out their hands in
    the midst of it,
    as swimmers spread out their hands
        to swim,
    their pride will be laid low despite
        the struggle[q] of their hands.
12 The high fortifications of his walls will
    be brought down,
    laid low, cast to the ground, even to
        the dust.

Judah's Song of Victory

26 On that day this song will be
sung in the land of Judah:
We have a strong city;
    he sets up victory
    like walls and bulwarks.
2 Open the gates,
    so that the righteous nation that
        keeps faith
    may enter in.
3 Those of steadfast mind you keep in
        peace—
    in peace because they trust in you.
4 Trust in the LORD forever,
    for in the LORD GOD[r]
    you have an everlasting rock.
5 For he has brought low
    the inhabitants of the height;
    the lofty city he lays low.
He lays it low to the ground,
    casts it to the dust.
6 The foot tramples it,
    the feet of the poor,
    the steps of the needy.

7 The way of the righteous is level;
    O Just One, you make smooth the
        path of the righteous.

8 In the path of your judgments,
    O LORD, we wait for you;
    your name and your renown
    are the soul's desire.
9 My soul yearns for you in the night,
    my spirit within me earnestly seeks
        you.
For when your judgments are in the
        earth,
    the inhabitants of the world learn
        righteousness.
10 If favor is shown to the wicked,
    they do not learn righteousness;
in the land of uprightness they deal
        perversely
    and do not see the majesty of the
        LORD.
11 O LORD, your hand is lifted up,
    but they do not see it.
Let them see your zeal for your people,
    and be ashamed.
    Let the fire for your adversaries
        consume them.
12 O LORD, you will ordain peace for us,
    for indeed, all that we have done,
    you have done for us.
13 O LORD our God,
    other lords besides you have ruled
        over us,
    but we acknowledge your name
        alone.
14 The dead do not live;
    shades do not rise—
because you have punished and
        destroyed them,
    and wiped out all memory of them.
15 But you have increased the nation, O
    LORD,
    you have increased the nation; you
        are glorified;
    you have enlarged all the borders of
        the land.

16 O LORD, in distress they sought you,
    they poured out a prayer[p]
    when your chastening was on them.

---

[p] Meaning of Heb uncertain   [q] Heb *in Yah, the*
LORD

¹⁷ Like a woman with child,
who writhes and cries out in her
pangs
when she is near her time,
so were we because of you, O LORD;
¹⁸ we were with child, we writhed,
but we gave birth only to wind.
We have won no victories on earth,
and no one is born to inhabit the
world.
¹⁹ Your dead shall live, their corpses[s] shall
rise.
O dwellers in the dust, awake and
sing for joy!
For your dew is a radiant dew,
and the earth will give birth to those
long dead.[t]

²⁰ Come, my people, enter your
chambers,
and shut your doors behind you;
hide yourselves for a little while
until the wrath is past.
²¹ For the LORD comes out from his place
to punish the inhabitants of the
earth for their iniquity;
the earth will disclose the blood shed
on it,
and will no longer cover its slain.

Israel's Redemption

27 On that day the LORD with his
cruel and great and strong sword
will punish Le·vī´a·than the fleeing serpent, Le·vī´a·than the twisting serpent, and
he will kill the dragon that is in the sea.

² On that day:
A pleasant vineyard, sing about it!
³ I, the LORD, am its keeper;
every moment I water it.
I guard it night and day
so that no one can harm it;
⁴ I have no wrath.
If it gives me thorns and briers,
I will march to battle against it.
I will burn it up.
⁵ Or else let it cling to me for protection,
let it make peace with me,
let it make peace with me.

⁶ In days to come[u] Jacob shall take root,
Israel shall blossom and put forth
shoots,
and fill the whole world with fruit.

⁷ Has he struck them down as he struck
down those who struck them?
Or have they been killed as their
killers were killed?
⁸ By expulsion,[v] by exile you struggled
against them;
with his fierce blast he removed
them in the day of the east wind.
⁹ Therefore by this the guilt of Jacob will
be expiated,
and this will be the full fruit of the
removal of his sin:
when he makes all the stones of the
altars
like chalkstones crushed to pieces,
no sacred poles[w] or incense altars
will remain standing.
¹⁰ For the fortified city is solitary,
a habitation deserted and forsaken,
like the wilderness;
the calves graze there,
there they lie down, and strip its
branches.
¹¹ When its boughs are dry, they are
broken;
women come and make a fire of
them.
For this is a people without
understanding;
therefore he that made them will not
have compassion on them,
he that formed them will show them
no favor.

12 On that day the LORD will thresh
from the channel of the Euphrates to the
Wadi of Egypt, and you will be gathered
one by one, O people of Israel. ¹³And on
that day a great trumpet will be blown, and
those who were lost in the land of Assyria
and those who were driven out to the land

---

[s] Cn Compare Syr Tg: Heb *my corpse*   [t] Heb *to the
shades*   [u] Heb *Those to come*   [v] Meaning of Heb
uncertain   [w] Heb *Asherim*

of Egypt will come and worship the LORD on the holy mountain at Jerusalem.

Judgment on Corrupt Rulers, Priests, and Prophets

28 Ah, the proud garland of the drunkards of Ē·phra·im,
and the fading flower of its glorious beauty,
which is on the head of those
bloated with rich food, of those
overcome with wine!
2 See, the Lord has one who is mighty and strong;
like a storm of hail, a destroying tempest,
like a storm of mighty, overflowing waters;
with his hand he will hurl them down to the earth.
3 Trampled under foot will be
the proud garland of the drunkards of Ē·phra·im.
4 And the fading flower of its glorious beauty,
which is on the head of those
bloated with rich food,
will be like a first-ripe fig before the summer;
whoever sees it, eats it up
as soon as it comes to hand.

5 In that day the LORD of hosts will be a garland of glory,
and a diadem of beauty, to the remnant of his people;
6 and a spirit of justice to the one who sits in judgment,
and strength to those who turn back the battle at the gate.

7 These also reel with wine
and stagger with strong drink;
the priest and the prophet reel with strong drink,
they are confused with wine,
they stagger with strong drink;
they err in vision,
they stumble in giving judgment.

8 All tables are covered with filthy vomit;
no place is clean.

9 "Whom will he teach knowledge,
and to whom will he explain the message?
Those who are weaned from milk,
those taken from the breast?
10 For it is precept upon precept, precept upon precept,
line upon line, line upon line,
here a little, there a little."[x]
11 Truly, with stammering lip
and with alien tongue
he will speak to this people,
12 to whom he has said,
"This is rest;
give rest to the weary;
and this is repose";
yet they would not hear.
13 Therefore the word of the LORD will be to them,
"Precept upon precept, precept upon precept,
line upon line, line upon line,
here a little, there a little;"[x]
in order that they may go, and fall backward,
and be broken, and snared, and taken.

14 Therefore hear the word of the LORD, you scoffers
who rule this people in Jerusalem.
15 Because you have said, "We have made a covenant with death,
and with Shēʼōl we have an agreement;
when the overwhelming scourge passes through
it will not come to us;
for we have made lies our refuge,
and in falsehood we have taken shelter";
16 therefore thus says the Lord GOD,
See, I am laying in Zion a foundation stone,

[x] Meaning of Heb of this verse uncertain

a tested stone,
a precious cornerstone, a sure
foundation:
"One who trusts will not panic."
¹⁷ And I will make justice the line,
and righteousness the plummet;
hail will sweep away the refuge of lies,
and waters will overwhelm the
shelter.
¹⁸ Then your covenant with death will be
annulled,
and your agreement with Shĕ´ŏl will
not stand;
when the overwhelming scourge
passes through
you will be beaten down by it.
¹⁹ As often as it passes through, it will
take you;
for morning by morning it will pass
through,
by day and by night;
and it will be sheer terror to
understand the message.
²⁰ For the bed is too short to stretch
oneself on it,
and the covering too narrow to wrap
oneself in it.
²¹ For the LORD will rise up as on Mount
Pe·rä´zim,
he will rage as in the valley of
Gib´ē·on
to do his deed—strange is his deed!—
and to work his work—alien is his
work!
²² Now therefore do not scoff,
or your bonds will be made
stronger;
for I have heard a decree of destruction
from the Lord GOD of hosts upon
the whole land.

²³ Listen, and hear my voice;
Pay attention, and hear my speech.
²⁴ Do those who plow for sowing plow
continually?
Do they continually open and har-
row their ground?
²⁵ When they have leveled its surface,
do they not scatter dill, sow cummin,

and plant wheat in rows
and barley in its proper place,
and spelt as the border?
²⁶ For they are well instructed;
their God teaches them.

²⁷ Dill is not threshed with a threshing
sledge,
nor is a cart wheel rolled over
cummin;
but dill is beaten out with a stick,
and cummin with a rod.
²⁸ Grain is crushed for bread,
but one does not thresh it forever;
one drives the cart wheel and horses
over it,
but does not pulverize it.
²⁹ This also comes from the LORD of
hosts;
he is wonderful in counsel,
and excellent in wisdom.

The Siege of Jerusalem

29 Ah, Ar´i·el, Ar´i·el,
the city where David encamped!
Add year to year;
let the festivals run their round.
² Yet I will distress Ar´i·el,
and there shall be moaning and
lamentation,
and Jerusalem^y shall be to me like
an Ar´i·el .^z
³ And like David^a I will encamp against
you;
I will besiege you with towers
and raise siegeworks against you.
⁴ Then deep from the earth you shall
speak,
from low in the dust your words
shall come;

People in ancient
times often used the
seeds of the cummin
plant to season food.

^y Heb *she*   ^z Probable meaning, *altar hearth*; com-
pare Ezek 43.15   ^a Gk: Meaning of Heb uncertain

your voice shall come from the ground
  like the voice of a ghost,
  and your speech shall whisper out
    of the dust.

5 But the multitude of your foes[b] shall be
    like small dust,
  and the multitude of tyrants like
    flying chaff.
And in an instant, suddenly,
6   you will be visited by the LORD of
      hosts
with thunder and earthquake and great
    noise,
  with whirlwind and tempest, and
    the flame of a devouring fire.
7 And the multitude of all the nations
      that fight against Ar′i·el,
  all that fight against her and her
    stronghold, and who distress her,
  shall be like a dream, a vision of the
    night.
8 Just as when a hungry person dreams
      of eating
  and wakes up still hungry,
  or a thirsty person dreams of drinking
    and wakes up faint, still thirsty,
  so shall the multitude of all the nations
      be
  that fight against Mount Zion.

9 Stupefy yourselves and be in a stupor,
    blind yourselves and be blind!
Be drunk, but not from wine;
    stagger, but not from strong drink!
10 For the LORD has poured out upon you
      a spirit of deep sleep;
  he has closed your eyes, you prophets,
    and covered your heads, you seers.
11 The vision of all this has become for
you like the words of a sealed document. If
it is given to those who can read, with the
command, "Read this," they say, "We cannot, for it is sealed." 12And if it is given to
those who cannot read, saying, "Read this,"
they say, "We cannot read."

13 The Lord said:
Because these people draw near with
      their mouths

and honor me with their lips,
    while their hearts are far from me,
  and their worship of me is a human
      commandment learned by rote;
14 so I will again do
    amazing things with this people,
    shocking and amazing.
The wisdom of their wise shall perish,
    and the discernment of the
      discerning shall be hidden.

15 Ha! You who hide a plan too deep for
      the LORD,
  whose deeds are in the dark,
    and who say, "Who sees us? Who
      knows us?"
16 You turn things upside down!
  Shall the potter be regarded as the
      clay?
  Shall the thing made say of its maker,
    "He did not make me";
  or the thing formed say of the one who
      formed it,
    "He has no understanding"?

Hope for the Future

17 Shall not Lebanon in a very little while
    become a fruitful field,
  and the fruitful field be regarded as
    a forest?
18 On that day the deaf shall hear
    the words of a scroll,
  and out of their gloom and darkness
    the eyes of the blind shall see.
19 The meek shall obtain fresh joy in the
      LORD,
  and the neediest people shall exult
    in the Holy One of Israel.
20 For the tyrant shall be no more,
    and the scoffer shall cease to be;
  all those alert to do evil shall be cut
      off—
21 those who cause a person to lose a
      lawsuit,
  who set a trap for the arbiter in the
      gate,
  and without grounds deny justice to
    the one in the right.

b Cn: Heb strangers

22 Therefore thus says the LORD, who redeemed Abraham, concerning the house of Jacob:
No longer shall Jacob be ashamed,
no longer shall his face grow pale.
23 For when he sees his children,
the work of my hands, in his midst,
they will sanctify my name;
they will sanctify the Holy One of Jacob,
and will stand in awe of the God of Israel.
24 And those who err in spirit will come to understanding,
and those who grumble will accept instruction.

The Futility of Reliance on Egypt

30 Oh, rebellious children, says the LORD, who carry out a plan, but not mine;
who make an alliance, but against my will,
adding sin to sin;
2 who set out to go down to Egypt
without asking for my counsel,
to take refuge in the protection of Pharaoh,
and to seek shelter in the shadow of Egypt;
3 Therefore the protection of Pharaoh shall become your shame,
and the shelter in the shadow of Egypt your humiliation.
4 For though his officials are at Zō'an
and his envoys reach Hā'nēs,
5 everyone comes to shame
through a people that cannot profit them,
that brings neither help nor profit,
but shame and disgrace.

6 An oracle concerning the animals of the Neg'eb.
Through a land of trouble and distress,
of lioness and roaring lion,
of viper and flying serpent,
they carry their riches on the backs of donkeys,
and their treasures on the humps of camels,
to a people that cannot profit them.
7 For Egypt's help is worthless and empty,
therefore I have called her,
"Rā'hab who sits still."d

In the Old Testament, the word "seer" refers to a person who had vision and could predict the future. A vision was like a dream in which God or God's will was revealed. Prophets were sometimes called seers in everyday language.

A Rebellious People

8 Go now, write it before them on a tablet,
and inscribe it in a book,
so that it may be for the time to come
as a witness forever.
9 For they are a rebellious people,
faithless children,
children who will not hear
the instruction of the LORD;
10 who say to the seers, "Do not see";
and to the prophets, "Do not prophesy to us what is right;
speak to us smooth things,
prophesy illusions,
11 leave the way, turn aside from the path,
let us hear no more about the Holy One of Israel."
12 Therefore thus says the Holy One of Israel:
Because you reject this word,
and put your trust in oppression and deceit,
and rely on them;
13 therefore this iniquity shall become for you

c Cn: Heb *from them* d Meaning of Heb uncertain

like a break in a high wall, bulging
out, and about to collapse,
whose crash comes suddenly, in an
instant;
¹⁴ its breaking is like that of a potter's
vessel
that is smashed so ruthlessly
that among its fragments not a sherd is
found
for taking fire from the hearth,
or dipping water out of the cistern.

¹⁵ For thus said the Lord GOD, the Holy
One of Israel:
In returning and rest you shall be
saved;
in quietness and in trust shall be
your strength.
But you refused ¹⁶and said,
"No! We will flee upon horses"—
therefore you shall flee!
and, "We will ride upon swift
steeds"—
therefore your pursuers shall be
swift!
¹⁷ A thousand shall flee at the threat of
one,
at the threat of five you shall flee,
until you are left
like a flagstaff on the top of a
mountain,
like a signal on a hill.

God's Promise to Zion

¹⁸ Therefore the LORD waits to be
gracious to you;
therefore he will rise up to show
mercy to you.
For the LORD is a God of justice;
blessed are all those who wait for
him.
¹⁹ Truly, O people in Zion, inhabitants
of Jerusalem, you shall weep no more. He
will surely be gracious to you at the sound
of your cry; when he hears it, he will
answer you. ²⁰Though the Lord may give
you the bread of adversity and the water of
affliction, yet your Teacher will not hide
himself any more, but your eyes shall see
your Teacher. ²¹And when you turn to the
right or when you turn to the left, your
ears shall hear a word behind you, saying,
"This is the way; walk in it." ²²Then you
will defile your silver-covered idols and
your gold-plated images. You will scatter
them like filthy rags; you will say to them,
"Away with you!"

23 He will give rain for the seed with
which you sow the ground, and grain, the
produce of the ground, which will be rich
and plenteous. On that day your cattle will
graze in broad pastures; ²⁴and the oxen
and donkeys that till the ground will eat
silage, which has been winnowed with
shovel and fork. ²⁵On every lofty mountain and every high hill there will be
brooks running with water—on a day of
the great slaughter, when the towers fall.
²⁶Moreover the light of the moon will be
like the light of the sun, and the light of the
sun will be sevenfold, like the light of
seven days, on the day when the LORD
binds up the injuries of his people, and
heals the wounds inflicted by his blow.

Judgment on Assyria

²⁷ See, the name of the LORD comes from
far away,
burning with his anger, and in thick
rising smoke;ᵉ
his lips are full of indignation,
and his tongue is like a devouring
fire;
²⁸ his breath is like an overflowing stream
that reaches up to the neck—
to sift the nations with the sieve of
destruction,
and to place on the jaws of the peoples a bridle that leads them
astray.

29 You shall have a song as in the night
when a holy festival is kept; and gladness
of heart, as when one sets out to the sound
of the flute to go to the mountain of the
LORD, to the Rock of Israel. ³⁰And the LORD
will cause his majestic voice to be heard

ᵉ Meaning of Heb uncertain

"Like birds hovering overhead, so the LORD of hosts will protect Jerusalem; he will protect and deliver it, he will spare and rescue it." Isaiah 31:5

and the descending blow of his arm to be seen, in furious anger and a flame of devouring fire, with a cloudburst and tempest and hailstones. ³¹The Assyrian will be terror-stricken at the voice of the LORD, when he strikes with his rod. ³²And every stroke of the staff of punishment that the LORD lays upon him will be to the sound of timbrels and lyres; battling with brandished arm he will fight with him. ³³For his burning place*f* has long been prepared; truly it is made ready for the king,*g* its pyre made deep and wide, with fire and wood in abundance; the breath of the LORD, like a stream of sulfur, kindles it.

Alliance with Egypt Is Futile

31 Alas for those who go down to Egypt for help
and who rely on horses,
who trust in chariots because they are many
and in horsemen because they are very strong,
but do not look to the Holy One of Israel
or consult the LORD!
² Yet he too is wise and brings disaster;
he does not call back his words,
but will rise against the house of the evildoers,
and against the helpers of those who work iniquity.
³ The Egyptians are human, and not God;
their horses are flesh, and not spirit.
When the LORD stretches out his hand,
the helper will stumble, and the one helped will fall,
and they will all perish together.

⁴ For thus the LORD said to me,
As a lion or a young lion growls over its prey,
and—when a band of shepherds is called out against it—
is not terrified by their shouting
or daunted at their noise,
so the LORD of hosts will come down
to fight upon Mount Zion and upon its hill.
⁵ Like birds hovering overhead, so the LORD of hosts
will protect Jerusalem;
he will protect and deliver it,
he will spare and rescue it.

6 Turn back to him whom you*h* have deeply betrayed, O people of Israel. ⁷For on that day all of you shall throw away your idols of silver and idols of gold, which your hands have sinfully made for you.
⁸ "Then the Assyrian shall fall by a sword, not of mortals;
and a sword, not of humans, shall devour him;
he shall flee from the sword,
and his young men shall be put to forced labor.
⁹ His rock shall pass away in terror,
and his officers desert the standard in panic,"
says the LORD, whose fire is in Zion,
and whose furnace is in Jerusalem.

Government with Justice Predicted

32 See, a king will reign in righteousness, and princes will rule with justice.
² Each will be like a hiding place from the wind,
a covert from the tempest,
like streams of water in a dry place,
like the shade of a great rock in a weary land.
³ Then the eyes of those who have sight will not be closed,

f Or *Topheth*   *g* Or *Molech*   *h* Heb *they*

Iniquity is another word for sin. Sin is any action that separates people from God or destroys relationships between people.

and the ears of those who have
hearing will listen.
4 The minds of the rash will have good
judgment,
and the tongues of stammerers will
speak readily and distinctly.
5 A fool will no longer be called noble,
nor a villain said to be honorable.
6 For fools speak folly,
and their minds plot iniquity:
to practice ungodliness,
to utter error concerning the LORD,
to leave the craving of the hungry
unsatisfied,
and to deprive the thirsty of drink.
7 The villainies of villains are evil;
they devise wicked devices
to ruin the poor with lying words,
even when the plea of the needy is
right.
8 But those who are noble plan noble
things,
and by noble things they stand.

Complacent Women
Warned of Disaster

9 Rise up, you women who are at ease,
hear my voice;
you complacent daughters, listen to
my speech.
10 In little more than a year
you will shudder, you complacent
ones;
for the vintage will fail,
the fruit harvest will not come.
11 Tremble, you women who are at ease,
shudder, you complacent ones;
strip, and make yourselves bare,
and put sackcloth on your loins.
12 Beat your breasts for the pleasant
fields,

for the fruitful vine,
13 for the soil of my people
growing up in thorns and briers;
yes, for all the joyous houses
in the jubilant city.
14 For the palace will be forsaken,
the populous city deserted;
the hill and the watchtower
will become dens forever,
the joy of wild asses,
a pasture for flocks;
15 until a spirit from on high is poured
out on us,
and the wilderness becomes a
fruitful field,
and the fruitful field is deemed a
forest.

The Peace of God's Reign

16 Then justice will dwell in the
wilderness,
and righteousness abide in the
fruitful field.
17 The effect of righteousness will be
peace,
and the result of righteousness,
quietness and trust forever.
18 My people will abide in a peaceful
habitation,
in secure dwellings, and in quiet
resting places.
19 The forest will disappear completely,[i]
and the city will be utterly laid low.
20 Happy will you be who sow beside
every stream,
who let the ox and the donkey
range freely.

A Prophecy of Deliverance
from Foes

33 Ah, you destroyer,
who yourself have not been
destroyed;
you treacherous one,
with whom no one has dealt
treacherously!
When you have ceased to destroy,
you will be destroyed;

i Cn: Heb *And it will hail when the forest comes down*

and when you have stopped dealing
treacherously,
you will be dealt with treacherously.

2 O LORD, be gracious to us; we wait for
you.
Be our arm every morning,
our salvation in the time of trouble.
3 At the sound of tumult, peoples fled;
before your majesty, nations
scattered.
4 Spoil was gathered as the caterpillar
gathers;
as locusts leap, they leaped[j] upon it.
5 The LORD is exalted, he dwells on
high;
he filled Zion with justice and
righteousness;
6 he will be the stability of your times,
abundance of salvation, wisdom,
and knowledge;
the fear of the LORD is Zion's
treasure.[k]

7 Listen! the valiant[j] cry in the streets;
the envoys of peace weep bitterly.
8 The highways are deserted,
travelers have quit the road.
The treaty is broken,
its oaths[l] are despised,
its obligation[m] is disregarded.
9 The land mourns and languishes;
Lebanon is confounded and withers
away;
Sharon is like a desert;
and Ba'shan and Car'mel shake off
their leaves.

10 "Now I will arise," says the LORD,
"now I will lift myself up;
now I will be exalted.
11 You conceive chaff, you bring forth
stubble;
your breath is a fire that will consume you.
12 And the peoples will be as if burned to
lime,
like thorns cut down, that are
burned in the fire."

13 Hear, you who are far away, what I
have done;
and you who are near, acknowledge
my might.
14 The sinners in Zion are afraid;
trembling has seized the godless:
"Who among us can live with the
devouring fire?
Who among us can live with
everlasting flames?"
15 Those who walk righteously and speak
uprightly,
who despise the gain of oppression,
who wave away a bribe instead of
accepting it,
who stop their ears from hearing of
bloodshed
and shut their eyes from looking on
evil,
16 they will live on the heights;
their refuge will be the fortresses of
rocks;
their food will be supplied, their
water assured.

The Land of the Majestic King

17 Your eyes will see the king in his
beauty;
they will behold a land that stretches
far away.
18 Your mind will muse on the terror:
"Where is the one who counted?
Where is the one who weighed the
tribute?
Where is the one who counted the
towers?"
19 No longer will you see the insolent
people,
the people of an obscure speech that
you cannot comprehend,
stammering in a language that you
cannot understand.
20 Look on Zion, the city of our
appointed festivals!
Your eyes will see Jerusalem,
a quiet habitation, an immovable
tent,

[j] Meaning of Heb uncertain   [k] Heb his treasure;
meaning of Heb uncertain   [l] Q Ms: MT cities
[m] Or everyone

whose stakes will never be pulled up,
and none of whose ropes will be
broken.
21 But there the LORD in majesty will be
for us
a place of broad rivers and streams,
where no galley with oars can go,
nor stately ship can pass.
22 For the LORD is our judge, the LORD is
our ruler,
the LORD is our king; he will save us.

23 Your rigging hangs loose;
it cannot hold the mast firm in its
place,
or keep the sail spread out.

Then prey and spoil in abundance will
be divided;
even the lame will fall to plundering.
24 And no inhabitant will say, "I am sick";
the people who live there will be
forgiven their iniquity.

Judgment on the Nations

34 Draw near, O nations, to hear;
O peoples, give heed!
Let the earth hear, and all that fills it;
the world, and all that comes from
it.
2 For the LORD is enraged against all the
nations,
and furious against all their hordes;
he has doomed them, has given
them over for slaughter.
3 Their slain shall be cast out,
and the stench of their corpses shall
rise;
the mountains shall flow with their
blood.
4 All the host of heaven shall rot away,
and the skies roll up like a scroll.
All their host shall wither
like a leaf withering on a vine,
or fruit withering on a fig tree.

5 When my sword has drunk its fill in
the heavens,
lo, it will descend upon Ēdom,

A scroll was a roll of papyrus or parchment sometimes called the "roll of a book." Scrolls were made of sheets fastened together and rolled around a rod. Scrolls were usually nine to eleven inches wide and thirty feet long. The writing was in columns, and because Hebrew is read from right to left, the scroll was rolled from right to left as it was read.

In 1947 about five hundred scrolls were found in caves at Qumran, near the Dead Sea. Some of the scrolls contained copies of parts of the Old Testament. One scroll was a complete copy of Isaiah. These scrolls were the library of a religious group that had lived at Qumran. When the members were forced to leave Qumran about 70 AD, they stored their scrolls in pottery jars and hid them in the caves. The dry air of the Dead Sea region kept the scrolls in good condition. These scrolls are still being examined and studied today.

upon the people I have doomed to
judgment.
6 The LORD has a sword; it is sated with
blood,
it is gorged with fat,
with the blood of lambs and goats,
with the fat of the kidneys of rams.
For the LORD has a sacrifice in Boz´rah,
a great slaughter in the land of
Ē´dom.
7 Wild oxen shall fall with them,
and young steers with the mighty
bulls.
Their land shall be soaked with blood,
and their soil made rich with fat.

"The wilderness and the dry land shall be glad, the desert shall rejoice and blossom; like the crocus it shall blossom abundantly and rejoice with joy and singing."

Isaiah 40:31*a*

8 For the LORD has a day of vengeance,
 a year of vindication by Zion's
  cause.[n]
9 And the streams of Ē′dom[o] shall be
  turned into pitch,
 and her soil into sulfur;
  her land shall become burning
   pitch.
10 Night and day it shall not be
  quenched;
 its smoke shall go up forever.
 From generation to generation it shall
  lie waste;
  no one shall pass through it forever
   and ever.
11 But the hawk[p] and the hedgehog[p]
  shall possess it;
 the owl[p] and the raven shall live in
  it.
 He shall stretch the line of confusion
  over it,
  and the plummet of chaos over[q] its
   nobles.
12 They shall name it No Kingdom There,
 and all its princes shall be nothing.
13 Thorns shall grow over its strongholds,
 nettles and thistles in its fortresses.
 It shall be the haunt of jackals,
  an abode for ostriches.
14 Wildcats shall meet with hyenas,
 goat-demons shall call to each other;
 there too Lil′ith shall repose,
  and find a place to rest.
15 There shall the owl nest
 and lay and hatch and brood in its
  shadow;
 there too the buzzards shall gather,
  each one with its mate.
16 Seek and read from the book of the
 LORD:

Not one of these shall be missing;
 none shall be without its mate.
For the mouth of the LORD has
  commanded,
 and his spirit has gathered them.
17 He has cast the lot for them,
 his hand has portioned it out to
  them with the line;
they shall possess it forever,
 from generation to generation they
  shall live in it.

The Return of the Redeemed to Zion

35 The wilderness and the dry land
   shall be glad,
 the desert shall rejoice and blossom;
like the crocus 2it shall blossom
  abundantly,
 and rejoice with joy and singing.
The glory of Lebanon shall be given to
  it,
 the majesty of Car′mel and Sharon.
They shall see the glory of the LORD,
 the majesty of our God.

3 Strengthen the weak hands,
 and make firm the feeble knees.
4 Say to those who are of a fearful heart,
 "Be strong, do not fear!
Here is your God.
 He will come with vengeance,
with terrible recompense.
 He will come and save you."

5 Then the eyes of the blind shall be
  opened,
 and the ears of the deaf unstopped;
6 then the lame shall leap like a deer,
 and the tongue of the speechless
  sing for joy.
For waters shall break forth in the
  wilderness,
 and streams in the desert;
7 the burning sand shall become a pool,
 and the thirsty ground springs of
  water;

[n] Or *of recompense by Zion's defender*   [o] Heb *her streams*   [p] Identification uncertain   [q] Heb lacks *over*

the haunt of jackals shall become a
  swamp,[r]
  the grass shall become reeds and
  rushes.
[8] A highway shall be there,
  and it shall be called the Holy Way;
  the unclean shall not travel on it,[s]
  but it shall be for God's people;[t]
  no traveler, not even fools, shall go
  astray.
[9] No lion shall be there,
  nor shall any ravenous beast come
  up on it;
  they shall not be found there,
  but the redeemed shall walk there.
[10] And the ransomed of the LORD shall
  return,
  and come to Zion with singing;
  everlasting joy shall be upon their
  heads;
  they shall obtain joy and gladness,
  and sorrow and sighing shall flee
  away.

Sennacherib Threatens Jerusalem

36 In the fourteenth year of King
Hez·e·kī´ah, King Sen·nach´e·rib
of Assyria came up against all the fortified
cities of Judah and captured them. [2]The
king of Assyria sent the Rab´sha·keh from
Lā´chish to King Hez·e·kī´ah at Jerusalem,
with a great army. He stood by the conduit
of the upper pool on the highway to the
Fuller's Field. [3]And there came out to him
E·lī´a·kim son of Hil·kī´ah, who was in
charge of the palace, and Sheb´na the secretary, and Jō´ah son of Ā´saph, the
recorder.

4 The Rab´sha·keh said to them, "Say to
Hez·e·kī´ah: Thus says the great king, the
king of Assyria: On what do you base this
confidence of yours? [5]Do you think that
mere words are strategy and power for
war? On whom do you now rely, that you
have rebelled against me? [6]See, you are
relying on Egypt, that broken reed of a
staff, which will pierce the hand of anyone
who leans on it. Such is Pharaoh king of

Egypt to all who rely on him. [7]But if you
say to me, 'We rely on the LORD our God,'
is it not he whose high places and altars
Hez·e·kī´ah has removed, saying to Judah
and to Jerusalem, 'You shall worship before
this altar'? [8]Come now, make a wager with
my master the king of Assyria: I will give
you two thousand horses, if you are able
on your part to set riders on them. [9]How
then can you repulse a single captain
among the least of my master's servants,
when you rely on Egypt for chariots and
for horsemen? [10]Moreover, is it without the
LORD that I have come up against this land
to destroy it? The LORD said to me, Go up
against this land, and destroy it."

11 Then E·lī´a·kim, Sheb´na, and Jō´ah
said to the Rab´sha·keh, "Please speak to
your servants in Ar·a·mā´ic, for we understand it; do not speak to us in the language
of Judah within the hearing of the people
who are on the wall." [12]But the Rab´-
sha·keh said, "Has my master sent me to
speak these words to your master and to
you, and not to the people sitting on the
wall, who are doomed with you to eat their
own dung and drink their own urine?"

13 Then the Rab´sha·keh stood and
called out in a loud voice in the language
of Judah, "Hear the words of the great
king, the king of Assyria! [14]Thus says the
king: 'Do not let Hez·e·kī´ah deceive you,
for he will not be able to deliver you. [15]Do
not let Hez·e·kī´ah make you rely on the
LORD by saying, The LORD will surely
deliver us; this city will not be given into
the hand of the king of Assyria.' [16]Do not
listen to Hez·e·kī´ah; for thus says the king
of Assyria: 'Make your peace with me and
come out to me; then everyone of you will
eat from your own vine and your own fig
tree and drink water from your own cistern, [17]until I come and take you away to a
land like your own land, a land of grain
and wine, a land of bread and vineyards.
[18]Do not let Hez·e·kī´ah mislead you by
saying, The LORD will save us. Has any of

[r] Cn: Heb *in the haunt of jackals is her resting place*
[s] Or *pass it by*   [t] Cn: Heb *for them*

the gods of the nations saved their land out of the hand of the king of Assyria? [19]Where are the gods of Hā´math and Ar´pad? Where are the gods of Seph·ar·vā´im? Have they delivered Sa·mār´i·a out of my hand? [20]Who among all the gods of these countries have saved their countries out of my hand, that the LORD should save Jerusalem out of my hand?' "

21 But they were silent and answered him not a word, for the king's command was, "Do not answer him." [22]Then E·lī´a·kim son of Hil·kī´ah, who was in charge of the palace, and Sheb´na the secretary, and Jō´ah son of Ā´saph, the recorder, came to Hez·e·kī´ah with their clothes torn, and told him the words of the Rab´sha·keh.

The prophets spoke for God. They were inspired to speak God's message of purpose and judgment to the people. Prophecies were often in the form of poems, parables, stories, or pantomimes (drama without words).

Hezekiah Consults Isaiah

37 When King Hez·e·kī´ah heard it, he tore his clothes, covered himself with sackcloth, and went into the house of the LORD. [2]And he sent E·lī´a·kim, who was in charge of the palace, and Sheb´na the secretary, and the senior priests, covered with sackcloth, to the prophet Ī·sāi´ah son of Ā´moz. [3]They said to him, "Thus says Hez·e·kī´ah, This day is a day of distress, of rebuke, and of disgrace; children have come to the birth, and there is no strength to bring them forth. [4]It may be that the LORD your God heard the words of the Rab´sha·keh, whom his master the king of Assyria has sent to mock the living God, and will rebuke the words that the LORD your God has heard; therefore lift up your prayer for the remnant that is left."

5 When the servants of King Hez·e·kī´ah came to Ī·sāi´ah, [6]Ī·sāi´ah said to them,

"Say to your master, 'Thus says the LORD: Do not be afraid because of the words that you have heard, with which the servants of the king of Assyria have reviled me. [7]I myself will put a spirit in him, so that he shall hear a rumor, and return to his own land; I will cause him to fall by the sword in his own land.' "

8 The Rab´sha·keh returned, and found the king of Assyria fighting against Lib´nah; for he had heard that the king had left Lā´chish. [9]Now the king[u] heard concerning King Tir·hā´kah of Ethiopia,[v] "He has set out to fight against you." When he heard it, he sent messengers to Hez·e·kī´ah, saying, [10]"Thus shall you speak to King Hez·e·kī´ah of Judah: Do not let your God on whom you rely deceive you by promising that Jerusalem will not be given into the hand of the king of Assyria. [11]See, you have heard what the kings of Assyria have done to all lands, destroying them utterly. Shall you be delivered? [12]Have the gods of the nations delivered them, the nations that my predecessors destroyed, Gō´zan, Har´an, Rē´zeph, and the people of Eden who were in Te·las´sar? [13]Where is the king of Hā´math, the king of Ar´pad, the king of the city of Seph·ar·vā´im, the king of Hē´na, or the king of Iv´vah?"

Hezekiah's Prayer

14 Hez·e·kī´ah received the letter from the hand of the messengers and read it; then Hez·e·kī´ah went up to the house of the LORD and spread it before the LORD. [15]And Hez·e·kī´ah prayed to the LORD, saying: [16]"O LORD of hosts, God of Israel, who are enthroned above the cherubim, you are God, you alone, of all the kingdoms of the earth; you have made heaven and earth. [17]Incline your ear, O LORD, and hear; open your eyes, O LORD, and see; hear all the words of Sen·nach´e·rib, which he has sent to mock the living God. [18]Truly, O LORD, the kings of Assyria have laid waste all the nations and their lands, [19]and have hurled their gods into the fire, though they

[u] Heb *he*   [v] Or *Nubia*; Heb *Cush*

were no gods, but the work of human hands—wood and stone—and so they were destroyed. [20]So now, O LORD our God, save us from his hand, so that all the kingdoms of the earth may know that you alone are the LORD."

21 Then I·sāi´ah son of Ā´moz sent to Hez·e·kī´ah, saying: "Thus says the LORD, the God of Israel: Because you have prayed to me concerning King Sen·nach´e·rib of Assyria, [22]this is the word that the LORD has spoken concerning him:

She despises you, she scorns you—
    virgin daughter Zion;
she tosses her head—behind your
        back,
    daughter Jerusalem.

[23] "Whom have you mocked and reviled?
    Against whom have you raised your
        voice
    and haughtily lifted your eyes?
    Against the Holy One of Israel!
[24] By your servants you have mocked the
        Lord,
    and you have said, 'With my many
        chariots
I have gone up the heights of the
        mountains,
    to the far recesses of Lebanon;
I felled its tallest cedars,
    its choicest cypresses;
I came to its remotest height,
    its densest forest.
[25] I dug wells
    and drank waters,
I dried up with the sole of my foot
    all the streams of Egypt.'

[26] "Have you not heard
    that I determined it long ago?
I planned from days of old
    what now I bring to pass,
    that you should make fortified cities
    crash into heaps of ruins,
[27] while their inhabitants, shorn of
        strength,
    are dismayed and confounded;
they have become like plants of the field

and like tender grass,
    like grass on the housetops,
    blighted[w] before it is grown.

[28] "I know your rising up[x] and your
        sitting down,
    your going out and coming in,
    and your raging against me.
[29] Because you have raged against me
    and your arrogance has come to my
        ears,
I will put my hook in your nose
    and my bit in your mouth;
I will turn you back on the way
    by which you came.

30 "And this shall be the sign for you: This year eat what grows of itself, and in the second year what springs from that; then in the third year sow, reap, plant vineyards, and eat their fruit. [31]The surviving remnant of the house of Judah shall again take root downward, and bear fruit upward; [32]for from Jerusalem a remnant shall go out, and from Mount Zion a band of survivors. The zeal of the LORD of hosts will do this.

33 "Therefore thus says the LORD concerning the king of Assyria: He shall not come into this city, shoot an arrow there, come before it with a shield, or cast up a siege ramp against it. [34]By the way that he came, by the same he shall return; he shall not come into this city, says the LORD. [35]For I will defend this city to save it, for my own sake and for the sake of my servant David."

Sennacherib's Defeat and Death

36 Then the angel of the LORD set out and struck down one hundred eighty-five thousand in the camp of the Assyrians; when morning dawned, they were all dead bodies. [37]Then King Sen·nach´e·rib of Assyria left, went home, and lived at Nin´e·veh. [38]As he was worshiping in the house of his god Nis´roch, his sons A·dram´me·lech and Sha·rē´zer killed him

[w] With 2 Kings 19.26: Heb *field*   [x] Q Ms Gk: MT lacks *your rising up*

with the sword, and they escaped into the land of Ar·a·rat. His son Ē′sar-had′don succeeded him.

Hezekiah's Illness

38 In those days Hez·e·kī′ah became sick and was at the point of death. The prophet Ī·sāi′ah son of Ā′moz came to him, and said to him, "Thus says the LORD: Set your house in order, for you shall die; you shall not recover." ²Then Hez·e·kī′ah turned his face to the wall, and prayed to the LORD: ³"Remember now, O LORD, I implore you, how I have walked before you in faithfulness with a whole heart, and have done what is good in your sight." And Hez·e·kī′ah wept bitterly.

4 Then the word of the LORD came to Ī·sāi′ah: ⁵"Go and say to Hez·e·kī′ah, Thus says the LORD, the God of your ancestor David: I have heard your prayer, I have seen your tears; I will add fifteen years to your life. ⁶I will deliver you and this city out of the hand of the king of Assyria, and defend this city.

7 "This is the sign to you from the LORD, that the LORD will do this thing that he has promised: ⁸See, I will make the shadow cast by the declining sun on the dial of Ā′haz turn back ten steps." So the sun turned back on the dial the ten steps by which it had declined.*y*

9 A writing of King Hez·e·kī′ah of Judah, after he had been sick and had recovered from his sickness:

¹⁰ I said: In the noontide of my days
   I must depart;
   I am consigned to the gates of Shē′ōl
      for the rest of my years.
¹¹ I said, I shall not see the LORD
      in the land of the living;
   I shall look upon mortals no more
      among the inhabitants of the world.

¹² My dwelling is plucked up and removed from me
      like a shepherd's tent;
   like a weaver I have rolled up my life;
      he cuts me off from the loom;
   from day to night you bring me to an end;*y*
¹³   I cry for help*z* until morning;
   like a lion he breaks all my bones;
      from day to night you bring me to an end.*y*

¹⁴ Like a swallow or a crane*y* I clamor,
      I moan like a dove.
   My eyes are weary with looking upward.
      O Lord, I am oppressed; be my security!
¹⁵ But what can I say? For he has spoken to me,
      and he himself has done it.
   All my sleep has fled*a*
      because of the bitterness of my soul.
¹⁶ O Lord, by these things people live,
      and in all these is the life of my spirit.*y*
   Oh, restore me to health and make me live!
¹⁷ Surely it was for my welfare
      that I had great bitterness;
   but you have held back*b* my life
      from the pit of destruction,
   for you have cast all my sins
      behind your back.
¹⁸ For Shē′ōl cannot thank you,
      death cannot praise you;
   those who go down to the Pit cannot hope
      for your faithfulness.
¹⁹ The living, the living, they thank you,
      as I do this day;
   fathers make known to children
      your faithfulness.

---

y Meaning of Heb uncertain *z* Cn: Meaning of Heb uncertain *a* Cn Compare Syr: Heb *I will walk slowly all my years* *b* Cn Compare Gk Vg: Heb *loved*

"The LORD will save me, and we will sing to stringed instruments all the days of our lives, at the house of the LORD." Isaiah 38:20

²⁰ The LORD will save me,
  and we will sing to stringed
    instruments^c
all the days of our lives,
  at the house of the LORD.

21 Now Ī·sāi´ah had said, "Let them take a lump of figs, and apply it to the boil, so that he may recover." ²² Hez·e·kī´ah also had said, "What is the sign that I shall go up to the house of the LORD?"

Envoys from Babylon Welcomed

39 At that time King Mer´o·dach-bal´a·dan son of Bal´a·dan of Babylon sent envoys with letters and a present to Hez·e·kī´ah, for he heard that he had been sick and had recovered. ²Hez·e·kī´ah welcomed them; he showed them his treasure house, the silver, the gold, the spices, the precious oil, his whole armory, all that was found in his storehouses. There was nothing in his house or in all his realm that Hez·e·kī´ah did not show them. ³Then the prophet Ī·sāi´ah came to King Hez·e·kī´ah and said to him, "What did these men say? From where did they come to you?" Hez·e·kī´ah answered, "They have come to me from a far country, from Babylon." ⁴He said, "What have they seen in your house?" Hez·e·kī´ah answered, "They have seen all that is in my house; there is nothing in my storehouses that I did not show them."

5 Then Ī·sāi´ah said to Hez·e·kī´ah, "Hear the word of the LORD of hosts: ⁶Days are coming when all that is in your house, and that which your ancestors have stored up until this day, shall be carried to Babylon; nothing shall be left, says the LORD. ⁷Some of your own sons who are born to you shall be taken away; they shall be eunuchs in the palace of the king of Babylon." ⁸Then Hez·e·kī´ah said to Ī·sāi´ah, "The word of the LORD that you have spoken is good." For he thought, "There will be peace and security in my days."

God's People Are Comforted

40 Comfort, O comfort my people,
  says your God.
² Speak tenderly to Jerusalem,
  and cry to her
that she has served her term,
  that her penalty is paid,
that she has received from the LORD's
    hand
  double for all her sins.

³ A voice cries out:
"In the wilderness prepare the way of
    the LORD,
  make straight in the desert a
    highway for our God.
⁴ Every valley shall be lifted up,
  and every mountain and hill be
    made low;
the uneven ground shall become level,
  and the rough places a plain.
⁵ Then the glory of the LORD shall be
    revealed,
  and all people shall see it together,
  for the mouth of the LORD has
    spoken."

⁶ A voice says, "Cry out!"
  And I said, "What shall I cry?"
All people are grass,
  their constancy is like the flower of
    the field.
⁷ The grass withers, the flower fades,
  when the breath of the LORD blows
    upon it;
  surely the people are grass.
⁸ The grass withers, the flower fades;
  but the word of our God will stand
    forever.
⁹ Get you up to a high mountain,
  O Zion, herald of good tidings;^d
lift up your voice with strength,
  O Jerusalem, herald of good tidings,^e
  lift it up, do not fear;
say to the cities of Judah,
  "Here is your God!"

^c Heb my stringed instruments   ^d Or O herald of good tidings to Zion   ^e Or O herald of good tidings to Jerusalem

¹⁰ See, the Lord GOD comes with might,
    and his arm rules for him;
his reward is with him,
    and his recompense before him.
¹¹ He will feed his flock like a shepherd;
    he will gather the lambs in his arms,
and carry them in his bosom,
    and gently lead the mother sheep.

¹² Who has measured the waters in the
    hollow of his hand
    and marked off the heavens with a
      span,
enclosed the dust of the earth in a
    measure,
    and weighed the mountains in scales
    and the hills in a balance?
¹³ Who has directed the spirit of the
    LORD,
    or as his counselor has instructed
      him?
¹⁴ Whom did he consult for his
    enlightenment,
    and who taught him the path of
      justice?
Who taught him knowledge,
    and showed him the way of
      understanding?
¹⁵ Even the nations are like a drop from a
    bucket,
    and are accounted as dust on the
      scales;
    see, he takes up the isles like fine
      dust.
¹⁶ Lebanon would not provide fuel
    enough,
    nor are its animals enough for a
      burnt offering.
¹⁷ All the nations are as nothing before
    him;
    they are accounted by him as less
      than nothing and emptiness.

¹⁸ To whom then will you liken God,
    or what likeness compare with him?
¹⁹ An idol? —A workman casts it,
    and a goldsmith overlays it with
      gold,
    and casts for it silver chains.

²⁰ As a gift one chooses mulberry wood*
    —wood that will not rot—
then seeks out a skilled artisan
    to set up an image that will not
      topple.

²¹ Have you not known? Have you not
    heard?
    Has it not been told you from the
      beginning?
Have you not understood from the
    foundations of the earth?
²² It is he who sits above the circle of the
    earth,
    and its inhabitants are like
      grasshoppers;
who stretches out the heavens like a
    curtain,
    and spreads them like a tent to live
      in;
²³ who brings princes to naught,
    and makes the rulers of the earth as
      nothing.
²⁴ Scarcely are they planted, scarcely
    sown,
    scarcely has their stem taken root in
      the earth,
when he blows upon them, and they
    wither,
    and the tempest carries them off like
      stubble.

²⁵ To whom then will you compare me,
    or who is my equal? says the Holy
      One.
²⁶ Lift up your eyes on high and see:
    Who created these?

> Look through a hymnal or songbook to see how many songs you can find that use some images from Isaiah. Many songs have a Bible verse reference printed at the top or the bottom of the page. Look up each verse in your Bible to see how closely it matches the song.

f Meaning of Heb uncertain

He who brings out their host and
    numbers them,
    calling them all by name;
because he is great in strength,
    mighty in power,
    not one is missing.

27 Why do you say, O Jacob,
    and speak, O Israel,
"My way is hidden from the LORD,
    and my right is disregarded by my
    God"?
28 Have you not known? Have you not
    heard?
The LORD is the everlasting God,
    the Creator of the ends of the earth.
He does not faint or grow weary;
    his understanding is unsearchable.
29 He gives power to the faint,
    and strengthens the powerless.
30 Even youths will faint and be weary,
    and the young will fall exhausted;
31 but those who wait for the LORD shall
    renew their strength,
    they shall mount up with wings like
    eagles,
they shall run and not be weary,
    they shall walk and not faint.

Israel Assured of God's Help

41 Listen to me in silence,
    O coastlands;
    let the peoples renew their strength;
let them approach, then let them
    speak;
    let us together draw near for
    judgment.

2 Who has roused a victor from the east,
    summoned him to his service?
He delivers up nations to him,
    and tramples kings under foot;
he makes them like dust with his
    sword,
    like driven stubble with his bow.
3 He pursues them and passes on safely,
    scarcely touching the path with his
    feet.
4 Who has performed and done this,

"Those who wait for the
LORD shall renew their
strength, they shall mount
up with wings like eagles,
they shall run and not be weary,
they shall walk and not faint."
    Isaiah 40:31

calling the generations from the
    beginning?
I, the LORD, am first,
    and will be with the last.
5 The coastlands have seen and are
    afraid,
    the ends of the earth tremble;
    they have drawn near and come.
6 Each one helps the other,
    saying to one another, "Take
    courage!"
7 The artisan encourages the goldsmith,
    and the one who smooths with the
    hammer encourages the one who
    strikes the anvil,
saying of the soldering, "It is good";
    and they fasten it with nails so that
    it cannot be moved.
8 But you, Israel, my servant,
    Jacob, whom I have chosen,
    the offspring of Abraham, my friend;
9 you whom I took from the ends of the
    earth,
    and called from its farthest corners,
saying to you, "You are my servant,
    I have chosen you and not cast you
    off";
10 do not fear, for I am with you,
    do not be afraid, for I am your God;
I will strengthen you, I will help you,
    I will uphold you with my
    victorious right hand.

11 Yes, all who are incensed against you
    shall be ashamed and disgraced;
those who strive against you
    shall be as nothing and shall perish.
12 You shall seek those who contend with
    you,
    but you shall not find them;

Winnowing is the process of separating the kernel of the grain from the chaff. To do this, people would throw the cut stalks of grain into the air with a long-handled fork. The grain seeds would fall back into a pile, and the light straw chaff would be carried away by the wind. The word "winnowing" is used to mean the sweeping away of evil.

those who war against you
    shall be as nothing at all.
¹³ For I, the LORD your God,
    hold your right hand;
it is I who say to you, "Do not fear,
    I will help you."

¹⁴ Do not fear, you worm Jacob,
    you insect[g] Israel!
I will help you, says the LORD;
    your Redeemer is the Holy One of
        Israel.
¹⁵ Now, I will make of you a threshing
        sledge,
    sharp, new, and having teeth;
you shall thresh the mountains and
        crush them,
    and you shall make the hills like
        chaff.
¹⁶ You shall winnow them and the wind
        shall carry them away,
    and the tempest shall scatter them.
Then you shall rejoice in the LORD;
    in the Holy One of Israel you shall
        glory.

¹⁷ When the poor and needy seek water,
    and there is none,
    and their tongue is parched with
        thirst,
I the LORD will answer them,
    I the God of Israel will not forsake
        them.

¹⁸ I will open rivers on the bare heights,[h]
    and fountains in the midst of the
        valleys;
I will make the wilderness a pool of
        water,
    and the dry land springs of water.
¹⁹ I will put in the wilderness the cedar,
    the acacia, the myrtle, and the olive;
I will set in the desert the cypress,
    the plane and the pine together,
²⁰ so that all may see and know,
    all may consider and understand,
that the hand of the LORD has done
        this,
    the Holy One of Israel has created it.

The Futility of Idols

²¹ Set forth your case, says the LORD;
    bring your proofs, says the King of
        Jacob.
²² Let them bring them, and tell us
    what is to happen.
Tell us the former things, what they
        are,
    so that we may consider them,
and that we may know their outcome;
    or declare to us the things to come.
²³ Tell us what is to come hereafter,
    that we may know that you are
        gods;
do good, or do harm,
    that we may be afraid and terrified.
²⁴ You, indeed, are nothing
    and your work is nothing at all;
    whoever chooses you is an
        abomination.

²⁵ I stirred up one from the north, and he
        has come,

When the Israelites escaped from Egypt, they suffered from thirst. Here, God promised that when they left Babylon, there would be enough water in the desert for them to plant trees. "I will not forsake my people," says God.

[g] Syr: Heb *men of*   [h] Or *trails*

from the rising of the sun he was
  summoned by name.[i]
He shall trample[j] on rulers as on
  mortar,
  as the potter treads clay.
[26] Who declared it from the beginning,
  so that we might know,
  and beforehand, so that we might
  say, "He is right"?
There was no one who declared it,
  none who proclaimed,
  none who heard your words.
[27] I first have declared it to Zion,[k]
  and I give to Jerusalem a herald of
  good tidings.
[28] But when I look there is no one;
  among these there is no counselor
  who, when I ask, gives an answer.
[29] No, they are all a delusion;
  their works are nothing;
  their images are empty wind.

The Servant, a Light to the Nations

42 Here is my servant, whom I
  uphold, my chosen, in whom
  my soul delights;
I have put my spirit upon him;
  he will bring forth justice to the
  nations.
[2] He will not cry or lift up his voice,
  or make it heard in the street;
[3] a bruised reed he will not break,
  and a dimly burning wick he will
  not quench;
  he will faithfully bring forth justice.
[4] He will not grow faint or be crushed
  until he has established justice in the
  earth;
  and the coastlands wait for his
  teaching.

[5] Thus says God, the LORD,
  who created the heavens and
  stretched them out,

who spread out the earth and what
  comes from it,
who gives breath to the people upon
  it
  and spirit to those who walk in it:
[6] I am the LORD, I have called you in
  righteousness,
  I have taken you by the hand and
  kept you;
I have given you as a covenant to the
  people,[l]
  a light to the nations,
[7] to open the eyes that are blind,
  to bring out the prisoners from the
  dungeon,
  from the prison those who sit in
  darkness.
[8] I am the LORD, that is my name;
  my glory I give to no other,
  nor my praise to idols.
[9] See, the former things have come to
  pass,
  and new things I now declare;
  before they spring forth,
  I tell you of them.

A Hymn of Praise

[10] Sing to the LORD a new song,
  his praise from the end of the earth!
Let the sea roar[m] and all that fills it,
  the coastlands and their inhabitants.
[11] Let the desert and its towns lift up
  their voice,
  the villages that Kḗ´dar inhabits;
let the inhabitants of Sē´la sing for joy,
  let them shout from the tops of the
  mountains.
[12] Let them give glory to the LORD,
  and declare his praise in the coastlands.
[13] The LORD goes forth like a soldier,
  like a warrior he stirs up his fury;
he cries out, he shouts aloud,
  he shows himself mighty against his
  foes.

"Sing to the LORD a new
song, his praise from the
end of the earth!"
Isaiah 42:10

[i] Cn Compare Q Ms Gk: MT *and he shall call on my
name*   [j] Cn: Heb *come*   [k] Cn: Heb *First to Zion—
Behold, behold them*   [l] Meaning of Heb uncertain
[m] Cn Compare Ps 96.11; 98.7: Heb *Those who go
down to the sea*

14 For a long time I have held my peace,
  I have kept still and restrained
    myself;
  now I will cry out like a woman in
    labor,
  I will gasp and pant.
15 I will lay waste mountains and hills,
  and dry up all their herbage;
  I will turn the rivers into islands,
  and dry up the pools.
16 I will lead the blind
  by a road they do not know,
  by paths they have not known
    I will guide them.
  I will turn the darkness before them
    into light,
  the rough places into level ground.
  These are the things I will do,
  and I will not forsake them.
17 They shall be turned back and utterly
    put to shame—
  those who trust in carved images,
  who say to cast images,
  "You are our gods."

18 Listen, you that are deaf;
  and you that are blind, look up and
    see!
19 Who is blind but my servant,
  or deaf like my messenger whom I
    send?
  Who is blind like my dedicated one,
  or blind like the servant of the LORD?
20 He sees many things, but does[n] not
    observe them;
  his ears are open, but he does not
    hear.

Israel's Disobedience

21 The LORD was pleased, for the sake of
    his righteousness,
  to magnify his teaching and make it
    glorious.
22 But this is a people robbed and
    plundered,
  all of them are trapped in holes
  and hidden in prisons;
  they have become a prey with no one
    to rescue,

  a spoil with no one to say, "Restore!"
23 Who among you will give heed to this,
  who will attend and listen for the
    time to come?
24 Who gave up Jacob to the spoiler,
  and Israel to the robbers?
  Was it not the LORD, against whom we
    have sinned,
  in whose ways they would not walk,
  and whose law they would not
    obey?
25 So he poured upon him the heat of his
    anger
  and the fury of war;
  it set him on fire all around, but he did
    not understand;
  it burned him, but he did not take it
    to heart.

Restoration and Protection Promised

43 But now thus says the LORD,
  he who created you, O Jacob,
  he who formed you, O Israel:
  Do not fear, for I have redeemed you;
  I have called you by name, you are
    mine.
2 When you pass through the waters, I
    will be with you;
  and through the rivers, they shall
    not overwhelm you;
  when you walk through fire you shall
    not be burned,
  and the flame shall not consume
    you.
3 For I am the LORD your God,
  the Holy One of Israel, your Savior.
  I give Egypt as your ransom,
  Ethiopia[o] and Sē'ba in exchange for
    you.
4 Because you are precious in my sight,
  and honored, and I love you,
  I give people in return for you,
  nations in exchange for your life.
5 Do not fear, for I am with you;
  I will bring your offspring from the
    east,

_____
[n] Heb _You see many things but do_   [o] Or Nubia; Heb
Cush

and from the west I will gather you;
[6] I will say to the north, "Give them up,"
and to the south, "Do not withhold;
bring my sons from far away
and my daughters from the end of
the earth—
[7] everyone who is called by my name,
whom I created for my glory,
whom I formed and made."

[8] Bring forth the people who are blind,
yet have eyes,
who are deaf, yet have ears!
[9] Let all the nations gather together,
and let the peoples assemble.
Who among them declared this,
and foretold to us the former things?
Let them bring their witnesses to
justify them,
and let them hear and say, "It is
true."
[10] You are my witnesses, says the LORD,
and my servant whom I have
chosen,
so that you may know and believe me
and understand that I am he.
Before me no god was formed,
nor shall there be any after me.
[11] I, I am the LORD,
and besides me there is no savior.
[12] I declared and saved and proclaimed,
when there was no strange god
among you;
and you are my witnesses, says the
LORD.
[13] I am God, and also henceforth I am
He;
there is no one who can deliver
from my hand;
I work and who can hinder it?
[14] Thus says the LORD,
your Redeemer, the Holy One of
Israel:
For your sake I will send to Babylon
and break down all the bars,
and the shouting of the Chal·dē′ans
will be turned to lamentation.[p]
[15] I am the LORD, your Holy One,
the Creator of Israel, your King.

[16] Thus says the LORD,
who makes a way in the sea,
a path in the mighty waters,
[17] who brings out chariot and horse,
army and warrior;
they lie down, they cannot rise,
they are extinguished, quenched like
a wick:
[18] Do not remember the former things,
or consider the things of old.
[19] I am about to do a new thing;
now it springs forth, do you not
perceive it?
I will make a way in the wilderness
and rivers in the desert.
[20] The wild animals will honor me,
the jackals and the ostriches;
for I give water in the wilderness,
rivers in the desert,
to give drink to my chosen people,
[21]   the people whom I formed for
myself
so that they might declare my praise.

[22] Yet you did not call upon me, O Jacob;
but you have been weary of me, O
Israel!
[23] You have not brought me your sheep
for burnt offerings,
or honored me with your sacrifices.
I have not burdened you with offerings,
or wearied you with frankincense.
[24] You have not bought me sweet cane
with money,
or satisfied me with the fat of your
sacrifices.
But you have burdened me with your
sins;
you have wearied me with your
iniquities.

[25] I, I am He
who blots out your transgressions
for my own sake,
and I will not remember your sins.
[26] Accuse me, let us go to trial;
set forth your case, so that you may
be proved right.

[p] Meaning of Heb uncertain

27 Your first ancestor sinned,
and your interpreters transgressed
against me.
28 Therefore I profaned the princes of the
sanctuary,
I delivered Jacob to utter
destruction,
and Israel to reviling.

God's Blessing on Israel

44 But now hear, O Jacob my
servant,
Israel whom I have chosen!
2 Thus says the LORD who made you,
who formed you in the womb and
will help you:
Do not fear, O Jacob my servant,
Jesh′ū·run whom I have chosen.
3 For I will pour water on the thirsty
land,
and streams on the dry ground;
I will pour my spirit upon your
descendants,
and my blessing on your offspring.
4 They shall spring up like a green
tamarisk,
like willows by flowing streams.
5 This one will say, "I am the LORD's,"
another will be called by the name
of Jacob,
yet another will write on the hand,
"The LORD's,"
and adopt the name of Israel.

6 Thus says the LORD, the King of Israel,
and his Redeemer, the LORD of
hosts:
I am the first and I am the last;
besides me there is no god.
7 Who is like me? Let them proclaim it,
let them declare and set it forth
before me.
Who has announced from of old the
things to come?q
Let them tell usr what is yet to be.
8 Do not fear, or be afraid;
have I not told you from of old and
declared it?
You are my witnesses!

Is there any god besides me?
There is no other rock; I know not
one.

The Absurdity of Idol Worship

9 All who make idols are nothing, and
the things they delight in do not profit;
their witnesses neither see nor know. And
so they will be put to shame. 10Who would
fashion a god or cast an image that can do
no good? 11Look, all its devotees shall be
put to shame; the artisans too are merely
human. Let them all assemble, let them
stand up; they shall be terrified, they shall
all be put to shame.

12 The ironsmith fashions its and
works it over the coals, shaping it with
hammers, and forging it with his strong
arm; he becomes hungry and his strength
fails, he drinks no water and is faint. 13The
carpenter stretches a line, marks it out
with a stylus, fashions it with planes, and
marks it with a compass; he makes it in
human form, with human beauty, to be set
up in a shrine. 14He cuts down cedars or
chooses a holm tree or an oak and lets it
grow strong among the trees of the forest.
He plants a cedar and the rain nourishes it.
15Then it can be used as fuel. Part of it he
takes and warms himself; he kindles a fire
and bakes bread. Then he makes a god
and worships it, makes it a carved image
and bows down before it. 16Half of it he
burns in the fire; over this half he roasts
meat, eats it and is satisfied. He also warms
himself and says, "Ah, I am warm, I can
feel the fire!" 17The rest of it he makes into
a god, his idol, bows down to it and worships it; he prays to it and says, "Save me,
for you are my god!"

18 They do not know, nor do they
comprehend; for their eyes are shut, so
that they cannot see, and their minds as
well, so that they cannot understand. 19No
one considers, nor is there knowledge or
discernment to say, "Half of it I burned in
the fire; I also baked bread on its coals, I

---

q Cn: Heb *from my placing an eternal people and things
to come*   r Tg: Heb *them*   s Cn: Heb *an ax*

roasted meat and have eaten. Now shall I make the rest of it an abomination? Shall I fall down before a block of wood?" [20]He feeds on ashes; a deluded mind has led him astray, and he cannot save himself or say, "Is not this thing in my right hand a fraud?"

Israel Is Not Forgotten

[21] Remember these things, O Jacob,
　　and Israel, for you are my servant;
　I formed you, you are my servant;
　　O Israel, you will not be forgotten
　　　by me.
[22] I have swept away your transgressions
　　like a cloud,
　　and your sins like mist;
　return to me, for I have redeemed you.
[23] Sing, O heavens, for the LORD has
　　done it;
　　shout, O depths of the earth;
　break forth into singing, O mountains,
　　O forest, and every tree in it!
　For the LORD has redeemed Jacob,
　　and will be glorified in Israel.

[24] Thus says the LORD, your Redeemer,
　　who formed you in the womb:
　I am the LORD, who made all things,
　　who alone stretched out the heavens,
　　who by myself spread out the earth;
[25] who frustrates the omens of liars,
　　and makes fools of diviners;
　who turns back the wise,
　　and makes their knowledge foolish;
[26] who confirms the word of his servant,
　　and fulfills the prediction of his
　　　messengers;
　who says of Jerusalem, "It shall be
　　inhabited,"
　　and of the cities of Judah, "They
　　　shall be rebuilt,
　　and I will raise up their ruins";
[27] who says to the deep, "Be dry—
　　I will dry up your rivers";
[28] who says of Cyrus, "He is my
　　shepherd,
　　and he shall carry out all my
　　　purpose";

and who says of Jerusalem, "It shall be
　　rebuilt,"
　and of the temple, "Your foundation
　　shall be laid."

Cyrus, God's Instrument

45 Thus says the LORD to his
　　anointed, to Cyrus,
　whose right hand I have grasped
　to subdue nations before him
　　and strip kings of their robes,
　to open doors before him—
　　and the gates shall not be closed:
[2] I will go before you
　　and level the mountains,[t]
　I will break in pieces the doors of
　　bronze
　　and cut through the bars of iron,
[3] I will give you the treasures of darkness
　　and riches hidden in secret places,
　so that you may know that it is I, the
　　LORD,
　　the God of Israel, who call you by
　　　your name.
[4] For the sake of my servant Jacob,
　　and Israel my chosen,
　I call you by your name,
　　I surname you, though you do not
　　　know me.
[5] I am the LORD, and there is no other;
　　besides me there is no god.
　I arm you, though you do not know
　　me,
[6] so that they may know, from the rising
　　of the sun
　　and from the west, that there is no
　　　one besides me;
　I am the LORD, and there is no other.
[7] I form light and create darkness,
　　I make weal and create woe;
　　I the LORD do all these things.

[8] Shower, O heavens, from above,
　　and let the skies rain down
　　　righteousness;
　let the earth open, that salvation may
　　spring up,[u]

[t] Q Ms Gk: MT *the swellings* 　[u] Q Ms: MT *that they may bring forth salvation*

> "Turn to me and be saved, all the ends of the earth! For I am God, and there is no other."
>
> Isaiah 45:22

and let it cause righteousness to
   sprout up also;
I the LORD have created it.

9 Woe to you who strive with your
      Maker,
   earthen vessels with the potter!^v
Does the clay say to the one who fash-
      ions it, "What are you making"?
   or "Your work has no handles"?
10 Woe to anyone who says to a father,
      "What are you begetting?"
   or to a woman, "With what are you
      in labor?"
11 Thus says the LORD,
   the Holy One of Israel, and its
      Maker:
Will you question me^w about my
      children,
   or command me concerning the
      work of my hands?
12 I made the earth,
   and created humankind upon it;
it was my hands that stretched out the
      heavens,
   and I commanded all their host.
13 I have aroused Cyrus^x in
      righteousness,
   and I will make all his paths
      straight;
he shall build my city
   and set my exiles free,
not for price or reward,
   says the LORD of hosts.
14 Thus says the LORD:
The wealth of Egypt and the merchan-
      dise of Ethiopia,^y
   and the Sa·be´ans, tall of stature,
shall come over to you and be yours,
   they shall follow you;
they shall come over in chains and
      bow down to you.

They will make supplication to you,
      saying,
   "God is with you alone, and there is
      no other;
   there is no god besides him."
15 Truly, you are a God who hides
      himself,
   O God of Israel, the Savior.
16 All of them are put to shame and
      confounded,
   the makers of idols go in confusion
      together.
17 But Israel is saved by the LORD
   with everlasting salvation;
you shall not be put to shame or
      confounded
   to all eternity.

18 For thus says the LORD,
who created the heavens
   (he is God!),
who formed the earth and made it
   (he established it;
he did not create it a chaos,
   he formed it to be inhabited!):
I am the LORD, and there is no other.
19 I did not speak in secret,
   in a land of darkness;
I did not say to the offspring of Jacob,
   "Seek me in chaos."
I the LORD speak the truth,
   I declare what is right.

Idols Cannot Save Babylon
20 Assemble yourselves and come
      together,
   draw near, you survivors of the
      nations!
They have no knowledge—
   those who carry about their wooden
      idols,
and keep on praying to a god
   that cannot save.
21 Declare and present your case;
   let them take counsel together!

---

^v Cn: Heb *with the potsherds*, or *with the potters*
^w Cn: Heb *Ask me of things to come*   ^x Heb *him*
^y Or *Nubia*; Heb *Cush*

Who told this long ago?
  Who declared it of old?
Was it not I, the LORD?
  There is no other god besides me,
a righteous God and a Savior;
  there is no one besides me.

22 Turn to me and be saved,
  all the ends of the earth!
For I am God, and there is no other.
23 By myself I have sworn,
  from my mouth has gone forth in
    righteousness
  a word that shall not return:
"To me every knee shall bow,
  every tongue shall swear."

24 Only in the LORD, it shall be said of me,
  are righteousness and strength;
all who were incensed against him
  shall come to him and be ashamed.
25 In the LORD all the offspring of Israel
  shall triumph and glory.

46

Bel bows down, Nĕ′bō stoops,
  their idols are on beasts and
    cattle;
these things you carry are loaded
  as burdens on weary animals.
2 They stoop, they bow down together;
  they cannot save the burden,
  but themselves go into captivity.

3 Listen to me, O house of Jacob,
  all the remnant of the house of
    Israel,
who have been borne by me from your
    birth,
  carried from the womb;
4 even to your old age I am he,
  even when you turn gray I will carry
    you.
I have made, and I will bear;
  I will carry and will save.

5 To whom will you liken me and make
  me equal,
  and compare me, as though we
    were alike?

6 Those who lavish gold from the purse,
  and weigh out silver in the scales—
they hire a goldsmith, who makes it
  into a god;
  then they fall down and worship!
7 They lift it to their shoulders, they
  carry it,
  they set it in its place, and it stands
    there;
  it cannot move from its place.
If one cries out to it, it does not answer
  or save anyone from trouble.

8 Remember this and consider,ᶻ
  recall it to mind, you transgressors,
9   remember the former things of old;
for I am God, and there is no other;
  I am God, and there is no one like
    me,
10 declaring the end from the beginning
  and from ancient times things not
    yet done,
saying, "My purpose shall stand,
  and I will fulfill my intention,"
11 calling a bird of prey from the east,
  the man for my purpose from a far
    country.
I have spoken, and I will bring it to
    pass;
  I have planned, and I will do it.

12 Listen to me, you stubborn of heart,
  you who are far from deliverance:
13 I bring near my deliverance, it is not
  far off,
  and my salvation will not tarry;
I will put salvation in Zion,
  for Israel my glory.

The Humiliation of Babylon

47

Come down and sit in the dust,
  virgin daughter Babylon!
Sit on the ground without a throne,
  daughter Chal·dē′a!
For you shall no more be called
  tender and delicate.
2 Take the millstones and grind meal,
  remove your veil,

ᶻ Meaning of Heb uncertain

strip off your robe, uncover your legs,
    pass through the rivers.
3 Your nakedness shall be uncovered,
    and your shame shall be seen.
I will take vengeance,
    and I will spare no one.
4 Our Redeemer—the LORD of hosts is
       his name—
    is the Holy One of Israel.

5 Sit in silence, and go into darkness,
    daughter Chal·dē´a!
For you shall no more be called
    the mistress of kingdoms.
6 I was angry with my people,
    I profaned my heritage;
I gave them into your hand,
    you showed them no mercy;
on the aged you made your yoke
    exceedingly heavy.
7 You said, "I shall be mistress forever,"
    so that you did not lay these things
       to heart
    or remember their end.

8 Now therefore hear this, you lover of
       pleasures,
    who sit securely,
who say in your heart,
    "I am, and there is no one besides
       me;
I shall not sit as a widow
    or know the loss of children"—
9 both these things shall come upon you
    in a moment, in one day:
the loss of children and widowhood
    shall come upon you in full
       measure,
in spite of your many sorceries
    and the great power of your
       enchantments.

10 You felt secure in your wickedness;
    you said, "No one sees me."
Your wisdom and your knowledge
    led you astray,
and you said in your heart,
    "I am, and there is no one besides
       me."

11 But evil shall come upon you,
    which you cannot charm away;
disaster shall fall upon you,
    which you will not be able to ward
       off;
and ruin shall come on you suddenly,
    of which you know nothing.

12 Stand fast in your enchantments
    and your many sorceries,
    with which you have labored from
       your youth;
perhaps you may be able to succeed,
    perhaps you may inspire terror.
13 You are wearied with your many
       consultations;
    let those who study[a] the heavens
stand up and save you,
    those who gaze at the stars,
and at each new moon predict
    what[b] shall befall you.

14 See, they are like stubble,
    the fire consumes them;
they cannot deliver themselves
    from the power of the flame.
No coal for warming oneself is this,
    no fire to sit before!
15 Such to you are those with whom you
       have labored,
    who have trafficked with you from
       your youth;
they all wander about in their own
       paths;
    there is no one to save you.

God the Creator and Redeemer

48 Hear this, O house of Jacob,
    who are called by the name of
       Israel,
    and who came forth from the loins[c]
       of Judah;
who swear by the name of the LORD,
    and invoke the God of Israel,
    but not in truth or right.
2 For they call themselves after the holy
       city,

---

[a] Meaning of Heb uncertain   [b] Gk Syr Compare
Vg: Heb *from what*   [c] Cn: Heb *waters*

and lean on the God of Israel;
  the LORD of hosts is his name.

3 The former things I declared long ago,
  they went out from my mouth and I
    made them known;
  then suddenly I did them and they
    came to pass.
4 Because I know that you are obstinate,
  and your neck is an iron sinew
  and your forehead brass,
5 I declared them to you from long ago,
  before they came to pass I
    announced them to you,
  so that you would not say, "My idol
    did them,
  my carved image and my cast image
    commanded them."

6 You have heard; now see all this;
  and will you not declare it?
From this time forward I make you
  hear new things,
  hidden things that you have not
    known.
7 They are created now, not long ago;
  before today you have never heard
    of them,
  so that you could not say, "I already
    knew them."
8 You have never heard, you have never
    known,
  from of old your ear has not been
    opened.
For I knew that you would deal very
  treacherously,
  and that from birth you were called
    a rebel.

9 For my name's sake I defer my anger,
  for the sake of my praise I restrain it
    for you,
  so that I may not cut you off.
10 See, I have refined you, but not like[d]
    silver;
  I have tested you in the furnace of
    adversity.
11 For my own sake, for my own sake, I
    do it,

for why should my name[e] be
  profaned?
My glory I will not give to another.

12 Listen to me, O Jacob,
  and Israel, whom I called:
I am He; I am the first,
  and I am the last.
13 My hand laid the foundation of the
    earth,
  and my right hand spread out the
    heavens;
when I summon them,
  they stand at attention.

14 Assemble, all of you, and hear!
  Who among them has declared
    these things?
The LORD loves him;
  he shall perform his purpose on
    Babylon,
  and his arm shall be against the
    Chal·de′ans.
15 I, even I, have spoken and called him,
  I have brought him, and he will
    prosper in his way.
16 Draw near to me, hear this!
  From the beginning I have not
    spoken in secret,
  from the time it came to be I have
    been there.
And now the Lord GOD has sent me
  and his spirit.

17 Thus says the LORD,
  your Redeemer, the Holy One of
    Israel:
I am the LORD your God,
  who teaches you for your own good,
  who leads you in the way you
    should go.
18 O that you had paid attention to my
    commandments!
  Then your prosperity would have
    been like a river,
  and your success like the waves of
    the sea;

[d] Cn: Heb *with*   [e] Gk Old Latin: Heb *for why should it*

19 your offspring would have been like
the sand,
and your descendants like its grains;
their name would never be cut off
or destroyed from before me.

20 Go out from Babylon, flee from
Chal·dḗ′a,
declare this with a shout of joy,
proclaim it,
send it forth to the end of the earth;
say, "The LORD has redeemed his
servant Jacob!"

21 They did not thirst when he led them
through the deserts;
he made water flow for them from
the rock;
he split open the rock and the water
gushed out.

22 "There is no peace," says the LORD, "for
the wicked."

The Servant's Mission

49 Listen to me, O coastlands,
pay attention, you peoples
from far away!
The LORD called me before I was born,
while I was in my mother's womb
he named me.

2 He made my mouth like a sharp
sword,
in the shadow of his hand he hid me;
he made me a polished arrow,
in his quiver he hid me away.

3 And he said to me, "You are my
servant,
Israel, in whom I will be glorified."

4 But I said, "I have labored in vain,
I have spent my strength for nothing
and vanity;
yet surely my cause is with the LORD,
and my reward with my God."

5 And now the LORD says,
who formed me in the womb to be
his servant,
to bring Jacob back to him,
and that Israel might be gathered to
him,

for I am honored in the sight of the
LORD,
and my God has become my
strength—

6 he says,
"It is too light a thing that you should
be my servant
to raise up the tribes of Jacob
and to restore the survivors of Israel;
I will give you as a light to the nations,
that my salvation may reach to the
end of the earth."

7 Thus says the LORD,
the Redeemer of Israel and his Holy
One,
to one deeply despised, abhorred by
the nations,
the slave of rulers,
"Kings shall see and stand up,
princes, and they shall prostrate
themselves,
because of the LORD, who is faithful,
the Holy One of Israel, who has
chosen you."

Zion's Children
to Be Brought Home

8 Thus says the LORD:
In a time of favor I have answered you,
on a day of salvation I have helped
you;
I have kept you and given you
as a covenant to the people,ƒ
to establish the land,
to apportion the desolate heritages;

9 saying to the prisoners, "Come out,"
to those who are in darkness, "Show
yourselves."
They shall feed along the ways,
on all the bare heightsᵍ shall be their
pasture;

10 they shall not hunger or thirst,
neither scorching wind nor sun shall
strike them down,
for he who has pity on them will lead
them,
and by springs of water will guide
them.

ƒ Meaning of Heb uncertain   ᵍ Or *the trails*

11 And I will turn all my mountains into
　　　a road,
　　and my highways shall be raised up.
12 Lo, these shall come from far away,
　　and lo, these from the north and
　　　from the west,
　　and these from the land of Sy·ē´nē.[h]

13 Sing for joy, O heavens, and exult, O
　　　earth;
　　break forth, O mountains, into
　　　singing!
　For the LORD has comforted his
　　　people,
　　and will have compassion on his
　　　suffering ones.

14 But Zion said, "The LORD has forsaken
　　　me,
　　my Lord has forgotten me."
15 Can a woman forget her nursing child,
　　or show no compassion for the child
　　　of her womb?
　Even these may forget,
　　yet I will not forget you.
16 See, I have inscribed you on the palms
　　　of my hands;
　　your walls are continually before
　　　me.
17 Your builders outdo your destroyers,[i]
　　and those who laid you waste go
　　　away from you.
18 Lift up your eyes all around and see;
　　they all gather, they come to you.
　As I live, says the LORD,
　　you shall put all of them on like an
　　　ornament,
　　and like a bride you shall bind them
　　　on.
19 Surely your waste and your desolate
　　　places
　　and your devastated land—
　surely now you will be too crowded
　　　for your
　　　inhabitants,
　　and those who swallowed you up
　　　will be far away.
20 The children born in the time of your
　　　bereavement

> "Sing for joy, O heavens,
> and exult, O earth; break
> forth, O mountains, into
> singing!"   Isaiah 49:13a

　will yet say in your hearing:
　"The place is too crowded for me;
　　make room for me to settle."
21 Then you will say in your heart,
　　"Who has borne me these?
　I was bereaved and barren,
　　exiled and put away—
　　so who has reared these?
　I was left all alone—
　　where then have these come from?"

22 Thus says the Lord GOD:
　I will soon lift up my hand to the
　　　nations,
　　and raise my signal to the peoples;
　and they shall bring your sons in their
　　　bosom,
　　and your daughters shall be carried
　　　on their shoulders.
23 Kings shall be your foster fathers,
　　and their queens your nursing
　　　mothers.
　With their faces to the ground they
　　　shall bow down to you,
　　and lick the dust of your feet.
　Then you will know that I am the
　　　LORD;
　　those who wait for me shall not be
　　　put to shame.

24 Can the prey be taken from the
　　　mighty,
　　or the captives of a tyrant[j] be
　　　rescued?
25 But thus says the LORD:
　Even the captives of the mighty shall
　　　be taken,
　　and the prey of the tyrant be
　　　rescued;
　for I will contend with those who
　　　contend with you,

---

[h] Q Ms: MT *Sinim*　　[i] Or *Your children come swiftly;
your destroyers*　　[j] Q Ms Syr Vg: MT *of a righteous
person*

and I will save your children.
26 I will make your oppressors eat their
own flesh,
and they shall be drunk with their
own blood as with wine.
Then all flesh shall know
that I am the LORD your Savior,
and your Redeemer, the Mighty One
of Jacob.

50

Thus says the LORD:
Where is your mother's bill of
divorce
with which I put her away?
Or which of my creditors is it
to whom I have sold you?
No, because of your sins you were
sold,
and for your transgressions your
mother was put away.
2 Why was no one there when I came?
Why did no one answer when I
called?
Is my hand shortened, that it cannot
redeem?
Or have I no power to deliver?
By my rebuke I dry up the sea,
I make the rivers a desert;
their fish stink for lack of water,
and die of thirst.*k*
3 I clothe the heavens with blackness,
and make sackcloth their covering.

The Servant's Humiliation
and Vindication

4 The Lord GOD has given me
the tongue of a teacher,*l*
that I may know how to sustain
the weary with a word.
Morning by morning he wakens—
wakens my ear
to listen as those who are taught.
5 The Lord GOD has opened my ear,
and I was not rebellious,
I did not turn backward.
6 I gave my back to those who struck
me,
and my cheeks to those who pulled
out the beard;

I did not hide my face
from insult and spitting.

7 The Lord GOD helps me;
therefore I have not been disgraced;
therefore I have set my face like flint,
and I know that I shall not be put to
shame;
8 he who vindicates me is near.
Who will contend with me?
Let us stand up together.
Who are my adversaries?
Let them confront me.
9 It is the Lord GOD who helps me;
who will declare me guilty?
All of them will wear out like a
garment;
the moth will eat them up.

10 Who among you fears the LORD
and obeys the voice of his servant,
who walks in darkness
and has no light,
yet trusts in the name of the LORD
and relies upon his God?
11 But all of you are kindlers of fire,
lighters of firebrands.*m*
Walk in the flame of your fire,
and among the brands that you have
kindled!
This is what you shall have from my
hand:
you shall lie down in torment.

Blessings in Store
for God's People

51

Listen to me, you that pursue
righteousness,
you that seek the LORD.
Look to the rock from which you were
hewn,
and to the quarry from which you
were dug.
2 Look to Abraham your father
and to Sarah who bore you;

---

k Or *die on the thirsty ground*   *l* Cn: Heb *of those
who are taught*   *m* Syr: Heb *you gird yourselves with
firebrands*

for he was but one when I called him,
but I blessed him and made him
many.

3 For the LORD will comfort Zion;
he will comfort all her waste places,
and will make her wilderness like
Eden,
her desert like the garden of the
LORD;
joy and gladness will be found in her,
thanksgiving and the voice of song.

4 Listen to me, my people,
and give heed to me, my nation;
for a teaching will go out from me,
and my justice for a light to the
peoples.
5 I will bring near my deliverance swiftly,
my salvation has gone out
and my arms will rule the peoples;
the coastlands wait for me,
and for my arm they hope.
6 Lift up your eyes to the heavens,
and look at the earth beneath;
for the heavens will vanish like smoke,
the earth will wear out like a
garment,
and those who live on it will die like
gnats;[n]
but my salvation will be forever,
and my deliverance will never be
ended.

7 Listen to me, you who know
righteousness,
you people who have my teaching
in your hearts;
do not fear the reproach of others,
and do not be dismayed when they
revile you.
8 For the moth will eat them up like a
garment,
and the worm will eat them like
wool;
but my deliverance will be forever,
and my salvation to all generations.

9 Awake, awake, put on strength,
O arm of the LORD!

Awake, as in days of old,
the generations of long ago!
Was it not you who cut Rā′hab in
pieces,
who pierced the dragon?
10 Was it not you who dried up the sea,
the waters of the great deep;
who made the depths of the sea a way
for the redeemed to cross over?
11 So the ransomed of the LORD shall
return,
and come to Zion with singing;
everlasting joy shall be upon their
heads;
they shall obtain joy and gladness,
and sorrow and sighing shall flee
away.

12 I, I am he who comforts you;
why then are you afraid of a mere
mortal who must die,
a human being who fades like grass?
13 You have forgotten the LORD, your
Maker,
who stretched out the heavens
and laid the foundations of the
earth.
You fear continually all day long
because of the fury of the oppressor,
who is bent on destruction.
But where is the fury of the
oppressor?
14 The oppressed shall speedily be
released;
they shall not die and go down to
the Pit,
nor shall they lack bread.
15 For I am the LORD your God,
who stirs up the sea so that its
waves roar—
the LORD of hosts is his name.
16 I have put my words in your mouth,
and hidden you in the shadow of
my hand,
stretching out[o] the heavens
and laying the foundations of the
earth,

---

[n] Or *in like manner*   [o] Syr: Heb *planting*

> "How beautiful upon the mountains are the feet of the messenger who announces peace, who brings good news, who announces salvation, who says to Zion, 'Your God reigns.'" Isaiah 52:7

and saying to Zion, "You are my people."

17 Rouse yourself, rouse yourself!
  Stand up, O Jerusalem,
you who have drunk at the hand of the LORD
  the cup of his wrath,
who have drunk to the dregs
  the bowl of staggering.
18 There is no one to guide her
  among all the children she has borne;
there is no one to take her by the hand
  among all the children she has brought up.
19 These two things have befallen you
  —who will grieve with you?—
devastation and destruction, famine and sword—
  who will comfort you?ᵖ
20 Your children have fainted,
  they lie at the head of every street
  like an antelope in a net;
they are full of the wrath of the LORD,
  the rebuke of your God.

21 Therefore hear this, you who are wounded,�q
  who are drunk, but not with wine:
22 Thus says your Sovereign, the LORD,
  your God who pleads the cause of his people:
See, I have taken from your hand the cup of staggering;
  you shall drink no more
  from the bowl of my wrath.
23 And I will put it into the hand of your tormentors,
  who have said to you,
  "Bow down, that we may walk on you";

and you have made your back like the ground
  and like the street for them to walk on.

Let Zion Rejoice

52 Awake, awake,
  put on your strength, O Zion!
Put on your beautiful garments,
  O Jerusalem, the holy city;
for the uncircumcised and the unclean
  shall enter you no more.
2 Shake yourself from the dust, rise up,
  O captiveʳ Jerusalem;
loose the bonds from your neck,
  O captive daughter Zion!

3 For thus says the LORD: You were sold for nothing, and you shall be redeemed without money. 4For thus says the Lord GOD: Long ago, my people went down into Egypt to reside there as aliens; the Assyrian, too, has oppressed them without cause. 5Now therefore what am I doing here, says the LORD, seeing that my people are taken away without cause? Their rulers howl, says the LORD, and continually, all day long, my name is despised. 6Therefore my people shall know my name; therefore in that day they shall know that it is I who speak; here am I.

7 How beautiful upon the mountains
  are the feet of the messenger who announces peace,
who brings good news,
  who announces salvation,
  who says to Zion, "Your God reigns."
8 Listen! Your sentinels lift up their voices,
  together they sing for joy;
for in plain sight they see
  the return of the LORD to Zion.
9 Break forth together into singing,
  you ruins of Jerusalem;
for the LORD has comforted his people,
  he has redeemed Jerusalem.

ᵖ Q Ms Gk Syr Vg: MT *how may I comfort you?*
q Or *humbled* ʳ Cn: Heb *rise up, sit*

10 The LORD has bared his holy arm
    before the eyes of all the nations;
and all the ends of the earth shall see
    the salvation of our God.

11 Depart, depart, go out from there!
    Touch no unclean thing;
go out from the midst of it, purify
      yourselves,
    you who carry the vessels of the
      LORD.
12 For you shall not go out in haste,
    and you shall not go in flight;
for the LORD will go before you,
    and the God of Israel will be your
      rear guard.

The Suffering Servant

13 See, my servant shall prosper;
    he shall be exalted and lifted up,
    and shall be very high.
14 Just as there were many who were
      astonished at him[s]
    —so marred was his appearance,
      beyond human semblance,
    and his form beyond that of
      mortals—
15 so he shall startle[t] many nations;
    kings shall shut their mouths
      because of him;
for that which had not been told them
      they shall see,
    and that which they had not heard
      they shall contemplate.

53

Who has believed what we have
      heard?
    And to whom has the arm of the
      LORD been revealed?
2 For he grew up before him like a
      young plant,
    and like a root out of dry ground;
he had no form or majesty that we
      should look at him,
    nothing in his appearance that we
      should desire him.
3 He was despised and rejected by
      others;
    a man of suffering[u] and acquainted
      with infirmity;

The book of Isaiah has four "Servant Songs." You can find these songs in chapters 42, 49, 50, and 53. Christians believe that chapter 53 tells of the coming of Jesus Christ, who would suffer for us so that we could be saved.

    and as one from whom others hide
      their faces[v]
    he was despised, and we held him
      of no account.

4 Surely he has borne our infirmities
    and carried our diseases;
yet we accounted him stricken,
    struck down by God, and afflicted.
5 But he was wounded for our
      transgressions,
    crushed for our iniquities;
upon him was the punishment that
      made us whole,
    and by his bruises we are healed.
6 All we like sheep have gone astray;
    we have all turned to our own way,
and the LORD has laid on him
    the iniquity of us all.

7 He was oppressed, and he was
      afflicted,
    yet he did not open his mouth;
like a lamb that is led to the slaughter,
    and like a sheep that before its
      shearers is silent,
    so he did not open his mouth.
8 By a perversion of justice he was taken
      away.
    Who could have imagined his
      future?
For he was cut off from the land of the
      living,
    stricken for the transgression of my
      people.

[s] Syr Tg: Heb *you*   [t] Meaning of Heb uncertain
[u] Or *a man of sorrows*   [v] Or *as one who hides his face from us*

9 They made his grave with the wicked
and his tomb[w] with the rich,[x]
although he had done no violence,
and there was no deceit in his
mouth.

10 Yet it was the will of the LORD to crush
him with pain.[y]
When you make his life an offering for
sin,[z]
he shall see his offspring, and shall
prolong his days;
through him the will of the LORD shall
prosper.
11   Out of his anguish he shall see
light;[a]
he shall find satisfaction through his
knowledge.
The righteous one,[b] my servant,
shall make many righteous,
and he shall bear their iniquities.
12 Therefore I will allot him a portion
with the great,
and he shall divide the spoil with
the strong;
because he poured out himself to
death,
and was numbered with the
transgressors;
yet he bore the sin of many,
and made intercession for the
transgressors.

The Eternal Covenant of Peace

54 Sing, O barren one who did not
bear; burst into song and
shout,
you who have not been in labor!
For the children of the desolate
woman will be more
than the children of her that is
married, says the LORD.
2 Enlarge the site of your tent,
and let the curtains of your
habitations be stretched out;
do not hold back; lengthen your cords
and strengthen your stakes.
3 For you will spread out to the right
and to the left,

and your descendants will possess
the nations
and will settle the desolate towns.

4 Do not fear, for you will not be
ashamed;
do not be discouraged, for you will
not suffer disgrace;
for you will forget the shame of your
youth,
and the disgrace of your
widowhood you will remember
no more.
5 For your Maker is your husband,
the LORD of hosts is his name;
the Holy One of Israel is your
Redeemer,
the God of the whole earth he is
called.
6 For the LORD has called you
like a wife forsaken and grieved in
spirit,
like the wife of a man's youth when
she is cast off,
says your God.
7 For a brief moment I abandoned you,
but with great compassion I will
gather you.
8 In overflowing wrath for a moment
I hid my face from you,
but with everlasting love I will have
compassion on you,
says the LORD, your Redeemer.

9 This is like the days of Noah to me:
Just as I swore that the waters of
Noah
would never again go over the earth,
so I have sworn that I will not be
angry with you
and will not rebuke you.
10 For the mountains may depart
and the hills be removed,
but my steadfast love shall not depart
from you,

<hr>

[w] Q Ms: MT *and in his death*   [x] Cn: Heb *with a rich person*   [y] Or *by disease*; meaning of Heb uncertain
[z] Meaning of Heb uncertain   [a] Q Mss: MT lacks *light*   [b] Or *and he shall find satisfaction. Through his knowledge, the righteous one*

and my covenant of peace shall not
　　be removed,
　says the LORD, who has compassion
　　on you.

11 O afflicted one, storm-tossed, and not
　　comforted,
　I am about to set your stones in
　　antimony,
　and lay your foundations with
　　sapphires.ᶜ
12 I will make your pinnacles of rubies,
　　your gates of jewels,
　and all your wall of precious stones.
13 All your children shall be taught by the
　　LORD,
　and great shall be the prosperity of
　　your children.
14 In righteousness you shall be
　　established;
　you shall be far from oppression, for
　　you shall not fear;
　and from terror, for it shall not come
　　near you.
15 If anyone stirs up strife,
　　it is not from me;
　whoever stirs up strife with you
　　shall fall because of you.
16 See it is I who have created the smith
　　who blows the fire of coals,
　　and produces a weapon fit for its
　　purpose;
　I have also created the ravager to
　　destroy.
17 　No weapon that is fashioned against
　　you shall prosper,
　　and you shall confute every tongue
　　that rises against you in
　　judgment.
　This is the heritage of the servants of
　　the LORD
　and their vindication from me, says
　　the LORD.

An Invitation to Abundant Life

55 Ho, everyone who thirsts,
　　come to the waters;
and you that have no money,
　come, buy and eat!

Come, buy wine and milk
　without money and without price.
2 Why do you spend your money for
　　that which is not bread,
　and your labor for that which does
　　not satisfy?
　Listen carefully to me, and eat what is
　　good,
　and delight yourselves in rich food.
3 Incline your ear, and come to me;
　　listen, so that you may live.
　I will make with you an everlasting
　　covenant,
　　my steadfast, sure love for David.
4 See, I made him a witness to the
　　peoples,
　a leader and commander for the
　　peoples.
5 See, you shall call nations that you do
　　not know,
　and nations that do not know you
　　shall run to you,
　because of the LORD your God, the
　　Holy One of Israel,
　for he has glorified you.

6 Seek the LORD while he may be found,
　　call upon him while he is near;
7 let the wicked forsake their way,
　　and the unrighteous their thoughts;
　let them return to the LORD, that he
　　may have mercy on them,
　and to our God, for he will
　　abundantly pardon.
8 For my thoughts are not your
　　thoughts,
　nor are your ways my ways, says the
　　LORD.
9 For as the heavens are higher than the
　　earth,
　so are my ways higher than your ways
　and my thoughts than your
　　thoughts.

10 For as the rain and the snow come
　　down from heaven,
　and do not return there until they
　　have watered the earth,

ᶜ Or lapis lazuli

"For you shall go out in joy, and be led back in peace; the mountains and the hills before you shall burst into song, and all the trees of the field shall clap their hands." Isaiah 55:12

making it bring forth and sprout,
    giving seed to the sower and bread
        to the eater,
11 so shall my word be that goes out from
        my mouth;
    it shall not return to me empty,
but it shall accomplish that which I
        purpose,
    and succeed in the thing for which I
        sent it.

12 For you shall go out in joy,
    and be led back in peace;
the mountains and the hills before you
    shall burst into song,
    and all the trees of the field shall
        clap their hands.
13 Instead of the thorn shall come up the
        cypress;
    instead of the brier shall come up
        the myrtle;
and it shall be to the LORD for a
        memorial,
    for an everlasting sign that shall not
        be cut off.

The Covenant Extended to All Who Obey

56 Thus says the LORD:
    Maintain justice, and do what is
        right,
for soon my salvation will come,
    and my deliverance be revealed.

2 Happy is the mortal who does this,
    the one who holds it fast,
who keeps the sabbath, not profaning
        it,
    and refrains from doing any evil.

3 Do not let the foreigner joined to the
        LORD say,

"The LORD will surely separate me
    from his people";
and do not let the eunuch say,
    "I am just a dry tree."
4 For thus says the LORD:
To the eunuchs who keep my
        sabbaths,
    who choose the things that please me
    and hold fast my covenant,
5 I will give, in my house and within my
        walls,
    a monument and a name
    better than sons and daughters;
I will give them an everlasting name
    that shall not be cut off.

6 And the foreigners who join
        themselves to the LORD,
    to minister to him, to love the name
        of the LORD,
    and to be his servants,
all who keep the sabbath, and do not
        profane it,
    and hold fast my covenant—
7 these I will bring to my holy
        mountain,
    and make them joyful in my house
        of prayer;
their burnt offerings and their sacrifices
    will be accepted on my altar;
for my house shall be called a house of
        prayer
    for all peoples.
8 Thus says the Lord GOD,
    who gathers the outcasts of Israel,
I will gather others to them
    besides those already gathered.[d]

The Corruption of Israel's Rulers
9 All you wild animals,
    all you wild animals in the forest,
        come to devour!
10 Israel's[e] sentinels are blind,
    they are all without knowledge;
they are all silent dogs
    that cannot bark;
dreaming, lying down,
    loving to slumber.

[d] Heb *besides his gathered ones*   [e] Heb *His*

¹¹ The dogs have a mighty appetite;
  they never have enough.
The shepherds also have no
    understanding;
  they have all turned to their own
    way,
  to their own gain, one and all.
¹² "Come," they say, "let us[f] get wine;
  let us fill ourselves with strong
    drink.
And tomorrow will be like today,
  great beyond measure."

The word "devout" in the Hebrew Scriptures means "righteous," which means being free from wrong or sin.

Israel's Futile Idolatry

57 The righteous perish,
    and no one takes it to heart;
the devout are taken away,
  while no one understands.
For the righteous are taken away from
    calamity,
²   and they enter into peace;
those who walk uprightly
  will rest on their couches.
³ But as for you, come here,
  you children of a sorceress,
  you offspring of an adulterer and a
    whore.[g]
⁴ Whom are you mocking?
  Against whom do you open your
    mouth wide
  and stick out your tongue?
Are you not children of transgression,
  the offspring of deceit—
⁵ you that burn with lust among the oaks,
  under every green tree;
you that slaughter your children in the
    valleys,
  under the clefts of the rocks?
⁶ Among the smooth stones of the valley
  is your portion;
  they, they, are your lot;

to them you have poured out a drink
    offering,
  you have brought a grain offering.
  Shall I be appeased for these things?
⁷ Upon a high and lofty mountain
  you have set your bed,
  and there you went up to offer
    sacrifice.
⁸ Behind the door and the doorpost
  you have set up your symbol;
for, in deserting me,[h] you have
    uncovered your bed,
  you have gone up to it,
  you have made it wide;
and you have made a bargain for
    yourself with them,
  you have loved their bed,
  you have gazed on their nakedness.[i]
⁹ You journeyed to Mō′lech[j] with oil,
  and multiplied your perfumes;
you sent your envoys far away,
  and sent down even to Shē′ōl.
¹⁰ You grew weary from your many
    wanderings,
  but you did not say, "It is useless."
You found your desire rekindled,
  and so you did not weaken.

¹¹ Whom did you dread and fear
  so that you lied,
and did not remember me
  or give me a thought?
Have I not kept silent and closed my
    eyes,[k]
  and so you do not fear me?
¹² I will concede your righteousness and
    your works,
  but they will not help you.
¹³ When you cry out, let your collection
    of idols deliver you!
  The wind will carry them off,
  a breath will take them away.
But whoever takes refuge in me shall
    possess the land
  and inherit my holy mountain.

---

[f] Q Ms Syr Vg Tg: MT *me* [g] Heb *an adulterer and
she plays the whore* [h] Meaning of Heb uncertain
[i] Or *their phallus*; Heb *the hand* [j] Or *the king*
[k] Gk Vg: Heb *silent even for a long time*

A Promise of Help and Healing

14 It shall be said,
"Build up, build up, prepare the way,
 remove every obstruction from my
 people's way."
15 For thus says the high and lofty one
 who inhabits eternity, whose name
 is Holy:
I dwell in the high and holy place,
 and also with those who are contrite
 and humble in spirit,
to revive the spirit of the humble,
 and to revive the heart of the
 contrite.
16 For I will not continually accuse,
 nor will I always be angry;
for then the spirits would grow faint
 before me,
 even the souls that I have made.
17 Because of their wicked covetousness I
 was angry;
 I struck them, I hid and was angry;
 but they kept turning back to their
 own ways.
18 I have seen their ways, but I will heal
 them;
 I will lead them and repay them
 with comfort,
 creating for their mourners the fruit
 of the lips.[l]
19 Peace, peace, to the far and the near,
 says the LORD;
 and I will heal them.
20 But the wicked are like the tossing sea
 that cannot keep still;
 its waters toss up mire and mud.
21 There is no peace, says my God, for
 the wicked.

False and True Worship

58 Shout out, do not hold back!
 Lift up your voice like a trumpet!
Announce to my people their
 rebellion,
 to the house of Jacob their sins.
2 Yet day after day they seek me
 and delight to know my ways,
as if they were a nation that practiced
 righteousness

The prophets, especially Isaiah and Jeremiah, used the term "backsliding" to describe the people's rejection of and disobedience to God. The word means "sliding back from" or "turning away from" what they knew was right.

and did not forsake the ordinance of
 their God;
they ask of me righteous judgments,
 they delight to draw near to God.
3 "Why do we fast, but you do not see?
 Why humble ourselves, but you do
 not notice?"
Look, you serve your own interest on
 your fast day,
 and oppress all your workers.
4 Look, you fast only to quarrel and to
 fight
 and to strike with a wicked fist.
Such fasting as you do today
 will not make your voice heard on
 high.
5 Is such the fast that I choose,
 a day to humble oneself?
Is it to bow down the head like a
 bulrush,
 and to lie in sackcloth and ashes?
Will you call this a fast,
 a day acceptable to the LORD?

6 Is not this the fast that I choose:
 to loose the bonds of injustice,
 to undo the thongs of the yoke,
to let the oppressed go free,
 and to break every yoke?
7 Is it not to share your bread with the
 hungry,
 and bring the homeless poor into
 your house;
when you see the naked, to cover
 them,

l Meaning of Heb uncertain

and not to hide yourself from your
own kin?
⁸ Then your light shall break forth like
the dawn,
and your healing shall spring up
quickly;
your vindicator[m] shall go before you,
the glory of the LORD shall be your
rear guard.
⁹ Then you shall call, and the LORD will
answer;
you shall cry for help, and he will
say, Here I am.

If you remove the yoke from among
you,
the pointing of the finger, the
speaking of evil,
¹⁰ if you offer your food to the hungry
and satisfy the needs of the afflicted,
then your light shall rise in the darkness
and your gloom be like the noonday.
¹¹ The LORD will guide you continually,
and satisfy your needs in parched
places,
and make your bones strong;
and you shall be like a watered garden,
like a spring of water,
whose waters never fail.
¹² Your ancient ruins shall be rebuilt;
you shall raise up the foundations of
many generations;
you shall be called the repairer of the
breach,
the restorer of streets to live in.

¹³ If you refrain from trampling the
sabbath,
from pursuing your own interests
on my holy day;
if you call the sabbath a delight
and the holy day of the LORD
honorable;
if you honor it, not going your own
ways,
serving your own interests, or
pursuing your own affairs;[n]
¹⁴ then you shall take delight in the
LORD,

and I will make you ride upon the
heights of the earth;
I will feed you with the heritage of
your ancestor Jacob,
for the mouth of the LORD has
spoken.

Injustice and Oppression to Be Punished

59 See, the LORD's hand is not too
short to save,
nor his ear too dull to hear.
² Rather, your iniquities have been
barriers
between you and your God,
and your sins have hidden his face
from you
so that he does not hear.
³ For your hands are defiled with blood,
and your fingers with iniquity;
your lips have spoken lies,
your tongue mutters wickedness.
⁴ No one brings suit justly,
no one goes to law honestly;
they rely on empty pleas, they speak lies,
conceiving mischief and begetting
iniquity.
⁵ They hatch adders' eggs,
and weave the spider's web;
whoever eats their eggs dies,
and the crushed egg hatches out a
viper.
⁶ Their webs cannot serve as clothing;
they cannot cover themselves with
what they make.
Their works are works of iniquity,
and deeds of violence are in their
hands.
⁷ Their feet run to evil,
and they rush to shed innocent blood;
their thoughts are thoughts of iniquity,
desolation and destruction are in
their highways.
⁸ The way of peace they do not know,
and there is no justice in their paths.
Their roads they have made crooked;
no one who walks in them knows
peace.

---

[m] Or *vindication*   [n] Heb *or speaking words*

⁹ Therefore justice is far from us,
  and righteousness does not reach us;
we wait for light, and lo! there is
    darkness;
  and for brightness, but we walk in
    gloom.
¹⁰ We grope like the blind along a wall,
  groping like those who have no
    eyes;
we stumble at noon as in the twilight,
  among the vigorous⁰ as though we
    were dead.
¹¹ We all growl like bears;
  like doves we moan mournfully.
We wait for justice, but there is none;
  for salvation, but it is far from us.
¹² For our transgressions before you are
    many,
  and our sins testify against us.
Our transgressions indeed are with us,
  and we know our iniquities:
¹³ transgressing, and denying the LORD,
  and turning away from following
    our God,
talking oppression and revolt,
  conceiving lying words and uttering
    them from the heart.
¹⁴ Justice is turned back,
  and righteousness stands at a
    distance;
for truth stumbles in the public square,
  and uprightness cannot enter.
¹⁵ Truth is lacking,
  and whoever turns from evil is
    despoiled.

The LORD saw it, and it displeased him
  that there was no justice.
¹⁶ He saw that there was no one,
  and was appalled that there was no
    one to intervene;
so his own arm brought him victory,
  and his righteousness upheld him.
¹⁷ He put on righteousness like a
    breastplate,
  and a helmet of salvation on his
    head;
he put on garments of vengeance for
    clothing,

and wrapped himself in fury as in a
    mantle.
¹⁸ According to their deeds, so will he
    repay;
  wrath to his adversaries, requital to
    his enemies;
  to the coastlands he will render
    requital.
¹⁹ So those in the west shall fear the
    name of the LORD,
  and those in the east, his glory;
for he will come like a pent-up stream
  that the wind of the LORD drives on.

²⁰ And he will come to Zion as
    Redeemer,
  to those in Jacob who turn from
    transgression, says the LORD.
²¹And as for me, this is my covenant with
them, says the LORD: my spirit that is upon
you, and my words that I have put in your
mouth, shall not depart out of your
mouth, or out of the mouths of your children, or out of the mouths of your children's children, says the LORD, from now
on and forever.

The Ingathering of the Dispersed

60 Arise, shine; for your light has
    come, and the glory of the
    LORD has risen upon you.
² For darkness shall cover the earth,
  and thick darkness the peoples;
but the LORD will arise upon you,
  and his glory will appear over you.
³ Nations shall come to your light,
  and kings to the brightness of your
    dawn.

⁴ Lift up your eyes and look around;
  they all gather together, they come
    to you;
your sons shall come from far away,
  and your daughters shall be carried
    on their nurses' arms.
⁵ Then you shall see and be radiant;
  your heart shall thrill and rejoice,ᵖ
because the abundance of the sea shall
    be brought to you,

⁰ Meaning of Heb uncertain   ᵖ Heb *be enlarged*

the wealth of the nations shall come
to you.
6 A multitude of camels shall cover you,
the young camels of Mid·i·an and
Eʹphah;
all those from Sheʹba shall come.
They shall bring gold and
frankincense,
and shall proclaim the praise of the
LORD.
7 All the flocks of Keʹdar shall be
gathered to you,
the rams of Ne·baʹi·oth shall
minister to you;
they shall be acceptable on my altar,
and I will glorify my glorious house.

8 Who are these that fly like a cloud,
and like doves to their windows?
9 For the coastlands shall wait for me,
the ships of Tarʹshish first,
to bring your children from far away,
their silver and gold with them,
for the name of the LORD your God,
and for the Holy One of Israel,
because he has glorified you.
10 Foreigners shall build up your walls,
and their kings shall minister to you;
for in my wrath I struck you down,
but in my favor I have had mercy on
you.
11 Your gates shall always be open;
day and night they shall not be shut,
so that nations shall bring you their
wealth,
with their kings led in procession.
12 For the nation and kingdom
that will not serve you shall perish;
those nations shall be utterly laid
waste.
13 The glory of Lebanon shall come to
you,
the cypress, the plane, and the pine,
to beautify the place of my sanctuary;
and I will glorify where my feet rest.
14 The descendants of those who
oppressed you
shall come bending low to you,
and all who despised you

shall bow down at your feet;
they shall call you the City of the
LORD,
the Zion of the Holy One of Israel.
15 Whereas you have been forsaken and
hated,
with no one passing through,
I will make you majestic forever,
a joy from age to age.
16 You shall suck the milk of nations,
you shall suck the breasts of kings;
and you shall know that I, the LORD,
am your Savior
and your Redeemer, the Mighty One
of Jacob.

17 Instead of bronze I will bring gold,
instead of iron I will bring silver;
instead of wood, bronze,
instead of stones, iron.
I will appoint Peace as your overseer
and Righteousness as your taskmaster.
18 Violence shall no more be heard in
your land,
devastation or destruction within
your borders;
you shall call your walls Salvation,
and your gates Praise.

God the Glory of Zion

19 The sun shall no longer be
your light by day,
nor for brightness shall the moon
give light to you by night;[q]
but the LORD will be your everlasting
light,
and your God will be your glory.
20 Your sun shall no more go down,
or your moon withdraw itself;
for the LORD will be your everlasting
light,
and your days of mourning shall be
ended.
21 Your people shall all be righteous;
they shall possess the land forever.
They are the shoot that I planted, the
work of my hands,
so that I might be glorified.

[q] Q Ms Gk Old Latin Tg: MT lacks *by night*

22 The least of them shall become a clan,
and the smallest one a mighty
nation;
I am the LORD;
in its time I will accomplish it
quickly.

The Good News of Deliverance

61 The spirit of the Lord GOD is
upon me, because the LORD
has anointed me;
he has sent me to bring good news to
the oppressed,
to bind up the brokenhearted,
to proclaim liberty to the captives,
and release to the prisoners;
2 to proclaim the year of the LORD's
favor,
and the day of vengeance of our
God;
to comfort all who mourn;
3 to provide for those who mourn in
Zion—
to give them a garland instead of
ashes,
the oil of gladness instead of mourning,
the mantle of praise instead of a
faint spirit.
They will be called oaks of
righteousness,
the planting of the LORD, to display
his glory.
4 They shall build up the ancient ruins,
they shall raise up the former
devastations;
they shall repair the ruined cities,
the devastations of many
generations.

5 Strangers shall stand and feed your
flocks,
foreigners shall till your land and
dress your vines;
6 but you shall be called priests of the
LORD,
you shall be named ministers of our
God;
you shall enjoy the wealth of the
nations,

and in their riches you shall glory.
7 Because their^r shame was double,
and dishonor was proclaimed as
their lot,
therefore they shall possess a double
portion;
everlasting joy shall be theirs.

8 For I the LORD love justice,
I hate robbery and wrongdoing;^s
I will faithfully give them their
recompense,
and I will make an everlasting
covenant with them.
9 Their descendants shall be known
among the nations,
and their offspring among the
peoples;
all who see them shall acknowledge
that they are a people whom the
LORD has blessed.
10 I will greatly rejoice in the LORD,
my whole being shall exult in my
God;
for he has clothed me with the
garments of salvation,
he has covered me with the robe of
righteousness,
as a bridegroom decks himself with a
garland,
and as a bride adorns herself with
her jewels.
11 For as the earth brings forth its shoots,
and as a garden causes what is sown
in it to spring up,
so the Lord GOD will cause
righteousness and praise
to spring up before all the nations.

The Vindication and Salvation of Zion

62 For Zion's sake I will not keep
silent, and for Jerusalem's
sake I will not rest,
until her vindication shines out like
the dawn,
and her salvation like a burning
torch.

---

^r Heb *your*   ^s Or *robbery with a burnt offering*

2 The nations shall see your vindication,
 and all the kings your glory;
and you shall be called by a new name
 that the mouth of the LORD will give.
3 You shall be a crown of beauty in the
 hand of the LORD,
and a royal diadem in the hand of
 your God.
4 You shall no more be termed
 Forsaken,[t]
and your land shall no more be
 termed Desolate;[u]
but you shall be called My Delight Is
 in Her,[v]
and your land Married;[w]
for the LORD delights in you,
 and your land shall be married.
5 For as a young man marries a young
 woman,
so shall your builder[x] marry you,
and as the bridegroom rejoices over
 the bride,
so shall your God rejoice over you.
6 Upon your walls, O Jerusalem,
 I have posted sentinels;
all day and all night
 they shall never be silent.
You who remind the LORD,
 take no rest,
7 and give him no rest
 until he establishes Jerusalem
and makes it renowned throughout
 the earth.
8 The LORD has sworn by his right hand
 and by his mighty arm:
I will not again give your grain
 to be food for your enemies,
and foreigners shall not drink the wine
 for which you have labored;
9 but those who garner it shall eat it
 and praise the LORD,
and those who gather it shall drink it
 in my holy courts.

10 Go through, go through the gates,
 prepare the way for the people;
build up, build up the highway,
 clear it of stones,
lift up an ensign over the peoples.

11 The LORD has proclaimed
 to the end of the earth:
Say to daughter Zion,
 "See, your salvation comes;
his reward is with him,
 and his recompense before him."
12 They shall be called, "The Holy People,
 The Redeemed of the LORD";
and you shall be called, "Sought Out,
 A City Not Forsaken."

Vengeance on Edom

63 "Who is this that comes from
 E'dom, from Boz'rah in
 garments stained crimson?
Who is this so splendidly robed,
 marching in his great might?"

"It is I, announcing vindication,
 mighty to save."

2 "Why are your robes red,
 and your garments like theirs who
 tread the wine press?"

3 "I have trodden the wine press alone,
 and from the peoples no one was
 with me;
I trod them in my anger
 and trampled them in my wrath;
their juice spattered on my garments,
 and stained all my robes.
4 For the day of vengeance was in my
 heart,
and the year for my redeeming work
 had come.
5 I looked, but there was no helper;
 I stared, but there was no one to
 sustain me;
so my own arm brought me victory,
 and my wrath sustained me.
6 I trampled down peoples in my anger,
 I crushed them in my wrath,
and I poured out their lifeblood on
 the earth."

God's Mercy Remembered

7 I will recount the gracious deeds of the
 LORD,

[t] Heb Azubah   [u] Heb Shemamah   [v] Heb Hephzibah
[w] Heb Beulah   [x] Cn: Heb your sons

the praiseworthy acts of the Lord,
because of all that the Lord has done
for us,
and the great favor to the house of
Israel
that he has shown them according to
his mercy,
according to the abundance of his
steadfast love.
⁸ For he said, "Surely they are my
people,
children who will not deal falsely";
and he became their savior
⁹ in all their distress.
It was no messenger^y or angel
but his presence that saved them;^z
in his love and in his pity he redeemed
them;
he lifted them up and carried them
all the days of old.

¹⁰ But they rebelled
and grieved his holy spirit;
therefore he became their enemy;
he himself fought against them.
¹¹ Then they^a remembered the days of
old,
of Moses his servant.^b
Where is the one who brought them
up out of the sea
with the shepherds of his flock?
Where is the one who put within them
his holy spirit,
¹² who caused his glorious arm
to march at the right hand of Moses,
who divided the waters before them
to make for himself an everlasting
name,
¹³ who led them through the depths?
Like a horse in the desert,
they did not stumble.
¹⁴ Like cattle that go down into the valley,
the spirit of the Lord gave them rest.
Thus you led your people,
to make for yourself a glorious name.

A Prayer of Penitence

¹⁵ Look down from heaven and see,
from your holy and glorious
habitation.

Where are your zeal and your might?
The yearning of your heart and your
compassion?
They are withheld from me.
¹⁶ For you are our father,
though Abraham does not know us
and Israel does not acknowledge us;
you, O Lord, are our father;
our Redeemer from of old is your
name.
¹⁷ Why, O Lord, do you make us stray
from your ways
and harden our heart, so that we do
not fear you?
Turn back for the sake of your
servants,
for the sake of the tribes that are
your heritage.
¹⁸ Your holy people took possession for a
little while;
but now our adversaries have
trampled down your sanctuary.
¹⁹ We have long been like those whom
you do not rule,
like those not called by your name.

64 O that you would tear open the
heavens and come down,
so that the mountains would quake
at your presence—
²^c as when fire kindles brushwood
and the fire causes water to boil—
to make your name known to your
adversaries,
so that the nations might tremble at
your presence!
³ When you did awesome deeds that we
did not expect,
you came down, the mountains
quaked at your presence.
⁴ From ages past no one has heard,
no ear has perceived,
no eye has seen any God besides you,
who works for those who wait for
him.
⁵ You meet those who gladly do right,

---

^y Gk: Heb *anguish*   ^z Or *savior.* ⁹*In all their distress
he was distressed; the angel of his presence saved them;*
^a Heb *he*   ^b Cn: Heb *his people*   ^c Ch 64.1 in Heb

those who remember you in your
ways.
But you were angry, and we sinned;
because you hid yourself we
transgressed.[d]

6 We have all become like one who is
unclean,
and all our righteous deeds are like
a filthy cloth.
We all fade like a leaf,
and our iniquities, like the wind,
take us away.

7 There is no one who calls on your
name,
or attempts to take hold of you;
for you have hidden your face from us,
and have delivered[e] us into the hand
of our iniquity.

8 Yet, O LORD, you are our Father;
we are the clay, and you are our
potter;
we are all the work of your hand.

9 Do not be exceedingly angry, O LORD,
and do not remember iniquity
forever.
Now consider, we are all your people.

10 Your holy cities have become a
wilderness,
Zion has become a wilderness,
Jerusalem a desolation.

11 Our holy and beautiful house,
where our ancestors praised you,
has been burned by fire,
and all our pleasant places have
become ruins.

12 After all this, will you restrain yourself,
O LORD?
Will you keep silent, and punish us
so severely?

The Righteousness
of God's Judgment

65 I was ready to be sought out by
those who did not ask,
to be found by those who did not
seek me.
I said, "Here I am, here I am,"
to a nation that did not call on my
name.

2 I held out my hands all day long
to a rebellious people,
who walk in a way that is not good,
following their own devices;

3 a people who provoke me
to my face continually,
sacrificing in gardens
and offering incense on bricks;

4 who sit inside tombs,
and spend the night in secret places;
who eat swine's flesh,
with broth of abominable things in
their vessels;

5 who say, "Keep to yourself,
do not come near me, for I am too
holy for you."
These are a smoke in my nostrils,
a fire that burns all day long.

6 See, it is written before me:
I will not keep silent, but I will
repay;
I will indeed repay into their laps

7 their[f] iniquities and their[f] ancestors'
iniquities together, says the LORD;
because they offered incense on the
mountains
and reviled me on the hills,
I will measure into their laps
full payment for their actions.

8 Thus says the LORD:
As the wine is found in the cluster,
and they say, "Do not destroy it,
for there is a blessing in it,"
so I will do for my servants' sake,
and not destroy them all.

9 I will bring forth descendants[g] from
Jacob,
and from Judah inheritors[h] of my
mountains;
my chosen shall inherit it,
and my servants shall settle there.

10 Sharon shall become a pasture for
flocks,
and the Valley of A'chor a place for
herds to lie down,
for my people who have sought me.

---

[d] Meaning of Heb uncertain   [e] Gk Syr Old Latin
Tg: Heb *melted*   [f] Gk Syr: Heb *your*   [g] Or *a
descendant*   [h] Or *an inheritor*

11 But you who forsake the LORD,
   who forget my holy mountain,
who set a table for Fortune
   and fill cups of mixed wine for
      Destiny;
12 I will destine you to the sword,
   and all of you shall bow down to
      the slaughter;
because, when I called, you did not
   answer,
   when I spoke, you did not listen,
but you did what was evil in my sight,
   and chose what I did not delight in.
13 Therefore thus says the Lord GOD:
My servants shall eat,
   but you shall be hungry;
my servants shall drink,
   but you shall be thirsty;
my servants shall rejoice,
   but you shall be put to shame;
14 my servants shall sing for gladness of
      heart,
   but you shall cry out for pain of
      heart,
   and shall wail for anguish of spirit.
15 You shall leave your name to my
      chosen to use as a curse,
   and the Lord GOD will put you to
      death;
   but to his servants he will give a
      different name.
16 Then whoever invokes a blessing in
      the land
   shall bless by the God of faithfulness,
and whoever takes an oath in the land
   shall swear by the God of faithfulness;
because the former troubles are
      forgotten
   and are hidden from my sight.

The Glorious New Creation

17 For I am about to create new heavens
   and a new earth;
the former things shall not be
   remembered

or come to mind.
18 But be glad and rejoice forever
   in what I am creating;
for I am about to create Jerusalem as a
      joy,
   and its people as a delight.
19 I will rejoice in Jerusalem,
   and delight in my people;
no more shall the sound of weeping be
      heard in it,
   or the cry of distress.
20 No more shall there be in it
   an infant that lives but a few days,
   or an old person who does not live
      out a lifetime;
for one who dies at a hundred years
      will be considered a youth,
   and one who falls short of a
      hundred will be considered
      accursed.
21 They shall build houses and inhabit
      them;
   they shall plant vineyards and eat
      their fruit.
22 They shall not build and another
      inhabit;
   they shall not plant and another
      eat;
for like the days of a tree shall the days
      of my people be,
   and my chosen shall long enjoy the
      work of their hands.
23 They shall not labor in vain,
   or bear children for calamity;[i]
for they shall be offspring blessed by
      the LORD—
   and their descendants as well.
24 Before they call I will answer,
   while they are yet speaking I will
      hear.
25 The wolf and the lamb shall feed
      together,
   the lion shall eat straw like the ox;
   but the serpent—its food shall be
      dust!
They shall not hurt or destroy
   on all my holy mountain,
                    says the LORD.

**"Before they call I will
answer, while they are yet
speaking I will hear."**
Isaiah 65:24

i Or sudden terror

The Worship God Demands

66 Thus says the LORD:
Heaven is my throne
and the earth is my footstool;
what is the house that you would
build for me,
and what is my resting place?
² All these things my hand has made,
and so all these things are mine,ʲ
says the LORD.
But this is the one to whom I will look,
to the humble and contrite in spirit,
who trembles at my word.

³ Whoever slaughters an ox is like one
who kills a human being;
whoever sacrifices a lamb, like one
who breaks a dog's neck;
whoever presents a grain offering, like
one who offers swine's blood;ᵏ
whoever makes a memorial offering
of frankincense, like one who
blesses an idol.
These have chosen their own ways,
and in their abominations they take
delight;
⁴ I also will choose to mockˡ them,
and bring upon them what they
fear;
because, when I called, no one
answered,
when I spoke, they did not listen;
but they did what was evil in my
sight,
and chose what did not please me.

The Lord Vindicates Zion

⁵ Hear the word of the LORD,
you who tremble at his word:
Your own people who hate you
and reject you for my name's sake
have said, "Let the LORD be glorified,
so that we may see your joy";
but it is they who shall be put to
shame.

⁶ Listen, an uproar from the city!
A voice from the temple!
The voice of the LORD,
dealing retribution to his enemies!

⁷ Before she was in labor
she gave birth;
before her pain came upon her
she delivered a son.
⁸ Who has heard of such a thing?
Who has seen such things?
Shall a land be born in one day?
Shall a nation be delivered in one
moment?
Yet as soon as Zion was in labor
she delivered her children.
⁹ Shall I open the womb and not
deliver?
says the LORD;
shall I, the one who delivers, shut the
womb?
says your God.

¹⁰ Rejoice with Jerusalem, and be glad for
her,
all you who love her;
rejoice with her in joy,
all you who mourn over her—
¹¹ that you may nurse and be satisfied
from her consoling breast;
that you may drink deeply with delight
from her glorious bosom.

¹² For thus says the LORD:
I will extend prosperity to her like a
river,
and the wealth of the nations like an
overflowing stream;
and you shall nurse and be carried on
her arm,
and dandled on her knees.
¹³ As a mother comforts her child,
so I will comfort you;
you shall be comforted in Jerusalem.

The Reign and Indignation of God

¹⁴ You shall see, and your heart shall
rejoice;
your bodiesᵐ shall flourish like the
grass;
and it shall be known that the hand of
the LORD is with his servants,

ʲ Gk Syr: Heb *these things came to be*   ᵏ Meaning of
Heb uncertain   ˡ Or *to punish*   ᵐ Heb *bones*

and his indignation is against his
enemies.
[15] For the LORD will come in fire,
and his chariots like the whirlwind,
to pay back his anger in fury,
and his rebuke in flames of fire.
[16] For by fire will the LORD execute
judgment,
and by his sword, on all flesh;
and those slain by the LORD shall be
many.

17 Those who sanctify and purify
themselves to go into the gardens, following the one in the center, eating the flesh of
pigs, vermin, and rodents, shall come to an
end together, says the LORD.

18 For I know[n] their works and their
thoughts, and I am[o] coming to gather all
nations and tongues; and they shall come
and shall see my glory, [19]and I will set a
sign among them. From them I will send
survivors to the nations, to Tar′shish, Put,[p]
and Lud—which draw the bow—to Tu′bal
and Ja′van, to the coastlands far away that
have not heard of my fame or seen my
glory; and they shall declare my glory
among the nations. [20]They shall bring all
your kindred from all the nations as an
offering to the LORD, on horses, and in
chariots, and in litters, and on mules, and
on dromedaries, to my holy mountain
Jerusalem, says the LORD, just as the
Israelites bring a grain offering in a clean
vessel to the house of the LORD. [21]And I
will also take some of them as priests and
as Le′vites, says the LORD.

[22] For as the new heavens and the new
earth,
which I will make,
shall remain before me, says the LORD;
so shall your descendants and your
name remain.
[23] From new moon to new moon,
and from sabbath to sabbath,
all flesh shall come to worship before
me,
says the LORD.

24 And they shall go out and look at
the dead bodies of the people who have
rebelled against me; for their worm shall
not die, their fire shall not be quenched,
and they shall be an abhorrence to all flesh.

[n] Gk Syr: Heb lacks *know*   [o] Gk Syr Vg Tg: Heb *it is*
[p] Gk: Heb *Pul*

Jeremiah

The book of Jeremiah tells of the deeds and sermons of Jeremiah, one of the bravest prophets of Judah. He preached from 626 to 586 BC, during a period when Babylonia controlled Judah. In 621 BC he supported the reforms that began when King Josiah read some scrolls from Deuteronomy that had been found during repairs to the Temple.

Jeremiah taught that the Babylonian rule of Judah was caused by the sins of the people. Time after time, Jeremiah was put in prison or had to go into hiding because his message was so unpopular. Because Jeremiah's name was linked with the sad songs called Lamentations (the book of the Bible that follows this one), he is sometimes called the weeping prophet. The truth is that Jeremiah was hopeful about the future of the Hebrew people. Even while the Babylonian army threatened Jerusalem, Jeremiah bought some land to assure the people that he believed in the future of their nation.

Jeremiah taught that serving God is a personal matter and that each of us must take personal responsibility for serving God. Jeremiah looked forward to a new day when religion would be more than a set of outward rules to be kept. Religion must be deep within our hearts and lived out in our lives.

Jeremiah 38:1–13

"Now the word of the LORD came to me saying, 'Before I formed you in the womb I knew you, and before you were born I consecrated you; I appointed you a prophet to the nations.' Then I said, 'Ah, LORD GOD! Truly I do not know how to speak, for I am only a boy.' But the LORD said to me, 'Do not say, "I am only a boy"; for you shall go to all to whom I send you, and you shall speak whatever I command you.'"
Jeremiah 1:4–7

1 The words of Jer·e·mī´ah son of Hil·kī´ah, of the priests who were in An´a·thoth in the land of Benjamin, ²to whom the word of the LORD came in the days of King Jō·sī´ah son of Ā´mon of Judah, in the thirteenth year of his reign. ³It came also in the days of King Je·hoi´a·kim son of Jō·sī´ah of Judah, and until the end of the eleventh year of King Zed·e·kī´ah son of Jō·sī´ah of Judah, until the captivity of Jerusalem in the fifth month.

Jeremiah's Call and Commission

4 Now the word of the LORD came to me saying,
⁵ "Before I formed you in the womb I knew you,
and before you were born I consecrated you;
I appointed you a prophet to the nations."
⁶Then I said, "Ah, Lord GOD! Truly I do not know how to speak, for I am only a boy."
⁷But the LORD said to me,
"Do not say, 'I am only a boy';
for you shall go to all to whom I send you,
and you shall speak whatever I command you.
⁸ Do not be afraid of them,
for I am with you to deliver you,
says the LORD."
⁹Then the LORD put out his hand and touched my mouth; and the LORD said to me,
"Now I have put my words in your mouth.
¹⁰ See, today I appoint you over nations and over kingdoms,
to pluck up and to pull down,
to destroy and to overthrow,
to build and to plant."
11 The word of the LORD came to me, saying, "Jer·e·mī´ah, what do you see?" And I said, "I see a branch of an almond tree."ᵃ ¹²Then the LORD said to me, "You have seen well, for I am watchingᵇ over my word to perform it." ¹³The word of the LORD came to me a second time, saying, "What do you see?" And I said, "I see a boiling pot, tilted away from the north."

Jeremiah's hometown was Anathoth, a city in the land of the tribe of Benjamin. Anathoth was given to the Levites to serve as a priestly city.

14 Then the LORD said to me: Out of the north disaster shall break out on all the inhabitants of the land. ¹⁵For now I am calling all the tribes of the kingdoms of the north, says the LORD; and they shall come and all of them shall set their thrones at the entrance of the gates of Jerusalem, against all its surrounding walls and against all the cities of Judah. ¹⁶And I will utter my judgments against them, for all their wickedness in forsaking me; they have made offerings to other gods, and worshiped the works of their own hands. ¹⁷But you, gird up your loins; stand up and tell them everything that I command you. Do not break down before them, or I will break you before them. ¹⁸And I for my part have made you today a fortified city, an iron pillar, and a bronze wall, against the whole land—against the kings of Judah, its princes, its priests, and the people of the

ᵃ Heb *shaqed*   ᵇ Heb *shoqed*

land. [19]They will fight against you; but they shall not prevail against you, for I am with you, says the LORD, to deliver you.

God Pleads with Israel to Repent

2 The word of the LORD came to me, saying: [2]Go and proclaim in the hearing of Jerusalem, Thus says the LORD:

I remember the devotion of your
　　youth,
　your love as a bride,
how you followed me in the
　　wilderness,
　in a land not sown.
[3] Israel was holy to the LORD,
　the first fruits of his harvest.
All who ate of it were held guilty;
　disaster came upon them,
　　　　　　　　　says the LORD.

4 Hear the word of the LORD, O house of Jacob, and all the families of the house of Israel. [5]Thus says the LORD:

What wrong did your ancestors find in
　　me
　that they went far from me,
and went after worthless things, and
　　became worthless themselves?
[6] They did not say, "Where is the LORD
　who brought us up from the land of
　　Egypt,
who led us in the wilderness,
　in a land of deserts and pits,
in a land of drought and deep
　　darkness,
in a land that no one passes
　　through,
　where no one lives?"
[7] I brought you into a plentiful land
　to eat its fruits and its good things.
But when you entered you defiled my
　　land,
　and made my heritage an
　　abomination.
[8] The priests did not say, "Where is the
　　LORD?"
　Those who handle the law did not
　　know me;
　the rulers[c] transgressed against me;
　the prophets prophesied by Bā´al,

and went after things that do not
　profit.

[9] Therefore once more I accuse you,
　　says the LORD,
　and I accuse your children's
　　children.
[10] Cross to the coasts of Cyprus and look,
　send to Kē´dar and examine with
　　care;
　see if there has ever been such a
　　thing.
[11] Has a nation changed its gods,
　even though they are no gods?
But my people have changed their
　　glory
　for something that does not profit.
[12] Be appalled, O heavens, at this,
　be shocked, be utterly desolate,
　　　　　　　　　says the LORD,
[13] for my people have committed two
　　evils:
　they have forsaken me,
the fountain of living water,
　and dug out cisterns for themselves,
cracked cisterns
　that can hold no water.

[14] Is Israel a slave? Is he a homeborn
　　servant?
　Why then has he become plunder?
[15] The lions have roared against him,
　they have roared loudly.
They have made his land a waste;
　his cities are in ruins, without
　　inhabitant.
[16] Moreover, the people of Memphis and
　　Tah´pan·hēs
　have broken the crown of your
　　head.
[17] Have you not brought this upon
　　yourself
　by forsaking the LORD your God,
　while he led you in the way?
[18] What then do you gain by going to
　　Egypt,
　to drink the waters of the Nile?

---

[c] Heb *shepherds*

Or what do you gain by going to
Assyria,
to drink the waters of the
Euphrates?
¹⁹ Your wickedness will punish you,
and your apostasies will convict you.
Know and see that it is evil and bitter
for you to forsake the LORD your God;
the fear of me is not in you,
says the Lord GOD of hosts.

²⁰ For long ago you broke your yoke
and burst your bonds,
and you said, "I will not serve!"
On every high hill
and under every green tree
you sprawled and played the whore.
²¹ Yet I planted you as a choice vine,
from the purest stock.
How then did you turn degenerate
and become a wild vine?
²² Though you wash yourself with lye
and use much soap,
the stain of your guilt is still before
me,
says the Lord GOD.
²³ How can you say, "I am not defiled,
I have not gone after the Ba'als"?
Look at your way in the valley;
know what you have done—
a restive young camel interlacing her
tracks,
²⁴ a wild ass at home in the
wilderness,
in her heat sniffing the wind!
Who can restrain her lust?
None who seek her need weary
themselves;
in her month they will find her.
²⁵ Keep your feet from going unshod
and your throat from thirst.
But you said, "It is hopeless,
for I have loved strangers,
and after them I will go."

²⁶ As a thief is shamed when caught,
so the house of Israel shall be
shamed—
they, their kings, their officials,
their priests, and their prophets,

²⁷ who say to a tree, "You are my father,"
and to a stone, "You gave me birth."
For they have turned their backs to
me,
and not their faces.
But in the time of their trouble they
say,
"Come and save us!"
²⁸ But where are your gods
that you made for yourself?
Let them come, if they can save you,
in your time of trouble;
for you have as many gods
as you have towns, O Judah.

²⁹ Why do you complain against me?
You have all rebelled against me,
says the LORD.
³⁰ In vain I have struck down your
children;
they accepted no correction.
Your own sword devoured your
prophets
like a ravening lion.
³¹ And you, O generation, behold the
word of the LORD!^d
Have I been a wilderness to Israel,
or a land of thick darkness?
Why then do my people say, "We are
free,
we will come to you no more"?
³² Can a girl forget her ornaments,
or a bride her attire?
Yet my people have forgotten me,
days without number.

³³ How well you direct your course
to seek lovers!
So that even to wicked women
you have taught your ways.
³⁴ Also on your skirts is found
the lifeblood of the innocent poor,
though you did not catch them
breaking in.
Yet in spite of all these things^d
³⁵ you say, "I am innocent;
surely his anger has turned from
me."

^d Meaning of Heb uncertain

Now I am bringing you to judgment
  for saying, "I have not sinned."
[36] How lightly you gad about,
  changing your ways!
You shall be put to shame by Egypt
  as you were put to shame by
  Assyria.
[37] From there also you will come away
  with your hands on your head;
for the LORD has rejected those in
  whom you trust,
  and you will not prosper through
  them.

Unfaithful Israel

3 If[e] a man divorces his wife
  and she goes from him
and becomes another man's wife,
  will he return to her?
  Would not such a land be greatly
  polluted?
You have played the whore with many
  lovers;
  and would you return to me?
                    says the LORD.
[2] Look up to the bare heights,[f] and see!
  Where have you not been lain with?
By the waysides you have sat waiting
  for lovers,
  like a nomad in the wilderness.
You have polluted the land
  with your whoring and wickedness.
[3] Therefore the showers have been
  withheld,
  and the spring rain has not come;
yet you have the forehead of a whore,
  you refuse to be ashamed.
[4] Have you not just now called to me,
  "My Father, you are the friend of my
  youth—
[5] will he be angry forever,
  will he be indignant to the end?"
This is how you have spoken,
  but you have done all the evil that
  you could.

A Call to Repentance

6 The LORD said to me in the days of
King Jō·sīʹah: Have you seen what she did,
that faithless one, Israel, how she went up

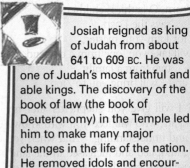

Josiah reigned as king of Judah from about 641 to 609 BC. He was one of Judah's most faithful and able kings. The discovery of the book of law (the book of Deuteronomy) in the Temple led him to make many major changes in the life of the nation. He removed idols and encouraged the worship of God.

on every high hill and under every green
tree, and played the whore there? [7]And I
thought, "After she has done all this she
will return to me"; but she did not return,
and her false sister Judah saw it. [8]She[g] saw
that for all the adulteries of that faithless
one, Israel, I had sent her away with a
decree of divorce; yet her false sister Judah
did not fear, but she too went and played
the whore. [9]Because she took her whoredom so lightly, she polluted the land, committing adultery with stone and tree. [10]Yet
for all this her false sister Judah did not
return to me with her whole heart, but
only in pretense, says the LORD.

11 Then the LORD said to me: Faithless
Israel has shown herself less guilty than
false Judah. [12]Go, and proclaim these
words toward the north, and say:
  Return, faithless Israel,
                    says the LORD.
  I will not look on you in anger,
  for I am merciful,
                    says the LORD;
  I will not be angry forever.
[13] Only acknowledge your guilt,
  that you have rebelled against the
  LORD your God,
and scattered your favors among
  strangers under every green tree,
  and have not obeyed my voice,
                    says the LORD.

---

[e] Q Ms Gk Syr: MT *Saying, If*   [f] Or *the trails*
[g] Q Ms Gk Mss Syr: MT *I*

¹⁴ Return, O faithless children,
  says the Lord,
  for I am your master;
I will take you, one from a city and
  two from a family,
and I will bring you to Zion.

15 I will give you shepherds after my
own heart, who will feed you with knowledge and understanding. ¹⁶And when you
have multiplied and increased in the land,
in those days, says the Lord, they shall no
longer say, "The ark of the covenant of the
Lord." It shall not come to mind, or be
remembered, or missed; nor shall another
one be made. ¹⁷At that time Jerusalem
shall be called the throne of the Lord, and
all nations shall gather to it, to the presence
of the Lord in Jerusalem, and they shall no
longer stubbornly follow their own evil
will. ¹⁸In those days the house of Judah
shall join the house of Israel, and together
they shall come from the land of the north
to the land that I gave your ancestors for a
heritage.

¹⁹ I thought
  how I would set you among my
    children,
and give you a pleasant land,
  the most beautiful heritage of all the
    nations.
And I thought you would call me, My
    Father,
  and would not turn from following
    me.
²⁰ Instead, as a faithless wife leaves her
    husband,
  so you have been faithless to me,
    O house of Israel,
                    says the Lord.

²¹ A voice on the bare heights^h is heard,
  the plaintive weeping of Israel's
    children,
because they have perverted their way,
  they have forgotten the Lord their
    God:
²² Return, O faithless children,
  I will heal your faithlessness.

> "I will give you shepherds
> after my own heart, who will
> feed you with knowledge
> and understanding."
> Jeremiah 3:15

"Here we come to you;
  for you are the Lord our God.
²³ Truly the hills areⁱ a delusion,
  the orgies on the mountains.
Truly in the Lord our God
  is the salvation of Israel.
24 "But from our youth the shameful
thing has devoured all for which our
ancestors had labored, their flocks and
their herds, their sons and their daughters.
²⁵Let us lie down in our shame, and let our
dishonor cover us; for we have sinned
against the Lord our God, we and our
ancestors, from our youth even to this day;
and we have not obeyed the voice of the
Lord our God."

4 If you return, O Israel,
                    says the Lord,
  if you return to me,
if you remove your abominations from
  my presence,
    and do not waver,
² and if you swear, "As the Lord lives!"
  in truth, in justice, and in
    uprightness,
then nations shall be blessed^j by him,
  and by him they shall boast.

3 For thus says the Lord to the people
of Judah and to the inhabitants of
Jerusalem:
  Break up your fallow ground,
    and do not sow among thorns.
⁴ Circumcise yourselves to the Lord,
  remove the foreskin of your hearts,
    O people of Judah and inhabitants
      of Jerusalem,
or else my wrath will go forth like fire,
  and burn with no one to quench it,
    because of the evil of your doings.

^h Or *the trails*   ⁱ Gk Syr Vg: Heb *Truly from the hills
is*   ^j Or *shall bless themselves*

Invasion and Desolation of Judah Threatened

5 Declare in Judah, and proclaim in Jerusalem, and say:

Blow the trumpet through the land;
  shout aloud[k] and say,
"Gather together, and let us go
  into the fortified cities!"

[6] Raise a standard toward Zion,
  flee for safety, do not delay,
for I am bringing evil from the north,
  and a great destruction.

[7] A lion has gone up from its thicket,
  a destroyer of nations has set out;
  he has gone out from his place
to make your land a waste;
  your cities will be ruins
  without inhabitant.

[8] Because of this put on sackcloth,
  lament and wail:
"The fierce anger of the LORD
  has not turned away from us."

The biblical writers often used the term "the destroyer" to warn the people that death or destruction would come to them if they did not turn back to God. Jeremiah compares the approaching army to a hungry lion that will destroy or eat up everything in its path. He was telling the people that God wanted them to return to God's ways of living.

[9]On that day, says the LORD, courage shall fail the king and the officials; the priests shall be appalled and the prophets astounded. [10]Then I said, "Ah, Lord GOD, how utterly you have deceived this people and Jerusalem, saying, 'It shall be well with you,' even while the sword is at the throat!"

11 At that time it will be said to this people and to Jerusalem: A hot wind comes from me out of the bare heights[l] in the desert toward my poor people, not to winnow or cleanse— [12]a wind too strong for that. Now it is I who speak in judgment against them.

[13] Look! He comes up like clouds,
  his chariots like the whirlwind;
his horses are swifter than eagles—
  woe to us, for we are ruined!

[14] O Jerusalem, wash your heart clean of
  wickedness
  so that you may be saved.
How long shall your evil schemes
  lodge within you?

[15] For a voice declares from Dan
  and proclaims disaster from Mount
    E´phra·im.

[16] Tell the nations, "Here they are!"
  Proclaim against Jerusalem,
"Besiegers come from a distant land;
  they shout against the cities of Judah.

[17] They have closed in around her like
  watchers of a field,
  because she has rebelled against me,
                    says the LORD.

[18] Your ways and your doings
  have brought this upon you.
This is your doom; how bitter it is!
  It has reached your very heart."

Sorrow for a Doomed Nation

[19] My anguish, my anguish! I writhe in
  pain!
  Oh, the walls of my heart!
My heart is beating wildly;
  I cannot keep silent;
for I[m] hear the sound of the trumpet,
  the alarm of war.

[20] Disaster overtakes disaster,
  the whole land is laid waste.
Suddenly my tents are destroyed,
  my curtains in a moment.

[21] How long must I see the standard,
  and hear the sound of the trumpet?

[22] "For my people are foolish,
  they do not know me;
they are stupid children,
  they have no understanding.

[k] Or shout, take your weapons: Heb shout, fill (your hand)   [l] Or the trails   [m] Another reading is for you, O my soul,

They are skilled in doing evil,
  but do not know how to do good."

23 I looked on the earth, and lo, it was
     waste and void;
  and to the heavens, and they had no
     light.
24 I looked on the mountains, and lo,
     they were quaking,
  and all the hills moved to and fro.
25 I looked, and lo, there was no one at all,
  and all the birds of the air had fled.
26 I looked, and lo, the fruitful land was a
     desert,
  and all its cities were laid in ruins
     before the LORD, before his fierce
     anger.
  27 For thus says the LORD: The whole
     land shall be a desolation; yet I
     will not make a full end.

28 Because of this the earth shall mourn,
  and the heavens above grow black;
  for I have spoken, I have purposed;
  I have not relented nor will I turn
     back.
29 At the noise of horseman and archer
     every town takes to flight;
  they enter thickets; they climb among
     rocks;
  all the towns are forsaken,
  and no one lives in them.
30 And you, O desolate one,
  what do you mean that you dress in
     crimson,
  that you deck yourself with
     ornaments of gold,
  that you enlarge your eyes with
     paint?
  In vain you beautify yourself.
  Your lovers despise you;
  they seek your life.
31 For I heard a cry as of a woman in
     labor,
  anguish as of one bringing forth her
     first child,
  the cry of daughter Zion gasping for
     breath,
  stretching out her hands,

"Woe is me! I am fainting before
  killers!"

The Utter Corruption of God's People

5 Run to and fro through the streets
  of Jerusalem,
  look around and take note!
  Search its squares and see
  if you can find one person
  who acts justly
  and seeks truth—
  so that I may pardon Jerusalem.[n]
2 Although they say, "As the LORD lives,"
  yet they swear falsely.
3 O LORD, do your eyes not look for
     truth?
  You have struck them,
  but they felt no anguish;
  you have consumed them,
  but they refused to take correction.
  They have made their faces harder
     than rock;
  they have refused to turn back.

4 Then I said, "These are only the poor,
  they have no sense;
  for they do not know the way of the
     LORD,
  the law of their God.
5 Let me go to the rich[o]
  and speak to them;
  surely they know the way of the LORD,
  the law of their God."
  But they all alike had broken the
     yoke,
  they had burst the bonds.

6 Therefore a lion from the forest shall
     kill them,
  a wolf from the desert shall destroy
     them.
  A leopard is watching against their
     cities;
  everyone who goes out of them shall
     be torn in pieces—
  because their transgressions are many,
  their apostasies are great.

n Heb it   o Or the great

7 How can I pardon you?
    Your children have forsaken me,
    and have sworn by those who are
        no gods.
    When I fed them to the full,
        they committed adultery
    and trooped to the houses of
        prostitutes.
8 They were well-fed lusty stallions,
    each neighing for his neighbor's
        wife.
9 Shall I not punish them for these
        things?
                        says the LORD;
    and shall I not bring retribution
    on a nation such as this?

10 Go up through her vine-rows and
        destroy,
    but do not make a full end;
    strip away her branches,
        for they are not the LORD's.
11 For the house of Israel and the house
        of Judah
    have been utterly faithless to me,
                        says the LORD.
12 They have spoken falsely of the LORD,
        and have said, "He will do nothing.
    No evil will come upon us,
        and we shall not see sword or
        famine."
13 The prophets are nothing but wind,
        for the word is not in them.
    Thus shall it be done to them!

14 Therefore thus says the LORD, the God
        of hosts:
    Because theyᵖ have spoken this word,
    I am now making my words in your
        mouth a fire,
        and this people wood, and the fire
        shall devour them.
15 I am going to bring upon you
    a nation from far away, O house of
        Israel,
                        says the LORD.
    It is an enduring nation,
        it is an ancient nation,
    a nation whose language you do not
        know,

nor can you understand what they
        say.
16 Their quiver is like an open tomb;
    all of them are mighty warriors.
17 They shall eat up your harvest and
        your food;
    they shall eat up your sons and your
        daughters;
    they shall eat up your flocks and your
        herds;
    they shall eat up your vines and
        your fig trees;
    they shall destroy with the sword
        your fortified cities in which you
        trust.

18 But even in those days, says the
LORD, I will not make a full end of you.
19 And when your people say, "Why has the
LORD our God done all these things to us?"
you shall say to them, "As you have forsaken me and served foreign gods in your
land, so you shall serve strangers in a land
that is not yours."

20 Declare this in the house of Jacob,
    proclaim it in Judah:
21 Hear this, O foolish and senseless
        people,
    who have eyes, but do not see,
    who have ears, but do not hear.
22 Do you not fear me? says the LORD;
    Do you not tremble before me?
    I placed the sand as a boundary for the
        sea,
    a perpetual barrier that it cannot
        pass;
    though the waves toss, they cannot
        prevail,
        though they roar, they cannot pass
        over it.
23 But this people has a stubborn and
        rebellious heart;
    they have turned aside and gone
        away.
24 They do not say in their hearts,
    "Let us fear the LORD our God,
    who gives the rain in its season,

ᵖ Heb *you*

the autumn rain and the spring rain,
and keeps for us
>the weeks appointed for the
>>harvest."

25 Your iniquities have turned these away,
>and your sins have deprived you of
>good.

26 For scoundrels are found among my
>people;
>they take over the goods of others.
Like fowlers they set a trap;q
>they catch human beings.

27 Like a cage full of birds,
>their houses are full of treachery;
therefore they have become great and
>rich,

28 >they have grown fat and sleek.
They know no limits in deeds of
>wickedness;
>they do not judge with justice
the cause of the orphan, to make it
>prosper,
>and they do not defend the rights of
>the needy.

29 Shall I not punish them for these
>things?
>>>>says the LORD,
>and shall I not bring retribution
>on a nation such as this?

30 An appalling and horrible thing
>has happened in the land:

31 the prophets prophesy falsely,
>and the priests rule as the prophets
>direct;r
>my people love to have it so,
>but what will you do when the end
>comes?

The Imminence and Horror
of the Invasion

6 Flee for safety, O children of Benjamin,
>from the midst of Jerusalem!
Blow the trumpet in Te·ko̅'a,
>and raise a signal on Beth-hac·che̅-
>rem;
for evil looms out of the north,
>and great destruction.

2 I have likened daughter Zion
>to the loveliest pasture.s

3 Shepherds with their flocks shall come
>against her.
>They shall pitch their tents around
>her;
>they shall pasture, all in their places.

4 "Prepare war against her;
>up, and let us attack at noon!"
"Woe to us, for the day declines,
>the shadows of evening lengthen!"

5 "Up, and let us attack by night,
>and destroy her palaces!"

6 For thus says the LORD of hosts:
Cut down her trees;
>cast up a siege ramp against
>Jerusalem.
This is the city that must be punished;t
>there is nothing but oppression
>within her.

7 As a well keeps its water fresh,
>so she keeps fresh her wickedness;
violence and destruction are heard
>within her;
>sickness and wounds are ever before
>me.

8 Take warning, O Jerusalem,
>or I shall turn from you in disgust,
and make you a desolation,
>an uninhabited land.

9 Thus says the LORD of hosts:
Gleanu thoroughly as a vine
>the remnant of Israel;
like a grape-gatherer, pass your hand
>again
>over its branches.

10 To whom shall I speak and give
>warning,
>that they may hear?
See, their ears are closed,v
>they cannot listen.
The word of the LORD is to them an
>object of scorn;
>they take no pleasure in it.

q Meaning of Heb uncertain   r Or rule by their
own authority   s Or I will destroy daughter Zion, the
loveliest pasture   t Or the city of license   u Cn: Heb
They shall glean   v Heb are uncircumcised

¹¹ But I am full of the wrath of the LORD;
    I am weary of holding it in.

Pour it out on the children in the
    street,
    and on the gatherings of young men
        as well;
both husband and wife shall be taken,
    the old folk and the very aged.
¹² Their houses shall be turned over to
        others,
    their fields and wives together;
for I will stretch out my hand
    against the inhabitants of the land,
                    says the LORD.

¹³ For from the least to the greatest of
        them,
    everyone is greedy for unjust gain;
and from prophet to priest,
    everyone deals falsely.
¹⁴ They have treated the wound of my
        people carelessly,
    saying, "Peace, peace,"
    when there is no peace.
¹⁵ They acted shamefully, they committed
        abomination;
    yet they were not ashamed,
    they did not know how to blush.
Therefore they shall fall among those
        who fall;
    at the time that I punish them, they
        shall be overthrown,
                    says the LORD.
¹⁶ Thus says the LORD:
Stand at the crossroads, and look,
    and ask for the ancient paths,
where the good way lies; and walk in it,
    and find rest for your souls.
But they said, "We will not walk in it."
¹⁷ Also I raised up sentinels for you:
    "Give heed to the sound of the
        trumpet!"
But they said, "We will not give heed."
¹⁸ Therefore hear, O nations,
    and know, O congregation, what
        will happen to them.
¹⁹ Hear, O earth; I am going to bring
    disaster on this people,
    the fruit of their schemes,

because they have not given heed to
    my words;
    and as for my teaching, they have
        rejected it.
²⁰ Of what use to me is frankincense that
    comes from Shēʹba,
    or sweet cane from a distant land?
Your burnt offerings are not acceptable,
    nor are your sacrifices pleasing to
        me.
²¹ Therefore thus says the LORD:
See, I am laying before this people
    stumbling blocks against which they
        shall stumble;
parents and children together,
    neighbor and friend shall perish.

²² Thus says the LORD:
See, a people is coming from the land
    of the north,
    a great nation is stirring from the
        farthest parts of the earth.
²³ They grasp the bow and the javelin,
    they are cruel and have no mercy,
    their sound is like the roaring sea;
they ride on horses,
    equipped like a warrior for battle,
    against you, O daughter Zion!

²⁴ "We have heard news of them,
    our hands fall helpless;
anguish has taken hold of us,
    pain as of a woman in labor.
²⁵ Do not go out into the field,
    or walk on the road;
for the enemy has a sword,
    terror is on every side."

²⁶ O my poor people, put on sackcloth,
    and roll in ashes;
make mourning as for an only child,
    most bitter lamentation:
for suddenly the destroyer
    will come upon us.

²⁷ I have made you a tester and a refiner[w]
    among my people
    so that you may know and test their
ways.

───────────
[w] Or *a fortress*

²⁸ They are all stubbornly rebellious,
　going about with slanders;
they are bronze and iron,
　all of them act corruptly.
²⁹ The bellows blow fiercely,
　the lead is consumed by the fire;
in vain the refining goes on,
　for the wicked are not removed.
³⁰ They are called "rejected silver,"
　for the LORD has rejected them.

Jeremiah Proclaims God's Judgment on the Nation

7 The word that came to Jer·e·mi´ah from the LORD: ²Stand in the gate of the LORD's house, and proclaim there this word, and say, Hear the word of the LORD, all you people of Judah, you that enter these gates to worship the LORD. ³Thus says the LORD of hosts, the God of Israel: Amend your ways and your doings, and let me dwell with you^x in this place. ⁴Do not trust in these deceptive words: "This is^y the temple of the LORD, the temple of the LORD, the temple of the LORD."

5 For if you truly amend your ways and your doings, if you truly act justly one with another, ⁶if you do not oppress the alien, the orphan, and the widow, or shed innocent blood in this place, and if you do not go after other gods to your own hurt, ⁷then I will dwell with you in this place, in the land that I gave of old to your ancestors forever and ever.

8 Here you are, trusting in deceptive words to no avail. ⁹Will you steal, murder, commit adultery, swear falsely, make offerings to Ba´al, and go after other gods that you have not known, ¹⁰and then come and stand before me in this house, which is called by my name, and say, "We are safe!"—only to go on doing all these abominations? ¹¹Has this house, which is called by my name, become a den of robbers in your sight? You know, I too am watching, says the LORD. ¹²Go now to my place that was in Shi´loh, where I made my name dwell at first, and see what I did to it for the wickedness of my people Israel. ¹³And now, because you have done all these things, says the LORD, and when I spoke to you persistently, you did not listen, and when I called you, you did not answer, ¹⁴therefore I will do to the house that is called by my name, in which you trust, and to the place that I gave to you and to your ancestors, just what I did to Shi´loh. ¹⁵And I will cast you out of my sight, just as I cast out all your kinsfolk, all the offspring of E´phra·im.

The People's Disobedience

16 As for you, do not pray for this people, do not raise a cry or prayer on their behalf, and do not intercede with me, for I will not hear you. ¹⁷Do you not see what they are doing in the towns of Judah and in the streets of Jerusalem? ¹⁸The children gather wood, the fathers kindle fire, and the women knead dough, to make cakes for the queen of heaven; and they pour out drink offerings to other gods, to provoke me to anger. ¹⁹Is it I whom they provoke? says the LORD. Is it not themselves, to their own hurt? ²⁰Therefore thus says the Lord GOD: My anger and my wrath shall be poured out on this place, on human beings and

The queen of heaven was a foreign goddess—an object of worship in Judah during the time of Jeremiah. Jeremiah condemned people for worshiping this idol and for showing devotion to this false god instead of to the one true God.

Sometimes things in our lives look so inviting that we let them take up time we should be spending in worship, in doing acts of kindness, or with our families. Can you think of things in your life that take up so much of your time they seem almost like an idol or a god to you? Talk with your family about how you might make better use of your time.

^x Or *and I will let you dwell*　^y Heb *They are*

animals, on the trees of the field and the fruit of the ground; it will burn and not be quenched.

21 Thus says the LORD of hosts, the God of Israel: Add your burnt offerings to your sacrifices, and eat the flesh. ²²For in the day that I brought your ancestors out of the land of Egypt, I did not speak to them or command them concerning burnt offerings and sacrifices. ²³But this command I gave them, "Obey my voice, and I will be your God, and you shall be my people; and walk only in the way that I command you, so that it may be well with you." ²⁴Yet they did not obey or incline their ear, but, in the stubbornness of their evil will, they walked in their own counsels, and looked backward rather than forward. ²⁵From the day that your ancestors came out of the land of Egypt until this day, I have persistently sent all my servants the prophets to them, day after day; ²⁶yet they did not listen to me, or pay attention, but they stiffened their necks. They did worse than their ancestors did.

27 So you shall speak all these words to them, but they will not listen to you. You shall call to them, but they will not answer you. ²⁸You shall say to them: This is the nation that did not obey the voice of the LORD their God, and did not accept discipline; truth has perished; it is cut off from their lips.

²⁹ Cut off your hair and throw it away;
  raise a lamentation on the bare
    heights,^z
for the LORD has rejected and forsaken
  the generation that provoked his
    wrath.

30 For the people of Judah have done evil in my sight, says the LORD; they have set their abominations in the house that is called by my name, defiling it. ³¹And they go on building the high place^a of To´pheth, which is in the valley of the son of Hin´nom, to burn their sons and their daughters in the fire—which I did not command, nor did it come into my mind. ³²Therefore, the days are surely coming,

says the LORD, when it will no more be called To´pheth, or the valley of the son of Hin´nom, but the valley of Slaughter: for they will bury in To´pheth until there is no more room. ³³The corpses of this people will be food for the birds of the air, and for the animals of the earth; and no one will frighten them away. ³⁴And I will bring to an end the sound of mirth and gladness, the voice of the bride and bridegroom in the cities of Judah and in the streets of Jerusalem; for the land shall become a waste.

8 At that time, says the LORD, the bones of the kings of Judah, the bones of its officials, the bones of the priests, the bones of the prophets, and the bones of the inhabitants of Jerusalem shall be brought out of their tombs; ²and they shall be spread before the sun and the moon and all the host of heaven, which they have loved and served, which they have followed, and which they have inquired of and worshiped; and they shall not be gathered or buried; they shall be like dung on the surface of the ground. ³Death shall be preferred to life by all the remnant that remains of this evil family in all the places where I have driven them, says the LORD of hosts.

The Blind Perversity of the Whole Nation

⁴ You shall say to them, Thus says the
  LORD:
When people fall, do they not get up
    again?
  If they go astray, do they not turn
    back?
⁵ Why then has this people^b turned away
  in perpetual backsliding?
They have held fast to deceit,
  they have refused to return.
⁶ I have given heed and listened,
  but they do not speak honestly;
no one repents of wickedness,
  saying, "What have I done!"

^z Or *the trails*   ^a Gk Tg: Heb *high places*   ^b One Ms Gk: MT *this people, Jerusalem,*

All of them turn to their own course,
 like a horse plunging headlong into
 battle.
7 Even the stork in the heavens
 knows its times;
and the turtledove, swallow, and crane[c]
 observe the time of their coming;
but my people do not know
 the ordinance of the LORD.

8 How can you say, "We are wise,
 and the law of the LORD is with us,"
when, in fact, the false pen of the
 scribes
 has made it into a lie?
9 The wise shall be put to shame,
 they shall be dismayed and taken;
since they have rejected the word of
 the LORD,
 what wisdom is in them?
10 Therefore I will give their wives to
 others
 and their fields to conquerors,
because from the least to the greatest
 everyone is greedy for unjust gain;
from prophet to priest
 everyone deals falsely.
11 They have treated the wound of my
 people carelessly,
 saying, "Peace, peace,"
 when there is no peace.
12 They acted shamefully, they committed
 abomination;
 yet they were not at all ashamed,
 they did not know how to blush.
Therefore they shall fall among those
 who fall;
 at the time when I punish them,
 they shall be overthrown,
 says the LORD.
13 When I wanted to gather them, says
 the LORD,
 there are[d] no grapes on the vine,
 nor figs on the fig tree;
even the leaves are withered,
 and what I gave them has passed
 away from them.[c]

14 Why do we sit still?

Gather together, let us go into the
 fortified cities
 and perish there;
for the LORD our God has doomed us
 to perish,
 and has given us poisoned water to
 drink,
 because we have sinned against the
 LORD.
15 We look for peace, but find no good,
 for a time of healing, but there is
 terror instead.

16 The snorting of their horses is heard
 from Dan;
 at the sound of the neighing of their
 stallions
 the whole land quakes.
They come and devour the land and
 all that fills it,
 the city and those who live in it.
17 See, I am letting snakes loose among
 you,
 adders that cannot be charmed,
 and they shall bite you,
 says the LORD.

The Prophet Mourns
for the People

18 My joy is gone, grief is upon me,
 my heart is sick.
19 Hark, the cry of my poor people
 from far and wide in the land:
"Is the LORD not in Zion?
 Is her King not in her?"
("Why have they provoked me to
 anger with their images,
 with their foreign idols?")
20 "The harvest is past, the summer is
 ended,
 and we are not saved."
21 For the hurt of my poor people I am
 hurt,
 I mourn, and dismay has taken hold
 of me.

22 Is there no balm in Gil'e·ad?
 Is there no physician there?

[c] Meaning of Heb uncertain   [d] Or I will make an
end of them, says the LORD. There are

Why then has the health of my poor
people
not been restored?

9 ^{e}O that my head were a spring of
water,
and my eyes a fountain of tears,
so that I might weep day and night
for the slain of my poor people!
^{2f}O that I had in the desert
a traveler's lodging place,
that I might leave my people
and go away from them!
For they are all adulterers,
a band of traitors.
^{3} They bend their tongues like bows;
they have grown strong in the land
for falsehood, and not for truth;
for they proceed from evil to evil,
and they do not know me, says the
LORD.

^{4} Beware of your neighbors,
and put no trust in any of your kin;^{g}
for all your kin^h are supplanters,
and every neighbor goes around like
a slanderer.
^{5} They all deceive their neighbors,
and no one speaks the truth;
they have taught their tongues to
speak lies;
they commit iniquity and are too
weary to repent.^{i}
^{6} Oppression upon oppression, deceit^j
upon deceit!
They refuse to know me, says the
LORD.

^{7} Therefore thus says the LORD of hosts:
I will now refine and test them,
for what else can I do with my sinful
people?^{k}
^{8} Their tongue is a deadly arrow;
it speaks deceit through the mouth.
They all speak friendly words to their
neighbors,
but inwardly are planning to lay an
ambush.
^{9} Shall I not punish them for these
things? says the LORD;

and shall I not bring retribution
on a nation such as this?

^{10} Take up^l weeping and wailing for the
mountains,
and a lamentation for the pastures of
the wilderness,
because they are laid waste so that no
one passes through,
and the lowing of cattle is not heard;
both the birds of the air and the animals
have fled and are gone.
^{11} I will make Jerusalem a heap of ruins,
a lair of jackals;
and I will make the towns of Judah a
desolation,
without inhabitant.

12 Who is wise enough to understand
this? To whom has the mouth of the LORD
spoken, so that they may declare it? Why
is the land ruined and laid waste like a
wilderness, so that no one passes through?
^{13}And the LORD says: Because they have
forsaken my law that I set before them,
and have not obeyed my voice, or walked
in accordance with it, ^{14}but have stubbornly followed their own hearts and have
gone after the Bāʹals, as their ancestors
taught them. ^{15}Therefore thus says the
LORD of hosts, the God of Israel: I am feeding this people with wormwood, and giving them poisonous water to drink. ^{16}I will
scatter them among nations that neither
they nor their ancestors have known; and
I will send the sword after them, until I
have consumed them.

The People Mourn in Judgment
^{17} Thus says the LORD of hosts:
Consider, and call for the mourning
women to come;
send for the skilled women to come;
^{18} let them quickly raise a dirge over us,

^{e} Ch 8.23 in Heb ^{f} Ch 9.1 in Heb ^{g} Heb *in a
brother* ^{h} Heb *for every brother* ^{i} Cn Compare
Gk: Heb *they weary themselves with iniquity.* ^{6}*Your
dwelling* ^{j} Cn: Heb *Your dwelling in the midst of
deceit* ^{k} Or *my poor people* ^{l} Gk Syr: Heb *I will
take up*

so that our eyes may run down with
tears,
and our eyelids flow with water.
[19] For a sound of wailing is heard from
Zion:
"How we are ruined!
We are utterly shamed,
because we have left the land,
because they have cast down our
dwellings."

[20] Hear, O women, the word of the LORD,
and let your ears receive the word of
his mouth;
teach to your daughters a dirge,
and each to her neighbor a lament.
[21] "Death has come up into our
windows,
it has entered our palaces,
to cut off the children from the streets
and the young men from the
squares."
[22] Speak! Thus says the LORD:
"Human corpses shall fall
like dung upon the open field,
like sheaves behind the reaper,
and no one shall gather them."

23 Thus says the LORD: Do not let the
wise boast in their wisdom, do not let the
mighty boast in their might, do not let the
wealthy boast in their wealth; [24]but let
those who boast boast in this, that they
understand and know me, that I am the
LORD; I act with steadfast love, justice, and
righteousness in the earth, for in these
things I delight, says the LORD.
25 The days are surely coming, says the
LORD, when I will attend to all those who
are circumcised only in the foreskin:
[26]Egypt, Judah, Ē´dom, the Am´mon·ītes,
Mō´ab, and all those with shaven temples
who live in the desert. For all these nations
are uncircumcised, and all the house of
Israel is uncircumcised in heart.

Idolatry Has Brought Ruin
on Israel

10 Hear the word that the LORD
speaks to you, O house of Israel.

"Thus says the LORD: Do
not let the wise boast in
their wisdom, do not let
the mighty boast in their
might, do not let the wealthy boast in
their wealth; but let those who boast
boast in this, that they understand
and know me, that I am the LORD; I
act with steadfast love, justice, and
righteousness in the earth, for in
these things I delight, says the LORD."
Jeremiah 9:23–24

[2]Thus says the LORD:
Do not learn the way of the nations,
or be dismayed at the signs of the
heavens;
for the nations are dismayed at
them.
[3] For the customs of the peoples are
false:
a tree from the forest is cut down,
and worked with an ax by the hands
of an artisan;
[4] people deck it with silver and gold;
they fasten it with hammer and nails
so that it cannot move.
[5] Their idols[m] are like scarecrows in a
cucumber field,
and they cannot speak;
they have to be carried,
for they cannot walk.
Do not be afraid of them,
for they cannot do evil,
nor is it in them to do good.

[6] There is none like you, O LORD;
you are great, and your name is
great in might.
[7] Who would not fear you, O King of
the nations?
For that is your due;
among all the wise ones of the nations
and in all their kingdoms
there is no one like you.
[8] They are both stupid and foolish;
the instruction given by idols
is no better than wood![n]

[m] Heb *They*   [n] Meaning of Heb uncertain

9 Beaten silver is brought from Tar´shish,
   and gold from Ū´phaz.
They are the work of the artisan and of
   the hands of the goldsmith;
   their clothing is blue and purple;
   they are all the product of skilled
      workers.
10 But the LORD is the true God;
   he is the living God and the
      everlasting King.
At his wrath the earth quakes,
   and the nations cannot endure his
      indignation.

11 Thus shall you say to them: The
gods who did not make the heavens and
the earth shall perish from the earth and
from under the heavens.*

12 It is he who made the earth by his
      power,
   who established the world by his
      wisdom,
   and by his understanding stretched
      out the heavens.
13 When he utters his voice, there is a
      tumult of waters in the heavens,
   and he makes the mist rise from the
      ends of the earth.
He makes lightnings for the rain,
   and he brings out the wind from his
      storehouses.
14 Everyone is stupid and without
      knowledge;
   goldsmiths are all put to shame by
      their idols;
for their images are false,
   and there is no breath in them.
15 They are worthless, a work of
      delusion;
   at the time of their punishment they
      shall perish.
16 Not like these is the LORD,ᵖ the portion
      of Jacob,
   for he is the one who formed all
      things,
and Israel is the tribe of his
      inheritance;
   the LORD of hosts is his name.

> Gold was probably the first metal known to humans. A goldsmith is a person who makes things out of gold.

The Coming Exile

17 Gather up your bundle from the
      ground,
   O you who live under siege!
18 For thus says the LORD:
I am going to sling out the inhabitants
      of the land
   at this time,
and I will bring distress on them,
   so that they shall feel it.
19 Woe is me because of my hurt!
   My wound is severe.
But I said, "Truly this is my
      punishment,
   and I must bear it."
20 My tent is destroyed,
   and all my cords are broken;
my children have gone from me,
   and they are no more;
there is no one to spread my tent
      again,
   and to set up my curtains.
21 For the shepherds are stupid,
   and do not inquire of the LORD;
therefore they have not prospered,
   and all their flock is scattered.

22 Hear, a noise! Listen, it is coming—
   a great commotion from the land of
      the north
to make the cities of Judah a
      desolation,
   a lair of jackals.

23 I know, O LORD, that the way of human
      beings is not in their control,
   that mortals as they walk cannot
      direct their steps.

*This verse is in Aramaic   ᵖ Heb lacks *the* LORD

²⁴ Correct me, O LORD, but in just
measure;
  not in your anger, or you will bring
  me to nothing.

²⁵ Pour out your wrath on the nations
that do not know you,
  and on the peoples that do not call
  on your name;
  for they have devoured Jacob;
  they have devoured him and
  consumed him,
  and have laid waste his habitation.

Israel and Judah
Have Broken the Covenant

11 The word that came to Jer·e·mi´ah from the LORD: ²Hear the words of this covenant, and speak to the people of Judah and the inhabitants of Jerusalem. ³You shall say to them, Thus says the LORD, the God of Israel: Cursed be anyone who does not heed the words of this covenant, ⁴which I commanded your ancestors when I brought them out of the land of Egypt, from the iron-smelter, saying, Listen to my voice, and do all that I command you. So shall you be my people, and I will be your God, ⁵that I may perform the oath that I swore to your ancestors, to give them a land flowing with milk and honey, as at this day. Then I answered, "So be it, LORD."

6 And the LORD said to me: Proclaim all these words in the cities of Judah, and in the streets of Jerusalem: Hear the words of this covenant and do them. ⁷For I solemnly warned your ancestors when I brought them up out of the land of Egypt, warning them persistently, even to this day, saying, Obey my voice. ⁸Yet they did not obey or incline their ear, but everyone walked in the stubbornness of an evil will. So I brought upon them all the words of this covenant, which I commanded them to do, but they did not.

9 And the LORD said to me: Conspiracy exists among the people of Judah and the inhabitants of Jerusalem. ¹⁰They have turned back to the iniquities of their ancestors of old, who refused to heed my words;

they have gone after other gods to serve them; the house of Israel and the house of Judah have broken the covenant that I made with their ancestors. ¹¹Therefore, thus says the LORD, assuredly I am going to bring disaster upon them that they cannot escape; though they cry out to me, I will not listen to them. ¹²Then the cities of Judah and the inhabitants of Jerusalem will go and cry out to the gods to whom they make offerings, but they will never save them in the time of their trouble. ¹³For your gods have become as many as your towns, O Judah; and as many as the streets of Jerusalem are the altars to shame you have set up, altars to make offerings to Ba´al.

14 As for you, do not pray for this people, or lift up a cry or prayer on their behalf, for I will not listen when they call to me in the time of their trouble. ¹⁵What right has my beloved in my house, when she has done vile deeds? Can vows^q and sacrificial flesh avert your doom? Can you then exult? ¹⁶The LORD once called you, "A green olive tree, fair with goodly fruit"; but with the roar of a great tempest he will set fire to it, and its branches will be consumed. ¹⁷The LORD of hosts, who planted you, has pronounced evil against you, because of the evil that the house of Israel and the house of Judah have done, provoking me to anger by making offerings to Ba´al.

Jeremiah's Life Threatened

¹⁸ It was the LORD who made it known to
me, and I knew;
  then you showed me their evil
  deeds.
¹⁹ But I was like a gentle lamb
  led to the slaughter.
  And I did not know it was against me
  that they devised schemes, saying,
  "Let us destroy the tree with its fruit,
  let us cut him off from the land of
  the living,
  so that his name will no longer be
  remembered!"

^q Gk: Heb *Can many*

²⁰ But you, O LORD of hosts, who judge
     righteously,
  who try the heart and the mind,
let me see your retribution upon them,
  for to you I have committed my
     cause.

21 Therefore thus says the LORD concerning the people of An´a·thoth, who seek your life, and say, "You shall not prophesy in the name of the LORD, or you will die by our hand"— ²²therefore thus says the LORD of hosts: I am going to punish them; the young men shall die by the sword; their sons and their daughters shall die by famine; ²³and not even a remnant shall be left of them. For I will bring disaster upon the people of An´a·thoth, the year of their punishment.

Jeremiah Complains to God

12 You will be in the right, O LORD,
       when I lay charges against you;
  but let me put my case to you.
Why does the way of the guilty
     prosper?
  Why do all who are treacherous
     thrive?
² You plant them, and they take root;
  they grow and bring forth fruit;
you are near in their mouths
  yet far from their hearts.
³ But you, O LORD, know me;
  You see me and test me—my heart
     is with you.
Pull them out like sheep for the
     slaughter,
  and set them apart for the day of
     slaughter.
⁴ How long will the land mourn,
  and the grass of every field wither?
For the wickedness of those who live
     in it
  the animals and the birds are swept
     away,
  and because people said, "He is
     blind to our ways."ʳ

God Replies to Jeremiah

⁵ If you have raced with foot-runners
  and they have wearied you,

how will you compete with horses?
And if in a safe land you fall down,
  how will you fare in the thickets of
     the Jordan?
⁶ For even your kinsfolk and your own
     family,
  even they have dealt treacherously
     with you;
  they are in full cry after you;
do not believe them,
  though they speak friendly words to
     you.

⁷ I have forsaken my house,
  I have abandoned my heritage;
I have given the beloved of my heart
  into the hands of her enemies.
⁸ My heritage has become to me
  like a lion in the forest;
she has lifted up her voice against
     me—
  therefore I hate her.
⁹ Is the hyena greedyˢ for my heritage at
     my command?
  Are the birds of prey all around her?
Go, assemble all the wild animals;
  bring them to devour her.
¹⁰ Many shepherds have destroyed my
     vineyard,
  they have trampled down my
     portion,
they have made my pleasant portion
  a desolate wilderness.
¹¹ They have made it a desolation;
  desolate, it mourns to me.
The whole land is made desolate,
  but no one lays it to heart.
¹² Upon all the bare heightsᵗ in the desert
     spoilers have come;
for the sword of the LORD devours
  from one end of the land to the
     other;
  no one shall be safe.
¹³ They have sown wheat and have
     reaped thorns,
  they have tired themselves out but
     profit nothing.

ʳ Gk: Heb *to our future*   ˢ Cn: Heb *Is the hyena, the
bird of prey*   ᵗ Or *the trails*

They shall be ashamed of their[u]
    harvests
  because of the fierce anger of the
    LORD.

14 Thus says the LORD concerning all my evil neighbors who touch the heritage that I have given my people Israel to inherit: I am about to pluck them up from their land, and I will pluck up the house of Judah from among them. [15]And after I have plucked them up, I will again have compassion on them, and I will bring them again to their heritage and to their land, everyone of them. [16]And then, if they will diligently learn the ways of my people, to swear by my name, "As the LORD lives," as they taught my people to swear by Bāʹal, then they shall be built up in the midst of my people. [17]But if any nation will not listen, then I will completely uproot it and destroy it, says the LORD.

The Linen Loincloth

13 Thus said the LORD to me, "Go and buy yourself a linen loincloth, and put it on your loins, but do not dip it in water." [2]So I bought a loincloth according to the word of the LORD, and put it on my loins. [3]And the word of the LORD came to me a second time, saying, [4]"Take the loincloth that you bought and are wearing, and go now to the Euphrates,[v] and hide it there in a cleft of the rock." [5]So I went, and hid it by the Euphrates,[v] as the LORD commanded me. [6]And after many days the LORD said to me, "Go now to the Euphrates,[v] and take from there the loincloth that I commanded you to hide there." [7]Then I went to the Euphrates,[v] and dug, and I took the loincloth from the place where I had hidden it. But now the loincloth was ruined; it was good for nothing.

8 Then the word of the LORD came to me: [9]Thus says the LORD: Just so I will ruin the pride of Judah and the great pride of Jerusalem. [10]This evil people, who refuse to hear my words, who stubbornly follow their own will and have gone after other gods to serve them and worship them, shall be like this loincloth, which is good for nothing. [11]For as the loincloth clings to one's loins, so I made the whole house of Israel and the whole house of Judah cling to me, says the LORD, in order that they might be for me a people, a name, a praise, and a glory. But they would not listen.

A loincloth was an inner garment made of leather or linen and worn around the waist. While working, workmen would remove their outer garments and wear only a loincloth. The linen loincloth Jeremiah bought would have clung tightly to him. When he buried it, it was ruined.

The people of Israel should have clung to God, but they refused. Despite God's great love for them, Jeremiah said they would be ruined just like the cloth. And yet time after time God offered them the chance to return and be the people God loves. The unchangeable God still waits for God's children today. When we make a wrong choice and turn away from God, God is sad. When we turn back to God, God is forgiving and welcomes us back as if we had never been away.

Symbol of the Wine-Jars

12 You shall speak to them this word: Thus says the LORD, the God of Israel: Every wine-jar should be filled with wine. And they will say to you, "Do you think we do not know that every wine-jar should be filled with wine?" [13]Then you shall say to them: Thus says the LORD: I am about to fill all the inhabitants of this land—the kings who sit on David's throne, the priests, the prophets, and all the inhabitants of Jerusalem—with drunkenness. [14]And I will dash them one against another, parents and children together,

[u] Heb *your*   [v] Or *by Parah*; Heb *perath*

says the LORD. I will not pity or spare or have compassion when I destroy them.

Exile Threatened

15 Hear and give ear; do not be haughty,
    for the LORD has spoken.
16 Give glory to the LORD your God
    before he brings darkness,
and before your feet stumble
    on the mountains at twilight;
while you look for light,
    he turns it into gloom
    and makes it deep darkness.
17 But if you will not listen,
    my soul will weep in secret for your
    pride;
my eyes will weep bitterly and run
    down with tears,
    because the LORD's flock has been
    taken captive.

18 Say to the king and the queen mother:
    "Take a lowly seat,
for your beautiful crown
    has come down from your head."ʷ
19 The towns of the Neg´eb are shut up
    with no one to open them;
all Judah is taken into exile,
    wholly taken into exile.

20 Lift up your eyes and see
    those who come from the north.
Where is the flock that was given you,
    your beautiful flock?
21 What will you say when they set as
    head over you
those whom you have trained
    to be your allies?
Will not pangs take hold of you,
    like those of a woman in labor?
22 And if you say in your heart,
    "Why have these things come upon
    me?"
it is for the greatness of your iniquity
    that your skirts are lifted up,
    and you are violated.
23 Can Ethiopiansˣ change their skin
    or leopards their spots?
Then also you can do good

who are accustomed to do evil.
24 I will scatter youʸ like chaff
    driven by the wind from the desert.
25 This is your lot,
    the portion I have measured out to
    you, says the LORD,
because you have forgotten me
    and trusted in lies.
26 I myself will lift up your skirts over
    your face,
    and your shame will be seen.
27 I have seen your abominations,
    your adulteries and neighings, your
    shameless prostitutions
    on the hills of the countryside.
Woe to you, O Jerusalem!
    How long will it be
    before you are made clean?

The Great Drought

14 The word of the LORD that came
to Jer·e·mi´ah concerning the
drought:
2 Judah mourns
    and her gates languish;
they lie in gloom on the ground,
    and the cry of Jerusalem goes up.
3 Her nobles send their servants for
    water;
    they come to the cisterns,
they find no water,
    they return with their vessels empty.
They are ashamed and dismayed
    and cover their heads,
4 because the ground is cracked.
    Because there has been no rain on
    the land
the farmers are dismayed;
    they cover their heads.
5 Even the doe in the field forsakes her
    newborn fawn
    because there is no grass.
6 The wild asses stand on the bare
    heights,ᶻ
    they pant for air like jackals;
their eyes fail
    because there is no herbage.

ʷ Gk Syr Vg: Meaning of Heb uncertain   ˣ Or
Nubians; Heb Cushites   ʸ Heb them   ᶻ Or the trails

7 Although our iniquities testify
   against us,
      act, O LORD, for your name's sake;
   our apostasies indeed are many,
      and we have sinned against you.
8 O hope of Israel,
      its savior in time of trouble,
   why should you be like a stranger in
      the land,
         like a traveler turning aside for the
         night?
9 Why should you be like someone
      confused,
      like a mighty warrior who cannot
      give help?
   Yet you, O LORD, are in the midst
      of us,
      and we are called by your name;
      do not forsake us!

10 Thus says the LORD concerning this
    people:
   Truly they have loved to wander,
      they have not restrained their feet;
   therefore the LORD does not accept
      them,
      now he will remember their iniquity
      and punish their sins.

11 The LORD said to me: Do not pray
for the welfare of this people. 12Although
they fast, I do not hear their cry, and
although they offer burnt offering and
grain offering, I do not accept them; but by
the sword, by famine, and by pestilence I
consume them.

Denunciation of Lying Prophets

13 Then I said: "Ah, Lord GOD! Here
are the prophets saying to them, 'You shall
not see the sword, nor shall you have
famine, but I will give you true peace in
this place.'" 14And the LORD said to me:
The prophets are prophesying lies in my
name; I did not send them, nor did I command them or speak to them. They are
prophesying to you a lying vision, worthless divination, and the deceit of their own
minds. 15Therefore thus says the LORD
concerning the prophets who prophesy in

Divination is trying to
communicate with
supernatural powers
or to tell the future with the help
of natural events such as
dreams, the position of the stars,
cloud formations, and unexpected storms. In Jeremiah's
time, people practiced divination
by shooting arrows, casting lots,
or examining the insides of sacrificed animals. Divination was
forbidden in Israel, and the
prophets preached against it.

my name though I did not send them, and
who say, "Sword and famine shall not
come on this land": By sword and famine
those prophets shall be consumed. 16And
the people to whom they prophesy shall
be thrown out into the streets of Jerusalem,
victims of famine and sword. There shall
be no one to bury them—themselves, their
wives, their sons, and their daughters. For
I will pour out their wickedness upon
them.

17 You shall say to them this word:
   Let my eyes run down with tears night
      and day,
      and let them not cease,
   for the virgin daughter—my people—
      is struck down with a crushing
      blow,
   with a very grievous wound.
18 If I go out into the field,
      look—those killed by the sword!
   And if I enter the city,
      look—those sick with^a famine!
   For both prophet and priest ply their
      trade throughout the land,
      and have no knowledge.

The People Plead for Mercy

19 Have you completely rejected Judah?
   Does your heart loathe Zion?

^{a} Heb look—the sicknesses of

Why have you struck us down
    so that there is no healing for us?
We look for peace, but find no good;
    for a time of healing, but there is
        terror instead.
20 We acknowledge our wickedness, O
      LORD,
    the iniquity of our ancestors,
    for we have sinned against you.
21 Do not spurn us, for your name's sake;
    do not dishonor your glorious
        throne;
    remember and do not break your
        covenant with us.
22 Can any idols of the nations bring rain?
    Or can the heavens give showers?
Is it not you, O LORD our God?
    We set our hope on you,
    for it is you who do all this.

Punishment Is Inevitable

15 Then the LORD said to me: Though Moses and Samuel stood before me, yet my heart would not turn toward this people. Send them out of my sight, and let them go! ²And when they say to you, "Where shall we go?" you shall say to them: Thus says the LORD:
Those destined for pestilence, to
      pestilence,
    and those destined for the sword, to
      the sword;
    those destined for famine, to famine,
    and those destined for captivity, to
      captivity.
³And I will appoint over them four kinds of destroyers, says the LORD: the sword to kill, the dogs to drag away, and the birds of the air and the wild animals of the earth to devour and destroy. ⁴I will make them a horror to all the kingdoms of the earth because of what King Ma·nas´seh son of Hez·e·kī´ah of Judah did in Jerusalem.

⁵ Who will have pity on you, O
      Jerusalem,
    or who will bemoan you?
Who will turn aside
    to ask about your welfare?

⁶ You have rejected me, says the LORD,
    you are going backward;
so I have stretched out my hand
      against you and destroyed you—
    I am weary of relenting.
⁷ I have winnowed them with a
      winnowing fork
    in the gates of the land;
I have bereaved them, I have destroyed
      my people;
    they did not turn from their ways.
⁸ Their widows became more numerous
    than the sand of the seas;
I have brought against the mothers of
      youths
    a destroyer at noonday;
I have made anguish and terror
    fall upon her suddenly.
⁹ She who bore seven has languished;
    she has swooned away;
her sun went down while it was yet
      day;
    she has been shamed and disgraced.
And the rest of them I will give to the
      sword
    before their enemies,
                 says the LORD.

Jeremiah Complains Again and Is Reassured

10 Woe is me, my mother, that you ever bore me, a man of strife and contention to the whole land! I have not lent, nor have I borrowed, yet all of them curse me. ¹¹The LORD said: Surely I have intervened in your life[b] for good, surely I have imposed enemies on you in a time of trouble and in a time of distress.[c] ¹²Can iron and bronze break iron from the north?

13 Your wealth and your treasures I will give as plunder, without price, for all your sins, throughout all your territory. ¹⁴I will make you serve your enemies in a land that you do not know, for in my anger a fire is kindled that shall burn forever.

[b] Heb *intervened with you*   [c] Meaning of Heb uncertain

¹⁵ O Lord, you know;
  remember me and visit me,
  and bring down retribution for me
    on my persecutors.
In your forbearance do not take me
    away;
  know that on your account I suffer
    insult.
¹⁶ Your words were found, and I ate
    them,
  and your words became to me a
    joy
  and the delight of my heart;
for I am called by your name,
  O Lord, God of hosts.
¹⁷ I did not sit in the company of
    merrymakers,
  nor did I rejoice;
under the weight of your hand I sat
    alone,
  for you had filled me with
    indignation.
¹⁸ Why is my pain unceasing,
  my wound incurable,
  refusing to be healed?
Truly, you are to me like a deceitful
    brook,
  like waters that fail.

¹⁹ Therefore thus says the Lord:
If you turn back, I will take you
    back,
  and you shall stand before me.
If you utter what is precious, and not
    what is worthless,
  you shall serve as my mouth.
It is they who will turn to you,
  not you who will turn to them.
²⁰ And I will make you to this people
  a fortified wall of bronze;
they will fight against you,
  but they shall not prevail over you,
for I am with you
  to save you and deliver you,
                    says the Lord.
²¹ I will deliver you out of the hand of
    the wicked,
  and redeem you from the grasp of
    the ruthless.

Jeremiah's Celibacy and Message

16 The word of the Lord came to me: ²You shall not take a wife, nor shall you have sons or daughters in this place. ³For thus says the Lord concerning the sons and daughters who are born in this place, and concerning the mothers who bear them and the fathers who beget them in this land: ⁴They shall die of deadly diseases. They shall not be lamented, nor shall they be buried; they shall become like dung on the surface of the ground. They shall perish by the sword and by famine, and their dead bodies shall become food for the birds of the air and for the wild animals of the earth.

5 For thus says the Lord: Do not enter the house of mourning, or go to lament, or bemoan them; for I have taken away my peace from this people, says the Lord, my steadfast love and mercy. ⁶Both great and small shall die in this land; they shall not be buried, and no one shall lament for them; there shall be no gashing, no shaving of the head for them. ⁷No one shall break bread[d] for the mourner, to offer comfort for the dead; nor shall anyone give them the cup of consolation to drink for their fathers or their mothers. ⁸You shall not go into the house of feasting to sit with them, to eat and drink. ⁹For thus says the Lord of hosts, the God of Israel: I am going to banish from this place, in your days and before your eyes, the voice of mirth and the voice of gladness, the voice of the bridegroom and the voice of the bride.

10 And when you tell this people all these words, and they say to you, "Why has the Lord pronounced all this great evil against us? What is our iniquity? What is the sin that we have committed against the Lord our God?" ¹¹then you shall say to them: It is because your ancestors have forsaken me, says the Lord, and have gone after other gods and have served and worshiped them, and have forsaken me and have not kept my law; ¹²and because you have behaved worse than your ancestors,

---

ᵈ Two Mss Gk: MT *break for them*

for here you are, every one of you, following your stubborn evil will, refusing to listen to me. [13]Therefore I will hurl you out
of this land into a land that neither you nor
your ancestors have known, and there you
shall serve other gods day and night, for I
will show you no favor.

God Will Restore Israel

14 Therefore, the days are surely coming, says the LORD, when it shall no longer
be said, "As the LORD lives who brought
the people of Israel up out of the land of
Egypt," [15]but "As the LORD lives who
brought the people of Israel up out of the
land of the north and out of all the lands
where he had driven them." For I will
bring them back to their own land that I
gave to their ancestors.

16 I am now sending for many fishermen, says the LORD, and they shall catch
them; and afterward I will send for many
hunters, and they shall hunt them from
every mountain and every hill, and out of
the clefts of the rocks. [17]For my eyes are on
all their ways; they are not hidden from my
presence, nor is their iniquity concealed
from my sight. [18]And[e] I will doubly repay
their iniquity and their sin, because they
have polluted my land with the carcasses
of their detestable idols, and have filled my
inheritance with their abominations.

[19] O LORD, my strength and my
           stronghold,
    my refuge in the day of trouble,
to you shall the nations come
    from the ends of the earth and say:
Our ancestors have inherited nothing
           but lies,
    worthless things in which there is
           no profit.
[20] Can mortals make for themselves
           gods?
    Such are no gods!

21 "Therefore I am surely going to
teach them, this time I am going to teach
them my power and my might, and they
shall know that my name is the LORD."

Judah's Sin and Punishment

17 The sin of Judah is written with
        an iron pen; with a diamond
point it is engraved on the tablet of their
hearts, and on the horns of their altars,
[2]while their children remember their altars
and their sacred poles,[f] beside every green
tree, and on the high hills, [3]on the mountains in the open country. Your wealth and
all your treasures I will give for spoil as the
price of your sin[g] throughout all your territory. [4]By your own act you shall lose the
heritage that I gave you, and I will make
you serve your enemies in a land that you
do not know, for in my anger a fire is kindled[h] that shall burn forever.

[5] Thus says the LORD:
    Cursed are those who trust in mere
           mortals
       and make mere flesh their strength,
       whose hearts turn away from the
           LORD.
[6] They shall be like a shrub in the
           desert,
       and shall not see when relief comes.
    They shall live in the parched places of
           the wilderness,
       in an uninhabited salt land.

[7] Blessed are those who trust in the
           LORD,
       whose trust is the LORD.
[8] They shall be like a tree planted by
           water,
       sending out its roots by the stream.
    It shall not fear when heat comes,
       and its leaves shall stay green;
    in the year of drought it is not anxious,
       and it does not cease to bear fruit.

[9] The heart is devious above all else;
       it is perverse—
       who can understand it?
[10] I the LORD test the mind
       and search the heart,

---

[e] Gk: Heb And first   [f] Heb Asherim   [g] Cn: Heb
spoil your high places for sin   [h] Two Mss
Theodotion: you kindled

to give to all according to their ways,
   according to the fruit of their
      doings.

11 Like the partridge hatching what it did
      not lay,
   so are all who amass wealth
      unjustly;
   in mid-life it will leave them,
   and at their end they will prove to
      be fools.

12 O glorious throne, exalted from the
      beginning,
   shrine of our sanctuary!
13 O hope of Israel! O LORD!
   All who forsake you shall be put to
      shame;
   those who turn away from you[i] shall
      be recorded in the underworld,[j]
   for they have forsaken the fountain
      of living water, the LORD.

Jeremiah Prays for Vindication

14 Heal me, O LORD, and I shall be
      healed;
   save me, and I shall be saved;
   for you are my praise.
15 See how they say to me,
   "Where is the word of the LORD?
   Let it come!"
16 But I have not run away from being a
      shepherd[k] in your service,
   nor have I desired the fatal day.
   You know what came from my lips;
   it was before your face.
17 Do not become a terror to me;
   you are my refuge in the day of
      disaster;
18 Let my persecutors be shamed,
   but do not let me be shamed;
   let them be dismayed,
   but do not let me be dismayed;
   bring on them the day of disaster;
   destroy them with double
      destruction!

Hallow the Sabbath Day

19 Thus said the LORD to me: Go and
stand in the People's Gate, by which the
kings of Judah enter and by which they go

"Blessed are those who trust in the LORD, whose trust is the LORD. They shall be like a tree planted by water, sending out its roots by the stream. It shall not fear when heat comes, and its leaves shall stay green; in the year of drought it is not anxious, and it does not cease to bear fruit." Jeremiah 17:7–8

out, and in all the gates of Jerusalem, 20and
say to them: Hear the word of the LORD,
you kings of Judah, and all Judah, and all
the inhabitants of Jerusalem, who enter by
these gates. 21Thus says the LORD: For the
sake of your lives, take care that you do not
bear a burden on the sabbath day or bring
it in by the gates of Jerusalem. 22And do
not carry a burden out of your houses on
the sabbath or do any work, but keep the
sabbath day holy, as I commanded your
ancestors. 23Yet they did not listen or
incline their ear; they stiffened their necks
and would not hear or receive instruction.

24 But if you listen to me, says the
LORD, and bring in no burden by the gates
of this city on the sabbath day, but keep the
sabbath day holy and do no work on it,
25then there shall enter by the gates of this
city kings[l] who sit on the throne of David,
riding in chariots and on horses, they and
their officials, the people of Judah and the
inhabitants of Jerusalem; and this city shall
be inhabited forever. 26And people shall
come from the towns of Judah and the
places around Jerusalem, from the land of
Benjamin, from the She·phē′lah, from the
hill country, and from the Neg′eb, bringing
burnt offerings and sacrifices, grain offerings and frankincense, and bringing thank
offerings to the house of the LORD. 27But if
you do not listen to me, to keep the sabbath day holy, and to carry in no burden
through the gates of Jerusalem on the sabbath day, then I will kindle a fire in its

i Heb me   j Or in the earth   k Meaning of Heb
uncertain   l Cn: Heb kings and officials

gates; it shall devour the palaces of Jerusalem and shall not be quenched.

> Every village in Bible times had a potter. Potters made many useful things including jugs, pots, bowls, storage jars, lamps, toys, and seals for letters. Potters would dig clay out of the ground and leave it outside until it was ready for use. Then, they would stomp on the clay to get all the air out and mix it with water and limestone. Early potters shaped clay into an object by hand, smoothed the sides, and then left it to dry. Finally, they would "fire," or bake, the object in a special oven called a "kiln." Some kilns were shelves above an open fire. Other kilns were dome-shaped ovens in the bottom of a shallow well or hole in the ground. Potters would place shaped objects under the dome, set branches on top of the dome, and then set the branches on fire.

The Potter and the Clay

18 The word that came to Jer·e·mī'-ah from the LORD: [2]"Come, go down to the potter's house, and there I will let you hear my words." [3]So I went down to the potter's house, and there he was working at his wheel. [4]The vessel he was making of clay was spoiled in the potter's hand, and he reworked it into another vessel, as seemed good to him.

5 Then the word of the LORD came to me: [6]Can I not do with you, O house of Israel, just as this potter has done? says the LORD. Just like the clay in the potter's hand, so are you in my hand, O house of Israel. [7]At one moment I may declare concerning a nation or a kingdom, that I will pluck up and break down and destroy it, [8]but if that

nation, concerning which I have spoken, turns from its evil, I will change my mind about the disaster that I intended to bring on it. [9]And at another moment I may declare concerning a nation or a kingdom that I will build and plant it, [10]but if it does evil in my sight, not listening to my voice, then I will change my mind about the good that I had intended to do to it. [11]Now, therefore, say to the people of Judah and the inhabitants of Jerusalem: Thus says the LORD: Look, I am a potter shaping evil against you and devising a plan against you. Turn now, all of you from your evil way, and amend your ways and your doings.

Israel's Stubborn Idolatry

12 But they say, "It is no use! We will follow our own plans, and each of us will act according to the stubbornness of our evil will."

[13] Therefore thus says the LORD:
Ask among the nations:
   Who has heard the like of this?
The virgin Israel has done
   a most horrible thing.
[14] Does the snow of Lebanon leave
   the crags of Sir'i·on?[m]
Do the mountain[n] waters run dry,[o]
   the cold flowing streams?
[15] But my people have forgotten me,
   they burn offerings to a delusion;
they have stumbled[p] in their ways,
   in the ancient roads,
and have gone into bypaths,
   not the highway,
[16] making their land a horror,
   a thing to be hissed at forever.
All who pass by it are horrified
   and shake their heads.
[17] Like the wind from the east,
   I will scatter them before the enemy.
I will show them my back, not my face,
   in the day of their calamity.

[m] Cn: Heb *of the field*   [n] Cn: Heb *foreign*   [o] Cn: Heb *Are . . . plucked up?*   [p] Gk Syr Vg: Heb *they made them stumble*

A Plot against Jeremiah

18 Then they said, "Come, let us make plots against Jer·e·mī´ah—for instruction shall not perish from the priest, nor counsel from the wise, nor the word from the prophet. Come, let us bring charges against him,[q] and let us not heed any of his words."

19 Give heed to me, O LORD,
    and listen to what my adversaries say!
20 Is evil a recompense for good?
    Yet they have dug a pit for my life.
Remember how I stood before you
    to speak good for them,
    to turn away your wrath from them.
21 Therefore give their children over to famine;
    hurl them out to the power of the sword,
let their wives become childless and widowed.
    May their men meet death by pestilence,
    their youths be slain by the sword in battle.
22 May a cry be heard from their houses,
    when you bring the marauder suddenly upon them!
For they have dug a pit to catch me,
    and laid snares for my feet.
23 Yet you, O LORD, know
    all their plotting to kill me.

When was the last time you saw snow? Do you live in a place where it snows every year, or do you live in a place where it hardly ever snows? Snow is rare in Palestine. In the hills, there are usually three days of snow each year, and there are many snow-capped mountains. The coldness, cleanness, and beauty of snow were a wonder to the people of Bible times.

Do not forgive their iniquity,
    do not blot out their sin from your sight.
Let them be tripped up before you;
    deal with them while you are angry.

In Bible times, people used broken pieces of pottery, called potshards, for writing tablets, receipts, lists, or notes. Sometimes prophets used the word "potsherd" to mean dryness and worthlessness.

The Broken Earthenware Jug

19 Thus said the LORD: Go and buy a potter's earthenware jug. Take with you[r] some of the elders of the people and some of the senior priests, 2and go out to the valley of the son of Hin´nom at the entry of the Potsherd Gate, and proclaim there the words that I tell you. 3You shall say: Hear the word of the LORD, O kings of Judah and inhabitants of Jerusalem. Thus says the LORD of hosts, the God of Israel: I am going to bring such disaster upon this place that the ears of everyone who hears of it will tingle. 4Because the people have forsaken me, and have profaned this place by making offerings in it to other gods whom neither they nor their ancestors nor the kings of Judah have known, and because they have filled this place with the blood of the innocent, 5and gone on building the high places of Bā´al to burn their children in the fire as burnt offerings to Bā´al, which I did not command or decree, nor did it enter my mind; 6therefore the days are surely coming, says the LORD, when this place shall no more be called Tō´pheth, or the valley of the son of Hin´nom, but the valley of Slaughter. 7And in this place I will make void the plans of Judah and Jerusalem, and will make them

[q] Heb strike him with the tongue   [r] Syr Tg Compare Gk: Heb lacks take with you

fall by the sword before their enemies, and by the hand of those who seek their life. I will give their dead bodies for food to the birds of the air and to the wild animals of the earth. ⁸And I will make this city a horror, a thing to be hissed at; everyone who passes by it will be horrified and will hiss because of all its disasters. ⁹And I will make them eat the flesh of their sons and the flesh of their daughters, and all shall eat the flesh of their neighbors in the siege, and in the distress with which their enemies and those who seek their life afflict them.

10 Then you shall break the jug in the sight of those who go with you, ¹¹and shall say to them: Thus says the LORD of hosts: So will I break this people and this city, as one breaks a potter's vessel, so that it can never be mended. In Tŏ´pheth they shall bury until there is no more room to bury. ¹²Thus will I do to this place, says the LORD, and to its inhabitants, making this city like Tŏ´pheth. ¹³And the houses of Jerusalem and the houses of the kings of Judah shall be defiled like the place of Tŏ´pheth—all the houses upon whose roofs offerings have been made to the whole host of heaven, and libations have been poured out to other gods.

14 When Jer·e·mi´ah came from Tŏ´pheth, where the LORD had sent him to prophesy, he stood in the court of the LORD's house and said to all the people: ¹⁵Thus says the LORD of hosts, the God of Israel: I am now bringing upon this city and upon all its towns all the disaster that I have pronounced against it, because they have stiffened their necks, refusing to hear my words.

Jeremiah Persecuted by Pashhur

20 Now the priest Pash´hur son of Im´mer, who was chief officer in the house of the LORD, heard Jer·e·mi´ah prophesying these things. ²Then Pash´hur struck the prophet Jer·e·mi´ah, and put him in the stocks that were in the upper Benjamin Gate of the house of the LORD. ³The next morning when Pash´hur released

Jer·e·mi´ah from the stocks, Jer·e·mi´ah said to him, The LORD has named you not Pash´hur but "Terror-all-around." ⁴For thus says the LORD: I am making you a terror to yourself and to all your friends; and they shall fall by the sword of their enemies while you look on. And I will give all Judah into the hand of the king of Babylon; he shall carry them captive to Babylon, and shall kill them with the sword. ⁵I will give all the wealth of this city, all its gains, all its prized belongings, and all the treasures of the kings of Judah into the hand of their enemies, who shall plunder them, and seize them, and carry them to Babylon. ⁶And you, Pash´hur, and all who live in your house, shall go into captivity, and to Babylon you shall go; there you shall die, and there you shall be buried, you and all your friends, to whom you have prophesied falsely.

Jeremiah Denounces His Persecutors

⁷ O LORD, you have enticed me,
    and I was enticed;
you have overpowered me,
    and you have prevailed.
I have become a laughingstock all day
        long;
    everyone mocks me.
⁸ For whenever I speak, I must cry out,
    I must shout, "Violence and
        destruction!"
For the word of the LORD has become
        for me
    a reproach and derision all day
        long.
⁹ If I say, "I will not mention him,
    or speak any more in his name,"
then within me there is something like
        a burning fire
    shut up in my bones;
I am weary with holding it in,
    and I cannot.
¹⁰ For I hear many whispering:
    "Terror is all around!
Denounce him! Let us denounce him!"
    All my close friends
    are watching for me to stumble.

"Perhaps he can be enticed,
and we can prevail against him,
and take our revenge on him."
[11] But the LORD is with me like a
dread warrior;
therefore my persecutors will
stumble,
and they will not prevail.
They will be greatly shamed,
for they will not succeed.
Their eternal dishonor
will never be forgotten.
[12] O LORD of hosts, you test the
righteous,
you see the heart and the mind;
let me see your retribution upon
them,
for to you I have committed my
cause.
[13] Sing to the LORD;
praise the LORD!
For he has delivered the life of the
needy
from the hands of evildoers.

[14] Cursed be the day
on which I was born!
The day when my mother bore
me,
let it not be blessed!
[15] Cursed be the man
who brought the news to my
father, saying,
"A child is born to you, a son,"
making him very glad.
[16] Let that man be like the cities
that the LORD overthrew without
pity;
let him hear a cry in the morning
and an alarm at noon,
[17] because he did not kill me in the
womb;
so my mother would have been
my grave,
and her womb forever great.
[18] Why did I come forth from the
womb
to see toil and sorrow,
and spend my days in shame?

Jerusalem Will Fall to Nebuchadrezzar

21 This is the word that came to Jer·e·mi´ah from the LORD, when King Zed·e·ki´ah sent to him Pash´hur son of Mal·chi´ah and the priest Zeph·a·ni´ah son of Mā·a·sēi´ah, saying, [2]"Please inquire of the LORD on our behalf, for King Ne·bū́ chad·rez´zar of Babylon is making war against us; perhaps the LORD will perform a wonderful deed for us, as he has often done, and will make him withdraw from us."

3 Then Jer·e·mi´ah said to them: [4]Thus you shall say to Zed·e·ki´ah: Thus says the LORD, the God of Israel: I am going to turn back the weapons of war that are in your hands and with which you are fighting against the king of Babylon and against the Chal·dē´ans who are besieging you outside the walls; and I will bring them together into the center of this city. [5]I myself will fight against you with outstretched hand and mighty arm, in anger, in fury, and in great wrath. [6]And I will strike down the inhabitants of this city, both human beings and animals; they shall die of a great pestilence. [7]Afterward, says the LORD, I will give King Zed·e·ki´ah of Judah, and his servants, and the people in this city—those who survive the pestilence, sword, and famine—into the hands of King Ne·bū́ chad·rez´zar of Babylon, into the hands of their enemies, into the hands of those who seek their lives. He shall strike them down with the edge of the sword; he shall not pity them, or spare them, or have compassion.

8 And to this people you shall say: Thus says the LORD: See, I am setting before you the way of life and the way of death. [9]Those who stay in this city shall die by the sword, by famine, and by pestilence; but those who go out and surrender to the Chal·dē´ans who are besieging you shall live and shall have their lives as a prize of war. [10]For I have set my face against this city for evil and not for good, says the LORD: it shall be given into the

hands of the king of Babylon, and he shall burn it with fire.

Message to the House of David

11 To the house of the king of Judah say: Hear the word of the LORD, [12]O house of David! Thus says the LORD:

Execute justice in the morning,
and deliver from the hand of the
oppressor
anyone who has been robbed,
or else my wrath will go forth like
fire,
and burn, with no one to quench
it,
because of your evil doings.

[13] See, I am against you, O inhabitant of
the valley,
O rock of the plain,
says the LORD;
you who say, "Who can come down
against us,
or who can enter our places of
refuge?"
[14] I will punish you according to the fruit
of your doings,
says the LORD;
I will kindle a fire in its forest,
and it shall devour all that is around
it.

Exhortation to Repent

22 Thus says the LORD: Go down to the house of the king of Judah, and speak there this word, [2]and say: Hear the word of the LORD, O King of Judah sitting on the throne of David—you, and your servants, and your people who enter these gates. [3]Thus says the LORD: Act with justice and righteousness, and deliver from the hand of the oppressor anyone who has been robbed. And do no wrong or violence to the alien, the orphan, and the widow, or shed innocent blood in this place. [4]For if you will indeed obey this word, then through the gates of this house shall enter kings who sit on the throne of David, riding in chariots and on horses, they, and their servants, and their people. [5]But if you will not heed these words, I swear by myself, says the LORD, that this house shall become a desolation. [6]For thus says the LORD concerning the house of the king of Judah:

You are like Gil′e·ad to me,
like the summit of Lebanon;
but I swear that I will make you a
desert,
an uninhabited city.[s]
[7] I will prepare destroyers against you,
all with their weapons;
they shall cut down your choicest
cedars
and cast them into the fire.

8 And many nations will pass by this city, and all of them will say one to another, "Why has the LORD dealt in this way with that great city?" [9]And they will answer, "Because they abandoned the covenant of the LORD their God, and worshiped other gods and served them."

[10] Do not weep for him who is dead,
nor bemoan him;
weep rather for him who goes away,
for he shall return no more
to see his native land.

King Josiah's son Jehoahaz (also called Shallum) was king of Judah about 609 BC. He reigned in Jerusalem for three months before he was taken to Egypt in captivity. His brother Jehoiakim became the next king. Jehoiakim had to live under the control of King Nebuchadnezzar of Babylon. After three years of paying tribute (taxes), Jehoiakim ignored the advice of Jeremiah, rebelled against Nebuchadnezzar, and lost his life. His son Jehoiachin became king but served only three months before being taken into exile.

[s] Cn: Heb *uninhabited cities*

Message to the Sons of Josiah

11 For thus says the LORD concerning Shal′lum son of King Jō·sī′ah of Judah, who succeeded his father Jō·sī′ah, and who went away from this place: He shall return here no more, [12]but in the place where they have carried him captive he shall die, and he shall never see this land again.

[13] Woe to him who builds his house by unrighteousness,
    and his upper rooms by injustice;
who makes his neighbors work for nothing,
    and does not give them their wages;
[14] who says, "I will build myself a spacious house
    with large upper rooms,"
and who cuts out windows for it,
    paneling it with cedar,
    and painting it with vermilion.
[15] Are you a king
    because you compete in cedar?
Did not your father eat and drink
    and do justice and righteousness?
    Then it was well with him.
[16] He judged the cause of the poor and needy;
    then it was well.
Is not this to know me?
    says the LORD.
[17] But your eyes and heart
    are only on your dishonest gain,
for shedding innocent blood,
    and for practicing oppression and violence.

18 Therefore thus says the LORD concerning King Je·hoi′a·kim son of Jō·sī′ah of Judah:
They shall not lament for him, saying,
    "Alas, my brother!" or "Alas, sister!"
They shall not lament for him, saying,
    "Alas, lord!" or "Alas, his majesty!"
[19] With the burial of a donkey he shall be buried—
    dragged off and thrown out beyond the gates of Jerusalem.

[20] Go up to Lebanon, and cry out,
    and lift up your voice in Bā′shan;
cry out from Ab′a·rim,
    for all your lovers are crushed.
[21] I spoke to you in your prosperity,
    but you said, "I will not listen."
This has been your way from your youth,
    for you have not obeyed my voice.
[22] The wind shall shepherd all your shepherds,
    and your lovers shall go into captivity;
then you will be ashamed and dismayed
    because of all your wickedness.
[23] O inhabitant of Lebanon,
    nested among the cedars,
how you will groan[f] when pangs come upon you,
    pain as of a woman in labor!

Judgment on Coniah (Jehoiachin)

24 As I live, says the LORD, even if King Cō·nī′ah son of Je·hoi′a·kim of Judah were the signet ring on my right hand, even from there I would tear you off [25]and give you into the hands of those who seek your life, into the hands of those of whom you are afraid, even into the hands of King Ne·bū·chad·rez′zar of Babylon and into the hands of the Chal·dē′ans. [26]I will hurl you and the mother who bore you into another country, where you were not born, and there you shall die. [27]But they shall not return to the land to which they long to return.
[28] Is this man Cō·nī′ah a despised broken pot,
    a vessel no one wants?
Why are he and his offspring hurled out
    and cast away in a land that they do not know?
[29] O land, land, land,
    hear the word of the LORD!
[30] Thus says the LORD:
Record this man as childless,

[f] Gk Vg Syr: Heb will be pitied

"The days are surely coming, says the LORD, when I will raise up for David a righteous Branch, and he shall reign as king and deal wisely, and shall execute justice and righteousness in the land. In his days Judah will be saved and Israel will live in safety. And this is the name by which he will be called: 'The LORD is our righteousness.'" Jeremiah 23:5–6

a man who shall not succeed in his days;
for none of his offspring shall succeed
in sitting on the throne of David,
and ruling again in Judah.

Restoration after Exile

23 Woe to the shepherds who destroy and scatter the sheep of my pasture! says the LORD. ²Therefore thus says the LORD, the God of Israel, concerning the shepherds who shepherd my people: It is you who have scattered my flock, and have driven them away, and you have not attended to them. So I will attend to you for your evil doings, says the LORD. ³Then I myself will gather the remnant of my flock out of all the lands where I have driven them, and I will bring them back to their fold, and they shall be fruitful and multiply. ⁴I will raise up shepherds over them who will shepherd them, and they shall not fear any longer, or be dismayed, nor shall any be missing, says the LORD.

The Righteous Branch of David

5 The days are surely coming, says the LORD, when I will raise up for David a righteous Branch, and he shall reign as king and deal wisely, and shall execute justice and righteousness in the land. ⁶In his days Judah will be saved and Israel will live in safety. And this is the name by which he will be called: "The LORD is our righteousness."

7 Therefore, the days are surely coming, says the LORD, when it shall no longer be said, "As the LORD lives who brought the people of Israel up out of the land of Egypt," ⁸but "As the LORD lives who brought out and led the offspring of the house of Israel out of the land of the north and out of all the lands where heᵘ had driven them." Then they shall live in their own land.

False Prophets of Hope Denounced

9 Concerning the prophets:
My heart is crushed within me,
all my bones shake;
I have become like a drunkard,
like one overcome by wine,
because of the LORD
and because of his holy words.

10 For the land is full of adulterers;
because of the curse the land mourns,
and the pastures of the wilderness are dried up.
Their course has been evil,
and their might is not right.

11 Both prophet and priest are ungodly;
even in my house I have found their wickedness,
says the LORD.

12 Therefore their way shall be to them
like slippery paths in the darkness,
into which they shall be driven and fall;
for I will bring disaster upon them
in the year of their punishment,
says the LORD.

13 In the prophets of Sa·mar′i·a
I saw a disgusting thing:
they prophesied by Ba′al
and led my people Israel astray.

14 But in the prophets of Jerusalem
I have seen a more shocking thing:
they commit adultery and walk in lies;
they strengthen the hands of evildoers,
so that no one turns from wickedness;
all of them have become like Sod′om to me,

ᵘ Gk: Heb *I*

and its inhabitants like Go·mor´rah.
¹⁵ Therefore thus says the LORD of hosts
concerning the prophets:
"I am going to make them eat
wormwood,
and give them poisoned water to
drink;
for from the prophets of Jerusalem
ungodliness has spread throughout
the land."

16 Thus says the LORD of hosts: Do not listen to the words of the prophets who prophesy to you; they are deluding you. They speak visions of their own minds, not from the mouth of the LORD. ¹⁷They keep saying to those who despise the word of the LORD, "It shall be well with you"; and to all who stubbornly follow their own stubborn hearts, they say, "No calamity shall come upon you."

¹⁸ For who has stood in the council of
the LORD
so as to see and to hear his word?
Who has given heed to his word so
as to proclaim it?
¹⁹ Look, the storm of the LORD!
Wrath has gone forth,
a whirling tempest;
it will burst upon the head of the
wicked.
²⁰ The anger of the LORD will not turn
back
until he has executed and
accomplished
the intents of his mind.
In the latter days you will understand
it clearly.

²¹ I did not send the prophets,
yet they ran;
I did not speak to them,
yet they prophesied.
²² But if they had stood in my council,
then they would have proclaimed
my words to my people,
and they would have turned them
from their evil way,
and from the evil of their doings.

23 Am I a God near by, says the LORD, and not a God far off? ²⁴Who can hide in secret places so that I cannot see them? says the LORD. Do I not fill heaven and earth? says the LORD. ²⁵I have heard what the prophets have said who prophesy lies in my name, saying, "I have dreamed, I have dreamed!" ²⁶How long? Will the hearts of the prophets ever turn back—those who prophesy lies, and who prophesy the deceit of their own heart? ²⁷They plan to make my people forget my name by their dreams that they tell one another, just as their ancestors forgot my name for Ba´al. ²⁸Let the prophet who has a dream tell the dream, but let the one who has my word speak my word faithfully. What has straw in common with wheat? says the LORD. ²⁹Is not my word like fire, says the LORD, and like a hammer that breaks a rock in pieces? ³⁰See, therefore, I am against the prophets, says the LORD, who steal my words from one another. ³¹See, I am against the prophets, says the LORD, who use their own tongues and say, "Says the LORD." ³²See, I am against those who prophesy lying dreams, says the LORD, and who tell them, and who lead my people astray by their lies and their recklessness, when I did not send them or appoint them; so they do not profit this people at all, says the LORD.

33 When this people, or a prophet, or a priest asks you, "What is the burden of the LORD?" you shall say to them, "You are the burden,ᵛ and I will cast you off, says the LORD." ³⁴And as for the prophet, priest, or the people who say, "The burden of the LORD," I will punish them and their households. ³⁵Thus shall you say to one another, among yourselves, "What has the LORD answered?" or "What has the LORD spoken?" ³⁶But "the burden of the LORD" you shall mention no more, for the burden is everyone's own word, and so you pervert the words of the living God, the LORD of hosts, our God. ³⁷Thus you shall ask the prophet, "What has the LORD answered

ᵛ Gk Vg: Heb *What burden*

"I will give them a heart to know that I am the LORD; and they shall be my people and I will be their God, for they shall return to me with their whole heart."

Jeremiah 24:7

you?" or "What has the LORD spoken?" [38]But if you say, "the burden of the LORD," thus says the LORD: Because you have said these words, "the burden of the LORD," when I sent to you, saying, You shall not say, "the burden of the LORD," [39]therefore, I will surely lift you up[w] and cast you away from my presence, you and the city that I gave to you and your ancestors. [40]And I will bring upon you everlasting disgrace and perpetual shame, which shall not be forgotten.

The Good and the Bad Figs

24 The LORD showed me two baskets of figs placed before the temple of the LORD. This was after King Ne·bu·chad·rez´zar of Babylon had taken into exile from Jerusalem King Jec·o·ni´ah son of Je·hoi´a·kim of Judah, together with the officials of Judah, the artisans, and the smiths, and had brought them to Babylon. [2]One basket had very good figs, like first-ripe figs, but the other basket had very bad figs, so bad that they could not be eaten. [3]And the LORD said to me, "What do you see, Jer·e·mi´ah?" I said, "Figs, the good figs very good, and the bad figs very bad, so bad that they cannot be eaten."

4 Then the word of the LORD came to me: [5]Thus says the LORD, the God of Israel: Like these good figs, so I will regard as good the exiles from Judah, whom I have sent away from this place to the land of the Chal·de´ans. [6]I will set my eyes upon them for good, and I will bring them back to this land. I will build them up, and not tear them down; I will plant them, and not pluck them up. [7]I will give them a heart to know that I am the LORD; and they shall be my people and I will be their God, for they

shall return to me with their whole heart.

8 But thus says the LORD: Like the bad figs that are so bad they cannot be eaten, so will I treat King Zed·e·ki´ah of Judah, his officials, the remnant of Jerusalem who remain in this land, and those who live in the land of Egypt. [9]I will make them a horror, an evil thing, to all the kingdoms of the earth—a disgrace, a byword, a taunt, and a curse in all the places where I shall drive them. [10]And I will send sword, famine, and pestilence upon them, until they are utterly destroyed from the land that I gave to them and their ancestors.

The Babylonian Captivity Foretold

25 The word that came to Jer·e·mi´ah concerning all the people of Judah, in the fourth year of King Je·hoi´a·kim son of Jo·si´ah of Judah (that was the first year of King Ne·bu-chad·rez´zar of Babylon), [2]which the prophet Jer·e·mi´ah spoke to all the people of Judah and all the inhabitants of Jerusalem: [3]For twenty-three years, from the thirteenth year of King Jo·si´ah son of A´mon of Judah, to this day, the word of the LORD has come to me, and I have spoken persistently to you, but you have not listened. [4]And though the LORD persistently sent you all his servants the prophets, you have neither listened nor inclined your ears to hear [5]when they said, "Turn now, everyone of you, from your evil way and wicked doings, and you will remain upon the land that the LORD has given to you and your ancestors from of old and forever; [6]do not go after other gods to serve and worship them, and do not provoke me to anger with the work of your hands. Then I will do you no harm." [7]Yet you did not listen to me, says the LORD, and so you have provoked me to anger with the work of your hands to your own harm.

8 Therefore thus says the LORD of hosts: Because you have not obeyed my words, [9]I am going to send for all the tribes of the

[w] Heb Mss Gk Vg: MT *forget you*

north, says the LORD, even for King Ne·bū´ chad·rez´zar of Babylon, my servant, and I will bring them against this land and its inhabitants, and against all these nations around; I will utterly destroy them, and make them an object of horror and of hissing, and an everlasting disgrace.ˣ ¹⁰And I will banish from them the sound of mirth and the sound of gladness, the voice of the bridegroom and the voice of the bride, the sound of the millstones and the light of the lamp. ¹¹This whole land shall become a ruin and a waste, and these nations shall serve the king of Babylon seventy years. ¹²Then after seventy years are completed, I will punish the king of Babylon and that nation, the land of the Chal·de´ans, for their iniquity, says the LORD, making the land an everlasting waste. ¹³I will bring upon that land all the words that I have uttered against it, everything written in this book, which Jer·e·mī´ah prophesied against all the nations. ¹⁴For many nations and great kings shall make slaves of them also; and I will repay them according to their deeds and the work of their hands.

The Cup of God's Wrath

15 For thus the LORD, the God of Israel, said to me: Take from my hand this cup of the wine of wrath, and make all the nations to whom I send you drink it. ¹⁶They shall drink and stagger and go out of their minds because of the sword that I am sending among them.

17 So I took the cup from the LORD's hand, and made all the nations to whom the LORD sent me drink it: ¹⁸Jerusalem and the towns of Judah, its kings and officials, to make them a desolation and a waste, an object of hissing and of cursing, as they are today; ¹⁹Pharaoh king of Egypt, his servants, his officials, and all his people; ²⁰all the mixed people;ʸ all the kings of the land of Uz; all the kings of the land of the Phi·lis´tines—Ash´ke·lon, Gā´za, Ek´ron, and the remnant of Ash´dod; ²¹E´dom, Mō´ab, and the Am´mon·ites; ²²all the kings of Tyre, all the kings of Sī´don, and

the kings of the coastland across the sea; ²³Dē´dan, Tē´ma, Buz, and all who have shaven temples; ²⁴all the kings of Arabia and all the kings of the mixed peoplesʸ that live in the desert; ²⁵all the kings of Zim´rī, all the kings of Ē´lam, and all the kings of Mēd´i·a; ²⁶all the kings of the north, far and near, one after another, and all the kingdoms of the world that are on the face of the earth. And after them the king of Shē´shachᶻ shall drink.

27 Then you shall say to them, Thus says the LORD of hosts, the God of Israel: Drink, get drunk and vomit, fall and rise no more, because of the sword that I am sending among you.

28 And if they refuse to accept the cup from your hand to drink, then you shall say to them: Thus says the LORD of hosts: You must drink! ²⁹See, I am beginning to bring disaster on the city that is called by my name, and how can you possibly avoid punishment? You shall not go unpunished, for I am summoning a sword against all the inhabitants of the earth, says the LORD of hosts.

30 You, therefore, shall prophesy against them all these words, and say to them:

The LORD will roar from on high,
    and from his holy habitation utter
        his voice;
he will roar mightily against his fold,
    and shout, like those who tread
        grapes,
    against all the inhabitants of the earth.
31 The clamor will resound to the ends of
        the earth,
    for the LORD has an indictment
        against the nations;
he is entering into judgment with all
        flesh,
    and the guilty he will put to the
        sword,

says the LORD.

32 Thus says the LORD of hosts:

ˣ Gk Compare Syr: Heb *and everlasting desolations*
ʸ Meaning of Heb uncertain   ᶻ *Sheshach* is a cryptogram for *Babel*, Babylon

See, disaster is spreading
 from nation to nation,
and a great tempest is stirring
 from the farthest parts of the earth!
33 Those slain by the LORD on that day
shall extend from one end of the earth to
the other. They shall not be lamented, or
gathered, or buried; they shall become
dung on the surface of the ground.
34 Wail, you shepherds, and cry out;
 roll in ashes, you lords of the flock,
for the days of your slaughter have
 come—and your dispersions,ᵃ
and you shall fall like a choice
 vessel.
35 Flight shall fail the shepherds,
 and there shall be no escape for the
 lords of the flock.
36 Hark! the cry of the shepherds,
 and the wail of the lords of the
 flock!
For the LORD is despoiling their
 pasture,
37 and the peaceful folds are
 devastated,
because of the fierce anger of the
 LORD.
38 Like a lion he has left his covert;
 for their land has become a waste
because of the cruel sword,
 and because of his fierce anger.

Jeremiah's Prophecies in the Temple

26 At the beginning of the reign of
King Je·hoi′a·kim son of Jō·sī′ah
of Judah, this word came from the LORD:
2Thus says the LORD: Stand in the court of
the LORD's house, and speak to all the cities
of Judah that come to worship in the
house of the LORD; speak to them all the
words that I command you; do not hold
back a word. 3It may be that they will listen, all of them, and will turn from their
evil way, that I may change my mind about
the disaster that I intend to bring on them
because of their evil doings. 4You shall say
to them: Thus says the LORD: If you will
not listen to me, to walk in my law that I

have set before you, 5and to heed the
words of my servants the prophets whom
I send to you urgently—though you have
not heeded— 6then I will make this house
like Shī′lōh, and I will make this city a
curse for all the nations of the earth.

7 The priests and the prophets and all
the people heard Jer·e·mī′ah speaking
these words in the house of the LORD. 8And
when Jer·e·mī′ah had finished speaking all
that the LORD had commanded him to
speak to all the people, then the priests
and the prophets and all the people laid
hold of him, saying, "You shall die! 9Why
have you prophesied in the name of the
LORD, saying, 'This house shall be like Shī′-
lōh, and this city shall be desolate, without
inhabitant'?" And all the people gathered
around Jer·e·mī′ah in the house of the
LORD.

10 When the officials of Judah heard
these things, they came up from the king's
house to the house of the LORD and took
their seat in the entry of the New Gate of
the house of the LORD. 11Then the priests
and the prophets said to the officials and to
all the people, "This man deserves the sentence of death because he has prophesied
against this city, as you have heard with
your own ears."

12 Then Jer·e·mī′ah spoke to all the
officials and all the people, saying, "It is the
LORD who sent me to prophesy against this
house and this city all the words you have
heard. 13Now therefore amend your ways
and your doings, and obey the voice of the
LORD your God, and the LORD will change
his mind about the disaster that he has
pronounced against you. 14But as for me,
here I am in your hands. Do with me as
seems good and right to you. 15Only know
for certain that if you put me to death, you
will be bringing innocent blood upon
yourselves and upon this city and its
inhabitants, for in truth the LORD sent me
to you to speak all these words in your
ears."

ᵃ Meaning of Heb uncertain

16 Then the officials and all the people said to the priests and the prophets, "This man does not deserve the sentence of death, for he has spoken to us in the name of the LORD our God." 17And some of the elders of the land arose and said to all the assembled people, 18"Mĭ′cah of Mŏ′re·sheth, who prophesied during the days of King Hez·e·kī′ah of Judah, said to all the people of Judah: 'Thus says the LORD of hosts,

Zion shall be plowed as a field;
   Jerusalem shall become a heap of
      ruins,
   and the mountain of the house a
      wooded height.'

19Did King Hez·e·kī′ah of Judah and all Judah actually put him to death? Did he not fear the LORD and entreat the favor of the LORD, and did not the LORD change his mind about the disaster that he had pronounced against them? But we are about to bring great disaster on ourselves!"

20 There was another man prophesying in the name of the LORD, Ū·rī′ah son of She·māi′ah from Kir′i·ath-jē′a·rim. He prophesied against this city and against this land in words exactly like those of Jer·e·mī′ah. 21And when King Je·hoi′a·kim, with all his warriors and all the officials, heard his words, the king sought to put him to death; but when Ū·rī′ah heard of it, he was afraid and fled and escaped to Egypt. 22Then King Je·hoi′a·kim sent[b] El·nā′than son of Ach′bor and men with him to Egypt, 23and they took Ū·rī′ah from Egypt and brought him to King Je·hoi′a·kim, who struck him down with the sword and threw his dead body into the burial place of the common people.

24 But the hand of A·hī′kam son of Shā′phan was with Jer·e·mī′ah so that he was not given over into the hands of the people to be put to death.

The Sign of the Yoke

27 In the beginning of the reign of King Zed·e·kī′ah[c] son of Jŏ·sī′ah of Judah, this word came to Jer·e·mī′ah

from the LORD. 2Thus the LORD said to me: Make yourself a yoke of straps and bars, and put them on your neck. 3Send word[d] to the king of Ē′dom, the king of Mŏ′ab, the king of the Am′mon·ites, the king of Tÿre, and the king of Sī′don by the hand of the envoys who have come to Jerusalem to King Zed·e·kī′ah of Judah. 4Give them this charge for their masters: Thus says the LORD of hosts, the God of Israel: This is what you shall say to your masters: 5It is I who by my great power and my outstretched arm have made the earth, with the people and animals that are on the earth, and I give it to whomever I please. 6Now I have given all these lands into the hand of King Ne·bū·chad·nez′zar of Babylon, my servant, and I have given him even the wild animals of the field to serve him. 7All the nations shall serve him and his son and his grandson, until the time of his own land comes; then many nations and great kings shall make him their slave.

8 But if any nation or kingdom will not serve this king, Ne·bū·chad·nez′zar of Babylon, and put its neck under the yoke of the king of Babylon, then I will punish that nation with the sword, with famine, and with pestilence, says the LORD, until I have completed its[e] destruction by his hand. 9You, therefore, must not listen to your prophets, your diviners, your dreamers,[f] your soothsayers, or your sorcerers, who are saying to you, "You shall not serve the king of Babylon." 10For they are prophesying a lie to you, with the result that you will be removed far from your land; I will drive you out, and you will perish. 11But any nation that will bring its neck under the yoke of the king of Babylon and serve him, I will leave on its own land, says the LORD, to till it and live there.

12 I spoke to King Zed·e·kī′ah of Judah in the same way: Bring your necks under the yoke of the king of Babylon, and serve him and his people, and live. 13Why

b Heb adds men to Egypt   c Another reading is Jehoiakim   d Cn: Heb send them   e Heb their f Gk Syr Vg: Heb dreams should you and your people die by the sword, by famine, and by pestilence, as the LORD has spoken concerning any nation that will not serve the king of Babylon? [14]Do not listen to the words of the prophets who are telling you not to serve the king of Babylon, for they are prophesying a lie to you. [15]I have not sent them, says the LORD, but they are prophesying falsely in my name, with the result that I will drive you out and you will perish, you and the prophets who are prophesying to you.

16 Then I spoke to the priests and to all this people, saying, Thus says the LORD: Do not listen to the words of your prophets who are prophesying to you, saying, "The vessels of the LORD's house will soon be brought back from Babylon," for they are prophesying a lie to you. [17]Do not listen to them; serve the king of Babylon and live. Why should this city become a desolation? [18]If indeed they are prophets, and if the word of the LORD is with them, then let them intercede with the LORD of hosts, that the vessels left in the house of the LORD, in the house of the king of Judah, and in Jerusalem may not go to Babylon. [19]For thus says the LORD of hosts concerning the pillars, the sea, the stands, and the rest of the vessels that are left in this city, [20]which King Ne·bu·chad·nez´zar of Babylon did not take away when he took into exile from Jerusalem to Babylon King Jec·o·ni´ah son of Je·hoi´a·kim of Judah, and all the nobles of Judah and Jerusalem— [21]thus says the LORD of hosts, the God of Israel, concerning the vessels left in the house of the LORD, in the house of the king of Judah, and in Jerusalem: [22]They shall be carried to Babylon, and there they shall stay, until the day when I give attention to them, says the LORD. Then I will bring them up and restore them to this place.

Hananiah Opposes Jeremiah and Dies

28 In that same year, at the beginning of the reign of King Zed·e·ki´-ah of Judah, in the fifth month of the fourth year, the prophet Han·a·ni´ah son of Az´zur, from Gib´e·on, spoke to me in the house of the LORD, in the presence of the priests and all the people, saying, [2]"Thus says the LORD of hosts, the God of Israel: I have broken the yoke of the king of Babylon. [3]Within two years I will bring back to this place all the vessels of the LORD's house, which King Ne·bu·chad·nez´zar of Babylon took away from this place and carried to Babylon. [4]I will also bring back to this place King Jec·o·ni´ah son of Je·hoi´-a·kim of Judah, and all the exiles from Judah who went to Babylon, says the LORD, for I will break the yoke of the king of Babylon."

5 Then the prophet Jer·e·mi´ah spoke to the prophet Han·a·ni´ah in the presence of the priests and all the people who were standing in the house of the LORD; [6]and the prophet Jer·e·mi´ah said, "Amen! May the LORD do so; may the LORD fulfill the words that you have prophesied, and bring back to this place from Babylon the vessels of the house of the LORD, and all the exiles. [7]But listen now to this word that I speak in your hearing and in the hearing of all the people. [8]The prophets who preceded you and me from ancient times prophesied war, famine, and pestilence against many countries and great kingdoms. [9]As for the prophet who prophesies peace, when the word of that prophet comes true, then it will be known that the LORD has truly sent the prophet."

10 Then the prophet Han·a·ni´ah took the yoke from the neck of the prophet Jer·e·mi´ah, and broke it. [11]And Han·a·ni´-ah spoke in the presence of all the people, saying, "Thus says the LORD: This is how I will break the yoke of King Ne·bu·chad·nez´zar of Babylon from the neck of all the nations within two years." At this, the prophet Jer·e·mi´ah went his way.

12 Sometime after the prophet Han·a·ni´ah had broken the yoke from the neck of the prophet Jer·e·mi´ah, the word of the LORD came to Jer·e·mi´ah: [13]Go, tell Han·a·ni´ah, Thus says the LORD: You have

broken wooden bars only to forge iron bars in place of them! ¹⁴For thus says the LORD of hosts, the God of Israel: I have put an iron yoke on the neck of all these nations so that they may serve King Ne·bū·chad·nez´zar of Babylon, and they shall indeed serve him; I have even given him the wild animals. ¹⁵And the prophet Jer·e·mī´ah said to the prophet Han·a·nī´ah, "Listen, Han·a·nī´ah, the LORD has not sent you, and you made this people trust in a lie. ¹⁶Therefore thus says the LORD: I am going to send you off the face of the earth. Within this year you will be dead, because you have spoken rebellion against the LORD."

17 In that same year, in the seventh month, the prophet Han·a·nī´ah died.

Jeremiah's Letter to the Exiles in Babylon

29 These are the words of the letter that the prophet Jer·e·mī´ah sent from Jerusalem to the remaining elders among the exiles, and to the priests, the prophets, and all the people, whom Ne·bū·chad·nez´zar had taken into exile from Jerusalem to Babylon. ²This was after King Jec·o·nī´ah, and the queen mother, the court officials, the leaders of Judah and Jerusalem, the artisans, and the smiths had departed from Jerusalem. ³The letter was sent by the hand of El·ā´sah son of Shā´phan and Gem·a·rī´ah son of Hil·kī´ah, whom King Zed·e·kī´ah of Judah sent to Babylon to King Ne·bū·chad·nez´zar of Babylon. It said: ⁴Thus says the LORD of hosts, the God of Israel, to all the exiles whom I have sent into exile from Jerusalem to Babylon: ⁵Build houses and live in them; plant gardens and eat what they produce. ⁶Take wives and have sons and daughters; take wives for your sons, and give your daughters in marriage, that they may bear sons and daughters; multiply there, and do not decrease. ⁷But seek the welfare of the city where I have sent you into exile, and pray to the LORD on its behalf, for in its welfare you will find your welfare. ⁸For thus says the LORD of hosts,

> "Then when you call upon me and come and pray to me, I will hear you. When you search for me, you will find me; if you seek me with all your heart."
>
> Jeremiah 29:12–13

the God of Israel: Do not let the prophets and the diviners who are among you deceive you, and do not listen to the dreams that they dream,ᵍ ⁹for it is a lie that they are prophesying to you in my name; I did not send them, says the LORD.

10 For thus says the LORD: Only when Babylon's seventy years are completed will I visit you, and I will fulfill to you my promise and bring you back to this place. ¹¹For surely I know the plans I have for you, says the LORD, plans for your welfare and not for harm, to give you a future with hope. ¹²Then when you call upon me and come and pray to me, I will hear you. ¹³When you search for me, you will find me; if you seek me with all your heart, ¹⁴I will let you find me, says the LORD, and I will restore your fortunes and gather you from all the nations and all the places where I have driven you, says the LORD, and I will bring you back to the place from which I sent you into exile.

15 Because you have said, "The LORD has raised up prophets for us in Babylon,"— ¹⁶Thus says the LORD concerning the king who sits on the throne of David, and concerning all the people who live in this city, your kinsfolk who did not go out with you into exile: ¹⁷Thus says the LORD of hosts, I am going to let loose on them sword, famine, and pestilence, and I will make them like rotten figs that are so bad they cannot be eaten. ¹⁸I will pursue them with the sword, with famine, and with pestilence, and will make them a horror to all the kingdoms of the earth, to be an object of cursing, and horror, and hissing, and a derision among all the nations where I have driven them, ¹⁹because they

---

ᵍ Cn: Heb *your dreams that you cause to dream*

did not heed my words, says the LORD, when I persistently sent to you my servants the prophets, but they[h] would not listen, says the LORD. [20]But now, all you exiles whom I sent away from Jerusalem to Babylon, hear the word of the LORD: [21]Thus says the LORD of hosts, the God of Israel, concerning Āʹhab son of Kōʹlaiʹah and Zed·e·kiʹah son of Mā·a·seiʹah, who are prophesying a lie to you in my name: I am going to deliver them into the hand of King Ne·bū·chad·rezʹzar of Babylon, and he shall kill them before your eyes. [22]And on account of them this curse shall be used by all the exiles from Judah in Babylon: "The LORD make you like Zed·e·kiʹah and Āʹhab, whom the king of Babylon roasted in the fire," [23]because they have perpetrated outrage in Israel and have committed adultery with their neighbors' wives, and have spoken in my name lying words that I did not command them; I am the one who knows and bears witness, says the LORD.

The Letter of Shemaiah

24 To She·māiʹah of Ne·helʹam you shall say: [25]Thus says the LORD of hosts, the God of Israel: In your own name you sent a letter to all the people who are in Jerusalem, and to the priest Zeph·a·niʹah son of Māa·seiʹah, and to all the priests, saying, [26]The LORD himself has made you priest instead of the priest Je·hoiʹa·da, so that there may be officers in the house of the LORD to control any madman who plays the prophet, to put him in the stocks and the collar. [27]So now why have you not rebuked Jer·e·miʹah of Anʹa·thoth who plays the prophet for you? [28]For he has actually sent to us in Babylon, saying, "It will be a long time; build houses and live in them, and plant gardens and eat what they produce."

29 The priest Zeph·a·niʹah read this letter in the hearing of the prophet Jer·e·miʹah. [30]Then the word of the LORD came to Jer·e·miʹah: [31]Send to all the exiles, saying, Thus says the LORD concerning She·māiʹah of Ne·helʹam: Because She·māiʹah has prophesied to you, though I did not send

him, and has led you to trust in a lie, [32]therefore thus says the LORD: I am going to punish She·māiʹah of Ne·helʹam and his descendants; he shall not have anyone living among this people to see[i] the good that I am going to do to my people, says the LORD, for he has spoken rebellion against the LORD.

Restoration Promised for Israel and Judah

30 The word that came to Jer·e·miʹah from the LORD: [2]Thus says the LORD, the God of Israel: Write in a book all the words that I have spoken to you. [3]For the days are surely coming, says the LORD, when I will restore the fortunes of my people, Israel and Judah, says the LORD, and I will bring them back to the land that I gave to their ancestors and they shall take possession of it.

4 These are the words that the LORD spoke concerning Israel and Judah:
5 Thus says the LORD:
We have heard a cry of panic,
    of terror, and no peace.
6 Ask now, and see,
    can a man bear a child?
Why then do I see every man
    with his hands on his loins like a
        woman in labor?
Why has every face turned pale?
7 Alas! that day is so great
    there is none like it;
it is a time of distress for Jacob;
    yet he shall be rescued from it.

8 On that day, says the LORD of hosts, I will break the yoke from off his[j] neck, and I will burst his[j] bonds, and strangers shall no more make a servant of him. [9]But they shall serve the LORD their God and David their king, whom I will raise up for them.
10 But as for you, have no fear, my
        servant Jacob, says the LORD,
    and do not be dismayed, O Israel;
for I am going to save you from far
        away,

---

[h] Syr: Heb you   [i] Gk: Heb and he shall not see
[j] Cn: Heb your

and your offspring from the land of
their captivity.
Jacob shall return and have quiet and
ease,
and no one shall make him afraid.
11 For I am with you, says the LORD, to
save you;
I will make an end of all the nations
among which I scattered you,
but of you I will not make an end.
I will chastise you in just measure,
and I will by no means leave you
unpunished.

12 For thus says the LORD:
Your hurt is incurable,
your wound is grievous.
13 There is no one to uphold your cause,
no medicine for your wound,
no healing for you.
14 All your lovers have forgotten you;
they care nothing for you;
for I have dealt you the blow of an
enemy,
the punishment of a merciless foe,
because your guilt is great,
because your sins are so numerous.
15 Why do you cry out over your hurt?
Your pain is incurable.
Because your guilt is great,
because your sins are so numerous,
I have done these things to you.
16 Therefore all who devour you shall be
devoured,
and all your foes, everyone of them,
shall go into captivity;
those who plunder you shall be
plundered,
and all who prey on you I will make
a prey.
17 For I will restore health to you,
and your wounds I will heal,
says the LORD,
because they have called you an outcast:
"It is Zion; no one cares for her!"

18 Thus says the LORD:
I am going to restore the fortunes of
the tents of Jacob,

and have compassion on his
dwellings;
the city shall be rebuilt upon its
mound,
and the citadel set on its rightful site.
19 Out of them shall come thanksgiving,
and the sound of merrymakers.
I will make them many, and they shall
not be few;
I will make them honored, and they
shall not be disdained.
20 Their children shall be as of old,
their congregation shall be
established before me;
and I will punish all who oppress
them.
21 Their prince shall be one of their own,
their ruler shall come from their
midst;
I will bring him near, and he shall
approach me,
for who would otherwise dare to
approach me?
says the LORD.
22 And you shall be my people,
and I will be your God.

23 Look, the storm of the LORD!
Wrath has gone forth,
a whirling[k] tempest;
it will burst upon the head of the
wicked.
24 The fierce anger of the LORD will not
turn back
until he has executed and
accomplished
the intents of his mind.
In the latter days you will understand
this.

The Joyful Return of the Exiles

31 At that time, says the LORD, I will
be the God of all the families of
Israel, and they shall be my people.
2 Thus says the LORD:
The people who survived the sword
found grace in the wilderness;
when Israel sought for rest,

[k] One Ms: Meaning of MT uncertain

3 the LORD appeared to him[l] from far
away.[m]
I have loved you with an everlasting
love;
therefore I have continued my
faithfulness to you.
4 Again I will build you, and you shall
be built,
O virgin Israel!
Again shall take[n] your tambourines,
go forth in the dance of the
merrymakers.
5 Again you shall plant vineyards
on the mountains of Sa·mār´i·a;
the planters shall plant,
and shall enjoy the fruit.
6 For there shall be a day when sentinels
will call
in the hill country of Ē´phra·im:
"Come, let us go up to Zion,
to the LORD our God."

7 For thus says the LORD:
Sing aloud with gladness for Jacob,
and raise shouts for the chief of the
nations;
proclaim, give praise, and say,
"Save, O LORD, your people,
the remnant of Israel."
8 See, I am going to bring them from the
land of the north,
and gather them from the farthest
parts of the earth,
among them the blind and the lame,
those with child and those in labor,
together;
a great company, they shall return
here.
9 With weeping they shall come,
and with consolations[o] I will lead
them back,
I will let them walk by brooks of water,
in a straight path in which they shall
not stumble;
for I have become a father to Israel,
and Ē´phra·im is my firstborn.

10 Hear the word of the LORD, O nations,
and declare it in the coastlands far
away;

say, "He who scattered Israel will
gather him,
and will keep him as a shepherd a
flock."
11 For the LORD has ransomed Jacob,
and has redeemed him from hands
too strong for him.
12 They shall come and sing aloud on the
height of Zion,
and they shall be radiant over the
goodness of the LORD,
over the grain, the wine, and the oil,
and over the young of the flock and
the herd;
their life shall become like a watered
garden,
and they shall never languish again.
13 Then shall the young women rejoice in
the dance,
and the young men and the old
shall be merry.
I will turn their mourning into joy,
I will comfort them, and give them
gladness for sorrow.
14 I will give the priests their fill of
fatness,
and my people shall be satisfied
with my bounty,
                              says the LORD.

15 Thus says the LORD:
A voice is heard in Rā´mah,
lamentation and bitter weeping.
Rachel is weeping for her children;
she refuses to be comforted for her
children,
because they are no more.
16 Thus says the LORD:
Keep your voice from weeping,
and your eyes from tears;
for there is a reward for your work,
                              says the LORD:
they shall come back from the land
of the enemy;
17 there is hope for your future,
                              says the LORD:

---

[l] Gk: Heb *me*   [m] Or *to him long ago*   [n] Or *adorn
yourself with*   [o] Gk Compare Vg Tg: Heb *supplications*

your children shall come back to
their own country.

¹⁸ Indeed I heard Ē´phra·im pleading:
"You disciplined me, and I took the
discipline;
I was like a calf untrained.
Bring me back, let me come back,
for you are the LORD my God.
¹⁹ For after I had turned away I repented;
and after I was discovered, I struck
my thigh;
I was ashamed, and I was dismayed
because I bore the disgrace of my
youth."
²⁰ Is Ē´phra·im my dear son?
Is he the child I delight in?
As often as I speak against him,
I still remember him.
Therefore I am deeply moved for him;
I will surely have mercy on him,
says the LORD.

²¹ Set up road markers for yourself,
make yourself guideposts;
consider well the highway,
the road by which you went.
Return, O virgin Israel,
return to these your cities.
²² How long will you waver,
O faithless daughter?
For the LORD has created a new thing
on the earth:
a woman encompasses^p a man.

23 Thus says the LORD of hosts, the
God of Israel: Once more they shall use
these words in the land of Judah and in its
towns when I restore their fortunes:
"The LORD bless you, O abode of
righteousness,
O holy hill!"
²⁴And Judah and all its towns shall live
there together, and the farmers and those
who wander^q with their flocks.
²⁵ I will satisfy the weary,
and all who are faint I will replenish.
26 Thereupon I awoke and looked, and
my sleep was pleasant to me.

Individual Retribution

27 The days are surely coming, says the
LORD, when I will sow the house of Israel
and the house of Judah with the seed of
humans and the seed of animals. ²⁸And
just as I have watched over them to pluck
up and break down, to overthrow, destroy,
and bring evil, so I will watch over them to
build and to plant, says the LORD. ²⁹In
those days they shall no longer say:
"The parents have eaten sour grapes,
and the children's teeth are set on
edge."
³⁰But all shall die for their own sins; the
teeth of everyone who eats sour grapes
shall be set on edge.

A New Covenant

31 The days are surely coming, says the
LORD, when I will make a new covenant
with the house of Israel and the house of
Judah. ³²It will not be like the covenant
that I made with their ancestors when I
took them by the hand to bring them out
of the land of Egypt—a covenant that they
broke, though I was their husband,^r says
the LORD. ³³But this is the covenant that I
will make with the house of Israel after
those days, says the LORD: I will put my
law within them, and I will write it on their
hearts; and I will be their God, and they
shall be my people. ³⁴No longer shall they
teach one another, or say to each other,
"Know the LORD," for they shall all know
me, from the least of them to the greatest,
says the LORD; for I will forgive their iniquity, and remember their sin no more.
³⁵ Thus says the LORD,
who gives the sun for light by day
and the fixed order of the moon and
the stars for light by night,
who stirs up the sea so that its waves
roar—
the LORD of hosts is his name:
³⁶ If this fixed order were ever to cease
from my presence, says the LORD,

---

^p Meaning of Heb uncertain   ^q Cn Compare Syr
Vg Tg: Heb *and they shall wander*   ^r Or *master*

then also the offspring of Israel would
    cease
  to be a nation before me forever.

³⁷ Thus says the LORD:
  If the heavens above can be measured,
    and the foundations of the earth
      below can be explored,
  then I will reject all the offspring of
    Israel
  because of all they have done,
                              says the LORD.

Jerusalem to Be Enlarged

38 The days are surely coming, says the
LORD, when the city shall be rebuilt for the
LORD from the tower of Ha·nan´el to the
Corner Gate. ³⁹And the measuring line
shall go out farther, straight to the hill
Gā´reb, and shall then turn to Gõ´ah. ⁴⁰The
whole valley of the dead bodies and the
ashes, and all the fields as far as the Wadi
Kid´ron, to the corner of the Horse Gate
toward the east, shall be sacred to the
LORD. It shall never again be uprooted or
overthrown.

Jeremiah Buys a Field During the Siege

32 The word that came to Jer·e·mī´-
ah from the LORD in the tenth
year of King Zed·e·kī´ah of Judah, which
was the eighteenth year of Ne·bū-
chad·rez´zar. ²At that time the army of the
king of Babylon was besieging Jerusalem,
and the prophet Jer·e·mī´ah was confined
in the court of the guard that was in the
palace of the king of Judah, ³where King
Zed·e·kī´ah of Judah had confined him.
Zed·e·kī´ah had said, "Why do you prophesy and say: Thus says the LORD: I am
going to give this city into the hand of the
king of Babylon, and he shall take it; ⁴King
Zed·e·kī´ah of Judah shall not escape out of
the hands of the Chal·dē´ans, but shall
surely be given into the hands of the king
of Babylon, and shall speak with him face
to face and see him eye to eye; ⁵and he
shall take Zed·e·kī´ah to Babylon, and
there he shall remain until I attend to him,

says the LORD; though you fight against the
Chal·dē´ans, you shall not succeed?"

6 Jer·e·mī´ah said, The word of the
LORD came to me: ⁷Han´a·mel son of your
uncle Shal´lum is going to come to you
and say, "Buy my field that is at An´a·thoth,
for the right of redemption by purchase is
yours." ⁸Then my cousin Han´a·mel came
to me in the court of the guard, in accordance with the word of the LORD, and said
to me, "Buy my field that is at An´a·thoth
in the land of Benjamin, for the right of
possession and redemption is yours; buy it
for yourself." Then I knew that this was the
word of the LORD.

9 And I bought the field at An´a·thoth
from my cousin Han´a·mel, and weighed
out the money to him, seventeen shekels
of silver. ¹⁰I signed the deed, sealed it, got
witnesses, and weighed the money on
scales. ¹¹Then I took the sealed deed of
purchase, containing the terms and conditions, and the open copy; ¹²and I gave the
deed of purchase to Bar´uch son of Ne·rī´-
ah son of Mah´sēi·ah, in the presence of my
cousin Han´a·mel, in the presence of the
witnesses who signed the deed of purchase, and in the presence of all the
Judeans who were sitting in the court of the
guard. ¹³In their presence I charged Bar´-
uch, saying, ¹⁴Thus says the LORD of hosts,
the God of Israel: Take these deeds, both
this sealed deed of purchase and this open
deed, and put them in an earthenware jar,
in order that they may last for a long time.
¹⁵For thus says the LORD of hosts, the God
of Israel: Houses and fields and vineyards
shall again be bought in this land.

We don't often know
who wrote down the
prophets' speeches,
but Jeremiah had a secretary: a
scribe named Baruch. It is likely
that Jeremiah dictated parts of
the book of Jeremiah to Baruch
and that Baruch wrote some of
the scrolls himself.

Jeremiah Prays for Understanding

16 After I had given the deed of purchase to Bar´uch son of Ne·ri´ah, I prayed to the LORD, saying: [17]Ah Lord GOD! It is you who made the heavens and the earth by your great power and by your outstretched arm! Nothing is too hard for you. [18]You show steadfast love to the thousandth generation,[s] but repay the guilt of parents into the laps of their children after them, O great and mighty God whose name is the LORD of hosts, [19]great in counsel and mighty in deed; whose eyes are open to all the ways of mortals, rewarding all according to their ways and according to the fruit of their doings. [20]You showed signs and wonders in the land of Egypt, and to this day in Israel and among all humankind, and have made yourself a name that continues to this very day. [21]You brought your people Israel out of the land of Egypt with signs and wonders, with a strong hand and outstretched arm, and with great terror; [22]and you gave them this land, which you swore to their ancestors to give them, a land flowing with milk and honey; [23]and they entered and took possession of it. But they did not obey your voice or follow your law; of all you commanded them to do, they did nothing. Therefore you have made all these disasters come upon them. [24]See, the siege ramps have been cast up against the city to take it, and the city, faced with sword, famine, and pestilence, has been given into the hands of the Chal·de´ans who are fighting against it. What you spoke has happened, as you yourself can see. [25]Yet you, O Lord GOD, have said to me, "Buy the field for money and get witnesses"— though the city has been given into the hands of the Chal·de´ans.

God's Assurance of the People's Return

26 The word of the LORD came to Jer·e·mi´ah: [27]See, I am the LORD, the God of all flesh; is anything too hard for me? [28]Therefore, thus says the LORD: I am going to give this city into the hands of the Chal·de´ans and into the hand of King Ne·bu·chad·rez´zar of Babylon, and he shall take it. [29]The Chal·de´ans who are fighting against this city shall come, set it on fire, and burn it, with the houses on whose roofs offerings have been made to Ba´al and libations have been poured out to other gods, to provoke me to anger. [30]For the people of Israel and the people of Judah have done nothing but evil in my sight from their youth; the people of Israel have done nothing but provoke me to anger by the work of their hands, says the LORD. [31]This city has aroused my anger and wrath, from the day it was built until this day, so that I will remove it from my sight [32]because of all the evil of the people of Israel and the people of Judah that they did to provoke me to anger—they, their kings and their officials, their priests and their prophets, the citizens of Judah and the inhabitants of Jerusalem. [33]They have turned their backs to me, not their faces; though I have taught them persistently, they would not listen and accept correction. [34]They set up their abominations in the house that bears my name, and defiled it. [35]They built the high places of Ba´al in the valley of the son of Hin´nom, to offer up their sons and daughters to Mo´lech, though I did not command them, nor did

Molech was a Canaanite god. People would offer their children as sacrifices to Molech by forcing them to pass through fire. Although it was forbidden by their law, some Israelites offered their children as sacrifices. Most of these sacrifices took place in the Valley of Hinnon, southwest of Jerusalem. During King Josiah's reign, the place of sacrifice was destroyed.

[s] Or *to thousands*

it enter my mind that they should do this abomination, causing Judah to sin.

36 Now therefore thus says the LORD, the God of Israel, concerning this city of which you say, "It is being given into the hand of the king of Babylon by the sword, by famine, and by pestilence": ³⁷See, I am going to gather them from all the lands to which I drove them in my anger and my wrath and in great indignation; I will bring them back to this place, and I will settle them in safety. ³⁸They shall be my people, and I will be their God. ³⁹I will give them one heart and one way, that they may fear me for all time, for their own good and the good of their children after them. ⁴⁰I will make an everlasting covenant with them, never to draw back from doing good to them; and I will put the fear of me in their hearts, so that they may not turn from me. ⁴¹I will rejoice in doing good to them, and I will plant them in this land in faithfulness, with all my heart and all my soul.

42 For thus says the LORD: Just as I have brought all this great disaster upon this people, so I will bring upon them all the good fortune that I now promise them. ⁴³Fields shall be bought in this land of which you are saying, It is a desolation, without human beings or animals; it has been given into the hands of the Chal·de´ans. ⁴⁴Fields shall be bought for money, and deeds shall be signed and sealed and witnessed, in the land of Benjamin, in the places around Jerusalem, and in the cities of Judah, of the hill country, of the She·phe´lah, and of the Neg´eb; for I will restore their fortunes, says the LORD.

Healing after Punishment

33 The word of the LORD came to Jer·e·mi´ah a second time, while he was still confined in the court of the guard: ²Thus says the LORD who made the earth,ᵗ the LORD who formed it to establish it—the LORD is his name: ³Call to me and I will answer you, and will tell you great and hidden things that you have not known. ⁴For thus says the LORD, the God of Israel, concerning the houses of this city and the houses of the kings of Judah that were torn down to make a defense against the siege ramps and before the sword:ᵘ ⁵The Chal·de´ans are coming in to fightᵛ and to fill them with the dead bodies of those whom I shall strike down in my anger and my wrath, for I have hidden my face from this city because of all their wickedness. ⁶I am going to bring it recovery and healing; I will heal them and reveal to them abundanceᵘ of prosperity and security. ⁷I will restore the fortunes of Judah and the fortunes of Israel, and rebuild them as they were at first. ⁸I will cleanse them from all the guilt of their sin against me, and I will forgive all the guilt of their sin and rebellion against me. ⁹And this cityʷ shall be to me a name of joy, a praise and a glory before all the nations of the earth who shall hear of all the good that I do for them; they shall fear and tremble because of all the good and all the prosperity I provide for it.

10 Thus says the LORD: In this place of which you say, "It is a waste without human beings or animals," in the towns of Judah and the streets of Jerusalem that are desolate, without inhabitants, human or

The Negeb was an area of the southern part of Canaan with many cities and good pastureland. The original people who lived in Negeb were the Amalekites. David brought the entire area of Negeb into the kingdom of Judah. After biblical times, due to the devastation of war and the neglect of the land, the Negeb became a desert. Now a part of modern Israel, the land has been restored.

ᵗ Gk: Heb *it*　　ᵘ Meaning of Heb uncertain
ᵛ Cn: Heb *They are coming in to fight against the Chaldeans*　　ʷ Heb *And it*

animal, there shall once more be heard [11]the voice of mirth and the voice of gladness, the voice of the bridegroom and the voice of the bride, the voices of those who sing, as they bring thank offerings to the house of the LORD:

"Give thanks to the LORD of hosts,
　for the LORD is good,
　for his steadfast love endures
　　forever!"

For I will restore the fortunes of the land as at first, says the LORD.

12 Thus says the LORD of hosts: In this place that is waste, without human beings or animals, and in all its towns there shall again be pasture for shepherds resting their flocks. [13]In the towns of the hill country, of the She·phe'lah, and of the Neg'eb, in the land of Benjamin, the places around Jerusalem, and in the towns of Judah, flocks shall again pass under the hands of the one who counts them, says the LORD.

The Righteous Branch and the Covenant with David

14 The days are surely coming, says the LORD, when I will fulfill the promise I made to the house of Israel and the house of Judah. [15]In those days and at that time I will cause a righteous Branch to spring up for David; and he shall execute justice and righteousness in the land. [16]In those days Judah will be saved and Jerusalem will live in safety. And this is the name by which it will be called: "The LORD is our righteousness."

17 For thus says the LORD: David shall never lack a man to sit on the throne of the house of Israel, [18]and the levitical priests shall never lack a man in my presence to offer burnt offerings, to make grain offerings, and to make sacrifices for all time.

19 The word of the LORD came to Jer·e·mi'ah: [20]Thus says the LORD: If any of you could break my covenant with the day and my covenant with the night, so that day and night would not come at their appointed time, [21]only then could my covenant with my servant David be broken, so that he would not have a son to reign on his throne, and my covenant with my ministers the Le'vites. [22]Just as the host of heaven cannot be numbered and the sands of the sea cannot be measured, so I will increase the offspring of my servant David, and the Le'vites who minister to me.

23 The word of the LORD came to Jer·e·mi'ah: [24]Have you not observed how these people say, "The two families that the LORD chose have been rejected by him," and how they hold my people in such contempt that they no longer regard them as a nation? [25]Thus says the LORD: Only if I had not established my covenant with day and night and the ordinances of heaven and earth, [26]would I reject the offspring of Jacob and of my servant David and not choose any of his descendants as rulers over the offspring of Abraham, Isaac, and Jacob. For I will restore their fortunes, and will have mercy upon them.

Death in Captivity Predicted for Zedekiah

34 The word that came to Jer·e·mi'-ah from the LORD, when King Ne·bu·chad·rez'zar of Babylon and all his army and all the kingdoms of the earth and all the peoples under his dominion were fighting against Jerusalem and all its cities: [2]Thus says the LORD, the God of Israel: Go and speak to King Zed·e·ki'ah of Judah and say to him: Thus says the LORD: I am going to give this city into the hand of the king of Babylon, and he shall burn it with fire. [3]And you yourself shall not escape from his hand, but shall surely be captured and handed over to him; you shall see the king of Babylon eye to eye and speak with him face to face; and you shall go to Babylon. [4]Yet hear the word of the LORD, O King Zed·e·ki'ah of Judah! Thus says the LORD concerning you: You shall not die by the sword; [5]you shall die in peace. And as spices were burned[x] for your ancestors, the earlier kings who preceded you, so they shall burn spices[y] for you and lament for

---

[x] Heb *as there was burning*　[y] Heb *shall burn*

you, saying, "Alas, lord!" For I have spoken the word, says the LORD.

6 Then the prophet Jer·e·mī´ah spoke all these words to Zed·e·kī´ah king of Judah, in Jerusalem, 7when the army of the king of Babylon was fighting against Jerusalem and against all the cities of Judah that were left, Lā´chish and A·zē´kah; for these were the only fortified cities of Judah that remained.

Treacherous Treatment of Slaves

8 The word that came to Jer·e·mī´ah from the LORD, after King Zed·e·kī´ah had made a covenant with all the people in Jerusalem to make a proclamation of liberty to them— 9that all should set free their Hebrew slaves, male and female, so that no one should hold another Judean in slavery. 10And they obeyed, all the officials and all the people who had entered into the covenant that all would set free their slaves, male or female, so that they would not be enslaved again; they obeyed and set them free. 11But afterward they turned around and took back the male and female slaves they had set free, and brought them again into subjection as slaves. 12The word of the LORD came to Jer·e·mī´ah from the LORD: 13Thus says the LORD, the God of Israel: I myself made a covenant with your ancestors when I brought them out of the land of Egypt, out of the house of slavery, saying, 14"Every seventh year each of you must set free any Hebrews who have been sold to you and have served you six years; you must set them free from your service." But your ancestors did not listen to me or incline their ears to me. 15You yourselves recently repented and did what was right in my sight by proclaiming liberty to one another, and you made a covenant before me in the house that is called by my name; 16but then you turned around and profaned my name when each of you took back your male and female slaves, whom you had set free according to their desire, and you brought them again into subjection to be your slaves. 17Therefore, thus says the LORD: You have not obeyed me by

granting a release to your neighbors and friends; I am going to grant a release to you, says the LORD—a release to the sword, to pestilence, and to famine. I will make you a horror to all the kingdoms of the earth. 18And those who transgressed my covenant and did not keep the terms of the covenant that they made before me, I will make like*z* the calf when they cut it in two and passed between its parts: 19the officials of Judah, the officials of Jerusalem, the eunuchs, the priests, and all the people of the land who passed between the parts of the calf 20shall be handed over to their enemies and to those who seek their lives. Their corpses shall become food for the birds of the air and the wild animals of the earth. 21And as for King Zed·e·kī´ah of Judah and his officials, I will hand them over to their enemies and to those who seek their lives, to the army of the king of Babylon, which has withdrawn from you. 22I am going to command, says the LORD, and will bring them back to this city; and they will fight against it, and take it, and burn it with fire. The towns of Judah I will make a desolation without inhabitant.

The Rechabites Commended

35 The word that came to Jer·e·mī´ah from the LORD in the days of King Je·hoi´a·kim son of Jō·sī´ah of Judah: 2Go to the house of the Rē´chab·ītes, and speak with them, and bring them to the house of the LORD, into one of the chambers; then offer them wine to drink. 3So I took Jā·az·a·nī´ah son of Jer·e·mī´ah son of Ha·baz·zi·nī´ah, and his brothers, and all his sons, and the whole house of the Rē´chab·ītes. 4I brought them to the house of the LORD into the chamber of the sons of Hā´nan son of Ig·da·lī´ah, the man of God, which was near the chamber of the officials, above the chamber of Mā·a·sēi´ah son of Shal´lum, keeper of the threshold. 5Then I set before the Rē´chab·ītes pitchers full of wine, and cups; and I said to them, "Have some wine." 6But they answered,

z Cn: Heb lacks *like*

"We will drink no wine, for our ancestor Jon·a·dab son of Rē′chab commanded us, 'You shall never drink wine, neither you nor your children; [7]nor shall you ever build a house, or sow seed; nor shall you plant a vineyard, or even own one; but you shall live in tents all your days, that you may live many days in the land where you reside.' [8]We have obeyed the charge of our ancestor Jon·a·dab son of Rē′chab in all that he commanded us, to drink no wine all our days, ourselves, our wives, our sons, or our daughters, [9]and not to build houses to live in. We have no vineyard or field or seed; [10]but we have lived in tents, and have obeyed and done all that our ancestor Jon·a·dab commanded us. [11]But when King Ne·bū·chad·rez′zar of Babylon came up against the land, we said, 'Come, and let us go to Jerusalem for fear of the army of the Chal·dē′ans and the army of the Ar·a·mē′ans.' That is why we are living in Jerusalem."

12 Then the word of the LORD came to Jer·e·mī′ah: [13]Thus says the LORD of hosts, the God of Israel: Go and say to the people of Judah and the inhabitants of Jerusalem, Can you not learn a lesson and obey my words? says the LORD. [14]The command has been carried out that Jon·a·dab son of Rē′chab gave to his descendants to drink no wine; and they drink none to this day, for they have obeyed their ancestor's command. But I myself have spoken to you persistently, and you have not obeyed me. [15]I have sent to you all my servants the prophets, sending them persistently, saying, "Turn now everyone of you from your evil way, and amend your doings, and do not go after other gods to serve them, and then you shall live in the land that I gave to you and your ancestors." But you did not incline your ear or obey me. [16]The descendants of Jon·a·dab son of Rē′chab have carried out the command that their ancestor gave them, but this people has not obeyed me. [17]Therefore, thus says the LORD, the God of hosts, the God of Israel: I am going to bring on Judah and on all the inhabi-

tants of Jerusalem every disaster that I have pronounced against them; because I have spoken to them and they have not listened, I have called to them and they have not answered.

18 But to the house of the Rē′chab·ites Jer·e·mī′ah said: Thus says the LORD of hosts, the God of Israel: Because you have obeyed the command of your ancestor Jon·a·dab, and kept all his precepts, and done all that he commanded you, [19]therefore thus says the LORD of hosts, the God of Israel: Jon·a·dab son of Rē′chab shall not lack a descendant to stand before me for all time.

The Scroll Read in the Temple

36 In the fourth year of King Je·hoi′a·kim son of Jō·sī′ah of Judah, this word came to Jer·e·mī′ah from the LORD: [2]Take a scroll and write on it all the words that I have spoken to you against Israel and Judah and all the nations, from the day I spoke to you, from the days of Jō·sī′ah until today. [3]It may be that when the house of Judah hears of all the disasters that I intend to do to them, all of them may turn from their evil ways, so that I may forgive their iniquity and their sin.

4 Then Jer·e·mī′ah called Bar′uch son of Ne·rī′ah, and Bar′uch wrote on a scroll at Jer·e·mī′ah's dictation all the words of the LORD that he had spoken to him. [5]And Jer·e·mī′ah ordered Bar′uch, saying, "I am prevented from entering the house of the LORD; [6]so you go yourself, and on a fast day in the hearing of the people in the LORD's house you shall read the words of the LORD from the scroll that you have written at my dictation. You shall read them also in the hearing of all the people of Judah who come up from their towns. [7]It may be that their plea will come before the LORD, and that all of them will turn from their evil ways, for great is the anger and wrath that the LORD has pronounced against this people." [8]And Bar′uch son of Ne·rī′ah did all that the prophet Jer·e·mī′ah

ordered him about reading from the scroll the words of the LORD in the LORD's house.

9 In the fifth year of King Je·hoi´a·kim son of Jō·sī´ah of Judah, in the ninth month, all the people in Jerusalem and all the people who came from the towns of Judah to Jerusalem proclaimed a fast before the LORD. ¹⁰Then, in the hearing of all the people, Bar´uch read the words of Jer·e·mī´ah from the scroll, in the house of the LORD, in the chamber of Gem·a·rī´ah son of Shā´phan the secretary, which was in the upper court, at the entry of the New Gate of the LORD's house.

The Scroll Read in the Palace

11 When Mī·cāi´ah son of Gem·a·rī´ah son of Shā´phan heard all the words of the LORD from the scroll, ¹²he went down to the king's house, into the secretary's chamber; and all the officials were sitting there: E·lish´a·ma the secretary, De·lai´ah son of She·māi´ah, El·nā´than son of Ach´bor, Gem·a·rī´ah son of Shā´phan, Zed·e·kī´ah son of Han·a·nī´ah, and all the officials. ¹³And Mī·cāi´ah told them all the words that he had heard, when Bar´uch read the scroll in the hearing of the people. ¹⁴Then all the officials sent Je·hū´dī son of Neth·a·nī´ah son of Shel·e·mī´ah son of Cū´shī to say to Bar´uch, "Bring the scroll that you read in the hearing of the people, and come." So Bar´uch son of Ne·rī´ah took the scroll in his hand and came to them. ¹⁵And they said to him, "Sit down and read it to us." So Bar´uch read it to them. ¹⁶When they heard all the words, they turned to one another in alarm, and said to Bar´uch, "We certainly must report all these words to the king." ¹⁷Then they questioned Bar´uch, "Tell us now, how did you write all these words? Was it at his dictation?" ¹⁸Bar´uch answered them, "He dictated all these words to me, and I wrote them with ink on the scroll." ¹⁹Then the officials said to Bar´uch, "Go and hide, you and Jer·e·mī´ah, and let no one know where you are."

Jehoiakim Burns the Scroll

20 Leaving the scroll in the chamber of E·lish´a·ma the secretary, they went to the court of the king; and they reported all the words to the king. ²¹Then the king sent Je·hū´dī to get the scroll, and he took it from the chamber of E·lish´a·ma the secretary; and Je·hū´dī read it to the king and all the officials who stood beside the king. ²²Now the king was sitting in his winter apartment (it was the ninth month), and there was a fire burning in the brazier before him. ²³As Je·hū´dī read three or four columns, the king[a] would cut them off with a penknife and throw them into the fire in the brazier, until the entire scroll was consumed in the fire that was in the brazier. ²⁴Yet neither the king, nor any of his servants who heard all these words, was alarmed, nor did they tear their garments. ²⁵Even when El·nā´than and De·lai´ah and Gem·a·rī´ah urged the king not to burn the scroll, he would not listen to them. ²⁶And the king commanded Je·rah´mē·el the king's son and Se·rāi´ah son of Az´ri·el and Shel·e·mī´ah son of Ab·dē´el to arrest the secretary Bar´uch and the prophet Jer·e·mī´ah. But the LORD hid them.

Jeremiah Dictates Another

27 Now, after the king had burned the scroll with the words that Bar´uch wrote at Jer·e·mī´ah's dictation, the word of the LORD came to Jer·e·mī´ah: ²⁸Take another scroll and write on it all the former words that were in the first scroll, which King Je·hoi´a·kim of Judah has burned. ²⁹And concerning King Je·hoi´a·kim of Judah you shall say: Thus says the LORD, You have dared to burn this scroll, saying, Why have you written in it that the king of Babylon will certainly come and destroy this land, and will cut off from it human beings and animals? ³⁰Therefore thus says the LORD concerning King Je·hoi´a·kim of Judah: He shall have no one to sit upon the throne of David, and his dead body shall be cast out to the heat by day and the frost by night.

_a_ Heb _he_

³¹And I will punish him and his offspring and his servants for their iniquity; I will bring on them, and on the inhabitants of Jerusalem, and on the people of Judah, all the disasters with which I have threatened them—but they would not listen.

32 Then Jer·e·mī´ah took another scroll and gave it to the secretary Bar´uch son of Ne·rī´ah, who wrote on it at Jer·e·mī´ah's dictation all the words of the scroll that King Je·hoi´a·kim of Judah had burned in the fire; and many similar words were added to them.

Zedekiah's Vain Hope

37 Zed·e·kī´ah son of Jō·sī´ah, whom King Ne·bū·chad·rez´zar of Babylon made king in the land of Judah, succeeded Cō·nī´ah son of Je·hoi´a·kim. ²But neither he nor his servants nor the people of the land listened to the words of the LORD that he spoke through the prophet Jer·e·mī´ah.

3 King Zed·e·kī´ah sent Je·hū´cal son of Shel·e·mī´ah and the priest Zeph·a·nī´ah son of Mā·a·sēi´ah to the prophet Jer·e·mī´ah saying, "Please pray for us to the LORD our God." ⁴Now Jer·e·mī´ah was still going in and out among the people, for he had not yet been put in prison. ⁵Meanwhile, the army of Pharaoh had come out of Egypt; and when the Chal·dē´ans who were besieging Jerusalem heard news of them, they withdrew from Jerusalem.

6 Then the word of the LORD came to the prophet Jer·e·mī´ah: ⁷Thus says the LORD, God of Israel: This is what the two of you shall say to the king of Judah, who sent you to me to inquire of me: Pharaoh's army, which set out to help you, is going to return to its own land, to Egypt. ⁸And the Chal·dē´ans shall return and fight against this city; they shall take it and burn it with fire. ⁹Thus says the LORD: Do not deceive yourselves, saying, "The Chal·dē´ans will surely go away from us," for they will not go away. ¹⁰Even if you defeated the whole army of Chal·dē´ans who are fighting against you, and there remained of them only wounded men in their tents, they would rise up and burn this city with fire.

Jeremiah Is Imprisoned

11 Now when the Chal·dē´an army had withdrawn from Jerusalem at the approach of Pharaoh's army, ¹²Jer·e·mī´ah set out from Jerusalem to go to the land of Benjamin to receive his share of property*ᵇ* among the people there. ¹³When he reached the Benjamin Gate, a sentinel there named I·rī´jah son of Shel·e·mī´ah son of Han·a·nī´ah arrested the prophet Jer·e·mī´ah saying, "You are deserting to the Chal·dē´ans." ¹⁴And Jer·e·mī´ah said, "That is a lie; I am not deserting to the Chal·dē´ans." But I·rī´jah would not listen to him, and arrested Jer·e·mī´ah and brought him to the officials. ¹⁵The officials were enraged at Jer·e·mī´ah, and they beat him and imprisoned him in the house of the secretary Jonathan, for it had been made a prison. ¹⁶Thus Jer·e·mī´ah was put in the cistern house, in the cells, and remained there many days.

17 Then King Zed·e·kī´ah sent for him, and received him. The king questioned him secretly in his house, and said, "Is there any word from the LORD?" Jer·e·mī´ah said, "There is!" Then he said, "You shall be handed over to the king of Babylon." ¹⁸Jer·e·mī´ah also said to King Zed·e·kī´ah, "What wrong have I done to you or your servants or this people, that you have put me in prison? ¹⁹Where are your prophets who prophesied to you, saying, 'The king of Babylon will not come against you and against this land'? ²⁰Now please hear me, my lord king: be good enough to listen to my plea, and do not send me back to the house of the secretary Jonathan to die there." ²¹So King Zed·e·kī´ah gave orders, and they committed Jer·e·mī´ah to the court of the guard; and a loaf of bread was given him daily from the bakers' street, until all the bread of the city was gone. So Jer·e·mī´ah remained in the court of the guard.

ᵇ Meaning of Heb uncertain

Jeremiah in the Cistern

38 Now Sheph·a·tī´ah son of Mat´tan, Ged·a·lī´ah son of Pash´hur, Jū´cal son of Shel·e·mī´ah, and Pash´hur son of Mal·chī´ah heard the words that Jer·e·mī´ah was saying to all the people, ²Thus says the LORD, Those who stay in this city shall die by the sword, by famine, and by pestilence; but those who go out to the Chal·dē´ans shall live; they shall have their lives as a prize of war, and live. ³Thus says the LORD, This city shall surely be handed over to the army of the king of Babylon and be taken. ⁴Then the officials said to the king, "This man ought to be put to death, because he is discouraging the soldiers who are left in this city, and all the people, by speaking such words to them. For this man is not seeking the welfare of this people, but their harm." ⁵King Zed·e·kī´ah said, "Here he is; he is in your hands; for the king is powerless against you." ⁶So they took Jer·e·mī´ah and threw him into the cistern of Mal·chī´ah, the king's son, which was in the court of the guard, letting Jer·e·mī´ah down by ropes. Now there was no water in the cistern, but only mud, and Jer·e·mī´ah sank in the mud.

Jeremiah Is Rescued by Ebed-melech

7 Ē´bed-mē´lech the Ethiopian,ᶜ a eunuch in the king's house, heard that they had put Jer·e·mī´ah into the cistern. The king happened to be sitting at the Benjamin Gate, ⁸So Ē´bed-mē´lech left the king's house and spoke to the king, ⁹"My lord king, these men have acted wickedly in all they did to the prophet Jer·e·mī´ah by throwing him into the cistern to die there of hunger, for there is no bread left in the city." ¹⁰Then the king commanded Ē´bed-mē´lech the Ethiopian,ᶜ "Take three men with you from here, and pull the prophet Jer·e·mī´ah up from the cistern before he dies." ¹¹So Ē´bed-mē´lech took the men with him and went to the house of the king, to a wardrobe ofᵈ the storehouse, and took from there old rags and worn-out clothes, which he let down to Jer·e·mī´ah in the cistern by ropes. ¹²Then Ē´bed-mē´lech the Ethiopianᶜ said to Jer·e·mī´ah, "Just put the rags and clothes between your armpits and the ropes." Jer·e·mī´ah did so. ¹³Then they drew Jer·e·mī´ah up by the ropes and pulled him out of the cistern. And Jer·e·mī´ah remained in the court of the guard.

Zedekiah Consults Jeremiah Again

14 King Zed·e·kī´ah sent for the prophet Jer·e·mī´ah and received him at the third entrance of the temple of the LORD. The king said to Jer·e·mī´ah, "I have something to ask you; do not hide anything from me." ¹⁵Jer·e·mī´ah said to Zed·e·kī´ah, "If I tell you, you will put me to death, will you not? And if I give you advice, you will not listen to me." ¹⁶So King Zed·e·kī´ah swore an oath in secret to Jer·e·mī´ah, "As the LORD lives, who gave us our lives, I will not put you to death or hand you over to these men who seek your life."

17 Then Jer·e·mī´ah said to Zed·e·kī´ah, "Thus says the LORD, the God of hosts, the God of Israel, If you will only surrender to

Whenever it rained in the desert lands, people collected water and stored it for later use. They kept the water in cisterns—pits that had been dug into the earth and lined with lime plaster. When Jeremiah said that Jerusalem would fall to Babylon, the city officials were so angry that they asked the king for permission to silence Jeremiah. Using ropes, they lowered him into a cistern. Luckily there was no water in the cistern, but Jeremiah sank down in the muddy bottom.

ᶜ Or *Nubian*; Heb *Cushite*　　ᵈ Cn: Heb *to under*

the officials of the king of Babylon, then your life shall be spared, and this city shall not be burned with fire, and you and your house shall live. ¹⁸But if you do not surrender to the officials of the king of Babylon, then this city shall be handed over to the Chal·dēʹans, and they shall burn it with fire, and you yourself shall not escape from their hand." ¹⁹King Zed·e·kīʹ-ah said to Jer·e·mīʹah, "I am afraid of the Judeans who have deserted to the Chal·dēʹ-ans, for I might be handed over to them and they would abuse me." ²⁰Jer·e·mīʹah said, "That will not happen. Just obey the voice of the LORD in what I say to you, and it shall go well with you, and your life shall be spared. ²¹But if you are determined not to surrender, this is what the LORD has shown me— ²²a vision of all the women remaining in the house of the king of Judah being led out to the officials of the king of Babylon and saying,

'Your trusted friends have seduced you
　　and have overcome you;
Now that your feet are stuck in the
　　mud,
　　they desert you.'

²³All your wives and your children shall be led out to the Chal·dēʹans, and you yourself shall not escape from their hand, but shall be seized by the king of Babylon; and this city shall be burned with fire."

24 Then Zed·e·kīʹah said to Jer·e·mīʹah, "Do not let anyone else know of this conversation, or you will die. ²⁵If the officials should hear that I have spoken with you, and they should come and say to you, 'Just tell us what you said to the king; do not conceal it from us, or we will put you to death. What did the king say to you?' ²⁶then you shall say to them, 'I was presenting my plea to the king not to send me back to the house of Jonathan to die there.'" ²⁷All the officials did come to Jer·e·mīʹah and questioned him; and he answered them in the very words the king had commanded. So they stopped questioning him, for the conversation had not been overheard. ²⁸And Jer·e·mīʹah remained in

the court of the guard until the day that Jerusalem was taken.

In 586 BC, King Nebuchadrezzar of Babylon captured the city of Jerusalem and sent many of the people away from their homeland into exile.

The Fall of Jerusalem

39 In the ninth year of King Zed·e·kīʹah of Judah, in the tenth month, King Ne·bū·chad·rezʹzar of Babylon and all his army came against Jerusalem and besieged it; ²in the eleventh year of Zed·e·kīʹah, in the fourth month, on the ninth day of the month, a breach was made in the city. ³When Jerusalem was taken,ᵉ all the officials of the king of Babylon came and sat in the middle gate: Nerʹgal-sha·rēʹzer, Samʹgar-nēʹbo, Sarʹ-se·chim the Rab-sarʹis, Nerʹgal-sha·rēʹzer the Rab-mag, with all the rest of the officials of the king of Babylon. ⁴When King Zed·e·kīʹah of Judah and all the soldiers saw them, they fled, going out of the city at night by way of the king's garden through the gate between the two walls; and they went toward the Arʹa·bah. ⁵But the army of the Chal·dēʹans pursued them, and overtook Zed·e·kīʹah in the plains of Jericho; and when they had taken him, they brought him up to King Ne·bū·chad-rezʹzar of Babylon, at Ribʹlah, in the land of Hāʹmath; and he passed sentence on him. ⁶The king of Babylon slaughtered the sons of Zed·e·kīʹah at Ribʹlah before his eyes; also the king of Babylon slaughtered all the nobles of Judah. ⁷He put out the eyes of Zed·e·kīʹah, and bound him in fetters to take him to Babylon. ⁸The Chal·dēʹans burned the king's house and the houses of the people, and broke down the walls of Jerusalem. ⁹Then Ne·bū·za·radʹan the captain of the guard exiled to Babylon the rest

---

ᵉ This clause has been transposed from 38.28

of the people who were left in the city, those who had deserted to him, and the people who remained. ¹⁰Ne·bū·za·rad´an the captain of the guard left in the land of Judah some of the poor people who owned nothing, and gave them vineyards and fields at the same time.

Jeremiah, Set Free, Remembers Ebed-melech

11 King Ne·bū·chad·rez´zar of Babylon gave command concerning Jer·e·mī´ah through Ne·bū·za·rad´an, the captain of the guard, saying, ¹²"Take him, look after him well and do him no harm, but deal with him as he may ask you." ¹³So Ne·bū·za·rad´an the captain of the guard, Ne·bū·za·rad´an the Rab-sar´is, Ner´gal-sha·rē´zer the Rab-mag, and all the chief officers of the king of Babylon sent ¹⁴and took Jer·e·mī´ah from the court of the guard. They entrusted him to Ged·a·lī´ah son of A·hī´kam son of Shā´phan to be brought home. So he stayed with his own people.

15 The word of the LORD came to Jer·e·mī´ah while he was confined in the court of the guard: ¹⁶Go and say to Ē´bed-mē´lech the Ethiopian:ᶠ Thus says the LORD of hosts, the God of Israel: I am going to fulfill my words against this city for evil and not for good, and they shall be accomplished in your presence on that day. ¹⁷But

I will save you on that day, says the LORD, and you shall not be handed over to those whom you dread. ¹⁸For I will surely save you, and you shall not fall by the sword; but you shall have your life as a prize of war, because you have trusted in me, says the LORD.

Jeremiah with Gedaliah the Governor

40 The word that came to Jer·e·mī´ah from the LORD after Ne·bū·za·rad´an the captain of the guard had let him go from Rā´mah, when he took him bound in fetters along with all the captives of Jerusalem and Judah who were being exiled to Babylon. ²The captain of the guard took Jer·e·mī´ah and said to him, "The LORD your God threatened this place with this disaster; ³and now the LORD has brought it about, and has done as he said, because all of you sinned against the LORD and did not obey his voice. Therefore this thing has come upon you. ⁴Now look, I have just released you today from the fetters on your hands. If you wish to come with me to Babylon, come, and I will take good care of you; but if you do not wish to come with me to Babylon, you need not come. See, the whole land is before you; go wherever you think it good and right to go. ⁵If you remain,ᵍ then return to Ged·a·lī´ah son of A·hī´kam son of Shā´phan, whom the king of Babylon appointed governor of the towns of Judah, and stay with him among the people; or go wherever you think it right to go." So the captain of the guard gave him an allowance of food and a present, and let him go. ⁶Then Jer·e·mī´ah went to Ged·a·lī´ah son of A·hī´kam at Miz´pah, and stayed with him among the people who were left in the land.

7 When all the leaders of the forces in the open country and their troops heard that the king of Babylon had appointed Ged·a·lī´ah son of A·hī´kam governor in the land, and had committed to him men,

Ebed-melech, whose name means "servant of the king," served in the court of King Zedekiah. Ebed-melech also served the Lord. He was an African slave who risked his own life to save the prophet Jeremiah. He used rags from the king's clothing to make ropes to lift Jeremiah out of the cistern. (For the full story, see chapter 38.) The story of Ebed-melech tells us that we can look for help from unexpected rescuers. We can also look for ways to help others who may not expect us to help them. Who can you help?

ᶠ Or *Nubian* ; Heb *Cushite*   ᵍ Syr: Meaning of Heb uncertain women, and children, those of the poorest of the land who had not been taken into exile to Babylon, [8]they went to Ged·a·lī´ah at Miz´pah—Ish´ma·el son of Neth·a·nī´ah, Jō·hā´nan son of Ka·rē´ah, Ser·āi´ah son of Tan´hu·meth, the sons of Ē´phaī the Ne·toph´a·thīte, Jez·a·nī´ah son of the Mā·a·ca·thīte, they and their troops. [9]Ged·a·lī´ah son of A·hī´kam son of Shā´phan swore to them and their troops, saying, "Do not be afraid to serve the Chal·dē´ans. Stay in the land and serve the king of Babylon, and it shall go well with you. [10]As for me, I am staying at Miz´pah to represent you before the Chal·dē´ans who come to us; but as for you, gather wine and summer fruits and oil, and store them in your vessels, and live in the towns that you have taken over." [11]Likewise, when all the Judeans who were in Mō´ab and among the Am´mon·ītes and in Ē´dom and in other lands heard that the king of Babylon had left a remnant in Judah and had appointed Ged·a·lī´ah son of A·hī´kam son of Shā´phan as governor over them, [12]then all the Judeans returned from all the places to which they had been scattered and came to the land of Judah, to Ged·a·lī´ah at Miz´pah; and they gathered wine and summer fruits in great abundance.

13 Now Jō·hā´nan son of Ka·rē´ah and all the leaders of the forces in the open country came to Ged·a·lī´ah at Miz´pah [14]and said to him, "Are you at all aware that Bā´a·lis king of the Am´mon·ītes has sent Ish´ma·el son of Neth·a·nī´ah to take your life?" But Ged·a·lī´ah son of A·hī´kam would not believe them. [15]Then Jō·hā´nan son of Ka·rē´ah spoke secretly to Ged·a·lī´ah at Miz´pah, "Please let me go and kill Ish´ma·el son of Neth·a·nī´ah, and no one else will know. Why should he take your life, so that all the Judeans who are gathered around you would be scattered, and the remnant of Judah would perish?" [16]But Ged·a·lī´ah son of A·hī´kam said to Jō·hā´nan son of Ka·rē´ah, "Do not do such a thing, for you are telling a lie about Ish´ma·el."

Insurrection against Gedaliah

41 In the seventh month, Ish´ma·el son of Neth·a·nī´ah son of E·lish´a·ma, of the royal family, one of the chief officers of the king, came with ten men to Ged·a·lī´ah son of A·hī´kam, at Miz´pah. As they ate bread together there at Miz´pah, [2]Ish´ma·el son of Neth·a·nī´ah and the ten men with him got up and struck down Ged·a·lī´ah son of A·hī´kam son of Shā´phan with the sword and killed him, because the king of Babylon had appointed him governor in the land. [3]Ish´ma·el also killed all the Judeans who were with Ged·a·lī´ah at Miz´pah, and the Chal·dē´an soldiers who happened to be there.

4 On the day after the murder of Ged·a·lī´ah, before anyone knew of it, [5]eighty men arrived from Shē´chem and Shī´lōh and Sa·mār´i·a, with their beards shaved and their clothes torn, and their bodies gashed, bringing grain offerings and incense to present at the temple of the LORD. [6]And Ish´ma·el son of Neth·a·nī´ah came out from Miz´pah to meet them, weeping as he came. As he met them, he said to them, "Come to Ged·a·lī´ah son of A·hī´kam." [7]When they reached the middle of the city, Ish´ma·el son of Neth·a·nī´ah and the men with him slaughtered them, and threw them[h] into a cistern. [8]But there were ten men among them who said to Ish´ma·el, "Do not kill us, for we have stores of wheat, barley, oil, and honey hidden in the fields." So he refrained, and did not kill them along with their companions.

9 Now the cistern into which Ish´ma·el had thrown all the bodies of the men whom he had struck down was the large cistern[i] that King Asa had made for defense against King Bā´a·sha of Israel; Ish´ma·el son of Neth·a·nī´ah filled that cistern with those whom he had killed. [10]Then Ish´ma·el took captive all the rest of the people who were in Miz´pah, the king's daughters and all the people who were left

[h] Syr: Heb lacks *and threw them*; compare verse 9
[i] Gk: Heb *whom he had killed by the hand of Gedaliah*

at Miz´pah, whom Ne·bū´za·rad´an, the captain of the guard, had committed to Ged·a·lī´ah son of A·hī´kam. Ish´ma·el son of Neth·a·nī´ah took them captive and set out to cross over to the Am´mon·ites.

11 But when Jō·hā´nan son of Ka·rē´ah and all the leaders of the forces with him heard of all the crimes that Ish´ma·el son of Neth·a·nī´ah had done, [12]they took all their men and went to fight against Ish´ma·el son of Neth·a·nī´ah. They came upon him at the great pool that is in Gib´e·on. [13]And when all the people who were with Ish´ma·el saw Jō·hā´nan son of Ka·rē´ah and all the leaders of the forces with him, they were glad. [14]So all the people whom Ish´ma·el had carried away captive from Miz´pah turned around and came back, and went to Jō·hā´nan son of Ka·rē´ah. [15]But Ish´ma·el son of Neth·a·nī´ah escaped from Ka·rē´ah with eight men, and went to the Am´mon·ites. [16]Then Jō·hā´nan son of Ka·rē´ah and all the leaders of the forces with him took all the rest of the people whom Ish´ma·el son of Neth·a·nī´ah had carried away captive[j] from Miz´pah after he had slain Ged·a·lī´ah son of A·hī´kam—soldiers, women, children, and eunuchs, whom Jō·hā´nan brought back from Gib´e·on.[k] [17]And they set out, and stopped at Gē´rūth Chim´ham near Bethlehem, intending to go to Egypt [18]because of the Chal·dē´ans; for they were afraid of them, because Ish´ma·el son of Neth·a·nī´ah had killed Ged·a·lī´ah son of A·hī´kam, whom the king of Babylon had made governor over the land.

Jeremiah Advises Survivors Not to Migrate

42 Then all the commanders of the forces, and Jō·hā´nan son of Ka·rē´ah and Az·a·rī´ah[l] son of Hō·shaī´ah, and all the people from the least to the greatest, approached [2]the prophet Jer·e·mī´ah and said, "Be good enough to listen to our plea, and pray to the LORD your God for us—for all this remnant. For there are only a few of us left out of many, as your

eyes can see. [3]Let the LORD your God show us where we should go and what we should do." [4]The prophet Jer·e·mī´ah said to them, "Very well: I am going to pray to the LORD your God as you request, and whatever the LORD answers you I will tell you; I will keep nothing back from you." [5]They in their turn said to Jer·e·mī´ah, "May the LORD be a true and faithful witness against us if we do not act according to everything that the LORD your God sends us through you. [6]Whether it is good or bad, we will obey the voice of the LORD our God to whom we are sending you, in order that it may go well with us when we obey the voice of the LORD our God."

7 At the end of ten days the word of the LORD came to Jer·e·mī´ah. [8]Then he summoned Jō·hā´nan son of Ka·rē´ah and all the commanders of the forces who were with him, and all the people from the least to the greatest, [9]and said to them, "Thus says the LORD, the God of Israel, to whom you sent me to present your plea before him: [10]If you will only remain in this land, then I will build you up and not pull you down; I will plant you, and not pluck you up; for I am sorry for the disaster that I have brought upon you. [11]Do not be afraid of the king of Babylon, as you have been; do not be afraid of him, says the LORD, for I am with you, to save you and to rescue you from his hand. [12]I will grant you mercy, and he will have mercy on you and restore you to your native soil. [13]But if you continue to say, 'We will not stay in this land,' thus disobeying the voice of the LORD your God [14]and saying, 'No, we will go to the land of Egypt, where we shall not see war, or hear the sound of the trumpet, or be hungry for bread, and there we will stay,' [15]then hear the word of the LORD, O remnant of Judah. Thus says the LORD of hosts, the God of Israel: If you are determined to enter Egypt and go to settle there, [16]then the sword that you fear shall overtake

---

[j] Cn: Heb *whom he recovered from Ishmael son of Nethaniah*　　[k] Meaning of Heb uncertain
[l] Gk: Heb *Jezaniah*

you there, in the land of Egypt; and the famine that you dread shall follow close after you into Egypt; and there you shall die. [17]All the people who have determined to go to Egypt to settle there shall die by the sword, by famine, and by pestilence; they shall have no remnant or survivor from the disaster that I am bringing upon them.

18 "For thus says the LORD of hosts, the God of Israel: Just as my anger and my wrath were poured out on the inhabitants of Jerusalem, so my wrath will be poured out on you when you go to Egypt. You shall become an object of execration and horror, of cursing and ridicule. You shall see this place no more. [19]The LORD has said to you, O remnant of Judah, Do not go to Egypt. Be well aware that I have warned you today [20]that you have made a fatal mistake. For you yourselves sent me to the LORD your God, saying, 'Pray for us to the LORD our God, and whatever the LORD our God says, tell us and we will do it.' [21]So I have told you today, but you have not obeyed the voice of the LORD your God in anything that he sent me to tell you. [22]Be well aware, then, that you shall die by the sword, by famine, and by pestilence in the place where you desire to go and settle."

Taken to Egypt, Jeremiah Warns of Judgment

43 When Jer·e·mī´ah finished speaking to all the people all these words of the LORD their God, with which the LORD their God had sent him to them, [2]Az·a·rī´ah son of Hō·shaī´ah and Jō·hā´nan son of Ka·rē´ah and all the other insolent men said to Jer·e·mī´ah, "You are telling a lie. The LORD our God did not send you to say, 'Do not go to Egypt to settle there'; [3]but Bar´uch son of Ne·rī´ah is inciting you against us, to hand us over to the Chal·dē´ans, in order that they may kill us or take us into exile in Babylon." [4]So Jō·hā´nan son of Ka·rē´ah and all the commanders of the forces and all the people did not obey the voice of the LORD, to stay in the land of Judah. [5]But Jō·hā´nan son of

Ka·rē´ah and all the commanders of the forces took all the remnant of Judah who had returned to settle in the land of Judah from all the nations to which they had been driven— [6]the men, the women, the children, the princesses, and everyone whom Ne·bū·za·rad´an the captain of the guard had left with Ged·a·lī´ah son of A·hī´kam son of Shā´phan; also the prophet Jer·e·mī´ah and Bar´uch son of Ne·rī´ah. [7]And they came into the land of Egypt, for they did not obey the voice of the LORD. And they arrived at Tah´pan·hēs.

8 Then the word of the LORD came to Jer·e·mī´ah in Tah´pan·hēs: [9]Take some large stones in your hands, and bury them in the clay pavement[m] that is at the entrance to Pharaoh's palace in Tah´pan·hēs. Let the Judeans see you do it, [10]and say to them, Thus says the LORD of hosts, the God of Israel: I am going to send and take my servant King Ne·bū·chad·rez´zar of Babylon, and he[n] will set his throne above these stones that I have buried, and he will spread his royal canopy over them. [11]He shall come and ravage the land of Egypt, giving

those who are destined for pestilence,
to pestilence,
and those who are destined for
captivity, to captivity,
and those who are destined for the
sword, to the sword.

[12]He[o] shall kindle a fire in the temples of the gods of Egypt; and he shall burn them and carry them away captive; and he shall pick clean the land of Egypt, as a shepherd picks his cloak clean of vermin; and he shall depart from there safely. [13]He shall break the obelisks of Hē·li·op´o·lis, which is in the land of Egypt; and the temples of the gods of Egypt he shall burn with fire.

Denunciation of Persistent Idolatry

44 The word that came to Jer·e·mī´ah for all the Judeans living in

---

[m] Meaning of Heb uncertain   [n] Gk Syr: Heb I
[o] Gk Syr Vg: Heb I

the land of Egypt, at Mig´dol, at Tah´-pan·hes, at Memphis, and in the land of Path´ros, ²Thus says the LORD of hosts, the God of Israel: You yourselves have seen all the disaster that I have brought on Jerusalem and on all the towns of Judah. Look at them; today they are a desolation, without an inhabitant in them, ³because of the wickedness that they committed, provoking me to anger, in that they went to make offerings and serve other gods that they had not known, neither they, nor you, nor your ancestors. ⁴Yet I persistently sent to you all my servants the prophets, saying, "I beg you not to do this abominable thing that I hate!" ⁵But they did not listen or incline their ear, to turn from their wickedness and make no offerings to other gods. ⁶So my wrath and my anger were poured out and kindled in the towns of Judah and in the streets of Jerusalem; and they became a waste and a desolation, as they still are today. ⁷And now thus says the LORD God of hosts, the God of Israel: Why are you doing such great harm to yourselves, to cut off man and woman, child and infant, from the midst of Judah, leaving yourselves without a remnant? ⁸Why do you provoke me to anger with the works of your hands, making offerings to other gods in the land of Egypt where you have come to settle? Will you be cut off and become an object of cursing and ridicule among all the nations of the earth? ⁹Have you forgotten the crimes of your ancestors, of the kings of Judah, of theirᵖ wives, your own crimes and those of your wives, which they committed in the land of Judah and in the streets of Jerusalem? ¹⁰They have shown no contrition or fear to this day, nor have they walked in my law and my statutes that I set before you and before your ancestors.

11 Therefore thus says the LORD of hosts, the God of Israel: I am determined to bring disaster on you, to bring all Judah to an end. ¹²I will take the remnant of Judah who are determined to come to the land of Egypt to settle, and they shall per-ish, everyone; in the land of Egypt they shall fall; by the sword and by famine they shall perish; from the least to the greatest, they shall die by the sword and by famine; and they shall become an object of execration and horror, of cursing and ridicule. ¹³I will punish those who live in the land of Egypt, as I have punished Jerusalem, with the sword, with famine, and with pestilence, ¹⁴so that none of the remnant of Judah who have come to settle in the land of Egypt shall escape or survive or return to the land of Judah. Although they long to go back to live there, they shall not go back, except some fugitives.

15 Then all the men who were aware that their wives had been making offerings to other gods, and all the women who stood by, a great assembly, all the people who lived in Path´ros in the land of Egypt, answered Jer·e·mi´ah: ¹⁶"As for the word that you have spoken to us in the name of the LORD, we are not going to listen to you. ¹⁷Instead, we will do everything that we have vowed, make offerings to the queen of heaven and pour out libations to her, just as we and our ancestors, our kings and our officials, used to do in the towns of Judah and in the streets of Jerusalem. We used to have plenty of food, and prospered, and saw no misfortune. ¹⁸But from the time we stopped making offerings to the queen of heaven and pouring out libations to her, we have lacked everything and have perished by the sword and by famine." ¹⁹And the women said,�q "Indeed we will go on making offerings to the queen of heaven and pouring out libations to her; do you think that we made cakes for her, marked with her image, and poured out libations to her without our husbands' being involved?"

20 Then Jer·e·mi´ah said to all the people, men and women, all the people who were giving him this answer: ²¹"As for the offerings that you made in the towns of Judah and in the streets of Jerusalem, you

ᵖ Heb *his*   q Compare Syr: Heb lacks *And the women said*

and your ancestors, your kings and your officials, and the people of the land, did not the LORD remember them? Did it not come into his mind? ²²The LORD could no longer bear the sight of your evil doings, the abominations that you committed; therefore your land became a desolation and a waste and a curse, without inhabitant, as it is to this day. ²³It is because you burned offerings, and because you sinned against the LORD and did not obey the voice of the LORD or walk in his law and in his statutes and in his decrees, that this disaster has befallen you, as is still evident today."

24 Jer·e·mi´ah said to all the people and all the women, "Hear the word of the LORD, all you Judeans who are in the land of Egypt, ²⁵Thus says the LORD of hosts, the God of Israel: You and your wives have accomplished in deeds what you declared in words, saying, 'We are determined to perform the vows that we have made, to make offerings to the queen of heaven and to pour out libations to her.' By all means, keep your vows and make your libations! ²⁶Therefore hear the word of the LORD, all you Judeans who live in the land of Egypt: Lo, I swear by my great name, says the LORD, that my name shall no longer be pronounced on the lips of any of the people of Judah in all the land of Egypt, saying, 'As the Lord GOD lives.' ²⁷I am going to watch over them for harm and not for good; all the people of Judah who are in the land of Egypt shall perish by the sword and by famine, until not one is left. ²⁸And those who escape the sword shall return from the land of Egypt to the land of Judah, few in number; and all the remnant of Judah, who have come to the land of Egypt to settle, shall know whose words will stand, mine or theirs! ²⁹This shall be the sign to you, says the LORD, that I am going to punish you in this place, in order that you may know that my words against you will surely be carried out: ³⁰Thus says the LORD, I am going to give Pharaoh Hoph´ra, king of Egypt, into the hands of

his enemies, those who seek his life, just as I gave King Zed·e·ki´ah of Judah into the hand of King Ne·bu·chad·rez´zar of Babylon, his enemy who sought his life."

A Word of Comfort to Baruch

45 The word that the prophet Jer·e·mi´ah spoke to Bar´uch son of Ne·ri´ah, when he wrote these words in a scroll at the dictation of Jer·e·mi´ah, in the fourth year of King Je·hoi´a·kim son of Jō·si´ah of Judah: ²Thus says the LORD, the God of Israel, to you, O Bar´uch: ³You said, "Woe is me! The LORD has added sorrow to my pain; I am weary with my groaning, and I find no rest." ⁴Thus you shall say to him, "Thus says the LORD: I am going to break down what I have built, and pluck up what I have planted—that is, the whole land. ⁵And you, do you seek great things for yourself? Do not seek them; for I am going to bring disaster upon all flesh, says the LORD; but I will give you your life as a prize of war in every place to which you may go."

Judgment on Egypt

46 The word of the LORD that came to the prophet Jer·e·mi´ah concerning the nations.

2 Concerning Egypt, about the army of Pharaoh Nē´cō, king of Egypt, which was by the river Euphrates at Car´chem·ish and which King Ne·bu·chad·rez´zar of Babylon defeated in the fourth year of King Je·hoi´a·kim son of Jō·si´ah of Judah:
³ Prepare buckler and shield,
    and advance for battle!
⁴ Harness the horses;
    mount the steeds!
Take your stations with your helmets,
    whet your lances,
    put on your coats of mail!
⁵ Why do I see them terrified?
    They have fallen back;
their warriors are beaten down,
    and have fled in haste.
They do not look back—
    terror is all around!
                    says the LORD.

⁶ The swift cannot flee away,
  nor can the warrior escape;
in the north by the river Euphrates
  they have stumbled and fallen.

⁷ Who is this, rising like the Nile,
  like rivers whose waters surge?
⁸ Egypt rises like the Nile,
  like rivers whose waters surge.
It said, Let me rise, let me cover the
  earth,
  let me destroy cities and their
  inhabitants.
⁹ Advance, O horses,
  and dash madly, O chariots!
Let the warriors go forth:
  Ethiopiaʳ and Put who carry the
  shield,
  the Lūʹdim, who drawˢ the bow.
¹⁰ That day is the day of the Lord GOD of
  hosts,
  a day of retribution,
  to gain vindication from his foes.
The sword shall devour and be sated,
  and drink its fill of their blood.
For the Lord GOD of hosts holds a
  sacrifice
  in the land of the north by the river
  Euphrates.
¹¹ Go up to Gilʹeʹad, and take balm,
  O virgin daughter Egypt!
In vain you have used many
  medicines;
  there is no healing for you.
¹² The nations have heard of your shame,
  and the earth is full of your cry;
for warrior has stumbled against
  warrior;
  both have fallen together.

Babylonia Will Strike Egypt

13 The word that the LORD spoke to the
prophet Jerʹeʹmiʹah about the coming of
King Neʹbuʹchadʹrezʹzar of Babylon to
attack the land of Egypt:
¹⁴ Declare in Egypt, and proclaim in
  Migʹdŏl;
  proclaim in Memphis and
  Tahʹpanʹhēs;

Say, "Take your stations and be ready,
  for the sword shall devour those
  around you."
¹⁵ Why has Āʹpis fled?ᵗ
  Why did your bull not stand?
  —because the LORD thrust him
  down.
¹⁶ Your multitude stumbledᵘ and fell,
  and one said to another,ᵛ
"Come, let us go back to our own
  people
  and to the land of our birth,
  because of the destroying sword."
¹⁷ Give Pharaoh, king of Egypt, the name
  "Braggart who missed his chance."

¹⁸ As I live, says the King,
  whose name is the LORD of hosts,
one is coming
  like Tāʹbor among the mountains,
  and like Carʹmel by the sea.
¹⁹ Pack your bags for exile,
  sheltered daughter Egypt!
For Memphis shall become a waste,
  a ruin, without inhabitant.

²⁰ A beautiful heifer is Egypt—
  a gadfly from the north lights upon
  her.
²¹ Even her mercenaries in her midst
  are like fatted calves;
they too have turned and fled together,
  they did not stand;
for the day of their calamity has come
  upon them,
  the time of their punishment.

²² She makes a sound like a snake gliding
  away;
  for her enemies march in force,
and come against her with axes,
  like those who fell trees.
²³ They shall cut down her forest,
                    says the LORD,
  though it is impenetrable,
  because they are more numerous

ʳ Or *Nubia*; Heb *Cush*   ˢ Cn: Heb *who grasp, who
draw*   ᵗ Gk: Heb *Why was it swept away*   ᵘ Gk:
Meaning of Heb uncertain   ᵛ Gk: Heb *and fell one
to another and they said*

than locusts;
they are without number.
24 Daughter Egypt shall be put to shame;
she shall be handed over to a people
from the north.

25 The LORD of hosts, the God of Israel,
said: See, I am bringing punishment upon
Ā́mon of Thēbes, and Pharaoh, and Egypt
and her gods and her kings, upon Pharaoh
and those who trust in him. 26I will hand
them over to those who seek their life, to
King Ne·bū·chad·rez´zar of Babylon and his
officers. Afterward Egypt shall be inhabited
as in the days of old, says the LORD.

God Will Save Israel

27 But as for you, have no fear, my
servant Jacob,
and do not be dismayed, O Israel;
for I am going to save you from far
away,
and your offspring from the land of
their captivity.
Jacob shall return and have quiet and
ease,
and no one shall make him afraid.
28 As for you, have no fear, my servant
Jacob,
says the LORD,
for I am with you.
I will make an end of all the nations
among which I have banished you,
but I will not make an end of you!
I will chastise you in just measure,
and I will by no means leave you
unpunished.

Judgment on the Philistines

47 The word of the LORD that came
to the prophet Jer·e·mī´ah concerning the Phi·lis´tines, before Pharaoh
attacked Gā´za:
2 Thus says the LORD:
See, waters are rising out of the north
and shall become an overflowing
torrent;
they shall overflow the land and all
that fills it,
the city and those who live in it.

People shall cry out,
and all the inhabitants of the land
shall wail.
3 At the noise of the stamping of the
hoofs of his stallions,
at the clatter of his chariots, at the
rumbling of their wheels,
parents do not turn back for children,
so feeble are their hands,
4 because of the day that is coming
to destroy all the Phi·lis´tines,
to cut off from Tyre and Sī´don
every helper that remains.
For the LORD is destroying the
Phi·lis´tines,
the remnant of the coastland of
Caph´tor.
5 Baldness has come upon Gā´za,
Ash´ke·lon is silenced.
O remnant of their power!w
How long will you gash yourselves?
6 Ah, sword of the LORD!
How long until you are quiet?
Put yourself into your scabbard,
rest and be still!
7 How can itx be quiet,
when the LORD has given it an order?
Against Ash´ke·lon and against the
seashore—
there he has appointed it.

Judgment on Moab

48 Concerning Mŏ´ab.

Thus says the LORD of hosts, the God of
Israel:
Alas for Nē´bō, it is laid waste!
Kir·i·a·thā´im is put to shame, it is
taken;
the fortress is put to shame and broken
down;
2 the renown of Mŏ´ab is no more.
In Hesh´bon they planned evil against
her:
"Come, let us cut her off from being
a nation!"

---

w Gk: Heb *their valley*   x Gk Vg: Heb *you*   y The
place-name *Madmen* sounds like the Hebrew verb *to
be silent*

You also, O Madmen, shall be brought
    to silence;[y]
    the sword shall pursue you.

3 Hark! a cry from Hor·ō·nā´im,
    "Desolation and great destruction!"
4 "Mō´ab is destroyed!"
    her little ones cry out.
5 For at the ascent of Lū´hith
    they go[z] up weeping bitterly;
for at the descent of Hor·ō·nā´im
    they have heard the distressing cry
        of anguish.
6 Flee! Save yourselves!
    Be like a wild ass[a] in the desert!

7 Surely, because you trusted in your
    strongholds[b] and your treasures,
    you also shall be taken;
Chē´mosh shall go out into exile,
    with his priests and his attendants.
8 The destroyer shall come upon every
    town,
    and no town shall escape;
the valley shall perish,
    and the plain shall be destroyed,
    as the LORD has spoken.

9 Set aside salt for Mō´ab,
    for she will surely fall;
her towns shall become a desolation,
    with no inhabitant in them.

10 Accursed is the one who is slack in
doing the work of the LORD; and accursed
is the one who keeps back the sword from
bloodshed.

11 Mō´ab has been at ease from his youth,
    settled like wine[c] on its dregs;
he has not been emptied from vessel to
    vessel,
    nor has he gone into exile;
therefore his flavor has remained
    and his aroma is unspoiled.
12 Therefore, the time is surely coming, says the LORD, when I shall send to
him decanters to decant him, and empty
his vessels, and break his[c] jars in pieces.
13 Then Mō´ab shall be ashamed of Chē-

mosh, as the house of Israel was ashamed
of Beth´el, their confidence.

14 How can you say, "We are heroes
    and mighty warriors"?
15 The destroyer of Mō´ab and his towns
    has come up,
    and the choicest of his young men
        have gone down to slaughter,
    says the King, whose name is the
        LORD of hosts.
16 The calamity of Mō´ab is near at hand
    and his doom approaches swiftly.
17 Mourn over him, all you his
    neighbors,
    and all who know his name;
say, "How the mighty scepter is
    broken,
    the glorious staff!"

18 Come down from glory,
    and sit on the parched ground,
    enthroned daughter Dī´bon!
For the destroyer of Mō´ab has come
    up against you;
    he has destroyed your strongholds.
19 Stand by the road and watch,
    you inhabitant of A·rō´er!
Ask the man fleeing and the woman
    escaping;
    say, "What has happened?"
20 Mō´ab is put to shame, for it is broken
    down;
    wail and cry!
Tell it by the Ar´non,
    that Mō´ab is laid waste.

21 Judgment has come upon the tableland, upon Hō´lon, and Jah´zah, and
Meph´a·ath, 22and Dī´bon, and Nē´bō, and
Beth-dib·la·thā´im, 23and Kir·i·a·thā´im,
and Beth-gā´mul, and Beth-mē´on, 24and
Ker´i·oth, and Boz´rah, and all the towns of
the land of Mō´ab, far and near. 25The horn
of Mō´ab is cut off, and his arm is broken,
says the LORD.
26 Make him drunk, because he magnified

[z] Cn: Heb *he goes*   [a] Gk Aquila: Heb *like Aroer*
[b] Gk: Heb *works*   [c] Heb lacks *like wine*   [d] Gk
Aquila: Heb *their*

himself against the LORD; let Mŏ'ab wallow in his vomit; he too shall become a laughingstock. ²⁷Israel was a laughingstock for you, though he was not caught among thieves; but whenever you spoke of him you shook your head!

²⁸ Leave the towns, and live on the rock,
O inhabitants of Mŏ'ab!
Be like the dove that nests
on the sides of the mouth of a gorge.
²⁹ We have heard of the pride of Mŏ'ab—
he is very proud—
of his loftiness, his pride, and his
arrogance,
and the haughtiness of his heart.
³⁰ I myself know his insolence, says the
LORD;
his boasts are false,
his deeds are false.
³¹ Therefore I wail for Mŏ'ab;
I cry out for all Mŏ'ab;
for the people of Kir-hē'res I mourn.
³² More than for Jā'zer I weep for you,
O vine of Sib'mah!
Your branches crossed over the sea,
reached as far as Jā'zer;ᵉ
upon your summer fruits and your
vintage
the destroyer has fallen.
³³ Gladness and joy have been taken
away
from the fruitful land of Mŏ'ab;
I have stopped the wine from the wine
presses;
no one treads them with shouts of joy;
the shouting is not the shout of joy.

34 Hesh'bon and Ē'le·ā'leh cry out;ᶠ as far as Jā'haz they utter their voice, from Zō'ar to Hor·ō·nā'im and Eg'lath-shelish'i·yah. For even the waters of Nim'rim have become desolate. ³⁵And I will bring to an end in Mŏ'ab, says the LORD, those who offer sacrifice at a high place and make offerings to their gods. ³⁶Therefore my heart moans for Mŏ'ab like a flute, and my heart moans like a flute for the people of Kir-hē'res; for the riches they gained have perished.

37 For every head is shaved and every beard cut off; on all the hands there are gashes, and on the loins sackcloth. ³⁸On all the housetops of Mŏ'ab and in the squares there is nothing but lamentation; for I have broken Mŏ'ab like a vessel that no one wants, says the LORD. ³⁹How it is broken! How they wail! How Mŏ'ab has turned his back in shame! So Mŏ'ab has become a derision and a horror to all his neighbors.
⁴⁰ For thus says the LORD:
Look, he shall swoop down like an
eagle,
and spread his wings against Mŏ'ab;
⁴¹ the townsᵍ shall be taken
and the strongholds seized.
The hearts of the warriors of Mŏ'ab, on
that day,
shall be like the heart of a woman in
labor.
⁴² Mŏ'ab shall be destroyed as a people,
because he magnified himself
against the LORD.
⁴³ Terror, pit, and trap
are before you, O inhabitants of
Mŏ'ab!
says the LORD.
⁴⁴ Everyone who flees from the terror
shall fall into the pit,
and everyone who climbs out of the pit
shall be caught in the trap.
For I will bring these thingsʰ upon Mŏ'ab
in the year of their punishment,
says the LORD.

⁴⁵ In the shadow of Hesh'bon
fugitives stop exhausted;
for a fire has gone out from Hesh'bon,
a flame from the house of Sī'hon;
it has destroyed the forehead of Mŏ'ab,
the scalp of the people of tumult.ⁱ
⁴⁶ Woe to you, O Mŏ'ab!
The people of Chē'mosh have
perished,
for your sons have been taken captive,
and your daughters into captivity.

ᵉ Two Mss and Isa 16.8: MT *the sea of Jazer*   ᶠ Cn:
Heb *From the cry of Heshbon to Elealeh*   ᵍ Or *Kerioth*
ʰ Gk Syr: Heb *bring upon it*   ⁱ Or *of Shaon*

⁴⁷ Yet I will restore the fortunes of Mōʹab
    in the latter days, says the LORD.
Thus far is the judgment on Mōʹab.

Judgment on the Ammonites

49 Concerning the Amʹmon·ītes.
      Thus says the LORD:
Has Israel no sons?
    Has he no heir?
Why then has Milʹcom dispossessed
        Gad,
    and his people settled in its towns?
² Therefore, the time is surely coming,
        says the LORD,
when I will sound the battle alarm
    against Rabʹbah of the Amʹmon·ītes;
it shall become a desolate mound,
    and its villages shall be burned with
        fire;
then Israel shall dispossess those who
        dispossessed him,
    says the LORD.

³ Wail, O Heshʹbon, for Aī is laid waste!
    Cry out, O daughtersʲ of Rabʹbah!
Put on sackcloth,
    lament, and slash yourselves with
        whips!ᵏ
For Milʹcom shall go into exile,
    with his priests and his attendants.
⁴ Why do you boast in your strength?
    Your strength is ebbing,
O faithless daughter.
    You trusted in your treasures, saying,
    "Who will attack me?"
⁵ I am going to bring terror upon you,
    says the Lord GOD of hosts,
    from all your neighbors,
and you will be scattered, each
        headlong,
    with no one to gather the fugitives.
6 But afterward I will restore the fortunes
of the Amʹmon·ītes, says the LORD.

Judgment on Edom

7 Concerning Ēʹdom.

Thus says the LORD of hosts:
    Is there no longer wisdom in Tēʹman?
    Has counsel perished from the prudent?

Has their wisdom vanished?
⁸ Flee, turn back, get down low,
    inhabitants of Dēʹdan!
For I will bring the calamity of Esau
        upon him,
    the time when I punish him.
⁹ If grape-gatherers came to you,
    would they not leave gleanings?
If thieves came by night,
    even they would pillage only what
        they wanted.
¹⁰ But as for me, I have stripped Esau
        bare,
    I have uncovered his hiding places,
    and he is not able to conceal
        himself.
His offspring are destroyed, his
        kinsfolk
    and his neighbors; and he is no
        more.
¹¹ Leave your orphans, I will keep them
        alive;
    and let your widows trust in me.

12 For thus says the LORD: If those who
do not deserve to drink the cup still have
to drink it, shall you be the one to go
unpunished? You shall not go unpunished;
you must drink it. ¹³For by myself I have
sworn, says the LORD, that Bozʹrah shall
become an object of horror and ridicule, a
waste, and an object of cursing; and all her
towns shall be perpetual wastes.
¹⁴ I have heard tidings from the LORD,
    and a messenger has been sent
        among the nations:
    "Gather yourselves together and come
        against her,
    and rise up for battle!"
¹⁵ For I will make you least among the
        nations,
    despised by humankind.
¹⁶ The terror you inspire
    and the pride of your heart have
        deceived you,
you who live in the clefts of the rock,ˡ
    who hold the height of the hill.

ʲ Or villages   ᵏ Cn: Meaning of Heb uncertain
ˡ Or of Sela

Although you make your nest as high
  as the eagle's,
from there I will bring you down,
  says the LORD.

17 Ē′dom shall become an object of horror; everyone who passes by it will be horrified and will hiss because of all its disasters. [18]As when Sod′om and Go·mor′rah and their neighbors were overthrown, says the LORD, no one shall live there, nor shall anyone settle in it. [19]Like a lion coming up from the thickets of the Jordan against a perennial pasture, I will suddenly chase Ē′dom[m] away from it; and I will appoint over it whomever I choose.[n] For who is like me? Who can summon me? Who is the shepherd who can stand before me? [20]Therefore hear the plan that the LORD has made against Ē′dom and the purposes that he has formed against the inhabitants of Tē′man: Surely the little ones of the flock shall be dragged away; surely their fold shall be appalled at their fate. [21]At the sound of their fall the earth shall tremble; the sound of their cry shall be heard at the Red Sea.[o] [22]Look, he shall mount up and swoop down like an eagle, and spread his wings against Boz′rah, and the heart of the warriors of Ē′dom in that day shall be like the heart of a woman in labor.

Judgment on Damascus

23 Concerning Damascus.

Hā′math and Ar′pad are confounded,
  for they have heard bad news;
they melt in fear, they are troubled like
    the sea[p]
  that cannot be quiet.
[24] Damascus has become feeble, she
    turned to flee,
  and panic seized her;
anguish and sorrows have taken hold
    of her,
  as of a woman in labor.
[25] How the famous city is forsaken,[q]
  the joyful town![r]
[26] Therefore her young men shall fall in
    her squares,

and all her soldiers shall be
    destroyed in that day,
        says the LORD of hosts.
[27] And I will kindle a fire at the wall of
    Damascus,
  and it shall devour the strongholds
    of Ben-hā′dad.

Judgment on Kedar and Hazor

28 Concerning Kē′dar and the kingdoms of Hā′zor that King Ne·bū·chad·rez′zar of Babylon defeated.

Thus says the LORD:
Rise up, advance against Kē′dar!
  Destroy the people of the east!
[29] Take their tents and their flocks,
  their curtains and all their goods;
carry off their camels for yourselves,
  and a cry shall go up: "Terror is all
    around!"
[30] Flee, wander far away, hide in deep
    places,
  O inhabitants of Hā′zor!
        says the LORD.
For King Ne·bū·chad·rez′zar of
    Babylon
  has made a plan against you
  and formed a purpose against you.

[31] Rise up, advance against a nation at
    ease,
  that lives secure,
        says the LORD,
that has no gates or bars,
  that lives alone.
[32] Their camels shall become booty,
  their herds of cattle a spoil.
I will scatter to every wind
  those who have shaven temples,
and I will bring calamity
  against them from every side,
        says the LORD.
[33] Hā′zor shall become a lair of jackals,
  an everlasting waste;
no one shall live there,
  nor shall anyone settle in it.

---

[m] Heb him   [n] Or and I will single out the choicest of his rams: Meaning of Heb uncertain   [o] Or Sea of Reeds
[p] Cn: Heb there is trouble in the sea   [q] Vg: Heb is not forsaken   [r] Syr Vg Tg: Heb the town of my joy

Judgment on Elam

34 The word of the LORD that came to the prophet Jer·e·mī´ah concerning Ē´lam, at the beginning of the reign of King Zed·e·kī´ah of Judah.

35 Thus says the LORD of hosts: I am going to break the bow of Ē´lam, the mainstay of their might; [36]and I will bring upon Ē´lam the four winds from the four quarters of heaven; and I will scatter them to all these winds, and there shall be no nation to which the exiles from Ē´lam shall not come. [37]I will terrify Ē´lam before their enemies, and before those who seek their life; I will bring disaster upon them, my fierce anger, says the LORD. I will send the sword after them, until I have consumed them; [38]and I will set my throne in Ē´lam, and destroy their king and officials, says the LORD.

39 But in the latter days I will restore the fortunes of Ē´lam, says the LORD.

Judgment on Babylon

50 The word that the LORD spoke concerning Babylon, concerning the land of the Chal·dē´ans, by the prophet Jer·e·mī´ah:

2 Declare among the nations and
   proclaim,
   set up a banner and proclaim,
   do not conceal it, say:
Babylon is taken,
   Bel is put to shame,
   Mer´o·dach is dismayed.
Her images are put to shame,
   her idols are dismayed.

3 For out of the north a nation has come up against her; it shall make her land a desolation, and no one shall live in it; both human beings and animals shall flee away.

4 In those days and in that time, says the LORD, the people of Israel shall come, they and the people of Judah together; they shall come weeping as they seek the LORD their God. [5]They shall ask the way to Zion, with faces turned toward it, and they shall come and join[s] themselves to the LORD by an everlasting covenant that will never be forgotten.

6 My people have been lost sheep; their shepherds have led them astray, turning them away on the mountains; from mountain to hill they have gone, they have forgotten their fold. [7]All who found them have devoured them, and their enemies have said, "We are not guilty, because they have sinned against the LORD, the true pasture, the LORD, the hope of their ancestors."

8 Flee from Babylon, and go out of the land of the Chal·dē´ans, and be like male goats leading the flock. [9]For I am going to stir up and bring against Babylon a company of great nations from the land of the north; and they shall array themselves against her; from there she shall be taken. Their arrows are like the arrows of a skilled warrior who does not return empty-handed. [10]Chal·dē´a shall be plundered; all who plunder her shall be sated, says the LORD.

11 Though you rejoice, though you exult,
     O plunderers of my heritage,
   though you frisk about like a heifer on
        the grass,
     and neigh like stallions,

Jeremiah said that Babylon's walls and bulwarks would soon fall down and that the people of Israel could return home with joy. Bulwarks were special walls or barriers built for defense purposes. At some places in the Old Testament "bulwark" is used as a symbol to describe God's protection. The church is sometimes called a bulwark of truth.

Can you think of ways knowing the truth about a situation would create a "bulwark," or wall of protection? When you are worried or afraid, remember that God cares for you. God doesn't always make our troubles disappear, but God is always there to help us be strong.

[s] Gk: Heb *toward it. Come! They shall join*

12 your mother shall be utterly shamed,
  and she who bore you shall be
    disgraced.
Lo, she shall be the last of the nations,
  a wilderness, dry land, and a desert.
13 Because of the wrath of the LORD she
    shall not be inhabited,
  but shall be an utter desolation;
everyone who passes by Babylon shall
    be appalled
  and hiss because of all her wounds.
14 Take up your positions around
    Babylon,
  all you that bend the bow;
shoot at her, spare no arrows,
  for she has sinned against the LORD.
15 Raise a shout against her from all sides,
  "She has surrendered;
her bulwarks have fallen,
  her walls are thrown down."
For this is the vengeance of the LORD:
  take vengeance on her,
  do to her as she has done.
16 Cut off from Babylon the sower,
  and the wielder of the sickle in time
    of harvest;
because of the destroying sword
  all of them shall return to their own
    people,
  and all of them shall flee to their
    own land.

17 Israel is a hunted sheep driven away
by lions. First the king of Assyria devoured
it, and now at the end King Ne·bū´-
chad·rez´zar of Babylon has gnawed its
bones. 18Therefore, thus says the LORD of
hosts, the God of Israel: I am going to punish the king of Babylon and his land, as I
punished the king of Assyria. 19I will
restore Israel to its pasture, and it shall feed
on Car´mel and in Bā´shan, and on the hills
of E´phra·im and in Gil´e·ad its hunger
shall be satisfied. 20In those days and at
that time, says the LORD, the iniquity of
Israel shall be sought, and there shall be
none; and the sins of Judah, and none shall
be found; for I will pardon the remnant
that I have spared.

21 Go up to the land of Mer·a·thā´im;[t]
  go up against her,
and attack the inhabitants of Pe´kod[u]
  and utterly destroy the last of them,[v]
                        says the LORD;
  do all that I have commanded you.
22 The noise of battle is in the land,
  and great destruction!
23 How the hammer of the whole earth
  is cut down and broken!
How Babylon has become
  a horror among the nations!
24 You set a snare for yourself and you
    were caught, O Babylon,
  but you did not know it;
you were discovered and seized,
  because you challenged the LORD.
25 The LORD has opened his armory,
  and brought out the weapons of his
    wrath,
for the Lord GOD of hosts has a task
    to do
  in the land of the Chal·dē´ans.
26 Come against her from every quarter;
  open her granaries;
pile her up like heaps of grain, and
    destroy her utterly;
  let nothing be left of her.
27 Kill all her bulls,
  let them go down to the slaughter.
Alas for them, their day has come,
  the time of their punishment!

28 Listen! Fugitives and refugees from
the land of Babylon are coming to declare
in Zion the vengeance of the LORD our
God, vengeance for his temple.

29 Summon archers against Babylon,
all who bend the bow. Encamp all around
her; let no one escape. Repay her according to her deeds; just as she has done, do
to her—for she has arrogantly defied the
LORD, the Holy One of Israel. 30Therefore
her young men shall fall in her squares,
and all her soldiers shall be destroyed on
that day, says the LORD.

[t] Or *of Double Rebellion*   [u] Or *of Punishment*   [v] Tg:
Heb *destroy after them*

³¹ I am against you, O arrogant one,
  says the Lord GOD of hosts;
for your day has come,
  the time when I will punish you.
³² The arrogant one shall stumble and
    fall,
  with no one to raise him up,
and I will kindle a fire in his cities,
  and it will devour everything around
    him.

33 Thus says the LORD of hosts: The people of Israel are oppressed, and so too are the people of Judah; all their captors have held them fast and refuse to let them go. ³⁴Their Redeemer is strong; the LORD of hosts is his name. He will surely plead their cause, that he may give rest to the earth, but unrest to the inhabitants of Babylon.

³⁵ A sword against the Chal·dē´ans, says
      the LORD,
  and against the inhabitants of
    Babylon,
  and against her officials and her
    sages!
³⁶ A sword against the diviners,
  so that they may become fools!
A sword against her warriors,
  so that they may be destroyed!
³⁷ A sword against her[w] horses and
      against her[w] chariots,
  and against all the foreign troops in
    her midst,
  so that they may become women!
A sword against all her treasures,
  that they may be plundered!
³⁸ A drought[x] against her waters,
  that they may be dried up!
For it is a land of images,
  and they go mad over idols.

39 Therefore wild animals shall live with hyenas in Babylon,[y] and ostriches shall inhabit her; she shall never again be peopled, or inhabited for all generations. ⁴⁰As when God overthrew Sod´om and Go·mor´rah and their neighbors, says the LORD, so no one shall live there, nor shall anyone settle in her.
⁴¹ Look, a people is coming from the
      north;
  a mighty nation and many kings
    are stirring from the farthest parts of
      the earth.
⁴² They wield bow and spear,
  they are cruel and have no mercy.
The sound of them is like the roaring
      sea;
  they ride upon horses,
set in array as a warrior for battle,
  against you, O daughter Babylon!

⁴³ The king of Babylon heard news of
      them,
  and his hands fell helpless;
anguish seized him,
  pain like that of a woman in labor.

44 Like a lion coming up from the thickets of the Jordan against a perennial pasture, I will suddenly chase them away from her; and I will appoint over her whomever I choose.[z] For who is like me? Who can summon me? Who is the shepherd who can stand before me? ⁴⁵Therefore hear the plan that the LORD has made against Babylon, and the purposes that he has formed against the land of the Chal·dē´ans: Surely the little ones of the flock shall be dragged away; surely their[a] fold shall be appalled at their fate. ⁴⁶At the sound of the capture of Babylon the earth shall tremble, and her cry shall be heard among the nations.

51 Thus says the LORD:
    I am going to stir up a destructive
      wind[b]
  against Babylon
  and against the inhabitants of
    Leb-qā´maī;[c]
² and I will send winnowers to Babylon,
  and they shall winnow her.

---

[w] Cn: Heb *his*   [x] Another reading is *A sword*
[y] Heb lacks *in Babylon*   [z] Or *and I will single out the choicest of her rams*: Meaning of Heb uncertain
[a] Syr Gk Tg Compare 49.20: Heb lacks *their*   [b] Or *stir up the spirit of a destroyer*

They shall empty her land
  when they come against her from
      every side
  on the day of trouble.
³ Let not the archer bend his bow,
  let him not array himself in his coat
      of mail.
Do not spare her young men;
  utterly destroy her entire army.
⁴ They shall fall down slain in the land
      of the Chal·dē'ans,
  and wounded in her streets.
⁵ Israel and Judah have not been
      forsaken
  by their God, the LORD of hosts,
though their land is full of guilt
  before the Holy One of Israel.

⁶ Flee from the midst of Babylon,
  save your lives, each of you!
Do not perish because of her guilt,
  for this is the time of the LORD's
      vengeance;
  he is repaying her what is due.
⁷ Babylon was a golden cup in the
      LORD's hand,
  making all the earth drunken;
the nations drank of her wine,
  and so the nations went mad.
⁸ Suddenly Babylon has fallen and is
      shattered;
  wail for her!
Bring balm for her wound;
  perhaps she may be healed.
⁹ We tried to heal Babylon,
  but she could not be healed.
Forsake her, and let each of us go
  to our own country;
for her judgment has reached up to
      heaven
  and has been lifted up even to the
      skies.
¹⁰ The LORD has brought forth our
      vindication;
  come, let us declare in Zion
the work of the LORD our God.

¹¹ Sharpen the arrows!
  Fill the quivers!
The LORD has stirred up the spirit of the

"It is he [God] who made
the earth by his power,
who established the world
by his wisdom, and by his
understanding stretched out the
heavens."   Jeremiah 51:15

kings of the Mēdes, because his purpose
concerning Babylon is to destroy it, for that
is the vengeance of the LORD, vengeance
for his temple.
¹² Raise a standard against the walls of
      Babylon;
  make the watch strong;
post sentinels;
  prepare the ambushes;
for the LORD has both planned and
      done
  what he spoke concerning the
      inhabitants of Babylon.
¹³ You who live by mighty waters,
  rich in treasures,
your end has come,
  the thread of your life is cut.
¹⁴ The LORD of hosts has sworn by
      himself:
Surely I will fill you with troops like a
      swarm of locusts,
  and they shall raise a shout of
      victory over you.

¹⁵ It is he who made the earth by his
      power,
  who established the world by his
      wisdom,
and by his understanding stretched out
      the heavens.
¹⁶ When he utters his voice there is a
      tumult of waters in the heavens,
  and he makes the mist rise from the
      ends of the earth.
He makes lightnings for the rain,
  and he brings out the wind from his
      storehouses.
¹⁷ Everyone is stupid and without
      knowledge;
  goldsmiths are all put to shame by
      their idols;

ᶜ *Leb-qamai* is a cryptogram for *Kasdim*, Chaldea

for their images are false,
and there is no breath in them.
¹⁸ They are worthless, a work of
delusion;
at the time of their punishment they
shall perish.
¹⁹ Not like these is the LORD,[d] the portion
of Jacob,
for he is the one who formed all
things,
and Israel is the tribe of his
inheritance;
the LORD of hosts is his name.

Israel the Creator's Instrument

²⁰ You are my war club, my weapon of
battle:
with you I smash nations;
with you I destroy kingdoms;
²¹ with you I smash the horse and its
rider;
with you I smash the chariot and
the charioteer;
²² with you I smash man and woman;
with you I smash the old man and
the boy;
with you I smash the young man and
the girl;
²³ with you I smash shepherds and
their flocks;
with you I smash farmers and their
teams;
with you I smash governors and
deputies.

The Doom of Babylon

24 I will repay Babylon and all the
inhabitants of Chal·dē′a before your very
eyes for all the wrong that they have done
in Zion, says the LORD.

²⁵ I am against you, O destroying
mountain,
says the LORD,
that destroys the whole earth;

I will stretch out my hand against you,
and roll you down from the crags,
and make you a burned-out
mountain.
²⁶ No stone shall be taken from you for a
corner
and no stone for a foundation,
but you shall be a perpetual waste,
says the LORD.

²⁷ Raise a standard in the land,
blow the trumpet among the
nations;
prepare the nations for war against her,
summon against her the kingdoms,
Ar′a·rat, Min′nī, and Ash′ke·naz;
appoint a marshal against her,
bring up horses like bristling
locusts.
²⁸ Prepare the nations for war against her,
the kings of the Mēdes, with their
governors and deputies,
and every land under their
dominion.
²⁹ The land trembles and writhes,
for the LORD's purposes against
Babylon stand,
to make the land of Babylon a
desolation,
without inhabitant.
³⁰ The warriors of Babylon have given up
fighting,
they remain in their strongholds;
their strength has failed,
they have become women;
her buildings are set on fire,
her bars are broken.
³¹ One runner runs to meet another,
and one messenger to meet
another,
to tell the king of Babylon
that his city is taken from end to
end:
³² the fords have been seized,
the marshes have been burned with
fire,
and the soldiers are in panic.

[d] Heb lacks *the LORD*

33 For thus says the LORD of hosts, the
   God of Israel:
Daughter Babylon is like a threshing
   floor
   at the time when it is trodden;
yet a little while
   and the time of her harvest will
      come.
34 "King Ne·bu·chad·rez´zar of Babylon
   has devoured me,
   he has crushed me;
he has made me an empty vessel,
   he has swallowed me like a monster;
he has filled his belly with my
      delicacies,
   he has spewed me out.
35 May my torn flesh be avenged on
      Babylon,"
   the inhabitants of Zion shall say.
"May my blood be avenged on the
      inhabitants of Chal·de´a,"
   Jerusalem shall say.
36 Therefore thus says the LORD:
I am going to defend your cause
   and take vengeance for you.
I will dry up her sea
   and make her fountain dry;
37 and Babylon shall become a heap of
      ruins,
   a den of jackals,
an object of horror and of hissing,
   without inhabitant.

38 Like lions they shall roar together;
   they shall growl like lions' whelps.
39 When they are inflamed, I will set out
      their drink
   and make them drunk, until they
      become merry
and then sleep a perpetual sleep
   and never wake, says the LORD.
40 I will bring them down like lambs to
      the slaughter,
   like rams and goats.

41 How She´shach[e] is taken,
   the pride of the whole earth seized!
How Babylon has become
   an object of horror among the nations!

42 The sea has risen over Babylon;
   she has been covered by its
      tumultuous waves.
43 Her cities have become an object of
      horror,
   a land of drought and a desert,
a land in which no one lives,
   and through which no mortal passes.
44 I will punish Bel in Babylon,
   and make him disgorge what he has
      swallowed.
The nations shall no longer stream to
      him;
   the wall of Babylon has fallen.

45 Come out of her, my people!
   Save your lives, each of you,
   from the fierce anger of the LORD!
46 Do not be fainthearted or fearful
   at the rumors heard in the land—
one year one rumor comes,
   the next year another,
rumors of violence in the land
   and of ruler against ruler.

47 Assuredly, the days are coming
   when I will punish the images of
      Babylon;
her whole land shall be put to shame,
   and all her slain shall fall in her midst.
48 Then the heavens and the earth,
   and all that is in them,
shall shout for joy over Babylon;
   for the destroyers shall come against
      them out of the north,
                     says the LORD.
49 Babylon must fall for the slain of Israel,
   as the slain of all the earth have
      fallen because of Babylon.

50 You survivors of the sword,
   go, do not linger!
Remember the LORD in a distant land,
   and let Jerusalem come into your
      mind:
51 We are put to shame, for we have
      heard insults;
   dishonor has covered our face,
   for aliens have come

e *Sheshach* is a cryptogram for *Babel*, Babylon

into the holy places of the LORD's house.

52 Therefore the time is surely coming,
    says the LORD,
when I will punish her idols,
and through all her land
    the wounded shall groan.
53 Though Babylon should mount up to
    heaven,
    and though she should fortify her
      strong height,
from me destroyers would come upon
    her,
    says the LORD.

54 Listen!—a cry from Babylon!
    A great crashing from the land of the
      Chal·dē´ans!
55 For the LORD is laying Babylon waste,
    and stilling her loud clamor.
Their waves roar like mighty waters,
    the sound of their clamor resounds;
56 for a destroyer has come against her,
    against Babylon;
her warriors are taken,
    their bows are broken;
for the LORD is a God of recompense,
    he will repay in full.
57 I will make her officials and her sages
    drunk,
    also her governors, her deputies,
    and her warriors;
they shall sleep a perpetual sleep and
    never wake,
    says the King, whose name is the
      LORD of hosts.

58 Thus says the LORD of hosts:
The broad wall of Babylon
    shall be leveled to the ground,
and her high gates
    shall be burned with fire.
The peoples exhaust themselves for
    nothing,
    and the nations weary themselves
      only for fire.[j]

Jeremiah's Command to Seraiah

59 The word that the prophet Jer·e·mī´-ah commanded Se·rāi´ah son of Ne·rī´ah son of Mah´sēi·ah, when he went with King Zed·e·kī´ah of Judah to Babylon, in the fourth year of his reign. Se·rāi´ah was the quartermaster. 60Jer·e·mī´ah wrote in a[g] scroll all the disasters that would come on Babylon, all these words that are written concerning Babylon. 61And Jer·e·mī´ah said to Se·rāi´ah: "When you come to Babylon, see that you read all these words, 62and say, 'O LORD, you yourself threatened to destroy this place so that neither human beings nor animals shall live in it, and it shall be desolate forever.' 63When you finish reading this scroll, tie a stone to it, and throw it into the middle of the Euphrates, 64and say, 'Thus shall Babylon sink, to rise no more, because of the disasters that I am bringing on her.' "[h]

Thus far are the words of Jer·e·mī´ah.

The Destruction of Jerusalem Reviewed

52 Zed·e·kī´ah was twenty-one years old when he began to reign; he reigned eleven years in Jerusalem. His mother's name was Ha·mū´tal daughter of Jer·e·mī´ah of Lib´nah. 2He did what was evil in the sight of the LORD, just as Je·hoi´a·kim had done. 3Indeed, Jerusalem and Judah so angered the LORD that he expelled them from his presence.

Zed·e·kī´ah rebelled against the king of Babylon. 4And in the ninth year of his reign, in the tenth month, on the tenth day of the month, King Ne·bū·chad·rez´zar of Babylon came with all his army against Jerusalem, and they laid siege to it; they built siegeworks against it all around. 5So the city was besieged until the eleventh year of King Zed·e·kī´ah. 6On the ninth day of the fourth month the famine became so severe in the city that there was no food for the people of the land. 7Then a breach was made in the city wall;[i] and all

---

[j] Gk Syr Compare Hab 2.13: Heb *and the nations for fire, and they are weary*   [g] Or *one*   [h] Gk: Heb *on her. And they shall weary themselves*   [i] Heb lacks *wall*

Zedekiah was the last king of the southern kingdom of Judah. He ruled from about 597 to 586 BC. Nebuchadnezzar, king of Babylon, placed him on the throne after King Jehoiachin had been sent into exile. Zedekiah rebelled against Nebuchadnezzar, which led to the attack and destruction of Jerusalem. Zedekiah was taken prisoner and was forced to watch as his two sons were killed. Zedekiah's eyes were put out, and he was led in chains to Babylon.

the soldiers fled and went out from the city by night by the way of the gate between the two walls, by the king's garden, though the Chal·dē´ans were all around the city. They went in the direction of the Ar´a·bah. ⁸But the army of the Chal·dē´ans pursued the king, and overtook Zed·e·kī´ah in the plains of Jericho; and all his army was scattered, deserting him. ⁹Then they captured the king, and brought him up to the king of Babylon at Rib´lah in the land of Hā´math, and he passed sentence on him. ¹⁰The king of Babylon killed the sons of Zed·e·kī´ah before his eyes, and also killed all the officers of Judah at Rib´lah. ¹¹He put out the eyes of Zed·e·kī´ah, and bound him in fetters, and the king of Babylon took him to Babylon, and put him in prison until the day of his death.

12 In the fifth month, on the tenth day of the month—which was the nineteenth year of King Ne·bū·chad·rez´zar, king of Babylon—Ne·bū·za·rad´an the captain of the bodyguard who served the king of Babylon, entered Jerusalem. ¹³He burned the house of the LORD, the king's house, and all the houses of Jerusalem; every great house he burned down. ¹⁴All the army of the Chal·dē´ans, who were with the captain of the guard, broke down all the walls

around Jerusalem. ¹⁵Ne·bū·za·rad´an the captain of the guard carried into exile some of the poorest of the people and the rest of the people who were left in the city and the deserters who had defected to the king of Babylon, together with the rest of the artisans. ¹⁶But Ne·bū·za·rad´an the captain of the guard left some of the poorest people of the land to be vinedressers and tillers of the soil.

17 The pillars of bronze that were in the house of the LORD, and the stands and the bronze sea that were in the house of the LORD, the Chal·dē´ans broke in pieces, and carried all the bronze to Babylon. ¹⁸They took away the pots, the shovels, the snuffers, the basins, the ladles, and all the vessels of bronze used in the temple service. ¹⁹The captain of the guard took away the small bowls also, the firepans, the basins, the pots, the lampstands, the ladles, and the bowls for libation, both those of gold and those of silver. ²⁰As for the two pillars, the one sea, the twelve bronze bulls that were under the sea, and the stands,ʲ which King Solomon had made for the house of the LORD, the bronze of all these vessels was beyond weighing. ²¹As for the pillars, the height of the one pillar was eighteen cubits, its circumference was twelve cubits; it was hollow and its thickness was four fingers. ²²Upon it was a capital of bronze; the height of the capital was five cubits; latticework and pomegranates, all of bronze, encircled the top of the capital. And the second pillar had the same, with pomegranates. ²³There were ninety-six pomegranates on the sides; all the pomegranates encircling the latticework numbered one hundred.

24 The captain of the guard took the chief priest Se·rāi´ah, the second priest Zeph·a·nī´ah, and the three guardians of the threshold; ²⁵and from the city he took an officer who had been in command of the soldiers, and seven men of the king's council who were found in the city; the

ʲ Cn: Heb *that were under the stands*

Hamath was a town on the Orontes River north of Damascus in Syria. For long periods of time, Hamath was the center of an independent kingdom to the north of the Israelite kingdom.

secretary of the commander of the army who mustered the people of the land; and sixty men of the people of the land who were found inside the city. [26]Then Ne·bū·za·rad´an the captain of the guard took them, and brought them to the king of Babylon at Rib´lah. [27]And the king of Babylon struck them down, and put them to death at Rib´lah in the land of Hā´math. So Judah went into exile out of its land.

28 This is the number of the people whom Ne·bū·chad·rez´zar took into exile: in the seventh year, three thousand twenty-three Judeans; [29]in the eighteenth year of Ne·bū·chad·rez´zar he took into exile from Jerusalem eight hundred thirty-two persons; [30]in the twenty-third year of Ne·bū·chad·rez´zar, Ne·bū·za·rad´an the captain of the guard took into exile of the Judeans seven hundred forty-five persons; all the persons were four thousand six hundred.

Jehoiachin Favored in Captivity

31 In the thirty-seventh year of the exile of King Je·hoi´a·chin of Judah, in the twelfth month, on the twenty-fifth day of the month, King Ē´vil-me·rō´dach of Babylon, in the year he began to reign, showed favor to King Je·hoi´a·chin of Judah and brought him out of prison; [32]he spoke kindly to him, and gave him a seat above the seats of the other kings who were with him in Babylon. [33]So Je·hoi´a·chin put aside his prison clothes, and every day of his life he dined regularly at the king's table. [34]For his allowance, a regular daily allowance was given him by the king of Babylon, as long as he lived, up to the day of his death.

Lamentations

When Jerusalem was conquered for the second time by the Babylonians in 586 BC, most of the Jewish leaders were taken to Babylon as prisoners. The book of Lamentations contains songs of sorrow for the Jewish nation. They describe the people's sadness over the destruction of Jerusalem, their beloved city. The book was probably completed by about 300 BC. Because there are laments in the book of Jeremiah, Jeremiah's name has often been linked with the sad songs called Lamentations.

The book of Lamentations is a collection of five poems in acrostic form. Chapters 1 and 2 are composed of three-line stanzas. The first word of each stanza begins with one of the 22 letters of the Hebrew alphabet, in alphabetical order—the first word of the first stanza begins with the letter *Alef* (the first letter of the Hebrew alphabet), the first word of the second stanza begins with the letter *Bet* (the second letter of the Hebrew alphabet), and so on. Chapter 3 uses the same letter to begin the lines in each stanza—the first stanza uses the letter *Alef* to begin each of its three lines, the second stanza uses the letter *Bet* to begin each of its three lines, and so on. Chapter 4 has the same style as chapters 1 and 2 but in two-line stanzas. Chapter 5 is not alphabetized but has twenty-two lines.

While the songs call for the people to repent of their sinful ways, they also express unshakable trust in God and in God's love and forgiveness.

Lamentations 3:22–24

The poems in the book of Lamentations tell about how God's people have rejected God and are being destroyed. Because they are sad poems, they are called laments.

The Deserted City

1 How lonely sits the city
    that once was full of people!
How like a widow she has become,
    she that was great among the
        nations!
She that was a princess among the
        provinces
    has become a vassal.

2 She weeps bitterly in the night,
    with tears on her cheeks;
among all her lovers
    she has no one to comfort her;
all her friends have dealt
        treacherously with her,
    they have become her enemies.

3 Judah has gone into exile with
        suffering
    and hard servitude;
she lives now among the nations,
    and finds no resting place;
her pursuers have all overtaken her
    in the midst of her distress.

4 The roads to Zion mourn,
    for no one comes to the festivals;
all her gates are desolate,
    her priests groan;
her young girls grieve,[a]
    and her lot is bitter.

5 Her foes have become the masters,
    her enemies prosper,
because the LORD has made her suffer
    for the multitude of her
        transgressions;
her children have gone away,
    captives before the foe.

6 From daughter Zion has departed
    all her majesty.
Her princes have become like stags
    that find no pasture;
they fled without strength
    before the pursuer.

7 Jerusalem remembers,
    in the days of her affliction and
        wandering,
all the precious things
    that were hers in days of old.
When her people fell into the hand
        of the foe,
    and there was no one to help her,
the foe looked on mocking
    over her downfall.

8 Jerusalem sinned grievously,
    so she has become a mockery;
all who honored her despise her,
    for they have seen her nakedness;
she herself groans,
    and turns her face away.

9 Her uncleanness was in her skirts;
    she took no thought of her future;
her downfall was appalling,
    with none to comfort her.
"O LORD, look at my affliction,
    for the enemy has triumphed!"

10 Enemies have stretched out their hands
    over all her precious things;
she has even seen the nations
    invade her sanctuary,
those whom you forbade
    to enter your congregation.

11 All her people groan
    as they search for bread;
they trade their treasures for food
    to revive their strength.
Look, O LORD, and see
    how worthless I have become.

12 Is it nothing to you,[a] all you who
        pass by?
    Look and see

[a] Meaning of Heb uncertain

if there is any sorrow like my sorrow,
  which was brought upon me,
which the LORD inflicted
  on the day of his fierce anger.

13 From on high he sent fire;
    it went deep into my bones;
  he spread a net for my feet;
    he turned me back;
  he has left me stunned,
    faint all day long.

14 My transgressions were bound[b] into
    a yoke;
    by his hand they were fastened
      together;
  they weigh on my neck,
    sapping my strength;
  the Lord handed me over
    to those whom I cannot
      withstand.

15 The LORD has rejected
    all my warriors in the midst of
      me;
  he proclaimed a time against me
    to crush my young men;
  the Lord has trodden as in a wine
    press
    the virgin daughter Judah.

16 For these things I weep;
    my eyes flow with tears;
  for a comforter is far from me,
    one to revive my courage;
  my children are desolate,
    for the enemy has prevailed.

17 Zion stretches out her hands,
    but there is no one to comfort
      her;
  the LORD has commanded against
    Jacob
    that his neighbors should become
      his foes;
  Jerusalem has become
    a filthy thing among them.

18 The LORD is in the right,

for I have rebelled against his
    word;
but hear, all you peoples,
  and behold my suffering;
my young women and young men
  have gone into captivity.

19 I called to my lovers
    but they deceived me;
  my priests and elders
    perished in the city
  while seeking food
    to revive their strength.

20 See, O LORD, how distressed I am;
    my stomach churns,
  my heart is wrung within me,
    because I have been very
      rebellious.
  In the street the sword bereaves;
    in the house it is like death.

21 They heard how I was groaning,
    with no one to comfort me.
  All my enemies heard of my trouble;
    they are glad that you have done it.
  Bring on the day you have
    announced,
    and let them be as I am.

22 Let all their evil doing come before
    you;
    and deal with them
  as you have dealt with me
    because of all my transgressions;
  for my groans are many
    and my heart is faint.

God's Warnings Fulfilled

2 How the Lord in his anger
    has humiliated[b] daughter Zion!
He has thrown down from heaven to
    earth
    the splendor of Israel;
he has not remembered his
    footstool
    in the day of his anger.

[b] Meaning of Heb uncertain

2 The Lord has destroyed without
        mercy
    all the dwellings of Jacob;
in his wrath he has broken down
    the strongholds of daughter Judah;
he has brought down to the ground in
        dishonor
    the kingdom and its rulers.

3 He has cut down in fierce anger
    all the might of Israel;
he has withdrawn his right hand from
        them
    in the face of the enemy;
he has burned like a flaming fire in
        Jacob,
    consuming all around.

4 He has bent his bow like an enemy,
    with his right hand set like a foe;
he has killed all in whom we took
        pride
    in the tent of daughter Zion;
he has poured out his fury like fire.

5 The Lord has become like an enemy;
    he has destroyed Israel;
He has destroyed all its palaces,
    laid in ruins its strongholds,
and multiplied in daughter Judah
    mourning and lamentation.

6 He has broken down his booth like a
        garden,
    he has destroyed his tabernacle;
the LORD has abolished in Zion
    festival and sabbath,
and in his fierce indignation has
        spurned
    king and priest.

7 The Lord has scorned his altar,
    disowned his sanctuary;
he has delivered into the hand of the
        enemy
    the walls of her palaces;
a clamor was raised in the house of
        the LORD
    as on a day of festival.

8 The LORD determined to lay in ruins
    the wall of daughter Zion;
he stretched the line;
    he did not withhold his hand from
        destroying;
he caused rampart and wall to lament;
    they languish together.

9 Her gates have sunk into the ground;
    he has ruined and broken her
        bars;
her king and princes are among the
        nations;
    guidance is no more,
and her prophets obtain
    no vision from the LORD.

10 The elders of daughter Zion
    sit on the ground in silence;
they have thrown dust on their
        heads
    and put on sackcloth;
the young girls of Jerusalem
    have bowed their heads to the
        ground.

11 My eyes are spent with weeping;
    my stomach churns;
my bile is poured out on the ground
    because of the destruction of my
        people,
because infants and babes faint
    in the streets of the city.

12 They cry to their mothers,
    "Where is bread and wine?"
as they faint like the wounded
    in the streets of the city,
as their life is poured out
    on their mothers' bosom.

13 What can I say for you, to what
        compare you,
    O daughter Jerusalem?
To what can I liken you, that I may
        comfort you,
    O virgin daughter Zion?
For vast as the sea is your ruin;
    who can heal you?

14 Your prophets have seen for you
    false and deceptive visions;
they have not exposed your iniquity
    to restore your fortunes,
but have seen oracles for you
    that are false and misleading.

15 All who pass along the way
    clap their hands at you;
they hiss and wag their heads
    at daughter Jerusalem;
"Is this the city that was called
    the perfection of beauty,
    the joy of all the earth?"

16 All your enemies
    open their mouths against you;
they hiss, they gnash their teeth,
    they cry: "We have devoured her!
Ah, this is the day we longed for;
    at last we have seen it!"

17 The LORD has done what he
        purposed,
    he has carried out his threat;
as he ordained long ago,
    he has demolished without pity;
he has made the enemy rejoice over
        you,
    and exalted the might of your foes.

18 Cry aloudᶜ to the Lord!
    O wall of daughter Zion!
Let tears stream down like a torrent
    day and night!
Give yourself no rest,
    your eyes no respite!

19 Arise, cry out in the night,
    at the beginning of the watches!
Pour out your heart like water
    before the presence of the Lord!
Lift your hands to him
    for the lives of your children,
who faint for hunger
    at the head of every street.

20 Look, O LORD, and consider!
    To whom have you done this?

Should women eat their offspring,
    the children they have borne?
Should priest and prophet be killed
    in the sanctuary of the Lord?

21 The young and the old are lying
    on the ground in the streets;
my young women and my young
        men
    have fallen by the sword;
in the day of your anger you have
        killed them,
    slaughtering without mercy.

22 You invited my enemies from all
        around
    as if for a day of festival;
and on the day of the anger of the
    LORD
    no one escaped or survived;
those whom I bore and reared
    my enemy has destroyed.

God's Steadfast Love Endures

3 I am one who has seen affliction
        under the rod of God'sᵈ wrath;
2 he has driven and brought me
    into darkness without any light;
3 against me alone he turns his hand,
    again and again, all day long.

4 He has made my flesh and my skin
        waste away,
    and broken my bones;
5 he has besieged and enveloped me
    with bitterness and tribulation;
6 he has made me sit in darkness
    like the dead of long ago.

Although the people were very sad and were suffering greatly, the poet told them to cry out to God. In difficult times, we too can cry out to God for forgiveness and help. God will always listen and will always forgive. God loves us and cares for us.

ᶜ Cn: Heb *Their heart cried*   ᵈ Heb *his*

⁷ He has walled me about so that I
cannot escape;
he has put heavy chains on me;
⁸ though I call and cry for help,
he shuts out my prayer;
⁹ he has blocked my ways with hewn
stones,
he has made my paths crooked.

¹⁰ He is a bear lying in wait for me,
a lion in hiding;
¹¹ he led me off my way and tore me to
pieces;
he has made me desolate;
¹² he bent his bow and set me
as a mark for his arrow.

¹³ He shot into my vitals
the arrows of his quiver;
¹⁴ I have become the laughingstock of all
my people,
the object of their taunt-songs all
day long.
¹⁵ He has filled me with bitterness,
he has sated me with wormwood.

¹⁶ He has made my teeth grind on gravel,
and made me cower in ashes;
¹⁷ my soul is bereft of peace;
I have forgotten what happiness is;
¹⁸ so I say, "Gone is my glory,
and all that I had hoped for from
the LORD."

¹⁹ The thought of my affliction and my
homelessness
is wormwood and gall!
²⁰ My soul continually thinks of it
and is bowed down within me.
²¹ But this I call to mind,
and therefore I have hope:

²² The steadfast love of the LORD never
ceases,ᵉ
his mercies never come to an end;
²³ they are new every morning;
great is your faithfulness.
²⁴ "The LORD is my portion," says my
soul,
"therefore I will hope in him."

> "The steadfast love of the LORD never ceases, his mercies never come to an end; they are new every morning; great is your faithfulness. 'The LORD is my portion,' says my soul, 'therefore I will hope in him.' The LORD is good to those who wait for him, to the soul that seeks him."
> Lamentations 3:22–25

²⁵ The LORD is good to those who wait
for him,
to the soul that seeks him.
²⁶ It is good that one should wait
quietly
for the salvation of the LORD.
²⁷ It is good for one to bear
the yoke in youth,
²⁸ to sit alone in silence
when the Lord has imposed it,
²⁹ to put one's mouth to the dust
(there may yet be hope),
³⁰ to give one's cheek to the smiter,
and be filled with insults.

³¹ For the Lord will not
reject forever.
³² Although he causes grief, he will
have compassion
according to the abundance of his
steadfast love;
³³ for he does not willingly afflict
or grieve anyone.

³⁴ When all the prisoners of the land
are crushed under foot,
³⁵ when human rights are perverted
in the presence of the Most High,

Gall is the juice of a bitter herb. The word is also used as a symbol to describe a feeling of bitterness.

ᵉ Syr Tg: Heb LORD, *we are not cut off*

36 when one's case is subverted
—does the Lord not see it?

37 Who can command and have it done,
if the Lord has not ordained it?
38 Is it not from the mouth of the Most
High
that good and bad come?
39 Why should any who draw breath
complain
about the punishment of their sins?

40 Let us test and examine our ways,
and return to the LORD.
41 Let us lift up our hearts as well as our
hands
to God in heaven.
42 We have transgressed and rebelled,
and you have not forgiven.

43 You have wrapped yourself with anger
and pursued us,
killing without pity;
44 you have wrapped yourself with a cloud
so that no prayer can pass through.
45 You have made us filth and rubbish
among the peoples.

46 All our enemies
have opened their mouths against
us;
47 panic and pitfall have come upon us,
devastation and destruction.
48 My eyes flow with rivers of tears
because of the destruction of my
people.

49 My eyes will flow without ceasing,
without respite,
50 until the LORD from heaven
looks down and sees.
51 My eyes cause me grief
at the fate of all the young women
in my city.

52 Those who were my enemies without
cause
have hunted me like a bird;
53 they flung me alive into a pit

and hurled stones on me;
54 water closed over my head;
I said, "I am lost."

55 I called on your name, O LORD,
from the depths of the pit;
56 you heard my plea, "Do not close your
ear
to my cry for help, but give me
relief!"
57 You came near when I called on you;
you said, "Do not fear!"

58 You have taken up my cause, O Lord,
you have redeemed my life.
59 You have seen the wrong done to me,
O LORD;
judge my cause.
60 You have seen all their malice,
all their plots against me.

61 You have heard their taunts, O LORD,
all their plots against me.
62 The whispers and murmurs of my
assailants
are against me all day long.
63 Whether they sit or rise—see,
I am the object of their taunt-songs.

64 Pay them back for their deeds, O
LORD,
according to the work of their
hands!
65 Give them anguish of heart;
your curse be on them!
66 Pursue them in anger and destroy
them
from under the LORD's heavens.

The Punishment of Zion

4 How the gold has grown dim,
how the pure gold is changed!
The sacred stones lie scattered
at the head of every street.

2 The precious children of Zion,
worth their weight in fine gold—
how they are reckoned as earthen pots,
the work of a potter's hands!

³ Even the jackals offer the breast
   and nurse their young,
but my people has become cruel,
   like the ostriches in the wilderness.

⁴ The tongue of the infant sticks
   to the roof of its mouth for thirst;
the children beg for food,
   but no one gives them anything.

⁵ Those who feasted on delicacies
   perish in the streets;
those who were brought up in purple
   cling to ash heaps.

⁶ For the chastisement*ᶠ* of my people has
   been greater
   than the punishmentᵍ of Sod´om,
which was overthrown in a moment,
   though no hand was laid on it.ʰ

⁷ Her princes were purer than snow,
   whiter than milk;
their bodies were more ruddy than
   coral,
   their hairʰ like sapphire.ⁱ

⁸ Now their visage is blacker than soot;
   they are not recognized in the
   streets.
Their skin has shriveled on their
   bones;
   it has become as dry as wood.

⁹ Happier were those pierced by the
   sword
   than those pierced by hunger,
whose life drains away, deprived
   of the produce of the field.

¹⁰ The hands of compassionate women
   have boiled their own children;
they became their food
   in the destruction of my people.

¹¹ The LORD gave full vent to his wrath;
   he poured out his hot anger,
and kindled a fire in Zion
   that consumed its foundations.

¹² The kings of the earth did not believe,
   nor did any of the inhabitants of the
   world,
that foe or enemy could enter
   the gates of Jerusalem.

¹³ It was for the sins of her prophets
   and the iniquities of her priests,
who shed the blood of the righteous
   in the midst of her.

¹⁴ Blindly they wandered through the
   streets,
   so defiled with blood
that no one was able
   to touch their garments.

¹⁵ "Away! Unclean!" people shouted at
   them;
   "Away! Away! Do not touch!"
So they became fugitives and
   wanderers;
   it was said among the nations,
   "They shall stay here no longer."

¹⁶ The LORD himself has scattered them,
   he will regard them no more;
no honor was shown to the priests,
   no favor to the elders.

¹⁷ Our eyes failed, ever watching
   vainly for help;
we were watching eagerly
   for a nation that could not save.

¹⁸ They dogged our steps
   so that we could not walk in our
   streets;
our end drew near; our days were
   numbered;
   for our end had come.

¹⁹ Our pursuers were swifter
   than the eagles in the heavens;
they chased us on the mountains,
   they lay in wait for us in the
   wilderness.

*ᶠ Or iniquity   ᵍ Or sin   ʰ Meaning of Heb
uncertain   ⁱ Or lapis lazuli*

> "Restore us to yourself, O
> LORD, that we may be
> restored; renew our days as
> of old."
>
> Lamentations 5:21

20 The LORD's anointed, the breath of
  our life,
    was taken in their pits—
  the one of whom we said, "Under
    his shadow
  we shall live among the nations."

21 Rejoice and be glad, O daughter
  E´dom,
    you that live in the land of Uz;
  but to you also the cup shall pass;
    you shall become drunk and strip
    yourself bare.

22 The punishment of your iniquity, O
  daughter Zion, is
  accomplished,
    he will keep you in exile no
    longer;
  but your iniquity, O daughter
  E´dom, he will punish,
    he will uncover your sins.

A Plea for Mercy

5 Remember, O LORD, what has
  befallen us;
    look, and see our disgrace!
2 Our inheritance has been turned
  over to strangers,
    our homes to aliens.
3 We have become orphans, fatherless;
    our mothers are like widows.
4 We must pay for the water we drink;
    the wood we get must be bought.
5 With a yoke[j] on our necks we are
  hard driven;
    we are weary, we are given no
    rest.
6 We have made a pact with[k] Egypt
  and Assyria,
    to get enough bread.

7 Our ancestors sinned; they are no
  more,
    and we bear their iniquities.
8 Slaves rule over us;
    there is no one to deliver us from
    their hand.
9 We get our bread at the peril of our
  lives,
    because of the sword in the
    wilderness.
10 Our skin is black as an oven
    from the scorching heat of famine.
11 Women are raped in Zion,
    virgins in the towns of Judah.
12 Princes are hung up by their hands;
    no respect is shown to the elders.
13 Young men are compelled to grind,
    and boys stagger under loads of
    wood.
14 The old men have left the city gate,
    the young men their music.
15 The joy of our hearts has ceased;
    our dancing has been turned to
    mourning.
16 The crown has fallen from our head;
    woe to us, for we have sinned!
17 Because of this our hearts are sick,
    because of these things our eyes
    have grown dim:
18 because of Mount Zion, which lies
    desolate;
    jackals prowl over it.

19 But you, O LORD, reign forever;
    your throne endures to all
    generations.
20 Why have you forgotten us
    completely?
    Why have you forsaken us these
    many days?
21 Restore us to yourself, O LORD, that
    we may be restored;
    renew our days as of old—
22 unless you have utterly rejected us,
    and are angry with us beyond
    measure.

j Symmachus: Heb lacks *With a yoke*   k Heb *have
given the hand to*

Ezekiel

Ezekiel was the son of a priest and had grown up close to the Temple in Jerusalem. He was carried off to exile in Babylon in 597 BC. Ezekiel had a vision of God and received the call to be a prophet to Israel. Ezekiel seems to have been a spiritual leader for the Jews at least part of the time while they were living in exile. He preached to them and prepared them for the time when God would restore them to their homeland. Much of the book of Ezekiel was completed by 550 BC.

The book of Ezekiel contains some of Ezekiel's speeches (or sermons). Some of the language and the symbols are hard for us to understand today. One of his most important messages to the Jews was that being separated from their land and from the Temple in Jerusalem did not separate them from God. There is no distance that can separate people from the love of God.

In the first part of the book, Ezekiel told about the punishment for God's people. He gave no hope that the city of Jerusalem would survive. He said that God's glory had left the Temple and had left Jerusalem. Ezekiel spoke out against the sins of the people and the sins of their leaders. He taught that each person is responsible to God for living a godly, righteous life. He talked about the judgement of God.

At the same time, Ezekiel did not abandon his faith in God. In chapters 33–48, Ezekiel spoke of restoration. Ezekiel believed that the Jews would not be in exile forever. He believed that God would gather the people and allow them to return to their homeland. He believed that God's people and God's glory would return to a new Temple in Jerusalem.

Ezekiel 1:15–16

Ezekiel had a vision of four living creatures that each had four faces (human, lion, ox, and eagle) and four wings. In chapter 10, he calls the creatures "cherubim." Cherubim were heavenly beings often associated with the worship of God. They used two of their wings to fly and two to cover their bodies. Beside each creature was a glowing wheel that moved as the creature moved—the spirit of each creature was in the wheels, and that spirit was the life-giving presence of God.

The Vision of the Chariot

1 In the thirtieth year, in the fourth month, on the fifth day of the month, as I was among the exiles by the river Chē´bar, the heavens were opened, and I saw visions of God. [2]On the fifth day of the month (it was the fifth year of the exile of King Je·hoi´a·chin), [3]the word of the LORD came to the priest E·zēk´i·el son of Bū´zī, in the land of the Chal·dē´ans by the river Chē´bar; and the hand of the LORD was on him there.

4 As I looked, a stormy wind came out of the north: a great cloud with brightness around it and fire flashing forth continually, and in the middle of the fire, something like gleaming amber. [5]In the middle of it was something like four living creatures. This was their appearance: they were of human form. [6]Each had four faces, and each of them had four wings. [7]Their legs were straight, and the soles of their feet were like the sole of a calf's foot; and they sparkled like burnished bronze. [8]Under their wings on their four sides they had human hands. And the four had their faces and their wings thus: [9]their wings touched one another; each of them moved straight ahead, without turning as

they moved. [10]As for the appearance of their faces: the four had the face of a human being, the face of a lion on the right side, the face of an ox on the left side, and the face of an eagle; [11]such were their faces. Their wings were spread out above; each creature had two wings, each of which touched the wing of another, while two covered their bodies. [12]Each moved straight ahead; wherever the spirit would go, they went, without turning as they went. [13]In the middle of[a] the living creatures there was something that looked like burning coals of fire, like torches moving to and fro among the living creatures; the fire was bright, and lightning issued from the fire. [14]The living creatures darted to and fro, like a flash of lightning.

15 As I looked at the living creatures, I saw a wheel on the earth beside the living creatures, one for each of the four of them.[b] [16]As for the appearance of the wheels and their construction: their appearance was like the gleaming of beryl; and the four had the same form, their construction being something like a wheel within a wheel. [17]When they moved, they moved in any of the four directions without veering as they moved. [18]Their rims were tall and awesome, for the rims of all four were full of eyes all around. [19]When the living creatures moved, the wheels moved beside them; and when the living creatures rose from the earth, the wheels rose. [20]Wherever the spirit would go, they went, and the wheels rose along with them; for the spirit of the living creatures was in the wheels. [21]When they moved, the others moved; when they stopped, the others stopped; and when they rose from the earth, the wheels rose along with them; for the spirit of the living creatures was in the wheels.

22 Over the heads of the living creatures there was something like a dome, shining like crystal,[c] spread out above their heads. [23]Under the dome their wings

---

[a] Gk OL: Heb *And the appearance of*　[b] Heb *of their faces*　[c] Gk: Heb *like the awesome crystal*

were stretched out straight, one toward another; and each of the creatures had two wings covering its body. [24]When they moved, I heard the sound of their wings like the sound of mighty waters, like the thunder of the Almighty,[d] a sound of tumult like the sound of an army; when they stopped, they let down their wings. [25]And there came a voice from above the dome over their heads; when they stopped, they let down their wings.

26 And above the dome over their heads there was something like a throne, in appearance like sapphire;[e] and seated above the likeness of a throne was something that seemed like a human form. [27]Upward from what appeared like the loins I saw something like gleaming amber, something that looked like fire enclosed all around; and downward from what looked like the loins I saw something that looked like fire, and there was a splendor all around. [28]Like the bow in a cloud on a rainy day, such was the appearance of the splendor all around. This was the appearance of the likeness of the glory of the LORD.

When I saw it, I fell on my face, and I heard the voice of someone speaking.

The Vision of the Scroll

2 He said to me: O mortal,[f] stand up on your feet, and I will speak with you. [2]And when he spoke to me, a spirit entered into me and set me on my feet; and I heard him speaking to me. [3]He said to me, Mortal, I am sending you to the people of Israel, to a nation[g] of rebels who have rebelled against me; they and their ancestors have transgressed against me to this very day. [4]The descendants are impudent and stubborn. I am sending you to them, and you shall say to them, "Thus says the Lord GOD." [5]Whether they hear or refuse to hear (for they are a rebellious house), they shall know that there has been a prophet among them. [6]And you, O mortal, do not be afraid of them, and do not be afraid of their words, though briers and thorns surround you and you live

among scorpions; do not be afraid of their words, and do not be dismayed at their looks, for they are a rebellious house. [7]You shall speak my words to them, whether they hear or refuse to hear; for they are a rebellious house.

8 But you, mortal, hear what I say to you; do not be rebellious like that rebellious house; open your mouth and eat what I give you. [9]I looked, and a hand was stretched out to me, and a written scroll was in it. [10]He spread it before me; it had writing on the front and on the back, and written on it were words of lamentation and mourning and woe.

Scrolls usually had writing on only one side, but the scroll Ezekiel saw had so many troubles written on it that both sides had to be used. God commanded Ezekiel to eat the scroll, and it tasted sweet. Isn't it strange that the scroll with so many troubles would taste sweet? Perhaps it meant that if the people heard Ezekiel and would listen to the words of the Lord, they would be fed.

3 He said to me, O mortal, eat what is offered to you; eat this scroll, and go, speak to the house of Israel. [2]So I opened my mouth, and he gave me the scroll to eat. [3]He said to me, Mortal, eat this scroll that I give you and fill your stomach with it. Then I ate it; and in my mouth it was as sweet as honey.

4 He said to me: Mortal, go to the house of Israel and speak my very words to them. [5]For you are not sent to a people of obscure speech and difficult language, but to the house of Israel— [6]not to many peoples of obscure speech and difficult

[d] Traditional rendering of Heb *Shaddai*   [e] Or *lapis lazuli*   [f] Or *son of man*; Heb *ben adam* (and so throughout the book when Ezekiel is addressed)   [g] Syr: Heb *to nations*

language, whose words you cannot understand. Surely, if I sent you to them, they would listen to you. [7]But the house of Israel will not listen to you, for they are not willing to listen to me; because all the house of Israel have a hard forehead and a stubborn heart. [8]See, I have made your face hard against their faces, and your forehead hard against their foreheads. [9]Like the hardest stone, harder than flint, I have made your forehead; do not fear them or be dismayed at their looks, for they are a rebellious house. [10]He said to me: Mortal, all my words that I shall speak to you receive in your heart and hear with your ears; [11]then go to the exiles, to your people, and speak to them. Say to them, "Thus says the Lord GOD"; whether they hear or refuse to hear.

Ezekiel at the River Chebar

12 Then the spirit lifted me up, and as the glory of the LORD rose[h] from its place, I heard behind me the sound of loud rumbling; [13]it was the sound of the wings of the living creatures brushing against one another, and the sound of the wheels beside them, that sounded like a loud rumbling. [14]The spirit lifted me up and bore me away; I went in bitterness in the heat of my spirit, the hand of the LORD being strong upon me. [15]I came to the exiles at Tel-a·bib´, who lived by the river Chē´bar.[i] And I sat there among them, stunned, for seven days.

16 At the end of seven days, the word of the LORD came to me: [17]Mortal, I have made you a sentinel for the house of Israel; whenever you hear a word from my mouth, you shall give them warning from me. [18]If I say to the wicked, "You shall surely die," and you give them no warning, or speak to warn the wicked from their wicked way, in order to save their life, those wicked persons shall die for their iniquity; but their blood I will require at your hand. [19]But if you warn the wicked, and they do not turn from their wickedness, or from their wicked way, they shall die for their iniquity; but

you will have saved your life. [20]Again, if the righteous turn from their righteousness and commit iniquity, and I lay a stumbling block before them, they shall die; because you have not warned them, they shall die for their sin, and their righteous deeds that they have done shall not be remembered; but their blood I will require at your hand. [21]If, however, you warn the righteous not to sin, and they do not sin, they shall surely live, because they took warning; and you will have saved your life.

Ezekiel Isolated and Silenced

22 Then the hand of the LORD was upon me there; and he said to me, Rise up, go out into the valley, and there I will speak with you. [23]So I rose up and went out into the valley; and the glory of the LORD stood there, like the glory that I had seen by the river Chē´bar; and I fell on my face. [24]The spirit entered into me, and set me on my feet; and he spoke with me and said to me: Go, shut yourself inside your house. [25]As for you, mortal, cords shall be placed on you, and you shall be bound with them, so that you cannot go out among the people; [26]and I will make your tongue cling to the roof of your mouth, so that you shall be speechless and unable to reprove them; for they are a rebellious house. [27]But when I speak with you, I will open your mouth, and you shall say to them, "Thus says the Lord GOD"; let those who will hear, hear; and let those who refuse to hear, refuse; for they are a rebellious house.

The Siege of Jerusalem Portrayed

4 And you, O mortal, take a brick and set it before you. On it portray a city, Jerusalem; [2]and put siegeworks against it, and build a siege-wall against it, and cast up a ramp against it; set camps also against it, and plant battering rams against it all around. [3]Then take an iron plate and place

---

h Cn: Heb *and blessed be the glory of the LORD*   *i* Two Mss Syr: Heb *Chebar, and to where they lived.* Another reading is *Chebar, and I sat where they sat* it as an iron wall between you and the city; set your face toward it, and let it be in a state of siege, and press the siege against it. This is a sign for the house of Israel.

4 Then lie on your left side, and place the punishment of the house of Israel upon it; you shall bear their punishment for the number of the days that you lie there. [5]For I assign to you a number of days, three hundred ninety days, equal to the number of the years of their punishment; and so you shall bear the punishment of the house of Israel. [6]When you have completed these, you shall lie down a second time, but on your right side, and bear the punishment of the house of Judah; forty days I assign you, one day for each year. [7]You shall set your face toward the siege of Jerusalem, and with your arm bared you shall prophesy against it. [8]See, I am putting cords on you so that you cannot turn from one side to the other until you have completed the days of your siege.

A hin is a liquid measure about equal to a gallon. A gallon is equal to four quarts. If Ezekiel was drinking one-sixth of a hin of water, that means he was drinking about two-thirds of a quart of water a day, which is not very much. God wanted to prepare the people for the time when there would not be a lot of food or water.

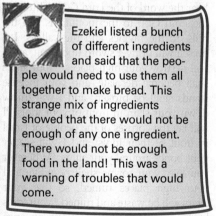

Ezekiel listed a bunch of different ingredients and said that the people would need to use them all together to make bread. This strange mix of ingredients showed that there would not be enough of any one ingredient. There would not be enough food in the land! This was a warning of troubles that would come.

9 And you, take wheat and barley, beans and lentils, millet and spelt; put them into one vessel, and make bread for yourself. During the number of days that you lie on your side, three hundred ninety days, you shall eat it. [10]The food that you eat shall be twenty shekels a day by weight; at fixed times you shall eat it. [11]And you shall drink water by measure, one-sixth of a hin; at fixed times you shall drink. [12]You shall eat it as a barley-cake, baking it in their sight on human dung. [13]The LORD said, "Thus shall the people of Israel eat their bread, unclean, among the nations to which I will drive them." [14]Then I said, "Ah Lord GOD! I have never defiled myself; from my youth up until now I have never eaten what died of itself or was torn by animals, nor has carrion flesh come into my mouth." [15]Then he said to me, "See, I will let you have cow's dung instead of human dung, on which you may prepare your bread."

16 Then he said to me, Mortal, I am going to break the staff of bread in Jerusalem; they shall eat bread by weight and with fearfulness; and they shall drink water by measure and in dismay. [17]Lacking bread and water, they will look at one another in dismay, and waste away under their punishment.

A Sword against Jerusalem

5 And you, O mortal, take a sharp sword; use it as a barber's razor and run it over your head and your beard; then take balances for weighing, and divide the hair. [2]One third of the hair you shall burn in the fire inside the city, when the days of the siege are completed; one third you shall take and strike with the sword all around the city;[j] and one third you shall scatter to the wind, and I will

[j] Heb *it*

unsheathe the sword after them. ³Then you shall take from these a small number, and bind them in the skirts of your robe. ⁴From these, again, you shall take some, throw them into the fire and burn them up; from there a fire will come out against all the house of Israel.

5 Thus says the Lord GOD: This is Jerusalem; I have set her in the center of the nations, with countries all around her. ⁶But she has rebelled against my ordinances and my statutes, becoming more wicked than the nations and the countries all around her, rejecting my ordinances and not following my statutes. ⁷Therefore thus says the Lord GOD: Because you are more turbulent than the nations that are all around you, and have not followed my statutes or kept my ordinances, but have acted according to the ordinances of the nations that are all around you; ⁸therefore thus says the Lord GOD: I, I myself, am coming against you; I will execute judgments among you in the sight of the nations. ⁹And because of all your abominations, I will do to you what I have never yet done, and the like of which I will never do again. ¹⁰Surely, parents shall eat their children in your midst, and children shall eat their parents; I will execute judgments on you, and any of you who survive I will scatter to every wind. ¹¹Therefore, as I live, says the Lord GOD, surely, because you have defiled my sanctuary with all your detestable things and with all your abominations—therefore I will cut you down;[k] my eye will not spare, and I will have no pity. ¹²One third of you shall die of pestilence or be consumed by famine among you; one third shall fall by the sword around you; and one third I will scatter to every wind and will unsheathe the sword after them.

13 My anger shall spend itself, and I will vent my fury on them and satisfy myself; and they shall know that I, the LORD, have spoken in my jealousy, when I spend my fury on them. ¹⁴Moreover I will make you a desolation and an object of

mocking among the nations around you, in the sight of all that pass by. ¹⁵You shall be[l] a mockery and a taunt, a warning and a horror, to the nations around you, when I execute judgments on you in anger and fury, and with furious punishments—I, the LORD, have spoken— ¹⁶when I loose against you[m] my deadly arrows of famine, arrows for destruction, which I will let loose to destroy you, and when I bring more and more famine upon you, and break your staff of bread. ¹⁷I will send famine and wild animals against you, and they will rob you of your children; pestilence and bloodshed shall pass through you; and I will bring the sword upon you. I, the LORD, have spoken.

Judgment on Idolatrous Israel

6 The word of the LORD came to me: ²O mortal, set your face toward the mountains of Israel, and prophesy against them, ³and say, You mountains of Israel, hear the word of the Lord GOD! Thus says the Lord GOD to the mountains and the hills, to the ravines and the valleys: I, I myself will bring a sword upon you, and I will destroy your high places. ⁴Your altars shall become desolate, and your incense stands shall be broken; and I will throw down your slain in front of your idols. ⁵I will lay the corpses of the people of Israel in front of their idols; and I will scatter your bones around your altars. ⁶Wherever you live, your towns shall be waste and your high places ruined, so that your altars will be waste and ruined,[n] your idols broken and destroyed, your incense stands cut down, and your works wiped out. ⁷The slain shall fall in your midst; then you shall know that I am the LORD.

8 But I will spare some. Some of you shall escape the sword among the nations and be scattered through the countries. ⁹Those of you who escape shall remember me among the nations where they are car-

---

[k] Another reading is *I will withdraw*   [l] Gk Syr Vg Tg: Heb *It shall be*   [m] Heb *them*   [n] Syr Vg Tg: Heb *and be made guilty*

ried captive, how I was crushed by their wanton heart that turned away from me, and their wanton eyes that turned after their idols. Then they will be loathsome in their own sight for the evils that they have committed, for all their abominations. [10]And they shall know that I am the LORD; I did not threaten in vain to bring this disaster upon them.

11 Thus says the Lord GOD: Clap your hands and stamp your foot, and say, Alas for all the vile abominations of the house of Israel! For they shall fall by the sword, by famine, and by pestilence. [12]Those far off shall die of pestilence; those nearby shall fall by the sword; and any who are left and are spared shall die of famine. Thus I will spend my fury upon them. [13]And you shall know that I am the LORD, when their slain lie among their idols around their altars, on every high hill, on all the mountain tops, under every green tree, and under every leafy oak, wherever they offered pleasing odor to all their idols. [14]I will stretch out my hand against them, and make the land desolate and waste, throughout all their settlements, from the wilderness to Rib´lah.[o] Then they shall know that I am the LORD.

Impending Disaster

7 The word of the LORD came to me: [2]You, O mortal, thus says the Lord GOD to the land of Israel:
An end! The end has come
    upon the four corners of the land.
[3] Now the end is upon you,
    I will let loose my anger upon you;
I will judge you according to your
        ways,
    I will punish you for all your
        abominations.
[4] My eye will not spare you, I will have
        no pity.
    I will punish you for your ways,
    while your abominations are among
        you.
Then you shall know that I am the LORD.
[5] Thus says the Lord GOD:
Disaster after disaster! See, it comes.
[6]   An end has come, the end has come.
It has awakened against you; see, it
        comes!
[7] Your doom[p] has come to you,
    O inhabitant of the land.
The time has come, the day is near—
    of tumult, not of reveling on the
        mountains.
[8] Soon now I will pour out my wrath
        upon you;
    I will spend my anger against you.
I will judge you according to your ways,
    and punish you for all your
        abominations.
[9] My eye will not spare; I will have no
        pity.
    I will punish you according to your
        ways,
    while your abominations are among
        you.

When the people worshiped in Old Testament times, they would burn sacrifices and offerings. The sight and smell of the smoke reminded the people that their prayers were rising to God. We know that God hears our prayers no matter when or how we pray. We don't have to close our eyes. We don't have to be in church. All we need to do is open our hearts, speak to God, and listen for God's response.

So that we will remember to pray, it is helpful to set aside a certain time every day. As we pray, we can give thanks and praise to God and ask God to care for us. Do you have a certain time to pray? Sit quietly for a few minutes and think about your day. When would be the best time? In the morning when you first get up, or at night before you go to bed? Another time? Try to spend a few minutes with God at the same time every day.

[o] Another reading is *Diblah*   [p] Meaning of Heb uncertain

Then you shall know that it is I the LORD who strike.

[10] See, the day! See, it comes!
Your doom[q] has gone out.
The rod has blossomed, pride has budded.
[11] Violence has grown into a rod of wickedness.
None of them shall remain,
not their abundance, not their wealth;
no pre-eminence among them.[q]
[12] The time has come, the day draws near;
let not the buyer rejoice, nor the seller mourn,
for wrath is upon all their multitude.

[13]For the sellers shall not return to what has been sold as long as they remain alive. For the vision concerns all their multitude; it shall not be revoked. Because of their iniquity, they cannot maintain their lives.[q]

[14] They have blown the horn and made everything ready;
but no one goes to battle,
for my wrath is upon all their multitude.
[15] The sword is outside, pestilence and famine are inside;
those in the field die by the sword;
those in the city—famine and pestilence devour them.
[16] If any survivors escape,
they shall be found on the mountains
like doves of the valleys,
all of them moaning over their iniquity.
[17] All hands shall grow feeble,
all knees turn to water.
[18] They shall put on sackcloth,
horror shall cover them.
Shame shall be on all faces,
baldness on all their heads.
[19] They shall fling their silver into the streets,
their gold shall be treated as unclean.

Their silver and gold cannot save them on the day of the wrath of the LORD. They shall not satisfy their hunger or fill their stomachs with it. For it was the stumbling block of their iniquity. [20]From their[r] beautiful ornament, in which they took pride, they made their abominable images, their detestable things; therefore I will make of it an unclean thing to them.

[21] I will hand it over to strangers as booty,
to the wicked of the earth as plunder;
they shall profane it.
[22] I will avert my face from them,
so that they may profane my treasured[s] place;
the violent shall enter it,
they shall profane it.
[23] Make a chain![q]
For the land is full of bloody crimes;
the city is full of violence.
[24] I will bring the worst of the nations
to take possession of their houses.
I will put an end to the arrogance of the strong,
and their holy places shall be profaned.
[25] When anguish comes, they will seek peace,
but there shall be none.
[26] Disaster comes upon disaster,
rumor follows rumor;
they shall keep seeking a vision from the prophet;
instruction shall perish from the priest,
and counsel from the elders.
[27] The king shall mourn,
the prince shall be wrapped in despair,
and the hands of the people of the land shall tremble.
According to their way I will deal with them;
according to their own judgments I will judge them.
And they shall know that I am the LORD.

[q] Meaning of Heb uncertain   [r] Syr Symmachus: Heb *its*   [s] Or *secret*

Abominations in the Temple

8 In the sixth year, in the sixth month, on the fifth day of the month, as I sat in my house, with the elders of Judah sitting before me, the hand of the Lord GOD fell upon me there. [2]I looked, and there was a figure that looked like a human being;[t] below what appeared to be its loins it was fire, and above the loins it was like the appearance of brightness, like gleaming amber. [3]It stretched out the form of a hand, and took me by a lock of my head; and the spirit lifted me up between earth and heaven, and brought me in visions of God to Jerusalem, to the entrance of the gateway of the inner court that faces north, to the seat of the image of jealousy, which provokes to jealousy. [4]And the glory of the God of Israel was there, like the vision that I had seen in the valley.

5 Then God[u] said to me, "O mortal, lift up your eyes now in the direction of the north." So I lifted up my eyes toward the north, and there, north of the altar gate, in the entrance, was this image of jealousy. [6]He said to me, "Mortal, do you see what they are doing, the great abominations that the house of Israel are committing here, to drive me far from my sanctuary? Yet you will see still greater abominations."

7 And he brought me to the entrance of the court; I looked, and there was a hole in the wall. [8]Then he said to me, "Mortal, dig through the wall"; and when I dug through the wall, there was an entrance. [9]He said to me, "Go in, and see the vile abominations that they are committing here." [10]So I went in and looked; there, portrayed on the wall all around, were all kinds of creeping things, and loathsome animals, and all the idols of the house of Israel. [11]Before them stood seventy of the elders of the house of Israel, with Jā·az·a·nī´ah son of Shā´phan standing among them. Each had his censer in his hand, and the fragrant cloud of incense was ascending. [12]Then he said to me, "Mortal, have you seen what the eld-ers of the house of Israel are doing in the dark, each in his room of images? For they say, 'The LORD does not see us, the LORD has forsaken the land.' " [13]He said also to me, "You will see still greater abominations that they are committing."

14 Then he brought me to the entrance of the north gate of the house of the LORD; women were sitting there weeping for Tam´mūz. [15]Then he said to me, "Have you seen this, O mortal? You will see still greater abominations than these."

16 And he brought me into the inner court of the house of the LORD; there, at the entrance of the temple of the LORD, between the porch and the altar, were about twenty-five men, with their backs to the temple of the LORD, and their faces toward the east, prostrating themselves to the sun toward the east. [17]Then he said to me, "Have you seen this, O mortal? Is it not bad enough that the house of Judah commits the abominations done here? Must they fill the land with violence, and provoke my anger still further? See, they are putting the branch to their nose! [18]Therefore I will act in wrath; my eye will not spare, nor will I have pity; and though they cry in my hearing with a loud voice, I will not listen to them."

The Slaughter of the Idolaters

9 Then he cried in my hearing with a loud voice, saying, "Draw near, you executioners of the city, each with his destroying weapon in his hand." [2]And six men came from the direction of the upper gate, which faces north, each with his weapon for slaughter in his hand; among them was a man clothed in linen, with a writing case at his side. They went in and stood beside the bronze altar.

3 Now the glory of the God of Israel had gone up from the cherub on which it rested to the threshold of the house. The LORD called to the man clothed in linen, who had the writing case at his side; [4]and said to him, "Go through the city, through

---

[t] Gk: Heb *like fire*   [u] Heb *he*

Jerusalem, and put a mark on the foreheads of those who sigh and groan over all the abominations that are committed in it." ⁵To the others he said in my hearing, "Pass through the city after him, and kill; your eye shall not spare, and you shall show no pity. ⁶Cut down old men, young men and young women, little children and women, but touch no one who has the mark. And begin at my sanctuary." So they began with the elders who were in front of the house. ⁷Then he said to them, "Defile the house, and fill the courts with the slain. Go!" So they went out and killed in the city. ⁸While they were killing, and I was left alone, I fell prostrate on my face and cried out, "Ah Lord GOD! will you destroy all who remain of Israel as you pour out your wrath upon Jerusalem?" ⁹He said to me, "The guilt of the house of Israel and Judah is exceedingly great; the land is full of bloodshed and the city full of perversity; for they say, 'The LORD has forsaken the land, and the LORD does not see.' ¹⁰As for me, my eye will not spare, nor will I have pity, but I will bring down their deeds upon their heads."

11 Then the man clothed in linen, with the writing case at his side, brought back word, saying, "I have done as you commanded me."

God's Glory Leaves Jerusalem

10 Then I looked, and above the dome that was over the heads of the cherubim there appeared above them something like a sapphire,ᵛ in form resembling a throne. ²He said to the man clothed in linen, "Go within the wheelwork underneath the cherubim; fill your hands with burning coals from among the cherubim, and scatter them over the city." He went in as I looked on. ³Now the cherubim were standing on the south side of the house when the man went in; and a cloud filled the inner court. ⁴Then the glory of the LORD rose up from the cherub to the threshold of the house; the house was filled with the cloud, and the court was full of the brightness of the glory of

the LORD. ⁵The sound of the wings of the cherubim was heard as far as the outer court, like the voice of God Almightyʷ when he speaks.

6 When he commanded the man clothed in linen, "Take fire from within the wheelwork, from among the cherubim," he went in and stood beside a wheel. ⁷And a cherub stretched out his hand from among the cherubim to the fire that was among the cherubim, took some of it and put it into the hands of the man clothed in linen, who took it and went out. ⁸The cherubim appeared to have the form of a human hand under their wings.

9 I looked, and there were four wheels beside the cherubim, one beside each cherub; and the appearance of the wheels was like gleaming beryl. ¹⁰And as for their appearance, the four looked alike, something like a wheel within a wheel. ¹¹When they moved, they moved in any of the four directions without veering as they moved; but in whatever direction the front wheel faced, the others followed without veering as they moved. ¹²Their entire body, their rims, their spokes, their wings, and the wheels—the wheels of the four of them—were full of eyes all around. ¹³As for the wheels, they were called in my hearing "the wheelwork." ¹⁴Each one had four faces: the first face was that of the cherub, the second face was that of a human being, the third that of a lion, and the fourth that of an eagle.

15 The cherubim rose up. These were the living creatures that I saw by the river Chē´bar. ¹⁶When the cherubim moved, the wheels moved beside them; and when the cherubim lifted up their wings to rise up from the earth, the wheels at their side did not veer. ¹⁷When they stopped, the others stopped, and when they rose up, the others rose up with them; for the spirit of the living creatures was in them.

18 Then the glory of the LORD went out from the threshold of the house and

ᵛ Or *lapis lazuli*   ʷ Traditional rendering of Heb *El Shaddai* stopped above the cherubim. ¹⁹The cherubim lifted up their wings and rose up from the earth in my sight as they went out with the wheels beside them. They stopped at the entrance of the east gate of the house of the LORD; and the glory of the God of Israel was above them.

20 These were the living creatures that I saw underneath the God of Israel by the river Chē′bar; and I knew that they were cherubim. ²¹Each had four faces, each four wings, and underneath their wings something like human hands. ²²As for what their faces were like, they were the same faces whose appearance I had seen by the river Chē′bar. Each one moved straight ahead.

Judgment on Wicked Counselors

11 The spirit lifted me up and brought me to the east gate of the house of the LORD, which faces east. There, at the entrance of the gateway, were twenty-five men; among them I saw Jā·az·a·nī′ah son of Az′zur, and Pel·a·tī′ah son of Be·nā′i·ah, officials of the people. ²He said to me, "Mortal, these are the men who devise iniquity and who give wicked counsel in this city; ³they say, 'The time is not near to build houses; this city is the pot, and we are the meat.' ⁴Therefore prophesy against them; prophesy, O mortal."

5 Then the spirit of the LORD fell upon me, and he said to me, "Say, Thus says the LORD: This is what you think, O house of Israel; I know the things that come into your mind. ⁶You have killed many in this city, and have filled its streets with the slain. ⁷Therefore thus says the Lord GOD: The slain whom you have placed within it are the meat, and this city is the pot; but you shall be taken out of it. ⁸You have feared the sword; and I will bring the sword upon you, says the Lord GOD. ⁹I will take you out of it and give you over to the hands of foreigners, and execute judgments upon you. ¹⁰You shall fall by the sword; I will judge you at the border of Israel. And you shall know that I am the LORD. ¹¹This city shall not be your pot, and you shall not be the meat inside it; I will judge you at the border of Israel. ¹²Then you shall know that I am the LORD, whose statutes you have not followed, and whose ordinances you have not kept, but you have acted according to the ordinances of the nations that are around you."

13 Now, while I was prophesying, Pel·a·tī′ah son of Be·nā′i·ah died. Then I fell down on my face, cried with a loud voice, and said, "Ah Lord GOD! will you make a full end of the remnant of Israel?"

God Will Restore Israel

14 Then the word of the LORD came to me: ¹⁵Mortal, your kinsfolk, your own kin, your fellow exiles,ˣ the whole house of Israel, all of them, are those of whom the inhabitants of Jerusalem have said, "They have gone far from the LORD; to us this land is given for a possession." ¹⁶Therefore say: Thus says the Lord GOD: Though I removed them far away among the nations, and though I scattered them among the countries, yet I have been a sanctuary to them for a little whileʸ in the countries where they have gone. ¹⁷Therefore say: Thus says the Lord GOD: I will gather you from the peoples, and assemble you out of the countries where you have been scattered, and I will give you the land of Israel. ¹⁸When they come there, they will remove from it all its detestable things and all its abominations. ¹⁹I will give them oneᶻ heart, and put a new spirit within them; I will remove the heart of stone from their flesh and give them a heart of flesh, ²⁰so that they may follow my statutes and keep my ordinances and obey them. Then they shall be my people, and I will be their God. ²¹But as for those whose heart goes after their detestable things and their abominations,ᵃ I will bring their deeds upon their own heads, says the Lord GOD.

ˣ Gk Syr: Heb *people of your kindred*   ʸ Or *to some extent*   ᶻ Another reading is *a new*   ᵃ Cn: Heb *And to the heart of their detestable things and their abominations their heart goes*

22 Then the cherubim lifted up their wings, with the wheels beside them; and the glory of the God of Israel was above them. ²³And the glory of the LORD ascended from the middle of the city, and stopped on the mountain east of the city. ²⁴The spirit lifted me up and brought me in a vision by the spirit of God into Chal·dē´a, to the exiles. Then the vision that I had seen left me. ²⁵And I told the exiles all the things that the LORD had shown me.

Judah's Captivity Portrayed

12 The word of the LORD came to me: ²Mortal, you are living in the midst of a rebellious house, who have eyes to see but do not see, who have ears to hear but do not hear; ³for they are a rebellious house. Therefore, mortal, prepare for yourself an exile's baggage, and go into exile by day in their sight; you shall go like an exile from your place to another place in their sight. Perhaps they will understand, though they are a rebellious house. ⁴You shall bring out your baggage by day in their sight, as baggage for exile; and you shall go out yourself at evening in their sight, as those do who go into exile. ⁵Dig through the wall in their sight, and carry the baggage through it. ⁶In their sight you shall lift the baggage on your shoulder, and carry it out in the dark; you shall cover your face, so that you may not see the land; for I have made you a sign for the house of Israel.

7 I did just as I was commanded. I brought out my baggage by day, as baggage for exile, and in the evening I dug through the wall with my own hands; I brought it out in the dark, carrying it on my shoulder in their sight.

8 In the morning the word of the LORD came to me: ⁹Mortal, has not the house of Israel, the rebellious house, said to you, "What are you doing?" ¹⁰Say to them, "Thus says the Lord GOD: This oracle concerns the prince in Jerusalem and all the house of Israel in it." ¹¹Say, "I am a sign for you: as I have done, so shall it be done to

> "I will give them one heart, and put a new spirit within them; I will remove the heart of stone from their flesh and give them a heart of flesh, so that they may follow my statutes and keep my ordinances and obey them. Then they shall be my people, and I will be their God." Ezekiel 11:19

them; they shall go into exile, into captivity." ¹²And the prince who is among them shall lift his baggage on his shoulder in the dark, and shall go out; he^b shall dig through the wall and carry it through; he shall cover his face, so that he may not see the land with his eyes. ¹³I will spread my net over him, and he shall be caught in my snare; and I will bring him to Babylon, the land of the Chal·dē´ans, yet he shall not see it; and he shall die there. ¹⁴I will scatter to every wind all who are around him, his helpers and all his troops; and I will unsheathe the sword behind them. ¹⁵And they shall know that I am the LORD, when I disperse them among the nations and scatter them through the countries. ¹⁶But I will let a few of them escape from the sword, from famine and pestilence, so that they may tell of all their abominations among the nations where they go; then they shall know that I am the LORD.

Judgment Not Postponed

17 The word of the LORD came to me: ¹⁸Mortal, eat your bread with quaking, and drink your water with trembling and with fearfulness; ¹⁹and say to the people of the land, Thus says the Lord GOD concerning the inhabitants of Jerusalem in the land of Israel: They shall eat their bread with fearfulness, and drink their water in dismay, because their land shall be stripped of all it contains, on account of the violence of all those who live in it. ²⁰The inhabited cities shall be laid waste, and the land shall become a desolation; and you shall know that I am the LORD.

^{b} Gk Syr: Heb *they*

21 The word of the LORD came to me: ²²Mortal, what is this proverb of yours about the land of Israel, which says, "The days are prolonged, and every vision comes to nothing"? ²³Tell them therefore, "Thus says the Lord GOD: I will put an end to this proverb, and they shall use it no more as a proverb in Israel." But say to them, The days are near, and the fulfillment of every vision. ²⁴For there shall no longer be any false vision or flattering divination within the house of Israel. ²⁵But I the LORD will speak the word that I speak, and it will be fulfilled. It will no longer be delayed; but in your days, O rebellious house, I will speak the word and fulfill it, says the Lord GOD.

26 The word of the LORD came to me: ²⁷Mortal, the house of Israel is saying, "The vision that he sees is for many years ahead; he prophesies for distant times." ²⁸Therefore say to them, Thus says the Lord GOD: None of my words will be delayed any longer, but the word that I speak will be fulfilled, says the Lord GOD.

False Prophets Condemned

13 The word of the LORD came to me: ²Mortal, prophesy against the prophets of Israel who are prophesying; say to those who prophesy out of their own imagination: "Hear the word of the LORD!" ³Thus says the Lord GOD, Alas for the senseless prophets who follow their own spirit, and have seen nothing! ⁴Your prophets have been like jackals among ruins, O Israel. ⁵You have not gone up into the breaches, or repaired a wall for the house of Israel, so that it might stand in battle on the day of the LORD. ⁶They have envisioned falsehood and lying divination; they say, "Says the LORD," when the LORD has not sent them, and yet they wait for the fulfillment of their word! ⁷Have you not seen a false vision or uttered a lying divination, when you have said, "Says the LORD," even though I did not speak?

8 Therefore thus says the Lord GOD: Because you have uttered falsehood and

Ezekiel compared the idea of whitewashed walls to false prophets. When the people built weak walls, the false prophets covered the walls with a thin coat of whitewash to make them look stronger. The walls looked good, but the first rainstorm could cause them to fall down! Although people might look good on the outside, their inward character might not be strong. Read what Paul had to say about someone like this in Acts 23:3. What about you? Are you strong on the inside?

envisioned lies, I am against you, says the Lord GOD. ⁹My hand will be against the prophets who see false visions and utter lying divinations; they shall not be in the council of my people, nor be enrolled in the register of the house of Israel, nor shall they enter the land of Israel; and you shall know that I am the Lord GOD. ¹⁰Because, in truth, because they have misled my people, saying, "Peace," when there is no peace; and because, when the people build a wall, these prophets^c smear whitewash on it. ¹¹Say to those who smear whitewash on it that it shall fall. There will be a deluge of rain,^d great hailstones will fall, and a stormy wind will break out. ¹²When the wall falls, will it not be said to you, "Where is the whitewash you smeared on it?" ¹³Therefore thus says the Lord GOD: In my wrath I will make a stormy wind break out, and in my anger there shall be a deluge of rain, and hailstones in wrath to destroy it. ¹⁴I will break down the wall that you have smeared with whitewash, and bring it to the ground, so that its foundation will be laid bare; when it falls, you shall perish within it; and you shall know that I am the LORD. ¹⁵Thus I will spend my wrath upon the wall, and upon those who have smeared it with whitewash; and I will say to you, The wall

^c Heb *they* 　　^d Heb *rain and you*

is no more, nor those who smeared it—[16]the prophets of Israel who prophesied concerning Jerusalem and saw visions of peace for it, when there was no peace, says the Lord GOD.

17 As for you, mortal, set your face against the daughters of your people, who prophesy out of their own imagination; prophesy against them [18]and say, Thus says the Lord GOD: Woe to the women who sew bands on all wrists, and make veils for the heads of persons of every height, in the hunt for human lives! Will you hunt down lives among my people, and maintain your own lives? [19]You have profaned me among my people for handfuls of barley and for pieces of bread, putting to death persons who should not die and keeping alive persons who should not live, by your lies to my people, who listen to lies.

20 Therefore thus says the Lord GOD: I am against your bands with which you hunt lives;[e] I will tear them from your arms, and let the lives go free, the lives that you hunt down like birds. [21]I will tear off your veils, and save my people from your hands; they shall no longer be prey in your hands; and you shall know that I am the LORD. [22]Because you have disheartened the righteous falsely, although I have not disheartened them, and you have encouraged the wicked not to turn from their wicked way and save their lives; [23]therefore you shall no longer see false visions or practice divination; I will save my people from your hand. Then you will know that I am the LORD.

God's Judgments Justified

14 Certain elders of Israel came to me and sat down before me. [2]And the word of the LORD came to me: [3]Mortal, these men have taken their idols into their hearts, and placed their iniquity as a stumbling block before them; shall I let myself be consulted by them? [4]Therefore speak to them, and say to them, Thus says the Lord GOD: Any of those of the house of Israel who take their idols into their hearts and place their iniquity as a stumbling block before them, and yet come to the prophet—I the LORD will answer those who come with the multitude of their idols, [5]in order that I may take hold of the hearts of the house of Israel, all of whom are estranged from me through their idols.

6 Therefore say to the house of Israel, Thus says the Lord GOD: Repent and turn away from your idols; and turn away your faces from all your abominations. [7]For any of those of the house of Israel, or of the aliens who reside in Israel, who separate themselves from me, taking their idols into their hearts and placing their iniquity as a stumbling block before them, and yet come to a prophet to inquire of me by him, I the LORD will answer them myself. [8]I will set my face against them; I will make them a sign and a byword and cut them off from the midst of my people; and you shall know that I am the LORD.

9 If a prophet is deceived and speaks a word, I, the LORD, have deceived that prophet, and I will stretch out my hand against him, and will destroy him from the midst of my people Israel. [10]And they shall bear their punishment—the punishment of the inquirer and the punishment of the prophet shall be the same— [11]so that the house of Israel may no longer go astray from me, nor defile themselves any more with all their transgressions. Then they shall be my people, and I will be their God, says the Lord GOD.

12 The word of the LORD came to me: [13]Mortal, when a land sins against me by acting faithlessly, and I stretch out my hand against it, and break its staff of bread and send famine upon it, and cut off from it human beings and animals, [14]even if Noah, Daniel,[f] and Jōb, these three, were in it, they would save only their own lives by their righteousness, says the Lord GOD. [15]If I send wild animals through the land to ravage it, so that it is made desolate,

e Gk Syr: Heb *lives for birds*   f Or, as otherwise read, *Danel* and no one may pass through because of the animals; ¹⁶even if these three men were in it, as I live, says the Lord GOD, they would save neither sons nor daughters; they alone would be saved, but the land would be desolate. ¹⁷Or if I bring a sword upon that land and say, 'Let a sword pass through the land,' and I cut off human beings and animals from it; ¹⁸though these three men were in it, as I live, says the Lord GOD, they would save neither sons nor daughters, but they alone would be saved. ¹⁹Or if I send a pestilence into that land, and pour out my wrath upon it with blood, to cut off humans and animals from it; ²⁰even if Noah, Daniel,^g and Jōb were in it, as I live, says the Lord GOD, they would save neither son nor daughter; they would save only their own lives by their righteousness.

21 For thus says the Lord GOD: How much more when I send upon Jerusalem my four deadly acts of judgment, sword, famine, wild animals, and pestilence, to cut off humans and animals from it! ²²Yet, survivors shall be left in it, sons and daughters who will be brought out; they will come out to you. When you see their ways and their deeds, you will be consoled for the evil that I have brought upon Jerusalem, for all that I have brought upon it. ²³They shall console you, when you see their ways and their deeds; and you shall know that it was not without cause that I did all that I have done in it, says the Lord GOD.

The Useless Vine

15 The word of the LORD came to me:

² O mortal, how does the wood of the vine surpass all other wood—
the vine branch that is among the trees of the forest?
³ Is wood taken from it to make anything?
Does one take a peg from it on which to hang any object?
⁴ It is put in the fire for fuel;

when the fire has consumed both ends of it
and the middle of it is charred, is it useful for anything?
⁵ When it was whole it was used for nothing;
how much less—when the fire has consumed it,
and it is charred—
can it ever be used for anything!

6 Therefore thus says the Lord GOD: Like the wood of the vine among the trees of the forest, which I have given to the fire for fuel, so I will give up the inhabitants of Jerusalem. ⁷I will set my face against them; although they escape from the fire, the fire shall still consume them; and you shall know that I am the LORD, when I set my face against them. ⁸And I will make the land desolate, because they have acted faithlessly, says the Lord GOD.

God's Faithless Bride

16 The word of the LORD came to me: ²Mortal, make known to Jerusalem her abominations, ³and say, Thus says the Lord GOD to Jerusalem: Your origin and your birth were in the land of the Cā´naan·ītes; your father was an Am´o·rīte, and your mother a Hit´tīte. ⁴As for your birth, on the day you were born your navel cord was not cut, nor were you washed with water to cleanse you, nor rubbed with salt, nor wrapped in cloths. ⁵No eye pitied you, to do any of these things for you out of compassion for you; but you were thrown out in the open field, for you were abhorred on the day you were born.

6 I passed by you, and saw you flailing about in your blood. As you lay in your blood, I said to you, "Live! ⁷and grow up^h like a plant of the field." You grew up and became tall and arrived at full womanhood;ⁱ your breasts were formed, and your hair had grown; yet you were naked and bare.

^g Or, as otherwise read, *Danel*   ^h Gk Syr: Heb *Live! I made you a myriad*   ⁱ Cn: Heb *ornament of ornaments*

8 I passed by you again and looked on you; you were at the age for love. I spread the edge of my cloak over you, and covered your nakedness: I pledged myself to you and entered into a covenant with you, says the Lord GOD, and you became mine. ⁹Then I bathed you with water and washed off the blood from you, and anointed you with oil. ¹⁰I clothed you with embroidered cloth and with sandals of fine leather; I bound you in fine linen and covered you with rich fabric.ʲ ¹¹I adorned you with ornaments: I put bracelets on your arms, a chain on your neck, ¹²a ring on your nose, earrings in your ears, and a beautiful crown upon your head. ¹³You were adorned with gold and silver, while your clothing was of fine linen, rich fabric,ʲ and embroidered cloth. You had choice flour and honey and oil for food. You grew exceedingly beautiful, fit to be a queen. ¹⁴Your fame spread among the nations on account of your beauty, for it was perfect because of my splendor that I had bestowed on you, says the Lord GOD.

15 But you trusted in your beauty, and played the whore because of your fame, and lavished your whorings on any passer-by.ᵏ ¹⁶You took some of your garments, and made for yourself colorful shrines, and on them played the whore; nothing like this has ever been or ever shall be.ʲ ¹⁷You also took your beautiful jewels of my gold and my silver that I had given you, and made for yourself male images, and with them played the whore; ¹⁸and you took your embroidered garments to cover them, and set my oil and my incense before them. ¹⁹Also my bread that I gave you—I fed you with choice flour and oil and honey—you set it before them as a pleasing odor; and so it was, says the Lord GOD. ²⁰You took your sons and your daughters, whom you had borne to me, and these you sacrificed to them to be devoured. As if your whorings were not enough! ²¹You slaughtered my children and delivered them up as an offering

to them. ²²And in all your abominations and your whorings you did not remember the days of your youth, when you were naked and bare, flailing about in your blood.

23 After all your wickedness (woe, woe to you! says the Lord GOD), ²⁴you built yourself a platform and made yourself a lofty place in every square; ²⁵at the head of every street you built your lofty place and prostituted your beauty, offering yourself to every passer-by, and multiplying your whoring. ²⁶You played the whore with the Egyptians, your lustful neighbors, multiplying your whoring, to provoke me to anger. ²⁷Therefore I stretched out my hand against you, reduced your rations, and gave you up to the will of your enemies, the daughters of the Phi·lis´tines, who were ashamed of your lewd behavior. ²⁸You played the whore with the Assyrians, because you were insatiable; you played the whore with them, and still you were not satisfied. ²⁹You multiplied your whoring with Chal·dé´a, the land of merchants; and even with this you were not satisfied.

30 How sick is your heart, says the Lord GOD, that you did all these things, the deeds of a brazen whore; ³¹building your platform at the head of every street, and making your lofty place in every square! Yet you were not like a whore, because you scorned payment. ³²Adulterous wife, who receives strangers instead of her husband! ³³Gifts are given to all whores; but you gave your gifts to all your lovers, bribing them to come to you from all around for your whorings. ³⁴So you were different from other women in your whorings: no one solicited you to play the whore; and you gave payment, while no payment was given to you; you were different.

35 Therefore, O whore, hear the word of the LORD: ³⁶Thus says the Lord GOD, Because your lust was poured out and

ʲ Meaning of Heb uncertain   ᵏ Heb adds let it be his

your nakedness uncovered in your whoring with your lovers, and because of all your abominable idols, and because of the blood of your children that you gave to them, [37]therefore, I will gather all your lovers, with whom you took pleasure, all those you loved and all those you hated; I will gather them against you from all around, and will uncover your nakedness to them, so that they may see all your nakedness. [38]I will judge you as women who commit adultery and shed blood are judged, and bring blood upon you in wrath and jealousy. [39]I will deliver you into their hands, and they shall throw down your platform and break down your lofty places; they shall strip you of your clothes and take your beautiful objects and leave you naked and bare. [40]They shall bring up a mob against you, and they shall stone you and cut you to pieces with their swords. [41]They shall burn your houses and execute judgments on you in the sight of many women; I will stop you from playing the whore, and you shall also make no more payments. [42]So I will satisfy my fury on you, and my jealousy shall turn away from you; I will be calm, and will be angry no longer. [43]Because you have not remembered the days of your youth, but have enraged me with all these things; therefore, I have returned your deeds upon your head, says the Lord GOD.

Have you not committed lewdness beyond all your abominations? [44]See, everyone who uses proverbs will use this proverb about you, "Like mother, like daughter." [45]You are the daughter of your mother, who loathed her husband and her children; and you are the sister of your sisters, who loathed their husbands and their children. Your mother was a Hit′tīte and your father an Am′o·rīte. [46]Your elder sister is Sa·mār′i·a, who lived with her daughters to the north of you; and your younger sister, who lived to the south of you, is Sod′om with her daughters. [47]You not only followed their ways, and acted according to their abominations; within a

very little time you were more corrupt than they in all your ways. [48]As I live, says the Lord GOD, your sister Sod′om and her daughters have not done as you and your daughters have done. [49]This was the guilt of your sister Sod′om: she and her daughters had pride, excess of food, and prosperous ease, but did not aid the poor and needy. [50]They were haughty, and did abominable things before me; therefore I removed them when I saw it. [51]Sa·mār′i·a has not committed half your sins; you have committed more abominations than they, and have made your sisters appear righteous by all the abominations that you have committed. [52]Bear your disgrace, you also, for you have brought about for your sisters a more favorable judgment; because of your sins in which you acted more abominably than they, they are more in the right than you. So be ashamed, you also, and bear your disgrace, for you have made your sisters appear righteous.

53 I will restore their fortunes, the fortunes of Sod′om and her daughters and the fortunes of Sa·mār′i·a and her daughters, and I will restore your own fortunes along with theirs, [54]in order that you may bear your disgrace and be ashamed of all that you have done, becoming a consolation to them. [55]As for your sisters, Sod′om and her daughters shall return to their former state, Sa·mār′i·a and her daughters shall return to their former state, and you and your daughters shall return to your former state. [56]Was not your sister Sod′om a byword in your mouth in the day of your pride, [57]before your wickedness was uncovered? Now you are a mockery to the daughters of Ar′am[l] and all her neighbors, and to the daughters of the Phi·lis′tines, those all around who despise you. [58]You must bear the penalty of your lewdness and your abominations, says the LORD.

An Everlasting Covenant

59 Yes, thus says the Lord GOD: I will deal with you as you have done, you who

[l] Another reading is *Edom*

have despised the oath, breaking the covenant; [60]yet I will remember my covenant with you in the days of your youth, and I will establish with you an everlasting covenant. [61]Then you will remember your ways, and be ashamed when I[m] take your sisters, both your elder and your younger, and give them to you as daughters, but not on account of my[n] covenant with you. [62]I will establish my covenant with you, and you shall know that I am the LORD, [63]in order that you may remember and be confounded, and never open your mouth again because of your shame, when I forgive you all that you have done, says the Lord GOD.

Although God's people had broken the promises they made to God, God was faithful and kept the promise made to Abraham long ago. That was good news for the people in Old Testament times, and it is good news for us today. Even when we make wrong choices and do not follow God's ways, God's mercy and grace cover us. God's love causes us to remember and to come back to the right way of living. God is always ready to welcome us back.

The Two Eagles and the Vine

17 The word of the LORD came to me: [2]O mortal, propound a riddle, and speak an allegory to the house of Israel. [3]Say: Thus says the Lord GOD:
A great eagle, with great wings and
long pinions,
rich in plumage of many colors,
came to the Lebanon.
He took the top of the cedar,
[4]   broke off its topmost shoot;
he carried it to a land of trade,
set it in a city of merchants.
[5] Then he took a seed from the land,
placed it in fertile soil;
a plant[o] by abundant waters,

he set it like a willow twig.
[6] It sprouted and became a vine
spreading out, but low;
Its branches turned toward him,
its roots remained where it stood.
So it became a vine;
it brought forth branches,
put forth foliage.

[7] There was another great eagle,
with great wings and much
plumage.
And see! This vine stretched out
its roots toward him;
it shot out its branches toward him,
so that he might water it.
From the bed where it was planted
[8]   it was transplanted
to good soil by abundant waters,
so that it might produce branches
and bear fruit
and become a noble vine.
[9]Say: Thus says the Lord GOD:
Will it prosper?
Will he not pull up its roots,
cause its fruit to rot[o] and wither,
its fresh sprouting leaves to fade?
No strong arm or mighty army will be
needed
to pull it from its roots.
[10] When it is transplanted, will it thrive?
When the east wind strikes it,
will it not utterly wither,
wither on the bed where it grew?

[11] Then the word of the LORD came to me: [12]Say now to the rebellious house: Do you not know what these things mean? Tell them: The king of Babylon came to Jerusalem, took its king and its officials, and brought them back with him to Babylon. [13]He took one of the royal offspring and made a covenant with him, putting him under oath (he had taken away the chief men of the land), [14]so that the kingdom might be humble and not lift itself up, and that by keeping his covenant it might stand. [15]But he rebelled against

[m] Syr: Heb *you*   [n] Heb lacks *my*   [o] Meaning of Heb uncertain

him by sending ambassadors to Egypt, in order that they might give him horses and a large army. Will he succeed? Can one escape who does such things? Can he break the covenant and yet escape? ¹⁶As I live, says the Lord GOD, surely in the place where the king resides who made him king, whose oath he despised, and whose covenant with him he broke—in Babylon he shall die. ¹⁷Pharaoh with his mighty army and great company will not help him in war, when ramps are cast up and siege-walls built to cut off many lives. ¹⁸Because he despised the oath and broke the covenant, because he gave his hand and yet did all these things, he shall not escape. ¹⁹Therefore thus says the Lord GOD: As I live, I will surely return upon his head my oath that he despised, and my covenant that he broke. ²⁰I will spread my net over him, and he shall be caught in my snare; I will bring him to Babylon and enter into judgment with him there for the treason he has committed against me. ²¹All the pick^p of his troops shall fall by the sword, and the survivors shall be scattered to every wind; and you shall know that I, the LORD, have spoken.

Israel Exalted at Last

22 Thus says the Lord GOD:
    I myself will take a sprig
        from the lofty top of a cedar;
        I will set it out.
    I will break off a tender one
        from the topmost of its young twigs;
    I myself will plant it
        on a high and lofty mountain.
²³ On the mountain height of Israel
    I will plant it,
    in order that it may produce boughs
        and bear fruit,
    and become a noble cedar.
    Under it every kind of bird will live;
        in the shade of its branches will
           nest
    winged creatures of every kind.
²⁴ All the trees of the field shall know
    that I am the LORD.

    I bring low the high tree,
        I make high the low tree;
    I dry up the green tree
        and make the dry tree flourish.
    I the LORD have spoken;
        I will accomplish it.

Individual Retribution

18 The word of the LORD came to me: ²What do you mean by repeating this proverb concerning the land of Israel, "The parents have eaten sour grapes, and the children's teeth are set on edge"? ³As I live, says the Lord GOD, this proverb shall no more be used by you in Israel. ⁴Know that all lives are mine; the life of the parent as well as the life of the child is mine: it is only the person who sins that shall die.

5 If a man is righteous and does what is lawful and right— ⁶if he does not eat upon the mountains or lift up his eyes to the idols of the house of Israel, does not defile his neighbor's wife or approach a woman during her menstrual period, ⁷does not oppress anyone, but restores to the debtor his pledge, commits no robbery, gives his bread to the hungry and covers the naked with a garment, ⁸does not take advance or accrued interest, withholds his hand from iniquity, executes true justice between contending parties, ⁹follows my statutes, and is careful to observe my ordinances, acting faithfully— such a one is righteous; he shall surely live, says the Lord GOD.

10 If he has a son who is violent, a shedder of blood, ¹¹who does any of these things (though his father^q does none of them), who eats upon the mountains, defiles his neighbor's wife, ¹²oppresses the poor and needy, commits robbery, does not restore the pledge, lifts up his eyes to the idols, commits abomination, ¹³takes advance or accrued interest; shall he then live? He shall not. He has done all these abominable things; he shall surely die; his blood shall be upon himself.

^p Another reading is *fugitives*   ^q Heb *he*

14 But if this man has a son who sees all the sins that his father has done, considers, and does not do likewise, [15]who does not eat upon the mountains or lift up his eyes to the idols of the house of Israel, does not defile his neighbor's wife, [16]does not wrong anyone, exacts no pledge, commits no robbery, but gives his bread to the hungry and covers the naked with a garment, [17]withholds his hand from iniquity,[r] takes no advance or accrued interest, observes my ordinances, and follows my statutes; he shall not die for his father's iniquity; he shall surely live. [18]As for his father, because he practiced extortion, robbed his brother, and did what is not good among his people, he dies for his iniquity.

19 Yet you say, "Why should not the son suffer for the iniquity of the father?" When the son has done what is lawful and right, and has been careful to observe all my statutes, he shall surely live. [20]The person who sins shall die. A child shall not suffer for the iniquity of a parent, nor a parent suffer for the iniquity of a child; the righteousness of the righteous shall be his own, and the wickedness of the wicked shall be his own.

21 But if the wicked turn away from all their sins that they have committed and keep all my statutes and do what is lawful and right, they shall surely live; they shall not die. [22]None of the transgressions that they have committed shall be remembered against them; for the righteousness

that they have done they shall live. [23]Have I any pleasure in the death of the wicked, says the Lord GOD, and not rather that they should turn from their ways and live? [24]But when the righteous turn away from their righteousness and commit iniquity and do the same abominable things that the wicked do, shall they live? None of the righteous deeds that they have done shall be remembered; for the treachery of which they are guilty and the sin they have committed, they shall die.

25 Yet you say, "The way of the Lord is unfair." Hear now, O house of Israel: Is my way unfair? Is it not your ways that are unfair? [26]When the righteous turn away from their righteousness and commit iniquity, they shall die for it; for the iniquity that they have committed they shall die. [27]Again, when the wicked turn away from the wickedness they have committed and do what is lawful and right, they shall save their life. [28]Because they considered and turned away from all the transgressions that they had committed, they shall surely live; they shall not die. [29]Yet the house of Israel says, "The way of the Lord is unfair." O house of Israel, are my ways unfair? Is it not your ways that are unfair?

30 Therefore I will judge you, O house of Israel, all of you according to your ways, says the Lord GOD. Repent and turn from all your transgressions; otherwise iniquity will be your ruin.[s] [31]Cast away from you all the transgressions that you have committed against me, and get yourselves a new heart and a new spirit! Why will you die, O house of Israel? [32]For I have no pleasure in the death of anyone, says the Lord GOD. Turn, then, and live.

Israel Degraded

19 As for you, raise up a lamentation for the princes of Israel, [2]and say:

What a lioness was your mother
among lions!

Sometimes people feel that their actions have caused such a break in their relationships with other people and with God that these relationships can never be healed. But Ezekiel tells us that we can leave the path we have been on and choose instead the way of righteousness and life. When we ask for God's forgiveness, God forgets the past. God always looks at our hearts.

[r] Gk: Heb *the poor*   [s] Or *so that they shall not be a stumbling block of iniquity to you*

She lay down among young lions,
  rearing her cubs.
3 She raised up one of her cubs;
  he became a young lion,
and he learned to catch prey;
  he devoured humans.
4 The nations sounded an alarm against
    him;
  he was caught in their pit;
and they brought him with hooks
  to the land of Egypt.
5 When she saw that she was thwarted,
  that her hope was lost,
she took another of her cubs
  and made him a young lion.
6 He prowled among the lions;
  he became a young lion,
and he learned to catch prey;
  he devoured people.
7 And he ravaged their strongholds,[t]
  and laid waste their towns;
the land was appalled, and all in it,
  at the sound of his roaring.
8 The nations set upon him
  from the provinces all around;
they spread their net over him;
  he was caught in their pit.
9 With hooks they put him in a cage,
  and brought him to the king of
    Babylon;
they brought him into custody,
so that his voice should be heard no
    more
  on the mountains of Israel.
10 Your mother was like a vine in a
    vineyard[u]
  transplanted by the water,
fruitful and full of branches
  from abundant water.
11 Its strongest stem became
  a ruler's scepter;[v]
it towered aloft
  among the thick boughs;
it stood out in its height
  with its mass of branches.
12 But it was plucked up in fury,
  cast down to the ground;
the east wind dried it up;
  its fruit was stripped off,

its strong stem was withered;
  the fire consumed it.
13 Now it is transplanted into the
    wilderness,
  into a dry and thirsty land.
14 And fire has gone out from its stem,
  has consumed its branches and
    fruit,
so that there remains in it no strong
    stem,
  no scepter for ruling.

This is a lamentation, and it is used as a
lamentation.

Israel's Continuing Rebellion

20 In the seventh year, in the fifth
month, on the tenth day of the
month, certain elders of Israel came to
consult the LORD, and sat down before
me. [2]And the word of the LORD came to
me: [3]Mortal, speak to the elders of Israel,
and say to them: Thus says the Lord GOD:
Why are you coming? To consult me? As I
live, says the Lord GOD, I will not be consulted by you. [4]Will you judge them, mortal, will you judge them? Then let them
know the abominations of their ancestors,
[5]and say to them: Thus says the Lord GOD:
On the day when I chose Israel, I swore to
the offspring of the house of Jacob—making myself known to them in the land of
Egypt—I swore to them, saying, I am the
LORD your God. [6]On that day I swore to
them that I would bring them out of the
land of Egypt into a land that I had
searched out for them, a land flowing with
milk and honey, the most glorious of all
lands. [7]And I said to them, Cast away the
detestable things your eyes feast on, every
one of you, and do not defile yourselves
with the idols of Egypt; I am the LORD
your God. [8]But they rebelled against me
and would not listen to me; not one of
them cast away the detestable things their
eyes feasted on, nor did they forsake the
idols of Egypt.

[t] Heb *his widows*   [u] Cn: Heb *in your blood*
[v] Heb *Its strongest stems became rulers' scepters*

Then I thought I would pour out my wrath upon them and spend my anger against them in the midst of the land of Egypt. ⁹But I acted for the sake of my name, that it should not be profaned in the sight of the nations among whom they lived, in whose sight I made myself known to them in bringing them out of the land of Egypt. ¹⁰So I led them out of the land of Egypt and brought them into the wilderness. ¹¹I gave them my statutes and showed them my ordinances, by whose observance everyone shall live. ¹²Moreover I gave them my sabbaths, as a sign between me and them, so that they might know that I the LORD sanctify them. ¹³But the house of Israel rebelled against me in the wilderness; they did not observe my statutes but rejected my ordinances, by whose observance everyone shall live; and my sabbaths they greatly profaned.

Then I thought I would pour out my wrath upon them in the wilderness, to make an end of them. ¹⁴But I acted for the sake of my name, so that it should not be profaned in the sight of the nations, in whose sight I had brought them out. ¹⁵Moreover I swore to them in the wilderness that I would not bring them into the land that I had given them, a land flowing with milk and honey, the most glorious of all lands, ¹⁶because they rejected my ordinances and did not observe my statutes, and profaned my sabbaths; for their heart went after their idols. ¹⁷Nevertheless my eye spared them, and I did not destroy them or make an end of them in the wilderness.

18 I said to their children in the wilderness, Do not follow the statutes of your parents, nor observe their ordinances, nor defile yourselves with their idols. ¹⁹I the LORD am your God; follow my statutes, and be careful to observe my ordinances, ²⁰and hallow my sabbaths that they may be a sign between me and you, so that you may know that I the LORD am your God. ²¹But the children rebelled against me; they did not follow my statutes, and were not careful to observe my ordinances, by whose observance everyone shall live; they profaned my sabbaths.

Then I thought I would pour out my wrath upon them and spend my anger against them in the wilderness. ²²But I withheld my hand, and acted for the sake of my name, so that it should not be profaned in the sight of the nations, in whose sight I had brought them out. ²³Moreover I swore to them in the wilderness that I would scatter them among the nations and disperse them through the countries, ²⁴because they had not executed my ordinances, but had rejected my statutes and profaned my sabbaths, and their eyes were set on their ancestors' idols. ²⁵Moreover I gave them statutes that were not good and ordinances by which they could not live. ²⁶I defiled them through their very gifts, in their offering up all their firstborn, in order that I might horrify them, so that they might know that I am the LORD.

27 Therefore, mortal, speak to the house of Israel and say to them, Thus says the Lord GOD: In this again your ancestors blasphemed me, by dealing treacherously with me. ²⁸For when I had brought them into the land that I swore to give them, then wherever they saw any high hill or any leafy tree, there they offered their sacrifices and presented the provocation of their offering; there they sent up their pleasing odors, and there they poured out their drink offerings. ²⁹(I said to them, What is the high place to which you go? So it is called Bāʹmahʷ to this day.) ³⁰Therefore say to the house of Israel, Thus says the Lord GOD: Will you defile yourselves after the manner of your ancestors and go astray after their detestable things? ³¹When you offer your gifts and make your children pass through the fire, you defile yourselves with all your idols to this day. And shall I be consulted by you, O house of Israel? As I live, says the Lord GOD, I will not be consulted by you.

ʷ That is *High Place*

32 What is in your mind shall never happen—the thought, "Let us be like the nations, like the tribes of the countries, and worship wood and stone."

God Will Restore Israel

33 As I live, says the Lord GOD, surely with a mighty hand and an outstretched arm, and with wrath poured out, I will be king over you. [34]I will bring you out from the peoples and gather you out of the countries where you are scattered, with a mighty hand and an outstretched arm, and with wrath poured out; [35]and I will bring you into the wilderness of the peoples, and there I will enter into judgment with you face to face. [36]As I entered into judgment with your ancestors in the wilderness of the land of Egypt, so I will enter into judgment with you, says the Lord GOD. [37]I will make you pass under the staff, and will bring you within the bond of the covenant. [38]I will purge out the rebels among you, and those who transgress against me; I will bring them out of the land where they reside as aliens, but they shall not enter the land of Israel. Then you shall know that I am the LORD.

39 As for you, O house of Israel, thus says the Lord GOD: Go serve your idols, everyone of you now and hereafter, if you will not listen to me; but my holy name you shall no more profane with your gifts and your idols.

40 For on my holy mountain, the mountain height of Israel, says the Lord GOD, there all the house of Israel, all of them, shall serve me in the land; there I will accept them, and there I will require your contributions and the choicest of your gifts, with all your sacred things. [41]As a pleasing odor I will accept you, when I bring you out from the peoples, and gather you out of the countries where you have been scattered; and I will manifest my holiness among you in the sight of the nations. [42]You shall know that I am the LORD, when I bring you into the land of Israel, the country that I swore to give to your ancestors. [43]There you shall remember your ways and all the deeds by which you have polluted yourselves; and you shall loathe yourselves for all the evils that you have committed. [44]And you shall know that I am the LORD, when I deal with you for my name's sake, not according to your evil ways, or corrupt deeds, O house of Israel, says the Lord GOD.

A Prophecy against the Negeb

45[x] The word of the LORD came to me: [46]Mortal, set your face toward the south, preach against the south, and prophesy against the forest land in the Neg´eb; [47]say to the forest of the Neg´eb, Hear the word of the LORD: Thus says the Lord GOD, I will kindle a fire in you, and it shall devour every green tree in you and every dry tree; the blazing flame shall not be quenched, and all faces from south to north shall be scorched by it. [48]All flesh shall see that I the LORD have kindled it; it shall not be quenched. [49]Then I said, "Ah Lord GOD! they are saying of me, 'Is he not a maker of allegories?' "

The Drawn Sword of God

21 [y]The word of the LORD came to me: [2]Mortal, set your face toward Jerusalem and preach against the sanctuaries; prophesy against the land of Israel [3]and say to the land of Israel, Thus says the LORD: I am coming against you, and will draw my sword out of its sheath, and will cut off from you both righteous and wicked. [4]Because I will cut off from you both righteous and wicked, therefore my sword shall go out of its sheath against all flesh from south to north; [5]and all flesh shall know that I the LORD have drawn my sword out of its sheath; it shall not be sheathed again. [6]Moan therefore, mortal; moan with breaking heart and bitter grief before their eyes. [7]And when they say to you, "Why do you moan?" you shall say, "Because of the news that has come. Every heart will melt and all hands will be feeble, every spirit will faint and all knees will

---

[x] Ch 21.1 in Heb   [y] Ch 21.6 in Heb

turn to water. See, it comes and it will be fulfilled," says the Lord GOD.

8 And the word of the LORD came to me: [9]Mortal, prophesy and say: Thus says the Lord; Say:

A sword, a sword is sharpened,
    it is also polished;
[10] It is sharpened for slaughter,
    honed to flash like lightning!
How can we make merry?
    You have despised the rod,
    and all discipline.[z]
[11] The sword[a] is given to be polished,
    to be grasped in the hand;
it is sharpened, the sword is polished,
    to be placed in the slayer's hand.
[12] Cry and wail, O mortal,
    for it is against my people;
it is against all Israel's princes;
    they are thrown to the sword,
    together with my people.
    Ah! Strike the thigh!
[13]For consider: What! If you despise the rod, will it not happen?[z] says the Lord GOD.
[14] And you, mortal, prophesy;
    strike hand to hand.
Let the sword fall twice, thrice;
    it is a sword for killing.
A sword for great slaughter—
    it surrounds them;
[15] therefore hearts melt
    and many stumble.
At all their gates I have set
    the point[z] of the sword.
Ah! It is made for flashing,
    it is polished[b] for slaughter.
[16] Attack to the right!
    Engage to the left!
    Wherever your edge is directed.
[17] I too will strike hand to hand,
    I will satisfy my fury;
    I the LORD have spoken.

18 The word of the LORD came to me: [19]Mortal, mark out two roads for the sword of the king of Babylon to come; both of them shall issue from the same land. And make a signpost, make it for a fork in the road leading to a city; [20]mark

out the road for the sword to come to Rab'bah of the Am'mon·ites or to Judah and to[c] Jerusalem the fortified. [21]For the king of Babylon stands at the parting of the way, at the fork in the two roads, to use divination; he shakes the arrows, he consults the teraphim,[d] he inspects the liver. [22]Into his right hand comes the lot for Jerusalem, to set battering rams, to call out for slaughter, for raising the battle cry, to set battering rams against the gates, to cast up ramps, to build siege-towers. [23]But to them it will seem like a false divination; they have sworn solemn oaths; but he brings their guilt to remembrance, bringing about their capture.

24 Therefore thus says the Lord GOD: Because you have brought your guilt to remembrance, in that your transgressions are uncovered, so that in all your deeds your sins appear—because you have come to remembrance, you shall be taken in hand.[e]
[25] As for you, vile, wicked prince of
    Israel,
    you whose day has come,
    the time of final punishment,
[26] thus says the Lord GOD:
    Remove the turban, take off the
      crown;
    things shall not remain as they are.
    Exalt that which is low,
    abase that which is high.
[27] A ruin, a ruin, a ruin—
    I will make it!
    (Such has never occurred.)
Until he comes whose right it is;
    to him I will give it.

28 As for you, mortal, prophesy, and say, Thus says the Lord GOD concerning the Am'mon·ites, and concerning their reproach; say:

A sword, a sword! Drawn for slaughter,
    polished to consume,[f] to flash like
      lightning.

---

[z] Meaning of Heb uncertain   [a] Heb *It*   [b] Tg: Heb *wrapped up*   [c] Gk Syr: Heb *Judah in*   [d] Or *the household gods*   [e] Or *be taken captive*   [f] Cn: Heb *to contain*

²⁹ Offering false visions for you,
 divining lies for you,
 they place you over the necks
 of the vile, wicked ones—
 those whose day has come,
 the time of final punishment.
³⁰ Return it to its sheath!
 In the place where you were created,
 in the land of your origin,
 I will judge you.
³¹ I will pour out my indignation upon
 you,
 with the fire of my wrath
 I will blow upon you.
 I will deliver you into brutish hands,
 those skillful to destroy.
³² You shall be fuel for the fire,
 your blood shall enter the earth;
 you shall be remembered no more,
 for I the LORD have spoken.

The Bloody City

22 The word of the LORD came to me: ²You, mortal, will you judge, will you judge the bloody city? Then declare to it all its abominable deeds. ³You shall say, Thus says the Lord GOD: A city! Shedding blood within itself; its time has come; making its idols, defiling itself. ⁴You have become guilty by the blood that you have shed, and defiled by the idols that you have made; you have brought your day near, the appointed time of your years has come. Therefore I have made you a disgrace before the nations, and a mockery to all the countries. ⁵Those who are near and those who are far from you will mock you, you infamous one, full of tumult.

6 The princes of Israel in you, everyone according to his power, have been bent on shedding blood. ⁷Father and mother are treated with contempt in you; the alien residing within you suffers extortion; the orphan and the widow are wronged in you. ⁸You have despised my holy things, and profaned my sabbaths. ⁹In you are those who slander to shed blood, those in you who eat upon the mountains, who commit lewdness in your midst. ¹⁰In you they uncover their fathers' nakedness; in you they violate women in their menstrual periods. ¹¹One commits abomination with his neighbor's wife; another lewdly defiles his daughter-in-law; another in you defiles his sister, his father's daughter. ¹²In you, they take bribes to shed blood; you take both advance interest and accrued interest, and make gain of your neighbors by extortion; and you have forgotten me, says the Lord GOD.

13 See, I strike my hands together at the dishonest gain you have made, and at the blood that has been shed within you. ¹⁴Can your courage endure, or can your hands remain strong in the days when I shall deal with you? I the LORD have spoken, and I will do it. ¹⁵I will scatter you among the nations and disperse you through the countries, and I will purge your filthiness out of you. ¹⁶And I[g] shall be profaned through you in the sight of the nations; and you shall know that I am the LORD.

17 The word of the LORD came to me: ¹⁸Mortal, the house of Israel has become dross to me; all of them, silver,[h] bronze, tin, iron, and lead. In the smelter they have become dross. ¹⁹Therefore thus says the Lord GOD: Because you have all become dross, I will gather you into the midst of Jerusalem. ²⁰As one gathers silver, bronze, iron, lead, and tin into a smelter, to blow the fire upon them in order to melt them; so I will gather you in my anger and in my wrath, and I will put you in and melt you. ²¹I will gather you and blow upon you with the fire of my wrath, and you shall be melted within it. ²²As silver is melted in a smelter, so you shall be melted in it; and you shall know that I the LORD have poured out my wrath upon you.

23 The word of the LORD came to me: ²⁴Mortal, say to it: You are a land that is not cleansed, not rained upon in the day

[g] Gk Syr Vg: Heb *you*   [h] Transposed from the end of the verse; compare verse 20

of indignation. ²⁵Its princes[i] within it are like a roaring lion tearing the prey; they have devoured human lives; they have taken treasure and precious things; they have made many widows within it. ²⁶Its priests have done violence to my teaching and have profaned my holy things; they have made no distinction between the holy and the common, neither have they taught the difference between the unclean and the clean, and they have disregarded my sabbaths, so that I am profaned among them. ²⁷Its officials within it are like wolves tearing the prey, shedding blood, destroying lives to get dishonest gain. ²⁸Its prophets have smeared whitewash on their behalf, seeing false visions and divining lies for them, saying, "Thus says the Lord GOD," when the LORD has not spoken. ²⁹The people of the land have practiced extortion and committed robbery; they have oppressed the poor and needy, and have extorted from the alien without redress. ³⁰And I sought for anyone among them who would repair the wall and stand in the breach before me on behalf of the land, so that I would not destroy it; but I found no one. ³¹Therefore I have poured out my indignation upon them; I have consumed them with the fire of my wrath; I have returned their conduct upon their heads, says the Lord GOD.

Oholah and Oholibah

23 The word of the LORD came to me: ²Mortal, there were two women, the daughters of one mother; ³they played the whore in Egypt; they played the whore in their youth; their breasts were caressed there, and their virgin bosoms were fondled. ⁴Ō·hō′lah was the name of the elder and Ō·hol′i·bah the name of her sister. They became mine, and they bore sons and daughters. As for their names, Ō·hō′lah is Sa·mār′i·a, and Ō·hol′i·bah is Jerusalem.

5 Ō·hō′lah played the whore while she was mine; she lusted after her lovers the Assyrians, warriors[j] ⁶clothed in blue, governors and commanders, all of them

handsome young men, mounted horsemen. ⁷She bestowed her favors upon them, the choicest men of Assyria all of them; and she defiled herself with all the idols of everyone for whom she lusted. ⁸She did not give up her whorings that she had practiced since Egypt; for in her youth men had lain with her and fondled her virgin bosom and poured out their lust upon her. ⁹Therefore I delivered her into the hands of her lovers, into the hands of the Assyrians, for whom she lusted. ¹⁰These uncovered her nakedness; they seized her sons and her daughters; and they killed her with the sword. Judgment was executed upon her, and she became a byword among women.

11 Her sister Ō·hol′i·bah saw this, yet she was more corrupt than she in her lusting and in her whorings, which were worse than those of her sister. ¹²She lusted after the Assyrians, governors and commanders, warriors[j] clothed in full armor, mounted horsemen, all of them handsome young men. ¹³And I saw that she was defiled; they both took the same way. ¹⁴But she carried her whorings further; she saw male figures carved on the wall, images of the Chal·dē′ans portrayed in vermilion, ¹⁵with belts around their waists, with flowing turbans on their heads, all of them looking like officers—a picture of Babylonians whose native land was Chal·dē′a. ¹⁶When she saw them she lusted after them, and sent messengers to them in Chal·dē′a. ¹⁷And the Babylonians came to her into the bed of love, and they defiled her with their lust; and after she defiled herself with them, she turned from them in disgust. ¹⁸When she carried on her whorings so openly and flaunted her nakedness, I turned in disgust from her, as I had turned from her sister. ¹⁹Yet she increased her whorings, remembering the days of her youth, when she played the whore in the land of Egypt ²⁰and lusted after her paramours there, whose members

---

[i] Gk: Heb *indignation.* ²⁵*A conspiracy of its prophets*
[j] Meaning of Heb uncertain

were like those of donkeys, and whose emission was like that of stallions. [21]Thus you longed for the lewdness of your youth, when the Egyptians[k] fondled your bosom and caressed[l] your young breasts.

22 Therefore, O Ō·hol´i·bah, thus says the Lord GOD: I will rouse against you your lovers from whom you turned in disgust, and I will bring them against you from every side: [23]the Babylonians and all the Chal·dē´ans, Pē´kod and Shō´a and Kō´a, and all the Assyrians with them, handsome young men, governors and commanders all of them, officers and warriors,[m] all of them riding on horses. [24]They shall come against you from the north[n] with chariots and wagons and a host of peoples; they shall set themselves against you on every side with buckler, shield, and helmet, and I will commit the judgment to them, and they shall judge you according to their ordinances. [25]I will direct my indignation against you, in order that they may deal with you in fury. They shall cut off your nose and your ears, and your survivors shall fall by the sword. They shall seize your sons and your daughters, and your survivors shall be devoured by fire. [26]They shall also strip you of your clothes and take away your fine jewels. [27]So I will put an end to your lewdness and your whoring brought from the land of Egypt; you shall not long for them, or remember Egypt any more. [28]For thus says the Lord GOD: I will deliver you into the hands of those whom you hate, into the hands of those from whom you turned in disgust; [29]and they shall deal with you in hatred, and take away all the fruit of your labor, and leave you naked and bare, and the nakedness of your whorings shall be exposed. Your lewdness and your whorings [30]have brought this upon you, because you played the whore with the nations, and polluted yourself with their idols. [31]You have gone the way of your sister; therefore I will give her cup into your hand. [32]Thus says the Lord GOD:

You shall drink your sister's cup,
    deep and wide;
you shall be scorned and derided,
    it holds so much.
[33] You shall be filled with drunkenness
    and sorrow.
A cup of horror and desolation
    is the cup of your sister Sa·mār´i·a;
[34] you shall drink it and drain it out,
    and gnaw its sherds,
    and tear out your breasts;

for I have spoken, says the Lord GOD. [35]Therefore thus says the Lord GOD: Because you have forgotten me and cast me behind your back, therefore bear the consequences of your lewdness and whorings.

36 The LORD said to me: Mortal, will you judge Ō·hō´lah and Ō·hol´i·bah? Then declare to them their abominable deeds. [37]For they have committed adultery, and blood is on their hands; with their idols they have committed adultery; and they have even offered up to them for food the children whom they had borne to me. [38]Moreover this they have done to me: they have defiled my sanctuary on the same day and profaned my sabbaths. [39]For when they had slaughtered their children for their idols, on the same day they came into my sanctuary to profane it. This is what they did in my house.

40 They even sent for men to come from far away, to whom a messenger was sent, and they came. For them you bathed yourself, painted your eyes, and decked yourself with ornaments; [41]you sat on a stately couch, with a table spread before it on which you had placed my incense and my oil. [42]The sound of a raucous multitude was around her, with many of the rabble brought in drunken from the wilderness; and they put bracelets on the arms[o] of the women, and beautiful crowns upon their heads.

[k] Two Mss: MT *from Egypt*   [l] Cn: Heb *for the sake of*   [m] Compare verses 6 and 12: Heb *officers and called ones*   [n] Gk: Meaning of Heb uncertain   [o] Heb *hands*

43 Then I said, Ah, she is worn out with adulteries, but they carry on their sexual acts with her. ⁴⁴For they have gone in to her, as one goes in to a whore. Thus they went in to Ō·hŏʹlah and to Ō·holʹi·bah, wanton women. ⁴⁵But righteous judges shall declare them guilty of adultery and of bloodshed; because they are adulteresses and blood is on their hands.

46 For thus says the Lord GOD: Bring up an assembly against them, and make them an object of terror and of plunder. ⁴⁷The assembly shall stone them and with their swords they shall cut them down; they shall kill their sons and their daughters, and burn up their houses. ⁴⁸Thus will I put an end to lewdness in the land, so that all women may take warning and not commit lewdness as you have done. ⁴⁹They shall repay you for your lewdness, and you shall bear the penalty for your sinful idolatry; and you shall know that I am the Lord GOD.

The Boiling Pot

24 In the ninth year, in the tenth month, on the tenth day of the month, the word of the LORD came to me: ²Mortal, write down the name of this day, this very day. The king of Babylon has laid siege to Jerusalem this very day. ³And utter an allegory to the rebellious house and say to them, Thus says the Lord GOD:

Set on the pot, set it on,
    pour in water also;
⁴ put in it the pieces,
    all the good pieces, the thigh and
        the shoulder;
    fill it with choice bones.
⁵ Take the choicest one of the flock,
    pile the logs^p under it;
boil its pieces,^q
    seethe^r also its bones in it.

6 Therefore thus says the Lord GOD:
Woe to the bloody city,
    the pot whose rust is in it,
    whose rust has not gone out of it!
Empty it piece by piece,
    making no choice at all.^s

⁷ For the blood she shed is inside it;
    she placed it on a bare rock;
she did not pour it out on the ground,
    to cover it with earth.
⁸ To rouse my wrath, to take vengeance,
    I have placed the blood she shed
        on a bare rock,
    so that it may not be covered.
⁹Therefore thus says the Lord GOD:
    Woe to the bloody city!
    I will even make the pile great.
¹⁰ Heap up the logs, kindle the fire;
    boil the meat well, mix in the
        spices,
    let the bones be burned.
¹¹ Stand it empty upon the coals,
    so that it may become hot, its
        copper glow,
    its filth melt in it, its rust be
        consumed.
¹² In vain I have wearied myself;^t
    its thick rust does not depart.
    To the fire with its rust!^u
¹³ Yet, when I cleansed you in your filthy
        lewdness,
    you did not become clean from
        your filth;
    you shall not again be cleansed
        until I have satisfied my fury upon
            you.
¹⁴I the LORD have spoken; the time is coming, I will act. I will not refrain, I will not spare, I will not relent. According to your ways and your doings I will judge you, says the Lord GOD.

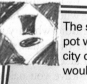

The story of the boiling pot was a sign that the city of Jerusalem soon would be destroyed.

Ezekiel's Bereavement

15 The word of the LORD came to me: ¹⁶Mortal, with one blow I am about to

---

^p Compare verse 10: Heb *the bones*   ^q Two Mss: Heb *its boilings*   ^r Cn: Heb *its bones seethe*   ^s Heb *piece, no lot has fallen on it*   ^t Cn: Meaning of Heb uncertain   ^u Meaning of Heb uncertain take away from you the delight of your eyes; yet you shall not mourn or weep, nor shall your tears run down. [17]Sigh, but not aloud; make no mourning for the dead. Bind on your turban, and put your sandals on your feet; do not cover your upper lip or eat the bread of mourners.[v] [18]So I spoke to the people in the morning, and at evening my wife died. And on the next morning I did as I was commanded.

19 Then the people said to me, "Will you not tell us what these things mean for us, that you are acting this way?" [20]Then I said to them: The word of the LORD came to me: [21]Say to the house of Israel, Thus says the Lord GOD: I will profane my sanctuary, the pride of your power, the delight of your eyes, and your heart's desire; and your sons and your daughters whom you left behind shall fall by the sword. [22]And you shall do as I have done; you shall not cover your upper lip or eat the bread of mourners.[v] [23]Your turbans shall be on your heads and your sandals on your feet; you shall not mourn or weep, but you shall pine away in your iniquities and groan to one another. [24]Thus E·zek´i·el shall be a sign to you; you shall do just as he has done. When this comes, then you shall know that I am the Lord GOD.

25 And you, mortal, on the day when I take from them their stronghold, their joy and glory, the delight of their eyes and their heart's affection, and also[w] their sons and their daughters, [26]on that day, one who has escaped will come to you to report to you the news. [27]On that day your mouth shall be opened to the one who has escaped, and you shall speak and no longer be silent. So you shall be a sign to them; and they shall know that I am the LORD.

Proclamation against Ammon

25 The word of the LORD came to me: [2]Mortal, set your face toward the Am´mon·ites and prophesy against them. [3]Say to the Am´mon·ites, Hear the word of the Lord GOD: Thus says the Lord GOD, Because you said, "Aha!"

over my sanctuary when it was profaned, and over the land of Israel when it was made desolate, and over the house of Judah when it went into exile; [4]therefore I am handing you over to the people of the East for a possession. They shall set their encampments among you and pitch their tents in your midst; they shall eat your fruit, and they shall drink your milk. [5]I will make Rab´bah a pasture for camels and Am´mon a fold for flocks. Then you shall know that I am the LORD. [6]For thus says the Lord GOD: Because you have clapped your hands and stamped your feet and rejoiced with all the malice within you against the land of Israel, [7]therefore I have stretched out my hand against you, and will hand you over as plunder to the nations. I will cut you off from the peoples and will make you perish out of the countries; I will destroy you. Then you shall know that I am the LORD.

Proclamation against Moab

8 Thus says the Lord GOD: Because Mō´ab[x] said, The house of Judah is like all the other nations, [9]therefore I will lay open the flank of Mō´ab from the towns[y] on its frontier, the glory of the country, Beth-jesh´i·moth, Bā´al-mē´on, and Kir·i·a·thā´-im. [10]I will give it along with Am´mon to the people of the East as a possession. Thus Am´mon shall be remembered no more among the nations, [11]and I will execute judgments upon Mō´ab. Then they shall know that I am the LORD.

Proclamation against Edom

12 Thus says the Lord GOD: Because Ē´dom acted revengefully against the house of Judah and has grievously offended in taking vengeance upon them, [13]therefore thus says the Lord GOD, I will stretch out my hand against Ē´dom, and cut off from it humans and animals, and I will make it desolate; from Tē´man even to Dē´dan they shall fall by the sword. [14]I will

v Vg Tg: Heb *of men*   w Heb lacks *and also*   x Gk Old Latin: Heb *Moab and Seir*   y Heb *towns from its towns* lay my vengeance upon Ē·dom by the hand of my people Israel; and they shall act in Ē·dom according to my anger and according to my wrath; and they shall know my vengeance, says the Lord GOD.

Proclamation against Philistia

15 Thus says the Lord GOD: Because with unending hostilities the Phi·lis´tines acted in vengeance, and with malice of heart took revenge in destruction; [16]therefore thus says the Lord GOD, I will stretch out my hand against the Phi·lis´tines, cut off the Cher´e·thītes, and destroy the rest of the seacoast. [17]I will execute great vengeance on them with wrathful punishments. Then they shall know that I am the LORD, when I lay my vengeance on them.

Proclamation against Tyre

26 In the eleventh year, on the first day of the month, the word of the LORD came to me: [2]Mortal, because Tyre said concerning Jerusalem,
"Aha, broken is the gateway of the peoples;
    it has swung open to me;
I shall be replenished,
    now that it is wasted,"
[3]therefore, thus says the Lord GOD:
See, I am against you, O Tyre!
    I will hurl many nations against you,
        as the sea hurls its waves.
[4] They shall destroy the walls of Tyre
    and break down its towers.
I will scrape its soil from it
    and make it a bare rock.
[5] It shall become, in the midst of the sea,
    a place for spreading nets.
I have spoken, says the Lord GOD.
    It shall become plunder for the nations,
[6]   and its daughter-towns in the country
        shall be killed by the sword.
Then they shall know that I am the LORD.
    7 For thus says the Lord GOD: I will bring against Tyre from the north King

Ne·bū·chad·rez´zar of Babylon, king of kings, together with horses, chariots, cavalry, and a great and powerful army.
[8] Your daughter-towns in the country
    he shall put to the sword.
He shall set up a siege-wall against you,
    cast up a ramp against you,
    and raise a roof of shields against you.
[9] He shall direct the shock of his battering rams against your walls
    and break down your towers with his axes.
[10] His horses shall be so many
    that their dust shall cover you.
At the noise of cavalry, wheels, and chariots
    your very walls shall shake,
when he enters your gates
    like those entering a breached city.
[11] With the hoofs of his horses
    he shall trample all your streets.
He shall put your people to the sword,
    and your strong pillars shall fall to the ground.
[12] They will plunder your riches
    and loot your merchandise.
they shall break down your walls
    and destroy your fine houses.
Your stones and timber and soil
    they shall cast into the water.
[13] I will silence the music of your songs;
    the sound of your lyres shall be heard no more.
[14] I will make you a bare rock;
    you shall be a place for spreading nets.
You shall never again be rebuilt,
    for I the LORD have spoken,
    says the Lord GOD.

15 Thus says the Lord GOD to Tyre: Shall not the coastlands shake at the sound of your fall, when the wounded groan, when slaughter goes on within you? [16]Then all the princes of the sea shall step down from their thrones; they shall remove their robes and strip off their embroidered garments. They shall clothe

themselves with trembling, and shall sit on the ground; they shall tremble every moment, and be appalled at you. [17]And they shall raise a lamentation over you, and say to you:

How you have vanished[z] from the seas,
　O city renowned,
once mighty on the sea,
　you and your inhabitants,[a]
who imposed your[b] terror
　on all the mainland![c]
[18] Now the coastlands tremble
　on the day of your fall;
the coastlands by the sea
　are dismayed at your passing.

[19] For thus says the Lord GOD: When I make you a city laid waste, like cities that are not inhabited, when I bring up the deep over you, and the great waters cover you, [20]then I will thrust you down with those who descend into the Pit, to the people of long ago, and I will make you live in the world below, among primeval ruins, with those who go down to the Pit, so that you will not be inhabited or have a place[d] in the land of the living. [21]I will bring you to a dreadful end, and you shall be no more; though sought for, you will never be found again, says the Lord GOD.

Lamentation over Tyre

27 The word of the LORD came to me: [2]Now you, mortal, raise a lamentation over Tyre, [3]and say to Tyre, which sits at the entrance to the sea, merchant of the peoples on many coastlands, Thus says the Lord GOD:

O Tyre, you have said,
　"I am perfect in beauty."
[4] Your borders are in the heart of the
　　seas;
　your builders made perfect your
　　beauty.
[5] They made all your planks
　of fir trees from Sē´nir;
they took a cedar from Lebanon
　to make a mast for you.
[6] From oaks of Bā´shan
　they made your oars;
they made your deck of pines[e]

from the coasts of Cyprus,
　inlaid with ivory.
[7] Of fine embroidered linen from Egypt
　was your sail,
　serving as your ensign;
blue and purple from the coasts of
　E·li´shah
　was your awning.
[8] The inhabitants of Sī´don and Ar´vad
　were your rowers;
skilled men of Zē´mer[f] were within
　you,
　they were your pilots.
[9] The elders of Gē´bal and its artisans
　were within you,
　caulking your seams;
all the ships of the sea with their
　　mariners were within you,
　to barter for your wares.
[10] Par´as[g] and Lud and Put
　were in your army,
　your mighty warriors;
they hung shield and helmet in you;
　they gave you splendor.
[11] Men of Ar´vad and Hē´lech[h]
　were on your walls all around;
men of Gā´mad were at your
　　towers.
They hung their quivers all around
　　your walls;
　they made perfect your beauty.

[12] Tar´shish did business with you out of the abundance of your great wealth; silver, iron, tin, and lead they exchanged for your wares. [13]Jā´van, Tū´bal, and Mē´shech traded with you; they exchanged human beings and vessels of bronze for your merchandise. [14]Beth-tō·gar´mah exchanged for your wares horses, war horses, and mules. [15]The Rhō´di·ans[i] traded with you; many coastlands were your own special markets; they brought you in payment ivory tusks and ebony. [16]Ē´dom[j] did busi-

---

[z] Gk OL Aquila: Heb *have vanished, O inhabited one,*
[a] Heb *it and its inhabitants* 　[b] Heb *their* 　[c] Cn:
Heb *its inhabitants* 　[d] Gk: Heb *I will give beauty*
[e] Or *boxwood* 　[f] Cn Compare Gen 10.18: Heb
your skilled men, O Tyre 　[g] Or *Persia* 　[h] Or *and
your army* 　[i] Gk: Heb *The Dedanites* 　[j] Another
reading is *Aram*

ness with you because of your abundant goods; they exchanged for your wares turquoise, purple, embroidered work, fine linen, coral, and rubies. ¹⁷Judah and the land of Israel traded with you; they exchanged for your merchandise wheat from Min′nith, millet,ᵏ honey, oil, and balm. ¹⁸Damascus traded with you for your abundant goods—because of your great wealth of every kind—wine of Hel′bon, and white wool. ¹⁹Vĕ′dan and Jā′van from Ū′zalᵏ entered into trade for your wares; wrought iron, cassia, and sweet cane were bartered for your merchandise. ²⁰Dĕ′dan traded with you in saddlecloths for riding. ²¹Arabia and all the princes of Kĕ′dar were your favored dealers in lambs, rams, and goats; in these they did business with you. ²²The merchants of Shĕ′ba and Rā′a·mah traded with you; they exchanged for your wares the best of all kinds of spices, and all precious stones, and gold. ²³Har′an, Can′neh, Eden, the merchants of Shĕ′ba, As′shur, and Chil′mad traded with you. ²⁴These traded with you in choice garments, in clothes of blue and embroidered work, and in carpets of colored material, bound with cords and made secure; in these they traded with you.ˡ ²⁵The ships of Tar′shish traveled for you in your trade.

So you were filled and heavily laden
in the heart of the seas.

²⁶ Your rowers have brought you
into the high seas.
The east wind has wrecked you
in the heart of the seas.

²⁷ Your riches, your wares, your
merchandise,
your mariners and your pilots,
your caulkers, your dealers in
merchandise,
and all your warriors within you,
with all the company
that is with you,
sink into the heart of the seas
on the day of your ruin.

²⁸ At the sound of the cry of your pilots
the countryside shakes,

²⁹ and down from their ships
come all that handle the oar.
The mariners and all the pilots of the
sea
stand on the shore

³⁰ and wail aloud over you,
and cry bitterly.
They throw dust on their heads
and wallow in ashes;

³¹ they make themselves bald for you,
and put on sackcloth,
and they weep over you in bitterness
of soul,
with bitter mourning.

³² In their wailing they raise a
lamentation for you,
and lament over you:
"Who was ever destroyedᵐ like Tyre
in the midst of the sea?

³³ When your wares came from the seas,
you satisfied many peoples;
with your abundant wealth and
merchandise
you enriched the kings of the earth.

³⁴ Now you are wrecked by the seas,
in the depths of the waters;
your merchandise and all your crew
have sunk with you.

³⁵ All the inhabitants of the coastlands
are appalled at you;
and their kings are horribly afraid,
their faces are convulsed.

³⁶ The merchants among the peoples
hiss at you;
you have come to a dreadful end
and shall be no more forever."

Proclamation against the King of Tyre

28 The word of the LORD came to me: ²Mortal, say to the prince of Tyre, Thus says the Lord GOD:
Because your heart is proud
and you have said, "I am a god;
I sit in the seat of the gods,
in the heart of the seas,"
yet you are but a mortal, and no god,

ᵏ Meaning of Heb uncertain   ˡ Cn: Heb *in your market*   ᵐ Tg Vg: Heb *like silence*

though you compare your mind
with the mind of a god.
[3] You are indeed wiser than Daniel;[n]
no secret is hidden from you;
[4] by your wisdom and your
understanding
you have amassed wealth for
yourself,
and have gathered gold and silver
into your treasuries.
[5] By your great wisdom in trade
you have increased your wealth,
and your heart has become proud
in your wealth.
[6] Therefore thus says the Lord GOD:
Because you compare your mind
with the mind of a god,
[7] therefore, I will bring strangers against
you,
the most terrible of the nations;
they shall draw their swords against
the beauty of your wisdom
and defile your splendor.
[8] They shall thrust you down to the Pit,
and you shall die a violent death
in the heart of the seas.
[9] Will you still say, "I am a god,"
in the presence of those who kill you,
though you are but a mortal, and no
god,
in the hands of those who wound
you?
[10] You shall die the death of the
uncircumcised
by the hand of foreigners;
for I have spoken, says the Lord GOD.

Lamentation over the King of Tyre

11 Moreover the word of the LORD
came to me: [12]Mortal, raise a lamentation
over the king of Tyre, and say to him, Thus
says the Lord GOD:
You were the signet of perfection,[o]
full of wisdom and perfect in
beauty.
[13] You were in Eden, the garden of God;
every precious stone was your
covering,

carnelian, chrysolite, and moonstone,
beryl, onyx, and jasper,
sapphire,[p] turquoise, and emerald;
and worked in gold were your
settings
and your engravings.[o]

On the day that you were created
they were prepared.
[14] With an anointed cherub as guardian I
placed you;[o]
you were on the holy mountain of
God;
you walked among the stones of
fire.
[15] You were blameless in your ways
from the day that you were created,
until iniquity was found in you.
[16] In the abundance of your trade
you were filled with violence, and
you sinned;
so I cast you as a profane thing from
the mountain of God,
and the guardian cherub drove you
out
from among the stones of fire.
[17] Your heart was proud because of your
beauty;
you corrupted your wisdom for the
sake of your splendor.
I cast you to the ground;
I exposed you before kings,
to feast their eyes on you.
[18] By the multitude of your iniquities,
in the unrighteousness of your
trade,
you profaned your sanctuaries.
So I brought out fire from within you;
it consumed you,
and I turned you to ashes on the
earth
in the sight of all who saw you.
[19] All who know you among the peoples
are appalled at you;
you have come to a dreadful end
and shall be no more forever.

---

[n] Or, as otherwise read, *Danel*　　　[o] Meaning of Heb
uncertain　　[p] Or *lapis lazuli*

Proclamation against Sidon

20 The word of the LORD came to me: ²¹Mortal, set your face toward Sī′don, and prophesy against it, ²²and say, Thus says the Lord GOD:

I am against you, O Sī′don,
and I will gain glory in your
midst.
They shall know that I am the LORD
when I execute judgments in it,
and manifest my holiness in it;
23 for I will send pestilence into it,
and bloodshed into its streets;
and the dead shall fall in its midst,
by the sword that is against it on
every side.
And they shall know that I am the
LORD.

24 The house of Israel shall no longer find a pricking brier or a piercing thorn among all their neighbors who have treated them with contempt. And they shall know that I am the Lord GOD.

Ezekiel said that God would gather God's people out of the lands where they had been exiled and would bring them back together. God would restore the people, giving them hope for the future.

Future Blessing for Israel

25 Thus says the Lord GOD: When I gather the house of Israel from the peoples among whom they are scattered, and manifest my holiness in them in the sight of the nations, then they shall settle on their own soil that I gave to my servant Jacob. ²⁶They shall live in safety in it, and shall build houses and plant vineyards. They shall live in safety, when I execute judgments upon all their neighbors who have treated them with contempt. And they shall know that I am the LORD their God.

Proclamation against Egypt

29 In the tenth year, in the tenth month, on the twelfth day of the month, the word of the LORD came to me: ²Mortal, set your face against Pharaoh king of Egypt, and prophesy against him and against all Egypt; ³speak, and say, Thus says the Lord GOD:

I am against you,
Pharaoh king of Egypt,
the great dragon sprawling
in the midst of its channels,
saying, "My Nile is my own;
I made it for myself."
4 I will put hooks in your jaws,
and make the fish of your channels
stick to your scales.
I will draw you up from your
channels,
with all the fish of your channels
sticking to your scales.
5 I will fling you into the wilderness,
you and all the fish of your channels;
you shall fall in the open field,
and not be gathered and buried.
To the animals of the earth and to the
birds of the air
I have given you as food.
6 Then all the inhabitants of Egypt shall
know
that I am the LORD
because you^q were a staff of reed
to the house of Israel;
7 when they grasped you with the hand,
you broke,
and tore all their shoulders;
and when they leaned on you, you
broke,
and made all their legs unsteady.^r

8 Therefore, thus says the Lord GOD: I will bring a sword upon you, and will cut off from you human being and animal; ⁹and the land of Egypt shall be a desolation and a waste. Then they shall know that I am the LORD.

Because you^s said, "The Nile is mine, and I made it," ¹⁰therefore, I am against you, and against your channels, and I will make the land of Egypt an utter waste and desolation, from Mig′dōl to Sȳ·ē′nē, as far

^q Gk Syr Vg: Heb *they*   ^r Syr: Heb *stand*   ^s Gk Syr Vg: Heb *he* as the border of Ethiopia.[t] [11]No human foot shall pass through it, and no animal foot shall pass through it; it shall be uninhabited forty years. [12]I will make the land of Egypt a desolation among desolated countries; and her cities shall be a desolation forty years among cities that are laid waste. I will scatter the Egyptians among the nations, and disperse them among the countries.

13 Further, thus says the Lord GOD: At the end of forty years I will gather the Egyptians from the peoples among whom they were scattered; [14]and I will restore the fortunes of Egypt, and bring them back to the land of Path′ros, the land of their origin; and there they shall be a lowly kingdom. [15]It shall be the most lowly of the kingdoms, and never again exalt itself above the nations; and I will make them so small that they will never again rule over the nations. [16]The Egyptians[u] shall never again be the reliance of the house of Israel; they will recall their iniquity, when they turned to them for aid. Then they shall know that I am the Lord GOD.

Babylonia Will Plunder Egypt

17 In the twenty-seventh year, in the first month, on the first day of the month, the word of the LORD came to me: [18]Mortal, King Ne·bū·chad·rez′zar of Babylon made his army labor hard against Tyre; every head was made bald and every shoulder was rubbed bare; yet neither he nor his army got anything from Tyre to pay for the labor that he had expended against it. [19]Therefore thus says the Lord GOD: I will give the land of Egypt to King Ne·bū·chad·rez′zar of Babylon; and he shall carry off its wealth and despoil it and plunder it; and it shall be the wages for his army. [20]I have given him the land of Egypt as his payment for which he labored, because they worked for me, says the Lord GOD.

21 On that day I will cause a horn to sprout up for the house of Israel, and I will open your lips among them. Then they shall know that I am the LORD.

Lamentation for Egypt

30 The word of the LORD came to me: [2]Mortal, prophesy, and say, Thus says the Lord GOD:
Wail, "Alas for the day!"
3   For a day is near,
        the day of the LORD is near;
    it will be a day of clouds,
        a time of doom[v] for the nations.
[4] A sword shall come upon Egypt,
        and anguish shall be in Ethiopia,[u]
    when the slain fall in Egypt,
        and its wealth is carried away,
        and its foundations are torn down.
[5]Ethiopia,[u] and Put, and Lud, and all Arabia, and Lib′ya,[w] and the people of the allied land[x] shall fall with them by the sword.

[6] Thus says the LORD:
    Those who support Egypt shall fall,
        and its proud might shall come
            down;
    from Mig′dōl to Sy̅·e̅′ne̅
        they shall fall within it by the
            sword,
    says the Lord GOD.
[7] They shall be desolated among other
            desolated countries,
        and their cities shall lie among cities
            laid waste.
[8] Then they shall know that I am the
            LORD,
    when I have set fire to Egypt,
        and all who help it are broken.

9 On that day, messengers shall go out from me in ships to terrify the unsuspecting Ethiopians;[y] and anguish shall come upon them on the day of Egypt's doom;[z] for it is coming!

10 Thus says the Lord GOD:
    I will put an end to the hordes of
            Egypt,
        by the hand of King Ne·bū·
            chad·rez′zar of Babylon.

[t] Or *Nubia*; Heb *Cush*   [u] Heb *It*   [v] Heb lacks *of doom*   [w] Compare Gk Syr Vg: Heb *Cub*   [x] Meaning of Heb uncertain   [y] Or *Nubians*; Heb *Cush*   [z] Heb *the day of Egypt*

11 He and his people with him, the most
  terrible of the nations,
    shall be brought in to destroy the
      land;
  and they shall draw their swords
      against Egypt,
  and fill the land with the slain.
12 I will dry up the channels,
    and will sell the land into the hand
      of evildoers;
  I will bring desolation upon the land
      and everything in it
    by the hand of foreigners;
  I the LORD have spoken.

13 Thus says the Lord GOD:
  I will destroy the idols
    and put an end to the images in
      Memphis;
  there shall no longer be a prince in the
      land of Egypt;
    so I will put fear in the land of
      Egypt.
14 I will make Path´ros a desolation,
    and will set fire to Zō´an,
    and will execute acts of judgment
      on Thēbes.
15 I will pour my wrath upon Pe·lū´-
      si·um,
    the stronghold of Egypt,
    and cut off the hordes of Thēbes.
16 I will set fire to Egypt;
  Pe·lū´si·um shall be in great agony;
  Thēbes shall be breached,
    and Memphis face adversaries by day.
17 The young men of On and of Pī-bē´-
      seth shall fall by the sword;
    and the cities themselves[a] shall go
      into captivity.
18 At Tehaph´ne·hēs the day shall be
      dark,
    when I break there the dominion of
      Egypt,
  and its proud might shall come to an
      end;
    the city[b] shall be covered by a
      cloud,
    and its daughter-towns shall go into
      captivity.

19 Thus I will execute acts of judgment
      on Egypt.
  Then they shall know that I am the
    LORD.

Proclamation against Pharaoh

20 In the eleventh year, in the first
month, on the seventh day of the month,
the word of the LORD came to me:
21Mortal, I have broken the arm of Pharaoh
king of Egypt; it has not been bound up for
healing or wrapped with a bandage, so
that it may become strong to wield the
sword. 22Therefore thus says the Lord
GOD: I am against Pharaoh king of Egypt,
and will break his arms, both the strong
arm and the one that was broken; and I
will make the sword fall from his hand. 23I
will scatter the Egyptians among the
nations, and disperse them throughout the
lands. 24I will strengthen the arms of the
king of Babylon, and put my sword in his
hand; but I will break the arms of Pharaoh,
and he will groan before him with the
groans of one mortally wounded. 25I will
strengthen the arms of the king of Babylon,
but the arms of Pharaoh shall fall. And
they shall know that I am the LORD, when
I put my sword into the hand of the king
of Babylon. He shall stretch it out against
the land of Egypt, 26and I will scatter the
Egyptians among the nations and disperse
them throughout the countries. Then they
shall know that I am the LORD.

The Lofty Cedar

31 In the eleventh year, in the third
month, on the first day of the
month, the word of the LORD came to me:
2Mortal, say to Pharaoh king of Egypt and
to his hordes:

  Whom are you like in your greatness?
3   Consider Assyria, a cedar of
      Lebanon,
    with fair branches and forest shade,
      and of great height,
    its top among the clouds.[c]

---

[a] Heb and they   [b] Heb she   [c] Gk: Heb thick boughs

⁴ The waters nourished it,
the deep made it grow tall,
making its rivers flow[d]
around the place it was planted,
sending forth its streams
to all the trees of the field.
⁵ So it towered high
above all the trees of the field;
its boughs grew large
and its branches long,
from abundant water in its shoots.
⁶ All the birds of the air
made their nests in its boughs;
under its branches all the animals of
the field
gave birth to their young;
and in its shade
all great nations lived.
⁷ It was beautiful in its greatness,
in the length of its branches;
for its roots went down
to abundant water.
⁸ The cedars in the garden of God could
not rival it,
nor the fir trees equal its boughs;
the plane trees were as nothing
compared with its branches;
no tree in the garden of God
was like it in beauty.
⁹ I made it beautiful
with its mass of branches,
the envy of all the trees of Eden
that were in the garden of God.

10 Therefore thus says the Lord GOD:
Because it[e] towered high and set its top
among the clouds,[f] and its heart was proud
of its height, ¹¹I gave it into the hand of the
prince of the nations; he has dealt with it
as its wickedness deserves. I have cast it
out. ¹²Foreigners from the most terrible of
the nations have cut it down and left it. On
the mountains and in all the valleys its

branches have fallen, and its boughs lie
broken in all the watercourses of the land;
and all the peoples of the earth went away
from its shade and left it. ¹³ On its fallen trunk settle
all the birds of the air,
and among its boughs lodge
all the wild animals.

¹⁴All this is in order that no trees by the
waters may grow to lofty height or set
their tops among the clouds,[f] and that no
trees that drink water may reach up to
them in height.
For all of them are handed over to
death,
to the world below;
along with all mortals,
with those who go down to the Pit.

15 Thus says the Lord GOD: On the
day it went down to Shēˊōl I closed the
deep over it and covered it; I restrained its
rivers, and its mighty waters were
checked. I clothed Lebanon in gloom for
it, and all the trees of the field fainted
because of it. ¹⁶I made the nations quake
at the sound of its fall, when I cast it down
to Shēˊōl with those who go down to the
Pit; and all the trees of Eden, the choice
and best of Lebanon, all that were well
watered, were consoled in the world
below. ¹⁷They also went down to Shēˊōl
with it, to those killed by the sword, along
with its allies,[g] those who lived in its shade
among the nations.

18 Which among the trees of Eden was
like you in glory and in greatness? Now
you shall be brought down with the trees
of Eden to the world below; you shall lie
among the uncircumcised, with those who
are killed by the sword. This is Pharaoh
and all his horde, says the Lord GOD.

Lamentation over Pharaoh and Egypt

32 In the twelfth year, in the twelfth
month, on the first day of the
month, the word of the LORD came to me:

The plane tree is a tall
tree with smooth bark,
wide branches, glossy
leaves, and spiky seed-
pods.

[d] Gk: Heb *rivers going*   [e] Syr Vg: Heb *you*   [f] Gk:
Heb *thick boughs*   [g] Heb *its arms*

²Mortal, raise a lamentation over Pharaoh king of Egypt, and say to him:

You consider yourself a lion among
the nations,
but you are like a dragon in the
seas;
you thrash about in your streams,
trouble the water with your feet,
and foul your*ʰ* streams.
³ Thus says the Lord GOD:
In an assembly of many peoples
I will throw my net over you;
and I*ⁱ* will haul you up in my
dragnet.
⁴ I will throw you on the ground,
on the open field I will fling you,
and will cause all the birds of the air
to settle on you,
and I will let the wild animals of the
whole earth gorge themselves
with you.
⁵ I will strew your flesh on the
mountains,
and fill the valleys with your
carcass.*ʲ*
⁶ I will drench the land with your
flowing blood
up to the mountains,
and the watercourses will be filled
with you.
⁷ When I blot you out, I will cover the
heavens,
and make their stars dark;
I will cover the sun with a cloud,
and the moon shall not give its
light.
⁸ All the shining lights of the heavens
I will darken above you,
and put darkness on your land,
says the Lord GOD.
⁹ I will trouble the hearts of many
peoples,
as I carry you captive*ᵏ* among the
nations,
into countries you have not known.
¹⁰ I will make many peoples appalled at
you;
their kings shall shudder because of
you.

When I brandish my sword before
them,
they shall tremble every moment
for their lives, each one of them,
on the day of your downfall.
¹¹ For thus says the Lord GOD:
The sword of the king of Babylon shall
come against you.
¹² I will cause your hordes to fall
by the swords of mighty ones,
all of them most terrible among the
nations.
They shall bring to ruin the pride of
Egypt,
and all its hordes shall perish.
¹³ I will destroy all its livestock
from beside abundant waters;
and no human foot shall trouble them
any more,
nor shall the hoofs of cattle trouble
them.
¹⁴ Then I will make their waters clear,
and cause their streams to run like
oil, says the Lord GOD.
¹⁵ When I make the land of Egypt
desolate
and when the land is stripped of all
that fills it,
when I strike down all who live
in it,
then they shall know that I am the
LORD.
¹⁶ This is a lamentation; it shall be
chanted.
The women of the nations shall
chant it.
Over Egypt and all its hordes they
shall chant it,
says the Lord GOD.

Dirge over Egypt

17 In the twelfth year, in the first month,*ˡ* on the fifteenth day of the month, the word of the LORD came to me: ¹⁸ Mortal, wail over the hordes of Egypt, and send them down,

---

ʰ Heb *their*   *ⁱ* Gk Vg: Heb *they*   *ʲ* Symmachus Syr Vg: Heb *your height*   *ᵏ* Gk: Heb *bring your destruction*   *ˡ* Gk: Heb lacks *in the first month*

with Egypt*[m]* and the daughters of
   majestic nations,
   to the world below,
   with those who go down to the Pit.
19 "Whom do you surpass in beauty?
   Go down! Be laid to rest with the
   uncircumcised!"

20They shall fall among those who are
killed by the sword. Egypt*[n]* has been
handed over to the sword; carry away
both it and its hordes. 21The mighty chiefs
shall speak of them, with their helpers,
out of the midst of She᷄·ōl: "They have
come down, they lie still, the uncircumcised, killed by the sword."

22 Assyria is there, and all its company,
their graves all around it, all of them
killed, fallen by the sword. 23Their graves
are set in the uttermost parts of the Pit. Its
company is all around its grave, all of
them killed, fallen by the sword, who
spread terror in the land of the living.

24 Ē᷄lam is there, and all its hordes
around its grave; all of them killed, fallen
by the sword, who went down uncircumcised into the world below, who spread
terror in the land of the living. They bear
their shame with those who go down to
the Pit. 25They have made Ē᷄lam*[m]* a bed
among the slain with all its hordes, their
graves all around it, all of them uncircumcised, killed by the sword; for terror of
them was spread in the land of the living,
and they bear their shame with those who
go down to the Pit; they are placed among
the slain.

26 Mē᷄shech and Tū᷄bal are there, and
all their multitude, their graves all around
them, all of them uncircumcised, killed by
the sword; for they spread terror in the
land of the living. 27And they do not lie
with the fallen warriors of long ago*[o]* who
went down to She᷄·ōl with their weapons of
war, whose swords were laid under their
heads, and whose shields*[p]* are upon their
bones; for the terror of the warriors was in
the land of the living. 28So you shall be
broken and lie among the uncircumcised,
with those who are killed by the sword.

29 Ē᷄dom is there, its kings and all its
princes, who for all their might are laid
with those who are killed by the sword;
they lie with the uncircumcised, with
those who go down to the Pit.

30 The princes of the north are there,
all of them, and all the Sī·dō᷄ni·ans, who
have gone down in shame with the slain,
for all the terror that they caused by their
might; they lie uncircumcised with those
who are killed by the sword, and bear
their shame with those who go down to
the Pit.

31 When Pharaoh sees them, he will
be consoled for all his hordes—Pharaoh
and all his army, killed by the sword, says
the Lord GOD. 32For he*[q]* spread terror in
the land of the living; therefore he shall be
laid to rest among the uncircumcised,
with those who are slain by the sword—
Pharaoh and all his multitude, says the
Lord GOD.

Ezekiel Israel's Sentry

33 The word of the LORD came to
me: 2O Mortal, speak to your
people and say to them,
If I bring the sword upon a land, and
the people of the land take one of their
number as their sentinel; 3and if the sentinel sees the sword coming upon the
land and blows the trumpet and warns
the people; 4then if any who hear the
sound of the trumpet do not take warning, and the sword comes and takes them
away, their blood shall be upon their own
heads. 5They heard the sound of the
trumpet and did not take warning; their
blood shall be upon themselves. But if
they had taken warning, they would have
saved their lives. 6But if the sentinel sees
the sword coming and does not blow the
trumpet, so that the people are not
warned, and the sword comes and takes
any of them, they are taken away in their
iniquity, but their blood I will require at
the sentinel's hand.

[m] Heb *it*   *[n]* Heb *It*   *[o]* Gk Old Latin: Heb *of the uncircumcised*   *[p]* Cn: Heb *iniquities*   *[q]* Cn: Heb *I*

7 So you, mortal, I have made a sentinel for the house of Israel; whenever you hear a word from my mouth, you shall give them warning from me. [8]If I say to the wicked, "O wicked ones, you shall surely die," and you do not speak to warn the wicked to turn from their ways, the wicked shall die in their iniquity, but their blood I will require at your hand. [9]But if you warn the wicked to turn from their ways, and they do not turn from their ways, the wicked shall die in their iniquity, but you will have saved your life.

God's Justice and Mercy

10 Now you, mortal, say to the house of Israel, Thus you have said: "Our transgressions and our sins weigh upon us, and we waste away because of them; how then can we live?" [11]Say to them, As I live, says the Lord God, I have no pleasure in the death of the wicked, but that the wicked turn from their ways and live; turn back, turn back from your evil ways; for why will you die, O house of Israel? [12]And you, mortal, say to your people, The righteousness of the righteous shall not save them when they transgress; and as for the wickedness of the wicked, it shall not make them stumble when they turn from their wickedness; and the righteous shall not be able to live by their righteousness[r] when they sin. [13]Though I say to the righteous that they shall surely live, yet if they trust in their righteousness and commit iniquity, none of their righteous deeds shall be remembered; but in the iniquity that they have committed they shall die. [14]Again, though I say to the wicked, "You shall surely die," yet if they turn from their sin and do what is lawful and right— [15]if the wicked restore the pledge, give back what they have taken by robbery, and walk in the statutes of life, committing no iniquity—they shall surely live, they shall not die. [16]None of the sins that they have committed shall be remembered against them; they have done what is lawful and right, they shall surely live.

17 Yet your people say, "The way of the Lord is not just," when it is their own way that is not just. [18]When the righteous turn from their righteousness, and commit iniquity, they shall die for it.[s] [19]And when the wicked turn from their wickedness, and do what is lawful and right, they shall live by it.[s] [20]Yet you say, "The way of the Lord is not just." O house of Israel, I will judge all of you according to your ways!

The Babylonians took control of the city of Jerusalem in 586 BC. They burned the Temple and sent the Jewish people into exile away from their land.

The Fall of Jerusalem

21 In the twelfth year of our exile, in the tenth month, on the fifth day of the month, someone who had escaped from Jerusalem came to me and said, "The city has fallen." [22]Now the hand of the Lord had been upon me the evening before the fugitive came; but he had opened my mouth by the time the fugitive came to me in the morning; so my mouth was opened, and I was no longer unable to speak.

The Survivors in Judah

23 The word of the Lord came to me: [24]Mortal, the inhabitants of these waste places in the land of Israel keep saying, "Abraham was only one man, yet he got possession of the land; but we are many; the land is surely given us to possess." [25]Therefore say to them, Thus says the Lord God: You eat flesh with the blood, and lift up your eyes to your idols, and shed blood; shall you then possess the land? [26]You depend on your swords, you commit abominations, and each of you defiles his neighbor's wife; shall you then possess the land? [27]Say this to them, Thus

[r] Heb *by it*   [s] Heb *them*

says the Lord GOD: As I live, surely those who are in the waste places shall fall by the sword; and those who are in the open field I will give to the wild animals to be devoured; and those who are in strongholds and in caves shall die by pestilence. [28]I will make the land a desolation and a waste, and its proud might shall come to an end; and the mountains of Israel shall be so desolate that no one will pass through. [29]Then they shall know that I am the LORD, when I have made the land a desolation and a waste because of all their abominations that they have committed.

30 As for you, mortal, your people who talk together about you by the walls, and at the doors of the houses, say to one another, each to a neighbor, "Come and hear what the word is that comes from the LORD." [31]They come to you as people come, and they sit before you as my people, and they hear your words, but they will not obey them. For flattery is on their lips, but their heart is set on their gain. [32]To them you are like a singer of love songs,[t] one who has a beautiful voice and plays well on an instrument; they hear what you say, but they will not do it. [33]When this comes—and come it will!—then they shall know that a prophet has been among them.

> "I myself will search for my sheep, and will seek them out. As shepherds seek out their flocks when they are among their scattered sheep, so I will seek out my sheep. I will rescue them from all the places to which they have been scattered...I myself will be the shepherd of my sheep, and I will make them lie down, says the LORD GOD. I will seek the lost, and I will bring back the strayed, and I will bind up the injured, and I will strengthen the weak."
> Ezekiel 34:11–12, 15–16

Israel's False Shepherds

34 The word of the LORD came to me: [2]Mortal, prophesy against the shepherds of Israel: prophesy, and say to them—to the shepherds: Thus says the Lord GOD: Ah, you shepherds of Israel who have been feeding yourselves! Should not shepherds feed the sheep? [3]You eat the fat, you clothe yourselves with the wool, you slaughter the fatlings; but you do not feed the sheep. [4]You have not strengthened the weak, you have not healed the sick, you have not bound up the injured, you have not brought back the strayed, you have not sought the lost, but with force and harshness you have ruled them. [5]So they were scattered, because there was no shepherd; and scattered, they became food for all the wild animals. [6]My sheep were scattered, they wandered over all the mountains and on every high hill; my sheep were scattered over all the face of the earth, with no one to search or seek for them.

7 Therefore, you shepherds, hear the word of the LORD: [8]As I live, says the Lord GOD, because my sheep have become a prey, and my sheep have become food for all the wild animals, since there was no shepherd; and because my shepherds have not searched for my sheep, but the shepherds have fed themselves, and have not fed my sheep; [9]therefore, you shepherds, hear the word of the LORD: [10]Thus says the Lord GOD, I am against the shepherds; and I will demand my sheep at their hand, and put a stop to their feeding the sheep; no longer shall the shepherds feed themselves. I will rescue my sheep from their mouths, so that they may not be food for them.

God, the True Shepherd

11 For thus says the Lord GOD: I myself will search for my sheep, and will seek them out. [12]As shepherds seek out their flocks when they are among their scattered sheep, so I will seek out my

---

[t] Cn: Heb *like a love song*

sheep. I will rescue them from all the places to which they have been scattered on a day of clouds and thick darkness. ¹³I will bring them out from the peoples and gather them from the countries, and will bring them into their own land; and I will feed them on the mountains of Israel, by the watercourses, and in all the inhabited parts of the land. ¹⁴I will feed them with good pasture, and the mountain heights of Israel shall be their pasture; there they shall lie down in good grazing land, and they shall feed on rich pasture on the mountains of Israel. ¹⁵I myself will be the shepherd of my sheep, and I will make them lie down, says the Lord GOD. ¹⁶I will seek the lost, and I will bring back the strayed, and I will bind up the injured, and I will strengthen the weak, but the fat and the strong I will destroy. I will feed them with justice.

17 As for you, my flock, thus says the Lord GOD: I shall judge between sheep and sheep, between rams and goats: ¹⁸Is it not enough for you to feed on the good pasture, but you must tread down with your feet the rest of your pasture? When you drink of clear water, must you foul the rest with your feet? ¹⁹And must my sheep eat what you have trodden with your feet, and drink what you have fouled with your feet?

20 Therefore, thus says the Lord GOD to them: I myself will judge between the fat sheep and the lean sheep. ²¹Because you pushed with flank and shoulder, and butted at all the weak animals with your horns until you scattered them far and wide, ²²I will save my flock, and they shall no longer be ravaged; and I will judge between sheep and sheep.

23 I will set up over them one shepherd, my servant David, and he shall feed them: he shall feed them and be their shepherd. ²⁴And I, the LORD, will be their God, and my servant David shall be prince among them; I, the LORD, have spoken.

25 I will make with them a covenant of peace and banish wild animals from the

> "I will make them and the region around my hill a blessing; and I will send down the showers in their season; they shall be showers of blessing. The trees of the field shall yield their fruit, and the earth shall yield its increase."
>
> Ezekiel 34:26–27

land, so that they may live in the wild and sleep in the woods securely. ²⁶I will make them and the region around my hill a blessing; and I will send down the showers in their season; they shall be showers of blessing. ²⁷The trees of the field shall yield their fruit, and the earth shall yield its increase. They shall be secure on their soil; and they shall know that I am the LORD, when I break the bars of their yoke, and save them from the hands of those who enslaved them. ²⁸They shall no more be plunder for the nations, nor shall the animals of the land devour them; they shall live in safety, and no one shall make them afraid. ²⁹I will provide for them a splendid vegetation so that they shall no more be consumed with hunger in the land, and no longer suffer the insults of the nations. ³⁰They shall know that I, the LORD their God, am with them, and that they, the house of Israel, are my people, says the Lord GOD. ³¹You are my sheep, the sheep of my pasture[u] and I am your God, says the Lord GOD.

Judgment on Mount Seir

35 The word of the LORD came to me: ²Mortal, set your face against Mount Sēʾir, and prophesy against it, ³and say to it, Thus says the Lord GOD:
I am against you, Mount Sēʾir;
   I stretch out my hand against you
   to make you a desolation and a
      waste.
⁴ I lay your towns in ruins;
   you shall become a desolation,
   and you shall know that I am the
      LORD.

[u] Gk OL: Heb *pasture, you are people*

⁵Because you cherished an ancient enmity, and gave over the people of Israel to the power of the sword at the time of their calamity, at the time of their final punishment; ⁶therefore, as I live, says the Lord GOD, I will prepare you for blood, and blood shall pursue you; since you did not hate bloodshed, bloodshed shall pursue you. ⁷I will make Mount Se͞ir a waste and a desolation; and I will cut off from it all who come and go. ⁸I will fill its mountains with the slain; on your hills and in your valleys and in all your watercourses those killed with the sword shall fall. ⁹I will make you a perpetual desolation, and your cities shall never be inhabited. Then you shall know that I am the LORD.

10 Because you said, "These two nations and these two countries shall be mine, and we will take possession of them,"—although the LORD was there— ¹¹therefore, as I live, says the Lord GOD, I will deal with you according to the anger and envy that you showed because of your hatred against them; and I will make myself known among you,ᵛ when I judge you. ¹²You shall know that I, the LORD, have heard all the abusive speech that you uttered against the mountains of Israel, saying, "They are laid desolate, they are given us to devour." ¹³And you magnified yourselves against me with your mouth, and multiplied your words against me; I heard it. ¹⁴Thus says the Lord GOD: As the whole earth rejoices, I will make you desolate. ¹⁵As you rejoiced over the inheritance of the house of Israel, because it was desolate, so I will deal with you; you shall be desolate, Mount Se͞ir, and all E͞dom, all of it. Then they shall know that I am the LORD.

Blessing on Israel

36 And you, mortal, prophesy to the mountains of Israel, and say: O mountains of Israel, hear the word of the LORD. ²Thus says the Lord GOD: Because the enemy said of you, "Aha!" and, "The ancient heights have become our possession," ³therefore prophesy, and say: Thus

says the Lord GOD: Because they made you desolate indeed, and crushed you from all sides, so that you became the possession of the rest of the nations, and you became an object of gossip and slander among the people; ⁴therefore, O mountains of Israel, hear the word of the Lord GOD: Thus says the Lord GOD to the mountains and the hills, the watercourses and the valleys, the desolate wastes and the deserted towns, which have become a source of plunder and an object of derision to the rest of the nations all around; ⁵therefore thus says the Lord GOD: I am speaking in my hot jealousy against the rest of the nations, and against all E͞dom, who, with wholehearted joy and utter contempt, took my land as their possession, because of its pasture, to plunder it. ⁶Therefore prophesy concerning the land of Israel, and say to the mountains and hills, to the watercourses and valleys, Thus says the Lord GOD: I am speaking in my jealous wrath, because you have suffered the insults of the nations; ⁷therefore thus says the Lord GOD: I swear that the nations that are all around you shall themselves suffer insults.

8 But you, O mountains of Israel, shall shoot out your branches, and yield your fruit to my people Israel; for they shall soon come home. ⁹See now, I am for you; I will turn to you, and you shall be tilled and sown; ¹⁰and I will multiply your population, the whole house of Israel, all of it; the towns shall be inhabited and the waste places rebuilt; ¹¹and I will multiply human beings and animals upon you. They shall increase and be fruitful; and I will cause you to be inhabited as in your former times, and will do more good to you than ever before. Then you shall know that I am the LORD. ¹²I will lead people upon you—my people Israel—and they shall possess you, and you shall be their inheritance. No longer shall you bereave them of children.

13 Thus says the Lord GOD: Because they say to you, "You devour people, and

ᵛ Gk: Heb *them*

you bereave your nation of children," [14]therefore you shall no longer devour people and no longer bereave your nation of children, says the Lord GOD; [15]and no longer will I let you hear the insults of the nations, no longer shall you bear the disgrace of the peoples; and no longer shall you cause your nation to stumble, says the Lord GOD.

The Renewal of Israel

16 The word of the LORD came to me: [17]Mortal, when the house of Israel lived on their own soil, they defiled it with their ways and their deeds; their conduct in my sight was like the uncleanness of a woman in her menstrual period. [18]So I poured out my wrath upon them for the blood that they had shed upon the land, and for the idols with which they had defiled it. [19]I scattered them among the nations, and they were dispersed through the countries; in accordance with their conduct and their deeds I judged them. [20]But when they came to the nations, wherever they came, they profaned my holy name, in that it was said of them, "These are the people of the LORD, and yet they had to go out of his land." [21]But I had concern for my holy name, which the house of Israel had profaned among the nations to which they came.

22 Therefore say to the house of Israel, Thus says the Lord GOD: It is not for your sake, O house of Israel, that I am about to act, but for the sake of my holy name, which you have profaned among the nations to which you came. [23]I will sanctify my great name, which has been profaned among the nations, and which you have profaned among them; and the nations shall know that I am the LORD, says the Lord GOD, when through you I display my holiness before their eyes. [24]I will take you from the nations, and gather you from all the countries, and bring you into your own land. [25]I will sprinkle clean water upon you, and you shall be clean from all your uncleannesses, and from all your idols I will cleanse you. [26]A new

heart I will give you, and a new spirit I will put within you; and I will remove from your body the heart of stone and give you a heart of flesh. [27]I will put my spirit within you, and make you follow my statutes and be careful to observe my ordinances. [28]Then you shall live in the land that I gave to your ancestors; and you shall be my people, and I will be your God. [29]I will save you from all your uncleannesses, and I will summon the grain and make it abundant and lay no famine upon you. [30]I will make the fruit of the tree and the produce of the field abundant, so that you may never again suffer the disgrace of famine among the nations. [31]Then you shall remember your evil ways, and your dealings that were not good; and you shall loathe yourselves for your iniquities and your abominable deeds. [32]It is not for your sake that I will act, says the Lord GOD; let that be known to you. Be ashamed and dismayed for your ways, O house of Israel.

33 Thus says the Lord GOD: On the day that I cleanse you from all your iniquities, I will cause the towns to be inhabited, and the waste places shall be rebuilt. [34]The land that was desolate shall be tilled, instead of being the desolation that it was in the sight of all who passed by. [35]And they will say, "This land that was desolate has become like the garden of Eden; and the waste and desolate and ruined towns are now inhabited and fortified." [36]Then the nations that are left all around you shall know that I, the LORD, have rebuilt the ruined places, and replanted that which was desolate; I, the LORD, have spoken, and I will do it.

37 Thus says the Lord GOD: I will also let the house of Israel ask me to do this for them: to increase their population like a flock. [38]Like the flock for sacrifices,[w] like the flock at Jerusalem during her appointed festivals, so shall the ruined towns be filled with flocks of people. Then they shall know that I am the LORD.

[w] Heb *flock of holy things*

"'I will put my spirit within you, and you shall live, and I will place you on your own soil; then you shall know that I, the LORD, have spoken and will act,' says the LORD."

Ezekiel 37:14

The Valley of Dry Bones

37 The hand of the LORD came upon me, and he brought me out by the spirit of the LORD and set me down in the middle of a valley; it was full of bones. [2]He led me all around them; there were very many lying in the valley, and they were very dry. [3]He said to me, "Mortal, can these bones live?" I answered, "O Lord GOD, you know." [4]Then he said to me, "Prophesy to these bones, and say to them: O dry bones, hear the word of the LORD. [5]Thus says the Lord GOD to these bones: I will cause breath[x] to enter you, and you shall live. [6]I will lay sinews on you, and will cause flesh to come upon you, and cover you with skin, and put breath[x] in you, and you shall live; and you shall know that I am the LORD."

[7] So I prophesied as I had been commanded; and as I prophesied, suddenly there was a noise, a rattling, and the bones came together, bone to its bone. [8]I looked, and there were sinews on them, and flesh had come upon them, and skin had covered them; but there was no breath in them. [9]Then he said to me, "Prophesy to the breath, prophesy, mortal, and say to the breath:[y] Thus says the Lord GOD: Come from the four winds, O breath,[y] and breathe upon these slain, that they may live." [10]I prophesied as he commanded me, and the breath came into them, and they lived, and stood on their feet, a vast multitude.

[11] Then he said to me, "Mortal, these bones are the whole house of Israel. They say, 'Our bones are dried up, and our hope is lost; we are cut off completely.' [12]Therefore prophesy, and say to them, Thus says

the Lord GOD: I am going to open your graves, and bring you up from your graves, O my people; and I will bring you back to the land of Israel. [13]And you shall know that I am the LORD, when I open your graves, and bring you up from your graves, O my people. [14]I will put my spirit within you, and you shall live, and I will place you on your own soil; then you shall know that I, the LORD, have spoken and will act, says the LORD."

Ezekiel saw a vision of a valley filled with dry bones that came to life again. This is not a foretelling of our resurrection, but a promise that God will make us new people when we invite the Lord's spirit to live in us.

The Two Sticks

[15] The word of the LORD came to me: [16]Mortal, take a stick and write on it, "For Judah, and the Israelites associated with it"; then take another stick and write on it, "For Joseph (the stick of Ē′phra·im) and all the house of Israel associated with it"; [17]and join them together into one stick, so that they may become one in your hand. [18]And when your people say to you, "Will you not show us what you mean by these?" [19]say to them, Thus says the Lord GOD: I am about to take the stick of Joseph (which is in the hand of Ē′phra·im) and the tribes of Israel associated with it; and I will put the stick of Judah upon it,[z] and make them one stick, in order that they may be one in my hand. [20]When the sticks on which you write are in your hand before their eyes, [21]then say to them, Thus says the Lord GOD: I will take the people of Israel from the nations among which they have gone, and will gather them from every quarter, and bring them to their own land. [22]I will make them one nation in the land, on the mountains of

[x] Or *spirit*   [y] Or *wind* or *spirit*   [z] Heb *I will put them upon it*

Israel; and one king shall be king over them all. Never again shall they be two nations, and never again shall they be divided into two kingdoms. ²³They shall never again defile themselves with their idols and their detestable things, or with any of their transgressions. I will save them from all the apostasies into which they have fallen,ᵃ and will cleanse them. Then they shall be my people, and I will be their God.

24 My servant David shall be king over them; and they shall all have one shepherd. They shall follow my ordinances and be careful to observe my statutes. ²⁵They shall live in the land that I gave to my servant Jacob, in which your ancestors lived; they and their children and their children's children shall live there forever; and my servant David shall be their prince forever. ²⁶I will make a covenant of peace with them; it shall be an everlasting covenant with them; and I will blessᵇ them and multiply them, and will set my sanctuary among them forevermore. ²⁷My dwelling place shall be with them; and I will be their God, and they shall be my people. ²⁸Then the nations shall know that I the LORD sanctify Israel, when my sanctuary is among them forevermore.

Invasion by Gog

38 The word of the LORD came to me: ²Mortal, set your face toward Gog, of the land of Māʹgog, the chief prince of Mēʹshech and Tūʹbal. Prophesy against him ³and say: Thus says the Lord GOD: I am against you, O Gog, chief prince of Mēʹshech and Tūʹbal; ⁴I will turn you around and put hooks into your jaws, and I will lead you out with all your army, horses and horsemen, all of them clothed in full armor, a great company, all of them with shield and buckler, wielding swords. ⁵Persia, Ethiopia,ᶜ and Put are with them, all of them with buckler and helmet; ⁶Gōʹmer and all its troops; Beth-tō-garʹmah from the remotest parts of the north with all its troops—many peoples are with you.

> "My dwelling place shall be with them; and I will be their God, and they shall be my people."
>
> Ezekiel 37:27

7 Be ready and keep ready, you and all the companies that are assembled around you, and hold yourselves in reserve for them. ⁸After many days you shall be mustered; in the latter years you shall go against a land restored from war, a land where people were gathered from many nations on the mountains of Israel, which had long lain waste; its people were brought out from the nations and now are living in safety, all of them. ⁹You shall advance, coming on like a storm; you shall be like a cloud covering the land, you and all your troops, and many peoples with you.

10 Thus says the Lord GOD: On that day thoughts will come into your mind, and you will devise an evil scheme. ¹¹You will say, "I will go up against the land of unwalled villages; I will fall upon the quiet people who live in safety, all of them living without walls, and having no bars or gates"; ¹²to seize spoil and carry off plunder; to assail the waste places that are now inhabited, and the people who were gathered from the nations, who are acquiring cattle and goods, who live at the centerᵈ of the earth. ¹³Sheʹba and Deʹdan and the merchants of Tarʹshish and all its young warriorsᵉ will say to you, "Have you come to seize spoil? Have you assembled your horde to carry off plunder, to carry away silver and gold, to take away cattle and goods, to seize a great amount of booty?"

14 Therefore, mortal, prophesy, and say to Gog: Thus says the Lord GOD: On that day when my people Israel are living securely, you will rouse yourselfᶠ ¹⁵and

---

ᵃ Another reading is *from all the settlements in which they have sinned*   ᵇ Tg: Heb *give*   ᶜ Or *Nubia*; Heb *Cush*   ᵈ Heb *navel*   ᵉ Heb *young lions*   ᶠ Gk: Heb *will you not know?*

come from your place out of the remotest parts of the north, you and many peoples with you, all of them riding on horses, a great horde, a mighty army; ¹⁶you will come up against my people Israel, like a cloud covering the earth. In the latter days I will bring you against my land, so that the nations may know me, when through you, O Gog, I display my holiness before their eyes.

Judgment on Gog

17 Thus says the Lord GOD: Are you he of whom I spoke in former days by my servants the prophets of Israel, who in those days prophesied for years that I would bring you against them? ¹⁸On that day, when Gog comes against the land of Israel, says the Lord GOD, my wrath shall be aroused. ¹⁹For in my jealousy and in my blazing wrath I declare: On that day there shall be a great shaking in the land of Israel; ²⁰the fish of the sea, and the birds of the air, and the animals of the field, and all creeping things that creep on the ground, and all human beings that are on the face of the earth, shall quake at my presence, and the mountains shall be thrown down, and the cliffs shall fall, and every wall shall tumble to the ground. ²¹I will summon the sword against Gog[g] in[h] all my mountains, says the Lord GOD; the swords of all will be against their comrades. ²²With pestilence and bloodshed I will enter into judgment with him; and I will pour down torrential rains and hailstones, fire and sulfur, upon him and his troops and the many peoples that are with him. ²³So I will display my greatness and my holiness and make myself known in the eyes of many nations. Then they shall know that I am the LORD.

Gog's Armies Destroyed

39 And you, mortal, prophesy against Gog, and say: Thus says the Lord GOD: I am against you, O Gog, chief prince of Me´shech and Tu´bal! ²I will turn you around and drive you forward, and bring you up from the remotest parts

of the north, and lead you against the mountains of Israel. ³I will strike your bow from your left hand, and will make your arrows drop out of your right hand. ⁴You shall fall upon the mountains of Israel, you and all your troops and the peoples that are with you; I will give you to birds of prey of every kind and to the wild animals to be devoured. ⁵You shall fall in the open field; for I have spoken, says the Lord GOD. ⁶I will send fire on Ma´gog and on those who live securely in the coastlands; and they shall know that I am the LORD.

7 My holy name I will make known among my people Israel; and I will not let my holy name be profaned any more; and the nations shall know that I am the LORD, the Holy One in Israel. ⁸It has come! It has happened, says the Lord GOD. This is the day of which I have spoken.

9 Then those who live in the towns of Israel will go out and make fires of the weapons and burn them—bucklers and shields, bows and arrows, handpikes and spears—and they will make fires of them for seven years. ¹⁰They will not need to take wood out of the field or cut down any trees in the forests, for they will make their fires of the weapons; they will despoil those who despoiled them, and plunder those who plundered them, says the Lord GOD.

The Burial of Gog

11 On that day I will give to Gog a place for burial in Israel, the Valley of the Travelers[i] east of the sea; it shall block the path of the travelers, for there Gog and all his horde will be buried; it shall be called the Valley of Ha´mon-gog.[j] ¹²Seven months the house of Israel shall spend burying them, in order to cleanse the land. ¹³All the people of the land shall bury them; and it will bring them honor on the day that I show my glory, says the Lord GOD. ¹⁴They will set apart men to

[g] Heb *him*   [h] Heb *to* or *for*   [i] Or *of the Abarim*   [j] That is, *the Horde of Gog*

pass through the land regularly and bury any invaders[k] who remain on the face of the land, so as to cleanse it; for seven months they shall make their search. [15]As the searchers[k] pass through the land, anyone who sees a human bone shall set up a sign by it, until the buriers have buried it in the Valley of Hā´mon-gog.[l] [16](A city Ha·mō´nah[m] is there also.) Thus they shall cleanse the land.

17 As for you, mortal, thus says the Lord GOD: Speak to the birds of every kind and to all the wild animals: Assemble and come, gather from all around to the sacrificial feast that I am preparing for you, a great sacrificial feast on the mountains of Israel, and you shall eat flesh and drink blood. [18]You shall eat the flesh of the mighty, and drink the blood of the princes of the earth—of rams, of lambs, and of goats, of bulls, all of them fatlings of Bā´shan. [19]You shall eat fat until you are filled, and drink blood until you are drunk, at the sacrificial feast that I am preparing for you. [20]And you shall be filled at my table with horses and charioteers,[n] with warriors and all kinds of soldiers, says the Lord GOD.

Israel Restored to the Land

21 I will display my glory among the nations; and all the nations shall see my judgment that I have executed, and my hand that I have laid on them. [22]The house of Israel shall know that I am the LORD their God, from that day forward. [23]And the nations shall know that the house of Israel went into captivity for their iniquity, because they dealt treacherously with me. So I hid my face from them and gave them into the hand of their adversaries, and they all fell by the sword. [24]I dealt with them according to their uncleanness and their transgressions, and hid my face from them.

25 Therefore thus says the Lord GOD: Now I will restore the fortunes of Jacob, and have mercy on the whole house of Israel; and I will be jealous for my holy name. [26]They shall forget[o] their shame,

and all the treachery they have practiced against me, when they live securely in their land with no one to make them afraid, [27]when I have brought them back from the peoples and gathered them from their enemies' lands, and through them have displayed my holiness in the sight of many nations. [28]Then they shall know that I am the LORD their God because I sent them into exile among the nations, and then gathered them into their own land. I will leave none of them behind; [29]and I will never again hide my face from them, when I pour out my spirit upon the house of Israel, says the Lord GOD.

The Vision of the New Temple

40 In the twenty-fifth year of our exile, at the beginning of the year, on the tenth day of the month, in the fourteenth year after the city was struck down, on that very day, the hand of the LORD was upon me, and he brought me there. [2]He brought me, in visions of God, to the land of Israel, and set me down upon a very high mountain, on which was a structure like a city to the south. [3]When he brought me there, a man was there, whose appearance shone like bronze, with a linen cord and a measuring reed in his hand; and he was standing in the gateway. [4]The man said to me, "Mortal, look closely and listen attentively, and set your mind upon all that I shall show you, for you were brought here in order that I might show it to you; declare all that you see to the house of Israel."

5 Now there was a wall all around the outside of the temple area. The length of the measuring reed in the man's hand was six long cubits, each being a cubit and a handbreadth in length; so he measured the thickness of the wall, one reed; and the height, one reed. [6]Then he went into the gateway facing east, going up its steps, and measured the threshold of the gate, one reed deep.[p] There were [7]recesses, and

k Heb *travelers*   l That is, *the Horde of Gog*   m That is *The Horde*   n Heb *chariots*   o Another reading is *They shall bear*   p Heb *deep, and one threshold, one reed deep* each recess was one reed wide and one reed deep; and the space between the recesses, five cubits; and the threshold of the gate by the vestibule of the gate at the inner end was one reed deep. [8]Then he measured the inner vestibule of the gateway, one cubit. [9]Then he measured the vestibule of the gateway, eight cubits; and its pilasters, two cubits; and the vestibule of the gate was at the inner end. [10]There were three recesses on either side of the east gate; the three were of the same size; and the pilasters on either side were of the same size. [11]Then he measured the width of the opening of the gateway, ten cubits; and the width of the gateway, thirteen cubits. [12]There was a barrier before the recesses, one cubit on either side; and the recesses were six cubits on either side. [13]Then he measured the gate from the back[q] of the one recess to the back[q] of the other, a width of twenty-five cubits, from wall to wall.[r] [14]He measured[s] also the vestibule, twenty cubits; and the gate next to the pilaster on every side of the court.[t] [15]From the front of the gate at the entrance to the end of the inner vestibule of the gate was fifty cubits. [16]The recesses and their pilasters had windows, with shutters[t] on the inside of the gateway all around, and the vestibules also had windows on the inside all around; and on the pilasters were palm trees.

17 Then he brought me into the outer court; there were chambers there, and a pavement, all around the court; thirty chambers fronted on the pavement. [18]The pavement ran along the side of the gates, corresponding to the length of the gates; this was the lower pavement. [19]Then he measured the distance from the inner front of[u] the lower gate to the outer front of the inner court, one hundred cubits.[v]

20 Then he measured the gate of the outer court that faced north—its depth and width. [21]Its recesses, three on either side, and its pilasters and its vestibule were of the same size as those of the first gate; its depth was fifty cubits, and its

width twenty-five cubits. [22]Its windows, its vestibule, and its palm trees were of the same size as those of the gate that faced toward the east. Seven steps led up to it; and its vestibule was on the inside.[w] [23]Opposite the gate on the north, as on the east, was a gate to the inner court; he measured from gate to gate, one hundred cubits.

24 Then he led me toward the south, and there was a gate on the south; and he measured its pilasters and its vestibule; they had the same dimensions as the others. [25]There were windows all around in it and in its vestibule, like the windows of the others; its depth was fifty cubits, and its width twenty-five cubits. [26]There were seven steps leading up to it; its vestibule was on the inside.[w] It had palm trees on its pilasters, one on either side. [27]There was a gate on the south of the inner court; and he measured from gate to gate toward the south, one hundred cubits.

28 Then he brought me to the inner court by the south gate, and he measured the south gate; it was of the same dimensions as the others. [29]Its recesses, its pilasters, and its vestibule were of the same size as the others; and there were windows all around in it and in its vestibule; its depth was fifty cubits, and its width twenty-five cubits. [30]There were vestibules all around, twenty-five cubits deep and five cubits wide. [31]Its vestibule faced the outer court, and palm trees were on its pilasters, and its stairway had eight steps.

32 Then he brought me to the inner court on the east side, and he measured the gate; it was of the same size as the others. [33]Its recesses, its pilasters, and its vestibule were of the same dimensions as the others; and there were windows all around in it and in its vestibule; its depth was fifty cubits, and its width twenty-five cubits. [34]Its vestibule faced the outer court, and it had

[q] Gk: Heb roof   [r] Heb opening facing opening
[s] Heb made   [t] Meaning of Heb uncertain
[u] Compare Gk: Heb from before   [v] Heb adds the east and the north   [w] Gk: Heb before them

palm trees on its pilasters, on either side; and its stairway had eight steps.

35 Then he brought me to the north gate, and he measured it; it had the same dimensions as the others. ³⁶Its recesses, its pilasters, and its vestibule were of the same size as the others;[x] and it had windows all around. Its depth was fifty cubits, and its width twenty-five cubits. ³⁷Its vestibule[y] faced the outer court, and it had palm trees on its pilasters, on either side; and its stairway had eight steps.

38 There was a chamber with its door in the vestibule of the gate,[z] where the burnt offering was to be washed. ³⁹And in the vestibule of the gate were two tables on either side, on which the burnt offering and the sin offering and the guilt offering were to be slaughtered. ⁴⁰On the outside of the vestibule[a] at the entrance of the north gate were two tables; and on the other side of the vestibule of the gate were two tables. ⁴¹Four tables were on the inside, and four tables on the outside of the side of the gate, eight tables, on which the sacrifices were to be slaughtered. ⁴²There were also four tables of hewn stone for the burnt offering, a cubit and a half long, and one cubit and a half wide, and one cubit high, on which the instruments were to be laid with which the burnt offerings and the sacrifices were slaughtered. ⁴³There were pegs, one handbreadth long, fastened all around the inside. And on the tables the flesh of the offering was to be laid.

44 On the outside of the inner gateway there were chambers for the singers in the inner court, one[b] at the side of the north gate facing south, the other at the side of the east gate facing north. ⁴⁵He said to me, "This chamber that faces south is for the priests who have charge of the temple, ⁴⁶and the chamber that faces north is for the priests who have charge of the altar; these are the descendants of Zāʹdok, who alone among the descendants of Levi may come near to the LORD to minister to him." ⁴⁷He measured the court, one hundred cubits deep, and one hundred cubits wide, a square; and the altar was in front of the temple.

The Temple

48 Then he brought me to the vestibule of the temple and measured the pilasters of the vestibule, five cubits on either side; and the width of the gate was fourteen cubits; and the sidewalls of the gate were three cubits[c] on either side. ⁴⁹The depth of the vestibule was twenty cubits, and the width twelve[d] cubits; ten steps led up[e] to it; and there were pillars beside the pilasters on either side.

41 Then he brought me to the nave, and measured the pilasters; on each side six cubits was the width of the pilasters.[f] ²The width of the entrance was ten cubits; and the sidewalls of the entrance were five cubits on either side. He measured the length of the nave, forty cubits, and its width, twenty cubits. ³Then he went into the inner room and measured the pilasters of the entrance, two cubits; and the width of the entrance, six cubits; and the sidewalls[g] of the entrance, seven cubits. ⁴He measured the depth of the room, twenty cubits, and its width, twenty cubits, beyond the nave. And he said to me, This is the most holy place.

5 Then he measured the wall of the temple, six cubits thick; and the width of the side chambers, four cubits, all around the temple. ⁶The side chambers were in three stories, one over another, thirty in each story. There were offsets[h] all around the wall of the temple to serve as supports for the side chambers, so that they should not be supported by the wall of the temple. ⁷The passageway[i] of the side chambers

^x One Ms: Compare verses 29 and 33: MT lacks *were of the same size as the others*   ^y Gk Vg Compare verses 26, 31, 34: Heb *pilasters*   ^z Cn: Heb *at the pilasters of the gates*   ^a Cn: Heb *to him who goes up*   ^b Heb lacks *one*   ^c Gk: Heb *and the width of the gate was three cubits*   ^d Gk: Heb *eleven*   ^e Gk: Heb *and by steps that went up*   ^f Compare Gk: Heb *tent*   ^g Gk: Heb *width*   ^h Gk Compare 1 Kings 6.6: Heb *they entered*   ⁱ Cn: Heb *it was surrounded*

widened from story to story; for the structure was supplied with a stairway all around the temple. For this reason the structure became wider from story to story. One ascended from the bottom story to the uppermost story by way of the middle one. [8]I saw also that the temple had a raised platform all around; the foundations of the side chambers measured a full reed of six long cubits. [9]The thickness of the outer wall of the side chambers was five cubits; and the free space between the side chambers of the temple [10]and the chambers of the court was a width of twenty cubits all around the temple on every side. [11]The side chambers opened onto the area left free, one door toward the north, and another door toward the south; and the width of the part that was left free was five cubits all around.

12 The building that was facing the temple yard on the west side was seventy cubits wide; and the wall of the building was five cubits thick all around, and its depth ninety cubits.

13 Then he measured the temple, one hundred cubits deep; and the yard and the building with its walls, one hundred cubits deep; [14]also the width of the east front of the temple and the yard, one hundred cubits.

15 Then he measured the depth of the building facing the yard at the west, together with its galleries[j] on either side, one hundred cubits.

The nave of the temple and the inner room and the outer[k] vestibule [16]were paneled,[l] and, all around, all three had windows with recessed[m] frames. Facing the threshold the temple was paneled with wood all around, from the floor up to the windows (now the windows were covered), [17]to the space above the door, even to the inner room, and on the outside. And on all the walls all around in the inner room and the nave there was a pattern.[n] [18]It was formed of cherubim and palm trees, a palm tree between cherub and cherub. Each cherub had two faces:

Ezekiel saw a vision of how the new Temple should be built. In this vision he saw a pattern of palm trees and cherubim. The palm trees represent prosperity and the cherubim represent security. What symbols represent prosperity and security for us?

[19]a human face turned toward the palm tree on the one side, and the face of a young lion turned toward the palm tree on the other side. They were carved on the whole temple all around; [20]from the floor to the area above the door, cherubim and palm trees were carved on the wall.[o]

21 The doorposts of the nave were square. In front of the holy place was something resembling [22]an altar of wood, three cubits high, two cubits long, and two cubits wide;[p] its corners, its base,[q] and its walls were of wood. He said to me, "This is the table that stands before the LORD." [23]The nave and the holy place had each a double door. [24]The doors had two leaves apiece, two swinging leaves for each door. [25]On the doors of the nave were carved cherubim and palm trees, such as were carved on the walls; and there was a canopy of wood in front of the vestibule outside. [26]And there were recessed windows and palm trees on either side, on the sidewalls of the vestibule.[r]

The Holy Chambers and the Outer Wall

42 Then he led me out into the outer court, toward the north, and he brought me to the chambers that were opposite the temple yard and oppo-

[j] Cn: Meaning of Heb uncertain   [k] Gk: Heb *of the court*   [l] Gk: Heb *the thresholds*   [m] Cn Compare Gk 1 Kings 6.4: Meaning of Heb uncertain   [n] Heb *measures*   [o] Cn Compare verse 25: Heb *and the wall*   [p] Gk: Heb lacks *two cubits wide*   [q] Gk: Heb *length*   [r] Cn: Heb *vestibule. And the side chambers of the temple and the canopies*

site the building on the north. ²The length of the building that was on the north side[s] was[t] one hundred cubits, and the width fifty cubits. ³Across the twenty cubits that belonged to the inner court, and facing the pavement that belonged to the outer court, the chambers rose[u] gallery[v] by gallery[v] in three stories. ⁴In front of the chambers was a passage on the inner side, ten cubits wide and one hundred cubits deep,[w] and its[x] entrances were on the north. ⁵Now the upper chambers were narrower, for the galleries[v] took more away from them than from the lower and middle chambers in the building. ⁶For they were in three stories, and they had no pillars like the pillars of the outer[y] court; for this reason the upper chambers were set back from the ground more than the lower and the middle ones. ⁷There was a wall outside parallel to the chambers, toward the outer court, opposite the chambers, fifty cubits long. ⁸For the chambers on the outer court were fifty cubits long, while those opposite the temple were one hundred cubits long. ⁹At the foot of these chambers ran a passage that one entered from the east in order to enter them from the outer court. ¹⁰The width of the passage[z] was fixed by the wall of the court.

On the south[a] also, opposite the vacant area and opposite the building, there were chambers ¹¹with a passage in front of them; they were similar to the chambers on the north, of the same length and width, with the same exits[b] and arrangements and doors. ¹²So the entrances of the chambers to the south were entered through the entrance at the head of the corresponding passage, from the east, along the matching wall.[v]

13 Then he said to me, "The north chambers and the south chambers opposite the vacant area are the holy chambers, where the priests who approach the LORD shall eat the most holy offerings; there they shall deposit the most holy offerings—the grain offering, the sin offering,

and the guilt offering—for the place is holy. ¹⁴When the priests enter the holy place, they shall not go out of it into the outer court without laying there the vestments in which they minister, for these are holy; they shall put on other garments before they go near to the area open to the people."

15 When he had finished measuring the interior of the temple area, he led me out by the gate that faces east, and measured the temple area all around. ¹⁶He measured the east side with the measuring reed, five hundred cubits by the measuring reed. ¹⁷Then he turned and measured[c] the north side, five hundred cubits by the measuring reed. ¹⁸Then he turned and measured[c] the south side, five hundred cubits by the measuring reed. ¹⁹Then he turned to the west side and measured, five hundred cubits by the measuring reed. ²⁰He measured it on the four sides. It had a wall around it, five hundred cubits long and five hundred cubits wide, to make a separation between the holy and the common.

The Divine Glory Returns to the Temple

43 Then he brought me to the gate, the gate facing east. ²And there, the glory of the God of Israel was coming from the east; the sound was like the sound of mighty waters; and the earth shone with his glory. ³The[d] vision I saw was like the vision that I had seen when he came to destroy the city, and[e] like the vision that I had seen by the river Chē'bar; and I fell upon my face. ⁴As the glory of the LORD entered the temple by the gate facing east, ⁵the spirit lifted me up, and brought me into the inner court; and the glory of the LORD filled the temple.

[s] Gk: Heb *door*   [t] Gk: Heb *before the length*
[u] Heb lacks *the chambers rose*   [v] Meaning of Heb uncertain   [w] Gk Syr: Heb *a way of one cubit*
[x] Heb *their*   [y] Gk: Heb lacks *outer*   [z] Heb lacks *of the passage*   [a] Gk: Heb *east*   [b] Heb *and all their exits*   [c] Gk: Heb *measuring reed all around. He measured*   [d] Gk: Heb *Like the vision*   [e] Syr: Heb *and the visions*

6 While the man was standing beside me, I heard someone speaking to me out of the temple. ⁷He said to me: Mortal, this is the place of my throne and the place for the soles of my feet, where I will reside among the people of Israel forever. The house of Israel shall no more defile my holy name, neither they nor their kings, by their whoring, and by the corpses of their kings at their death./ ⁸When they placed their threshold by my threshold and their doorposts beside my doorposts, with only a wall between me and them, they were defiling my holy name by their abominations that they committed; therefore I have consumed them in my anger. ⁹Now let them put away their idolatry and the corpses of their kings far from me, and I will reside among them forever.

10 As for you, mortal, describe the temple to the house of Israel, and let them measure the pattern; and let them be ashamed of their iniquities. ¹¹When they are ashamed of all that they have done, make known to them the plan of the temple, its arrangement, its exits and its entrances, and its whole form—all its ordinances and its entire plan and all its laws; and write it down in their sight, so that they may observe and follow the entire plan and all its ordinances. ¹²This is the law of the temple: the whole territory on the top of the mountain all around shall be most holy. This is the law of the temple.

The Altar

13 These are the dimensions of the altar by cubits (the cubit being one cubit and a handbreadth): its base shall be one cubit high,ᵍ and one cubit wide, with a rim of one span around its edge. This shall be the height of the altar: ¹⁴From the base on the ground to the lower ledge, two cubits, with a width of one cubit; and from the smaller ledge to the larger ledge, four cubits, with a width of one cubit; ¹⁵and the altar hearth, four cubits; and from the altar hearth projecting upward, four horns. ¹⁶The altar hearth shall be

square, twelve cubits long by twelve wide. ¹⁷The ledge also shall be square, fourteen cubits long by fourteen wide, with a rim around it half a cubit wide, and its surrounding base, one cubit. Its steps shall face east.

18 Then he said to me: Mortal, thus says the Lord GOD: These are the ordinances for the altar: On the day when it is erected for offering burnt offerings upon it and for dashing blood against it, ¹⁹you shall give to the levitical priests of the family of Zā´dok, who draw near to me to minister to me, says the Lord GOD, a bull for a sin offering. ²⁰And you shall take some of its blood, and put it on the four horns of the altar, and on the four corners of the ledge, and upon the rim all around; thus you shall purify it and make atonement for it. ²¹You shall also take the bull of the sin offering, and it shall be burnt in the appointed place belonging to the temple, outside the sacred area.

22 On the second day you shall offer a male goat without blemish for a sin offering; and the altar shall be purified, as it was purified with the bull. ²³When you have finished purifying it, you shall offer a bull without blemish and a ram from the flock without blemish. ²⁴You shall present them before the LORD, and the priests shall throw salt on them and offer them up as a burnt offering to the LORD. ²⁵For seven days you shall provide daily a goat for a sin offering; also a bull and a ram from the flock, without blemish, shall be provided. ²⁶Seven days shall they make atonement for the altar and cleanse it, and so consecrate it. ²⁷When these days are over, then from the eighth day onward the priests shall offer upon the altar your burnt offerings and your offerings of well-being; and I will accept you, says the Lord GOD.

The Closed Gate

44 Then he brought me back to the outer gate of the sanctuary, which faces east; and it was shut. ²The

---

ᶠ Or on their high places　　ᵍ Gk: Heb lacks high

LORD said to me: This gate shall remain shut; it shall not be opened, and no one shall enter by it; for the LORD, the God of Israel, has entered by it; therefore it shall remain shut. ³Only the prince, because he is a prince, may sit in it to eat food before the LORD; he shall enter by way of the vestibule of the gate, and shall go out by the same way.

Admission to the Temple

4 Then he brought me by way of the north gate to the front of the temple; and I looked, and lo! the glory of the LORD filled the temple of the LORD; and I fell upon my face. ⁵The LORD said to me: Mortal, mark well, look closely, and listen attentively to all that I shall tell you concerning all the ordinances of the temple of the LORD and all its laws; and mark well those who may be admitted to^h the temple and all those who are to be excluded from the sanctuary. ⁶Say to the rebellious house,^{i} to the house of Israel, Thus says the Lord GOD: O house of Israel, let there be an end to all your abominations ⁷in admitting foreigners, uncircumcised in heart and flesh, to be in my sanctuary, profaning my temple when you offer to me my food, the fat and the blood. You^j have broken my covenant with all your abominations. ⁸And you have not kept charge of my sacred offerings; but you have appointed foreigners^k to act for you in keeping my charge in my sanctuary.

9 Thus says the Lord GOD: No foreigner, uncircumcised in heart and flesh, of all the foreigners who are among the people of Israel, shall enter my sanctuary. ¹⁰But the Lĕʹvītes who went far from me, going astray from me after their idols when Israel went astray, shall bear their punishment. ¹¹They shall be ministers in my sanctuary, having oversight at the gates of the temple, and serving in the temple; they shall slaughter the burnt offering and the sacrifice for the people, and they shall attend on them and serve them. ¹²Because they ministered to them before their idols and made the house of Israel stumble into

iniquity, therefore I have sworn concerning them, says the Lord GOD, that they shall bear their punishment. ¹³They shall not come near to me, to serve me as priest, nor come near any of my sacred offerings, the things that are most sacred; but they shall bear their shame, and the consequences of the abominations that they have committed. ¹⁴Yet I will appoint them to keep charge of the temple, to do all its chores, all that is to be done in it.

Zadok was a high priest in the time of David. Zadok was known for his faithfulness to the king. His family remained faithful to God through all the troubles the Jews faced. In Ezekiel's vision, the family of Zadok will care for the new Temple.

The Levitical Priests

15 But the levitical priests, the descendants of Zāʹdok, who kept the charge of my sanctuary when the people of Israel went astray from me, shall come near to me to minister to me; and they shall attend me to offer me the fat and the blood, says the Lord GOD. ¹⁶It is they who shall enter my sanctuary, it is they who shall approach my table, to minister to me, and they shall keep my charge. ¹⁷When they enter the gates of the inner court, they shall wear linen vestments; they shall have nothing of wool on them, while they minister at the gates of the inner court, and within. ¹⁸They shall have linen turbans on their heads, and linen undergarments on their loins; they shall not bind themselves with anything that causes sweat. ¹⁹When they go out into the outer court to the people, they shall remove the vestments in which they have

^{h} Cn: Heb *the entrance of* ^{i} Gk: Heb lacks *house*
^{j} Gk Syr Vg: Heb *They* ^{k} Heb lacks *foreigners*

In Old Testament times, both people and things were set apart to be used only for God. They were said to be "devoted." During war all men, animals, and objects that were captured were "devoted" to God and were usually destroyed. Sometimes, however, precious metals captured in battle were taken to the sanctuary, or holy place. Captured sheep might be used for burnt offerings to the Lord.

been ministering, and lay them in the holy chambers; and they shall put on other garments, so that they may not communicate holiness to the people with their vestments. [20]They shall not shave their heads or let their locks grow long; they shall only trim the hair of their heads. [21]No priest shall drink wine when he enters the inner court. [22]They shall not marry a widow, or a divorced woman, but only a virgin of the stock of the house of Israel, or a widow who is the widow of a priest. [23]They shall teach my people the difference between the holy and the common, and show them how to distinguish between the unclean and the clean. [24]In a controversy they shall act as judges, and they shall decide it according to my judgments. They shall keep my laws and my statutes regarding all my appointed festivals, and they shall keep my sabbaths holy. [25]They shall not defile themselves by going near to a dead person; for father or mother, however, and for son or daughter, and for brother or unmarried sister they may defile themselves. [26]After he has become clean, they shall count seven days for him. [27]On the day that he goes into the holy place, into the inner court, to minister in the holy place, he shall offer his sin offering, says the Lord GOD.

28 This shall be their inheritance: I am their inheritance; and you shall give them no holding in Israel; I am their holding. [29]They shall eat the grain offering, the sin offering, and the guilt offering; and every devoted thing in Israel shall be theirs. [30]The first of all the first fruits of all kinds, and every offering of all kinds from all your offerings, shall belong to the priests; you shall also give to the priests the first of your dough, in order that a blessing may rest on your house. [31]The priests shall not eat of anything, whether bird or animal, that died of itself or was torn by animals.

The Holy District

45 When you allot the land as an inheritance, you shall set aside for the LORD a portion of the land as a holy district, twenty-five thousand cubits long and twenty[l] thousand cubits wide; it shall be holy throughout its entire extent. [2]Of this, a square plot of five hundred by five hundred cubits shall be for the sanctuary, with fifty cubits for an open space around it. [3]In the holy district you shall measure off a section twenty-five thousand cubits long and ten thousand wide, in which shall be the sanctuary, the most holy place. [4]It shall be a holy portion of the land; it shall be for the priests, who minister in

In Ezekiel's vision, the holy district is the piece of land devoted to the Lord—25,000 cubits long and 20,000 cubits wide. A cubit is the distance from a man's elbow to his fingertip—about eighteen inches. Some of Ezekiel's measurements are in "long" cubits—the regular cubit plus the width of a man's hand. In today's measures, the holy district would be about eight miles square.

[l] Gk: Heb *ten*

the sanctuary and approach the Lord to minister to him; and it shall be both a place for their houses and a holy place for the sanctuary. [5]Another section, twenty-five thousand cubits long and ten thousand cubits wide, shall be for the Lē´vītes who minister at the temple, as their holding for cities to live in.[m]

6 Alongside the portion set apart as the holy district you shall assign as a holding for the city an area five thousand cubits wide, and twenty-five thousand cubits long; it shall belong to the whole house of Israel.

7 And to the prince shall belong the land on both sides of the holy district and the holding of the city, alongside the holy district and the holding of the city, on the west and on the east, corresponding in length to one of the tribal portions, and extending from the western to the eastern boundary [8]of the land. It is to be his property in Israel. And my princes shall no longer oppress my people; but they shall let the house of Israel have the land according to their tribes.

9 Thus says the Lord God: Enough, O princes of Israel! Put away violence and oppression, and do what is just and right. Cease your evictions of my people, says the Lord God.

Weights and Measures

10 You shall have honest balances, an honest ephah, and an honest bath.[n] [11]The ephah and the bath shall be of the same measure, the bath containing one-tenth of a homer, and the ephah one-tenth of a homer; the homer shall be the standard measure. [12]The shekel shall be twenty gerahs. Twenty shekels, twenty-five shekels, and fifteen shekels shall make a mina for you.

Offerings

13 This is the offering that you shall make: one-sixth of an ephah from each homer of wheat, and one-sixth of an ephah from each homer of barley, [14]and as the fixed portion of oil,[o] one-tenth of a bath

from each cor (the cor,[p] like the homer, contains ten baths); [15]and one sheep from every flock of two hundred, from the pastures of Israel. This is the offering for grain offerings, burnt offerings, and offerings of well-being, to make atonement for them, says the Lord God. [16]All the people of the land shall join with the prince in Israel in making this offering. [17]But this shall be the obligation of the prince regarding the burnt offerings, grain offerings, and drink offerings, at the festivals, the new moons, and the sabbaths, all the appointed festivals of the house of Israel: he shall provide the sin offerings, grain offerings, the burnt offerings, and the offerings of well-being, to make atonement for the house of Israel.

Festivals

18 Thus says the Lord God: In the first month, on the first day of the month, you shall take a young bull without blemish,

> Ezekiel told the people that they needed to have honest measures and weights. Because there were many different standards, buying and selling in the marketplace was often not fair. One person's scale might weigh things too light, and another person's scale might weigh those same things too heavy. Ezekiel gave guidelines so that all measurements would be the same. The *ephah* and the *homer* (probably the load one donkey could carry) were units of dry measure, while the *bath* was a unit of liquid measure. The *shekel*, the *gerah*, and the *mina* were all units of weight. How do we measure things today?

m Gk: Heb *as their holding, twenty chambers* *n* A Heb measure of volume *o* Cn: Heb *oil, the bath the oil* *p* Vg: Heb *homer* and purify the sanctuary. [19]The priest shall take some of the blood of the sin offering and put it on the doorposts of the temple, the four corners of the ledge of the altar, and the posts of the gate of the inner court. [20]You shall do the same on the seventh day of the month for anyone who has sinned through error or ignorance; so you shall make atonement for the temple.

21 In the first month, on the fourteenth day of the month, you shall celebrate the festival of the passover, and for seven days unleavened bread shall be eaten. [22]On that day the prince shall provide for himself and all the people of the land a young bull for a sin offering. [23]And during the seven days of the festival he shall provide as a burnt offering to the LORD seven young bulls and seven rams without blemish, on each of the seven days; and a male goat daily for a sin offering. [24]He shall provide as a grain offering an ephah for each bull, an ephah for each ram, and a hin of oil to each ephah. [25]In the seventh month, on the fifteenth day of the month and for the seven days of the festival, he shall make the same provision for sin offerings, burnt offerings, and grain offerings, and for the oil.

Miscellaneous Regulations

46 Thus says the Lord GOD: The gate of the inner court that faces east shall remain closed on the six working days; but on the sabbath day it shall be opened and on the day of the new moon it shall be opened. [2]The prince shall enter by the vestibule of the gate from outside, and shall take his stand by the post of the gate. The priests shall offer his burnt offering and his offerings of well-being, and he shall bow down at the threshold of the gate. Then he shall go out, but the gate shall not be closed until evening. [3]The people of the land shall bow down at the entrance of that gate before the LORD on the sabbaths and on the new moons. [4]The burnt offering that the prince offers to the LORD on the sabbath day shall be six lambs without blemish and a ram without blemish; [5]and the grain offering with the ram shall be an ephah, and the grain offering with the lambs shall be as much as he wishes to give, together with a hin of oil to each ephah. [6]On the day of the new moon he shall offer a young bull without blemish, and six lambs and a ram, which shall be without blemish; [7]as a grain offering he shall provide an ephah with the bull and an ephah with the ram, and with the lambs as much as he wishes, together with a hin of oil to each ephah. [8]When the prince enters, he shall come in by the vestibule of the gate, and he shall go out by the same way.

9 When the people of the land come before the LORD at the appointed festivals, whoever enters by the north gate to worship shall go out by the south gate; and whoever enters by the south gate shall go out by the north gate: they shall not return by way of the gate by which they entered, but shall go out straight ahead. [10]When they come in, the prince shall come in with them; and when they go out, he shall go out.

11 At the festivals and the appointed seasons the grain offering with a young bull shall be an ephah, and with a ram an ephah, and with the lambs as much as one wishes to give, together with a hin of oil to an ephah. [12]When the prince provides a freewill offering, either a burnt offering or offerings of well-being as a freewill offering to the LORD, the gate facing east shall be opened for him; and he shall offer his burnt offering or his offerings of well-being as he does on the sabbath day. Then he shall go out, and after he has gone out the gate shall be closed.

13 He shall provide a lamb, a yearling, without blemish, for a burnt offering to the LORD daily; morning by morning he shall provide it. [14]And he shall provide a grain offering with it morning by morning regularly, one-sixth of an ephah, and one-third of a hin of oil to moisten the choice flour, as a grain offering to the LORD; this is the ordinance for all time. [15]Thus the

lamb and the grain offering and the oil shall be provided, morning by morning, as a regular burnt offering.

16 Thus says the Lord GOD: If the prince makes a gift to any of his sons out of his inheritance,[q] it shall belong to his sons, it is their holding by inheritance. [17]But if he makes a gift out of his inheritance to one of his servants, it shall be his to the year of liberty; then it shall revert to the prince; only his sons may keep a gift from his inheritance. [18]The prince shall not take any of the inheritance of the people, thrusting them out of their holding; he shall give his sons their inheritance out of his own holding, so that none of my people shall be dispossessed of their holding.

19 Then he brought me through the entrance, which was at the side of the gate, to the north row of the holy chambers for the priests; and there I saw a place at the extreme western end of them. [20]He said to me, "This is the place where the priests shall boil the guilt offering and the sin offering, and where they shall bake the grain offering, in order not to bring them out into the outer court and so communicate holiness to the people."

21 Then he brought me out to the outer court, and led me past the four corners of the court; and in each corner of the court there was a court—[22]in the four corners of the court were small[r] courts, forty cubits long and thirty wide; the four were of the same size. [23]On the inside, around each of the four courts[s] was a row of masonry, with hearths made at the bottom of the rows all around. [24]Then he said to me, "These are the kitchens where those who serve at the temple shall boil the sacrifices of the people."

Water Flowing from the Temple

47 Then he brought me back to the entrance of the temple; there, water was flowing from below the threshold of the temple toward the east (for the temple faced east); and the water was flowing down from below the south end

of the threshold of the temple, south of the altar. [2]Then he brought me out by way of the north gate, and led me around on the outside to the outer gate that faces toward the east;[t] and the water was coming out on the south side.

3 Going on eastward with a cord in his hand, the man measured one thousand cubits, and then led me through the water; and it was ankle-deep. [4]Again he measured one thousand, and led me through the water; and it was knee-deep. Again he measured one thousand, and led me through the water; and it was up to the waist. [5]Again he measured one thousand, and it was a river that I could not cross, for the water had risen; it was deep enough to swim in, a river that could not be crossed. [6]He said to me, "Mortal, have you seen this?"

Then he led me back along the bank of the river. [7]As I came back, I saw on the bank of the river a great many trees on the one side and on the other. [8]He said to me, "This water flows toward the eastern region and goes down into the Ar′a·bah; and when it enters the sea, the sea of stagnant waters, the water will become fresh. [9]Wherever the river goes,[u] every living creature that swarms will live, and there will be very many fish, once these waters

> **Arabah** is one of the main regions of Israel lying below sea level. It contains the Jordan Valley, the Sea of Galilee, the Dead Sea, and the land south to the Gulf of Aqaba. In the Bible "the Arabah" means any part of this long valley. The southern Arabah was one of the areas the Israelites went through on their journey from Egypt to Canaan.

[q] Gk: Heb *it is his inheritance* Meaning of Heb uncertain   [r] Gk Syr Vg: [s] Heb *the four of them*   [t] Meaning of Heb uncertain   [u] Gk Syr Vg Tg: Heb *the two rivers go*

reach there. It will become fresh; and everything will live where the river goes. [10]People will stand fishing beside the sea[v] from En-ge´di to En-eg´la·im; it will be a place for the spreading of nets; its fish will be of a great many kinds, like the fish of the Great Sea. [11]But its swamps and marshes will not become fresh; they are to be left for salt. [12]On the banks, on both sides of the river, there will grow all kinds of trees for food. Their leaves will not wither nor their fruit fail, but they will bear fresh fruit every month, because the water for them flows from the sanctuary. Their fruit will be for food, and their leaves for healing."

The New Boundaries of the Land

13 Thus says the Lord GOD: These are the boundaries by which you shall divide the land for inheritance among the twelve tribes of Israel. Joseph shall have two portions. [14]You shall divide it equally; I swore to give it to your ancestors, and this land shall fall to you as your inheritance.

15 This shall be the boundary of the land: On the north side, from the Great Sea by way of Heth´lon to Lē´bō-hā´math, and on to Zē´dad,[w] [16]Be·rō´thah, Sib´rā·im (which lies between the border of Damascus and the border of Hā´math), as far as Hā´zer-hat´ti·con, which is on the border of Hau´ran. [17]So the boundary shall run from the sea to Hā´zar-ē´non, which is north of the border of Damascus, with the border of Ha´math to the north.[x] This shall be the north side.

18 On the east side, between Hau´ran and Damascus; along the Jordan between Gil´e·ad and the land of Israel; to the eastern sea and as far as Tā´mar.[y] This shall be the east side.

19 On the south side, it shall run from Tā´mar as far as the waters of Mer´i·bath-kā´desh, from there along the Wadi of Egypt[z] to the Great Sea. This shall be the south side.

20 On the west side, the Great Sea shall be the boundary to a point opposite Lē´bo-hā´math. This shall be the west side.

21 So you shall divide this land among you according to the tribes of Israel. [22]You shall allot it as an inheritance for yourselves and for the aliens who reside among you and have begotten children among you. They shall be to you as citizens of Israel; with you they shall be allotted an inheritance among the tribes of Israel. [23]In whatever tribe aliens reside, there you shall assign them their inheritance, says the Lord GOD.

The Tribal Portions

48 These are the names of the tribes: Beginning at the northern border, on the Heth´lon road,[a] from Lē´bō-hā´math, as far as Hā´zar-ē´non (which is on the border of Damascus, with Hā´math to the north), and[b] extending from the east side to the west,[c] Dan, one portion. [2]Adjoining the territory of Dan, from the east side to the west, Ash´er, one portion. [3]Adjoining the territory of Ash´er, from the east side to the west, Naph´ta·lī, one portion. [4]Adjoining the territory of Naph´ta·lī, from the east side to the west, Ma·nas´seh, one portion. [5]Adjoining the territory of Ma·nas´seh, from the east side to the west, Ē´phra·im, one portion. [6]Adjoining the territory of Ē´phra·im, from the east side to the west, Reuben, one portion. [7]Adjoining the territory of Reuben, from the east side to the west, Judah, one portion.

8 Adjoining the territory of Judah, from the east side to the west, shall be the portion that you shall set apart, twenty-five thousand cubits in width, and in length equal to one of the tribal portions, from the east side to the west, with the sanctuary in the middle of it. [9]The portion that you shall set apart for the LORD shall be twenty-five thousand cubits in length, and twenty[d] thousand in width. [10]These

---

[v] Heb it   [w] Gk: Heb *Lebo-zedad,* [16]Hamath
[x] Meaning of Heb uncertain   [y] Compare Syr: Heb *you shall measure*   [z] Heb lacks *of Egypt*   [a] Compare 47.15: Heb *by the side of the way*   [b] Cn: Heb *and they shall be his*   [c] Gk Compare verses 2-8: Heb *the east side the west*   [d] Compare 45.1: Heb *ten*

shall be the allotments of the holy portion: the priests shall have an allotment measuring twenty-five thousand cubits on the northern side, ten thousand cubits in width on the western side, ten thousand in width on the eastern side, and twenty-five thousand in length on the southern side, with the sanctuary of the LORD in the middle of it. [11]This shall be for the consecrated priests, the descendants[e] of Zā´dok, who kept my charge, who did not go astray when the people of Israel went astray, as the Lē´vītes did. [12]It shall belong to them as a special portion from the holy portion of the land, a most holy place, adjoining the territory of the Lē´vītes. [13]Alongside the territory of the priests, the Lē´vītes shall have an allotment twenty-five thousand cubits in length and ten thousand in width. The whole length shall be twenty-five thousand cubits and the width twenty[f] thousand. [14]They shall not sell or exchange any of it; they shall not transfer this choice portion of the land, for it is holy to the LORD.

15 The remainder, five thousand cubits in width and twenty-five thousand in length, shall be for ordinary use for the city, for dwellings and for open country. In the middle of it shall be the city; [16]and these shall be its dimensions: the north side four thousand five hundred cubits, the south side four thousand five hundred, the east side four thousand five hundred, and the west side four thousand five hundred. [17]The city shall have open land: on the north two hundred fifty cubits, on the south two hundred fifty, on the east two hundred fifty, on the west two hundred fifty. [18]The remainder of the length alongside the holy portion shall be ten thousand cubits to the east, and ten thousand to the west, and it shall be alongside the holy portion. Its produce shall be food for the workers of the city. [19]The workers of the city, from all the tribes of Israel, shall cultivate it. [20]The whole portion that you shall set apart shall be twenty-five thousand cubits square, that is, the holy portion together with the property of the city.

21 What remains on both sides of the holy portion and of the property of the city shall belong to the prince. Extending from the twenty-five thousand cubits of the holy portion to the east border, and westward from the twenty-five thousand cubits to the west border, parallel to the tribal portions, it shall belong to the prince. The holy portion with the sanctuary of the temple in the middle of it, [22]and the property of the Lē´vītes and of the city, shall be in the middle of that which belongs to the prince. The portion of the prince shall lie between the territory of Judah and the territory of Benjamin.

23 As for the rest of the tribes: from the east side to the west, Benjamin, one portion. [24]Adjoining the territory of Benjamin, from the east side to the west, Sim´ē·on, one portion. [25]Adjoining the territory of Sim´ē·on, from the east side to the west, Is´sa·char, one portion. [26]Adjoining the territory of Is´sa·char, from the east side to the west, Zeb´ū·lun, one portion. [27]Adjoining the territory of Zeb´ū·lun, from the east side to the west, Gad, one portion. [28]And adjoining the territory of Gad to the south, the boundary shall run from Tā´mar to the waters of Mer´i·bath-kā´desh, from there along the Wadi of Egypt[g] to the Great Sea. [29]This is the land that you shall allot as an inheritance among the tribes of Israel, and these are their portions, says the Lord GOD.

30 These shall be the exits of the city: On the north side, which is to be four thousand five hundred cubits by measure, [31]three gates, the gate of Reuben, the gate of Judah, and the gate of Levi, the gates of the city being named after the tribes of Israel. [32]On the east side, which is to be four thousand five hundred cubits, three gates, the gate of Joseph, the gate of Benjamin, and the gate of Dan. [33]On the south side, which is to be four thousand five hundred cubits by measure, three

gates, the gate of Sim´ē·on, the gate of Is´sa·char, and the gate of Zeb´ū·lun. ³⁴On the west side, which is to be four thousand five hundred cubits, three gates,ʰ the gate of Gad, the gate of Ash´er, and the gate of Naph´ta·lī. ³⁵The circumference of the city shall be eighteen thousand cubits. And the name of the city from that time on shall be, The LORD is There.

Ezekiel's visions are hopeful in the end. He tells of a new city that will be called "The LORD is There."

ʰ One Ms Gk Syr: MT *their gates three*

Daniel

Less than two hundred years before the birth of Jesus, a Greek king named Antiochus Epiphanes demanded that the Jews accept Greek ideas and religion. The book of Daniel was written to encourage the Jews to be faithful to their God and to their own people. Parts of it were written in the second century BC.

The book of Daniel tells about a man who was faithful to God even though he lived in Babylon (far away from his homeland) between 597 and 538 BC. The stories of his visions gave a message of hope to the Jewish people that in spite of their troubles, they would be triumphant. The stories were in a kind of secret language. This form of writing is called apocalyptic, which means uncovered or revealed, and it is similar to the book of Revelation. The writer knew his Jewish readers would be able to uncover the meaning of the stories. Chapters 1–6 tell stories of Daniel and his friends. Chapters 7–12 tell about strange visions with symbolic pictures that encouraged the Jews to resist the power of the king.

Both Jews and Christians have turned to the book of Daniel whenever they have been persecuted for their faith. The stories in this book remind us that God gives us the courage to do the right thing even when it is very hard to do so.

Daniel 6:10–28

Four Young Israelites at the Babylonian Court

1 In the third year of the reign of King Je·hoi´a·kim of Judah, King Ne·būchad·nez´zar of Babylon came to Jerusalem and besieged it. ²The Lord let King Je·hoi´a·kim of Judah fall into his power, as well as some of the vessels of the house of God. These he brought to the land of Shī´nar,ᵃ and placed the vessels in the treasury of his gods.

3 Then the king commanded his palace master Ash´pe·naz to bring some of the Israelites of the royal family and of the nobility, ⁴young men without physical defect and handsome, versed in every branch of wisdom, endowed with knowledge and insight, and competent to serve in the king's palace; they were to be taught the literature and language of the Chal·dē´ans. ⁵The king assigned them a daily portion of the royal rations of food and wine. They were to be educated for three years, so that at the end of that time they could be stationed in the king's court. ⁶Among them were Daniel, Han·a·nī´ah, Mish´a·el, and Az·a·rī´ah, from the tribe of Judah. ⁷The palace master gave them other names: Daniel he called Bel·te·shaz´zar, Han·a·nī´ah he called Shad´rach, Mish´a·el he called Mē´shach, and Az·a·rī´ah he called A·bed´ne·gō.

The name Daniel means "God is my judge." While at the palace, Daniel was given a Babylonian name. His new name, Belteshazzar, means "protect his life." Though he did not know what would happen in his life, both names seem to be good ones for this man!

8 But Daniel resolved that he would not defile himself with the royal rations of food and wine; so he asked the palace master to allow him not to defile himself. ⁹Now God

Daniel and his friends refused to eat food the Jewish people thought was unclean. If they had eaten the food, they would have been unclean and unfit to worship. But they remained faithful to God. What are some ways that you can remain faithful to God today?

allowed Daniel to receive favor and compassion from the palace master. ¹⁰The palace master said to Daniel, "I am afraid of my lord the king; he has appointed your food and your drink. If he should see you in poorer condition than the other young men of your own age, you would endanger my head with the king." ¹¹Then Daniel asked the guard whom the palace master had appointed over Daniel, Han·a·nī´ah, Mish´a·el, and Az·a·rī´ah: ¹²"Please test your servants for ten days. Let us be given vegetables to eat and water to drink. ¹³You can then compare our appearance with the appearance of the young men who eat the royal rations, and deal with your servants according to what you observe." ¹⁴So he agreed to this proposal and tested them for ten days. ¹⁵At the end of ten days it was observed that they appeared better and fatter than all the young men who had been eating the royal rations. ¹⁶So the guard continued to withdraw their royal rations and the wine they were to drink, and gave them vegetables. ¹⁷To these four young men God gave knowledge and skill in every aspect of literature and wisdom; Daniel also had insight into all visions and dreams.

18 At the end of the time that the king had set for them to be brought in, the palace master brought them into the presence of Ne·bū·chad·nez´zar, ¹⁹and the king spoke with them. And among them all, no one was found to compare with Daniel, Han·a·nī´ah, Mish´a·el, and Az·a·rī´ah; therefore they were stationed in the king's

ᵃ Gk Theodotion: Heb adds *to the house of his own gods*

court. ²⁰In every matter of wisdom and understanding concerning which the king inquired of them, he found them ten times better than all the magicians and enchanters in his whole kingdom. ²¹And Daniel continued there until the first year of King Cyrus.

Nebuchadnezzar's Dream

2 In the second year of Ne·bu·chad·nez´zar's reign, Ne·bu·chad·nez´zar dreamed such dreams that his spirit was troubled and his sleep left him. ²So the king commanded that the magicians, the enchanters, the sorcerers, and the Chal·dē´ans be summoned to tell the king his dreams. When they came in and stood before the king, ³he said to them, "I have had such a dream that my spirit is troubled by the desire to understand it." ⁴The Chal·dē´ans said to the king (in Ar·a·mā´ic),ᵇ "O king, live forever! Tell your servants the dream, and we will reveal the interpretation." ⁵The king answered the Chal·dē´ans, "This is a public decree: if you do not tell me both the dream and its interpretation, you shall be torn limb from limb, and your houses shall be laid in ruins. ⁶But if you do tell me the dream and its interpretation, you shall receive from me gifts and rewards and great honor. Therefore tell me the dream and its interpretation." ⁷They answered a second time, "Let the king first tell his servants the dream, then we can give its interpretation." ⁸The king answered, "I know with certainty that you are trying to gain time, because you see I have firmly decreed: ⁹if you do not tell me the dream, there is but one verdict for you. You have agreed to speak lying and misleading words to me until things take a turn. Therefore, tell me the dream, and I shall know that you can give me its interpretation." ¹⁰The Chal·dē´ans answered the

king, "There is no one on earth who can reveal what the king demands! In fact no king, however great and powerful, has ever asked such a thing of any magician or enchanter or Chal·dē´an. ¹¹The thing that the king is asking is too difficult, and no one can reveal it to the king except the gods, whose dwelling is not with mortals."

12 Because of this the king flew into a violent rage and commanded that all the wise men of Babylon be destroyed. ¹³The decree was issued, and the wise men were about to be executed; and they looked for Daniel and his companions, to execute them. ¹⁴Then Daniel responded with prudence and discretion to Ar´i·och, the king's chief executioner, who had gone out to execute the wise men of Babylon; ¹⁵he asked Ar´i·och, the royal official, "Why is the decree of the king so urgent?" Ar´i·och then explained the matter to Daniel. ¹⁶So Daniel went in and requested that the king give him time and he would tell the king the interpretation.

God Reveals
Nebuchadnezzar's Dream

17 Then Daniel went to his home and informed his companions, Han·a·nī´ah, Mish´a·el, and Az·a·rī´ah, ¹⁸and told them to seek mercy from the God of heaven concerning this mystery, so that Daniel and his companions with the rest of the wise men of Babylon might not perish. ¹⁹Then the mystery was revealed to Daniel in a vision of the night, and Daniel blessed the God of heaven.
²⁰ Daniel said:
"Blessed be the name of God from age to age,
    for wisdom and power are his.
²¹ He changes times and seasons,
    deposes kings and sets up kings;
he gives wisdom to the wise
    and knowledge to those who have understanding.

"Blessed be the name of God from age to age, for wisdom and power are his." Daniel 2:20

ᵇ The text from this point to the end of chapter 7 is in Aramaic

22 He reveals deep and hidden things;
    he knows what is in the darkness,
    and light dwells with him.
23 To you, O God of my ancestors,
    I give thanks and praise,
for you have given me wisdom and
    power,
    and have now revealed to me what
      we asked of you,
    for you have revealed to us what the
      king ordered."

King Nebuchadnezzar dreamed of a huge statue. When none of his wise men could tell him what the dream meant, Daniel said that he could explain the dream to the king. Daniel explained that the statue was a symbol for the four empires that ruled the world throughout ancient history—Babylon, Media, Persia, and Greece.

Daniel Interprets the Dream

24 Therefore Daniel went to Ar·i·och, whom the king had appointed to destroy the wise men of Babylon, and said to him, "Do not destroy the wise men of Babylon; bring me in before the king, and I will give the king the interpretation." 25 Then Ar·i·och quickly brought Daniel before the king and said to him: "I have found among the exiles from Judah a man who can tell the king the interpretation." 26 The king said to Daniel, whose name was Bel·te·shaz´zar, "Are you able to tell me the dream that I have seen and its interpretation?" 27 Daniel answered the king, "No wise men, enchanters, magicians, or diviners can show to the king the mystery that the king is asking, 28 but there is a God in heaven who reveals mysteries, and he has disclosed to King Ne·bū-chad·nez´zar what will happen at the end of days. Your dream and the visions of your head as you lay in bed were these:

29 To you, O king, as you lay in bed, came thoughts of what would be hereafter, and the revealer of mysteries disclosed to you what is to be. 30 But as for me, this mystery has not been revealed to me because of any wisdom that I have more than any other living being, but in order that the interpretation may be known to the king and that you may understand the thoughts of your mind.

31 "You were looking, O king, and lo! there was a great statue. This statue was huge, its brilliance extraordinary; it was standing before you, and its appearance was frightening. 32 The head of that statue was of fine gold, its chest and arms of silver, its middle and thighs of bronze, 33 its legs of iron, its feet partly of iron and partly of clay. 34 As you looked on, a stone was cut out, not by human hands, and it struck the statue on its feet of iron and clay and broke them in pieces. 35 Then the iron, the clay, the bronze, the silver, and the gold, were all broken in pieces and became like the chaff of the summer threshing floors; and the wind carried them away, so that not a trace of them could be found. But the stone that struck the statue became a great mountain and filled the whole earth.

36 "This was the dream; now we will tell the king its interpretation. 37 You, O king, the king of kings—to whom the God of heaven has given the kingdom, the power, the might, and the glory, 38 into whose hand he has given human beings, wherever they live, the wild animals of the field, and the birds of the air, and whom he has established as ruler over them all—you are the head of gold. 39 After you shall arise another kingdom inferior to yours, and yet a third kingdom of bronze, which shall rule over the whole earth. 40 And there shall be a fourth kingdom, strong as iron; just as iron crushes and smashes everything,[c] it shall crush and shatter all these. 41 As you saw the feet and toes partly of potter's clay and partly of iron, it shall be a divided

[c] Gk Theodotion Syr Vg: Aram adds *and like iron that crushes*

kingdom; but some of the strength of iron shall be in it, as you saw the iron mixed with the clay. [42]As the toes of the feet were part iron and part clay, so the kingdom shall be partly strong and partly brittle. [43]As you saw the iron mixed with clay, so will they mix with one another in marriage,[d] but they will not hold together, just as iron does not mix with clay. [44]And in the days of those kings the God of heaven will set up a kingdom that shall never be destroyed, nor shall this kingdom be left to another people. It shall crush all these kingdoms and bring them to an end, and it shall stand forever; [45]just as you saw that a stone was cut from the mountain not by hands, and that it crushed the iron, the bronze, the clay, the silver, and the gold. The great God has informed the king what shall be hereafter. The dream is certain, and its interpretation trustworthy."

Daniel and His Friends Promoted

46 Then King Ne·bu·chad·nez´zar fell on his face, worshiped Daniel, and commanded that a grain offering and incense be offered to him. [47]The king said to Daniel, "Truly, your God is God of gods and Lord of kings and a revealer of mysteries, for you have been able to reveal this mystery!" [48]Then the king promoted Daniel, gave him many great gifts, and made him ruler over the whole province of Babylon and chief prefect over all the wise men of Babylon. [49]Daniel made a request of the king, and he appointed Shad´rach, Me´shach, and A·bed´ne·go over the affairs of the province of Babylon. But Daniel remained at the king's court.

The Golden Image

3 King Ne·bu·chad·nez´zar made a golden statue whose height was sixty cubits and whose width was six cubits; he set it up on the plain of Du´ra in the province of Babylon. [2]Then King Ne·bu chad·nez´zar sent for the satraps, the prefects, and the governors, the counselors, the treasurers, the justices, the magistrates, and all the officials of the provinces, to assemble and come to the dedication of the statue that King Ne·bu·chad·nez´zar had set up. [3]So the satraps, the prefects, and the governors, the counselors, the treasurers, the justices, the magistrates, and all the officials of the provinces, assembled for the dedication of the statue that King Ne·bu·chad·nez´zar had set up. When they were standing before the statue that Ne·bu·chad·nez´zar had set up, [4]the herald proclaimed aloud, "You are commanded, O peoples, nations, and languages, [5]that when you hear the sound of the horn, pipe, lyre, trigon, harp, drum, and entire musical ensemble, you are to fall down and worship the golden statue that King Ne·bu·chad·nez´zar has set up. [6]Whoever does not fall down and worship shall immediately be thrown into a furnace of blazing fire." [7]Therefore, as soon as all the peoples heard the sound of the horn, pipe, lyre, trigon, harp, drum, and entire musical ensemble, all the peoples, nations, and languages fell down and worshiped the golden statue that King Ne·bu·chad·nez´zar had set up.

8 Accordingly, at this time certain Chal·de´ans came forward and denounced the Jews. [9]They said to King Ne·bu·chad·nez´zar, "O king, live forever! [10]You, O king, have made a decree, that everyone who hears the sound of the horn, pipe, lyre, trigon, harp, drum, and entire musical ensemble, shall fall down and worship the golden statue, [11]and whoever does not fall down and worship shall be thrown into a furnace of blazing fire. [12]There are certain Jews whom you have appointed over the affairs of the province of Babylon:

You do the math! If King Nebuchadnezzar's statue was 60 cubits tall, how many feet and inches would it be? (Hint: 1 cubit is 18 inches.)

[d] Aram *by human seed*

Shad′rach, Mē′shach, and A·bed′ne·gō. These pay no heed to you, O king. They do not serve your gods and they do not worship the golden statue that you have set up."

13 Then Ne·bū·chad·nez′zar in furious rage commanded that Shad′rach, Mē′shach, and A·bed′ne·gō be brought in; so they brought those men before the king. ¹⁴Ne·bū·chad·nez′zar said to them, "Is it true, O Shad′rach, Mē′shach, and A·bed′ne·gō, that you do not serve my gods and you do not worship the golden statue that I have set up? ¹⁵Now if you are ready when you hear the sound of the horn, pipe, lyre, trigon, harp, drum, and entire musical ensemble to fall down and worship the statue that I have made, well and good.ᵉ But if you do not worship, you shall immediately be thrown into a furnace of blazing fire, and who is the god that will deliver you out of my hands?"

16 Shad′rach, Mē′shach, and A·bed′ne·gōanswered the king, "O Ne·bū·chad·nez′zar, we have no need to present a defense to you in this matter. ¹⁷If our God whom we serve is able to deliver us from the furnace of blazing fire and out of your hand, O king, let him deliver us.ᶠ ¹⁸But if not, be it known to you, O king, that we will not serve your gods and we will not worship the golden statue that you have set up."

The Fiery Furnace

19 Then Ne·bū·chad·nez′zar was so filled with rage against Shad′rach, Mē′shach, and A·bed′ne·gō that his face was distorted. He ordered the furnace heated up seven times more than was customary, ²⁰and ordered some of the strongest guards in his army to bind Shad′rach, Mē′shach, and A·bed′ne·gō and to throw them into the furnace of blazing fire. ²¹So the men were bound, still wearing their tunics,ᵍ their trousers,ᵍ their hats, and their other garments, and they were thrown into the furnace of blazing fire. ²²Because the king's command was urgent and the furnace was so overheated, the raging flames killed the

Shadrach, Meshach, and Abednego were friends with Daniel. Along with Daniel, they became favorites of the king. When these men refused to worship an idol (something that gets in the way of our relationship with God by pulling us away from God), they knew they were choosing to face death. They were put in a fiery furnace, but they were not harmed by the fire!

Sometimes it is very easy to be faithful to God. Other times it is very hard. God is always faithful to us. Read the following verses and pray that God will help you be faithful: Psalm 85:8–11, Proverbs 3:3–4, Matthew 24:45–47, Luke 16:10, and 1 Corinthians 10:13.

men who lifted Shad′rach, Mē′shach, and A·bed′ne·gō. ²³But the three men, Shad′rach, Mē′shach, and A·bed′ne·gō, fell down, bound, into the furnace of blazing fire.

24 Then King Ne·bū·chad·nez′zar was astonished and rose up quickly. He said to his counselors, "Was it not three men that we threw bound into the fire?" They answered the king, "True, O king." ²⁵He replied, "But I see four men unbound, walking in the middle of the fire, and they are not hurt; and the fourth has the appearance of a god."ʰ ²⁶Ne·bū·chad·nez′zar then approached the door of the furnace of blazing fire and said, "Shad′rach, Mē′shach, and A·bed′ne·gō, servants of the Most High God, come out! Come here!" So Shad′rach, Mē′shach, and A·bed′ne·gō came out from the fire. ²⁷And the satraps, the prefects, the governors, and the king's counselors gathered together and saw that the fire had not had any power over the bodies of those men;

ᵉ Aram lacks *well and good*   ᶠ Or *If our God whom we serve is able to deliver us, he will deliver us from the furnace of blazing fire and out of your hand, O king.*   ᵍ Meaning of Aram word uncertain   ʰ Aram *a son of the gods* the hair of their heads was not singed, their tunics[i] were not harmed, and not even the smell of fire came from them. [28]Ne·bu·chad·nez´zar said, "Blessed be the God of Shad´rach, Me´shach, and A·bed´ne·go, who has sent his angel and delivered his servants who trusted in him. They disobeyed the king's command and yielded up their bodies rather than serve and worship any god except their own God. [29]Therefore I make a decree: Any people, nation, or language that utters blasphemy against the God of Shad´rach, Me´shach, and A·bed´ne·go shall be torn limb from limb, and their houses laid in ruins; for there is no other god who is able to deliver in this way." [30]Then the king promoted Shad´rach, Me´shach, and A·bed´ne·go in the province of Babylon.

Nebuchadnezzar's Second Dream

4 [j]King Ne·bu·chad·nez´zar to all peoples, nations, and languages that live throughout the earth: May you have abundant prosperity! [2]The signs and wonders that the Most High God has worked for me I am pleased to recount.

[3] How great are his signs,
 how mighty his wonders!
His kingdom is an everlasting
  kingdom,
 and his sovereignty is from
  generation to generation.

[4][k] I, Ne·bu·chad·nez´zar, was living at ease in my home and prospering in my palace. [5]I saw a dream that frightened me; my fantasies in bed and the visions of my head terrified me. [6]So I made a decree that all the wise men of Babylon should be brought before me, in order that they might tell me the interpretation of the dream. [7]Then the magicians, the enchanters, the Chal·de´ans, and the diviners came in, and I told them the dream, but they could not tell me its interpretation. [8]At last Daniel came in before me—he who was named Bel·te·shaz´zar after the name of my god, and who is endowed with a spirit of the holy gods[l]—and I told him the dream: [9]"O Bel·te·shaz´zar, chief of

the magicians, I know that you are endowed with a spirit of the holy gods[l] and that no mystery is too difficult for you. Hear[m] the dream that I saw; tell me its interpretation.

[10][n] Upon my bed this is what I saw;
  there was a tree at the center of the
   earth,
  and its height was great.
[11] The tree grew great and strong,
  its top reached to heaven,
  and it was visible to the ends of the
   whole earth.
[12] Its foliage was beautiful,
  its fruit abundant,
  and it provided food for all.
The animals of the field found shade
  under it,
  the birds of the air nested in its
   branches,
  and from it all living beings were fed.

[13] "I continued looking, in the visions of my head as I lay in bed, and there was a holy watcher, coming down from heaven. [14]He cried aloud and said:

'Cut down the tree and chop off its
   branches,
  strip off its foliage and scatter its
   fruit.
Let the animals flee from beneath it
  and the birds from its branches.
[15] But leave its stump and roots in the
   ground,
  with a band of iron and bronze,
  in the tender grass of the field.
Let him be bathed with the dew of
   heaven,
  and let his lot be with the animals of
   the field
  in the grass of the earth.
[16] Let his mind be changed from that of a
   human,
  and let the mind of an animal be
   given to him.

[i] Meaning of Aram word uncertain [j] Ch 3.31 in Aram [k] Ch 4.1 in Aram [l] Or *a holy, divine spirit* [m] Theodotion: Aram *The visions of* [n] Theodotion Syr Compare Gk: Aram adds *The visions of my head*

And let seven times pass over him.
[17] The sentence is rendered by decree of
      the watchers,
    the decision is given by order of the
      holy ones,
  in order that all who live may know
    that the Most High is sovereign over
      the kingdom of mortals;
  he gives it to whom he will
    and sets over it the lowliest of
      human beings.'

18 "This is the dream that I, King Ne·bū-
chad·nez´zar, saw. Now you, Bel·te-
shaz´zar, declare the interpretation, since
all the wise men of my kingdom are unable
to tell me the interpretation. You are able,
however, for you are endowed with a spirit
of the holy gods."[o]

Daniel Interprets the
Second Dream

19 Then Daniel, who was called
Bel·te·shaz´zar, was severely distressed for
a while. His thoughts terrified him. The
king said, "Bel·te·shaz´zar, do not let the
dream or the interpretation terrify you."
Bel·te·shaz´zar answered, "My lord, may
the dream be for those who hate you, and
its interpretation for your enemies! [20]The
tree that you saw, which grew great and
strong, so that its top reached to heaven
and was visible to the end of the whole
earth, [21]whose foliage was beautiful and
its fruit abundant, and which provided
food for all, under which animals of the
field lived, and in whose branches the
birds of the air had nests— [22]it is you, O
king! You have grown great and strong.
Your greatness has increased and reaches
to heaven, and your sovereignty to the
ends of the earth. [23]And whereas the king
saw a holy watcher coming down from
heaven and saying, 'Cut down the tree and
destroy it, but leave its stump and roots in
the ground, with a band of iron and
bronze, in the grass of the field; and let
him be bathed with the dew of heaven,
and let his lot be with the animals of the
field, until seven times pass over him'—

[24]this is the interpretation, O king, and it
is a decree of the Most High that has come
upon my lord the king: [25]You shall be
driven away from human society, and
your dwelling shall be with the wild animals. You shall be made to eat grass like
oxen, you shall be bathed with the dew of
heaven, and seven times shall pass over
you, until you have learned that the Most
High has sovereignty over the kingdom of
mortals, and gives it to whom he will. [26]As
it was commanded to leave the stump and
roots of the tree, your kingdom shall be
reestablished for you from the time that
you learn that Heaven is sovereign.
[27]Therefore, O king, may my counsel be
acceptable to you: atone for[p] your sins
with righteousness, and your iniquities
with mercy to the oppressed, so that your
prosperity may be prolonged."

Nebuchadnezzar's Humiliation

28 All this came upon King Ne·bū-
chad·nez´zar. [29]At the end of twelve
months he was walking on the roof of
the royal palace of Babylon, [30]and the
king said, "Is this not magnificent
Babylon, which I have built as a royal
capital by my mighty power and for my
glorious majesty?" [31]While the words
were still in the king's mouth, a voice
came from heaven: "O King Ne·bū-
chad·nez´zar, to you it is declared: The
kingdom has departed from you! [32]You
shall be driven away from human society, and your dwelling shall be with the
animals of the field. You shall be made to
eat grass like oxen, and seven times shall
pass over you, until you have learned
that the Most High has sovereignty over
the kingdom of mortals and gives it to
whom he will." [33]Immediately the sentence was fulfilled against Ne·bū-
chad·nez´zar. He was driven away from
human society, ate grass like oxen, and his
body was bathed with the dew of heaven,
until his hair grew as long as eagles' feath-
ers and his nails became like birds' claws.

---

[o] Or *a holy, divine spirit*   [p] Aram *break off*

"Now I, Nebuchadnezzar, praise and extol and honor the King of heaven, for all his works are truth, and his ways are justice; and he is able to bring low those who walk in pride."   Daniel 4:37

Nebuchadnezzar Praises God

34 When that period was over, I, Ne·bū-chad·nez´zar, lifted my eyes to heaven, and my reason returned to me.

I blessed the Most High,
    and praised and honored the one
        who lives forever.
For his sovereignty is an everlasting
        sovereignty,
    and his kingdom endures from
        generation to generation.
[35] All the inhabitants of the earth are
        accounted as nothing,
    and he does what he wills with the
        host of heaven
    and the inhabitants of the earth.
There is no one who can stay his hand
    or say to him, "What are you
        doing?"

[36]At that time my reason returned to me; and my majesty and splendor were restored to me for the glory of my kingdom. My counselors and my lords sought me out, I was reestablished over my kingdom, and still more greatness was added to me. [37]Now I, Ne·bū·chad·nez´zar, praise and extol and honor the King of heaven,
    for all his works are truth,
        and his ways are justice;
    and he is able to bring low
        those who walk in pride.

Belshazzar's Feast

5 King Bel·shaz´zar made a great festival for a thousand of his lords, and he was drinking wine in the presence of the thousand.

2 Under the influence of the wine, Bel·shaz´zar commanded that they bring in the vessels of gold and silver that his father Ne·bū·chad·nez´zar had taken out of the

temple in Jerusalem, so that the king and his lords, his wives, and his concubines might drink from them. [3]So they brought in the vessels of gold and silver[q] that had been taken out of the temple, the house of God in Jerusalem, and the king and his lords, his wives, and his concubines drank from them. [4]They drank the wine and praised the gods of gold and silver, bronze, iron, wood, and stone.

The Writing on the Wall

5 Immediately the fingers of a human hand appeared and began writing on the plaster of the wall of the royal palace, next to the lampstand. The king was watching the hand as it wrote. [6]Then the king's face turned pale, and his thoughts terrified him. His limbs gave way, and his knees knocked together. [7]The king cried aloud to bring in the enchanters, the Chal·dē´ans, and the diviners; and the king said to the wise men of Babylon, "Whoever can read this writing and tell me its interpretation shall be clothed in purple, have a chain of gold around his neck, and rank third in the kingdom." [8]Then all the king's wise men came in, but they could not read the writing or tell the king the interpretation. [9]Then King Bel·shaz´zar became greatly

King Belshazzar had a huge party. He and his guests drank wine from the golden cups that came from God's Temple in Jerusalem. In the middle of their fun and laughter, they suddenly saw a hand writing on the wall. No one at the party could read this writing, but the queen knew that Daniel would be able to. Daniel read the writing on the wall and told the king that his kingdom would be taken over by the Medes and Persians.

[q] Theodotion Vg: Aram lacks and silver

terrified and his face turned pale, and his lords were perplexed.

10 The queen, when she heard the discussion of the king and his lords, came into the banqueting hall. The queen said, "O king, live forever! Do not let your thoughts terrify you or your face grow pale. ¹¹There is a man in your kingdom who is endowed with a spirit of the holy gods.ʳ In the days of your father he was found to have enlightenment, understanding, and wisdom like the wisdom of the gods. Your father, King Ne·bu·chad·nez´zar, made him chief of the magicians, enchanters, Chal·de´ans, and diviners,ˢ ¹²because an excellent spirit, knowledge, and understanding to interpret dreams, explain riddles, and solve problems were found in this Daniel, whom the king named Bel·te·shaz´zar. Now let Daniel be called, and he will give the interpretation."

The Writing on the Wall Interpreted

13 Then Daniel was brought in before the king. The king said to Daniel, "So you are Daniel, one of the exiles of Judah, whom my father the king brought from Judah? ¹⁴I have heard of you that a spirit of the godsᵗ is in you, and that enlightenment, understanding, and excellent wisdom are found in you. ¹⁵Now the wise men, the enchanters, have been brought in before me to read this writing and tell me its interpretation, but they were not able to give the interpretation of the matter. ¹⁶But I have heard that you can give interpretations and solve problems. Now if you are able to read the writing and tell me its interpretation, you shall be clothed in purple, have a chain of gold around your neck, and rank third in the kingdom."

17 Then Daniel answered in the presence of the king, "Let your gifts be for yourself, or give your rewards to someone else! Nevertheless I will read the writing to the king and let him know the interpretation. ¹⁸O king, the Most High God gave your father Ne·bu·chad·nez´zar kingship, greatness, glory, and majesty. ¹⁹And

because of the greatness that he gave him, all peoples, nations, and languages trembled and feared before him. He killed those he wanted to kill, kept alive those he wanted to keep alive, honored those he wanted to honor, and degraded those he wanted to degrade. ²⁰But when his heart was lifted up and his spirit was hardened so that he acted proudly, he was deposed from his kingly throne, and his glory was stripped from him. ²¹He was driven from human society, and his mind was made like that of an animal. His dwelling was with the wild asses, he was fed grass like oxen, and his body was bathed with the dew of heaven, until he learned that the Most High God has sovereignty over the kingdom of mortals, and sets over it whomever he will. ²²And you, Bel·shaz´zar his son, have not humbled your heart, even though you knew all this! ²³You have exalted yourself against the Lord of heaven! The vessels of his temple have been brought in before you, and you and your lords, your wives and your concubines have been drinking wine from them. You have praised the gods of silver and gold, of bronze, iron, wood, and stone, which do not see or hear or know; but the God in whose power is your very breath, and to whom belong all your ways, you have not honored.

24 "So from his presence the hand was sent and this writing was inscribed. ²⁵And this is the writing that was inscribed: MENE, MENE, TEKEL, and PARSIN. ²⁶This is the interpretation of the matter: MENE, God has numbered the days ofᵘ your kingdom and brought it to an end; ²⁷TEKEL, you have been weighed on the scales and found wanting; ²⁸PERES,ᵛ your kingdom is divided and given to the Medes and Persians."

29 Then Bel·shaz´zar gave the command, and Daniel was clothed in purple, a chain of gold was put around his neck, and a proclamation was made concerning him

---

ʳ Or *a holy, divine spirit*   ˢ Aram adds *the king your father*   ᵗ Or *a holy, divine spirit*   ᵘ Aram lacks *the days of*   ᵛ The singular of *Parsin* that he should rank third in the kingdom.

30 That very night Bel·shaz´zar, the Chal·de´an king, was killed. [31]w And Da·rī´us the Mēde received the kingdom, being about sixty-two years old.

The Plot against Daniel

6 It pleased Da·rī´us to set over the kingdom one hundred twenty satraps, stationed throughout the whole kingdom, [2]and over them three presidents, including Daniel; to these the satraps gave account, so that the king might suffer no loss. [3]Soon Daniel distinguished himself above all the other presidents and satraps because an excellent spirit was in him, and the king planned to appoint him over the whole kingdom. [4]So the presidents and the satraps tried to find grounds for complaint against Daniel in connection with the kingdom. But they could find no grounds for complaint or any corruption, because he was faithful, and no negligence or corruption could be found in him. [5]The men said, "We shall not find any ground for complaint against this Daniel unless we find it in connection with the law of his God."

6 So the presidents and satraps conspired and came to the king and said to him, "O King Da·rī´us, live forever! [7]All the presidents of the kingdom, the prefects and the satraps, the counselors and the governors are agreed that the king should establish an ordinance and enforce an interdict, that whoever prays to anyone, divine or human, for thirty days, except to you, O king, shall be thrown into a den of lions. [8]Now, O king, establish the interdict and sign the document, so that it cannot be changed, according to the law of the Mēdes and the Persians, which cannot be revoked." [9]Therefore King Da·rī´us signed the document and interdict.

Daniel in the Lions' Den

10 Although Daniel knew that the document had been signed, he continued to go to his house, which had windows in its upper room open toward Jerusalem, and to get down on his knees three times a day to pray to his God and praise him, just as he had done previously. [11]The conspirators came and found Daniel praying and seeking mercy before his God. [12]Then they approached the king and said concerning the interdict, "O king! Did you not sign an interdict, that anyone who prays to anyone, divine or human, within thirty days except to you, O king, shall be thrown into a den of lions?" The king answered, "The thing stands fast, according to the law of the Mēdes and Persians, which cannot be revoked." [13]Then they responded to the king, "Daniel, one of the exiles from Judah, pays no attention to you, O king, or to the interdict you have signed, but he is saying his prayers three times a day."

14 When the king heard the charge, he was very much distressed. He was determined to save Daniel, and until the sun went down he made every effort to rescue him. [15]Then the conspirators came to the king and said to him, "Know, O king, that it is a law of the Mēdes and Persians that no interdict or ordinance that the king establishes can be changed."

16 Then the king gave the command, and Daniel was brought and thrown into the den of lions. The king said to Daniel, "May your God, whom you faithfully serve, deliver you!" [17]A stone was brought and laid on the mouth of the den, and the king sealed it with his own signet and with the signet of his lords, so that nothing might be changed concerning Daniel.

Daniel went to a quiet place to pray three times a day. The windows in Daniel's room probably faced toward Jerusalem. Read Psalm 55:17. At what times of the day did the writer of this psalm pray? Do you think those were the only times he prayed? When do you pray?

In ancient times, people made seals by carving a design into clay, bone, metal, stone, or precious gems. They would then press this design into clay to serve as a type of signature. People used seals to close letters or official documents. A king's seal was one of the signs of his authority.

Today a person called a notary public uses a metal instrument to put his or her seal on official documents. This seal shows that what is written in the document is true. You can also buy small instruments made from plastic or metal to press into wax as a way to decorate an envelope when you send a letter.

18Then the king went to his palace and spent the night fasting; no food was brought to him, and sleep fled from him.

Daniel Saved from the Lions

19 Then, at break of day, the king got up and hurried to the den of lions. 20When he came near the den where Daniel was, he cried out anxiously to Daniel, "O Daniel, servant of the living God, has your God whom you faithfully serve been able to deliver you from the lions?" 21Daniel then said to the king, "O king, live forever! 22My God sent his angel and shut the lions' mouths so that they would not hurt me, because I was found blameless before him; and also before you, O king, I have done no wrong." 23Then the king was exceedingly glad and commanded that Daniel be taken up out of the den. So

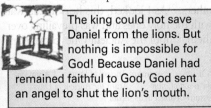

The king could not save Daniel from the lions. But nothing is impossible for God! Because Daniel had remained faithful to God, God sent an angel to shut the lion's mouth.

Daniel was taken up out of the den, and no kind of harm was found on him, because he had trusted in his God. 24The king gave a command, and those who had accused Daniel were brought and thrown into the den of lions—they, their children, and their wives. Before they reached the bottom of the den the lions overpowered them and broke all their bones in pieces.

25 Then King Da·rī´us wrote to all peoples and nations of every language throughout the whole world: "May you have abundant prosperity! 26I make a decree, that in all my royal dominion people should tremble and fear before the God of Daniel:

For he is the living God,
    enduring forever.
His kingdom shall never be destroyed,
    and his dominion has no end.
27 He delivers and rescues,
    he works signs and wonders in
        heaven and on earth;
for he has saved Daniel
    from the power of the lions."
28So this Daniel prospered during the reign of Da·rī´us and the reign of Cyrus the Persian.

Visions of the Four Beasts

7 In the first year of King Bel·shaz´zar of Babylon, Daniel had a dream and visions of his head as he lay in bed. Then he wrote down the dream:*x* 2I,*y* Daniel, saw in my vision by night the four winds of heaven stirring up the great sea, 3and four

"Then King Darius wrote ... 'For he is the living God, enduring forever. His kingdom shall never be destroyed, and his dominion has no end. He delivers and rescues, he works signs and wonders in heaven and on earth; for he has saved Daniel from the power of the lions.'" Daniel 6:26*b*–27

x Q Ms Theodotion: MT adds *the beginning of the words; he said* *y* Theodotion: Aram *Daniel answered and said, "I* great beasts came up out of the sea, different from one another. ⁴The first was like a lion and had eagles' wings. Then, as I watched, its wings were plucked off, and it was lifted up from the ground and made to stand on two feet like a human being; and a human mind was given to it. ⁵Another beast appeared, a second one, that looked like a bear. It was raised up on one side, had three tusks² in its mouth among its teeth and was told, "Arise, devour many bodies!" ⁶After this, as I watched, another appeared, like a leopard. The beast had four wings of a bird on its back and four heads; and dominion was given to it. ⁷After this I saw in the visions by night a fourth beast, terrifying and dreadful and exceedingly strong. It had great iron teeth and was devouring, breaking in pieces, and stamping what was left with its feet. It was different from all the beasts that preceded it, and it had ten horns. ⁸I was considering the horns, when another horn appeared, a little one coming up among them; to make room for it, three of the earlier horns were plucked up by the roots. There were eyes like human eyes in this horn, and a mouth speaking arrogantly.

Judgment before the Ancient One

⁹ As I watched,
thrones were set in place,
    and an Ancient One*ᵃ* took his
        throne,
his clothing was white as snow,
    and the hair of his head like pure
        wool;
his throne was fiery flames,
    and its wheels were burning fire.
¹⁰ A stream of fire issued
    and flowed out from his presence.
A thousand thousands served him,
    and ten thousand times ten
        thousand stood attending him.
The court sat in judgment,
    and the books were opened.

¹¹I watched then because of the noise of the arrogant words that the horn was speaking. And as I watched, the beast was put to death, and its body destroyed and

given over to be burned with fire. ¹²As for the rest of the beasts, their dominion was taken away, but their lives were prolonged for a season and a time. ¹³As I watched in the night visions,

I saw one like a human being*ᵇ*
    coming with the clouds of heaven.
And he came to the Ancient One*ᶜ*
    and was presented before him.
¹⁴ To him was given dominion
    and glory and kingship,
that all peoples, nations, and languages
    should serve him.
His dominion is an everlasting
        dominion
    that shall not pass away,
and his kingship is one
    that shall never be destroyed.

Daniel's Visions Interpreted

15 As for me, Daniel, my spirit was troubled within me,*ᵈ* and the visions of my head terrified me. ¹⁶I approached one of the attendants to ask him the truth concerning all this. So he said that he would disclose to me the interpretation of the matter: ¹⁷"As for these four great beasts, four kings shall arise out of the earth. ¹⁸But the holy ones of the Most High shall receive the kingdom and possess the kingdom forever—forever and ever."

19 Then I desired to know the truth concerning the fourth beast, which was different from all the rest, exceedingly terrifying, with its teeth of iron and claws of bronze, and which devoured and broke in pieces, and stamped what was left with its feet; ²⁰and concerning the ten horns that were on its head, and concerning the other horn, which came up and to make room for which three of them fell out—the horn that had eyes and a mouth that spoke arrogantly, and that seemed greater than the others. ²¹As I looked, this horn made war with the holy ones and was prevailing over them, ²²until the Ancient One*ᶜ* came; then

---

² Or ribs *ᵃ Aram* an Ancient of Days *ᵇ Aram* one
like a son of man *ᶜ Aram* the Ancient of Days
ᵈ Aram troubled in its sheath

judgment was given for the holy ones of the Most High, and the time arrived when the holy ones gained possession of the kingdom.

23 This is what he said: "As for the fourth beast,

there shall be a fourth kingdom on
    earth
    that shall be different from all the
        other kingdoms;
it shall devour the whole earth,
    and trample it down, and break it to
        pieces.

24 As for the ten horns,
out of this kingdom ten kings shall
    arise,
    and another shall arise after them.
This one shall be different from the
    former ones,
    and shall put down three kings.

25 He shall speak words against the Most
    High,
    shall wear out the holy ones of the
        Most High,
    and shall attempt to change the
        sacred seasons and the law;
and they shall be given into his
    power
    for a time, two times,[e] and half a
        time.

26 Then the court shall sit in
    judgment,
    and his dominion shall be taken
        away,
    to be consumed and totally
        destroyed.

27 The kingship and dominion
    and the greatness of the kingdoms
        under the whole heaven
    shall be given to the people of the
        holy ones of the Most High;
    their kingdom shall be an everlasting
        kingdom,
    and all dominions shall serve and
        obey them."

28 Here the account ends. As for me, Daniel, my thoughts greatly terrified me, and my face turned pale; but I kept the matter in my mind.

Vision of a Ram and a Goat

8 In the third year of the reign of King Bel·shaz′zar a vision appeared to me, Daniel, after the one that had appeared to me at first. [2]In the vision I was looking and saw myself in Su′sa the capital, in the province of E′lam,[f] and I was by the river U′lai[g] [3]I looked up and saw a ram standing beside the river.[h] It had two horns. Both horns were long, but one was longer than the other, and the longer one came up second. [4]I saw the ram charging westward and northward and southward. All beasts were powerless to withstand it, and no one could rescue from its power; it did as it pleased and became strong.

5 As I was watching, a male goat appeared from the west, coming across the face of the whole earth without touching the ground. The goat had a horn[i] between its eyes. [6]It came toward the ram with the two horns that I had seen standing beside the river,[h] and it ran at it with savage force. [7]I saw it approaching the ram. It was enraged against it and struck the ram, breaking its two horns. The ram did not have power to withstand it; it threw the ram down to the ground and trampled upon it, and there was no one who could rescue the ram from its power. [8]Then the male goat grew exceedingly great; but at the height of its power, the great horn was broken, and in its place there came up four prominent horns toward the four winds of heaven.

9 Out of one of them came another[j] horn, a little one, which grew exceedingly great toward the south, toward the east, and toward the beautiful land. [10]It grew as high as the host of heaven. It threw down to the earth some of the host and some of the stars, and trampled on them. [11]Even against the prince of the host it acted arrogantly; it took the regular burnt offering away from him and overthrew the place of

[e] Aram *a time, times*   [f] Gk Theodotion: MT Q Ms repeat *in the vision I was looking*   [g] Or *the Ulai Gate*   [h] Or *gate*   [i] Theodotion: Gk *one horn*; Heb *a horn of vision*   [j] Cn Compare 7.8: Heb *one*

his sanctuary. [12]Because of wickedness, the host was given over to it together with the regular burnt offering;[k] it cast truth to the ground, and kept prospering in what it did. [13]Then I heard a holy one speaking, and another holy one said to the one that spoke, "For how long is this vision concerning the regular burnt offering, the transgression that makes desolate, and the giving over of the sanctuary and host to be trampled?"[k] [14]And he answered him,[l] "For two thousand three hundred evenings and mornings; then the sanctuary shall be restored to its rightful state."

Daniel had been able to interpret dreams for kings, but he had a strange vision he could not understand. Suddenly he heard a voice telling someone named Gabriel to help him understand. Gabriel is a messenger angel whose name means "man of God." Gabriel explained Daniel's vision—the ram he saw was a symbol for Antiochus, who had treated God's Temple with great disrespect.

Gabriel Interprets the Vision

15 When I, Daniel, had seen the vision, I tried to understand it. Then someone appeared standing before me, having the appearance of a man, [16]and I heard a human voice by the Ūlaī, calling, "Gabriel, help this man understand the vision." [17]So he came near where I stood; and when he came, I became frightened and fell prostrate. But he said to me, "Understand, O mortal,[m] that the vision is for the time of the end."

18 As he was speaking to me, I fell into a trance, face to the ground; then he touched me and set me on my feet. [19]He said, "Listen, and I will tell you what will take place later in the period of wrath; for it refers to the appointed time of the end. [20]As for the ram that you saw with the two

horns, these are the kings of Mēd·i·a and Persia. [21]The male goat[n] is the king of Greece, and the great horn between its eyes is the first king. [22]As for the horn that was broken, in place of which four others arose, four kingdoms shall arise from his[o] nation, but not with his power.

[23] At the end of their rule,
  when the transgressions have
    reached their full measure,
 a king of bold countenance shall arise,
    skilled in intrigue.
[24] He shall grow strong in power,[p]
    shall cause fearful destruction,
    and shall succeed in what he does.
 He shall destroy the powerful
    and the people of the holy ones.
[25] By his cunning
  he shall make deceit prosper under
    his hand,
    and in his own mind he shall be
      great.
 Without warning he shall destroy
      many
    and shall even rise up against the
      Prince of princes.
 But he shall be broken, and not by
      human hands.
[26]The vision of the evenings and the mornings that has been told is true. As for you, seal up the vision, for it refers to many days from now."

27 So I, Daniel, was overcome and lay sick for some days; then I arose and went about the king's business. But I was dismayed by the vision and did not understand it.

Daniel's Prayer for the People

9 In the first year of Da·rī´us son of A·has·u·ē´rus, by birth a Mēde, who became king over the realm of the Chal·dē´ans— [2]in the first year of his reign, I, Daniel, perceived in the books the number of years that, according to the word of the

[k] Meaning of Heb uncertain   [l] Gk Theodotion Syr Vg: Heb me   [m] Heb son of man   [n] Or shaggy male goat   [o] Gk Theodotion Vg: Heb the
[p] Theodotion and one Gk Ms: Heb repeats (from 8.22) but not with his power

LORD to the prophet Jer·e·mi´ah, must be fulfilled for the devastation of Jerusalem, namely, seventy years.

3 Then I turned to the Lord God, to seek an answer by prayer and supplication with fasting and sackcloth and ashes. ⁴I prayed to the LORD my God and made confession, saying,

"Ah, Lord, great and awesome God, keeping covenant and steadfast love with those who love you and keep your commandments, ⁵we have sinned and done wrong, acted wickedly and rebelled, turning aside from your commandments and ordinances. ⁶We have not listened to your servants the prophets, who spoke in your name to our kings, our princes, and our ancestors, and to all the people of the land.

7 "Righteousness is on your side, O Lord, but open shame, as at this day, falls on us, the people of Judah, the inhabitants of Jerusalem, and all Israel, those who are near and those who are far away, in all the lands to which you have driven them, because of the treachery that they have committed against you. ⁸Open shame, O LORD, falls on us, our kings, our officials, and our ancestors, because we have sinned against you. ⁹To the Lord our God belong mercy and forgiveness, for we have rebelled against him, ¹⁰and have not obeyed the voice of the LORD our God by following his laws, which he set before us by his servants the prophets.

11 "All Israel has transgressed your law and turned aside, refusing to obey your voice. So the curse and the oath written in the law of Moses, the servant of God, have been poured out upon us, because we have sinned against you. ¹²He has confirmed his words, which he spoke against us and against our rulers, by bringing upon us a calamity so great that what has been done against Jerusalem has never before been done under the whole heaven. ¹³Just as it is written in the law of Moses, all this calamity has come upon us. We did not entreat the favor of the LORD our God, turning from our iniquities and reflecting on his*q* fidelity. ¹⁴So the LORD kept watch over this calamity until he brought it upon us. Indeed, the LORD our God is right in all that he has done; for we have disobeyed his voice.

15 "And now, O Lord our God, who brought your people out of the land of Egypt with a mighty hand and made your name renowned even to this day—we have sinned, we have done wickedly. ¹⁶O Lord, in view of all your righteous acts, let your anger and wrath, we pray, turn away from your city Jerusalem, your holy mountain; because of our sins and the iniquities of our ancestors, Jerusalem and your people have become a disgrace among all our neighbors. ¹⁷Now therefore, O our God, listen to the prayer of your servant and to his supplication, and for your own sake, Lord,*r* let your face shine upon your desolated sanctuary. ¹⁸Incline your ear, O my God, and hear. Open your eyes and look at our desolation and the city that bears your name. We do not present our supplication before you on the ground of our righteousness, but on the ground of your great mercies. ¹⁹O Lord, hear; O Lord, forgive; O Lord, listen and act and do not delay! For your own sake, O my God, because your city and your people bear your name!"

Daniel confessed the sins of the people to God and asked that God show mercy and forgive them. While he was praying, Gabriel came to Daniel to give him comfort and strength and to assure Daniel that God loved him.

Has anyone ever come to give you comfort and strength when you were worried or afraid? If so, say a prayer of thanks to God for that person. If not, ask your family members if this has happened to any of them. Pray together as a family, giving thanks for the person who helped.

q Heb *your*   *r* Theodotion Vg Compare Syr: Heb *for the Lord's sake*

The Seventy Weeks

20 While I was speaking, and was praying and confessing my sin and the sin of my people Israel, and presenting my supplication before the LORD my God on behalf of the holy mountain of my God— [21]while I was speaking in prayer, the man Gabriel, whom I had seen before in a vision, came to me in swift flight at the time of the evening sacrifice. [22]He came[s] and said to me, "Daniel, I have now come out to give you wisdom and understanding. [23]At the beginning of your supplications a word went out, and I have come to declare it, for you are greatly beloved. So consider the word and understand the vision:

24 "Seventy weeks are decreed for your people and your holy city: to finish the transgression, to put an end to sin, and to atone for iniquity, to bring in everlasting righteousness, to seal both vision and prophet, and to anoint a most holy place.[t] [25]Know therefore and understand: from the time that the word went out to restore and rebuild Jerusalem until the time of an anointed prince, there shall be seven weeks; and for sixty-two weeks it shall be built again with streets and moat, but in a troubled time. [26]After the sixty-two weeks, an anointed one shall be cut off and shall have nothing, and the troops of the prince who is to come shall destroy the city and the sanctuary. Its[u] end shall come with a flood, and to the end there shall be war. Desolations are decreed. [27]He shall make a strong covenant with many for one week, and for half of the week he shall make sacrifice and offering cease; and in their place[v] shall be an abomination that desolates, until the decreed end is poured out upon the desolator."

Conflict of Nations and Heavenly Powers

10 In the third year of King Cyrus of Persia a word was revealed to Daniel, who was named Bel·te·shaz´zar. The word was true, and it concerned a great conflict. He understood the word, having received understanding in the vision.

2 At that time I, Daniel, had been mourning for three weeks. [3]I had eaten no rich food, no meat or wine had entered my mouth, and I had not anointed myself at all, for the full three weeks. [4]On the twenty-fourth day of the first month, as I was standing on the bank of the great river (that is, the Tigris), [5]I looked up and saw a man clothed in linen, with a belt of gold from U̅phaz around his waist. [6]His body was like beryl, his face like lightning, his eyes like flaming torches, his arms and legs like the gleam of burnished bronze, and the sound of his words like the roar of a multitude. [7]I, Daniel, alone saw the vision; the people who were with me did not see the vision, though a great trembling fell upon them, and they fled and hid themselves. [8]So I was left alone to see this great vision. My strength left me, and my complexion grew deathly pale, and I retained no strength. [9]Then I heard the sound of his words; and when I heard the sound of his words, I fell into a trance, face to the ground.

10 But then a hand touched me and roused me to my hands and knees. [11]He said to me, "Daniel, greatly beloved, pay attention to the words that I am going to speak to you. Stand on your feet, for I have now been sent to you." So while he was speaking this word to me, I stood up trembling. [12]He said to me, "Do not fear, Daniel, for from the first day that you set your mind to gain understanding and to humble yourself before your God, your words have been heard, and I have come because of your words. [13]But the prince of the kingdom of Persia opposed me twenty-one days. So Michael, one of the chief princes, came to help me, and I left him there with the prince of the kingdom of Persia,[w] [14]and have come to help you

[s] Gk Syr: Heb *He made to understand*   [t] Or *thing or one*   [u] Or *His*   [v] Cn: Meaning of Heb uncertain   [w] Gk Theodotion: Heb *I was left there with the kings of Persia*

understand what is to happen to your people at the end of days. For there is a further vision for those days."

15 While he was speaking these words to me, I turned my face toward the ground and was speechless. [16]Then one in human form touched my lips, and I opened my mouth to speak, and said to the one who stood before me, "My lord, because of the vision such pains have come upon me that I retain no strength. [17]How can my lord's servant talk with my lord? For I am shaking,[x] no strength remains in me, and no breath is left in me."

18 Again one in human form touched me and strengthened me. [19]He said, "Do not fear, greatly beloved, you are safe. Be strong and courageous!" When he spoke to me, I was strengthened and said, "Let my lord speak, for you have strengthened me." [20]Then he said, "Do you know why I have come to you? Now I must return to fight against the prince of Persia, and when I am through with him, the prince of Greece will come. [21]But I am to tell you what is inscribed in the book of truth. There is no one with me who contends against these princes except Michael, your prince.

11 As for me, in the first year of Da·rī´-us the Mēde, I stood up to support and strengthen him.

2 "Now I will announce the truth to you. Three more kings shall arise in Persia. The fourth shall be far richer than all of them, and when he has become strong through his riches, he shall stir up all against the kingdom of Greece. [3]Then a warrior king shall arise, who shall rule with great dominion and take action as he pleases. [4]And while still rising in power, his kingdom shall be broken and divided toward the four winds of heaven, but not to his posterity, nor according to the dominion with which he ruled; for his kingdom shall be uprooted and go to others besides these.

5 "Then the king of the south shall grow strong, but one of his officers shall grow stronger than he and shall rule a realm greater than his own realm. [6]After some years they shall make an alliance, and the daughter of the king of the south shall come to the king of the north to ratify the agreement. But she shall not retain her power, and his offspring shall not endure. She shall be given up, she and her attendants and her child and the one who supported her.

"In those times [7]a branch from her roots shall rise up in his place. He shall come against the army and enter the fortress of the king of the north, and he shall take action against them and prevail. [8]Even their gods, with their idols and with their precious vessels of silver and gold, he shall carry off to Egypt as spoils of war. For some years he shall refrain from attacking the king of the north; [9]then the latter shall invade the realm of the king of the south, but will return to his own land.

10 "His sons shall wage war and assemble a multitude of great forces, which shall advance like a flood and pass through, and again shall carry the war as far as his fortress. [11]Moved with rage, the king of the south shall go out and do battle against the king of the north, who shall muster a great multitude, which shall, however, be defeated by his enemy. [12]When the multitude has been carried off, his heart shall be exalted, and he shall overthrow tens of thousands, but he shall not prevail. [13]For the king of the north shall again raise a multitude, larger than the former, and after some years[y] he shall advance with a great army and abundant supplies.

14 "In those times many shall rise against the king of the south. The lawless among your own people shall lift themselves up in order to fulfill the vision, but they shall fail. [15]Then the king of the north shall come and throw up siegeworks, and take a well-fortified city. And the forces of the south shall not stand, not even his picked troops, for there shall be no

---

[x] Gk: Heb *from now*   [y] Heb *and at the end of the times years*

strength to resist. ¹⁶But he who comes against him shall take the actions he pleases, and no one shall withstand him. He shall take a position in the beautiful land, and all of it shall be in his power. ¹⁷He shall set his mind to come with the strength of his whole kingdom, and he shall bring terms of peace^z and perform them. In order to destroy the kingdom,^a he shall give him a woman in marriage; but it shall not succeed or be to his advantage. ¹⁸Afterward he shall turn to the coastlands, and shall capture many. But a commander shall put an end to his insolence; indeed,^b he shall turn his insolence back upon him. ¹⁹Then he shall turn back toward the fortresses of his own land, but he shall stumble and fall, and shall not be found.

20 "Then shall arise in his place one who shall send an official for the glory of the kingdom; but within a few days he shall be broken, though not in anger or in battle. ²¹In his place shall arise a contemptible person on whom royal majesty had not been conferred; he shall come in without warning and obtain the kingdom through intrigue. ²²Armies shall be utterly swept away and broken before him, and the prince of the covenant as well. ²³And after an alliance is made with him, he shall act deceitfully and become strong with a small party. ²⁴Without warning he shall come into the richest parts^c of the province and do what none of his predecessors had ever done, lavishing plunder, spoil, and wealth on them. He shall devise plans against strongholds, but only for a time. ²⁵He shall stir up his power and determination against the king of the south with a great army, and the king of the south shall wage war with a much greater and stronger army. But he shall not succeed, for plots shall be devised against him ²⁶by those who eat of the royal rations. They shall break him, his army shall be swept away, and many shall fall slain. ²⁷The two kings, their minds bent on evil, shall sit at one table and exchange lies. But it shall not succeed, for there remains an end at the time appointed. ²⁸He shall return to his land with great wealth, but his heart shall be set against the holy covenant. He shall work his will, and return to his own land.

29 "At the time appointed he shall return and come into the south, but this time it shall not be as it was before. ³⁰For ships of Kit′tim shall come against him, and he shall lose heart and withdraw. He shall be enraged and take action against the holy covenant. He shall turn back and pay heed to those who forsake the holy covenant. ³¹Forces sent by him shall occupy and profane the temple and fortress. They shall abolish the regular burnt offering and set up the abomination that makes desolate. ³²He shall seduce with intrigue those who violate the covenant; but the people who are loyal to their God shall stand firm and take action. ³³The wise among the people shall give understanding to many; for some days, however, they shall fall by sword and flame, and suffer captivity and plunder. ³⁴When they fall victim, they shall receive a little help, and many shall join them insincerely. ³⁵Some of the wise shall fall, so that they may be refined, purified, and cleansed,^d until the time of the end, for there is still an interval until the time appointed.

36 "The king shall act as he pleases. He shall exalt himself and consider himself greater than any god, and shall speak horrendous things against the God of gods. He shall prosper until the period of wrath is completed, for what is determined shall be done. ³⁷He shall pay no respect to the gods of his ancestors, or to the one beloved by women; he shall pay no respect to any other god, for he shall consider himself greater than all. ³⁸He shall honor the god of fortresses instead of these; a god whom his ancestors did not know he shall honor with gold and silver, with precious stones and costly gifts. ³⁹He shall deal with the

---

^z Gk: Heb *kingdom, and upright ones with him*
^a Heb *it* ^b Meaning of Heb uncertain ^c Or *among the richest men* ^d Heb *made them white*

strongest fortresses by the help of a foreign god. Those who acknowledge him he shall make more wealthy, and shall appoint them as rulers over many, and shall distribute the land for a price.

The Time of the End

40 "At the time of the end the king of the south shall attack him. But the king of the north shall rush upon him like a whirlwind, with chariots and horsemen, and with many ships. He shall advance against countries and pass through like a flood. ⁴¹He shall come into the beautiful land, and tens of thousands shall fall victim, but Ēʹdom and Mōʹab and the main part of the Amʹmon-ītes shall escape from his power. ⁴²He shall stretch out his hand against the countries, and the land of Egypt shall not escape. ⁴³He shall become ruler of the treasures of gold and of silver, and all the riches of Egypt; and the Libyans and the Ethiopiansᵉ shall follow in his train. ⁴⁴But reports from the east and the north shall alarm him, and he shall go out with great fury to bring ruin and complete destruction to many. ⁴⁵He shall pitch his palatial tents between the sea and the beautiful holy mountain. Yet he shall come to his end, with no one to help him.

The Resurrection of the Dead

12 "At that time Michael, the great prince, the protector of your people, shall arise. There shall be a time of anguish, such as has never occurred since nations first came into existence. But at that time your people shall be delivered, everyone who is found written in the book. ²Many of those who sleep in the dust of the earthᶠ shall awake, some to everlasting life, and some to shame and everlasting contempt. ³Those who are wise shall shine like the brightness of the sky,ᵍ and those who lead many to righteousness, like the stars forever and ever. ⁴But you, Daniel, keep the words secret and the book sealed until the time of the end. Many shall be running back and forth, and evilʰ shall increase."

5 Then I, Daniel, looked, and two others appeared, one standing on this bank of the stream and one on the other. ⁶One of them said to the man clothed in linen, who was upstream, "How long shall it be until the end of these wonders?" ⁷The man clothed in linen, who was upstream, raised his right hand and his left hand toward heaven. And I heard him swear by the one who lives forever that it would be for a time, two times, and half a time,ⁱ and that when the shattering of the power of the holy people comes to an end, all these things would be accomplished. ⁸I heard but could not understand; so I said, "My lord, what shall be the outcome of these things?" ⁹He said, "Go your way, Daniel, for the words are to remain secret and sealed until the time of the end. ¹⁰Many shall be purified, cleansed, and refined, but the wicked shall continue to act wickedly. None of the wicked shall understand, but those who are wise shall understand. ¹¹From the time that the regular burnt offering is taken away and the abomination that desolates is set up, there shall be one thousand two hundred ninety days. ¹²Happy are those who persevere and attain the thousand three hundred thirty-five days. ¹³But you, go your way,ʲ and rest; you shall rise for your reward at the end of the days."

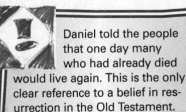

Daniel told the people that one day many who had already died would live again. This is the only clear reference to a belief in resurrection in the Old Testament.

ᵉ Or *Nubians;* Heb *Cushites*   ᶠ Or *the land of dust*
ᵍ Or *dome*   ʰ Cn Compare Gk: Heb *knowledge*
ⁱ Heb *a time, times, and a half*   ʲ Gk Theodotion:
Heb adds *to the end*

Hosea

About eight hundred years before Jesus was born, Assyria was a strong and powerful nation. Because of the strength and power of this nearby nation, some of the Jews wanted to worship Assyrian gods and copy Assyrian religious customs. Four prophets—Amos, Hosea, Isaiah, and Micah—began to preach against the wicked ways of the people. Hosea spoke out against the terrible sins and unfaithfulness of the people, but he also said that God was wonderfully loving and forgiving. He taught that if the people would repent, God would forgive and restore them.

The sermons that make up the book of Hosea were preached in the northern kingdom of Israel about 747 BC, around the same time Amos was preaching.

Both of these prophets warned that Assyria would defeat Israel because of the sins of God's people. Not only were they worshiping false gods, they were also being cruel and dishonest to one another. Amos preached that the anger of God would destroy Israel, but Hosea had an insight through his personal life. Although Hosea's wife had been unfaithful, he still loved her and wanted to win her back. He realized that if a man like himself could be loving and forgiving toward an unfaithful wife, God was even more patient and forgiving with God's chosen people.

Hosea 1:1

Hosea was a prophet in Israel in the eighth century BC and the only one of the writing prophets who lived in the northern kingdom of Israel. There were other prophets in Israel, but they were generally unreliable and had seen better days. Hosea criticized the prophets and also the priests for failing to lead the people, for giving them poor advice, and for not knowing the true nature of God. He accused these leaders of guiding the people into pagan worship rather than into the true faith.

1 The word of the LORD that came to Hō·sē´a son of Be·ē´rī, in the days of Kings Uz·zī´ah, Jō´tham, Ā´haz, and Hez·e·kī´ah of Judah, and in the days of King Jer·o·bō´am son of Jō´ash of Israel.

The Family of Hosea

2 When the LORD first spoke through Hō·sē´a, the LORD said to Hō·sē´a, "Go, take for yourself a wife of whoredom and have children of whoredom, for the land commits great whoredom by forsaking the LORD." ³So he went and took Gō´mer daughter of Dib·lā´im, and she conceived and bore him a son.

4 And the LORD said to him, "Name him Jez´rē·el;[a] for in a little while I will punish the house of Jē´hū for the blood of Jez´rē·el, and I will put an end to the kingdom of the house of Israel. ⁵On that day I will break the bow of Israel in the valley of Jez´rē·el."

6 She conceived again and bore a daughter. Then the LORD said to him, "Name her Lō·rū·ha´mah,[b] for I will no longer have pity on the house of Israel or forgive them. ⁷But I will have pity on the house of Judah, and I will save them by the LORD their God; I will not save them by

bow, or by sword, or by war, or by horses, or by horsemen."

8 When she had weaned Lō·rū·ha´mah, she conceived and bore a son. ⁹Then the LORD said, "Name him Lō-am´mī,[c] for you are not my people and I am not your God."[d]

The Restoration of Israel

10[e] Yet the number of the people of Israel shall be like the sand of the sea, which can be neither measured nor numbered; and in the place where it was said to them, "You are not my people," it shall be said to them, "Children of the living God." ¹¹The people of Judah and the people of Israel shall be gathered together, and they shall appoint for themselves one head; and they shall take possession of[f] the land, for great shall be the day of Jez´rē·el.

2[g] Say to your brother,[h] Am´mī,[i] and to your sister,[j] Rū·ha´mah.[k]

Israel's Infidelity, Punishment, and Redemption

2 Plead with your mother, plead—
   for she is not my wife,
   and I am not her husband—
that she put away her whoring from
      her face,
   and her adultery from between her
      breasts,

God was sad because Israel had turned away from worshiping God. God told Hosea to marry a woman he knew would be unfaithful and to give his children symbolic names. Hosea used his family life to show the people that they had been unfaithful to God.

---

[a] That is *God sows*   [b] That is *Not pitied*   [c] That is *Not my people*   [d] Heb *I am not yours*   [e] Ch 2.1 in Heb   [f] Heb *rise up from*   [g] Ch 2.3 in Heb   [h] Gk: Heb *brothers*   [i] That is *My people*   [j] Gk Vg: Heb *sisters*   [k] That is *Pitied*

3 or I will strip her naked
and expose her as in the day she
was born,
and make her like a wilderness,
and turn her into a parched land,
and kill her with thirst.
4 Upon her children also I will have no
pity,
because they are children of
whoredom.
5 For their mother has played the
whore;
she who conceived them has acted
shamefully.
For she said, "I will go after my lovers;
they give me my bread and my
water,
my wool and my flax, my oil and
my drink."
6 Therefore I will hedge up her[l] way
with thorns;
and I will build a wall against her,
so that she cannot find her paths.
7 She shall pursue her lovers,
but not overtake them;
and she shall seek them,
but shall not find them.
Then she shall say, "I will go
and return to my first husband,
for it was better with me then than
now."
8 She did not know
that it was I who gave her
the grain, the wine, and the oil,
and who lavished upon her silver
and gold that they used for Ba´al.
9 Therefore I will take back
my grain in its time,
and my wine in its season;
and I will take away my wool and my
flax,
which were to cover her nakedness.
10 Now I will uncover her shame
in the sight of her lovers,
and no one shall rescue her out of
my hand.
11 I will put an end to all her mirth,
her festivals, her new moons, her
sabbaths,

and all her appointed festivals.
12 I will lay waste her vines and her fig
trees,
of which she said,
"These are my pay,
which my lovers have given me."
I will make them a forest,
and the wild animals shall devour
them.
13 I will punish her for the festival days of
the Ba´als,
when she offered incense to them
and decked herself with her ring and
jewelry,
and went after her lovers,
and forgot me, says the LORD.

14 Therefore, I will now allure her,
and bring her into the wilderness,
and speak tenderly to her.
15 From there I will give her her
vineyards,
and make the Valley of A´chor a
door of hope.
There she shall respond as in the days
of her youth,
as at the time when she came out of
the land of Egypt.
16 On that day, says the LORD, you will call
me, "My husband," and no longer will you
call me, "My Ba´al."[m] 17 For I will remove

In Joshua 7, the people found out that Achan had stolen some things that should have been set apart for God. Only after Achan was punished were the Israelites able to defeat the city of Ai. Hosea reminded the people of this story and said that God had opened a "door of hope" in the valley. If the Israelites would repent, their relationship with God would be restored.

---

l Gk Syr: Heb *your*   m That is, *"My master"*

the names of the Bā́als from her mouth, and they shall be mentioned by name no more. [18]I will make for you[n] a covenant on that day with the wild animals, the birds of the air, and the creeping things of the ground; and I will abolish[o] the bow, the sword, and war from the land; and I will make you lie down in safety. [19]And I will take you for my wife forever; I will take you for my wife in righteousness and in justice, in steadfast love, and in mercy. [20]I will take you for my wife in faithfulness; and you shall know the LORD.

[21] On that day I will answer, says the
　　LORD,
　　I will answer the heavens
　　and they shall answer the earth;
[22] and the earth shall answer the grain,
　　the wine, and the oil,
　　and they shall answer Jez′re·el;[p]
[23]　and I will sow him[q] for myself in the
　　land.
　And I will have pity on
　　Lō-rū·ha′mah,[r]
　and I will say to Lō-am′mī,[s] "You are
　　my people";
　and he shall say, "You are my God."

Further Assurances of God's Redeeming Love

3 The LORD said to me again, "Go, love a woman who has a lover and is an adulteress, just as the LORD loves the people of Israel, though they turn to other gods and love raisin cakes." [2]So I bought her for fifteen shekels of silver and a homer of barley and a measure of wine.[t] [3]And I said to her, "You must remain as mine for many days; you shall not play the whore, you shall not have intercourse with a man, nor I with you." [4]For the Israelites shall remain many days without king or prince, without sacrifice or pillar, without ephod or teraphim. [5]Afterward the Israelites shall return and seek the LORD their God, and David their king; they shall come in awe to the LORD and to his goodness in the latter days.

Israel had not followed the Ten Commandments—a guide for living God's way. Not only would people suffer, but all creation (even the land and the animals) would suffer. God wants humankind to care for the earth and all that is in it. Make a list of ways you and your family can take care of the earth. Here are a few to get you started: Turn off the water while you are brushing your teeth, turn off lights in empty rooms, walk or ride a bike when you are only going a short distance, and recycle soda cans and newspapers.

God Accuses Israel

4 Hear the word of the LORD, O people of Israel;
　　for the LORD has an indictment
　　against the inhabitants of the
　　land.
　There is no faithfulness or loyalty,
　　and no knowledge of God in the
　　land.
[2] Swearing, lying, and murder,
　　and stealing and adultery break out;
　　bloodshed follows bloodshed.
[3] Therefore the land mourns,
　　and all who live in it languish;
　together with the wild animals
　　and the birds of the air,
　　even the fish of the sea are
　　perishing.

[4] Yet let no one contend,
　　and let none accuse,
　for with you is my contention, O
　　priest.[u]
[5] You shall stumble by day;
　　the prophet also shall stumble with
　　you by night,
　　and I will destroy your mother.

[n] Heb *them*　　[o] Heb *break*　　[p] That is *God sows*
[q] Cn: Heb *her*　　[r] That is *Not pitied*　　[s] That is *Not my people*　　[t] Gk: Heb *a homer of barley and a lethech of barley*　　[u] Cn: Meaning of Heb uncertain

6 My people are destroyed for lack of
  knowledge;
    because you have rejected
      knowledge,
    I reject you from being a priest to
      me.
  And since you have forgotten the law
    of your God,
    I also will forget your children.

7 The more they increased,
    the more they sinned against me;
    they changed[v] their glory into
      shame.
8 They feed on the sin of my people;
    they are greedy for their iniquity.
9 And it shall be like people, like priest;
    I will punish them for their ways,
    and repay them for their deeds.
10 They shall eat, but not be satisfied;
    they shall play the whore, but not
      multiply;
  because they have forsaken the LORD
    to devote themselves to
      11whoredom.

The Idolatry of Israel

Wine and new wine
    take away the understanding.
12 My people consult a piece of wood,
    and their divining rod gives them
      oracles.
  For a spirit of whoredom has led them
    astray,
    and they have played the whore,
      forsaking their God.
13 They sacrifice on the tops of the
      mountains,
    and make offerings upon the hills,
  under oak, poplar, and terebinth,
    because their shade is good.

  Therefore your daughters play the
    whore,
    and your daughters-in-law commit
      adultery.
14 I will not punish your daughters when
      they play the whore,
    nor your daughters-in-law when
      they commit adultery;

for the men themselves go aside with
    whores,
    and sacrifice with temple prostitutes;
  thus a people without understanding
    comes to ruin.

15 Though you play the whore, O Israel,
    do not let Judah become guilty.
  Do not enter into Gil'gal,
    or go up to Beth-a'ven,
    and do not swear, "As the LORD lives."
16 Like a stubborn heifer,
    Israel is stubborn;
  can the LORD now feed them
    like a lamb in a broad pasture?

17 E'phra·im is joined to idols—
    let him alone.
18 When their drinking is ended, they
      indulge in sexual orgies;
    they love lewdness more than their
      glory.[w]
19 A wind has wrapped them[x] in its wings,
    and they shall be ashamed because
      of their altars.[y]

Impending Judgment on Israel and Judah

5 Hear this, O priests!
    Give heed, O house of Israel!
  Listen, O house of the king!
    For the judgment pertains to you;
  for you have been a snare at Miz'pah,
    and a net spread upon Ta'bor,
2 and a pit dug deep in Shit'tim;[z]
    but I will punish all of them.

3 I know E'phra·im,
    and Israel is not hidden from me;
  for now, O E'phra·im, you have played
    the whore;
    Israel is defiled.
4 Their deeds do not permit them
    to return to their God.
  For the spirit of whoredom is within
    them,
    and they do not know the LORD.

v Ancient Heb tradition: MT *I will change*   w Cn
Compare Gk: Meaning of Heb uncertain   x Heb
her   y Gk Syr: Heb *sacrifices*   z Cn: Meaning of
Heb uncertain

⁵ Israel's pride testifies against him;
  Ē′phra·im[a] stumbles in his guilt;
  Judah also stumbles with them.
⁶ With their flocks and herds they shall
    go
    to seek the LORD,
  but they will not find him;
    he has withdrawn from them.
⁷ They have dealt faithlessly with the
    LORD;
    for they have borne illegitimate
      children.
  Now the new moon shall devour
    them along with their fields.

⁸ Blow the horn in Gib′e·ah,
    the trumpet in Rā′mah.
  Sound the alarm at Beth-a′ven;
    look behind you, Benjamin!
⁹ Ē′phra·im shall become a desolation
    in the day of punishment;
  among the tribes of Israel
    I declare what is sure.
¹⁰ The princes of Judah have become
    like those who remove the
      landmark;
  on them I will pour out
    my wrath like water.
¹¹ Ē′phra·im is oppressed, crushed in
      judgment,
    because he was determined to go
      after vanity.[b]
¹² Therefore I am like maggots to
    Ē′phra·im,
    and like rottenness to the house of
      Judah.
¹³ When Ē′phra·im saw his sickness,
    and Judah his wound,
  then Ē′phra·im went to Assyria,
    and sent to the great king.[c]
  But he is not able to cure you
    or heal your wound.
¹⁴ For I will be like a lion to Ē′phra·im,
    and like a young lion to the house
      of Judah.
  I myself will tear and go away;
    I will carry off, and no one shall
      rescue.
¹⁵ I will return again to my place

> "Come, let us return to the
> LORD; for it is he who has
> torn, and he will heal us; he
> has struck down, and he
> will bind us up." Hosea 6:1

  until they acknowledge their guilt
    and seek my face.
  In their distress they will beg my
    favor:

A Call to Repentance

6 "Come, let us return to the LORD;
    for it is he who has torn, and he
      will heal us;
  he has struck down, and he will
    bind us up.
² After two days he will revive us;
    on the third day he will raise us up,
    that we may live before him.
³ Let us know, let us press on to know
      the LORD;
    his appearing is as sure as the dawn;
  he will come to us like the showers,
    like the spring rains that water the
      earth."

Impenitence of Israel and Judah

⁴ What shall I do with you, O Ē′phra·im?
    What shall I do with you, O Judah?
  Your love is like a morning cloud,
    like the dew that goes away early.
⁵ Therefore I have hewn them by the
      prophets,
    I have killed them by the words of
      my mouth,
    and my[d] judgment goes forth as the
      light.

> "Let us know, let us press on to
> know the LORD; his appearing is as
> sure as the dawn; he will
> come to us like the show-
> ers, like the spring rains
> that water the earth."
> Hosea 6:3

---

[a] Heb *Israel and Ephraim*   [b] Gk: Meaning of Heb
uncertain   [c] Cn: Heb *to a king who will contend*
[d] Gk Syr: Heb *your*

⁶ For I desire steadfast love and not
    sacrifice,
  the knowledge of God rather than
    burnt offerings.

⁷ But at[e] Adam they transgressed the
    covenant;
  there they dealt faithlessly with me.
⁸ Gil´ē·ad is a city of evildoers,
  tracked with blood.
⁹ As robbers lie in wait[f] for someone,
  so the priests are banded together;[g]
they murder on the road to Shē´chem,
  they commit a monstrous crime.
¹⁰ In the house of Israel I have seen a
    horrible thing;
  Ē´phra·im's whoredom is there,
  Israel is defiled.

¹¹ For you also, O Judah, a harvest is
    appointed.
  When I would restore the fortunes of
    my people,

7 ¹when I would heal Israel,
    the corruption of Ē´phra·im is
    revealed,
  and the wicked deeds of Sa·mar´i·a;
for they deal falsely,
  the thief breaks in,
  and the bandits raid outside.
² But they do not consider
  that I remember all their
    wickedness.
Now their deeds surround them,
  they are before my face.
³ By their wickedness they make the
    king glad,
  and the officials by their treachery.
⁴ They are all adulterers;
  they are like a heated oven,

whose baker does not need to stir the
    fire,
  from the kneading of the dough
    until it is leavened.
⁵ On the day of our king the officials
  became sick with the heat of wine;
  he stretched out his hand with
    mockers.
⁶ For they are kindled[h] like an oven,
    their heart burns within them;
  all night their anger smolders;
  in the morning it blazes like a
    flaming fire.
⁷ All of them are hot as an oven,
  and they devour their rulers.
All their kings have fallen;
  none of them calls upon me.

⁸ Ē´phra·im mixes himself with the
    peoples;
  Ē´phra·im is a cake not turned.
⁹ Foreigners devour his strength,
  but he does not know it;
gray hairs are sprinkled upon him,
  but he does not know it.
¹⁰ Israel's pride testifies against[i] him;
  yet they do not return to the LORD
    their God,
  or seek him, for all this.

Futile Reliance on the Nations

¹¹ Ē´phra·im has become like a dove,
  silly and without sense;
  they call upon Egypt, they go to
    Assyria.
¹² As they go, I will cast my net over them;
  I will bring them down like birds of
    the air;
  I will discipline them according to the
    report made to their assembly.[j]
¹³ Woe to them, for they have strayed
    from me!
  Destruction to them, for they have
    rebelled against me!
  I would redeem them,
  but they speak lies against me.

[e] Cn: Heb *like*   [f] Cn: Meaning of Heb uncertain
[g] Syr: Heb *are a company*   [h] Gk Syr: Heb *brought
near* [i] Or *humbles* [j] Meaning of Heb uncertain

Have you ever heard
the term "half-baked"?
It means that some-
thing isn't quite finished or
ready. Hosea says that Israel is
like a half-baked cake that falls
apart when it is turned.

14 They do not cry to me from the heart,
　　but they wail upon their beds;
　they gash themselves for grain and
　　　wine;
　　they rebel against me.
15 It was I who trained and strengthened
　　　their arms,
　　yet they plot evil against me.
16 They turn to that which does not
　　　profit;[k]
　　they have become like a defective
　　　bow;
　their officials shall fall by the sword
　　because of the rage of their tongue.
　So much for their babbling in the land
　　of Egypt.

Israel's Apostasy

8 Set the trumpet to your lips!
　　　One like a vulture[l] is over the
　　　house of the LORD,
　because they have broken my
　　　covenant,
　　and transgressed my law.
2 Israel cries to me,
　　"My God, we—Israel—know you!"
3 Israel has spurned the good;
　　the enemy shall pursue him.

4 They made kings, but not through me;
　　they set up princes, but without my
　　　knowledge.
　With their silver and gold they made
　　　idols
　　for their own destruction.
5 Your calf is rejected, O Sa·mār´i·a.
　　My anger burns against them.
　How long will they be incapable of
　　　innocence?
6　　For it is from Israel,
　an artisan made it;
　　it is not God.
　The calf of Sa·mār´i·a
　　shall be broken to pieces.[m]

7 For they sow the wind,
　　and they shall reap the whirlwind.
　The standing grain has no heads,
　　it shall yield no meal;

　if it were to yield,
　　foreigners would devour it.
8 Israel is swallowed up;
　　now they are among the nations
　　as a useless vessel.
9 For they have gone up to Assyria,
　　a wild ass wandering alone;
　　Ē´phra·im has bargained for lovers.
10 Though they bargain with the nations,
　　I will now gather them up.
　They shall soon writhe
　　under the burden of kings and
　　　princes.

11 When Ē´phra·im multiplied altars to
　　　expiate sin,
　　they became to him altars for
　　　sinning.
12 Though I write for him the multitude
　　of my instructions,
　　they are regarded as a strange thing.
13 Though they offer choice sacrifices,[n]
　　though they eat flesh,
　　the LORD does not accept them.
　Now he will remember their iniquity,
　　and punish their sins;
　　they shall return to Egypt.
14 Israel has forgotten his Maker,
　　and built palaces;
　and Judah has multiplied fortified cities;
　　but I will send a fire upon his cities,
　　and it shall devour his strongholds.

Punishment for Israel's Sin

9 Do not rejoice, O Israel!
　　　Do not exult[o] as other nations do;
　for you have played the whore,
　　　departing from your God.
　　You have loved a prostitute's pay
　　on all threshing floors.
2 Threshing floor and wine vat shall not
　　　feed them,
　　and the new wine shall fail them.
3 They shall not remain in the land of
　　　the LORD;

k Cn: Meaning of Heb uncertain　　l Meaning of
Heb uncertain　　m Or shall go up in flames
n Meaning of Heb uncertain　　o Gk: Heb To exultation

but Ē′phra·im shall return to Egypt,
and in Assyria they shall eat unclean
food.

4 They shall not pour drink offerings of
wine to the LORD,
and their sacrifices shall not please
him.
Such sacrifices shall be like mourners'
bread;
all who eat of it shall be defiled;
for their bread shall be for their hunger
only;
it shall not come to the house of the
LORD.

5 What will you do on the day of
appointed festival,
and on the day of the festival of the
LORD?
6 For even if they escape destruction,
Egypt shall gather them,
Memphis shall bury them.
Nettles shall possess their precious
things of silver;[p]
thorns shall be in their tents.

7 The days of punishment have come,
the days of recompense have come;
Israel cries,[q]
"The prophet is a fool,
the man of the spirit is mad!"
Because of your great iniquity,
your hostility is great.
8 The prophet is a sentinel for my God
over Ē′phra·im,
yet a fowler's snare is on all his ways,
and hostility in the house of his God.
9 They have deeply corrupted
themselves
as in the days of Gib′e·ah;
he will remember their iniquity,
he will punish their sins.

10 Like grapes in the wilderness,
I found Israel.
Like the first fruit on the fig tree,
in its first season,
I saw your ancestors.

But they came to Bā′al-pē′or,
and consecrated themselves to a
thing of shame,
and became detestable like the thing
they loved.
11 Ē′phra·im's glory shall fly away like a
bird—
no birth, no pregnancy, no
conception!
12 Even if they bring up children,
I will bereave them until no one is
left.
Woe to them indeed
when I depart from them!
13 Once I saw Ē′phra·im as a young palm
planted in a lovely meadow,[p]
but now Ē′phra·im must lead out
his children for slaughter.
14 Give them, O LORD—
what will you give?
Give them a miscarrying womb
and dry breasts.

15 Every evil of theirs began at Gil′gal;
there I came to hate them.
Because of the wickedness of their
deeds
I will drive them out of my house.
I will love them no more;
all their officials are rebels.

16 Ē′phra·im is stricken,
their root is dried up,
they shall bear no fruit.
Even though they give birth,
I will kill the cherished offspring of
their womb.
17 Because they have not listened to him,
my God will reject them;
they shall become wanderers among
the nations.

Israel's Sin and Captivity

10 Israel is a luxuriant vine
that yields its fruit.
The more his fruit increased
the more altars he built;

---

[p] Meaning of Heb uncertain   [q] Cn Compare Gk:
Heb *shall know*

as his country improved,
    he improved his pillars.
2 Their heart is false;
    now they must bear their guilt.
The LORD[r] will break down their altars,
    and destroy their pillars.

3 For now they will say:
    "We have no king,
for we do not fear the LORD,
    and a king—what could he do for
        us?"
4 They utter mere words;
    with empty oaths they make
        covenants;
so litigation springs up like poisonous
        weeds
    in the furrows of the field.
5 The inhabitants of Sa·mār´i·a tremble
    for the calf[s] of Beth-ā´ven.
Its people shall mourn for it,
    and its idolatrous priests shall wail[t]
        over it,
        over its glory that has departed from
            it.
6 The thing itself shall be carried to
        Assyria
    as tribute to the great king.[u]
Ē´phra·im shall be put to shame,
    and Israel shall be ashamed of his
        idol.[v]

7 Sa·mār´i·a's king shall perish
    like a chip on the face of the waters.
8 The high places of Ā´ven, the sin of
        Israel,
    shall be destroyed.
Thorn and thistle shall grow up
    on their altars.
They shall say to the mountains, Cover
        us,
    and to the hills, Fall on us.

9 Since the days of Gib´ē·ah you have
        sinned, O Israel;
    there they have continued.
    Shall not war overtake them in
        Gib´ē·ah?
10 I will come[w] against the wayward

people to punish them;
    and nations shall be gathered against
        them
    when they are punished[x] for their
        double iniquity.

11 Ē´phra·im was a trained heifer
    that loved to thresh,
    and I spared her fair neck;
but I will make Ē´phra·im break the
        ground;
    Judah must plow;
    Jacob must harrow for himself.
12 Sow for yourselves righteousness;
    reap steadfast love;
    break up your fallow ground;
for it is time to seek the LORD,
    that he may come and rain
        righteousness upon you.

13 You have plowed wickedness,
    you have reaped injustice,
    you have eaten the fruit of lies.
Because you have trusted in your
        power
    and in the multitude of your
        warriors,
14 therefore the tumult of war shall rise
        against your people,
    and all your fortresses shall be
        destroyed,
as Shal´man destroyed Beth-ar´bel on
        the day of battle
    when mothers were dashed in
        pieces with their children.
15 Thus it shall be done to you, O
        Beth´el,
    because of your great wickedness.
At dawn the king of Israel
    shall be utterly cut off.

God's Compassion Despite Israel's Ingratitude

11 When Israel was a child, I loved
        him,
    and out of Egypt I called my son.

[r] Heb he   [s] Gk Syr: Heb calves   [t] Cn: Heb exult
[u] Cn: Heb to a king who will contend   [v] Cn: Heb
counsel   [w] Cn Compare Gk: Heb In my desire
[x] Gk: Heb bound

"When Israel was a child, I loved him, and out of Egypt I called my son."
Hosea 11:1

2 The more I[y] called them,
   the more they went from me;[z]
they kept sacrificing to the Bā′als,
   and offering incense to idols.

3 Yet it was I who taught E̅′phra·im to
      walk,
   I took them up in my[a] arms;
   but they did not know that I healed
      them.
4 I led them with cords of human
      kindness,
   with bands of love.
I was to them like those
   who lift infants to their cheeks.[b]
   I bent down to them and fed them.

5 They shall return to the land of Egypt,
   and Assyria shall be their king,
   because they have refused to return
      to me.
6 The sword rages in their cities,
   it consumes their oracle-priests,
   and devours because of their
      schemes.
7 My people are bent on turning away
      from me.
   To the Most High they call,
   but he does not raise them up at all.[c]

8 How can I give you up, E̅′phra·im?
   How can I hand you over, O Israel?
How can I make you like Ad′mah?
   How can I treat you like Ze·boi′im?
My heart recoils within me;
   my compassion grows warm and
      tender.

"I led them with cords of human kindness, with bands of love. I was

to them like those who lift infants to their cheeks. I bent down to them and fed them." Hosea 11:4

9 I will not execute my fierce anger;
   I will not again destroy E̅′phra·im;
for I am God and no mortal,
   the Holy One in your midst,
   and I will not come in wrath.[c]

10 They shall go after the LORD,
   who roars like a lion;
when he roars,
   his children shall come trembling
      from the west.
11 They shall come trembling like birds
      from Egypt,
   and like doves from the land of
      Assyria;
   and I will return them to their
      homes, says the LORD.

12[d] E̅′phra·im has surrounded me with lies,
   and the house of Israel with deceit;
but Judah still walks[e] with God,
   and is faithful to the Holy One.

12

E̅′phra·im herds the wind,
      and pursues the east wind all
         day long;
they multiply falsehood and violence;
   they make a treaty with Assyria,
   and oil is carried to Egypt.

The Long History of Rebellion

2 The LORD has an indictment against
      Judah,
   and will punish Jacob according to
      his ways,
   and repay him according to his deeds.
3 In the womb he tried to supplant his
      brother,
   and in his manhood he strove with
      God.
4 He strove with the angel and prevailed,
   he wept and sought his favor;
he met him at Beth′el,
   and there he spoke with him.[f]
5 The LORD the God of hosts,
   the LORD is his name!

y Gk: Heb they   z Gk: Heb them   a Gk Syr Vg:
Heb his   b Or who ease the yoke on their jaws
c Meaning of Heb uncertain   d Ch 12.1 in Heb
e Heb roams or rules   f Gk Syr: Heb us

6 But as for you, return to your God,
    hold fast to love and justice,
    and wait continually for your God.

7 A trader, in whose hands are false
        balances,
    he loves to oppress.
8 Eʹphra·im has said, "Ah, I am rich,
    I have gained wealth for myself;
in all of my gain

    no offense has been found in me
    that would be sin."[g]
9 I am the LORD your God
    from the land of Egypt;
I will make you live in tents again,
    as in the days of the appointed
        festival.

10 I spoke to the prophets;
    it was I who multiplied visions,
    and through the prophets I will
        bring destruction.
11 In Gilʹe·ad[h] there is iniquity,
    they shall surely come to nothing.
In Gilʹgal they sacrifice bulls,
    so their altars shall be like stone
        heaps
    on the furrows of the field.
12 Jacob fled to the land of Arʹam,
    there Israel served for a wife,
    and for a wife he guarded sheep.[i]
13 By a prophet the LORD brought Israel
        up from Egypt,
    and by a prophet he was guarded.
14 Eʹphra·im has given bitter offense,
    so his Lord will bring his crimes
        down on him
    and pay him back for his insults.

Relentless Judgment on Israel

13 When Eʹphra·im spoke, there
        was trembling;
    he was exalted in Israel;
    but he incurred guilt through Baʹal
        and died.
2 And now they keep on sinning
    and make a cast image for
        themselves,

idols of silver made according to their
        understanding,
    all of them the work of artisans.
"Sacrifice to these," they say.[j]
    People are kissing calves!
3 Therefore they shall be like the
        morning mist
    or like the dew that goes away early,
like chaff that swirls from the threshing
        floor
    or like smoke from a window.

4 Yet I have been the LORD your God
    ever since the land of Egypt;
you know no God but me,
    and besides me there is no savior.
5 It was I who fed[k] you in the
        wilderness,
    in the land of drought.
6 When I fed[l] them, they were satisfied;
    they were satisfied, and their heart
        was proud;
    therefore they forgot me.
7 So I will become like a lion to them,
    like a leopard I will lurk beside the
        way.
8 I will fall upon them like a bear robbed
    of her cubs,
    and will tear open the covering of
        their heart;

Chaff is the outer shell that covers seeds of grain. In Bible times the people would separate the chaff from the grain in a process called threshing. The chaff would blow away, and only the good parts of the grain would be left. Chaff is a symbol for something that is useless or worthless.

---

g Meaning of Heb uncertain   h Compare Syr: Heb
Gilead   i Heb lacks sheep   j Cn Compare Gk:
Heb To these they say sacrifices of people   k Gk Syr:
Heb knew   l Cn: Heb according to their pasture

there I will devour them like a lion,
as a wild animal would mangle
them.

9 I will destroy you, O Israel;
who can help you?[m]
10 Where now is[n] your king, that he may
save you?
Where in all your cities are your
rulers,
of whom you said,
"Give me a king and rulers"?
11 I gave you a king in my anger,
and I took him away in my wrath.

12 E′phra·im's iniquity is bound up;
his sin is kept in store.
13 The pangs of childbirth come for
him,
but he is an unwise son;
for at the proper time he does not
present himself
at the mouth of the womb.

14 Shall I ransom them from the power of
She′ol?
Shall I redeem them from Death?
O Death, where are[o] your plagues?
O She′ol, where is[o] your
destruction?
Compassion is hidden from my eyes.

15 Although he may flourish among
rushes,[p]
the east wind shall come, a blast
from the LORD,
rising from the wilderness;
and his fountain shall dry up,
his spring shall be parched.
It shall strip his treasury
of every precious thing.
16q Sa·mar′i·a shall bear her guilt,
because she has rebelled against her
God;
they shall fall by the sword,
their little ones shall be dashed in
pieces,
and their pregnant women ripped
open.

A Plea for Repentance

14 Return, O Israel, to the LORD
your God,
for you have stumbled because of
your iniquity.
2 Take words with you
and return to the LORD;
say to him,
"Take away all guilt;
accept that which is good,
and we will offer
the fruit[r] of our lips.
3 Assyria shall not save us;
we will not ride upon horses;
we will say no more, 'Our God,'
to the work of our hands.
In you the orphan finds mercy."

Assurance of Forgiveness

4 I will heal their disloyalty;
I will love them freely,
for my anger has turned from them.
5 I will be like the dew to Israel;
he shall blossom like the lily,
he shall strike root like the forests of
Lebanon.[s]
6 His shoots shall spread out;
his beauty shall be like the olive
tree,
and his fragrance like that of
Lebanon.
7 They shall again live beneath my[t]
shadow,
they shall flourish as a garden;[u]
they shall blossom like the vine,
their fragrance shall be like the wine
of Lebanon.

8 O E′phra·im, what have I[v] to do with
idols?
It is I who answer and look after
you.[w]
I am like an evergreen cypress;
your faithfulness[x] comes from me.

m Gk Syr: Heb *for in me is your help*   n Gk Syr Vg:
Heb *I will be*   o Gk Syr: Heb *I will be*   p Or *among
brothers*   q Ch 14.1 in Heb   r Gk Syr: Heb *bulls*
s Cn: Heb *like Lebanon*   t Heb *his*   u Cn: Heb *they
shall grow grain*   v Or *What more has Ephraim*
w Heb *him*   x Heb *your fruit*

9 Those who are wise understand these
things;
those who are discerning know
them.
For the ways of the LORD are right,
and the upright walk in them,
but transgressors stumble in them.

"Those who are wise
understand these things;
those who are discerning
know them. For the ways of
the LORD are right, and the
upright walk in them, but transgressors stumble in them." Hosea 14:9

Joel

The book of Joel was written after millions of locusts (grasshopper-like insects) had invaded Jerusalem. These locusts moved across the land like an army, eating every last bit of the crops. After the locusts, there was a terrible drought (shortage of water) and famine (shortage of food), which meant that the people did not have enough to drink or to eat.

The prophet Joel taught that these awful disasters were God's punishment for the sins of the people—a warning from God to the people of even worse disaster that would come at the day of judgment. He asked the people to repent and promised that God would forgive them. He predicted that they would be forgiven and that their land would be restored. The prophet Joel called God's people to return to God and God's way of living.

Joel 2:12–15

1 The word of the LORD that came to
Jŏ·el son of Pe·thŭ·el:

Lament over the Ruin
of the Country

2 Hear this, O elders,
    give ear, all inhabitants of the land!
Has such a thing happened in your
        days,
    or in the days of your ancestors?
3 Tell your children of it,
    and let your children tell their
        children,
    and their children another
        generation.

> A locust is a type of
> grasshopper that can
> destroy crops like
> grain, fruit, and vegetables.
> The prophet Joel speaks of
> four different kinds of locusts
> that came one after the other
> and ate up everything in their
> paths. Joel compares these
> insects to an invading army.

4 What the cutting locust left,
    the swarming locust has eaten.
What the swarming locust left,
    the hopping locust has eaten,
and what the hopping locust left,
    the destroying locust has eaten.

5 Wake up, you drunkards, and weep;
    and wail, all you wine-drinkers,
over the sweet wine,
    for it is cut off from your mouth.
6 For a nation has invaded my land,
    powerful and innumerable;
its teeth are lions' teeth,
    and it has the fangs of a lioness.
7 It has laid waste my vines,
    and splintered my fig trees;
it has stripped off their bark and
        thrown it down;
    their branches have turned white.

8 Lament like a virgin dressed in
        sackcloth
    for the husband of her youth.
9 The grain offering and the drink
        offering are cut off
    from the house of the LORD.
The priests mourn,
    the ministers of the LORD.
10 The fields are devastated,
    the ground mourns;
for the grain is destroyed,
    the wine dries up,
    the oil fails.

11 Be dismayed, you farmers,
    wail, you vinedressers,
over the wheat and the barley;
    for the crops of the field are ruined.
12 The vine withers,
    the fig tree droops.
Pomegranate, palm, and apple—
    all the trees of the field are dried up;
surely, joy withers away
    among the people.

A Call to Repentance and Prayer

13 Put on sackcloth and lament, you
        priests;
    wail, you ministers of the altar.
Come, pass the night in sackcloth,
    you ministers of my God!
Grain offering and drink offering
    are withheld from the house of your
        God.

14 Sanctify a fast,
    call a solemn assembly.
Gather the elders
    and all the inhabitants of the land
to the house of the LORD your God,
    and cry out to the LORD.
15 Alas for the day!
For the day of the LORD is near,
    and as destruction from the
        Almighty[a] it comes.
16 Is not the food cut off
    before our eyes,
joy and gladness
    from the house of our God?

[a] Traditional rendering of Heb *Shaddai*

> "Rend your hearts and not your clothing. Return to the LORD, your God, for he is gracious and merciful, slow to anger, and abounding in steadfast love, and relents from punishing." Joel 2:13

17 The seed shrivels under the clods,[b]
the storehouses are desolate;
the granaries are ruined
because the grain has failed.
18 How the animals groan!
The herds of cattle wander about
because there is no pasture for them;
even the flocks of sheep are dazed.[c]

19 To you, O LORD, I cry.
For fire has devoured
the pastures of the wilderness,
and flames have burned
all the trees of the field.
20 Even the wild animals cry to you
because the watercourses are dried
up,
and fire has devoured
the pastures of the wilderness.

2 Blow the trumpet in Zion;
sound the alarm on my holy
mountain!
Let all the inhabitants of the land
tremble,
for the day of the LORD is coming, it
is near—
2 a day of darkness and gloom,
a day of clouds and thick darkness!
Like blackness spread upon the
mountains
a great and powerful army comes;
their like has never been from of old,
nor will be again after them
in ages to come.
3 Fire devours in front of them,
and behind them a flame burns.
Before them the land is like the garden
of Eden,
but after them a desolate wilderness,
and nothing escapes them.

4 They have the appearance of horses,
and like war-horses they charge.
5 As with the rumbling of chariots,
they leap on the tops of the
mountains,
like the crackling of a flame of fire
devouring the stubble,
like a powerful army
drawn up for battle.

6 Before them peoples are in anguish,
all faces grow pale.[b]
7 Like warriors they charge,
like soldiers they scale the wall.
Each keeps to its own course,
they do not swerve from[d] their
paths.
8 They do not jostle one another,
each keeps to its own track;
they burst through the weapons
and are not halted.
9 They leap upon the city,
they run upon the walls;
they climb up into the houses,
they enter through the windows like
a thief.

10 The earth quakes before them,
the heavens tremble.
The sun and the moon are darkened,
and the stars withdraw their shining.
11 The LORD utters his voice
at the head of his army;
how vast is his host!
Numberless are those who obey his
command.
Truly the day of the LORD is great;
terrible indeed—who can endure it?

12 Yet even now, says the LORD,
return to me with all your heart,
with fasting, with weeping, and with
mourning;
13 rend your hearts and not your
clothing.
Return to the LORD, your God,
for he is gracious and merciful,

---

[b] Meaning of Heb uncertain [c] Compare Gk Syr
Vg: Meaning of Heb uncertain [d] Gk Syr Vg: Heb
they do not take a pledge along

In Bible times people tore their clothes as a sign of grief or sadness. Joel told the people to rend (which means tear) their hearts and not their clothes—in other words to repent and be sorry for their sins. God wanted the people to care more about their hearts than about how they looked.

slow to anger, and abounding in
     steadfast love,
   and relents from punishing.
14 Who knows whether he will not turn
     and relent,
   and leave a blessing behind him,
 a grain offering and a drink offering
   for the LORD, your God?

15 Blow the trumpet in Zion;
   sanctify a fast;
 call a solemn assembly;
16   gather the people.
 Sanctify the congregation;
   assemble the aged;
 gather the children,
   even infants at the breast.
 Let the bridegroom leave his room,
   and the bride her canopy.

17 Between the vestibule and the altar
   let the priests, the ministers of the
     LORD, weep.
 Let them say, "Spare your people,
   O LORD,
   and do not make your heritage a
     mockery,
   a byword among the nations.
 Why should it be said among the
     peoples,
 'Where is their God?' "

God's Response and Promise
18 Then the LORD became jealous for his
     land,
   and had pity on his people.
19 In response to his people the LORD
     said:

I am sending you
   grain, wine, and oil,
   and you will be satisfied;
 and I will no more make you
   a mockery among the nations.

20 I will remove the northern army far
     from you,
   and drive it into a parched and
     desolate land,
 its front into the eastern sea,
   and its rear into the western sea;
 its stench and foul smell will rise up.
   Surely he has done great things!

21 Do not fear, O soil;
   be glad and rejoice,
   for the LORD has done great things!
22 Do not fear, you animals of the field,
   for the pastures of the wilderness are
     green;
 the tree bears its fruit,
   the fig tree and vine give their full
     yield.

23 O children of Zion, be glad
   and rejoice in the LORD your God;
 for he has given the early rain[e] for your
     vindication,
   he has poured down for you
     abundant rain,
 the early and the later rain, as
     before.
24 The threshing floors shall be full of
     grain,
   the vats shall overflow with wine
     and oil.

25 I will repay you for the years
   that the swarming locust has eaten,
 the hopper, the destroyer, and the
     cutter,
   my great army, which I sent against
     you.

26 You shall eat in plenty and be satisfied,
   and praise the name of the LORD
     your God,
   who has dealt wondrously with you.

e Meaning of Heb uncertain

> "Then afterward I will pour out my spirit on all flesh; your sons and your daughters shall prophesy, your old men shall dream dreams, and your young men shall see visions." Joel 2:28

And my people shall never again be
   put to shame.
27 You shall know that I am in the midst
      of Israel,
   and that I, the LORD, am your God
      and there is no other.
And my people shall never again
   be put to shame.

God's Spirit Poured Out

28f Then afterward
   I will pour out my spirit on all flesh;
   your sons and your daughters shall
      prophesy,
   your old men shall dream dreams,
   and your young men shall see
      visions.
29 Even on the male and female slaves,
   in those days, I will pour out my
      spirit.

30 I will show portents in the heavens and on the earth, blood and fire and columns of smoke. 31The sun shall be turned to darkness, and the moon to blood, before the great and terrible day of the LORD comes. 32Then everyone who calls on the name of the LORD shall be saved; for in Mount Zion and in Jerusalem there shall be those who escape, as the LORD has said, and among the survivors shall be those whom the LORD calls.

3 gFor then, in those days and at that time, when I restore the fortunes of Judah and Jerusalem, 2I will gather all the nations and bring them down to the valley of Je·hosh´a·phat, and I will enter into judgment with them there, on account of my people and my heritage Israel, because they have scattered them among the nations. They have divided my land, 3and

cast lots for my people, and traded boys for prostitutes, and sold girls for wine, and drunk it down.

4 What are you to me, O Tyre and Si·-don, and all the regions of Phi·lis´ti·a? Are you paying me back for something? If you are paying me back, I will turn your deeds back upon your own heads swiftly and speedily. 5For you have taken my silver and my gold, and have carried my rich treasures into your temples.h 6You have sold the people of Judah and Jerusalem to the Greeks, removing them far from their own border. 7But now I will rouse them to leave the places to which you have sold them, and I will turn your deeds back upon your own heads. 8I will sell your sons and your daughters into the hand of the people of Judah, and they will sell them to the Sa·be´ans, to a nation far away; for the LORD has spoken.

Judgment in the Valley of Jehoshaphat

9 Proclaim this among the nations:
   Prepare war,i
      stir up the warriors.
   Let all the soldiers draw near,
      let them come up.
10 Beat your plowshares into swords,
      and your pruning hooks into spears;
   let the weakling say, "I am a
      warrior."
11 Come quickly,j
      all you nations all around,
      gather yourselves there.
   Bring down your warriors, O LORD.
12 Let the nations rouse themselves,
      and come up to the valley of
         Je·hosh´a·phat;
   for there I will sit to judge
      all the neighboring nations.

13 Put in the sickle,
      for the harvest is ripe.
   Go in, tread,
      for the wine press is full.

---

f Ch 3.1 in Heb   g Ch 4.1 in Heb   h Or *palaces*
i Heb *sanctify war*   j Meaning of Heb uncertain

The vats overflow,
for their wickedness is great.

14 Multitudes, multitudes,
in the valley of decision!
For the day of the LORD is near
in the valley of decision.
15 The sun and the moon are darkened,
and the stars withdraw their shining.

16 The LORD roars from Zion,
and utters his voice from Jerusalem,
and the heavens and the earth
shake.

But the LORD is a refuge for his people,
a stronghold for the people of Israel.

The Glorious Future of Judah

17 So you shall know that I, the LORD
your God,
dwell in Zion, my holy mountain.
And Jerusalem shall be holy,
and strangers shall never again pass
through it.
18 In that day
the mountains shall drip sweet wine,

"But the LORD is a refuge for his people, a stronghold for the people of Israel." Joel 3:16b

the hills shall flow with milk,
and all the stream beds of Judah
shall flow with water;
a fountain shall come forth from the
house of the LORD
and water the Wadi Shit′tim.

19 Egypt shall become a desolation
and E′dom a desolate wilderness,
because of the violence done to the
people of Judah,
in whose land they have shed
innocent blood.
20 But Judah shall be inhabited forever,
and Jerusalem to all generations.
21 I will avenge their blood, and I will not
clear the guilty,[k]
for the LORD dwells in Zion.

[k] Gk Syr: Heb *I will hold innocent their blood that I have not held innocent*

Amos

The book of Amos, made up of sermons, was probably the first book of the Bible to be written down. The prophet Amos preached and wrote these sermons about 750 BC. This was a time of great wealth for both the southern kingdom of Judah and the northern kingdom of Israel. Even though the people seemed to be doing well, Amos challenged their sins. He told them that God would punish them for doing wrong over and over again.

Amos was a prophet who lived in Tekoa, a town in Judah. He was a shepherd, and he also took care of sycamore trees. When Amos went into the cities of his day, he saw the dishonesty of the people. He saw that the rich mistreated the poor. He saw that the legal and religious systems were corrupt. He saw that some people brought fine gifts to the Temple but then continued to be mean and unfair.

When Amos realized these things, he went to the city of Bethel. There he taught that God was a just God who should not be disobeyed. He began by preaching against the evils of enemy countries like Syria, Edom, Ammon, and Moab. He preached against the sins of Judah, his own nation. At last, when he had everyone's attention, he preached against Israel itself and said that it would be judged more sternly than its enemies because God had given it so many blessings.

Amos 1:1–2

1 The words of Ā´mos, who was among the shepherds of Te·kō´a, which he saw concerning Israel in the days of King Uz·zī´ah of Judah and in the days of King Jer·o·bō´am son of Jō´ash of Israel, two years[a] before the earthquake.

Judgment on Israel's Neighbors

2 And he said:

The LORD roars from Zion,
and utters his voice from Jerusalem;
the pastures of the shepherds wither,
and the top of Car´mel dries up.

On the surface, the country of Israel was at peace. The people were wealthy. There seemed to be plenty of food for everyone. No other nation was threatening them. But God saw beyond all these things. God knows that even though things may look peaceful on the outside, there is no true peace where there is no justice.

3 Thus says the LORD:
For three transgressions of
Damascus,
and for four, I will not revoke the
punishment;[b]
because they have threshed Gil´e·ad
with threshing sledges of iron.
4 So I will send a fire on the house of
Haz´a·el,
and it shall devour the
strongholds of Ben-hā´dad.
5 I will break the gate bars of
Damascus,
and cut off the inhabitants from
the Valley of Ā´ven,
and the one who holds the scepter
from Beth-e´den;
and the people of Ar´am shall go
into exile to Kir,
says the LORD.

6 Thus says the LORD:
For three transgressions of Gā´za,
and for four, I will not revoke the
punishment;[b]
because they carried into exile entire
communities,
to hand them over to E´dom.
7 So I will send a fire on the wall of
Gā´za,
fire that shall devour its
strongholds.
8 I will cut off the inhabitants from
Ash´dod,

and the one who holds the scepter
from Ash´ke·lon;
I will turn my hand against
Ek´ron,
and the remnant of the
Phi·lis´tines shall perish,
says the Lord GOD.
9 Thus says the LORD:
For three transgressions of Tyre,
and for four, I will not revoke the
punishment;[b]
because they delivered entire
communities over to E´dom,
and did not remember the
covenant of kinship.
10 So I will send a fire on the wall of
Tyre,
fire that shall devour its
strongholds.

11 Thus says the LORD:
For three transgressions of E´dom,
and for four, I will not revoke the
punishment;[b]
because he pursued his brother with
the sword
and cast off all pity;
he maintained his anger
perpetually,[c]
and kept his wrath[d] forever.
12 So I will send a fire on Tē´man,
and it shall devour the
strongholds of Boz´rah.

[a] Or *during two years* [b] Heb *cause it to return*
[c] Syr Vg: Heb *and his anger tore perpetually*
[d] Gk Syr Vg: Heb *and his wrath kept*

13 Thus says the LORD:
  For three transgressions of the
    Am´mon·ites,
      and for four, I will not revoke the
        punishment;*e*
  because they have ripped open
    pregnant women in Gil´e·ad
      in order to enlarge their territory.
14 So I will kindle a fire against the wall
    of Rab´bah,
  fire that shall devour its
    strongholds,
      with shouting on the day of battle,
        with a storm on the day of the
          whirlwind;
15 then their king shall go into exile,
    he and his officials together,
                                   says the LORD.

2 Thus says the LORD:
  For three transgressions of Mō´ab,
    and for four, I will not revoke the
      punishment;*e*
  because he burned to lime
    the bones of the king of Ē´dom.
2 So I will send a fire on Mō´ab,
    and it shall devour the
      strongholds of Ker´i·oth,
  and Mō´ab shall die amid uproar,
    amid shouting and the sound of
      the trumpet;
3 I will cut off the ruler from its midst,
    and will kill all its officials with
      him,
                              says the LORD.

Judgment on Judah

4 Thus says the LORD:
  For three transgressions of Judah,
    and for four, I will not revoke the
      punishment;*e*
  because they have rejected the law of
    the LORD,
      and have not kept his statutes,
  but they have been led astray by the
    same lies
      after which their ancestors walked.
5 So I will send a fire on Judah,
    and it shall devour the
      strongholds of Jerusalem.

Judgment on Israel

6 Thus says the LORD:
  For three transgressions of Israel,
    and for four, I will not revoke the
      punishment;*e*
  because they sell the righteous for
    silver,
      and the needy for a pair of
        sandals—
7 they who trample the head of the
      poor into the dust of the earth,
    and push the afflicted out of the
      way;
  father and son go in to the same girl,
    so that my holy name is profaned;
8 they lay themselves down beside
      every altar
    on garments taken in pledge;
  and in the house of their God they
      drink
    wine bought with fines they imposed.

9 Yet I destroyed the Am´o·rīte before
      them,
    whose height was like the height
      of cedars,
      and who was as strong as oaks;
  I destroyed his fruit above,
    and his roots beneath.
10 Also I brought you up out of the
      land of Egypt,
    and led you forty years in the
      wilderness,
      to possess the land of the Am´o·rīte.

The prophet Amos spoke out against both Judah and Israel. The people of Judah had forgotten the commandments of God and were worshiping idols. The people of Israel were not treating the poor fairly and were selling them into slavery to pay off very small amounts of money.

e Heb *cause it to return*

11 And I raised up some of your chil-
　　dren to be prophets
　　and some of your youths to be
　　　nazirites.*f*
　　Is it not indeed so, O people of
　　　Israel?
　　　　　　　　　　　says the LORD.

12 But you made the Nazirites*f* drink
　　　wine,
　　and commanded the prophets,
　　　saying, "You shall not prophesy."
13 So, I will press you down in your
　　　place,
　　just as a cart presses down
　　　when it is full of sheaves.*g*
14 Flight shall perish from the swift,
　　and the strong shall not retain
　　　their strength,
　　nor shall the mighty save their lives;
15 those who handle the bow shall not
　　　stand,
　　and those who are swift of foot
　　　shall not save themselves,
　　nor shall those who ride horses
　　　save their lives;
16 and those who are stout of heart
　　　among the mighty
　　shall flee away naked in that day,
　　　　　　　　　says the LORD.

Israel's Guilt and Punishment

3 Hear this word that the LORD has
　spoken against you, O people of
Israel, against the whole family that I
brought up out of the land of Egypt:
2 You only have I known
　　　of all the families of the earth;
　　therefore I will punish you
　　　for all your iniquities.

3 Do two walk together
　　unless they have made an
　　　appointment?
4 Does a lion roar in the forest,
　　when it has no prey?
　Does a young lion cry out from its
　　　den,
　　if it has caught nothing?

5 Does a bird fall into a snare on the
　　　earth,
　　when there is no trap for it?
　Does a snare spring up from the
　　　ground,
　　when it has taken nothing?
6 Is a trumpet blown in a city,
　　and the people are not afraid?
　Does disaster befall a city,
　　unless the LORD has done it?
7 Surely the Lord GOD does
　　　nothing,
　　without revealing his secret
　　　to his servants the prophets.
8 The lion has roared;
　　who will not fear?
　The Lord GOD has spoken;
　　who can but prophesy?

9 Proclaim to the strongholds in
　　　Ash′dod,
　　and to the strongholds in the land
　　　of Egypt,
　and say, "Assemble yourselves on
　　　Mount*h* Sa·mār′i·a,
　　and see what great tumults are
　　　within it,
　　and what oppressions are in its
　　　midst."
10 They do not know how to do right,
　　　says the LORD,
　　those who store up violence and
　　　robbery in their strongholds.
11 Therefore thus says the Lord
　　　GOD:
　　An adversary shall surround the
　　　land,
　　and strip you of your defense;
　　and your strongholds shall be
　　　plundered.
12 Thus says the LORD: As the shepherd rescues from the mouth of the lion
two legs, or a piece of an ear, so shall the
people of Israel who live in Sa·mār′i·a be
rescued, with the corner of a couch and
part*g* of a bed.

f That is, *those separated* or *those consecrated*
g Meaning of Heb uncertain　　*h* Gk Syr: Heb *the
mountains of*

13 Hear, and testify against the house of
Jacob,
  says the Lord GOD, the God of
  hosts:
14 On the day I punish Israel for its
  transgressions,
    I will punish the altars of Beth′el,
  and the horns of the altar shall be
  cut off
  and fall to the ground.
15 I will tear down the winter house as
  well as the summer house;
    and the houses of ivory shall perish,
  and the great houses[i] shall come to
  an end,
                    says the LORD.

4 Hear this word, you cows of
  Bā′shan
      who are on Mount Sa·mār′i·a,
  who oppress the poor, who crush
  the needy,
      who say to their husbands, "Bring
  something to drink!"
2 The Lord GOD has sworn by his
  holiness:
    The time is surely coming upon
  you,
  when they shall take you away with
  hooks,
      even the last of you with fishhooks.
3 Through breaches in the wall you
  shall leave,
    each one straight ahead;
  and you shall be flung out into
  Har′mon,[j]
                    says the LORD.
4 Come to Beth′el—and transgress;
  to Gil′gal—and multiply
  transgression;
    bring your sacrifices every morning,
    your tithes every three days;
5 bring a thank offering of leavened
  bread,
    and proclaim freewill offerings,
    publish them;
  for so you love to do, O people of
  Israel!
                    says the Lord GOD.

Israel Rejects Correction

6 I gave you cleanness of teeth in all
  your cities,
    and lack of bread in all your
  places,
  yet you did not return to me,
                    says the LORD.

7 And I also withheld the rain from you
    when there were still three
    months to the harvest;
  I would send rain on one city,
    and send no rain on another city;
  one field would be rained upon,
    and the field on which it did not
    rain withered;
8 so two or three towns wandered to
  one town
    to drink water, and were not
    satisfied;
  yet you did not return to me,
                    says the LORD.
9 I struck you with blight and mildew;
    I laid waste[k] your gardens and
    your vineyards;
    the locust devoured your fig trees
    and your olive trees;
  yet you did not return to me,
                    says the LORD.

10 I sent among you a pestilence after
    the manner of Egypt;
    I killed your young men with the
    sword;
  I carried away your horses;[l]
    and I made the stench of your
    camp go up into your nostrils;
  yet you did not return to me,
                    says the LORD.

11 I overthrew some of you,
    as when God overthrew Sod′om
    and Go·mor′rah,
    and you were like a brand
    snatched from the fire;
  yet you did not return to me,
                    says the LORD.

[i] Or *many houses*   [j] Meaning of Heb uncertain
[k] Cn: Heb *the multitude of*   [l] Heb *with the captivity of your horses*

12 Therefore thus I will do to you, O
　　Israel;
　　　because I will do this to you,
　　　prepare to meet your God, O
　　　Israel!
13 For lo, the one who forms the
　　　mountains, creates the wind,
　　　reveals his thoughts to mortals,
　　makes the morning darkness,
　　　and treads on the heights of the
　　　　earth—
　　　the LORD, the God of hosts, is his
　　　　name!

A Lament for Israel's Sin

5 Hear this word that I take up over
　you in lamentation, O house of
Israel:

2 Fallen, no more to rise,
　　is maiden Israel;
　forsaken on her land,
　　with no one to raise her up.

3 For thus says the Lord GOD:
　The city that marched out a
　　　thousand
　　shall have a hundred left,
　and that which marched out a
　　　hundred
　　shall have ten left.ᵐ

4 For thus says the LORD to the house
　　of Israel:
　Seek me and live;
5 　but do not seek Beth´el,
　and do not enter into Gil´gal
　　or cross over to Bē´er-shē´ba;
　for Gil´gal shall surely go into
　　　exile,
　　and Beth´el shall come to nothing.

6 Seek the LORD and live,
　　or he will break out against the
　　　house of Joseph like fire,
　　and it will devour Beth´el, with no
　　　one to quench it.
7 Ah, you that turn justice to
　　　wormwood,
　　and bring righteousness to the
　　　ground!

> "For lo, the one who forms
> the mountains, creates the
> wind, reveals his thoughts
> to mortals, makes the
> morning darkness, and
> treads on the heights of the earth—
> the LORD, the God of hosts, is his
> name!"　　　　　　Amos 4:13

8 The one who made the Plēi´a·dēs
　　　and Ō·rī´on,
　　and turns deep darkness into the
　　　morning,
　　and darkens the day into night,
　who calls for the waters of the
　　　sea,
　　and pours them out on the surface
　　　of the earth,
　the LORD is his name,
9 who makes destruction flash out
　　　against the strong,
　　so that destruction comes upon
　　　the fortress.

10 They hate the one who reproves in
　　　the gate,
　　and they abhor the one who
　　　speaks the truth.
11 Therefore because you trample on
　　　the poor
　　and take from them levies of
　　　grain,
　you have built houses of hewn stone,
　　but you shall not live in them;
　you have planted pleasant
　　　vineyards,
　　but you shall not drink their wine.

> "The one who made the Pleiades
> and Orion, and turns deep darkness
> into the morning, and darkens the
> day into night, who calls for the
> waters of the sea, and
> pours them out on the sur-
> face of the earth, the LORD
> is his name." Amos 5:8

ᵐ Heb adds *to the house of Israel*

Because God cares for all people, God wants to be sure that no one is overlooked. And so God gave the people rules for taking care of the poor. Read Leviticus 19:9–10. "Gleanings" were the food left behind on the fields for the poor when the workers were finished. In the book of Ruth, Ruth provided for Naomi and herself by gleaning.

12 For I know how many are your
        transgressions,
    and how great are your sins—
    you who afflict the righteous, who
        take a bribe,
        and push aside the needy in the
        gate.
13 Therefore the prudent will keep
        silent in such a time;
    for it is an evil time.
14 Seek good and not evil,
        that you may live;
    and so the LORD, the God of hosts,
        will be with you,
        just as you have said.
15 Hate evil and love good,
        and establish justice in the gate;
    it may be that the LORD, the God of
        hosts,
        will be gracious to the remnant of
        Joseph.

16 Therefore thus says the LORD, the
        God of hosts, the Lord:
    In all the squares there shall be
        wailing;
    and in all the streets they shall say,
        "Alas! alas!"
    They shall call the farmers to
        mourning,
    and those skilled in lamentation,
        to wailing;

"Hate evil and love good, and establish justice in the gate." Amos 5:15

17 in all the vineyards there shall be
        wailing,
    for I will pass through the midst
        of you,
                        says the LORD.

The Day of the Lord a Dark Day

18 Alas for you who desire the day of
        the LORD!
    Why do you want the day of the
        LORD?
    It is darkness, not light;
19   as if someone fled from a lion,
        and was met by a bear;
    or went into the house and rested a
        hand against the wall,
        and was bitten by a snake.
20 Is not the day of the LORD darkness,
        not light,
    and gloom with no brightness in it?

21 I hate, I despise your festivals,
    and I take no delight in your
        solemn assemblies.
22 Even though you offer me your burnt
        offerings and grain offerings,
    I will not accept them;
    and the offerings of well-being of
        your fatted animals
    I will not look upon.
23 Take away from me the noise of your
        songs;
    I will not listen to the melody of
        your harps.
24 But let justice roll down like waters,
    and righteousness like an
        ever-flowing stream.
    25 Did you bring to me sacrifices and
offerings the forty years in the wilderness, O house of Israel? 26You shall take

Amos told the Israelites that God would not accept their worship unless they learned to treat others with kindness and justice. Read the following passages and think about how you can build peace by working for justice. Genesis 6:9, 2 Samuel 22:3–4, Psalm 11:7, Psalm 140:12–13, and Amos 5:24.

up Sak´kuth your king, and Kaī´wan your star-god, your images,[n] which you made for yourselves; [27]therefore I will take you into exile beyond Damascus, says the LORD, whose name is the God of hosts.

Complacent Self-Indulgence Will Be Punished

6 Alas for those who are at ease in Zion,
     and for those who feel secure on Mount Sa·mar´i·a,
     the notables of the first of the nations,
       to whom the house of Israel resorts!
2 Cross over to Cal´neh, and see;
     from there go to Hā´math the great;
     then go down to Gath of the Phi·lis´tines.
     Are you better[o] than these kingdoms?
     Or is your[p] territory greater than their[q] territory,
3 O you that put far away the evil day,
     and bring near a reign of violence?

4 Alas for those who lie on beds of ivory,
     and lounge on their couches,
     and eat lambs from the flock,
     and calves from the stall;
5 who sing idle songs to the sound of the harp,
     and like David improvise on instruments of music;
6 who drink wine from bowls,
     and anoint themselves with the finest oils,
     but are not grieved over the ruin of Joseph!
7 Therefore they shall now be the first to go into exile,
     and the revelry of the loungers shall pass away.
8 The Lord GOD has sworn by himself (says the LORD, the God of hosts):
     I abhor the pride of Jacob
     and hate his strongholds;
     and I will deliver up the city and all that is in it.

9 If ten people remain in one house, they shall die. [10]And if a relative, one who burns the dead,[r] shall take up the body to bring it out of the house, and shall say to someone in the innermost parts of the house, "Is anyone else with you?" the answer will come, "No." Then the relative[s] shall say, "Hush! We must not mention the name of the LORD."

11 See, the LORD commands,
     and the great house shall be shattered to bits,
     and the little house to pieces.
12 Do horses run on rocks?
     Does one plow the sea with oxen?[t]
     But you have turned justice into poison
     and the fruit of righteousness into wormwood—
13 you who rejoice in Lō-dē´bar,[u]
     who say, "Have we not by our own strength
     taken Kar·nā´im[v] for ourselves?"
14 Indeed, I am raising up against you a nation,
     O house of Israel, says the LORD, the God of hosts,
     and they shall oppress you from Lē´bō-hā´math
     to the Wadi Ar´a·bah.

Locusts, Fire, and a Plumb Line

7 This is what the Lord GOD showed me: he was forming locusts at the time the latter growth began to sprout (it was the latter growth after the king's mowings). [2]When they had finished eating the grass of the land, I said,
     "O Lord GOD, forgive, I beg you!
     How can Jacob stand?
     He is so small!"

---

[n] Heb your images, your star-god   [o] Or Are they better   [p] Heb their   [q] Heb your   [r] Or who makes a burning for him   [s] Heb he   [t] Or Does one plow them with oxen   [u] Or in a thing of nothingness   [v] Or horns

"See, I am setting a plumb line in the midst of my people Israel; I will never again pass them by."

Amos 7:8b

3 The LORD relented concerning this;
"It shall not be," said the LORD.

4 This is what the Lord GOD showed me: the Lord GOD was calling for a shower of fire,[w] and it devoured the great deep and was eating up the land. [5]Then I said,

"O Lord GOD, cease, I beg you!
How can Jacob stand?
He is so small!"

6 The LORD relented concerning this;
"This also shall not be," said the Lord GOD.

7 This is what he showed me: the Lord was standing beside a wall built with a plumb line, with a plumb line in his hand. [8]And the LORD said to me, "Ā´mos, what do you see?" And I said, "A plumb line." Then the Lord said,

"See, I am setting a plumb line
in the midst of my people Israel;
I will never again pass them by;
9 the high places of Isaac shall be
made desolate,
and the sanctuaries of Israel shall
be laid waste,
and I will rise against the house of
Jer·o·bō´am with the sword."

Amaziah Complains to the King

10 Then Am·a·zī´ah, the priest of Beth´el, sent to King Jer·o·bō´am of Israel, saying, "Ā´mos has conspired against you in the very center of the house of Israel; the land is not able to bear all his words. [11]For thus Ā´mos has said,

'Jer·o·bō´am shall die by the sword,
and Israel must go into exile
away from his land.'"

[12]And Am·a·zī´ah said to Ā´mos, "O seer, go, flee away to the land of Judah, earn your bread there, and prophesy there; [13]but never again prophesy at Beth´el, for it is the king's sanctuary, and it is a temple of the kingdom."

14 Then Ā´mos answered Am·a·zī´ah, "I am[x] no prophet, nor a prophet's son; but I am[x] a herdsman, and a dresser of sycamore trees, [15]and the LORD took me from following the flock, and the LORD said to me, 'Go, prophesy to my people Israel.'

16 "Now therefore hear the word of the
LORD.
You say, 'Do not prophesy against
Israel,
and do not preach against the
house of Isaac.'
17 Therefore thus says the LORD:
'Your wife shall become a prostitute
in the city,
and your sons and your daughters
shall fall by the sword,
and your land shall be parceled
out by line;

In Bible times, builders used a plumb line to see if a wall was straight. A plumb line is a string with a small weight tied to one end. When the builder held up the other end of the string, the plumb line was straight. The builder could immediately see if the wall behind the string was crooked. The more often we do the things that God expects us to do, the straighter the wall we are building with our lives.

Think about the sentences below. Are they true in your life? How straight is your wall?

I am honest.
I am kind.
I am fair to others.
I am thoughtful of others.
I respect others' rights.
I share with others.
I treat everyone equally.
I obey God.

[w] Or *for a judgment by fire*   [x] Or *was*

you yourself shall die in an unclean
land,
   and Israel shall surely go into exile
      away from its land.' "

The Basket of Fruit

8 This is what the Lord GOD showed
me—a basket of summer fruit.[y]
[2]He said, "Āʹmos, what do you see?" And
I said, "A basket of summer fruit."[y] Then
the LORD said to me,
   "The end[z] has come upon my people
      Israel;
   I will never again pass them by.
3 The songs of the temple[a] shall
      become wailings in that day,"
            says the Lord GOD;
   "the dead bodies shall be many,
      cast out in every place. Be silent!"

4 Hear this, you that trample on the
      needy,
   and bring to ruin the poor of the
      land,
5 saying, "When will the new moon be
      over
   so that we may sell grain;
and the sabbath,

so that we may offer wheat for
   sale?
We will make the ephah small and
   the shekel great,
   and practice deceit with false
      balances,
6 buying the poor for silver
   and the needy for a pair of
      sandals,
   and selling the sweepings of the
      wheat."

7 The LORD has sworn by the pride of
      Jacob:
   Surely I will never forget any of their
      deeds.
8 Shall not the land tremble on this
      account,
   and everyone mourn who lives in
      it,
   and all of it rise like the Nile,
      and be tossed about and sink
         again, like the Nile of Egypt?

9 On that day, says the Lord GOD,
   I will make the sun go down at
      noon,
      and darken the earth in broad
         daylight.
10 I will turn your feasts into
      mourning,
   and all your songs into
      lamentation;
   I will bring sackcloth on all loins,
      and baldness on every head;
   I will make it like the mourning for
      an only son,
      and the end of it like a bitter
         day.

11 The time is surely coming, says the
      Lord GOD,
   when I will send a famine on the
      land;
   not a famine of bread, or a thirst for
      water,
      but of hearing the words of the
         LORD.

[y] Heb *qayits*   [z] Heb *qets*   [a] Or *palace*

Many things happen that are not fair or just. Sometimes we can make a difference. Sometimes we can't. But we never know until we try. Scientists have learned that how well people learn is affected by whether they get enough good food to eat. In a world where there is enough food for every single person, why should anyone be hungry? Even in the United States, nearly nine million people do not have enough food to eat each day. Over three million of the hungry are children. On the Internet or at the library, find out about some programs that are reaching out to help others. Look for "Bread for the World" and "The Heifer Project." Talk to your family about how you can get involved with helping others.

12 They shall wander from sea to sea,
> and from north to east;
> they shall run to and fro, seeking the
> word of the LORD,
> but they shall not find it.

13 In that day the beautiful young
> women and the young men
> shall faint for thirst.

14 Those who swear by Ash·i·mah of
> Sa·mār´i·a,
> and say, "As your god lives, O
> Dan,"
> and, "As the way of Bē´er·shē´ba
> lives"—
> they shall fall, and never rise again.

The Destruction of Israel

9 I saw the LORD standing beside[b] the
altar, and he said:
> Strike the capitals until the
> thresholds shake,
> and shatter them on the heads of
> all the people;[c]
> and those who are left I will kill with
> the sword;
> not one of them shall flee away,
> not one of them shall escape.

2 Though they dig into Shē´ōl,
> from there shall my hand take
> them;
> though they climb up to heaven,
> from there I will bring them
> down.

3 Though they hide themselves on the
> top of Car´mel,
> from there I will search out and
> take them;
> and though they hide from my sight
> at the bottom of the sea,
> there I will command the sea-
> serpent, and it shall bite them.

**"I will plant them upon their land, and
they shall never again be plucked up
out of the land that I have
given them, says the LORD
your God." Amos 9:15**

---

4 And though they go into captivity in
> front of their enemies,
> there I will command the sword,
> and it shall kill them;
> and I will fix my eyes on them
> for harm and not for good.

5 The Lord, GOD of hosts,
> he who touches the earth and it
> melts,
> and all who live in it mourn,
> and all of it rises like the Nile,
> and sinks again, like the Nile of
> Egypt;

6 who builds his upper chambers in
> the heavens,
> and founds his vault upon the
> earth;
> who calls for the waters of the sea,
> and pours them out upon the sur-
> face of the earth—
> the LORD is his name.

7 Are you not like the Ethiopians[d] to
> me,
> O people of Israel? says the LORD.
> Did I not bring Israel up from the
> land of Egypt,
> and the Phi·lis´tines from Caph´tor
> and the Ar·a·mē´ans from Kir?

8 The eyes of the Lord GOD are upon
> the sinful kingdom,
> and I will destroy it from the face
> of the earth
> —except that I will not utterly
> destroy the house of Jacob,
> says the LORD.

9 For lo, I will command,
> and shake the house of Israel
> among all the nations
> as one shakes with a sieve,
> but no pebble shall fall to the
> ground.

10 All the sinners of my people shall die
> by the sword,
> who say, "Evil shall not overtake
> or meet us."

[b] Or *on* [c] Heb *all of them* [d] Or *Nubians*;
Heb *Cushites*

The Restoration
of David's Kingdom

11 On that day I will raise up
  the booth of David that is fallen,
  and repair its[e] breaches,
   and raise up its[f] ruins,
   and rebuild it as in the days of
    old;
12 in order that they may possess the
    remnant of Edom
   and all the nations who are called
    by my name,
   says the LORD who does this.

13 The time is surely coming, says the
   LORD,
   when the one who plows shall
    overtake the one who reaps,
   and the treader of grapes the one
    who sows the seed;

the mountains shall drip sweet
    wine,
   and all the hills shall flow with
    it.
14 I will restore the fortunes of my
    people Israel,
   and they shall rebuild the ruined
    cities and inhabit them;
  they shall plant vineyards and drink
    their wine,
   and they shall make gardens and
    eat their fruit.
15 I will plant them upon their land,
   and they shall never again be
    plucked up
   out of the land that I have given
    them,
                    says the LORD your God.

e Gk: Heb *their*   f Gk: Heb *his*

Obadiah

Obadiah was a prophet who lived in Jerusalem about 586 BC during the days when Babylon controlled Judah, the southern kingdom. However, parts of the book of Obadiah were added as late as 450 BC. This little book, like much of the writing of the prophets, is poetry. Beginning with verse 12, there are eight parallel lines that begin with the phrase "You should not have" and then list the sins of Edom.

The Edomites, long-time enemies of the Israelites, had threatened to invade Judah. At this time, however, the Edomites themselves were facing enemy tribes from the Arabian desert. Obadiah believed that these troubles were a fair punishment to the Edomites. He spoke of how Jerusalem would triumph and all her enemies would be destroyed.

Obadiah 1

Proud Edom
Will Be Brought Low

1 The vision of Ō·ba·dī´ah.

Thus says the Lord GOD concerning
Ē´dom:
We have heard a report from the
LORD,
and a messenger has been sent
among the nations:
"Rise up! Let us rise against it for
battle!"
2 I will surely make you least among
the nations;
you shall be utterly despised.
3 Your proud heart has deceived you,
you that live in the clefts of the
rock,[a]
whose dwelling is in the heights.
You say in your heart,
"Who will bring me down to the
ground?"
4 Though you soar aloft like the eagle,
though your nest is set among the
stars,
from there I will bring you down,
says the LORD.

Pillage and Slaughter
Will Repay Edom's Cruelty

5 If thieves came to you,
if plunderers by night
—how you have been
destroyed!—
would they not steal only what
they wanted?
If grape-gatherers came to you,
would they not leave gleanings?
6 How Esau has been pillaged,
his treasures searched out!
7 All your allies have deceived you,
they have driven you to the border;
your confederates have prevailed
against you;
those who ate[b] your bread have
set a trap for you—
there is no understanding of it.
8 On that day, says the LORD,
I will destroy the wise out of
Ē´dom,
and understanding out of Mount
Esau.
9 Your warriors shall be shattered, O
Tē´man,
so that everyone from Mount Esau
will be cut off.

Edom Mistreated His Brother

10 For the slaughter and violence done
to your brother Jacob,
shame shall cover you,
and you shall be cut off forever.
11 On the day that you stood aside,
on the day that strangers carried
off his wealth,
and foreigners entered his gates
and cast lots for Jerusalem,
you too were like one of them.
12 But you should not have gloated[c]
over[d] your brother
on the day of his misfortune;
you should not have rejoiced over
the people of Judah
on the day of their ruin;
you should not have boasted
on the day of distress.
13 You should not have entered the gate
of my people
on the day of their calamity;
you should not have joined in the
gloating over Judah's[e] disaster
on the day of his calamity;
you should not have looted his goods
on the day of his calamity.

> Obadiah is the short-
> est book in the Old
> Testament. The book
> describes the suffering of the
> Israelites and the awful way
> the nation of Edom acted
> toward Judah. The prophet
> Obadiah said that Edom would
> be punished and Judah would
> be restored.

[a] Or *clefts of Sela*   [b] Cn: Heb lacks *those who ate*
[c] Heb *But do not gloat* (and similarly through verse
14)   [d] Heb *on the day of*   [e] Heb *his*

> "Those who have been
> saved shall go up to
> Mount Zion to rule
> Mount Esau; and the
> kingdom shall be the LORD's."
>
> Obadiah 21

¹⁴ You should not have stood at the
 crossings
  to cut off his fugitives;
 you should not have handed over
  his survivors
  on the day of distress.

¹⁵ For the day of the LORD is near
  against all the nations.
 As you have done, it shall be done to
  you;
  your deeds shall return on your
  own head.
¹⁶ For as you have drunk on my holy
  mountain,
  all the nations around you shall
  drink;
 they shall drink and gulp
  down,ᶠ
  and shall be as though they had
  never been.

Israel's Final Triumph
¹⁷ But on Mount Zion there shall be
  those that escape,
  and it shall be holy;
 and the house of Jacob shall take
  possession of those who
  dispossessed them.
¹⁸ The house of Jacob shall be a fire,
  the house of Joseph a flame,
  and the house of Esau stubble;
 they shall burn them and consume
  them,
  and there shall be no survivor of
  the house of Esau;
     for the LORD has spoken.
¹⁹ Those of the Negʹeb shall possess
  Mount Esau,
  and those of the She·phēʹlah the
  land of the Phi·lisʹtines;
 they shall possess the land of
  Ēʹphra·im and the land of
  Sa·mārʹi·a,
  and Benjamin shall possess
  Gilʹe·ad.
²⁰ The exiles of the Israelites who are in
  Hāʹlahᵍ
  shall possessʰ Phoe·niʹci·a as far as
  Zarʹe·phath;
 and the exiles of Jerusalem who are
  in Se·pharʹad
  shall possess the towns of the
  Negʹeb.
²¹ Those who have been savedⁱ shall go
  up to Mount Zion
  to rule Mount Esau;
  and the kingdom shall be the LORD's.

ᶠ Meaning of Heb uncertain   ᵍ Cn: Heb *in this army*   ʰ Cn: Meaning of Heb uncertain   ⁱ Or *Saviors*

Jonah

The book of Jonah is a story about a prophet named Jonah. When God told Jonah to go to the city of Nineveh and preach to the people there, Jonah did not want to go. Instead, he tried to run from God and got on a ship headed the opposite direction. While on the ship, a mighty storm came over the sea. The crew of the ship believed that Jonah was the cause of the storm, and so they threw Jonah overboard. A large fish swallowed Jonah, and he lived in the belly of that fish for three days and three nights. Jonah prayed to God, and the fish spit Jonah out on dry land.

God told Jonah a second time to go to Nineveh. This time, Jonah went and preached the message God had told him to preach. The king and all the people of Nineveh fasted and prayed that they would be saved. God saw that they were truly sorry for the way they had been living, so God decided not to destroy the city. The people of Nineveh believed God, and God showed mercy to them.

Even though Jonah did what God asked him to do, he became angry! He didn't think God should have let the people of Nineveh live. But God reminded Jonah that while Jonah worried about small things, God's love is for all people. The book of Jonah teaches that God is "a gracious God and merciful, slow to anger, and abounding in steadfast love" (see Jonah 4:2). Just like God, we too should care for all people.

Jonah 1:17

Jonah 1

When God told Jonah to go to Nineveh, Jonah tried to run away. He went in the opposite direction of Nineveh—toward Tarshish. Do you ever do the opposite of what you are supposed to do? Pray that God will help you do what God wants you to do.

Jonah Tries to Run Away from God

1 Now the word of the LORD came to Jonah son of A·mit´taī, saying, [2]"Go at once to Nin´e·veh, that great city, and cry out against it; for their wickedness has come up before me." [3]But Jonah set out to flee to Tar´shish from the presence of the LORD. He went down to Jop´pa and found a ship going to Tar´shish; so he paid his fare and went on board, to go with them to Tar´shish, away from the presence of the LORD.

4 But the LORD hurled a great wind upon the sea, and such a mighty storm came upon the sea that the ship threatened to break up. [5]Then the mariners were afraid, and each cried to his god. They threw the cargo that was in the ship into the sea, to lighten it for them. Jonah, meanwhile, had gone down into the hold of the ship and had lain down, and was fast asleep. [6]The captain came and said to him, "What are you doing sound asleep? Get up, call on your god! Perhaps the god will spare us a thought so that we do not perish."

7 The sailors[a] said to one another, "Come, let us cast lots, so that we may know on whose account this calamity has come upon us." So they cast lots, and the lot fell on Jonah. [8]Then they said to him, "Tell us why this calamity has come upon us. What is your occupation? Where do you come from? What is your country? And of what people are you?" [9]"I am a Hebrew," he replied. "I worship the LORD, the God of heaven, who made the sea and the dry land." [10]Then the men were even more afraid, and said to him, "What is this that you have done!" For the men knew that he was fleeing from the presence of the LORD, because he had told them so.

11 Then they said to him, "What shall we do to you, that the sea may quiet down for us?" For the sea was growing more and more tempestuous. [12]He said to them, "Pick me up and throw me into the sea; then the sea will quiet down for you; for I know it is because of me that this great storm has come upon you." [13]Nevertheless the men rowed hard to bring the ship back to land, but they could not, for the sea grew more and more stormy against them. [14]Then they cried out to the LORD, "Please, O LORD, we pray, do not let us perish on account of this man's life. Do not make us guilty of innocent blood; for you, O LORD, have done as it pleased you." [15]So they picked Jonah up and threw him into the sea; and the sea ceased from its raging. [16]Then the men feared the LORD even more, and they offered a sacrifice to the LORD and made vows.

17[b] But the LORD provided a large fish to swallow up Jonah; and Jonah was in the belly of the fish three days and three nights.

When the sailors threw Jonah overboard, God sent a huge fish to swallow him. Unlike Jonah, the fish did what God told it to do!

A Psalm of Thanksgiving

2 Then Jonah prayed to the LORD his God from the belly of the fish, [2]saying,

"I called to the LORD out of my distress,
 and he answered me;
out of the belly of Shē´ōl I cried,
 and you heard my voice.

---

[a] Heb *They* [b] Ch 2.1 in Heb

³ You cast me into the deep,
   into the heart of the seas,
   and the flood surrounded me;
all your waves and your billows
   passed over me.
⁴ Then I said, 'I am driven away
   from your sight;
how*ᶜ* shall I look again
   upon your holy temple?'
⁵ The waters closed in over me;
   the deep surrounded me;
weeds were wrapped around my head
⁶   at the roots of the mountains.
I went down to the land
   whose bars closed upon me forever;
yet you brought up my life from the
      Pit,
   O LORD my God.
⁷ As my life was ebbing away,
   I remembered the LORD;
and my prayer came to you,
   into your holy temple.
⁸ Those who worship vain idols
   forsake their true loyalty.
⁹ But I with the voice of thanksgiving
   will sacrifice to you;
what I have vowed I will pay.
   Deliverance belongs to the LORD!"
¹⁰Then the LORD spoke to the fish, and it
spewed Jonah out upon the dry land.

Nineveh was the capital of the Assyrian empire. One of the oldest cities of Mesopotamia, Nineveh dates back to prehistoric times. It reached its greatest fame in the eighth century BC. The Israelites feared Nineveh because it represented the constant threat of danger from Assyria.

Conversion of Nineveh

3 The word of the LORD came to Jonah a second time, saying, ²"Get up, go to Nin´e·veh, that great city, and proclaim to it the message that I tell you." ³So Jonah set out and went to Nin´e·veh, according to the word of the LORD. Now Nin´e·veh was an exceedingly large city, a three days' walk across. ⁴Jonah began to go into the city, going a day's walk. And he cried out, "Forty days more, and Nin´e·veh shall be overthrown!" ⁵And the people of Nin´e·veh believed God; they proclaimed a fast, and everyone, great and small, put on sackcloth.

6 When the news reached the king of Nin´e·veh, he rose from his throne, removed his robe, covered himself with sackcloth, and sat in ashes. ⁷Then he had a proclamation made in Nin´e·veh: "By the decree of the king and his nobles: No human being or animal, no herd or flock, shall taste anything. They shall not feed, nor shall they drink water. ⁸Human beings and animals shall be covered with sackcloth, and they shall cry mightily to God. All shall turn from their evil ways and from the violence that is in their hands. ⁹Who knows? God may relent and change his mind; he may turn from his fierce anger, so that we do not perish."

10 When God saw what they did, how they turned from their evil ways, God changed his mind about the calamity that he had said he would bring upon them; and he did not do it.

Jonah's Anger

4 But this was very displeasing to Jonah, and he became angry. ²He prayed to the LORD and said, "O LORD! Is not this what I said while I was still in my own country? That is why I fled to Tar´shish at the beginning; for I knew that you are a gracious God and merciful, slow to anger, and abounding in steadfast love, and ready to relent from punishing. ³And now, O LORD, please take my life from me, for it is better for me to die than to live." ⁴And the LORD said, "Is it right for you to be angry?"

ᶜ Theodotion: Heb *surely*

"You are a gracious God and merciful, slow to anger, and abounding in steadfast love."

Jonah 4:2

[5] Then Jonah went out of the city and sat down east of the city, and made a booth for himself there. He sat under it in the shade, waiting to see what would become of the city.

6 The LORD God appointed a bush,[d] and made it come up over Jonah, to give shade over his head, to save him from his discomfort; so Jonah was very happy about the bush. [7]But when dawn came up the next day, God appointed a worm that attacked the bush, so that it withered. [8]When the sun rose, God prepared a sultry east wind, and the sun beat down on the head of Jonah so that he was faint and asked that he might die. He said, "It is better for me to die than to live."

Jonah did what God asked him to do but instead of being happy, Jonah was so angry he was ready to die! God arranged for a bush to grow over Jonah's head to shade him from the sun. Then God sent a worm to cut the bush down. God wanted Jonah to realize that his concern for the bush was nothing compared to God's concern for the people of Nineveh.

Jonah Is Reproved

9 But God said to Jonah, "Is it right for you to be angry about the bush?" And he said, "Yes, angry enough to die." [10]Then the LORD said, "You are concerned about the bush, for which you did not labor and which you did not grow; it came into being in a night and perished in a night. [11]And should I not be concerned about Nin´e·veh, that great city, in which there are more than a hundred and twenty thousand persons who do not know their right hand from their left, and also many animals?"

Although he didn't really want to, Jonah made a big difference in the lives of the people of Nineveh. God wants us to be concerned about others whether they are just like us or very different. What are some things you can do to make a difference in the lives of the people in your community?

[d] Heb *qiqayon,* possibly *the castor bean plant*

Micah

More than seven hundred years before Jesus was born, God called Micah to be a prophet. At this same time Isaiah was preaching in Jerusalem. Micah was from a small village in Palestine. He loved the country people and their ways, and he thought that many people who lived in the city were corrupt. He saw the northern kingdom of Israel fall to the Assyrians in 722 BC. Because of this, Micah warned the southern kingdom of Judah to return to the law of God and to pure worship of God so that Judah would not also fall.

The book of Micah is a collection of his sermons written about 690 BC. The Assyrian armies were destroying Samaria (capital of the northern king-

dom of Israel) and threatened to invade Jerusalem (capital of the southern kingdom of Judah). Micah preached against the selfishness of the Israelite leaders and spoke out against the way they mistreated the poor. For this reason, he has often been called "the prophet of the poor." The people had started to worship idols on hilltops, following the ways of their neighbors. Micah said that God was punishing the people by letting Assyria destroy both Samaria and Jerusalem. Beginning with chapter 4, the sermons become more hopeful and talk about God's forgiveness and mercy.

Micah 4:3

1 The word of the LORD that came to Mī´cah of Mō´re·sheth in the days of Kings Jō´tham, Ā´haz, and Hez·e·kī´ah of Judah, which he saw concerning Sa·mār´i·a and Jerusalem.

Judgment Pronounced against Samaria

2 Hear, you peoples, all of you;
  listen, O earth, and all that is in it;
and let the Lord GOD be a witness
      against you,
  the Lord from his holy temple.
3 For lo, the LORD is coming out of his
      place,
  and will come down and tread upon
      the high places of the earth.
4 Then the mountains will melt under
      him
  and the valleys will burst open,
like wax near the fire,
  like waters poured down a steep
      place.
5 All this is for the transgression of Jacob
  and for the sins of the house of
      Israel.
What is the transgression of Jacob?
  Is it not Sa·mār´i·a?
And what is the high place*a* of Judah?
  Is it not Jerusalem?
6 Therefore I will make Sa·mār´i·a a heap
      in the open country,
  a place for planting vineyards.
I will pour down her stones into the
      valley,
  and uncover her foundations.
7 All her images shall be beaten to
      pieces,
  all her wages shall be burned with fire,
  and all her idols I will lay waste;
for as the wages of a prostitute she
      gathered them,
  and as the wages of a prostitute they
      shall again be used.

The Doom of the Cities of Judah

8 For this I will lament and wail;
  I will go barefoot and naked;
I will make lamentation like the
      jackals,

and mourning like the ostriches.
9 For her wound*b* is incurable.
  It has come to Judah;
it has reached to the gate of my
      people,
  to Jerusalem.

10 Tell it not in Gath,
    weep not at all;
  in Beth-le·aph´rah
    roll yourselves in the dust.
11 Pass on your way,
    inhabitants of Shā´phir,
    in nakedness and shame;
  the inhabitants of Zā´a·nan
    do not come forth;
  Beth-e´zel is wailing
    and shall remove its support from
        you.
12 For the inhabitants of Mā´roth
    wait anxiously for good,
  yet disaster has come down from the
      LORD
    to the gate of Jerusalem.
13 Harness the steeds to the chariots,
    inhabitants of Lā´chish;
  it was the beginning of sin
    to daughter Zion,
  for in you were found
    the transgressions of Israel.
14 Therefore you shall give parting gifts
    to Mō´re·sheth-gath;
  the houses of Ach´zib shall be a
      deception
    to the kings of Israel.
15 I will again bring a conqueror upon
      you,
    inhabitants of Ma·rē´shah;
  the glory of Israel
    shall come to A·dul´lam.
16 Make yourselves bald and cut off your
      hair
    for your pampered children;
  make yourselves as bald as the eagle,
    for they have gone from you into
        exile.

a Heb *what are the high places*   *b* Gk Syr Vg: Heb *wounds*

Social Evils Denounced

2 Alas for those who devise wickedness
and evil deeds[c] on their beds!
When the morning dawns, they
perform it,
because it is in their power.

2 They covet fields, and seize them;
houses, and take them away;
they oppress householder and house,
people and their inheritance.

3 Therefore thus says the LORD:
Now, I am devising against this family
an evil
from which you cannot remove your
necks;
and you shall not walk haughtily,
for it will be an evil time.

4 On that day they shall take up a taunt
song against you,
and wail with bitter lamentation,
and say, "We are utterly ruined;
the LORD[d] alters the inheritance of
my people;
how he removes it from me!
Among our captors[e] he parcels out
our fields."

5 Therefore you will have no one to cast
the line by lot
in the assembly of the LORD.

6 "Do not preach"—thus they preach—
"one should not preach of such
things;
disgrace will not overtake us."

7 Should this be said, O house of Jacob?
Is the LORD's patience exhausted?
Are these his doings?
Do not my words do good
to one who walks uprightly?

> "I will surely gather all of you, O
> Jacob, I will gather the survivors of
> Israel; I will set them together like
> sheep in a fold, like a
> flock in its pasture; it will
> resound with people."
> Micah 2:12

8 But you rise up against my people[f] as
an enemy;
you strip the robe from the
peaceful,[g]
from those who pass by trustingly
with no thought of war.

9 The women of my people you drive out
from their pleasant houses;
from their young children you take away
my glory forever.

10 Arise and go;
for this is no place to rest,
because of uncleanness that destroys
with a grievous destruction.[h]

11 If someone were to go about uttering
empty falsehoods,
saying, "I will preach to you of wine
and strong drink,"
such a one would be the preacher
for this people!

A Promise for the
Remnant of Israel

12 I will surely gather all of you, O Jacob,
I will gather the survivors of Israel;
I will set them together
like sheep in a fold,
like a flock in its pasture;
it will resound with people.

13 The one who breaks out will go up
before them;
they will break through and pass the
gate,
going out by it.
Their king will pass on before them,
the LORD at their head.

Wicked Rulers and Prophets

3 And I said:
Listen, you heads of Jacob
and rulers of the house of Israel!
Should you not know justice?—

2 you who hate the good and love the
evil,
who tear the skin off my people,[i]
and the flesh off their bones;

---

[c] Cn: Heb *work evil*   [d] Heb *he*   [e] Cn: Heb *the
rebellious*   [f] Cn: Heb *But yesterday my people rose*
[g] Cn: Heb *from before a garment*   [h] Meaning of
Heb uncertain   [i] Heb *from them*

Micah reminds us that some day all nations will live in peace following the ways of God. Read these Scripture passages to remind you of how you are called to be a peace builder: Ecclesiastes 3:8, John 14:25–27, Romans 2:10, Galatians 5:22–23, Hebrews 13:20–21, and James 3:18.

Pray for the men and women who serve in the military and for all people everywhere who live in countries that are at war.

³ who eat the flesh of my people,
  flay their skin off them,
break their bones in pieces,
  and chop them up like meat* in a kettle,
  like flesh in a caldron.

⁴ Then they will cry to the LORD,
  but he will not answer them;
he will hide his face from them at that time,
  because they have acted wickedly.

⁵ Thus says the LORD concerning the prophets
  who lead my people astray,
who cry "Peace"
  when they have something to eat,
but declare war against those
  who put nothing into their mouths.
⁶ Therefore it shall be night to you, without vision,
  and darkness to you, without revelation.
The sun shall go down upon the prophets,
  and the day shall be black over them;
⁷ the seers shall be disgraced,
  and the diviners put to shame;
they shall all cover their lips,
  for there is no answer from God.
⁸ But as for me, I am filled with power,
  with the spirit of the LORD,
and with justice and might,
  to declare to Jacob his transgression
  and to Israel his sin.

⁹ Hear this, you rulers of the house of Jacob
  and chiefs of the house of Israel,
who abhor justice
  and pervert all equity,
¹⁰ who build Zion with blood
  and Jerusalem with wrong!
¹¹ Its rulers give judgment for a bribe,
  its priests teach for a price,
  its prophets give oracles for money;
yet they lean upon the LORD and say,
  "Surely the LORD is with us!
  No harm shall come upon us."
¹² Therefore because of you
  Zion shall be plowed as a field;
Jerusalem shall become a heap of ruins,
  and the mountain of the house a wooded height.

Peace and Security through Obedience

4 In days to come
  the mountain of the LORD's house
shall be established as the highest of the mountains,
  and shall be raised up above the hills.
Peoples shall stream to it,
² and many nations shall come and say:
"Come, let us go up to the mountain of the LORD,
  to the house of the God of Jacob;
that he may teach us his ways
  and that we may walk in his paths."
For out of Zion shall go forth instruction,
  and the word of the LORD from Jerusalem.
³ He shall judge between many peoples,
  and shall arbitrate between strong nations far away;

j Gk: Heb *as*

In the country Kampuchea (also known as Cambodia), children pick up shell casings left in the fields from war in their country. Shell casings are covers on bullets shot from guns. The children take the shells to foundries, places that melt and shape metal. In the foundries, the shells are melted and shaped into bells. The people of Kampuchea put these bells on the harnesses of their oxen. The people depend on their oxen to help them farm the land and carry them from place to place. How does the making of bells from shells remind you of Micah's hope for "beating swords into plowshares?"

they shall beat their swords into
    plowshares,
  and their spears into pruning hooks;
nation shall not lift up sword against
    nation,
  neither shall they learn war any
    more;
4 but they shall all sit under their own
    vines and under their own fig
    trees,
  and no one shall make them
    afraid;
  for the mouth of the LORD of hosts
    has spoken.

5 For all the peoples walk,
  each in the name of its god,
but we will walk in the name of the
    LORD our God
  forever and ever.

Restoration Promised after Exile

6 In that day, says the LORD,
  I will assemble the lame
and gather those who have been
    driven away,
  and those whom I have afflicted.

7 The lame I will make the remnant,
  and those who were cast off, a
    strong nation;
and the LORD will reign over them in
    Mount Zion
  now and forevermore.

8 And you, O tower of the flock,
  hill of daughter Zion,
to you it shall come,
  the former dominion shall come,
  the sovereignty of daughter
    Jerusalem.

9 Now why do you cry aloud?
  Is there no king in you?
Has your counselor perished,
  that pangs have seized you like a
    woman in labor?
10 Writhe and groan,[k] O daughter Zion,
  like a woman in labor;
for now you shall go forth from the
    city
  and camp in the open country;
  you shall go to Babylon.
There you shall be rescued,
  there the LORD will redeem you
  from the hands of your enemies.

11 Now many nations
  are assembled against you,
saying, "Let her be profaned,
  and let our eyes gaze upon Zion."
12 But they do not know
  the thoughts of the LORD;
they do not understand his plan,
  that he has gathered them as sheaves
    to the threshing floor.
13 Arise and thresh,
  O daughter Zion,
for I will make your horn iron
  and your hoofs bronze;
you shall beat in pieces many peoples,
  and shall[l] devote their gain to the
    LORD,
  their wealth to the Lord of the
    whole earth.

k Meaning of Heb uncertain   l Gk Syr Tg: Heb
and I will

5 ᵐNow you are walled around with a wall;ⁿ
siege is laid against us;
with a rod they strike the ruler of Israel
upon the cheek.

The Ruler from Bethlehem

²⁰ But you, O Bethlehem of Eph´ra·thah,
who are one of the little clans of Judah,
from you shall come forth for me
one who is to rule in Israel,
whose origin is from of old,
from ancient days.

³ Therefore he shall give them up until the time
when she who is in labor has brought forth;
then the rest of his kindred shall return
to the people of Israel.

⁴ And he shall stand and feed his flock
in the strength of the LORD,
in the majesty of the name of the LORD his God.
And they shall live secure, for now he shall be great
to the ends of the earth;

⁵ and he shall be the one of peace.

If the Assyrians come into our land
and tread upon our soil,ᵖ
we will raise against them seven shepherds
and eight installed as rulers.

⁶ They shall rule the land of Assyria with the sword,
and the land of Nim´rod with the drawn sword;�q

Micah tells of a new king who would come from the small village of Bethlehem to bring peace to the earth. Christians believe the verse tells of the coming of Jesus.

theyʳ shall rescue us from the Assyrians
if they come into our land
or tread within our border.

The Future Role of the Remnant

⁷ Then the remnant of Jacob,
surrounded by many peoples,
shall be like dew from the LORD,
like showers on the grass,
which do not depend upon people
or wait for any mortal.

⁸ And among the nations the remnant of Jacob,
surrounded by many peoples,
shall be like a lion among the animals of the forest,
like a young lion among the flocks of sheep,
which, when it goes through, treads down
and tears in pieces, with no one to deliver.

⁹ Your hand shall be lifted up over your adversaries,
and all your enemies shall be cut off.

¹⁰ In that day, says the LORD,
I will cut off your horses from among you
and will destroy your chariots;

¹¹ and I will cut off the cities of your land
and throw down all your strongholds;

¹² and I will cut off sorceries from your hand,
and you shall have no more soothsayers;

¹³ and I will cut off your images
and your pillars from among you,
and you shall bow down no more
to the work of your hands;

¹⁴ and I will uproot your sacred polesˢ
from among you
and destroy your towns.

ᵐ Ch 4.14 in Heb   ⁿ Cn Compare Gk: Meaning
of Heb uncertain   ᵒ Ch 5.1 in Heb   ᵖ Gk:
Heb *in our palaces*   q Cn: Heb *in its entrances*
ʳ Heb *he*   ˢ Heb *Asherim*

> "He has told you, O
> mortal, what is good;
> and what does the LORD
> require of you but to do
> justice, and to love kindness, and
> to walk humbly with your God?"
>   Micah 6:8

15 And in anger and wrath I will execute
     vengeance
     on the nations that did not obey.

God Challenges Israel

6 Hear what the Lord says:
     Rise, plead your case before the
        mountains,
     and let the hills hear your voice.
2 Hear, you mountains, the controversy
        of the LORD,
     and you enduring foundations of
        the earth;
   for the LORD has a controversy with his
        people,
     and he will contend with Israel.

3 "O my people, what have I done to
        you?
     In what have I wearied you? Answer
        me!
4 For I brought you up from the land of
        Egypt,
     and redeemed you from the house
        of slavery;
   and I sent before you Moses,
        Aaron, and Miriam.
5 O my people, remember now what
        King Bāʹlak of Mōʹab devised,
     what Bāʹlaam son of Bēʹor answered
        him,
   and what happened from Shitʹtim to
        Gilʹgal,
     that you may know the saving acts
        of the LORD."

What God Requires

6 "With what shall I come before the
     LORD,
     and bow myself before God on
        high?

Shall I come before him with burnt
     offerings,
     with calves a year old?
7 Will the LORD be pleased with
     thousands of rams,
     with ten thousands of rivers of oil?
Shall I give my firstborn for my
     transgression,
     the fruit of my body for the sin of
        my soul?"
8 He has told you, O mortal, what is
     good;
     and what does the LORD require of
        you
   but to do justice, and to love kindness,
     and to walk humbly with your God?

Cheating and Violence
to Be Punished

9 The voice of the LORD cries to the city
     (it is sound wisdom to fear your
        name):
   Hear, O tribe and assembly of the city!ᵗ
10   Can I forgetᵘ the treasures of
        wickedness in the house of the
        wicked,
     and the scant measure that is
        accursed?
11 Can I tolerate wicked scales
     and a bag of dishonest weights?
12 Yourᵛ wealthy are full of violence;
     yourʷ inhabitants speak lies,
     with tongues of deceit in their
        mouths.
13 Therefore I have begunˣ to strike you
        down,
     making you desolate because of
        your sins.
14 You shall eat, but not be satisfied,
     and there shall be a gnawing hunger
        within you;
   you shall put away, but not save,
     and what you save, I will hand over
        to the sword.
15 You shall sow, but not reap;

ᵗ Cn Compare Gk: Heb *tribe, and who has
appointed it yet?*   ᵘ Cn: Meaning of Heb uncertain   ᵛ Heb *Whose*   ʷ Heb *whose*
ˣ Gk Syr Vg: Heb *have made sick*

you shall tread olives, but not anoint
yourselves with oil;
you shall tread grapes, but not drink
wine.
[16] For you have kept the statutes of
Om´ri[y]
and all the works of the house of
Ā´hab,
and you have followed their
counsels.
Therefore I will make you a desolation,
and your[z] inhabitants an object
of hissing;
so you shall bear the scorn of my
people.

The Total Corruption
of the People

7 Woe is me! For I have become like
one who,
after the summer fruit has been
gathered,
after the vintage has been gleaned,
finds no cluster to eat;
there is no first-ripe fig for which I
hunger.
[2] The faithful have disappeared from the
land,
and there is no one left who is
upright;
they all lie in wait for blood,
and they hunt each other with
nets.
[3] Their hands are skilled to do evil;
the official and the judge ask for a
bribe,
and the powerful dictate what they
desire;
thus they pervert justice.[a]
[4] The best of them is like a brier,
the most upright of them a thorn
hedge.
The day of their[b] sentinels, of their[b]
punishment, has come;
now their confusion is at hand.
[5] Put no trust in a friend,
have no confidence in a loved one;
guard the doors of your mouth
from her who lies in your embrace;

[6] for the son treats the father with
contempt,
the daughter rises up against her
mother,
the daughter-in-law against her
mother-in-law;
your enemies are members of your
own household.
[7] But as for me, I will look to the LORD,
I will wait for the God of my
salvation;
my God will hear me.

Penitence and Trust in God

[8] Do not rejoice over me, O my
enemy;
when I fall, I shall rise;
when I sit in darkness,
the LORD will be a light to me.
[9] I must bear the indignation of the
LORD,
because I have sinned against him,
until he takes my side
and executes judgment for me.
He will bring me out to the light;
I shall see his vindication.
[10] Then my enemy will see,
and shame will cover her who said
to me,
"Where is the LORD your God?"
My eyes will see her downfall;[c]
now she will be trodden down
like the mire of the streets.

A Prophecy of Restoration

[11] A day for the building of your walls!
In that day the boundary shall be far
extended.
[12] In that day they will come to you
from Assyria to[d] Egypt,
and from Egypt to the River,
from sea to sea and from mountain
to mountain.
[13] But the earth will be desolate
because of its inhabitants,
for the fruit of their doings.

[y] Gk Syr Vg Tg: Heb *the statutes of Omri are kept*
[z] Heb *its*   [a] Cn: Heb *they weave it*   [b] Heb *your*
[c] Heb lacks *downfall*   [d] One Ms: MT *Assyria and
cities of*

14 Shepherd your people with your staff,
   the flock that belongs to you,
which lives alone in a forest
   in the midst of a garden land;
let them feed in Bā´shan and Gil´e·ad
   as in the days of old.
15 As in the days when you came out of
     the land of Egypt,
   show us*e* marvelous things.
16 The nations shall see and be ashamed
     of all their might;
they shall lay their hands on their
     mouths;
   their ears shall be deaf;
17 they shall lick dust like a snake,
   like the crawling things of the earth;
they shall come trembling out of their
     fortresses;
   they shall turn in dread to the LORD
     our God,
   and they shall stand in fear of you.

God's Compassion and Steadfast Love

18 Who is a God like you, pardoning
     iniquity
   and passing over the transgression
     of the remnant of your*f* possession?
He does not retain his anger forever,
   because he delights in showing
     clemency.
19 He will again have compassion upon
     us;
   he will tread our iniquities under
     foot.
You will cast all our*g* sins
   into the depths of the sea.
20 You will show faithfulness to Jacob
     and unswerving loyalty to Abraham,
as you have sworn to our ancestors
   from the days of old.

e Cn: Heb *I will show him*   *f* Heb *his*   *g* Gk Syr
Vg Tg: Heb *their*

Nahum

Nahum was a prophet in the southern kingdom of Judah in the seventh century BC, about the same time the prophets Zephaniah, Habakkuk, and Jeremiah were preaching. The book of Nahum was written close to the time when Babylonia's armies destroyed the nation of Assyria in 605 BC. Nahum saw the fall of the Assyrian enemy as a great blessing from God to Israel.

One hundred years earlier, Assyria's armies had destroyed the northern kingdom of Israel. So the people of the southern kingdom of Judah hated and feared Assyria's capital city, Nineveh. When the Babylonian armies defeated Nineveh, Nahum believed the defeat was the triumph of God over an enemy of God's people.

The book of Nahum teaches that those who turn away from God and trust in themselves are in danger. The book also teaches that God will punish the enemies of those who trust in God. There is no enemy that can destroy God's people.

Nahum 1:1

1

An oracle concerning Nin´e·veh. The book of the vision of Nā´hum of El´kosh.

The Consuming Wrath of God

2 A jealous and avenging God is the
LORD,
the LORD is avenging and wrathful;
the LORD takes vengeance on his
adversaries
and rages against his enemies.
3 The LORD is slow to anger but great in
power,
and the LORD will by no means clear
the guilty.

His way is in whirlwind and storm,
and the clouds are the dust of his
feet.
4 He rebukes the sea and makes it dry,
and he dries up all the rivers;
Bā´shan and Car´mel wither,
and the bloom of Lebanon fades.
5 The mountains quake before him,
and the hills melt;
the earth heaves before him,
the world and all who live in it.

6 Who can stand before his indignation?
Who can endure the heat of his
anger?
His wrath is poured out like fire,
and by him the rocks are broken in
pieces.
7 The LORD is good,
a stronghold in a day of trouble;
he protects those who take refuge in
him,
8 even in a rushing flood.
He will make a full end of his
adversaries,[a]
and will pursue his enemies into
darkness.
9 Why do you plot against the LORD?
He will make an end;
no adversary will rise up twice.
10 Like thorns they are entangled,
like drunkards they are drunk;
they are consumed like dry straw.

> "The LORD is good, a stronghold in a day of trouble; he protects those who take refuge in him, even in a rushing flood." Nahum 1:7–8a

11 From you one has gone out
who plots evil against the LORD,
one who counsels wickedness.

Good News for Judah

12 Thus says the LORD,
"Though they are at full strength and
many,[b]
they will be cut off and pass away.
Though I have afflicted you,
I will afflict you no more.
13 And now I will break off his yoke from
you
and snap the bonds that bind you."

14 The LORD has commanded concerning
you:
"Your name shall be perpetuated no
longer;
from the house of your gods I will cut
off
the carved image and the cast image.
I will make your grave, for you are
worthless."

15c Look! On the mountains the feet of
one
who brings good tidings,
who proclaims peace!
Celebrate your festivals, O Judah,
fulfill your vows,
for never again shall the wicked invade
you;
they are utterly cut off.

The Destruction of
the Wicked City

2

A shatterer[d] has come up against
you.
Guard the ramparts;

---

a Gk: Heb *of her place*   b Meaning of Heb uncertain   c Ch 2.1 in Heb   d Cn: Heb *scatterer*

watch the road;
gird your loins;
collect all your strength.

2 (For the LORD is restoring the majesty
of Jacob,
as well as the majesty of Israel,
though ravagers have ravaged them
and ruined their branches.)

3 The shields of his warriors are red;
his soldiers are clothed in crimson.
The metal on the chariots flashes
on the day when he musters them;
the chargers*e* prance.

4 The chariots race madly through the
streets,
they rush to and fro through the
squares;
their appearance is like torches,
they dart like lightning.

5 He calls his officers;
they stumble as they come forward;
they hasten to the wall,
and the mantelet*f* is set up.

6 The river gates are opened,
the palace trembles.

7 It is decreed*f* that the city*g* be exiled,
its slave women led away,
moaning like doves
and beating their breasts.

8 Nin´e·veh is like a pool
whose waters*h* run away.
"Halt! Halt!"—
but no one turns back.

9 "Plunder the silver,
plunder the gold!
There is no end of treasure!
An abundance of every precious
thing!"

10 Devastation, desolation, and destruction!
Hearts faint and knees tremble,
all loins quake,
all faces grow pale!

11 What became of the lions' den,
the cave*i* of the young lions,
where the lion goes,
and the lion's cubs, with no one to
disturb them?

12 The lion has torn enough for his
whelps
and strangled prey for his lionesses;
he has filled his caves with prey
and his dens with torn flesh.

13 See, I am against you, says the
LORD of hosts, and I will burn your*j* chariots in smoke, and the sword shall devour
your young lions; I will cut off your prey
from the earth, and the voice of your messengers shall be heard no more.

In 1 Samuel 1:3 God is
called "the LORD of
hosts." Other verses in 1
Samuel and Numbers, as
well as here in Nahum, use that
name to describe God as the
leader of a divine army that will
battle for God's people. In the book
of Revelation, Jesus is depicted as
the leader of a heavenly army that
battles for the Church.

Ruin Imminent and Inevitable

3 Ah! City of bloodshed,
utterly deceitful, full of booty—
no end to the plunder!

2 The crack of whip and rumble of
wheel,
galloping horse and bounding
chariot!

3 Horsemen charging,
flashing sword and glittering
spear,
piles of dead,
heaps of corpses,
dead bodies without end—
they stumble over the bodies!

4 Because of the countless debaucheries
of the prostitute,
gracefully alluring, mistress of
sorcery,

e Cn Compare Gk Syr: Heb *cypresses*   *f* Meaning
of Heb uncertain   *g* Heb *it*   *h* Cn Compare
Gk: Heb *a pool, from the days that she has become,
and they*   *i* Cn: Heb *pasture*   *j* Heb *her*

who enslaves[k] nations through her
    debaucheries,
and peoples through her sorcery,
5 I am against you,
    says the LORD of hosts,
and will lift up your skirts over your
    face;
and I will let nations look on your
    nakedness
and kingdoms on your shame.
6 I will throw filth at you
    and treat you with contempt,
    and make you a spectacle.
7 Then all who see you will shrink from
    you and say,
"Nin′e·veh is devastated; who will
    bemoan her?"
    Where shall I seek comforters for
    you?

8 Are you better than Thē′bes[l]
    that sat by the Nile,
with water around her,
    her rampart a sea,
    water her wall?
9 Ethiopia[m] was her strength,
    Egypt too, and that without limit;
    Put and the Libyans were her[n]
    helpers.

10 Yet she became an exile,
    she went into captivity;
even her infants were dashed in pieces
    at the head of every street;
lots were cast for her nobles,
    all her dignitaries were bound in
    fetters.
11 You also will be drunken,
    you will go into hiding;[o]
you will seek
    a refuge from the enemy.
12 All your fortresses are like fig trees
    with first-ripe figs—
if shaken they fall
    into the mouth of the eater.

13 Look at your troops:
    they are women in your midst.
The gates of your land
    are wide open to your foes;
    fire has devoured the bars of your
    gates.

14 Draw water for the siege,
    strengthen your forts;
trample the clay,
    tread the mortar,
    take hold of the brick mold!
15 There the fire will devour you,
    the sword will cut you off.
    It will devour you like the locust.

Multiply yourselves like the locust,
    multiply like the grasshopper!
16 You increased your merchants
    more than the stars of the heavens.
    The locust sheds its skin and flies
    away.
17 Your guards are like grasshoppers,
    your scribes like swarms[o] of locusts
settling on the fences
    on a cold day—
when the sun rises, they fly away;
    no one knows where they have
    gone.

18 Your shepherds are asleep,
    O king of Assyria;
    your nobles slumber.
Your people are scattered on the
    mountains
    with no one to gather them.
19 There is no assuaging your hurt,
    your wound is mortal.
All who hear the news about you
    clap their hands over you.
For who has ever escaped
    your endless cruelty?

[k] Heb *sells*   [l] Heb *No-amon*   [m] Or *Nubia*; Heb
Cush   [n] Gk: Heb *your*   [o] Meaning of Heb
uncertain

Habakkuk

The book of Habakkuk, written about 695 BC, searches for the reason why God allows so much evil in the world. Along with the prophets Zephaniah, Nahum, and Jeremiah, the prophet Habakkuk knew that Assyria was about to fall under the military power of Babylonia. He also knew that his own small country of Judah was in danger.

As Habakkuk thought about the history of God's people, he noticed that each time a new ruler took over, that ruler was even more evil than the one who came before. Habakkuk complained to God about the power and cruelty of the Babylonian empire. He wondered how long his country would continue to be mistreated by large neighbor nations. He wondered how long there would be war and defeat for his people.

The answer to Habakkuk's question is given in chapter 2, especially verses 2–4. Habakkuk admitted that the wicked often seem to succeed. At the same time, he saw that people are able to follow God because of the strength of their faith and loyalty to God. The book of Habakkuk ends with a beautiful song that tells of the writer's trust in God as the true source of happiness.

Habakkuk 1:1

1 The oracle that the prophet Ha·bak′kuk saw.

The Prophet's Complaint

2 O Lord, how long shall I cry for help,
  and you will not listen?
 Or cry to you "Violence!"
  and you will not save?
3 Why do you make me see wrongdoing
  and look at trouble?
 Destruction and violence are before
  me;
  strife and contention arise.
4 So the law becomes slack
  and justice never prevails.
 The wicked surround the righteous—
  therefore judgment comes forth
  perverted.

5 Look at the nations, and see!
  Be astonished! Be astounded!
 For a work is being done in your days
  that you would not believe if you
  were told.
6 For I am rousing the Chal·dē′ans,
  that fierce and impetuous nation,
 who march through the breadth of the
  earth
  to seize dwellings not their own.
7 Dread and fearsome are they;
  their justice and dignity proceed
  from themselves.
8 Their horses are swifter than leopards,
  more menacing than wolves at dusk;
  their horses charge.
 Their horsemen come from far away;
  they fly like an eagle swift to devour.
9 They all come for violence,
  with faces pressing[a] forward;
  they gather captives like sand.

Habakkuk said that God the creator has made people like the fish of the sea. He asked why God had allowed the Babylonians to catch God's own people.

10 At kings they scoff,
  and of rulers they make sport.
 They laugh at every fortress,
  and heap up earth to take it.
11 Then they sweep by like the wind;
  they transgress and become guilty;
  their own might is their god!

12 Are you not from of old,
  O Lord my God, my Holy One?
 You[b] shall not die.
 O Lord, you have marked them for
  judgment;
  and you, O Rock, have established
  them for punishment.
13 Your eyes are too pure to behold evil,
  and you cannot look on
  wrongdoing;
 why do you look on the treacherous,
  and are silent when the wicked
  swallow
  those more righteous than they?
14 You have made people like the fish of
  the sea,
  like crawling things that have no
  ruler.

15 The enemy[c] brings all of them up with
  a hook;
  he drags them out with his net,
 he gathers them in his seine;
  so he rejoices and exults.
16 Therefore he sacrifices to his net
  and makes offerings to his seine;
 for by them his portion is lavish,
  and his food is rich.
17 Is he then to keep on emptying his net,
  and destroying nations without
  mercy?

God's Reply to the Prophet's Complaint

2 I will stand at my watchpost,
  and station myself on the
  rampart;
 I will keep watch to see what he will
  say to me,

---

a Meaning of Heb uncertain   *b* Ancient Heb tradition: MT *We*   *c* Heb *He*

and what he[d] will answer
concerning my complaint.
² Then the LORD answered me and said:
Write the vision;
make it plain on tablets,
so that a runner may read it.
³ For there is still a vision for the
appointed time;
it speaks of the end, and does not lie.
If it seems to tarry, wait for it;
it will surely come, it will not delay.
⁴ Look at the proud!
Their spirit is not right in them,
but the righteous live by their faith.[e]
⁵ Moreover, wealth[f] is treacherous;
the arrogant do not endure.
They open their throats wide as Shēʾōl;
like Death they never have enough.
They gather all nations for themselves,
and collect all peoples as their own.

The Woes of the Wicked

6 Shall not everyone taunt such people and, with mocking riddles, say about
them,
"Alas for you who heap up what is not
your own!"
How long will you load yourselves
with goods taken in pledge?
⁷ Will not your own creditors suddenly
rise,
and those who make you tremble
wake up?
Then you will be booty for them.
⁸ Because you have plundered many
nations,
all that survive of the peoples shall
plunder you—
because of human bloodshed, and
violence to the earth,
to cities and all who live in them.

⁹ "Alas for you who get evil gain for
your houses,
setting your nest on high
to be safe from the reach of harm!"
¹⁰ You have devised shame for your
house
by cutting off many peoples;
you have forfeited your life.

When Habakkuk com-
plained about the power
and the evil of Babylon,
God reminded him that
people who do not keep God's
laws will lose their lives in the end.
Although Babylon was strong for a
while, their wicked ways would
cause them to be defeated.

¹¹ The very stones will cry out from the
wall,
and the plaster[g] will respond from
the woodwork.

¹² "Alas for you who build a town by
bloodshed,
and found a city on iniquity!"
¹³ Is it not from the LORD of hosts
that peoples labor only to feed the
flames,
and nations weary themselves for
nothing?
¹⁴ But the earth will be filled
with the knowledge of the glory of
the LORD,
as the waters cover the sea.

¹⁵ "Alas for you who make your
neighbors drink,
pouring out your wrath[h] until they
are drunk,
in order to gaze on their nakedness!"
¹⁶ You will be sated with contempt
instead of glory.
Drink, you yourself, and stagger![i]
The cup in the LORD's right hand
will come around to you,
and shame will come upon your
glory!
¹⁷ For the violence done to Lebanon will
overwhelm you;
the destruction of the animals will
terrify you—[j]

[d] Syr: Heb I   [e] Or *faithfulness*   [f] Other Heb
Mss read *wine*   [g] Or *beam*   [h] Or *poison*
[i] Q Ms Gk: MT *be uncircumcised*   [j] Gk Syr:
Meaning of Heb uncertain

because of human bloodshed and
     violence to the earth,
     to cities and all who live in them.

18 What use is an idol
     once its maker has shaped it—
     a cast image, a teacher of lies?
For its maker trusts in what has been
     made,
     though the product is only an idol
          that cannot speak!
19 Alas for you who say to the wood,
     "Wake up!"
     to silent stone, "Rouse yourself!"
     Can it teach?
See, it is gold and silver plated,
     and there is no breath in it at all.

20 But the LORD is in his holy temple;
     let all the earth keep silence before
          him!

3 A prayer of the prophet Ha·bak´-
     kuk according to Shig·i·ōn´oth.

The Prophet's Prayer

2 O LORD, I have heard of your renown,
     and I stand in awe, O LORD, of your
          work.
In our own time revive it;
     in our own time make it known;
     in wrath may you remember mercy.
3 God came from Tē´man,
     the Holy One from Mount Par´an.
                                   Sēlah

His glory covered the heavens,
     and the earth was full of his praise.
4 The brightness was like the sun;
     rays came forth from his hand,
     where his power lay hidden.
5 Before him went pestilence,
     and plague followed close behind.
6 He stopped and shook the earth;
     he looked and made the nations
          tremble.
The eternal mountains were shattered;
     along his ancient pathways
     the everlasting hills sank low.
7 I saw the tents of Cū´shan under
          affliction;

> "The LORD is in his holy temple; let all the earth keep silence before him!"   Habakkuk 2:20

     the tent-curtains of the land of
          Mid´i·an trembled.
8 Was your wrath against the rivers,[k] O
          LORD?
     Or your anger against the rivers,[k]
     or your rage against the sea,[l]
when you drove your horses,
     your chariots to victory?
9 You brandished your naked bow,
     sated[m] were the arrows at your
          command.[n]   *Sēlah*
     You split the earth with rivers.
10 The mountains saw you, and writhed;
     a torrent of water swept by;
     the deep gave forth its voice.
     The sun[o] raised high its hands;
11 the moon[p] stood still in its exalted
          place,
     at the light of your arrows speeding
          by,
     at the gleam of your flashing spear.
12 In fury you trod the earth,
     in anger you trampled nations.
13 You came forth to save your people,
     to save your anointed.
You crushed the head of the wicked
     house,
     laying it bare from foundation to
          roof.[n]   *Sēlah*
14 You pierced with his[q] own arrows the
          head[r] of his warriors,[s]
who came like a whirlwind to
     scatter us,[t]
     gloating as if ready to devour the
          poor who were in hiding.

15 You trampled the sea with your horses,
     churning the mighty waters.

---

[k] Or *against River*   [l] Or *against Sea*   [m] Cn: Heb
oaths   [n] Meaning of Heb uncertain   [o] Heb *It*
[p] Heb *sun, moon*   [q] Heb *his*   [r] Or *leader*
[s] Vg Compare Gk Syr: Meaning of Heb uncertain
[t] Heb *me*

"GOD, the Lord, is my strength; he makes my feet like the feet of a deer, and makes me tread upon the heights."

Habakkuk 3:19

16 I hear, and I tremble within;
my lips quiver at the sound.
Rottenness enters into my bones,
and my steps tremble[u] beneath me.
I wait quietly for the day of calamity
to come upon the people who attack
us.

Trust and Joy in the Midst of Trouble

17 Though the fig tree does not blossom,
and no fruit is on the vines;
though the produce of the olive
fails,
and the fields yield no food;
though the flock is cut off from the
fold,
and there is no herd in the stalls,
18 yet I will rejoice in the LORD;
I will exult in the God of my
salvation.
19 GOD, the Lord, is my strength;
he makes my feet like the feet of a
deer,
and makes me tread upon the
heights.[v]

To the leader: with stringed[w]
instruments.

[u] Cn Compare Gk: Meaning of Heb uncertain
[v] Heb *my heights*   [w] Heb *my stringed*

Zephaniah

Zephaniah was the great-great-grandson of King Hezekiah, a godly man who had restored the Temple and made Jerusalem strong. Zephaniah was a prophet during the reign of King Josiah, another good and godly king. Zephaniah spoke of the evils of idolatry and warned that the day of the Lord would bring judgment on God's people and on the surrounding nations. The book of Zephaniah was written about 627 BC.

The book opens with a dramatic picture of the coming of "the day of the LORD." This is the day when God will be fully revealed and will judge all the people according to their faith and their actions. Zephaniah talked about more than just judgment. He told the people to ask for God's forgiveness for their sins. And he finished with a song of joy, showing that he believed the people would repent and be saved by God.

Zephaniah 1:1

1 The word of the LORD that came to Zeph·a·nī´ah son of Cū´shī son of Ged·a·lī´ah son of Am·a·rī´ah son of Hez·e·kī´ah, in the days of King Jō·sī´ah son of Ā´mon of Judah.

The Coming Judgment on Judah

² I will utterly sweep away everything
from the face of the earth, says the
LORD.
³ I will sweep away humans and
animals;
I will sweep away the birds of the air
and the fish of the sea.
I will make the wicked stumble.[a]
I will cut off humanity
from the face of the earth, says the
LORD.
⁴ I will stretch out my hand against
Judah,
and against all the inhabitants of
Jerusalem;
and I will cut off from this place every
remnant of Bā´al
and the name of the idolatrous
priests;[b]
⁵ those who bow down on the roofs
to the host of the heavens;
those who bow down and swear to the
LORD,
but also swear by Mil´com;[c]
⁶ those who have turned back from
following the LORD,
who have not sought the LORD or
inquired of him.

The day of the LORD is the day when God will appear to judge all the people. There were many ideas about this day. Many people thought of it as a day of punishment for the enemies of God's people. But Zephaniah points out that God's people deserve judgment as well.

On the day of the LORD, God will search Jerusalem and bring hidden sins into the light. Like many of the other prophets, Zephaniah points to those people who do not share their wealth with the poor and who believe they will escape God's judgment.

⁷ Be silent before the Lord GOD!
For the day of the LORD is at hand;
the LORD has prepared a sacrifice,
he has consecrated his guests.
⁸ And on the day of the LORD's sacrifice
I will punish the officials and the king's
sons
and all who dress themselves in
foreign attire.
⁹ On that day I will punish
all who leap over the threshold,
who fill their master's house
with violence and fraud.

¹⁰ On that day, says the LORD,
a cry will be heard from the Fish
Gate,
a wail from the Second Quarter,
a loud crash from the hills.
¹¹ The inhabitants of the Mortar wail,
for all the traders have perished;
all who weigh out silver are cut
off.
¹² At that time I will search Jerusalem
with lamps,
and I will punish the people
who rest complacently[d] on their
dregs,
those who say in their hearts,
"The LORD will not do good,
nor will he do harm."

^a Cn: Heb *sea, and those who cause the wicked to stumble*   ^b Compare Gk: Heb *the idolatrous priests with the priests*   ^c Gk Mss Syr Vg: Heb *Malcam* (or, *their king*)   ^d Heb *who thicken*

13 Their wealth shall be plundered,
  and their houses laid waste.
Though they build houses,
  they shall not inhabit them;
though they plant vineyards,
  they shall not drink wine from
    them.

The Great Day of the Lord

14 The great day of the LORD is near,
  near and hastening fast;
the sound of the day of the LORD is
    bitter,
  the warrior cries aloud there.
15 That day will be a day of wrath,
  a day of distress and anguish,
a day of ruin and devastation,
  a day of darkness and gloom,
  a day of clouds and thick darkness,
16   a day of trumpet blast and battle cry
against the fortified cities
  and against the lofty battlements.

17 I will bring such distress upon people
  that they shall walk like the blind;
  because they have sinned against the
    LORD,
their blood shall be poured out like
    dust,
  and their flesh like dung.
18 Neither their silver nor their gold
  will be able to save them
  on the day of the LORD's wrath;
in the fire of his passion
  the whole earth shall be consumed;
for a full, a terrible end
  he will make of all the inhabitants of
    the earth.

Judgment on Israel's Enemies

2 Gather together, gather,
    O shameless nation,
2 before you are driven away
  like the drifting chaff,[e]
before there comes upon you
  the fierce anger of the LORD,
before there comes upon you
  the day of the LORD's wrath.
3 Seek the LORD, all you humble of the
    land,

who do his commands;
seek righteousness, seek humility;
  perhaps you may be hidden
  on the day of the LORD's wrath.
4 For Ga´za shall be deserted,
  and Ash´ke·lon shall become a
    desolation;
Ash´dod's people shall be driven out at
    noon,
  and Ek´ron shall be uprooted.

5 Ah, inhabitants of the seacoast,
  you nation of the Cher´e·thites!
The word of the LORD is against you,
  O Ca´naan, land of the Phi·lis´tines;
  and I will destroy you until no
    inhabitant is left.
6 And you, O seacoast, shall be pastures,
  meadows for shepherds
  and folds for flocks.
7 The seacoast shall become the
    possession
  of the remnant of the house of
    Judah,
  on which they shall pasture,
and in the houses of Ash´ke·lon
  they shall lie down at evening.
For the LORD their God will be mindful
    of them
  and restore their fortunes.

8 I have heard the taunts of Mo´ab
  and the revilings of the
    Am´mon·ites,
how they have taunted my people
  and made boasts against their
    territory.
9 Therefore, as I live, says the LORD of
    hosts,
  the God of Israel,
Mo´ab shall become like Sod´om
  and the Am´mon·ites like
    Go·mor´rah,
a land possessed by nettles and salt
    pits,
  and a waste forever.

e Cn Compare Gk Syr: Heb *before a decree is born;
like chaff a day has passed away*

The remnant of my people shall
plunder them,
and the survivors of my nation shall
possess them.
10 This shall be their lot in return for
their pride,
because they scoffed and boasted
against the people of the LORD of
hosts.
11 The LORD will be terrible against them;
he will shrivel all the gods of the
earth,
and to him shall bow down,
each in its place,
all the coasts and islands of the
nations.

12 You also, O Ethiopians,[j]
shall be killed by my sword.

13 And he will stretch out his hand
against the north,
and destroy Assyria;
and he will make Nin′e·veh a
desolation,
a dry waste like the desert.
14 Herds shall lie down in it,
every wild animal;[g]
the desert owl[h] and the screech owl[h]
shall lodge on its capitals;
the owl[i] shall hoot at the window,
the raven[j] croak on the threshold;
for its cedar work will be laid bare.
15 Is this the exultant city
that lived secure,
that said to itself,
"I am, and there is no one else"?
What a desolation it has become,
a lair for wild animals!
Everyone who passes by it
hisses and shakes the fist.

The Wickedness of Jerusalem

3 Ah, soiled, defiled,
oppressing city!
2 It has listened to no voice;
it has accepted no correction.
It has not trusted in the LORD;
it has not drawn near to its God.

3 The officials within it
are roaring lions;
its judges are evening wolves
that leave nothing until the
morning.
4 Its prophets are reckless,
faithless persons;
its priests have profaned what is
sacred,
they have done violence to the law.
5 The LORD within it is righteous;
he does no wrong.
Every morning he renders his
judgment,
each dawn without fail;
but the unjust knows no shame.

6 I have cut off nations;
their battlements are in ruins;
I have laid waste their streets
so that no one walks in them;
their cities have been made desolate,
without people, without inhabitants.
7 I said, "Surely the city[k] will fear me,
it will accept correction;
it will not lose sight[l]
of all that I have brought upon it."
But they were the more eager
to make all their deeds corrupt.

Punishment and Conversion of the Nations

8 Therefore wait for me, says the LORD,
for the day when I arise as a witness.
For my decision is to gather nations,
to assemble kingdoms,
to pour out upon them my
indignation,
all the heat of my anger;
for in the fire of my passion
all the earth shall be consumed.

9 At that time I will change the speech of
the peoples
to a pure speech,

j Or Nubians; Heb Cushites   g Tg Compare Gk:
Heb nation   h Meaning of Heb uncertain   i Cn:
Heb a voice   j Gk Vg: Heb desolation   k Heb it
l Gk Syr: Heb its dwelling will not be cut off

"The LORD, your God, is in your midst, a warrior who gives victory; he will rejoice over you with gladness, he will renew you in his love." Zephaniah 3:17

that all of them may call on the name
of the LORD
and serve him with one accord.
¹⁰ From beyond the rivers of Ethiopia^m
my suppliants, my scattered ones,
shall bring my offering.

¹¹ On that day you shall not be put to
shame
because of all the deeds by which
you have rebelled against me;
for then I will remove from your midst
your proudly exultant ones,
and you shall no longer be haughty
in my holy mountain.
¹² For I will leave in the midst of you
a people humble and lowly.
They shall seek refuge in the name of
the LORD—
¹³ the remnant of Israel;
they shall do no wrong
and utter no lies,
nor shall a deceitful tongue
be found in their mouths.
Then they will pasture and lie down,
and no one shall make them afraid.

A Song of Joy

¹⁴ Sing aloud, O daughter Zion;
shout, O Israel!
Rejoice and exult with all your heart,
O daughter Jerusalem!
¹⁵ The LORD has taken away the
judgments against you,
he has turned away your enemies.
The king of Israel, the LORD, is in your
midst;
you shall fear disaster no more.
¹⁶ On that day it shall be said to
Jerusalem:
Do not fear, O Zion;
do not let your hands grow weak.

¹⁷ The LORD, your God, is in your midst,
a warrior who gives victory;
he will rejoice over you with gladness,
he will renew youⁿ in his love;
he will exult over you with loud
singing
¹⁸ as on a day of festival.^o
I will remove disaster from you,^p
so that you will not bear reproach
for it.
¹⁹ I will deal with all your oppressors
at that time.
And I will save the lame
and gather the outcast,
and I will change their shame into
praise
and renown in all the earth.

> God will save God's people in the end. Zephaniah ends his book by telling the people to have hope. God has not forsaken them!

²⁰ At that time I will bring you home,
at the time when I gather you;
for I will make you renowned and
praised
among all the peoples of the earth,
when I restore your fortunes
before your eyes, says the LORD.

> Read the following Bible passages and think of the great works of God: Jeremiah 17:7, 1 Samuel 2:1–2, Matthew 19:26, Mark 6:35–42, Acts 19:11–12, and Philippians 4:13! Just as God was with people during hard times long ago, we can depend on God to be with us today when things seem impossible.

---

^m Or *Nubia*; Heb *Cush*   ⁿ Gk Syr: Heb *he will be silent*   ^o Gk Syr: Meaning of Heb uncertain   ^p Cn: Heb *I will remove from you; they were*

Haggai

In 538 BC, Cyrus the Great (king of Persia) conquered Babylon and freed the Jews who had been prisoners there. Some of the people who were set free went back to their country, Judah, where they planned to rebuild Jerusalem and the Temple. The prophet Haggai was one of the people who returned home. Haggai is mentioned in the book of Ezra as being active during the early efforts to rebuild the Temple after the Babylonian exile (see Ezra 5:1).

The book of Haggai is made up of four sermons that were written about 520 BC. These sermons reminded the Jews that they had been working so hard to build houses for themselves that they had forgotten to rebuild the Temple. Haggai's words helped the people return to their work on the Temple.

Haggai 1:13–15

When the people returned to Jerusalem after their exile in Babylon, Haggai was one of the leaders who encouraged them to continue rebuilding the Temple.

The Command to Rebuild the Temple

1 In the second year of King Da·rī´us, in the sixth month, on the first day of the month, the word of the LORD came by the prophet Hag´gaī to Ze·rub´ba·bel son of She·al´ti·el, governor of Judah, and to Joshua son of Je·hoz´a·dak, the high priest: ²Thus says the LORD of hosts: These people say the time has not yet come to rebuild the LORD's house. ³Then the word of the LORD came by the prophet Hag´gaī, saying: ⁴Is it a time for you yourselves to live in your paneled houses, while this house lies in ruins? ⁵Now therefore thus says the LORD of hosts: Consider how you have fared. ⁶You have sown much, and harvested little; you eat, but you never have enough; you drink, but you never have your fill; you clothe yourselves, but no one is warm; and you that earn wages earn wages to put them into a bag with holes.

7 Thus says the LORD of hosts: Consider how you have fared. ⁸Go up to the hills and bring wood and build the house, so that I may take pleasure in it and be honored, says the LORD. ⁹You have looked for much, and, lo, it came to little; and when you brought it home, I blew it away. Why? says the LORD of hosts. Because my house lies in ruins, while all of you hurry off to your own houses. ¹⁰Therefore the heavens above you have withheld the dew, and the earth has withheld its produce. ¹¹And I have called for a drought on the land and the hills, on the grain, the new wine, the oil, on what the soil produces, on human beings and animals, and on all their labors.

12 Then Ze·rub´ba·bel son of She·al´ti·el, and Joshua son of Je·hoz´a·dak, the high priest, with all the remnant of the people, obeyed the voice of the LORD their God, and the words of the prophet Hag´gaī, as the LORD their God had sent him; and the people feared the LORD. ¹³Then Hag´gaī, the messenger of the LORD, spoke to the people with the LORD's message, saying, I am with you, says the LORD. ¹⁴And the LORD stirred up the spirit of Ze·rub´ba·bel son of She·al´ti·el, governor of Judah, and the spirit of Joshua son of Je·hoz´a·dak, the high priest, and the spirit of all the remnant of the people; and they came and worked on the house of the LORD of hosts, their God, ¹⁵on the twenty-fourth day of the month, in the sixth month.

More than fifteen years earlier, the people had started to rebuild the Temple, but they lost interest. Instead of working on the Temple, they went about the business of farming and building houses for themselves. Haggai brought a message from God that they needed to continue their work on the Temple. He told the people that their crops had suffered because they put them before the work of the Lord. Is there anything in your life that you sometimes put before God? What are some things that you can do to help you remember to put God's work first in your life?

The Future Glory of the Temple

2 In the second year of King Da·rī´us, ¹in the seventh month, on the twenty-first day of the month, the word of the LORD came by the prophet Hag´gaī, saying: [2]Speak now to Ze·rub′ba·bel son of She·al′ti·el, governor of Judah, and to Joshua son of Je·hoz′a·dak, the high priest, and to the remnant of the people, and say, [3]Who is left among you that saw this house in its former glory? How does it look to you now? Is it not in your sight as nothing? [4]Yet now take courage, O Ze·rub′ba·bel, says the LORD; take courage, O Joshua, son of Je·hoz′a·dak, the high priest; take courage, all you people of the land, says the LORD; work, for I am with you, says the LORD of hosts, [5]according to the promise that I made you when you came out of Egypt. My spirit abides among you; do not fear. [6]For thus says the LORD of hosts: Once again, in a little while, I will shake the heavens and the earth and the sea and the dry land; [7]and I will shake all the nations, so that the treasure of all nations shall come, and I will fill this house with splendor, says the LORD of hosts. [8]The silver is mine, and the gold is mine, says the LORD of hosts. [9]The latter splendor of this house shall be greater than the former, says the LORD of hosts; and in this place I will give prosperity, says the LORD of hosts.

A Rebuke and a Promise

10 On the twenty-fourth day of the ninth month, in the second year of Da·ri′-us, the word of the LORD came by the prophet Hag′gai, saying: [11]Thus says the LORD of hosts: Ask the priests for a ruling: [12]If one carries consecrated meat in the fold of one's garment, and with the fold touches bread, or stew, or wine, or oil, or any kind of food, does it become holy? The priests answered, "No." [13]Then Hag′gai said, "If one who is unclean by contact with a dead body touches any of these, does it become unclean?" The priests answered, "Yes, it becomes unclean." [14]Hag′gai then said, So is it with this people, and with this nation before me, says the LORD; and so with every work of their hands; and

what they offer there is unclean. [15]But now, consider what will come to pass from this day on. Before a stone was placed upon a stone in the LORD's temple, [16]how did you fare?[a] When one came to a heap of twenty measures, there were but ten; when one came to the winevat to draw fifty measures, there were but twenty. [17]I struck you and all the products of your toil with blight and mildew and hail; yet you did not return to me, says the LORD. [18]Consider from this day on, from the twenty-fourth day of the ninth month. Since the day that the foundation of the LORD's temple was laid, consider: [19]Is there any seed left in the barn? Do the vine, the fig tree, the pomegranate, and the olive tree still yield nothing? From this day on I will bless you.

The people listened to Haggai and began to rebuild the Temple. God was pleased and promised that they would be blessed.

God's Promise to Zerubbabel

20 The word of the LORD came a second time to Hag′gai on the twenty-fourth day of the month: [21]Speak to Ze·rub′ba·bel, governor of Judah, saying, I am about to shake the heavens and the earth, [22]and to overthrow the throne of kingdoms; I am about to destroy the strength of the kingdoms of the nations, and overthrow the chariots and their riders; and the horses and their riders shall fall, every one by the sword of a comrade. [23]On that day, says the LORD of hosts, I will take you, O Ze·rub′ba·bel my servant, son of She·al′ti·el, says the LORD, and make you like a signet ring; for I have chosen you, says the LORD of hosts.

_____

[a] Gk: Heb _since they were_

Zechariah

Zechariah was a prophet who preached about 520 BC. This was after the Jews had returned home to Jerusalem after their exile in Babylon. At the time, the people were trying to rebuild Jerusalem. Zechariah was very concerned that they return to their work of rebuilding the Temple.

The prophet Zechariah (and also the prophet Haggai) finally persuaded the people to work at rebuilding the Temple.

The sermons in the book of Zechariah are in the form of visions that came to the prophet Zechariah. The visions told of a time when the people would repent and would rebuild Jerusalem and the Temple under the leadership of Joshua and Zerubbabel. The last six chapters of the book of Zechariah may have been written by later prophets and added to the first part of the collection.

Zechariah 4:1–2

Israel Urged to Repent

1 In the eighth month, in the second year of Da·ri´us, the word of the LORD came to the prophet Zech·a·ri´ah son of Ber·e·chi´ah son of Id´do, saying: ²The LORD was very angry with your ancestors. ³Therefore say to them, Thus says the LORD of hosts: Return to me, says the LORD of hosts, and I will return to you, says the LORD of hosts. ⁴Do not be like your ancestors, to whom the former prophets proclaimed, "Thus says the LORD of hosts, Return from your evil ways and from your evil deeds." But they did not hear or heed me, says the LORD. ⁵Your ancestors, where are they? And the prophets, do they live forever? ⁶But my words and my statutes, which I commanded my servants the prophets, did they not overtake your ancestors? So they repented and said, "The LORD of hosts has dealt with us according to our ways and deeds, just as he planned to do."

Zechariah had a vision of an angel and a man on a red horse. In this vision, the man on the horse spoke to the angel and told him that the earth was at peace. This was a sign that the exile was ending and God was showing mercy to Jerusalem.

First Vision: The Horsemen

7 On the twenty-fourth day of the eleventh month, the month of She·bat´, in the second year of Da·ri´us, the word of the LORD came to the prophet Zech·a·ri´ah son of Ber·e·chi´ah son of Id´do; and Zech·a·ri´ah[a] said, ⁸In the night I saw a man riding on a red horse! He was standing among the myrtle trees in the glen; and behind him were red, sorrel, and white horses. ⁹Then I said, "What are these, my lord?" The angel who talked with me said to me, "I will show you what they are." ¹⁰So the man who was standing among the myrtle trees answered, "They are those whom the LORD has sent to patrol the earth." ¹¹Then they spoke to the angel of the LORD who was standing among the myrtle trees, "We have patrolled the earth, and lo, the whole earth remains at peace." ¹²Then the angel of the LORD said, "O LORD of hosts, how long will you withhold mercy from Jerusalem and the cities of Judah, with which you have been angry these seventy years?" ¹³Then the LORD replied with gracious and comforting words to the angel who talked with me. ¹⁴So the angel who talked with me said to me, Proclaim this message: Thus says the LORD of hosts; I am very jealous for Jerusalem and for Zion. ¹⁵And I am extremely angry with the nations that are at ease; for while I was only a little angry, they made the disaster worse. ¹⁶Therefore, thus says the LORD, I have returned to Jerusalem with compassion; my house shall be built in it, says the LORD of hosts, and the measuring line shall be stretched out over Jerusalem. ¹⁷Proclaim further: Thus says the LORD of hosts: My cities shall again overflow with prosperity; the LORD will again comfort Zion and again choose Jerusalem.

Second Vision: The Horns and the Smiths

18[b] And I looked up and saw four horns. ¹⁹I asked the angel who talked with me, "What are these?" And he answered me, "These are the horns that have scattered Judah, Israel, and Jerusalem." ²⁰Then the LORD showed me four blacksmiths. ²¹And I asked, "What are they coming to do?" He answered, "These are the horns that scattered Judah, so that no head could be raised; but these have come to terrify them, to strike down the horns of the nations that lifted up their horns against the land of Judah to scatter its people."[c]

---

a Heb *and he*   *b* Ch 2.1 in Heb   *c* Heb *it*

The measuring line was a symbol that Jerusalem would be rebuilt, the people would return, and the Temple would be restored.

Third Vision: The Man with a Measuring Line

2 [d]I looked up and saw a man with a measuring line in his hand. [2]Then I asked, "Where are you going?" He answered me, "To measure Jerusalem, to see what is its width and what is its length." [3]Then the angel who talked with me came forward, and another angel came forward to meet him, [4]and said to him, "Run, say to that young man: Jerusalem shall be inhabited like villages without walls, because of the multitude of people and animals in it. [5]For I will be a wall of fire all around it, says the LORD, and I will be the glory within it."

Interlude: An Appeal to the Exiles

6 Up, up! Flee from the land of the north, says the LORD; for I have spread you abroad like the four winds of heaven, says the LORD. [7]Up! Escape to Zion, you that live with daughter Babylon. [8]For thus said the LORD of hosts (after his glory[e] sent me) regarding the nations that plundered you: Truly, one who touches you touches the apple of my eye.[f] [9]See now, I am going to raise[g] my hand against them, and they shall become plunder for their own slaves. Then you will know that the LORD of hosts has sent me. [10]Sing and rejoice, O daughter Zion! For lo, I will come and dwell in your midst, says the LORD. [11]Many nations shall join themselves to the LORD on that day, and shall be my people; and I will dwell in your midst. And you shall know that the LORD of hosts has sent me to you. [12]The LORD will inherit Judah as his portion in the holy land, and will again choose Jerusalem.

13 Be silent, all people, before the LORD; for he has roused himself from his holy dwelling.

Fourth Vision: Joshua and Satan

3 Then he showed me the high priest Joshua standing before the angel of the LORD, and Satan[h] standing at his right hand to accuse him. [2]And the LORD said to Satan,[h] "The LORD rebuke you, O Satan![h] The LORD who has chosen Jerusalem rebuke you! Is not this man a brand plucked from the fire?" [3]Now Joshua was dressed with filthy clothes as he stood before the angel. [4]The angel said to those who were standing before him, "Take off his filthy clothes." And to him he said, "See, I have taken your guilt away from you, and I will clothe you with festal apparel." [5]And I said, "Let them put a clean turban on his head." So they put a clean turban on his head and clothed him with the apparel; and the angel of the LORD was standing by.

6 Then the angel of the LORD assured Joshua, saying [7]"Thus says the LORD of hosts: If you will walk in my ways and keep my requirements, then you shall rule my house and have charge of my courts, and I will give you the right of access among those who are standing

Joshua stood before the heavenly council—Satan and the angel of the Lord. The angel gave Joshua clean clothes as a sign showing that he was ready to serve in the restored community. Joshua's new duties included giving legal judgments, teaching the Torah, and collecting the tithes.

[d] Ch 2.5 in Heb   [e] Cn: Heb *after glory he*
[f] Heb *his eye*   [g] Or *wave*   [h] Or *the Accuser;* Heb *the Adversary*

here. ⁸Now listen, Joshua, high priest, you and your colleagues who sit before you! For they are an omen of things to come: I am going to bring my servant the Branch. ⁹For on the stone that I have set before Joshua, on a single stone with seven facets, I will engrave its inscription, says the LORD of hosts, and I will remove the guilt of this land in a single day. ¹⁰On that day, says the LORD of hosts, you shall invite each other to come under your vine and fig tree."

Fifth Vision: The Lampstand and Olive Trees

4 The angel who talked with me came again, and wakened me, as one is wakened from sleep. ²He said to me, "What do you see?" And I said, "I see a lampstand all of gold, with a bowl on the top of it; there are seven lamps on it, with seven lips on each of the lamps that are on the top of it. ³And by it there are two olive trees, one on the right of the bowl and the other on its left." ⁴I said to the angel who talked with me, "What are these, my lord?" ⁵Then the angel who talked with me answered me, "Do you not know what these are?" I said, "No, my lord." ⁶He said to me, "This is the word of the LORD to Ze·rub´ba·bel: Not by might, nor by power, but by my spirit, says the LORD of hosts. ⁷What are you, O great mountain? Before Ze·rub´ba·bel you shall become a plain; and he shall bring out the top stone amid shouts of 'Grace, grace to it!' "

8 Moreover the word of the LORD came to me, saying, ⁹"The hands of Ze·rub´ba·bel have laid the foundation of this house; his hands shall also complete it. Then you will know that the LORD of hosts has sent me to you. ¹⁰For whoever has despised the day of small things shall rejoice, and shall see the plummet in the hand of Ze·rub´ba·bel.

"These seven are the eyes of the LORD, which range through the whole earth." ¹¹Then I said to him, "What are these two olive trees on the right and the left

> "Not by might, nor by power, but by my spirit, says the LORD of hosts."
> Zechariah 4:5b

of the lampstand?" ¹²And a second time I said to him, "What are these two branches of the olive trees, which pour out the oilⁱ through the two golden pipes?" ¹³He said to me, "Do you not know what these are?" I said, "No, my lord." ¹⁴Then he said, "These are the two anointed ones who stand by the Lord of the whole earth."

Sixth Vision: The Flying Scroll

5 Again I looked up and saw a flying scroll. ²And he said to me, "What do you see?" I answered, "I see a flying scroll; its length is twenty cubits, and its width ten cubits." ³Then he said to me, "This is the curse that goes out over the face of the whole land; for everyone who steals shall be cut off according to the writing on one side, and everyone who swears falselyʲ shall be cut off according to the writing on the other side. ⁴I have sent it out, says the LORD of hosts, and it shall enter the house of the thief, and the house of anyone who swears falsely by my name; and it shall abide in that house and consume it, both timber and stones."

The vision of the woman in a basket showed that wickedness would be sealed away and the land would be cleansed.

Seventh Vision: The Woman in a Basket

5 Then the angel who talked with me came forward and said to me, "Look up and see what this is that is coming out."

ⁱ Cn: Heb *gold*   ʲ The word *falsely* added from verse 4

⁶I said, "What is it?" He said, "This is a basket[k] coming out." And he said, "This is their iniquity[l] in all the land." ⁷Then a leaden cover was lifted, and there was a woman sitting in the basket![k] ⁸And he said, "This is Wickedness." So he thrust her back into the basket,[k] and pressed the leaden weight down on its mouth. ⁹Then I looked up and saw two women coming forward. The wind was in their wings; they had wings like the wings of a stork, and they lifted up the basket[k] between earth and sky. ¹⁰Then I said to the angel who talked with me, "Where are they taking the basket?"[k] ¹¹He said to me, "To the land of Shĭ´nar, to build a house for it; and when this is prepared, they will set the basket[k] down there on its base."

The name "Branch" refers to the coming Messiah. (This name is also used in Jeremiah 23:5–6.) King David's family line is referred to as a tree. Zechariah said that when God's chosen Messiah came, the tree would be fruitful again.

Have you ever drawn a family tree? Talk to your parents or other adults in your family about your ancestors. Where did they live? What language did they speak? What type of work did they do? Use the library or the Internet to learn how to make your own family tree. Write a special prayer to use with your family this week giving thanks for God's love and care for God's people through many generations.

Eighth Vision: Four Chariots

6 And again I looked up and saw four chariots coming out from between two mountains—mountains of bronze. ²The first chariot had red horses, the second black horses, ³the third chariot white horses, and the fourth chariot dappled gray[m] horses. ⁴Then I said to the angel who talked with me, "What are these, my lord?" ⁵The angel answered me, "These are the four winds[n] of heaven going out, after presenting themselves before the Lord of all the earth. ⁶The chariot with the black horses goes toward the north country, the white ones go toward the west country,[o] and the dappled ones go toward the south country." ⁷When the steeds came out, they were impatient to get off and patrol the earth. And he said, "Go, patrol the earth." So they patrolled the earth. ⁸Then he cried out to me, "Lo, those who go toward the north country have set my spirit at rest in the north country."

The Coronation of the Branch

9 The word of the Lord came to me: ¹⁰Collect silver and gold[p] from the exiles—from Hel´daī, Tō·bī´jah, and Je·daī´ah—who have arrived from Babylon; and go the same day to the house of Jō·sī´ah son of Zeph·a·nī´ah. ¹¹Take the silver and gold and make a crown,[q] and set it on the head of the high priest Joshua son of Je·hoz´a·dak; ¹²say to him: Thus says the Lord of hosts: Here is a man whose name is Branch: for he shall branch out in his place, and he shall build the temple of the Lord. ¹³It is he that shall build the temple of the Lord; he shall bear royal honor, and shall sit and rule on his throne. There shall be a priest by his throne, with peaceful understanding between the two of them. ¹⁴And the crown[r] shall be in the care of Hel´daī,[s] Tō·bī´jah, Je·daī´ah, and Jō·sī´ah[t] son of Zeph·a·nī´ah, as a memorial in the temple of the Lord.

15 Those who are far off shall come and help to build the temple of the Lord; and you shall know that the Lord

---

[k] Heb *ephah*   [l] Gk Compare Syr: Heb *their eye*   [m] Compare Gk: Meaning of Heb uncertain   [n] Or *spirits*   [o] Cn: Heb *go after them*   [p] Cn Compare verse 11: Heb lacks *silver and gold*   [q] Gk Mss Syr Tg: Heb *crowns*   [r] Gk Syr: Heb *crowns*   [s] Syr Compare verse 10: Heb *Helem*   [t] Syr Compare verse 10: Heb *Hen*

of hosts has sent me to you. This will happen if you diligently obey the voice of the LORD your God.

Hypocritical Fasting Condemned

7 In the fourth year of King Da·ri′us, the word of the LORD came to Zech·a·ri′ah on the fourth day of the ninth month, which is Chis′lev. ²Now the people of Beth′el had sent Sha·re′zer and Reg′em-mel′ech and their men, to entreat the favor of the LORD, ³and to ask the priests of the house of the LORD of hosts and the prophets, "Should I mourn and practice abstinence in the fifth month, as I have done for so many years?" ⁴Then the word of the LORD of hosts came to me: ⁵Say to all the people of the land and the priests: When you fasted and lamented in the fifth month and in the seventh, for these seventy years, was it for me that you fasted? ⁶And when you eat and when you drink, do you not eat and drink only for yourselves? ⁷Were not these the words that the LORD proclaimed by the former prophets, when Jerusalem was inhabited and in prosperity, along with the towns around it, and when the Neg′eb and the She·phe′lah were inhabited?

Punishment for Rejecting God's Demands

8 The word of the LORD came to Zech·a·ri′ah, saying: ⁹Thus says the LORD of hosts: Render true judgments, show kindness and mercy to one another; ¹⁰do not oppress the widow, the orphan, the alien, or the poor; and do not devise evil in your hearts against one another. ¹¹But they refused to listen, and turned a stubborn shoulder, and stopped their ears in order not to hear. ¹²They made their hearts adamant in order not to hear the law and the words that the LORD of hosts had sent by his spirit through the former prophets. Therefore great wrath came from the LORD of hosts. ¹³Just as, when I[u] called, they would not hear, so, when they called, I would not hear, says the

LORD of hosts, ¹⁴and I scattered them with a whirlwind among all the nations that they had not known. Thus the land they left was desolate, so that no one went to and fro, and a pleasant land was made desolate.

God's Promises to Zion

8 The word of the LORD of hosts came to me, saying: ²Thus says the LORD of hosts: I am jealous for Zion with great jealousy, and I am jealous for her with great wrath. ³Thus says the LORD: I will return to Zion, and will dwell in the midst of Jerusalem; Jerusalem shall be called the faithful city, and the mountain of the LORD of hosts shall be called the holy mountain. ⁴Thus says the LORD of hosts: Old men and old women shall again sit in the streets of Jerusalem, each with staff in hand because of their great age. ⁵And the streets of the city shall be full of boys and girls playing in its streets. ⁶Thus says the LORD of hosts: Even though it seems impossible to the remnant of this people in these days, should it also seem impossible to me, says the LORD of hosts? ⁷Thus says the LORD of hosts: I will save my people from the east country and from the west country; ⁸and I will bring them to live in Jerusalem. They shall be my people and I will be their God, in faithfulness and in righteousness.

9 Thus says the LORD of hosts: Let your hands be strong—you that have recently been hearing these words from the mouths of the prophets who were present when the foundation was laid for the rebuilding of the temple, the house of the LORD of hosts. ¹⁰For before those days there were no wages for people or for animals, nor was there any safety from the foe for those who went out or came in, and I set them all against one other. ¹¹But now I will not deal with the remnant of this people as in the former days, says the LORD of hosts. ¹²For there shall be a sowing of peace; the vine

[u] Heb he

"For there shall be a sowing of peace; the vine shall yield its fruit, the ground shall give its produce, and the skies shall give their dew." Zechariah 8:12

shall yield its fruit, the ground shall give its produce, and the skies shall give their dew; and I will cause the remnant of this people to possess all these things. ¹³Just as you have been a cursing among the nations, O house of Judah and house of Israel, so I will save you and you shall be a blessing. Do not be afraid, but let your hands be strong.

14 For thus says the LORD of hosts: Just as I purposed to bring disaster upon you, when your ancestors provoked me to wrath, and I did not relent, says the LORD of hosts, ¹⁵so again I have purposed in these days to do good to Jerusalem and to the house of Judah; do not be afraid. ¹⁶These are the things that you shall do: Speak the truth to one another, render in your gates judgments that are true and make for peace, ¹⁷do not devise evil in your hearts against one another, and love no false oath; for all these are things that I hate, says the LORD.

Joyful Fasting

18 The word of the LORD of hosts came to me, saying: ¹⁹Thus says the LORD of hosts: The fast of the fourth month, and the fast of the fifth, and the fast of the seventh, and the fast of the tenth, shall be seasons of joy and gladness, and cheerful festivals for the house of Judah: therefore love truth and peace.

Many Peoples Drawn to Jerusalem

20 Thus says the LORD of hosts: Peoples shall yet come, the inhabitants of many cities; ²¹the inhabitants of one city shall go to another, saying, "Come, let us go to entreat the favor of the LORD, and to seek the LORD of hosts; I myself am going."

²²Many peoples and strong nations shall come to seek the LORD of hosts in Jerusalem, and to entreat the favor of the LORD. ²³Thus says the LORD of hosts: In those days ten men from nations of every language shall take hold of a Jew, grasping his garment and saying, "Let us go with you, for we have heard that God is with you."

Judgment on Israel's Enemies

9 An Oracle.

The word of the LORD is against the
　　land of Had′rach
and will rest upon Damascus.
For to the LORD belongs the capital^v of
　　Ar′am,^w
　　as do all the tribes of Israel;
² Ha′math also, which borders on it,
　　Tyre and Si′don, though they are
　　　very wise.
³ Tyre has built itself a rampart,
　　and heaped up silver like dust,
　　and gold like the dirt of the streets.
⁴ But now, the Lord will strip it of its
　　possessions
　　and hurl its wealth into the sea,
　　and it shall be devoured by fire.

⁵ Ash′ke·lon shall see it and be afraid;
　　Ga′za too, and shall writhe in
　　　anguish;
　　Ek′ron also, because its hopes are
　　　withered.
The king shall perish from Ga′za;
　　Ash′ke·lon shall be uninhabited;
⁶ a mongrel people shall settle in
　　Ash′dod,
　　and I will make an end of the pride
　　of Phi·lis′ti·a.
⁷ I will take away its blood from its
　　mouth,
　　and its abominations from between
　　its teeth;
it too shall be a remnant for our God;
　　it shall be like a clan in Judah,
　　and Ek′ron shall be like the Jeb·u′sites.

ᵛ Heb *eye*　　ʷ Cn: Heb *of Adam* (or *of humankind*)

8 Then I will encamp at my house as a
guard,
so that no one shall march to and
fro;
no oppressor shall again overrun them,
for now I have seen with my own
eyes.

The Coming Ruler
of God's People

9 Rejoice greatly, O daughter Zion!
Shout aloud, O daughter Jerusalem!
Lo, your king comes to you;
triumphant and victorious is he,
humble and riding on a donkey,
on a colt, the foal of a donkey.
10 He[x] will cut off the chariot from
Ē′phra·im
and the war-horse from Jerusalem;
and the battle bow shall be cut off,
and he shall command peace to the
nations;
his dominion shall be from sea to sea,
and from the River to the ends of
the earth.

11 As for you also, because of the blood
of my covenant with you,
I will set your prisoners free from
the waterless pit.
12 Return to your stronghold, O prisoners
of hope;
today I declare that I will restore to
you double.
13 For I have bent Judah as my bow;
I have made Ē′phra·im its arrow.
I will arouse your sons, O Zion,
against your sons, O Greece,
and wield you like a warrior's sword.

14 Then the LORD will appear over them,
and his arrow go forth like lightning;
the Lord GOD will sound the trumpet
and march forth in the whirlwinds
of the south.
15 The LORD of hosts will protect them,
and they shall devour and tread
down the slingers;[y]

"On that day the LORD
their God will save them
for they are the flock of
his people; for like the
jewels of a crown they
shall shine on his land."
Zechariah 9:16

they shall drink their blood[z] like wine,
and be full like a bowl,
drenched like the corners of the
altar.

16 On that day the LORD their God will
save them
for they are the flock of his people;
for like the jewels of a crown
they shall shine on his land.
17 For what goodness and beauty are his!
Grain shall make the young men
flourish,
and new wine the young women.

Restoration of Judah and Israel

10 Ask rain from the LORD
in the season of the spring rain,
from the LORD who makes the storm
clouds,
who gives showers of rain to you,[a]
the vegetation in the field to everyone.
2 For the teraphim[b] utter nonsense,
and the diviners see lies;
the dreamers tell false dreams,
and give empty consolation.
Therefore the people wander like
sheep;
they suffer for lack of a shepherd.

3 My anger is hot against the shepherds,
and I will punish the leaders;[c]
for the LORD of hosts cares for his
flock, the house of Judah,
and will make them like his proud
war-horse.

[x] Gk: Heb *I*   [y] Cn: Heb *the slingstones*   [z] Gk:
Heb *shall drink*   [a] Heb *them*   [b] Or *household
gods*   [c] Or *male goats*

Read Judges 20:2, Psalm 118:22, Isaiah 19:13, and Zechariah 10:4. The word "cornerstone" is a symbol for royalty. The cornerstone of a building in Bible times helped the whole building stand. Christians believe that Jesus is the cornerstone, the king who will rule all the earth. When we put our trust in Jesus, our whole life is tied to him. The apostle Peter quoted Psalm 118:22 and said that Jesus is the chief cornerstone for all of life (see Acts 4:11).

⁴ Out of them shall come the
        cornerstone,
    out of them the tent peg,
    out of them the battle bow,
        out of them every commander.
⁵ Together they shall be like warriors in
        battle,
    trampling the foe in the mud of the
        streets;
they shall fight, for the LORD is with
        them,
    and they shall put to shame the
        riders on horses.

⁶ I will strengthen the house of Judah,
    and I will save the house of Joseph.
I will bring them back because I have
        compassion on them,
    and they shall be as though I had
        not rejected them;
    for I am the LORD their God and I
        will answer them.
⁷ Then the people of Ē´phra·im shall
        become like warriors,
    and their hearts shall be glad as with
        wine.
Their children shall see it and rejoice,
    their hearts shall exult in the LORD.
⁸ I will signal for them and gather them
        in,
    for I have redeemed them,
    and they shall be as numerous as
        they were before.

⁹ Though I scattered them among the
        nations,
    yet in far countries they shall
        remember me,
    and they shall rear their children
        and return.
¹⁰ I will bring them home from the land
        of Egypt,
    and gather them from Assyria;
    I will bring them to the land of
        Gil´e·ad and to Lebanon,
    until there is no room for them.
¹¹ They^d shall pass through the sea of
        distress,
    and the waves of the sea shall be
        struck down,
    and all the depths of the Nile dried
        up.
The pride of Assyria shall be laid low,
    and the scepter of Egypt shall depart.
¹² I will make them strong in the LORD,
    and they shall walk in his name,
                    says the LORD.

11 Open your doors, O Lebanon,
        so that fire may devour your
            cedars!
² Wail, O cypress, for the cedar has fallen,
    for the glorious trees are ruined!
Wail, oaks of Ba´shan,
    for the thick forest has been felled!
³ Listen, the wail of the shepherds,
    for their glory is despoiled!
Listen, the roar of the lions,
    for the thickets of the Jordan are
        destroyed!

Two Kinds of Shepherds

4 Thus said the LORD my God: Be a shepherd of the flock doomed to slaughter. ⁵Those who buy them kill them and go unpunished; and those who sell them say, "Blessed be the LORD, for I have become rich"; and their own shepherds have no pity on them. ⁶For I will no longer have pity on the inhabitants of the earth, says the LORD. I will cause them, every one, to

^d Gk: Heb *He*

fall each into the hand of a neighbor, and each into the hand of the king; and they shall devastate the earth, and I will deliver no one from their hand.

7 So, on behalf of the sheep merchants, I became the shepherd of the flock doomed to slaughter. I took two staffs; one I named Favor, the other I named Unity, and I tended the sheep. ⁸In one month I disposed of the three shepherds, for I had become impatient with them, and they also detested me. ⁹So I said, "I will not be your shepherd. What is to die, let it die; what is to be destroyed, let it be destroyed; and let those that are left devour the flesh of one another!" ¹⁰I took my staff Favor and broke it, annulling the covenant that I had made with all the peoples. ¹¹So it was annulled on that day, and the sheep merchants, who were watching me, knew that it was the word of the LORD. ¹²I then said to them, "If it seems right to you, give me my wages; but if not, keep them." So they weighed out as my wages thirty shekels of silver. ¹³Then the LORD said to me, "Throw it into the treasury"ᵉ—this lordly price at which I was valued by them. So I took the thirty shekels of silver and threw them into the treasuryᵉ in the house of the LORD. ¹⁴Then I broke my second staff Unity, annulling the family ties between Judah and Israel.

15 Then the LORD said to me: Take once more the implements of a worthless shepherd. ¹⁶For I am now raising up in the land a shepherd who does not care for the perishing, or seek the wandering,ᶠ or heal the maimed, or nourish the healthy,ᵍ but devours the flesh of the fat ones, tearing off even their hoofs.

¹⁷ Oh, my worthless shepherd,
   who deserts the flock!
May the sword strike his arm
   and his right eye!
Let his arm be completely withered,
   his right eye utterly blinded!

Jerusalem's Victory

12

An Oracle.

The word of the LORD concerning Israel: Thus says the LORD, who stretched out the heavens and founded the earth and formed the human spirit within: ²See, I am about to make Jerusalem a cup of reeling for all the surrounding peoples; it will be against Judah also in the siege against Jerusalem. ³On that day I will make Jerusalem a heavy stone for all the peoples; all who lift it shall grievously hurt themselves. And all the nations of the earth shall come together against it. ⁴On that day, says the LORD, I will strike every horse with panic, and its rider with madness. But on the house of Judah I will keep a watchful eye, when I strike every horse of the peoples with blindness. ⁵Then the clans of Judah shall say to themselves, "The inhabitants of Jerusalem have strength through the LORD of hosts, their God."

6 On that day I will make the clans of Judah like a blazing pot on a pile of wood, like a flaming torch among sheaves; and they shall devour to the right and to the left all the surrounding peoples, while Jerusalem shall again be inhabited in its place, in Jerusalem.

7 And the LORD will give victory to the tents of Judah first, that the glory of the house of David and the glory of the inhabitants of Jerusalem may not be exalted over that of Judah. ⁸On that day the LORD will shield the inhabitants of Jerusalem so that the feeblest among them on that day shall be like David, and the house of David shall be like God, like the angel of the LORD, at their head. ⁹And on that day I will seek to destroy all the nations that come against Jerusalem.

Mourning for the Pierced One

10 And I will pour out a spirit of compassion and supplication on the house of David and the inhabitants of Jerusalem,

---

ᵉ Syr: Heb *it to the potter*   ᶠ Syr Compare Gk Vg: Heb *the youth*   ᵍ Meaning of Heb uncertain

> "They will call on my name, and I will answer them. I will say, 'They are my people'; and they will say, 'The LORD is our God.'"
>
> Zechariah 13:9b

so that, when they look on the one[h] whom they have pierced, they shall mourn for him, as one mourns for an only child, and weep bitterly over him, as one weeps over a firstborn. [11]On that day the mourning in Jerusalem will be as great as the mourning for Ha´dad-rim´mon in the plain of Me·gid´do. [12]The land shall mourn, each family by itself; the family of the house of David by itself, and their wives by themselves; the family of the house of Nathan by itself, and their wives by themselves; [13]the family of the house of Levi by itself, and their wives by themselves; the family of the Shim´e·ites by itself, and their wives by themselves; [14]and all the families that are left, each by itself, and their wives by themselves.

13 On that day a fountain shall be opened for the house of David and the inhabitants of Jerusalem, to cleanse them from sin and impurity.

Idolatry Cut Off

2 On that day, says the LORD of hosts, I will cut off the names of the idols from the land, so that they shall be remembered no more; and also I will remove from the land the prophets and the unclean spirit. [3]And if any prophets appear again, their fathers and mothers who bore them will say to them, "You shall not live, for you speak lies in the name of the LORD"; and their fathers and their mothers who bore them shall pierce them through when they prophesy. [4]On that day the prophets will be ashamed, every one, of their visions when they prophesy; they will not put on a hairy mantle in order to deceive, [5]but each of them will say, "I am no prophet, I am a tiller of the soil; for the land has been

my possession[i] since my youth." [6]And if anyone asks them, "What are these wounds on your chest?"[j] the answer will be "The wounds I received in the house of my friends."

The Shepherd Struck, the Flock Scattered

[7] "Awake, O sword, against my shepherd,
 against the man who is my associate,"
      says the LORD of hosts.
Strike the shepherd, that the sheep
 may be scattered;
 I will turn my hand against the little
 ones.
[8] In the whole land, says the LORD,
 two-thirds shall be cut off and perish,
 and one-third shall be left alive.
[9] And I will put this third into the fire,
 refine them as one refines silver,
 and test them as gold is tested.
They will call on my name,
 and I will answer them.
I will say, "They are my people";
 and they will say, "The LORD is our
 God."

Future Warfare and Final Victory

14 See, a day is coming for the LORD, when the plunder taken from you will be divided in your midst. [2]For I will gather all the nations against Jerusalem to battle, and the city shall be taken and the houses looted and the women raped; half the city shall go into exile, but the rest of the people shall not be cut off from the city. [3]Then the LORD will go forth and fight against those nations as when he fights on a day of battle. [4]On that day his feet shall stand on the Mount of Olives, which lies before Jerusalem on the east; and the Mount of Olives shall be split in two from east to west by a very wide valley; so that one half of the Mount shall withdraw northward, and the other half southward.

---

[h] Heb *on me*
[i] Cn: Heb *for humankind has caused me to possess*
[j] Heb *wounds between your hands*

5And you shall flee by the valley of the LORD's mountain,*k* for the valley between the mountains shall reach to A´zal;*l* and you shall flee as you fled from the earthquake in the days of King Uz·zi´ah of Judah. Then the LORD my God will come, and all the holy ones with him.

6 On that day there shall not be*m* either cold or frost.*n* 7And there shall be continuous day (it is known to the LORD), not day and not night, for at evening time there shall be light.

8 On that day living waters shall flow out from Jerusalem, half of them to the eastern sea and half of them to the western sea; it shall continue in summer as in winter.

9 And the LORD will become king over all the earth; on that day the LORD will be one and his name one.

10 The whole land shall be turned into a plain from Ge´ba to Rim´mon south of Jerusalem. But Jerusalem shall remain aloft on its site from the Gate of Benjamin to the place of the former gate, to the Corner Gate, and from the Tower of Ha·nan´el to the king's wine presses. 11And it shall be inhabited, for never again shall it be doomed to destruction; Jerusalem shall abide in security.

12 This shall be the plague with which the LORD will strike all the peoples that wage war against Jerusalem: their flesh shall rot while they are still on their feet; their eyes shall rot in their sockets, and their tongues shall rot in their mouths. 13On that day a great panic from the LORD shall fall on them, so that each will seize the hand of a neighbor, and the hand of the one will be raised against the hand of the other; 14even Judah will fight at Jerusalem. And the wealth of all the surrounding nations shall be collected— gold, silver, and garments in great abundance. 15And a plague like this plague shall fall on the horses, the mules, the camels, the donkeys, and whatever animals may be in those camps.

16 Then all who survive of the nations

> "And the LORD will become king over all the earth; on that day the LORD will be one and his name one."
> Zechariah 14:9

that have come against Jerusalem shall go up year after year to worship the King, the LORD of hosts, and to keep the festival of booths.*o* 17If any of the families of the earth do not go up to Jerusalem to worship the King, the LORD of hosts, there will be no rain upon them. 18And if the family of Egypt do not go up and present themselves, then on them shall*p* come the plague that the LORD inflicts on the nations that do not go up to keep the festival of booths.*o* 19Such shall be the punishment of Egypt and the punishment of all the nations that do not go up to keep the festival of booths.*o*

20 On that day there shall be inscribed on the bells of the horses, "Holy to the LORD." And the cooking pots in the house of the LORD shall be as holy as*q* the bowls in front of the altar; 21and every cooking pot in Jerusalem and Judah shall be sacred to the LORD of hosts, so that all who sacrifice may come and use them to boil the flesh of the sacrifice. And there shall no longer be traders*r* in the house of the LORD of hosts on that day.

God created the world and all the people in the world. The time will come when all people will worship God and there will be peace in the world. Pray every day that God's peace will come soon.

k Heb *my mountains*   *l* Meaning of Heb uncertain
m Cn: Heb *there shall not be light*   *n* Compare Gk
Syr Vg Tg: Meaning of Heb uncertain   *o* Or *tabernacles*; Heb *succoth*   *p* Gk Syr: Heb *shall not*
q Heb *shall be like*   *r* Or *Canaanites*

Malachi

When the Jews returned from exile in Babylon, the prophets Haggai and Zechariah were able to get them to rebuild the Temple from 520 to 516 BC. After the Temple was rebuilt, the people were once again interested in worship. About sixty years later, the prophet Malachi spoke to the people of Jerusalem. Malachi lived in Jerusalem just before Ezra and Nehemiah came back from Babylon to direct the rebuilding of the city walls.

The book of Malachi protests the sinful way the people lived and the careless worship at the Temple. Although Malachi describes many evils, the closing passages of the book show that the prophet believed the people would repent and God would save them. The book of Malachi was written about 460 BC.

Malachi 1:1

1

An oracle. The word of the LORD to Israel by Mal′a·chī.[a]

Israel Preferred to Edom

2 I have loved you, says the LORD. But you say, "How have you loved us?" Is not Esau Jacob's brother? says the LORD. Yet I have loved Jacob ³but I have hated Esau; I have made his hill country a desolation and his heritage a desert for jackals. ⁴If Ē′dom says, "We are shattered but we will rebuild the ruins," the LORD of hosts says: They may build, but I will tear down, until they are called the wicked country, the people with whom the LORD is angry forever. ⁵Your own eyes shall see this, and you shall say, "Great is the LORD beyond the borders of Israel!"

Corruption of the Priesthood

6 A son honors his father, and servants their master. If then I am a father, where is the honor due me? And if I am a master, where is the respect due me? says the LORD of hosts to you, O priests, who despise my name. You say, "How have we despised your name?" ⁷By offering polluted food on my altar. And you say, "How have we polluted it?"[b] By thinking that the LORD's table may be despised.

We should always give God our very best. God's people had been giving God animals that were not perfect as a sacrifice. They had been keeping the best for themselves. Even today we sometimes want to give God what we have left over instead of giving God our best. Think about the way you spend your day. Do you set aside special time to pray and praise God, or do you sometimes forget God entirely because you are so busy with other things? Talk with your family about the best way to spend your time. Draw a picture of a clock, and decide to give God the first and best use of your time.

⁸When you offer blind animals in sacrifice, is that not wrong? And when you offer those that are lame or sick, is that not wrong? Try presenting that to your governor; will he be pleased with you or show you favor? says the LORD of hosts. ⁹And now implore the favor of God, that he may be gracious to us. The fault is yours. Will he show favor to any of you? says the LORD of hosts. ¹⁰Oh, that someone among you would shut the temple[c] doors, so that you would not kindle fire on my altar in vain! I have no pleasure in you, says the LORD of hosts, and I will not accept an offering from your hands. ¹¹For from the rising of the sun to its setting my name is great among the nations, and in every place incense is offered to my name, and a pure offering; for my name is great among the nations, says the LORD of hosts. ¹²But you profane it when you say that the Lord's table is polluted, and the food for it[d] may be despised. ¹³"What a weariness this is," you say, and you sniff at me,[e] says the LORD of hosts. You bring what has been taken by violence or is lame or sick, and this you bring as your offering! Shall I accept that from your hand? says the LORD. ¹⁴Cursed be the cheat who has a male in the flock and vows to give it, and yet sacrifices to the Lord what is blemished; for I am a great King, says the LORD of hosts, and my name is reverenced among the nations.

2

And now, O priests, this command is for you. ²If you will not listen, if you will not lay it to heart to give glory to my name, says the LORD of hosts, then I will send the curse on you and I will curse your blessings; indeed I have already cursed them,[f] because you do not lay it to heart. ³I will rebuke your offspring, and spread dung on your faces, the dung of your offerings, and I will put you out of my presence.[g]

---

[a] Or by my messenger   [b] Gk: Heb you   [c] Heb lacks temple   [d] Compare Syr Tg: Heb its fruit, its food   [e] Another reading is at it   [f] Heb it   [g] Cn Compare Ck Syr: Heb and he shall bear you to it

4 Know, then, that I have sent this command to you, that my covenant with Levi may hold, says the LORD of hosts. 5My covenant with him was a covenant of life and well-being, which I gave him; this called for reverence, and he revered me and stood in awe of my name. 6True instruction was in his mouth, and no wrong was found on his lips. He walked with me in integrity and uprightness, and he turned many from iniquity. 7For the lips of a priest should guard knowledge, and people should seek instruction from his mouth, for he is the messenger of the LORD of hosts. 8But you have turned aside from the way; you have caused many to stumble by your instruction; you have corrupted the covenant of Levi, says the LORD of hosts, 9and so I make you despised and abased before all the people, inasmuch as you have not kept my ways but have shown partiality in your instruction.

The Covenant Profaned by Judah

10 Have we not all one father? Has not one God created us? Why then are we faithless to one another, profaning the covenant of our ancestors? 11Judah has been faithless, and abomination has been committed in Israel and in Jerusalem; for Judah has profaned the sanctuary of the LORD, which he loves, and has married the daughter of a foreign god. 12May the LORD cut off from the tents of Jacob anyone who does this—any to witness[h] or answer, or to bring an offering to the LORD of hosts.

13 And this you do as well: You cover the LORD's altar with tears, with weeping and groaning because he no longer regards the offering or accepts it with favor at your hand. 14You ask, "Why does he not?" Because the LORD was a witness between you and the wife of your youth, to whom you have been faithless, though she is your companion and your wife by covenant. 15Did not one God make her?[i] Both flesh and spirit are his.[j] And what does the one God[k] desire? Godly off-

spring. So look to yourselves, and do not let anyone be faithless to the wife of his youth. 16For I hate[l] divorce, says the LORD, the God of Israel, and covering one's garment with violence, says the LORD of hosts. So take heed to yourselves and do not be faithless.

17 You have wearied the LORD with your words. Yet you say, "How have we wearied him?" By saying, "All who do evil are good in the sight of the LORD, and he delights in them." Or by asking, "Where is the God of justice?"

The Coming Messenger

3 See, I am sending my messenger to prepare the way before me, and the Lord whom you seek will suddenly come to his temple. The messenger of the covenant in whom you delight— indeed, he is coming, says the LORD of hosts. 2But who can endure the day of his coming, and who can stand when he appears?

For he is like a refiner's fire and like fullers' soap; 3he will sit as a refiner and purifier of silver, and he will purify the descendants of Levi and refine them like gold and silver, until they present offerings to the LORD in righteousness.[m] 4Then the offering of Judah and Jerusalem will be pleasing to the LORD as in the days of old and as in former years.

5 Then I will draw near to you for judgment; I will be swift to bear witness against the sorcerers, against the adulterers, against those who swear falsely, against those who oppress the hired workers in their wages, the widow and the orphan, against those who thrust aside the alien, and do not fear me, says the LORD of hosts.

6 For I the LORD do not change; therefore you, O children of Jacob, have not perished. 7Ever since the days of your ancestors you have turned aside

h Cn Compare Gk: Heb arouse   i Or Has he not made one?   j Cn: Heb and a remnant of spirit was his   k Heb he   l Cn: Heb he hates   m Or right offerings to the LORD from my statutes and have not kept them. Return to me, and I will return to you, says the LORD of hosts. But you say, "How shall we return?"

Do Not Rob God

8 Will anyone rob God? Yet you are robbing me! But you say, "How are we robbing you?" In your tithes and offerings! [9]You are cursed with a curse, for you are robbing me—the whole nation of you! [10]Bring the full tithe into the storehouse, so that there may be food in my house, and thus put me to the test, says the LORD of hosts; see if I will not open the windows of heaven for you and pour down for you an overflowing blessing. [11]I will rebuke the locust[n] for you, so that it will not destroy the produce of your soil; and your vine in the field shall not be barren, says the LORD of hosts. [12]Then all nations will count you happy, for you will be a land of delight, says the LORD of hosts.

13 You have spoken harsh words against me, says the LORD. Yet you say, "How have we spoken against you?" [14]You have said, "It is vain to serve God. What do we profit by keeping his command or by going about as mourners before the LORD of hosts? [15]Now we count the arrogant happy; evildoers not only prosper, but when they put God to the test they escape."

The Reward of the Faithful

16 Then those who revered the LORD spoke with one another. The LORD took note and listened, and a book of remembrance was written before him of those who revered the LORD and thought on his name. [17]They shall be mine, says the LORD of hosts, my special possession on

"But for you who revere my name the sun of righteousness shall rise, with healing in its wings. You shall go out leaping like calves from the stall." Malachi 4:2

the day when I act, and I will spare them as parents spare their children who serve them. [18]Then once more you shall see the difference between the righteous and the wicked, between one who serves God and one who does not serve him.

The Great Day of the Lord

4 [o]See, the day is coming, burning like an oven, when all the arrogant and all evildoers will be stubble; the day that comes shall burn them up, says the LORD of hosts, so that it will leave them neither root nor branch. [2]But for you who revere my name the sun of righteousness shall rise, with healing in its wings. You shall go out leaping like calves from the stall. [3]And you shall tread down the wicked, for they will be ashes under the soles of your feet, on the day when I act, says the LORD of hosts.

4 Remember the teaching of my servant Moses, the statutes and ordinances that I commanded him at Hōʹreb for all Israel.

5 Lo, I will send you the prophet E·līʹ-jah before the great and terrible day of the LORD comes. [6]He will turn the hearts of parents to their children and the hearts of children to their parents, so that I will not come and strike the land with a curse.[p]

[n] Heb *devourer*   [o] Ch 4.1-6 are Ch 3.19-24 in Heb   [p] Or *a ban of utter destruction*

Some of the things you read about in the Bible, like the "shofar", you might not see today. Other things, like a coin, look different today from how they looked during Bible times.

shofar

drum

lyre

pipes

coin

date

perfume or oil jar

fig

pomegranate

sling
and
stone

rod and
staff

scroll

potter's wheel

fishing net

high priest's breastplate

Ark of the Covenant

golden calf

10 Commandments tablets

The Lord's Prayer

Jesus prayed often and taught his followers about prayer. Through his teachings on prayer we can learn how to pray.

My caring Parent who is heavenly
(but not far away),
Absolutely great is your name.
Bring us the best life together with you,
And what you would have us do,
let us get on with it in this world!
May no one go hungry (including me):
food for the body and food for our spirits.
Forgive all of us for the hurts we cause
others (and you). Help us forgive others
who have hurt us as well. May we be
spared the temptation to do wrong,
and, in spite of the worst that can
happen, get through this life knowing
that you will be there for us, with us, and in
us. When all is said and done, it is your
world, you have the loving power, and
you are forever! Amen!

(see Matthew 6:9-13)

The Beatitudes

Jesus taught people how to be happy.

Happy are those people who depend only upon God,
  for they belong to the kingdom of heaven.
Happy are those who are sad now,
  because God will comfort them.
Happy are those people who are humble,
  for the earth belongs to them.
Happy are those who seek to obey God,
  for they will be given what they want.
Happy are those who show mercy,
  for mercy will be shown to them.
Happy are those whose hearts are pure,
  for they will see God.
Happy are those who make peace,
  for they will be called children of God.
Happy are those who are treated badly for doing right,
  for God's kingdom belongs to them.

(see Matthew 5:1-12)

Lesser-Known Bible Folks

Joanna (Luke 8:1–3; 24:1–12)

Joanna was one of the women who traveled with Jesus and the twelve disciples, helping proclaim the good news of God's kingdom. When Jesus was arrested, the other disciples ran away in fear, but she and some other women stayed with Jesus all the way to the cross. She was among the women who discovered the empty tomb and ran to tell the disciples that Jesus was alive.

Matthias (Acts 1:15–26)

After Judas betrayed Jesus, there were only eleven disciples left. Matthias was chosen to replace Judas. This was an honor and a great responsibility for Matthias, because it meant he was entrusted with spreading the good news about Jesus's love to as many people as he could.

Huldah (2 Kgs 22:14; 2 Chron 32:22)

Huldah was a prophetess who lived in Jerusalem during the reign of King Josiah. The king sent some men to her, and she told them that God would soon punish the people because they had been making offerings to other gods. Huldah listened to God and told the truth, even though it was not what the king's men wanted to hear.

Apostles

There were many other people called "apostles" who were not counted among the Twelve: Andronicus and Junia (Rom. 16:7), Apollos (1 Cor. 4:6–9), Barnabas (1 Cor. 9:5–6), James (Gal. 1:19), Epaphroditus (Phil. 2:25), Silvanus and Timothy (1 Thess. 2:7), and Paul (Rom. 1:1; 1 Cor. 1:1). There were many people who were not called "apostles," but who did what apostles do: tell others about Jesus. You can read about the Samaritan woman (John 4:4–42), Mary Magdalene (John 20:1–2; 11–18), and other women who saw the empty tomb and ran to tell others (Luke 24:10).

Balaam and his Donkey (Num 22:23–24)

Balaam was a prophet who did not always pay very close attention to what God was trying to tell him. Once, while Balaam was riding his donkey down the road, God sent an angel to stand in the road with his sword drawn to block Balaam's way. The donkey saw the angel and turned off the road in fear, but Balaam did not see the angel, so he hit his donkey to make him go. This happened two more times until God gave the donkey a voice. The donkey said, "Why have you hit me three times?" Balaam must have been very surprised to hear his donkey speaking, and he finally saw the angel. The angel told Balaam that it was wrong to strike the poor donkey, who was only trying to save his life. From then on, Balaam paid more attention to what God was telling him.

Eutychus (Acts 20:9–10)

Eutychus was sitting in the window listening to Paul preach. Paul spoke on and on, late into the night, and Eutychus drifted off to sleep. He was so sleepy that he fell out the window! He landed on the ground three floors below, and everyone thought he was surely dead. But Paul held him in his arms and said he was still alive. Everyone was very relieved and happy. Eutychus is probably the first person in recorded history to fall asleep during a sermon. He was well named: Eutychus means "lucky."

Anna (Luke 2:36–40)

Anna was a very old prophetess who had spent her whole life praying and hoping to see the promised Messiah. When she saw the baby Jesus, she recognized him immediately and began joyfully telling everyone about him.

The Gerasene Demoniac (Mark 5:1–20)

A "demoniac" is someone who has been possessed by demons or evil spirits. In Jesus's time, people thought that both physical and mental illnesses were caused by demons. There was a man who lived "on the other side of the sea" in the Gerasenes. He was so ill that he had to be bound in chains, because he would cut himself with rocks and try to harm others. Jesus crossed the sea and healed this man, and the man was so grateful that he wanted to follow Jesus. But Jesus told him to go tell his friends what the Lord had done for him. He is an example of thinking globally but acting locally. Sometimes you can serve the Lord best in your own neighborhood.

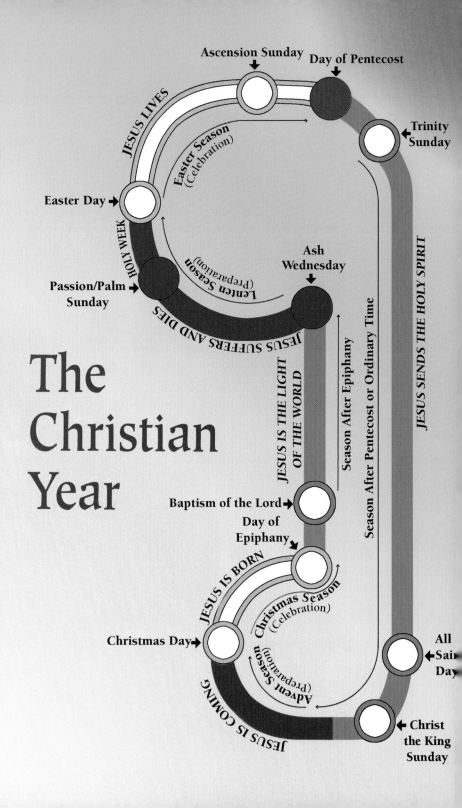

THE NEW COVENANT
commonly called

THE NEW TESTAMENT

of
OUR LORD AND SAVIOR
JESUS CHRIST

New Revised Standard Version

Matthew

The first four books of the New Testament are called Gospels. The word *gospel* means "good news." These books tell us the good news that Jesus came to earth to live as a human and to show us how we ought to live as the children of God. Each of the four books was written for a different group of readers, and the Gospel of Matthew was especially for Jews. This Gospel was written about 85 AD and was named for Matthew because he had collected some of the information about Jesus that went into the book.

Although the Gospel of Matthew is the first book in the New Testament, many people believe it was the third Gospel to be written. The writer used the Gospel of Mark as the main outline of the events of Jesus's life. In fact, the Gospel of Matthew quotes much of the Gospel of Mark.

The Gospel of Matthew tells the story of Jesus—his birth, life as an adult (including his ministry and teaching), crucifixion, and resurrection. This Gospel was written to encourage readers to have faith in Jesus as the Messiah (or "Christ," in Greek). The Gospel often makes connections between Jesus's teachings and the Hebrew Scriptures, which are what we call the Old Testament. The writer of the Gospel of Matthew wanted those who read or heard the Gospel to understand Jesus based on their knowledge of the Hebrew Scriptures.

Matthew 14:13–21

The Genealogy of Jesus the Messiah

1 An account of the genealogy[a] of Jesus the Messiah,[b] the son of David, the son of Abraham.

2 Abraham was the father of Isaac, and Isaac the father of Jacob, and Jacob the father of Judah and his brothers, ³and Judah the father of Per′ez and Ze′rah by Ta′mar, and Per′ez the father of Hez′ron, and Hez′ron the father of Ar′am, ⁴and Ar′am the father of A·min′a·dab, and A·min′a·dab the father of Nah′shon, and Nah′shon the father of Sal′mon, ⁵and Sal′mon the father of Bō′az by Ra′hab, and Bō′az the father of Ō′bed by Ruth, and Ō′bed the father of Jesse, ⁶and Jesse the father of King David.

And David was the father of Solomon by the wife of U·ri′ah, ⁷and Solomon the father of Re·ho·bō′am, and Re·ho·bō′am the father of A·bi′jah, and A·bi′jah the father of A′saph,[c] ⁸and A′saph[c] the father of Je·hosh′a·phat, and Je·hosh′a·phat the father of Jō′ram, and Jō′ram the father of Uz·zi′ah, ⁹and Uz·zi′ah the father of Jō′tham, and Jō′tham the father of A′haz, and A′haz the father of Hez·e·ki′ah, ¹⁰and Hez·e·ki′ah the father of Ma·nas′seh, and Ma·nas′seh the father of A′mos,[d] and A′mos[d] the father of Jō·si′ah, ¹¹and Jō·si′ah the father of Jech·o·ni′ah and his brothers, at the time of the deportation to Babylon.

12 And after the deportation to Babylon: Jech·o·ni′ah was the father of Sa·la′thi·el, and Sa·la′thi·el the father of Ze·rub′ba·bel, ¹³and Ze·rub′ba·bel the father of A·bi′ud, and A·bi′ud the father of E·li′a·kim, and E·li′a·kim the father of A′zor, ¹⁴and A′zor the father of Za′dok, and Za′dok the father of A′chim, and A′chim the father of E·li′ud, ¹⁵and E·li′ud the father of El·e·a′zar, and El·e·a′zar the father of Mat′than, and Mat′than the father of Jacob, ¹⁶and Jacob the father of Joseph the husband of Mary, of whom Jesus was born, who is called the Messiah.[e]

17 So all the generations from Abraham to David are fourteen generations; and from David to the deportation to Babylon, fourteen generations; and from the deportation to Babylon to the Messiah,[e] fourteen generations.

The Gospel of Matthew begins with a list of Jesus's ancestors. God had made covenants (or promises) with Abraham and David. Now God makes a new covenant with the descendants of Abraham and David by sending Jesus, the Messiah.

The Birth of Jesus the Messiah

18 Now the birth of Jesus the Messiah[b] took place in this way. When his mother Mary had been engaged to Joseph, but before they lived together, she was found to be with child from the Holy Spirit. ¹⁹Her husband Joseph, being a righteous man and unwilling to expose her to public disgrace, planned to dismiss her quietly. ²⁰But just when he had resolved to do this, an angel of the Lord appeared to him in a dream and said, "Joseph, son of David, do not be afraid to take Mary as your wife, for the child conceived in her is from the Holy Spirit. ²¹She will bear a son, and you are to name him Jesus, for he will save his people from their sins." ²²All this took place to fulfill what had been spoken by the Lord through the prophet:

23 "Look, the virgin shall conceive and
    bear a son,
  and they shall name him
    Em·man′u·el,"

which means, "God is with us." ²⁴When Joseph awoke from sleep, he did as the angel of the Lord commanded him; he took her as his wife, ²⁵but had no marital relations with her until she had borne a son;[f] and he named him Jesus.

[a] Or birth   [b] Or Jesus Christ   [c] Other ancient authorities read Asa   [d] Other ancient authorities read Amon   [e] Or the Christ   [f] Other ancient authorities read her firstborn son

Even though the Bible does not tell us how many wise men there were, we generally speak of three wise men because the Bible tells us about the three gifts the wise men brought to Jesus. Their gifts were very expensive items, fit for a king. Gold was the most precious metal. Frankincense was burned in temples as a sign of prayer. Myrrh was used as a medicine, especially to treat cuts or bruises.

The Visit of the Wise Men

2 In the time of King Her´od, after Jesus was born in Bethlehem of Judea, wise men[g] from the East came to Jerusalem, [2]asking, "Where is the child who has been born king of the Jews? For we observed his star at its rising,[h] and have come to pay him homage." [3]When King Her´od heard this, he was frightened, and all Jerusalem with him; [4]and calling together all the chief priests and scribes of the people, he inquired of them where the Messiah[i] was to be born. [5]They told him, "In Bethlehem of Judea; for so it has been written by the prophet:

[6] 'And you, Bethlehem, in the land of Judah,
  are by no means least among the rulers of Judah;
 for from you shall come a ruler
  who is to shepherd[j] my people Israel.' "

[7] Then Her´od secretly called for the wise men[g] and learned from them the exact time when the star had appeared. [8]Then he sent them to Bethlehem, saying, "Go and search diligently for the child; and when you have found him, bring me word so that I may also go and pay him homage." [9]When they had heard the king, they set out; and there, ahead of them, went the star that they had seen at its rising,[h] until it stopped over the place where the child was. [10]When they saw that the star had stopped,[k] they were overwhelmed with joy. [11]On entering the house, they saw the child with Mary his mother; and they knelt down and paid him homage. Then, opening their treasure chests, they offered him gifts of gold, frankincense, and myrrh. [12]And having been warned in a dream not to return to Her´od, they left for their own country by another road.

The Escape to Egypt

[13] Now after they had left, an angel of the Lord appeared to Joseph in a dream and said, "Get up, take the child and his mother, and flee to Egypt, and remain there until I tell you; for Her´od is about to search for the child, to destroy him." [14]Then Joseph[l] got up, took the child and his mother by night, and went to Egypt, [15]and remained there until the death of Her´od. This was to fulfill what had been spoken by the Lord through the prophet, "Out of Egypt I have called my son."

The Massacre of the Infants

[16] When Her´od saw that he had been tricked by the wise men,[g] he was infuriated, and he sent and killed all the children in and around Bethlehem who were two years old or under, according to the time that he had learned from the wise men.[g] [17]Then was fulfilled what had been spoken through the prophet Jer·e·mī´ah:

[18] "A voice was heard in Rā´mah,
  wailing and loud lamentation,
 Rachel weeping for her children;
  she refused to be consoled, because they are no more."

"Where is the child who has been born king of the Jews? For we observed his star at its rising, and have come to pay him homage." Matthew 2:2

[g] Or *astrologers*; Gk *magi*   [h] Or *in the East*   [i] Or *the Christ*   [j] Or *rule*   [k] Gk *saw the star*   [l] Gk *he*

The Return from Egypt

19 When Her'od died, an angel of the Lord suddenly appeared in a dream to Joseph in Egypt and said, 20"Get up, take the child and his mother, and go to the land of Israel, for those who were seeking the child's life are dead." 21Then Joseph[m] got up, took the child and his mother, and went to the land of Israel. 22But when he heard that Ar·che·lā'us was ruling over Judea in place of his father Her'od, he was afraid to go there. And after being warned in a dream, he went away to the district of Galilee. 23There he made his home in a town called Nazareth, so that what had been spoken through the prophets might be fulfilled, "He will be called a Naz·o·rē'an."

The Proclamation of John the Baptist

3 In those days John the Baptist appeared in the wilderness of Judea, proclaiming, 2"Repent, for the kingdom of heaven has come near."[n] 3This is the one of whom the prophet Ī·sāi'ah spoke when he said,

"The voice of one crying out in the wilderness:
'Prepare the way of the Lord,
make his paths straight.' "

4Now John wore clothing of camel's hair with a leather belt around his waist, and his food was locusts and wild honey. 5Then the people of Jerusalem and all Judea were going out to him, and all the region along the Jordan, 6and they were baptized by him in the river Jordan, confessing their sins.

7 But when he saw many Phar'i·sees and Sad'dū·cees coming for baptism, he said to them, "You brood of vipers! Who warned you to flee from the wrath to come? 8Bear fruit worthy of repentance. 9Do not presume to say to yourselves, 'We have Abraham as our ancestor'; for I tell you, God is able from these stones to raise up children to Abraham. 10Even now the ax is lying at the root of the trees; every tree therefore that does not bear good fruit is cut down and thrown into the fire.

11"I baptize you with[q] water for repentance, but one who is more powerful than I is coming after me; I am not worthy to carry his sandals. He will baptize you with[o] the Holy Spirit and fire. 12His winnowing fork is in his hand, and he will clear his threshing floor and will gather his wheat into the granary; but the chaff he will burn with unquenchable fire."

The dove is a symbol of the Holy Spirit because the Holy Spirit is said to have descended "like a dove" at the baptism of Jesus.

The Baptism of Jesus

13 Then Jesus came from Galilee to John at the Jordan, to be baptized by him. 14John would have prevented him, saying, "I need to be baptized by you, and do you come to me?" 15But Jesus answered him, "Let it be so now; for it is proper for us in this way to fulfill all righteousness." Then he consented. 16And when Jesus had been baptized, just as he came up from the water, suddenly the heavens were opened to him and he saw the Spirit of God descending like a dove and alighting on him. 17And a voice from heaven said, "This is my Son, the Beloved,[p] with whom I am well pleased."

The Temptation of Jesus

4 Then Jesus was led up by the Spirit into the wilderness to be tempted

"This is my Son, the Beloved, with whom I am well pleased."

Matthew 3:17

[m] Gk he [n] Or is at hand [o] Or in [p] Or my beloved Son

"And he said to them, 'Follow me, and I will make you fish for people.' Immediately they left their nets and followed him." Matthew 4:19–20

by the devil. ²He fasted forty days and forty nights, and afterwards he was famished. ³The tempter came and said to him, "If you are the Son of God, command these stones to become loaves of bread." ⁴But he answered, "It is written,

'One does not live by bread alone,
   but by every word that comes from
      the mouth of God.' "

5 Then the devil took him to the holy city and placed him on the pinnacle of the temple, ⁶saying to him, "If you are the Son of God, throw yourself down; for it is written,

'He will command his angels
      concerning you,'
   and 'On their hands they will bear
      you up,
so that you will not dash your foot
      against a stone.' "

⁷Jesus said to him, "Again it is written, 'Do not put the Lord your God to the test.' "

8 Again, the devil took him to a very high mountain and showed him all the kingdoms of the world and their splendor; ⁹and he said to him, "All these I will give you, if you will fall down and worship me." ¹⁰Jesus said to him, "Away with you, Satan! for it is written,

'Worship the Lord your God,
   and serve only him.' "

¹¹Then the devil left him, and suddenly angels came and waited on him.

Jesus Begins His Ministry in Galilee

12 Now when Jesus^q heard that John had been arrested, he withdrew to Galilee. ¹³He left Nazareth and made his home in Ca·per´na·um by the sea, in the territory of Zeb´u·lun and Naph´ta·li, ¹⁴so that what had been spoken through

the prophet I·sai´ah might be fulfilled:
¹⁵ "Land of Zeb´u·lun, land of Naph´ta·li,
      on the road by the sea, across the
         Jordan, Galilee of the Gentiles—
¹⁶ the people who sat in darkness
      have seen a great light,
and for those who sat in the region
      and shadow of death
   light has dawned."

¹⁷From that time Jesus began to proclaim, "Repent, for the kingdom of heaven has come near."^r

Jesus Calls the First Disciples

18 As he walked by the Sea of Galilee, he saw two brothers, Simon, who is called Peter, and Andrew his brother, casting a net into the sea—for they were fishermen. ¹⁹And he said to them, "Follow me, and I will make you fish for people." ²⁰Immediately they left their nets and followed him. ²¹As he went from there, he saw two other brothers, James son of Zeb´e·dee and his brother John, in the boat with their father Zeb´e·dee, mending their nets, and he called them. ²²Immediately they left the boat and their father, and followed him.

Jesus Ministers to Crowds of People

23 Jesus^s went throughout Galilee, teaching in their synagogues and proclaiming the good news^t of the kingdom

Almost all of Jesus's ministry took place in a tiny region called Galilee. The region lay in northern Palestine, east of the Mediterranean Sea. In Old Testament times its boundaries changed many times, and for centuries it was ruled by one nation after another. In 63 BC Galilee was under Roman rule.

^q Gk he   ^r Or is at hand   ^s Gk He   ^t Gk gospel

and curing every disease and every sickness among the people. [24]So his fame spread throughout all Syria, and they brought to him all the sick, those who were afflicted with various diseases and pains, demoniacs, epileptics, and paralytics, and he cured them. [25]And great crowds followed him from Galilee, the De·cap´o·lis, Jerusalem, Judea, and from beyond the Jordan.

The Beatitudes

5 When Jesus[u] saw the crowds, he went up the mountain; and after he sat down, his disciples came to him. [2]Then he began to speak, and taught them, saying:

3 "Blessed are the poor in spirit, for theirs is the kingdom of heaven.

4 "Blessed are those who mourn, for they will be comforted.

5 "Blessed are the meek, for they will inherit the earth.

6 "Blessed are those who hunger and thirst for righteousness, for they will be filled.

7 "Blessed are the merciful, for they will receive mercy.

8 "Blessed are the pure in heart, for they will see God.

9 "Blessed are the peacemakers, for they will be called children of God.

10 "Blessed are those who are persecuted for righteousness' sake, for theirs is the kingdom of heaven.

11 "Blessed are you when people revile you and persecute you and utter all kinds of evil against you falsely[v] on my account. [12]Rejoice and be glad, for your reward is great in heaven, for in the same way they persecuted the prophets who were before you.

Salt and Light

13 "You are the salt of the earth; but if salt has lost its taste, how can its saltiness be restored? It is no longer good for anything, but is thrown out and trampled under foot.

14 "You are the light of the world. A

> "No one after lighting a lamp puts it under the bushel basket, but on the lampstand, and it gives light to all in the house. In the same way, let your light shine before others, so that they may see your good works and give glory to your Father in heaven."
>
> **Matthew 5:14–16**

city built on a hill cannot be hid. [15]No one after lighting a lamp puts it under the bushel basket, but on the lampstand, and it gives light to all in the house. [16]In the same way, let your light shine before others, so that they may see your good works and give glory to your Father in heaven.

The Law and the Prophets

17 "Do not think that I have come to abolish the law or the prophets; I have come not to abolish but to fulfill. [18]For truly I tell you, until heaven and earth pass away, not one letter,[w] not one stroke of a letter, will pass from the law until all is accomplished. [19]Therefore, whoever breaks[x] one of the least of these commandments, and teaches others to do the same, will be called least in the kingdom of heaven; but whoever does them and teaches them will be called great in the kingdom of heaven. [20]For I tell you, unless your righteousness exceeds that of the scribes and Phar´i·sees, you will never enter the kingdom of heaven.

Concerning Anger

21 "You have heard that it was said to those of ancient times, 'You shall not murder'; and 'whoever murders shall be liable to judgment.' [22]But I say to you that if you are angry with a brother or sister,[y] you will be liable to judgment; and if you insult[z] a brother or sister,[a] you

[u] Gk *he* [v] Other ancient authorities lack *falsely* [w] Gk *one iota* [x] Or *annuls* [y] Gk *a brother* ; other ancient authorities add *without cause* [z] Gk *say Raca to* (an obscure term of abuse) [a] Gk *a brother*

will be liable to the council; and if you say, 'You fool,' you will be liable to the hell*[b]* of fire. ²³So when you are offering your gift at the altar, if you remember that your brother or sister*[c]* has something against you, ²⁴leave your gift there before the altar and go; first be reconciled to your brother or sister,*[c]* and then come and offer your gift. ²⁵Come to terms quickly with your accuser while you are on the way to court*[d]* with him, or your accuser may hand you over to the judge, and the judge to the guard, and you will be thrown into prison. ²⁶Truly I tell you, you will never get out until you have paid the last penny.

Concerning Adultery

27 "You have heard that it was said, 'You shall not commit adultery.' ²⁸But I say to you that everyone who looks at a woman with lust has already committed adultery with her in his heart. ²⁹If your right eye causes you to sin, tear it out and throw it away; it is better for you to lose one of your members than for your whole body to be thrown into hell.*[b]* ³⁰And if your right hand causes you to sin, cut it off and throw it away; it is better for you to lose one of your members than for your whole body to go into hell.*[b]*

Concerning Divorce

31 "It was also said, 'Whoever divorces his wife, let him give her a certificate of divorce.' ³²But I say to you that anyone who divorces his wife, except on the ground of unchastity, causes her to commit adultery; and whoever marries a divorced woman commits adultery.

Concerning Oaths

33 "Again, you have heard that it was said to those of ancient times, 'You shall not swear falsely, but carry out the vows you have made to the Lord.' ³⁴But I say to you, Do not swear at all, either by heaven, for it is the throne of God, ³⁵or by the earth, for it is his footstool, or by Jerusalem, for it is the city of the great

King. ³⁶And do not swear by your head, for you cannot make one hair white or black. ³⁷Let your word be 'Yes, Yes' or 'No, No'; anything more than this comes from the evil one.*[e]*

Concerning Retaliation

38 "You have heard that it was said, 'An eye for an eye and a tooth for a tooth.' ³⁹But I say to you, Do not resist an evildoer. But if anyone strikes you on the right cheek, turn the other also; ⁴⁰and if anyone wants to sue you and take your coat, give your cloak as well; ⁴¹and if anyone forces you to go one mile, go also the second mile. ⁴²Give to everyone who begs from you, and do not refuse anyone who wants to borrow from you.

Love for Enemies

43 "You have heard that it was said, 'You shall love your neighbor and hate your enemy.' ⁴⁴But I say to you, Love your enemies and pray for those who persecute you, ⁴⁵so that you may be children of your Father in heaven; for he makes his sun rise on the evil and on the good, and sends rain on the righteous and on the unrighteous. ⁴⁶For if you love those who love you, what reward do you have? Do not even the tax collectors do the same? ⁴⁷And if you greet only your brothers and sisters,*[f]* what more are you doing than others? Do not even the Gentiles do the same? ⁴⁸Be perfect, therefore, as your heavenly Father is perfect.

Concerning Almsgiving

6 "Beware of practicing your piety before others in order to be seen by them; for then you have no reward from your Father in heaven.

2 "So whenever you give alms, do not sound a trumpet before you, as the hypocrites do in the synagogues and in the streets, so that they may be praised by

[b] Gk *Gehenna*   *[c]* Gk *your brother*   *[d]* Gk lacks *to court*   *[e]* Or *evil*   *[f]* Gk *your brothers*

Jesus spoke out against people who made sure the way they followed God was noticed by others. He called these people hypocrites. Hypocrites are people who pretend to be something they are not, like acting a part in a play. Jesus said that we should not pretend to follow God so that others will notice and praise us. We should follow God because we love God.

others. Truly I tell you, they have received their reward. ³But when you give alms, do not let your left hand know what your right hand is doing, ⁴so that your alms may be done in secret; and your Father who sees in secret will reward you.ᵍ

Concerning Prayer

5 "And whenever you pray, do not be like the hypocrites; for they love to stand and pray in the synagogues and at the street corners, so that they may be seen by others. Truly I tell you, they have received their reward. ⁶But whenever you pray, go into your room and shut the door and pray to your Father who is in secret; and your Father who sees in secret will reward you.ᵍ

7 "When you are praying, do not heap up empty phrases as the Gentiles do; for they think that they will be heard because of their many words. ⁸Do not be like them, for your Father knows what you need before you ask him.

9 "Pray then in this way:
Our Father in heaven,
    hallowed be your name.
10   Your kingdom come.
    Your will be done,
      on earth as it is in heaven.
11   Give us this day our daily bread.ʰ
12   And forgive us our debts,

as we also have forgiven our debtors.
13   And do not bring us to the time of trial,ⁱ
    but rescue us from the evil one.ʲ
¹⁴For if you forgive others their trespasses, your heavenly Father will also forgive you; ¹⁵but if you do not forgive others, neither will your Father forgive your trespasses.

Concerning Fasting

16 "And whenever you fast, do not look dismal, like the hypocrites, for they disfigure their faces so as to show others that they are fasting. Truly I tell you, they have received their reward. ¹⁷But when you fast, put oil on your head and wash your face, ¹⁸so that your fasting may be seen not by others but by your Father who is in secret; and your Father who sees in secret will reward you.ᵍ

Concerning Treasures

19 "Do not store up for yourselves treasures on earth, where moth and rustᵏ consume and where thieves break in and steal; ²⁰but store up for yourselves treasures in heaven, where neither moth nor rustᵏ consumes and where thieves do not break in and steal. ²¹For where your treasure is, there your heart will be also.

The Sound Eye

22 "The eye is the lamp of the body. So, if your eye is healthy, your whole

When Jesus taught the people to pray, he used the name "father" when speaking of God. God cares for people just as a parent on earth cares for his or her child. We can speak to God just as we speak to our own mothers and fathers.

ᵍ Other ancient authorities add *openly*   ʰ Or *our bread for tomorrow*   ⁱ Or *us into temptation* ʲ Or *from evil*. Other ancient authorities add, in some form, *For the kingdom and the power and the glory are yours forever. Amen.*   ᵏ Gk *eating*

"Strive first for the kingdom of God and his righteousness, and all these things will be given to you as well." Matthew 6:33

body will be full of light; [23]but if your eye is unhealthy, your whole body will be full of darkness. If then the light in you is darkness, how great is the darkness!

Serving Two Masters

24 "No one can serve two masters; for a slave will either hate the one and love the other, or be devoted to the one and despise the other. You cannot serve God and wealth.[l]

Do Not Worry

25 "Therefore I tell you, do not worry about your life, what you will eat or what you will drink,[m] or about your body, what you will wear. Is not life more than food, and the body more than clothing? [26]Look at the birds of the air; they neither sow nor reap nor gather into barns, and yet your heavenly Father feeds them. Are you not of more value than they? [27]And can any of you by worrying add a single hour to your span of life?[n] [28]And why do you worry about clothing? Consider the lilies of the field, how they grow; they neither toil nor spin, [29]yet I tell you, even Solomon in all his glory was not clothed like one of these. [30]But if God so clothes the grass of the field, which is alive today and tomorrow is thrown into the oven, will he not much more clothe you—you of little faith? [31]Therefore do not worry, saying, 'What will we eat?' or 'What will we drink?' or 'What will we wear?' [32]For it is the Gentiles who strive for all these things; and indeed your heavenly Father knows that you need all these things. [33]But strive first for the kingdom of God[o] and his[p] righteousness, and all these things will be given to you as well.

34 "So do not worry about tomorrow, for tomorrow will bring worries of its own. Today's trouble is enough for today.

Judging Others

7 "Do not judge, so that you may not be judged. [2]For with the judgment you make you will be judged, and the measure you give will be the measure you get. [3]Why do you see the speck in your neighbor's[q] eye, but do not notice the log in your own eye? [4]Or how can you say to your neighbor,[r] 'Let me take the speck out of your eye,' while the log is in your own eye? [5]You hypocrite, first take the log out of your own eye, and then you will see clearly to take the speck out of your neighbor's[q] eye.

Profaning the Holy

6 "Do not give what is holy to dogs; and do not throw your pearls before swine, or they will trample them under foot and turn and maul you.

Ask, Search, Knock

7 "Ask, and it will be given you; search, and you will find; knock, and the door will be opened for you. [8]For everyone who asks receives, and everyone who searches finds, and for everyone who knocks, the door will be opened. [9]Is there anyone among you who, if your child asks for bread, will give a stone? [10]Or if the child asks for a fish, will give a snake? [11]If you then, who are evil, know how to give good gifts to your children, how much more will your Father in heaven give good things to those who ask him!

"To strive" means to give serious effort or energy toward doing something. Jesus tells us to put our energy toward living as God would have us live.

[l] Gk mammon   [m] Other ancient authorities lack or what you will drink   [n] Or add one cubit to your height   [o] Other ancient authorities lack of God   [p] Or its   [q] Gk brother's   [r] Gk brother

The Golden Rule

12 "In everything do to others as you would have them do to you; for this is the law and the prophets.

The Narrow Gate

13 "Enter through the narrow gate; for the gate is wide and the road is easy[s] that leads to destruction, and there are many who take it. [14]For the gate is narrow and the road is hard that leads to life, and there are few who find it.

A Tree and Its Fruit

15 "Beware of false prophets, who come to you in sheep's clothing but inwardly are ravenous wolves. [16]You will know them by their fruits. Are grapes gathered from thorns, or figs from thistles? [17]In the same way, every good tree bears good fruit, but the bad tree bears bad fruit. [18]A good tree cannot bear bad fruit, nor can a bad tree bear good fruit. [19]Every tree that does not bear good fruit is cut down and thrown into the fire. [20]Thus you will know them by their fruits.

Concerning Self-Deception

21 "Not everyone who says to me, 'Lord, Lord,' will enter the kingdom of heaven, but only the one who does the will of my Father in heaven. [22]On that day many will say to me, 'Lord, Lord, did we not prophesy in your name, and cast out demons in your name, and do many deeds of power in your name?' [23]Then I will declare to them, 'I never knew you; go away from me, you evildoers.'

"Ask, and it will be given you; search, and you will find; knock, and the door will be opened for you. For everyone who asks receives, and everyone who searches finds, and for everyone who knocks, the door will be opened." Matthew 7:7–8

Hearers and Doers

24 "Everyone then who hears these words of mine and acts on them will be like a wise man who built his house on rock. [25]The rain fell, the floods came, and the winds blew and beat on that house, but it did not fall, because it had been founded on rock. [26]And everyone who hears these words of mine and does not act on them will be like a foolish man who built his house on sand. [27]The rain fell, and the floods came, and the winds blew and beat against that house, and it fell—and great was its fall!"

28 Now when Jesus had finished saying these things, the crowds were astounded at his teaching, [29]for he taught them as one having authority, and not as their scribes.

Jesus Cleanses a Leper

8 When Jesus[t] had come down from the mountain, great crowds followed him; [2]and there was a leper[u] who came to him and knelt before him, saying, "Lord, if you choose, you can make me clean." [3]He stretched out his hand and touched him, saying, "I do choose. Be made clean!" Immediately his leprosy[u] was cleansed. [4]Then Jesus said to him, "See that you say nothing to anyone; but go, show yourself to the priest, and offer the gift that Moses commanded, as a testimony to them."

God knows the things we need even before we ask. God loves us and is ready to answer our prayers. So when we pray, we don't have to coax, pester, or try to persuade God into answering. God knows us and knows what is best for us. Do you ever find yourself begging God for something? Can you trust God to take care of you?

[s] Other ancient authorities read *for the road is wide and easy*   [t] Gk *he*   [u] The terms *leper* and *leprosy* can refer to several diseases

Jesus Heals a Centurion's Servant

5 When he entered Ca·per′na·um, a centurion came to him, appealing to him [6]and saying, "Lord, my servant is lying at home paralyzed, in terrible distress." [7]And he said to him, "I will come and cure him." [8]The centurion answered, "Lord, I am not worthy to have you come under my roof; but only speak the word, and my servant will be healed. [9]For I also am a man under authority, with soldiers under me; and I say to one, 'Go,' and he goes, and to another, 'Come,' and he comes, and to my slave, 'Do this,' and the slave does it." [10]When Jesus heard him, he was amazed and said to those who followed him, "Truly I tell you, in no one[v] in Israel have I found such faith. [11]I tell you, many will come from east and west and will eat with Abraham and Isaac and Jacob in the kingdom of heaven, [12]while the heirs of the kingdom will be thrown into the outer darkness, where there will be weeping and gnashing of teeth." [13]And to the centurion Jesus said, "Go; let it be done for you according to your faith." And the servant was healed in that hour.

Jesus Heals Many at Peter's House

14 When Jesus entered Peter's house, he saw his mother-in-law lying in bed with a fever; [15]he touched her hand, and the fever left her, and she got up and began to serve him. [16]That evening they brought to him many who were possessed with demons; and he cast out the spirits with a word, and cured all who were sick. [17]This was to fulfill what had been spoken through the prophet Ī·sāi′ah, "He took our infirmities and bore our diseases."

Would-Be Followers of Jesus

18 Now when Jesus saw great crowds around him, he gave orders to go over to the other side. [19]A scribe then approached and said, "Teacher, I will follow you wherever you go." [20]And Jesus said to him, "Foxes have holes, and birds of the air have nests; but the Son of Man has nowhere to lay his head." [21]Another of his disciples said to him, "Lord, first let me go and bury my father." [22]But Jesus said to him, "Follow me, and let the dead bury their own dead."

Jesus Stills the Storm

23 And when he got into the boat, his disciples followed him. [24]A windstorm arose on the sea, so great that the boat was being swamped by the waves; but he was asleep. [25]And they went and woke him up, saying, "Lord, save us! We are perishing!" [26]And he said to them, "Why are you afraid, you of little faith?" Then he got up and rebuked the winds and the sea; and there was a dead calm. [27]They were amazed, saying, "What sort of man is this, that even the winds and the sea obey him?"

Jesus Heals the Gadarene Demoniacs

28 When he came to the other side, to the country of the Gad′a·rēnes,[w] two demoniacs coming out of the tombs met

Jesus chose Matthew to be one of his disciples. Matthew was a tax collector, a man employed by the Romans to collect money for them. No one liked paying taxes to the Romans, and so they didn't like those who collected the taxes. Tax collectors made their living by charging more money for taxes than the Romans expected and keeping the difference for themselves. But from the day that Jesus spoke to him, Matthew left his tax table and followed Jesus. What would it be like to leave everything to go with Jesus?

[v] Other ancient authorities read *Truly I tell you, not even* [w] Other ancient authorities read *Gergesenes*; others, *Gerasenes*

him. They were so fierce that no one could pass that way. ²⁹Suddenly they shouted, "What have you to do with us, Son of God? Have you come here to torment us before the time?" ³⁰Now a large herd of swine was feeding at some distance from them. ³¹The demons begged him, "If you cast us out, send us into the herd of swine." ³²And he said to them, "Go!" So they came out and entered the swine; and suddenly, the whole herd rushed down the steep bank into the sea and perished in the water. ³³The swineherds ran off, and on going into the town, they told the whole story about what had happened to the demoniacs. ³⁴Then the whole town came out to meet Jesus; and when they saw him, they begged him to leave their neighborhood.

9 ¹And after getting into a boat he crossed the sea and came to his own town.

Jesus Heals a Paralytic

2 And just then some people were carrying a paralyzed man lying on a bed. When Jesus saw their faith, he said to the paralytic, "Take heart, son; your sins are forgiven." ³Then some of the scribes said to themselves, "This man is blaspheming." ⁴But Jesus, perceiving their thoughts, said, "Why do you think evil in your hearts? ⁵For which is easier, to say, 'Your sins are forgiven,' or to say, 'Stand up and walk'? ⁶But so that you may know that the Son of Man has authority on earth to forgive sins"—he then said to the paralytic—"Stand up, take your bed and go to your home." ⁷And he stood up and went to his home. ⁸When the crowds saw it, they were filled with awe, and they glorified God, who had given such authority to human beings.

The Call of Matthew

9 As Jesus was walking along, he saw a man called Matthew sitting at the tax booth; and he said to him, "Follow me." And he got up and followed him.

10 And as he sat at dinnerˣ in the

Pharisees were Jewish religious leaders committed to following the laws set down in the Torah (the first five books of what we call the Old Testament). The Pharisees opposed Jesus because they thought he wanted Jews to stop following these laws and because he spent time with people considered to be sinners.

house, many tax collectors and sinners came and were sittingʸ with him and his disciples. ¹¹When the Phar′i·sees saw this, they said to his disciples, "Why does your teacher eat with tax collectors and sinners?" ¹²But when he heard this, he said, "Those who are well have no need of a physician, but those who are sick. ¹³Go and learn what this means, 'I desire mercy, not sacrifice.' For I have come to call not the righteous but sinners."

The Question about Fasting

14 Then the disciples of John came to him, saying, "Why do we and the Phar′i·sees fast often,ᶻ but your disciples do not fast?" ¹⁵And Jesus said to them, "The wedding guests cannot mourn as long as the bridegroom is with them, can they? The days will come when the bridegroom is taken away from them, and then they will fast. ¹⁶No one sews a piece of unshrunk cloth on an old cloak, for the patch pulls away from the cloak, and a worse tear is made. ¹⁷Neither is new wine put into old wineskins; otherwise, the skins burst, and the wine is spilled, and the skins are destroyed; but new wine is put into fresh wineskins, and so both are preserved."

ˣ Gk reclined   ʸ Gk were reclining   ᶻ Other ancient authorities lack often

"When he saw the crowds, he had compassion for them, because they were harassed and helpless, like sheep without a shepherd." Matthew 9:36

A Girl Restored to Life and a Woman Healed

18 While he was saying these things to them, suddenly a leader of the synagogue[a] came in and knelt before him, saying, "My daughter has just died; but come and lay your hand on her, and she will live." [19]And Jesus got up and followed him, with his disciples. [20]Then suddenly a woman who had been suffering from hemorrhages for twelve years came up behind him and touched the fringe of his cloak, [21]for she said to herself, "If I only touch his cloak, I will be made well." [22]Jesus turned, and seeing her he said, "Take heart, daughter; your faith has made you well." And instantly the woman was made well. [23]When Jesus came to the leader's house and saw the flute players and the crowd making a commotion, [24]he said, "Go away; for the girl is not dead but sleeping." And they laughed at him. [25]But when the crowd had been put outside, he went in and took her by the hand, and the girl got up. [26]And the report of this spread throughout that district.

Jesus Heals Two Blind Men

27 As Jesus went on from there, two blind men followed him, crying loudly, "Have mercy on us, Son of David!" [28]When he entered the house, the blind men came to him; and Jesus said to them, "Do you believe that I am able to do this?" They said to him, "Yes, Lord." [29]Then he touched their eyes and said, "According to your faith let it be done to you." [30]And their eyes were opened. Then Jesus sternly ordered them, "See that no one knows of this." [31]But they went away and spread the news about him throughout that district.

Jesus Heals One Who Was Mute

32 After they had gone away, a demoniac who was mute was brought to him. [33]And when the demon had been cast out, the one who had been mute spoke; and the crowds were amazed and said, "Never has anything like this been seen in Israel." [34]But the Phar·i·sees said, "By the ruler of the demons he casts out the demons."[b]

The Harvest Is Great, the Laborers Few

35 Then Jesus went about all the cities and villages, teaching in their synagogues, and proclaiming the good news of the kingdom, and curing every disease and every sickness. [36]When he saw the crowds, he had compassion for them, because they were harassed and helpless, like sheep without a shepherd. [37]Then he said to his disciples, "The harvest is plentiful, but the laborers are few; [38]therefore ask the Lord of the harvest to send out laborers into his harvest."

The Twelve Apostles

10 Then Jesus[c] summoned his twelve disciples and gave them authority over unclean spirits, to cast them out, and to cure every disease and

Sheep were important to life in Bible times, but they could not live on their own. Without the care of a shepherd, they could wander off and be eaten by wild animals, or fall over cliffs and be killed. Jesus knew that the crowds of people who came to listen to him needed someone to care for them as a shepherd cares for sheep. The idea that God or Jesus cares for us as a shepherd is also found in Psalm 23 and John 10.

---

[a] Gk lacks *of the synagogue* [b] Other ancient authorities lack this verse [c] Gk *he*

every sickness. ²These are the names of the twelve apostles: first, Simon, also known as Peter, and his brother Andrew; James son of Zeb´e·dee, and his brother John; ³Philip and Bartholomew; Thomas and Matthew the tax collector; James son of Al·phae´us, and Thad·dae´us;*d* ⁴Simon the Cā·na·nae´an, and Judas Is·car´i·ot, the one who betrayed him.

The Mission of the Twelve

5 These twelve Jesus sent out with the following instructions: "Go nowhere among the Gentiles, and enter no town of the Sa·mār´i·tans, ⁶but go rather to the lost sheep of the house of Israel. ⁷As you go, proclaim the good news, 'The kingdom of heaven has come near.'*e* ⁸Cure the sick, raise the dead, cleanse the lepers,*f* cast out demons. You received without payment; give without payment. ⁹Take no gold, or silver, or copper in your belts, ¹⁰no bag for your journey, or two tunics, or sandals, or a staff; for laborers deserve their food. ¹¹Whatever town or village you enter, find out who in it is worthy, and stay there until you leave. ¹²As you enter the house, greet it. ¹³If the house is worthy, let your peace come upon it; but if it is not worthy, let your peace return to you. ¹⁴If anyone will not welcome you or listen to your words, shake off the dust from your feet as you leave that house or town. ¹⁵Truly I tell you, it will be more tolerable for the land of Sod´om and Go·mor´rah on the day of judgment than for that town.

Coming Persecutions

16 "See, I am sending you out like sheep into the midst of wolves; so be wise as serpents and innocent as doves. ¹⁷Beware of them, for they will hand you over to councils and flog you in their synagogues; ¹⁸and you will be dragged before governors and kings because of me, as a testimony to them and the Gentiles. ¹⁹When they hand you over, do not worry about how you are to speak or what you are to say; for what you are to say will be given to you at that time; ²⁰for it is not you who speak, but the Spirit of your Father speaking through you. ²¹Brother will betray brother to death, and a father his child, and children will rise against parents and have them put to death; ²²and you will be hated by all because of my name. But the one who endures to the end will be saved. ²³When they persecute you in one town, flee to the next; for truly I tell you, you will not have gone through all the towns of Israel before the Son of Man comes.

24 "A disciple is not above the teacher, nor a slave above the master; ²⁵it is enough for the disciple to be like the teacher, and the slave like the master. If they have called the master of the house Bē·el´ze·bul, how much more will they malign those of his household!

Whom to Fear

26 "So have no fear of them; for nothing is covered up that will not be uncovered, and nothing secret that will not become known. ²⁷What I say to you in the dark, tell in the light; and what you hear whispered, proclaim from the housetops. ²⁸Do not fear those who kill the body but cannot kill the soul; rather fear him who can destroy both soul and body in hell.*g* ²⁹Are not two sparrows sold for a penny? Yet not one of them will fall to the ground apart from your Father. ³⁰And even the hairs of your head are all counted. ³¹So do not be afraid; you are of more value than many sparrows.

32 "Everyone therefore who acknowledges me before others, I also will acknowledge before my Father in heaven; ³³but whoever denies me before others, I also will deny before my Father in heaven.

Not Peace, but a Sword

34 "Do not think that I have come to bring peace to the earth; I have not come to bring peace, but a sword.

---

d Other ancient authorities read *Lebbaeus,* or *Lebbaeus called Thaddaeus*   *e* Or *is at hand*
f The terms *leper* and *leprosy* can refer to several diseases   *g* Gk *Gehenna*

"Come to me, all you that are weary and are carrying heavy burdens, and I will give you rest. Take my yoke upon you, and learn from me; for I am gentle and humble in heart, and you will find rest for your souls."   Matthew 11:28–29a

³⁵ For I have come to set a man against his father,
  and a daughter against her mother,
  and a daughter-in-law against her mother-in-law;
³⁶ and one's foes will be members of one's own household.

³⁷Whoever loves father or mother more than me is not worthy of me; and whoever loves son or daughter more than me is not worthy of me; ³⁸and whoever does not take up the cross and follow me is not worthy of me. ³⁹Those who find their life will lose it, and those who lose their life for my sake will find it.

Rewards

40 "Whoever welcomes you welcomes me, and whoever welcomes me welcomes the one who sent me. ⁴¹Whoever welcomes a prophet in the name of a prophet will receive a prophet's reward; and whoever welcomes a righteous person in the name of a righteous person will receive the reward of the righteous; ⁴²and whoever gives even a cup of cold water to one of these little ones in the name of a disciple—truly I tell you, none of these will lose their reward."

11 Now when Jesus had finished instructing his twelve disciples, he went on from there to teach and proclaim his message in their cities.

Messengers from John the Baptist

2 When John heard in prison what the Messiah[h] was doing, he sent word by his[i] disciples ³and said to him, "Are you the one who is to come, or are we to wait for another?" ⁴Jesus answered them, "Go and tell John what you hear and see: ⁵the blind receive their sight, the lame walk, the lepers[j] are cleansed, the deaf hear, the dead are raised, and the poor have good news brought to them. ⁶And blessed is anyone who takes no offense at me."

Jesus Praises John the Baptist

7 As they went away, Jesus began to speak to the crowds about John: "What did you go out into the wilderness to look at? A reed shaken by the wind? ⁸What then did you go out to see? Someone[k] dressed in soft robes? Look, those who wear soft robes are in royal palaces. ⁹What then did you go out to see? A prophet?[l] Yes, I tell you, and more than a prophet. ¹⁰This is the one about whom it is written,

'See, I am sending my messenger ahead of you,
  who will prepare your way before you.'

¹¹Truly I tell you, among those born of women no one has arisen greater than John the Baptist; yet the least in the kingdom of heaven is greater than he. ¹²From the days of John the Baptist until now the kingdom of heaven has suffered violence,[m] and the violent take it by force. ¹³For all the prophets and the law prophesied until John came; ¹⁴and if you are willing to accept it, he is E·li′jah who is to come. ¹⁵Let anyone with ears[n] listen!

16 "But to what will I compare this generation? It is like children sitting in the marketplaces and calling to one another,

¹⁷ 'We played the flute for you, and you did not dance;
  we wailed, and you did not mourn.'

¹⁸For John came neither eating nor drinking, and they say, 'He has a demon'; ¹⁹the

---

[h] Or the Christ   [i] Other ancient authorities read two of his   [j] The terms leper and leprosy can refer to several diseases   [k] Or Why then did you go out? To see someone   [l] Other ancient authorities read Why then did you go out? To see a prophet?   [m] Or has been coming violently   [n] Other ancient authorities add to hear

Son of Man came eating and drinking, and they say, 'Look, a glutton and a drunkard, a friend of tax collectors and sinners!' Yet wisdom is vindicated by her deeds."[o]

Woes to Unrepentant Cities

20 Then he began to reproach the cities in which most of his deeds of power had been done, because they did not repent. [21]"Woe to you, Chō·ra´zin! Woe to you, Beth·sā´i·da! For if the deeds of power done in you had been done in Tyre and Sī´don, they would have repented long ago in sackcloth and ashes. [22]But I tell you, on the day of judgment it will be more tolerable for Tyre and Sī´don than for you. [23]And you, Ca·per´na·um,

will you be exalted to heaven?

No, you will be brought down to Hades.

For if the deeds of power done in you had been done in Sod´om, it would have remained until this day. [24]But I tell you that on the day of judgment it will be more tolerable for the land of Sod´om than for you."

Jesus Thanks His Father

25 At that time Jesus said, "I thank[p] you, Father, Lord of heaven and earth, because you have hidden these things from the wise and the intelligent and have revealed them to infants; [26]yes, Father, for such was your gracious will.[q] [27]All things have been handed over to me by my Father; and no one knows the Son except the Father, and no one knows the Father except the Son and anyone to whom the Son chooses to reveal him.

28 "Come to me, all you that are weary and are carrying heavy burdens, and I will give you rest. [29]Take my yoke upon you, and learn from me; for I am gentle and humble in heart, and you will find rest for your souls. [30]For my yoke is easy, and my burden is light."

Plucking Grain on the Sabbath

12 At that time Jesus went through the grainfields on the sabbath; his disciples were hungry, and they began to pluck heads of grain and to eat. [2]When the Phar´i·sees saw it, they said to him, "Look, your disciples are doing what is not lawful to do on the sabbath." [3]He said to them, "Have you not read what David did when he and his companions were hungry? [4]He entered the house of God and ate the bread of the Presence, which it was not lawful for him or his companions to eat, but only for the priests. [5]Or have you not read in the law that on the sabbath the priests in the temple break the sabbath and yet are guiltless? [6]I tell you, something greater than the temple is here. [7]But if you had known what this means, 'I desire mercy and not sacrifice,' you would not have condemned the guiltless. [8]For the Son of Man is lord of the sabbath."

Some religious leaders did not like the fact that Jesus healed people on the sabbath. They believed that no one should do any work on the day God had commanded them to rest. But Jesus recognized that anyone would know it was important to help an animal even if it was the sabbath. So in the same way, Jesus taught them that no one should turn away from a person who needed help, no matter what day it was.

The Man with a Withered Hand

9 He left that place and entered their synagogue; [10]a man was there with a withered hand, and they asked him, "Is it lawful to cure on the sabbath?" so that they might accuse him. [11]He said to them, "Suppose one of you has only one sheep and it falls into a pit on the sabbath; will you not lay hold of it and lift it out? [12]How much more valuable is a human being than a sheep! So it is lawful to do good on the sabbath." [13]Then he

[o] Other ancient authorities read *children*   [p] Or *praise*   [q] Or *for so it was well-pleasing in your sight*

said to the man, "Stretch out your hand." He stretched it out, and it was restored, as sound as the other. ¹⁴But the Phar′i·sees went out and conspired against him, how to destroy him.

God's Chosen Servant

15 When Jesus became aware of this, he departed. Many crowds[r] followed him, and he cured all of them, ¹⁶and he ordered them not to make him known. ¹⁷This was to fulfill what had been spoken through the prophet I·sai′ah:

¹⁸ "Here is my servant, whom I have chosen,
 my beloved, with whom my soul is well pleased.
 I will put my Spirit upon him,
 and he will proclaim justice to the Gentiles.
¹⁹ He will not wrangle or cry aloud,
 nor will anyone hear his voice in the streets.
²⁰ He will not break a bruised reed
 or quench a smoldering wick
 until he brings justice to victory.
²¹ And in his name the Gentiles will hope."

Jesus and Beelzebul

22 Then they brought to him a demoniac who was blind and mute; and he cured him, so that the one who had been mute could speak and see. ²³All the crowds were amazed and said, "Can this be the Son of David?" ²⁴But when the Phar′i·sees heard it, they said, "It is only by Be·el′ze·bul, the ruler of the demons, that this fellow casts out the demons." ²⁵He knew what they were thinking and said to them, "Every kingdom divided against itself is laid waste, and no city or house divided against itself will stand. ²⁶If Satan casts out Satan, he is divided against himself; how then will his kingdom stand? ²⁷If I cast out demons by Be·el′ze·bul, by whom do your own exorcists[s] cast them out? Therefore they will be your judges. ²⁸But if it is by the Spirit of God that I cast out demons, then the kingdom

of God has come to you. ²⁹Or how can one enter a strong man's house and plunder his property, without first tying up the strong man? Then indeed the house can be plundered. ³⁰Whoever is not with me is against me, and whoever does not gather with me scatters. ³¹Therefore I tell you, people will be forgiven for every sin and blasphemy, but blasphemy against the Spirit will not be forgiven. ³²Whoever speaks a word against the Son of Man will be forgiven, but whoever speaks against the Holy Spirit will not be forgiven, either in this age or in the age to come.

A Tree and Its Fruit

33 "Either make the tree good, and its fruit good; or make the tree bad, and its fruit bad; for the tree is known by its fruit. ³⁴You brood of vipers! How can you speak good things, when you are evil? For out of the abundance of the heart the mouth speaks. ³⁵The good person brings good things out of a good treasure, and the evil person brings evil things out of an evil treasure. ³⁶I tell you, on the day of judgment you will have to give an account for every careless word you utter; ³⁷for by your words you will be justified, and by your words you will be condemned."

The Sign of Jonah

38 Then some of the scribes and Phar′i·sees said to him, "Teacher, we wish to see a sign from you." ³⁹But he answered them, "An evil and adulterous generation asks for a sign, but no sign will be given to it except the sign of the prophet Jonah. ⁴⁰For just as Jonah was three days and three nights in the belly of the sea monster, so for three days and three nights the Son of Man will be in the heart of the earth. ⁴¹The people of Nin′e·veh will rise up at the judgment with this generation and condemn it, because they repented at the proclamation of Jonah, and see, something greater than Jonah is here! ⁴²The queen of the

---

[r] Other ancient authorities lack *crowds* [s] Gk *sons*

South will rise up at the judgment with this generation and condemn it, because she came from the ends of the earth to listen to the wisdom of Solomon, and see, something greater than Solomon is here!

The Return of the Unclean Spirit

43 "When the unclean spirit has gone out of a person, it wanders through waterless regions looking for a resting place, but it finds none. [44]Then it says, 'I will return to my house from which I came.' When it comes, it finds it empty, swept, and put in order. [45]Then it goes and brings along seven other spirits more evil than itself, and they enter and live there; and the last state of that person is worse than the first. So will it be also with this evil generation."

The True Kindred of Jesus

46 While he was still speaking to the crowds, his mother and his brothers were standing outside, wanting to speak to him. [47]Someone told him, "Look, your mother and your brothers are standing outside, wanting to speak to you."[t] [48]But to the one who had told him this, Jesus[u] replied, "Who is my mother, and who are my brothers?" [49]And pointing to his disciples, he said, "Here are my mother and my brothers! [50]For whoever does the will of my Father in heaven is my brother and sister and mother."

The Parable of the Sower

13 That same day Jesus went out of the house and sat beside the sea. [2]Such great crowds gathered around him that he got into a boat and sat there, while the whole crowd stood on the beach. [3]And he told them many things in parables, saying: "Listen! A sower went out to sow. [4]And as he sowed, some seeds fell on the path, and the birds came and ate them up. [5]Other seeds fell on rocky ground, where they did not have much soil, and they sprang up quickly, since they had no depth of soil. [6]But when the sun rose, they were scorched; and since they had no root, they withered away. [7]Other seeds fell among thorns, and the thorns grew up and choked them. [8]Other seeds fell on good soil and brought forth grain, some a hundredfold, some sixty, some thirty. [9]Let anyone with ears[v] listen!"

A parable is a short story that teaches an important lesson. Jesus used parables to teach about God and God's kingdom in ways that his listeners could understand. He often began parables by saying, "The kingdom of heaven is like..." or "The kingdom of heaven may be compared to..."

The Purpose of the Parables

10 Then the disciples came and asked him, "Why do you speak to them in parables?" [11]He answered, "To you it has been given to know the secrets[w] of the kingdom of heaven, but to them it has not been given. [12]For to those who have, more will be given, and they will have an abundance; but from those who have nothing, even what they have will be taken away. [13]The reason I speak to them in parables is that 'seeing they do not perceive, and hearing they do not listen, nor do they understand.' [14]With them indeed is fulfilled the prophecy of Ī·saī´ah that says:

'You will indeed listen, but never understand,
　and you will indeed look, but never perceive.
[15] For this people's heart has grown dull,
　and their ears are hard of hearing,
　　and they have shut their eyes;
　so that they might not look with their eyes,
　and listen with their ears,
　and understand with their heart and turn—

---

[t] Other ancient authorities lack verse 47　　[u] Gk *he*　[v] Other ancient authorities add *to hear*　[w] Or *mysteries*

and I would heal them.'

[16]But blessed are your eyes, for they see, and your ears, for they hear. [17]Truly I tell you, many prophets and righteous people longed to see what you see, but did not see it, and to hear what you hear, but did not hear it.

The Parable of the Sower Explained

18 "Hear then the parable of the sower. [19]When anyone hears the word of the kingdom and does not understand it, the evil one comes and snatches away what is sown in the heart; this is what was sown on the path. [20]As for what was sown on rocky ground, this is the one who hears the word and immediately receives it with joy; [21]yet such a person has no root, but endures only for a while, and when trouble or persecution arises on account of the word, that person immediately falls away.[x] [22]As for what was sown among thorns, this is the one who hears the word, but the cares of the world and the lure of wealth choke the word, and it yields nothing. [23]But as for what was sown on good soil, this is the one who hears the word and understands it, who indeed bears fruit and yields, in one case a hundredfold, in another sixty, and in another thirty."

The Parable of Weeds among the Wheat

24 He put before them another parable: "The kingdom of heaven may be compared to someone who sowed good seed in his field; [25]but while everybody was asleep, an enemy came and sowed weeds among the wheat, and then went away. [26]So when the plants came up and bore grain, then the weeds appeared as well. [27]And the slaves of the householder came and said to him, 'Master, did you not sow good seed in your field? Where, then, did these weeds come from?' [28]He answered, 'An enemy has done this.' The slaves said to him, 'Then do you want us to go and gather them?' [29]But he replied, 'No; for in gathering the weeds you would uproot the wheat along with them. [30]Let both of them grow together until the harvest; and at harvest time I will tell the reapers, Collect the weeds first and bind them in bundles to be burned, but gather the wheat into my barn.' "

The Parable of the Mustard Seed

31 He put before them another parable: "The kingdom of heaven is like a mustard seed that someone took and sowed in his field; [32]it is the smallest of all the seeds, but when it has grown it is the greatest of shrubs and becomes a tree, so that the birds of the air come and make nests in its branches."

The Parable of the Yeast

33 He told them another parable: "The kingdom of heaven is like yeast that a woman took and mixed in with[y] three measures of flour until all of it was leavened."

The Use of Parables

34 Jesus told the crowds all these things in parables; without a parable he told them nothing. [35]This was to fulfill what had been spoken through the prophet:[z]

Jesus talked often about the kingdom of heaven, also called the kingdom of God. The kingdom comes on earth whenever people follow God, who is the ruler of this kingdom. When Jesus came to live on earth, he announced, "The kingdom of God has come near" (see Mark 1:15). He taught that his life, work, and death were necessary for the coming of the kingdom. When we believe in Jesus, we become part of the kingdom of God here and now. And we can also look forward to a place in the kingdom of the future.

[x] Gk *stumbles*   [y] Gk *hid in*   [z] Other ancient authorities read *the prophet Isaiah*

"I will open my mouth to speak in parables;
I will proclaim what has been hidden from the foundation of the world."[a]

Jesus Explains the Parable of the Weeds

36 Then he left the crowds and went into the house. And his disciples approached him, saying, "Explain to us the parable of the weeds of the field." [37]He answered, "The one who sows the good seed is the Son of Man; [38]the field is the world, and the good seed are the children of the kingdom; the weeds are the children of the evil one, [39]and the enemy who sowed them is the devil; the harvest is the end of the age, and the reapers are angels. [40]Just as the weeds are collected and burned up with fire, so will it be at the end of the age. [41]The Son of Man will send his angels, and they will collect out of his kingdom all causes of sin and all evildoers, [42]and they will throw them into the furnace of fire, where there will be weeping and gnashing of teeth. [43]Then the righteous will shine like the sun in the kingdom of their Father. Let anyone with ears[b] listen!

Three Parables

44 "The kingdom of heaven is like treasure hidden in a field, which someone found and hid; then in his joy he goes and sells all that he has and buys that field.

45 "Again, the kingdom of heaven is like a merchant in search of fine pearls; [46]on finding one pearl of great value, he went and sold all that he had and bought it.

47 "Again, the kingdom of heaven is like a net that was thrown into the sea and caught fish of every kind; [48]when it was full, they drew it ashore, sat down, and put the good into baskets but threw out the bad. [49]So it will be at the end of the age. The angels will come out and separate the evil from the righteous [50]and throw them into the furnace of fire, where there will be weeping and gnashing of teeth.

Treasures New and Old

51 "Have you understood all this?" They answered, "Yes." [52]And he said to them, "Therefore every scribe who has been trained for the kingdom of heaven is like the master of a household who brings out of his treasure what is new and what is old." [53]When Jesus had finished these parables, he left that place.

The Rejection of Jesus at Nazareth

54 He came to his hometown and began to teach the people[c] in their synagogue, so that they were astounded and said, "Where did this man get this wisdom and these deeds of power? [55]Is not this the carpenter's son? Is not his mother called Mary? And are not his brothers James and Joseph and Simon and Judas? [56]And are not all his sisters with us? Where then did this man get all this?" [57]And they took offense at him. But Jesus said to them, "Prophets are not without honor except in their own country and in their own house." [58]And he did not do many deeds of power there, because of their unbelief.

The Death of John the Baptist

14 At that time Her´od the ruler[d] heard reports about Jesus; [2]and he said to his servants, "This is John the Baptist; he has been raised from the dead, and for this reason these powers are at work in him." [3]For Her´od had

Being a follower of Jesus is not always easy. Jesus was even rejected by the people of his hometown. But God is always with us even in the most difficult situations, just as God was with Jesus. Why do you think the people who grew up with Jesus rejected him?

---

[a] Other ancient authorities lack *of the world*
[b] Other ancient authorities add *to hear*   [c] Gk *them*   [d] Gk *tetrarch*

arrested John, bound him, and put him in prison on account of He·rō′di·as, his brother Philip's wife,[e] ⁴because John had been telling him, "It is not lawful for you to have her." ⁵Though Her′od[f] wanted to put him to death, he feared the crowd, because they regarded him as a prophet. ⁶But when Her′od's birthday came, the daughter of He·rō′di·as danced before the company, and she pleased Her′od ⁷so much that he promised on oath to grant her whatever she might ask. ⁸Prompted by her mother, she said, "Give me the head of John the Baptist here on a platter." ⁹The king was grieved, yet out of regard for his oaths and for the guests, he commanded it to be given; ¹⁰he sent and had John beheaded in the prison. ¹¹The head was brought on a platter and given to the girl, who brought it to her mother. ¹²His disciples came and took the body and buried it; then they went and told Jesus.

Feeding the Five Thousand

13 Now when Jesus heard this, he withdrew from there in a boat to a deserted place by himself. But when the crowds heard it, they followed him on foot from the towns. ¹⁴When he went ashore, he saw a great crowd; and he had compassion for them and cured their sick. ¹⁵When it was evening, the disciples came to him and said, "This is a deserted place, and the hour is now late; send the crowds away so that they may go into the villages and buy food for themselves." ¹⁶Jesus said to them, "They need not go away; you give them something to eat." ¹⁷They replied, "We have nothing here but five loaves and two fish." ¹⁸And he said, "Bring them here to me." ¹⁹Then he ordered the crowds to sit down on the grass. Taking the five loaves and the two fish, he looked up to heaven, and blessed and broke the loaves, and gave them to the disciples, and the disciples gave them to the crowds. ²⁰And all ate and were filled; and they took up what was left over of the broken pieces, twelve baskets full. ²¹And those who ate were about five thousand men, besides women and children.

Crowds of people followed Jesus everywhere he went. Jesus taught the people and often healed those who were sick. Sometimes the people stayed until late in the day, listening to him teach. Jesus knew that they needed to eat before traveling home. Jesus fed five thousand people with only five loaves of bread and two fish!

Jesus Walks on the Water

22 Immediately he made the disciples get into the boat and go on ahead to the other side, while he dismissed the crowds. ²³And after he had dismissed the crowds, he went up the mountain by himself to pray. When evening came, he was there alone, ²⁴but by this time the boat, battered by the waves, was far from the land,[g] for the wind was against them. ²⁵And early in the morning he came walking toward them on the sea. ²⁶But when the disciples saw him walking on the sea, they were terrified, saying, "It is a ghost!" And they cried out in fear. ²⁷But immediately Jesus spoke to them and said, "Take heart, it is I; do not be afraid."

28 Peter answered him, "Lord, if it is you, command me to come to you on the water." ²⁹He said, "Come." So Peter got out of the boat, started walking on the water, and came toward Jesus. ³⁰But when he noticed the strong wind,[h] he became frightened, and beginning to sink, he cried out, "Lord, save me!" ³¹Jesus immediately reached out his hand and caught him, saying to him, "You of little faith, why did you doubt?" ³²When they got into the boat, the wind ceased. ³³And those in the boat worshiped him, saying, "Truly you are the Son of God."

[e] Other ancient authorities read *his brother's wife* [f] Gk *he* [g] Other ancient authorities read *was out on the sea* [h] Other ancient authorities read *the wind*

Jesus Heals the Sick in Gennesaret

34 When they had crossed over, they came to land at Gen·nes´a·ret. [35]After the people of that place recognized him, they sent word throughout the region and brought all who were sick to him, [36]and begged him that they might touch even the fringe of his cloak; and all who touched it were healed.

The Tradition of the Elders

15 Then Phar´i·sees and scribes came to Jesus from Jerusalem and said, [2]"Why do your disciples break the tradition of the elders? For they do not wash their hands before they eat." [3]He answered them, "And why do you break the commandment of God for the sake of your tradition? [4]For God said,[i] 'Honor your father and your mother,' and, 'Whoever speaks evil of father or mother must surely die.' [5]But you say that whoever tells father or mother, 'Whatever support you might have had from me is given to God,'[j] then that person need not honor the father.[k] [6]So, for the sake of your tradition, you make void the word[l] of God. [7]You hypocrites! I·sai´ah prophesied rightly about you when he said:

[8] 'This people honors me with their lips,
　　but their hearts are far from me;
[9] in vain do they worship me,
　　teaching human precepts as
　　　　doctrines.' "

In the Old Testament, "defile" meant to make persons, foods, places, or objects unclean in a religious sense, so that they were unfit for worship in the Temple. Priests in the Old Testament gave instructions on how to clean whatever had been defiled. Jesus used "defile" in a deeper sense to mean that people's words, thoughts, and actions might be unclean and might defile them in the sight of God.

Things That Defile

10 Then he called the crowd to him and said to them, "Listen and understand: [11]it is not what goes into the mouth that defiles a person, but it is what comes out of the mouth that defiles." [12]Then the disciples approached and said to him, "Do you know that the Phar´i·sees took offense when they heard what you said?" [13]He answered, "Every plant that my heavenly Father has not planted will be uprooted. [14]Let them alone; they are blind guides of the blind.[m] And if one blind person guides another, both will fall into a pit." [15]But Peter said to him, "Explain this parable to us." [16]Then he said, "Are you also still without understanding? [17]Do you not see that whatever goes into the mouth enters the stomach, and goes out into the sewer? [18]But what comes out of the mouth proceeds from the heart, and this is what defiles. [19]For out of the heart come evil intentions, murder, adultery, fornication, theft, false witness, slander. [20]These are what defile a person, but to eat with unwashed hands does not defile."

The Canaanite Woman's Faith

21 Jesus left that place and went away to the district of Tyre and Si´don. [22]Just then a Ca´naan·ite woman from that region came out and started shouting, "Have mercy on me, Lord, Son of David; my daughter is tormented by a demon." [23]But he did not answer her at all. And his disciples came and urged him, saying, "Send her away, for she keeps shouting after us." [24]He answered, "I was sent only to the lost sheep of the house of Israel." [25]But she came and knelt before him, saying, "Lord, help me." [26]He answered, "It is not fair to take the children's food and throw it to the dogs." [27]She said, "Yes, Lord, yet even

---

[i] Other ancient authorities read *commanded, saying*　[j] Or *is an offering*　[k] Other ancient authorities add *or the mother*　[l] Other ancient authorities read *law*; others, *commandment*　[m] Other ancient authorities lack *of the blind*

the dogs eat the crumbs that fall from their masters' table." [28]Then Jesus answered her, "Woman, great is your faith! Let it be done for you as you wish." And her daughter was healed instantly.

Jesus Cures Many People

29 After Jesus had left that place, he passed along the Sea of Galilee, and he went up the mountain, where he sat down. [30]Great crowds came to him, bringing with them the lame, the maimed, the blind, the mute, and many others. They put them at his feet, and he cured them, [31]so that the crowd was amazed when they saw the mute speaking, the maimed whole, the lame walking, and the blind seeing. And they praised the God of Israel.

Feeding the Four Thousand

32 Then Jesus called his disciples to him and said, "I have compassion for the crowd, because they have been with me now for three days and have nothing to eat; and I do not want to send them away hungry, for they might faint on the way." [33]The disciples said to him, "Where are we to get enough bread in the desert to feed so great a crowd?" [34]Jesus asked them, "How many loaves have you?" They said, "Seven, and a few small fish." [35]Then ordering the crowd to sit down on the ground, [36]he took the seven loaves and the fish; and after giving thanks he broke them and gave them to the disciples, and the disciples gave them to the crowds. [37]And all of them ate and were filled; and they took up the broken pieces left over, seven baskets full. [38]Those who had eaten were four thousand men, besides women and children. [39]After sending away the crowds, he got into the boat and went to the region of Mag´a·dan.[n]

The Demand for a Sign

16 The Phar´i·sees and Sad´du·cees came, and to test Jesus[o] they asked him to show them a sign from heaven. [2]He answered them, "When it is evening, you say, 'It will be fair weather, for the sky is red.' [3]And in the morning, 'It will be stormy today, for the sky is red and threatening.' You know how to interpret the appearance of the sky, but you cannot interpret the signs of the times.[p] [4]An evil and adulterous generation asks for a sign, but no sign will be given to it except the sign of Jonah." Then he left them and went away.

The Yeast of the Pharisees and Sadducees

5 When the disciples reached the other side, they had forgotten to bring any bread. [6]Jesus said to them, "Watch out, and beware of the yeast of the Phar´i·sees and Sad´du·cees." [7]They said to one another, "It is because we have brought no bread." [8]And becoming aware of it, Jesus said, "You of little faith, why are you talking about having no bread? [9]Do you still not perceive? Do you not remember the five loaves for the five thousand, and how many baskets you gathered? [10]Or the seven loaves for the four thousand, and how many baskets you gathered? [11]How could you fail to perceive that I was not speaking about bread? Beware of the yeast of the Phar´i·sees and Sad´du·cees!" [12]Then they understood that he had not told them to beware of the yeast of bread, but of the teaching of the Phar´i·sees and Sad´du·cees.

Peter's Declaration about Jesus

13 Now when Jesus came into the district of Caes·a·re´a Phi·lip´pi, he asked his disciples, "Who do people say that the Son of Man is?" [14]And they said, "Some say John the Baptist, but others E·li´jah, and still others Jer·e·mi´ah or one of the prophets." [15]He said to them, "But who do you say that I am?" [16]Simon Peter answered, "You are the Messiah,[q] the Son of the living God." [17]And Jesus

[n] Other ancient authorities read *Magdala* or *Magdalan* [o] Gk *him* [p] Other ancient authorities lack [2]*When it is . . . of the times* [q] Or *the Christ*

Peter's given name was Simon. He was also called Cephas. Jesus renamed him Peter, which means "rock." He was the most outspoken of all Jesus's disciples. His natural leadership qualities made him the spokesperson of the Twelve. Peter was one of the first of Jesus's followers to recognize that Jesus was the Messiah sent from God. Jesus recognized Peter's deep faith as an important quality for building God's church here on earth. He declared, "You are Peter, and on this rock I will build my church." But soon after, Jesus calls Peter a "stumbling block." Even the strongest and most faithful people sometimes make mistakes.

answered him, "Blessed are you, Simon son of Jonah! For flesh and blood has not revealed this to you, but my Father in heaven. [18]And I tell you, you are Peter,[r] and on this rock[s] I will build my church, and the gates of Hades will not prevail against it. [19]I will give you the keys of the kingdom of heaven, and whatever you bind on earth will be bound in heaven, and whatever you loose on earth will be loosed in heaven." [20]Then he sternly ordered the disciples not to tell anyone that he was[t] the Messiah.

Jesus Foretells His Death and Resurrection

21 From that time on, Jesus began to show his disciples that he must go to Jerusalem and undergo great suffering at the hands of the elders and chief priests and scribes, and be killed, and on the third day be raised. [22]And Peter took him aside and began to rebuke him, saying, "God forbid it, Lord! This must never happen to you." [23]But he turned and said to Peter, "Get behind me, Satan! You are a stumbling block to me; for you are setting your mind not on divine things but on human things."

The Cross and Self-Denial

24 Then Jesus told his disciples, "If any want to become my followers, let them deny themselves and take up their cross and follow me. [25]For those who want to save their life will lose it, and those who lose their life for my sake will find it. [26]For what will it profit them if they gain the whole world but forfeit their life? Or what will they give in return for their life?

27 "For the Son of Man is to come with his angels in the glory of his Father, and then he will repay everyone for what has been done. [28]Truly I tell you, there are some standing here who will not taste death before they see the Son of Man coming in his kingdom."

The Transfiguration

17 Six days later, Jesus took with him Peter and James and his brother John and led them up a high mountain, by themselves. [2]And he was transfigured before them, and his face shone like the sun, and his clothes became dazzling white. [3]Suddenly there appeared to them Moses and Elijah, talking with him. [4]Then Peter said to Jesus, "Lord, it is good for us to be here; if you wish, I[u] will make three dwellings[v] here, one for you, one for Moses, and one for Elijah." [5]While he was still speaking, suddenly a bright cloud overshadowed them, and from the cloud a voice said, "This is my Son, the Beloved;[w] with him I am well pleased; listen to him!" [6]When the disciples heard this, they fell to the ground and were overcome by fear. [7]But Jesus came and touched them, saying, "Get up and do not be afraid." [8]And when they looked up, they saw no one except Jesus himself alone.

[r] Gk Petros   [s] Gk petra   [t] Other ancient authorities add Jesus   [u] Other ancient authorities read we   [v] Or tents   [w] Or my beloved Son

9 As they were coming down the mountain, Jesus ordered them, "Tell no one about the vision until after the Son of Man has been raised from the dead." [10]And the disciples asked him, "Why, then, do the scribes say that E·lī´jah must come first?" [11]He replied, "E·lī´jah is indeed coming and will restore all things; [12]but I tell you that E·lī´jah has already come, and they did not recognize him, but they did to him whatever they pleased. So also the Son of Man is about to suffer at their hands." [13]Then the disciples understood that he was speaking to them about John the Baptist.

Jesus Cures a Boy with a Demon

14 When they came to the crowd, a man came to him, knelt before him, [15]and said, "Lord, have mercy on my son, for he is an epileptic and he suffers terribly; he often falls into the fire and often into the water. [16]And I brought him to your disciples, but they could not cure him." [17]Jesus answered, "You faithless and perverse generation, how much longer must I be with you? How much longer must I put up with you? Bring him here to me." [18]And Jesus rebuked the demon,[x] and it[y] came out of him, and the boy was cured instantly. [19]Then the disciples came to Jesus privately and said, "Why could we not cast it out?" [20]He said to them, "Because of your little faith. For truly I tell you, if you have faith the size of a[z] mustard seed, you will say to this mountain, 'Move from here to there,' and it will move; and nothing will be impossible for you."[a]

Jesus Again Foretells His Death and Resurrection

22 As they were gathering[b] in Galilee, Jesus said to them, "The Son of Man is going to be betrayed into human hands, [23]and they will kill him, and on the third day he will be raised." And they were greatly distressed.

Jesus and the Temple Tax

24 When they reached Ca·per´na·um, the collectors of the temple tax[c] came to Peter and said, "Does your teacher not pay the temple tax?"[c] [25]He said, "Yes, he does." And when he came home, Jesus spoke of it first, asking, "What do you think, Simon? From whom do kings of the earth take toll or tribute? From their children or from others?" [26]When Peter[d] said, "From others," Jesus said to him, "Then the children are free. [27]However, so that we do not give offense to them, go to the sea and cast a hook; take the first fish that comes up; and when you open its mouth, you will find a coin;[e] take that and give it to them for you and me."

True Greatness

18 At that time the disciples came to Jesus and asked, "Who is the greatest in the kingdom of heaven?" [2]He called a child, whom he put among them, [3]and said, "Truly I tell you, unless you change and become like children, you will never enter the kingdom of heaven. [4]Whoever becomes humble like this child is the greatest in the kingdom of heaven. [5]Whoever welcomes one such child in my name welcomes me.

Temptations to Sin

6 "If any of you put a stumbling block before one of these little ones who believe in me, it would be better for you if a great millstone were fastened around your neck and you were drowned in the depth of the sea. [7]Woe to the world because of stumbling blocks! Occasions for stumbling are bound to come, but woe to the one by whom the stumbling block comes!

8 "If your hand or your foot causes you to stumble, cut it off and throw it away; it is better for you to enter life maimed or lame than to have two hands or two feet and to be thrown into the

---

[x] Gk it or him [y] Gk the demon [z] Gk faith as a grain of [a] Other ancient authorities add verse 21, But this kind does not come out except by prayer and fasting [b] Other ancient authorities read living [c] Gk didrachma [d] Gk he [e] Gk stater; the stater was worth two didrachmas

Jesus reminds his disciples that God expects us to take care of all people, especially those who are helpless and have no one else to care for them. What are some ways we can care for people in need?

eternal fire. [9]And if your eye causes you to stumble, tear it out and throw it away; it is better for you to enter life with one eye than to have two eyes and to be thrown into the hell[f] of fire.

The Parable of the Lost Sheep

[10] "Take care that you do not despise one of these little ones; for, I tell you, in heaven their angels continually see the face of my Father in heaven.[g] [12]What do you think? If a shepherd has a hundred sheep, and one of them has gone astray, does he not leave the ninety-nine on the mountains and go in search of the one that went astray? [13]And if he finds it, truly I tell you, he rejoices over it more than over the ninety-nine that never went astray. [14]So it is not the will of your[h] Father in heaven that one of these little ones should be lost.

Reproving Another Who Sins

[15] "If another member of the church[i] sins against you,[j] go and point out the fault when the two of you are alone. If the member[k] listens to you, you have regained that one. [16]But if you are not listened to, take one or two others along with you, so that every word may be confirmed by the evidence of two or three witnesses. [17]If the member refuses to listen to them, tell it to the church; and if the offender refuses to listen even to the church, let such a one be to you as a Gentile and a tax collector. [18]Truly I tell you, whatever you bind on earth will be bound in heaven, and whatever you loose on earth will be loosed in heaven. [19]Again, truly I tell you, if two of you agree on earth about anything you ask, it will be done for you by my Father

in heaven. [20]For where two or three are gathered in my name, I am there among them."

Forgiveness

[21] Then Peter came and said to him, "Lord, if another member of the church[l] sins against me, how often should I forgive? As many as seven times?" [22]Jesus said to him, "Not seven times, but, I tell you, seventy-seven[m] times.

The Parable of the Unforgiving Servant

[23] "For this reason the kingdom of heaven may be compared to a king who wished to settle accounts with his slaves. [24]When he began the reckoning, one who owed him ten thousand talents[n] was brought to him; [25]and, as he could not pay, his lord ordered him to be sold, together with his wife and children and all his possessions, and payment to be made. [26]So the slave fell on his knees before him, saying, 'Have patience with me, and I will pay you everything.' [27]And out of pity for him, the lord of that slave released him and forgave him the debt. [28]But that same slave, as he went out, came upon one of his fellow slaves who owed him a hundred denarii;[o] and seizing him by the throat, he said, 'Pay what you owe.' [29]Then his fellow slave fell down and pleaded with him, 'Have patience with me, and I will pay you.' [30]But he refused; then he went and threw him into prison until he would pay the debt. [31]When his fellow slaves saw what had happened, they were greatly distressed, and they went and reported to their lord all that had taken place. [32]Then his lord summoned

[f] Gk Gehenna   [g] Other ancient authorities add verse 11, *For the Son of Man came to save the lost*
[h] Other ancient authorities read *my*   [i] Gk *If your brother*   [j] Other ancient authorities lack *against you*   [k] Gk *the brother*   [l] Gk *if my brother*
[m] Or *seventy times seven*   [n] A talent was worth more than fifteen years' wages of a laborer
[o] The denarius was the usual day's wage for a laborer

"Let the little children come to me, and do not stop them; for it is to such as these that the kingdom of heaven belongs."
Matthew 19:14

him and said to him, 'You wicked slave! I forgave you all that debt because you pleaded with me. [33]Should you not have had mercy on your fellow slave, as I had mercy on you?' [34]And in anger his lord handed him over to be tortured until he would pay his entire debt. [35]So my heavenly Father will also do to every one of you, if you do not forgive your brother or sister[p] from your heart."

Teaching about Divorce

19 When Jesus had finished saying these things, he left Galilee and went to the region of Judea beyond the Jordan. [2]Large crowds followed him, and he cured them there.

3 Some Phar'i·sees came to him, and to test him they asked, "Is it lawful for a man to divorce his wife for any cause?" [4]He answered, "Have you not read that the one who made them at the beginning 'made them male and female,' [5]and said, 'For this reason a man shall leave his father and mother and be joined to his wife, and the two shall become one flesh'? [6]So they are no longer two, but one flesh. Therefore what God has joined together, let no one separate." [7]They said to him, "Why then did Moses command us to give a certificate of dismissal and to divorce her?" [8]He said to them, "It was because you were so hard-hearted that Moses allowed you to divorce your wives, but from the beginning it was not so. [9]And I say to you, whoever divorces his wife, except for unchastity, and marries another commits adultery."[q]

10 His disciples said to him, "If such is the case of a man with his wife, it is better not to marry." [11]But he said to them, "Not everyone can accept this teaching, but only those to whom it is given. [12]For there are eunuchs who have been so from birth, and there are eunuchs who have been made eunuchs by others, and there are eunuchs who have made themselves eunuchs for the sake of the kingdom of heaven. Let anyone accept this who can."

Jesus Blesses Little Children

13 Then little children were being brought to him in order that he might lay his hands on them and pray. The disciples spoke sternly to those who brought them; [14]but Jesus said, "Let the little children come to me, and do not stop them; for it is to such as these that the kingdom of heaven belongs." [15]And he laid his hands on them and went on his way.

The Rich Young Man

16 Then someone came to him and said, "Teacher, what good deed must I do to have eternal life?" [17]And he said to him, "Why do you ask me about what is good? There is only one who is good. If you wish to enter into life, keep the commandments." [18]He said to him, "Which ones?" And Jesus said, "You shall not murder; You shall not commit adultery; You shall not steal; You shall not bear false witness; [19]Honor your father and mother; also, You shall love your neighbor as yourself." [20]The young man said to him, "I have kept all these;[r] what do I still lack?" [21]Jesus said to him, "If you wish to be perfect, go, sell your possessions, and give the money[s] to the poor, and you will have treasure in heaven; then come, follow me." [22]When the young man heard this word, he went away grieving, for he had many possessions.

23 Then Jesus said to his disciples, "Truly I tell you, it will be hard for a rich person to enter the kingdom of heaven.

[p] Gk brother　　[q] Other ancient authorities read except on the ground of unchastity, causes her to commit adultery; others add at the end of the verse and he who marries a divorced woman commits adultery
[r] Other ancient authorities add from my youth
[s] Gk lacks the money

²⁴Again I tell you, it is easier for a camel to go through the eye of a needle than for someone who is rich to enter the kingdom of God." ²⁵When the disciples heard this, they were greatly astounded and said, "Then who can be saved?" ²⁶But Jesus looked at them and said, "For mortals it is impossible, but for God all things are possible."

27 Then Peter said in reply, "Look, we have left everything and followed you. What then will we have?" ²⁸Jesus said to them, "Truly I tell you, at the renewal of all things, when the Son of Man is seated on the throne of his glory, you who have followed me will also sit on twelve thrones, judging the twelve tribes of Israel. ²⁹And everyone who has left houses or brothers or sisters or father or mother or children or fields, for my name's sake, will receive a hundredfold,ᵗ and will inherit eternal life. ³⁰But many who are first will be last, and the last will be first.

The Laborers in the Vineyard

20 "For the kingdom of heaven is like a landowner who went out early in the morning to hire laborers for his vineyard. ²After agreeing with the laborers for the usual daily wage,ᵘ he sent them into his vineyard. ³When he went out about nine o'clock, he saw others standing idle in the marketplace; ⁴and he said to them, 'You also go into the vineyard, and I will pay you whatever is right.' So they went. ⁵When he went out again about noon and about three o'clock, he did the same. ⁶And about five o'clock he went out and found others standing around; and he said to them, 'Why are you standing here idle all day?' ⁷They said to him, 'Because no one has hired us.' He said to them, 'You also go into the vineyard.' ⁸When evening came, the owner of the vineyard said to his manager, 'Call the laborers and give them their pay, beginning with the last and then going to the first.' ⁹When those hired about five o'clock came, each of them received the usual daily wage.ᵘ ¹⁰Now when the first came, they thought they would receive more; but each of them also received the usual daily wage.ᵘ ¹¹And when they received it, they grumbled against the landowner, ¹²saying, 'These last worked only one hour, and you have made them equal to us who have borne the burden of the day and the scorching heat.' ¹³But he replied to one of them, 'Friend, I am doing you no wrong; did you not agree with me for the usual daily wage?ᵘ ¹⁴Take what belongs to you and go; I choose to give to this last the same as I give to you. ¹⁵Am I not allowed to do what I choose with what belongs to me? Or are you envious because I am generous?'ᵛ ¹⁶So the last will be first, and the first will be last."ʷ

A Third Time Jesus Foretells His Death and Resurrection

17 While Jesus was going up to Jerusalem, he took the twelve disciples aside by themselves, and said to them on the way, ¹⁸"See, we are going up to Jerusalem, and the Son of Man will be handed over to the chief priests and scribes, and they will condemn him to death; ¹⁹then they will hand him over to the Gentiles to be mocked and flogged and crucified; and on the third day he will be raised."

The Request of the Mother of James and John

20 Then the mother of the sons of Zeb´e·dee came to him with her sons, and kneeling before him, she asked a favor of him. ²¹And he said to her, "What do you want?" She said to him, "Declare that these two sons of mine will sit, one at your right hand and one at your left, in your kingdom." ²²But Jesus answered, "You do not know what you are asking. Are you able to drink the cup that I am

---

ᵗ Other ancient authorities read *manifold*   ᵘ Gk *a denarius*   ᵛ Gk *is your eye evil because I am good?*   ʷ Other ancient authorities add *for many are called but few are chosen* about to drink?"[x] They said to him, "We are able." [23]He said to them, "You will indeed drink my cup, but to sit at my right hand and at my left, this is not mine to grant, but it is for those for whom it has been prepared by my Father."

24 When the ten heard it, they were angry with the two brothers. [25]But Jesus called them to him and said, "You know that the rulers of the Gentiles lord it over them, and their great ones are tyrants over them. [26]It will not be so among you; but whoever wishes to be great among you must be your servant, [27]and whoever wishes to be first among you must be your slave; [28]just as the Son of Man came not to be served but to serve, and to give his life a ransom for many."

Jesus Heals Two Blind Men

29 As they were leaving Jericho, a large crowd followed him. [30]There were two blind men sitting by the roadside. When they heard that Jesus was passing by, they shouted, "Lord,[y] have mercy on us, Son of David!" [31]The crowd sternly ordered them to be quiet; but they shouted even more loudly, "Have mercy on us, Lord, Son of David!" [32]Jesus stood still and called them, saying, "What do you want me to do for you?" [33]They said to him, "Lord, let our eyes be opened." [34]Moved with compassion, Jesus touched their eyes. Immediately they regained their sight and followed him.

Jesus' Triumphal Entry into Jerusalem

21 When they had come near Jerusalem and had reached Beth′pha·ge, at the Mount of Olives, Jesus sent two disciples, [2]saying to them,

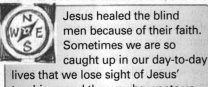

Jesus healed the blind men because of their faith. Sometimes we are so caught up in our day-to-day lives that we lose sight of Jesus' teachings and the way he wants us to live.

Jesus rode into Jerusalem on a donkey rather than a horse as a conquering king would have done. He wanted people to know that he was the Prince of Peace.

"Go into the village ahead of you, and immediately you will find a donkey tied, and a colt with her; untie them and bring them to me. [3]If anyone says anything to you, just say this, 'The Lord needs them.' And he will send them immediately.[z]" [4]This took place to fulfill what had been spoken through the prophet, saying,

[5] "Tell the daughter of Zion,
   Look, your king is coming to you,
      humble, and mounted on a donkey,
         and on a colt, the foal of a donkey."

[6]The disciples went and did as Jesus had directed them; [7]they brought the donkey and the colt, and put their cloaks on them, and he sat on them. [8]A very large crowd[a] spread their cloaks on the road, and others cut branches from the trees and spread them on the road. [9]The crowds that went ahead of him and that followed were shouting,

"Hosanna to the Son of David!
   Blessed is the one who comes in the name of the Lord!
Hosanna in the highest heaven!"

[10]When he entered Jerusalem, the whole city was in turmoil, asking, "Who is this?" [11]The crowds were saying, "This is the prophet Jesus from Nazareth in Galilee."

Jesus Cleanses the Temple

12 Then Jesus entered the temple[b] and drove out all who were selling and buying in the temple, and he overturned the tables of the money changers and the seats of those who sold doves. [13]He said to them, "It is written,

x Other ancient authorities add *or to be baptized with the baptism that I am baptized with?*   y Other ancient authorities lack *Lord*   z Or *'The Lord needs them and will send them back immediately.'*   a Or *Most of the crowd*   b Other ancient authorities add *of God*

'My house shall be called a house of
prayer';
but you are making it a den of
robbers."

14 The blind and the lame came to
him in the temple, and he cured them.
[15]But when the chief priests and the scribes
saw the amazing things that he did, and
heard[c] the children crying out in the temple, "Hosanna to the Son of David," they
became angry [16]and said to him, "Do you
hear what these are saying?" Jesus said to
them, "Yes; have you never read,
'Out of the mouths of infants and
nursing babies
you have prepared praise for
yourself'?"
[17]He left them, went out of the city to
Beth´a·ny, and spent the night there.

Jesus Curses the Fig Tree

18 In the morning, when he returned
to the city, he was hungry. [19]And seeing a
fig tree by the side of the road, he went to
it and found nothing at all on it but
leaves. Then he said to it, "May no fruit
ever come from you again!" And the fig
tree withered at once. [20]When the disciples saw it, they were amazed, saying,
"How did the fig tree wither at once?"
[21]Jesus answered them, "Truly I tell you, if
you have faith and do not doubt, not only
will you do what has been done to the fig
tree, but even if you say to this mountain,
'Be lifted up and thrown into the sea,' it
will be done. [22]Whatever you ask for in
prayer with faith, you will receive."

The Authority of Jesus Questioned

23 When he entered the temple, the
chief priests and the elders of the people came to him as he was teaching,
and said, "By what authority are you
doing these things, and who gave you
this authority?" [24]Jesus said to them, "I
will also ask you one question; if you
tell me the answer, then I will also tell
you by what authority I do these
things. [25]Did the baptism of John come
from heaven, or was it of human origin?" And they argued with one
another, "If we say, 'From heaven,' he
will say to us, 'Why then did you not
believe him?' [26]But if we say, 'Of human
origin,' we are afraid of the crowd; for
all regard John as a prophet." [27]So they
answered Jesus, "We do not know."
And he said to them, "Neither will I tell
you by what authority I am doing these
things.

The Parable of the Two Sons

28 "What do you think? A man had
two sons; he went to the first and said,
'Son, go and work in the vineyard today.'
[29]He answered, 'I will not'; but later he
changed his mind and went. [30]The
father[d] went to the second and said the
same; and he answered, 'I go, sir'; but he
did not go. [31]Which of the two did the
will of his father?" They said, "The first."
Jesus said to them, "Truly I tell you, the
tax collectors and the prostitutes are
going into the kingdom of God ahead of
you. [32]For John came to you in the way
of righteousness and you did not believe
him, but the tax collectors and the prostitutes believed him; and even after you
saw it, you did not change your minds
and believe him.

The temple in this
story was built by King
Herod the Great. It was
the same size as the original one
built by Solomon, but it was
much more spectacular. The
temple was made of polished
white stone and trimmed with
gold. This temple was completed in 63 AD but destroyed by
the Romans in 70 AD. One wall,
known as the "Wailing Wall,"
remains, and Jews still travel to
Jerusalem to pray there.

[c] Gk lacks *heard*   [d] Gk *He*

The Parable of the Wicked Tenants

33 "Listen to another parable. There was a landowner who planted a vineyard, put a fence around it, dug a wine press in it, and built a watchtower. Then he leased it to tenants and went to another country. ³⁴When the harvest time had come, he sent his slaves to the tenants to collect his produce. ³⁵But the tenants seized his slaves and beat one, killed another, and stoned another. ³⁶Again he sent other slaves, more than the first; and they treated them in the same way. ³⁷Finally he sent his son to them, saying, 'They will respect my son.' ³⁸But when the tenants saw the son, they said to themselves, 'This is the heir; come, let us kill him and get his inheritance.' ³⁹So they seized him, threw him out of the vineyard, and killed him. ⁴⁰Now when the owner of the vineyard comes, what will he do to those tenants?" ⁴¹They said to him, "He will put those wretches to a miserable death, and lease the vineyard to other tenants who will give him the produce at the harvest time."

42 Jesus said to them, "Have you never read in the scriptures:

'The stone that the builders rejected
    has become the cornerstone;ᵉ
this was the Lord's doing,
    and it is amazing in our eyes'?

⁴³Therefore I tell you, the kingdom of God will be taken away from you and given to a people that produces the fruits of the kingdom.ᶠ ⁴⁴The one who falls on this stone will be broken to pieces; and it will crush anyone on whom it falls."ᵍ

45 When the chief priests and the Phar·i·sees heard his parables, they realized that he was speaking about them. ⁴⁶They wanted to arrest him, but they feared the crowds, because they regarded him as a prophet.

The Parable of the Wedding Banquet

22 Once more Jesus spoke to them in parables, saying: ²"The kingdom of heaven may be compared to a king who gave a wedding banquet for his son. ³He sent his slaves to call those who had been invited to the wedding banquet, but they would not come. ⁴Again he sent other slaves, saying, 'Tell those who have been invited: Look, I have prepared my dinner, my oxen and my fat calves have been slaughtered, and everything is ready; come to the wedding banquet.' ⁵But they made light of it and went away, one to his farm, another to his business, ⁶while the rest seized his slaves, mistreated them, and killed them. ⁷The king was enraged. He sent his troops, destroyed those murderers, and burned their city. ⁸Then he said to his slaves, 'The wedding is ready, but those invited were not worthy. ⁹Go therefore into the main streets, and invite everyone you find to the wedding banquet.' ¹⁰Those slaves went out into the streets and gathered all whom they found, both good and bad; so the wedding hall was filled with guests.

11 "But when the king came in to see the guests, he noticed a man there who was not wearing a wedding robe, ¹²and he said to him, 'Friend, how did you get in here without a wedding robe?' And he was speechless. ¹³Then the king said to the attendants, 'Bind him hand and foot, and throw him into the outer darkness, where there will be weeping and gnashing of teeth.' ¹⁴For many are called, but few are chosen."

The Question about Paying Taxes

15 Then the Phar·i·sees went and plotted to entrap him in what he said. ¹⁶So they sent their disciples to him, along with the He·rō´di·ans, saying, "Teacher, we know that you are sincere, and teach the way of God in accordance with truth, and show deference to no one; for you do not regard people with partiality. ¹⁷Tell us, then, what you think.

ᵉ Or *keystone*   ᶠ Gk *the fruits of it*   ᵍ Other ancient authorities lack verse 44

Is it lawful to pay taxes to the emperor, or not?" [18]But Jesus, aware of their malice, said, "Why are you putting me to the test, you hypocrites? [19]Show me the coin used for the tax." And they brought him a denarius. [20]Then he said to them, "Whose head is this, and whose title?" [21]They answered, "The emperor's." Then he said to them, "Give therefore to the emperor the things that are the emperor's, and to God the things that are God's." [22]When they heard this, they were amazed; and they left him and went away.

The Question about the Resurrection

23 The same day some Sad′du·cees came to him, saying there is no resurrection;[h] and they asked him a question, saying, [24]"Teacher, Moses said, 'If a man dies childless, his brother shall marry the widow, and raise up children for his brother.' [25]Now there were seven brothers among us; the first married, and died childless, leaving the widow to his brother. [26]The second did the same, so also the third, down to the seventh. [27]Last of all, the woman herself died. [28]In the resurrection, then, whose wife of the seven will she be? For all of them had married her."

29 Jesus answered them, "You are wrong, because you know neither the scriptures nor the power of God. [30]For in the resurrection they neither marry nor are given in marriage, but are like angels[i] in heaven. [31]And as for the resurrection of the dead, have you not read what was said to you by God, [32]'I am the God of Abraham, the God of Isaac, and the God of Jacob'? He is God not of the dead, but of the living." [33]And when the crowd heard it, they were astounded at his teaching.

The Greatest Commandment

34 When the Phar′i·sees heard that he had silenced the Sad′du·cees, they gathered together, [35]and one of them, a lawyer, asked him a question to test him. [36]"Teacher, which commandment in the

"'You shall love the Lord your God with all your heart, and with all your soul, and with all your mind.' This is the greatest and first commandment. And a second is like it: 'You shall love your neighbor as yourself.' On these two commandments hang all the law and the prophets." Matthew 22:37–40

law is the greatest?" [37]He said to him, "'You shall love the Lord your God with all your heart, and with all your soul, and with all your mind.' [38]This is the greatest and first commandment. [39]And a second is like it: 'You shall love your neighbor as yourself.' [40]On these two commandments hang all the law and the prophets."

The Question about David's Son

41 Now while the Phar′i·sees were gathered together, Jesus asked them this question: [42]"What do you think of the Messiah?[j] Whose son is he?" They said to him, "The son of David." [43]He said to them, "How is it then that David by the Spirit[k] calls him Lord, saying,
44 'The Lord said to my Lord,
"Sit at my right hand,
until I put your enemies under your feet"'?
[45]If David thus calls him Lord, how can he be his son?" [46]No one was able to give him an answer, nor from that day did anyone dare to ask him any more questions.

Jesus Denounces Scribes and Pharisees

23 Then Jesus said to the crowds and to his disciples, [2]"The scribes and the Phar′i·sees sit on Moses' seat; [3]therefore, do whatever they teach you and follow it; but do not do as they do, for they do not practice what they teach. [4]They tie up heavy burdens, hard to bear,[l] and lay them on the shoulders of

[h] Other ancient authorities read *who say that there is no resurrection* [i] Other ancient authorities add *of God* [j] Or *Christ* [k] Gk *in spirit*

others; but they themselves are unwilling to lift a finger to move them. [5]They do all their deeds to be seen by others; for they make their phylacteries broad and their fringes long. [6]They love to have the place of honor at banquets and the best seats in the synagogues, [7]and to be greeted with respect in the marketplaces, and to have people call them rabbi. [8]But you are not to be called rabbi, for you have one teacher, and you are all students.[m] [9]And call no one your father on earth, for you have one Father—the one in heaven. [10]Nor are you to be called instructors, for you have one instructor, the Messiah.[n] [11]The greatest among you will be your servant. [12]All who exalt themselves will be humbled, and all who humble themselves will be exalted.

13 "But woe to you, scribes and Phar'i·sees, hypocrites! For you lock people out of the kingdom of heaven. For you do not go in yourselves, and when others are going in, you stop them.[o] [15]Woe to you, scribes and Phar'i·sees, hypocrites! For you cross sea and land to make a single convert, and you make the new convert twice as much a child of hell[p] as yourselves.

16 "Woe to you, blind guides, who say, 'Whoever swears by the sanctuary is bound by nothing, but whoever swears by the gold of the sanctuary is bound by the oath.' [17]You blind fools! For which is greater, the gold or the sanctuary that has made the gold sacred? [18]And you say, 'Whoever swears by the altar is bound by nothing, but whoever swears by the gift that is on the altar is bound by the oath.' [19]How blind you are! For which is greater, the gift or the altar that makes the gift sacred? [20]So whoever swears by the altar, swears by it and by everything on it; [21]and whoever swears by the sanctuary, swears by it and by the one who dwells in it; [22]and whoever swears by heaven, swears by the throne of God and by the one who is seated upon it.

23 "Woe to you, scribes and Phar'-

i·sees, hypocrites! For you tithe mint, dill, and cummin, and have neglected the weightier matters of the law: justice and mercy and faith. It is these you ought to have practiced without neglecting the others. [24]You blind guides! You strain out a gnat but swallow a camel!

25 "Woe to you, scribes and Phar'-i·sees, hypocrites! For you clean the outside of the cup and of the plate, but inside they are full of greed and self-indulgence. [26]You blind Phar'i·see! First clean the inside of the cup,[q] so that the outside also may become clean.

27 "Woe to you, scribes and Phar'-i·sees, hypocrites! For you are like white-washed tombs, which on the outside look beautiful, but inside they are full of the bones of the dead and of all kinds of filth. [28]So you also on the outside look righteous to others, but inside you are full of hypocrisy and lawlessness.

29 "Woe to you, scribes and Phar'-i·sees, hypocrites! For you build the tombs of the prophets and decorate the graves of the righteous, [30]and you say, 'If we had lived in the days of our ancestors, we would not have taken part with them in shedding the blood of the prophets.' [31]Thus you testify against yourselves that you are descendants of those who murdered the prophets. [32]Fill up, then, the measure of your ancestors. [33]You snakes, you brood of vipers! How can you escape being sentenced to hell?[r] [34]Therefore I send you prophets, sages, and scribes, some of whom you will kill and crucify, and some you will flog in your synagogues and pursue from town to town, [35]so that upon you may come all the righteous blood shed on earth,

---

[l] Other ancient authorities lack *hard to bear*   [m] Gk *brothers*   [n] Or *the Christ*   [o] Other authorities add here (or after verse 12) verse 14, *Woe to you, scribes and Pharisees, hypocrites! For you devour widows' houses and for the sake of appearance you make long prayers; therefore you will receive the greater condemnation*   [p] Gk *Gehenna*   [q] Other ancient authorities add *and of the plate*

from the blood of righteous Abel to the blood of Zech·a·rī´ah son of Bar·a·chī´ah, whom you murdered between the sanctuary and the altar. ³⁶Truly I tell you, all this will come upon this generation.

The Lament over Jerusalem

37 "Jerusalem, Jerusalem, the city that kills the prophets and stones those who are sent to it! How often have I desired to gather your children together as a hen gathers her brood under her wings, and you were not willing! ³⁸See, your house is left to you, desolate.�q ³⁹For I tell you, you will not see me again until you say, 'Blessed is the one who comes in the name of the Lord.' "

The Destruction of the Temple Foretold

24 As Jesus came out of the temple and was going away, his disciples came to point out to him the buildings of the temple. ²Then he asked them, "You see all these, do you not? Truly I tell you, not one stone will be left here upon another; all will be thrown down."

Signs of the End of the Age

3 When he was sitting on the Mount of Olives, the disciples came to him privately, saying, "Tell us, when will this be, and what will be the sign of your coming and of the end of the age?" ⁴Jesus answered them, "Beware that no one leads you astray. ⁵For many will come in my name, saying, 'I am the Messiah!'ʳ and they will lead many astray. ⁶And you will hear of wars and rumors of wars; see that you are not alarmed; for this must take place, but the end is not yet. ⁷For nation will rise against nation, and kingdom against kingdom, and there will be faminesˢ and earthquakes in various places: ⁸all this is but the beginning of the birth pangs.

Persecutions Foretold

9 "Then they will hand you over to be tortured and will put you to death, and you will be hated by all nations because of my name. ¹⁰Then many will fall away,ᵗ and they will betray one another and hate one another. ¹¹And many false prophets will arise and lead many astray. ¹²And because of the increase of lawlessness, the love of many will grow cold. ¹³But the one who endures to the end will be saved. ¹⁴And this good newsᵘ of the kingdom will be proclaimed throughout the world, as a testimony to all the nations; and then the end will come.

The Desolating Sacrilege

15 "So when you see the desolating sacrilege standing in the holy place, as was spoken of by the prophet Daniel (let the reader understand), ¹⁶then those in Judea must flee to the mountains; ¹⁷the one on the housetop must not go down to take what is in the house; ¹⁸the one in the field must not turn back to get a coat. ¹⁹Woe to those who are pregnant and to those who are nursing infants in those days! ²⁰Pray that your flight may not be in winter or on a sabbath. ²¹For at that time there will be great suffering, such as has not been from the beginning of the world until now, no, and never will be. ²²And if those days had not been cut short, no one would be saved; but for the sake of the elect those days will be cut short. ²³Then if anyone says to you, 'Look! Here is the Messiah!'ʳ or 'There he is!'— do not believe it. ²⁴For false messiahsᵛ and false prophets will appear and produce great signs and omens, to lead astray, if possible, even the elect. ²⁵Take note, I have told you beforehand. ²⁶So, if they say to you, 'Look! He is in the wilderness,' do not go out. If they say, 'Look! He is in the inner rooms,' do not believe it. ²⁷For as the lightning comes from the east and flashes as far as the west, so will be the coming of the Son of

---

q Other ancient authorities lack *desolate*   r Or *the Christ*   s Other ancient authorities add *and pestilences*   t Or *stumble*   u Or *gospel*   v Or *christs*

Man. [28]Wherever the corpse is, there the vultures will gather.

The Coming of the Son of Man

29 "Immediately after the suffering of those days

the sun will be darkened,
and the moon will not give its
light;
the stars will fall from heaven,
and the powers of heaven will be
shaken.

[30]Then the sign of the Son of Man will appear in heaven, and then all the tribes of the earth will mourn, and they will see 'the Son of Man coming on the clouds of heaven' with power and great glory. [31]And he will send out his angels with a loud trumpet call, and they will gather his elect from the four winds, from one end of heaven to the other.

The Lesson of the Fig Tree

32 "From the fig tree learn its lesson: as soon as its branch becomes tender and puts forth its leaves, you know that summer is near. [33]So also, when you see all these things, you know that he[w] is near, at the very gates. [34]Truly I tell you, this generation will not pass away until all these things have taken place. [35]Heaven and earth will pass away, but my words will not pass away.

The Necessity for Watchfulness

36 "But about that day and hour no one knows, neither the angels of heaven, nor the Son,[x] but only the Father. [37]For as the days of Noah were, so will be the coming of the Son of Man. [38]For as in those days before the flood they were eating and drinking, marrying and giving in marriage, until the day Noah entered the ark, [39]and they knew nothing until the flood came and swept them all away, so too will be the coming of the Son of Man. [40]Then two will be in the field; one will be taken and one will be left. [41]Two women will be grinding meal together; one will be taken and one will be left.

[42]Keep awake therefore, for you do not know on what day[y] your Lord is coming. [43]But understand this: if the owner of the house had known in what part of the night the thief was coming, he would have stayed awake and would not have let his house be broken into. [44]Therefore you also must be ready, for the Son of Man is coming at an unexpected hour.

The Faithful or the Unfaithful Slave

45 "Who then is the faithful and wise slave, whom his master has put in charge of his household, to give the other slaves[z] their allowance of food at the proper time? [46]Blessed is that slave whom his master will find at work when he arrives. [47]Truly I tell you, he will put that one in charge of all his possessions. [48]But if that wicked slave says to himself, 'My master is delayed,' [49]and he begins to beat his fellow slaves, and eats and drinks with drunkards, [50]the master of that slave will come on a day when he does not expect him and at an hour that he does not know. [51]He will cut him in pieces[a] and put him with the hypocrites, where there will be weeping and gnashing of teeth.

The Parable of the Ten Bridesmaids

25 "Then the kingdom of heaven will be like this. Ten bridesmaids[b] took their lamps and went to meet the bridegroom.[c] [2]Five of them were foolish, and five were wise. [3]When the foolish took their lamps, they took no oil with them; [4]but the wise took flasks of oil with their lamps. [5]As the bridegroom was delayed, all of them became drowsy and slept. [6]But at midnight there was a shout, 'Look! Here is the bridegroom! Come out to meet him.' [7]Then all those bridesmaids[b] got up and trimmed their lamps. [8]The foolish said to

w Or it   x Other ancient authorities lack *nor the Son*   y Other ancient authorities read *at what hour*   z Gk *to give them*   a Or *cut him off*   b Gk *virgins*   c Other ancient authorities add *and the bride*

Before there was electricity, people used oil lamps for light. In this parable, ten bridesmaids took lamps when they went to meet the bridegroom. Five of the bridesmaids also took oil. But five of them did not take any oil, and they had to leave to go buy some. When they left, the bridegroom arrived, and they missed out on the wedding banquet. Only those who had taken oil in the first place were able to join in the banquet. Just as the bridesmaids should have been ready with their oil, Jesus wants his followers to be ready for his return.

the wise, 'Give us some of your oil, for our lamps are going out.' ⁹But the wise replied, 'No! there will not be enough for you and for us; you had better go to the dealers and buy some for yourselves.' ¹⁰And while they went to buy it, the bridegroom came, and those who were ready went with him into the wedding banquet; and the door was shut. ¹¹Later the other bridesmaids*d* came also, saying, 'Lord, lord, open to us.' ¹²But he replied, 'Truly I tell you, I do not know you.' ¹³Keep awake therefore, for you know neither the day nor the hour.*e*

The Parable of the Talents

14 "For it is as if a man, going on a journey, summoned his slaves and entrusted his property to them; ¹⁵to one he gave five talents,*f* to another two, to another one, to each according to his ability. Then he went away. ¹⁶The one who had received the five talents went off at once and traded with them, and made five more talents. ¹⁷In the same way, the one who had the two talents made two more talents. ¹⁸But the one who had received the one talent went off and dug a hole in the ground and hid his master's money. ¹⁹After a long time the master of those slaves came and settled accounts with them. ²⁰Then the one who had received the five talents

came forward, bringing five more talents, saying, 'Master, you handed over to me five talents; see, I have made five more talents.' ²¹His master said to him, 'Well done, good and trustworthy slave; you have been trustworthy in a few things, I will put you in charge of many things; enter into the joy of your master.' ²²And the one with the two talents also came forward, saying, 'Master, you handed over to me two talents; see, I have made two more talents.' ²³His master said to him, 'Well done, good and trustworthy slave; you have been trustworthy in a few things, I will put you in charge of many things; enter into the joy of your master.' ²⁴Then the one who had received the one talent also came forward, saying, 'Master, I knew that you were a harsh man, reaping where you did not sow, and gathering where you did not scatter seed; ²⁵so I was afraid, and I went and hid your talent in the ground. Here you have what is yours.' ²⁶But his master replied, 'You wicked and lazy slave! You knew, did you, that I reap where I did not sow, and gather where I did not scatter? ²⁷Then you ought to have invested my money with the bankers, and on my return I would have received what was my own with interest. ²⁸So take the talent from him, and give it to the one with the ten talents. ²⁹For to all those who have, more will be given, and they will have an abundance; but from those who have nothing, even what they have will be taken away. ³⁰As for this worthless slave, throw him into the outer darkness, where there will be weeping and gnashing of teeth.'

The Judgment of the Nations

31 "When the Son of Man comes in his glory, and all the angels with him, then he will sit on the throne of his glory. ³²All the nations will be gathered before him, and he will separate people one from another as a shepherd separates the sheep from the goats, ³³and he will put

d Gk virgins   *e* Other ancient authorities add in which the Son of Man is coming   *f* A talent was worth more than fifteen years' wages of a laborer the sheep at his right hand and the goats at the left. [34]Then the king will say to those at his right hand, 'Come, you that are blessed by my Father, inherit the kingdom prepared for you from the foundation of the world; [35]for I was hungry and you gave me food, I was thirsty and you gave me something to drink, I was a stranger and you welcomed me, [36]I was naked and you gave me clothing, I was sick and you took care of me, I was in prison and you visited me.' [37]Then the righteous will answer him, 'Lord, when was it that we saw you hungry and gave you food, or thirsty and gave you something to drink? [38]And when was it that we saw you a stranger and welcomed you, or naked and gave you clothing? [39]And when was it that we saw you sick or in prison and visited you?' [40]And the king will answer them, 'Truly I tell you, just as you did it to one of the least of these who are members of my family,[g] you did it to me.' [41]Then he will say to those at his left hand, 'You that are accursed, depart from me into the eternal fire prepared for the devil and his angels; [42]for I was hungry and you gave me no food, I was thirsty and you gave me nothing to drink, [43]I was a stranger and you did not welcome me, naked and you did not give me clothing, sick and in prison and you did not visit me.' [44]Then they also will answer, 'Lord, when was it that we saw you hungry or thirsty or a stranger or naked or sick or in prison, and did not take care of you?' [45]Then he will answer them, 'Truly I tell you, just as you did not do it to one of the least of these, you did not do it to me.' [46]And these will go away into eternal punishment, but the righteous into eternal life."

The Plot to Kill Jesus

26 When Jesus had finished saying all these things, he said to his disciples, [2]"You know that after two days the Passover is coming, and the Son of Man will be handed over to be crucified."

3 Then the chief priests and the eld-ers of the people gathered in the palace of the high priest, who was called Cā′-i·a·phas, [4]and they conspired to arrest Jesus by stealth and kill him. [5]But they said, "Not during the festival, or there may be a riot among the people."

The Anointing at Bethany

6 Now while Jesus was at Beth′a·ny in the house of Simon the leper,[h] [7]a woman came to him with an alabaster jar of very costly ointment, and she poured it on his head as he sat at the table. [8]But when the disciples saw it, they were angry and said, "Why this waste? [9]For this ointment could have been sold for a large sum, and the money given to the poor." [10]But Jesus, aware of this, said to them, "Why do you trouble the woman? She has performed a good service for me. [11]For you always have the poor with you, but you will not always have me. [12]By pouring this ointment on my body she has prepared me for burial. [13]Truly I tell you, wherever this good news[i] is proclaimed in the whole world, what she has done will be told in remembrance of her."

Judas Agrees to Betray Jesus

14 Then one of the twelve, who was called Judas Is·car′i·ot, went to the chief priests [15]and said, "What will you give me if I betray him to you?" They paid him thirty pieces of silver. [16]And from that moment he began to look for an opportunity to betray him.

The Passover with the Disciples

17 On the first day of Unleavened Bread the disciples came to Jesus, saying, "Where do you want us to make the preparations for you to eat the Passover?" [18]He said, "Go into the city to a certain man, and say to him, 'The Teacher says, My time is near; I will keep the Passover at your house with my disciples.' " [19]So the disciples did as Jesus

---

[g] Gk *these my brothers*   [h] The terms *leper* and *leprosy* can refer to several diseases   [i] Or *gospel*

Each year, the Jews ate a special meal called Passover to remember their flight out of Egypt and their rescue from slavery (this story is told in the book of Exodus). Jesus ate this meal with his disciples and used broken pieces of bread and a cup of wine to explain to the disciples that God would use his coming death to bring about God's kingdom. Today, we remember the Last Supper in the Communion service, also called the Eucharist or the Lord's Supper.

had directed them, and they prepared the Passover meal.

20 When it was evening, he took his place with the twelve;[j] [21]and while they were eating, he said, "Truly I tell you, one of you will betray me." [22]And they became greatly distressed and began to say to him one after another, "Surely not I, Lord?" [23]He answered, "The one who has dipped his hand into the bowl with me will betray me. [24]The Son of Man goes as it is written of him, but woe to that one by whom the Son of Man is betrayed! It would have been better for that one not to have been born." [25]Judas, who betrayed him, said, "Surely not I, Rabbi?" He replied, "You have said so."

The Institution of the Lord's Supper

26 While they were eating, Jesus took a loaf of bread, and after blessing it he broke it, gave it to the disciples, and said, "Take, eat; this is my body." [27]Then he took a cup, and after giving thanks he gave it to them, saying, "Drink from it, all of you; [28]for this is my blood of the[k] covenant, which is poured out for many for the forgiveness of sins. [29]I tell you, I will never again drink of this fruit of the vine until that day when I drink it new with you in my Father's kingdom."

30 When they had sung the hymn, they went out to the Mount of Olives.

Peter's Denial Foretold

31 Then Jesus said to them, "You will all become deserters because of me this night; for it is written,

'I will strike the shepherd,
and the sheep of the flock will be scattered.'

[32]But after I am raised up, I will go ahead of you to Galilee." [33]Peter said to him, "Though all become deserters because of you, I will never desert you." [34]Jesus said to him, "Truly I tell you, this very night, before the cock crows, you will deny me three times." [35]Peter said to him, "Even though I must die with you, I will not deny you." And so said all the disciples.

The garden where Jesus went to pray was called Gethsemane, which means, "oil press." It was here that his disciple Judas betrayed him.

Jesus Prays in Gethsemane

36 Then Jesus went with them to a place called Geth·sem´a·nē; and he said to his disciples, "Sit here while I go over there and pray." [37]He took with him Peter and the two sons of Zeb´e·dee, and began to be grieved and agitated. [38]Then he said to them, "I am deeply grieved, even to death; remain here, and stay awake with me." [39]And going a little farther, he threw himself on the ground and prayed, "My Father, if it is possible, let this cup pass from me; yet not what I want but what you want." [40]Then he came to the disciples and found them sleeping; and he said to Peter, "So, could you not stay awake with me one hour? [41]Stay awake and pray that you may not come into the time of trial;[l] the spirit indeed is willing, but the flesh is weak." [42]Again he went away for the second time

[j] Other ancient authorities add *disciples* [k] Other ancient authorities add *new* [l] Or *into temptation*

Judas Iscariot was one of Jesus's disciples, but he also betrayed Jesus. For thirty pieces of silver (Matthew 16:15), Judas agreed to help some religious leaders arrest Jesus in a quiet place where not many people could see. He betrayed Jesus by giving him a kiss, a usual way of greeting another person. There are many puzzling questions about Judas: Why did he spend time with Jesus? Why did Jesus include him as a disciple? Why did he turn against Jesus?

and prayed, "My Father, if this cannot pass unless I drink it, your will be done." [43]Again he came and found them sleeping, for their eyes were heavy. [44]So leaving them again, he went away and prayed for the third time, saying the same words. [45]Then he came to the disciples and said to them, "Are you still sleeping and taking your rest? See, the hour is at hand, and the Son of Man is betrayed into the hands of sinners. [46]Get up, let us be going. See, my betrayer is at hand."

The Betrayal and Arrest of Jesus

47 While he was still speaking, Judas, one of the twelve, arrived; with him was a large crowd with swords and clubs, from the chief priests and the elders of the people. [48]Now the betrayer had given them a sign, saying, "The one I will kiss is the man; arrest him." [49]At once he came up to Jesus and said, "Greetings, Rabbi!" and kissed him. [50]Jesus said to him, "Friend, do what you are here to do." Then they came and laid hands on Jesus and arrested him. [51]Suddenly, one of those with Jesus put his hand on his sword, drew it, and struck the slave of the high priest, cutting off his ear. [52]Then Jesus said to him, "Put your sword back into its place; for all who take the sword will perish by the sword. [53]Do you think that I cannot appeal to my Father, and he will at once send me more than twelve legions of angels? [54]But how then would the scriptures be fulfilled, which say it must happen in this way?" [55]At that hour Jesus said to the crowds, "Have you come out with swords and clubs to arrest me as though I were a bandit? Day after day I sat in the temple teaching, and you did not arrest me. [56]But all this has taken place, so that the scriptures of the prophets may be fulfilled." Then all the disciples deserted him and fled.

Jesus before the High Priest

57 Those who had arrested Jesus took him to Cā́·i·a·phas the high priest, in whose house the scribes and the elders had gathered. [58]But Peter was following him at a distance, as far as the courtyard of the high priest; and going inside, he sat with the guards in order to see how this would end. [59]Now the chief priests and the whole council were looking for false testimony against Jesus so that they might put him to death, [60]but they found none, though many false witnesses came forward. At last two came forward [61]and said, "This fellow said, 'I am able to destroy the temple of God and to build it in three days.'" [62]The high priest stood up and said, "Have you no answer? What is it that they testify against you?" [63]But Jesus was silent. Then the high priest said to him, "I put you under oath before the living God, tell us if you are the Messiah,[m] the Son of God." [64]Jesus said to him, "You have said so. But I tell you,

From now on you will see the Son of Man
   seated at the right hand of Power
   and coming on the clouds of
      heaven."

[m] Or *Christ*

[65]Then the high priest tore his clothes and said, "He has blasphemed! Why do we still need witnesses? You have now heard his blasphemy. [66]What is your verdict?" They answered, "He deserves death." [67]Then they spat in his face and struck him; and some slapped him, [68]saying, "Prophesy to us, you Messiah![n] Who is it that struck you?"

Peter's Denial of Jesus

69 Now Peter was sitting outside in the courtyard. A servant-girl came to him and said, "You also were with Jesus the Galilean." [70]But he denied it before all of them, saying, "I do not know what you are talking about." [71]When he went out to the porch, another servant-girl saw him, and she said to the bystanders, "This man was with Jesus of Nazareth."[o] [72]Again he denied it with an oath, "I do not know the man." [73]After a little while the bystanders came up and said to Peter, "Certainly you are also one of them, for your accent betrays you." [74]Then he began to curse, and he swore an oath, "I do not know the man!" At that moment the cock crowed. [75]Then Peter remembered what Jesus had said: "Before the cock crows, you will deny me three times." And he went out and wept bitterly.

Jesus Brought before Pilate

27 When morning came, all the chief priests and the elders of the people conferred together against Jesus in order to bring about his death. [2]They bound him, led him away, and handed him over to Pilate the governor.

The Suicide of Judas

3 When Judas, his betrayer, saw that Jesus[p] was condemned, he repented and brought back the thirty pieces of silver to the chief priests and the elders. [4]He said, "I have sinned by betraying innocent[q] blood." But they said, "What is that to us? See to it yourself." [5]Throwing down the pieces of silver in the temple, he departed; and he went and hanged himself. [6]But the chief priests, taking the pieces of silver, said, "It is not lawful to put them into the treasury, since they are blood money." [7]After conferring together, they used them to buy the potter's field as a place to bury foreigners. [8]For this reason that field has been called the Field of Blood to this day. [9]Then was fulfilled what had been spoken through the prophet Jer·e·mi´ah,[r] "And they took[s] the thirty pieces of silver, the price of the one on whom a price had been set,[t] on whom some of the people of Israel had set a price, [10]and they gave[u] them for the potter's field, as the Lord commanded me."

Pilate Questions Jesus

11 Now Jesus stood before the governor; and the governor asked him, "Are you the King of the Jews?" Jesus said, "You say so." [12]But when he was accused by the chief priests and elders, he did not answer. [13]Then Pilate said to him, "Do you not hear how many accusations they make against you?" [14]But he gave him no answer, not even to a single charge, so that the governor was greatly amazed.

Barabbas or Jesus?

15 Now at the festival the governor was accustomed to release a prisoner for the crowd, anyone whom they wanted. [16]At that time they had a notorious prisoner, called Jesus[v] Ba·rab´bas. [17]So after they had gathered, Pilate said to them, "Whom do you want me to release for you, Jesus[v] Ba·rab´bas or Jesus who is called the Messiah?"[w] [18]For he realized that it was out of jealousy that they had handed him over. [19]While he was sitting on the judgment seat, his wife sent word to him, "Have nothing to do with that innocent man, for today I have suffered

[n] Or *Christ* [o] Gk *the Nazorean* [p] Gk *he*
[q] Other ancient authorities read *righteous*
[r] Other ancient authorities read *Zechariah* or *Isaiah*
[s] Or *I took* [t] Or *the price of the precious One*
[u] Other ancient authorities read *I gave* [w] Other ancient authorities lack *Jesus* [w] Or *the Christ*

a great deal because of a dream about him." ²⁰Now the chief priests and the elders persuaded the crowds to ask for Ba·rab'bas and to have Jesus killed. ²¹The governor again said to them, "Which of the two do you want me to release for you?" And they said, "Ba·rab'bas." ²²Pilate said to them, "Then what should I do with Jesus who is called the Messiah?"ˣ All of them said, "Let him be crucified!" ²³Then he asked, "Why, what evil has he done?" But they shouted all the more, "Let him be crucified!"

Pilate Hands Jesus over to Be Crucified

24 So when Pilate saw that he could do nothing, but rather that a riot was beginning, he took some water and washed his hands before the crowd, saying, "I am innocent of this man's blood;ʸ see to it yourselves." ²⁵Then the people as a whole answered, "His blood be on us and on our children!" ²⁶So he released Ba·rab'bas for them; and after flogging Jesus, he handed him over to be crucified.

The Soldiers Mock Jesus

27 Then the soldiers of the governor took Jesus into the governor's headquarters,ᶻ and they gathered the whole cohort around him. ²⁸They stripped him and put a scarlet robe on him, ²⁹and after twisting some thorns into a crown, they put it on his head. They put a reed in his right hand and knelt before him and mocked him, saying, "Hail, King of the Jews!" ³⁰They spat on him, and took the reed and struck him on the head. ³¹After mocking him, they stripped him of the robe and put his own clothes on him. Then they led him away to crucify him.

The Crucifixion of Jesus

32 As they went out, they came upon a man from Cy·re'ne named Simon; they compelled this man to carry his cross. ³³And when they came to a place called Gol'go·tha (which means Place of a Skull), ³⁴they offered him wine to drink, mixed with gall; but when he tasted it, he

would not drink it. ³⁵And when they had crucified him, they divided his clothes among themselves by casting lots;ᵃ ³⁶then they sat down there and kept watch over him. ³⁷Over his head they put the charge against him, which read, "This is Jesus, the King of the Jews."

38 Then two bandits were crucified with him, one on his right and one on his left. ³⁹Those who passed by deridedᵇ him, shaking their heads ⁴⁰and saying, "You who would destroy the temple and build it in three days, save yourself! If you are the Son of God, come down from the cross." ⁴¹In the same way the chief priests also, along with the scribes and elders, were mocking him, saying, ⁴²"He saved others; he cannot save himself.ᶜ He is the King of Israel; let him come down from the cross now, and we will believe in him. ⁴³He trusts in God; let God deliver him now, if he wants to; for he said, 'I am God's Son.' " ⁴⁴The bandits who were crucified with him also taunted him in the same way.

The Death of Jesus

45 From noon on, darkness came over the whole landᵈ until three in the afternoon. ⁴⁶And about three o'clock Jesus cried with a loud voice, "E'li, E'li, le·ma' sa·bach'tha·ni?" that is, "My God, my God, why have you forsaken me?" ⁴⁷When some of the bystanders heard it, they said, "This man is calling for E·li'jah."

The wine offered to Jesus was supposed to ease his pain, but he refused to drink it.

⁴⁸At once one of them ran and got a sponge, filled it with sour wine, put it on a stick, and gave it to him to drink. ⁴⁹But the others said, "Wait, let us see whether E·lī´jah will come to save him."ᵉ ⁵⁰Then Jesus cried again with a loud voice and breathed his last.ᶠ ⁵¹At that moment the curtain of the temple was torn in two, from top to bottom. The earth shook, and the rocks were split. ⁵²The tombs also were opened, and many bodies of the saints who had fallen asleep were raised. ⁵³After his resurrection they came out of the tombs and entered the holy city and appeared to many. ⁵⁴Now when the centurion and those with him, who were keeping watch over Jesus, saw the earthquake and what took place, they were terrified and said, "Truly this man was God's Son!"ᵍ

55 Many women were also there, looking on from a distance; they had followed Jesus from Galilee and had provided for him. ⁵⁶Among them were Mary Mag´da·lēne, and Mary the mother of James and Joseph, and the mother of the sons of Zeb´e·dee.

Joseph of Arimathea was a wealthy man and disciple of Jesus. He asked Pilate for Jesus' body so he could bury it in his own tomb.

The Burial of Jesus

57 When it was evening, there came a rich man from Ar·i·ma·thē´a, named Joseph, who was also a disciple of Jesus. ⁵⁸He went to Pilate and asked for the body of Jesus; then Pilate ordered it to be given to him. ⁵⁹So Joseph took the body and wrapped it in a clean linen cloth ⁶⁰and laid it in his own new tomb, which he had hewn in the rock. He then rolled a great stone to the door of the tomb and went away. ⁶¹Mary Mag´da·lēne

and the other Mary were there, sitting opposite the tomb.

The Guard at the Tomb

62 The next day, that is, after the day of Preparation, the chief priests and the Phar´i·sees gathered before Pilate ⁶³and said, "Sir, we remember what that impostor said while he was still alive, 'After three days I will rise again.' ⁶⁴Therefore command the tomb to be made secure until the third day; otherwise his disciples may go and steal him away, and tell the people, 'He has been raised from the dead,' and the last deception would be worse than the first." ⁶⁵Pilate said to them, "You have a guardʰ of soldiers; go, make it as secure as you can."ⁱ

Jewish funerals almost always took place on the same day a person died. People would prepare the body for burial by closing the eyes, washing the body with perfumes and ointments, such as myrrh, tying the hands and feet with strips of cloth, covering the face with a linen square, and then wrapping the body in white linen. They then carried the body to the family tomb, which was usually a cave with a small, narrow opening that could be covered by a stone. Because funerals did not take place on the Sabbath, Jesus' friends were not able to prepare his body for burial. So the women came to do the job as soon as the Sabbath was over. To their surprise, they found the tomb was empty. Jesus was alive! He had risen, just as he had said he would.

ᵉ Other ancient authorities add *And another took a spear and pierced his side, and out came water and blood*   ᶠ Or *gave up his spirit*   ᵍ Or *a son of God*   ʰ Or *Take a guard*   ⁱ Gk *you know how*

[66]So they went with the guard and made the tomb secure by sealing the stone.

The Resurrection of Jesus

28 After the sabbath, as the first day of the week was dawning, Mary Mag·da·lēne and the other Mary went to see the tomb. [2]And suddenly there was a great earthquake; for an angel of the Lord, descending from heaven, came and rolled back the stone and sat on it. [3]His appearance was like lightning, and his clothing white as snow. [4]For fear of him the guards shook and became like dead men. [5]But the angel said to the women, "Do not be afraid; I know that you are looking for Jesus who was crucified. [6]He is not here; for he has been raised, as he said. Come, see the place where he[j] lay. [7]Then go quickly and tell his disciples, 'He has been raised from the dead,[k] and indeed he is going ahead of you to Galilee; there you will see him.' This is my message for you." [8]So they left the tomb quickly with fear and great joy, and ran to tell his disciples. [9]Suddenly Jesus met them and said, "Greetings!" And they came to him, took hold of his feet, and worshiped him. [10]Then Jesus said to them, "Do not be afraid; go and tell my brothers to go to Galilee; there they will see me."

The Report of the Guard

11 While they were going, some of the guard went into the city and told the chief priests everything that had happened. [12]After the priests[l] had assembled with the elders, they devised a plan to give a large sum of money to the soldiers, [13]telling them, "You must say, 'His disciples came by night and stole him away while we were asleep.' [14]If this comes to the governor's ears, we will satisfy him and keep you out of trouble." [15]So they took the money and did as

> The Resurrection is the central truth of the Christian gospel. It is the reality that Jesus was alive after the Crucifixion. This was the event that the disciples preached to the world to show that Jesus was the Christ, the Son of God. Not only did the Resurrection demonstrate Jesus's defeat of death, but it also gave to all believers a hope for personal resurrection, or everlasting life.

they were directed. And this story is still told among the Jews to this day.

The Commissioning of the Disciples

16 Now the eleven disciples went to Galilee, to the mountain to which Jesus had directed them. [17]When they saw him, they worshiped him; but some doubted. [18]And Jesus came and said to them, "All authority in heaven and on earth has been given to me. [19]Go therefore and make disciples of all nations, baptizing them in the name of the Father and of the Son and of the Holy Spirit, [20]and teaching them to obey everything that I have commanded you. And remember, I am with you always, to the end of the age."[m]

> "Go therefore and make disciples of all nations, baptizing them in the name of the Father and of the Son and of the Holy Spirit, and teaching them to obey everything that I have commanded you."
> Matthew 28:19–20

[j] Other ancient authorities read *the Lord* [k]Other ancient authorities lack *from the dead* [l] Gk *they* [m] Other ancient authorities add *Amen*

Mark

The Gospel of Mark was written sometime between 65–70 AD, before any of the other Gospels in the New Testament. It was probably written for the Christians at Rome, but nothing in Mark's Gospel tells us for sure. Many believe a man named John Mark (not the disciple Mark) wrote the Gospel.

Like all the early writings about Jesus, copies of the Gospel of Mark were sent to many different churches. This book was one of the main sources used by writers who wrote down other accounts of the good news that Jesus was the long-awaited Christ (or Messiah). When you read the Gospels of Matthew and Luke, you will find much of Mark's Gospel included.

The book of Mark does not tell us anything about Jesus's birth or childhood. The story begins with Jesus as an adult going to be baptized by John the Baptist and ends with the Resurrection. The book shows Jesus as a person of action and power. He called the disciples, taught, performed miracles, and healed the sick. Jesus reminded the people of God's commandment to Moses and the Israelites (see Deuteronomy 5:5) and told them that the greatest commandment is to "love the Lord your God with all your heart, and with all your soul, and with all your mind, and with all your strength" (Mark 12:30).

Mark 3:13–19

The Proclamation of John the Baptist

1 The beginning of the good news[a] of Jesus Christ, the Son of God.[b] 2 As it is written in the prophet I·sāi´ah,[c]

"See, I am sending my messenger
  ahead of you,[d]
who will prepare your way;
[3] the voice of one crying out in the
  wilderness:
'Prepare the way of the Lord,
  make his paths straight,' "

[4]John the baptizer appeared[e] in the wilderness, proclaiming a baptism of repentance for the forgiveness of sins. [5]And people from the whole Judean countryside and all the people of Jerusalem were going out to him, and were baptized by him in the river Jordan, confessing their sins. [6]Now John was clothed with camel's hair, with a leather belt around his waist, and he ate locusts and wild honey. [7]He proclaimed, "The one who is more powerful than I is coming after me; I am not worthy to stoop down and untie the thong of his sandals. [8]I have baptized you with[f] water; but he will baptize you with[f] the Holy Spirit."

The Baptism of Jesus

9 In those days Jesus came from Nazareth of Galilee and was baptized by John in the Jordan. [10]And just as he was

When people came to John to be baptized, he told them that someone else would come after him. He said that he did not deserve to untie the sandals of the one coming. John was talking about the coming of Jesus, and he was saying that he did not deserve even to be a servant to Jesus. Later in his ministry, Jesus himself would wash the disciples' feet (see John 13:1–20). In this way, Jesus showed that those who follow God must always be looking for ways to serve other people.

coming up out of the water, he saw the heavens torn apart and the Spirit descending like a dove on him. [11]And a voice came from heaven, "You are my Son, the Beloved;[g] with you I am well pleased."

The Temptation of Jesus

12 And the Spirit immediately drove him out into the wilderness. [13]He was in the wilderness forty days, tempted by Satan; and he was with the wild beasts; and the angels waited on him.

The Beginning of the Galilean Ministry

14 Now after John was arrested, Jesus came to Galilee, proclaiming the good news[a] of God,[h] [15]and saying, "The time is fulfilled, and the kingdom of God has come near;[i] repent, and believe in the good news."[a]

The first people Jesus called to be his followers were fishermen on the Sea of Galilee, a heart-shaped, inland lake that empties into the Jordan River.

Jesus Calls the First Disciples

16 As Jesus passed along the Sea of Galilee, he saw Simon and his brother Andrew casting a net into the sea—for they were fishermen. [17]And Jesus said to them, "Follow me and I will make you fish for people." [18]And immediately they left their nets and followed him. [19]As he went a little farther, he saw James son of Zeb´e·dee and his brother John, who were in their boat mending the nets. [20]Immediately he called them; and they left their father Zeb´e·dee in the boat with the hired men, and followed him.

[a] Or gospel   [b] Other ancient authorities lack the Son of God [c] Other ancient authorities read in the prophets   [d] Gk before your face   [e] Other ancient authorities read John was baptizing   [f] Or in   [g] Or my beloved Son   [h] Other ancient authorities read of the kingdom   [i] Or is at hand

"And Jesus said to them, 'Follow me and I will make you fish for people.' And immediately they left their nets and followed him."
Mark 1:17-18

The Man with an Unclean Spirit

21 They went to Ca·per′na·um; and when the sabbath came, he entered the synagogue and taught. [22]They were astounded at his teaching, for he taught them as one having authority, and not as the scribes. [23]Just then there was in their synagogue a man with an unclean spirit, [24]and he cried out, "What have you to do with us, Jesus of Nazareth? Have you come to destroy us? I know who you are, the Holy One of God." [25]But Jesus rebuked him, saying, "Be silent, and come out of him!" [26]And the unclean spirit, convulsing him and crying with a loud voice, came out of him. [27]They were all amazed, and they kept on asking one another, "What is this? A new teaching—with authority! He[j] commands even the unclean spirits, and they obey him." [28]At once his fame began to spread throughout the surrounding region of Galilee.

Jesus Heals Many at Simon's House

29 As soon as they[k] left the synagogue, they entered the house of Simon and Andrew, with James and John. [30]Now Simon's mother-in-law was in bed with a fever, and they told him about her at once. [31]He came and took her by the hand and lifted her up. Then the fever left her, and she began to serve them.

32 That evening, at sundown, they brought to him all who were sick or possessed with demons. [33]And the whole city was gathered around the door. [34]And he cured many who were sick with various diseases, and cast out many demons; and he would not permit the demons to speak, because they knew him.

A Preaching Tour in Galilee

35 In the morning, while it was still very dark, he got up and went out to a deserted place, and there he prayed. [36]And Simon and his companions hunted for him. [37]When they found him, they said to him, "Everyone is searching for you." [38]He answered, "Let us go on to the neighboring towns, so that I may proclaim the message there also; for that is what I came out to do." [39]And he went throughout Galilee, proclaiming the message in their synagogues and casting out demons.

Jesus Cleanses a Leper

40 A leper[l] came to him begging him, and kneeling[m] he said to him, "If you choose, you can make me clean." [41]Moved with pity,[n] Jesus[o] stretched out his hand and touched him, and said to him, "I do choose. Be made clean!" [42]Immediately the leprosy[l] left him, and he was made clean. [43]After sternly warning him he sent him away at once, [44]saying to him, "See that you say nothing to anyone; but go, show yourself to the priest, and offer for your cleansing what Moses commanded, as a testimony to them." [45]But he went out and began to proclaim it freely, and to spread the word, so that Jesus[o] could no longer go into a town openly, but stayed out in the country; and people came to him from every quarter.

Jesus Heals a Paralytic

2 When he returned to Ca·per′na·um after some days, it was reported that he was at home. [2]So many gathered around that there was no longer room for them, not even in front of the door; and he was speaking the word to them. [3]Then some people[p] came, bringing to him a paralyzed man, carried by four of

[j] Or A new teaching! With authority he [k] Other ancient authorities read he [l] The terms leper and leprosy can refer to several diseases [m] Other ancient authorities lack kneeling [n] Other ancient authorities read anger [o] Gk he [p] Gk they

them. [4]And when they could not bring him to Jesus because of the crowd, they removed the roof above him; and after having dug through it, they let down the mat on which the paralytic lay. [5]When Jesus saw their faith, he said to the paralytic, "Son, your sins are forgiven." [6]Now some of the scribes were sitting there, questioning in their hearts, [7]"Why does this fellow speak in this way? It is blasphemy! Who can forgive sins but God alone?" [8]At once Jesus perceived in his spirit that they were discussing these questions among themselves; and he said to them, "Why do you raise such questions in your hearts? [9]Which is easier, to say to the paralytic, 'Your sins are forgiven,' or to say, 'Stand up and take your mat and walk'? [10]But so that you may know that the Son of Man has authority on earth to forgive sins"—he said to the paralytic— [11]"I say to you, stand up, take your mat and go to your home." [12]And he stood up, and immediately took the mat and went out before all of them; so that they were all amazed and glorified God, saying, "We have never seen anything like this!"

Jesus Calls Levi

13 Jesus[q] went out again beside the sea; the whole crowd gathered around him, and he taught them. [14]As he was walking along, he saw Levi son of Al·phaē´us sitting at the tax booth, and he said to him, "Follow me." And he got up and followed him.

15 And as he sat at dinner[r] in Levi's[s] house, many tax collectors and sinners were also sitting[t] with Jesus and his disciples—for there were many who followed him. [16]When the scribes of[u] the Phar´i·sees saw that he was eating with sinners and tax collectors, they said to his disciples, "Why does he eat[v] with tax collectors and sinners?" [17]When Jesus heard this, he said to them, "Those who are well have no need of a physician, but those who are sick; I have come to call not the righteous but sinners."

Levi (also called Matthew) was a tax collector—an official who collected and kept track of taxes paid to the government. Tax collectors reminded the people of Roman rule. Tax collectors made their living by charging more money for taxes than the Romans expected and keeping the difference for themselves. Matthew must have known that his life would change if he left to follow Jesus, but he did not pause for even one minute. Matthew left behind everything to follow Jesus.

The Question about Fasting

18 Now John's disciples and the Phar´i·sees were fasting; and people[w] came and said to him, "Why do John's disciples and the disciples of the Phar´i·sees fast, but your disciples do not fast?" [19]Jesus said to them, "The wedding guests cannot fast while the bridegroom is with them, can they? As long as they have the bridegroom with them, they cannot fast. [20]The days will come when the bridegroom is taken away from them, and then they will fast on that day.

21 "No one sews a piece of unshrunk cloth on an old cloak; otherwise, the patch pulls away from it, the new from the old, and a worse tear is made. [22]And no one puts new wine into old wineskins; otherwise, the wine will burst the skins, and the wine is lost, and so are the skins; but one puts new wine into fresh wineskins."[x]

Pronouncement about the Sabbath

23 One sabbath he was going through the grainfields; and as they made their

[q] Gk he   [r] Gk reclined   [s] Gk his   [t] Gk reclining
[u] Other ancient authorities read and   [v] Other ancient authorities add and drink   [w] Gk they
[x] Other ancient authorities lack but one puts new wine into fresh wineskins

When Jesus healed a man's hand, some religious leaders thought that Jesus should have waited until the day after the Sabbath. This attitude must have made Jesus very sad. He believed that it is important to follow the Law, but he knew that the most important thing in life is to take care of the needs of others.

way his disciples began to pluck heads of grain. 24The Phar´i·sees said to him, "Look, why are they doing what is not lawful on the sabbath?" 25And he said to them, "Have you never read what David did when he and his companions were hungry and in need of food? 26He entered the house of God, when A·bī´a·thar was high priest, and ate the bread of the Presence, which it is not lawful for any but the priests to eat, and he gave some to his companions." 27Then he said to them, "The sabbath was made for humankind, and not humankind for the sabbath; 28so the Son of Man is lord even of the sabbath."

The Man with a Withered Hand

3 Again he entered the synagogue, and a man was there who had a withered hand. 2They watched him to see whether he would cure him on the sabbath, so that they might accuse him. 3And he said to the man who had the withered hand, "Come forward." 4Then he said to them, "Is it lawful to do good or to do harm on the sabbath, to save life or to kill?" But they were silent. 5He looked around at them with anger; he was grieved at their hardness of heart and said to the man, "Stretch out your hand." He stretched it out, and his hand was restored. 6The Phar´i·sees went out and immediately conspired with the He·rō´di·ans against him, how to destroy him.

A Multitude at the Seaside

7 Jesus departed with his disciples to the sea, and a great multitude from Galilee

followed him; 8hearing all that he was doing, they came to him in great numbers from Judea, Jerusalem, Id·ū·mē´a, beyond the Jordan, and the region around Tyre and Sī´don. 9He told his disciples to have a boat ready for him because of the crowd, so that they would not crush him; 10for he had cured many, so that all who had diseases pressed upon him to touch him. 11Whenever the unclean spirits saw him, they fell down before him and shouted, "You are the Son of God!" 12But he sternly ordered them not to make him known.

There were many people who followed Jesus, but Jesus called twelve to be an inner circle with him and to tell others the Good News. We call these twelve men "disciples," or "apostles."

Jesus Appoints the Twelve

13 He went up the mountain and called to him those whom he wanted, and they came to him. 14And he appointed twelve, whom he also named apostles,y to be with him, and to be sent out to proclaim the message, 15and to have authority to cast out demons. 16So he appointed the twelve:z Simon (to whom he gave the name Peter); 17James son of Zeb´e·dee and John the brother of James (to whom he gave the name Bō·a·ner´gēs, that is, Sons of Thunder); 18and Andrew, and Philip, and Bartholomew, and Matthew, and Thomas, and James son of Al·phae´us, and Thad·dae´us, and Simon the Cā·na·nae´an, 19and Judas Is·car´i·ot, who betrayed him.

Jesus and Beelzebul

Then he went home; 20and the crowd came together again, so that they could not even eat. 21When his family heard it, they went out to restrain him, for people

y Other ancient authorities lack *whom he also named apostles*　z Other ancient authorities lack *So he appointed the twelve* were saying, "He has gone out of his mind." [22]And the scribes who came down from Jerusalem said, "He has Bē·el´ze·bul, and by the ruler of the demons he casts out demons." [23]And he called them to him, and spoke to them in parables, "How can Satan cast out Satan? [24]If a kingdom is divided against itself, that kingdom cannot stand. [25]And if a house is divided against itself, that house will not be able to stand. [26]And if Satan has risen up against himself and is divided, he cannot stand, but his end has come. [27]But no one can enter a strong man's house and plunder his property without first tying up the strong man; then indeed the house can be plundered.

28 "Truly I tell you, people will be forgiven for their sins and whatever blasphemies they utter; [29]but whoever blasphemes against the Holy Spirit can never have forgiveness, but is guilty of an eternal sin"— [30]for they had said, "He has an unclean spirit."

The True Kindred of Jesus

31 Then his mother and his brothers came; and standing outside, they sent to him and called him. [32]A crowd was sitting around him; and they said to him, "Your mother and your brothers and sisters[a] are outside, asking for you." [33]And he replied, "Who are my mother and my brothers?" [34]And looking at those who sat around him, he said, "Here are my mother and my brothers! [35]Whoever does the will of God is my brother and sister and mother."

The Parable of the Sower

4 Again he began to teach beside the sea. Such a very large crowd gathered around him that he got into a boat on the sea and sat there, while the whole crowd was beside the sea on the land. [2]He began to teach them many things in parables, and in his teaching he said to them: [3]"Listen! A sower went out to sow. [4]And as he sowed, some seed fell on the path, and the birds came and ate it up. [5]Other seed fell on rocky ground, where it did not have much soil, and it sprang

up quickly, since it had no depth of soil. [6]And when the sun rose, it was scorched; and since it had no root, it withered away. [7]Other seed fell among thorns, and the thorns grew up and choked it, and it yielded no grain. [8]Other seed fell into good soil and brought forth grain, growing up and increasing and yielding thirty and sixty and a hundredfold." [9]And he said, "Let anyone with ears to hear listen!"

The Purpose of the Parables

10 When he was alone, those who were around him along with the twelve asked him about the parables. [11]And he said to them, "To you has been given the secret[b] of the kingdom of God, but for those outside, everything comes in parables; [12]in order that
'they may indeed look, but not
  perceive,
and may indeed listen, but not
  understand;
so that they may not turn again and be
  forgiven.' "
13 And he said to them, "Do you not understand this parable? Then how will you understand all the parables? [14]The sower sows the word. [15]These are the ones on the path where the word is sown: when they hear, Satan immediately comes and takes away the word that is sown in them. [16]And these are the ones sown on rocky ground: when they hear the word, they immediately receive it with joy. [17]But they have no root, and endure only for a while; then, when trouble or persecution arises on account of the word, immediately they fall away.[c] [18]And others are those sown among the thorns: these are the ones who hear the word, [19]but the cares of the world, and the lure of wealth, and the desire for other things come in and choke the word, and it yields nothing. [20]And these are the ones sown on the good soil: they hear the word and accept

[a] Other ancient authorities lack *and sisters*   [b] Or *mystery*   [c] Or *stumble*

"And he said to them, 'Pay attention to what you hear; the measure you give will be the measure you get, and still more will be given you." Mark 4:24

it and bear fruit, thirty and sixty and a hundredfold."

A Lamp under a Bushel Basket

21 He said to them, "Is a lamp brought in to be put under the bushel basket, or under the bed, and not on the lampstand? ²²For there is nothing hidden, except to be disclosed; nor is anything secret, except to come to light. ²³Let anyone with ears to hear listen!" ²⁴And he said to them, "Pay attention to what you hear; the measure you give will be the measure you get, and still more will be given you. ²⁵For to those who have, more will be given; and from those who have nothing, even what they have will be taken away."

The Parable of the Growing Seed

26 He also said, "The kingdom of God is as if someone would scatter seed on the ground, ²⁷and would sleep and rise night and day, and the seed would sprout and grow, he does not know how. ²⁸The earth produces of itself, first the stalk, then the head, then the full grain in the head. ²⁹But when the grain is ripe, at once he goes in with his sickle, because the harvest has come."

The mustard seed is a very small seed, but it can grow into a very tall tree! Jesus said that the kingdom of God is like a mustard seed. Though at first it may appear small, it can grow into something very big.

The Parable of the Mustard Seed

30 He also said, "With what can we compare the kingdom of God, or what parable will we use for it? ³¹It is like a mustard seed, which, when sown upon the ground, is the smallest of all the seeds on earth; ³²yet when it is sown it grows up and becomes the greatest of all shrubs, and puts forth large branches, so that the birds of the air can make nests in its shade."

The Use of Parables

33 With many such parables he spoke the word to them, as they were able to hear it; ³⁴he did not speak to them except in parables, but he explained everything in private to his disciples.

Jesus Stills a Storm

35 On that day, when evening had come, he said to them, "Let us go across to the other side." ³⁶And leaving the crowd behind, they took him with them in the boat, just as he was. Other boats were with him. ³⁷A great windstorm arose, and the waves beat into the boat, so that the boat was already being swamped. ³⁸But he was in the stern, asleep on the cushion; and they woke him up and said to him, "Teacher, do you not care that we are perishing?" ³⁹He woke up and rebuked the wind, and said to the sea, "Peace! Be still!" Then the wind ceased, and there was a dead calm. ⁴⁰He said to them, "Why are you afraid? Have you still no faith?" ⁴¹And they were filled with great awe and said to one another, "Who then is this, that even the wind and the sea obey him?"

Jesus Heals the Gerasene Demoniac

5 They came to the other side of the sea, to the country of the Ger-a·sēnes.^d ²And when he had stepped out of the boat, immediately a man out of the tombs with an unclean spirit met him. ³He lived among the tombs; and no one could restrain him any more, even with a chain; ⁴for he had often been restrained with shackles and chains, but the chains he wrenched apart, and the shackles he broke in pieces; and no one

^d Other ancient authorities read *Gergesenes*; others, *Gadarenes*

had the strength to subdue him. ⁵Night and day among the tombs and on the mountains he was always howling and bruising himself with stones. ⁶When he saw Jesus from a distance, he ran and bowed down before him; ⁷and he shouted at the top of his voice, "What have you to do with me, Jesus, Son of the Most High God? I adjure you by God, do not torment me." ⁸For he had said to him, "Come out of the man, you unclean spirit!" ⁹Then Jesus*ᵉ* asked him, "What is your name?" He replied, "My name is Legion; for we are many." ¹⁰He begged him earnestly not to send them out of the country. ¹¹Now there on the hillside a great herd of swine was feeding; ¹²and the unclean spirits*ᶠ* begged him, "Send us into the swine; let us enter them." ¹³So he gave them permission. And the unclean spirits came out and entered the swine; and the herd, numbering about two thousand, rushed down the steep bank into the sea, and were drowned in the sea.

14 The swineherds ran off and told it in the city and in the country. Then people came to see what it was that had happened. ¹⁵They came to Jesus and saw the demoniac sitting there, clothed and in his right mind, the very man who had had the legion; and they were afraid. ¹⁶Those who had seen what had happened to the demoniac and to the swine reported it. ¹⁷Then they began to beg Jesus*ᵍ* to leave their neighborhood. ¹⁸As he was getting into the boat, the man who had been possessed by demons begged him that he might be with him. ¹⁹But Jesus*ᵉ* refused, and said to him, "Go home to your friends, and tell them how much the Lord

has done for you, and what mercy he has shown you." ²⁰And he went away and began to proclaim in the De·cap'o·lis how much Jesus had done for him; and everyone was amazed.

A Girl Restored to Life and a Woman Healed

21 When Jesus had crossed again in the boat*ʰ* to the other side, a great crowd gathered around him; and he was by the sea. ²²Then one of the leaders of the synagogue named Jā·ī'rus came and, when he saw him, fell at his feet ²³and begged him repeatedly, "My little daughter is at the point of death. Come and lay your hands on her, so that she may be made well, and live." ²⁴So he went with him.

And a large crowd followed him and pressed in on him. ²⁵Now there was a woman who had been suffering from hemorrhages for twelve years. ²⁶She had endured much under many physicians, and had spent all that she had; and she was no better, but rather grew worse. ²⁷She had heard about Jesus, and came up behind him in the crowd and touched his cloak, ²⁸for she said, "If I but touch his clothes, I will be made well." ²⁹Immediately her hemorrhage stopped; and she felt in her body that she was healed of her disease. ³⁰Immediately aware that power had gone forth from him, Jesus turned about in the crowd and said, "Who touched my clothes?" ³¹And his disciples said to him, "You see the crowd pressing in on you; how can you say, 'Who touched me?'" ³²He looked all around to see who had done it. ³³But the woman, knowing what had happened to her, came in fear and trembling, fell down before him, and told him the whole truth. ³⁴He said to her, "Daughter, your faith has made you well; go in peace, and be healed of your disease."

35 While he was still speaking, some people came from the leader's house to

Decapolis means "ten cities." In Jesus's time, the Decapolis was a group of ten cities in an area near the Sea of Galilee in the Roman province of Syria.

ᵉ Gk *he*   *ᶠ* Gk *they*   *ᵍ* Gk *him*   *ʰ* Other ancient authorities lack *in the boat* say, "Your daughter is dead. Why trouble the teacher any further?" [36]But overhearing[i] what they said, Jesus said to the leader of the synagogue, "Do not fear, only believe." [37]He allowed no one to follow him except Peter, James, and John, the brother of James. [38]When they came to the house of the leader of the synagogue, he saw a commotion, people weeping and wailing loudly. [39]When he had entered, he said to them, "Why do you make a commotion and weep? The child is not dead but sleeping." [40]And they laughed at him. Then he put them all outside, and took the child's father and mother and those who were with him, and went in where the child was. [41]He took her by the hand and said to her, "Tal·i·tha cūm," which means, "Little girl, get up!" [42]And immediately the girl got up and began to walk about (she was twelve years of age). At this they were overcome with amazement. [43]He strictly ordered them that no one should know this, and told them to give her something to eat.

The Rejection of Jesus at Nazareth

6 He left that place and came to his hometown, and his disciples followed him. [2]On the sabbath he began to teach in the synagogue, and many who heard him were astounded. They said, "Where did this man get all this? What is this wisdom that has been given to him? What deeds of power are being done by his hands! [3]Is not this the carpenter, the son of Mary[j] and brother of James and Jo·sēs and Judas and Simon, and are not his sisters here with us?" And they took offense[k] at him. [4]Then Jesus said to them, "Prophets are not without honor, except in their hometown, and among their own kin, and in their own house." [5]And he could do no deed of power there, except that he laid his hands on a few sick people and cured them. [6]And he was amazed at their unbelief.

The Mission of the Twelve

Then he went about among the villages teaching. [7]He called the twelve and began to send them out two by two, and gave them authority over the unclean spirits. [8]He ordered them to take nothing for their journey except a staff; no bread, no bag, no money in their belts; [9]but to wear sandals and not to put on two tunics. [10]He said to them, "Wherever you enter a house, stay there until you leave the place. [11]If any place will not welcome you and they refuse to hear you, as you leave, shake off the dust that is on your feet as a testimony against them." [12]So they went out and proclaimed that all should repent. [13]They cast out many demons, and anointed with oil many who were sick and cured them.

The Death of John the Baptist

[14] King Her·od heard of it, for Jesus'[l] name had become known. Some were[m] saying, "John the baptizer has been raised from the dead; and for this reason these powers are at work in him." [15]But others said, "It is E·lī´jah." And others said, "It is a prophet, like one of the prophets of old." [16]But when Her·od heard of it, he said, "John, whom I beheaded, has been raised."

[17] For Her´od himself had sent men who arrested John, bound him, and put him in prison on account of He·rō´di·as, his brother Philip's wife, because Her´od[n]

Jesus sent out the twelve disciples to carry out his ministry. When he told them not to take bread, money, or a bag, he was saying that they should depend on the hospitality of the people they would meet along the way and trust God to provide for them.

[i] Or *ignoring* ; other ancient authorities read *hearing*   [j] Other ancient authorities read *son of the carpenter and of Mary*   [k] Or *stumbled*   [l] Gk *his*   [m] Other ancient authorities read *He was*   [n] Gk *he*

A denarius was a Roman silver coin about the size of a dime. A person would usually receive one denarius for one day of work. The disciples said it would cost two hundred denarii (almost a year's salary) to buy enough food to feed the people who had come to hear Jesus teach!

had married her. ¹⁸For John had been telling Her·od, "It is not lawful for you to have your brother's wife." ¹⁹And He·rō·di·as had a grudge against him, and wanted to kill him. But she could not, ²⁰for Her·od feared John, knowing that he was a righteous and holy man, and protected him. When he heard him, he was greatly perplexed;ᵒ and yet he liked to listen to him. ²¹But an opportunity came when Her·od on his birthday gave a banquet for his courtiers and officers and for the leaders of Galilee. ²²When his daughter He·rō·di·asᵖ came in and danced, she pleased Her·od and his guests; and the king said to the girl, "Ask me for whatever you wish, and I will give it." ²³And he solemnly swore to her, "Whatever you ask me, I will give you, even half of my kingdom." ²⁴She went out and said to her mother, "What should I ask for?" She replied, "The head of John the baptizer." ²⁵Immediately she rushed back to the king and requested, "I want you to give me at once the head of John the Baptist on a platter." ²⁶The king was deeply grieved; yet out of regard for his oaths and for the guests, he did not want to refuse her. ²⁷Immediately the king sent a soldier of the guard with orders to bring John's�q head. He went and beheaded him in the prison, ²⁸brought his head on a platter, and gave it to the girl. Then the girl gave it to her mother. ²⁹When his disciples heard about it, they came and took his body, and laid it in a tomb.

Feeding the Five Thousand

30 The apostles gathered around Jesus, and told him all that they had done and taught. ³¹He said to them, "Come away to a deserted place all by yourselves and rest a while." For many were coming and going, and they had no leisure even to eat. ³²And they went away in the boat to a deserted place by themselves. ³³Now many saw them going and recognized them, and they hurried there on foot from all the towns and arrived ahead of them. ³⁴As he went ashore, he saw a great crowd; and he had compassion for them, because they were like sheep without a shepherd; and he began to teach them many things. ³⁵When it grew late, his disciples came to him and said, "This is a deserted place, and the hour is now very late; ³⁶send them away so that they may go into the surrounding country and villages and buy something for themselves to eat." ³⁷But he answered them, "You give them something to eat." They said to him, "Are we to go and buy two hundred denariiʳ worth of bread, and give it to them to eat?" ³⁸And he said to them, "How many loaves have you? Go and see." When they had found

There are often large storms around the Sea of Galilee. These storms come quickly and turn the deep, clear waters of the sea into crashing waves. Fishermen in small boats can suddenly find themselves in great danger!

Sometimes things happen suddenly in our lives that make us feel as if we are caught in a storm. But God is always with us through the storms of life. Whenever we are afraid or discouraged, we can trust God to help us. We can turn to God in prayer and know that God is there.

ᵒ Other ancient authorities read *he did many things*
ᵖ Other ancient authorities read *the daughter of Herodias herself*   q Gk *his*   ʳ The denarius was the usual day's wage for a laborer

out, they said, "Five, and two fish." ³⁹Then he ordered them to get all the people to sit down in groups on the green grass. ⁴⁰So they sat down in groups of hundreds and of fifties. ⁴¹Taking the five loaves and the two fish, he looked up to heaven, and blessed and broke the loaves, and gave them to his disciples to set before the people; and he divided the two fish among them all. ⁴²And all ate and were filled; ⁴³and they took up twelve baskets full of broken pieces and of the fish. ⁴⁴Those who had eaten the loaves numbered five thousand men.

Jesus Walks on the Water

45 Immediately he made his disciples get into the boat and go on ahead to the other side, to Beth·sa´i·da, while he dismissed the crowd. ⁴⁶After saying farewell to them, he went up on the mountain to pray.

47 When evening came, the boat was out on the sea, and he was alone on the land. ⁴⁸When he saw that they were straining at the oars against an adverse wind, he came towards them early in the morning, walking on the sea. He intended to pass them by. ⁴⁹But when they saw him walking on the sea, they thought it was a ghost and cried out; ⁵⁰for they all saw him and were terrified. But immediately he spoke to them and said, "Take heart, it is I; do not be afraid." ⁵¹Then he got into the boat with them and the wind ceased. And they were utterly astounded, ⁵²for they did not understand about the loaves, but their hearts were hardened.

Healing the Sick in Gennesaret

53 When they had crossed over, they came to land at Gen·nes´a·ret and moored the boat. ⁵⁴When they got out of the boat, people at once recognized him, ⁵⁵and rushed about that whole region and began to bring the sick on mats to wherever they heard he was. ⁵⁶And wherever he went, into villages or cities or farms, they laid the sick in the marketplaces, and begged him that they might touch even the fringe of his cloak; and all who touched it were healed.

The Tradition of the Elders

7 Now when the Phar´i·sees and some of the scribes who had come from Jerusalem gathered around him, ²they noticed that some of his disciples were eating with defiled hands, that is, without washing them. ³(For the Phar´i·sees, and all the Jews, do not eat unless they thoroughly wash their hands,ˢ thus observing the tradition of the elders; ⁴and they do not eat anything from the market unless they wash it;ᵗ and there are also many other traditions that they observe, the washing of cups, pots, and bronze kettles.ᵘ) ⁵So the Phar´i·sees and the scribes asked him, "Why do your disciples not liveᵛ according to the tradition of the elders, but eat with defiled hands?" ⁶He said to them, "I·sai´ah prophesied rightly about you hypocrites, as it is written,

'This people honors me with their lips,
  but their hearts are far from me;
⁷ in vain do they worship me,
  teaching human precepts as
    doctrines.'

⁸You abandon the commandment of God and hold to human tradition."

9 Then he said to them, "You have a fine way of rejecting the commandment of God in order to keep your tradition! ¹⁰For Moses said, 'Honor your father and your mother'; and, 'Whoever speaks evil of father or mother must surely die.' ¹¹But you say that if anyone tells father or mother, 'Whatever support you might have had from me is Cor´ban' (that is, an offering to Godʷ)— ¹²then you no longer permit doing anything for a father or mother, ¹³thus making void the word of God through your tradition that you have handed on. And you do many things like this."

14 Then he called the crowd again and said to them, "Listen to me, all of you, and

ˢ Meaning of Gk uncertain   ᵗ Other ancient authorities read *and when they come from the marketplace, they do not eat unless they purify themselves*   ᵘ Other ancient authorities add *and beds*   ᵛ Gk *walk*   ʷ Gk lacks *to God* understand: ¹⁵there is nothing outside a person that by going in can defile, but the things that come out are what defile."ˣ

17 When he had left the crowd and entered the house, his disciples asked him about the parable. ¹⁸He said to them, "Then do you also fail to understand? Do you not see that whatever goes into a person from outside cannot defile, ¹⁹since it enters, not the heart but the stomach, and goes out into the sewer?" (Thus he declared all foods clean.) ²⁰And he said, "It is what comes out of a person that defiles. ²¹For it is from within, from the human heart, that evil intentions come: fornication, theft, murder, ²²adultery, avarice, wickedness, deceit, licentiousness, envy, slander, pride, folly. ²³All these evil things come from within, and they defile a person."

A Gentile woman knew that Jesus could heal. She came and bowed before Jesus, asking his help for her daughter. Jesus recognized the woman's great faith and healed her daughter. This is an example of God's loving care for all people.

The Syrophoenician Woman's Faith

24 From there he set out and went away to the region of Tyre.ʸ He entered a house and did not want anyone to know he was there. Yet he could not escape notice, ²⁵but a woman whose little daughter had an unclean spirit immediately heard about him, and she came and bowed down at his feet. ²⁶Now the woman was a Gentile, of Sȳ·rō·-phoe·ni´ci·an origin. She begged him to cast the demon out of her daughter. ²⁷He said to her, "Let the children be fed first, for it is not fair to take the children's food and throw it to the dogs." ²⁸But she answered him, "Sir,ᶻ even the dogs under the table eat the children's crumbs." ²⁹Then he said to her, "For saying that, you may go—the demon has left your

When healing a man who could not hear, Jesus used the word *Ephphatha*. This is an Aramaic word that means "be opened."

daughter." ³⁰So she went home, found the child lying on the bed, and the demon gone.

Jesus Cures a Deaf Man

31 Then he returned from the region of Tyre, and went by way of Si´don towards the Sea of Galilee, in the region of the De·cap´o·lis. ³²They brought to him a deaf man who had an impediment in his speech; and they begged him to lay his hand on him. ³³He took him aside in private, away from the crowd, and put his fingers into his ears, and he spat and touched his tongue. ³⁴Then looking up to heaven, he sighed and said to him, "Eph´pha·tha," that is, "Be opened." ³⁵And immediately his ears were opened, his tongue was released, and he spoke plainly. ³⁶Then Jesusᵃ ordered them to tell no one; but the more he ordered them, the more zealously they proclaimed it. ³⁷They were astounded beyond measure, saying, "He has done everything well; he even makes the deaf to hear and the mute to speak."

Feeding the Four Thousand

8 In those days when there was again a great crowd without anything to eat, he called his disciples and said to them, ²"I have compassion for the crowd, because they have been with me now for three days and have nothing to eat. ³If I send them away hungry to their homes, they will faint on the way—and some of them have come from a great distance." ⁴His disciples replied, "How

---

ˣ Other ancient authorities add verse 16, *"Let any-one with ears to hear listen"*   ʸ Other ancient authorities add *and Sidon*   ᶻ Or *Lord*; other ancient authorities prefix *Yes*   ᵃ Gk *he* can one feed these people with bread here in the desert?" [5]He asked them, "How many loaves do you have?" They said, "Seven." [6]Then he ordered the crowd to sit down on the ground; and he took the seven loaves, and after giving thanks he broke them and gave them to his disciples to distribute; and they distributed them to the crowd. [7]They had also a few small fish; and after blessing them, he ordered that these too should be distributed. [8]They ate and were filled; and they took up the broken pieces left over, seven baskets full. [9]Now there were about four thousand people. And he sent them away. [10]And immediately he got into the boat with his disciples and went to the district of Dal·ma·nū́tha.[b]

The Demand for a Sign

11 The Phar·i·sees came and began to argue with him, asking him for a sign from heaven, to test him. [12]And he sighed deeply in his spirit and said, "Why does this generation ask for a sign? Truly I tell you, no sign will be given to this generation." [13]And he left them, and getting into the boat again, he went across to the other side.

The Yeast of the Pharisees and of Herod

14 Now the disciples[c] had forgotten to bring any bread; and they had only one loaf with them in the boat. [15]And he cautioned them, saying, "Watch out—beware of the yeast of the Phar·i·sees and the yeast of Her·od."[d] [16]They said to one another, "It is because we have no bread." [17]And becoming aware of it, Jesus said to them, "Why are you talking about having no bread? Do you still not perceive or understand? Are your hearts hardened? [18]Do you have eyes, and fail to see? Do you have ears, and fail to hear? And do you not

remember? [19]When I broke the five loaves for the five thousand, how many baskets full of broken pieces did you collect?" They said to him, "Twelve." [20]"And the seven for the four thousand, how many baskets full of broken pieces did you collect?" And they said to him, "Seven." [21]Then he said to them, "Do you not yet understand?"

Jesus Cures a Blind Man at Bethsaida

22 They came to Beth·sā́i·da. Some people[e] brought a blind man to him and begged him to touch him. [23]He took the blind man by the hand and led him out of the village; and when he had put saliva on his eyes and laid his hands on him, he asked him, "Can you see anything?" [24]And the man[f] looked up and said, "I can see people, but they look like trees, walking." [25]Then Jesus[f] laid his hands on his eyes again; and he looked intently and his sight was restored, and he saw everything clearly. [26]Then he sent him away to his home, saying, "Do not even go into the village."[g]

Peter's Declaration about Jesus

27 Jesus went on with his disciples to the villages of Caes·a·rḗa Phi·liṕpī; and on the way he asked his disciples, "Who do people say that I am?" [28]And they answered him, "John the Baptist; and others, E·lī́jah; and still others, one of the prophets." [29]He asked them, "But who do you say that I am?" Peter answered him, "You are the Messiah."[h] [30]And he sternly ordered them not to tell anyone about him.

Jesus Foretells His Death and Resurrection

31 Then he began to teach them that the Son of Man must undergo great suffering, and be rejected by the elders, the

"He [Jesus] asked them, 'But who do you say that I am?' Peter answered him, 'You are the Messiah.'"

Mark 8:29

[b] Other ancient authorities read *Mageda* or *Magdala*   [c] Gk *they*   [d] Other ancient authorities read *the Herodians*   [e] Gk *They*   [f] Gk *he*   [g] Other ancient authorities add *or tell anyone in the village*   [h] Or *the Christ*

chief priests, and the scribes, and be killed, and after three days rise again. [32]He said all this quite openly. And Peter took him aside and began to rebuke him. [33]But turning and looking at his disciples, he rebuked Peter and said, "Get behind me, Satan! For you are setting your mind not on divine things but on human things."

34 He called the crowd with his disciples, and said to them, "If any want to become my followers, let them deny themselves and take up their cross and follow me. [35]For those who want to save their life will lose it, and those who lose their life for my sake, and for the sake of the gospel,[i] will save it. [36]For what will it profit them to gain the whole world and forfeit their life? [37]Indeed, what can they give in return for their life? [38]Those who are ashamed of me and of my words[j] in this adulterous and sinful generation, of them the Son of Man will also be ashamed when he comes in the glory of his Father with the holy angels."

9 [1]And he said to them, "Truly I tell you, there are some standing here who will not taste death until they see that the kingdom of God has come with[k]power."

The Transfiguration

2 Six days later, Jesus took with him Peter and James and John, and led them up a high mountain apart, by themselves. And he was transfigured before them, [3]and his clothes became dazzling white, such as no one[l] on earth could bleach

Imagine how the disciples must have felt when they saw Jesus with Elijah and Moses, people who had died hundreds of years earlier! Do you think the disciples were afraid? They heard the voice of God, telling them to listen to God's son. God was telling the disciples that Jesus is God's son and that they should listen to him.

them. [4]And there appeared to them E·li′jah with Moses, who were talking with Jesus. [5]Then Peter said to Jesus, "Rabbi, it is good for us to be here; let us make three dwellings,[m] one for you, one for Moses, and one for E·li′jah." [6]He did not know what to say, for they were terrified. [7]Then a cloud overshadowed them, and from the cloud there came a voice, "This is my Son, the Beloved;[n] listen to him!" [8]Suddenly when they looked around, they saw no one with them any more, but only Jesus.

The Coming of Elijah

9 As they were coming down the mountain, he ordered them to tell no one about what they had seen, until after the Son of Man had risen from the dead. [10]So they kept the matter to themselves, questioning what this rising from the dead could mean. [11]Then they asked him, "Why do the scribes say that E·li′jah must come first?" [12]He said to them, "E·li′jah is indeed coming first to restore all things. How then is it written about the Son of Man, that he is to go through many sufferings and be treated with contempt? [13]But I tell you that E·li′jah has come, and they did to him whatever they pleased, as it is written about him."

The Healing of a Boy with a Spirit

14 When they came to the disciples, they saw a great crowd around them, and some scribes arguing with them. [15]When the whole crowd saw him, they were immediately overcome with awe, and they ran forward to greet him. [16]He asked them, "What are you arguing about with them?" [17]Someone from the crowd answered him, "Teacher, I brought you my son; he has a spirit that makes him unable to speak; [18]and whenever it seizes him, it dashes him down; and he foams and grinds his teeth and becomes rigid;

[i] Other ancient authorities read *lose their life for the sake of the gospel*   [j] Other ancient authorities read *and of mine*   [k] Or in   [l] Gk *no fuller*   [m] Or *tents*   [n] Or *my beloved Son*

and I asked your disciples to cast it out, but they could not do so." [19]He answered them, "You faithless generation, how much longer must I be among you? How much longer must I put up with you? Bring him to me." [20]And they brought the boy[o] to him. When the spirit saw him, immediately it convulsed the boy,[o] and he fell on the ground and rolled about, foaming at the mouth. [21]Jesus[p] asked the father, "How long has this been happening to him?" And he said, "From childhood. [22]It has often cast him into the fire and into the water, to destroy him; but if you are able to do anything, have pity on us and help us." [23]Jesus said to him, "If you are able!—All things can be done for the one who believes." [24]Immediately the father of the child cried out,[q] "I believe; help my unbelief!" [25]When Jesus saw that a crowd came running together, he rebuked the unclean spirit, saying to it, "You spirit that keeps this boy from speaking and hearing, I command you, come out of him, and never enter him again!" [26]After crying out and convulsing him terribly, it came out, and the boy was like a corpse, so that most of them said, "He is dead." [27]But Jesus took him by the hand and lifted him up, and he was able to stand. [28]When he had entered the house, his disciples asked him privately, "Why could we not cast it out?" [29]He said to them, "This kind can come out only through prayer."[r]

Jesus Again Foretells His Death and Resurrection

30 They went on from there and passed through Galilee. He did not want anyone to know it; [31]for he was teaching his disciples, saying to them, "The Son of Man is to be betrayed into human hands, and they will kill him, and three days after being killed, he will rise again." [32]But they did not understand what he was saying and were afraid to ask him.

Who Is the Greatest?

33 Then they came to Ca·per´na·um; and when he was in the house he asked

Capernaum was a large fishing village on the Sea of Galilee and the place where Jesus did much of his teaching and healing. Capernaum was the home of Peter, Andrew, James, and John, and it was probably the home of Matthew.

them, "What were you arguing about on the way?" [34]But they were silent, for on the way they had argued with one another who was the greatest. [35]He sat down, called the twelve, and said to them, "Whoever wants to be first must be last of all and servant of all." [36]Then he took a little child and put it among them; and taking it in his arms, he said to them, [37]"Whoever welcomes one such child in my name welcomes me, and whoever welcomes me welcomes not me but the one who sent me."

Another Exorcist

38 John said to him, "Teacher, we saw someone[s] casting out demons in your name, and we tried to stop him, because he was not following us." [39]But Jesus said, "Do not stop him; for no one who does a deed of power in my name will be able soon afterward to speak evil of me. [40]Whoever is not against us is for us. [41]For truly I tell you, whoever gives you a cup of water to drink because you bear the name of Christ will by no means lose the reward.

Temptations to Sin

42 "If any of you put a stumbling block before one of these little ones who believe in me,[t] it would be better for you if a great millstone were hung around your neck

[o] Gk him   [p] Gk He   [q] Other ancient authorities add *with tears*   [r] Other ancient authorities add *and fasting*   [s] Other ancient authorities add *who does not follow us*   [t] Other ancient authorities lack *in me*

and you were thrown into the sea. [43]If your hand causes you to stumble, cut it off; it is better for you to enter life maimed than to have two hands and to go to hell,[u] to the unquenchable fire.[v] [45]And if your foot causes you to stumble, cut it off; it is better for you to enter life lame than to have two feet and to be thrown into hell.[u,w] [47]And if your eye causes you to stumble, tear it out; it is better for you to enter the kingdom of God with one eye than to have two eyes and to be thrown into hell,[u] [48]where their worm never dies, and the fire is never quenched.

49 "For everyone will be salted with fire.[x] [50]Salt is good; but if salt has lost its saltiness, how can you season it?[y] Have salt in yourselves, and be at peace with one another."

Teaching about Divorce

10 He left that place and went to the region of Judea and[z] beyond the Jordan. And crowds again gathered around him; and, as was his custom, he again taught them.

2 Some Phar·i·sees came, and to test him they asked, "Is it lawful for a man to divorce his wife?" [3]He answered them, "What did Moses command you?" [4]They said, "Moses allowed a man to write a certificate of dismissal and to divorce her." [5]But Jesus said to them, "Because of your hardness of heart he wrote this commandment for you. [6]But from the beginning of creation, 'God made them male and female.' [7]For this reason a man shall leave his father and mother and be joined to his wife,[a] [8]and the two shall become one flesh.' So they are no longer two, but one flesh. [9]Therefore what God has joined together, let no one separate."

10 Then in the house the disciples asked him again about this matter. [11]He said to them, "Whoever divorces his wife and marries another commits adultery against her; [12]and if she divorces her husband and marries another, she commits adultery."

Jesus gathered the children close to him and placed his hands on them to bless them. He taught that all people—even grown-ups—must come to God like little children.

Jesus Blesses Little Children

13 People were bringing little children to him in order that he might touch them; and the disciples spoke sternly to them. [14]But when Jesus saw this, he was indignant and said to them, "Let the little children come to me; do not stop them; for it is to such as these that the kingdom of God belongs. [15]Truly I tell you, whoever does not receive the kingdom of God as a little child will never enter it." [16]And he took them up in his arms, laid his hands on them, and blessed them.

The Rich Man

17 As he was setting out on a journey, a man ran up and knelt before him, and asked him, "Good Teacher, what must I do to inherit eternal life?" [18]Jesus said to him, "Why do you call me good? No one is good but God alone. [19]You know the commandments: 'You shall not murder; You shall not commit adultery; You shall not steal; You shall not bear false witness; You shall not defraud; Honor your father and mother.' " [20]He said to him, "Teacher, I have kept all these since my youth." [21]Jesus, looking at him, loved him and said, "You lack one thing; go, sell what you own, and give the money[b] to the poor, and you will have treasure in heaven; then come, follow me." [22]When he heard this, he

---

[u] Gk *Gehenna*   [v] Verses 44 and 46 (which are identical with verse 48) are lacking in the best ancient authorities   [w] Verses 44 and 46 (which are identical with verse 48) are lacking in the best ancient authorities   [x] Other ancient authorities either add or substitute *and every sacrifice will be salted with salt*   [y] Or *how can you restore its saltiness?*   [z] Other ancient authorities lack *and*   [a] Other ancient authorities lack *and be joined to his wife*   [b] Gk lacks *the money*

was shocked and went away grieving, for he had many possessions.

23 Then Jesus looked around and said to his disciples, "How hard it will be for those who have wealth to enter the kingdom of God!" 24And the disciples were perplexed at these words. But Jesus said to them again, "Children, how hard it is*c* to enter the kingdom of God! 25It is easier for a camel to go through the eye of a needle than for someone who is rich to enter the kingdom of God." 26They were greatly astounded and said to one another,*d* "Then who can be saved?" 27Jesus looked at them and said, "For mortals it is impossible, but not for God; for God all things are possible."

28 Peter began to say to him, "Look, we have left everything and followed you." 29Jesus said, "Truly I tell you, there is no one who has left house or brothers or sisters or mother or father or children or fields, for my sake and for the sake of the good news,*e* 30who will not receive a hundredfold now in this age—houses, brothers and sisters, mothers and children, and fields, with persecutions—and in the age to come eternal life. 31But many who are first will be last, and the last will be first."

A Third Time Jesus Foretells His Death and Resurrection

32 They were on the road, going up to Jerusalem, and Jesus was walking ahead of them; they were amazed, and those who followed were afraid. He took the twelve aside again and began to tell them what was to happen to him, 33saying, "See, we are going up to Jerusalem, and the Son of Man will be handed over to the chief priests and the scribes, and they will condemn him to death; then they will hand him over to the Gentiles; 34they will mock him, and spit upon him, and flog him, and kill him; and after three days he will rise again."

The Request of James and John

35 James and John, the sons of Zeb′e·dee, came forward to him and said to him, "Teacher, we want you to do for us whatever we ask of you." 36And he said to them, "What is it you want me to do for you?" 37And they said to him, "Grant us to sit, one at your right hand and one at your left, in your glory." 38But Jesus said to them, "You do not know what you are asking. Are you able to drink the cup that I drink, or be baptized with the baptism that I am baptized with?" 39They replied, "We are able." Then Jesus said to them, "The cup that I drink you will drink; and with the baptism with which I am baptized, you will be baptized; 40but to sit at my right hand or at my left is not mine to grant, but it is for those for whom it has been prepared."

41 When the ten heard this, they began to be angry with James and John. 42So Jesus called them and said to them, "You know that among the Gentiles those whom they recognize as their rulers lord it over them, and their great ones are tyrants over them. 43But it is not so among you; but whoever wishes to become great among you must be your servant, 44and whoever wishes to be first among you must be slave of all. 45For the Son of Man came not to be served but to serve, and to give his life a ransom for many."

Read Mark 10:29–31. The good news is Jesus—his birth, loving deeds, and resurrection! His words and actions have fulfilled the promises of God. This is good news for the people of Jesus's day and good news for us! This is what the word gospel means. When we trust in Jesus and his works, we are saved from the sin and weakness that all people have. We can enjoy a life filled with the goodness of God.

c Other ancient authorities add *for those who trust in riches*   *d* Other ancient authorities read *to him*   *e* Or *gospel*

Bartimaeus knew Jesus could heal him. Although others tried to get him to be quiet, Bartimaeus was not afraid. He kept calling out to Jesus. Jesus healed Bartimaeus and pointed out his great faith. Then Bartimaeus joined the disciples in following Jesus. We do not need to be aftraid of calling on Jesus for help, no matter what anyone else says.

The Healing of Blind Bartimaeus

46 They came to Jericho. As he and his disciples and a large crowd were leaving Jericho, Bar·ti·maē´us son of Ti·maē´us, a blind beggar, was sitting by the roadside. [47]When he heard that it was Jesus of Nazareth, he began to shout out and say, "Jesus, Son of David, have mercy on me!" [48]Many sternly ordered him to be quiet, but he cried out even more loudly, "Son of David, have mercy on me!" [49]Jesus stood still and said, "Call him here." And they called the blind man, saying to him, "Take heart; get up, he is calling you." [50]So throwing off his cloak, he sprang up and came to Jesus. [51]Then Jesus said to him, "What do you want me to do for you?" The blind man said to him, "My teacher,[f] let me see again." [52]Jesus said to him, "Go; your faith has made you well." Immediately he regained his sight and followed him on the way.

Jesus' Triumphal Entry into Jerusalem

11 When they were approaching Jerusalem, at Beth´pha·gē and Beth´a·ny, near the Mount of Olives, he sent two of his disciples [2]and said to them, "Go into the village ahead of you, and immediately as you enter it, you will find tied there a colt that has never been ridden; untie it and bring it. [3]If anyone says to you, 'Why are you doing this?' just say this, 'The Lord needs it and will send it back here immediately.' " [4]They went away and found a colt tied near a door,

outside in the street. As they were untying it, [5]some of the bystanders said to them, "What are you doing, untying the colt?" [6]They told them what Jesus had said; and they allowed them to take it. [7]Then they brought the colt to Jesus and threw their cloaks on it; and he sat on it. [8]Many people spread their cloaks on the road, and others spread leafy branches that they had cut in the fields. [9]Then those who went ahead and those who followed were shouting,

"Hosanna!
Blessed is the one who comes in the name of the Lord!
[10] Blessed is the coming kingdom of our ancestor David!
Hosanna in the highest heaven!"

11 Then he entered Jerusalem and went into the temple; and when he had looked around at everything, as it was already late, he went out to Beth´a·ny with the twelve.

Jesus Curses the Fig Tree

12 On the following day, when they came from Beth´a·ny, he was hungry. [13]Seeing in the distance a fig tree in leaf, he went to see whether perhaps he would find anything on it. When he came to it, he found nothing but leaves, for it was not the season for figs. [14]He said to it, "May no

The Old Testament prophets told the people that God wanted the Temple to be used only to worship God (read Isaiah 56:7 and Jeremiah 7:11). But in order for visitors to obtain the animals necessary for sacrifice, merchants sold them at the Temple. It may be that by Jesus's time a few of these merchants were overcharging for the items necessary for proper Temple worship. Jesus wanted to return the focus of worship to God, not on buying and selling.

[f] Aramaic *Rabbouni*

one ever eat fruit from you again." And his disciples heard it.

Jesus Cleanses the Temple

15 Then they came to Jerusalem. And he entered the temple and began to drive out those who were selling and those who were buying in the temple, and he overturned the tables of the money changers and the seats of those who sold doves; [16]and he would not allow anyone to carry anything through the temple. [17]He was teaching and saying, "Is it not written,

'My house shall be called a house of
prayer for all the nations'?
But you have made it a den of
robbers."

[18]And when the chief priests and the scribes heard it, they kept looking for a way to kill him; for they were afraid of him, because the whole crowd was spellbound by his teaching. [19]And when evening came, Jesus and his disciples[g] went out of the city.

The Lesson from the Withered Fig Tree

20 In the morning as they passed by, they saw the fig tree withered away to its roots. [21]Then Peter remembered and said to him, "Rabbi, look! The fig tree that you cursed has withered." [22]Jesus answered them, "Have[h] faith in God. [23]Truly I tell you, if you say to this mountain, 'Be taken up and thrown into the sea,' and if you do not doubt in your heart, but believe that what you say will come to pass, it will be done for you. [24]So I tell you, whatever you ask for in prayer, believe that you have received[i] it, and it will be yours.

25 "Whenever you stand praying, forgive, if you have anything against anyone; so that your Father in heaven may also forgive you your trespasses."[j]

Jesus' Authority Is Questioned

27 Again they came to Jerusalem. As he was walking in the temple, the chief priests, the scribes, and the elders came to him [28]and said, "By what authority are you doing these things? Who gave you this authority to do them?" [29]Jesus said to them, "I will ask you one question; answer me, and I will tell you by what authority I do these things. [30]Did the baptism of John come from heaven, or was it of human origin? Answer me." [31]They argued with one another, "If we say, 'From heaven,' he will say, 'Why then did you not believe him?' [32]But shall we say, 'Of human origin'?"—they were afraid of the crowd, for all regarded John as truly a prophet. [33]So they answered Jesus, "We do not know." And Jesus said to them, "Neither will I tell you by what authority I am doing these things."

The Parable of the Wicked Tenants

12 Then he began to speak to them in parables. "A man planted a vineyard, put a fence around it, dug a pit for the wine press, and built a watchtower; then he leased it to tenants and went to another country. [2]When the season came, he sent a slave to the tenants to collect from them his share of the produce of the vineyard. [3]But they seized him, and beat him, and sent him away emptyhanded. [4]And again he sent another slave to them; this one they beat over the head and insulted. [5]Then he sent another, and that one they killed. And so it was with many others; some they beat, and others they killed. [6]He had still one other, a beloved son. Finally he sent him to them, saying, 'They will respect my son.' [7]But those tenants said to one another, 'This is the heir; come, let us kill him, and the inheritance will be ours.' [8]So they seized him, killed him, and threw him out of the vineyard. [9]What then will the owner of the vineyard do? He will come and destroy the tenants and give the vineyard to others. [10]Have you not read this scripture:

---

[g] Gk *they*: other ancient authorities read *he*
[h] Other ancient authorities read *"If you have*
[i] Other ancient authorities read *are receiving*
[j] Other ancient authorities add verse 26, *"But if you do not forgive, neither will your Father in heaven forgive your trespasses."*

'The stone that the builders rejected
has become the cornerstone;[k]
[11] this was the Lord's doing,
and it is amazing in our eyes'?"

12 When they realized that he had told this parable against them, they wanted to arrest him, but they feared the crowd. So they left him and went away.

The Question about Paying Taxes

13 Then they sent to him some Phar'i·sees and some He·ro'di·ans to trap him in what he said. [14]And they came and said to him, "Teacher, we know that you are sincere, and show deference to no one; for you do not regard people with partiality, but teach the way of God in accordance with truth. Is it lawful to pay taxes to the emperor, or not? [15]Should we pay them, or should we not?" But knowing their hypocrisy, he said to them, "Why are you putting me to the test? Bring me a denarius and let me see it." [16]And they brought one. Then he said to them, "Whose head is this, and whose title?" They answered, "The emperor's." [17]Jesus said to them, "Give to the emperor the things that are the emperor's, and to God the things that are God's." And they were utterly amazed at him.

The Question about the Resurrection

18 Some Sad'du·cees, who say there is no resurrection, came to him and asked him a question, saying, [19]"Teacher, Moses wrote for us that if a man's brother dies, leaving a wife but no child, the man[l] shall marry the widow and raise up children for his brother. [20]There were seven brothers; the first married and, when he died, left no children; [21]and the second married the widow[m] and died, leaving no children; and the third likewise; [22]none of the seven left children. Last of all the woman herself died. [23]In the resurrection[n] whose wife will she be? For the seven had married her."

24 Jesus said to them, "Is not this the reason you are wrong, that you know nei-

> When some religious leaders asked Jesus a question about paying taxes, he told them to look at a coin. The coin had a picture of the Roman emperor on it. So Jesus told them to give to the emperor the things that belong to the emperor—in other words, pay taxes. But more importantly, he told them to give to God the things that belong to God. Because we are made in the image of God, it is as if there is a picture of God on us! We should give ourselves to God because we belong to God.

ther the scriptures nor the power of God? [25]For when they rise from the dead, they neither marry nor are given in marriage, but are like angels in heaven. [26]And as for the dead being raised, have you not read in the book of Moses, in the story about the bush, how God said to him, 'I am the God of Abraham, the God of Isaac, and the God of Jacob'? [27]He is God not of the dead, but of the living; you are quite wrong."

The First Commandment

28 One of the scribes came near and heard them disputing with one another, and seeing that he answered them well, he asked him, "Which commandment is the first of all?" [29]Jesus answered, "The first is, 'Hear, O Israel: the Lord our God, the Lord is one; [30]you shall love the Lord your God with all your heart, and with all your soul, and with all your mind, and with all your strength.' [31]The second is this, 'You shall love your neighbor as yourself.' There is no other commandment greater than these." [32]Then the scribe said to him, "You are right, Teacher; you have truly said that 'he is one, and besides him there is no other'; [33]and 'to love him with all the heart, and with all the understanding, and with all the strength,' and 'to love one's neighbor as oneself,'—this is much more

[k] Or *keystone*   [l] Gk *his brother*   [m] Gk *her*
[n] Other ancient authorities add *when they rise*

important than all whole burnt offerings and sacrifices." [34]When Jesus saw that he answered wisely, he said to him, "You are not far from the kingdom of God." After that no one dared to ask him any question.

The Question about David's Son

35 While Jesus was teaching in the temple, he said, "How can the scribes say that the Messiah[o] is the son of David? [36]David himself, by the Holy Spirit, declared,

'The Lord said to my Lord,
"Sit at my right hand,
    until I put your enemies under your feet." '

[37]David himself calls him Lord; so how can he be his son?" And the large crowd was listening to him with delight.

Jesus Denounces the Scribes

38 As he taught, he said, "Beware of the scribes, who like to walk around in long robes, and to be greeted with respect in the marketplaces, [39]and to have the best seats in the synagogues and places of honor at banquets! [40]They devour widows' houses and for the sake of appearance say long prayers. They will receive the greater condemnation."

The Widow's Offering

41 He sat down opposite the treasury, and watched the crowd putting money into the treasury. Many rich people put in large sums. [42]A poor widow came and put in two small copper coins, which are worth a penny. [43]Then he called his disciples and said to them, "Truly I tell you, this poor widow has put in more than all those who are contributing to the treasury. [44]For all of them have contributed out of their abundance; but she out of her poverty has put in everything she had, all she had to live on."

The Destruction of the Temple Foretold

13 As he came out of the temple, one of his disciples said to him, "Look, Teacher, what large stones and what large buildings!" [2]Then Jesus asked him, "Do you see these great buildings? Not one stone will be left here upon another; all will be thrown down."

3 When he was sitting on the Mount of Olives opposite the temple, Peter, James, John, and Andrew asked him privately, [4]"Tell us, when will this be, and what will be the sign that all these things are about to be accomplished?" [5]Then Jesus began to say to them, "Beware that no one leads you astray. [6]Many will come in my name and say, 'I am he!'[p] and they will lead many astray. [7]When you hear of wars and rumors of wars, do not be alarmed; this must take place, but the end is still to come. [8]For nation will rise against nation, and kingdom against kingdom; there will be earthquakes in various places; there will be famines. This is but the beginning of the birth pangs.

Persecution Foretold

9 "As for yourselves, beware; for they will hand you over to councils; and you will be beaten in synagogues; and you will stand before governors and kings because of me, as a testimony to them. [10]And the good news[q] must first be proclaimed to all nations. [11]When they bring you to trial and hand you over, do not worry beforehand about what you are to say; but say

> When the widow gave two small coins as an offering, she gave all that she had. Although her coins were not worth very much money, the woman gave from her heart. God wants us to give and to serve from our hearts like the widow in this story. We don't have to have a lot of money or a lot of things. We don't have to be the very best at doing something. God wants us to give and to serve with our whole hearts, doing the best we can.

[o] Or *the Christ*   [p] Gk *I am*   [q] Gk *gospel*

whatever is given you at that time, for it is not you who speak, but the Holy Spirit. [12]Brother will betray brother to death, and a father his child, and children will rise against parents and have them put to death; [13]and you will be hated by all because of my name. But the one who endures to the end will be saved.

The Desolating Sacrilege

14 "But when you see the desolating sacrilege set up where it ought not to be (let the reader understand), then those in Judea must flee to the mountains; [15]the one on the housetop must not go down or enter the house to take anything away; [16]the one in the field must not turn back to get a coat. [17]Woe to those who are pregnant and to those who are nursing infants in those days! [18]Pray that it may not be in winter. [19]For in those days there will be suffering, such as has not been from the beginning of the creation that God created until now, no, and never will be. [20]And if the Lord had not cut short those days, no one would be saved; but for the sake of the elect, whom he chose, he has cut short those days. [21]And if anyone says to you at that time, 'Look! Here is the Messiah!'[r] or 'Look! There he is!'—do not believe it. [22]False messiahs[s] and false prophets will appear and produce signs and omens, to lead astray, if possible, the elect. [23]But be alert; I have already told you everything.

The Coming of the Son of Man

24 "But in those days, after that suffering,
>   the sun will be darkened,
>   and the moon will not give its
>   light,
[25] and the stars will be falling from
>   heaven,
>   and the powers in the heavens will
>   be shaken.

[26]Then they will see 'the Son of Man coming in clouds' with great power and glory. [27]Then he will send out the angels, and gather his elect from the four winds, from the ends of the earth to the ends of heaven.

The Lesson of the Fig Tree

28 "From the fig tree learn its lesson: as soon as its branch becomes tender and puts forth its leaves, you know that summer is near. [29]So also, when you see these things taking place, you know that he[t] is near, at the very gates. [30]Truly I tell you, this generation will not pass away until all these things have taken place. [31]Heaven and earth will pass away, but my words will not pass away.

The Necessity for Watchfulness

32 "But about that day or hour no one knows, neither the angels in heaven, nor the Son, but only the Father. [33]Beware, keep alert;[u] for you do not know when the time will come. [34]It is like a man going on a journey, when he leaves home and puts his slaves in charge, each with his work, and commands the doorkeeper to be on the watch. [35]Therefore, keep awake—for you do not know when the master of the house will come, in the evening, or at midnight, or at cockcrow, or at dawn, [36]or else he may find you asleep when he comes suddenly. [37]And what I say to you I say to all: Keep awake."

The Plot to Kill Jesus

14 It was two days before the Passover and the festival of Unleavened Bread. The chief priests and the scribes were looking for a way to arrest Jesus[v] by stealth and kill him; [2]for they said, "Not during the festival, or there may be a riot among the people."

The Anointing at Bethany

3 While he was at Beth·a·ny in the house of Simon the leper,[w] as he sat at the

"Heaven and earth will pass away, but my words will not pass away."
Mark 13:31

[r] Or *the Christ*   [s] Or *christs*   [t] Or *it*   [u] Other ancient authorities add *and pray*   [v] Gk *him*   [w] The terms *leper* and *leprosy* can refer to several diseases

table, a woman came with an alabaster jar of very costly ointment of nard, and she broke open the jar and poured the ointment on his head. ⁴But some were there who said to one another in anger, "Why was the ointment wasted in this way? ⁵For this ointment could have been sold for more than three hundred denarii,ˣ and the money given to the poor." And they scolded her. ⁶But Jesus said, "Let her alone; why do you trouble her? She has performed a good service for me. ⁷For you always have the poor with you, and you can show kindness to them whenever you wish; but you will not always have me. ⁸She has done what she could; she has anointed my body beforehand for its burial. ⁹Truly I tell you, wherever the good newsʸ is proclaimed in the whole world, what she has done will be told in remembrance of her."

Judas Agrees to Betray Jesus

10 Then Judas Is·car′i·ot, who was one of the twelve, went to the chief priests in order to betray him to them. ¹¹When they heard it, they were greatly pleased, and promised to give him money. So he began to look for an opportunity to betray him.

The Passover with the Disciples

12 On the first day of Unleavened Bread, when the Passover lamb is sacrificed, his disciples said to him, "Where do you want us to go and make the preparations for you to eat the Passover?" ¹³So he sent two of his disciples, saying to them, "Go into the city, and a man carrying a jar of water will meet you; follow him, ¹⁴and wherever he enters, say to the owner of the house, 'The Teacher asks, Where is my guest room where I may eat the Passover with my disciples?' ¹⁵He will show you a large room upstairs, furnished and ready. Make preparations for us there." ¹⁶So the disciples set out and went to the city, and found everything as he had told them; and they prepared the Passover meal.

17 When it was evening, he came with the twelve. ¹⁸And when they had taken

their places and were eating, Jesus said, "Truly I tell you, one of you will betray me, one who is eating with me." ¹⁹They began to be distressed and to say to him one after another, "Surely, not I?" ²⁰He said to them, "It is one of the twelve, one who is dipping breadᶻ into the bowlᵃ with me. ²¹For the Son of Man goes as it is written of him, but woe to that one by whom the Son of Man is betrayed! It would have been better for that one not to have been born."

The Institution of the Lord's Supper

22 While they were eating, he took a loaf of bread, and after blessing it he broke it, gave it to them, and said, "Take; this is my body." ²³Then he took a cup, and after giving thanks he gave it to them, and all of them drank from it. ²⁴He said to them, "This is my blood of theᵇ covenant, which is poured out for many. ²⁵Truly I tell you, I will never again drink of the fruit of the vine until that day when I drink it new in the kingdom of God."

Peter's Denial Foretold

26 When they had sung the hymn, they went out to the Mount of Olives.

When a woman anointed Jesus with some expensive oil, he was thankful. Some people complained, saying that she should have sold the oil and given the money to the poor. Jesus wanted his followers to take care of the poor, but he also knew that he would not be on the earth much longer. He told the people that the woman had done a good thing for him. She showed love and kindness to Jesus.

ˣ The denarius was the usual day's wage for a laborer   ʸ Or gospel   ᶻ Gk lacks bread
ᵃ Other ancient authorities read same bowl
ᵇ Other ancient authorities add new

²⁷And Jesus said to them, "You will all become deserters; for it is written,

'I will strike the shepherd,
    and the sheep will be scattered.'

²⁸But after I am raised up, I will go before you to Galilee." ²⁹Peter said to him, "Even though all become deserters, I will not." ³⁰Jesus said to him, "Truly I tell you, this day, this very night, before the cock crows twice, you will deny me three times." ³¹But he said vehemently, "Even though I must die with you, I will not deny you." And all of them said the same.

Jesus Prays in Gethsemane

32 They went to a place called Geth·sem´a·nē; and he said to his disciples, "Sit here while I pray." ³³He took with him Peter and James and John, and began to be distressed and agitated. ³⁴And he said to them, "I am deeply grieved, even to death; remain here, and keep awake." ³⁵And going a little farther, he threw himself on the ground and prayed that, if it were possible, the hour might pass from him. ³⁶He said, "Abba,^c Father, for you all things are possible; remove this cup from me; yet, not what I want, but what you want." ³⁷He came and found them sleeping; and he said to Peter, "Simon, are you asleep? Could you not keep awake one hour? ³⁸Keep awake and pray that you may not come into the time of trial;^d the spirit indeed is willing, but the flesh is weak." ³⁹And again he went away and prayed, saying the same words. ⁴⁰And once more he came and found them sleeping, for their eyes were very heavy; and they did not know what to say to him. ⁴¹He came a third time and said to them, "Are you still sleeping and taking your rest? Enough! The hour has come; the Son of Man is betrayed into the hands of sinners. ⁴²Get up, let us be going. See, my betrayer is at hand."

The Betrayal and Arrest of Jesus

43 Immediately, while he was still speaking, Judas, one of the twelve, arrived; and with him there was a crowd with

> "He said, 'Abba, Father, for you all things are possible; remove the cup from me; yet, not what I want, but what you want.'"
>
> Mark 14:36

swords and clubs, from the chief priests, the scribes, and the elders. ⁴⁴Now the betrayer had given them a sign, saying, "The one I will kiss is the man; arrest him and lead him away under guard." ⁴⁵So when he came, he went up to him at once and said, "Rabbi!" and kissed him. ⁴⁶Then they laid hands on him and arrested him. ⁴⁷But one of those who stood near drew his sword and struck the slave of the high priest, cutting off his ear. ⁴⁸Then Jesus said to them, "Have you come out with swords and clubs to arrest me as though I were a bandit? ⁴⁹Day after day I was with you in the temple teaching, and you did not arrest me. But let the scriptures be fulfilled." ⁵⁰All of them deserted him and fled.

51 A certain young man was following him, wearing nothing but a linen cloth. They caught hold of him, ⁵²but he left the linen cloth and ran off naked.

Jesus before the Council

53 They took Jesus to the high priest; and all the chief priests, the elders, and the scribes were assembled. ⁵⁴Peter had followed him at a distance, right into the courtyard of the high priest; and he was sitting with the guards, warming himself at the fire. ⁵⁵Now the chief priests and the whole council were looking for testimony against Jesus to put him to death; but they found none. ⁵⁶For many gave false testimony against him, and their testimony did not agree. ⁵⁷Some stood up and gave false testimony against him, saying, ⁵⁸"We heard him say, 'I will destroy this temple that is made with hands, and in three days I will build another, not made with hands.' " ⁵⁹But even on this point their testimony did not agree. ⁶⁰Then the high

^c Aramaic for *Father*   ^d Or *into temptation*

priest stood up before them and asked Jesus, "Have you no answer? What is it that they testify against you?" [61]But he was silent and did not answer. Again the high priest asked him, "Are you the Messiah,[e] the Son of the Blessed One?" [62]Jesus said, "I am; and

> 'you will see the Son of Man
> seated at the right hand of the Power,'
> and 'coming with the clouds of
> heaven.' "

[63]Then the high priest tore his clothes and said, "Why do we still need witnesses? [64]You have heard his blasphemy! What is your decision?" All of them condemned him as deserving death. [65]Some began to spit on him, to blindfold him, and to strike him, saying to him, "Prophesy!" The guards also took him over and beat him.

Peter Denies Jesus

66 While Peter was below in the courtyard, one of the servant-girls of the high priest came by. [67]When she saw Peter warming himself, she stared at him and said, "You also were with Jesus, the man from Nazareth." [68]But he denied it, saying, "I do not know or understand what you are talking about." And he went out into the forecourt.[f] Then the cock crowed.[g] [69]And the servant-girl, on seeing him, began again to say to the bystanders, "This man is one of them." [70]But again he

After Jesus was arrested, a servant-girl saw Peter and knew that he had been with Jesus.

Completely forgetting the promise he had made to Jesus only hours earlier (read Mark 14:26–31), Peter said that he was not a follower of Jesus and that he did not even know Jesus.

Sometimes it is hard to follow Jesus. Sometimes we make mistakes like Peter, who broke his promise and did not tell the truth. Pray to God, asking for help as you try your best to follow Jesus. Ask God to help you be strong and have courage.

denied it. Then after a little while the bystanders again said to Peter, "Certainly you are one of them; for you are a Galilean." [71]But he began to curse, and he swore an oath, "I do not know this man you are talking about." [72]At that moment the cock crowed for the second time. Then Peter remembered that Jesus had said to him, "Before the cock crows twice, you will deny me three times." And he broke down and wept.

Jesus before Pilate

15 As soon as it was morning, the chief priests held a consultation with the elders and scribes and the whole council. They bound Jesus, led him away, and handed him over to Pilate. [2]Pilate asked him, "Are you the King of the Jews?" He answered him, "You say so." [3]Then the chief priests accused him of many things. [4]Pilate asked him again, "Have you no answer? See how many charges they bring against you." [5]But Jesus made no further reply, so that Pilate was amazed.

Pilate Hands Jesus over to Be Crucified

6 Now at the festival he used to release a prisoner for them, anyone for whom they asked. [7]Now a man called Ba·rab´bas was in prison with the rebels who had committed murder during the insurrection. [8]So the crowd came and began to ask Pilate to do for them according to his custom. [9]Then he answered them, "Do you want me to release for you the King of the Jews?" [10]For he realized that it was out of jealousy that the chief priests had handed him over. [11]But the chief priests stirred up the crowd to have him release Ba·rab´bas for them instead. [12]Pilate spoke to them again, "Then what do you wish me to do[h] with the man you call[i] the King of the Jews?" [13]They shouted back, "Crucify

[e] Or the Christ [f] Or gateway [g] Other ancient authorities lack Then the cock crowed [h] Other ancient authorities read what should I do [i] Other ancient authorities lack the man you call

him!" ¹⁴Pilate asked them, "Why, what evil has he done?" But they shouted all the more, "Crucify him!" ¹⁵So Pilate, wishing to satisfy the crowd, released Ba·rab′bas for them; and after flogging Jesus, he handed him over to be crucified.

The Soldiers Mock Jesus

16 Then the soldiers led him into the courtyard of the palace (that is, the governor's headquarters[j]); and they called together the whole cohort. ¹⁷And they clothed him in a purple cloak; and after twisting some thorns into a crown, they put it on him. ¹⁸And they began saluting him, "Hail, King of the Jews!" ¹⁹They struck his head with a reed, spat upon him, and knelt down in homage to him. ²⁰After mocking him, they stripped him of the purple cloak and put his own clothes on him. Then they led him out to crucify him.

A man named Simon from the city of Cyrene had to carry the cross on which Jesus was later crucified. Simon was probably a visitor to the city of Jerusalem for the festival of the Passover.

The Crucifixion of Jesus

21 They compelled a passer-by, who was coming in from the country, to carry his cross; it was Simon of Cy·re′ne, the father of Alexander and Rufus. ²²Then they brought Jesus[k] to the place called Gol′go·tha (which means the place of a skull). ²³And they offered him wine mixed with myrrh; but he did not take it. ²⁴And they crucified him, and divided his clothes among them, casting lots to decide what each should take.

25 It was nine o'clock in the morning when they crucified him. ²⁶The inscription of the charge against him read, "The King of the Jews." ²⁷And with him they crucified two bandits, one on his right and one on his left.[l] ²⁹Those who passed by

derided[m] him, shaking their heads and saying, "Aha! You who would destroy the temple and build it in three days, ³⁰save yourself, and come down from the cross!" ³¹In the same way the chief priests, along with the scribes, were also mocking him among themselves and saying, "He saved others; he cannot save himself. ³²Let the Messiah,[n] the King of Israel, come down from the cross now, so that we may see and believe." Those who were crucified with him also taunted him.

The Death of Jesus

33 When it was noon, darkness came over the whole land[o] until three in the afternoon. ³⁴At three o'clock Jesus cried out with a loud voice, "E′lo·i, E′lo·i, le·ma′ sa·bach′tha·ni?" which means, "My God, my God, why have you forsaken me?"[p] ³⁵When some of the bystanders heard it, they said, "Listen, he is calling for E·li′jah." ³⁶And someone ran, filled a sponge with sour wine, put it on a stick, and gave it to him to drink, saying, "Wait, let us see whether E·li′jah will come to take him down." ³⁷Then Jesus gave a loud cry and breathed his last. ³⁸And the curtain of the temple was torn in two, from top to bottom. ³⁹Now when the centurion, who stood facing him, saw that in this way he[q] breathed his last, he said, "Truly this man was God's Son!"[r]

40 There were also women looking on from a distance; among them were Mary Mag′da·lene, and Mary the mother of James the younger and of Jo′ses, and Sa·lo′me. ⁴¹These used to follow him and provided for him when he was in Galilee; and there were many other women who had come up with him to Jerusalem.

The Burial of Jesus

42 When evening had come, and since it was the day of Preparation, that is, the

[j] Gk the praetorium   [k] Gk him   [l] Other ancient authorities add verse 28, *And the scripture was fulfilled that says, "And he was counted among the lawless."*   [m] Or *blasphemed*   [n] Or *the Christ*   [o] Or *earth*   [p] Other ancient authorities read *made me a reproach*   [q] Other ancient authorities add *cried out and*   [r] Or *a son of God*

day before the sabbath, ⁴³Joseph of Ar·i·ma·thē´a, a respected member of the council, who was also himself waiting expectantly for the kingdom of God, went boldly to Pilate and asked for the body of Jesus. ⁴⁴Then Pilate wondered if he were already dead; and summoning the centurion, he asked him whether he had been dead for some time. ⁴⁵When he learned from the centurion that he was dead, he granted the body to Joseph. ⁴⁶Then Joseph⁵ bought a linen cloth, and taking down the body,ᵗ wrapped it in the linen cloth, and laid it in a tomb that had been hewn out of the rock. He then rolled a stone against the door of the tomb. ⁴⁷Mary Mag´da·lēne and Mary the mother of Jō´sēs saw where the bodyᵗ was laid.

> In Jesus's day, people were buried in caves in the rock of a hillside. Their bodies were laid on shelves that had been cut into the walls of the caves. The tombs were then sealed with round, flat stones that rolled in front of the entrance.

The Resurrection of Jesus

16 When the sabbath was over, Mary Mag´da·lēne, and Mary the mother of James, and Sa·lō´mē bought spices, so that they might go and anoint him. ²And very early on the first day of the week, when the sun had risen, they went to the tomb. ³They had been saying to one another, "Who will roll away the stone for us from the entrance to the tomb?" ⁴When they looked up, they saw that the stone, which was very large, had already been rolled back. ⁵As they entered the tomb, they saw a young man, dressed in a white robe, sitting on the right side; and they were alarmed. ⁶But he said to them, "Do not be alarmed; you are looking for Jesus of

Nazareth, who was crucified. He has been raised; he is not here. Look, there is the place they laid him. ⁷But go, tell his disciples and Peter that he is going ahead of you to Galilee; there you will see him, just as he told you." ⁸So they went out and fled from the tomb, for terror and amazement had seized them; and they said nothing to anyone, for they were afraid.ᵘ

> After Jesus's death, Mary, Mary, and Salome went to anoint his body. But when they got to the tomb, the stone that covered the entrance had been rolled away! There was a young man sitting in the tomb. He was a messenger sent from God. He told the women to tell the disciples that they would see Jesus again.

THE SHORTER ENDING OF MARK

[[And all that had been commanded them they told briefly to those around Peter. And afterward Jesus himself sent out through them, from east to west, the sacred and imperishable proclamation of eternal salvation.ᵛ]]

THE LONGER ENDING OF MARK
Jesus Appears to Mary Magdalene

9 [[Now after he rose early on the first day of the week, he appeared first to Mary Mag´da·lēne, from whom he had cast out seven demons. ¹⁰She went out and told those who had been with him, while they were mourning and weeping. ¹¹But when they heard that he was alive and had been seen by her, they would not believe it.

ˢ Gk *he*   ᵗ Gk *it*   ᵘ Some of the most ancient authorities bring the book to a close at the end of verse 8. One authority concludes the book with the shorter ending; others include the shorter ending and then continue with verses 9-20. In most authorities verses 9-20 follow immediately after verse 8, though in some of these authorities the passage is marked as being doubtful.   ᵛ Other ancient authorities add *Amen*

Jesus Appears to Two Disciples

12 After this he appeared in another form to two of them, as they were walking into the country. [13]And they went back and told the rest, but they did not believe them.

Jesus Commissions the Disciples

14 Later he appeared to the eleven themselves as they were sitting at the table; and he upbraided them for their lack of faith and stubbornness, because they had not believed those who saw him after he had risen.[w] [15]And he said to them, "Go into all the world and proclaim the good news[x] to the whole creation. [16]The one who believes and is baptized will be saved; but the one who does not believe will be condemned. [17]And these signs will accompany those who believe: by using my name they will cast out demons; they will speak in new tongues; [18]they will pick up snakes in their hands,[y] and if they drink any deadly thing, it will not hurt them; they will lay their hands on the sick, and they will recover."

The Ascension of Jesus

19 So then the Lord Jesus, after he had spoken to them, was taken up into heaven and sat down at the right hand of God. [20]And they went out and proclaimed the good news everywhere, while the Lord worked with them and confirmed the message by the signs that accompanied it.[z]]]

[w] Other ancient authorities add, in whole or in part, *And they excused themselves, saying, "This age of lawlessness and unbelief is under Satan, who does not allow the truth and power of God to prevail over the unclean things of the spirits. Therefore reveal your righteousness now"—thus they spoke to Christ. And Christ replied to them, "The term of years of Satan's power has been fulfilled, but other terrible things draw near. And for those who have sinned I was handed over to death, that they may return to the truth and sin no more, that they may inherit the spiritual and imperishable glory of righteousness that is in heaven."*   [x] Or *gospel*   [y] Other ancient authorities lack *in their hands*   [z] Other ancient authorities add *Amen*

Luke

The Gospel of Luke begins by telling us how Luke came to write the story of Jesus. There were people who had known Jesus and had seen his actions and listened to his words. These people, called eyewitnesses, remembered and told others what they had seen. And so people began to write down the stories about Jesus. Although others had written down the stories, Luke probably wanted to tell the story for Gentiles (non-Jews) like Theophilus. The purpose of the Gospel of Luke was to tell the truth about Jesus's life, death, and resurrection for a man named Theophilus (see Luke 1:1–4).

The Gospel of Luke was written about 80–90 AD. To help as he wrote his Gospel, Luke used information that included the Gospel of Mark and a small collection of Jesus's sayings. There are some parts of the story of Jesus that are told only in the Gospel of Luke. For instance, only in Luke do we find the birth of John the Baptist, the song of the angels at the birth of Jesus, and the visit of the shepherds to the stable. Also, Luke is the only Gospel that tells about the prodigal son, the shepherd who lost a sheep, and the woman who lost a coin. In addition to his Gospel, Luke also wrote the Acts of the Apostles, which continues the story he began in his Gospel. Through these two books, Luke tells the marvelous story of God's love in Christ as the Good News began to spread to all people everywhere.

Luke 8:4–21

An angel brought a message from God to a priest named Zechariah, promising that his wife Elizabeth would give birth to a son. The angel told him to name the child John. God kept the promise, and Elizabeth gave birth to John (read Luke 1:57–66). When he grew older, John (who we call John the Baptist) helped the people be ready for the arrival of Jesus.

Dedication to Theophilus

1 Since many have undertaken to set down an orderly account of the events that have been fulfilled among us, [2]just as they were handed on to us by those who from the beginning were eyewitnesses and servants of the word, [3]I too decided, after investigating everything carefully from the very first,[a] to write an orderly account for you, most excellent Thē·oph´i·lus, [4]so that you may know the truth concerning the things about which you have been instructed.

The Birth of John the Baptist Foretold

5 In the days of King Her´od of Judea, there was a priest named Zech·a·rī´ah, who belonged to the priestly order of A·bī´jah. His wife was a descendant of Aaron, and her name was Elizabeth. [6]Both of them were righteous before God, living blamelessly according to all the commandments and regulations of the Lord. [7]But they had no children, because Elizabeth was barren, and both were getting on in years.

8 Once when he was serving as priest before God and his section was on duty, [9]he was chosen by lot, according to the custom of the priesthood, to enter the sanctuary of the Lord and offer incense. [10]Now at the time of the incense offering, the whole assembly of the people was praying outside. [11]Then there appeared to him an angel of the Lord, standing at the right side of the altar of incense. [12]When Zech·a·rī´ah saw him, he was terrified; and fear overwhelmed him. [13]But the angel said to him, "Do not be afraid, Zech·a·rī´ah, for your prayer has been heard. Your wife Elizabeth will bear you a son, and you will name him John. [14]You will have joy and gladness, and many will rejoice at his birth, [15]for he will be great in the sight of the Lord. He must never drink wine or strong drink; even before his birth he will be filled with the Holy Spirit. [16]He will turn many of the people of Israel to the Lord their God. [17]With the spirit and power of E·lī´jah he will go before him, to turn the hearts of parents to their children, and the disobedient to the wisdom of the righteous, to make ready a people prepared for the Lord." [18]Zech·a·rī´ah said to the angel, "How will I know that this is so? For I am an old man, and my wife is getting on in years." [19]The angel replied, "I am Gabriel. I stand in the presence of God, and I have been sent to speak to you and to bring you this good news. [20]But now, because you did not believe my words, which will be fulfilled in their time, you will become mute, unable to speak, until the day these things occur."

21 Meanwhile the people were waiting for Zech·a·rī´ah, and wondered at his delay in the sanctuary. [22]When he did come out, he could not speak to them, and they realized that he had seen a vision in the sanctuary. He kept motioning to them and remained unable to speak. [23]When his time of service was ended, he went to his home.

24 After those days his wife Elizabeth conceived, and for five months she remained in seclusion. She said, [25]"This is what the Lord has done for me when he looked favorably on me and took away the disgrace I have endured among my people."

[a] Or *for a long time*

"My soul magnifies the Lord, and my spirit rejoices in God my Savior." Luke 1:47

The Birth of Jesus Foretold

26 In the sixth month the angel Gabriel was sent by God to a town in Galilee called Nazareth, ²⁷to a virgin engaged to a man whose name was Joseph, of the house of David. The virgin's name was Mary. ²⁸And he came to her and said, "Greetings, favored one! The Lord is with you."ᵇ ²⁹But she was much perplexed by his words and pondered what sort of greeting this might be. ³⁰The angel said to her, "Do not be afraid, Mary, for you have found favor with God. ³¹And now, you will conceive in your womb and bear a son, and you will name him Jesus. ³²He will be great, and will be called the Son of the Most High, and the Lord God will give to him the throne of his ancestor David. ³³He will reign over the house of Jacob forever, and of his kingdom there will be no end." ³⁴Mary said to the angel, "How can this be, since I am a virgin?"ᶜ ³⁵The angel said to her, "The Holy Spirit will come upon you, and the power of the Most High will overshadow you; therefore the child to be bornᵈ will be holy; he will be called Son of God. ³⁶And now, your relative Elizabeth in her old age has also conceived a son; and this is the sixth month for her who was said to be barren. ³⁷For nothing will be impossible with God." ³⁸Then Mary said, "Here am I, the servant of the Lord; let it be with me according to your word." Then the angel departed from her.

Mary Visits Elizabeth

39 In those days Mary set out and went with haste to a Judean town in the hill country, ⁴⁰where she entered the house of Zech·a·rī́ah and greeted Elizabeth. ⁴¹When Elizabeth heard Mary's greeting, the child leaped in her womb. And Elizabeth was filled with the Holy Spirit ⁴²and exclaimed with a loud cry, "Blessed are you among women, and blessed is the fruit of your womb. ⁴³And why has this happened to me, that the mother of my Lord comes to me? ⁴⁴For as soon as I heard the sound of your greeting, the child in my womb leaped for joy. ⁴⁵And blessed is she who believed that there would beᵉ a fulfillment of what was spoken to her by the Lord."

Mary's Song of Praise

46 And Maryᶠ said,

⁴⁷ "My soul magnifies the Lord,
    and my spirit rejoices in God my
        Savior,
⁴⁸ for he has looked with favor on the
        lowliness of his servant.
    Surely, from now on all generations
        will call me blessed;
⁴⁹ for the Mighty One has done great
        things for me,
    and holy is his name.
⁵⁰ His mercy is for those who fear him
        from generation to generation.
⁵¹ He has shown strength with his arm;
    he has scattered the proud in the
        thoughts of their hearts.
⁵² He has brought down the powerful
        from their thrones,
    and lifted up the lowly;
⁵³ he has filled the hungry with good
        things,
    and sent the rich away empty.
⁵⁴ He has helped his servant Israel,
    in remembrance of his mercy,
⁵⁵ according to the promise he made to
        our ancestors,
    to Abraham and to his descendants
        forever."

56 And Mary remained with her about three months and then returned to her home.

ᵇ Other ancient authorities add *Blessed are you among women*   ᶜ Gk *I do not know a man*   ᵈ Other ancient authorities add *of you*   ᵉ Or *believed, for there will be*   ᶠ Other ancient authorities read *Elizabeth*

The Birth of John the Baptist

57 Now the time came for Elizabeth to give birth, and she bore a son. [58]Her neighbors and relatives heard that the Lord had shown his great mercy to her, and they rejoiced with her.

59 On the eighth day they came to circumcise the child, and they were going to name him Zech·a·ri´ah after his father. [60]But his mother said, "No; he is to be called John." [61]They said to her, "None of your relatives has this name." [62]Then they began motioning to his father to find out what name he wanted to give him. [63]He asked for a writing tablet and wrote, "His name is John." And all of them were amazed. [64]Immediately his mouth was opened and his tongue freed, and he began to speak, praising God. [65]Fear came over all their neighbors, and all these things were talked about throughout the entire hill country of Judea. [66]All who heard them pondered them and said, "What then will this child become?" For, indeed, the hand of the Lord was with him.

Zechariah's Prophecy

67 Then his father Zech·a·ri´ah was filled with the Holy Spirit and spoke this prophecy:
[68] "Blessed be the Lord God of Israel,
   for he has looked favorably on his
      people and redeemed them.
[69] He has raised up a mighty savior[g] for
      us
   in the house of his servant David,
[70] as he spoke through the mouth of his
      holy prophets from of old,
[71]   that we would be saved from our
      enemies and from the hand of all
      who hate us.
[72] Thus he has shown the mercy prom-
      ised to our ancestors,
   and has remembered his holy
      covenant,
[73] the oath that he swore to our ancestor
      Abraham,
      to grant us [74]that we, being rescued
      from the hands of our enemies,

might serve him without fear,
[75]in holiness and righteousness
   before him all our days.
[76] And you, child, will be called the
      prophet of the Most High;
   for you will go before the Lord to
      prepare his ways,
[77] to give knowledge of salvation to his
      people
   by the forgiveness of their sins.
[78] By the tender mercy of our God,
   the dawn from on high will break
      upon[h] us,
[79] to give light to those who sit in dark-
      ness and in the shadow of death,
   to guide our feet into the way of
      peace."

80 The child grew and became strong in spirit, and he was in the wilderness until the day he appeared publicly to Israel.

The town of Bethlehem is in the hill country just a few miles south of the city walls of Jerusalem. Bethlehem means "house of bread."

The Birth of Jesus

2 In those days a decree went out from Emperor Augustus that all the world should be registered. [2]This was the first registration and was taken while Qui·rin´i·us was governor of Syria. [3]All went to their own towns to be registered. [4]Joseph also went from the town of Nazareth in Galilee to Judea, to the city of David called Bethlehem, because he was descended from the house and family of David. [5]He went to be registered with Mary, to whom he was engaged and who was expecting a child. [6]While they were there, the time came for her to deliver her child. [7]And she gave birth to her firstborn son and

[g] Gk *a horn of salvation*   [h] Other ancient authorities read *has broken upon*

"Glory to God in the highest heaven, and on earth peace among those whom he favors." Luke 2:14

wrapped him in bands of cloth, and laid him in a manger, because there was no place for them in the inn.

The Shepherds and the Angels

8 In that region there were shepherds living in the fields, keeping watch over their flock by night. [9]Then an angel of the Lord stood before them, and the glory of the Lord shone around them, and they were terrified. [10]But the angel said to them, "Do not be afraid; for see—I am bringing you good news of great joy for all the people: [11]to you is born this day in the city of David a Savior, who is the Messiah,[i] the Lord. [12]This will be a sign for you: you will find a child wrapped in bands of cloth and lying in a manger." [13]And suddenly there was with the angel a multitude of the heavenly host,[j] praising God and saying,

[14] "Glory to God in the highest heaven,
and on earth peace among those
whom he favors!"[k]

15 When the angels had left them and gone into heaven, the shepherds said to one another, "Let us go now to Bethlehem and see this thing that has taken place, which the Lord has made known to us." [16]So they went with haste and found Mary and Joseph, and the child lying in the

Shepherds were the first people to hear about Jesus's birth. Shepherds did not have a lot of power or money. They were not famous or well-known. But God wanted everyone, everywhere, to know the gospel, or the Good News, of Jesus. Just as shepherds spent their lives caring for sheep, Jesus would grow up to spend his life caring for the people God had sent him to save.

manger. [17]When they saw this, they made known what had been told them about this child; [18]and all who heard it were amazed at what the shepherds told them. [19]But Mary treasured all these words and pondered them in her heart. [20]The shepherds returned, glorifying and praising God for all they had heard and seen, as it had been told them.

Jesus Is Named

21 After eight days had passed, it was time to circumcise the child; and he was called Jesus, the name given by the angel before he was conceived in the womb.

God's Holy Spirit had promised a man named Simeon that he would see the Messiah before he died. As soon as Simeon saw Jesus, he knew that this baby was the long-awaited Savior. He took the baby Jesus in his arms and blessed him. A prophet named Anna also recognized Jesus as the Messiah. She was one of the first people to tell others that Jesus would bring redemption to God's people.

Jesus Is Presented in the Temple

22 When the time came for their purification according to the law of Moses, they brought him up to Jerusalem to present him to the Lord [23](as it is written in the law of the Lord, "Every firstborn male shall be designated as holy to the Lord"), [24]and they offered a sacrifice according to what is stated in the law of the Lord, "a pair of turtledoves or two young pigeons."

25 Now there was a man in Jerusalem whose name was Sim´e·on;[l] this man was righteous and devout, looking forward to the consolation of Israel, and the Holy

---

[i] Or *the Christ*   [j] Gk *army*   [k] Other ancient authorities read *peace, goodwill among people*
[l] Gk *Symeon*

Spirit rested on him. [26]It had been revealed to him by the Holy Spirit that he would not see death before he had seen the Lord's Messiah.[m] [27]Guided by the Spirit, Sim´e·on[n] came into the temple; and when the parents brought in the child Jesus, to do for him what was customary under the law, [28]Sim´e·on[o] took him in his arms and praised God, saying,

[29] "Master, now you are dismissing your
        servant[p] in peace,
    according to your word;
[30] for my eyes have seen your salvation,
[31]   which you have prepared in the
        presence of all peoples,
[32] a light for revelation to the Gentiles
    and for glory to your people Israel."

33 And the child's father and mother were amazed at what was being said about him. [34]Then Sim´e·on[q] blessed them and said to his mother Mary, "This child is destined for the falling and the rising of many in Israel, and to be a sign that will be opposed [35]so that the inner thoughts of many will be revealed—and a sword will pierce your own soul too."

36 There was also a prophet, Anna[r] the daughter of Phan´u·el, of the tribe of Ash´er. She was of a great age, having lived with her husband seven years after her marriage, [37]then as a widow to the age of eighty-four. She never left the temple but worshiped there with fasting and prayer night and day. [38]At that moment she came, and began to praise God and to speak about the child[s] to all who were looking for the redemption of Jerusalem.

The Return to Nazareth

39 When they had finished everything required by the law of the Lord, they returned to Galilee, to their own town of Nazareth. [40]The child grew and became strong, filled with wisdom; and the favor of God was upon him.

The Boy Jesus in the Temple

41 Now every year his parents went to Jerusalem for the festival of the Passover. [42]And when he was twelve years old, they went up as usual for the festival. [43]When the festival was ended and they started to return, the boy Jesus stayed behind in Jerusalem, but his parents did not know it. [44]Assuming that he was in the group of travelers, they went a day's journey. Then they started to look for him among their relatives and friends. [45]When they did not find him, they returned to Jerusalem to search for him. [46]After three days they found him in the temple, sitting among the teachers, listening to them and asking them questions. [47]And all who heard him were amazed at his understanding and his answers. [48]When his parents[t] saw him they were astonished; and his mother said to him, "Child, why have you treated us like this? Look, your father and I have been searching for you in great anxiety." [49]He said to them, "Why were you searching for me? Did you not know that I must be in my Father's house?"[u] [50]But they did not understand what he said to them. [51]Then he went down with them and came to Nazareth, and was obedient to

Faithful Jewish families traveled to Jerusalem as often as they could to take part in the Jewish festivals. Jesus and his family traveled to Jerusalem for the festival of Passover. When the time came to leave, Jesus remained behind in Jerusalem. After looking among their friends and family, his parents went back to the city and found Jesus sitting with the teachers in the Temple, listening and asking questions. The people were amazed at what he understood. This was the first time Jesus spoke about his understanding that his life would be one of service to God and to others. In what ways can your life be one of service to God and to others?

[m] Or *the Lord's Christ*   [n] Gk *In the Spirit, he*
[o] Gk *he*   [p] Gk *slave*   [q] Gk *Symeon*   [r] Gk
Hanna   [s] Gk *him*   [t] Gk *they*   [u] Or *be about my Father's interests?*

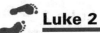
them. His mother treasured all these things in her heart.

52 And Jesus increased in wisdom and in years,ᵛ and in divine and human favor.

The Proclamation of John the Baptist

3 In the fifteenth year of the reign of Emperor Tī·bē´ri·us, when Pon´ti·us Pilate was governor of Judea, and Her´od was rulerʷ of Galilee, and his brother Philip rulerʷ of the region of Ī·tu·raē´a and Trach·o·nī´tis, and Lȳ·sā´ni·as rulerʷ of Ab·i·lē´nē, ²during the high priesthood of An´nas and Cā´i·a·phas, the word of God came to John son of Zech·a·rī´ah in the wilderness. ³He went into all the region around the Jordan, proclaiming a baptism of repentance for the forgiveness of sins, ⁴as it is written in the book of the words of the prophet Ī·sāi´ah,

"The voice of one crying out in the
wilderness:
'Prepare the way of the Lord,
make his paths straight.
⁵ Every valley shall be filled,
and every mountain and hill shall be
made low,
and the crooked shall be made
straight,
and the rough ways made smooth;
⁶ and all flesh shall see the salvation of
God.' "

7 John said to the crowds that came out to be baptized by him, "You brood of vipers! Who warned you to flee from the wrath to come? ⁸Bear fruits worthy of repentance. Do not begin to say to yourselves, 'We have Abraham as our ancestor'; for I tell you, God is able from these stones to raise up children to Abraham. ⁹Even now the ax is lying at the root of the trees; every tree therefore that does not bear good fruit is cut down and thrown into the fire."

10 And the crowds asked him, "What then should we do?" ¹¹In reply he said to them, "Whoever has two coats must share with anyone who has none; and whoever

has food must do likewise." ¹²Even tax collectors came to be baptized, and they asked him, "Teacher, what should we do?" ¹³He said to them, "Collect no more than the amount prescribed for you." ¹⁴Soldiers also asked him, "And we, what should we do?" He said to them, "Do not extort money from anyone by threats or false accusation, and be satisfied with your wages."

15 As the people were filled with expectation, and all were questioning in their hearts concerning John, whether he might be the Messiah,ˣ ¹⁶John answered all of them by saying, "I baptize you with water; but one who is more powerful than I is coming; I am not worthy to untie the thong of his sandals. He will baptize you withʸ the Holy Spirit and fire. ¹⁷His winnowing fork is in his hand, to clear his threshing floor and to gather the wheat into his granary; but the chaff he will burn with unquenchable fire."

18 So, with many other exhortations, he proclaimed the good news to the people. ¹⁹But Her´od the ruler,ʷ who had been rebuked by him because of He·rō´di·as, his brother's wife, and because of all the evil things that Her´od had done, ²⁰added to them all by shutting up John in prison.

The Baptism of Jesus

21 Now when all the people were baptized, and when Jesus also had been baptized and was praying, the heaven was opened, ²²and the Holy Spirit descended

Without water, no living thing could exist. We drink water to live. We cool ourselves with water on hot, summer days. We use water to clean things and to clean ourselves. And we baptize with water. The water in baptism reminds us that we are made new in our lives with God. Baptism is a sign that God is with us.

ᵛ Or in *stature* ʷ Gk *tetrarch* ˣ Or *the Christ*
ʸ Or *in*

When Jesus was baptized, the Holy Spirit came down like a dove upon him. Today, we use the dove as a symbol of the Holy Spirit. We also use the dove as a symbol for peace and forgiveness.

upon him in bodily form like a dove. And a voice came from heaven, "You are my Son, the Beloved;[z] with you I am well pleased."[a]

The Ancestors of Jesus

23 Jesus was about thirty years old when he began his work. He was the son (as was thought) of Joseph son of Hē′lī, [24]son of Mat′that, son of Levi, son of Mel′chī, son of Jan′naī, son of Joseph, [25]son of Mat·ta·thī′as, son of Ā′mos, son of Nā′hum, son of Es′lī, son of Nag′ga·ī, [26]son of Mā′ath, son of Mat·ta·thī′as, son of Sem′ē·in, son of Jō′sech, son of Jō′da, [27]son of Jō·an′an, son of Rhē′sa, son of Ze·rub′-ba·bel, son of She·al′ti·el,[b] son of Nē′rī, [28]son of Mel′chī, son of Ad′dī, son of Cō′sam, son of El·mā′dam, son of Er, [29]son of Joshua, son of El·i·ē′zer, son of Jō′rim, son of Mat′that, son of Levi, [30]son of Sim′ē·on, son of Judah, son of Joseph, son of Jō′nam, son of E·lī′a·kim, [31]son of Mē′le·a, son of Men′na, son of Mat′ta·tha, son of Nathan, son of David, [32]son of Jesse, son of Ō′bed, son of Bō′az, son of Sā′la,[c] son of Nah′shon, [33]son of Am·min′-a·dab, son of Ad·min, son of Ar′nī,[d] son of Hez′ron, son of Per′ez, son of Judah, [34]son of Jacob, son of Isaac, son of Abraham, son of Tē′rah, son of Nā′hor, [35]son of Sē′rug, son of Rē′ū, son of Pē′leg, son of Ē′ber, son of Shē′lah, [36]son of Cā·ī′nan, son of Ar·phā′-xad, son of Shem, son of Noah, son of Lā′mech, [37]son of Me·thū′se·lah, son of Ē′noch, son of Jar′ed, son of Mā·ha·la′le·el, son of Cā·ī′nan, [38]son of Ē′nos, son of Seth, son of Adam, son of God.

The Temptation of Jesus

4 Jesus, full of the Holy Spirit, returned from the Jordan and was led by the Spirit in the wilderness, [2]where for forty days he was tempted by the devil. He ate nothing at all during those days, and when they were over, he was famished. [3]The devil said to him, "If you are the Son of God, command this stone to become a loaf of bread." [4]Jesus answered him, "It is written, 'One does not live by bread alone.' "

5 Then the devil[e] led him up and showed him in an instant all the kingdoms of the world. [6]And the devil[e] said to him, "To you I will give their glory and all this authority; for it has been given over to me, and I give it to anyone I please. [7]If you, then, will worship me, it will all be yours." [8]Jesus answered him, "It is written,

'Worship the Lord your God,
    and serve only him.' "

9 Then the devil[e] took him to Jerusalem, and placed him on the pinnacle of the temple, saying to him, "If you are the Son of God, throw yourself down from here, [10]for it is written,

Before Jesus began his ministry, God led Jesus into the wilderness where he was tested for forty days. To help himself resist temptation, Jesus quoted the Scriptures he had learned as a boy. Look up the passages he used to help him during this time: Deuteronomy 8:3, Deuteronomy 6:13, and Deuteronomy 6:16. In many New Testament stories, Jesus quoted verses from the Hebrew Scriptures.

[z] Or *my beloved Son*   [a] Other ancient authorities read *You are my Son, today I have begotten you*   [b] Gk *Salathiel*   [c] Other ancient authorities read *Salmon*   [d] Other ancient authorities read *Amminadab, son of Aram*; others vary widely   [e] Gk *he*

'He will command his angels
concerning you,
to protect you,'
¹¹and
'On their hands they will bear you up,
so that you will not dash your foot
against a stone.'"
¹²Jesus answered him, "It is said, 'Do not put the Lord your God to the test.'"
¹³When the devil had finished every test, he departed from him until an opportune time.

The Beginning of the Galilean Ministry

14 Then Jesus, filled with the power of the Spirit, returned to Galilee, and a report about him spread through all the surrounding country. ¹⁵He began to teach in their synagogues and was praised by everyone.

Synagogues are places of worship for Jewish congregations. The word synagogue means a gathering or an assembly. Many people believe that synagogues were first built during the Babylonian exile when the people could no longer worship in the Temple. In Jesus's time, people gathered together for worship and for teaching the Scriptures and the Law.

The Rejection of Jesus at Nazareth

16 When he came to Nazareth, where he had been brought up, he went to the synagogue on the sabbath day, as was his custom. He stood up to read, ¹⁷and the scroll of the prophet I·sa·i'ah was given to him. He unrolled the scroll and found the place where it was written:
¹⁸ "The Spirit of the Lord is upon me,
because he has anointed me to bring
good news to the poor.

He has sent me to proclaim release to
the captives
and recovery of sight to the blind,
to let the oppressed go free,
¹⁹ to proclaim the year of the Lord's
favor."
²⁰And he rolled up the scroll, gave it back to the attendant, and sat down. The eyes of all in the synagogue were fixed on him. ²¹Then he began to say to them, "Today this scripture has been fulfilled in your hearing." ²²All spoke well of him and were amazed at the gracious words that came from his mouth. They said, "Is not this Joseph's son?" ²³He said to them, "Doubtless you will quote to me this proverb, 'Doctor, cure yourself!' And you will say, 'Do here also in your hometown the things that we have heard you did at Ca·per'na·um.'" ²⁴And he said, "Truly I tell you, no prophet is accepted in the prophet's hometown. ²⁵But the truth is, there were many widows in Israel in the time of E·li'jah, when the heaven was shut up three years and six months, and there was a severe famine over all the land; ²⁶yet E·li'jah was sent to none of them except to a widow at Zar'e·phath in Si'don. ²⁷There were also many lepers′ in Israel in the time of the prophet E·li'sha, and none of them was cleansed except Na'a·man the Syrian." ²⁸When they heard this, all in the synagogue were filled with rage. ²⁹They got up, drove him out of the town, and led him to the brow of the hill on which their town was built, so that they might hurl him off the cliff. ³⁰But he passed through the midst of them and went on his way.

The Man with an Unclean Spirit

31 He went down to Ca·per'na·um, a city in Galilee, and was teaching them on the sabbath. ³²They were astounded at his teaching, because he spoke with authority. ³³In the synagogue there was a man who had the spirit of an unclean demon, and he cried out with a loud voice, ³⁴"Let us

───

ʲ The terms *leper* and *leprosy* can refer to several diseases alone! What have you to do with us, Jesus of Nazareth? Have you come to destroy us? I know who you are, the Holy One of God." ³⁵But Jesus rebuked him, saying, "Be silent, and come out of him!" When the demon had thrown him down before them, he came out of him without having done him any harm. ³⁶They were all amazed and kept saying to one another, "What kind of utterance is this? For with authority and power he commands the unclean spirits, and out they come!" ³⁷And a report about him began to reach every place in the region.

Simon and the other men working with him fished all night long and did not catch any fish. But when Jesus told them to put their nets into the water again, they did. They caught so many fish that their nets were beginning to break! They were amazed at what Jesus had done. When they got back to the shore, they left everything behind and followed Jesus.

Peter's house was located at Capernaum, a fishing village on Lake Galilee. He and his brother Andrew, along with James and John, ran a fishing business.

Healings at Simon's House

38 After leaving the synagogue he entered Simon's house. Now Simon's mother-in-law was suffering from a high fever, and they asked him about her. ³⁹Then he stood over her and rebuked the fever, and it left her. Immediately she got up and began to serve them.

40 As the sun was setting, all those who had any who were sick with various kinds of diseases brought them to him; and he laid his hands on each of them and cured them. ⁴¹Demons also came out of many, shouting, "You are the Son of God!" But he rebuked them and would not allow them to speak, because they knew that he was the Messiah.ᵍ

Jesus Preaches in the Synagogues

42 At daybreak he departed and went into a deserted place. And the crowds were looking for him; and when they reached him, they wanted to prevent him from leaving them. ⁴³But he said to them, "I must proclaim the good news of the

kingdom of God to the other cities also; for I was sent for this purpose." ⁴⁴So he continued proclaiming the message in the synagogues of Judea.ʰ

Jesus Calls the First Disciples

5 Once while Jesusⁱ was standing beside the lake of Gen·nes´a·ret, and the crowd was pressing in on him to hear the word of God, ²he saw two boats there at the shore of the lake; the fishermen had gone out of them and were washing their nets. ³He got into one of the boats, the one belonging to Simon, and asked him to put out a little way from the shore. Then he sat down and taught the crowds from the boat. ⁴When he had finished speaking, he said to Simon, "Put out into the deep water and let down your nets for a catch." ⁵Simon answered, "Master, we have worked all night long but have caught nothing. Yet if you say so, I will let down the nets." ⁶When they had done this, they caught so many fish that their nets were beginning to break. ⁷So they signaled their partners in the other boat to come and help them. And they came and filled both boats, so that they began to sink. ⁸But when Simon Peter saw it, he fell down at Jesus' knees, saying, "Go away from me, Lord, for I am a sinful man!" ⁹For he and all who were with him were amazed at the catch of fish that they had taken; ¹⁰and so also were James and

ᵍ Or the Christ   ʰ Other ancient authorities read Galilee   ⁱ Gk he

John, sons of Zeb´e·dee, who were partners with Simon. Then Jesus said to Simon, "Do not be afraid; from now on you will be catching people." [11]When they had brought their boats to shore, they left everything and followed him.

Jesus Cleanses a Leper

12 Once, when he was in one of the cities, there was a man covered with leprosy.[j] When he saw Jesus, he bowed with his face to the ground and begged him, "Lord, if you choose, you can make me clean." [13]Then Jesus[k] stretched out his hand, touched him, and said, "I do choose. Be made clean." Immediately the leprosy[j] left him. [14]And he ordered him to tell no one. "Go," he said, "and show yourself to the priest, and, as Moses commanded, make an offering for your cleansing, for a testimony to them." [15]But now more than ever the word about Jesus[l] spread abroad; many crowds would gather to hear him and to be cured of their diseases. [16]But he would withdraw to deserted places and pray.

Jesus Heals a Paralytic

17 One day, while he was teaching, Phar´i·sees and teachers of the law were sitting near by (they had come from every village of Galilee and Judea and from Jerusalem); and the power of the Lord was with him to heal.[m] [18]Just then some men came, carrying a paralyzed man on a bed. They were trying to bring him in and lay him before Jesus;[l] [19]but finding no way to bring him in because of the crowd, they went up on the roof and let him down with his bed through the tiles into the middle of the crowd[n] in front of Jesus. [20]When he saw their faith, he said, "Friend,[o] your sins are forgiven you." [21]Then the scribes and the Phar´i·sees

began to question, "Who is this who is speaking blasphemies? Who can forgive sins but God alone?" [22]When Jesus perceived their questionings, he answered them, "Why do you raise such questions in your hearts? [23]Which is easier, to say, 'Your sins are forgiven you,' or to say, 'Stand up and walk'? [24]But so that you may know that the Son of Man has authority on earth to forgive sins"—he said to the one who was paralyzed—"I say to you, stand up and take your bed and go to your home." [25]Immediately he stood up before them, took what he had been lying on, and went to his home, glorifying God. [26]Amazement seized all of them, and they glorified God and were filled with awe, saying, "We have seen strange things today."

Jesus Calls Levi

27 After this he went out and saw a tax collector named Levi, sitting at the tax booth; and he said to him, "Follow me." [28]And he got up, left everything, and followed him.

29 Then Levi gave a great banquet for him in his house; and there was a large crowd of tax collectors and others sitting at the table[p] with them. [30]The Phar´i·sees and their scribes were complaining to his disciples, saying, "Why do you eat and drink with tax collectors and sinners?" [31]Jesus answered, "Those who are well have no need of a physician, but those who are sick; [32]I have come to call not the righteous but sinners to repentance."

The Question about Fasting

33 Then they said to him, "John's disciples, like the disciples of the Phar´i·sees, frequently fast and pray, but your disciples eat and drink." [34]Jesus said to them, "You cannot make wedding guests fast while the bridegroom is with them, can you? [35]The days will come when the bridegroom will be taken away from them, and

"Those who are well have no need of a physician, but those who are sick; I have come to call not the righteous but sinners to repentance." Luke 5:31

[j] The terms *leper* and *leprosy* can refer to several diseases   [k] Gk *he*   [l] Gk *him*   [m] Other ancient authorities read *was present to heal them*   [n] Gk *into the midst*   [o] Gk *Man*   [p] Gk *reclining*

Fasting is going without food (and sometimes water) for a period of time. In Bible times, people fasted to show devotion to God, grief or sadness. Fasting was also an act of repentance for sin. After the Exile, days of fasting were set at regular times during the year. Jesus taught that fasting should be done in sincerity and for the glory of God.

ered. [7]The scribes and the Phar′i·sees watched him to see whether he would cure on the sabbath, so that they might find an accusation against him. [8]Even though he knew what they were thinking, he said to the man who had the withered hand, "Come and stand here." He got up and stood there. [9]Then Jesus said to them, "I ask you, is it lawful to do good or to do harm on the sabbath, to save life or to destroy it?" [10]After looking around at all of them, he said to him, "Stretch out your hand." He did so, and his hand was restored. [11]But they were filled with fury and discussed with one another what they might do to Jesus.

then they will fast in those days." [36]He also told them a parable: "No one tears a piece from a new garment and sews it on an old garment; otherwise the new will be torn, and the piece from the new will not match the old. [37]And no one puts new wine into old wineskins; otherwise the new wine will burst the skins and will be spilled, and the skins will be destroyed. [38]But new wine must be put into fresh wineskins. [39]And no one after drinking old wine desires new wine, but says, 'The old is good.' "[q]

Many times Jesus went alone to pray. Sometimes he spent the whole night talking and listening to God! These times of prayer helped him to be ready for the days of teaching and healing. We too can be ready for our days by talking and listening to God. Talk to your family about making a commitment to pray together every day.

The Question about the Sabbath

6 One sabbath[r] while Jesus[s] was going through the grainfields, his disciples plucked some heads of grain, rubbed them in their hands, and ate them. [2]But some of the Phar′i·sees said, "Why are you doing what is not lawful[t] on the sabbath?" [3]Jesus answered, "Have you not read what David did when he and his companions were hungry? [4]He entered the house of God and took and ate the bread of the Presence, which it is not lawful for any but the priests to eat, and gave some to his companions?" [5]Then he said to them, "The Son of Man is lord of the sabbath."

The Man with a Withered Hand

6 On another sabbath he entered the synagogue and taught, and there was a man there whose right hand was with-

Jesus Chooses
the Twelve Apostles

12 Now during those days he went out to the mountain to pray; and he spent the night in prayer to God. [13]And when day came, he called his disciples and chose twelve of them, whom he also named apostles: [14]Simon, whom he named Peter, and his brother Andrew, and James, and John, and Philip, and Bartholomew, [15]and Matthew, and Thomas, and James son of Al·phae′us, and Simon, who was called the Zealot, [16]and Judas son of James, and Judas Is·car′i·ot, who became a traitor.

[q] Other ancient authorities read *better*; others lack verse 39   [r] Other ancient authorities read *On the second first sabbath*   [s] Gk he   [t] Other ancient authorities add *to do*

Luke 6

Jesus Teaches and Heals

17 He came down with them and stood on a level place, with a great crowd of his disciples and a great multitude of people from all Judea, Jerusalem, and the coast of Tyre and Si′don. 18They had come to hear him and to be healed of their diseases; and those who were troubled with unclean spirits were cured. 19And all in the crowd were trying to touch him, for power came out from him and healed all of them.

Blessings and Woes

20 Then he looked up at his disciples and said:

"Blessed are you who are poor,
for yours is the kingdom of God.

21 "Blessed are you who are hungry now,
for you will be filled.

"Blessed are you who weep now,
for you will laugh.

22 "Blessed are you when people hate you, and when they exclude you, revile you, and defame you[u] on account of the Son of Man. 23Rejoice in that day and leap for joy, for surely your reward is great in heaven; for that is what their ancestors did to the prophets.

24 "But woe to you who are rich,
for you have received your consolation.

25 "Woe to you who are full now,
for you will be hungry.

"Woe to you who are laughing now,
for you will mourn and weep.

26 "Woe to you when all speak well of you, for that is what their ancestors did to the false prophets.

Love for Enemies

27 "But I say to you that listen, Love your enemies, do good to those who hate you, 28bless those who curse you, pray for those who abuse you. 29If anyone strikes you on the cheek, offer the other also; and from anyone who takes away your coat do not withhold even your shirt. 30Give to everyone who begs from you; and if anyone takes away your goods, do not ask for them again. 31Do to others as you would have them do to you.

32 "If you love those who love you, what credit is that to you? For even sinners love those who love them. 33If you do good to those who do good to you, what credit is that to you? For even sinners do the same. 34If you lend to those from whom you hope to receive, what credit is that to you? Even sinners lend to sinners, to receive as much again. 35But love your enemies, do good, and lend, expecting nothing in return.[v] Your reward will be great, and you will be children of the Most High; for he is kind to the ungrateful and the wicked. 36Be merciful, just as your Father is merciful.

Judging Others

37 "Do not judge, and you will not be judged; do not condemn, and you will not be condemned. Forgive, and you will be forgiven; 38give, and it will be given to you. A good measure, pressed down, shaken together, running over, will be put into your lap; for the measure you give will be the measure you get back."

39 He also told them a parable: "Can a blind person guide a blind person? Will not both fall into a pit? 40A disciple is not above the teacher, but everyone who is fully qualified will be like the teacher. 41Why do you see the speck in your neighbor's[w] eye, but do not notice the log in your own eye? 42Or how can you say to your neighbor,[x] 'Friend,[x] let me take out the speck in your eye,' when you yourself do not see the log in your own eye? You hypocrite, first take the log out of your own eye, and then you will see clearly to take the speck out of your neighbor's[w] eye.

A Tree and Its Fruit

43 "No good tree bears bad fruit, nor

"Do to others as you would have them do to you." Luke 6:31

---

u Gk cast out your name as evil   v Other ancient authorities read despairing of no one   w Gk brother's   x Gk brother again does a bad tree bear good fruit; ⁴⁴for each tree is known by its own fruit. Figs are not gathered from thorns, nor are grapes picked from a bramble bush. ⁴⁵The good person out of the good treasure of the heart produces good, and the evil person out of evil treasure produces evil; for it is out of the abundance of the heart that the mouth speaks.

The Two Foundations

46 "Why do you call me 'Lord, Lord,' and do not do what I tell you? ⁴⁷I will show you what someone is like who comes to me, hears my words, and acts on them. ⁴⁸That one is like a man building a house, who dug deeply and laid the foundation on rock; when a flood arose, the river burst against that house but could not shake it, because it had been well built.ʸ ⁴⁹But the one who hears and does not act is like a man who built a house on the ground without a foundation. When the river burst against it, immediately it fell, and great was the ruin of that house."

Jesus Heals a Centurion's Servant

7 After Jesusᶻ had finished all his sayings in the hearing of the people, he entered Ca·per′na·um. ²A centurion there had a slave whom he valued highly, and who was ill and close to death. ³When he heard about Jesus, he sent some Jewish elders to him, asking him to come and heal his slave. ⁴When they came to Jesus, they appealed to him earnestly, saying, "He is worthy of having you do this for him, ⁵for he loves our people, and it is he who built our synagogue for us." ⁶And Jesus went with them, but when he was not far from the house, the centurion sent friends to say to him, "Lord, do not trouble yourself, for I am not worthy to have you come under my roof; ⁷therefore I did not presume to come to you. But only speak the word, and let my servant be healed. ⁸For I also am a man set under authority, with soldiers under me; and I say to one, 'Go,' and he goes, and to another, 'Come,' and he

comes, and to my slave, 'Do this,' and the slave does it." ⁹When Jesus heard this he was amazed at him, and turning to the crowd that followed him, he said, "I tell you, not even in Israel have I found such faith." ¹⁰When those who had been sent returned to the house, they found the slave in good health.

Jesus Raises the Widow's Son at Nain

11 Soon afterwardsᵃ he went to a town called Nā′in, and his disciples and a large crowd went with him. ¹²As he approached the gate of the town, a man who had died was being carried out. He was his mother's only son, and she was a widow; and with her was a large crowd from the town. ¹³When the Lord saw her, he had compassion for her and said to her, "Do not weep." ¹⁴Then he came forward and touched the bier, and the bearers stood still. And he said, "Young man, I say to you, rise!" ¹⁵The dead man sat up and began to speak, and Jesusᶻ gave him to his mother. ¹⁶Fear seized all of them; and they glorified God, saying, "A great prophet has risen among us!" and "God has looked favorably on his people!" ¹⁷This word about him spread throughout Judea and all the surrounding country.

Messengers from John the Baptist

18 The disciples of John reported all these things to him. So John summoned

Jesus had been teaching that people must love not only their friends but also their enemies! Then he showed them how to live out that kind of love by healing the servant of a centurion, a member of the Roman army. Jesus not only healed the man's servant, but also pointed out that the man had great faith.

ʸ Other ancient authorities read *founded upon the rock*　ᶻ Gk *he*　ᵃ Other ancient authorities read *Next day* two of his disciples ¹⁹and sent them to the Lord to ask, "Are you the one who is to come, or are we to wait for another?" ²⁰When the men had come to him, they said, "John the Baptist has sent us to you to ask, 'Are you the one who is to come, or are we to wait for another?' " ²¹Jesus*ᵇ* had just then cured many people of diseases, plagues, and evil spirits, and had given sight to many who were blind. ²²And he answered them, "Go and tell John what you have seen and heard: the blind receive their sight, the lame walk, the lepers*ᶜ* are cleansed, the deaf hear, the dead are raised, the poor have good news brought to them. ²³And blessed is anyone who takes no offense at me."

24 When John's messengers had gone, Jesus*ᵈ* began to speak to the crowds about John:*ᵉ* "What did you go out into the wilderness to look at? A reed shaken by the wind? ²⁵What then did you go out to see? Someone*ᶠ* dressed in soft robes? Look, those who put on fine clothing and live in luxury are in royal palaces. ²⁶What then did you go out to see? A prophet? Yes, I tell you, and more than a prophet. ²⁷This is the one about whom it is written,

'See, I am sending my messenger ahead
   of you,
   who will prepare your way before you.'

²⁸I tell you, among those born of women no one is greater than John; yet the least in the kingdom of God is greater than he." ²⁹(And all the people who heard this, including the tax collectors, acknowledged the justice of God,*ᵍ* because they had been baptized with John's baptism. ³⁰But by refusing to be baptized by him, the Phar'i·sees and the lawyers rejected God's purpose for themselves.)

31 "To what then will I compare the people of this generation, and what are they like? ³²They are like children sitting in the marketplace and calling to one another,

'We played the flute for you, and you
   did not dance;
   we wailed, and you did not weep.'

³³For John the Baptist has come eating no bread and drinking no wine, and you say, 'He has a demon'; ³⁴the Son of Man has come eating and drinking, and you say, 'Look, a glutton and a drunkard, a friend of tax collectors and sinners!' ³⁵Nevertheless, wisdom is vindicated by all her children."

A Sinful Woman Forgiven

36 One of the Phar'i·sees asked Jesus*ᵈ* to eat with him, and he went into the Phar'i·see's house and took his place at the table. ³⁷And a woman in the city, who was a sinner, having learned that he was eating in the Phar'i·see's house, brought an alabaster jar of ointment. ³⁸She stood behind him at his feet, weeping, and began to bathe his feet with her tears and to dry them with her hair. Then she continued kissing his feet and anointing them with the ointment. ³⁹Now when the Phar'i·see who had invited him saw it, he said to himself, "If this man were a prophet, he would have known who and what kind of woman this is who is touching him—that she is a sinner." ⁴⁰Jesus spoke up and said to him, "Simon, I have something to say to you." "Teacher," he replied, "speak." ⁴¹"A certain creditor had two debtors; one owed five hundred denarii,*ʰ* and the other fifty. ⁴²When they could not pay, he canceled the debts for both of them. Now which of them will love him more?" ⁴³Simon answered, "I suppose the one for whom he canceled the greater debt." And Jesus*ⁱ* said to him, "You have judged rightly." ⁴⁴Then turning toward the woman, he said to Simon, "Do you see this woman? I entered your house; you gave me no water for my feet, but she has bathed my feet with her tears and dried them with her hair. ⁴⁵You gave me no kiss, but from the time I came in she has not stopped kissing my feet. ⁴⁶You did not anoint my head with oil, but she

ᵇ Gk He   *ᶜ* The terms *leper* and *leprosy* can refer to several diseases   *ᵈ* Gk he   *ᵉ* Gk him
ᶠ Or *Why then did you go out? To see someone*
ᵍ Or *praised God*   *ʰ* The denarius was the usual day's wage for a laborer   *ⁱ* Gk he

has anointed my feet with ointment. ⁴⁷Therefore, I tell you, her sins, which were many, have been forgiven; hence she has shown great love. But the one to whom little is forgiven, loves little." ⁴⁸Then he said to her, "Your sins are forgiven." ⁴⁹But those who were at the table with him began to say among themselves, "Who is this who even forgives sins?" ⁵⁰And he said to the woman, "Your faith has saved you; go in peace."

The inner circle of twelve disciples were all men, but Jesus also had disciples who were women. Jesus came for all people. And Jesus calls us today to be his followers. He asks us to show love and kindness to everyone. This isn't easy, but Jesus will help us if we ask him.

Some Women Accompany Jesus

8 Soon afterwards he went on through cities and villages, proclaiming and bringing the good news of the kingdom of God. The twelve were with him, ²as well as some women who had been cured of evil spirits and infirmities: Mary, called Mag'da·lēne, from whom seven demons had gone out, ³and Jō·an'na, the wife of Herod's steward Chū'za, and Susanna, and many others, who provided for them^j out of their resources.

The Parable of the Sower

4 When a great crowd gathered and people from town after town came to him, he said in a parable: ⁵"A sower went out to sow his seed; and as he sowed, some fell on the path and was trampled on, and the birds of the air ate it up. ⁶Some fell on the rock; and as it grew up, it withered for lack of moisture. ⁷Some fell among thorns, and the thorns grew with it and choked it. ⁸Some fell into good soil, and when it grew, it produced a hundredfold." As he said this, he called out, "Let anyone with ears to hear listen!"

The Purpose of the Parables

9 Then his disciples asked him what this parable meant. ¹⁰He said, "To you it has been given to know the secrets^k of the kingdom of God; but to others I speak^l in parables, so that

'looking they may not perceive,
and listening they may not
understand.'

The Parable of the Sower Explained

11 "Now the parable is this: The seed is the word of God. ¹²The ones on the path are those who have heard; then the devil comes and takes away the word from their hearts, so that they may not believe and be saved. ¹³The ones on the rock are those who, when they hear the word, receive it with joy. But these have no root; they believe only for a while and in a time of testing fall away. ¹⁴As for what fell among the thorns, these are the ones who hear; but as they go on their way, they are choked by the cares and riches and pleasures of life, and their fruit does not mature. ¹⁵But as for that in the good soil, these are the ones who, when they hear the word, hold it fast in an honest and good heart, and bear fruit with patient endurance.

A Lamp under a Jar

16 "No one after lighting a lamp hides it under a jar, or puts it under a bed, but puts it on a lampstand, so that those who enter may see the light. ¹⁷For nothing is hidden that will not be disclosed, nor is anything secret that will not become known and come to light. ¹⁸Then pay attention to how you listen; for to those

"No one after lighting a lamp hides it under a jar, or puts it under a bed, but puts it on a lampstand, so that those who enter may see the light."   Luke 8:16

^j Other ancient authorities read *him*   ^k Or *mysteries*   ^l Gk lacks *I speak*

who have, more will be given; and from those who do not have, even what they seem to have will be taken away."

The True Kindred of Jesus

19 Then his mother and his brothers came to him, but they could not reach him because of the crowd. ²⁰And he was told, "Your mother and your brothers are standing outside, wanting to see you." ²¹But he said to them, "My mother and my brothers are those who hear the word of God and do it."

Jesus Calms a Storm

22 One day he got into a boat with his disciples, and he said to them, "Let us go across to the other side of the lake." So they put out, ²³and while they were sailing he fell asleep. A windstorm swept down on the lake, and the boat was filling with water, and they were in danger. ²⁴They went to him and woke him up, shouting, "Master, Master, we are perishing!" And he woke up and rebuked the wind and the raging waves; they ceased, and there was a calm. ²⁵He said to them, "Where is your faith?" They were afraid and amazed, and said to one another, "Who then is this, that he commands even the winds and the water, and they obey him?"

Jesus Heals
the Gerasene Demoniac

26 Then they arrived at the country of the Ger´a·senes,ᵐ which is opposite Galilee. ²⁷As he stepped out on land, a man of the city who had demons met him. For a long time he had wornⁿ no clothes, and he did not live in a house but in the tombs. ²⁸When he saw Jesus, he fell down before him and shouted at the top of his voice, "What have you to do with me, Jesus, Son of the Most High God? I beg you, do not torment me"— ²⁹for Jesusᵒ had commanded the unclean spirit to come out of the man. (For many times it had seized him; he was kept under guard and bound with chains and shackles, but he would break the bonds and be driven by the demon into the wilds.) ³⁰Jesus then

asked him, "What is your name?" He said, "Legion"; for many demons had entered him. ³¹They begged him not to order them to go back into the abyss.

32 Now there on the hillside a large herd of swine was feeding; and the demonsᵖ begged Jesus�q to let them enter these. So he gave them permission. ³³Then the demons came out of the man and entered the swine, and the herd rushed down the steep bank into the lake and was drowned.

34 When the swineherds saw what had happened, they ran off and told it in the city and in the country. ³⁵Then people came out to see what had happened, and when they came to Jesus, they found the man from whom the demons had gone sitting at the feet of Jesus, clothed and in his right mind. And they were afraid. ³⁶Those who had seen it told them how the one who had been possessed by demons had been healed. ³⁷Then all the people of the surrounding country of the Ger´a·senesᵐ asked Jesusq to leave them; for they were seized with great fear. So he got into the boat and returned. ³⁸The man from whom the demons had gone begged that he might be with him; but Jesusᵒ sent him away, saying, ³⁹"Return to your home, and declare how much God has done for you." So he went away, proclaiming throughout the city how much Jesus had done for him.

A Girl Restored to Life and
a Woman Healed

40 Now when Jesus returned, the crowd welcomed him, for they were all waiting for him. ⁴¹Just then there came a man named Ja´i´rus, a leader of the synagogue. He fell at Jesus' feet and begged him to come to his house, ⁴²for he had an only daughter, about twelve years old, who was dying.

As he went, the crowds pressed in on

ᵐ Other ancient authorities read *Gadarenes*; others, *Gergesenes* ⁿ Other ancient authorities read *a man of the city who had had demons for a long time met him. He wore* ᵒ Gk *he* ᵖ Gk *they* q Gk *him*

him. [43]Now there was a woman who had been suffering from hemorrhages for twelve years; and though she had spent all she had on physicians,[r] no one could cure her. [44]She came up behind him and touched the fringe of his clothes, and immediately her hemorrhage stopped. [45]Then Jesus asked, "Who touched me?" When all denied it, Peter[s] said, "Master, the crowds surround you and press in on you." [46]But Jesus said, "Someone touched me; for I noticed that power had gone out from me." [47]When the woman saw that she could not remain hidden, she came trembling; and falling down before him, she declared in the presence of all the people why she had touched him, and how she had been immediately healed. [48]He said to her, "Daughter, your faith has made you well; go in peace."

[49] While he was still speaking, someone came from the leader's house to say, "Your daughter is dead; do not trouble the teacher any longer." [50]When Jesus heard this, he replied, "Do not fear. Only believe, and she will be saved." [51]When he came to the house, he did not allow anyone to enter with him, except Peter, John, and James, and the child's father and mother. [52]They were all weeping and wailing for her; but he said, "Do not weep; for she is not dead but sleeping." [53]And they laughed at him, knowing that she was dead. [54]But he took her by the hand and called out, "Child, get up!" [55]Her spirit returned, and she got up at once. Then he directed them to give her something to eat. [56]Her parents were astounded; but he ordered them to tell no one what had happened.

The Mission of the Twelve

9 Then Jesus[t] called the twelve together and gave them power and authority over all demons and to cure diseases, [2]and he sent them out to proclaim the kingdom of God and to heal. [3]He said to them, "Take nothing for your journey, no staff, nor bag, nor bread, nor money—not even an extra tunic. [4]Whatever house you enter, stay there, and

leave from there. [5]Wherever they do not welcome you, as you are leaving that town shake the dust off your feet as a testimony against them." [6]They departed and went through the villages, bringing the good news and curing diseases everywhere.

Herod's Perplexity

[7] Now Her'od the ruler[u] heard about all that had taken place, and he was perplexed, because it was said by some that John had been raised from the dead, [8]by some that E-li'jah had appeared, and by others that one of the ancient prophets had arisen. [9]Her'od said, "John I beheaded; but who is this about whom I hear such things?" And he tried to see him.

Feeding the Five Thousand

[10] On their return the apostles told Jesus[v] all they had done. He took them with him and withdrew privately to a city called Beth-sa'i-da. [11]When the crowds found out about it, they followed him; and he welcomed them, and spoke to them about the kingdom of God, and healed those who needed to be cured.

[12] The day was drawing to a close, and the twelve came to him and said, "Send the crowd away, so that they they may go into the surrounding villages and countryside, to lodge and get provisions; for we are here in a deserted place." [13]But he said to them, "You give them something to eat." They said, "We have no more than five loaves and two fish—unless we are to go and buy food for all these people." [14]For there were about five thousand men. And he said to his disciples, "Make them sit down in groups of about fifty each." [15]They did so and made them all sit down. [16]And taking the five loaves and the two fish, he looked up to heaven, and blessed

---

[r] Other ancient authorities lack *and though she had spent all she had on physicians*   [s] Other ancient authorities add *and those who were with him*   [t] Gk *he*   [u] Gk *tetrarch*   [v] Gk *him*

and broke them, and gave them to the disciples to set before the crowd. ¹⁷And all ate and were filled. What was left over was gathered up, twelve baskets of broken pieces.

Peter's Declaration about Jesus

18 Once when Jesus^w was praying alone, with only the disciples near him, he asked them, "Who do the crowds say that I am?" ¹⁹They answered, "John the Baptist; but others, E·lī′jah; and still others, that one of the ancient prophets has arisen." ²⁰He said to them, "But who do you say that I am?" Peter answered, "The Messiah^x of God."

Jesus Foretells His Death and Resurrection

21 He sternly ordered and commanded them not to tell anyone, ²²saying, "The Son of Man must undergo great suffering, and be rejected by the elders, chief priests, and scribes, and be killed, and on the third day be raised."

23 Then he said to them all, "If any want to become my followers, let them deny themselves and take up their cross daily and follow me. ²⁴For those who want to save their life will lose it, and those who lose their life for my sake will save it. ²⁵What does it profit them if they gain the whole world, but lose or forfeit themselves? ²⁶Those who are ashamed of me and of my words, of them the Son of Man will be ashamed when he comes in his glory and the glory of the Father and of the holy angels. ²⁷But truly I tell you, there are some standing here who will not taste death before they see the kingdom of God."

The Transfiguration

28 Now about eight days after these sayings Jesus^w took with him Peter and John and James, and went up on the mountain to pray. ²⁹And while he was praying, the appearance of his face changed, and his clothes became dazzling white. ³⁰Suddenly they saw two men, Moses and E·lī′jah, talking to him. ³¹They appeared in glory and were speaking of his departure, which he was about to accomplish at Jerusalem. ³²Now Peter and his companions were weighed down with sleep; but since they had stayed awake,^y they saw his glory and the two men who stood with him. ³³Just as they were leaving him, Peter said to Jesus, "Master, it is good for us to be here; let us make three dwellings,^z one for you, one for Moses, and one for E·lī′jah"—not knowing what he said. ³⁴While he was saying this, a cloud came and overshadowed them; and they were terrified as they entered the cloud. ³⁵Then from the cloud came a voice that said, "This is my Son, my Chosen;^a listen to him!" ³⁶When the voice had spoken, Jesus was found alone. And they kept silent and in those days told no one any of the things they had seen.

Jesus Heals a Boy with a Demon

37 On the next day, when they had come down from the mountain, a great crowd met him. ³⁸Just then a man from the crowd shouted, "Teacher, I beg you to look at my son; he is my only child. ³⁹Suddenly a spirit seizes him, and all at once he^b shrieks. It convulses him until he foams at the mouth; it mauls him and will scarcely leave him. ⁴⁰I begged your disciples to cast it out, but they could not." ⁴¹Jesus answered, "You faithless and perverse generation, how much longer must I be with you and bear with you? Bring your son here." ⁴²While he was coming, the demon dashed him to the ground in convulsions. But Jesus rebuked the unclean spirit, healed the boy, and gave him back to his father. ⁴³And all were astounded at the greatness of God.

Jesus Again Foretells His Death

While everyone was amazed at all that he was doing, he said to his disciples, ⁴⁴"Let these words sink into your ears: The Son of Man is going to be betrayed into human hands." ⁴⁵But they did not under-

^w Gk he ^x Or The Christ ^y Or but when they were fully awake ^z Or tents ^a Other ancient authorities read my Beloved ^b Or it stand this saying; its meaning was concealed from them, so that they could not perceive it. And they were afraid to ask him about this saying.

True Greatness

46 An argument arose among them as to which one of them was the greatest. [47]But Jesus, aware of their inner thoughts, took a little child and put it by his side, [48]and said to them, "Whoever welcomes this child in my name welcomes me, and whoever welcomes me welcomes the one who sent me; for the least among all of you is the greatest."

Another Exorcist

49 John answered, "Master, we saw someone casting out demons in your name, and we tried to stop him, because he does not follow with us." [50]But Jesus said to him, "Do not stop him; for whoever is not against you is for you."

A Samaritan Village Refuses to Receive Jesus

51 When the days drew near for him to be taken up, he set his face to go to Jerusalem. [52]And he sent messengers ahead of him. On their way they entered a village of the Sa·mar´i·tans to make ready for him; [53]but they did not receive him, because his face was set toward Jerusalem. [54]When his disciples James and John saw it, they said, "Lord, do you want us to command fire to come down from heaven and consume them?"[c] [55]But he turned and rebuked them. [56]Then[d] they went on to another village.

Would-Be Followers of Jesus

57 As they were going along the road, someone said to him, "I will follow you wherever you go." [58]And Jesus said to him, "Foxes have holes, and birds of the air have nests; but the Son of Man has nowhere to lay his head." [59]To another he said, "Follow me." But he said, "Lord, first let me go and bury my father." [60]But Jesus[e] said to him, "Let the dead bury their own dead; but as for you, go and proclaim the kingdom of

> "Jesus...took a little child and put it by his side and said to them, 'Whoever welcomes this child in my name welcomes me and whoever welcomes me welcomes the one who sent me; for the least among all of you is the greatest.'"
> Luke 9:46

God." [61]Another said, "I will follow you, Lord; but let me first say farewell to those at my home." [62]Jesus said to him, "No one who puts a hand to the plow and looks back is fit for the kingdom of God."

The Mission of the Seventy

10 After this the Lord appointed seventy[f] others and sent them on ahead of him in pairs to every town and place where he himself intended to go. [2]He said to them, "The harvest is plentiful, but the laborers are few; therefore ask the Lord of the harvest to send out laborers into his harvest. [3]Go on your way. See, I am sending you out like lambs into the midst of wolves. [4]Carry no purse, no bag, no sandals; and greet no one on the road. [5]Whatever house you enter, first say, 'Peace to this house!' [6]And if anyone is there who shares in

Jesus sent out his disciples to tell the Good News. Today, we too are his disciples sent to tell about Jesus. When telling people the Good News about Jesus, remember these things: God's grace is available to all people. God loves all people. People can respond to God's love by becoming disciples. Disciples are recognized by their actions.

[c] Other ancient authorities add *as Elijah did*
[d] Other ancient authorities read *rebuked them, and said, "You do not know what spirit you are of, [56]for the Son of Man has not come to destroy the lives of human beings but to save them." Then*　[e] Gk *he*
[f] Other ancient authorities read *seventy-two*

"You shall love the Lord your God with all your heart, and with all your soul, and with all your strength, and with all your mind; and your neighbor as yourself." Luke 10:27

peace, your peace will rest on that person; but if not, it will return to you. [7]Remain in the same house, eating and drinking whatever they provide, for the laborer deserves to be paid. Do not move about from house to house. [8]Whenever you enter a town and its people welcome you, eat what is set before you; [9]cure the sick who are there, and say to them, 'The kingdom of God has come near to you.'[g] [10]But whenever you enter a town and they do not welcome you, go out into its streets and say, [11]'Even the dust of your town that clings to our feet, we wipe off in protest against you. Yet know this: the kingdom of God has come near.'[h] [12]I tell you, on that day it will be more tolerable for Sod'om than for that town.

Woes to Unrepentant Cities

13 "Woe to you, Chō·rā'zin! Woe to you, Beth·sā'i·da! For if the deeds of power done in you had been done in Tyre and Sī'don, they would have repented long ago, sitting in sackcloth and ashes. [14]But at the judgment it will be more tolerable for Tyre and Sī'don than for you. [15]And you, Ca·per'na·um,

will you be exalted to heaven?

No, you will be brought down to Hades.

16 "Whoever listens to you listens to me, and whoever rejects you rejects me, and whoever rejects me rejects the one who sent me."

The Return of the Seventy

17 The seventy[i] returned with joy, saying, "Lord, in your name even the demons submit to us!" [18]He said to them, "I watched Satan fall from heaven like a flash of lightning. [19]See, I have given you authority to tread on snakes and scorpions, and over all the power of the enemy; and nothing will hurt you. [20]Nevertheless, do not rejoice at this, that the spirits submit to you, but rejoice that your names are written in heaven."

Jesus Rejoices

21 At that same hour Jesus[j] rejoiced in the Holy Spirit[k] and said, "I thank[l] you, Father, Lord of heaven and earth, because you have hidden these things from the wise and the intelligent and have revealed them to infants; yes, Father, for such was your gracious will.[m] [22]All things have been handed over to me by my Father; and no one knows who the Son is except the Father, or who the Father is except the Son and anyone to whom the Son chooses to reveal him."

23 Then turning to the disciples, Jesus[j] said to them privately, "Blessed are the eyes that see what you see! [24]For I tell you that many prophets and kings desired to see what you see, but did not see it, and to hear what you hear, but did not hear it."

A parable is a short story that makes a point. Jesus used parables to help people understand his message. He told the parable of the good Samaritan to teach people how to love others. Read Luke 10:27 and Deuteronomy 6:4–5. These verses are alike, but Jesus added something else. The people had always heard that they should love God, but Jesus told them they must love others, even enemies, as well.

What can you do to show love to others? Consider some of these ideas: Offer to take care of a neighbor's pet while the neighbor is away. Send cards to someone who is sick. Make friends with someone at school who appears lonely.

---

[g] Or is at hand for you   [h] Or is at hand   [i] Other ancient authorities read seventy-two   [j] Gk he
[k] Other authorities read in the spirit   [l] Or praise
[m] Or for so it was well-pleasing in your sight

The Parable of the Good Samaritan

25 Just then a lawyer stood up to test Jesus.[n] "Teacher," he said, "what must I do to inherit eternal life?" [26]He said to him, "What is written in the law? What do you read there?" [27]He answered, "You shall love the Lord your God with all your heart, and with all your soul, and with all your strength, and with all your mind; and your neighbor as yourself." [28]And he said to him, "You have given the right answer; do this, and you will live."

29 But wanting to justify himself, he asked Jesus, "And who is my neighbor?" [30]Jesus replied, "A man was going down from Jerusalem to Jericho, and fell into the hands of robbers, who stripped him, beat him, and went away, leaving him half dead. [31]Now by chance a priest was going down that road; and when he saw him, he passed by on the other side. [32]So likewise a Lē'vīte, when he came to the place and saw him, passed by on the other side. [33]But a Sa·mār'i·tan while traveling came near him; and when he saw him, he was moved with pity. [34]He went to him and bandaged his wounds, having poured oil and wine on them. Then he put him on his own animal, brought him to an inn, and took care of him. [35]The next day he took out two denarii,[o] gave them to the innkeeper, and said, 'Take care of him; and when I come back, I will repay you whatever more you spend.' [36]Which of these three, do you think, was a neighbor to the man who fell into the hands of the robbers?" [37]He said, "The one who showed him mercy." Jesus said to him, "Go and do likewise."

Jesus Visits Martha and Mary

38 Now as they went on their way, he entered a certain village, where a woman named Martha welcomed him into her home. [39]She had a sister named Mary, who sat at the Lord's feet and listened to what he was saying. [40]But Martha was distracted by her many tasks; so she came to him and asked, "Lord, do you not care that my sister has left me to do all the work by myself? Tell her then to help me." [41]But the Lord answered her, "Martha, Martha, you are worried and distracted by many things; [42]there is need of only one thing.[p] Mary has chosen the better part, which will not be taken away from her."

The Lord's Prayer

11 He was praying in a certain place, and after he had finished, one of his disciples said to him, "Lord, teach us to pray, as John taught his disciples." [2]He said to them, "When you pray, say:
Father,[q] hallowed be your name.
Your kingdom come.[r]
3 Give us each day our daily bread.[s]
4 And forgive us our sins,
for we ourselves forgive everyone indebted to us.
And do not bring us to the time of trial."[t]

Perseverance in Prayer

5 And he said to them, "Suppose one of you has a friend, and you go to him at midnight and say to him, 'Friend, lend me three loaves of bread; [6]for a friend of mine has arrived, and I have nothing to set before him.' [7]And he answers from within, 'Do not bother me; the door has already been locked, and my children are with me in bed; I cannot get up and give you anything.' [8]I tell you, even though he will not get up and give him anything because he is his friend, at least because of his persistence he will get up and give him whatever he needs.

9 "So I say to you, Ask, and it will be given you; search, and you will find;

[n] Gk him [o] The denarius was the usual day's wage for a laborer [p] Other ancient authorities read *few things are necessary, or only one* [q] Other ancient authorities read *Our Father in heaven* [r] A few ancient authorities read *Your Holy Spirit come upon us and cleanse us.* Other ancient authorities add *Your will be done, on earth as in heaven* [s] Or *our bread for tomorrow* [t] Or *us into temptation.* Other ancient authorities add *but rescue us from the evil one* (or *from evil*)

"Ask, and it will be given you; search, and you will find; knock, and the door will be opened for you. For everyone who asks receives, and everyone who searches finds, and for everyone who knocks, the door will be opened."

Luke 11:9–10

knock, and the door will be opened for you. [10]For everyone who asks receives, and everyone who searches finds, and for everyone who knocks, the door will be opened. [11]Is there anyone among you who, if your child asks for[u] a fish, will give a snake instead of a fish? [12]Or if the child asks for an egg, will give a scorpion? [13]If you then, who are evil, know how to give good gifts to your children, how much more will the heavenly Father give the Holy Spirit[v] to those who ask him!"

Jesus and Beelzebul

14 Now he was casting out a demon that was mute; when the demon had gone out, the one who had been mute spoke, and the crowds were amazed. [15]But some of them said, "He casts out demons by Bē·el´ze·bul, the ruler of the demons." [16]Others, to test him, kept demanding from him a sign from heaven. [17]But he knew what they were thinking and said to them, "Every kingdom divided against itself becomes a desert, and house falls on house. [18]If Satan also is divided against himself, how will his kingdom stand? — for you say that I cast out the demons by Bē·el´ze·bul. [19]Now if I cast out the demons by Bē·el´ze·bul, by whom do your exorcists[w] cast them out? Therefore they will be your judges. [20]But if it is by the finger of God that I cast out the demons, then the kingdom of God has come to you. [21]When a strong man, fully armed, guards his castle, his property is safe. [22]But when one stronger than he attacks him and overpowers him, he takes away his armor in which he trusted and divides his plunder. [23]Whoever is not with me is

against me, and whoever does not gather with me scatters.

The Return of the Unclean Spirit

24 "When the unclean spirit has gone out of a person, it wanders through waterless regions looking for a resting place, but not finding any, it says, 'I will return to my house from which I came.' [25]When it comes, it finds it swept and put in order. [26]Then it goes and brings seven other spirits more evil than itself, and they enter and live there; and the last state of that person is worse than the first."

True Blessedness

27 While he was saying this, a woman in the crowd raised her voice and said to him, "Blessed is the womb that bore you and the breasts that nursed you!" [28]But he said, "Blessed rather are those who hear the word of God and obey it!"

The Sign of Jonah

29 When the crowds were increasing, he began to say, "This generation is an evil generation; it asks for a sign, but no sign will be given to it except the sign of Jonah. [30]For just as Jonah became a sign to the people of Nin´e·veh, so the Son of Man will be to this generation. [31]The queen of the South will rise at the judgment with the people of this generation and condemn them, because she came from the ends of the earth to listen to the wisdom of Solomon, and see, something greater than Solomon is here! [32]The people of Nin´e·veh will rise up at the judgment with this generation and condemn it, because they repented at the proclamation of Jonah, and see, something greater than Jonah is here!

The Light of the Body

33 "No one after lighting a lamp puts it in a cellar,[x] but on the lampstand so that

[u] Other ancient authorities add *bread, will give a stone; or if your child asks for* [v] Other ancient authorities read *the Father give the Holy Spirit from heaven* [w] Gk *sons* [x] Other ancient authorities add *or under the bushel basket*

those who enter may see the light. ³⁴Your eye is the lamp of your body. If your eye is healthy, your whole body is full of light; but if it is not healthy, your body is full of darkness. ³⁵Therefore consider whether the light in you is not darkness. ³⁶If then your whole body is full of light, with no part of it in darkness, it will be as full of light as when a lamp gives you light with its rays."

Jesus Denounces Pharisees and Lawyers

37 While he was speaking, a Phar·i·see invited him to dine with him; so he went in and took his place at the table. ³⁸The Phar·i·see was amazed to see that he did not first wash before dinner. ³⁹Then the Lord said to him, "Now you Phar·i·sees clean the outside of the cup and of the dish, but inside you are full of greed and wickedness. ⁴⁰You fools! Did not the one who made the outside make the inside also? ⁴¹So give for alms those things that are within; and see, everything will be clean for you.

42 "But woe to you Phar·i·sees! For you tithe mint and rue and herbs of all kinds, and neglect justice and the love of God; it is these you ought to have practiced, without neglecting the others. ⁴³Woe to you Phar·i·sees! For you love to have the seat of honor in the synagogues and to be greeted with respect in the marketplaces. ⁴⁴Woe to you! For you are like unmarked graves, and people walk over them without realizing it."

45 One of the lawyers answered him, "Teacher, when you say these things, you insult us too." ⁴⁶And he said, "Woe also to you lawyers! For you load people with burdens hard to bear, and you yourselves do not lift a finger to ease them. ⁴⁷Woe to you! For you build the tombs of the prophets whom your ancestors killed. ⁴⁸So you are witnesses and approve of the deeds of your ancestors; for they killed them, and you build their tombs. ⁴⁹Therefore also the Wisdom of God said, 'I will send them prophets and apostles,

some of whom they will kill and persecute,' ⁵⁰so that this generation may be charged with the blood of all the prophets shed since the foundation of the world, ⁵¹from the blood of Abel to the blood of Zech·a·rī´ah, who perished between the altar and the sanctuary. Yes, I tell you, it will be charged against this generation. ⁵²Woe to you lawyers! For you have taken away the key of knowledge; you did not enter yourselves, and you hindered those who were entering."

53 When he went outside, the scribes and the Phar·i·sees began to be very hostile toward him and to cross-examine him about many things, ⁵⁴lying in wait for him, to catch him in something he might say.

A Warning against Hypocrisy

12 Meanwhile, when the crowd gathered by the thousands, so that they trampled on one another, he began to speak first to his disciples, "Beware of the yeast of the Phar·i·sees, that is, their hypocrisy. ²Nothing is covered up that will not be uncovered, and nothing secret that will not become known. ³Therefore whatever you have said in the dark will be heard in the light, and what you have whispered behind closed doors will be proclaimed from the housetops.

Exhortation to Fearless Confession

4 "I tell you, my friends, do not fear those who kill the body, and after that can do nothing more. ⁵But I will warn you whom to fear: fear him who, after he has killed, has authority* to cast into hell.ᶻ Yes, I tell you, fear him! ⁶Are not five sparrows sold for two pennies? Yet not one of them is forgotten in God's sight. ⁷But even the hairs of your head are all counted. Do not be afraid; you are of more value than many sparrows.

8 "And I tell you, everyone who acknowledges me before others, the Son of Man also will acknowledge before the

Or power ᶻ *Gk Gehenna*

angels of God; [9]but whoever denies me before others will be denied before the angels of God. [10]And everyone who speaks a word against the Son of Man will be forgiven; but whoever blasphemes against the Holy Spirit will not be forgiven. [11]When they bring you before the synagogues, the rulers, and the authorities, do not worry about how[a] you are to defend yourselves or what you are to say; [12]for the Holy Spirit will teach you at that very hour what you ought to say."

The Parable of the Rich Fool

13 Someone in the crowd said to him, "Teacher, tell my brother to divide the family inheritance with me." [14]But he said to him, "Friend, who set me to be a judge or arbitrator over you?" [15]And he said to them, "Take care! Be on your guard against all kinds of greed; for one's life does not consist in the abundance of possessions." [16]Then he told them a parable: "The land of a rich man produced abundantly. [17]And he thought to himself, 'What should I do, for I have no place to store my crops?' [18]Then he said, 'I will do this: I will pull down my barns and build larger ones, and there I will store all my grain and my goods. [19]And I will say to my soul, Soul, you have ample goods laid up for many years; relax, eat, drink, be merry.' [20]But God said to him, 'You fool! This very night your life is being demanded of you. And the things you have prepared, whose will they be?' [21]So it is with those who store up treasures for themselves but are not rich toward God."

Do Not Worry

22 He said to his disciples, "Therefore I tell you, do not worry about your life, what you will eat, or about your body, what you will wear. [23]For life is more than food, and the body more than clothing. [24]Consider the ravens: they neither sow nor reap, they have neither storehouse nor barn, and yet God feeds them. Of how much more value are you than the birds! [25]And can any of you by worrying add a single hour to your span of life?[b] [26]If then you are not able to do so small a thing as that, why do you worry about the rest? [27]Consider the lilies, how they grow: they neither toil nor spin;[c] yet I tell you, even Solomon in all his glory was not clothed like one of these. [28]But if God so clothes the grass of the field, which is alive today and tomorrow is thrown into the oven, how much more will he clothe you—you of little faith! [29]And do not keep striving for what you are to eat and what you are to drink, and do not keep worrying. [30]For it is the nations of the world that strive after all these things, and your Father knows that you need them. [31]Instead, strive for his[d] kingdom, and these things will be given to you as well.

32 "Do not be afraid, little flock, for it is your Father's good pleasure to give you the kingdom. [33]Sell your possessions, and give alms. Make purses for yourselves that do not wear out, an unfailing treasure in heaven, where no thief comes near and no moth destroys. [34]For where your treasure is, there your heart will be also.

Watchful Slaves

35 "Be dressed for action and have your lamps lit; [36]be like those who are waiting for their master to return from the wedding banquet, so that they may open the door for him as soon as he comes and knocks. [37]Blessed are those slaves whom the master finds alert when he comes; truly I tell you, he will fasten his belt and have them sit down to eat, and he will come and serve them. [38]If he comes during the middle of the night, or near dawn, and finds them so, blessed are those slaves.

39 "But know this: if the owner of the house had known at what hour the thief was coming, he[e] would not have let his house be broken into. [40]You also must be

---

[a] Other ancient authorities add *or what*   [b] Or *add a cubit to your stature*   [c] Other ancient authorities read *Consider the lilies; they neither spin nor weave*   [d] Other ancient authorities read *God's*   [e] Other ancient authorities add *would have watched and*

ready, for the Son of Man is coming at an unexpected hour."

The Faithful or the Unfaithful Slave

41 Peter said, "Lord, are you telling this parable for us or for everyone?" [42]And the Lord said, "Who then is the faithful and prudent manager whom his master will put in charge of his slaves, to give them their allowance of food at the proper time? [43]Blessed is that slave whom his master will find at work when he arrives. [44]Truly I tell you, he will put that one in charge of all his possessions. [45]But if that slave says to himself, 'My master is delayed in coming,' and if he begins to beat the other slaves, men and women, and to eat and drink and get drunk, [46]the master of that slave will come on a day when he does not expect him and at an hour that he does not know, and will cut him in pieces,[f] and put him with the unfaithful. [47]That slave who knew what his master wanted, but did not prepare himself or do what was wanted, will receive a severe beating. [48]But the one who did not know and did what deserved a beating will receive a light beating. From everyone to whom much has been given, much will be required; and from the one to whom much has been entrusted, even more will be demanded.

Jesus the Cause of Division

49 "I came to bring fire to the earth, and how I wish it were already kindled! [50]I have a baptism with which to be baptized, and what stress I am under until it is completed! [51]Do you think that I have come to bring peace to the earth? No, I tell you, but rather division! [52]From now on five in one household will be divided, three against two and two against three; [53]they will be divided:

father against son
 and son against father,
mother against daughter
 and daughter against mother,
mother-in-law against her
 daughter-in-law

and daughter-in-law against
 mother-in-law."

Interpreting the Time

54 He also said to the crowds, "When you see a cloud rising in the west, you immediately say, 'It is going to rain'; and so it happens. [55]And when you see the south wind blowing, you say, 'There will be scorching heat'; and it happens. [56]You hypocrites! You know how to interpret the appearance of earth and sky, but why do you not know how to interpret the present time?

Settling with Your Opponent

57 "And why do you not judge for yourselves what is right? [58]Thus, when you go with your accuser before a magistrate, on the way make an effort to settle the case,[g] or you may be dragged before the judge, and the judge hand you over to the officer, and the officer throw you in prison. [59]I tell you, you will never get out until you have paid the very last penny."

Repent or Perish

13 At that very time there were some present who told him about the Galileans whose blood Pilate had mingled with their sacrifices. [2]He asked them, "Do you think that because these Galileans suffered in this way they were worse sinners than all other Galileans? [3]No, I tell you; but unless you repent, you will all perish as they did. [4]Or those eighteen who were killed when the tower of Sĭ·lŏ'am fell on them—do you think that they were worse offenders than all the others living in Jerusalem? [5]No, I tell you; but unless you repent, you will all perish just as they did."

The Parable of the Barren Fig Tree

6 Then he told this parable: "A man had a fig tree planted in his vineyard; and he came looking for fruit on it and found none. [7]So he said to the gardener, 'See

[f] Or *cut him off*   [g] Gk *settle with him*

here! For three years I have come looking for fruit on this fig tree, and still I find none. Cut it down! Why should it be wasting the soil?' [8]He replied, 'Sir, let it alone for one more year, until I dig around it and put manure on it. [9]If it bears fruit next year, well and good; but if not, you can cut it down.' "

Jesus Heals a Crippled Woman

10 Now he was teaching in one of the synagogues on the sabbath. [11]And just then there appeared a woman with a spirit that had crippled her for eighteen years. She was bent over and was quite unable to stand up straight. [12]When Jesus saw her, he called her over and said, "Woman, you are set free from your ailment." [13]When he laid his hands on her, immediately she stood up straight and began praising God. [14]But the leader of the synagogue, indignant because Jesus had cured on the sabbath, kept saying to the crowd, "There are six days on which work ought to be done; come on those days and be cured, and not on the sabbath day." [15]But the Lord answered him and said, "You hypocrites! Does not each of you on the sabbath untie his ox or his donkey from the manger, and lead it away to give it water? [16]And ought not this woman, a daughter of Abraham whom Satan bound for eighteen long years, be set free from this bondage on the sabbath day?" [17]When he said this, all his opponents were put to shame; and the entire crowd was rejoicing at all the wonderful things that he was doing.

The Parable of the Mustard Seed

18 He said therefore, "What is the kingdom of God like? And to what should I compare it? [19]It is like a mustard seed that someone took and sowed in the garden; it grew and became a tree, and the birds of the air made nests in its branches."

The Parable of the Yeast

20 And again he said, "To what should I compare the kingdom of God? [21]It is like yeast that a woman took and mixed in with[h] three measures of flour until all of it was leavened."

The Narrow Door

22 Jesus[i] went through one town and village after another, teaching as he made his way to Jerusalem. [23]Someone asked him, "Lord, will only a few be saved?" He said to them, [24]"Strive to enter through the narrow door; for many, I tell you, will try to enter and will not be able. [25]When once the owner of the house has got up and shut the door, and you begin to stand outside and to knock at the door, saying, 'Lord, open to us,' then in reply he will say to you, 'I do not know where you come from.' [26]Then you will begin to say, 'We ate and drank with you, and you taught in our streets.' [27]But he will say, 'I do not know where you come from; go away from me, all you evildoers!' [28]There will be weeping and gnashing of teeth when you see Abraham and Isaac and Jacob and all the prophets in the kingdom of God, and you yourselves thrown out. [29]Then people will come from east and west, from north and south, and will eat in the kingdom of God. [30]Indeed, some are last who will be first, and some are first who will be last."

The Lament over Jerusalem

31 At that very hour some Phar′i·sees came and said to him, "Get away from here, for Her′od wants to kill you." [32]He said to them, "Go and tell that fox for me,[j] 'Listen, I am casting out demons and performing cures today and tomorrow, and on the third day I finish my work. [33]Yet today, tomorrow, and the next day I must be on my way, because it is impossible for a prophet to be killed outside of Jerusalem.' [34]Jerusalem, Jerusalem, the city that kills the prophets and stones those who are sent to it! How often have I desired to gather your children together as a hen gathers her brood under her wings, and you were not willing! [35]See, your house is left to you. And I tell you, you

[h] Gk hid in   [i] Gk He   [j] Gk lacks for me

will not see me until the time comes when[k] you say, 'Blessed is the one who comes in the name of the Lord.' "

Jesus Heals the Man with Dropsy

14 On one occasion when Jesus[l] was going to the house of a leader of the Phar´i·sees to eat a meal on the sabbath, they were watching him closely. [2]Just then, in front of him, there was a man who had dropsy. [3]And Jesus asked the lawyers and Phar´i·sees, "Is it lawful to cure people on the sabbath, or not?" [4]But they were silent. So Jesus[l] took him and healed him, and sent him away. [5]Then he said to them, "If one of you has a child[m] or an ox that has fallen into a well, will you not immediately pull it out on a sabbath day?" [6]And they could not reply to this.

Humility and Hospitality

7 When he noticed how the guests chose the places of honor, he told them a parable. [8]"When you are invited by someone to a wedding banquet, do not sit down at the place of honor, in case someone more distinguished than you has been invited by your host; [9]and the host who invited both of you may come and say to you, 'Give this person your place,' and then in disgrace you would start to take the lowest place. [10]But when you are invited, go and sit down at the lowest place, so that when your host comes, he may say to you, 'Friend, move up higher'; then you will be honored in the presence of all who sit at the table with you. [11]For all who exalt themselves will be humbled, and those who humble themselves will be exalted."

12 He said also to the one who had invited him, "When you give a luncheon or a dinner, do not invite your friends or your brothers or your relatives or rich neighbors, in case they may invite you in return, and you would be repaid. [13]But when you give a banquet, invite the poor, the crippled, the lame, and the blind. [14]And you will be blessed, because they cannot repay you, for you will be repaid at the resurrection of the righteous."

The Parable of the Great Dinner

15 One of the dinner guests, on hearing this, said to him, "Blessed is anyone who will eat bread in the kingdom of God!" [16]Then Jesus[l] said to him, "Someone gave a great dinner and invited many. [17]At the time for the dinner he sent his slave to say to those who had been invited, 'Come; for everything is ready now.' [18]But they all alike began to make excuses. The first said to him, 'I have bought a piece of land, and I must go out and see it; please accept my regrets.' [19]Another said, 'I have bought five yoke of oxen, and I am going to try them out; please accept my regrets.' [20]Another said, 'I have just been married, and therefore I cannot come.' [21]So the slave returned and reported this to his master. Then the owner of the house became angry and said to his slave, 'Go out at once into the streets and lanes of the town and bring in the poor, the crippled, the blind, and the lame.' [22]And the slave said, 'Sir, what you ordered has been done, and there is still room.' [23]Then the master said to the slave, 'Go out into the roads and lanes, and compel people to come in, so that my house may be filled. [24]For I tell you,[n] none of those who were invited will taste my dinner.' "

The Cost of Discipleship

25 Now large crowds were traveling with him; and he turned and said to them, [26]"Whoever comes to me and does not hate father and mother, wife and children, brothers and sisters, yes, and even life itself, cannot be my disciple. [27]Whoever does not carry the cross and follow me cannot be my disciple. [28]For which of

> "Whoever does not carry the cross and follow me cannot be my disciple."
> Luke 14:27

---

[k] Other ancient authorities lack *the time comes when* [l] Gk *he* [m] Other ancient authorities read *a donkey* [n] The Greek word for *you* here is plural

you, intending to build a tower, does not first sit down and estimate the cost, to see whether he has enough to complete it? ²⁹Otherwise, when he has laid a foundation and is not able to finish, all who see it will begin to ridicule him, ³⁰saying, 'This fellow began to build and was not able to finish.' ³¹Or what king, going out to wage war against another king, will not sit down first and consider whether he is able with ten thousand to oppose the one who comes against him with twenty thousand? ³²If he cannot, then, while the other is still far away, he sends a delegation and asks for the terms of peace. ³³So therefore, none of you can become my disciple if you do not give up all your possessions.

About Salt

34 "Salt is good; but if salt has lost its taste, how can its saltiness be restored?ᵒ ³⁵It is fit neither for the soil nor for the manure pile; they throw it away. Let anyone with ears to hear listen!"

The Parable of the Lost Sheep

15 Now all the tax collectors and sinners were coming near to listen to him. ²And the Phar′i·sees and the scribes were grumbling and saying, "This fellow welcomes sinners and eats with them."

3 So he told them this parable: ⁴"Which one of you, having a hundred sheep and losing one of them, does not leave the ninety-nine in the wilderness and go after the one that is lost until he finds it? ⁵When he has found it, he lays it on his shoulders and rejoices. ⁶And when he comes home, he calls together his friends and neighbors, saying to them, 'Rejoice with me, for I have found my sheep that was lost.' ⁷Just so, I tell you, there will be more joy in heaven over one sinner who repents than over ninety-nine righteous persons who need no repentance.

The Parable of the Lost Coin

8 "Or what woman having ten silver coins,ᵖ if she loses one of them, does not light a lamp, sweep the house, and search carefully until she finds it? ⁹When she has found it, she calls together her friends and neighbors, saying, 'Rejoice with me, for I have found the coin that I had lost.' ¹⁰Just so, I tell you, there is joy in the presence of the angels of God over one sinner who repents."

The Parable of the Prodigal and His Brother

11 Then Jesus�q said, "There was a man who had two sons. ¹²The younger of them said to his father, 'Father, give me the share of the property that will belong to me.' So he divided his property between them. ¹³A few days later the younger son gathered all he had and traveled to a distant country, and there he squandered his property in dissolute living. ¹⁴When he had spent everything, a severe famine took place throughout that country, and he began to be in need. ¹⁵So he went and hired himself out to one of the citizens of that country, who sent him to his fields to feed the pigs. ¹⁶He would gladly have filled himself withʳ the pods that the pigs

 Jesus told several "lost" stories—the parable of the lost sheep, the parable of the lost coin, and the parable of the prodigal and his brother. Each of these stories tells about finding something that was lost. These stories help us to understand how important it is to come back to God.

What can you do to help others find their way to God? Think about these ideas: Invite a friend to one of your church activities. Encourage your parents to attend church with you. Pray for a person you know who is having troubles.

ᵒ Or how can it be used for seasoning?   ᵖ Gk drachmas, each worth about a day's wage for a laborer   �q Gk he   ʳ Other ancient authorities read filled his stomach with were eating; and no one gave him anything. ¹⁷But when he came to himself he said, 'How many of my father's hired hands have bread enough and to spare, but here I am dying of hunger! ¹⁸I will get up and go to my father, and I will say to him, "Father, I have sinned against heaven and before you; ¹⁹I am no longer worthy to be called your son; treat me like one of your hired hands." ' ²⁰So he set off and went to his father. But while he was still far off, his father saw him and was filled with compassion; he ran and put his arms around him and kissed him. ²¹Then the son said to him, 'Father, I have sinned against heaven and before you; I am no longer worthy to be called your son.'ˢ ²²But the father said to his slaves, 'Quickly, bring out a robe—the best one—and put it on him; put a ring on his finger and sandals on his feet. ²³And get the fatted calf and kill it, and let us eat and celebrate; ²⁴for this son of mine was dead and is alive again; he was lost and is found!' And they began to celebrate.

25 "Now his elder son was in the field; and when he came and approached the house, he heard music and dancing. ²⁶He called one of the slaves and asked what was going on. ²⁷He replied, 'Your brother has come, and your father has killed the fatted calf, because he has got him back

> "Just so, I tell you, there is joy in the presence of the angels of God over one sinner who repents."
> Luke 15:10

safe and sound.' ²⁸Then he became angry and refused to go in. His father came out and began to plead with him. ²⁹But he answered his father, 'Listen! For all these years I have been working like a slave for you, and I have never disobeyed your command; yet you have never given me even a young goat so that I might celebrate with my friends. ³⁰But when this son of yours came back, who has devoured your property with prostitutes, you killed the fatted calf for him!' ³¹Then the father' said to him, 'Son, you are always with me, and all that is mine is yours. ³²But we had to celebrate and rejoice, because this brother of yours was dead and has come to life; he was lost and has been found.' "

The Parable of the Dishonest Manager

16 Then Jesus' said to the disciples, "There was a rich man who had a manager, and charges were brought to him that this man was squandering his property. ²So he summoned him and said to him, 'What is this that I hear about you? Give me an accounting of your management, because you cannot be my manager any longer.' ³Then the manager said to himself, 'What will I do, now that my master is taking the position away from me? I am not strong enough to dig, and I am ashamed to beg. ⁴I have decided what to do so that, when I am dismissed as manager, people may welcome me into their homes.' ⁵So, summoning his master's debtors one by one, he asked the first, 'How much do you owe my master?' ⁶He answered, 'A hundred jugs of olive oil.' He said to him, 'Take your bill, sit down quickly, and make it fifty.' ⁷Then he asked

In Jesus's day, a son only received his father's property as an inheritance after his father had died. But Jesus told a story about a son who asked for his inheritance early so that he could leave his family. The father gave his son his share of the property because he loved him. Later, the son returned, and the father once again showed his love by welcoming the son home. Jesus wanted his listeners to know that God never forgets God's children. God is always waiting for us to return.

ˢ Other ancient authorities add *Treat me like one of your hired servants*　　ᵗ Gk *he* another, 'And how much do you owe?' He replied, 'A hundred containers of wheat.' He said to him, 'Take your bill and make it eighty.' [8]And his master commended the dishonest manager because he had acted shrewdly; for the children of this age are more shrewd in dealing with their own generation than are the children of light. [9]And I tell you, make friends for yourselves by means of dishonest wealth[u] so that when it is gone, they may welcome you into the eternal homes.[v]

10 "Whoever is faithful in a very little is faithful also in much; and whoever is dishonest in a very little is dishonest also in much. [11]If then you have not been faithful with the dishonest wealth,[u] who will entrust to you the true riches? [12]And if you have not been faithful with what belongs to another, who will give you what is your own? [13]No slave can serve two masters; for a slave will either hate the one and love the other, or be devoted to the one and despise the other. You cannot serve God and wealth."[u]

The Law and the Kingdom of God

14 The Phar'i·sees, who were lovers of money, heard all this, and they ridiculed him. [15]So he said to them, "You are those who justify yourselves in the sight of others; but God knows your hearts; for what is prized by human beings is an abomination in the sight of God.

16 "The law and the prophets were in effect until John came; since then the good news of the kingdom of God is proclaimed, and everyone tries to enter it by force.[w] [17]But it is easier for heaven and earth to pass away, than for one stroke of a letter in the law to be dropped.

18 "Anyone who divorces his wife and marries another commits adultery, and whoever marries a woman divorced from her husband commits adultery.

The Rich Man and Lazarus

19 "There was a rich man who was dressed in purple and fine linen and who feasted sumptuously everyday. [20]And at his gate lay a poor man named Laz'a·rus, covered with sores, [21]who longed to satisfy his hunger with what fell from the rich man's table; even the dogs would come and lick his sores. [22]The poor man died and was carried away by the angels to be with Abraham.[x] The rich man also died and was buried. [23]In Hades, where he was being tormented, he looked up and saw Abraham far away with Laz'a·rus by his side.[y] [24]He called out, 'Father Abraham, have mercy on me, and send Laz'a·rus to dip the tip of his finger in water and cool my tongue; for I am in agony in these flames.' [25]But Abraham said, 'Child, remember that during your lifetime you received your good things, and Laz'a·rus in like manner evil things; but now he is comforted here, and you are in agony. [26]Besides all this, between you and us a great chasm has been fixed, so that those who might want to pass from here to you cannot do so, and no one can cross from there to us.' [27]He said, 'Then, father, I beg you to send him to my father's house— [28]for I have five brothers—that he may warn them, so that they will not also come into this place of torment.' [29]Abraham replied, 'They have Moses and the prophets; they should listen to them.' [30]He said, 'No, father Abraham; but if someone goes to them from the dead, they will repent.' [31]He said to him, 'If they do not listen to Moses and the prophets, neither will they be convinced even if someone rises from the dead.' "

Some Sayings of Jesus

17 Jesus[z] said to his disciples, "Occasions for stumbling are bound to come, but woe to anyone by whom they come! [2]It would be better for you if a millstone were hung around your neck and you were thrown into the

---

[u] Gk mammon   [v] Gk tents   [w] Or everyone is strongly urged to enter it   [x] Gk to Abraham's bosom   [y] Gk in his bosom   [z] Gk He

Faith is believing in God, trusting in God, and being loyal to God. Jesus said that people can do amazing things with faith the size of a mustard seed. The mustard seed was the smallest seed known in Jesus's day. Jesus taught that with even a small amount of faith, we can do things that seem impossible. Think of some small things you can do that might have big results.

sea than for you to cause one of these little ones to stumble. ³Be on your guard! If another disciple[a] sins, you must rebuke the offender, and if there is repentance, you must forgive. ⁴And if the same person sins against you seven times a day, and turns back to you seven times and says, 'I repent,' you must forgive."

5 The apostles said to the Lord, "Increase our faith!" ⁶The Lord replied, "If you had faith the size of a[b] mustard seed, you could say to this mulberry tree, 'Be uprooted and planted in the sea,' and it would obey you.

7 "Who among you would say to your slave who has just come in from plowing or tending sheep in the field, 'Come here at once and take your place at the table'? ⁸Would you not rather say to him, 'Prepare supper for me, put on your apron and serve me while I eat and drink; later you may eat and drink'? ⁹Do you thank the slave for doing what was commanded? ¹⁰So you also, when you have done all that you were ordered to do, say, 'We are worthless slaves; we have done only what we ought to have done!' "

Jesus Cleanses Ten Lepers

11 On the way to Jerusalem Jesus[c] was going through the region between Sa·mār´-i·a and Galilee. ¹²As he entered a village, ten lepers[d] approached him. Keeping their distance, ¹³they called out, saying, "Jesus, Master, have mercy on us!" ¹⁴When he saw them, he said to them, "Go and show yourselves to the priests." And as they went, they were made clean. ¹⁵Then one of them, when he saw that he was healed, turned back, praising God with a loud voice. ¹⁶He prostrated himself at Jesus'[e] feet and thanked him. And he was a Sa·mār´i·tan. ¹⁷Then Jesus asked, "Were not ten made clean? But the other nine, where are they? ¹⁸Was none of them found to return and give praise to God except this foreigner?" ¹⁹Then he said to him, "Get up and go on your way; your faith has made you well."

The Coming of the Kingdom

20 Once Jesus[c] was asked by the Phar´i·sees when the kingdom of God was coming, and he answered, "The kingdom of God is not coming with things that can be observed; ²¹nor will they say, 'Look, here it is!' or 'There it is!' For, in fact, the kingdom of God is among[f] you."

22 Then he said to the disciples, "The days are coming when you will long to see one of the days of the Son of Man, and you will not see it. ²³They will say to you, 'Look there!' or 'Look here!' Do not go, do

In Bible times, people who had leprosy (a type of skin disease) were seen as "unclean" and had to live apart from everyone else, including their families. People who did not have leprosy believed they might also become unclean if they came too close to someone with the disease. But Jesus was not afraid. As he traveled to Jerusalem, Jesus healed ten people who had leprosy! One of the ten came back to thank Jesus, but the other nine went on their way and did not say thanks. We need to remember to thank Jesus for what he has done in our lives.

---

[a] Gk *your brother*   [b] Gk *faith as a grain of*
[c] Gk *he*   [d] The terms *leper* and *leprosy* can refer to several diseases   [e] Gk *his*   [f] Gk *within*

not set off in pursuit. ²⁴For as the lightning flashes and lights up the sky from one side to the other, so will the Son of Man be in his day.ᵍ ²⁵But first he must endure much suffering and be rejected by this generation. ²⁶Just as it was in the days of Noah, so too it will be in the days of the Son of Man. ²⁷They were eating and drinking, and marrying and being given in marriage, until the day Noah entered the ark, and the flood came and destroyed all of them. ²⁸Likewise, just as it was in the days of Lot: they were eating and drinking, buying and selling, planting and building, ²⁹but on the day that Lot left Sod′om, it rained fire and sulfur from heaven and destroyed all of them ³⁰—it will be like that on the day that the Son of Man is revealed. ³¹On that day, anyone on the housetop who has belongings in the house must not come down to take them away; and likewise anyone in the field must not turn back. ³²Remember Lot's wife. ³³Those who try to make their life secure will lose it, but those who lose their life will keep it. ³⁴I tell you, on that night there will be two in one bed; one will be taken and the other left. ³⁵There will be two women grinding meal together; one will be taken and the other left."ʰ ³⁷Then they asked him, "Where, Lord?" He said to them, "Where the corpse is, there the vultures will gather."

The Parable of the Widow and the Unjust Judge

18 Then Jesusⁱ told them a parable about their need to pray always and not to lose heart. ²He said, "In a certain city there was a judge who neither feared God nor had respect for people. ³In that city there was a widow who kept coming to him and saying, 'Grant me justice against my opponent.' ⁴For a while he refused; but later he said to himself, 'Though I have no fear of God and no respect for anyone, ⁵yet because this widow keeps bothering me, I will grant her justice, so that she may not wear me out by continually coming.' "ʲ ⁶And the Lord said, "Listen to what the unjust judge

says. ⁷And will not God grant justice to his chosen ones who cry to him day and night? Will he delay long in helping them? ⁸I tell you, he will quickly grant justice to them. And yet, when the Son of Man comes, will he find faith on earth?"

The Parable of the Pharisee and the Tax Collector

9 He also told this parable to some who trusted in themselves that they were righteous and regarded others with contempt: ¹⁰"Two men went up to the temple to pray, one a Phar′i·see and the other a tax collector. ¹¹The Phar′i·see, standing by himself, was praying thus, 'God, I thank you that I am not like other people: thieves, rogues, adulterers, or even like this tax collector. ¹²I fast twice a week; I give a tenth of all my income.' ¹³But the tax collector, standing far off, would not even look up to heaven, but was beating his breast and saying, 'God, be merciful to me, a sinner!' ¹⁴I tell you, this man went down to his home justified rather than the other; for all who exalt themselves will be humbled, but all who humble themselves will be exalted."

> When we are humble, we do not think of ourselves as being better than we are. We are not proud or boastful. We do not put ourselves above others.

Jesus Blesses Little Children

15 People were bringing even infants to him that he might touch them; and when the disciples saw it, they sternly ordered them not to do it. ¹⁶But Jesus called for them and said, "Let the little children come to me, and do not stop

ᵍ Other ancient authorities lack *in his day*
ʰ Other ancient authorities add verse 36, *"Two will be in the field; one will be taken and the other left."*
ⁱ Gk he ʲ Or *so that she may not finally come and slap me in the face*

them; for it is to such as these that the kingdom of God belongs. [17]Truly I tell you, whoever does not receive the kingdom of God as a little child will never enter it."

"Let the little children come to me, and do not stop them; for it is to such as these that the kingdom of God belongs." Luke 18:17

The Rich Ruler

18 A certain ruler asked him, "Good Teacher, what must I do to inherit eternal life?" [19]Jesus said to him, "Why do you call me good? No one is good but God alone. [20]You know the commandments: 'You shall not commit adultery; You shall not murder; You shall not steal; You shall not bear false witness; Honor your father and mother.'" [21]He replied, "I have kept all these since my youth." [22]When Jesus heard this, he said to him, "There is still one thing lacking. Sell all that you own and distribute the money[k] to the poor, and you will have treasure in heaven; then come, follow me." [23]But when he heard this, he became sad; for he was very rich. [24]Jesus looked at him and said, "How hard it is for those who have wealth to enter the kingdom of God! [25]Indeed, it is easier for a camel to go through the eye of a needle than for someone who is rich to enter the kingdom of God."

26 Those who heard it said, "Then who can be saved?" [27]He replied, "What is impossible for mortals is possible for God."

28 Then Peter said, "Look, we have left our homes and followed you." [29]And he said to them, "Truly I tell you, there is no one who has left house or wife or brothers or parents or children, for the sake of the kingdom of God, [30]who will not get back very much more in this age, and in the age to come eternal life."

A Third Time Jesus Foretells His Death and Resurrection

31 Then he took the twelve aside and said to them, "See, we are going up to Jerusalem, and everything that is written about the Son of Man by the prophets will be accomplished. [32]For he will be handed over to the Gentiles; and he will be

mocked and insulted and spat upon. [33]After they have flogged him, they will kill him, and on the third day he will rise again." [34]But they understood nothing about all these things; in fact, what he said was hidden from them, and they did not grasp what was said.

Jesus Heals a Blind Beggar Near Jericho

35 As he approached Jericho, a blind man was sitting by the roadside begging. [36]When he heard a crowd going by, he asked what was happening. [37]They told him, "Jesus of Nazareth[l] is passing by." [38]Then he shouted, "Jesus, Son of David, have mercy on me!" [39]Those who were in front sternly ordered him to be quiet; but he shouted even more loudly, "Son of David, have mercy on me!" [40]Jesus stood still and ordered the man to be brought to him; and when he came near, he asked him, [41]"What do you want me to do for you?" He said, "Lord, let me see again." [42]Jesus said to him, "Receive your sight; your faith has saved you." [43]Immediately he regained his sight and followed him, glorifying God; and all the people, when they saw it, praised God.

Jesus and Zacchaeus

19 He entered Jericho and was passing through it. [2]A man was there named Zac·chae'us; he was a chief tax collector and was rich. [3]He was trying to see who Jesus was, but on account of the crowd he could not, because he was short in stature. [4]So he ran ahead and climbed a sycamore tree to see him, because he was going to pass that way. [5]When Jesus came to the place, he looked up and said to him, "Zac·chae'us,

[k] Gk lacks *the money*   [l] Gk *the Nazorean*

> Zacchaeus was the chief tax collector of Jericho. When he met and talked with Jesus, his life was changed! Like many other people who met Jesus, Zacchaeus made a complete turn-around in the way he treated other people.

hurry and come down; for I must stay at your house today." ⁶So he hurried down and was happy to welcome him. ⁷All who saw it began to grumble and said, "He has gone to be the guest of one who is a sinner." ⁸Zac·chae´us stood there and said to the Lord, "Look, half of my possessions, Lord, I will give to the poor; and if I have defrauded anyone of anything, I will pay back four times as much." ⁹Then Jesus said to him, "Today salvation has come to this house, because he too is a son of Abraham. ¹⁰For the Son of Man came to seek out and to save the lost."

The Parable of the Ten Pounds

11 As they were listening to this, he went on to tell a parable, because he was near Jerusalem, and because they supposed that the kingdom of God was to appear immediately. ¹²So he said, "A nobleman went to a distant country to get royal power for himself and then return. ¹³He summoned ten of his slaves, and gave them ten pounds,ᵐ and said to them, 'Do business with these until I come back.' ¹⁴But the citizens of his country hated him and sent a delegation after him, saying, 'We do not want this man to rule over us.' ¹⁵When he returned, having received royal power, he ordered these slaves, to whom he had given the money, to be summoned so that he might find out what they had gained by trading. ¹⁶The first came forward and said, 'Lord, your pound has made ten more pounds.' ¹⁷He said to

him, 'Well done, good slave! Because you have been trustworthy in a very small thing, take charge of ten cities.' ¹⁸Then the second came, saying, 'Lord, your pound has made five pounds.' ¹⁹He said to him, 'And you, rule over five cities.' ²⁰Then the other came, saying, 'Lord, here is your pound. I wrapped it up in a piece of cloth, ²¹for I was afraid of you, because you are a harsh man; you take what you did not deposit, and reap what you did not sow.' ²²He said to him, 'I will judge you by your own words, you wicked slave! You knew, did you, that I was a harsh man, taking what I did not deposit and reaping what I did not sow? ²³Why then did you not put my money into the bank? Then when I returned, I could have collected it with interest.' ²⁴He said to the bystanders, 'Take the pound from him and give it to the one who has ten pounds.' ²⁵(And they said to him, 'Lord, he has ten pounds!') ²⁶'I tell you, to all those who have, more will be given; but from those who have nothing, even what they have will be taken away. ²⁷But as for these enemies of mine who did not want me to be king over them—bring them here and slaughter them in my presence.' "

Jesus' Triumphal Entry into Jerusalem

28 After he had said this, he went on ahead, going up to Jerusalem.

29 When he had come near Beth´-pha·gē and Beth´a·ny, at the place called the Mount of Olives, he sent two of the disciples, ³⁰saying, "Go into the village ahead of you, and as you enter it you will find tied there a colt that has never been ridden. Untie it and bring it here. ³¹If anyone asks you, 'Why are you untying it?' just say this, 'The Lord needs it.' " ³²So those who were sent departed and found it as he had told them. ³³As they were untying the colt, its owners asked them, "Why are you untying the colt?" ³⁴They

ᵐ The mina, rendered here by *pound*, was about three months' wages for a laborer said, "The Lord needs it." [35]Then they brought it to Jesus; and after throwing their cloaks on the colt, they set Jesus on it. [36]As he rode along, people kept spreading their cloaks on the road. [37]As he was now approaching the path down from the Mount of Olives, the whole multitude of the disciples began to praise God joyfully with a loud voice for all the deeds of power that they had seen, [38]saying,

"Blessed is the king
who comes in the name of the Lord!
Peace in heaven,
and glory in the highest heaven!"

[39]Some of the Phar′i·sees in the crowd said to him, "Teacher, order your disciples to stop." [40]He answered, "I tell you, if these were silent, the stones would shout out."

Jesus Weeps over Jerusalem

41 As he came near and saw the city, he wept over it, [42]saying, "If you, even you, had only recognized on this day the things that make for peace! But now they are hidden from your eyes. [43]Indeed, the days will come upon you, when your enemies will set up ramparts around you and surround you, and hem you in on every side. [44]They will crush you to the ground, you and your children within you, and they will not leave within you one stone upon another; because you did not recognize the time of your visitation from God."[n]

Jesus Cleanses the Temple

45 Then he entered the temple and began to drive out those who were selling things there; [46]and he said, "It is written,

'My house shall be a house of prayer';
but you have made it a den of
robbers."

47 Every day he was teaching in the temple. The chief priests, the scribes, and the leaders of the people kept looking for a way to kill him; [48]but they did not find anything they could do, for all the people were spellbound by what they heard.

The Authority of Jesus Questioned

20 One day, as he was teaching the people in the temple and telling the good news, the chief priests and the scribes came with the elders [2]and said to him, "Tell us, by what authority are you doing these things? Who is it who gave you this authority?" [3]He answered them, "I will also ask you a question, and you tell me: [4]Did the baptism of John come from heaven, or was it of human origin?" [5]They discussed it with one another, saying, "If we say, 'From heaven,' he will say, 'Why did you not believe him?' [6]But if we say, 'Of human origin,' all the people will stone us; for they are convinced that John was a prophet." [7]So they answered that they did not know where it came from. [8]Then Jesus said to them, "Neither will I tell you by what authority I am doing these things."

The Parable of the Wicked Tenants

9 He began to tell the people this parable: "A man planted a vineyard, and leased it to tenants, and went to another country for a long time. [10]When the season came, he sent a slave to the tenants in order that they might give him his share of the produce of the vineyard; but the tenants beat him and sent him away empty-handed. [11]Next he sent another slave; that one also they beat and insulted and sent away empty-handed. [12]And he sent still a third; this one also they wounded and threw out. [13]Then the owner of the vineyard said, 'What shall I do? I will send my beloved son; perhaps they will respect him.' [14]But when the tenants saw him, they discussed it among themselves and said, 'This is the heir; let us kill him so that the inheritance may be ours.' [15]So they threw him out of the vineyard and killed him. What then will the owner of the vineyard do to them? [16]He will come and destroy those tenants and give the vineyard

[n] Gk lacks *from God*

to others." When they heard this, they said, "Heaven forbid!" ¹⁷But he looked at them and said, "What then does this text mean:

'The stone that the builders rejected
    has become the cornerstone'?ᵒ
¹⁸Everyone who falls on that stone will be broken to pieces; and it will crush anyone on whom it falls." ¹⁹When the scribes and chief priests realized that he had told this parable against them, they wanted to lay hands on him at that very hour, but they feared the people.

The Question about Paying Taxes

20 So they watched him and sent spies who pretended to be honest, in order to trap him by what he said, so as to hand him over to the jurisdiction and authority of the governor. ²¹So they asked him, "Teacher, we know that you are right in what you say and teach, and you show deference to no one, but teach the way of God in accordance with truth. ²²Is it lawful for us to pay taxes to the emperor, or not?" ²³But he perceived their craftiness and said to them, ²⁴"Show me a denarius. Whose head and whose title does it bear?" They said, "The emperor's." ²⁵He said to them, "Then give to the emperor the things that are the emperor's, and to God the things that are God's." ²⁶And they were not able in the presence of the people to trap him by what he said; and being amazed by his answer, they became silent.

The Question about the Resurrection

27 Some Sad'du-cees, those who say there is no resurrection, came to him ²⁸and asked him a question, "Teacher, Moses wrote for us that if a man's brother dies, leaving a wife but no children, the manᵖ shall marry the widow and raise up children for his brother. ²⁹Now there were seven brothers; the first married, and died childless; ³⁰then the second ³¹and the third married her, and so in the same way

all seven died childless. ³²Finally the woman also died. ³³In the resurrection, therefore, whose wife will the woman be? For the seven had married her."

34 Jesus said to them, "Those who belong to this age marry and are given in marriage; ³⁵but those who are considered worthy of a place in that age and in the resurrection from the dead neither marry nor are given in marriage. ³⁶Indeed they cannot die anymore, because they are like angels and are children of God, being children of the resurrection. ³⁷And the fact that the dead are raised Moses himself showed, in the story about the bush, where he speaks of the Lord as the God of Abraham, the God of Isaac, and the God of Jacob. ³⁸Now he is God not of the dead, but of the living; for to him all of them are alive." ³⁹Then some of the scribes answered, "Teacher, you have spoken well." ⁴⁰For they no longer dared to ask him another question.

The Question about David's Son

41 Then he said to them, "How can they say that the Messiah�q is David's son? ⁴²For David himself says in the book of Psalms,

'The Lord said to my Lord,
    "Sit at my right hand,
⁴³   until I make your enemies your
        footstool."'
⁴⁴David thus calls him Lord; so how can he be his son?"

Jesus Denounces the Scribes

45 In the hearing of all the people he said to theʳ disciples, ⁴⁶"Beware of the scribes, who like to walk around in long robes, and love to be greeted with respect in the marketplaces, and to have the best seats in the synagogues and places of honor at banquets. ⁴⁷They devour widows' houses and for the sake of appearance say long prayers. They will receive the greater condemnation."

ᵒ Or keystone   ᵖ Gk his brother   q Or the Christ
ʳ Other ancient authorities read his

The Widow's Offering

21 He looked up and saw rich people putting their gifts into the treasury; ²he also saw a poor widow put in two small copper coins. ³He said, "Truly I tell you, this poor widow has put in more than all of them; ⁴for all of them have contributed out of their abundance, but she out of her poverty has put in all she had to live on."

The Destruction of the Temple Foretold

5 When some were speaking about the temple, how it was adorned with beautiful stones and gifts dedicated to God, he said, ⁶"As for these things that you see, the days will come when not one stone will be left upon another; all will be thrown down."

Signs and Persecutions

7 They asked him, "Teacher, when will this be, and what will be the sign that this is about to take place?" ⁸And he said, "Beware that you are not led astray; for many will come in my name and say, 'I am he!'ˢ and, 'The time is near!'ᵗ Do not go after them. 9 "When you hear of wars and insurrections, do not be terrified; for these things must take place first, but the end will not follow immediately." ¹⁰Then he said to them, "Nation will rise against nation, and kingdom against kingdom; ¹¹there will be great earthquakes, and in various places famines and plagues; and there will be dreadful portents and great signs from heaven.

12 "But before all this occurs, they will arrest you and persecute you; they will hand you over to synagogues and prisons, and you will be brought before kings and governors because of my name. ¹³This will give you an opportunity to testify. ¹⁴So make up your minds not to prepare your defense in advance; ¹⁵for I will give you wordsᵘ and a wisdom that none of your opponents will be able to withstand or contradict. ¹⁶You will be betrayed even by parents and brothers, by relatives and friends; and they will put some of you to death. ¹⁷You will be hated by all because of my name. ¹⁸But not a hair of your head will perish. ¹⁹By your endurance you will gain your souls.

The Destruction of Jerusalem Foretold

20 "When you see Jerusalem surrounded by armies, then know that its desolation has come near.ᵛ ²¹Then those in Judea must flee to the mountains, and those inside the city must leave it, and those out in the country must not enter it; ²²for these are days of vengeance, as a fulfillment of all that is written. ²³Woe to those who are pregnant and to those who are nursing infants in those days! For there will be great distress on the earth and wrath against this people; ²⁴they will fall by the edge of the sword and be taken away as captives among all nations; and Jerusalem will be trampled on by the Gentiles, until the times of the Gentiles are fulfilled.

The Coming of the Son of Man

25 "There will be signs in the sun, the moon, and the stars, and on the earth distress among nations confused by the roaring of the sea and the waves. ²⁶People will faint from fear and foreboding of what is coming upon the world, for the powers of the heavens will be shaken. ²⁷Then they will see 'the Son of Man coming in a cloud' with power and great glory. ²⁸Now when these things begin to take place, stand up and raise your heads, because your redemption is drawing near."

The Lesson of the Fig Tree

29 Then he told them a parable: "Look at the fig tree and all the trees; ³⁰as soon as they sprout leaves you can see for yourselves and know that summer is already near. ³¹So also, when you see these things taking place, you know that the kingdom

ˢ Gk I am　ᵗ Or at hand　ᵘ Gk a mouth　ᵛ Or is at hand

> "Heaven and earth will pass away, but my words will not pass away." Luke 21:33

of God is near. [32]Truly I tell you, this generation will not pass away until all things have taken place. [33]Heaven and earth will pass away, but my words will not pass away.

Exhortation to Watch

34 "Be on guard so that your hearts are not weighed down with dissipation and drunkenness and the worries of this life, and that day does not catch you unexpectedly, [35]like a trap. For it will come upon all who live on the face of the whole earth. [36]Be alert at all times, praying that you may have the strength to escape all these things that will take place, and to stand before the Son of Man."

37 Every day he was teaching in the temple, and at night he would go out and spend the night on the Mount of Olives, as it was called. [38]And all the people would get up early in the morning to listen to him in the temple.

The Plot to Kill Jesus

22 Now the festival of Unleavened Bread, which is called the Passover, was near. [2]The chief priests and the scribes were looking for a way to put Jesus[w] to death, for they were afraid of the people.

3 Then Satan entered into Judas called Is·car'i·ot, who was one of the twelve; [4]he went away and conferred with the chief priests and officers of the temple police about how he might betray him to them. [5]They were greatly pleased and agreed to give him money. [6]So he consented and began to look for an opportunity to betray him to them when no crowd was present.

The Preparation of the Passover

7 Then came the day of Unleavened Bread, on which the Passover lamb had to be sacrificed. [8]So Jesus[x] sent Peter and John, saying, "Go and prepare the Passover meal for us that we may eat it." [9]They asked him, "Where do you want us to make preparations for it?" [10]"Listen," he said to them, "when you have entered the city, a man carrying a jar of water will meet you; follow him into the house he enters [11]and say to the owner of the house, 'The teacher asks you, "Where is the guest room, where I may eat the Passover with my disciples?" ' [12]He will show you a large room upstairs, already furnished. Make preparations for us there." [13]So they went and found everything as he had told them; and they prepared the Passover meal.

The Institution of the Lord's Supper

14 When the hour came, he took his place at the table, and the apostles with him. [15]He said to them, "I have eagerly desired to eat this Passover with you before I suffer; [16]for I tell you, I will not eat it[y] until it is fulfilled in the kingdom of God." [17]Then he took a cup, and after giving thanks he said, "Take this and divide it among yourselves; [18]for I tell you that from now on I will not drink of the fruit of the vine until the kingdom of God comes." [19]Then he took a loaf of bread, and when he had given thanks, he broke it and gave it to them, saying, "This is my body, which is given for you. Do this in remembrance of me." [20]And he did the same with the cup after supper, saying, "This cup that is poured out for you is the new covenant in my blood.[z] [21]But see, the one who betrays me is with me, and his hand is on the table. [22]For the Son of Man is going as it has been determined, but woe to that one by whom he is betrayed!" [23]Then they began to ask one another which one of them it could be who would do this.

The Dispute about Greatness

24 A dispute also arose among them as to which one of them was to be regarded

[w] Gk *him*   [x] Gk *he*   [y] Other ancient authorities read *never eat it again*   [z] Other ancient authorities lack, in whole or in part, verses 19b-20 (*which is given . . . . in my blood*)

During the Passover meal that Jesus ate with his disciples, Jesus took bread and broke it, saying "This is my body, which is given for you." He also took a cup of wine and poured it, saying, "This is the cup that is poured out for you." This was the first Lord's Supper. When we celebrate the Lord's Supper (also called Holy Communion, or the Eucharist), we remember that Jesus gave himself for us.

as the greatest. ²⁵But he said to them, "The kings of the Gentiles lord it over them; and those in authority over them are called benefactors. ²⁶But not so with you; rather the greatest among you must become like the youngest, and the leader like one who serves. ²⁷For who is greater, the one who is at the table or the one who serves? Is it not the one at the table? But I am among you as one who serves.

28 "You are those who have stood by me in my trials; ²⁹and I confer on you, just as my Father has conferred on me, a kingdom, ³⁰so that you may eat and drink at my table in my kingdom, and you will sit on thrones judging the twelve tribes of Israel.

Jesus Predicts Peter's Denial

31 "Simon, Simon, listen! Satan has demanded[a] to sift all of you like wheat, ³²but I have prayed for you that your own faith may not fail; and you, when once you have turned back, strengthen your brothers." ³³And he said to him, "Lord, I am ready to go with you to prison and to death!" ³⁴Jesus[b] said, "I tell you, Peter, the cock will not crow this day, until you have denied three times that you know me."

Purse, Bag, and Sword

35 He said to them, "When I sent you out without a purse, bag, or sandals, did you lack anything?" They said, "No, not a thing." ³⁶He said to them, "But now, the one who has a purse must take it, and likewise a bag. And the one who has no sword must sell his cloak and buy one. ³⁷For I tell you, this scripture must be fulfilled in me, 'And he was counted among the lawless'; and indeed what is written about me is being fulfilled." ³⁸They said, "Lord, look, here are two swords." He replied, "It is enough."

Jesus Prays on the Mount of Olives

39 He came out and went, as was his custom, to the Mount of Olives; and the disciples followed him. ⁴⁰When he reached the place, he said to them, "Pray that you may not come into the time of trial."[c] ⁴¹Then he withdrew from them about a stone's throw, knelt down, and prayed, ⁴²"Father, if you are willing, remove this cup from me; yet, not my will but yours be done." [[⁴³Then an angel from heaven appeared to him and gave him strength. ⁴⁴In his anguish he prayed more earnestly, and his sweat became like great drops of blood falling down on the ground.]][d] ⁴⁵When he got up from prayer, he came to the disciples and found them sleeping because of grief, ⁴⁶and he said to them, "Why are you sleeping? Get up and pray that you may not come into the time of trial."[c]

The Betrayal and Arrest of Jesus

47 While he was still speaking, suddenly a crowd came, and the one called Judas, one of the twelve, was leading them. He approached Jesus to kiss him; ⁴⁸but Jesus said to him, "Judas, is it with a kiss that you are betraying the Son of Man?" ⁴⁹When those who were around

"Father, if you are willing, remove this cup from me; yet, not my will but yours be done." Luke 22:42

---

[a] Or *has obtained permission*   [b] Gk *He*   [c] Or *into temptation*   [d] Other ancient authorities lack verses 43 and 44

him saw what was coming, they asked, "Lord, should we strike with the sword?" [50]Then one of them struck the slave of the high priest and cut off his right ear. [51]But Jesus said, "No more of this!" And he touched his ear and healed him. [52]Then Jesus said to the chief priests, the officers of the temple police, and the elders who had come for him, "Have you come out with swords and clubs as if I were a bandit? [53]When I was with you day after day in the temple, you did not lay hands on me. But this is your hour, and the power of darkness!"

Peter Denies Jesus

54 Then they seized him and led him away, bringing him into the high priest's house. But Peter was following at a distance. [55]When they had kindled a fire in the middle of the courtyard and sat down together, Peter sat among them. [56]Then a servant-girl, seeing him in the firelight, stared at him and said, "This man also was with him." [57]But he denied it, saying, "Woman, I do not know him." [58]A little later someone else, on seeing him, said, "You also are one of them." But Peter said, "Man, I am not!" [59]Then about an hour later still another kept insisting, "Surely this man also was with him; for he is a Galilean." [60]But Peter said, "Man, I do not know what you are talking about!" At that moment, while he was still speaking, the cock crowed. [61]The Lord turned and looked at Peter. Then Peter remembered the word of the Lord, how he had said to him, "Before the cock crows today, you will deny me three times." [62]And he went out and wept bitterly.

The Mocking and Beating of Jesus

63 Now the men who were holding Jesus began to mock him and beat him; [64]they also blindfolded him and kept asking him, "Prophesy! Who is it that struck you?" [65]They kept heaping many other insults on him.

Jesus before the Council

66 When day came, the assembly of the elders of the people, both chief priests and scribes, gathered together, and they brought him to their council. [67]They said, "If you are the Messiah,[e] tell us." He replied, "If I tell you, you will not believe; [68]and if I question you, you will not answer. [69]But from now on the Son of Man will be seated at the right hand of the power of God." [70]All of them asked, "Are you, then, the Son of God?" He said to them, "You say that I am." [71]Then they said, "What further testimony do we need? We have heard it ourselves from his own lips!"

Jesus before Pilate

23 Then the assembly rose as a body and brought Jesus[f] before Pilate. [2]They began to accuse him, saying, "We found this man perverting our nation, forbidding us to pay taxes to the emperor, and saying that he himself is the Messiah, a king."[g] [3]Then Pilate asked him, "Are you the king of the Jews?" He answered, "You say so." [4]Then Pilate said to the chief priests and the crowds, "I find no basis for an accusation against this man." [5]But they were insistent and said, "He stirs up the people by teaching throughout all Judea, from Galilee where he began even to this place."

Jesus before Herod

6 When Pilate heard this, he asked whether the man was a Galilean. [7]And

Peter was sorry that he had not been loyal to his friend and teacher Jesus. Sometimes we say, "I don't know Jesus," by the way we treat others and by the things we do. Whenever we do this, we should ask Jesus to forgive us and commit ourselves to living as Jesus wants us live.

[e] Or *the Christ*   [f] Gk *him*   [g] Or *is an anointed king*

when he learned that he was under Her´od's jurisdiction, he sent him off to Her´od, who was himself in Jerusalem at that time. [8]When Her´od saw Jesus, he was very glad, for he had been wanting to see him for a long time, because he had heard about him and was hoping to see him perform some sign. [9]He questioned him at some length, but Jesus[h] gave him no answer. [10]The chief priests and the scribes stood by, vehemently accusing him. [11]Even Her´od with his soldiers treated him with contempt and mocked him; then he put an elegant robe on him, and sent him back to Pilate. [12]That same day Her´od and Pilate became friends with each other; before this they had been enemies.

Jesus Sentenced to Death

13 Pilate then called together the chief priests, the leaders, and the people, [14]and said to them, "You brought me this man as one who was perverting the people; and here I have examined him in your presence and have not found this man guilty of any of your charges against him. [15]Neither has Her´od, for he sent him back to us. Indeed, he has done nothing to deserve death. [16]I will therefore have him flogged and release him."[i]

18 Then they all shouted out together, "Away with this fellow! Release Ba·rab´bas for us!" [19](This was a man who had been put in prison for an insurrection that had taken place in the city, and for murder.) [20]Pilate, wanting to release Jesus, addressed them again; [21]but they kept shouting, "Crucify, crucify him!" [22]A third time he said to them, "Why, what evil has he done? I have found in him no ground for the sentence of death; I will therefore have him flogged and then release him." [23]But they kept urgently demanding with loud shouts that he should be crucified; and their voices prevailed. [24]So Pilate gave his verdict that their demand should be granted. [25]He released the man they asked for, the one who had been put in prison for insurrection and murder, and he handed Jesus over as they wished.

The Crucifixion of Jesus

26 As they led him away, they seized a man, Simon of Cy·re´ne, who was coming from the country, and they laid the cross on him, and made him carry it behind Jesus. [27]A great number of the people followed him, and among them were women who were beating their breasts and wailing for him. [28]But Jesus turned to them and said, "Daughters of Jerusalem, do not weep for me, but weep for yourselves and for your children. [29]For the days are surely coming when they will say, 'Blessed are the barren, and the wombs that never bore, and the breasts that never nursed.' [30]Then they will begin to say to the mountains, 'Fall on us'; and to the hills, 'Cover us.' [31]For if they do this when the wood is green, what will happen when it is dry?"

32 Two others also, who were criminals, were led away to be put to death with him. [33]When they came to the place that is called The Skull, they crucified Jesus[j] there with the criminals, one on his right and one on his left. [[[34]Then Jesus said, "Father, forgive them; for they do not know what they are doing."]][k] And they cast lots to divide his clothing. [35]And the people stood by, watching; but the leaders scoffed at him, saying, "He saved others; let him save himself if he is the Messiah[l] of God, his chosen one!" [36]The soldiers also mocked him, coming up and offering him sour wine, [37]and saying, "If you are the King of the Jews, save yourself!" [38]There was also an inscription over him,[m] "This is the King of the Jews."

"Then Jesus said, 'Father, forgive them; for they do not know what they are doing.'" Luke 23:34

---

[h] Gk he   [i] Here, or after verse 19, other ancient authorities add verse 17, *Now he was obliged to release someone for them at the festival*   [j] Gk him   [k] Other ancient authorities lack the sentence *Then Jesus . . . what they are doing*   [l] Or *the Christ*   [m] Other ancient authorities add *written in Greek and Latin and Hebrew* (that is, *Aramaic*)

39 One of the criminals who were hanged there kept deriding[n] him and saying, "Are you not the Messiah?[o] Save yourself and us!" 40But the other rebuked him, saying, "Do you not fear God, since you are under the same sentence of condemnation? 41And we indeed have been condemned justly, for we are getting what we deserve for our deeds, but this man has done nothing wrong." 42Then he said, "Jesus, remember me when you come into[p] your kingdom." 43He replied, "Truly I tell you, today you will be with me in Paradise."

The Death of Jesus

44 It was now about noon, and darkness came over the whole land[q] until three in the afternoon, 45while the sun's light failed;[r] and the curtain of the temple was torn in two. 46Then Jesus, crying with a loud voice, said, "Father, into your hands I commend my spirit." Having said this, he breathed his last. 47When the centurion saw what had taken place, he praised God and said, "Certainly this man was innocent."[s] 48And when all the crowds who had gathered there for this spectacle saw what had taken place, they returned home, beating their breasts. 49But all his acquaintances, including the women who had followed him from Galilee, stood at a distance, watching these things.

The Burial of Jesus

50 Now there was a good and righteous man named Joseph, who, though a member of the council, 51had not agreed to their plan and action. He came from the Jewish town of Ar·i·ma·thē′a, and he was waiting expectantly for the kingdom of God. 52This man went to Pilate and asked for the body of Jesus. 53Then he took it down, wrapped it in a linen cloth, and laid it in a rock-hewn tomb where no one had ever been laid. 54It

was the day of Preparation, and the sabbath was beginning.[t] 55The women who had come with him from Galilee followed, and they saw the tomb and how his body was laid. 56Then they returned, and prepared spices and ointments.

On the sabbath they rested according to the commandment.

The Resurrection of Jesus

24 But on the first day of the week, at early dawn, they came to the tomb, taking the spices that they had prepared. 2They found the stone rolled away from the tomb, 3but when they went in, they did not find the body.[u] 4While they were perplexed about this, suddenly two men in dazzling clothes stood beside them. 5The women[v] were terrified and bowed their faces to the ground, but the men[w] said to them, "Why do you look for the living among the dead? He is not here, but has risen.[x] 6Remember how he told you, while he was still in Galilee, 7that the Son of Man must be handed over to sinners, and be crucified, and on the third day rise again." 8Then they remembered his words, 9and returning from the tomb, they told all this to the eleven and to all the rest. 10Now it was Mary Mag′da·lēne, Jō·an′na, Mary the mother of James, and the other women with them who told this to the apostles. 11But these words seemed to them an idle tale, and they did not believe them. 12But Peter got up and ran to the tomb; stooping and looking in, he saw the linen cloths by themselves; then he went home, amazed at what had happened.[y]

The Walk to Emmaus

13 Now on that same day two of them were going to a village called Em·mā′us,

[n] Or blaspheming   [o] Or the Christ   [p] Other ancient authorities read in   [q] Or earth   [r] Or the sun was eclipsed. Other ancient authorities read the sun was darkened   [s] Or righteous   [t] Gk was dawning   [u] Other ancient authorities add of the Lord Jesus   [v] Gk They   [w] Gk but they   [x] Other ancient authorities lack He is not here, but has risen   [y] Other ancient authorities lack verse 12

"Why do you look for the living among the dead? He is not here, but has risen." Luke 24:5b

The two disciples on the road recognized Jesus when they sat down and ate a meal together. Sharing food is one way of sharing the Good News of Jesus. With your family, find ways to help give food to your local community as well as send food around the world.

about seven miles[z] from Jerusalem, [14]and talking with each other about all these things that had happened. [15]While they were talking and discussing, Jesus himself came near and went with them, [16]but their eyes were kept from recognizing him. [17]And he said to them, "What are you discussing with each other while you walk along?" They stood still, looking sad.[a] [18]Then one of them, whose name was Clē′o·pas, answered him, "Are you the only stranger in Jerusalem who does not know the things that have taken place there in these days?" [19]He asked them, "What things?" They replied, "The things about Jesus of Nazareth,[b] who was a prophet mighty in deed and word before God and all the people, [20]and how our chief priests and leaders handed him over to be condemned to death and crucified him. [21]But we had hoped that he was the one to redeem Israel.[c] Yes, and besides all this, it is now the third day since these things took place. [22]Moreover, some women of our group astounded us. They were at the tomb early this morning, [23]and when they did not find his body there, they came back and told us that they had indeed seen a vision of angels who said that he was alive. [24]Some of those who were with us went to the tomb and found it just as the women had said; but they did not see him." [25]Then he said to them, "Oh, how foolish you are, and how slow of heart to believe all that the prophets have declared! [26]Was it not necessary that the Messiah[d] should suffer these things and then enter into his glory?" [27]Then begin-

ning with Moses and all the prophets, he interpreted to them the things about himself in all the scriptures.

28 As they came near the village to which they were going, he walked ahead as if he were going on. [29]But they urged him strongly, saying, "Stay with us, because it is almost evening and the day is now nearly over." So he went in to stay with them. [30]When he was at the table with them, he took bread, blessed and broke it, and gave it to them. [31]Then their eyes were opened, and they recognized him; and he vanished from their sight. [32]They said to each other, "Were not our hearts burning within us[e] while he was talking to us on the road, while he was opening the scriptures to us?" [33]That same hour they got up and returned to Jerusalem; and they found the eleven and their companions gathered together. [34]They were saying, "The Lord has risen indeed, and he has appeared to Simon!" [35]Then they told what had happened on the road, and how he had been made known to them in the breaking of the bread.

Jesus Appears to His Disciples

36 While they were talking about this, Jesus himself stood among them and said to them, "Peace be with you."[f] [37]They were startled and terrified, and thought that they were seeing a ghost. [38]He said to them, "Why are you frightened, and why do doubts arise in your hearts? [39]Look at my hands and my feet; see that it is I myself. Touch me and see; for a ghost does not have flesh and bones as you see that I have." [40]And when he had said this, he showed them his hands and his feet.[g] [41]While in their joy they were disbelieving

[z] Gk sixty stadia; other ancient authorities read a hundred sixty stadia   [a] Other ancient authorities read walk along, looking sad?"   [b] Other ancient authorities read Jesus the Nazorean   [c] Or to set Israel free   [d] Or the Christ   [e] Other ancient authorities lack within us   [f] Other ancient authorities lack and said to them, "Peace be with you."   [g] Other ancient authorities lack verse 40

and still wondering, he said to them, "Have you anything here to eat?" [42]They gave him a piece of broiled fish, [43]and he took it and ate in their presence.

44 Then he said to them, "These are my words that I spoke to you while I was still with you—that everything written about me in the law of Moses, the prophets, and the psalms must be fulfilled." [45]Then he opened their minds to understand the scriptures, [46]and he said to them, "Thus it is written, that the Messiah[h] is to suffer and to rise from the dead on the third day, [47]and that repentance and forgiveness of sins is to be proclaimed in his name to all nations,[i] beginning from Jerusalem. [48]You are witnesses of these things. [49]And see, I am sending upon you

what my Father promised; so stay here in the city until you have been clothed with power from on high."

The Ascension of Jesus

50 Then he led them out as far as Beth´a·ny, and, lifting up his hands, he blessed them. [51]While he was blessing them, he withdrew from them and was carried up into heaven.[j] [52]And they worshiped him, and[k] returned to Jerusalem with great joy; [53]and they were continually in the temple blessing God.[l]

[h] Or the Christ   [i] Or nations. Beginning from Jerusalem [48]you are witnesses   [j] Other ancient authorities lack and was carried up into heaven   [k] Other ancient authorities lack worshiped him, and   [l] Other ancient authorities add Amen

John

Of the four Gospels, John was the last to be written, probably around 90–100 AD. We are not sure who wrote this Gospel because John was a very common name, and the book does not clearly state which John wrote it. Whoever the author was, it was someone who knew and understood Jesus Christ and the meaning of his life and work.

Like the other Gospels, the Gospel of John tells the story of Jesus—his life, death, and resurrection. In this Gospel, we read that Jesus spent time teaching his disciples as well as others whom he met. He often told the people who he was, using words they could picture. He told them he was "the living bread" (John 6:51), "the light of the world" (John 8:12), "the gate" (John 10:9), "the good shepherd" (John 10:11), "the resurrection and the life" (John 11:25), "the way, and the truth, and the life" (John 14:6), and "the true vine" (John 15:1). Some of the most wonderful statements in the Bible are found in the Gospel of John. Perhaps the most important is, "For God so loved the world that he gave his only Son, so that everyone who believes in him may not perish but may have eternal life." (John 3:16).

John 10:1–18

The Word Became Flesh

1 In the beginning was the Word, and the Word was with God, and the Word was God. ²He was in the beginning with God. ³All things came into being through him, and without him not one thing came into being. What has come into being ⁴in him was life,ᵃ and the life was the light of all people. ⁵The light shines in the darkness, and the darkness did not overcome it.

6 There was a man sent from God, whose name was John. ⁷He came as a witness to testify to the light, so that all might believe through him. ⁸He himself was not the light, but he came to testify to the light. ⁹The true light, which enlightens everyone, was coming into the world.ᵇ

10 He was in the world, and the world came into being through him; yet the world did not know him. ¹¹He came to what was his own,ᶜ and his own people did not accept him. ¹²But to all who received him, who believed in his name, he gave power to become children of God, ¹³who were born, not of blood or of the will of the flesh or of the will of man, but of God.

14 And the Word became flesh and lived among us, and we have seen his glory, the glory as of a father's only son,ᵈ full of grace and truth. ¹⁵(John testified to him and cried out, "This was he of whom I said, 'He who comes after me ranks ahead of me because he was before me.' ") ¹⁶From his fullness we have all received, grace upon grace. ¹⁷The law indeed was given through Moses; grace and truth came through Jesus Christ. ¹⁸No one has ever seen God. It is God the only Son,ᵉ who is close to the Father's heart,ᶠ who has made him known.

The Testimony of John the Baptist

19 This is the testimony given by John when the Jews sent priests and Lē´vītes from Jerusalem to ask him, "Who are you?" ²⁰He confessed and did not deny it, but confessed, "I am not the Messiah."ᵍ ²¹And they asked him, "What then? Are

Have you ever thought about how many light bulbs it takes to light a house? Walk through your home, and count how many light bulbs there are! Think about how dark it would be at night without those lights.

John called Jesus "the light of the world." Jesus often told stories that had to do with light. Read Matthew 5:14–16, Matthew 6:22–23, and Luke 8:16–18. What do you think "light" stands for in each passage? Thank God for sending Jesus to be the light for our world.

you E·lī´jah?" He said, "I am not." "Are you the prophet?" He answered, "No." ²²Then they said to him, "Who are you? Let us have an answer for those who sent us. What do you say about yourself?" ²³He said,

"I am the voice of one crying out in the
 wilderness,
'Make straight the way of the Lord,' "
as the prophet Ī·sāi´ah said.

24 Now they had been sent from the Phar´i·sees. ²⁵They asked him, "Why then are you baptizing if you are neither the Messiah,ᵍ nor E·lī´jah, nor the prophet?" ²⁶John answered them, "I baptize with water. Among you stands one whom you do not know, ²⁷the one who is coming after me; I am not worthy to untie the thong of his sandal." ²⁸This took place in Beth´a·ny across the Jordan where John was baptizing.

The Lamb of God

29 The next day he saw Jesus coming toward him and declared, "Here is the Lamb of God who takes away the sin of

ᵃ Or ³through him. And without him not one thing came into being that has come into being. ⁴In him was life   ᵇ Or He was the true light that enlightens everyone coming into the world   ᶜ Or to his own home   ᵈ Or the Father's only Son   ᵉ Other ancient authorities read It is an only Son, God, or It is the only Son   ᶠ Gk bosom   ᵍ Or the Christ

In Bible times, people would take lambs to the priest to be sacrificed. The priest would hold up the lamb and say, "Behold the lamb of [family name] who takes away the sins of [family name]." When John saw Jesus, he said, "Here is the Lamb of God who takes away the sin of the world!" In other words, John was saying that Jesus would take away the sin of all of God's family!

the world! [30]This is he of whom I said, 'After me comes a man who ranks ahead of me because he was before me.' [31]I myself did not know him; but I came baptizing with water for this reason, that he might be revealed to Israel." [32]And John testified, "I saw the Spirit descending from heaven like a dove, and it remained on him. [33]I myself did not know him, but the one who sent me to baptize with water said to me, 'He on whom you see the Spirit descend and remain is the one who baptizes with the Holy Spirit.' [34]And I myself have seen and have testified that this is the Son of God."[h]

The First Disciples of Jesus

35 The next day John again was standing with two of his disciples, [36]and as he watched Jesus walk by, he exclaimed, "Look, here is the Lamb of God!" [37]The two disciples heard him say this, and they followed Jesus. [38]When Jesus turned and saw them following, he said to them, "What are you looking for?" They said to him, "Rabbi" (which translated means Teacher), "where are you staying?" [39]He said to them, "Come and see." They came and saw where he was staying, and they remained with him that day. It was about four o'clock in the afternoon. [40]One of the two who heard John speak and followed him was Andrew, Simon Peter's brother. [41]He first found his brother Simon and said to him, "We have found

the Messiah" (which is translated Anointed[i]). [42]He brought Simon[j] to Jesus, who looked at him and said, "You are Simon son of John. You are to be called Cēphas" (which is translated Peter[k]).

Jesus Calls Philip and Nathanael

43 The next day Jesus decided to go to Galilee. He found Philip and said to him, "Follow me." [44]Now Philip was from Beth·sā·i·da, the city of Andrew and Peter. [45]Philip found Na·than'a·el and said to him, "We have found him about whom Moses in the law and also the prophets wrote, Jesus son of Joseph from Nazareth." [46]Na·than'a·el said to him, "Can anything good come out of Nazareth?" Philip said to him, "Come and see." [47]When Jesus saw Na·than'a·el coming toward him, he said of him, "Here is truly an Israelite in whom there is no deceit!" [48]Na·than'a·el asked him, "Where did you get to know me?" Jesus answered, "I saw you under the fig tree before Philip called you." [49]Na·than'a·el replied, "Rabbi, you are the Son of God! You are the King of Israel!" [50]Jesus answered, "Do you believe because I told you that I saw you under the fig tree? You will see greater things than these." [51]And he said to him, "Very truly, I tell you,[l] you will see heaven opened and the angels of God ascending and descending upon the Son of Man."

Andrew was a fisherman and the brother of Simon Peter. Andrew is not mentioned many times in the Bible, but he was one of the first people to recognize that Jesus was the long-awaited Messiah.

[h] Other ancient authorities read is God's chosen one [i] Or Christ [j] Gk him [k] From the word for rock in Aramaic (kepha) and Greek (petra), respectively [l] Both instances of the Greek word for you in this verse are plural

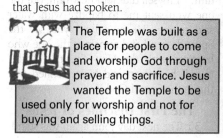

Jesus went to a wedding where he changed water into wine! This miracle was the first act of Jesus's ministry in John's Gospel. John called the miracle a "sign."

The Wedding at Cana

2 On the third day there was a wedding in Cā′na of Galilee, and the mother of Jesus was there. ²Jesus and his disciples had also been invited to the wedding. ³When the wine gave out, the mother of Jesus said to him, "They have no wine." ⁴And Jesus said to her, "Woman, what concern is that to you and to me? My hour has not yet come." ⁵His mother said to the servants, "Do whatever he tells you." ⁶Now standing there were six stone water jars for the Jewish rites of purification, each holding twenty or thirty gallons. ⁷Jesus said to them, "Fill the jars with water." And they filled them up to the brim. ⁸He said to them, "Now draw some out, and take it to the chief steward." So they took it. ⁹When the steward tasted the water that had become wine, and did not know where it came from (though the servants who had drawn the water knew), the steward called the bridegroom ¹⁰and said to him, "Everyone serves the good wine first, and then the inferior wine after the guests have become drunk. But you have kept the good wine until now." ¹¹Jesus did this, the first of his signs, in Cā′na of Galilee, and revealed his glory; and his disciples believed in him.

12 After this he went down to Ca·per′na·um with his mother, his brothers, and his disciples; and they remained there a few days.

Jesus Cleanses the Temple

13 The Passover of the Jews was near, and Jesus went up to Jerusalem. ¹⁴In the temple he found people selling cattle, sheep, and doves, and the money changers seated at their tables. ¹⁵Making a whip of cords, he drove all of them out of the temple, both the sheep and the cattle. He also poured out the coins of the money changers and overturned their tables. ¹⁶He told those who were selling the doves, "Take these things out of here! Stop making my Father's house a marketplace!" ¹⁷His disciples remembered that it was written, "Zeal for your house will consume me." ¹⁸The Jews then said to him, "What sign can you show us for doing this?" ¹⁹Jesus answered them, "Destroy this temple, and in three days I will raise it up." ²⁰The Jews then said, "This temple has been under construction for forty-six years, and will you raise it up in three days?" ²¹But he was speaking of the temple of his body. ²²After he was raised from the dead, his disciples remembered that he had said this; and they believed the scripture and the word that Jesus had spoken.

The Temple was built as a place for people to come and worship God through prayer and sacrifice. Jesus wanted the Temple to be used only for worship and not for buying and selling things.

23 When he was in Jerusalem during the Passover festival, many believed in his name because they saw the signs that he was doing. ²⁴But Jesus on his part would not entrust himself to them, because he knew all people ²⁵and needed no one to testify about anyone; for he himself knew what was in everyone.

Nicodemus Visits Jesus

3 Now there was a Phar′i·see named Nic·o·dē′mus, a leader of the Jews. ²He came to Jesus^m by night and said to him, "Rabbi, we know that you are a teacher who has come from God; for no

^{m} Gk *him*

one can do these signs that you do apart from the presence of God." ³Jesus answered him, "Very truly, I tell you, no one can see the kingdom of God without being born from above."ⁿ ⁴Nic·o·dē´mus said to him, "How can anyone be born after having grown old? Can one enter a second time into the mother's womb and be born?" ⁵Jesus answered, "Very truly, I tell you, no one can enter the kingdom of God without being born of water and Spirit. ⁶What is born of the flesh is flesh, and what is born of the Spirit is spirit.ᵒ ⁷Do not be astonished that I said to you, 'Youᵖ must be born from above.'�q ⁸The windᵒ blows where it chooses, and you hear the sound of it, but you do not know where it comes from or where it goes. So it is with everyone who is born of the Spirit." ⁹Nic·o·dē´mus said to him, "How can these things be?" ¹⁰Jesus answered him, "Are you a teacher of Israel, and yet you do not understand these things?

11 "Very truly, I tell you, we speak of what we know and testify to what we have seen; yet youʳ do not receive our testimony. ¹²If I have told you about earthly things and you do not believe, how can you believe if I tell you about heavenly things? ¹³No one has ascended into heaven except the one who descended from heaven, the Son of Man.ˢ ¹⁴And just as Moses lifted up the serpent in the wilderness, so must the Son of Man be lifted up, ¹⁵that whoever believes in him may have eternal life.ᵗ

16 "For God so loved the world that he gave his only Son, so that everyone who believes in him may not perish but may have eternal life.

17 "Indeed, God did not send the Son into the world to condemn the world, but

Nicodemus was a member of the Sanhedrin, a group of Jewish religious leaders who functioned as a court. Jesus was often at odds with the Sanhedrin, so Nicodemus came to Jesus secretly at night to ask questions and to hear more of Jesus's teachings. Nicodemus became a follower of Jesus. Read where he is mentioned again in John 7:45–52 and John 19:38–42.

in order that the world might be saved through him. ¹⁸Those who believe in him are not condemned; but those who do not believe are condemned already, because they have not believed in the name of the only Son of God. ¹⁹And this is the judgment, that the light has come into the world, and people loved darkness rather than light because their deeds were evil. ²⁰For all who do evil hate the light and do not come to the light, so that their deeds may not be exposed. ²¹But those who do what is true come to the light, so that it may be clearly seen that their deeds have been done in God."ᵗ

Jesus and John the Baptist

22 After this Jesus and his disciples went into the Judean countryside, and he spent some time there with them and baptized. ²³John also was baptizing at Aē´non near Sā´lim because water was abundant there; and people kept coming and were being baptized ²⁴—John, of course, had not yet been thrown into prison.

"For God so loved the world that he gave his only Son, so that everyone who believes in him may not perish but may have eternal life."
John 3:16

ⁿ Or *born anew*   ᵒ The same Greek word means both *wind* and *spirit*   ᵖ The Greek word for *you* here is plural   q Or *anew*   ʳ The Greek word for *you* here and in verse 12 is plural   ˢ Other ancient authorities add *who is in heaven*   ᵗ Some interpreters hold that the quotation concludes with verse 15

25 Now a discussion about purification arose between John's disciples and a Jew.ᵘ ²⁶They came to John and said to him, "Rabbi, the one who was with you across the Jordan, to whom you testified, here he is baptizing, and all are going to him." ²⁷John answered, "No one can receive anything except what has been given from heaven. ²⁸You yourselves are my witnesses that I said, 'I am not the Messiah,ᵛ but I have been sent ahead of him.' ²⁹He who has the bride is the bridegroom. The friend of the bridegroom, who stands and hears him, rejoices greatly at the bridegroom's voice. For this reason my joy has been fulfilled. ³⁰He must increase, but I must decrease."ʷ

The One Who Comes from Heaven

31 The one who comes from above is above all; the one who is of the earth belongs to the earth and speaks about earthly things. The one who comes from heaven is above all. ³²He testifies to what he has seen and heard, yet no one accepts his testimony. ³³Whoever has accepted his testimony has certifiedˣ this, that God is true. ³⁴He whom God has sent speaks the words of God, for he gives the Spirit without measure. ³⁵The Father loves the Son and has placed all things in his hands. ³⁶Whoever believes in the Son has eternal life; whoever disobeys the Son will not see life, but must endure God's wrath.

Jesus and the Woman of Samaria

4 Now when Jesusʸ learned that the Pharisees had heard, "Jesus is making and baptizing more disciples than John" ²— although it was not Jesus himself but his disciples who baptized— ³he left Judea and started back to Galilee. ⁴But he had to go through Samaria. ⁵So he came to a Samaritan city called Sychar, near the plot of ground that Jacob had given to his son Joseph. ⁶Jacob's well was there, and Jesus, tired out by his journey, was sitting by the well. It was about noon.

7 A Samaritan woman came to draw water, and Jesus said to her, "Give me a drink." ⁸(His disciples had gone to the city to buy food.) ⁹The Samaritan woman said to him, "How is it that you, a Jew, ask a drink of me, a woman of Samaria?" (Jews do not share things in common with Samaritans.)ᶻ ¹⁰Jesus answered her, "If you knew the gift of God, and who it is that is saying to you, 'Give me a drink,' you would have asked him, and he would have given you living water." ¹¹The woman said to him, "Sir, you have no bucket, and the well is deep. Where do you get that living water? ¹²Are you greater than our ancestor Jacob, who gave us the well, and with his sons and his flocks drank from it?" ¹³Jesus said to her, "Everyone who drinks of this water will be thirsty again, ¹⁴but those who drink of the water that I will give them will never be thirsty. The water that I will give will become in them a spring of water gushing up to eternal life." ¹⁵The woman said to him, "Sir, give me this water, so that I may never be thirsty or have to keep coming here to draw water."

16 Jesus said to her, "Go, call your husband, and come back." ¹⁷The woman answered him, "I have no husband." Jesus said to her, "You are right in saying, 'I have

> Like people in many parts of the world today (including parts of the United States), people in Bible times used wells as a source of water. The people would get water out of the wells with jars or waterskins attached to ropes. They had to return often to draw water from the well.

ᵘ Other ancient authorities read *the Jews*   ᵛ Or *the Christ*   ʷ Some interpreters hold that the quotation continues through verse 36   ˣ Gk *set a seal to*   ʸ Other ancient authorities read *the Lord*   ᶻ Other ancient authorities lack this sentence no husband'; [18]for you have had five husbands, and the one you have now is not your husband. What you have said is true!" [19]The woman said to him, "Sir, I see that you are a prophet. [20]Our ancestors worshiped on this mountain, but you[a] say that the place where people must worship is in Jerusalem." [21]Jesus said to her, "Woman, believe me, the hour is coming when you will worship the Father neither on this mountain nor in Jerusalem. [22]You worship what you do not know; we worship what we know, for salvation is from the Jews. [23]But the hour is coming, and is now here, when the true worshipers will worship the Father in spirit and truth, for the Father seeks such as these to worship him. [24]God is spirit, and those who worship him must worship in spirit and truth." [25]The woman said to him, "I know that Messiah is coming" (who is called Christ). "When he comes, he will proclaim all things to us." [26]Jesus said to her, "I am he,[b] the one who is speaking to you."

27 Just then his disciples came. They were astonished that he was speaking with a woman, but no one said, "What do you want?" or, "Why are you speaking with her?" [28]Then the woman left her water jar and went back to the city. She said to the people, [29]"Come and see a man who told me everything I have ever done! He cannot be the Messiah,[c] can he?" [30]They left the city and were on their way to him.

31 Meanwhile the disciples were urging him, "Rabbi, eat something." [32]But he said to them, "I have food to eat that you do not know about." [33]So the disciples said to one another, "Surely no one has brought him something to eat?" [34]Jesus said to them, "My food is to do the will of him who sent me and to complete his work. [35]Do you not say, 'Four months more, then comes the harvest'? But I tell you, look around you, and see how the fields are ripe for harvesting. [36]The reaper is already receiving[d] wages and is gathering fruit for eternal life, so that sower and reaper may rejoice together. [37]For here the saying holds true, 'One sows and another reaps.' [38]I sent you to reap that for which you did not labor. Others have labored, and you have entered into their labor."

39 Many Sa·mār´i·tans from that city believed in him because of the woman's testimony, "He told me everything I have ever done." [40]So when the Sa·mār´i·tans came to him, they asked him to stay with them; and he stayed there two days. [41]And many more believed because of his word. [42]They said to the woman, "It is no longer because of what you said that we believe, for we have heard for ourselves, and we know that this is truly the Savior of the world."

Jesus Returns to Galilee

43 When the two days were over, he went from that place to Galilee [44](for Jesus himself had testified that a prophet has no honor in the prophet's own country). [45]When he came to Galilee, the Galileans welcomed him, since they had seen all that he had done in Jerusalem at the festival; for they too had gone to the festival.

Jesus Heals an Official's Son

46 Then he came again to Cā´na in Galilee where he had changed the water into wine. Now there was a royal official

As Jesus traveled to Galilee, he stopped in the city of Sychar and talked with a Samaritan woman at a well. Jesus talked with her about eternal life and about worship. She said she knew the Messiah would be coming. Jesus told her that he was the Messiah! After the woman left the well and went back to the city, she told people about meeting Jesus. Because of what she said, many people believed in him. Who can you tell about Jesus?

---

[a] The Greek word for *you* here and in verses 21 and 22 is plural　　[b] Gk *I am*　　[c] Or *the Christ*
[d] Or [35]. . . *the fields are already ripe for harvesting.*
[36]*The reaper is receiving*

whose son lay ill in Ca·per′na·um. [47]When he heard that Jesus had come from Judea to Galilee, he went and begged him to come down and heal his son, for he was at the point of death. [48]Then Jesus said to him, "Unless you[e] see signs and wonders you will not believe." [49]The official said to him, "Sir, come down before my little boy dies." [50]Jesus said to him, "Go; your son will live." The man believed the word that Jesus spoke to him and started on his way. [51]As he was going down, his slaves met him and told him that his child was alive. [52]So he asked them the hour when he began to recover, and they said to him, "Yesterday at one in the afternoon the fever left him." [53]The father realized that this was the hour when Jesus had said to him, "Your son will live." So he himself believed, along with his whole household. [54]Now this was the second sign that Jesus did after coming from Judea to Galilee.

Jesus Heals on the Sabbath

5 After this there was a festival of the Jews, and Jesus went up to Jerusalem.

2 Now in Jerusalem by the Sheep Gate there is a pool, called in Hebrew[f] Beth-za′tha,[g] which has five porticoes. [3]In these lay many invalids—blind, lame, and paralyzed.[h] [5]One man was there who had been ill for thirty-eight years. [6]When Jesus saw him lying there and knew that he had been there a long time, he said to him, "Do you want to be made well?" [7]The sick man answered him, "Sir, I have no one to put me into the pool when the water is stirred up; and while I am making my way, someone else steps down ahead of me." [8]Jesus said to him, "Stand up, take your mat and walk." [9]At once the man was made well, and he took up his mat and began to walk.

Now that day was a sabbath. [10]So the Jews said to the man who had been cured, "It is the sabbath; it is not lawful for you to carry your mat." [11]But he answered them, "The man who made me well said to me, 'Take up your mat and walk.'" [12]They

> "Jesus said to him, 'Stand up, take your mat and walk.' At once the man was made well, and he took up his mat and began to walk." John 5:8–9

asked him, "Who is the man who said to you, 'Take it up and walk'?" [13]Now the man who had been healed did not know who it was, for Jesus had disappeared in[i] the crowd that was there. [14]Later Jesus found him in the temple and said to him, "See, you have been made well! Do not sin any more, so that nothing worse happens to you." [15]The man went away and told the Jews that it was Jesus who had made him well. [16]Therefore the Jews started persecuting Jesus, because he was doing such things on the sabbath. [17]But Jesus answered them, "My Father is still working, and I also am working." [18]For this reason the Jews were seeking all the more to kill him, because he was not only breaking the sabbath, but was also calling God his own Father, thereby making himself equal to God.

The way we spend our time tells a lot about what is important to us. Jesus spent time being kind to others. In this story, he healed a man who could not walk. Some religious people thought that Jesus was breaking God's laws by healing on the Sabbath, a day of rest. But Jesus knew that doing good—every day of the week—was important to God.

---

[e] Both instances of the Greek word for *you* in this verse are plural   [f] That is, *Aramaic*   [g] Other ancient authorities read *Bethesda*, others *Bethsaida*   [h] Other ancient authorities add, wholly or in part, *waiting for the stirring of the water;* [4]*for an angel of the Lord went down at certain seasons into the pool, and stirred up the water; whoever stepped in first after the stirring of the water was made well from whatever disease that person had.*   [i] Or *had left because of*

The Authority of the Son

19 Jesus said to them, "Very truly, I tell you, the Son can do nothing on his own, but only what he sees the Father doing; for whatever the Father[j] does, the Son does likewise. 20The Father loves the Son and shows him all that he himself is doing; and he will show him greater works than these, so that you will be astonished. 21Indeed, just as the Father raises the dead and gives them life, so also the Son gives life to whomever he wishes. 22The Father judges no one but has given all judgment to the Son, 23so that all may honor the Son just as they honor the Father. Anyone who does not honor the Son does not honor the Father who sent him. 24Very truly, I tell you, anyone who hears my word and believes him who sent me has eternal life, and does not come under judgment, but has passed from death to life.

25 "Very truly, I tell you, the hour is coming, and is now here, when the dead will hear the voice of the Son of God, and those who hear will live. 26For just as the Father has life in himself, so he has granted the Son also to have life in himself; 27and he has given him authority to execute judgment, because he is the Son of Man. 28Do not be astonished at this; for the hour is coming when all who are in their graves will hear his voice 29and will come out—those who have done good, to the resurrection of life, and those who have done evil, to the resurrection of con- demnation.

Witnesses to Jesus

30 "I can do nothing on my own. As I hear, I judge; and my judgment is just, because I seek to do not my own will but the will of him who sent me.

31 "If I testify about myself, my testi- mony is not true. 32There is another who testifies on my behalf, and I know that his testimony to me is true. 33You sent mes- sengers to John, and he testified to the truth. 34Not that I accept such human tes- timony, but I say these things so that you

may be saved. 35He was a burning and shining lamp, and you were willing to rejoice for a while in his light. 36But I have a testimony greater than John's. The works that the Father has given me to complete, the very works that I am doing, testify on my behalf that the Father has sent me. 37And the Father who sent me has himself testified on my behalf. You have never heard his voice or seen his form, 38and you do not have his word abiding in you, because you do not believe him whom he has sent.

39 "You search the scriptures because you think that in them you have eternal life; and it is they that testify on my behalf. 40Yet you refuse to come to me to have life. 41I do not accept glory from human beings. 42But I know that you do not have the love of God in[k] you. 43I have come in my Father's name, and you do not accept me; if another comes in his own name, you will accept him. 44How can you believe when you accept glory from one another and do not seek the glory that comes from the one who alone is God? 45Do not think that I will accuse you before the Father; your accuser is Moses, on whom you have set your hope. 46If you believed Moses, you would believe me, for he wrote about me. 47But if you do not believe what he wrote, how will you believe what I say?"

Feeding the Five Thousand

6 After this Jesus went to the other side of the Sea of Galilee, also called the Sea of Tī·bē'ri·as.[l] 2A large crowd kept following him, because they saw the signs that he was doing for the sick. 3Jesus went up the mountain and sat down there with his disciples. 4Now the Passover, the festival of the Jews, was near. 5When he looked up and saw a large crowd coming toward him, Jesus said to Philip, "Where are we to buy bread for these people to eat?" 6He said

[j] Gk that one [k] Or among [l] Gk of Galilee of Tiberius

this to test him, for he himself knew what he was going to do. [7]Philip answered him, "Six months' wages[m] would not buy enough bread for each of them to get a little." [8]One of his disciples, Andrew, Simon Peter's brother, said to him, [9]"There is a boy here who has five barley loaves and two fish. But what are they among so many people?" [10]Jesus said, "Make the people sit down." Now there was a great deal of grass in the place; so they[n] sat down, about five thousand in all. [11]Then Jesus took the loaves, and when he had given thanks, he distributed them to those who were seated; so also the fish, as much as they wanted. [12]When they were satisfied, he told his disciples, "Gather up the fragments left over, so that nothing may be lost." [13]So they gathered them up, and from the fragments of the five barley loaves, left by those who had eaten, they filled twelve baskets. [14]When the people saw the sign that he had done, they began to say, "This is indeed the prophet who is to come into the world."

15 When Jesus realized that they were about to come and take him by force to make him king, he withdrew again to the mountain by himself.

Jesus Walks on the Water

16 When evening came, his disciples went down to the sea, [17]got into a boat, and started across the sea to Ca·per´-na·um. It was now dark, and Jesus had not yet come to them. [18]The sea became rough because a strong wind was blowing. [19]When they had rowed about three or four miles,[o] they saw Jesus walking on the sea and coming near the boat, and they were terrified. [20]But he said to them, "It is I;[p] do not be afraid." [21]Then they wanted to take him into the boat, and immediately the boat reached the land toward which they were going.

The Bread from Heaven

22 The next day the crowd that had stayed on the other side of the sea saw that there had been only one boat there. They also saw that Jesus had not got into the boat with his disciples, but that his disciples had gone away alone. [23]Then some boats from Ti·be´ri·as came near the place where they had eaten the bread after the Lord had given thanks.[q] [24]So when the crowd saw that neither Jesus nor his disciples were there, they themselves got into the boats and went to Ca·per´na·um looking for Jesus.

25 When they found him on the other side of the sea, they said to him, "Rabbi, when did you come here?" [26]Jesus answered them, "Very truly, I tell you, you are looking for me, not because you saw signs, but because you ate your fill of the loaves. [27]Do not work for the food that perishes, but for the food that endures for eternal life, which the Son of Man will give you. For it is on him that God the Father has set his seal." [28]Then they said to him, "What must we do to perform the works of God?" [29]Jesus answered them, "This is the work of God, that you believe in him whom he has sent." [30]So they said to him, "What sign are you going to give us then, so that we may see it and believe you? What work are you performing? [31]Our ancestors ate the manna in the wilderness; as it is written, 'He gave them bread from heaven to eat.' " [32]Then Jesus said to them, "Very truly, I tell you, it was not Moses who gave you the bread from heaven, but it is my Father who gives you the true bread from heaven. [33]For the bread of God is that which[r] comes down from heaven and gives life to the world." [34]They said to him, "Sir, give us this bread always."

35 Jesus said to them, "I am the bread of life. Whoever comes to me will never be hungry, and whoever believes in me will never be thirsty. [36]But I said to you that

---

[m] Gk *Two hundred denarii*; the denarius was the usual day's wage for a laborer   [n] Gk *the men*
[o] Gk *about twenty-five or thirty stadia*   [p] Gk *I am*
[q] Other ancient authorities lack *after the Lord had given thanks*   [r] Or *he who*

"Jesus said to them, 'I am the bread of life. Whoever comes to me will never be hungry, and whoever believes in me will never be thirsty.'" John 6:35

you have seen me and yet do not believe. [37]Everything that the Father gives me will come to me, and anyone who comes to me I will never drive away; [38]for I have come down from heaven, not to do my own will, but the will of him who sent me. [39]And this is the will of him who sent me, that I should lose nothing of all that he has given me, but raise it up on the last day. [40]This is indeed the will of my Father, that all who see the Son and believe in him may have eternal life; and I will raise them up on the last day."

41 Then the Jews began to complain about him because he said, "I am the bread that came down from heaven." [42]They were saying, "Is not this Jesus, the son of Joseph, whose father and mother we know? How can he now say, 'I have come down from heaven'?" [43]Jesus answered them, "Do not complain among yourselves. [44]No one can come to me unless drawn by the Father who sent me; and I will raise that person up on the last day. [45]It is written in the prophets, 'And they shall all be taught by God.' Everyone

Jesus said, "I am the bread of life" (John 6:35). In Bible times, bread was an important food item. The people made bread from scratch—grinding flour, mixing ingredients, and then baking that mixture. When Jesus compared himself to this most basic of foods, his listeners understood that he was saying that believing in him was simply all they needed.

who has heard and learned from the Father comes to me. [46]Not that anyone has seen the Father except the one who is from God; he has seen the Father. [47]Very truly, I tell you, whoever believes has eternal life. [48]I am the bread of life. [49]Your ancestors ate the manna in the wilderness, and they died. [50]This is the bread that comes down from heaven, so that one may eat of it and not die. [51]I am the living bread that came down from heaven. Whoever eats of this bread will live forever; and the bread that I will give for the life of the world is my flesh."

52 The Jews then disputed among themselves, saying, "How can this man give us his flesh to eat?" [53]So Jesus said to them, "Very truly, I tell you, unless you eat the flesh of the Son of Man and drink his blood, you have no life in you. [54]Those who eat my flesh and drink my blood have eternal life, and I will raise them up on the last day; [55]for my flesh is true food and my blood is true drink. [56]Those who eat my flesh and drink my blood abide in me, and I in them. [57]Just as the living Father sent me, and I live because of the Father, so whoever eats me will live because of me. [58]This is the bread that came down from heaven, not like that which your ancestors ate, and they died. But the one who eats this bread will live forever." [59]He said these things while he was teaching in the synagogue at Ca·per′na·um.

The Words of Eternal Life

60 When many of his disciples heard it, they said, "This teaching is difficult; who can accept it?" [61]But Jesus, being aware that his disciples were complaining about it, said to them, "Does this offend you? [62]Then what if you were to see the Son of Man ascending to where he was before? [63]It is the spirit that gives life; the flesh is useless. The words that I have spoken to you are spirit and life. [64]But among you there are some who do not believe." For Jesus knew from the first who were the ones that did not believe, and who

was the one that would betray him. ⁶⁵And he said, "For this reason I have told you that no one can come to me unless it is granted by the Father."

66 Because of this many of his disciples turned back and no longer went about with him. ⁶⁷So Jesus asked the twelve, "Do you also wish to go away?" ⁶⁸Simon Peter answered him, "Lord, to whom can we go? You have the words of eternal life. ⁶⁹We have come to believe and know that you are the Holy One of God."ˢ ⁷⁰Jesus answered them, "Did I not choose you, the twelve? Yet one of you is a devil." ⁷¹He was speaking of Judas son of Simon Is·car′i·ot,ᵗ for he, though one of the twelve, was going to betray him.

The Unbelief of Jesus' Brothers

7 After this Jesus went about in Galilee. He did not wishᵘ to go about in Judea because the Jews were looking for an opportunity to kill him. ²Now the Jewish festival of Boothsᵛ was near. ³So his brothers said to him, "Leave here and go to Judea so that your disciples also may see the works you are doing; ⁴for no one who wantsʷ to be widely known acts in secret. If you do these things, show yourself to the world." ⁵(For not even his brothers believed in him.) ⁶Jesus said to them, "My time has not yet come, but your time is always here. ⁷The world cannot hate you, but it hates me because I testify against it that its works are evil. ⁸Go to the festival yourselves. I am notˣ going to this festival, for my time has not yet fully come." ⁹After saying this, he remained in Galilee.

Jesus at the Festival of Booths

10 But after his brothers had gone to the festival, then he also went, not publicly but as it wereʸ in secret. ¹¹The Jews were looking for him at the festival and saying, "Where is he?" ¹²And there was considerable complaining about him among the crowds. While some were say-

ing, "He is a good man," others were saying, "No, he is deceiving the crowd." ¹³Yet no one would speak openly about him for fear of the Jews.

14 About the middle of the festival Jesus went up into the temple and began to teach. ¹⁵The Jews were astonished at it, saying, "How does this man have such learning,ᶻ when he has never been taught?" ¹⁶Then Jesus answered them, "My teaching is not mine but his who sent me. ¹⁷Anyone who resolves to do the will of God will know whether the teaching is from God or whether I am speaking on my own. ¹⁸Those who speak on their own seek their own glory; but the one who seeks the glory of him who sent him is true, and there is nothing false in him.

19 "Did not Moses give you the law? Yet none of you keeps the law. Why are you looking for an opportunity to kill me?" ²⁰The crowd answered, "You have a demon! Who is trying to kill you?" ²¹Jesus answered them, "I performed one work, and all of you are astonished. ²²Moses gave you circumcision (it is, of course, not from Moses, but from the patriarchs), and you circumcise a man on the sabbath. ²³If a man receives circumcision on the sabbath in order that the law of Moses may not be broken, are you angry with me because I healed a man's whole body on the sabbath? ²⁴Do not judge by appearances, but judge with right judgment."

Is This the Christ?

25 Now some of the people of Jerusalem were saying, "Is not this the man whom they are trying to kill? ²⁶And here he is, speaking openly, but they say nothing to him! Can it be that the author-

ˢ Other ancient authorities read *the Christ, the Son of the living God*   ᵗ Other ancient authorities read *Judas Iscariot son of Simon*; others, *Judas son of Simon from Karyot* (Kerioth)   ᵘ Other ancient authorities read *was not at liberty*   ᵛ Or *Tabernacles*
ʷ Other ancient authorities read *wants it*
ˣ Other ancient authorities add *yet*   ʸ Other ancient authorities lack *as it were*   ᶻ Or *this man know his letters*

ities really know that this is the Messiah?[a] [27]Yet we know where this man is from; but when the Messiah[a] comes, no one will know where he is from." [28]Then Jesus cried out as he was teaching in the temple, "You know me, and you know where I am from. I have not come on my own. But the one who sent me is true, and you do not know him. [29]I know him, because I am from him, and he sent me." [30]Then they tried to arrest him, but no one laid hands on him, because his hour had not yet come. [31]Yet many in the crowd believed in him and were saying, "When the Messiah[a] comes, will he do more signs than this man has done?"[b]

Officers Are Sent to Arrest Jesus

32 The Phar´i·sees heard the crowd muttering such things about him, and the chief priests and Phar´i·sees sent temple police to arrest him. [33]Jesus then said, "I will be with you a little while longer, and then I am going to him who sent me. [34]You will search for me, but you will not find me; and where I am, you cannot come." [35]The Jews said to one another, "Where does this man intend to go that we will not find him? Does he intend to go to the Dispersion among the Greeks and teach the Greeks? [36]What does he mean by saying, 'You will search for me and you will not find me' and 'Where I am, you cannot come'?"

Rivers of Living Water

37 On the last day of the festival, the great day, while Jesus was standing there, he cried out, "Let anyone who is thirsty come to me, [38]and let the one who believes in me drink. As[c] the scripture has said, 'Out of the believer's heart[d] shall flow rivers of living water.'" [39]Now he said this about the Spirit, which believers in him were to receive; for as yet there was no Spirit,[e] because Jesus was not yet glorified.

Division among the People

40 When they heard these words, some in the crowd said, "This is really the

prophet." [41]Others said, "This is the Messiah."[a] But some asked, "Surely the Messiah[a] does not come from Galilee, does he? [42]Has not the scripture said that the Messiah[a] is descended from David and comes from Bethlehem, the village where David lived?" [43]So there was a division in the crowd because of him. [44]Some of them wanted to arrest him, but no one laid hands on him.

The Unbelief of Those in Authority

45 Then the temple police went back to the chief priests and Phar´i·sees, who asked them, "Why did you not arrest him?" [46]The police answered, "Never has anyone spoken like this!" [47]Then the Phar´i·sees replied, "Surely you have not been deceived too, have you? [48]Has any one of the authorities or of the Phar´i·sees believed in him? [49]But this crowd, which does not know the law—they are accursed." [50]Nic·o·dē´mus, who had gone to Jesus[f] before, and who was one of them, asked, [51]"Our law does not judge people without first giving them a hearing to find out what they are doing, does it?" [52]They replied, "Surely you are not also from Galilee, are you? Search and you will see that no prophet is to arise from Galilee."

People often made jokes about people from Galilee. The religious leaders did not expect a prophet to come from Galilee—especially not the Messiah, God's own Son.

[a] Or *the Christ*   [b] Other ancient authorities read *is doing*   [c] Or *come to me and drink.* [38]*The one who believes in me, as*   [d] Gk *out of his belly*   [e] Other ancient authorities read *for as yet the Spirit* (others, *Holy Spirit*) *had not been given*   [f] Gk *him*

The Woman Caught in Adultery

[[⁵³Then each of them went home, ¹while Jesus went to the Mount of Olives. ²Early in the morning he came again to the temple. All the people came to him and he sat down and began to teach them. ³The scribes and the Phar′i·sees brought a woman who had been caught in adultery; and making her stand before all of them, ⁴they said to him, "Teacher, this woman was caught in the very act of committing adultery. ⁵Now in the law Moses commanded us to stone such women. Now what do you say?" ⁶They said this to test him, so that they might have some charge to bring against him. Jesus bent down and wrote with his finger on the ground. ⁷When they kept on questioning him, he straightened up and said to them, "Let anyone among you who is without sin be the first to throw a stone at her." ⁸And once again he bent down and wrote on the ground.^g ⁹When they heard it, they went away, one by one, beginning with the elders; and Jesus was left alone with the woman standing before him. ¹⁰Jesus straightened up and said to her, "Woman, where are they? Has no one condemned you?" ¹¹She said, "No one, sir."^h And Jesus said, "Neither do I condemn you. Go your way, and from now on do not sin again."]]ⁱ

Jesus the Light of the World

12 Again Jesus spoke to them, saying, "I am the light of the world. Whoever follows me will never walk in darkness but will have the light of life." ¹³Then the Phar′i·sees said to him, "You are testifying on your own behalf; your testimony is not

> "Again Jesus spoke to them, saying, 'I am the light of the world. Whoever follows me will never walk in darkness but will have the light of life.'" John 8:12

valid." ¹⁴Jesus answered, "Even if I testify on my own behalf, my testimony is valid because I know where I have come from and where I am going, but you do not know where I come from or where I am going. ¹⁵You judge by human standards;^j I judge no one. ¹⁶Yet even if I do judge, my judgment is valid; for it is not I alone who judge, but I and the Father^k who sent me. ¹⁷In your law it is written that the testimony of two witnesses is valid. ¹⁸I testify on my own behalf, and the Father who sent me testifies on my behalf." ¹⁹Then they said to him, "Where is your Father?" Jesus answered, "You know neither me nor my Father. If you knew me, you would know my Father also." ²⁰He spoke these words while he was teaching in the treasury of the temple, but no one arrested him, because his hour had not yet come.

Jesus Foretells His Death

21 Again he said to them, "I am going away, and you will search for me, but you will die in your sin. Where I am going, you cannot come." ²²Then the Jews said, "Is he going to kill himself? Is that what he means by saying, 'Where I am going, you cannot come'?" ²³He said to them, "You are from below, I am from above; you are of this world, I am not of this world. ²⁴I told you that you would die in your sins, for you will die in your sins unless you believe that I am he."^l ²⁵They said to him, "Who are you?" Jesus said to them, "Why

Jesus said, "I am the light of the world" (John 8:12). He also said, "Let your light shine before others" (Matthew 5:16). As Christians, we are called to reflect the light of Jesus Christ. What are some ways that you can be a reflection of Christ's love?

^g Other ancient authorities add *the sins of each of them* ^h Or *Lord* ⁱ The most ancient authorities lack 7.53—8.11; other authorities add the passage here or after 7.36 or after 21.25 or after Luke 21.38, with variations of text; some mark the passage as doubtful. ^j Gk *according to the flesh* ^k Other ancient authorities read *he* ^l Gk *I am*

do I speak to you at all?[m] [26]I have much to say about you and much to condemn; but the one who sent me is true, and I declare to the world what I have heard from him." [27]They did not understand that he was speaking to them about the Father. [28]So Jesus said, "When you have lifted up the Son of Man, then you will realize that I am he,[n] and that I do nothing on my own, but I speak these things as the Father instructed me. [29]And the one who sent me is with me; he has not left me alone, for I always do what is pleasing to him." [30]As he was saying these things, many believed in him.

True Disciples

31 Then Jesus said to the Jews who had believed in him, "If you continue in my word, you are truly my disciples; [32]and you will know the truth, and the truth will make you free." [33]They answered him, "We are descendants of Abraham and have never been slaves to anyone. What do you mean by saying, 'You will be made free'?"

34 Jesus answered them, "Very truly, I tell you, everyone who commits sin is a slave to sin. [35]The slave does not have a permanent place in the household; the son has a place there forever. [36]So if the Son makes you free, you will be free indeed. [37]I know that you are descendants of Abraham; yet you look for an opportunity to kill me, because there is no place in you for my word. [38]I declare what I have seen in the Father's presence; as for you, you should do what you have heard from the Father."[o]

Jesus and Abraham

39 They answered him, "Abraham is our father." Jesus said to them, "If you were Abraham's children, you would be doing[p] what Abraham did, [40]but now you are trying to kill me, a man who has told you the truth that I heard from God. This is not what Abraham did. [41]You are indeed doing what your father does." They said to him, "We are not illegitimate

children; we have one father, God himself." [42]Jesus said to them, "If God were your Father, you would love me, for I came from God and now I am here. I did not come on my own, but he sent me. [43]Why do you not understand what I say? It is because you cannot accept my word. [44]You are from your father the devil, and you choose to do your father's desires. He was a murderer from the beginning and does not stand in the truth, because there is no truth in him. When he lies, he speaks according to his own nature, for he is a liar and the father of lies. [45]But because I tell the truth, you do not believe me. [46]Which of you convicts me of sin? If I tell the truth, why do you not believe me? [47]Whoever is from God hears the words of God. The reason you do not hear them is that you are not from God."

48 The Jews answered him, "Are we not right in saying that you are a Sa·mār′i·tan and have a demon?" [49]Jesus answered, "I do not have a demon; but I honor my Father, and you dishonor me. [50]Yet I do not seek my own glory; there is one who seeks it and he is the judge. [51]Very truly, I tell you, whoever keeps my word will never see death." [52]The Jews said to him, "Now we know that you have a demon. Abraham died, and so did the prophets; yet you say, 'Whoever keeps my word will never taste death.' [53]Are you greater than our father Abraham, who died? The prophets also died. Who do you claim to be?" [54]Jesus answered, "If I glorify myself, my glory is nothing. It is my Father who glorifies me, he of whom you say, 'He is our God,' [55]though you do not know him. But I know him; if I would say that I do not know him, I would be a liar like you. But I do know him and I keep his word. [56]Your ancestor Abraham rejoiced that he would see my day; he saw

---

[m] Or *What I have told you from the beginning*
[n] Gk *I am*   [o] Other ancient authorities read *you do what you have heard from your father*   [p] Other ancient authorities read *If you are Abraham's children, then do*

it and was glad." [57]Then the Jews said to him, "You are not yet fifty years old, and have you seen Abraham?"[q] [58]Jesus said to them, "Very truly, I tell you, before Abraham was, I am." [59]So they picked up stones to throw at him, but Jesus hid himself and went out of the temple.

A Man Born Blind Receives Sight

9 As he walked along, he saw a man blind from birth. [2]His disciples asked him, "Rabbi, who sinned, this man or his parents, that he was born blind?" [3]Jesus answered, "Neither this man nor his parents sinned; he was born blind so that God's works might be revealed in him. [4]We[r] must work the works of him who sent me[s] while it is day; night is coming when no one can work. [5]As long as I am in the world, I am the light of the world." [6]When he had said this, he spat on the ground and made mud with the saliva and spread the mud on the man's eyes, [7]saying to him, "Go, wash in the pool of Sī·lō′am" (which means Sent). Then he went and washed and came back able to see. [8]The neighbors and those who had seen him before as a beggar began to ask, "Is this not the man who used to sit and beg?" [9]Some were saying, "It is he." Others were saying, "No, but it is someone like him." He kept saying, "I am the man." [10]But they kept asking him, "Then how were your eyes opened?" [11]He answered, "The man called Jesus made mud, spread it on my eyes, and said to me, 'Go to Sī·lō′am and wash.' Then I went and washed and received my sight." [12]They said to him, "Where is he?" He said, "I do not know."

The Pharisees Investigate the Healing

13 They brought to the Phar′i·sees the man who had formerly been blind. [14]Now it was a sabbath day when Jesus made the mud and opened his eyes. [15]Then the Phar′i·sees also began to ask him how he had received his sight. He said to them, "He put mud on my eyes. Then I washed,

and now I see." [16]Some of the Phar′i·sees said, "This man is not from God, for he does not observe the sabbath." But others said, "How can a man who is a sinner perform such signs?" And they were divided. [17]So they said again to the blind man, "What do you say about him? It was your eyes he opened." He said, "He is a prophet."

18 The Jews did not believe that he had been blind and had received his sight until they called the parents of the man who had received his sight [19]and asked them, "Is this your son, who you say was born blind? How then does he now see?" [20]His parents answered, "We know that this is our son, and that he was born blind; [21]but we do not know how it is that now he sees, nor do we know who opened his eyes. Ask him; he is of age. He will speak for himself." [22]His parents said this because they were afraid of the Jews; for the Jews had already agreed that anyone who confessed Jesus[t] to be the Messiah[u] would be put out of the synagogue. [23]Therefore his parents said, "He is of age; ask him."

24 So for the second time they called the man who had been blind, and they said to him, "Give glory to God! We know that this man is a sinner." [25]He answered, "I do not know whether he is a sinner.

> Jesus healed a man who had been blind all his life. He gave the gift of sight to the man who could not see! You too can give the gift of sight. Ask members of your family or some adults at your church to help you collect eyeglasses that people no longer use. Donate the eyeglasses to a local organization that provides the gift of better vision to people in need.

[q] Other ancient authorities read *has Abraham seen you?* [r] Other ancient authorities read *I* [s] Other ancient authorities read *us* [t] Gk *him* [u] Or *the Christ*

One thing I do know, that though I was blind, now I see." ²⁶They said to him, "What did he do to you? How did he open your eyes?" ²⁷He answered them, "I have told you already, and you would not listen. Why do you want to hear it again? Do you also want to become his disciples?" ²⁸Then they reviled him, saying, "You are his disciple, but we are disciples of Moses. ²⁹We know that God has spoken to Moses, but as for this man, we do not know where he comes from." ³⁰The man answered, "Here is an astonishing thing! You do not know where he comes from, and yet he opened my eyes. ³¹We know that God does not listen to sinners, but he does listen to one who worships him and obeys his will. ³²Never since the world began has it been heard that anyone opened the eyes of a person born blind. ³³If this man were not from God, he could do nothing." ³⁴They answered him, "You were born entirely in sins, and are you trying to teach us?" And they drove him out.

Spiritual Blindness

35 Jesus heard that they had driven him out, and when he found him, he said, "Do you believe in the Son of Man?"^v ³⁶He answered, "And who is he, sir?^w Tell me, so that I may believe in him." ³⁷Jesus said to him, "You have seen him, and the one speaking with you is he." ³⁸He said, "Lord,^w I believe." And he worshiped him. ³⁹Jesus said, "I came into this world for judgment so that those who do not see may see, and those who do see may become blind." ⁴⁰Some of the Phar·i·sees near him heard this and said to him, "Surely we are not blind, are we?" ⁴¹Jesus said to them, "If you were blind, you would not have sin. But now that you say, 'We see,' your sin remains.

"I am the good shepherd. The good shepherd lays down his life for the sheep." John 10:11

Jesus the Good Shepherd

10 "Very truly, I tell you, anyone who does not enter the sheepfold by the gate but climbs in by another way is a thief and a bandit. ²The one who enters by the gate is the shepherd of the sheep. ³The gatekeeper opens the gate for him, and the sheep hear his voice. He calls his own sheep by name and leads them out. ⁴When he has brought out all his own, he goes ahead of them, and the sheep follow him because they know his voice. ⁵They will not follow a stranger, but they will run from him because they do not know the voice of strangers." ⁶Jesus used this figure of speech with them, but they did not understand what he was saying to them.

7 So again Jesus said to them, "Very truly, I tell you, I am the gate for the sheep. ⁸All who came before me are thieves and bandits; but the sheep did not listen to them. ⁹I am the gate. Whoever enters by me will be saved, and will come in and go out and find pasture. ¹⁰The thief comes only to steal and kill and destroy. I came that they may have life, and have it abundantly.

11 "I am the good shepherd. The good shepherd lays down his life for the sheep. ¹²The hired hand, who is not the shepherd and does not own the sheep, sees the wolf coming and leaves the sheep and runs away—and the wolf snatches them and scatters them. ¹³The hired hand runs away because a hired hand does not care for the sheep. ¹⁴I am the good shepherd. I know my own and my own know me, ¹⁵just as the Father knows me and I know the Father. And I lay down my life for the sheep. ¹⁶I have other sheep that do not belong to this fold. I must bring them also, and they will listen to my voice. So there will be one flock, one shepherd. ¹⁷For this reason the Father loves me, because I lay down my life in order to take it up again. ¹⁸No one takes^x it from me, but I lay it

^v Other ancient authorities read *the Son of God*
^w *Sir* and *Lord* translate the same Greek word
^x Other ancient authorities read *has taken*

down of my own accord. I have power to lay it down, and I have power to take it up again. I have received this command from my Father."

19 Again the Jews were divided because of these words. ²⁰Many of them were saying, "He has a demon and is out of his mind. Why listen to him?" ²¹Others were saying, "These are not the words of one who has a demon. Can a demon open the eyes of the blind?"

Jesus Is Rejected by the Jews

22 At that time the festival of the Dedication took place in Jerusalem. It was winter, ²³and Jesus was walking in the temple, in the portico of Solomon. ²⁴So the Jews gathered around him and said to him, "How long will you keep us in suspense? If you are the Messiah,ʸ tell us plainly." ²⁵Jesus answered, "I have told you, and you do not believe. The works that I do in my Father's name testify to me; ²⁶but you do not believe, because you do not belong to my sheep. ²⁷My sheep hear my voice. I know them, and they follow me. ²⁸I give them eternal life, and they will never perish. No one will snatch them out of my hand. ²⁹What my Father has given me is greater than all else, and no one can snatch it out of the Father's hand.ᶻ ³⁰The Father and I are one."

31 The Jews took up stones again to stone him. ³²Jesus replied, "I have shown you many good works from the Father. For which of these are you going to stone me?" ³³The Jews answered, "It is not for a good work that we are going to stone you, but for blasphemy, because you, though only a human being, are making yourself God." ³⁴Jesus answered, "Is it not written in your law,ᵃ 'I said, you are gods'? ³⁵If those to whom the word of God came were called 'gods'—and the scripture cannot be annulled— ³⁶can you say that the one whom the Father has sanctified and sent into the world is blaspheming because I said, 'I am God's Son'? ³⁷If I am not doing the works of my Father, then do not believe me. ³⁸But if I do them, even

though you do not believe me, believe the works, so that you may know and understandᵇ that the Father is in me and I am in the Father." ³⁹Then they tried to arrest him again, but he escaped from their hands.

40 He went away again across the Jordan to the place where John had been baptizing earlier, and he remained there. ⁴¹Many came to him, and they were saying, "John performed no sign, but everything that John said about this man was true." ⁴²And many believed in him there.

The Death of Lazarus

11 Now a certain man was ill, Lazʹa·rus of Bethʹa·ny, the village of Mary and her sister Martha. ²Mary was the one who anointed the Lord with perfume and wiped his feet with her hair; her brother Lazʹa·rus was ill. ³So the sisters sent a message to Jesus,ᶜ "Lord, he whom you love is ill." ⁴But when Jesus heard it, he said, "This illness does not lead to death; rather it is for God's glory, so that the Son of God may be glorified through it." ⁵Accordingly, though Jesus loved Martha and her sister and Lazʹa·rus, ⁶after having heard that Lazʹa·rusᵈ was ill, he stayed two days longer in the place where he was.

7 Then after this he said to the disciples, "Let us go to Judea again." ⁸The disciples said to him, "Rabbi, the Jews were just now trying to stone you, and are you going there again?" ⁹Jesus answered, "Are there not twelve hours of daylight? Those who walk during the day do not stumble, because they see the light of this world. ¹⁰But those who walk at night stumble, because the light is not in them." ¹¹After saying this, he told them, "Our friend Lazʹa·rus has fallen asleep, but I am going there to awaken him." ¹²The disciples said

---

ʸ Or *the Christ*   ᶻ Other ancient authorities read *My Father who has given them to me is greater than all, and no one can snatch them out of the Father's hand*   ᵃ Other ancient authorities read *in the law*   ᵇ Other ancient authorities lack *and understand;* others read *and believe*   ᶜ Gk *him*   ᵈ Gk *he*

John 11

to him, "Lord, if he has fallen asleep, he will be all right." [13]Jesus, however, had been speaking about his death, but they thought that he was referring merely to sleep. [14]Then Jesus told them plainly, "Laz′a·rus is dead. [15]For your sake I am glad I was not there, so that you may believe. But let us go to him." [16]Thomas, who was called the Twin,[e] said to his fellow disciples, "Let us also go, that we may die with him."

Jesus the Resurrection and the Life

17 When Jesus arrived, he found that Laz′a·rus[f] had already been in the tomb four days. [18]Now Beth′a·ny was near Jerusalem, some two miles[g] away, [19]and many of the Jews had come to Martha and Mary to console them about their brother. [20]When Martha heard that Jesus was coming, she went and met him, while Mary stayed at home. [21]Martha said to Jesus, "Lord, if you had been here, my brother would not have died. [22]But even now I know that God will give you whatever you ask of him." [23]Jesus said to her, "Your brother will rise again." [24]Martha said to him, "I know that he will rise again in the resurrection on the last day." [25]Jesus said to her, "I am the resurrection and the life.[h]Those who believe in me, even though they die, will live, [26]and everyone who lives and believes in me will never die. Do you believe this?" [27]She said to

When Jesus's friend Lazarus was sick, Lazarus's sisters, Mary and Martha, sent for Jesus. By the time Jesus arrived, Lazarus had died. Mary and Martha were very sad, and Jesus was too. Even though Jesus was God, he was also human. He shared the same emotions of love, joy, anger, and sadness as we do. When someone we love dies, we can remember that Jesus knows how we feel.

him, "Yes, Lord, I believe that you are the Messiah,[i] the Son of God, the one coming into the world."

Jesus Weeps

28 When she had said this, she went back and called her sister Mary, and told her privately, "The Teacher is here and is calling for you." [29]And when she heard it, she got up quickly and went to him. [30]Now Jesus had not yet come to the village, but was still at the place where Martha had met him. [31]The Jews who were with her in the house, consoling her, saw Mary get up quickly and go out. They followed her because they thought that she was going to the tomb to weep there. [32]When Mary came where Jesus was and saw him, she knelt at his feet and said to him, "Lord, if you had been here, my brother would not have died." [33]When Jesus saw her weeping, and the Jews who came with her also weeping, he was greatly disturbed in spirit and deeply moved. [34]He said, "Where have you laid him?" They said to him, "Lord, come and see." [35]Jesus began to weep. [36]So the Jews said, "See how he loved him!" [37]But some of them said, "Could not he who opened the eyes of the blind man have kept this man from dying?"

Jesus Raises Lazarus to Life

38 Then Jesus, again greatly disturbed, came to the tomb. It was a cave, and a stone was lying against it. [39]Jesus said, "Take away the stone." Martha, the sister of the dead man, said to him, "Lord, already there is a stench because he has been dead four days." [40]Jesus said to her, "Did I not tell you that if you believed, you would see the glory of God?" [41]So they took away the stone. And Jesus looked upward and said, "Father, I thank you for having heard me. [42]I knew that you always hear me, but I have said this for the sake of the crowd standing here, so that

[e] Gk Didymus   [f] Gk he   [g] Gk fifteen stadia
[h] Other ancient authorities lack and the life   [i] Or the Christ

they may believe that you sent me." [43]When he had said this, he cried with a loud voice, "Laz′a·rus, come out!" [44]The dead man came out, his hands and feet bound with strips of cloth, and his face wrapped in a cloth. Jesus said to them, "Unbind him, and let him go."

The Plot to Kill Jesus

45 Many of the Jews therefore, who had come with Mary and had seen what Jesus did, believed in him. [46]But some of them went to the Phar′i·sees and told them what he had done. [47]So the chief priests and the Phar′i·sees called a meeting of the council, and said, "What are we to do? This man is performing many signs. [48]If we let him go on like this, everyone will believe in him, and the Romans will come and destroy both our holy place[j] and our nation." [49]But one of them, Ca′-i·a·phas, who was high priest that year, said to them, "You know nothing at all! [50]You do not understand that it is better for you to have one man die for the people than to have the whole nation destroyed." [51]He did not say this on his own, but being high priest that year he prophesied that Jesus was about to die for the nation, [52]and not for the nation only, but to gather into one the dispersed children of God. [53]So from that day on they planned to put him to death.

54 Jesus therefore no longer walked about openly among the Jews, but went from there to a town called E′phra·im in the region near the wilderness; and he remained there with the disciples.

55 Now the Passover of the Jews was near, and many went up from the country to Jerusalem before the Passover to purify themselves. [56]They were looking for Jesus and were asking one another as they stood in the temple, "What do you think? Surely he will not come to the festival, will he?" [57]Now the chief priests and the Phar′i·sees had given orders that anyone who knew where Jesus[k] was should let them know, so that they might arrest him.

Mary Anoints Jesus

12 Six days before the Passover Jesus came to Beth′a·ny, the home of Laz′a·rus, whom he had raised from the dead. [2]There they gave a dinner for him. Martha served, and Laz′a·rus was one of those at the table with him. [3]Mary took a pound of costly perfume made of pure nard, anointed Jesus' feet, and wiped them[l] with her hair. The house was filled with the fragrance of the perfume. [4]But Judas Is·car′i·ot, one of his disciples (the one who was about to betray him), said, [5]"Why was this perfume not sold for three hundred denarii[m] and the money given to the poor?" [6](He said this not because he cared about the poor, but because he was a thief; he kept the common purse and used to steal what was put into it.) [7]Jesus said, "Leave her alone. She bought it[n] so that she might keep it for the day of my burial. [8]You always have the poor with you, but you do not always have me."

The Plot to Kill Lazarus

9 When the great crowd of the Jews learned that he was there, they came not only because of Jesus but also to see Laz′a·rus, whom he had raised from the dead. [10]So the chief priests planned to put Laz′a·rus to death as well, [11]since it was on account of him that many of the Jews were deserting and were believing in Jesus.

Jesus' Triumphal Entry into Jerusalem

12 The next day the great crowd that had come to the festival heard that Jesus was coming to Jerusalem. [13]So they took branches of palm trees and went out to meet him, shouting,

"Hosanna!
Blessed is the one who comes in the name of the Lord—
the King of Israel!"

[j] Or *our temple*; Greek *our place* [k] Gk *he* [l] Gk *his feet* [m] Three hundred denarii would be nearly a year's wages for a laborer [n] Gk lacks *She bought it*

[14]Jesus found a young donkey and sat on it; as it is written:

[15] "Do not be afraid, daughter of Zion.
Look, your king is coming,
    sitting on a donkey's colt!"

[16]His disciples did not understand these things at first; but when Jesus was glorified, then they remembered that these things had been written of him and had been done to him. [17]So the crowd that had been with him when he called Laz·a·rus out of the tomb and raised him from the dead continued to testify.[o] [18]It was also because they heard that he had performed this sign that the crowd went to meet him. [19]The Phar·i·sees then said to one another, "You see, you can do nothing. Look, the world has gone after him!"

Some Greeks Wish to See Jesus

20 Now among those who went up to worship at the festival were some Greeks. [21]They came to Philip, who was from Beth·sa·i·da in Galilee, and said to him, "Sir, we wish to see Jesus." [22]Philip went and told Andrew; then Andrew and Philip went and told Jesus. [23]Jesus answered them, "The hour has come for the Son of Man to be glorified. [24]Very truly, I tell you, unless a grain of wheat falls into the earth and dies, it remains just a single grain; but if it dies, it bears much fruit. [25]Those who love their life lose it, and those who hate their life in this world will keep it for eternal life. [26]Whoever serves me must follow me, and where I am, there will my servant be also. Whoever serves me, the Father will honor.

Jesus Speaks about His Death

27 "Now my soul is troubled. And what should I say—'Father, save me from this hour'? No, it is for this reason that I have come to this hour. [28]Father, glorify

your name." Then a voice came from heaven, "I have glorified it, and I will glorify it again." [29]The crowd standing there heard it and said that it was thunder. Others said, "An angel has spoken to him." [30]Jesus answered, "This voice has come for your sake, not for mine. [31]Now is the judgment of this world; now the ruler of this world will be driven out. [32]And I, when I am lifted up from the earth, will draw all people[p] to myself." [33]He said this to indicate the kind of death he was to die. [34]The crowd answered him, "We have heard from the law that the Messiah[q] remains forever. How can you say that the Son of Man must be lifted up? Who is this Son of Man?" [35]Jesus said to them, "The light is with you for a little longer. Walk while you have the light, so that the darkness may not overtake you. If you walk in the darkness, you do not know where you are going. [36]While you have the light, believe in the light, so that you may become children of light."

The Unbelief of the People

After Jesus had said this, he departed and hid from them. [37]Although he had performed so many signs in their presence, they did not believe in him. [38]This was to fulfill the word spoken by the prophet I·sai·ah:

"Lord, who has believed our message,
    and to whom has the arm of the
        Lord been revealed?"

[39]And so they could not believe, because I·sai·ah also said,

[40] "He has blinded their eyes
    and hardened their heart,
so that they might not look with their
      eyes,
and understand with their heart and
      turn—
and I would heal them."

[41]I·sai·ah said this because[r] he saw his glory and spoke about him. [42]Nevertheless

"Whoever serves me must follow me, and where I am, there will my servant be also. Whoever serves me, the Father will honor."
John 12:26

---

[o] Other ancient authorities read *with him began to testify that he had called . . . from the dead*
[p] Other ancient authorities read *all things*   [q] Or *the Christ*   [r] Other ancient witnesses read *when*

many, even of the authorities, believed in him. But because of the Phar'i·sees they did not confess it, for fear that they would be put out of the synagogue; ⁴³for they loved human glory more than the glory that comes from God.

Summary of Jesus' Teaching

44 Then Jesus cried aloud: "Whoever believes in me believes not in me but in him who sent me. ⁴⁵And whoever sees me sees him who sent me. ⁴⁶I have come as light into the world, so that everyone who believes in me should not remain in the darkness. ⁴⁷I do not judge anyone who hears my words and does not keep them, for I came not to judge the world, but to save the world. ⁴⁸The one who rejects me and does not receive my word has a judge; on the last day the word that I have spoken will serve as judge, ⁴⁹for I have not spoken on my own, but the Father who sent me has himself given me a commandment about what to say and what to speak. ⁵⁰And I know that his commandment is eternal life. What I speak, therefore, I speak just as the Father has told me."

Jesus Washes the Disciples' Feet

13 Now before the festival of the Passover, Jesus knew that his hour had come to depart from this world and go to the Father. Having loved his own who were in the world, he loved them to the end. ²The devil had already put it into the heart of Judas son of Simon Is·car'i·ot to betray him. And during supper ³Jesus, knowing that the Father had given all things into his hands, and that he had come from God and was going to God, ⁴got up from the table,ˢ took off his outer robe, and tied a towel around himself. ⁵Then he poured water into a basin and began to wash the disciples' feet and to wipe them with the towel that was tied around him. ⁶He came to Simon Peter, who said to him, "Lord, are you going to wash my feet?" ⁷Jesus answered, "You do not know now what I am doing, but later you will

understand." ⁸Peter said to him, "You will never wash my feet." Jesus answered, "Unless I wash you, you have no share with me." ⁹Simon Peter said to him, "Lord, not my feet only but also my hands and my head!" ¹⁰Jesus said to him, "One who has bathed does not need to wash, except for the feet,ᵗ but is entirely clean. And youᵘ are clean, though not all of you." ¹¹For he knew who was to betray him; for this reason he said, "Not all of you are clean."

12 After he had washed their feet, had put on his robe, and had returned to the table, he said to them, "Do you know what I have done to you? ¹³You call me Teacher and Lord—and you are right, for that is what I am. ¹⁴So if I, your Lord and Teacher, have washed your feet, you also ought to wash one another's feet. ¹⁵For I have set you an example, that you also should do as I have done to you. ¹⁶Very truly, I tell you, servantsᵛ are not greater than their master, nor are messengers greater than the one who sent them. ¹⁷If you know these things, you are blessed if you do them. ¹⁸I am not speaking of all of you; I know whom I have chosen. But it is to fulfill the scripture, 'The one who ate my breadʷ has lifted his heel against me.' ¹⁹I tell you this now, before it occurs, so that when it does occur, you may believe that I am he.ˣ ²⁰Very truly, I tell you,

> Foot washing was an act of hospitality for guests when they arrived at the home of their host. Usually, a servant washed the feet of the guests. Jesus used foot washing as an example of humble service. When he washed the feet of the disciples, he showed them that following him means serving others.

ˢ Gk *from supper*   ᵗ Other ancient authorities lack *except for the feet*   ᵘ The Greek word for *you* here is plural   ᵛ Gk *slaves*   ʷ Other ancient authorities read *ate bread with me*   ˣ Gk *I am*

"Jesus said to him, 'I am the way, and the truth, and the life. No one comes to the Father except through me.'" John 14:6

whoever receives one whom I send receives me; and whoever receives me receives him who sent me."

Jesus Foretells His Betrayal

21 After saying this Jesus was troubled in spirit, and declared, "Very truly, I tell you, one of you will betray me." ²²The disciples looked at one another, uncertain of whom he was speaking. ²³One of his disciples—the one whom Jesus loved—was reclining next to him; ²⁴Simon Peter therefore motioned to him to ask Jesus of whom he was speaking. ²⁵So while reclining next to Jesus, he asked him, "Lord, who is it?" ²⁶Jesus answered, "It is the one to whom I give this piece of bread when I have dipped it in the dish."*y* So when he had dipped the piece of bread, he gave it to Judas son of Simon Is·car´i·ot.*z* ²⁷After he received the piece of bread,*a* Satan entered into him. Jesus said to him, "Do quickly what you are going to do." ²⁸Now no one at the table knew why he said this to him. ²⁹Some thought that, because Judas had the common purse, Jesus was telling him, "Buy what we need for the festival"; or, that he should give something to the poor. ³⁰So, after receiving the piece of bread, he immediately went out. And it was night.

The New Commandment

31 When he had gone out, Jesus said, "Now the Son of Man has been glorified, and God has been glorified in him. ³²If God has been glorified in him,*b* God will also glorify him in himself and will glorify him at once. ³³Little children, I am with you only a little longer. You will look for me; and as I said to the Jews so now I say to you, 'Where I am going, you cannot come.' ³⁴I give you a new commandment, that you love one another. Just as I have loved you, you also should love one another. ³⁵By this everyone will know that you are my disciples, if you have love for one another."

Jesus Foretells Peter's Denial

36 Simon Peter said to him, "Lord, where are you going?" Jesus answered, "Where I am going, you cannot follow me now; but you will follow afterward." ³⁷Peter said to him, "Lord, why can I not follow you now? I will lay down my life for you." ³⁸Jesus answered, "Will you lay down your life for me? Very truly, I tell you, before the cock crows, you will have denied me three times.

Jesus the Way to the Father

14 "Do not let your hearts be troubled. Believe*c* in God, believe also in me. ²In my Father's house there are many dwelling places. If it were not so, would I have told you that I go to prepare a place for you?*d* ³And if I go and prepare a place for you, I will come again and will take you to myself, so that where I am, there you may be also. ⁴And you know the way to the place where I am going."*e* ⁵Thomas said to him, "Lord, we do not know where you are going. How can we know the way?" ⁶Jesus said to him, "I am the way, and the truth, and the life. No one comes to the Father except through me. ⁷If you know me, you will know*f* my Father also. From now on you do know him and have seen him."

8 Philip said to him, "Lord, show us the Father, and we will be satisfied." ⁹Jesus said to him, "Have I been with you all this time, Philip, and you still do not know me? Whoever has seen me has seen the

---

y Gk dipped it   *z* Other ancient authorities read *Judas Iscariot son of Simon;* others, *Judas son of Simon from Karyot* (Kerioth)   *a* Gk *After the piece of bread*   *b* Other ancient authorities lack *If God has been glorified in him*   *c* Or *You believe*   *d* Or *If it were not so, I would have told you; for I go to prepare a place for you*   *e* Other ancient authorities read *Where I am going you know, and the way you know*   *f* Other ancient authorities read *If you had known me, you would have known*

Father. How can you say, 'Show us the Father'? [10]Do you not believe that I am in the Father and the Father is in me? The words that I say to you I do not speak on my own; but the Father who dwells in me does his works. [11]Believe me that I am in the Father and the Father is in me; but if you do not, then believe me because of the works themselves. [12]Very truly, I tell you, the one who believes in me will also do the works that I do and, in fact, will do greater works than these, because I am going to the Father. [13]I will do whatever you ask in my name, so that the Father may be glorified in the Son. [14]If in my name you ask me[g] for anything, I will do it.

The Promise of the Holy Spirit

15 "If you love me, you will keep[h] my commandments. [16]And I will ask the Father, and he will give you another Advocate,[i] to be with you forever. [17]This is the Spirit of truth, whom the world cannot receive, because it neither sees him nor knows him. You know him, because he abides with you, and he will be in[j] you.

18 "I will not leave you orphaned; I am coming to you. [19]In a little while the world will no longer see me, but you will see me; because I live, you also will live. [20]On that day you will know that I am in my Father, and you in me, and I in you. [21]They who have my commandments and keep them are those who love me; and those who love me will be loved by my Father, and I will love them and reveal myself to them." [22]Judas (not Is·car´i·ot) said to him, "Lord, how is it that you will reveal yourself to us, and not to the world?" [23]Jesus answered him, "Those who love me will keep my word, and my Father will love them, and we will come to them and make our home with them. [24]Whoever does not love me does not keep my words; and the word that you hear is not mine, but is from the Father who sent me.

25 "I have said these things to you while I am still with you. [26]But the Advocate,[i] the Holy Spirit, whom the Father will send in my name, will teach you everything, and remind you of all that I have said to you. [27]Peace I leave with you; my peace I give to you. I do not give to you as the world gives. Do not let your hearts be troubled, and do not let them be afraid. [28]You heard me say to you, 'I am going away, and I am coming to you.' If you loved me, you would rejoice that I am going to the Father, because the Father is greater than I. [29]And now I have told you this before it occurs, so that when it does occur, you may believe. [30]I will no longer talk much with you, for the ruler of this world is coming. He has no power over me; [31]but I do as the Father has commanded me, so that the world may know that I love the Father. Rise, let us be on our way.

Jesus the True Vine

15 "I am the true vine, and my Father is the vinegrower. [2]He removes every branch in me that bears no fruit. Every branch that bears fruit he prunes[k] to make it bear more fruit. [3]You have already been cleansed[k] by the word that I have spoken to you. [4]Abide in me as I abide in you. Just as the branch cannot bear fruit by itself unless it abides in the vine, neither can you unless you abide in me. [5]I am the vine, you are the branches.

Jesus promised to send the Holy Spirit to be a Comforter or Helper after he went back to be with God. Even now, the Holy Spirit lives in all Christians to help them live as God wants them to live. When you have a difficult decision to make, ask the Holy Spirit to guide you. Remember to sit quietly for a while and listen. If the answer does not come, try again later. You may want to try praying with an adult in your family or church.

---

[g] Other ancient authorities lack *me*   [h] Other ancient authorities read *me, keep*   [i] Or *Helper*   [j] Or *among*   [k] The same Greek root refers to pruning and cleansing

"This is my commandment, that you love one another as I have loved you."   John 15:12

Those who abide in me and I in them bear much fruit, because apart from me you can do nothing. [6]Whoever does not abide in me is thrown away like a branch and withers; such branches are gathered, thrown into the fire, and burned. [7]If you abide in me, and my words abide in you, ask for whatever you wish, and it will be done for you. [8]My Father is glorified by this, that you bear much fruit and become[l] my disciples. [9]As the Father has loved me, so I have loved you; abide in my love. [10]If you keep my commandments, you will abide in my love, just as I have kept my Father's commandments and abide in his love. [11]I have said these things to you so that my joy may be in you, and that your joy may be complete.

12 "This is my commandment, that you love one another as I have loved you. [13]No one has greater love than this, to lay down one's life for one's friends. [14]You are my friends if you do what I command you. [15]I do not call you servants[m] any longer, because the servant[n] does not know what the master is doing; but I have called you friends, because I have made known to you everything that I have heard from my Father. [16]You did not choose me but I chose you. And I appointed you to go and bear fruit, fruit that will last, so that the Father will give you whatever you ask him in my name. [17]I am giving you these commands so that you may love one another.

The World's Hatred

18 "If the world hates you, be aware that it hated me before it hated you. [19]If you belonged to the world,[o] the world would love you as its own. Because you do not belong to the world, but I have chosen you out of the world—therefore the world hates you. [20]Remember the word that I said to you, 'Servants[m] are not greater than their master.' If they persecuted me, they will persecute you; if they kept my word, they will keep yours also. [21]But they will do all these things to you on account of my name, because they do not know him who sent me. [22]If I had not come and spoken to them, they would not have sin; but now they have no excuse for their sin. [23]Whoever hates me hates my Father also. [24]If I had not done among them the works that no one else did, they would not have sin. But now they have seen and hated both me and my Father. [25]It was to fulfill the word that is written in their law, 'They hated me without a cause.'

26 "When the Advocate[p] comes, whom I will send to you from the Father, the Spirit of truth who comes from the Father, he will testify on my behalf. [27]You also are to testify because you have been with me from the beginning.

16 "I have said these things to you to keep you from stumbling. [2]They will put you out of the synagogues. Indeed, an hour is coming when those who kill you will think that by doing so they are offering worship to God. [3]And they will do this because they have not known the Father or me. [4]But I have said these things to you so that when their hour comes you may remember that I told you about them.

The Work of the Spirit

"I did not say these things to you from the beginning, because I was with you. [5]But now I am going to him who sent me; yet none of you asks me, 'Where are you going?' [6]But because I have said these things to you, sorrow has filled your hearts. [7]Nevertheless I tell you the truth: it is to your advantage that I go away, for if I do not go away, the Advocate[p] will not come to you; but if I go, I will send him to you. [8]And when he comes, he will prove the world wrong about[q] sin and

[l] Or be   [m] Gk slaves   [n] Gk slave   [o] Gk were of the world   [p] Or Helper   [q] Or convict the world of

righteousness and judgment: [9]about sin, because they do not believe in me; [10]about righteousness, because I am going to the Father and you will see me no longer; [11]about judgment, because the ruler of this world has been condemned.

12 "I still have many things to say to you, but you cannot bear them now. [13]When the Spirit of truth comes, he will guide you into all the truth; for he will not speak on his own, but will speak whatever he hears, and he will declare to you the things that are to come. [14]He will glorify me, because he will take what is mine and declare it to you. [15]All that the Father has is mine. For this reason I said that he will take what is mine and declare it to you.

Sorrow Will Turn into Joy

16 "A little while, and you will no longer see me, and again a little while, and you will see me." [17]Then some of his disciples said to one another, "What does he mean by saying to us, 'A little while, and you will no longer see me, and again a little while, and you will see me'; and 'Because I am going to the Father'?" [18]They said, "What does he mean by this 'a little while'? We do not know what he is talking about." [19]Jesus knew that they wanted to ask him, so he said to them, "Are you discussing among yourselves what I meant when I said, 'A little while, and you will no longer see me, and again a little while, and you will see me'? [20]Very truly, I tell you, you will weep and mourn, but the world will rejoice; you will have pain, but your pain will turn into joy. [21]When a woman is in labor, she has pain, because her hour has come. But when her child is born, she no longer remembers the anguish because of the joy of having brought a human being into the world. [22]So you have pain now; but I will see you again, and your hearts will rejoice, and no one will take your joy from you. [23]On that day you will ask nothing of me.[r] Very truly, I tell you, if you ask anything of the Father in my name, he will give it to you.[s] [24]Until now you have not asked for anything in my name. Ask and you will receive, so that your joy may be complete.

Peace for the Disciples

25 "I have said these things to you in figures of speech. The hour is coming when I will no longer speak to you in figures, but will tell you plainly of the Father. [26]On that day you will ask in my name. I do not say to you that I will ask the Father on your behalf; [27]for the Father himself loves you, because you have loved me and have believed that I came from God.[t] [28]I came from the Father and have come into the world; again, I am leaving the world and am going to the Father."

29 His disciples said, "Yes, now you are speaking plainly, not in any figure of speech! [30]Now we know that you know all things, and do not need to have anyone question you; by this we believe that you came from God." [31]Jesus answered them, "Do you now believe? [32]The hour is coming, indeed it has come, when you will be scattered, each one to his home, and you will leave me alone. Yet I am not alone because the Father is with me. [33]I have said this to you, so that in me you may have peace. In the world you face persecution. But take courage; I have conquered the world!"

Jesus Prays for His Disciples

17 After Jesus had spoken these words, he looked up to heaven and said, "Father, the hour has come; glorify your Son so that the Son may glorify you, [2]since you have given him authority over all people,[u] to give eternal

> "I have said this to you, so that in me you may have peace.
> In the world you face persecution. But take courage;
> I have conquered the world!" John 16:33

---

[r] Or *will ask me no question* [s] Other ancient authorities read *Father, he will give it to you in my name* [t] Other ancient authorities read *the Father* [u] Gk *flesh*

life to all whom you have given him. ³And this is eternal life, that they may know you, the only true God, and Jesus Christ whom you have sent. ⁴I glorified you on earth by finishing the work that you gave me to do. ⁵So now, Father, glorify me in your own presence with the glory that I had in your presence before the world existed.

6 "I have made your name known to those whom you gave me from the world. They were yours, and you gave them to me, and they have kept your word. ⁷Now they know that everything you have given me is from you; ⁸for the words that you gave to me I have given to them, and they have received them and know in truth that I came from you; and they have believed that you sent me. ⁹I am asking on their behalf; I am not asking on behalf of the world, but on behalf of those whom you gave me, because they are yours. ¹⁰All mine are yours, and yours are mine; and I have been glorified in them. ¹¹And now I am no longer in the world, but they are in the world, and I am coming to you. Holy Father, protect them in your name that you have given me, so that they may be one, as we are one. ¹²While I was with them, I protected them in your name that* you have given me. I guarded them, and not one of them was lost except the one destined to be lost,* so that the scripture might be fulfilled. ¹³But now I am coming to you, and I speak these things in the world so that they may have my joy made complete in themselves.* ¹⁴I have given them your word, and the world has hated them because they do not belong to the world, just as I do not belong to the world. ¹⁵I am not asking you to take them out of the world, but I ask you to protect them from the evil one.* ¹⁶They do not belong to the world, just as I do not belong to the world. ¹⁷Sanctify them in the truth; your word is truth. ¹⁸As you have sent me into the world, so I have sent them into the world. ¹⁹And for their sakes I sanctify myself, so that they also may be sanctified in truth.

20 "I ask not only on behalf of these, but also on behalf of those who will believe in me through their word, ²¹that they may all be one. As you, Father, are in me and I am in you, may they also be in us,ᶻ so that the world may believe that you have sent me. ²²The glory that you have given me I have given them, so that they may be one, as we are one, ²³I in them and you in me, that they may become completely one, so that the world may know that you have sent me and have loved them even as you have loved me. ²⁴Father, I desire that those also, whom you have given me, may be with me where I am, to see my glory, which you have given me because you loved me before the foundation of the world.

25 "Righteous Father, the world does not know you, but I know you; and these know that you have sent me. ²⁶I made your name known to them, and I will make it known, so that the love with which you have loved me may be in them, and I in them."

Jesus prayed that the followers he left behind would come together and love each other in the same way that he loved them and loved God.

The Betrayal and Arrest of Jesus

18 After Jesus had spoken these words, he went out with his disciples across the Kid´ron valley to a place where there was a garden, which he and his disciples entered. ²Now Judas, who betrayed him, also knew the place, because Jesus often met there with his disciples. ³So Judas brought a detachment of soldiers together with police from the chief priests and the Phar´i·sees, and they came there with lanterns

---

ᵛ Other ancient authorities read *protected in your name those whom*   ʷ Gk *except the son of destruction*   ˣ Or *among themselves*   ʸ Or *from evil*
ᶻ Other ancient authorities read *be one in us*

and torches and weapons. ⁴Then Jesus, knowing all that was to happen to him, came forward and asked them, "Whom are you looking for?" ⁵They answered, "Jesus of Nazareth."ᵃ Jesus replied, "I am he."ᵇ Judas, who betrayed him, was standing with them. ⁶When Jesusᶜ said to them, "I am he,"ᵇ they stepped back and fell to the ground. ⁷Again he asked them, "Whom are you looking for?" And they said, "Jesus of Nazareth."ᵃ ⁸Jesus answered, "I told you that I am he.ᵇ So if you are looking for me, let these men go." ⁹This was to fulfill the word that he had spoken, "I did not lose a single one of those whom you gave me." ¹⁰Then Simon Peter, who had a sword, drew it, struck the high priest's slave, and cut off his right ear. The slave's name was Mal´chus. ¹¹Jesus said to Peter, "Put your sword back into its sheath. Am I not to drink the cup that the Father has given me?"

Jesus before the High Priest

12 So the soldiers, their officer, and the Jewish police arrested Jesus and bound him. ¹³First they took him to An´nas, who was the father-in-law of Cā´i·a·phas, the high priest that year. ¹⁴Cā´i·a·phas was the one who had advised the Jews that it was better to have one person die for the people.

Peter Denies Jesus

15 Simon Peter and another disciple followed Jesus. Since that disciple was known to the high priest, he went with Jesus into the courtyard of the high priest, ¹⁶but Peter was standing outside at the gate. So the other disciple, who was known to the high priest, went out, spoke to the woman who guarded the gate, and brought Peter in. ¹⁷The woman said to Peter, "You are not also one of this man's disciples, are you?" He said, "I am not." ¹⁸Now the slaves and the police had made a charcoal fire because it was cold, and they were standing around it and warming themselves. Peter also was standing with them and warming himself.

The High Priest Questions Jesus

19 Then the high priest questioned Jesus about his disciples and about his teaching. ²⁰Jesus answered, "I have spoken openly to the world; I have always taught in synagogues and in the temple, where all the Jews come together. I have said nothing in secret. ²¹Why do you ask me? Ask those who heard what I said to them; they know what I said." ²²When he had said this, one of the police standing nearby struck Jesus on the face, saying, "Is that how you answer the high priest?" ²³Jesus answered, "If I have spoken wrongly, testify to the wrong. But if I have spoken rightly, why do you strike me?" ²⁴Then An´nas sent him bound to Cā´i·a·phas the high priest.

Peter Denies Jesus Again

25 Now Simon Peter was standing and warming himself. They asked him, "You are not also one of his disciples, are you?" He denied it and said, "I am not." ²⁶One of the slaves of the high priest, a relative of the man whose ear Peter had cut off, asked, "Did I not see you in the garden with him?" ²⁷Again Peter denied it, and at that moment the cock crowed.

Jesus before Pilate

28 Then they took Jesus from Cā´i·a·phas to Pilate's headquarters.ᵈ It was early in the morning. They themselves did not enter the headquarters,ᵈ so as to avoid ritual defilement and to be able to eat the Passover. ²⁹So Pilate went out to them and said, "What accusation do you bring against this man?" ³⁰They answered, "If this man were not a criminal, we would not have handed him over to you." ³¹Pilate said to them, "Take him yourselves and judge him according to your law." The Jews replied, "We are not permitted to put anyone to death." ³²(This was to fulfill what Jesus had said when he indicated the kind of death he was to die.)

ᵃ Gk the Nazorean   ᵇ Gk I am   ᶜ Gk he
ᵈ Gk the praetorium

33 Then Pilate entered the headquarters[e] again, summoned Jesus, and asked him, "Are you the King of the Jews?" [34]Jesus answered, "Do you ask this on your own, or did others tell you about me?" [35]Pilate replied, "I am not a Jew, am I? Your own nation and the chief priests have handed you over to me. What have you done?" [36]Jesus answered, "My kingdom is not from this world. If my kingdom were from this world, my followers would be fighting to keep me from being handed over to the Jews. But as it is, my kingdom is not from here." [37]Pilate asked him, "So you are a king?" Jesus answered, "You say that I am a king. For this I was born, and for this I came into the world, to testify to the truth. Everyone who belongs to the truth listens to my voice." [38]Pilate asked him, "What is truth?"

Jesus Sentenced to Death

After he had said this, he went out to the Jews again and told them, "I find no case against him. [39]But you have a custom that I release someone for you at the Passover. Do you want me to release for you the King of the Jews?" [40]They shouted in reply, "Not this man, but Ba·rab'bas!" Now Ba·rab'bas was a bandit.

19 Then Pilate took Jesus and had him flogged. [2]And the soldiers wove a crown of thorns and put it on his head, and they dressed him in a purple robe. [3]They kept coming up to him, saying, "Hail, King of the Jews!" and striking him on the face. [4]Pilate went out again and said to them, "Look, I am bringing him out to you to let you know that I find no case against him." [5]So Jesus came out, wearing the crown of thorns and the purple robe. Pilate said to them, "Here is the man!" [6]When the chief priests and the police saw him, they shouted, "Crucify him! Crucify him!" Pilate said to them, "Take him yourselves and crucify him; I find no case against him." [7]The Jews answered him, "We have a law, and according to

that law he ought to die because he has claimed to be the Son of God."

8 Now when Pilate heard this, he was more afraid than ever. [9]He entered his headquarters[e] again and asked Jesus, "Where are you from?" But Jesus gave him no answer. [10]Pilate therefore said to him, "Do you refuse to speak to me? Do you not know that I have power to release you, and power to crucify you?" [11]Jesus answered him, "You would have no power over me unless it had been given you from above; therefore the one who handed me over to you is guilty of a greater sin." [12]From then on Pilate tried to release him, but the Jews cried out, "If you release this man, you are no friend of the emperor. Everyone who claims to be a king sets himself against the emperor."

13 When Pilate heard these words, he brought Jesus outside and sat[f] on the judge's bench at a place called The Stone Pavement, or in Hebrew[g] Gab'ba·tha. [14]Now it was the day of Preparation for the Passover; and it was about noon. He said to the Jews, "Here is your King!" [15]They cried out, "Away with him! Away with him! Crucify him!" Pilate asked them, "Shall I crucify your King?" The chief priests answered, "We have no king but the emperor." [16]Then he handed him over to them to be crucified.

The Crucifixion of Jesus

So they took Jesus; [17]and carrying the cross by himself, he went out to what is called The Place of the Skull, which in Hebrew[g] is called Gol'go·tha. [18]There they crucified him, and with him two others, one on either side, with Jesus between them. [19]Pilate also had an inscription written and put on the cross. It read, "Jesus of Nazareth,[h] the King of the Jews." [20]Many of the Jews read this inscription, because the place where Jesus was crucified was near the city; and it was written in Hebrew,[g] in Latin, and in Greek. [21]Then

[e] Gk *the praetorium*   [f] Or *seated him*   [g] That is, *Aramaic*   [h] Gk *the Nazorean*

Jesus was crucified at a place called Golgotha, which means "skull." Golgotha was probably outside the city wall of Jerusalem, but we do not know exactly where it was.

the chief priests of the Jews said to Pilate, "Do not write, 'The King of the Jews,' but, 'This man said, I am King of the Jews.' " ²²Pilate answered, "What I have written I have written." ²³When the soldiers had crucified Jesus, they took his clothes and divided them into four parts, one for each soldier. They also took his tunic; now the tunic was seamless, woven in one piece from the top. ²⁴So they said to one another, "Let us not tear it, but cast lots for it to see who will get it." This was to fulfill what the scripture says,

"They divided my clothes among
themselves,
and for my clothing they cast lots."
²⁵And that is what the soldiers did.

When Jesus was crucified, a sign that read "Jesus of Nazareth, King of the Jews" was nailed above his head.

Meanwhile, standing near the cross of Jesus were his mother, and his mother's sister, Mary the wife of Clō´pas, and Mary Mag´da·lēne. ²⁶When Jesus saw his mother and the disciple whom he loved standing beside her, he said to his mother, "Woman, here is your son." ²⁷Then he said to the disciple, "Here is your mother." And from that hour the disciple took her into his own home.

28 After this, when Jesus knew that all was now finished, he said (in order to fulfill the scripture), "I am thirsty." ²⁹A jar full of sour wine was standing there. So they

put a sponge full of the wine on a branch of hyssop and held it to his mouth. ³⁰When Jesus had received the wine, he said, "It is finished." Then he bowed his head and gave up his spirit.

Jesus' Side Is Pierced

31 Since it was the day of Preparation, the Jews did not want the bodies left on the cross during the sabbath, especially because that sabbath was a day of great solemnity. So they asked Pilate to have the legs of the crucified men broken and the bodies removed. ³²Then the soldiers came and broke the legs of the first and of the other who had been crucified with him. ³³But when they came to Jesus and saw that he was already dead, they did not break his legs. ³⁴Instead, one of the soldiers pierced his side with a spear, and at once blood and water came out. ³⁵(He who saw this has testified so that you also may believe. His testimony is true, and he knows[i] that he tells the truth.) ³⁶These things occurred so that the scripture might be fulfilled, "None of his bones shall be broken." ³⁷And again another passage of scripture says, "They will look on the one whom they have pierced."

The Burial of Jesus

38 After these things, Joseph of Ar·i·ma·thē´a, who was a disciple of Jesus, though a secret one because of his fear of the Jews, asked Pilate to let him take away the body of Jesus. Pilate gave him permission; so he came and removed his body. ³⁹Nic·o·dē´mus, who had at first come to Jesus by night, also came, bringing a mixture of myrrh and aloes, weighing about a hundred pounds. ⁴⁰They took the body of Jesus and wrapped it with the spices in linen cloths, according to the burial custom of the Jews. ⁴¹Now there was a garden in the place where he was crucified, and in the garden there was a new tomb in which no one had ever been laid. ⁴²And so, because it was the Jewish day of Preparation, and the tomb was nearby, they laid Jesus there.

---
[i] Or *there is one who knows*

The Resurrection of Jesus

20 Early on the first day of the week, while it was still dark, Mary Mag·da·lēne came to the tomb and saw that the stone had been removed from the tomb. ²So she ran and went to Simon Peter and the other disciple, the one whom Jesus loved, and said to them, "They have taken the Lord out of the tomb, and we do not know where they have laid him." ³Then Peter and the other disciple set out and went toward the tomb. ⁴The two were running together, but the other disciple outran Peter and reached the tomb first. ⁵He bent down to look in and saw the linen wrappings lying there, but he did not go in. ⁶Then Simon Peter came, following him, and went into the tomb. He saw the linen wrappings lying there, ⁷and the cloth that had been on Jesus' head, not lying with the linen wrappings but rolled up in a place by itself. ⁸Then the other disciple, who reached the tomb first, also went in, and he saw and believed; ⁹for as yet they did not understand the scripture, that he must rise from the dead. ¹⁰Then the disciples returned to their homes.

When Mary Magdalene saw Jesus for the first time after the Resurrection, she did not recognize him. But when he called her by name, she knew that he was her Lord. Read John 10:3–4. Jesus had said that his sheep would know his voice. At the tomb, Jesus, the good shepherd, called out to Mary Magdalene, one of his sheep, who responded in joy.

Jesus Appears to Mary Magdalene

11 But Mary stood weeping outside the tomb. As she wept, she bent over to look^j into the tomb; ¹²and she saw two angels in white, sitting where the body of Jesus had been lying, one at the head and the other at the feet. ¹³They said to her, "Woman, why are you weeping?" She said to them, "They have taken away my Lord, and I do not know where they have laid him." ¹⁴When she had said this, she turned around and saw Jesus standing there, but she did not know that it was Jesus. ¹⁵Jesus said to her, "Woman, why are you weeping? Whom are you looking for?" Supposing him to be the gardener, she said to him, "Sir, if you have carried him away, tell me where you have laid him, and I will take him away." ¹⁶Jesus said to her, "Mary!" She turned and said to him in Hebrew,^k "Rab·boū·nī!" (which means Teacher). ¹⁷Jesus said to her, "Do not hold on to me, because I have not yet ascended to the Father. But go to my brothers and say to them, 'I am ascending to my Father and your Father, to my God and your God.' " ¹⁸Mary Mag·da·lēne went and announced to the disciples, "I have seen the Lord"; and she told them that he had said these things to her.

Jesus Appears to the Disciples

19 When it was evening on that day, the first day of the week, and the doors of the house where the disciples had met were locked for fear of the Jews, Jesus came and stood among them and said, "Peace be with you." ²⁰After he said this, he showed them his hands and his side. Then the disciples rejoiced when they saw the Lord. ²¹Jesus said to them again, "Peace be with you. As the Father has sent me, so I send you." ²²When he had said this, he breathed on them and said to them, "Receive the Holy Spirit. ²³If you forgive the sins of any, they are forgiven them; if you retain the sins of any, they are retained."

Jesus and Thomas

24 But Thomas (who was called the Twin^l), one of the twelve, was not with them when Jesus came. ²⁵So the other disciples told him, "We have seen the Lord."

^j Gk lacks *to look*   ^k That is, *Aramaic*   ^l Gk *Didymus*

To believe is to accept something as true or real. Thomas did not believe that Jesus was alive until Jesus came to the disciples and Thomas saw him. Today, even though we can't see Jesus with our eyes or touch him with our hands, we can remember what Jesus said to Thomas, "Blessed are those who have not seen and yet have come to believe."

But he said to them, "Unless I see the mark of the nails in his hands, and put my finger in the mark of the nails and my hand in his side, I will not believe."

26 A week later his disciples were again in the house, and Thomas was with them. Although the doors were shut, Jesus came and stood among them and said, "Peace be with you." [27]Then he said to Thomas, "Put your finger here and see my hands. Reach out your hand and put it in my side. Do not doubt but believe." [28]Thomas answered him, "My Lord and my God!" [29]Jesus said to him, "Have you believed because you have seen me? Blessed are those who have not seen and yet have come to believe."

The Purpose of This Book

30 Now Jesus did many other signs in the presence of his disciples, which are not written in this book. [31]But these are written so that you may come to believe[m] that Jesus is the Messiah,[n] the Son of God, and that through believing you may have life in his name.

Jesus Appears to Seven Disciples

21 After these things Jesus showed himself again to the disciples by the Sea of Tĭ·bē´ri·as; and he showed himself in this way. [2]Gathered there together were Simon Peter, Thomas called the Twin,[o] Na·than´a·el of Cā´na in Galilee, the sons of Zeb´e·dee, and two others of his disciples. [3]Simon Peter said to them, "I am going fishing." They said to him, "We will go with you." They went out and got into the boat, but that night they caught nothing.

4 Just after daybreak, Jesus stood on the beach; but the disciples did not know that it was Jesus. [5]Jesus said to them, "Children, you have no fish, have you?" They answered him, "No." [6]He said to them, "Cast the net to the right side of the boat, and you will find some." So they cast it, and now they were not able to haul it in because there were so many fish. [7]That disciple whom Jesus loved said to Peter, "It is the Lord!" When Simon Peter heard that it was the Lord, he put on some clothes, for he was naked, and jumped into the sea. [8]But the other disciples came in the boat, dragging the net full of fish, for they were not far from the land, only about a hundred yards[p] off.

9 When they had gone ashore, they saw a charcoal fire there, with fish on it, and bread. [10]Jesus said to them, "Bring some of the fish that you have just caught." [11]So Simon Peter went aboard and hauled the net ashore, full of large fish, a hundred fifty-three of them; and though there were so many, the net was not torn. [12]Jesus said to them, "Come and have breakfast." Now none of the disciples dared to ask him, "Who are you?" because they knew it was the Lord. [13]Jesus came and took the bread and gave it to them, and did the same with the fish. [14]This was now the third time that Jesus appeared to the disciples after he was raised from the dead.

Jesus and Peter

15 When they had finished breakfast, Jesus said to Simon Peter, "Simon son of John, do you love me more than these?" He said to him, "Yes, Lord; you know that I love you." Jesus said to him, "Feed my lambs." [16]A second time he said to him, "Simon son of John, do you love me?" He said to him, "Yes, Lord; you know that I love you." Jesus said to him, "Tend my

---

[m] Other ancient authorities read *may continue to believe*   [n] Or *the Christ*   [o] Gk *Didymus*
[p] Gk *two hundred cubits*

sheep." [17]He said to him the third time, "Simon son of John, do you love me?" Peter felt hurt because he said to him the third time, "Do you love me?" And he said to him, "Lord, you know everything; you know that I love you." Jesus said to him, "Feed my sheep. [18]Very truly, I tell you, when you were younger, you used to fasten your own belt and to go wherever you wished. But when you grow old, you will stretch out your hands, and someone else will fasten a belt around you and take you where you do not wish to go." [19](He said this to indicate the kind of death by which he would glorify God.) After this he said to him, "Follow me."

Jesus and the Beloved Disciple

20 Peter turned and saw the disciple whom Jesus loved following them; he was the one who had reclined next to Jesus at the supper and had said, "Lord, who is it that is going to betray you?" [21]When Peter saw him, he said to Jesus, "Lord, what about him?" [22]Jesus said to him, "If it is my will that he remain until I come, what is that to you? Follow me!" [23]So the rumor spread in the community[q] that this disciple would not die. Yet Jesus did not say to him that he would not die, but, "If it is my will that he remain until I come, what is that to you?"[r]

24 This is the disciple who is testifying to these things and has written them, and we know that his testimony is true. [25]But there are also many other things that Jesus did; if every one of them were written down, I suppose that the world itself could not contain the books that would be written.

Jesus called Peter to serve. When Jesus told Peter to feed the sheep, he meant more than sharing food. Today, Jesus also calls us to serve. What can you do to share the love of God with others? Here are some suggestions: Take clothing you cannot wear to a shelter. Donate toys to a local charity. Give books to the local library. Spend time reading to children or older adults at the hospital. Visit someone who is unable to get to church on Sunday mornings. Make cookies and share them with your neighbor.

[q] Gk *among the brothers*   [r] Other ancient authorities lack *what is that to you*

Acts

The Acts of the Apostles was written by Luke, the author of the Gospel of Luke. Acts was written about 90 AD. Beginning with the risen Christ, Acts shows us how God brought the church into being through the first Christians. They told the Good News of Jesus Christ and did mighty acts in Jesus's name.

As the book of Acts opens, Jesus's followers were joyful over his resurrection. They often met together to pray, study the Scriptures, and talk about God's actions as demonstrated in Jesus's life, death, and resurrection. On a Jewish feast day called Pentecost, they received from God the gift of the Holy Spirit—the Comforter Jesus had promised to send.

Beginning in chapter 7, the book of Acts tells the story of Paul, the Pharisee from Tarsus who became a follower of Christ and a great missionary. After preaching in Syria and parts of what is now Turkey, Paul crossed over to Europe. He preached in Greece and finally in Rome, where he had been taken as a prisoner. There the book of Acts ends, but the church of Jesus Christ was only just beginning to spread.

Paul was later put to death in Rome, but God used Paul's preaching, witnessing, and writing. God used the work of many others who shared the Good News as well. The first Christians shared their faith with all sorts of people—Jews and Gentiles, men and women, slaves and people who were free. What they shared changed lives. People in many different places began to follow Jesus Christ, Son of God.

Acts 2:1–4

For forty days after his resurrection, Jesus appeared to his disciples. It must have been a happy time for them, but Jesus told them he could not stay. His place was with God. But he promised that the Holy Spirit would come to help them continue his work. And so, as they watched, he was carried up into heaven. Today we know that we have the Holy Spirit with us, and we know that Christ will come again. While we wait for him to come again, we must tell others about Jesus and how he wants us to live.

The Promise of the Holy Spirit

1 In the first book, Thē·oph′i·lus, I wrote about all that Jesus did and taught from the beginning ²until the day when he was taken up to heaven, after giving instructions through the Holy Spirit to the apostles whom he had chosen. ³After his suffering he presented himself alive to them by many convincing proofs, appearing to them during forty days and speaking about the kingdom of God. ⁴While staying*ᵃ* with them, he ordered them not to leave Jerusalem, but to wait there for the promise of the Father. "This," he said, "is what you have heard from me; ⁵for John baptized with water, but you will be baptized with*ᵇ* the Holy Spirit not many days from now."

The Ascension of Jesus

6 So when they had come together, they asked him, "Lord, is this the time when you will restore the kingdom to Israel?" ⁷He replied, "It is not for you to know the times or periods that the Father has set by his own authority. ⁸But you will receive power when the Holy Spirit has come upon you; and you will be my witnesses in Jerusalem, in all Judea and Sa·mār′i·a, and to the ends of the earth." ⁹When he had said this, as they were watching, he was lifted up, and a cloud took him out of their sight. ¹⁰While he

was going and they were gazing up toward heaven, suddenly two men in white robes stood by them. ¹¹They said, "Men of Galilee, why do you stand looking up toward heaven? This Jesus, who has been taken up from you into heaven, will come in the same way as you saw him go into heaven."

Matthias Chosen to Replace Judas

12 Then they returned to Jerusalem from the mount called Ol′i·vet, which is near Jerusalem, a sabbath day's journey away. ¹³When they had entered the city, they went to the room upstairs where they were staying, Peter, and John, and James, and Andrew, Philip and Thomas, Bartholomew and Matthew, James son of Al·phae′us, and Simon the Zealot, and Judas son of*ᶜ* James. ¹⁴All these were constantly devoting themselves to prayer, together with certain women, including Mary the mother of Jesus, as well as his brothers.

15 In those days Peter stood up among the believers*ᵈ* (together the crowd numbered about one hundred twenty persons) and said, ¹⁶"Friends,*ᵉ* the scripture had to be fulfilled, which the Holy Spirit through David foretold concerning Judas, who became a guide for those who arrested Jesus— ¹⁷for he was numbered among us and was allotted his share in this ministry." ¹⁸(Now this man acquired a field with the reward of his wickedness; and falling headlong,*ᶠ* he burst open in the middle and all his bowels gushed out. ¹⁹This became known to all the residents of Jerusalem, so that the field was called in

"But you will receive power when the Holy Spirit has come upon you; and you will be my witnesses in Jerusalem, in all Judea and Samaria, and to the ends of the earth." **Acts 1:8**

ᵃ Or *eating*   *ᵇ* Or *by*   *ᶜ* Or *the brother of*   *ᵈ* Gk *brothers*   *ᵉ* Gk *Men, brothers*   *ᶠ* Or *swelling up*

The disciples cast lots to choose the person who would fill the spot left by Judas Iscariot. The man chosen was Matthias.

their language Ha·kel´da·ma, that is, Field of Blood.) [20]"For it is written in the book of Psalms,

'Let his homestead become desolate,
    and let there be no one to live in it';
and

'Let another take his position of over-
    seer.'

[21]So one of the men who have accompanied us during all the time that the Lord Jesus went in and out among us, [22]beginning from the baptism of John until the day when he was taken up from us—one of these must become a witness with us to his resurrection." [23]So they proposed two, Joseph called Bar·sab´bas, who was also known as Justus, and Mat·thi´as. [24]Then they prayed and said, "Lord, you know everyone's heart. Show us which one of these two you have chosen [25]to take the place[g] in this ministry and apostleship from which Judas turned aside to go to his own place." [26]And they cast lots for them, and the lot fell on Mat·thi´as; and he was added to the eleven apostles.

The Coming of the Holy Spirit

2 When the day of Pentecost had come, they were all together in one place. [2]And suddenly from heaven there came a sound like the rush of a violent wind, and it filled the entire house where they were sitting. [3]Divided tongues, as of fire, appeared among them, and a tongue rested on each of them. [4]All of them were filled with the Holy Spirit and began to speak in other languages, as the Spirit gave them ability.

5 Now there were devout Jews from every nation under heaven living in Jerusalem. [6]And at this sound the crowd gathered and was bewildered, because each one heard them speaking in the native language of each. [7]Amazed and astonished, they asked, "Are not all these who are speaking Galileans? [8]And how is it that we hear, each of us, in our own native language? [9]Par´thi·ans, Medes, E´lam·ites, and residents of Mes·o·po·tā´mi·a, Judea and Cap·pa·dō´ci·a, Pon´tus and Asia, [10]Phryg´i·a and Pam·phyl´i·a, Egypt and the parts of Lib´ya belonging to Cȳ·rē´nē, and visitors from Rome, both Jews and proselytes, [11]Crē´tans and Arabs—in our own languages we hear them speaking about God's deeds of power." [12]All were amazed and perplexed, saying to one another, "What does this mean?" [13]But others sneered and said, "They are filled with new wine."

Peter Addresses the Crowd

14 But Peter, standing with the eleven, raised his voice and addressed them,

"Now there were devout Jews from every nation under heaven living in Jerusalem. And at this sound the crowd gathered and was bewildered because each heard them [the apostles] speaking in the native language of each." Acts 2:5–6

Pentecost is the Greek name for the Jewish Festival of Weeks. This special celebration was held fifty days after Passover. On the day of Pentecost, Jews would travel to Jerusalem to mark the end of the grain harvest. During the Pentecost mentioned in Acts, Jesus's followers were filled with the Holy Spirit. Today, as Christians, we think of Pentecost as the birthday of the church.

[g] Other ancient authorities read *the share*

The Holy Spirit is the helper that Jesus sent after he left his disciples and went back to God. The Holy Spirit lives within each of us to help us live as God wants us to live. Even though we cannot see, touch, or hear the Holy Spirit, we can see the work of the Holy Spirit in the lives of those who follow Jesus. The Holy Spirit inspires us to do good works, gives us the power to stand up for Jesus, helps us to choose what is right, comforts us when we are sad, and fills us with God's love.

"Men of Judea and all who live in Jerusalem, let this be known to you, and listen to what I say. [15]Indeed, these are not drunk, as you suppose, for it is only nine o'clock in the morning. [16]No, this is what was spoken through the prophet Jōel:

[17] 'In the last days it will be, God declares,
that I will pour out my Spirit upon all flesh,
and your sons and your daughters shall prophesy,
and your young men shall see visions, and your old men shall dream dreams.
[18] Even upon my slaves, both men and women,
in those days I will pour out my Spirit;
and they shall prophesy.
[19] And I will show portents in the heaven above
and signs on the earth below,
blood, and fire, and smoky mist.
[20] The sun shall be turned to darkness and the moon to blood,
before the coming of the Lord's great and glorious day.
[21] Then everyone who calls on the name of the Lord shall be saved.'

[22] "You that are Israelites,[h] listen to what I have to say: Jesus of Nazareth,[i] a man attested to you by God with deeds of power, wonders, and signs that God did through him among you, as you yourselves know— [23]this man, handed over to you according to the definite plan and foreknowledge of God, you crucified and killed by the hands of those outside the law. [24]But God raised him up, having freed him from death,[j] because it was impossible for him to be held in its power. [25]For David says concerning him,

'I saw the Lord always before me,
for he is at my right hand so that I will not be shaken;
[26] therefore my heart was glad, and my tongue rejoiced;
moreover my flesh will live in hope.
[27] For you will not abandon my soul to Hades,
or let your Holy One experience corruption.
[28] You have made known to me the ways of life;
you will make me full of gladness with your presence.'

[29] "Fellow Israelites,[k] I may say to you confidently of our ancestor David that he both died and was buried, and his tomb is with us to this day. [30]Since he was a prophet, he knew that God had sworn with an oath to him that he would put one of his descendants on his throne. [31]Foreseeing this, David[l] spoke of the resurrection of the Messiah,[m] saying,

'He was not abandoned to Hades,
nor did his flesh experience corruption.'

[32]This Jesus God raised up, and of that all of us are witnesses. [33]Being therefore exalted at[n] the right hand of God, and having received from the Father the promise of the Holy Spirit, he has poured out this that you both see and hear. [34]For David did not ascend into the heavens, but he himself says,

---

[h] Gk *Men, Israelites* [i] Gk *the Nazorean* [j] Gk *the pains of death* [k] Gk *Men, brothers* [l] Gk *he* [m] Or *the Christ* [n] Or *by*

'The Lord said to my Lord,
"Sit at my right hand,
35 until I make your enemies your
footstool." ' '

³⁶Therefore let the entire house of Israel know with certainty that God has made him both Lord and Messiah,° this Jesus whom you crucified."

The First Converts

37 Now when they heard this, they were cut to the heart and said to Peter and to the other apostles, "Brothers,ᵖ what should we do?" ³⁸Peter said to them, "Repent, and be baptized every one of you in the name of Jesus Christ so that your sins may be forgiven; and you will receive the gift of the Holy Spirit. ³⁹For the promise is for you, for your children, and for all who are far away, everyone whom the Lord our God calls to him." ⁴⁰And he testified with many other arguments and exhorted them, saying, "Save yourselves from this corrupt generation." ⁴¹So those who welcomed his message were baptized, and that day about three thousand persons were added. ⁴²They devoted themselves to the apostles' teaching and fellowship, to the breaking of bread and the prayers.

Life among the Believers

43 Awe came upon everyone, because many wonders and signs were being done by the apostles. ⁴⁴All who believed were together and had all things in common; ⁴⁵they would sell their possessions and goods and distribute the proceeds�q to all, as any had need. ⁴⁶Day by day, as they spent much time together in the temple, they broke bread at homeʳ and ate their food with glad and generousˢ hearts, ⁴⁷praising God and having the goodwill of all the people. And day by day the Lord added to their number those who were being saved.

Peter Heals a Crippled Beggar

3 One day Peter and John were going up to the temple at the

As Peter and John went to the Temple to pray, they saw a man who had never been able to walk. The man was lying near a large gate called "the Beautiful Gate." He asked for money, but Peter knew he had something worth more than money to give the man. Peter had the power to heal in Jesus's name. When he was healed, the man recognized that the power came from God, not from the two disciples. He entered the Temple, walking and leaping and praising God.

hour of prayer, at three o'clock in the afternoon. ²And a man lame from birth was being carried in. People would lay him daily at the gate of the temple called the Beautiful Gate so that he could ask for alms from those entering the temple. ³When he saw Peter and John about to go into the temple, he asked them for alms. ⁴Peter looked intently at him, as did John, and said, "Look at us." ⁵And he fixed his attention on them, expecting to receive something from them. ⁶But Peter said, "I have no silver or gold, but what I have I give you; in the name of Jesus Christ of Nazareth,ᵗ stand up and walk." ⁷And he took him by the right hand and raised him up; and immediately his feet and ankles were made strong. ⁸Jumping up, he stood and began to walk, and he entered the temple with them, walking and leaping and praising God. ⁹All the people saw him walking and praising God, ¹⁰and they recognized him as the one who used to sit and ask for alms at the Beautiful Gate of the temple; and they were filled with wonder and amazement at what had happened to him.

° Or Christ   ᵖ Gk Men, brothers   q Gk them
ʳ Or from house to house   ˢ Or sincere   ᵗ Gk
the Nazorean

Peter Speaks in Solomon's Portico

11 While he clung to Peter and John, all the people ran together to them in the portico called Solomon's Portico, utterly astonished. [12]When Peter saw it, he addressed the people, "You Israelites,[u] why do you wonder at this, or why do you stare at us, as though by our own power or piety we had made him walk? [13]The God of Abraham, the God of Isaac, and the God of Jacob, the God of our ancestors has glorified his servant[v] Jesus, whom you handed over and rejected in the presence of Pilate, though he had decided to release him. [14]But you rejected the Holy and Righteous One and asked to have a murderer given to you, [15]and you killed the Author of life, whom God raised from the dead. To this we are witnesses. [16]And by faith in his name, his name itself has made this man strong, whom you see and know; and the faith that is through Jesus[w] has given him this perfect health in the presence of all of you.

17 "And now, friends,[x] I know that you acted in ignorance, as did also your rulers. [18]In this way God fulfilled what he had foretold through all the prophets, that his Messiah[y] would suffer. [19]Repent therefore, and turn to God so that your sins may be wiped out, [20]so that times of refreshing may come from the presence of the Lord, and that he may send the Messiah[z] appointed for you, that is, Jesus, [21]who must remain in heaven until the time of universal restoration that God announced long ago through his holy prophets. [22]Moses said, 'The Lord your God will raise up for you from your own people[x] a prophet like me. You must listen to whatever he tells you. [23]And it will be that everyone who does not listen to that prophet will be utterly rooted out of the people.' [24]And all the prophets, as many as have spoken, from Samuel and those after him, also predicted these days. [25]You are the descendants of the prophets and of the covenant that God gave to your ancestors, saying to Abraham, 'And in your descendants all the families of the earth shall be blessed.' [26]When God raised up his servant,[a] he sent him first to you, to bless you by turning each of you from your wicked ways."

Peter and John before the Council

4 While Peter and John[b] were speaking to the people, the priests, the captain of the temple, and the Sad'du cees came to them, [2]much annoyed because they were teaching the people and proclaiming that in Jesus there is the resurrection of the dead. [3]So they arrested them and put them in custody until the next day, for it was already evening. [4]But many of those who heard the word believed; and they numbered about five thousand.

5 The next day their rulers, elders, and scribes assembled in Jerusalem, [6]with An'nas the high priest, Ca'i·a·phas, John,[c] and Alexander, and all who were of the high-priestly family. [7]When they had made the prisoners[d] stand in their midst, they inquired, "By what power or by what name did you do this?" [8]Then Peter, filled with the Holy Spirit, said to them, "Rulers of the people and elders, [9]if we are questioned today because of a good deed done to someone who was sick and are asked how this man has been healed, [10]let it be known to all of you, and to all the people of Israel, that this man is standing before you in good health by the name of Jesus Christ of Nazareth,[e] whom you crucified, whom God raised from the dead. [11]This Jesus[f] is

'the stone that was rejected by you, the builders;
    it has become the cornerstone.'[g]

[12]There is salvation in no one else, for there is no other name under heaven

[u] Gk Men, Israelites   [v] Or child   [w] Gk him
[x] Gk brothers   [y] Or his Christ   [z] Or the Christ
[a] Or child   [b] Gk While they   [c] Other ancient authorities read Jonathan   [d] Gk them   [e] Gk the Nazorean   [f] Gk This   [g] Or keystone

given among mortals by which we must be saved."

13 Now when they saw the boldness of Peter and John and realized that they were uneducated and ordinary men, they were amazed and recognized them as companions of Jesus. [14]When they saw the man who had been cured standing beside them, they had nothing to say in opposition. [15]So they ordered them to leave the council while they discussed the matter with one another. [16]They said, "What will we do with them? For it is obvious to all who live in Jerusalem that a notable sign has been done through them; we cannot deny it. [17]But to keep it from spreading further among the people, let us warn them to speak no more to anyone in this name." [18]So they called them and ordered them not to speak or teach at all in the name of Jesus. [19]But Peter and John answered them, "Whether it is right in God's sight to listen to you rather than to God, you must judge; [20]for we cannot keep from speaking about what we have seen and heard." [21]After threatening them again, they let them go, finding no way to punish them because of the people, for all of them praised God for what had happened. [22]For the man on whom this sign of healing had been performed was more than forty years old.

The Believers Pray for Boldness

23 After they were released, they went to their friends[h] and reported what the chief priests and the elders had said to them. [24]When they heard it, they raised their voices together to God and said, "Sovereign Lord, who made the heaven and the earth, the sea, and everything in them, [25]it is you who said by the Holy Spirit through our ancestor David, your servant:[i]

'Why did the Gentiles rage,
   and the peoples imagine vain
      things?
[26] The kings of the earth took their stand,
   and the rulers have gathered
      together
      against the Lord and against his
         Messiah.'[j]

[27]For in this city, in fact, both Her'od and Pon'ti·us Pilate, with the Gentiles and the peoples of Israel, gathered together against your holy servant[i] Jesus, whom you anointed, [28]to do whatever your hand and your plan had predestined to take place. [29]And now, Lord, look at their threats, and grant to your servants[k] to speak your word with all boldness, [30]while you stretch out your hand to heal, and signs and wonders are performed through the name of your holy servant[i] Jesus." [31]When

The followers of Jesus knew that they might face the same problems Jesus faced, so they prayed for strength. Jesus taught that a person can pray to God at any time of day, using any words, about anything.

Looking at your hand can help you remember what to pray for:

(1) Your thumb is closest to your heart. Use this finger to remember to pray for your friends and family.

(2) Your index finger is the finger you point with. Use this finger to remember to pray for people who point you in the right direction—pastors, teachers, parents.

(3) The middle finger is the tallest finger. Use this finger to remember to pray for the leaders of our nation and of the whole world.

(4) The ring finger is not very strong. Use this finger to remember to pray for people who need help.

(5) The pinkie finger is the last finger. Use this finger to remember to pray for yourself, asking God to help you live as God wants you to live.

---

h Gk *their own*   i Or *child*   j Or *his Christ*
k Gk *slaves*

Barnabas, whose name meant "son of encouragement," was one of the first people in Jerusalem to become a believer. Barnabas worked with the apostles and later became a leader of the church in Antioch. He introduced Paul to the disciples in Jerusalem and traveled with Paul on several missionary journeys.

they had prayed, the place in which they were gathered together was shaken; and they were all filled with the Holy Spirit and spoke the word of God with boldness.

The Believers Share Their Possessions

32 Now the whole group of those who believed were of one heart and soul, and no one claimed private ownership of any possessions, but everything they owned was held in common. [33]With great power the apostles gave their testimony to the resurrection of the Lord Jesus, and great grace was upon them all. [34]There was not a needy person among them, for as many as owned lands or houses sold them and brought the proceeds of what was sold. [35]They laid it at the apostles' feet, and it was distributed to each as any had need. [36]There was a Le´vite, a native of Cyprus, Joseph, to whom the apostles gave the name Bar´na·bas (which means "son of encouragement"). [37]He sold a field that belonged to him, then brought the money, and laid it at the apostles' feet.

Ananias and Sapphira

5 But a man named An·a·ni´as, with the consent of his wife Sap·phi´ra, sold a piece of property; [2]with his wife's knowledge, he kept back some of the proceeds, and brought only a part and laid it at the apostles' feet. [3]"An·a·ni´as," Peter asked, "why has Satan filled your heart to lie to the Holy Spirit and to keep back part of the proceeds of the land? [4]While it remained unsold, did it not remain your own? And after it was sold, were not the proceeds at your disposal? How is it that you have contrived this deed in your heart? You did not lie to us[l] but to God!" [5]Now when An·a·ni´as heard these words, he fell down and died. And great fear seized all who heard of it. [6]The young men came and wrapped up his body,[m] then carried him out and buried him.

7 After an interval of about three hours his wife came in, not knowing what had happened. [8]Peter said to her, "Tell me whether you and your husband sold the land for such and such a price." And she said, "Yes, that was the price." [9]Then Peter said to her, "How is it that you have agreed together to put the Spirit of the Lord to the test? Look, the feet of those who have buried your husband are at the door, and they will carry you out." [10]Immediately she fell down at his feet and died. When the young men came in they found her dead, so they carried her out and buried her beside her husband. [11]And great fear seized the whole church and all who heard of these things.

The Apostles Heal Many

12 Now many signs and wonders were done among the people through the

Ananias and Sapphira sold their land and gave part of the money to the community of believers. There was no rule that they had to give all of the money, but they pretended to do so! They did not sin by keeping part of the money. They sinned by lying to their fellow believers. The writer of Acts reminds us that people see our actions, but God sees our hearts.

[l] Gk to men   [m] Meaning of Gk uncertain

apostles. And they were all together in Solomon's Portico. [13]None of the rest dared to join them, but the people held them in high esteem. [14]Yet more than ever believers were added to the Lord, great numbers of both men and women, [15]so that they even carried out the sick into the streets, and laid them on cots and mats, in order that Peter's shadow might fall on some of them as he came by. [16]A great number of people would also gather from the towns around Jerusalem, bringing the sick and those tormented by unclean spirits, and they were all cured.

The Apostles Are Persecuted

17 Then the high priest took action; he and all who were with him (that is, the sect of the Sad'du·cees), being filled with jealousy, [18]arrested the apostles and put them in the public prison. [19]But during the night an angel of the Lord opened the prison doors, brought them out, and said, [20]"Go, stand in the temple and tell the people the whole message about this life." [21]When they heard this, they entered the temple at daybreak and went on with their teaching.

When the high priest and those with him arrived, they called together the council and the whole body of the elders of Israel, and sent to the prison to have them brought. [22]But when the temple police went there, they did not find them in the prison; so they returned and reported, [23]"We found the prison securely locked and the guards standing at the doors, but when we opened them, we found no one inside." [24]Now when the captain of the temple and the chief priests heard these words, they were perplexed about them, wondering what might be going on. [25]Then someone arrived and announced, "Look, the men whom you put in prison are standing in the temple and teaching the people!" [26]Then the captain went with the temple police and brought them, but without violence, for they were afraid of being stoned by the people.

27 When they had brought them, they had them stand before the council. The high priest questioned them, [28]saying, "We gave you strict orders not to teach in this name,[n] yet here you have filled Jerusalem with your teaching and you are determined to bring this man's blood on us." [29]But Peter and the apostles answered, "We must obey God rather than any human authority.[o] [30]The God of our ancestors raised up Jesus, whom you had killed by hanging him on a tree. [31]God exalted him at his right hand as Leader and Savior that he might give repentance to Israel and forgiveness of sins. [32]And we are witnesses to these things, and so is the Holy Spirit whom God has given to those who obey him."

33 When they heard this, they were enraged and wanted to kill them. [34]But a Phar'i·see in the council named Ga·ma'·li·el, a teacher of the law, respected by all the people, stood up and ordered the men to be put outside for a short time. [35]Then he said to them, "Fellow Israelites,[p] consider carefully what you propose to do to these men. [36]For some time ago Theu'das rose up, claiming to be somebody, and a

> Gamaliel was an important Pharisee and a member of the Sanhedrin, a council of religious leaders in Jerusalem. Gamaliel spoke to his fellow council members, telling them to be careful about standing against the apostles who preached and healed in the name of Jesus Christ. He pointed out that if the apostles' teaching were false, it would fade away. If it were true, the council would be working against God.

[n] Other ancient authorities read *Did we not give you strict orders not to teach in this name?*
[o] Gk *than men*   [p] Gk *Men, Israelites*

number of men, about four hundred, joined him; but he was killed, and all who followed him were dispersed and disappeared. [37]After him Judas the Galilean rose up at the time of the census and got people to follow him; he also perished, and all who followed him were scattered. [38]So in the present case, I tell you, keep away from these men and let them alone; because if this plan or this undertaking is of human origin, it will fail; [39]but if it is of God, you will not be able to overthrow them—in that case you may even be found fighting against God!"

They were convinced by him, [40]and when they had called in the apostles, they had them flogged. Then they ordered them not to speak in the name of Jesus, and let them go. [41]As they left the council, they rejoiced that they were considered worthy to suffer dishonor for the sake of the name. [42]And every day in the temple and at home[q] they did not cease to teach and proclaim Jesus as the Messiah.[r]

The early Christian community was made up mostly of Jews. Some of them spoke Greek. They were called "Hellenists" because "Hellene" is an ancient name for Greece. Others spoke Aramaic and Hebrew. Because the groups were from different places, they sometimes didn't get along. The Greek-speaking Christians felt their widows were not being cared for. To solve the problem, seven people were chosen to make sure no one was overlooked.

Seven Chosen to Serve

6 Now during those days, when the disciples were increasing in number, the Hellenists complained against the Hebrews because their widows were being neglected in the daily distribution of food. [2]And the twelve called together the whole community of the disciples and said, "It is not right that we should

neglect the word of God in order to wait on tables.[s] [3]Therefore, friends,[t] select from among yourselves seven men of good standing, full of the Spirit and of wisdom, whom we may appoint to this task, [4]while we, for our part, will devote ourselves to prayer and to serving the word." [5]What they said pleased the whole community, and they chose Stephen, a man full of faith and the Holy Spirit, together with Philip, Proch´o·rus, Nī·cā´nor, Tī´mon, Par´me·nas, and Nic·o·lā´us, a proselyte of An´ti·och. [6]They had these men stand before the apostles, who prayed and laid their hands on them.

7 The word of God continued to spread; the number of the disciples increased greatly in Jerusalem, and a great many of the priests became obedient to the faith.

The Arrest of Stephen

8 Stephen, full of grace and power, did great wonders and signs among the people. [9]Then some of those who belonged to the synagogue of the Freedmen (as it was called), Cȳ·rē´ni·ans, Alexandrians, and others of those from Ci·li´ci·a and Asia, stood up and argued with Stephen. [10]But they could not withstand the wisdom and the Spirit[u] with which he spoke. [11]Then they secretly instigated some men to say, "We have heard him speak blasphemous words against Moses and God." [12]They stirred up the people as well as the elders and the scribes; then they suddenly confronted him, seized him, and brought him before the council. [13]They set up false witnesses who said, "This man never stops saying things against this holy place and the law; [14]for we have heard him say that this Jesus of Nazareth[v] will destroy this place and will change the customs that Moses handed on to us." [15]And all who sat in the council looked intently at him, and

---

[q] Or *from house to house*   [r] Or *the Christ*
[s] Or *keep accounts*   [t] Gk *brothers*   [u] Or *spirit*
[v] Gk *the Nazorean*

they saw that his face was like the face of an angel.

Stephen's Speech to the Council

7 Then the high priest asked him, "Are these things so?" [2]And Stephen replied:

"Brothers[w] and fathers, listen to me. The God of glory appeared to our ancestor Abraham when he was in Mes·o·po·tā´mi·a, before he lived in Har´an, [3]and said to him, 'Leave your country and your relatives and go to the land that I will show you.' [4]Then he left the country of the Chal·dē´ans and settled in Har´an. After his father died, God had him move from there to this country in which you are now living. [5]He did not give him any of it as a heritage, not even a foot's length, but promised to give it to him as his possession and to his descendants after him, even though he had no child. [6]And God spoke in these terms, that his descendants would be resident aliens in a country belonging to others, who would enslave them and mistreat them during four hundred years. [7]'But I will judge the nation that they serve,' said God, 'and after that they shall come out and worship me in this place.' [8]Then he gave him the covenant of circumcision. And so Abraham[x] became the father of Isaac and circumcised him on the eighth day; and Isaac became the father of Jacob, and Jacob of the twelve patriarchs.

9 "The patriarchs, jealous of Joseph, sold him into Egypt; but God was with him, [10]and rescued him from all his afflictions, and enabled him to win favor and to show wisdom when he stood before Pharaoh, king of Egypt, who appointed him ruler over Egypt and over all his household. [11]Now there came a famine throughout Egypt and Cā´naan, and great suffering, and our ancestors could find no food. [12]But when Jacob heard that there was grain in Egypt, he sent our ancestors there on their first visit. [13]On the second visit Joseph made himself known to his brothers, and Joseph's family became

known to Pharaoh. [14]Then Joseph sent and invited his father Jacob and all his relatives to come to him, seventy-five in all; [15]so Jacob went down to Egypt. He himself died there as well as our ancestors, [16]and their bodies[y] were brought back to Shē´chem and laid in the tomb that Abraham had bought for a sum of silver from the sons of Hā´mor in Shē´chem.

17 "But as the time drew near for the fulfillment of the promise that God had made to Abraham, our people in Egypt increased and multiplied [18]until another king who had not known Joseph ruled over Egypt. [19]He dealt craftily with our race and forced our ancestors to abandon their infants so that they would die. [20]At this time Moses was born, and he was beautiful before God. For three months he was brought up in his father's house; [21]and when he was abandoned, Pharaoh's daughter adopted him and brought him up as her own son. [22]So Moses was instructed in all the wisdom of the Egyptians and was powerful in his words and deeds.

23 "When he was forty years old, it came into his heart to visit his relatives, the Israelites.[z] [24]When he saw one of them being wronged, he defended the oppressed man and avenged him by striking down the Egyptian. [25]He supposed that his kinsfolk would understand that God through him was rescuing them, but they did not understand. [26]The next day he came to some of them as they were quarreling and tried to reconcile them, saying, 'Men, you are brothers; why do you wrong each other?' [27]But the man who was wronging his neighbor pushed Moses[a] aside, saying, 'Who made you a ruler and a judge over us? [28]Do you want to kill me as you killed the Egyptian yesterday?' [29]When he heard this, Moses fled and became a resident alien in the land of Mid´i·an. There he became the father of two sons.

[w] Gk *Men, brothers* [x] Gk *he* [y] Gk *they* [z] Gk *his brothers, the sons of Israel* [a] Gk *him*

30 "Now when forty years had passed, an angel appeared to him in the wilderness of Mount Sinai, in the flame of a burning bush. ³¹When Moses saw it, he was amazed at the sight; and as he approached to look, there came the voice of the Lord: ³²'I am the God of your ancestors, the God of Abraham, Isaac, and Jacob.' Moses began to tremble and did not dare to look. ³³Then the Lord said to him, 'Take off the sandals from your feet, for the place where you are standing is holy ground. ³⁴I have surely seen the mistreatment of my people who are in Egypt and have heard their groaning, and I have come down to rescue them. Come now, I will send you to Egypt.'

35 "It was this Moses whom they rejected when they said, 'Who made you a ruler and a judge?' and whom God now sent as both ruler and liberator through the angel who appeared to him in the bush. ³⁶He led them out, having performed wonders and signs in Egypt, at the Red Sea, and in the wilderness for forty years. ³⁷This is the Moses who said to the Israelites, 'God will raise up a prophet for you from your own people*ᵇ* as he raised me up.' ³⁸He is the one who was in the congregation in the wilderness with the angel who spoke to him at Mount Sinai, and with our ancestors; and he received living oracles to give to us. ³⁹Our ancestors were unwilling to obey him; instead, they pushed him aside, and in their hearts they turned back to Egypt, ⁴⁰saying to Aaron, 'Make gods for us who will lead the way for us; as for this Moses who led us out from the land of Egypt, we do not know what has happened to him.' ⁴¹At that time they made a calf, offered a sacrifice to the idol, and reveled in the works of their hands. ⁴²But God turned away from them and handed them over to worship the host of heaven, as it is written in the book of the prophets:

'Did you offer to me slain victims and
      sacrifices
   forty years in the wilderness, O
      house of Israel?

⁴³ No; you took along the tent of
      Mŏ'loch,
   and the star of your god Rē'phan,
      the images that you made to
         worship;
   so I will remove you beyond
      Babylon.'

44 "Our ancestors had the tent of testimony in the wilderness, as God*ᶜ* directed when he spoke to Moses, ordering him to make it according to the pattern he had seen. ⁴⁵Our ancestors in turn brought it in with Joshua when they dispossessed the nations that God drove out before our ancestors. And it was there until the time of David, ⁴⁶who found favor with God and asked that he might find a dwelling place for the house of Jacob.*ᵈ* ⁴⁷But it was Solomon who built a house for him. ⁴⁸Yet the Most High does not dwell in houses made with human hands;*ᵉ* as the prophet says,

49 'Heaven is my throne,
      and the earth is my footstool.
   What kind of house will you build
      for me, says the Lord,
         or what is the place of my rest?
50 Did not my hand make all these things?'

51 "You stiff-necked people, uncircumcised in heart and ears, you are

Stephen was one of the seven chosen to serve tables and supervise those giving help to the poor. He also carried the Good News about Jesus Christ to others. Later, Stephen was stoned to death. He was the first disciple to be killed. Just as Jesus prayed for forgiveness for those who killed him, so Stephen asked that God not punish those who stoned him.

ᵇ Gk *your brothers*   *ᶜ* Gk *he*   *ᵈ* Other ancient authorities read *for the God of Jacob*   *ᵉ* Gk *with hands* forever opposing the Holy Spirit, just as your ancestors used to do. [52]Which of the prophets did your ancestors not persecute? They killed those who foretold the coming of the Righteous One, and now you have become his betrayers and murderers. [53]You are the ones that received the law as ordained by angels, and yet you have not kept it."

The Stoning of Stephen

54 When they heard these things, they became enraged and ground their teeth at Stephen.[f] [55]But filled with the Holy Spirit, he gazed into heaven and saw the glory of God and Jesus standing at the right hand of God. [56]"Look," he said, "I see the heavens opened and the Son of Man standing at the right hand of God!" [57]But they covered their ears, and with a loud shout all rushed together against him. [58]Then they dragged him out of the city and began to stone him; and the witnesses laid their coats at the feet of a young man named Saul. [59]While they were stoning Stephen, he prayed, "Lord Jesus, receive my spirit." [60]Then he knelt down and cried out in a loud voice, "Lord, do not hold this sin against them." When he had said this, he died.[g]

8 And Saul approved of their killing him.

Saul Persecutes the Church

That day a severe persecution began against the church in Jerusalem, and all except the apostles were scattered throughout the countryside of Judea and Sa·mar´i·a. [2]Devout men buried Stephen and made loud lamentation over him. [3]But Saul was ravaging the church by entering house after house; dragging off both men and women, he committed them to prison.

Philip Preaches in Samaria

4 Now those who were scattered went from place to place, proclaiming the word. [5]Philip went down to the city[h] of Sa·mar´i·a and proclaimed the Messiah[i] to them. [6]The crowds with one accord listened eagerly to what was said by Philip, hearing and seeing the signs that he did, [7]for unclean spirits, crying with loud shrieks, came out of many who were possessed; and many others who were paralyzed or lame were cured. [8]So there was great joy in that city.

9 Now a certain man named Simon had previously practiced magic in the city and amazed the people of Sa·mar´i·a, saying that he was someone great. [10]All of them, from the least to the greatest, listened to him eagerly, saying, "This man is the power of God that is called Great." [11]And they listened eagerly to him because for a long time he had amazed them with his magic. [12]But when they believed Philip, who was proclaiming the good news about the kingdom of God and the name of Jesus Christ, they were baptized, both men and women. [13]Even Simon himself believed. After being baptized, he stayed constantly with Philip and was amazed when he saw the signs and great miracles that took place.

14 Now when the apostles at Jerusalem heard that Sa·mar´i·a had accepted the word of God, they sent Peter and John to them. [15]The two went down and prayed for them that they might receive the Holy Spirit [16](for as yet the Spirit had not come[j] upon any of them; they had only been baptized in the name of the Lord Jesus). [17]Then Peter and John[k] laid their hands on them, and they received the Holy Spirit. [18]Now when Simon saw that the Spirit was given through the laying on of the apostles' hands, he offered them money, [19]saying, "Give me also this power so that anyone on whom I lay my hands may receive the Holy Spirit." [20]But Peter said to him, "May your silver perish with you, because you thought you could obtain God's gift with money! [21]You have no part or share in this, for your heart is not right before God. [22]Repent therefore

---

[f] Gk *him*   [g] Gk *fell asleep*   [h] Other ancient authorities read *a city*   [i] Or *the Christ*   [j] Gk *fallen*   [k] Gk *they*

Philip met an Ethiopian official who was reading from the book of Isaiah. Philip and the Ethiopian discussed the Scripture, and Philip shared the Good News about Jesus Christ. There are many verses in the book of Isaiah that Christians believe to be about Christ. Find Isaiah in your Bible. Then look up Isaiah 53:7–8. Compare it to Acts 8:32–33. Do you see why Philip believed these verses talk about Jesus? In this story, Luke wants us to remember that Jesus came for all people everywhere and that we are the ones who must tell others the Good News about Jesus.

of this wickedness of yours, and pray to the Lord that, if possible, the intent of your heart may be forgiven you. ²³For I see that you are in the gall of bitterness and the chains of wickedness." ²⁴Simon answered, "Pray for me to the Lord, that nothing of what you*l* have said may happen to me."

25 Now after Peter and John*m* had testified and spoken the word of the Lord, they returned to Jerusalem, proclaiming the good news to many villages of the Sa·mar´i·tans.

Philip and the Ethiopian Eunuch

26 Then an angel of the Lord said to Philip, "Get up and go toward the south*n* to the road that goes down from Jerusalem to Ga´za." (This is a wilderness road.) ²⁷So he got up and went. Now there was an Ethiopian eunuch, a court official of the Can·da´ce, queen of the Ethiopians, in charge of her entire treasury. He had come to Jerusalem to worship ²⁸and was returning home; seated in his chariot, he was reading the prophet I·sai´ah. ²⁹Then the Spirit said to Philip, "Go over to this chariot and join it." ³⁰So Philip ran up to it and heard him reading the prophet I·sai´ah. He asked, "Do you understand what you are reading?" ³¹He replied, "How can I,

unless someone guides me?" And he invited Philip to get in and sit beside him. ³²Now the passage of the scripture that he was reading was this:

"Like a sheep he was led to the
    slaughter,
  and like a lamb silent before its
    shearer,
    so he does not open his mouth.
³³ In his humiliation justice was denied
    him.
  Who can describe his generation?
    For his life is taken away from the
    earth."

³⁴The eunuch asked Philip, "About whom, may I ask you, does the prophet say this, about himself or about someone else?" ³⁵Then Philip began to speak, and starting with this scripture, he proclaimed to him the good news about Jesus. ³⁶As they were going along the road, they came to some water; and the eunuch said, "Look, here is water! What is to prevent me from being baptized?"*o* ³⁸He commanded the chariot to stop, and both of them, Philip and the eunuch, went down into the water, and Philip*p* baptized him. ³⁹When they came up out of the water, the Spirit of the Lord snatched Philip away; the eunuch saw him no more, and went on his way rejoicing. ⁴⁰But Philip found himself at A·zo´tus, and as he was passing through the region, he proclaimed the good news to all the towns until he came to Caes·a·re´a.

The Conversion of Saul

9 Meanwhile Saul, still breathing threats and murder against the disciples of the Lord, went to the high priest ²and asked him for letters to the synagogues at Damascus, so that if he found any who belonged to the Way, men or women, he might bring them bound to Jerusalem. ³Now as he was

l The Greek word for *you* and the verb *pray* are plural   *m* Gk *after they*   *n* Or *go at noon*   *o* Other ancient authorities add all or most of verse 37, *And Philip said, "If you believe with all your heart, you may." And he replied, "I believe that Jesus Christ is the Son of God."*   *p* Gk *he*

Damascus, the capital of Syria, was an important city in Bible times and was also an important center for early Christians.

going along and approaching Damascus, suddenly a light from heaven flashed around him. ⁴He fell to the ground and heard a voice saying to him, "Saul, Saul, why do you persecute me?" ⁵He asked, "Who are you, Lord?" The reply came, "I am Jesus, whom you are persecuting. ⁶But get up and enter the city, and you will be told what you are to do." ⁷The men who were traveling with him stood speechless because they heard the voice but saw no one. ⁸Saul got up from the ground, and though his eyes were open, he could see nothing; so they led him by the hand and brought him into Damascus. ⁹For three days he was without sight, and neither ate nor drank.

10 Now there was a disciple in Damascus named An·a·ni´as. The Lord said to him in a vision, "An·a·ni´as." He answered, "Here I am, Lord." ¹¹The Lord said to him, "Get up and go to the street called Straight, and at the house of Judas look for a man of Tar´sus named Saul. At this moment he is praying, ¹²and he has seen in a vision^q a man named An·a·ni´as come in and lay his hands on him so that he might regain his sight." ¹³But An·a·ni´as answered, "Lord, I have heard from many about this man, how much evil he has done to your saints in Jerusalem; ¹⁴and here he has authority from the chief priests to bind all who invoke your name." ¹⁵But the Lord said to him, "Go, for he is an instrument whom I have chosen to bring my name before Gentiles and kings and before the people of Israel; ¹⁶I myself will show him how much he must suffer for the sake of my name." ¹⁷So An·a·ni´as went and entered the house. He laid his

hands on Saul^r and said, "Brother Saul, the Lord Jesus, who appeared to you on your way here, has sent me so that you may regain your sight and be filled with the Holy Spirit." ¹⁸And immediately something like scales fell from his eyes, and his sight was restored. Then he got up and was baptized, ¹⁹and after taking some food, he regained his strength.

Paul (whose name was at first Saul) persecuted the followers of Christ (see Acts 9:1–2), but he repented after he met Jesus on the road to Damascus. To repent is to change one's heart, mind, and direction. Paul repented by leaving behind his whole life and becoming a follower of Jesus. Paul became a witness for Jesus Christ when he told others how Jesus changed his life. To witness is to see or hear something and then tell others about it.

Saul Preaches in Damascus

For several days he was with the disciples in Damascus, ²⁰and immediately he began to proclaim Jesus in the synagogues, saying, "He is the Son of God." ²¹All who heard him were amazed and said, "Is not this the man who made havoc in Jerusalem among those who invoked this name? And has he not come here for the purpose of bringing them bound before the chief priests?" ²²Saul became increasingly more powerful and confounded the Jews who lived in Damascus by proving that Jesus^s was the Messiah.^t

Saul Escapes from the Jews

23 After some time had passed, the Jews plotted to kill him, ²⁴but their plot became known to Saul. They were watching the gates day and night so that they

^q Other ancient authorities lack *in a vision*   ^r Gk *him*   ^s Gk *that this*   ^t Or *the Christ*

might kill him; [25]but his disciples took him by night and let him down through an opening in the wall,[u] lowering him in a basket.

Saul in Jerusalem

26 When he had come to Jerusalem, he attempted to join the disciples; and they were all afraid of him, for they did not believe that he was a disciple. [27]But Bar'na·bas took him, brought him to the apostles, and described for them how on the road he had seen the Lord, who had spoken to him, and how in Damascus he had spoken boldly in the name of Jesus. [28]So he went in and out among them in Jerusalem, speaking boldly in the name of the Lord. [29]He spoke and argued with the Hellenists; but they were attempting to kill him. [30]When the believers[v] learned of it, they brought him down to Caes·a·re'a and sent him off to Tar'sus.

31 Meanwhile the church throughout Judea, Galilee, and Sa·mar'i·a had peace and was built up. Living in the fear of the Lord and in the comfort of the Holy Spirit, it increased in numbers.

The Healing of Aeneas

32 Now as Peter went here and there among all the believers,[w] he came down also to the saints living in Lyd'da. [33]There he found a man named Aē·nē'as, who had been bedridden for eight years, for he was paralyzed. [34]Peter said to him, "Aē·nē'as, Jesus Christ heals you; get up and make your bed!" And immediately he got up. [35]And all the residents of Lyd'da and Sharon saw him and turned to the Lord.

Peter in Lydda and Joppa

36 Now in Jop'pa there was a disciple whose name was Tab'i·tha, which in Greek is Dor'cas.[x] She was devoted to good works and acts of charity. [37]At that time she became ill and died. When they had washed her, they laid her in a room upstairs. [38]Since Lyd'da was near Jop'pa, the disciples, who heard that Peter was there, sent two men to him with the request, "Please come to us without delay." [39]So Peter got up and went with them; and when he arrived, they took him to the room upstairs. All the widows stood beside him, weeping and showing tunics and other clothing that Dor'cas had made while she was with them. [40]Peter put all of them outside, and then he knelt down and prayed. He turned to the body and said, "Tab'i·tha, get up." Then she opened her eyes, and seeing Peter, she sat up. [41]He gave her his hand and helped her up. Then calling the saints and widows, he showed her to be alive. [42]This became known throughout Jop'pa, and many believed in the Lord. [43]Meanwhile he stayed in Jop'pa for some time with a certain Simon, a tanner.

Peter and Cornelius

10 In Caes·a·re'a there was a man named Cornelius, a centurion of the Italian Cohort, as it was called. [2]He was a devout man who feared God with all his household; he gave alms generously to the people and prayed constantly to God. [3]One afternoon at about three o'clock he had a vision in which he clearly saw an angel of God coming in and saying to him, "Cornelius." [4]He stared at him in terror and said, "What is it, Lord?" He answered, "Your prayers and your alms have ascended as a memorial before God. [5]Now send men to Jop'pa for a certain Simon who is called Peter; [6]he is lodging with Simon,

Tabitha (also called Dorcas) was a disciple who lived in the city of Joppa. She was known for her good deeds, especially among widows. When Tabitha died, the disciples sent for Peter, and he raised her from the dead.

[u] Gk through the wall   [v] Gk brothers   [w] Gk all of them   [x] The name Tabitha in Aramaic and the name Dorcas in Greek mean a gazelle

a tanner, whose house is by the seaside." [7]When the angel who spoke to him had left, he called two of his slaves and a devout soldier from the ranks of those who served him, [8]and after telling them everything, he sent them to Jop´pa.

9 About noon the next day, as they were on their journey and approaching the city, Peter went up on the roof to pray. [10]He became hungry and wanted something to eat; and while it was being prepared, he fell into a trance. [11]He saw the heaven opened and something like a large sheet coming down, being lowered to the ground by its four corners. [12]In it were all kinds of four-footed creatures and reptiles and birds of the air. [13]Then he heard a voice saying, "Get up, Peter; kill and eat." [14]But Peter said, "By no means, Lord; for I have never eaten anything that is profane or unclean." [15]The voice said to him again, a second time, "What God has made clean, you must not call profane." [16]This happened three times, and the thing was suddenly taken up to heaven.

17 Now while Peter was greatly puzzled about what to make of the vision that he had seen, suddenly the men sent by Cornelius appeared. They were asking for Simon's house and were standing by the gate. [18]They called out to ask whether Simon, who was called Peter, was staying there. [19]While Peter was still thinking about the vision, the Spirit said to him, "Look, three[y] men are searching for you. [20]Now get up, go down, and go with them without hesitation; for I have sent them." [21]So Peter went down to the men and said, "I am the one you are looking for; what is the reason for your coming?" [22]They answered, "Cornelius, a centurion, an upright and God-fearing man, who is well spoken of by the whole Jewish nation, was directed by a holy angel to send for you to come to his house and to hear what you have to say." [23]So Peter[z] invited them in and gave them lodging.

The next day he got up and went with them, and some of the believers[a] from

The book of Leviticus lists the rules God gave to Moses and the people of Israel about the foods that were clean (could be eaten) and unclean (could not be eaten). Peter had a vision and heard the voice of God telling him that everything God had created was clean. Peter came to understand that God was not just talking about food, but about people as well. God created all people and sent Jesus to save all people.

Jop´pa accompanied him. [24]The following day they came to Caes·a·re´a. Cornelius was expecting them and had called together his relatives and close friends. [25]On Peter's arrival Cornelius met him, and falling at his feet, worshiped him. [26]But Peter made him get up, saying, "Stand up; I am only a mortal." [27]And as he talked with him, he went in and found that many had assembled; [28]and he said to them, "You yourselves know that it is unlawful for a Jew to associate with or to visit a Gentile; but God has shown me that I should not call anyone profane or unclean. [29]So when I was sent for, I came without objection. Now may I ask why you sent for me?"

30 Cornelius replied, "Four days ago at this very hour, at three o'clock, I was praying in my house when suddenly a man in dazzling clothes stood before me. [31]He said, 'Cornelius, your prayer has been heard and your alms have been remembered before God. [32]Send therefore to Jop´pa and ask for Simon, who is called Peter; he is staying in the home of Simon, a tanner, by the sea.' [33]Therefore I sent for you immediately, and you have been kind enough to come. So now all of us are here in the presence of God to listen to all that the Lord has commanded you to say."

[y] One ancient authority reads *two*; others lack the word   [z] Gk *he*   [a] Gk *brothers*

Gentiles Hear the Good News

34 Then Peter began to speak to them: "I truly understand that God shows no partiality, 35but in every nation anyone who fears him and does what is right is acceptable to him. 36You know the message he sent to the people of Israel, preaching peace by Jesus Christ—he is Lord of all. 37That message spread throughout Judea, beginning in Galilee after the baptism that John announced: 38how God anointed Jesus of Nazareth with the Holy Spirit and with power; how he went about doing good and healing all who were oppressed by the devil, for God was with him. 39We are witnesses to all that he did both in Judea and in Jerusalem. They put him to death by hanging him on a tree; 40but God raised him on the third day and allowed him to appear, 41not to all the people but to us who were chosen by God as witnesses, and who ate and drank with him after he rose from the dead. 42He commanded us to preach to the people and to testify that he is the one ordained by God as judge of the living and the dead. 43All the prophets testify about him that everyone who believes in him receives forgiveness of sins through his name."

Gentiles Receive the Holy Spirit

44 While Peter was still speaking, the Holy Spirit fell upon all who heard the word. 45The circumcised believers who had come with Peter were astounded that the gift of the Holy Spirit had been poured out even on the Gentiles, 46for they heard them speaking in tongues and extolling God. Then Peter said, 47"Can anyone withhold the water for baptizing these people who have received the Holy Spirit just as we have?" 48So he ordered them to be baptized in the name of Jesus Christ. Then they invited him to stay for several days.

Peter's Report to the Church at Jerusalem

11 Now the apostles and the believers[b] who were in Judea heard that the Gentiles had also accepted the word of God. 2So when Peter went up to Jerusalem, the circumcised believers[c] criticized him, 3saying, "Why did you go to uncircumcised men and eat with them?" 4Then Peter began to explain it to them, step by step, saying, 5"I was in the city of Jop'pa praying, and in a trance I saw a vision. There was something like a large sheet coming down from heaven, being lowered by its four corners; and it came close to me. 6As I looked at it closely I saw four-footed animals, beasts of prey, reptiles, and birds of the air. 7I also heard a voice saying to me, 'Get up, Peter; kill and eat.' 8But I replied, 'By no means, Lord; for nothing profane or unclean has ever entered my mouth.' 9But a second time the voice answered from heaven, 'What God has made clean, you must not call profane.' 10This happened three times; then everything was pulled up again to heaven. 11At that very moment three men, sent to me from Caes·a·rē'a, arrived at the house where we were. 12The Spirit told me to go with them and not to make a distinction between them and us.[d] These six brothers also accompanied me, and we entered the man's house. 13He told us how he had seen the angel standing in his house and saying, 'Send to Jop'pa and bring Simon, who is called Peter; 14he will give you a message by which you and your entire household will be saved.' 15And as I began to speak, the Holy Spirit fell upon them just as it had upon us at the beginning. 16And I remembered the word of the Lord, how he had said, 'John baptized with water, but you will be baptized with the Holy Spirit.' 17If then God gave them the same gift that he gave us when we believed in the Lord Jesus Christ, who was I that I could hinder God?" 18When they heard this, they were silenced. And they praised God, saying, "Then God has given even to the Gentiles the repentance that leads to life."

[b] Gk brothers   [c] Gk lacks believers   [d] Or not to hesitate

After the stoning of Stephen (Acts 7:54–60), many of the believers left Jerusalem and went to Phoenicia, Cyprus, Antioch, and many places in between. Those who went to Antioch told the Good News not only to the Jews, but also to the Gentiles. Many people trusted in Jesus and began meeting with the believers. Back in Jerusalem, the believers who had been in hiding heard about the community in Antioch. They sent Barnabas to find out what was happening there. Barnabas was so excited about what he saw that he immediately went to get Paul in Tarsus, and brought him back to Antioch. Paul and Barnabas stayed in Antioch for about a year, helping the community grow. It was in Antioch that the believers were first called "Christians" because they worshiped Jesus Christ.

The Church in Antioch

19 Now those who were scattered because of the persecution that took place over Stephen traveled as far as Phoe·-ni´ci·a, Cyprus, and An´ti·och, and they spoke the word to no one except Jews. ²⁰But among them were some men of Cyprus and Cy̅·re̅·ne̅ who, on coming to An´ti·och, spoke to the Hellenists[e] also, proclaiming the Lord Jesus. ²¹The hand of the Lord was with them, and a great number became believers and turned to the Lord. ²²News of this came to the ears of the church in Jerusalem, and they sent Bar´na·bas to An´ti·och. ²³When he came and saw the grace of God, he rejoiced, and he exhorted them all to remain faithful to the Lord with steadfast devotion; ²⁴for he was a good man, full of the Holy Spirit

and of faith. And a great many people were brought to the Lord. ²⁵Then Bar´na·bas went to Tar´sus to look for Saul, ²⁶and when he had found him, he brought him to An´ti·och. So it was that for an entire year they met with[f] the church and taught a great many people, and it was in An´ti·och that the disciples were first called "Christians."

27 At that time prophets came down from Jerusalem to An´ti·och. ²⁸One of them named Ag´a·bus stood up and pre-dicted by the Spirit that there would be a severe famine over all the world; and this took place during the reign of Clau´di·us. ²⁹The disciples determined that according to their ability, each would send relief to the believers[g] living in Judea; ³⁰this they did, sending it to the elders by Bar´na·bas and Saul.

James Killed and Peter Imprisoned

12 About that time King Her´od laid violent hands upon some who belonged to the church. ²He had James, the brother of John, killed with the sword. ³After he saw that it pleased the Jews, he proceeded to arrest Peter also. (This was during the festival of Unleavened Bread.) ⁴When he had seized him, he put him in prison and handed him over to four squads of sol-diers to guard him, intending to bring him out to the people after the Passover. ⁵While Peter was kept in prison, the church prayed fervently to God for him.

Peter Delivered from Prison

6 The very night before Her´od was going to bring him out, Peter, bound with two chains, was sleeping between two sol-diers, while guards in front of the door were keeping watch over the prison. ⁷Sud-denly an angel of the Lord appeared and a light shone in the cell. He tapped Peter on the side and woke him, saying, "Get up quickly." And the chains fell off his wrists.

---

[e] Other ancient authorities read *Greeks* [f] Or *were guests of* [g] Gk *brothers*

[8]The angel said to him, "Fasten your belt and put on your sandals." He did so. Then he said to him, "Wrap your cloak around you and follow me." [9]Peter[h] went out and followed him; he did not realize that what was happening with the angel's help was real; he thought he was seeing a vision. [10]After they had passed the first and the second guard, they came before the iron gate leading into the city. It opened for them of its own accord, and they went outside and walked along a lane, when suddenly the angel left him. [11]Then Peter came to himself and said, "Now I am sure that the Lord has sent his angel and rescued me from the hands of Her'od and from all that the Jewish people were expecting."

12 As soon as he realized this, he went to the house of Mary, the mother of John whose other name was Mark, where many had gathered and were praying. [13]When he knocked at the outer gate, a maid named Rho'da came to answer. [14]On recognizing Peter's voice, she was so overjoyed that, instead of opening the gate, she ran in and announced that Peter was standing at the gate. [15]They said to her, "You are out of your mind!" But she insisted that it was so. They said, "It is his angel." [16]Meanwhile Peter continued knocking; and when they opened the gate, they saw him and were amazed. [17]He motioned to them with his hand to be silent, and described for them how the Lord had brought him out of the prison. And he added, "Tell this to James and to the believers.[i]" Then he left and went to another place.

18 When morning came, there was no small commotion among the soldiers over what had become of Peter. [19]When Her'od had searched for him and could not find him, he examined the guards and ordered them to be put to death. Then Peter[j] went down from Judea to Caes·a·re'a and stayed there.

The Death of Herod

20 Now Her'od was angry with the people of Tyre and Si'don. So they came to him in a body; and after winning over Blas'tus, the king's chamberlain, they asked for a reconciliation, because their country depended on the king's country for food. [21]On an appointed day Her'od put on his royal robes, took his seat on the platform, and delivered a public address to them. [22]The people kept shouting, "The voice of a god, and not of a mortal!" [23]And immediately, because he had not given the glory to God, an angel of the Lord struck him down, and he was eaten by worms and died.

24 But the word of God continued to advance and gain adherents. [25]Then after completing their mission Bar'na·bas and Saul returned to[k] Jerusalem and brought with them John, whose other name was Mark.

Barnabas and Saul Commissioned

13 Now in the church at An'ti·och there were prophets and teachers: Bar'na·bas, Sim'e·on who was called Ni'ger, Lucius of Cy·re'ne, Man'a·en a member of the court of Her'od the ruler,[l] and Saul. [2]While they were worshiping the Lord and fasting, the Holy Spirit said, "Set apart for me Bar'na·bas and Saul for the work to which I have called them." [3]Then after fasting and praying

Peter, who had been thrown in prison, was released by an angel. He went to a home where his friends were staying. When he arrived at the home and knocked at the gate, a servant named Rhoda answered. She was so excited to hear Peter's voice that she ran to tell his friends and left Peter standing outside!

[h] Gk He [i] Gk brothers [j] Gk he [k] Other ancient authorities read *from* [l] Gk tetrarch

they laid their hands on them and sent them off.

The Apostles Preach in Cyprus

4 So, being sent out by the Holy Spirit, they went down to Se·leū'ci·a; and from there they sailed to Cyprus. [5]When they arrived at Sal'a·mis, they proclaimed the word of God in the synagogues of the Jews. And they had John also to assist them. [6]When they had gone through the whole island as far as Pā'phos, they met a certain magician, a Jewish false prophet, named Bar-Jesus. [7]He was with the proconsul, Ser'gi·us Paul'us, an intelligent man, who summoned Bar'na·bas and Saul and wanted to hear the word of God. [8]But the magician El'y·mas (for that is the translation of his name) opposed them and tried to turn the proconsul away from the faith. [9]But Saul, also known as Paul, filled with the Holy Spirit, looked intently at him [10]and said, "You son of the devil, you enemy of all righteousness, full of all deceit and villainy, will you not stop making crooked the straight paths of the Lord? [11]And now listen—the hand of the Lord is against you, and you will be blind for a while, unable to see the sun." Immediately mist and darkness came over him, and he went about groping for someone to lead him by the hand. [12]When the proconsul saw what had happened, he believed, for he was astonished at the teaching about the Lord.

Paul and Barnabas in Antioch of Pisidia

13 Then Paul and his companions set sail from Pā'phos and came to Per'ga in Pam·phyl'i·a. John, however, left them and returned to Jerusalem; [14]but they went on from Per'ga and came to An'ti·och in Pi·sid'i·a. And on the sabbath day they went into the synagogue and sat down. [15]After the reading of the law and the prophets, the officials of the synagogue sent them a message, saying, "Brothers, if you have any word of exhortation for the people, give it." [16]So Paul stood up and with a gesture began to speak:

"You Israelites,[m] and others who fear God, listen. [17]The God of this people Israel chose our ancestors and made the people great during their stay in the land of Egypt, and with uplifted arm he led them out of it. [18]For about forty years he put up with[n] them in the wilderness. [19]After he had destroyed seven nations in the land of Cā'naan, he gave them their land as an inheritance [20]for about four hundred fifty years. After that he gave them judges until the time of the prophet Samuel. [21]Then they asked for a king; and God gave them Saul son of Kish, a man of the tribe of Benjamin, who reigned for forty years. [22]When he had removed him, he made David their king. In his testimony about him he said, 'I have found David, son of Jesse, to be a man after my heart, who will carry out all my wishes.' [23]Of this man's posterity God has brought to Israel a Savior, Jesus, as he promised; [24]before his coming John had already proclaimed a baptism of repentance to all the people of Israel. [25]And as John was finishing his work, he said, 'What do you suppose that I am? I am not he. No, but one is coming after me; I am not worthy to untie the thong of the sandals[o] on his feet.'

26 "My brothers, you descendants of Abraham's family, and others who fear God, to us[p] the message of this salvation has been sent. [27]Because the residents of Jerusalem and their leaders did not recognize him or understand the words of the prophets that are read every sabbath, they fulfilled those words by condemning him. [28]Even though they found no cause for a sentence of death, they asked Pilate to have him killed. [29]When they had carried out everything that was written about him, they took him down from the tree and laid him in a tomb. [30]But God raised him from the dead; [31]and for many days

---

[m] Gk Men, Israelites   [n] Other ancient authorities read cared for   [o] Gk untie the sandals   [p] Other ancient authorities read you

he appeared to those who came up with him from Galilee to Jerusalem, and they are now his witnesses to the people. ³²And we bring you the good news that what God promised to our ancestors ³³he has fulfilled for us, their children, by raising Jesus; as also it is written in the second psalm,

'You are my Son;
  today I have begotten you.'

³⁴As to his raising him from the dead, no more to return to corruption, he has spoken in this way,

'I will give you the holy promises made
  to David.'

³⁵Therefore he has also said in another psalm,

'You will not let your Holy One experience corruption.'

³⁶For David, after he had served the purpose of God in his own generation, died,�q was laid beside his ancestors, and experienced corruption; ³⁷but he whom God raised up experienced no corruption. ³⁸Let it be known to you therefore, my brothers, that through this man forgiveness of sins is proclaimed to you; ³⁹by this Jesusʳ everyone who believes is set free from all those sinsˢ from which you could not be freed by the law of Moses. ⁴⁰Beware, therefore, that what the prophets said does not happen to you:

⁴¹ 'Look, you scoffers!
  Be amazed and perish,
  for in your days I am doing a work,
    a work that you will never believe,
    even if someone tells you.' "

42 As Paul and Bar′na·basᵗ were going out, the people urged them to speak about these things again the next sabbath. ⁴³When the meeting of the synagogue broke up, many Jews and devout converts to Ju̅′da·ism followed Paul and Bar′na·bas, who spoke to them and urged them to continue in the grace of God.

44 The next sabbath almost the whole city gathered to hear the word of the Lord.ᵘ ⁴⁵But when the Jews saw the crowds, they were filled with jealousy;

> "Let it be known to you therefore, my brothers, that through this man forgiveness of sins is proclaimed to you; by this Jesus everyone who believes is set free from all those sins from which you could not be freed by the law of Moses." Acts 13:38–39

and blaspheming, they contradicted what was spoken by Paul. ⁴⁶Then both Paul and Bar′na·bas spoke out boldly, saying, "It was necessary that the word of God should be spoken first to you. Since you reject it and judge yourselves to be unworthy of eternal life, we are now turning to the Gentiles. ⁴⁷For so the Lord has commanded us, saying,

'I have set you to be a light for the
  Gentiles,
  so that you may bring salvation to
    the ends of the earth.' "

48 When the Gentiles heard this, they were glad and praised the word of the Lord; and as many as had been destined for eternal life became believers. ⁴⁹Thus the word of the Lord spread throughout the region. ⁵⁰But the Jews incited the devout women of high standing and the leading men of the city, and stirred up persecution against Paul and Bar′na·bas, and drove them out of their region. ⁵¹So they shook the dust off their feet in protest against them, and went to I̅·co̅′ni·um. ⁵²And the disciples were filled with joy and with the Holy Spirit.

Paul and Barnabas in Iconium

14 The same thing occurred in I̅·co̅′ni·um, where Paul and Bar′na·basᵗ went into the Jewish synagogue and spoke in such a way that a great number of both Jews and Greeks became believers. ²But the unbelieving Jews stirred up the Gentiles and poisoned their minds against the brothers.

�q Gk fell asleep   ʳ Gk this   ˢ Gk all   ᵗ Gk they   ᵘ Other ancient authorities read God

"So they remained for a long time, speaking boldly for the Lord, who testified to the word of his grace by granting signs and wonders to be done through them." Acts 14:3

³So they remained for a long time, speaking boldly for the Lord, who testified to the word of his grace by granting signs and wonders to be done through them. ⁴But the residents of the city were divided; some sided with the Jews, and some with the apostles. ⁵And when an attempt was made by both Gentiles and Jews, with their rulers, to mistreat them and to stone them, ⁶the apostles^v learned of it and fled to Lys´tra and Der´bē, cities of Lyc·a·ō´ni·a, and to the surrounding country; ⁷and there they continued proclaiming the good news.

Paul and Barnabas in Lystra and Derbe

8 In Lys´tra there was a man sitting who could not use his feet and had never walked, for he had been crippled from birth. ⁹He listened to Paul as he was speaking. And Paul, looking at him intently and seeing that he had faith to be healed, ¹⁰said in a loud voice, "Stand upright on your feet." And the man^w sprang up and began to walk. ¹¹When the crowds saw what Paul had done, they shouted in the Lyc·a·ō´ni·an language, "The gods have come down to us in human form!" ¹²Bar´na·bas they called Zeūs, and Paul they called Hēr´mēs, because he was the chief speaker. ¹³The priest of Zeūs, whose temple was just outside the city,^x brought oxen and garlands to the gates; he and the crowds wanted to offer sacrifice. ¹⁴When the apostles Bar´na·bas and Paul heard of it, they tore their clothes and rushed out into the crowd, shouting, ¹⁵"Friends,^y why are you doing this? We are mortals just like you, and we bring you good news, that you should turn from these worthless things to

the living God, who made the heaven and the earth and the sea and all that is in them. ¹⁶In past generations he allowed all the nations to follow their own ways; ¹⁷yet he has not left himself without a witness in doing good—giving you rains from heaven and fruitful seasons, and filling you with food and your hearts with joy." ¹⁸Even with these words, they scarcely restrained the crowds from offering sacrifice to them.

19 But Jews came there from An´ti·och and Ī·cō´ni·um and won over the crowds. Then they stoned Paul and dragged him out of the city, supposing that he was dead. ²⁰But when the disciples surrounded him, he got up and went into the city. The next day he went on with Bar´na·bas to Der´bē.

The Return to Antioch in Syria

21 After they had proclaimed the good news to that city and had made many disciples, they returned to Lys´tra, then on to Ī·cō´ni·um and An´ti·och. ²²There they strengthened the souls of the disciples and encouraged them to continue in the faith, saying, "It is through many persecutions that we must enter the kingdom of God." ²³And after they had appointed elders for them in each church, with prayer and fasting they entrusted them to the Lord in whom they had come to believe.

24 Then they passed through Pi·sid´i·a and came to Pam·phyl´i·a. ²⁵When they had spoken the word in Per´ga, they went down to At·ta·lī´a. ²⁶From there they sailed back to An´ti·och, where they had been commended to the grace of God for the work^z that they had completed. ²⁷When they arrived, they called the church together and related all that God had done with them, and how he had opened a door of faith for the Gentiles. ²⁸And they stayed there with the disciples for some time.

---

^v Gk they   ^w Gk he   ^x Or The priest of Zeus-Outside-the-City   ^y Gk Men   ^z Or committed in the grace of God to the work

The Council at Jerusalem

15 Then certain individuals came down from Judea and were teaching the brothers, "Unless you are circumcised according to the custom of Moses, you cannot be saved." ²And after Paul and Bar´na·bas had no small dissension and debate with them, Paul and Bar´na·bas and some of the others were appointed to go up to Jerusalem to discuss this question with the apostles and the elders. ³So they were sent on their way by the church, and as they passed through both Phoe·ni´ci·a and Sa·mar´i·a, they reported the conversion of the Gentiles, and brought great joy to all the believers.[a] ⁴When they came to Jerusalem, they were welcomed by the church and the apostles and the elders, and they reported all that God had done with them. ⁵But some believers who belonged to the sect of the Phar´i·sees stood up and said, "It is necessary for them to be circumcised and ordered to keep the law of Moses."

6 The apostles and the elders met together to consider this matter. ⁷After there had been much debate, Peter stood up and said to them, "My brothers,[b] you know that in the early days God made a choice among you, that I should be the one through whom the Gentiles would hear the message of the good news and become believers. ⁸And God, who knows the human heart, testified to them by giving them the Holy Spirit, just as he did to us; ⁹and in cleansing their hearts by faith he has made no distinction between them and us. ¹⁰Now therefore why are you putting God to the test by placing on the neck of the disciples a yoke that neither our ancestors nor we have been able to bear? ¹¹On the contrary, we believe that we will be saved through the grace of the Lord Jesus, just as they will."

12 The whole assembly kept silence, and listened to Bar´na·bas and Paul as they told of all the signs and wonders that God had done through them among the Gen-

tiles. ¹³After they finished speaking, James replied, "My brothers,[b] listen to me. ¹⁴Sim´e·on has related how God first looked favorably on the Gentiles, to take from among them a people for his name. ¹⁵This agrees with the words of the prophets, as it is written,

¹⁶ 'After this I will return,
and I will rebuild the dwelling of
David, which has fallen;
from its ruins I will rebuild it,
and I will set it up,
¹⁷ so that all other peoples may seek the
Lord—
even all the Gentiles over whom my
name has been called.
Thus says the Lord, who has been
making these things ¹⁸known
from long ago.'[c]

¹⁹Therefore I have reached the decision that we should not trouble those Gentiles who are turning to God, ²⁰but we should write to them to abstain only from things polluted by idols and from fornication and from whatever has been strangled[d] and from blood. ²¹For in every city, for generations past, Moses has had those who proclaim him, for he has been read aloud every sabbath in the synagogues."

The Council's Letter to Gentile Believers

22 Then the apostles and the elders, with the consent of the whole church, decided to choose men from among their members[e] and to send them to An´ti·och with Paul and Bar´na·bas. They sent Judas called Bar·sab´bas, and Silas, leaders among the brothers, ²³with the following letter: "The brothers, both the apostles and the elders, to the believers[a] of Gentile origin in An´ti·och and Syria and Ci·li´ci·a, greetings. ²⁴Since we have heard that certain persons who have gone out from us,

[a] Gk brothers   [b] Gk Men, brothers   [c] Other ancient authorities read *things.* ¹⁸*Known to God from of old are all his works.'*   [d] Other ancient authorities lack *and from whatever has been strangled*   [e] Gk *from among them*

though with no instructions from us, have said things to disturb you and have unsettled your minds,ʲ ²⁵we have decided unanimously to choose representativesᵍ and send them to you, along with our beloved Barʹnaʹbas and Paul, ²⁶who have risked their lives for the sake of our Lord Jesus Christ. ²⁷We have therefore sent Judas and Silas, who themselves will tell you the same things by word of mouth. ²⁸For it has seemed good to the Holy Spirit and to us to impose on you no further burden than these essentials: ²⁹that you abstain from what has been sacrificed to idols and from blood and from what is strangledʰ and from fornication. If you keep yourselves from these, you will do well. Farewell."

> John Mark had traveled with Barnabas and Paul on their first missionary journey. But John Mark had not stayed to the end of that journey. Later when Barnabas wanted John Mark to go on the next trip, Paul refused to take him. Paul and Barnabas disagreed so sharply that they went separate ways—Barnabas returned to Cyprus, and Paul chose Silas to go with him.

30 So they were sent off and went down to Anʹtiʹoch. When they gathered the congregation together, they delivered the letter. ³¹When its membersⁱ read it, they rejoiced at the exhortation. ³²Judas and Silas, who were themselves prophets, said much to encourage and strengthen the believers.ʲ ³³After they had been there for some time, they were sent off in peace by the believersʲ to those who had sent them.ᵏ ³⁵But Paul and Barʹnaʹbas remained in Anʹtiʹoch, and there, with many others, they taught and proclaimed the word of the Lord.

Paul and Barnabas Separate

36 After some days Paul said to Barʹnaʹbas, "Come, let us return and visit

> Silas was a leading member of the church in Jerusalem. Both the Aramaic form of his name (Silas) and the Latin form (Silvanus) are found in the New Testament. He was connected to both Paul and Peter in the mission of the early church.

the believersⁱ in every city where we proclaimed the word of the Lord and see how they are doing." ³⁷Barʹnaʹbas wanted to take with them John called Mark. ³⁸But Paul decided not to take with them one who had deserted them in Pamʹphylʹiʹa and had not accompanied them in the work. ³⁹The disagreement became so sharp that they parted company; Barʹnaʹbas took Mark with him and sailed away to Cyprus. ⁴⁰But Paul chose Silas and set out, the believersⁱ commending him to the grace of the Lord. ⁴¹He went through Syria and Ciʹliʹciʹa, strengthening the churches.

Timothy Joins Paul and Silas

16 Paulˡ went on also to Derʹbē and to Lysʹtra, where there was a disciple named Timothy, the son of a Jewish woman who was a believer; but his father was a Greek. ²He was well spoken of by the believersⁱ in Lysʹtra and Iʹcōʹniʹum. ³Paul wanted Timothy to accompany him; and he took him and had him circumcised because of the Jews who were in those places, for they all knew that his father was a Greek. ⁴As they went from town to town, they delivered to them for observance the decisions that had been reached by the

ʲ Other ancient authorities add *saying, 'You must be circumcised and keep the law,'* ᵍ Gk *men*
ʰ Other ancient authorities lack *and from what is strangled* ⁱ Gk *When they* ʲ Gk *brothers*
ᵏ Other ancient authorities add verse 34, *But it seemed good to Silas to remain there* ˡ Gk *He*

apostles and elders who were in Jerusalem. [5]So the churches were strengthened in the faith and increased in numbers daily.

Paul's Vision of the Man of Macedonia

6 They went through the region of Phryg'i·a and Galatia, having been forbidden by the Holy Spirit to speak the word in Asia. [7]When they had come opposite My'si·a, they attempted to go into Bi·thyn'i·a, but the Spirit of Jesus did not allow them; [8]so, passing by My'si·a, they went down to Trō'as. [9]During the night Paul had a vision: there stood a man of Mac·e·dō'ni·a pleading with him and saying, "Come over to Mac·e·dō'ni·a and help us." [10]When he had seen the vision, we immediately tried to cross over to Mac·e·dō'ni·a, being convinced that God had called us to proclaim the good news to them.

The Conversion of Lydia

11 We set sail from Trō'as and took a straight course to Sam'o·thrāce, the following day to Nē·ap'o·lis, [12]and from there to Phi·lip'pī, which is a leading city of the district[m] of Mac·e·dō'ni·a and a Roman colony. We remained in this city for some days. [13]On the sabbath day we went outside the gate by the river, where we supposed there was a place of prayer; and we sat down and spoke to the women who had gathered there. [14]A certain woman named Lyd'i·a, a worshiper of God, was listening to us; she was from the city of Thȳ·a·tī'ra and a dealer in purple cloth. The Lord opened her heart to listen eagerly to what was said by Paul. [15]When she and her household were baptized, she urged us, saying, "If you have judged me to be faithful to the Lord, come and stay at my home." And she prevailed upon us.

Paul and Silas in Prison

16 One day, as we were going to the place of prayer, we met a slave girl who had a spirit of divination and brought her owners a great deal of money by fortune-telling. [17]While she followed Paul and us, she would cry out, "These men are slaves of the Most High God, who proclaim to you[n] a way of salvation." [18]She kept doing this for many days. But Paul, very much annoyed, turned and said to the spirit, "I order you in the name of Jesus Christ to come out of her." And it came out that very hour.

19 But when her owners saw that their hope of making money was gone, they seized Paul and Silas and dragged them into the marketplace before the authorities. [20]When they had brought them before the magistrates, they said, "These men are disturbing our city; they are Jews [21]and are advocating customs that are not lawful for us as Romans to adopt or observe." [22]The crowd joined in attacking them, and the magistrates had them stripped of their clothing and ordered them to be beaten with rods. [23]After they had given them a severe flogging, they threw them into prison and ordered the jailer to keep them securely. [24]Following these instructions, he put them in the innermost cell and fastened their feet in the stocks.

25 About midnight Paul and Silas were praying and singing hymns to God, and the prisoners were listening to them. [26]Suddenly there was an earthquake, so violent that the foundations of the prison were shaken; and immediately all the doors were opened and everyone's chains

After Lydia heard Paul speak about the Good News of Jesus Christ, she and her whole family were baptized. She was faithful and committed, even opening her home to Paul as a guest. Talk with your family about how you can be more like Lydia, who showed dedication to God and hospitality to others.

[m] Other authorities read *a city of the first district*
[n] Other ancient authorities read *to us*

Earthquakes occur when pieces of land (or plates) that "float" on the surface of the earth move against each other. This causes the earth to shake, quickly sending energy through the land like ripples from a pebble dropped in a pond. Earthquakes are among the most destructive forces in all nature. We need to remember to pray for and help people who are victims of earthquakes. In this story, God used an earthquake to free Paul and Silas from their prison and give them an opportunity to witness to the jailer and help him find Christ.

were unfastened. ²⁷When the jailer woke up and saw the prison doors wide open, he drew his sword and was about to kill himself, since he supposed that the prisoners had escaped. ²⁸But Paul shouted in a loud voice, "Do not harm yourself, for we are all here." ²⁹The jailer⁰ called for lights, and rushing in, he fell down trembling before Paul and Silas. ³⁰Then he brought them outside and said, "Sirs, what must I do to be saved?" ³¹They answered, "Believe on the Lord Jesus, and you will be saved, you and your household." ³²They spoke the word of the Lordᵖ to him and to all who were in his house. ³³At the same hour of the night he took them and washed their wounds; then he and his entire family were baptized without delay. ³⁴He brought them up into the house and set food before them; and he and his entire household rejoiced that he had become a believer in God.

35 When morning came, the magistrates sent the police, saying, "Let those men go." ³⁶And the jailer reported the message to Paul, saying, "The magistrates sent word to let you go; therefore come

out now and go in peace." ³⁷But Paul replied, "They have beaten us in public, uncondemned, men who are Roman citizens, and have thrown us into prison; and now are they going to discharge us in secret? Certainly not! Let them come and take us out themselves." ³⁸The police reported these words to the magistrates, and they were afraid when they heard that they were Roman citizens; ³⁹so they came and apologized to them. And they took them out and asked them to leave the city. ⁴⁰After leaving the prison they went to Lyd′i·a′s home; and when they had seen and encouraged the brothers and sisters�q there, they departed.

The Uproar in Thessalonica

17 After Paul and Silasʳ had passed through Am·phip′o·lis and Ap·ol·lo′ni·a, they came to Thes·sa·lo·nī′-ca, where there was a synagogue of the Jews. ²And Paul went in, as was his custom, and on three sabbath days argued with them from the scriptures, ³explaining and proving that it was necessary for the Messiahˢ to suffer and to rise from the dead, and saying, "This is the Messiah,ˢ Jesus whom I am proclaiming to you." ⁴Some of them were persuaded and joined Paul and Silas, as did a great many of the devout Greeks and not a few of the leading women. ⁵But the Jews became jealous, and with the help of some ruffians in the marketplaces they formed a mob and set the city in an uproar. While they were searching for Paul and Silas to bring them out to the assembly, they attacked Jason's house. ⁶When they could not find them, they dragged Jason and some believersq before the city authorities,ᵗ shouting, "These people who have been turning the world upside down have come here also, ⁷and Jason has entertained them as guests. They are all acting contrary to

⁰ Gk He   ᵖ Other ancient authorities read *word of God*   q Gk *brothers*   ʳ Gk *they*   ˢ Or *the Christ*   ᵗ Gk *politarchs*

Beroea was a city in Macedonia about forty-five miles west of Thessalonica. The people of Beroea were excited to hear the gospel. Not only did they listen to the disciples, but they also studied the Scriptures so that they could understand how Jesus could be the Messiah.

the decrees of the emperor, saying that there is another king named Jesus." [8]The people and the city officials were disturbed when they heard this, [9]and after they had taken bail from Jason and the others, they let them go.

Paul and Silas in Beroea

10 That very night the believers[u] sent Paul and Silas off to Be·roe´a; and when they arrived, they went to the Jewish synagogue. [11]These Jews were more receptive than those in Thes·sa·lo·ni´ca, for they welcomed the message very eagerly and examined the scriptures every day to see whether these things were so. [12]Many of them therefore believed, including not a few Greek women and men of high standing. [13]But when the Jews of Thes·sa·lo·ni´ca learned that the word of God had been proclaimed by Paul in Be·roe´a as well, they came there too, to stir up and incite the crowds. [14]Then the believers[u] immediately sent Paul away to the coast, but Silas and Timothy remained behind. [15]Those who conducted Paul brought him as far as Athens; and after receiving instructions to have Silas and Timothy join him as soon as possible, they left him.

Paul in Athens

16 While Paul was waiting for them in Athens, he was deeply distressed to see that the city was full of idols. [17]So he argued in the synagogue with the Jews and the devout persons, and also in the marketplace[v] every day with those who

happened to be there. [18]Also some Ep·i·cu·re´an and Stoic philosophers debated with him. Some said, "What does this babbler want to say?" Others said, "He seems to be a proclaimer of foreign divinities." (This was because he was telling the good news about Jesus and the resurrection.) [19]So they took him and brought him to the Ar·e·op´a·gus and asked him, "May we know what this new teaching is that you are presenting? [20]It sounds rather strange to us, so we would like to know what it means." [21]Now all the Athenians and the foreigners living there would spend their time in nothing but telling or hearing something new.

22 Then Paul stood in front of the Ar·e·op´a·gus and said, "Athenians, I see how extremely religious you are in every way. [23]For as I went through the city and looked carefully at the objects of your worship, I found among them an altar with the inscription, 'To an unknown god.' What therefore you worship as unknown, this I proclaim to you. [24]The God who made the world and everything in it, he who is Lord of heaven and earth, does not live in shrines made by human hands, [25]nor is he served by human hands, as though he needed anything, since he himself gives to all mortals life and breath and all things. [26]From one ancestor[w] he made all nations to inhabit the whole earth, and he allotted the times of their existence and the boundaries of the places where they would live, [27]so that they would search for God[x] and perhaps grope for him and find him—though indeed he is not far from each one of us. [28]For 'In him we live and move and have our being'; as even some of your own poets have said,

'For we too are his offspring.'

[29]Since we are God's offspring, we ought not to think that the deity is like gold, or silver, or stone, an image formed by the art

[u] Gk brothers   [v] Or civic center; Gk agora   [w] Gk From one; other ancient authorities read From one blood   [x] Other ancient authorities read the Lord

and imagination of mortals. ³⁰While God has overlooked the times of human ignorance, now he commands all people everywhere to repent, ³¹because he has fixed a day on which he will have the world judged in righteousness by a man whom he has appointed, and of this he has given assurance to all by raising him from the dead."

32 When they heard of the resurrection of the dead, some scoffed; but others said, "We will hear you again about this." ³³At that point Paul left them. ³⁴But some of them joined him and became believers, including Dī·o·nys´i·us the Ar·e·op´a·gīte and a woman named Dam´a·ris, and others with them.

Paul in Corinth

18 After this Paul[y] left Athens and went to Corinth. ²There he found a Jew named A·qui´la, a native of Pon´tus, who had recently come from Italy with his wife Priscilla, because Clau´di·us had ordered all Jews to leave Rome. Paul[z] went to see them, ³and, because he was of the same trade, he stayed with them, and they worked together—by trade they were tentmakers. ⁴Every sabbath he would argue in the synagogue and would try to convince Jews and Greeks.

5 When Silas and Timothy arrived from Mac·e·dō´ni·a, Paul was occupied with proclaiming the word,[a] testifying to the Jews that the Messiah[b] was Jesus. ⁶When they opposed and reviled him, in protest he shook the dust from his clothes[c] and said to them, "Your blood be on your own heads! I am innocent. From now on I will go to the Gentiles." ⁷Then he left the synagogue[d] and went to the house of a man named Tit´i·us[e] Justus, a worshiper of God; his house was next door to the synagogue. ⁸Cris´pus, the official of the synagogue, became a believer in the Lord, together with all his household; and many of the Corinthians who heard Paul became believers and were baptized. ⁹One night the Lord said to Paul in a vision, "Do

A missionary is a person who is sent to tell the good news about Jesus Christ. Paul was one of the first missionaries. Aquila and Priscilla, husband and wife, were friends of Paul in Corinth. They became partners with Paul in his missionary work, possibly as teachers.

not be afraid, but speak and do not be silent; ¹⁰for I am with you, and no one will lay a hand on you to harm you, for there are many in this city who are my people." ¹¹He stayed there a year and six months, teaching the word of God among them.

12 But when Gal´li·ō was proconsul of A·chā´i·a, the Jews made a united attack on Paul and brought him before the tribunal. ¹³They said, "This man is persuading people to worship God in ways that are contrary to the law." ¹⁴Just as Paul was about to speak, Gal´li·ō said to the Jews, "If it were a matter of crime or serious villainy, I would be justified in accepting the complaint of you Jews; ¹⁵but since it is a matter of questions about words and names and your own law, see to it yourselves; I do not wish to be a judge of these matters." ¹⁶And he dismissed them from the tribunal. ¹⁷Then all of them[f] seized Sos´the·nēs, the official of the synagogue, and beat him in front of the tribunal. But Gal´li·ō paid no attention to any of these things.

Paul's Return to Antioch

18 After staying there for a considerable time, Paul said farewell to the believers[g] and sailed for Syria, accompanied by Priscilla and A·qui´la. At Cen´chre·ae he had his hair

---

[y] Gk he   [z] Gk He   [a] Gk with the word   [b] Or the Christ   [c] Gk reviled him, he shook out his clothes   [d] Gk left there   [e] Other ancient authorities read Titus   [f] Other ancient authorities read all the Greeks   [g] Gk brothers

cut, for he was under a vow. [19]When they reached Eph´e·sus, he left them there, but first he himself went into the synagogue and had a discussion with the Jews. [20]When they asked him to stay longer, he declined; [21]but on taking leave of them, he said, "I[h] will return to you, if God wills." Then he set sail from Eph´e·sus.

22 When he had landed at Caes·a·re´a, he went up to Jerusalem[i] and greeted the church, and then went down to An´ti·och. [23]After spending some time there he departed and went from place to place through the region of Galatia[j] and Phryg´i·a, strengthening all the disciples.

Ministry of Apollos

24 Now there came to Eph´e·sus a Jew named A·pol´los, a native of Alexandria. He was an eloquent man, well-versed in the scriptures. [25]He had been instructed in the Way of the Lord; and he spoke with burning enthusiasm and taught accurately the things concerning Jesus, though he knew only the baptism of John. [26]He began to speak boldly in the synagogue; but when Priscilla and A·qui´la heard him, they took him aside and explained the Way of God to him more accurately. [27]And when he wished to cross over to A·cha´i·a, the believers[k] encouraged him and wrote to the disciples to welcome him. On his arrival he greatly helped those who through grace had become believers, [28]for he powerfully refuted the Jews in public, showing by the scriptures that the Messiah[l] is Jesus.

Paul in Ephesus

19 While A·pol´los was in Corinth, Paul passed through the interior regions and came to Eph´e·sus, where he found some disciples. [2]He said to them, "Did you receive the Holy Spirit when you became believers?" They replied, "No, we have not even heard that there is a Holy Spirit." [3]Then he said, "Into what then were you baptized?" They answered, "Into John's baptism." [4]Paul said, "John baptized with the baptism of repentance, telling the people to believe in the one who was to come after him, that is, in Jesus." [5]On hearing this, they were baptized in the name of the Lord Jesus. [6]When Paul had laid his hands on them, the Holy Spirit came upon them, and they spoke in tongues and prophesied—[7]altogether there were about twelve of them.

8 He entered the synagogue and for three months spoke out boldly, and argued persuasively about the kingdom of God. [9]When some stubbornly refused to believe and spoke evil of the Way before the congregation, he left them, taking the disciples with him, and argued daily in the lecture hall of Ty·ran´nus.[m] [10]This continued for two years, so that all the residents of Asia, both Jews and Greeks, heard the word of the Lord.

The Sons of Sceva

11 God did extraordinary miracles through Paul, [12]so that when the handkerchiefs or aprons that had touched his skin were brought to the sick, their diseases left them, and the evil spirits came out of them. [13]Then some itinerant Jewish exorcists tried to use the name of the Lord Jesus over those who had evil spirits, saying, "I adjure you by the Jesus whom Paul proclaims." [14]Seven sons of a Jewish high priest named Sce´va were doing this. [15]But the evil spirit said to them in reply, "Jesus I know, and Paul I know; but who are you?" [16]Then the man with the evil spirit leaped on them, mastered them all, and so overpowered them that they fled out of the house naked and wounded. [17]When this became known to all residents of Eph´e·sus, both Jews and Greeks, everyone was awestruck; and the name of the Lord Jesus was praised. [18]Also many of those who became believers confessed

---

[h] Other ancient authorities read *I must at all costs keep the approaching festival in Jerusalem, but I* [i] Gk *went up* [j] Gk *the Galatian region* [k] Gk *brothers* [l] Or *the Christ* [m] Other ancient authorities read *of a certain Tyrannus, from eleven o'clock in the morning to four in the afternoon*

and disclosed their practices. [19]A number of those who practiced magic collected their books and burned them publicly; when the value of these books[n] was calculated, it was found to come to fifty thousand silver coins. [20]So the word of the Lord grew mightily and prevailed.

The Riot in Ephesus

21 Now after these things had been accomplished, Paul resolved in the Spirit to go through Mac·e·dō'ni·a and A·chā'i·a, and then to go on to Jerusalem. He said, "After I have gone there, I must also see Rome." [22]So he sent two of his helpers, Timothy and E·ras'tus, to Mac·e·dō'ni·a, while he himself stayed for some time longer in Asia.

23 About that time no little disturbance broke out concerning the Way. [24]A man named De·mē'tri·us, a silversmith who made silver shrines of Ar'te·mis, brought no little business to the artisans. [25]These he gathered together, with the workers of the same trade, and said, "Men, you know that we get our wealth from this business. [26]You also see and hear that not only in Eph'e·sus but in almost the whole of Asia this Paul has persuaded and drawn away a considerable number of people by saying that gods made with hands are not gods. [27]And there is danger not only that this trade of ours may come into disrepute but also that the temple of the great goddess Ar'te·mis will be scorned, and she will be deprived of her majesty that brought all Asia and the world to worship her."

28 When they heard this, they were enraged and shouted, "Great is Ar'te·mis of the E·phē'si·ans!" [29]The city was filled with the confusion; and people[o] rushed together to the theater, dragging with them Gā'i·us and Ar·is·tar'chus, Mac·e·dō'ni·ans who were Paul's travel companions. [30]Paul wished to go into the crowd, but the disciples would not let him; [31]even some officials of the province of Asia,[p] who were friendly to him, sent him a mes-sage urging him not to venture into the theater. [32]Meanwhile, some were shouting one thing, some another; for the assembly was in confusion, and most of them did not know why they had come together. [33]Some of the crowd gave instructions to Alexander, whom the Jews had pushed forward. And Alexander motioned for silence and tried to make a defense before the people. [34]But when they recognized that he was a Jew, for about two hours all of them shouted in unison, "Great is Ar'te·mis of the E·phē'si·ans!" [35]But when the town clerk had quieted the crowd, he said, "Citizens of Eph'e·sus, who is there that does not know that the city of the E·phē'si·ans is the temple keeper of the great Ar'te·mis and of the statue that fell from heaven?[q] [36]Since these things cannot be denied, you ought to be quiet and do nothing rash. [37]You have brought these men here who are neither temple robbers nor blasphemers of our[r] goddess. [38]If therefore De·mē'tri·us and the artisans with him have a complaint against anyone, the courts are open, and there are proconsuls; let them bring charges there against one another. [39]If there is anything further[s] you want to know, it must be settled in the regular assembly. [40]For we are in danger of being charged with rioting today, since there is no cause that we can give to justify this commotion." [41]When he had said this, he dismissed the assembly.

Paul Goes to Macedonia and Greece

20 After the uproar had ceased, Paul sent for the disciples; and after encouraging them and saying farewell, he left for Mac·e·dō'ni·a. [2]When he had gone through those regions and had given the believers[t] much encouragement, he came to Greece, [3]where he stayed for three months. He was about to set sail for Syria when a plot was made

[n] Gk them [o] Gk they [p] Gk some of the Asiarchs
[q] Meaning of Gk uncertain [r] Other ancient authorities read your [s] Other ancient authorities read about other matters [t] Gk given them

against him by the Jews, and so he decided to return through Mac·e·dō̂ni·a. ⁴He was accompanied by Sop´a·ter son of Pyr´rhus from Be·roē´a, by Ar·is·tar´chus and Se·cun´dus from Thes·sa·lo·nī´ca, by Gā´i·us from Der´bē, and by Timothy, as well as by Tych´i·cus and Troph´i·mus from Asia. ⁵They went ahead and were waiting for us in Trō̂as; ⁶but we sailed from Phi·lip´pī after the days of Unleavened Bread, and in five days we joined them in Trō̂as, where we stayed for seven days.

Paul's Farewell Visit to Troas

7 On the first day of the week, when we met to break bread, Paul was holding a discussion with them; since he intended to leave the next day, he continued speaking until midnight. ⁸There were many lamps in the room upstairs where we were meeting. ⁹A young man named Eū´ty·chus, who was sitting in the window, began to sink off into a deep sleep while Paul talked still longer. Overcome by sleep, he fell to the ground three floors below and was picked up dead. ¹⁰But Paul went down, and bending over him took him in his arms, and said, "Do not be alarmed, for his life is in him." ¹¹Then Paul went upstairs, and after he had broken bread and eaten, he continued to converse with them until dawn; then he left. ¹²Meanwhile they had taken the boy away alive and were not a little comforted.

The Voyage from Troas to Miletus

13 We went ahead to the ship and set sail for As´sos, intending to take Paul on board there; for he had made this arrangement, intending to go by land himself. ¹⁴When he met us in As´sos, we took him on board and went to Mit·y·lē´nē. ¹⁵We sailed from there, and on the following day we arrived opposite Chī´os. The next day we touched at Sā´mos, andᵘ the day after that we came to Mī·lē´tus. ¹⁶For Paul had decided to sail past Eph´e·sus, so that he might not have to spend time in Asia;

he was eager to be in Jerusalem, if possible, on the day of Pentecost.

Paul Speaks to the Ephesian Elders

17 From Mī·lē´tus he sent a message to Eph´e·sus, asking the elders of the church to meet him. ¹⁸When they came to him, he said to them:

"You yourselves know how I lived among you the entire time from the first day that I set foot in Asia, ¹⁹serving the Lord with all humility and with tears, enduring the trials that came to me through the plots of the Jews. ²⁰I did not shrink from doing anything helpful, proclaiming the message to you and teaching you publicly and from house to house, ²¹as I testified to both Jews and Greeks about repentance toward God and faith toward our Lord Jesus. ²²And now, as a captive to the Spirit,ᵛ I am on my way to Jerusalem, not knowing what will happen to me there, ²³except that the Holy Spirit testifies to me in every city that imprisonment and persecutions are waiting for me. ²⁴But I do not count my life of any value to myself, if only I may finish my course and the ministry that I received from the Lord Jesus, to testify to the good news of God's grace.

25 "And now I know that none of you, among whom I have gone about proclaiming the kingdom, will ever see my face again. ²⁶Therefore I declare to you this day that I am not responsible for the blood of any of you, ²⁷for I did not shrink from declaring to you the whole purpose of God. ²⁸Keep watch over yourselves and over all the flock, of which the Holy Spirit has made you overseers, to shepherd the church of Godʷ that he obtained with the blood of his own Son.ˣ ²⁹I know that after I have gone, savage wolves will come in

---

ᵘ Other ancient authorities add *after remaining at Trogyllium*　　ᵛ Or *And now, bound in the spirit*
ʷ Other ancient authorities read *of the Lord*
ˣ Or *with his own blood*; Gk *with the blood of his Own*

"In all this I have given you an example that by such work we must support the weak, remembering the words of the Lord Jesus, for he himself said, 'It is more blessed to give than to receive.'" Acts 20:35

among you, not sparing the flock. [30]Some even from your own group will come distorting the truth in order to entice the disciples to follow them. [31]Therefore be alert, remembering that for three years I did not cease night or day to warn everyone with tears. [32]And now I commend you to God and to the message of his grace, a message that is able to build you up and to give you the inheritance among all who are sanctified. [33]I coveted no one's silver or gold or clothing. [34]You know for yourselves that I worked with my own hands to support myself and my companions. [35]In all this I have given you an example that by such work we must support the weak, remembering the words of the Lord Jesus, for he himself said, 'It is more blessed to give than to receive.' "

36 When he had finished speaking, he knelt down with them all and prayed. [37]There was much weeping among them all; they embraced Paul and kissed him, [38]grieving especially because of what he had said, that they would not see him again. Then they brought him to the ship.

Paul's Journey to Jerusalem

21 When we had parted from them and set sail, we came by a straight course to Cōs, and the next day to Rhōdes, and from there to Pat´a·ra.[y] [2]When we found a ship bound for Phoe·ni´ci·a, we went on board and set sail. [3]We came in sight of Cyprus; and leaving it on our left, we sailed to Syria and landed at Tȳre, because the ship was to unload its cargo there. [4]We looked up the disciples and stayed there for seven days. Through the Spirit they told Paul not to go on to Jerusalem. [5]When our

days there were ended, we left and proceeded on our journey; and all of them, with wives and children, escorted us outside the city. There we knelt down on the beach and prayed [6]and said farewell to one another. Then we went on board the ship, and they returned home.

7 When we had finished[z] the voyage from Tȳre, we arrived at Ptol·e·ma´is; and we greeted the believers[a] and stayed with them for one day. [8]The next day we left and came to Caes·a·re´a; and we went into the house of Philip the evangelist, one of the seven, and stayed with him. [9]He had four unmarried daughters[b] who had the gift of prophecy. [10]While we were staying there for several days, a prophet named Ag´a·bus came down from Judea. [11]He came to us and took Paul's belt, bound his own feet and hands with it, and said, "Thus says the Holy Spirit, 'This is the way the Jews in Jerusalem will bind the man who owns this belt and will hand him over to the Gentiles.' " [12]When we heard this, we and the people there urged him not to go up to Jerusalem. [13]Then Paul answered, "What are you doing, weeping and breaking my heart? For I am ready not only to be bound but even to die in Jerusalem for the name of the Lord Jesus." [14]Since he would not be persuaded, we remained silent except to say, "The Lord's will be done."

15 After these days we got ready and started to go up to Jerusalem. [16]Some of the disciples from Caes·a·re´a also came along and brought us to the house of Mnā´son of Cyprus, an early disciple, with whom we were to stay.

Paul Visits James at Jerusalem

17 When we arrived in Jerusalem, the brothers welcomed us warmly. [18]The next day Paul went with us to visit James; and all the elders were present. [19]After greeting them, he related one by one the things

---

[y] Other ancient authorities add *and Myra*   [z] Or *continued*   [a] Gk *brothers*   [b] Gk *four daughters, virgins,*

that God had done among the Gentiles through his ministry. [20]When they heard it, they praised God. Then they said to him, "You see, brother, how many thousands of believers there are among the Jews, and they are all zealous for the law. [21]They have been told about you that you teach all the Jews living among the Gentiles to forsake Moses, and that you tell them not to circumcise their children or observe the customs. [22]What then is to be done? They will certainly hear that you have come. [23]So do what we tell you. We have four men who are under a vow. [24]Join these men, go through the rite of purification with them, and pay for the shaving of their heads. Thus all will know that there is nothing in what they have been told about you, but that you yourself observe and guard the law. [25]But as for the Gentiles who have become believers, we have sent a letter with our judgment that they should abstain from what has been sacrificed to idols and from blood and from what is strangled[c] and from fornication." [26]Then Paul took the men, and the next day, having purified himself, he entered the temple with them, making public the completion of the days of purification when the sacrifice would be made for each of them.

Paul Arrested in the Temple

27 When the seven days were almost completed, the Jews from Asia, who had seen him in the temple, stirred up the whole crowd. They seized him, [28]shouting, "Fellow Israelites, help! This is the man who is teaching everyone everywhere against our people, our law, and this place; more than that, he has actually brought Greeks into the temple and has defiled this holy place." [29]For they had previously seen Troph'i·mus the E·phe'si·an with him in the city, and they supposed that Paul had brought him into the temple. [30]Then all the city was aroused, and the people rushed together. They seized Paul and dragged him out of the temple, and immediately the doors were shut. [31]While

they were trying to kill him, word came to the tribune of the cohort that all Jerusalem was in an uproar. [32]Immediately he took soldiers and centurions and ran down to them. When they saw the tribune and the soldiers, they stopped beating Paul. [33]Then the tribune came, arrested him, and ordered him to be bound with two chains; he inquired who he was and what he had done. [34]Some in the crowd shouted one thing, some another; and as he could not learn the facts because of the uproar, he ordered him to be brought into the barracks. [35]When Paul[d] came to the steps, the violence of the mob was so great that he had to be carried by the soldiers. [36]The crowd that followed kept shouting, "Away with him!"

Paul Defends Himself

37 Just as Paul was about to be brought into the barracks, he said to the tribune, "May I say something to you?" The tribune[e] replied, "Do you know Greek? [38]Then you are not the Egyptian who recently stirred up a revolt and led the four thousand assassins out into the wilderness?" [39]Paul replied, "I am a Jew, from Tar'sus in Ci·li'ci·a, a citizen of an important city; I beg you, let me speak to the people." [40]When he had given him permission, Paul stood on the steps and motioned to the people for silence; and when there was a great hush, he addressed them in the Hebrew[f] language, saying:

22 "Brothers and fathers, listen to the defense that I now make before you."

2 When they heard him addressing them in Hebrew,[g] they became even more quiet. Then he said:

3 "I am a Jew, born in Tar'sus in Ci·li'ci·a, but brought up in this city at the feet of Ga·ma'li·el, educated strictly according to our ancestral law, being zealous for God, just as all of you are today.

---

[c] Other ancient authorities lack *and from what is strangled*   [d] Gk *he*   [e] Gk *He*   [f] That is, Aramaic   [g] That is, *Aramaic*

[4]I persecuted this Way up to the point of death by binding both men and women and putting them in prison, [5]as the high priest and the whole council of elders can testify about me. From them I also received letters to the brothers in Damascus, and I went there in order to bind those who were there and to bring them back to Jerusalem for punishment.

Paul Tells of His Conversion

[6]"While I was on my way and approaching Damascus, about noon a great light from heaven suddenly shone about me. [7]I fell to the ground and heard a voice saying to me, 'Saul, Saul, why are you persecuting me?' [8]I answered, 'Who are you, Lord?' Then he said to me, 'I am Jesus of Nazareth[h] whom you are persecuting.' [9]Now those who were with me saw the light but did not hear the voice of the one who was speaking to me. [10]I asked, 'What am I to do, Lord?' The Lord said to me, 'Get up and go to Damascus; there you will be told everything that has been assigned to you to do.' [11]Since I could not see because of the brightness of that light, those who were with me took my hand and led me to Damascus.

[12]"A certain An·a·nī´as, who was a devout man according to the law and well spoken of by all the Jews living there, [13]came to me; and standing beside me, he said, 'Brother Saul, regain your sight!' In that very hour I regained my sight and saw him. [14]Then he said, 'The God of our ancestors has chosen you to know his will, to see the Righteous One and to hear his own voice; [15]for you will be his witness to all the world of what you have seen and heard. [16]And now why do you delay? Get up, be baptized, and have your sins washed away, calling on his name.'

Paul Sent to the Gentiles

[17]"After I had returned to Jerusalem and while I was praying in the temple, I fell into a trance [18]and saw Jesus[i] saying to me, 'Hurry and get out of Jerusalem quickly, because they will not accept your testimony about me.' [19]And I said, 'Lord, they themselves know that in every synagogue I imprisoned and beat those who believed in you. [20]And while the blood of your witness Stephen was shed, I myself was standing by, approving and keeping the coats of those who killed him.' [21]Then he said to me, 'Go, for I will send you far away to the Gentiles.' "

Paul and the Roman Tribune

[22]Up to this point they listened to him, but then they shouted, "Away with such a fellow from the earth! For he should not be allowed to live." [23]And while they were shouting, throwing off their cloaks, and tossing dust into the air, [24]the tribune directed that he was to be brought into the barracks, and ordered him to be examined by flogging, to find out the reason for this outcry against him. [25]But when they had tied him up with thongs,[j] Paul said to the centurion who was standing by, "Is it legal for you to flog a Roman citizen who is uncondemned?" [26]When the centurion heard that, he went to the tribune and said to him, "What are you about to do? This man is a Roman citizen." [27]The tribune came and asked Paul,[i] "Tell me, are you a Roman citizen?" And he said, "Yes." [28]The tribune answered, "It cost me a large sum of money to get my citizenship." Paul said, "But I was born a citizen." [29]Immediately those who were about to examine him drew back from him; and the tribune also was afraid, for he realized that Paul was a Roman citizen and that he had bound him.

Paul before the Council

[30]Since he wanted to find out what Paul[k] was being accused of by the Jews, the next day he released him and ordered the chief priests and the entire council to meet. He brought Paul down and had him stand before them.

23 While Paul was looking intently at the council he said,

[h] Gk the Nazorean   [i] Gk him   [j] Or up for the lashes   [k] Gk he

"Brothers,[l] up to this day I have lived my life with a clear conscience before God." [2]Then the high priest An·a·nī́as ordered those standing near him to strike him on the mouth. [3]At this Paul said to him, "God will strike you, you whitewashed wall! Are you sitting there to judge me according to the law, and yet in violation of the law you order me to be struck?" [4]Those standing nearby said, "Do you dare to insult God's high priest?" [5]And Paul said, "I did not realize, brothers, that he was high priest; for it is written, 'You shall not speak evil of a leader of your people.'"

6 When Paul noticed that some were Sad́dū·cees and others were Phaŕi·sees, he called out in the council, "Brothers, I am a Phaŕi·see, a son of Phaŕi·sees. I am on trial concerning the hope of the resurrection[m] of the dead." [7]When he said this, a dissension began between the Phaŕi·sees and the Sad́dū·cees, and the assembly was divided. [8](The Sad́dū·cees say that there is no resurrection, or angel, or spirit; but the Phaŕi·sees acknowledge all three.) [9]Then a great clamor arose, and certain scribes of the Phaŕi·sees' group stood up and contended, "We find nothing wrong with this man. What if a spirit or an angel has spoken to him?" [10]When the dissension became violent, the tribune, fearing that they would tear Paul to pieces, ordered the soldiers to go down, take him by force, and bring him into the barracks.

11 That night the Lord stood near him and said, "Keep up your courage! For just as you have testified for me in Jerusalem, so you must bear witness also in Rome."

The Plot to Kill Paul

12 In the morning the Jews joined in a conspiracy and bound themselves by an oath neither to eat nor drink until they had killed Paul. [13]There were more than forty who joined in this conspiracy. [14]They went to the chief priests and elders and said, "We have strictly bound ourselves by an oath to taste no food until we have killed Paul. [15]Now then, you and the council must notify the tribune to bring him down to you, on the pretext that you want to make a more thorough examination of his case. And we are ready to do away with him before he arrives."

16 Now the son of Paul's sister heard about the ambush; so he went and gained entrance to the barracks and told Paul. [17]Paul called one of the centurions and said, "Take this young man to the tribune, for he has something to report to him." [18]So he took him, brought him to the tribune, and said, "The prisoner Paul called me and asked me to bring this young man to you; he has something to tell you." [19]The tribune took him by the hand, drew him aside privately, and asked, "What is it that you have to report to me?" [20]He answered, "The Jews have agreed to ask you to bring Paul down to the council tomorrow, as though they were going to inquire more thoroughly into his case. [21]But do not be persuaded by them, for more than forty of their men are lying in ambush for him. They have bound themselves by an oath neither to eat nor drink until they kill him. They are ready now and are waiting for your consent." [22]So the tribune dismissed the young man, ordering him, "Tell no one that you have informed me of this."

Paul Sent to Felix the Governor

23 Then he summoned two of the centurions and said, "Get ready to leave by nine o'clock tonight for Caes·a·rḗa with two hundred soldiers, seventy horsemen, and two hundred spearmen. [24]Also provide mounts for Paul to ride, and take him safely to Felix the governor." [25]He wrote a letter to this effect:

26 "Clauʹdiʹus Lysʹiʹas to his Excellency the governor Felix, greetings. [27]This man was seized by the Jews and was about to be killed by them, but when I had

[l] Gk Men, brothers   [m] Gk concerning hope and resurrection

learned that he was a Roman citizen, I came with the guard and rescued him. [28]Since I wanted to know the charge for which they accused him, I had him brought to their council. [29]I found that he was accused concerning questions of their law, but was charged with nothing deserving death or imprisonment. [30]When I was informed that there would be a plot against the man, I sent him to you at once, ordering his accusers also to state before you what they have against him.[n]."

31 So the soldiers, according to their instructions, took Paul and brought him during the night to An·tip′a·tris. [32]The next day they let the horsemen go on with him, while they returned to the barracks. [33]When they came to Caes·a·re′a and delivered the letter to the governor, they presented Paul also before him. [34]On reading the letter, he asked what province he belonged to, and when he learned that he was from Ci·li′ci·a, [35]he said, "I will give you a hearing when your accusers arrive." Then he ordered that he be kept under guard in Herod's headquarters.[o]

Paul before Felix at Caesarea

24 Five days later the high priest An·a·ni′as came down with some elders and an attorney, a certain Ter·tul′lus, and they reported their case against Paul to the governor. [2]When Paul[p] had been summoned, Ter·tul′lus began to accuse him, saying:

"Your Excellency,[q] because of you we have long enjoyed peace, and reforms have been made for this people because of your foresight. [3]We welcome this in every way and everywhere with utmost gratitude. [4]But, to detain you no further, I beg you to hear us briefly with your customary graciousness. [5]We have, in fact, found this man a pestilent fellow, an agitator among all the Jews throughout the world, and a ringleader of the sect of the Naz′a·renes.[r] [6]He even tried to profane the temple, and so we seized him.[s] [8]By

examining him yourself you will be able to learn from him concerning everything of which we accuse him."

9 The Jews also joined in the charge by asserting that all this was true.

Paul's Defense before Felix

10 When the governor motioned to him to speak, Paul replied:

"I cheerfully make my defense, knowing that for many years you have been a judge over this nation. [11]As you can find out, it is not more than twelve days since I went up to worship in Jerusalem. [12]They did not find me disputing with anyone in the temple or stirring up a crowd either in the synagogues or throughout the city. [13]Neither can they prove to you the charge that they now bring against me. [14]But this I admit to you, that according to the Way, which they call a sect, I worship the God of our ancestors, believing everything laid down according to the law or written in the prophets. [15]I have a hope in God—a hope that they themselves also accept—that there will be a resurrection of both[t] the righteous and the unrighteous. [16]Therefore I do my best always to have a clear conscience toward God and all people. [17]Now after some years I came to bring alms to my nation and to offer sacrifices. [18]While I was doing this, they found me in the temple, completing the rite of purification, without any crowd or disturbance. [19]But there were some Jews from Asia—they ought to be here before you to make an accusation, if they have anything against me. [20]Or let these men here tell what crime they had found when I stood before the council, [21]unless it was this one sentence that I called out while standing before them, 'It is about the resurrection

[n] Other ancient authorities add *Farewell* [o] Gk *praetorium* [p] Gk *he* [q] Gk lacks *Your Excellency* [r] Gk *Nazoreans* [s] Other ancient authorities add *and we would have judged him according to our law.* [7]*But the chief captain Lysias came and with great violence took him out of our hands,* [8]*commanding his accusers to come before you.* [t] Other ancient authorities read *of the dead, both of*

of the dead that I am on trial before you today.' "

22 But Felix, who was rather well informed about the Way, adjourned the hearing with the comment, "When Lysʹi·as the tribune comes down, I will decide your case." 23Then he ordered the centurion to keep him in custody, but to let him have some liberty and not to prevent any of his friends from taking care of his needs.

Paul Held in Custody

24 Some days later when Felix came with his wife Drūʹsilʹla, who was Jewish, he sent for Paul and heard him speak concerning faith in Christ Jesus. 25And as he discussed justice, self-control, and the coming judgment, Felix became frightened and said, "Go away for the present; when I have an opportunity, I will send for you." 26At the same time he hoped that money would be given him by Paul, and for that reason he used to send for him very often and converse with him.

27 After two years had passed, Felix was succeeded by Porʹci·us Fesʹtus; and since he wanted to grant the Jews a favor, Felix left Paul in prison.

Paul Appeals to the Emperor

25 Three days after Fesʹtus had arrived in the province, he went up from Caes·a·reʹa to Jerusalem 2where the chief priests and the leaders of the Jews gave him a report against Paul. They appealed to him 3and requested, as a favor to them against Paul,ᵘ to have him transferred to Jerusalem. They were, in fact, planning an ambush to kill him along the way. 4Fesʹtus replied that Paul was being kept at Caes·a·reʹa, and that he himself intended to go there shortly. 5"So," he said, "let those of you who have the authority come down with me, and if there is anything wrong about the man, let them accuse him."

6 After he had stayed among them not more than eight or ten days, he went down to Caes·a·reʹa; the next day he took

Felix was the Roman governor of Judea from about 52–60 AD. When Paul visited and was arrested in Jerusalem, he was brought to Caesarea for trial. Felix kept him in prison for two years, hoping that Paul would pay for his freedom.

After Felix, Festus became the Roman governor of Judea, probably from 60–62 AD. When Paul (still in prison) appealed to Caesar as a Roman citizen, Festus had to send Paul to Rome for trial.

his seat on the tribunal and ordered Paul to be brought. 7When he arrived, the Jews who had gone down from Jerusalem surrounded him, bringing many serious charges against him, which they could not prove. 8Paul said in his defense, "I have in no way committed an offense against the law of the Jews, or against the temple, or against the emperor." 9But Fesʹtus, wishing to do the Jews a favor, asked Paul, "Do you wish to go up to Jerusalem and be tried there before me on these charges?" 10Paul said, "I am appealing to the emperor's tribunal; this is where I should be tried. I have done no wrong to the Jews, as you very well know. 11Now if I am in the wrong and have committed something for which I deserve to die, I am not trying to escape death; but if there is nothing to their charges against me, no one can turn me over to them. I appeal to the emperor." 12Then Fesʹtus, after he had conferred with his council, replied, "You have appealed to the emperor; to the emperor you will go."

Festus Consults King Agrippa

13 After several days had passed, King A·gripʹpa and Ber·nīʹcē arrived at

ᵘ Gk him

Caes·a·rē´a to welcome Fes´tus. [14]Since they were staying there several days, Fes´tus laid Paul's case before the king, saying, "There is a man here who was left in prison by Felix. [15]When I was in Jerusalem, the chief priests and the elders of the Jews informed me about him and asked for a sentence against him. [16]I told them that it was not the custom of the Romans to hand over anyone before the accused had met the accusers face to face and had been given an opportunity to make a defense against the charge. [17]So when they met here, I lost no time, but on the next day took my seat on the tribunal and ordered the man to be brought. [18]When the accusers stood up, they did not charge him with any of the crimes[v] that I was expecting. [19]Instead they had certain points of disagreement with him about their own religion and about a certain Jesus, who had died, but whom Paul asserted to be alive. [20]Since I was at a loss how to investigate these questions, I asked whether he wished to go to Jerusalem and be tried there on these charges.[w] [21]But when Paul had appealed to be kept in custody for the decision of his Imperial Majesty, I ordered him to be held until I could send him to the emperor." [22]A·grip´pa said to Fes´tus, "I would like to hear the man myself." "Tomorrow," he said, "you will hear him."

Paul Brought before Agrippa

23 So on the next day A·grip´pa and Ber·nī´cē came with great pomp, and they entered the audience hall with the military tribunes and the prominent men of the city. Then Fes´tus gave the order and Paul was brought in. [24]And Fes´tus said, "King A·grip´pa and all here present with us, you see this man about whom the whole Jewish community petitioned me, both in Jerusalem and here, shouting that he ought not to live any longer. [25]But I found that he had done nothing deserving death; and when he appealed to his Imperial Majesty, I decided to send him. [26]But I have nothing definite to write to our sovereign about him. Therefore I have brought him before all of you, and especially before you, King A·grip´pa, so that, after we have examined him, I may have something to write— [27]for it seems to me unreasonable to send a prisoner without indicating the charges against him."

Paul Defends Himself before Agrippa

26 A·grip´pa said to Paul, "You have permission to speak for yourself." Then Paul stretched out his hand and began to defend himself:

2 "I consider myself fortunate that it is before you, King A·grip´pa, I am to make my defense today against all the accusations of the Jews, [3]because you are especially familiar with all the customs and controversies of the Jews; therefore I beg of you to listen to me patiently.

4 "All the Jews know my way of life from my youth, a life spent from the beginning among my own people and in Jerusalem. [5]They have known for a long time, if they are willing to testify, that I have belonged to the strictest sect of our religion and lived as a Phar´i·see. [6]And now I stand here on trial on account of my hope in the promise made by God to our ancestors, [7]a promise that our twelve tribes hope to attain, as they earnestly worship day and night. It is for this hope, your Excellency,[x] that I am accused by Jews! [8]Why is it thought incredible by any of you that God raises the dead?

9 "Indeed, I myself was convinced that I ought to do many things against the name of Jesus of Nazareth.[y] [10]And that is what I did in Jerusalem; with authority received from the chief priests, I not only locked up many of the saints in prison, but I also cast my vote against them when they were being condemned to death. [11]By punishing them often in all the synagogues I tried to force them to blaspheme; and

---

[v] Other ancient authorities read *with anything*
[w] Gk *on them*   [x] Gk *O king*   [y] Gk *the Nazorean*

since I was so furiously enraged at them, I pursued them even to foreign cities.

Paul Tells of His Conversion

12 "With this in mind, I was traveling to Damascus with the authority and commission of the chief priests, [13]when at midday along the road, your Excellency,[v] I saw a light from heaven, brighter than the sun, shining around me and my companions. [14]When we had all fallen to the ground, I heard a voice saying to me in the Hebrew[z] language, 'Saul, Saul, why are you persecuting me? It hurts you to kick against the goads.' [15]I asked, 'Who are you, Lord?' The Lord answered, 'I am Jesus whom you are persecuting. [16]But get up and stand on your feet; for I have appeared to you for this purpose, to appoint you to serve and testify to the things in which you have seen me[a] and to those in which I will appear to you. [17]I will rescue you from your people and from the Gentiles—to whom I am sending you [18]to open their eyes so that they may turn from darkness to light and from the power of Satan to God, so that they may receive forgiveness of sins and a place among those who are sanctified by faith in me.'

Paul Tells of His Preaching

19 "After that, King A·grip´pa, I was not disobedient to the heavenly vision, [20]but declared first to those in Damascus, then in Jerusalem and throughout the countryside of Judea, and also to the Gentiles, that they should repent and turn to God and do deeds consistent with repentance. [21]For this reason the Jews seized me in the temple and tried to kill me. [22]To this day I have had help from God, and so I stand here, testifying to both small and great, saying nothing but what the prophets and Moses said would take place: [23]that the Messiah[b] must suffer, and that, by being the first to rise from the dead, he would proclaim light both to our people and to the Gentiles."

> "I will rescue you from your people and from the Gentiles—to whom I am sending you to open their eyes so that they may turn from darkness to light." Acts 26:17a

Paul Appeals to Agrippa to Believe

24 While he was making this defense, Fes´tus exclaimed, "You are out of your mind, Paul! Too much learning is driving you insane!" [25]But Paul said, "I am not out of my mind, most excellent Fes´tus, but I am speaking the sober truth. [26]Indeed the king knows about these things, and to him I speak freely; for I am certain that none of these things has escaped his notice, for this was not done in a corner. [27]King A·grip´pa, do you believe the prophets? I know that you believe." [28]A·grip´pa said to Paul, "Are you so quickly persuading me to become a Christian?"[c] [29]Paul replied, "Whether quickly or not, I pray to God that not only you but also all who are listening to me today might become such as I am—except for these chains."

30 Then the king got up, and with him the governor and Ber·ni´cē and those who had been seated with them; [31]and as they were leaving, they said to one another, "This man is doing nothing to deserve death or imprisonment." [32]A·grip´pa said to Fes´tus, "This man could have been set free if he had not appealed to the emperor."

Paul Sails for Rome

27 When it was decided that we were to sail for Italy, they transferred Paul and some other prisoners to a centurion of the Augustan Cohort, named Julius. [2]Embarking on a ship of Ad·ra·myt´ti·um that was about to set

---

[z] That is, *Aramaic*   [a] Other ancient authorities read *the things that you have seen*   [b] Or *the Christ*   [c] Or *Quickly you will persuade me to play the Christian*

sail to the ports along the coast of Asia, we put to sea, accompanied by Ar·is·tar´chus, a Mac·e·dō´ni·an from Thes·sa·lo·nī´ca. [3]The next day we put in at Sī´don; and Julius treated Paul kindly, and allowed him to go to his friends to be cared for. [4]Putting out to sea from there, we sailed under the lee of Cyprus, because the winds were against us. [5]After we had sailed across the sea that is off Ci·li´ci·a and Pam·phyl´i·a, we came to Mȳ´ra in Ly´ci·a. [6]There the centurion found an Alexandrian ship bound for Italy and put us on board. [7]We sailed slowly for a number of days and arrived with difficulty off Cnī´dus, and as the wind was against us, we sailed under the lee of Crete off Sal·mō´nē. [8]Sailing past it with difficulty, we came to a place called Fair Havens, near the city of La·sē´a.

9 Since much time had been lost and sailing was now dangerous, because even the Fast had already gone by, Paul advised them, [10]saying, "Sirs, I can see that the voyage will be with danger and much heavy loss, not only of the cargo and the ship, but also of our lives." [11]But the centurion paid more attention to the pilot and to the owner of the ship than to what Paul said. [12]Since the harbor was not suitable for spending the winter, the majority was in favor of putting to sea from there, on the chance that somehow they could reach Phoenix, where they could spend the winter. It was a harbor of Crete, facing southwest and northwest.

The Storm at Sea

13 When a moderate south wind began to blow, they thought they could achieve their purpose; so they weighed anchor and began to sail past Crete, close to the shore. [14]But soon a violent wind, called the northeaster, rushed down from Crete.[d] [15]Since the ship was caught and could not be turned head-on into the wind, we gave way to it and were driven. [16]By running under the lee of a small island called Cau´da[e] we were scarcely able to get the ship's boat under control.

> Courage is an inside strength that allows a person to face danger or fear with confidence. Paul, through his faith in Jesus, had great courage. When his ship was caught in a storm, he helped the crew to save themselves when they wanted to give up.

[17]After hoisting it up they took measures[f] to undergird the ship; then, fearing that they would run on the Syr´tis, they lowered the sea anchor and so were driven. [18]We were being pounded by the storm so violently that on the next day they began to throw the cargo overboard, [19]and on the third day with their own hands they threw the ship's tackle overboard. [20]When neither sun nor stars appeared for many days, and no small tempest raged, all hope of our being saved was at last abandoned.

21 Since they had been without food for a long time, Paul then stood up among them and said, "Men, you should have listened to me and not have set sail from Crete and thereby avoided this damage and loss. [22]I urge you now to keep up your courage, for there will be no loss of life among you, but only of the ship. [23]For last night there stood by me an angel of the God to whom I belong and whom I worship, [24]and he said, 'Do not be afraid, Paul; you must stand before the emperor; and indeed, God has granted safety to all those who are sailing with you.' [25]So keep up your courage, men, for I have faith in God that it will be exactly as I have been told. [26]But we will have to run aground on some island."

27 When the fourteenth night had come, as we were drifting across the sea of Ā´dri·a, about midnight the sailors sus-

[d] Gk it [e] Other ancient authorities read *Clauda* [f] Gk *helps*

pected that they were nearing land. ^{28}So they took soundings and found twenty fathoms; a little farther on they took soundings again and found fifteen fathoms. ^{29}Fearing that we might run on the rocks, they let down four anchors from the stern and prayed for day to come. ^{30}But when the sailors tried to escape from the ship and had lowered the boat into the sea, on the pretext of putting out anchors from the bow, ^{31}Paul said to the centurion and the soldiers, "Unless these men stay in the ship, you cannot be saved." ^{32}Then the soldiers cut away the ropes of the boat and set it adrift.

33 Just before daybreak, Paul urged all of them to take some food, saying, "Today is the fourteenth day that you have been in suspense and remaining without food, having eaten nothing. ^{34}Therefore I urge you to take some food, for it will help you survive; for none of you will lose a hair from your heads." ^{35}After he had said this, he took bread; and giving thanks to God in the presence of all, he broke it and began to eat. ^{36}Then all of them were encouraged and took food for themselves. ^{37}(We were in all two hundred seventy-six^g persons in the ship.) ^{38}After they had satisfied their hunger, they lightened the ship by throwing the wheat into the sea.

The Shipwreck

39 In the morning they did not recognize the land, but they noticed a bay with a beach, on which they planned to run the ship ashore, if they could. ^{40}So they cast off the anchors and left them in the sea. At the same time they loosened the ropes that tied the steering-oars; then hoisting the foresail to the wind, they made for the beach. ^{41}But striking a reef,^{h} they ran the ship aground; the bow stuck and remained immovable, but the stern was being broken up by the force of the waves. ^{42}The soldiers' plan was to kill the prisoners, so that none might swim away

and escape; ^{43}but the centurion, wishing to save Paul, kept them from carrying out their plan. He ordered those who could swim to jump overboard first and make for the land, ^{44}and the rest to follow, some on planks and others on pieces of the ship. And so it was that all were brought safely to land.

Paul on the Island of Malta

28 After we had reached safety, we then learned that the island was called Malta. ^{2}The natives showed us unusual kindness. Since it had begun to rain and was cold, they kindled a fire and welcomed all of us around it. ^{3}Paul had gathered a bundle of brushwood and was putting it on the fire, when a viper, driven out by the heat, fastened itself on his hand. ^{4}When the natives saw the creature hanging from his hand, they said to one another, "This man must be a murderer; though he has escaped from the sea, justice has not allowed him to live." ^{5}He, however, shook off the creature into the fire and suffered no harm. ^{6}They were expecting him to swell up or drop dead, but after they had waited a long time and saw that nothing unusual had happened to him, they changed their minds and began to say that he was a god.

7 Now in the neighborhood of that place were lands belonging to the leading man of the island, named Pub·li·us, who received us and entertained us hospitably for three days. ^{8}It so happened that the father of Pub·li·us lay sick in bed with fever and dysentery. Paul visited him and cured him by praying and putting his hands on him. ^{9}After this happened, the rest of the people on the island who had diseases also came and were cured. ^{10}They bestowed many honors on us, and when we were about to sail, they put on board all the provisions we needed.

Paul Arrives at Rome

11 Three months later we set sail on a

^{g} Other ancient authorities read *seventy-six*; others, *about seventy-six* ^{h} Gk *place of two seas* ship that had wintered at the island, an Alexandrian ship with the Twin Brothers as its figurehead. [12]We put in at Syracuse and stayed there for three days; [13]then we weighed anchor and came to Rhē´gi·um. After one day there a south wind sprang up, and on the second day we came to Pū·tē´o·lǐ. [14]There we found believers[i] and were invited to stay with them for seven days. And so we came to Rome. [15]The believers[i] from there, when they heard of us, came as far as the Forum of Ap´pi·us and Three Taverns to meet us. On seeing them, Paul thanked God and took courage.

16 When we came into Rome, Paul was allowed to live by himself, with the soldier who was guarding him.

Paul and Jewish Leaders in Rome

17 Three days later he called together the local leaders of the Jews. When they had assembled, he said to them, "Brothers, though I had done nothing against our people or the customs of our ancestors, yet I was arrested in Jerusalem and handed over to the Romans. [18]When they had examined me, the Romans[j] wanted to release me, because there was no reason for the death penalty in my case. [19]But when the Jews objected, I was compelled to appeal to the emperor—even though I had no charge to bring against my nation. [20]For this reason therefore I have asked to see you and speak with you,[k] since it is for the sake of the hope of Israel that I am bound with this chain." [21]They replied, "We have received no letters from Judea about you, and none of the brothers coming here has reported or spoken anything evil about you. [22]But we would like to hear from you what you think, for with regard to this sect we know that everywhere it is spoken against."

Paul Preaches in Rome

23 After they had set a day to meet with him, they came to him at his lodgings in great numbers. From morning until evening he explained the matter to them, testifying to the kingdom of God and trying to convince them about Jesus both from the law of Moses and from the prophets. [24]Some were convinced by what he had said, while others refused to believe. [25]So they disagreed with each other; and as they were leaving, Paul made one further statement: "The Holy Spirit was right in saying to your ancestors through the prophet Ī·sāi´ah,

[26] 'Go to this people and say,
You will indeed listen, but never understand,
and you will indeed look, but never perceive.
[27] For this people's heart has grown dull,
and their ears are hard of hearing,
and they have shut their eyes;
so that they might not look with their eyes,
and listen with their ears,
and understand with their heart and turn—
and I would heal them.'

[28]Let it be known to you then that this salvation of God has been sent to the Gentiles; they will listen."[l]

30 He lived there two whole years at his own expense[m] and welcomed all who came to him, [31]proclaiming the kingdom of God and teaching about the Lord Jesus Christ with all boldness and without hindrance.

---

[i] Gk brothers   [j] Gk they   [k] Or I have asked you to see me and speak with me   [l] Other ancient authorities add verse 29, And when he had said these words, the Jews departed, arguing vigorously among themselves   [m] Or in his own hired dwelling

Romans

This letter to the Romans is a letter from the apostle Paul to Christians in Rome. Paul wrote this letter about 57–58 AD probably from Corinth, where he had helped to start a church. It appears Paul planned to visit the Christians in Rome and wrote the letter to the Romans to explain his views on the Christian faith as he believed and preached it in hopes that they would welcome him as an apostle and would support his ministry. (You can read the story of Paul in the book of Acts.)

In the letter to the Romans, Paul taught that all people are guilty of sin. He explained that both Jews and Gentiles (a Gentile is a non-Jewish person) are sinful and cannot save themselves. But, he said, God sent Jesus Christ to be the Savior of all people everywhere. "While we still were sinners Christ died for us" (Romans 5:8). Salvation is the free gift of God given through Jesus. This gift shows us the great love of God, and there is nothing in all creation that is more powerful than God's love.

When people receive the gift of salvation through faith, they have new life in Christ. Paul told the believers to offer their lives as living sacrifices to God. He explained that faith in Jesus Christ must involve loyalty to God and God's purposes. Christians are to turn away from bad, hold onto good, and treat one another with love. New life and love for God in Christ helps Christians behave with goodness and love toward others.

Romans 11:1–32

Rome was the capital of the world in the first century AD. The mighty Roman Empire included the whole Mediterranean world and parts of what is now Europe. Christianity came to Rome before 50 AD. Paul visited the Christian church in Rome and was later imprisoned there. There is a strong ancient church tradition that Peter visited Rome and that he and Paul were both killed there.

Salutation

1 Paul, a servant*a* of Jesus Christ, called to be an apostle, set apart for the gospel of God, ²which he promised beforehand through his prophets in the holy scriptures, ³the gospel concerning his Son, who was descended from David according to the flesh ⁴and was declared to be Son of God with power according to the spirit*b* of holiness by resurrection from the dead, Jesus Christ our Lord, ⁵through whom we have received grace and apostleship to bring about the obedience of faith among all the Gentiles for the sake of his name, ⁶including yourselves who are called to belong to Jesus Christ,

7 To all God's beloved in Rome, who are called to be saints:

Grace to you and peace from God our Father and the Lord Jesus Christ.

Prayer of Thanksgiving

8 First, I thank my God through Jesus Christ for all of you, because your faith is

proclaimed throughout the world. ⁹For God, whom I serve with my spirit by announcing the gospel*c* of his Son, is my witness that without ceasing I remember you always in my prayers, ¹⁰asking that by God's will I may somehow at last succeed in coming to you. ¹¹For I am longing to see you so that I may share with you some spiritual gift to strengthen you— ¹²or rather so that we may be mutually encouraged by each other's faith, both yours and mine. ¹³I want you to know, brothers and sisters,*d* that I have often intended to come to you (but thus far have been prevented), in order that I may reap some harvest among you as I have among the rest of the Gentiles. ¹⁴I am a debtor both to Greeks and to barbarians, both to the wise and to the foolish ¹⁵— hence my eagerness to proclaim the gospel to you also who are in Rome.

The Power of the Gospel

16 For I am not ashamed of the gospel; it is the power of God for salvation to everyone who has faith, to the Jew first and also to the Greek. ¹⁷For in it the righteousness of God is revealed through faith for faith; as it is written, "The one who is righteous will live by faith."*e*

The Guilt of Humankind

18 For the wrath of God is revealed from heaven against all ungodliness and wickedness of those who by their wickedness suppress the truth. ¹⁹For what can be known about God is plain to them, because God has shown it to them. ²⁰Ever since the creation of the world his eternal power and divine nature, invisible though they are, have been understood and seen through the things he has made. So they are without excuse; ²¹for though they knew God, they did not honor him as God or give thanks to him, but they became futile in their thinking, and their senseless minds were darkened. ²²Claiming to be

"For I am not ashamed of the gospel; it is the power of God for salvation to everyone who has faith, to the Jew first and also to the Greek." Romans 1:16

a Gk *slave*   *b* Or *Spirit*   *c* Gk *my spirit in the gospel*   *d* Gk *brothers*   *e* Or *The one who is righteous through faith will live* wise, they became fools; ²³and they exchanged the glory of the immortal God for images resembling a mortal human being or birds or four-footed animals or reptiles.

24 Therefore God gave them up in the lusts of their hearts to impurity, to the degrading of their bodies among themselves, ²⁵because they exchanged the truth about God for a lie and worshiped and served the creature rather than the Creator, who is blessed forever! Amen.

26 For this reason God gave them up to degrading passions. Their women exchanged natural intercourse for unnatural, ²⁷and in the same way also the men, giving up natural intercourse with women, were consumed with passion for one another. Men committed shameless acts with men and received in their own persons the due penalty for their error.

28 And since they did not see fit to acknowledge God, God gave them up to a debased mind and to things that should not be done. ²⁹They were filled with every kind of wickedness, evil, covetousness, malice. Full of envy, murder, strife, deceit, craftiness, they are gossips, ³⁰slanderers, God-haters,ᶠ insolent, haughty, boastful, inventors of evil, rebellious toward parents, ³¹foolish, faithless, heartless, ruthless. ³²They know God's decree, that those who practice such things deserve to die— yet they not only do them but even applaud others who practice them.

The Righteous Judgment of God

2 Therefore you have no excuse, whoever you are, when you judge others; for in passing judgment on another you condemn yourself, because you, the judge, are doing the very same things. ²You say,ᵍ "We know that God's judgment on those who do such things is in accordance with truth." ³Do you imagine, whoever you are, that when you judge those who do such things and yet do them yourself, you will escape the judgment of God? ⁴Or do you despise the riches of his kindness and forbear-

God alone judges our actions. God has the power and wisdom to judge with righteousness and truth.

ance and patience? Do you not realize that God's kindness is meant to lead you to repentance? ⁵But by your hard and impenitent heart you are storing up wrath for yourself on the day of wrath, when God's righteous judgment will be revealed. ⁶For he will repay according to each one's deeds: ⁷to those who by patiently doing good seek for glory and honor and immortality, he will give eternal life; ⁸while for those who are self-seeking and who obey not the truth but wickedness, there will be wrath and fury. ⁹There will be anguish and distress for everyone who does evil, the Jew first and also the Greek, ¹⁰but glory and honor and peace for everyone who does good, the Jew first and also the Greek. ¹¹For God shows no partiality.

12 All who have sinned apart from the law will also perish apart from the law, and all who have sinned under the law will be judged by the law. ¹³For it is not the hearers of the law who are righteous in God's sight, but the doers of the law who will be justified. ¹⁴When Gentiles, who do not possess the law, do instinctively what the law requires, these, though not having the law, are a law to themselves. ¹⁵They show that what the law requires is written on their hearts, to which their own conscience also bears witness; and their conflicting thoughts will accuse or perhaps excuse them ¹⁶on the day when, according to my gospel, God, through Jesus Christ, will judge the secret thoughts of all.

The Jews and the Law

17 But if you call yourself a Jew and rely on the law and boast of your relation to God ¹⁸and know his will and determine what is best because you are instructed in

ᶠ Or *God-hated*   ᵍ Gk lacks *You say*

the law, [19]and if you are sure that you are a guide to the blind, a light to those who are in darkness, [20]a corrector of the foolish, a teacher of children, having in the law the embodiment of knowledge and truth, [21]you, then, that teach others, will you not teach yourself? While you preach against stealing, do you steal? [22]You that forbid adultery, do you commit adultery? You that abhor idols, do you rob temples? [23]You that boast in the law, do you dishonor God by breaking the law? [24]For, as it is written, "The name of God is blasphemed among the Gentiles because of you."

25 Circumcision indeed is of value if you obey the law; but if you break the law, your circumcision has become uncircumcision. [26]So, if those who are uncircumcised keep the requirements of the law, will not their uncircumcision be regarded as circumcision? [27]Then those who are physically uncircumcised but keep the law will condemn you that have the written code and circumcision but break the law. [28]For a person is not a Jew who is one outwardly, nor is true circumcision something external and physical. [29]Rather, a person is a Jew who is one inwardly, and real circumcision is a matter of the heart—it is spiritual and not literal. Such a person receives praise not from others but from God.

3 Then what advantage has the Jew? Or what is the value of circumcision? [2]Much, in every way. For in the first place the Jews[h] were entrusted with the oracles of God. [3]What if some were unfaithful? Will their faithlessness nullify the faithfulness of God? [4]By no means! Although everyone is a liar, let God be proved true, as it is written,
"So that you may be justified in your words,
and prevail in your judging."[i]
[5]But if our injustice serves to confirm the justice of God, what should we say? That God is unjust to inflict wrath on us? (I speak in a human way.) [6]By no means! For then how could God judge the world? [7]But if through my falsehood God's truth-

fulness abounds to his glory, why am I still being condemned as a sinner? [8]And why not say (as some people slander us by saying that we say), "Let us do evil so that good may come"? Their condemnation is deserved!

None Is Righteous

9 What then? Are we any better off?[j] No, not at all; for we have already charged that all, both Jews and Greeks, are under the power of sin, [10]as it is written:
"There is no one who is righteous, not even one;
[11] there is no one who has understanding,
there is no one who seeks God.
[12] All have turned aside, together they have become worthless;
there is no one who shows kindness,
there is not even one."
[13] "Their throats are opened graves;
they use their tongues to deceive."
"The venom of vipers is under their lips."
[14] "Their mouths are full of cursing and bitterness."
[15] "Their feet are swift to shed blood;
[16] ruin and misery are in their paths,
[17] and the way of peace they have not known."
[18] "There is no fear of God before their eyes."

19 Now we know that whatever the law says, it speaks to those who are under the law, so that every mouth may be silenced, and the whole world may be held accountable to God. [20]For "no human being will be justified in his sight" by deeds prescribed by the law, for through the law comes the knowledge of sin.

Righteousness through Faith

21 But now, apart from law, the righteousness of God has been disclosed, and is attested by the law and the prophets, [22]the righteousness of God through faith

---

[h] Gk *they*   [i] Gk *when you are being judged*
[j] Or *at any disadvantage?*

God created human beings with the freedom to remain close to God or to go our own way. When we choose to go our own way, we sin. Sin is a separation from God.

in Jesus Christ[k] for all who believe. For there is no distinction, [23]since all have sinned and fall short of the glory of God; [24]they are now justified by his grace as a gift, through the redemption that is in Christ Jesus, [25]whom God put forward as a sacrifice of atonement[l] by his blood, effective through faith. He did this to show his righteousness, because in his divine forbearance he had passed over the sins previously committed; [26]it was to prove at the present time that he himself is righteous and that he justifies the one who has faith in Jesus.[m]

27 Then what becomes of boasting? It is excluded. By what law? By that of works? No, but by the law of faith. [28]For we hold that a person is justified by faith apart from works prescribed by the law. [29]Or is God the God of Jews only? Is he not the God of Gentiles also? Yes, of Gentiles also, [30]since God is one; and he will justify the circumcised on the ground of faith and the uncircumcised through that same faith. [31]Do we then overthrow the law by this faith? By no means! On the contrary, we uphold the law.

The Example of Abraham

4 What then are we to say was gained by[n] Abraham, our ancestor according to the flesh? [2]For if Abraham was justified by works, he has something to boast about, but not before

"For the promise that he would inherit the world did not come to Abraham or to his descendants through the law but through the righteousness of faith." Romans 4:13

God. [3]For what does the scripture say? "Abraham believed God, and it was reckoned to him as righteousness." [4]Now to one who works, wages are not reckoned as a gift but as something due. [5]But to one who without works trusts him who justifies the ungodly, such faith is reckoned as righteousness. [6]So also David speaks of the blessedness of those to whom God reckons righteousness apart from works:

7 "Blessed are those whose iniquities are forgiven,
   and whose sins are covered;
8 blessed is the one against whom the
   Lord will not reckon sin."

9 Is this blessedness, then, pronounced only on the circumcised, or also on the uncircumcised? We say, "Faith was reckoned to Abraham as righteousness." [10]How then was it reckoned to him? Was it before or after he had been circumcised? It was not after, but before he was circumcised. [11]He received the sign of circumcision as a seal of the righteousness that he had by faith while he was still uncircumcised. The purpose was to make him the ancestor of all who believe without being circumcised and who thus have righteousness reckoned to them, [12]and likewise the ancestor of the circumcised who are not only circumcised but who also follow the example of the faith that our ancestor Abraham had before he was circumcised.

God's Promise Realized through Faith

13 For the promise that he would inherit the world did not come to Abraham or to his descendants through the law but through the righteousness of faith. [14]If it is the adherents of the law who are to be the heirs, faith is null and the promise is void. [15]For the law brings wrath; but where there is no law, neither is there violation.

---

[k] Or *through the faith of Jesus Christ*   [l] Or *a place of atonement*   [m] Or *who has the faith of Jesus*
[n] Other ancient authorities read *say about*

16 For this reason it depends on faith, in order that the promise may rest on grace and be guaranteed to all his descendants, not only to the adherents of the law but also to those who share the faith of Abraham (for he is the father of all of us, ¹⁷as it is written, "I have made you the father of many nations")—in the presence of the God in whom he believed, who gives life to the dead and calls into existence the things that do not exist. ¹⁸Hoping against hope, he believed that he would become "the father of many nations," according to what was said, "So numerous shall your descendants be." ¹⁹He did not weaken in faith when he considered his own body, which was already° as good as dead (for he was about a hundred years old), or when he considered the barrenness of Sarah's womb. ²⁰No distrust made him waver concerning the promise of God, but he grew strong in his faith as he gave glory to God, ²¹being fully convinced that God was able to do what he had promised. ²²Therefore his faithᵖ "was reckoned to him as righteousness." ²³Now the words, "it was reckoned to him," were written not for his sake alone, ²⁴but for ours also. It will be reckoned to us who believe in him who raised Jesus our Lord from the dead, ²⁵who was handed over to death for our trespasses and was raised for our justification.

Results of Justification

5 Therefore, since we are justified by faith, we�q have peace with God through our Lord Jesus Christ, ²through whom we have obtained accessʳ to this grace in which we stand; and weˢ boast in our hope of sharing the glory of God. ³And not only that, but weˢ also boast in our sufferings, knowing that suffering produces endurance, ⁴and endurance produces character, and character produces hope, ⁵and hope does not disappoint us, because God's love has been poured into our hearts through the Holy Spirit that has been given to us.

> Being justified is being made right with God. When Paul used the word "justify," he spoke of the action of God that forgives and restores people to goodness and righteousness. Several ideas come together in this thought: (1) God is holy and righteous. (2) God demands holiness and righteousness of God's people. (3) Humans are not holy; they are sinners. (4) This sinfulness deserves punishment. (5) God sent a solution to this problem—God's Son Jesus. Through Jesus Christ, God offers forgiveness to people.

6 For while we were still weak, at the right time Christ died for the ungodly. ⁷Indeed, rarely will anyone die for a righteous person—though perhaps for a good person someone might actually dare to die. ⁸But God proves his love for us in that while we still were sinners Christ died for us. ⁹Much more surely then, now that we have been justified by his blood, will we be saved through him from the wrath of God.ᵗ ¹⁰For if while we were enemies, we were reconciled to God through the death of his Son, much more surely, having been reconciled, will we be saved by his life. ¹¹But more than that, we even boast in God through our Lord Jesus Christ, through whom we have now received reconciliation.

Adam and Christ

12 Therefore, just as sin came into the world through one man, and death came

> "But God proves his love for us in that while we still were sinners Christ died for us." Romans 5:8

° Other ancient authorities lack *already*   ᵖ Gk *Therefore it* �q Other ancient authorities read *let us* ʳ Other ancient authorities add *by faith* ˢ Or *let us* ᵗ Gk *the wrath* through sin, and so death spread to all because all have sinned— [13]sin was indeed in the world before the law, but sin is not reckoned when there is no law. [14]Yet death exercised dominion from Adam to Moses, even over those whose sins were not like the transgression of Adam, who is a type of the one who was to come.

15 But the free gift is not like the trespass. For if the many died through the one man's trespass, much more surely have the grace of God and the free gift in the grace of the one man, Jesus Christ, abounded for the many. [16]And the free gift is not like the effect of the one man's sin. For the judgment following one trespass brought condemnation, but the free gift following many trespasses brings justification. [17]If, because of the one man's trespass, death exercised dominion through that one, much more surely will those who receive the abundance of grace and the free gift of righteousness exercise dominion in life through the one man, Jesus Christ.

18 Therefore just as one man's trespass led to condemnation for all, so one man's act of righteousness leads to justification and life for all. [19]For just as by the one man's disobedience the many were made sinners, so by the one man's obedience the many will be made righteous. [20]But law came in, with the result that the trespass multiplied; but where sin increased, grace abounded all the more, [21]so that, just as sin exercised dominion in death, so grace might also exercise dominion through justification[u] leading to eternal life through Jesus Christ our Lord.

Dying and Rising with Christ

6 What then are we to say? Should we continue in sin in order that grace may abound? [2]By no means! How can we who died to sin go on living in it? [3]Do you not know that all of us who have been baptized into Christ Jesus were baptized into his death? [4]Therefore we have been buried with him by baptism into death, so that, just as Christ

Grace is God's great love for us. We cannot earn that love—it is a free gift from God. In the Old Testament, God's "steadfast love" is a love that never changes or ends (read Psalm 136:1–26). In the New Testament, the grace of God is one of the most important parts of the Christian gospel. God's grace is seen as divine power flowing through Jesus Christ into our lives. This grace makes it possible for us to think, act, and speak according to God's will. Paul reminds us that although God's love never ends and God will continue to forgive us, we should not keep sinning. Instead, we should do our best to live as close to Jesus's example as we can.

was raised from the dead by the glory of the Father, so we too might walk in newness of life.

5 For if we have been united with him in a death like his, we will certainly be united with him in a resurrection like his. [6]We know that our old self was crucified with him so that the body of sin might be destroyed, and we might no longer be enslaved to sin. [7]For whoever has died is freed from sin. [8]But if we have died with Christ, we believe that we will also live with him. [9]We know that Christ, being raised from the dead, will never die again; death no longer has dominion over him. [10]The death he died, he died to sin, once for all; but the life he lives, he lives to God. [11]So you also must consider yourselves dead to sin and alive to God in Christ Jesus.

12 Therefore, do not let sin exercise dominion in your mortal bodies, to make you obey their passions. [13]No longer present your members to sin as instruments[v] of wickedness, but present yourselves to God as those who have been brought from

[u] Or *righteousness*   [v] Or *weapons*

death to life, and present your members to God as instruments[w] of righteousness. [14]For sin will have no dominion over you, since you are not under law but under grace.

Slaves of Righteousness

15 What then? Should we sin because we are not under law but under grace? By no means! [16]Do you not know that if you present yourselves to anyone as obedient slaves, you are slaves of the one whom you obey, either of sin, which leads to death, or of obedience, which leads to righteousness? [17]But thanks be to God that you, having once been slaves of sin, have become obedient from the heart to the form of teaching to which you were entrusted, [18]and that you, having been set free from sin, have become slaves of righteousness. [19]I am speaking in human terms because of your natural limitations.[x] For just as you once presented your members as slaves to impurity and to greater and greater iniquity, so now present your members as slaves to righteousness for sanctification.

20 When you were slaves of sin, you were free in regard to righteousness. [21]So what advantage did you then get from the things of which you now are ashamed? The end of those things is death. [22]But now that you have been freed from sin and enslaved to God, the advantage you get is sanctification. The end is eternal life. [23]For the wages of sin is death, but the free gift of God is eternal life in Christ Jesus our Lord.

An Analogy from Marriage

7 Do you not know, brothers and sisters[y]—for I am speaking to those who know the law—that the law is binding on a person only during that person's lifetime? [2]Thus a married woman is bound by the law to her husband as long as he lives; but if her husband dies, she is discharged from the law concerning the husband. [3]Accordingly, she will be called an adulteress if she lives with another man while her husband is alive. But if her husband dies, she is free from that law, and if she marries another man, she is not an adulteress.

4 In the same way, my friends,[y] you have died to the law through the body of Christ, so that you may belong to another, to him who has been raised from the dead in order that we may bear fruit for God. [5]While we were living in the flesh, our sinful passions, aroused by the law, were at work in our members to bear fruit for death. [6]But now we are discharged from the law, dead to that which held us captive, so that we are slaves not under the old written code but in the new life of the Spirit.

The Law and Sin

7 What then should we say? That the law is sin? By no means! Yet, if it had not been for the law, I would not have known sin. I would not have known what it is to covet if the law had not said, "You shall not covet." [8]But sin, seizing an opportunity in the commandment, produced in me all kinds of covetousness. Apart from the law sin lies dead. [9]I was once alive apart from the law, but when the commandment came, sin revived [10]and I died, and the very commandment that promised life proved to be death to me. [11]For sin, seizing an opportunity in the commandment, deceived me and through it killed me. [12]So the law is holy, and the commandment is holy and just and good.

13 Did what is good, then, bring death to me? By no means! It was sin, working death in me through what is good, in order that sin might be shown to be sin, and through the commandment might become sinful beyond measure.

The Inner Conflict

14 For we know that the law is spiritual; but I am of the flesh, sold into slavery under sin.[z] [15]I do not understand my own actions. For I do not do what I want,

---

[w] Or *weapons*   [x] Gk *the weakness of your flesh*
[y] Gk *brothers*   [z] Gk *sold under sin*

When we become Christians, we do not automatically stop doing wrong things. We are still human, and humans often make bad choices. But God is faithful. God not only forgives us when we ask, God rejoices each time we make the right choice. We need to try to think carefully, pray, and rely on God to help us make good choices.

but I do the very thing I hate. ¹⁶Now if I do what I do not want, I agree that the law is good. ¹⁷But in fact it is no longer I that do it, but sin that dwells within me. ¹⁸For I know that nothing good dwells within me, that is, in my flesh. I can will what is right, but I cannot do it. ¹⁹For I do not do the good I want, but the evil I do not want is what I do. ²⁰Now if I do what I do not want, it is no longer I that do it, but sin that dwells within me.

21 So I find it to be a law that when I want to do what is good, evil lies close at hand. ²²For I delight in the law of God in my inmost self, ²³but I see in my members another law at war with the law of my mind, making me captive to the law of sin that dwells in my members. ²⁴Wretched man that I am! Who will rescue me from this body of death? ²⁵Thanks be to God through Jesus Christ our Lord!

So then, with my mind I am a slave to the law of God, but with my flesh I am a slave to the law of sin.

Life in the Spirit

8 There is therefore now no condemnation for those who are in Christ Jesus. ²For the law of the Spirit*ᵃ* of life in Christ Jesus has set you*ᵇ* free from the law of sin and of death. ³For God has done what the law, weakened by the

flesh, could not do: by sending his own Son in the likeness of sinful flesh, and to deal with sin,*ᶜ* he condemned sin in the flesh, ⁴so that the just requirement of the law might be fulfilled in us, who walk not according to the flesh but according to the Spirit.*ᵃ* ⁵For those who live according to the flesh set their minds on the things of the flesh, but those who live according to the Spirit*ᵃ* set their minds on the things of the Spirit.*ᵃ* ⁶To set the mind on the flesh is death, but to set the mind on the Spirit*ᵃ* is life and peace. ⁷For this reason the mind that is set on the flesh is hostile to God; it does not submit to God's law—indeed it cannot, ⁸and those who are in the flesh cannot please God.

9 But you are not in the flesh; you are in the Spirit,*ᵃ* since the Spirit of God dwells in you. Anyone who does not have the Spirit of Christ does not belong to him. ¹⁰But if Christ is in you, though the body is dead because of sin, the Spirit*ᵃ* is life because of righteousness. ¹¹If the Spirit of him who raised Jesus from the dead dwells in you, he who raised Christ*ᵈ* from the dead will give life to your mortal bodies also through*ᵉ* his Spirit that dwells in you.

12 So then, brothers and sisters,*ᶠ* we are debtors, not to the flesh, to live according to the flesh— ¹³for if you live according to the flesh, you will die; but if by the Spirit you put to death the deeds of the body, you will live. ¹⁴For all who are led by the Spirit of God are children of God. ¹⁵For you did not receive a spirit of slavery to fall back into fear, but you have received a spirit of adoption. When we cry, "Abba!*ᵍ* Father!" ¹⁶it is that very Spirit bearing witness*ʰ* with our spirit that we are children of God, ¹⁷and if children,

"For all who are led by the Spirit of God are children of God."   Romans 8:14

ᵃ Or *spirit*   *ᵇ* Here the Greek word *you* is singular number; other ancient authorities read *me* or *us*   *ᶜ* Or *and as a sin offering*   *ᵈ* Other ancient authorities read *the Christ* or *Christ Jesus* or *Jesus Christ*   *ᵉ* Other ancient authorities read *on account of*   *ᶠ* Gk *brothers*   *ᵍ* Aramaic for *Father*   *ʰ* Or *¹⁵a spirit of adoption, by which we cry, "Abba! Father!" ¹⁶The Spirit itself bears witness* then heirs, heirs of God and joint heirs with Christ—if, in fact, we suffer with him so that we may also be glorified with him.

Future Glory

18 I consider that the sufferings of this present time are not worth comparing with the glory about to be revealed to us. [19]For the creation waits with eager longing for the revealing of the children of God; [20]for the creation was subjected to futility, not of its own will but by the will of the one who subjected it, in hope [21]that the creation itself will be set free from its bondage to decay and will obtain the freedom of the glory of the children of God. [22]We know that the whole creation has been groaning in labor pains until now; [23]and not only the creation, but we ourselves, who have the first fruits of the Spirit, groan inwardly while we wait for adoption, the redemption of our bodies. [24]For in[i] hope we were saved. Now hope that is seen is not hope. For who hopes[j] for what is seen? [25]But if we hope for what we do not see, we wait for it with patience.

26 Likewise the Spirit helps us in our weakness; for we do not know how to pray as we ought, but that very Spirit intercedes[k] with sighs too deep for words. [27]And God,[l] who searches the heart, knows what is the mind of the Spirit, because the Spirit[m] intercedes for the saints according to the will of God.[n]

28 We know that all things work together for good[o] for those who love God, who are called according to his purpose. [29]For those whom he foreknew he also predestined to be conformed to the image of his Son, in order that he might be the firstborn within a large family.[p] [30]And those whom he predestined he also called; and those whom he called he also justified; and those whom he justified he also glorified.

God's Love in Christ Jesus

31 What then are we to say about these things? If God is for us, who is against us? [32]He who did not withhold his own Son, but gave him up for all of us, will he not with him also give us everything else? [33]Who will bring any charge against God's elect? It is God who justifies. [34]Who is to condemn? It is Christ Jesus, who died, yes, who was raised, who is at the right hand of God, who indeed intercedes for us.[q] [35]Who will separate us from the love of Christ? Will hardship, or distress, or persecution, or famine, or nakedness, or peril, or sword? [36]As it is written,

"For your sake we are being killed all
    day long;
we are accounted as sheep to be
    slaughtered."

> Nothing can separate us from Christ's love—not even death. This is a very powerful promise!

[37]No, in all these things we are more than conquerors through him who loved us. [38]For I am convinced that neither death, nor life, nor angels, nor rulers, nor things present, nor things to come, nor powers, [39]nor height, nor depth, nor anything else in all creation, will be able to separate us from the love of God in Christ Jesus our Lord.

God's Election of Israel

9 I am speaking the truth in Christ— I am not lying; my conscience confirms it by the Holy Spirit— [2]I have great sorrow and unceasing anguish in my heart. [3]For I could wish that I myself were accursed and cut off from Christ for the sake of my own people,[r] my kindred according to the flesh. [4]They are Israelites, and to them belong the adoption, the glory, the covenants, the giving of the law, the worship, and the promises;

[i] Or by   [j] Other ancient authorities read *awaits*
[k] Other ancient authorities add *for us*   [l] Gk *the one*   [m] Gk *he* or *it*   [n] Gk *according to God*
[o] Other ancient authorities read *God makes all things work together for good*, or *in all things God works for good*   [p] Gk *among many brothers*
[q] Or *Is it Christ Jesus . . . for us?*   [r] Gk *my brothers*

5to them belong the patriarchs, and from them, according to the flesh, comes the Messiah,[s] who is over all, God blessed forever.[t] Amen.

6 It is not as though the word of God had failed. For not all Israelites truly belong to Israel, 7and not all of Abraham's children are his true descendants; but "It is through Isaac that descendants shall be named for you." 8This means that it is not the children of the flesh who are the children of God, but the children of the promise are counted as descendants. 9For this is what the promise said, "About this time I will return and Sarah shall have a son." 10Nor is that all; something similar happened to Rebecca when she had conceived children by one husband, our ancestor Isaac. 11Even before they had been born or had done anything good or bad (so that God's purpose of election might continue, 12not by works but by his call) she was told, "The elder shall serve the younger." 13As it is written,

"I have loved Jacob,
but I have hated Esau."

14 What then are we to say? Is there injustice on God's part? By no means! 15For he says to Moses,

"I will have mercy on whom I have mercy,
and I will have compassion on whom I have compassion."

16So it depends not on human will or exertion, but on God who shows mercy. 17For the scripture says to Pharaoh, "I have raised you up for the very purpose of showing my power in you, so that my name may be proclaimed in all the earth." 18So then he has mercy on whomever he chooses, and he hardens the heart of whomever he chooses.

God's Wrath and Mercy

19 You will say to me then, "Why then does he still find fault? For who can resist his will?" 20But who indeed are you, a human being, to argue with God? Will what is molded say to the one who molds

it, "Why have you made me like this?" 21Has the potter no right over the clay, to make out of the same lump one object for special use and another for ordinary use? 22What if God, desiring to show his wrath and to make known his power, has endured with much patience the objects of wrath that are made for destruction; 23and what if he has done so in order to make known the riches of his glory for the objects of mercy, which he has prepared beforehand for glory— 24including us whom he has called, not from the Jews only but also from the Gentiles? 25As indeed he says in Hō·sē´a,

"Those who were not my people I will
call 'my people,'
and her who was not beloved I will
call 'beloved.' "
26 "And in the very place where it was
said to them, 'You are not my
people,'
there they shall be called children of
the living God."

27 And Ī·sāi´ah cries out concerning Israel, "Though the number of the children of Israel were like the sand of the sea, only a remnant of them will be saved; 28for the Lord will execute his sentence on the earth quickly and decisively."[u] 29And as Ī·sāi´ah predicted,

"If the Lord of hosts had not left
survivors[v] to us,
we would have fared like Sod´om
and been made like Go·mor´rah."

Israel's Unbelief

30 What then are we to say? Gentiles, who did not strive for righteousness, have attained it, that is, righteousness through faith; 31but Israel, who did strive for the righteousness that is based on the law, did not succeed in fulfilling that law. 32Why not? Because they did not strive for it on

s Or the Christ   t Or Messiah, who is God over all, blessed forever; or Messiah. May he who is God over all be blessed forever   u Other ancient authorities read for he will finish his work and cut it short in righteousness, because the Lord will make the sentence shortened on the earth   v Or descendants; Gk seed the basis of faith, but as if it were based on works. They have stumbled over the stumbling stone, [33]as it is written,

"See, I am laying in Zion a stone that
will make people stumble, a rock
that will make them fall,
and whoever believes in him[w] will
not be put to shame."

10 Brothers and sisters,[x] my heart's desire and prayer to God for them is that they may be saved. [2]I can testify that they have a zeal for God, but it is not enlightened. [3]For, being ignorant of the righteousness that comes from God, and seeking to establish their own, they have not submitted to God's righteousness. [4]For Christ is the end of the law so that there may be righteousness for everyone who believes.

Salvation Is for All

5 Moses writes concerning the righteousness that comes from the law, that "the person who does these things will live by them." [6]But the righteousness that comes from faith says, "Do not say in your heart, 'Who will ascend into heaven?'" (that is, to bring Christ down) [7]"or 'Who will descend into the abyss?'" (that is, to bring Christ up from the dead). [8]But what does it say?

"The word is near you,
on your lips and in your heart"
(that is, the word of faith that we proclaim); [9]because[y] if you confess with your lips that Jesus is Lord and believe in your heart that God raised him from the dead, you will be saved. [10]For one believes with the heart and so is justified, and one confesses with the mouth and so is saved. [11]The scripture says, "No one who believes in him will be put to shame." [12]For there is no distinction between Jew and Greek; the same Lord is Lord of all and is generous to all who call on him. [13]For, "Everyone who calls on the name of the Lord shall be saved."

14 But how are they to call on one in whom they have not believed? And how are they to believe in one of whom they

"So faith comes from what is heard, and what is heard comes through the word of Christ."
Romans 10:17

have never heard? And how are they to hear without someone to proclaim him? [15]And how are they to proclaim him unless they are sent? As it is written, "How beautiful are the feet of those who bring good news!" [16]But not all have obeyed the good news;[z] for I·sāi´ah says, "Lord, who has believed our message?" [17]So faith comes from what is heard, and what is heard comes through the word of Christ.[a]

18 But I ask, have they not heard? Indeed they have; for

"Their voice has gone out to all the earth,
and their words to the ends of the world."

[19]Again I ask, did Israel not understand? First Moses says,

"I will make you jealous of those who
are not a nation;
with a foolish nation I will make
you angry."

[20]Then I·sāi´ah is so bold as to say,

"I have been found by those who did
not seek me;
I have shown myself to those who
did not ask for me."

[21]But of Israel he says, "All day long I have held out my hands to a disobedient and contrary people."

Paul reminds us that God works through us. Draw a picture of yourself, and think about your family, your friends, other people you know, and then the whole world. How can you be the messenger of God to others? Make notes on your drawing about how you might serve God with your head, mouth, hands, and feet.

---

[w] Or *trusts in it*   [x] Gk *Brothers*   [y] Or *namely, that*   [z] Or *gospel*   [a] Or *about Christ*; other ancient authorities read *of God*

Israel's Rejection Is Not Final

11 I ask, then, has God rejected his people? By no means! I myself am an Israelite, a descendant of Abraham, a member of the tribe of Benjamin. [2]God has not rejected his people whom he foreknew. Do you not know what the scripture says of E·li′jah, how he pleads with God against Israel? [3]"Lord, they have killed your prophets, they have demolished your altars; I alone am left, and they are seeking my life." [4]But what is the divine reply to him? "I have kept for myself seven thousand who have not bowed the knee to Ba′al." [5]So too at the present time there is a remnant, chosen by grace. [6]But if it is by grace, it is no longer on the basis of works, otherwise grace would no longer be grace.[b]

7 What then? Israel failed to obtain what it was seeking. The elect obtained it, but the rest were hardened, [8]as it is written,

"God gave them a sluggish spirit,
    eyes that would not see
    and ears that would not hear,
down to this very day."
[9]And David says,
"Let their table become a snare and a
    trap,
    a stumbling block and a retribution
    for them;
[10] let their eyes be darkened so that they
    cannot see,
    and keep their backs forever bent."

The Salvation of the Gentiles

11 So I ask, have they stumbled so as to fall? By no means! But through their stumbling[c] salvation has come to the Gentiles, so as to make Israel[d] jealous. [12]Now if their stumbling[c] means riches for the world, and if their defeat means riches for Gentiles, how much more will their full inclusion mean!

13 Now I am speaking to you Gentiles. Inasmuch then as I am an apostle to the Gentiles, I glorify my ministry [14]in order to make my own people[e] jealous, and thus save some of them. [15]For if their rejection is the reconciliation of the world, what will their acceptance be but life from the dead! [16]If the part of the dough offered as first fruits is holy, then the whole batch is holy; and if the root is holy, then the branches also are holy.

17 But if some of the branches were broken off, and you, a wild olive shoot, were grafted in their place to share the rich root[f] of the olive tree, [18]do not boast over the branches. If you do boast, remember that it is not you that support the root, but the root that supports you. [19]You will say, "Branches were broken off so that I might be grafted in." [20]That is true. They were broken off because of their unbelief, but you stand only through faith. So do not become proud, but stand in awe. [21]For if God did not spare the natural branches, perhaps he will not spare you.[g] [22]Note then the kindness and the severity of God: severity toward those who have fallen, but God's kindness toward you, provided you continue in his kindness; otherwise you also will be cut off. [23]And even those of Israel,[h] if they do not persist in unbelief, will be grafted in, for God has the power to graft them in again. [24]For if you have been cut from what is by nature a wild olive tree and grafted, contrary to nature, into a cultivated olive tree, how much more will these natural branches be grafted back into their own olive tree.

All Israel Will Be Saved

25 So that you may not claim to be wiser than you are, brothers and sisters,[i] I want you to understand this mystery: a hardening has come upon part of Israel, until the full number of the Gentiles has come in. [26]And so all Israel will be saved; as it is written,

[b] Other ancient authorities add *But if it is by works, it is no longer on the basis of grace, otherwise work would no longer be work*   [c] Gk *transgression*   [d] Gk *them*   [e] Gk *my flesh*   [f] Other ancient authorities read *the richness*   [g] Other ancient authorities read *neither will he spare you*   [h] Gk lacks *of Israel*   [i] Gk *brothers*

"Out of Zion will come the Deliverer;
he will banish ungodliness from
Jacob."
²⁷ "And this is my covenant with them,
when I take away their sins."
²⁸As regards the gospel they are enemies of
God^j for your sake; but as regards election
they are beloved, for the sake of their
ancestors; ²⁹for the gifts and the calling of
God are irrevocable. ³⁰Just as you were
once disobedient to God but have now
received mercy because of their disobedience, ³¹so they have now been disobedient
in order that, by the mercy shown to you,
they too may now^k receive mercy. ³²For
God has imprisoned all in disobedience so
that he may be merciful to all.

33 O the depth of the riches and wisdom and knowledge of God! How unsearchable are his judgments and how
inscrutable his ways!
³⁴ "For who has known the mind of the
Lord?
Or who has been his counselor?"
³⁵ "Or who has given a gift to him,
to receive a gift in return?"
³⁶For from him and through him and to
him are all things. To him be the glory forever. Amen.

The New Life in Christ

12 I appeal to you therefore, brothers and sisters,^l by the mercies
of God, to present your bodies as a living sacrifice, holy and acceptable to
God, which is your spiritual^m worship.
²Do not be conformed to this world,ⁿ
but be transformed by the renewing of
your minds, so that you may discern
what is the will of God—what is good
and acceptable and perfect.^o

3 For by the grace given to me I say to
everyone among you not to think of yourself more highly than you ought to think,
but to think with sober judgment, each
according to the measure of faith that God
has assigned. ⁴For as in one body we have
many members, and not all the members
have the same function, ⁵so we, who are
many, are one body in Christ, and indi-

> "O the depth of the riches
> and wisdom and knowl-
> edge of God! How un-
> searchable are his
> judgments and how
> inscrutable his ways!"
> **Romans 11:33**

vidually we are members one of another.
⁶We have gifts that differ according to the
grace given to us: prophecy, in proportion
to faith; ⁷ministry, in ministering; the
teacher, in teaching; ⁸the exhorter, in
exhortation; the giver, in generosity; the
leader, in diligence; the compassionate, in
cheerfulness.

Marks of the True Christian

9 Let love be genuine; hate what is evil,
hold fast to what is good; ¹⁰love one
another with mutual affection; outdo one
another in showing honor. ¹¹Do not lag in
zeal, be ardent in spirit, serve the Lord.^p
¹²Rejoice in hope, be patient in suffering,
persevere in prayer. ¹³Contribute to the
needs of the saints; extend hospitality to
strangers.

14 Bless those who persecute you;
bless and do not curse them. ¹⁵Rejoice
with those who rejoice, weep with those
who weep. ¹⁶Live in harmony with one

> "I appeal to you therefore, brothers
> and sisters, by the mercies of God, to
> present your bodies as a living sacri-
> fice, holy and acceptable to God,
> which is your spiritual worship. Do not
> be conformed to this world, but be
> transformed by the renewing of your
> minds, so that you may
> discern what is the will of
> God—what is good and
> acceptable and perfect."
> **Romans 12:1–2**

---

^j Gk lacks of God   ^k Other ancient authorities
lack now   ^l Gk brothers   ^m Or reasonable
ⁿ Gk age   ^o Or what is the good and acceptable
and perfect will of God   ^p Other ancient authorities read serve the opportune time

another; do not be haughty, but associate with the lowly;[q] do not claim to be wiser than you are. [17]Do not repay anyone evil for evil, but take thought for what is noble in the sight of all. [18]If it is possible, so far as it depends on you, live peaceably with all. [19]Beloved, never avenge yourselves, but leave room for the wrath of God;[r] for it is written, "Vengeance is mine, I will repay, says the Lord." [20]No, "if your enemies are hungry, feed them; if they are thirsty, give them something to drink; for by doing this you will heap burning coals on their heads." [21]Do not be overcome by evil, but overcome evil with good.

Being Subject to Authorities

13 Let every person be subject to the governing authorities; for there is no authority except from God, and those authorities that exist have been instituted by God. [2]Therefore whoever resists authority resists what God has appointed, and those who resist will incur judgment. [3]For rulers are not a terror to good conduct, but to bad. Do you wish to have no fear of the authority? Then do what is good, and you will receive its approval; [4]for it is God's servant for your good. But if you do what is wrong, you should be afraid, for the authority[s] does not bear the sword in vain! It is the servant of God to execute wrath on the wrongdoer. [5]Therefore one must be subject, not only because of wrath but also because of conscience. [6]For the same reason you also pay taxes, for the authorities are God's servants, busy with this very thing. [7]Pay to all what is due them—taxes to whom taxes are due, revenue to whom revenue is due, respect to whom respect is due, honor to whom honor is due.

> God's love is completely selfless. When we decide to be disciples of Jesus Christ, we commit ourselves to that kind of love. We begin to look for ways to do good things for all people—not just people who already love us. Paul tells us that we must try especially hard to do good things for people who do not like us! This is how God wants us to live.

Love for One Another

8 Owe no one anything, except to love one another; for the one who loves another has fulfilled the law. [9]The commandments, "You shall not commit adultery; You shall not murder; You shall not steal; You shall not covet"; and any other commandment, are summed up in this word, "Love your neighbor as yourself." [10]Love does no wrong to a neighbor; therefore, love is the fulfilling of the law.

An Urgent Appeal

11 Besides this, you know what time it is, how it is now the moment for you to wake from sleep. For salvation is nearer to us now than when we became believers; [12]the night is far gone, the day is near. Let us then lay aside the works of darkness and put on the armor of light; [13]let us live honorably as in the day, not in reveling and drunkenness, not in debauchery and licentiousness, not in quarreling and jealousy. [14]Instead, put on the Lord Jesus Christ, and make no provision for the flesh, to gratify its desires.

Do Not Judge Another

14 Welcome those who are weak in faith,[t] but not for the purpose of quarreling over opinions. [2]Some believe in eating anything, while the weak eat only vegetables. [3]Those who eat must not despise those who abstain, and those

> "Love does no wrong to a neighbor; therefore, love is the fulfilling of the law."
> Romans 13:10

[q] Or give yourselves to humble tasks   [r] Gk the wrath   [s] Gk it   [t] Or conviction

who abstain must not pass judgment on those who eat; for God has welcomed them. [4]Who are you to pass judgment on servants of another? It is before their own lord that they stand or fall. And they will be upheld, for the Lord[u] is able to make them stand.

5 Some judge one day to be better than another, while others judge all days to be alike. Let all be fully convinced in their own minds. [6]Those who observe the day, observe it in honor of the Lord. Also those who eat, eat in honor of the Lord, since they give thanks to God; while those who abstain, abstain in honor of the Lord and give thanks to God.

7 We do not live to ourselves, and we do not die to ourselves. [8]If we live, we live to the Lord, and if we die, we die to the Lord; so then, whether we live or whether we die, we are the Lord's. [9]For to this end Christ died and lived again, so that he might be Lord of both the dead and the living.

10 Why do you pass judgment on your brother or sister?[v] Or you, why do you despise your brother or sister?[v] For we will all stand before the judgment seat of God.[w] [11]For it is written,

"As I live, says the Lord, every knee
    shall bow to me,
and every tongue shall give praise
    to[x] God."

Because Jews and Gentiles (non-Jewish people) did not follow all the same rules (such as rules about eating certain foods), they sometimes argued about the correct way to live as Christ's followers. Paul asked both groups not to judge each other but to come together in faith to worship. God wants believers to treat one another with love, even though they may not always agree. This applies to disagreements everywhere, whether they are at church, school, or home.

[12]So then, each of us will be accountable to God.[y]

Do Not Make Another Stumble

13 Let us therefore no longer pass judgment on one another, but resolve instead never to put a stumbling block or hindrance in the way of another.[z] [14]I know and am persuaded in the Lord Jesus that nothing is unclean in itself; but it is unclean for anyone who thinks it unclean. [15]If your brother or sister[v] is being injured by what you eat, you are no longer walking in love. Do not let what you eat cause the ruin of one for whom Christ died. [16]So do not let your good be spoken of as evil. [17]For the kingdom of God is not food and drink but righteousness and peace and joy in the Holy Spirit. [18]The one who thus serves Christ is acceptable to God and has human approval. [19]Let us then pursue what makes for peace and for mutual upbuilding. [20]Do not, for the sake of food, destroy the work of God. Everything is indeed clean, but it is wrong for you to make others fall by what you eat; [21]it is good not to eat meat or drink wine or do anything that makes your brother or sister[v] stumble.[a] [22]The faith that you have, have as your own conviction before God. Blessed are those who have no reason to condemn themselves because of what they approve. [23]But those who have doubts are condemned if they eat, because they do not act from faith;[b] for whatever does not proceed from faith[b] is sin.[c]

Please Others, Not Yourselves

15 We who are strong ought to put up with the failings of the weak, and not to please ourselves. [2]Each of us must please our neighbor for the good purpose of building up the neighbor. [3]For Christ did not please himself; but,

---

[u] Other ancient authorities read *for God*   [v] Gk *brother*   [w] Other ancient authorities read *of Christ*   [x] Or *confess*   [y] Other ancient authorities lack *to God*   [z] Gk *of a brother*   [a] Other ancient authorities add *or be upset or be weakened*   [b] Or *conviction*   [c] Other authorities, some ancient, add here 16.25-27

as it is written, "The insults of those who insult you have fallen on me." [4]For whatever was written in former days was written for our instruction, so that by steadfastness and by the encouragement of the scriptures we might have hope. [5]May the God of steadfastness and encouragement grant you to live in harmony with one another, in accordance with Christ Jesus, [6]so that together you may with one voice glorify the God and Father of our Lord Jesus Christ.

The Gospel for Jews and Gentiles Alike

7 Welcome one another, therefore, just as Christ has welcomed you, for the glory of God. [8]For I tell you that Christ has become a servant of the circumcised on behalf of the truth of God in order that he might confirm the promises given to the patriarchs, [9]and in order that the Gentiles might glorify God for his mercy. As it is written,

"Therefore I will confess[d] you among
    the Gentiles,
    and sing praises to your name";
[10]and again he says,

"Rejoice, O Gentiles, with his people";
[11]and again,

"Praise the Lord, all you Gentiles,
    and let all the peoples praise him";
[12]and again Ī·saī'ah says,

"The root of Jesse shall come,
    the one who rises to rule the Gentiles;
    in him the Gentiles shall hope."
[13]May the God of hope fill you with all joy and peace in believing, so that you may abound in hope by the power of the Holy Spirit.

> "May the God of steadfastness and encouragement grant you to live in harmony with one another, in accordance with Christ Jesus, so that together you may with one voice glorify the God and Father of our Lord Jesus Christ."
> Romans 15:5–6

Paul's Reason for Writing So Boldly

14 I myself feel confident about you, my brothers and sisters,[e] that you yourselves are full of goodness, filled with all knowledge, and able to instruct one another. [15]Nevertheless on some points I have written to you rather boldly by way of reminder, because of the grace given me by God [16]to be a minister of Christ Jesus to the Gentiles in the priestly service of the gospel of God, so that the offering of the Gentiles may be acceptable, sanctified by the Holy Spirit. [17]In Christ Jesus, then, I have reason to boast of my work for God. [18]For I will not venture to speak of anything except what Christ has accomplished[f] through me to win obedience from the Gentiles, by word and deed, [19]by the power of signs and wonders, by the power of the Spirit of God,[g] so that from Jerusalem and as far around as Il·lyr´i·cum I have fully proclaimed the good news[h] of Christ. [20]Thus I make it my ambition to proclaim the good news,[h] not where Christ has already been named, so that I do not build on someone else's foundation, [21]but as it is written,

"Those who have never been told of
    him shall see,
    and those who have never heard of
    him shall understand."

Paul's Plan to Visit Rome

22 This is the reason that I have so often been hindered from coming to you. [23]But now, with no further place for me in these regions, I desire, as I have for many years, to come to you [24]when I go to Spain. For I do hope to see you on my journey and to be sent on by you, once I have enjoyed your company for a little while. [25]At present, however, I am going to Jerusalem in a ministry to the saints; [26]for Mac·e·dõ'ni·a and A·chā'i·a have been pleased to share their resources with

---

[d] Or thank   [e] Gk brothers   [f] Gk speak of those things that Christ has not accomplished   [g] Other ancient authorities read of the Spirit or of the Holy Spirit   [h] Or gospel

Paul believed in the power of prayer and asked the believers to pray for him so that he might share God's love with others. When do you pray? At night before you go to bed? In the morning when you get up? At mealtimes? During the day? Do you have a special prayer you use? Jesus taught that a person can pray to God at any time of day, using any words, about anything. Still, having a certain time to pray can help us form a good habit. If your family does not have a time to pray together, talk to them about when might be the best time to pray as a family. Then choose a time to pray on your own. Make a reminder to hang in your room.

the poor among the saints at Jerusalem. ²⁷They were pleased to do this, and indeed they owe it to them; for if the Gentiles have come to share in their spiritual blessings, they ought also to be of service to them in material things. ²⁸So, when I have completed this, and have delivered to them what has been collected,ⁱ I will set out by way of you to Spain; ²⁹and I know that when I come to you, I will come in the fullness of the blessingʲ of Christ.

30 I appeal to you, brothers and sisters,ᵏ by our Lord Jesus Christ and by the love of the Spirit, to join me in earnest prayer to God on my behalf, ³¹that I may be rescued from the unbelievers in Judea, and that my ministryˡ to Jerusalem may be acceptable to the saints, ³²so that by God's will I may come to you with joy and be refreshed in your company. ³³The God of peace be with all of you.ᵐ Amen.

Personal Greetings

16 I commend to you our sister Phoē´bē, a deaconⁿ of the church at Cen´chrē·ae, ²so that you may welcome her in the Lord as is fitting for the saints, and help her in whatever she may require from you, for she has been a

benefactor of many and of myself as well.

3 Greet Pris´ca and A·qui´la, who work with me in Christ Jesus, ⁴and who risked their necks for my life, to whom not only I give thanks, but also all the churches of the Gentiles. ⁵Greet also the church in their house. Greet my beloved E·paē´-ne·tus, who was the first convertᵒ in Asia for Christ. ⁶Greet Mary, who has worked very hard among you. ⁷Greet An-dron´i·cus and Jū´ni·a,ᵖ my relativesᑫ who were in prison with me; they are prominent among the apostles, and they were in Christ before I was. ⁸Greet Am·pli·ā´tus, my beloved in the Lord. ⁹Greet Ur·bā´nus, our co-worker in Christ, and my beloved Stā´chys. ¹⁰Greet Apel´lēs, who is approved in Christ. Greet those who belong to the family of Ar·is·tob´ū·lus. ¹¹Greet my relativeʳ He·rō´di·on. Greet those in the Lord who belong to the family of Nar·cis´sus. ¹²Greet those workers in the Lord, Trȳ·phaē´na and Trȳ·phō´sa. Greet the beloved Per´sis, who has worked hard in the Lord. ¹³Greet Rufus, chosen in the Lord; and greet his mother—a mother to me also. ¹⁴Greet A·syn´cri·tus, Phlē´gon, Her´mēs, Pat´ro·bas, Her´mas, and the brothers and sistersˢ who are with them. ¹⁵Greet Phi·lol´o·gus, Julia, Nē´re·us and his sister, and Ō·lym´pas, and all the saints who are with them. ¹⁶Greet one another with a holy kiss. All the churches of Christ greet you.

Final Instructions

17 I urge you, brothers and sisters,ˢ to keep an eye on those who cause dissensions and offenses, in opposition to the teaching that you have learned; avoid them.¹⁸For such people do not serve our Lord Christ, but their own appetites,ᵗ and

---

ⁱ Gk *have sealed to them this fruit*   ʲ Other ancient authorities add *of the gospel*   ᵏ Gk *brothers*   ˡ Other ancient authorities read *my bringing of a gift*   ᵐ One ancient authority adds 16.25-27 here   ⁿ Or *minister*   ᵒ Gk *first fruits*   ᵖ Or *Junias;* other ancient authorities read *Julia*   ᑫ Or *compatriots*   ʳ Or *compatriot*   ˢ Gk *brothers* by smooth talk and flattery they deceive the hearts of the simple-minded. [19]For while your obedience is known to all, so that I rejoice over you, I want you to be wise in what is good and guileless in what is evil. [20]The God of peace will shortly crush Satan under your feet. The grace of our Lord Jesus Christ be with you.[u]

21 Timothy, my co-worker, greets you; so do Lucius and Jason and Sō·sip'a·ter, my relatives.[v]

22 I Ter'ti·us, the writer of this letter, greet you in the Lord.[w]

23 Gā'i·us, who is host to me and to the whole church, greets you. E·ras'tus, the city treasurer, and our brother Quar'tus, greet you.[x]

Final Doxology

25 Now to God[y] who is able to strengthen you according to my gospel and the proclamation of Jesus Christ, according to the revelation of the mystery that was kept secret for long ages [26]but is now disclosed, and through the prophetic writings is made known to all the Gentiles, according to the command of the eternal God, to bring about the obedience of faith— [27]to the only wise God, through Jesus Christ, to whom[z] be the glory forever! Amen.[a]

---

[t] Gk their own belly   [u] Other ancient authorities lack this sentence   [v] Or compatriots   [w] Or I Tertius, writing this letter in the Lord, greet you   [x] Other ancient authorities add verse 24, The grace of our Lord Jesus Christ be with all of you. Amen.   [y] Gk the one   [z] Other ancient authorities lack to whom. The verse then reads, to the only wise God be the glory through Jesus Christ forever. Amen.   [a] Other ancient authorities lack 16.25-27 or include it after 14.23 or 15.33; others put verse 24 after verse 27

1 Corinthians

Paul preached and had started a church in the city of Corinth, Greece. Later, while he was preaching in the city of Ephesus, about 51 AD, he wrote at least four letters (maybe more) to the Christians at Corinth. We do not have copies of the original letters Paul wrote (nor do we have them from any of the other letter writers), but they were written to encourage new Christians. These letters were fragile, and as they began to show wear, scribes copied them down to preserve them. These scribes may have rearranged and combined the letters into the two letters that we now call First and Second Corinthians.

Paul wrote chapters 1–4 to help the Corinthian Christians overcome argu-

ments among the members of the church. Some were bragging about who had baptized them. Paul said that all spiritual blessings come from God. Preachers and missionaries are simply helpers for God. Chapters 5–11 gave careful guidance to some of the questions the Corinthians had about how Christians should live. Chapters 12–14 contain teaching about spiritual gifts—the ability to teach, to preach, to heal the sick, and so on. Chapter 13 is a poem about Christian love. Paul said that without true love, all actions count for nothing. Chapter 15 shows Paul's belief that true Christians have eternal life through the resurrection of Jesus Christ. Chapter 16 contains final words and greetings.

1 Corinthians 1:1–2

Salutation

1 Paul, called to be an apostle of Christ Jesus by the will of God, and our brother Sos´the·nēs,

2 To the church of God that is in Corinth, to those who are sanctified in Christ Jesus, called to be saints, together with all those who in every place call on the name of our Lord Jesus Christ, both their Lord[a] and ours:

3 Grace to you and peace from God our Father and the Lord Jesus Christ.

4 I give thanks to my[b] God always for you because of the grace of God that has been given you in Christ Jesus, 5for in every way you have been enriched in him, in speech and knowledge of every kind— 6just as the testimony of[c] Christ has been strengthened among you— 7so that you are not lacking in any spiritual gift as you wait for the revealing of our Lord Jesus Christ. 8He will also strengthen you to the end, so that you may be blameless on the day of our Lord Jesus Christ. 9God is faithful; by him you were called into the fellowship of his Son, Jesus Christ our Lord.

> Corinth's location made it an important trading center between Rome and the East. Corinth was famous for its bronze, pottery, and shipbuilding. The Romans destroyed Corinth in 146 BC, and Julius Caesar restored it in 44 BC. He brought in a large number of people from all over the known world to live there. The Corinthian population was made up of people from all over the Roman empire. These people brought their own customs to the port city. This diversity was also reflected in the Corinthian church. It should not be a surprise that sometimes these new Christians had trouble getting along.

Divisions in the Church

10 Now I appeal to you, brothers and sisters,[d] by the name of our Lord Jesus Christ, that all of you be in agreement and that there be no divisions among you, but that you be united in the same mind and the same purpose. 11For it has been reported to me by Chloe's people that there are quarrels among you, my brothers and sisters.[e] 12What I mean is that each of you says, "I belong to Paul," or "I belong to A·pol´los," or "I belong to Cē´phas," or "I belong to Christ." 13Has Christ been divided? Was Paul crucified for you? Or were you baptized in the name of Paul? 14I thank God[f] that I baptized none of you except Cris´pus and Gā´i·us, 15so that no one can say that you were baptized in my name. 16(I did baptize also the household of Steph´a·nas; beyond that, I do not know whether I baptized anyone else.) 17For Christ did not send me to baptize but to proclaim the gospel, and not with eloquent wisdom, so that the cross of Christ might not be emptied of its power.

Christ the Power and Wisdom of God

18 For the message about the cross is foolishness to those who are perishing, but to us who are being saved it is the power of God. 19For it is written,

"I will destroy the wisdom of the wise,

and the discernment of the discerning I will thwart."

20Where is the one who is wise? Where is the scribe? Where is the debater of this age? Has not God made foolish the wisdom of the world? 21For since, in the wisdom of God, the world did not know God through wisdom, God decided, through the foolishness of our proclamation, to save those who believe. 22For Jews demand signs and Greeks desire wisdom, 23but we proclaim Christ crucified, a

---

[a] Gk theirs   [b] Other ancient authorities lack my
[c] Or to   [d] Gk brothers   [e] Gk my brothers
[f] Other ancient authorities read I am thankful

"For God's foolishness is wiser than human wisdom, and God's weakness is stronger than human strength." 1 Corinthians 1:25

stumbling block to Jews and foolishness to Gentiles, [24]but to those who are the called, both Jews and Greeks, Christ the power of God and the wisdom of God. [25]For God's foolishness is wiser than human wisdom, and God's weakness is stronger than human strength.

26 Consider your own call, brothers and sisters:[g] not many of you were wise by human standards,[h] not many were powerful, not many were of noble birth. [27]But God chose what is foolish in the world to shame the wise; God chose what is weak in the world to shame the strong; [28]God chose what is low and despised in the world, things that are not, to reduce to nothing things that are, [29]so that no one[i] might boast in the presence of God. [30]He is the source of your life in Christ Jesus, who became for us wisdom from God, and righteousness and sanctification and redemption, [31]in order that, as it is written, "Let the one who boasts, boast in[j] the Lord."

Proclaiming Christ Crucified

2 When I came to you, brothers and sisters,[k] I did not come proclaiming the mystery[l] of God to you in lofty words or wisdom. [2]For I decided to know nothing among you except Jesus Christ, and him crucified. [3]And I came to you in weakness and in fear and in much trembling. [4]My speech and my proclamation were not with plausible words of wisdom,[m] but with a demonstration of the Spirit and of power, [5]so that your faith might rest not on human wisdom but on the power of God.

The True Wisdom of God

6 Yet among the mature we do speak wisdom, though it is not a wisdom of this age or of the rulers of this age, who are doomed to perish. [7]But we speak God's wisdom, secret and hidden, which God decreed before the ages for our glory. [8]None of the rulers of this age understood this; for if they had, they would not have crucified the Lord of glory. [9]But, as it is written,

"What no eye has seen, nor ear heard,
    nor the human heart conceived,
what God has prepared for those
    who love him"—

[10]these things God has revealed to us through the Spirit; for the Spirit searches everything, even the depths of God. [11]For what human being knows what is truly human except the human spirit that is within? So also no one comprehends what is truly God's except the Spirit of God. [12]Now we have received not the spirit of the world, but the Spirit that is from God, so that we may understand the gifts bestowed on us by God. [13]And we speak of these things in words not taught by human wisdom but taught by the Spirit, interpreting spiritual things to those who are spiritual.[n]

14 Those who are unspiritual[o] do not receive the gifts of God's Spirit, for they are foolishness to them, and they are unable to understand them because they are spiritually discerned. [15]Those who are spiritual discern all things, and they are themselves subject to no one else's scrutiny.
16 "For who has known the mind of the Lord
    so as to instruct him?"
But we have the mind of Christ.

On Divisions in the Corinthian Church

3 And so, brothers and sisters,[k] I could not speak to you as spiritual people, but rather as people of the flesh,

[g] Gk brothers [h] Gk according to the flesh [i] Gk no flesh [j] Or of [k] Gk brothers [l] Other ancient authorities read testimony [m] Other ancient authorities read the persuasiveness of wisdom [n] Or interpreting spiritual things in spiritual language, or comparing spiritual things with spiritual [o] Or natural

as infants in Christ. ²I fed you with milk, not solid food, for you were not ready for solid food. Even now you are still not ready, ³for you are still of the flesh. For as long as there is jealousy and quarreling among you, are you not of the flesh, and behaving according to human inclinations? ⁴For when one says, "I belong to Paul," and another, "I belong to A·pol′los," are you not merely human?

5 What then is A·pol′los? What is Paul? Servants through whom you came to believe, as the Lord assigned to each. ⁶I planted, A·pol′los watered, but God gave the growth. ⁷So neither the one who plants nor the one who waters is anything, but only God who gives the growth. ⁸The one who plants and the one who waters have a common purpose, and each will receive wages according to the labor of each. ⁹For we are God's servants, working together; you are God's field, God's building.

10 According to the grace of God given to me, like a skilled master builder I laid a foundation, and someone else is building on it. Each builder must choose with care how to build on it. ¹¹For no one can lay any foundation other than the one that has been laid; that foundation is Jesus Christ. ¹²Now if anyone builds on the foundation with gold, silver, precious stones, wood, hay, straw— ¹³the work of each builder will become visible, for the Day will disclose it, because it will be revealed with fire, and the fire will test what sort of work each has done. ¹⁴If what has been built on the foundation survives, the builder will receive a reward. ¹⁵If the work is burned up, the builder will suffer loss; the builder will be saved, but only as through fire.

> "For we are God's servants, working together; you are God's field, God's building." 1 Corinthians 3:9

16 Do you not know that you are God's temple and that God's Spirit dwells in you?ᵖ ¹⁷If anyone destroys God's temple, God will destroy that person. For God's temple is holy, and you are that temple.

18 Do not deceive yourselves. If you think that you are wise in this age, you should become fools so that you may become wise. ¹⁹For the wisdom of this world is foolishness with God. For it is written,

> "He catches the wise in their
> craftiness,"

²⁰and again,

> "The Lord knows the thoughts
> of the wise,
> that they are futile."

²¹So let no one boast about human leaders. For all things are yours, ²²whether Paul or A·pol′los or Ce′phas or the world or life or death or the present or the future—all belong to you, ²³and you belong to Christ, and Christ belongs to God.

The Ministry of the Apostles

4 Think of us in this way, as servants of Christ and stewards of God's

Paul told the Christians at Corinth that they were to work for Christ as servants and stewards. Servants are helpers and caregivers. Jesus showed us the best example of how to be a servant when he washed the disciples' feet (see John 13:1–17). Stewards are managers of a household. God calls us to care for the earth and all that is in it. This includes not only other people, but also all of God's creation. What are some ways that you can be a servant and a steward?

The wonderful thing about becoming a Christian is that we become a part of God's family. No matter how we came to be a Christian or who showed us the way, the end result is that we belong to Christ and Christ belongs to God!

ᵖ In verses 16 and 17 the Greek word for *you* is plural

mysteries. [2]Moreover, it is required of stewards that they be found trustworthy. [3]But with me it is a very small thing that I should be judged by you or by any human court. I do not even judge myself. [4]I am not aware of anything against myself, but I am not thereby acquitted. It is the Lord who judges me. [5]Therefore do not pronounce judgment before the time, before the Lord comes, who will bring to light the things now hidden in darkness and will disclose the purposes of the heart. Then each one will receive commendation from God.

[6]I have applied all this to A·pol´los and myself for your benefit, brothers and sisters,[q] so that you may learn through us the meaning of the saying, "Nothing beyond what is written," so that none of you will be puffed up in favor of one against another. [7]For who sees anything different in you?[r] What do you have that you did not receive? And if you received it, why do you boast as if it were not a gift?

[8]Already you have all you want! Already you have become rich! Quite apart from us you have become kings! Indeed, I wish that you had become kings, so that we might be kings with you! [9]For I think that God has exhibited us apostles as last of all, as though sentenced to death, because we have become a spectacle to the world, to angels and to mortals. [10]We are fools for the sake of Christ, but you are wise in Christ. We are weak, but you are strong. You are held in honor, but we in disrepute. [11]To the present hour we are hungry and thirsty, we are poorly clothed and beaten and homeless, [12]and we grow weary from the work of our own hands. When reviled, we bless; when persecuted, we endure; [13]when slandered, we speak kindly. We have become like the rubbish of the world, the dregs of all things, to this very day.

Fatherly Admonition

[14]I am not writing this to make you ashamed, but to admonish you as my beloved children. [15]For though you might have ten thousand guardians in Christ,

In Bible times, bread was an important food. One of the ingredients used to make bread is yeast, which makes the dough rise. Each day the baker kept a pinch of that day's dough to use as a "starter" for the next day. That little pinch would cause the whole batch of new dough to rise. Paul warned the Corinthians that even a tiny bit of the evil left from their old lives could ruin their new lives. Clean out malice and evil, he said, and replace them with sincerity and truth.

you do not have many fathers. Indeed, in Christ Jesus I became your father through the gospel. [16]I appeal to you, then, be imitators of me. [17]For this reason I sent[s] you Timothy, who is my beloved and faithful child in the Lord, to remind you of my ways in Christ Jesus, as I teach them everywhere in every church. [18]But some of you, thinking that I am not coming to you, have become arrogant. [19]But I will come to you soon, if the Lord wills, and I will find out not the talk of these arrogant people but their power. [20]For the kingdom of God depends not on talk but on power. [21]What would you prefer? Am I to come to you with a stick, or with love in a spirit of gentleness?

Sexual Immorality Defiles the Church

5 It is actually reported that there is sexual immorality among you, and of a kind that is not found even among pagans; for a man is living with his father's wife. [2]And you are arrogant! Should you not rather have mourned, so that he who has done this would have been removed from among you?

[3]For though absent in body, I am present in spirit; and as if present I have already pronounced judgment [4]in the

[q] Gk brothers   [r] Or Who makes you different from another?   [s] Or am sending

name of the Lord Jesus on the man who has done such a thing.[t] When you are assembled, and my spirit is present with the power of our Lord Jesus, [5]you are to hand this man over to Satan for the destruction of the flesh, so that his spirit may be saved in the day of the Lord.[u]

6 Your boasting is not a good thing. Do you not know that a little yeast leavens the whole batch of dough? [7]Clean out the old yeast so that you may be a new batch, as you really are unleavened. For our paschal lamb, Christ, has been sacrificed. [8]Therefore, let us celebrate the festival, not with the old yeast, the yeast of malice and evil, but with the unleavened bread of sincerity and truth.

Sexual Immorality Must Be Judged

9 I wrote to you in my letter not to associate with sexually immoral persons— [10]not at all meaning the immoral of this world, or the greedy and robbers, or idolaters, since you would then need to go out of the world. [11]But now I am writing to you not to associate with anyone who bears the name of brother or sister[v] who is sexually immoral or greedy, or is an idolater, reviler, drunkard, or robber. Do not even eat with such a one. [12]For what have I to do with judging those outside? Is it not those who are inside that you are to judge? [13]God will judge those outside. "Drive out the wicked person from among you."

Lawsuits among Believers

6 When any of you has a grievance against another, do you dare to take it to court before the unrighteous, instead of taking it before the saints? [2]Do you not know that the saints will judge the world? And if the world is to be judged by you, are you incompetent to try trivial cases? [3]Do you not know that we are to judge angels—to say nothing of ordinary matters? [4]If you have ordinary cases, then, do you appoint as judges those who have no standing in the church? [5]I say this to your shame.

Can it be that there is no one among you wise enough to decide between one believer[v] and another, [6]but a believer[v] goes to court against a believer[v]—and before unbelievers at that?

7 In fact, to have lawsuits at all with one another is already a defeat for you. Why not rather be wronged? Why not rather be defrauded? [8]But you yourselves wrong and defraud—and believers[w] at that.

9 Do you not know that wrongdoers will not inherit the kingdom of God? Do not be deceived! Fornicators, idolaters, adulterers, male prostitutes, sodomites, [10]thieves, the greedy, drunkards, revilers, robbers—none of these will inherit the kingdom of God. [11]And this is what some of you used to be. But you were washed, you were sanctified, you were justified in the name of the Lord Jesus Christ and in the Spirit of our God.

Glorify God in Body and Spirit

12 "All things are lawful for me," but not all things are beneficial. "All things are lawful for me," but I will not be dominated by anything. [13]"Food is meant for the stomach and the stomach for food,"[x] and God will destroy both one and the other. The body is meant not for fornication but for the Lord, and the Lord for the body. [14]And God raised the Lord and will also raise us by his power. [15]Do you not know that your bodies are members of Christ? Should I therefore take the members of Christ and make them members of a prostitute? Never! [16]Do you not know that whoever is united to a prostitute becomes one body with her? For it is said, "The two shall be one flesh." [17]But anyone united to the Lord becomes one spirit with him. [18]Shun fornication! Every sin that a person commits is outside the body; but the fornicator sins against the body itself. [19]Or do you not know that your body is a temple[y]

---

[t] Or *on the man who has done such a thing in the name of the Lord Jesus*   [u] Other ancient authorities add *Jesus*   [v] Gk *brother*   [w] Gk *brothers*   [x] The quotation may extend to the word *other*   [y] Or *sanctuary*

"Or do you not know that your body is a temple of the Holy Spirit within you, which you have from God, and that you are not your own? For you were bought with a price; therefore glorify God in your body."   1 Corinthians 6:19

of the Holy Spirit within you, which you have from God, and that you are not your own? ²⁰For you were bought with a price; therefore glorify God in your body.

Directions concerning Marriage

7 Now concerning the matters about which you wrote: "It is well for a man not to touch a woman." ²But because of cases of sexual immorality, each man should have his own wife and each woman her own husband. ³The husband should give to his wife her conjugal rights, and likewise the wife to her husband. ⁴For the wife does not have authority over her own body, but the husband does; likewise the husband does not have authority over his own body, but the wife does. ⁵Do not deprive one another except perhaps by agreement for a set time, to devote yourselves to prayer, and then come together again, so that Satan may not tempt you because of your lack of self-control. ⁶This I say by way of concession, not of command. ⁷I wish that all were as I myself am. But each has a particular gift from God, one having one kind and another a different kind.

8 To the unmarried and the widows I say that it is well for them to remain unmarried as I am. ⁹But if they are not practicing self-control, they should marry. For it is better to marry than to be aflame with passion.

10 To the married I give this command—not I but the Lord—that the wife should not separate from her husband ¹¹(but if she does separate, let her remain unmarried or else be reconciled to her husband), and that the husband should not divorce his wife.

12 To the rest I say—I and not the Lord—that if any believer^z has a wife who is an unbeliever, and she consents to live with him, he should not divorce her. ¹³And if any woman has a husband who is an unbeliever, and he consents to live with her, she should not divorce him. ¹⁴For the unbelieving husband is made holy through his wife, and the unbelieving wife is made holy through her husband. Otherwise, your children would be unclean, but as it is, they are holy. ¹⁵But if the unbelieving partner separates, let it be so; in such a case the brother or sister is not bound. It is to peace that God has called you.^{a} ¹⁶Wife, for all you know, you might save your husband. Husband, for all you know, you might save your wife.

The Life That the Lord Has Assigned

17 However that may be, let each of you lead the life that the Lord has assigned, to which God called you. This is my rule in all the churches. ¹⁸Was anyone at the time of his call already circumcised? Let him not seek to remove the marks of circumcision. Was anyone at the time of his call uncircumcised? Let him not seek circumcision. ¹⁹Circumcision is nothing, and uncircumcision is nothing; but obeying the commandments of God is everything. ²⁰Let each of you remain in the condition in which you were called.

21 Were you a slave when called? Do not be concerned about it. Even if you can gain your freedom, make use of your present condition now more than ever.^{b} ²²For whoever was called in the Lord as a slave is a freed person belonging to the Lord, just as whoever was free when called is a slave of Christ. ²³You were bought with a price; do not become slaves of human masters. ²⁴In whatever condition you were called, brothers and sisters,^{c} there remain with God.

---

^{z} Gk brother ^{a} Other ancient authorities read us
^{b} Or avail yourself of the opportunity ^{c} Gk brothers

The Unmarried and the Widows

25 Now concerning virgins, I have no command of the Lord, but I give my opinion as one who by the Lord's mercy is trustworthy. [26]I think that, in view of the impending[d] crisis, it is well for you to remain as you are. [27]Are you bound to a wife? Do not seek to be free. Are you free from a wife? Do not seek a wife. [28]But if you marry, you do not sin, and if a virgin marries, she does not sin. Yet those who marry will experience distress in this life,[e] and I would spare you that. [29]I mean, brothers and sisters,[f] the appointed time has grown short; from now on, let even those who have wives be as though they had none, [30]and those who mourn as though they were not mourning, and those who rejoice as though they were not rejoicing, and those who buy as though they had no possessions, [31]and those who deal with the world as though they had no dealings with it. For the present form of this world is passing away.

32 I want you to be free from anxieties. The unmarried man is anxious about the affairs of the Lord, how to please the Lord; [33]but the married man is anxious about the affairs of the world, how to please his wife, [34]and his interests are divided. And the unmarried woman and the virgin are anxious about the affairs of the Lord, so that they may be holy in body and spirit; but the married woman is anxious about the affairs of the world, how to please her husband. [35]I say this for your own benefit, not to put any restraint upon you, but to promote good order and unhindered devotion to the Lord.

36 If anyone thinks that he is not behaving properly toward his fiancée,[g] if his passions are strong, and so it has to be, let him marry as he wishes; it is no sin. Let them marry. [37]But if someone stands firm in his resolve, being under no necessity but having his own desire under control, and has determined in his own mind to keep her as his fiancée,[g] he will do well. [38]So then, he who marries his fiancée[g] does

An idol was an image of a god made out of wood, stone, or metal—or any other symbol that was an object of worship. People who worshiped idols would sacrifice animals at temples dedicated to the gods. Later, the meat that had been sacrificed was sold in the market. Corinthian Christians were not sure whether or not it was acceptable to buy and eat that meat. Paul said to do as their hearts led them—if it bothered them to eat the meat, then they should not. Otherwise it was okay. But Paul reminded the people who had been Christians longer that it was important to think about their actions, so that people who had not been Christians very long would have a good example. What do you do to set an example for others?

well; and he who refrains from marriage will do better.

39 A wife is bound as long as her husband lives. But if the husband dies,[h] she is free to marry anyone she wishes, only in the Lord. [40]But in my judgment she is more blessed if she remains as she is. And I think that I too have the Spirit of God.

Food Offered to Idols

8 Now concerning food sacrificed to idols: we know that "all of us possess knowledge." Knowledge puffs up, but love builds up. [2]Anyone who claims to know something does not yet have the necessary knowledge; [3]but anyone who loves God is known by him.

4 Hence, as to the eating of food offered to idols, we know that "no idol in the world really exists," and that "there is no God but one." [5]Indeed, even though there may be so-called gods in heaven or on earth—as in fact there are many gods and many lords— [6]yet for us there is one God,

[d] Or *present*   [e] Gk *in the flesh*   [f] Gk *brothers*
[g] Gk *virgin*   [h] Gk *falls asleep*

the Father, from whom are all things and for whom we exist, and one Lord, Jesus Christ, through whom are all things and through whom we exist.

7 It is not everyone, however, who has this knowledge. Since some have become so accustomed to idols until now, they still think of the food they eat as food offered to an idol; and their conscience, being weak, is defiled. [8]"Food will not bring us close to God."[i] We are no worse off if we do not eat, and no better off if we do. [9]But take care that this liberty of yours does not somehow become a stumbling block to the weak. [10]For if others see you, who possess knowledge, eating in the temple of an idol, might they not, since their conscience is weak, be encouraged to the point of eating food sacrificed to idols? [11]So by your knowledge those weak believers for whom Christ died are destroyed.[j] [12]But when you thus sin against members of your family,[k] and wound their conscience when it is weak, you sin against Christ. [13]Therefore, if food is a cause of their falling,[l] I will never eat meat, so that I may not cause one of them[m] to fall.

The Rights of an Apostle

9 Am I not free? Am I not an apostle? Have I not seen Jesus our Lord? Are you not my work in the Lord? [2]If I am not an apostle to others, at least I am to you; for you are the seal of my apostleship in the Lord.

3 This is my defense to those who would examine me. [4]Do we not have the right to our food and drink? [5]Do we not have the right to be accompanied by a believing wife,[n] as do the other apostles and the brothers of the Lord and Cē′phas? [6]Or is it only Bar′na·bas and I who have no right to refrain from working for a living? [7]Who at any time pays the expenses for doing military service? Who plants a vineyard and does not eat any of its fruit? Or who tends a flock and does not get any of its milk?

8 Do I say this on human authority? Does not the law also say the same? [9]For it is written in the law of Moses, "You shall not muzzle an ox while it is treading out the grain." Is it for oxen that God is concerned? [10]Or does he not speak entirely for our sake? It was indeed written for our sake, for whoever plows should plow in hope and whoever threshes should thresh in hope of a share in the crop. [11]If we have sown spiritual good among you, is it too much if we reap your material benefits? [12]If others share this rightful claim on you, do not we still more?

Nevertheless, we have not made use of this right, but we endure anything rather than put an obstacle in the way of the gospel of Christ. [13]Do you not know that those who are employed in the temple service get their food from the temple, and those who serve at the altar share in what is sacrificed on the altar? [14]In the same way, the Lord commanded that those who proclaim the gospel should get their living by the gospel.

15 But I have made no use of any of these rights, nor am I writing this so that they may be applied in my case. Indeed, I would rather die than that—no one will deprive me of my ground for boasting! [16]If I proclaim the gospel, this gives me no ground for boasting, for an obligation is laid on me, and woe to me if I do not proclaim the gospel! [17]For if I do this of my own will, I have a reward; but if not of my own will, I am entrusted with a commission. [18]What then is my reward? Just this: that in my proclamation I may make the gospel free of charge, so as not to make full use of my rights in the gospel.

19 For though I am free with respect to all, I have made myself a slave to all, so that I might win more of them. [20]To the Jews I became as a Jew, in order to win Jews. To those under the law I became as one under the law (though I myself am not under the law) so that I might win those under the

---

[i] The quotation may extend to the end of the verse
[j] Gk the weak brother . . . is destroyed   [k] Gk against the brothers   [l] Gk my brother's falling   [m] Gk cause my brother   [n] Gk a sister as wife

law. ²¹To those outside the law I became as one outside the law (though I am not free from God's law but am under Christ's law) so that I might win those outside the law. ²²To the weak I became weak, so that I might win the weak. I have become all things to all people, that I might by all means save some. ²³I do it all for the sake of the gospel, so that I may share in its blessings.

24 Do you not know that in a race the runners all compete, but only one receives the prize? Run in such a way that you may win it. ²⁵Athletes exercise self-control in all things; they do it to receive a perishable wreath, but we an imperishable one. ²⁶So I do not run aimlessly, nor do I box as though beating the air; ²⁷but I punish my body and enslave it, so that after proclaiming to others I myself should not be disqualified.

Warnings from Israel's History

10 I do not want you to be unaware, brothers and sisters,^o that our ancestors were all under the cloud, and all passed through the sea, ²and all were baptized into Moses in the cloud and in the sea, ³and all ate the same spiritual food, ⁴and all drank the same spiritual drink. For they drank from the spiritual rock that followed them, and the rock was Christ. ⁵Nevertheless, God was not pleased with most of them, and they were struck down in the wilderness.

6 Now these things occurred as examples for us, so that we might not desire evil as they did. ⁷Do not become idolaters as some of them did; as it is written, "The people sat down to eat and drink, and they rose up to play." ⁸We must not indulge in sexual immorality as some of them did, and twenty-three thousand fell in a single day. ⁹We must not put Christ^p to the test, as some of them did, and were destroyed by serpents. ¹⁰And do not complain as some of them did, and were destroyed by the destroyer. ¹¹These things happened to them to serve as an example, and they were written down to instruct us, on

> "No testing has overtaken you that is not common to everyone. God is faithful, and he will not let you be tested beyond your strength, but with the testing he will also provide the way out so that you may be able to endure it."
> **1 Corinthians 10:13**

whom the ends of the ages have come. ¹²So if you think you are standing, watch out that you do not fall. ¹³No testing has overtaken you that is not common to everyone. God is faithful, and he will not let you be tested beyond your strength, but with the testing he will also provide the way out so that you may be able to endure it.

14 Therefore, my dear friends,^q flee from the worship of idols. ¹⁵I speak as to sensible people; judge for yourselves what I say. ¹⁶The cup of blessing that we bless, is it not a sharing in the blood of Christ? The bread that we break, is it not a sharing in the body of Christ? ¹⁷Because there is one bread, we who are many are one body, for we all partake of the one bread. ¹⁸Consider the people of Israel;^r are not those who eat the sacrifices partners in the altar? ¹⁹What do I imply then? That food sacrificed to idols is anything, or that an idol is anything? ²⁰No, I imply that what pagans sacrifice, they sacrifice to demons and not to God. I do not want you to be partners with demons. ²¹You cannot drink the cup of the Lord and the cup of demons. You cannot partake of the table of the Lord and the

> "Do you not know that in a race the runners all compete, but only one receives the prize? Run in such a way that you may win it."
> **1 Corinthians 9:24**

---

^o Gk brothers　　^p Other ancient authorities read the Lord　　^q Gk my beloved　　^r Gk Israel according to the flesh

table of demons. ²²Or are we provoking the Lord to jealousy? Are we stronger than he?

Do All to the Glory of God

23 "All things are lawful," but not all things are beneficial. "All things are lawful," but not all things build up. ²⁴Do not seek your own advantage, but that of the other. ²⁵Eat whatever is sold in the meat market without raising any question on the ground of conscience, ²⁶for "the earth and its fullness are the Lord's." ²⁷If an unbeliever invites you to a meal and you are disposed to go, eat whatever is set before you without raising any question on the ground of conscience. ²⁸But if someone says to you, "This has been offered in sacrifice," then do not eat it, out of consideration for the one who informed you, and for the sake of conscience— ²⁹I mean the other's conscience, not your own. For why should my liberty be subject to the judgment of someone else's conscience? ³⁰If I partake with thankfulness, why should I be denounced because of that for which I give thanks?

31 So, whether you eat or drink, or whatever you do, do everything for the glory of God. ³²Give no offense to Jews or to Greeks or to the church of God, ³³just as I try to please everyone in everything I do, not seeking my own advantage, but that of many, so that that may be saved. ¹Be imitators of me, as I am of Christ.

11

Head Coverings

2 I commend you because you remember me in everything and maintain the traditions just as I handed them on to you. ³But I want you to understand that Christ is the head of every man, and the husband^s is the head of his wife,^t and God is the head of Christ. ⁴Any man who prays or prophesies with something on his head

disgraces his head, ⁵but any woman who prays or prophesies with her head unveiled disgraces her head—it is one and the same thing as having her head shaved. ⁶For if a woman will not veil herself, then she should cut off her hair; but if it is disgraceful for a woman to have her hair cut off or to be shaved, she should wear a veil. ⁷For a man ought not to have his head veiled, since he is the image and reflection^u of God; but woman is the reflection^u of man. ⁸Indeed, man was not made from woman, but woman from man. ⁹Neither was man created for the sake of woman, but woman for the sake of man. ¹⁰For this reason a woman ought to have a symbol of^v authority on her head,^w because of the angels. ¹¹Nevertheless, in the Lord woman is not independent of man or man independent of woman. ¹²For just as woman came from man, so man comes through woman; but all things come from God. ¹³Judge for yourselves: is it proper for a woman to pray to God with her head unveiled? ¹⁴Does not nature itself teach you that if a man wears long hair, it is degrading to him, ¹⁵but if a woman has long hair, it is her glory? For her hair is given to her for a covering. ¹⁶But if anyone is disposed to be contentious—we have no such custom, nor do the churches of God.

Abuses at the Lord's Supper

17 Now in the following instructions I do not commend you, because when you come together it is not for the better but for the worse. ¹⁸For, to begin with, when you come together as a church, I hear that there are divisions among you; and to some extent I believe it. ¹⁹Indeed, there have to be factions among you, for only so will it become clear who among you are genuine. ²⁰When you come together, it is not really to eat the Lord's supper. ²¹For when the time comes to eat, each of you

"Do everything for the glory of God."
1 Corinthians 10:31*b*

^s The same Greek word means *man* or *husband*
^t Or *head of the woman*   ^u Or *glory*   ^v Gk lacks *a symbol of*   ^w Or *have freedom of choice regarding her head*

goes ahead with your own supper, and one goes hungry and another becomes drunk. ²²What! Do you not have homes to eat and drink in? Or do you show contempt for the church of God and humiliate those who have nothing? What should I say to you? Should I commend you? In this matter I do not commend you!

The Institution of the Lord's Supper

23 For I received from the Lord what I also handed on to you, that the Lord Jesus on the night when he was betrayed took a loaf of bread, ²⁴and when he had given thanks, he broke it and said, "This is my body that is for˟ you. Do this in remembrance of me." ²⁵In the same way he took the cup also, after supper, saying, "This cup is the new covenant in my blood. Do this, as often as you drink it, in remembrance of me." ²⁶For as often as you eat this bread and drink the cup, you proclaim the Lord's death until he comes.

Partaking of the Supper Unworthily

27 Whoever, therefore, eats the bread or drinks the cup of the Lord in an unworthy manner will be answerable for the body and blood of the Lord. ²⁸Examine yourselves, and only then eat of the bread and drink of the cup. ²⁹For all who eat and drinkʸ without discerning the body,ᶻ eat

When the believers who made up the Corinthian church met to remember Jesus in the Lord's Supper, they had a full meal together. Unfortunately, the believers did not wait for everyone to gather before they began to eat. Each person ate his or her fill so that those who arrived later received very little. God wants us to remember the needs of others. What are some ways you can put someone else's needs before your own? How can you make sure that person is not left out?

and drink judgment against themselves. ³⁰For this reason many of you are weak and ill, and some have died.ᵃ ³¹But if we judged ourselves, we would not be judged. ³²But when we are judged by the Lord, we are disciplinedᵇ so that we may not be condemned along with the world.

33 So then, my brothers and sisters,ᶜ when you come together to eat, wait for one another. ³⁴If you are hungry, eat at home, so that when you come together, it will not be for your condemnation. About the other things I will give instructions when I come.

God gives each person special gifts to use in service to others. Not everyone has the same gifts, and we need everyone working together so that all gifts help the church.

What special gift has God given you? Are you kind? Are you a good friend? Are you good at taking care of other people? Do people like the way you inspire them to be better at something? Ask God to help you use your special gift in the best way you can.

Spiritual Gifts

12 Now concerning spiritual gifts,ᵈ brothers and sisters,ᶜ I do not want you to be uninformed. ²You know that when you were pagans, you were enticed and led astray to idols that could not speak. ³Therefore I want you to understand that no one speaking by the Spirit of God ever says "Let Jesus be cursed!" and no one can say "Jesus is Lord" except by the Holy Spirit.

4 Now there are varieties of gifts, but the same Spirit; ⁵and there are varieties of

---

˟ Other ancient authorities read *is broken for*
ʸ Other ancient authorities add *in an unworthy manner,* ᶻ Other ancient authorities read *the Lord's body* ᵃ Gk *fallen asleep* ᵇ Or *When we are judged, we are being disciplined by the Lord* ᶜ Gk *brothers* ᵈ Or *spiritual persons*

services, but the same Lord; [6]and there are varieties of activities, but it is the same God who activates all of them in everyone. [7]To each is given the manifestation of the Spirit for the common good. [8]To one is given through the Spirit the utterance of wisdom, and to another the utterance of knowledge according to the same Spirit, [9]to another faith by the same Spirit, to another gifts of healing by the one Spirit, [10]to another the working of miracles, to another prophecy, to another the discernment of spirits, to another various kinds of tongues, to another the interpretation of tongues. [11]All these are activated by one and the same Spirit, who allots to each one individually just as the Spirit chooses.

One Body with Many Members

12 For just as the body is one and has many members, and all the members of the body, though many, are one body, so it is with Christ. [13]For in the one Spirit we were all baptized into one body—Jews or Greeks, slaves or free—and we were all made to drink of one Spirit.

14 Indeed, the body does not consist of one member but of many. [15]If the foot would say, "Because I am not a hand, I do not belong to the body," that would not make it any less a part of the body. [16]And if the ear would say, "Because I am not an eye, I do not belong to the body," that would not make it any less a part of the body. [17]If the whole body were an eye, where would the hearing be? If the whole body were hearing, where would the sense of smell be? [18]But as it is, God arranged the members in the body, each one of them, as he chose. [19]If all were a single member, where would the body be? [20]As it is, there are many members, yet one body. [21]The eye cannot say to the hand, "I have no need of you," nor again the head to the feet, "I have no need of you." [22]On the contrary, the members of the body that seem to be weaker are indispensable, [23]and those members of the body that we think less honorable we clothe with greater honor, and our less respectable members

1 Corinthians 13 is often called "The Love Chapter." Read this chapter with your family. Then write each of these words or phrases on a piece of paper: kind, patient, not jealous, not rude, doesn't brag, doesn't demand its own way, doesn't get angry quickly, doesn't hold grudges, happy about good things, sad about bad things, loyal, hopeful, trusting. Put these pieces of paper in a basket or a jar. Each night at dinner or bedtime, pull out one piece of paper. Have each family member tell about a time when they acted like the word on the paper, or when someone acted that way toward them. Then pray together: Dear God, help us to love others as you have loved us. Amen.

are treated with greater respect; [24]whereas our more respectable members do not need this. But God has so arranged the body, giving the greater honor to the inferior member, [25]that there may be no dissension within the body, but the members may have the same care for one another. [26]If one member suffers, all suffer together with it; if one member is honored, all rejoice together with it.

27 Now you are the body of Christ and individually members of it. [28]And God has appointed in the church first apostles, second prophets, third teachers; then deeds of power, then gifts of healing, forms of assistance, forms of leadership, various kinds of tongues. [29]Are all apostles? Are all prophets? Are all teachers? Do all work miracles? [30]Do all possess gifts of healing? Do all speak in tongues? Do all interpret? [31]But strive for the greater gifts. And I will show you a still more excellent way.

The Gift of Love

13 If I speak in the tongues of mortals and of angels, but do not have love, I am a noisy gong or a clanging cymbal. [2]And if I have prophetic

powers, and understand all mysteries and all knowledge, and if I have all faith, so as to remove mountains, but do not have love, I am nothing. ³If I give away all my possessions, and if I hand over my body so that I may boast,ᵉ but do not have love, I gain nothing.

4 Love is patient; love is kind; love is not envious or boastful or arrogant ⁵or rude. It does not insist on its own way; it is not irritable or resentful; ⁶it does not rejoice in wrongdoing, but rejoices in the truth. ⁷It bears all things, believes all things, hopes all things, endures all things.

8 Love never ends. But as for prophecies, they will come to an end; as for tongues, they will cease; as for knowledge, it will come to an end. ⁹For we know only in part, and we prophesy only in part; ¹⁰but when the complete comes, the partial will come to an end. ¹¹When I was a child, I spoke like a child, I thought like a child, I reasoned like a child; when I became an adult, I put an end to childish ways. ¹²For now we see in a mirror, dimly,ᶠ but then we will see face to face. Now I know only in part; then I will know fully, even as I have been fully known. ¹³And now faith, hope, and love abide, these three; and the greatest of these is love.

Gifts of Prophecy and Tongues

14 Pursue love and strive for the spiritual gifts, and especially that you may prophesy. ²For those who speak in a tongue do not speak to other people but to God; for nobody understands them, since they are speaking mysteries in the Spirit. ³On the other hand, those who prophesy speak to other people for their upbuilding and encouragement and consolation. ⁴Those who speak in a tongue build up themselves, but those who prophesy build up the church. ⁵Now I would like all of you to speak in tongues, but even more to prophesy. One who prophesies is greater than one who speaks in tongues, unless someone interprets, so that the church may be built up.

6 Now, brothers and sisters,ᵍ if I come to you speaking in tongues, how will I benefit you unless I speak to you in some revelation or knowledge or prophecy or teaching? ⁷It is the same way with lifeless instruments that produce sound, such as the flute or the harp. If they do not give distinct notes, how will anyone know what is being played? ⁸And if the bugle gives an indistinct sound, who will get ready for battle? ⁹So with yourselves; if in a tongue you utter speech that is not intelligible, how will anyone know what is being said? For you will be speaking into the air. ¹⁰There are doubtless many different kinds of sounds in the world, and nothing is without sound. ¹¹If then I do not know the meaning of a sound, I will be a foreigner to the speaker and the speaker a foreigner to me. ¹²So with yourselves; since you are eager for spiritual gifts, strive to excel in them for building up the church.

13 Therefore, one who speaks in a tongue should pray for the power to interpret. ¹⁴For if I pray in a tongue, my spirit prays but my mind is unproductive. ¹⁵What should I do then? I will pray with the spirit, but I will pray with the mind also; I will sing praise with the spirit, but I will sing praise with the mind also. ¹⁶Otherwise, if you say a blessing with the spirit, how can anyone in the position of an outsider say the "Amen" to your thanksgiving, since the outsider does not know what you are saying? ¹⁷For you may give thanks well enough, but the other person is not built up. ¹⁸I thank God that I speak in tongues more than all of you; ¹⁹nevertheless, in church I would rather speak five words with my mind, in order to instruct others also, than ten thousand words in a tongue.

20 Brothers and sisters,ᶠ do not be children in your thinking; rather, be infants in

> "And now faith, hope, and love abide, these three; and the greatest of these is love." 1 Corinthians 13:13

ᵉ Other ancient authorities read *body to be burned*
ᶠ Gk *in a riddle*   ᵍ Gk *brothers*

evil, but in thinking be adults. [21]In the law it is written,

> "By people of strange tongues
>   and by the lips of foreigners
> I will speak to this people;
>   yet even then they will not listen
>   to me,"

says the Lord. [22]Tongues, then, are a sign not for believers but for unbelievers, while prophecy is not for unbelievers but for believers. [23]If, therefore, the whole church comes together and all speak in tongues, and outsiders or unbelievers enter, will they not say that you are out of your mind? [24]But if all prophesy, an unbeliever or outsider who enters is reproved by all and called to account by all. [25]After the secrets of the unbeliever's heart are disclosed, that person will bow down before God and worship him, declaring, "God is really among you."

Orderly Worship

26 What should be done then, my friends?[h] When you come together, each one has a hymn, a lesson, a revelation, a tongue, or an interpretation. Let all things be done for building up. [27]If anyone speaks in a tongue, let there be only two or at most three, and each in turn; and let one interpret. [28]But if there is no one to interpret, let them be silent in church and speak to themselves and to God. [29]Let two or three prophets speak, and let the others weigh what is said. [30]If a revelation is made to someone else sitting nearby, let the first person be silent. [31]For you can all prophesy one by one, so that all may learn and all be encouraged. [32]And the spirits of prophets are subject to the prophets, [33]for God is a God not of disorder but of peace.

(As in all the churches of the saints, [34]women should be silent in the churches. For they are not permitted to speak, but should be subordinate, as the law also says. [35]If there is anything they desire to know, let them ask their husbands at home. For it is shameful for a woman to speak in church.[i] [36]Or did the word of God originate with you? Or are you the only ones it has reached?)

37 Anyone who claims to be a prophet, or to have spiritual powers, must acknowledge that what I am writing to you is a command of the Lord. [38]Anyone who does not recognize this is not to be recognized. [39]So, my friends,[j] be eager to prophesy, and do not forbid speaking in tongues; [40]but all things should be done decently and in order.

The Resurrection of Christ

15 Now I would remind you, brothers and sisters,[h] of the good news[k] that I proclaimed to you, which you in turn received, in which also you stand, [2]through which also you are being saved, if you hold firmly to the message that I proclaimed to you—unless you have come to believe in vain.

3 For I handed on to you as of first importance what I in turn had received: that Christ died for our sins in accordance with the scriptures, [4]and that he was buried, and that he was raised on the third day in accordance with the scriptures, [5]and that he appeared to Cē´phas, then to the twelve. [6]Then he appeared to more than five hundred brothers and sisters[h] at one time, most of whom are still alive, though some have died.[l] [7]Then he appeared to James, then to all the apostles. [8]Last of all, as to one untimely born, he appeared also to me. [9]For I am the least of the apostles, unfit to be called an apostle, because I persecuted the church of God. [10]But by the grace of God I am what I am, and his grace toward me has not been in vain. On the contrary, I worked harder than any of them—though it was not I, but the grace of God that is with me. [11]Whether then it was I or they, so we proclaim and so you have come to believe.

The Resurrection of the Dead

12 Now if Christ is proclaimed as

---

[h] Gk brothers   [i] Other ancient authorities put verses 34-35 after verse 40   [j] Gk my brothers   [k] Or gospel   [l] Gk fallen asleep

raised from the dead, how can some of you say there is no resurrection of the dead? [13]If there is no resurrection of the dead, then Christ has not been raised; [14]and if Christ has not been raised, then our proclamation has been in vain and your faith has been in vain. [15]We are even found to be misrepresenting God, because we testified of God that he raised Christ—whom he did not raise if it is true that the dead are not raised. [16]For if the dead are not raised, then Christ has not been raised. [17]If Christ has not been raised, your faith is futile and you are still in your sins. [18]Then those also who have died[m] in Christ have perished. [19]If for this life only we have hoped in Christ, we are of all people most to be pitied.

20 But in fact Christ has been raised from the dead, the first fruits of those who have died.[m] [21]For since death came through a human being, the resurrection of the dead has also come through a human being; [22]for as all die in Adam, so all will be made alive in Christ. [23]But each in his own order: Christ the first fruits, then at his coming those who belong to Christ. [24]Then comes the end,[n] when he hands over the kingdom to God the Father, after he has destroyed every ruler and every authority and power. [25]For he must reign until he has put all his enemies under his feet. [26]The last enemy to be destroyed is death. [27]For "God[o] has put all things in subjection under his feet." But when it says, "All things are put in subjection," it is plain that this does not include the one who put all things in subjection under him. [28]When all things are subjected to him, then the Son himself will also be subjected to the one who put all things in subjection under him, so that God may be all in all.

29 Otherwise, what will those people do who receive baptism on behalf of the dead? If the dead are not raised at all, why are people baptized on their behalf?

30 And why are we putting ourselves in danger every hour? [31]I die every day! That

is as certain, brothers and sisters,[p] as my boasting of you—a boast that I make in Christ Jesus our Lord. [32]If with merely human hopes I fought with wild animals at Eph´e·sus, what would I have gained by it? If the dead are not raised,

"Let us eat and drink,
for tomorrow we die."

[33]Do not be deceived:

"Bad company ruins good morals."

[34]Come to a sober and right mind, and sin no more; for some people have no knowledge of God. I say this to your shame.

The Resurrection Body

35 But someone will ask, "How are the dead raised? With what kind of body do they come?" [36]Fool! What you sow does not come to life unless it dies. [37]And as for what you sow, you do not sow the body that is to be, but a bare seed, perhaps of wheat or of some other grain. [38]But God gives it a body as he has chosen, and to each kind of seed its own body. [39]Not all flesh is alike, but there is one flesh for human beings, another for animals, another for birds, and another for fish. [40]There are both heavenly bodies and earthly bodies, but the glory of the heavenly is one thing, and that of the earthly is another. [41]There is one glory of the sun, and another glory of the moon, and another glory of the stars; indeed, star differs from star in glory.

42 So it is with the resurrection of the dead. What is sown is perishable, what is raised is imperishable. [43]It is sown in dishonor, it is raised in glory. It is sown in weakness, it is raised in power. [44]It is sown a physical body, it is raised a spiritual body. If there is a physical body, there is also a spiritual body. [45]Thus it is written, "The first man, Adam, became a living being"; the last Adam became a life-giving spirit. [46]But it is not the spiritual that is first, but the physical, and then the spiritual. [47]The first man was from the earth, a man of

[m] Gk fallen asleep   [n] Or Then come the rest   [o] Gk he   [p] Gk brothers

> "The sting of death is sin, and the power of sin is the law. But thanks be to God, who gives us the victory through our Lord Jesus Christ." 1 Corinthians 15:56–57

dust; the second man is[q] from heaven. [48]As was the man of dust, so are those who are of the dust; and as is the man of heaven, so are those who are of heaven. [49]Just as we have borne the image of the man of dust, we will[r] also bear the image of the man of heaven.

50 What I am saying, brothers and sisters,[s] is this: flesh and blood cannot inherit the kingdom of God, nor does the perishable inherit the imperishable. [51]Listen, I will tell you a mystery! We will not all die,[t] but we will all be changed, [52]in a moment, in the twinkling of an eye, at the last trumpet. For the trumpet will sound, and the dead will be raised imperishable, and we will be changed. [53]For this perishable body must put on imperishability, and this mortal body must put on immortality. [54]When this perishable body puts on imperishability, and this mortal body puts on immortality, then the saying that is written will be fulfilled:

"Death has been swallowed up in
victory."
[55] "Where, O death, is your victory?
Where, O death, is your sting?"
[56]The sting of death is sin, and the power of sin is the law. [57]But thanks be to God, who gives us the victory through our Lord Jesus Christ.

58 Therefore, my beloved,[u] be steadfast, immovable, always excelling in the work of the Lord, because you know that in the Lord your labor is not in vain.

> "Keep alert, stand firm in your faith, be courageous, be strong. Let all that you do be done in love." 1 Corinthians 6:13–14

The Collection for the Saints

16 Now concerning the collection for the saints: you should follow the directions I gave to the churches of Galatia. [2]On the first day of every week, each of you is to put aside and save whatever extra you earn, so that collections need not be taken when I come. [3]And when I arrive, I will send any whom you approve with letters to take your gift to Jerusalem. [4]If it seems advisable that I should go also, they will accompany me.

Plans for Travel

5 I will visit you after passing through Mac·e·dō′ni·a—for I intend to pass through Mac·e·dō′ni·a—[6]and perhaps I will stay with you or even spend the winter, so that you may send me on my way, wherever I go. [7]I do not want to see you now just in passing, for I hope to spend some time with you, if the Lord permits. [8]But I will stay in Eph′e·sus until Pentecost, [9]for a wide door for effective work has opened to me, and there are many adversaries.

10 If Timothy comes, see that he has nothing to fear among you, for he is doing the work of the Lord just as I am; [11]therefore let no one despise him. Send him on his way in peace, so that he may come to me; for I am expecting him with the brothers.

12 Now concerning our brother A·pol′los, I strongly urged him to visit you with the other brothers, but he was not at all willing[v] to come now. He will come when he has the opportunity.

Final Messages and Greetings

13 Keep alert, stand firm in your faith, be courageous, be strong. [14]Let all that you do be done in love.

15 Now, brothers and sisters,[s] you know that members of the household of

[q] Other ancient authorities add *the Lord* [r] Other ancient authorities read *let us* [s] Gk *brothers* [t] Gk *fall asleep* [u] Gk *beloved brothers* [v] Or *it was not at all God's will for him*

Steph′a·nas were the first converts in A·chā′i·a, and they have devoted themselves to the service of the saints; [16]I urge you to put yourselves at the service of such people, and of everyone who works and toils with them. [17]I rejoice at the coming of Steph′a·nas and For·tu·nā′tus and A·chā′i·cus, because they have made up for your absence; [18]for they refreshed my spirit as well as yours. So give recognition to such persons.

19 The churches of Asia send greetings. A·qui′la and Pris′ca, together with the church in their house, greet you warmly in the Lord. [20]All the brothers and sisters[w] send greetings. Greet one another with a holy kiss.

21 I, Paul, write this greeting with my own hand. [22]Let anyone be accursed who has no love for the Lord. Our Lord, come![x] [23]The grace of the Lord Jesus be with you. [24]My love be with all of you in Christ Jesus.[y]

[w] Gk brothers　　[x] Gk Marana tha. These Aramaic words can also be read Maran atha, meaning Our Lord has come　　[y] Other ancient authorities add Amen

2 Corinthians

Paul wrote several letters to the Christians at Corinth in about 51 AD. The books of First and Second Corinthians that are in our Bible today are probably made up of parts of these letters. For more information, read the introduction to the book of First Corinthians. Second Corinthians demonstrates the problems that faced the new church at Corinth and the tasks of leadership placed on the apostle Paul.

Although they appear at the end of this letter, Paul wrote chapters 10–13 before he wrote chapters 1–9. This part of the letter was written after Timothy

2 Corinthians 2:1–5

visited Corinth and found the Corinthians arguing and criticizing Paul, the one who had first told them the good news of Christ. In chapters 10–13, Paul defended his ministry and spoke out against false apostles. He shared his concern for the Corinthian church and warned those who were sinning. Paul said that he would visit Corinth again and would demand high standards of all the churchís members. These chapters end with the thought that the harsh words came out of love and that the conflict between Paul and the Corinthians would not last forever. These chapters point out that we must test ourselves not by the standards of other human beings but by Jesus Christ.

Chapters 1–9 (except 6:14–7:1) were written after the harsh letter that is now found in chapters 10–13. Paul gave thanks and told the Corinthians to trust in Christ and to have hope. He encouraged them to forgive one another and to keep living the way that God wanted them to live, even when times were tough. As Christians, they were to walk by faith and not by sight. Titus brought news that the Corinthians had read Paul's earlier letter, repented, and changed their ways. This made Paul joyful. He encouraged the Corinthians to be generous—giving to those who were in need—and suggested that they help with the fund for Jewish Christians in Jerusalem who did not have enough food to eat.

Salutation

1 Paul, an apostle of Christ Jesus by the will of God, and Timothy our brother,

To the church of God that is in Corinth, including all the saints throughout A·chā'i·a:

2 Grace to you and peace from God our Father and the Lord Jesus Christ.

Paul's Thanksgiving after Affliction

3 Blessed be the God and Father of our Lord Jesus Christ, the Father of mercies and the God of all consolation, [4]who consoles us in all our affliction, so that we may be able to console those who are in any affliction with the consolation with which we ourselves are consoled by God. [5]For just as the sufferings of Christ are abundant for us, so also our consolation is abundant through Christ. [6]If we are being afflicted, it is for your consolation and salvation; if we are being consoled, it is for your consolation, which you experience when you patiently endure the same sufferings that we are also suffering. [7]Our hope for you is unshaken; for we know that as you share in our sufferings, so also you share in our consolation.

8 We do not want you to be unaware, brothers and sisters,[a] of the affliction we experienced in Asia; for we were so utterly, unbearably crushed that we despaired of life itself. [9]Indeed, we felt that we had received the sentence of death so that we would rely not on ourselves but on God who raises the dead. [10]He who rescued us from so deadly a peril will continue to rescue us; on him we have set our hope that he will rescue us again, [11]as you also join in helping us by your prayers, so that many will give thanks on our[b] behalf for the blessing granted us through the prayers of many.

The Postponement of Paul's Visit

12 Indeed, this is our boast, the testimony of our conscience: we have behaved in the world with frankness[c] and godly sin-

When we pray to God and ask for something, God may not respond in ways that we hope for. Sometimes we must wait for a response. Sometimes we cannot recognize the answer, or the answer is one that we did not want. Sometimes the answer is "no." Whether God's answer to our prayers is "yes," "no," or "wait," God loves us and wants the very best for our lives.

Suppose you had a friend, but you spoke to this friend only when you wanted him or her to do something for you. What kind of friendship would that be? In the same way it's important to keep our friendship with God by praying often, even when we have no urgent need. We don't always have to ask God for things when we pray. We can also praise and thank God for who God is and how God loves us.

cerity, not by earthly wisdom but by the grace of God—and all the more toward you. [13]For we write you nothing other than what you can read and also understand; I hope you will understand until the end— [14]as you have already understood us in part—that on the day of the Lord Jesus we are your boast even as you are our boast.

15 Since I was sure of this, I wanted to come to you first, so that you might have a double favor;[d] [16]I wanted to visit you on my way to Mac·e·dō'ni·a, and to come back to you from Mac·e·dō'ni·a and have you send me on to Judea. [17]Was I vacillating when I wanted to do this? Do I make my plans according to ordinary human standards,[e] ready to say "Yes, yes" and "No, no" at the same time? [18]As surely as God is faithful, our word to you has not been "Yes

---

[a] Gk brothers   [b] Other ancient authorities read your   [c] Other ancient authorities read holiness   [d] Other ancient authorities read pleasure   [e] Gk according to the flesh

and No." [19]For the Son of God, Jesus Christ, whom we proclaimed among you, Sil·vā´nus and Timothy and I, was not "Yes and No"; but in him it is always "Yes." [20]For in him every one of God's promises is a "Yes." For this reason it is through him that we say the "Amen," to the glory of God. [21]But it is God who establishes us with you in Christ and has anointed us, [22]by putting his seal on us and giving us his Spirit in our hearts as a first installment.

23 But I call on God as witness against me: it was to spare you that I did not come again to Corinth. [24]I do not mean to imply that we lord it over your faith; rather, we are workers with you for your joy, because you stand firm in the faith. [1]So I made up my mind not to make you another pain-

2 ful visit. [2]For if I cause you pain, who is there to make me glad but the one whom I have pained? [3]And I wrote as I did, so that when I came, I might not suffer pain from those who should have made me rejoice; for I am confident about all of you, that my joy would be the joy of all of you. [4]For I

Sometimes even best friends have disagreements. That happened to Paul and the church at Corinth! At least one person was causing pain between Paul and the Corinthian Christians. But Paul forgave him and asked the others to forgive him as well. Just as God forgives us, so God wants us to forgive one another. Forgiving means that if someone has caused us pain, we excuse that person and count their wrong as if it had never happened.

Forgiving those who hurt us can be very difficult. If you are having a hard time forgiving someone, try talking with someone in your family or with your pastor. They may be able to give you a new way to think about the situation.

wrote you out of much distress and anguish of heart and with many tears, not to cause you pain, but to let you know the abundant love that I have for you.

Forgiveness for the Offender

5 But if anyone has caused pain, he has caused it not to me, but to some extent—not to exaggerate it—to all of you. [6]This punishment by the majority is enough for such a person; [7]so now instead you should forgive and console him, so that he may not be overwhelmed by excessive sorrow. [8]So I urge you to reaffirm your love for him. [9]I wrote for this reason: to test you and to know whether you are obedient in everything. [10]Anyone whom you forgive, I also forgive. What I have forgiven, if I have forgiven anything, has been for your sake in the presence of Christ. [11]And we do this so that we may not be outwitted by Satan; for we are not ignorant of his designs.

Paul's Anxiety in Troas

12 When I came to Trō´as to proclaim the good news of Christ, a door was opened for me in the Lord; [13]but my mind could not rest because I did not find my brother Titus there. So I said farewell to them and went on to Mac·ē·do´ni·a.

14 But thanks be to God, who in Christ always leads us in triumphal procession, and through us spreads in every place the fragrance that comes from knowing him. [15]For we are the aroma of Christ to God among those who are being saved and among those who are perishing; [16]to the one a fragrance from death to death, to the other a fragrance from life to life. Who is sufficient for these things? [17]For we are not peddlers of God's word like so many;[f] but in Christ we speak as persons of sincerity, as persons sent from God and standing in his presence.

Ministers of the New Covenant

3 Are we beginning to commend ourselves again? Surely we do not

[f] Other ancient authorities read *like the others*

need, as some do, letters of recommendation to you or from you, do we? ²You yourselves are our letter, written on our^g hearts, to be known and read by all; ³and you show that you are a letter of Christ, prepared by us, written not with ink but with the Spirit of the living God, not on tablets of stone but on tablets of human hearts.

4 Such is the confidence that we have through Christ toward God. ⁵Not that we are competent of ourselves to claim anything as coming from us; our competence is from God, ⁶who has made us competent to be ministers of a new covenant, not of letter but of spirit; for the letter kills, but the Spirit gives life.

7 Now if the ministry of death, chiseled in letters on stone tablets,^h came in glory so that the people of Israel could not gaze at Moses' face because of the glory of his face, a glory now set aside, ⁸how much more will the ministry of the Spirit come in glory? ⁹For if there was glory in the ministry of condemnation, much more does the ministry of justification abound in glory! ¹⁰Indeed, what once had glory has lost its glory because of the greater glory; ¹¹for if what was set aside came through glory, much more has the permanent come in glory!

12 Since, then, we have such a hope, we act with great boldness, ¹³not like Moses, who put a veil over his face to keep

> "For we are the aroma of Christ to God among those who are being saved and among those who are perishing." 2 Corinthians 2:15

the people of Israel from gazing at the end of the glory thatⁱ was being set aside. ¹⁴But their minds were hardened. Indeed, to this very day, when they hear the reading of the old covenant, that same veil is still there, since only in Christ is it set aside. ¹⁵Indeed, to this very day whenever Moses is read, a veil lies over their minds; ¹⁶but when one turns to the Lord, the veil is removed. ¹⁷Now the Lord is the Spirit, and where the Spirit of the Lord is, there is freedom. ¹⁸And all of us, with unveiled faces, seeing the glory of the Lord as though reflected in a mirror, are being transformed into the same image from one degree of glory to another; for this comes from the Lord, the Spirit.

Treasure in Clay Jars

4 Therefore, since it is by God's mercy that we are engaged in this ministry, we do not lose heart. ²We have renounced the shameful things that one hides; we refuse to practice cunning or to falsify God's word; but by the open statement of the truth we commend ourselves to the conscience of everyone in the sight of God. ³And even if our gospel is veiled, it is veiled to those who are perishing. ⁴In their case the god of this world has blinded the minds of the unbelievers, to keep them from seeing the light of the gospel of the glory of Christ, who is the image of God. ⁵For we do not proclaim ourselves; we proclaim Jesus Christ as Lord and ourselves as your slaves for Jesus' sake. ⁶For it is the God who said, "Let light shine out of darkness," who has shone in our hearts to give the light of the knowledge of the glory of God in the face of Jesus Christ.

When someone hopes to get into a college or to be hired for a job, they have to send in letters of recommendation. A letter of recommendation tells the school or the workplace that the person is a good student or worker, an honest person, and has many wonderful qualities. Paul says that the believers in Corinth are his "letters" because their actions are a good reflection of him and his teaching.

^g Other ancient authorities read *your*   ^h Gk *on stones*   ⁱ Gk *of what*

> "So we do not lose heart. Even though our outer nature is wasting away, our inner nature is being renewed day by day."
>
> 2 Corinthians 4:16

7 But we have this treasure in clay jars, so that it may be made clear that this extraordinary power belongs to God and does not come from us. ⁸We are afflicted in every way, but not crushed; perplexed, but not driven to despair; ⁹persecuted, but not forsaken; struck down, but not destroyed; ¹⁰always carrying in the body the death of Jesus, so that the life of Jesus may also be made visible in our bodies. ¹¹For while we live, we are always being given up to death for Jesus' sake, so that the life of Jesus may be made visible in our mortal flesh. ¹²So death is at work in us, but life in you.

13 But just as we have the same spirit of faith that is in accordance with scripture— "I believed, and so I spoke"—we also believe, and so we speak, ¹⁴because we know that the one who raised the Lord Jesus will raise us also with Jesus, and will bring us with you into his presence. ¹⁵Yes, everything is for your sake, so that grace, as it extends to more and more people, may increase thanksgiving, to the glory of God.

Living by Faith

16 So we do not lose heart. Even though our outer nature is wasting away, our inner nature is being renewed day by day. ¹⁷For this slight momentary affliction is preparing us for an eternal weight of glory beyond all measure, ¹⁸because we look not at what can be seen but at what cannot be seen; for what can be seen is temporary, but what cannot be seen is eternal.

5 For we know that if the earthly tent we live in is destroyed, we have a building from God, a house not made with hands, eternal in the heavens. ²For in this tent we groan, longing to be clothed with our heavenly dwelling— ³if

indeed, when we have taken it off[j] we will not be found naked. ⁴For while we are still in this tent, we groan under our burden, because we wish not to be unclothed but to be further clothed, so that what is mortal may be swallowed up by life. ⁵He who has prepared us for this very thing is God, who has given us the Spirit as a guarantee.

6 So we are always confident; even though we know that while we are at home in the body we are away from the Lord— ⁷for we walk by faith, not by sight. ⁸Yes, we do have confidence, and we would rather be away from the body and at home with the Lord. ⁹So whether we are at home or away, we make it our aim to please him. ¹⁰For all of us must appear before the judgment seat of Christ, so that each may receive recompense for what has been done in the body, whether good or evil.

The Ministry of Reconciliation

11 Therefore, knowing the fear of the Lord, we try to persuade others; but we ourselves are well known to God, and I hope that we are also well known to your consciences. ¹²We are not commending ourselves to you again, but giving you an opportunity to boast about us, so that you may be able to answer those who boast in outward appearance and not in the heart. ¹³For if we are beside ourselves, it is for God; if we are in our right mind, it is for you. ¹⁴For the love of Christ urges us on, because we are convinced that one has died for all; therefore all have died. ¹⁵And he died for all, so that those who live might

Christ came into the world to show love for us all. That love meant that he was willing to die on the cross so that we could be saved from our sins. Because of his example, we should not live for ourselves but for Jesus.

^j Other ancient authorities read *put it on*

live no longer for themselves, but for him who died and was raised for them.

16 From now on, therefore, we regard no one from a human point of view;[k] even though we once knew Christ from a human point of view,[k] we know him no longer in that way. [17]So if anyone is in Christ, there is a new creation: everything old has passed away; see, everything has become new! [18]All this is from God, who reconciled us to himself through Christ, and has given us the ministry of reconciliation; [19]that is, in Christ God was reconciling the world to himself,[l] not counting their trespasses against them, and entrusting the message of reconciliation to us. [20]So we are ambassadors for Christ, since God is making his appeal through us; we entreat you on behalf of Christ, be reconciled to God. [21]For our sake he made him to be sin who knew no sin, so that in him we might become the righteousness of God.

6 As we work together with him,[m] we urge you also not to accept the grace of God in vain. [2]For he says,

> "At an acceptable time I have listened
>   to you,
> and on a day of salvation I have
>   helped you."

See, now is the acceptable time; see, now is the day of salvation! [3]We are putting no obstacle in anyone's way, so that no fault may be found with our ministry, [4]but as servants of God we have commended ourselves in every way: through great endurance, in afflictions, hardships, calamities, [5]beatings, imprisonments, riots, labors, sleepless nights, hunger; [6]by purity, knowledge, patience, kindness, holiness of spirit, genuine love, [7]truthful speech, and the power of God; with the weapons of righteousness for the right hand and for the left; [8]in honor and dishonor, in ill repute and good repute. We are treated as impostors, and yet are true; [9]as unknown, and yet are well known; as dying, and see—we are alive; as punished, and yet not killed;

> "So if anyone is in Christ, there is a new creation; everything old has passed away; see everything has become new!"
> **2 Corinthians 5:17**

[10]as sorrowful, yet always rejoicing; as poor, yet making many rich; as having nothing, and yet possessing everything.

11 We have spoken frankly to you Corinthians; our heart is wide open to you. [12]There is no restriction in our affections, but only in yours. [13]In return—I speak as to children—open wide your hearts also.

The Temple of the Living God

14 Do not be mismatched with unbelievers. For what partnership is there between righteousness and lawlessness? Or what fellowship is there between light and darkness? [15]What agreement does Christ have with Bēʹli·ar? Or what does a believer share with an unbeliever? [16]What agreement has the temple of God with idols? For we[n] are the temple of the living God; as God said,

> "I will live in them and walk among
>   them,
> and I will be their God,
> and they shall be my people.
> [17] Therefore come out from them,
>   and be separate from them, says the
>   Lord,
> and touch nothing unclean;
>   then I will welcome you,
> [18] and I will be your father,
>   and you shall be my sons and
>   daughters,
> says the Lord Almighty."

7 Since we have these promises, beloved, let us cleanse ourselves from every defilement of body and of spirit, making holiness perfect in the fear of God.

[k] Gk *according to the flesh*   [l] Or *God was in Christ reconciling the world to himself*   [m] Gk *As we work together*   [n] Other ancient authorities read *you*

Paul's Joy at the Church's Repentance

2 Make room in your hearts° for us; we have wronged no one, we have corrupted no one, we have taken advantage of no one. ³I do not say this to condemn you, for I said before that you are in our hearts, to die together and to live together. ⁴I often boast about you; I have great pride in you; I am filled with consolation; I am overjoyed in all our affliction.

5 For even when we came into Mac·e·dō′ni·a, our bodies had no rest, but we were afflicted in every way—disputes without and fears within. ⁶But God, who consoles the downcast, consoled us by the arrival of Titus, ⁷and not only by his coming, but also by the consolation with which he was consoled about you, as he told us of your longing, your mourning, your zeal for me, so that I rejoiced still more. ⁸For even if I made you sorry with my letter, I do not regret it (though I did regret it, for I see that I grieved you with that letter, though only briefly). ⁹Now I rejoice, not because you were grieved, but because your grief led to repentance; for you felt a godly grief, so that you were not harmed in any way by us. ¹⁰For godly grief produces a repentance that leads to salvation and brings no regret, but worldly grief produces death. ¹¹For see what earnestness this godly grief has produced in you, what eagerness to clear yourselves, what indignation, what alarm, what longing, what zeal, what punishment! At every point you have proved yourselves guiltless in the matter. ¹²So although I wrote to you, it was not on account of the one who did the wrong, nor on account of the one who was wronged, but in order that your zeal for us might be made known to you before God. ¹³In this we find comfort.

In addition to our own consolation, we rejoiced still more at the joy of Titus, because his mind has been set at rest by all of you. ¹⁴For if I have been somewhat boastful about you to him, I was not disgraced; but just as everything we said to you was true, so our boasting to Titus has proved true as well. ¹⁵And his heart goes out all the more to you, as he remembers the obedience of all of you, and how you welcomed him with fear and trembling. ¹⁶I

Titus resumed the collection for the Jerusalem church. Paul reminded the church he started in Corinth that their mission extended to helping those in need. Paul persuaded them to give by reminding them that they were good at other forms of discipleship. He said they should be just as good at giving as they were at believing in Christ, in speaking and learning about their faith, and in their love for Paul. We should also do the same. Think about the things you have and ask yourself this question: How much is enough?

Make a list of what you have (clothes, shoes, toys, games, books, music, money, and so on), and think about each thing on the list in this way: __I could use more; __I have enough; __I have more than enough. Think about your love and concern for others and the time you give to help others in the same way. Now make a list of ways that you can share not only the things you have, but also your time and your love. Pray, asking Jesus to help you know the best way to give to people in need.

Titus was a Gentile Christian and one of Paul's co-workers. Paul thanks the Corinthians for warmly welcoming Titus to their church.

° Gk lacks *in your hearts*

rejoice, because I have complete confidence in you.

Encouragement to Be Generous

8 We want you to know, brothers and sisters,[p] about the grace of God that has been granted to the churches of Mac·e·dō′ni·a; [2]for during a severe ordeal of affliction, their abundant joy and their extreme poverty have overflowed in a wealth of generosity on their part. [3]For, as I can testify, they voluntarily gave according to their means, and even beyond their means, [4]begging us earnestly for the privilege[q] of sharing in this ministry to the saints— [5]and this, not merely as we expected; they gave themselves first to the Lord and, by the will of God, to us, [6]so that we might urge Titus that, as he had already made a beginning, so he should also complete this generous undertaking[r] among you. [7]Now as you excel in everything—in faith, in speech, in knowledge, in utmost eagerness, and in our love for you[s]—so we want you to excel also in this generous undertaking.[r]

8 I do not say this as a command, but I am testing the genuineness of your love against the earnestness of others. [9]For you know the generous act[t] of our Lord Jesus Christ, that though he was rich, yet for your sakes he became poor, so that by his poverty you might become rich. [10]And in this matter I am giving my advice: it is appropriate for you who began last year not only to do something but even to desire to do something— [11]now finish doing it, so that your eagerness may be matched by completing it according to your means. [12]For if the eagerness is there, the gift is acceptable according to what one has—not according to what one does not have. [13]I do not mean that there should be relief for others and pressure on you, but it is a question of a fair balance between [14]your present abundance and their need, so that their abundance may be for your need, in order that there may be a fair balance. [15]As it is written,

"The one who had much did not have too much,
and the one who had little did not have too little."

Commendation of Titus

16 But thanks be to God who put in the heart of Titus the same eagerness for you that I myself have. [17]For he not only accepted our appeal, but since he is more eager than ever, he is going to you of his own accord. [18]With him we are sending the brother who is famous among all the churches for his proclaiming the good news;[u] [19]and not only that, but he has also been appointed by the churches to travel with us while we are administering this generous undertaking[v] for the glory of the Lord himself[w] and to show our goodwill. [20]We intend that no one should blame us about this generous gift that we are administering, [21]for we intend to do what is right not only in the Lord's sight but also in the sight of others. [22]And with them we are sending our brother whom we have often tested and found eager in many matters, but who is now more eager than ever because of his great confidence in you. [23]As for Titus, he is my partner and co-worker in your service; as for our brothers, they are messengers[x] of the churches, the glory of Christ. [24]Therefore openly before the churches, show them the proof of your love and of our reason for boasting about you.

> "Each of you must give as you have made up your mind, not reluctantly or under compulsion, for God loves a cheerful giver."
>
> 2 Corinthians 9:7

---

[p] Gk brothers   [q] Gk grace   [r] Gk this grace
[s] Other ancient authorities read your love for us
[t] Gk the grace   [u] Or the gospel   [v] Gk this grace
[w] Other ancient authorities lack himself   [x] Gk apostles

The Collection for Christians at Jerusalem

9 Now it is not necessary for me to write you about the ministry to the saints, [2]for I know your eagerness, which is the subject of my boasting about you to the people of Mac·e·do̅ni·a, saying that A·cha̅i·a has been ready since last year; and your zeal has stirred up most of them. [3]But I am sending the brothers in order that our boasting about you may not prove to have been empty in this case, so that you may be ready, as I said you would be; [4]otherwise, if some Mac·e·do̅ni·ans come with me and find that you are not ready, we would be humiliated—to say nothing of you—in this undertaking.[y] [5]So I thought it necessary to urge the brothers to go on ahead to you, and arrange in advance for this bountiful gift that you have promised, so that it may be ready as a voluntary gift and not as an extortion.

6 The point is this: the one who sows sparingly will also reap sparingly, and the one who sows bountifully will also reap bountifully. [7]Each of you must give as you have made up your mind, not reluctantly or under compulsion, for God loves a cheerful giver. [8]And God is able to provide you with every blessing in abundance, so that by always having enough of everything, you may share abundantly in every good work. [9]As it is written,

"He scatters abroad, he gives to the
     poor;
     his righteousness[z] endures forever."

[10]He who supplies seed to the sower and bread for food will supply and multiply your seed for sowing and increase the harvest of your righteousness.[z] [11]You will be enriched in every way for your great generosity, which will produce thanksgiving to God through us; [12]for the rendering of this ministry not only supplies the needs of the saints but also overflows with many thanksgivings to God. [13]Through the testing of this ministry you glorify God by your obedience to the confession of the gospel of Christ and by the generosity of your sharing with them and with all others, [14]while they long for you and pray for you because of the surpassing grace of God that he has given you. [15]Thanks be to God for his indescribable gift!

Paul Defends His Ministry

10 I myself, Paul, appeal to you by the meekness and gentleness of Christ— I who am humble when face to face with you, but bold toward you when I am away!— [2]I ask that when I am present I need not show boldness by daring to oppose those who think we are acting according to human standards.[a] [3]Indeed, we live as human beings,[b] but we do not wage war according to human standards;[a] [4]for the weapons of our warfare are not merely human,[c] but they have divine power to destroy strongholds. We destroy arguments [5]and every proud obstacle raised up against the knowledge of God, and we take every thought captive to obey Christ. [6]We are ready to punish every disobedience when your obedience is complete.

7 Look at what is before your eyes. If you are confident that you belong to Christ, remind yourself of this, that just as you belong to Christ, so also do we. [8]Now, even if I boast a little too much of our authority, which the Lord gave for building you up and not for tearing you down, I will not be ashamed of it. [9]I do not want to seem as though I am trying to frighten you with my letters. [10]For they say, "His letters are weighty and strong, but his bodily presence is weak, and his speech contemptible." [11]Let such people understand that what we say by letter when absent, we will also do when present.

12 We do not dare to classify or compare ourselves with some of those who commend themselves. But when they measure themselves by one another, and compare themselves with one another, they do not show good sense. [13]We, however,

[y] Other ancient authorities add *of boasting*   [z] Or *benevolence*   [a] Gk *according to the flesh*   [b] Gk *in the flesh*   [c] Gk *fleshly*

will not boast beyond limits, but will keep within the field that God has assigned to us, to reach out even as far as you. [14]For we were not overstepping our limits when we reached you; we were the first to come all the way to you with the good news[d] of Christ. [15]We do not boast beyond limits, that is, in the labors of others; but our hope is that, as your faith increases, our sphere of action among you may be greatly enlarged, [16]so that we may proclaim the good news[d] in lands beyond you, without boasting of work already done in someone else's sphere of action. [17]"Let the one who boasts, boast in the Lord." [18]For it is not those who commend themselves that are approved, but those whom the Lord commends.

Paul and the False Apostles

11 I wish you would bear with me in a little foolishness. Do bear with me! [2]I feel a divine jealousy for you, for I promised you in marriage to one husband, to present you as a chaste virgin to Christ. [3]But I am afraid that as the serpent deceived Eve by its cunning, your thoughts will be led astray from a sincere and pure[e] devotion to Christ. [4]For if someone comes and proclaims another Jesus than the one we proclaimed, or if you receive a different spirit from the one you received, or a different gospel from the one you accepted, you submit to it readily enough. [5]I think that I am not in the least inferior to these super-apostles. [6]I may be untrained in speech, but not in knowledge; certainly in every way and in all things we have made this evident to you.

7 Did I commit a sin by humbling myself so that you might be exalted, because I proclaimed God's good news[f] to you free of charge? [8]I robbed other churches by accepting support from them in order to serve you. [9]And when I was with you and was in need, I did not burden anyone, for my needs were supplied by the friends[g] who came from Mac·e·do·ni·a. So I refrained and will continue to refrain from burdening you in any way.

[10]As the truth of Christ is in me, this boast of mine will not be silenced in the regions of A·cha´i·a. [11]And why? Because I do not love you? God knows I do!

12 And what I do I will also continue to do, in order to deny an opportunity to those who want an opportunity to be recognized as our equals in what they boast about. [13]For such boasters are false apostles, deceitful workers, disguising themselves as apostles of Christ. [14]And no wonder! Even Satan disguises himself as an angel of light. [15]So it is not strange if his ministers also disguise themselves as ministers of righteousness. Their end will match their deeds.

Paul's Sufferings as an Apostle

16 I repeat, let no one think that I am a fool; but if you do, then accept me as a fool, so that I too may boast a little. [17]What I am saying in regard to this boastful confidence, I am saying not with the Lord's authority, but as a fool; [18]since many boast according to human standards,[h] I will also boast. [19]For you gladly put up with fools, being wise yourselves! [20]For you put up with it when someone makes slaves of you, or preys upon you, or takes advantage of you, or puts on airs, or gives you a slap in the face. [21]To my shame, I must say, we were too weak for that!

But whatever anyone dares to boast of— I am speaking as a fool—I also dare to boast of that. [22]Are they Hebrews? So am I. Are they Israelites? So am I. Are they descendants of Abraham? So am I. [23]Are they ministers of Christ? I am talking like a madman—I am a better one: with far greater labors, far more imprisonments, with countless floggings, and often near death. [24]Five times I have received from the Jews the forty lashes minus one. [25]Three times I was beaten with rods. Once I received a stoning. Three times I was shipwrecked; for a night and a day I was

---

[d] Or the gospel   [e] Other ancient authorities lack and pure   [f] Gk the gospel of God   [g] Gk brothers   [h] Gk according to the flesh

adrift at sea; ²⁶on frequent journeys, in danger from rivers, danger from bandits, danger from my own people, danger from Gentiles, danger in the city, danger in the wilderness, danger at sea, danger from false brothers and sisters;ⁱ ²⁷in toil and hardship, through many a sleepless night, hungry and thirsty, often without food, cold and naked. ²⁸And, besides other things, I am under daily pressure because of my anxiety for all the churches. ²⁹Who is weak, and I am not weak? Who is made to stumble, and I am not indignant?

30 If I must boast, I will boast of the things that show my weakness. ³¹The God and Father of the Lord Jesus (blessed be he forever!) knows that I do not lie. ³²In Damascus, the governor^j under King Ar·e·tas guarded the city of Damascus in order to^k seize me, ³³but I was let down in a basket through a window in the wall,^l and escaped from his hands.

Paul's Visions and Revelations

12 It is necessary to boast; nothing is to be gained by it, but I will go on to visions and revelations of the Lord. ²I know a person in Christ who fourteen years ago was caught up to the third heaven—whether in the body or out of the body I do not know; God knows. ³And I know that such a person—whether in the body or out of the body I do not know; God knows— ⁴was caught up into Paradise and heard things that are not to be told, that no mortal is permitted to repeat. ⁵On behalf of such a one I will boast, but on my own behalf I will not boast, except of my weaknesses. ⁶But if I wish to boast, I will not be a fool, for I will be

 Paul suffered greatly from something he called "a thorn in my flesh" (we do not know what it was). Paul prayed and prayed that God would remove it, but the answer he got was that God's grace was enough and that God's power was made perfect in Paul's weakness. When we have to rely on God's power because we cannot do something ourselves, we are made stronger.

speaking the truth. But I refrain from it, so that no one may think better of me than what is seen in me or heard from me, ⁷even considering the exceptional character of the revelations. Therefore, to keep^m me from being too elated, a thorn was given me in the flesh, a messenger of Satan to torment me, to keep me from being too elated.ⁿ ⁸Three times I appealed to the Lord about this, that it would leave me, ⁹but he said to me, "My grace is sufficient for you, for power^o is made perfect in weakness." So, I will boast all the more gladly of my weaknesses, so that the power of Christ may dwell in me. ¹⁰Therefore I am content with weaknesses, insults, hardships, persecutions, and calamities for the sake of Christ; for whenever I am weak, then I am strong.

Paul's Concern for the Corinthian Church

11 I have been a fool! You forced me to it. Indeed you should have been the ones commending me, for I am not at all inferior to these super-apostles, even though I am nothing. ¹²The signs of a true apostle were performed among you with utmost patience, signs and wonders and mighty works. ¹³How have you been worse off

"But he said to me, 'My grace is sufficient for you, for power is made perfect in weakness.' So, I will boast all the more gladly of my weaknesses, so that the power of Christ may dwell in me." 2 Corinthians 12:9

ⁱ Gk *brothers*   ^j Gk *ethnarch*   ^k Other ancient authorities read *and wanted to*   ^l Gk *through the wall*   ^m Other ancient authorities read *To keep*   ⁿ Other ancient authorities lack *to keep me from being too elated*   ^o Other ancient authorities read *my power*

than the other churches, except that I myself did not burden you? Forgive me this wrong!

14 Here I am, ready to come to you this third time. And I will not be a burden, because I do not want what is yours but you; for children ought not to lay up for their parents, but parents for their children. [15]I will most gladly spend and be spent for you. If I love you more, am I to be loved less? [16]Let it be assumed that I did not burden you. Nevertheless (you say) since I was crafty, I took you in by deceit. [17]Did I take advantage of you through any of those whom I sent to you? [18]I urged Titus to go, and sent the brother with him. Titus did not take advantage of you, did he? Did we not conduct ourselves with the same spirit? Did we not take the same steps?

19 Have you been thinking all along that we have been defending ourselves before you? We are speaking in Christ before God. Everything we do, beloved, is for the sake of building you up. [20]For I fear that when I come, I may find you not as I wish, and that you may find me not as you wish; I fear that there may perhaps be quarreling, jealousy, anger, selfishness, slander, gossip, conceit, and disorder. [21]I fear that when I come again, my God may humble me before you, and that I may have to mourn over many who previously sinned and have not repented of the impurity, sexual immorality, and licentiousness that they have practiced.

Further Warning

13 This is the third time I am coming to you. "Any charge must be sustained by the evidence of two or three witnesses." [2]I warned those who sinned previously and all the others, and I warn them now while absent, as I did when present on my second visit, that if I come again, I will not be lenient— [3]since you desire proof that Christ is speaking in me. He is not weak in dealing with you, but is powerful in you. [4]For he was crucified in weakness, but lives by the power of God. For we are weak in him,[p] but in dealing with you we will live with him by the power of God.

5 Examine yourselves to see whether you are living in the faith. Test yourselves. Do you not realize that Jesus Christ is in you?—unless, indeed, you fail to meet the test! [6]I hope you will find out that we have not failed. [7]But we pray to God that you may not do anything wrong—not that we may appear to have met the test, but that you may do what is right, though we may seem to have failed. [8]For we cannot do anything against the truth, but only for the truth. [9]For we rejoice when we are weak and you are strong. This is what we pray for, that you may become perfect. [10]So I write these things while I am away from you, so that when I come, I may not have to be severe in using the authority that the Lord has given me for building up and not for tearing down.

Final Greetings and Benediction

11 Finally, brothers and sisters,[q] farewell.[r] Put things in order, listen to my appeal,[s] agree with one another, live in peace; and the God of love and peace will be with you. [12]Greet one another with a holy kiss. [13]All the saints greet you.

14 The grace of the Lord Jesus Christ, the love of God, and the communion of[t] the Holy Spirit be with all of you.

[p] Other ancient authorities read *with him*   [q] Gk *brothers*   [r] Or *rejoice*   [s] Or *encourage one another*   [t] Or *and the sharing in*

Galatians

The book of Galatians is a letter Paul wrote to several churches in Galatia about 50–56 AD. Paul learned that another group made up of Jewish Christians was trying to convince the Galatian Gentile Christians that they must accept and follow Jewish law before embracing faith in Jesus Christ. Paul wrote to the Galatian church saying that there was no need to follow Jewish law if you had not been a Jew before hearing about Jesus. Paul taught that those who believe in Jesus are saved by that alone. Paul sounds angry in this letter and he was!

He did not want anyone to confuse those who had become Christians by teaching them the wrong message about Jesus.

In this letter, Paul tells about his life before he met Jesus. His experience changed him dramatically, and he became convinced that Christian faith and life must be open to everyone who receives Christ with faith. The letter ends with a beautiful description of the kind of goodness that comes from the life of a person who truly believes in and follows Jesus Christ.

Galatians 1:1–5

Salutation

1 Paul an apostle—sent neither by human commission nor from human authorities, but through Jesus Christ and God the Father, who raised him from the dead— [2]and all the members of God's family[a] who are with me,

To the churches of Galatia:

3 Grace to you and peace from God our Father and the Lord Jesus Christ, [4]who gave himself for our sins to set us free from the present evil age, according to the will of our God and Father, [5]to whom be the glory forever and ever. Amen.

There Is No Other Gospel

6 I am astonished that you are so quickly deserting the one who called you in the grace of Christ and are turning to a different gospel— [7]not that there is another gospel, but there are some who are confusing you and want to pervert the gospel of Christ. [8]But even if we or an angel[b] from heaven should proclaim to you a gospel contrary to what we proclaimed to you, let that one be accursed! [9]As we have said before, so now I repeat, if anyone proclaims to you a gospel contrary to what you received, let that one be accursed!

10 Am I now seeking human approval, or God's approval? Or am I trying to please people? If I were still pleasing people, I would not be a servant[c] of Christ.

Paul's Vindication of His Apostleship

11 For I want you to know, brothers and sisters,[d] that the gospel that was proclaimed by me is not of human origin; [12]for I did not receive it from a human source, nor was I taught it, but I received it through a revelation of Jesus Christ.

13 You have heard, no doubt, of my earlier life in Jū·da·ism. I was violently persecuting the church of God and was trying to destroy it. [14]I advanced in Jū·da·ism beyond many among my people

of the same age, for I was far more zealous for the traditions of my ancestors. [15]But when God, who had set me apart before I was born and called me through his grace, was pleased [16]to reveal his Son to me,[e] so that I might proclaim him among the Gentiles, I did not confer with any human being, [17]nor did I go up to Jerusalem to those who were already apostles before me, but I went away at once into Arabia, and afterwards I returned to Damascus.

18 Then after three years I did go up to Jerusalem to visit Cē'phas and stayed with him fifteen days; [19]but I did not see any other apostle except James the Lord's brother. [20]In what I am writing to you, before God, I do not lie! [21]Then I went into the regions of Syria and Ci·li'ci·a, [22]and I was still unknown by sight to the churches of Judea that are in Christ; [23]they only heard it said, "The one who formerly was persecuting us is now proclaiming the faith he once tried to destroy." [24]And they glorified God because of me.

Paul and the Other Apostles

2 Then after fourteen years I went up again to Jerusalem with Bar'na·bas, taking Titus along with me. [2]I went up in response to a revelation. Then I laid before them (though only in a private meeting with the acknowledged leaders) the gospel that I proclaim among the Gentiles, in order to make sure that I was not running, or had not run, in vain. [3]But even Titus, who was with me, was not compelled to be circumcised, though he was a Greek. [4]But because of false believers[f] secretly brought in, who slipped in to spy on the freedom we have in Christ Jesus, so that they might enslave us— [5]we did not submit to them even for a moment, so that the truth of the gospel might always remain with you. [6]And from those who were supposed

a Gk *all the brothers*   *b* Or *a messenger*   *c* Gk *slave*   *d* Gk *brothers*   *e* Gk *in me*   *f* Gk *false brothers*

Paul talks about giving to the poor several times in the letters he wrote. Read Acts 24:17; Romans 15:25–28; 1 Corinthians 16:1–4; and 2 Corinthians 8–9. What do you think life would be like if everyone gave to the poor?

to be acknowledged leaders (what they actually were makes no difference to me; God shows no partiality)—those leaders contributed nothing to me. ⁷On the contrary, when they saw that I had been entrusted with the gospel for the uncircumcised, just as Peter had been entrusted with the gospel for the circumcised ⁸(for he who worked through Peter making him an apostle to the circumcised also worked through me in sending me to the Gentiles), ⁹and when James and Cē´phas and John, who were acknowledged pillars, recognized the grace that had been given to me, they gave to Bar´na·bas and me the right hand of fellowship, agreeing that we should go to the Gentiles and they to the circumcised. ¹⁰They asked only one thing, that we remember the poor, which was actually what I was⁸ eager to do.

Paul Rebukes Peter at Antioch

11 But when Cē´phas came to An´ti·och, I opposed him to his face, because he stood self-condemned; ¹²for until certain people came from James, he used to eat with the Gentiles. But after they came, he drew back and kept himself separate for fear of the circumcision faction. ¹³And the other Jews joined him in this hypocrisy, so that even Bar´na·bas was led astray by their hypocrisy. ¹⁴But when I saw that they were not acting consistently with the truth of the gospel, I said to Cē´phas before them all, "If you, though a Jew, live like a Gentile and not like a Jew, how can you compel the Gentiles to live like Jews?"ʰ

Jews and Gentiles Are Saved by Faith

15 We ourselves are Jews by birth and not Gentile sinners; ¹⁶yet we know that a person is justifiedⁱ not by the works of the law but through faith in Jesus Christ.ʲ And we have come to believe in Christ Jesus, so that we might be justified by faith in Christ,ᵏ and not by doing the works of the law, because no one will be justified by the works of the law. ¹⁷But if, in our effort to be justified in Christ, we ourselves have been found to be sinners, is Christ then a servant of sin? Certainly not! ¹⁸But if I build up again the very things that I once tore down, then I demonstrate that I am a transgressor. ¹⁹For through the law I died to the law, so that I might live to God. I have been crucified with Christ; ²⁰and it is no longer I who live, but it is Christ who lives in me. And the life I now live in the flesh I live by faith in the Son of God,ˡ who loved me and gave himself for me. ²¹I do not nullify the grace of God; for if justificationᵐ comes through the law, then Christ died for nothing.

Law or Faith

3 You foolish Galatians! Who has bewitched you? It was before your eyes that Jesus Christ was publicly

⁸ Or *had been*　ʰ Some interpreters hold that the quotation extends into the following paragraph　ⁱ Or *reckoned as righteous; and so elsewhere* ʲ Or *the faith of Jesus Christ*　ᵏ Or *the faith of Christ*　ˡ Or *by the faith of the Son of God*　ᵐ Or *righteousness*

Following the law was Paul's faithful and thankful response to God. He didn't follow the law to be saved, but as a way to be mindful of his connection to God. Paul says that faith alone is enough for those who follow Jesus Christ.

exhibited as crucified! [2]The only thing I want to learn from you is this: Did you receive the Spirit by doing the works of the law or by believing what you heard? [3]Are you so foolish? Having started with the Spirit, are you now ending with the flesh? [4]Did you experience so much for nothing?—if it really was for nothing. [5]Well then, does God[n] supply you with the Spirit and work miracles among you by your doing the works of the law, or by your believing what you heard?

6 Just as Abraham "believed God, and it was reckoned to him as righteousness," [7]so, you see, those who believe are the descendants of Abraham. [8]And the scripture, foreseeing that God would justify the Gentiles by faith, declared the gospel beforehand to Abraham, saying, "All the Gentiles shall be blessed in you." [9]For this reason, those who believe are blessed with Abraham who believed.

10 For all who rely on the works of the law are under a curse; for it is written, "Cursed is everyone who does not observe and obey all the things written in the book of the law." [11]Now it is evident that no one is justified before God by the law; for "The one who is righteous will live by faith."[o] [12]But the law does not rest on faith; on the contrary, "Whoever does the works of the law[p] will live by them." [13]Christ redeemed us from the curse of the law by becoming a curse for us—for it is written, "Cursed is everyone who hangs on a tree"— [14]in order that in Christ Jesus the blessing of Abraham might come to the Gentiles, so that we might receive the promise of the Spirit through faith.

The Promise to Abraham

15 Brothers and sisters,[q] I give an example from daily life: once a person's will[r] has been ratified, no one adds to it or annuls it. [16]Now the promises were made to Abraham and to his offspring;[s] it does not say, "And to offsprings,"[t] as of many; but it says, "And to your off-spring,"[s] that is, to one person, who is Christ. [17]My point is this: the law, which came four hundred thirty years later, does not annul a covenant previously ratified by God, so as to nullify the promise. [18]For if the inheritance comes from the law, it no longer comes from the promise; but God granted it to Abraham through the promise.

The Purpose of the Law

19 Why then the law? It was added because of transgressions, until the offspring[s] would come to whom the promise had been made; and it was ordained through angels by a mediator. [20]Now a mediator involves more than one party; but God is one.

21 Is the law then opposed to the promises of God? Certainly not! For if a law had been given that could make alive, then righteousness would indeed come through the law. [22]But the scripture has imprisoned all things under the power of sin, so that what was promised through faith in Jesus Christ[u] might be given to those who believe.

23 Now before faith came, we were imprisoned and guarded under the law until faith would be revealed. [24]Therefore the law was our disciplinarian until Christ came, so that we might be justified by faith. [25]But now that faith has come, we are no longer subject to a disciplinarian, [26]for in Christ Jesus you are all children of God through faith. [27]As many of you as were baptized into Christ have clothed yourselves with Christ. [28]There is no longer Jew or Greek, there is no longer slave or free, there is no longer male and female; for all of you are one in Christ Jesus. [29]And if you belong to Christ, then you are Abraham's offspring,[s] heirs according to the promise.

---

[n] Gk he   [o] Or The one who is righteous through faith will live [p] Gk does them   [q] Gk Brothers [r] Or covenant (as in verse 17)   [s] Gk seed [t] Gk seeds   [u] Or through the faith of Jesus Christ

"There is no longer Jew or Greek, there is no longer slave or free, there is no longer male and female; for all of you are one in Christ Jesus." Galatians 3:28

4 My point is this: heirs, as long as they are minors, are no better than slaves, though they are the owners of all the property; ²but they remain under guardians and trustees until the date set by the father. ³So with us; while we were minors, we were enslaved to the elemental spirits[v] of the world. ⁴But when the fullness of time had come, God sent his Son, born of a woman, born under the law, ⁵in order to redeem those who were under the law, so that we might receive adoption as children. ⁶And because you are children, God has sent the Spirit of his Son into our[w] hearts, crying, "Abba![x] Father!" ⁷So you are no longer a slave but a child, and if a child then also an heir, through God.[y]

Paul Reproves the Galatians

8 Formerly, when you did not know God, you were enslaved to beings that by nature are not gods. ⁹Now, however, that you have come to know God, or rather to be known by God, how can you turn back again to the weak and beggarly elemental spirits?[z] How can you want to be enslaved to them again? ¹⁰You are observing special days, and months, and seasons, and years. ¹¹I am afraid that my work for you may have been wasted.

Paul said that we are "children of God," because God's son came into our hearts and said, "Abba! Father!" Jesus shows us how we are sons and daughters of God, and can talk to God as a loving parent.

12 Friends,[a] I beg you, become as I am, for I also have become as you are. You have done me no wrong. ¹³You know that it was because of a physical infirmity that I first announced the gospel to you; ¹⁴though my condition put you to the test, you did not scorn or despise me, but welcomed me as an angel of God, as Christ Jesus. ¹⁵What has become of the good will you felt? For I testify that, had it been possible, you would have torn out your eyes and given them to me. ¹⁶Have I now become your enemy by telling you the truth? ¹⁷They make much of you, but for no good purpose; they want to exclude you, so that you may make much of them. ¹⁸It is good to be made much of for a good purpose at all times, and not only when I am present with you. ¹⁹My little children, for whom I am again in the pain of childbirth until Christ is formed in you, ²⁰I wish I were present with you now and could change my tone, for I am perplexed about you.

The Allegory of Hagar and Sarah

21 Tell me, you who desire to be subject to the law, will you not listen to the law? ²²For it is written that Abraham had two sons, one by a slave woman and the other by a free woman. ²³One, the child of the slave, was born according to the flesh; the other, the child of the free woman, was born through the promise. ²⁴Now this is an allegory: these women are two covenants. One woman, in fact, is Haʹgar, from Mount Sinai, bearing children for slavery. ²⁵Now Haʹgar is Mount Sinai in Arabia[c] and corresponds to the present Jerusalem, for she is in slavery with her children. ²⁶But the other woman corresponds to the Jerusalem above; she is free, and she is our mother. ²⁷For it is written,

---

[v] Or *the rudiments*   [w] Other ancient authorities read *your*   [x] Aramaic for *Father*   [y] Other ancient authorities read *an heir of God through Christ*   [z] Or *beggarly rudiments*   [a] Gk *Brothers*   [b] Other ancient authorities read *For Sinai is a mountain in Arabia*

"Rejoice, you childless one, you who
   bear no children,
burst into song and shout, you
   who endure no birth pangs;
for the children of the desolate
   woman are more numerous
than the children of the one who
   is married."

[28]Now you,[c] my friends,[d] are children of
the promise, like Isaac. [29]But just as at
that time the child who was born
according to the flesh persecuted the
child who was born according to the
Spirit, so it is now also. [30]But what does
the scripture say? "Drive out the slave
and her child; for the child of the slave
will not share the inheritance with the
child of the free woman." [31]So then,
friends,[d] we are children, not of the slave
but of the free woman.

5 [1]For freedom Christ has set us free.
   Stand firm, therefore, and do not
submit again to a yoke of slavery.

The Nature of Christian Freedom

2 Listen! I, Paul, am telling you that if
you let yourselves be circumcised, Christ
will be of no benefit to you. [3]Once again
I testify to every man who lets himself be
circumcised that he is obliged to obey the
entire law. [4]You who want to be justified
by the law have cut yourselves off from
Christ; you have fallen away from grace.
[5]For through the Spirit, by faith, we
eagerly wait for the hope of righteousness. [6]For in Christ Jesus neither circumcision nor uncircumcision counts for
anything; the only thing that counts is
faith working[e] through love.

7 You were running well; who prevented you from obeying the truth?
[8]Such persuasion does not come from
the one who calls you. [9]A little yeast
leavens the whole batch of dough. [10]I am
confident about you in the Lord that you
will not think otherwise. But whoever it
is that is confusing you will pay the
penalty. [11]But my friends,[g] why am I still

being persecuted if I am still preaching
circumcision? In that case the offense of
the cross has been removed. [12]I wish
those who unsettle you would castrate
themselves!

13 For you were called to freedom,
brothers and sisters;[d] only do not use
your freedom as an opportunity for self-
indulgence,[f] but through love become
slaves to one another. [14]For the whole
law is summed up in a single commandment, "You shall love your neighbor as
yourself." [15]If, however, you bite and
devour one another, take care that you
are not consumed by one another.

The Works of the Flesh

16 Live by the Spirit, I say, and do
not gratify the desires of the flesh. [17]For
what the flesh desires is opposed to the
Spirit, and what the Spirit desires is
opposed to the flesh; for these are
opposed to each other, to prevent you
from doing what you want. [18]But if you
are led by the Spirit, you are not subject
to the law. [19]Now the works of the flesh
are obvious: fornication, impurity, licentiousness, [20]idolatry, sorcery, enmities,
strife, jealousy, anger, quarrels, dissensions, factions, [21]envy,[g] drunkenness,
carousing, and things like these. I am
warning you, as I warned you before:
those who do such things will not
inherit the kingdom of God.

Good, healthy fruit trees
bear good, healthy fruit!
In the same way, God's
Spirit moves in the
hearts of believers and
fills them with good things. When
people look at the life of a Christian, they should see good, healthy
fruit (see Galatians 5:22-23a) in the
Christian's words and actions.

[c] Other ancient authorities read *we*   [d] Grk
brothers   [e] Or *made effective*   [f] Gk *the flesh*
[g] Other ancient authorities add *murder*

> "The fruit of the Spirit is love, joy, peace, patience, kindness, generosity, faithfulness, gentleness, and self-control."
>
> Galatians 5:22–23a

The Fruit of the Spirit

22 By contrast, the fruit of the Spirit is love, joy, peace, patience, kindness, generosity, faithfulness, [23]gentleness, and self-control. There is no law against such things. [24]And those who belong to Christ Jesus have crucified the flesh with its passions and desires. [25]If we live by the Spirit, let us also be guided by the Spirit. [26]Let us not become conceited, competing against one another, envying one another.

Bear One Another's Burdens

6 My friends,[h] if anyone is detected in a transgression, you who have received the Spirit should restore such a one in a spirit of gentleness. Take care that you yourselves are not tempted. [2]Bear one another's burdens, and in this way you will fulfill[i] the law of Christ. [3]For if those who are nothing think they are something, they deceive themselves. [4]All must test their own work; then that work, rather than their neighbor's work, will become a cause for pride. [5]For all must carry their own loads.

6 Those who are taught the word must share in all good things with their teacher.

> "So let us not grow weary in doing what is right, for we will reap at harvest-time, if we do not give up."
>
> Galatians 6:9

7 Do not be deceived; God is not mocked, for you reap whatever you sow. [8]If you sow to your own flesh, you will reap corruption from the flesh; but if you sow to the Spirit, you will reap eternal life from the Spirit. [9]So let us not grow weary in doing what is right, for we will reap at harvest-time, if we do not give up. [10]So then, whenever we have an opportunity, let us work for the good of all, and especially for those of the family of faith.

Final Admonitions and Benediction

11 See what large letters I make when I am writing in my own hand! [12]It is those who want to make a good showing in the flesh that try to compel you to be circumcised—only that they may not be persecuted for the cross of Christ. [13]Even the circumcised do not themselves obey the law, but they want you to be circumcised so that they may boast about your flesh. [14]May I never boast of anything except the cross of our Lord Jesus Christ, by which[j] the world has been crucified to me, and I to the world. [15]For[k] neither circumcision nor uncircumcision is anything; but a new creation is everything! [16]As for those who will follow this rule—peace be upon them, and mercy, and upon the Israel of God.

17 From now on, let no one make trouble for me; for I carry the marks of Jesus branded on my body.

18 May the grace of our Lord Jesus Christ be with your spirit, brothers and sisters.[h] Amen.

---

[h] Gk *Brothers*   [i] Other ancient authorities read *in this way fulfill* [j] Or *through whom*   [k] Other ancient authorities add *in Christ Jesus*

Ephesians

Most scholars believe the letter to the Ephesians was not written by Paul but by one of his disciples. This does not mean someone was trying to steal Paul's authority. It means that the person writing the letter was trying to sound like Paul in order to teach the readers Paul's most important ideas about Jesus and the Christian life.

The letter was probably written toward the end of the first century AD. There are some very old copies of this letter that are not addressed to Ephesus. Also, although Paul lived in the city of Ephesus for three years, this letter does not have any personal greetings to friends in Ephesus. Therefore, the letter to the Ephesians was probably a "circular" letter—a letter that was copied and sent to several churches rather than only to the church at Ephesus.

Ephesians appears to be written to churches having problems between the Jewish and Gentile members. The author wanted them to know Paul's belief that both Jew and Gentile were unified through faith in Jesus's life, death, and resurrection.

Ephesians 1:1–2

In New Testament times, Ephesus was a large Roman city. It was a commercial seaport and a religious center for the worship of the goddess Artemis. Paul lived for a while in Ephesus, where he taught in the synagogue.

Salutation

1 Paul, an apostle of Christ Jesus by the will of God,

To the saints who are in Eph´e·sus and are faithful[a] in Christ Jesus:

2 Grace to you and peace from God our Father and the Lord Jesus Christ.

Spiritual Blessings in Christ

3 Blessed be the God and Father of our Lord Jesus Christ, who has blessed us in Christ with every spiritual blessing in the heavenly places, [4]just as he chose us in Christ[b] before the foundation of the world to be holy and blameless before him in love. [5]He destined us for adoption as his children through Jesus Christ, according to the good pleasure of his will, [6]to the praise of his glorious grace that he freely bestowed on us in the Beloved. [7]In him we have redemption through his blood, the forgiveness of our trespasses, according to the riches of his grace [8]that he lavished on us. With all wisdom and insight [9]he has made known to us the mystery of his will, according to his good pleasure that he set forth in Christ, [10]as a plan for the fullness of time, to gather up all things in him, things in heaven and things on earth. [11]In Christ we have also obtained an inheritance,[c] having been destined according to the purpose of him who accomplishes all things according to his counsel and will, [12]so that we, who were the first to set our hope on Christ, might live for the praise of his glory. [13]In him

you also, when you had heard the word of truth, the gospel of your salvation, and had believed in him, were marked with the seal of the promised Holy Spirit; [14]this[d] is the pledge of our inheritance toward redemption as God's own people, to the praise of his glory.

Paul's Prayer

15 I have heard of your faith in the Lord Jesus and your love[e] toward all the saints, and for this reason [16]I do not cease to give thanks for you as I remember you in my prayers. [17]I pray that the God of our Lord Jesus Christ, the Father of glory, may give you a spirit of wisdom and revelation as you come to know him, [18]so that, with the eyes of your heart enlightened, you may know what is the hope to which he has called you, what are the riches of his glorious inheritance among the saints, [19]and what is the immeasurable greatness of his power for us who believe, according to the working of his great power. [20]God[f] put this power to work in Christ when he raised him from the dead and seated him at his right hand in the heavenly places,

> "I pray that the God of our Lord Jesus Christ, the Father of glory, may give you a spirit of wisdom and revelation as you come to know him, so that, with the eyes of your heart enlightened, you may know what is the hope to which he has called you, what are the riches of his glorious inheritance among the saints, and what is the immeasurable greatness of his power for us who believe, according to the working of his great power."
> Ephesians 1:17–19

[a] Other ancient authorities lack *in Ephesus*, reading *saints who are also faithful* [b] Gk *in him* [c] Or *been made a heritage* [d] Other ancient authorities read *who* [e] Other ancient authorities lack *and your love* [f] Gk *He*

[21]far above all rule and authority and power and dominion, and above every name that is named, not only in this age but also in the age to come. [22]And he has put all things under his feet and has made him the head over all things for the church, [23]which is his body, the fullness of him who fills all in all.

From Death to Life

2 You were dead through the trespasses and sins [2]in which you once lived, following the course of this world, following the ruler of the power of the air, the spirit that is now at work among those who are disobedient. [3]All of us once lived among them in the passions of our flesh, following the desires of flesh and senses, and we were by nature children of wrath, like everyone else. [4]But God, who is rich in mercy, out of the great love with which he loved us [5]even when we were dead through our trespasses, made us alive together with Christ[g]—by grace you have been saved— [6]and raised us up with him and seated us with him in the heavenly places in Christ Jesus, [7]so that in the ages to come he might show the immeasurable riches of his grace in kindness toward us in Christ Jesus. [8]For by grace you have been saved through faith, and this is not your own doing; it is the gift of God—[9]not the result of works, so that no one may boast. [10]For we are what he has made us, created in Christ Jesus for good works, which God prepared beforehand to be our way of life.

One in Christ

11 So then, remember that at one time you Gentiles by birth,[h] called "the uncircumcision" by those who are called "the circumcision"—a physical circum-cision made in the flesh by human hands— [12]remember that you were at that time without Christ, being aliens from the commonwealth of Israel, and strangers to the covenants of promise, having no hope and without God in the world. [13]But now in Christ Jesus you who once were far off have been brought near by the blood of Christ. [14]For he is our peace; in his flesh he has made both groups into one and has broken down the dividing wall, that is, the hostility between us. [15]He has abolished the law with its commandments and ordinances, that he might create in himself one new humanity in place of the two, thus making peace, [16]and might reconcile both groups to God in one body[i] through the cross, thus putting to death that hostility through it.[j] [17]So he came and proclaimed peace to you who were far off and peace to those who were near; [18]for through him both of us have access in one Spirit to the Father. [19]So then you are no longer strangers and aliens, but you are citizens with the saints and also members of the household of God, [20]built upon the foundation of the apostles and prophets, with Christ Jesus himself as the cornerstone.[k] [21]In him the whole structure is joined together and grows into a holy temple in the Lord; [22]in whom you also are built together spiritually[l] into a dwelling place for God.

Paul's Ministry to the Gentiles

3 This is the reason that I Paul am a prisoner for[m] Christ Jesus for the sake of you Gentiles— [2]for surely you have already heard of the commission of God's grace that was given me for you, [3]and how the mystery was made known to me by revelation, as I wrote above in a few words, [4]a reading of which will enable you to perceive my understanding of the mystery of Christ. [5]In former

You do not have to earn God's love—in fact, you cannot earn God's love! God's love is a gift to you.

---

[g] Other ancient authorities read *in Christ*　　[h] Gk *in the flesh*　　[i] Or *reconcile both of us in one body for God*　　[j] Or *in him, or in himself*　　[k] Or *keystone*　　[l] Gk *in the Spirit*　　[m] Or *of*

generations this mystery[n] was not made known to humankind, as it has now been revealed to his holy apostles and prophets by the Spirit: [6]that is, the Gentiles have become fellow heirs, members of the same body, and sharers in the promise in Christ Jesus through the gospel.

7 Of this gospel I have become a servant according to the gift of God's grace that was given me by the working of his power. [8]Although I am the very least of all the saints, this grace was given to me to bring to the Gentiles the news of the boundless riches of Christ, [9]and to make everyone see[o] what is the plan of the mystery hidden for ages in[p] God who created all things; [10]so that through the church the wisdom of God in its rich variety might now be made known to the rulers and authorities in the heavenly places. [11]This was in accordance with the eternal purpose that he has carried out in Christ Jesus our Lord, [12]in whom we have access to God in boldness and confidence through faith in him.[q] [13]I pray therefore that you[r] may not lose heart over my sufferings for you; they are your glory.

Prayer for the Readers

14 For this reason I bow my knees before the Father,[s] [15]from whom every family[t] in heaven and on earth takes its name. [16]I pray that, according to the riches of his glory, he may grant that you may be strengthened in your inner being with power through his Spirit, [17]and that Christ may dwell in your hearts through faith, as you are being rooted and grounded in love. [18]I pray that you may have the power to comprehend, with all the saints, what is the breadth and length and height and depth, [19]and to know the love of Christ that surpasses knowledge, so that you may be filled with all the fullness of God.

20 Now to him who by the power at work within us is able to accomplish abundantly far more than all we can ask

"Now to him who by the power at work within us is able to accomplish abundantly far more than all we can ask or imagine, to him be glory in the church and in Christ Jesus to all generations, forever and ever. Amen."

Ephesians 3:20

or imagine, [21]to him be glory in the church and in Christ Jesus to all generations, forever and ever. Amen.

Unity in the Body of Christ

4 I therefore, the prisoner in the Lord, beg you to lead a life worthy of the calling to which you have been called, [2]with all humility and gentleness, with patience, bearing with one another in love, [3]making every effort to maintain the unity of the Spirit in the bond of peace. [4]There is one body and one Spirit, just as you were called to the one hope of your calling, [5]one Lord, one faith, one baptism, [6]one God and Father of all, who is above all and through all and in all.

7 But each of us was given grace according to the measure of Christ's gift. [8]Therefore it is said,

"When he ascended on high he
made captivity itself a captive;
he gave gifts to his people."

[9](When it says, "He ascended," what does it mean but that he had also descended[u] into the lower parts of the

"There is one body and one Spirit, just as you were called to the one hope of your calling, one Lord, one faith, one baptism, one God and Father of all, who is above all and through all and in all."

Ephesians 4:4–6

[n] Gk it [o] Other ancient authorities read *to bring to light* [p] Or *by* [q] Or *the faith of him* [r] Or *I* [s] Other ancient authorities add *of our Lord Jesus Christ* [t] Gk *fatherhood* [u] Other ancient authorities add *first*

earth? ¹⁰He who descended is the same one who ascended far above all the heavens, so that he might fill all things.) ¹¹The gifts he gave were that some would be apostles, some prophets, some evangelists, some pastors and teachers, ¹²to equip the saints for the work of ministry, for building up the body of Christ, ¹³until all of us come to the unity of the faith and of the knowledge of the Son of God, to maturity, to the measure of the full stature of Christ. ¹⁴We must no longer be children, tossed to and fro and blown about by every wind of doctrine, by people's trickery, by their craftiness in deceitful scheming. ¹⁵But speaking the truth in love, we must grow up in every way into him who is the head, into Christ, ¹⁶from whom the whole body, joined and knit together by every ligament with which it is equipped, as each part is working properly, promotes the body's growth in building itself up in love.

The Old Life and the New

17 Now this I affirm and insist on in the Lord: you must no longer live as the Gentiles live, in the futility of their minds. ¹⁸They are darkened in their understanding, alienated from the life of God because of their ignorance and hardness of heart. ¹⁹They have lost all sensitivity and have abandoned themselves to licentiousness, greedy to practice every kind of impurity. ²⁰That is not the way you learned Christ! ²¹For surely you have heard about him and were taught in him, as truth is in Jesus. ²²You were taught to put away your former way of life, your old self, corrupt and deluded by its lusts, ²³and to be renewed in the spirit of your minds, ²⁴and to clothe yourselves with the new self, created according to the likeness of God in true righteousness and holiness.

Rules for the New Life

25 So then, putting away falsehood, let all of us speak the truth to our neighbors, for we are members of one another.

²⁶Be angry but do not sin; do not let the sun go down on your anger, ²⁷and do not make room for the devil. ²⁸Thieves must give up stealing; rather let them labor and work honestly with their own hands, so as to have something to share with the needy. ²⁹Let no evil talk come out of your mouths, but only what is useful for building up,ᵛ as there is need, so that your words may give grace to those who hear. ³⁰And do not grieve the Holy Spirit of God, with which you were marked with a seal for the day of redemption. ³¹Put away from you all bitterness and wrath and anger and wrangling and slander, together with all malice, ³²and be kind to one another, tenderhearted, forgiving one another, as God in Christ has forgiven you.ʷ

5 ¹Therefore be imitators of God, as beloved children, ²and live in love, as Christ loved usˣ and gave himself up for us, a fragrant offering and sacrifice to God.

Renounce Pagan Ways

3 But fornication and impurity of any kind, or greed, must not even be mentioned among you, as is proper among saints. ⁴Entirely out of place is obscene, silly, and vulgar talk; but instead, let there be thanksgiving. ⁵Be sure of this, that no fornicator or impure person, or one who is greedy (that is, an idolater), has any inheritance in the kingdom of Christ and of God.

6 Let no one deceive you with empty words, for because of these things the wrath of God comes on those who are disobedient. ⁷Therefore do not be associated with them. ⁸For once you were darkness, but now in the Lord you are light. Live as children of light— ⁹for the fruit of the light is found in all that is good and right and true. ¹⁰Try to find out what is pleasing to the Lord. ¹¹Take no part in the unfruitful works of darkness,

ᵛ Other ancient authorities read *building up faith*
ʷ Other ancient authorities read *us*   ˣ Other ancient authorities read *you*

but instead expose them. ¹²For it is shameful even to mention what such people do secretly; ¹³but everything exposed by the light becomes visible, ¹⁴for everything that becomes visible is light. Therefore it says,

"Sleeper, awake!
    Rise from the dead,
        and Christ will shine on you."

15 Be careful then how you live, not as unwise people but as wise, ¹⁶making the most of the time, because the days are evil. ¹⁷So do not be foolish, but understand what the will of the Lord is. ¹⁸Do not get drunk with wine, for that is debauchery; but be filled with the Spirit, ¹⁹as you sing psalms and hymns and spiritual songs among yourselves, singing and making melody to the Lord in your hearts, ²⁰giving thanks to God the Father at all times and for everything in the name of our Lord Jesus Christ.

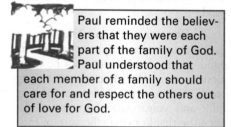

Paul reminded the believers that they were each part of the family of God. Paul understood that each member of a family should care for and respect the others out of love for God.

The Christian Household

21 Be subject to one another out of reverence for Christ.

22 Wives, be subject to your husbands as you are to the Lord. ²³For the husband is the head of the wife just as Christ is the head of the church, the body of which he is the Savior. ²⁴Just as the church is subject to Christ, so also wives ought to be, in everything, to their husbands.

25 Husbands, love your wives, just as Christ loved the church and gave himself up for her, ²⁶in order to make her holy by cleansing her with the washing of water by the word, ²⁷so as to present the church to himself in splendor, without a spot or wrinkle or anything of

the kind—yes, so that she may be holy and without blemish. ²⁸In the same way, husbands should love their wives as they do their own bodies. He who loves his wife loves himself. ²⁹For no one ever hates his own body, but he nourishes and tenderly cares for it, just as Christ does for the church, ³⁰because we are members of his body.ʸ ³¹"For this reason a man will leave his father and mother and be joined to his wife, and the two will become one flesh." ³²This is a great mystery, and I am applying it to Christ and the church. ³³Each of you, however, should love his wife as himself, and a wife should respect her husband.

To show respect for their parents, children should do what their parents tell them to do. Parents should never harm their children or try to make them angry but should be wise, responsible, and caring (see also Colossians 3:20–21).

Children and Parents

6 Children, obey your parents in the Lord,ᶻ for this is right. ²"Honor your father and mother"—this is the first commandment with a promise: ³"so that it may be well with you and you may live long on the earth."

4 And, fathers, do not provoke your children to anger, but bring them up in the discipline and instruction of the Lord.

Slaves and Masters

5 Slaves, obey your earthly masters with fear and trembling, in singleness of heart, as you obey Christ; ⁶not only while being watched, and in order to please them, but as slaves of Christ, doing the will of God from the heart. ⁷Render service with enthusiasm, as to the Lord and not to men and women, ⁸knowing that whatever good we do, we

ʸ Other ancient authorities add *of his flesh and of his bones*   ᶻ Other ancient authorities lack *in the Lord*

Armor is a covering that protects soldiers in battle. In Bible times, armor included a helmet, a girdle, a shield, a breastplate, mail, and leg guards. These protected the soldier during an enemy attack. Paul used the pieces of armor to refer to truth, righteousness, peace, faith, and prayer. When we wear the "armor of God," it gives us strength us to stand against evil. Are you wearing any of the pieces of God's armor right now?

will receive the same again from the Lord, whether we are slaves or free.

9 And, masters, do the same to them. Stop threatening them, for you know that both of you have the same Master in heaven, and with him there is no partiality.

The Whole Armor of God

10 Finally, be strong in the Lord and in the strength of his power. [11]Put on the whole armor of God, so that you may be able to stand against the wiles of the devil. [12]For our[a] struggle is not against enemies of blood and flesh, but against the rulers, against the authorities, against the cosmic powers of this present darkness, against the spiritual forces of evil in the heavenly places. [13]Therefore take up the whole armor of God, so that you may be able to withstand on that evil day, and having done everything, to stand firm. [14]Stand therefore, and fasten the belt of truth around your waist, and

put on the breastplate of righteousness. [15]As shoes for your feet put on whatever will make you ready to proclaim the gospel of peace. [16]With all of these,[b] take the shield of faith, with which you will be able to quench all the flaming arrows of the evil one. [17]Take the helmet of salvation, and the sword of the Spirit, which is the word of God.

18 Pray in the Spirit at all times in every prayer and supplication. To that end keep alert and always persevere in supplication for all the saints. [19]Pray also for me, so that when I speak, a message may be given to me to make known with boldness the mystery of the gospel,[c] [20]for which I am an ambassador in chains. Pray that I may declare it boldly, as I must speak.

Personal Matters and Benediction

21 So that you also may know how I am and what I am doing, Tych´i·cus will tell you everything. He is a dear brother and a faithful minister in the Lord. [22]I am sending him to you for this very purpose, to let you know how we are, and to encourage your hearts.

23 Peace be to the whole community,[d] and love with faith, from God the Father and the Lord Jesus Christ. [24]Grace be with all who have an undying love for our Lord Jesus Christ.[e]

[a] Other ancient authorities read *your*   [b] Or *In all circumstances*   [c] Other ancient authorities lack *of the gospel*   [d] Gk *to the brothers*   [e] Other ancient authorities add *Amen*

Philippians

The apostle Paul, along with fellow missionaries, left Asia to do missionary work in Europe. In the city of Philippi, several people heard the Good News and became Christians. These included a woman named Lydia, the local jailer, and their families. Acts 16 tells of Paul's experiences in Philippi. We do not know exactly when Paul wrote the letter to the Philippians or where he was when he wrote it. Some people believe that two letters may have been put together to form this letter.

In this letter, Paul expressed love for the Christians at Philippi. He also expressed thanks for a gift of money they had sent to pay for his expenses in prison. He encouraged them to treat one another with kindness and humility and to live as Jesus lived. Even though he was in prison, Paul did not give up or turn away from God. He knew that his strength gave others the courage to stand up for their faith in Jesus Christ. This letter shows Paul's strong personal faith and teaches us how to live as Christians. As Paul wrote this letter, he realized that he would probably be killed because of his faith in Christ. But he was not sad or afraid. Paul knew that if he escaped death, he would resume his missionary work. If he did not escape death, he would "depart and be with Christ" (Philippians 1:23). Paul knew that every follower of Jesus could have the same deep joy that he had, and so he wrote, "Rejoice in the Lord always; again I will say, Rejoice" (Philippians 4:4).

Philippians 1:1–2

Salutation

1 Paul and Timothy, servants[a] of Christ Jesus,

To all the saints in Christ Jesus who are in Phi·lip′pī, with the bishops[b] and deacons:[c]

2 Grace to you and peace from God our Father and the Lord Jesus Christ.

Paul's Prayer for the Philippians

3 I thank my God every time I remember you, [4]constantly praying with joy in every one of my prayers for all of you, [5]because of your sharing in the gospel from the first day until now. [6]I am confident of this, that the one who began a good work among you will bring it to completion by the day of Jesus Christ. [7]It is right for me to think this way about all of you, because you hold me in your heart,[d] for all of you share in God's grace[e] with me, both in my imprisonment and in the defense and confirmation of the gospel. [8]For God is my witness, how I long for all of you with the compassion of Christ Jesus. [9]And this is my prayer, that your love may overflow more and more with knowledge and full insight [10]to help you to determine what is best, so that in the day of Christ you may be pure and blameless, [11]having produced the harvest of righteousness that comes through Jesus Christ for the glory and praise of God.

Paul's Present Circumstances

12 I want you to know, beloved,[f] that what has happened to me has actually helped to spread the gospel, [13]so that it has become known throughout the whole imperial guard[g] and to everyone else that my imprisonment is for Christ; [14]and most of the brothers and sisters,[f] having been made confident in the Lord by my imprisonment, dare to speak the word[h] with greater boldness and without fear.

15 Some proclaim Christ from envy and rivalry, but others from goodwill. [16]These proclaim Christ out of love, knowing that I have been put here for the defense of the gospel; [17]the others proclaim Christ out of selfish ambition, not sincerely but intending to increase my suffering in my imprisonment. [18]What does it matter? Just this, that Christ is proclaimed in every way, whether out of false motives or true; and in that I rejoice.

Yes, and I will continue to rejoice, [19]for I know that through your prayers and the help of the Spirit of Jesus Christ this will turn out for my deliverance. [20]It is my eager expectation and hope that I will not be put to shame in any way, but that by my speaking with all boldness, Christ will be exalted now as always in my body, whether by life or by death. [21]For to me, living is Christ and dying is gain. [22]If I am to live in the flesh, that means fruitful labor for me; and I do not know which I prefer. [23]I am hard pressed between the two: my desire is to depart and be with Christ, for that is far better;

Paul was in prison for proclaiming the gospel. Christianity is so commonly accepted in many parts of the world today that it is hard to imagine that people still sometimes go to jail for believing that Jesus is the Messiah, even now.

Though Paul felt close to death in prison (conditions were harsh, and he probably wondered if he would be killed), he was happy because the guards, prisoners, and others knew about Jesus through him. Instead of feeling sorry for himself, Paul was glad for others.

[a] Gk slaves   [b] Or overseers   [c] Or overseers and helpers   [d] Or because I hold you in my heart   [e] Gk in grace   [f] Gk brothers   [g] Gk whole praetorium   [h] Other ancient authorities read word of God

> "So that at the name of Jesus every knee should bend, in heaven and on earth and under the earth, and every tongue should confess that Jesus Christ is Lord, to the glory of God the Father."
>
> Philippians 2:10

²⁴but to remain in the flesh is more necessary for you. ²⁵Since I am convinced of this, I know that I will remain and continue with all of you for your progress and joy in faith, ²⁶so that I may share abundantly in your boasting in Christ Jesus when I come to you again.

27 Only, live your life in a manner worthy of the gospel of Christ, so that, whether I come and see you or am absent and hear about you, I will know that you are standing firm in one spirit, striving side by side with one mind for the faith of the gospel, ²⁸and are in no way intimidated by your opponents. For them this is evidence of their destruction, but of your salvation. And this is God's doing. ²⁹For he has graciously granted you the privilege not only of believing in Christ, but of suffering for him as well—³⁰since you are having the same struggle that you saw I had and now hear that I still have.

Imitating Christ's Humility

2 If then there is any encouragement in Christ, any consolation from love, any sharing in the Spirit, any compassion and sympathy, ²make my joy

The "Christ Hymn" (Philippians 2:5–11) is a beautiful poem or hymn about Jesus deciding to be like a slave to serve God's people. Jesus once said, "The first will be last, and the last will be first" (see Matthew 20:16, Mark 10:21, and Luke 13:30). What do you think this means?

complete: be of the same mind, having the same love, being in full accord and of one mind. ³Do nothing from selfish ambition or conceit, but in humility regard others as better than yourselves. ⁴Let each of you look not to your own interests, but to the interests of others. ⁵Let the same mind be in you that was[i] in Christ Jesus,

⁶ who, though he was in the form of
    God,
        did not regard equality with God
            as something to be exploited,
⁷ but emptied himself,
        taking the form of a slave,
        being born in human likeness.
    And being found in human form,
⁸   he humbled himself
        and became obedient to the point
            of death—
        even death on a cross.

⁹ Therefore God also highly exalted
    him
        and gave him the name
        that is above every name,
¹⁰ so that at the name of Jesus
        every knee should bend,
        in heaven and on earth and under
            the earth,
¹¹ and every tongue should confess
        that Jesus Christ is Lord,
        to the glory of God the Father.

Shining as Lights in the World

12 Therefore, my beloved, just as you have always obeyed me, not only in my presence, but much more now in my absence, work out your own salvation with fear and trembling; ¹³for it is God who is at work in you, enabling you both to will and to work for his good pleasure.

14 Do all things without murmuring and arguing, ¹⁵so that you may be blameless and innocent, children of God without blemish in the midst of a crooked and perverse generation, in

---

[i] Or *that you have*

which you shine like stars in the world. [16]It is by your holding fast to the word of life that I can boast on the day of Christ that I did not run in vain or labor in vain. [17]But even if I am being poured out as a libation over the sacrifice and the offering of your faith, I am glad and rejoice with all of you— [18]and in the same way you also must be glad and rejoice with me.

Timothy and Epaphroditus

19 I hope in the Lord Jesus to send Timothy to you soon, so that I may be cheered by news of you. [20]I have no one like him who will be genuinely concerned for your welfare. [21]All of them are seeking their own interests, not those of Jesus Christ. [22]But Timothy's[j] worth you know, how like a son with a father he has served with me in the work of the gospel. [23]I hope therefore to send him as soon as I see how things go with me; [24]and I trust in the Lord that I will also come soon.

25 Still, I think it necessary to send to you E·paph·ro·di´tus—my brother and co-worker and fellow soldier, your messenger[k] and minister to my need; [26]for he has been longing for[l] all of you, and has been distressed because you heard that he was ill. [27]He was indeed so ill that he nearly died. But God had mercy on him, and not only on him but on me also, so that I would not have one sorrow after another. [28]I am the more eager to send him, therefore, in order that you may rejoice at seeing him again, and that I may be less anxious. [29]Welcome him then in the Lord with all joy, and honor such people, [30]because he came close to death for the work of Christ,[m] risking his life to make up for those services that you could not give me.

3 Finally, my brothers and sisters,[n] rejoice[o] in the Lord.

Breaking with the Past

To write the same things to you is not troublesome to me, and for you it is a safeguard.

2 Beware of the dogs, beware of the evil workers, beware of those who mutilate the flesh![p] [3]For it is we who are the circumcision, who worship in the Spirit of God[q] and boast in Christ Jesus and have no confidence in the flesh— [4]even though I, too, have reason for confidence in the flesh.

If anyone else has reason to be confident in the flesh, I have more: [5]circumcised on the eighth day, a member of the people of Israel, of the tribe of Benjamin, a Hebrew born of Hebrews; as to the law, a Phar´i·see; [6]as to zeal, a persecutor of the church; as to righteousness under the law, blameless.

7 Yet whatever gains I had, these I have come to regard as loss because of Christ. [8]More than that, I regard everything as loss because of the surpassing value of knowing Christ Jesus my Lord. For his sake I have suffered the loss of all things, and I regard them as rubbish, in order that I may gain Christ [9]and be found in him, not having a righteousness of my own that comes from the law, but one that comes through faith in Christ,[r] the righteousness from God based on faith. [10]I want to know Christ[s] and the power of his resurrection and the sharing of his sufferings by becoming like him in his death, [11]if somehow I may attain the resurrection from the dead.

 As Christians our goal is to know Jesus Christ and to do our best to become like him. Read Philippians 2:5–11 to find out more about how Jesus lived his life. How can we have this same type of attitude?

j Gk *his*   *k* Gk *apostle*   *l* Other ancient authorities read *longing to see*   *m* Other ancient authorities read *of the Lord*   *n* Gk *my brothers*   *o* Or *farewell*   *p* Gk *the mutilation*   *q* Other ancient authorities read *worship God in spirit*   *r* Or *through the faith of Christ*   *s* Gk *him*

> "But this one thing I do: forgetting what lies behind and straining forward to what lies ahead, I press on toward the goal for the prize of the heavenly call of God in Christ Jesus." Philippians 3:13*b*

Pressing toward the Goal

12 Not that I have already obtained this or have already reached the goal;[t] but I press on to make it my own, because Christ Jesus has made me his own. [13]Beloved,[u] I do not consider that I have made it my own;[v] but this one thing I do: forgetting what lies behind and straining forward to what lies ahead, [14]I press on toward the goal for the prize of the heavenly[w] call of God in Christ Jesus. [15]Let those of us then who are mature be of the same mind; and if you think differently about anything, this too God will reveal to you. [16]Only let us hold fast to what we have attained.

17 Brothers and sisters,[u] join in imitating me, and observe those who live according to the example you have in us. [18]For many live as enemies of the cross of Christ; I have often told you of them, and now I tell you even with tears. [19]Their end is destruction; their god is the belly; and their glory is in their shame; their minds are set on earthly things. [20]But our citizenship[x] is in heaven, and it is from there that we are expecting a Savior, the Lord Jesus Christ. [21]He will transform the body of our humiliation[y] that it may be conformed to the body of his glory,[z] by the power that also enables him to make all things subject to himself. [1]Therefore, my brothers and sisters,[a] whom I love and long for, my joy and crown, stand firm in the Lord in this way, my beloved.

Exhortations

2 I urge Eū·ŏ′di·a and I urge Syn′-ty·chē to be of the same mind in the Lord. [3]Yes, and I ask you also, my loyal companion,[b] help these women, for they have struggled beside me in the work of the gospel, together with Clement and the rest of my co-workers, whose names are in the book of life.

4 Rejoice[c] in the Lord always; again I will say, Rejoice.[c] [5]Let your gentleness be known to everyone. The Lord is near. [6]Do not worry about anything, but in everything by prayer and supplication with thanksgiving let your requests be made known to God. [7]And the peace of God, which surpasses all understanding, will guard your hearts and your minds in Christ Jesus.

8 Finally, beloved,[d] whatever is true, whatever is honorable, whatever is just, whatever is pure, whatever is pleasing, whatever is commendable, if there is any excellence and if there is anything worthy of praise, think about[e] these things. [9]Keep on doing the things that you have learned and received and heard and seen in me, and the God of peace will be with you.

 Paul says we should not worry about anything, but pray to God with thanks. Sometimes it is hard to remember to talk to God when we are very worried. But God will give us peace of mind if we ask.

Acknowledgment of the Philippians' Gift

10 I rejoice[f] in the Lord greatly that now at last you have revived your concern for me; indeed, you were concerned for me, but had no opportunity to show it.[g] [11]Not that I am referring to

---

[t] Or *have already been made perfect*   [u] Gk *Brothers*   [v] Other ancient authorities read *my own yet*   [w] Gk *upward*   [x] Or *commonwealth*   [y] Or *our humble bodies*   [z] Or *his glorious body*   [a] Gk *my brothers*   [b] Or *loyal Syzygus*   [c] Or *Farewell*   [d] Gk *brothers*   [e] Gk *take account*   [f] Gk *I rejoiced*   [g] Gk lacks *to show it*

being in need; for I have learned to be content with whatever I have. [12]I know what it is to have little, and I know what it is to have plenty. In any and all circumstances I have learned the secret of being well-fed and of going hungry, of having plenty and of being in need. [13]I can do all things through him who strengthens me. [14]In any case, it was kind of you to share my distress.

15 You Phi·lip´pi·ans indeed know that in the early days of the gospel, when I left Mac·e·dō´ni·a, no church shared with me in the matter of giving and receiving, except you alone. [16]For even when I was in Thes·sa·lo·nī´ca, you sent me help for my needs more than once. [17]Not that I seek the gift, but I seek the profit that accumulates to your account. [18]I have been paid in full and have more than enough; I am fully satisfied, now that I have received from E·paph·ro·dī´tus the gifts you sent, a fragrant offering, a sacrifice acceptable and pleasing to God. [19]And my God will fully satisfy every need of yours according to his riches in glory

"Finally, beloved, whatever is true, whatever is honorable, whatever is just, whatever is pure, whatever is pleasing, whatever is commendable, if there is any excellence and if there is anything worthy of praise, think about these things."   Philippians 4:8

in Christ Jesus. [20]To our God and Father be glory forever and ever. Amen.

Final Greetings and Benediction

21 Greet every saint in Christ Jesus. The friends[h] who are with me greet you. [22]All the saints greet you, especially those of the emperor's household.

23 The grace of the Lord Jesus Christ be with your spirit.[i]

"I can do all things through him who strengthens me."
Philippians 4:13

[h] Gk *brothers*   [i] Other ancient authorities add *Amen*

Colossians

Colossae was a city about 100 miles from Ephesus. It formed a triangle with Hierapolis and Laodicea, two other cities mentioned in the New Testament. Colossae was once a wealthy city, but it eventually declined to a small town. Paul did not found the church at Colossae but had heard of the love and faith of the Christians there through his friend Epaphras. At one point there was some sort of false teaching going on, and some of the believers were listening to things that were not true. We do not know if Paul wrote the letter to the Colossians, but the letter teaches that people are saved only through faith in Jesus Christ.

The author of the letter to the Colossians did not want the believers at Colossae to be misled but to know the truth about Jesus Christ. Christians should know the true mystery of having the spirit of Christ in their hearts by faith: "the riches of the glory of this mystery, which is Christ in you, the hope of glory" (Colossians 1:27). The letter tells the believers that trust in Christ is the one thing that matters, and encourages them to remain strong in their devotion to Christ. "And whatever you do, in word or deed, do everything in the name of the Lord Jesus, giving thanks to God the Father through him" (Colossians 3:17).

Colossians 1:1–2

Salutation

1 Paul, an apostle of Christ Jesus by the will of God, and Timothy our brother,

2 To the saints and faithful brothers and sisters*a* in Christ in Co·los´saē:

Grace to you and peace from God our Father.

Paul Thanks God for the Colossians

3 In our prayers for you we always thank God, the Father of our Lord Jesus Christ, [4]for we have heard of your faith in Christ Jesus and of the love that you have for all the saints, [5]because of the hope laid up for you in heaven. You have heard of this hope before in the word of the truth, the gospel [6]that has come to you. Just as it is bearing fruit and growing in the whole world, so it has been bearing fruit among yourselves from the day you heard it and truly comprehended the grace of God. [7]This you learned from Ep´a·phras, our beloved fellow servant.*b* He is a faithful minister of Christ on your*c* behalf, [8]and he has made known to us your love in the Spirit.

9 For this reason, since the day we heard it, we have not ceased praying for you and asking that you may be filled with the knowledge of God's*d* will in all spiritual wisdom and understanding, [10]so that you may lead lives worthy of the Lord, fully pleasing to him, as you bear fruit in every good work and as you grow in the knowledge of God. [11]May you be made strong with all the strength that comes from his glorious power, and may you be prepared to endure everything with patience, while joyfully [12]giving thanks to the Father, who has enabled*e* you*f* to share in the inheritance of the saints in the light. [13]He has rescued us from the power of darkness and transferred us into the kingdom of his beloved Son, [14]in whom we have redemption, the forgiveness of sins.*g*

Through Christ, God created the world and everything in it (see also John 1:1–5). God was pleased with creation and especially with humanity, whom God loved. But we often turn away from God's love. Although we turn away from God, God never turns away from us. Instead, God sent Jesus to die for our sins. When we have faith in Jesus, we are once more God's perfect creation.

The Supremacy of Christ

15 He is the image of the invisible God, the firstborn of all creation; [16]for in*h* him all things in heaven and on earth were created, things visible and invisible, whether thrones or dominions or rulers or powers—all things have been created through him and for him. [17]He himself is before all things, and in*i* him all things hold together. [18]He is the head of the body, the church; he is the beginning, the firstborn from the dead, so that he might come to have first place in everything. [19]For in him all the fullness of God was pleased to dwell, [20]and through him God was pleased to reconcile to himself all things, whether on earth or in heaven, by making peace through the blood of his cross.

21 And you who were once estranged and hostile in mind, doing evil deeds, [22]he has now reconciled*i* in his fleshly body*j* through death, so as to present you holy and blameless and irreproachable before him— [23]provided that you continue securely established and steadfast in the faith, without shifting from the hope promised by the gospel that

a Gk brothers *b* Gk slave *c* Other ancient authorities read our *d* Gk his *e* Other ancient authorities read called *f* Other ancient authorities read us *g* Other ancient authorities add through his blood *h* Or by *i* Other ancient authorities read you have now been reconciled *j* Gk in the body of his flesh you heard, which has been proclaimed to every creature under heaven. I, Paul, became a servant of this gospel.

Paul's Interest in the Colossians

24 I am now rejoicing in my sufferings for your sake, and in my flesh I am completing what is lacking in Christ's afflictions for the sake of his body, that is, the church. [25]I became its servant according to God's commission that was given to me for you, to make the word of God fully known, [26]the mystery that has been hidden throughout the ages and generations but has now been revealed to his saints. [27]To them God chose to make known how great among the Gentiles are the riches of the glory of this mystery, which is Christ in you, the hope of glory. [28]It is he whom we proclaim, warning everyone and teaching everyone in all wisdom, so that we may present everyone mature in Christ. [29]For this I toil and struggle with all the energy that he powerfully inspires within me.

2 For I want you to know how much I am struggling for you, and for those in Lā·o·di·cē′a, and for all who have not seen me face to face. [2]I want their hearts to be encouraged and united in love, so that they may have all the riches of assured understanding and have the knowledge of God's mystery, that is, Christ himself,[k] [3]in whom are hidden all the treasures of wisdom and knowledge. [4]I am saying this so that no one may deceive you with plausible arguments. [5]For though I am absent in body, yet I am with you in spirit, and I rejoice to see your morale and the firmness of your faith in Christ.

"As you therefore have received Christ Jesus the Lord, continue to live your lives in him and established in the faith, just as you were taught, abounding in thanksgiving."

Colossians 2:6

Fullness of Life in Christ

6 As you therefore have received Christ Jesus the Lord, continue to live your lives[l] in him, [7]rooted and built up in him and established in the faith, just as you were taught, abounding in thanksgiving.

8 See to it that no one takes you captive through philosophy and empty deceit, according to human tradition, according to the elemental spirits of the universe,[m] and not according to Christ. [9]For in him the whole fullness of deity dwells bodily, [10]and you have come to fullness in him, who is the head of every ruler and authority. [11]In him also you were circumcised with a spiritual circumcision,[n] by putting off the body of the flesh in the circumcision of Christ; [12]when you were buried with him in baptism, you were also raised with him through faith in the power of God, who raised him from the dead. [13]And when you were dead in trespasses and the uncircumcision of your flesh, God[o] made you[p] alive together with him, when he forgave us all our trespasses, [14]erasing the record that stood against us with its legal demands. He set this aside, nailing it to the cross. [15]He disarmed[q] the rulers and authorities and made a public example of them, triumphing over them in it.

16 Therefore do not let anyone condemn you in matters of food and drink or of observing festivals, new moons, or sabbaths. [17]These are only a shadow of what is to come, but the substance belongs to Christ. [18]Do not let anyone disqualify you, insisting on self-abasement and worship of angels, dwelling[r] on visions,[s] puffed up without cause by a human way of thinking,[t] [19]and not holding fast

[k] Other ancient authorities read *of the mystery of God, both of the Father and of Christ* [l] Gk *to walk* [m] Or *the rudiments of the world* [n] Gk *a circumcision made without hands* [o] Gk *he* [p] Other ancient authorities read *made us*; others, *made* [q] Or *divested himself of* [r] Other ancient authorities read *not dwelling* [s] Meaning of Gk uncertain [t] Gk *by the mind of his flesh*

to the head, from whom the whole body, nourished and held together by its ligaments and sinews, grows with a growth that is from God.

Warnings against False Teachers

20 If with Christ you died to the elemental spirits of the universe,[u] why do you live as if you still belonged to the world? Why do you submit to regulations, [21]"Do not handle, Do not taste, Do not touch"? [22]All these regulations refer to things that perish with use; they are simply human commands and teachings. [23]These have indeed an appearance of wisdom in promoting self-imposed piety, humility, and severe treatment of the body, but they are of no value in checking self-indulgence.[v]

The New Life in Christ

3 So if you have been raised with Christ, seek the things that are above, where Christ is, seated at the right hand of God. [2]Set your minds on things that are above, not on things that are on earth, [3]for you have died, and your life is hidden with Christ in God. [4]When Christ who is your[w] life is revealed, then you also will be revealed with him in glory.

5 Put to death, therefore, whatever in you is earthly: fornication, impurity, passion, evil desire, and greed (which is idolatry). [6]On account of these the wrath of God is coming on those who are disobedient.[x] [7]These are the ways you also once followed, when you were living that life.[y] [8]But now you must get rid of all such things—anger, wrath, malice, slander, and abusive[z] language from your mouth. [9]Do not lie to one another, seeing that you have stripped off the old self with its practices [10]and have clothed yourselves with the new self, which is being renewed in knowledge according to the image of its creator. [11]In that renewal[a] there is no longer Greek and Jew, circumcised and uncircumcised, barbarian, Scyth'i·an, slave and free; but Christ is all and in all!

"Set your mind on things that are above, not on things that are on earth, for you have died, and your life is hidden with Christ in God."
Colossians 3:2

12 As God's chosen ones, holy and beloved, clothe yourselves with compassion, kindness, humility, meekness, and patience. [13]Bear with one another and, if anyone has a complaint against another, forgive each other; just as the Lord[b] has forgiven you, so you also must forgive. [14]Above all, clothe yourselves with love, which binds everything together in perfect harmony. [15]And let the peace of Christ rule in your hearts, to which indeed you were called in the one body. And be thankful. [16]Let the word of Christ[c] dwell in you richly; teach and admonish one another in all wisdom; and with gratitude in your hearts sing psalms, hymns, and spiritual songs to God.[d] [17]And whatever you do, in word or deed, do everything in the name of the Lord Jesus, giving thanks to God the Father through him.

Colossians 3:12–17 is a beautiful expression of how God wants us to live together in community. We are to forgive one another, be at peace with one another, and treat one another with kindness and love.

Rules for Christian Households

18 Wives, be subject to your husbands, as is fitting in the Lord. [19]Husbands, love your wives and never treat them harshly.

[u] Or *the rudiments of the world*   [v] Or *are of no value, serving only to indulge the flesh*   [w] Other authorities read *our*   [x] Other ancient authorities lack *on those who are disobedient* (Gk *the children of disobedience*)   [y] Or *living among such people*   [z] Or *filthy*   [a] Gk *its creator,* [11]*where*   [b] Other ancient authorities read *just as Christ*   [c] Other ancient authorities read *of God,* or *of the Lord*   [d] Other ancient authorities read *to the Lord*

> "Devote yourselves to prayer, keeping alert in it with thanksgiving."
>
> Colossians 4:2

20 Children, obey your parents in everything, for this is your acceptable duty in the Lord. [21]Fathers, do not provoke your children, or they may lose heart. [22]Slaves, obey your earthly masters[e] in everything, not only while being watched and in order to please them, but wholeheartedly, fearing the Lord.[e] [23]Whatever your task, put yourselves into it, as done for the Lord and not for your masters,[f] [24]since you know that from the Lord you will receive the inheritance as your reward; you serve[g] the Lord Christ. [25]For the wrongdoer will be paid back for whatever wrong has been done, and there is no partiality. [1]Masters, treat your slaves justly and fairly, for you

4 know that you also have a Master in heaven.

Further Instructions

2 Devote yourselves to prayer, keeping alert in it with thanksgiving. [3]At the same time pray for us as well that God will open to us a door for the word, that we may declare the mystery of Christ, for which I am in prison, [4]so that I may reveal it clearly, as I should.

5 Conduct yourselves wisely toward outsiders, making the most of the time.[h] [6]Let your speech always be gracious, seasoned with salt, so that you may know how you ought to answer everyone.

Final Greetings and Benediction

7 Tych·i·cus will tell you all the news about me; he is a beloved brother, a faithful minister, and a fellow servant[i] in the Lord. [8]I have sent him to you for this very purpose, so that you may know how we are[j] and that he may encourage your hearts; [9]he is coming with O·nes´i·mus,

the faithful and beloved brother, who is one of you. They will tell you about everything here.

10 Ar·is·tar´chus my fellow prisoner greets you, as does Mark the cousin of Bar´na·bas, concerning whom you have received instructions—if he comes to you, welcome him. [11]And Jesus who is called Justus greets you. These are the only ones of the circumcision among my co-workers for the kingdom of God, and they have been a comfort to me. [12]Ep´a·phras, who is one of you, a servant[i] of Christ Jesus, greets you. He is always wrestling in his prayers on your behalf, so that you may stand mature and fully assured in everything that God wills. [13]For I testify for him that he has worked hard for you and for those in Lā·o·di·cē´a and in Hī·er·ap´o·lis. [14]Luke, the beloved physician, and Dē´mas greet you. [15]Give my greetings to the brothers and sisters[k] in Lā·o·di·cē´a, and to Nym´pha and the church in her house. [16]And when this letter has been read among you, have it read also in the church of the Lā·o·di·cē´ans; and see that you read also the letter from Lā·o·di·cē´a. [17]And say to Ar·chip´pus, "See that you complete the task that you have received in the Lord."

> We should always live so that other people will see Christ at work in our lives. When we talk to people, we should be kind, gracious, and polite.

18 I, Paul, write this greeting with my own hand. Remember my chains. Grace be with you.[l]

---

[e] In Greek the same word is used for *master* and *Lord* [f] Gk *not for men* [g] Or *you are slaves of,* or *be slaves of* [h] Or *opportunity* [i] Gk *slave* [j] Other authorities read *that I may know how you are* [k] Gk *brothers* [l] Other ancient authorities add *Amen*

1 Thessalonians

The book of First Thessalonians is a letter Paul wrote to the Christians in Thessalonica, a city in Greece where Paul had preached and had formed a church (Acts 17:1–4). He wrote this letter about 50 AD from Corinth, Greece, where he was carrying on his missionary work. This book is the earliest letter we have from Paul and also the earliest book in the New Testament.

In the first letter to the Thessalonians, Paul complimented the Christians at Thessalonica on their faith and gave directions for how followers of Jesus should live—with faith, love, and hope. He encouraged them to live lives that were pleasing to God. Because some of the Christians there believed the risen Christ would return to earth very soon, they were worried when Jesus did not immediately return. Paul told them not to worry about when Jesus would return. He told them to remain faithful, encourage one another, and have hope in the salvation that comes through faith in Christ.

1 Thessalonians 1:1–2

Salutation

1 Paul, Sil·va´nus, and Timothy,
To the church of the Thes·sa·lo̅´-
ni·ans in God the Father and the Lord
Jesus Christ:
Grace to you and peace.

The Thessalonians' Faith and Example

2 We always give thanks to God for all
of you and mention you in our prayers,
constantly ³remembering before our God
and Father your work of faith and labor of
love and steadfastness of hope in our Lord
Jesus Christ. ⁴For we know, brothers and
sisters*a* beloved by God, that he has chosen you, ⁵because our message of the
gospel came to you not in word only, but
also in power and in the Holy Spirit and
with full conviction; just as you know
what kind of persons we proved to be
among you for your sake. ⁶And you
became imitators of us and of the Lord, for
in spite of persecution you received the
word with joy inspired by the Holy Spirit,
⁷so that you became an example to all the
believers in Mac·e·do̅´ni·a and in A·cha̅´i·a.
⁸For the word of the Lord has sounded
forth from you not only in Mac·e·do̅´ni·a
and A·cha̅´i·a, but in every place your faith
in God has become known, so that we
have no need to speak about it. ⁹For the
people of those regions*b* report about us
what kind of welcome we had among
you, and how you turned to God from
idols, to serve a living and true God, ¹⁰and
to wait for his Son from heaven, whom he
raised from the dead—Jesus, who rescues
us from the wrath that is coming.

Paul's Ministry in Thessalonica

2 You yourselves know, brothers and
sisters,*a* that our coming to you
was not in vain, ²but though we had
already suffered and been shamefully
mistreated at Phi·lip´pi, as you know, we
had courage in our God to declare to
you the gospel of God in spite of great
opposition. ³For our appeal does not
spring from deceit or impure motives or

In New Testament times, Thessalonica was an important trading city and seaport. Paul established a Christian church in this city. Today, it is called Salonica and is still an important city in Greece.

trickery, ⁴but just as we have been
approved by God to be entrusted with
the message of the gospel, even so we
speak, not to please mortals, but to
please God who tests our hearts. ⁵As you
know and as God is our witness, we
never came with words of flattery or
with a pretext for greed; ⁶nor did we
seek praise from mortals, whether from
you or from others, ⁷though we might
have made demands as apostles of
Christ. But we were gentle*c* among you,
like a nurse tenderly caring for her own
children. ⁸So deeply do we care for you
that we are determined to share with you
not only the gospel of God but also our
own selves, because you have become
very dear to us.

9 You remember our labor and toil,
brothers and sisters;*a* we worked night
and day, so that we might not burden
any of you while we proclaimed to you

When Paul lived and taught in Thessalonica, he probably worked in a shop in the marketplace, making and repairing tents. When people came into the shop, he was able to share God's love for them not only through his words but also through his actions.

a Gk *brothers*   *b* Gk *For they*   *c* Other ancient authorities read *infants* the gospel of God. [10]You are witnesses, and God also, how pure, upright, and blameless our conduct was toward you believers. [11]As you know, we dealt with each one of you like a father with his children, [12]urging and encouraging you and pleading that you lead a life worthy of God, who calls you into his own kingdom and glory.

13 We also constantly give thanks to God for this, that when you received the word of God that you heard from us, you accepted it not as a human word but as what it really is, God's word, which is also at work in you believers. [14]For you, brothers and sisters,[d] became imitators of the churches of God in Christ Jesus that are in Judea, for you suffered the same things from your own compatriots as they did from the Jews, [15]who killed both the Lord Jesus and the prophets,[e] and drove us out; they displease God and oppose everyone [16]by hindering us from speaking to the Gentiles so that they may be saved. Thus they have constantly been filling up the measure of their sins; but God's wrath has overtaken them at last.[f]

Paul's Desire to Visit the Thessalonians Again

17 As for us, brothers and sisters,[d] when, for a short time, we were made orphans by being separated from you—in person, not in heart—we longed with great eagerness to see you face to face. [18]For we wanted to come to you—certainly I, Paul, wanted to again and again—but Satan blocked our way. [19]For what is our hope or joy or crown of boasting before our Lord Jesus at his coming? Is it not you? [20]Yes, you are our glory and joy!

3 Therefore when we could bear it no longer, we decided to be left alone in Athens; [2]and we sent Timothy, our brother and co-worker for God in proclaiming[g] the gospel of Christ, to strengthen and encourage you for the sake of your faith, [3]so that no one would be shaken by these persecutions. Indeed, you yourselves know that this is what we are destined for. [4]In fact, when we were with you, we told you beforehand that we were to suffer persecution; so it turned out, as you know. [5]For this reason, when I could bear it no longer, I sent to find out about your faith; I was afraid that somehow the tempter had tempted you and that our labor had been in vain.

Timothy's Encouraging Report

6 But Timothy has just now come to us from you, and has brought us the good news of your faith and love. He has told us also that you always remember us kindly and long to see us—just as we long to see you. [7]For this reason, brothers and sisters,[d] during all our distress and persecution we have been encouraged about you through your faith. [8]For we now live, if you continue to stand firm in the Lord. [9]How can we thank God enough for you in return for all the joy that we feel before our God because of you? [10]Night and day we pray most earnestly that we may see you face to face and restore whatever is lacking in your faith.

11 Now may our God and Father himself and our Lord Jesus direct our

Paul had warned the Christians at Thessalonica that they might have difficulties. Following Jesus wasn't easy then, and it isn't easy now! Sometimes people make fun of Christians. The wonderful thing is that God is always with us and will help us through tough times. Read chapter 3, and then read Psalm 121:1–2. God's love for us is amazing!

---

[d] Gk brothers   [e] Other ancient authorities read their own prophets   [f] Or completely or forever
[g] Gk lacks proclaiming

way to you. [12]And may the Lord make you increase and abound in love for one another and for all, just as we abound in love for you. [13]And may he so strengthen your hearts in holiness that you may be blameless before our God and Father at the coming of our Lord Jesus with all his saints.

A Life Pleasing to God

4 Finally, brothers and sisters,[h] we ask and urge you in the Lord Jesus that, as you learned from us how you ought to live and to please God (as, in fact, you are doing), you should do so more and more. [2]For you know what instructions we gave you through the Lord Jesus. [3]For this is the will of God, your sanctification: that you abstain from fornication; [4]that each one of you know how to control your own body[i] in holiness and honor, [5]not with lustful passion, like the Gentiles who do not know God; [6]that no one wrong or exploit a brother or sister[j] in this matter, because the Lord is an avenger in all these things, just as we have already told you beforehand and solemnly warned you. [7]For God did not call us to impurity but in holiness. [8]Therefore whoever rejects this rejects not human authority but God, who also gives his Holy Spirit to you.

9 Now concerning love of the brothers and sisters,[h] you do not need to have anyone write to you, for you yourselves have been taught by God to love one another; [10]and indeed you do love all the brothers and sisters[h] throughout Mac·e·dō'ni·a. But we urge you, beloved,[h] to do so more and more, [11]to aspire to live quietly, to mind your own affairs, and to work with your hands, as we directed you, [12]so that you

may behave properly toward outsiders and be dependent on no one.

The Coming of the Lord

13 But we do not want you to be uninformed, brothers and sisters,[h] about those who have died,[k] so that you may not grieve as others do who have no hope. [14]For since we believe that Jesus died and rose again, even so, through Jesus, God will bring with him those who have died.[k] [15]For this we declare to you by the word of the Lord, that we who are alive, who are left until the coming of the Lord, will by no means precede those who have died.[k] [16]For the Lord himself, with a cry of command, with the archangel's call and with the sound of God's trumpet, will descend from heaven, and the dead in Christ will rise first. [17]Then we who are alive, who are left, will be caught up in the clouds together with them to meet the Lord in the air; and so we will be with the Lord forever. [18]Therefore encourage one another with these words.

Paul reminds us that we do not have to worry that we will never see our loved ones again when they die. We will be together with our loved ones in the Resurrection.

5 Now concerning the times and the seasons, brothers and sisters,[h] you do not need to have anything written to you. [2]For you yourselves know very well that the day of the Lord will come like a thief in the night. [3]When they say, "There is peace and security," then sudden destruction will come upon them, as labor pains come upon a pregnant woman, and there will be no escape! [4]But you, beloved,[h] are not in darkness,

What can you do today, right where you are, to show God's love? Surprise someone today with an act of kindness.

[h] Gk brothers [i] Or how to take a wife for himself [j] Gk brother [k] Gk fallen asleep

for that day to surprise you like a thief; [5]for you are all children of light and children of the day; we are not of the night or of darkness. [6]So then let us not fall asleep as others do, but let us keep awake and be sober; [7]for those who sleep sleep at night, and those who are drunk get drunk at night. [8]But since we belong to the day, let us be sober, and put on the breastplate of faith and love, and for a helmet the hope of salvation. [9]For God has destined us not for wrath but for obtaining salvation through our Lord Jesus Christ, [10]who died for us, so that whether we are awake or asleep we may live with him. [11]Therefore encourage one another and build up each other, as indeed you are doing.

Final Exhortations, Greetings, and Benediction

12 But we appeal to you, brothers and sisters,[l] to respect those who labor among you, and have charge of you in the Lord and admonish you; [13]esteem them very highly in love because of their work. Be at peace among yourselves. [14]And we urge you, beloved,[l] to admonish the idlers, encourage the faint hearted, help the weak, be patient with all of them. [15]See that none of you repays evil for evil, but always seek to do good to one another and to all. [16]Rejoice always, [17]pray without ceasing, [18]give thanks in all circumstances; for this is the will of God in Christ Jesus for you. [19]Do not quench the Spirit. [20]Do not despise the words of prophets,[m] [21]but test everything; hold fast to what is good; [22]abstain from every form of evil.

23 May the God of peace himself sanctify you entirely; and may your spirit and soul and body be kept sound[n] and blameless at the coming of our Lord Jesus Christ. [24]The one who calls you is faithful, and he will do this.

25 Beloved,[l] pray for us.

26 Greet all the brothers and sisters[l] with a holy kiss. [27]I solemnly command you by the Lord that this letter be read to all of them.[o]

28 The grace of our Lord Jesus Christ be with you.[p]

"Rejoice always, pray withut ceasing, give thanks in all circumstances; for this is the will of God in Christ Jesus for you."
1 Thessalonians 5:16–17

[l] Gk brothers   [m] Gk despise prophecies   [n] Or complete   [o] Gk to all the brothers   [p] Other ancient authorities add Amen

2 Thessalonians

We are not exactly sure who wrote the second letter to the Thessalonians. Some believe that one of Paul's disciples wrote it to update teaching on the second coming of Christ. Others believe that Paul wrote the second letter to the Thessalonians from Corinth in 50 AD, shortly after he wrote the first letter. Maybe the church at Thessalonica had not understood his first letter, or maybe someone misled them with a letter Paul did not really write that wrongly said Jesus would return immediately. No matter who wrote the letter or what had happened, many of the Christians at Thessalonica were very upset. Some of them were even refusing to work for a living because they thought Jesus would return any day! To those who had quit working, the author wrote, "Anyone unwilling to work should not eat" (2 Thessalonians 3:10).

The second letter to the Thessalonians encouraged the believers to be loyal to the true gospel they had been taught. The author warned that they should guard against false teaching in any letters written to appear as though they were from Paul. At the end of the letter, the author called attention to the letter's signature and handwriting, which indicate that Paul wrote the letter (see 2 Thessalonians 3:17), so that the believers would not be misled again.

2 Thessalonians 1:1–2

Salutation

1 Paul, Sil·vā´nus, and Timothy,
To the church of the Thes·sa·lō´-ni·ans in God our Father and the Lord Jesus Christ:

2 Grace to you and peace from God our[a] Father and the Lord Jesus Christ.

Thanksgiving

3 We must always give thanks to God for you, brothers and sisters,[b] as is right, because your faith is growing abundantly, and the love of everyone of you for one another is increasing. [4]Therefore we ourselves boast of you among the churches of God for your steadfastness and faith during all your persecutions and the afflictions that you are enduring.

The Judgment at Christ's Coming

5 This is evidence of the righteous judgment of God, and is intended to make you worthy of the kingdom of God, for which you are also suffering. [6]For it is indeed just of God to repay with affliction those who afflict you, [7]and to give relief to the afflicted as well as to us, when the Lord Jesus is revealed from heaven with his mighty angels [8]in flaming fire, inflicting vengeance on those who do not know God and on those who do not obey the gospel of our Lord Jesus. [9]These will suffer the punishment of eternal destruction, separated from the presence of the Lord and from the glory of his might, [10]when he comes to be glorified by his saints and to be marveled at on that day among all who have believed, because our testimony to you was believed. [11]To this end we always pray for you, asking that our God will make you worthy of his call and will fulfill by his power every good resolve and work of faith, [12]so that the name of our Lord Jesus may be glorified in you, and you in him, according to the grace of our God and the Lord Jesus Christ.

The Man of Lawlessness

2 As to the coming of our Lord Jesus Christ and our being gathered together to him, we beg you, brothers and sisters,[b] [2]not to be quickly shaken in mind or alarmed, either by spirit or by word or by letter, as though from us, to the effect that the day of the Lord is already here. [3]Let no one deceive you in any way; for that day will not come unless the rebellion comes first and the lawless one[c] is revealed, the one destined for destruction.[d] [4]He opposes and exalts himself above every so-called god or object of worship, so that he takes his seat in the temple of God, declaring himself to be God. [5]Do you not remember that I told you these things when I was still with you? [6]And you know what is now restraining him, so that he may be revealed when his time comes. [7]For the mystery of lawlessness is already at work, but only until the one who now restrains it is removed. [8]And then the lawless one will be revealed, whom the Lord Jesus[e] will destroy[f] with the breath of his mouth, annihilating him by the manifestation of his coming. [9]The coming of the lawless one is apparent in the working of Satan, who uses all power, signs, lying wonders, [10]and every kind of

Paul told the believers to let the name of Jesus be glorified in them—in other words, to give honor and praise to Jesus. Think about the many names of Jesus: Miracle Worker, Comforter, Healer, Savior, Son of God, and many others. When we put our faith in Jesus, he gives us strength and comfort for living. When we share our faith with others so that they can believe and have that same comfort and strength, we glorify Jesus. How can you share Jesus with someone today?

---

[a] Other ancient authorities read *the*   [b] Gk *brothers*   [c] Gk *the man of lawlessness*; other ancient authorities read *the man of sin*   [d] Gk *the son of destruction*   [e] Other ancient authorities lack *Jesus*   [f] Other ancient authorities read *consume*

> "So then, brothers and sisters, stand firm and hold fast to the traditions that you were taught by us, either by word of mouth or by our letter." 2 Thessalonians 2:15

wicked deception for those who are perishing, because they refused to love the truth and so be saved. [11]For this reason God sends them a powerful delusion, leading them to believe what is false, [12]so that all who have not believed the truth but took pleasure in unrighteousness will be condemned.

Chosen for Salvation

13 But we must always give thanks to God for you, brothers and sisters[g] beloved by the Lord, because God chose you as the first fruits[h] for salvation through sanctification by the Spirit and through belief in the truth. [14]For this purpose he called you through our proclamation of the good news,[i] so that you may obtain the glory of our Lord Jesus Christ. [15]So then, brothers and sisters,[g] stand firm and hold fast to the traditions that you were taught by us, either by word of mouth or by our letter.

16 Now may our Lord Jesus Christ himself and God our Father, who loved us and through grace gave us eternal comfort and good hope, [17]comfort your hearts and strengthen them in every good work and word.

Request for Prayer

3 Finally, brothers and sisters,[g] pray for us, so that the word of the Lord may spread rapidly and be glorified everywhere, just as it is among you, [2]and that we may be rescued from wicked and evil people; for not all have faith. [3]But the Lord is faithful; he will strengthen you

> "May the Lord direct your hearts to the love of God and to the steadfastness of Christ." 2 Thessalonians 3:5

and guard you from the evil one.[j] [4]And we have confidence in the Lord concerning you, that you are doing and will go on doing the things that we command. [5]May the Lord direct your hearts to the love of God and to the steadfastness of Christ.

Warning against Idleness

6 Now we command you, beloved,[g] in the name of our Lord Jesus Christ, to keep away from believers who are[k] living in idleness and not according to the tradition that they[l] received from us. [7]For you yourselves know how you ought to imitate us; we were not idle when we were with you, [8]and we did not eat anyone's bread without paying for it; but with toil and labor we worked night and day, so that we might not burden any of you. [9]This was not because we do not have that right, but in order to give you an example to imitate. [10]For even when we were with you, we gave you this command: Anyone unwilling to work should not eat. [11]For we hear that some of you are living in idleness, mere busybodies, not doing any work. [12]Now such persons we command and exhort in the Lord Jesus Christ to do their work quietly and to earn their own living. [13]Brothers and sisters,[g] do not be weary in doing what is right.

14 Take note of those who do not obey what we say in this letter; have

 Paul told the Christians at Thessalonica to do their share of the work that needed to be done and never be tired of doing what is right. Paul urged the church at Thessalonica to stand up for their values and beliefs. What are some ways that you can do what is right? How can you stand up for your values and beliefs?

[g] Gk brothers [h] Other ancient authorities read from the beginning [i] Or through our gospel [j] Or from evil [k] Gk from every brother who is [l] Other ancient authorities read you

nothing to do with them, so that they may be ashamed. [15]Do not regard them as enemies, but warn them as believers.[m]

Final Greetings and Benediction

16 Now may the Lord of peace himself give you peace at all times in all ways. The Lord be with all of you.

17 I, Paul, write this greeting with my own hand. This is the mark in every letter of mine; it is the way I write. [18]The grace of our Lord Jesus Christ be with all of you.[n]

[m] Gk a brother   [n] Other ancient authorities add Amen

1 Timothy

The book of First Timothy is a letter said to have been written by Paul to his young helper and friend Timothy. If Paul wrote the letter, he would have written it sometime before his death, during the 60s AD. But there are many good reasons to think that a later Christian wrote the letter in order to give advice to a young church leader—the same kind of advice Paul would have given to Timothy. If this is the case, the letter may have been written as late as 125 AD. Although we are not exactly sure who wrote the letter or when it was written, God still speaks to us through its words.

First Timothy reflects the kind of trust and love Paul had for Timothy. The letter encourages those who are young to be examples for all believers (1 Timothy 4:12). It warns against false teaching and encourages Christians to live according to God's ways. The letter says that Christians should treat one another as brothers and sisters in one loving family. They are to show God's love to people both inside and outside of the church. First Timothy also contains guidance for how to organize and lead the church. The last chapter of the letter reminds Christians to be strong and stand firm in the faith, setting their hope not on uncertain things, but on God alone.

1 Timothy 1:1–2

In New Testament times when Paul wrote letters, there was no organized mail service. People had to make their own arrangements for having mail delivered. Families and friends living near each other might hire a messenger to deliver a letter. Or, if travelers were heading in the right direction, they might take a letter along with them. Since travel was difficult and dangerous, it could take months or even years for a letter to be delivered!

Salutation

1 Paul, an apostle of Christ Jesus by the command of God our Savior and of Christ Jesus our hope,

2 To Timothy, my loyal child in the faith:

Grace, mercy, and peace from God the Father and Christ Jesus our Lord.

Warning against False Teachers

3 I urge you, as I did when I was on my way to Mac·e·dõ'ni·a, to remain in Eph'e·sus so that you may instruct certain people not to teach any different doctrine, 4and not to occupy themselves with myths and endless genealogies that promote speculations rather than the divine training[a] that is known by faith. 5But the aim of such instruction is love that comes from a pure heart, a good conscience, and sincere faith. 6Some people have deviated from these and turned to meaningless talk, 7desiring to be teachers of the law, without understanding either what they are saying or the things about which they make assertions.

8 Now we know that the law is good, if one uses it legitimately. 9This means understanding that the law is laid down not for the innocent but for the lawless and disobedient, for the godless and sin-ful, for the unholy and profane, for those who kill their father or mother, for murderers, 10fornicators, sodomites, slave traders, liars, perjurers, and whatever else is contrary to the sound teaching 11that conforms to the glorious gospel of the blessed God, which he entrusted to me.

Gratitude for Mercy

12 I am grateful to Christ Jesus our Lord, who has strengthened me, because he judged me faithful and appointed me to his service, 13even though I was formerly a blasphemer, a persecutor, and a man of violence. But I received mercy because I had acted ignorantly in unbelief, 14and the grace of our Lord overflowed for me with the faith and love that are in Christ Jesus. 15The saying is sure and worthy of full acceptance, that Christ Jesus came into the world to save sinners—of whom I am the foremost. 16But for that very reason I received mercy, so that in me, as the foremost,

Blasphemy is any action that insults or dishonors the name of God. For the people of Israel, the name of God was so sacred that they never pronounced it but used the word *adonai*, which means "lord." Referring to God for a wrong or foolish purpose was a sin. In the New Testament, some of the religious leaders accused Jesus of blasphemy because he spoke of God as his father. When Paul said that he was guilty of blasphemy, he meant that in his own life he had spoken against Jesus and did not at first believe Jesus was God's son. It was only later that Paul had his own encounter with Jesus and realized Jesus was truly divine.

[a] Or *plan*

> "The saying is sure and worthy of full acceptance that Christ Jesus came into the world to save sinners."
> 1 Timothy 1:15

Jesus Christ might display the utmost patience, making me an example to those who would come to believe in him for eternal life. [17]To the King of the ages, immortal, invisible, the only God, be honor and glory forever and ever.[b] Amen.

18 I am giving you these instructions, Timothy, my child, in accordance with the prophecies made earlier about you, so that by following them you may fight the good fight, [19]having faith and a good conscience. By rejecting conscience, certain persons have suffered shipwreck in the faith; [20]among them are Hy·me·naēʹus and Alexander, whom I have turned over to Satan, so that they may learn not to blaspheme.

Instructions concerning Prayer

2 First of all, then, I urge that supplications, prayers, intercessions, and thanksgivings be made for everyone, [2]for kings and all who are in high positions, so that we may lead a quiet and peaceable life in all godliness and dignity. [3]This is right and is acceptable in the sight of God our Savior, [4]who desires everyone to be saved and to come to the knowledge of the truth. [5]For

there is one God;
there is also one mediator
between God and humankind,
Christ Jesus, himself human,
[6]   who gave himself a ransom for
all—this was attested at the
right time.

[7]For this I was appointed a herald and an apostle (I am telling the truth,[c] I am not lying), a teacher of the Gentiles in faith and truth.

8 I desire, then, that in every place the men should pray, lifting up holy hands without anger or argument; [9]also that the women should dress themselves modestly and decently in suitable cloth-

ing, not with their hair braided, or with gold, pearls, or expensive clothes, [10]but with good works, as is proper for women who profess reverence for God. [11]Let a woman[d] learn in silence with full submission. [12]I permit no woman[d] to teach or to have authority over a man;[e] she is to keep silent. [13]For Adam was formed first, then Eve; [14]and Adam was not deceived, but the woman was deceived and became a transgressor. [15]Yet she will be saved through childbearing, provided they continue in faith and love and holiness, with modesty.

When we pray, we should remember to pray for everyone—not only ourselves, but also friends, family, teachers, leaders, and even people we have trouble getting along with. Make a list of the people you want to pray for, and pray for at least one person on the list every day.

Qualifications of Bishops

3 The saying is sure:[f] whoever aspires to the office of bishop[g] desires a noble task. [2]Now a bishop[h] must be above reproach, married only once,[i] temperate, sensible, respectable, hospitable, an apt teacher, [3]not a drunkard, not violent but gentle, not quarrelsome, and not a lover of money. [4]He must manage his own household well, keeping his children submissive and respectful in every way— [5]for if someone does not know how to manage his own household, how can he take care of God's church? [6]He must not be a recent convert, or he may be puffed up with conceit and fall into

[b] Gk to the ages of the ages   [c] Other ancient authorities add in Christ   [d] Or wife   [e] Or her husband   [f] Some interpreters place these words at the end of the previous paragraph. Other ancient authorities read The saying is commonly accepted   [g] Or overseer   [h] Or an overseer   [i] Gk the husband of one wife

the condemnation of the devil. [7]Moreover, he must be well thought of by outsiders, so that he may not fall into disgrace and the snare of the devil.

Qualifications of Deacons

8 Deacons likewise must be serious, not double-tongued, not indulging in much wine, not greedy for money; [9]they must hold fast to the mystery of the faith with a clear conscience. [10]And let them first be tested; then, if they prove themselves blameless, let them serve as deacons. [11]Women[j] likewise must be serious, not slanderers, but temperate, faithful in all things. [12]Let deacons be married only once,[k] and let them manage their children and their households well; [13]for those who serve well as deacons gain a good standing for themselves and great boldness in the faith that is in Christ Jesus.

The Mystery of Our Religion

14 I hope to come to you soon, but I am writing these instructions to you so that, [15]if I am delayed, you may know how one ought to behave in the household of God, which is the church of the living God, the pillar and bulwark of the truth. [16]Without any doubt, the mystery of our religion is great:

He[l] was revealed in flesh,
vindicated[m] in spirit,[n]
seen by angels,
proclaimed among Gentiles,
believed in throughout the world,
taken up in glory.

False Asceticism

4 Now the Spirit expressly says that in later[o] times some will renounce the faith by paying attention to deceitful spirits and teachings of demons, [2]through the hypocrisy of liars whose consciences are seared with a hot iron. [3]They forbid marriage and demand abstinence from foods, which God created to be received with thanksgiving by those who believe and know the truth. [4]For everything created by God is good,

> "Let no one despise your youth, but set the believers an example in speech and conduct, in love, in faith, in purity." 1 Timothy 4:12

and nothing is to be rejected, provided it is received with thanksgiving; [5]for it is sanctified by God's word and by prayer.

A Good Minister of Jesus Christ

6 If you put these instructions before the brothers and sisters,[p] you will be a good servant[q] of Christ Jesus, nourished on the words of the faith and of the sound teaching that you have followed. [7]Have nothing to do with profane myths and old wives' tales. Train yourself in godliness, [8]for, while physical training is of some value, godliness is valuable in every way, holding promise for both the present life and the life to come. [9]The saying is sure and worthy of full acceptance. [10]For to this end we toil and struggle,[r] because we have our hope set on the living God, who is the Savior of all people, especially of those who believe.

11 These are the things you must insist on and teach. [12]Let no one despise your youth, but set the believers an example in speech and conduct, in love, in faith, in purity. [13]Until I arrive, give attention to the public reading of scripture,[s] to exhorting, to teaching. [14]Do not neglect the gift that is in you, which was given to you through prophecy with the laying on of hands by the council of elders.[t] [15]Put these things into practice, devote yourself to them, so that all may see your progress. [16]Pay close attention to yourself and to your teaching; continue in these things, for in doing this you will save both yourself and your hearers.

[j] Or *Their wives,* or *Women deacons*   [k] Gk *be husbands of one wife*   [l] Gk *Who;* other ancient authorities read *God;* others, *Which*   [m] Or *justified*   [n] Or *by the Spirit*   [o] Or *the last*   [p] Gk *brothers*   [q] Or *deacon*   [r] Other ancient authorities read *suffer reproach*   [s] Gk *to the reading*   [t] Gk *by the presbytery*

Duties toward Believers

5 Do not speak harshly to an older man,[u] but speak to him as to a father, to younger men as brothers, [2]to older women as mothers, to younger women as sisters—with absolute purity.

3 Honor widows who are really widows. [4]If a widow has children or grandchildren, they should first learn their religious duty to their own family and make some repayment to their parents; for this is pleasing in God's sight. [5]The real widow, left alone, has set her hope on God and continues in supplications and prayers night and day; [6]but the widow[v] who lives for pleasure is dead even while she lives. [7]Give these commands as well, so that they may be above reproach. [8]And whoever does not provide for relatives, and especially for family members, has denied the faith and is worse than an unbeliever.

9 Let a widow be put on the list if she is not less than sixty years old and has been married only once;[w] [10]she must be well attested for her good works, as one who has brought up children, shown hospitality, washed the saints' feet, helped the afflicted, and devoted herself to doing good in every way. [11]But refuse to put younger widows on the list; for when their sensual desires alienate them from Christ, they want to marry, [12]and so they incur condemnation for having violated their first pledge. [13]Besides that, they learn to be idle, gadding about from house to house; and they are not merely idle, but also gossips and busybodies, saying what they should not say. [14]So I would have younger widows marry, bear children, and manage their households, so as to give the adversary no occasion to revile us. [15]For some have already turned away to follow Satan. [16]If any believing woman[x] has relatives who are really widows, let her assist them; let the church not be burdened, so that it can assist those who are real widows.

17 Let the elders who rule well be considered worthy of double honor,[y] especially those who labor in preaching and teaching; [18]for the scripture says, "You shall not muzzle an ox while it is treading out the grain," and, "The laborer deserves to be paid." [19]Never accept any accusation against an elder except on the evidence of two or three witnesses. [20]As for those who persist in sin, rebuke them in the presence of all, so that the rest also may stand in fear. [21]In the presence of God and of Christ Jesus and of the elect angels, I warn you to keep these instructions without prejudice, doing nothing on the basis of partiality. [22]Do not ordain[z] anyone hastily, and do not participate in the sins of others; keep yourself pure.

23 No longer drink only water, but take a little wine for the sake of your stomach and your frequent ailments.

24 The sins of some people are conspicuous and precede them to judgment, while the sins of others follow them there. [25]So also good works are conspicuous; and even when they are not, they cannot remain hidden.

6 Let all who are under the yoke of slavery regard their masters as worthy of all honor, so that the name of God and the teaching may not be blasphemed. [2]Those who have believing masters must not be disrespectful to them on the ground that they are members of the church;[a] rather they must serve them all the more, since those who benefit by their service are believers and beloved.[b]

False Teaching and True Riches

Teach and urge these duties. [3]Whoever teaches otherwise and does not agree with the sound words of our Lord Jesus Christ and the teaching that is in

[u] Or *an elder*, or *a presbyter*   [v] Gk *she*   [w] Gk *the wife of one husband*   [x] Other ancient authorities read *believing man or woman*; others, *believing man*   [y] Or *compensation*   [z] Gk *Do not lay hands on*   [a] Gk *are brothers*   [b] Or *since they are believers and beloved, who devote themselves to good*

accordance with godliness, [4]is conceited, understanding nothing, and has a morbid craving for controversy and for disputes about words. From these come envy, dissension, slander, base suspicions, [5]and wrangling among those who are depraved in mind and bereft of the truth, imagining that godliness is a means of gain.[c] [6]Of course, there is great gain in godliness combined with contentment; [7]for we brought nothing into the world, so that[d] we can take nothing out of it; [8]but if we have food and clothing, we will be content with these. [9]But those who want to be rich fall into temptation and are trapped by many senseless and harmful desires that plunge people into ruin and destruction. [10]For the love of money is a root of all kinds of evil, and in their eagerness to be rich some have wandered away from the faith and pierced themselves with many pains.

The Good Fight of Faith

11 But as for you, man of God, shun all this; pursue righteousness, godliness, faith, love, endurance, gentleness. [12]Fight the good fight of the faith; take hold of the eternal life, to which you were called and for which you made[e] the good confession in the presence of many witnesses. [13]In the presence of God, who gives life to all things, and of Christ Jesus, who in his testimony before Pon'ti·us Pilate made the good confession, I charge you [14]to keep the commandment without spot or blame until the manifestation of our Lord Jesus Christ, [15]which he will bring about at the right time—he who is the blessed and only Sovereign, the King of kings

and Lord of lords. [16]It is he alone who has immortality and dwells in unapproachable light, whom no one has ever seen or can see; to him be honor and eternal dominion. Amen.

17 As for those who in the present age are rich, command them not to be haughty, or to set their hopes on the uncertainty of riches, but rather on God who richly provides us with everything for our enjoyment. [18]They are to do good, to be rich in good works, generous, and ready to share, [19]thus storing up for themselves the treasure of a good foundation for the future, so that they may take hold of the life that really is life.

Personal Instructions and Benediction

20 Timothy, guard what has been entrusted to you. Avoid the profane chatter and contradictions of what is falsely called knowledge; [21]by professing it some have missed the mark as regards the faith.

Grace be with you.[f]

Paul encouraged Timothy to stay away from sin, to keep himself pure, and to be strong in his beliefs. This is good advice for us too! We should try as hard as we can to turn away from sin and live as Jesus taught us.

[c] Other ancient authorities add *Withdraw yourself from such people* [d] Other ancient authorities read *world—it is certain that*   [e] Gk *confessed* [f] The Greek word for *you* here is plural; in other ancient authorities it is singular. Other ancient authorities add *Amen*

2 Timothy

We are not exactly sure who wrote Second Timothy or when this letter was written. (For more information, see the introduction to First Timothy.) No matter who the author was, this tender and inspiring letter reads like a goodbye message from the great apostle Paul to his trusted young helper Timothy.

The letter tells Timothy never to be ashamed of the gospel of Jesus Christ or of the suffering that comes as a result of following Christ. The letter tells about Paul's unashamed commitment to the gospel, even during his lonely last days in prison. It tells Timothy to join Paul in suffering for the gospel of Jesus, always relying on the power of God. The letter warns against false teaching and encourages Timothy to hold on to true teaching. Whatever happens in his life, he is to be strong, to endure, and to remain faithful to Christ. The letter tells him to pursue righteousness, faith, love, and peace. It tells him to stay away from silly arguments. And it warns him about tough days to come. Although there will be many who will not follow God's ways, Timothy is to continue in what he has learned and believed. At all times, he is to proclaim the message of Christ and to share the good news.

2 Timothy 1:1–2

Timothy's mother, Eunice, and his grandmother, Lois, shared their faith with him. Timothy became a strong Christian and helped Paul spread the good news. Who are the people who have shared their faith with you? Write them a thank-you letter and promise to pray for them each day.

Salutation

1 Paul, an apostle of Christ Jesus by the will of God, for the sake of the promise of life that is in Christ Jesus,

2 To Timothy, my beloved child:

Grace, mercy, and peace from God the Father and Christ Jesus our Lord.

Thanksgiving and Encouragement

3 I am grateful to God—whom I worship with a clear conscience, as my ancestors did—when I remember you constantly in my prayers night and day. [4]Recalling your tears, I long to see you so that I may be filled with joy. [5]I am reminded of your sincere faith, a faith that lived first in your grandmother Lōʹis and your mother Euʹnice and now, I am sure, lives in you. [6]For this reason I remind you to rekindle the gift of God that is within you through the laying on of my hands; [7]for God did not give us a spirit of cowardice, but rather a spirit of power and of love and of self-discipline.

8 Do not be ashamed, then, of the testimony about our Lord or of me his prisoner, but join with me in suffering for the gospel, relying on the power of God, [9]who saved us and called us with a holy calling, not according to our works but according to his own purpose and grace. This grace was given to us in Christ Jesus before the ages began, [10]but it has now been revealed through the appearing of our Savior Christ Jesus, who abolished death and brought life and immortality to light through the gospel. [11]For this gospel I was appointed

a herald and an apostle and a teacher,[a] [12]and for this reason I suffer as I do. But I am not ashamed, for I know the one in whom I have put my trust, and I am sure that he is able to guard until that day what I have entrusted to him.[b] [13]Hold to the standard of sound teaching that you have heard from me, in the faith and love that are in Christ Jesus. [14]Guard the good treasure entrusted to you, with the help of the Holy Spirit living in us.

15 You are aware that all who are in Asia have turned away from me, including Phyʹgeʹlus and Herʹmogʹeʹnēs. [16]May the Lord grant mercy to the household of Onʹeʹsiphʹoʹrus, because he often refreshed me and was not ashamed of my chain; [17]when he arrived in Rome, he eagerly[c] searched for me and found me [18]—may the Lord grant that he will find mercy from the Lord on that day! And you know very well how much service he rendered in Ephʹeʹsus.

Because of Paul's faith in Christ, he ended up as a prisoner in Rome. Even in prison his faith was strong, and he continued to follow God's ways. Paul encouraged others to trust in Jesus, hold to sound teaching, and rely on God's power.

A Good Soldier of Christ Jesus

2 You then, my child, be strong in the grace that is in Christ Jesus; [2]and what you have heard from me through many witnesses entrust to faithful people who will be able to teach others as well. [3]Share in suffering like a good soldier of Christ Jesus. [4]No one serving in the army gets entangled in everyday affairs; the soldier's aim is to please the enlisting officer. [5]And in the case of an athlete, no one is crowned without competing according to the rules. [6]It is the farmer who does

[a] Other ancient authorities add *of the Gentiles*
[b] Or *what has been entrusted to me*   [c] Or *promptly*

the work who ought to have the first share of the crops. ⁷Think over what I say, for the Lord will give you understanding in all things.

8 Remember Jesus Christ, raised from the dead, a descendant of David—that is my gospel, ⁹for which I suffer hardship, even to the point of being chained like a criminal. But the word of God is not chained. ¹⁰Therefore I endure everything for the sake of the elect, so that they may also obtain the salvation that is in Christ Jesus, with eternal glory. ¹¹The saying is sure:

If we have died with him, we will
　　also live with him;
¹² if we endure, we will also reign with
　　him;
if we deny him, he will also deny us;
¹³ if we are faithless, he remains
　　faithful—
for he cannot deny himself.

Paul was "chained," which means he was in prison. But the good news of God's power to save us through Jesus is never chained! It moves freely through the world and is available to everyone.

A Worker Approved by God

14 Remind them of this, and warn them before God[d] that they are to avoid wrangling over words, which does no good but only ruins those who are listening. ¹⁵Do your best to present yourself to God as one approved by him, a worker who has no need to be ashamed, rightly explaining the word of truth. ¹⁶Avoid profane chatter, for it will lead people into more and more impiety, ¹⁷and their talk will spread like gangrene. Among them are Hy·me·naeʹus and Phi·leʹtus, ¹⁸who have swerved from the truth by claiming that the resurrection has already taken place. They are upsetting the faith of some. ¹⁹But God's firm foundation stands, bearing this inscription: "The

Lord knows those who are his," and, "Let everyone who calls on the name of the Lord turn away from wickedness."

20 In a large house there are utensils not only of gold and silver but also of wood and clay, some for special use, some for ordinary. ²¹All who cleanse themselves of the things I have mentioned[e] will become special utensils, dedicated and useful to the owner of the house, ready for every good work. ²²Shun youthful passions and pursue righteousness, faith, love, and peace, along with those who call on the Lord from a pure heart. ²³Have nothing to do with stupid and senseless controversies; you know that they breed quarrels. ²⁴And the Lord's servant[f] must not be quarrelsome but kindly to everyone, an apt teacher, patient, ²⁵correcting opponents with gentleness. God may perhaps grant that they will repent and come to know the truth, ²⁶and that they may escape from the snare of the devil, having been held captive by him to do his will.[g]

Godlessness in the Last Days

3 You must understand this, that in the last days distressing times will come. ²For people will be lovers of themselves, lovers of money, boasters, arrogant, abusive, disobedient to their parents, ungrateful, unholy, ³inhuman, implacable, slanderers, profligates, brutes, haters of good, ⁴treacherous, reckless, swollen with conceit, lovers of pleasure rather than lovers of God, ⁵holding to the outward form of godliness but denying its power. Avoid them! ⁶For among them are those who make their way into households and captivate silly women, overwhelmed by their sins and swayed by all kinds of desires, ⁷who are always being instructed and can never arrive at a knowledge of the truth. ⁸As Janʹes and Jamʹbres opposed Moses, so these people, of corrupt mind

[d] Other ancient authorities read *the Lord*　[e] Gk *of these things*　[f] Gk *slave*　[g] Or *by him, to do his (that is, God's) will*

and counterfeit faith, also oppose the truth. [9]But they will not make much progress, because, as in the case of those two men,[h] their folly will become plain to everyone.

Paul's Charge to Timothy

10 Now you have observed my teaching, my conduct, my aim in life, my faith, my patience, my love, my steadfastness, [11]my persecutions, and my suffering the things that happened to me in An´ti·och, I·cō´ni·um, and Lys´tra. What persecutions I endured! Yet the Lord rescued me from all of them. [12]Indeed, all who want to live a godly life in Christ Jesus will be persecuted. [13]But wicked people and impostors will go from bad to worse, deceiving others and being deceived. [14]But as for you, continue in what you have learned and firmly believed, knowing from whom you learned it, [15]and how from childhood you have known the sacred writings that are able to instruct you for salvation through faith in Christ Jesus. [16]All scripture is inspired by God and is[i] useful for teaching, for reproof, for correction, and for training in righteousness, [17]so that everyone who belongs to God may be proficient, equipped for every good work.

4 In the presence of God and of Christ Jesus, who is to judge the living and the dead, and in view of his appearing and his kingdom, I solemnly urge you: [2]proclaim the message; be persistent whether the time is favorable or unfavorable; convince, rebuke, and encourage, with the utmost patience in

> "All scripture is inspired by God and is useful for teaching, for reproof, for correction, and for training in righteousness."
> 2 Timothy 3:16

teaching. [3]For the time is coming when people will not put up with sound doctrine, but having itching ears, they will accumulate for themselves teachers to suit their own desires, [4]and will turn away from listening to the truth and wander away to myths. [5]As for you, always be sober, endure suffering, do the work of an evangelist, carry out your ministry fully.

6 As for me, I am already being poured out as a libation, and the time of my departure has come. [7]I have fought the good fight, I have finished the race, I have kept the faith. [8]From now on there is reserved for me the crown of righteousness, which the Lord, the righteous judge, will give me on that day, and not only to me but also to all who have longed for his appearing.

After a long, hard struggle, the author says, "I have fought the good fight, I have finished the race, I have kept the faith" (see 2 Timothy 4:7). Ask God to help you "keep the faith"!

Personal Instructions

9 Do your best to come to me soon, [10]for Dē´mas, in love with this present world, has deserted me and gone to Thes·sa·lo·nī´ca; Cres´cens has gone to Galatia,[j] Titus to Dal·mā´tia. [11]Only Luke is with me. Get Mark and bring him with you, for he is useful in my ministry. [12]I have sent Tych´i·cus to Eph´e·sus. [13]When you come, bring the cloak that I left with

The letter warns that sometimes people have "itching ears;" that is, they decide to listen to people who tell them only what they want to hear instead of what is true. Do you ever feel like you have ears that "itch" to hear only what sounds good to you?

[h] Gk lacks *two men*   [i] Or *Every scripture inspired by God is also*   [j] Other ancient authorities read *Gaul*

Car´pus at Trō´as, also the books, and above all the parchments. [14]Alexander the coppersmith did me great harm; the Lord will pay him back for his deeds. [15]You also must beware of him, for he strongly opposed our message.

16 At my first defense no one came to my support, but all deserted me. May it not be counted against them! [17]But the Lord stood by me and gave me strength, so that through me the message might be fully proclaimed and all the Gentiles might hear it. So I was rescued from the lion's mouth. [18]The Lord will rescue me from every evil attack and save me for his heavenly kingdom. To him be the glory forever and ever. Amen.

Final Greetings and Benediction

19 Greet Pris´ca and A·qui´la, and the household of On·e·siph´o·rus. [20]E·ras´tus remained in Corinth; Troph´i·mus I left ill in Mī·lē´tus. [21]Do your best to come before winter. Eū·bū´lus sends greetings to you, as do Pū´dens and Lī´nus and Clau´di·a and all the brothers and sisters.[k]

22 The Lord be with your spirit. Grace be with you.[l]

[k] Gk all the brothers   [l] The Greek word for you here is plural. Other ancient authorities add Amen

Titus

Titus, like Timothy, was one of Paul's closest friends. Because this letter contains few of Paul's favorite teachings and has a different style and wording from Paul's other letters, many think Paul did not write it. The letter to Titus was probably written by one of Paul's co-workers as late as 125 AD.

Titus was a Gentile Christian and co-worker with Paul (see Galatians 2:1–10). When Paul first took Titus to Jerusalem, some Jewish Christians insisted that he could not become a Christian because he had not been born a Jew. Paul, however, used Titus's case to demonstrate that keeping the Law was not a requirement for being a Christian. The only thing necessary was faith in Jesus Christ. Titus was a young man, and his great faith helped him to become a leader in the church in Crete.

The letter to Titus gives guidance for the church on the island of Crete. It warns against false teaching and insists on the true teaching of the gospel. It speaks of the goodness and kindness of God and encourages the followers of God to do good works. The letter holds up the highest standards of life for all who have faith in Christ.

Titus 1:1–4

Crete is a small, beautiful island in the Mediterranean Sea. Paul told Titus to help organize the church in Crete and help the believers become strong in the true faith. It is important for both leaders and church members to lead lives of good behavior and to encourage each other to live like Jesus. How does your behavior encourage others to live like Christ?

Salutation

1 Paul, a servant[a] of God and an apostle of Jesus Christ, for the sake of the faith of God's elect and the knowledge of the truth that is in accordance with godliness, [2]in the hope of eternal life that God, who never lies, promised before the ages began— [3]in due time he revealed his word through the proclamation with which I have been entrusted by the command of God our Savior,

4 To Titus, my loyal child in the faith we share:

Grace[b] and peace from God the Father and Christ Jesus our Savior.

Titus in Crete

5 I left you behind in Crete for this reason, so that you should put in order what remained to be done, and should appoint elders in every town, as I directed you: [6]someone who is blameless, married only once,[c] whose children are believers, not accused of debauchery and not rebellious. [7]For a bishop,[d] as God's steward, must be blameless; he must not be arrogant or quick-tempered or addicted to wine or violent or greedy for gain; [8]but he must be hospitable, a lover of goodness, prudent, upright, devout, and self-controlled. [9]He must have a firm grasp of the word that is trustworthy in accordance with the teaching, so that he may be able both to preach with sound doctrine and to refute those who contradict it.

10 There are also many rebellious people, idle talkers and deceivers, especially those of the circumcision; [11]they must be silenced, since they are upsetting whole families by teaching for sordid gain what it is not right to teach. [12]It was one of them, their very own prophet, who said,

"Cre'tans are always liars, vicious brutes, lazy gluttons."

[13]That testimony is true. For this reason rebuke them sharply, so that they may become sound in the faith, [14]not paying attention to Jewish myths or to commandments of those who reject the truth. [15]To the pure all things are pure, but to the corrupt and unbelieving nothing is pure. Their very minds and consciences are corrupted. [16]They profess to know God, but they deny him by their actions. They are detestable, disobedient, unfit for any good work.

Teach Sound Doctrine

2 But as for you, teach what is consistent with sound doctrine. [2]Tell the older men to be temperate, serious, prudent, and sound in faith, in love, and in endurance.

3 Likewise, tell the older women to be reverent in behavior, not to be slanderers or slaves to drink; they are to teach what is good, [4]so that they may encourage the young women to love their husbands, to love their children, [5]to be self-controlled, chaste, good managers of the household, kind, being submissive to their husbands, so that the word of God may not be discredited.

6 Likewise, urge the younger men to be self-controlled. [7]Show yourself in all respects a model of good works, and in your teaching show integrity, gravity, [8]and sound speech that cannot be censured; then any opponent will be put to shame, having nothing evil to say of us.

---

[a] Gk slave   [b] Other ancient authorities read Grace, mercy,   [c] Gk husband of one wife   [d] Or an overseer

9 Tell slaves to be submissive to their masters and to give satisfaction in every respect; they are not to talk back, [10]not to pilfer, but to show complete and perfect fidelity, so that in everything they may be an ornament to the doctrine of God our Savior.

11 For the grace of God has appeared, bringing salvation to all,[e] [12]training us to renounce impiety and worldly passions, and in the present age to live lives that are self-controlled, upright, and godly, [13]while we wait for the blessed hope and the manifestation of the glory of our great God and Savior,[f] Jesus Christ. [14]He it is who gave himself for us that he might redeem us from all iniquity and purify for himself a people of his own who are zealous for good deeds.

15 Declare these things; exhort and reprove with all authority.[g] Let no one look down on you.

Maintain Good Deeds

3 Remind them to be subject to rulers and authorities, to be obedient, to be ready for every good work, [2]to speak evil of no one, to avoid quarreling, to be gentle, and to show every courtesy to everyone. [3]For we ourselves were once foolish, disobedient, led astray, slaves to various passions and pleasures, passing our days in malice and envy, despicable, hating one another. [4]But when the goodness and loving kindness of God our Savior appeared, [5]he saved us, not because of any works of righteousness that we had done, but according to his mercy, through the water[h] of rebirth and renewal by the Holy Spirit. [6]This Spirit he poured out on us richly through Jesus Christ our Savior, [7]so that, having been justified by his grace, we

> "But when the goodness and loving kindness of God our Savior appeared, he saved us, not because of any works of righteousness that we had done, but according to his mercy." **Titus 3:4a**

> Paul encouraged the believers to spend time doing good works— things that are kind and helpful for others. God wants us to live in harmony with all people.

might become heirs according to the hope of eternal life. [8]The saying is sure.

I desire that you insist on these things, so that those who have come to believe in God may be careful to devote themselves to good works; these things are excellent and profitable to everyone. [9]But avoid stupid controversies, genealogies, dissensions, and quarrels about the law, for they are unprofitable and worthless. [10]After a first and second admonition, have nothing more to do with anyone who causes divisions, [11]since you know that such a person is perverted and sinful, being self-condemned.

Final Messages and Benediction

12 When I send Ar·te·mas to you, or Tych´i·cus, do your best to come to me at Ni·cop´o·lis, for I have decided to spend the winter there. [13]Make every effort to send Zē´nas the lawyer and A·pol´los on their way, and see that they lack nothing. [14]And let people learn to devote themselves to good works in order to meet urgent needs, so that they may not be unproductive.

15 All who are with me send greetings to you. Greet those who love us in the faith.

Grace be with all of you.[i]

> Zenas and Apollos were Christian workers who had been in Crete. Paul told the Christians there to offer these workers money so that they could continue their travels.

e Or has appeared to all, bringing salvation   f Or of the great God and our Savior   g Gk commandment   h Gk washing   i Other ancient authorities add Amen

Philemon

The letter to Philemon is one of the shortest books in the Bible. The apostle Paul may have written many such personal letters, but this is the one that has come down to us. Paul wrote the letter to a man named Philemon who probably lived in Colossae. Philemon was a friend who had come to faith in Christ as a result of Paul's teaching. Although we are not sure when the letter was written, many believe that Paul wrote the letter from prison in Rome about 50–60 AD.

Philemon owned a slave named Onesimus, who went to visit Paul. We do not know if Onesimus ran away, if he was sent to Paul as a messenger, or if he left to take care of some other business.

Whatever the case, Onesimus joined Paul wherever he was and the two men became friends. Soon Paul was telling him the Good News about Jesus Christ, and Onesimus became a believer.

Not wanting his master Philemon to be angry, Onesimus apparently asked for Paul's help in explaining why he (Onesimus) had been away for longer than expected. Paul gave Onesimus this letter to take back with him when he returned to his owner, Philemon. In the letter, Paul asked Philemon to receive Onesimus as a fellow Christian, "no longer as a slave but more than a slave, a beloved brother" (Philemon 16).

Philemon
15–16

Salutation

1 Paul, a prisoner of Christ Jesus, and Timothy our brother,[a]

To Phī·le´mon our dear friend and co-worker, [2]to Ap´phi·a our sister,[b] to Ar·chip´pus our fellow soldier, and to the church in your house:

3 Grace to you and peace from God our Father and the Lord Jesus Christ.

Philemon's Love and Faith

4 When I remember you[c] in my prayers, I always thank my God [5]because I hear of your love for all the saints and your faith toward the Lord Jesus. [6]I pray that the sharing of your faith may become effective when you perceive all the good that we[d] may do for Christ. [7]I have indeed received much joy and encouragement from your love, because the hearts of the saints have been refreshed through you, my brother.

Paul's Plea for Onesimus

8 For this reason, though I am bold enough in Christ to command you to do your duty, [9]yet I would rather appeal to you on the basis of love—and I, Paul, do this as an old man, and now also as a prisoner of Christ Jesus.[e] [10]I am appealing to you for my child, Ō·nes´i·mus, whose father I have become during my imprisonment. [11]Formerly he was useless to you, but now he is indeed useful[f] both to you and to me. [12]I am sending him, that is, my own heart, back to you. [13]I wanted to keep him with me, so that

> "When I remember you in my prayers, I always thank my God because I hear of your love for all the saints and your faith toward the Lord Jesus." **Philemon 4**

he might be of service to me in your place during my imprisonment for the gospel; [14]but I preferred to do nothing without your consent, in order that your good deed might be voluntary and not something forced. [15]Perhaps this is the reason he was separated from you for a while, so that you might have him back forever, [16]no longer as a slave but more than a slave, a beloved brother—especially to me but how much more to you, both in the flesh and in the Lord.

17 So if you consider me your partner, welcome him as you would welcome me. [18]If he has wronged you in any way, or owes you anything, charge that to my account. [19]I, Paul, am writing this with my own hand: I will repay it. I say nothing about your owing me even your own self. [20]Yes, brother, let me have this benefit from you in the Lord! Refresh my heart in Christ. [21]Confident of your

A slave who ran away from a slave owner was usually punished when he or she returned. Paul begged Philemon not to punish Onesimus but to do what is right. As Christians, we are called to do the right thing, even though it may not be usual or popular. How difficult do you think it would have been for Philemon to treat his slave like a brother?

A slave is a person who is owned by another person. During the time of the Roman Empire, slavery was a way of life. Slaves worked many different jobs. They were potters, household servants, silversmiths, farmers, shepherds, builders, and scribes. Some slaves were able to save enough money to buy their freedom.

[a] Gk the brother [b] Gk the sister [c] From verse 4 through verse 21, you is singular [d] Other ancient authorities read you (plural) [e] Or as an ambassador of Christ Jesus, and now also his prisoner [f] The name Onesimus means useful or (compare verse 20) beneficial

obedience, I am writing to you, knowing that you will do even more than I say.

22 One thing more—prepare a guest room for me, for I am hoping through your prayers to be restored to you.

Final Greetings and Benediction

23 Ep´a·phras, my fellow prisoner in Christ Jesus, sends greetings to you,[g] [24]and so do Mark, Ar·is·tar´chus, De¯-mas, and Luke, my fellow workers.

25 The grace of the Lord Jesus Christ be with your spirit.[h]

[g] Here *you* is singular [h] Other ancient authorities add *Amen*

Hebrews

The letter to the Hebrews reads more like a sermon than a letter. It teaches that Jesus is the Jewish Messiah and the Savior of all people who have faith in him. We do not know who wrote the letter, when it was written, or for whom it was written. Hebrews encourages Christians to be faithful, to be holy, and not to give up.

The letter contains many references to the Old Testament and to Jewish customs and teachings. The main idea of the letter is that Jesus is the high priest who gave his own life as the perfect sacrifice to take away the sins of the world. As the true high priest and sacrifice sent by God for all people, Jesus takes the place of all other priests and sacrifices. Hebrews 11 tells stories of people who had faith in God. Then, the next chapter explains that Christians must also have faith and must keep their eyes on Jesus, the one who is "the pioneer and perfecter of our faith" (12:2).

Hebrews 13:22

God Has Spoken by His Son

1 Long ago God spoke to our ancestors in many and various ways by the prophets, [2]but in these last days he has spoken to us by a Son,[a] whom he appointed heir of all things, through whom he also created the worlds. [3]He is the reflection of God's glory and the exact imprint of God's very being, and he sustains[b] all things by his powerful word. When he had made purification for sins, he sat down at the right hand of the Majesty on high, [4]having become as much superior to angels as the name he has inherited is more excellent than theirs.

The Son Is Superior to Angels

5 For to which of the angels did God ever say,

"You are my Son;
today I have begotten you"?

Or again,

"I will be his Father,
and he will be my Son"?

[6]And again, when he brings the firstborn into the world, he says,

"Let all God's angels worship him."

[7]Of the angels he says,

"He makes his angels winds,
and his servants flames of fire."

[8]But of the Son he says,

"Your throne, O God,[c] is forever and ever,
and the righteous scepter is the scepter of your[d] kingdom.
[9] You have loved righteousness and hated wickedness;
therefore God, your God, has anointed you
with the oil of gladness beyond your companions."

[10]And,

"In the beginning, Lord, you founded the earth,
and the heavens are the work of your hands;
[11] they will perish, but you remain;
they will all wear out like clothing;
[12] like a cloak you will roll them up,
and like clothing[e] they will be changed.
But you are the same,
and your years will never end."

[13]But to which of the angels has he ever said,

"Sit at my right hand
until I make your enemies a footstool for your feet"?

[14]Are not all angels[f] spirits in the divine service, sent to serve for the sake of those who are to inherit salvation?

Warning to Pay Attention

2 Therefore we must pay greater attention to what we have heard, so that we do not drift away from it. [2]For if the message declared through angels was valid, and every transgression or disobedience received a just penalty, [3]how can we escape if we neglect so great a salvation? It was declared at first through the Lord, and it was attested to us by those who heard him, [4]while God added his testimony by signs and wonders and various miracles, and by gifts of the Holy Spirit, distributed according to his will.

Exaltation through Abasement

5 Now God[g] did not subject the coming world, about which we are speaking, to angels. [6]But someone has testified somewhere,

"What are human beings that you are mindful of them,[h]
or mortals, that you care for them?[i]

[a] Or *the Son*   [b] Or *bears along*   [c] Or *God is your throne*   [d] Other ancient authorities read *his*
[e] Other ancient authorities lack *like clothing*
[f] Gk *all of them*   [g] Gk *he*   [h] Gk *What is man that you are mindful of him?*   [i] Gk *or the son of man that you care for him?* In the Hebrew of Psalm 8.4-6 both *man* and *son of man* refer to all humankind

Christ was present at Creation. Everything that God created at the beginning of time will perish, but God's Son will remain forever.

[7] You have made them for a little while
    lower[j] than the angels;
  you have crowned them with glory
    and honor,[k]
[8] subjecting all things under their feet."
Now in subjecting all things to them,
God[l] left nothing outside their control.
As it is, we do not yet see everything in
subjection to them, [9]but we do see Jesus,
who for a little while was made lower[m]
than the angels, now crowned with glory
and honor because of the suffering of
death, so that by the grace of God[n] he
might taste death for everyone.

> Jesus was born as a human baby, and grew up just as we do. He knows how it feels to be hungry and tired. He knows how it feels to be hurt by his friends. He knows how it feels to be hurt physically. Because he was, he is able to help us when we have troubles.

[10] It was fitting that God,[l] for whom
and through whom all things exist, in
bringing many children to glory, should
make the pioneer of their salvation perfect through sufferings. [11]For the one
who sanctifies and those who are sanctified all have one Father.[o] For this reason
Jesus[l] is not ashamed to call them brothers and sisters,[p] [12]saying,
  "I will proclaim your name to my
    brothers and sisters,[p]
  in the midst of the congregation I
    will praise you."
[13]And again,
  "I will put my trust in him."
And again,
  "Here am I and the children whom
    God has given me."

> "Yet Jesus is worthy of more glory than Moses, just as the builder of a house has more honor than the house itself." Hebrews 3:3

[14] Since, therefore, the children share
flesh and blood, he himself likewise
shared the same things, so that through
death he might destroy the one who has
the power of death, that is, the devil,
[15]and free those who all their lives were
held in slavery by the fear of death. [16]For
it is clear that he did not come to help
angels, but the descendants of Abraham.
[17]Therefore he had to become like his
brothers and sisters[p] in every respect, so
that he might be a merciful and faithful
high priest in the service of God, to make
a sacrifice of atonement for the sins of the
people. [18]Because he himself was tested
by what he suffered, he is able to help
those who are being tested.

Moses a Servant, Christ a Son

3 Therefore, brothers and sisters,[p] holy
partners in a heavenly calling, consider that Jesus, the apostle and high
priest of our confession, [2]was faithful to
the one who appointed him, just as Moses
also "was faithful in all[q] God's[r] house." [3]Yet
Jesus[s] is worthy of more glory than Moses,
just as the builder of a house has more
honor than the house itself. [4](For every
house is built by someone, but the builder
of all things is God.) [5]Now Moses was
faithful in all God's[r] house as a servant, to
testify to the things that would be spoken
later. [6]Christ, however, was faithful over
God's[r] house as a son, and we are his
house if we hold firm[t] the confidence and
the pride that belong to hope.

Warning against Unbelief

[7] Therefore, as the Holy Spirit says,
  "Today, if you hear his voice,
[8] do not harden your hearts as in the
    rebellion,
  as on the day of testing in the
    wilderness,

[j] Or *them only a little lower*   [k] Other ancient
authorities add *and set them over the works of your
hands*   [l] Gk *he*   [m] Or *who was made a little lower*
[n] Other ancient authorities read *apart from God*
[o] Gk *are all of one*   [p] Gk *brothers*   [q] Other
ancient authorities lack *all*   [r] Gk *his*   [s] Gk *this
one*   [t] Other ancient authorities add *to the end*

[9] where your ancestors put me to the
test,
though they had seen my works
[10]for forty years.
Therefore I was angry with that
generation,
and I said, 'They always go astray in
their hearts,
and they have not known my ways.'
[11] As in my anger I swore,
'They will not enter my rest.' "
[12]Take care, brothers and sisters,[u] that
none of you may have an evil, unbelieving
heart that turns away from the living God.
[13]But exhort one another every day, as
long as it is called "today," so that none of
you may be hardened by the deceitfulness
of sin. [14]For we have become partners of
Christ, if only we hold our first confidence
firm to the end. [15]As it is said,
"Today, if you hear his voice,
do not harden your hearts as in the
rebellion."
[16]Now who were they who heard and yet
were rebellious? Was it not all those who
left Egypt under the leadership of Moses?
[17]But with whom was he angry forty
years? Was it not those who sinned,
whose bodies fell in the wilderness? [18]And
to whom did he swear that they would
not enter his rest, if not to those who were
disobedient? [19]So we see that they were
unable to enter because of unbelief.

The Rest That God Promised

4 Therefore, while the promise of
entering his rest is still open, let us
take care that none of you should seem
to have failed to reach it. [2]For indeed the
good news came to us just as to them;
but the message they heard did not benefit them, because they were not united
by faith with those who listened.[v] [3]For
we who have believed enter that rest,
just as God[w] has said,
"As in my anger I swore,
'They shall not enter my rest,' "
though his works were finished at the
foundation of the world. [4]For in one
place it speaks about the seventh day as

follows, "And God rested on the seventh
day from all his works." [5]And again in
this place it says, "They shall not enter
my rest." [6]Since therefore it remains
open for some to enter it, and those who
formerly received the good news failed
to enter because of disobedience, [7]again
he sets a certain day—"today"—saying
through David much later, in the words
already quoted,
"Today, if you hear his voice,
do not harden your hearts."
[8]For if Joshua had given them rest, God[w]
would not speak later about another day.
[9]So then, a sabbath rest still remains for
the people of God; [10]for those who enter
God's rest also cease from their labors as
God did from his. [11]Let us therefore
make every effort to enter that rest, so
that no one may fall through such disobedience as theirs.

12 Indeed, the word of God is living
and active, sharper than any two-edged
sword, piercing until it divides soul from
spirit, joints from marrow; it is able to
judge the thoughts and intentions of the
heart. [13]And before him no creature is
hidden, but all are naked and laid bare
to the eyes of the one to whom we must
render an account.

Jesus the Great High Priest

14 Since, then, we have a great high
priest who has passed through the heavens, Jesus, the Son of God, let us hold fast
to our confession. [15]For we do not have a
high priest who is unable to sympathize
with our weaknesses, but we have one
who in every respect has been tested[x] as
we are, yet without sin. [16]Let us therefore

"Let us therefore approach the throne
of grace with boldness, so
that we may receive mercy
and find grace to help in
time of need."

Hebrews 4:16

[u] Gk *brothers*   [v] Other ancient authorities read
it did not meet with faith in those who listened
[w] Gk *he*   [x] Or *tempted*

approach the throne of grace with boldness, so that we may receive mercy and find grace to help in time of need.

Jesus is always our example. Even though he was God's Son, he still prayed to God for comfort and strength. Prayer is a powerful force, a way to talk and listen to God, and a response to God's love. Ask some people you know, "When do you pray? Where do you pray? How do you pray?" Their answers may help you with your own prayer life.

5 Every high priest chosen from among mortals is put in charge of things pertaining to God on their behalf, to offer gifts and sacrifices for sins. [2]He is able to deal gently with the ignorant and wayward, since he himself is subject to weakness; [3]and because of this he must offer sacrifice for his own sins as well as for those of the people. [4]And one does not presume to take this honor, but takes it only when called by God, just as Aaron was.

5 So also Christ did not glorify himself in becoming a high priest, but was appointed by the one who said to him,

"You are my Son,
today I have begotten you";

[6]as he says also in another place,

"You are a priest forever,
according to the order of
Mel·chiz′e·dek."

7 In the days of his flesh, Jesus[y] offered up prayers and supplications, with loud cries and tears, to the one who was able to save him from death, and he was heard because of his reverent submission. [8]Although he was a Son, he learned obedience through what he suffered; [9]and having been made perfect, he became the source of eternal salvation for all who obey him,

[10]having been designated by God a high priest according to the order of Mel·chiz′e·dek.

Warning against Falling Away

11 About this[z] we have much to say that is hard to explain, since you have become dull in understanding. [12]For though by this time you ought to be teachers, you need someone to teach you again the basic elements of the oracles of God. You need milk, not solid food; [13]for everyone who lives on milk, being still an infant, is unskilled in the word of righteousness. [14]But solid food is for the mature, for those whose faculties have been trained by practice to distinguish good from evil.

The Peril of Falling Away

6 Therefore let us go on toward perfection,[a] leaving behind the basic teaching about Christ, and not laying again the foundation: repentance from dead works and faith toward God, [2]instruction about baptisms, laying on of hands, resurrection of the dead, and eternal judgment. [3]And we will do[b] this, if God permits. [4]For it is impossible to restore again to repentance those who have once been enlightened, and have tasted the heavenly gift, and have shared in the Holy Spirit, [5]and have tasted the goodness of the word of God and the powers of the age to come, [6]and then have fallen away, since on their own they are crucifying again the Son of God and are holding him up to contempt. [7]Ground that drinks up the rain falling on it repeatedly, and that produces a crop useful to those for whom it is cultivated, receives a blessing from God. [8]But if it produces thorns and thistles, it is worthless and on the verge of being cursed; its end is to be burned over.

9 Even though we speak in this way, beloved, we are confident of better things in your case, things that belong to

y Gk he   z Or him   a Or toward maturity
b Other ancient authorities read let us do

salvation. ¹⁰For God is not unjust; he will not overlook your work and the love that you showed for his sake^c in serving the saints, as you still do. ¹¹And we want each one of you to show the same diligence so as to realize the full assurance of hope to the very end, ¹²so that you may not become sluggish, but imitators of those who through faith and patience inherit the promises.

The Certainty of God's Promise

13 When God made a promise to Abraham, because he had no one greater by whom to swear, he swore by himself, ¹⁴saying, "I will surely bless you and multiply you." ¹⁵And thus Abraham,^d having patiently endured, obtained the promise. ¹⁶Human beings, of course, swear by someone greater than themselves, and an oath given as confirmation puts an end to all dispute. ¹⁷In the same way, when God desired to show even more clearly to the heirs of the promise the unchangeable character of his purpose, he guaranteed it by an oath, ¹⁸so that through two unchangeable things, in which it is impossible that God would prove false, we who have taken refuge might be strongly encouraged to seize the hope set before us. ¹⁹We have this hope, a sure and steadfast anchor of the soul, a hope that enters the inner shrine behind the curtain, ²⁰where Jesus, a forerunner on our behalf, has

> "For God is not unjust; he will not overlook your work and the love that you showed for his sake in serving the saints, as you still do."   Hebrews 6:10

entered, having become a high priest forever according to the order of Mel·chiz´e·dek.

The Priestly Order of Melchizedek

7 This "King Mel·chiz´e·dek of Salem, priest of the Most High God, met Abraham as he was returning from defeating the kings and blessed him"; ²and to him Abraham apportioned "one-tenth of everything." His name, in the first place, means "king of righteousness"; next he is also king of Salem, that is, "king of peace." ³Without father, without mother, without genealogy, having neither beginning of days nor end of life, but resembling the Son of God, he remains a priest forever.

4 See how great he is! Even^e Abraham the patriarch gave him a tenth of the spoils. ⁵And those descendants of Levi who receive the priestly office have a commandment in the law to collect tithes^f from the people, that is, from their kindred,^g though these also are descended from Abraham. ⁶But this man, who does not belong to their ancestry, collected tithes^f from Abraham and blessed him who had received the promises. ⁷It is beyond dispute that the inferior is blessed by the superior. ⁸In the one case, tithes are received by those who are mortal; in the other, by one of whom it is testified that he lives. ⁹One might even say that Levi himself, who receives tithes, paid tithes through Abraham, ¹⁰for he was still in the loins of his ancestor when Mel·chiz´e·dek met him.

Melchizedek lived at the same time Abraham lived. Melchizedek was a king and priest who prepared a meal for Abraham and blessed him. Since Melchizedek had both royal and priestly authority in the city of Jerusalem before the Israelites came, David claimed to be his successor.

Melchizedek became the symbol of an ideal priest-king.

^c Gk for his name   ^d Gk he   ^e Other ancient authorities lack Even   ^f Or a tenth   ^g Gk brothers

Another Priest, Like Melchizedek

11 Now if perfection had been attainable through the levitical priesthood—for the people received the law under this priesthood—what further need would there have been to speak of another priest arising according to the order of Mel·chiz´e·dek, rather than one according to the order of Aaron? 12For when there is a change in the priesthood, there is necessarily a change in the law as well. 13Now the one of whom these things are spoken belonged to another tribe, from which no one has ever served at the altar. 14For it is evident that our Lord was descended from Judah, and in connection with that tribe Moses said nothing about priests.

15 It is even more obvious when another priest arises, resembling Mel·chiz´e·dek, 16one who has become a priest, not through a legal requirement concerning physical descent, but through the power of an indestructible life. 17For it is attested of him,

"You are a priest forever,
according to the order of
Mel·chiz´e·dek."

18There is, on the one hand, the abrogation of an earlier commandment because it was weak and ineffectual 19(for the law made nothing perfect); there is, on the other hand, the introduction of a better hope, through which we approach God.

20 This was confirmed with an oath; for others who became priests took their office without an oath, 21but this one became a priest with an oath, because of the one who said to him,

"The Lord has sworn
and will not change his mind,
'You are a priest forever' "—

22accordingly Jesus has also become the guarantee of a better covenant.

23 Furthermore, the former priests were many in number, because they were prevented by death from continuing in office; 24but he holds his priesthood permanently, because he continues forever. 25Consequently he is able for all time to save[h] those who approach God through him, since he always lives to make intercession for them.

26 For it was fitting that we should have such a high priest, holy, blameless, undefiled, separated from sinners, and exalted above the heavens. 27Unlike the other[i] high priests, he has no need to offer sacrifices day after day, first for his own sins, and then for those of the people; this he did once for all when he offered himself. 28For the law appoints as high priests those who are subject to weakness, but the word of the oath, which came later than the law, appoints a Son who has been made perfect forever.

Mediator of a Better Covenant

8 Now the main point in what we are saying is this: we have such a high priest, one who is seated at the right hand of the throne of the Majesty in the heavens, 2a minister in the sanctuary and the true tent[j] that the Lord, and not any mortal, has set up. 3For every high priest is appointed to offer gifts and sacrifices; hence it is necessary for this priest also to have something to offer. 4Now if he were on earth, he would not be a priest at all,

Can you remember a time when you made a promise? Was it serious and important? How did you feel? A covenant is a promise made between two people. God has made a covenant with us through Jesus. To help you keep this covenant with God, remember these suggestions: Read your Bible every day. Pray for yourself and for others every day. Attend a worship service at least once a week. Get involved with a service project or activity that helps someone in need. Spend time with others who will do these same things, and support one another.

---

[h] Or *able to save completely*   [i] Gk lacks *other*
[j] Or *tabernacle*

since there are priests who offer gifts according to the law. [5]They offer worship in a sanctuary that is a sketch and shadow of the heavenly one; for Moses, when he was about to erect the tent,[k] was warned, "See that you make everything according to the pattern that was shown you on the mountain." [6]But Jesus[l] has now obtained a more excellent ministry, and to that degree he is the mediator of a better covenant, which has been enacted through better promises. [7]For if that first covenant had been faultless, there would have been no need to look for a second one.

8 God[l] finds fault with them when he says:

"The days are surely coming, says the
    Lord,
  when I will establish a new covenant
      with the house of Israel
    and with the house of Judah;
[9] not like the covenant that I made with
        their ancestors,
    on the day when I took them by the
        hand to lead them out of the
        land of Egypt;
  for they did not continue in my
        covenant,
    and so I had no concern for them,
        says the Lord.
[10] This is the covenant that I will make
        with the house of Israel
    after those days, says the Lord:
  I will put my laws in their minds,
    and write them on their hearts,
  and I will be their God,
    and they shall be my people.
[11] And they shall not teach one another
    or say to each other, 'Know the Lord,'
  for they shall all know me,
    from the least of them to the greatest.
[12] For I will be merciful toward their
        iniquities,
    and I will remember their sins no
        more."

[13]In speaking of "a new covenant," he has made the first one obsolete. And what is obsolete and growing old will soon disappear.

The Earthly and the Heavenly Sanctuaries

9 Now even the first covenant had regulations for worship and an earthly sanctuary. [2]For a tent[k] was constructed, the first one, in which were the lampstand, the table, and the bread of the Presence;[m] this is called the Holy Place. [3]Behind the second curtain was a tent[k] called the Holy of Holies. [4]In it stood the golden altar of incense and the ark of the covenant overlaid on all sides with gold, in which there were a golden urn holding the manna, and Aaron's rod that budded, and the tablets of the covenant; [5]above it were the cherubim of glory overshadowing the mercy seat.[n] Of these things we cannot speak now in detail.

6 Such preparations having been made, the priests go continually into the first tent[k] to carry out their ritual duties; [7]but only the high priest goes into the second, and he but once a year, and not without taking the blood that he offers for himself and for the sins committed unintentionally by the people. [8]By this the Holy Spirit indicates that the way into the sanctuary has not yet been disclosed as long as the first tent[k] is still standing. [9]This is a symbol[o] of the present time, during which gifts and sacrifices are offered that cannot perfect the conscience of the worshiper, [10]but deal only with food and drink and various baptisms, regulations for the body imposed until the time comes to set things right.

11 But when Christ came as a high priest of the good things that have come,[p] then through the greater and perfect[q] tent[k] (not made with hands, that is,

God is slow to anger, full of love for us, and merciful to us when we make wrong choices.

[k] Or *tabernacle*   [l] Gk *he*   [m] Gk *the presentation of the loaves*   [n] Or *the place of atonement*   [o] Gk *parable*   [p] Other ancient authorities read *good things to come*   [q] Gk *more perfect*

not of this creation), [12]he entered once for all into the Holy Place, not with the blood of goats and calves, but with his own blood, thus obtaining eternal redemption. [13]For if the blood of goats and bulls, with the sprinkling of the ashes of a heifer, sanctifies those who have been defiled so that their flesh is purified, [14]how much more will the blood of Christ, who through the eternal Spirit[r] offered himself without blemish to God, purify our[s] conscience from dead works to worship the living God!

15 For this reason he is the mediator of a new covenant, so that those who are called may receive the promised eternal inheritance, because a death has occurred that redeems them from the transgressions under the first covenant.[t] [16]Where a will[t] is involved, the death of the one who made it must be established. [17]For a will[t] takes effect only at death, since it is not in force as long as the one who made it is alive. [18]Hence not even the first covenant was inaugurated without blood. [19]For when every commandment had been told to all the people by Moses in accordance with the law, he took the blood of calves and goats,[u] with water and scarlet wool and hyssop, and sprinkled both the scroll itself and all the people, [20]saying, "This is the blood of the covenant that God has ordained for you." [21]And in the same way he sprinkled with the blood both the tent[v] and all the vessels used in worship. [22]Indeed, under the law almost everything is purified with blood, and without the shedding of blood there is no forgiveness of sins.

> "For Christ did not enter a sanctuary made by human hands, a mere copy of the true one, but he entered into heaven itself, now to appear in the presence of God on our behalf."
> Hebrews 9:24

Christ's Sacrifice Takes Away Sin

23 Thus it was necessary for the sketches of the heavenly things to be purified with these rites, but the heavenly things themselves need better sacrifices than these. [24]For Christ did not enter a sanctuary made by human hands, a mere copy of the true one, but he entered into heaven itself, now to appear in the presence of God on our behalf. [25]Nor was it to offer himself again and again, as the high priest enters the Holy Place year after year with blood that is not his own; [26]for then he would have had to suffer again and again since the foundation of the world. But as it is, he has appeared once for all at the end of the age to remove sin by the sacrifice of himself. [27]And just as it is appointed for mortals to die once, and after that the judgment, [28]so Christ, having been offered once to bear the sins of many, will appear a second time, not to deal with sin, but to save those who are eagerly waiting for him.

Christ's Sacrifice Once for All

10 Since the law has only a shadow of the good things to come and not the true form of these realities, it[w] can never, by the same sacrifices that are continually offered year after year, make perfect those who approach. [2]Otherwise, would they not have ceased being offered, since the worshipers, cleansed once for all, would no longer have any consciousness of sin? [3]But in these sacrifices there is a reminder of sin year after year. [4]For it is impossible for the blood of bulls and goats to take away sins. [5]Consequently, when Christ[x] came into the world, he said,

"Sacrifices and offerings you have not desired,

[r] Other ancient authorities read *Holy Spirit*
[s] Other ancient authorities read *your*   [t] The Greek word used here means both *covenant* and *will*   [u] Other ancient authorities lack *and goats*
[v] Gk *tabernacle*   [w] Other ancient authorities read *they*   [x] Gk *he*

but a body you have prepared for me;

[6] in burnt offerings and sin offerings you have taken no pleasure.

[7] Then I said, 'See, God, I have come to do your will, O God'
(in the scroll of the book[y] it is written of me).' "

[8] When he said above, "You have neither desired nor taken pleasure in sacrifices and offerings and burnt offerings and sin offerings" (these are offered according to the law), [9] then he added, "See, I have come to do your will." He abolishes the first in order to establish the second. [10] And it is by God's will[z] that we have been sanctified through the offering of the body of Jesus Christ once for all.

11 And every priest stands day after day at his service, offering again and again the same sacrifices that can never take away sins. [12] But when Christ[a] had offered for all time a single sacrifice for sins, "he sat down at the right hand of God," [13] and since then has been waiting "until his enemies would be made a footstool for his feet." [14] For by a single offering he has perfected for all time those who are sanctified. [15] And the Holy Spirit also testifies to us, for after saying,

[16] "This is the covenant that I will make with them
after those days, says the Lord:
I will put my laws in their hearts,
and I will write them on their minds,"

[17] he also adds,

"I will remember[b] their sins and their lawless deeds no more."

[18] Where there is forgiveness of these, there is no longer any offering for sin.

A Call to Persevere

19 Therefore, my friends,[c] since we have confidence to enter the sanctuary by the blood of Jesus, [20] by the new and living way that he opened for us through the curtain (that is, through his flesh), [21] and since we have a great priest over the house of God, [22] let us approach with a true heart in full assurance of faith, with our hearts sprinkled clean from an evil conscience and our bodies washed with pure water. [23] Let us hold fast to the confession of our hope without wavering, for he who has promised is faithful. [24] And let us consider how to provoke one another to love and good deeds, [25] not neglecting to meet together, as is the habit of some, but encouraging one another, and all the more as you see the Day approaching.

26 For if we willfully persist in sin after having received the knowledge of the truth, there no longer remains a sacrifice for sins, [27] but a fearful prospect of judgment, and a fury of fire that will consume the adversaries. [28] Anyone who has violated the law of Moses dies without mercy "on the testimony of two or three witnesses." [29] How much worse punishment do you think will be deserved by those who have spurned the Son of God, profaned the blood of the covenant by which they were sanctified, and outraged the Spirit of grace? [30] For we know the one who said, "Vengeance is mine, I will repay." And again, "The Lord will judge his people." [31] It is a fearful thing to fall into the hands of the living God.

32 But recall those earlier days when, after you had been enlightened, you endured a hard struggle with sufferings, [33] sometimes being publicly exposed to abuse and persecution, and sometimes being partners with those so treated. [34] For you had compassion for those who were in prison, and you cheerfully accepted the plundering of your possessions, knowing that you yourselves possessed something better and more lasting. [35] Do not, therefore, abandon that confidence of yours; it brings a great reward. [36] For you need endurance, so that when you have done the will of God, you may receive what was promised. [37] For yet

[y] Meaning of Gk uncertain [z] Gk by that will
[a] Gk this one [b] Gk on their minds and I will remember [c] Gk Therefore, brothers

"in a very little while,
the one who is coming will come
and will not delay;
[38] but my righteous one will live by faith.
My soul takes no pleasure in anyone
who shrinks back."
[39]But we are not among those who shrink back and so are lost, but among those who have faith and so are saved.

The Meaning of Faith

11 Now faith is the assurance of things hoped for, the conviction of things not seen. [2]Indeed, by faith[d] our ancestors received approval. [3]By faith we understand that the worlds were prepared by the word of God, so that what is seen was made from things that are not visible. [e]

The Examples of Abel, Enoch, and Noah

4 By faith Abel offered to God a more acceptable[f] sacrifice than Cain's. Through this he received approval as righteous, God himself giving approval to his gifts; he died, but through his faith[g] he still speaks. [5]By faith Enoch was taken so that he did not experience death; and "he was not found, because God had taken him." For it was attested before he was taken away that "he had pleased God." [6]And without faith it is impossible to please God, for whoever would approach him must believe that he exists and that he rewards those who seek him. [7]By faith Noah, warned by God about events as yet unseen, respected the warning and built an ark to save his household; by this he condemned the world and became an heir to the righteousness that is in accordance with faith.

"Now faith is the assurance of things hoped for, the conviction of things not seen." Hebrews 11:1

One way to think of the Bible is as a family album that contains stories of God's family. These are the stories of our family, and the people in the stories are like us in many ways. Sometimes the people tried their best to follow God. Sometimes the people did not. The stories in the Bible teach us about ourselves and about God. They show us who God is and how God wants us to live.

The Faith of Abraham

8 By faith Abraham obeyed when he was called to set out for a place that he was to receive as an inheritance; and he set out, not knowing where he was going. [9]By faith he stayed for a time in the land he had been promised, as in a foreign land, living in tents, as did Isaac and Jacob, who were heirs with him of the same promise. [10]For he looked forward to the city that has foundations, whose architect and builder is God. [11]By faith he received power of procreation, even though he was too old—and Sarah herself was barren—because he considered him faithful who had promised.[h] [12]Therefore from one person, and this one as good as dead, descendants were born, "as many as the stars of heaven and as the innumerable grains of sand by the seashore."

13 All of these died in faith without having received the promises, but from a distance they saw and greeted them. They confessed that they were strangers and foreigners on the earth, [14]for people who speak in this way make it clear that they are seeking a homeland. [15]If they had been thinking of the land that they

d Gk *by this*   *e* Or *was not made out of visible things*   *f* Gk *greater*   *g* Gk *through it*   *h* Other ancient authorities read *By faith Sarah herself, though barren, received power to conceive, even when she was too old, because she considered him faithful who had promised* had left behind, they would have had opportunity to return. ¹⁶But as it is, they desire a better country, that is, a heavenly one. Therefore God is not ashamed to be called their God; indeed, he has prepared a city for them.

17 By faith Abraham, when put to the test, offered up Isaac. He who had received the promises was ready to offer up his only son, ¹⁸of whom he had been told, "It is through Isaac that descendants shall be named for you." ¹⁹He considered the fact that God is able even to raise someone from the dead—and figuratively speaking, he did receive him back. ²⁰By faith Isaac invoked blessings for the future on Jacob and Esau. ²¹By faith Jacob, when dying, blessed each of the sons of Joseph, "bowing in worship over the top of his staff." ²²By faith Joseph, at the end of his life, made mention of the exodus of the Israelites and gave instructions about his burial.ⁱ

The Faith of Moses

23 By faith Moses was hidden by his parents for three months after his birth, because they saw that the child was beautiful; and they were not afraid of the king's edict.^j ²⁴By faith Moses, when he was grown up, refused to be called a son of Pharaoh's daughter, ²⁵choosing rather to share ill-treatment with the people of God than to enjoy the fleeting pleasures of sin. ²⁶He considered abuse suffered for the Christ^k to be greater wealth than the treasures of Egypt, for he was looking ahead to the reward. ²⁷By faith he left Egypt, unafraid of the king's anger; for he persevered as though^l he saw him who is invisible. ²⁸By faith he kept the Passover and the sprinkling of blood, so that the destroyer of the firstborn would not touch the firstborn of Israel.^m

The Faith of Other Israelite Heroes

29 By faith the people passed through the Red Sea as if it were dry land, but when the Egyptians attempted

to do so they were drowned. ³⁰By faith the walls of Jericho fell after they had been encircled for seven days. ³¹By faith Rā'hab the prostitute did not perish with those who were disobedient,ⁿ because she had received the spies in peace.

32 And what more should I say? For time would fail me to tell of Gideon, Bar'ak, Samson, Jeph'thah, of David and Samuel and the prophets— ³³who through faith conquered kingdoms, administered justice, obtained promises, shut the mouths of lions, ³⁴quenched raging fire, escaped the edge of the sword, won strength out of weakness, became mighty in war, put foreign armies to flight. ³⁵Women received their dead by resurrection. Others were tortured, refusing to accept release, in order to obtain a better resurrection. ³⁶Others suffered mocking and flogging, and even chains and imprisonment. ³⁷They were stoned to death, they were sawn in two,^o they were killed by the sword; they went about in skins of sheep and goats, destitute, persecuted, tormented— ³⁸of whom the world was not worthy. They wandered in deserts and mountains, and in caves and holes in the ground.

39 Yet all these, though they were commended for their faith, did not receive what was promised, ⁴⁰since God had provided something better so that they would not, apart from us, be made perfect.

The Example of Jesus

12 Therefore, since we are surrounded by so great a cloud of witnesses, let us also lay aside every weight and the sin that clings so closely,^p and let us run with perseverance the race

ⁱ Gk his bones ^jOther ancient authorities add By faith Moses, when he was grown up, killed the Egyptian, because he observed the humiliation of his people (Gk brothers) ^k Or the Messiah ^l Or because ^m Gk would not touch them ⁿ Or unbelieving ^o Other ancient authorities add they were tempted ^p Other ancient authorities read sin that easily distracts

It is easy to listen to Jesus's words but much harder to live in the way he taught. We must keep our eyes on Jesus and put our faith in him into action.

that is set before us, [2]looking to Jesus the pioneer and perfecter of our faith, who for the sake of[q] the joy that was set before him endured the cross, disregarding its shame, and has taken his seat at the right hand of the throne of God.

3 Consider him who endured such hostility against himself from sinners,[r] so that you may not grow weary or lose heart. [4]In your struggle against sin you have not yet resisted to the point of shedding your blood. [5]And you have forgotten the exhortation that addresses you as children—

"My child, do not regard lightly the discipline of the Lord,
    or lose heart when you are punished by him;
[6] for the Lord disciplines those whom he loves,
    and chastises every child whom he accepts."

[7]Endure trials for the sake of discipline. God is treating you as children; for what child is there whom a parent does not discipline? [8]If you do not have that discipline in which all children share, then you are illegitimate and not his children. [9]Moreover, we had human parents to discipline us, and we respected them. Should we not be even more willing to be subject to the Father of spirits and live? [10]For they disciplined us for a short time as seemed best to them, but he disciplines us for our good, in order that we may share his holiness. [11]Now, discipline always seems painful rather than pleasant at the time, but later it yields the peaceful fruit of righteousness to those who have been trained by it.

12 Therefore lift your drooping hands and strengthen your weak knees, [13]and make straight paths for your feet, so that what is lame may not be put out of joint, but rather be healed.

Warnings against Rejecting God's Grace

14 Pursue peace with everyone, and the holiness without which no one will see the Lord. [15]See to it that no one fails to obtain the grace of God; that no root of bitterness springs up and causes trouble, and through it many become defiled. [16]See to it that no one becomes like Esau, an immoral and godless person, who sold his birthright for a single meal. [17]You know that later, when he wanted to inherit the blessing, he was rejected, for he found no chance to repent,[s] even though he sought the blessing[t] with tears.

18 You have not come to something[u] that can be touched, a blazing fire, and darkness, and gloom, and a tempest, [19]and the sound of a trumpet, and a voice whose words made the hearers beg that not another word be spoken to them. [20](For they could not endure the order that was given, "If even an animal touches the mountain, it shall be stoned to death." [21]Indeed, so terrifying was the sight that Moses said, "I tremble with fear.") [22]But you have come to Mount Zion and to the city of the living God, the heavenly Jerusalem, and to innumerable angels in festal gathering, [23]and to the assembly[v] of the firstborn who are enrolled in heaven, and to God the judge of all, and to the spirits of the righteous made perfect, [24]and to Jesus, the mediator of a new covenant, and to the sprinkled blood that speaks a better word than the blood of Abel.

25 See that you do not refuse the one who is speaking; for if they did not escape when they refused the one who warned them on earth, how much less will we

[q] Or *who instead of*   [r] Other ancient authorities read *such hostility from sinners against themselves*
[s] Or *no chance to change his father's mind*   [t] Gk *it*
[u] Other ancient authorities read *a mountain*
[v] Or *angels, and to the festal gathering* [23]*and assembly*

escape if we reject the one who warns from heaven! [26]At that time his voice shook the earth; but now he has promised, "Yet once more I will shake not only the earth but also the heaven." [27]This phrase, "Yet once more," indicates the removal of what is shaken—that is, created things—so that what cannot be shaken may remain. [28]Therefore, since we are receiving a kingdom that cannot be shaken, let us give thanks, by which we offer to God an acceptable worship with reverence and awe; [29]for indeed our God is a consuming fire.

Service Well-Pleasing to God

13 Let mutual love continue. [2]Do not neglect to show hospitality to strangers, for by doing that some have entertained angels without knowing it. [3]Remember those who are in prison, as though you were in prison with them; those who are being tortured, as though you yourselves were being tortured.[w] [4]Let marriage be held in honor by all, and let the marriage bed be kept undefiled; for God will judge fornicators and adulterers. [5]Keep your lives free from the love of money, and be content with what you have; for he has said, "I will never leave you or forsake you." [6]So we can say with confidence,

"The Lord is my helper;
I will not be afraid.
What can anyone do to me?"

[7] Remember your leaders, those who spoke the word of God to you; consider the outcome of their way of life, and imitate their faith. [8]Jesus Christ is the same yesterday and today and forever. [9]Do not be carried away by all kinds of strange teachings; for it is well for the heart to be strengthened by grace, not by regulations about food,[x] which have not benefited those who observe them. [10]We have an altar from which those who officiate in the tent[y] have no right to eat. [11]For the bodies of those animals whose blood is brought into the sanctuary by the high priest as a sacrifice for sin are burned

outside the camp. [12]Therefore Jesus also suffered outside the city gate in order to sanctify the people by his own blood. [13]Let us then go to him outside the camp and bear the abuse he endured. [14]For here we have no lasting city, but we are looking for the city that is to come. [15]Through him, then, let us continually offer a sacrifice of praise to God, that is, the fruit of lips that confess his name. [16]Do not neglect to do good and to share what you have, for such sacrifices are pleasing to God.

17 Obey your leaders and submit to them, for they are keeping watch over your souls and will give an account. Let them do this with joy and not with sighing—for that would be harmful to you.

18 Pray for us; we are sure that we have a clear conscience, desiring to act honorably in all things. [19]I urge you all the more to do this, so that I may be restored to you very soon.

Benediction

20 Now may the God of peace, who brought back from the dead our Lord Jesus, the great shepherd of the sheep, by the blood of the eternal covenant, [21]make you complete in everything good so that you may do his will, working among us[z] that which is pleasing in his sight, through Jesus Christ, to whom be the glory forever and ever. Amen.

Final Exhortation and Greetings

22 I appeal to you, brothers and sisters,[a] bear with my word of exhortation, for I have written to you briefly. [23]I want you to know that our brother Timothy has been set free; and if he comes in time, he will be with me when I see you. [24]Greet all your leaders and all the saints. Those from Italy send you greetings. [25]Grace be with all of you.[b]

---

[w] Gk were in the body   [x] Gk not by foods   [y] Or tabernacle   [z] Other ancient authorities read you   [a] Gk brothers   [b] Other ancient authorities add Amen

James

The letter of James begins with the words "James, a servant of God and of the Lord Jesus Christ." Some people think the writer was James, the brother of Jesus. Others think some other man named James wrote the letter much later.

The letter of James is written to "the twelve tribes in the Dispersion." This refers to Jews who had scattered throughout the empire. The main pur-pose of the letter was to strengthen Jewish Christians in times of trouble and to insist that they do good with every part of their lives, including their words and actions. The theme of this book is expressed in two of the best-known verses: "But be doers of the word, and not merely hearers who deceive them-selves" (1:22) and "So faith by itself, if it has no works, is dead" (2:17).

James 1:1

Salutation

1 James, a servant[a] of God and of the Lord Jesus Christ,
To the twelve tribes in the Dispersion: Greetings.

Faith and Wisdom

2 My brothers and sisters,[b] whenever you face trials of any kind, consider it nothing but joy, [3]because you know that the testing of your faith produces endurance; [4]and let endurance have its full effect, so that you may be mature and complete, lacking in nothing.

5 If any of you is lacking in wisdom, ask God, who gives to all generously and ungrudgingly, and it will be given you. [6]But ask in faith, never doubting, for the one who doubts is like a wave of the sea, driven and tossed by the wind; [7, 8]for the doubter, being double-minded and unstable in every way, must not expect to receive anything from the Lord.

Poverty and Riches

9 Let the believer[c] who is lowly boast in being raised up, [10]and the rich in being brought low, because the rich will disappear like a flower in the field. [11]For the sun rises with its scorching heat and withers the field; its flower falls, and its beauty perishes. It is the same way with the rich; in the midst of a busy life, they will wither away.

Trial and Temptation

12 Blessed is anyone who endures temptation. Such a one has stood the test and will receive the crown of life that the Lord[d] has promised to those who love him. [13]No one, when tempted, should say, "I am being tempted by God"; for God cannot be tempted by evil and he himself tempts no one. [14]But one is tempted by one's own desire, being lured and enticed by it; [15]then, when that desire has conceived, it gives birth to sin, and that sin, when it is fully grown, gives birth to death. [16]Do not be deceived, my beloved.[e]

> "Every generous act of giving, with every perfect gift, is from above, coming down from the Father of lights, with whom there is no variation or shadow due to change." James 1:17

17 Every generous act of giving, with every perfect gift, is from above, coming down from the Father of lights, with whom there is no variation or shadow due to change.[f] [18]In fulfillment of his own purpose he gave us birth by the word of truth, so that we would become a kind of first fruits of his creatures.

Hearing and Doing the Word

19 You must understand this, my beloved:[e] let everyone be quick to listen, slow to speak, slow to anger; [20]for your anger does not produce God's righteousness. [21]Therefore rid yourselves of all sordidness and rank growth of wickedness, and welcome with meekness the implanted word that has the power to save your souls.

22 But be doers of the word, and not merely hearers who deceive themselves. [23]For if any are hearers of the word and not doers, they are like those who look at themselves[g] in a mirror; [24]for they look at themselves and, on going away, immediately forget what they were like. [25]But those who look into the perfect law, the law of liberty, and persevere, being not hearers who forget but doers who act—they will be blessed in their doing.

26 If any think they are religious, and do not bridle their tongues but deceive their hearts, their religion is worthless. [27]Religion that is pure and undefiled before God, the Father, is this: to care for orphans and widows in their distress, and to keep oneself unstained by the world.

a Gk *slave*   b Gk *brothers*   c Gk *brother*
d Gk *he*; other ancient authorities read *God*
e Gk *my beloved brothers*   f Other ancient authorities read *variation due to a shadow of turning*
g Gk *at the face of his birth*

Warning against Partiality

2 My brothers and sisters,[h] do you with your acts of favoritism really believe in our glorious Lord Jesus Christ?[i] [2]For if a person with gold rings and in fine clothes comes into your assembly, and if a poor person in dirty clothes also comes in, [3]and if you take notice of the one wearing the fine clothes and say, "Have a seat here, please," while to the one who is poor you say, "Stand there," or, "Sit at my feet,"[j] [4]have you not made distinctions among yourselves, and become judges with evil thoughts? [5]Listen, my beloved brothers and sisters.[k] Has not God chosen the poor in the world to be rich in faith and to be heirs of the kingdom that he has promised to those who love him? [6]But you have dishonored the poor. Is it not the rich who oppress you? Is it not they who drag you into court? [7]Is it not they who blaspheme the excellent name that was invoked over you?

8 You do well if you really fulfill the royal law according to the scripture, "You shall love your neighbor as yourself." [9]But if you show partiality, you commit sin and are convicted by the law as transgressors. [10]For whoever keeps the whole law but fails in one point has become accountable for all of it. [11]For the one who said, "You shall not commit adultery," also said, "You shall not murder." Now if you do not commit adultery but if you murder, you have become a transgressor of the law. [12]So speak and so act as those who are to be judged by the law of liberty. [13]For judgment will be without mercy to anyone who has shown no mercy; mercy triumphs over judgment.

Faith without Works Is Dead

14 What good is it, my brothers and sisters,[k] if you say you have faith but do

"I by my works will show you my faith."
James 2:18b

James wrote to his fellow Jewish Christians that they should not choose favorites but should show love and mercy to all.

not have works? Can faith save you? [15]If a brother or sister is naked and lacks daily food, [16]and one of you says to them, "Go in peace; keep warm and eat your fill," and yet you do not supply their bodily needs, what is the good of that? [17]So faith by itself, if it has no works, is dead.

18 But someone will say, "You have faith and I have works." Show me your faith apart from your works, and I by my works will show you my faith. [19]You believe that God is one; you do well. Even the demons believe—and shudder. [20]Do you want to be shown, you senseless person, that faith apart from works is barren? [21]Was not our ancestor Abraham justified by works when he offered his son Isaac on the altar? [22]You see that faith was active along with his works, and faith was brought to completion by the works. [23]Thus the scripture was fulfilled that says, "Abraham believed God, and it was reckoned to him as righteousness," and he was called the friend of God. [24]You see that a person is justified

God expects us to care for others. Good works are not an express ticket to heaven but a part of the life of those who love God. Being followers of Jesus means that we do good works like sharing, caring, helping, and reaching out to others. Jesus's example is the path we follow. By following his ways, discipleship becomes a way of life.

[h] Gk My brothers   [i] Or hold the faith of our glorious Lord Jesus Christ without acts of favoritism   [j] Gk Sit under my footstool   [k] Gk brothers

by works and not by faith alone. [25]Likewise, was not Rāʾhab the prostitute also justified by works when she welcomed the messengers and sent them out by another road? [26]For just as the body without the spirit is dead, so faith without works is also dead.

Taming the Tongue

3 Not many of you should become teachers, my brothers and sisters,[l] for you know that we who teach will be judged with greater strictness. [2]For all of us make many mistakes. Anyone who makes no mistakes in speaking is perfect, able to keep the whole body in check with a bridle. [3]If we put bits into the mouths of horses to make them obey us, we guide their whole bodies. [4]Or look at ships: though they are so large that it takes strong winds to drive them, yet they are guided by a very small rudder wherever the will of the pilot directs. [5]So also the tongue is a small member, yet it boasts of great exploits.

How great a forest is set ablaze by a small fire! [6]And the tongue is a fire. The tongue is placed among our members as a world of iniquity; it stains the whole body, sets on fire the cycle of nature,[m] and is itself set on fire by hell.[n] [7]For every species of beast and bird, of reptile and sea creature, can be tamed and has been tamed by the human species, [8]but no one can tame the tongue—a restless evil, full of deadly poison. [9]With it we bless the Lord and Father, and with it we curse those who are made in the likeness of God. [10]From the same mouth come blessing and cursing. My brothers and sisters,[l] this ought not to be so. [11]Does a spring pour forth from the same opening both fresh and brackish water? [12]Can a fig tree, my brothers and sisters,[l] yield olives, or a grapevine figs? No more can salt water yield fresh.

Two Kinds of Wisdom

13 Who is wise and understanding among you? Show by your good life that

We need to be very careful about what we say, because words have the power to hurt. We all say things that disappoint God. If we go to church every Sunday but use bad words and call people bad names during the week, then we are not living the way God wants us to live. If we say "Jesus loves you just the way you are" and then make fun of someone's clothes or hairstyle, then we are not living the way God wants us to live. James reminds us that what we say (and even the way we say it), might keep others from seeing Jesus in our lives.

your works are done with gentleness born of wisdom. [14]But if you have bitter envy and selfish ambition in your hearts, do not be boastful and false to the truth. [15]Such wisdom does not come down from above, but is earthly, unspiritual, devilish. [16]For where there is envy and selfish ambition, there will also be disorder and wickedness of every kind. [17]But the wisdom from above is first pure, then peaceable, gentle, willing to yield, full of mercy and good fruits, without a trace of partiality or hypocrisy. [18]And a harvest of righteousness is sown in peace for[o] those who make peace.

Friendship with the World

4 Those conflicts and disputes among you, where do they come from? Do they not come from your cravings that are at war within you? [2]You want something and do not have it; so you commit murder. And you covet[p]

"And a harvest of righteousness is sown in peace for those who make peace."
James 3:18

[l] Gk brothers   [m] Or wheel of birth   [n] Gk Gehenna   [o] Or by   [p] Or you murder and you covet

> "Draw near to God, and he
> will draw near to you."
>   James 4:8a

something and cannot obtain it; so you engage in disputes and conflicts. You do not have, because you do not ask. ³You ask and do not receive, because you ask wrongly, in order to spend what you get on your pleasures. ⁴Adulterers! Do you not know that friendship with the world is enmity with God? Therefore whoever wishes to be a friend of the world becomes an enemy of God. ⁵Or do you suppose that it is for nothing that the scripture says, "God^q yearns jealously for the spirit that he has made to dwell in us"? ⁶But he gives all the more grace; therefore it says,

"God opposes the proud,
    but gives grace to the humble."

⁷Submit yourselves therefore to God. Resist the devil, and he will flee from you. ⁸Draw near to God, and he will draw near to you. Cleanse your hands, you sinners, and purify your hearts, you double-minded. ⁹Lament and mourn and weep. Let your laughter be turned into mourning and your joy into dejection. ¹⁰Humble yourselves before the Lord, and he will exalt you.

Warning against Judging Another

11 Do not speak evil against one another, brothers and sisters.^r Whoever speaks evil against another or judges another, speaks evil against the law and judges the law; but if you judge the law, you are not a doer of the law but a judge. ¹²There is one lawgiver and judge who is able to save and to destroy. So who, then, are you to judge your neighbor?

Boasting about Tomorrow

13 Come now, you who say, "Today or tomorrow we will go to such and such a town and spend a year there, doing business and making money." ¹⁴Yet you do not even know what tomorrow will bring.

What is your life? For you are a mist that appears for a little while and then vanishes. ¹⁵Instead you ought to say, "If the Lord wishes, we will live and do this or that." ¹⁶As it is, you boast in your arrogance; all such boasting is evil. ¹⁷Anyone, then, who knows the right thing to do and fails to do it, commits sin.

Warning to Rich Oppressors

5 Come now, you rich people, weep and wail for the miseries that are coming to you. ²Your riches have rotted, and your clothes are moth-eaten. ³Your gold and silver have rusted, and their rust will be evidence against you, and it will eat your flesh like fire. You have laid up treasure^s for the last days. ⁴Listen! The wages of the laborers who mowed your fields, which you kept back by fraud, cry out, and the cries of the harvesters have reached the ears of the Lord of hosts. ⁵You have lived on the earth in luxury and in pleasure; you have fattened your hearts in a day of slaughter. ⁶You have condemned and murdered the righteous one, who does not resist you.

Patience in Suffering

7 Be patient, therefore, beloved,^r until the coming of the Lord. The farmer waits for the precious crop from the earth, being patient with it until it receives the early and the late rains. ⁸You also must be patient. Strengthen your hearts, for the coming of the Lord is near.^t ⁹Beloved,^r do not grumble against one another, so that you may not be judged. See, the Judge is standing at the doors! ¹⁰As an example of suffering and patience, beloved,^r take the prophets who spoke in the name of the Lord. ¹¹Indeed we call blessed those who showed endurance. You have heard of the endurance of Jōb, and you have seen the purpose of the Lord, how the Lord is compassionate and merciful.

^q Gk He   ^r Gk brothers   ^s Or will eat your flesh, since you have stored up fire   ^t Or is at hand

12 Above all, my beloved,[u] do not swear, either by heaven or by earth or by any other oath, but let your "Yes" be yes and your "No" be no, so that you may not fall under condemnation.

The Prayer of Faith

13 Are any among you suffering? They should pray. Are any cheerful? They should sing songs of praise. [14]Are any among you sick? They should call for the elders of the church and have them pray over them, anointing them with oil in the name of the Lord. [15]The prayer of faith will save the sick, and the Lord will raise them up; and anyone who has committed sins will be forgiven. [16]Therefore confess your sins to one another, and pray for one another, so that you may be healed. The prayer of the righteous is powerful and effective. [17]E·li´jah was a human being like us, and he prayed fervently that it might not rain, and for three years and six months it did not rain on the earth. [18]Then he prayed again, and the heaven gave rain and the earth yielded its harvest.

19 My brothers and sisters,[v] if anyone among you wanders from the truth and is brought back by another, [20]you should know that whoever brings back a sinner from wandering will save the sinner's[w] soul from death and will cover a multitude of sins.

James told the believers they should pray with faith. Do you spend time in prayer? You may want to try these ideas: Set a regular prayer time—early in the morning, after school, or in the evening. Choose the time seems to work best for you. Find a quiet place. It can be anywhere, as long as it is easy to get to and has a comfortable place to sit. Keep a prayer journal, and write words or thoughts that come to you as you talk and listen to God. Look back through your journal to see how God has been working in your life.

[u] Gk *My brothers*   [v] Gk *My brothers*   [w] Gk *his*

1 Peter

First Peter was probably written in the later part of the first century AD. The letter tells us that it is a message from the apostle Peter (see 1:1) but that Silvanus is the person who actually wrote it down (see 5:12). First Peter is a message meant to encourage Christians tempted to deny their faith in Jesus Christ because of threats, lies, and hatred from enemies. Peter told the believers to continue following God, living the way that Christ had shown them.

The letter speaks of salvation through the death and resurrection of Jesus. It reminds the readers to have hope in that salvation and to live holy lives. Peter told the people to rejoice and to endure suffering just as Christ had done. No matter how difficult things became, the readers were to hold tight to their faith—loving one another deeply, doing what is good, and telling about the mighty acts of God. Peter told the people that their suffering was a "fire" that would test their faith (1 Peter 1:7). If their faith was real, it would survive suffering in the same way that gold is made pure when heated with fire. He encouraged them saying, "After you have suffered for a little while, the God of all grace, who has called you to his eternal glory in Christ, will himself restore, support, strengthen, and establish you" (1 Peter 5:10).

1 Peter 1:1–2

Jesus is alive, and through him we have hope for the future. There may be suffering in this world, but God shows us mercy by giving us a chance at a new life.

Salutation

1 Peter, an apostle of Jesus Christ,
To the exiles of the Dispersion in Pon´tus, Galatia, Cap·pa·dō´ci·a, Asia, and Bi·thyn´i·a, [2]who have been chosen and destined by God the Father and sanctified by the Spirit to be obedient to Jesus Christ and to be sprinkled with his blood:
May grace and peace be yours in abundance.

A Living Hope

3 Blessed be the God and Father of our Lord Jesus Christ! By his great mercy he has given us a new birth into a living hope through the resurrection of Jesus Christ from the dead, [4]and into an inheritance that is imperishable, undefiled, and unfading, kept in heaven for you, [5]who are being protected by the power of God through faith for a salvation ready to be revealed in the last time. [6]In this you rejoice,[a] even if now for a little while you have had to suffer various trials, [7]so that the genuineness of your faith—being more precious than gold that, though perishable, is tested by fire—may be found to result in praise and glory and honor when Jesus Christ is revealed. [8]Although you have not seen[b] him, you love him; and even though you do not see him now, you believe in him and rejoice with an indescribable and glorious joy, [9]for you are receiving the outcome of your faith, the salvation of your souls.

10 Concerning this salvation, the prophets who prophesied of the grace that was to be yours made careful search and inquiry, [11]inquiring about the person or time that the Spirit of Christ within them indicated when it testified in advance to the sufferings destined for Christ and the

subsequent glory. [12]It was revealed to them that they were serving not themselves but you, in regard to the things that have now been announced to you through those who brought you good news by the Holy Spirit sent from heaven—things into which angels long to look!

A Call to Holy Living

13 Therefore prepare your minds for action;[c] discipline yourselves; set all your hope on the grace that Jesus Christ will bring you when he is revealed. [14]Like obedient children, do not be conformed to the desires that you formerly had in ignorance. [15]Instead, as he who called you is holy, be holy yourselves in all your conduct; [16]for it is written, "You shall be holy, for I am holy."

17 If you invoke as Father the one who judges all people impartially according to their deeds, live in reverent fear during the time of your exile. [18]You know that you were ransomed from the futile ways inherited from your ancestors, not with perishable things like silver or gold, [19]but with the precious blood of Christ, like that of a lamb without defect or blemish. [20]He was destined before the foundation of the world, but was revealed at the end of the ages for your sake. [21]Through him you have come to trust in God, who raised him from the dead and gave him glory, so that your faith and hope are set on God.

22 Now that you have purified your souls by your obedience to the truth[d] so that you have genuine mutual love, love one another deeply[e] from the heart.[f]

"He was destined before the foundation of the world, but was revealed at the end of the ages for your sake."
1 Peter 1:20

[a] Or *Rejoice in this*   [b] Other ancient authorities read *known*   [c] Gk *gird up the loins of your mind*
[d] Other ancient authorities add *through the Spirit*
[e] Or *constantly*   [f] Other ancient athorities read *a pure heart*

[23]You have been born anew, not of perishable but of imperishable seed, through the living and enduring word of God.[g] [24]For

"All flesh is like grass
and all its glory like the flower of
grass.
The grass withers,
and the flower falls,
[25] but the word of the Lord endures
forever."

That word is the good news that was announced to you.

The Living Stone and a Chosen People

2 Rid yourselves, therefore, of all malice, and all guile, insincerity, envy, and all slander. [2]Like newborn infants, long for the pure, spiritual milk, so that by it you may grow into salvation— [3]if indeed you have tasted that the Lord is good.

4 Come to him, a living stone, though rejected by mortals yet chosen and precious in God's sight, and [5]like living stones, let yourselves be built[h] into a spiritual house, to be a holy priesthood, to offer spiritual sacrifices acceptable to God through Jesus Christ. [6]For it stands in scripture:

Jesus is the cornerstone of the church and of our lives. A cornerstone is a strong foundation that cannot be moved. Like a cornerstone, Jesus is fixed in place, and he is eternal. With Christ as the cornerstone, we form the rest of the building! This letter encourages Christians to be "living stones"—stones placed upon the cornerstone to build a spiritual house. Read Psalm 118:22; 1 Corinthians 3:16–17; 2 Corinthians 6:16; and Ephesians 2:20–22 to see what other biblical writers said about the cornerstone and the spiritual house.

"See, I am laying in Zion a stone,
a cornerstone chosen and precious;
and whoever believes in him[i] will
not be put to shame."
[7]To you then who believe, he is precious; but for those who do not believe,
"The stone that the builders rejected
has become the very head of the
corner,"
[8]and
"A stone that makes them stumble,
and a rock that makes them fall."
They stumble because they disobey the word, as they were destined to do.

9 But you are a chosen race, a royal priesthood, a holy nation, God's own people,[j] in order that you may proclaim the mighty acts of him who called you out of darkness into his marvelous light. [10] Once you were not a people,
but now you are God's people;
once you had not received mercy,
but now you have received mercy.

Live as Servants of God

11 Beloved, I urge you as aliens and exiles to abstain from the desires of the flesh that wage war against the soul. [12]Conduct yourselves honorably among the Gentiles, so that, though they malign you as evildoers, they may see your honorable deeds and glorify God when he comes to judge.[k]

13 For the Lord's sake accept the authority of every human institution,[l] whether of the emperor as supreme, [14]or of governors, as sent by him to punish those who do wrong and to praise those who do right. [15]For it is God's will that by doing right you should silence the ignorance of the foolish. [16]As servants[m] of God, live as free people, yet do not use your freedom as a pretext for evil. [17]Honor

[g] Or through the word of the living and enduring God
[h] Or you yourselves are being built   [i] Or it
[j] Gk a people for his possession   [k] Gk God on the day of visitation   [l] Or every institution ordained for human beings   [m] Gk slaves

everyone. Love the family of believers.[n] Fear God. Honor the emperor.

The Example of Christ's Suffering

18 Slaves, accept the authority of your masters with all deference, not only those who are kind and gentle but also those who are harsh. [19]For it is a credit to you if, being aware of God, you endure pain while suffering unjustly. [20]If you endure when you are beaten for doing wrong, what credit is that? But if you endure when you do right and suffer for it, you have God's approval. [21]For to this you have been called, because Christ also suffered for you, leaving you an example, so that you should follow in his steps.
[22] "He committed no sin,
     and no deceit was found in his
          mouth."
[23]When he was abused, he did not return abuse; when he suffered, he did not threaten; but he entrusted himself to the one who judges justly. [24]He himself bore our sins in his body on the cross,[o] so that, free from sins, we might live for righteousness; by his wounds[p] you have been healed. [25]For you were going astray like sheep, but now you have returned to the shepherd and guardian of your souls.

Wives and Husbands

3 Wives, in the same way, accept the authority of your husbands, so that, even if some of them do not obey the word, they may be won over without a word by their wives' conduct, [2]when they see the purity and reverence of your lives. [3]Do not adorn yourselves outwardly by braiding your hair, and by wearing gold ornaments or fine clothing; [4]rather, let your adornment be the inner self with the lasting beauty of a gentle and quiet spirit, which is very precious in God's sight. [5]It was in this way long ago that the holy women who hoped in God used to adorn themselves by accepting the authority of their hus-

> "He himself bore out sins in his body on the cross, so that, free from sins, we might live for righteousness; by his wounds you have been healed."   1 Peter 2:24

bands. [6]Thus Sarah obeyed Abraham and called him lord. You have become her daughters as long as you do what is good and never let fears alarm you.

7 Husbands, in the same way, show consideration for your wives in your life together, paying honor to the woman as the weaker sex,[q] since they too are also heirs of the gracious gift of life—so that nothing may hinder your prayers.

Suffering for Doing Right

8 Finally, all of you, have unity of spirit, sympathy, love for one another, a tender heart, and a humble mind. [9]Do not repay evil for evil or abuse for abuse; but, on the contrary, repay with a blessing. It is for this that you were called— that you might inherit a blessing. [10]For
"Those who desire life
     and desire to see good days,
     let them keep their tongues from evil
          and their lips from speaking
               deceit;
[11] let them turn away from evil and do
          good;
     let them seek peace and pursue it.
[12] For the eyes of the Lord are on the
          righteous,
     and his ears are open to their
          prayer.
But the face of the Lord is against
     those who do evil."
13 Now who will harm you if you are eager to do what is good? [14]But even if you do suffer for doing what is right, you are blessed. Do not fear what they fear,[r] and do not be intimidated, [15]but in your hearts sanctify Christ as Lord. Always be ready to make your defense to anyone

[n] Gk Love the brotherhood   [o] Or carried up our sins in his body to the tree   [p] Gk bruise   [q] Gk vessel   [r] Gk their fear

> Christians are called to love one another. When someone does wrong against us, we should not do wrong against them. We should run from the things that are bad and try our very best to do good. In our homes, communities, and churches, we should always treat one another with kindness and respect. Pray that God will help you to live this way.

who demands from you an accounting for the hope that is in you; [16]yet do it with gentleness and reverence.[s] Keep your conscience clear, so that, when you are maligned, those who abuse you for your good conduct in Christ may be put to shame. [17]For it is better to suffer for doing good, if suffering should be God's will, than to suffer for doing evil. [18]For Christ also suffered[t] for sins once for all, the righteous for the unrighteous, in order to bring you[u] to God. He was put to death in the flesh, but made alive in the spirit, [19]in which also he went and made a proclamation to the spirits in prison, [20]who in former times did not obey, when God waited patiently in the days of Noah, during the building of the ark, in which a few, that is, eight persons, were saved through water. [21]And baptism, which this prefigured, now saves you—not as a removal of dirt from the body, but as an appeal to God for[v] a good conscience, through the resurrection of Jesus Christ, [22]who has gone into heaven and is at the right hand of God, with angels, authorities, and powers made subject to him.

Good Stewards of God's Grace

4 Since therefore Christ suffered in the flesh,[w] arm yourselves also with the same intention (for whoever has suffered in the flesh has finished with sin), [2]so as to live for the rest of your earthly life[x] no longer by human desires but by the will of God. [3]You have already spent enough

time in doing what the Gentiles like to do, living in licentiousness, passions, drunkenness, revels, carousing, and lawless idolatry. [4]They are surprised that you no longer join them in the same excesses of dissipation, and so they blaspheme.[y] [5]But they will have to give an accounting to him who stands ready to judge the living and the dead. [6]For this is the reason the gospel was proclaimed even to the dead, so that, though they had been judged in the flesh as everyone is judged, they might live in the spirit as God does.

7 The end of all things is near;[z] therefore be serious and discipline yourselves for the sake of your prayers. [8]Above all, maintain constant love for one another, for love covers a multitude of sins. [9]Be hospitable to one another without complaining. [10]Like good stewards of the manifold grace of God, serve one another with whatever gift each of you has received. [11]Whoever speaks must do so as one speaking the very words of God; whoever serves must do so with the strength that God supplies, so that God may be glorified in all things through Jesus Christ. To him belong the glory and the power forever and ever. Amen.

Suffering as a Christian

12 Beloved, do not be surprised at the fiery ordeal that is taking place among you to test you, as though something strange were happening to you. [13]But rejoice insofar as you are sharing Christ's sufferings, so that you may also be glad and shout for joy when his glory is revealed. [14]If you are reviled for the name of Christ, you are blessed, because the spirit of glory,[a] which is the Spirit of God, is resting on you.[b] [15]But let none of

---

[s] Or respect   [t] Other ancient authorities read died   [u] Other ancient authorities read us   [v] Or a pledge to God from   [w] Other ancient authorities add for us; others, for you   [x] Gk rest of the time in the flesh   [y] Or they malign you   [z] Or is at hand   [a] Other ancient authorities add and of power   [b] Other ancient authorities add On their part he is blasphemed, but on your part he is glorified

you suffer as a murderer, a thief, a criminal, or even as a mischief maker. [16]Yet if any of you suffers as a Christian, do not consider it a disgrace, but glorify God because you bear this name. [17]For the time has come for judgment to begin with the household of God; if it begins with us, what will be the end for those who do not obey the gospel of God? [18]And

> "If it is hard for the righteous to be
>   saved,
>   what will become of the ungodly
>   and the sinners?"

[19]Therefore, let those suffering in accordance with God's will entrust themselves to a faithful Creator, while continuing to do good.

The author of this letter told the Christian leaders to "tend the flock of God," which means to take care of the people of God. Jesus told his disciples that they could care for others like a shepherd cares for sheep. The shepherd leads the sheep to safety, good pasture, water, and food.

Being Christians doesn't mean that our lives will be easy. In fact, 1 Peter tells us that hard times and troubles will come our way because we follow Christ. But we know that God will always be with us. We have the promise of God's faithfulness to us, and so we must continue to follow God's ways at all times.

Tending the Flock of God

5 Now as an elder myself and a witness of the sufferings of Christ, as well as one who shares in the glory to be revealed, I exhort the elders among you [2]to tend the flock of God that is in your charge, exercising the oversight,[c] not under compulsion but willingly, as God would have you do it[d]—not for sordid gain but eagerly. [3]Do not lord it over those in your charge, but be examples to the flock. [4]And when the chief shepherd appears, you will win the crown of glory that never fades away. [5]In the same way, you who are younger must accept the authority of the elders.[e] And all of you must clothe yourselves with humility in your dealings with one another, for

> "God opposes the proud,
>   but gives grace to the humble."

6 Humble yourselves therefore under the mighty hand of God, so that he may exalt you in due time. [7]Cast all your anxiety on him, because he cares for you. [8]Discipline yourselves, keep alert.[f] Like a roaring lion your adversary the devil prowls around, looking for someone to devour. [9]Resist him, steadfast in your faith, for you know that your brothers and sisters[g] in all the world are undergoing the same kinds of suffering. [10]And after you have suffered for a little while, the God of all grace, who has called you to his eternal glory in Christ, will himself restore, support, strengthen, and establish you. [11]To him be the power forever and ever. Amen.

Final Greetings and Benediction

12 Through Sil·vā´nus, whom I consider a faithful brother, I have written this short letter to encourage you and to testify that this is the true grace of God. Stand fast in it. [13]Your sister church[h] in Babylon, chosen together with you, sends you greetings; and so does my son Mark. [14]Greet one another with a kiss of love.

Peace to all of you who are in Christ.[i]

"Cast all your anxiety on him, because he cares for you."   1 Peter 5:7

[c] Other ancient authorities lack *exercising the oversight*   [d] Other ancient authorities lack *as God would have you do it*   [e] Or *of those who are older*   [f] Or *be vigilant*   [g] Gk *your brotherhood*   [h] Gk *She who is*   [i] Other ancient authorities add *Amen*

2 Peter

Second Peter is a letter written to strengthen Christians who were in great danger from their enemies and in great danger of misunderstanding Christianity. The letter claims to be written by the apostle Peter, who was killed about 64 AD. But because this letter deals with situations Christians did not face until 125–150 AD, many people believe it was written many years after Peter's death. If this is the case, we do not know who wrote the letter.

The writer wanted to give the kind of advice Peter would have given if he had been living at that time. Christians were being persecuted and killed for their faith. They were worried because Christ had not returned to the earth to overcome all their troubles. The writer assured the people that Jesus would return, but that no one knows when that day will be. The letter encouraged the people to hold tight to the teaching of the prophets and the apostles and to reject the lies of false teachers. It urged Christians to trust in the promises of God and to live good lives no matter what happens. It closes by saying, "Grow in the grace and knowledge of our Lord and Savior Jesus Christ. To him be the glory both now and to the day of eternity" (3:18).

2 Peter 1:1

Salutation

1 Si′mē·on[a] Peter, a servant[b] and apostle of Jesus Christ,

To those who have received a faith as precious as ours through the righteousness of our God and Savior Jesus Christ:[c]

2 May grace and peace be yours in abundance in the knowledge of God and of Jesus our Lord.

The Christian's Call and Election

3 His divine power has given us everything needed for life and godliness, through the knowledge of him who called us by[d] his own glory and goodness. [4]Thus he has given us, through these things, his precious and very great promises, so that through them you may escape from the corruption that is in the world because of lust, and may become participants of the divine nature. [5]For this very reason, you must make every effort to support your faith with goodness, and goodness with knowledge, [6]and knowledge with self-control, and self-control with endurance, and endurance with godliness, [7]and godliness with mutual[e] affection, and mutual[e] affection with love. [8]For if these things are yours and are increasing among you, they keep you from being ineffective and unfruitful in the knowledge of our Lord Jesus Christ. [9]For anyone who lacks these things is nearsighted and blind, and is forgetful of the cleansing of past sins. [10]Therefore, brothers and sisters,[f] be all the more eager to confirm your call and election, for if you do this, you will never stumble. [11]For in this way, entry into the eternal kingdom of our Lord and Savior Jesus Christ will be richly provided for you.

12 Therefore I intend to keep on reminding you of these things, though you know them already and are established in the truth that has come to you. [13]I think it right, as long as I am in this body,[g] to refresh your memory,

> "For this very reason, you must make every effort to support your faith with goodness, and goodness with knowledge, and knowledge with self-control, and self-control with endurance, and endurance with godliness, and godliness with mutual affection, and mutual affection with love."   2 Peter 1:5

[14]since I know that my death[h] will come soon, as indeed our Lord Jesus Christ has made clear to me. [15]And I will make every effort so that after my departure you may be able at any time to recall these things.

Eyewitnesses of Christ's Glory

16 For we did not follow cleverly devised myths when we made known to you the power and coming of our Lord Jesus Christ, but we had been eyewitnesses of his majesty. [17]For he received honor and glory from God the Father when that voice was conveyed to him by the Majestic Glory, saying, "This is my Son, my Beloved,[i] with whom I am well pleased." [18]We ourselves heard this voice come from heaven, while we were with him on the holy mountain.

19 So we have the prophetic message more fully confirmed. You will do well to be attentive to this as to a lamp shining in a dark place, until the day dawns and the morning star rises in your hearts. [20]First of all you must understand this, that no prophecy of scripture is a matter of one's own interpretation, [21]because no prophecy ever came by human will, but men and women moved by the Holy Spirit spoke from God.[j]

[a] Other ancient authorities read *Simon*   [b] Gk *slave*   [c] Or *of our God and the Savior Jesus Christ*   [d] Other ancient authorities read *through*   [e] Gk *brotherly*   [f] Gk *brothers*   [g] Gk *tent*   [h] Gk *the putting off of my tent*   [i] Other ancient authorities read *my beloved Son*   [j] Other ancient authorities read *but moved by the Holy Spirit saints of God spoke*

False Prophets and Their Punishment

2 But false prophets also arose among the people, just as there will be false teachers among you, who will secretly bring in destructive opinions. They will even deny the Master who bought them—bringing swift destruction on themselves. [2]Even so, many will follow their licentious ways, and because of these teachers[k] the way of truth will be maligned. [3]And in their greed they will exploit you with deceptive words. Their condemnation, pronounced against them long ago, has not been idle, and their destruction is not asleep.

4 For if God did not spare the angels when they sinned, but cast them into hell[l] and committed them to chains[m] of deepest darkness to be kept until the judgment; [5]and if he did not spare the ancient world, even though he saved Noah, a herald of righteousness, with seven others, when he brought a flood on a world of the ungodly; [6]and if by turning the cities of Sod'om and Go·mor'rah to ashes he condemned them to extinction[n] and made them an example of what is coming to the ungodly;[o] [7]and if he rescued Lot, a righteous man greatly distressed by the licentiousness of the lawless [8](for that righteous man, living among them day after day, was tormented in his righteous soul by their lawless deeds that he saw and heard), [9]then the Lord knows how to rescue the godly from trial, and to keep the unrighteous under punishment until the day of judgment [10]—especially those who indulge their flesh in depraved lust, and who despise authority.

Bold and willful, they are not afraid to slander the glorious ones,[p] [11]whereas angels, though greater in might and power, do not bring against them a slanderous judgment from the Lord.[q] [12]These people, however, are like irrational animals, mere creatures of instinct, born to be caught and killed. They slander what they do not understand, and when those creatures are destroyed,[r] they also will be destroyed, [13]suffering[s] the penalty for doing wrong. They count it a pleasure to revel in the daytime. They are blots and blemishes, reveling in their dissipation[t] while they feast with you. [14]They have eyes full of adultery, insatiable for sin. They entice unsteady souls. They have hearts trained in greed. Accursed children! [15]They have left the straight road and have gone astray, following the road of Ba'laam son of Bo'sor,[u] who loved the wages of doing wrong, [16]but was rebuked for his own transgression; a speechless donkey spoke with a human voice and restrained the prophet's madness.

17 These are waterless springs and mists driven by a storm; for them the deepest darkness has been reserved. [18]For they speak bombastic nonsense, and with licentious desires of the flesh they entice people who have just[v] escaped from those who live in error. [19]They promise them freedom, but they themselves are slaves of corruption; for people are slaves to whatever masters them. [20]For if, after they have escaped the defilements of the world through the knowledge of our Lord and Savior Jesus Christ, they are again entangled in them and overpowered, the last state has become worse for them than the first. [21]For it would have been better for them never to have known the way of righteousness than, after knowing it, to turn back from the holy commandment that was passed on to them. [22]It has happened to them according to the true proverb,

k Gk because of them   l Gk Tartaros   m Other ancient authorities read pits   n Other ancient authorities lack to extinction   o Other ancient authorities read an example to those who were to be ungodly   p Or angels; Gk glories   q Other ancient authorities read before the Lord; others lack the phrase   r Gk in their destruction   s Other ancient authorities read receiving   t Other ancient authorities read love feasts   u Other ancient authorities read Beor   v Other ancient authorities read actually

"The dog turns back to its own
vomit,"
and,
"The sow is washed only to wallow
in the mud."

The Promise of
the Lord's Coming

3 This is now, beloved, the second letter I am writing to you; in them I am trying to arouse your sincere intention by reminding you ²that you should remember the words spoken in the past by the holy prophets, and the commandment of the Lord and Savior spoken through your apostles. ³First of all you must understand this, that in the last days scoffers will come, scoffing and indulging their own lusts ⁴and saying, "Where is the promise of his coming? For ever since our ancestors died,ʷ all things continue as they were from the beginning of creation!" ⁵They deliberately ignore this fact, that by the word of God heavens existed long ago and an earth was formed out of water and by means of water, ⁶through which the world of that time was deluged with water and perished. ⁷But by the same word the present heavens and earth have been reserved for fire, being kept until the day of judgment and destruction of the godless.

8 But do not ignore this one fact, beloved, that with the Lord one day is like a thousand years, and a thousand years are like one day. ⁹The Lord is not slow about his promise, as some think of slowness, but is patient with you,ˣ not wanting any to perish, but all to come to repentance. ¹⁰But the day of the Lord will come like a thief, and then the heavens will pass away with a loud noise, and the elements will be dissolved with fire, and the earth and everything that is done on it will be disclosed.ʸ

11 Since all these things are to be dissolved in this way, what sort of persons ought you to be in leading lives of holiness and godliness, ¹²waiting for and hasteningᶻ the coming of the day of God, because of

"But do not ignore this one fact, beloved, that with the Lord one day is like a thousand years, and a thousand years are like one day." 2 Peter 3:8

which the heavens will be set ablaze and dissolved, and the elements will melt with fire? ¹³But, in accordance with his promise, we wait for new heavens and a new earth, where righteousness is at home.

Final Exhortation and Doxology

14 Therefore, beloved, while you are waiting for these things, strive to be found by him at peace, without spot or blemish; ¹⁵and regard the patience of our Lord as salvation. So also our beloved brother Paul wrote to you according to the wisdom given him, ¹⁶speaking of this as he does in all his letters. There are some things in them hard to understand, which the ignorant and unstable twist to their own destruction, as they do the other scriptures. ¹⁷You therefore, beloved, since you are forewarned, beware that you are not carried away with the error of the lawless and lose your own stability. ¹⁸But grow in the grace and knowledge of our Lord and Savior Jesus Christ. To him be the glory both now and to the day of eternity. Amen.ᵃ

God has promised us that Jesus will return a second time, and we can be sure that God will keep that promise. See Matthew 24:43–44 and 1 Thessalonians 5:1.

ʷ Gk *our fathers fell asleep*   ˣ Other ancient authorities read *on your account*   ʸ Other ancient authorities read *will be burned up*   ᶻ Or *earnestly desiring*   ᵃ Other ancient authorities lack *Amen*

1 John

Although we can't be sure who wrote First, Second, and Third John, many believe that the same person who wrote the Gospel of John wrote these three letters. Others believe that the writer of the letters lived in the same community as the writer of the Gospel, but at a later time. The author was clearly influenced by the same materials as the Gospel writer. Both the Gospel of John and the three letters of John have similar themes—Christians are beloved children of God who are called to love others and point them to God.

First John was written in the same way a parent would write to a child (2:1). The writer taught that God is light, God is love, and God is the giver of eternal life through the saving work of Jesus Christ. He wrote, "In this the love of God was made manifest among us, that God sent his only Son into the world, so that we might live through him" (4:9).

First John also teaches Christians how they are to live. Christians are children of God, called to walk in the light and follow God's ways. The writer told the readers to believe in Jesus, to do what is right, and to love one another. He taught that Christians must overcome evil and hate and must live pure, good lives. That is why he wrote, "Beloved, let us love one another; for love is from God; everyone who loves is born of God and knows God. Whoever does not love does not know God, for God is love" (4:7–8). The letter assures Christians that they can endure (or overcome) all their troubles and inherit eternal life by having faith in Christ.

1 John 3:1

The Word of Life

1 We declare to you what was from the beginning, what we have heard, what we have seen with our eyes, what we have looked at and touched with our hands, concerning the word of life— ²this life was revealed, and we have seen it and testify to it, and declare to you the eternal life that was with the Father and was revealed to us— ³we declare to you what we have seen and heard so that you also may have fellowship with us; and truly our fellowship is with the Father and with his Son Jesus Christ. ⁴We are writing these things so that our*ᵃ* joy may be complete.

John told the believers to think of God's Word as a light to help guide them in right living. Read Psalm 27:1 and Psalm 119:105 to see how some Old Testament writers spoke of God and God's Word.

God Is Light

5 This is the message we have heard from him and proclaim to you, that God is light and in him there is no darkness at all. ⁶If we say that we have fellowship with him while we are walking in darkness, we lie and do not do what is true; ⁷but if we walk in the light as he himself is in the light, we have fellowship with one another, and the blood of Jesus his Son cleanses us from all sin. ⁸If we say that we have no sin, we deceive ourselves, and the truth is not in us. ⁹If we confess our sins, he who is faithful and just will forgive us our sins and cleanse us from all unrighteousness. ¹⁰If we say that we have not sinned, we make him a liar, and his word is not in us.

Christ Our Advocate

2 My little children, I am writing these things to you so that you may not sin. But if anyone does sin, we have

"Whoever says, 'I abide in him,' ought to walk just as he walked." 1 John 2:6

an advocate with the Father, Jesus Christ the righteous; ²and he is the atoning sacrifice for our sins, and not for ours only but also for the sins of the whole world.

3 Now by this we may be sure that we know him, if we obey his commandments. ⁴Whoever says, "I have come to know him," but does not obey his commandments, is a liar, and in such a person the truth does not exist; ⁵but whoever obeys his word, truly in this person the love of God has reached perfection. By this we may be sure that we are in him: ⁶whoever says, "I abide in him," ought to walk just as he walked.

A New Commandment

7 Beloved, I am writing you no new commandment, but an old commandment that you have had from the beginning; the old commandment is the word that you have heard. ⁸Yet I am writing you a new commandment that is true in him and in you, because*ᵇ* the darkness is passing away and the true light is already shining. ⁹Whoever says, "I am in the light," while hating a brother or sister,*ᶜ* is still in the darkness. ¹⁰Whoever loves a brother or sister*ᵈ* lives in the light, and in such a person*ᵉ* there is no cause for stumbling. ¹¹But whoever hates another believer*ᶠ* is in the darkness, walks in the darkness, and does not know the way to go, because the darkness has brought on blindness.

12 I am writing to you, little children,
    because your sins are forgiven on
        account of his name.
13 I am writing to you, fathers,
    because you know him who is
        from the beginning.

ᵃ Other ancient authorities read *your*   *ᵇ* Or *that*
ᶜ Gk *hating a brother*   *ᵈ* Gk *loves a brother*
ᵉ Or *in it*   *ᶠ* Gk *hates a brother*

I am writing to you, young people,
  because you have conquered the
  evil one.
[14] I write to you, children,
  because you know the Father.
I write to you, fathers,
  because you know him who is
  from the beginning.
I write to you, young people,
  because you are strong
  and the word of God abides in
    you,
  and you have overcome the evil
    one.
15 Do not love the world or the things in the world. The love of the Father is not in those who love the world; [16]for all that is in the world—the desire of the flesh, the desire of the eyes, the pride in riches—comes not from the Father but from the world. [17]And the world and its desire[g] are passing away, but those who do the will of God live forever.

Warning against Antichrists

18 Children, it is the last hour! As you have heard that antichrist is coming, so now many antichrists have come. From this we know that it is the last hour. [19]They went out from us, but they did not belong to us; for if they had belonged to us, they would have remained with us. But by going out they made it plain that none of them belongs to us. [20]But you have been anointed by the Holy One, and all of you have knowledge.[h] [21]I write to you, not because you do not know the truth, but because you know it, and you know that no lie comes from the truth. [22]Who is the liar but the one who denies that Jesus is the Christ?[i] This is the antichrist, the one who denies the Father and the Son. [23]No one who denies the Son has the Father; everyone who confesses the Son has the Father also. [24]Let what you heard from the beginning abide in you. If what you heard from the beginning

abides in you, then you will abide in the Son and in the Father. [25]And this is what he has promised us,[j] eternal life.

26 I write these things to you concerning those who would deceive you. [27]As for you, the anointing that you received from him abides in you, and so you do not need anyone to teach you. But as his anointing teaches you about all things, and is true and is not a lie, and just as it has taught you, abide in him.[k]

28 And now, little children, abide in him, so that when he is revealed we may have confidence and not be put to shame before him at his coming.

Children of God

29 If you know that he is righteous, you may be sure that everyone who does right has been born of him. [1]See what love the Father has given us, that we should be called children of God; and that is what we are. The reason the world does not know us is that it did not know him. [2]Beloved, we are God's children now; what we will be has not yet been revealed. What we do know is this: when he[k] is revealed, we will be like him, for we will see him as he is. [3]And all who have this hope in him purify themselves, just as he is pure.

4 Everyone who commits sin is guilty of lawlessness; sin is lawlessness. [5]You know that he was revealed to take away sins, and in him there is no sin. [6]No one who abides in him sins; no one who sins has either seen him or known him. [7]Little children, let no one deceive you. Everyone who does what is right is righteous, just as he is righteous. [8]Everyone who commits sin is a child of the devil; for the devil has been sinning from the beginning. The Son of God was revealed for this purpose, to destroy the works of the devil. [9]Those who have

---

[g] Or *the desire for it*   [h] Other ancient authorities read *you know all things*   [i] Or *the Messiah*   [j] Other ancient authorities read *you*   [k] Or *it*

When asked about the greatest commandment, Jesus talked about love (see Matthew 22:34–40). John also talks about love. He makes clear that love is not just a warm, fuzzy feeling. Love is helping others and treating them with kindness. If you are able to help someone in need but choose not to do so, then you don't have the kind of love John is talking about. John tells us not to say that we love but to show that we love with our actions.

been born of God do not sin, because God's seed abides in them;[l] they cannot sin, because they have been born of God. [10]The children of God and the children of the devil are revealed in this way: all who do not do what is right are not from God, nor are those who do not love their brothers and sisters.[m]

Love One Another

[11] For this is the message you have heard from the beginning, that we should love one another. [12]We must not be like Cain who was from the evil one and murdered his brother. And why did he murder him? Because his own deeds were evil and his brother's righteous. [13]Do not be astonished, brothers and sisters,[n] that the world hates you. [14]We know that we have passed from death to life because we love one another. Whoever does not love abides in death. [15]All who hate a brother or sister[m] are murderers, and you know that murderers do not have eternal life abiding in them. [16]We know love by this, that he laid down his life for us—and we ought to lay down our lives for one another. [17]How does God's love abide in anyone who has the world's goods and sees a brother or sister[o] in need and yet refuses help?

[18] Little children, let us love, not in word or speech, but in truth and action.

[19]And by this we will know that we are from the truth and will reassure our hearts before him [20]whenever our hearts condemn us; for God is greater than our hearts, and he knows everything. [21]Beloved, if our hearts do not condemn us, we have boldness before God; [22]and we receive from him whatever we ask, because we obey his commandments and do what pleases him.

[23] And this is his commandment, that we should believe in the name of his Son Jesus Christ and love one another, just as he has commanded us. [24]All who obey his commandments abide in him, and he abides in them. And by this we know that he abides in us, by the Spirit that he has given us.

Testing the Spirits

4 Beloved, do not believe every spirit, but test the spirits to see whether

God expects us to treat others with love. Do you show love with your actions? Here is one simple way to show God's love to others. In a small gift box or bag, put together some or all of these things with an explanation for each one: cotton ball—to cushion the rough roads; rubber band—for flexibility; sweet and tart candy—a reminder to appreciate the differences in others; happy face stickers—smiling is contagious; candle—a reminder to share your light with others; eraser—a reminder that we can start each day over with no mistakes; button—a reminder to keep quiet when you have nothing kind or good to say; gum—a reminder that friends stick together. Who will you give these gifts to? Can you think of other items you might add?

[l] Or because the children of God abide in him
[m] Gk his brother   [n] Gk brothers   [o] Gk brother

they are from God; for many false prophets have gone out into the world. ²By this you know the Spirit of God: every spirit that confesses that Jesus Christ has come in the flesh is from God, ³and every spirit that does not confess Jesus*ᵖ* is not from God. And this is the spirit of the antichrist, of which you have heard that it is coming; and now it is already in the world. ⁴Little children, you are from God, and have conquered them; for the one who is in you is greater than the one who is in the world. ⁵They are from the world; therefore what they say is from the world, and the world listens to them. ⁶We are from God. Whoever knows God listens to us, and whoever is not from God does not listen to us. From this we know the spirit of truth and the spirit of error.

God Is Love

7 Beloved, let us love one another, because love is from God; everyone who loves is born of God and knows God. ⁸Whoever does not love does not know God, for God is love. ⁹God's love was revealed among us in this way: God sent his only Son into the world so that we might live through him. ¹⁰In this is love, not that we loved God but that he loved us and sent his Son to be the atoning sacrifice for our sins. ¹¹Beloved, since God loved us so much, we also ought to love one another. ¹²No one has ever seen God; if we love one another, God lives in us, and his love is perfected in us.

13 By this we know that we abide in him and he in us, because he has given us of his Spirit. ¹⁴And we have seen and do testify that the Father has sent his Son as the Savior of the world. ¹⁵God abides in those who confess that Jesus is the Son of God, and they abide in God. ¹⁶So we have known and believe the love that God has for us.

God is love, and those who abide in love abide in God, and God abides in them. ¹⁷Love has been perfected among us in this: that we may have boldness on the day of judgment, because as he is, so are we in this world. ¹⁸There is no fear in love, but perfect love casts out fear; for fear has to do with punishment, and whoever fears has not reached perfection in love. ¹⁹We love*�q* because he first loved us. ²⁰Those who say, "I love God," and hate their brothers or sisters,*ʳ* are liars; for those who do not love a brother or sister*ˢ* whom they have seen, cannot love God whom they have not seen. ²¹The commandment we have from him is this: those who love God must love their brothers and sisters*ʳ* also.

Faith Conquers the World

5 Everyone who believes that Jesus is the Christ*ᵗ* has been born of God, and everyone who loves the parent loves the child. ²By this we know that we love the children of God, when we love God and obey his commandments. ³For the love of God is this, that we obey his commandments. And his commandments are not burdensome, ⁴for whatever is born of God conquers the world. And this is the victory that conquers the world, our faith. ⁵Who is it that conquers the world but the one who believes that Jesus is the Son of God?

Testimony concerning the Son of God

6 This is the one who came by water and blood, Jesus Christ, not with the water only but with the water and the blood. And the Spirit is the one that testifies, for the Spirit is the truth. ⁷There are three that testify:*ᵘ* ⁸the Spirit and the

---

ᵖ Other ancient authorities read *does away with Jesus* (Gk *dissolves Jesus*)   *q* Other ancient authorities add *him*; others add *God*   *ʳ* Gk *brothers*   *ˢ* Gk *brother*   *ᵗ* Or *the Messiah*   *ᵘ* A few other authorities read (with variations) *⁷There are three that testify in heaven, the Father, the Word, and the Holy Spirit, and these three are one. ⁸And there are three that testify on earth:*

"Beloved, since God loved us so much, we also ought to love one another."   1 John 4:11

Jesus is God's own Son. He came from heaven and became a human being just like us. When we have faith in him, we inherit eternal life through him.

water and the blood, and these three agree. [9]If we receive human testimony, the testimony of God is greater; for this is the testimony of God that he has testified to his Son. [10]Those who believe in the Son of God have the testimony in their hearts. Those who do not believe in God[v] have made him a liar by not believing in the testimony that God has given concerning his Son. [11]And this is the testimony: God gave us eternal life, and this life is in his Son. [12]Whoever has the Son has life; whoever does not have the Son of God does not have life.

Epilogue

13 I write these things to you who believe in the name of the Son of God, so that you may know that you have eternal life.

14 And this is the boldness we have in him, that if we ask anything according to his will, he hears us. [15]And if we know that he hears us in whatever we ask, we know that we have obtained the requests made of him. [16]If you see your brother or sister[w] committing what is not a mortal sin, you will ask, and God[x] will give life to such a one—to those whose sin is not mortal. There is sin that is mortal; I do not say that you should pray about that. [17]All wrongdoing is sin, but there is sin that is not mortal.

18 We know that those who are born of God do not sin, but the one who was born of God protects them, and the evil one does not touch them. [19]We know that we are God's children, and that the whole world lies under the power of the evil one. [20]And we know that the Son of God has come and has given us understanding so that we may know him who is true;[y] and we are in him who is true, in his Son Jesus Christ. He is the true God and eternal life.

21 Little children, keep yourselves from idols.[z]

[v] Other ancient authorities read *in the Son*
[w] Gk *your brother*   [x] Gk *he*   [y] Other ancient authorities read *know the true God*   [z] Other ancient authorities add *Amen*

2 John

Although we can't be sure who wrote First, Second, and Third John, many believe that the same person who wrote the Gospel of John wrote these three letters. Others believe that the writer of the letters lived in the same community as the writer of the Gospel, but at a later time. The author was clearly influenced by the same materials as the Gospel writer. Both the Gospel of John and the three letters of John have similar themes—Christians are beloved children of God who are called to love others and point them to God.

The first verse of Second John tells us that "the elder" wrote the letter to "the elect lady and her children." The writer may have been referring to an actual woman who the church very much respected, but more likely he is referring to the church and its members as if the church were a woman and the members her children. Most of this letter is made up of word-for-word quotations from First John. It warns against false teachers who do not really believe that Jesus is the Christ. It stresses love as the true mark of a Christian. The letter encourages the believers not to be discouraged but to hold to the teaching of Christ and follow the commands of God. It ends with a friendly word from the members of the writer's church: "The children of your elect sister greet you" (verse 13).

2 John 6

Salutation

1 The elder to the elect lady and her children, whom I love in the truth, and not only I but also all who know the truth, ²because of the truth that abides in us and will be with us forever:

3 Grace, mercy, and peace will be with us from God the Father and from*ᵃ* Jesus Christ, the Father's Son, in truth and love.

Truth and Love

4 I was overjoyed to find some of your children walking in the truth, just as we have been commanded by the Father. ⁵But now, dear lady, I ask you, not as though I were writing you a new commandment, but one we have had from the beginning, let us love one another. ⁶And this is love, that we walk according to his commandments; this is the commandment just as you have heard it from the beginning—you must walk in it.

7 Many deceivers have gone out into the world, those who do not confess that Jesus Christ has come in the flesh; any such person is the deceiver and the antichrist! ⁸Be on your guard, so that you do not lose what we*ᵇ* have worked

> "Let us love one another. And this is love, that we walk according to his commandments; this is the commandment just as you have heard it from the beginning— you must walk in it." 2 John 5b–6

for, but may receive a full reward. ⁹Everyone who does not abide in the teaching of Christ, but goes beyond it, does not have God; whoever abides in the teaching has both the Father and the Son. ¹⁰Do not receive into the house or welcome anyone who comes to you and does not bring this teaching; ¹¹for to welcome is to participate in the evil deeds of such a person.

Final Greetings

12 Although I have much to write to you, I would rather not use paper and ink; instead I hope to come to you and talk with you face to face, so that our joy may be complete.

13 The children of your elect sister send you their greetings.*ᶜ*

ᵃ Other ancient authorities add *the Lord*
ᵇ Other ancient authorities read *you*   *ᶜ* Other ancient authorities add *Amen*

3 John

Although we can't be sure who wrote First, Second, and Third John, many believe that the same person who wrote the Gospel of John wrote these three letters. Others believe that the writer of the letters lived in the same community as the writer of the Gospel, but at a later time. The author was clearly influenced by the same materials as the Gospel writer. Both the Gospel of John and the three letters of John have similar themes—Christians are beloved children of God who are called to love others and point them to God.

The first verse of Third John tells us that "the elder" wrote the letter to "the beloved Gaius." This is a letter of introduction for a group of missionaries who probably brought the letter with them to a Christian man named Gaius. The writer wanted Gaius and his friends to help these missionaries, even though a man named Diotrephes opposed them. Diotrephes was a false teacher who chose not to show hospitality to those who were teaching and preaching about Jesus.

Third John shows the troubles that can sometimes come between members of Christian congregations. The writer spoke out against Diotrephes, the person who was causing problems in the church that received this letter. He said that his greatest joy is hearing that believers follow the ways of God. He wrote, "I have no greater joy than this, to hear that my children are walking in the truth" (verse 4). The letter tells the Christians not to imitate evil, but to do what is good.

3 John 4

Salutation

1 The elder to the beloved Gā´i·us, whom I love in truth.

Gaius Commended for His Hospitality

2 Beloved, I pray that all may go well with you and that you may be in good health, just as it is well with your soul. [3]I was overjoyed when some of the friends[a] arrived and testified to your faithfulness to the truth, namely how you walk in the truth. [4]I have no greater joy than this, to hear that my children are walking in the truth.

5 Beloved, you do faithfully whatever you do for the friends,[a] even though they are strangers to you; [6]they have testified to your love before the church. You will do well to send them on in a manner worthy of God; [7]for they began their journey for the sake of Christ,[b] accepting no support from non-believers.[c] [8]Therefore we ought to support such people, so that we may become co-workers with the truth.

Gaius was a leader in the church who worked hard to show God's love to everyone—friends and strangers alike. Talk to your family or your Sunday school class about putting together a care package for a college student who is away from home or for someone at a homeless shelter. What would you need to include in the kit? How is this showing God's love as Gaius did?

"Beloved, do not imitate what is evil but imitate what is good."
3 John 11*a*

Diotrephes and Demetrius

9 I have written something to the church; but Dī·ot´re·phēs, who likes to put himself first, does not acknowledge our authority. [10]So if I come, I will call attention to what he is doing in spreading false charges against us. And not content with those charges, he refuses to welcome the friends,[a] and even prevents those who want to do so and expels them from the church.

11 Beloved, do not imitate what is evil but imitate what is good. Whoever does good is from God; whoever does evil has not seen God. [12]Everyone has testified favorably about De·mē´tri·us, and so has the truth itself. We also testify for him,[d] and you know that our testimony is true.

Final Greetings

13 I have much to write to you, but I would rather not write with pen and ink; [14]instead I hope to see you soon, and we will talk together face to face.

15 Peace to you. The friends send you their greetings. Greet the friends there, each by name.

[a] Gk *brothers*   [b] Gk *for the sake of the name*
[c] Gk *the Gentiles*   [d] Gk lacks *for him*

Jude

The person who wrote the letter of Jude refers to himself as "a servant of Jesus Christ and brother of James." He wrote the letter during the end of the first century AD. We know little about the writer except that he lived over a hundred years after the death of Jesus. Although we do not know to whom the letter was written, it was obviously written to warn Christians about false teachers and to encourage and strengthen their faith.

Jude contains many ideas found in Second Peter, which was written about the same time. Many people think that at that time some Christians were being misled by false teachers who did not understand the gospel. Today, it is almost impossible for us to understand some parts of Jude because we do not know exactly what some of the words meant during the difficult times when the letter was written. But although we may not understand all of the symbols, what shines through is Jude's clear message of an unshakable faith in God as revealed in Jesus Christ, who will be victorious over all evil.

Jude 1

The first verse of this letter tells us that a man named Jude wrote it. Over the centuries some people believed that Jude was the brother of Jesus. See Matthew 13:55 and Mark 6:3.

Salutation

1 Jude,[a] a servant[b] of Jesus Christ and brother of James,

To those who are called, who are beloved[c] in[d] God the Father and kept safe for[d] Jesus Christ:

2 May mercy, peace, and love be yours in abundance.

Occasion of the Letter

3 Beloved, while eagerly preparing to write to you about the salvation we share, I find it necessary to write and appeal to you to contend for the faith that was once for all entrusted to the saints. [4]For certain intruders have stolen in among you, people who long ago were designated for this condemnation as ungodly, who pervert the grace of our God into licentiousness and deny our only Master and Lord, Jesus Christ.[e]

Judgment on False Teachers

5 Now I desire to remind you, though you are fully informed, that the Lord, who once for all saved[f] a people out of the land of Egypt, afterward destroyed those who did not believe. [6]And the angels who did not keep their own position, but left their proper dwelling, he has kept in eternal chains in deepest darkness for the judgment of the great day. [7]Likewise, Sod'om and Go·mor'rah and the surrounding cities, which, in the same manner as they, indulged in sexual immorality and pursued unnatural lust,[g] serve as an example by undergoing a punishment of eternal fire.

8 Yet in the same way these dreamers also defile the flesh, reject authority, and slander the glorious ones.[h] [9]But when the archangel Michael contended with the devil and disputed about the body of Moses, he did not dare to bring a condemnation of slander[i] against him, but said, "The Lord rebuke you!" [10]But these people slander whatever they do not understand, and they are destroyed by those things that, like irrational animals, they know by instinct. [11]Woe to them! For they go the way of Cain, and abandon themselves to Bā'laam's error for the sake of gain, and perish in Kō'rah's rebellion. [12]These are blemishes[j] on your love-feasts, while they feast with you without fear, feeding themselves.[k] They are waterless clouds carried along by the winds; autumn trees without fruit, twice dead, uprooted; [13]wild waves of the sea, casting up the foam of their own shame; wandering stars, for whom the deepest darkness has been reserved forever.

14 It was also about these that Ē'noch, in the seventh generation from Adam, prophesied, saying, "See, the Lord is coming[l] with ten thousands of his holy ones, [15]to execute judgment on all, and to convict everyone of all the deeds of ungodliness that they have committed in such an ungodly way, and of all the harsh things that ungodly sinners have spoken against him." [16]These are grumblers and malcontents; they indulge their own lusts; they are bombastic in speech, flattering people to their own advantage.

Warnings and Exhortations

17 But you, beloved, must remember the predictions of the apostles of our Lord Jesus Christ; [18]for they said to you,

[a] Gk *Judas* [b] Gk *slave* [c] Other ancient authorities read *sanctified* [d] Or *by* [e] Or *the only Master and our Lord Jesus Christ* [f] Other ancient authorities read *though you were once for all fully informed, that Jesus* (or *Joshua*) *who saved* [g] Gk *went after other flesh* [h] Or *angels*; Gk *glories* [i] Or *condemnation for blasphemy* [j] Or *reefs* [k] Or *without fear. They are shepherds who care only for themselves* [l] Gk *came*

"In the last time there will be scoffers, indulging their own ungodly lusts." [19]It is these worldly people, devoid of the Spirit, who are causing divisions. [20]But you, beloved, build yourselves up on your most holy faith; pray in the Holy Spirit; [21]keep yourselves in the love of God; look forward to the mercy of our Lord Jesus Christ that leads to[m] eternal life. [22]And have mercy on some who are wavering; [23]save others by snatching them out of the fire; and have mercy on still others with fear, hating even the tunic defiled by their bodies.[n]

Benediction

24 Now to him who is able to keep you from falling, and to make you stand without blemish in the presence of his glory with rejoicing, [25]to the only God

Prayer strengthens our faith. Do you pray to God each day? When we pray, we should praise God and confess to God anything we have done wrong. We should pray for others—that they will know God's love. And we should also remember to listen. Each day, try to spend five minutes in silence, just being with God and listening for God's message.

our Savior, through Jesus Christ our Lord, be glory, majesty, power, and authority, before all time and now and forever. Amen.

[m] Gk *Christ to*   [n] Gk *by the flesh*. The Greek text of verses 22-23 is uncertain at several points

Revelation

The book of Revelation was written about 95 AD. During this time, the Roman emperor Domitian was persecuting Christians. Many followers of Christ were put into prison or killed because they would not worship images of the Roman emperor as a god. Although many believe that the apostle John, the son of Zebedee, wrote the book of Revelation, this is very unlikely. The book does not tell which John was the author, but it does say that he was an exile on the island of Patmos in the Mediterranean Sea, close to Ephesus.

The book of Revelation is a type of writing called an apocalypse. Apocalypse means "to uncover" or "to reveal." This type of writing usually describes a battle between good and evil by using strange images, codes, and symbols. "Revelation" is another word for "apocalypse." It contains many visions and symbols similar to those found in parts of Isaiah, Ezekiel, and Daniel. Symbolic books such as Revelation have sometimes been used to try to predict future events, including the end of the world. But Jesus warned against trying to do so. Speaking about the end of the world, he said, "but of that day or that hour no one knows, not even the angels in heaven, nor the Son, but only the Father" (Mark 13:32).

John wrote to encourage Christians of the Roman Empire to be faithful to Christ even while suffering. He wanted them to know that the worst possible persecution could not defeat God's plan for Jesus Christ and his followers. He did not criticize Rome by name because anyone found with the book would have been in great danger. Instead, he used code words. He referred to Rome with the word "Babylon," the ancient enemy of the people of Israel and Judah. The Romans would not have understood, but the Christians, who were familiar with Old Testament writings, would have. We have trouble understanding some parts of this book because we do not know what all of the symbolic words and images mean. But there is no doubt about the main message: God will finally triumph over every evil here on earth and in the world to come.

Revelation 1:12

Introduction and Salutation

1 The revelation of Jesus Christ, which God gave him to show his servants[a] what must soon take place; he made[b] it known by sending his angel to his servant[c] John, 2 who testified to the word of God and to the testimony of Jesus Christ, even to all that he saw.

3 Blessed is the one who reads aloud the words of the prophecy, and blessed are those who hear and who keep what is written in it; for the time is near.

4 John to the seven churches that are in Asia:

Grace to you and peace from him who is and who was and who is to come, and from the seven spirits who are before his throne, 5and from Jesus Christ, the faithful witness, the firstborn of the dead, and the ruler of the kings of the earth.

To him who loves us and freed[d] us from our sins by his blood, 6and made[b] us to be a kingdom, priests serving[e] his God and Father, to him be glory and dominion forever and ever. Amen.

7 Look! He is coming with the clouds;
　　every eye will see him,
　even those who pierced him;
　　and on his account all the tribes
　　of the earth will wail.
So it is to be. Amen.

8 "I am the Alpha and the Omega," says the Lord God, who is and who was and who is to come, the Almighty.

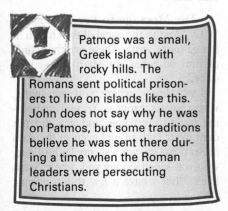

Patmos was a small, Greek island with rocky hills. The Romans sent political prisoners to live on islands like this. John does not say why he was on Patmos, but some traditions believe he was sent there during a time when the Roman leaders were persecuting Christians.

John describes a figure called the Son of Man, whose face was so bright that it looked like the sun. While he does not say this is Jesus, the description of the figure makes many people believe John is writing about Jesus.

A Vision of Christ

9 I, John, your brother who share with you in Jesus the persecution and the kingdom and the patient endurance, was on the island called Pat´mos because of the word of God and the testimony of Jesus.[f] 10I was in the spirit[g] on the Lord's day, and I heard behind me a loud voice like a trumpet 11saying, "Write in a book what you see and send it to the seven churches, to Eph´e·sus, to Smyrna, to Per´ga·mum, to Thy·a·tī´ra, to Sar´dis, to Philadelphia, and to Lā·o·di·cē´a."

12 Then I turned to see whose voice it was that spoke to me, and on turning I saw seven golden lampstands, 13and in the midst of the lampstands I saw one like the Son of Man, clothed with a long robe and with a golden sash across his chest. 14His head and his hair were white as white wool, white as snow; his eyes were like a flame of fire, 15his feet were like burnished bronze, refined as in a furnace, and his voice was like the sound of many waters. 16In his right hand he held seven stars, and from his mouth came a sharp, two-edged sword, and his face was like the sun shining with full force.

17 When I saw him, I fell at his feet as though dead. But he placed his right hand on me, saying, "Do not be afraid; I am the first and the last, 18and the living one. I was dead, and see, I am alive forever and ever; and I have the keys of Death and of Hades. 19Now write what

[a] Gk slaves　　[b] Gk and he made　　[c] Gk slave
[d] Other ancient authorities read washed　　[e] Gk priests to　　[f] Or testimony to Jesus　　[g] Or in the Spirit

you have seen, what is, and what is to take place after this. ²⁰As for the mystery of the seven stars that you saw in my right hand, and the seven golden lampstands: the seven stars are the angels of the seven churches, and the seven lampstands are the seven churches.

The Message to Ephesus

2 "To the angel of the church in Eph´e·sus write: These are the words of him who holds the seven stars in his right hand, who walks among the seven golden lampstands:

2 "I know your works, your toil and your patient endurance. I know that you cannot tolerate evildoers; you have tested those who claim to be apostles but are not, and have found them to be false. ³I also know that you are enduring patiently and bearing up for the sake of my name, and that you have not grown weary. ⁴But I have this against you, that you have abandoned the love you had at first. ⁵Remember then from what you have fallen; repent, and do the works you did at first. If not, I will come to you and remove your lampstand from its place, unless you repent. ⁶Yet this is to your credit: you hate the works of the Nic·ō·lā´i·tans, which I also hate. ⁷Let

Revelation 2–3 contains seven messages to churches in seven cities. The Son of Man told these churches that he knew how they had been living and what was in their hearts. To some churches, he gave words of warning. To others, he gave words of encouragement. These words were meant to encourage the people of these churches to stay faithful to God. Like the people of the seven churches, we must also be faithful to God. Pray that God will give you strength and courage to remain faithful at all times.

anyone who has an ear listen to what the Spirit is saying to the churches. To everyone who conquers, I will give permission to eat from the tree of life that is in the paradise of God.

The word "paradise" means "garden." The same word describes Eden in Genesis 2. Here, the word refers to the place where the righteous continue to live after death in this world.

The Message to Smyrna

8 "And to the angel of the church in Smyrna write: These are the words of the first and the last, who was dead and came to life:

9 "I know your affliction and your poverty, even though you are rich. I know the slander on the part of those who say that they are Jews and are not, but are a synagogue of Satan. ¹⁰Do not fear what you are about to suffer. Beware, the devil is about to throw some of you into prison so that you may be tested, and for ten days you will have affliction. Be faithful until death, and I will give you the crown of life. ¹¹Let anyone who has an ear listen to what the Spirit is saying to the churches. Whoever conquers will not be harmed by the second death.

The Message to Pergamum

12 "And to the angel of the church in Per´ga·mum write: These are the words of him who has the sharp two-edged sword:

13 "I know where you are living, where Satan's throne is. Yet you are holding fast to my name, and you did not deny your faith in me[h] even in the days of An´ti·pas my witness, my faithful one, who was killed among you, where Satan lives. ¹⁴But I have a few things against

[h] Or *deny my faith*

you: you have some there who hold to the teaching of Bāʹlaam, who taught Bāʹlak to put a stumbling block before the people of Israel, so that they would eat food sacrificed to idols and practice fornication. ¹⁵So you also have some who hold to the teaching of the Nic·ōʹlā·i·tans. ¹⁶Repent then. If not, I will come to you soon and make war against them with the sword of my mouth. ¹⁷Let anyone who has an ear listen to what the Spirit is saying to the churches. To everyone who conquers I will give some of the hidden manna, and I will give a white stone, and on the white stone is written a new name that no one knows except the one who receives it.

The Message to Thyatira

18 "And to the angel of the church in Thȳ·a·tīʹra write: These are the words of the Son of God, who has eyes like a flame of fire, and whose feet are like burnished bronze:

19 "I know your works—your love, faith, service, and patient endurance. I know that your last works are greater than the first. ²⁰But I have this against you: you tolerate that woman Jezʹe·bel, who calls herself a prophet and is teaching and beguiling my servants[i] to practice fornication and to eat food sacrificed to idols. ²¹I gave her time to repent, but she refuses to repent of her fornication. ²²Beware, I am throwing her on a bed, and those who commit adultery with her I am throwing into great distress, unless they repent of her doings; ²³and I will strike her children dead. And all the churches will know that I am the one who searches minds and hearts, and I will give to each of you as your works deserve. ²⁴But to the rest of you in Thȳ·a·tīʹra, who do not hold this teaching, who have not learned what some call 'the deep things of Satan,' to you I say, I do not lay on you any other burden; ²⁵only hold fast to what you have until I come. ²⁶To everyone who conquers and continues to do my works to the end,

I will give authority over the nations;
²⁷ to rule[j] them with an iron rod,
    as when clay pots are shattered—
²⁸even as I also received authority from my Father. To the one who conquers I will also give the morning star. ²⁹Let anyone who has an ear listen to what the Spirit is saying to the churches.

The Message to Sardis

3 "And to the angel of the church in Sarʹdis write: These are the words of him who has the seven spirits of God and the seven stars:

"I know your works; you have a name of being alive, but you are dead. ²Wake up, and strengthen what remains and is on the point of death, for I have not found your works perfect in the sight of my God. ³Remember then what you received and heard; obey it, and repent. If you do not wake up, I will come like a thief, and you will not know at what hour I will come to you. ⁴Yet you have still a few persons in Sarʹdis who have not soiled their clothes; they will walk with me, dressed in white, for they are worthy. ⁵If you conquer, you will be clothed like them in white robes, and I will not blot your name out of the book of life; I will confess your name before my Father and before his angels. ⁶Let anyone who has an ear listen to what the Spirit is saying to the churches.

The Message to Philadelphia

7 "And to the angel of the church in Philadelphia write:
These are the words of the holy one,
    the true one,
    who has the key of David,
    who opens and no one will shut,
        who shuts and no one opens:
8 "I know your works. Look, I have set before you an open door, which no one is able to shut. I know that you have but little power, and yet you have kept my word and have not denied my name. ⁹I will make those of the synagogue of

---

i Gk slaves   j Or to shepherd

Satan who say that they are Jews and are not, but are lying—I will make them come and bow down before your feet, and they will learn that I have loved you. [10]Because you have kept my word of patient endurance, I will keep you from the hour of trial that is coming on the whole world to test the inhabitants of the earth. [11]I am coming soon; hold fast to what you have, so that no one may seize your crown. [12]If you conquer, I will make you a pillar in the temple of my God; you will never go out of it. I will write on you the name of my God, and the name of the city of my God, the new Jerusalem that comes down from my God out of heaven, and my own new name. [13]Let anyone who has an ear listen to what the Spirit is saying to the churches.

The Message to Laodicea

14 "And to the angel of the church in Lā·o·di·cē′a write: The words of the Amen, the faithful and true witness, the origin[k] of God's creation:

15 "I know your works; you are neither cold nor hot. I wish that you were either cold or hot. [16]So, because you are lukewarm, and neither cold nor hot, I am about to spit you out of my mouth. [17]For you say, 'I am rich, I have prospered, and I need nothing.' You do not realize that you are wretched, pitiable, poor, blind, and naked. [18]Therefore I counsel you to buy from me gold refined by fire so that you may be rich; and white robes to clothe you and to keep the shame of your nakedness from being seen; and salve to anoint your eyes so that you may see. [19]I reprove and discipline those whom I love. Be earnest, therefore, and repent. [20]Listen! I am

> "Listen! I am standing at the door, knocking; if you hear my voice and open the door, I will come in to you and eat with you, and you with me."
> Revelation 3:20

standing at the door, knocking; if you hear my voice and open the door, I will come in to you and eat with you, and you with me. [21]To the one who conquers I will give a place with me on my throne, just as I myself conquered and sat down with my Father on his throne. [22]Let anyone who has an ear listen to what the Spirit is saying to the churches."

The Heavenly Worship

4 After this I looked, and there in heaven a door stood open! And the first voice, which I had heard speaking to me like a trumpet, said, "Come up here, and I will show you what must take place after this." [2]At once I was in the spirit,[l] and there in heaven stood a throne, with one seated on the throne! [3]And the one seated there looks like jasper and carnelian, and around the throne is a rainbow that looks like an emerald. [4]Around the throne are twenty-four thrones, and seated on the thrones are twenty-four elders, dressed in white robes, with golden crowns on their heads. [5]Coming from the throne are flashes of lightning, and rumblings and peals of thunder, and in front of the throne burn seven flaming torches, which are the seven spirits of God; [6]and in front of the throne there is something like a sea of glass, like crystal.

Around the throne, and on each side of the throne, are four living creatures, full of eyes in front and behind: [7]the first living creature like a lion, the second living creature like an ox, the third living creature with a face like a human face, and the fourth living creature like a flying eagle. [8]And the four living creatures, each of them with six wings, are full of eyes all around and inside. Day and night without ceasing they sing,

"Holy, holy, holy,
the Lord God the Almighty,
who was and is and is to come."

[k] Or *beginning* [l] Or *in the Spirit*

9And whenever the living creatures give glory and honor and thanks to the one who is seated on the throne, who lives forever and ever, 10the twenty-four elders fall before the one who is seated on the throne and worship the one who lives forever and ever; they cast their crowns before the throne, singing,

11 "You are worthy, our Lord and God,
　　to receive glory and honor and power,
　for you created all things,
　　and by your will they existed and were created."

The Scroll and the Lamb

5 Then I saw in the right hand of the one seated on the throne a scroll written on the inside and on the back, sealed[m] with seven seals; 2and I saw a mighty angel proclaiming with a loud voice, "Who is worthy to open the scroll and break its seals?" 3And no one in heaven or on earth or under the earth was able to open the scroll or to look into it. 4And I began to weep bitterly because no one was found worthy to open the scroll or to look into it. 5Then one of the elders said to me, "Do not weep. See, the Lion of the tribe of Judah, the Root of David, has conquered, so that he can open the scroll and its seven seals."

6 Then I saw between the throne and the four living creatures and among the elders a Lamb standing as if it had been slaughtered, having seven horns and seven eyes, which are the seven spirits of God sent out into all the earth. 7He went and took the scroll from the right hand of the one who was seated on the throne. 8When he had taken the scroll, the four living creatures and the twenty-four elders fell before the Lamb, each holding a harp and golden bowls full of incense, which are the prayers of the saints. 9They sing a new song:

"You are worthy to take the scroll
　　and to open its seals,
　for you were slaughtered and by your
　　blood you ransomed for God

saints from[n] every tribe and language and people and nation;
10 you have made them to be a kingdom
　　and priests serving[o] our God,
　　and they will reign on earth."

11 Then I looked, and I heard the voice of many angels surrounding the throne and the living creatures and the elders; they numbered myriads of myriads and thousands of thousands, 12singing with full voice,

"Worthy is the Lamb that was slaughtered
to receive power and wealth and wisdom and might
and honor and glory and blessing!"

13Then I heard every creature in heaven and on earth and under the earth and in the sea, and all that is in them, singing,

"To the one seated on the throne and to the Lamb
be blessing and honor and glory and might
forever and ever!"

14And the four living creatures said, "Amen!" And the elders fell down and worshiped.

The Seven Seals

6 Then I saw the Lamb open one of the seven seals, and I heard one of the four living creatures call out, as with a voice of thunder, "Come!"[p] 2I looked, and there was a white horse! Its rider had a bow; a crown was given to him, and he came out conquering and to conquer.

3 When he opened the second seal, I heard the second living creature call out,

---

m Or written on the inside, and sealed on the back
n Gk ransomed for God from　　o Gk priests to
p Or "Go!"

"Come!"q 4And out camer another horse, bright red; its rider was permitted to take peace from the earth, so that people would slaughter one another; and he was given a great sword.

5 When he opened the third seal, I heard the third living creature call out, "Come!"q I looked, and there was a black horse! Its rider held a pair of scales in his hand, 6and I heard what seemed to be a voice in the midst of the four living creatures saying, "A quart of wheat for a day's pay,s and three quarts of barley for a day's pay,s but do not damage the olive oil and the wine!"

7 When he opened the fourth seal, I heard the voice of the fourth living creature call out, "Come!"q 8I looked and there was a pale green horse! Its rider's name was Death, and Hades followed with him; they were given authority over a fourth of the earth, to kill with sword, famine, and pestilence, and by the wild animals of the earth.

9 When he opened the fifth seal, I saw under the altar the souls of those who had been slaughtered for the word of God and for the testimony they had given; 10they cried out with a loud voice, "Sovereign Lord, holy and true, how long will it be before you judge and avenge our blood on the inhabitants of the earth?" 11They were each given a white robe and told to rest a little longer, until the number would be complete both of their fellow servantst and of their brothers and sisters,u who were soon to be killed as they themselves had been killed.

12 When he opened the sixth seal, I looked, and there came a great earthquake; the sun became black as sackcloth, the full moon became like blood, 13and the stars of the sky fell to the earth as the fig tree drops its winter fruit when shaken by a gale. 14The sky vanished like a scroll rolling itself up, and every mountain and island was removed from its place. 15Then the kings of the earth and the magnates and the generals and the rich and the powerful, and everyone, slave and free, hid in the caves and among the rocks of the mountains, 16calling to the mountains and rocks, "Fall on us and hide us from the face of the one seated on the throne and from the wrath of the Lamb; 17for the great day of their wrath has come, and who is able to stand?"

Like writers of many other books in the Bible, John used numbers as symbols. Four is a symbol for the universe, the earth, the world, and creation. Seven is a symbol for perfection, completion, fullness, and holiness. Twelve is a symbol for the twelve tribes of Israel, the people of God (12 X 1,000 = 12,000 and 12 X 12,000 = 144,000).

The 144,000 of Israel Sealed

7 After this I saw four angels standing at the four corners of the earth, holding back the four winds of the earth so that no wind could blow on earth or sea or against any tree. 2I saw another angel ascending from the rising of the sun, having the seal of the living God, and he called with a loud voice to the four angels who had been given power to damage earth and sea, 3saying, "Do not damage the earth or the sea or the trees, until we have marked the servantst of our God with a seal on their foreheads."

4 And I heard the number of those who were sealed, one hundred forty-four thousand, sealed out of every tribe of the people of Israel:

q Or "Go!"   r Or went   s Gk a denarius
t Gk slaves   u Gk brothers

From the tribe of Judah twelve
    thousand sealed,
5 from the tribe of Reuben twelve
    thousand,
  from the tribe of Gad twelve
    thousand,
6 from the tribe of Ash´er twelve
    thousand,
  from the tribe of Naph´ta·li twelve
    thousand,
  from the tribe of Ma·nas´seh
    twelve thousand,
7 from the tribe of Sim´e·on twelve
    thousand,
  from the tribe of Levi twelve
    thousand,
  from the tribe of Is´sa·char twelve
    thousand,
8 from the tribe of Zeb´u·lun twelve
    thousand,
  from the tribe of Joseph twelve
    thousand,
  from the tribe of Benjamin twelve
    thousand sealed.

The Multitude from Every Nation

9 After this I looked, and there was a great multitude that no one could count, from every nation, from all tribes and peoples and languages, standing before the throne and before the Lamb, robed in white, with palm branches in their hands. ¹⁰They cried out in a loud voice, saying,

"Salvation belongs to our God who
    is seated on the throne, and to
    the Lamb!"

¹¹And all the angels stood around the throne and around the elders and the four living creatures, and they fell on their faces before the throne and worshiped God, ¹²singing,

"Amen! Blessing and glory and wis-
    dom
and thanksgiving and honor
and power and might
be to our God forever and ever!
    Amen."

13 Then one of the elders addressed me, saying, "Who are these, robed in

> "Amen! Blessing and glory and wisdom and thanksgiving and honor and power and might be to our God forever and ever! Amen." **Revelation 7:12**

white, and where have they come from?" ¹⁴I said to him, "Sir, you are the one that knows." Then he said to me, "These are they who have come out of the great ordeal; they have washed their robes and made them white in the blood of the Lamb.

¹⁵ For this reason they are before the
    throne of God,
  and worship him day and night
    within his temple,
  and the one who is seated on the
    throne will shelter them.
¹⁶ They will hunger no more, and thirst
    no more;
  the sun will not strike them,
    nor any scorching heat;
¹⁷ for the Lamb at the center of the
    throne will be their shepherd,
  and he will guide them to springs
    of the water of life,
  and God will wipe away every tear
    from their eyes."

The Seventh Seal and the Golden Censer

8 When the Lamb opened the seventh seal, there was silence in heaven for about half an hour. ²And I saw the seven angels who stand before God, and seven trumpets were given to them.

3 Another angel with a golden censer came and stood at the altar; he was given a great quantity of incense to offer with the prayers of all the saints on the golden altar that is before the throne. ⁴And the smoke of the incense, with the prayers of the saints, rose before God from the hand of the angel. ⁵Then the angel took the censer and filled it with fire from the altar and threw it on the earth; and there

Wormwood is a type of shrub with bitter-tasting leaves that were used to make medicine in Bible times. The prophets used the word "wormwood" as a symbol to describe something hard to accept. "Wormwood" refers to the results of evil and to the judgment of God. John emphasizes that God's judgment will be painful and difficult for people to accept.

were peals of thunder, rumblings, flashes of lightning, and an earthquake.

The Seven Trumpets

6 Now the seven angels who had the seven trumpets made ready to blow them.

7 The first angel blew his trumpet, and there came hail and fire, mixed with blood, and they were hurled to the earth; and a third of the earth was burned up, and a third of the trees were burned up, and all green grass was burned up.

8 The second angel blew his trumpet, and something like a great mountain, burning with fire, was thrown into the sea. 9A third of the sea became blood, a third of the living creatures in the sea died, and a third of the ships were destroyed.

10 The third angel blew his trumpet, and a great star fell from heaven, blazing like a torch, and it fell on a third of the rivers and on the springs of water. 11The name of the star is Wormwood. A third of the waters became wormwood, and many died from the water, because it was made bitter.

12 The fourth angel blew his trumpet, and a third of the sun was struck, and a third of the moon, and a third of the stars, so that a third of their light was darkened; a third of the day was kept from shining, and likewise the night.

13 Then I looked, and I heard an eagle crying with a loud voice as it flew in midheaven, "Woe, woe, woe to the inhabitants of the earth, at the blasts of the other trumpets that the three angels are about to blow!"

9 And the fifth angel blew his trumpet, and I saw a star that had fallen from heaven to earth, and he was given the key to the shaft of the bottomless pit; 2he opened the shaft of the bottomless pit, and from the shaft rose smoke like the smoke of a great furnace, and the sun and the air were darkened with the smoke from the shaft. 3Then from the smoke came locusts on the earth, and they were given authority like the authority of scorpions of the earth. 4They were told not to damage the grass of the earth or any green growth or any tree, but only those people who do not have the seal of God on their foreheads. 5They were allowed to torture them for five months, but not to kill them, and their torture was like the torture of a scorpion when it stings someone. 6And in those days people will seek death but will not find it; they will long to die, but death will flee from them.

7 In appearance the locusts were like horses equipped for battle. On their heads were what looked like crowns of gold; their faces were like human faces, 8their hair like women's hair, and their teeth like lions' teeth; 9they had scales like iron breastplates, and the noise of their wings was like the noise of many chariots with horses rushing into battle. 10They have tails like scorpions, with stingers, and in their tails is their power to harm people for five months. 11They have as king over them the angel of the bottomless pit; his name in Hebrew is A·bad'·don,v and in Greek he is called A·pol'lyon.w

12 The first woe has passed. There are still two woes to come.

v That is, *Destruction*   w That is, *Destroyer*

13 Then the sixth angel blew his trumpet, and I heard a voice from the four[x] horns of the golden altar before God, [14]saying to the sixth angel who had the trumpet, "Release the four angels who are bound at the great river Euphrates." [15]So the four angels were released, who had been held ready for the hour, the day, the month, and the year, to kill a third of humankind. [16]The number of the troops of cavalry was two hundred million; I heard their number. [17]And this was how I saw the horses in my vision: the riders wore breastplates the color of fire and of sapphire[y] and of sulfur; the heads of the horses were like lions' heads, and fire and smoke and sulfur came out of their mouths. [18]By these three plagues a third of humankind was killed, by the fire and smoke and sulfur coming out of their mouths. [19]For the power of the horses is in their mouths and in their tails; their tails are like serpents, having heads; and with them they inflict harm.

20 The rest of humankind, who were not killed by these plagues, did not repent of the works of their hands or give up worshiping demons and idols of gold and silver and bronze and stone and wood, which cannot see or hear or walk. [21]And they did not repent of their murders or their sorceries or their fornication or their thefts.

The Angel with the Little Scroll

10 And I saw another mighty angel coming down from heaven, wrapped in a cloud, with a rainbow over his head; his face was like the sun, and his legs like pillars of fire. [2]He held a little scroll open in his hand. Setting his right foot on the sea and his left foot on the land, [3]he gave a great shout, like a lion roaring. And when he shouted, the seven thunders sounded. [4]And when the seven thunders had sounded, I was about to write, but I heard a voice from heaven saying, "Seal up what the seven

thunders have said, and do not write it down." [5]Then the angel whom I saw standing on the sea and the land
    raised his right hand to heaven
[6]   and swore by him who lives
        forever and ever,
who created heaven and what is in it, the earth and what is in it, and the sea and what is in it: "There will be no more delay, [7]but in the days when the seventh angel is to blow his trumpet, the mystery of God will be fulfilled, as he announced to his servants[z] the prophets."

8 Then the voice that I had heard from heaven spoke to me again, saying, "Go, take the scroll that is open in the hand of the angel who is standing on the sea and on the land." [9]So I went to the angel and told him to give me the little scroll; and he said to me, "Take it, and eat; it will be bitter to your stomach, but sweet as honey in your mouth." [10]So I took the little scroll from the hand of the angel and ate it; it was sweet as honey in my mouth, but when I had eaten it, my stomach was made bitter.

11 Then they said to me, "You must prophesy again about many peoples and nations and languages and kings."

The Two Witnesses

11 Then I was given a measuring rod like a staff, and I was told, "Come and measure the temple of God and the altar and those who worship there, [2]but do not measure the court outside the temple; leave that out, for it is given over to the nations, and they will trample over the holy city for forty-two months. [3]And I will grant my two witnesses authority to prophesy for one thousand two hundred sixty days, wearing sackcloth."

4 These are the two olive trees and the two lampstands that stand before the Lord of the earth. [5]And if anyone wants to harm them, fire pours from their

---

[x] Other ancient authorities lack *four*   [y] Gk *hyacinth*   [z] Gk *slaves*

mouth and consumes their foes; anyone who wants to harm them must be killed in this manner. [6]They have authority to shut the sky, so that no rain may fall during the days of their prophesying, and they have authority over the waters to turn them into blood, and to strike the earth with every kind of plague, as often as they desire.

7 When they have finished their testimony, the beast that comes up from the bottomless pit will make war on them and conquer them and kill them, [8]and their dead bodies will lie in the street of the great city that is prophetically[a] called Sod´om and Egypt, where also their Lord was crucified. [9]For three and a half days members of the peoples and tribes and languages and nations will gaze at their dead bodies and refuse to let them be placed in a tomb; [10]and the inhabitants of the earth will gloat over them and celebrate and exchange presents, because these two prophets had been a torment to the inhabitants of the earth.

11 But after the three and a half days, the breath[b] of life from God entered them, and they stood on their feet, and those who saw them were terrified. [12]Then they[c] heard a loud voice from heaven saying to them, "Come up here!" And they went up to heaven in a cloud while their enemies watched them. [13]At that moment there was a great earthquake, and a tenth of the city fell; seven thousand people were killed in the earthquake, and the rest were terrified and gave glory to the God of heaven.

14 The second woe has passed. The third woe is coming very soon.

The Seventh Trumpet

15 Then the seventh angel blew his trumpet, and there were loud voices in heaven, saying,

"The kingdom of the world has
　　become the kingdom of our
　　Lord
　and of his Messiah,[d]
　and he will reign forever and ever."

16 Then the twenty-four elders who sit on their thrones before God fell on their faces and worshiped God, [17]singing,

"We give you thanks, Lord God
　　Almighty,
　who are and who were,
　for you have taken your great power
　　and begun to reign.
[18] The nations raged,
　　but your wrath has come,
　　and the time for judging the dead,
　for rewarding your servants,[e] the
　　prophets
　　and saints and all who fear your
　　name,
　　both small and great,
　and for destroying those who
　　destroy the earth."

19 Then God's temple in heaven was opened, and the ark of his covenant was seen within his temple; and there were flashes of lightning, rumblings, peals of thunder, an earthquake, and heavy hail.

Chapter 12 talks about the battle between good and evil. In John's vision, a dragon (Satan), was thrown down from heaven to earth, where he tries to destroy those who follow God.

The Woman and the Dragon

12 A great portent appeared in heaven: a woman clothed with the sun, with the moon under her feet, and on her head a crown of twelve stars. [2]She was pregnant and was crying out in birth pangs, in the agony of giving birth. [3]Then another portent appeared in heaven: a great red dragon, with seven heads and ten horns, and seven diadems

---

[a] Or *allegorically*; Gk *spiritually*　　[b] Or *the spirit*
[c] Other ancient authorities read *I*　　[d] Gk *Christ*
[e] Gk *slaves*

on his heads. [4]His tail swept down a third of the stars of heaven and threw them to the earth. Then the dragon stood before the woman who was about to bear a child, so that he might devour her child as soon as it was born. [5]And she gave birth to a son, a male child, who is to rule[f] all the nations with a rod of iron. But her child was snatched away and taken to God and to his throne; [6]and the woman fled into the wilderness, where she has a place prepared by God, so that there she can be nourished for one thousand two hundred sixty days.

Michael Defeats the Dragon

7 And war broke out in heaven; Michael and his angels fought against the dragon. The dragon and his angels fought back, [8]but they were defeated, and there was no longer any place for them in heaven. [9]The great dragon was thrown down, that ancient serpent, who is called the Devil and Satan, the deceiver of the whole world—he was thrown down to the earth, and his angels were thrown down with him. 10 Then I heard a loud voice in heaven, proclaiming,

"Now have come the salvation and
        the power
and the kingdom of our God
and the authority of his Messiah,[g]
for the accuser of our comrades[h] has
        been thrown down,
who accuses them day and night
        before our God.
[11] But they have conquered him by the
        blood of the Lamb
and by the word of their testimony,
for they did not cling to life even in
        the face of death.
[12] Rejoice then, you heavens
        and those who dwell in them!
But woe to the earth and the sea,
        for the devil has come down to you
        with great wrath,
        because he knows that his time is
        short!"

The Dragon Fights Again on Earth

13 So when the dragon saw that he had been thrown down to the earth, he pursued[i] the woman who had given birth to the male child. [14]But the woman was given the two wings of the great eagle, so that she could fly from the serpent into the wilderness, to her place where she is nourished for a time, and times, and half a time. [15]Then from his mouth the serpent poured water like a river after the woman, to sweep her away with the flood. [16]But the earth came to the help of the woman; it opened its mouth and swallowed the river that the dragon had poured from his mouth. [17]Then the dragon was angry with the woman, and went off to make war on the rest of her children, those who keep the commandments of God and hold the testimony of Jesus.

The First Beast

18 Then the dragon[j] took his stand on the sand of the seashore. [1]And I saw a beast rising out of the sea, having ten

13 horns and seven heads; and on its horns were ten diadems, and on its heads were blasphemous names. [2]And the beast that I saw was like a leopard, its feet were like a bear's, and its mouth was like a lion's mouth. And the dragon gave it his power and his throne and great authority. [3]One of its heads seemed to have received a death-blow, but its mortal wound[k] had been healed. In amazement the whole earth followed the beast. [4]They worshiped the dragon, for he had given his authority to the beast, and they worshiped the beast, saying, "Who is like the beast, and who can fight against it?"

5 The beast was given a mouth uttering haughty and blasphemous words,

[f] Or to shepherd   [g] Gk Christ   [h] Gk brothers
[i] Or persecuted   [j] Gk Then he; other ancient
authorities read Then I stood   [k] Gk the plague of
its death

and it was allowed to exercise authority for forty-two months. [6]It opened its mouth to utter blasphemies against God, blaspheming his name and his dwelling, that is, those who dwell in heaven. [7]Also it was allowed to make war on the saints and to conquer them.[l] It was given authority over every tribe and people and language and nation, [8]and all the inhabitants of the earth will worship it, everyone whose name has not been written from the foundation of the world in the book of life of the Lamb that was slaughtered.[m]

9 Let anyone who has an ear listen:
[10] If you are to be taken captive,
  into captivity you go;
 if you kill with the sword,
  with the sword you must be
   killed.

Here is a call for the endurance and faith of the saints.

The Second Beast

11 Then I saw another beast that rose out of the earth; it had two horns like a lamb and it spoke like a dragon. [12]It exercises all the authority of the first beast on its behalf, and it makes the earth and its inhabitants worship the first beast, whose mortal wound[n] had been healed. [13]It performs great signs, even making fire come down from heaven to earth in the sight of all; [14]and by the signs that it is allowed to perform on behalf of the beast, it deceives the inhabitants of earth, telling them to make an image for the beast that had been wounded by the sword[o] and yet lived; [15]and it was allowed to give breath[p] to the image of the beast so that the image of the beast could even speak and cause those who would not worship the image of the beast to be killed. [16]Also it causes all, both small and great, both rich and poor, both free and slave, to be marked on the right hand or the forehead, [17]so that no one can buy or sell who does not have the mark, that is, the name of the beast or the number of its name. [18]This calls for wisdom: let anyone with understanding calculate the number of the beast, for it is the number of a person. Its number is six hundred sixty-six.[q]

Have you ever heard people say that "666" is an evil number? When John wrote about a great "beast" whose number was 666, he was probably referring to the emperor Nero Caesar. The numerical value of Nero's name in Hebrew letters was 666. This is one of John's secret codes, meant to keep the Romans from understanding.

The Lamb and the 144,000

14 Then I looked, and there was the Lamb, standing on Mount Zion! And with him were one hundred forty-four thousand who had his name and his Father's name written on their foreheads. [2]And I heard a voice from heaven like the sound of many waters and like the sound of loud thunder; the voice I heard was like the sound of harpists playing on their harps, [3]and they sing a new song before the throne and before the four living creatures and before the elders. No one could learn that song except the one hundred forty-four thousand who have been redeemed from the earth. [4]It is these who have not defiled themselves with women, for they are virgins; these follow the Lamb wherever he goes. They have been redeemed from humankind as first fruits for God and the Lamb, [5]and in their mouth no lie was found; they are blameless.

[l] Other ancient authorities lack this sentence
[m] Or written in the book of life of the Lamb that was slaughtered from the foundation of the world
[n] Gk whose plague of its death   [o] Or that had received the plague of the sword   [p] Or spirit
[q] Other ancient authorities read six hundred sixteen

The Messages of the Three Angels

6 Then I saw another angel flying in midheaven, with an eternal gospel to proclaim to those who live[r] on the earth—to every nation and tribe and language and people. [7]He said in a loud voice, "Fear God and give him glory, for the hour of his judgment has come; and worship him who made heaven and earth, the sea and the springs of water."

8 Then another angel, a second, followed, saying, "Fallen, fallen is Babylon the great! She has made all nations drink of the wine of the wrath of her fornication."

9 Then another angel, a third, followed them, crying with a loud voice, "Those who worship the beast and its image, and receive a mark on their foreheads or on their hands, [10]they will also drink the wine of God's wrath, poured unmixed into the cup of his anger, and they will be tormented with fire and sulfur in the presence of the holy angels and in the presence of the Lamb. [11]And the smoke of their torment goes up forever and ever. There is no rest day or night for those who worship the beast and its image and for anyone who receives the mark of its name."

12 Here is a call for the endurance of the saints, those who keep the commandments of God and hold fast to the faith of[s] Jesus.

13 And I heard a voice from heaven saying, "Write this: Blessed are the dead who from now on die in the Lord." "Yes," says the Spirit, "they will rest from their labors, for their deeds follow them."

Reaping the Earth's Harvest

14 Then I looked, and there was a white cloud, and seated on the cloud was one like the Son of Man, with a golden crown on his head, and a sharp sickle in his hand! [15]Another angel came out of the temple, calling with a loud voice to the one who sat on the cloud, "Use your sickle and reap, for the hour to reap has come, because the harvest of

Revelation calls for the people of God to keep God's commandments and to hold on to their faith in Christ. Whatever happens in life, we are to be strong and have faith. God is always faithful to us.

Have you been through a hard time in your life? Have any of your friends or family members been through hard times? Talk about these times together. Did you have faith in God? Did they? If hard times come again, what will help you to stay faithful?

the earth is fully ripe." [16]So the one who sat on the cloud swung his sickle over the earth, and the earth was reaped.

17 Then another angel came out of the temple in heaven, and he too had a sharp sickle. [18]Then another angel came out from the altar, the angel who has authority over fire, and he called with a loud voice to him who had the sharp sickle, "Use your sharp sickle and gather the clusters of the vine of the earth, for its grapes are ripe." [19]So the angel swung his sickle over the earth and gathered the vintage of the earth, and he threw it into the great wine press of the wrath of God. [20]And the wine press was trodden outside the city, and blood flowed from the wine press, as high as a horse's bridle, for a distance of about two hundred miles.[t]

The Angels with the Seven Last Plagues

15 Then I saw another portent in heaven, great and amazing: seven angels with seven plagues, which are the last, for with them the wrath of God is ended.

2 And I saw what appeared to be a sea of glass mixed with fire, and those who had conquered the beast and its image and the number of its name,

[r] Gk sit   [s] Or *to their faith in*   [t] Gk *one thousand six hundred stadia*

standing beside the sea of glass with harps of God in their hands. ³And they sing the song of Moses, the servant[u] of God, and the song of the Lamb:

"Great and amazing are your deeds,
Lord God the Almighty!
Just and true are your ways,
King of the nations![v]
⁴ Lord, who will not fear
and glorify your name?
For you alone are holy.
All nations will come
and worship before you,
for your judgments have been
revealed."

5 After this I looked, and the temple of the tent[w] of witness in heaven was opened, ⁶and out of the temple came the seven angels with the seven plagues, robed in pure bright linen,[x] with golden sashes across their chests. ⁷Then one of the four living creatures gave the seven angels seven golden bowls full of the wrath of God, who lives forever and ever; ⁸and the temple was filled with smoke from the glory of God and from his power, and no one could enter the temple until the seven plagues of the seven angels were ended.

The Bowls of God's Wrath

16 Then I heard a loud voice from the temple telling the seven angels, "Go and pour out on the earth the seven bowls of the wrath of God."

2 So the first angel went and poured his bowl on the earth, and a foul and painful sore came on those who had the mark of the beast and who worshiped its image.

3 The second angel poured his bowl into the sea, and it became like the blood of a corpse, and every living thing in the sea died.

4 The third angel poured his bowl into the rivers and the springs of water, and they became blood. ⁵And I heard the angel of the waters say,

"You are just, O Holy One, who are and were,
for you have judged these things;
⁶ because they shed the blood of
saints and prophets,
you have given them blood to
drink.
It is what they deserve!"
⁷And I heard the altar respond,
"Yes, O Lord God, the Almighty,
your judgments are true and just!"

8 The fourth angel poured his bowl on the sun, and it was allowed to scorch people with fire; ⁹they were scorched by the fierce heat, but they cursed the name of God, who had authority over these plagues, and they did not repent and give him glory.

10 The fifth angel poured his bowl on the throne of the beast, and its kingdom was plunged into darkness; people gnawed their tongues in agony, ¹¹and cursed the God of heaven because of their pains and sores, and they did not repent of their deeds.

12 The sixth angel poured his bowl on the great river Euphrates, and its water was dried up in order to prepare the way for the kings from the east. ¹³And I saw three foul spirits like frogs coming from the mouth of the dragon, from the mouth of the beast, and from the mouth of the false prophet. ¹⁴These are demonic spirits, performing signs, who go abroad to the kings of the whole world, to assemble them for battle on the great day of God the Almighty. ¹⁵("See, I am coming like a thief! Blessed is the one who stays awake and is clothed,[y] not going about naked and exposed to shame.") ¹⁶And they assembled them at the place that in Hebrew is called Har·ma·ged´on.

17 The seventh angel poured his bowl into the air, and a loud voice came out of the temple, from the throne, say-

[u] Gk slave   [v] Other ancient authorities read the ages   [w] Or tabernacle   [x] Other ancient authorities read stone   [y] Gk and keeps his robes

ing, "It is done!" [18]And there came flashes of lightning, rumblings, peals of thunder, and a violent earthquake, such as had not occurred since people were upon the earth, so violent was that earthquake. [19]The great city was split into three parts, and the cities of the nations fell. God remembered great Babylon and gave her the wine-cup of the fury of his wrath. [20]And every island fled away, and no mountains were to be found; [21]and huge hailstones, each weighing about a hundred pounds,[z] dropped from heaven on people, until they cursed God for the plague of the hail, so fearful was that plague.

The Great Whore and the Beast

17 Then one of the seven angels who had the seven bowls came and said to me, "Come, I will show you the judgment of the great whore who is seated on many waters, [2]with whom the kings of the earth have committed fornication, and with the wine of whose fornication the inhabitants of the earth have become drunk." [3]So he carried me away in the spirit[a] into a wilderness, and I saw a woman sitting on a scarlet beast that was full of blasphemous names, and it had seven heads and ten horns. [4]The woman was clothed in purple and scarlet, and adorned with gold and jewels and pearls, holding in her hand a golden cup full of abominations and the impurities of her fornication; [5]and on her forehead was written a name, a mystery: "Babylon the great, mother of whores and of earth's abominations." [6]And I saw that the woman was drunk with the blood of the saints and the blood of the witnesses to Jesus.

When I saw her, I was greatly amazed. [7]But the angel said to me, "Why are you so amazed? I will tell you the mystery of the woman, and of the beast with seven heads and ten horns that carries her. [8]The beast that you saw was, and is not, and is about to ascend from the bottomless pit and go to destruction. And the inhabitants of the earth, whose names have not been written in the book of life from the foundation of the world, will be amazed when they see the beast, because it was and is not and is to come.

9 "This calls for a mind that has wisdom: the seven heads are seven mountains on which the woman is seated; also, they are seven kings, [10]of whom five have fallen, one is living, and the other has not yet come; and when he comes, he must remain only a little while. [11]As for the beast that was and is not, it is an eighth but it belongs to the seven, and it goes to destruction. [12]And the ten horns that you saw are ten kings who have not yet received a kingdom, but they are to receive authority as kings for one hour, together with the beast. [13]These are united in yielding their power and authority to the beast; [14]they will make war on the Lamb, and the Lamb will conquer them, for he is Lord of lords and King of kings, and those with him are called and chosen and faithful."

15 And he said to me, "The waters that you saw, where the whore is seated, are peoples and multitudes and nations and languages. [16]And the ten horns that you saw, they and the beast will hate the whore; they will make her desolate and naked; they will devour her flesh and burn her up with fire. [17]For God has put it into their hearts to carry out his purpose by agreeing to give their kingdom to the beast, until the words of God will be fulfilled. [18]The woman you saw is the great city that rules over the kings of the earth."

The Fall of Babylon

18 After this I saw another angel coming down from heaven, having great authority; and the earth was made bright with his splendor. [2]He called out with a mighty voice,

---

[z] Gk *weighing about a talent*   [a] Or *in the Spirit*

"Babylon" is a symbol for the Roman Empire. During the time when John wrote Revelation, the Roman leaders were persecuting and killing Christians because of their faith in Christ. In John's vision, God will punish and defeat Babylon (Rome).

"Fallen, fallen is Babylon the great!
    It has become a dwelling place of
        demons,
    a haunt of every foul spirit,
    a haunt of every foul bird,
    a haunt of every foul and hateful
        beast.*b*
3 For all the nations have drunk*c*
    of the wine of the wrath of her
        fornication,
    and the kings of the earth have com-
        mitted fornication with her,
    and the merchants of the earth
        have grown rich from the pow-
        er*d* of her luxury."
4 Then I heard another voice from
heaven saying,
"Come out of her, my people,
    so that you do not take part in her
        sins,
    and so that you do not share in her
        plagues;
5 for her sins are heaped high as
        heaven,
    and God has remembered her
        iniquities.
6 Render to her as she herself has ren-
        dered,
    and repay her double for her
        deeds;
    mix a double draught for her in
        the cup she mixed.
7 As she glorified herself and lived
        luxuriously,
    so give her a like measure of tor-
        ment and grief.

Since in her heart she says,
    'I rule as a queen;
    I am no widow,
    and I will never see grief,'
8 therefore her plagues will come in a
        single day—
    pestilence and mourning and
        famine—
    and she will be burned with fire;
    for mighty is the Lord God who
        judges her."
9 And the kings of the earth, who
committed fornication and lived in luxury with her, will weep and wail over
her when they see the smoke of her
burning; 10they will stand far off, in fear
of her torment, and say,
"Alas, alas, the great city,
    Babylon, the mighty city!
    For in one hour your judgment has
        come."
11 And the merchants of the earth
weep and mourn for her, since no one
buys their cargo anymore, 12cargo of
gold, silver, jewels and pearls, fine linen,
purple, silk and scarlet, all kinds of
scented wood, all articles of ivory, all
articles of costly wood, bronze, iron, and
marble, 13cinnamon, spice, incense,
myrrh, frankincense, wine, olive oil,
choice flour and wheat, cattle and sheep,
horses and chariots, slaves—and human
lives.*e*
14 "The fruit for which your soul
        longed
    has gone from you,
    and all your dainties and your splen-
        dor
    are lost to you,
    never to be found again!"
15The merchants of these wares, who
gained wealth from her, will stand far
off, in fear of her torment, weeping and
mourning aloud,

b Other ancient authorities lack the words *a haunt
of every foul beast* and attach the words *and hateful*
to the previous line so as to read *a haunt of every
foul and hateful bird*   *c* Other ancient authorities
read *She has made all nations drink*   *d* Or *resources*
e Or *chariots, and human bodies and souls*

16 "Alas, alas, the great city,
  clothed in fine linen,
    in purple and scarlet,
  adorned with gold,
    with jewels, and with pearls!
17 For in one hour all this wealth has
    been laid waste!"
And all shipmasters and seafarers,
sailors and all whose trade is on the sea,
stood far off 18and cried out as they saw
the smoke of her burning,
  "What city was like the great city?"
19And they threw dust on their heads, as
they wept and mourned, crying out,
  "Alas, alas, the great city,
    where all who had ships at sea
    grew rich by her wealth!
  For in one hour she has been laid
    waste."
20 Rejoice over her, O heaven, you
saints and apostles and prophets! For God
has given judgment for you against her.
21 Then a mighty angel took up a
stone like a great millstone and threw it
into the sea, saying,
  "With such violence Babylon the
    great city
  will be thrown down,
    and will be found no more;
22 and the sound of harpists and min-
    strels and of flutists and trum-
    peters
  will be heard in you no more;
  and an artisan of any trade
  will be found in you no more;
  and the sound of the millstone
  will be heard in you no more;
23 and the light of a lamp
  will shine in you no more;
  and the voice of bridegroom and bride
  will be heard in you no more;
  for your merchants were the mag-
    nates of the earth,
  and all nations were deceived by
    your sorcery.
24 And in you*f* was found the blood of
    prophets and of saints,
    and of all who have been slaugh-
    tered on earth."

The Rejoicing in Heaven

19 After this I heard what seemed
  to be the loud voice of a great
multitude in heaven, saying,
  "Hallelujah!
Salvation and glory and power to
    our God,
2   for his judgments are true and
      just;
  he has judged the great whore
    who corrupted the earth with her
      fornication,
  and he has avenged on her the blood
      of his servants."*g*
3Once more they said,
  "Hallelujah!
The smoke goes up from her forever
    and ever."
4And the twenty-four elders and the four
living creatures fell down and worshiped
God who is seated on the throne, saying,
  "Amen. Hallelujah!"
5 And from the throne came a voice
saying,
  "Praise our God,
    all you his servants,*g*
  and all who fear him,
    small and great."
6Then I heard what seemed to be the
voice of a great multitude, like the sound
of many waters and like the sound of
mighty thunderpeals, crying out,
  "Hallelujah!
  For the Lord our God
    the Almighty reigns.
7 Let us rejoice and exult
    and give him the glory,
  for the marriage of the Lamb has
    come,
  and his bride has made herself
    ready;
8 to her it has been granted to be
    clothed
  with fine linen, bright and
    pure"—
for the fine linen is the righteous deeds
of the saints.

f Gk her   *g* Gk slaves

Have you ever ridden a horse? In Bible times, powerful people rode horses. In his vision, John saw Jesus riding on a white horse. Jesus, who is called "Faithful and True," is the one with all power and authority.

9 And the angel said[h] to me, "Write this: Blessed are those who are invited to the marriage supper of the Lamb." And he said to me, "These are true words of God." [10]Then I fell down at his feet to worship him, but he said to me, "You must not do that! I am a fellow servant[i] with you and your comrades[j] who hold the testimony of Jesus.[k] Worship God! For the testimony of Jesus[k] is the spirit of prophecy."

The Rider on the White Horse

11 Then I saw heaven opened, and there was a white horse! Its rider is called Faithful and True, and in righteousness he judges and makes war. [12]His eyes are like a flame of fire, and on his head are many diadems; and he has a name inscribed that no one knows but himself. [13]He is clothed in a robe dipped in[l] blood, and his name is called The Word of God. [14]And the armies of heaven, wearing fine linen, white and pure, were following him on white horses. [15]From his mouth comes a sharp sword with which to strike down the nations, and he will rule[m] them with a rod of iron; he will tread the wine press of the fury of the wrath of God the Almighty. [16]On his robe and on his thigh

John called Jesus "Word" and "Word of God" to mean that Jesus Christ himself is God's clearest word to humankind. Jesus lived on earth as God wants us to live, sharing God's love with others.

he has a name inscribed, "King of kings and Lord of lords."

The Beast and Its Armies Defeated

17 Then I saw an angel standing in the sun, and with a loud voice he called to all the birds that fly in midheaven, "Come, gather for the great supper of God, [18]to eat the flesh of kings, the flesh of captains, the flesh of the mighty, the flesh of horses and their riders—flesh of all, both free and slave, both small and great." [19]Then I saw the beast and the kings of the earth with their armies gathered to make war against the rider on the horse and against his army. [20]And the beast was captured, and with it the false prophet who had performed in its presence the signs by which he deceived those who had received the mark of the beast and those who worshiped its image. These two were thrown alive into the lake of fire that burns with sulfur. [21]And the rest were killed by the sword of the rider on the horse, the sword that came from his mouth; and all the birds were gorged with their flesh.

The Thousand Years

20 Then I saw an angel coming down from heaven, holding in his hand the key to the bottomless pit and a great chain. [2]He seized the dragon, that ancient serpent, who is the Devil and Satan, and bound him for a thousand years, [3]and threw him into the pit, and locked and sealed it over him, so that he would deceive the nations no more, until the thousand years were ended. After that he must be let out for a little while.

4 Then I saw thrones, and those seated on them were given authority to judge. I also saw the souls of those who had been beheaded for their testimony to Jesus[n] and for the word of God. They

[h] Gk he said   [i] Gk slave   [j] Gk brothers   [k] Or to Jesus   [l] Other ancient authorities read sprinkled with   [m] Or will shepherd   [n] Or for the testimony of Jesus

had not worshiped the beast or its image and had not received its mark on their foreheads or their hands. They came to life and reigned with Christ a thousand years. [5](The rest of the dead did not come to life until the thousand years were ended.) This is the first resurrection. [6]Blessed and holy are those who share in the first resurrection. Over these the second death has no power, but they will be priests of God and of Christ, and they will reign with him a thousand years.

Satan's Doom

7 When the thousand years are ended, Satan will be released from his prison [8]and will come out to deceive the nations at the four corners of the earth, Gog and Māʹgog, in order to gather them for battle; they are as numerous as the sands of the sea. [9]They marched up over the breadth of the earth and surrounded the camp of the saints and the beloved city. And fire came down from heaven[o] and consumed them. [10]And the devil who had deceived them was thrown into the lake of fire and sulfur, where the beast and the false prophet were, and they will be tormented day and night forever and ever.

The Dead Are Judged

11 Then I saw a great white throne and the one who sat on it; the earth and the heaven fled from his presence, and no place was found for them. [12]And I saw the dead, great and small, standing before the throne, and books were opened. Also another book was opened, the book of life. And the dead were judged according to their works, as recorded in the books. [13]And the sea gave up the dead that were in it, Death and Hades gave up the dead that were in them, and all were judged according to what they had done. [14]Then Death and Hades were thrown into the lake of fire. This is the second death, the lake of fire; [15]and anyone whose name was not found written in the book of life was thrown into the lake of fire.

> "Then I saw a new heaven and a new earth; for the first heaven and the first earth had passed away, and the sea was no more."   Revelation 21:1

The New Heaven and the New Earth

21 Then I saw a new heaven and a new earth; for the first heaven and the first earth had passed away, and the sea was no more. [2]And I saw the holy city, the new Jerusalem, coming down out of heaven from God, prepared as a bride adorned for her husband. [3]And I heard a loud voice from the throne saying,

> John describes God living among us. God will wipe away all our tears, and we will no longer suffer pain and death. All things will be made new. This is a beautiful vision of life with God.

"See, the home[p] of God is among mortals.
He will dwell[q] with them;
they will be his peoples,[r]
and God himself will be with them;[s]

> John described his vision of the new heavens and new earth restored (or made new) by God. Coming down from the new heaven will be the city of new Jerusalem, the beautiful home of the people of God. This city will not need the light of the sun or the moon—God will be its light.

[o] Other ancient authorities read *from God, out of heaven,* or *out of heaven from God*   [p] Gk *the tabernacle*   [q] Gk *will tabernacle*   [r] Other ancient authorities read *people*   [s] Other ancient authorities add *and be their God*

> "It is done! I am the Alpha and the Omega, the beginning and the end."
> Revelation 21:6

⁴ he will wipe every tear from their eyes.
Death will be no more;
mourning and crying and pain will
be no more,
for the first things have passed
away."

5 And the one who was seated on the throne said, "See, I am making all things new." Also he said, "Write this, for these words are trustworthy and true." ⁶Then he said to me, "It is done! I am the Alpha and the Omega, the beginning and the end. To the thirsty I will give water as a gift from the spring of the water of life. ⁷Those who conquer will inherit these things, and I will be their God and they will be my children. ⁸But as for the cowardly, the faithless,ᵗ the polluted, the murderers, the fornicators, the sorcerers, the idolaters, and all liars, their place will be in the lake that burns with fire and sulfur, which is the second death."

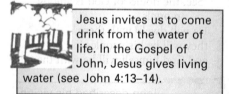
Jesus invites us to come drink from the water of life. In the Gospel of John, Jesus gives living water (see John 4:13–14).

Vision of the New Jerusalem

9 Then one of the seven angels who had the seven bowls full of the seven last plagues came and said to me, "Come, I will show you the bride, the wife of the Lamb." ¹⁰And in the spiritᵘ he carried me away to a great, high mountain and showed me the holy city Jerusalem coming down out of heaven from God. ¹¹It has the glory of God and a radiance like a very rare jewel, like jasper, clear as crystal. ¹²It has a great, high wall with twelve gates, and at the gates twelve angels, and on the gates are inscribed the names of the twelve tribes of the Israelites; ¹³on the east three gates, on the north three gates, on the south three gates, and on the west three gates. ¹⁴And the wall of the city has twelve foundations, and on them are the twelve names of the twelve apostles of the Lamb.

15 The angelᵛ who talked to me had a measuring rod of gold to measure the city and its gates and walls. ¹⁶The city lies foursquare, its length the same as its width; and he measured the city with his rod, fifteen hundred miles;ʷ its length and width and height are equal. ¹⁷He also measured its wall, one hundred forty-four cubitsˣ by human measurement, which the angel was using. ¹⁸The wall is built of jasper, while the city is pure gold, clear as glass. ¹⁹The foundations of the wall of the city are adorned with every jewel; the first was jasper, the second sapphire, the third agate, the fourth emerald, ²⁰the fifth onyx, the sixth carnelian, the seventh chrysolite, the eighth beryl, the ninth topaz, the tenth chrysoprase, the eleventh jacinth, the twelfth amethyst. ²¹And the twelve gates are twelve pearls, each of the gates is a single pearl, and the street of the city is pure gold, transparent as glass.

22 I saw no temple in the city, for its temple is the Lord God the Almighty and the Lamb. ²³And the city has no need of sun or moon to shine on it, for the glory of God is its light, and its lamp is the Lamb. ²⁴The nations will walk by its light, and the kings of the earth will bring their glory into it. ²⁵Its gates will never be shut by day—and there will be no night there. ²⁶People will bring into it the glory and the honor of the nations. ²⁷But nothing unclean will enter it, nor anyone who practices abomination or falsehood, but only those who are written in the Lamb's book of life.

ᵗ Or *the unbelieving*   ᵘ Or *in the Spirit*   ᵛ Gk *He*
ʷ Gk *twelve thousand stadia*   ˣ That is, almost
seventy-five yards

The River of Life

22 Then the angel[y] showed me the river of the water of life, bright as crystal, flowing from the throne of God and of the Lamb [2]through the middle of the street of the city. On either side of the river is the tree of life[z] with its twelve kinds of fruit, producing its fruit each month; and the leaves of the tree are for the healing of the nations. [3]Nothing accursed will be found there any more. But the throne of God and of the Lamb will be in it, and his servants[a] will worship him; [4]they will see his face, and his name will be on their foreheads. [5]And there will be no more night; they need no light of lamp or sun, for the Lord God will be their light, and they will reign forever and ever.

6 And he said to me, "These words are trustworthy and true, for the Lord, the God of the spirits of the prophets, has sent his angel to show his servants[a] what must soon take place."

7 "See, I am coming soon! Blessed is the one who keeps the words of the prophecy of this book."

Epilogue and Benediction

8 I, John, am the one who heard and saw these things. And when I heard and saw them, I fell down to worship at the feet of the angel who showed them to me; [9]but he said to me, "You must not do that! I am a fellow servant[b] with you and your comrades[c] the prophets, and with those who keep the words of this book. Worship God!"

10 And he said to me, "Do not seal up the words of the prophecy of this book, for the time is near. [11]Let the evildoer still do evil, and the filthy still be filthy, and the righteous still do right, and the holy still be holy."

12 "See, I am coming soon; my reward is with me, to repay according to everyone's work. [13]I am the Alpha and the Omega, the first and the last, the beginning and the end."

"Alpha" is the first letter and "Omega" is the last letter of the Greek alphabet. Put together, the two letters are a symbol for Jesus Christ. We know that Jesus has always been present, is now present, and always will be present. Jesus will live forever! This is what we mean when we say Jesus is "the Alpha and the Omega, the first and the last, the beginning and the end" (22:13).

14 Blessed are those who wash their robes,[d] so that they will have the right to the tree of life and may enter the city by the gates. [15]Outside are the dogs and sorcerers and fornicators and murderers and idolaters, and everyone who loves and practices falsehood.

16 "It is I, Jesus, who sent my angel to you with this testimony for the churches. I am the root and the descendant of David, the bright morning star."

17 The Spirit and the bride say,
   "Come."
And let everyone who hears say,
   "Come."
And let everyone who is thirsty
   come.
Let anyone who wishes take the
   water of life as a gift.

18 I warn everyone who hears the words of the prophecy of this book: if anyone adds to them, God will add to that person the plagues described in this book; [19]if anyone takes away from the words of the book of this prophecy, God will take away that person's share in the tree of life and in the holy city, which are described in this book.

[y] Gk he   [z] Or the Lamb. [2]In the middle of the street of the city, and on either side of the river, is the tree of life   [a] Gk slaves   [b] Gk slave   [c] Gk brothers   [d] Other ancient authorities read do his commandments

Before people made printed books, they would sometimes add or take away pages from letters or manuscripts sent around for many people to read. When John told the people not to add or take away from the words of his letter, he was speaking only of his own letter, not the Bible. The Bible as we know it did not exist at that time! But John considered his letter a message from God to the churches and wanted them to handle it with respect.

20 The one who testifies to these things says, "Surely I am coming soon."

Amen. Come, Lord Jesus!

21 The grace of the Lord Jesus be with all the saints. Amen.[e]

[e] Other ancient authorities lack *all*; others lack *the saints*; others lack *Amen*

Dictionary

A

Abba—An Aramaic word meaning "the father," "my father," or "our father." Jesus used this word as a familiar name for God, the Father.

abyss—An unmeasured, deep, bottomless pit.

adultery—Intimate and sinful physical relations between a married man and a woman who is not his wife, or between a married woman and a man who is not her husband.

alabaster—A soft stone, light and creamy in color and often having a striped appearance. In Bible times, people used alabaster for vases and flasks or for boxes to hold perfume and precious ointments.

allotment—In early Old Testament times, the portion of land given to each of the tribes occupying Canaan.

Almighty—Having all power. A name used to describe God's greatness, power, and might.

alms—Gifts given to the poor.

Alpha and Omega—The first and last letters of the Greek alphabet. In the New Testament, the letters are used together as symbols for God and Jesus Christ.

altar—A stone or pile of stones on which sacrifices were offered to God.

ambush—Waiting in a hiding place in order to attack an enemy by surprise.

Amen—A Hebrew word meaning "truly" or "surely." This word is often used at the end of songs or prayers.

angel—A spiritual being or messenger from God sometimes said to appear in human form.

anoint—To pour oil on the head or body of a person or on an object. In biblical times, anointing was often part of a religious ceremony showing that a person had been set apart for the service of the Lord.

antichrist—An enemy of Christ.

apostle—A title meaning "messenger" or "someone who is sent." The title given to the twelve disciples sent out by Jesus. Also refers to Paul and to other leaders in the early church. See also **disciple**.

Aramaic—A language closely related to Hebrew. During the time of Jesus, Aramaic was the everyday language of the Jews.

archangel—A chief angel.

Ark of the Covenant—A wooden box covered with gold that held the stone tablets containing the Ten Commandments. The Israelites carried the Ark with them during their wanderings in the wilderness, and they later placed the Ark in the Temple.

ark of Noah—A floating vessel like a houseboat in which Noah, his family, and at least one pair each of all living creatures took refuge during the Great Flood.

armlet—A metal ring or band worn on the upper arm as jewelry. Kings and other persons in authority wore armlets.

armor—Protective equipment given to soldiers to protect them during battle. The phrase "armor of God" is a way of speaking of the protection God gives people to stand against evil.

ascend—To go up. Forty days after Jesus's resurrection, he ascended into heaven.

atonement—The achievement of a state of harmony, or the overcoming of conflict or separation. People are separated from God due to their sin, and atonement (or reconciliation) brings agreement and restoration between people and God.

Atonement, Day of—A Jewish holy day of fasting and repentance. It is also called Yom Kippur.

B

Baal—The name of the chief god of the Canaanites.

Babylon—An ancient city of Mesopotamia that was the capital city of the great Babylonian Empire under King Nebuchadnezzar. When Nebuchadnezzar captured Judah, the Hebrew people were taken as captives to Babylon.

balances—A type of scale made by hanging one pan from each end of a beam balanced on a cord or from a shaft. To weigh metal or grain, blocks or stones of a given size were put in one pan, and the material to be weighed was put in the other. Material or weights were added until the pans hung evenly.

banner—A sign or symbol held high on a pole as the emblem of a tribe. Soldiers used banners like flags to rally the troops. They sounded trumpets when the banners were raised.

banquet—A large meal with many rich foods.

baptism—A ceremonial act using water to symbolize washing or making pure in the sight of God.

barley—An important grain that was cheaper and ripened earlier than wheat. Barley was used as food for animals and humans and was especially important to the poor.

barren—Not able to have children; not able to grow crops.

basin—A bowl-like vessel of any size.

battering ram—A large pole with a heavy head supported in a framework set on wheels so it could be rammed against the gates and walls of a city to break them down. See also **siege**.

beatitude—A form of writing that begins with the word "blessed."

Bethlehem—A town in Judah about six miles north of Jerusalem. It is best known as the birthplace of Jesus.

birthright—The special rights and privileges of the first-born (or oldest) son. In Old Testament times, the oldest son inherited more of his father's wealth than did his younger brothers and became head of the family after his father's death.

blasphemy—Any dishonoring of the name of God by slandering, cursing, or an act of irreverence.

blessed—To be favored with spiritual happiness. When "blessed" is applied to God, it is an exclamation of worship.

blind—Without sight. Not able to see.

body—In the Old Testament, "body" refers to the whole physical makeup of a person. In the New Testament, the word has added meanings. Jesus used bread as a symbol of his body. The church is often called the body of Christ.

bread—An important food made from wheat or barley flour, mixed with water, kneaded, and baked.

Bread of the Presence—Also called showbread. Twelve loaves of bread made of fine flour, arranged in two rows on a table in the Temple or sanctuary as an offering to God.

breastpiece—A decorated piece of material attached by golden rings to the ephod, a garment worn by the high priest in the sanctuary.

breastplate—A piece of armor made of solid metal, attached to, or worn over, a tunic to protect the chest, soldiers, and back of a soldier.

C

calf, golden—In the Old Testament, an image of a bull made of wood and covered with gold.

Canaan—The land God promised to the people of Israel. Canaan is also called "The Promised Land."

captivity—Being taken and kept imprisoned or enslaved by force, especially being taken from one's own country and made to live in another land. During the Babylonian captivity, the people of Judah were conquered by Nebuchadnezzar and carried off to Babylon.

caravan—A group of people, especially merchants with pack animals, traveling together, often through dangerous areas.

carpenter—A person who repairs or makes things out of wood.

census—A count of all people in a land.

centurion—The commanding officer of one hundred foot soldiers, part of a division in the Roman army.

chaff—The useless dry husks of grain that were blown away from the good seed in the process of winnowing. See also **winnow**.

chariot—A two-wheeled, horse-drawn vehicle used in war and for travel, especially by kings and officials.

cherub, cherubim—Winged, angelic creatures. There were images of two cherubim on the Ark of the Covenant.

children of God—The spiritual family of God.

Christ—Greek word meaning "the Anointed One," "the Messiah." A title given to the king expected by the Jews. It became a name or surname for Jesus.

Christian—A person who follows Jesus.

church—A fellowship of believers in Jesus Christ gathered together for the purpose of worship, prayer, instruction, and fellowship. "Church" also refers to the whole group of believers in Jesus Christ from every land and continent.

circumcision—The act of cutting off the foreskin of a baby boy. This act dedicated the child and was a sign of the covenant between God and the Israelites.

cistern—A lined pit dug in the earth for the storage of water.

citadel—A fortified building or stronghold within a city for the purpose of defense. See also **stronghold**.

city—In Old Testament times, a walled town.

cloak—An outer garment worn over a coat.

coat—A long tunic-like shirt with long sleeves worn as an undergarment.

colt—A young horse or donkey.

commandment—A law or order from someone in authority.

communion—The act of sharing. It is important in the covenant relationship between God and humanity. This relationship is remembered in the sacrament of the Lord's Supper, which is also called Communion. See also **covenant**.

confession—An act in the worship of God in which a person humbly admits sins and asks for God's forgiveness.

congregation—A gathering or assembly. A term used for all the Israelites living in the wilderness. The term is also used for the assembly of people before God for worship or judgment.

consecrate—See **dedicate**.

cornerstone—A stone at the corner of a building that holds two walls together. New Testament writers referred to Jesus as the cornerstone of the Christian life.

council—An assembly made up of people of authority.

covenant—An agreement or solemn promise binding people together in a firm relationship. "Covenant" was the word used for the special relationship between God and Israel. God was to be their God, and they were to be God's people. The early Christians in the New Testament thought of their relationships to one another and to Jesus as a covenant binding them together.

covet—To want something that belongs to someone else or to want more than one already has.

cross—A large beam set in the ground as a way to kill criminals. Often, a crossbar was attached to the beam to form a "T." Jesus was put to death on a cross, and this event is described in all four Gospels.

crown—A headdress often made of rich material and decorated with designs or jewels. There were also simple metal headbands that served as crowns.

crown of thorns—A circle of thorny briers made by Roman soldiers and pushed down on Jesus's head as part of their torture and mockery of him. They teased Jesus with this make-believe crown.

crucifixion—Nailing or tying a person to a cross or sometimes to a tree as a means of death.

cubit—A unit of measurement based on the length from the elbow to the tip of the middle finger—about eighteen inches.

curtain of the Temple—See **veil of the Temple**.

D

Day of Judgment—See **Day of the Lord**.

Day of the Lord—The day when God will be fully revealed and will judge all the people. This day is also called Day of Judgment, Day of God, and the Day.

deacon—Meaning "servant, attendant, minister." An officer in the early Christian church who was responsible for collecting and distributing the offerings of money or goods and for caring for the sick, needy, and elderly.

Dead Sea—A lake fed by the Jordan River. This lake is over 1,200 feet below sea level and has the highest percentage of salt in any water in the world.

debt—Something owed by one person to another.

decree—Something a king would declare or proclaim. A decree was usually written down and then read aloud to the people to let them know what they were supposed to do.

dedicate—To set apart an offering, a building, or a person for some sacred purpose.

defile—To make people, foods, places, or objects unclean in a religious sense. Priests in the Old Testament gave instructions on how to clean whatever had been defiled. Jesus used the word defile in a deeper sense to mean that people's words, thoughts, and actions might be unclean and might defile them in the sight of God.

demon—In the Old Testament, a nameless god or spirit that might be friendly or unfriendly. In the New Testament, "demon" refers only to evil spirits who are the cause of all kinds of misfortunes.

denarius—An ancient Roman silver coin, about the size of a dime. A person would usually receive one denarius for one day of work.

devil—A term used when speaking of evil as if it were a person. One who leads people to sin and disturbs their relationship with God. In the New Testament, it often refers to Satan. See also **Satan**.

devoted—Things forbidden for common use. Set apart for God.

devout—Being free from wrong or sin. Devoted to God.

disciple—A student or learner. One who accepts and follows a certain teaching or teacher. In the Bible, the term most often means those who follow Jesus. See also **apostle**.

discipline—In the Bible this word refers to training and instruction. It also means correction and punishment.

dispersion—A word used for the settlement of the Jewish people away from their own land after the time of the Assyrian and Babylonian exiles.

dominion—To have power over. Authority. Rule. The word is used to mean the supreme rule of God, humanity's rule over nature, or power gained by conquest.

door, doorkeeper—An entrance and one who watches or guards it.

Also indicates the authors of the New Testament Gospels.

evil—Sinful. Wicked. Something that causes harm.

Exile, The—The time in biblical history when the Babylonians conquered the city of Jerusalem and carried many of the Jews away to live in Babylonia.

Exodus, The—Means "a going out." Refers to the people "going out" from Egypt under the leadership of Moses. The deliverance of the people from slavery and the journey to the land of Canaan.

E

earth—In Bible times, dry land.

Eden—The name given for the garden where Adam and Eve lived.

edict—A public proclamation or ruling that was written, sealed with the king's ring, and read aloud before all the people.

Egypt—A land on the southern coast of the Mediterranean Sea in northwest Africa. Egyptians had many contacts with the Israelites, sometimes friendly and sometimes not. It was from Egypt that Moses led the Israelites into the land of Canaan.

elder—The leader of a family, tribe, synagogue, or community.

ephod—The upper garment of plain linen worn by a priest. The high priest wore a more elaborate ephod embroidered in colors of gold, blue, crimson, and purple.

epistle—A letter, especially the letters included the New Testament. See also **letter**.

eternal life—Life with God that is not destroyed by death. Eternal life can begin here and now.

evangelist—"One who announces good news." A title of early Christian missionaries and preachers of the gospel.

F

faith—Believing in and trusting in God. Faith is the confident response people make to God's love and care.

family—A group of people related to each other by kinship or marriage.

famine—A time when there is not enough food.

fast—To go without food and water for a period of time for a religious reason.

fear—Panic, worry, or dread. "Fear of God" and "fear of the Lord" mean having awe, respect, love, trust, and faith.

feast—A religious celebration to remember an event from the past and/or to thank and honor God. Jewish feasts include the Feast of Booths, Feast of Hanukkah, Feast of Weeks (or Feast of Pentecost), Feast of Passover, and Feast of Unleavened Bread.

fellowship—Friendship. Communion. See also **communion**.

fig—A sweet fruit that grows on trees. An important food in Bible times.

first-born—The first child born to a family. See also **birthright**.

first fruits—The sacrificial offering of giving the first and best from the yearly crop of vegetables, grain, and animals to God.

flask—A small, bottle-like container for oil, water, perfume, or ointment. In ancient times, flasks were made of pottery or alabaster; later they were made of glass.

flog—To whip.

footstool—The footrest for a king's throne or steps leading to the throne.

forgiveness—The pardoning of an offender, the giving up of a claim to a debt, or the release from an obligation. Forgiveness is God's gracious taking away of the barriers that separate people from God.

fortress—See **stronghold**.

foundation—The base on which a structure is built.

fountain—A spring of water flowing from an opening in a hillside or valley. An important source of water in Bible times.

fragrant—Having a sweet or pleasant odor. See also **odor**.

frankincense—A fragrant gum taken from tree bark that was an important ingredient in incense. One of the gifts the wise men brought to Jesus. See also **incense**.

G

Galilee—A small region east of the Mediterranean Sea. Almost all of Jesus's life took place within the borders of this tiny region.

Galilee, Sea of—A lake that empties into the Jordan River. Many people and places associated with Jesus came from this area.

gall—The juice of a bitter herb. "Gall" is also used as a symbol to describe a feeling of bitterness.

gate—An opening in the wall of a city. There were usually an outer gate and an inner gate built at angles to the wall, with a lookout tower. Near the gate was the center of interest in the town, and most business was carried

on there. Just inside the gate was the busy marketplace.

genealogy—A list of names that tells the family history of a person. A genealogy can also show the relationships of families, clans, tribes, or nations.

Gentile—In the New Testament, a word for a person who was not a Jew. In the plural it meant "nations" in general. See also **Jew**.

girdle—A piece of clothing like a belt or a sash. People used girdles to hold in their long, flowing robes. They also used girdles to carry money pouches and weapons. Messengers and travelers who wanted to move more easily would bring their robes through their legs toward the front and tuck it into their girdle. This was called "girding up the loins."

gleaning—The practice of picking up what had been left behind in the fields after harvesting. The law said that the poor must be allowed to glean.

glory—Honor and praise. The word describes the presence of God. People glorify, or magnify, God by praising and honoring God.

God (names of)—For the Israelites, every person's name represented who he or she was inside. It was the same for the name of God. This name expressed power and holiness. The fact that God had revealed this name to the Israelites was a sign of God's special care for them. Other ways of referring to God are: Lord, the Rock, Father, Savior, King, Judge, Shepherd, Creator, Redeemer, Maker, Almighty, and such descriptive expressions as the Living God, the Everlasting God, the First and the Last, the Ancient of Days, the God of our Fathers, the God of Abraham.

God (nature of)—To the Israelites, God was the living God who was the LORD, the ruler of their lives. The Old Testament reports the historical events of the Israelites as the acts of God. The

Israelites lived out their special history as the people with whom God had made a covenant. In the New Testament, God was revealed in Jesus Christ, and humanity's relationship with God was made richer because it could be experienced in a very personal way. It can be compared to a relationship with an earthly parent or beloved friend.

goldsmith—A person who works with and makes things out of gold.

gospel—The Good News about Jesus Christ: that his birth, life, death, and resurrection have accomplished salvation. Gospel is also the name given to each of the first four books of the New Testament.

governor—A ruler appointed by a king to govern a specific territory or province.

grace—God's great love for humanity that cannot be earned but is offered as a free gift. Grace makes it possible for people to think, act, and speak according to God's will.

graven image—An image carved from stone, metal, or wood. These idols were used in ancient times to represent gods.

H

Hades—The New Testament name for the place of the dead.

Hallelujah—A Hebrew word meaning "praise the Lord."

hallow—To make holy, to set apart, to treat with reverence.

handbreadth—A measure based on the width of the hand at the base of the fingers, about three inches.

harp—A stringed musical instrument small enough to be carried.

harvest—The gathering of ripe crops.

heaven—This word is used in two ways in the Bible. The first and most important meaning is the place where God lives. It is also used to refer to the sky.

Hebrew—The ancient language of the Jews. Most of the Old Testament books were written in Hebrew. "Hebrew" also refers to the people descended from Abraham and Sarah.

hell—The New Testament name for the place under the earth for the punishment of the dead.

herald—An officer making public proclamations for the nation or ruler, or one who bears ceremonial messages between countries or between royal persons.

heritage—Possessions passed down from one generation to another.

high place—A religious place of sacrifice, worship, and festival.

high priest—Chief of the priests in the Temple at Jerusalem. He acted as the representative of the people before God.

highway—A road built up higher than the land on either side.

hireling—A servant or other worker paid wages.

holiness—More than any other word, "holiness" suggests the nature of God. Includes some sense of a tremendous and mysterious energy that is above and beyond humanity.

holy—Sacred. Set apart for God. See also **sacred**.

Holy of Holies—The innermost room of the Temple, the place of the presence of God. The high priest entered the Holy of Holies only on the Day of Atonement. See also **Atonement, Day of** and **high priest**.

Holy One—In the Old Testament, a name for God that emphasizes that God is absolute holiness and the source of holiness in all other things. In the New Testament, "Holy One" refers to the Messiah, the one who would appear on earth among people and who would be holy as God is holy. See also **holy** and **Messiah**.

Holy Place—In the Tabernacle, the courts with the inner and outer rooms. In the Temple, the rooms and the surrounding courts.

Holy Spirit—The mysterious power of God. Sometimes called the Spirit or the Spirit of the Lord.

homer—An ancient measure for dry materials. It was probably the load that a donkey could carry.

Hosanna—A term meaning, "Save us, we ask you." At Jesus's triumphal entry into Jerusalem, the people waved palm branches and sang, "Hosanna!"

hospitality—Welcoming strangers or guests as if they were family members, giving them food, shelter, protection, and much more.

host, host of heaven—As a military word, "a body of men organized for war." In the Bible, God is often called "God of hosts." The "host of heaven" includes the sun, moon, stars, and particularly angels. These forces are at God's command to carry out God's purpose for the world.

household of God—A group of believers or the members of the church.

hymn—A song of praise.

hypocrisy, hypocrite—A person who pretends to be something he or she is not. From a Greek word meaning the act of playing a part.

I

idol, idolatry—An image of a god made of wood, stone, or metal. It may also be any other symbol of the supernatural that is an object of worship. Idolatry is worshipping an idol.

incense—A mixture of gums and spices made into a powder and burned so that the smell of the smoke would rise in the air as an offering to God or to the "gods."

inheritance—A possession handed down from the past. The word refers to material possessions, such as land, cattle and wealth. In the New Testament the word more often refers to spiritual gifts from God, such as eternal life or the kingdom of God.

iniquity—Another word for sin. Any action that separates people from God or destroys a person's relationship with another person.

inn—A shelter for travelers and their animals.

iron—A type of very strong metal. "Iron" is used in the Bible as a symbol for hardness, strength, and harshness.

ironsmith—One who works with, and makes things out of, iron.

Israel, Israelites—A name given to Jacob after his vision of God. The descendants of Jacob are called Israelites. Israel was the name of the kingdom under Saul, David, and Solomon. When the kingdom split into two parts, the northern part continued to be called Israel. It came to an end in 722 BC. The name "Israel" is used not only for the land, but also for the people as a whole in their exodus from Egypt, their desert wanderings, and their entrance into Canaan. See also **Judah**.

ivory—A white bonelike substance that makes up the tusks of elephants and walruses. In Bible times, people carved ivory to make decorations for thrones and houses. Ivory was a sign of great wealth.

J

jealousy—In the Bible this word has two meanings. "Jealousy" can mean strong hatred and suspicion that grows out of envy and greed. "Jealousy" can also mean the single-minded devotion of humanity to God. God is also said to be jealous, and this means that God demands complete obedience and loyalty from God's people.

Jerusalem—The capital city under King David, who brought the Ark of the Covenant to the city and made it the religious center of the Israelites. David's son Solomon built the Temple there, and Jerusalem became a holy city. When the kingdom was divided, Jerusalem was the capital of the southern kingdom, Judah. The city was finally conquered and burned by Nebuchadnezzar, and its important leaders were taken to Babylon. The city of Jerusalem is also called Salem, Zion, city of David, and Jebus.

Jesus Christ—The central person in the New Testament. Both God and human, Jesus is the one in whom the whole of Old Testament history takes on a new and deeper meaning. Jesus was the personal name of one whose title is "the Christ," from which the Christian religion gets its name. The name Jesus in the original Hebrew is a form of the name Joshua meaning, "God saves." See also **Christ**.

Jew—A word that refers to members of the southern kingdom of Judah who were in Babylon during the time of exile. Later, it was used to refer to people who were not Gentiles and who lived in the province of Judah. Any person who worships God and follows Judaism. See also **Gentile**.

Jubilee, Year of—The "year of liberty." Every fiftieth year was set by law as the time when all slaves were to be released and all property was to be returned to its original owners.

Judah—The fourth son of Jacob and leader of the tribe descended from him that took his name. The tribes and territory of Judah became the southern kingdom of Judah after the death of King Solomon. The kingdom of Judah came to an end in 586 BC.

judge—A military leader who delivered the Israelites from their enemies. Judges ruled Israel before the days of the kings. "Judge" is also used as a title for God, who is the Judge of all the earth, and for Jesus, who set a new standard of judgment.

Judaism—The belief and total way of life of the Jewish community.

Justice—Fairness. Righteousness. See also **righteousness**.

justify—The action of God that forgives people and restores them to goodness and righteousness.

K

king—A male ruler who has power over a nation.

kingdom of God, of heaven—The rule or reign of God. A kingdom that is not only in the world that we know, but includes all places and all times. A kingdom designed to carry out the purposes of God.

knead—To pound or press dough with the hands until it forms a well-mixed mass.

L

lamb—A young sheep. In Old Testament times, the lamb was used for food and for sacrifices in the Temple. In the New Testament, Jesus is called the "Lamb of God."

lamentation—An expression of sorrow or grief. See also **mourn**.

lamp—A pottery saucer filled with olive oil that had a wick of twisted threads resting on the edge or held in a spout.

lampstand—A device used for raising a lamp high so that its light will cover a large area.

landmark—A mark showing the boundaries of an area of land. In Bible times, stones were piled to mark the boundaries between the fields of two neighbors. They also marked districts and nations.

Last Supper—The final meal Jesus ate with his disciples on the night before his death.

laver—A large metal basin or bowl for water in the Tabernacle or Temple.

law—Rules for living together in community. The Old Testament law was based on a covenant, or agreement, between God and the Israelites. The first five books of the Old Testament contain most of the laws, including the Ten Commandments. Jesus taught that the most important law is the law of love.

lawyer—In New Testament times, one who knew and interpreted the law, especially the law of Moses.

leather—Animal skins prepared for use as clothes, shoes, tent coverings, bottles for water or wine, and writing materials.

leaven—Any substance, such as yeast, that was added to bread dough to make it rise. During the Passover festival each year, Jews eat bread that has been made without leaven to remind them of the exodus from Egypt. See also **Exodus** and **Passover**.

legion—The main unit of the Roman army. In the New Testament, the word is used to refer to a large number or group.

leprosy—A serious skin disease. In Bible times, people who had leprosy were thought to be unclean and had to live apart from others.

letter—A written message sent to a person or people at a distance. Many of the books in the New Testament were written in the form of letters.

leviathan—In the Old Testament, the name of a dragon, a symbol of disorder and evil, subdued by God at the time of creation. The name is also used to refer to any sea monster.

liberty—Freedom from bondage, slavery, or the control of another.

lily—A general term for a variety of springtime flowers that grew in Bible lands.

locust—A flying grasshopper-like insect. Locusts travel in large groups and can destroy crops.

Lord—A title for anyone who commands respect or has authority over others. "Lord" is a title of honor and majesty for God and also for Jesus.

Lord's Prayer—The title given to the prayer Jesus taught his disciples. This prayer is recorded in Matthew 6:9–13 and Luke 11:2–4.

Lord's Supper—A sacrament, or sacred observance, that continues the fellowship Jesus began with his disciples at the Last Supper. Also called Holy Communion or Eucharist. This meal is a time when Christians remember Jesus Christ. See also **Communion** and **Last Supper**.

lots—Small stones or cubes used to make choices. Casting lots (throwing them on the ground) is similar to how we throw dice today.

love—The deep personal attachment that includes loyalty, goodwill, devotion, and responsibility. People are the object of God's love; humanity's love for God is the response people make to God's love.

lute—A stringed instrument made of gut strings on a wooden frame.

lyre—A stringed instrument similar to a harp.

M

Magi—See **wise men**.

magic, magician—In ancient times, power that was believed to be supernatural.

magistrate—A judge or governing official in the Roman provinces.

magnify—See **glory**.

manger—A box made of stones or hollowed out of rock, used for feeding cattle. The first bed of the baby Jesus was a manger.

manna—The substance the Israelites gathered and ate for part of their food during the long journey through the wilderness. The Hebrew word *manna* means "What is it?".

mantle—A loose, sleeveless coat.

meal—A course type of flour ground from whole kernels of wheat or barley.

meekness—Complete dependence upon God rather than on oneself. The opposite of pride. The quality of a person with a gentle and quiet spirit of thoughtful courtesy in dealing with others.

mercy seat—A slab of gold with a cherub at each end on top of the Ark of the Covenant. It was reverenced as God's throne, the symbol of God's presence in the Temple.

Messiah—Meaning "anointed one." The Israelites looked forward to the coming of an ideal king who they believed God would send to restore a kingdom to Israel. Some who recognized Jesus as the long-awaited king gave him the title of Messiah.

midwife—A woman skilled in helping during childbirth.

mill, millstones—Hard, rough stones used to grind grain to make flour. People would hold one stone in their hand and push it back and forth against another, crushing the grain between them. Because they were heavy and strong, millstones could also be used as weapons.

minister—As a noun it means "one who serves." In the Old Testament, the word was used most often as a verb meaning "to serve," especially to serve God in worship and carrying out sacrifices. In the New Testament, Jesus showed by his own life the importance of humble service.

miracle—Any event in which a person sees the supernatural power of God at work. Other words used in the Bible to mean "miracle" are "signs," "wonders," and "mighty acts."

molten image—A representation of a god made from melted metal.

money—Something accepted as payment for goods.

money-changers—People who carried on many of the duties of a modern banker. One important duty was exchanging coins of one country or province for those of another. At Passover time money-changers set up their tables in the Temple courts. On one of his visits to the Temple, Jesus drove out the money-changers.

mortar—A building material, usually clay mixed with straw, used while damp and soft to bind bricks or stones together. Also, a bowl in which grain, herbs, spices, and dyes were crushed with a tool called a pestle.

Most Holy Place—The innermost room of the Tabernacle and Temple in which the Ark of the Covenant was placed.

mourning—An expression of grief or sadness.

mustard seed—The seed from a mustard plant. This seed is known for being tiny in size.

myrrh—A sweet-smelling, gumlike substance made from certain plants and trees. An important ingredient in the sacred anointing oil and in perfumes. Myrrh mixed with wine was given to relieve pain.

mystery—A hidden truth. In the New Testament, the word refers to the plan and purpose of God hidden from all except those who see it revealed in the life and ministry of Jesus.

myth—A story told to explain an event or happening that is not understood or to explain the beginning of a custom or practice that has been forgotten.

N

name—The title by which a person is known. In the Bible, a person's name was an expression of his or her character or personality. When a name was changed, it meant a change in character or a change in relationship with God.

nard—An expensive, fragrant ointment prepared from the roots and stems of the spikenard plant. The ointment was used to anoint the head. See also **anoint**.

nations—The whole of humanity divided into kinship groups, not into countries or states as we know them today. The nation of Israel made a covenant with God to be God's people. See also **covenant** and **Israel**.

nave—The main room of the Temple between the vestibule and the inner room.

Nazareth—The village where Jesus lived as a child and where he grew to adulthood.

Nazirite—A person who took a vow of dedication to serve God. Nazirites promised not to cut their hair, drink wine, or have anything to do with dead bodies. Samson, Samuel, and John the Baptist were all Nazirites.

nettle—A fast-growing wild plant with thorns that sting when touched. Nettles grow quickly in fields that are not taken care of.

nets—Mesh traps woven of twine or cord and used for catching fish, birds, and animals.

new moon—The beginning of the month. It was observed as a holy day of rejoicing, special feasting, and sacrifices.

O

oath—A promise made and often accompanied by formal words and actions. People often called upon God as a witness to an oath. Breaking an oath was a serious matter.

obeisance—In the Old Testament the word means "to bow down" or "to touch one's face to the ground" as a sign of submission or an act of worship or honor.

odor—Scent or fragrance. During worship in Old Testament times, the sacrifices and offerings were burned so that the smoke could rise as a pleasant odor before God. In the New Testament, one's acts of love are spoken of as a fragrant offering to God in the name of Christ.

offering—A gift given to God as an act of worship.

officer—In Bible times, a servant or minister of the king, the army, or the Temple.

oil—A liquid substance used during anointing. People often made oil by pressing olives, the fruit of the olive tree. See also **anoint** and **olive tree**.

olive tree—An evergreen tree with fruit good for eating and rich in oil. The olive branch is a symbol of peace and well-being.

Omega—See **Alpha and Omega**.

omer—A measure for dry substances equal to a little more than two quarts.

oracle—A speech or pronouncement given by an inspired prophet, king, or priest as a message from God. The prophets often used the words, "Thus says the Lord."

ordinance—A law or rule for governing social and religious customs. The word has the same meaning as "commandment." See also **commandment**.

oven—In Biblical times, an outdoor baking device. It was a large round jar of burnt clay with the fire built on pebbles at the bottom. Flat cakes of dough were stuck against the hot inner wall or laid on the pebbles after the fire was down. The fuel was usually dried grass or bushes.

overlay—In Old Testament times, a layer of metal laid over various objects.

overseer—One who supervise a work gang, a household, or a group performing some special task.

ox goad—A pointed stick used for driving or guiding cattle, especially oxen when plowing.

P

Palestine—In today's usage, the name for the land occupied by the twelve tribes of Israel during Old Testament times. The common Hebrew name for the land was Canaan. See also **Canaan**.

palm—A tall, thin tree with a group of branches at the top. People ate its fruit, called dates, and they wove mats from its leaves. They often used the palm tree as a symbol for righteousness.

papyrus—A tall, reed plant that grows in watery places. In ancient times, people used papyrus to make paper, baskets, and small boats. Moses's mother put him in a basket made of papyrus to keep him safe.

parable—A short story that teaches an important lesson. Jesus used parables to teach about God and God's kingdom in ways that his listeners could understand.

paradise—The New Testament name for the place of the righteous after death.

parapet—A railing or low wall built around the edge of a roof to prevent people from falling off.

parchment—A writing material made from the skins of sheep or goats. Parchment replaced papyrus because it could last longer.

Paschal Lamb—The lamb sacrificed at the Passover festival. See also **Passover, the**.

Passion, the—A term used for the suffering and death of Jesus. It refers to the last days of Jesus's life and includes such events as the Last Supper, the agony in Gethsemane, the arrest, trial, crucifixion, death, and burial.

Passover, the—The first of three great religious festivals in the Jewish year. The Passover and Feast of Unleavened Bread were celebrated in the spring to mark the deliverance of the Israelites from Egyptian slavery. See also **feast** and **unleavened**.

pastor—Meaning "shepherd." In the New Testament, a leader in the early church whose work was closely connected with teaching.

penny—A Roman coin of Old Testament times, probably equal to about one fourth of a cent.

Pentecost—The Greek term for the Jewish Feast of Weeks held fifty days after Passover. It marked the beginning of the offering of first fruits of the harvest. It was on the day of Pentecost that the Holy Spirit came upon Jesus's disciples gathered in Jerusalem after he ascended. See also **ascension**, **feast**, and **Passover**.

people of God—One of the many Old Testament expressions that refer to the special covenant relationship between God and the people of Israel. The New Testament meaning identifies "people of God" with the church grounded upon faith in Jesus Christ. See also **covenant** and **Israel**.

perdition—A word that refers to death and destruction.

perfume—Sweet-smelling substances used in cosmetics, in preparing the dead for burial, in scenting furniture and clothing, and in incense for worship.

persecute—To cause someone to suffer because of his or her beliefs, especially religious beliefs.

pestilence—A disease that spreads quickly from person to person.

Pharaoh—A title given to the king of Egypt.

Pharisees—Jewish religious leaders committed to following the laws set down in the Torah (the first five books of what we call the Old Testament).

phylacteries—Small leather boxes that Jewish men tie to their foreheads and arms. The head phylactery has four small parts that contains copies of Exodus 13:1–6 and Deuteronomy 6:4–9; 11:13–21.

pillar—Rough, uncut stone with a round top set up as a monument to help people remember an important event or as an object of worship. A pillar is also a support column for a roof.

plague—A destructive event, such as a disease, that spreads quickly, causes great suffering, and kills many people.

plow, plowshare—A tool used for breaking up the ground.

potsherd—A piece of broken pottery. A symbol of dryness and worthlessness.

potter—A person who makes things out of clay. A potter often uses a wheel to shape clay into bowls, jars, and plates.

praetorium—In the New Testament, the official residence or palace of a Roman governor.

prayer—Any attempt to communicate with God. Prayer may be spoken or silent. It may include praise, confession, thanksgiving, repentance, or meditation on behalf of oneself or another person.

priest—One who took care of the Temple, taught the law, and took part in the sacrifices. See also **high priest**, **Temple**, and **law**.

prince—A ruler, such as a king, military officer, leader of a tribe or of the Temple, or any man of noble birth.

profane—To treat a holy person, place, or institution as if it were not holy. To make unclean or defile a name. See also **defile**.

prophecy—A message from God.

prophesy—To give a message from God.

prophet—A spokesperson for God. One who was inspired to speak God's message of purpose and judgment to the people. See also **prophecy** and **prophesy**.

proselyte—In the New Testament, a person who was converted to Judaism, accepting all its customs and requirements.

province—A division of an empire ruled by an appointed official.

pruning hook—A curved blade attached to a handle, used for removing surplus twigs and trimming vines.

psalms—Poems, prayers, and hymns for use in public and private worship. Psalms tell of joy and sorrow, sin and suffering, evil and righteousness.

Promised Land, the—See **Canaan**.

purify—To make clean.

Purim—A two-day Jewish festival celebrating the deliverance of the Jews in Persia from Haman's plot to kill them. The story is told in the book of Esther.

Q

quail—A reddish-brown bird used in Bible times for food. The Israelites ate quail on their journey from Egypt to Canaan.

quiver—A container for carrying arrows.

R

Rabbi, Rabboni—Hebrew word meaning "master." A title of respect for a teacher.

rampart—The outer defense around a city that consists of a broad, sloping embankment usually made of earth.

raven—A large, crowlike bird that travels in flocks and scavenges for food.

reap—To harvest grain. See also **sow**.

reconcile, reconciliation—To bring agreement. The restoration of harmony and love between people and God.

redeem, redeemer, redemption—Redeem means to reclaim, to get back, or to buy back. A redeemer is the person who performs these acts. Redemption is the act of liberating or getting back.

reed—The flowering stem of several tall grasses that grow in marshy places. Reeds are sometimes called rushes. People in Bible times used reeds to make many things, including measuring rods, writing pens, baskets and mats.

refine, refining—To strain or filter out impurities from metals by melting them in large containers in a hot furnace. The act of purifying. "Refine" is used as a figure of speech to describe the way God cleanses or purifies God's people. See also **purify**.

refuge—A place of escape, a stronghold. The word is used to describe God's protection. See also **stronghold**.

remnant—That part of a community that is left after a disaster and is responsible for the future of the community. The word is used specifically to refer to those Jews who returned to Jerusalem after the Exile. See also **Exile, the**.

renewal—The act of reforming completely, being made new spiritually.

repent, repentance—Turning away from sin and back to God.

resurrection—Coming back to life after being dead. Resurrection is the central truth of the Christian gospel. It is the reality that Jesus was alive after the Crucifixion. This was the event the disciples preached to the world to show that Jesus was the Christ, the Son of God.

revelation—Making known the nature and will of God. In the Bible, God is represented as becoming known by God's actions in history and especially in Jesus Christ. The Bible is a record of this revelation and also one of the ways in which God becomes known to humans.

righteous, righteousness—Being free from sin and doing what is right. Having a right relationship with God.

rod—A staff. A stick cut from a branch of a tree. Shepherds and travelers who journeyed by foot used staffs. Rods were also used as measuring sticks and as poles for carrying things.

Rome—The capital of the world in New Testament times.

S

sabbath—From a word meaning "to cease" or "to be at an end." The Ten Commandments provided that the last day of the seven-day week be a day set aside to rest and to worship God.

sackcloth—Rough cloth made of animal hair. People wore sackcloth as a sign of mourning or repentance. See also **mourn**. See also **repent**.

sacrifice—Something presented as a gift, or offering, to God. In the Old Testament, a sacrifice involved the killing, burning, and sometimes eating of an animal at the altar. A person could make an offering of grain, flour, fruit, or vegetables. Such things were presented with symbolic gestures such as waving, lifting up, or burning. See also **offering**.

sacred—Holy; set apart for God. See also **holy**.

sacrilege—The abuse or defiling of something sacred or holy.

Sadducees—Jewish religious leaders who did not believe in the resurrection of the dead.

saint—Meaning "holy" or "set apart" for God's use. In the Old Testament, the word is used to describe Israel as God's holy people. In the New Testament, the word is used for members of the Christian church. The word was particularly associated with the love Christians showed to one another.

salvation—The saving, redeeming, or delivering of something. Salvation is the central theme of the whole Bible. See also **Savior**.

sanctify, sanctification—To set apart something so that it might belong to God. To be made clean or acceptable to God.

sanctuary—The holy place set apart for the worship of God by the people.

Sanhedrin—The supreme Jewish council in Jerusalem following the Exile. It consisted of seventy-one members chosen from the priests, scribes, Sadducees, and Pharisees. The Sanhedrin made laws for the Jews and judged those who broke the laws. See also **Exile, Pharisees, priest, Sadducees,** and **scribe**.

sandals—Flat soles of leather or wood tied to the feet with strips of leather. Sandals were the usual shoes of Bible times.

Satan—The chief of the devils, the enemy of God.

satrap—A governor of a province in the Persian Empire.

Savior—One who saves. Savior is a name for Jesus. See also **salvation**.

scepter—A rod or staff carried by a king or queen as a sign of authority and power. The word is also used as a figure of speech to mean "rule" or "ruler."

scribe—Originally a person who could write. Old Testament scribes studied, interpreted, and taught the Jewish law. They came from the families of priests and were probably responsible for gathering together and writing down many of the sacred writings that make up the Old Testament we have today. New Testament scribes were a professional group that defended and taught the law. They were important in the Sanhedrin. Some were members of the Pharisees. See also **Pharisees** and **Sanhedrin**.

Scripture—As it is used in the New Testament, "scripture" refers to the sacred writings of the Jews, or what we call the Old Testament. Today, the Christian Bible, which contains the Old Testament and the New Testament, is often called "the Scriptures." "Scripture" is sometimes used to refer to a verse or passage from the Bible.

scroll—Meaning "book." A roll of papyrus or parchment made by fastening the sheets together and rolling them around a rod. Writing was done in columns, and the scroll was rolled from right to left as it was read. See also **papyrus**.

seal—Bone, metal, stone, or precious gems that had been carved with a design. This design was pressed into clay or wax to serve as a person's signature. Seals were used to close letters or official documents.

seer—One who sees. In the Old Testament, a seer was usually a person who had visions and could predict the future. Prophets were sometimes called seers in everyday language.

selah—A word of uncertain meaning. Probably a musical direction to choirs or musicians.

seraphim—Six-winged heavenly beings seen by the prophet Isaiah in a vision. Like the cherubim, they are associated with the glory of God.

servant of the Lord, the—One who serves God, as a devoted slave or servant works for a master. Israel, the nation, was often called the servant of the Lord. The book of Isaiah tells of a suffering servant whose labor costs him pain and humiliation. The servant willingly accepts the suffering and through it accomplishes salvation. Christians have recognized in this description the likeness of Jesus Christ.

shades—In the Old Testament, a word that refers to the ghosts, or spirits, of the dead.

sheath—the case or covering for a sword or bow.

shepherd—One who takes care of sheep. The shepherd's care of sheep is often used as a figure of speech to show God's love, mercy, and compassion for God's people.

shekel—A coin, or the weight of a coin, used as money.

Sheol—The Old Testament name for the place under the earth where the spirits of the dead lived.

shroud—A linen sheet wrapped around a dead body to prepare it for burial.

sickle—A tool for reaping grain. See also **reap**.

siege—A military blockade in which attackers tried to cut off a city's water and food supply and weaken the city walls by tunneling under them or smashing them with battering rams. A method of warfare used to capture cities or land. See also **battering ram**.

sieve—A tool for sifting or cleaning grain after it has been winnowed. In the Old Testament the word was often used as a figure of speech to refer to the Day of Judgment, when God would "sift the nations." See also **Day of Judgment** and **winnow**.

signs and wonders—Refer to the acts of God throughout history. In the Old Testament, the phrase is mostly connected to the events surrounding the exodus from Egypt. In the New Testament, the phrase refers to the miracles of Jesus Christ and the works of the apostles, which revealed God's will and purpose. See also **apostle**, **Exodus**, and **miracle**.

silversmith—One who works with silver.

sin—Any action that separates people from God or destroys relationships between people. Sin is also called an **iniquity**, **transgression**, or **trespass**.

slavery—The ownership of one person by another. In Bible times, slavery was a common practice.

sling—A weapon for hurling small stones or clay pellets. A sling was made of two pieces of leather or cloth joined to a pouch-shaped piece of leather that held a stone. One end was tied to the wrist and the other end was held with the hand. The stone was swung over the head in a circle and then let go.

slothful—Lazy.

sluggard—One who is lazy or idle.

snare—A device used to catch birds and animals.

sojourner—A person living for a while in an unfamiliar community among unfamiliar people. The Israelites had laws that protected the rights of sojourners.

Son of God—In the Old Testament, a phrase used to refer to divine beings, angels, or godlike persons. Israel was called God's son because God had chosen the nation to be God's people. In the New Testament, the term refers to Jesus as the special or unique Son of God. The plural "sons (or children) of God" refers to followers of Jesus.

Son of Man—In the Old Testament, a word for a human being. In the New Testament, a title for Jesus.

soothsayer—One who predicts future events by observing signs.

sorcery—The use of power that was supposedly gained through the use of charms, magic, or divination. The Israelites were not supposed to practice sorcery.

soul—Life, the self, or person. In biblical use the soul was not considered to be separate from the body.

sow—To plant seeds. See also **reap**.

span—A measure based on the distance between the end of the thumb and the little finger when the hand is spread. "Span" sometimes refers to length of life.

sparrow—A perching, seed-eating bird that did not have much value in Bible times.

spice—The sweet-smelling leaves, roots, and gums of certain vegetables and herbs that were used in cosmetics, oil, incense, perfume, and preparing a body for burial. In Bible times spices were not generally used for cooking as they are today.

spirit—A term applied to God, gods, bodiless beings, and to the divine element in humans. It was sometimes used to indicate God's power in humans. The phrase "the Spirit of God" refers to God's activity and God's power in the world.

spoil—Loot or plunder taken as a right of conquest. In Bible times, warfare involved the right to possess anything that belonged to the conquered enemy.

staff—A long pole used by shepherd and travelers for climbing and defense. See **rod**.

steadfastness—Patient endurance.

steward—An official responsible for the affairs of a large household. In the New Testament, Christians were spoken of as stewards of God's affairs. Their stewardship involved the use of time, talents, possessions, and themselves on behalf of God.

stiff-necked—A word used to mean rebellious, stubborn, or unteachable.

stone—To kill someone by throwing rocks.

stronghold—A fortress for refuge or defense against military attacks. The word is also used as a figure. See also **refuge**.

swaddling—Wrapping a newborn baby in a square of cloth.

synagogue—A place of assembly for worship used by Jewish communities.

T

Tabernacle—A portable sanctuary for the worship of God carried by the Israelites during their wilderness journey from Egypt to Canaan. The Ark of the Covenant was kept in it, and for the Israelites it was a symbol of the presence of God. The Tabernacle was also called the "tent of meeting." See also **Ark of the Covenant, Canaan, Egypt, Exile,** and **Israel**.

tablet—A writing surface made from stone, wood, metal, wax, or clay.

talent—A unit of weight used for payment.

tanner, tanning—One who prepares leather from the skins of animals. Tanning is the process of tanning skins.

tax—Payment that people make to support the government. The tax in Bible times was paid in money, treasure, farm products, hours of labor, and other means.

tax collector—An official who collects and keeps accounts of taxes.

teacher—Anyone who instructs.

Temple—The great sacred building in Jerusalem where the Jewish people gathered to worship God. It was also called the house of the Lord, or the house of God.

Ten Commandments—Laws that summarize the covenant between God and God's people, making clear the people's duty to God and to others. The Ten Commandments are found in Exodus 20:1–17.

Tent of Meeting—Another name for the Tabernacle. See **Tabernacle**.

tentmaker—One who makes tents.

testimony—Evidence given by a witness to the action and demands of God.

tetrarch—The title for a ruler of a part of a Roman province.

thistles, thorns—Wild plants with sharp spines on their stems and leaves.

threshing, threshing floor—The process of separating the kernels of grain from the straw. The stalks of grain were beaten with a stick or trampled by oxen on the threshing floor.

throne—The ceremonial chair or seat of someone in authority.

Thummim—See **Urim**.

timbrel—A musical instrument like a tambourine.

tithe—A tenth part. In Bible times people acknowledged God's ownership of the land by giving one-tenth of the produce to God. Jesus criticized people who tithed only material possessions but did not practice justice or show love to others.

tomb—A cave cut into the rock of a hillside and used as a burial place for the dead.

tongues, gift of—Also referred to as "speaking in tongues." An experience in which a person considered possessed by the Holy Spirit utters sounds that often cannot be understood.

tower—A high, narrow structure generally higher than things around it. Built of brick or stone, towers served as places of refuge or defense against military attack.

transgression—See **sin**.

trap—A device used to catch birds and animals.

trespass—See **sin**.

tribe—A group of clans or families held together by bonds of blood and kinship. The people of Israel consisted of twelve tribes who were the descendants of Jacob. The names of the tribes were also given to the land the people lived on.

tribulation—Suffering, distress, and affliction.

tribunal—Also called judgment seat. The official place from which the Roman governor heard and judged cases brought before him.

tribune—A Roman military officer in charge of an army division.

tribute—Another word for tax. A payment one nation made to another for protection or after defeat.

trigon—A musical instrument, a triangular lyre or harp.

trumpet—A musical instrument.

tunic—A kind of coat. A long, shirtlike undergarment draped over one shoulder.

turban—A head covering. A cloth wrapped around the head.

turtledove—A small type of pigeon used in sacrificial offerings.

U

uncircumcised—All people who did not keep the law of circumcision. In the Old Testament, it referred usually to the Philistines. In the New Testament, it referred to all Gentiles. See also **circumcision**.

unclean—Not pure according to religious laws. Old Testament laws declared that certain animals, foods, places, objects, and persons were unclean. To come in contact with any of these things made a person unclean. To be clean, one had to go through a cleansing ritual.

unleavened bread—Bread or cakes baked without yeast. See also **leaven**.

Upper Room—A room in the upper floor of a house or a room on the roof, usually for guests. In the New Testament, an upper room was the place chosen by Jesus for his last meal with his disciples.

Urim and Thummim—Objects used to determine the will of God. These objects may have been stones or pieces of metal. The priests would shake them in a container and throw them on the ground like dice. How the Urim and the Thummim landed would tell the priests what to do.

V

vanity, vain—The quality of being empty or worthless; having no real value.

vassal—One in a subordinate position who has promised loyalty to an overlord.

veil—A head covering worn usually by women.

veil of the Temple or Tabernacle—The curtain that hung at the entrance to the most holy place.

vestments—Special clothes worn by the priests conducting religious ceremonies.

village—A small grouping of houses and other buildings.

vineyard—A planting of grapevines.

vision—An experience similar to a dream in which God reveals the presence of God or the will of God to someone.

votive offering—A gift given to God as part of a promise made in a vow. See also **vow**.

vow—A sacred promise or pledge made to God.

W

wafers—Thin, unleavened cakes made of flour, sometimes mixed with honey. See also **unleavened**.

walls—Enclosure of bricks, wood, stone, or other materials for privacy or protection. Stone walls were built around cities for defense against enemy attack. They were usually tall and thick, with watchtowers and a gate.

watchman—A sentry or guard. A watchman was placed in the fields and vineyards during the time of the ripening and harvesting of crops to frighten away thieves, birds, and animals. The watchman of a city patrolled the walls of the city at night and was especially helpful during times of attack.

way—A path, road, or street along which a person passes to get from one place to another.

well—A source or storage place for water.

wheat—A grain crop that produced some of the most important foods in Bible times. Wheat was made into flour for bread or was roasted and eaten as parched grain.

whirlwind—Several kinds of winds: a high, destructive wind, a tornado, or spinning clouds of dust.

widow, widower—A woman whose husband has died; or a man whose wife has died.

wilderness—A word that refers to sandy deserts, rocky plateaus, barren pasturelands, and desolate mountain regions.

winepress—A vat in which the juice was pressed from grapes. The vat was usually hollowed-out rock on a hill near the vineyard. Grapes were spread over the floor, and barefoot people walked and jumped on the grapes to press out the juice. A hole in the rock allowed the juice to trickle down to a lower vat where it was left to become vine. The wine was then put into jars and wineskins.

winnow—The process of separating the kernel of grain from the chaff by throwing the cut stalks of grain into the air with a long-handled fork. The grain seeds would fall back into a pile, and the light straw chaff would be carried away by the wind. "Winnowing" is used as a figure of speech to describe the sweeping away of evil. See also **chaff**.

wise men—Magicians and interpreters of the stars. In the Gospel of Matthew, it is reported that wise men came from the East to worship the baby Jesus. These wise men had studied the stars to learn of the birth of Jesus and also how to find him.

wither—To shrivel or dry up.

witness—A person who has firsthand knowledge of a fact or an event. In the New Testament, those who testified to the truth of God and those who testified to what they had seen or heard about Jesus were called witnesses.

woe—Deep trouble or distress.

Word, the—In the Old Testament, God's declaration of God's will and purpose. God's word and God's act were the same. In some places in the New Testament, "the word" still has this meaning. In other places, it becomes "the Word of Christ," the gospel that he first preached. In the Gospel of John and in Revelation, "Word" or "Word of God" is used to mean Jesus Christ himself as God's clearest word to humanity.

world—In the Old Testament, "world" most often referred to the lands around the Mediterranean Sea. By New Testament times, the known world was as large as the Roman Empire. "World" was also used to mean not so much lands and nations but the concerns and actions of humans. The word "world" in this sense shows the difference between the concerns and actions of humans from the kingdom of God.

worship—An acknowledgment of worthiness, respect, and reverence. In the Bible, worship is an act or attitude intended to recognize the worth of God, to honor God.

Y

Yahweh (YHWH)—An English-language version of the probable name by which the Hebrews thought of God. It is believed that the name would have been pronounced, "Yahweh," but it was seldom spoken.

yeast—See **leaven**.

yoke—A wooden frame placed over the necks of two oxen to harness them together. To the middle of the yoke bar was connected a single shaft, which pulled a plow, sled, or cart.

youth—The time between a person's birth and his or her years of greatest vigor and opportunity, but not years of greatest maturity and judgment. The prophets called the early years of Israel the nation's youth.

Z

Zealot—A member of a patriotic group of Jews who rebelled against all foreign rulers, especially the Romans.

Zion—Another name for the city of Jerusalem, where the Temple was built.

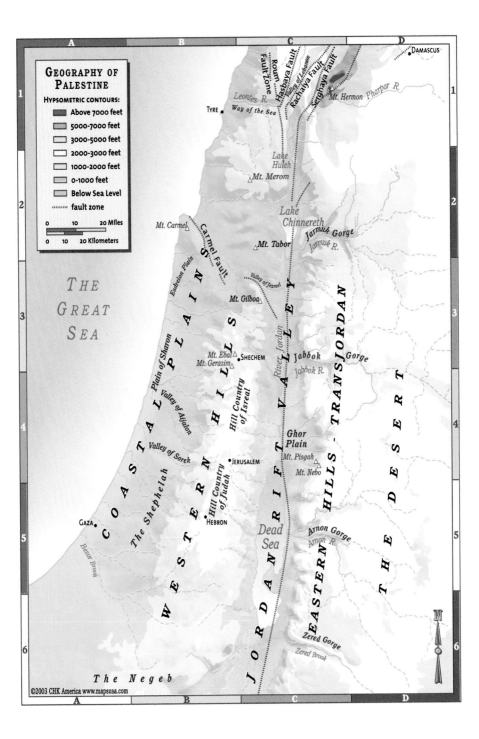

GEOGRAPHY OF PALESTINE

HYPSOMETRIC CONTOURS:

- Above 7000 feet
- 5000-7000 feet
- 3000-5000 feet
- 2000-3000 feet
- 1000-2000 feet
- 0-1000 feet
- Below Sea Level
- fault zone

0   10   20 Miles
0   10   20 Kilometers

DAMASCUS

Roum Fault Zone
Hasbaya Fault
Valley of Lebanon
Rachaiya Fault
Serghaya Fault

Leontes R.
TYRE
Way of the Sea
Mt. Hermon   Pharpar R.

Lake Huleh
Mt. Merom

Lake Chinnereth
Mt. Carmel
Carmel Fault
Jarmuk Gorge
Mt. Tabor
Jarmuk R.

THE GREAT SEA

Esdrelon Plain
Valley of Jezreel
Mt. Gilboa

WESTERN HILLS

Plain of Sharon
Mt. Ebal
Mt. Gerazim
SHECHEM
Hill Country of Isreal

Jabbok
Jabbok R.
Gorge

River Jordan

TRANSJORDAN

Valley of Aijalon

Valley of Sorek

JORDAN RIFT VALLEY

Ghor Plain
Mt. Pisgah
Mt. Nebo

JERUSALEM

COASTAL PLAINS

The Shephelah

Hill Country of Judah

GAZA
HEBRON

Dead Sea

EASTERN HILLS

Arnon Gorge
Arnon R.

THE DESERT

Besor Brook

Zered Gorge
Zered Brook

N

The Negeb

©2003 CHK America www.mapsusa.com

THE EXODUS

- ☐ Area controlled by ancient Israel
- ← Probable route of wandering in the Sinai
- ← Entry into and conquest of Canaan
- ✕ Battle

0   25   50 Miles
0   25   50 Kilometers

THE GREAT SEA

SIDON
DAMASCUS
TYRE
KEDESH
MEROM ● HAZOR
BASHAN
Mt. Tabor
Edrei
SHECHEM
R. Jordan
CANAAN
Bethel Shiloh Shittim
Gibeah Gilgal? AMMON
Beth-horon Ai Jericho Heshbon
Jarmuth Jerusalem Mt. Nebo
Azekah Libnah? Dibon
PHILISTIA Lachish Hebron Jahaz?
Eglon? Makkedah? Salt Sea
Debir? MOAB
Besor Br. Beer-sheba
Zered Br. Iye Abarim?
WILDERNESS OF ZIN
LOWER EGYPT
Oboth? Punon
RAMESES GOSHEN
Kadesh EDOM
Pithom Succoth Barnea
WILDERNESS OF SHUR
WILDERNESS OF PARAN
Heliopolis (On)
Memphis (Noph)
Ezion-geber
Marah?
SINAI
Elim?
Dophkah?
WILDERNESS OF SIN Hazeroth?
River Nile
UPPER EGYPT
(Gulf of Suez)
Wadi Feiran
(Gulf of Aqaba)
Rephidim?
Mt. Sinai (traditonal location)
MIDIAN

N

RED SEA

©2003 CHK America www.mapsusa.com

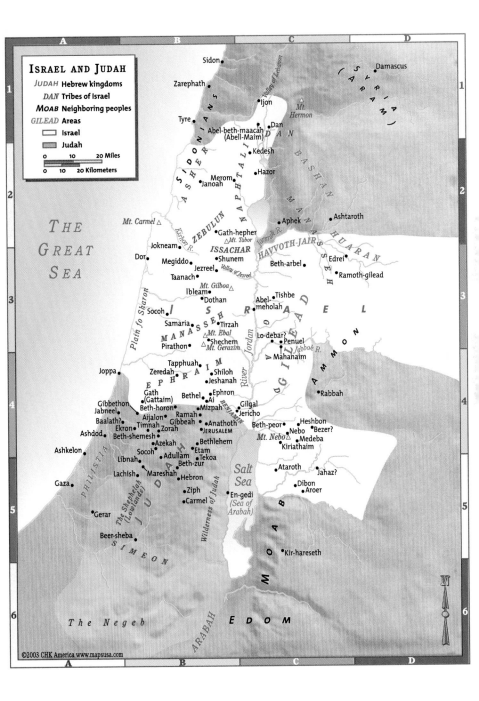

ISRAEL AND JUDAH

JUDAH Hebrew kingdoms
DAN Tribes of Israel
MOAB Neighboring peoples
GILEAD Areas

Israel
Judah

0   10   20 Miles
0   10   20 Kilometers

THE
GREAT
SEA

Sidon
Zarephath
Ijon
Tyre
Abel-beth-maacah (Abell-Maim)
Dan
Kedesh
Merom
Janoah
Hazor
Mt. Carmel △
Mt. Hermon △
Aphek
Ashtaroth
ZEBULUN
Gath-hepher
Mt. Tabor △
Jokneam
ISSACHAR
Beth-arbel
Dor
Megiddo
Shunem
Edrei
Jezreel
Taanach
Valley of Jezreel
Ramoth-gilead
Ibleam
Mt. Gilboa △
Tishbe
Dothan
Abel-meholah
Socoh
Samaria
Tirzah
Lo-debar?
Penuel
Pirathon
Mt. Ebal △
Shechem
Mahanaim
Mt. Gerazim △
Tappuah
Joppa
Zeredah
Shiloh
Jeshanah
Gath (Gattaim)
Bethel
Ephron
Gibbethon
Beth-horon
Ai
Gilgal
Rabbah
Jabneel
Mizpah
Jericho
Aijalon
Ramah
Baalath?
Gibeah
Anathoth
Beth-peor
Heshbon
Ekron
Timnah
Zorah
JERUSALEM
Nebo
Bezer?
Ashdod
Beth-shemesh
Azekah
Bethlehem
Mt. Nebo △
Medeba
Ashkelon
Socoh
Etam
Kiriathaim
Libnah
Adullam
Tekoa
Lachish
Mareshah
Beth-zur
Ataroth
Jahaz?
Gaza
Hebron
Dibon
Ziph
Aroer
Gerar
Carmel of Judah
En-gedi (Sea of Arabah)
Beer-sheba
SIMEON
Kir-hareseth
The Negeb
EDOM

©2003 CHK America www.mapsusa.com

ISRAEL, JUDAH AND THE
ASSYRIAN EMPIRE AT
THE TIME OF ISRAEL'S
FALL, 722-21 BCE

Assyrian Kingdom

0   50   100 Miles
0   100   200 Kilometers

©2003 CHK America www.mapsusa.com

Judah and Babylonia at the Time of Jerusalem's Fall

THE ROMAN WORLD

Corinth• Christian communities by
        the end of the second century

EPHESUS• "Seven Churches of Asia" (Rev 1-3)

DACIA Roman province

©2003 CHK America www.mapsusa.com

0   50   100 Miles
0   50   100 Kilometers

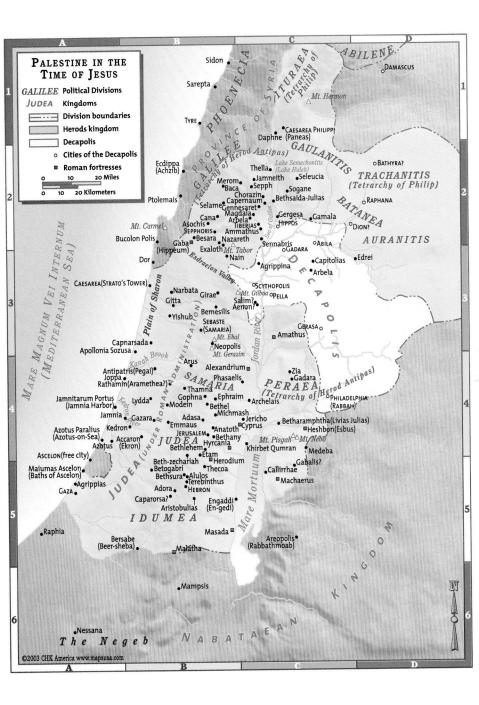

PALESTINE IN THE TIME OF JESUS

GALILEE Political Divisions
JUDEA Kingdoms

Division boundaries
Herods kingdom
Decapolis

○ Cities of the Decapolis
■ Roman fortresses

0   10   20 Miles
0   10   20 Kilometers

Sidon

Sarepta

TYRE

PHOENECIA

PROVINCE OF SYRIA

GALILEE *(Tetrarchy of Herod Antipas)*

ITURAEA *(Tetrarchy of Philip)*

ABILENE

DAMASCUS

Mt. Hermon

CAESAREA PHILIPPI

Daphne (Paneas)

GAULANITIS

Ecdippa (Achzib)

Thella

Lake Semechonitis *(Lake Huleh)*

BATHYRA?

TRACHANITIS *(Tetrarchy of Philip)*

Merom
Baca
Sepph
Jamneith
Seleucia
Sogane

BATANEA

RAPHANA

Ptolemais

Selame
Capernaum
Bethsaida-Julias

Asochis
Cana
Gennesaret
Magdala
Arbela
TIBERIAS
Ammathus
Nazareth

SEPPHORIS
Gergesa
Gamala
HIPPOS
DION?

AURANITIS

Mt. Carmel

Bucolon Polis
Gaba (Hippeum)
Besara
Exaloth
Mt. Tabor
Nain

Sennabris
GADARA
ABILA

DECAPOLIS

Capitolias
Arbela

Edrei

Dor

Agrippina

CAESAREA (STRATO'S TOWER)

Plain of Sharon

Narbata
Gitta
Girae
Yishub

SCYTHOPOLIS
Mt. Gilboa
Salim
Aenon?
PELLA

Bemesilis
SEBASTE (SAMARIA)

Jordan River

GERASA

Capnarsada
Apollonia Sozusa

Kanah Brook

Arus
Alexandrium

Mt. Ebal
Neopolis
Mt. Gerazim

Amathus

Antipatris(Pegai)
Joppa
Rathamin(Aramethea?)

SAMARIA *(UNDER ROMAN ADMINISTRATION)*

Thamna
Gophna
Modein
Phasaelis
Ephraim
Archelais

Zia
Gadara

PERAEA *(Tetrarchy of Herod Antipas)*

PHILADELPHIA (RABBAH)

Jamnitarum Portus (Jamnia Harbor)
Jamnia
Lydda
Gazara
Kedron
Adasa
Emmaus
Bethel
Michmash
Anatoth
Jericho
Cyprus
Betharamphtha(Livias Julias)
Heshbon(Esbus)

Azotus Paralius (Azotus-on-Sea)
Azotus
Accaron (Ekron)
JERUSALEM
Bethany
Hyrcania
Mt. Pisgah
Mt. Nebo
Medeba

ASCELON(free city)
Bethlehem
Etam
Herodium
Khirbet Qumran
Gabalis?

Maiumas Ascelon (Baths of Ascelon)
Agrippias
GAZA
Beth-zechariah
Betogabri
Bethsura
Adora
HEBRON
Thecoa
Terebinthus
Alulos
Callirrhae
Machaerus

Caparorsa?
Aristobulias
Engaddi (En-gedi)

IDUMEA

JUDEA *(UNDER ROMAN ADMINISTRATION)*

Kedron River

MARE MAGNUM VEI INTERNUM *(MEDITERRANEAN SEA)*

Raphia

Bersabe (Beer-sheba)
Malatha
Masada

Areopolis (Rabbathmoab)

Mare Mortuum

NABATAEAN KINGDOM

Mampsis

Nessana

The Negeb

©2003 CHK America www.mapsusa.com

N

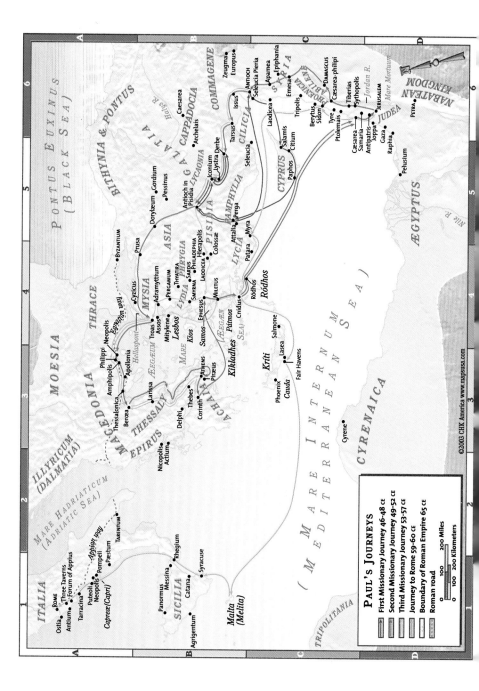

PAUL'S JOURNEYS

First Missionary Journey 46-48 CE
Second Missionary Journey 49-52 CE
Third Missionary Journey 53-57 CE
Journey to Rome 59-60 CE
Boundary of Roman Empire 65 CE
Roman road

0   100   200 Miles
0   100   200 Kilometers

©2003 CHK America www.mapsusa.com